ENCYCLOPEDIA OF WORLD ART

Vol. IX

LANDSCAPE IN ART – MICRONESIAN CULTURES

ENCICLOPEDIA UNIVERSALE DELL'ARTE

Sotto gli auspici della Fondazione Giorgio Cini

ISTITUTO PER LA COLLABORAZIONE CULTURALE
VENEZIA-ROMA

ENCYCLOPEDIA OF WORLD ART

McGRAW-HILL BOOK COMPANY, INC.
NEW YORK, TORONTO, LONDON

ENCYCLOPEDIA OF WORLD ART: VOLUME IX

Copyright © 1964 in England by McGraw-Hill Publishing Company Limited, London. All rights reserved. Italian language edition, including all texts and plates, copyrighted © 1958 by the Istituto per la Collaborazione Culturale, Rome, under the Universal Copyright Convention. All plates herein are the property of the Istituto per la Collaborazione Culturale. Except for brief quotations in reviews no part of this book may be reproduced without permission in writing from the publishers.

Paper for plates and text supplied by Cartiere Burgo, Turin — Engraving by Zincotipia Altimani, Milan — Black-and-white and color plates printed by Tipocolor, Florence — Text printed by "L'Impronta," Florence — Binding by Stabilimento Stianti, San Casciano Val di Pesa, Florence — Book cloth supplied by Kohorn Ltd., Egerton, near Bolton, England.

Printed in Italy

Library of Congress Catalog Card Number 59-13433
19466

INTERNATIONAL COUNCIL OF SCHOLARS

Mario Salmi, University of Rome, President

Marcel Aubert, Membre de l'Institut; Director, Société Française d'Archéologie, Paris, Vice President
Ernst Kühnel, formerly, Director, Islamic Section, Berlin Museum, Berlin-Dahlem, Vice President
† Amedeo Maiuri, late Accademico dei Lincei, Naples
Gisela M. A. Richter, Honorary Curator, Metropolitan Museum of Art, New York, Vice President
Giuseppe Tucci, University of Rome; President, Istituto Italiano per il Medio ed Estremo Oriente, Vice President

Alvar Aalto, Architect, Helsinki, Finland
Jean Alazard, University of Algiers
Andrew Alföldi, University of Basel; Institute for Advanced Study, Princeton, N.J.
† Carlo Anti, University of Padua
Gilbert Archey, Director, Auckland Institute and Museum, Auckland, New Zealand
A. S. Ardojo, Jakarta, Indonesia
Bernard Ashmole, Oxford University
Jeannine Auboyer, Curator, Musée Guimet, Paris
Ludwig Baldass, formerly, Director, Kunsthistorisches Museum, Vienna
Sir John D. Beazley, formerly, Oxford University
† Bernard Berenson
W. Blawatsky, University of Moscow
† Albert Boeckler, late Staatsbibliothekar, Munich
Axel Boëthius, formerly, University of Göteborg; Director, Swedish Institute, Rome
† Helmut T. Bossert, University of Istanbul
Cesare Brandi, University of Palermo
† Henri Breuil, late Membre de l'Institut; Collège de France, Paris
Peter H. Brieger, University of Toronto
Joseph Burke, University of Melbourne
A. W. Byvanck, University of Leiden
Guido Calogero, University of Rome
Alfonso Caso, Escuela Nacional de Arqueología e Historia, Mexico City
† Carlo Cecchelli, University of Rome
Enrico Cerulli, Accademico dei Lincei, Rome
Jean Charbonneaux, Curator in Chief, Musée du Louvre, Paris
† Gino Chierici, late Superintendent of Monuments, Pavia
Fernando Chueca y Goitia, Architect, Madrid
Sir Kenneth Clark, Chairman, Arts Council of Great Britain, London
Giuseppe Cocchiara, University of Palermo
George Cœdès, Honorary Director, Ecole Française d'Extrême-Orient, Paris
Paul Collart, Director, Swiss Institute, Rome
W. G. Constable, formerly, Boston Museum of Fine Arts
Paolo D'Ancona, University of Milan
Sir Percival David, London
Guglielmo De Angelis D'Ossat, University of Rome
Otto Demus, President, Bundesdenkmalamt, Vienna
Paul Deschamps, Director, Musée des Monuments Français, Paris
Roland de Vaux, Director, Ecole Française, Jerusalem
Prince Dhaninivat, President, Siam Society, Bangkok
Adrian Digby, Keeper of the Department of Ethnography, British Museum, London
† Einar Dyggve, late Director, Ny Carlsberg Foundation, Copenhagen
Gustav Ecke, Curator of Chinese Art, Honolulu Academy of Arts; University of Hawaii
Vadime Elisséeff, Curator, Musée Cernuschi, Paris
A. P. Elkin, University of Sydney
Richard Ettinghausen, Freer Gallery of Art, Washington, D.C.
Bishr Farès, Institut d'Egypte, Cairo
† Paul Fierens, late Curator in Chief, Musées Royaux des Beaux-Arts de Belgique, Brussels
Giuseppe Fiocco, University of Padua; Director, Istituto di Storia dell'Arte, Venice
Pierre Francastel, Director, Ecole des Hautes Etudes, Paris
† Giuseppe Furlani, University of Rome
Albert Gabriel, Director, Institut Français d'Archéologie, Istanbul
O. C. Gangoly, Calcutta
Antonio García y Bellido, University of Madrid
Alberto Giuganino, Vice President, Istituto Italiano per il Medio ed Estremo Oriente, Rome
Albert Rex Gonzales, Director, Museo de La Plata, Argentina

L. Carrington GOODRICH, Universities of Buenos Aires and Montevideo; Columbia University, New York
Lloyd GOODRICH, Director, Whitney Museum of American Art, New York
André GRABAR, Collège de France, Paris
Basil GRAY, Keeper of the Department of Oriental Antiquities, British Museum, London
Paolo GRAZIOSI, University of Florence
† Albert GRENIER, late Membre de l'Institut; Collège de France, Paris
Will GROHMANN, Berlin
Walter GROPIUS, The Architects' Collaborative, Cambridge, Mass.
José GUDIOL, University of Barcelona; Director, Instituto Amatller de Arte Hispánico
Robert H. VAN GULIK, The Hague
Hans HAHNLOSER, Bern
Charles HENTZE, Trautheim, Darmstadt, Germany
† Reinhard HERBIG, late Director, German Archaeological Institute, Rome
† Melville J. HERSKOVITS, Northwestern University, Evanston, Ill.
L. H. HEYDENREICH, University of Munich; Director, Zentralinstitut für Kunstgeschichte, Munich
Henry-Russell HITCHCOCK, Smith College, Northampton, Mass.
Jean HUBERT, Director, Ecole Nationale des Chartes, Paris
René HUYGHE, Collège de France, Paris
José IMBELLONI, University of Buenos Aires
† Guido VON KASCHNITZ-WEINBERG, University of Frankfort on the Main
Ahmed Ali KHOZAD KHAN, formerly, Director, Archaeological Museum of Kabul
Carl KJERSMEIER, Copenhagen
† Elie LAMBERT, late Membre de l'Institut; University of Paris
Ernst LANGLOTZ, University of Bonn
Raymond LANTIER, Membre de l'Institut; Curator in Chief, Musée des Antiquités Nationales, Saint-Germain-en-Laye
Oliver W. LARKIN, Smith College, Northampton, Mass.
Sherman E. LEE, Director, The Cleveland Museum of Art
† Paul LEMERLE, late Directeur d'Etudes, Ecole des Hautes Etudes, Paris
Doro LEVI, Director, Scuola Archeologica Italiana, Athens
Roberto LONGHI, University of Florence
Hans Peter L'ORANGE, University of Oslo; Director, Norwegian Archaeological Institute, Rome
Stanislaw LORENTZ, Director, National Museum, Warsaw
Otto J. MAENCHEN-HELFEN, University of California, Berkeley
Arif Müfid MANSEL, University of Istanbul
Millard MEISS, Institute for Advanced Study, Princeton, N.J.
Osvaldo F. A. MENGHIN, University of Buenos Aires; Director, Ethnographic Museum of the University
Alfred MERLIN, Membre de l'Institut, Paris
Bruno MOLAJOLI, Direttore Generale delle Antichità e Belle Arti, Roma
Théodore MONOD, Director, Institut Français d'Afrique Noire, Dakar
Bernard S. MYERS, formerly, The City College, New York
Pier Luigi NERVI, Architect, Rome
† Frans M. OLBRECHTS, University of Ghent; late Director, Musée Royal du Congo Belge, Tervueren, Belgium
Rodolfo PALLUCCHINI, University of Padua
Erwin PANOFSKY, Institute for Advanced Study, Princeton, N.J.
Senarat PARANAVITANA, University of Ceylon, Paradeniya, Ceylon
Luciano PETECH, University of Rome
Helmut PETRI, University of Cologne
† Carlo Alberto PETRUCCI, late President, Accademia di San Luca, Rome
Sir Herbert READ, President, Institute of Contemporary Art, London
D. C. RÖELL, Director, Rijksmuseum, Amsterdam
Jorge ROMERO BREST, Universities of Buenos Aires and Montevideo
Andreas RUMPF, University of Cologne
Edouard SALIN, Membre de l'Institut; Director, Musée Historique Lorrain, Nancy
† Alfred SALMONY, Institute of Fine Arts, New York University
Meyer SCHAPIRO, Columbia University, New York
Daniel SCHLUMBERGER, University of Strasbourg; Director, Délégation Archéologique Française en Afghanistan
Antonio SERRANO, formerly, University of Córdoba, Argentina
Osvald SIRÉN, formerly, Curator, National Museum, Stockholm
Calambur SIVARAMAMURTI, Director, National Museum of India, New Delhi
Werner SPEISER, University of Cologne; Director, Museum für Ostasiatische Kunst
Ugo SPIRITO, University of Rome
Alfred STEINMANN, Director, Sammlung für Völkerkunde der Universität, Zurich
Philippe STERN, Curator in Chief, Musée Guimet, Paris
† William SUIDA, Samuel H. Kress Foundation, New York
Charles DE TOLNAY, Columbia University, New York
Paolo TOSCHI, University of Rome
Arthur D. TRENDALL, Australian National University, Canberra
Naoteru UENO, President, Bijutsu Daigaku, Tokyo
Luís E. VALCÁRCEL, Director, Museo Nacional de Historia, Lima, Peru
† Lionello VENTURI, University of Rome
Ernst WALDSCHMIDT, University of Göttingen
Kurt WEITZMANN, Princeton University, Princeton, N.J.
Sir Mortimer WHEELER, University of London
Paul S. WINGERT, Columbia University, New York
Rudolf WITTKOWER, Columbia University, New York
Yukio YASHIRO, Deputy Chairman, National Commission for Protection of Cultural Properties, Tokyo
Paola ZANCANI MONTUORO, Accademia dei Lincei, Rome

ITALIAN EDITORIAL BOARD

Editor in Chief, Massimo PALLOTTINO, University of Rome. Section Directors: *Modern Art*, Giulio Carlo ARGAN, University of Rome; *Oriental Art*, Mario BUSSAGLI, University of Rome; *Ancient Art*, Michelangelo CAGIANO DE AZEVEDO, Università Cattolica del S. Cuore, Milan; *Medieval Art*, Géza DE' FRANCOVICH, University of Rome; *Primitive Art*, Vinigi L. GROTTANELLI, Pontificium Athenaeum Urbanianum de Propaganda Fide, Rome. Consulting Director, Sabatino MOSCATI, University of Rome. Coordinating Committee: Mario SALMI, President of the International Council of Scholars; Giuseppe TUCCI, Vice President of the International Council of Scholars; Massimo PALLOTTINO; Giulio Carlo ARGAN.

AMERICAN EDITORIAL ADVISORY COMMITTEE

W. G. CONSTABLE, formerly, Boston Museum of Fine Arts; Lloyd GOODRICH, Director, Whitney Museum of American Art; Henry-Russell HITCHCOCK, Smith College; Oliver W. LARKIN, Smith College; Bernard S. MYERS, formerly, The City College, New York; Gisela M. A. RICHTER, Honorary Curator, Metropolitan Museum of Art; Paul S. WINGERT, Columbia University.

EDITORIAL STAFF FOR THE ISTITUTO

Secretary General: Prof. Alberto Mario CIRESE. *Section Editors*: Dr. Catia CAPRINO; Dr. Ernesta CERULLI; Dr. Paolo DAFFINÀ; Dr. Fernanda DE' MAFFEI; Dr. Luciana FERRARA; Prof. Luigi SALERNO. *Consulting Editor*: Prof. Eugenio BATTISTI. *Editorial Assistants*: Dr. Margherita ABBRUZZESE; Dr. Margherita ALOSI CATELLI; Dr. Tea MARTINELLI COCO; Dr. Anna Maria ROVERI; Dr. Italo SIGNORINI.
Illustrations. Editor: Prof. Alessandro MARABOTTINI MARABOTTI. *Consultants*: Maria CALANDRA, Architect; Dr. Enzo CREA. *Assistants*: Dr. Assunta BOSCHETTI ALBANESI; Dr. Gemma CORTESE DI DOMENICO; Prof. Raniero GNOLI; Dr. Romolo STACCIOLI; Dr. Anna Maria TAMASSIA; Paola VERGARA CAFFARELLI.
Copy Editing and Index. Editor: Dr. Nicola TERRANOVA. *Assistants*: Dr. Gigliola BONUCCI CAPORALI; Dr. Maria BORSELLINO DE LORENZO; Dr. Emilia BOSCHERINI GIANCOTTI; Adriana CARINI; Dr. Marco CHIARINI; Dr. Giovanni CRAPULLI; Dr. Elsa FUBINI; Prof. Alberto GIANQUINTO; Elena GRILLO; Dr. Elena OTTOLENGHI; Dr. Giorgio STACUL; Dr. Mario TRONTI; Dr. Franco VOLTAGGIO.
Secretary: Dr. Bianca Laura DE VITA FASANI.

STAFF FOR THE McGRAW-HILL EDITION

Managing Editor: Theresa C. BRAKELEY. *Associate Managing Editor and Translation Editor*: Ronald STROM.
Editorial Advisor: Mamie HARMON. *Assistant Translation Editor*: Richard WADLEIGH.
Office Manager: Letizia BARONE DAMIANI.
Research Editors: Edmée BUSCH; George G. MARCUS. *Assistants*: Per-Olof LUTHMAN; Susan TWIGG; Hope WEISHAAR.
Illustrations: Erika BIZZARRI; Françoise CHIARINI; Sally Lee COOK; Linda PERLMAN. *Bibliography*: Neil THOMPSON.
Copy and Proof Editors: Robert BRAINERD; Ruth EISENSTEIN; John KREMITSKE. *Assistants*: Barbara ANGELILLO; Florence DANKO; Clodagh M. FLAHERTY; Pamela JONES; Anne PHALON; Betsy REIN.
Consulting Editor: Bernard S. MYERS.
Executive Editor: George A. HOY. *Administrative Editor*: M. Barat Kerr SPARKS.

TECHNICAL STAFF

Technical Director: Dr. Matilde GIACHETTI, Casa Editrice G. C. Sansoni. *Technical Assistants*: Dr. Catervo BLASI FOGLIETTI; Giulio GIUFFRIDA RUGGERI. *Photographic Archives. Director*: Dr. Enzo CREA. *Assistant*: Dr. Paola DE GASPERI. *Maps*: Prof. Mario RICCARDI; Giuliana CAPORALI. *Drawings*: Bruno BARINCI, Architect. *Plate layout*: Piero BERTA; Paolo BUDASSI.

Production and Technical Direction, English and Italian Editions

CASA EDITRICE G. C. SANSONI

Florence

ABBREVIATIONS

Museums, Galleries, Libraries, and Other Institutions

Antikensamml.	— Antikensammlungen
Antiq.	— Antiquarium
Bib. Nat.	— Bibliothèque Nationale
Bib. Naz.	— Biblioteca Nazionale
Brera	— Pinacoteca di Brera
Br. Mus.	— British Museum
Cab. Méd.	— Cabinet des Médailles (Paris, Bibliothèque Nationale)
Cleve. Mus.	— Cleveland Museum
Conserv.	— Palazzo dei Conservatori
Gall. Arte Mod.	— Galleria di Arte Moderna
IsMEO	— Istituto Italiano per il Medio ed Estremo Oriente
Kunstgewerbemus.	— Kunstgewerbemuseum
Kunsthist. Mus.	— Kunsthistorisches Museum
Louvre	— Musée du Louvre
Medagl.	— Medagliere
Met. Mus.	— Metropolitan Museum
Mus. Ant.	— Museo di Antichità
Mus. Arch.	— Museo Archeologico
Mus. B. A.	— Musée des Beaux-Arts
Mus. Cap.	— Musei Capitolini
Mus. Civ.	— Museo Civico
Mus. Com.	— Museo Comunale
Mus. Etn.	— Museo Etnologico
Mus. Naz.	— Museo Nazionale
Mus. Vat.	— Musei Vaticani, Vatican Museums
Nat. Gall.	— National Gallery
Öst. Gall.	— Österreichische Galerie
Pin. Naz.	— Pinacoteca Nazionale
Prado	— Museo del Prado
Rijksmus.	— Rijksmuseum
Samml.	— Sammlung
Staat. Mus.	— Staatliche Museen
Staatsbib.	— Staatsbibliothek
Städt. Mus.	— Städtisches Museum
Tate Gall.	— Tate Gallery
Uffizi	— Uffizi Gallery
Vict. and Alb.	— Victoria and Albert Museum
Villa Giulia	— Museo di Villa Giulia

Reviews and Miscellanies

AAE	— Archivio per la Antropologia e la Etnologia, Florence
AAnz	— Archäologischer Anzeiger, Berlin
AAs	— Artibus Asiae, Ascona, Switzerland
AB	— Art Bulletin, New York
AbhAkMünchen	— Abhandlungen der Bayerischen Akademie der Wissenschaften, Munich
AbhBerlAk	— Abhandlungen der Berliner Akademie der Wissenschaften, Berlin
AbhPreussAk	— Abhandlungen der preussischen Akademie der Wissenschaften, Berlin; after 1945, Abhandlungen der Deutschen Akademie der Wissenschaften zu Berlin, Berlin
ABIA	— Annual Bibliography of Indian Archaeology, Leiden
ABMAB	— Anales y Boletín de los Museos de Arte de Barcelona
ABME	— 'Αρχεῖον τῶν Βυζαντινῶν Μνημείων τῆς Ἑλλάδος, Athens
AC	— Archeologia Classica, Rome
ACCV	— Anales del Centro de Cultura Valenciana, Valencia
ActaA	— Acta Archaeologica, Copenhagen
ActaO	— Acta Orientalia, Leiden, The Hague
AD	— Antike Denkmäler, Deutsches Archäologisches Institut, Berlin, Leipzig
AE	— Arte Español, Madrid
AEA	— Archivo Español de Arqueología, Madrid
AEAA	— Archivo Español de Arte y Arqueología, Madrid
AEArte	— Archivio Español de Arte, Madrid
AErt	— Archaeologiai Értesitö, Budapest
AfA	— Archiv für Anthropologie, Brunswick
AfO	— Archiv für Orientforschung, Berlin
AfrIt	— Africa Italiana, Bergamo
AGS	— American Guide Series, U.S. Federal Writer's Project, Works Progress Administration, Washington, D.C., 1935–41
AIEC	— Anuari de l'Institut d'Estudies Catalans, Barcelona
AIEG	— Anales del Instituto de Estudios Gerundenses, Gerona
AJA	— American Journal of Archaeology, Baltimore
AM	— Mitteilungen des deutschen archäologischen Instituts, Athenische Abteilung, Athens, Stuttgart
AmA	— American Anthropologist, Menasha, Wis.
AmAnt	— American Antiquity, Menasha, Wis.
AN	— Art News, New York
AnnInst	— Annali dell'Instituto di Corrispondenza Archeologica, Rome
AnnSAntEg	— Annales du Service des Antiquités de l'Egypte, Cairo
AntC	— L'Antiquité Classique, Louvain
AntJ	— The Antiquaries Journal, London
AnzAlt	— Anzeiger für die Altertumswissenschaft, Innsbruck, Vienna
AnzÖAk	— Anzeiger der Österreichischen Akademie der Wissenschaften, Vienna
APAmM	— Anthropological Papers of the American Museum of Natural History, New York
AQ	— Art Quarterly, Detroit
ArndtBr	— P. Arndt, F. Bruckmann, Griechische und römische Porträts, Munich, 1891 ff.
ARSI	— Annual Report of the Smithsonian Institution, Bureau of Ethnology, Washington, D.C.
ArtiFig	— Arti Figurative, Rome
ASAtene	— Annuario della Scuola Archeologica Italiana di Atene, Bergamo
ASI	— Archivio Storico Italiano, Florence
ASWI	— Archaeological Survey of Western India, Hyderabad
AttiDeSPa	— Atti e Memorie della Deputazione di Storia Patria
AttiPontAcc	— Atti della Pontificia Accademia Romana di Archeologia, Rome
Atti3StArch	— Atti del III Convegno Nazionale di Storia dell'Architettura, Rome, 1938
Atti5StArch	— Atti del V Convegno Nazionale di Storia dell'Architettura, Florence, 1957

AZ	— Archäologische Zeitung, Berlin	BRABASF	— Boletín de la Real Academia de Bellas Artes de San Fernando, Madrid
BA	— Baessler Archiv, Leipzig, Berlin		
BABsch	— Bulletin van de Vereeniging tot bevordering der kennis van de antieke Beschaving, The Hague	BRABLB	— Boletín de la Real Academia de Buenas Letras de Barcelona
BAC	— Bulletin du Comité des Travaux Historiques et Scientifiques, Section d'Archéologie, Paris	BRAH	— Boletín de la Real Academia de la Historia, Madrid
BAcBelg	— Bulletin de l'Académie Royale de Belgique, Cl. des Lettres, Brussels	BrBr	— H. Brunn, F. Bruckmann, Denkmäler griechischer und römischer Skulptur, Munich
BACr	— Bollettino di Archeologia Cristiana, Rome	Brunn, GGK	— H. Brunn, Geschichte der griechischen Künstler, 2d ed., Stuttgart, 1889
BAEB	— Bureau of American Ethnology, Bulletins, Washington, D.C.	Brunn, GK	— H. Brunn, Griechische Kunstgeschichte, Munich, I, 1893; II, 1897
BAER	— Bureau of American Ethnology, Reports, Washington, D.C.	BSA	— Annual of the British School at Athens, London
BAFr	— Bulletin de la Société Nationale des Antiquaires de France, Paris	BSCC	— Boletín de la Sociedad Castellonense de Cultura, Castellón de la Plana
BAmSOR	— Bulletin of the American Schools of Oriental Research, South Hadley, Mass.	BSCE	— Boletín de la Sociedad Castellana de Excursiones, Valladolid
BArte	— Bollettino d'Arte del Ministero della Pubblica Istruzione, Rome	BSEAAV	— Boletín del Seminario de Estudios de Arte y Arqueología, Universidad de Valladolid
BAT	— Boletín Arqueológico Tarragona	BSEE	— Boletín de la Sociedad Española de Excursiones, Madrid
BBMP	— Boletín de la Biblioteca Menéndez Pelayo, Santander	BSEI	— Bulletin de la Société des Etudes Indochinoises, Saigon
BByzI	— The Bulletin of the Byzantine Institute, Paris	BSOAS	— Bulletin of the School of Oriental and African Studies, London
BCH	— Bulletin de Correspondance Hellénique, Paris		
BCom	— Bullettino della Commissione Archeologica Comunale, Rome	BSPF	— Bulletin de la Société Préhistorique Française, Paris
BCPMB	— Boletín de la Comision Provincial de Monumentos de Burgos	BSR	— Papers of the British School at Rome, London
		BuNedOud	— Bulletin van de Koninklijke Nederlandse Oudheikundige Bond, Leiden
BCPML	— Boletín de la Comision Provincial de Monumentos de Lugo	Cabrol-Leclercq	— F. Cabrol, H. Leclercq, Dictionnaire d'archéologie chrétienne et de liturgie, Paris, 1907
BCPMO	— Boletín de la Comision Provincial de Monumentos de Orense	CAF	— Congrès Archéologique de France, Paris, 1841–1935
Beazley, ABV	— J. D. Beazley, Attic Black-figure Vase-painters, Oxford, 1956	CahA	— Cahiers Archéologiques, Fin de l'Antiquité et Moyen-Age, Paris
Beazley, ARV	— J. D. Beazley, Attic Red-figure Vase-painters, Oxford, 1942	CahArt	— Cahiers d'art, Paris
		CAJ	— Central Asiatic Journal, Wiesbaden
Beazley, EVP	— J. D. Beazley, Etruscan Vase-painting, Oxford, 1947	CAUG	— Cuadernos de Arte de la Universidad de Granada
Beazley, VA	— J. D. Beazley, Attic Red-figured Vases in American Museums, Cambridge, 1918	CEFEO	— Cahiers de l'Ecole Française d'Extrême-Orient, Paris
Beazley, VRS	— J. D. Beazley, Attische Vasenmaler des rotfigurigen Stils, Tübingen, 1925	CEG	— Cuadernos de Estudios Gallegos, Santiago de Compostela
BEFEO	— Bulletin de l'Ecole Française d'Extrême-Orient, Hanoi, Saigon, Paris	CIE	— Corpus Inscriptionum Etruscarum, Lipsiae
BerlNZ	— Berliner Numismatische Zeitschrift, Berlin	CIG	— Corpus Inscriptionum Graecarum, Berolini
Bernoulli, GI	— J. J. Bernoulli, Griechische Ikonographie, Munich, 1901	CIL	— Corpus Inscriptionum Latinarum, Berolini
		CIS	— Corpus Inscriptionum Semiticarum, Parisiis
Bernoulli, RI	— J. J. Bernoulli, Römische Ikonographie, I, Stuttgart, 1882; II, 1, Berlin, Stuttgart, 1886; II, 2, Stuttgart, Berlin, Leipzig, 1891; II, 3, Stuttgart, Berlin, Leipzig, 1894	Coh	— H. Cohen, Description historique des Monnaies frappées sous l'Empire Romain, Paris
		Collignon, SG	— M. Collignon, Histoire de la sculpture grecque, Paris, I, 1892; II, 1897
BHAcRoum	— Bulletin Historique, Académie Roumaine, Bucharest	Comm	— Commentari, Florence, Rome
		Cr	— La Critica, Bari
BICR	— Bollettino dell'Istituto Centrale del Restauro, Rome	CRAI	— Comptes Rendus de l'Académie des Inscriptions et Belles-Lettres, Paris
BIE	— Bulletin de l'Institut de l'Egypte, Cairo	CrArte	— La Critica d'Arte, Florence
BIFAN	— Bulletin de l'Institut Français d'Afrique Noire, Dakar	CVA	— Corpus Vasorum Antiquorum
		DA	— N. Daremberg, N. Saglio, Dictionnaire des antiquités grecques et romaines, Paris, 1877–1912
BIFAO	— Bulletin de l'Institut Français d'Archéologie Orientale, Cairo		
BInst	— Bullettino dell'Instituto di Corrispondenza Archeologica, Rome	Dehio, I-V	— G. Dehio, Handbuch der deutschen Kunstdenkmäler, Berlin, I, Mitteldeutschland, 1927; II, Nordostdeutschland, 1926; III, Süddeutschland, 1933; IV, Südwestdeutschland, 1933; V, Nordwestdeutschland, 1928
BJ	— Bonner Jahrbücher, Bonn, Darmstadt		
BM	— Burlington Magazine, London		
BMBeyrouth	— Bulletin du Musée de Beyrouth, Beirut		
BMC	— British Museum, Catalogue of Greek Coins, London	Dehio, DtK	— G. Dehio, Geschichte der deutschen Kunst, 4 vols., Berlin, 1930–34
BMCEmp	— H. Mattingly, Coins of the Roman Empire in the British Museum, London	Dehio-VonBezold	— G. Dehio, G. von Bezold, Die kirchliche Baukunst des Abendlandes, Stuttgart, 1892–1901
BMFA	— Museum of Fine Arts, Bulletin, Boston		
BMFEA	— Museum of Far-Eastern Antiquities, Bulletin, Stockholm	DissPontAcc	— Dissertazioni della Pontificia Accademia Romana di Archeologia, Rome
BMImp	— Bullettino del Museo dell'Impero, Rome	EA	— Photographische Einzelaufnahmen, Munich, 1893 ff.
BMMA	— Bulletin of the Metropolitan Museum of Art, New York	EAA	— Enciclopedia dell'Arte Antica, Rome, I, 1958; II, 1959; III, 1960; IV, 1961
BMN	— Boletín Monumentos Navarra		
BMQ	— The British Museum Quarterly, London	EArt	— Eastern Art, London
BNedOud	— Bulletin van de Koninklijke Nederlandse Oudheidkundige Bond, Leiden	EB	— Encyclopaedia Britannica
		’ΕΕΒΣ	— ’Επετερὶς ’Εταιρεία Βυζαντινῶν Σπουδῶν, Athens
BPI	— Bullettino di Paletnologia Italiana, Rome		
BRA	— Boletín de la Real Academia de Ciencias, Bellas Letras y Nobles Artes de Córdoba, Córdoba	’Εφημ	— ’Αρχαιολογικὴ ’Εφημερίς, Athens
		EI	— Enciclopedia Italiana, Rome, 1929 ff.

EphDR	— Ephemeris Dacoromana, Rome	JIAN	— Journal International d'Archéologie Numismatique, Athens
Ἔργον	— Τὸ ἔργον τῆς ἀρχαιολογικῆς ἑταιρείας, ed. A. K. Orlandos, Athens	JISOA	— Journal of the India Society of Oriental Art, Calcutta
ES	— Estudios Segovianos, Segovia	JNES	— Journal of Near Eastern Studies, Chicago
ESA	— Eurasia Septentrionalis Antiqua, Helsinki	JPS	— Journal of the Polynesian Society, Wellington, New Zealand
Espér	— E. Espérandieu, R. Lantier, Recueil général des Bas-Reliefs de la Gaule Romaine, Paris	JRAI	— Journal of the Royal Anthropological Institute of Great Britain and Ireland, London
EUC	— Estudis Universitaris Catalans, Barcelona	JRAS	— Journal of the Royal Asiatic Society, London
FA	— Fasti Archaeologici, Florence	JRS	— Journal of Roman Studies, London
FD	— Fouilles de Delphes, Paris	JS	— Journal des Savants, Paris
Friedländer	— Max Friedländer, Altniederländische Malerei, Berlin, 1924-37	JSA	— Journal de la Société des Africanistes, Paris
Furtwängler, AG	— A. Furtwängler, Antiken Gemmen, Leipzig, Berlin, 1900	JSAH	— Journal of the Society of Architectural Historians, Charlottesville, Va.
Furtwängler, BG	— A. Furtwängler, Beschreibung der Glyptothek König Ludwig I zu München, Munich, 1900	JSAm	— Journal de la Société des Americanistes, Paris
		JSO	— Journal de la Société des Océanistes, Paris
Furtwängler, KlSchr	— A. Furtwängler, Kleine Schriften, Munich, 1912	KbNed	— Kunstreisboek voor Nederland, Amsterdam, 1960
Furtwängler, MP	— A. Furtwängler, Masterpieces of Greek Sculpture, London, 1895	Klein, GrK	— W. Klein, Geschichte der griechischen Kunst, Leipzig, 1904-07
Furtwängler, MW	— A. Furtwängler, Meisterwerke der griechischen Plastik, Leipzig, Berlin, 1893	KS	— Communications on the Reports and Field Research of the Institute of Material Culture, Moscow, Leningrad
Furtwängler Reichhold	— A. Furtwängler, K. Reichhold, Griechische Vasenmalerei, Munich	Lippold, GP	— G. Lippold, Die griechische Plastik (W. Otto, Handbuch der Archäologie, II, 1), Munich, 1950
FWP	— U.S. Federal Writer's Project, Works Progress Administration, Washington, D.C., 1935-1941	Löwy, IGB	— E. Löwy, Inschriften griechischer Bildhauer, Leipzig, 1885
GBA	— Gazette des Beaux-Arts, Paris	MAAccIt	— Monumenti Antichi dell'Accademia d'Italia, Milan
GJ	— The Geographical Journal, London		
HA	— Handbuch der Archäologie in Rahmen des Handbuchs der Altertumswissenschaft..., herausgegeben von Walter Otto, Munich, 1939-53	MAARome	— Memoirs of the American Academy in Rome, Rome, New York
		MAF	— Mémoires de la Société Nationale des Antiquaires de France, Paris
HABS	— Historic American Buildings Survey, U.S. Library of Congress, Washington, D.C.	MAGWien	— Mitteilungen der anthropologischen Gesellschaft in Wien, Vienna
HBr	— P. Herrmann, F. Bruckmann, Denkmäler der Malerei des Altertums, Munich, 1907	Mâle, I	— E. Mâle, L'art religieux du XIIe siècle en France, Paris, 1928
Helbig-Amelung	— W. Helbig, W. Amelung, E. Reisch, F. Weege, Führer durch die öffentlichen Sammlungen klassischer Altertümer in Rom, Leipzig, 1912-13	Mâle, II	— E. Mâle, L'art religieux du XIIIe siècle en France, Paris, 1925
		Mâle, III	— E. Mâle, L'art religieux de la fin du moyen-âge en France, Paris, 1925
HIPBC	— A Handbook for Travellers in India, Pakistan, Burma and Ceylon, London, 1955	Mâle, IV	— E. Mâle, L'art religieux après le Concile de Trente, Paris, 1932
HJAS	— Harvard Journal of Asiatic Studies, Cambridge, Mass.	MALinc	— Monumenti Antichi dell'Accademia dei Lincei, Milan, Rome
Hoppin, Bf	— J. C. Hoppin, A Handbook of Greek Black-figured Vases with a Chapter on the Red-figured Southern Italian Vases, Paris, 1924	Mattingly-Sydenham	— H. Mattingly, E. Sydenham, C. H. V. Sutherland, The Roman Imperial Coinage, London
Hoppin, Rf	— J. C. Hoppin, A Handbook of Attic Red-figured Vases Signed by or Attributed to the Various Masters of the Sixth and Fifth Centuries B.C., Cambridge, 1919	MdI	— Mitteilungen des deutschen archäologischen Instituts, Munich
		MdIK	— Mitteilungen des deutschen Instituts für ägyptische Altertumskunde in Kairo, Wiesbaden
HSAI	— J. H. Steward, ed., Handbook of South American Indians, 6 vols., Bureau of American Ethnology, Bull. 143, Washington, D.C., 1946-50	Mél	— Mélanges d'Archéologie et d'Histoire (Ecole Française de Rome), Paris
		Mem. Junta Sup. Exc.	— Memoria de la Junta Superior de Excavaciones y Antigüedades, Madrid
IAE	— Internationales Archiv für Ethnographie, Leiden	MemLinc	— Memorie dell'Accademia dei Lincei, Rome
		MGH	— Monumenta Germaniae Historica, Berlin
IBAI	— Bulletin de l'Institut Archéologique Bulgare, Sofia	MIA	— Material and Research in Archaeology of the U.S.S.R., Moscow, Leningrad
IFAN	— Institut Français Afrique Noire	Michel	— A. Michel, Histoire de l'art depuis les premiers temps chrétiens jusqu'à nos jours, Paris, 1905-29
IG	— Inscriptiones Graecae, Berolini		
ILN	— Illustrated London News, London		
IPEK	— Ipek, Jahrbuch für prähistorische und ethnographische Kunst, Berlin	MInst	— Monumenti dell'Instituto di Corrispondenza Archeologica, Rome
ITTM	— Instituto Tello Tellez de Meneses, Palencia	MJhb	— Münchner Jahrbuch der bildenden Kunst, Munich
JA	— Journal Asiatique, Paris		
JAF	— Journal of American Folklore, Lancaster, Pa.	MLJ	— Modern Language Journal, St. Louis, Mo.
JAOS	— Journal of the American Oriental Society, Baltimore	MnbKw	— Monatsberichte über Kunstwissenschaft
		MPA	— Monumenti della pittura antica scoperti in Italia, Rome
JAS	— Journal of the African Society, London		
JBORS	— Journal of the Bihar and Orissa Research Society, Patna, India	MPiot	— Fondation Eugène Piot, Monuments et Mémoires, Paris
JdI	— Jahrbuch des deutschen archäologischen Instituts, Berlin	MPontAcc	— Memorie della Pontificia Accademia Romana di Archeologia, Rome
JEA	— Journal of Egyptian Archaeology, London	NBACr	— Nuovo Bullettino di Archeologia Cristiana, Rome
JhbKhSammlWien	— Jahrbuch der kunsthistorischen Sammlungen in Wien, Vienna	NChr	— Numismatic Chronicle and Journal of the Royal Numismatic Society, London
JhbPreussKSamml	— Jahrbuch der preussischen Kunstsammlungen, Berlin	NedKhJb	— Nederlandsch Kunsthistorisch Jaarboek, 1945ff.
JHS	— Journal of Hellenic Studies, London	NedMon	— De Nederlandse Monumenten van Geschiedenis en Kunst, 1911 ff.
JIAI	— Journal of Indian Art and Industry, London		

NIFAN	— Notes de l'Institut Français d'Afrique Noire, Dakar	Reinach, RV	— S. Reinach, Répertoire des Vases peints, grecs et étrusques, Paris, I, 1899; II, 1900
NR	— Numismatic Review, New York	REL	— Revue des Etudes Latines, Paris
NSc	— Notizie degli Scavi di Antichità, Rome	RendAccIt	— Rendiconti della R. Accademia d'Italia, Rome
NZ	— Numismatische Zeitschrift, Vienna	RendLinc	— Rendiconti dell'Accademia dei Lincei, Rome
OAZ	— Ostasiatische Zeitschrift, Vienna	RendNapoli	— Rendiconti dell'Accademia di Archeologia di Napoli, Naples
OIP	— Oriental Institute Publications, Chicago	RendPontAcc	— Rendiconti della Pontificia Accademia Romana di Archeologia, Rome
ÖJh	— Jahreshefte des Österreichischen archäologischen Instituts, Vienna		
ÖKT	— Österreichische Kunsttopographie, Vienna	RepfKw	— Repertorium für Kunstwissenschaft, Berlin, Stuttgart
OMLeiden	— Oudheidkundige Mededeelingen van het Rijksmuseum van Oudheten te Leiden, Leiden	REthn	— Revue d'Ethnographie, Paris
OpA	— Opuscola Archaeologica, Lund	RhMus	— Rheinisches Museum für Philologie, Frankfort on the Main
OTNE	— Old Time New England; the Bulletin of the Society for the Preservation of New England Antiquities, Boston, Massachusetts, I, 1910	RIASA	— Rivista dell'Istituto d'Archeologia e Storia dell'Arte, Rome
		RIE	— Revista de Ideas Estéticas, Madrid
OudJb	— Oudheidkundig Jaarboek, Leiden	RIN	— Rivista Italiana di Numismatica, Rome
Overbeck, SQ	— J. Overbeck, Die antiken Schriftquellen zur Geschichte der bildenden Künste bei den Griechen, Leipzig, 1868; reprint, Hildesheim, 1958	RlDKg	— Reallexicon zur deutschen Kunstgeschichte, Stuttgart, 1937
		RLV	— M. Ebert, Real-Lexicon der Vorgeschichte, Berlin, 1924-32
Oxy. Pap.	— The Oxyrhynchus Papyri, by B. P. Grenfell, A. S. Hunt, H. I. Bell et al., eds., London, 1898 ff.	RM	— Mitteilungen des deutschen archäologischen Instituts, Römische Abteilung, Berlin
ΠΑΕ	— Πρακτικά τῆς ἐν Ἀθήναις Ἀρχαιολογικῆς Ἑταιρίας, Athens	RN	— Revue Numismatique, Paris
		RNA	— Revista Nacional de Arquitectura, Madrid
PEQ	— Palestine Exploration Quarterly, London	Robert, SR	— C. Robert, Die antiken Sarkophag-Reliefs, Berlin, 1890 ff.
Perrot-Chipiez	— G. Perrot, C. Chipiez, Histoire de l'art dans l'Antiquité, Paris, I, 1882; II, 1884; III, 1885; IV, 1887; V, 1890; VI, 1894; VII, 1898; VIII, 1903; IX, 1911	Roscher	— W. H. Roscher, Ausführliches Lexikon der griechischen und römischen Mythologie, Leipzig, 1884-86; 1924-37
Pfuhl	— E. Pfuhl, Malerei und Zeichnung der Griechen, Munich, 1923	RQ	— Römische Quartalschrift, Freiburg
PG	— J. P. Migne, Patrologiae cursus completus, Series Graeca, 162 vols., with Latin trans., Paris, 1857-66	RScPr	— Rivista di Scienze Preistoriche, Florence
		RSLig	— Rivista di Studi Liguri, Bordighera, Italy
		RSO	— Rivista degli Studi Orientali, Rome
		Rumpf, MZ	— A. Rumpf, Malerei und Zeichnung (W. Otto, Handbuch der Archäologie, IV, 1), Munich, 1953
Picard	— C. Picard, Manuel d'Archéologie, La Sculpture, Paris, I, 1935; II, 1939; III, 1948; IV, 1, 1954	RUO	— Revista de la Universidad de Oviedo
PL	— J. P. Migne, Patrologiae cursus completus, Series Latina, 221 vols., Paris, 1844-64	SA	— Soviet Archaeology, Moscow, Leningrad
		SAA	— Seminario de Arte Aragonés, Zaragoza
PM	— B. Porter and R. L. B. Moss, Topographical Bibliography of Ancient Egyptian Hieroglyphic Texts, Reliefs and Paintings, 7 vols., Oxford, 1927-51, 2d ed., 1960 ff.	SbBerlin	— Sitzungsberichte der preussischen Akademie der Wissenschaften, Berlin
		SbHeidelberg	— Sitzungsberichte der Akademie der Wissenschaften zu Heidelberg, Heidelberg
Porter	— A. Kingsley Porter, Romanesque Sculpture of the Pilgrimage Roads, Boston, 1923	SbMünchen	— Sitzungsberichte der bayerischen Akademie der Wissenschaften zu München, Munich
Post	— Charles Post, A History of Spanish Painting, 10 vols., Cambridge, Mass., 1930 ff.	SbWien	— Sitzungsberichte der Akademie der Wissenschaften in Wien, Vienna
ProcPrSoc	— Proceedings of the Prehistoric Society, Cambridge	Schlosser	— J. Schlosser, La letteratura artistica, Florence, 1956
PSI	— Pubblicazioni della Società Italiana per la ricerca dei papiri greci e latini in Egitto, Florence, 1912 ff.	Scranton, Greek Walls	— R. L. Scranton, Greek Walls, Cambridge, Mass., 1941
		SEtr	— Studi Etruschi, Florence
QCr	— Quaderni della Critica, Bari	SNR	— Sudan Notes and Records, Khartoum
RA	— Revue Archéologique, Paris	SPA	— A Survey of Persian Art, ed. A. U. Pope and P. Ackerman, Oxford, 1938
RAA	— Revue des Arts Asiatiques, Paris		
RAAB	— Revista de la Asociacion Artístico-Arqueológica Barcelonesa, Barcelona	SymbOsl	— Symbolae Osloenses, Oslo
		Tebtunis	— The Tebtunis Papyri, B. P. Grenfell, A. S. Hunt, et al., eds., London, 1902 ff.
RABM	— Revista de Archivos, Bibliotecas y Museos, Madrid	ThB	— U. Thieme, F. Becker, Künstler Lexikon, Leipzig, 1907-50
RACr	— Rivista di Archeologia Cristiana, Rome	TitAM	— Tituli Asiae Minoris, Vindobonae, 1901-44
RArte	— Rivista d'Arte, Florence	TNR	— Tanganyika Notes and Records, Dar-es-Salaam
RArts	— Revue des arts, Paris	Toesca, Md	— P. Toesca, Il Medioevo, 2 vols., Turin, 1927
RBib	— Revue Biblique, Paris	Toesca, Tr	— P. Toesca, Il Trecento, Turin, 1951
RCHS	— Records of the Columbia Historical Society, Washington, D.C., I, 1897	TP	— T'oung Pao, Leiden
		UCalPAAE	— University of California, Publications in American Archaeology and Ethnology, Berkeley
RDK	— Reallexicon zur deutschen Kunstgeschichte, Stuttgart, 1937 ff.	USMB	— United States National Museum, Bulletin, Washington, D.C.
RE	— A. Pauly, G. Wissowa, Real-Enzyklopädie der klassischen Altertumswissenschaft, Stuttgart, 1894 ff.	Van Marle	— R. van Marle, The Development of the Italian Schools of Painting, The Hague, 1923-38
REA	— Revue des Etudes Anciennes, Bordeaux	Vasari	— G. Vasari, Vite, ed. Milanesi, Florence, 1878 ff. (Am. ed., trans. E. H. and E. W. Blashfield and A. A. Hopkins, 4 vols., New York, 1913)
REByz	— Revue des Etudes Byzantines, Paris		
REE	— Revista des Estudios Extremesios, Badajoz		
REG	— Revue des Etudes Grecques, Paris	Venturi	— A. Venturi, Storia dell'Arte Italiana, Milan, 1901 ff.
Reinach, RP	— S. Reinach, Répertoire des Peintures Grecques et Romaines, Paris, 1922	VFPA	— Viking Fund Publications in Anthropology, New York
Reinach, RR	— S. Reinach, Répertoire des Reliefs Grecs et Romains, Paris, I, 1909; II and III, 1912	Vollmer	— H. Vollmer, Allgemeines Lexikon der bildenden Künstler des XX. Jahrhunderts, Leipzig, 1953
Reinach, RS	— S. Reinach, Répertoire de la Statuaire Grecque et Romaine, Paris, I, 1897; II, 1, 1897; II, 2, 1898; III, 1904; IV, 1910	Warburg	— Journal of the Warburg and Courtauld Institutes, London

Weickert, Archaische Architektur	C. Weickert, Typen der archaischen Architektur in Griechenland und Kleinasien, Augsburg, 1929
Wpr	— Winckelmannsprogramm, Berlin
WürzbJ	— Würzburger Jahrbücher für die Altertumswissenschaft, Würzburg
WVDOG	— Wissenschaftliche Veröffentlichungen der Deutschen Orient-Gesellschaft, Leipzig, Berlin
ZäS	— Zeitschrift für ägyptische Sprache und Altertumskunde, Berlin, Leipzig
ZfAssyr	— Zeitschrift für Assyriologie, Strasbourg
ZfbK	— Zeitschrift für bildende Kunst, Leipzig
ZfE	— Zeitschrift für Ethnologie, Berlin
ZfKg	— Zeitschrift für Kunstgeschichte, Munich
ZfKw	— Zeitschrift für Kunstwissenschaft, Munich
ZfN	— Zeitschrift für Numismatik, Berlin
ZfSAKg	— Zeitschrift für schweizerische Archäologie und Kunstgeschichte, Basel
ZMG	— Zeitschrift der deutschen morgenländischen Gesellschaft, Leipzig
ZSAKg	— Zeitschrift für schweizerische Archäologie und Kunstgeschichte, Basel

Languages and Ethnological Descriptions

Alb.	— Albanian
Am.	— American
Ang.	— Anglice, Anglicized
Ar.	— Arabic
Arm.	— Armenian
AS.	— Anglo-Saxon
Bab.	— Babylonian
Br.	— British
Bulg.	— Bulgarian
Chin.	— Chinese
D.	— Dutch
Dan.	— Danish
Eg.	— Egyptian
Eng.	— English
Finn.	— Finnish
Fr.	— French
Ger.	— German
Gr.	— Greek
Heb.	— Hebrew
Hung.	— Hungarian
It.	— Italian
Jap.	— Japanese
Jav.	— Javanese
Lat.	— Latin
Mod. Gr.	— Modern Greek
Nor.	— Norwegian
Per.	— Persian
Pol.	— Polish
Port.	— Portuguese
Rum.	— Rumanian
Rus.	— Russian
Skr.	— Sanskrit
Sp.	— Spanish
Swed.	— Swedish
Yugo.	— Yugoslav

Other Abbreviations (Standard abbreviations in common usage are omitted.)

Abh.	— Abhandlungen
Acad.	— Academy, Académie
Acc.	— Accademia
Adm.	— Administration
Ak.	— Akademie
Allg.	— Allgemein
Alm.	— Almanacco
Amm.	— Amministrazione
Ann.	— Annals, Annali, Annuario, Annual, etc.
Ant.	— Antiquity, Antico, Antiquaire, etc.
Anthr.	— Anthropology, etc.
Antr.	— Antropologia, etc.
Anz.	— Anzeiger
Arch.	— Architecture, Architettura, Architettonico, etc.; Archives
Archaeol.	— Archaeology, etc.
attrib.	— attributed
Aufl.	— Auflage
Aufn.	— Aufnahme
B.	— Bulletin, Bollettino, etc.
b.	— born
Belg.	— Belgian, Belga, etc.
Berl.	— Berlin, Berliner
Bern.	— Berner
Bib.	— Bible, Biblical, Bibliothèque, etc.
Bibliog.	— Bibliography, etc.
Bur.	— Bureau
Byz.	— Byzantine
C.	— Corpus
ca.	— circa
Cah.	— Cahiers
Cal.	— Calendar
Cap.	— Capital, Capitolium
Cat.	— Catalogue, Catalogo, etc.
Chr.	— Chronicle, Chronik
Civ.	— Civiltà, Civilization, etc.
cod.	— codex
col., cols.	— column, columns
Coll.	— Collection, Collana, Collationes, Collectanea, Collezione, etc.
Comm.	— Commentaries, Commentari, Communications, etc.
Cong.	— Congress, Congresso, etc.
Cr.	— Critica
Cron.	— Cronaca
Cuad.	— Cuadernos
Cult.	— Culture, Cultura, etc.
D.	— Deutsch
d.	— died
Diss.	— Dissertation, Dissertazione
Doc.	— Documents, etc.
E.	— Encyclopedia, etc.
Eccl.	— Ecclesiastic, Ecclesia, etc.
Ep.	— Epigraphy
Esp.	— España, Español
Est.	— Estudios
Et.	— Etudes
Ethn.	— Ethnology, Ethnography, Ethnographie, etc.
Etn.	— Etnico, Etnografia, etc.
Etnol.	— Etnologia
Eur.	— Europe, Europa, etc.
ext.	— extract
f.	— für
fasc.	— fascicle
Fil.	— Filologia
Filos.	— Filosofia, Filosofico
fol.	— folio
Forsch.	— Forschung, Forschungen
Gal.	— Galerie
Gall.	— Gallery, Galleria
Geog.	— Geography, Geografia, Geographical, etc.
Giorn.	— Giornale
H.	— History, Historie, etc.
hl.	— heilig, heilige
Holl.	— Hollandisch, etc.
Hum.	— Humanity, Humana, etc.
I.	— Istituto
Ill.	— Illustration, Illustrato, Illustrazione, etc.
Ind.	— Index, Indice, Indicatore, etc.
Inf.	— Information, Informazione, etc.
Inst.	— Institute, Institut, Instituto, etc.
Int.	— International, etc.
Ist.	— Istituto
J.	— Journal
Jb.	— Jaarboek
Jhb.	— Jahrbuch
Jhrh.	— Jahreshefte
K.	— Kunst
Kat.	— Katalog
Kchr.	— Kunstchronik
Kg.	— Kunstgeschichte
Kunsthist.	— Kunsthistorische
Kw.	— Kunstwissenschaft
Lett.	— Letteratura, Lettere
Lib.	— Library
ling.	— linguistica, lingua, etc.
Lit.	— Literary, Literarische, Littéraire, etc.
Mag.	— Magazine
Med.	— Medieval, Medievale, etc.
Meded.	— Mededeelingen
Mél.	— Mélanges
Mém.	— Mémoire

Mem.	— Memorie, Memoirs	Rend.	— Rendiconti
Min.	— Minerva	Rép.	— Répertoire
Misc.	— Miscellany, Miscellanea, etc.	Rep.	— Report, Repertorio, Repertorium
Mit.	— Mitteilungen	Rev.	— Review, Revue, etc.
Mnb.	— Monatsberichte	Rl.	— Reallexicon
Mnbl.	— Monatsblätter	Rom.	— Roman, Romano, Romanico, etc.
Mnh.	— Monatshefte	rv.	— reverse
Mod.	— Modern, Moderno, etc.	S.	— San, Santo, Santa (saint)
Mon.	— Monuments, Monumento	S.	— Studi, Studies, etc.
Münch.	— München, Münchner	Samml.	— Sammlung, Sammlungen
Mus.	— Museum, Museo, Musée, Museen, etc.	Sc.	— Science, Scienza, Scientific, etc.
Muz.	— Muzeum	Schr.	— Schriften
N.	— New, Notizia, etc.	Schw.	— Schweitzer
Nachr.	— Nachrichten	Script.	— Scriptorium
Nat.	— National, etc.	Sitzb.	— Sitzungsberichte
Naz.	— Nazionale	s.l.	— in its place
Notit. dign.	— Notitia Dignitatum	Soc.	— Social, Society, Società, Sociale, etc.
N.S.	— new series	Spec.	— Speculum
O.	— Oriental, Orient, etc.	SS.	— Saints, Sante, Santi, Santissima
Ö.	— Österreichische	St.	— Saint
obv.	— obverse	Sta	— Santa (holy)
öffentl.	— öffentlich	Ste	— Sainte
Op.	— Opuscolo	Sto	— Santo (holy)
Pap.	— Papers, Papyrus	Sup.	— Supplement, Supplemento
per.	— period	s.v.	— under the word
Per.	— Periodical, Periodico	Tech.	— Technical, Technology, etc.
Pin.	— Pinacoteca	Tecn.	— Tecnica, Tecnico
Pr.	— Prehistory, Preistoria, Preystori, Préhistoire	Tr.	— Transactions
Proc.	— Proceedings	trans.	— translator, translated, etc.
Pub.	— Publication, Publicación	Trav.	— Travaux
Pubbl.	— Pubblicazione	u.	— und
Q.	— Quarterly, Quaderno	Um.	— Umanesimo
Quel.	— Quellen	Univ.	— University, Università, Université, etc.
R.	— Rivista	Urb.	— Urban, Urbanistica
r	— recto	v	— verso
r.	— reigned	VAT	— Vorderasiatische Tafen
Racc.	— Raccolta	Verh.	— Verhandlungen, Verhandelingen
Rass.	— Rassegna	Verz.	— Verzeichnis
Rec.	— Recueil	Vf.	— Verfasser
Recens.	— Recensione	Wien.	— Wiener
Rech.	— Recherches	Yb.	— Yearbook
Rel.	— Relazione	Z.	— Zeitschrift, Zeitung, etc.

NOTES ON THE ENGLISH EDITION

Standards of Translation. Contributors to the Encyclopedia, drawn from the outstanding authorities of over 35 different countries, have written in many languages — Italian, Spanish, French, German, Russian, etc. To ensure faithful translation of the author's thought, all articles have been translated into English from the original language, checked for the accuracy of technical terms and accepted English forms of nomenclature by English and American art historians, and correlated with the final editorial work of the Italian edition for uniformity and coherence of the over-all presentation. Naturally the McGraw-Hill Book Company, Inc., assumes full responsibility for the accuracy and completeness of all translations. Those articles written in English appear in the words and style of the authors, within the bounds of editorial attention to consistency and stylistic and organizational unity of the work as a whole. Article titles are in most cases parallel to those in the Italian edition, though occasionally they have been simplified, as *Dravidian Art* for *Dravidiche Correnti e Tradizioni*.

New Features. Although generally the English-language edition corresponds to the Italian version, a small number of purely editorial changes have been made in the interest of clear English-language alphabetization and occasional deletions or amplifications solely in the interest of clarity. Three major differences between the two editions do exist, however:

A considerable number of cross-references have been added in many places where it was felt that relating the subject under consideration to other pertinent articles would be of value to the reader.

A more extensive article on the Art of the Americas was projected for Volume One of the English edition with an entirely new text and many plates in black and white and color. This article was designed to give the completest possible coverage within the existing space of some 100,000 words to a subject which, because of its interest to the English-speaking public, was entrusted to a group of well-known American scholars, each expert in his respective area.

Some 300 separate short biographies have been added to the English edition to provide ready access to data on the lives, works, and critical acceptance of certain artists identified with schools, movements, and broad categories of historical development that are treated in the longer monographic articles. These articles are unillustrated, but works of the artists are represented in the plates accompanying the longer articles.

Bibliographies. The bibliographies of the original Italian edition have been amplified at times to include titles of special interest to the English-speaking world and English-language editions of works originally published in other languages.

In undertaking these adaptations of the Italian text and preparing original material for the English edition, the publisher has been aided by the generous advice and, in many cases, collaboration of the members of the Editorial Advisory Committee.

CONTRIBUTORS TO VOLUME IX

Bianca Maria ALFIERI, University of Rome
Rosalba AMERIO, Soprintendenza ai Monumenti del Piemonte
Olga AMMAN, Rome
Paolo Enrico ARIAS, University of Pisa
Umberto BALDINI, Director, Soprintendenza alle Gallerie di Firenze
Luisa BECHERUCCI, Director, Galleria degli Uffizi, Florence
John BECKWITH, Deputy Keeper, Department of Architecture and Sculpture, Victoria and Albert Museum, London
Fernand BENOIT, Membre de l'Institut; Director, Antiquités de Provence; Curator, Musée Borély, Marseilles
Ignacio BERNAL, Instituto Nacional de Antropologia e Historia, Cordova
Maurice BESSET, Curator, Musée National d'Art Moderne, Paris
Vincenzo BONELLO, Valletta, Malta
Karel G. BOON, Curator, Cabinet des Estampes, Rijksmuseum, Amsterdam
Evelina BOREA, Rome
Sergio BOSTICCO, University of Florence
Ernest H. BRANDL, University of Notre Dame, South Bend, Ind.
Luigi BERNABÒ BREA, Superintendent of Antiquities, Syracuse, Sicily
Anna Maria BRIZIO, University of Milan
Allen BROOKS, University of Toronto
Mario BUSSAGLI, University of Rome
Michelangelo CAGIANO DE AZEVEDO, Università Cattolica del Sacro Cuore, Milan
James CAHILL, Associate Curator of Chinese Art, Freer Gallery of Art, Washington, D.C.
Ernesta CERULLI, University of Rome
Marco CHIARINI, Rome
Sir Kenneth CLARK, Chairman, Arts Council of Great Britain, London
George CŒDÈS, Honorary Director, Ecole Française d'Extrême-Orient, Paris
Herbert H. COGHLAN, Curator, Borough Museum, Newbury, England
Paul COLLART, Director, Swiss Institute, Rome
Enrico CRISPOLTI, Rome
Valentin DENIS, University of Louvain
† Waldemar DEONNA, Geneva
Dario DURBÉ, Rome
Mircea ELIADE, University of Chicago
William FAGG, Department of Ethnography, British Museum, London
Otto H. FÖRSTER, University of Cologne, Generaldirektor der Museen
Francesco GABRIELI, University of Rome
Giovanni GARBINI, University of Rome
Eugenio GARIN, University of Florence
Kenneth GARLICK, Assistant Curator, The Barber Institute of Fine Arts, Birmingham, England
Hermann GOETZ, University of Heidelberg
Vinigi L. GROTTANELLI, Pontificium Athenaeum Urbanianum de Propaganda Fide, Rome
Bo GYLLENSVÄRD, Museum of Far Eastern Antiquities, Stockholm
Madeleine HALLADE, Musée Guimet, Paris
Louis HAMBIS, Ecole Pratique des Hautes-Etudes, Sorbonne, Paris
† Gustav F. HARTLAUB, late Director Emeritus, Städtische Kunsthalle, Mannheim
Louis HAUTECOEUR, Secretary, Institut de France; Académie des Beaux-Arts, Paris
John F. HAYWARD, Deputy Keeper, Victoria and Albert Museum, London

Hamilton HAZLEHURST, University of Georgia, Athens, Ga.
Julius S. HELD, Barnard College, Columbia University, New York
Robert L. HERBERT, Yale University, New Haven, Conn.
Ludwig H. HEYDENREICH, University of Munich; Director, Zentralinstitut für Kunstgeschichte, Munich
Henry-Russell HITCHCOCK, Smith College, Northampton, Mass.
Henry R. Hope, Indiana University, Bloomington, Ind.
Thomas HOWARTH, Director, School of Architecture, University of Toronto
Michael KITSON, Courtauld Institute of Art, London
Carlo KOVACEVICH, Rome
Niko KURET, Slovenian Folklore Institute, Ljubljana, Yugoslavia
Sherman E. LEE, Director, Cleveland Museum of Art
Lionello LANCIOTTI, University of Rome
Jean LEYMARIE, Universities of Geneva and Lausanne
Giovanni LILLIU, University of Cagliari, Sardinia
Hans Peter L'ORANGE, University of Oslo; Director, Norwegian Institute of Rome
Bates LOWRY, Brown University, Providence, R.I.
John W. McCOUBREY, University of Pennsylvania, Philadelphia
Corrado MALTESE, University of Cagliari, Sardinia
Juan MALUQUER DE MOTES, University of Barcelona
Caterina MARCENARO, Director, Belle Arti del Comune, Genoa
Leonard MASON, Chairman, Department of Anthropology, University of Hawaii, Honolulu
Paolo MATTHIAE, Rome
A. Hyatt MAYOR, Metropolitan Museum of Art, New York
Jennifer MONTAGU, Campden Hill, England
Anton MOORTGAT, Freie Universität, Berlin
Sabatino MOSCATI, University of Rome
Peter MURRAY, Courtauld Institute of Art, London
Bernard S. MYERS, formerly, The City College, New York
Francesco NEGRI ARNOLDI, Rome
Paul F. NORTON, University of Massachusetts, Amherst
Giovanni PACCAGNINI, Superintendent of Galleries for the provinces of Mantua, Verona, and Cremona
François-Georges PARISET, University of Bordeaux
Nikolaus PEVSNER, Birbeck College, University of London
Mary PITTALUGA, University of Florence
Nello PONENTE, Rome
Jean PORCHER, Curator in Chief, Cabinet des Manuscrits, Paris
Antonio PRIORI, Rome
Margaretta M. SALINGER, Metropolitan Museum of Art, New York
Mario SALMI, University of Rome
Fritz SCHACHERMEYR, University of Vienna
Karl SCHEFOLD, University of Basel
Dominik SCHRÖDER, Nanzan University, Nagoya, Japan
Farid SHĀFI'Ī, Cairo
Curtis SHELL, Wellesley College, Wellesley, Mass.
Erik SJÖQVIST, Princeton University, Princeton, N.J.
Michael SULLIVAN, School of Oriental and African Studies, University of London
Adolfo TAMBURELLO, Istituto Italiano per il Medio ed Estremo Oriente, Rome
Herbert TISCHNER, Curator of Oceanic Art, Museum für Völkerkunde und Vorgeschichte, Hamburg
Charles DE TOLNAY, Columbia University, New York
Francesco VALCANOVER, Director, Gallerie dell'Accademia, Venice
Martin WEINBERGER, Institute of Fine Arts, New York University, New York
Allen S. WELLER, University of Illinois, Urbana, Ill.
Paul S. WINGERT, Columbia University, New York

ACKNOWLEDGMENTS

The Institute for Cultural Collaboration and the publishers express their thanks to the collectors and to the directors of the museums and galleries listed below for permission to reproduce works in their collections and for the photographs supplied.

The Institute also acknowledges the kind permission of H. M. Queen Elizabeth II to reproduce works belonging to the Crown.

AGRIGENTO, Sicily, Museo Civico Archeologico
AIX-EN-PROVENCE, France, Musée Granet
ALEPPO, Syria, Musée National
AMMAN, Jordan, Museum
AMSTERDAM, Koninklijk Instituut voor de Tropen
AMSTERDAM, Rijksmuseum
AMSTERDAM, Stedelijk Museum
ANKARA, Archaeological Museum
ANTWERP, Ethnografisch Museum
ANTWERP, Musée Royal des Beaux-Arts
AREZZO, Italy, Museo Archeologico
ATHENS, National Museum

BAGHDAD, Iraq Museum
BALTIMORE, Museum of Art, Cone Coll.
BALTIMORE, Walters Art Gallery
BARCELONA, Gabinete Numismático de Cataluña
BARCELONA, Museo Arqueológico
BASEL, A. G. Ciba Foundation
BASEL, Coll. Marguerite Arp-Hagenbach
BASEL, Kunstmuseum, Kupferstichkabinett
BASEL, Museum für Völkerkunde
BASEL, Öffentliche Kunstsammlung
BASEL, Schweizerisches Museum für Volkskunde
BERGAMO, Italy, Accademia Carrara
BERLIN, Kupferstichkabinett
BERLIN, Museum für Völkerkunde
BERLIN, Staatliche Museen
BERN, Historisches Museum
BOLOGNA, Metropolitana
BOLOGNA, Museo Civico
BOLOGNA, Palazzo dell'Università, Accademia delle Scienze
BOLOGNA, Pinacoteca Nazionale
BOMBAY, Prince of Wales Museum
BOSTON, Museum of Fine Arts
BREMEN, Kunsthalle
BREMEN, Übersee-Museum
BRESCIA, Italy, Museo Cristiano
BRUGES, Musée Memling
BRUSSELS, Musées Royaux d'Art et d'Histoire
BUCHAREST, Archaeological Museum
BUDAPEST, National Museum
BUFFALO, N. Y., Albright-Knox Art Gallery

CAGLIARI, Sardinia, Museo Archeologico Nazionale
CAIRO, Museum of Islamic Art
CALCUTTA, Indian Museum

CAMBRIDGE, England, University Museum of Archaeology and Ethnology
CAMBRIDGE, Mass., Peabody Museum of Archaeology and Ethnology
CHANTILLY, France, Musée Condé
CHARTRES, Cathedral Treasury
CHICAGO, Art Institute
CHICAGO, A. Maremont Coll.
CINCINNATI, Art Museum
CITTÀ DI CASTELLO, Italy, Museo Capitolare
COLOGNE, Wallraf-Richartz-Museum
COLORADO SPRINGS, Fine Arts Center, Taylor Museum
COPENHAGEN, Nationalmuseet
COPENHAGEN, Ny Carlsberg Glyptotek
COPENHAGEN, Statens Museum for Kunst
CORINTH, Archaeological Museum
CORTONA, Italy, Museo dell'Accademia Etrusca
CRACOW, Poland, Czartoryski Museum
CREMA, Italy, Coll. Stramezzi

DARMSTADT, Germany, Landesmuseum
DELPHI, Greece, Archaeological Museum
DENVER, Art Museum
DETROIT, Institute of Arts

EDINBURGH, Royal Scottish Museum

FLORENCE, Accademia
FLORENCE, Casa Buonarroti
FLORENCE, Coll. Contini Bonacossi
FLORENCE, Coll. Nardini
FLORENCE, Coll. Ojetti
FLORENCE, Galleria d'Arte Moderna
FLORENCE, Museo Archeologico
FLORENCE, Museo Nazionale
FLORENCE, Museo Nazionale di Antropologia e Etnologia
FLORENCE, Museo dell'Opera del Duomo
FLORENCE, Museo Stibbert
FLORENCE, Pitti
FLORENCE, Uffizi
FRANKFORT ON THE MAIN, Städelsches Kunstinstitut

GENOA, Galleria di Palazzo Bianco
GENOA, Palazzo Doria-Pamphili
GLASGOW, Art Gallery and Museum
GÖTEBORG, Sweden, Coll. G. Trädgårdh

HAMBURG, Museum für Kunst und Gewerbe
HAMBURG, Museum für Völkerkunde
HAMPTON COURT, England, Royal Colls.
HANOI, North Vietnam, Museum
HANOVER, Germany, Kestner-Museum
HERAKLION, Crete, Archaeological Museum
HILDESHEIM, Germany, Cathedral Treasury
HONOLULU, Bernice P. Bishop Museum
HONOLULU, L. Mason Coll.
HONOLULU, R. Sparks Coll.

IESI, Italy, Pinacoteca Comunale
ISTANBUL, Archaeological Museums

JERUSALEM, Jordan, Palestine Archaeological Museum

LA SPEZIA, Italy, Museo Archeologico Lunense
LEIDEN, Netherlands, Rijksmuseum
LEIDEN, Stedelijk Museum "De Lakenhal"
LEIPZIG, Museum der bildenden Künste
LEIPZIG, Museum des Kunsthandwerks
LENINGRAD, The Hermitage
LIPARI, Italy, Museo Eoliano
LISBON (Belém), Museu Etnológico
LJUBLJANA, Yugoslavia, National Museum
LONDON, British Museum
LONDON, Courtauld Institute Galleries
LONDON, National Gallery
LONDON, Royal Academy of Arts
LONDON, Tate Gallery
LONDON, Victoria and Albert Museum
LONDON, Wallace Coll.
LYONS, Musée des Beaux-Arts

MADRID, Museo Arqueológico Nacional
MADRID, Prado
MARSEILLES, Musée Archéologique
MATERA, Italy, Museo Nazionale
MATHURA, India, Archaeological Museum
MESSINA, Sicily, Museo Nazionale
MEXICO CITY, Museo Nacional de Antropologia
MILAN, Museo di S. Ambrogio
MILAN, Biblioteca Ambrosiana
MILAN, Brera
MILAN, Castello Sforzesco
MILAN, Coll. Cavallini
MILAN, Coll. Falck
MILAN, Coll. Jucker
MILAN, Museo Poldi Pezzoli
MILAN, Museo Teatrale alla Scala
MIYAGINO, Kanagawa, Japan, Hakone Art Museum
MODENA, Italy, Galleria Estense
MONZA, Italy, Cathedral Treasury
MONZA, Italy, Coll. M. Modorati
MUNICH, Alte Pinakothek
MUNICH, Bayerisches Nationalmuseum
MUNICH, Museum für Völkerkunde
MUNICH, Residenzmuseum

NANCY, France, Musée Historique Lorrain
NANTES, France, Musée des Beaux-Arts
NAPLES, Museo di Capodimonte
NAPLES, Museo Nazionale
NARA, Japan, Hōryūji
NARA, Tōdaiji
NEW DELHI, National Museum of India
NEW YORK, American Museum of Natural History
NEW YORK, Brooklyn Museum
NEW YORK, Coll. W. P. Chrysler, Jr.
NEW YORK, Metropolitan Museum
NEW YORK, Metropolitan Museum, the Cloisters
NEW YORK, Minkenhof Coll.
NEW YORK, Museum of the American Indian, Heye Foundation
NEW YORK, Museum of Modern Art
NEW YORK, Pierpont Morgan Library
NEW YORK, H. C. Weng Coll.
NICE, Musée Masséna (depôt de l'État)
NÜRNBERG, Germany, Germanisches National-Museum

ORVIETO, Italy, Museo dell'Opera del Duomo
OXFORD, England, Ashmolean Museum
OXFORD, England, Pitt Rivers Museum

PADUA, A. Sartori
PADUA, Museo Civico
PALERMO, Sicily, Cappella Palatina
PALERMO, Sicily, Museo Nazionale Archeologico
PARIS, Bibliothèque de l'Arsenal
PARIS, Bibliothèque Nationale
PARIS, Cabinet des Médailles
PARIS, Coll. D.B.C.
PARIS, Coll. Fukushima
PARIS, C. T. Loo & Cie
PARIS, Louvre
PARIS, Musée d'Art Moderne
PARIS, Musée des Arts Decoratifs
PARIS, Musée de Cluny
PARIS, Musée de l'Homme
PARIS, Musée Guimet
PARMA, Italy, Galleria Nazionale
PEKING, Hui-hua-kuan
PEKING, Palace Museum
PERUGIA, Italy, Musei Civici
PHILADELPHIA, University Museum
PIACENZA, Italy, Museo Civico
PISA, Museo Nazionale
POMPEII, Antiquarium

REIMS, Cathedral Treasury
REIMS, Musée des Beaux-Arts
RENNES, France, Musée des Beaux-Arts
ROME, Capitoline Museum
ROME, Coll. Giustiniani-Scola-Camerini
ROME, Gabinetto Nazionale delle Stampe
ROME, Galleria d'Arte Moderna
ROME, Galleria Borghese
ROME, Galleria Colonna
ROME, Galleria Doria Pamphili
ROME, Galleria Nazionale
ROME, Galleria Spada
ROME, Lateran Museums
ROME, Museo della Civiltà Romana
ROME, Museo dei Conservatori
ROME, Museo Nazionale delle Arti e Tradizioni Popolari
ROME, Museo Nazionale Romano
ROME, Museo Pigorini
ROME, Museo di Villa Giulia
ROME, Palazzo Pallavicini-Rospigliosi
ROME, Pinacoteca Capitolina
ROME, Vatican Library
ROME, Vatican Museums

ST. LOUIS, Coll. Washington University
SALEM, Mass., Peabody Museum
SEATTLE, Thomas Burke Memorial Washington State Museum
SHIGA, Japan, Jinshoji
SIENA, Italy, Museo dell'Opera del Duomo
SIENA, Italy, Palazzo Pubblico
SIENA, Italy, Pinacoteca
SITGES, Barcelona, Spain, Museo del Cau Ferrat
SOLSONA, Spain, Museo Diocesano
STOCKHOLM, Nationalmuseum
STOCKHOLM, Statens Etnografiska Museum
STUTTGART, Linden-Museum
SULMONA, Italy, Cathedral Treasury
SYRACUSE, Sicily, Museo Archeologico Nazionale

TAICHUNG, Formosa, National Central Museum
TAICHUNG, Formosa, National Palace Museum
TARANTO, Italy, Museo Nazionale
TBILISI, U.S.S.R., Museum
TEHERAN, Foroughi Coll.
TEHERAN, Gulistan Palace, Imperial Library
THE HAGUE, Mauritshuis
TOKYO, Muromachi Coll.
TOKYO, National Museum
TOKYO, Seikado Foundation
TURIN, Galleria Sabauda
TURIN, Museo Egizio
TURVUEREN, Belgium, Musée Royal de l'Afrique Centrale

VALLETTA, Malta, Museum
VATHY, Samos, Museum
VENICE, Accademia
VENICE, Galleria Querini Stampalia

VENICE, Treasury of S. Marco
VIENNA, Albertina
VIENNA, Kunsthistorisches Museum
VIENNA, Museum für Völkerkunde
VIENNA, Nationalbibliothek
VIENNA, Nationalbibliothek, Theatersammlung
VIENNA, Naturhistorisches Museum

WASHINGTON, D.C., Freer Gallery of Art
WASHINGTON, D.C., National Gallery
WINDSOR, England, Royal Library
WOBURN ABBEY, Bedfordshire, Coll. Duke of Bedford

YOKOHAMA, K. Hara Coll.

ZAGREB, Yugoslavia, Archaeological Museum
ZURICH, Kunsthaus

PHOTOGRAPHIC CREDITS

The numbers refer to the plates. Those within parentheses indicate the sequence of subjects in composite plate pages. Italic numbers refer to photographs owned by the Institute for Cultural Collaboration.

A.C.L., Brussels: 11 (1); 250 (3); 338; 461; 462 (1, 2)
ALINARI, Florence: 5 (2); 7 (1, 2); 18 (3); 21 (2, 3); 22 (2, 3); 35 (2); 36 (1); 37 (1); 40 (1); 46; 50; 54 (1); 60; 75; 83; 87; 96; 97 (1, 3); 103 (2); 104 (2); 117 (1, 2); *144*; 145 (1, 2); *147 (1, 2)*; *149*; 158 (3); 161 (2, 3); 162 (4); 165 (3); 166 (2, 3); 167 (4); 168 (1, 2, 4); 169; 170 (4); 174 (1, 2); 186 (2); *190*; 191; *194*; 195; 196; 197; 198; *199*; 200; 201 (1, 2); 202 (2); 209 (2); 210; 219; 222 (1); 224; 225; 231 (2); 232 (2); 233 (1); 234; 260 (1); *261*; 266; 267 (1, 2); 269 (1, 2); *289*; *290*; 293 (1–3); 294 (2); *295*; 297 (4); 298 (2); 301 (2); 302 (1–4); 303 (1, 2); 307 (1–3); 308 (1, 3); 311 (2); 312 (1–3); 313 (1, 2); 314 (2); 327 (2); *334*; 335; *339*; *349*; *350*; *360* (1); 365 (1, 2, 4); *371*; *372*; 395 (2–4); 401 (2); 402; *430*; *437* (2); 488 (1); 505 (1–3); 508 (3, 4); 512 (3); 516 (2, 3); 519 (1); 524; *527*; 538 (1, 3); 539 (1)
ANDERSON, Rome: 2 (3); 3; 4 (1); 5 (1); 6 (2); 18 (2); 21 (4); 40 (2); 54 (2); 99; 115; 116; 161 (1); 192; 203 (2); 268; 297 (1, 2); 311 (1); 312 (4); 314 (1), 322 (1–3); 360 (3); 365 (3); 506; 508 (2); 518 (2); 525 (2); 526 (1, 2); 530; 531 (1–3); 532; 535 (1–3); 536 (1–3); 537; 540; 541; 542 (2)
ARCHIVIO FOTOGRAFICO DEGLI SCAVI DI POMPEI: 248 (3)
ARMONI MORETTI, Orvieto, Italy: 265
ARTE E COLORE, Milan: *121*; *122*; *125*; *126*; *176 (1, 2)*; 177 (2); *178* (4); *187*; 193; *280*; *323*; 365 (5)

BALZARINI, Milan: *172*; *227*; *228*; *235*; *236*; *237*
BANDIERI, Modena, Italy: 301 (1)
BAYERISCHE STAATSGEMÄLDESAMMLUNGEN, Munich: 374 (1)
BILDARCHIV FOTO MARBURG, Marburg: 37 (3); 162 (3); 167 (1, 2); 168 (3); 170 (3); 425; 487 (1); 507; 508 (1); 511 (3); 519 (3)
BÖHM, Osvaldo, Venice: 88 (4)
BONACASA, N., Palermo: 418 (1, 2)
BROGI, Florence: 21 (1); 191 (2); 529 (1)
BUSCH-HAUCK, Frankfort on the Main: 257 (3)

CACCO, Venice: 325 (1)
CAISSE NATIONALE DES MONUMENTS HISTORIQUES, Paris: 73 (1); 77 (2); 104 (1); 165 (2); 170 (2); 276 (2); 277 (2); 291; 317 (1, 2); 318; 319; 320 (2); 327 (1); 467; 470 (1); 474 (1, 3); 475 (3); 476; 477; 480 (1–3); 484; 509; 512 (1, 2); 520
CALZOLARI, Mantua: 298 (1)
CAMPONOGARA, Lyons: 90 (2); 103 (3)
CASKEY, John L., University of Cincinnati: 423 (1); 424 (2)
COMON PERINO, Turin: 296

DE ANTONIS, Rome: 8 (2); 9; *10*; *15 (1, 3, 4)*; 19; 20; 52; *84 (1)*; *157 (2)*; *205*; 229 (1, 2); *230*; 249 (3, 4); *279*; *300*; *309*; *324*; *329*; *330*; *343*; *344*; 359 (1); *368*; *375*; *376*; 422 (1–3); *458* (3); *459*; *460*; 500 (2); *502*; 521
DEPARTMENT OF ARCHAEOLOGY, GOVERNMENT OF INDIA, New Delhi: 178 (1)
DEUTSCHES ARCHÄOLOGISCHES INSTITUT, Athens: 49 (1, 2); 420; 500 (3); 503 (2)
DEUTSCHES ARCHÄOLOGISCHES INSTITUT, Rome: 35 (1); 55 (1); 59 (2); 80 (3)
DINGJAN, A., The Hague: 14 (1)
DRÄYER, Walter, Zurich: 352 (2)

EKBERG, O., Stockholm: 357 (2); 513
EMILE, Athens: 423 (3)
EMMER, Claudio, Milan: 232 (1); *238*; *262*
ENCICLOPEDIA DELLO SPETTACOLO, Rome: 366 (1, 2)

FARID SHAFEI: 271; 272 (1, 2); 273; 274 (1–3); 275 (1)
FARINA, Monza, Italy: 163 (1)
FIORENTINI, Venice: 213
FLEMING, London: *206*
FOTO-ATELIER BIJL, Amsterdam: 306 (1)
FOTO CELERE, Turin: 426
FOTOCIELO, Rome: 401 (1)
FOTOMERO, Urbino, Italy: 97 (2); 98
FOTOTECA ASAC BIENNALE, Venice: 398 (1, 2)
FOTOTECA UNIONE, Rome: 37 (2)
FRANCESCHI-ZODIAQUE, La Pierre Qui Vire (Yonne), France: 411 (1)

GABINETTO FOTOGRAFICO NAZIONALE, Rome: 14 (2); 15 (2); 17 (1–3); 22 (1); 70; 73 (2); 100; 146 (3); 163 (3); 204; 244 (1); 378; 379; 383 (2); 384; 538 (4)
GASPARINI, Genoa: 263 (1, 2); 264 (2)
GIACOMELLI, Venice: 396; 397 (1)
GIRAUDON, Paris: 2 (2); 8 (1); 24 (1, 2); 25 (1); 58 (1); 59 (1); 76 (3); 77 (1); 85 (4); *91*; 93 (1, 2); 94 (2); *101*; *102*; 103 (1); 110; *111*; *112*; 114; 119 (1); 124 (2); 137; 138; 139; 140; 158 (2); 160; 164 (3); *171*; 175 (3); 278; 305 (1); 306 (2); 315; 320 (1); 325 (2); 352 (1, 4); 360 (2); 385 (2); 386 (1, 2); 421 (1); 424 (1); 470 (2); *472*; 479; *481*; *482*; 485 (4); 486 (1, 2); 489 (2); 490 (1); 491 (1, 2); 496 (7); 510 (3); 517 (2); 518 (1); 529 (2); *547*

HADI, Teheran: 497 (3)
HERVÉ, Lucien, Paris: 105 (2); 106 (1–3); 107 (1, 3); 108
HEWICKER, Friederich, Kaltenkirchen, Germany: 442 (3); 445 (2); 446 (1, 2); 448 (2); 451 (1); 457 (1)
HIRMER VERLAG, Munich: 38 (1, 2); 43; 44; 45; 48; 53; 55 (2); 56; 57 (1–3); 58 (2); 59 (3, 4); 62; 63 (1); 64 (1, 2); 65 (1–3); 66; 67; 72; 74; 80 (2); 81; 84 (2, 3); 85 (2, 3); 86 (1, 2); 89 (4); 162 (1); 164 (1)

IDEAL STUDIO, Edinburgh: 248 (2)
ISTITUTO CENTRALE DEL RESTAURO, Rome: 332

KEMPTER, Munich: 12 (1); *182*; *217*; 255
KONINGSVELD, Leiden: 245

LEE, S. E., Cleveland Museum of Art: 130 (1); 389; 391
LEHNERT & LANDROCK, Cairo: 1 (2); 351

MALTA GOVERNMENT TOURIST BOARD: 427 (2–4)
MAS, Barcelona: 12 (3); 13 (1); 166 (1); 170 (1); 297 (1); 326; 406 (1, 2); 407; 408 (1–4); 409; 410 (1–5); 431; 432 (1–3); 436 (1); 516 (1); 522 (1)
MASON, Leonard, Honolulu: 543 (2); 544 (2); 548 (1)
MELLEMA, R. L., Amsterdam: 363
MEYER, Vienna: *82*; *299*; *316*; *367*
MUSÉE GUIMET, Paris: 29 (1, 2); 30; 31 (1, 2); 32 (1, 2)

Museo Correr, Venice: 185 (3)
Museum of Art, Cleveland: 130 (2); 131; 389; 390; 391; 392

Oriental Institute, University of Chicago: 468 (1, 2); 473; 475 (1); 485 (3)
Österreichische Nationalbibliothek, Vienna: 291 (2)

Perotti, Mario, Milan: 239 (1)
Photo Studios Limited, London: 123; 208
Pontificia Commissione d'Arte Sacra, Vatican City: 68 (1-3)
Pracownia Fotograficzna Museum Narodwego w Krakowie: 124 (1)

Rampazzi, Turin: 248 (1); 353
Rheinisches Bildarchiv, Cologne: 167 (3); 179 (1-3); 180 (1, 2)
Rossi, Venice: 186 (1)

Sakamoto, M., Tokyo: 128
Salcow, Cologne: 416 (1); 417 (1, 2)
Savio, Oscar, Rome: 4 (2); 33; 36 (2); 39; 41; 42; 49 (3); 51; 61; 71; 72; 81; 127; 143; 148 (2, 3); 150; 173 (1, 2); 188; 189; 211 (1, 2); 212; 216 (1-3); 222 (2); 223 (2); 250 (2); 256; 297 (3); 310; 333; 355 (2); 356 (2); 359 (2); 364; 380; 381; 382; 383 (1); 414 (2, 3); 419 (3); 429 (1, 2); 432 (4); 434 (2); 438 (2, 3); 444 (2-4); 450; 501; 523 (3); 542 (1, 3)
Scala, Florence: 183; 246; 399; 400
Schwenk, E., Vienna: 308 (4)
Scichilone, Giovanni, Rome: 69; 76 (2)
Scuola Archeologica Italiana, Athens: 422 (4)
Soprintendenza alle Antichità, Bologna: 253 (2)
Soprintendenza alle Antichità, Palermo: 440
Soprintendenza alle Antichità, Rome: 457 (2, 3)
Soprintendenza alle Antichità, Syracuse, Sicily: 434 (3); 435 (2-4); 437 (1, 3)
Soprintendenza alle Antichità, Taranto, Italy: 434 (1)
Soprintendenza alle Antichità, Turin: 158 (6); 248 (1)
Soprintendenza alle Antichità della Campania, Naples: 226
Soprintendenza alle Antichità dell'Etruria, Florence: 80 (1)
Soprintendenza alla Galleria Nazionale d'Arte Moderna, Rome: 231 (1); 240 (3)
Soprintendenza alle Gallerie, Florence: 11 (2); 141; 142 (1, 2); 147 (3); 148 (1); 202 (1); 209 (1); 233 (2); 288; 341; 345; 347 (1, 2); 348; 370 (1, 2); 374 (3); 525 (1)
Soprintendenza alle Gallerie, Naples: 207; 336; 374 (2)
Soprintendenza alle Gallerie di Mantova-Verona-Cremona: 328 (1, 2)
Soprintendenza ai Monumenti, Florence: 147 (1)
Staatliche Museen, Berlin: 463 (1, 2); 464
Stamm, Liselotte, Basel; 453; 454
Steinkopf, Walter, Berlin (Dahlem): 92; 215 (1); 285; 286
Stickelmann, Bremen: 215 (2)
Sunami, Soichi, New York: 105 (1); 385 (3); 397 (2)

Thomas Burke Memorial Washington State Museum, Seattle: 522 (2)
Tombasi, V. & N., Athens: 421 (4); 424 (3); 503 (1)
Towne Studio, Buffalo, N. Y.: 385 (1)

Uht, Charles, New York City: 415 (1)
Urbanistički Biko, Split, Yugoslavia: 34 (1, 2)

Vasari, Rome: 294 (1)
Vatican Museums, Rome: 528; 533; 534
Veroft Lode, Antwerp: 522 (3)
Vigneau, André, Paris; 250 (4); 474 (2); 478; 489 (1)

Walz, Kurt, Cologne: 181
Wells, Bergamo, Italy: 184
Widmer, Basel: 394
Wolfslag, Jan, Leiden: 218

Zancolli, La Spezia, Italy: 405 (3)

CONTENTS - VOLUME IX

	Col.	Pls.		Col.	Pls.
Landscape in Art	1	1–28	Magic	370	241–260
Laos	49		Magnasco, Alessandro	396	261–264
Laotian Art	53	29–32	Maitani, Lorenzo	399	265–269
Largillière, Nicolas de	59		Malagasy Republic	402	
Late-antique and Early Christian Art	60	33–90	Malaya	407	
La Tour, Georges de	161	91–95	Malevich, Kazimir	410	
Latour, Maurice Quentin de	165		Malta	411	
Latrobe, Benjamin	166		Mameluke Art	419	270–275
Laurana, Luciano	167	96–100	Manet, Edouard	428	276–280
Lawrence, Thomas	171		Manichaean Art	433	281–287
Lebanon	172		Mannerism	443	288–316
Lebrun, Charles	187	101–104	Mansart, François and Jules Hardouin	478	317–320
Le Corbusier	190	105–108	Mantegna, Andrea	486	321–330
Ledoux, Claude Nicolas	196		Manuhar	498	331
Léger, Fernand	197		Marc, Franz	499	
Lehmbruck, Wilhelm	198		Marin, John	500	
Lely, Peter	199		Marini, Marino	501	
Le Nain, Antoine, Louis, Mathieu	200	109–114	Martini, Simone	502	332–340
Le Nôtre, André	205		Masaccio	509	341–350
Leonardo da Vinci	206	115–126	Masks	520	351–368
Lescot, Pierre	238		Maso di Banco	571	369–373
Le Vau, Louis	238		Masolino	574	374–378
Liang K'ai	239	127–131	Massys (Metsys), Quentin	578	
Liberia	244		Mathura	579	379–384
Li Kung-lin	247	132–136	Matisse, Henri	586	385–388
Limbourg, Pol, Herman, Jehanequin de	251	137–140	Ma Yüan	590	389–392
Lipchitz, Jacques	256		McKim, Mead & White	594	
Lippi, Filippo and Filippino	257	141–150	Media, Composite	595	393–398
Li Ssŭ-hsün and Li Chao-tao	266	151–155	Mediterranean, Ancient Western	600	399–412
Liturgical and Ritual Objects	270	156–178	Mediterranean Protohistory	632	413–438
Lochner, Stefan	315	179–182	Meidias Painter	690	439–440
Longhena, Baldassarre	317		Melanesia	691	
Longhi, Pietro and Alessandro	318	183–187	Melanesian Cultures	697	441–458
Loos, Adolf	323		Melozzo da Forlì	728	
Lorenzetti, Ambrogio and Pietro	324	188–198	Memling, Hans	729	459–462
Lorenzo Monaco	337	199–202	Mendelsohn, Eric	735	
Lorrain, Claude	340	203–206	Meryon, Charles	735	
Lotto, Lorenzo	344	207–213	Mesopotamia	736	463–496
Lucas van Leyden	349	214–218	Metalwork	790	497–523
Lutyens, Edwin L.	353		Metsu, Gabriel	827	
Luxembourg	354		Mexico	828	
Lysippos	357	219–226	Michelangelo Buonarroti	861	524–542
Macchiaioli	362	227–240	Michelozzo	914	
Mackintosh, Charles Rennie	367		Micronesia	915	
Maderno, Carlo	368		Micronesian Cultures	918	543–548
Maes, Nicolaes	369				

LANDSCAPE IN ART. The term "landscape" refers to that type of pictorial representation in which natural scenery is the subject or at least prevails over the action of the figures. In many civilizations landscape was a subordinate art form (e.g., in ancient Greece and during the medieval period), retaining this position even when great proficiency had been achieved in the depiction of nature (as in late Gothic and Renaissance art). In Western art from the 17th century on, landscape gained a place as an independent form of pictorial art, even though initially it was considered inferior to figure painting. Outside Europe on the other hand, especially in China, landscape art has long flourished as a respected and autonomous form of artistic expression.

SUMMARY. Introduction (col. 1). Antiquity (col. 3): *Ancient Near East; Mediterranean world.* Medieval and modern periods (col. 10): *Landscape of symbols; Landscape of fact; Landscape of fantasy; Ideal landscape; The natural vision; From Turner to the present.* The East (col. 38): *India and Southeast Asia; China; Japan.*

INTRODUCTION. The continued lack of autonomy of landscape as an art form delayed the formulation of theoretical principles of landscape art. Moreover, when these finally did appear, they were formulated in terms of theories of nature or vision. Throughout the Renaissance, for example, apart from the *Treatise on Painting* and other writings of Leonardo da Vinci, no explicit literature appeared on the subject of landscape — neither treating it theoretically nor reflecting upon its value in painting hitherto. Even Leonardo's writings are concerned with nature rather than with landscape as an independent art form. The treatises of the 17th century set forth the canons of landscape as an art form, establishing the classifications of "ideal" (ancient or heroic) and "pastoral" (rustic or picturesque) landscape; later the *veduta*, or view, a faithful reproduction of a real and specific place, was added to this classification. But such formal categories resulted only in a strengthening of academic prejudices, which, springing from classicist theories, considered landscape an inferior art form. The eventual change in opinion came about through the increasing interest in landscape on the part of artists, connoisseurs, and collectors who disregarded official esthetics in cultivating and even favoring this type of art. Their response encouraged the critical discernment of Roger de Piles, a passionate collector of Flemish and Dutch paintings. After Leonardo, his were the first truly perceptive observations on light, colors, and *valeurs* (tones); he resolutely opposed the then current prejudices against landscape as an art form. Because the art of landscape was born in conflict with the contemporary esthetic, there developed in the 18th century new and autonomous esthetic ideals. The picturesque (q.v.) and the sublime (see TRAGEDY AND THE SUBLIME) were posited by Burke (1756) and Uvedale Price (1794) as two categories of the beautiful. Moreover, notwithstanding its well-known relationship with the classical ideal, even the great French *Encyclopédie* (1751–80) defined landscape painting as one of the "richest, most agreeable, and most fruitful" art forms. In somewhat picturesque disorder the *Encyclopédie* reviewed, for the first time, the notable landscape artists of every school, even those who did not satisfy classic norms. The selection of artists evidently reflected the taste of the great collectors of that period, and the English water-colorists were singled out for high praise.

One of the first modern theories of landscape art was expounded by the English painter John Constable (q.v.). In the celebrated introduction to a book of his landscape pictures published in 1833 and in his lectures on the history of landscape (1833–36), he was among the first to propose, in opposition to the ideal of "beautiful nature," the principle that under no circumstances should nature undergo correction. He accounted for and justified diversity of style by stating that just as in nature, where "no two days are alike, not even two hours, neither were there ever two leaves alike since the creation of the world," so in art each valid work is distinct from every other. Although stated with a different ethical nuance, Constable's observation repeats Leonardo's concept of the affinity of the creative principle of the artist with that of nature. Twenty years later, the realist French critic Théophile Thoré-Burger again noted this affinity. The reiteration was not altogether fortuitous, for both the abandonment of panoramic effects and the growing disinterest in the actual site depicted were derived from a more extreme interpretation of this position. Ruskin devoted much of his writing to landscape, rejecting both stylization and the concept of composed and ideal nature. Instead he articulates the 19th-century feeling for nature in all its aspects — an appeal to the senses that may be interpreted as a flight from urban civilization or simply as the abiding, instinctive response of man to nature. As a consequence of this characteristic attitude, the importance of landscape extended far beyond the limits of the artistic genre, and sensibility to nature was refined to the extreme. In a related development, theories concerning color and its separation were propagated and became increasingly complex. These were elaborated by Goethe, Delacroix (q.v.), by impressionists (see IMPRESSIONISM) such as Seurat and Signac, and in the writings of the Macchiaioli (q.v.), but such color theories can hardly be termed scientific.

More and more, art historians have tended to investigate the relationship between landscape painting and the development of modern concepts of nature. Since the publication of Woermann's studies of ancient landscape art (1876) and with the subsequent research on landscape in German, Dutch, and French art, an ever-increasing amount of critical writing on the subject has appeared. In France, where the tradition of landscape painting is strong, many specialized studies have been published, and major exhibitions of landscape were held in 1926 and 1949. The "ideal" landscape of the 17th century has been treated in much critical writing (e.g., Gerstenberg, 1923; Waetzold, 1927), as have the "capriccio," the "vedutismo," and the numerous other specific classifications of this genre. Because of its importance, English landscape painting has been the subject of a number of general studies and exhibitions. Another topic that has been investigated, sometimes with the aid of the camera, is the influence of actual landscape on the work of certain painters. The ideal of Italian landscape as a phenomenon in the development of English taste has been the subject of a monograph by Elizabeth Manwaring (*Italian Landscape in Eighteenth Century England*, New York, 1925). The relation between landscape and astrology in late medieval art and in the illuminations of the Limbourg brothers (q.v.) has been studied by Otto Pächt and Guy de Tervarent. According to Charles de Tolnay, magic and alchemy enter into the "afflatus of sympathetic animation" in the landscapes of Grünewald (q.v.) and certain romantic German painters of the 16th century. Flemish mysticism and ideas about alchemy in the 14th and 15th centuries have been suggested as the key to interpretation of the fantastic landscapes of Bosch (q.v.).

* *

ANTIQUITY. *Ancient Near East.* Landscape representations are found in Mesopotamian art of the earliest period; these are limited, however, to the decoration on cylinder seals, since larger art forms of that period are lacking. In the glyptics of the Uruk period (early 3d millennium B.C.; VI, PL. 33) landscape elements are depicted in a manner appropriate to the aims of the artist. In Mesopotamia a detailed representation of landscape was not an end in itself; landscape depiction was limited to more or less summary indications intended to suggest the setting of the scene. Rows of animals appear with plant elements, and hunters are seen in a mountain landscape. The mountains are represented schematically by closely spaced rows of segmental circles. This type of landscape representation continued through the first half of the 3d millennium, but it does not seem to have been used in sculpture, or at least does not appear in the few extant fragments from this period. On the other hand, a seal from Susa is remarkable in that it is decorated with a pure landscape and therefore is completely different in emphasis from the Uruk works. For this reason the piece elicits interest beyond the unquestionable excellence of its narrative treatment and style. In its depiction of a river abounding in fish and following a sinuous course among the trees, a notable feature is the schematic upside-down representation of the trees on the lower bank.

During the Akkadian period the landscape element in the representation of scenes diminished. In the stele of Naram-Sin (I, PL. 507) the mountain terrain is barely indicated by a light, undulating line, and two trees represent the vegetation. These elements are rendered very tenuously, but they may possibly indicate that landscape was present in the reliefs of the preceding period. That landscape began to appear in reliefs only at the same time it vanished from glyptics, which always paralleled but never presaged the other arts, is a highly questionable premise; in fact, a few examples of landscape elements do occur and are similar to those of the preceding period, although in the typical compositions of the Akkadian period the background is nearly always blank. Bits of landscape are found in mythological scenes, but here they are essential, since hey are intrinsic parts of the myth: a mountain from which emerges the god who had been buried there, the tree symbolizing vegetation in representations of the fertility myth. In the succeeding Neo-Sumerian period even these last vestiges of landscape vanish, and only a few stylized plants recall the more detailed motifs of the earlier period.

In Assyrian art landscape again assumed importance, initially in the glyptics of the last centuries of the 2d millennium B.C., in which animals are depicted surrounded by vegetation. With new iconographic themes, there was a return to the conception of landscape prevalent in the first half of the 3d millennium. Later, the value of landscape was enhanced in historical reliefs (see HISTORICAL SUBJECTS). Nonetheless, though here the landscape element is often central, it is not free of the iconographic conventions that persisted from the earliest period: mountains continued to be represented by rows of small squares or ovals, water by wavy lines, and so on. Perspective continued to be governed by rules that gave it a rudimentary serviceable aspect. In the oldest reliefs (those of Ashurnasirpal II) the landscape is more complete and fulfills the narrative requirements. The rivers are shown by stylized waves (in a manner that was to last throughout the Assyrian period) and the vegetation with an extensive repertory of forms. Nevertheless, it cannot be said that the rendering of landscape is the primary concern of the creator of these reliefs; he executes it with a masterful hand, but only when it is essential to his main purpose. The same concept applies to the bronze reliefs of Balawat; here, however, the expanded narrative demands a richer, more varied repertory of landscape motifs. Examples of these new devices are the city built on an island (PL. 2) and the underground course of the Tigris, which is rendered in a fashion suggesting that the side of the mountain from which it flows is opened with a series of windows (PL. 490). In the few surviving reliefs of Tiglathpileser III, on the contrary, landscape elements are almost completely absent. Landscape details — sometimes highly effective, as in the scene of a forest hunt — reappeared in the reliefs of the palace of Sargon II at Dur Sharrukin (mod. Khorsabad). The figures in the hunting scene move about in a space filled with trees similar in form but varying in dimensions; birds in flight appear in other scenes. A high point in Assyrian landscape art is marked by the Sennacherib reliefs (Br. Mus.), in which a military scene seems almost a pretext for surrounding figures with marshes, forests, and mountains. The convention of a neutral background has all but disappeared in favor of a naturalistic setting suitable to the action. In the reign of Ashurbanipal (PL. 2) there arose many new tendencies, ranging from complete absence of landscape — corresponding to the new conception of an immaterial space enveloping the figures (especially in reliefs of hunting scenes; PL. 493) — to its explicit use as a narrative element (as in the subsidiary scenes of the hunt, which show a hill crowded with spectators, and in the battle scenes at the edge of a river). Landscape also appears as an autonomous and purely descriptive element, as in a relief showing the city of Susa surrounded by trees and with a river flowing around it. It is present as well in a relief representing the flight of the Elamites below a park crossed by brooks and filled with shrines and altars. The sense of narrative is also present in the reliefs depicting the king in his garden (VIII, PL. 423); here the interlacing of vines among the trees is an elegant play of lines, the last and highest expression of landscape in Mesopotamian art.

Outside of Mesopotamia and Egypt, representation of landscape does not exist in the ancient Near East. Neither the background of the Nimrud ivory showing a lion attacking a Negro (I, PL. 510) nor the design on a plate of uncertain significance, also from Nimrud, can be classified as landscape.

Giovanni GARBINI

In Egyptian art landscape appears only as a subordinate element, in scenes representing the actions of men and beasts, never as an independent element. Nevertheless, such landscape details are frequently indispensable to the comprehension of the scene. They are indicated in monuments as early as the predynastic period, for example, in the ceremonial scene on the macehead of the Scorpion King (IV, PL. 325), where there are shrubs, trees, water, islands, and a reed enclosure. The three fundamental divisions of the Egyptian landscape — the savanna, the agricultural zone, and the marshes — afforded great expressive opportunities to artists of the 4th, 5th, and 6th dynasties, and these elements figure prominently in their reliefs and paintings of scenes from Egyptian daily life (IV, PL. 335). The theme of the seasons particularly stimulated the evocation and composition of landscapes, and those activities connected with the cycle of the seasons were favorite subjects. These scenes appeared first on royal reliefs and later on those executed for private persons. In hunting scenes the savanna is rendered as a series of undulating dunes of varied height, with sparse shrubbery and an occasional thicket. The composition is generally organized on a single plane; but in exceptional cases, such as the painting in the tomb of Sembi near Meir, the composition is distributed over various superimposed planes. In the scenes of agrarian life the environmental element is more limited and remains subordinate to the figures; in a harvest scene there is spare indication of a field where the crops are being harvested, while pastoral scenes are suggested by a few shrubs. In this type of scene, deviations from the single plane are rare and, for the most part, appear only in works of a later period. An example is the agricultural scene in the tomb of Nakht, where an upper plane depicts a winding canal flanked by trees and encircling a small island. The landscape in the hunting scene generally comprises dense groups of papyrus plants growings at the edge of a pond, with appropriate fauna represented as a collection of types. The papyrus plants are shown in section and set in a single row, forming a kind of compact barrier of slender vertical elements.

In tomb paintings of the New Kingdom, in addition to the motifs described above, the residences of great functionaries are frequently depicted, complemented with gardens, orchards, and pools (IV, PL. 371; see LANDSCAPE ARCHITECTURE). During this period there developed a new type of landscape representation, one which evoked life in the world of the dead. Such subjects appear in vignettes illustrated in papyrus funerary texts. The Elysian fields are represented as a series of level zones, particularly in the form of small islands having canals, fields, trees, small temples, and kiosks. In such settings the dead are shown at work in the fields, either sowing or harvesting, or else they are seen in attitudes of prayer; they are sometimes depicted in boats, crossing the channels from one island to another.

An identifiable landscape element of the New Kingdom is the Theban necropolis depicted in murals, sarcophagi, and wooden steles. The mountain on the west bank is rendered as a high hill with descending wavy lines of a reddish color, dotted with yellow to represent sand. Halfway down the mountain are shown the entrances to the hypogea, with their steles and a few fruit trees dedicated to the dead.

Sergio BOSTICCO

Mediterranean world. In modern times a romantic, and even sentimental, approach to nature has become so ingrained that it is difficult to understand the wholly different attitude of the ancient world. The easiest way to achieve such an understanding is to find out how the ancient approach to the natural world has been transformed.

In the early Bronze Age in Greece religion assumed a markedly ecstatic character that was manifested in many ways, particularly in the dynamic pottery forms, which were often animalistic in character and decorated with spirals and cordons. There were signs of the vital, rhythmic sense of nature that was to find its fullest expression in the Dionysiac thiasos. During the middle Bronze Age in Crete this awareness brought about the creation of the primeval and fundamental forms of nature which have persisted to the present: the palmette and a series of waves sprouting from the spiral, symbolizing the genesis or earliest form of life (the *Urpflanze* of Goethe). In the late Bronze Age in Crete, images of land and marine flora and fauna derived from this basic motive rhythm began to prevail. The marine forms were clearly the attributes of the great sea-born goddess of life, later identified with Aphrodite. A peculiarity of Cretan landscape art is the placement of natural features and flora not only below the animal figures but above them as well — a convention signifying that life is immersed in nature and is one with it (VIII, PL. 423). The gods are forces of nature and appear to man only as visions; the men to whom they manifest themselves must therefore cover their eyes. Such attitudes of *aposkopeia* appear in later Greek art, in the depiction of satyrs and other nature demons dazzled by the appearance of their godly masters. Sometimes Egyptian elements appear in the landscape, for even at that time Egypt was regarded essentially as a divine land. Lions, sphinxes, and sirens in a landscape are an indication of its daemonic character.

By the Mycenaean phase of Cretan civilization, landscape was already represented in a more rigid and schematic manner. On Geometric pottery plant motifs were replaced by concentric circles, rings, crosshatching, and meander patterns. In no other period has the primordial rhythm of life been expressed with such severity. At the same time, a more varied repertory of ornament developed, including rows of deer, birds, horses, and decorative fillers. Nor were indications of landscape lacking, particularly in the Cretan Geometric. In the late Geometric period the palmetto reappeared, and in Greek ornamental art thereafter the human feeling of unity with a natural environment as a manifestation of divine power was expressed in an ever-increasing variety of ways: zoomorphic friezes, decorative fillers, and the classic, organic acanthus ornament.

In the archaic period, however, these images of nature became accessory elements rather than the primary expressions of religious sentiment they had been in Cretan landscapes. The deities, no longer abstract forces of nature, manifested themselves not as visions but as real beings. In place of wild animals, birds, and flowers, there appeared satyrs and maenads; octopuses and shells were replaced by Nereids and Tritons. Temples and other edifices that are dwellings of the gods served to emphasize the three-dimensional character of the landscape. The world was thus observed in its concrete aspects, and the background peculiar to each event was revealed. In the "Chigi oinochoe" (XI, PL. 70), the hunters are depicted hiding behind a bush, and Achilles attacks Troilus near a spring and a sacred grove. The landscape is represented by means of very spare indications, but these suffice to set the scene for the event. The same approach is particularly evident in Ionian art, as well as in the Etruscan art derived from it. The interior of a Samian cup is completely covered with two trees containing birds' nests; between them is a running man. The intimate contact with nature here acquires a more personal character, reminiscent of the archaic poetry of Sappho and Alcman.

This newly developed ability to depict individual landscape backgrounds was further used to convey a lighthearted enjoyment of life amid nature in the hunting and fishing scenes of the Etruscan grave painting (PL. 2). The natural setting also assumed strong expressive values in the works of the Attic ceramist Exekias (q.v.) and his school. In an amphora depicting Eos mourning the death of Memnon (Mus. Vat.), the figures are set within a sinister environment that includes a stark forest, a solitary bird, and a still life of weapons.

In the art of the classical period, landscape not only provides atmospheric background but also contributes more directly to the fate of the beings dominating the image. Already in the transition from the late archaic to the classical period, the Berlin cup of the Brygos Painter shows Night plunging into the ocean, while at the first light of day the lightning of Zeus annihilates the giants. In the Ilioupersis hydria (Naples, Mus. Naz.) of the Kleophrades Painter (Epiktetos the Second), the palm separating the temple where Ajax violates Cassandra and Neoptolemos slays Priam droops meaningfully. According to Pausanias, the painter Polygnotos (q.v.) used spare and allusive landscape elements in his mural paintings at Delphi. In the east pediment of the Parthenon, sunrise and nightfall frame the cosmic event of the birth of Athena, embodiment of the intellect, while the nature gods Dionysos and Aphrodite are shown reposing on a rocky mound. In a white-ground cup, landscape lends a lyric atmosphere to a scene in which one of the Hesperides plucks an apple from a tree with a bowed trunk as graceful and slender as the maiden herself. Another dramatic background is the high mountain looming over the seashore where Pelops carries off Hippodameia after a breathless chase. The fluttering garb and the waves breaking on the shore suggest the sea breeze, and the doves perched nearby on a sapling echo the sentiments of the lovers.

It is but a short step then to the extended landscape backgrounds of the friezes carved by Greek artists at Xanthos, Gjölbaschi, Tlos, and elsewhere for the Lycian kings. Here the Near Eastern tradition of the historical tableau is fused with the classical aim of fixing the event within a well-organized setting. The panels of the Lycian reliefs are reminiscent of the illustrated books, with or without text, that were probably widely disseminated throughout the ancient world; in these the scenes were arranged in coherent sequence, so that even a person unable to read could follow the narrative. The Homeric goblets, the Tabulae Iliacae (Rome, Mus. Cap.), and the Joshua Roll (II, PL. 447) are derived from these books, as are certain Roman wall friezes (especially in Pompeian Style II) and the column friezes of Trajan (VII, PL. 263) and Marcus Aurelius. The Column of Trajan is classical in character not only in its figures but also for its landscape backgrounds. Recalling the compositional style reputed to have been that of the painter Polygnotos, these contrast sharply with the spatial-illusionistic pictorial manner of older Roman art. The historical realism of the triumphal reliefs became stylized in an ideal programmatic idiom through the incorporation of such classic elements. The Trojan frieze in the House of the Cryptoporticus in Pompeii is a more faithful reproduction of a Greek model of the late 4th century B.C. As far as it is possible to determine, the landscape backgrounds in all these works did not have the expressive force of the tightly composed symbols of the high classical period described above, or even of the bare tree in the mosaic *The Battle of Alexander* (VII, PL. 154). This tree stands out in an uncanny manner near the victorious king, as like a bolt of lightning he shatters the venerable Persian empire.

Landscape was of greater importance in theatrical scenery. The Prometheus of Aeschylus was chained to a rock; and according to Vitruvius (Introduction, vii, 11), Agatharchos painted for Aeschylus a set that furnished incentive for Vitruvius himself — and for Democritus and Anaxagoras — in his theoretical research on optical perspective. Greek perspective, however, is completely different from the central perspective of Renaissance art, which places the single elements in a fixed position within a wide space, leading in well-ordered fashion to a church or other imposing building. Greek perspective is a single-unit, corporeal perspective. The Greeks reiterated again and again that the mission of art was to depict things as they are, not as it appears they should be. Therefore separate images were treated perspectively, but the organization of a whole picture was never based on a unified central perspective. The Greeks naturally studied perspective in theory and regarded it as a means of realizing the organic unity of a body; but they worshiped and depicted the divine corporeally, as a single entity, not as part of a spatial construct. In the classic compositional unity, Apollodoros appears to have attained a level far above that of Agatharchos. The ultimate goal of the Greek landscape artists is best exemplified in the paintings of sacred places and rocky landscapes inserted among the architectural elements in the cubiculum and its alcove in the villa at Boscoreale (VIII, PL. 424). As in the theater sets of late Hellenistic type mentioned by Vitruvius (vii, 5, 2), all the resources of perspective are used with complete mastery but in such a way as to promote autonomy for the single elements by giving them individual viewing points. The sacred groves on the lateral walls are represented in a freer Roman manner, giving a feeling of space and atmosphere; whereas the scenery in the alcove, copied more faithfully from Greek prototypes, has a peculiarly dry and isolated quality. How far back this Greek ability in perspective design goes is affirmed by the architectural elements in late classical vase painting.

In Hellenistic art, landscape — like all Roman art — became a free synthesis of Greek elements, greatly elaborated. Actual copies from the Greek are rare and therefore take on more importance, since the degree of faithfulness can then be measured against the few surviving originals. The "yellow frieze" of the House of Livia on the Palatine, like certain other works of the type, is stylistically so different from the prevailing Roman art of its period that it can be explained only as a copy from some illustrated book of the early Hellenistic period. The frieze depicts the kingdom of Ptolemy in the form of an idealized landscape with shrines of Isis-Tyche, and Isis-Neith, in the guise of Athena, and of Dionysos, Priapus, and Poseidon. Scattered among them are worshipers, shepherds, and pilgrims. The somewhat angular, insubstantial, yet graceful appearance of the human figures is similar to that found in works dating from about 300 B.C., but the rhythmic arrangement of the deities rather suggests work of the late classical period. The landscape background consists of forms rendered three-dimensionally, but there are no images filling the intervening spaces. Where the attention of the viewer is directed to the background of the scene, as in the Munich offering relief (late 3d cent. B.C.), by contrast the three-dimensional forms are more closely grouped in the foreground. The two deities in this relief are unidentified and mysterious; however, Hellenistic variants from Rhodes indicate that they represent Isis and Serapis.

The mission of Isis, a theme known through inscriptions, presented the Egyptian element in a Greek manner in order to be more understandable to the public. Because of this intent, on the Munich relief Isis and Serapis are barely indicated, and on the yellow frieze of Livia, Isis-Neith is assimilated into Athena; also, Isis is often hidden behind Hecate, Artemis, or Aphrodite. The great number of landscapes of Egyptian type in Roman art (PL. 3; VII, PL. 197) unquestionably proceed from the image of Egypt, as a land sacred to the gods, conveyed by books illustrating the mission of Isis. Such illustrations readily served as models for the new type of mural decoration of Roman private houses. Settings were rendered in depth in many examples of early Hellenistic art, but this spatial treatment disappeared in the 2d century B.C. The most important example, the Telephos frieze of the great Pergamon altar (VII, PL. 174), undoubtedly inspired by an illustrated book, has a landscape background that differs very little from those of the late classical period.

Knowledge of landscape representations used as settings for the deeds of great men in the art of the Roman republican era derives only from literary sources. The surviving funerary images suggest that the figural components were dominant.

The advances in illusionistic perspective of Pompeian Style II (beginning ca. 80 B.C.) offered far greater possibilities for landscape in mural decoration. Artists not only copied Hellenistic landscapes, as in the yellow frieze in the House of Livia and — even more notably — the atrium scene in the Villa of the Mysteries in Pompeii, but they controlled and enhanced the sense of space to such a degree as to convey even the monumental scale of Roman vaulting. The most accomplished examples of this illusionistic style are the sacred groves painted at the center of the long sides of the cubiculum at Boscoreale and the Vatican Odyssey landscapes (VII, PL. 180). The latter cycle, like all the similar Roman painted friezes, was derived from an illustrated book in which the figural style supports a date of about 320 B.C. The landscape type was probably similar to the frieze in the House of the Cryptoporticus in Pompeii. In the Roman Odyssey frieze the landscape acquires an independent value in relation to the figures; it is rendered more spacious by means of perspective techniques that make the figures appear to be deployed in the distance. The "continuous narration," that is, the sequence of different scenes in the same landscape, thus achieved the significance Wickhoff has recognized as characteristically Roman. The landscape surrounding the human figures suggests a supernatural realm. In the central panel with Odysseus and Circe is a palace, with an exedra and a baetulus indicating a sanctuary of Isis. The great goddess guides the wanderings of Odysseus, whose descendants, together with those of Circe, were later to found the cities of Praeneste and Tusculum. The spatial depth of the composition is used effectively to mark out the progress of the action; as in the *Aeneid*, the hero is presented in a sequence of cosmic events.

In mythological landscapes, of which the oldest known is the Io painting in the House of Livia, book illustrations are reproduced on a larger scale. They reveal themselves clearly as copies after classical originals, since it became customary to give wall decorations the aspect of a collection of paintings. But the small scale of the figures and the sequential narration in many of these landscapes clearly reveal the fact that the original models were in the small format of picture books. Often the grandeur of nature imparts an awesome or violent tone to the scene; at other times the natural elements reflect the good fortune vouchsafed to the favorite of the gods. The stringent organization of all the paintings within the decorative scheme suggests that the hero acts in accordance with a higher natural order. The art of the early and middle imperial era reveals an almost irrational submission to divine will, which, together with the motifs of the sacred mysteries found in the surviving decoration, heightens the supernatural aspect of this order.

Roman landscape art was not limited to single paintings and frieze panels, for the decoration throughout the house was related to its landscape setting. The wainscots of the walls were adorned with plant patterns, thus relating them to the garden and the image of the sacred grove. The upper sections and the spaces between the principal panels were treated as apertures disclosing sacred groves; sometimes such areas of landscape became the principal decorative element, as in the Villa of Livia at Prima Porta (VII, PL. 208). Subjects favored for the large landscapes decorating the walls adjoining the garden of the house include zoological gardens modeled after the gardens of Hellenistic nobles, Orpheus as the lord of nature, painted statues, water nymphs, and other motifs related to the sacred groves. All these elements were framed within grandiose landscape layouts for villas and sanctuaries derived from Hellenistic structures. The circular and rectangular temples at Tivoli, built on the edge of a gorge, represent one such idealized Alexandrian landscape.

An original contribution of Roman art is the decorative landscape relief in which are fused pictorial motifs and elements of Greek landscape votive reliefs, used as in the paintings described above. The Dolon relief (Vienna, Kunsthist. Mus.; Rome, Mus. Naz. Rom.) corresponds to early Pompeian Style II painting, the Icarus relief to late Style II, and the Polyphemus relief (Rome, Villa Albani) to the Neronian Style IV. Landscape motifs appear on silver vessels (VII, PL. 216), cameos, and cameo-carved crystals. Particularly fine examples are the silver cup of Egyed (Hungary), depicting a landscape of Egyptian type, and the scrollwork on the silver cups from the Hildesheim Treasure (Städt. Mus.), reminiscent of the Ara Pacis. Propitiatory landscape symbols, executed in more modest forms, are found on clay pottery and terra-cotta lamps. Such images survived until the Christian Era, when they assumed definite symbolic significance. This intent is confirmed by the fact that images of shepherds and flocks, sacred enclosures, *paradeisoi*, and votive landscape paintings were already regarded as propitiatory images in the earliest years of the Empire, though not yet linked to any explicit dogma.

The most important sources for the study of landscape motifs of the middle imperial period are the Column of Trajan and that of Marcus Aurelius. Since they are classical in style, their landscape component has less importance than it had in the art of the early Empire. Nevertheless landscape is significantly present in the initial scenes on the Column of Trajan — the river, with the solitary sentries on the banks, and the sinister-looking forests from which the barbarians emerge. On the Column of Marcus Aurelius, the effect of supernatural elements is heightened through a faint, almost expressionistic treatment of rivers, encampments, and especially the figure of the rain god. The finest example of landscape in the painting of the same period is found in the paradisiac aquatic scenes in the building lying below the Church of SS. Giovanni e Paolo in Rome. Landcapes of this type were to assume more and more the symbolic purpose of a promise of heavenly felicity. In funerary art this intention was anticipated in the early Empire, as shown by paintings from the columbarium of Villa Doria-Pamphili (VI, PL. 60), the tombs on the Via Latina (Rome), and the Caivano tomb (north of Naples). Beginning in the 3d century these motifs were used in catacomb paintings, and the Hellenistic protective image of the shepherd became common in the decoration of sarcophagi.

Notable landscapes are preserved in mosaic pavements, particularly in Antioch and North Africa (I, PLS. 23, 24, 26). The most elaborate mosaic landscapes are those in the Great Palace of the Emperors in Istanbul, works that can be dated no earlier than the 5th century. In Christian art the same motifs were adopted in mosaics on the walls and ceilings of churches. Examples worthy of note include the mosaic of S. Costanza and the nave mosaics in S. Maria Maggiore (mid-5th cent.) in Rome, the Good Shepherd in the so-called "Mausoleum of Galla Placidia" in Ravenna (X, PL. 179), and the mosaics in the Great Mosque in Damascus (X, PLS. 379, 380, 386). The last-named mosaics, executed for the caliphs, are in a sumptuous and aniconic Byzantine style: no living being appears in them, and the buildings and gardens on the banks of the river are a splendid array. Their decided three-dimensional treatment, derived from the Greek tradition apparent in the yellow frieze of Livia, is in strong contrast to the expressionistic style of the S. Maria Maggiore mosaics. Their style is reminiscent not only of illustrated manuscripts of Homer and Virgil but also of the Roman triumphal columns. The landscape of the Good Shepherd in the "Mausoleum of Galla Placidia" and of the Vienna Genesis (PL. 6) is purely Greek in style. These general stylistic differences were to persist throughout the course of medieval art.

While the works of the classic artists, for the most part, evidence profound awareness of nature, only those of the Romans presented nature to man in the guise of a paradisiac ideal of fulfillment. This sentimental approach, joined with an effort toward a deeper comprehension that is closer to the Greek concept of nature, mark the modern attitude toward landscape and the place of nature in art.

Karl Schefold

MEDIEVAL AND MODERN PERIODS. *Landscape of symbols.* In the art of the early Middle Ages the existence of natural forms was at first acknowledged by symbols that bore little relation to actual appearance. Why did these symbols satisfy the medieval mind? To some extent they were the outcome of medieval Christian philosophy. If our earthly life is no more than a brief and squalid interlude, then the surroundings in which it is lived need not absorb our attention. If ideas are Godlike and sensations debased, then our rendering of appearances must be as far as possible symbolic, and nature, which we perceive through our senses, becomes categorically sinful.

Parallel with this mistrust of nature was the symbolizing faculty of the medieval mind: the power of immediately substituting an idea for an object, or an object for an idea, which allowed men to accept without question even unconvincing equivalences. Although this attitude toward nature could never produce landscape painting in the modern sense, it did, in two ways, prepare the way for the kind of art that may be called the "landscape of symbols."

The less an artifact interests the eye as imitation, the more it must delight the eye as pattern, and an art of symbols always evolves a language of decoration. More important still, when men begin to look with pleasure at the actual details of nature, the symbolizing habit of mind gives to their observation an unusual intensity, for they look at flowers and trees not only as delightful objects but as prototypes of the divine. It is this attitude, no doubt, that gives to the earliest naturalism of the Middle Ages its beauty. The leaves, flowers, and tendrils of Reims and Southwell Minster have the clarity of newly created things.

Natural objects were first perceived individually, as pleasing in themselves and symbolic of divine qualities. The next step in the direction of landscape painting was to see them as forming some tangible whole that would be a symbol of perfection within the compass of the imagination. This end was satisfied by the discovery of the garden. In a sense "discovery" is the wrong word, for the enchanted garden — be it Eden, the Hesperides, or TirnanOg — has been one of humanity's most constant, widespread, and consoling myths; and its reappearance in the 12th century was only a part of the general reawakening of the imaginative faculty.

One of the first garden scenes with figures in painting is a 14th-century fresco in the Camposanto in Pisa, once renowned as the work of Orcagna but actually a fresco by an unknown follower of the Lorenzettis. It represents a number of solid-looking revelers making music under the trees, a carpet of flowers at their feet. This work is an offshoot of Sienese art, for landscape had no tradition in Florentine painting. The stark, economical rocks that serve as background in the paintings of Giotto admirably complement the sculptural balance of each group; but Giotto, who was so great an observer of human gesture and expression, disdained to record his observations of plants and trees.

Thus, it is to Sienese painting that one must look for the sense of natural beauty which occurs in the poetry of the early 14th century; and the pictorial counterpart is found in the work of Simone Martini and the Lorenzettis (PL. 9). The first surviving landscapes, in the modern sense, are in Ambrogio Lorenzetti's frescoes of Good and Bad Government in the Palazzo

Pubblico in Siena (PLS. 194, 195; VI, PL. 378). These are so factual that they hardly belong to the landscape of symbol, and they remained unique for almost a century. Simone, on the other hand, was the born interpreter of heavenly beauty in sensuous terms. In this gift he was at one with the finest Gothic art of France, and it was no accident that, in 1339, he found his way to Avignon.

It was presumably in Avignon that Simone met the man whose name has come to stand for the juncture of the medieval and modern worlds, Petrarch. Petrarch figures in all history books as the first modern man; and rightly, for in his curiosity, his skepticism, his restlessness, his ambition, and his self-consciousness, he is certainly akin to the modern temper. He was probably the first man to express the sentiment on which the existence of landscape painting so largely depends — the desire to escape from the turmoil of cities into the peace of the countryside. Then, too, Petrarch was an incipient botanist, not merely delighting in the decorative profusion of flowers, but minutely studying their characteristics and keeping a daybook to record their progress. Finally, he was the first to climb a mountain for its own sake, to enjoy the view from the top and relate the experience. These modern traits continue nonetheless to be dominated by a monastic philosophy, and so it is with Petrarch's responsiveness to nature: for him, and for the landscape painters of the late Middle Ages, nature as a whole was disturbing, vast, and fearful, laying open the mind to many dangerous thoughts.

Even in such wild country man may enclose a garden, however; it is, appropriately enough, at Avignon that the first pictorial expression of this new gratification is to be found, in the landscape frescoes that decorate the wardrobe room of the Papal Palace (VI, PL. 325). They were begun in 1343, and there are indications that they represent a well-established style, of which no other trace remains. The Avignon frescoes are the first complete examples of the landscape of symbols, both in subject and in style. They present an untroubled enjoyment of open-air life — people fishing in a garden pool, hawking, and ferreting — and still preserve from the more constrained, symbolic vision of the Middle Ages the full mastery of decoration. Interest in naturalistic detail has not yet overpowered the feeling for texture that was the legacy of Byzantine art. This taste for decorative richness in landscape, first significantly evident in these tapestrylike frescoes of Avignon, is apparent throughout the 15th century in the tapestries themselves, which have survived in great numbers.

In religious art, the beautiful subject of the *hortus conclusus*, the enclosed garden where the Madonna can sit on the ground and the Christ child play with the birds, achieved great popularity during the 15th century. At first the garden is very small, only a conventional symbol of enclosure, as in the charming paintings of Stefan Lochner. But sometimes there are large enclosures: a flowery orchard is seen in the Stefano da Zevio *Madonna in the Rose Garden* (VI, PL. 372) — and here the source of inspiration was undoubtedly a Persian miniature. Of all paradise gardens, the jewel and crown — it is indeed like the enameled crown of a Gothic goldsmith — is the little school of Cologne picture in Frankfurt (VI, PL. 345). It contains the elements of late medieval landscape in their most perfect form and distills a world of delicate perception where flowers exist to please the senses of sight and smell, fruit to satisfy the taste, and the sound of a zither, mingled with that of falling water, to delight the hearing. Still, all these sensations have some immaterial value, for they are conceived as testimonies of heavenly joy, and the picture is full of Christian symbols: the fountain, the birds on the battlements, the Holy Child making music, and the tiny dragon of evil lying with his belly in the air.

Outside the garden wall were mountain and forest, and for each the Middle Ages had contrived a symbol. The mountains of Gothic landscapes, those strange, twisted rocks that rise so abruptly from the plain, are part of a very ancient pictorial tradition that goes back to Hellenistic painting. Surviving in manuscripts based on antique models, they were common in Byzantine art and became the central motif of icons representing the desert of Sinai. But they do not survive solely as symbols of desert places; they were a convenient symbol for any mountain. Why did it remain the practice to use a sort of ideogram for mountains when other natural objects were treated realistically? One answer might be that mountains were large and inapprehensible. Perhaps another reason for the unreal mountains of Gothic landscape was that medieval man did not explore them: he was not interested. The forests outside the garden wall, on the other hand, were different in appeal. Dark woods had always stirred the medieval imagination, and in the 14th century man penetrated their depths in partaking of activities such as hunting.

The Avignon frescoes portray hunting, fishing, and falconry; and the earliest pictures concerned entirely with observation of nature are in manuscripts on sport. Hunting is traditionally the occupation, often the sole occupation, of the aristocracy, and the painting style that made hunting one of its chief subjects was an aristocratic one. It grew up in the courts of France and Burgundy about 1400, and its most perfect expression survives in the manuscripts illuminated for the great bibliophile the Duc de Berry. One of these, the *Très Riches Heures*, to which the Limbourg brothers made their contribution from about 1409 to 1415, is crucial in the history of landscape painting, for it stands halfway between symbol and fact (PLS. 8, 137–140; VI, PL. 65). Pol de Limbourg and all the other artists who created this style, though they were employed by princes, came from the predominantly bourgeois Low Countries, from a land of work and fact. The calendar of the *Très Riches Heures*, with the occupations of the months, provides a comprehensive illustration of everyday life in the Middle Ages; and although several scenes are devoted to the pleasures of the chase, more than half represent the work of the fields. In these depictions one is aware of an eye for fact so keen that the symbolic inheritance of the Middle Ages is almost forgotten.

Aristocratic landscape painting originated in the courts of France and Burgundy but quickly spread to Italy, where Gentile da Fabriano gave the International Gothic style a fullness, and Pisanello a finality, beyond the range of the illustrators for the Duc de Berry. Pisanello's drawings evidence his almost Leonardesque curiosity about nature, and one of his few surviving pictures, *St. Eustache* (London, Nat. Gall.), shows his feeling for forest life. It is so dark in this wood that only after a few minutes can one discern all the animals. This murky atmosphere was part of the imaginative perception of the time, as is evident from several other *sous-bois* of the 15th century, above all the superb hunt scene by Paolo Uccello (XI, PL. 44). It is known that Pisanello painted many wall decorations, in the Palazzo Ducale of Mantua and elsewhere, with small figures in landscapes; of these works, which must have developed the style of the Limbourg calendar, nothing remains except some preparatory drawings.

The most elaborate and extensive landscape of symbols, however, comes not from the manuscript but from the tapestry tradition. This is *The Procession of the Magi* by Benozzo Gozzoli (VIII, PL. 193), where all the details of late Gothic landscape — the carpets of flowers, the little woods, the fantastic rocks, the formalized trees, and the cypresses already stylized by nature — are combined to decorate and delight. But by 1459, when this fresco was painted, the landscape of symbols had become somewhat self-conscious and had already ceased to reflect the true creative impulse of the time.

What was it that made men no longer content to put together the precious fragments of nature into some decorative whole? It was a new idea of space and a new perception of light. In the landscape of symbols the nexus of unity was the flat surface of the wall, panel, or tapestry. About 1420 some change in the working of the human mind demanded a new nexus of unity, the enclosed space. In a very extended sense of the term, this new way of thinking about the world may be called scientific, for it involved relation and comparison as well as the measurement on which science is based. But this new awareness antedates the real rise of science by almost 200 years, and it is found in the work of artists who seem untroubled by the mathematics of perspective, notably Fra Angelico and the manuscript illuminators of the north. This spatial sense is combined with another unifying medium, light. It has often been said that the sun first shines in the landscape of *The Flight into Egypt* that Gentile da Fabriano painted in the predella to his *Adoration of the Magi* of 1423 (VI, PLS. 84, 85). To a great extent his style is still symbolic, for the rising sun itself is a solid disk of gold, and the light it sheds on the hillside is rendered by allowing the gold ground to show through the paint. But Gentile, with a sure sense of values, fused this golden light with the rest of his landscape, with the shadows cast by the olive trees and with the cool tone of the valley. Here for the first time the details of landscape are united by light, not solely by decorative arrangement. A similar beauty of morning or evening light pervades the landscape backgrounds of Fra Angelico.

Despite these moments of enchantment, it was not in Italian art that light became the *primum mobile* of painting. As early as 1410 Pol de Limbourg, in his eagerness to record with truth the country life, had achieved a new unity of tone; and in 1425 Hubert van Eyck, in the *Adoration of the Holy Lamb*, painted the first great modern landscape (PL. 11; for opinions on the dating and attribution of this work, see V, cols. 325–326).

Landscape of fact. The first modern landscapes were painted between 1414 and 1417, probably by Hubert van Eyck, in a manuscript known as the *Heures de Turin* (Turin, Mus. Civ.) executed for the Count of Holland (see also V, cols. 327–328). In these miniature landscapes Van Eyck achieved by masterful color a sense of the saturation of light. The landscape has a subtle tone hardly observed again until the 19th century, and the reflection of the evening sky in the water is exactly the kind of effect that was to become part of the popular landscape imagery after the mid-19th century. Historically, they are among the most original and astonishing works of art in the world, without clear precursors. If they are indeed by Hubert van Eyck, and if one accepts the inscription on the Ghent Altarpiece saying that it was largely his work, then it must be that he was responsible for the remarkable distance effects in the *Adoration of the Holy Lamb*, where the landscape melts into light as in a work of Claude Lorrain. In the pictures painted after Hubert's death in 1426, which are certainly by Jan van Eyck, the landscapes are more factual, more urban, and less imaginative.

The other tradition of painting in the Low Countries, that which springs from Tournai and from the artist whom historians call either Robert Campin or the Master of Flémalle, was also concerned with the facts of landscape but was closer to the tradition of the Limbourg brothers. Campin's backgrounds, as sharp and crystalline as the view through the wrong end of a telescope, show little of the Van Eycks' rapture at the all-enriching envelopment of light. Painters of this group seem to have preferred landscapes of winter — a season in which the forms of nature have the angularity and the linear clarity characteristic of this sober late Gothic style.

The resolute search for truth in these early Flemish landscapes, the eagerness with which the artist's eye fed on each object, raises the question of how they were done. They could hardly have been painted from memory. But were they put together from preliminary drawings, or are they portraits of actual places? Hubert's miniatures display so sure a sense of color values that they must be based on studies made directly from nature, probably in water colors. Jan's townscapes were probably based on silverpoint drawings made on the spot. The first indisputable piece of topography in art, however, is by a follower of Campin, the Swiss Konrad Witz. This is his background for *The Miraculous Draught of Fishes* (1444; Geneva, Mus. d'Art et d'Histoire), which portrays the shores of the Lake of Geneva — a work that remained unique for 50 years.

The interest in the precise character of a particular spot, which was part of the general curiosity of the 15th century, culminated in the topographical water colors of Dürer. The earliest date from 1494, and the drawing of Innsbruck (Vienna, Albertina) is the first portrait of a town. It evidences a delicate perception of light, but most of Dürer's water-color landscapes are remarkable less for esthetic qualities than for dexterity and curiosity that, by its intense concentration, has an almost hypnotic effect.

One condition of the landscape of fact was a new sense of space. This appears simultaneously in Flemish and Italian art, and though it produces a similar result, it is different in means and intention. In Van Eyck it is instinctive, a by-product of the perception of light; and throughout the course of Flemish painting it remains empirical. This empirical rendering of space, this tracing as it were on a transparent screen, fulfills the requisites of naturalistic painting. But it could not satisfy the mathematical-minded Florentines, who demanded, in the words of Luca Pacioli, that art be concerned with "certainties," not with "opinions"; and they believed that such certainties could be established only by mathematics. They defined the real as that which could be proved to occupy a given position in space. The result of this thirst for certainty was scientific perspective, invented, it is said, by Brunelleschi, first put into words by Leon Battista Alberti, and given its fullest exposition by Piero della Francesca.

Scientific perspective is clearly not a basis for naturalism, and its abstract character was not fully understood even in 15th-century Florence. Alberti himself fluctuates between a mathematical and a realistic approach to appearances, without recognizing that the two are incompatible. He had come to take pleasure in the spectacle of nature and, in order to concentrate the visual appearances that delighted him, had invented a device that was a sort of camera obscura. Alberti has described the vast and varied panoramas obtained in his magic box, and it is evident that his conception of landscape is related to the first realistic backgrounds of Italian art, which appear about 1460 in the work of Baldovinetti and the brothers Pollaiuolo. The notion of a distant view from a high terrace must owe something to Flemish influence, but the literal manner in which these artists depict their native Valdarno suggests that their real motive was scientific naturalism. The landscape in Pollaiuolo's *Martyrdom of St. Sebastian* (1475; XI, PL. 182) is of astonishing sweep and truth. Of very high order as topography, it discloses a curiosity and sharpness of vision strong enough to make the landscape in the picture as important as the nude. But masterful as this background is, Pollaiuolo has not overcome the difficulty of a smooth transition into space, which was solved instinctively by Van Eyck: there is still the jump from foreground to background, an uneasy middle distance. It is this shortcoming which mars the first Italian picture in which landscape is not incidental but essential, Pollaiuolo's *Rape of Deianira* (XI, PL. 181).

These paintings show how difficult it was for the Florentines to combine a mathematical with a realistic position. The panorama of the camera obscura demanded a high point of view, but Brunelleschian perspective was feasible only when the receding plane was at right angles to the plane of vision. In the two most beautiful distance views of the 1460s this fact is recognized, and the traditional device of a high ledge is adopted; the works in question are the reverse panels of Piero della Francesca's portraits of the Duke of Urbino and his wife (PL. 11). Piero, the greatest living master of perspective, was also a friend of Alberti and must have known his camera obscura. But when it came to the painting of light, he realized the superiority of the north and, of all his contemporaries, made the most intelligent use of the late-14th-century fashion for Flemish painting.

The naturalism of Alberti's magic box and the Pollaiuolo panoramas was a freak, an experiment without roots, as was so much of 15th-century art and thought. It was not in Tuscany but in Venice, in the art of Giovanni Bellini, that the revelation of the Van Eycks was thoroughly understood and expanded upon. Bellini was by nature one of the great landscape painters of all time. How far he was directly influenced by Flemish art is impossible to say. In portraiture, he certainly studied the Van Eycks and Memling; and he was probably affected by the mysterious and powerful personality of Antonello da Messina, who was in Venice in 1475 and who, through Petrus Christus, was the direct heir of the Van Eyck tradition. Antonello's landscapes have all the dispassionate precision of his Flemish masters; moreover, he was a master not only of Flemish realism but also of systematic perspective.

Bellini's responsiveness to nature required no great stimulus from outside, however, for he was born with the landscape painter's greatest gift: an emotional response to light. In his early work he had loved the poignant light of sunrise and sunset, and he continued to portray such moments of heightened emotion when they could intensify the meaning of his subject, as in the *Resurrection* in Berlin (Staat. Mus.). As he grew older, he became more in love with the full light of day, in which all things can expand and be completely themselves. This is the attitude which pervades his *St. Francis in Ecstasy* (II, PL. 253); although full of light and natural details, it is painted with a rigorous sense of the individual identity of forms. In many of Bellini's later works, forms are more fused in the general atmosphere. He loved especially the soft, palpable air of a summer evening, a time when forms seem to give back the light they have absorbed all day. Bellini's landscapes are the supreme instance of natural facts transfigured through love. Few artists have been capable of such universal love embracing every twig and stone, the humblest detail as well as the most grandiose perspective; it is a state of being that can be reached only through profound humility.

After Bellini the landscape of fact disappears from Italy, and — with one great exception — from northern Europe, not to reappear until the mid-17th century. The notable exception is Pieter Bruegel the Elder. This master of naturalistic landscape was probably born in the 1520s, after the death of Bosch, one of the great geniuses of fantasy, from whom he learned much. Italian landscape painting at the time was entirely dominated by the elaborate fantasies of mannerism, in which the essential ingredients were a high viewpoint, a range of craggy mountains, and a distant prospect of river and seacoast. Bruegel mastered this mannerist style, and it remains the scaffolding for much of his work. Many of his paintings are, indeed, landscapes of fantasy. But he was so continuously excited by what he saw, and possessed such prodigious powers of observation and memory, that his true place is with the masters of fact.

In so far as a progression can be traced in Bruegel's short career, it is in his ability to make his criticism of life implicit rather than explicit. He begins with proverbs and allegories in which landscape is a setting and an accessory, and proceeds to the great landscapes in which the accidents of human life are one with the weather and the seasons. Few works of art are less in need of commentary. His compositions are full of reminiscences of early Flemish painting — of Hugo van der Goes (PL. 10), the Van Eycks, and even the Limbourg brothers; but he was also capable of anticipating the Dutch landscape painters of the 17th century. The confidence with which he looks back and forward in time and seizes any weapon that comes to hand is almost Shakespearean and is used for a similar end: the expression of an all-embracing sympathy with humanity. For although his human beings, their faces simplified to mere disks, seem sometimes to lose their individuality and become part of the mechanism of the universe, in the end it is the struggles and scant animal pleasures of their lives that really absorb him and dictate the character of his landscapes. Bruegel's work remains unique; though he had many imitators, none was able to use his style for a fresh creative purpose. The course of landscape painting was then set toward a totality of impression and away from the rich accumulation of incidents with which Bruegel's landscapes were filled.

The landscape of fact that directly influenced, or even created, 19th-century vision was the landscape painting of 17th-century Holland. It bears no resemblance to that of Bruegel, and its kinship with the backgrounds of Bellini and Pollaiuolo depends solely on similarity of aim, for these early Italian landscape painters were entirely unknown in Holland. It can be accounted for in no single way, but answers in three different modes may aid in understanding the situation.

The first basis is sociological. The landscape of fact, like portraiture, is a bourgeois form of art. Seventeenth-century Holland was the great, the heroic epoch of the *bourgeoisie*, and its art reflected the desire to see recognizable experiences portrayed. The Dutch felt the need for identifiable, unidealized views of their own country, the character of which they had recently fought so hard to defend. The second answer is philosophical. This was an age in which men once more felt free to ask questions about the workings of nature. The curiosity of the Renaissance had been repressed by the Counter Reformation, though never quite destroyed. Now that wars of religion were over — in Holland at least — a revival of science was possible. Landscape painting may also be seen as a symptom of quietism; after the pandemonium of religious war, men needed an interval of calm. The third answer lies within the art itself. By 1600 the tradition of mannerist landscape was exhausted, and the old Netherlandish love of representing the thing as seen, which had never been completely smothered, was ready to reassert itself.

It would be a mistake to suppose that Dutch landscape painting is admirable in proportion to the degree of fact it contains. The most naturalistic painters — Adriaen van der Velde, for one — are by no means the most inspired, and some of the greatest pictures of the period are ideal landscapes, such as Rembrandt's *The Mill* (Washington, D. C., Nat. Gall.) and Hercules Seghers' mountain prospect in the Uffizi (II, PL. 214). As a painter, Seghers must be reckoned as one of the great masters of the landscape of fantasy, but his etchings and drawings show him to have been the first acute observer of the distinctive Dutch scenery, both its oak woods with grassy paths and its panoramic views over flat country (IV, PL. 435; V, PL. 310). Thirty years later Hobbema (V, PL. 309) and De Koninck were to carry out these graphic observations in paint.

This difference in approach between drawings and paintings substantiates the immense prestige of ideal landscape, a disparity seen nowhere so clearly as in the work of Rembrandt. One of the most sensitive and accurate observers of fact who has ever lived, as time went on he could immediately find a graphic equivalent for everything he saw. In his landscape drawings of the 1650s, every dot and scribble contributes to an effect of space and light; problems that had baffled earlier landscape painters — for example, the difficulty of the middle distance, of getting into a picture smoothly from a low point of view — did not exist for him. Yet, when he came to paint, he felt that all these observations were no more than the raw material of art. To Rembrandt, as to Rubens, landscape painting meant the creation of an imaginary world, vaster, more dramatic, and more fraught with associations than the world we can perceive for ourselves. His greatest landscapes, with their solemn, legendary atmosphere, in the end may seem more satisfying than the transparent records of perception, however miraculous their precision and delicacy.

Holland is a country of great skies, and it was the sky that inspired those Dutch painters who first made an impression of landscape their entire subject. The oldest of this group, Jan van Goyen (PL. 14), had inherited the mannered picturesque of "Velvet" Brueghel and Jodocus (Joos) de Momper; but the loving delicacy with which he observed every nuance of a cloudscape gradually extended to the scene as a whole, and an initially artificial style became true landscape painting. When sky was reflected in water (II, PL. 215), there was achieved that unity of luminous atmosphere which is one of the chief qualities of Albert Cuyp (PL. 14) and the essence of Jan van de Cappelle and Jan van de Velde. A second-rate painter of sea and sky may enchant us, while an artist as painstaking and skillful as Hobbema may grow tedious because, to cite one aspect, the elaborately described trees in his woodland scenes are not subordinated to a general principle of light. To this judgment there is one exception: Jacob van Ruisdael, who must be reckoned the greatest master of the natural vision before Constable. Though in fits of depression he worked without a spark of feeling or vitality, when his emotions were rekindled he felt the grandeur and pathos of simple nature with Wordsworthian force. This feeling he expressed — as all the greatest landscape painters have done — through the telling disposition of large areas of light and dark, so that even before viewing his pictures at short range one is aware of their dramatic power (PL. 14); only upon close scrutiny does one find them full of observed facts. Once more light removes these observations to a new plane of reality. Here, however, light has a new character: it is no longer static and saturating, as in the work of Bellini but, rather, is in continual movement.

In the mid-17th century the Dutch school also perfected the painting of towns and buildings. This was part of a curious revival of classic principles of design, as opposed to the mannerist principles of the earlier genre painters. Of this revival Jan Vermeer was the most distinguished and consistent representative, but for a time it also affected De Hooch, Terborch, Metsu, and even Steen, and it is the basis of such exercises in perspective as the architectural pieces of Saenredam, Berckheyde, and De Witte (V, PL. 317). Within an over-all geometrical structure the Dutch could introduce as much detail as they liked without appearing trivial, in addition to a greater or lesser realization of atmosphere. The rendering of atmosphere reached a point of perfection that, for sheer accuracy, has never been surpassed: the Vermeer *View of Delft* (PL. 20). Not only does Vermeer display an astonishing subtlety of tone in this uncanny approximation of a color photograph, but he has used it with almost inhuman detachment. He has not allowed any one point in the scene to engage his interest and has set everything down with a complete evenness of focus. But the more one studies the *View of Delft* the more artful it appears, the more carefully calculated its design, and the more consistent all its components. No doubt truth of tone adds to the viewer's delight, but mere accuracy could not sustain one long without other qualities.

By the end of the 17th century the painting of light had become a trick, and that underlying sense of the importance of nature in daily life — which gave value to statements about natural appearances — had disappeared. Landscape painting was mere picture-making according to certain formulas; fact was confined to topography. Occasionally, when the topographer-artist could not suppress his interest in the beauty of atmosphere, the landscape of fact was once more raised to the condition of art. The impact of a fresh scene roused Canaletto to transcend his ordinary style. He painted *The Stonemason's Yard* (London, Nat. Gall.) because the scene appealed to him, not for sale to some traveling Englishman; his first views of the Thames express his pleasure in a new kind of light. Canaletto's rival Francesco Guardi had an impressionist's quickness of eye. He could catch the most delicate tone of a sail against the sky, the most tremulous light reflected from a canal on the faded plaster of a Venetian palace. But he was committed to a rococo principle of composition and a brilliant calligraphic style of drawing that, seductive as it is, belongs to the world of artifice. Naturalistic painting was impossible in the 18th century, as the case of Gainsborough confirms. In a letter to a patron he states that he has "... never seen any place that affords a subject equal to the poorest imitations of Gasper or Claude."

Landscape of fantasy. Regarding previous landscape painting as too tame and domesticated, artists began as early as the 15th century to explore the mysterious and the unsubdued aspects of nature. Working for an urban population that had long since learned to control natural forces, they could view former menaces such as flood with a kind of detachment and use them purposefully to excite a pleasing horror. Painting an aspect of nature that expressed the dark convolutions of the human spirit, making conscious use of disturbing shapes and symbols, they are what are now called "expressionist" artists. Expressionist art is fundamentally a northern and anticlassical form, which prolongs in both its imagery and complex rhythms the restless, organic art of the epoch of the folk migrations. It is forest-born, and even when it does not actually represent fir trees and undergrowth — as in German painting it almost invariably does — their gnarled and shaggy forms dominate the design.

The two painters who expressed this attitude to nature in its purest form came from the forests bordering the Rhine and the Danube: Grünewald and Altdorfer. Of the two, Grünewald is the greater and the more disturbing; his Isenheim Altar (VII, PLS. 85–89) is perhaps the most phenomenal picture ever painted. He was profoundly influenced by the mystical writings of his time and by the revivalism that preceded and accompanied Luther's reforms. As with all revivalist art, everything in his pictures is designed to have the most jarring and immediate effect upon the emotions. The landscapes on the outer wings of the altarpiece are terrifying. The wilderness in which St. Paul has found release from the world is of a desolation never again achieved in painting; and Grünewald has discovered, in the ragged fingers of moss that drip from every leafless twig, a perfect symbol of decay. Their repeated verticals impose a ghastly stillness broken only by the fall of a rotten branch. The landscape behind St. Anthony's hideous ordeal is more supportable only because it is really too extravagant in its manipulations of the machinery of horror (IV, PL. 180).

Altdorfer, though on a lesser scale than Grünewald, is more representative of the German spirit; in fact, he is the most German of all painters, for although his eye penetrates deeply into the northern forest, with its twisting tendrils and undergrowth, its pools and mosses glowing like enamel, he views them with a certain *Gemütlichkeit* — a snugness, as though from a cottage window — whereas Grünewald walks abroad among his terrors with starting eyes. Altdorfer's little *St. George and the Dragon* (ca. 1511; Munich, Alte Pin.) is at the opposite pole to the great figure pieces that were being painted at this time in Italy. In it man, even though he be St. George, almost disappears amid the luxuriance of the forest. Trees fill every inch of the picture: they are not the orderly decorative trees of tapestry landscape, with their gifts of fruit and blossom, but menacing organic growth, ready to smother and strangle any intruder.

In these landscapes of Grünewald and Altdorfer one sometimes has the feeling that the world has been newly created, and they were, in fact, painted at a time when men were again taking an interest in their origins. The most imaginative interpretation of primitive life was made by a Florentine, Piero di Cosimo, in a series of decorative panels, one of which, *The Forest Fire* (Oxford, Ashmolean Mus.), was the first Italian landscape in which man is of no importance. In this series the pattern for the representation of trees and hills was taken from Flemish models; but the lonely and neurasthenic Piero di Cosimo, although he affected an extreme conventionality in moments of depression, was capable of turning these formulas into personal symbols. He was obsessed by pendent cliffs and bulbous trees, which are an unusually direct and overt expression of his unconscious mind.

The emotive effect of flaming light, or actual flames, seems to have been recognized in the 1490s, and it was part of the repertoire of Hieronymus Bosch. In this, as in so much of his work, he may have been inspired by medieval miniatures or, more probably, by the frequent representation of Hell in miracle plays. The esthetic effectiveness of unexpected red and orange in a pool of darkness added to its popularity; and in the next 30 years the characteristic flames of Bosch break out in almost every landscape. In particular, the paintings associated with the name of Joachim Patinir, which constitute the first series of pure landscapes, rely on Bosch's fire device to alleviate their somewhat prosaic character.

The appearance of fire in Italian painting was in most cases traceable to the direct influence of Bosch, for much of his work was in Italian collections, particularly in that of Cardinal Grimani in Venice. There it was seen by the ardent young romantic Giorgione; immediately fire breaks out in his backgrounds, and he chooses subjects that justify its presence, such as the story of Orpheus and Eurydice. Another Giorgione design that shows very markedly the influence of Bosch, a work surviving only in an engraving by Marcantonio Raimondi, is the sinister piece which used to be known as *The Dream of Raphael*. Two naked women, of full Venetian sensuality, lie sleeping at the edge of a lake. Beyond them the sky is menacing and a castle has broken out in flames. The sleepers are undisturbed, but they are soon to be the victims of four disgusting monsters, which advance toward them along the bank. Here the supreme interpreter of harmony between man and nature materializes those mysterious and malevolent forces which, in man's mind no less than in nature itself, lie in wait to poison his dreams of epicurean tranquillity. Giorgione must have inspired such mannerist romantics as Lorenzo Lotto, Dosso Dossi, and even Domenico Beccafumi (PL. 295), who injected fire effects into their paintings from 1520 to 1550. But there is no doubt that Lotto had direct contact with German painters as well. In his earliest painting, *A Maiden's Dream* (ca. 1498; Washington, D. C., Nat. Gall.), the trees and their relation to the distant landscape show unmistakably the influence of Dürer, who was in Venice in 1494–95, and foreshadow the forest landscapes of Altdorfer and Cranach. Lotto's *St. Jerome in the Wilderness* (1506; Louvre) contains rocks and trees remarkably similar to those in the drawings Dürer did on his journey home from Italy in 1495.

Whereas in the north fantastic form was dominated by the knotted shapes of trees, in Mediterranean art a similar formal impulse was expressed through the old Byzantine tradition of jagged rocks. The strange Gothic mountains of Melchior Broederlam (V, PL. 277) and Lorenzo Monaco (PLS. 199, 201) continued far into the 15th century, and in its decadence this trend achieved a point of unreality that has not been equaled since. One of the earliest attempts to retain and justify the iconographic motif of fantastic rocks by means of science and reason was made by Mantegna in his *Virgin of the Quarries* (Uffizi).

The culmination of this union of science and fantasy is to be found in the work of Leonardo da Vinci. The direction of Leonardo's scientific researches was generally established by his esthetic appetites. He loved certain forms, he wanted to draw them, and while drawing them he began to ask questions: why were they that shape and what were the laws of their growth? This is true of his interest in fantastic rocks. He began, in *The Annunciation* (PL. 116) and in *The Virgin with the Flowers* (Munich, Alte Pin.), by accepting the rocks of convention, and about 1483 his love of fantastic rock forms led to that peculiar sample of personal iconography, *The Virgin of the Rocks* (PL. 121). At this date he had no particular interest in science: the first scientific entries in his notebooks date from a few years later. But, as time went on, his insatiable curiosity prompted him to ask more and more questions about the character and origins of rocks, until finally his researches into geology led to the most original of all his scientific speculations. His studies of strata show a genuine understanding of the forces leading to their formation. This empirical knowledge is implicit in his later landscapes, but it is used in the service of his imagination. In his *Treatise on Painting* Leonardo advises the painter to look at stains on walls, stones of uneven color, embers of the fire, clouds, and mud and then allow the imagination free play. Mountain landscapes, figures in violent action, expressions of faces, clothes, and "an infinity of things which you will be able to reduce to their complete and proper forms" will at once be suggested to the inventive spirit. This famous passage illustrates an important element in the landscape of fantasy: the manner in which it evolves from a chaos of forms — out of the undergrowth, the firelight, or the clouds — through an interplay of the conscious and the unconscious mind. The backgrounds of the *Mona Lisa* (PL. 126) and *The Virgin and Child with St. Anne* (PL. 122) conform entirely to this character, landscape of a primitive world in which man has hardly established a foothold.

Later in life the scientific subject that occupied his mind until it became an obsession was the movement of water. The rhythmic qualities of moving water first fascinated him esthetically, and this interest led to an analytic approach. And again, he ultimately used his researches to enhance his imaginative fantasies. The drawings of the deluges, in which Leonardo concentrated all his knowledge of rock forms and hydrodynamics, present a most disturbing juncture of the medieval and modern worlds. In these the landscape of fantasy is not nature before man has tamed it but the forces of nature rising in revolt against man, with his absurd pretense to ignore them or use them for his advantage. Leonardo had arrived at a vision of destruction in which symbol and reality seem to be at one.

The feeling for the independent life of nature that was the mainspring of Leonardo was soon to be lost in mannerism. Sixteenth-century mannerism employs the exciting elements of picturemaking regardless of their truth or relevance; and although it uses the forms of classicism as far as possible, it reveals in accent and rhythm that great deposit of Gothicism which the Renaissance had not strained out of Italian art. It was characteristic of the mannerists that they should take pleasure in the fantastic rocks of Gothic painting, but should justify this taste by using forms derived from the decorative landscapes of antiquity. From such landscapes in Hellenistic style comes the compositional scheme of mannerist landscape, with its high point of view, its distant prospect of mountains and hills on one side of the picture, and a seacoast or estuary on the other. It is a scheme foreshadowed in Altdorfer and present in the frankly antiquarian decorations of Polidoro da Caravaggio in S. Silvestro al Quirinale, Rome. The pure mannerist landscape, with its complete repertoire of tricks and a minimum of firsthand observation, is exemplified in the work of Niccolò dell'Abate, who subordinates everything to an ideal of elegant picturemaking. Naturally this superficial style was at its best when used for its original purpose of interior decoration; and nowhere is it more charming than in the room of landscapes that Paolo Veronese painted about 1560 in Palladio's Villa Barbaro at Maser. In most of them he has followed the antique model, with its elaborate architecture, bridges, and jetties and a dark foreground tree; but he has also allowed himself the expansive Venetian skies that irradiate all his work.

This decorative use of landscape is the most harmless form of wall decoration ever devised, and so has continued to be fashionable. But it is an approach to the subject at the furthest remove from that of Bellini, Constable, Cézanne, and the other patient quarriers of natural appearances. In fact only two of the great mannerists produced landscapes of any significance — Tintoretto and El Greco. With Tintoretto, nature was caught up in the rushing wind of his genius and made to serve the purpose of his colossal invention. The background of his *Flight into Egypt* is a drama of light and shade as exciting as an Altdorfer; the desert landscapes of the two panels of Mary Magdalene and St. Mary of Egypt (Venice, Scuola di S. Rocco; XII, PL. 372) are made up of twisted forms that communicate the artist's creative energy through the representation of organic life. Switch off this current of energy, leave only the nervous gestures, and one has those minor picturesque landscape painters Mola, Testa, and Magnasco, whose caves, ravines, and beaches are found diverting in an age of decadence. El Greco has left us one unforgettable landscape, his *View of Toledo* (New York, Met. Mus.). It is a true expressionist work, a picture of the artist's own mood, and an exception to all rules. Far removed from the spirit of Mediterranean art and from the rest of 17th-century landscape painting, it has more the character of 19th-century romanticism.

The compositional scheme of mannerism also provided a scaffolding for one of the greatest of all landscape painters, Peter Paul Rubens. He cannot, of course, be classed with the painters just considered. Tintoretto probably never paused to draw the correct form of a single leaf; whereas the drawings Rubens did from nature are among the most sensitive and observant ever made. But although this prodigious power of recording natural details was often transferred to his pictures, Rubens cannot be called a painter of fact. Nor have his landscapes the literary character and the backward glance to a golden age that one may call Virgilian. They must therefore be discussed here, although the word "fantasy" is altogether too weak to describe their imaginative richness and warmth (PL. 19; XII, PL. 332). Just as Shakespeare reworked the stock themes and situations of Elizabethan drama, so Rubens, by the wealth of his imagination, his unfailing vitality, and the richness of his pictorial vocabulary, has forced the worn-out scheme of mannerist landscape to yield new splendor. His earlier landscapes, such as the *Shipwreck of Aeneas* (Berlin, Staat. Mus.) and the *Philemon and Baucis* (Vienna, Kunsthist. Mus.), conform superficially to the pattern that is found, for example, in the engravings of Bruegel, but his variant has become more complex and more dynamic. The mannerist desire to keep all forms in perpetual flux has never been more marvelously realized in landscape than in *Philemon and Baucis*. But these breath-taking arcs and spirals are based on a series of horizontals, calculated with a classic sense of interval.

The Watering Place (London, Nat. Gall.) introduces a different scheme of composition. It is seen from a low point of view, and the construction of the towering central mass is a perfect example of the baroque: it has the sweeping movement, the twist and countertwist which are the essence of baroque architecture and which give it a unity and power that transcend the perverse rhythms of the preceding style. As a reading of nature, however, it still belongs to the romantic tradition of the north. The trees and undergrowth are of an overwhelming luxuriance. Part of the primeval forest, they writhe and surge like monsters. Rubens himself recognized the character of his romanticism and captured it fully in the painting *Tournament before a Castle* (Louvre). Like Altdorfer seeing the connection between the landscape of fantasy and the Gothic past, he filled the foreground of his picture with knights in armor. Beyond the castle, hanging low over the landscape, is one of the large red suns with which Rubens, in his later work, is so prodigal. No one, before Turner, has painted richer and more varied sunsets, ranging from fiery orange to the mysterious milky sun of the *Birdcatcher* (Louvre). Rubens was also a master of raging skies. In the *Philemon and Baucis* the clouds portend a deluge; in the *Shipwreck of Aeneas* their darkness is made more lurid by a flaming beacon on the distant promontory. Here, and in the moonlight landscape in the Seilern Collection (London), Rubens returns to the night scenes that had so stirred the imaginations of Altdorfer, Leonardo, and Giorgione.

Night is not a subject for naturalistic painting. A large area of dark paint cannot be made to look convincing by optical processes alone; it has to be transmuted through the medium of the poetic imagination. About 1600, when darkness was much in vogue, there appeared in Rome a landscape painter whose work was a strange and evocative concentration of poetry, the Frankfurt-born Adam Elsheimer (PL. 13). Like Edgar Allan Poe, he was one of those artists whose influence was much beyond his own achievement. Rubens, Rembrandt, and Claude each took from him something decisive in their development, and — what is more extraordinary — each took something different. Elsheimer died in Rome in 1610, after having worked there for the preceding ten years. He therefore used the current Roman landscape style, that of Brill and Domenichino (PL. 15), but his spirit is that of Altdorfer. He paints classical scenery, but with a strangeness and intensity of light, an enameled quality which is entirely German and which takes one back beyond Altdorfer to Lukas Moser of Tiefenbronn. It was Elsheimer who brought to a new stage of realization the nocturnal fantasies of a hundred years earlier. In his *Flight into Egypt* (VI, PL. 159), he carried them as near to the limits of truth as such subjects can go without entirely sacrificing the element of decoration that must exist in any picture.

Just as in the 18th century, that winter of the imagination, the landscape of fact degenerated into topography, so the landscape of fantasy degenerated into the picturesque, more particularly into that strain of the picturesque which derived from Salvator Rosa (PL. 16). He was, in a minor degree, a kind of Byron who opened a new vein of sentiment and discovered the rhetorical form by which it could be conveyed. His sentiments were exaggerated and his means of expressing them often commonplace; his enormous popularity only affirms that the 18th century needed some escape from its own oppressive rationalism.

Ideal landscape. Before landscape painting could be made an end in itself, it had to be fitted into the ideal concept to which every artist and writer on art subscribed for 300 years after the Renaissance. The delight in imitation, which had satisfied Alberti and Bellini, was not enough for Lomazzo and the Carraccis. In both content and design, landscape must aspire to those higher kinds of painting which illustrate a theme — religious, historical, or poetic. And this cannot be done simply by introducing a small group of figures enacting the Flight into Egypt or the story of Eurydice but must be effected through the mood and character of the entire scene. The features of which it is composed must be chosen from nature, as poetic diction is chosen from ordinary speech, for their elegance, their ancient associations, and their faculty of harmonious combination: *Ut pictura poesis*.

Two poets of antiquity, Ovid and Virgil, furnished the imagination of the Renaissance artists. Ovid, with his clear and detailed descriptions of the fabulous, was the favorite of figure painters; but Virgil was the inspiration of landscape. The reason lies not only in the delicate suggestions of scenery that occur in the *Aeneid* but also in the myth of ideal rusticity, of which he was the master. This was the most enchanting dream that has ever consoled mankind, the myth of a golden age in which man lived on the fruits of the earth, peacefully, piously, and with primitive simplicity. As a conception of the early history of mankind, it is the exact opposite of that which produced the landscape of fantasy.

Virgilian landscape is essentially an evocation of the antique world, with all its fullness of life and its confidence in the body, but also with some qualities the ancient world lacked, some half-lights, some backward glances to the dreams of the late Gothic period. Foreshadowing this new prospect is the beautiful *Allegory of Souls* by Giovanni Bellini (Uffizi); this is a descendant of the paradise garden, but one in which the figures breathe the palpable atmosphere of a warm summer evening. The foreground is occupied by saints, but cupids (however Christianized) play around the Tree of Life, and in the landscape a centaur is lurking near the Cross.

In spite of its sacred theme, this is really the first example of that kind of painting which the Venetians called "poesie." Such pictures must have been a formative influence on the youthful Giorgione, whose earliest landscapes — backgrounds of religious works painted when he can have been no more than a boy — show astonishing skill. The eye is led into the background firmly and smoothly, but with some complexity. Natural objects, leaves, and stones are rendered with extraordinary precision, but already they are removed from the landscape of fact. Giorgione inherited Bellini's sense of precious light, and it is the golden light and the flowing rhythm in the lines of trees and contours that make his earliest landscapes poetical. Giorgione's natural lyricism was developed by association with the group of poets of the so-called "Arcadian movement" at the court of Caterina Cornaro in Asolo, near his native Castelfranco, and in particular with that arbiter of classic elegance Pietro Bembo. An Arcadian spirit is present in Italian poetry as early as Boccaccio, but its great popularity was due to Jacopo Sannazaro, whose *Arcadia* appeared in the 1490s. Apart from the general charm of its subject matter to a landscape painter, the *Arcadia* is full of pictures, the kind of subject that was to delight the painters of Venice during the next 50 years.

The structure of the new Arcadian landscape follows a regular pattern. On either side are dark masses of trees and rock, like wings of a theatrical scene, which leave the center of the picture free. Even the figures, which are completely at one with the landscape, are sometimes placed at the side; sky and distance take the principal place. It is the composition that, with every refinement of variation, was to form the basis of Claude Lorrain's work. It occurred in one of Giorgione's earliest paintings, *The Finding of Paris* (now lost), and it also underlies his one essential and indubitable work, that quintessence of poetic landscape, *The Tempest* (VI, PL. 186). *The Tempest* is one of those works before which the scholar had best remain silent. No one knows what it represents; even Marcantonio Michiel, writing almost in Giorgione's day, could offer no better title than "a gypsy and a soldier." There is little doubt that it is a free fantasy which grew as Giorgione painted it; X rays have shown that he was an improviser, who changed his pictures as he went along, and that this composition originally contained another naked woman, bathing her feet in the stream.

In a masterly essay on the school of Giorgione, Walter Pater points out that many pictures of that school have musical themes; and it is precisely this musical quality, this feeling that "life itself is conceived as a sort of listening," which distinguishes Giorgione from his younger contemporary Titian. The most complete and satisfying of Titian's early landscapes are those that lie on either side of the *Sacred and Profane Love* (Rome, Gall. Borghese). But in the heads of the twin Venuses (for that is what they are) is seen a proud, sensual look entirely different from the pure, gentle, abstracted expression of Giorgione's women. The appeal of this picture to the emotions is due very largely to the mood of the landscape, achieved by the beauty of the evening light; and this mood dominates the painting of the time. The very group of buildings that lies behind the earthly Venus appears in two other pictures, the *Sleeping Venus* by Giorgione (VI, PL. 195) and the still-debated *Noli me tangere* in London (Nat. Gall.), and in each case it gives the keynote of the entire picture.

Although Titian was primarily a painter of portraits and figure compositions, the trees and mountains with which he enriched his backgrounds are of great importance in the history of ideal landscape, for they provided the forms of vegetation employed by Claude and Poussin. Anyone who has visited Cadore will recognize that the impressions of Titian's native place remained with him all his life. The rocky hills with their thick clusters of trees, the rushing streams, and blue mountain distances are seized upon with Titian's sensual power and crowded into the small background of a portrait. Occasionally they are given more space, and one recognizes the origin of all Carracciesque landscape. The great hunting landscapes by the Carraccis in the Louvre are no more than freer and more crowded versions of Titian's *Vènus du Pardo*, which hangs opposite them; and from the lost *St. Peter Martyr* — perhaps the most copied picture in the world — there flowed an unending series of landscape compositions during the 17th century. Titian's appetite for nature gives to his landscapes a magnificent fullness. His trees, in particular, have a weight of leaf and roundness of trunk never surpassed, and it is not surprising that Poussin and Rubens, Constable and Turner, all looked on him as a source of inspiration. But he has not enlarged the field of landscape composition as Giorgione has. His planes lie behind one another in a purely theatrical manner, and he is not greatly concerned with tone, although in such late works as the *Rape of Europa* (Boston, Gardner Mus.) his distances are painted with a glorious freedom. To find the Titianesque scheme of ideal landscape, one must look in the numerous drawings and engravings associated with the name of Campagnola, in which these characteristic traits persisted without a break to the time of the Carraccis. Through these works, no less than through the study of Titian's paintings, the Bolognese continued uninterruptedly the tradition of the first ideal landscapes.

At their best, as in the lunettes in the Galleria Doria Pamphili (III, PL. 89), the landscapes of Annibale Carracci are admirable pieces of picturemaking, in which agreeably stylized parts are built up into a harmonious whole. There is even at times a note of authentic poetry, though it is faint and guarded compared with the poetry that, at almost the same date, Elsheimer was able to infuse into the same stylistic materials. But, in the end, these eclectic landscapes are of interest only to historians. The landscapes of Brill (PL. 13; V, PL. 304) and Domenichino (PL. 15) are without joy in the perception of fact, without an imaginative sense of the force and mystery of nature, and above all they lack feeling for the unifying element of light. Without these life-giving qualities, no amount of idealization will justify landscape painting as an art form.

It is by these qualities, no less than by his sense of Arcadian poetry, that Claude can make the formal vocabulary of his predecessors fresh and vivid to the present day. Claude Gellée, called Lorrain, the true heir to the poetry of Giorgione, was born in 1600 in Lorraine, but went to Rome as a youth and remained there almost uninterruptedly until his death in 1682. Very little is known about his life, apart from a short biographical note by a fellow painter, Joachim von Sandrart, who accompanied him on his early painting expeditions. He tells that at that time Claude's study of nature was limited to contemplation, particularly of sunrise and sunset. "Seeing that I worked from nature," he adds, "he began to do the same himself"; and Sandrart later makes it clear that Claude not only drew but painted from nature, especially for his distance effects. This is contrary to anything one is told about the landscapes of the old masters, and it is not a method suggested by a first impression of the paintings themselves, although careful scrutiny of Claude's work shows effects that could hardly have been carried in the memory. No great painter ever lived so completely within his resources as Claude. Unlike those of such splendid prodigals as Rubens, his pictures always suggest a tactful and farsighted economy. At first sight their extreme simplicity may suggest a certain lack of resource; it is only upon becoming familiar with them and comparing them with the work of imitators that one realizes how rich is the observation Claude has put into every branch, how extremely subtle the tonality of his foregrounds, and how delicately drawn the waves and ripples which catch the light of his golden skies.

Behind these seemingly simple pictures there was an immense amount of preparation. First came the sketches from nature, the works of Claude that most clearly disclose the gulf which separates him from the Carraccis, for these show a visual responsiveness hardly different from that of the impressionists. Sometimes they are careful studies of detail, sometimes entirely impressionist in their sense of light; sometimes they have a Chinese delicacy of accent (PL. 204). In all of them the general disposition of mass is masterly, and no one will deny their ravishing beauty, freshness, and variety. But it is important to remember that Claude never thought of the sketches as ends in themselves. His mind was always looking forward to their use as part of a whole composition; and parallel with detail studies from observation, he made sketches of ideas that could be used as the basis of fully developed pictures. Then came the actual studies for pictures carried far toward the final composition, some — such as the *Ascanius and the Stag* (Oxford, Ashmolean Mus.), done when Claude was eighty-two — setting the completed version down exactly. These are the drawings which Claude himself valued and which were collected by his contemporaries, and if studied with something of the patience that went into their composition, their poetic fullness is extremely impressive. Finally come the finished paintings themselves, about which there is little to say, for anyone who looks at them in a receptive frame of mind must surely be touched by their exquisite poetry. There is never a false note. Claude could subordinate all his powers of perception and knowledge of natural appearances to the poetic feeling of the whole. The world of his imagination is so clear and consistent that nothing obtrudes, nothing is commonplace, nothing is done just for effect. As with the plays of Racine, which give the same feeling of devotion to an ideal whole, this is not so much the result of self-discipline — an act of will — as of a natural habit of mind.

Claude nearly always conformed to an underlying scheme of composition. This involved a dark coulisse on one side (hardly ever on two), the shadow of which extended across the first plane of the foreground; a middle plane with a large central feature, usually a group of trees; and finally, two planes, one behind the other, the second being that luminous distance for which he has always been famous, and which he painted directly from nature. Much art was necessary to lead the eye from one plane to the next, and Claude employed bridges, rivers, cattle fording a stream, and similar devices; but these are less important than his sure sense of tone, which allowed him to achieve an effect of recession even in pictures where every plane is parallel. Naturally he used many variants of this compositional scheme. Often he dispensed with the central feature, as in that enchanting work which by its title alone evokes the spirit of Claude, *The Decline of the Roman Empire* (Trustees of the Late Duke of Westminster). More rarely he dispensed with the coulisse, as in *Morning* (Leningrad, The Hermitage) or *Jacob with Laban and His Daughters* (London, Dulwich College Picture Gall.). This method of designing by successive planes that sometimes, at first sight, seem little more than silhouettes gave unusual prominence to the shape of his dark masses. Yet, however refined and carefully balanced in the final picture are the shapes of his trees and rocks, they always retain their natural character. In spite of the extreme formality, nothing in Claude is reduced to formula.

Only when Claude was past middle age do spirit and design attain their full expression. His greatest poems — the *Times of the Day* (Leningrad, The Hermitage) and *Acis and Galatea* (Dresden, Gemäldegalerie) — were painted when he was over sixty. It is these later works that, whatever their ostensible subject, are fullest of the Virgilian spirit. His seaports (PL. 205), painted in the 1640s, may evoke that moment when Aeneas leaves the grandeur and certainty of Carthage for a shining unknown distance. But the Virgilian element in Claude is, above all, his sense of a golden age: grazing flocks, unruffled waters, and a calm luminous sky, images of perfect harmony between man and nature but, as he combines them, touched with a Mozartean wistfulness, as if this perfection could last no longer than the moment in which it takes possession of the mind.

The great figures in history have a curious way of appearing in complementary pairs. The complement to the gentle, inarticulate Claude is the stern Cartesian, Nicolas Poussin. Unlike Claude, much is known about Poussin, and everything that is known proves that the intellectual content of his pictures cannot be exaggerated. Every incident, no less than the disposition of every form, is the result of profound meditation. No art could be further from the inspired improvisation and lyric flow of Giorgione; yet the early Poussin landscapes, the backgrounds of his bacchanalian scenes (XI, PL. 231), go back to Titian's mythological paintings for Alfonso d'Este (Prado; London, Nat. Gall.), which the French master is said to have copied.

Poussin did not paint pure landscapes until about 1648, when he was fifty-four, and one may wonder why, holding the opinions he did about the inherently moral character of painting, he should have attempted the subject at all. But in spite of his theories, Poussin had an immense appetite for nature; and one may also guess that he was ambitious of achieving a fresh conquest for the intellect by giving logical form even to the disorder of natural scenery. Poussin conceived that the basis of landscape painting lay in the harmonious balance of the horizontal and vertical elements in his design. He recognized that the spacing of these horizontals and verticals and their rhythmic relation to one another could have an effect exactly like the rhythmic trave or other harmonic devices of architecture; and in fact, he often disposed them according to the golden section. The chief difficulty of imposing this geometric scheme on nature lies, of course, in the absence of verticals. Landscape is essentially horizontal, and such verticals as exist are not always at right angles to the ground. To meet this difficulty Poussin, in his more schematic compositions, was fond of introducing architecture, which assisted his secondary purpose of giving an antique air to his subjects. His groups of buildings are of great importance in providing a modulus to the scheme of proportion on which the design is constructed; and sometimes, by means of blocks of masonry from a ruined temple, he is able to carry this pure geometry right through the composition. It was essential to Poussin's design that his verticals and horizontals should meet at right angles: indeed, if any upright line inclines slightly from the vertical, one may be sure to find another slightly off the horizontal that is at right angles to it. This insistence on the right angle is only possible when the main axis of the composition is parallel to the picture plane, and it thus accounts for the frontality of Poussin's landscape, a condition equally at variance with ordinary vision and with the serpentine recession of mannerism.

Since penetration into space is the essence of landscape, Poussin had to devise means of leading the eye back into the distance. No doubt the way most congenial to his mathematical mind was the central point of perspective, but he saw this as too rigid and artificial to be anything more than an occasional solution. He therefore fitted into his scaffolding of horizontals a subsidiary scheme of diagonals to conduct the eye smoothly and rhythmically into the background, and he was particularly fond of a diagonal path turning back on itself after about two-thirds of its journey. In the great myths Poussin painted between 1658 and 1665 this extreme geometrical ardor was relaxed or at least concealed. Although their subjects were often drawn from the myths of antiquity — Orpheus and Eurydice, Polyphemus, the giant Orion — and were no doubt inspired by fervid reading of the classics, they do not at all suggest the imaginative worlds of Ovid and Virgil. They are too grave, too weighted down with thought and the consciousness of original sin. In contemplating the work of Poussin, it is Milton who most often comes to mind, and the four famous landscapes of the seasons (XI, PL. 147), it might be noted, were painted during the years of the composition of *Paradise Lost*. Although Milton lacked Poussin's extreme rationalism, one finds in both the same early delight in pagan richness of color and imagery, the same strenuous and didactic middle period, and the same old age of renunciation and remoteness, which gave a new depth of poetic vision.

Poussin is one of those rare artists whose influence was wholly beneficial. He combined in full measure the real and the ideal; his scrupulous sense of design was nourished on observation, and his most exalted visions always remain concrete. Without his sense of truth, Sébastian Bourdon would have become a mere picturemaker; without his sense of form, Gaspard Dughet would have become a sort of Charles Jacques. As it is, they both produced fine landscapes. Dughet had a gift of straightforward naturalism that makes him the true precursor of the Barbizon school (PL. 15). Even the romantic side of Poussin was perpetuated in the work of Francisque Millet. That the influence of Poussin should have declined in the rococo period was inevitable, but in the more heroic age of classicism his spirit was revived. Through Pierre Henri de Valenciennes (PL. 22) it dominated the early work of Corot; and although Corot himself was to discover that his true affinities were with Claude, the shadow of Poussin still falls across the landscapes of Millet and Pissarro, long before Cézanne made a more spectacular return to his principles.

In England Poussin has had few followers, for Claude gave to English painting a simpler scaffolding on which the native school could build. There was something in Claude's gentle poetry, in his wistful glances at a vanished civilization, and his feeling that all nature could be laid out for man's delight, which appealed particularly to the English connoisseurs of the 18th century. Sometimes his principles of composition, with their wings and stage trees, offered too easy a formula; but Richard Wilson (VI, PL. 440), at his best, understood the two chief lessons of Claude — that the center of a landscape is an area of light, and that everything must be subordinate to a single mood. As a result, although by no means a skillful artist, Wilson was a true minor poet.

Ideal landscape was closely connected with the landscape of symbols; both were inspired by a dream of the earthly paradise, and both sought to create a harmony between man and nature. By the 19th century the myth of a golden age lost its hold on the imaginations of poets and painters, and with this annihilation of an ideal past there vanished the concept of ideal landscape. William Blake's illustrations for R. J. Thornton's edition of Virgil's *Pastorals* may fitly bring the story to an end. These 17 tiny woodcuts, full of a most powerful poetry, inspired the visionary landscape that Samuel Palmer painted between 1825 and 1830, when he was living at Shoreham, remote from the world. Palmer invested nature with a spiritual quality and found every blade of grass and leaf and cloud was designed according to God's pattern. It was the vision of the Middle Ages and thus created a style very close to the landscape of symbols. In his use of decorative symbols and in the freedom and unconventionality of his means, Palmer surpasses that other romantic landscape painter whose brooding on nature is in many respects similar to his, Caspar David Friedrich. Palmer remains the last painter of Virgilian landscape, and with him there ends that beautiful episode in European art which from Giorgione's day had been a source of enchantment and consolation.

The natural vision. Early in the 19th century it was recognized that the status of landscape painting was changing, and very soon landscapes that at least purported to be close imitations of nature came to hold a more secure place in popular affection than any other form of art. Such changes or expansions of popular taste usually have their origins in the vision of some great artist or group of artists; and although the wider appreciation of landscape arose from complex causes, in the end it was the genius of Constable that first discovered — and still justifies — the art of unquestioning naturalism.

No artist, of course, is entirely original. As a native of East Anglia, where he was born in 1776, John Constable had certainly seen Dutch landscapes in the local collections. His feeling for moving light, for shadows cast by clouds in a vast windy sky, must have derived from Ruisdael, as well as from his own observations, for Constable like all revolutionaries was an eager student of tradition. He had the capacity, found only in great artists, of entering into a way of painting apparently alien to his own and drawing from it those elements which are eternally vital and nourishing: that is, he could absorb without imitating. His letters are full of understanding of Titian, Claude, Richard Wilson, and Dughet, and quite late in life he would give up any commission in order to copy a Poussin or a Claude. This deep understanding of the tradition of European landscape was one of the reasons why Constable was able to present such a quantity of normal observation without the banality of later realists. Another reason was the importance Constable attached to what he called the "chiaroscuro of nature," a phrase he used repeatedly to describe two rather different effects. First he meant the sparkle of light, and this was the aspect of his work which is usually considered most original. The technical devices by which it was achieved, the broken touches and flicks of pure white applied with a palette knife, were a decisive influence on French painting. But by "chiaroscuro of nature" Constable also meant that some drama of light and shade must underlie all landscape compositions and give the keynote of feeling in which the scene was painted.

It is this sense of dramatic unity, as much as his feeling for the freshness of nature, which distinguishes Constable from his contemporaries. He recognized the fundamental truth that art must be based on a single dominating idea and that the test of an artist is his ability to carry this idea through, to enrich and expand it, but never to lose sight of it and never to include any incidents, however seductive in themselves, which are not ultimately subordinate to his initial main conception. Such an aim was relatively simple to achieve in classic landscape painting, where ideal forms could be used to prevent the multiplication of distracting details. But it is exceedingly difficult in the naturalistic landscape, Constable's discovery, where the impressions received from actual objects are the essential point of departure, and where the means of simplification have not already been shaped by generations of taste and style. Perhaps no other painter (except Rubens) has succeeded as Constable did in subordinating the infinite visual data of landscape to a single pictorial idea. Later painters have either killed the idea by embellishing it or have merely offered the first sensation without daring to build on it. The second course, though it produced much of the finest painting of the 19th century, restricts both scale and sense of permanence.

Constable has left a full record of his sensations in oil sketches that have become the most admired part of his work. But the struggle came, as he well knew, when first impressions had to be turned into large pictures. Of this process, for several of his compositions, there is evidence at every stage: there are the first tiny oils stating the theme of the pictures in terms of light and shade, the pencil studies that begin the definition of form, the detailed drawings from nature, and the larger oil sketches.

In Constable's greatest work naturalism is raised to a higher mold by the artist's belief that, since nature was the clearest revelation of God's will, the painting of landscape could be a means of conveying moral ideas. The final stage has been reached in the development of man's relations with nature, in an evolution that began with the timid confidence of the Middle Ages. Just as the last section might have been called "Virgilian landscape," so might this have been called "Wordsworthian," although Constable alone was a conscious exponent of the poet's beliefs. Both poet and painter found nature transformed by the philosophy of the 18th century into a mechanical universe working under the dictates of common sense; and both believed that there was something in trees, flowers, meadows, and mountains which was so full of the divine that, if contemplated with sufficient devotion, it would reveal a moral and spiritual quality of its own. Both men turned to rustic life because, to quote Wordsworth, "in that condition our elementary feelings co-exist in a state of greater simplicity, and consequently may be more accurately contemplated and more forcibly communicated." Both drew practically the whole of their emotive power from the scenes of their boyhood. Constable felt that his paintings of Dedham (PL. 23), the Stour River (III, PLS. 443, 444), and the surrounding country reached a higher emotional temperature than his other work. Above all, Wordsworth and Constable were united by their rapture in all created things. "I never saw an ugly thing in my life," said Constable.

Although a Wordsworthian attitude toward nature lies at the root of Constable's greatness, his immediate importance was due to pictorial rather than philosophical causes. His influence in England, the country of philosophical naturalism, was practically nonexistent, whereas in France it was immense. Contemporary critics speak of his influence on a school of French landscape painters, but little evidence of this survives before the rise of the Barbizon school in the late 1830s. Théodore Rousseau (PL. 22), who had seen *The Hay Wain* (III, PL. 441) and other Constables, had fundamentally the same aim as the English painter. He wished to make great compositions out of observed facts, and said: "J'entends par composition ce qui est en nous, entrant le plus possible dans la réalité extérieure des choses." His responses to nature, however, were very different: it was the static and not the dynamic that appealed to him, and his most genuine emotions were aroused by the absolute stillness of a summer day. Rousseau was an important painter; he created the academism of naturalistic landscape painting, which became the standard style for serious exhibition pieces at the official Salons. Perhaps if we knew more of his direct studies from nature, he would be rated more highly. But even so, he seems to have lacked the unself-conscious abandonment to nature on which the new vision depended; and this was the great gift of Corot.

Corot went to Rome as a student in 1825, the year after Constable's triumph at the Paris Salon. He does not seem to have participated in the general excitement, and never in his recorded sayings refers to Constable. His tastes were entirely classic, and he went to Rome with the intention of following in the steps of Poussin and that more recent master of classic landscape Pierre Henri de Valenciennes. The sketches he made from nature were undertaken simply as material for later compositions. All the classic landscape painters of the time made such studies, but they were not considered of more than private or professional interest and were generally destroyed. From the first, Corot brought to a current form certain qualities his fellow students lacked. He had a natural power of simplification that prevented his studies from ever becoming mere topography. He aided his powers of selection, as Claude had done, by the simple means of choosing as his main motif quite distant objects. This would have produced feeble results had it not been supported by a perfectly true sense of tone, inseparable from an equally unerring sense of design. On his first visit to Rome, the forms and colors of classic landscape had induced in him a state of passionate receptivity, and he had been able to absorb principles of composition that lasted him all his life. The sketches made on this first journey are, in some ways, the most remarkable he ever did, for his excitement engendered a freedom of handling he did not allow himself again until his last years; in those from subsequent visits, although there is a greater measure of observed fact, the touch is more discreet and the color less resonant.

Looking at these crystalline visions, it is hard to believe that they were practically never seen in Corot's lifetime and were intended only as material for large compositions which, by an irony of history, are never seen today. Corot's studies are in many respects more complete than those of Constable.

Fundamentally a classic artist, Corot had at the back of his mind a feeling for generalized form that allowed him to compose his sketches in larger and simpler units. But he seldom succeeded, as Constable had, in making them into exhibition pictures. His large compositions bear no relation to his sketches. Only one of Corot's Italian pictures, the *View near Volterra* (Washington, D. C., Nat. Gall.), retains the virtues of his studies; but in France, particularly in the pictures painted in the Morvan Mountains, he arrived at a satisfactory compromise, pictures of moderate size, firmly constructed and seen with absolute naturalness.

In the 1840s Corot gradually evolved a means of making his Salon pictures more his own. In *Le Vallon* (1855; Louvre) he brought to the creation of a new vision his fine sense of composition and tone and some of the lyric flow that was to fill his later work; at the same time there began the series of nymphs dancing among feathery trees, the subject that was to increase so disastrously the number of his admirers. One cannot blame Corot for adopting a genre which pleased both fashionable and critical opinion, for his own tastes inclined him in the same direction. From all his range of delicate visual experiences Corot came to be satisfied with one: shimmery light reflected from water and passing through the delicate leaves of birches and willows (III, PL. 459).

It is interesting to find that Corot, whose mind was anything but philosophic, had instinctively absorbed the esthetic philosophy of his time and assumed that art consists in conveying a sensation, not in persuading us to accept a truth. He was far nearer to pure estheticism than was Constable. Constable chose his subjects with a sense of their moral grandeur and worked over them to make them nobler and more dramatic. Corot had no such Protestant preoccupation with morals but was confident that, if he submitted with sincere humility to his sensations, *le bon Dieu* would do the rest. The point that unites them is unquestioning belief in the natural vision as the basis of art. By the mid-19th century this belief had evidently become widespread, and it found a born popularizer in the person of Courbet. For him, "Le beau est dans la nature, et s'y rencontre dans la réalité sous les formes les plus diverses." Beauty is there awaiting discovery by the artist, who has no right to amplify what he finds. "Le beau donné par la nature est supérieur à toutes les conventions de l'artiste." Although these statements have become the stock-in-trade of art teaching, in Courbet's day it was still postulated in academic circles that nature must be improved in the interest of the ideal. To paint merely what one saw was "vulgar." The widespread use of this word shows that the conflict between realism and academism, like most conflicts in the 19th century, has a social basis. Realist painting was called "the painting of democrats, of those who don't change their linen," and the provocative personality of a Courbet, tough and arrogant, was necessary to establish the new style.

Courbet's answer to rejection by the official Salon was his monster one-man show of 1855. It contained 14 landscapes, the earliest of which was dated 1841. These were truly popular paintings. One does not sense behind them, as with Constable, the study of landscape tradition; still less does one feel the admiration for Claude with which Corot gives a classic accent even to his Second Empire reveries. Courbet chose subjects with an immediate appeal and dwelt on them with relish; the grass is very green — greener than it has ever been in good painting before or since, the sunset skies are very pink, the sea is very blue. At their best Courbet's landscapes are great painting, not only because his skill and productive power are exhilarating, but because the wave of faith in nature is still at its crest. In them is witnessed the creation of a popular imagery that was to serve for almost a hundred years. When Courbet is true to his declared aims and does not aggrandize the expression, as in some of his smaller snow scenes, he remains a great landscape painter. But sometimes he is seduced by nature's more extravagant effects, occasions when only understatement could carry conviction; and sometimes, as in the embarrassing series of dying stags in the snow, he entirely forgets his principles in satisfaction at having produced an emotional effect. Such pictures are inescapably "vulgar," and it must be asked what, in relation to landscape, this word means. All forms of expression have within them the seeds of their own destruction, and just as classicism tends to emptiness and lack of vitality, so naturalism tends to vulgarity. It is the popular style, the style that can be understood without effort or education. Any art of recognition spares the effort of concentrating on formal relationships; but quite soon, recognition itself becomes an effort, and the popular taste demands ready-made equivalents for its favorite themes. In general, the popular landscapes are those in which the lazy or uninterested eye is suddenly jerked into responsiveness by an usually resonant contrast of tone or color. It is extremely difficult for a naturalistic painter to make true works of art from such crude effects, and to an artist with a less robust appetite than Courbet, seeking the popular effect is exceedingly dangerous.

To realize how such ready-made naturalism corrupts the eye, one has only to consider the early history of the impressionists (see IMPRESSIONISM). Until 1869 they were simple naturalistic painters: Sisley and Pissarro were devoted followers of Corot; and Monet was inspired by Daubigny, though he had first of all felt the more refreshing influence of Boudin. A glance at the early work of these fine artists makes it seem inconceivable that they should have been thought offensive. Bourgeois taste was already so debauched by pseudo naturalism, however, that the fresh vision of a Monet or Pissarro was an unpleasant shock. How far were the freshness and the shock due to the fact that these painters worked in the open air? On this point opinion has fluctuated. At one time it was usual to attribute great advantages to the method; but in truth, when an artist has evolved a consistent personal style, it is difficult to know when he has painted directly from nature. It was a mode of vision, not the physical fact of being out of doors, that made the impressionist scale of tones seem so startling.

Monet, Sisley (PL. 24), and Pissarro, during the 1860s and even as late as 1874, achieved the most complete naturalism that has ever been made into art. A picture could scarcely be much truer to a visual impression, with all its implications of light and tone, than the Sisley paintings of Hampton Court, or Pissarro's of Norwood. This perfect moment of impressionism, like all other points of balance in the history of art, could not be maintained for long. After about ten years the impressionists, like Constable fifty years before them, reached the crisis of the natural vision, the point at which it either relapses into the commonplace or ceases to satisfy the creative needs of the artist. To go on producing clear, objective transcripts of natural appearance without loss of freshness requires rare gifts of simpleheartedness and calm; and no artist of the first rank, except Corot, has succeeded in doing so. Even such an admirably endowed painter as Sisley suffered a gradual decline in sensibility and conviction. Monet and Pissarro, being more conscious of their dilemma, took a different course. They forced themselves to see in nature what the average eye cannot see, the web of pure color of which light is composed. Theoretically they were maintaining the principle of naturalism or even carrying it a stage further, but actually they were rejecting the limitations of the natural vision in favor of a transposition that would allow them greater creative freedom.

In 1870 the Franco-Prussian War temporarily broke up the partnership of the impressionist painters. Monet, Pissarro, and Sisley took refuge in England, where they painted their most completely "natural" pictures. This exile is mere coincidence; the war and the Paris Commune coincided with the naturalistic stage of their development, and England, as Monet afterward realized, is the setting for romantic rather than realistic painting. They do not seem to have been interested in Constable, whose work was then disregarded and whose sketches were not yet accessible. It is known from Pissarro's letters that they were impressed by Turner, though they saw only his big machines. When Monet returned to France in 1871 and once more began painting with Renoir, his palette grew more brilliant; but so did that of Renoir. A comparison of the pictures they painted together at Argenteuil shows that Monet still renders sparkle by contrasts of light and dark, whereas Renoir dissolves the whole scene in broken touches of pure color, and in consequence loses some of the certainty of tone in which Monet excelled. In the pictures of Argenteuil by Monet and Renoir, done between 1871 and 1874, the painting of sensation yielded its most perfect fruits. These show an unquestioning joy in the visible world, as well as an unquestioning belief that the new technique alone can convey it. The balance between subject, vision, and technique was so complete that it not only captivated such sympathetic spirits as Sisley and Pissarro but even imposed itself on painters to whom it was quite alien. Manet, for example, whose own range of responsiveness to tone and color was similar to that of Goya — or even darker — was bewitched into trying his hand at an Argenteuil picture. Even Gauguin and Van Gogh, who were to destroy impressionism, painted some of their most beautiful pictures in this style.

By the middle of the 1880s the great moment of impressionism had passed. At first Renoir and Monet tried to keep up their excitement by choosing more and more brilliant subjects. Renoir painted flower-laden gardens, which gave the added problem of bright local colors, and Monet painted coast scenes that have the most intense light which can be put on canvas. Monet later moved to the French Riviera, where, in the garish sunshine of that hitherto unpaintable region, not only his forms but his color tones were dissolved in incandescence. It was the crisis of "sensational" painting, and each member of the group responded in a different manner. Renoir, with his fundamentally classical outlook, was inspired by the antique painting in Naples and by Raphael's frescoes in the Vatican to recapture the firm outline, and thereafter he gave up naturalistic landscape painting entirely. Pissarro, who had always taken more interest than the others in the architectural composition of his pictures, joined the return to order. Sisley, the least intellectual and self-critical of the group, went on painting in the same way with declining confidence. His last pictures are a warning that simple perception of nature is not enough.

It was Monet, the real inventor of impressionism, who alone had the courage to push its doctrines on to their conclusion. Not content with the sparkle of his Riviera scenes, he undertook to prove that the object painted was of no importance, that the sensation of light was the only true subject. Actually, Monet's technique made him particularly dependent on the nature of his subjects; and these were limited. Only sun on water and sun on snow could give full play to the prismatic vision and the sparkling touch. In such pictures Monet has remained without equal. In order to prove his point he chose for the subjects of his experiments cathedrals and haystacks. No doubt he did so intentionally, in order to show that the most articulate works of man and the most formless were pictorially of equal importance to the painter of light. But the choice, especially that of cathedrals, was perverse, because gray Gothic façades do not sparkle. In these muffled, obstinate pictures impressionism departed altogether from the natural vision from which it sprang. The arbitrary color of the cathedrals — now pink, now mauve, now orange — is less beautiful than the truly perceived color of the Argenteuil pictures; and the dialectical basis on which these subjects were painted prevented Monet from abandoning himself to such poetic fantasies or musical harmonies of color as Turner's *Interior at Petworth* (London, Tate Gall.).

Looking back over the years from the beginning of impressionism, one may feel that this unqualified confidence in the physical world was a fundamental weakness. Art is concerned with our whole being — our knowledge, our memories, our associations. To confine painting to purely visual sensations is to touch only the surface of our spirits. Perhaps in the end the idealist doctrine is right: we are more impressed by concepts than by sensations, as any child's drawing will show. The supreme creation of art is the compelling image. An image is a "thing," and impressionism aimed at abolishing things. In painting, the simplest and most enduring images are things with lines around them; and impressionism abolished line.

This is only a way of saying in pictorial terms that impressionism did not address itself to the imagination. One cannot call it the art of materialism, for that word carries too gross an implication; nor can one (as many critics have done) call it pagan, for paganism involves the idea of remote country superstition, spring festivals, and Dionysiac rites. Paganism has precisely that element of magic which impressionism excludes. That is the price one must pay for the happiness of here and now, on which it is founded.

From Turner to the present. The splendid procession of naturalistic painters that passes through the 19th century from Constable to Pissarro may lead one to believe that for a hundred years landscape painting took no other form. In reality, however, two artists of genius — Turner at the beginning of the century and Van Gogh at the end — show that the landscape of fantasy was still a valid and potent means of expression. Both were fundamentally northern artists; yet both were inspired by the landscape of Mediterranean countries, because only in these could they find that delirium of light which was the release of their emotions. It is through this passion for light that the landscape of fantasy is linked with the history of 19th-century painting. The great imaginative painters of the early 16th century had made effects of flame and sunset the chief weapons in their assault on our emotions and, with great powers of observation and memory, had rendered effects of light that could never have been achieved by a purely factual approach. So it is not surprising that, in the pursuit of light which was to culminate in impressionism, it was a master of imaginative landscape — a romantic and not a realist — who made the decisive step. It was Turner who raised the whole key of color, so that his pictures not only represented light but were also symbolic of its nature. Among his many achievements, this is the one that associates him with the great painters who succeeded him.

Turner had been painting supposed views of Italy for about twenty years before he visited that country in 1819, but these had all been copies from the drawings of J. R. Cozens or pastiches based on Claude. When he saw Italy with his own eyes, he might have said, as did Ingres when he went to Rome, "Comme ils m'ont trompé!" As if in reaction against the formal, twilight vision of his predecessors, he was conscious chiefly of the heat, glitter, and profusion. He made a large number of detailed drawings and water colors in which he was content to record his pleasure in the classic landscape with almost the simplicity of Corot. But when he returned to England and began to re-create his impressions in his studio, the memories of Italy were like fumes of wine to his mind, and the landscape seemed to swim before his eyes in a sea of light. Shadows became scarlet and yellow, distances mother-of-pearl, and the trees lapis lazuli; and figures floated in the heat-engendered haze, like diaphanous tropical fish.

Turner's visit to Italy also had the paradoxical effect of intensifying the anticlassical element in his art. From then on, he did not attempt sham Claudes and Poussins, and his compositions gave up all pretense of classical construction. Based on an extension of the mannerist scheme, rather similar to that evolved by Bruegel, they often involve serpentine recession along an inner and outer circle. They are also anticlassical in their staffage: monks, maidens, troubadours, balconies, guitars, and other properties of the "keepsake style," reminding one that the antique landscape of Corot was also the Italy of *Childe Harold's Pilgrimage*. For this reason Turner was happiest not in the classic locales of Naples and the campagna but in the wholly romantic setting of Venice, which effected the final release of his imagination. It was the confirmation of all the sunset-cloud architecture he had ever built in his mind's eye, and in consequence he could paint it directly, without the rhetoric with which he felt bound to embellish less dreamlike subjects.

The theory of color had long occupied Turner's mind; his annotated copy of Goethe's treatise on color exists, and his sketchbooks are full of completely abstract color combinations in which he put his ideas to the test. In his late paintings the transitions of color are as considered and elaborate as the transitions of form in a Poussin and, like them, represent an alliance of thought, sensibility, and imagination. Whereas

Poussin's compositions of form were conceived with a high sense of literature, and were in fact subservient to some literary or didactic intention, Turner's compositions of color existed for their own sake. Turner was completely devoid of literary sense, and his exhibition pictures are always weakened by their ostensible subject. In spite of this, one can feel the immense symbolic and expressive importance of color for his imagination; and when the human and historical elements were removed, Turner could distill from light and color a poetry as delicate as that of Shelley. Such are the pale opalescent visions of rivers and estuaries, of which perhaps the most beautiful are those which take their point of departure from Norham Castle. To say that they "represent" Norham Castle is as misleading as to say that a picture by Braque represents a woman at a piano. The logical connection between what we should have seen if we had been there and the faint touches of pink, blue, and yellow with which Turner has stained his canvas does exist: it is the essence of their beauty, but it is extremely complex and could be discovered only by reliving Turner's experience. And it is inseparable from the technique by which he floats onto the canvas the most delicate films and mists of color, a technique which Turner by elaborate precautions kept a secret in his own day, and which has remained a secret ever since.

These landscapes are almost as abstract coloristically as a great piece of classic architecture is abstract formally; yet they give a more vivid feeling of nature than do his earlier works, in which the shapes and colors of nature are so minutely described. Just as the grammar of language always defeated Turner when he wrote, so the articulation of style seems to have hindered that pure synthesis which his later paintings achieve. In the vast range of his work Turner fulfills practically every aim that the earlier romantics foreshadowed. He was penetrated by a sense of nature's unsubduable, destructive force and of man's impotence before it. He painted those elements of nature which supported this conviction, which were in fact the same as those which had expressed the romantic fears of the 16th century — the crags and tempests and "fire in the flood." It is Turner's devotion to this last motif which shows decisively his kinship with Grünewald, Altdorfer, and Bosch.

With the death of Turner it must have seemed that the romantic response to nature, the obsessive fears and the sudden glory, had vanished from landscape painting and could not reappear in a material world. But when, at the end of the century, the tide of naturalism began to turn, there emerged an artist who embodied all the impulses of Grünewald, Altdorfer, and Huber. Van Gogh was truly such a northern artist. Throughout his work there runs a restless flowing line, curling and uncurling in endless agitated spirals, as it does in the earliest ornament of the migrations period or in the convoluted draperies of German Gothic (PL. 25). This linear character is best seen in astonishing landscape drawings, where Van Gogh uses the style of Altdorfer and Huber with added truth and richness. One is dazzled by the color and saturation of light he is able to convey by a sort of hailstorm of dots and dashes. The particular recurrent images found in Van Gogh are the enormous suns, the gnarled and hollow trees, and the pierced and twisted rocks. Since he was oblivious of earlier expressionists and drew his inspiration from such utterly unlike sources as Millet and Hiroshige, it may be assumed that these images are really part of the permanent furniture of the unconscious. Above all, like Turner, Van Gogh had the northern sense of light as a source of magic; yet Van Gogh's light is very different from the pearly radiance of Turner. It is fierce, fitful, and distracting (once more one sees the analogy between light and love); it beats upon the brain and can be exorcised only by the most violent symbols — wheels and whorls of fire — and by the brightest, crudest colors that can be squeezed with frenzied urgency from the tube.

Thus, in spite of his passion for nature, Van Gogh was forced more and more to twist what he saw into an expression of his own despair. It was Van Gogh who brought the sense of tragedy back into modern art; and like Nietzsche and Ruskin, he found in madness the only escape from the materialism of the 19th century. Cézanne, when shown one of Van Gogh's pictures, said with characteristic brusqueness, "Sincèrement, vous faites une peinture de fou"; and looking at *The Road with Cypresses* or *The Ravine* (both Otterlo, Rijksmus. Kröller-Müller), one must reluctantly agree with him. Expressionist art involves a dangerous tension of the spirit. One feels that Grünewald cannot have been entirely sane; but the frenzied writhings, the Catherine-wheel convolutions of Van Gogh are further out of control than anything in El Greco and are in fact painfully similar to the paintings of actual madmen.

Impressionism, like all genuine art forms, created its own order by consistency of vision and texture, but it was the unity of sensation deriving from the glance or snapshot. The measured interplay of horizontals and verticals; the use of a house, a window, or a block of masonry as a modulus of proportion; the diagonal that turns back on itself after two-thirds of its journey; and the arc whose ideated center is a nodal point in the composition — all these devices brought to perfection by Poussin were foreign to the impressionists and may have seemed irreconcilable with their technique. As a result, they could achieve neither the scale nor the air of permanence of their greatest predecessors.

An exception must be made in the case of Pissarro. As the pupil of Corot he had learned the laws of classic landscape painting, and these are apparent in the village scenes he painted before 1870. They are even perceptible in purely impressionist pictures of the early 1870s, and it is not surprising that, when the group split up, Pissarro should have become an imitator of Seurat. Monet, on the other hand, was the pupil of two painters to whom the rules of construction meant little: Daubigny and Boudin. And it was Monet whose desire for total immersion in a bath of appearance led him to leave the firm ground of traditional design. Not that his compositions were feeble, but they tended to be loose and hearty, and by the 1880s this bent occasionally degenerated into sloppiness.

This is the point at which Seurat appeared, concentrating in himself all the intellectual currents of the time: the belief in science, the interest in primitive and Oriental art, and even the beginnings of Art Nouveau. He and Cézanne represent the two prime traditions in 19th-century French painting. Delacroix was Cézanne's god, whereas Seurat's earliest paintings are wonderfully perceptive copies of Ingres. After these classical exercises of Seurat, there occurred a gap in his career while he completed his military service. Stationed at Brest, he spent the long hours of sentry duty gazing at the sea and gained the intimate knowledge of its light and color that was the basis of his finest landscapes. The landscapes Seurat did on his return to Paris show without question that he was influenced by the tonality of impressionism, and in particular that of Pissarro. They also show that he was a man of delicate poetic sensibility coupled with the French passion for intellectual tidiness. He must have studied the Uccello battle scene in the Louvre (XI, PL. 43), feeling some instinctive sympathy with this earlier disciple of theory, and he took from Uccello the idea of arranging simple masses of light and dark so that one is always set off by, or even framed in, the other. This involved reducing the modeling of his figures to a minimum and placing them in profile, so that they did not upset the stability of the design by moving from one plane to another. But these simplified elements were subject to the most complex laws of composition. Seurat was a great master of the mathematical laws of harmony by which all the greatest architects of the past, and some of the greatest painters, have secured their effects. The arsenal of geometry, of which the golden section was only one important weapon, was at Seurat's command, and perhaps no painter other than Poussin and Piero della Francesca has used it with greater precision.

Seurat's finest work, nonetheless, depends on his emotional response to what he has seen. He was particularly moved by the seaside, by the immense whiteness of water and sky, by the precision of seaside architecture, and by the interval of proportion between sky and jetty, or sea and distant sail (PL. 24). That space should be both uneventful yet full of movement, architectural yet tremulous with light, was the first necessity of his spirit, as can be seen from his simplest drawings. In these seascapes Seurat has taken the archetypal impressionist subject — sailboats on sparkling water — and has used it for anti-impressionist ends, plotting every inch of surface with the industry of a coral insect and the logic of a mathematician. Seurat's ambitions were very great. He wished not only to tidy up impressionism but to employ its luminous technique and contemporary vision in the creation of pictures that had the scale and timelessness of Renaissance frescoes. This aim involved great difficulties of style, of scale, and of vision, but Seurat succeeded at the first attempt. The *Bathers* (VII, PLS. 436, 437) remains a triumph of the will, and one of those great works which immediately convince us of their authority, from which each succeeding age will draw its own conclusions.

The *Bathers* is painted in an extension of the impressionist technique, which Seurat called *balayé*, meaning that touches of pure color were swept on by a broad brush. But as the requirements of Seurat's sense of design became more exacting, he felt that the touches, in order to be more easily controlled, must be smaller. This belief coincided with the crystallization in his mind of a pseudoscientific theory of color, which was applied in his next great picture, *La Grande Jatte*, together with all the other principles of composition that went into the *Bathers*. Here the preliminary studies were even more numerous and elaborate than those for the earlier picture, for in addition to drawings and small color sketches he made a number of large preparatory paintings (IV, PL. 280; V, PL. 115).

Without comparing the two men as painters, there is no doubt that Cézanne possessed the richer and more abundant temperament. Painters with disparate aims can find in him inspiration and support for their own endeavors, and as a result he has often been considered in his several aspects — which is exactly how he should not be considered. One runs the risk of doing this by treating Cézanne landscapes as a part of a return to order; to correct the balance, one should first recall the sumptuous, thundery picnics and bathing parties, of which the Pellerin Collection in Paris has several examples. These Baudelairean orgies show that Cézanne's genius was based on a colossal sensuality. They essay the only style in which an exuberant young romantic could express such violent emotions, the style of Delacroix. But Cézanne's peculiar limitations as an artist, his inability to paint from memory or to use the stylistic tricks of other painters, led to a complete travesty of his model. In particular, he was quite incapable of using the traditional devices by which postbaroque artists had achieved the illusion of depth. In the Pellerin *Bathers*, serpentine recessions have been rolled flat. Yet his power to reduce what he sees to interesting shapes is already very impressive, and one sees how he felt that a picture must exist as a design of flat patterns even before it creates an illusion of depth.

Cézanne's earliest important landscape, *The Cutting* (Munich, Neue Staatsgalerie), gives a clear idea of his strength and weakness at this time. Compared with Seurat's exquisitely neat and lucid compositions, it is very crude; but it has stunning boldness and a largeness of vision. It also foreshadows one of the chief characteristics separating Cézanne from the impressionists: the frontality of his attack. The powerful horizontals running parallel to the picture plane and supporting the simplified mass produce an immediate assault on the eye, differing both from the carefully contrived "lead in" of the baroque landscape and from the balanced design of the classical. In another landscape done at this period, *Les Quais de Bercy* (Paris, Coll. Lecomte), Cézanne subdues his imagination in the interest of facts — a process that was to occupy him during the next twenty years.

Although he was friendly with the impressionist group and interested in their coloristic experiments, Cézanne was troubled by the changeable conditions of open air. Much of his time was spent in the Louvre making copies of Rubens and Delacroix, as well as the innumerable pencil studies of antique and baroque sculpture presumably unknown to those critics who have maintained he could not draw. These studies show a progressive mastery in realizing form without sacrificing flat pattern, but Cézanne had not yet found a means of carrying this over to his painting. He recognized that he could not express his grand conception of the world through imagery half-invented, half-remembered from the old masters; he could do so only by setting down with complete truth the visual sensations conveyed to him by natural objects. The technique of his friends the impressionists offered him a means of registering every shade of visual sensation, but for a time Cézanne thought they were too much concerned with the surface of things. Such a judgment could not survive acquaintance with Pissarro's sober and thoughtful work, which even as late as 1872 retained the elements of classical composition. Moreover, Pissarro, the oldest of the group, had lulled Cézanne's suspicions by the understanding he had shown of his crude beginnings; and in 1873 Cézanne was persuaded to join Pissarro at Auvers. The humble spirit in which Cézanne attempted to learn the impressionist style is shown by the fact that he made a careful copy of a Pissarro in which the composition is contrary to his usual practice. He has followed Pissarro's scheme of perspective, with the road running diagonally into the background. This was the conventional scheme of landscape composition taught in schools, but it was foreign to Cézanne's direct and frontal approach to nature — how foreign can be seen by comparing it with an authentic Cézanne composition of almost the same date, the landscape *Chestnut Trees at the Jas de Bouffan* (Minneapolis, Inst. of Arts). The lines of the foreground run parallel to the picture plane, and the composition is broken almost in the middle by a strong vertical line; yet Cézanne achieves an effect of depth by perfect understanding of color value.

As with anyone learning a new style, Cézanne's first impressionist pictures are less satisfactory than those which immediately preceded them, but quite soon he was able to adapt the new language to his own purpose. In *The Enclosure Wall* (New York, Coll. Durand-Ruel) he uses a broken touch to give the vibration of light, but the architectural composition might belong to his work of any period. It is the beginning of the famous attempt to "do Poussin over again from nature," and in fact it is by no means dissimilar from a Poussin composition in its balance of verticals against a parallel horizon and in its use of distant architecture as a nucleus. It is, however, less closely knit in design than his subsequent landscapes, and much less closely painted. Ten years later a rough statement like the foliage of the overhanging branch would not have been allowed to stand; and although the sense of light in the background is vividly rendered, Cézanne is not yet able to give every inch of his canvas a beautiful and vivid texture.

This aim he achieved through a struggle to integrate his natural sense of flat pattern with his consciousness of solid form, a struggle so fiercely sustained that it gives a feeling of tension to every part of his pictures. As a result the objects depicted — no less than the brush strokes — begin to take on some dominating shape, like trees on the coast that have all bent before the same relentless wind, or rocks twisted into a unity of rhythm by the same seismic upheaval. Such unifying distortions are common to all art, but they are usually concealed; whereas in Cézanne's work they are presented with the uncompromising directness of all his utterances. Critics have not agreed how far such distortions were calculated, how far instinctive, and perhaps the question is unanswerable. All art involves selection and control of natural appearances, which must reflect the artist's whole temperament, and in the choice of his dominant forms Cézanne was simply expressing his own vision of nature. But in the use of these forms he was, no doubt, perfectly conscious of his intentions. For this strange man, whose views on life seem to have been simple and orthodox to the point of absurdity, was where art was concerned a profound and original thinker; and even in this period of prevailing naturalism he had the insight to define painting as a harmony parallel with nature.

It is easiest to apprehend Cézanne's principles of design, as he himself learned them, from his paintings of still life. Very soon, however, he was able to transfer them to the more complex and evasive subject of landscape. As his design becomes more intellectual, his compositions are built up on straight lines rather than curves. But these straight lines — for example, in the trunks of trees — are frequently interrupted. It is as if Cézanne put them up as a scaffolding but then feared that they would arrest the movement of the picture and lead to a too great insistence on contours. He recognized that an uninterrupted line implies a point of focus on the edge of the object and so makes impossible any movement in space, forward or backward, and even in his first pencil notes he always interrupts an outline and starts it again a fraction farther in or out.

Cézanne's interest in the problems of construction is seen most clearly in those landscapes of Provence in which he gave the scenery of his native country the eternal harmonies of classical landscape. But this triumph of vision is inseparable from a triumph of style. The landscapes of L'Estaque (III, PLS. 184, 190) and the farmhouses near Mt. Sainte-Victoire (III, PL. 191) show for the first time one direction that Cézanne's mature style was to take — the direction that after his death was to lead to cubism. The motives that prompted him to adopt this way of painting are quite simple and are latent in all his early work. He wished to render the solidity of objects without degrading his color or weakening his design by continuous modeling. The only means of doing this was to split his planes into many small facets, each of which could, by its color, make one aware of a new direction of the planes. This cubist, or perhaps prismatic, approach to individual forms was also inherent in his compositions as a whole. It is this attitude which distinguishes him from the impressionists, for impressionism also offers a means of rendering continuous modeling by color, a means developed by Seurat. But underlying all impressionism is the belief that the unity of a picture depends on the enveloping atmosphere rendered by a continuous weft of color; whereas Cézanne wished forms to retain their identity and cohere in an architectural relationship. To achieve this, he began by choosing subjects in which the forms went some way to meet this kind of simplification.

In 1895 the art dealer Vollard, on Pissarro's advice, arranged for the first time a comprehensive exhibition of Cézanne's work, and immediately the great French painters of the day recognized Cézanne as their master. Monet, Renoir, Degas, and Pissarro himself spent what little money they could afford in buying his pictures. Nevertheless, the fame for which Cézanne had striven so vigorously in his youth came too late to give him pleasure. He had aged prematurely and had become almost insanely suspicious of interference. The struggle to solve so many problems of painting and thereby express himself had cost him his friends and everything else life had to offer; and when he was almost in sight of realization of his goals, he became terrified lest some outside influence should deflect him. His inner life at this time was evidently of great turbulence, and his state of mind expressed itself in agitated, cursive handling very similar to that of his earliest work, in complete contrast to the delicacy and precision of his middle period. This turmoil is evident in his water colors and is intensified in his oils, where the paint is applied with disturbing ferocity. His concentration involved a narrow choice of subjects. His landscapes were virtually confined to the quarry of Bibémus, a motif that seems to have provoked the greatest violence; a building known as the Château Noir, which he used as a studio; and Mt. Sainte-Victoire. Of the mountain he made innumerable studies, and one feels that the painting of this motif became for him like a ritual act of worship, in which he could achieve perfect self-realization.

In one of his letters, Cézanne writes that he believes these late works, if exhibited, "will give a correct notion of progress of my studies"; and anyone who understands his intentions will agree with him. It is more surprising to realize that these are the works in which he believed himself to have the clearest understanding of nature. "Je deviens comme peintre," he writes in 1906, "plus lucide devant la nature." By this he surely meant that his own passionate imaginative life, which as a young man he had tried to express by creating fantastic images, could now be revealed in every stroke with which he recorded his visual sensations. He had brought his inner and outer vision into uniform focus and had created a harmony parallel with nature. The unifying factor was his own temperament; but this could exert itself only unconsciously on the raw material of things seen, experienced as shape and color and wrestled with to secure their maximum realization. In so far as modern art involves a readiness to override nature, to defy appearances in the interests of emotion, Cézanne was far from being a modern, for no one ever looked at nature more earnestly. In this pursuit he was at one with the great landscape painters of the past, with Bellini, Rubens, and Poussin; and it is with them that he belongs.

Kenneth CLARK

For a discussion of landscape painting in the Americas, see I, cols. 280, 285, 287 ff., 305, 344.

THE EAST. *India and Southeast Asia.* The character of landscape art in India has been determined by the topography of the country: an immense plain rising gradually from sea level to a highland, occasionally interrupted by low ranges of hills and broken with ravines near the large rivers. The most salient features are the innumerable shallow ponds and lakes; whether natural depressions — dammed wherever possible — or man-made excavations, these are covered with water lilies and lotus and swarm with geese, ducks, herons, and other aquatic birds. The dams, a favorite resort of the people, are surrounded with bathing ghats, pavilions, temples, country houses, and luxuriant gardens irrigated by channels from the lake. These waters and landscaped embankments are cool retreats in a tropical climate where the distance is veiled by waves of heat. Neither the mountains of central and southern India, long inhabited by primitive tribes, nor the higher ranges of the Himalaya, visited only by Hindu pilgrims who frequently have renounced the world, have contributed significantly to the inspiration of Indian landscape art. Although their snow-covered peaks occasionally figure in the Rajput miniatures of the Pahari school (18th–19th cent.), these paintings ordinarily depict their more accessible surroundings — the river valleys, lakes, and undulating hills of the outer Himalaya.

Thus it is typical of landscape in Indian art (q.v.) that it is for the most part without broad vistas; instead there are generally found painstaking reproductions of details of the immediate environment. Within this prevailing tendency, however, wide variations in approach are to be noted, for although scenery was in some periods reduced to summary indications of trees or houses, in others one may find attempts to encompass perhaps several miles of landscape.

The oldest fragments of crude paintings on shards of the Indus, or Harappa, civilization (3d–2d millenium B.C.; see INDUS VALLEY ART) present just a few hints of vegetation, along river banks where deer are grazing. Early Buddhist art, on the other hand, aspired to a more comprehensive treatment of the natural environment. In the reliefs from Bharhut (VII, PL. 442), scenery continues to be artificially disposed: the over-all ground plan is rendered from a bird's-eye view, while the individual elements are viewed from the side. The 1st-century B.C. reliefs from the cave monasteries of Bhaja (near Bombay) and Udayagiri (near Orissa) depict real landscapes based on empirical — though naïve — observation. The components are many and diverse: sacred trees protected by railings and hung with votive gifts, lotus-banked ponds and rivers with bathing elephants, various tame animals, the rude huts of ascetics, and men and women playing musical instruments, dancing, or courting. The land appears to slope upward from foreground to background, perhaps a visual convention, since the setting is probably meant to be a plain. Where mountains appear, they are oddly stylized and resemble grotesque cliffs, a strange conformation actually found in many parts of India. The abundant caves of these mountains attracted both pious ascetics and amorous couples during the torrid season. In the gateway reliefs of a stupa at Sanchi (2d–1st cent. B.C.; VII, PL. 441) the landscape, though it has become a more elaborate and balanced backdrop, has retained its naïve charm and its detailed observation of nature. The stupa reliefs (2d–early 3d cent.) of the Sātavāhana and Ikṣvāku dynasties, from the Andhra littoral, reveal an almost illusionistic, yet empirical perspective. In these, because the culture had become predominantly an urban one, the subjects in turn become episodes in the life of cities and sizable villages, as well as at pilgrimage spots, and the open countryside is but rarely depicted.

In the provincial Hellenistic art of Gandhara (1st–5th cent.; q.v.), along the Indo-Afghan frontier, landscape is rarely depicted, being confined largely to representations of the Buddha sitting in a mountain cave; overhead are grouped bodhisattvas, monks, lay followers, and various animals. Unlike earlier art of the country, this recurrent compositional scheme has almost no peculiarly Indian features; rather, it belongs to the Alexandrian tradition.

In the decoration of the Hindu temple, from the Gupta period (4th cent.; see GUPTA, SCHOOL OF) through medieval times (13th cent.; in the south, 16th–17th cent.), landscape backgrounds or motifs are virtually nonexistent. Figures of gods, heavenly nymphs, men, and animals are ranged in essentially flat friezes about the walls of both freestanding and cave temples. Individual figures may have pronounced depth, or the conventional overlapping of groups of figures may create a suggestion of depth; but there is no systematic attempt to achieve the effect of a truly spatial setting. Even where some indication of setting is indispensable to the purpose, such elements are reduced to a minimum: a bed, a portal, a diminutive palace, a tree, or some rocks. During this era it is only in the cave temples of Ellora and, to some degree, in those of Elephanta (6th–8th cent.) that a little more in the way of setting is presented: a mountain scene, with Śiva and Pārvatī surrounded by gods and demons; a lotus pond spreading at the feet of Lakṣmī; a lake from which rises the stem of a huge lotus held by *nāgarājas* (snake kings), whereon the Buddha or Śiva as Lakuliśa is seated in the yoga posture. The most ambitious landscape, the representation of Mount Kailasa, occurs in the episodes where Śiva, merely by pressing down with his toe, subdues the rebellious demon king Rāvaṇa, imprisoned and quaking within the mountain throne of the gods. This scene, well known from the large group in the Kailāsanātha at Ellora (IV, PL. 171), recurs as the sole landscape motif on the walls of many freestanding temples, especially in southern India. This mountain, essential to the narrative but stylized almost to a thronelike conformation, is often represented in various tiers filled with animals, gods, and godlings.

The murals at Bagh, Ajanta (q.v.; PL. 6), and similar sites prove that such restrictive use of landscape can be attributed to purely religious considerations implicit in the magic symbolism of the Hindu temple. In these frescoes, which reflect the character of the lost secular paintings of the time, the landscape of earlier Buddhist art persists, though in a very refined guise. Scenes are of minimal depth and include streets, views into houses, gardens, and pavilions, sometimes disposed over a slope with geometrically stylized cliffs but with admirably lifelike plants, animals, and richly dressed people as well.

Hindu art in Indonesia and Indochina was less inhibited in this respect. Delicate descriptions of nature occur at Borobudur and Prambanam (9th–10th cent.), but once more it is the immediate milieu that is reproduced: forests populated with monkeys and birds and all varieties of tame and wild animals, lotus ponds, villages, palaces, and views of the sea with sailing ships. In Eastern Javanese and Balinese art, when the indigenous Malay sentiment came to the fore again, landscape motifs became increasingly important. There were attempts at depicting an extended landscape, even with a primitive perspective, incorporating palaces and water pavilions, rivers and mountains, temples on slopes, and bridges. Some, such as the reliefs of the central temple of the Majapahit kingdom at Panataran, are rather clumsy; later representations are more naturalistic in appearance, for example, the relief from Travulan. Ultimately, in the art of Bali, landscape dissolved into a general background of ornamental rocks and leaves.

In Khmer art (q.v.) the all-pervasive primeval forest of Cambodia forms the background of many scenes, but in general it remains simply background — a mass of treetops emerging from behind mythological scenes, historical processions, and battle scenes. Its execution evidences careful observation of details, in the diverse trees, birds, deer, and beasts of prey. Perhaps the best of these landscapes are a *Rāmāyaṇa* scene at Banteay Srei (10th cent.) and a series of reliefs in the Bayon at Angkor Thom, with their descriptive treatment of a river (boats, fish, crocodiles, etc.) and the life along its shores. In the later art of Burma, Siam, and Cambodia, strong Chinese influences became particularly apparent in the landscapes.

In India proper, the advent of the Moslems introduced a new style of landscape art. Early Indo-Moslem painting — only few fragments of which have been brought to light — seems to have confined itself to spare indications of background, just as is found in contemporaneous Jain miniatures. Thereafter, the introduction of Timurid painting in the late 15th century, especially through the work of the Moghuls, brought with it the semi-Chinese landscape and its combination of bizarre cliff formations and naturalistic trees, flowers, and animals. This style of landscape was again seen with bird's-eye perspective as a whole, but individual details were rendered as if viewed from ground level. Often the artists also tried to compress all the landscape details into several compact groups establishing the foreground, middle ground, and background of the picture. Houses and towns were treated much like stage wings, resembling cardboard panels rather than substantial structures. This tendency to organize a composition in depth like a sequence of scenery panels became more pronounced after Moghul painting became Indianized during the 17th century (VII, PLS. 499, 500; see MOGHUL SCHOOL). The landscape was interpreted as if seen from atop a one- or two-storied house. The principal event — usually occurring on a terrace, meadow, or court — was set between a foreground consisting of flower beds, a seashore, or other elements and a dual background comprising first a garden, lake, pavilion, or gateway and then the outlines of trees and palaces, as well as a splendid post-monsoon sky of red and golden clouds. In the 18th century, partly because of acquaintance with European painting, there developed a convincing landscape setting. Especially in pictures of the school of Oudh (second half of 18th cent.), one finds broad vistas of enclosed gardens, towns, fields, lakes, rivers, and hills, frequently with caravans or armies moving across the scene. Erratic perspective is common in this late eclectic style, however, and is the result of combining several pictures into a single more comprehensive landscape, without properly adjusting the components to a consistent viewpoint. Only toward the end of the 18th century was uniform perspective achieved in such landscapes.

The early painting of the Rajput school (q.v.) does not evidence any spatially convincing landscape. The subjects were conceived quite two-dimensionally, and the scenery constituted merely a sort of flat backdrop. When scenic elements were taken over from Moghul painting, the figures were often apparently suspended in mid-air, without contact or relation with either ground or background. After Moghul painters emigrated to the Rajput courts in the second and third quarters of the 18th century, true landscape art developed; but in the Rajasthani branch of the school, the art of the plains, depiction of landscape remained rudimentary. In Pahari art, the Himalayan or hills branch of Rajput, however, especially in Kangra painting, scenery became a rather well-developed accessory. Here it was also quite carefully observed but tended toward an ornamental stylization.

Modern Indian landscape art has not yet developed a distinctive style. Artists working in an impressionistic technique treat the Indian scenery in the same way as European painters might; for those working in an expressionistic vein the problem of landscape is not a prime concern. Nonetheless, the relation and the emotional response of Indian artists to their native landscape differs noticeably from a Western attitude to the same milieu (see ORIENTAL MODERN MOVEMENTS). The Indian landscape is not for them a source of exoticism; it is an intimate environment saturated with the sentiments of a common, inherited religious and national tradition.

Hermann GOETZ

China. The profound veneration of the Chinese for the forces of nature is the base upon which their landscape art was formed (see CHINESE ART). Its principles are rooted in the concept of Tao (see TAOISM) as expressed in *Tao-tê-ching* (Chap. XXV), wherein the Tao "is something without form, although complete, which existed before heaven and earth, without sound, without substance, dependent upon nothing, immutable, permeating all things, infallible...." It was this formulation of the Tao as the supreme concept of spirit and matter which pervaded the creative imagination, subject, and interpretation in Chinese landscape art. Taoist philosophy profoundly influenced Chinese painters and taught them to lose themselves in the immensity of nature in order to find themselves once more, thereby identifying themselves with the spirit permeating the universe, which is the Tao.

The Tao is manifested in the eternal flow of being and becoming; it is never static. Forms appear and disappear in water, in clouds, and in the mists, and their rhythm palpitates in a perpetual becoming. It is in this unceasing movement that the Tao is manifest. "The Tao does not create, but there is nothing which is not created." This is the most subtle and fruitful aspect of the Tao in its relation to art, for it inspires the unique interior dynamism: this manifestation of activity in the midst of quiet was conveyed by Chinese artists in their reproduction of static forms, which generally arise from the resolution of the opposing principles yin and yang. The Chinese artist has been subject to this resolution of opposites in the ordering of his composition and in the creative process. Landscape art — which in Chinese is descriptively called *shan-shui* (mountains and water) — is none other than a representation of mountains and streams in which these opposites complete each other. Taoist mysticism and then Ch'an Buddhism (see BUDDHISM) were thus the principal intellectual and spiritual forces that raised landscape art to the heights attained in the Sung period (960–1279).

Aside from mountains and water, a third element, the tree, was indispensable to the representation of landscape. The tree most favored by Chinese artists was the pine: its straight trunk, with knotty and twisting branches, personified the wise man who, buffeted by the winds of calumny and misfortune, remained steadfast in his profound faith in the Confucian virtues. Also favored was the bamboo (to which an entire branch of painting is dedicated), the symbol of lasting friendship and of the *chu-jên* (gentleman) who bows before the tempest but rises again when it has subsided. The pine, the bamboo, and the plum — the herald of spring — were termed "the three friends of the cold season"; other varieties represented include the willow, the elm, the oak, and the mulberry. Rocks, flowers, and shrubs were further components of landscape art, and waterfalls and gorges were features chosen to evoke the awesome and more violent aspects of nature.

This exaltation of pure landscape is characteristic of Chinese painting (in contrast with Western painting, where landscape customarily furnishes a background for human activity), in which man is clearly subordinate to the immensity of nature. Particularly in the Sung and Ming periods, in the midst of his presentation of natural phenomena, the artist would depict a tiny hut with one or two sages lost in contemplation of the infinity and beauty of the landscape. In painting scenes of this type, the artist accepted in principle that he must identify himself with the landscape and become completely one with the Tao. He was concerned not with the outward appearance of nature but with its inner spirit; therefore he limited himself to the essential elements, since only within such strictures could he attain the universal spirit. Chinese literary-artistic sources repeatedly tell of great painters who spent months and even years in mountain regions, immersed in the spectacle of nature and searching for its essence. When they had achieved this mystical identification, they recaptured the vision and with their mastery of the brush immediately reproduced it without hesitation and without the preparatory sketches common to Western painting. Although the landscapes were often identified with a name, and certain subjects were depicted many times, this does not signify that the paintings were actual representations of particular scenes. Chinese artists rarely painted from life, but instead created ideal landscapes, expressions of a cultural ideal that dominated the production of the Chinese literati painters of the Sung and subsequent periods. Chinese artists did not attempt to depict landscape in realistic and detailed terms but gave more a unitary impression of the whole scene. Perhaps it is this ability to bring together many details in an expressive and unified entity, animated by the true spirit of nature, that distinguishes the masters of landscape from their many followers and imitators. Undoubtedly Hsieh Ho, the great 5th-century critic, had this in mind when he laid down the first and most important of the "Six Principles" of painting, the *ch'i-yün shêng-tung* (the consonance of the spirit and the dynamism of life); this principle represented the most profound concept of Chinese art. In other words, even the greatest inspiration was without value if the artist did not possess the ability to bring it to life; on the other hand, even the greatest technical proficiency was of little account if the artist lacked genuine inspiration.

There is some knowledge of the earliest landscapes of the Han period (206 B.C.–221 A.D.), when the principal compositional elements first appeared on textiles, carvings, mirrors, and objects of inlaid metal. Nature, however, was depicted in abstract and highly symbolic terms. The reason for this lies in the scant interest of the artists of this period in landscape painting; they preferred to concentrate on figural painting that depicted myths, legends, history, and stories of filial piety. Landscape painting in the true sense of the term did not come into being until the period of the Six Dynasties (A.D. 220–590). It was the great painter and calligrapher Ku K'ai-chih (q.v.; III, PL. 235) who first gave value to this art form, although in his work the proportions of the figures, too large in relation to the mountains, are not natural, and the mountains are so stylized as to be almost unrecognizable. Tsung Ping, a contemporary of Ku K'ai-chih, was reputed to be a famous landscape painter, but unfortunately none of his works have survived.

In the 4th century, landscape painting apparently underwent profound stylistic changes, but no authenticated originals of this period have survived; the only painting that could possibly be attributed to the 4th century is a mural in Cave 110 at Tun-huang (q.v.), on the western edge of China. The subject, a mountain landscape that is part of a Jātaka, is treated in a highly decorative manner, with the very stylized mountains placed one beside the other in rhythmic groups. The Tun-huang paintings, the work of provincial craftsmen, were but distant copies of the style in favor at the imperial court. In the 6th century, however, a true form of landscape art was developed: for the first time, figures were rendered more correctly in proportion with their natural setting, and composition began to convey a sense of space (III, PL. 244).

The T'ang period (618–906) saw landscape art emerge as an art form wholly independent of the human figure (q.v.), acquiring an importance equal to figure painting. This is the merit of two great artists, Li Ssŭ-hsün (q.v.) and his son Li Chao-tao, who were the first to use a technique known as *kung-pi*, characterized by a palette of blue and green malachite colors and gold, with delicate brushwork. Unfortunately no certain originals of these two artists exist, but two works of a later date, paintings on silk, are known to reflect their style: *Travelers in the Mountains in Spring* (formerly, Peking, Palace Coll.) and *The Chiu-ch'êng Summer Palace* (PL. 152). The meticulous painting, precision of detail, and the brilliance of the colors make them excellent examples of that style of painting of the T'ang period known as *ch'ing-lü shan-shui* ("blue-and-green" landscape). The dominant artistic figure of the 8th century was Wu Tao-tzŭ (q.v.), one of the pioneers in the evolution of landscape painting. Another famous artist of the period was Wang Wei (q.v.), who used the *p'o-mo* ("broken ink") technique. T'ang painting represented the natural elements of the landscape in a clearly defined manner, but the human figure nonetheless remained the focus of artistic interest during the period.

Substantial changes in landscape painting occurred in the 10th century, when the artists, differing from their predecessors of the T'ang period, created a type of landscape no longer subordinate to the human figure. The first of these artists was Ching Hao, active in the early 10th century, to whom two paintings are attributed, a view of the K'uan-lu Mountains (formerly, Peking, Palace Coll.) and a scroll of landscapes (Washington, D.C., Freer Gall. of Art). A contemporary of Ching Hao was Kuan T'ung, to whom is attributed the scroll *Ford across the Mountain Stream* (formerly, Peking, Palace Coll.). His brush stroke is more spontaneous and the composition has a greater sense of depth and space, obtained by deft use of fog and aerial perspective. The major artistic figure of the mid-10th century was Li Ch'êng, whose painting *Travelers amid the Snowy Hills* exhibits a different treatment of the background and includes trees of bizarre and contorted forms. Another artist who influenced later generations was Tung Yüan, in whose hands landscape acquired effective depth by means of a balanced use of clouds among the mountains. Although he also worked in the monochrome style of Wang Wei and in the polychrome style of Li Ssŭ-hsün, he was chiefly famous for his use of Chinese ink.

The landscape art that flourished in the 11th century, during the period of the Northern Sung dynasty (III, PLS. 262, 269), was based on and continued the artistic development of the 10th cent. The most eminent painter was Kuo Hsi, whose fame rests on his activity both as a painter (PL. 26) and as the author of a famous treatise on landscape painting, the *Lin-ch'üan kao-chih* ("The Great Message of Forests and Streams"). His concepts of landscape, in relation to the artist who elaborates them and transmutes them into painting, arise from his profound comprehension of nature and its subtler aspects beyond external appearance. Another noted artist of the 11th century was Mi Fei (q.v.; or Mi Fu), whose reputation proceeds from his being a leading exponent of the Southern school. His style was carried on by his son Mi Yu-jên, who painted the scroll *Misty Mountains and River Landscape*, in which the mountains swathed in mist are placed within a composition that is extremely simple. Two renowned artists of the first half of the 12th century were Li T'ang and Chao Po-chü. The former is noted for his scenes of village life; the latter for his manner of painting with blues, brilliant greens, and white (*ch'ing-lü-pai*).

The Southern Sung period saw the rise, about the year 1200, of a school of monochrome painting that may be considered the highest point attained by Chinese landscape painters. The two great artists of this school were Ma Yüan and Hsia Kuei (qq.v.; III, PLS. 263, 265). In the work of Ma Yüan, mountains lost the structural clarity of the older masters and were depicted with a transparent outline that increased the spatial effect. In the last decades of the Sung dynasty (960–1279) a new school of landscape art, based on Ch'an Buddhism and its teachings, was founded. One of the famous Ch'an artists was Liang K'ai (q.v.), who adopted the "summary" manner (*chien-pi*) in which the brush strokes were reduced to a minimum. Another remarkable artist was the monk Ying Yü-chien, who with the *p'o-mo* technique handled the brush so freely that the ink often appears to have been sprayed on the paper. Another contemporaneous artist was the monk Mu-ch'i (q.v.), whose very simple landscapes are without unnecessary detail or ornament.

Under the Yüan dynasty (1260–1368), a radical stylistic change took place in Chinese landscape art. The interest of the artist turned exclusively upon the external appearance of the natural scene, landscape wholly without figures (III, PL. 276). The exponents of the Southern school regarded these artists as the ideal literati painters (*wên-jên-hua*). Belonging to no academy, they lived a free life dedicated entirely to art and assumed the title of *tao-jên* or *shan-jên*. The most eminent of these artists was Huang Kung-wang, who wandered through the mountains to observe the changing moods of nature. He often painted — contrary to Chinese tradition — at the actual scene. His *Mountains of Fu-ch'un* (formerly, Peking, Palace Coll.), is typical of his work, which emphasizes forms with areas of light and shade, to create a feeling of space and atmosphere. Another painter, much admired in the West, was Ni Tsan (q.v.), originator of the *kan-pi* ("dry brush") style, by means of which the artist, using very little ink, was able to produce extremely fine brush strokes. The last notable artist of the Yüan period was Kao K'o-kung, whose manner of painting differed greatly from that of his contemporaries, for his style was closer to the Sung tradition and modeled on the works of Mi Fei.

The advent of the Ming dynasty (1368–1644) saw a revival of the arts. The styles of painting once again underwent a change, and landscape art expressed a new set of ideals. Notwithstanding these changes, regard for tradition was maintained: the Ming artists claimed to follow the Sung and Yüan masters in the two schools of the period, the Wu and the Chê. A master of the Wu school and one of the great Ming painters was Shên Chou (III, PL. 283); the chief painter of the Chê school was Tai Chin, who followed the precepts of the Sung period. The two leading artists of the early 16th century were Wên Chêng-ming (q.v.; III, PLS., 282, 283) and T'ang Yin, according to Chinese tradition both followers of the Wu school. A pupil of T'ang Yin was Ch'iu Ying, who revived the *kung-pi* method, the so-called "blue-and-green" landscape. The works of these artists are marked by exquisite detail; the ink was applied with moderation, and brilliant touches of color emphasized the decorative design (III, PL. 287).

After the death of Wên Chêng-ming and Ch'iu Ying there was a noticeable decline in the art of landscape painting, which lasted until the mid-17th century. With the Ch'ing period (1644–1912) came new trends derived from the art of the T'ang, Sung, and Yüan eras. One of the best-known painters of the late 17th century was Wang Hui (see WANG SHIH-MIN, etc.), a gifted man but lacking in originality. Although painters of this tendency dominated the artistic scene, another group of artists appeared who created works of very different type. Termed the "Great Individualists," the majority of them were Taoist monks. The most famous of these was Tao-chi, better known as Shih-t'ao (PL. 27; III, PL. 292), whose pictorial style was both spontaneous and highly expressive. Another artist of this group was the monk Chu Ta, better known under the name of Pa-ta-shan-jên (q.v.; III, PL. 290).

During the 18th and 19th centuries eclecticism became very pronounced, and no new elements appeared in landscape painting. Imitative tendencies and a strong attachment to tradition persisted throughout the 19th century (III, PLS. 295, 296). An excellent example of such tendencies is furnished by a landscape (1812) of Wang Chêng-kuo, a work executed in the style of Wang Hui. In the 20th century, the natural scene has continued to be the favorite subject of Chinese painters, and both traditionalists and those artists who adopted Occidental styles have produced landscapes in large numbers. While it is not possible to give a detailed account of the many landscape artists of the 20th century, mention should at least be made of Wang Chi-ch'üan, who has brought fresh insight to traditional Chinese subjects. His scroll *Rocks and Water* presents a fusion of Western perspective, obtained by the use of varied planes, with a typical Chinese landscape executed in strongly contrasting tones of ink.

Japan. The love of nature so characteristic of the Japanese people has long encouraged the practice of landscape art in Japan (see JAPANESE ART). Before the introduction of Buddhism in 552, the only form of painting known there was concerned with abstract designs composed of very simple geometric devices. Only in the second half of the 6th century, when Japan entered the Chinese cultural ambient, did a veritable cultural and artistic revolution take place; among other developments, it vitalized the art of painting. The oldest Japanese landscapes are found in the paintings on the Tamamushi shrine at Hōryūji (VIII, PL. 418), whose probable date (determined on the basis of stylistic affinity with Chinese sculpture of the Sui period) is the first half of the 7th century, toward the end of the Asuka period (552–ca. 645). The paintings, which depict Jātaka scenes, are typical of this period: the landscape is reduced to a few abstract, greatly simplified elements, and space is two-dimensional. Although it is no longer possible to compare these paintings with the Chinese or Korean models from which they were undoubtedly copied, the restriction to only those elements indispensable to landscape — mountains and trees — is definitely peculiar to the Chinese painting of the same period.

The only detail suggesting anything typically Japanese is the manner in which the mountains are represented, with rounded forms and rhythmic disposition.

Other early landscapes, about a century later in date, occur in the *Kako-Genzai-Inga-kyō* (fragments in Tokyo, University of Arts; Wakayama; and Kyoto), illustrations of the Sūtra episodes from the life of the Buddha before his Illumination. This work is of great historic interest as the forerunner of the Japanese school of narrative painting on horizontal scrolls (*emakimono*). The landscape is but a crude representation of natural scenes in vivid and fresh colors, and mountains and trees are the only elements forming the background. Still other examples of early landscape painting are preserved among the treasures in the Shōsōin of Nara: excellent landscapes, which reflect the T'ang style, are found on the backs of mirrors and on metal vessels, utensils, lacquered objects, and musical instruments. The most interesting design on a musical instrument is a painting on a *biwa*, depicting three musicians and a dancer on the back of an elephant, all set against a mountainous landscape. As far as can be inferred from the few surviving examples, it would appear that the Nara period produced a great many landscape paintings, which undoubtedly followed styles then fashionable in China as well as those of preceding periods.

Although no direct artistic evidence exists, landscape painting is known to have developed rapidly during the first half of the Heian period (9th cent.), for numerous literary sources contain the names of famous artists such as Kudara-no-Kawanari and Kose-no-Kanaoka. The latter painter is believed to have executed landscapes on the walls of the Seiryōden of the imperial palace of Kyoto.

A violent civil war that broke out in China interrupted relations between the T'ang court and Japan and led to a marked decrease in Chinese influence on Japanese art. The resulting cultural isolation had the effect of stimulating the development of a purely Japanese style, known as Yamato-e (q.v.), characterized by landscape paintings depicting indigenous Japanese scenes. No 10th-century originals exist today, but the mural paintings in the Hōōdō (Phoenix Hall) of the Byōdōin (Uji, prefecture of Kyoto) give some idea of landscapes painted in the 11th century. Although these present Buddhist subjects, landscape once again forms the most important element of the composition. Green is the predominant color, and the gently rounded hills differ from the towering mountains of Chinese landscapes. The outstanding example of Heian landscape art is the six-paneled screen preserved in the Tōji of Kyoto (VIII, PL. 277). According to the tradition of the temple, this screen was brought from China in the 9th century by Kūkai (Kōbō Daishi); however, another tradition attributes it to the 12th-century monk Chinkai, and several authorities favor such later dating (11th–12th cent.). In any case, this screen shows unmistakable T'ang characteristics in the figures and costumes, while the use of color and the treatment of the landscape is definitely Japanese.

The works most typical of this period are the *emakimono*. One of the finest of these is the *Shigisan Engi* (Chōgosonshiji, Nara prefecture), or history of Mount Shigi, which illustrates the most salient characteristic of Yamato-e painting: namely, emphasis on the narrative rather than on the majesty of the landscape (cf. VIII, PL. 300).

The high point in the development of the Yamato-e style was reached during the Kamakura period (1185–1333), from which many paintings have been preserved. For the most part, in the earlier years of the period the figures still dominated the composition too much and the landscape was reduced to mere setting (VIII, PLS. 293, 296, 297); it was only at the end of the Kamakura period that landscape attained a more pure form, as a result of Chinese influence (VIII, PL. 298). Kamakura pure landscapes are found only on the *sansui-byōbu* (folding screens) and on the *kakemono* (vertical scrolls). The finest of the *sansui-byōbu* is probably the pair in the Jingoji of Kyoto, in the style of the Yamato-e school of the 13th century. Of the *kakemono* from this period, the most notable is the *Nachi Waterfall* (VIII, PL. 299), which symbolizes the deity of the great Shinto shrine of Kumano. Despite the religious significance of the composition, this is pure landscape in a style that is strictly Japanese in character — clearly apparent when it is compared with contemporary Chinese painting.

During the Muromachi period (1334–1573) landscape art, influenced by Zen Buddhism, flourished in a remarkable fashion. Renewed contact with China brought into favor ink painting in the Chinese style, known in Japanese as *suiboku-ga* ("black-and-white" art) or *sumi-e*, a technique that had been introduced to Japan during the second half of the Kamakura period. The Zen artists, in an attempt to discover the true essence of reality, moved away from superficial color effects and stress on detail in order to produce highly stylized black-and-white works. Among the earliest noteworthy *suiboku-ga* landscapists were Minchō (Chōdensu) and Josetsu, artists of the late 14th and early 15th centuries. The importance of Josetsu in the history of Japanese landscape painting is based more upon his activity as a teacher than upon his own artistic output (VIII, PL. 305).

Shūbun (mid-15th cent.), a disciple of Josetsu, perfected the Chinese style of landscape. His work is marked by a straightforward expression that was to influence the work of later artists: the mysterious aspect of Chinese landscape disappears, foreground and background become flat planes, and the entire painting is rendered more dramatic with stronger brush strokes. Of various works attributed to him, the most probable is a representation of a mountainous landscape (VIII, PL. 306).

While the work of Shūbun and his contemporaries was merely in emulation of the Chinese style, Japanese ink painting continued to acquire a distinctive character, under the impulse of the greatest *sumi-e* painter, the Zen monk Sesshū (q.v.). About 1468 he went to China to study the works of the great Chinese masters of the past. His simple composition, subtly varied tones of black, and his fresh, open perception of reality signify a vital art attainable only by an artist drawing his inspiration directly from nature. Among the many paintings attributed to him, the most famous is an *emakimono* that begins with a spring scene and ends with a winter landscape (1486; Yamaguchi, Mōri Motomichi Coll.). The style and subject reveal the influence of Hsia Kuei, the handling of ink tones that of Li T'ang. In spite of such clear Chinese influences, Sesshū brought to his work characteristics both individual and typically Japanese. Another of his works, a *kakemono* entitled *Winter Landscape* (VIII, PL. 307) painted in 1495, when the artist was about seventy-five years old, is in the technique of the Southern Chinese school known as "splashed ink" (Jap., *hatsubo-ku*) and shows affinity with the work of the Chinese painter Ying Yü-chien. In this work, deeply pervaded with the spirit of Zen, much of the composition is left empty, and the void becomes highly expressive in relation to the gray and black of the ink. A contemporary of Sesshū was Sōami (q.v.), whose artistic career was passed at the court of the shogun Ashikaga Yoshimasa; his style recalls the manner of Mu-ch'i. The rounded hills and increased depth characteristic of Sōami's work are in sharp contrast with the style of Sesshū.

A school of painting which originated during the late Muromachi period but which rose to importance during the Edo period (1615–1867) was the Kanō school (q.v.), named for its founder, the Zen monk Kanō Motonobu. Although Kanō Motonobu dedicated himself to the study of Chinese painting, his style was typically Japanese, the salient characteristics being its highly decorative character and the pronounced realism of details (VIII, PL. 313). These qualities are clearly seen in his painting *The Monk Ling-yün Contemplating Lotus Blossoms* (Tokyo, Nat. Mus.).

During the Momoyama period (1573–1615), Chinese influence vanished almost completely and gave way to a strictly Japanese style emphasizing the decorative character of landscape painting. The painters were no longer Zen monks but professional artists who worked for the great military lords, decorating their castles with large landscapes, either in monochrome or in brilliant colors on a gold-leaf ground (VIII, PLS. 319, 320). This type of painting, known as *shōheki-ga*, was executed on *byōbu*, *fusuma*, and *shōji*, as well as directly on the interior walls of edifices.

One of the famous artists of this period was Kanō Eitoku, the grandson of Kanō Motonobu; diverging from the monochrome work of his grandfather, he developed a highly individual manner in brilliant colors, with simplified forms set against a flat ground. He also painted monochrome panels, and among these should be noted his series of *fusuma* in Kyoto (VIII, PL. 318). Works in his own — that is, the colored — style include the screen *Cypress Trees* (Tokyo, Nat. Mus.) and the six-paneled screen *Hawks on Pine Trees* (VIII, PL. 353). Although the subjects are of Chinese inspiration, they are executed in a completely different manner and in a decidedly Japanese style.

Other painters of the Momoyama period drew their inspiration from the works of Sesshū instead of following the style of the Kanō school. The most prominent of this group, Hasegawa Tōhaku, founded the school named for him and painted in the *suiboku-ga* style. His finest work is undoubtedly a screen with pine trees (VIII, PL. 309), a work using the technique of the Zen artists but blending the best qualities of both the Chinese and the Japanese tradition.

The Kanō school was the official school followed by artists of the Edo period. The most authoritative of these, Kanō Naonobu, was especially noted for his landscapes, the finest of which are on a pair of screens in Tokyo (VIII, PL. 355). The style is like that of the Chinese artist Ying Yü-chien, but the brushwork is more varied, sometimes free, at times precise and detailed. Nonetheless, despite the prestige of the Kanō school, the artists who actually created new and interesting work belonged to rival schools. The school that most closely followed Japanese tradition in this period was the Sōtatsu school — based on the principles of Yamato-e — named for its founder Tawaraya (Nonomura) Sōtatsu, to whom is attributed a screen representing the Bay of Matsushima and its rocky isles (Washington, D.C., Freer Gall. of Art). The work most typical of Sōtatsu's style is a pair of screens (Tokyo, Seikadō Bunko) depicting episodes of the *Genji Monogatari*. Somewhat later another great artist, Ogata Kōrin (q.v.), adopted Sōtatsu's style. A painter of great talent, he produced remarkable compositions in the decorative polychrome style.

The notable school of landscape painting that arose in 17th-century Japan was influenced by Chinese art. This new style, known as Nanga and based on the canons of the Southern school of Chinese painting, was also called *bunjin-ga* ("literati" or "gentlemen's" painting) and was the work of scholars, officials, and writers. The most famous of these literati was Ike-no-Taiga, a student of Zen and of calligraphy who spent his life in the mountains. There he produced works of great artistic merit, among which are the series of album leaves in Kamakura (Kawabata Coll.). The simple, almost abstract style resembles the manner of the Ch'ing painters.

Perhaps the most representative of the 18th-century painters was Maruyama Ōkyo, who began painting in the Kanō style but later studied Western perspective and the realistic manner of the Ming painters. This preparation resulted in a decorative, realistic mode of painting (VIII, PL. 327) which had great influence throughout the remainder of the Edo period. An excellent example of his style is a folding screen on which are represented the rapids of Hozu (Kyoto, Nishimura Sōzaemon Coll.), a work with a great number of naturalistic details and realistic vigor. Among the followers of Ōkyo was Goshun (Matsumura Gekkei), the founder of the Shijō school. Typical of his work is the *Landscape under Snow* (Tokyo, Nat. Mus.), combining the realism of Ōkyo with the more poetic spirit of the Nanga school.

In the two and a half centuries spanned by the Edo period, a great variety of styles and an imposing number of distinct schools were developed — trends ranging from the decorative Sōtatsu to the realistic Maruyama school, and from the traditionalist Kanō style to the *bunjin-ga* of the Nanga school (cf. VIII, PL. 329). Of all Japanese landscapes, perhaps the most famous in the West are those of Hokusai and Hiroshige (qq.v.), exponents of the Ukiyo-e school (q.v.). Katsushika Hokusai studied the works of the Kanō and Tosa schools, as well as the principles of Western perspective. Fusing these techniques, he evolved an original style that is magnificently exemplified in the series of views of Mount Fuji (IV, PL. 447; VII, PL. 297), executed between 1823 and 1835. Although the mastery of perspective testifies to Western contacts, the spirit of his work is purely Japanese. The painting, marked by an intimate understanding of nature, is at the same time decorative and abstract. The prolific activity of this artist was truly phenomenal. He produced a total of at least 35,000 drawings, but his major achievement was the series of views mentioned above. Hiroshige, the other great Ukiyo-e landscape artist, may be regarded as the last of the great masters of this school. His style, more realistic and lyrical, is seen at its best in his most important work, *Fifty-three Stages on the Tōkaidō Highway* (IV, PL. 447).

With Hiroshige, landscape painting in a recognizably Japanese tradition, and with some degree of artistic originality, was virtually brought to an end. After his death, with a few notable exceptions, there was an absence of creative landscape until well into the present century, when landscape subjects began to reappear in markedly Western guise, frequently executed in the nontraditional medium of oils.

Antonio PRIORI

BIBLIOG. *Antiquity*: a. *General works*: K. Woermann, Die Landschaft in der Kunst der alten Völker, Munich, 1876; W. S. Smith, A History of Egyptian Sculpture and Painting in the Old Kingdom, 2d ed., London, Boston, 1949, pp. 333-34, 347-50; Pfuhl, p. 327 ff., 589, 409 ff., 969 ff., pls. 59, 109, 164, 174, 290, 378, 527, 583, 648, 721 ff. b. *Crete*: K. Schefold, Griechische Kunst als religiöses Phenomen, Hamburg, 1959. c. *Greece*: M. Heinemann, Landschaftliche Elemente in der griechischen Kunst bis Polygnot, Bonn, 1910; E. Kunze, Ionische Kleinmeister, AM, LIX, 1934, pp. 81-122. d. *Hellenism and Rome*: M. Rostovtsev, Die hellenistisch-römische Architekturlandschaft, RM, XXVI, 1911, pp. 1-185; C. M. Dawson, Romano-Campanian Mythological Landscape Painting (Yale Classical S., IX), New Haven, London, 1954; K. Schefold, Vorbilder römischer Landschaftsmalerei, AM, LXXI, 1956, pp. 24-31; K. Schefold, Origins of Roman Landscape Painting, AB, XLII, 1960, pp. 86-96. e. *Perspective*: E. Panofsky, Perspektive als symbolische Form, Vorträge Bib. Warburg, 1924-25, pp. 258-330; B. Schweitzer, Vom Sinn der Perspektive, Tübingen, 1953 (bibliog.); J. White, Perspective in Ancient Drawing and Painting, London, 1956; F. Gioseffi, Perspectiva artificialis, Trieste, 1957.

Medieval and modern period: T. B. Deperthes, Histoire de l'art du paysage, Paris, 1822; C. Baudelaire, Salon de 1845, Curiosités esthétiques, Paris, 1954, pp. 585-91 (Paysages), 664-71; W. Bode, Studien zur Geschichte der holländischen Malerei, Brunswick, 1883; L. Kämmerer, Die Landschaft in der deutschen Kunst, Leipzig, 1886; E. Michel, Hobbema et les paysagistes de son temps en Hollande, Paris, 1890; J. Ruskin, Lectures on Landscape Delivered at Oxford, London, 1897; G. Lanoë and T. Brice, Histoire de l'école française de paysage depuis le Poussin jusqu'à Millet, Paris, 1901; J. Guthmann, Die Landschaftsmalerei der toskanischen und umbrischen Kunst, Leipzig, 1902; F. Rosen, Die Natur in der Kunst, Leipzig, 1903; J. de Jongh, Die holländische Landschaftsmalerei: ihre Entstehung und Entwicklung, Berlin, 1905; F. Armenter, L'illusion du mouvement dans le paysage, Paris, 1907; F. Benoit et al., Histoire du paysage en France, Paris, 1908; P. Dorbec, Les premiers peintres du paysage parisien, GBA, XL, 1908, pp. 441-70; L. Ozzola, Cenni sui precursori del paesaggio secentesco, Ausonia, II, 1908, pp. 303-14; H. Höhn, Studien zur Entwicklung der Münchener Landschaftsmalerei, Strasbourg, 1909; J. Gramm, Ideal-Landschaftsmalerei, 2 vols., Freiburg, 1912; A. Massara, Scuola d'arte del paesaggio, Bologna, 1912; T. Leclère, Hubert Robert et les paysagistes français du XVIIIe siècle, Paris, 1913; F. Paulhan, L'esthétique du paysage, Paris, 1913; M. Moore, Del paesaggio nella pittura di Raffaello, Naples, 1920; A. Foratti, Il paesaggio dei Carracci e la loro scuola, L'Archiginnasio, XVI, 1921, pp. 19-21; G. Rouchès, Le paysage dans les peintures de l'école bolognaise, GBA, LXVIII, 1921, pp. 7-32, 119-32; A. Arentz, Holländische Landschaftsmalerei des 17. Jahrhunderts, Leipzig, 1923; K. Gerstenberg, Die ideale Landschaftsmalerei, Halle, 1923; C. L. Hind, Landscape Painting from Giotto to the Present Day, 2 vols., London, 1923; R. A. Pelzer, Niederländische-venezianische Landschaftsmalerei, Münch. Jhb. der bildenden K., N.S., I, 1924, pp. 37-70; F. Pfister, La scuola di Posillipo, BArte, N.S., IV, 1924-25, pp. 163-83; P. Dorbec, L'art du paysage en France, Paris, 1925; M. H. Grant, A Chronological History of the Old English Landscape Painters, 3 vols., London, 1925; R. Grosse, Die holländische Landschaftkunst, 1600-1650, Berlin, 1925; W. J. James, The Development of Modern Landscape, Oxford, 1925; L. Hourticq, Le paysage français de Poussin à Corot à l'exposition du Petit Palais, Paris, 1926; H. Voss, Studien zur venezianischen Vedutenmalerei des 18. Jahrhunderts, RepfKw, XLVII, 1926, pp. 10-45; I. Haumann, Das oberitalienische Landschaftbild des Settecento, Strasbourg, 1927; C. Hussey, The Picturesque: Studies in a Point of View, London, New York, 1927; W. Waetzold, Das klassische Land, Leipzig, 1927; C. Zervos, Paysages français du XVe siècle, Paris, 1927; J. Magnin, Le paysage français: Dès enlumineurs à Corot, Paris, 1928; Paesaggio umbro (cat.), Orvieto, 1930; Giardino italiano (cat.), Florence, 1931; J. Havelaar, De nederlandsche Landschapskunst, Amsterdam, 1931; Winterlandschappen (cat.), Amsterdam, 1932; Dessins des paysagistes français du XIXe siècle (cat.), Paris, 1933; R. Buscaroli, La pittura di paesaggio in Italia, Bologna, 1935; L. Richmond, The Art of Landscape Painting, London, 1935 (New York, 1946); E. Waldmann, Albrecht Dürer und die deutsche Landschaft,

Pantheon, V, 1935, pp. 130–36; R. Eisen, Die deutsche Landschaftsmalerei des Spätbarock, Leipzig, 1936; W. Gaunt, Bandits in a Landscape: A Study of Romantic Painting from Caravaggio to Delacroix, London, 1937; Le paysage français avant les impressionnistes (cat.), Geneva, 1937; S. Stelling-Michaud, Unbekannte Schweizer Landschaften aus dem 17. Jahrhundert, Zürich, 1937; P. Jamot, Sur la naissance du paysage dans l'art moderne: Du paysage abstrait au paysage humaniste, Paris, 1938; G. Bell, Invaded Landscape, The Studio, CXX, 1940, pp. 34–51; K. Klitgaard, Through the American Landscape, Chapel Hill, N.C., 1941; J. López Jiménez, El paisaje y los paisajistas españoles, Madrid, 1943; J. H. Pleasants, Four Late 18th Century Anglo-American Landscape Painters, Worcester, Mass., 1943; J. Wilhelm, Les peintres du paysage parisien du XVe siècle à nos jours, Paris, 1944; A. G. Roth, Die Gestirne in der Landschaftsmalerei des Abendlandes, Bern, 1945; F. Weitenkampf, Early American Landscape Prints, AQ, VIII, 1945, pp. 40–67; A. Lhote, Traité du paysage, 3d ed., Paris, 1946 (Eng. trans., W. L. Strachan, London, 1950); A. Dragone, I paesisti piemontesi dell'Ottocento, Milan, 1947; J. L. Vaudoyer, Paysages d'Italie (cat.), Paris, 1947; W. Born, American Landscape Painting: An Interpretation, New Haven, 1948; W. Born, The Sentiment of Nature in American Landscape Painting, GBA, XXXIII, 1948, pp. 219–38; K. Clark, Landscape Into Art, London, 1949 (pub. as Landscape Painting, New York, 1950); Delacroix et le paysage romantique (cat.), Paris, 1949; B. Dorival, Landscape in French Art (cat.), London, 1949; M. J. Friedländer, Landscape, Portrait, Still-Life, Oxford, New York, 1949; Le paysage hollandais au XVIIe siècle (cat.), Paris, 1949; An Exhibition of English Landscape: Watercolours from English and American Private Collections (cat.), London, 1950; E. Seaver, Landscape Paintings, Art in Am., XXXVIII, 1950, pp. 81–90; Het Franse Landschap van Poussin tot Cézanne (cat.), Amsterdam, 1951; Å. Bengtsson, Studies on the Rise of Realistic Landscape Painting in Holland, 1610–25, Stockholm, 1952; A. L. Cummings, The Beginnings of American Landscape Painting, BMMA, XI, 1952, pp. 93–99; C. Gilbert, Francesco Corradi e la tipologia del paesaggio del Seicento, Comm, III, 1952, pp. 175–85; H. A. Fedorov-Davydov, Russkii peisazh 18-nachala 19 veka (Russian Landscapes of the 18th and Early 19th Centuries), Moscow, 1953; H. Gerson, Dutch Landscape, BM, XCV, 1953, pp. 47–52; Le paysage anglais (cat.), London, 1953; Y. Thiéry, Le paysage flamand au XVIIe siècle, Brussels, 1953; R. D. Dunlop, Landscape Painting, London, 1954; Meisterwerke holländischer Landschaftsmalerei des 17. Jahrhunderts (cat.), Munich, 1954; R. Seddon, British Landscape, The Studio, CXLVIII, 1954, pp. 97–103; H. Lemaître, Le paysage anglais à l'aquarelle, 1760–1851, Paris, 1955; R. Longhi, Viviano Codazzi e l'invenzione della veduta realistica, Paragone, VI, 71, 1955, pp. 40–47; H. V. S. and M. S. Ogden, English Taste in Landscape in the 17th Century, Ann Arbor, Mich., 1955; N. Di Carpegna, Mostra dei paesisti e vedutisti a Roma nel Seicento e Settecento (cat.), Rome, 1956; M. Schefold, Alte Ansichten aus Württemberg, 2 vols., Stuttgart, 1956–57; Paisagistas e animalistas do século XVII (cat.), Lisbon, 1957; P. Camarnesco, Le paysage à l'Exposition interrégional, in L'art dans la République populaire roumaine, 1958, pp. 33–44; Monuments et sites d'Italie vues par les dessinateurs français de Callot à Degas (cat.), Paris, 1958; Ideal and Classical Landscape (cat.), Cardiff, 1959; D. Sutton, Il paesaggio classico e ideale, Arti-Fig, 44,1960, pp. 17–27; M. Soria, Velázquez and Vedute Painting in Italy and Spain 1620–1750, Arte ant. e mod., IV, 1961, pp. 439–47; L'ideale classico del Seicento in Italia e la pittura di paesaggio (cat.), Bologna, 1962.

The East: a. India: J. Auboyer, L'influence chinoise sur le paysage dans la peinture de l'Orient et dans la sculpture de l'Insulinde, RAA, IX, 1935, pp. 228–34 (see also INDIAN ART). *b. China*: A. Salmony, Chinesische Landschaftsmalerei, Berlin, 1921; O. Sirén, History of Early Chinese Art, 4 vols., London, 1929–30; Kuo Hsi, An Essay on Landscape Painting (ed. S. Sakanishi), London, 1935; S. Sakanishi, The Spirit of the Brush, London, 1939; E. Dietz, Shan Shui, Vienna, 1943; O. Fischer, Chinesische Landschaftsmalerei, 3d ed., Vienna, 1943; G. Rowley, Principles of Chinese Painting, Princeton, 1947; W. Speiser, Meisterwerke chinesischer Malerei, Berlin, 1947 (3d ed., 1958); W. Cohn, Chinese Painting, London, 1948; S. E. Lee, Chinese Landscape Painting, Cleveland, O., 1954; V. Contag, Zwei Meister chinesischer Landschaftsmalerei, Baden-Baden, 1955; A. Waley, Introduction to the Study of Chinese Painting, London, 1958; J. Cahill, Chinese Painting, New York, 1960; D. M. Sullivan, The Birth of Landscape Painting in China, London, 1961 (Berkeley, Calif., 1962). *c. Japan*: E. de Goncourt, Hokusai, Paris, 1896; W. Cohn, Stilanalysen als Einführung in die japanische Malerei, Berlin, 1908; H. P. Bowie, On the Laws of Japanese Painting, San Francisco, 1911; Y. Yashiro, Japanische Malerei der Gegenwart, Berlin, 1931; Y. Noguchi, Hiroshige and Japanese Landscapes, Tokyo, 1934; N. Tsuda, Ideals of Japanese Painting, Tokyo, 1940; J. C. Covell, Under the Seal of Sesshū, New York, 1941; Pageant of Japanese Art, I–II, Tokyo, 1952; H. Okuhira, E no rekishi (History of Painting), 2 vols., Tokyo, 1953; H. Munsterberg, The Landscape Painting of China and Japan, Tokyo, Rutland, Vt., 1955; T. Hasumi, Zen in Japanese Art, London, 1962.

Illustrations: PLS. 1–28.

LAOS. A kingdom of southeast Asia, founded in A.D. 1353, Laos is bounded by Vietnam, Cambodia, Thailand, Burma, and China. Much of its western border follows the course of the Mekong River. The administrative capital is at Vientiane, the residence of the court at Luangprabang. Together with its predominant Buddhist religion, Laos received artistic inspiration from India. There has been little contact with Western culture, and the area has continued to produce religious architecture and sculpture in archaicizing styles and techniques dependent on the earlier cultures.

SUMMARY. Historical sketch (col. 50). Art centers (col. 50): *Province of Tranninh; Luangprabang; Vientiane; Mekong Valley.*

HISTORICAL SKETCH. In the valley of the Mekong River, which from the most remote times was a migration route for peoples originally from China and Tibet, are preserved numerous traces of prehistoric and protohistoric life — at Luangprabang, at Tranninh (the "Plaine des Jarres"), and in the province of Cammon. In the recorded history of the territory, the Khmer Empire (see KHMER ART) gradually extended its dominion from south to north, along the length of the valley, on the Korat Plateau, and, toward the end of the 12th century, up to the heights of Vientiane. At the end of the 13th century the Tai (Thai) kingdom of Sukhotai incorporated the lands to the west of the Mekong as far as Vientiane and the site of Luangprabang.

The formation of the Laotian kingdom was the work of Prince Fa Ngum, who had been raised at the Khmer court of Angkor. Following a military expedition that lasted from 1340 to 1350, he was proclaimed king (1353) in the city later to be called Luangprabang. His successors continued to reside there until the reign of Pothisarat, who provisionally established himself at Vientiane, which was better situated from the commercial standpoint. His son Setthathirat made the move permanent in 1560 and was responsible for building the temple of Wat Phra Keo (Ho Phra Keo) and the That Luang (1586). The wars with Burma during the second half of the 16th century resulted in the occupation of Laotian territory by the Burmese toward the end of that century, a circumstance that had some influence on the culture and art of the country. Following a period of confused succession to the throne, which began in 1694, the country was divided into two kingdoms, with Luangprabang and Vientiane as the dual capitals. The latter city sustained two Siamese invasions at fifty-year intervals: the first (1778) despoiled Wat Phra Keo, where the celebrated "Emerald Buddha" was located, and the second (1828) reduced the city to ruins. The oldest Laotian monuments that have survived date only from the 16th century. Nevertheless, since they are known to conserve a tradition with its roots in the more distant past, such works provide reliable approximations of earlier Laotian architecture.

ART CENTERS. *Province of Tranninh*. The plateau of Tranninh is the site of the architecture that most rigorously adheres to the traditional canons of Laotian art.

Xieng Khuang. At Xieng Khuang, the principal town of Tranninh province, and in the vicinity the outstanding monuments number: Wat Bun Ko, notable for the elaborate roof decoration, the gable of its façade, and the triple entrance on its front porch; Wat Si Phum, where the shrine (partially ruined) rises from a base similar to that of the That Luang at Vientiane; That Phuen, enclosing an earlier octagonal stupa with its own bell-shaped, square-based stupa having recessed corners; and That Phong Peng, one of the tallest shrines of Tranninh. Its three traditional components (base, main body, and terminal bulb) are of the narrowest diameter possible and create an extremely tapered silhouette.

Muong Sui. In this district, in addition to the Plaine des Jarres with its funerary monoliths, there are four architectural landmarks of note: Wat Thong Hak, covered by a roof of an angular severity that contrasts with the usual curve of Laotian roofs; Wat Visai, with an ornate portal on its front porch and a rear wall painted with an interesting array of Buddhas; Wat Ban Phong, a diverse group of buildings comprising a monastery, including a meeting hall of five aisles and nine bays (the two end bays separated from the others by walls in order to form front and back porches), a chapel with a sharply pitched roof (PL. 29), a library, and living quarters for the monks; and Wat Ban Mang, another important complex, with a shrine, less tapered than the one of That Phong Peng, that is one of the finest-proportioned buildings of Tranninh.

Luangprabang. This city is situated at the confluence of the Nam Khan and Mekong rivers, which have parallel currents but run in opposite directions, and the northeast sector is bounded by the two rivers. The southern part is protected by a city wall that runs from the left bank of the Mekong to the left bank of the Nam Khan. At the center of the city rises the sacred hill of Phu Si, on the summit of which is a notable Laotian monument, That Chom Si, a gilded pyramid constructed over the ruins of an older building, enlarged in 1796 and restored in 1914. Wat Xieng Thong (PL. 29), a monastery to the north of the city, is of legendary origin lost in the remote past; it was rebuilt in 1561 by King Chei Chettha. Its several buildings include a meeting hall, chapels, shrine, and library. Wat Mai, south of the Royal Palace, was built in 1796 on the site of an earlier building in order to receive a statue of the Buddha (PL. 30). The present building comprises an aisle seven bays long, terminated at front and back by porches resting on double colonnades (perhaps added later, at the same time as the lateral pavilions). The central portal is richly embellished and surmounted by graduated tiers in a crownlike arrangement (PL. 31). Wat That, where relics are known to have been deposited in 1548, was rebuilt in 1907. The meeting hall is surrounded by a veranda. East of this is the shrine, rising from a high foundation of three tiers. Its main body, on a square plan with indented corners, is decorated with four blind doors, each serving as a niche for an image of a standing Buddha. Above this level is superimposed a gradually diminishing series of stages, crowned by a tiny stupa.

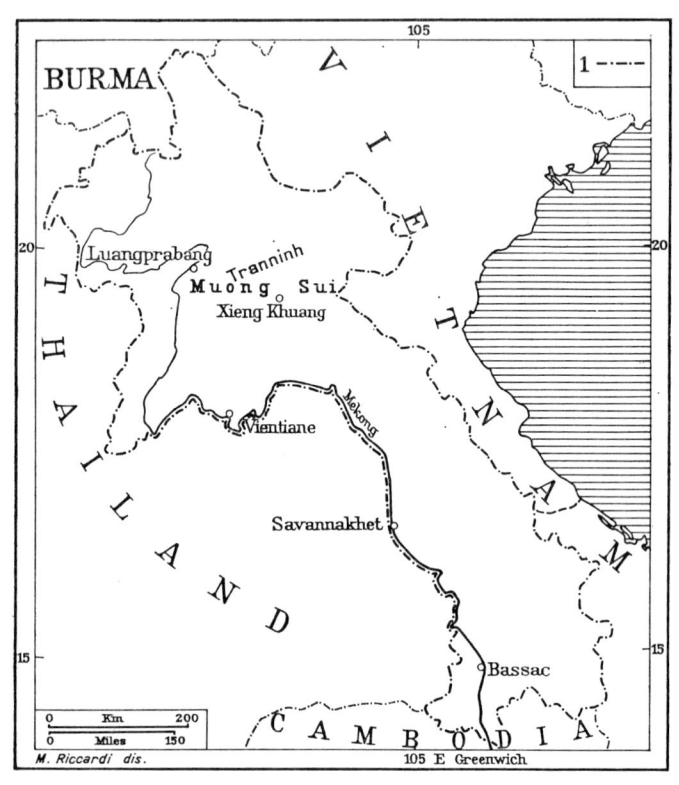

The precincts of Wat That Luang, south of the city, contain a three-aisled meeting hall divided longitudinally into nine bays by tall square pillars, which are decorated with capitals in the form of a double row of lotus blossoms. Because there is no ceiling within, the details of the roof construction are plainly visible. South of the meeting hall a shrine was built in 1818; square in plan and with corner recesses, it enclosed an older building. It has a notable three-tiered base and a small terminal bulb resting on a bulky support. Now in ruins, Wat Manorom was built in 1372 by King Sam Sen Tai to house a colossal bronze image of the Buddha, of which only the head (ca. 6 ft.) and the torso (13 ft.) remain. Wat Visun, built by King Visun in 1503, was seen — if not wholly in its original form, at least in an older aspect than the present one — and recorded in 1867 by members of an exploratory mission to the region of the Mekong. A sketch attributed to Louis Delaporte (F. Garnier, *Voyage d'Exploration en Indochine*, Paris, 1885) illustrates the meeting hall of the complex, a beautiful building with flaring contours that recall Laotian caskets. Its wooden walls were delicately carved; but the whole was unfortunately destroyed in 1887, when the city was pillaged by Chinese pirates. The masonry hall on the site, which reproduces the earlier building with great care, was erected in 1898. The shrine, consisting of a hemispheric stupa surmounted by a conical flamelike ornament, collapsed in 1914 but was rebuilt in 1937.

Vientiane. The city of Vientiane, formerly enclosed by a defensive brick wall, extends in an arc along the left bank of the Mekong River for more than 3 miles.

Phya Wat, once a great complex of buildings, is at present largely in ruins. The three-aisled meeting hall was divided lengthwise into five bays, with porches at both the ends. The roofing has disappeared, but within remain eight tapered pillars with indented corners and a gigantic masonry Buddha on a heavily decorated pedestal. Behind this hall are vestiges of a large octagonal shrine, as well as the ruins of diverse other buildings. Wat In Peng is worthy of note for its small library (restored), which is covered with a double roof and has splayed walls. Another small and well-preserved building is a chapel with a steep masonry roof. The principal shrine is raised on a high base, formed of tiers of diminishing size.

Wat Sisaket, which dates from 1820, was restored in 1921–23 and turned into an archaeological museum. In the manner of the great temples of Bangkok, the meeting hall is surrounded by a cloister which is closed toward the outside but which opens onto an interior court; formed by a double colonnade, this enclosure is interrupted by a doorway on each of its four sides. The gallery of the cloister, with a ceiling of wooden planks painted red and decorated with golden rosettes, protects the collection of 120 lacquered-masonry Buddha images and four bronze Buddhas that stand in the corners. Along the walls are disposed a total of 3,372 niches, each containing two figures of the Buddha. The meeting hall, in the center of the court, is surrounded by a veranda that is formed by a colonnade supporting the lower roof; the walls of the hall itself support the double upper roof. The interior plan is extremely simple; the walls are ornamented with frescoes, and near the top are seven rows of ogival niches, each containing two small Buddhas of gilded terra cotta. The shutters of the doors and windows are lacquered and gilded. On the exterior of the cloister, near the western corner, rise two square shrines, with corner recesses, and a library. This square library building is raised off the ground and is surrounded by a hip-roofed veranda with four columns to a side. Supporting the veranda is a low parapet pierced with ogival openings. The interior chamber has a superstructure composed of three distinct levels, each successive stage decreasing in span. On the exterior this ceiling structure is repeated in three superimposed roofs which rise above the veranda roof and which are partly supported by the veranda columns. The terminal spire of this high roof, reminiscent of Burmese architecture, is in the form of a bulblike miniature shrine.

On the site of Wat Phra Keo (Ho Phra Keo), constructed in the 16th century to hold the famous Emerald Buddha (now in Bangkok), nothing remains except the meeting hall, which has been restored (PL. 32). This hall rises atop a three-tiered base, within a narrow square court enclosed by a low, decorated wall. The end of the hall is occupied by a large altar on which the statue of Phra Keo was once enthroned. The walls are pierced by three doors on the entry side and by two on the rear wall behind the altar, as well as by five windows on each of the other sides. These openings are framed by a motif which imitates the various elements of a building: base, pilasters, capitals, and two graduated tiers that terminate in a reliquary finial. Between the openings, the walls are covered with a coat of black lacquer decorated with gilt designs; the interior pilasters are aligned with the pillars of the veranda and the end porches. Above the quadriform roof that shelters the veranda, two receding multilayer roofs span the porches and the hall itself. These are surmounted by a third roof corresponding to the center segment of the hall.

That Luang, a monument unique in the Laotian tradition, was built in the second half of the 16th century; its original name was Lokacūḷāmani, "the crowning jewel at the summit of the universe." Like the Khmer pyramidal temples, it symbolizes the cosmic mountain that marks the center of the world and is purported to contain a relic of the Buddha. It was restored in 1898, but the pinnacle of the central shrine, which did not correspond in silhouette to that of an earlier state represented in a sketch made by Delaporte (Garnier, *op. cit.*, II, p. 291), was rebuilt in 1934, when various other parts of the building were reconstructed. Its main stupa, rising from an enclosed platform, is roofed with a square-based, domelike vault, which, as the restoration of 1934 revealed, had encompassed an older construction. At the base of each face of the stupa are shrines — a total of 30, including the taller corner structures. This number corresponds to the Ten Perfections of Buddhism (*pāramitā*), each of which has three degrees. The principal shrine rises from the summit of the stupa; the finial rests on a base composed of three tiers, the lowest of which is decorated with large lotus petals of gilded stucco. The temple is set within a square gallery entirely decorated on the exterior faces with large lotus petals. At the center of each side this gallery is broken by an arched portal crowned with the characteristic tiered roof and slender spire. Outside and concentric with this gallery is a lower wall with a small pavilion at the center of its eastern face. This wall in turn rests on a platform that has four axial chapels. The brick-paved court surrounding the whole complex is enclosed by a great cloister (ca. 260 ft. on a side), which has a triple-roofed entry pavilion at the middle of each side.

Mekong Valley. Because two of the most important monuments of the Mekong Valley, the That Phanom and the shrine of Lakhon Kao, are located in Siamese territory on the right bank of the river.

they will not be discussed here (see SIAMESE ART; THAILAND). Mention will be made of two other monuments, however, which are located farther downstream within Laotian territory but which are stylistically linked with Khmer art.

That Ing Rang, a little more than 10 miles from the modern city of Savannakhet, is a sanctuary in pre-Angkorian style that has been disfigured by restorations, which included whitewashing and the imposition of Laotian taste on the true and blind doorways. Similar changes were made in the superstructure, rebuilt to satisfy the line of a flagon-shaped reliquary spire. That the original sanctuary was consecrated to the cult of some Hindu god is confirmed by the *somasūtra* preserved within the spire. It was later transformed into a Buddhist chapel, but its purpose did not deter the Laotians from carving erotic scenes on the exterior, at both sides of the façade entry.

Wat Phu, the last of the Mekong Valley monuments before the Cambodian frontier, is the northernmost of the significant monuments of Khmer art. Some 10 miles from the city of Bassac, on the right bank of the Mekong, the temple precinct is built into the east side of a mountain, formerly named Liṅgapārvata, that was a cult and pilgrimage site throughout the history of the Khmer empire. Farther to the east extends a large rectangular pool, bounded on its western edge by a terrace from which a long causeway (ca. 900 ft.) leads toward the sanctuary. Flanked by two rows of boundary posts, this causeway rises in a gentle slope to another terrace, where it meets two quadrangular galleries (improperly known as the "palace"). Farther west the pathway continues to rise between two more galleries, after which the plan encompasses a cruciform terrace, a stairway, and a narrow terrace occupied by six small temples aligned from north to south. A final stairway, punctuated with seven landings, leads to the esplanade where the sanctuary is situated. Behind the sanctuary is still another gallery, built about a spring at the foot of the mountain. The water is conducted to the sanctuary, where it bathes the idol and a kind of linga within.

BIBLIOG. H. Parmentier, L'art du Laos, Paris, Hanoi, 1954.

George Cœdès

Illustrations: 1 fig. in text.

LAOTIAN ART. Artistically, Laos belongs to the southeast Asian area of Indian culture; but since the country was not founded until the mid-14th century, it was unable to benefit directly from the contributions of Indian art during the great period coeval with the first centuries of the Christian Era. Laos assimilated Indian influences from its neighbors to the south and west — Cambodia (q.v.), Thailand (see SIAMESE ART), and Burma (see BURMESE ART) — during the period when they had already adopted Singhalese Buddhism (see BUDDHISM).

There is evidence that at a relatively early period Indian architectural styles, transmitted by way of Burma, permanently influenced Laotian light architecture — that is, the corpus of architecture constructed of perishable materials, no longer available for direct comparison with possible Indian prototypes. From the time of its 14th-century foundation and from the century following, there remains only some of the sculpture of the Laotian kingdom.

SUMMARY. Introduction (col. 53). Sculpture (col. 54). Architecture (col. 54): *General characteristics; Types of buildings; Architectural styles; Conclusion.*

INTRODUCTION. It is impossible to make a study of the art of Laos comparable with those which have been made of the other schools of southeast Asia, because the surviving art of Laos is of too late a date to permit tracing its course over a period of equally significant length. The most that can be done is to distinguish certain stylistic variants in the art of different regions. Laotian art has up to the present been the object of only one ambitious study, that of Henri Parmentier (1954); it deals primarily with architecture, the sole art of Laos that has substantial interest and esthetic value and is worth while relating to other southeast Asian art.

In its treatment of architecture the present article will be limited to giving some very general notions of the different types of Laotian buildings and their principal components, in the process attempting to isolate the distinct qualities in the work of each region and to determine the various influences that may have affected it. Laotian sculpture, on the whole quite mediocre, will be dealt with first, in summary fashion.

SCULPTURE. The vast majority of Laotian statues are images of the Buddha. Large works were most often executed in masonry, very rarely in solid stone; the small images were frequently of bronze (PL. 31).

In most instances the Buddha is represented seated. His hands, inordinately large, have fingers of uniform length. The head is covered with little knots of hair resembling the thorns of a breadfruit tree; the *uṣṇīṣa* is very pronounced and is surmounted by a flamelike ornament; the *ūrṇā* is either absent or merely a token indication in silver wire incrusted on the forehead. The ears are extremely stylized. The garment is completely conventional: the outer robe, which leaves the right shoulder uncovered, appears to vanish beneath the undergarment at the belt level. The rare statues of a standing Buddha have both shoulders covered, but the undergarment unexplainably remains visible. There are also some images of the Buddha adorned, that is, dressed in royal regalia.

Bronze images are often dated, but the Laotian practice of omitting the ciphers indicating thousands, and even those for hundreds, occasionally makes the calculation of dates rather difficult. None of these figures is dated much before the 17th century; but at the Wat Manorom of Luangprabang there are colossal remnants of a much older image, assigned a date of 1372 by tradition. The head of this image indicates that the characteristic type of Laotian Buddha was already established at that time, evidencing the stylized hair and ears described above and the aquiline nose found in much later versions.

Aside from the representations of the Buddha, another prevalent type in Laotian sculpture was the *dvārapāla*, or portal guardian, taking the form of a monstrous or grotesque kneeling figure. Laotian statuary also includes lions inspired by those created by the Khmer sculptors. Bas-relief sculpture, which most often decorated door panels, posts, and lintels, is as a whole superior in quality to the sculpture in the round. Principally it consists of rinceaux and leaf ornament, which sometimes frame depictions of divine or mythological beings (PL. 31).

ARCHITECTURE. *General characteristics.* Laotian architecture differs from Khmer architecture in that it did not utilize sandstone; occasionally huge blocks of laterite were the chief material, but brick was used in the great majority of structures. The bricks were held together by a lime mortar so adhesive that the builders were able to achieve a sort of compromise between keystone and corbeled vaults. However, such vaulting was used only for very small buildings. Wood generally served both for the framework and as a finishing material; tile was the usual roof covering.

Certain buildings, such as the more modestly scaled reliquary shrines, lent themselves to complete masonry construction; others, such as dwellings and some temple annexes, were built completely of wood. In the great religious structures, however, the walls were commonly of brick masonry and the roofs of wood, supported by a framework of wooden beams. "It is thus the form of covering and the distribution of its supports that dictates the plan of the building, and it is also this roof which practically by itself gives to the exterior its characteristic appearance" (Parmentier).

The Laotian architects used two methods of covering: the saddleback (or double-pitched) roof, and the four-sided roof. In the first type the ridge of the roof, following the main axis of the chamber it covers, extends far beyond the gable ends and side walls in order to furnish protection from the sun and bad weather. The appearance of such a building may be compared to a tent slightly elevated from the ground. The second type of structure comprises a main chamber surrounded by a gallery or veranda sheltered on all four sides, but with a roof on a lower level than the double-sloped covering of the central hall and generally of a more gentle pitch.

The Laotian timberwork did not permit uninterrupted spanning of large spaces; the architects were obliged to sustain roofs with pillars fitted into the beam system. The result was

LAOTIAN ART

a chamber divided lengthwise into three aisles, subdivided into as many bays as the number of supports made necessary.

The decoration of walls and moldings was executed in a plaster finish, the work being accomplished in two stages: first the mason outlined the general scheme and roughly executed the masses; then followed the artists, working with threads

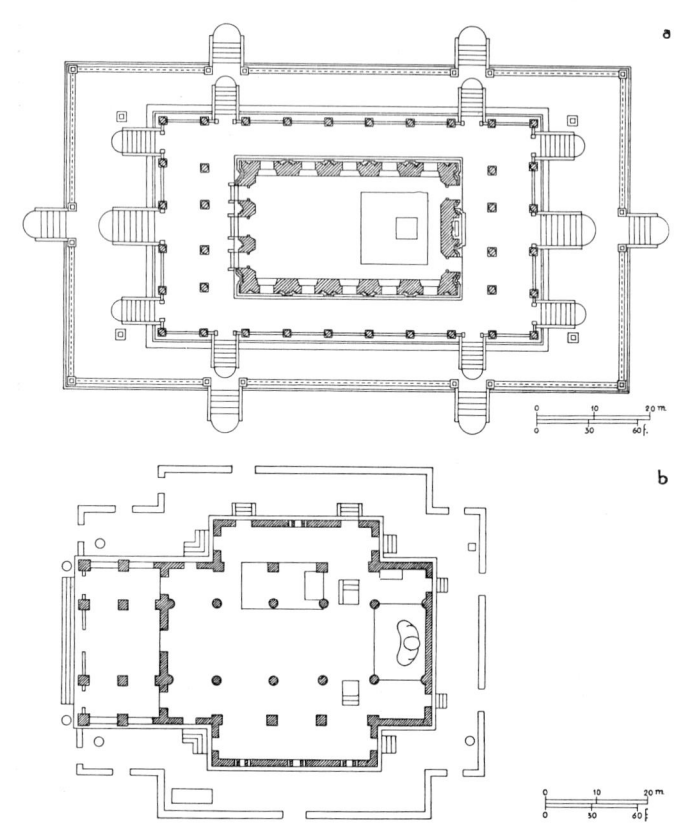

Types of *wat*: (*a*) Vientiane, Wat Phra Keo, 16th cent.; (*b*) Luangprabang, Wat Xieng Thong, first rebuilt 1561 (*from Parmentier, 1954*).

of nearly dry lime that they applied over the layer of wet plaster. Finally, small beads and pieces of glass-enameled lead were sometimes added for surface enrichment.

Types of buildings. The only Laotian architectural type that has evidenced a degree of artistic genius is the Buddhist monastery, or *wat* (FIG. 55). The essential building of the complex is the hall — in Laotian, the *bot* (Skr., *uposathāgāra*) or *vihan* (Skr., *vihāra*) — where religious rites are celebrated by the monks of the community and where laymen come at each quarter of the moon to hear the monks expound doctrine and to celebrate the great holy days. In the simplest monasteries this hall is supplemented only by monks' quarters of wood and thatch. The more important monasteries contain in addition, whether or not enclosed by walls, various subsidiary buildings: reliquary shrines (*that*) similar to the Indian stupas, chapels, and libraries.

On the basis of plan, the meeting halls erected by Laotian architects can be divided into three principal types: a simple hall covered by a saddleback roof; a hall surrounded by a veranda, from which it is separated by an interior wall supporting the roof; and a hall with a surrounding gallery, the roof of which is supported by an exterior wall. Access to the hall is commonly through one or three portals in the front wall and occasionally by two other doors situated in the rear wall, one on each side of the altar on which the throne of the great cult statue of the Buddha is placed, his back to the wall.

The hall is given its characteristic appearance by the two-sided, double-pitched roof. The gables take the form of an acute angle, resulting from the inward curve of the roof line, which also determines the aspect of the end façades. In the examples at Tranninh and Luangprabang, where the side walls are very low, the roof declivity is excessive and, because of this condition, takes on great importance in the over-all appearance; the outline has been compared to the wings of a laying hen (PL. 29). In the Wat Phra Keo at Vientiane, where the walls are much higher and the veranda is roofed on four sides, the effect is quite opposite; the proportion of the roof to the whole of the building is less striking (PL. 32). When the meeting hall is of the simple type, as it most often is at Tranninh and Luangprabang, it is generally divided into three aisles by two rows of pillars and is extended by a porch on both end façades. At Vientiane, on the contrary, the hall is most often surrounded by a covered veranda, the roof of which is supported on pillars. In the case of the triple-aisled hall, this interior division is reflected on the façade by the four pillars supporting the wooden gable, which in turn sustains the end projection of the roof.

This long roof, the horizontal arris of which is slightly concave and rises at the extremities, is without doubt the most characteristic architectural element of the meeting hall. It is related to a type well known in the Far East and in southeastern Asia, occasionally termed "telescopic"; that is to say, it consists of successive detached elements and projections over the various parts of the substructure. "These roofs, which are extremely heavy because the careful tiling is always put down in double layers, are sustained by raised trusses of a flexible type. In other words, all the pressure resolves on an enormous horizontal beam, holding up the entire weight by means of a series of small struts and tie beams. There are almost never rafters.... This roof is borne by the walls and the pillars that frequently divide the aisles" (Parmentier). On the exterior the roof is further characterized by the hornlike ornaments that terminate the peaks at each end and the shepherd's-crook forms at the eaves of the front and rear façades. It should be noted that in the Laotian structures, unlike those in Cambodia and Thai-

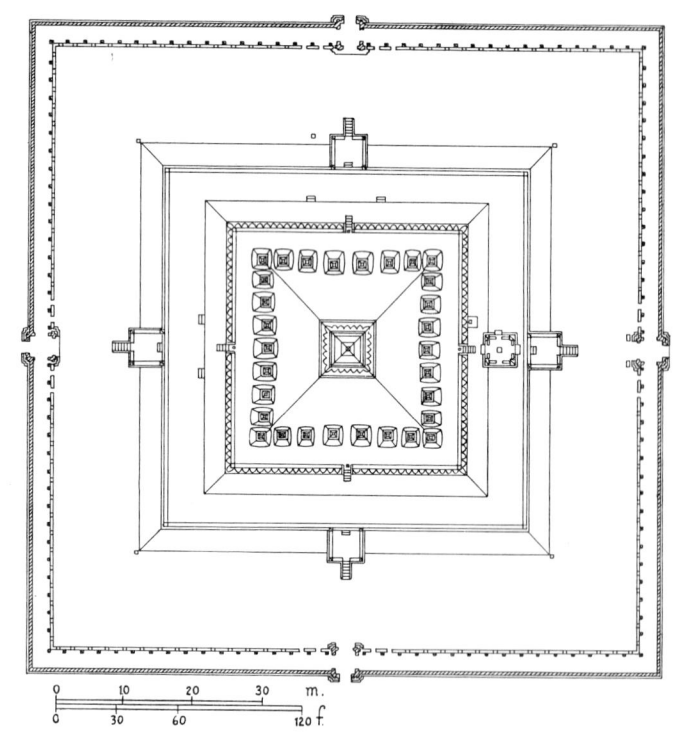

Vientiane, That Luang, ground plan, 1586 (*from Parmentier, 1954*).

land, there are never transverse roofs corresponding to a transept. From this point of view the Laotian roof appears much simpler, or more primitive. On the other hand, as has been noted, some Laotian meeting halls are elaborated with porches on the façades, an architectural feature unknown in Cambodia.

Inside the hall the framework of the roof is supported by pillars that taper slightly toward the top. These supports are never set on bases. The capitals, purely decorative, in most instances resemble large-petaled lotus flowers. While the architects of Tranninh and Luangprabang used only round columns, those at Vientiane used square pillars with recessed corners. Most hall interiors are without ceilings, except over the last bay at the rear, where the large image of the Buddha on a pedestal is located. When there is a ceiling, it is composed of square coffers of red-lacquered wood, ornamented with gold rosettes.

In the meeting halls of Tranninh and Luangprabang, where the walls are not high, the windows are small and the interior is poorly lighted; but at Vientiane, where the walls are much higher, the windows are more important elements. In general, the openings in the walls, whether for windows or doors, are of two types: either arched or rectangular and slightly trapezoidal. The exterior framing of these apertures resembles the silhouette of a building placed in relief against the wall. It comprises a base beneath the opening, decorative supporting elements at the sides, and a cornice topped with crownlike ornamentation — a very rich composition, further embellished with small pieces of glass set into the plaster surface. The window shutters are soberly decorated; those of the doors are much richer and are frequently carved with rinceaux or leaf patterns framing human or divine figures.

It is obligatory for the meeting hall to contain, in the segment farthest from the entrance, a great statue of the Buddha. It is a seated, frontal image that rests on a decorated pedestal, with its back against the rear wall or separated from it by a small passage (PL. 30). Before the pedestal is an altar where offerings are deposited. To the left of the Buddha image, in a bay adjacent to that containing the statue, there is a pulpit, a small construction of gilded wood on a masonry base. Among other furnishings, many halls contain seats for ecclesiastical dignitaries, cabinets, and chests for storing manuscripts. The chests are made in the form of inverted pyramids, similar in appearance to Laotian sarcophagi. The most distinctive furnishing, and that which most inspired the metalworkers, is the candelabrum (PL. 32): its armature consists of a horizontal arc of iron representing the bodies of two reptiles, their backs bristling with points, their tails knotted at the center, and their heads raised at the extremities of the piece. The knot formed by the interlaced tails is supported by fifteen vertical shafts that, above the knot, terminate in flamelike points which serve to hold the candles. The center vertical is the tallest, and from it those on each side diminish in height, so that the whole forms a decorative, comblike triangle resting on the knot. Another object peculiar to the meeting halls of Luangprabang is a type of water vessel called *hang-lin*, a wooden barrel topped on one side by a funnel and on the other by a spout in the form of a monster's head. It was used for the purification of images of the Buddha.

Among the buildings annexed to a Laotian monastery the most significant is certainly the reliquary shrine, rarely absent even in the poorest monasteries. Its importance should not be measured by its dimensions, which can be comparatively small, but by its religious value. It is, in effect, the Laotian version of the stupa, an important feature of Indian, Singhalese, and Burmese religious architecture, or the chaitya of Khmer or Siamese art. Such structures are objects of fervent veneration from faithful Buddhists, whether the building constitutes a true reliquary containing remains of the Buddha or some holy person or whether it is simply a commemorative monument.

The reliquary shrine, or *that* (Skr., *dhātugarbha*), is designed in a great variety of forms. Apparently the architects were receptive of diverse influences that combined to inspire small buildings of almost infinite variety. The only common characteristics are the complete masonry construction and a distinctive element, derived from the stupa, that always appears between the foundations and the terminal spire. This essential element can assume either the original hemispherical stupa shape or that of a bell, bulb, flask, or the like. Each of these is in turn subject to many variations; nonetheless, three principal types of reliquary may be discerned, among which the innumerable transmutations can be found. The first, derived directly from the stupa, is characterized by the curves of its profile and is set upon a base that has been subordinated to the structure as a whole. The second type gives the base a value equal to the main body of the stupa, which retains the typical curvilinear profile. The base thereby becomes a cubic mass forecasting the development of the third type, in which the base becomes the principal component of the building. In this third variant, the stupa is simply a terminal accessory integrated with the spire; the building takes on the aspect of a Khmer tower with four blind apertures, rising from a substantial base and surmounted by a pyramid of gradually diminishing stages. All that remains of the original stupa form is a subsidiary element with a curved outline.

After the reliquary shrine, in order of significance among the other buildings of the monastery complex, come the chapels built to hold images, structures that are most prevalent at Luangprabang. As a rule, these are low masonry buildings containing a long hall covered with an ogival vault. The façade, with a single entrance and rich decoration in plaster, has a roughly spadelike contour. The libraries, built either of wood or of wood and brick, are raised on a high base with moldings, intended to protect them from the dampness of the ground and from gnawing insects. The walls spread out toward the top, recalling the inverted-pyramid shape of the manuscript chests and the sarcophagi.

Finally, mention should be made of the enclosure walls for the precincts of the important monasteries. There are sometimes several successive circuits of such walls, quite imposing in extent; however, the gateways are not so richly decorated as those of Cambodia and Champa.

Architectural styles. After this brief analysis of the architectural elements of the Laotian Buddhist monastery, it is appropriate to indicate the distinguishing characteristics of the various building types from the three major regions into which the country is divided: namely, Tranninh, Luangprabang, and Vientiane.

The Tranninh Buddhist temples (PL. 29) reflect a type of building characteristic of the region as a whole. They are composed, almost consistently, of a simple hall of three aisles formed by two rows of round columns. At each of the two ends of the building there is a porch covered by a roof separate from that over the main body of the hall; the roof of the aisle rests on the porch roof. Access to the hall is through two doors, one on the front porch, the other in the posterior wall, to the left of the great statue of the Buddha at the end of the hall. The interior is lighted by windows with wooden balustrades. On the sides the roof descends very low and has a wide, sheltering overhang. The projecting roofs of the hall and the porches, one above the other, are sometimes accented by another small roof element set above the center of the hall roof.

The buildings of Luangprabang (PL. 29) differ little from those of Tranninh, except that masonry is used more generously and the roofs often become less prominent because of the greater height of the walls. The meeting halls in general have only one porch, sheltering the entrance on the main façade.

The style of the buildings at Vientiane, many of which are in ruins, is quite homogeneous. The meeting halls (PL. 32), generally of vast dimensions, have walls of masonry that rise to a great height, while the roofs never descend so low as those at Luangprabang and Tranninh. These buildings are sometimes amplified with a veranda around all four sides; in other instances they are closer to the system usual at Tranninh, that is, three aisles terminating in two porches. The columns are never round as at Tranninh and Luangprabang but are square in section, with notched or recessed corners. Their great height makes it possible to mask the wooden roof supports with a ceiling, at the level of the top of the outside walls. This system of support generally remains visible in the other two main regions. The doors and windows are trapezoidal; their frames, composed of pilasters disposed on multiple planes and capped with a series of superimposed tiers, differ distinctly from those of the other regions, which use the blind *prasat* style of decoration for their apertures.

Conclusion. The essential elements of Laotian architecture, in the north as well as in the south, aside from occasional Burmese or Siamese nuances, present a mixture of two different styles: the first is the light construction with simple steep roofs characteristic of the building of all primitive peoples of southeast Asia; the second reflects an ancient Hindu tradition of medium-weight architecture, characterized by the curvilinear roof, which in Laos has left traces in the design of apertures, and in several monuments very archaic in appearance, either in their over-all composition or their ornamentation.

To the question of how such Hindu influence in Laos — which must have come through Buddhism, inasmuch as no traces of Hinduism itself have been remarked — could have been introduced, Parmentier answers that there must have been a penetration from the north, from Burma; but it is a hypothesis yet to be substantiated. The continuance of a light autochthonous architecture, with walls that flare at the top, a feature common in the architecture of most southeast Asian countries, can be explained more readily. "The impermanence of the materials in which the forms were realized guaranteed the preservation of the traditions followed when they were originally executed. By the very fact that such buildings demanded continual maintenance and frequent rebuilding, the workers kept alive the skill" (Parmentier). It should be added that this Laotian light architecture never developed a counterpart in stone because the country never gained sufficient power and eminence for its kings to have the means to erect monuments comparable with those of Cambodia and Burma.

BIBLIOG. H. Parmentier, L'art du Laos, Paris, Hanoi, 1954.

George CŒDÈS

Illustrations: PLS. 29-32; 2 figs. in text.

LARGILLIÈRE, NICOLAS DE. Painter of the French school (b. Paris, Oct. 10, 1656; d. Mar. 20, 1746). Although born in Paris, Largillière was brought up in Antwerp, where at the age of twelve he entered the studio of Antoine Goubaud, a painter of peasant scenes and still life. By 1672 Largillière had become a master of the painters' guild in that city. From about 1674 until 1680 he worked in London, painting draperies and still-life accessories for Lely (q.v.). In London Largillière painted his first portraits, but none of his early work survives. Because of anti-Catholic sentiment in England he returned to Paris after Lely's death, and by 1682 he had established himself among the many Flemish artists of that city. With the aid of Adam van der Meulen, a Flemish painter resident in Paris, Largillière met Charles Lebrun (q.v.); he then presented himself at the Académie Royale and was admitted in 1683. In the Académie Largillière rose steadily and became director in 1728, retaining that post until he resigned in 1742. His residence in Paris was continuous except for a visit to London in 1685, where he painted James II and his queen at the time of their coronation. In 1699 he married Marie-Elizabeth Forest, daughter of a landscape painter.

Although Largillière occasionally painted religious subjects and still life for his own satisfaction, he made his reputation as a portraitist of the Parisian *bourgeoisie*. As official painter to the *corps de ville* of Paris, he executed five group portraits of them, which were his most important commissions. Of this series, commemorating notable public occasions, only one survives — *Échevins of the City of Paris before Ste-Geneviève* (1696; Paris, Church of St-Etienne-du-Mont). His enormous production (P. J. Mariette mentions some 1,500 works by him in and around Paris alone) included types ranging from imposing state portraits and the great groups executed for the city to more intimate, and often more profound, portraits of artists and friends. Largillière's style was fully developed within the tradition of Rubens and Van Dyck, in London as well as in Antwerp, before his arrival in Paris. When in Paris — like J.-B. Jouvenet, C. de Lafosse, and Hyacinthe Rigaud (q.v.) — he promoted the colorism of the north. According to an account left by his pupil J.-B. Oudry, Largillière encouraged in his pupils great sensitivity to color; he was among the first to recognize this gift in Chardin. His delicacy of touch and fondness for the fleeting effects of light and color, already apparent in some of his 17th-century work, anticipate the rococo lightness soon to prevail.

REPRESENTATIVE WORKS. *Charles Lebrun* (his diploma picture, 1686; Louvre); *Mme de Thorigny* (1696; Met. Mus.); *Louis XIV and the Royal Family* (1708; London, Wallace Coll.); *President de Laage* (Louvre); *Mme de Gueydan as Flora* (V, PL. 406); *Portrait of the Artist with His Wife and Daughter* (XII, PL. 160).

BIBLIOG. G. Pascal, Nicolas Largillière, Paris, 1928.

John W. MCCOUBREY

LATE-ANTIQUE AND EARLY CHRISTIAN ART. This article concerns the art and architecture of the Mediterranean world from the second half of the 3d to the first half of the 6th century. With reference to the development of the Roman Empire, which unified the area politically and juridically, the late-antique period begins in the Severan age and ends in the reign of Justinian. On occasion it will be necessary to overstep these limits in order to study artistic developments anticipating the late-antique period proper, as well as to note others that extended its characteristic qualities beyond the era of Justinian (see AFRICAN-ROMAN ART; BYZANTINE ART; COPTIC ART; DANUBIAN-ROMAN ART; EGYPT; EGYPTIAN ART; EUROPE, BARBARIAN; GALLO-ROMAN ART; HISPANO-ROMAN ART; ISLAM; ITALO-ROMAN FOLK ART; PARTHIAN ART; ROMAN ART OF THE EASTERN EMPIRE; SASSANIAN ART).

The unfolding of the late-antique "life cycle" required about the same length of time — some three centuries — as did that of the Hellenistic period (see HELLENISTIC ART). The geographical scope of the work involved was much greater, however, comprising south-central and western Europe and North Africa, in addition to the Hellenized East. The multiplicity of peoples and cultural traditions within this vast area gave rise to fruitful blendings of artistic taste, which contributed decisively to the formation of the medieval world.

SUMMARY. Introduction (col. 60). Architecture (col. 68): *Introduction; Architectural elements; Interior layout; Development of the religious sanctuary: a. Pagan; b. Jewish; c. Christian. Regional development of late-antique architecture: a. The West; b. The East. Secular structures: a. Domestic architecture; b. Official buildings; c. Palaces and villas; d. Commemorative monuments and funerary architecture; e. Functional structures (aqueducts, cisterns). Late-antique city planning.* Sculpture (col. 99): *Sculpture in the round; Portraiture; Relief; Porphyry; Stucco.* Painting and mosaics (col. 118): *From Septimius Severus to the era of the Tetrarchy (193–286); From the Tetrarchy to Arcadius (286–408): a. Court style; b. Rome; c. Alexandria; d. Syria-Mesopotamia; e. North Africa, Sicily, and Iberia; f. Other European centers. From Theodosius II to Justinian I (408–565): a. Rome and Italy in the 5th century; b. The East during the 5th century; c. Constantinople from Zeno the Isaurian to Justinian the Great; d. Manuscripts.* Minor arts (col. 137): *Coins and medals; Jewelry; Glyptics; Silverwork; Ivories; Textiles; Glassware.*

INTRODUCTION. The concept of a distinguishable late-antique art was introduced in the scholarly literature by Alois Riegl in 1901 in the more limited formulation of *spätromisch*; Riegl's analyses contributed importantly to the rejection of the outmoded view that the art of the 4th and succeeding centuries was merely a debased form of classical art. Riegl's Viennese colleague Franz Wickhoff, in his *Die Wiener Genesis* (1895) — the full title of the English translation, *Roman Art: Some of Its Principles and Their Application to Early Christian Painting*, gives a truer idea of the work's scope — had previously informed his contemporaries of the fact that absence of "academic correctness" and the departure from the "classical manner" did not signify an involution or regression of art but rather corresponded to a new and consistent attitude in the visual arts, an attitude that provided the foundation for the ensuing medieval art cycle. Subsequently, understanding of late-antique art was significantly advanced by the work of four scholars: Gerhard Rodenwaldt, Guido von Kaschnitz-Weinberg, Hans Peter L'Orange, and Richard Delbrück.

* *

The study of late-antique art is inseparable from a study of the history of the period. In the mid-3d century the Roman Empire was on the verge of destruction. Under the emperor Gallienus (260–68) there had been so many separatist movements that the era of his reign became known as that of the "Thirty Tyrants." Postumus and his successors were supreme in Gaul, Spain, and Britain (258–73); Zenobia commanded the Asiatic provinces from her capital at Palmyra (267–73). Only by the superhuman effort of the Illyrian emperors, culminating in the reigns of Diocletian (284–305) and Constantine the Great (306–37), was disaster averted. In a sense, the unity of the Empire was recovered by the discipline of a glorified sergeant-major who affected the trappings of an Oriental despot, supported by an enormous army and efficient civil service financed by crushing taxes. Moreover, it was realized that the Empire could no longer be controlled and defended by a single emperor; the porphyry group of the Tetrarchs (PL. 56), once at Acre and then built into the wall of S. Marco in Venice, is testimony to this change in the system of rule. The decision to rule the Empire with coemperors and Caesars, formulated under Valerian (253–60), was given renewed force by Diocletian and by Constantine's insistence on the "felix progenies Constantini"; it became systematized under Valentinian I (364–75) and endured until the capitulation of Romulus Augustulus to Odoacer the Ostrogoth in 476.

In the 4th century Rome ceased to be the capital of the Empire to which it had given its name. Realizing that the West might prove strategically untenable before the barbarian invasions, Constantine I determined after the official recognition of Christianity (A.D. 313) — clearly one of the most significant events in the evolution of late-antique art — to set up a "New Rome" in opposition to the recalcitrant paganism of the old capital. Diocletian had ruled for a time from Nicomedia, but Constantine founded his new capital (consecrated in 330) on the opposite shore of the Sea of Marmara, on the site of the little town of Byzantium. At various times Vienne in southern Gaul, Trier in Germany, Sirmium in Pannonia, Milan, and Ravenna all became imperial residences and seats of government. When the West finally succumbed to the barbarians, the foresight of Constantine was vindicated. The wealth and manpower of Asia Minor, controlled from Constantinople, was to preserve the Eastern Roman Empire for nearly a thousand years more. Nevertheless, until the end of the 5th century, Rome continued to enjoy great prestige; and it would be a mistake to consider, as some scholars have done, the first sack of Rome in 410 by Alaric as an overwhelming catastrophe and the decisive event in the fall of the Western Empire. It aroused prophetic groans from St. Jerome and encouraged St. Augustine to write *De Civitate Dei*, but the city was more grievously plundered by the Vandals in 455 and also suffered greatly from the entry of Ricimer in 472.

John Beckwith

In general, the formal development of the late-antique period may be characterized as a transition from detailed articulation to an intense simplification of forms. This over-all tendency holds true for the evolution of forms in the very widest application of the term — not merely in art but also throughout the political, economic, and social life of the time.

Under the early Roman Empire human existence, both in the cities and in the countryside, presented a seemingly infinite spectrum of local variation and was marked by advanced economic development of the individual regions and by autonomy of the community of citizens. During the late-antique period these autonomous local units disappeared; instead of independent individuals forming natural groups, there were disciplined men integrated into the cadres of the state. Members of all classes, and especially those of less privileged economic levels, were bound to their professions and trades under strict supervision. What was true for the individual was also true for the social unit: municipalities were no longer free to manage themselves but were firmly harnessed to the needs of the state. The result of this all-pervasive centralized control was a general "immobilization" of the social life.

The soldier-emperors' simplification of the machinery of state along the lines of the military was accompanied by militarization of the civil service and by assimilation of military law by the civil code. Men submitted en bloc to the commands of the state. On this massive and unconditional obedience was superimposed a soldierly order that introduced military terminology and organization into every aspect of life. Militarism became the pattern of the new society, and therein lay the essential difference from earlier times. The contrast between the civil and the military order is the contrast between the organic, natural grouping of individuals and the mechanical coordination of masses, between the free formations of nature and masses composed of files, columns, and squares.

The formation of blocs in the life of the state found a close parallel in the compact structure characteristic of the art and architecture of the time. The retreat from organically developed details within the sculptural mass corresponded to a new sense of compactness of mass elsewhere. Architecture was dominated by massive walls that dispensed increasingly with traditional ornament; the classical sense that each architectural detail merited its own identity, its own esthetic value and expressiveness, was extinguished in these overpowering masses. Thus it was an accepted canon that constructional elements which are not homogeneous may coexist in a single building, and the reuse of "spoils" taken from older buildings became a commonplace. The eye of the observer traveled over the great expanses of wall, unbroken by striking details; his gaze was directed to the breathtaking, uninterrupted ascent of the vaulting and met with an interminable succession of wall surfaces articulated in a repetitive and monotone manner.

The transition from differentiated to compact, simplified mass was accompanied by a change in treatment of subject, from the concrete to the abstract, from the corporeal to the symbolic. The general tendency was away from the organic movement of natural forms toward the abstract rigidity of types. Still, at the same time that artists began to produce works ever more schematic and generalized, they endowed them with a content more profound and inherent. The art object became a kind of receptacle for a kernel that embodied an idea; made into a conventional formula, the object became more and more a sign which pointed to a thought and which, as a sign, remained always equal to (i.e., capable of being perceived as) itself. The late-antique rinceau, for example, was no longer a living tendril as in classical times but became instead a lifeless band: the volutes are uniformly circular, and the whole plant is an abstract ornament lacking organic vitality and truth to nature. Moreover, such ornament possessed a new "inwardness," a life that seems to subsist outside the order of nature. When a plant grows in the form of a cross or springs from an altar chalice, it is filled with new meaning, it becomes a symbol of Christ and the Sacrament. In the late-antique period, the objects of art forfeited their substance, their corporeal nature, and in turn were transformed into symbols and conceptual images, with enhanced intellectual and spiritual content and powers of suggestion.

Human figures are presented not as individuals but as fixed types. The martyrs in the processional mosaic of S. Apollinare Nuovo in Ravenna (III, PL. 301) float as incorporeal spirits against a background of the palms symbolic of victory. The most striking feature of these grave figures is their enlarged and staring eyes, which the ancients associated with the idea of the divine and which give them a rapt expression. Individuals have yielded to stereotypes, with a conceptual significance concerning the nature of sainthood and its place in the eternal order. Similarly, in images of the emperor distinct personal traits give way to a *typos hieros* appropriate to the imperial dignity. Like the saints, the emperors become "semblances,"

Dioceses and provinces of the Western Roman Empire. *Key*: (1) boundary between Western and Eastern Empires in A.D. 395; (2) boundaries of dioceses organized by Diocletian; (3) boundaries of provinces organized by Diocletian; (4) residences of the Praetorian Prefect; (5) diocesan capitals; (6) patriarchates; (7) ecclesiastical metropolises (archdioceses). Dioceses organized by Diocletian: (VIII) Illyricum (after 395, Pannonia; Prefecture of Illyricum); (IX) Italia Annonaria, (X) Italia Suburbicaria, (XI) Africa (Prefecture of Italia); (XII) Britannia, (XIII) Gallia, (XIV) the "Seven Provinces," (XV) Hispania (Prefecture of Galliae). (*From F. van der Meer, C. Mohrmann, Atlas of the Early Christian World, London, Edinburgh, 1958*).

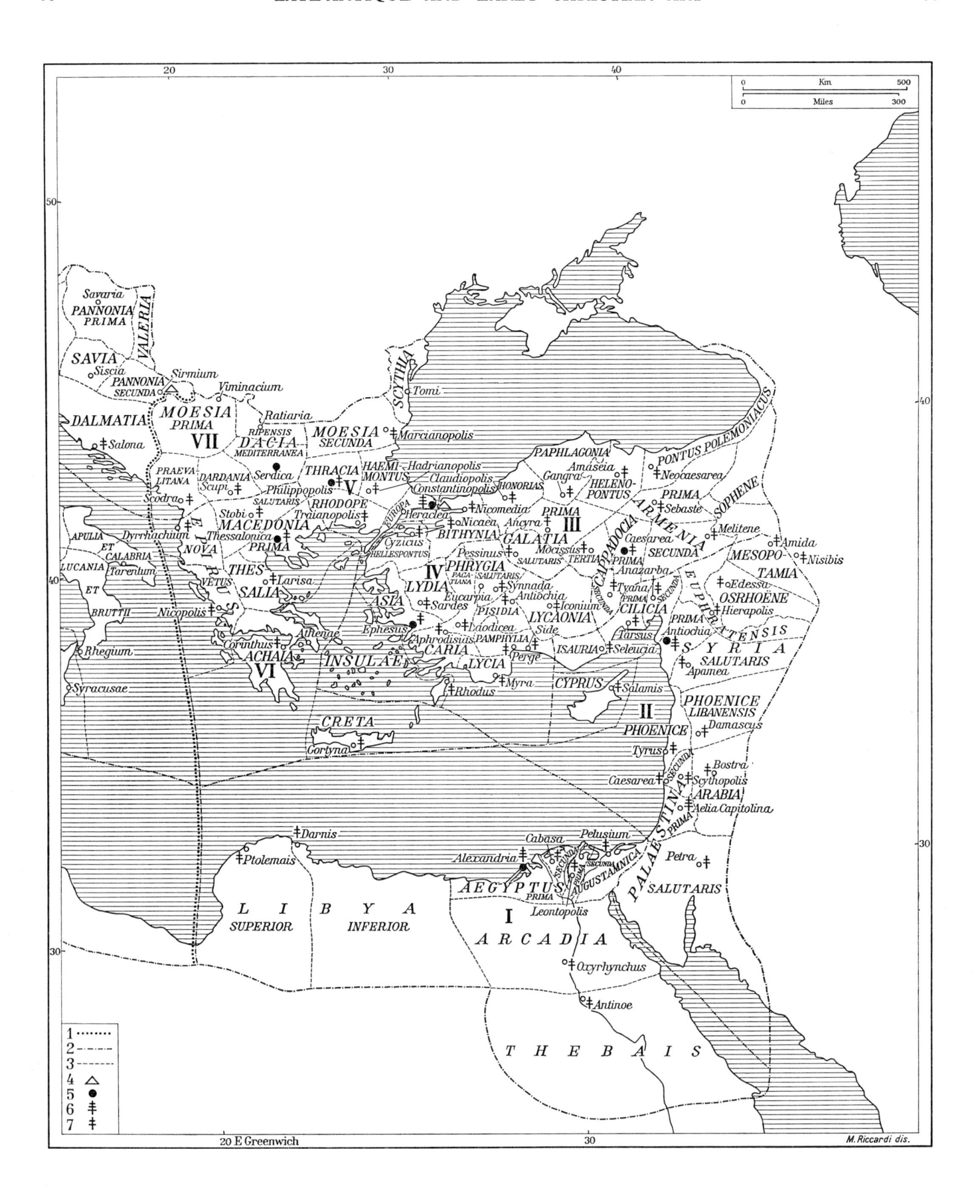

Dioceses and provinces of the Eastern Roman Empire. Key: (1) Boundary between Eastern and Western Empires in A.D. 395; (2) boundaries of dioceses organized by Diocletian; (3) boundaries of provinces organized by Diocletian; (4) residences of the Praetorian Prefect; (5) diocesan capitals; (6) patriarchates; (7) ecclesiastical metropolises (archdioceses). Dioceses organized by Diocletian: (I) Aegyptus, (II) Oriens, (III) Pontus, (IV) Asiana, (V) Thracia (Prefecture of the East), (VI) Macedonia, (VII) Dacia (Prefecture of Illyricum). (From F. van der Meer, C. Mohrmann, Atlas of the Early Christian World, London, Edinburgh, 1958.)

and their faces are expressive types conveying qualities more lofty and more elemental than their human identities. These late-antique facial types may be compared to ancient theater masks, which "represented" the part played by the actor and also served to conceal his own features. Inner meaning supersedes the natural appearance of things and is schematized in new modes of expression and compositional types. Figures are no longer depicted in varied natural groupings but are collected into a whole that has a fixed organization corresponding to some essential inner meaning. Characteristic of late-antique art are symmetrical compositions in which an array of figures is as if choreographed around the dominant central figure of the emperor. Typical also is the disposition of figures in registers, one above the other, according to rank in the imperial or celestial hierarchy. The scale of the figures is freed from the laws of empirical observation, for the relative size of the figure does not correspond to its true dimensions but to the importance of the individual represented.

The same shift from outer to inner qualities is found in esthetic ideals as well. The beautiful no longer resides in perfectly proportioned bodies, as the classical tradition maintained, but in the "inner light" of form, that is, in the spiritual intent and expressiveness. According to Plotinus, the body is beautiful only when illuminated by a soul; the beautiful is thus the consequence of inner form or essence. This esthetic is closely related to the representative philosophical currents of the late-antique period, according to which the natural life of the senses, the life "of the flesh," is merely an inferior form of existence. The soul is celestial essence that must be freed from matter and made independent of corporeal nature and concepts induced by the senses. Man must withdraw from the external world of appearance, from the natural world and the "beautiful body," to the verities of inward contemplation and to the world of symbols and ideas. This philosophical and spiritual withdrawal into the realm of abstraction is strongly reflected in the art of the late-antique era. Beyond the fleeting and unstable natural world, the artists and theorists glimpsed the broad, regular outlines of an immutable hierarchy of forces and ideas, of substance and essence; and they strove to capture this eternal order with new abstract modes of expression, through conventional expressive types and fixed forms of composition.

Everywhere there is the same denial or negation of the concrete, of the plastically determined and limited. Gods and myths lose their corporeal reality and acquire new, more profound content in allegory and symbol. The myth is a human contrivance or falsity, but an illusion that holds some truth.

There is an ineluctable attraction toward simple absolutes: for example, in triumphal art the historical victory becomes "eternal victory," and the historical victor the absolute victor (*victor omnium gentium*). The reliefs on the Arch of Constantine in Rome include not only representatives of the peoples actually conquered by Constantine but representatives of all Rome's enemies. Such abstract humanity is clearly present in late-antique portrait sculpture, where from the end of the 3d century the gaze acquired a new expressiveness. Not focused on surrounding things, the subject looks out beyond space and time, toward some distant object outside the reality of the senses. As mirror of the soul, the eye became the most significant physiognomic feature in late-antique art.

Late-antique architecture may also be examined from the standpoint of this turn toward inner values. It is significant that the great expanses of wall surface convey an idea of spatial unity altogether at variance with that of the finely differentiated forms of the architecture which had gone before. The attention is focused upon the space enclosed rather than on the tectonic units. The ancient way of building, that well-ordered system of architectural ornament which artists such as Vitruvius had conceived as the *dignitas* of architecture, was abandoned in favor of effects of incorporeal space and elusive depths of light and shade. The increasing immobilization of social life was matched by contemporaneous efforts in art and architecture, in philosophy and religion, to fix individual components within the framework of an immutable system. A geometrical system of coordinates dominated the planning of building complexes such as the Palace of Diocletian at Spalato and the caravan city of Palmyra. Faith and doctrine were combined in rigorous schemata that when fully developed were diametrically opposed to the multiplicity of the ancient religions and their dialectical conception of life. In the realm of thought, there was a general movement from the dialectic attitude toward the dogmatic and authoritarian, from empirical knowledge and relativism toward theology and theosophy. Neoplatonism broadened into a speculative theology that sought to comprehend all the cults of antiquity except Christianity. Christian doctrine itself manifested a stability that eventually concretized in Catholic dogma. The tendencies encountered under the Christian emperors, the striving to bring all religious life within the bounds of a "state church," were already discernible in the time of Aurelian and under the Tetrarchy.

In all aspects of collective life there was an evolution (and an involution) toward simple, massive forms and statically compact wholes. It is as if life itself, in the process of the gigantic, perilous, and all-embracing transformation leading from antiquity to the Middle Ages, put on armor and took refuge within the solid blocs and impregnable systems of the state, as well as those of art and religion. Indeed, at this time the cities of Rome and Constantinople — and the entire Roman Empire behind the limes — were enclosed within the most powerful fortifications known to the ancient world. The life of the period seemed ready to sacrifice liberty and mobility for security and stability. And who can say whether the seed of future development would have been able to survive without this protective shell?

Hans Peter L'Orange

ARCHITECTURE. *Introduction.* The late-antique period cannot be easily circumscribed with firm chronological limits. For the history of architecture, the period of the Tetrarchy has come to be commonly regarded as the beginning date for the earliest phase, though a number of elements characteristic of late-antique architectural style can be traced back to an even earlier time. The great transformation of the style can first be discerned in the monumental Christian buildings undertaken in the reign of Constantine the Great. The line of demarcation separating late antiquity from the Middle Ages is equally difficult to fix with precision. Although the second half of the 6th century may be said to mark a definite break in the political continuity of the West, and especially in Italy, Roman architecture at the beginning of the 7th century evidenced no substantial change with respect to established tradition. In the East, however, the progressive Arab conquest of large areas of Christian territory in the mid-7th century clearly initiated a new epoch, as was to become gradually but decidedly evident. It might be maintained, hence, that the effective transition between late antiquity and the Middle Ages came about in the course of the 7th century.

The geographical extent of the late-antique period comprises those areas marked by Hellenistic-Roman culture. Contemporary developments within the Sassanian and Arab empires are not included in this definition, and the influences exerted by these cultural spheres upon the late-antique development, and vice versa, is consequently looked upon as a separate problem. Historically and geographically, therefore, the study of late antiquity treats of the areas constituting the late Roman Empire proper and its sphere of influence. It also encompasses the various ephemeral barbarian states that had been established within the bounds of the Empire, particularly in the western segment, regardless of whether they were *foederati* of Rome or fully autonomous political bodies.

Although, in a broad historical perspective, the late-antique synthesis was founded in the heritage of Hellenistic-Roman culture, it also included the contributions of many peoples, often very distinctive and strongly contrasting in character, each with a lengthy history and traditions of its own. The decided differences between East and West were manifested in the division of the Empire in A.D. 395, which was but a final resolution of divergencies whose roots were much older than the late-antique era. In the development of architecture, this contrast was already to be detected below the surface of the seemingly homogeneous art of the early Roman Empire. Moreover, the two halves of the Empire were in no sense closed and self-consistent entities, for within each there were numerous, even if sometimes only transitory, opposing tendencies at work.

Almost everywhere, local traditions asserted themselves more strongly than in previous epochs, and distinct provincial styles developed. Lines of demarcation tended to be fluid, and specific historical factors often generated novel trends that bypassed traditional practice. These observations are applicable to both the eastern and the western spheres of late-antique culture. In the 3d and at the beginning of the 4th century an official imperial architecture, not restricted to one specific center, had been a common denominator of style. From A.D. 312 until the founding of Constantinople in 330, the architectural enterprises of Constantine the Great were concentrated in Rome. Thereafter, the focus of building activity shifted to the new eastern capital, which in the 5th and 6th centuries became the undisputed architectural center of the Eastern Empire and exerted a manifold influence on all the provincial styles.

From the 3d to the 6th century of our era, the architecture of the Italian mainland was characterized by great variety. In the 3d century Rome still occupied a commanding position, with a style based primarily on its own architectural heritage; but from the Severan period onward, Oriental elements were to be observed in an ever-increasing degree, variously in details such as capitals or in whole architectural complexes such as the great nymphaea (e.g., the Septizonium on the Palatine, Rome). Roman architecture enjoyed a resurgence under the Tetrarchy and in the reigns of Maxentius and Constantine the Great. After the founding of Constantinople, however, this creative impulse weakened, very likely as a consequence of the general decline in building activity in the western areas. Along with this loss of vitality in Roman architecture, Eastern influence became pronounced, especially during the 6th century. Southern Italy was linked not only with Rome but with the eastern and southern outposts of the Empire as well, the latter connection being most apparent in Sicily through its close relations with North Africa.

From the second half of the 3d century on, northern Italy gained steadily in importance. Milan, an imperial residence, became the leading cultural and artistic center for the whole of Italy during the 4th century of the Christian Era, to be supplanted in the 5th century by Ravenna. Ravenna was within easy distance of the outlying Aquileia, which in turn had ties with the territories of Istria and Dalmatia, where artistic influence from Asia Minor was strong, following upon the construction of Diocletian's Palace at Spalato. Northern Italy and the Adriatic areas as a unit can clearly be distinguished from central and southern Italy. Relations between upper Italy and the East, largely communicated through the Adriatic Sea, not only were intensive but were also more direct than anywhere else on the Italian peninsula.

Forms native to Asia Minor were widely adopted in these northerly sections, whereas Roman influence was proportionately weakened. In time, the architectural style of Constantinople became the principal influence, but not to the point of eliminating entirely those elements derived from Asia Minor and perhaps from Syria as well. Moreover, also common in upper Italy was an emphasis on verticality, a tendency reaching beyond to Gaul and Germany; its extent is demonstrated by the strong similarity of the so-called "Basilica" of Trier (Augusta Treverorum) to that of S. Simpliciano in Milan. As in earlier times, close relations must have continued to exist between Liguria and the province of Gallia Narbonensis, where the city of Arelate (Arles) had gradually risen in importance. Roman influence was also perceptible in 4th-century Arelate, as revealed for instance by the architectonic sculpture.

Late-antique architecture in Spain was of a marked provincial character. Along the southern shores of Iberia, there had long been contact with North Africa, where an indigenous style of architectonic sculpture generally impervious to outside influences developed. Among the regions of North Africa, the historical position of Mauretania and Numidia differed from that of Libya, where ties with Egypt were of long standing; Numidia, on the other hand, was oriented more toward the Italian peninsula, and Mauretania toward the Iberian.

In the East, the territories in which the older Oriental cultures still held sway stood in contrast to those dominated by Greek culture, subsequently reinforced by other Hellenist and Roman colonization. The term "East Roman" is most appropriately applied to the coast lands and their leading cities such as Ephesus, Antioch, and Alexandria, artistically in close contact with one another. The influence of the interior regions was another appreciable factor, producing great variety in the evolution of styles; the role of western Asia Minor was of particular significance, and not only in the late-antique period proper. The importance of this region had early been established, in the 3d century, through the productive schools of architectonic sculpture of Sidamara and of Aphrodisias, with influence that extended to Leptis Magna in Libya as well as to Rome and northern Italy. The increasing use of brick brought with it the development of true brick vaulting. The architectonic sculpture and the building technique of this region were to form one of the basic constituents in the architectural style of Constantinople, the new imperial seat, and thus during the 5th and 6th centuries assumed decisive importance for the entire late-antique world.

Elsewhere in the Near East, a rich architectural tradition is evident in Syria from the beginning of the imperial epoch, favored by the generally stable conditions that prevailed until the end of the late-antique period. This Syrian tradition was characterized by the use of a refined ashlar technique, inherited from Hellenistic times. From the 5th century on, in northern Syria there developed a tendency toward highly decorated exteriors, incorporating moldings, pilaster strips, pilasters, elaborate window and door frames, and engaged columns (e.g., apses of Qal'at Sim'ān, Qalb Lauzeh, and Basufan; PL. 47). In eastern Syria (the basalt region and the Hauran), there evolved another provincial strain, with pronounced Orientalizing tendencies especially in the architectural ornament. Even more strongly than at Palmyra, the distinctly Oriental forms of Parthian art appeared in the northern Mesopotamian city of Dura-Europos in the 3d century; geographically, however, the sphere of influence of this Orientalizing current seems to have been limited. The architecture of eastern Asia Minor and Armenia was closely related to north Syrian construction.

During the 4th century Palestine, in the south the gateway from the Near East to Egypt, acquired particular importance as a melting pot for diverse architectural styles. In large measure, this stemmed from the presence of many pilgrimage sites within its borders. Egyptian architecture underwent a separate development during the late-antique era; provincial in character, it exhibited a return to older Egyptian traditions and, in the architectonic sculpture, an increased stylization of the ornamental elements. Then, through Alexandrian architecture came the penetration first of East Roman influences and afterward of the style of Constantinople.

Very gradual in the beginning, the process leading toward development of a recognizable late-antique architecture, through a fusion of the varied traditions of Rome, Hellenistic culture, and the Near East, quickened after the middle of the 3d century. On the whole a process of internal development, it was little affected by outside contributions as it emerged, in essence a style clearly distinguishable from the individual preceding styles of antiquity.

Late-antique architecture was above all an architecture of interior space, concerned primarily with the organization and articulation of space rather than with the elaboration of individual members, which were progressively subordinated to over-all spatial and compositional aims. Elements that had been fundamentally structural therefore tended to acquire a more purely ornamental character, and sculpture and painting as such were relegated to an ancillary role in the total aspect of late-antique structures. Light as a factor in the architectural ensemble assumed new importance, as shown by the planned use of contrasts of light and shadow, of bright and dark tones. These qualities characteristic of late-antique architecture were to reach a fully developed state in the monumental Christian structures erected after the conversion of Constantine.

Architectural elements. The simplification and gradual transformation of classical forms was a process already under way in pre-Constantinian times. Leading in this development was the art of the provinces, especially those of the Near East (Syria, Palestine, northern Arabia, central Asia Minor, and other regions). Similar tendencies were remarked in the West as well but, in all likelihood, were due in part to Eastern influence. An ornamental tradition specifically Hellenistic and Roman continued to dominate in imperial and other official architecture, particularly in western Asia Minor and also in Rome. In Constantinople, the 5th and 6th centuries witnessed an impressive development of ornamental sculpture; and in the regions farther east, the late-antique repertory of forms to some degree absorbed older Oriental Hellenistic idioms. The clear split between East and West in ornamental style became, despite repeated absorption of Eastern elements in the West, one of the salient features of late-antique art.

Although still treated with great naturalism before the middle of the 3d century in the works of the school of Aphrodisias (Asia Minor), the animal and vegetal forms constituting the vocabulary of ornament were elsewhere to be transformed through progressive denaturalization and schematization into stylized patterns, in which the real model was rendered all but unrecognizable. The acanthus became the basic and ubiquitous motif on capitals, impost blocks, cornices, and consoles — to such an extent that even the other vegetal ornaments tended to take on its appearance.

In this evolution, thus, the rendering of natural forms became more and more nonnaturalistic and moved toward abstract and pure geometric ornament. This kind of abstract decorative style — particularly diffused in the Near East (e.g., in eastern Syria), though it occurs in all parts of the late-antique world — frequently had a symbolic purpose as well. Ultimately, the fully developed ornamentation presented to the eye a unified surface in which background, blank space, and frame all became integral parts of the decorative scheme and were of equal value with the specifically ornamental elements. This typically late-antique phenomenon, first perceptible in pure form in western Asia Minor (related to the Sidamara sculpture) and in certain Syrian structures of the late 2d and the 3d century, achieved full expression in the openwork architectural decoration of the age of Justinian in Constantinople. The ornamental field here consisted entirely of a play of raised and depressed areas, of light and shadow (*Tiefendunkel*), the design having become fully abstracted from its natural model. In the 6th century this mature late-antique ornamentation was disseminated in all directions from Constantinople, and it exerted significant influence on the development of architectonic decoration especially in the Near East (Asia Minor, Syria, Armenia, Mesopotamia, and Egypt).

A peculiar phenomenon of late antiquity was that architectural elements such as bases, shafts, capitals, architraves, and decorated friezes were frequently removed from older buildings and reused for the same function in new constructions. Such reemployed parts were used both by themselves and in combination with elements made expressly for the building at hand. This somewhat puzzling practice may appear more understandable in the light of the fact that during the late-antique period many architectural elements, including entire columns with their bases and capitals, were mass-produced in standard sizes by specialized workshops and were thus interchangeable in various buildings. Among the most productive of such workshops were those of Constantinople and its surroundings (the Propontis), which manufactured building parts for export to virtually all lands around the Mediterranean and for all types of construction, private as well as official.

The most important of the individual architectural elements is the column. The Attic base, with square (and only rarely octagonal) plinth, at times raised on a pedestal, came into general use. A simplified version of the standard Ionic base is found only in rare instances. Individual parts of the column and base such as the shaft, fillet, torus, and echinus were simplified and no longer were distinctly separated from one another. Sporadically in the 4th and 5th centuries, but more frequently in the 6th century, a type of embossed base in which the neck molding and torus were replaced by a single flared tier was produced in workshops on Proconnesus and employed in Constantinople and Ephesus, in Greece, and in Ravenna and Salona (Dalmatia). Certain octagonal stepped bases of the 6th century found in S. Vitale in Ravenna appear to have retained little of the antecedent classical form.

A sizable proportion of column shafts were reused material. The late-antique shafts have no entasis; they are smooth-surfaced and only slightly tapered. The neck and foot normally have a smooth shaft ring without grooving. Great value was placed on luxurious quality and variety of materials for column shafts. In addition to marble quarried in Italy and Africa, stone from Greece and Asia Minor, such as the marble from Phrygian Synnada and the Propontic littoral and the green conglomerate of Thessaly, was in widespread use. Granite was less common, and porphyry was reserved for official constructions (e.g., Temple of Venus and Roma in Rome, Hagia Sophia and the Great Palace in Constantinople). In many provincial regions — among them, Dalmatia, Gaul, upper Italy, Spain, North Africa, Egypt, and Syria — local varieties of stone were employed in the carving of shafts. As early as the 4th century, shafts of variegated colors were combined within a single building scheme (Rome, S. Costanza). This practice had particular vogue during the 6th century, as perhaps best exemplified in Hagia Sophia.

Shafts that were fluted, twisted, or covered with ornament were chiefly used for decorative purposes in constructions such as ciboria and balustrades. Tendril-covered shafts were, however, frequently found even in monumental architecture during the 3d century. In place of columns, piers of square or rectangular section were also commonly employed; these were generally masonry constructions and only seldom monolithic units. Monolithic piers with engaged half columns on two faces served as supporting elements for windows in territories around the Aegean and were also exported to sites along the Adriatic. In central Asia Minor such compound supports were introduced into arcades.

Without doubt, the one element most subject to variation in design during the late-antique period was the capital. In the 3d and 4th centuries the continuity of imperial Roman and provincial types was maintained; the great break in the late-antique transformation of the capital did not become apparent until the 5th and 6th centuries. Ionic, Composite, but primarily Corinthian capitals were still in general use during the 4th and 5th centuries, the Eastern version of the Corinthian capital having been widely adopted and elaborated in the West (e.g., the compact calathus form, the closed garland, the short calyx and stem). In Rome and other western localities, however, Ionic, Corinthian, and Composite capitals representing a continuation or a revival of Western tradition were still to be found in the 4th century (Rome, S. Paolo fuori le Mura; Carthage); and in some provinces, capitals in prevailing use f.om the 3d to the 5th centuries reflected local traditional prototypes in their forms. The most important local schools developed in northern Syria, Egypt, North Africa, Dalmatia, and Rome itself.

In the late-antique evolution of the capital the general tendency was also toward simplification. The calathus, abacus, and other ornamentation were combined into single compact blocks. The introduction of the impost block, the one truly new element inserted in the Hellenistic-Roman system of support during late antiquity, constituted an important occurrence in the further development of the capital. The impost block was an additional supporting member inserted between the capital and the arch and, larger on its upper surface than on its lower, had trapezoidal faces. Appearing first in areas near the Aegean, including Constantinople, it became an indispensable feature of architecture there in the 5th and 6th centuries and afterward found its way to other provinces, especially in coastal regions such as those along the upper Adriatic. The front and side surfaces were frequently embellished with ornamental motifs, sometimes based on those of Corinthian and Composite capitals.

The impost block was in some types directly incorporated with the capital, and there arose toward the end of the 4th century the Ionic impost-capital, in which the abacus was organically joined to the inverted trapezoidal slab. This new type of capital came into widespread use in the Aegean area during the 5th and 6th centuries. At the end of the 5th or in the early years of the 6th century, in Constantinople, closer junction of impost block and capital produced the true impost-capital and its variations such as kettle, basket, fluted, trapezoidal, and border capitals. This marked the culmination of the development of the capital in late-antique architecture. The structure and decoration of these capitals, in which a compact mass was uniformly covered with an ornamental pattern, no longer owed anything to the tradition of the classical orders.

The importance of the impost-capital throughout the late-antique world was considerable. In addition to its regular use in Constantinople and its immediate sphere of influence, great numbers of such capitals were exported ready-made to many lands bordering the Mediterranean, where they exerted decisive influence on the architectonic sculpture of various coastal centers and the hinterlands (for instance, in Armenia, Mesopotamia, Syria, Palestine, and Egypt). In the Proconnesus workshops, in addition, capitals with figural motifs continued to be produced. These were principally carvings of the so-called "two-zone" type, with representations in the upper zone of birds and animal protomas (usually four in number) or, more rarely, capitals with impost blocks decorated with leaf masks, theater masks, or Medusa masks. The mask motifs were most likely intended for secular buildings, while others such as angels or Evangelist symbols were destined for religious structures.

The architrave, an architectural element encountered less frequently in the late-antique period than earlier times, still ordinarily had three flat fasciae, often embellished with a stringcourse, astragal, or a pearl band. Friezes were framed with various kinds of cymae, with acanthus and tendril ornament used in the more lavish constructions. The Lesbian cyma became increasingly rare and fell into disuse after the 6th century, whereupon the Ionic cyma was used exclusively. Pictorial friezes are known to have existed even in Christian buildings, as is shown by a frieze of lambs symbolizing the apostles, in the narthex of the Theodosian church of Hagia Sophia in Constantinople.

The architrave and frieze, however, were at times almost displaced by archivolts with elaborate soffits in the intrados and with fasciae and friezes on the face; yet, in other examples, these decorative elements were often worked out only in rudimentary form, and ornament was restricted to a simple frontal profile. A combination of architrave and archivolts appeared principally in propylaea with gabled pediments, where the central intercolumniation was surmounted by an arch and the four lateral ones by an architrave. The earliest examples of this type are generally attributed to Syria, although it is more probable that the idea originated in western Asia Minor toward the end of the 2d century. Major monuments in which such a combination occurred were the propylaea of Damascus, of Miletus, and of the Theodosian Hagia Sophia; another example is found in the mosaic representation of a palace façade in the Church of S. Apollinare Nuovo in Ravenna.

Cornices, often equipped with consoles, appeared as the crowning element both of the entire architectural system and of individual wall surfaces. Especially favored for the sloping sides of pediments, on the exterior these forms consisted predominantly of stuccoed or plastered masonry.

Classical orders (i.e., Ionic, Corinthian, and Composite) remained essentially unchanged only in the form of the capitals. Traditional usage of the orders was supplanted by a variety of canons strongly marked by regional peculiarities. Most frequently used was the Corinthian or the Composite order alone. Even when reused materials were involved, these orders were preferred over the Ionic and the extremely rare Doric (e.g., Rome, S. Pietro in Vincoli). Whereas uniformity of order tended to prevail within a single building, a group of structures was sometimes characterized by the use of varied orders, a device to separate clearly or give emphasis to individual parts of the complex. The choice of orders thus became a means of expressing spatial relationships in terms of correspondences and contrasts. In the mature phase of late-antique architecture, varying orders were employed even within the two rows of a single colonnade; however, the principle of the identity of parts centered upon a single axis was consistently observed. A particular canon was followed in East Roman structures with galleries, in which the Corinthian order was applied to the lower arcade level and the Ionic was used for the galleries above.

The colonnade and arcade became the most important elements of the interior space during late antiquity and served both in connecting and in separating the various components of the entire spatial complex. Arcading supported on columns or piers assumed other important functions in the triumphal arch, crossing arches, and transverse diaphragm arches. In vaulted structures of Constantinopolitan type, there developed an arcade system of alternate columns and piers, whereby in general the intermediate (gallery) level was supported on the columns, the roof vaults and the crossing arches beneath the dome rested on the piers. The round arch, generally somewhat elevated or stilted, was most widely employed, while the horseshoe arch was confined to a few regions such as central Asia Minor, northern Mesopotamia, and Spain. On the inside, the fusion of colonnade or arcade with wall surface, another characteristic development of late-antique architecture, made its appearance in the course of the 3d century of the Christian Era. This engagement of the columns or piers resulted in various combinations: piered arcade topped by a clerestory level (i.e., light source); colonnade with architrave and clerestory; and columned arcade with clerestory.

Wall articulation and decoration tended to be more developed in interiors than on the exterior. On the outside walls, the various levels were most frequently marked off by cornices; and in East Roman architecture an over-all horizontal articulation of wall surfaces predominated. In certain areas a "blind architecture" was the prevalent mode for exteriors, and the exterior walls were embellished by arrangements of pilaster strips, with or without horizontal subdivisions, or by blind arcades springing from pilasters or pilaster strips, as found about the clerestory openings and on the aisle walls of basilicas of the north Italian and Adriatic regions. Sometimes such blind arcades were elongated and embraced several stories without horizontal interruption, thus creating the strong sense of verticality that was to characterize Western architecture (Trier, the Constantinian "Basilica"; Milan, S. Simpliciano). Rich decoration of the outer walls — comprising cornices, pilasters, and strongly modeled window and door frames — prevailed in Syrian hewn-stone structures until the 7th century.

Brick buildings were generally plastered on the exterior during the late-antique era; also, in contrast to preceding periods, marble revetments were applied to exterior walls, though only in rare instances. The façades of the so-called "Temple of Minerva Medica" in Rome (PL. 37) and Hagia Sophia in Constantinople provide examples of this last practice, while the portal façade of the Roman villa at Casale, near Piazza Armerina, was painted in imitation of marble incrustation. Façades and pediments were also occasionally embellished with glass mosaics: Poreč (Parenzo), Yugoslavia, Cathedral; the Forum of Naples (cf. Procopius, Bell. Goth., 5, 24, 82).

Interior wall surfaces were richly decorated and articulated, primarily according to Roman tradition. The wall was generally divided into horizontal zones, comprised of one or two lower bands, which served as a base, and an upper zone. The base portions of the wall in all monumental edifices were marble or polychrome stone revetments, while the upper zones were stuccoed or plastered. In religious and palace architecture this upper band was reserved for pictorial cycles, either painted or executed in mosaic. From the 3d century on, the latter technique enjoyed increasing popularity and became the preferred and characteristic decorative medium for walls in late-antique architecture.

Late in the century, from the period of the Tetrarchy, an extraordinary refinement was achieved in the technique of stone incrustation, employed in structures undertaken for the imperial court and later in church architecture. Buildings such as the "Temple of Minerva Medica" or the Basilica of Junius Bassus in Rome possessed not only incrusted wall decoration but also pictorial schemes in *opus sectile* (PL. 70; VIII, PL. 79). Examples of rich incrustation, with vegetal and geometric motifs, from the 5th and 6th centuries have survived in the Lateran Baptistery in Rome and in the 6th-century buildings of Constantinople, Ravenna, and Poreč (VIII, PL. 81). Inlay, stucco, and plaster were not confined to the interior walls of brick constructions, for those of hewn-stone structures in Syria and northern Mesopotamia were plastered and stuccoed; some luxurious buildings were even faced with colored stone, such as the churches of Rusafa and Qal'at Sim'ān. The Roman wall mosaic was also employed in the East, even beyond the boundaries of the Empire (e.g., Ctesiphon, the Ṭāq-i-Kisrā complex). The interior wall might also be articulated with blind arcades and half columns, and with blind arches or aediculae around the windows. The strong — and at least seemingly structural — relief thus given to the wall surfaces was particularly in evidence in such 4th-century edifices as the Mausoleum of Diocletian in Spalato and the Temple of Venus and Roma (as rebuilt by Maxentius) in Rome, as well as in the 5th-century S. Maria Maggiore (PL. 40) and the Baptistery of the Orthodox in Ravenna (PL. 45). Having the appearance of rectilinear paneling, the 6th-century wall incrustation of Hagia Sophia in Constantinople, on the other hand, served more to hide the system of support than to give it visual expression.

While most doors had rectilinear lintels, windows were chiefly roundheaded, a form analogous to the arcades that was almost uniformly adopted in monumental architecture in the 5th and 6th centuries. Rectangular openings, nearly always of small dimensions, usually served particular purposes (e.g., the slit windows found in staircases and funeral structures) but were also the characteristic wall openings of the architecture of individual provinces such as Egypt. In Syria, the rectangular window was commonly employed in the 4th century but was replaced in the 5th by the roundheaded type. As a rule, doors and windows were set into the walls singly; however, paired windows occurred with some frequency, and even whole window arcades were known, with shutters or screens installed between columns or monolithic piers. In the same way, doors were installed within colonnades, the successive arch openings being closed either entirely by means of stone slabs or only partially by gates or screens. Screens of this kind existed in the Lateran Baptistery, and probably in the narthexes of the churches of SS. Giovanni e Paolo, S. Clemente, S. Maria Maggiore, and S. Pietro in Vincoli, all in Rome. In the narthex of the baptistery of Hagia Sophia, the doorposts and accompanying column shafts were carved in a single piece.

In vaulted buildings, the lunettes under barrel vaults were occasionally pierced to serve as windows, and a substantial amount of light was thereby admitted to the vaulting level. Such a system of fenestration, which was elaborated in the great thermae of the 3d and early 4th centuries, had its most notable application in Hagia Sophia (I, PLS. 378, 379). These apertures were closed with latticework or pierced screens (*transennae*) fitted with glass. Such transennae were made of wood, stucco, stone (marble), or bronze, and employed numerous ornamental patterns composed of squares, rhomboids, circles, or varied combinations of basic geometric shapes, as well as scalelike and star motifs. For large openings reaching to ground level, as found in Hagia Sophia, the window area was usually subdivided vertically by piers and horizontally by lintels, and grilles were inserted. Monumental structures were generally provided with solid double doors, often of wood; those of the Church of S. Sabina in Rome have been preserved. Continuing the antique traditions, there were also doors of gilded bronze, such as those of the 4th-century vestibule of the Temple of Romulus in the Forum Romanum (PL. 41), of the Lateran Baptistery, and of Hagia Sophia. Doorways were usually given further prominence through high-relief jambs and lintels; in the decoration of brick buildings, costly materials (especially marble) were employed for such purposes.

The various types of pavement known in Roman architecture continued in use during the late-antique period. There were simple pavements, inlays of *opus signinum* and *opus sectile* (geometric patterns made by piecing together varied fragments of marble), and above all the mosaic proper, predominantly with stone tesserae but occasionally in glass. Mosaic pavements enjoyed great vogue during late antiquity, and excavations have brought to light numerous examples of the technique. Moreover, mosaic and *opus sectile* were sometimes combined within the same pavement (Ravenna, S. Vitale).

All the types of roofing forms and construction current in late antiquity may be traced back to earlier periods. In buildings with sloping wooden roofs, crossbeams and trusswork might be left exposed in the interior, but they were perhaps painted and even gilded. The beams were sometimes decorated with coffers or lacunars (*laquearia*). Often a flat ceiling of wood (*contignatio*) or of plastered canework (*camerae canitiae, camera cannae*) was inserted. Flat wooden ceilings with undersupports were also employed between stories and for false (inserted) floors; these were decorated on the underside with coffers, either given a strong relief effect by means of wood or stucco construction or merely suggested through painting. A particular form of the flat coffered ceiling, consisting of a wooden grid holding coffers constructed with painted bricks, has been found in the Synagogue of Dura-Europos; and coffered ceilings wholly of marble still existed in the 3d century. Flat ceilings composed of stone slabs or beams were a standard type in Syria (Hauran, Qalb Lauzeh), following an old tradition.

As it had in Roman architecture in general, vaulting continued to play a role of capital importance. Because of the preeminence of Constantinopolitan architecture, brick vaulting, originally developed in western Asia Minor, appeared in the farthest reaches of the Empire. In Rome, however, from the 3d century vaults were constructed in *opus caementicium*, usually reinforced by brick ribs. At the end of the century, lighter vaults were achieved through the introduction of large clay vases into the structural fabric. Known in Numidia and Sicily earlier in the the 3d century, the technique of vaulting involving the use of clay vessels set end to end — thereby avoiding the need for outer scaffolding during construction — came increasingly into vogue in the West, beginning with the 4th century, for the erection of all types of vaults and especially of domes.

Apart from the dome rising directly from a round drum or octagonal base and the domelike raised crossing vault set on a square, which were forms previously known, the dome on squinches and the dome on true pendentives, both resting on square podia, constitute the late-antique contributions to and customary types of domical construction. While the earlier of these types had probably originated in Sassanid Persia (palaces of Sarvistan and Firuzabad), though widely diffused in the West as well (Naples, Cathedral Baptistery; Vicenza, S. Maria Mater Domini), the latter forms were undoubtedly the great original developments of late-antique architecture. The dome on pendentives in all likelihood made its appearance first in East Roman territories of the Aegean region, although the oldest preserved example is found in the shrine of St. Mennas near Alexandria, dating from the beginning of the 5th century. The imposing second dome of Hagia Sophia in Constantinople, from the Justinianic epoch, marks the culmination of this mode of construction (II, PLS. 427, 428). Moreover, it is the first example in late-antique architecture of a dome in which a distinction between load-bearing and covering functions was achieved through the use of ribs. In the decoration of the underside of the vaults, the formerly standard coffers became rarer (though a coffered vault existed in the narthex of the first Hagia Sophia, erected in the reign of Theodosius). Increasingly, vault decoration was executed in glass mosaic, and to a lesser extent with painting and stuccowork, which nevertheless remained in use until the 6th century.

The principal Hellenistic and Roman types of roofing were maintained by late-antique architects. Following long-standing Near Eastern tradition, however, flat roofs were constructed in parts of Syria and Egypt, not only in domestic architecture but also on a larger scale in public buildings. With stone or brick masonry the shed (pent) roof was used for the special purposes of porticoes and side aisles; but as may be inferred from the existence of so many gabled frontals, the span roof was the most widely employed type of sloping roof. In public buildings, the hip roof was also adopted. In wooden constructions, the triangular trussed roof developed by the Romans was virtually the only type in use. Conical, pyramidal, and tent roofs were constructed not only in wood but also in stone, as practiced in Syrian funerary buildings. Similar constructions were also erected over domes, especially those built of lighter materials; a drum ringing the circumference of the dome removed from it the added weight of the roofing.

For the most part, roofs were covered with clay tiles (*tegulae et imbrices*). In vaulted buildings, the tiles were generally laid directly on the surface of vaults or over the surface covering them. Marble or bronze tiling, the latter sometimes gilded, was customary in more important edifices; lead tiles were in more ordinary use for vault covering.

high point in the development of this form, the interior disposition of space was visible on the exterior only at roof level, for the lower parts formed a closed, tightly knit unit. It should be noted that, despite the equal emphasis given to the two main axes, central-plan buildings wholly nonoriented in direction within were rare.

Development of the religious sanctuary. a. Pagan. Construction of pagan religious shrines, which had declined sharply by the beginning of the 4th century, disappeared altogether at the end of the century. The typical temple dedicated to the cult of official deities continued to adhere to the Hellenistic-Roman tradition during the 3d century and even at the beginning of the 4th century (as shown by the 4th-century rebuilding of the Temple of Venus and Roma in Rome, a podium temple with peristyle, and the Temple of Jupiter in Spalato, with prostyle). The cellae, however, were generally vaulted. The Temple of the Sun built by Aurelian in Rome may have been circular in plan.

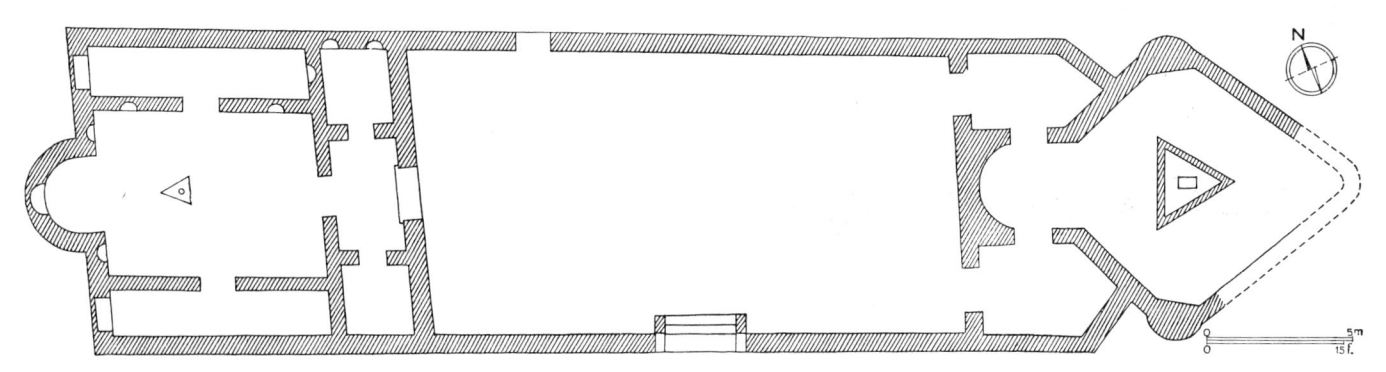

Rome, mystery sanctuary of the Syrian gods, on the Janiculum, plan of the 4th-century structure (*from B. M. Felletti Mai, BCom, LXXV, 1953-55, p. 137*)

The temple roof richly decorated with acroteria and antefixes was to find only a modest echo in the Christian church of late antiquity. The cross replaced the central acroteria at the summit of pediments and pitched roofs, while funerary buildings were occasionally adorned with appropriate symbols such as the pine cone.

Interior layout. In both religious and secular structures, the late-antique preference was for spatial arrangements in which individual rooms or spaces were not functionally combined with each other but were subordinated to geometric schemes laid out along horizontal and vertical axes. The Roman system of axial symmetry in layout was further elaborated, and the development of the centralized plan may be cited as a characteristic example of this taste. The central-plan buildings of the 3d century consisted of a single spatial unit, either round or polygonal and sometimes surrounded on the exterior by a portico. The Constantinian period, however, saw the advent of centralized structures with single or double ambulatories, a new form that was to have broad application in the following centuries. Such enlargement and elaboration of space led gradually to the interpenetration of individual units, in particular through the addition of niches to the central core and the alternation of concentric forms such as squares, circles, and polygons.

In longitudinal buildings, the principal type of spatial arrangement was the basilican plan. In such structures, involving a larger basic unit with subordinate elements attached, the transverse axis often constituted a secondary base for organization of the spatial elements; thus, the basilica with transept was gradually developed. By making the arms of the crossing equal in value with the bisected nave, late-antique architects created a new variation of the centralized plan, the Greek cross, which was to play a significant role in the subsequent history of architecture. Besides the simple square crossing, there appeared — though more infrequently — round or polygonal central elements (e.g., Qal'at Sim'ān). The cruciform central plan was further elaborated through the imposition of circular or polygonal elements upon the basic cross. In the 6th century, the

Far more important, until well into the 4th century, were the official sanctuaries of the Oriental mystery cults, such as those of Isis, Jupiter Dolichenus, and especially Mithras, which were spread out over the entire late Empire. In addition to the predominant single-aisled type, there also existed Mithraea with a three-aisled division of the space, for example, the Mithraeum of the Baths of Caracalla in Rome and the Mithraeum in Dura-Europos. The 4th-century mystery sanctuary of the Syrian gods on the Janiculum in Rome had two cult chambers placed on opposite sides of a courtyard: one a tripartite longitudinal structure, the other a polygonal central-plan construction (FIG. 77). Such a spatial disposition is similar to certain arrangements of Christian architecture. Nothing has been preserved of the sanctuaries of the Manichaean cult, which existed in all large cities; and the development of the Persian fire temple of the Sassanian period lies outside the compass of the late-antique period.

b. Jewish. For a discussion of late-antique synagogues, see the article JEWISH ART.

c. Christian. Early Christian architecture lent a distinctive aspect to the entire late-antique period, notable not only because of its wide diffusion but also for the significance these structures were to have as the basis of medieval church architecture in both West and East, including the Slavic countries. Little is known concerning forms of church construction in the period before the reign of Constantine. The *domus ecclesiae*, or "house church," in Dura-Europos (second quarter of 3d cent.; FIG. 79) consisted of a chamber for worship, improvised by combining two small rooms in a residential building with courtyard, and an adjoining room that served as a baptistery. The house church at Qirk Bize in northern Syria, probably dating from the beginning of the 4th century, does not differ from the typical farmhouse of this region and focuses upon a room two stories in height that served as the church. It is clear that the prototype of later churches cannot be identified with structures such as these; the monumental churches erected during and after the Constantinian period — in some instances, under the direct patronage of the emperor — were based stylistically on the tradition of official secular architecture, not on domestic architecture or the pre-Constantinian house churches, which merely contributed functional (i.e., ritual) schemata.

Until well into the 4th century, diocesan and parish churches, to which a separate baptistery was more or less closely linked, constituted the prime concern of Christian architecture. From

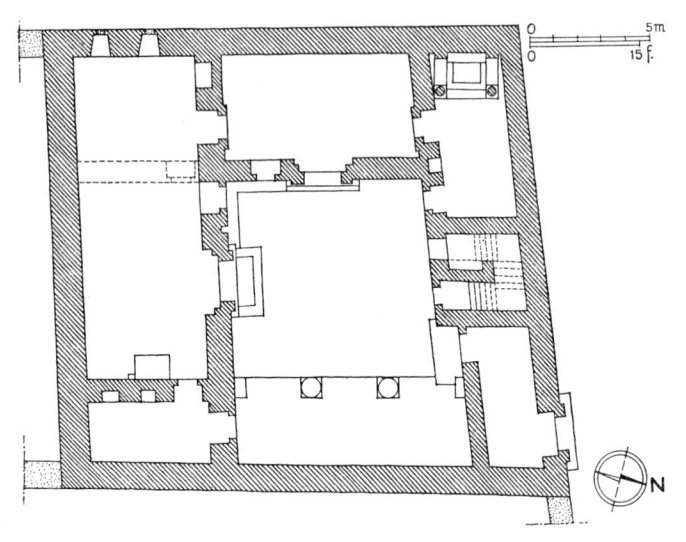

Dura-Europos (Syria), ground plan of house church (*domus ecclesiae*) (*from U. Monneret de Villard, Chiese della Mesopotamia, Rome, 1940*).

the Constantinian period on, the commemorative church, erected on sacred sites or in memory of martyrs, assumed major significance. In the 5th century and thereafter, especially in eastern parts of the Empire such as Egypt, Syria, and Palestine, the monastic church gained steadily in importance. Depending on the specific religious purpose, many variations of central and longitudinal plans were adopted. Chapels, oratories, and mausoleums, frequently constructed by private individuals, were sometimes annexed to the churches, but isolated and freestanding structures of these types were also built.

The plan of the Early Christian church in general consisted of the following elements. Preceding the church proper was an atrium, narthex, portico, or merely portals, usually on the western side, although in Rome these could be located on the eastern side and in northern Syria on the southern side of the main body. Access was thus gained to the main structure, housing the congregation and a sanctuary with the altar and space for the clergy. The bishop's throne, surrounded by the bench (*subsellium*) of the presbyters, was generally located in the apse, behind the altar and facing the nave. The apse, especially in the eastern provinces, was flanked by side chambers, the so-called "pastophoria," designated as prothesis and diaconicon but occasionally adapted to serve as a baptistery. In northern Syria the chamber of the southern side of the apse was used, almost without exception after the early 5th century, as a martyr's chapel, where sarcophagi with venerated relics were kept.

Baptisteries did not conform to any single type of plan. In some instances, a room at the front or to the side of the church (*consignatorium*) was used in preparation for the ceremony. The baptistery itself might consist of a central-plan structure with a baptismal font in the middle; or a font might simply be located within the church proper, in the apse, which as an alternative might be depressed to serve as a piscina itself, as was notably the case in the Syrian apse baptisteries.

The arrangement of commemorative churches and martyriums, which followed the same general lines as parish churches, was not uniform and changed in the course of time in response to the significant growth of the cult of martyrs. In Constantinian times there were two kinds of commemorative churches: the structure housing at its center some venerated site, and that located in the vicinity of such sacred sites. The first type was represented by the holy places in Palestine and by St. Peter's in Rome, and the second particularly by the Roman funerary basilicas near the tombs of the Early Christian martyrs and sites honoring the apostles along the Via Appia. In none of the Constantinian martyriums did the altar stand immediately over the venerated spot, for the direct association of altar and tomb had not yet arisen. As late as the 5th century, in the majority of commemorative churches the altar stood in front or to the side of, but not actually on, the honored site, as in the apsidal mausoleum of St. Anastasius at Marusinac, near Solin (Salona) in Dalmatia. The altar tomb did not become an obligatory form until the 6th century. Soon thereafter, during the reign of Gregory the Great (ca. 600), the sanctuary of St. Peter's in Rome was reconstructed and the altar installed directly above the tomb of the martyred first Pope.

The two fundamental spatial layouts for church structures were the central and the longitudinal plans, employed concurrently as early as the Constantinian period. The longitudinal plan, of which the Early Christian basilica was the most recurrent type, had the widest diffusion, with elaborate variations of form and a complex evolution that lasted until the twilight of late antiquity.

In tracing the origin of the Christian basilica, the following formal antecedents have at one time or another been mentioned: (1) the peristyle of the ancient private house or the house church; (2) the Hellenistic heroon, sometimes regarded as the prototype of the transept in the martyr basilicas; (3) the ancient colonnaded street, with its flanking porticoes considered as the model of the Heavenly City; (4) the imperial palace-basilica and especially the throne room, regarded as the throne room of Christ; (5) the public or secular basilica, such as the *basilica forensis*.

The origin of the Christian basilica is, however, purely a problem of form, not one of function; thus some of the foregoing hypotheses are from the outset based on false premises. The plan of the Christian basilica was undoubtedly derived from the numerous basilican halls of secular architecture, the most representative variety of which was the *basilica forensis*. Whereas the latter form was generally marked by an emphasis on width, the Christian basilica was characterized by a longitudinal axis focusing on the sanctuary. The adaptation of an

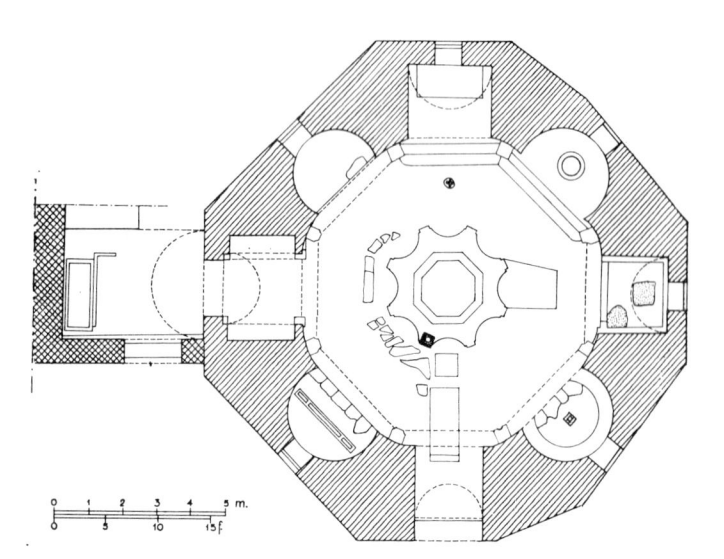

Albenga (Liguria), Baptistery (5th cent.), plan (*from G. De Angelis, I Battisteri d'Albenga e di Ventimiglia, Alassio, 1936*).

existing type of structure for an entirely new purpose therefore resulted in a decided spatial change, which makes it useless to seek definite antecedents in diverse earlier types, even though this new orientation of space is of course inexplicable without reference to preceding formal developments. The transformation of Christianity from a private, even secret, religious community in pre-Constantinian times to an official state religion during the reign of Constantine constitutes the decisive event, the factor motivating the change from a small-scaled to a monumental architecture.

The following types of Christian basilicas can be distinguished: (1) Three-aisled basilicas, such as that with nave and two side aisles: (a) *basilica discoperta*, with its central aisle open to the sky, a controversial type not recognized by all scholars; (b) basilica without galleries, the side aisles having shed roofs and the central aisle a span roof set above a clerestory zone; (c) basilica with galleries above the aisles reserved for women, that is, gynaecea (γυναικωνῖτις), a type found chiefly around the Aegean. (2) Many-aisled basilicas: (a) five-aisled basilicas, with or without galleries; (b) seven- or nine-aisled basilicas, found particularly in North Africa. These varied types of basilican structures might also have either an uninterrupted transept preceding the apse or a transept subdivided by the aisle supports. A particularly complex form of basilica, developed about the beginning of the 5th century, was the cruciform type in which the aisles run continuously around the transept arms. (Latin-cross plan: St. John's, Ephesus; the St. Mennas shrine, near Alexandria; St. Demetrius, Salonika. Greek-cross plan: Thasos, Gerasa, and Salona. Cf. FIG. 86; II, FIGS. 763, 765, 766, 772.)

The diversity of architectural types evolved during the Constantinian period provided a rich basis for further development in the centuries thereafter. The undertakings of the Emperor and his retinue undoubtedly exerted great influence; by way of example, it was in imperial circles that the five-aisled, colonnaded basilica appears to have been adopted for church use, the oldest of this type being the diocesan church of St. John Lateran in Rome, founded by Constantine himself. That the five-aisled basilica was also known in the provinces during the reign of Constantine is apparent from the basilica of Orléansville in North Africa. In Rome, some cemeterial churches were three-aisled basilicas terminating in exedrae. The most important commemorative church and martyrium of the Holy Land, the Church of the Nativity in Bethlehem and that of the Holy Sepulcher in Jerusalem, were five-aisled basilicas in combination with centralized plans (FIG. 83). The main church of Antioch, another edifice founded by Constantine himself, was an octagonal central-plan building with galleries.

The canonical basilica with a nave proper, two lateral aisles, and apse does not appear to have been developed until the post-Constantinian period, wherein the formal elaboration of the basilica continued throughout the 4th century and into the first half of the 5th century. This development was marked by intricate plans such as the above-mentioned continuous-aisled cruciform basilica, with great emphasis thus placed upon the complex transept. An over-all tendency toward centrality of ground plan prevailing about the middle of the 5th century also affected the layout of the basilica. Thus there were constructed numerous basilicas in the Greek-cross form, with either square or polygonal crossing. The basilica with a dome over the crossing was another new type, originating in Constantinople, as did the octagonal plan with the central ring of support in the form of niches. This last variant had wide diffusion in the provinces of the Empire.

The architecture of the age of Justinian marks the high point in late-antique basilican development, testifying to the undisputed architectural leadership of Constantinople at this time. The oblong basilica, combined with an inscribed cross, formed the basic scheme of the domed cruciform church, which was to become an important type in middle Byzantine architecture. Basilicas with transepts were fully vaulted and had a dome over the crossing. Hagia Sophia embodied the grandiose synthesis of a vaulted longitudinal structure and a central-plan building with a domed crossing at the mid-point of the principal axis (II, FIG. 774). These developments in the new capital affected primarily the eastern provinces and furnished the basis for a rich stream of variations on the central and centralizing plans. However, the older types — among them, the plain three-aisled basilica and the standard basilica with transept, as well as the simple central-plan structure — continued in use everywhere, though especially in provincial centers, side by side with the new variations of Constantinopolitan architecture. This continuity of older types was observed in the East and remained a vital aspect of religious architecture in Byzantium until the Islamic conquest; such recourse to tradition was even more persistent in the West, where it was apparent in church architecture well beyond late antiquity.

Regional development of late-antique architecture. a. The West.
In the Constantinian period, Rome was the center of architectural development in the West. The patronage of Constantine and his retinue resulted in the construction of the five-aisled diocesan church of St. John Lateran, the commemorative churches at the tombs of the martyrs Peter and Marcellinus, Lawrence, and Agnes, and the memorial shrine dedicated to the apostles on the Via Appia (probably at the present-day S. Sebastiano); these last-named memorials were all three-aisled basilicas with exedrae. The Constantinian commemorative churches for St. Peter (the old basilica of St. Peter's; FIG. 83) and St. Paul (S. Paolo fuori le Mura) were five-aisled basilicas with transepts. Subsequent construction on the church dedicated to St. Paul, occurring on the site of the saint's tomb a little before the year 400, followed the plan of Old St. Peter's. From the end of the 4th until the 6th century, the conventional three-aisled basilica dominated the Roman scene, as shown by such structures as S. Clemente, SS. Giovanni e Paolo, S. Sabina, S. Maria Maggiore, and S. Giovanni a Porta Latina. In the 5th-century construction of S. Pietro in Vincoli, there appeared a three-aisled basilica with tripartite transept, and in the same century also appeared the central-plan, circular building with inscribed cross, as once exemplified by the Church of S. Stefano Rotondo (PL. 39), before the 15th-century reconstruction by Nicholas V. The 6th century witnessed the introduction to Rome of the Eastern basilica type with galleries (e.g., S. Lorenzo fuori le Mura, S. Agnese fuori le Mura).

Only a few scattered Early Christian structures in southern Italy and Sicily can be cited — among them, the basilica of Salemi (4th–5th cent.), a central-plan structure in Canosa di Puglia, the baptistery (S. Maria Maggiore, 5th cent?) of Nocera Superiore, and the cruciform church of Casaranello. However, no less than three important centers of architectural development can be clearly distinguished in upper Italy: namely, Milan, Ravenna, and Aquileia. Stylistically, these were all more closely connected with the East Roman provinces than with Rome. Milan offered a rich variety of formal types: the old cathedral, a simple basilica with transept; S. Simpliciano, a basilica with three aisles of equal height and a two-aisled transept (FIG. 83); S. Nazaro Maggiore, a cruciform building; S. Lorenzo Maggiore, an octagonal central-plan edifice lobed on four alternate sides, one of the greatest monuments of its kind, displaying Eastern influence (PL. 43); and the adjoining Chapel of St. Aquilinus, a simple octagonal building with eight interior niches. A special form of three-aisled basilica with chambers or chapels alongside the apse was favored in Ravenna, undoubtedly because of strong Eastern influence (S. Giovanni Evangelista, FIG. 86; S. Apollinare in Classe, FIG. 87; II, PLS. 430, 431). S. Vitale, another octagonal building, with eight niches spanning the interior ring of piers, was the most important central-plan structure built in the West during the 6th century and was in all probability dependent on Constantinopolitan architecture (I, PLS. 384, 411; II, PL. 430, FIG. 775). In Aquileia are located the remains of one of the oldest Christian sanctuaries, consisting of two parallel three-aisled halls, dating from the second decade of the 4th century. During the following period, both in Aquileia and in nearby Grado the basilica was the preferred form. A particular regional type of church, found also in Istria and Dalmatia and markedly influential in the architecture of the eastern Alpine areas, was a structure without apse but with a semicircular bench for the clergy placed in the central aisle. In Salona, chief city of the Roman province of Dalmatia, the *basilica discoperta* of Marusinac was perhaps the most notable early structure, followed in importance by the cruciform church of the 6th century and the 4th-century *basilica urbana*, which reveals a connection with the East.

The northern territories, from the Danube and the Rhine to northern Gaul, were characterized by very simple structures

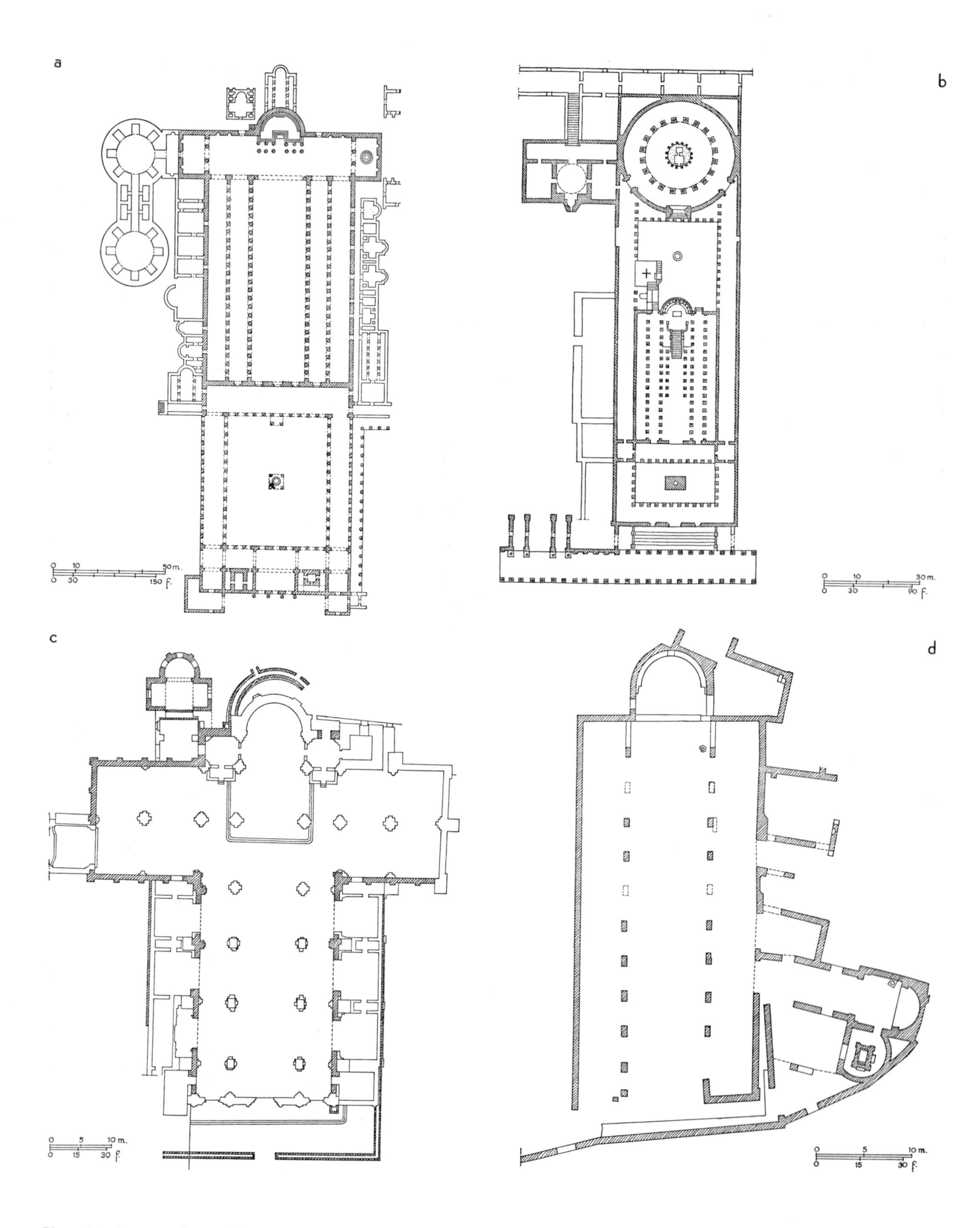

Plans of basilican complexes of the 4th century, partly reconstructed: (*a*) Rome, St. Peter's; (*b*) Jerusalem, Church of the Holy Sepulcher (cross indicates the location of Calvary); (*c*) Milan, S. Simpliciano; (*d*) Bône (Hippo), Algeria, the Great Basilica.

that consisted of modest-scaled rectangular halls, often without apse. In strongly Romanized centers, nonetheless, the architectural types of the Mediterranean littoral were present, such as at Trier, with its cathedral complex composed of two three-aisled basilicas of the 4th century. St. Gereon in Cologne, with an elliptical interior ringed by eight niches, dates from the second half of the 4th century and may reflect a Roman prototype. It may be assumed that in other leading Roman cities of Gaul, buildings of Mediterranean Roman character were also present, although no examples have been preserved.

North Africa, especially Numidia (Tunisia) and western Mauretania (Algeria), was one of the most important regions for the development of late-antique architecture. The local variant of the three-aisled basilica was the commonly favored monumental type. From the Constantinian period, to a lesser extent, there were also some basilicas of five (Orléansville) to nine aisles (Damus el-Karita in Carthage; Tipasa). Further distinctive details of North African architecture were coupled supports (either columns or piers with columns) and double apses, often elevated above the pavement level of the aisles.

Spain, where the three-aisled basilican type can also be traced, was undoubtedly influenced by the western sectors of North Africa. Architecture in western Libya (Tripolitania) was closely connected with the Numidian style, whereas that of the Cyrenaic region tended to follow Egypt, in accordance with ancient tradition.

b. The East. Constantinople became the foremost architectural center of the Eastern Empire with the construction of a number of monumental religious edifices after A.D. 330, begun under the auspices of the emperor Constantine and completed by his successor Constantius. None of these has survived to the present day. The oldest surviving construction, dating from the end of the 4th century, is the lower story of the martyrium dedicated to SS. Karpos and Papylos, a round domed building with ambulatory and apse. The façade of the first Hagia Sophia, as rebuilt by Theodosius II, dates from the early 5th century. It consisted of a pedimented propylaeum (excavated by Schneider in front of the present-day façade) flanked by porticoes, with sculptural decoration that was the basis of a subsequent line of stylistic development (II, PL. 429). The Church of St. John in Studion (ca. 463) is the earliest remaining example of the canonical three-aisled East Roman basilica, with galleries and the rounded apse with polygonal exterior that was characteristic of Constantinople and later widely adopted (II, PL. 423; FIG. 762). The age of Justinian marked the culmination in the development of Constantinopolitan architecture and architectonic decoration. The most significant buildings preserved from this period are SS. Sergius and Bacchus (II, PL. 426, FIGS. 770, 771), St. Irene (II, PL. 433, FIG. 774; VII, PL. 408), and the most notable, Hagia Sophia.

Closely connected with the capital in architectural style were the regions around the Aegean and the bordering Balkan territories. In Greece often furnished with transept and crossing, the three-aisled basilica constituted the most common type in these areas. As in Constantinople, such structures usually had the galleries reserved for women. The most important structures extant in these regions are the Church of St. Demetrius in Salonika (II, FIG. 763), a five-aisled basilica with transept; St. John in Ephesus, a three-aisled basilica, cruciform and domed as reconstructed under Justinian (II, FIG. 772); and central-plan structures in Hierapolis and Thasos, similar to the cruciform basilicas of Gerasa and Salona.

In central Asia Minor basilican structures were not unknown, but single-aisled cruciform buildings, frequently with domed crossings, were the characteristic type of the region. Farther south, especially in Cilicia, the basilican plan was the more prevalent. In Syria numerous structures have been well preserved, primarily in open country but sometimes as part of ancient settlements; thus, the late-antique evolution of the architecture of this region can be clearly traced. In the metropolis of Antioch, where an octagonal building with an ambulatory surmounted by galleries is known to have been constructed in the reign of Constantine, St. Babilas is the only example of the single-aisled cruciform structure preserved (II, FIG. 764). The areas around Antioch and Apamea, the basalt region to the east, and the Hauran in the south were the chief architectural subdivisions of Syria. The greatest number of churches were three-aisled basilicas with tripartite sanctuary. In the Hauran, where local tradition favored simple hall-type structures, the basilica did not appear until the late 5th century. The most significant central-plan structures in Syria were the cruciform pilgrimage church of St. Simeon Stylites at Qal'at Sim'ān (PL. 47; FIG. 89); the so-called "martyrium" at Seleucia Pieria (mod. Süveydiye,

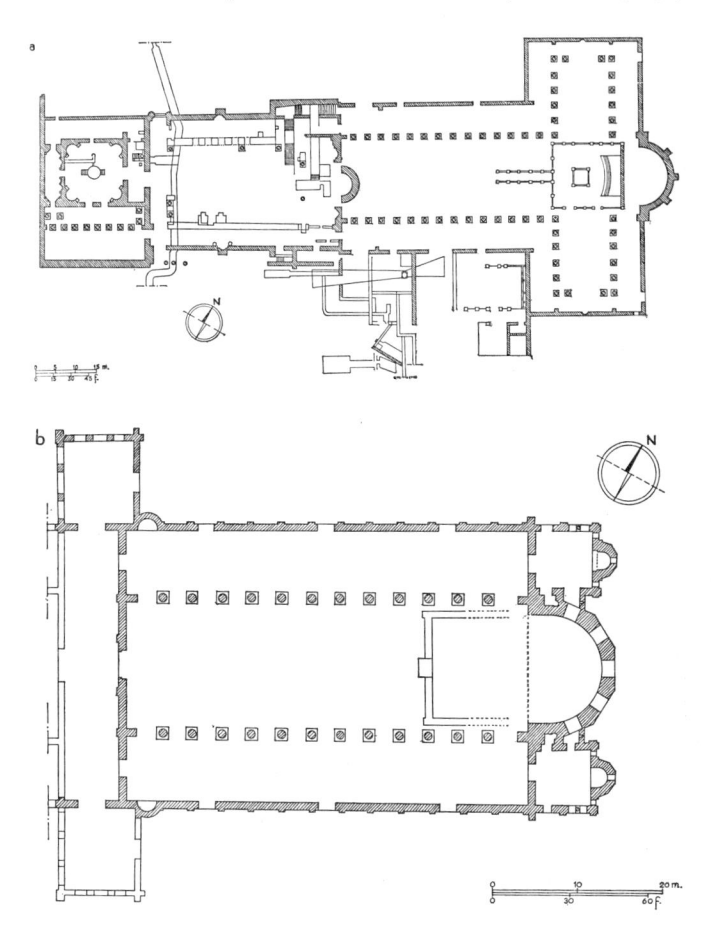

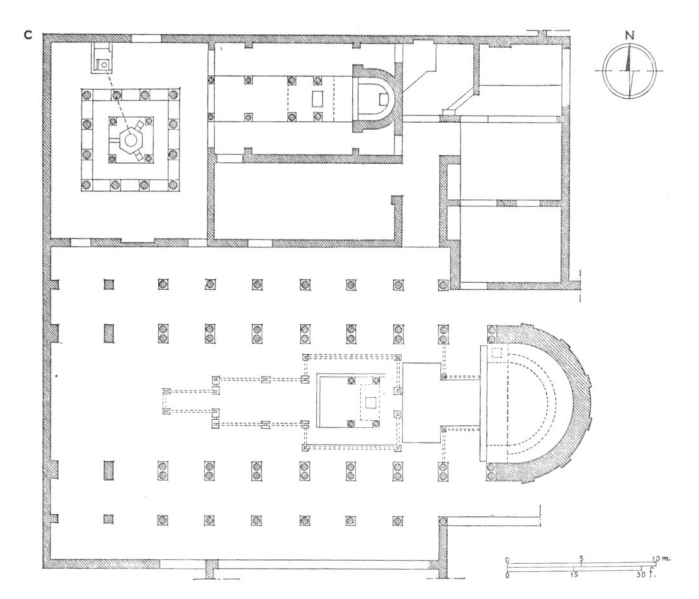

Plans of basilican complexes of the 5th century, partly reconstructed: (*a*) St. Mennas, near Alexandria (Egypt), reign of Arcadius (395-408); (*b*) Ravenna, S. Giovanni Evangelista, reign of Galla Placidia (425-50); (*c*) Carthage, Basilica of Douimes (late 5th cent.).

Turkey), similar in plan to the Cathedral of Bosra; and the Church of St. George in Zorava (mod. Ezraa). The churches of northern Mesopotamia are clearly related to Syrian types, and the so-called "martyrium" (probably the diocesan church) of the important complex of Rusafa-Sergiopolis (FIG. 87) is stylistically very much like the group of central-plan Syrian structures just mentioned. Central-plan buildings in Maiyafarikin and Amida (mod. Diryarbekir, Turkey), on the other hand, reflect the influence of Constantinople; whereas the extramural cemetery church of Rusafa may perhaps have been related to Sassanian architecture. The Armenian churches can also be linked with those of Syria and eastern Asia Minor.

In Palestine, almost nothing remains of the original church of the Holy Sepulcher, but its general appearance is known through ancient descriptions. In Bethlehem, the site of the Grotto of the Nativity was occupied by a five-aisled basilica attached to an octagonal structure, which was then replaced by a basilica with transept during the reign of Justinian. The three-aisled basilica with transept commemorating the Multiplication of the Loaves at the Sea of Galilee is somewhat later in date. Outside the metropolitan areas, the three-aisled basilican plan was the customary type. In the 5th and 6th centuries the development of architectural history was still strongly affected by the imperial foundations, only one of which, the octagonal sanctuary dedicated to the Virgin on Mount Garizim, has been excavated. In Gerasa, another important center, three-aisled basilicas were favored, but central-plan structures were also in evidence.

In Egypt, unfortunately, all traces of the ecclesiastical architecture of Alexandria have disappeared. The church architecture of this metropolis, nevertheless, is probably reflected in the buildings of the nearby shrine of St. Mennas, which has a basilica with transept marking the site of the tomb of the martyr, as well as other basilican structures. The oldest true dome on pendentives extant, located in one of these, dates from the beginning of the 5th century. A three-aisled, galleried basilica terminating in a triconchal sanctuary was an important type in Middle and Upper Egypt from the 5th century on (Deir el-Abiad, Deir el-Ahmar, Dendera). A church closely linked with the architecture of the St. Mennas complex, and hence with the Alexandrian style, is the basilica with transept at Hermopolis.

Secular structures. a. Domestic architecture. As far as it has been possible to establish, existing local traditions persisted during late antiquity, and the architecture of the private house was marked by a great variety of regional types. Thus, certain types of houses in existence in the ancient Near East — forms still found in modern times in Asia Minor, Syria, Mesopotamia, and Egypt — were continued in the late-antique era. This was largely the case with the archetypal private house in the plains country, which also, as shown by excavations, made increasingly frequent appearances in the cities, perhaps as some indication of an impoverishment or regression of urban culture in a number of regions (Greece, Sicily, etc.). In the countryside the farmhouse, fortified in frontier areas, assumed added importance, especially in regions where productive land was not only maintained but even augmented as late as the 3d to 6th century (Syria, Palestine, North Africa). Elsewhere, in the Alpine regions, southern Germany, the areas along the Rhine, and Britain, substantial building activity was abruptly brought to an end with the barbaric invasions of the last years of the 4th century. In general, the late-antique farmhouses appear to have followed prototypes from earlier periods. In the cities, besides the more modest kinds of private houses mentioned earlier, the elaborate Hellenistic peristyle house and multistoried dwellings for several families, with provision for shops at the street level, continued in use throughout late antiquity.

b. Official buildings. Late-antique official and public architecture was also marked by continuity of tradition, particularly in the Roman imperial enterprises. The leading architectural centers were the great metropolises of the Empire and the capitals of the individual provinces. Compared with the preceding epoch, however, official architecture on the whole declined and in some localities came to a virtual halt. Various factors were responsible for this phenomenon. Established centers such as Rome declined in importance as a consequence of the founding of new ones (Constantinople). Entire regions became impoverished, either through the migration of peoples, the expansion of the latifundia, the barbarian incursions, or a pervasive insecurity. Public edifices already standing — moreover, sometimes reduced in scale — were found sufficient to meet the limited demands of the new times. In some areas, where the population increased and urban civilization continued to flourish (e.g., Syria), civic architecture evidenced a rich development that extended even to centers in the hinterlands. After the period of political disorder that followed the end of Severan rule, a new flowering of official architecture took place in Rome, beginning tentatively with Aurelian, accelerating under the Tetrarchy and Maxentius, and continuing during the reign of Constantine the Great until the founding of Constantinople in A.D. 330. Thereupon the center of imperial architectural undertakings gradually shifted to the new eastern capital.

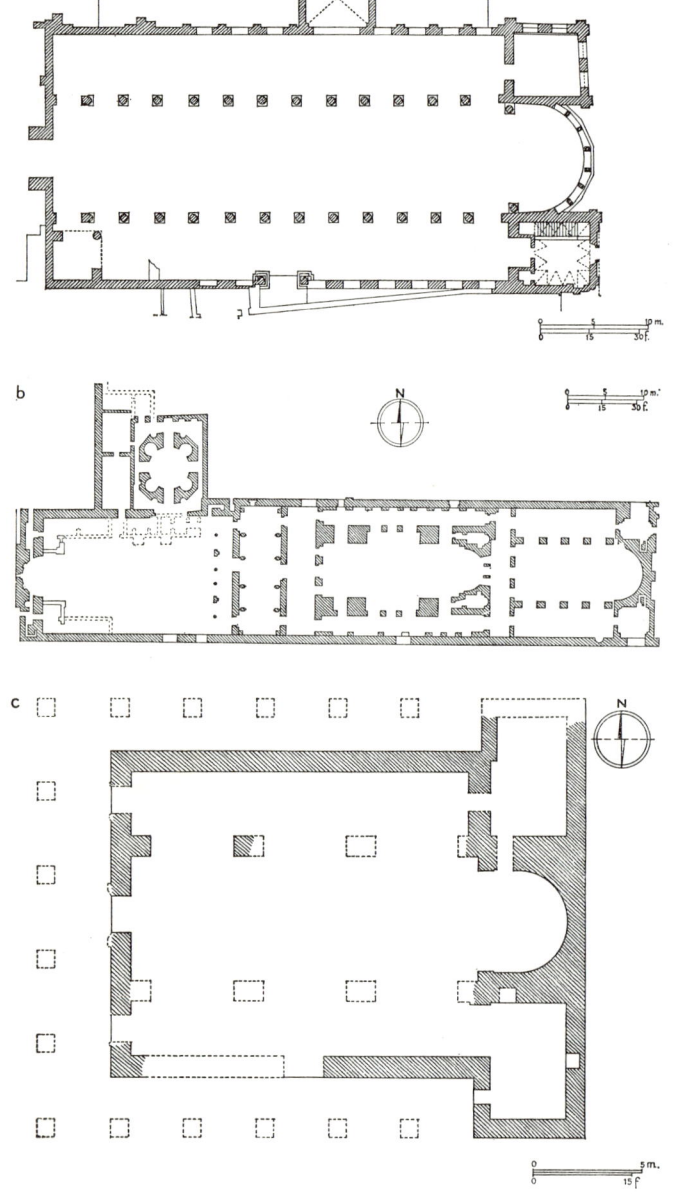

Plans of basilican complexes of the 6th century, partly reconstructed: (*a*) Ravenna, S. Apollinare in Classe (549); (*b*) Ephesus, Church of the Virgin or of the Council (second half of 6th cent.); (*c*) Rusafa, St. Sergius (probably second half of 6th cent.).

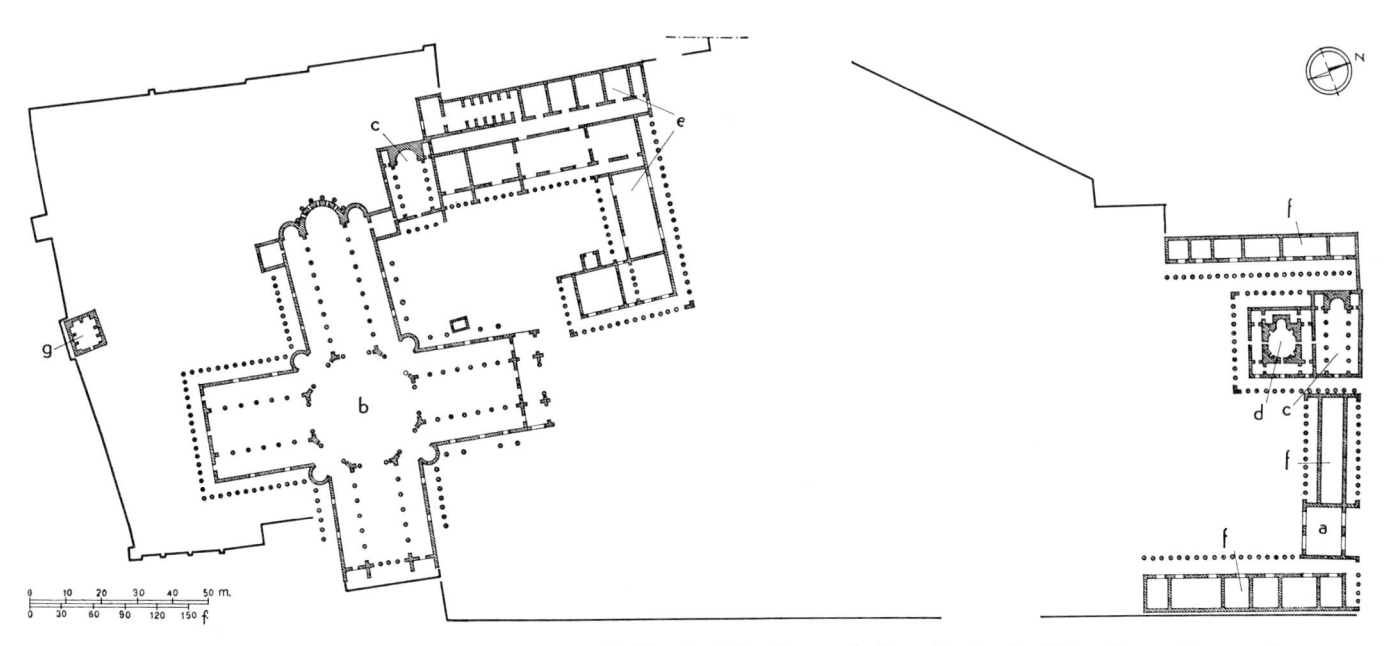

Qal'at Sim'ān (Syria), plan of monastic complex: (*a*) Entrance; (*b*) Church of St. Simeon Stylites; (*c*) chapels; (*d*) baptistery; (*e*) monastic quarters; (*f*) guest quarters; (*g*) tomb (*from G. Tchalenko, Villages antiques de la Syrie du Nord, Paris, 1953–58*).

The most notable surviving example of a senatorial assembly hall (*curia*), that in the Forum Romanum constructed for Diocletian, is in the form of a high, rectilinear, and once probably vaulted hall (PL. 33). The three-aisled Basilica Nova of the Forum, begun under Maxentius and finished under Constantine, is an example of a vaulted *basilica forensis* and constitutes one of the greatest achievements in vaulted construction during all antiquity (PL. 36). Its interior layout can be directly related to the frigidaria of Roman imperial thermae. Unfortunately, no examples of such large-scale civic architecture have survived from this era in Constantinople; but commercial towns in northern Syria offer many, albeit more modest, examples of public buildings such as market halls, bazaars, "town halls," and lodging places, dating from the 3d to the 6th century.

The Baths of Diocletian (PL. 37) and those built on the Quirinal by Constantine represented the continuation and further development of the urban type of Roman imperial thermal structure in the late-antique period. Of the thermae of Constantinople, nothing has survived; however, a monumental thermal construction has recently been excavated in Ephesus. In what measure such thermal establishments were a vital feature of even small rural settlements is demonstrated by the thermae of Babisqa in northern Syria (5th or 6th cent.), where the peristyle courtyard reveals a clear connection with older building tradition. A 5th-century thermal building within the pilgrimage sanctuary of St. Mennas near Alexandria was probably used for therapeutic purposes.

c. Palaces and villas. Because of the political decentralization that began in the 3d century, and the consequent establishment of imperial residences in cities other than Rome in both the eastern and western sectors of the Empire, construction of palaces flourished in this period (Trier, Paris, Milan, Aquileia, and later Ravenna, Sirmium, Salonika, Nicomedia, and Antioch). While only parts of the residence of Galerius in Salonika (PL. 44; FIG. 90) are extant (from the period of the Tetrarchy; porticoed streets, triumphal arch, and mausoleum), major elements of the palace complex of Spalato, constructed for Diocletian near Salona in Dalmatia by workmen from Asia Minor, still stand (PL. 34; FIG. 91). This imperial residence, built as a place of retirement, was a self-sufficient fortified city (*castrum*), with a peristyle at the intersection of the main axes and four portals looking toward the sea. These vantage points were accessible from the central peristyle of the palace, a court flanked by the Temple of Jupiter and the imperial mausoleum. This disposition, through which the imperial palace and the confronted temple and mausoleum were intended to create a single spatial unit, was undoubtedly a late-antique innovation. Of the imperial palace of Trier, which probably dates from the first years of the reign of Constantine, a large single-aisled, apsidal hall with great blind arcades on the exterior has been preserved. Originally flanked by porticoed courtyards, this structure (the so-called "Basilica"; FIG. 93) was probably the throne room, the only one of its kind surviving from the period.

The palatial villa of Maxentius, on the Via Appia near Rome, was joined with the mausoleum of his son Romulus and a large circus. From either the beginning or the end of

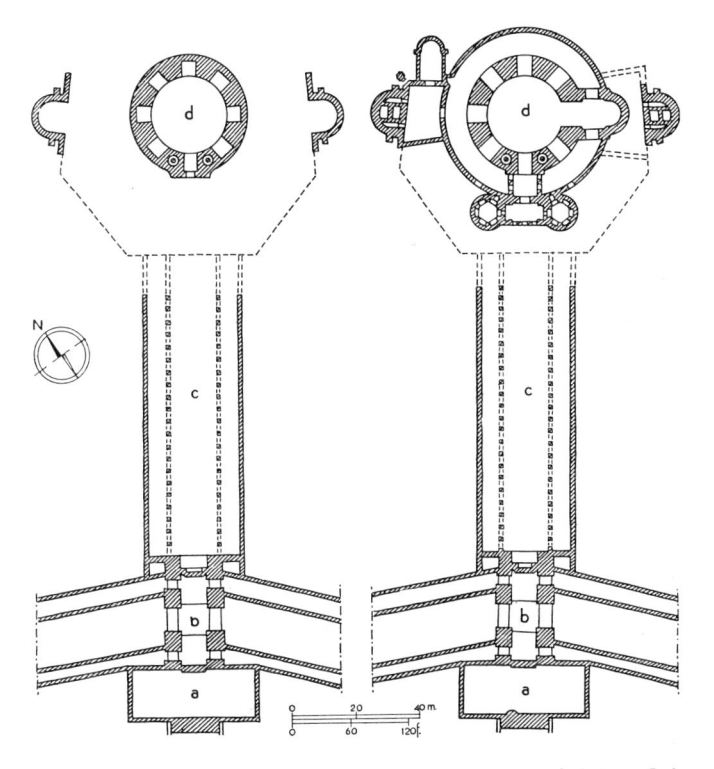

Salonika, structures forming part of the palace complex of Galerius. *Left*: Ground plan at the time of Galerius. (*a*) Atrium of the palace; (*b*) tetrapylon over the public street; (*c*) colonnaded street; (*d*) mausoleum. *Right*: Ground plan of the same complex, with the Mausoleum of Galerius as transformed into the Church of St. George during the reign of Theodosius.

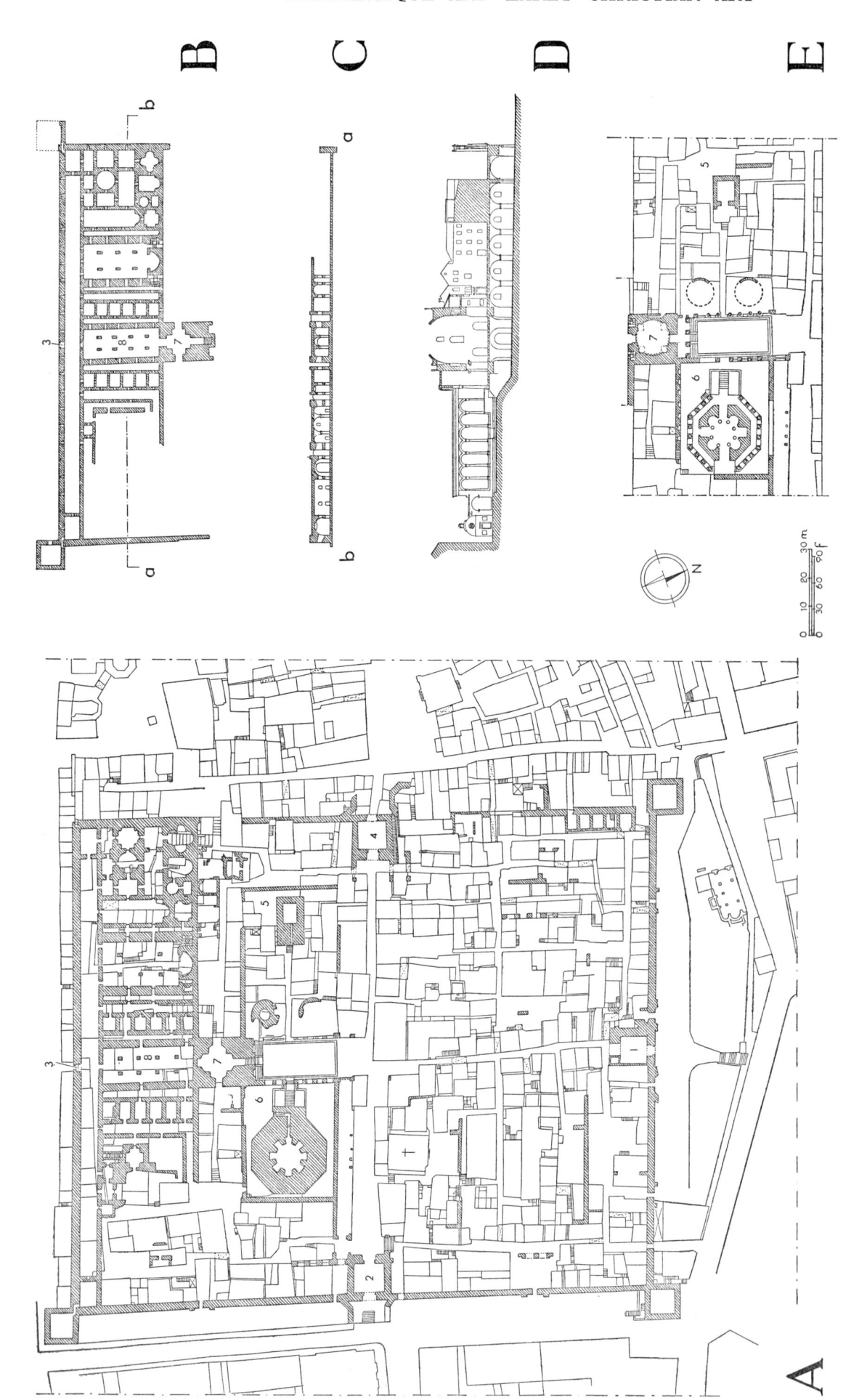

Spalato (mod. Split), Palace of Diocletian: *A*, plan of ruins at ground level (as of January, 1963; prepared by T. Marasovic, Urbanisticki biro, Split); *B*, plan of remains below ground level in the south zone; *C*, east–west sectional view of remains below ground level in the south zone; *D*, north–south sectional view along the axis of the peristyle facing the sea; *E*, plan of ruins of the central complex (*from Urbs, 1957*). Principal structures: (1) Porta Aurea; (2) Porta Argentea; (3) Porta Aenea; (4) Porta Ferrea; (5) sacred precinct with Temple of Jupiter; (6) precinct with Mausoleum; (7) vestibulum; (8) so-called "tablinum."

the 4th century is the vast and luxurious villa at Casale (FIG. 95), near Piazza Armerina in Sicily, which some scholars have attributed — though probably erroneously — to Maximianus Herculius. In addition to a central peristyle, which connected directly with the monumental entrance unit and also led to the main rooms, the villa contained a reception or guest suite comprising a large oval courtyard and a hall in triconch form on one side and baths on the other. Since their incorporation in the Villa of Hadrian at Tivoli, the last-named chambers had become an important part of such princely dwellings. Sumptuous country residences were constructed not only for rulers

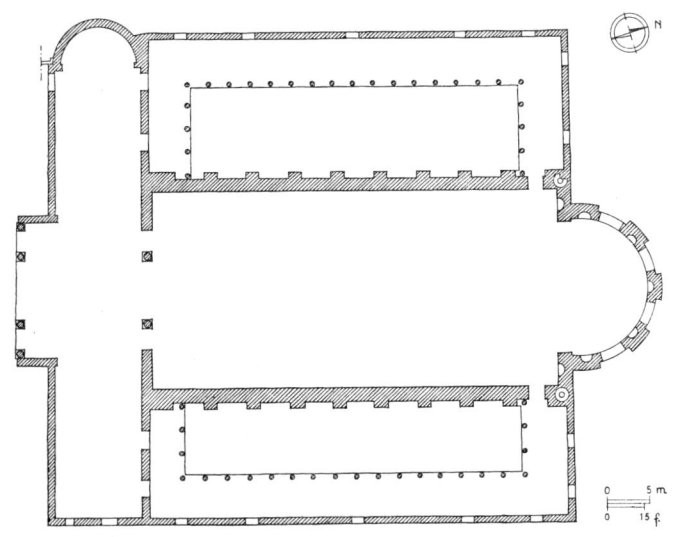

Trier (Germany), imperial hall or so-called "Basilica," plan (*from L. Crema, Architettura Romana, Turin, 1959*).

but also for the wealthy owners of latifundia, who in late antiquity had generally become members of a newly rich and powerful artistocracy.

The palace for the new capital on the Bosporus, a structure no doubt planned from the ground up for Constantine's purposes, was completed and further enlarged by his successors well into the Middle Ages. Despite the wealth of literary sources, however, no clear archaeological picture of this totally destroyed structure has yet emerged. This Great Palace of the Emperors (Sacrum Palatium; II, FIG. 759) in Constantinople was not only the imperial residence but also the seat of the highest political authority; as such, it became the model for all late-antique seats of government, even certain barbarian ones. Thus, more than the nomenclature of some of the principal parts of the Palace of Theodoric in Ravenna must have been derived from its prototype in Constantinople. In the evolution of palace planning, the palace church ultimately replaced the temple within the residential complex, as is demonstrated by the present S. Apollinare Nuovo in Ravenna, the former palace chapel. Undoubtedly, the highest officials in the leading cities of the Empire also occupied residences of a palatial character.

From the reign of Constantine, the palace of the bishop (*episcopium*) acquired increasing importance. Constantine himself donated the Palace of Fausta (Lateran) to the bishop of Rome as his seat. Corresponding to the importance of the diocese, the forms of episcopal residence ranged from sumptuous palaces to structures hardly distinguishable from conventional dwellings or even farmhouses. Traces of extensive episcopal palaces have been discovered in Bosra, Djemila, Salona, and elsewhere; in Ravenna, only the chapel (5th–6th cent.), which was in an upper story, has survived the over-all remodeling of the episcopal palace. Monastic structures, traceable in North Africa and Syria from the 5th century onward, presented a building scheme new to late antiquity. In North Africa, the complex at Tebessa is an imposing example of a fortified monastery: at the center is the monastery church, with atrium and martyrium, which was joined on the west with the cloister and the monastic quarters proper. Because of the large number of extant monuments, the development of monastic architecture in Syria is especially clear. Here the monastic buildings, including the church, were generally situated around irregular-shaped courtyards. The guesthouse, refectory, living quarters of the monks, and other buildings were usually preceded by multistoried porticoes. A mausoleum for the monks, located very near the monastery, was another standard element. In Egypt, traces of such monastic communities (hospices, cells, chapels) have been discovered at Bawit, as well as in the area of Wadi Natrun.

d. Commemorative monuments and funerary architecture. The triumphal arch remained one of the principal types of honorific structures during the late-antique period, as seen in such examples as the Arch of Galerius in Salonika and the Arch of Constantine in Rome (PL. 35). The freestanding column, however, appears to have enjoyed the greatest favor: surviving examples include that of Phocas in the Forum Romanum, composed of salvaged materials; the simple honorific columns of Constantine and of Claudius II, commemorating his victory over the Goths, both of which date from the 4th century; and the Column of Marcianus from the 5th century (last-named three in Constantinople). The colossal Roman imperial columns with spiraling bands of historical reliefs were imitated in Constantinople in the honorific columns of Theodosius and Arcadius; the base of the latter, with a chamber and part of a winding stairway, survives.

The central-plan structure with niches made its appearance for funerary purposes as early as the end of the 2d century (e.g., round mausoleum near Old St. Peter's, Rome), but it was not adopted as the characteristic form for the aristocratic mausoleum until sometime in the 3d century. The more imposing structures had a lower story for burial purposes and an exterior colonnaded ambulatory (the round peripteral temple of Porto; the so-called "Mausoleum of Gallienus" on the Via Appia). The mausoleums of the Villa of the Gordians, from the period of the Tetrarchy, and of Romulus (son of Maxentius) on the Via Appia are without ambulatories; the upper story was accessible through a pedimented propylaeum. The mausoleum near Rome (Tor Pignattara), originally destined for Constantine himself and subsequently for his mother Helena, was not provided with a distinct lower story. A wholly new development with this mausoleum was its junction with the church of the martyrs Peter and Marcellinus, which was placed on the same axis. Also in Rome, the Mausoleum of Constantina (S. Costanza; PL. 38), daughter of Constantine the Great, on the south flank of the memorial church of the martyr Agnes (FIG. 98), is the oldest existing central-plan edifice with an inner ring of columns separating the low-roofed ambulatory from the domed space within, which is lighted by twelve windows. Throughout the late-antique period, however, simple funerary cellae, usually with an apse, continued to be built. Cruciform and triconch mausoleums were also common forms during late antiquity, for example, the Catacomb of Callixtus in Rome and the "Mausoleum of Galla Placidia" in Ravenna (II, PL. 425; IV, PL. 458). From the 4th century, the mausoleum was invariably annexed to a church.

Traditions of pronounced local character continued to be manifest in a number of provinces of the Empire, above all in Syria. Besides the commemorative column, still used in the 3d century, the most common type in Syria until the 6th century was a quadrangular mausoleum of ashlar blocks, rectangular in plan and with a pyramidal stone roof. Multistoried funerary towers, as well as underground mortuary chambers, existed in Palmyra into the 3d century. In Egypt (q.v.) the late-antique, partly Christian cemetery of el-Bagawat has mausoleums of crude, sun-dried brick, for the most part domed and rectilinear in plan and sometimes decorated with blind arcades.

In addition to surface cemeteries, the extensive underground burial complexes known as catacombs (q.v.) were adopted in certain localities, notably in Rome and Alexandria, as early as the 3d century. Originally not exclusively Christian, from the 4th century such underground burial grounds in Rome, Syracuse, Naples, and elsewhere came to be used chiefly by the

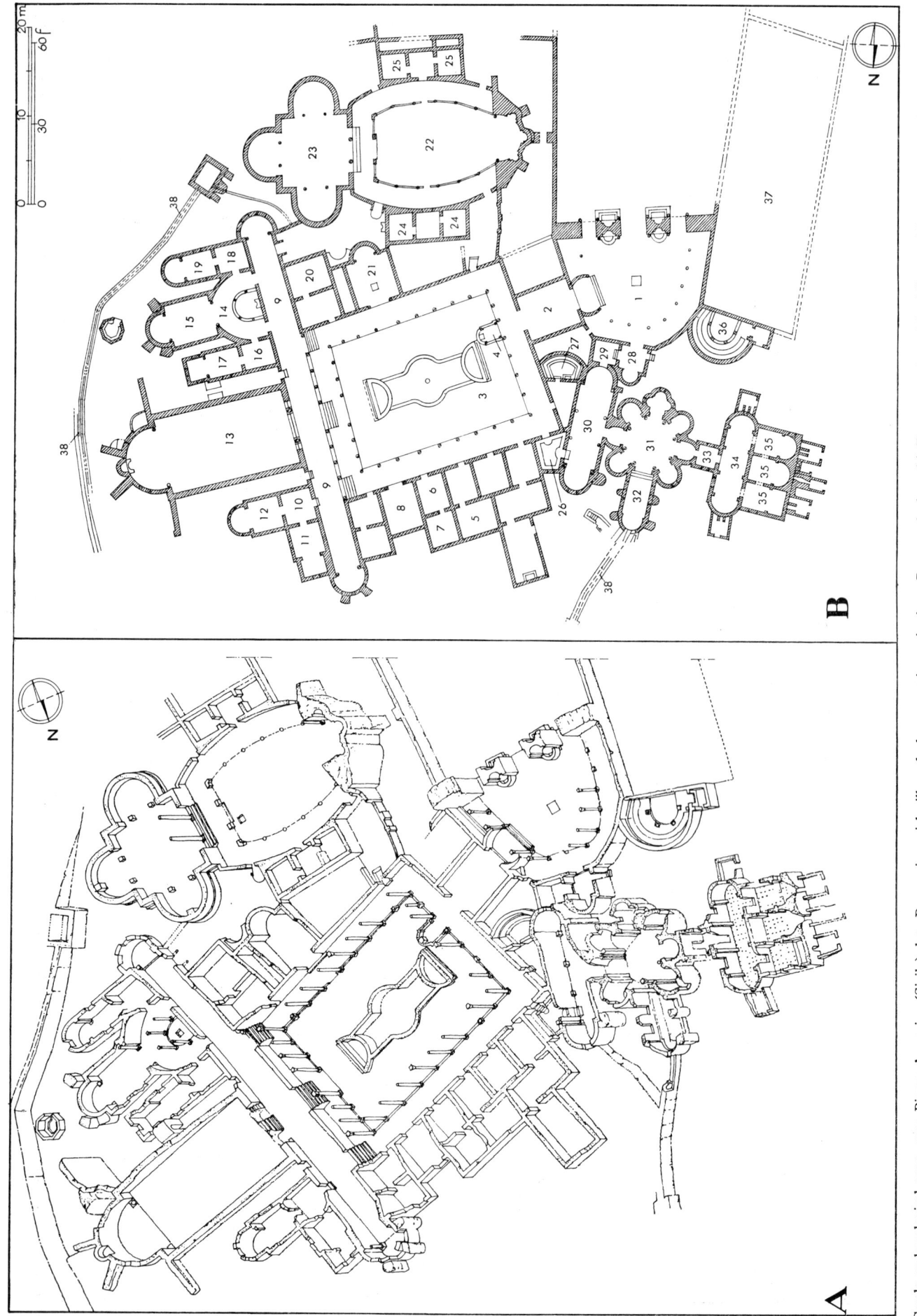

Casale archaeological zone, near Piazza Armerina (Sicily), late Roman imperial villa. *A*, Axonometric projection; *B*, ground plan: (1) Entrance atrium; (2) tablinum with adventus; (3) peristyle; (4) apsidal shrine; (5) room with dance scenes; (6) room with representations of the seasons; (7) room with fishing Cupids; (8) diaeta with the Small Hunt; (9) ambulacrum with the Great Hunt; (10) vestibule with Polyphemus; (11) cubiculum with erotic scene; (12) cubiculum with fruit decoration; (13) basilican hall; (14) porticoed atrium with exedra, decorated with marine scenes; (15) diaeta with Arion; (16) vestibule with Cupid and Pan; (17) cubiculum with young hunters; (18) vestibule with the Small Circus; (19) cubiculum with musicians and actors; (20) room with the Ten Girls; (21) diaeta with Orpheus; (22) xystus; (23) triconchal hall with Labors of Hercules; (24) oecus with vintage scenes; (25) oecus with fishing Cupids; (26) vestibule; (27) small latrine; (28) aedicula of bath; (29) vestibule to bath; (30) ambulacrum with circus scenes; (31) frigidarium with marine scenes; (32) piscina; (33) room with anointing scenes; (34) tepidarium; (35) caldarium; (36) large latrine; (37) probable area of hygienic services, unexcavated; (38) aqueduct.

Christians. In these catacombs, the spatial arrangements conventionally employed for single funerary chambers (cubicula) above ground were mainly employed.

e. Functional structures (aqueducts, cisterns). In the late-antique era, functional structures undoubtedly had less significance within the total architectural activity than they had had at the time of the greatest expansion and succeeding consolidation of the Empire; nevertheless, it would be erroneous to infer thereby that the technical capacity for great undertakings of this kind had disappeared. Such may often have been the case in the West, where, as in Rome, it was deemed sufficient to maintain the existing facilities and few new projects were initiated. In regions that were still being developed, however, much work of prime importance was accomplished in this field. The water supply of Constantinople was secured by means of new aqueducts, a reservoir, and distribution system. The most important of these aqueducts, that built by Valens, is still preserved (II, PL. 421). Under the auspices of Justinian, Ephesus was also provided with a new aqueduct. In Constantinople the water carried by the aqueducts, as well as rain water, was collected in numerous cisterns and reservoirs, the largest of which were open to the sky. Others, such as the great reservoirs of Binbirdirek and Yerebatan Saray, were vaulted over on colonnades. The dimensions of these cisterns surpassed all such previous structures. Large cisterns were also characteristic features of most settlements in Syria and Mesopotamia.

Late-antique city planning. The transition toward the typical late-antique city layout was a gradual process that is revealed primarily in details of organization. The city of Philippopolis (mod. Shahba, Syria), founded in the mid-3d century by Philip the Arabian in the Auranitis region, was substantially a traditional Roman urban settlement: a somewhat irregular, wall-enclosed rectangle; porticoed main streets (*cardo* and *decumanus maximus*), with their intersection marked by a tetrapylon; numerous temples, a theater, thermae, and other public buildings, perhaps including a palace near the center of the town. That this entire undertaking followed a set plan conceived elsewhere rather than *in situ* is indicated by the prevailing application of methods of construction foreign to the region (mortar walls, *opus caementicium* vaults).

The founding of Constantinople, and the consequent transformation of the Hellenistic-Roman settlement of Byzantium, served to establish the model for the large late-antique city. Not far from the old acropolis, the Great Palace of the Emperors formed the heart of the new city. Nearby were the principal church, in which great events in the history of the Empire were solemnized, and the Hippodrome, the center of entertainment for the people. The public life of the city focused on the Forum of Constantine, at some distance from the palace complex. With the column in honor of the Emperor in its midst, this space was surrounded by porticoes. The Church of the Holy Apostles, erected jointly with the imperial mausoleum, was situated on the periphery of the city. Like Rome, the city was divided into districts, with the important central tract consisting of the palace, the Hippodrome, and the major churches.

Having begun to make its presence known in the ancient city in the 3d century, Christianity gained importance, through its steadily multiplying religious edifices, in the organization and general aspect of the late-antique city from the 4th century onward. On the outskirts of the cities, Christian cemeteries and memorial sites appeared side by side with pagan burial grounds. The important Christian sites seem always to have been located on the margins of urban centers in this early period. In Rome, the Church received its episcopal seat through the donation of the Lateran — at that time, also located on the edge of the city — by Constantine, after the Edict of Milan in A.D. 313. The focus of Christian life in Rome was thus clearly established on the periphery of the city. A similar situation arose in other cities: for example, Ravenna, Salona, Carthage, Timgad, Tipasa, Seleucia, Basra, Umm el-Jemāl, Palmyra, Thugga, and Djemila. This phenomenon may be explained by the shortage of space at the center of older cities, a zone usually occupied by public buildings and temples; even in the 4th century, these could not be freely disposed of to the Church, and there remained little room for the often extensive church complexes. Thus the advance of Christianity toward the heart of most cities was necessarily a slow process in many instances. Nevertheless, Constantinople was not the only city where the urban center was won over by Christianity at the very outset, for a number of large cities in the eastern segment of the Empire witnessed a like development (e.g., Jerusalem, Gerasa, Miletus, Ephesus, Athens). As early as the 4th century, moreover, the

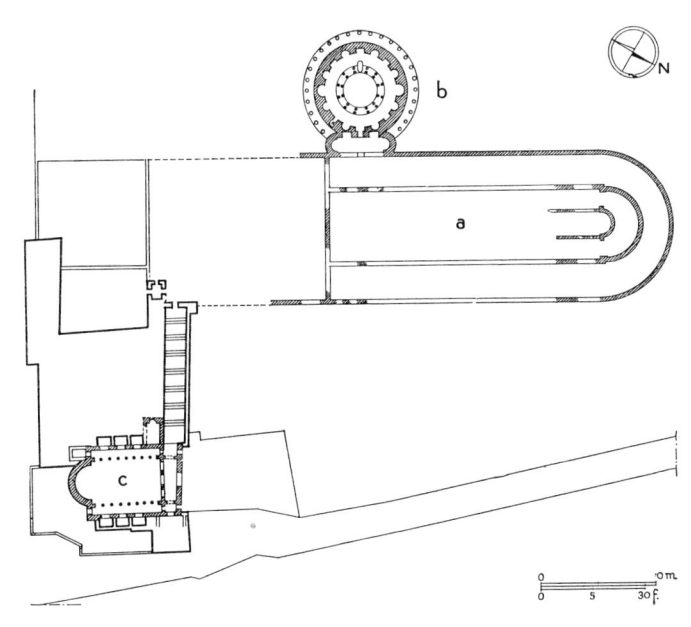

Rome, complex of S. Agnese, plan: (*a*) 4th-century basilica; (*b*) Mausoleum of Constantina (S. Costanza); (*c*) 7th-century basilica.

struggle against paganism led, particularly in eastern locales, to the destruction of temples and their replacement by churches.

Legal measures, the first ever enacted for the protection of monuments, were introduced in an effort to halt the destruction and deterioration of earlier constructions, and the old cities of the Empire reveal much evidence of restoration undertaken during late antiquity. Pagan statuary on public display was sometimes removed, but sometimes assigned new meanings or allusions, and great works of art were thereby respected and preserved from destruction. In Constantinople, works of art from all parts of the Empire were collected and exhibited in the palace, the Hippodrome, and the forums, and it may be assumed that the center of a great city such as Rome must have taken on a somewhat museumlike appearance in late antiquity.

In comparison with the preceding period, however, aspects of life in the late-antique city must have changed but little. Among the amusements, it is certain that the theater disappeared, but enjoyment of the circus and the baths continued uninterrupted, as is confirmed not only by the new constructions but also by evidence of the continued use of older structures for these purposes.

In contrast with the first centuries of the Roman Empire, the construction of fortifications assumed prime importance during late antiquity, for barbarian and foreign peoples were breaking deeply into the European, Asian, and African boundaries of the Empire. Consequently, cities theretofore unfortified began to be provided with protective walls during the 3d century. The massive new walls of Rome, for example, were constructed under Aurelian, and those of Nicaea under Claudius Gothicus. At the beginning of the 5th century, under Theodosius II, the land walls of Constantinople were extended toward Thrace (II, PLS. 420, 421); these fortifications served as a model for the entire Eastern Empire. Under Justinian, the frontier between Armenia and Mesopotamia was reinforced with an impressive new series of fortified cities, presumably according to plans formulated in Constantinople (e.g., Balis-Meskene, Sergiopolis-Rusafa, Zenobia-Zalebiya).

For the strongly fortified outposts (e.g., the Syrian limes), the Roman square castrum with corner towers was retained. In the layout of the interior, the *cardo* and *decumanus* were no longer obligatory features. At the center, in place of the *praetorium* or the sanctuary of the standard, there was often a chapel. A particular type of military residence along the Syrian-Arabian frontier is exemplified by the castrum of Qaṣr ibn-Wardan, probably erected by masons from Constantinople in the service of the military. The barracks forming the castrum proper, a palace serving as residence for the commanding officer of the territory, and an immediately adjoining church were the most prominent elements. Residences of this type were probably the models for comparable Ommiad castles built in the desert.

Friedrich W. Deichmann

SCULPTURE. In the 4th and 5th centuries, as in preceding periods, marble remained the material principally employed for sculpture, and marble sculpture was an especially prominent feature of the great cities. In provincial areas the sculptors, like their predecessors, continued to use local stones such as limestone and tufa. Increasing steadily in favor were marbles from the eastern sectors of the Empire, especially those with large crystals of gray-blue veining which were exported from Proconnesus, in the Propontis, throughout the Mediterranean. Luna marble, on the contrary, was continually more limited in use during the 3d century, so much so that regular exploitation of the Apuan quarries eventually ceased. Porphyry, a material that had special status, was taken from quarries near the Red Sea belonging exclusively to the imperial house. Fine bronzework persisted, and its high quality is attested by the gigantic Capitoline head (PL. 51), presumed to be Constantinus II, and by the Colossus of Barletta (PL. 60). Sculpture in stucco also acquired importance during this era.

Sculpture in the round. A major characteristic of the transition period from antiquity to the Middle Ages is the fact that sculpture, relief, and sculptural ornament in general gave way increasingly to mosaic, fresco, and inlay as decorative media. In imperial times the cult statue tended to recede gradually toward the rear of the temple, at last being placed within an apsidal space and thence losing its previously dominant position. With the emergence of Christianity, volumetric representation of divinity disappeared; the divinity was present in the sanctuary only in the sacraments and on the altar, or in relics of the witnesses of divinity contained within or under the altar. Religious art was altered in scope and intent: effort was no longer expended on creating the divine image that is the cult focus, an imposing mass to occupy the ritual space, but rather on the sanctuary surrounding the divine. The artists of the classical period materialized the divine image in space, whereas those of the late-antique period and the Middle Ages were employed in creating a fitting ambient for worship of the divine. Large-scale plastic — or space-filling — religious art vanished, to be replaced by relief sculpture, mosaic, frescoes, and intarsia, which surrounded and gave devotional character to the new sanctuaries.

It is a fact of great importance that, with the exception of the portrait, the making of statuary was generally abandoned in the late 3d and early 4th centuries, in conscious disavowal of what had been the central preoccupation of the Greco-Roman artistic tradition. The idealized statue disappeared; this was true not only for the gods, heroes, demons, and personifications of evil to be combatted by Christianity but even for figures that might be considered religiously neutral. The new Christian types that were evolving were also outside the classical tradition.

Late testimonies of a bygone ideal are such statues as the Capitoline Dioscuri, the Hercules of Piazza Armerina, and a group of statues at Ostia similarly idealized — survivals of a host that had once filled the ancient world. The last significant cult statues erected in the city of Rome were those of Venus and Roma in the Velia temple, which were made of porphyry and alabaster in the time of Maxentius to replace a pair destroyed by fire. In relief sculpture, however, as in mosaic, painting, and minor arts, the ancient world of images lived on, and not solely in iconographical forms that were neutral in religious aspect but also in deities and personifications taken from the ancient mythology. Thus, throughout the 4th and the 5th centuries, the reliefs on triumphal monuments bore representations of Victory with trophies, Eros with wreaths and garlands, river gods, tutelary goddesses, the Sun, and the Moon.

Wherein lies the explanation for these phenomena? A general regression, affecting the will and ability to create full-bodied forms, played a major part in but cannot fully account for the late-antique situation, inasmuch as portrait sculpture continued in the traditional full-round form (e.g., the so-called "Seneca" and "Menander" of the Capitoline Museum). One of the prime factors was the widespread Early Christian abhorrence of anything that might suggest an idol. A two-dimensional representation (including reliefs), however, has neither the corporeal reality of a statue nor its power of substitution. In order to understand this Christian fear of idols, one must bear in mind the way in which the ancient world — in late antiquity as well — felt the presence of the god in the statue. "When images are set up, the habits of the people do the rest," says the 4th-century dogmatist Epiphanius. As early as Constantine's reign there began the struggle against pagan sacrifices and against the ancient religious imagery; every idol was regarded as a possible dwelling or hiding place for the daemon it represented. The execration was then extended from the diabolical statues of the gods to the whole range of idealized statues resembling those of the gods. In some respects, Byzantine iconoclasm was prefigured in the condemnation of pagan images and idealized statuary by the Early Christian rigorists (see IMAGES AND ICONOCLASM). It should be added that the use of older statues in the ornamentation of contemporary monuments was still an accepted practice, for instance, the 2d-century statuary of the conquered nations on the Arch of Constantine.

The earliest Christian art showed a decided resistance to direct representation of Christ; instead, symbolic images such as the Good Shepherd were preferred. When Constantia wrote to Eusebius asking for a depiction of Christ, he rejected the request, though it came from the Emperor's own sister. She would never, said Eusebius, have seen such a depiction in any church; this was absolutely out of the question, for it was a well-known fact that any representation of this sort was forbidden to Christians everywhere. It should be observed that Eusebius did not extend his condemnation (*Life of Constantine*, iii, 49) to the symbolic representations. Again according to Eusebius (*History of the Church*, vii, 18), an image of Christ erected at Paneas must have reflected pagan custom; this was probably an image of a pagan deity which had been brought into relation with the Saviour through a local Christian legend. References to images of Christ in later literature, and in the 6th century to the adoration of such images, are always to be identified with figures in relief; images in the round were strongly repudiated, both by the Christian polemicists and in practice. Thus, aside from a few lost pagan images known from literary sources and some Christian statuettes, such as the *Good Shepherd* and the *Christ as Teacher* (III, PL. 304), the history of late-antique sculpture in the round becomes essentially that of the portrait sculpture of the era.

Portraiture. During the first three centuries of the Empire, still following in the tradition of Hellenistic art, the Roman portrait always — despite the variety of styles — found its point of departure in the individual personality. The likeness of the subject was strongly individualized, "alive." About the year 300, however, this situation was radically transformed.

The beginnings of the new tendencies may be discerned in that remarkable portraiture, so full of restlessness and movement, which flourished about the mid-3d century. This art may be appraised in imperial portraits, particularly those of Philip the Arabian and Decius, in private portraits that may be linked with these, and in the portrait (known through four replicas) of a philosopher, in all likehood to be identified with Plotinus. All these portraits — and the same is true of female subjects — were designed both to reproduce exactly the features of a particular physiognomy and to convey the very pulse of life, the mutations of expression governed by the nervous facial muscles and the inner gleam of personality. The effect of movement, in the turning of a head for instance, is achieved through the shaping of the face. A characteristic method is an asymmetrical construction, emphasized in the musculature of the forehead and mouth through undulating furrows and folds of flesh. Clearly the artist seeks to capture a physiognomic state subject to instant change, a fleet expression stressed by a certain indeterminacy in the sculptural forms. As an example, the forehead of the portrait of Decius is furrowed by deep, yet draftsmanlike incisions of the chisel; the resulting forms are not facial furrows themselves but are those created by the play of light bringing tremulous shadows to them. The hair and beard are formed in a similar manner — not a precision chiseling of the forms of individual locks but a sketch consisting of scratches and points, so that the illusion of a mass of hair is obtained only at a certain distance through the play of light.

These works mark the high point of the major trend in the art of the 3d century, tendencies that were eventually to change the configuration of the antique tradition. About 250–70 this trend was opposed by another, justly termed the "Gallienic renaissance," which tended to conserve the classical integrity of the sculptural forms from such illusionistic disintegration. The two main types of Gallienus portraits serve as the basis for an examination of the sculptural mode during his reign (253–68): the youthful Gallienus depicted in the late 250s and the older Gallienus of the 260s. The first type clearly shows the reaction to the earlier impressionistic portraiture. The restless vitality of the skin surface and musculature has subsided, facial asymmetry yields to a firmly balanced construction, the evanescence of expression is stabilized with a more organic articulation, and the hair and beard are more copious and flowing, with the single components strongly defined. In this art there is revealed a classicizing reaction that was deeply rooted in the whole Gallienic interlude. This taste had its first great exponent in the person of the Emperor, a philhellene and friend of Plotinus who had himself elected an Athenian archon and initiated into the Eleusinian mysteries. In the transition to the portraits of the older Gallienus there occurs a reduction of the organic sculptural form, a change in which the head becomes more massive and simplified, the surface loses the subtle delineation of details, and the hair becomes much longer and is articulated in a single compact mass, with individual locks modeled only lightly on the surface. This treatment is in strong contrast to the loose, deeply chased mass of hair and beard typical in Antonine and Severan portraits, with which those of Gallienus have on occasion been confused. A somewhat ornamental or schematic tendency also characterizes the late Gallienic phase of late-antique portraiture, for instance, in the symmetric lines of the forehead, in the arrangement of the locks, parted in the middle, and in the forms composing the beard.

After this brief Gallienic episode, the artists rapidly returned to the impressionistic illusionism that was the most pronounced trend in the 3d century, and during the last three decades of the century a curious, almost complete dissolution of the traditional portrait forms came about. Representative of this development are two male heads datable about the turn of the century (Naples, Mus. Naz.; Copenhagen, Ny Carlsberg Glyptotek). The almost pained disquiet of the expressions, an agitation curiously restricted to certain parts of the freely asymmetrical faces, is particularly evident in the musculature of the forehead. These details do not proceed from an organic whole; rather, the physiognomy of the figures has been fragmented, and the tense play of features has been fixed in spasms and convulsions. These heads may be compared with the disintegrated compositions typical of the contemporary reliefs, in which the gradual dissolution of form perhaps reflects the anarchic situation found in other aspects of the life of the time, both spiritual and material.

This return to the fragmented, impressionistic style was accompanied, however, by the first signs of another strain of portraiture favoring the compact mass. Four portrait heads dating from about A.D. 300, from both the Roman and the Greek sectors of the Empire, evidence this blocklike simplification of organic form. Within this compact block the individual features became less significant, and in place of deeper, more naturalistic modeling they constituted merely a surface layer. Seen in the effigies on coins, this new portraiture first appeared in the eastern part of the Empire, in coinage from Nicomedia, Kyzikos, Antiochia, and Alexandria. This style soon became common in all imperial provinces, though the West Roman and, even more so, the local styles of Greek portraits generally conserved more of the traditional organic structure.

Characteristic of the development during the following two decades is a tendency to give the head a more regular, conventional form, stereometric in character, as evidenced by the forceful porphyry of an emperor in Cairo, in which the structure of the head and the facial features are marked out in simple flat and curved surfaces of great breadth and clarity, while individual folds, furrows, and locks of hair were rigorously symmetrical in relation to the vertical axis of the face. The hair and beard are schematically rendered with points and incised lines. As may also be seen in relief figures, this evolves into an abstract system for organizing the forms mechanically, gradually superseding the organic basis of modeling.

After those of Gallienus, there is no longer a continuous series of imperial portraits that can be securely identified and dated to provide a comparative base for the history of art. Moreover, the formerly widespread practice of making replicas and copies of notable portraits and types became much rarer in the post-Gallienic period, thereby lessening the effectiveness of the method used to establish an iconography for the earlier Roman emperors, that is, through comparison of numerous replicas. There are other useful criteria, however, such as the study of imperial insignia, the specialized use of porphyry, and the presence of certain attributes or colossal dimensions, indicating an emperor portrait. Through these means a whole series of imperial portraits can be identified from the Tetrarchic era (broadly, ca. 285–312). Sure portraits of Diocletian, Maximian, Galerius, and Constantius Chlorus are found among the famous porphyry groups of the Vatican Library (VII, PL. 371) and S. Marco in Venice (PL. 56). Portraits in a provincial mode are those of Diocletian and his wife Prisca on a frieze in the imperial mausoleum of Spalato. To these verified works and the previously mentioned porphyry portraits may be added two double herms in Salona, also provincial in style, which undoubtedly reproduce the features of the emperors of the early Tetrarchic period. In all likelihood, the Cairo bust represents Licinius. This whole group of works exemplifies the Eastern taste in Tetrarchic portraiture, affirmed in some instances by definite Eastern provenance and also by the use of porphyry for the masterworks of the era. The simplified heads and the schematic, ornamental detail correspond to the images on Eastern coins of this time. To this general taste of the epoch, some reliefs on the Arch of Galerius in Salonika may also be ascribed (PL. 49).

Of the more organic West Roman portraits of the Tetrarchic period, one has survived in two replicas. This represents an emperor who, as comparison with effigies on coins suggests, may be Constantius Chlorus. (The older identification with Maximinus Thrax must be rejected for reasons of style.) Three closely related portraits, one larger than life-sized, probably reproduce the emperor Maxentius. A togaed statue of a sacrificing emperor in the Villa Doria-Pamphili, Rome, in all likelihood portrays Diocletian. Almost certainly another portrait of this emperor is a head in Sabratha, Tripoli; also referable to Diocletian is a double herm combining a Cronus-Saturn figure and a mortal. The so-called "Diocletian" of the Ny Carlsberg Glyptotek, Copenhagen, must be excluded from the accepted catalogue of Diocletian portraits.

Stylistically, the numerous Tetrarchic portrait sculptures may be divided into two broad groups: one of West Roman, the other of Eastern origin. The West Roman group is in turn divided into two subgroups. The early and proto-Tetrarchic portraits are still characterized by asymmetrical structure and agitated, almost convulsive facial muscles, lending a peculiar aspect that might well be termed schizophrenic and suggesting pain or inner conflict. The late Tetrarchic examples present a calmer expression and more stable forms, along with a greatly attenuated symmetry. The first of these subgroups roughly coincides with the Diocletian tetrarchate (292–305), and the second corresponds to the post-Diocletian tetrarchate (305–12). A number of West Roman portraits related to the first subgroup, and constituting a later reaction to the Gallienic style, also exhibit strong links with the illusionistic or impressionist pre-Gallienic tradition of the 240s. Of the emperors who came after Gallienus and before the Tetrarchy, Probus is represented by a colossal portrait in the Capitoline Museum and probably also by two heads of gilded bronze in Brescia (Mus. Romano). The likeness of Claudius Gothicus is perhaps to be identified in a relief depicting a sacrifice, in the Museo Nazionale Romano, and that of Carinus in a colossal head in the Palazzo dei Conservatori.

With these more or less datable West Roman works as a point of departure, a series of portraits of Eastern provenance — notwithstanding their more plastic style, evident especially in the rendering of the hair — can be attributed to the period from Gallienus to Constantine. A head in Athens (Nat. Mus.) and another in Istanbul (PL. 48), from Nicomedia, probably portray Diocletian or his imperial portrait type. Of particular interest is a group of heads of philosophers that ranges from the Gallienic phase into the 4th century; outstanding among these is a portrait (preserved in five replicas), dating from the first decades of the 4th century, which almost certainly represents Iamblichus, the major philosopher of that era.

Finally, comparison of a typical West Roman work, such as the statue of Diocletian in the Villa Doria-Pamphili, with representative Eastern-inspired works, such as the imperial groups of S. Marco and the Vatican Library, confirms that the stylistic contrast between East and West observed in portrait heads extends to the figure style as a whole. In contrast to the emphasis on undifferentiated mass in the Eastern works, which show a lack of sensitivity to ideal proportion, the Western work has preserved more of the proportions, the organic structure and symmetry, and the richly carved drapery of the classical tradition of Greco-Roman statuary. The abstraction and monolithic rigidity of this Eastern style are nonnaturalistic qualities more suggestive of medieval than of classical sculpture.

The beginning of the Constantinian period witnesses the disappearance of the impressionist tendency of the 3d century, with its manipulation of light, asymmetry, and flickering musculature and epidermis. The agitated folds and furrows become resolved in simplified, regular features that are masklike in expression. The gaze no longer seems uncertain but instead is as if fixed upon a distant object. Comparing a head of the Tetrarchic period with the famous Lateran portrait of Dogmatius, placed by inscription within the Constantinian period, one notes that, even though the general aspect of the pre-Constantinian head type with short hair and close-cropped beard has been preserved, there is clear indication of the gradual crystallization of form achieved during the age of Constantine. The whole is stereometrically simplified, and the individual elements are symmetrically ordered around the median axis of the face. The area covered by the short hair is bounded by carefully described contours, with the widow's peak over the forehead accenting the central axis. The lines of the brow undulate in easy, parallel curves. The transcendent gaze of this "mask of the spirit" — the eyes framed and highlighted by concentric curves — is the most significant characteristic of the portrait sculpture of the epoch. In this intense, fixed look there is perhaps a foretaste of the Byzantine icon.

As vital, organic structure gives way to canonical regularity, so the strongly individual portrait yields to the conventional type. Each of the emperors of the Vatican porphyry pairs is based on the same model, the image of the emperor-god. Subsequently, however, it was not this deified ruler figure from which the definitive hieratic type was derived but rather that of the sovereign Constantine, the heir of the Tetrarchy. In his reign and thereafter the images of Constantine created the *typos hieros* of the epoch, exemplified by portraits such as the colossal head of Constantine (PL. 53) formerly belonging to the huge enthroned statue in the Basilica of Maxentius or of Constantine. This imposing statue was originally situated on the main axis of the basilica; in its expression of divine majesty, it presents all the qualities of hieratic frontality, impassiveness, and stereometric form previously described as characteristic of the portraiture of the time.

This fixed gaze of the great eyes in such portraits, this remote stare into infinite space, is arresting and of heightened intensity, truly an attempt to project the "mirror of the soul." In order to grasp the significance of this gaze to contemporaries, one should recall the importance attached to the eye in the pursuit of knowledge and understanding by the people of antiquity, for whom the coexistence of man with divinity is realized in a visual symphysis, in a "connaturality" between the viewer and the being who is seen. In an identification of this type, man is exalted beyond his human limitations and participates in divine essence and actions, thereby acquiring superhuman powers. He is raised up to God and becomes "holy" himself. This inspired contemplation which fills a man with daemonic force is the quality with which late-antique artists sought to endow the visages of god-emperors, particularly through the accentuated concentric curves of the lids and brows. Ineffably calm and removed from time, the images have a quality of eternal repose. A suggestion of this sacred prototype also appears in nonofficial portraits: the fixed gaze of the visionary provides the formula for a purely spiritual idealization, one which is "pneumatic," in contrast to the idealization of physical beauty in the classical tradition.

Thus, with the portrait of Constantine there arose a durable imperial symbol, an iconographic formula for expressing divine kingship which posterity was to rework and vary but which, to some degree, was unfailingly present in late-antique representations of emperors. Just as the Constantinian order created the basis for the Byzantine state, so Constantinian taste, as a reflection of this organization, furnished the archetype of the late-antique and medieval imperial likenesses.

It is of passing significance that the new arrangement of the hair in the portraits of Constantine created a genuine "state coiffure" for the emperors, little subject to the usual changes of fashion. Although this coiffure was on occasion modified in details, its basic formula remained unchanged for centuries; it is related of the Eastern emperor Heraclius (610–41) that in preparing himself to rule he had his hair and beard cut according to this imperial mode (Cedrenus, Bonn ed., I, p. 714).

It is possible to assemble a catalogue of portraits which, from the time of Constantine, includes the likenesses of his sons and of the emperors of the second half of the 4th century and ends with a series of unidentified portraits that for stylistic reasons should be assigned to the 5th century. As the individual physical characteristics gradually disappear, the conventional schema of majesty, of a ritual personality, emerges like a mask in the facial features. A colossal head in the entrance hall of the Vatican Museums and a colossal bronze in the National Museum, Athens, attest to the persistence of this imperial type into the early Middle Ages. The historian Ammianus Marcellinus (xvi, 10) gave a notable description of Constantius II's solemn entry into Rome: "He gazed fixedly forward as if wearing an iron collar around the neck, turning his head neither to right nor to left. He was not as a living man, but the icon of a man." This hieratic imperial style, which, as an expression of divine majesty, gave its cast to portraits, palaces, and life in general during the era, came down via Byzantium to imperial Russia. A contemporary of Czar Alexander III described him in words surprisingly similar to those of Ammianus: "He looked out fixedly, directly forward, and his features were as still as those of a statue — a man of stone, a personification of power and destiny."

The history of portrait sculpture in the time of Constantine and his sons may be divided into an earlier phase, extending from 312 to 324, and a later period encompassing the era of world dominion of Constantine and his sons, firmly established after the victory over Licinius and the foundation of the new capital on the Bosporus (324–61).

The point of departure for the first period is provided by the portraits on the Arch of Constantine: specifically, the heads reworked in 312–15, including those on the medallions from the time of Hadrian and the two heads on the Trajanic reliefs placed within the main opening, and also a very fragmentary head in one of the Constantinian friezes, depicting his seige of Verona. This last-named and the two reworked Trajanic heads portray Constantine; those of the Hadrianic medallions, paired images of Constantine and Licinius representing the concept of imperial concord ("Fit amicitia, utriusque imagines simul locantur"; Lactantius, *De mortibus persecutorum*, XLIII, 3). As on the coins of the time, the effigy of Licinius is still of the Tetrarchic type, with short hair and beard. The portraits of Constantine — "turbator et novator omnium rerum" — reveal a radically new type, however: beardless, with pronounced features and thick locks of hair. This contrast between the two types, which has been the source of divergent opinions as to the dating of these imperial likenesses, is characteristic of the portraiture of the time and, for example, is found in all the anonymous heads in the historical friezes of the Arch of Constantine.

A group of colossal Roman statues dated about 320, among which are the figures of Constantine and Constantine II (X, PL. 145) presently on the balustrade of the Capitoline and the figure of Constantine in the atrium of St. John Lateran (PL. 50), substantiates a marked traditionalist and classicist constraint, which seems to revert to the taste of the Augustan age, both in Rome and throughout the Empire during the 4th century. All these statues are related to a conventional type: the emperor as an armed military commander. The proportions are somewhat distorted, with the robust body strongly emphasized and the head too small. The balance of the figure does not have the classic freedom, and the contours of the face are peculiarly sharp and linear.

In coin effigies the Tetrarchic type dominated in the East until about 324, whereas in the West the Constantinian type was predominant. There remained the distinction between the simplified and compact portrait of the East and the more individualized and naturalistic one typical of the West. In the late Constantinian period — that is, after 324 — the Constantinian type spread throughout the Empire, gradually leveling regional divergences of custom and taste, and in the process Eastern and Western elements interpenetrated. The Roman and Western type of Constantine invaded the East, just as Latin supplanted Greek as the official language of the East, with the founding of the "New Rome" on the Bosporus. The most significant outward indication of this development was the fact that Constantine began to exhibit a diadem and a longer, more sophisticated hair style in his images about the time of this assertion of his universal monarchy and the consolidation of the Empire.

A series of monumental portraits in this style forms a relatively cohesive group, a characteristic member of which is the above-mentioned colossal head of Constantine from the Basilica of Maxentius or of Constantine. The identification of this fragmented colossus with the statue of Constantine with the cross erected immediately after his entry into Rome (312), of which Eusebius speaks, does not seem compatible with the Constantinian iconography that is better documented, such as the reliefs on the Arch of Constantine, nor with their religious significance, namely, the motif of Sol Invictus. Very similar to this head is the colossal bronze portrait of the Palazzo dei Conservatori, which may well be a late head of Constantine, although it is customarily identified with one of his sons (PL. 51). An imperial bust in the Musée Lapidaire, Vienne (Isère), probably represents the Gallic usurper Magnentius, and thus it may be dated 350–53. A reflection of the colossal gilt statue of Constantine-Sol, a celebrated work which was erected on a porphyry column in his Forum in Constantinople and which became the object of general veneration, is quite likely found in a bronze statuette from Jutland (Copenhagen, Nationalmus.), depicting an emperor crowned with rays of the sun. The face and the hair style are clearly Constantinian, and the jewel placed at the center of the crown of rays also seems an appropriate token for an emperor. The right hand was raised in the magical gesture of the Sun-Emperor, while the left bore the globe, corresponding exactly to the famous image of the rising sun on a medallion of the Arch of Constantine.

Representations of the emperor with attributes such as the thunderbolt or the aureole, in many received directly from the hand of a god, were intended to affirm his divine ordination. In late-antique narrative reliefs and on coins the supreme god, be it Juipter or Sol, appears as the supernatural escort (*comes Augusti*) and inspiration of the deified emperor, oftentimes delivering to him the insignia of might and victory. Besides being honorific effigies of an emperor, these portrayals revive the concept of the emperor as divinely sanctioned intermediary between the gods and mortals.

After the conversion of Constantine, the supernatural association of Christ with the earthly ruler supersedes that between the emperor and the antique gods. The new link with Christ was conveyed by images that frequently bore striking resemblance to the pagan treatments of this theme. Typical presentations include: the Holy Spirit, in the form of a dove, hovering above the emperor and giving him divine inspiration; Christ or angels arraying the ruler with imperial insignia as the vicar of Christ in the world empire; the emperor being crowned victor in the name of Christ, either by Christ Himself or by angels. A corresponding expression of the theme is found also in the literature of the time, where the emperor of the early Middle Ages is referred to as "wreathed" or "crowned by God." The inscription on the base of the column statue of Phocas in the Forum Romanum (A.D. 608) designates Phocas "the eternal emperor crowned by God," thereby asserting the divine right and the presence of a supreme, eternal order within the temporal power.

To the Constantinian and post-Constantinian period may also be assigned a series of female portraits, both on grounds of general style and of coiffure. The female coiffure in the Tetrarchic sculpture is distinguished by having the hair drawn back to the nape of the neck in a flat plait, which is then pinned to the top of the head and above the forehead, where it stands up as if it were a diadem. Also characteristic are the side strands of hair at the neck, which are free of the plaits and which are gathered and pressed onto the nape of the neck almost like a roundel at the back of a battle helmet. Nor is this necessarily a chance comparison, for these were the times of the soldier emperors. Such a hair style appears on the coins of Severina, wife of Aurelian; Magna Urbica, wife of Carinus; and Valeria, daughter of Diocletian and wife of Galerius. Its use continued until the time of Constantine, when it was worn by Fausta (d. 326), wife of Constantine, and by his mother Helena. A variant of this style, about the turn of the century, was the coiffure in which the wide plait was divided and arranged atop the head like a crown or turban. These two hair styles were typical of the late-antique era and subsequently became the "state coiffure" of the empresses; though on occasion altered in particulars, like the official male hair style they retained their fundamental shape. In rare instances, there are female adaptations of the emperor's own hair style.

A place of prime importance among the female figures with turban coiffures is given to a seated statue that has survived through several replicas (Mus. Cap.; Uffizi), a subject that has been rightly identified with Helena, the mother of Constantine. In this figure the late-antique taste in drapery is revealed by a certain hardness in the *ductus* of the lines and a rather monotonous composition, especially in the cornucopia-shaped folds along the lower border of the *apoptygma*. Whereas these statues are close enough to classic models to be confused with them, another standing female figure (Ostia Antica, Mus. Ostiense) that reproduces a classic type, namely, the so-called "Pudicitia," reveals the late-antique touch much more strongly. The figure has completely lost its classic sculptural volume, the proportions are changed, the balance seems unsteady, and the rendering of the folds is quite harsh at the corners. Yet another female portrait of the imperial type, one that is markedly Constantinian, is located in Como (Mus. Civ.).

The last descendant of the Constantinian dynasty, Julian the Apostate, is represented by two datable statues in the Louvre that have wrongly been stigmatized as forgeries (PL. 57). The emperor-philosopher is shown according to the traditional scheme for philosophers, with a long beard, wearing the pallium, and carrying a rotulus in his left hand — a balanced, weighty figure in the classical spirit, belonging to the same line as the statue of Helena and the three imperial figures of the Lateran and the Capitoline. As shown by the sculpture on sarcophagi, this classicizing current opposed to the characteristic late-antique taste achieved its highest level in the 350s and 360s and was in vogue throughout the Valentinian-Theodosian period. This sculptural tendency parallels literary and religious attempts to restore paganism, which was still strongly supported by the senatorial class of Rome.

Important criteria for the determination of the Theodosian portrait may be derived from the reliefs on the base of the obelisk of Theodosius in Constantinople (PL. 57; II, PL. 467; VII, PL. 265), erected in the Hippodrome in 390. When compared with the reliefs on the Arch of Constantine, the Theodosian character of the sculpture on this base emerges clearly: the svelte, elongated proportions and the aristocratic, relaxed attitudes contrast with the rough, stocky, and rigid figures on the Constantinian monument. The soft, flowing drapery and the roundness in the modeling of the Theodosian examples is opposed to the harder, more angular forms of the Constantinian period. Consequently the Theodosian heads have a gentler, smoother, and less bony aspect; they have more elegant features and a free disposition of the abundant locks of hair. A slight smile diffuses a mood of affable grace over the faces of the Theodosian period, in contrast to the severity of the Constantinian ones; there breathes in the former expression a sense of ease and a relaxation of the human spirit, perhaps the visual realization of the renewed classicism characterizing the period from Julian through Theodosius. While the Constantinian form of the hair and the absence of the beard continue, without exception, in the relief images of the emperor as well, new forms develop in the subsidiary figures; in some the beard reappears and another layer of tresses frequently is displayed over the forehead and temples. Barbarian *foederati*, for example, have a distinctive coiffure that is shown on a series of herms in Trier and on a grave decoration in Bulgaria.

A group of portrait statues, closely related stylistically, belong to the Theodosian period: the togaed statue of Valentinian II from Aphrodisias (Istanbul, Archaeol. Mus.); a colossal head, splendidly preserved, in Rome (Gall. Borghese); a small cuirassed bust in Lyons (Mus. B. A.), which probably represents Maximus, the late-4th-century Gallic competitor of Theodosius; and a head in Trier, perhaps a portrait of Gratian, who had his capital there. Two other togaed statues in Rome (Pal. dei Conservatori) are linked with this group; the flat, arid rendering of their garments characterizes Roman in contrast to Greek work of the epoch, exemplified by a statuette of an empress from Cyprus that has been identified with Theodosius' consort Aelia Flacilla (PL. 57).

This Theodosian ambient seems to have provided the starting point for the creation of an unusual group of portraits, apparently executed sometime after A.D. 400, that is, during the time of Arcadius and Honorius. The oval form of the faces acquires an almost Gothic slenderness and is as smooth as an egg; the aquiline noses are long and thin, the eyes narrow and quasi-oblique, the fine lips faintly smiling, the chins elongated, and the hair indicated with shallow, sharp lines. In some instances there is an unobtrusive beard. The pronounced arc of hair in the tradition of Constantinian portraiture is broken up into pointed locks around the forehead; or else, as previously mentioned, the coiffure becomes crownlike, a form that was increasingly common during the 5th century. The finest examples of this group are a man and wife in Salonika (Archaeol. Mus.), and a male portrait in Rome (Mus. Naz. Romano) and another in Munich (Glyptothek).

The reliefs of the 5th century — the most extensive and useful basis available for continuing a chronology of portraiture during this period, since it lacks a sequence of surely identifiable emperor portraits — reveal an ever-increasing flatness and linearity, a rigidity and hardness in the treatment of forms, as evidenced in the ivory diptychs. The diptychs ascribed to the first half of the 5th century by R. Delbrück, for example, the so-called "Patricius" in the Cathedral of Novara (Bib. Capitolare), differ from preceding ones dated about 400 in the marked regression of sculptural volume and in the lack of rhythmic ponderance and harmony in their angular figures. At the same time, however, there is a new realism in portrait heads other than idealized emperors and saints. The hair takes the loose form of natural locks or else the crownlike coiffure, and as during the Tetrarchic period, the short beard becomes a general feature. The official Constantinian type, limited to probable portraits of emperors, gives way to a more sober, naturalistic characterization, in contrast to the rather academic classicism of the preceding period — perhaps indicating the recession of the pagan reaction.

These diptych portraits of the first half of the 5th century are related to a group of Eastern and Western portrait sculptures, the most important of which are the "magistrate" figures found at Aphrodisias (PL. 59; II, PL. 465), a togaed statue in Ostia, and two heads in Aquileia. All these likenesses of private individuals reveal a crude realism, owing in part to an emphasis on the irregular — and even the ugly — in facial features and in part to a lugubrious, almost exasperated expression. If these are compared with the portraits among the reliefs on the Theodosian base in Constantinople, the change is immediately apparent: a new human type, anguished and introverted, far removed from the classically beautiful form and its surroundings, has replaced the calm, relaxed humanity of the pedestal figures. Therefore it is reasonable to assume a certain chronological advance from the Theodosian age, probably into the second or third decade of the 5th century.

A clear typological relationship with this last group of works is revealed by a series of unusual portrait sculptures from Italy, Greece, and Asia Minor, which in style and technique, as well as in the forms of beard and hair, seem to form a homogeneous group. One of these portraits has survived in two copies, one of which, a head larger than life size with a long beard and the crownlike hair, is at Ostia. The expression is an ecstatic, uplifted gaze, doubtless a magnate of the era represented as *homo spiritualis*. Numerous other portraits of the time, including one at Ephesus, have the same fanatical, introspective aspect. The stereotyped spirituality of the expression, produced by the severe symmetry, the accentuated fixity of the gaze, and the upturned lines of the forehead, prefigures Byzantine icons. The head, both in frontal and profile views, is inscribed within a rectangle and reduced to an almost prismatic form. The orthogonal emphasis of the face is also recorded in contemporaneous literary descriptions of the rectangular facial type of the Neoplatonic philosopher Isidorus in the guise of Hermes Logeios. The relationship of these heads to those known to be from the beginning of the 5th century is again like that of the diptychs of the second half of the century (e.g., the Boethius diptych, A.D. 487) to those of the first half. The suggestion of mass in the later diptychs recedes even further, and the flattened figures become rigid as tree trunks. On the basis of this similarity, the sculpture in this rectilinear mode may also be attributed to the second half of the 5th century.

The formal shift observable in these works, from the Aphrodisian magistrates through the Aquileia heads to the portrait of Ephesus, is characterized by progressive simplification of organic form and concentration on the elements of spiritual expression, notably the eyes. This transformation appears all the more clearly inasmuch as the basic physiognomic type remains unaltered: long, thin, and ascetic face; narrow, tightly shut mouth surrounded by sharp lines; similar hair and beard forms. But organic structure gives way to a masklike formula for the spiritual life. The works under discussion enable one to follow the process by which the late-antique Greco-Roman portrait — the "Eugenius," for instance (PL. 59) — ultimately evolves into the Byzantine icon. The gradual growth of this spiritual stereotype is perhaps most clearly presented in the conventionalizing of the eyes and in the pronounced, schematic lines of the forehead. The intimate connection obvious between the Ephesus head and an icon of the early Middle Ages, such as that of the Bawit bishop, makes further comment superfluous.

Whereas in the 4th century the most extended series of portraits was that of the emperors, the works surely attributable to the 5th century do not include a single definite imperial portrait. This fact should not, however, encourage the false conclusion that the central theme of Roman portraiture, the imperial image, had disappeared. Rather, it signifies that post-Constantinian imperial portraiture constituted a wholly distinct category and that private portraits departed increasingly from the imperial type; consequently, portraits of individuals from this period are of little use in evaluating official images.

Because they are in poor accord with the free classicism distinguishing the latter part of the 4th century, certain heads of the Constantinian *typos hieros*, reduced to masklike simplicity, such as the so-called "Valens" of the Uffizi or that of Valentinian I in the Ny Carlsberg Glyptotek, are difficult to place within the development ranging from the Julian statues of the Louvre to that of Valentinian II in Constantinople and quite likely are not earlier than two emperor portraits in Berlin that may have been rightly identified as Arcadius and Honorius. The so-called "Honorius" of the Louvre (PL. 58) is an imperial portrait of later date; the delineation of the eyebrows and the slant eyes relate it to private portraits from the second half of the 5th century. In the Colossus of Barletta (PL. 60), the mask of the emperor yields to typical features of the late or mid-5th century, which would seem to support its identification with Marcian (450–57). The so-called "Eugenius" of the Louvre (PL. 59), with features also suggesting a date well into the 5th century, has perhaps been correctly linked with Theodosius II (408–50). An imperial portrait in the Castello Sforzesco in Milan, a compelling figure in which one would like to recognize the magnificent Theodora, discloses instead a stylization of the eyes and mouth that is closest to portraits of the second half of the 5th century.

The same distance existing between the imperial portrait and that of a private citizen also exists between the images of saints and those of ordinary mortals. The concept "beauteous as an envoy of God" is valid for the Christian world as well as for the pagan; the saint, too, becomes a *typos hieros*. Neoplatonic theosophs and Christian saints are distinguished from common men by means of "angelic" beauty, the reflection of divine qualities revealing a God-sent man. Therefore, the word "charis" for the Christian author has the double significance of beauty and supernatural grace; the visible beauty reflects the divine grace. In the same way, the emperor inspired by God partakes of celestial beauty: he is "dis simillimus princeps," and his individuality is hidden behind an ideal type. The human qualities in the portrait of an emperor or a saint are concealed behind an elevated mask, representing more sublime and heroic qualities than those of other individuals — just as the ancient stage masks conveyed qualities more sublime and essential than did the faces of the actors hidden behind them.

The common man, however, as he is seen in the portraits of the 5th century, and later in those of the early Middle Ages, is characterized as a natural being set apart from any sacred type, with his human failings, abnormalities, weaknesses, and ultimately his ugliness and misery. In ex-votos from the 5th to 8th century (e.g., mosaics in Salonika; frescoes in S. Maria Antiqua, Rome) the representation of human dedicants flanked by their celestial protectors clearly reveals the dualism between holy, eternal beauty and the imperfection of the natural world. Literary sources testify that throughout the 4th, 5th, and 6th centuries portrait statues continued to be erected publicly in honor both of emperors and of private citizens. Large equestrian images were erected in Constantinople as late as the time of Justinian, but many of these may have been earlier statues adapted or reworked. The equestrian statue of Theodoric the Great that Charlemagne took from Ravenna to Aachen probably belonged to this East Roman tradition. A series of headless statues, once portraits of individuals, discloses the same retreat from organic structure evidenced in the portrait heads of the 5th century. Details are compressed into a compact block, and the folds of the drapery fall vertically as if governed by a plumb line. An example of this nonorganic form is a togaed figure in the Selçuk Museum (Ephesus), which undoubtedly had a head of the same style described in the last portrait group. A *non plus ultra* of blocklike construction and severe linearity is found in certain statues from Corinth and Megara, some of which must be as late as the 6th century.

Yet another group of portrait heads evidences the continuation of late-antique portrait sculpture beyond the 5th century and into the early Middle Ages. The group — including three curious images of an empress or an Ostrogothic queen (PL. 59), some fragmentary male heads, and an emperor portrait — is characterized by extremely rounded faces with protuberant eyes, having prominent, concave pupils of hemispherical form, and by the softness of the fine mouth, which sometimes assumes a smile. These and other related examples probably date from the end of the 5th and first half of the 6th century. Of uncertain date is a porphyry portrait of an emperor, wearing a diadem, in S. Marco; because of the flattened nose, it has been identified with Justinian II Rhinotmetos by Delbrück and thus dated about 700.

Relief. Although there are frequent lacunae in the sequence of dated historical reliefs, the existing works range through the mid-5th century, whereas dated and identifiable portrait sculptures of emperors beyond the 4th-century examples are not known. The chief types in this category are commemorative historical reliefs and sarcophagus decoration. The latter form can oftentimes be reasonably dated by stylistic reference to dated commemorative reliefs or portraiture. On this basis, reliefs may also furnish a varied estimate of the development of late-antique sculpture.

Of the Arch of Galerius in Salonika (PL. 49), there remain only two piers, covered on each face by four superimposed relief panels bearing scenes of Galerius's military expedition against Sassanian Persia in 297. Scenes of battle, allocution, and marching alternate with scenes of homage to the emperor, such as the *adventus Augusti*. These friezes have not yet received a fully convincing interpretation.

The Diocletian decennial base in the Roman Forum (PL. 49) probably dates from the year 303. On the front are two Victories bearing a votive shield with the inscription recording the *decennalia*. The other faces display three related reliefs. The middle relief represents an imperial sacrifice, toward which a sacrificial procession advances from the left relief, while from the right there approaches a file of representatives of the senate and the army. This base once belonged to an honorific column topped with an imperial statue; along with four other similar units it formed a monument to the Tetrarchs, erected behind the Rostra in the Forum Romanum. The whole can be reconstructed on the basis of a Renaissance description of these socles and the depiction of the original monument in a relief on the Arch of Constantine. Four columns bearing statues of the Tetrarchic rulers were grouped around an image of Jupiter.

The Arch of Constantine in Rome, dated between 312 and 315, is the oldest Roman monument in which spoils were extensively used, for a large part of the architectural and sculptural ornament came from earlier monuments. Attention here will be centered on the late-antique portions, that is, those carved specifically for the arch. On the front of each of the eight column bases is a Victory; on two side faces are triumphal processions, including soldiers with standards, the *dei militares*, Victory and Sol Invictus, barbarian prisoners, and sometimes the captive families near a trophy. On the intrados of the lateral arches are headless busts of emperors and one of Sol Invictus, Constantine's protector. Eight rectangular fields above the two lateral arches contain reclining river gods; in the four corners of the central intrados are winged Victories and genii of the seasons. Among the various medallions, those of the short sides are late-antique: one shows the rising Sol Invictus, the other the setting moon. The most important part of the late-antique relief decoration is the historical frieze that, in six large sections and four smaller ones, girds the arch. In a chronological presentation are shown the departure of Constantine's army in the war against Maxentius (*profectio*), the siege of Susa, the Battle of Milvian Bridge (VII, PL. 265), Constantine's entry into Rome, his allocution at the Rostra of the Forum (*oratio*), and his largesse to the Roman people (*liberalitas*; PL. 54). In reliefs taken from earlier monuments, the heads of emperors were transformed into those of the reigning sovereigns Constantine and Licinius, and the spoils were thereby fitted to the contemporaneous situation.

The porphyry base relief of the Column of Constantine in the Constantinian forum of Constantinople (A.D. 328), which originally bore the gilded colossal statue of Constantine-Sol, is known through Melchior Lorch's drawing of 1561. An *imago clipeata* of Constantine is flanked by two Victories, who escort young men offering gifts to a female personification (Rome or Constantinople) beneath the clipeus of the emperor. At the tips of the wings are an Eastern barbarian and a German.

The reliefs of the base of the Egyptian obelisk set up by Theodosius in the Hippodrome of Constantinople date from about 390. They are distributed over an upper, almost cubical block and a lower, narrower block. The four faces of the upper block exhibit public ceremonies in the Hippodrome (PL. 57; II, PL. 467; VII, PL. 265); Theodosius and Valentinian II, Arcadius and Honorius, all appear standing or seated on thrones in the imperial box high above the arena. Flanking this dominant central group are bodyguards, senators, and officials; and below are varied scenes of the crowded Hippodrome, among others, the offering of gifts to the rulers by barbarian peoples and the appearance of singers and dancers before a large crowd. The lower block bears reliefs on two sides — one a race scene, the other showing the erection of the obelisk. The historiated column of Theodosius in the Forum Tauri in Constantinople, only a few fragments of which have been preserved, is datable about 386–94. Of the same type as the columns of Trajan (VII, PL. 263; X, PL. 152) and Marcus Aurelius (VII, PL. 264) in Rome, it had a spiral relief depicting the battles and victories of the Emperor. Also of the same type was the historiated column of Arcadius, situated in his forum in Constantinople, probably begun in 401–02 and perhaps completed about 421. The reliefs of the spiral and of the base were reproduced several times in drawings (PL. 58), notably those of Freshfield of 1574. The relief of the base of the Column of Marcianus in Constantinople is dated 450–52. On the front of the base are two Victories holding a votive shield; the other faces display a Christogram within a corona.

Compared with the reliefs of the base of the Column of Theodosius of about 390, the fragments from the Column of Arcadius of about a decade later evidence a stiffening of form; the rounded folds of the earlier monument become sharper and the undulating curves less flexible. Even more pronounced in their hard, draftsmanly style are the reliefs of the Column of Marcianus and its base. The sculptural character of the Victories is due essentially to the vigorous contour enclosing the compact, simplified figures. A kindred linearity of form is found in a well-preserved relief Victory in Istanbul (Archaeol. Mus.).

The art of relief also bears witness to the change in taste that has been observed in sculpture in the round. The full volume of forms, the sense of bodily form contained by the garments, and the vitality and tension of musculature, that is, all the classical traits, declined steadily in reliefs as well. The organic development of form and movement was gradually lost, as were the details, in surfaces more and more smooth and generalized. The dark holes and grooves left by the drill, now favored over the chisel, evidence a decided modification in the technique of marbleworking, as true for architectural decoration as for sculpture. In contrast to the chisel, the drill lends itself more to incorporeal and illusionistic effects; rather than strongly molded forms it creates an active surface of luminous edges and shaded furrows. A parallel to the drill technique is provided by mosaic designs, executed about the same time, in which white lines were traced on a black ground; the important element was not so much the essential forms delineated but the changing reflections of light. Rome was the center of this style of mosaics and reliefs, as it was the arbiter in portraiture, and its influence radiated throughout the provinces of the Western Empire.

The history of 3d-century relief after the Severan age is divided into three main periods, roughly corresponding to the phases of development in portraiture. The reliefs of the decade 230–40 are characterized by a restlessness, a nervous excitement, that is revealed in the composition, the pose and movement of the figures, the drapery, and the form of the hair. Lions' and horses' manes, for example, are agitated like windblown flames, so much so that this has been dubbed the "style of the flaming mane." The expression of both men and animals is anguished and preoccupied. This mood of anxiety, and the sculptural manner used to convey it, corresponds to the preferred themes of the time: battles and lion hunts. Moreover, because the sarcophagus itself and the principal relief become taller, the ideal proportions of the classical frieze are no longer retained.

During the ensuing Gallienic renaissance the general artistic temper became quieter. In the sarcophagus reliefs, battles and lion hunts gave way to scenes with philosophers and muses, suggesting that it was not only military and hunting prowess which led a man successfully through life and beyond, but culture and education, the appreciation of art and philosophy as well. Hence the dead are oftentimes represented as philosophers, poets, or others occupied with some spiritual pursuit. A splendid example of this type is the sarcophagus of Plotinus in the Vatican Museums. The philosopher, flanked by two female figures, has a head that is closely related to the youthful Gallienus type in hair style and beard. Since this so-called "Plotinus" lacks the long beard with which the true philosopher is ordinarily depicted, it most likely portrays some dilettante of philosophy who chose to be presented in a traditional philosopher guise. Although their relaxed attitudes enounce the renewed classicism of this phase, the lack of truly sculptural volume and organic form in these figures reveals a lingering tendency toward the characteristic late-antique taste. The conventional frontality of the focal figure at the center and the symmetric deployment of the subsidiary personages about him is also typically late-antique.

The earliest Christian sarcophagi — those of La Gayolle, the Via Salaria (Vat. Mus.), and S. Maria Antiqua — are commonly ascribed to the time of Gallienus, on the basis of both style and iconography, for they partake of an artistic tendency seeking to regain the effect of full-bodied mass and, like contemporaneous pagan sarcophagi, they favor the philosopher type as their central motif. Their relaxed and balanced figures follow classical models and are freed from the unitary group and the background elements. As in pagan sarcophagi, the seated philosopher is shown in the act of teaching, holding a rotulus and wearing the pallium. The rotulus, an emblem of philosophy, in subsequent Christian versions of the theme becomes indicative of the Gospel, denoting Christianity as the true philosophy. Such a personification of Christian philosophy is found on several sarcophagi, where the figure is significantly placed between the orant and the Good Shepherd, that is, between the personified prayer for salvation and the symbolic identity of the Saviour. About 300 this image of Christian philosophy underwent a transformation and became that of the evangelical Christ, first encountered on a fragmentary polychrome sarcophagus (Mus. Naz. Romano) from the Tetrarchic period, showing the Sermon on the Mount. The Philosopher-Christ or "Christ as Teacher" — that is, Christ wearing the pallium, carrying a rotulus or book, and in the act of instructing (cf. III, PL. 304) — appeared at this time, going on to become a permanent form in the Christological repertory of later periods. During the persecutions and until the Edict of Milan, Christian sarcophagus reliefs carried a crypto-Christian language in order to avoid endangering the families of the deceased. Because of their accepted significance in pagan iconography, the good-shepherd figure with a lamb on his shoulders (*humanitas*) and the orant (*pietas*) were frequently adopted as motifs uncompromising to the well-being of the Christian faithful.

As has already been stated, the period from about 207 until 315 was the critical period of transition for ancient art: the classic tradition clearly began to disintegrate, and the late-antique style presaging the medieval tradition developed. The last three decades of the 3d century constituted a period of formal anarchy in the art of relief, as was true also of portraiture. Characteristic examples of this decomposition of form are a series of sarcophagi with Prometheus, Phaëthon, and circus and hunt scenes. The figures have lost their corporeal beauty and are no longer related to each other in natural groupings; interwoven and overlapping, they are no longer organic entities but instead form parts of confused clumps. Contours no longer flow softly and rhythmically but are rendered in angular and broken lines, so that there results a suggestion of disarticulated, marionettelike movements. Markedly disintegrated compositions present an eloquent parallel to the anarchy of the state and the violent social stresses of the time.

Contemporaneously with the collapse of the classical formal tradition, the great classical figural themes, now become seemingly empty and without valid content, also were increasingly abandoned. The reality of the epoch entered its visual arts, with a crowd of motifs drawn from ordinary life in the cities and the countryside. The sarcophagus figures are suffused with an ingenuous narrative *joie de vivre* that deals with life directly and tells simply what is happening, paying no heed to artistic conventions and tradition. The noble classic types are replaced by ordinary men of rough aspect, frequently ugly and grotesque. This widespread manifestation of Roman popular art was foreshadowed by the 3d-century development of strong realistic and anticlassical tendencies. Funerary art turned from the mythological themes of the hunt of Hippolytus or of Meleager to real hunts, with the deceased in the role of hunter; it turned from mythical battles to historical ones, with the deceased leading in the fight. In other words, there occurred a gradual Romanization of figural themes originally of Hellenistic character, as well as an association of them with the contemporary situation.

Even the earliest Roman art revealed a strain of popular realism that remained relatively untouched by classical influence; but such expressions had always been restricted to the most simple, utilitarian art forms and were not found, for example, in the craft of the funerary carver. The new situation characterizing the period under discussion (ca. 300) was that this popular inclination became the state style, which set the general tone and found expression on such official monuments as the Arch of Constantine. The reason for this lay in the great social changes effected during the 3d century, and then stabilized by Diocletian's sweeping reforms, through which a new class rose to power, a ruling class made up of elements that had always been inclined toward artistic expression conventionally termed "popular."

Similarly, in Christian art there took place in the post-Gallienic period an all-encompassing transformation, both in style and subject matter, marked by the appearance of a popular narrative character that sacrificed symbolism in favor of factual reality. The bucolic paradise that is the appropriate setting for the figures of the orant and the Good Shepherd became a vast natural landscape with scenes of agricultural and pastoral pursuits. Scenes of martyrdom were also rendered realistically (e.g., the sarcophagus lid of Aelia, Catacomb of Praetextatus). In place of the symbolic images of instruction and annunciation, there appeared miracle scenes from the New Testament and, of course, the figure of the historical Christ. And the personification of Christian philosophy was transformed into Christ preaching the Sermon on the Mount.

The new popular, narrative style had its center in Rome, and its chief use was on Roman sarcophagi. The sarcophagus workshops of Greece and Asia Minor declined greatly at this time, while in Trier and the surrounding area the art of relief came virtually to an end in the second half of the 3d century. When their own workshops were closed, Greek sculptors from Asia Minor, Syrians, and perhaps also Galatians came to Rome, where what survived of their tradition was blended into a lively popular art, fusing both Roman and Christian strains. In the course of the Constantinian age, pagan sarcophagi decreased sharply and Christian sarcophagi led the development thereafter.

With the "restoration of form" that set in about 300 — becoming more and more pronounced in the early decades of the 4th century — relief compositions which had been disintegrated in the preceding formal anarchy were again pulled together with a new mechanical order based on parallel placement and symmetry. In two famous reliefs on the Arch of Constantine, the *oratio* and the *liberalitas* (PL. 54), this new ordering was fully developed: the individual figures are not associated in free, natural groupings but are placed in coordinate rows. These files of individuals and the architecture framing them are rigorously subordinated to and symmetrically disposed about the figure of the Emperor, who dominates the center of the relief. The mechanical quality of this order is emphasized by the fact that the axes of the composition are coordinated with the orthogonal elements of the frame; thus, for example, the lines of the tops of the heads and of the feet coincide with or parallel the borders of the composition. At the two ends of the *oratio* each row of figures is closed into a rectangle that parallels the frame. Similarly, in individual figures such as the flying Victories with trophies, the strong influence exerted by the frame over the whole composition is evident. The upper part of their bodies usually follows a vertical axis, while the lower part conforms more closely to a horizontal; the trophy is bent into a curve that is concentric with the lower cornice of the arch. The weaker the organic integrity of the figures has become, the more adaptable are the single parts to the constraint of the frame. Among the numerous post-Constantinian examples of this total subordination of all the figural elements to such a system of coordinates, dictated by the frame, may be cited the reliefs of the Theodosian base of the obelisk in the Hippodrome of Constantinople. The mechanical ordering of form affects even the smallest details; in representations of hair or feathers, of water or stone, there is a schematic repetition of identical component motifs. This abstract regularity is most striking in the rendering of rocks, which are given uniform shapes resembling cakes of wax.

The centralized, symmetrical compositions evolved naturally from the stylistic development in Rome itself, which paralleled in expression but did not derive from a corresponding situation in Eastern art. Western liberation from the classical Greek tradition did signal a *rapprochement* with the East, where a similar transformation had occurred, but not a direct causal relationship.

An important group of early-4th-century sarcophagi is so closely related to the reliefs on the Arch of Constantine that it is reasonable to suppose they were produced by the same workshop. These are the so-called "frieze sarcophagi," which were the dominant form during the Constantinian period. The style has the following characteristic organization: a single register of reliefs or two superimposed registers; individual figures stiffly disposed with respect to each other; alignment of the heads paralleling the upper frame, and the feet paralleling the lower frame; pronounced verticality of the separate figures; and repetition of types almost as if mechanically reproduced in series. Even within this mechanical order, however, their narrative sense is lively. Scenes from the Old and New Testaments — including Adam and Eve after the Fall, the sacrifice of Isaac by Abraham, the healing of the paralytic, the resurrection of Lazarus, the denial of Peter — are treated with the spontaneity and the same sense of reality evident in the scenes of warfare and Roman urban life found in the friezes on the Arch of Constantine and in the preceding popular art. To the Biblical subjects were added the apocryphal legends of St. Peter, but the main theme became the miracle-working Christ. Instead of the philosopher's rotulus, He carries a *virga magica* betokening His powers; moreover, the philosopher's beard is gone, and the figure of the divine miracle worker radiates an angelic and youthful beauty. Abundant curls, variously arranged, fall about Christ's face. The idealized "Christus heroicus" modeled after divine beings of pre-Christian typology was introduced before the 4th century.

A series of porphyry sarcophagi from Rome and Constantinople are of Eastern type (PL. 55). Battle scenes decorated the supposed sarcophagus of Empress Helena from the mausoleum at Tor Pignattara, which originally was probably intended for Constantine. The sarcophagus of Constantina from the Constantinian mausoleum (S. Costanza) on the Via Nomentana bears figures of vintaging putti, a traditional pagan motif that had acquired a Christian meaning. With the exception of a single fragment, the porphyry sarcophagi of Constantinople are devoid of figural decoration and display only simple Christian symbols.

A reaction against this Constantinian popular, narrative taste was evident as early as 340. Inspired by pre-Christian prototypes, motifs of columns, niches, and trees began to enter or replace the figural scenes on sarcophagi. Instead of tight units of figures distributed over interconnected scenes or in continuous pictorial bands, there are isolated compositions and small groups alternating with niches or divided by columns and trees (III, PL. 304); instead of the flat, strongly outlined figures of the frieze sarcophagi, there is a return to well-rounded ones in lifelike groupings and set within a generous, convincing space. The figures once more acknowledge classical proportions, poise, and ponderation, and the drapery style becomes plastic and softly natural. This style, which approaches the classicism of the time of Julian the Apostate, was to be decisive throughout the second half of the 4th century.

In the course of this evolution new narrative themes appeared; most notably, the Miraculum Christi gave way to the Passio Christi. Christ is seen entering Jerusalem, taken prisoner in the garden, appearing before Pilate, wearing the crown of thorns; but the corporal punishments of the Saviour ordinarily are not represented, neither the torments of the scourge nor the Crucifixion itself. The scenes of Christ's Passion are supplemented by scenes from the lives of Peter and Paul. The stories of Cain and Abel and of Jonah are also adopted as Old Testament analogies for Christ's sacrifice and return from the grave. The subject of the Passion contributes other, more symbolic allusions to Christ's triumph over death: the Cross as *crux invicta* and the crown of thorns as *corona vitae*, since it is through the Passion that eternal victory is achieved. At the same time there was created the image of the celestial enthronement, the "Christus super caelum." The culmination of this development is exemplified by a sarcophagus in the Lateran Museums (no. 171) and the sarcophagus of Junius Bassus in the Vatican Grottoes (II, PL. 282). On the latter, in the reliefs of the principal side, is an enthroned Christ placed among various scenes of the Passion.

In the mid-4th century, there appeared a new type of Passion sarcophagus with Christ in Glory, between Peter and Paul, occupying the central niches and with scenes of the Passion at the sides. The central panel was devoted to a theme that was later to assume great importance, the Traditio Legis, showing Christ giving his *nova lex* to Peter (PL. 63). Gradually the Passion scenes were relegated to the sides, and Christ in Glory dominated the central relief of the sarcophagus. Such scenes appear in the columnar sarcophagi and in the "city gate" sarcophagi, such as that of S. Ambrogio in Milan (PL. 64), in which the gates symbolize the heavenly Jerusalem. Elevated before them stands Christ, flanked by the Twelve Apostles; His right arm is usually extended in the gesture of the Cosmocrator, and with the left He conveys the Law to the apostles. A similar type from this period, especially popular in Gaul, shows the heavenly council of the apostles with Christ enthroned in their midst. The iconographic progression is from the Passio Domini of the 4th century to the Majestas Domini of the Theodosian period. The quality of *majestas* is emphasized by the fact that Christ is invested with the imperial aureole.

The youthful beardless Christ was still dominant in the period of the Passion sarcophagi; a particularly fine example of this type is the Christ Enthroned found on a sarcophagus in the Lateran Museums (no. 174). Related to this type, because of the form of the face and the hair style, is the noted statue of Christ in the Museo Nazionale Romano, which reflects an image of Christ — probably in mosaic originally — widely known at the time. Toward the end of the 4th century the image underwent an important new modification in response to the emphasis on the majesty of Christ, whereby the figure assumed the solemn aspect of the images of Jupiter with beard and long hair.

A child's sarcophagus of the Theodosian period (II, PL. 468), stylistically close to the base reliefs of the Hippodrome obelisk, represents a widely diffused Eastern sarcophagus type and is particularly important for its iconography. On each of the long sides are two flying angels, holding between them a Christogram enclosed in a wreath; on the short sides are pairs of apostles flanking a cross. These angels bearing a monogram derive directly from the flying Victories, holding shields with the portrait of the deceased, on pagan sarcophagi. Among the other late-antique Christian reliefs of the East Roman ambient may be cited an ambo from Salonika (PL. 67) and a relief fragment with a procession of apostles and the Traditio Legis, both of the Theodosian period and both in Istanbul (Archaeol. Mus.); a relief with Christ among the apostles (Berlin, Staat. Mus.); and two fragmentary slabs with Nativity scenes (Carthage, Mus. Lavigérie), from the first half of the 5th century.

The Ravenna sarcophagi (PL. 65; III, PL. 304) dating from about 400 to the early Middle Ages are usually of Eastern type. In these the sarcophagus becomes an architectural construction having the form of a closed temple for the deceased. Intended to be placed in the open, they were decorated with reliefs on all four sides. Their reliefs generally conform to Greek taste — clarity and simplicity of composition, rhythmic balance, and strong suggestion of volume in the figures. Some of these sarcophagi were probably imported, but most of them seem to have been produced by foreign craftsmen who had set up workshops in Ravenna.

Figural sarcophagi of the Ravenna group are distributed over a period of about two centuries, from the late 4th through the mid-6th century. An example of the first phase is a sarcophagus in S. Francesco (PL. 64), with decoration that is closely related to the reliefs of the base of Theodosius. To the early or mid-5th century belongs the important group named after the Rinaldo sarcophagus (PL. 65). Among the later examples, that of St. Barbatianus (Ravenna, Cathedral) may belong to the 6th century. In the 5th and 6th centuries the symbolic Lamb and the peacock displaced the human figures (III, PL. 303). Together with other symbols these animals constituted the sole decoration of the 7th- and 8th-century sarcophagi. As contact with the Greek world ceased, the process of provincialization proceeded at a rapid pace. The barbarian infiltration brought to the relief style a peculiar uncertainty of proportion and anatomy; classical order and clarity, precise outlines and volumes, yielded to seemingly accidental compositions and coarsened figures and ornament.

With regard to bas-reliefs, mention should be made of the doors of S. Ambrogio in Milan (379-86) and those of S. Sabina in Rome (ca. 430), on which scenes from the Old and New Testaments are surrounded by rich borders of acanthus and vine tendrils. The sculptural fullness and ease of the figures on the S. Ambrogio doors is typical of the Ambrosian classicism, as opposed to the somewhat harsh style of the doors of S. Sabina.

Porphyry. The regular mining of porphyry at the imperial quarries of Mons Porphyrites in Egypt, near the Red Sea, ceased in the mid-4th century, probably for military or strategic reasons. From that time, only special expeditions were sent to procure the lustrous purple stone. The Tetrarchic-Constantinian period had witnessed the greatest development of porphyry sculpture. Besides the porphyry groups of S. Marco and the Vatican and the emperor bust in Cairo, there exists a series of headless statues that very likely belong to this period; these were carved in the East, in the vicinity of Mons Claudianus, where porphyry was also quarried. A colossal togaed statue is preserved in the Greco-Roman Museum in Alexandria. The emperor is seated like a pharaoh of the Old Kingdom on a jeweled cubic throne with a straight back; the over-all form is compact and blocklike, of great force and monumental in effect. A standing statue of a togaed emperor (Berlin, Staat. Mus.), approximately life-size, and a statue in a chlamys (Ravenna, Mus. Arcivescovile), over life-size and also representing an emperor, are characteristic examples of this porphyry mode, severe, cubiform, and of a linear simplicity, which may almost be termed a distinct style. The hardness of the material did not permit fine differentiation of details and thus favored the taste of the time, which was inclined toward forceful, simplified, and compact forms. A magnificent colossal togaed statue in porphyry, which stands behind the Curia of the Forum Romanum, and a related work preserved in fragments in the Vatican Museums may originally have surmounted columns of the great monument erected in honor of Diocletian near the Rostra of the Forum.

It was only during the late imperial age, however, that porphyry assumed its definite significance as a symbol of the imperial dignity. A visage carved in porphyry possessed a superhuman splendor for its late-antique viewers; and for this reason the celestial faces of the angels in late-antique mosaics are often purple in contrast to the white skin of the human figures. Thus porphyry entered the service of the imperial apotheosis, not only for statuary but also in architecture, for the revetment of walls, pavements, and certain items of furniture. It became solely a prerogative of majesty, just as purple cloth was reserved to the imperial wardrobe and the decoration of the imperial apartments. In the palace in the new capital of Constantinople, the emperors were surrounded with porphyry, just as the imperial medallions on the Arch of Constantine were framed with porphyry inlays. The first thing to meet the eye of the newborn son of the emperor was the purple decoration of the *porphyra*, the chamber lined with porphyry or draped in purple for the empress's delivery; from this tradition, the newborn child was called *porphyro genitus*. And after his death the ruler and his family were once again surrounded with porphyry, for it was the material chosen for imperial sarcophagi, some of which have been noted above (PL. 55).

From imperial use, the symbolic significance of purple descended to the Church. Baptismal fonts, for example, were made of porphyry: as the imperial newborn had been brought forth in a purple chamber, so the spiritual rebirth was signified by baptism in or from a purple font.

Stucco. The general economic decline in late antiquity, especially in the western regions, caused increasing difficulty in the importation of fine stone and, along with the deterioration of classical techniques of marbleworking, led to the widespread use of a substitute material, namely, stucco. In order to simulate the more costly material, the stucco was often covered with a thin layer of marble paste. Stucco decoration itself had an old tradition, but in the new economic situation it found new and extended application. Also in imitation of the possibilities of marble, stuccowork tended toward greater relief, even to full sculptural form, and was not limited to subsidiary ornament but was used for the principal figural themes. The fragility of the material and the indifference of later periods to preservation of works in this medium has meant that little of the great quantities of late-antique stucco has survived; however, what remains is sufficient to follow a line of development through the early Middle Ages.

The most important examples of late-antique stucco art are found in Ravenna. In the Baptistery of the Orthodox stucco decoration predominates in the zone of the windows, above the mosaic and stone incrustation of the "socle" zone. The stucco is applied to form a kind of relief architecture, including niches holding saints executed in high relief (PL. 66). In the corresponding stuccoed zone of the Baptistery of the Arians some of the architectural forms — columns, capitals, cornices — are made in the full round. Much later, in the Lombard tempietto of Cividale (mid-8th cent.), stucco sculpture continued dominant in the zone of the windows, with life-size figures of female saints in very high relief around the window niches, which in turn are framed by a stucco architecture of colonnettes, capitals, and richly decorated arches. A comparable development of stucco sculpture is seen in the East during this period. Elaborate architectural decoration in stucco work — with columns, architraves, archivolts, and niches with figures in high relief — is found in the Sassanian Empire and subsequently throughout Islam, where from the 8th century stucco sculpture reached its greatest heights in the Syrian palaces of the Ommiads.

The degree to which stucco sculpture was used as a substitute for stone sculpture in the early Middle Ages is attested by literary sources that speak of *signa* and *imagines* which were "ex gypso." Epigraphs accompanying the sculpture further attest to the connection with the statuary tradition of antiquity. Ambitious religious compositions such as the Nativity, the Passion, the Resurrection, and the Ascension were fully executed in stucco, and painting and gilding of this sculpture was an extensive practice.

Hans Peter L'ORANGE

PAINTING AND MOSAICS. *From Septimius Severus to the era of the Tetrarchy (193–286).* As the administrative and economic capital of a vast empire, Rome was of necessity an influential cultural center as well as the source of governmental directives. A long Hellenistic-Roman tradition conferred an unmistakable character on its art, and this was most pronounced in those works associated with the imperial court and the high officialdom. Typical are the mosaics from imperial villas such as those at Lorium (Vat. Mus.) and Baccano (X, PL. 176), which were too near Rome to permit their august occupants, the Severi (the oldest of the villas at Lorium was renovated by them), to manifest freely the taste they displayed in their African residences, particularly in Leptis Magna (near Homs, Libya), the birthplace of Septimius Severus. Marked changes that came about there had permanent effects on the further development of art, as evidenced by the reliefs on the Arch of Septimius Severus in Leptis Magna (III, PL. 387) and the mosaics from Zliten (Tripoli, Archaeol. Mus.), which range in time from the beginning of the Severan age (circus scene, ca. 200–25) to the end of the 3d century (Seasons mosaic). In these last, all fine detail is eradicated in brightness, and shadow effects no longer serve as darkening elements. Shadow is replaced by areas of heavier, more opaque color that is contrasted with the incandescent palette which is applied broadly to indicate the highlights. These innovations became permanent qualities, adopted by later artists who transformed the background from a simple identifying support for the figures into more evocative treatments of atmosphere, achieving new and fundamental effects characterizing a taste that, although to some degree "unclassical," was certainly not anticlassical.

At Leptis Magna great artists, who unfortunately remain unidentified, imparted new vitality to the Hellenistic style of Alexandria. From the Libyan city it was transmitted to Carthage and its sphere of influence, and eventually to Rome, which in turn transmitted these modes to Gaul, the Rhineland, and other parts of northern and central Europe. From habit long established, Rome was generally responsive to tendencies emanating from the Near East, and at this time developments of major significance were occurring in the Syro-Mesopotamian area, in part synchronous with developments in Africa. The importance of three-dimensional effect diminished constantly, so that the suggestion of mass within the figures was lost and space was conceived as atmosphere rather than measurable volume. The figures themselves, however, did not undergo a complete flattening against the background plane. A typical example is the mosaic of *Dionysus and Ariadne in Naxos* (Antioch, House of Dionysus and Ariadne), which can be dated between A.D. 210 and 220. The passive nature of the background, which no longer indicates a given space but only an atmosphere, is emphasized by the fact that no classical perspective systems are used. The figures are placed in several registers: those farther away are set on a higher level, and those parts more removed from the viewer are made larger, adopting what is known as "reverse perspective." This perspective system is exemplified by paintings from the so-called "Schola Praeconum" (220–40; Rome, Antiquarium Palatino). It is an even more evident feature in provincial centers such as Dura-Europos, where space, as it is usually understood, no longer exists, nor is the relation between space and figures that was an indispensable part of the classical prototypes made clear, so that some figures, such as those of patriarchs and prophets, seem to be crowded within frames too narrow to contain them. In the Roman ambient proper, however, the quality of defined space survived and was affirmed particularly in pictorial schemes that were imported to Rome. In the triclinium paintings of the Schola Praeconum the architectural elements, which are obviously derived from Asia Minor, divide the space into areas appropriate to the breadth of structure and the movement of the figures, and the same is true of the contemporary depictions of apostles (or philosophers) in the Hypogeum of the Aurelii. The manner of disposing the figures in a single row reveals an Eastern influence, and a rhythmic quality is achieved by alternating the suggested movement of the figures with the static intervals of the light, luminous background, which acquires a spatial vibrancy that has as palpable an existence as the figures themselves.

At this time Alexandria still played a preeminent role in the arts, in perpetuating and transmitting Hellenistic culture. It was from Alexandria that the more traditional North African paintings and mosaics and the Syro-Mesopotamian production derived. A wealth of Syro-Mesopotamian material has come to light, much of it at Antioch, as well as a substantial amount at Apamea (Syria) and fewer examples, of varying quality, in Lebanon. In all these regions, however, the artistic patrimony is limited almost entirely to pavement mosaics. Nonetheless, great innovations occurred within this tradition also; while they were not so pronounced as the developments in Leptis Magna, they were to have an even more lasting influence.

The mosaic panel of *Iphigenia in Aulis* (Antioch, House of Iphigenia; ca. 200–10) reproduces a theatrical scene probably taken from a codex, but with one difference that changes the entire effect of the composition: the temple, or at least that part which is depicted, is seen in a three-quarter view that sharply interrupts the line established by the portico in the background and blocks or displaces some of its components. Since a column of the temple is placed where the third column of the portico would be evident, the temple infringes upon the uniformity of the background and a broken or dual perspective results. In the *Ninus and Semiramis* pavement (Princeton, N.J., Univ. Art Mus.) from the House of the Man of Letters in Antioch, contemporary with the *Iphigenia* panel, the bird's-eye perspective of Ninus's couch is equally daring. This piece is related to the focal perspective of the standing female figure by means of a turn in the orthogonal arrangement of the tesserae of the background. The way the figures in the frieze of the *Battle of the Lapiths and Centaurs* (Antioch, House of the Buffet Supper) are composed of zones of solid color, eliminating all traces of contour lines, recalls Hellenistic antecedents. Since this mosaic dates from about 200–10, it significantly anticipates the painting of the Schola Praeconum of 220–40. The previously mentioned *Dionysus and Ariadne* mosaic in Antioch repeats the tripartite compositional scheme typical of Severan sarcophagi, with thiasos figures in the lateral compartments. The highlights on the drapery, however, especially that covering Ariadne's leg, evidence a decorative, calligraphic transformation which is a distant harbinger of the network of golden lines that was to be adopted in Byzantine art.

There are several interesting elements to note in an Antioch pavement in which small figures of Psyches are depicted pulling Eros's boat (Daphne-Harbie, House of the Boat of Psyches; 210–20): the novel way the figure of one of the Psyches is cut off at the thigh to suggest immersion in water, the delineation of the sea by means of dark streaks on a blue background, the diagonal composition, and the appearance of an iconographic motif that was to become part of the repertory at Dura-Europos to indicate the souls of the dead. Other devices used in figural representations at Dura-Europos are also based on usage at Antioch, such as the way the drowning Egyptians in the Moses cycle of the Synagogue are cut off across the thighs and the way the sea is rendered. Similarly, the artist of the Seasons mosaics at Leptis Magna drew upon prototypes such as the bust personifying luxury (Tryphe) in the House of Menander (Antioch; 230–50), though comparison shows him much inferior. In the House of the Buffet Supper, the rectangular panels with banqueting youths and hetaerae (portico pavement, intermediate level; ca. 260–80) again brought to the East the spaced, monumental figures characteristic of Roman art of the mid-3d century, which in simplified, almost incorporeal form were sketched by the painters of the catacombs.

At Dura-Europos the artistic situation is very different from circumstances in the other localities discussed. The destruction of the city about 256 or soon thereafter supplies a date *ante quem* for its monuments. From a purely visual point of view, it is justifiable to say that the two worlds — East and West — met in the works of Dura-Europos. In addition to the treatment of space, this confluence is illustrated in another sense by the paintings on the ceiling tiles (dated 245 by inscription) of the Synagogue. On these, some of the heads depicted are complete with neck, as is usual in Occidental practice, while others that follow the Oriental manner are without a neck. Also on the ceiling, the motif of an animal encircled with a garland was a decorative device that enjoyed great popularity in the West. On the other hand, the over-all arrangement of compositional elements in the decorations is Eastern. This decorative influence did not come directly from the East but was transmitted through Edessa (mod. Urfa, Turkey), where the sacred Hebrew texts were first translated into Syriac and where the codices used in other communities were made. Presumably the subjects — and more definitely, the style and composition — of the frescoes in the Synagogue (VIII, PLS. 333, 335–37) were taken from these illustrated codices. Whereas the source of the imagery must remain conjecture, there is evidence for the stylistic resemblance in the funerary mosaics from Edessa. These mosaics, though poorer in quality than the frescoes, provide dated documentation for the style: the *Orpheus* mosaic, 218–22; the *Phoenix*, 235–36; and the *Funerary Couch*, 277–78. Heavy dark outlines, frontal poses, and absence of regulated perspective are characteristic of both Edessa and Dura-Europos and confirm the common background. Evidence of contacts with the West is passing and superficial, such as in the Psyches mentioned above, the depiction of the Temple of Solomon, which recalls those found in the Delian reliefs, and the enclosure wall of the temple precinct, which repeats the architectural motifs of the *frontes scaenae* or of the views of the nymphaea so frequent in the East. Yet certain details at Dura-Europos — the gleaming lines of the highlights on David's purple mantle, for instance — are akin to devices used at Antioch and also foreshadow Byzantine art.

The new centers, therefore, from which the late-antique artistic currents emanated were the following cities, themselves receptive to and fertile in adapting innovations: Alexandria and Leptis Magna for the Hellenistic sphere; Antioch primarily, along with Edessa and Dura-Europos, for Syria; and Rome, where the results were particularly fruitful, for the Latin West. New artistic impulses that tended to disrupt the unity of surviving classical traditions were continually being introduced from the East by way of Mesopotamia. When the flow of influence was in the opposite direction, there came into being works such as the mosaics (largely destroyed during World War II) of Bishapur, Iran, in which the Eastern element was confined to details of clothing and local customs that captive Western craftsmen injected in order to Orientalize their schemes and techniques (X, PL. 177). Since these works are assuredly later than the defeat of Valerian, they may be dated between 260 and 280.

Stylistically distinct from regions immediately adjacent, the northern territories of the Roman Empire were permeated with North African artistic influences. Mosaic examples of this northern style exist in various locales: the *Bellerophon* panel in Reims (first half of 3d cent.), the circus scene at Nennig (Luxembourg) and the mosaic by Monnus in Trier (both ca. 250), and the *Charioteer*, also in Trier and slightly later in date (ca. 265). (The Monnus mosaic and the *Charioteer* are contained in the Rheinisches Landesmus.)

A new pictorial style, that which developed with the earliest Christian monuments, came into being in Rome about this time. More than ever before, didactic purpose took precedence over all other considerations. The fear of idolatry tended to turn the Early Christian artists from the supple and rich classical forms of 2d-century art, with its typical strongly modeled anatomy and wealth of detail; they strove for a figural synthesis that avoided naturalistic anatomical detail, in order to emphasize a spiritual significance in physical qualities. Moreover, the austere idiom of the sacred texts, especially that of the Gospels, where narrative is kept to the bare essentials, could not but encourage artists to seek a concise pictorial style and to eliminate all details that were not essential to the presentation of the narrative. The most significant catacomb paintings (see CATACOMBS) from the beginning of the 3d century, whether narrative or purely decorative, follow such didactic criteria: the Cubiculum of Ampliatus, the Good Shepherd and the Cupid and Psyche in the Catacomb of Domitilla, the Good Shepherd in the Catacomb of Callixtus, the series of the "Cubicula of the Sacraments" in the same catacomb, and the doves in the Catacomb of Praetextatus. The so-called "Greek Chapel" (III, PLS. 93, 95) and the Virgin with the prophet Balaam, both in the Catacomb of Priscilla, and the Multiplication of the Loaves, in the Catacomb of SS. Peter and Marcellinus, may be dated as late as the second decade of the 3d century. The so-called "Cubiculum of the Veiled One" in the Catacomb of Priscilla (III, PL. 94), the Woman with the Issue of Blood in the Catacomb of SS. Peter and Marcellinus, and figures of Christ and Orpheus in the Catacomb of Domitilla may all be dated between 220 and 250. The Susanna and the Elders in the Catacomb of Callixtus should be placed between 250 and 270, and the milking scene in an arcosolium in the Coemeterium Majus about 280.

It should be added that this mode is not the free expression of individual inspiration, of arbitrary and random innovations, that is, the work of untrained painters from the uneducated mass. The development of this painting style parallels cultural and philosophical currents described by Plotinus (205?-70), whose Alexandrian education was further refined in Asia Minor and Persia. As Plotinus explained it in the *Enneads*, form is light and color. He goes on to say that, in reproducing forms, it is not the drawing which establishes the form in space but that the form is made recognizable by its color in the atmosphere, which in itself is light. Since it is the object — or, more precisely, its color — that is seen, it diminishes when it comes nearer to the eye and enlarges as it moves farther away. Absence of detailed drawing, transformation of measurable space into atmosphere, and inverse perspective are the three formal elements corresponding to the Neoplatonic philosophy of Plotinus, according to which the work of art does not have existence as a fact of the purely visual capacity but in the action of the mind, which comprehends beauty in the whole and in the parts. The difference between this conception of art and that of mimesis reflects the essential contrast between the late-antique work of art and a classical or classicistic work.

In manuscript illumination the situation is even more complex. Later codices, surviving in scant numbers, and the qualities that can be deduced from contemporaneous paintings and mosaics confirm how great a development this medium must have had in Asia Minor and North Africa during the period in question. Unfortunately, not a single original seems to have survived. This was the period in which the codex began to compete in favor with the scroll, which eventually it was to supplant completely. The area extending from Mauretania to Syria seems to have played a leading part in this development, especially the Christian communities that recognized the advantages of the codex over the scroll for bringing several works together, being more readily illustrated, more easily consulted, and less fragile. Although the codex was extensively adopted first among Christians, it soon became preponderant in the pagan world as well, as evidenced in the works of the 4th century.

It is probable that a whole group of illustrations in the Milan *Iliad* (Bib. Ambrosiana, Ms. F.205, inf.), namely, R. Bianchi Bandinelli's "group B," is derived from a 3d-century Alexandrian prototype. Of similar derivation is the Vatican Ptolemy (Ms. gr. 1291), though some of its elements may be traced to Asia Minor, the place of origin of some herbariums that are reflected in the Vienna (II, PLS. 439, 479) and Naples (Bib. Naz., Cod. suppl. gr. 28) Dioscorides. An Eastern provenance may also be ascribed to the prototypes of the *Cynegetica* of Oppian, written at Apamea (Syria) and dedicated to Caracalla, which are best documented in an 11th-century manuscript in Venice (Bib. Marciana, Ms. gr. 479). Near Eastern, too, were the prototypes of the Octateuch manuscripts, in which the illustrations suggest Antioch as a source; their closest reflection is found in a Vatican Library manuscript (Ms. gr. 747). The Edessa codices mentioned earlier should be remembered in discussing the flow of influence in the manuscript illumination of the era.

From the Tetrarchy to Arcadius (286-408). a. Court style. The paintings of the Temple of the Imperial Cult in the legionary sacellum at Luxor were almost completely destroyed when archaeologists cleared the Egyptian structure beneath them. The paintings are known chiefly from 19th-century water colors that do not permit thorough critical evaluation. Dedicated to the Tetrarchs in A.D. 300, they seem to have been executed in an academic style that was stiff and hieratic, qualities substantiated by the fact that they were produced by workshops attached to a military outpost.

The "Barberini Goddess" (PL. 42), from the old Lateran Palace, having been painted in a niche that was bricked up when the palace became the papal residence in 313, was undoubtedly painted before that event; since it is known to have been patterned upon the statue of Venus placed in the Temple of Venus and Roma after the fire of 307, it must be dated between 307 and 312. The "Goddess" is typical of official painting, the mannered classicism revived in the chromatic style of this period, which remained unchanged for several decades because it was the mode peculiar to the court. This character may be seen in the allegorical figures (or portraits, according to some scholars) and cupids with symbols of imperium that were on the painted ceiling of the Constantinian hall beneath the Cathedral of Trier (III, PL. 387). These may be dated about 326 and are certainly of a higher caliber than the "Barberini Goddess." Painted with long, broad brush strokes, the figures are presented austerely and soberly, with very little stress on detail. The style is even more pronounced in the cupids than in the imposing allegorical figures.

The sumptuous mosaics from the Constantinian villa of Antioch (excavations at Daphne-Harbie; PL. 73) should be mentioned together with these works, for the various novel trends of this period were brought together there in a singular array. The way in which ceilings and floors were divided into decorative panels became so standard that it is almost characteristic of the period; and diagonal panels spanning the corners with decorative motifs also became a common feature. The allegorical figures of the seasons in the diagonals of the Constantinian villa at Daphne-Harbie are highly stylized according to formulas of a rigid classicism. However, the plant motifs are developed in strongly defined and fanciful shapes, deriving from a lively, free synthesis of the styles of the Zliten mosaics and of the earlier *Lapiths and Centaurs* frieze in Antioch (House of the Buffet Supper). The hunting and pastoral scenes of the Daphne-Harbie villa are more closely allied with traditional classicizing canons. In the mosaics of the Constantinian villa, Western culture predominates more clearly than in any other complex at Antioch.

The far-ranging locations of the finds — Rome, Trier, Centcelles (near Tarragona), Carthage, Antioch — indicate that the Roman world had again acquired a cultural and artistic koine, no less significant because it was so closely connected with imperial court circles. Although such official art is usually designated as "Roman," this conventional usage is accurate only in so far as Rome was the name of the capital of the Empire and its political and administrative center.

b. Rome. As soon as one looks beyond this official sphere, striking contrasts and correspondences, clashes and fusions of the diverse artistic currents may be observed. The sacellum of Dea Roma on the Via della Consolazione, which dated from the early decades of the 4th century, was characterized by paintings firm in composition but weak in execution and full of folk elements, thereby suggesting that their creator was an artist on the periphery of official art circles. The polychrome marble inlays of the Basilica of Junius Bassus are quite certainly imports of great artistic value (PL. 70; VIII, PL. 79). There is no longer any way of ascertaining whether the basilica was built by the Junius Bassus who became consul in 317 or by the senator Junius Bassus, buried in the sarcophagus of the Vatican Grottoes, who died in 359 — if by either of these historical figures — since the dedicatory inscription refers only to the building itself. Moreover, although these inlays have generally been placed in the first half of the 4th century, they are most likely of later origin and are not at all Roman — or, more precisely, are in neither the Italic nor the court style. Distinctly provincial in manner, they should be assigned to the North African sphere; they were not made before the last quarter of the 4th century, and even later dating would be reasonable.

In the aftermath of the Constantinian edict of tolerance (A.D. 313), many changes came about in catacomb painting. The works involved are many, and mention of but a few is made in this discussion: the frescoes of saints in the so-called "Cubiculum of the Five Saints," in the Catacomb of Callixtus; the loculus of Januarius, in the Catacomb of Domitilla; and the poorest of the Eucharistic banquets in the Agape region of the Catacomb of SS. Peter and Marcellinus. All these are works from the beginning of the 4th century and are in a popular vein that affected a classical garb. The paintings in the Hypogeum of Vibia and the Catacomb of the Jordani from the second decade of the 4th century, the orants in the Catacomb of Domitilla (with a grace all their own), the Madonna and Child in the Coemeterium Majus (320-30), which has a solid and monumental aspect, and the orants of the Catacomb of Thraso (III, PL. 97), which were painted some five years later and which reveal some connection with painters trained in the East (probably in Syria), all seem to aim toward removing the distinctive marks of traditional Christian art and assimilating the classicism of Constantinian court art. In this light, it is worth noting again the allegorical figures in the imperial hall beneath the Cathedral of Trier, which present the same classicizing impulses.

Certain works reveal other possibilities for this classical court tradition when developed outside the sometimes inhibiting official ambient. The hypogeum on the Via Latina, a large aristocratic tomb, is an excellent example of such varied strains. Aside from paintings having clear ties with court art and other catacomb painting, this burial chamber has diverse frescoes executed at various times by many artists. Most scholars date these frescoes between about 320 and 350, but some parts may actually be dated as much as half a century earlier. They would, on the whole, be indicative of the new development following Constantine's edict. The decorative arrangement of the sharp-cornered vaults is characteristic of the post-Constantinian era, as are the cupids in the tondos, which were so popular from this time onward. In the panels of the Samaritan Woman and the Resurrection of Lazarus, both dating from about the middle of the 4th century, either the old decorative schemes of the catacombs are enriched by adding new figures or the traditional figures are arranged in quieter, more balanced compositions.

A group of paintings in a catacomb (that discovered in 1955) on the Via Latina provide further examples of the transition. In the so-called "anatomy lesson" the composition used is the Christ among the Apostles motif, as found for example in the Catacomb of Domitilla a little after 350. The subject of Christ with SS. Peter and Paul was here for the first time presented in a monumental context, and this more elaborate composition was soon to find its logical situation in the apses of Early Christian basilicas. The depiction of the crossing of the Red Sea undoubtedly draws upon prototypes taken from illustrated codices, which are also reflected in some of the illustrations of the Ambrosian *Iliad*. The pagan cycles of Hercules and Alcestis (or the death of Cleopatra), in the hypogeum of the Via Latina, belong instead to a more conventional and commonplace repertory of subjects. The same may be said of the paintings in the Hypogeum of Trebius Justus (VII, PL. 218), from the beginning of the 4th century, in which the undeniable virtues of good composition, a sense of monumentality, and a lively observation do not, however, raise the painter above the level of a competent craftsman.

The roughly contemporaneous hypogeum of the Via Livenza gives a good idea of what wholly Roman painting was like during the early decades of the 4th century. Although the compositions are sketchy in execution, they have a monumental effect deriving from a careful balance between figures and space. Thus three-dimensional presentation, which during the preceding decades seems to have been rejected in some circles, was successfully adopted once more and developed in a manner analogous to that observed at Centcelles, for example. The monumentality of the dapifers n the decoration (ca. 330-50; partially Naples, Mus. Naz.) of a house near the Lateran, which may have been an adjunct or even an integral part of the palace, reveals true mural painting of a quality the "Barberini Goddess" does not equal.

It may be said that, in Rome at least, any difference between Christian painting and the pagan official tradition effectively disappeared in the second half of the 4th century. The Sacrifice of Abraham in the Catacomb of Callixtus, the Christ among the Apostles in the Cubiculum of Ampliatus in the Catacomb of Domitilla, the SS. Peter and Paul in the Catacomb of Domitilla, the arcosolium of Veneranda in the Catacomb of Domitilla (III, PL. 98), and the Cubiculum of Leo Officialis Annonae in the Catacomb of the Jordani (all done between 350 and 400) accord perfectly with the development of earlier and contemporaneous pagan decor as documented, for example, by many upper-class houses in Ostia and in outlying areas of the Empire. Just as the tomb of Durostorum (IV, PL. 111; second half of 4th cent.), a garrison town on the lower Danube, is a provincial reflection of the style exemplified in Rome by the dapifer paintings of the Lateran house, so the apostles at Niš (Yugoslavia; anc. Naissus) and Pécs (Hungary), which should also be dated about 360-70, repeat the monumental mass characteristic of the fresco figures in the Catacomb of Domitilla mentioned above. There is also the same mode of forming the hands in relation to the body, which makes them appear as if carved from a single block. Similarly, too, broad strokes of dark green or brown indicate the folds of the white togas and the limbs underneath. The brush is handled boldly, like a spatula for scraping the base substance. This style of painting, unique to Rome and the areas directly dependent on her, reached its apex in the two apostles in the Catacomb of Domitilla.

A survey of the truly Roman painting of this era would be incomplete without mention of the Calendar of 354 (or Calendar of the Sons of Constantine; known from 16th- and 17th-century copies of a Carolingian copy), the only work that transmits the style of Furius Dionysius Filocalus, whose art is known from the inscriptions he made for Pope Damasus I (366-84). Though Filocalus was in close touch with the contemporary taste, his drawing style does not seem as up-to-date as his epigraphy, which represented a new step for this art in Rome. In his draftmanship, he favored motifs and mannerisms of the Constantinian age — presumably, that is, the modes of his youth.

c. Alexandria. At this time, in an area forming a sweeping arc from Mauretania, through the Nile Delta, and on to Syria, there became established a broad artistic koine equally as influential as that of Rome but even richer in its possibilities of future development. The Hellenistic culture that had been the heritage of Alexandria for many centuries was disseminated through these lands with increased force and took on many new forms and qualities in the process, though the subjects and iconography still derived from age-old traditions. Alexandria itself, however, seems to have disappeared from the cultural scene, as if depleted by centuries of uninterrupted artistic endeavor. A portrait of a woman (Athens, Benaki Mus.) that must surely come from Egypt, and quite possibly from Alexandria, is symptomatic of this new lassitude. The iconographic scheme is one common to portraiture of all ages, but the pose is that used for the allegorical figures in Trier and for orants in the catacombs. The same may be remarked of the painting style, so that this work partakes of the classicizing tendency of the official style during the first three decades of the 4th century. Nor is this an isolated example, inasmuch as this manner of painting — a broad, assured brush technique, rich on the surface but empty and insubstantial in effect — can be seen in much sepulchral decoration of the time. It is found, for instance, in two tombs, both of which are closely related to the above-mentioned Athens portrait: one at Asgfa (anc. Cyrenaica), the other near Ashkelon (Ascalon, Israel). Other noteworthy portraits include one in Würzburg (Martin-von-Wagner-Mus. der Univ.), another in Vienna (Kunsthist. Mus.), and a third formerly in New York (Brummer Gall.); these works (Drerup nos. 26–28) can be attributed to the same hand as a portrait in Paris (formerly Coll. Sambon; Drerup no. 29). None, however, rises above the craftsman level, which proceeded from a strong dilution of the court style in adapting it to provincial circumstance.

d. Syria-Mesopotamia. An exceptional number of mosaics has been found at Antioch. There, in Bath E (330–40), a favored theme of the first half of the 4th century was elaborated in the mosaic representing Ge (Gaea) and the Karpoi: namely, the motif of putti bearing emblems or symbols. These putti recall the chubby cupids of the Trier hall. Wheat stalks protrude from the heavy garlands, with full kernels very like the single grapes of the clusters in the vintage mosaics at Cherchel (anc. Caesarea), which will be discussed below. In the mosaic of *Chresis* (ca. 350; House of the Triumph of Dionysus), the seated allegorical figure has the tall cylindrical form that in the East became a hallmark of the Madonna Enthroned a century later. The large allegorical scene on the floor of the Tomb of Mnemosyne (ca. 380–400), also in Antioch, may reflect motifs from miniatures or, even more likely, from textiles. The archetype was probably not very far removed in time or distance, since it has gradually become clear how active a textile production Syria had in this period. The similarities between the pavement mosaic from the Bath of Apolausis (Washington, D.C., Dumbarton Oaks Coll.), also from the end of the 4th century, and the mosaic pavements of many Early Christian basilicas affirm the origin of the iconographic motifs of the pavement.

Philippopolis (mod. Shahba, Syria) was another active center for mosaics; noteworthy among its works are the *Allegory of Earth* and the allegorical representations of justice (Eutekneia), education (Dikaiosyne), and philosophy (all mid-4th cent.; Damascus, Nat. Mus.), with harmonious composition, a rich palette, and an obvious Hellenistic tradition. Another important center was Apamea, from which the *Therapenides* mosaic (Brussels, Mus. Royaux d'Art et d'Histoire) presents a fusion of the two iconographic sources: a residue of Hellenistic tradition is evident in the architectural setting, but it is accompanied by awareness of those compositions which eliminated all systems of strict perspective and which, despite theories to the contrary, could have derived only from the Iranian sphere. The mosaic of *Socrates and the Wise Men* (Apamea, East Basilica), which like the preceding panel dates from about 350, is among those works, documented also in manuscript illustrations, which have as their subject a conversation engaging several persons. This iconographic type, transmitted to Christian from pagan art, is but one example of an extensive and complex transfer of artistic concepts and devices. The mosaic of the *Birth of Alexander* from Baalbek (Beirut, Nat. Mus.), dated about the middle of the 4th century, testifies to the persistence and assimilation of certain motifs, such as the figure cut off at the thighs to indicate its immersion in water (in this case, in a basin). It is significant that this survival occurred not far from Dura-Europos, where similar figures had been painted about a century earlier.

Mosaic remains in Lebanon are much more modest. The presence of Greco–Near Eastern workshops is indicated at Mount Nebo by a large Dionysiac composition. In Armenia, at Garni, local craftsmen imitated Hellenistic models transmitted to them by migratory artisans, even to the Greek inscriptions. The mosaics of the church of Mopsuestia (mod. Misis; near Adana, Turkey) are clearly related to those of Antioch, understandably in view of the geographical proximity of the two cities. Moreover, Theodore of Mopsuestia, the bishop (392–428) who commissioned the mosaics, was himself from Antioch. These mosaics mark a further point on the route of a cultural development that eventually spread from the Near East as far as northern Europe.

e. North Africa, Sicily, and Iberia. Two distinct stylistic tendencies are to be noted in North Africa (see AFRICAN-ROMAN ART), even though their origins are rather similar: one was derived from a mannered Hellenism undoubtedly Alexandrian, but also evidencing some awareness of Syrian developments; the opposing, more original strain impressed the elegance and grace of Alexandria on a Syro-Mesopotamian base. There was also a degree of influence from Italy and Rome proper. The first trend in painting was midway between the official (or court) style of Rome and its classicizing Alexandrian derivative discussed earlier. To this category belong a portrait in Sousse (Tunisia; anc. Hadrumetum), said to be that of Quintus Ennius; the *Triumph of Neptune and Amphitrite* (I, PL. 28), from Constantine (Algeria; anc. Cirta); the *Toilet of Venus* at Djemila (Algeria; anc. Cuicul); the popularizing mosaic from Lambiridi, which seems to depict a colloquy with a doctor; and the six slaves of Dougga (Tunisia; anc. Thugga). These examples, all from the first half of the 4th century, are but a few of a prolific output.

North Africa has another, quite distinctive strain to offer. The so-called "Dominus Julius" (ca. 350), a Carthaginian mosaic with a composition divided into three registers, presents a balanced narrative form in its juxtaposition of figures that is rarely found elsewhere. This compositional balance reappears in a group of mosaics at Cherchel (Algeria), to which various dates have been assigned but which must be Constantinian or post-Constantinian because of the clothing typical of this period. These mosaics depict scenes of agriculture, vintaging, and the arena, placed in several superimposed registers according to a scheme favored at this time. The figures are conceived as volumes in appearance only, for their suggestion of mass is merely the result of color resonance in light. The moduli of the figures, their interrelation, and their placement in space derive from a basically classical orientation, not pedantically applied, however, but intended as stimulus to new efforts and experiments. In the vintaging scene, for example, the glistening clusters of grapes are transformed into small dark circles with luminous halos, thus translating an observed natural phenomenon into a poetic, ornamental motif.

From this cultural background came the mosaicists who worked on the Roman villa at Casale, near Piazza Armerina in Sicily (PLS. 52, 73; X, PL. 178). There were many artisans involved, and they worked there for a number of years. Some were truly outstanding artists, such as the creators of the *Great Hunt* and the *Hercules* mosaics (PLS. 52, 73). Others, such as the creators of the *Small Hunt* and the festoons in the peristyle, were more aptly master technicians of a highly refined craft. A few, among them the mosaicist who executed the circus scenes in the atrium of the baths, revealed such exceptional individuality as to seem unrelated to the others who worked on the villa. On the basis of style, all the Piazza Armerina mosaics should be placed between 360 and 410 (which accords with historical considerations), even though some scholars have assigned them to the beginning of the 4th century. The later date is supported by similarities with the mosaics of the villa at Desenzano del Garda, which is structurally similar as well.

A mosaic depicting a she-ass nursing two lion cubs (Boston, Mus. of Fine Arts), found in Tunisia, exemplifies the subsequent development of the same artistic school (which this author believes can be assigned to a single workshop), which was afterward to influence the mosaics of the Great Palace of the Emperors in Constantinople (II, PL. 437; VII, PL. 372). If the Great Palace mosaics were made during the first half of the 5th century, they could very likely be the work of African artisans who had moved to the "New Rome," perhaps in the wake of the Vandal invasions. If they were made a century later, in the first half of the 6th century, as many scholars have believed, they might then be the work of the artistic descendants of such African immigrants.

The mosaics from the contemporaneous villa at Saint-Leu (Algeria; anc. Portus Magnus) are exact counterparts of the Piazza Armerina mosaics. The thematic material of both — the victorious gods, those who challenge the gods, and the triumphs of individual divinities — reflects the pagan revival at the end of the 4th century. Another link with Piazza Armerina is that at Saint-Leu, too, the artists — albeit not so highly skilled — reveal the same taste for opulence and ostentation that was the hallmark of the final outburst of Hellenism. The existence of very strong affinities between the mosaics at Piazza Armerina, others in Africa, and those of Misis, Gamzigrad, and Vicenza should not therefore be discounted, for these works document the new cultural koine of the Theodosian-Honorian age and testify to its broad dissemination.

A mosaic with Eros represented as a charioteer, found at Dougga, deserves particular consideration: the construction of the quadriga, the color fragmentation of the face, and the deliberate rejection of any indication of perspective are all definite points of departure identifying the ambient that produced the artist who did the stone inlays of the Basilica of Junius Bassus. This Dougga mosaic is presently assigned to the second half of the 4th century.

This mosaic school, which had a general effect that was incalculable, exerted strong influence in Coptic Egypt. This explains the affinities to Coptic art evident in another mosaic, that of Gafsa (Tunisia; anc. Capsa), also from the second half of the century and with scenes of the circus. The method of indicating the spectators by means of heads alone, repeated within the arcades composing the sides of the arena, and the outline style itself make this mosaic very like a tapestry cartoon.

The influence of the African mosaicists was also felt in the Iberian peninsula, as may be seen in several impressive mosaics. The circus mosaics found near Barcelona and Gerona (VII, PL. 248) and that from Italica (lost) which was signed Marcel[...] and Marcianus — the work of local artists — are early-4th-century examples fitting schemes from which there developed the many later mosaics with similar subjects in Piazza Armerina, as well as in Africa, where they were not at all infrequent. The mosaics from Alentejo, Portugal (PL. 76), evidence equally close relations with North African work and, on the basis of the scaly pattern of the background, should be assigned to the end of the 4th century. The similarity to the mosaics from Saint-Leu in general taste suggests a more direct connection in the cultural origins of the artists. The same antecedents are to be assumed for a more rigid mosaic with Tritons from the villa of La Cocosa (VII, FIG. 453) and *The Hunter Dulcitius* from the villa at Ramalete. At the latter site, however, the mosaic with thick, interlaced festoons is the achievement of an artisan of appreciable stature. These last examples are to be dated quite late in the 4th century. The mosaic signed by one "Felix" from the villa at Tossa (380–400), while extremely provincial, is related both in type and quality to the more modest funerary mosaics of North Africa — a type that is also common in Spain.

The mosaics of Christian structures should be allotted separate treatment, since many factors help to unite them despite the diversity arising from far-ranging and disparate cultural provenances. The uniformity promoted by the Christian tendency to follow the official artistic koine was further advanced by the fact that the Christian hierarchy supervised all artistic activity in religious edifices, dictating norms for the iconographic motifs and their execution that would preclude every possibility of idolatrous contamination. Furthermore, once the Christian architectural forms — basilica, rotunda, baptistery — became established, their decorative schemes also tended to become fixed within clearly defined rules. As a result, variation came to be limited to purely artistic means.

The mosaics of the rotunda of S. Costanza (1337–51; PL. 38) might almost be taken as a canon of Roman official, or court, taste of the middle of the century. Unfortunately, the extensive and fundamental restorations of the rotunda hinder a definitive appraisal of this notable monument and its decoration. The same difficulty occurs with the apse mosaic in S. Pudenziana (late 4th or early 5th cent.; III, PL. 305), where the entire right side is a reconstruction. Under such circumstances, judgment must be limited to stating that the execution may be ascribed to Roman workshops, primarily on the basis of the solemn, rhythmic deployment of the figures within the broad space created by the background buildings. Essential differences between East and West can be pinpointed in a comparison of the female figure representing *ecclesia ex gentibus* (i.e., Church of the Gentiles) in the S. Pudenziana mosaic with the female bust in the roughly contemporaneous *Samson* mosaic in the church at Misis. The latter figure has a strong decorative and pictorial emphasis, fragmenting the volume of the figure into bands of color; whereas in the Roman mosaic of S. Costanza, outline and color have a precise function, restricted to the modeling of the figure and its relation to the surrounding space.

Many decorative themes continued to pass from the pagan to the Christian world: for example, the floral motifs enclosing animals and the squares with animals or flowers at the center, both of which became frequent for mosaic pavements. These were common motifs in the East, whence they spread to Italy; the pavement of the basilica of Aquileia, with a pronounced degree of African influence as well, is one such case on the Italian mainland. These motifs continued at large in both areas of the Empire, as may be seen in the Djemila mosaic with the inscription "Asinus Nica," dating from the end of the 4th century.

The chance, scattered mosaic finds from the Near East make it impossible to locate the leading centers there, and only broad hypothetical conclusions can be formulated for these regions. Discoveries such as the Misis (i.e., Mopsuestia) mosaics suggest a flourishing artistic life in the cities of Asia Minor, especially those along the coast, which may also have transmitted the Pergamene motifs that survived in so many works of the second half of the 4th century. The lower quality of the mosaics from Zkruni and Kaoussie (Beirut, Nat. Mus.), as well as the purely decorative display of the oldest basilica at Kos, all from the end of the 4th century, indicates the existence of marginal production in which the artistic trends of the leading centers became uninspired and devitalized.

Unknown also are the origins of the mosaic artists who worked for the emperor Theodosius in transforming the Mausoleum of Galerius in Salonika into the Church of St. George (PL. 62). All that can yet be said is that they were definitely Eastern-oriented. The over-all figure style, bodies whose corporeal identity is obscured by the broad expanse of robes hanging from the outstretched arms, and an architectural background very like the *frontes scaenae* bring to mind both Syria and Asia Minor. Thus, their immediate artistic source remains a moot question.

Important remains from the Constantinian period in Spain have been found in the mausoleum at Centcelles (near Tarragona; 353–58), which was probably meant for Constans, son of Constantine the Great. The division into concentric circles, the subjects, and especially the manner of execution combine to make the dome mosaics of the tomb magnificent examples of the official court style. Nor was this an isolated example in Spain, for the mosaic pavement with the Muses from Arróniz (Madrid, Mus. Arqueológico Nacional) and the funerary mosaic with a Christ(?) in an attitude of benediction (Tarragona, Mus. Paleocristiano) belong to the same ambient. Although adaptations of Syrian schemata are evident in these works, the solidity of the figures and their relation to the surrounding space are Western qualities.

Some of the North African church and baptistery decorations also fit with the imperial koine, while others have a more decided provincial character. The former type includes the Great Basilica of Bône (Algeria; anc. Hippo), the baptistery of Sbeitla (Tunisia; anc. Sufetula), and the basilica of Cap Matifou (Algeria; anc. Rusguniae), which all seem to derive inspiration from Italy. To the second class belong the mosaic of Valentia in Thabraca and the many Algerian tomb mosaics, as well as the curious late sarcophagus with mosaic inlay from the cemetery of St. Salsa in Tipaza (Tipasa). The last-named work anticipates the mosaic design that was to be widely diffused in Palestine during the next century, for example, as seen in the mosaics of the Beth Alpha synagogue (VIII, PL. 337).

The importance of the Calendar of 354 has already been mentioned. Also from the second half of the 4th century is the Quedlinburg *Itala* (Berlin, Staatsbib., Ms. theol. lat. fol. 485), an original codex usually attributed to the Roman sphere, though it cannot with any certainty be included in the stylistic circle of Filocalus. Either Roman or Alexandrian in origin and of high quality, the manuscript must have been the prototype for the early-5th-century mosaics of S. Maria Maggiore in Rome. The papyrus with the rape of Briseis (Munich, Staatsbib., Pap. gr. 128), of uncertain origin, with its robust and powerful drawing, seems related to the more modest and simple paintings of the Tetrarchic sacellum in Luxor. One series of illustrations in the Ambrosian *Iliad* of Milan (R. Bianchi Bandinelli's "group D") may also hark back to Egyptian — or, more precisely, to Alexandrian — prototypes; this likelihood has given rise to a theory that the whole manuscript was of Alexandrian provenance. The archetypes for the numerous Eusebian Canon Tables, so widely diffused by Constantine himself, also originated in Eastern scriptoria. Finally, there should not be omitted from the list the curious pictorialism of the *technopaignion*, or calligram, a poem written so that its lines fill the shape of a relevant figure or object. The leading practitioner of this style was Constantine's court poet Publilius Optatianus Porfyrius.

f. Other European centers. The 4th-century mosaics with hunting scenes found at the Roman castrum of Gamzigrad in Yugoslavia mark one of the advance points in the spread of artistic tendencies from the Near East to northern and western Europe. This cultural development then progressed to the Po plain, where it left another significant marker in the mosaic of the wild-boar hunt in Vicenza (Mus. Civ.). From these regions the Eastern mosaic workshops carried their activities and influence not to the Danube territories, which were permeated with Roman influence, but instead toward the Rhine, northern Gaul, and even Brittany.

The 3d-century date usually given for the *Philosopher* mosaic from Cologne does not seem justified, since even in the East the treatment of the background as a scale pattern did not occur before the end of the 4th century. This mosaic has definite connections with the *Philosopher* mosaic at Shahba (Syria), not only in subject but also in iconographic details. Moreover, it is known that Syrian craftsmen were active in Cologne glassworks at this time. The Dionysian mosaic in Cologne may be assigned a similarly late date for much the same reason, and because it was laid down over an earlier pavement. The atmospheric scaly background is rendered in light and delicate colors, in which the contours of the figures lose some degree of sharpness. But the provincial rigidity of the figure style is in strong contrast to the continuous flow of light among figures and objects. For much the same reasons, a 4th-century date should be assigned to a mosaic found in Trier (Rheinisches Landesmus.; Süd-Allee, Schaab R.10), though more precise dating remains impossible. Undoubtedly of Eastern inspiration, it is a design composed of four sea shells joined in the shape of a four-leaf clover, a form to be remembered in connection with Byzantine mosaics. The late date for this mosaic is supported by the knowledge that the house in which it was found underwent alterations during the 4th century.

Because of its rarity, it is difficult to fix the date and source of the mosaic found at No. 21 Werberbachstrasse, Trier. At its center is a hexagon with a linear and stylized Medusa head, and this panel is surrounded by a series of hexagonal bands filled with fishes, birds, and plants. The outline curves seem to be inscribed with a compass, a drawing style for which there is no basis for comparison — though this simplicity of line may be partly due to extensive restorations. Only the *Rape of Europa* mosaic in the Lullingstone villa (Kent, Eng.) can be cited as in any way similar, both for its linearity and for its sea-monster motif. The emphasis on strong outlines and the peculiar colors that are somewhat like African mosaics of the period after the Vandal invasions suggest a late date, but for historical reasons no later than the end of the 4th century. The *Mysteries* mosaic in Trier, found in 1950 in what was presumably a collegium (No. 7 Johann-Philipstrasse), is to be dated about 370. Its essentially popular style is not without vitality, but artistic considerations are consistently subordinated to the narrative. Possible influences from northern Italy should be considered.

In Gaul, too, Eastern influences were generally tempered by elements derived from northern Italy. This is evident in a mosaic from Blanzy-les-Fismes (Aisne; Bib. de Laon, Inv. 77A), with a large panel depicting Orpheus surrounded by wild beasts. The *Diana and Callisto* mosaic from Villelaure and the *Apollo and Daphne* of Lillebonne should be assigned to the Constantinian era, because the compositions are divided in a manner reminiscent of those from the Constantinian villa in Antioch. That they appear more rigid and schematic may be either because they are provincial works or because they represent an actual cultural lag; in the latter case, they would be dated a few decades later. A mosaic from Sainte-Colombe (near Vienne) showing the punishment of Lycurgus is contemporaneous with the two just mentioned; whereas the *Battle of Eros and Pan* in Lyons (Mus. B. A.) should be dated much later. Though the subject of the last-named brings the Piazza Armerina mosaics to mind, it is quite different in execution.

The farthest outpost of these artistic currents emanating from the East was Britain. The mosaics of the Lullingstone villa mentioned above are good examples. Mosaics with Eastern subjects are often found, such as that of *Orpheus*, with the peculiar circular iconographic schemes that could only have been based on Eastern prototypes. An excellent example of the latter motif is the pavement at Horkstow (Lincolnshire). The walls of the very early Christian chapel (mid-4th cent.) on the upper floor of the Lullingstone villa were painted with a row of frontal orants, posed with arms upraised; in their attitudes and placement they recall the figures of the Catacomb of Thraso. Their repetitive deployment foreshadows the rhythmic files of figures that were to become typical of Byzantine art. Their painting style — as far as one can judge from the few fragments recovered — also seems to reflect a typically Eastern taste.

Developments in northern Italy require separate discussion (although little has survived there from this period), since the fusion of varied artistic tendencies seems to have been more common and to have had a richer outcome here than elsewhere. The secular mosaics at Aquileia (first half of 4th cent.), those from Oderzo (Treviso; anc. Opitergium), made a few decades later, and those of the villa at Desenzano del Garda (end of 4th cent.) constitute a group that, while it does not resolve stylistic problems, does pose many questions. Many Italic artisans contributed to these works, and influences from Rome and (via Rome) from North Africa are evident. A tendency toward the schematic in composition and a certain concern with volume, sometimes manifested in hardness and woodenness of features, are not necessarily the result of the artist's lack of experience but may sometimes reflect the ambient in which he was trained. Thus, the rigidity of the Dea Roma from the sacellum of Via della Consolazione, mentioned above, may clarify somewhat the mosaic style at Aquileia, where certain popularizing elements are probably the result of a craftsman having absorbed only the surface mannerisms of the official court painting without having grasped its deeper intent.

The North African element is very apparent in the hunt mosaic of Oderzo (Mus. Civ.). This quality is expressed in the richness and modulation of color, in a tendency toward irridescence that blurs the unemphasized outlines, and in compositional refinements which surpass the usual local standards and which can be associated with a specific place of origin — Carthage. The Desenzano mosaics can also be linked with this strain, although the possibility of some Eastern contribution must be kept in mind.

At least some manifestations of Eastern taste can be explained by the fact that in Italy at this time many Eastern artisans were active, particularly in producing silverwork. Such related crafts, if not the Syrian and other Near Eastern mosaicists themselves, may have brought about the introduction of these elements, which in the course of the 4th century entered increasingly into the production of the Po Valley. Artisans from the mosaic workshops of the Po Valley also crossed the Alps, and evidence of their work is clearly recognizable along the Danube and the Rhine.

From Theodosius II to Justinian I (408–565). The development of the cultural koine that had emerged from the period immediately preceding was intensified during the 5th century. This was the result of two complementary factors: on the one hand, the person of the emperor, his family, and court were imposed upon every aspect of public life, either as patrons or as ideal models; on the other, the Church, growing steadily in influence, gradually came in the West to a position equivalent to that of imperial authority, and secular as well as religious art was permeated with its standards. A constant interaction between these poles — Empire and Christianity — developed, so that the iconography of Christian themes was often inspired by court protocol, and conversely, representations of the emperor tended to assume the gestures and vestments identified with Christ. As a result, most works of art were associated with imperial palaces, official buildings, or the Church. Some of the last-mentioned have survived, but almost all the others have been destroyed.

From the end of the 5th century and throughout the 6th the production in this koine had a particular stamp reminiscent of Hellenistic art, and it can have had only one source: Constantinople. There, in the century and a half since its foundation as capital, artists, scholars, poets, and philosophers had come together from all over that world which had once been Roman, and they came into contact with others from Armenia, Persia, and even more distant places. The Hellenistic civilization of the Near East, the Syro-Mesopotamian civilization, the Alexandrian-Carthaginian civilization, and that evolved in Rome all found a particularly fertile soil in which new life could take root and spread. The resulting civilization — the Byzantine — had nothing eclectic about it, however, nothing of the mixed, but was distinct, independent, and brilliant.

a. Rome and Italy in the 5th century. In S. Sabina, Rome (422), important stone-inlay decorations have been preserved, and of the mosaics there remains the large panel with an inscription flanked by figures representing the early branches of Christianity — the Jewish and the Gentile (III, PL. 314). These static figures, solemn and regal, but not hieratic, have much in common with the same symbolic figures in S. Pudenziana in the continuation of the Roman tradition of sensitivity to volumes and their relation to space. The blue background, against which the figures are set on either side of a luminous gold inscription, is a well-composed space that has a consistency of its own. The same thoughtful composition is evident in the mosaic cycle in S. Maria Maggiore, Rome (II, PL. 283). Here there can be no doubt that the scenes are based upon a manuscript, but they are realized in an independent and original manner that makes them an outstanding artistic creation. The figures in the panels in the nave have rhythm even when they are compressed into large groups, and the rows of red or black tesserae outlining the most important parts of the composition serve to accentuate the design. Coherence is given to the lively color scheme by alternating repetition, and gold is used extensively, often to emphasize certain figures and groups. The space is conceived as a shallow area in which the figures move between the background and the frontal plane. In the scenes on the triumphal arch gold serves as a rich framework for the enlarged miniatures, which, because the transposition was so skillful, have retained the punctilious attention to detail of the originals. These mosaics are an example of a transposition of one art form into another, resulting in an outstanding work in its own right.

The mosaics in the two small apses of S. Costanza, dating from about the end of the 4th and the beginning of the 5th century, also are obviously of Roman workmanship. Finally, the mosaics of the Lateran Baptistery, from the time of Sixtus III (432–40), and especially the large acanthus scrolls on a blue background, are of interest in that they anticipate mosaics made a century later under Justinian for Hagia Sophia in Constantinople.

Contemporaneous painting in Campania, at least that still to be seen, is closely linked to the Roman school, though it is often decidedly popular in manner, as in several catacombs in Naples: the arcosolium of S. Severus in the Catacomb of S. Severus, datable to 408, the slightly later one depicting Theotecnus, Ilaria, and Nonnosa, and the one of Cominia and Nicatiola in the Catacomb of St. Januarius (III, PL. 99), and that of Pascentius in the Catacomb of St. Gaudiosus. The mosaics in the Chapel of Matrona in S. Prisco, not far from Santa Maria Capua Vetere, dating possibly from some decades earlier, have similar characteristics. The tomb of St. Gaudiosus, in the cemetery in Naples named for him, is noteworthy because of its mosaics, though unfortunately they are badly damaged. The clipeus with a portrait bust of Eleusinus in the Catacomb of St. Januarius is close in time and style. The two last-mentioned works evince Eastern influences that relate them to contemporaneous work in Ravenna. It is to be regretted that most of the mosaic decorations produced in Campania at this time — for example, those in the Basilica of Cimitile and of SS. Severino e Sosio in Naples — have been totally lost. The paintings in S. Gennaro extra Moenia, Naples, also belong to the 5th century. The date of the mosaics in the Baptistery at Naples is disputed. These softly modeled mosaics are clearly differentiated from Roman works by the fluid handling of robes. The uncertainty of the date is here accompanied by difficulties in determining the stylistic milieu, even though some contributions from the East, and particularly from Greece, are certain, as was true of the early work in Ravenna.

Similar influences, presumably, also Eastern, are evident in the right apse of S. Aquilino in Milan, in the mosaic of Christ enthroned amid the apostles. This subject, very popular in catacomb painting, is here distinguished by the fluid rhythm of the group, with each white figure of an apostle, alternately set in two different planes, accented against a gold background. The more rigid and sketchy small Biblical scenes recall some of the provincial mosaics in Antioch. The mosaics almost suggest a manuscript prototype, perhaps from Salonika, Asia Minor, or Syria, especially when one notes the differences between the Milanese and the Roman mosaics.

The earliest of the Ravenna monuments, the so-called "Mausoleum of Galla Placidia," identified by some as the Church of S. Lorenzo, was built between 425 and 450. Here a noticeable Hellenistic influence of the type evolved in Asia Minor — by this time perhaps transmitted through Greece — is evident, especially in the mosaic depicting the Good Shepherd, who is shown in a three-quarter view typical of Pergamene representations. Elements of Pergamene Hellenism also appear in the pastoral scenes in S. Aquilino in Milan, where, however, the poses are stiffer and the space more attenuated. Such elements recur later in the Paris Psalter (II, PL. 480), in which they were translated into the brilliant, vigorous idiom of the miniaturist. There are precise similarities between the apostles in the "Galla Placidia" monument and the saints in S. Vittore in Ciel d'Oro, Milan; and for neither can a Roman — or more generally, Western — descent be absolutely excluded. Thus Ravenna, for all its Eastern foundations, did not ignore or abjure certain fundamental Western modes, even in its earliest period.

The degree of traditional derivation in the iconography of the Baptistery of the Orthodox, or Cathedral Baptistery (PLS. 45, 66, 72; X, PL. 441), in Ravenna is a complicated question that would be of only superficial interest in defining the artistic environment. What is relevant in this respect is the intensity with which the motifs are handled; the clear separation between iconic and aniconic themes; the insistent rhythm imposed on disparate elements; and the narrative continuity without beginning or end, which demonstrates the particular value of a central plan in the interrelation of the structure and its pictorial decoration. The lesson transmitted from the rotunda of the Church of St. George in Salonika (PL. 44) could not be more explicit, and affinities with the modes of form and description of the figures in the small apses in S. Costanza were surely not accidental. Thus, here too the Western element is operative because of its contact with a vital contemporary current that had found expression in Greece.

b. The East during the 5th century. In this period Greece in general, and Salonika in particular, again rose to a position in mosaic art that seems not to have been fully appreciated. An imposing work of the period is Hosios David (Salonika), with its Majestas Domini, datable toward the middle of the century, which partakes of traditions from Pergamon and Asia Minor in the broad, seated figures and the symbolic animals, as well as of a tendency toward chromatic surfaces adapted from contemporary textiles, particularly from those from Syria. A new visual idiom grows out of this fusion, but its ties with Constantinople have not as yet been clarified and cannot be until other finds are added to the mosaics of the Great Palace (VII, PL. 372). It is possible that the Vandal invasions of Africa caused many inhabitants of the region to emigrate, and that the artisans among them chose to go to leading centers with an extensive building activity.

The large area between the sea and Mesopotamia at this time had close ties with Greece, but though it may seem that the stimulus came from Constantinople, this has not yet been demonstrated. The mosaic of the basilica of Shavei Zion (Palestine), which for historical reasons cannot be later than 427, shows a large cross set on Mount Golgotha, pomegranates, and fish; the whole composition exemplifies new representational modes (most pronounced in the handling of the pomegranate and fish motifs), which also appeared in Greece (e.g., church at Klausion). The same may be said of the pavement mosaics found in the Synagogue at Maon (Nirim). Elsewhere, however, typically Hellenistic motifs and representational means are employed — animals and plants that are clearly derived from Alexandria in their modeling and in their subtle and varied colors. A case in point is the Church of the Multiplication of the Loaves and Fishes, in Heptapegon (Tabgha).

A nonfigural trend (i.e, one with purely ornamental motifs) asserts itself toward and after the middle of the 5th century throughout the Greek-Mediterranean and the Syro-Palestinian world and Asia Minor. Good examples of mosaics are those from a house and the basilica at Epidauros, from the basilica at Lefkadia Nausis, from several basilicas in Kos and one in Samos, from the baths at Serjilla (473), those of the so-called "Glass Court" at Jerash, and those in Casaranello. The broad repertory of decorative geometric patterns, the variety of colors, and the effect of iridescence obtained by juxtaposing colors in narrow rows of tesserae placed so that only the corners touch — these are the characteristics of this production, which had an enormous diffusion.

In Antioch, mosaics in private houses became more common, even though the city seems steadily and progressively to have become more provincial, a sign that other centers were becoming culturally more important. However, the devitalization of schemata and the fossilization of certain types of representations were accompanied by a series of innovations, the value of which cannot be denied. To the first group belongs the House of the Masks (400–25). The mosaic of the Amazons in the House of the Amazonomachy (400–25), however, shows that a work in *opus sectile* (stone inlays) was translated into mosaic. That this was the inspiration of the artist in composing his picture is confirmed by the fact that he seems to have cut up fragments of mosaic of the same color, only to lay them side by side. The scene is thus intentionally and forcibly reduced to two dimensions, without suggesting a derivation from manuscript illustrations or from textiles. The House of the Green Carpet (ca. 450) has one of those monumental allegorical compositions that show how slowly classical sources dried up. In the Hall of Philia mosaics (Baltimore, Mus. of Art.), as well as in the House of the Rams' Heads (450–60), the Eastern world, with its predilection for heraldically affronted animals, is once more interjected into the Western sphere. Especially in the Hall of Philia, the Hellenistic representational tradition absorbs such sources to an exceptional degree into images that are thoroughly descriptive and anything but symbolic. The varied mosaic decoration of the Yakto complex (ca. 460), especially the composition known as the "Megalopsychia," shows a hunt in which the plants, animals, and hunter-heroes are disposed according to a composition synthesized from the schemata of the distant Constantinian era, with divisions along the axes and bisections of angles. The figures are set against a white, scale-patterned background that emphasizes the fragmental and isolated character of each scene. The topographical border is a valuable indication of a continued taste for representations of buildings, cities, and regions. Here, too, the scenes are broken up into a series of many episodes all disposed on the same plane in a "continuous narrative," inevitably recalling the use of this scheme on the columns of Theodosius and Arcadius in Constantinople. The strong preference for long-established iconographic and representational means is balanced by a frank and easy style: one punctuated by incandescent light marking time segments and situations, which cannot be traced farther back than the middle of the century.

The animal frieze in the "martyrium" at Seleucia Pieria, of the Justinian period, has animals scattered on a white, scale-patterned, background — almost as though they were decorative geometrical and floral elements on a rug. The relationship of rug and mosaic is also revealed in such contemporary compositions as the mosaic of the *Striding Lion* (Baltimore, Mus. of Art), or of those in the House of the Phoenix, and in the mosaic of the *Beribboned Parrots* (PL. 76). In contrast, the style that was reintroduced into North Africa after the departure of the Vandals is clearly revealed in the mosaics in Room 2 of the House of Ktisis (500–525). The hunt mosaics in Worcester, Mass. (Art Mus.), and Washington, D. C. (Dumbarton Oaks Coll.), in which the monumental figures of hunters are immersed in the scale-patterned background, mark the exact point at which the late-antique and Byzantine worlds meet. In these two mosaics the influence of Constantinople is decisive.

Apart from the mosaics of Antioch, certain others should be noted: the mosaic of mythological scenes found in a house at Epidaurus, the mosaics of the Palace at Stobi, and those of the House with the Double Apse, also at Stobi, all of the early 5th century. The mosaic at Low Ham (England), with Homeric subjects that undoubtedly derived from the Hellenistic iconography of Asia Minor, is from the middle of the century. Such works are not extensive, probably because the barbarian incursions put an end to such expensive artistic enterprises.

c. Constantinople from Zeno the Isaurian to Justinian the Great. The chief characteristic of paintings and mosaics of this period is the absence of any system of perspective. Since the background (whether gold, blue, or white) indicates atmosphere, the figures are each conceived independently and without a point of reference that postulates a general perspective. Concomitantly, the sense of time is lost and, with it, continuous narrative. As a result, even where scenes could be given narrative treatment, they are scattered about the surface without any representational link. The typical example is the mosaics of the Great Palace of the Emperors in Constantinople (II, PL. 372), variously dated to the reigns of Theodosius I or Justinian, but now generally assigned to the latter period. Groups and figures are scattered in calculated eurythmy on a scale-patterned background that is only rarely interrupted by indications of landscape. The mixing of real and imaginary animals emphasizes the nonrealistic character of the whole, which thus exists outside any logical dimensions (II, PL. 437). There is no perspective, but all the figures are seen in a three-quarter view or in a spiral attitude that makes them seem to rotate on an axis, so that they appear to be enveloped in deep space. The lights and shadows that articulate the figures are given the greatest emphasis, but in the plants the more pronounced lights and shadows are transformed into decorative motifs by means of a repetitive alternation of tesserae in orderly arrangements. The contours of each image are fluid, rapid, and only very rarely rendered in one strong line, but emerge from the fluctuations of color that describe the figure. The different sources are easily distinguished: the Hellenistic culture of Asia Minor, more specifically Pergamene, in the arrangement and pose of the figures; North African influence in the mosaic technique and in a certain exuberance in the use of color; Persian contributions, coming by way of Syria, in some iconographic motifs, especially in the wide borders with clusters of foliage and human faces. All these elements are enriched and transformed by the great anonymous artist who seems to dominate the Constantinople of Justinian, from which few other mosaics have survived the ravages of time. All that remains of the magnificence of Justinian's Hagia Sophia are a few floral scrolls and some fragments in the narthex, where the gold crosses on a gold ground look almost like intarsia work.

The way in which some of the figures of the mosaic in the Great Palace are drawn points up their connection with two well-known paintings, the icon of St. Peter from Sinai, and the *Madonna della Clemenza* in S. Maria in Trastevere, Rome (XII, PL. 142). The common ancestry of all three lies in the Hellenistic suggestion of mass in a space that has no dimensions, for neither the tympanum above the figure of St. Peter nor the enclosing frame of the Roman painting creates a limitation of space. In the former, the heavy frontality of the saint has something archaic about it in comparison with the mosaics in Constantinople. In the *Madonna della Clemenza* the forward thrust of the angels emerging at the sides of the throne and encircling the central figure (which is the pivot of the composition), in two spiraling movements, repeats a motif frequently used in the mosaics of the Great Palace. Whereas the 6th-century date assigned to the Sinai icon is acceptable, the 8th-century date given the *Madonna della Clemenza* — because it is the date of the frame and inscription — may not be justified, for the frame may well be a later replacement.

The most important group of Byzantine works in the west is in Ravenna. The series includes: Baptistery of the Arians, between 493 and 526; the chapel of the archiepiscopal palace, between 491 and 519; S. Apollinare Nuovo, between 493 and 525; S. Vitale, between 521 and 534; and S. Apollinare in Classe, before 549 (see BYZANTINE ART).

The Italo-Roman tradition, which set the pattern for the works in Campania and Lombardy, as well as in Rome, here manifests itself in the Christological cycle in S. Apollinare Nuovo. This cycle seems to postulate as model an illustrated text that was close in its cultural origins to the one that served as the prototype for the mosaics in the nave of S. Maria Maggiore, Rome, even though the corporal solidity of the figure of Christ seems to be diminished in the less definite modeling that is apparent in all Ravenna mosaics. The same Egyptian currents that had produced the Cotton Genesis (Br. Mus., Cotton Otho. B.vi), the manuscript with the illustration of charioteers (Oxford), and the drawing of Christ and the apostles on the Sea of Tiberias also influenced the scenes of the sacrifice of Abraham and the sacrifice of Melchizedek in S. Vitale (XI, PL. 86), where the setting is clearly reminiscent of the Alexandrian style; the same is true of the Biblical scenes with Jeremiah and Moses and of the four panels with the Evangelists (all in S. Vitale). In the eagle of St. John and in the figure of Christ in the apse there is a chromatic dissolution or fragmentation of surfaces, which supports the theory of an Eastern prototype, thus also explaining that mixture of tendencies that is common to so much of the production of Ravenna. Some of the richness of Constantinople erupts in the use of gold on gold in the halos of the saints in S. Apollinare Nuovo, in the rhythmic disposition of the long rows of saints, in the disregard for the modeling of the body, and in the bright colors of the robes. The taste of Constantinople is most pronounced in the two panels in S. Vitale showing Justinian and Theodora (II, PLS. 440, 446; IV, PL. 18). However, these are part of a traditional development that derives from the reliefs on the base of the Obelisk of Theodosius, and that, in Constantinople at this time, seems to have been superseded by the style represented by the mosaics of the Great Palace. Perhaps this archaism in Ravenna can be justified by the close relation to manuscript illumination.

All these mosaics have one thing in common — a definition of space that is neither incorporeal nor merely atmospheric but presents a shallow space in which the figures are forced to move within the narrow area between the surface and the background.

In Rome a similar but somewhat more Western development may be observed in the apse mosaic in SS. Cosma e Damiano (526–30), in which spatial breadth gives monumentality to the clouds dominated by the figure of Christ (PL. 75; III, PL. 305; X, PL. 178). In contrast, the earliest Annunciation, in S. Maria Antiqua, faithfully echoes the manner of Constantinople, but also conforms to the inevitable Roman monumentality; this preference for architecturally conceived structure underlies such works as the *Madonna and Child with the Donatrix Turtura*, in the crypt of SS. Felix and Adauctus in the Catacomb of Commodilla.

The trends in the East were very different. One reveals a predilection for decoration consisting of ornamental motifs with dense and intensely chromatic designs similar to those of textiles. This may be seen in the mosaic pavement of the court joining the churches of St. John, SS. Cosmas and Damian, and St. George, in Jerash (ancient Gerasa), all from the end of the third decade of the 6th century, as well as in the Church of St. John in Ephesus and in the church at Machouk, near Antioch.

Another tendency was an emphatic outlining of forms. This reaches an almost classical equilibrium in the rich and varied decoration of the sumptuous late-antique house at Agros (Greece), from the beginning of the 6th century. The same quality may be seen in the contemporaneous pavements of the Beth Guvrin Villa (Israel), but in Palestine the manner is accentuated to the extreme, as in the Beth Alpha Synagogue. The same preference for outlines is evident in some of the topographical mosaics with cities, such as those in the Church of SS. Peter and Paul in Jerash, which may be thought of as antecedents for the later, large "geographical" mosaics, such as the one in the Church of St. John at Madaba (III, PL. 494).

The style of Constantinople, translated into popular idiom, or rather transmitted by provincial centers (as Antioch was by then), was reintroduced into Africa after the Byzantine reconquest. The resultant works, such as the mosaics in the Baptistery of Kélibia, represent an attempt to assimilate the new culture. Other works are provincial echoes of Constantinople, for example, the mosaics in Gasr-el-Libia (ancient Theodorias) and of the Cathedral of Cyrene (Libya).

The great mosaics of the Justinianic period were also an inspiration to the Arabs, and the mosaics in the Great Mosque, Damascus (II, PL. 441; VII, PL. 407; VIII, PL. 145), and in the Dome of the Rock, Jerusalem (VIII, PL. 146), built during the Ommiad rule, derive from them. The Arabs took those schemata with them to Spain, where the effects survived even into the 9th century, for example, in the Church of Santullo, Asturias.

d. Manuscripts. It has been shown that illustrated manuscripts played a major and determining role in the development of contemporaneous mosaics. Fortunately, from the 5th century onward, original codices have survived that are of high enough quality to permit detailed stylistic analysis. The most important are the Vatican Virgil (Vergilius Vaticanus; PL. 78) and the "Roman" Virgil (Virgilius Romanus; Vat. lat. 3867), both dating from the end of the first quarter of the 5th century, and the Terence (Vat. lat. 3868) from the middle of the 5th century. The *Iliad* (Milan, Bib. Ambrosiana, Ms. F.205 inf.), which some date to the Justinianic age, should be dated to the end of the century. The fragment of a poem with the illustration of charioteers from Antinoë (Oxford, Johnson Coll.) can be dated about 500 on paleographic evidence, and the same is true of the scroll with the illustration of Christ and the apostles on the Sea of Tiberias (Florence, Bib. Laurenziana), which has the same origins. Important manuscripts of the Justinianic age are the Dioscorides in Vienna (ca. 512; Cod. vindob. med. gr. 1) and in Naples (Cod. suppl. gr. 28), the Cotton Genesis (Br. Mus., Cotton Otho. B.vi), and the Vienna Genesis (PL. 79). The Rossano Codex (Rossano, Mus. Arcivescovile), the Sinope fragment (Paris, Bib. Nat., Suppl. gr. 1286), and the *Christian Topography* of Cosmas Indicopleustes (Ms. Vat. gr. 699) are all from the 6th century.

The Vatican Virgil, which stands out even among these superior works, is attributed to the pagan Roman milieu around the Nicomachi and Symmachi (see below, MINOR ARTS). The style is compact and consistent and the compositions well balanced, qualities usually considered the hallmarks of the Alexandrian school. The Terence is also from Rome or Latium and belongs to a highly cultured milieu, whereas the style of the "Roman" Virgil is more popular. The origins of the Ambrosian *Iliad* are as uncertain as its date. In some respects it seems Eastern and in others more Western, in the line of descent from the Vatican Virgil. The attribution of the Cotton Genesis to Alexandria is certain. The fragments — the one with the charioteers in Oxford and the one in Florence — are both works of considerable quality and indicate how great an influence manuscripts could exercise on mosaics and wall painting. There are also well-founded reasons for assigning the Cosmas Indicopleustes to Alexandria. Constantinople was almost certainly the home of the Vienna Dioscorides. This manuscript was dedicated to Juliana Anicia, and even its dedicatory miniature has decidedly Eastern characteristics.

Michelangelo CAGIANO DE AZEVEDO

MINOR ARTS. Late-antique minor arts were predominantly — there were notable exceptions — the reflection of imperial patronage. Not only coins and medallions, which were as a matter of course regarded as imperial propaganda, but cameos, gems, silver dishes, carvings in ivory, glass, and, no doubt, textiles, all bore the imperial image or witnessed imperial benevolence. Although the surviving evidence suggests that Christian forms of art were established rapidly after the rise of the religion (for example, in Dura-Europos and Palmyra), and although it is known that from the beginning members of all classes of society had been attracted to the new faith, it is clear that, in order to raise the status of a creed so recently regarded as seditious, the driving force of imperial recognition was necessary. Only with the 4th century is it possible to begin to chart with any consistency the effect of aristocratic patronage on Christian sarcophagi, to note the intensive (and therefore undoubtedly imperial) building enterprises that entailed a proliferation of church decoration and furniture, and to see open devotion demanding icons, carvings in ivory, and Christian silver marriage caskets. The sign of the new era had appeared in the vision of Constantine before the Battle of Milvian Bridge (312), and the seal was set by his mother Helena's finding of the True Cross (ca. 327). Christianity was to confirm that which the imperial cult had predicated: the proper subject for art was not the precise notation of matter nor a summary evocation of the ideal, but a deliberate statement of the Intelligible Being — either as God in the human form of Christ, or as the Vicar of God in the person of the emperor. There were, of course, artifacts on different levels; and works of art executed for the pagan aristocracy in Rome were of comparable quality with those commissioned by the Christian court. In the late 4th century, however, pagan allegories and mythological subjects began to look academic and uninspired.

Coins and medals. The seeds of the style called "late-antique" are already to be seen in the coinage of the late 3d and early 4th centuries. The medallion equivalent of five *aurei* with a representation of Diocletian and Maximian, dating possibly from the year 287 (Berlin, Staat. Mus., Münzkabinett; Schlunk, 1939, pl. 1, no. 1), reveals that classical standards of proportion were being abandoned. Although the heads are depicted with the intention of verisimilitude, shoulders and hands have shrunk to a degree that would have been considered barbaric by a Hadrianic or Antonine connoisseur. From this time begins the gradual disintegration of the ideal forms postulated by the Greeks and the moderately precise statement of fact demanded by the Romans. Generally speaking, the heads on the Tetrarchic coinage still preserve this Roman interest in realistic representation. Diocletian (PL. 90), of lowly Dalmatian stock, Maximian, a Pannonian peasant, and Galerius, the son of a shepherd, are in no sense idealized. Their rugged features, closely cropped hair, and stubbly beards are presented factually and contrast forcibly with heads on some of the coins of Constantine, such as those, struck possibly in about 326, based on a portrait of Alexander the Great (Schlunk, 1939, pl. 1, no. 4), and with some of the coins of Constantius II (Toynbee, 1944, pls. II, 15; VI, 3; XX, 2; XXXIV, 1, 2; XXXV, 3). From the time of Constantine, realistic portraits are rare. Although it is possible to detect differences of physiognomy in the sequences of imperial coins, the image is usually depicted with an exaggeratedly youthful face and with hair curling over the nape of the neck and combed over the brow; rank is denoted by the imperial diadem and various attributes of power. Julian the Apostate (361–63) and, later, Eugenius were represented with beards, but, in spite of the Emperor Julian's retrograde tendencies, there was no attempt to return stylistically to the standards of the Antonines or of Augustus. A small gilt bronze bust of Valentinian II (375–92) or of Gratian (H. Peirce and R. Tyler, 1932–34, I, pl. 50a), from a private collection at Pécs (where after 375 Roman domination was weak) and now in the National Museum, Budapest, shows the continuity of the Constantinian models. But to return to the coins, it must be emphasized that quality does not necessarily vary with the metropolitan position of the mint. Coins struck in Antioch may be better than those from Constantinople; and even as late as the reign of Leo I (457–74), the coins minted at Salonika were superior to those of the new Rome on the Bosporus.

In spite of the disintegration of classical canons, there can be no denying the beauty of the majority of late-antique coins and medallions, such as that issued by Constantius II at Constantinople between 333 and 335, now in Vienna (Gnecchi, 1912, I, p. 30, no. 10); the medallion of the same emperor in a fragment of a gold girdle, dating possibly from the 5th century (Baltimore, Walters Art Gall., 1947, no. 421); the *aureus* of Valentinian I, issued at Constantinople between 364 and 375 (London, Br. Mus.); the medallion of Theodosius I (Washington, D.C., Freer Gall.; Toynbee, 1944, pl. XXXVI); and a medallion of Galla Placidia, from about 420 (Paris, Cab. Méd.; Peirce and Tyler, I, pl. 88b). Medallions and coins such as these were regarded at the time as works of art and were frequently mounted in gold to make bracelets, collars, and girdles. They served as models for the jewelry of the aristocracy, for example, the early-5th-century wedding ring of Aristophanes and Vigilantia from Rome (Washington, D.C., Dumbarton Oaks Coll.; *Handbook*, no. 166). But after Arcadius (395–408) the decline was rapid. Coins were badly designed and indifferently struck — although the image of the Empress Licinia Eudoxia is not without barbaric charm (cf. Delbrück, 1933, pl. 24, nos. 4–6) — and in spite of the great medallion of Justinian (lost) issued to celebrate the victory of Belisarius in 535 (Toynbee, 1944, pl. XLIV), the later sequences amount to little more than pictographs of imperial power.

Contorniates — coinlike pieces not issued to circulate as currency — were probably used in Rome as games counters. Of indifferent quality, struck with pagan legends or with portraits of emperors noted for their interest in the circus, such as Nero and Hadrian, these medals were produced for persons lacking in culture or refined taste. Nevertheless, an attempt has been made to establish such artifacts, ranging from the 4th into the 5th century, as pagan propaganda distributed during the New Year games by a group of Roman aristocratic families obstinately clinging to the old gods. But references to the New Year are scanty on the contorniates; and the illiterate inscriptions, slipshod technique, and rough facture make it unlikely that pagan families such as the Nicomachi or the Symmachi would have sponsored such an enterprise. Nor is there any real evidence that the contorniates represent deliberate anti-Christian propaganda.

Jewelry. Jewelry, even when it was not made up from coins and medallions, was likely to bear the imperial portrait or to stress rank. Thus, a gold brooch with three small pendent crosses (found at Ténès, Algeria) bears a frontal portrait of an empress, identified with Galla Placidia, and dates probably from the first quarter of the 5th century. The cruciform fibulas, all gold, from the same treasure (Heurgon, 1958, pl. II) were used to pin the chlamys at the right shoulder; they represent part of the uniform of the higher ranks of the army and of the imperial bureaucracy. It is known that there were strict rules governing the type of fibula worn: those decorated with precious stones were reserved for the use of the emperor, and the pinning of the fibula to the chlamys by the emperor became an important act of investiture. Belt ornaments, buckles, and bracelets, as represented in the Ténès treasure, suggest that by the early 5th century jewelry worked in an *à jour* technique had become fashionable. The gold is pierced to show patterns of interlace, small birds in vine-scrolls, or more complex figural scenes, as in a gold buckle, found at Coudray (Oise), which is in the Collection B. de Montesquiou-Fezensac (Heurgon, 1958, pl. XIX). On the other hand, bracelets and collars may consist of simple twisted strands of gold, ending in knobs or filigree. Earrings may combine many techniques — *à jour* work, filigree, plaited strands of gold, with or without precious stones; but typical of the period are those decorated with jewels or pearls suspended at the ends of gold strands, varying in number between three and five (for necklaces of this type, cf. Schlunk, 1939, pl. 15, no. 73; pl. 24, nos. 97 and 98).

Glyptics. Late-antique cameos and gems may be regarded as expressions of the personal taste of the emperor. Constantine the Great was particularly fond of giving them as presents, and the majority of surviving late-antique cameos were made for him or for his family (cf. Delbrück, 1933, pl. 73). The sequence begins, however, with a beautiful chalcedony cameo carved with the busts of Diocletian (284–305) and Maximianus Herculius (286–305), in the Dumbarton Oaks Collection (*Handbook*, no. 210). The most famous, the Rothschild chalcedony cameo (VI, PL. 40), has been identified as either the portrait of the emperor Honorius and the empress Maria or that of Constantius II and his empress and has been attributed to a Constantinopolitan workshop of about 335. Apart from imperial portraits and scenes of apotheosis, there may be represented battle scenes, as on the superb fragment in the National Museum in Belgrade (G. Bruns, 1948, p. 19, fig. 14), and Christian subjects such as the Good Shepherd (Schlunk, 1939, pl. 18, no. 180).

The carving of gems, largely confined to the imperial portrait in choice of subject (PL. 90), follows closely the style of the coins, as in the fine amethyst intaglio engraved with a bust of Constantius II in the British Museum (H. B. Watters, 1926, no. 2032; Delbrück, 1933, pl. 74, 2). A sapphire intaglio in the Trivulzio Collection in the Castello Sforzesco, Milan, depicting Constantius II spearing a boar (*ibid.*, pl. 74, 1), should be compared with gems bearing his portrait in Boston and Leipzig. A jasper intaglio with a representation of Mars and Venus, in the Cathedral Treasury at Cologne (Peirce and Tyler, 1932–34, I, pl. 9), may be slightly earlier in date than the gems engraved for the Constantinian house. An engraved sardonyx of Romulus (Leningrad, The Hermitage), which represents the emperor Honorius investing the young Valentinian III as Caesar in the presence of his father Constantius III, may be dated about 423 (Delbrück, 1933, fig. 73, and pl. III, 1). The style of this gem is a great deal coarser and more summary than those of the 4th century.

Carvings in rock crystal, almost certainly executed in Egypt, are extremely rare. A series of bowls, fish, and a miniature temple in this technique are in the collection of Mrs. W. H. Moore, New York (Baltimore, Walters Art Gall., *Catalogue of Early Christian and Byzantine Art*, nos. 536–40); but the finest of the rock-crystal carvings is a statuette of Hercules and the Erymanthian boar (PL. 89), dating probably from the early 4th century (*ibid*, no. 534). A statuette of a lady of the imperial house — represented without a diadem, however — in the Freer Gallery, Washington, D.C. (Dennison, pls. LIII, LIV), is coarser in quality. A fragment of an armored torso in the Louvre (Pierce and Tyler, 1932–34, I, pl. 7) and the head of a lion in the Musée de Cluny, Paris (*ibid*, I, pl. 17), would seem to date from the early 4th century.

Among carvings in agate, also very rare, the magnificent "Rubens Vase" (PL. 88), decorated with large vine leaves, grapes, and two heads of satyrs, has been assigned to Constantinople and dated about 400 (Baltimore, Walters Art Gall., *op. cit.*, no. 543). It should be compared with the Waddesdon Vase, carved in agate with spreading vine-scrolls, acanthus leaves, and heads of Pan, which is in the British Museum (C. H. Read, *The Waddesdon Bequest*, 1902, p. 32, no. 68, pl. 17); the "Rubens" may be slightly earlier in date.

Silverwork. The great sequence of silver dishes and other vessels of the late-antique period start with Constantius II. Two dishes found at Kerch (Leningrad, The Hermitage) refer to an anniversary of Constantius in 343. The style of these dishes and that of a third, with a representation of a mounted emperor preceded by a Victory and followed by a soldier, is provincial. Scholars have hesitated to assign them either to Constantinople or to Rome; a workshop in the Black Sea area has been suggested (cf. Matzulewitsch, 1929, pls. 23–25). Constantius celebrated his anniversary in his favorite city, Antioch; but if the standards of its mint are considered, it would seem unlikely that Antioch was the source of the dishes. Works in a provincial style are not unknown in Constantinople during the period from the founding of the city until the outbreak of iconoclasm (726), and it may be that these *largitio* dishes were made there. The imperial sequence continues with the silver dish of Valentinian I (364–75), found in the river Arve near Geneva (Mus. d'Art et d'Histoire; Delbrück, 1933, pl. 79). On the dish the emperor is represented standing; a Victory flies toward him from the left, and he is accompanied by six soldiers. The silver is badly rubbed, and the face of the emperor has at some time been covered. It seems reasonable to suppose that this dish was made in Rome. The third, and most splendid, piece of this type is the Missorium of Theodosius I (II, PL. 487), which celebrates the Decennalia (388); found in Estremadura, it is in the Real Academia de la Historia, Madrid. One of the key pieces of late-antique style, it was to be copied by Byzantine silversmiths in the early 7th century. Scholars differ over the situation of the workshop: Rome, Constantinople, and Salonika have all been mooted. The missorium shows the emperor Theodosius I seated before an arcaded screen between his nephew Valentinian II and his son Arcadius. The imperial family is flanked by bodyguards, and the emperor is in the act of presenting a diploma to an official. In the lower field a reclining figure of Earth, or Abundance, holds a cornucopia, and five Erotes lift the fruits of the earth toward the emperor. The supernatural aspect of the emperor is emphasized by depicting him twice the size of his guards and of the official receiving the diploma. The soft contours of the imperial face seem embalmed in eternal youth; the slim figure leans forward out of the plane in which his nephew, son, and guards are set, seemingly to hypnotize the beholder. The seated Augusti no longer appear to sit; they float above their stools and hover delicately in space. Their robes ripple over softly defined forms. There is no longer a precise statement of function: hands no longer grip, and the manner in which Earth holds the cornucopia is ill-defined. The intent is to portray not so much a historical event — the bestowal of a diploma at the time of the Decennalia — but a vision of imperium not wholly of this world, an epiphany of the Vicar of God.

Late-antique art constantly expressed a fusion of authorities and traditions — scholarly meditation on the antique, the stressing of imperial might, the perception of a new religious scheme. The change in esthetic vision had already been proposed by Plotinus: art should be a point of departure for metaphysical experience. Theories such as these favored Christianity, but for some time the old pagan cults were ranged beside the new faith. The Corbridge Lanx, from the Collection of the Duke of Northumberland (on loan to Br. Mus.), presents Ortygia-Delos as a cult center of the gods Apollo, Artemis, Athena, Leto, and Leto's sister, the local goddess Asteria. The last known official sacrifice to Apollo at Delos was made by Julian the Apostate before his unfortunate Persian war, which began in 363, and the Corbridge Lanx dates very likely from about 360. Also probably to be related to Julian the Apostate, from about 360, is the remarkable octagonal silver-gilt dish with scenes from the youth of Achilles, made by Pansylyppos in Thessalonika and found with a large hoard buried at Augst, once the fort Augusta Raurica and also once a base for operations against the Alamanni by Constantine II and Julian (354–61). In addition to 168 silver coins (Diocletian, Constantine I, Constantine II), 17 large medallions (Constantine I, Constans, Constantine II), and 3 silver ingots bearing the stamp of the Gallic usurper Magentius (350–53), the hoard contained a circular silver-gilt and niello dish showing Erotes fishing in front of a walled town; a rectangular silver-gilt and niello tray with Dionysos, Ariadne, and a satyr and a similar dish with the mark "Euticius Naisi" (of Niš, or Nish); a silver candelabrum; a statuette of Venus; dishes, bowls, cups, spoons, and one small eating implement with the "Chi-Rho" monogram. Among the silver vessels dating from the third quarter of the 4th century and into the 5th, there is a remarkable sequence of pagan and Christian subjects: the marriage casket of the Christians Projecta and Secondus (PL. 86), the Venus trulla, and four silver statuettes that personify Rome, Constantinople, Alexandria, and Antioch (all part of the Esquiline Treasure, Br. Mus.); the Parabiago dish (Castello Sforzesco, Milan), showing Cybele and Attis, in a chariot drawn by four lions, and their cortege; the reliquary casket in the Church of S. Nazaro Maggiore, Milan (PL. 81); the so-called "Personification of India" (Istanbul, Archaeol. Mus.); and a dish with Artemis and a stag (Berlin, Staat. Mus.). Included in this group is the treasure of Traprain Law (Edinburgh, Nat. Mus. of Antiquities of Scotland), with a dish showing a Nereid riding a sea monster; a flagon with Dionysiac scenes; and another depicting the Fall of Man, Moses Striking the Rock, the Adoration of the Magi, and what appears to be the Betrayal in the Garden. The magnificent Oceanus dish and two Dionysiac platters from Mildenhall (Br. Mus.) and the Cesena dish, found with a Gothic coin of Theodoric (454–526), are further examples. It seems probable that most of this silver was made in Rome.

A silver vase with Bacchic scenes and other vessels found in Syria (Cleve. Mus.), have been described as "Byzantine" and assigned to the 4th century. It is probable that an amphora, decorated with an Amazonomachy, hunting scenes, and Nereids on sea monsters, found at Concesti (Leningrad, The Hermitage), was also made at Constantinople in the early 5th century. By this century some Byzantine silver was stamped. A vase with mythological reliefs (Moscow, the Kremlin, Hall of Arms), dating from the 5th century, is stamped with the tyche of Constantinople. A series of vessels bears the control stamps of the emperor Anastasius I (491–518): a trulla with Nilotic scenes and the dish of Bishop Paternus (ca. 518), with alterations made at Tomi (both Leningrad, The Hermitage); a plate from Sutton Hoo (Br. Mus.); and a plate with a niello cross (Bulgaria, Razgrad Mus.).

Other centers are known to have produced silver vessels in the late-antique period. Probably among such local production was the Carthage Treasure (Br. Mus.), some of which is decorated with pastoral and animal scenes, including a dish bearing an inscription referring to the Cresconii, a well-known North African family. A silver ampulla found at Ténès, Algeria, decorated with the Christian monogram framed by a garland of laurel leaves, is probably a Carthaginian work dating from the first half of the 5th century. The silver dish of Aspar Ardabur (PL. 87), dated 434, and the "Capsella Africana" (Vat. Mus.) bear Carthaginian control stamps; and in the 6th century this series was continued with a silver plate decorated with a Nereid riding a sea lion (Turin, Gall. Sabauda; 534–542, or 557), and the "Shield of Gelimer," the Vandal king who was overcome by Belisarius in 533, and the "Shield of Hannibal" (both Paris, Cab. Méd.). A series of silver dishes containing medallions with scenes from the story of Ino and Melikertes (Athens, Benaki Mus.) may be representative of Alexandrian work, since they are presumed to have been acquired in Egypt. These include the Berlin dish, found at Thebes, with a shepherdess carrying a child on her back and holding a basket of fruit (Schlunk, 1939, no. 108), and a silver plate from the tombs of Ballana and Qustul (dated by coins from 364–640). Two pyxides with Christian subjects (Grado, Italy, Cathedral Treasury) have been assigned to the 5th century, but it is more likely that they are of the 6th century and were made in Ravenna. It is generally agreed that some part of the silver, of inferior quality, found at Mildenhall, Traprain Law, and other sites in northern Europe was made in Gaul; examples include a fragment of a vase with bacchanalian scenes and a Hercules dish, both from Traprain Law; the Risley Lanx and four bowls, with mythological heads on the base and hunting scenes on the rim, from the Mildenhall Treasure. Some of the less accomplished pieces found at Mildenhall may have been made in Britain.

Ivories. By a curious chance, one of the earliest Western carvings in ivory of the late-antique period is Christian. Most scholars agree that the date of the Brescia Casket (VIII, PL. 240) lies within the third quarter of the 4th century, although an attempt has been made to place it as early as the second quarter. Scenes from the Old and New Testaments are carved in a cold replica of many 4th-century sarcophagus reliefs, but the precise statement of form and the use of space suggest that the patron or artist was thinking in terms of past esthetic standards. There seems to be no doubt that toward the end of the 4th century there was in Rome an atmosphere of classic revival, partly as a result of patrician patronage. One of the most beautiful of all late-antique carvings in ivory, the Nicomachi-Symmachi diptych (I, PL. 301), was produced probably to celebrate the profession of a priestess — the two families, closely related, represented the hard core of paganism in Rome — but a marriage between the two houses, in 401, has also been suggested. This diptych and that (in Berlin) of Probianus, Vicar of Rome about 400, serve as the prime examples around which a number of distinguished carvings in ivory may be assembled: the Asklepios and Hygieia diptych (VIII, PL. 240); a small casket in Paris (Bib. de l'Arsenal); the Trivulzio relief with the Marys at the Sepulcher (VIII, PL. 240); the Ascension relief (Munich, Bayerisches Nationalmus.); and, somewhere within this ambiance, the Adam in Paradise and St. Paul diptych (Florence, Mus. Naz.), and the Querini diptych (Brescia, Mus. Cristiano), with representations of Hippolytus and Phaedra and, possibly, of Artemis and Endymion. It can be seen that, in spite of tenacious paganism in certain Roman circles, the workshops served both the old and the new religions. Slightly below the quality of the above-mentioned reliefs, the so-called diptych of "Stilicho and Serena" (PL. 84), may conceivably have been carved in Milan; and it is possible that the diptych of Probus (Aosta, Cathedral), with a representation of the emperor Honorius is also Milanese — though, stylistically, a Roman origin seems more likely.

Probably of slightly later date, but closely allied to the Probianus diptych, are the panels in the British Museum with scenes of the Passion and Resurrection of Christ. They may not be far removed in time from the diptych of the Lampadii (Brescia, Mus. Cristiano), probably from about 410. The diptych of Constantius III (Halberstadt, Cathedral Treasury), may perhaps be dated to 417, the diptych, so-called of "Patricius" (Novara, Bib. Capitolare) to 422, and that of Felix (Paris, Cab. Méd.) to 428. Assigned to the decade between 430 and 440 are the Berlin (Staat. Mus.), Paris (Louvre), and Nevers (Mus. Municipal) panels with scenes from the life of Christ; the Moses, St. Peter, and St. Thecla panels (Br. Mus.); and the Pola Casket (Pulj, Yugoslavia, Archaeol. Mus.), also with Christian subjects. This group should be compared stylistically with the wooden doors of S. Sabina (PL. 83) in

Rome, carved about 430. In the third quarter of the 5th century appear two superb panels with circus combats: the *venatio* panels in Liverpool and in Leningrad. Of approximately the same date are a Bellerophon panel (PL. 85), and another bearing an apotheosis, possibly commemorating the tercentenary (463) of the *consecratio* of Antoninus Pius (Br. Mus.); the Dionysus-Selene diptych (Sens, Cathedral Treasury); and the "Andrews Diptych" (PL. 85), with scenes depicting the Miracles of Christ. After the capitulation of the young emperor Romulus Augustulus to Odoacer, four authentic consular diptychs are known: that of Basilius (480), divided between Florence (Mus. Naz.) and Milan (Cathedral Treasury); that of Boethius (487), in Brescia; that of Sividius (488), in the Cabinet des Médailles, Paris — all showing a marked decline in quality; and lastly, that of Rufus Gennadius Probus Orestes (530), in London (Vict. and Alb. Mus.), which is a coarse copy of the Constantinopolitan diptych of Clementinus (513).

The ivory diptychs issued by consuls holding office in Constantinople as a rule reveal the consul as presiding over the games. They include those of Areobindus (506), who was responsible for the several versions in Zürich (Landesmus.), Besançon (Mus. B. A.), Paris (Mus. de Cluny, Louvre, and a private coll.), Leningrad (The Hermitage), and Lucca (Bib. Capitolare) and also that of Justinus (540) in Berlin (Staat. Mus.). The diptych of Clementinus (513) is in Liverpool (Public Mus.); that of Anthemius (515), which was in Limoges, is lost; some of those of Anastasius (517) are divided between Berlin (Staat. Mus.) and London (Vict. and Alb. Mus.), and some are in Leningrad (The Hermitage), in Verona (Bib. Capitolare), in Paris (Cab. Méd.), and in Rome (Mus. Vat.); the supposed diptych of Magnus, dated 518 (PL. 84), is divided between the Castello Sforzesco, Milan, and the Cabinet des Médailles, Paris. Diptychs issued by Justinian (521) are in the last two collections, and a third is in the Metropolitan Museum, New York; those issued by Philoxenus (525) are in the Cabinet des Médailles, Paris, and in the Dumbarton Oaks Collection, Washington, D.C.; that of Apion (539) is in the Cámara Santa of the Cathedral in Oviedo. In addition, a number of imperial diptychs appear to have been issued at Constantinople: the panels depicting an empress, probably Ariadne (d. 515), in the Museo Nazionale in Florence, and in the Kunsthistorisches Museum, Vienna; sections of a diptych, according to one scholar datable only to the years of the reign of Anastasius (491–518), in the Castello Sforzesco, Milan; and the much debated "Barberini Diptych" (PL. 85), variously assigned to Zeno (474–491), Anastasius, and Justinian (527–565).

Closely related to these ivory reliefs carved for officials in Constantinople in the first half of the 6th century, but strictly speaking outside the late-antique period, is the superb leaf of a diptych with a Greek inscription and a representation of the Archangel Michael (Br. Mus.); this has been tentatively identified as a commemoration of the reunion of Rome and Constantinople in the presence of the papal delegates in 519. The serene diptych with representations of Christ enthroned between SS. Peter and Paul and of the Virgin and Child between two angels, now in Berlin (Staat. Mus.), and the so-called "throne of Maximian" (V, PLS. 340, 432), dating probably from the middle of the 6th century and variously assigned to Constantinople, Alexandria, and Ravenna, seem to represent aspects of the Justinianic "renovatio," which should be seen as the first phase of Byzantine art. To this phase, also, should be assigned the Poet and the Muse diptych (Monza, Italy, Cathedral Treasury), dated in the past to the 4th, 5th, and 6th centuries, which, because of its similarity to Justinianic silver, should be assigned to Constantinople. The diptych now serving as a book cover in the Treasury of the Cathedral in Milan, with Christian scenes and embellished with enamels, is Italian work dating from the middle of the 6th century.

In addition to these reasonably datable carvings in ivory, there is a large group of reliefs and pyxides which has been ascribed to first one part of the Mediterranean world and then another, and which has been shifted from date to date. It is probable that most of the debatable pieces fall outside the late-antique period and must be looked upon as provincial artifacts. But there is a sequence of rather coarse, largely pagan carvings in bone and ivory, found on the outskirts of Alexandria and in Egyptian rubbish heaps, which would seem to be Egyptian work dating from the late 3d century to the 6th century. In quality some of the finest are a small ivory fragment of a Bacchic procession, found at Oxyrhynchus (Bahnasa), now in the Victoria and Albert Museum, London (Longhurst, *Catalogue*, I, p. 21, fig. 1); a statuette of Mars (?) and an ivory box with a representation of Dionysus with a maenad, a satyr, a Tyche, and an Eros — both in the Dumbarton Oaks Collection, Washington, D.C. (*Handbook*, nos. 223, 224); and, by analogy, some boxes with representations of Asklepios and Hygieia. A relief representing Apollo and Daphne (Ravenna, Mus. Naz.) and the figure of a naked girl (Baltimore, Walters Art Gall.; *op. cit.*, no. 177) suggest by comparison with Coptic sculpture in Herakleopolis Magna (Ahnas) an Egyptian provenance dating from the late 5th century. It may be that a carved ivory panel with the figure of a bearded saint in the Monastery of Kikko, Cyprus, is also Egyptian, but of the 6th century.

The assigning of groups of ivory carvings with certainty to other centers is difficult, but there seems no reason to doubt that carvings in ivory were made in various parts of the Empire. The cautious student will prefer, however, concrete evidence in the form of inscriptions or other unassailable archaeological detail to personal theories about Antiochian, Alexandrian, north Italian, and Gaulish styles or groups based on tendentious iconographical speculation.

Textiles. The problems set by late-antique textiles are in some respects less complex and in others more so. The majority of the textiles — they number many thousands — of this period have been found in Egyptian burial grounds; and although finds at Dura-Europos, which were produced presumably before 256, and at Palmyra, before 273, led to speculation on technical grounds that sequences of fragments found in Egypt were imported from elsewhere, the general conclusion, on both stylistic and technical evidence, must be that textiles found in Egypt were, on the whole, made in Egypt. As a result of prolonged Greek and Roman occupation, however, the patterns reflect Hellenistic and Roman influences, and may with reason be regarded as echoing Western fashion. Problems of workshop differentiation in Egypt, on the other hand, and problems of dating both stylistic and technical innovations are more difficult to resolve. The greater part of the textiles found in Egypt were almost certainly woven not in factories but in the home; and production of this sort is apt to resist any rigid attempt at classification. The main sequences have always been assumed to have begun in the second half of the 3d century, when mummification ceased to be a general practice, but there are few textiles which may be assigned with confidence to this early date. A roundel tapestry woven in purple wool and undyed linen thread, found at Hawara, is dated by coins to about A.D. 340, and this type of ornament is paralleled by the textile patterns of costumes depicted in the mosaic floors of the Tetrarchic villa in Piazza Armerina (X, PL. 178), believed to date from the early 4th century. But it is equally clear that such patterns continued to be used over a considerable period of time: they are reflected in the Missorium of Theodosius I and in 6th-century mosaics at Ravenna (II, PLS. 440, 446; IV, PL. 18). In general, when reviewing Egyptian textiles, the student must rely on broad principles of stylistic development, the application of which is apt to be subjective. From the technical point of view, one of the major developments of the craft was the invention of the drawloom, but the date and place of this discovery are still shrouded in mystery. Patterns on the chlamys worn by "Stilicho," represented on the ivory diptych in the Cathedral Treasury in Monza, suggest that this is a drawloom-woven fabric; thus it is probable that the invention had been made before the end of the 4th century. In the late-antique period the majority of textiles found in Egypt were made on a simple tapestry loom. The materials used were, for the most part, linen and wool. Gold thread was probably much more extensively used, both in tapestries and embroideries, than the surviving examples suggest. Although Chinese silks were found at Palmyra and cotton has been found in Syria and Nubia, examples of silk and cotton from the 4th and 5th centuries are extremely rare.

It is reasonable to assume that large-scale historiated hangings existed from early times, but few have survived. The fragment of a large woolen tapestry with a mask and a duck set in a network of jeweled bands, in the Dumbarton Oaks Collection (*Handbook*, no. 297), has been assigned to the 4th or 5th century, and there is a similar tapestry in the Textile Museum, Washington, D.C. The superb woolen tapestry woven with Nereids riding on sea monsters, also at Dumbarton Oaks (*Handbook*, no. 298; Peirce and Tyler 1932–34, I, pl. 141), has been assigned to the same period, but a late date is not unlikely. A fragment of a weft-loop woolen rug with geometrical ornament (Met. Mus.) may date from the 4th or 5th century. There seems no reason to doubt that a sizable weft-loop woolen panel with Erotes fishing from a boat (Br. Mus.) dates from the 4th century. But, generally speaking, curtains and other household fabrics have grounds of undyed linen decorated with occasional scattered ornament — roundels, squares containing mythological subjects, flowers, birds, rabbits, and other animals — woven at random intervals. The decoration of tunics at this time consists of shoulder bands that continued from shoulder to hem or end in a pendant ornament halfway down; roundels or squares at about knee level and on the shoulders; cuff bands, and sometimes neck and hem borders. Within these bands, roundels, squares, and borders may be depicted pastoral scenes, such as the elegant late-4th-century fragment (London, Vict. and Alb. Mus., no. 1028–1901); hunting scenes, warriors, heads of gods and allegorical figures, such as the beautiful Dionysiac head (Washington, D.C., Textile Mus. no. 71.106), or the Nile and the Earth (Leningrad, The Hermitage; Moscow, Mus. of Fine Arts); and Nereids, Tritons, and Erotes, as in the silk, gold, and wool tapestry (Boston, Mus. of Fine Arts, no. 46. 401), dating probably from the middle of the 5th century. The fashion for historiated scenes on clothing seems to have developed during the second half of the 4th century. Asterius, Bishop of Amasia in Pontus (d. 410), in a homily described with some indignation people wearing pictured garments and looking like painted walls; some even wore sacred scenes, such as Christ with the apostles or the Miracles of Christ. Surviving textiles decorated with Christian scenes attributable to the late-antique period are rare, and it is possible that they did not become common until the 6th century. A well-known tapestry fragment in linen and wool with the figure of a Victory holding a garlanded Cross (Vict. and Alb., no. 349–1887) has been assigned in the past to the 5th century, but on stylistic grounds a later date seems preferable. There can be no doubt that sequences of debased late-antique patterns continued into the early Islamic period.

Groups of drawloom-woven fabrics in wool, found in Egypt, have been assigned to the 3d century — for example, a fragment of compound tabby (Philadelphia, Mus. of Art), decorated with a hunting scene (Weibel, 1952, no. 37) — but it is unlikely that any group in this debased style existed before the 6th century. Drawloom-woven silks, either compound tabby or compound twill, assignable with any certainty to the 5th century are exceedingly rare. It is probable that the majority of those given in the past to the 5th century should be dated later. Likely candidates for the earliest "Western" silks are a compound tabby and a compound twill woven with a scenes from the life of Joseph, a maenad hunting twill and a goatherd twill, a series of twills with birds framed by acanthus leaves, and a series of allover lozenge patterns containing palmettes and small leafy sprays (all, Sens, Cathedral Treasury), a pastoral scene (Boston, Mus. of Fine Arts, no. 11.90); a Nereid silk divided between the Cathedral Treasury of Sion (Sitten), Berlin (Staat. Mus.), and Zürich; a pastoral scene with horses drinking from a trough and men plucking fruit (?) from a tree, in the Treasury of the Abbey of St-Maurice d'Agaune; an early twill-damask with a hunting scene, in the Basilica of S. Ambrogio, Milan; and a fragmentary silk twill with a representation of Daniel in the lions' den (Vict. and Alb. no. T.93-1937). The provenance of all these is uncertain, but Constantinople, Antioch, and Alexandria have all been suggested, and it is known that there was a factory at Carthage. A twill fragment decorated with parrots (Vict. and Alb., no. T.104-1949), a silk with peacocks, ducks, and parrots (New York, Cooper Union Mus., no. 1902-1-210), and a silk with griffins, ducks, and leafy sprays (Sens, Cathedral Treasury) approach the court dresses represented in the imperial mosaics in S. Vitale in Ravenna and thus may be of 6th-century date; but, if this is so, some of the silks previously mentioned should be dated about the same time.

Glassware. Glassware has survived in considerable quantities from various parts of the Empire, and it is probable that almost all the big cities of the ancient world had factories. Glass was made in Syria and North Africa; it is probable that there were factories in the Danube basin, in Greece and the Balkans, and in Asia Minor. Fine examples of glass were produced in Italy and in the Rhine-Moselle area, where Cologne was an important center.

Glass from Syria, ranging in date from the 3d to the 6th century, tends to be unfigured and is characterized by simple shapes decorated with fantastic whorls and spirals of drawn solid threads. Time and oxidization have formed a patina to which only the most rigid purist would object, and the colors range from murky white to iridescent greens and bronzed blues. Similar glass was made in the Rhineland. Flasks in the shape of human heads were made both in Syria and in the West. A fragment of enameled glass dating from the 3d century was found at Dura-Europos, and a group of painted glasses, typified by the Daphne Vase (found in the Crimea) and the Judgment of Paris dish (found near Damascus), both now in the Ray Winfield Smith Collection (Corning Glass Center, *Glass from the Ancient World*, 1957, nos. 341, 342), has been assigned to Antioch. Although a considerable amount of glass has been excavated at Karanis, and other finds have passed through the hands of dealers in Cairo, the general standard of production suggests that the importance of Alexandria as a glass-producing center had diminished before the late-antique period.

From an esthetic point of view, a series of cut and engraved glasses from a variety of finds are the most distinguished of the period. The series may be divided into various categories, and it is clear that the varied groups were made in factories in different parts of the Empire. The group known as *diatreta*, or "cage-cups," is of superb quality. The cage-cup was made by cutting and grinding openwork decoration out of a thick blank of cast or blown glass, the decoration being attached to the wall of the inner portion by small shanks or bridges left for this purpose by the glass cutter. Perhaps the finest example is the cup with a representation of Lycurgus (PL. 88), probably Roman work of the second half of the 4th century. It has been related to the Cagnola cup (Varese, Mus. Civ.); to a situla with a hunting scene (VI, PL. 221); to a fragmentary cup decorated with the Pharos of Alexandria, found in Begram in Afghanistan (Kabul Mus.), for which external evidence may demand a closing date in the middle of the 3d century; and to a cup with fish and snails, found in Szekszárd, in the Budapest Historical Museum. The presence of the Pharos of Alexandria suggests that Alexandria may also have been a center for this type of work, but it seems reasonable to suppose that many of the finds in the West are Roman. A Roman workshop has also been claimed for a fine, deeply engraved situla with Dionysiac scenes (PL. 88).

On the other hand, a group of glasses engraved with a type of hard-stone point (it is not known whether a diamond point was available at this period) would seem to have been made in Cologne in the 4th and 5th centuries. This sequence includes the Wint Hill hunting bowl (Oxford, Ashmolean Mus.); a bowl, found at Homblières (Aisne) and now in the Louvre, dating from about 400 and decorated with the sacred monogram and Biblical scenes; a cup engraved with the Raising of Lazarus (New York, Mrs. W. H. Moore Coll.), dating from the 4th century (Baltimore, Walters Art Gall., *op. cit.*, no. 625); and a goblet, found in Cologne, engraved with Adam and Eve, Moses Striking the Rock, and the Raising of Lazarus (Br. Mus. *Guide to Early Christian and Byzantine Antiquities*, 1921, p. 172). The list may be extended by a number of pieces found in or near Cologne, with representations of Susanna and the Elders, Poseidon, and scenes from the Old and New Testaments, all in Berlin (Staat. Mus.; cf. Schlunk, 1939, nos. 193-98).

Some glasses, dating apparently from the 3d to the 5th century, have rather rough designs executed with a wheel tracing lightly over the surface. There may have been both Eastern and Western schools producing this type of glass. The Highdown Hill (Worthing Mus.) goblet has been assigned to an Egyptian workshop, and a considerable number have been found in Egypt at Hawara, Karanis, and Oxyrhynchus. It is possible to argue that the examples found in the West are all imports, but it would be rash to be dogmatic. Painted glasses, found mainly in Scandinavia and Britain and dating from the 3d to the 4th century, are decorated with various kinds of animals and birds; these are believed to have been made in Cologne and other factories in the Rhine-Moselle area.

Rome would seem to have been the chief source of an extensive sequence of gilded glass. Large quantities, ranging in date from the 3d to the 5th century, have been found in Roman catacombs, with many examples bearing Christian subjects. Sometimes glass medallions, such as portrait miniatures, were made for their own sake; but as a rule they formed the bottoms of cups or plates or were fused into the sides of glass vessels. The majority were made for domestic use and, as the inscriptions show, were given as gifts on the occasion of weddings, birthdays, and various anniversaries. They were often used, too, as a seal in the mortar that closed a tomb. It has been suggested that, since the labels on the earliest of these glasses — for example, the family portrait in the Museo Cristiano, Brescia (VI, PL. 226) — show Egyptian and Greek peculiarities, and since there are iconographical similarities to the Fayum mummy portraits, a case can be made for Alexandrian influence and craftsmen at work in Italy. The Ficoroni medallion (Met. Mus.), bearing a portrait of a lady and her son, has been assigned to Alexandria in the second half of the 3d or the early 4th century. But family portraits in diverse media are common enough in Rome; and, since there is no doubt that Greek was written in the metropolis, the main sequences suggest indigenous patronage and workmanship. At the same time, there is every reason to believe that this type of work was produced in other centers, notably Cologne. It is probable that a dish with portraits of the sons of Constantine I, found in Cologne (Delbrück, 1933, pl. 45), and a gilded glass dish with scenes from the Old and New Testaments, also found in Cologne (Br. Mus., *Guide to the Early Christian and Byzantine Antiquities*, 1921, p. 141, fig. 91), among a number of examples found in northern France and the Rhineland, were made locally. Although undoubtedly the most beautiful are the stern, melancholy portraits of individuals or family groups (PL. 80), the later sequences with their mixtures of pagan, Jewish, and Christian symbolism reflect the popular taste of cosmopolitan but declining Rome. The mythological scenes, as on the contorniates, are coarse and stereotyped; the Jewish emblems are presented with considerable broadness of effect; and the Christan examples, although iconographically interesting, make it plain that the art of the common body of the faithful was seldom governed by high esthetic standards.

A study of other sequences of ceramics, terra cottas, and urns, and of household artifacts such as bronze lamps, candlesticks, and other furniture suggests that outside the court or the patronage of the great patricians, standards were low. Bronze counterpoise weights were still fashioned in the likeness of imperial busts, but they bear no comparison to the Missorium of Theodosius I or the ivory diptych of Probianus.

John BECKWITH

BIBLIOG. *General*. a. *Methodological studies and general accounts*: R. Garrucci, Storia dell'arte cristiana nei primi otto secoli della chiesa, 6 vols., Prato, 1872-81; F. Wickhoff (with W. von Härtel), Die Wiener Genesis, Vienna, 1895 (trans., E. Sellers Strong, Roman Art, London, 1900); A. Riegl, Die spätrömische Kunstindustrie nach dem Funden in Österreich-Ungarn, Vienna, 1901 (2d ed., 1927); O. Wulff, Altchristliche und byzantinische Kunst, 3 vols., Berlin, 1914-39; W. Neuss, Die Kunst der alten Christen, Augsburg, 1926; G, Rodenwaldt, Art from Nero to the Antonines, in Cambridge Ancient History, XI, Cambridge, 1936, pp. 775-805; W. Weisbach, Geschichtliche Voraussetzungen der Entstehung einer christlichen Kunst, Basel, 1937; G. Rodenwaldt, The Transition to Late-Classical Art, in Cambridge Ancient History, XII, Cambridge, 1939, pp. 544-70; A. Grabar, Martyrium: Recherches sur le culte des reliques et l'art chrétien antique, 3 vols., Paris, 1943-46; G. Rodenwaldt, Zur Begrenzung und Gliederung der Spätantike, JdI, LIX-LX, 1944-45, pp. 81-87; A. Grabar, Plotin et les origines de l'esthétique médiévale, CahA, I, 1945, pp. 15-34; S. Bettini, L'arte alla fine del mondo antico, Padua, 1948; B. Schweitzer, Die spätantike Grundlagen der mittelalterlichen Kunst, Leipzig, 1949; E. H. Swift, Roman Sources of Early Christian Art, New York, 1951; C. R. Morey, Early Christian Art, 2d ed., Princeton, 1953; A. Rumpf, Stilphasen der spätantiken Kunst: Ein Versuch, Cologne-Opladen, 1957; E. Auerbach, Literatursprache und Publikum in der lateinischen Spätantike und im Mittelalter, Bern, 1958; T. Klauser, Studien zur Entstehungsgeschichte der christlichen Kunst (I), Jhb. für Antike und Christentum, I, 1958, pp. 20-52; D. V. Ainalov, The Hellenistic Origins of Byzantine Art (trans. E. and S. Sobolevitch), New Brunswick, N.J., 1961; R. Bianchi Bandinelli, Archeologia e cultura, Milan, 1961; H. Jursch, Tradition und Neuschöpfung im altchristlichen Bilderkreis, Berlin, 1961.

b. *Handbooks*: O. Marucchi, Eléments d'archéologie chrétienne, 3 vols., Rome, 1902; L. von Sybel, Christliche Antike, 2 vols., Marburg, 1906-09; Cabrol-Leclercq; V. Schultze, Altchristliche Städte und Landschaften, 3 vols., Leipzig, Gütersloh, 1913-30; C. M. Kaufmann, Handbuch der christlichen Archäologie, 3d ed., Paderborn, 1923; G. Ferretto, Note storicobibliografiche di archeologia cristiana, Vatican City, 1942 (bibliog.); W. Lowrie, Art in the Early Church, New York, 1947; E. Kitzinger, Early Medieval Art in the British Museum, 2d ed., London, 1955; M. Laurent, L'art chrétien primitif des origines à Justinien, 2d ed., Brussels, 1957; P. Testini, Archeologia cristiana, I, Roma, 1958; F. van der Meer and C. Mohrmann, Atlas of the Early Christian World (trans. M. F. Hedlund and H. H. Rowley), London, 1959; M. Gough, The Early Christians, London, New York, 1961; W. F. Volbach, Early Christian Art (trans. S. Ligota), New York, London, 1961; E. Syndicus, Early Christian Art (trans. J. R. Foster), New York, 1962.

c. *Iconography and symbolism*: (1) *Architecture*: J. Sauer, Symbolik des Kirchengebäudes und seiner Ausstattung in der Auffassung des Mittelalters, 2d ed., Freiburg im Breisgau, 1924; K. Liesenberg, Der Einfluss der Liturgie auf die frühchristliche Basilika, Freiburg im Breisgau, 1928; L. Kitschelt, Die frühchristliche Basilika als Darstellung des himmlischen Jerusalem, Munich, 1938; D. F. Brown, The Arcuated Lintel and Its Symbolic Interpretation in Ancient Art, AJA, XLVI, 1942, pp. 389-99; R. Krautheimer, Introduction to an "Iconography of Medieval Architecture," Warburg, V, 1942, pp. 1-33; K. Lehmann, The Dome of Heaven, AB, XXVII, 1945, pp. 1-27; A. Grabar, Le témoignage d'une hymne syriaque sur l'architecture de la cathédrale d'Edesse au VIe siècle et sur la symbolique de l'édifice chrétien, CahA, II, 1947, pp. 41-67; A. M. Schneider, Liturgie und Kirchenbau in Syrien, Nachr. der Ak. der Wissenschaften in Göttingen, Philologisch-H. Klasse, 1949, 3, pp. 45-68; P. Underwood, The Fountain of Life in Manuscripts of the Gospels, Dumbarton Oaks Papers, V, 1950, pp. 43-138; A. Stange, Das frühchristliche Kirchengebäude als Bild des Himmels, Cologne, 1950; G. Bandmann, Mittelalterliche Architektur als Bedeutungsträger, Berlin, 1951 (bibliog.); R. Krautheimer, Sancta Maria Rotunda, in Arte del primo millennio (ed. E. Arslan), Turin, 1953, pp. 21-27; E. B. Smith, Architectural Symbolism of Imperial Rome and the Middle Ages, Princeton, 1956; T. Klauser, Das Ciborium in der älteren christlichen Buchmalerei, Nachr. der Ak. der Wissenschaften in Göttingen, I: Philologisch-H. Klasse, 1961, Nr. 7, pp. 191-208. (2) *The representational arts*: F. Cumont, Textes et monuments figurés relatifs aux mystères de Mithra, 2 vols., Brussels, 1894-96; K. Michel, Gebet und Bild in frühchristlichen Zeit, Leipzig, 1902; J. Reil, Die altchristliche Darstellungen der Kreuzigung Christi, Leipzig, 1904; A. Krücke, Der Nimbus und verwandte Attribute in der frühchristlichen Kunst, Strasbourg, 1905; H. L. Keher, Die heiligen drei Könige in Literatur und Kunst, 2 vols., Leipzig, 1908-09; E. Becker, Das Quellenwunder des Moses in der altchristlichen Kunst, Strasbourg, 1909; F. J. Dölger, ΙΧΘΥΣ, 5 vols., Münster in Westfalen, 1910-57; J. Reil, Die altchristlichen Bildzyklen des Lebens Jesu, Leipzig, 1910; E. B. Smith, Early Christian Iconography and a School of Ivory Carvers in Provence, Princeton, 1918; G. Stuhlfauth, Die apokryphen Petrusgeschichten in der alt-christlichen Kunst, Berlin, 1925; H. Schrade, Zur Ikonographie der Himmelfahrt Christi, Vorträge der Bib. Warburg, VIII, 1928-29, pp. 66-190; M. Huggler, Mythologie der altchristlichen Kunst, Strasbourg, 1929; F. Saxl, Mithras: Typengeschichtliche Untersuchungen, Berlin, 1930; F. Suehling, Die Taube als religiöses Symbol im christlichen Altertum, Freiburg im Breisgau, 1930; F. Gerke, Petrus und Paulus, RACr, X, 1933, pp. 307-29; F. Gerke, Der Ursprung der Lämmerallegorie, Z. für neutestamentliche Wissenschaft, XXXIII, 1934, pp. 160-96; A. C. M. Beck, Genien und Niken als Engel in der altchristlichen Kunst, Giessen, 1936; J. Kollwitz, Christus als Lehrer und die Gesetzübergabe an Petrus in der konstantinischen Kunst Roms, RQ, XLIV, 1936, pp. 45-66; F. Gerke, Ideengeschichte der ältesten christlichen Kunst, Z. für Kirchengeschichte, LX, 1940, pp. 1-102; F. Cumont, Recherches sur le symbolisme funéraire des Romains, Paris, 1942; T. Kempf, Christus der Hirt: Ursprung und Deutung einer altchristlichen Symbolgestalt, Rome, 1942; E. H. Kantorowicz, The "King's Advent" and the Enigmatic Panels in the Doors of Santa Sabina, AB, XXVI, 1944, pp. 207-32; J. Kollwitz, Das Bild von Christus dem König in Kunst und Liturgie der christlichen Frühzeit, Theologie und Glaube, XXXVIII, 1947-48, pp. 95-117; C. Leonardi, Ἄμπελος: Il simbolo della vita nell'arte pagana e paleocristiana, Rome, 1947; G. Vezin, L'adoration et le cycle des mages dans l'art chrétien primitif, Paris, 1950; U. Rapp, Das Mysterienbild, Münsterschwarzach, 1952; E. R. Goodenough, Jewish Symbols in the Greco-Roman Period, 8 vols., New York, 1953-58; C. Roth, Jewish Antecedents of Christian Art, Warburg, XVI, 1953, pp. 24-44; C. Cecchelli, Il trionfo della Croce, Rome, 1954; J. Fink, Noe: Der Ferechte in der frühchristlichen Kunst, Münster, Cologne, 1955; A. Grillmeier, Der

Logos am Kreuz, Munich, 1956; M. J. Vermaseren, Corpus inscriptionum et monumentorum religionis mithraicae, 2 vols., The Hague, 1956–60; K. Wessel, Der Sieg über den Tod: Die Passion Christi in der frühchristliche Kunst des Abendlandes, Berlin, 1956; J. Villette, La résurrection du Christ dans l'art chrétien du IIe au VIIe siècle, Paris, 1957; J. Fink, Bilderfolgen zu 5 Szenen in der Kunst der Spätantike, MdI, LXV, 1958, pp. 142–53; J. Doresse, Des hiéroglyphes à la croix: Ce que le passé pharaonique a légué au Christianisme, Istanbul, 1960; G.A.Wellen, Theotokos: Eine ikonographische Abhandlung über das Gottesmutterbild in frühchristlichen Zeit, Utrecht, Antwerp, 1960; M. Lawrence, Three Pagan Themes in Christian Art, in De artibus opuscula XL: Essays in Honor of Erwin Panofsky (ed. M. Meiss), New York, 1961, pp. 323–34; C. Weyer-Davis, Die Traditio-legis-Bild und seine Nachfolge, MJhb., 3d ser., XII, 1961, pp. 7–45.

d. Historical background: O. Seeck, Geschichte des Untergangs der antiken Welt, 6 vols. in 8, Berlin, 1895–1921; S. Dill, Roman Society in the Last Century of the Roman Empire, 2d ed., London, New York, 1899; J. B. Bury, History of the Later Roman Empire, London, 1923 (repr. New York, 1958); M. Lietzmann, Probleme der Spätantike, SbBerlin, 1927, pp. 342–58; F. Lot, La fin du monde antique et le début du moyen âge, Paris, 1927 (rev., ed., 1950; trans. P. and M. Leon, The End of the Ancient World and the Beginning of the Middle Ages, London, New York, 1931, rev. ed., New York, 1961); J. Geffcken, Der Ausgang des griechisch-römischen Heidentums, Heidelberg, 1929; R. Laqueur, H. Koch and W. Weber, Probleme der Spätantike, Stuttgart, 1930; A. Alföldi, A Festival of Isis in Rome under the Christian Emperors of the 4th Century, Budapest, 1937; W. Seston, Dioclétien et la Tétrarchie, Paris, 1946; A. Piganiol, L'empire chrétien, 325–395, Paris, 1947; A. Alföldi, The Conversion of Constantine and Pagan Rome (trans. H. Mattingly), Oxford, 1948; E. Stein, Histoire du Bas-Empire, 2 vols., Paris, 1949–59; J. Vogt, Constantin der Grosse und seiner Jahrhundert, Munich, 1949; A. Alföldi, A Conflict of Ideas in the Late Roman Empire, Oxford, 1952; The Age of Diocletian: A Symposium, December 14–16, 1951, The Metropolitan Museum of Art, New York, 1953; W. C. Bark, Origins of the Medieval World, Stanford, Calif., 1958; H. Dörries, Konstantin der Grosse, Stuttgart, 1958: P. W. A. Immink and H. J. Scheltema, At the Roots of Medieval Society, Oslo, Cambridge, Mass., 1958; H. P. L'Orange, Fra principat til dominat, Stockholm, 1958; P. E. Hübinger, Spätantike und frühes Mittelalter, Darmstadt, 1959; B. Rubin, Das Zeitalter Justinians, I, Berlin, 1960; G. Downey, A. History of Antioch in Syria from Seleucus to the Arab Conquest, Princeton, 1961; H. Lietzmann, A History of the Early Church (trans. B. L. Woolf), Cleveland, 1961; K. D. Schmidt and E. Wolf, eds., Die Kirche in ihrer Geschichte, I, Göttingen, 1961; G. Walser and T. Pekáry, Die Krise des römischen Reichs, Berlin, 1962; A. Momigliano, ed., The Conflict between Paganism and Christianity in the Fourth Century, Oxford, 1963; See also current bibliog. in Byzantinische Zeitschrift.

Architecture: *a. General*: J. Durm, Baukunst der Römer, 2d ed., Stuttgart, 1905; H. Holtzinger, Altchristliche und byzantinische Baukunst, 2d ed., Leipzig, 1908; G. F. Rivoira, Le origini dell'architettura lombarda, 2d ed., Rome, 1908 (trans. G. McN. Rushforth, Lombardic Architecture, 2 vols., London, 1910); G. F. Rivoira, Architettura romana, Milan, 1921 (trans., Roman Architecture and Its Principles of Construction under the Empire, Oxford, 1925); G. Rodenwaldt, Die letzte Blütezeit der römischen Architektur, Forsch. und Fortschritte, XV, 1939, pp. 244–45; P. H. von Blanckenhagen, Flavische Architektur und ihre Dekoration untersucht am Nervaforum, Berlin, 1940; F. W. Deichmann, Rl. für Ant. und Christentum, s.v. Architektur, I, 1950, cols. 604–13; L. Crema, L'architettura romana, Turin, 1959; W. L. MacDonald, Early Christian and Byzantine Architecture, New York, 1962.

b. Architectural structure: (1) *Reuse of earlier buildings and building materials*: F. W. Deichmann, Frühchristliche Kirchen in antiken Heiligtümern, JdI, LIV, 1939, pp. 105–36; F. W. Deichmann, Die Spolie in der frühchristlichen Architektur, Bericht VI. Int. Kong. für Archäol., 1939, Berlin, 1940, pp. 588–90; F. W. Deichmann, Rl. für Ant. und Christentum, s.v. Christianisierung, II, 1954, cols. 1228–41. (2) *Orders and columns*: R. Kautzsch, Kapitellstudien, Berlin, 1936; F. W. Deichmann and A. Tschira, Die frühchristlichen Basen und Kapitelle von S. Paolo fuori le mura, RM, LIV, 1939, pp. 99–111; F. W. Deichmann, Säule und Ordnung in der frühchristlichen Architektur, RM, LV, 1940, pp. 114–30; J. B. Ward Perkins, The Shrine of St. Peter and Its 12 Columns, JRS, XLII, 1952, pp. 21–33; P. Verzone, I capitelli del tipo corinzio dal IV all'VIII secolo, in Wandlungen christlicher Kunst in Mittelalter (Forsch. zur Kg. und christliche Archäol., II), Baden-Baden, 1953, pp. 87–97; I. Nikolajević-Stojković, La décoration architecturale sculptée de l'époque bas-romaine en Macédoine, en Serbie et au Montenegro, Belgrad, 1957 (Serb., with Fr. summary). (3) *Entablatures*: F. Töbelmann and H. Kähler, Römische Gebälke, 2 vols., Heidelberg, 1923–53. (4) *Architraves and archivolts*: E. Weigand, Propylon und Bogentor in der östlichen Reichskunst, Wiener Jhb. für Kg., V, 1928, pp. 71–114. (5) *Arcades and the baldachin system*: H. Sedlmayr, Das erste mittelalterliche Architektursystem, Kw. Forsch., II, 1933, pp. 25–62 (repr. in H. Sedlmayr, Epochen und Werke, Vienna, 1959, pp. 80–139); E. Weigand, Das spätrömische Architektursystem, Forsch. und Fortschritte, X, 1934, pp. 414–15. (6) *Walls*: T. Ashby and G. Lugli, La Basilica di Giunio Basso sull'Esquilino, RACr, IX, 1932, pp. 221–55; G. Becatti, Case ostiensi del Tardo Impero, Rome, 1948; H. Sedlmayr, Spätantike Wandsysteme, SbMünchen, 1958, 7 (repr. in H. Sedlmayr, Epochen und Werke, Vienna, 1959, pp. 31–79). (7) *Open entrances*: G. Matthiae, Basiliche paleocristiane con ingresso a polifora, BArte, XLII, 1957, pp. 107–21. (8) *Screens and doors*: R. Jäger, Die Bronzetüren von Bethlehem, JdI, XLV, 1930, pp. 91–115; M. D. Darsy, Bibliographie chronologique des études publiées sur les portes de Sainte Sabine, Rome, 1954; C. Bertelli, Notizia preliminare sul restauro di alcune porte di S. Sofia a Istanbul, B. Ist centrale del restauro, 34–35, 1958, pp. 95–115; G. Webster, Roman Windows and Grilles, Antiquity, XXXIII, 1959, pp. 10–14. (9) *Ceilings*: F. W. Deichmann, Copertura delle basiliche paleocristiane, Felix Ravenna, 3d ser., XXIV, 1957, pp. 63–73; F. W. Deichmann, Rl. für Ant. und Christentum, s.v. Decke, III, 1957, cols. 629–43; F. W. Deichmann, Untersuchungen zu Dach und Decke der Basilika, Charites, Bonn, 1957, pp. 249–64. (10) *Vaults*: H. Glück, Der Ursprung des römischen und abendländischen Wölbungsbaues, Vienna, 1933; F. W. Deichmann, Die Entdeckung von S. Stefano Rotondo, Misc. G. Belvederi, Vatican City, 1954, pp. 437–50; G. Lugli, La tecnica edilizia romana, I, Rome, 1957, pp. 659–93; G. Bovini, L'impiego dei tubi fittili nelle volte degli edifici di culto ravennati, Corsi di cultura sull'arte ravennate e bizantina, 1959, 1, pp. 27–43. (11) *Domes*: G. De Angelis d'Ossat, La forma e la costruzione delle cupole nell'architettura romana, Atti III Conv. naz. Storia Arch., Rome, 1940, pp. 223–50; M. Rumpler-Schlachter, Le triomphe de la coupole dans l'architecture byzantine, Strasbourg, 1947; G. De Angelis d'Ossat, Le origine e lo sviluppo degli edifici occidentali a cupola nell'antichità cristiana, Att IV Cong. int. Archeol. cristiana, II, Vatican City, 1948, pp. 17–28; S. Guyer, Les édifices à coupole de l'Orient, Atti IV Cong. int. Archeol. cristiana, II, Vatican City, 1948, pp. 1–15; E. B. Smith, The Dome, Princeton, 1950; J. Fink, Die Kuppel über den Viereck, Freiburg im Breisgau, 1958. (12) *Roofs*: F. W. Deichmann, Rl. für Ant. und Christentum, s.v. Dach, III, 1957, cols. 517–36.

c. Development of sacred architecture: (1) *Pagan*: G. Niemann, Der Palast Diokletians in Spalato, Vienna, 1910; P. Gauckler, Le sanctuaire syrien du Janicule, Paris, 1912; U. Monneret de Villard, The Temple of the Imperial Cult at Luxor, Archaeologia, XCV, 1953, pp. 85–105. (2) *Jewish*: H. Kohl and C. Watzinger, Antike Synagogen in Galiläa, Leipzig, 1916; H. L. Gordon, The Basilica and the Stoa in Early Rabbinical Literature, AB, XIII, 1931, pp. 353–75; E. L. Sukenik, The Ancient Synagogue of Beth Alpha, Jerusalem, 1932; E. L. Sukenik, Ancient Synagogues in Palestine and Greece, London, 1934; C. H. Kraeling, Excavations at Dura Europos: The Synagogue (Final Rep., VIII, 1), New Haven, 1956. (3) *Christian*: (α) *General*: Dehio-Von Bezold, I; J. G. Davies, The Origin and Development of Early Christian Church Architecture, London, 1952; A. K. Orlandos, Ἡ ξυλόστεγος παλαιοχριστιανικὴ βασιλικὴ τῆς μεσογειακῆς λεκάνης, 3 vols., Athens, 1952–57; P. Testini, Archeologia cristiana, Rome, 1959, pp. 547–751. (β) *Pastophories*: J. Lassus, Sanctuaires chrétiennes de Syrie, Paris, 1947; G. Bandmann, Über Pastophorien und verwandte Nebenräume im mittelalterlichen Kirchenbau, in Kg. S. für Hans Kauffmann, Berlin, 1958, pp. 19–58; D. Stričević, The Diakonikon and the Prothesis in Early Christian Churches, Starinar, IX–X, 1958–59, pp. 59–66 (Serb., with Eng. summary). (γ) *Baptisteries*: F. W. Deichmann, Rl. für Ant. Christentum, s.v. Baptisterium, I, 1950, cols. 1157–67; A. Khatchatrian, Les baptistères paléochrétiens: Plans, notices et bibliographie, Paris, 1962. (δ) *Martyria*: F. W. Deichmann and A. Tschira, Das Mausoleum der Kaiserin Helena und die Basilika der heiligen Marcellinus und Petrus and der Via Labicana vor Rom, JdI, LXXII, 1957, pp. 44–110; R. Krautheimer, Mensa — coemiterium — martyrium, CahA, XI, 1960, pp. 15–40. (ε) *Basilicas*: F. W. Deichmann, Rl. für Ant. und Christentum, s.v. Basilica (christlich), I, 1950, cols. 1249–59; L. Voelkl, Die Komplexanlagen im konstantinischen Kirchenbau, Das Münster, VI, 1953, pp. 301–11; L. Voelkl, Die konstantinischen Kirchenbauten nach Eusebius, RACr, XXIX, 1953, pp. 49–66, 187–206; C. Delvoye, Recherches récentes sur les origines de la basilique paléochrétienne, Ann. Inst. de Philol. et d'H. O. et Slaves, XIV, 1954–57, pp. 205–28 (bibliog.); J. B. Ward Perkins, Constantine and the Origins of the Christian Basilica, BSR, XXII, 1955, pp. 68–80; F. W. Deichmann, Religion in Geschichte und Gegenwart, s.v. Basilika, 3d ed., I, Tübingen, 1957, cols. 910–12; E. Dyggve, Aula sacra — aula sancta, Copenhagen, 1959. (ξ) *Transepts*: P. Lemerle, A propos d'une basilique de Thasos et de Saint-Jean d'Ephèse, Byzantion, XXIII, 1953, pp. 531–43; P. Lemerle, Saint-Démétrius de Thessalonique et les problèmes du martyrion et du transept, BCH, LXXVII, 1953, pp. 660–94; R. Krautheimer, Il transetto nella basilica paleocristiana, Actes Ve Cong. int. Archéol. chrétienne (1954), Vatican City, Paris, 1957, pp. 283–90; G. Egger, Römischer Kaiserkult und konstantinischer Kirchenbau, ÖJh, XLIII, 1958, pp. 120–32. (η) *Central-plan structures*: W. Altmann, Die italienischen Rundbauten, Berlin, 1906; M. Stettler, Vom römischen zum christlichen Rundbau, Mus. Helveticum, VIII, 1951, pp. 260–70. (ϑ) *Galleries*: F. W. Deichmann, Rl. für Ant. und Christentum, s.v. Empore, IV, 1959, cols. 1255–69.

d. Interregional relationships: E. Weigand, Baalbek und Rom: Die römische Reichskunst in ihrer Entwickelung und Differenzierung, JdI, XXIX, 1914, pp. 37–91; E. Weigand, Die Stellung Dalmatiens in der römischen Reichskunst, Strena Buliciana, Zagreb, 1924, pp. 77–105; R. Krautheimer, Santo Stefano Rotondo a Roma e la chiesa del Santo Sepolcro a Gerusalemme, RACr, XII, 1935, pp. 51–102; E. Weigand, Ist das "justinianische Architektursystem" mittelalterlich oder antik? B. Inst. Archéol. Bulgare, X, 1936, pp. 145–55; F. W. Deichmann, Versuch einer Darstellung der Grundrisstypen des Kirchenbaues in frühchristlicher und byzantinischer Zeit im Morgenlande, Halle, 1937; J. B. Ward Perkins, The Italian Element in Late Roman and Early Medieval Architecture, London, 1947; S.Guyer, Grundlagen mittelalterlicher abendländischer Baukunst, Einsiedeln, 1950; P. Lemerle, L'archéologie paléochrétienne in Italie: Milan et Castelseprio, "Orient ou Rome." Byzantion, XXII, 1952, pp. 165–206; D. Talbot Rice, Rome or the East, Byzantinoslavica, XIII, 1952–53, pp. 312–19; G. Tchalenko, Villages antiques de la Syrie du Nord, 3 vols., Paris, 1953–58; F. W. Deichmann, Studien zur Architektur Konstantinopels im 5. und 6. Jahrhundert nach Christus, Baden-Baden, 1956; J. B. Ward Perkins, in The Great Palace of the Byzantine Emperors, 2d report (ed. D. Talbot Rice), Edinburgh, 1958, pp. 52–104; P. Verzone, Rapporti fra l'architettura bizantina e quella italiana del V e VI secolo, Corsi di cultura ravennate e Bizantina, 1958, 2, pp. 127–39.

e. Development of the various regions: (1) *Rome*: J. P. Kirsch, Die römischen Titelkirchen im Altertum, Paderborn, 1918; R. Krautheimer,

Corpus Basilicarum Christianarum Romae, Rome, 1937 ff.; M. Armellini, Le chiese di Roma dal secolo IV al XIX, 2d ed., 2 vols., Rome, 1942; A. M. Colini, Storia e topografia del Celio nell'antichità, MPontAcc, 3d ser., VII, Vatican City, 1944; F. W. Deichmann, Frühchristliche Kirchen in Rom, Basel, 1947; R. Egger, Das Goldkreuz am Grabe Petri, AnzÖAk, 1959, pp. 182–202; R. Vielliard, Recherches sur les origines de Rome chrétienne, Rome, 1959; E. Mâle, The Early Churches of Rome, Chicago, 1960; R. Krautheimer, The Architecture of Sixtus III: A 5th Century Renascence? in De Artibus Opuscula XL: Essays in Honor of E. Panofsky (ed. M. Meiss), New York, 1961, pp. 291–302; E. Nash, Pictorial Dictionary of Ancient Rome, 2 vols., New York, 1961–62. (2) *Southern Italy*: E. Bertaux, L'art dans l'Italie méridionale, I, Paris, 1904; R. Bartoccini, Casaranello e i suoi mosaici, Felix Ravenna, N.S., IV, 1934, pp. 157–85; G. Chierici, Di alcuni risultati sui recenti lavori intorno alla basilica di San Lorenzo a Milano e alle basiliche Paoliniane di Cimitile, RACr, XVI, 1939, pp. 59–72; M. Stettler, Das Baptisterium zu Nocera Superiore, RACr, XVII, 1940, pp. 83–142; B. Pace, Arte e civiltà della Sicilia antica, IV, Milan, 1949; G. Chierici, Cimitile, Palladio, N.S., VII, 1957, pp. 69–73; S. L. Agnello, Architettura paleocristiana e bizantina della Sicilia, Corsi di cultura sull'arte ravennate e bizantina, 1961, pp. 53–108. (3) *Northern Italy*: P. Verzone, L'architettura religiosa dell'Alto Medio Evo nell'Italia settentrionale, Milan, 1942; G. Bovini, Le ultime scoperte d'antichità cristiane nell'Italia centro-settentrionale, Actes Ve Cong. int. Archéol. chrétienne (1954), Vatican City, Paris, 1957, pp. 125–46; M. Mirabella Roberti, Cinque anni di lavori per le antichità in Lombardia, Cisalpina, I, 1959, pp. 72–86; E. Arslan, Milano e Ravenna : Due momenti dell'architettura paleocristiana, Felix Ravenna, 3d ser., XXXIII, 1961, pp. 5–38; A. de Capitani d'Arzago, Architettura dei secoli IV e V in Alta Italia, Milan, n.d. (4) *Milan*: A. de Capitani d'Arzago, L'architettura cristiana di Milano, Actes VIe Cong. int. ét. byz., II, Paris, 1950, pp. 67–84; A. Calderini, G. Chierici and C. Ceccherelli, La basilica di S. Lorenzo Maggiore, Milan, 1951; A. de Capitani d'Arzago, La chiesa maggiore di Milano: S. Tecla, Milan, 1952; Storia di Milano, I, 1953, pp. 591–625, II, 1954, pp. 501–608; E. Villa, La "Basilica Apostolorum" sulla via romana a Milano, in Arte del primo millennio, Turin, 1953, pp. 77–90; E. Arslan, Nuovi ritrovamenti in S. Simpliciano a Milano, BArte, XLIII, 1958, pp. 199–212; E. Arslan, Ultime novità a San Simpliciano, Arte Lombarda, VI, 1961, pp. 149–64. (5) *Vicenza*: B. Tamaro Forlati, F. Forlati, and F. Barbieri, Il Duomo di Vicenza, Vicenza, 1956. (6) *Padua*: L. Micheletto, L'oratorio paleocristiano di "Opilione," Palladio, N.S., IV, 1954, pp. 179–84. (7) *Ravenna*: C. Ricci, Tavole storiche dei mosaici di Ravenna, 8 vols., Rome, 1930–37; M. Mazzotti, S. Apollinare in Classe, Vatican City, 1954; G. Bovini, I monumenti di Ravenna antica, 3d ed., Milan, 1955; F. W. Deichmann, Frühchristliche Bauten und Mosaiken von Ravenna, Baden-Baden, 1958; G. Bovini, Principale bibliografia su Ravenna romana, paleocristiana e paleobizantina, Corsi di cultura sull'arte ravennate e bizantina, 1962, pp. 7–42; G. De Angelis d'Ossat, Studi ravennati, Ravenna, 1962. (8) *Concordia*: P. L. Zovatto, Antichi monumenti cristiani di Iulia Concordia Sagittaria, Vatican City, 1950. (9) *Aquileia and its dependencies*: J. Fink, Der Ursprung der ältesten Kirchen am Domplatz von Aquileja, Münster, Cologne, 1954; G. Brusin and P. L. Zovatto, Monumenti paleocristiani di Aquileia e di Grado, Padua, 1957; H. Kähler, Die spätantiken Bauten unter dem Dom von Aquileia und ihre Stellung innerhalb der Geschichte des frühchristlichen Kirchenbaues, Saarbrücken, 1957; G. C. Menis, La basilica paleocristiana nelle diocesi settentrionali della metropoli d'Aquileia, Vatican City, 1958. (10) *Istria and Dalmatia*: T. G. Jackson, Dalmatia, the Quarnero and Istria, 3 vols., Oxford, 1887; W. Gerber, Altchristliche Kultbauten Istriens und Dalmatiens, Dresden, 1912; W. Gerber et al., Forschungen in Salona, 3 vols., Vienna, 1917–39; J. Brøndsted, E. Dyggve, and F. Weilbach, Recherches à Salone, 2 vols., Copenhagen, 1928–33; E. Dyggve, Die altchristlichen Kultbauten an der Westküste der Balkanhalbinsel, Atti IV Cong. int. Archeol. Cristiana, I, Vatican City, 1940, pp. 391–414; B. Molajoli, La basilica Eufrasiana di Parenzo, 2d ed., Padua, 1943; M. Mirabella Roberti, La sede paleocristiana di Orsera, Ann. triestini, XV, 1944, pp. 31–119; M. Mirabella Roberti, Indagini nel Duomo di Pola, RACr, XXIII–XXIV, 1947–48, pp. 209–29; E. Dyggve, History of Salonitan Christianity, Oslo, Cambridge, Mass., 1951; E. Dyggve, Nova Basilica discoperta u Solinu, Peristil, II, 1957, pp. 57–61; M. Prelog, Poreč: Grad i spomenici (Poreč: City and Monuments), Belgrade, 1957. (11) *Alpine regions and northern Danube basin*: R. Egger, Frühchristlichen Kirchenbauten im südlichen Norikum, Vienna, 1916; R. Egger, Teurnia: Die römischen und frühchristlichen Altertümer Oberkärntens, 3d ed., Klagenfurt, 1948; R. Noll, Frühes Christentum in Österreich, Vienna, 1954; F. Miltner, Die Grabungen auf dem Kirchbühl von Lavant – Osttirol, ÖJh, XLIII, 1956, Beiblatt, cols. 90–124; R. Egger, Bericht über die altchristlichen Funde in Österreich ab 1938, Actes Ve Cong. int. Archéol. chrétienne (1954), Vatican City, Paris, 1957, pp. 73–81. (12) *Hungary*: L. Nagy, Ricordi cristiano-romani trovati recentemente in Ungheria, Atti III Cong. int. Archeol. cristiana, Rome, 1934 pp. 293–310. (13) *Western Germany*: W. Neuss, Die Anfänge des Christentums in Rheinlande, 2d ed., Bonn, 1933; F. Fremersdorf, Altestes Christentum mit besonderen Berücksichtigung der Grabungsergebnisse unter der Severinskirche in Köln, Kölner Jhb. zur Vor- und Frühgeschichte, II, 1956, pp. 7–26; K. T. Kempf, Frühchristliche Funde und Forschungen in Deutschland, Actes Ve Cong. int. Archéol. chrétienne (1954), Vatican City, Paris, 1957, pp. 61–72; H. Borger, Die Ausgrabungen in Bereich des Xantener Domes, in Neue Ausgrabungen in Deutschland, Berlin, 1958, pp. 380–90; H. von Petrikovits, Das römische Rheinland: Archäologische Forschungen seit 1945, Cologne-Opladen, 1960. (14) *Switzerland*: L. Blondel, Aperçu sur les édifices chrétiens dans la Suisse occidentale avant l'an mille, in Frühmittelalterliche Kunst in den Alpenländern, Olten, Lausanne, 1954, pp. 271–307; E. Poeschel, Frühchristliche und frühmittelalterliche Architektur in Currätien, Frühmittelalterliche Kunst in den Alpenländern, Olten, Lausanne, 1954, pp. 119–32; B. Ita, Antiker Bau und frühmittelalterliche Kirche, Zürich, 1961. (15) *Gaul*: J. Hubert, L'art préroman, Paris, 1938; E. Mâle, La fin du paganisme en Gaule et les plus anciennes basiliques chrétiennes, Paris, 1950; J. Hubert, L'architecture religieuse du haut moyen âge en France, Paris, 1952. (16) *Spain*: A. S. Frischauer, Altspanischer Kirchenbau, Berlin, 1930; E. Junyent, I monumenti cristiani di Spagna studiati in questi ultimi anni, Atti III Cong. int. Archeol. cristiana, Rome, 1934, pp. 255–85; A. M. Schneider, Das neuentdeckte Coemeterium zu Tarragona (Span. Forsch. der Görres-Gesellschaft, V), Münster in Westfalen, 1935; P. Batlle Huguet, Arte paleocristiana: Monumentos arquitectónicos, Ars Hispaniae, II, Madrid, 1947, pp. 185–88; H. Schlunk, Arte visigodo: Arquitectura visigoda de los siglos V y VI, Ars Hispaniae, II, Madrid, 1947, pp. 299–32; G. Segni Vidal, La basilica descubierta en Son Bou y los origines del cristianismo en Menorca, Analecta Gregoriana, LXX, 1954, pp. 79–92; P. de Palol Salellas, Los monumentos paleocristianos y visigodos estudiados en España desde el año 1939 a 1954, Actes Ve Cong. int. Archéol. chrétienne (1954), Vatican City, Paris, 1957, pp. 87–95; J. Puig i Cadafalch, L'art wisigothique et ses survivances, Paris, 1961; F. Gerke and P. de Palol Salellas, Die Kunst im frühchristlichen und westgotischen Spanien (in press). (17) *North Africa*: S. Gsell, Les monuments antiques de l'Algérie, II, Paris, 1901; P. Gauckler, Basiliques chrétiennes de Tunisie, Paris, 1913; J. Vaultrin, Basiliques chrétiennes de Carthage, Algiers, 1933; P. G. Lapeyre, La basilique chrétienne de Tunisie, Atti IV Cong. int. Archeol. cristiana, I, Vatican City, 1940, pp. 169–244; L. Leschi, La basilique chrétienne en Algérie, Atti IV Cong. int. Archeol. cristiana, I, Vatican City, 1940, pp. 145–67; L. Leschi, Djemila: Antique Cuicul, Algiers, 1950; L. Leschi, Tipasa de Mauretania, Algiers, 1950; A. G. Luiks, Cathedra en Mensa, Francken, 1955; J. Lassus, Vingt-cinq ans d'histoire algérienne: Recherches et publications (1931–1956): L'antiquité, Rev. africaine, C, 1956, pp. 81–119; G. C. Picard, L'archéologie chrétienne en Afrique 1938–1953, Actes Ve Cong. int. Archéol. chrétienne (1954), Vatican City, Paris, 1957, pp. 45–59; E. Marec, Monuments chrétiens d'Hippone, ville épiscopale de Saint Augustin, Paris, 1958; M. Fendri, Basiliques chrétiennes de la Skhira, Paris, 1961. (18) *Libya*: P. Romanelli, La basilica cristiana nell'Africa settentrionale italiana, Atti IV Cong. int. Archeol. cristiana, I, Vatican City, 1940, pp. 245–89; J. B. Ward Perkins, Christian Antiquities of the Cyrenaican Pentapolis, B. Soc. d'Archéol. Copte, IX, 1943, pp. 123–39; J. B. Ward Perkins and R. G. Goodchild, The Christian Antiquities in Tripolitania, Archaeologia, XCV, 1953, pp. 1–82. (19) *Constantinople*: A. van Millingen, Byzantine Churches in Constantinople, London, 1912; A. M. Schneider, Byzanz: Vorarbeiten zur Topographie und Archäologie der Stadt, Berlin, 1936; R. Janin, Constantinople byzantine: Développement urbain et répertoire topographique, Paris, 1953; R. Janin, La géographie ecclésiastique de l'Empire byzantin, III: Les églises et les monastères, Paris, 1953; J. Kollwitz, Religion in Geschichte und Gegenwart, s.v. Byzantinische Kunst, 3d ed., I, Tübingen, 1957, cols. 1560–69; F. W. Deichmann, EAA, s.v. Costantinopoli, chiese, II, 1959, pp. 914–17. (20) *The Balkan peninsula*: I. Barnea, Nouvelles considérations sur les basiliques chrétiennes de Dobrudja, Dacia, XI–XII, 1945–47, pp. 221–41; A. Grabar, L'architecture balkanique avant et après les invasions à la lumière des découvertes recentes, CRAI, 1945, pp. 270–87. (21) *Romania*: D. Ciurea, La basilica cristiana in Romania, Atti IV Cong. int. Archeol. cristiana, I, Vatican City, 1940, pp. 381–89; I. Barnea, Douze ans d'archéologie chrétienne en Roumanie (1936–1948), Actes VIe Cong. int. ét. byz., II, Paris, 1950, pp. 25–34. (22) *Bulgaria*: V. Ivanova, Eglises et monastères en pays bulgares, IVe–XIIe siècles, Ann. Mus. nat. bulgare, IV, 1922–25, pp. 429–582; B. Filov, Geschichte der altbulgarischen Kunst, I, Berlin, 1932; S. J. Pokrovski, Christlichen Basilika an der Kamcijamündung, B. Inst. archéol. bulgare, XIV, 1940–42, pp. 252–55 (Bulg.); M. P. Chapenko, Arkhitektura Bolgarii (Bulgarian Architecture), Moscow, 1953; V. Beševliev and J. Irmscher, eds., Antike und Mittelalter in Bulgarien, Berlin, 1960. (23) *Yugoslavia*: E. Kitzinger, A Survey of the Early Christian Town of Stobi, Dumbarton Oaks Pap., III, 1946, pp. 81–162; V. R. Petković, Les fouilles de Tsaritchin Grad, CahA, III, 1948, pp. 40–48; A. Deroko and S. Radojčić, Otkopavanje Caričina Grada 1947: godine i vizantiske starine u Jablanici i Pustoj Reci (Archaeological Excavations at Tsaritsin Grad in 1947: Byzantine Archaeological Remains in the Region of Jablanica and Pusta Reka), Starinar, N.S., I, 1950, pp. 119–42; D. Mano-Zisi, Iskopavanje na Caričiny Grady 1949–52 god. (Excavations at Tsaritsin Grad in 1949–52), Starinar, N.S., III–IV, 1952–53, pp. 127–68; S. Radojčić, Crkva u Konjuhu (The Church at Konjuh), Zbornik Vizant. Inst. SAN, I, 1952, pp. 148–67; N. Spremo-Petrović, La basilique à crypte de Caricin Grad, Starinar, N.S., III–IV, 1952–53, pp. 169–80; C. A. Ralegh Radford, Justiniana Prima (Tsaritsin Grad), Antiquity, XXVIII, 1954, pp. 15–18; D. Stričević, Byzantine Archaeology in Yugoslavia, 1955–1958, Akten des XI. Internationalen Byzantinistischen-Kongresses 1958, Munich, 1960, pp. 586–94; D. Bošković, D. Stričević, and I. Nikolajević-Stojković, L'architecture de la Basse Antiquité et du Moyen Age dans les régions centrales des Balkans, Rapport XIIe Cong. int. ét. byz., Belgrade, Ohrid, 1961, pp. 155–247; D. Koco, Basiliques paléochrétiens dans la région du Lac d'Ohrid, Mus. nat. d'Ohrid, Rec. de Travaux, 1961, pp. 15–33; F. Hoddinott Early Byzantine Churches in Macedonia and Southern Serbia, London, 1962; (24) *Greece*: G. A. Sotiriou, *Ευρετήριοι τῶν μεσαιωνικῶν μνημείων τῆς 'Ελλαδος*, I, Athens, 1927; G. A. Sotiriou, *Αἱ χριστιανικαὶ βασιλικαὶ τῆς 'Ελλαδος, 'Εφημ*, 1929, pp. 161–248; H. Balducci, Basiliche proto-cristiane e bizantine a Coo, Pavia, 1936; G. A. Sotiriou, Die altchristlichen Basiliken Griechenlands, Atti IV Cong. int. Archeol. cristiana, I, Vatican City, 1940, pp. 355–80; P. Lemerle, Philippes et la Macédoine orientale, Paris, 1945; L. Morricone, Scavi e ricerche a Coo, BArte, XXXV, 1950, pp. 54–74, 219–46; G. A. and M. Sotiriou, *'Η βασιλικὴ τοῦ 'Αγίου Δημητρίου Θεσσαλονίκης*, 2 vols., Athens, 1952; *"Εργον*, 1954 ff.; N. Platon, *Αἱ ξυλόστεγαι παλαιοχριστιανικαὶ βασιλικαὶ τῆς Κρήτης Πεπραγμένα τοὺ θ' διεθνοὺς βυζαντινολογικὸυ Συνέδιου* (1953), I, Athens, 1955, pp. 415–32; A. C. Orlandos, Les monuments paléochrétiens découverts ou étudiés en Grèce de 1938 à 1954, Actes Ve Cong. int. Archéol. chrétienne (1954), Vatican City, Paris, 1957, pp. 109–16. (25) *Asia Minor*: E. Herzfeld and S. Guyer, Meriamlik und Korykos, Manchester, 1930; J. Keil and A. Wilhelm, Denkmäler aus dem Rauhen Kilikien, Manchester, 1931; S. Guyer, Les monuments chrétiens en Asie Mineure, Atti III Cong. int. Archeol. cristiana,

Rome, 1934, pp. 433–58; H. Swoboda, J. Keil, and F. Knoll, Denkmäler aus Lykaonien, Pamphylien und Isaurien, Vienna, 1935; M. Gough, Anazarbus, Anatolian S., II, 1952, pp. 85–150; M. Gough, A Temple and Church at Ayaş (Cilicia), Anatolian S., IV, 1954, pp. 49–64; P. Verzone, Alahan Monastir: Un monumento dell'arte tardo-romana in Isauria, Turin, 1956; P. Verzone, Le chiese di Hierapolis in Asia Minore, CahA, VIII, 1956, pp. 37–61; P. Verzone, Ausgrabungen von Hierapolis in Phrygien, Türk. Arkeol. Dergisi, VIII, 2, 1958–59, pp. 20–22; G. H. Forsyth, Jr., An Early Byzantine Church at Kanlī Divane in Cilicia, in De artibus opuscula XL: Essays in Honor of Erwin Panofsky (ed. M. Meiss), New York, 1961, pp. 127–37. (26) *Armenia*: J. Strzygowski, Die Baukunst der Armenier und Europa, 2 vols., Vienna, 1918; A. Khatchatrian, L'architecture arménienne, Paris, 1949; V. Harutiurian and S. A. Safarian, Monuments of Armenian Architecture, Moscow, 1951 (Rus.). (27) *Syria*: C. J. M. de Vogüé, La Syrie centrale, 2 vols., Paris, 1865–67; H. C. Butler, Publications of an American Archaeological Expedition to Syria in 1899–1900, II: Architecture and the Other Arts, New York, 1904; H. C. Butler, Ancient Architecture in Syria (Pub. Princeton Univ. Archaeol. Expedition to Syria in 1904–05 and 1909, IIA–IIB), 12 vols., Leiden, 1907–21; A. Birnbaum, Die Oktogone von Antiochia, Nazianz und Nyssa, RepfKw, XXXVI, 1913, pp. 181–209; H. W. Beyer, Der syrische Kirchenbau, Berlin, 1925; H. C. Butler and E. B. Smith, Early Christian Churches in Syria, Princeton, 1929; G. W. Elderkin and R. Stillwell, eds., Antioch on the Orontes, I–III, Princeton, 1934–41; D. Krencker, Die Wallfahrtskirche des Simeon Stylites in Kal 'at Sim'ân, Berlin, 1939; J. Lassus, Sanctuaires chrétiens de la Syrie, Paris, 1947; J. Kollwitz, Die Grabungen in Resefa, in Neue Deutsche Ausgrabungen im Mittelmeergebiet und im vorderen Orient, Berlin, 1959, pp. 45–70. (28) *Mesopotamia*: U. Monneret de Villard, Le chiese della Mesopotamia, Rome, 1940. (29) *Palestine*: H. Vincent and F.-M. Abel, Jérusalem, 2 vols., Paris, 1912–26; T. Wiegand, Sinai, Berlin, 1920; K. Watzinger, Denkmäler Palästinas, II, Leipzig, 1935; J. W. Crowfoot, Churches at Bosra and Samaria-Sebaste, London, 1937; A. M. Schneider, The Church of the Multiplication of Loaves and Fishes at Tabgha, London, 1937; C. H. Kraeling, ed., Gerasa, New Haven, 1938; A. M. Schneider, Südjüdäische Kirchen, Z. des d. Palästina-Vereins, LXI, 1938, pp. 96–108; J. W. Crowfoot, Early Churches in Palestine, London, 1941; L. H. Vincent, La cathédrale antique de Beisân-Scythopolis, Muséon, LIX, 1946, pp. 303–18; R. W. Hamilton, The Church of the Nativity, Bethlehem, Jerusalem, 1947; S. J. Saller and B. Bagatti, The Town of Nebo (Khirbet el-Mekhayyat), with a Brief Survey of Other Ancient Christian Monuments in Transjordan, Jerusalem, 1949; B. Bagatti, Gli antichi edifici sacri di Betlemme in seguito agli scavi e restauri praticati dalle Custodi di Terra Santa (1948–51), Jerusalem, 1952; E. Wistrand, Konstantins Kirche am heiligen Grab in Jerusalem nach dem ältesten literarischen Zeugnissen, Göteborg, 1952; K. J. Conant, The Original Buildings at the Holy Sepulchre in Jerusalem, Speculum, XXXI, 1956, pp. 1–48; M. Avi-Yonah, Christian Archaeology in Israel, 1948–1954, Actes Ve Cong. int. Archéol. chrétienne (1954), Vatican City, Paris, 1957, pp. 117–23; P. Benoît, Les découvertes paléochrétiennes en Palestine arabe entre 1939 et 1954, Actes Ve Cong. int. Archéol. chrétienne (1954), Vatican City, Paris, 1957, pp. 163–68; A. E. Mader, Mambre, Freiburg im Breisgau, 1957. (30) *Cyprus*: Dept. of Antiquities (Cyprus), Ann. Rep., Nicosia, 1934 ff.; G. A. Sotiriou, Τὰ βυζαντινὰ μνημεῖα τῆς Κύπρου, Athens, 1935. (31) *Egypt*: U. Monneret de Villard, Les couvents près de Sohag, 2 vols., Milan, 1925–26; U. Monneret de Villard, La basilica cristiana d'Egitto, Atti IV Cong. int. Archeol. cristiana, I, Vatican City, 1940, pp. 291–319; U. Monneret de Villard, Gli studi sull'archeologia cristiana d'Egitto, 1920–1940, Orientalia Christiana Periodica, VII, 1941, pp. 274–92; J. B. Ward Perkins, The Shrine of St. Menas in the Maryût, BSR, XVII, 1949, pp. 26–71; A. Badawy, Guide de l'Egypte chrétienne, Cairo, 1953; A. H. S. Megaw, Ἡ βασιλικὴ Ἑρμουπόλεως, Πεπραγμένα τοῦ θ' διεθνοῦς βυζαντινολογικοῦ Συνέδριου (1953), I, Athens, 1955, pp. 287–95; D. Russell, Medieval Cairo and the Monasteries of the Wādi Natrūn, London, 1962. (32) *Nubia*: U. Monneret de Villard, La Nubia medioevale, 2 vols., Cairo, 1935.

f. Secular structures: (1) *General*: L. de Beylié, L'habitation byzantine, Paris, 1902; A. Boëthius, The Golden House of Nero, Ann Arbor, Mich., 1960, pp. 129–85. (2) *Villas*: R. Paribeni, Le dimore dei potentiores nel Basso Impero, RM, LV, 1940, pp. 131–48; A. Garcia y Bellido, Dos "villae rusticae" romanas recientemente excavados, AEA, XXVI, 1953, pp. 207–17; H. Vetters, Ein in der Spätantike befestigtes Bauernhaus in Oberösterreich, Frühmittelalterliche Kunst in den Alpenländern, Olten, Lausanne, 1954, pp. 9–16; G. W. Meates, Lullingstone Roman Villa, London, 1955. (3) *Town planning*: G. Rodenwaldt, Römische Staatsarchitektur, Das Neue Bild der Antike, II, Berlin, 1942, pp. 356–73. (4) *Secular architecture in Rome*: G. Lugli, Roma antica: Il centro monumentale, Rome, 1946. (5) *Provincial work*: O Doppelfeld, Das Praetorium dem Kölner Rathaus, Neue Ausgrabungen in Deutschland, Berlin, 1958, pp. 313–21. (6) *Thermae*: D. Krenker, Die Trierer Kaiserthermen, Augsburg, 1929; S. Charitonidis and R. Ginouvès, Bain romain de Zevgolatio près de Corinthe, BCH, LXXIX, 1955, pp. 102–20; R. Ginouvès, Sur un aspect de l'évolution des bains en Grèce vers le IVe siècle de notre ère, BCH, LXXIX, 1955, pp. 135–52; F. Miltner, Vorläufiger Bericht über die Ausgrabungen in Ephesos, ÖJh, XLIII, 1956, Beiblatt, cols. 1–64. (7) *Palaces*: E. Hébrard and J. Zeiller, Spalato: Le palais de Dioclétien, Paris, 1912; K. M. Swoboda, Römische und romanische Paläste, 2d ed., Vienna, 1924; E. Dyggve, Ravennatum sacrum palatium, Copenhagen, 1941; H. P. L'Orange, È un palazzo di Massimiano Erculeo che gli scavi di Piazza Armerina portano alla luce? SymbOsl, XXIX, 1952, pp. 114–28; U. Monneret de Villard, Sul palazzo di Teodorico a Galatea, RendLinc, 8th ser., VII, 1952, pp. 26–32; E. Dyggve, Recherches sur le palais imperial de Thessalonike, S. orientalia J. Pedersen dicata, Copenhagen, 1953, pp. 59–70; G. V. Gentili, La villa imperiale di Piazza Armerina, 2d ed., Rome, 1954; W. Reusch, Die Aula Palatina in Trier, Germania, XXXIII, 1955, pp. 180–99; H. P. L'Orange, Il Palazzo di Massimiano Erculeo di Piazza Armerina, S. in onore di A. Calderini e R. Paribeni, III, Milan, 1956, pp. 593–600; N. Neuerburg, Some Considerations on the Architecture of the Imperial Villa at Piazza Armerina, Marsyas, VIII, 1957–58, pp. 22–29; B. Gabričević, Ultime scoperte entro il Palazzo di Diocleziano a Spalato, Atti VII Cong. int. di Archeol. Classica, Rome, 1958, pp. 411–20; M. Cagiano de Azevedo, Admiranda palatia: I palazzi imperiali e le residenze tetrarchiche, B. Centro di s. storia arch., XIV, 1959, pp. 3–24; C. Mango, The Brazen House: A Study of the Vestibule of the Imperial Palace of Constantinople, Copenhagen, 1959; N. Duval, Que savons-nous du Palais de Théodoric à Ravenne? Mél, LXXII, 1960, pp. 337–71; I. Lavin, The House of the Lord: Aspects of the Role of Palace Triclinia in the Architecture of Late Antiquity and the Early Middle Ages, AB, XLIV, 1962, pp. 1–27.

g. Monasteries: A. Ballu, Le monastère byzantin de Tébessa, Paris, 1897; J. Clédat, Le monastère et la nécropole de Baouît, 2 vols., Cairo, 1904; J. E. Quibell, The Monastery of Apa Jeremias (Excavations at Saqqara, IV), Cairo, 1912; A. C. Orlandos, Μοναστηριακὴ 'αρχιτεκτονική, 2 vols., Athens, 1927–55; W. Seston, Le monastère d'Aïn Tamda et les origines de l'architecture monastique en Afrique du Nord, Mél, LI, 1934, pp. 79–113; 'Umar Tusūn, Notes sur le désert Libyque: "Cellia" et ses couvents, Alexandria, 1935; G. Ferrari, Early Roman Monasteries, Vatican City, 1957.

h. Funerary architecture: (1) *Imperial mausoleums*: H. Koethe, Frühchristliche Nischenrundbauten, Marburg, 1928; E. Dyggve, Ein Mausoleum des frühen 4. Jahrhunderts in Salona, Serta Hoffilleriana, Zagreb, 1940, pp. 257–61; A. Fakhry, The Necropolis of el-Bagawāt in the Khārga Oasis, Cairo, 1951; A. Ferrua, Due mausolei di pagani cristiani presso S. Sebastiano, RACr, XXVIII, 1952, pp. 13–41; A. Calderini, Mausolei imperiali di Milano, Arte del primo Millennio, Turin, 1953, pp. 42–55. (2) *Tombs of the Apostles*: B. M. Apollonj Getti, A. Ferrua, E. Josi, and E. Kirschbaum, Esplorazioni sotto la confessione di San Pietro in Vaticano, 2 vols., 1951; G. Pacini, La basilica degli Apostoli, Rome, 1951; T. Klauser, Die römische Petrustradition im Lichte der neuen Ausgrabungen unter den Petruskirche, Cologne-Opladen, 1956; J. Toynbee and J. Ward Perkins, The Shrine of St. Peter and the Vatican Excavations, London, 1956; E. Kirschbaum, The Tombs of St. Peter and St. Paul, London, New York, 1959. (3) *Catacombs*: (α) *Rome*: G. B. De Rossi, La Roma sotterranea, 3 vols., Rome, 1864–67 (Eng. trans., J. S. Northcote and W. R. Brownlow, 3 vols., London, 1879); O. Marucchi, Le catacombe romane, 2d ed., Rome, 1903; P. Styger, Die römischen Katakomben, Berlin, 1933; L. Hertling and E.Kirschbaum, Die römischen Katakomben und ihre Märtyrer, 2d ed., Vienna, 1955 (trans. M. J. Costelloe, The Roman Catacombs and Their Martyrs, Milwaukee, 1956); M. H. Marrou, Une catacombe pagane-chrétienne récemment découverte à Rome, B. Soc. nat. ant. de France, 1956, pp. 77–81; A. Ferrua, Lavori e scoperte nelle catacombe, Triplice omaggio a S. S. Pio XII, II, Vatican City, 1958, pp. 49–64. (β) *Naples*: H. Achelis, Die Katakomben von Neapel, Leipzig, 1936. (γ) *Sicily*: J. Führer and V. Schultze, Die altchristlichen Grabstätten Siziliens, Berlin, 1907; G. Agnello, Sicilia paleocristiana: Catacombe inedite dell'altopiano ispicese, Misc. Giulio Belvederi, Vatican City, 1954–55, pp. 245–57; S. L. Agnello, Le catacombe di Vigna Cassia a Siracusa, Rome, 1956.

i. Utilitarian architecture: P. Forchheimer and J. Strzygowski, Die byzantinischen Wasserbehälter von Konstantinopel, Vienna, 1893; P. Forchheimer, Wasserleitungen, Forsch. in Ephesos, III, Vienna, 1923, pp. 224–55; H. Spanner and S. Guyer, Rusafa, Berlin, 1926, p. 69; G. Downey, The Water Supply of Antioch on the Orontes in Antiquity, Ann. archéol. de Syrie, I, 1951, pp. 171–87; F. Dirimtekin, Adduction de l'eau à Byzance dans la région dite "Bulgare," CahA, X, 1959, pp. 217–43.

Sculpture: *a. General*: J. Wiegand, Das altchristliche Hauptportal an der Kirche der heiligen Sabina, Trier, 1900; G. Galassi, Scultura romana e bizantina a Ravenna, L'arte, XVIII, 1915, pp. 29–57; G. Rodenwaldt, Eine spätantike Kunstströmung in Rom, RM, XXXVI–XXXVII, 1921–22, pp. 58–110; G. Rodenwaldt, AAnz, 1931, cols. 317–38; G. Rodenwaldt, Über den Stilwandel in der antoninischen Kunst, AbhPreussAk, Philos.-H. Klasse, 1935, 3; R. Hinks, Raum und Fläche im spätantiken Relief, AAnz, 1936, cols. 238–51; G. Rodenwaldt, Zur Kunstgeschichte der Jahre 220 bis 270, JdI, LI, 1936, pp. 82–113; G. Rodenwaldt, Römische Reliefs: Vorstufen zur Spätantike, JdI, LV, 1940, pp. 12–43; J. Kollwitz, Oströmische Plastik der theodosianischen Zeit, Berlin, 1941; M. Squarciapino, La scuola di Afrodisia, Rome, 1943; F. Gerke, Christus in der spätantike Plastik, 3d ed., Mainz, 1948; H. Kähler, Konstantin 313, JdI, LXVII, 1952, pp. 1–30; F. Saxl, Pagan and Jewish Elements in Early Christian Sculpture, in Lectures, London, 1957, pp. 45–57; G. Egger, Die Architekturdarstellungen im spätantiken Relief, JhbKhSammlWien, LV, 1959, pp. 7–30; F. Gerke, La scultura paleocristiana in Occidente: La scultura paleobizantina in Oriente: La scultura ravennate, Corsi di cultura sull'arte ravennate e bizantina, 1959, 2, pp. 49–121; G. Gullini, Maestri e botteghe in Roma da Gallieno alla Tetrarchia, Cuneo, 1960; E. Kitzinger, A Marble Relief of the Theodosian Period, Dumbarton Oaks Pap., XIV, 1960, pp. 17–42; C. Delvoye, La sculpture byzantine jusqu'à l'époque iconoclaste, Corsi di cultura sull'arte ravennate e bizantina, 1961, pp. 177–94; G. de Francovich, Osservazioni sull'altare di Ratchis a Cividale e sui rapporti tra occidente ed oriente nei secoli VII e VIII d.C., Scritti di storia dell'arte in onore di Mario Salmi, Rome, 1961, pp. 173–236; H. P. L'Orange, Der subtile Stil: Eine Kunstströmung um 400 n. Chr., Antike K., IV, 1961, pp. 68–75.

b. Portraiture: J. J. Bernoulli, Römische Ikonographie, 2 vols., Stuttgart, 1882–94; A. Riegl, Zur spätrömischen Porträtskulptur, in Strena Helbigiana, Leipzig, 1900, pp. 250–56; R. Delbrück, Bildnisse römischer Kaiser, Berlin, 1914; G. Rodenwaldt, Griechische Porträts aus dem Ausgang der Antike, Wpr, 76, 1919; G. Albizzati, Un ritratto di Licinia Eudoxia e gli ultimi statuari romani, DissPontAcc, 2d ser., XV, 1921, pp. 337–59; G. von Kaschnitz-Weinberg, Spätrömische Porträts, Die Antike, II, 1926, pp. 36–60; F. Poulsen, Porträtstudien in norditalienischen Provinzmuseen, Copenhagen, 1928; H. P. L'Orange, Ein Porträt des Kaisers Diokletian, R.M,

XLIV, 1929 pp. 180–93; H. P. L'Orange, Die Bildnisse der Tetrarchen, ActaA, II, 1931, pp. 29–52; R. Delbrück, Spätantike Kaiserporträts, Berlin, 1933; H. P. L'Orange, Studien zur Geschichte des spätantiken Porträts, Oslo, 1933; T. Dohrn, Ein spätantikes Platonporträt, AM, LXIII, LXIV, 1938–39, pp. 163–70; M. B. Mackeprang, Eine in Jütland vor 200 Jahren gefundene Kaiserstatuette, ActaA, IX, 1938, pp. 135–50; R. Delbrück, Die Münzbildnisse von Maximinus bis Carinus, Berlin, 1940; G. Bovini, Gallieno, MemLinc, 7th ser., II, 1941, pp. 115–65; H. P. L'Orange, Apotheosis in Ancient Portraiture, Oslo, Cambridge, Mass., 1947; R. Calza, Statua iconica femminile da Ostia, BArte, XXXV, 1950, pp. 201–07; H. P. L'Orange, The Portrait of Plotinus, CahA, V, 1951, pp. 15–30; R. Calza, Cronologia e identificazione dell'Agrippina Capitolina, MPontAcc, VIII, 2–3, 1955, pp. 107–36; H. von Heintze, Studien zu den Porträts des 3. Jahrhunderts nach Christus, RM, LXII, 1955, pp. 174–84, LXIII, 1956, pp. 56–65, LXIV, 1957, pp. 69–91; H. P. L'Orange, Plotinus-Paul, Byzantion, XXV–XXVII, 1955–57, pp. 473–85; N. Firatli, A Portrait of Constantine the Great, Ann. Istanbul Archaeol. Mus., VII, 1956, pp. 75–78; A. Giuliano, Catalogo dei ritratti romani nel Museo Profano Lateranense, Vatican City, 1957; H. P. L'Orange, The Antique Origin of Medieval Portraiture, Acta Cong. Madvigiani: Proc. 2d Int. Cong. of Classical S., III, Copenhagen, 1957, pp. 53–70; B. M. Felletti Maj, Iconografia romana imperiale da Severo Alessandro a M. Aurelio Carino, Rome, 1958; H. Jucker, Verkannte Köpfe, Mus. Helveticum, XVI, 1959, pp. 275–91; H. P. L'Orange, Ein Meisterwerk römischer Porträtkunst, SymbOsl, XXXV, 1959, pp. 88–97.

c. Monumental and official sculpture: K. F. Kinch, L'arc de triomphe de Salonique, Paris, 1890; A. J. B. Wace, The Base of the Obelisk of Theodosius, JHS, XXIX, 1909, pp. 60–69; W. Kluge and K. Lehmann-Hartleben, Die antike Grossbronzen, 3 vols., Berlin, Leipzig, 1927; R. Delbrück, Antike Porphyrwerke, Berlin, Leipzig, 1932; G. Bruns, Der Obelisk und seine Basis Auf dem Hippodrom zu Konstantinopel, Istanbul, 1935; H. Kähler, Zwei Sockel eines Triumphbogens in Boboli-Garten, Wpr, 96, 1936; J. Wytzes, ed., Der Streit um den Altar der Victoria, Amsterdam, 1936; L. Małunowiczówna, De Ara Victoriae in curia romana . . ., Vilnius, 1937; H. P. L'Orange, Ein tetrarchisches Ehrendenkmal auf dem Forum Romanum, RM, LIII, 1938, pp. 1–34; H. P. L'Orange and A. von Gerkan, Der spätantike Bildschmuck des Konstantinsbogens, Berlin, 1939; G. Q. Giglioli, La colonna di Arcadio a Costantinopoli, Naples, 1952; A. Giuliano, Arco di Costantino, Milan, 1955; M. Cassandro, Il Colosso di Barletta, Barletta, 1959; G. Becatti, La colonna coclide istoriata, Rome, 1960; G. Bovini, La statua di porfido del Museo Arcivescovile di Ravenna, Corsi di cultura sull'arte ravennate e bizentina, 1960, 1, pp. 39–56; A. W. Byvanck, De obelisk van Constantinopel (Meded. der koninklijke Nederlandse Ak. van Wetenschappen, Afd. Letterkunde, N.S., XXIII, 11), Amsterdam, 1960.

d. Sarcophagi: E. Le Blant, Etude sur les sarcophages chrétiens antiques de la ville d'Arles, Paris, 1878; E. Le Blant, Les sarcophages de la Gaule, Paris, 1886; C. R. Morey, The Christian Sarcophagus in Santa Maria Antiqua, in Sup. Pap. of the Am. School of Classical S., Rome, I, 1905, pp. 148–56; H. Dütschke, Ravennatische Studien, Leipzig, 1909; G. Rodenwaldt, Säulensarkophage, RM, XXXVIII–XXXIX, 1923–24, pp. 1–40; C. R. Morey, The Sarcophagus of Claudia Antonia Sabina and the Asiatic Sarcophagi (Sardis, V, 1), Princeton, 1924; M. Lawrence, City-Gate Sarcophagi, AB, X, 1927, pp. 1–45; J. Wilpert, I sarcofagi cristiani antichi, 4 vols., and sup., Rome, 1929–36; G. Rodenwaldt, Der Klinensarkophag von S. Lorenzo, JdI, XLV, 1930, pp. 116–89; M. Lawrence, Columnar Sarcophagi in the Latin West, AB, XIV, 1932, pp. 103–65; Arif Müfid Mansel, Ein Prinzensarkophag aus Istanbul, Istanbul, 1934; G. Rodenwaldt, Römische Löwen, CrArte, I, 1935–36, pp. 225–28; H. U. von Schoenebeck, Der Mailänder Sarkophag und seine Nachfolge, Vatican City, 1935; F. Gerke, Der Sarkophag des Iunius Bassus, Berlin, 1936; H. U. von Schoenebeck, Die christliche Sarkophagplastik unter Konstantin, RM, LI, 1936, pp. 241–336; M. Simon, Notes sur le sarcophage de Santa Maria Antiqua, Mél, LIII, 1936, pp. 131–50; H. U. von Schoenebeck, Die christlichen Paradeisossarkophage, RACr, XIV, 1937, pp. 289–343; A. C. Soper, The Latin Style on Christian Sarcophagi of the 4th Century, AB, XIX, 1937, pp. 148–202; M. Gütschow, Das Museum der Praetextat-Katakombe, MemPontAcc, 3d ser., IV, 2, 1938, pp. 29–268; H. I. Marrou, *Μουσικὸς 'Ανήρ*: Etude sur les scènes de la vie intellectuelle figurant sur les monuments funéraires romains, Grenoble, 1938; F. Gerke, Die christlichen Sarkophage der vorkonstantinische Zeit, Berlin, 1940; F. Gerke, Das Heilige Antlitz: Köpfe altchristlichen Platstik, Berlin, 1940; F. Gerke, Die Zeitbestimmung der Passionsarkophage, Budapest, 1940; K. Lehmann and E. C. Olsen, Dionysiac Sarcophagi in Baltimore, New York, Baltimore, 1942; M. Lawrence, The Sarcophagi of Ravenna, New York, 1945; A. Katzenellenbogen, The Sarcophagus in S. Ambrogio and St. Ambrose, AB, XXIX, 1947, pp. 249–59; A. A. Vasiliev, Imperial Porphyry Sarcophagi in Constantinople, Dumbarton Oaks Pap., IV, 1948, pp. 3–26; G. Bovini, I sarcofagi cristiani, Vatican City, 1949; F. Gerke, Der Trierer Agricius Sarcophag, Trier, 1949; G. M. A. Hanfmann, The Season Sarcophagus in Dumbarton Oaks, Cambridge, Mass., 1951; M. Lawrence, Additional Asiatic Sarcophagi, MAARome, XX, 1951, pp. 115–66; F. Bénoit, Sarcophages paléochrétiens d'Arles et de Marseille (Gallia, sup., 5), Paris, 1954; G. Bovini, Sarcofagi paleocristiani della Spagna, Vatican City, 1954; F. Bovini, Sarcofagi paleocristiani di Ravenna, Vatican City, 1954; E. Stommel, Beiträge zur Ikonographie der konstantinischen Sarkophagplastik, Bonn, 1954; S. L. Agnello, Il sarcofago di Adelfia, Vatican City, 1956; J.Kollwitz, Die Sarkophage Ravennas, Freiburg im Breisgau, 1958; M. Lawrence, Season Sarcophagi of Architectural Type, AJA, LXII, 1958, pp. 282–85; G. de Francovich, Studi sulla scultura ravennate, I: I sarcofagi, Felix Ravenna, 3d ser., 26–28, 1958–59; F. Matz, Ein römisches Meisterwerk: Der Jahreszeitsarcophag Badminton-New York (JdI, sup., XIX), Berlin, 1958; N. Firatli, Deux nouveau reliefs funéraires d'Istanbul et les reliefs similaires, CahA, XI, 1960, pp. 73–92, G. M. Gabrielli, I sarcofagi paleocristiani ed altomedioevali delle Marche, Ravenna, 1961; G. Bovini, Iconografia e cronologia del sarcofago paleocristiano per fanciullo del Museo Nazionale di Ravenna, Corsi di cultura sull'arte ravennate e bizantina, 1962, pp. 139–54; J. Doignon, Le monogramme cruciforme du sarcophage paléochrétien de Metz représentant le passage de la Mer Rouge, CahA, XII, 1962, pp. 65–87; R. Farioli, I sarcofagi paleocristiani e paleobizantini della Sicilia, Corsi di cultura sull'arte ravennate e bizantina, 1962, pp. 241–67.

Painting and mosaics: *a. General*: R. Kömstedt, Vormittelalterliche Malerei, Augsburg, 1929; R. Hinks, Catalogue of the Greek, Etruscan and Roman Paintings in the British Museum, London, 1933; F. Wirth, Römische Wandmalerei vom Untergang Pompejis bis ans Ende des dritten Jarhunderts, Berlin, 1934; F. Gerke, Das Verhältnis von Malerei und Plastik in der theodosianisch-honorischen Zeit, RACr, XII, 1935, pp. 119–63; R. Lantier, Les arts chrétiens de la péninsule ibérique et de l'Afrique du Nord, Anuario del Cuerpo Facultativo de Archiveros, Bibliotecarios y Arqueólogos, III, 1935, pp. 257–72; J. De Wit, Spätrömische Bildmalerei, Berlin, 1938; H. Häberlin, Grundzüge einer Nachantike Farbikonographie, Römisches Jhb. für Kg., III, 1939, pp. 75–126; D. Levi, The Allegories of the Months in Classical Art, AB, XXIII, 1941, pp. 250–91; E. W. Anthony, Romanesque Frescoes, Princeton, 1951; G. de Francovich, L'arte siriaca e il suo influsso sulla pittura medievale, Comm, II, 1951, pp. 3–16, 75–92, 143–52; G. Galassi, Roma o Bisanzio, 2 vols., Rome, 1953; E. Kitzinger, The Cult of Images in the Age before Iconoclasm, Dumbarton Oaks Pap., VIII, 1954, pp. 83–150; E. Will, De l'Euphrate au Rhin, Syria, XXXI, 1954, pp. 271–85; A. Grabar and C. Nordenfalk, Early Medieval Painting from the 4th to the 11th Century, Geneva, 1957 (rev. D. Wright, AB, XLIII, 1961, pp. 245–55); M. Borda, La pittura romana, Milan, 1958; A. Grabar, Peintures murales chrétiennes, Cah. de civ. méd., I, 1958, pp. 9–15; H. P. L'Orange and P. J. Nordhagen, Mosaik fra antikk til middelalter, Oslo, 1958 (Ger. ed., Munich, 1960); A. Grabar, Recherches sur les sources juives de l'art paléochrétien, CahA, XI, 1960, pp. 41–71, XII, 1962, pp. 115–52; C. Ihm, Die Programme der christlichen Apsismalerei vom 4. Jahrhundert bis zur Mitte des 8. Jahrhunderts, Wiesbaden, 1960.

b. Illustrated codices: O. von Gebhardt, The Miniatures of the Ashburnham Pentateuch, London, 1883; A. Haseloff, Codex purpureus rossanensis, Berlin, 1898; A. Muñoz, Il codice purpureo di Rossano, Rome, 1907; A. Minto, Cronaca delle Belle Arti, BArte, N.S., V, 1925–26, p. 190; A. M. Friend, Jr., The Portraits of the Evangelists in Greek and Latin Manuscripts, Art S., V, 1927, pp. 115–47, VII, 1929, pp. 3–29; C. R. Morey, Notes on East Christian Miniatures, AB, XI, 1929, pp. 5–103; S. J. Gasiorowski, A Fragment of a Greek Illustrated Papyrus from Antinoe, JEA, XVII, 1931, pp. 1–9; H. Gerstinger, Die Wiener Genesis, 2 vols., Vienna, 1931; H. Degering and A. Boeckler, Die Quedlinburger Italafragmente, Berlin, 1932; P. Buberl, Das Problem der Wiener Genesis, JhbKhSammlWien, N.S., X, 1936, pp. 9–58; A. W. Byvanck, Antike Buchmalerei, Mnemosyne, 3d ser., VI, 1938, pp. 241–51; W. Lameere, Apamée de Syrie et les Cynégétiques du Pseudo-Oppien dans la miniature byzantine, B. Inst. H. Belge de Rome, XIX, 1938, pp. 125–47; C. Nordenfalk, Die spätantiken Kanontafeln, 2 vols., Göteborg, 1938; E. Bethe, Buch und Bild im Altertum, Leipzig, 1945; M. V. Anastos, The Alexandrian Origin of the Christian Topography of Cosmas Indicopleustes, Dumbarton Oaks Pap., III, 1946, pp. 73–80; K. Weitzmann, Illustrations in Roll and Codex, Princeton, 1947; A. Grabar, Les peintures de l'Evangéliaire de Sinope, Paris, 1948; C. Nordenfalk, The Beginnings of Book Decoration, in Essays in Honor of Georg Swarzenski (ed. O. Goetz), Chicago, 1952, pp. 9–20; K. Weitzmann, Die Illustration der Septuaginta, Münch. Jhb. der bildenden K., 3d ser., III–IV, 1952–53, pp. 96–120; H. Stern, Le calendrier de 354, Paris, 1953; H. Gerstinger and H. E. Killy, Rl. für Ant. und Christentum, s.v. Buchmalerei, II, 1954, cols. 733–72; K. Weitzmann, Observations on the Milan Iliad, Nederlands Kh. Jb., V, 1954, pp. 241–64; F. Wormald, The Miniatures of the Gospels of St. Augustine, Cambridge, 1954; R. Bianchi Bandinelli, Hellenistic-Byzantine Miniatures of the Iliad (Ilias Ambrosiana), Olten, Lausanne, 1955; R. Bianchi Bandinelli, Il Dioscuride napoletano, La Parola del Passato, XI, 1956, pp. 48–51; K. Weitzmann, The Octateuch of the Seraglio and the History of Its Picture Recension, in Actes Xe Cong. int. ét. byz. (1955), Istanbul, 1957, pp. 183–86; K. Weitzmann, Observations on the Cotton Genesis Fragments, in Late Classical and Med. S. in Honor of A. M. Friend, Jr., Princeton, 1958, pp. 112–31; C. Cecchelli and M. Salmi, The Rabbula Gospels, Olten, Lausanne, 1959; C.-O. Nordström, Rabbinica in frühchristlichen und byzantinischen Illustrationen zum 4. Buch Mose, Figura, N.S., I, 1959, pp. 24–47; O. Pächt, Ephraimillustration, Haggadah, und Wiener Genesis, in Festschrift K. M. Swoboda, Vienna, 1959, pp. 213–21; K. Weitzmann, Ancient Book Illumination, Cambridge, Mass., 1959; J. de Wit, Die Miniaturen des Vergilius Vaticanus, Amsterdam, 1959.

c. Eastern provinces: (1) *Constantinople and Asia Minor*: G. Brett, The Mosaic of the Great Palace in Constantinople, Warburg, V, 1942, pp. 34–43; G. Brett and D. Talbot Rice, ed., The Great Palace of the Byzantine Emperors, 2 vols., Oxford, 1947, Edinburgh, 1958; L. Budde, Die rettende Arche Noes, RACr, XXXII, 1956, pp. 41–58; G. Bănăteanu, Ein vernachlässiges Zweig der armenischen Kunst, die Mosaik, Byzantinoslavica, XIX, 1958, pp. 107–18; L. Budde, Die frühchristlichen Mosaiken von Misis-Mopsuestia in Kilikien, Pantheon, XVIII, 1960, pp. 116–26. (2) *Syria and Palestine*: F.-M. Abel, Découvertes récentes à Beit-Djebrin, RBib, XXXIII, 1924, pp. 583–604; M. Avi-Yonah, Mosaic Pavements in Palestine, Q. Palestine Dept. of Ant., II, 1933, pp. 136–81, III, 1934, pp. 26–73; F. Mayence, La VIe campagne de fouilles à Apamée, B. Mus. royaux, X, 1938, pp. 99–113; G. M. A. Hanfmann, The Seasons in John of Gaza's "Tabula Mundi," Latomus, III, 1939, pp. 111–18; M. Avi-Yonah, Oriental Elements in the Art of Palestine in the Roman and Byzantine Periods, Q. Palestine Dept of Ant., X, 1940, pp. 105–51, XIII, 1947–49, pp. 128–65, XIV, 1950, pp. 49–80; H. Lacoste, La VIIe campagne de fouilles à Apamée, B. Mus. royaux, XII, 1940, pp. 2–12; D. Levi, Antioch Mosaic Pavements, 2 vols., Princeton, 1947; R. Wischnitzer, The Messianic Theme in the Paintings of the

Dura Synagogue, Chicago, 1948; M. Chéhab, Mosaïques de Beyrouth et de Baalbeck, Actes VIe Cong. int. ét. byz. (1948), II, Paris, 1951, pp. 89–92; G. M. A. Hanfmann, Socrates and Christ, Harvard S. of Classical Philology, LX, 1951, pp. 206–33; E. Kitzinger, Mosaic Pavements in the Greek East and the Question of a "Renaissance" under Justinian, Actes VIe Cong. int. ét. byz. (1948), II, Paris, 1951, pp. 209–23; J. B. Segal, Pagan Syriac Monuments in the Vilayet of Urfa, Anatolian S., III, 1953, pp. 97–119; M. Avi-Yonah, The Madaba Mosaic Map, Jerusalem, 1954; C. H. Kraeling, Excavations at Dura Europos: The Synagogue (Final Rep., VIII,1), New Haven, 1956; B. Bagatti, Il significato dei mosaici della scuola di Madaba, RACr, XXXIII, 1957, pp. 139–60; M. Chéhab, Mosaïques du Liban, B. Mus. de Beyrouth, XIV, 1959, pp. 5–189; O. Grabar, The Umayyad Dome of the Rock in Jerusalem, Ars Orientalis, III, 1959, pp. 33–62; J. B. Segal, New Mosaics from Edessa, Archaeology, XII, 1959, pp. 151–57; M. Schapiro and M. Avi-Yonah, Israel: Ancient Mosaics, Greenwich, Conn., 1960; S. Yeivin, A Decade of Archaeology in Israel, 1948–1958, Istanbul, 1960; P. Testini, The "Kathisma" Church and Monastery, Excavations at Ramat Rahel: Seasons 1959 and 1960, Rome, 1962. (3) *The Balkans*: A. Frova, Pittura romana in Bulgaria, Rome, 1943; E. Kitzinger, Mosaic at Nikopolis, Dumbarton Oaks Pap., VI, 1951, pp. 81–122; F. Gerke, Die Wandmalereien der neugefundenen Grabkammer in Pécs, Forsch. zur Kg. und christlichen Archäol.: Spätantike und Byzanz, Baden-Baden, 1952, pp. 115–37; A. Frova, Peinture romaine en Bulgarie, CahArt, XXIX, 1954, pp. 25–40, 246–59; D. Mano-Zisi, Le castrum de Gamzigrad et ses mosaïques, Archaeol. Jugoslavica, II, 1956, pp. 67–84; L. Mirkovič, La nécropole paléochrétienne de Niš, Archaeol., Jugoslavica, II, 1956, pp. 85–100; A. J. Festugière, La mosaïque de Philippopolis et le sarcophage au "Promethée," RArts, VII, 1957, pp. 194–202; J. Maximovič, Contributions à l'étude des fresques de Stobi, CahA, X, 1959, pp. 207–16. (4) *Greece*: A. M. Schneider, Samos in frühchristlicher und byzantinischer Zeit, AM, LIV, 1929, pp. 95–141; R. Ginouvès, Mosaïque de la maison Kalivinou, BCH, LXXX, 1956, pp. 396–98; R. Ginouvès, La mosaïque des mois à Argos, BCH, LXXXI, 1957, pp. 216–68; E. Dyggve, La région palatiale de Thessalonique, Acta Cong. Madvigiani: Proc. 2d Int. Cong. of Classical S., I, Copenhagen, 1958, pp. 353–65.

d. Italy: (1) *General*: M. van Berchem and E. Clouzot, Mosaïques chrétiennes du IVe au Xe siècle, Geneva, 1924; R. Huch and W. F. Volbach, Early Christian Mosaics, New York, 1946; A. W. Byvanck, Kerkelijke mozaïeken in Italië, uit de vijfde en uit de eerste helft van de zesde eeuw, Brussels, 1957. (2) *Rome and vicinity*: J. Wilpert, Die malereien der Katakomben Roms, 2 vols., Freiburg im Breisgau, 1903; W. de Grüneisen, Sainte-Marie-Antique, Rome, 1911; M. Avery, The Alexandrian Style at Santa Maria Antiqua, AB, VII, 1924–25, pp. 131–49; T. Ashby and G. Lugli, La basilica di Giunio Basso sull'Esquilino, RACr, IX, 1932, pp. 221–55; E. Kitzinger, Römische Malerei von Beginn des 7. bis zur Mitte des 8. Jahrhunderts, Munich, 1936; M. E. Blake, Mosaics of the Late Empire in Rome and Vicinity, MAARome, XVII, 1940, pp. 81–130; C. Cecchelli, Monumenti cristiano-eretici di Roma, Rome, 1944; M. Cagiano de Azevedo, Osservazioni sulle pitture romane di un edificio di Via dei Cerchi, RendPontAcc, XXII–XXIV, 1947–49, pp. 253–58; G. Matthiae, SS. Cosma e Damiano e S. Teodoro, Rome, 1948; G. Matthiae, Tradizione o reazione nei mosaici romani dei secoli VI e VII, Proporzioni, III, 1950, pp. 10–15; M. Cagiano de Azevedo, La dea Barberini, RIASA, N.S., III, 1954, pp. 108–46; C. Cecchelli, I mosaici della basilica di Santa Maria Maggiore, Turin, 1956; C. C. van Essen, Studio cronologico sulle pitture parietali di Ostia, BCom, LXXVI, 1956–58, pp. 155–81; C. Bertelli, Osservazioni sulla Madonna della Clemenza, RendPontAcc, XXX–XXXI, 1957–59, pp. 141–52; C. Cecchelli, Mosaici romani del V e VI secolo, Corsi di cultura sull'arte ravennate e bizantina, 1958, 2, pp. 37–44; C. Proskauer, The Significance to Medical History of the Newly Discovered 4th Century Roman Fresco, B. N.Y. Acad. of Medicine, 2d ser., XXXIV, 1958, pp. 672–86; H. Stern, Les mosaïques de l'église de Saint-Constance à Rome, Dumbarton Oaks Pap., XII, 1958, pp. 157–218; A. Ferrua, Le pitture della nuova catacomba di Via Latina, Vatican City, 1960; G. Becatti, Scavi di Ostia: I mosaici, Rome, 1961; C. Bertelli, La Madonna di Santa Maria in Trastevere, Rome, 1961; A. W. Byvanck, Das Problem der Mosaiken von Santa Maria Maggiore, in Festschrift Hans R. Hahnloser, Basel, Stuttgart, 1961, pp. 15–26. (3) *Ravenna*: C. Ricci, Monumenti: Tavole storiche dei mosaici di Ravenna, 8 vols., Rome, 1930–37; O. G. von Simson, Sacred Fortress: Byzantine Art and Statecraft in Ravenna, Chicago, 1948; G. Bovini, Il cosidetto mausoleo di Galla Placidia in Ravenna, Vatican City, 1950; C.-O. Nordström, Ravennastudien: Ideengeschichtliche und ikonographische Untersuchung über die Mosaiken von Ravenna (Figura, 4), Stockholm, 1953; G. Bovini, S. Vitale di Ravenna, Milan, 1955. (4) *Northern Italy*: A. Calderini, G. Chierici, and C. Cecchelli, La basilica di S. Lorenzo Maggiore in Milano, Milan, 1951; B. Forlati Tamaro, La basilica paleocristiana di Verona, RendPontAcc, XXX–XXXI, 1957–59, pp. 117–27; P. L. Zovatto, Mosaici opitergini con scene all'aria aperta, CrArte, N.S., IV, 1957, pp. 97–107; A. Degrassi, EAA, s.v. Desenzano, III, 1960, pp. 79–80. (5) *Sicily*: G. Agnello, La pittura paleocristiana della Sicilia, Vatican City, 1952; G. V. Gentili, La villa erculia di Piazza Armerina: I mosaici figurati, Milan, 1959.

e. North Africa: P. Gauckler, Mosaïques tombales d'une chapelle de martyrs à Thabarca, MPiot, XIII, 1906, pp. 175–227; Inventaire des mosaïques del a Gaule et de l'Afrique, II–IV, Paris, 1910–15; A. Merlin, La mosaïque du Seigneur Julius à Carthage, BAC, 1921, pp. 95–114; M. Drerup, Die Datierung der Mumienporträts, Paderborn, 1933; J. Bérard, Mosaïques inédites de Cherchel, Mél, LII, 1935, pp. 115–42; Y. Allais, Djemila, Paris, 1938; A. Merlin and L. Poinssot, Factions de cirque et saisons sur des mosaïques de la Tunisie, RA, 6th ser., XXXI–XXXII (Mél. Charles Picard, II), 1949, pp. 732–45; J. B. Ward Perkins and J. M. C. Toynbee, The Hunting Baths at Leptis Magna, Archaeologia, XCIII, 1949, pp. 165–95; G. Pesce, Pitture sabratensi, BArte, XXXVI, 1951, pp. 158–65; C. Courtois, L. and C. Poinssot, Sur un baptistère découvert dans la région de Kélibia (Cap Bon), Karthago, VI, 1955, pp. 98–123; E. Marec, Monuments chrétiens d'Hippone, Paris, 1958; J. B. Ward Perkins, A New Group of 6th-Century Mosaics from Cyrenaica, RACr, XXXIV, 1958, pp. 183–92; N. Duval and A. Lézine, Nécropole chrétienne et baptistère souterrain à Carthage, CahA, X, 1959, pp. 71–147; P. A. Février and C. Poinssot, Les cierges et l'abeille: Note sur l'iconographie du baptistère découvert dans la région de Kélibia (Tunisie), CahA, X, 1959, pp. 149–56; L. Foucher, Inventaire des mosaïques, feuille no. 57 de l'Atlas archéologique: Sousse, Tunis, 1960; R. Goodchild, A Byzantine Palace at Apollonia (Cyrenaica), Antiquity, XXXIX, 1960, pp. 246–58; G. Caputo and A. Driss, Tunisia: Ancient Mosaics, New York, 1962; M. Cagiano de Azevedo, La datazione dei mosaici di Zliten, Hommages à Albert Grenier, Brussels, 1962, pp. 374–80.

f. Western provinces: (1) *Spain*: J. Serra Vilaró, Excavaciones en la necrópolis romano-cristiana de Tarragona (Mem. Junta superior de excavaciones y ant., 93), Madrid, 1927; A. del Castillo, La Costa Brava en la antigüedad, Ampurias, I, 1939, pp. 186–267; A. Blanco Freijeiro, Mosaicos romanos con escenes de circo y anfiteatro en el Museo Arqueológico Nacional, AEA, XXIII, 1950–51, pp. 127–42; J. de C. Serra Ràfols, La "villa" romana de la dehesa de "La Cocosa," Badajoz, 1952; A. García y Bellido, Dos "villae rusticae" romanas recientemente excavadas, AEA, XXVI, 1953, pp. 207–17; O. Sargnon, A la jerme — villa romaine de Torre de Palma (Alentejo), RA, L, 1957, pp. 84–88; A. Balil, Consideraciones sobre el mosaico hispanoromano, Rev. de Guimaraes, LXVII, 1958, pp. 337–54; H. Schlunk, Untersuchungen im frühchristlichen Mausoleum von Centcelles, in Neue deutsche Ausgrabungen im Mittelmeerraum und im vorderen Orient, Berlin, 1959, pp. 344–65. (2) *Gaul*: Inventaire des mosaïques de la Gaule et de l'Afrique, I, Paris, 1909; H. Stern, Recueil général des mosaiques de la Gaule, I, 1–2, Paris, 1957–60. (3) *Germany and Switzerland*: F. Fremersdorf, Das römische Haus mit dem Dionysius-Mosaik vor dem Südportal des Kölner Domes, Berlin, 1956; M. Cagiano de Azevedo, Ritratti o personificazioni le figure del soffitto di Treviri?, AC, X, 1958, pp. 60–63; K. Parlasca, Die römischen Mosaiken in Deutschland (Römisch-germanische Forsch., 23), Berlin, 1959; V. von Gonzebach, Die römischen Mosaiken in der Schweiz, Basel, 1961. (4) *Britain*: T. Morgan, Romano-British Mosaic Pavements, London, 1886; C. A. Ralegh Radford and H. S. L. Dewar, The Roman Mosaics from Low Ham and East Coker, Taunton, 1954; G. W. Meates, Lullingstone Roman Villa, London, 1955.

Minor Arts: *a. General*: O. M. Dalton, Catalogue of Early Christian Antiquities in the British Museum, London, 1901; J. Strzygowski, Koptische Kunst (Cat. général des antiquités égyptiennes du Musée du Caire), Vienna, 1904; O. Wulff, Altchristliche und mittelalterliche byzantinische und italienische Bildwerke, 2 vols., Berlin, 1909–11; O. M. Dalton, Byzantine Art and Archaeology, Oxford, 1911 (repr. New York, 1961); O. M. Dalton, A Guide to the Early Christian and Byzantine Antiquities in the British Museum, 2d ed., London, 1921; O. Wulff and W. F. Volbach, Die altchristlichen und mittelalterlichen Bildwerke, Berlin, Leipzig, 1923; Burlington Fine Arts Club, Art in the Dark Ages in Europe, ca. 400–1000 A.D. (cat.), London, 1930; Catalogue de l'Exposition internationale d'art byzantin, Paris, 1931; H. Peirce and R. Tyler, L'art byzantin, 2 vols., Paris, 1932–34; W. F. Volbach, Das christliche Kunstgewerbe der Spätantike und des frühen Mittelalters im Mittelmeergebiet, Geschichte des Kunstgewerbes aller Zeiten und Völker (ed. H. T. Bossert), V, Berlin, 1932, pp. 46–125; H. Schlunk, Kunst der Spätantike in Mittelmeerraum (cat.), Berlin, 1939; Pagan and Christian Art: Catalogue of the Coptic Exhibition in the Brooklyn Museum, New York, 1941; Walters Art Gallery, Exhibition of Early Christian and Byzantine Art (cat.), Baltimore, 1947; Zürich Kunsthaus, Kunstschätze der Lombardei (cat.), Zürich, 1948–49; Handbook of the Dumbarton Oaks Collection, Washington, D.C., 1955; Villa Hügel, Werdendes Abendland an Rhein und Ruhr (cat.), Essen, 1956; E. Coche de la Ferté, L'antiquité chrétienne au Musée du Louvre, Paris, 1958; Masterpieces of Byzantine Art (cat.), Edinburgh, 1958; R. Noll, Vom Altertum zum Mittelalter (Führer durch das Kunsthist. Mus., Nr. 8), Vienna, 1958; K. Weitzmann, The survival of Mythological Representations in Early Christian and Byzantine Art and Their Impact on Christian Iconography, Dumbarton Oaks Pap., XIV, 1960, pp. 43–68; J. Beckwith, The Art of Constantinople: An Introduction to Byzantine Art 330–1453, London, New York, 1961; M. C. Ross, Catalogue of the Byzantine and Early Mediaeval Antiquities in the Dumbarton Oaks Collection, I, Washington, D. C., 1962.

b. Coins, medallions and jewelry: H. A. Grueber, Roman Medallions in the British Museum, London, 1874; J. Maurice, Numismatique constantinienne, 3 vols., Paris, 1908–12; W. W. Wroth, Catalogue of the Imperial Byzantine Coins in the British Museum, I, London, 1908; M. Rosenberg, Geschichte der Goldschmiedekunst, 11 vols., Frankfurt, 1908–24; F. Gnecchi, I medaglioni romani, 3 vols., Milan, 1912; I. I. Tolstoi, Monnaies byzantines, 4 vols., St. Petersburg, 1912–14 (Rus.); W. Dennison, A Gold Treasure of the Late Roman Period, New York, 1918; H. Goodacre, The Bronze Coinage of the Late Roman Empire, London, 1922; H. Goodacre, A Handbook of the Coinage of the Byzantine Empire, 3 vols., London, 1928–33; R. Delbrück, Der spätantike Kaiserornat, Die Antike, VIII, 1932, pp. 1–21; A. Alföldi, Insignien und Tracht der römischen Kaiser, RM, L, 1935, pp. 1–171; G. Castelfranco, L'arte della moneta nel tardo impero, CrArte, II, 1937, pp. 11–21; B. Segall, Katalog der Goldschmiedarbeiten, Benaki Mus., Athens, 1938; J. Babelon, Le portrait dans l'antiquité après les monnaies, Paris, 1942; A. Alföldi, Die Kontorniaten: Ein verkanntes Propagandamittel der stadt-römischen heidnischen Aristokratie in ihrem Kampf gegen das christliche Kaisertum, Budapest, 1943; J. M. C. Toynbee, Roman Medallions, New York, 1944; J. W. E. Pearce, Roman Imperial Coinage, IX, London, 1951; M. Grant, Roman Imperial Money, London, 1954; J. P. C. Kent, Notes on Some 4th Century Coin Types, NChr, 6th ser., XIV, 1954, pp. 216–17; M. C. Ross, Notes on Byzantine Gold and Silversmiths' Work, J. Walters Art Gall., XVIII, 1955, pp. 59–67; E. Coche de la Ferté, Les bijoux antiques, Paris, 1956; J. Heurgon, Le trésor de Ténès, Paris, 1958; P. W. Lehmann, Theodosius or Justinian? A Renaissance Drawing of a Byzantine Rider, AB, XLI, 1959, pp. 39–57; P. V. Hill, J. P. C. Kent, and R. A. G. Carson, Late Roman Bronze Coinage, A.D. 324–498, London, 1960; M. R. Alföldi, Die Hofkunst Constantins des Grossen im Spiegel der Goldprägung, Bonn, 1961; P. Bruun, Studies in Constantinian Chronology, New York, 1961; A. Lipinsky, Il gioiello di San Francesco, un diadema tardoromano perduto, Felix Ravenna, 3d ser., XXXIII, 1961, pp. 39–78; I. Maull, Le zecche dell'antica Ravenna, Felix Ravenna, 3d ser., XXXIII, 1961, pp. 79–134; M. R. Alföldi, Die Constantinische Goldprägung, Untersuchung zu ihrer Bedeutung für Kaiserpolitik und Hofkunst, Mainz, 1963.

c. Cameos, gems, and precious stones: E. Babelon, La gravure en pierre fine, Paris, 1894; E. Babelon, Catalogue des camées antiques et modernes de la Bibliothèque Nationale, Paris, 1897; Furtwängler, AG; C. H. Read, The Waddesdon Bequest, London, 1902; H. B. Walters, Catalogue of the Engraved Gems and Cameos, Greek, Etruscan, and Roman, in the British Museum, London, 1926; F. Eichler and E. Kris, Die Kameen im Kunsthistorisches Museum, Vienna, 1927; B. Segall, A Rock-Crystal Statuette of Herakles, J. Walters Art Gall., II, 1939, pp. 113–17; M. C. Ross, The Rubens Vase: Its History and Date, J. Walters Art Gall., VI, 1943, pp. 8–39; D. Miner and E. J. Edelstein, A Carving in Lapis Lazuli, J. Walters Art Gall., VII–VIII, 1944–45, pp. 82–103; G. Bruns, Staatskameen des 4. Jahrhunderts nach Christi Geburt, Wpr, 104, 1948; E. Coche de la Ferté, Le camée Rothschild, Paris, 1957.

d. Silverwork: G. B. de Rossi, Le insigne capselle reliquarie scoperte in Grado, BACr, 1872, pp. 155–58; A. de Longpérier, Le missorium de Geilamir, Roi des Vandales, Gazette Archéol., V, 1879, pp. 53–59; G. B. de Rossi, Capsella argentea africana, BACr, 1887, pp. 118–29; T. Schreiber, Die alexandrinische Toreutik, Leipzig, 1894; H. Graeven, Ein altchristlichen Silberkasten, Z. für christliche Kunst, XII, 1899, cols. 1–16; P. Lauer, Le trésor du Sancta Sanctorum, MPiot, XV, 1906, pp. 71–146; H. Grisar, Il Sancta Sanctorum ed il suo tesoro sacro, Rome, 1907; F. Drexel, Alexandrinische Silbergefässer der Kaiserzeit, BJ, CXVIII, 1909, pp. 176–235; F. Drexel, Über einen spätantiken Silberteller mit mythologischer Darstellung, JdI, XXX, 1915, pp. 192–211; R. Zahn, Spätantike Silbergefässe, Amtliche Berichte aus den königlichen Kunstsamml., XXXVIII, 1917, pp. 263–304; L. Brehier, Les trésors d'argenterie syrienne et l'école artistique d'Antioche, GBA, I, 1920, pp. 173–96; C. Diehl, Ecole artistique d'Antioche et les trésors d'argenterie syrienne, Syria, II, 1921, pp. 81–95; F. Drexel, Ein ägyptisches Silberinventar der Kaiserzeit, RM, XXXVI–XXXVII, 1921–22, pp. 34–57; W. F. Volbach, Metallarbeiten des christlichen Kultes, Mainz, 1921; H. B. Walters, Catalogue of the Silver Plate, Greek, Etruscan, and Roman, in the British Museum, London, 1921; A. O. Curle, The Treasure of Traprain, Glasgow, 1923; F. Drexel, Der Silberschatz von Traprain, Germania, IX, 1925, pp. 122–28; R. Jaeger, Ein Beitrag zur Geschichte der altchristlichen Silberarbeiten, AAnz, 1928, cols. 555–62; L. Matzulewitsch, Byzantinische Antike, Berlin, Leipzig, 1929; S. Poglayen-Neuwall, Über die ursprünglichen Besitzer des spätantiken Silberfundes vom Esquilin und seine Datierung, RM, XLV, 1930, pp. 124–36; M. T. Tozzi, Il tesoro di Projecta, RACr, IX, 1932, pp. 279–314; G. de Lamón, Il calice del Diacono Orso, Treviso, 1937; H. Mattingly, J. W. Pearce, and T. D. Kendrick, The Coleraine Hoard, Antiquity, XI, 1937, pp. 39–45; H. H. Arnason, Early Christian Silver of North Italy and Gaul, AB, XX, 1938, pp. 193–226; W. B. Emery, The Royal Tombs of Balluna and Qustul (Mission archéol. de Nubie, 1929–34), Cairo, 1938; G. L. Brett, Formal Ornament on Late Roman and Early Byzantine Silver, BSR, XV, 1939, pp. 33–41; E. Kitzinger, The Sutton Hoo Ship Burial, V: The Silver, Antiquity, XIV, 1940, pp. 40–63; O. Brendel, The Corbridge Lanx, JRS, XXXI, 1941, pp. 100–27; W. F. Volbach, Il tesoro della Cappella Sancta Sanctorum, Vatican City, 1941; S. Pelekanidis, *'Αργυρὰ πινάκια τοῦ Μουσείου Μπενάκη*, (Silver Plate in the Benake Museum) *'Εφημ*, 1942–44, pp. 37–62; E. Arias, Il piatto argenteo di Cesena, ASAtene, N.S., VIII–X, 1946–48, pp. 309–44; W. B. Emery, Nubian Treasure, London, 1948; A. J. B. Wace, Late Roman Pottery and Plate, B. Soc. royale d'archéol. d'Alexandrie, XXXVII, 1948, pp. 47–57; A. Alföldi, Die Spätantike in der Ausstellung "Kunstschätze der Lombardei" in Zürich, Atlantis, XXI, 1949, pp. 61–80; A. García y Bellido, Esculturas romanas di España y Portugal, I, Madrid, 1949, p. 470, no. 494, II, 1949, pls. 346–52; T. Dohrn, Spätantikes Silber aus Britannien, RM, N.S., II, 1949, pp. 67–139; P. L. Zovatto, La capsella argentea di Grado con le immagini "clipeatae," Aquileia nostra, XXIII, 1952, pp. 18–23; J. M. C. Toynbee, Some Notes on the Mildenhall Treasure, Wandlungen christlicher Kunst im Mittelalter (Forsch. zur Kg. und christlichen Archäol., II), Baden-Baden, 1953, pp. 41–57; P. L. Zovatto, La capsella di Grado con l'immagine di Maria Regina, Aquileia nostra, XXIV–XXV, 1953–54, pp. 121–28; J. W. Brailsford, The Mildenhall Treasure: A Handbook, 2d ed., London, 1955; R. L. S. Bruce-Mitford, The Sutton Hoo Ship Burial: A Provisional Guide, 5th ed., London, 1956; A. Grabar, Les ampoules de Terre Sainte, Paris, 1958; W. M. Milliken, Early Byzantine Silver, B. Cleve. Mus., XLV, 1958, pp. 35–41; W. F. Volbach, Argenterie dei secoli V e VI d.C., Corsi di cultura sull'arte ravennate e bizantina, 1958, 1, pp. 101–05; E. Cruikshank Dodd, Byzantine Silver Stamps, Washington, D.C., 1961 (bibliog.); E. Barbier, La signification du cortège représenté sur le couvercle du coffret de "Projecta," CahA, XII, 1962, pp. 7–33; R. Laur-Belart, A Swiss "Mildenhall Treasure"... discovered at Kaiseraugst, near Basel, ILN, CLXLI, 1962, pp. 70–71, 98–99; W. F. Volbach, Silver- und Elfenbeinarbeiten vom Ende der 4. bis zum Anfang des 7. Jahrhunderts, Akten zum VII. Int. Kong. fur Frühmittelalterforschung (1958), Graz, Cologne, 1962, pp. 21–36; P. L. Zovatto, Il piatto argenteo di Verona, Felix Ravenna, LXXXIV, 34, 1962, pp. 72–79.

e. Ivories: R. Delbrück, Die Consular-diptychen und verwandte Denkmäler, Berlin, 1929; C. Cecchelli, La cattedra di Massimiano ed altri avorii romano-orientali, Rome, 1937; A. C. Soper, The Italo-Gallic School of Early Christian Art, AB, XX, 1938, pp. 145–92; A. C. Soper, The Brescia Casket: A Problem in Late Antique Perspective, AJA, XLVII, 1943, pp. 278–90; E. P. de Loos-Dietz, Vroeg-Christelijke Ivoren, Assen, 1947; R. Delbrück, Probleme der Lipsanothek in Brescia, Bonn, 1952; R. Delbrück, Zu spätrömischen Elfenbeinen des Westreiche, BJ, CLII, 1952, pp. 165–89; R. Delbrück, Zwei christliche Elfenbeine des 5. Jahrhunderts, Spätantike und Byzanz, Neue Beiträge zur Kg. des l. Jahrhunderts (Forsch. zur Kg. und christlichen Archäol., I), I, Baden-Baden, 1952, pp. 167–88; W. F. Volbach, Elfenbeinarbeiten der Spätantike und des frühen Mittelalters, Mainz, 1952 (bibliog.); K. Wessel, Studien zur oströmischen Elfenbeinskulptur, Wissenschaftliche Z. der Univ. Greifswald, II, 1952–53, pp. 63–94, III, 1953–54, pp. 1–36; J. Natanson, Early Christian Ivories, London, 1953; K. Wessel, Der Liverpooler Venatio-Tafel, Wandlungen christlicher Kunst im Mittelalter (Forsch. zu Kg. und christlichen Archäol., II), Baden-Baden, 1953, pp. 59–73; E. Rosenbaum, The Andrews Diptych and Some Related Ivories, AB, XXXVI, 1954, pp. 253–61; British Museum, Liverpool Ivories: Special Exhibition (cat.), London, 1955; G. Bovini and L. Ottolenghi, Avori dell'alto Medio Evo (cat.), Faenza, 1956; K. Wessel, Das Diptychon Andrews, Byz. Z., L, 1957, pp. 99–126; J. Beckwith, The Andrews Diptych, London, 1958; J. Beckwith, The Werden Casket Reconsidered, AB, XL, 1958, pp. 1–11; T. Neumann, Die Elfenbeinpyxis von Xanten und ihr Umkreis, Berlin, 1958; T. Buddensieg, Le coffret en ivoire de Pola, Saint-Pierre et le Lateran, CahA, X, 1959, pp. 157–200; P. Metz, Elfenbein der Spätantike, Munich, 1962; J. Beckwith, Coptic Sculpture 300–1300, London, 1963.

f. Textiles: E. Chartraire, Inventaire du trésor de l'église principale et métropolitaine de Sens, Paris, 1897; E. Chartraire and M. Prou, Note sur un tissu byzantin, MAF, 6th ser., VIII, 1899, pp. 258–70; I. Errera, Catalogue d'étoffes anciennes et modernes, Brussels, 1907; J. Braun, Die spätrömischen Stoffe aus dem Sarcophag des heiligen Paulinus zu Trier, Z. für christliche K., XXIII, 1910, pp. 279–84, 347–50; E. Chartraire, Les tissus anciens du trésor de la Cathédrale de Sens, Rev. de l'art chrétien, LXI, 1911, pp. 261–80, 371–86, 452–68; O. von Falke, Kunstgeschichte der Seidenweberei, 2 vols., Berlin, 1913; I. Errera, Collection d'anciennes étoffes égyptiennes, Brussels, 1916; J. F. Flanagan, The Origin of the Drawloom Used in the Making of Early Byzantine Silks, BM, XXXV, 1919, pp. 167–72; A. F. Kendrick, Catalogue of Textiles from the Burying Grounds of Egypt, 3 vols., London, 1920–22; U. Monneret de Villard, Le transenne di S. Aspreno e le stoffe alessandrine, Aegyptus, IV, 1923, pp. 64–71; M. S. Dimand, Die Ornamentik der ägyptischen Wollwirkereien, Leipzig, 1924; E. A. Stückelberg, Unveröffentliche Walliser Gewebefunde, Anz. für schw. Altertumskunde, N.S., XXVI, 1924, pp. 95–115; O. Wulff and W. F. Volbach, Spätantike und koptische Stoffe aus ägyptischen Grabfunden in den staatlichen Museen, Berlin, 1926; R. Hinks, Ein hellenistische Bildteppiche in British Museum, Pantheon, II, 1928, pp. 588–89; M. S. Dimand, An Early Cut-pile Rug from Egypt, Met. Mus. S., IV, 1932–33, pp. 151–62; R. Pfister, Tissus coptes du Musée du Louvre, Paris, 1932; W. F. Volbach, Spätantike und frühmittelalterliche Stoffe, 2 vols., Mainz, 1932; R. M. Riefstahl, Ein Knüpfteppich spätantiker Tradition im Metropolitan Museum zu New York, RM, XLVIII, 1933, pp. 127–52; R. Pfister, Textiles de Palmyra, 3 vols., Paris, 1934–40; E. Vogt, Ein spätantike Gewebefund aus dem Wallis, Germania, XVIII, 1934, pp. 198–206; J. F. Flanagan, Early Figured Silks, BM, LXVIII, 1936, pp. 145–47; C. J. Lamm and R. J. Charleston, Some Early Egyptian Draw-loom Weavings, B. Soc. d'archéol. copte, V, 1939, pp. 193–99; A. de Capitani d'Arzago, Antichi tessuti della Basilica Ambrosiana, Milan, 1941; W. F. Volbach, Catalogo del Museo Sacro Vaticano, III, 1: I Tessuti, Vatican City, 1942; J. F. Flanagan, Textiles from Palmyra, BM, LXXXIV–LXXXV, 1944, pp. 179–81; R. S. Lopez, The Silk Industry in the Byzantine Empire, Speculum, XX, 1945, pp. 1–42; R. Pfister and L. Bellinger, The Excavations at Dura Europos, IV, 2: The Textiles, New Haven, 1945; J. F. Flanagan, The "Nature Goddess" Silk at Durham, BM, LXXXVIII, 1946, pp. 241–46; E. Kitzinger, The Horse and Lion Tapestry at Dumbarton Oaks, Dumbarton Oaks Pap., III, 1946, pp. 1–72; G. Townsend, Two Fragments of Late Hellenistic Tapestry, BMFA, XLVI, 1948, pp. 13–17; M. Mat'e and K. Lyapunova, Khudozhestvenniye tkani koptskogo Egipta (Decorative Textiles of Coptic Egypt), Moscow, 1951; E. Vogt, Frühmittelalterliche Seidenstoffe aus dem Hochaltar der Kathedrale Chur, ZfSAKg, XIII, 1952, pp. 1–23; A. C. Weibel, Two Thousand Years of Textiles, New York, 1952; J. F. Flanagan, The Figured Silks, in The Relics of St. Cuthbert (ed. C. F. Battiscombe), Oxford, 1956, pp. 484–525; L. Guerrini, Le stoffe copte del Museo Archeologico di Firenze, Rome, 1957; E. Vogt, Frühmittelalterliche Stoffe aus der Abtei-St. Maurice, ZfSAKg, XVIII, 1958, pp. 110–40; J. Beckwith, Coptic Textiles, CIBA Rev., XII, 133, 1959, pp. 2–27.

g. Glass: A. Kisa, Das Glas im Altertum, 3 vols., Leipzig, 1908; J. Morin (Morin-Jean), La verrerie en Gaule sous l'empire romain, Paris, 1913; G. Sangiorgi, Collezione di vetri antichi, Milan, Rome, 1914; C. D. Drew and K. C. Collingwood Selby, The Excavations at Colliton Park, Dorchester: 2d Interim Report, Proc. Dorset Natural H. and Archaeol. Soc., LX, 1939, pp. 51–65; D. B. Harden, Tomb-Groups of Glass of Roman Date from Syria and Palestine, Iraq, XI, 1949, pp. 151–59; F. Neuberg, Glass in Antiquity (trans. R. J. Charleston), London, 1949; E. Schuldt, Das spätrömische Grab von Jesendorf, Kreis Wismar, Hammaburg, III, 1949, pp. 225–30; F. Fremersdorff, Figurlich geschliffene Gläser: Einer Kölner Werkstatt des 3. Jahrhunderts, Berlin, 1951; F. Fremersdorff, Christliche Leibwächte auf einem geschliffenen Kölner Glasbecher des 4. Jahrhunderts, Festschrift für Rudolf Egger, I, Klagenfurt, 1952, pp. 66–83; J. Villette, Une coupe chrétienne en verre gravé trouvée à Carthage, MPiot, XLVI, 1952, pp. 131–51; N. Norling-Christensen, Vestlandskedler og Malede Glas, Kuml: Aarbog for Jydsk Arkaeol. Selskab, 1953, pp. 47–60; J. Hackin et al., Nouvelles recherches archéologiques à Begram, 2 vols., Paris, 1954; E. Coche de la Ferté, Le verre de Lycurgue, MPiot, XLVIII, 1956, pp. 131–62; Glass from the Ancient World: The R. W. Smith Collection (cat.), Corning, N.Y., 1957; D. B. Harden, The Highdown Hill Glass Goblet with Greek Inscription, Sussex Archaeol. Coll. XCVII, 1959, pp. 3–20; D. B. Harden and J. M. C. Toynbee, The Rothschild Lycurgus Cup, Archeologia, XCVII, 1959, pp. 179–212; C. R. Morey and G. Ferrari, The Gold Glass Collection of the Vatican Library, Vatican City, 1959; J. E. Crome, Due medaglioni di vetro dorato dell'anno 400, Felix Ravenna, LXXXI, 1960, pp. 115–24; D. B. Harden, The Wint Hill Hunting Bowl and Related Glasses, J. Glass S., II, 1960, pp. 45–81; U. H. Elbern, Ein christlicher Kultgefäss aus glas in der Dumbarton Oaks Collection, Jhb. Berliner Mus., IV, 1962, pp. 17–41.

h. Ceramics: A. L. Delattre, Lampes chrétiennes de Carthage, 2 vols., Lille, 1890–91; C. M. Kauffmann, Ägyptische Terrakotten der griechisch-römischen und koptischen Epoche, Cairo, 1913; F. O. Waagé, The American Excavations in the Athenian Agora, 1st Report: The Roman and Byzantine Pottery, Hesperia, II, 1933, pp. 279–328; J. H. Holwerda, Het Laat-Griekische en Romeinsche gebruiksaardwerke, The Hague, 1936; G. Chenet, La céramique gallo-romaine d'Argonne du IVe siècle et la terre sigillée decorée à la molette, Maçon, 1941; F. E. Day, Early Islamic and Christian Lamps, Berytus, VII, 1942, pp. 65–79; A. J. B. Wace, Late Roman Pottery and Plate, B. Soc. royale d'archéol. d'Alexandrie, XXXVII, 1948, pp. 47–57; P. de Palol Salettas, La ceramica estampada romana-cristiana, Crónica del IV Cong. arqueol. del Sudeste España (Elche, 1948), Cartagena, 1949, pp. 450–69; M. Floriani Squarciapino, Note per lo studio del vasellame fittile romano, RendLinc, ser. VIII, VI, 1951, pp. 133–43; R. J. Charleston, Roman Pottery, London, 1955.

i. Bronzes: F. Schottmüller, Bronze Statuette und Geräte, 2d ed., Berlin, 1921; A. Alföldi, Cornuti, Dumbarton Oaks Pap., XIII, 1959, pp. 169–83.

See also bibliogs. for ARMENIAN ART; BYZANTINE ART; CATACOMBS; COPTIC ART; IMAGES AND ICONOCLASM; MOSAICS; PRE-ROMANESQUE ART.

Illustrations: PLS. 33–90; 14 figs. in text.

LA TOUR, GEORGES DE. French painter (b. Vic, 1593; d. Lunéville, 1652). Sometime after his marriage in 1617, La Tour moved from Vic, the small capital of the bishopric of Metz in the duchy of Lorraine, to Lunéville, where by 1620 he appears to have had an active studio. Lunéville was the summer residence of the Duke of Lorraine, who commissioned from the artist a painting of St. Peter. In 1633 the duchy was occupied by the French. In that same year La Tour offered a painting of St. Sebastian to Louis XIII. In 1638 Lunéville was burned and sacked as it changed hands between the French and local partisans; during this period La Tour went to Nancy and perhaps to Vic and to Paris. He reappeared in Lunéville in 1641 as a rich court painter, detested by the people but protected by the royal governor of Nancy, who had Lunéville present him with some of La Tour's paintings, paid for by taxes.

The complexity of the artistic influences upon La Tour seems in part to explain the enigma of his genius. Although somewhat behind the times, the visual arts of Lorraine nevertheless influenced his style to some extent, for his religious night scenes follow an old Lorrainese tradition. The chiaroscuro paintings — of beggars with elongated faces and tapering fingers — by the mannerist Jacques Bellange, who dominated the court of Nancy from 1600 to 1617, also left their mark on La Tour.

From 1614 to 1616 La Tour was probably in Italy. His work, like that of Jean Jacques Tournier and Jean Tassel, is generally considered to be Caravaggesque, but the most obvious points of similarity between his style and the art of Caravaggio — interest in chiaroscuro and the popular pseudorealism of his religious scenes, secularized in order to make the holy figures more accessible to the faithful — are only superficial; La Tour's forms and colors are used for other ends (A. Malraux, 1953). Decidedly different from the *tenebrosi* — the somber painters — La Tour comes closer to the artists who blended some elements from the art of Caravaggio with others from that of Jacopo Bassano and of such painters of the school of Brescia as Carlo Saraceni and Paolo Piazza. The presumed influence of Luca Cambiaso — the mannerist who antedated Caravaggio — on La Tour during his supposed visit to Genoa is not substantiated by the few analogies to that artist's work found in La Tour's paintings; likewise, the nocturnal *Nativity* of J. Sánchez Cotán was an antecedent of, but not a source for, La Tour. The phrase "La Tour lorrain, élève de Guide," which appears in the chronicle of the monastery of Saint-Antoine-en-Viennois, is a more important clue, inasmuch as the monastery possessed original paintings by La Tour (e.g., *St. Jerome*; Grenoble, Mus. de Peinture et Sculpture); Guido Reni's influence on La Tour seems to have encompassed flawless technique, precise drawing, nobility and sweetness of expression, and balance in design.

The types of faces and figures, the lighting effects, and the subject matter in La Tour's paintings all reveal the influence of Dutch Caravaggesque painters, whose works La Tour may have known and with whom he might even have had direct contact. According to Blunt (1954), two trips made by La Tour determined the evolution of his art. The first (1620–30) exposed him to the school of Utrecht, which inspired him to paint realistic daylight scenes that reflect the influence of Terbrugghen's *The Four Evangelists* (1621; Deventer, Stadhuis) or even later works by the Dutch master. Blunt believes that La Tour subsequently painted nocturnes in which the source of light remained concealed, and that only after a second trip, in about 1640, did he begin to expose the source of light, in the manner of Gerrit van Honthorst (q.v.). It is also possible that La Tour painted both day and night scenes all along.

There was a marked Italian current in Lorraine. La Tour met both Jacques Callot (q.v.), who had formerly worked at the Medici court in Florence, and the disciple of Saraceni, Jean Le Clerc, who was no genius but had an inquiring mind and may have impelled Callot and La Tour to paint night scenes. Shortly before his death in 1632, Le Clerc engraved four night scenes, one of his own invention and three after works of La Tour, which helped to make La Tour's work known. Between 1631 and 1640 La Tour may have gone to Paris. In any case, he was aware of several of the currents in Parisian art, perhaps only because of his acquaintance with Callot, Israël Henriet, and the French artists active in Lorraine; he knew the work of the popular realists and of the Italianate religious painters, and he was responsive to the movement toward a classical style.

These Dutch, Italian, and French elements appear in each of La Tour's paintings in different combinations, which explains the tenuous classifications and contradictory interpretations characteristic of studies up to the present time. There are only two dated works by La Tour. Many are signed, but some of the signatures seem questionable. Frequent recurrence of themes and motifs and the problem of separating originals from studio replicas add to the confusion. The only connecting links are his technique, the manner in which he rendered forms colored by light, and the engravings that were made after his works.

Much uncertainty remains as to La Tour's earliest work; *The Peasant Family* (San Francisco, M. H. de Young Memorial Mus.) must be excluded, as well as the *Pièta* (Chancelade, Dordogne, parish church; copy in Amsterdam, Rijksmus.) and such other works as *The Young Girl with a Lamp* (San Francisco, Calif. Palace of the Legion of Honor).

The Cheat (or *The Sharper*) can be firmly dated about 1625 (Paris, Coll. Landry; copy in Geneva, Coll. Marie Pictet). It is a daylight scene, evidently influenced by Terbrugghen, but with a certain harshness; the palette is clear and varied, and the composition has been executed with patient precision. The scene is apparently an innocent one, but with latent drama. *The Fortune Teller* (New York, Met. Mus.) is of slightly earlier date, according to Sterling; this painting is signed, and Lunéville is mentioned in the inscription. It too is a daylight scene, related to *The Cheat* and to the paintings of Terbrugghen. In the development of La Tour's style, *The Fortune Teller* leads to his *Servant with the Flea* (PL. 95), discovered in 1954, which is similar in certain details but shows the attempt to build up masses in a haze of nocturnal light. The servant girl is shown crushing the flea with such concentration that the Honthorstian theme is completely transformed.

The Newborn or *The Nativity* (PL. 93) — painted no later than about 1630 — is a family scene but at the same time a devout work, enchanting in its melancholy tenderness and its luminous effects of blended reds and mauves. It approaches his composition *The Old Women*, which was engraved by Le Clerc before 1632 and to which a *St. Anne* (U.S.A., private coll.) may also be related. To a second engraving by Le Clerc, *St. Francis in Ecstasy* — a night scene, with striking contrasts in lighting, showing the saint with another monk in a cell — may be connected a fragment of a similar composition (Hartford, Conn., Wadsworth Atheneum) attributed to La Tour, as well as his *Two Monks* (Le Mans, Mus. B. A.), depicting a saint in ecstasy; the latter, having been repainted in part, is an uneven painting that has been much discussed and is later in date than the engraving. A third engraving by Le Clerc is of another candlelit scene with a half-length figure of Mary Magdalene; on a table a skull seen against the light is reflected in a mirror. Two copies of this work are known (Besançon, Mus. B. A.; private coll.), and there are subsequent interpretations by La Tour of the same theme.

His *Adoration of the Shepherds* (Paris, Louvre; copy in Albi) is a nocturne with as vibrant an atmosphere as that of *The Nativity*, but some of its characteristics — fuller composition, less emphasis on realistic detail, more concise yet lighter and freer execution — place it between 1630 and 1635. The painting of St. Sebastian which La Tour presented to Louis XIII in 1633 (preserved only in eight replicas, among them those located in: Orléans, Mus. B. A.; Rouen, Mus. B. A.; Detroit, Inst. of Arts) is an authoritative composition, organized in planes that are emphasized more than in earlier works, its realism underlined by the lantern and by the figure of St. Irene in contemporary middle-class dress.

After 1633 La Tour became more of a realist. For a lay clientele, which was in part French, he painted the *Souffleurs*: a young girl at the brazier — mysterious, tinted red by the light (three versions of this composition are known; signed one in Paris, Coll. Neger) — and a smoker with firebrand (also in several versions). Also in this category are some compositions known only through replicas or copies: *The Boy with the Cap*, *The Lute Player*, and *The Drinker*. Among his religious paintings are some strongly realistic daylight scenes: half-length representations of apostles dressed as peasants or as militiamen; one of these, a signed painting (private coll.), is a bold work with silver, green, and brown tonalities. To these works should be added a series of paintings of Christ and the apostles (Albi, Mus.; originally painted for the Capuchins), two of which are quite beautiful and may be originals, the others being surely replicas or copies. There are also a *St. Andrew* (Paris, private coll.) that appears to be an original and a replica of *The Brawl between Beggars and Strolling Musicians* (Chambéry, Mus. d'H. et d'Archéol.), which exaggerates the style of this period, confirming analogies with the French realists and the continuing influence of Dutch art, and revealing La Tour's austere irony.

These paintings prefigure La Tour's masterly daylight scenes with full-length figures of the period 1635-40. *The Hurdy-gurdy Player* (PL. 94) was at one time attributed to the Spanish school, but it is typically French in its realism, which is reminiscent of Callot, a realism that is sometimes extreme but not homogeneously applied. There are inert areas in the painting, as well as scumbling, occasional calligraphic drawing, and vivid colors. Connected with it are replicas of other compositions of the same subject (Bergues, Mus. Municipal; Nancy, Mus. Historique Lorrain; signed fragment of a painting of two or three figures, Brussels, Mus. Royaux d'Art et d'H.). Also in the same style and dating from the same period are two versions of *St. Jerome*, one in Stockholm (PL. 94), the other in Grenoble. In a third rendering (Paris, Louvre), the theme of St. Jerome becomes a pretext — as in the painting of the apostles — for a realistic representation, here showing a notary at his work table; there are also two additional versions of this theme, probably both replicas (London, Royal Colls.; U.S.A., private coll.).

La Tour's mystical night scenes dating from about 1640 are of monumental grandeur, often suggesting silent dialogues between two beings, an active figure dominating an apparently more passive one, or they may depict dreamy or bemused children in profile. In these, the palette becomes more severe, tending toward browns and violets, and great changes appear in the rendering of forms and in technique. His *St. Joseph the Carpenter* (II, PL. 185; copy in Besançon, Mus. B. A.) is an amplification, in a solemn tone, of a theme by Honthorst. The full-length *Magdalen with the Night Light* (PL. 91), a signed painting, is also broad in execution, but is rendered in a more flowing manner, with exacting detail and without geometric exaggeration. The subject is shown as a fervent penitent; but the type is the same as that used by La Tour throughout his life, at times realistically and at times ideally represented, to suggest wordly or heavenly themes. *The Magdalen with a Mirror* (Paris, Coll. Fabius), later in date, with chiaroscuro accents that produce an almost monochrome effect, again takes up, in part, motifs from the engraving, but the saint is a full-length figure and the fluid composition approaches that of the *Repentant St. Peter*, signed and dated 1645 (Cleveland, Mus. of Art), a painting of an almost too unrestrained virtuosity in its transparent effects and pathos.

Children recalling the *Souffleurs* or the Jesus in *St. Joseph the Carpenter* appear in some of his religious works, such as *The Angel Appearing to St. Joseph Asleep* (Nantes, Mus. B. A.), *The Education of the Virgin* (copies in Dijon, Mus. B. A.; New York, Frick Coll.), and *The Discovery of the Body of St. Alexis*, a painting noted in 1647 (PL. 95; also Belgium, private coll.).

Other night scenes indicate a growing tendency to lay bare the essential structure of the compositions. *St. Sebastian Mourned by St. Irene* (PL. 92; copy in Bois-Anzeray) — "a static tragedy," according to P. Fierens — is derived from Caravaggio's *Deposition* (Rome, Mus. Vat.) and seems to go back to the style of Reni and perhaps is even a repetition of the same subject, but La Tour paints in a more polished manner and is concerned with the illumination of every facet of spatial dimension in a colored atmosphere. This geometric stylization is exaggerated in *The Mocking of Job* (Épinal, Mus. Départemental des Vosges), and in *The Denial of St. Peter* (PL. 93) — a signed work dated 1651, commissioned in 1650.

La Tour's collaboration with his son may explain certain dissonances apparent in his later works. In his final years he occasionally reused former compositions or borrowed from foreign artists. For example, he drew upon an engraving after a work of Seghers of about 1630; although he was isolated in Lorraine from progressive art currents, La Tour still knew how to refine the animated and more vulgar Flemish subjects of that artist with delicacy, serenity, and dramatic tension, adopting his angular forms but rendering them in a rarified and coloristic atmosphere.

The works of La Tour are infused with an intelligent order, an essential calm, and a sobriety of purpose that link him to a French tradition of "classical" harmony and of the "integrity" of art. He had little interest in problems of composition and little desire to formulate new ideas, which resulted in a certain inflexibility, in a limited repertoire of subjects, in the frequent repetition of forms, but his technique was constantly shifting — cursive or painstaking, impetuous or relaxed, and finally cool and cautious. He delighted in color-light effects that recall medieval theories, and he progressed slowly toward abstraction; he rendered objects with a muted but luminous palette (centered about reddish tones) and used reflections and nuances of light to model volumes in a vibrant aura of color. These light effects are worked out with scientific precision but have little correspondence to actual reality; they suggest simultaneously reality and mystical abstraction. La Tour's is an unrealistic art that continually makes use of fragments of reality, combining and even distorting them, in order to express ideas and feelings.

The work of La Tour reveals little empathy with the world but rather a familiarity with the supernatural. There is a motionlessness that seems infinite. The silence, purity, sweetness, meditation, ecstasy, suffering, self-denial, penitence, and resignation that prevail in his paintings and, in the background, themes of the Crucifixion and of redemption, relate La Tour to certain religious orders, in particular the Capuchin monks, who were both his friends and clients. His art was wholly impregnated by Franciscan spiritualism, which, along with the religious humanism of the Jesuits and the strict codes of the Jansenists and Calvinists, contributed to shaping the French spirit of the 17th century.

La Tour has been cited by Michel de Marolles (*Livre des peintres et graveurs*, Paris, 1677) as among those artists honored by Lorraine, but he was soon forgotten in spite of continued admiration for some of his works. Thanks to the studies of some modern scholars — Voss (1914-15), Weisbach (1932), Sterling (1935), Isarlo (1941), Jamot (1948), and Bloch (1950), among others — La Tour has emerged with his proper stature, as one of the greatest of the 17th-century French artists.

BIBLIOG. H. Voss, G. Dumesnil de La Tour, Arch. für Kg., II, 1914–15, nos. 121–23; W. Weisbach, Französische Malerei des XVII. Jahrhunderts, Berlin, 1932; C. Sterling, Catalogue de l'exposition des peintres de la réalité en France au XVIIe siècle, 3d ed., Paris, 1935; G. Isarlo, Caravage et le caravagisme européen, Aix-en-Provence, 1941; A. Blunt, The "joueur de la veille" of Georges de La Tour, BM, LXXXVI, 1946, pp. 108–11; P. Jamot, Georges de La Tour, 2d ed., Paris, 1948; F.-G. Pariset, Georges de La Tour, Paris, 1948; S. M. M. Furness, Georges de La Tour of Lorraine, London, 1949 (bibliog.); V. Bloch, Georges de la Tour, Amsterdam, 1950 (rev. by C. Sterling, Observations à propos d'un livre récent, RArts, I, 1951, pp. 147–58); E. Orozco Díaz, Un importante antecedente de los nocturnos de Georges de La Tour, Arte español, XIX, 1952–53, pp. 69–74; M. Arland and A. Marsan, Georges de La Tour, Paris, 1953; A. Blunt, Art and Architecture in France, 1500–1700, Harmondsworth, 1954; A. Malraux, The Voices of Silence (Eng. trans., S. Gilbert), Garden City, N.Y., 1953, pp. 382–96; F.-G. Pariset, La servante à la puce, RArts, V, 1955, pp. 91–94; H. Tribou Morembert, Du nouveau sur le peintre des "Nuits," Figaro littéraire, Aug. 6, 1955; Il seicento europeo (exhibition cat.), Rome, 1956 (bibliog.); The Age of Louis XIV (exhibition cat.), London, 1958; P. Colman, Une nouvelle image de Saint Alexis, B. Inst. Royal du patrimoine artistique, I, 1958, pp. 103–10; F. Grossmann, A Painting by Georges de La Tour in the Collection of Archduke Leopold Wilhelm, BM, C, 1958, pp. 86–91, CI, 1959, p. 27; F.-G. Pariset, Note sur Jean Le Clerc, RArts, VIII, 1958, pp. 67–71; Le XVIIe siècle français (exhibition cat.), Paris, 1958; P. Grate, Quelques observations sur les Saint Jérôme de Georges de La Tour, RArts, IX, 1959, pp. 15–24; B. Nicolson, The "Candlelight Master": A Follower of Honthorst, Nederlandsch Kunsthist. Jb., XI, 1960, pp. 121–64; F.-G. Pariset, A Newly Discovered La Tour : "The Fortune Teller," BMMA, N.S., XIX, 1961, pp. 198–205; P. Bober, A Painting by Georges de la Tour, Art. J., XXII, 1962, pp. 28–32.

François-Georges PARISET

Illustrations: PLS. 91–95.

LATOUR, MAURICE QUENTIN DE. Pastel painter of the French school (b. Saint-Quentin, Sept. 5, 1704; d. Feb. 17, 1788). Little is known of Latour's early career. He went to Paris in 1723 and introduced himself to the engraver Nicolas Henri Tardieu, who placed him with Jean Jacques Spoede and Claude Dupouch, both members of the Académie de St-Luc. According to early sources, Latour was in London from 1724 until 1727, and upon his return to Paris first posed as an Englishman to draw attention to himself and his work. In 1737 he was accepted as a candidate for membership in the Académie Royale, but he did not become a full member until 1746, when he submitted a pastel portrait of Jean Restout. Within the Académie he attained only the rank of *conseiller*. He exhibited portraits in pastel regularly at the Salons from 1737 until 1773; his best work appeared between 1740 and 1760. Among Latour's sitters were members of the royal family, the nobility, and leading intellectuals of the period such as D'Alembert, Voltaire, and Rousseau.

Toward the end of his career, in 1778–79, he founded a free drawing school in his native city of Saint-Quentin. He established prizes for students at the Académie Royale in Paris and, in 1783, a scientific prize for the Académie des Sciences, Arts, et Belles-Lettres in Amiens. Interested in literature, politics, and science, he enjoyed a reputation as a witty, intelligent conversationalist. In 1784, however, he began to show symptoms of insanity and retired to Saint-Quentin, where he was welcomed as a benefactor by the townspeople. The following year he was legally declared not responsible for his actions. Although the works left by the artist at the time of his death were to have been sold to benefit his favorite charities, many of them remain in the Musée Lécuyer in Saint-Quentin.

Latour's *œuvre* consists entirely of portraits in pastel, a medium that enjoyed a great vogue in 18th-century France, where it was popularized in 1719–20 by the visit to Paris of Rosalba Carriera, a noted Venetian pastelist. From the beginning Latour's portraits were much admired by the Salon critics; they overshadow those of contemporaries such as J.-B. Perroneau who worked in the same medium. Latour's manipulation of the crayons, it was felt, conveyed not only an astonishingly frank, animated likeness of his sitters but also a genuine insight into their personalities. These effects were achieved, despite the apparent spontaneity of his technique in this difficult medium, by repeated changes and corrections. Among Latour's most ambitious compositions are *Mme de Pompadour* (ca. 1755) and *Philibert Orry* (1745), both in the Louvre. Also of interest are his self-portraits, one of unknown date (Louvre) and another of 1751 (V, PL. 411), and his preparatory sketches, such as that of *Mlle Fel* (1757; Saint-Quentin, Mus. Lécuyer).

BIBLIOG. Albert Besnard, Latour, la vie et l'œuvre de l'artiste, Paris, 1928.

John W. McCOUBREY

LATROBE, BENJAMIN. Architect (b. Fulneck, near Leeds 1764; d. New Orleans, 1820). The remarkable record of Latrobe as an architect in America was very likely not anticipated by his English friends and contemporaries, for he left England in the fall of 1795, dejected and bankrupt, having lost his wife in childbirth and having failed in private architectural practice. Latrobe's Moravian parents provided him with an excellent classical education, which he completed in Germany. Upon returning to London, he tried various jobs and eventually worked for three years in the office of the successful architect Samuel Pepys Cockerell.

Upon his arrival in America, Latrobe's talents were quickly recognized, and he was commissioned to build the penitentiary in Richmond, a number of private houses, and the Bank of Pennsylvania in Philadelphia (1798–1800). The last was doubtless the most handsome public building in the country at the time; its Ionic order and proportions were, on the whole, Greek, though the plan and interior vaulted spaces suggest a strong Roman influence.

In 1798 Latrobe persuaded the city of Philadelphia to use his steam-pump plan, rather than the proposed canal system, for providing good water. Though continually opposed by the canal interests, by 1801 he was able to have a wooden pipe system put into use, thereby fulfilling the city's needs. The pump station, known from paintings and engravings, comprised a structure with a square Doric base and a windowed cylinder topped with a dome. This was the first successful venture of the sort in America.

Latrobe was the first to introduce the Gothic style to residential architecture in America, in his design for Sedgeley (1798–99), the suburban Philadelphia home of William Crammond.

A fortunate meeting with Thomas Jefferson led to Latrobe's appointment in 1803 as architect of the U.S. Capitol in Washington (I, PL. 79). Originally designed by William Thornton and partially finished under the guidance of a succession of architects, the building had only its north wing prepared for Congress at the time Jefferson became President. Latrobe completed the south wing, using the original design for the exterior and making some changes on the interior. After the Capitol was burned by the British in 1814, the architect retained the exterior walls but redesigned and rebuilt the interiors of both the north and south wings. He also proposed a design for the central unit with a well-proportioned dome; but this segment was never built, and in 1817 he resigned because of disagreement over the nature of his position.

While supervising the Capitol, Latrobe was able to fulfill several other architectural commissions, most notably that for the Cathedral of the Assumption in Baltimore (I, PL. 81). The Cathedral, essentially in its original state, is one of the few Latrobe buildings still standing. Two sets of plans were offered to Bishop Carroll and the building committee in 1805 — one Neo-Gothic, the other neoclassic. The latter design was chosen, and construction was substantially completed when the Cathedral was dedicated in 1821.

The Baltimore Exchange (1816–20; destroyed 1904) was, on the the exterior, one of Latrobe's least interesting works. It was a monotonous design except for the imposing dome, which rose on pendentives to a height of 115 ft. over the floor of the Exchange — the most daring exercise in masonry in

America at the time. Only two other notable buildings of Latrobe exist essentially unchanged. The fine-proportioned "Old West" of Dickinson College (Carlisle, Pa.) was designed to replace a structure destroyed by fire in 1802 but was not seen by the architect until 1811. The Louisiana State Bank, New Orleans, was begun in 1819 but was not yet completed when Latrobe died the following year during an epidemic of yellow fever.

Latrobe brought a high standard of taste and beauty in the application of the neoclassic style, and contributed much to the knowledge of engineering and construction in the United States. Most important of all, he trained a number of architects of the next generation (including Robert Mills, William Strickland, and William Small) in the craft of building durably and tastefully.

BIBLIOG. S. Wilson, Jr., Impressions Respecting New Orleans, New York, 1951; T. Hamlin, Benjamin Henry Latrobe, New York, 1955.

Paul F. NORTON

LAURANA, LUCIANO. Architect (also called Luciano di Martino da Laurana, Lauranna, Dellaurana, and Luciano da Urbino). Although it is certain that Laurana came from Dalmatia, the date of his birth is unknown, and Lovrana, Vrana, Urana, and Zara (Zadar) have all been advanced as the location. He died in Pesaro in 1479. The Laurana problem is one of the most intricate in the history of early Renaissance architecture. Highly praised by his contemporaries in the years immediately following his death (Giovanni Santi, *Cronaca*, ed. H. Holtzinger, Stuttgart, 1893), his name was then forgotten for centuries. Vasari is chiefly responsible for this neglect, for he failed to mention Laurana in his *Lives* and ascribed to Francesco di Giorgio (q.v.) the creation of the Palazzo Ducale (PLS. 96–100; FIG. 168) at Urbino. Among the few monuments attributable to Laurana, this imposing construction seems most clearly to bear his imprint.

It was not until the 19th century that historical research began to reconstruct the artistic identity of Laurana. Newly discovered documents revealed that the palace at Urbino was not the conception of a single architect but the work of several, among them Laurana, whose role was substantial (G. Milanesi, in his comments for Vasari's *Lives*, II, *passim*). Early in the 20th century intensive stylistic analysis coordinated with the documentary evidence led to additional attributions, which included the much-discussed architectural perspectives in Urbino (Gall. Naz. delle Marche), Baltimore (Walters Art Gall.), and Berlin (Staat. Mus.). Finally, the hypothetical opera of Laurana were increased with ingenious but often unsupported and implausible attributions (A. Venturi). In reaction, there followed an elaborate reappraisal, wherein Roberto Papini, representing one tendency, went so far as to repudiate almost entirely the Laurana attributions of earlier critics and the very career they outlined. For the most part, however, such reevaluation took the form of careful definition and separation, of intensive analyses of related documents and the stylistic traits of the works in question. As awareness of the difficulties of the problem grew, the need for clarifying Laurana's role became unmistakable, along with the obstacles hindering the task: the lack of documents and their sometimes contradictory nature, the heterogeneous mass of the Urbino palace, and the inaccessibility of the fortress of Pesaro (still used as a penal institution), an authentic — and the final — work of Laurana. For these reasons, there is as yet no definitive conformation of the Laurana personality, from either a documentary or a stylistic point of view. Although Milanesi's hypothesis — that Laurana was the pupil of Brunelleschi — based on a passage from Vasari's *Lives* ("a Slovene who did a number of things in Venice") is provocative, it is corroborated neither by documentation nor by traces of such buildings. In the present state of the research, the attribution to Laurana of the gate of the Arsenal in Venice (on the landward side) remains purely an inference.

Some reflection of Alberti (q.v.) in Laurana's work, at least as an object of inspiration, is reinforced by his presence in Mantua before 1465, in the decade of the building of Alberti's first project for S. Sebastiano; by his adoption of Roman architectonic motifs in the courtyard of the Palazzo Ducale of Urbino, such as the tondos between the arches and the frieze inscription (derived from the Tempio Malatestiano at Rimini of Alberti; I, PLS. 51, 52); by his use of capitals nearly identical with ancient examples to be seen in Rome and Latium; and in the stately, harmonious proportions of his masterwork. Further

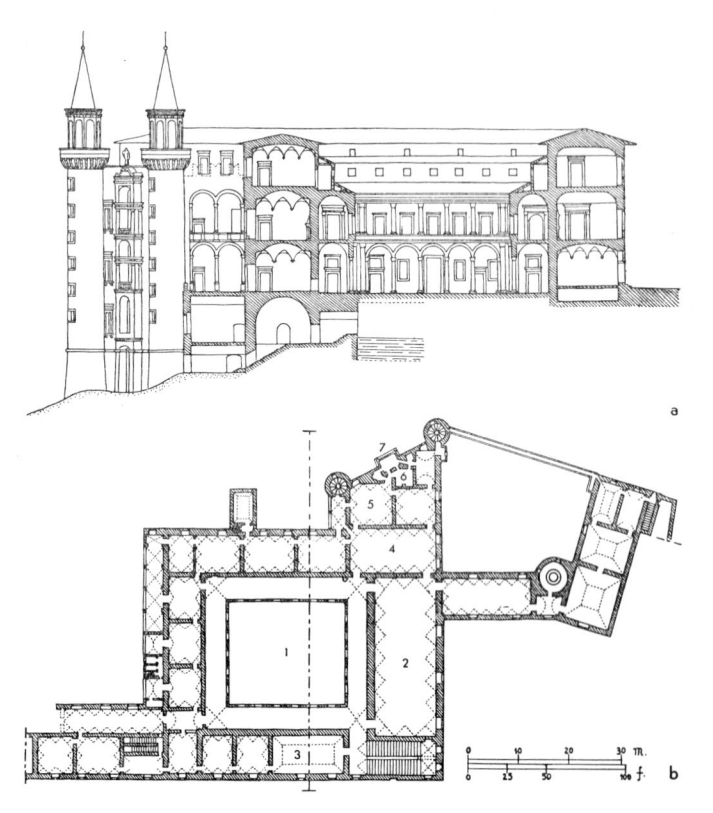

Urbino, Palazzo Ducale. (*a*) Section, east-west. (*b*) Plan of the first floor: (1) main courtyard; (2) Throne Room; (3) Sala della Jole; (4) Sala degli Angeli; (5) Sala delle Udienze; (6) *studiolo* of Federigo da Montefeltro; (7) loggia of the west façade.

suggestion of dependency on Alberti appears in the disposition of the loggias on the west façade of the palace (PL. 96), which recalls the favored Alberti device of superposed arches and apertures accenting the vertical axis of the façade — used first in the Rimini work and later in S. Sebastiano in Mantua (I, PL. 56). One must not be misled to another tenuous attribution by analogies between the Laurana façade for the Palazzo Ducale and the triumphal arch of the Castel Nuovo in Naples (III, PL. 390), which was built ten years earlier. In the Neapolitan structure the Albertian inspiration common to both monuments was implemented (probably by the Mallorcan Guillén Sagrera and assistants) with a poorly understood classicism, in imitation of the mere externals of antique models; whereas the loggias at Urbino were realized in purely architectonic terms, with subtly calculated proportions subordinated to considerations of perspective and light, so as to achieve coloristic effects across the façade.

Although Laurana was very likely indebted to Alberti, he declined to follow the Albertian propensity for masking the structure with marble incrustations or facings and with stucco painted or decorated in sgraffito. He turned instead to effects of light and shade achieved by the modeling of the building itself: the chromatic contrast of colored bricks with the limestone framework, the shadowed disks of the hollowed-out tondos between the arches of the main courtyard, the narrow rims above the windows, the absolute sobriety of the window framing, and the great dark hollows created by the loggias on the west façade. In this concern with light and shade and with perspective, Laurana demonstrates not only his relationship with Venetian art but also his unquestionable affinity with Piero della Francesca (Salmi, 1945; R. Longhi, *Piero della Francesca*, Rome, 1927). These characteristics alone would suffice to remove Laurana's name from consideration as the architect of the Mantegnesque courtyard of the Castello di S. Giorgio in Mantua, where the delicate ornamental garlands and painted surfaces of the spacious arcade create an effect more pictorial than architectural. Furthermore, documents suggest that the S. Giorgio courtyard was executed about 1472 by Luca Fancelli after the design of Mantegna (Cottafavi, 1939). The only link between the structures at Mantua and Urbino is their common Albertian inspiration.

Among the minor works assigned to Laurana in Mantua is the "occhio di portico," in the street leading to S. Andrea (Venturi, 1923), but the remnants are insufficient to permit definite attribution.

The documents attest to Laurana's stay for a brief period at the court of Alessandro Sforza in Pesaro during the early months of 1465. There is also reason to believe that he returned to Pesaro in January, 1466. It is likely that on the latter occasion Laurana presented some designs for the Palazzo Ducale at Pesaro, part of which were already in existence in 1462. The principal façade appears to have been near completion in 1472. The Pesaro palace manifests none of the strict proportion and classical simplicity of the courtyard at Urbino, thus suggesting that Laurana's plans were distorted in the execution. This conclusion is supported by documents lately brought to light (Franceschini, 1959), which indicate that in March of 1466 — shortly after his second journey to Pesaro — Laurana had already completed a model for the Palazzo Ducale. The discordant impression produced by the impossibility of aligning the six arches of the portico, raised on massive piers, with the five windows of the upper story may have been dictated by exigencies of perspective. A correspondence not noted heretofore is to be found in a contemporary illustrated text, the *Tavolette di Perugia* (1473), in which there appear façades arranged on noncoincident axes like those of the Pesaro palace. The sculptural decoration of the palace was executed in 1476 by Domenico Rosselli, in keeping with the practice of submitting every sizable edifice to copious, more or less legitimately architectonic embellishments. Such decorative overlays did not reflect Laurana's intentions.

Though Laurana had yielded to the imposition of such sculptural additions on other occasions, it is likely that in Urbino he firmly resisted the customary excesses of the army of stone masons and decorators swarming about the construction, in order to attain the absolute precision of proportion and carving which characterizes those parts of the Palazzo Ducale attributable to him. His refusal to accept their handiwork is implied by the litigations in which he was involved during 1467 at Urbino (where he had probably taken up residence the previous year), before he obtained from Duke Federigo da Montefeltro the well-known letter of patent as chief architect of the palace. Laurana directed the palace construction until about the middle of 1472, that is, for almost six years. Probably at the end of August of that year, for unknown reasons, he left Urbino, never to return. From there he went to Naples, where he served the house of Aragon in the position of "master of artillery."

Modern critics have exhaustively analyzed the structure of the Palazzo Ducale. Laurana's fundamental problem was to join two existing buildings: the Palazzetto della Jole, a proto-Renaissance palace added to and remodeled by Laurana, and a medieval keep known as the Castellare. His plan had to take account of a sharp incline of the land on the west, as far as the Mercatale sector of the city, as well as a difference in levels between the Palazzetto and the Castellare on the east. Esthetically he faced the problem of finding a suitable monumental façade for the complex exterior and a corresponding solution for the interior.

These were also the years when Cardinal Pietro Barbo (later to become Pope Paul II) was finishing in Rome the arcaded garden (1464) of Palazzetto Venezia and a sizable portion of the great palace of the same name. In 1468 the Cardinal was planning for the Palazzo Venezia a huge courtyard with a two-tiered arcade, which remained unfinished, however. For Federigo da Montefeltro — gonfalonier of the Church, *condottiere*, Humanist, and devotee of antiquity — Laurana was required to supply a residence more modest in size but equal, if not surpassing, in beauty that of the prince of the Church.

Laurana's conception of the tower façade was a striking innovation for Renaissance palaces; it was to be admired not from an adjacent piazza but from the streets leading to the countryside in the west and from the valley below. In the main courtyard (PL. 99), altered with a later superstructure, Laurana used modular ratios that establish a regular rhythm: arcs, circles, and squares distributed with vertical and horizontal interrelation. The sides of the court are terminated by double pilasters at the corners (PL. 100). In order to lend an immobile, crystalline purity to his geometry, Laurana slightly raised the round arches. To create an impression of greater space he exaggerated the perspective by resorting to entasis in the imposing monolithic columns and by placing the windows in shadowed recesses. Furthermore, to ensure appreciation of the courtyard from a perfectly centered approach, he placed the entrance hall very high and put the palace entrance on the same axis, considerably off center in respect to the east façade on Piazza Duca Federico (PL. 98). In so doing, Laurana renounced all conventional practices with regard to the principal portal, a decision that caused unavoidable anomalies in the design for the two east façades. Faced with an already compromised situation, the architect had to decide between a unified courtyard entered by way of an unpleasing façade or a harmonious exterior façade leading into an irregular courtyard. Laurana chose the "perfect" courtyard, adhering strictly to his own ideal.

Laurana's strong interest in perspective explains, and in part justifies, the above-noted attribution of the three perspective panels to him, though closer analysis has led to their inclusion in the ambit of the Sangallos (Sanpaolesi, 1949).

Before leaving Urbino, Laurana had probably planned and partially supervised work on the Throne Room (PL. 97), the Sala delle Veglie, the Sala degli Angeli, the Sala delle Udienze, the hanging gardens, and the grand staircase, in addition to other, minor elements. The details of Laurana's work on the Palazzo Ducale described above and the innumerable additions and modifications that followed are matters to which critical analysis must certainly turn again.

The second important project in which Laurana's participation has been verified is the citadel of Pesaro, the Rocca Costanza. By order of Costanza Sforza, the foundations of the fortress were laid in May, 1474. Although it has not been shown that Laurana was present at that time, he was certainly active in the construction in 1476, again in 1478, and finally in 1479, the year in which the courtyard was completed. Laurana's style is readily discernible in the austere form of the citadel, a four-sided structure of geometric regularity, with cylindrical corner towers that perhaps recall the Aragonese towers then to be seen in southern Italy and the neighboring islands. The characteristic juxtaposition of limestone and brick recurs, as does the extreme sobriety of the moldings, particularly in the functional cut of the crenels.

Laurana had some part in the building of another citadel, the Rocca of Senigallia, whose architect (possibly Baccio Pontelli) apparently borrowed from the design of the Rocca Costanza, but without striving for the same geometric purity. Laurana's contribution was restricted to the design of a connecting bridge, which documents testify was under construction at the end of 1479, the year of his death. Pontelli seems to have lived and worked in Urbino sometime between 1479 and 1482, when he went to Rome, thus making him — if he did design the citadel of Senigallia — the last military architect to employ Laurana's forms. Later, however, Pontelli worked in the less rigorous and more adaptable style of Francesco di Giorgio, who had trained under Laurana in Urbino. The style of Donato Bramante (q.v.), another decisive figure in Renaissance architecture, also reflects the influence of Laurana.

BIBLIOG. C. Budinich, Il Palazzo Ducale di Urbino, Trieste, 1904; A. Colasanti, Architetti dal XV al XVIII secolo: Luciano Laurana, Rome, 1922; G. Pacchioni, L'opera di Luciano Laurana a Mantova, BArte, N.S., III, 1923-24, pp. 97-111; Venturi, VIII, 1, 1923, pp. 669-704 (bibliog.); S. F. Kimball, Luciano Laurana and the "High Renaissance," AB, X, 1927, pp. 125-50; R. Filangieri di Candida, L'architettura della reggia aragonese in Napoli, L'Arte, XXX, 1928, pp. 32-35; L. Serra, Le varie fasi costruttive del Palazzo Ducale di Urbino, BArte, N.S., X, 1930-31, pp. 433-48; L. Serra, L'arte nelle Marche, II, Rome, 1934; C. Cottafavi, Ricerche e documenti sulla costruzione del Palazzo Ducale di Mantova, Atti e mem. Acc. Virgiliana di Mantova, XXV, 1939, pp. 171-229; M. Salmi, Piero della Francesca e il Palazzo Ducale di Urbino, Florence, 1945; R. Petrovich, Questi schiavoni, GBA, XXXI, 1947, pp. 65-80; R. Krautheimer, The Tragic and the Comic Scene of the Renaissance: The Baltimore and Urbino Panels, GBA, XXXIII, 1948, pp. 327-46; P. Sanpaolesi, Le prospettive architettoniche di Urbino, di Baltimora e di Berlino, BArte, XXXIV, 1949, pp. 322-37; P. Rotondi, Il Palazzo Ducale di Urbino, 2 vols., Urbino, 1950-51 (bibliog.); R. Causa, Sagrera, Laurana e l'arco di Castelnuovo, Paragone, V, 55, 1954, pp. 3-23; G. Marchini, Il Palazzo Ducale di Urbino, Rinascimento, IX, 1, 1958, pp. 43-78; G. Franceschini, Figure del Rinascimento urbinate, Urbino, 1959; L. Michelini-Tocci, I due manoscritti urbinati dei privilegi del Montefeltro con una appendice lauranesca, Florence, 1959; G. Marchini, Aggiunte al Palazzo Ducale di Urbino, BArte, XLV, 1960, pp. 73-80.

Corrado MALTESE

Illustrations: PLS. 96-100; 1 fig. in text.

LAWRENCE, THOMAS. English portrait painter (b. Bristol, 1769; d. London, 1830). Lawrence was the son of an excise official turned innkeeper, who in 1773 took over the Black Bear at Devizes. Here the boy Lawrence made pencil likenesses and acquired a reputation as a prodigy. In 1782 he moved with his family to Bath and practiced in pastel, and in 1787 he went to London, where he began to work in oil. Lawrence appears to have been almost entirely self-taught.

In 1789 he exhibited at the Royal Academy of Arts a full-length portrait of Lady Cremorne (Coll. Lt. Comdr. C. Windham), brilliantly modeled if somewhat gaudy in color, which led directly to an introduction to Queen Charlotte and to a commission to paint her portrait. The result was Lawrence's first masterwork; in it he toned down some of the vulgarities of *Lady Cremorne*, and in the background first revealed his decided gift for landscape painting. The royal portrait was exhibited at the Royal Academy in 1790, together with *Miss Farren*, a more vivid and more obviously romantic portrait that caught the public fancy. From this time on, Lawrence had consistent success. He became an associate of the Royal Academy in 1791, succeeded Reynolds as Painter-in-Ordinary to the King in 1792, and became a full member of the Royal Academy at the earliest admissable age in 1794.

Throughout the 1790s Lawrence produced portraits of sustained brilliance. He was a splendid draftsman, but facility was his weakness, and it is clear that his taste was very uncertain. He tended to work for surface effect, employing too many highlights and exaggerating the vitality of his sitters. In a mistaken if laudable belief that he should attempt narrative painting, he exhibited *Satan Calling His Legions* (Royal Acad. of Arts) in 1797, which he believed was his finest achievement. Sensitive to the almost unanimous criticism of the press, however, he attempted nothing else of the kind.

From about 1800 there was a noticeable sobering in Lawrence's style and more marked variation in the quality of his work. The good was better and more controlled than before (*Family of Sir Francis Baring*, 1807), but other work was inexplicably careless. About this time he was frequently in financial difficulties. With the death of John Hoppner in 1810, Lawrence was without a rival and had by then recovered the balance in his production. In 1815 the prince-regent knighted him, and in 1818 he was sent to Aachen and Vienna to paint the allied victors of the Napoleonic Wars. From Vienna Lawrence went to Rome; and on his return to England in 1820, he was elected president of the Royal Academy to succeed Benjamin West. The portraits painted on this European tour hang in the Waterloo Chamber of Windsor Castle; of these, *Pope Pius VII* and *Archduke Charles* are masterpieces of his mature style. Lawrence never ceased being ready to learn; the whole European series reveals his response to the works of Titian and Velázquez that he was able to study in the imperial collections in Vienna.

In the work of his last decade Lawrence often tended to sentimentalize, but these years also produced some of his strongest studies of character. His death at the age of sixty was an undoubted loss, for he continued to be prolific and had not ceased to develop. The artist was also a notable public figure and a great connoisseur. His collection of old-master drawings was perhaps the finest yet made. He never married, but his love affairs with the daughters of Mrs. Siddons were well known.

MAJOR WORKS. *Queen Charlotte*, 1790, London, Nat. Gall. – *Miss Farren*, 1790, New York, Met. Mus. – *Lord Mountstuart*, 1795, London, Coll. Marquess of Bute. – *The Family of Sir Francis Baring*, 1807, Coll. of Earl of Northbrook. – *Mrs. Wolff*, 1815, Chicago, Art Inst. – *Archduke Charles*, 1818, Windsor, Royal Colls. – *Pope Pius VII*, 1819, Windsor, Royal Colls. – *Portrait of George IV*, 1819 (VI, PL. 446).

BIBLIOG. D. E. Williams, Life and Correspondence of Sir Thomas Lawrence, Kt., London, 1831; Sir Walter Armstrong, Lawrence, London, 1913; Kenneth Garlick, Sir Thomas Lawrence, London, 1954.

Kenneth GARLICK

LEBANON. The Lebanese state was created in 1920 as a result of the dissolution of the Ottoman Empire. Placed under French mandate, it was known first as Great Lebanon (Fr., Grand Liban) and later (1926) as the Lebanese Republic, the name which it retained after achieving independence in 1944. From the art-historical point of view, Lebanon is closely bound to Syria (q.v.). In antiquity the area was included in the theater of Phoenician art (see PHOENICIAN-PUNIC ART) and entered into the history of the more comprehensive region lying between the Euphrates and the Nile valleys (see SYRO-PALESTINIAN ART), up to and throughout the Hellenistic period and after — first under Alexander, then under the Seleucids, and finally as part of the Roman province of Syria. Long contested by the Byzantines and Sassanids, the territory was later conquered by the Arabs. The Crusaders left behind numerous works of religious and military architecture; there are fewer monuments from the period of Turkish domination. In the 20th century Western influences have permeated the art and architecture, but they are sometimes overlaid with traditional Levantine characteristics.

SUMMARY. Artistic and cultural epochs (col. 172). Art centers and monuments (col. 178).

ARTISTIC AND CULTURAL EPOCHS. Because of its geographic position, Lebanon has been the meeting place and throughway of the land and sea routes of those regions where the first great cultures of the ancient world developed: Mesopotamia, the Nile Valley, and the Mediterranean basin. As a result it has preserved numerous vestiges of the past.

The antiquity of the primitive inhabitants of the land is attested by paleolithic and neolithic remains. From the 3d millennium B.C. successive waves of Semitic invaders superimposed and intermixed their cultures. These peoples, traditionally called Amorites and Canaanites, together with Aramaic peoples who appeared on the Biqa plain near the end of the 2d millennium B.C., gave the country its original physiognomy and formed its ancient linguistic, religious, cultural, and social traditions. The transformation of nomadic tribes into sedentary peoples, the beginning of building in stone, the early use of writing, and the development of a mythology emanating from the land gave this culture its essential characteristics.

The most thoroughly documented foreign influence in this early epoch is the Egyptian, as is shown by the excavations of Byblos (see below). As early as the 3d millennium B.C. Egyptian objects of the Old Kingdom were buried in a foundation deposit together with locally produced articles of Egyptian influence. These include various figurines and a seal with hieroglyphs and figures, on which the local goddess Baalat is depicted with the characteristics of an Egyptian deity.

The vitality of the artistic tradition of the Nile Valley in the territory is still more effectively proved by finds from the beginning of the 2d millennium. In this period an Aegean influence appears side by side with the Egyptian and, although more limited in scope, is just as decided. The royal tombs in Byblos (12th dynasty) have yielded pectorals decorated with falcons, bronze *harpés* (ceremonial axes) decorated with the uraeus or with Egyptian hieroglyphs, and scarab seals, as well as other objects bearing royal inscriptions of Amenemhet III. The coexistence of objects in the Aegean tradition reveals the presence of an eastern Mediterranean influence considerably prior to the invasion by the Peoples of the Sea (ca. 1200 B.C.), which populated the Phoenician coast with Philistines. These Aegean objects include a long-spouted silver pitcher and other vessels that are similar to Minoan teapot vases (see PL. 422); a basin decorated on the rim with a network of spirals; and a gold- and silver-inlaid dagger such as those found at Mycenae (IV, PL. 71). Much later, at the end of the 2d millennium, in the tomb of Aḥīrām, an ivory with Mycenaean decoration lay next to part of a vase with the cartouche of Ramses II. Even at the periphery of Egyptian influence, objects from the necropolis of Kfar el-Jarra — engraved stones, majolica tiles, gold rosettes — reveal that, among other influences, that of Aegean art was dominant in the first half of the 2d millennium.

From the middle of the 2d millennium, more numerous Egyptian documents and local sources — especially the Tell el'Amarna letters — show that the Pharaohs, in their politics of expansion after the expulsion of the Hyksos, succeeded in establishing dominion over Byblos, Beirut, Sidon, and Tyre. In the artistic field, although Egyptian influence is widely documented, elements of typically continental Asian tradition appeared and were disseminated by these cities, which were emporiums open to all commerce and consequently sensitive to artistic and cultural activity. Evidence of this is found in the use of the *harpé* as a royal emblem (even if of local make and with Egyptian decoration), in the Syro-Hittite cylinder seals, in the torques characteristic of the Caucasus, and in the style of the figures on the sarcophagus of Aḥīrām (IV, PL. 453). At the end of the 2d millennium, in the period following the Egyptian-Hittite struggle, the Egyptian lotus-flower motif was still used in the sculptured decoration of objects such as the famous sarcophagus of Aḥīrām. Egyptian influence is also evident in the temple architecture of the epoch at Byblos and in the colossal statues found there.

After the destructive invasion of the Peoples of the Sea, the great cities, such as Sidon and Tyre, revived in the early centuries of the 1st millennium. External artistic influences did not lose their vitality. In this epoch evidence of relations with Egypt is to be found chiefly in the stone sarcophagi discovered in the necropolises of Sidon and Byblos. This practice of inhumation in a sarcophagus, together with that of mummification, was certainly imported into Phoenicia from Egypt. In Sidon, in the early 5th century, the anthropomorphous sarcophagus of Egyptian origin replaced the ancient indigenous theca. The sarcophagus of King Tabnit (XI, PL. 132) is a reused Egyptian piece, while the 25 sarcophagi of the Ford Collection in the National Museum, Beirut, are local productions of Egyptian inspiration. The Phoenician convention of organizing relief decoration in horizontal registers comes from Asian, specifically Assyrian, models. Persian influences have been found, at Sidon, in capitals sculptured with double protomas of bulls; at Umm el-Aḥmād, in steles; and, at Khara'ib, less clearly, in terra-cotta figurines.

The abundance of Tanagra types in the last-named figurines, excavated from a favissa and datable from the 4th to the 1st century B.C., illustrates unequivocally the decline of Egyptian and Eastern influences to the advantage of the almost immediately dominant Hellenistic Greek. When the Lebanese territory (which had been annexed by Cyrus to the Achaemenid Empire in 539 B.C., becoming part of the Fifth Satrapy) fell to Alexander in 333 B.C., Greek art was already highly prized, as is shown by the series of fine, large sarcophagi of Greek marble, from Sidon, in the Archaeological Museum, Istanbul. Unquestionably executed within Phoenician lands by Greek sculptors, they include the "Sarcophagus of the Satrap" (mid-5th cent. B.C.); the Lycian sarcophagus (ca. 400 B.C.), decorated with lion- and boar-hunting scenes; the "Sarcophagus of the Mourning Women" (mid-4th cent. B.C.; III, PL. 379); and the famous "Alexander Sarcophagus" of the early Hellenistic period, with representations of hunting and war scenes (VII, PLS. 151, 152). The decoration of hypogea with paintings of flowers, birds, and mythological scenes can also be related to Greek art. At Alexander's death, after the battles of the Diadochi, the territory of what is today Lebanon fell into the hands of Seleucus I Nicator; it did not, however, remain a stable possession of the Seleucids, because the Ptolemies of Egypt had designs on it. The defeat of Antiochus III at Magnesia (190 B.C.) and the treaty of Apamea (ca. 188 B.C.) confirmed the triumph of Rome in the Syrian coastal territories.

Thereafter, Roman inspiration was manifest primarily in fine lead sarcophagi and in limestone sarcophagi decorated with garlands. Later the influence of imperial Rome was just as strong, fostered above all in the Roman colonies of Berytus (mod. Beirut) and Heliopolis (mod. Baalbek). Typical is the sculptured decoration of the temples at Baalbek. A stylistic study of the Corinthian capitals of the Great Temple and of the sculptured ceilings of the monumental altar in the rectangular court has identified the combined activity, in the 1st century of the Christian Era, of local workshops, with strong local traditions, and of Roman workshops, which had developed in the western Augustan tradition of the Ara Pacis. The Roman builders of the temples of Baalbek had to submit to the requirements of the ancient local rites.

In contrast, the introduction of Christianity in Lebanon was not marked, as it was in northern Syria, by a renewal of architecture and ornamental decoration. Moreover, architectural remains of early Christian buildings are rare. They were generally reused in later constructions, as in the basilica at Baalbek, the Great Mosque of Beirut, and the no longer extant basilica at Tyre. While the imperial edicts resulted in the building of a few early Christian basilicas, their application also did irreparable damage, of which the ruins of Baalbek offer sad testimony.

Paul COLLART

The transition to Byzantine rule took place smoothly in the east, but the Syrian territories were troubled, from 500 to 628, by the tenacious battle between the Byzantines and the Sassanids. After the Arab conquest (ca. 636) and with the decline of the Abbasside caliphate in the 9th century, the region fell successively into the hands of the Tulunids (868–905), the Ikhshidids (935–69), and the Fatimid caliphs of Cairo (969–1171). There was a parallel development of an Islamic type of art, of which, for the period preceding the Crusades, all trace has disappeared; Christian tradition and artistic activity, on the other hand, have remained constant elements in Lebanese history. The emperors of Byzantium, Nicephorus II Phocas and Basil I, attacked the coast of Lebanon and sacked the cities. With the final defeat of the Byzantines at Manzikert (mod. Malazkirt), in 1071, the safeguarding of eastern Christianity was taken up by the Crusaders; thereafter the Latin kingdom of Jerusalem was formed. With the annexation of Tripoli in 1109, Beirut in 1110, and Sidon at about the same time, Crusader buildings sprang up throughout the region.

Noteworthy are the remains of military architecture from this period along the coast. Imposing castles and fortresses dominate the strategic points of the region, and walls, towers, and city gates are still to be seen in almost all the coastal towns. The most important and best preserved are the castles of the Embriaco family in Byblos, of St. Louis in Sidon, of Raymond de Saint-Gilles in Tripoli, and of Beaufort (or Belfort; Ar., Qal'at al-Shaqīf). This last, built of large stone blocks in 1139, passed from Fulk V of Anjou, king of Jerusalem, to the lords of Sayette, who rebuilt it and sold it to the Knights Templars in 1260; it was greatly restored in the 17th century by the amir Fakhr ad-Dīn. Also notable is Toron, a circular castle near Tibnīn, which was erected in 1104 by Hugh de Saint-Omer, taken by Ṣalāḥ ad-Dīn (Saladin) in 1187, and dismantled in 1219 by the sultan Malik Mu'aẓẓam; rebuilt in 1229, it passed to the Montforts and then to al-Ẓāhir Baybars and was rebuilt once more in the 17th century. The Castle of Akkār (near Tripoli), erected in the 11th century by Muḥriz ibn-Akkār and considerably remodeled throughout the centuries, was held successively by the Fatimid caliphs of Egypt (1033–94), by the Turks, by the Franks (from 1109), and by al-Ẓāhir Baybars (from 1271). Many other fortresses are now mostly in ruins.

Examples of religious architecture of the period of the Crusades survive, for example, in the Great Mosque, the small Frankish chapel, and the Church of St. George in Beirut; in the Church of St. John the Baptist and adjoining baptistery in Byblos; in the churches of St. George (built on Roman walls) and Mār Fūqās (St. Phocas; late 12th cent. with Byzantine paintings), and others in ruins at Amyun; and in Notre-Dame-du-Vent at Enfe. A great many chapels, hermitages, and sanctuaries are scattered in the foothills of Qurnat al-Saada; many of them are decorated with wall paintings of Byzantine influence. Paintings of the 13th century are still extant in the Grotto of St. Marina near Tripoli. Among the many important monastic buildings of the Crusader period are the Cistercian Abbey of Belmont (Deir Balamand; founded 1157; now Orthodox), preserving the ancient church, bell tower, and parlor; the Monastery of Deir Qannūbīn, near Diman, apparently dating from the time of Theodosius the Great (379–95) and the residence of Maronite patriarchs from the 15th century on, in the church of which are 15th- and 16th-century paintings; the Maronite Monastery of Deir al-Qal'a, built on the remains of a Roman temple; the Monastery of Mār Elias near Shuwayr; and the Monastery of St. John above the village of Khunshara. Because of the difficult political and military situation, not much architecture was created in the following period, and that which remains is of little interest. As early as 1187 the army of Ṣalāḥ ad-Dīn recaptured the capital; only Tyre, under the guidance of Conrad of Montferrat, succeeded in resisting, but in the following century it too fell, as did

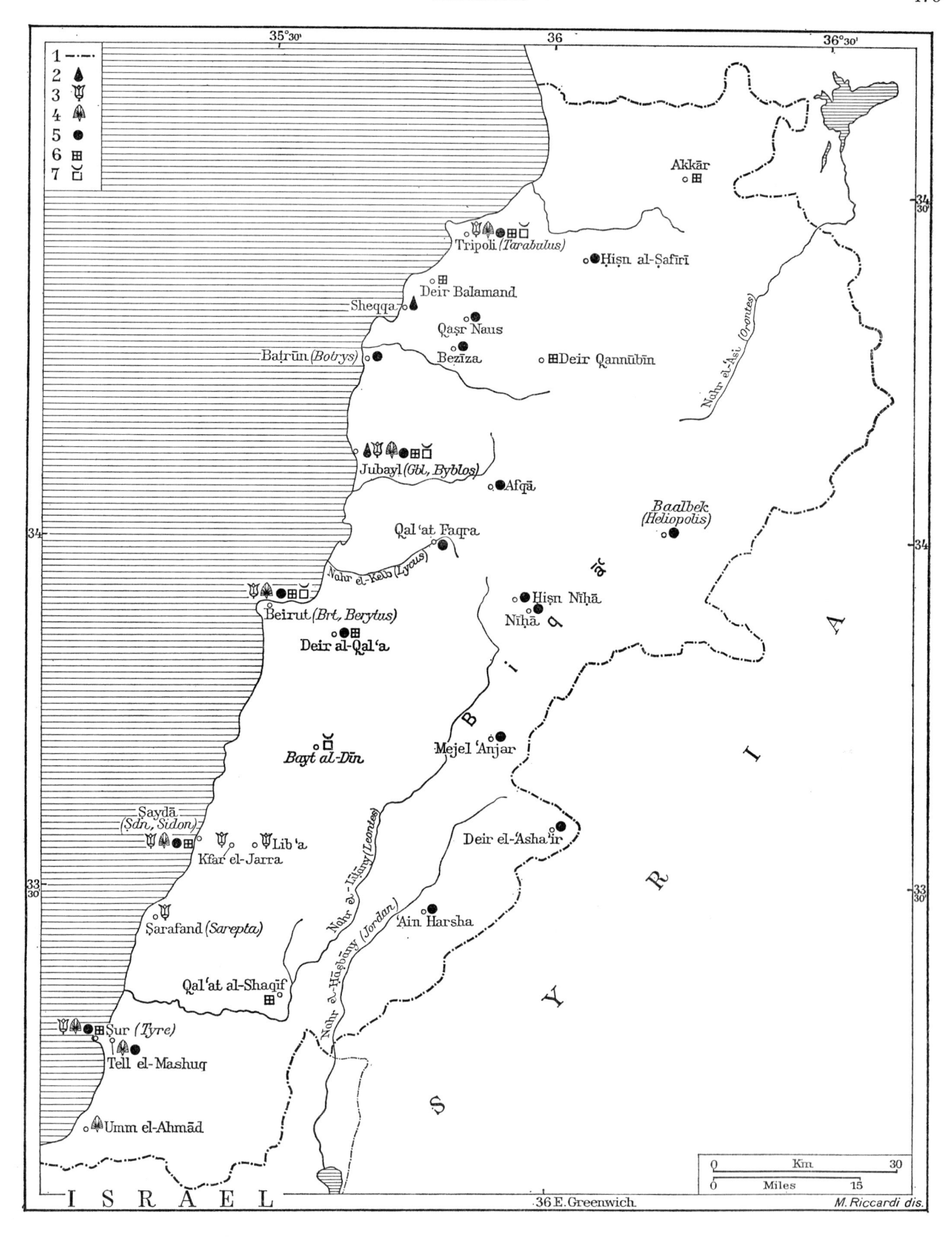

Lebanon, principal centers of archaeological and artistic interest. *Key*: (1) National boundaries; (2) monuments and prehistoric remains; (3) Phoenician and Aramaic centers; (4) Persian and Hellenistic centers; (5) Roman centers; (6) centers with Byzantine and medieval monuments; (7) centers with Islamic monuments.

other cities that had been reconquered by the Christians. In the 13th century the Mamelukes reached the coast and were not driven away until 1516, by the Ottoman prince Selim I. They did not succeed, however, in leaving an architectural imprint on the land, which always retained a certain independence from the Ottoman Empire.

Lebanon is in fact poor in Islamic monuments of any importance; the existing monuments are either remodelings of the period of the Crusades or additions and completely new constructions of the Mameluke and Ottoman periods. Moreover, this modest architectural heritage from Islam has no local stylistic characteristics whatsoever, since these buildings belong to the general development of Mameluke and Ottoman art of Syria.

In the early 17th century the amir Fakhr ad-Dīn, who traveled to Italy and visited the court of Cosimo II de' Medici, had the Sidon bridge built by Italian architects (1631) and requested "fountain

Manuel d'archéologie orientale, 4 vols., Paris, 1927–47; R. Dussaud, Topographie historique de la Syrie antique et médiévale, Paris, 1927; R. Dussaud, P. Deschamps and H. Seyrig, La Syrie antique et médiévale illustrée, Paris, 1931; R. Weill, La Phénicie et l'Asie occidentale, Paris, 1939 (Eng. trans., E. F. Row, London, 1940); V. G. Childe, The Dawn of European Civilization, 4th ed., London, 1947; G. Contenau, La civilisation phénicienne, 2d ed., Paris, 1949; R. Dussaud, L'art phénicien du IIe millénaire, Paris, 1949; P. K. Hitti, History of Syria, including Lebanon and Palestine, London, 1951; E. de Vaumas, Le Liban: Etude de géographique physique, 3 vols., Paris, 1954; P. K. Hitti, Lebanon in History, London, 1957; M. Chehab, Mosaïques au Liban (BMBeyrouth, XIV–XV), Paris, 1958–59. *Medieval and modern era*: M. von Baumgarten, Peregrinatio in ... Syriam, Nürnberg, 1594; Leandro di Santa Cecilia, Palestina, ovvero primo viaggio in Oriente, Rome, 1753; E. Poujade, Le Liban et la Syrie 1845–60, Paris, 1860; G. Rey, Etude sur les monuments de l'architecture militaire des Croisés en Syrie et dans l'île de Chypre, Paris, 1871; G. Rey, Les colonies franques de Syrie au XIIe et XIIIe siècles, Paris, 1883; H. Frauberger, Die Akropolis

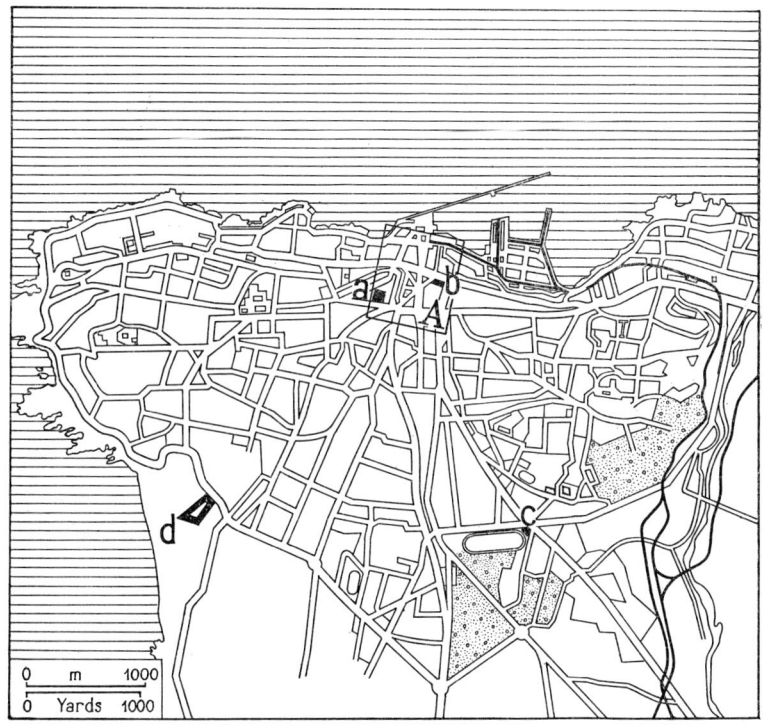

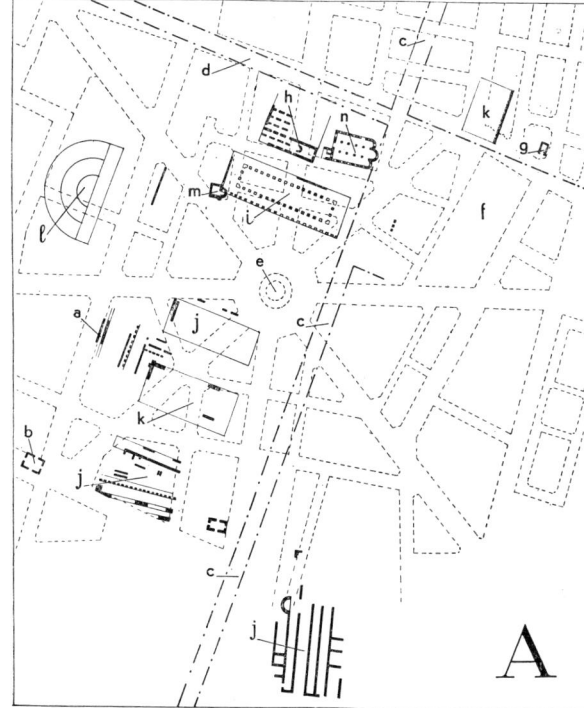

Beirut, plan of the modern city with major buildings. (*a*) Grand Seraglio; (*b*) Jāmi' al-Sarāyā; (*c*) National Museum; (*d*) UNESCO building. Inset *A*: Archaeological plan of the center of the city with Roman and medieval buildings. (*a*) Sustaining walls; (*b*) tetrapylon; (*c*) *cardo*; (*d*) *decumanus*; (*e*) western forum; (*f*) eastern forum; (*g*) tabernae; (*h*) baths; (*i*) basilica; (*j*) unidentified buildings of the Roman period; (*k*) temples (?); (*l*) theater (?); (*m*) Frankish chapel; (*n*) Church of St. John the Baptist, now the Great Mosque (Jāmi' al-'Omarī) (*from J. Lauffray*).

masters" and "inspired ... gardeners" from Italy. With the resurgence of building activity, arising from an intense economic development, European influences were assimilated and fused with traditional elements. Of particular note are the examples of Arab and Turkish military architecture, such as the Qal'at Jubayl, a fortress near Tibnin, and the Castle of Shema (in ruins), and those of Christian religious architecture, such as the monastery of Mār Abda at Deir el-Qamar and the Armenian monastery of Bzummār. The imposing palace at Bayt al-Dīn was built in the early 19th century. With its arcades, galleries, domes, and towers, the structure is without doubt Lebanon's major monument of Islamic secular art. The first government buildings of the principal cities were also built in the 19th century. The Turkish sultanate's concession, in the 1860s, of a greater degree of autonomy and a Christian military governor for Lebanon resulted in closer political and cultural contact with Europe. The Ottoman government, or Sublime Porte, ended in 1914. Industrial and commercial prosperity in the 20th century has brought about important urban development, particularly in the port cities, with the creation of whole new quarters and residential areas outside the old centers. The many buildings (scholastic complexes, ministries, banks, international organization offices such as FAO, UNESCO, and UNRRA in Beirut) that have been erected since World War II indicate a virtual abandonment of local traditions and the affirmation of an architecture bound to the most modern currents.

Francesco GABRIELI and Francesco NEGRI ARNOLDI

BIBLIOG. *Antiquity*: E. Renan, Mission de Phénicie, Paris, 1864; E. Reclus, La Phénicie et les Phéniciens, Neuchâtel, 1900; G. Contenau,

von Baalbek, Frankfurt am Main, 1892; C. Enlart, Les monuments des Croisés dans le Royaume de Jérusalem, 2 vols., Paris, 1925–28; H. Thiersch, Zu den Tempeln und der Basilika von Baalbek, Berlin, Leipzig, 1925; A. Geiger, En Syrie et au Liban, Grenoble, 1942; P. Collart and others, Lebanon: Suggestions for the Plan of Tripoli and for the Surroundings of the Baalbek Acropolis, Paris, 1954; R. Boulanger, Lebanon, Hachette World Guides, Paris, 1955.

ART CENTERS AND MONUMENTS. Beirut (Phoenician, Brt; Βηρυτός; Λαοδίκεια ἡ ἐν Φοινικίῃ; Colonia Iulia Augusta Felix Berytus; Beyrut). The ancient city, whose name appears in the letters of Tell el 'Amarna, was an important Phoenician port. Isolated finds from there are now in the National Museum. A sphinx of Amenemhet IV testifies to relations with Egypt. The Hellenistic-Roman city, destroyed at the time of Antiochus VII (ca. 138–129 B.C.), was rebuilt by the Romans when Marcus Agrippa founded a colony there in 15 B.C. Traces of the Roman city, destroyed by an earthquake in 551, have been found. Tentatively identified from the remains are the areas of an eastern and a western forum; the basilica, with an interior colonnade of the Ionic order and an exterior one of the Corinthian order; and baths. North of the eastern forum there are remains of private houses and of a building, perhaps a temple, from which came a monumental torso, now in the National Museum.

Seat of an archdiocese from the 4th century, Beirut was occupied by the Arabs in 635 and was repeatedly besieged during the Crusades. After the brief reign of Jean I d'Ibelin (1205–36) it again fell into the hands of the Mamelukes. The first settlements of French and Italian merchants date from the 15th century. In 1516 the city became part of the Ottoman Empire, though its amirs preserved a certain independence from the central power. Under the amir Fakhr ad-Dīn (1583–1635)

Beirut entered into commerce with Italian cities (Venice, Florence, etc.) and enjoyed a period of prosperity. Briefly falling under the Egyptian domination of Muḥammad ʿAlī in 1831, the city was bombarded and returned to Turkey in 1840 by an Anglo-Austro-Turkish fleet. In 1920 it became the capital of Lebanon under the French mandate. After Lebanon gained independence in 1944, there began a period of development that has made the city one of the principal port cities of the Middle East. Today the old city, lying between the sea and the heights of Ras Beirut, Mār Elias, and Ashrafiya, is surrounded by modern quarters (Christian and Moslem), which have grown up around the main highways to Tripoli, Sidon, and Damascus. Villas and parks are scattered over the surrounding heights. The only large ancient monument completely intact is the Great Mosque (Jāmiʿ al-ʿOmarī), a Moslem adaptation (1291) of the preceding Christian church dedicated to John the Baptist, built 1113–50 on a Byzantine building, which, in its turn, was constructed from the remains of an ancient temple; both Roman and Byzantine capitals were incorporated into the present structure. The Jāmiʿ al-Sarāyā (Mosque of the Seraglio) and the Jāmiʿ al-Naffāra (Mosque of the Fountain), with its octagonal minaret and white cupolas, complete Beirut's modest group of Moslem monuments. Interesting frescoes from a small Frankish chapel, discovered in 1941, are now in the National Museum. Among the other monuments in the old city are the Greek Catholic Cathedral of St. Elias and the Orthodox Cathedral of St. George, an ancient edifice with a women's gallery and a cloister (the frescoes within are modern). Fine examples of 19th- and 20th-century architecture are the parliament and town-hall buildings, the Catholic University, which has a rich library of precious manuscripts, and the great complex of American University (founded 1866). In recent years the National Museum, Hotel Biarritz, the American Embassy, National Library, Academy of Fine Arts, UNESCO, FAO, UNRRA, and other office buildings have been built. Other modern constructions include a large hospital complex on the outskirts of the city; the women's college (1957; M. Ecochard and C. Lecoeur, architects); a scholastic center, Amlié (1957; Hojeil); the Protestant College (1957; M. Ecochard and C. Lecoeur); the enlarged and modernized port; and the airport at Khalde.

BIBLIOG. *Antiquity*: I. Benzinger, RE, s.v. Berytos, V, 1897, cols. 321–23; M. Dunand, Les Egyptiens à Beyrouth, Syria, IX, 1928, pp. 300–02; J. Lauffray, Forums et monuments de Béryte, BMBeyrouth, VII, 1944–45, pp. 13–80, VIII, 1946–48, pp. 7–16; M. Floriani Squarciapino, EAA, s.v. Beirut, II, 1959, p. 38. *Medieval and modern era*: K. Baedeker, Palestine et Syrie, Leipzig, 1912; R. du Mesnil de Buisson, Les anciennes défenses de Beyrout, Syria, II, 1921, pp. 235–57, 317–27 (bibliog.); J. Lauffray and R. Mouterde, Beyrouth, ville romaine: Histoire et monuments, Beirut, 1952; R. Boulanger, Lebanon, Hachette World Guides, Paris, 1955; Collège protestant de jeunes filles à Beyrouth, Arch. d'aujourd'hui, 72, 1957, pp. 22–23; V. Elysséef, E. of Islam, 2d ed., s.v. Bayrūt, I, 1959, pp. 1137–38.

Afqa. In front of the cave of this name, near the sacred Spring of Adonis, are the remains of a Roman temple. The plan is highly uncertain, but it was built in part on artificially leveled ground and had a piscina to the northeast of the enclosing wall. This sanctuary, famous in antiquity, was dedicated to Venus. Tradition says the temple was destroyed by Constantine, but it is possible that the complex was still intact in the 5th century.

BIBLIOG. D. Krencker and W. Zschietzschmann, Römische Tempel in Syrien, I, Berlin, Leipzig, 1938, pp. 56–64.

ʿAin Harsha. On a height near this village is a well-preserved Roman temple, rather provincial in style, of the second half of the 3d century. It is a building *in antis* of modest proportions, interesting for the curvature of the entablature, supported by columns with Ionic capitals, at the entrance to the adytum.

BIBLIOG. D. Krencker and W. Zschietzschmann, Römische Tempel in Syrien, I, Berlin, Leipzig, 1938, pp. 245–55.

Baalbek (Ἡλιούπολις; Colonia Iulia Augusta Felix Heliopolis). The construction of the famous monumental complex here was begun in the 1st century and never completed. The Great Temple, dedicated to the Heliopolitan triad (Jupiter, Venus, and Mercury), was probably pseudodipteral; construction must have begun in the second half of the 1st century. It stands on a high terracelike base, and parts of the external colonnade, having unfluted shafts and frieze consoles with lion and bull protomas, are still standing. A large, complex, five-story altar and an interior staircase leading to an upper terrace were built in Flavian times. A minor altar, also on the sanctuary axis, rose between the major altar and the Corinthian decastyle façade of the temple. The vast rectangular court, dominated on the west side by the temple façade, was finished in the first half of the 2d century. It was surrounded on the other three sides by an inner colonnade and an outer enclosing wall, along which rectangular and semicircular exedrae alternated; between the column shafts of pink granite could be seen the decoration of a double tier of niches adorned with statues, both within and between the exedrae. This group was completed about the middle of the 3d century with the erection of the hexagonal forecourt, arcaded and encircled by large exedrae, and preceded by a wide propylaeum, the portico of which is flanked by two large towers decorated with pilasters in two superposed orders.

Possibly in the 1st, but more likely in the 2d, century another temple was erected, parallel to the long axis of the Great Temple, but on a lower level and structurally unrelated to it. Traditionally called the "Temple of Bacchus," this edifice was, according to recent

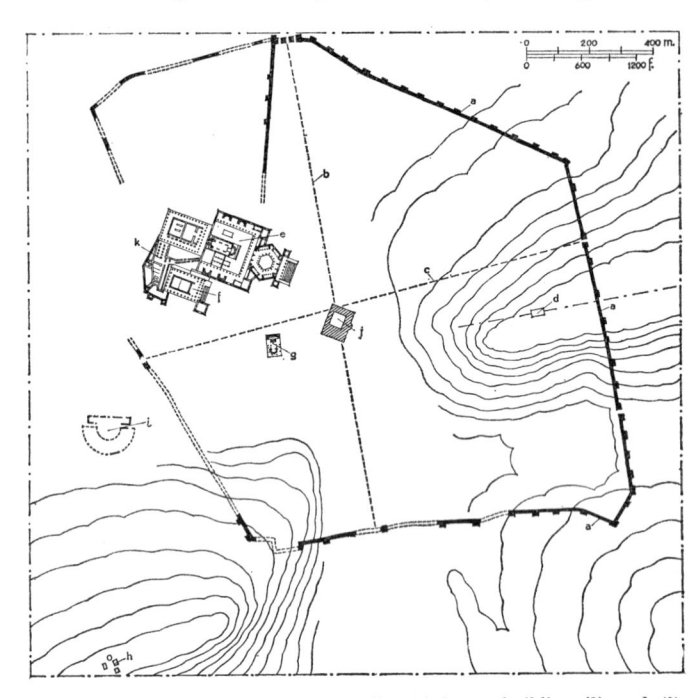

Baalbek, plan of the city. (a) Roman walls with later rebuilding; (b) cardo (?); (c) decumanus (?); (d) aqueduct; (e) Great Temple; (f) Temple of Bacchus; (g) Temple of Venus, or Round Temple; (h) probable site of the Temple of Mercury; (i) theater; (j) Great Mosque; (k) Moslem fortifications (*after* E. Honigmann, RE, Sup. IV, 1924, s.v. Heliupolis).

hypotheses, also dedicated to the Heliopolitan triad and intended for specific mystical rites. The building was raised on a high podium, and most of the colonnade, with its double row of columns in front of the pronaos, is still intact. A huge doorway leads into the cella, also in good condition; its walls are decorated with engaged columns, arched niches, and pedimented aediculae. The adytum, on a higher level, was reached by a short staircase. Not far from the monumental complex is the small central-plan Temple of Venus, or Round Temple (restored). An elegant example of the Hellenistic baroque, its base and entablature had a concave profile between the columns.

Occupied by the Moslems in 634, Baalbek was repeatedly destroyed during the Middle Ages. It became part of the Ottoman Empire in 1516. Two earthquakes, in 1667 and 1750, further damaged the ancient remains. The city encircles the artificial terrace on which the temples and the ruins of Crusader fortifications are found. At the center of the courtyard of the temple complex (described above) is a Christian basilica built on Roman foundations; it dates from the 4th or, perhaps, the 6th century.

BIBLIOG. *Antiquity*: R. Wood, The Ruins of Baalbek, London, 1757; E. Weigand, Baalbek und Rom, JdI, XXIX, 1914, pp. 37–91; T. Wiegand, Baalbek: Ergebnisse der Ausgrabungen und Untersuchungen in den Jahren 1898 bis 1905, 3 vols., Berlin, Leipzig, 1921–25; E. Weigand, Baalbek, Jhb. für Kw, 1924–25, pp. 77–99, 165–96; O. Eissfeldt, Tempel und Kulte syrischer Städte, Leipzig, 1941, p. 58; P. Collart, Baalbek et Rome, Mus. helveticum, VIII, 1951, pp. 241–59; P. Collart and P. Coupel, L'autel monumental de Baalbek, Paris, 1951; F. Castagnoli, EAA, s.v. Heliopolis, III, 1960, pp. 1137–40. *Medieval and modern era*: La Palestine: Guide... par les professeurs de Notre-Dame de France à Jérusalem, 1912, pp. 532–43; M. M. Alouf, Histoire de Baalbek, Beirut, 1938 (9th Eng. ed., Beirut, 1953); R. Boulanger, Lebanon, Hachette World Guides, Paris, 1955.

Batrun (Βότρυς; Botrys). Northeast of the modern city, the site of Greco-Roman Botrys, which is mentioned in the Tell elʿAmarna letters as Batruna, are the remains of a Roman amphitheater with fragments of elaborate sculptured decoration.

BIBLIOG. R. Dussaud, Topographie historique de la Syrie antique et médiévale, Paris, 1927, pp. 71, 82, 117.

Bayt al-Dīn. The famous palace here was built early in the 19th century for the amir Bashīr II (1788-1844). Now the residence of the president of the republic, it was built in pure Islamic style by architects from Damascus. Its arcaded courts, salons, and galleries were described by Lamartine, who stayed there for a time in the early 1830s.

BIBLIOG. R. Boulanger, Lebanon, Hachette World Guides, Paris, 1955; A. de Lamartine, Voyage en Orient (ed. Lotfy Fam), Paris, 1959.

Beziza (Bziza). In this hilltop town near Amyun rise the ruins of an Ionic prostyle temple, possibly of the Flavian period. The building, without a podium, has a handsome doorway and a cella enriched with shell-shaped niches.

BIBLIOG. D. Krencker and W. Zschietzschmann, Römische Tempel in Syrien, I, Berlin, Leipzig, 1938, pp. 4-7.

Byblos (mod. Jubayl; Phoenician, Gbl; Βύβλος; Βίβλος; Gebal; Jebeyl). The acropolis of Byblos occupies a promontory situated between the entrances to two valleys, approximately 25 miles north of Beirut. Stratigraphic excavations have permitted the identification of a succession of 15 periods from very ancient times to the Arab conquest. Up to the end of the 4th millennium B.C. three successive settlements can be distinguished, each of which is characterized by different types of dwellings and burials as well as by the evolution of stone tools and pottery. At the beginning of the 3d millennium an urban community was formed. Larger dwellings, the first temples, and a fortified wall were built, while the use of metal and wheel-turned fired pottery spread. The brilliant pre-Amorite period (ca. 2700-2150) was distinguished by spacious and well-built structures, by the remodeling of the temples and the defense system, and by the variety and elegance of its pottery. After a period of disturbance and destruction came the Amorite period (ca. 2150-1725), during which rich deposits of offerings were placed in sanctuaries, the Temple of Baalat Jubayl was reconstructed, and the temple with obelisks consecrated to Resheph and two other temples were built. Also contemporary are the four important hypogea in the royal necropolis, with limestone sarcophagi of the 12th dynasty and an abundant supply of funerary objects — pottery, pectorals, and weapons, often of precious materials. During the rule of the Hyksos (ca. 1725-1580) and the Egyptians (1580-1200) the temples remained in use and new tombs were added to the royal necropolis. The names of the princes of Byblos under the rule of Tyre (1200-734 B.C.), of Syria and Babylonia (734-539 B.C.), and of Achaemenid Persia (539-322 B.C.) have survived in inscriptions, among which is one, most important for its antiquity (ca. 1000 B.C.), found on the sarcophagus of Aḥīram. According to the inscription on the stele of Yeḥawmilk, the Temple of Baalat Jubayl was restored and cult objects added to it in the Persian period. The Hellenistic-Roman age was characterized by considerable building activity: a Roman temple, a basilica, a nymphaeum, and a theater, from which comes a fine mosaic with a bacchic scene (Beirut, Nat. Mus.).

Occupied in 1104 by the Crusaders under the command of Raymond de Saint-Gilles, the city (called Giblet by the Crusaders) was ceded in 1109 to the Genoese Embriaco family. It subsequently passed into the hands of Ṣalāh ad-Dīn, who dismantled the fortifications, and was returned to Frankish rule in 1199, under the lordship of Guy de Giblet. In 1266 Byblos fell to the Turks. The present-day city, which is surrounded by walls with towers and few openings, still partly preserves its medieval aspect; remains of towers are also still visible on the arms of the small harbor. At the southeast corner of the walls rises the rectangular castle of the Embriaco family (later Frankish), with a strong keep and surrounded by a moat. At the center of the city stands the triple-apsed Church of St. John the Baptist (begun 1115), the western half of which was entirely destroyed and only recently rebuilt; adjoining the church is a baptistery, dating from about 1200.

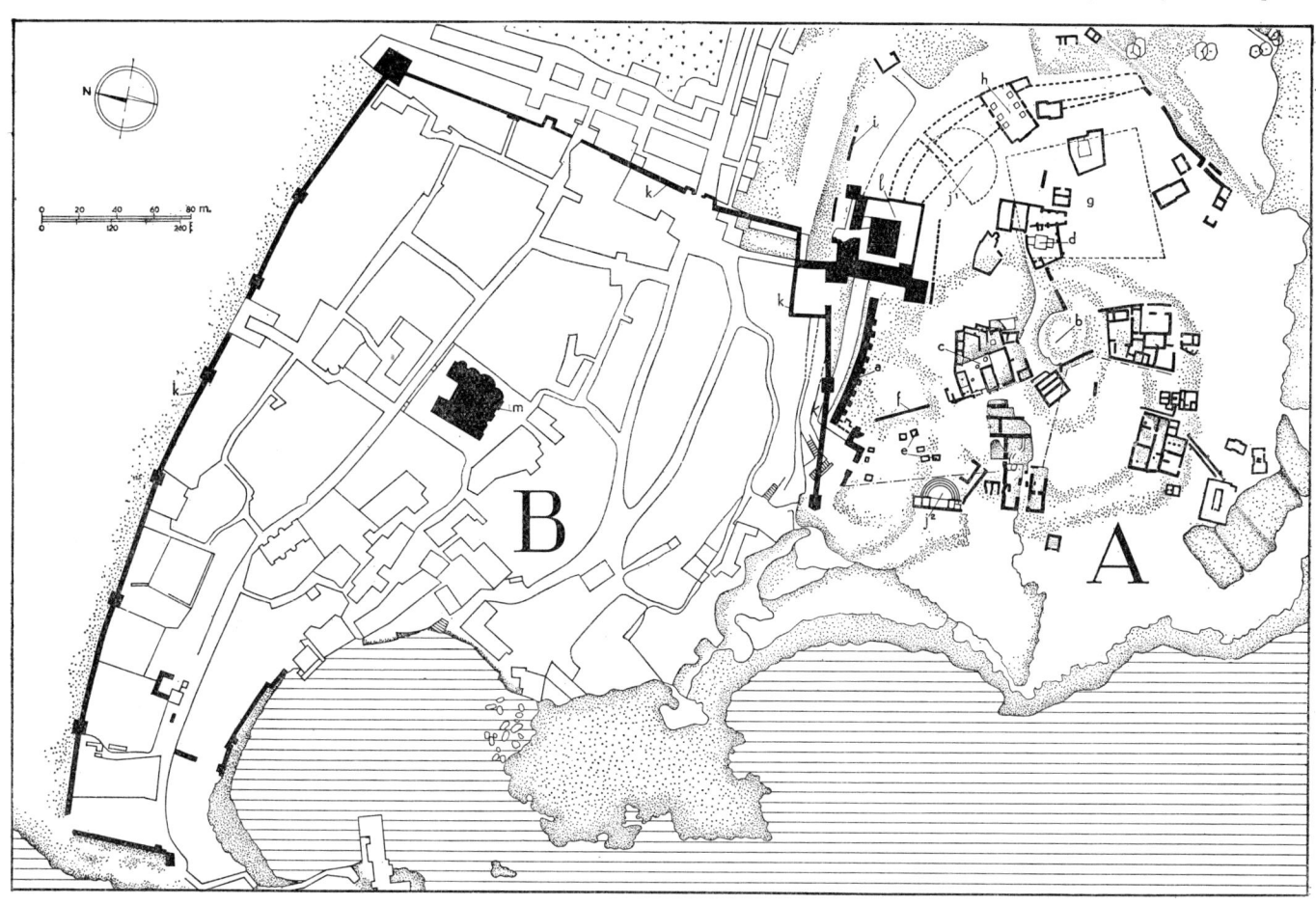

Byblos (mod Jubayl), plan (A = zone of ancient city; B = medieval and modern area). Principal monuments. Phoenician period: (a) bastions; (b) fortress; (c) Temple of Baalat Jubayl; (d) Temple of Resheph; (e) royal hypogea. Roman period: (f) colonnades; (g) temple; (h) basilica; (i) nymphaeum; (j¹) theater (moved now to j²). Medieval period: (k) walls; (l) castle of the Embriaco family (12th-13th cent.); (m) Church of St. John the Baptist and Baptistery (from M. Dunand, 1937).

LEBANON

BIBLIOG. *Antiquity*: M. Dunand, Rapports préliminaires sur les fouilles de Byblos, Syria, VIII, 1927 ff.; P. Montet, Byblos et l'Egypte, 2 vols. Paris, 1928–29; M. Dunand, Fouilles de Byblos, 2 vols., Paris, 1937–39; M. Dunand, Rapports préliminaires sur les fouilles de Byblos, BMBeyrouth, IX, 1949–50 ff.; M. Dunand and G. Furlani, EAA, s.v. Biblo, II, 1959, pp. 99–102. *Medieval and modern era*: R. Boulanger, Lebanon, Hachette World Guides, Paris, 1955.

Deir el-'Asha'ir. Near this village, on the frontier with Syria, are the ruins of a prostyle temple with a vast podium — which can be dated no later than A.D. 179 on the basis of an inscription — and a cella, whose portal is flanked by niches. Characteristic of the Mt. Hermon region are the complex crypt and the interior decoration of the cella with pilasters.

BIBLIOG. D. Krencker and W. Zschietzschmann, Römische Tempel in Syrien, I, Berlin, Leipzig, 1938, pp. 256–64.

Deir al-Qal'a. The remains of a Roman temple are still visible. Some of the structural elements indicate that it dates from the 1st century, or perhaps later. It is prostyle, with a pronaos extended by means of columns added at its sides; two of the colonnade shafts jut out at the corners. The interior is finished with engaged columns. A Maronite monastery now rises on the temple ruins.

BIBLIOG. D. Krencker and W. Zschietzschmann, Römische Tempel in Syrien, I, Berlin, Leipzig, 1938, pp. 1–3.

Ḥiṣn al-Safiri (Sfire). Of the three sacred Roman buildings now lying in ruins in this locality, the 1st-century Temple B, *in antis*, is characterized by an adytum on a higher level than the cella, from which it is separated by two columns. Temple C, also 1st-century, was decidedly smaller but of similar construction and enclosed an older sacellum. Temple A, the largest of the sanctuaries, was built at the beginning of the 3d century; on both outside and inside walls it has rhythmically alternated pilasters with jutting plinths.

BIBLIOG. D. Krencker and W. Zschietzschmann, Römische Tempel in Syrien, I, Berlin, Leipzig, 1938, pp. 20–34.

Kfar el-Jarra. On a small hill near this village has been found a complex of tombs dating from the first half of the 2d millennium B.C. The finds from the necropolis (necklaces, bronze daggers, pottery, lances, a scarab), which seems to have been in use for a long time, reveal relationships with the Aegean world, as well as Egypt (12th–18th dynasties).

BIBLIOG. P. E. Guigues, Nécropoles de la région sidonienne, BMBeyrouth, I, 1937, pp. 35–76, II, 1938, pp. 27–72.

Khara'ib. Trial digs have brought to light a favissa with numerous terra-cotta statuettes and some coins. Other small images were found under the paving of a building of rectangular plan, which was discovered in the vicinity of the village. The statuettes — representing divinities, youths, dancers, and musicians — reveal Egyptian, Persian, and, particularly, Hellenistic influences; they have been associated with local agrarian and fertility cults and with Greek mystery rites. As confirmed by presumably contemporary coins, they date from the late 4th to the late 1st century B.C.

BIBLIOG. M. Chehab, Les terres cuites de Kharayeb, BMBeyrouth, X–XI, 1951–54.

Lib'a. Near this village, about 9 miles east of Sidon, there are six extant tombs, which contain fragments of pottery and weapons. The tombs probably date from the 18th or the 17th century B.C.

BIBLIOG. P. E. Guigues, Nécropoles de la région sidonienne, BMBeyrouth, III, 1939, pp. 53–63.

Mejel 'Anjar. This village south of Baalbek is the site of a peripteral temple with flattened bosses on the exterior walls. In the interior there are engaged Ionic columns, semicircular niches, and aediculae with alternating curvilinear and triangular pediments.

BIBLIOG. D. Krencker and W. Zschietzschmann, Römische Tempel in Syrien, I, Berlin, Leipzig, 1938, pp. 182–91.

Nahr el-Kelb (Λύκος; Lycus). The sides of the canyon which this river has carved out of a steep promontory approximately 9½ miles north of Beirut are famous for the many rock-cut inscriptions left there through the ages by passing armies. On the right bank of the river only one inscription (No. 1) has been identified — that of Nebuchadnezzar II, the king of Babylonia (605–562 B.C.). On the left bank the oldest inscriptions are Nos. 14 and 16, which commemorate the passage of Ramses II (13th cent. B.C.). These also include a relief with the Pharaoh executing a prisoner before a statue of the sun god. Flanking inscription No. 14, which forms a rectangular slab, is an Assyrian inscription, not positively identifiable, curved on the top to reproduce the classic form of the Mesopotamian stele and depicting a king in prayer. Most important among the other Assyrian reliefs (Nos. 6, 7, 9, and 15) is that of Esarhaddon, with a monumental inscription referring to his Egyptian campaign. Other inscriptions on the rocks are both ancient (Latin, No. 3; Greek, No. 12) and modern (English and French).

BIBLIOG. H. Winckler, Das Vorgebirge am Nahr el-Kelb und seine Denkmäler, Leipzig, 1909; R. Mouterde, Le Nahr el-Kelb, Beirut, 1932.

Niha. Here are found the ruins of two prostyle temples: Temple B (1st cent.), with a single row of columns on the front, and the massive, tetrastyle Temple A, which has Ionic engaged columns with jutting bases and trabeation on the interior. The latter temple, which repeats the features of the interior of the oldest sacred building at Deir al-Qal'a, is attributed to the 2d century. Not far from Niha is Ḥiṣn Niha, particularly noteworthy for Great Temple A (2d cent.), with the pilasters projecting rhythmically from the walls, a device typical of other Syrian sanctuaries of the 2d and 3d centuries.

BIBLIOG. D. Krencker and W. Zschietzschmann, Römische Tempel in Syrien, I, Berlin, Leipzig, 1938, pp. 105–37.

Qal'at Faqra. In this locality are the remains of a large Roman temple (first half of 1st cent.), with a columned portico and a large court. The so-called "Mausoleum of Q.F." rises from a podium with a pseudoperipteral upper structure on which are inscriptions referring to the time of Claudius; it may have been used for worship, rather than as a tomb.

BIBLIOG. D. Krencker and W. Zschietzschmann, Römische Tempel in Syrien, I, Berlin, Leipzig, 1938, pp. 40–55.

Qaraya (Qraya). In this village, 5 miles southeast of Sidon, has been found a tomb from the time of Thutmosis III, containing pottery that clearly shows Mycenaean and Cypriote influence. These remains, found along with a type of pottery that is common in both Egypt and Syria, provide evidence of Aegean influence on the Phoenician coast about the middle of the 2d millennium B.C.

BIBLIOG. P. E. Guigues, Nécropoles de la région sidonienne, BMBeyrouth, III, 1939, pp. 53–63.

Qaṣr Naus. Here rise ruins of a Roman monumental complex, of which the most important sacred building is the prostyle temple (probably 2d cent.). The temple walls are decorated with protruding pilasters without bases, as well as arched niches and aediculae.

BIBLIOG. D. Krencker and W. Zschietzschmann, Römische Tempel in Syrien, I, Berlin, Leipzig, 1938, pp. 8–19.

Sarafand. Near this village is the ancient city of Sarepta (Akkadian, Ṣariptu; Heb., Sarefat; Σάρεπτα; Zarephath), where there was a fortified stronghold at the time of the Crusades. From it comes the torso of a statue now in the Louvre; an interesting aspect of this figure is the dress, with a skirt having ornamental motifs that terminate in the form of a uraeus.

BIBLIOG. G. Contenau, La civilisation phénicienne, 2d ed., Paris, 1949, pp. 157–58, fig. 18.

Sidon (Phoenician, Ṣdn; Σιδών; Ar., Sayda). The topography of the ancient port, which was divided into four sectors, has been discerned. One of the few extant sanctuaries of the Phoenician period is the Temple of Eshmun, the ruins of which, lying against the slope of a hill, suggest either a stepped construction or a massive bastion extending toward the valley. The sacred character of the building is verified by some inscriptions, found between the blocks of stone, which mention King Bodashtart. The tombs found in the necropolises around Sidon are sometimes very complex in their structure and plan. They have yielded many sarcophagi of great artistic interest; the oldest examples found there are in the shape of a theca. Of particular importance, because of their utterly Egyptian character, are those of King Tabnit (XI, PL. 132) and Eshmunazar II (Louvre), although Egyptian influence appears in other coffins dating back to the Persian period. In addition, four notable marble sarcophagi of Greek workmanship have been found. Funerary objects found in the tombs consist principally of pottery of the Seleucid epoch and lamps of Greek type. Tombs of the early Christian Era nearly always contain cippi; much more rarely they contain painted limestone steles, and in one case investigation has disclosed a large mosaic stele, probably of the 4th century. The first centuries of the Christian Era produced sarcophagi which greatly vary in form, appearance, and material; two fine examples, of lead, are in the Louvre.

Seat of a bishopric under the Byzantine government, Sidon was occupied in 637 by the Arabs, who changed its name to Sayda. Taken by the Frankish Crusaders in 1111, it surrendered in 1187 to Ṣalāḥ ad-Dīn, who razed the fortifications. Reoccupied by the Crusaders in 1197, the city was again destroyed by the Saracens in 1249 and then fell once more to the Franks, who definitely abandoned it in 1291. In the 17th century the amir Fakhr ad-Dīn attempted a reconstruction of the city, although he closed the port to keep out the Turkish fleet. The French settlers played an important role in the commercial life of the city until they were dismissed by the pasha Jezzar in 1791. After the earthquake of 1837 the city was rebuilt and encircled with new walls; in 1840 the harbor fortifications were once again destroyed by an Anglo-Austrian fleet. One of the city's oldest architectural monuments is the 13th-century fortress Qalʿat al-Baḥr, built on an island that is situated at the mouth of the harbor and composed of two large towers joined by a wall. Mostly in ruins, this building still shows architectural elements of pure 13th-century French style. The Castle of St. Louis — so called because, according to tradition, the saint once stayed there — dates back to the 12th century, but was almost completely rebuilt by the Arabs. The Great Mosque (Jāmiʿ al-Kabīr) rises on the site of the Church of the Knights of St. John. Many of the khans built by the amir Fakhr ad-Dīn during the 17th century are still extant. One of the most important of rectangular plan, surrounded by galleries and loggias, it was residence of the French consul in the 19th century.

BIBLIOG. G. Le Strange, Palestine under the Moslems, London, 1890, pp. 240–42; T. Reinach and Hamdy Bey, Une nécropole à Sidon, 4 vols., Paris, 1892–96; G. Contenau, Mission archéologique à Sidon (1914), Paris, 1921; G. Contenau, Deuxième mission archéologique à Sidon (1920), Paris, 1924; E. von Mercklin, Untersuchungen zu den antiken Bleisarkophagen, Berytus, III, 1936, pp. 51–75, V, 1938, pp. 27–46, VI, 1939–40, pp. 27–61; P. E. Guigues, Nécropoles de la région sidonienne, BMBeyrouth, I, 1937, pp. 35–76, II, 1938, pp. 27–72, III, 1939, pp. 53–63; M. Meurdrac and M. Albanèse, A travers les nécropoles gréco-romaines de Sidon, BMBeyrouth, II, 1938, pp. 73–98; J. Lauffray, Sidon, Beirut, 1951; R. Boulanger, Lebanon, Hachette World Guides, Paris, 1955; E. Kukahn, Anthropoide Sarkophage in Beyrouth und die Geschichte dieser sidonischen Sarkophagkunst, Berlin, 1955; BMBeyrouth, Chronique, passim.

Tripoli (Τρίπολις; anc. Tripolis; Ar., Tarabulus). Because of the lack of archaeological evidence, no secure data for the ancient city, already a flourishing port in Greco-Roman times, exist. A few ruins of little value and uncertain provenance were brought to light during work in the modern city. Some interesting facts, however, are furnished by Arrian and Strabo, who report that the city was divided into three large quarters, each fortified with a wall.

Occupied by the Moslems in 638, the city experienced a series of political vicissitudes until it was besieged by Raymond de Saint-Gilles and finally conquered by a coalition of Crusader forces in 1109; after this it became a Crusader stronghold for about 180 years. Under Frankish domination churches, monasteries, and hospitals were built, and it became the seat of a bishopric and an important industrial and commercial center. In 1187, with the extinction of the dynasty of Toulouse, the city passed to the ruling house of Antioch. With the fall of Antioch in 1289, Tripoli also fell into the hands of the Mameluke sultan Qalāʾūn, who through territorial concessions to the Moslems, built the present-day city on the banks of the Nahr Abū-ʿAlī, at the foot of the Frankish castle, as well as a series of fortifications on the sea, of which a few ruins are still extant today at el-Mina. Between 1516 and 1918, under the Ottoman Empire, the city slowly declined. After the city was joined to Lebanon in 1920, it became the administrative capital of the northern region. The aqueduct, the so-called "Arches of the Prince" (still partially standing), and a considerable number of 13th-century architectural remains in the medieval quarter of Hamman Izz ed-Dīn date from the Crusader period. While the Great Mosque rose on the site of the ancient cathedral, Ste-Marie de la Tour, and utilized its ruins, the 14th-century Mosque of Taylān seems to be a purely Islamic construction. Next to the Great Mosque there is a mausoleum of the same century with a magnificent monumental portal; nearby are the small mosque of Saqraqiya (now a residence) and the Qurṭāi Bey, with a large ablution basin. The castle of Raymond de Saint-Gilles (Qalʿat Sanjīl) was rebuilt in the 14th century by the amir Asandmīr Kurgī. Other Islamic monuments, in what is unquestionably the most interesting Lebanese center in this respect, are the Lion Tower (Burj es-Sibāʿ), built on the sea by the amir Aydamūsh (late 14th cent.); the monastery (tekke) of the Maulawiya dervishes; the Mosque and Madrasah al-ʿAṭṭār; the Mosque of the Tanners; and the Mosque al-Tūba. In the last decades modern quarters and residential centers with numerous office and store buildings of Western style have been built, and the harbor has also been enlarged.

BIBLIOG. G. Le Strange, Palestine under the Moslems, London, 1890, pp. 348–52; E. Honigmann, RE, s.v. Tripolis, no. 4, 2d ser., XIII, 1939, cols. 203–07; R. Boulanger, Lebanon, Hachette World Guides, Paris, 1955.

Tyre. (Phoenician, Ṣr; Akkadian, Ṣurru; Heb., Zor; Τύρος; Tyrus; Sur). Uncertainties still exist about the ancient topography of the great Phoenician city, approximately 53 miles south of Beirut. Although the present site is on a peninsula, it is known that the earliest settlement was on an island about a half mile from the shore, whence

Tyre, zone of ancient city. (1) Modern town. Principal archaeological remains; partly submerged: (a) southern or "Egyptian" harbor; (b) breakwaters, (c) entrance to the harbor; (d) west entrance; (e) ruins of the embankment; (f) the breakwater of the spring; (g) spring; (h) tomb; (i) northern or "Sidonian" harbor, submerged ruins of the breakwater (from A. Poidebard).

the Semitic names, meaning "rock," perhaps derived. Scylax noted, under the name Palaityros, the separate settlements that eventually developed on the adjacent coast because of the pressure of population growth. The ancient harbors were located through the underwater explorations conducted by A. Poidebard, who identified a northern and a southern port. Foundations of the breakwaters have been found and suggest construction in the period between the end of the Hellenistic era and Roman times. At Jel el-ʿAmad, in the immediate vicinity of the city, a hypogeum tomb with decorative paintings of the Roman period has been discovered. At Tell el-Maʿshuq stone slabs and parts of a stairway leading to a large building (probably a temple) have been found, in addition to many fragments of pottery, mosaics, and coins, which are datable from the 5th century B.C. to the early centuries of the Christian Era.

Occupied in 636 by the Arabs, Tyre became part of the Latin kingdom of Jerusalem in 1124. In 1231 the city was conquered by an expedition sent out by Frederick II, who held it until 1243. Abandoned by the Crusaders in 1291 and subsequently destroyed by the Moslems, its ruins were used as a quarry for building materials. In the 17th century the amir Fakhr ad-Dīn tried, unsuccessfully, to reconstruct the city. The sands have gradually covered the ruins and closed the port, though remains of the triple wall of the Crusader period and ruins of towers are visible here and there on the sandy dunes. Of the large basilica, begun in 1127 on the ruins of a 4th-century basilica, all that remains is part of the peripheral wall, which is stripped of its ancient facing. The modern-day development of the town has produced no notable constructions.

BIBLIOG. D. Le Lasseur, Mission archéologique à Tyr (1921), Syria, III, 1922, pp. 1–26, 116–33; A. Poidebard, Un grand port disparu: Tyr, Paris, 1939; R. Boulanger, Lebanon, Hachette World Guides, Paris, 1955.

Umm el-Aḥmād. This locality, south of Tyre, was excavated in 1860 by E. Renan and in 1921 by M. de Lorey, who brought to light remains of two Hellenistic temples. The excavations have yielded some fine funerary reliefs, among which are a stele in the Louvre, depicting a female figure making an offering, and that of Baalyaton in the Ny Carlsberg Glyptotek, Copenhagen.

BIBLIOG. G. Contenau, Musée du Louvre, Les antiquités orientales, II, Paris, 1927, pl. 34; G. Contenau, Manuel d'archéologie orientale, III, Paris, 1931, fig. 897.

The accounts of places are edited by Paul COLLART, with contributions by Paolo MATTHIAE for the ancient world, by Francesco GABRIELI for the Islamic period, and by Francesco NEGRI ARNOLDI for medieval and modern times.

Illustrations: 5 figs. in text.

LEBRUN (LE BRUN) CHARLES. French painter, designer, and decorator (b. Paris, 1619; d. Paris, 1690). His father, Nicolas, was a sculptor; his elder brother, Nicolas, was a painter; and one of his younger brothers, Gabriel, also painted but was best known as an engraver. The young Charles showed a precocious talent and was sent to study under François Perrier. He attracted the attention of the Chancellor of France, Pierre Séguier, on whose *hôtel* his father was working. Séguier sent him to Simon Vouet (q.v.) for further training. Lebrun was soon dissatisfied with the minor tasks he was given and left to pursue his own studies at Fontainebleau. The paintings of his early years show the influence of these two masters. *Hercules and Diomedes* (Nottingham, City Mus. and Art Gall.), painted for Cardinal Richelieu, is a vigorous composition reminiscent of Perrier and suggesting a familiarity with Rubens; *The Crucifixion* (Moscow, Pushkin Mus.) follows a Vouet type; while *The Martyrdom of St. John* (Church of St-Nicolas-du-Chardonnet) combines stylistic elements from both his masters in a work that is audacious in conception and brilliant in execution. The minor works (designs for frontispieces, theses etc.) show the same precocious ability to challenge his elders on their own ground. In his six etchings, particularly the four of a satyr family symbolizing the times of day, the physical types from Vouet's repertory are etched in the rough technique of Perrier. A lost *Annunciation* must have shown Lebrun working in a sober, somewhat heavy style, closer to that of Philippe de Champaigne (q.v.), and turning toward a simpler, more classic art.

In 1642 Séguier sent him with a pension to Rome. There he came under the influence of Nicolas Poussin (q.v.), who probably encouraged him to copy antique statues (sketchbook presented to Séguier; Paris, Bib. Nat., Ms. fonds fr. 17217), as well as the frescoes of Raphael and the Carraccis. He also painted a *Pietà* (Louvre; PL. 103) and a *Death of Cato* (Arras, Palais St-Vaast), a work of almost Caravaggesque intensity, with rugged, unclassical figures like those of the *Hercules and Diomedes*; his *Horatius Cocles Defending Rome* (London, Dulwich College Picture Gall.) and *Mucius Scaevola* (Mâcon, Mus. B. A.) reflect various aspects of Poussin's art.

On his return to Paris in 1646 he was occupied with numerous commissions, and by 1648 he was sufficiently established to play a prominent part in the foundation of the Académie Royale de Peinture et de Sculpture. Yet his style was not fully formed. His two altarpieces commissioned as May offerings for Notre-Dame, *The Martyrdom of St. Andrew* (1647) and *The Martyrdom of St. Stephen* (1651), both in Notre-Dame, show the influence of Domenichino (q.v.), while the small altarpiece for the Church of St-Paul et St-Louis, the *Bénédicité* (Louvre), has a monumental quality recalling the work of Andrea Sacchi. In the paintings for friends, such as *The Brazen Serpent* (Bristol, City Art Gall.) and *The Massacre of the Innocents* (London, Dulwich College Picture Gall.), Lebrun used numerous small figures and groups to show the psychological effects of an event on the various people involved, much as Poussin had done in *The Gathering of the Manna*.

During the 1650s Lebrun formed from these elements the style which can be noted in *The Feast in the House of Simon* (Venice, Accademia), *The Repentant Magdalen* (Louvre), *Christ in the Desert Served by Angels* (Louvre), all commissioned for the convent of the Carmelites in the Faubourg Saint-Jacques; in *The Crucifixion with Angels* (Louvre), commissioned by the Queen Mother for her oratory; and in *The Pentecost* (copy in Louvre) for St-Sulpice.

Soon after his return from Rome he began the series of decorations that was to culminate in his work at Versailles. Although its execution was spread over several years, the earliest design must be that of *The Apotheosis and Marriage of Hercules* for the gallery of the Hôtel Lambert. Here that standard baroque trick, the illusion of a ceiling broken through to show a sky peopled with gods and goddesses, increases the effect of height in a low gallery. The long, narrow shape necessitated subdivision into square fields, which are linked by flying figures below the dividing arches. By the use of imitation tapestries Lebrun was able to introduce into this scene two other scenes of Hercules' earthly triumphs, without violating the principle of the unities. In the two rooms of the Hôtel de la Rivière (now Mus. Carnavalet) that Lebrun painted in 1653 the sky scenes are surrounded by a deep coving, the decoration of which in one room includes eagles and putti modeled in relief. In the central scenes the illusionistic foreshortening, restrained in the Hôtel Lambert, is reduced to a minimum.

In Vaux-le-Vicomte, the château of Nicolas Fouquet, Lebrun showed his decorative talents to the full. His studied avoidance of steep foreshortening creates a classic harmony, accepting the architectural facts of wall and ceiling; in some rooms the richness of the coloring is enhanced by the combination of painted scenes with stucco supporting figures in full relief, a technique derived ultimately from Pietro da Cortona (q.v.). It was for Fouquet that Lebrun first demonstrated his versatility, designing tapestries for his patron's weavers at Maincy and preparing brilliant fêtes at Vaux.

In 1660 Lebrun was summoned to Fontainebleau by Louis XIV and ordered to paint a scene from the life of Alexander; he selected the theme of the magnanimous victor for his painting, *The Family of Darius before Alexander*. The scene takes place on a shallow stage, with only a brief glimpse into the distance; Alexander, Hephaestion, and the family of Darius with their servants form a double line, allowing the expression of each figure to be seen in succession (cf. etching version, IV, PL. 432). This combination of richness in the individual elements with a simple friezelike arrangement exemplifies Lebrun's compromise with classic severity. This picture was to become the foundation of Lebrun's career, and appropriately so, for it is his masterpiece as well as a manifestation of those elements most typically his own and most eagerly imitated by his successors.

The following year he painted another of his most successful works, the equestrian portrait of Chancellor Séguier (Louvre; PL. 102). The gold, white, and blue-gray coloring gives it a cool splendor, and in its quiet simple dignity and the severity of its composition it is the classical answer to the baroque equestrian portraits of Rubens and Van Dyck. In the handling of the paint it has a freshness and vigor which his later works too often lack.

The year 1661 marks a turning point in Lebrun's life. With the fall of Fouquet he entered the service of the King, and from then on his energies were devoted to the glorification of Louis XIV. In 1662 he was put in charge of the new Manufacture Royale des Meubles de la Couronne (the Gobelins manufactory). There he controlled the complete production of furnishings for the royal palaces, ensuring that uniformity of style which, even now, when so much has been lost (the silver furniture was afterward melted down), is such a striking feature of Versailles. The best-known of these Gobelins products are the tapestries, the *Elements, The Seasons, The Battles of Alexander* (reproducing Lebrun's paintings in the Louvre; PL. 101), *The Family of Darius, The History of Louis XIV* (cf. PL. 103), and *The Royal Palaces* (also known as "The Months"). All were intended, directly or indirectly, to celebrate Louis XIV, his victories, and his magnificence. The publication of engravings from these designs served to spread further the renown of Louis and, incidentally, that of his Premier Peintre.

The King set Lebrun to work first on the Palais des Tuileries (since destroyed) and on the Louvre, where the Galerie d'Apollon, which he never finished, remains one of the most splendid memorials to the Sun King. The varied use of white and gilded stucco to frame, support, and expand the painted scenes, interspersed with panels of arabesques, creates a rich three-dimensional effect.

But it is Versailles which provides the most united and complete example of Lebrun's work. The Grands Appartements were decorated between 1671 and 1681 under his direction, while Lebrun himself decorated the magnificent Escalier des Ambassadeurs (destroyed) and planned a ceiling painting for a chapel. In 1679 he began the designs of the Galerie des Glaces (Hall of Mirrors; II, PL. 212; V, PL. 409), on which he worked till 1684, and the ensemble was completed in 1686 with the Salon de la Paix and the Salon de la Guerre (PL. 104). Each scene on the ceiling of the Galerie is framed within an architectural structure and surrounded by putti, satyrs, caryatids, genii, and trophies, of which only a small part of the framework and the trophies on the heavy cornice are in actual relief. Here, as in several other rooms, the walls are covered with colored marble, arranged in rectilinear designs. This formal severity of the walls and the framework circumscribing the pomp and grandeur of the paintings reflects the rigid protocol that controlled the splendor of court life. The paintings are triumphs of 17th-century allegory, in which the King retains his majestic calm in the midst of battles fought for him by Hercules and Minerva and the full story of a campaign is compressed into a single picture.

Lebrun supplied designs for much of the garden sculpture of Versailles and for the decoration of the châteaux of Saint-Germain-en-Laye and Marly-le-Roi; he prepared decorations for state occasions and still had time for frontispieces and allegorical illustrations of theses and for religious paintings such as his *Louis XIV Adoring the Risen Christ* (1674, Lyons, Mus. B.A.; PL. 103). In the early 70s he decorated the chapel of Colbert's villa at Sceaux and the dome of the Pavillon de l'Aurore (PL. 104) in the garden.

To help with these tasks Lebrun built up a corps of artists; some were specialists in animal painting, in still life, or in landscape, living at the Gobelins and not aspiring to the Académie, but many of the academicians also cooperated with Lebrun and worked from his designs. With so much royal patronage dispensed by Lebrun, it was an advantage for artists to adopt the style he favored, but even a rival, such as Pierre Mignard, painted in the same manner. His rise in 1668 to life chancellor of the Académie and his assumption of the directorship in 1683 were in part the result of intrigue, but he was well suited for this authority, both as an artist and as an organizer, and the political ability by which he acquired power for himself was used with equal skill to steer the Académie through its difficult early years. In close cooperation with Colbert he raised the Académie's position to the point that he could negotiate for union on equal terms with the older Accademia di S. Luca in Rome; in both 1676 and 1677 the Roman academicians accorded him the honor of electing him *principe*.

He had a sound grasp of the purpose of the Académie, using it to ensure the dignity of painting and sculpture as liberal arts and to establish a doctrine, based on rational rules, comparable to the rules of grammar, rhetoric, and poetics that the Académie Française was devising for the French language. His discourses on the paintings of Raphael and Poussin and his defense of drawing as opposed to color are outstanding. His illustrated lecture of 1669 on the expression of the passions, a subject so important for the elaborate history paintings of the time, was printed in full in 1698 (*Méthode pour apprendre à dessiner les passions*, Paris; cf. III, PL. 206) and was widely used and reproduced many times during the next two centuries. His discourse on physiognomy, designed to complement it, was printed only in 1806, and then in a misleading form (*Dissertation sur un traité de Charles Le Brun concernant le rapport de la physionomie humaine avec celle des animaux*, Paris).

In 1683 Colbert died; since his successor, Louvois, favored the rival Mignard, Lebrun soon found his authority contested even at the Gobelins and Versailles. He needed the stimulus of large commissions, and the neglect he now experienced — in part deliberate, in part the inevitable result of Louis XIV's financial difficulties — hurt his pride and dried up his inspiration. He painted and presented to the King small-scale religious scenes, crowded, full of erudite incident, and prepared with great care, but pictorially dull. *Moses Defending Jethro's Daughters* (1686) and *Moses Marrying Sephora* (1687) are now in Modena (Gall. Estense); of the proposed series of the life of Christ only *The Raising of the Cross* (1685), *The Adoration of the Shepherds* (1688), *Christ Bearing the Cross* (1688), and *The Entry into Jerusalem* (1689) were completed (all in the Louvre).

The emergence of France during the second half of the 17th century as the dominant power in Europe produced a new self-consciousness and the need for an art that would reflect this new ascendency, create a setting fit for the court of the Sun King, and challenge the hitherto unquestioned superiority of Italy. The painter who achieved this was Lebrun; he created the style of Louis XIV, which was imitated by lesser princes and established the French artistic hegemony of Europe. Based on a study of Raphael, the Carraccis, Domenichino, and, above all, Poussin, but reflecting also the different tradition of Rubens and Pietro da Cortona, it was a compromise which avoided both the severity of the late Poussin and the flamboyant exuberance of the full baroque.

Immensely competent, a sure and sometimes brilliant draftsman, an intelligent and conscientious historian, Lebrun had little sense of color, and his interest in narrative values all too often submerged his esthetic sensibility. He deployed the figures in his pictures like actors; each must be viewed as a separate statement. For this reason it is not surprising that of the 2,000 or more of his drawings in the Louvre about three-fourths are figure studies.

By the time of his death Lebrun was a disappointed man; yet his achievements were great and lasting. He had built up one of the most successful bodies of artists and craftsmen in the history of art, which produced one of the most splendid palaces in the Western world, and he had created the most influential of academies, which controlled French art for more than two centuries.

BIBLIOG. H. Jouin, Charles Le Brun et les arts sous Louis XIV, Paris, 1889; P. Marcel, Charles Le Brun, Paris, 1909 (bibliog.); J. Cordey, Vaux-le-Vicomte, Paris, 1924; W. Baumeister, Zur Geschichte des Lebrunschen Jabachbildes, Wallraf-Richartz Jhb., III-IV, 1926-27, pp. 211-21; R. Josephson, Le Monument du Triomphe pour le Louvre, Rev. de l'art ancien et mod., LIII, 1928, pp. 21-34; A. F. Blunt, The Early Work of Charles Le Brun, BM, LXXXV, 1944, pp. 165-73, 186-94; J. Wilhelm, Les décorations de Charles Le Brun à l'Hôtel de la Rivière, B. du Mus. Carnavalet, II, 1949, pp. 6-15; D. Posner, Charles Lebrun's Triumphs of Alexander, AB, XLI, 1959, pp. 237-48; B. de Montgolfier, Charles Le Brun et les confréries parisiennes, GBA, LV, 1960, pp. 323-42; M. Florisoone, Charles Le Brun: Premier directeur de la Manufacture Royale des Gobelins (exhibition cat.), Paris, 1962.

Jennifer MONTAGU

Illustrations: PLS. 101-104.

LE CORBUSIER. Pseudonym of Charles-Edouard Jeanneret (b. La Chaux-de-Fonds, Switzerland, Oct. 6, 1887), architect and city planner. After studying printmaking at the local art scool, Le Corbusier was directed toward architecture by his first important teacher, the painter Charles L'Eplattenier, and his first buildings were erected in Switzerland in 1904-06. Soon thereafter he began a protracted period of travel. In 1907 he was in Italy; next he visited Budapest and then Vienna, where he met Josef Hoffman. At Lyons in 1908 he met Tony Garnier and afterward moved on to Paris, where he spent 15 months with Auguste Perret (q.v.). In 1910-11, years spent for the most part in Germany, he passed several months with Peter Behrens (q.v.) in Berlin and also participated in the Deutscher Werkbund exposition at Munich. During 1911 he traveled in the Balkans and Asia Minor and revisited Italy. In 1917 Le Corbusier settled in Paris, where he still lives; here

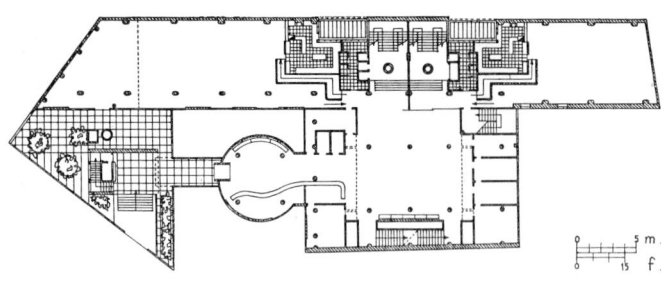

Paris, Salvation Army hospice, plan of reception areas (*from A. Sartoris, Gli elementi della architettura funzionale, Milan, 1941*).

he produced his first paintings (PL. 105), took part in his first exhibit in 1918, and initiated the Purist movement with Amédée Ozenfant. In 1920, again with Ozenfant, he founded *L'Esprit Nouveau*, a review they published until 1925; in 1922, with his cousin Pierre Jeanneret, he set up an architectural studio and also exhibited architectural projects at the Salon d'Automne (Citrohan houses, "Immeubles-Villas," and a contemporary city for 3,000,000 inhabitants). This early work was followed by extensive and uninterrupted activity on an international scale and dedicated participation in the solution of problems of avant-garde architecture. The principal organizer of the first International Congress of Modern Architecture (CIAM) in 1928 at La Sarraz, Switzerland, Le Corbusier was also the animating force in its subsequent gatherings; at the fourth Congress, held in Athens in 1933, the basic principles of modern architecture were articulated under his influence and were later published (*La Charte d'Athènes*, 1943). In 1930 he became a French citizen, and in 1935 he made his first trip to the United States, where his ideas had by then created a marked impression.

It is relatively easy to detect the component influences in the early development of Le Corbusier. The decorative rationalism of the Nancy school (V. Prouvé, Souriau) was instilled in him by L'Eplattenier. Perret must have sought to interest him in "harmonic structuralism." Behrens elicited his interest in the problems of architecture and form posed by industrial needs and methods. Garnier proposed ambitious solutions to the planning problems of industrial cities. Contact with the Werkbund must have provoked reflection on the social role of art and architecture in modern life. Acquaintance with the theories of Adolf Loos (q.v.) introduced an attitude of formal and decorative asceticism, while cubist developments assuredly influenced his own Purist efforts. But, far from inhibiting or diluting the creativity of Le Corbusier, these complex elements assimilated from contemporary culture merely served to accent his significant personal contribution. In the light of the marked originality of his ideas and total work, discerning appraisal of his extraordinary talent for synthesizing effectively what were often little more than diffuse theoretical outlines must strongly qualify the importance attached to these borrowings, for in the process of integrating them into a distinctive and fruitful architectural order Le Corbusier gave them new power and worth. In truth, his contribution to the contemporary renewal of architecture consisted not only of questioning the traditional rules but, above all, of rearranging them according to the rhythm of his own time. He reconstructed the family dwelling by defining the "machine for living" (*la machine à habiter*), with which he sought to replace the undifferentiated shelter that the traditional home offered. Seeking to reorganize the structure of cities, he began by classifying their functions and went on to inject an artistic element of grandeur into his urban scheme. In order to accomplish many of his new ideas, he even revised construction methods through industrializing building procedures

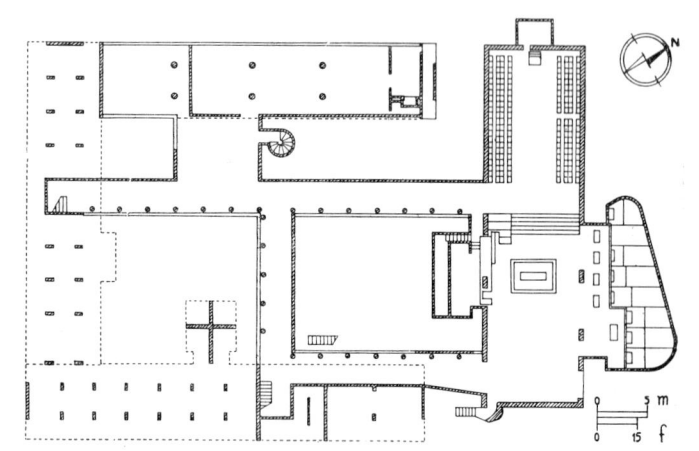

Eveux-sur-Arbresle, Dominican monastery of Ste-Marie de la Tourette, floor plan of the church (*from Casabella, no. 246, 1960*).

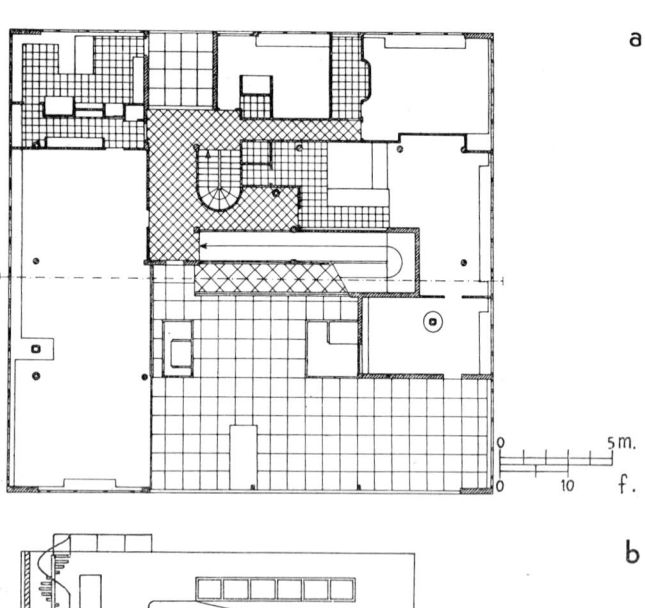

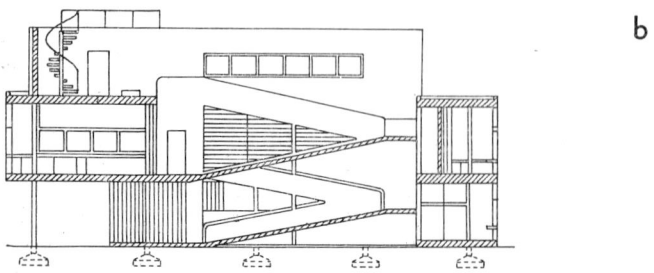

Poissy, Savoye house: (*a*) Floor plan; (*b*) cross section.

to correspond to the advances made in other industries. Finally, he created a new world of architectural forms by affirming, in opposition to the principles of historical and natural romanticism, the underlying geometry of structure and the preeminent role of mathematical proportion, both as a basis for theoretical study and as the effective means of creating architectural harmony.

Le Corbusier's radical rethinking of family dwellings and his innovations began with the Citrohan house (stilts, or *pilotis*; bands of windows and weightless screen walls; open, fluid plan; free façade; roof garden) and then the "Immeubles-Villas," which adapted similar structural elements to problems of communal living, and culminated in enormous housing blocks (*unité d'habitation*, Marseilles: PL. 107; I, PL. 388). These projects were meant to utilize in the optimum way the space allotted to each person in the crowded modern city, and the living unit was shaped to meet the functional demands of families within the industrialized civilization of the 1930s. Various buildings and projects mark the principal advances in his studies: in the 1920s, the Pavillon de l'Esprit Nouveau (Paris, Exposition des Arts Décoratifs), workers' housing for Pessac, and the houses of the Weissenhof quarter in Stuttgart (PL. 105; V, PL. 109); in the 1930s, the Clarté apartments and the Pavillon des Temps Nouveaux (Exposition Internationale). The reform of interior decoration and furniture that began in 1925, in collaboration with Charlotte Perriand and Pierre

Jeanneret, capped his efforts to promote spare and practical accessories for modern living.

In a parallel effort, Le Corbusier launched a vast inquiry into the urban problem, and by 1922 he had devised a theoretical solution from which his later plans derived. Contrary to Wright, who advocated diffusion of urban communities, Le Corbusier was opposed to horizontal spreading of the urban complex; at first sight, the principles he proposed for urban renovation might even seem contradictory — increased population density, improved methods of communication, and enlargement of green areas. This program could be implemented only by means of a radically new approach to the urban problem, involving innovations such as the "Cartesian skyscraper" (PL. 106); for residential areas, units of homes of a similar size; for the organization of traffic, the "7V" plan; and for industrial areas, the spacious landscaped "green factory." Classification by function extended to over-all zoning of the urban organism as well (*Les Trois Etablissements Humains*, 1944). Two projects exemplify these ideas: the plan for Saint-Dié (1945), which introduced a classic solution to the problem of the civic center, and the creation of Chandigarh (PL. 108; VII, FIG. 899), the new capital of Punjab, for which Le Corbusier laid out the general plan and constructed a monumental ensemble of exceptional importance.

Without industrialization and standardization of building techniques it would have been impossible to solve economically the social problem of producing lodgings *en masse*; nor would it have been possible to reinstate a genuine architectural discipline. The "Dom-ino" system of mass housing suggested as early as 1914 a principle of prefabricated construction that combined the advantages of standardization with the possibility of wide functional variation and esthetic satisfaction. Like Gropius, Le Corbusier saw as the most urgent task of modern architecture the definition of fundamental standards satisfying both the primordial needs of man and the demands of industrial production. His studies of such norms led to the concept of the "modulor," a scale of harmonic measures based on human stature. This system encouraged the ordering — that is, the unifying and humanizing — of basic forms in architecture and elsewhere in modern design.

The firm logic of the lyricism inherent in Le Corbusier's designs, set forth with a disciplined rhythm and proportion, escapes both the dryness of neoclassicism and dogmatic functionalism and the excesses of expressionism. The "correct and magnificent play of volumes in light" he postulated has been realized masterfully in his architecture. His manipulation of right angles and plane surfaces in the 1920s and 1930s is no less poetic than his use of sweeping curves and slanted surfaces in the 1950s at Ronchamp (I, PL. 381; IV, PL. 187). Although the free forms of the later works may appear highly irrational, they have a functional and acoustical logic (in his own words, *l'acoustique paysagiste*), as well founded as the austere functionalism of the early works. From 1925 to 1945, while his vocabulary of forms became more bold and varied, and gained a sculptural solidity, the spirit of his architectural aims remained

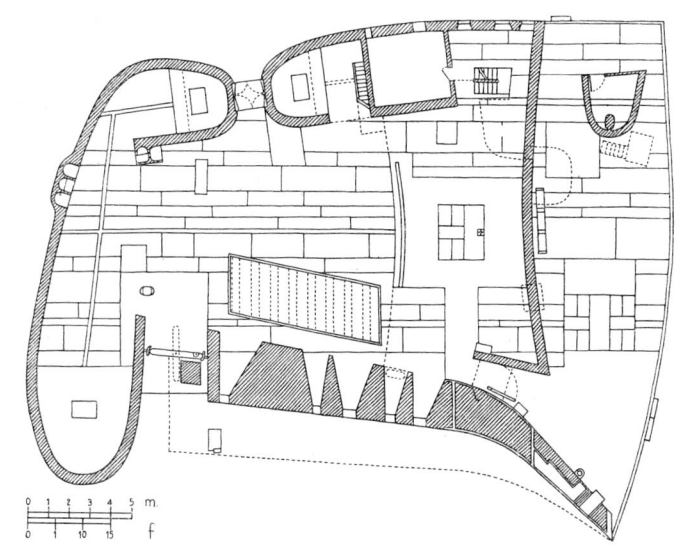

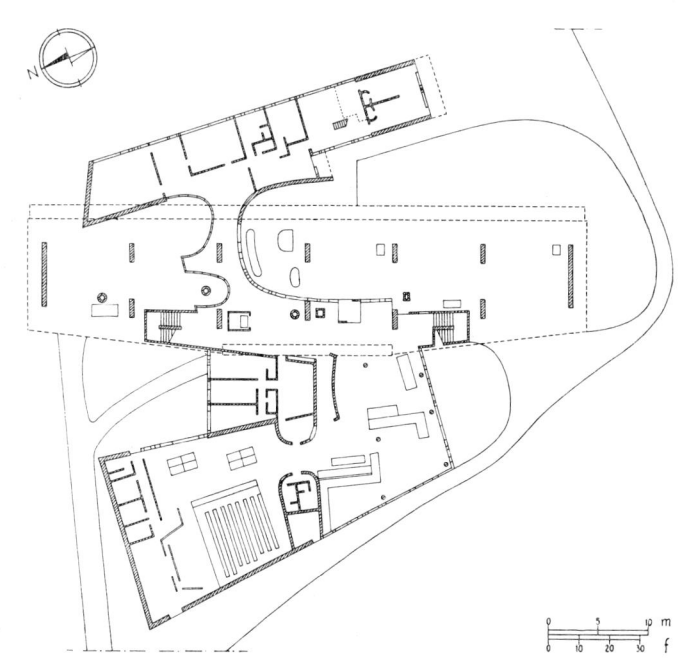

Ronchamp, Notre-Dame-du-Haut, ground plan (*from Œuvre complète*, Zurich, *1952–57*).

Paris, Cité Universitaire, Maison du Brésil, plan of the ground floor (in collaboration with L. Costa; *from Casabella, no. 248, 1961*).

unchanged. The "light-wall" of the Ronchamp chapel and the sections of undulant glass in the stark Dominican monastery of Ste-Marie de la Tourette are more lyrical realizations of the essentially functional *façade libre* (glass sections and *brises-soleil*, or sun shades) and of his preoccupation with ideal mathematical proportion.

The historical importance of Le Corbusier and the wide influence of his theories are universally acknowledged, though certain reactionary critics persist in denying the merits of his architecture in itself. Others who esteem most his cubist rationalism are disconcerted by Chandigarh and the Ronchamp chapel, which they prefer to view as lyric digressions from his fundamental principles. The housing units in Marseilles (PL. 107; I, PL. 388) revived the polemic incited in the 1930s by the Ville Radieuse, a scheme rejected by many urban planners and sociologists. For these critics Le Corbusier's response to mechanized civilization (enthusiasm according to some, distaste according to others) was purely subjective and thus without the value of critical method. The results, however, affirm the methodological worth of his ideas, which have proved a vital source for the innovations of 20th-century architecture.

PRINCIPAL WORKS. 1904–06: house at La Chaux-de-Fonds. – 1914–15: "Dom-ino" projects for prefabricated houses. – 1922–24: Paris, Ozenfant house; Auteil, double house for A. Jeanneret and La Roche; Boulogne-sur-Seine, double house for Lipchitz and Miestschaninoff. – 1925–26: Paris, Pavillon de l'Esprit Nouveau, displaying first "Voisin" plan for Paris; Pessac, workers' housing. – 1927: Stuttgart, two residences for Deutscher Werkbund exposition (PL. 105; V, PL. 109); villas at Garches (XI, PL. 354) and Carthage; project for League of Nations, Geneva. – 1929–33: Poissy, Savoye house (PL. 106; FIG. 191); Geneva, Clarté apartments; Moscow, Centrosoyus (completed 1935); first projects for the Ville Radieuse; Paris, Salvation Army hospice (Cité du Refuge; V, PL. 109; FIG. 191); Paris, Cité Universitaire, Swiss Hostel (PL. 106); project for "square spiral" museum with unlimited expansion capacity ("Musée à Croissance Illimitée"); project for Palace of the Soviets, Moscow; first city plan for Algiers; Boulogne-sur-Seine, apartment house; Macia plan for Barcelona; projects for apartment house and business center (Cité d'Affaires),

Algiers; Rentenanstalt project, Zurich; urban projects for Antwerp and Stockholm. – 1934–35: villa at Les Mathes; projects for the Algiers waterfront, Nemours (Algeria), and Barcelona; plans for a Ferme Radieuse and a cooperative village; project for workers' housing, Zurich. – 1936–37: consultant for Ministry of Education and Health, Rio de Janeiro (with L. Costa and O. Niemeyer; I, PL. 142); urban plan for Zlin, Czechoslovakia; projects for a museum of modern art (Paris), a university complex (Rio de Janeiro), and a housing unit for the Exposition Internationale of 1937 (Paris). – Paris, Pavillon des Temps Nouveaux; urban plan "Paris '37"; "Ilot Insalubre" city plan (no. 6); project for Centre National de Rejouissances Populaires for 100,000 persons. – 1938: urban scheme for Buenos Aires. – 1939: plans for a sports center and for refugee barracks. – 1940: armament factory ("Usine-verte"); designs for prefabricated Murondin buildings. – 1942–43: final plan for Algiers; studies concerning the employment of land and regional reorganization; founding of ASCORAL; publication of *La Charte d'Athènes*. – 1945–46: urban planning for Saint-Dié, Saint-Gaudens, and La Rochelle-Pallice. – 1946–47: Marseilles, large housing block (*unité d'habitation*; completed 1952); collaboration on project for seat of United Nations, New York. – 1948: project for subterranean basilica at Sainte-Baume; wood sculpture, in collaboration with the craftsman Savina. – 1950: city plans for Marseilles, Bogotá, and İzmir; studies for Ronchamp and Chandigarh; drawings for tapestries; publication of *Le Modulor*. – 1951–58: project for Quartier Rotterdam, Strasbourg; master plan for Chandigarh, capital of Punjab; Nantes-Rezé, apartment block; Ahmadabad, Shodhan house (PL. 107), Millowners' Association Building (I, PLS. 387, 424), and Museum of Knowledge (first realization of his "square spiral" plan); Chandigarh, High Courts of Justice (PL. 108); Ronchamp, completion of Notre-Dame-du-Haut (FIG. 193); Eveux-sur-Arbresle, Dominican monastery of Ste-Marie de la Tourette (FIG. 192); Neuilly, Jaoul houses; Tokyo, National Museum of Western Art; Meaux, five housing units; project for suburban housing (with J. Prouvé); Briey-en-Forêt, housing units; Berlin, Interbau housing block; Brussels, Philips Pavilion for International Exposition of 1958 (V, PL. 192, FIG. 291); Paris, Cité Universitaire, Maison du Brésil (with L. Costa; FIG. 194).

BIBLIOG. *Writings of Le Corbusier*: a. *Collections*: J. Badovici, ed., Œuvre complète, 8 vols., Paris, 1924–38 (discontinued); W. Boesinger et al., ed., Œuvre complète, 6 vols., Zurich, 1929–57 (in course of publication); Creation is a Patient Search, trans. J. Palmes, New York, 1960 (pub. as My Work, London, 1960). b. *Single works*: Étude sur le mouvement d'art décoratif en Allemagne, La Chaux-de-Fonds, 1911; Après le Cubisme, Paris, 1918 (with A. Ozenfant); Vers une architecture, Paris, 1923 (Eng. trans., F. Etchells, New York, 1927); L'art décoratif d'aujourd'hui, Paris, 1925 (2d ed., 1959); La peinture moderne, Paris, 1925 (with A. Ozenfant); Urbanisme, Paris, 1925 (Eng. trans., F. Etchells, The City of Tomorrow and Its Planning, New York, 1929); Almanach de l'architecture moderne, Paris, 1926; Une maison — un palais, Paris, 1928; Précisions sur un état présent de l'architecture et de l'urbanisme, Paris, 1930; Croisade ou Le crépuscule des académies, Paris, 1932; Aircraft, London, 1935; La ville radieuse, Boulogne-sur-Seine, 1935; Quand les cathédrales étaient blanches: Voyage aux pays des timides, Paris, 1937 (Eng. trans., F. E. Hyslop, New York, 1947); Des canons, des munitions? Merci! Des logis . . . s.v.p., Boulogne-sur-Seine, 1938; Le lyrisme des temps nouveaux et l'urbanisme, Colmar, 1939; Les constructions "Murondins," Paris, 1941; Destin de Paris, Paris, 1941; Sur les quatre routes, Paris, 1941 (Eng. trans., D. Todd, London, 1947); La maison des hommes, Paris, 1942 (with F. de Pierrefeu; Eng. trans., The Home of Man, London, 1948); La Charte d'Athènes, Paris, 1943 (introd. by J. Giraudoux; repr., Paris, 1957); Entretien avec les étudiants des écoles d'architecture, Paris, 1943 (Eng. trans., P. Chase, New York, 1961); Les trois établissements humains, Paris, 1944; Manière de penser d'urbanisme, Paris, 1945; Propos d'urbanisme, Paris, 1945 (Eng. trans., C. Entwistle, Concerning Town Planning, London, 1947); Plan Director para Buenos Aires, Buenos Aires, 1947; United Nations Headquarters, New York, 1947; New World of Space, New York, 1948; Le Modulor, Boulogne-sur-Seine, 1950 (Eng. trans., P. de Francia and A. Bostock, Cambridge, Mass., 1954); Poésie sur Alger, Paris, 1950; Une petite maison, Zurich, 1954; Le Modulor II, Boulogne-sur-Seine, 1955 (Eng. trans., P. de Francia and A. Bostock, Cambridge, Mass., 1958); Le poème de l'angle droit (19 lithographs in color), Paris, 1955; Les plans Le Corbusier de Paris, Paris, 1956; Von der Poesie des Bauens (selected texts), Zurich, 1957; Ronchamp, Zurich, 1957 (Eng. trans., J. Cullen, The Chapel at Ronchamp, London, 1957); Matisse, Léger, Le Corbusier: Moderne Kirchen (selected texts), Zurich, 1958. Among the prefaces, that to F. Cali and L. Hervé, La plus grande aventure du monde (l'architecture de Cîteaux), Grenoble, 1956, is of particular interest. Reviews edited by Le Corbusier with others: L'esprit nouveau, Paris, 1920–25 (28 nos.); Plans (1930–32).

Works on Le Corbusier: S. Giedion, Le Corbusier et l'architecture contemporaine, CahArt, V, 1930, pp. 204–15; F. de Pierrefeu, Le Corbusier et P. Jeanneret, Paris, 1932; L'arch. d'aujourd'hui, IV, 10, 1933, 38, 1948 (special nos.); A. Roth, Zwei Häuser in Stuttgart, Stuttgart, 1934; L. Mumford, The Culture of Cities, New York, 1938; J. M. Richards, An Introduction to Modern Architecture, Harmondsworth, 1940; M. Gauthier, Le Corbusier, or the Architect in the Service of Man, Paris, 1944; S. Giedion, Space, Time and Architecture, Cambridge, Mass., 1944 (3d ed. 1956); Unité d'habitation à Marseille de Le Corbusier, L'homme et l'architecture, 11–14, 1947, special no.; S. Papadaki et al., Le Corbusier: Architect, Painter, Writer, New York, 1948; B. Zevi, Saper vedere l'architettura, Turin, 1948; J. Alazard, Le Corbusier, Florence, Paris, 1950 (Eng. trans., New York, 1960); L'unité de habitation de Marseille (Point, 38), Mulhouse, 1950 (Eng. trans., G. Sainsbury, The Marseille Block, London, 1953); B. Zevi, Storia dell'architettura moderna, Turin, 1950; G. C. Argan, Walter Gropius e la Bauhaus, Turin, 1951; A. Gatti, L'abitazione nell'architettura di Le Corbusier, Rome, 1953; Architecture du bonheur, Forces vives, 5–7, 1955, special no. (with a text by Le Corbusier: L'urbanisme est une clé); Les Chapelles du Rosaire à Vence par Henri Matisse et de Notre-Dame-du-Haut à Ronchamp par Le Corbusier (L'art sacré, 1–2, special no.), Paris, 1955; E. M. Fry, Chandigarh: New Capital City, Arch. Record, CXVII, 1955, pp. 139–48; E. N. Rogers, Il metodo di Le Corbusier, e la forma nella "Chapelle de Ronchamp," Casabella, 207, 1955, pp. 2–30; A. E. Brinckmann, Baukunst, Tübingen, 1956; Chandigarh: Le Corbusier architecte, Aujourd'hui, VII, 1956, pp. 36–47; Construction en pays chauds: Chandigarh, Arch. d'aujourd'hui, XXVII, 66, 1956, pp. 172–76; P. Francastel, Art et technique, Paris, 1956; S. Giedion, Architektur und Gemeinschaft, Tagebuch einer Entwicklung, Hamburg, 1956 (Eng. trans., J. Tyrwhitt, Architecture, You and Me, Cambridge, Mass., 1958); A. Henze, Ronchamp, Recklinghausen, 1956; G. Samonà, Lettura della cappella a Ronchamp, L'Architettura, II, 1956, pp. 118–23; H. Baur, Ronchamp und die neuere kirchliche Architektur, Werk, 44, 1957, pp. 187–89; A. Henze, Le Corbusier, Berlin, 1957; Kunsthaus, Le Corbusier (cat.), Zürich, 1957 (biblio.); Le Corbusier: Chapelle Notre-Dame-du-Haut de Ronchamp, Cahiers Forces Vives, Paris, 1957; Unité d'habitation in Nantes-Rezé, Bauen und Wohnen, XII, 1957, pp. 1–7; H. Perruchot, Le Corbusier, Paris, 1958; P. Blake, The Master Builders, New York, 1960, pp. 3–150; W. Boesiger and E. Girsberger, Le Corbusier, Zurich, 1960; F. Choay, Le Corbusier, New York, 1960; J. Alazard and J. P. Hebert, De la fenêtre au pan de verre dans l'œuvre de Le Corbusier, Paris, 1961; Musée d'art moderne, Le Corbusier (cat.), Paris, 1962.

Maurice BESSET

Illustrations: PLS. 105–108; 5 figs. in text.

LEDOUX, CLAUDE NICOLAS. French architect (b. Dormans, Marne, 1736; d. Paris, Nov. 19, 1806.) From 1764 to 1789 Ledoux created buildings of a fresh style, impressive scale, and dramatic settings which appealed strongly to Parisian society (particularly Madame du Barry) and made his services, as one of France's foremost men of artistic genius, sought after by rulers in Germany and Russia. His early buildings reflect the doctrines of his teacher Jacques-François Blondel and the work of Ange-Jacques Gabriel (q.v.) at the Ministère de la Marine (cf. Ledoux's Hôtel Montmorency, Paris, 1765–70) and the Petit Trianon of Versailles (cf. Ledoux's series of small cube houses: Guimard, 1770; Louveciennes, 1771; St-Germain, 1772). In this sense Ledoux's style was similar to that of several contemporaries (J. Gondoin, J.-D. Antoine, F.-J. Bélanger), but his dramatic flair (illusionistic garden of Hôtel d'Hallwyl, Paris, 1764–67) and superior feeling for scale and unity of design (cf. Hôtel d'Hallwyl with Antoine's Hôtel de Fleury) makes his work distinctive even in this early period.

After 1775, however, Ledoux's designs became increasingly powerful and original, infused with a new spirit of fantasy which may be derived from his contemporary Etienne-Louis Boullée (particularly his Hôtel de Brunoy, 1772), but which only Ledoux was able to realize in major monuments. Ledoux's bolder style, appearing first in the buildings designed for the royal saltworks at Arc-et-Senans (1775–79), is exemplified by the differences remarked between his theater designs for Besançon and Marseilles (1775 and 1784, respectively) and between the above-mentioned early and the later cube houses (Jarnac, Espinchal, 1780; Saisseval, 1786). The richness of the new style is strikingly demonstrated in the 42 different designs produced for the tollhouses of Paris (1784–89; V, PL. 422), and its capacity for development is clear from a comparison of the Hôtel Thélusson (1780) with the Maisons Hosten (1787), both located in Paris. Further progress by Ledoux in developing this style was precluded by the Revolution, which enforced his permanent retirement from active practice.

With no commissions to stimulate and further shape his style, Ledoux spent the last seventeen years of his life creating an ideal and theoretical formulation of its principles, in the form of an ambitious publication entitled *L'Architecture considérée sous le rapport de l'Art, des Moeurs et de la Législation* (1804; a "second" volume published posthumously, 1847). In this literary effort, Ledoux idealized his past work both by changing the designs of his earlier buildings (pre-1775) to fit his new style and by embellishing and enlarging other past commissions (Maupertuis?; I, PL. 308), particularly the buildings at Arc-et-Senans, which became the nucleus of an enormous ideal city called Chaux.

Although both the designs and text are a romantic statement of ideas better expressed in his buildings, it was this book which rescued Ledoux from the general disregard history had accorded his generation of architects. Ledoux's fantastic designs for workers' houses and factories were perceived anew in terms of a Bauhaus functionalism, and he was consequently acclaimed as the first "modern" architect, the initiator of ideas culminating in the work of Le Corbusier (E. Kaufmann, *Von Ledoux bis Le Corbusier*, Vienna, 1933). Although sustained at a popular level, this theory has been discarded by latter-day historians in their attempt to characterize more accurately, and thereby restore, Ledoux's true genius.

BIBLIOG. L. Hautecoeur, Histoire de l'architecture classique en France, IV, Paris, 1952; E. Kaufmann, Three Revolutionary Architects, Boullée, Ledoux, and Lequeu, Tr. Am. Philosophical Soc., N.S., XLII, 3, 1952, pp. 431–554; W. Herrmann, The Problem of Chronology in Claude-Nicolas Ledoux's Engraved Work, AB, XLII, 1960, pp. 191–210; J. Langner Ledoux's Redaktion der eigenen Entwürfe für die Veröffentlichung, ZfKg, XXIII, 1960, pp. 136–166.

Bates LOWRY

LÉGER, FERNAND. French cubist and postcubist painter (b. Argentan, Normandy, Feb. 4, 1881; d. Gif-sur-Yvette, Seine-et-Oise, Aug. 17, 1955). In 1900 Léger moved to Paris, where he made his living as an architect's draftsman. After a year's military service in 1902–03, he studied informally in the studios of Léon Gérôme and Gabriel Ferrier and from 1906 to 1910 gave himself over almost entirely to painting. By 1911, having met the painters and writers of the cubist movement, Léger had defined his personal variant of cubism, made public the following year in a one-man exhibition at the Galerie Kahnweiler in Paris. Mobilized in 1914, he served as a stretcher-bearer until he was gassed and hospitalized for several months in 1917. His fame grew rapidly after the war with the development of his mature style, the mural-scale paintings incorporating machine motifs in a crisp, bas-relief manner of geometric clarity and strong color.

Léger's first major ventures outside the field of easel painting were his designs for the Swedish Ballet in 1921–22 and, in collaboration with Dudley Murphey, the famous film *Ballet mécanique* of 1923–24. Although Léger spent most of his life in Paris, he traveled widely and lived in the United States from 1940 to 1946. Soon after his death, his memorial and many major works were installed in the Musée Fernand Léger at Biot.

Léger was above all a painter of public scale, both in his social attitude and his broad decorative style. His special talents were recognized by Le Corbusier, for whom he did his first true murals in that architect's pavilion at the Exposition des Arts Décoratifs in Paris in 1925. After World War II he was given a number of major commissions, including mosaics for the façade of Notre-Dame in Assy (1949) and for the memorial at Bastogne (1950), stained glass for the Church of Sacré-Cœur in Audincourt (1951) and a church in Courfaivre, Switzerland (1954), and murals for the United Nations General Assembly auditorium (1952).

In spite of activity in other media, especially painted ceramics, Léger's reputation was established by his large oil paintings, among them *The Card Players* (1917; Otterlo, Rijksmus. Kröller-Müller), *The City* (1919; Philadelphia, Mus. of Art); *Three Women* (*Le Grand Déjeuner*; 1921; New York, Mus. of Mod. Art), *Divers on Yellow Background* (1941; Chicago, Art Inst.), *Leisure* (1944–49; Paris, Mus. d'Art Mod.), and *The Great Parade* (1954; New York, Guggenheim Mus.). One of the rare artists receptive to and genuinely inspired by popular taste, Léger embodied in his art both the iconography and the expression of modern urban and technological culture. Figures and abstract objects of his own creation float in the shallow spaces of what he called his "animated landscapes." The individual forms, planar and metallic in their modeling — he was heir to David and Ingres in this aspect of his work — and the intense primary colors produce a visual cacophony suggesting the dynamic qualities of the machine age (V, PL. 124).

MAJOR ARTICLES. Les origines de la peinture et sa valeur représentative, Montjoie, 8, 1913, p. 7; 9–10, 1913, p. 9 ff.; L'esthétique de la machine, Little Rev. 9, 1923, pp. 45–49.

BIBLIOG. M. Couturier et al., Fernand Léger, Montreal, 1945; D. Cooper, Fernand Léger et le nouvel espace, Geneva, 1949; K. Kuh, Léger, Urbana, Ill., 1953; P. Descargues, Fernand Léger, Paris, 1955.

Robert L. HERBERT

LEHMBRUCK, WILHELM. German sculptor (b. Meiderich, near Duisburg, Jan. 4, 1881; d. Mar. 25, 1919). Wilhelm Lehmbruck was the fourth of eight children born to a Rhineland miner. His artistic training began at the Kunstgewerbeschule in Düsseldorf (1895–99). From 1901 to 1907 he was an assistant in sculpture at the Düsseldorf Kunstakademie. A handsome, sensitive youth, his aristocratic bearing and dress belied his modest background. Successful from the beginning, he received numerous awards and, in 1905, won a first prize for sculpture, after which he traveled in Italy. In 1907 he sent several works to the Salon of the Société Nationale des Beaux-Arts in Paris and in 1910, with his young wife, went to Paris to live. Except for another trip to Italy in 1912, he remained in Paris until the outbreak of World War I, when he moved to Berlin.

His early work was in the academic tradition, but by 1905 he had come under the influence of Rodin, especially in his choice of subject matter and pose and in his treatment of surface. *The Bather* (1905; Düsseldorf, Kunstakademie) is a naturalistically modeled nude bending to touch her leg. To capture the fleeting gesture and convey varied emotions, he posed his figures unconventionally — bending, standing with one foot raised, kneeling, and even crawling. Lehmbruck's characteristic qualities began to appear in these early years, particularly his capacity for evoking mood and a sense of anxiety. *Mother and Child* (1907; Essen, Folkwang Mus.) depicts a crouching nude gazing with loving fondness at the infant on her lap. Emotion bordering on the sentimental is expressed in *Sorrowing Woman* (1909; Duisburg, Städt. Kunstmus. und Lehmbruck-Samml.) and *Memories* (1909; Essen, Folkwang Mus.). The life-size figure *Mankind* (1909) is reminiscent of a Michelangelo *Slave*. In Paris Lehmbruck became acquainted with and admired the classicism of Maillol. The *Standing Woman* of 1910 (New York, Mus. of Mod. Art), one of his most important works, is posed in the manner of the *Venus de Milo*, with inflected hips and draped thighs. The body is classically smooth and rounded, but the treatment of the head is delicately impressionistic, with soft curls and lowered eyelids. Although in a transitional style, this work marks Lehmbruck, at the age of 29, as a major sculptor. It was followed by the *Frau Lehmbruck* (1910; Stuttgart, Coll. Frau A. Lehmbruck), a bust in which his former classical restraint begins to be modified: in the torso, by subtle enlargement of the throat and breasts; in the head, by emphasis upon the prominent forehead, the deep-set eyes, and a moody, introspective expression. This portrait of his beautiful wife, at about the time of her first pregnancy (she bore Lehmbruck two sons, one of whom, Manfred, was to design a museum at Duisburg for his father's works), reveals the sculptor's strong attachment to his family, as do numerous drawings and two sculptures of infants (1910).

At this point in his career Lehmbruck's mature style began to emerge rapidly. The sentiment of the late German Gothic was part of his Rhenish heritage; moreover, he was influenced by the Art Nouveau sculpture of George Minne, and his drawings are suggestive of the winding, moodily expressive linear patterns of Munch. From such disparate influences, including the work of Rodin and Maillol, this hypersensitive and inner-oriented young sculptor produced a masterpiece in the over-life-size *Kneeling Woman* (1911; New York, Mus. of Mod. Art). An extremely tall figure, with gracefully posed arms, long neck, and bent head, the body retains the classical form of the *Standing Woman*, although here the proportions are gently attenuated. The bemused countenance inspires in the spectator a feeling of melancholy. Among many fine sculptures of the productive period that followed, perhaps the finest is the *Standing Youth* (1913; New York, Mus. of Mod. Art), a thin giant whose crossed arms, raised leg, and enigmatic frown invest him with great power. In Berlin during the war, Lehmbruck produced the tragic monument *The Fallen* (1915-16; Coll. Frau A. Lehmbruck), the figure of a crouching war hero whose lowered head touches the ground. The *Seated Youth* (1918; Düsseldorf, Kunstakademie), formerly a public monument and his last major work, is on a related theme. Deeply troubled in the aftermath of the war, and in poor health, Lehmbruck took his own life on Mar. 25, 1919. In addition to his sculpture, he left a large number of drawings and etchings.

BIBLIOG. P. Westheim, Wilhelm Lehmbruck, Potsdam, 1919; A. Hoff, Wilhelm Lehmbruck, Berlin, 1961.

Henry R. Hope

LELY, PETER. English painter (b. Soest, Westphalia, Oct. 14, 1618; d. London, Dec. 7, 1680). Lely was trained in Haarlem under Pieter Fransz. de Grebber, became a master in the Haarlem Guild of St. Luke (1637), and afterward went to England (1641 or 1643), where by the 1650s he had established the most extensive practice of any English portrait painter. Following the Restoration (1660), Lely became the first painter since Van Dyck to attain a position of social eminence, upon his appointment as principal court painter by Charles II; he was subsequently pensioned and knighted. By 1670 he was directing a large studio, in which the young Nicolas de Largillière worked as his assistant. The first painter in England whose work survives in great quantities, Lely was also one of the first nonprincely collectors of paintings and drawings. His collection, begun during the Commonwealth, was sold after his death at the first spectacular picture auction in the Western world.

Although nothing is known of Lely's earliest subjects, those painted in England were landscapes and historical pieces; his first portraits, such as the *Blind Harper* (Northamptonshire, Althorp, Coll. Earl Spencer), were influenced by William Dobson and Isaac Fuller. During the Commonwealth he painted what might be called "subject pieces," but after the Restoration confined himself to portraiture. Patronage by the Earl of Northumberland in the 1640s may have given Lely the opportunity to study the Earl's Van Dyck collection; Van Dyck's influence is marked, for instance, in *The Younger Children of Charles I* (1647; Sussex, Petworth House), embodying the "portrait in a landscape" motif that was to dominate English painting through the 18th century. In contrast to the Van Dyck style was Lely's "classical" pictorial manner (later taken up by Reynolds), initiated in his *Henry Sidney, later Earl of Romney* (1650-55; Kent, Penshurst Place, Coll. Viscount De L'Isle) — "classical" solely because of its introduction of antique attributes.

In the 1650s Lely produced a series of portraits in his so-called "austere Commonwealth style," characterized by subjects of somewhat gloomy countenance, often complemented by a large, decorative sculptural piece. During this period he began — at least in his female portraits — to generalize and flatter the sitter. At the same time he developed the group composition, which became a fixed tradition in English portrait painting. With the 1660s and the Restoration Lely evolved a new style, sustained for the rest of his career; its voluptuous and languorous tone, reflecting the fashionable court life of the period, was imparted with ever-refined and subtle technique and a formal catalogue of poses (which, in fact, he eventually numbered). The late portrait series such as the "Windsor Beauties" (1660s; Middlesex, Hampton Court Palace, Royal Colls.) and the "Admirals" (1666-67; Greenwich, London, Nat. Maritime Mus.) display loose, free brushwork, transparent color overlays, emphasis on chiaroscuro and decorative effects, and high color. Throughout his work Lely's style was decidedly international, rather than personal or English, and some of his portraits are indistinguishable from work done on the Continent about this time. Although technically proficient, he cannot be judged a truly creative artist; however, his businesslike approach toward his art established the cast of the successful portrait painter in England until the romantic period.

REPRESENTATIVE WORKS. *Charles I and James, Duke of York*, 1647, Middlesex, Syon House, Coll. Duke of Northumberland. - *Lady Dering*, 1651, Sussex, Parham Park, Coll. Hon. Clive Pearson. - *Sir William Compton*, ca. 1651, Surrey, Ham House. - *The Duet*, 1654, Gloucestershire, Batsford Park, Coll. Lord Dulverton. - *Europa and the Bull*, ca. 1655, Derbyshire, Trustees of the Chatsworth Settlement. - *Nymphs at a Fountain*, ca. 1655, London, Dulwich College Picture Gallery. - *The Perryer Family*, 1655, Kent, Chequers Court. - *The Family of Charles Dormer, Earl of Carnarvon*, ca. 1658-59, London, Coll. Sir John Coote. - *The Family of Sir John Cotton, Bart.*, 1660, Oxford, Brewis Coll. - *Elizabeth, Countess of Northumberland*, 1660s, Middlesex, Hampton Court Palace, Royal Colls. - *Admiral Sir Jeremy Smith*, 1666-67, Greenwich, London, Nat. Maritime Mus. - *Sir John Harman*, 1666-67 (VI, PL. 438).

BIBLIOG. C. H. Collins Baker, Sir Peter Lely, Art J., 1911, pp. 304-09; C. H. Collins Baker, Lely and the Stuart Portrait Painters, London, 1912; C. King, The "Flaggmen," Naval Portraits by Sir Peter Lely, Connoisseur, November, 1938, pp. 227-33; T. Borenius, H. Ogden, and M. Ogden, Sir Peter Lely's Collection (with lists), BM, August, 1943, pp. 185-91, June, 1944, p. 154; Lely (English Master Painters Series), London, 1951; R. B. Beckett, Peter Lely, London, 1951; E. K. Waterhouse, Painting in Britain, 1530 to 1750, Harmondsworth, 1953, pp. 62-67.

* *

LE NAIN, ANTOINE (1588-1648), LOUIS (1593-1648), MATHIEU (1607-77). Family of painters, born at Laon-en-Vermandois (Picardy), between Paris and Flanders. The sons of a *sergent royal*, "they were trained by a foreign painter... at Laon... for a year. From there, they went to Paris where they perfected their art, and established themselves... living in the same house... in a perfect union" (Claude L'Eleu, Histoire de Laon, 1711-23, ms. in Laon library; cf. Valabrègue, 1904, pp. 9-11). P. J. Mariette noted that the brothers Le Nain "were so similar in their work that it was practically impossible to distinguish what each had done on a particular painting, inasmuch as they all worked together" (*Abecedario...*, ed. P. de Chennevières and A. de Montaiglon, Paris, 1851-60). An idea of the appearance of their studio is conveyed in a painting, *The Studio* (ca. 1630; London, Coll. Marquess of Bute; also, drawing in Leningrad, The Hermitage). The painter represented appears to be Mathieu; the model, Louis; the seated man, Antoine; and the portrait of an old man, that of their father. The attribution of this painting to Antoine is uncertain.

There are neither many nor particularly significant dates for a biography of the Le Nain brothers. In 1629 Antoine was a master painter at Saint-Germain-des-Prés, then a suburb of Paris; in 1630 he was again cited as "maître," his brothers being mentioned as fellow painters; L'Eleu gives 1632 as the year in which they began to achieve wider repute; and in 1633 Mathieu was a master painter of the city of Paris and a lieutenant in the city militia. In 1646, the three men agreed to leave all their property to the last to survive. In March, 1648, the newly founded Royal Academy of Painting and Sculpture received the brothers as academicians of the second class; Louis and Antoine were mentioned as "peintres de bambochades." But in May both Louis, 55, and Antoine, 60, died. In the following year, Mathieu was mentioned as a portraitist when he was twice noted as in arrears with his dues for the Academy. L'Eleu mentions that in 1662 Mathieu corresponded with other artists of the Academy, but in 1663 he no longer appeared on the list of the members. In 1667 Mathieu was referred to as the owner of La Jumelle, a small farm he had inherited. In 1668 he willed his substantial property to a nephew, but he later annulled this bequest. Chevalier of the Order of St. Michael, "Peintre du Roi," and member of the Academy, Mathieu Le Nain died in 1677 at the age of seventy. The inventory of his house revealed an austere interior with many pictures, both finished and incomplete, predominantly on religious themes.

The Le Nains pose a complex problem for art historians. Definition of three separate but intimately related artistic personalities is understandably difficult. Their life spans, ranging from 1588 to 1677, comprehend a century of rapid evolution in painting, and the problem is therefore complicated further. The attribution of works is also extremely involved, for their activity encompassed both works painted by a single brother and close collaborations.

Moreover, the early critics are divided in their opinion. Mariette said "they painted *bamboches* in the French style. They had beautiful brush technique and were able to blend their colors artfully and to produce paintings that were as pleasing by their technique as by the naïveté of the characters which they introduced." On the other hand, André Félibien considered them portraitists and historical painters, "but in a manner with little nobility, frequently representing simple subjects without beauty... subjects of common and often ridiculous activities" (*Entretiens sur les vies et les ouvrages des plus excellens peintres...*, London, new ed., 1705, pp. 170-71). Finally, for L'Eleu, the Le Nains "had different personalities. Antoine excelled in miniatures and in portraits *en raccourcis*. Louis, the younger brother, was successful with half-length and bust portraits. Mathieu... was for the grand tableaux, such as those representing religious mysteries, the martyrdom of saints, battles, and the like." In addition to problems arising from the discordant early criticism, there are others created by the disappearance of many works, some fully documented. There are known only 15 paintings dated and signed "Le Nain"; none is signed with a first name. Certain of the signatures are disputed, and some of the dates are incomplete or doubtful. Ten works dated between 1641 and 1648, which must be variously assigned among the brothers, are the reference points about which the obscure artistic activities of this family must be reconstructed.

The influence of the foreign painter in Laon (who was not necessarily Flemish, but perhaps Italianate in his art) mentioned by L'Eleu should not be exaggerated. Nor should it even be assumed that he was any more influential over Antoine because he was the eldest brother. This early tutelage in Laon was less important to the formation of the style of the Le Nains than was the period of their studies in Paris, before and after 1629. Saint-Germain-des-Prés was the center of a colony of artists, in part Dutch and Flemish, including numerous engravers, whose work presented varied influences. These realistic engravers copied or interpreted works by Villamena, Valentin, Callot, Rembrandt, Both, Vorsterman, and Adriaen van Ostade, in somewhat awkward fashion but with much freedom and animation. This style can also be seen in the compositions of Hulpeau, which were more expressive than those of the Le Nains, and in the work of Jacques Lagniet (later, ca. 1660), who was more vulgar. Abraham Bosse was closer to the Le Nain brothers by reason of his careful attention to composition and execution, his honest realism, and his bourgeois sobriety. Like their contemporary Baugin, who painted both still lifes and larger religious works, the Le Nains painted subjects of various types. Their portraits, such as the signed likeness of a noblewoman — perhaps the Marquise de Forbin — in Avignon (1644?; Mus. Calvet; copy?), have a frankness of characterization that brings to mind the contemporaneous, but more Flemish, Philippe de Champaigne. There are also similarities with the provincial art of Richard Tassel of Langres, whose *Cathérine de Montholon* (Dijon, Mus. B.A.) is, however, a more incisive portrait than the Le Nain in the Musée Calvet.

The influence of the Netherlands on the environment of the Le Nains is illustrated by certain works of, for example, Sébastien Bourdon, who painted genre scenes in Flemish style, and of the pseudo-De Vlieger, who was surely French. The relationship of Spanish art, despite some arguable similarities to Velázquez, cannot be established; and similarly, the Italian: one of the brothers — Louis according to P. Jamot (1929), Mathieu to Thuillier (1958) — was nicknamed "le Romain," but, as for all French art of the period, the problem of Italian influence remains equally unresolved.

The personality of Antoine is connected with the art of the Netherlands; Blunt (1954) cites the influence of A. Pietersz. van de Venne and Hendrick Avercamp. G. Isarlo (1938) dates *The Supper at Emmaus* (Louvre) and *The Studio* (London, Coll. Marquess of Bute) in the Laon period. The decade 1630-40 (with patent influence from Brouwer, Van Craesbeeck, and Hals) has been cited by Isarlo as the period of the small paintings of children on wood or copper, *The Grace* (*Bénédicité*; Paris, Coll. David-Weill), some group scenes (London, Nat. Gall.; Lugano, Thyssen-Bornemisza Coll.), the *Family Gathering* (PL. 112), and the *Portraits in an Interior*, both in the Louvre (Isarlo does not accept the dates 1642 and 1647 for the last two). In these pictures the perspective is unconvincing. The figures of a group, bunched before a neutral ground in one or two rows, face the viewer directly or assume degrees of profile that create a slight illusion of depth. They are individually stiff, often awkwardly seated; the hands are too small; the rough-hewn faces are too large in proportion to the bodies; and the eyes are set too far from the noses. All the figures, whether peasants or townspeople, are posed as if sitting for portraits, even when the scene represents a concert, a dance, or a meal. These group studies often include authentic portraits, ingenuous and good-humored, but at times they approach caricature. The manner is miniaturist, though it is varied by broad accents. The color scale, predominantly in gradations of brown, also includes pinks, lively reds, and white.

After 1640 (under the influence of Teniers, according to Isarlo) the lighting in Antoine's works is rendered with greater contrast. The draperies are frequently more ample and arranged with more elegant folds, as in the cape of *The Flageolet Player* (London, Vict. and Alb.) or the sumptuous materials of the costumes in *The Young Musicians* (London, Coll. Lord Aldenham). Antoine was impelled toward a new style by his brothers, who may have collaborated in some of his works. As he grew more audacious, he increased the size of his paintings. Yet the large full-length portrait of the Marquis de Troisvilles (1644; Rueil, Seine-et-Oise, Coll. Comtesse de Montréal), in the manner of Frans Pourbus the Younger, is still minutely executed and lacks vitality. Essentially, Antoine must be considered an artist in the old style, *petit-bourgeois* in taste, and of limited range.

Louis Le Nain, in the opinion of Isarlo, was certainly influenced by Pieter Aertsen, Bruegel, and Bassano in the Laon period and later, in Italy, by Caravaggesque and Bassanesque painters. Blunt has indicated possible contact with Pieter van Laer, in Paris (ca. 1626) or in Italy (between 1626 and 1630?), and with Italians who had worked in Paris, such as O. Gentileschi (1626). Certain Italianate works available to Louis in Paris, for example those of Valentin, have also been suggested as an influence.

The genius of Louis is attested by the solidity, sincerity, and warmth of his works, such as the 1644 portrait in Avignon, mentioned above, the *Young Men* in Brussels, and especially the genre scenes, so different from the typical anecdotal pictures of the period.

The paintings from 1630 to 1640, of medium size and representing religious subjects (*The Supper at Emmaus* and *The Last Supper* in the Louvre), reveal an Italian influence in the strong lighting, the movement, the studio models, and in details taken from the antique such as sandals and amphoras. *The Forge* (Louvre) is a night scene with a slight suggestion of Bassano; the pale flames of the hearth set the tone of the picture against a deep background, with a play of rose, blond tints, browns, blues, and greenish tones. All the figures are relaxed and waiting. The execution is fluid, with visible retouching and erasures as if the painting were an improvisation.

The Cart of 1641 (PL. 111) is kind of pendant to *The Forge*: the dimensions are similar, and the possibilities of color and lighting are again investigated. Here, however, the scene is outdoors, with a wan sunlight in humid atmosphere picking out light reflections in the shadow of the shed. The color harmonies range from blond to gray, red, or pink. The execution, vigorous in the foreground, is modulated into bare suggestions of form in other areas. Treated in a style reminiscent of miniatures, this is one of the first French landscapes; its poetry foreshadows that of Corot. The clusters of figures are ably disposed around a central void, and the girl with the brass caldron anticipates the mood of Chardin. Other larger and later paintings are connected with *The Cart: Peasants in front of a House* (Boston, Mus. of Fine Arts), *The Resting Chevalier* (London, Vict. and Alb.), *The Dairywoman's Family* (Leningrad, The Hermitage; PL. 109) with its monumental figures, and the small painting in the same genre, the *Peasants in a Landscape* (Hartford, Wadsworth Atheneum).

About 1640 Louis painted large interior scenes such as *The Peasant Supper* (Louvre; II, PL. 182), almost a monochrome with a reddish tonality relieved by touches of blue, a puzzle pattern of spots and crisp details. In the background a child is silhouetted against the fire on the hearth; another, a little girl, is outlined in pink, her face catching the light of the fire under the shadow of her cap. The other figures, lighted from a side source, are posed on several planes facing outward. Similar lighting effects may be seen in the *Venus in Vulcan's Forge* and other works.

The Peasant Family (1642?; Louvre) is more ample and studied. The brownish tone is picked up with grays and pinks. The execution is more careful, at times drier, than in other scenes of the kind, and the lighting is more evenly distributed. There is no uniformity in the furnishings, which include crude chairs along with a fine bed in the background, nor in the social standing of the various figures placed irregularly around the table. The meal proceeds with a religious solemnity, as noted by the 19th-century critic Théophile Thoré-Burger, and the central figure, with his gaunt, dedicated face, seems to be conducting a sacred rite. In other family groups the content is less grave, for example, *The Visit to Grandmother* (Leningrad, The Hermitage; PL. 109) and *The Return from a Baptism* (1642?; Louvre).

Some works on which Louis was assisted by his brothers can be dated sometime after 1640. *The Bird Catchers* (lost; copy in Leningrad) may be one such painting or it may be largely by Mathieu, who must have had to finish the works of his older brothers, make copies of them, or execute compositions in their style. Typical instances of these inextricable collaborations are two large paintings conceived as pendants, which, though of Flemish inspiration, are of a French stiffness and boldness of style. Against a gray-blue sky and a low-lying chalky landscape, the procession of the ram (Philadelphia, Mus. of Art) and that of the wine or of the fattened calf (Paris, Gall. Simon) advance; the figures are arranged as if in a frieze: bourgeois, peasants, lively children, a violinist, a blind hurdy-gurdy player. The first and the better of the two paintings, with a fine landscape and silvery color harmonies, is by Louis and Mathieu; the second and later is harder, more cursory in execution and garish in color; it is by Mathieu. The *Bacchus and Ariadne* (Paris, private coll.), recently discovered, is almost certainly by Louis. Both Louis and Mathieu worked on the *Venus in Vulcan's Forge* of 1641 (PL. 114); the luminosity is Louis's; the varied and vigorous tonality is Mathieu's; and certain seminude figures showing the influence of Simon Vouet constitute a new direction, probably on the part of Mathieu. The same tendencies occur in *The Birth of the Virgin* (Paris, St-Etienne-du-Mont), in which Isarlo distinguished elements from all three brothers, and in *The Nativity* (Louvre), by Louis and Mathieu. Other recently found works are akin to the preceding two: a *Visitation* (Saint-Denis-de-Piles, near Libourne, Gironde) a *Presentation of the Virgin* (Limon, Seine-et-Oise, St-Louis-du-Temple) and a rather saccharine *St. Michael* (Nevers, St-Pierre), perhaps also collaborative works. Certain details are beautiful, but there are other parts that are heavy-handed.

For certain scholars (e.g., Thuillier, 1958) the painter of religious and historical subjects was Mathieu, not Louis. Mathieu Le Nain was the most eclectic of the brothers, the one most open to new ideas. Even before 1640 he was noted for his portraits, and the later (1646?) *Portrait of a Young Man* in the style of Van Dyck (Laon, Mus. Municipal) is an example of his work in this genre. In this period he also executed religious works, not yet in the Caravaggesque manner of *The Nativity* (New York, George Farkas Coll.), but on the order of *The Virgin and Child with St. Anne and Angels* (Rennes, Mus. B.A.), the ashen tonalities of which recall the school of Utrecht. About 1640 his personality reveals a marked sensitivity to baroque and classic traditions in painting, perhaps indicating a visit to Italy. At the same time, his work shows points of contact with Dutch genre painters such as Palamedesz, Metsu, and the Italianate Dutch artists of the court.

A Tavern Quarrel (Highnam Court, Gloucester, England, Gambier-Parry Coll.), the *Peasants' Meal* (PL. 113), and the *Young Gamblers* (Louvre; London, Royal Colls.) are rustic scenes in the style of Louis but with a baroque animation conveyed by facial expressions and bold lighting effects. In the bourgeois genre, *Le Corps de Garde* (1643?; Paris, Coll. Baroness de Berckheim) is a striking virtuoso piece (for example, the carpet), close-knit in detail and sustained in color. This work is not coherent throughout but is notable for its complicated sources of illumination: the flame in the background, the candle-light that recalls Honthorst's work, the Negro servant lighted from below, eyes gleaming in the shadow. The *Family Reunion* (Louvre), once attributed to a Dutch painter, is less intense but minutely detailed under a cold light.

After 1648 Mathieu continued in this genre with *The Backgammon Players* (PL. 110), a more emphatic work, in which the forms are modeled with black shadows, and the strong red of a cape is played against more muted tones. *The Dice Throwers* (Amsterdam, Rijksmus.), the *Youths at a Meal* (Magdeburg), and *The Family Dinner* (Toledo, Ohio, Mus. of Art) are in a similar style. In *The Dancing Lesson* (Paris, Coll. Bérard) and the *Farandole* (U.S.A., private coll.) a certain negligence in execution is compensated by the harmony of grays, pinks, and blond tints and the graceful garlands. *The Dancing Lesson* and other works of Mathieu were, in the 18th century, grouped with other paintings, including *The Piper* and *The Vintage*; these two, however, are not by Mathieu but later imitators. These superficial *bambochades* may be said to "anticipate" the 18th century, in much the same way as the work of Jean Michelin, a mediocre disciple of the Le Nains, and the somewhat younger Pierre Montallier.

By about 1660 Mathieu was following the fashion that preferred historical subjects to contemporary realism, as L'Eleu's inventory affirms. A *Nativity* (Le Bourget, Coll. Mary), formerly thought to be dated 1674 and therefore attributed to him, is now moved back to 1644, thus posing the possibility of a collaboration. A recently discovered *Entombment*, for a time attributed to Louis alone, may also be a collaboration. After 1648 religious themes recur in Mathieu's painting but with less successful effect.

The work of the Le Nain brothers must be considered within the framework of French painting from Fouquet to our time and in the light of the trends carried on by Chardin, Corot, Courbet, and Cézanne. Champfleury saw in the brothers' compositions "the austerity of Poussin"; they aspired to classicism both instinctively and in response to Italian influence, the classical ideal being more that of the bourgeoisie than of the court. They were realists both in the manner of the Dutch artists and of the French "little" masters. Their bent for improvisation resulted not only in certain faults in their works, but also in productive discoveries and a striking spontaneity. They set themselves problems, seeking better composition and rendering of light with effective gray harmonies. Louis, with his light effects, his beautiful landscapes, and his cameo faces, was the most gifted, but Mathieu, with his vigor and his clear or pearly colors, is not far inferior. Their figures vary from the ridiculous, to the monumental, to the highly animated (in the last works). The expressions — pensive, sweetly or sadly smiling — carry conviction. In the French art devoted to children the Le Nains created an appealing type. Their children, whether bourgeois or peasant, are grave, attentive, or dreamy, bringing a poetic note to the scenes of everyday life. The Le Nains conceived of the French family as a circumscribed group in which each individual, though isolated, may suggest, by a gesture or a glance, the affection that unites them all. These families clearly belong to well-defined social classes, and from servant to master each person is differentiated by dress. Although the Le Nains certainly were aware of the terrible poverty of the peasants, they preferred to paint them with an air of good health, occasionally prosperous and never extremely poor. Their scenes are inspired not by reality but by an ideal conception of peasant life. On the other hand, when they painted the bourgeoisie, they were more precise, for the subjects are actual or seeming portraits. Antoine's *petits bourgeois* contrast with those by Mathieu — aware of their power, cultivated, and at their ease. The abrupt disappearance of this art of the bourgeoisie occurred when all France was dazzled by the splendor of the court. The Le Nains liked to combine peasants and bourgeoisie in harmony, not as opposed groups but as two aspects of the Third Estate. The figures in these paintings are relaxed in body and soul, now and then to the point of lassitude, but heavy fatigue, laughter, and wild joy are absent. The poetry of the Le Nains lies in the expression of prudence, dignity, seriousness, good will, and harmony.

About 1850 the reputation of the Le Nains soared. Previously, since the 18th century, they had been considered in the category of the Dutch minor masters. Then, quite suddenly, for social and political rather than artistic reasons, there was a complete reevaluation. Champfleury particularly, who was also a native of Laon, took an interest in these forgotten provincial painters, declaring them the champions of a democratic and social realism (1862). On the basis of newly discovered documents, among which were those of Claude L'Eleu, a canon of Laon in the 18th century, Champfleury compiled the first catalogue of their works (1861). In 1904 appeared Valabrègue's monograph, carrying on Champfleury's theories. In 1910 Robert Witt organized an exhibition at the Burlington Fine Arts Club in London and collected indispensable documentary material, now at the Courtauld Institute. In his fundamental work of 1929 P. Jamot emphasized the poetry and the benevolence of the brothers Le Nain, provided a new criterion of judgment, and essayed the difficult task of separating their personalities. This task was continued by P. Fierens (1933), while W. Weisbach (1932) clarified their position in the history of French painting. The Paris "Peintres de la réalité" exhibition (1934) confirmed their significance. The Reims Le Nain exhibition (1953) revealed the insecurity of many attributions, and recent critics, particularly G. Isarlo, have tried to elucidate some of the problems presented by the brothers' collaboration and by the various influences on their art. Wildenstein published (in 1955) the inventory compiled after the death of Mathieu. Investigation of the legal archives is bit by bit expanding and clarifying knowledge of the brothers' *œuvre*.

BIBLIOG. Champfleury (pseud. J. Fleury), Catalogue des tableaux des Le Nain (repr. from Rev. universelle des arts), Brussels, 1861; Champfleury, Les peintres de la réalité sous Louis XIII: Les frères Le Nain, Paris, 1862; A. Valabrègue, Les frères Le Nain, Paris, 1904; P. Jamot, Les Le Nain, Paris, 1929; W. Weisbach, Französische Malerei des XVII. Jahrhunderts, Berlin, 1932; P. Fierens, Les Le Nain, Paris, 1933; C. Sterling, Les peintres de la réalité en France au XVIIᵉ siècle (exhibition cat.), Paris, 1934; M. Davies, Signed Le Nains, BM, LXVI, 1935, pp. 293-94; V. N. Lazarev, Brat'ia Lenen (The Brothers Le Nain), Moscow, Leningrad, 1936; G. Isarlo, Les trois Le Nain et leur suite, La Renaissance, XXI, 1938, pp. 1-58; S. Meltzoff, The Revival of the Le Nain, AB, XXIV, 1942, pp. 259-86; A. Blunt, Art and Architecture in France, 1500-1700, Harmondsworth, 1954; G. Wildenstein, L'inventaire de Mathieu Le Nain, GBA, XLV, 1955, pp. 197-210; P. Gaudibert, Louis Le Nain et les paysans de l'ancien régime français, Europe, 123, 1956, pp. 63-79; Il Seicento europeo (exhibition cat.), Rome, 1956; The Age of Louis XIV (exhibition cat.), London, 1958; Le XVIIᵉ siècle français (exhibition cat.), Paris, 1958 (bibliog.); B. de Montgolfier, Nouveaux documents sur les frères Le Nain, GBA, LII, 1958, pp. 267-88; J. Thuillier, Le Nain Studies, BM, C, 1958, pp. 54-61, 91-97; J. Thuillier, Les frères Le Nain: Une nouvelle œuvre religieuse, Art de France, I, 1961, pp. 327-28.

François-Georges PARISET

Illustrations: PLS. 109-114.

LE NÔTRE (LE NOSTRE), ANDRÉ. French landscape architect and gardener (b. Paris, Mar. 12, 1613; d. Sept. 15, 1700). Son of Jean Le Nôtre, "jardinier en chef" to Louis XIII, and grandson of Pierre Le Nôtre, also a royal master gardener, André Le Nôtre's style developed logically from a complex of influences: his family background, the classic tradition, French rational thought, and the canons of gardening established earlier in the century by the landscape architects and theorists Claude Mollet and Jacques Boyceau. Under the tutelage of the painter Simon Vouet (q.v.), to whom he was apprenticed at the age of thirteen, and from the writings of Salomon de Caus, Le Nôtre learned the laws of perspective and optical foreshortening. This knowledge and his study of the academic architecture of his day both served him well in the composition of his geometric, architecturally conceived garden schemes.

Although he succeeded his father as "jardinier en chef des Tuileries" in 1637, it was not until about 1655 that Le Nôtre's significant place in the history of architecture was finally assured, for it was then he began to design the gardens of Nicolas Fouquet's Vaux-le-Vicomte. At Vaux the direction that 17th-century landscape architecture was ultimately to follow became clearly defined: in the geometric formality of the axial composition, in the careful proportioning of the many and diverse parts, and in the perfect equilibrium and subtle relationship of sculpture, fountains, parterres, and architectural elements. The garden becomes a logical architectural extension of the château and, at the same time, a pleasing, carefully ordered frame for it. Optical foreshortening and the many subtle changes in level contribute the significant element of "surprise," providing relief from what might otherwise be too rigorous a geometry. Already in the water parterres at Vaux, which were treated like luminous mirrors in accord with theories of light propounded by Descartes (*La Dioptrique*), yet another aspect of Le Nôtre's definitive formula was established.

In the grandiose plan for Versailles (II, FIG. 299), begun in 1662, the Le Nôtre principles of garden design attained full realization. The imposing scale and visual splendor provided the ideal backdrop for the elaborate fetes of the court of Louis XIV. At Versailles, marked by numerous vistas opening to infinity, the landscape designer further refined his manipulation of optical illusion, the balance of parts, and his use of planes of water (canals, pools, basins) as sources of luminosity. Within the wooded areas bordering the axially conceived avenues, a myriad of surprises awaited the spectator in the form of topiary and architectural chambers, with jetting fountains, intriguing in their seemingly endless variety (VIII, PLS. 437, 438).

During Le Nôtre's long life, his creative genius was manifest not only in extensive royal parks throughout France but also in more intimate gardens both at home and abroad. Soon after the park at Versailles was begun, he was commissioned to design the gardens at Chantilly, and later those at Clagny, Sceaux, and the Grand Trianon (V, FIG. 674). He was equally facile in adapting and modifying existing garden sites, to which his landscape renderings for Saint-Germain-en-Laye, Meudon, Fontainebleau, Saint-Cloud, and the Tuileries all attest. As Le Nôtre's fame spread, his counsel was sought by the sovereigns of Europe, among them Charles II of England and the rulers of the Low Countries, Denmark, and Sweden.

The gardens he designed proclaim Le Nôtre's ingenuity and skill, but it remained for his collaborators and pupils to record his theories of landscape design. As his epitaph states, Le Nôtre "invented significant beauties and carried all others to their utmost perfection." (See also LANDSCAPE ARCHITECTURE.)

BIBLIOG. J. Guiffrey, André Le Nostre, Paris, 1912; E. de Ganay, André Le Nostre, 1613-1700, Paris, 1962.

Hamilton HAZLEHURST

LEONARDO DA VINCI. Illegitimate son of the Florentine notary Ser Piero da Vinci, Leonardo was born Apr. 15, 1452, in Vinci, near Empoli; he died May 2, 1519, at Cloux near Amboise. At the age of fifteen he was taken by his father to Florence, to the studio of Andrea del Verrocchio. There Leonardo received a broad training, which included painting, sculpture, and the technical aspects of art. He also frequented the neighboring atelier of the Pollaiuolo brothers, where he became especially interested in anatomy. In 1472 he was accepted as a member of the Florentine painters' guild; he remained, however, an additional four years in the workshop of Verrocchio. Leonardo's early works were produced in this period of collaboration with his teacher and included one of the angels and the landscape background in Verrocchio's *Baptism of Christ* (Florence, Uffizi), two paintings of the Annunciation (Florence, Uffizi, PL. 116; Paris, Louvre), and a *Virgin and Child* (Munich, Alte Pin.). About 1478 Leonardo became an independent master, remaining for another five years in Florence. From this period of activity stem the so-called "Portrait of Ginevra Benci" (Vaduz, Liechtenstein Coll.), the unfinished *St. Jerome* (PL. 115), and the large incomplete panel with *The Adoration of the Magi* (PL. 117; IV, PL. 266); the panel was commissioned by the Monastery of S. Donato a Scopeto but remained unfinished when Leonardo left Florence in 1481 to enter into the service of Lodovico Sforza, duke of Milan.

A petition written by Leonardo (1481–82), which resulted in his call to the court of the Sforzas in Milan, is the earliest indication of the artist's many-sided interests and skills. Preserved now only in outline among Leonardo's manuscripts, the petition presented his qualifications in ten points. Nine of these dealt with his competence as a civil and military engineer, and only the tenth expressed his capacity as a painter. Leonardo was employed as court painter and engineer in Milan for nearly twenty years. During that time he completed the first version of *The Virgin of the Rocks* (Louvre; PL. 121), begun in 1483; a second version (London, Nat. Gall.; PL. 120), begun about 1497 and completed in 1511; *The Last Supper*, painted between 1495 and 1497 for the Convent of S. Maria delle Grazie in Milan (PL. 125); the portrait of Cecilia Gallerani (PL. 124); and *Portrait of a Musician* (Milan, Ambrosiana). Other works from this period have disappeared.

An important reason for the artist's call to Milan was the commission for a monumental bronze equestrian statue of Francesco Sforza, the first duke, which occupied Leonardo for a number of years. The full-size clay model of the horse, now lost, was executed and then displayed in 1493, but the work was never cast, because the bronze intended for this purpose was needed for casting cannons in the war against the French. The defeat of Duke Lodovico sealed the fate of the projected monument of his ancestor.

Leonardo's architectural projects from the Milanese period are known only through documents and drawings. He executed a model for the dome of the Cathedral of Milan (1487–90), made plans for a palace, and supervised the construction of the new cathedral of Pavia. Leonardo's advice was solicited in the construction of fortifications. Also undertaken during this period were Leonardo's first systematic theoretical and scientific studies in anatomy, botany, mathematics, optics, and mechanics. At this time as well, he composed important parts of his treatise on painting and laid the basis for various other tracts on architecture, anatomy, and mechanics. At the court of Lodovico, Leonardo was an esteemed member of a circle of outstanding learned men concerned with the sciences, somewhat like the academies of Florence and Urbino. Here the artist met the mathematician Luca Pacioli, for whose *De divina proportione* he drew illustrations of geometric bodies.

The end of Sforza rule in 1499 terminated Leonardo's stay in Milan. He returned to Florence in April of 1500 by way of Mantua, where he made a preparatory drawing for a portrait of Isabella d'Este (PL. 119), and Venice, where he executed a plan of defense against the threatened attack of the Turks. At this time he began painting *The Virgin and Child with St. Anne* (PL. 122; cartoon, PL. 123, now displayed in London, Nat. Gall.). In May, 1502, Leonardo became military engineer in the service of Cesare Borgia and traveled for 10 months in Romagna, Umbria, and parts of Tuscany — the operational area of the leader of the papal forces. A good number of the artist's geographical maps and city plans, which are masterpieces of their kind and incunabula of modern cartography, were produced in the course of this activity. After his return to Florence, Leonardo was employed as a military engineer; he proposed a plan to divert the course of the Arno (cf. IV, PL. 268) in order to deprive the city of Pisa of its leading artery of communication in the war against Florence. This strategic undertaking led Leonardo to devise a project for the canalization of the Arno, which would have made the river navigable from Florence to the sea, rendering the adjoining regions profitable. These plans — and another project sent at this time to Sultan Bāyazīd II, for a bridge across the Bosporus — must be reckoned as Utopian conceptions. Nevertheless they were surprisingly farsighted for their time and were based on clear, correct constructional principles.

In 1503 Leonardo was commissioned by the Florentine Signoria to paint a fresco for the large audience hall of the Palazzo Vecchio, which was to represent a famous event from the history of Florence. His partner was Michelangelo, who selected for the opposite wall the theme of the Battle of Cascina. Leonardo's composition represented the Battle of Anghiari, depicting the struggle of the rival armies for possession of the standard. Hurriedly dried by means of a technically unsound process, Leonardo's painting suffered serious damage. It was never completed and was ultimately lost through the redecoration of the hall by Vasari. The composition is known only through copies and drawings by Rubens (PL. 119) and others, based on the original cartoon. At about the same time Leonardo painted the *Mona Lisa* (PL. 126) and the lost *Leda and the Swan*, known only through copies.

Leonardo was then at the height of his artistic reputation; he was greatly admired by Raphael and somewhat more reluctantly recognized by Michelangelo. Yet he produced relatively few paintings. Many commissions extended by famous persons remained unfulfilled, as Leonardo devoted himself increasingly to scientific endeavors. In addition to mathematical investigations he carried out systematic studies in anatomy, performing dissections on cadavers from the hospital of S. Maria Nuova. He recorded his findings in a detailed treatise on the construction of the human body, in which equal importance was given to the text and the accompanying anatomical illustrations. Leonardo's studies in biology and physics are equally impressive. Experiments concerning man's ability to fly led him to a study of bird flight, which he recorded in the Codice sul volo degli uccelli (Turin, Bib. Reale). Observations on the principles governing air currents and water were included in a work on theoretical and practical hydrology (Cod. Leicester, Norfolk, Holkham Hall, Earl of Leicester Coll.). But this period of activity was primarily devoted to the planning of Leonardo's comprehensive volumes on the primary forces of nature, comprising an entire cosmology.

In 1506 Leonardo interrupted work on *The Battle of Anghiari* in the Palazzo Vecchio and, released by the Signoria from his contractual obligations, moved once more to Milan, this time at the invitation of the King of France. Until 1513 he was active at the court of Charles d'Amboise, the French governor of Milan, for whom he designed a large residential palace and drew plans for the Chapel of S. Maria alla Fontana in the church of the same name. The preliminary studies for the monumental equestrian funerary monument of the military commander Gian Giacomo Trivulzio also date from this period, although, as in the case of the Sforza monument, the work was never carried out. Two nearly completed Madonnas "for the most Christian king" have disappeared without trace. While in Milan, Leonardo also devoted much of his time to scientific studies. His writings on anatomy in this period may have benefited from his acquaintance with the anatomist Marc Antonio della Torre of Pavia. Leonardo's hydraulic and geophysical experiments became more searching, as is shown by his important project for the Adda canal, which was to connect Milan with Lake Como, and by his astounding geological observations on the development of fossils. Finally, his precise graphic observations of botanical phenomena rank him, in this field as in others, the founder of modern scientific illustration.

Toward the end of 1513, after Giovanni de' Medici had ascended the papal throne as Leo X, the sixty-year-old Leonardo went to Rome, where he expected to receive commissions from his patron, Cardinal Giuliano de' Medici. However, apparently no great commissions such as were extended to

Raphael, Bramante, and Michelangelo were offered. Tangible traces of Leonardo's artistic activity are lacking for this period, although it is known that he had a workshop in the Palazzo Belvedere. The Roman years were occupied with scientific endeavors, particularly mechanics and anatomy, except for such archaeological studies as the attempt to reconstruct the plan of the antique harbor of Civitavecchia. There is only one painting, his last, that may have been a product of the artist's stay in Rome — the problematic *John the Baptist* (PL. 124).

In January, 1517, Leonardo changed his place of residence for the last time. He left Rome for France at the invitation of the French king, Francis I, who gave him the country house of Cloux near Amboise and granted him the title "Premier Peintre, Architecte, et Mechanicien du Roi." The infirmity of one hand, however, prevented Leonardo from painting, though the artist continued his scientific studies, especially in the field of anatomy. The only documented project of these later years is a plan for a large castle with gardens, intended as a residence in Romorantin for the Queen Mother. The building was not constructed, but Leonardo's plan is to some extent reflected in the castle of Chambord, begun under Francis I during Leonardo's lifetime. The most impressive documents of Leonardo's last years are the *Deluge* series (Windsor Castle, Royal Lib.), drawings in which are summarized the experience and experiments of a lifetime of investigating natural phenomena.

Leonardo was buried in the Church of St-Florentin in Amboise. His tomb, however, vanished in the destruction of the church during the French Revolution.

SUMMARY. Literary works (col. 209). Painting (col. 210). Sculpture (col. 217). Architecture and fortification (col. 219). Court art (col. 222). Scientific works (col. 223): *Mathematics, optics, and mechanics; Anatomy and physiology; Zoology and botany; Cosmology and other physical sciences.* Leonardo's thought (col. 233).

LITERARY WORKS. To the care of his loyal disciple and friend Francesco Melzi, Leonardo left his paintings, drawings, and entire literary works, including a vast number of notes on various subjects. Several large notebooks and numerous individual leaves amounting to a total of some thirty-five hundred densely filled sheets have come down to the present time. Yet this imposing mass of work represents only a part of the total of Leonardo's recorded activity. Other notebooks, known through documents, have disappeared or have survived only in a mutilated and incomplete state. A great many single leaves have also disappeared.

Nineteen books of Leonardo's work are known at the present time. These are either small sketchbooks, which the artist carried suspended from his waist for quick sketches of everyday events or scientific observations, or larger notebooks intended for scientific studies. One of the latter is devoted to the flight of birds, another to optics, another to architecture, another to the study of the properties of water; but these books were often, in the course of time, filled with notes not pertinent to the subject at hand. One manuscript, the Codex Arundel (London, Br. Mus.), contains writings and sketches on various subjects treated in separate folios but bound into one volume. Countless single leaves are dispersed in collections throughout the world. To this body of material must also be added the Codex Atlanticus (Milan, Bib. Ambrosiana), so named for its large dimensions, which stems from the collection of the 17th-century Milanese collector Pompeo Leoni. A sister volume found its way to England and is one of the major treasures of the Royal Library at Windsor Castle.

This vast *œuvre* constitutes the basic foundation and seemingly inexhaustible source of our knowledge of Leonardo's thought. It encompasses — in addition to biographical notes such as diary entries, accounts, snatches of correspondence, and excerpts from literary works read by the artist — the sum of his artistic and scientific studies. Leonardo habitually used reverse, or mirror-image, script and seldom wrote in the conventional manner. The easiest explanation for this preference lies in the fact that he was left-handed. Yet since even the most carefully written documents are in mirror writing, a better explanation is needed. The desire for secrecy has only limited validity; while it is true that Leonardo also arbitrarily broke up words and sentences and deliberately interpolated misleading punctuation, which makes reading of the text even more difficult than simple mirror writing, these additional mannerisms are relatively rare. The writing is clearly legible with the help of a mirror, and with some practice the reader will find Leonardo's script as accessible as any conventional one. His manuscripts are carefully executed, and text and drawings combine to form an admirable esthetic entity. There can thus be no question of an undecipherable code in his script. Perhaps the best explanation is that Leonardo did not intend these pages to be read by others but rather considered them a kind of personal written monologue that he wished to protect somewhat from the unwelcome glances of the curious; perhaps he was expressing his strong individuality. As he wrote in his *Treatise on Painting* (Rome, Vat. Lib., Cod. Urbinas lat. 1270, 31v), "If you are alone, you belong to yourself completely." Special methods, including the "paleografia vinciana," have been devised to analyze the literary works of Leonardo with the aim of establishing a chronology. A pioneer in these studies was Gerolamo Calvi, whose work (1925) was the point of departure for all subsequent investigations.

Leonardo often referred to himself as "omo sanza lettere," an ignorant man; nevertheless, his education, which was surely more extensive than that of a common artisan, and, above all, his great intelligence gave to his work a cultural scope that is truly exceptional. Although Leonardo's knowledge has unmistakable limits (it has been too customary to consider him a wizard in all branches of science), it would be erroneous to present a totally negative view, as has Leonardo Olschki (1919), and to deny the originality of his self-education. The more objective judgment of Eugenio Garin (1952) concerning Leonardo's philosophical principles and the factual presentation of Leonardo's language and style by Augusto Marinoni (1944-52) provide surer and more fruitful guides. The work of Pierre Duhem (1906-13), together with that of Edmondo Solmi (1908), constituted the most comprehensive statement of Leonardo's cultural scope for the preceding generations but should now be superseded by an entirely new investigation of the subject. Leonardo's manifold interests and achievements still need to be examined in their historical context and reevaluated. That the underlying basis of both his artistic and scientific activity constitutes a unified whole, informing every aspect of his thought, is repeatedly demonstrated in his work.

PAINTING. Leonardo's output of paintings was unusually small. A total of seventeen commonly accepted works has been preserved, and of this total, four are unfinished. Five or ten additional compositions have been documented, and a fraction of this number has come down through the medium of contemporary copies. The majority of Leonardo's paintings were executed in the earlier part of his life, in the period 1473/75 to 1500. *The Virgin and Child with St. Anne* (PL. 122) and the *Mona Lisa* (PL. 126) were painted between 1500 and 1507, while in the same years the *Madonna with the Yarn Reel, Christ among the Doctors, The Battle of Anghiari, Leda and the Swan, Bacchus, Salvator Mundi,* and *Angel of the Annunciation* were begun but remained unfinished; they are known to us only through drawings and copies.

In addition to these few and often fragmentary works, a large number of sketches and composition projects is known. These studies, which extend from the artist's earliest youth until his last years and are climaxed by the grandiose invention embodied in the series of *Deluge* drawings, demonstrate that Leonardo considered drawing to be an independent and self-sufficient medium. In fact, the appraisal of Leonardo's significance as a painter depends in large measure on the evaluation of his work as a draftsman.

At the time of Leonardo's collaboration with Verrocchio on *The Baptism of Christ*, he had just achieved the status of master. At the age of twenty his remarkable gifts were already apparent. The seemingly effortless mastery of technical and representational means is accompanied by an expressive quality that sets his angel apart from the other figures in the painting. The pose of the kneeling angel is relaxed, introducing a diagonal movement of the body that later became characteristic in Leonardo's work, and is composed along a number of axes that create a multiplicity of movements. The fine quality of form, the delicacy of the modeling through soft shading, and the organically articulated folds of the drapery of Leonardo's figure stand out from the rest of the painting. Leonardo's touch is also visible in the *Baptism* in the section of landscape above the angels. This small portion of nature is pervaded by a new artistic vision. The same qualities can also be seen in a remarkable pen drawing (IV, PL. 271) made in 1473, a subtle combination of imaginative fantasy and observation of nature, which can be regarded as the first truly modern landscape rendering. Although the composition shows traces of traditional schemes of landscape representation, such as the rocky elements in the foreground and the precipices in the distance, there is a new interest in the precise recording of optical sensations. This is apparent in the atmospheric space that unifies the landscape and separates the observer from the object of his vision, imparting to the latter an authenticity of its own. The effect of light and humidity upon the material world is carefully recorded; some forms are sharply delineated, others consumed in haze.

This interest in the appearance of the natural world in the 1473 drawing was conditioned by Leonardo's striving toward comprehension of natural phenomena, which he had recorded objectively since youth. He sought an artistic means whereby the new perceptions could be represented, a graphic language that could provide an adequate reflection of his intense observation. In both the drawing of 1473 and the landscape in Verrocchio's *Baptism* he succeeded.

The harmonious combination of movement and expression that distinguishes the angel in the *Baptism* is also found in the later works of the master. The gestures and expression in the *St. Jerome* (PL. 115) produce a convincing pathos. In his *Treatise on Painting* Leonardo repeatedly emphasizes the expressive character of movement and gesture: "A good painter has two subjects of primary importance: man and the state of his mind. The first is easy; the latter difficult, since it must be conveyed by means of the gestures and movements of various parts of the body. This one should learn from the deaf-mutes, for they express themselves better in this way than any other group of human beings" (Rome, Vat. Lib., Cod. Urbinas lat. 1270, 60v).

In their attempt to capture the external appearance and inner essence of every phenomenon, Leonardo's studies of nature differ from those of other artists of his time. He became interested at an early date in the emotive potentiality of certain expressions of the face. A leaf of sketches drawn about 1480 shows the head of a screaming man with a wide-open mouth juxtaposed with the snarling heads of a lion and a dog; the similarity in the expression of rage in man and beast is recorded here perhaps for the first time. An entire theory of physiognomy grew out of such systematic studies.

A large number of extant preparatory sketches for *The Adoration of the Magi* (PL. 117) permits an insight into Leonardo's method of work. These sketches include studies of the movement of individual figures, a detailed construction of the setting in central perspective, and a trial drawing for the entire composition. All these preparatory sketches are reflected in the final, although unfinished, version. The rocky projection in front of which Mary is seated divides the setting of the action into a foreground and a background, thus resolving the problem of an open central space that must be filled with figures or remain uncomfortably empty. Formally and thematically the elements of the painting are disposed from the center to the edges in a descending rhythm. The classic triangular composition of the central group, which Leonardo used here for the first time, helps coordinate all individual action into a cohesive whole. The two figures standing at the lower corners of the painting — the older one immersed in the contemplation of the event, while the younger stares out of the picture — seem to connect the real world with the pictorial space. Our eye is led through these flanking figures to the main participants in the action, and from these to the shadowy surrounding figures seen as a multitude rather than as separate individuals. In the interplay of expressions and gestures the seemingly uncoordinated mass of hands echoes every shade of emotion shown in the faces of the shepherds. In the unfinished state in which it was left, the painting is a demonstration of Leonardo's chiaroscuro technique. The artist did not introduce color, which remained of secondary interest to him, until a late stage in the execution of a painting. His vital concern was for modeling in light and shade, the representation of the substance and weight of objects in terms of their proper tonal value in relation to the surrounding space.

"...ber, 1478, I began the two Virgin Marys," Leonardo wrote on one of his early sheets of sketches (Florence, Uffizi). In an inventory of works in his atelier made toward the end of 1481, in connection with his departure for the court of Milan, he noted, "a Virgin Mary, almost completed" and "a Virgin Mary." Of these paintings, on which the artist worked during the last years of his stay in Florence, only one has been preserved: the so-called "Benois Madonna" (Leningrad, The Hermitage). Even though unfinished and uneven in execution, this small work is an eloquent witness of the rich creative gifts of the twenty-six-year-old master and a new, imaginative interpretation of one of the oldest themes of Christian art. The youthful Madonna offers her Son a flower taken from a bouquet in her hand. The representation of the Child in the act of reaching for the flower shows great insight and observation. Beneath this simple and playful gesture, and in the face of the Christ child, there is an earnestness which reveals once more the artist's interest in the dramatic content of gesture and facial expression.

In addition to the above-mentioned works, other early paintings of the artist include the small "Dreyfus Madonna" (Washington, D.C., Nat. Gall.), as well as the *Virgin and Child* (Munich, Alte Pin.), the two Annunciations (Uffizi and Louvre), and the "Portrait of Ginevra Benci." Of varying quality and states of preservation, these paintings are characteristic products of Verrocchio's workshop, where, side by side with Leonardo, other young painters, including Botticelli, Lorenzo di Credi, and Perugino, were active. Yet each of these early paintings, qualitatively far above typical renditions of similar subjects, reveals the hand of the artist. The most important work of the group is the portrait (in all likelihood Ginevra Benci) that Leonardo painted in Florence, according to a contemporaneous source. The panel has been cut down; it originally extended almost 8 in. beyond the present lower edge. As indicated by traces under the layer of overpainting below the lace of the bodice, the missing strip showed the hands of the sitter, probably in the same quiet and graceful pose illustrated in a drawing now in Windsor Castle (12558). As originally completed, the portrait fits naturally into the tradition of late-15th-century portraiture, although set apart by the unconventional composition. The roundness of the head, the arrangement of the hair, the curious slant of the eyes, and the restrained seriousness of the expression relate to the style of Verrocchio. However, the execution of the painting, the soft yet precise modeling, especially of the forehead and cheeks, has a rich chiaroscuro unique with Leonardo. The juniper bushes (*ginepro*, or *ginevro*) that serve as a dense, dark foil for the head, enhancing its luminous quality, are masterfully conceived. This apparently opaque foliated background has a delicate quality that creates not a wall but a translucent curtain leading the eye smoothly into the distance. The beautifully formed spaces in the bushes at the left are islands of light, the lower one with its network of brush shielding the foreground. As in the "Benois Madonna," Leonardo has transformed a conventional and well-established pictorial type into a personal statement of great originality.

Immediately following *The Adoration of the Magi*, which had been left behind unfinished in Florence, Leonardo painted *The Virgin of the Rocks*. The first of the two versions (Louvre; PL. 121) was painted by Leonardo about 1483–86 as the center panel of an altarpiece. The wings, showing angel musicians

(London, Nat. Gall.), were executed by Ambrogio de Predis. The painting was removed from its intended place, the Chapel of the Order of the Immaculate Conception in the Church of S. Francesco in Milan, perhaps by the Duke of Milan, who either kept it himself or gave it away. The painting is known to have been in the possession of the French royal house in 1625, having perhaps been acquired by Louis XII. To replace this picture in the chapel, Leonardo and Ambrogio de Predis painted a second, slightly different version, begun about 1494. This painting was the subject of a 10-year lawsuit concerning the fee, brought against the order by the artists. The dispute was finally settled in the artists' favor in 1506, whereupon the picture was delivered to the patrons. This second version of *The Virgin of the Rocks* (PL. 120) remained in the chapel in S. Francesco until the dissolution of the order in 1871. It was acquired by the National Gallery in London in 1880 after several changes of ownership.

The first version of the picture shows Leonardo's art in its mature phase, depicting the legend of an encounter in the desert between the young St. John and the infant Christ on the journey home from Egypt. The legend arose during the Middle Ages, probably on the basis of an apocryphal source. It did not make its appearance in art, however, until the 15th century, when it became a part of the infancy cycle of John the Baptist, especially in certain towns of central Italy, where the Baptist was venerated as patron saint. In Florence after the middle of the 15th century, the little St. John (S. Giovannino) began to be represented in paintings of the Virgin. Leonardo's version is a classical rendition of this theme. The pyramidal grouping of the figures, first employed in an early drawing and in the Uffizi *Adoration*, reappears in *The Virgin of the Rocks*. Later it became one of the most popular compositional devices of the Cinquecento and was repeatedly used by Raphael.

The effectiveness of Leonardo's *Virgin of the Rocks* is in large part due to a visionary quality that removes this painting from the realm of pure reality. Since true form for Leonardo is always modified by effects of light and atmosphere, every optical impression is in a certain sense also a vision. Leonardo creates this effect in *The Virgin of the Rocks* through aerial perspective, by suffusing his composition with a misty atmosphere. In the dim light of the cave, each form seems to emerge from a fine mist. The group of figures stands between two sources of light. One source, originating in the distance, brightens the rear of the cave but is too weak to illuminate the figures in the foreground. A second source, shining from the front, is trained on the figures and distributed in fine gradations over each. No brighter than the first, its most intense shafts are directed to the head of Mary and the body of the Child, while St. John and the angel receive slightly less illumination. The expressive blessing hand of the Virgin, emerging from the darkness, appears to float in space. The gossamer veil that seems to separate the viewer from the pictorial stage is a technical effect achieved through *sfumato* painting — the eradication of the hard outlines of objects by means of soft gradations of tones, which renders form primarily through the play of surface and light. The head of the Virgin is delicately modeled in tones from dark to light, the forms articulated without the aid of outlines. That Leonardo often consciously avoided sharp outlines but articulated surface areas to produce form is shown in a study for this painting (Turin, Bib. Reale). Within the softly modeled contours of the angel's head, the inner forms in this study are defined by a dense system of hatching that is peculiarly Leonardo's. The tightly massed strokes manipulated by a sure hand are subtly varied in strength and density, some broad, some broken, and the total effect is a clear, relieflike definition of form. A successful interplay of graphic and painterly means has been employed. The precise linearity of the plants and of certain folds of the garments contrasts strongly with the more painterly effects of the broadly modeled areas. This contrast is evident in the figure of the infant St. John, modeled primarily by means of chiaroscuro and thus set off from the precise graphic treatment of the surrounding foliage.

Leonardo's painting *The Lady with an Ermine* (PL. 124) is believed to be the portrait of the youthful Cecilia Gallerani mentioned in contemporary letters. Because of heavy repainting and poor preservation, however, the identification cannot be absolutely certain. Yet no Milanese painter other than Leonardo could have conceived such a masterful pictorial conception. The original quality of the execution is still evident in the delicate face and in the graceful hand that rests on the back of the ermine. Cecilia was the mistress of Lodovico Sforza at the time Leonardo painted her portrait, and the ermine, often used as an emblem by Lodovico, is added evidence for the identification of the painting. The *Portrait of a Musician* (Milan, Ambrosiana), rightly attributed to Leonardo in view of its outstanding quality, may also be placed in the 1490s in the artist's Milanese period.

Ten years after *The Virgin of the Rocks*, Leonardo painted his *Last Supper* (PL. 125; XII, PL. 61). He began working on the fresco in the refectory of the Convent of S. Maria delle Grazie in 1495, at the request of Duke Lodovico. Three years later the work was completed. Leonardo's slow, meditative working process was entirely at odds with the existing technique of fresco painting. In order to maintain his own work habits, Leonardo invented a new technique consisting of a mixture of oil and tempera on stone, necessitating the prior treatment of the wall surface with a ground capable of receiving oil paint while insulating the wall against humidity. Contrived by Leonardo from a mixture of mastic and pitch, the ground did not hold, and soon the paint began to peel from the wall. As early as 1517 the painting was described by the Cardinal of Aragon as seriously damaged, and by the middle of the century it was in ruinous condition. The process of disintegration could not be halted. The work was often retouched in the course of time, and by the beginning of the 19th century only a few traces of its former greatness could still be seen. It was not until the 20th century that it became possible to arrest further disintegration through modern methods of restoration. Freed from later overpainting, the little that remains of the work still creates a powerful and unforgettable impression and in part retains the splendid luminosity of its colors.

The group of *The Last Supper* is placed in a somewhat confined space, the monumental figures crowded around the table. The use of figures seemingly too large for the space they occupy — one of the principles of classical composition — appears here for the first time in Leonardo's work. The perspective is an illusionistic continuation of the refectory where the fresco is situated, expanding the real space in which the viewer stands. The illusion is heightened by the imitation of linens and utensils actually in use in the monastery. Yet within this realistic space the figures are represented larger than life, and through their presence the space itself seems to expand. In the later work of Leonardo and of many who came after him, including Raphael and Michelangelo, this space-creating principle became one of the tenets of classicism in painting. Leonardo's composition is a skillfully coordinated and rhythmically compelling statement of its theme. The pause between two phases of an action, the momentary shock that freezes the disciples for an instant before they break into violent motion, is in *The Last Supper* presented in its most consummate form. The play of gesture, expression, and movement and the response of each of the figures in a manner appropriate to his inward disposition have contributed to make this first work of Renaissance classicism, despite its tragically deteriorated state, one of the most perfect artistic creations of all time.

Immediately following completion of *The Last Supper*, Leonardo conceived the design of *The Virgin and Child with St. Anne* (PL. 122), which was to become a model for the most outstanding Italian masters. The painting was executed after the artist's return to Florence after the fall of Duke Lodovico of Milan in 1499–1500. The painter resided in the Monastery of the SS. Annunziata as a guest of the Servite monks, and it was here that he worked on his new picture, apparently without commission. According to Vasari, the entire city of Florence watched the progress of the work of the artist, who, almost fifty years of age, stood at the peak of his reputation. Historically the picture marks a turning point in Italian painting. Not easily resolved pictorially, the theme is presented by Leonardo in an entirely new form. In a break with existing iconographical tradition, the Virgin is shown seated on the lap of St. Anne. With a graceful forward motion she tries to restrain the Christ child from playfully riding the lamb. The dynamic tension that invests the picture was sensed in Florence as something new. The figures are shown in a relatively confined spatial setting which lacks a middle ground, and the depth of the space is less the result of perspective illusion than of the great space-creating volume of the figures themselves. The background landscape is little more than a distant prospect, lacking direct connection with the sphere of action of the figures. The influence of this painting on the art of the following generations was enormous, and for masters such as Raphael, Andrea del Sarto, Fra Bartolommeo, and Michelangelo, as well as for the mannerists, it became the ideal example of a classical composition. Even in the north, Massys' elaboration of the composition testifies to the far-reaching interest aroused by Leonardo's painting.

In *The Battle of Anghiari*, begun in Florence in 1503, Leonardo attempted a grandiose evocation of a historical event documented in detail in literary sources. A number of trial studies for the work reveal his basic intention to represent within a single composition several episodes of the battle. The thematic and compositional high point was to be the struggle over the flag, which took place on the approaches of a bridge. The studies for the composition show a gradual increase in the importance given to the combat over the flag. The group of fighting riders, which occupies the center of the wide narrative composition, was continually simplified until in its final state, as seen in Rubens's copy (PL. 119) and finally executed on the wall, the four riders entangled in fierce combat became the classic model for battle representation. Leonardo's composition, which served as a study piece for painters from Raphael to Delacroix, has come down in numerous copies of the 16th and 17th centuries. The fury of battle is represented as an uncontrolled animal instinct in which man and beast show the same frightful distortions of distended upper lip and bared teeth, a similarity already studied by the artist in earlier sketches. The heads of the fighting riders show an expressive distortion of the facial muscles also seen on the heads of a horse and a lion on an earlier leaf of sketches in Windsor Castle; these examples show how Leonardo combined scientific study and artistic expression in this later painting. As a composition the group of fighting riders is characterized by the same quality of balance found in *The Virgin and Child with St. Anne*. In contrast to the restrained calm of the latter, however, the struggling group in *The Battle of Anghiari* is full of harsh movements confined within a tightly bound form. The boundaries of this form not only describe the shape assumed by the action but serve to imprison its explosive energy, to prevent any escape of intensity. The energy presses inward as if bound to a gravitational center. The opposing horses appear locked in hermetic and motionless combat. As in *The Virgin and Child with St. Anne*, an understanding of the physical principles of force and counterforce is applied in the formulation of *The Battle of Anghiari*, and both works show a moment of arrested action rendered with great sense of strength and plasticity. It is not surprising that in preparation for the latter Leonardo made, according to his own testimony, a number of small three-dimensional sketches in wax, and that the finished work inspired a series of sculptures of equestrian combats — the terra-cotta groups of the Florentine sculptor Giovan Francesco Rustici.

During the years in which Leonardo worked on *The Battle of Anghiari* he also painted the *Mona Lisa* (PL. 126). This is the work most closely identified with the art and spirit of the artist. All that is known about the background of this painting is based on the brief note of a contemporary stating that Leonardo painted the portrait of the wife of the Florentine merchant Francesco di Bartolommeo del Giocondo; hence the picture's other name, *La Gioconda*. Although the painting has darkened and lost its original delicacy and lightness of color, the fine execution and the simplicity of pose take on more meaning and subtlety with closer scrutiny. Body and head, hands and arms, are related to one another by almost imperceptibly varied directional axes of movement, resulting in a harmonious and lively effect that has served as a model for portraiture up to our own time. The famous and oft-discussed smile of the sitter is the key to the apparent "mystery" of the *Mona Lisa*. It represents the subtlest stage in the transition between a motionless, expressionless human face and the first delicate enlivening. All expressive possibilities are open, and much has been read into the smile. Yet it produces no specific emotion, neither rejecting nor inviting, reflecting rather a state between nearness and distance, a sense of being apart. Thus questions concerning the sitter's personality are of doubtful value. The *Mona Lisa* represents the ideal female portrait, a type continued from Raphael to Corot.

For the lost *Leda and the Swan*, it has been surmised that the cartoon for the painting must have been made in Florence; a *Leda* has been found among Raphael's drawings executed in Florence about 1505, after works of Leonardo. However, since all later preserved copies of the painting stem from Leonardo's Milanese following, it may be surmised that the artist took the work from Florence to Milan and completed it there, as he did with *The Virgin and Child with St. Anne*. In his *Leda*, Leonardo created the classic type of standing nude figure for Italian art. Few other works by great masters have exercised such a profound influence on succeeding generations. Standing in the classical *contrapposto*, the lovely female body was constructed on many varied directional axes and presented a rich variety of aspects. Through Raphael, who based the standing pose of one of the philosophers in his *School of Athens* on the Leda, this figure became a model type in High Renaissance art. In addition, the gentle turn of the torso to one side, contrasting with the turn of the head in the opposite direction, while the arm is elegantly stretched across the body, provided the archetype for the famous *figura serpentinata*, the ideal mannerist figure, designed to combine in one pose as many viewpoints as possible, imparting to the body a spiral effect. More animated than the classical *contrapposto* stance, yet more classically constructed than the serpentine figures of mannerism, Leonardo's Leda has a statuesque quality which might well impress a sculptor. It is possible that the change in Michelangelo's style that separated the still classical pose of the *David* from the early figures executed for the tomb of Pope Julius and the vehemently animated *Matthew* may have been partly influenced by Leonardo's Leda. The so-called "David Apollo" (Florence, Mus. Naz.) indeed seems like her sculptural brother.

The soft, dense modeling on a sheet of preparatory drawings for the *Leda* (Windsor Castle, 12516), suggests the same gently swelling forms seen in all the preserved copies of the painting. Leonardo's original probably had a strongly sensuous quality. With the exception of a *Bacchus* which Leonardo was commissioned to paint for the Duke of Ferrara but which was probably never executed (the *Bacchus* in the Louvre is the poor work of an unknown follower), *Leda and the Swan* represents the only subject drawn from classical mythology treated by Leonardo. Those who believe that the painting carries a hidden meaning are probably not mistaken. Leonardo may have used the myth to represent the symbol of female creation. The double embrace and softly yielding pose of the figure suggest surrender; and the children, just emerged from the egg, are a symbol of fertility. Perhaps Leda should be interpreted as the mother-earth goddess Gaea. Here even more than in the *Mona Lisa* Leonardo has presented an enigma. For the first time he has combined an open sensuousness with a veiled, symbolic meaning.

After this Florentine period, Leonardo gave most of his time to scientific research and seldom again made use of the brush. Commissions extended to him by the King of France through his governor in Milan were undertaken only with reluctance. The two Madonnas, which in a letter to the governor he designated as near completion and soon to be delivered, were probably not new creations but reworkings of the earlier compositions of the "Benois Madonna" and the *Madonna with the Yarn Reel*. During his stay in Rome (1513–17) as well, the artist apparently painted little. *John the Baptist* (PL. 124), the one extant painting of Leonardo's late years, shows a mysterious figure that appears at the same time to emerge from and retreat into the dark background. Once again Leonardo created for one of the most frequently represented themes in Christian art a spiritual and formal interpretation that has no known prototype. While in the past Leonardo had habitually gone beyond the traditional limits of Christian iconography, this last work represents his freest and boldest elaboration of a religious pictorial theme. Outwardly St. John remains faithful to the figure of the Gospel; he carries the attributes of the preacher in the wilderness. Yet his bearing suggests that his message is not the prophecy of deliverance, and his smile suggests not transfiguration but the inscrutable secret of divine intention, the eternal mystery which hangs over human destiny.

In the same period during which he painted *John the Baptist*, Leonardo also began to draw his visions of the end of the world. Though based on the theme of the Deluge, these drawings constitute a complete break with traditional representations of the Biblical episode; Leonardo's artistic and scientific imagination are fused in a great synthesis that symbolizes his entire cosmology.

SCULPTURE. That Leonardo worked in sculpture from his youth onward is known from his own statements and through other sources. In the workshop of Verrocchio he became acquainted with such techniques of this art as modeling in wax and clay, stone carving, and bronze casting. He may have participated in Verrocchio's project for the Medici tomb in the Old Sacristy of S. Lorenzo. He must also have witnessed the execution of the Forteguerri monument for the Cathedral of Pistoia and the St. Thomas group for Orsanmichele in Florence. Undoubtedly Leonardo saw and thoroughly studied the model of Verrocchio's monument to Bartolommeo Colleoni, which was taken from Florence to Venice in the summer of 1481.

In his petition to the Duke of Milan (1481–82) Leonardo mentioned his ability to work in marble, bronze, or clay and offered to execute the equestrian monument of Duke Francesco. In a draft of a letter of about 1498, he urged the building commissioners of the Cathedral of Piacenza to select an able master for the task of creating the great bronze doors of the Cathedral, then being planned. He stressed his own qualifications in bronze casting and seemed himself to be bidding for the commission. In his *Treatise on Painting*, weighting the merits of painting against those of sculpture to the advantage of the former, he wrote, "As I practice myself the art of sculpture no less than that of painting, and doing both the one and the other in the same degree, it seems to me that, without being suspected of unfairness, I may venture to give an opinion as to which of the two is more intellectual and of greater difficulty and perfection" (Paris, Inst. de France, Ms. 2038, 24, 25).

Of Leonardo's sculpture nothing is preserved, if in fact any of his projects was ever carried beyond the stage of clay or plaster models. All attempts thus far to attribute to him various objects in bronze or stone must be rejected. The only work which has been related with any plausibility to Leonardo's art, specifically to the works of his early Florentine period, is the beautiful terra-cotta *Madonna and Child* (London, Vict. and Alb.), which has recently, however, been more convincingly attributed to Antonio Rossellino. Leonardo's achievement as a sculptor can thus be inferred only from the influence of his projects on other artists and from his relationship with his student G. F. Rustici, one of Leonardo's most talented followers, who became especially interested in equestrian sculptures.

Leonardo was called to Milan to execute a colossal equestrian statue of Duke Francesco Sforza, on which he worked with extended interruptions from 1483 to 1498. In the first period of work (1483–89) he designed a composition which completely broke with tradition, representing a departure from the classical type of equestrian monument transmitted from the *Marcus Aurelius* on the Capitoline hill (X, PL. 148) to Verrocchio's Colleoni monument. The rider was not shown quietly seated on his horse but was mounted on a rearing one, a plan which was not only new but was also unusually difficult to execute. Many drawings, among them a fine silverpoint study in Windsor Castle, have transmitted to us his first plan, which resembled, and may have been inspired by, an earlier design made by Antonio Pollaiuolo for the Sforza monument (Pope-Hennessy, 1958). Leonardo made a thorough study of the difficult technical problems involved and apparently found a workable solution not only for the casting procedure but also for the resolution of the static stresses. A sketch in Windsor Castle (12349r) shows the design of the mold as well as the inner iron framework destined to be inserted within the mold for reinforcement. Calculations of the stresses made by Leonardo show his thorough understanding of the principles of mechanics and his ability to apply them in the service of his art. He also had explored the possibility of an outer support in the form of a fallen warrior trampled under the hoofs of the horse.

Leonardo did not, however, carry through this first design and, beginning in 1490, returned to the type of the quietly standing horse. The trial sketches of the following years are intensive studies after nature of horses from the stables of the Duke and other noblemen, including an entire series of motion studies and systematic investigations of individual parts of the animal. He also turned his attention to existing equestrian monuments, not merely the *Gattamelata* and the Colleoni monument but also the so-called "Regisole," the late-antique equestrian monument in Pavia, which he admired for its beauty, the natural quality of its motion, the trot which had "almost the quality of a free horse" (Milan, Ambrosiana, Cod. Atlanticus, 147r). The final version of the design for the Sforza monument and a clay model were thus eventually completed, and in November, 1493, on the occasion of the wedding of Bianca Maria Sforza to the emperor Maximilian, the model was publicly exhibited, arousing great admiration. It remained on view in the courtyard of the castle and was still seen there in 1498 by Luca Pacioli, who noted its colossal proportions — over 20 ft. from head to foot, or about twice the size of the Colleoni monument. A sketchy drawing by Leonardo of the wooden crating that was probably used to transport the model to its place of public exhibition gives some impression of the powerful tension in the mighty body of the horse, in which the massive, compact forms of the *Gattamelata* appear to be combined with the animated intensity of the Colleoni work to form a monumental new conception. However, with the downfall of Lodovico and his expulsion from Milan, this project along with many others had to be abandoned.

A more specific idea of the intended final form of the Sforza monument can be obtained from the preparatory sketches for a second equestrian statue on which Leonardo began working between 1511 and 1513. The *condottiere* Gian Giacomo Trivulzio, who in 1499, while in the service of the King of France, had wrested Milan from the usurper Lodovico Sforza, commissioned Leonardo to execute his funerary monument, which was to stand in the family mortuary chapel in the Church of S. Celso in Milan. A precise description of the projected work can be found among Leonardo's papers. The life-size equestrian statue was to stand on a richly decorated base that was toho use the sarcophagus of the deceased. Even though considerably smaller than the Sforza monument and differing from it in function, the basic conception behind the two works is the same. A large number of life and motion studies again attest to the concentrated effort leading up to the formulation of Leonardo's unconventional solution. Like the Sforza monument, the project for the Trivulzio tomb was never executed in final form, and thus two of the boldest designs on the equestrian theme in Renaissance sculpture did not materialize.

Leonardo was almost sixty years of age when he began work on this project. As in the studies for the Sforza statue, he appears in time to have abandoned his plan for a rearing horse in favor of a striding one for the Trivulzio monument. His preparatory sketches (PL. 118), distinguished by the powerful, curving, form-defining lines of his mature style, show the experience gained by the artist in his work on *The Battle of Anghiari*, which helps to account for the differences in the drawings for the two equestrian works. The second series of preparatory studies shows a greater feeling for volume. The forward movement of the horse is checked by the bridle. In comparison to the Sforza project, the potential motion of the animal seems to be constrained within the posture of the tightly reined head, heightening the effect of tension. At the same time the design of the rider shows, despite its indebtedness to the Sforza type, an effort to stress the domination of the human figure over that of the horse. The influence of the "Regisole," with its livelier gait emphasized in the raised rear leg, seems to predominate over that of the *Marcus Aurelius*, *Gattamelata*, and the Colleoni monument.

Leonardo's impressive drawings for his equestrian monuments must have had a strong impact. A number of sculpture groups from the beginning of the Cinquecento employing the motif of the mounted rider are derived from his designs, although it cannot be determined whether they were transmitted through drawings or through models in clay or wax. Among these are a beautiful bronze group in Budapest and the terra-cotta groups by Rustici in Paris and Florence. The influence of Leonardo's doctrines can be felt in other types of sculpture as well — for example, in Rustici's three larger-than-life bronze figures of the preaching John the Baptist flanked by two doubting priests, above the north door of the Baptistery in Florence (XII, PL. 57). Vasari, who must have known Rustici personally, wrote in his life of Leonardo concerning the modeling of these figures: "They were executed by Giovan Francesco Rustici, but under Leonardo's direction, and are the finest casts for design and general perfection that have yet been seen." In his life of Rustici, Vasari amplified this account: "While engaged upon this work Rustici would allow no one near except Leonardo da Vinci, who never left him while he was modeling in clay and casting, until the work was finished. Many therefore believe, though nothing definite is known, that Leonardo worked at them himself, or at least helped Rustici with his advice and judgment." On the basis of a note in Leonardo's own hand in the Codex Arundel (263; London, Br. Mus.) it is known that he and Rustici shared a house for a period of six months at the most crucial time during the execution of the figures.

The composition of Rustici's group as well as the structure of the individual figures must undoubtedly be credited to a large extent to Leonardo. The stance of the so-called "Levite," a thickset, muscular figure; the organic fall of the drapery; and the contrast between the coarse expression of the Levite and the refined gaze of the Pharisee all point to Leonardo's spiritual participation. This sculptural group of three figures is the single instance, although largely obscured by the hand of another artist, of a completed piece from which some insight can be gained into Leonardo's work in this medium. With the exception of the equestrian statue, sculpture apparently interested him little, and sculpture in stone not at all. His criticism of sculpture in the *Treatise on Painting*, which repeats arguments found in Lucian, was aimed primarily at work in stone. A decisive factor in Leonardo's attitude is the irrevocable nature of stone sculpture, which does not permit the artist continually to formulate new ideas in the very process of the work. The only form of sculpture possible for Leonardo was modeling in wax, clay, or plaster, which allowed a slow, continuous, and always alterable development of an idea until a final model could be achieved and then cast in bronze.

ARCHITECTURE AND FORTIFICATION. In Leonardo's famous letter of petition to the Duke of Milan he itemized his experience as an architect. "In time of peace I believe that I can give perfect satisfaction, and to the equal of any other, in architecture, in the design of buildings public and private, and in guiding water from one place to the other" (Milan, Ambrosiana, Cod. Atlanticus, 391r). A document dated 1490 mentions Leonardo, along with Bramante and other masters, as "ingeniarius et pinctor." The account books of the building operations for the Cathedral of Milan also show that Leonardo participated in the competition for the design of the dome of the Cathedral between 1487 and 1490, having entered a model of his proposed project; however, he withdrew before the decision of the judges was announced. His services as an adviser were often sought. He was consulted by the builders of the new Cathedral of Pavia (1490) and in connection with damage suffered by the Church of S. Salvatore al Monte in Florence (1500). About 1502 he devised a plan for a gigantic bridge across the Bosporus for Sultan Bāyazīd II. In 1506 Charles d'Amboise, the French governor of Milan, had high words of praise for certain architectural projects which Leonardo had designed for him, probably a palace and the Chapel of S. Maria alla Fontana. During his last years in France the artist made plans for a large castle intended for the mother of King Francis I, which was to be constructed in Romorantin (1518). Despite this activity, however, not a single finished building can with certainty be attributed to Leonardo.

His sketchbooks, on the other hand, and some independent leaves were filled with architectural designs from all periods of his life, including military constructions, city plans, buildings for sacred and secular purposes, architectural details, and theoretical studies. With the exception of a few individual studies and rather modest illustrations in architectural treatises of the middle of the century, Leonardo's designs (PL. 118; I, PL. 406; III, PL. 485) are the first architectural drawings of the Renaissance which to a significant extent reveal the architectural climate of the time.

Whenever Leonardo became involved with a specific building project, he evolved from the task at hand principles of a general application far beyond the immediate requirements of the problem. In the design for the dome of the Cathedral of Milan, the problem was to invent a suitable crowning element for the crossing of the huge late Gothic structure which would at once be structurally consonant with the Gothic piers and in esthetic harmony with the elaborate decorative style of the building. In contrast to the works of his Lombard competitors, Leonardo's project called for a freestanding dome in the Tuscan manner which was to consist of a bold, double-shell construction. This design, however, conflicted with the Milanese tradition, which favored towers over the crossing; this may have been the reason for his withdrawal from the competition. From his systematic investigation of the problems connected with the construction of this dome, however, Leonardo was able to broaden his understanding with a series of studies on dome construction and design in general. His studies reveal that he was generally more inclined toward theoretical than practical architectural problems; and in actual construction he was called upon to advise rather than to serve as working architect.

It is significant that for 17 years, while at the court of the Sforzas, Leonardo lived and worked side by side with Bramante, one of the greatest architects of his time. This contact stimulated Leonardo's interest in important artistic problems of the period, including the centralized building plan and the designing of monumental palace and church façades, as well as his concern for the technical aspects of construction, which represented the practical application of those principles of statics and mechanics that had interested him as a theoretician.

The idea of systematizing his thoughts and studies on architecture seems to have occurred to Leonardo at an early date. One of his sketchbooks, Manuscript B in the Institut de France, was originally intended as a pattern book of architectural types. In addition, other studies (in Mss. A and B and in the Cod. Atlanticus, Arundel, and Trivulzio) reveal a planned organization and can in all likelihood be recognized as preparatory studies for a treatise on architecture. Taken as a whole, these studies form the outlines of an ambitious architectural theory, which was to have given to the collective knowledge of construction of the period a coherent and systematic form. Numerous individual sketches may be regarded as preparatory for this project, which would undoubtedly also have included Leonardo's work in connection with specific constructions. The plans include all varieties of urban construction and designs for ideal centralized or longitudinal buildings employing innumerable combinations of spatial arrangement. In this realm Leonardo proved himself a gifted mediator between northern and central Italian architectural traditions. His drawings show efforts to transform, through architectural clarity and tectonic severity, the rich forms of Lombard centralized buildings into a more coherent and sober mode. Thus arose a veritable catalogue of designs. The intended treatise forms an important link between the simple spatial complexes and architectural theories of the early Renaissance and the intricate constructions of the High Renaissance and provides a unique representational survey of the great development which Italian architecture underwent at the end of the 15th century. The style of the early Renaissance, based upon the principles of Brunelleschi, Filarete, Francesco di Giorgio Martini, Alberti, and Laurana, entered its classical phase in the work of Bramante and Leonardo. Not a single drawing by Bramante from his Milanese period has been preserved to record the transition from his buildings in Milan, which are still completely in the early Renaissance tradition, and his post-1500 "Roman style." This gap is filled by Leonardo's drawings, and for this reason their importance as documentary evidence for the architectural preoccupations of their time cannot be overestimated. The drawings also serve another function. They demonstrate for the first time the basic forms of architectural representation employed during the Renaissance. This includes the exploration of perspective representation of exterior and interior, as well as the fully developed cross section. The use of central perspective as a means of visualizing an architectural composition was perfected by Leonardo to the point of competing with a three-dimensional model.

While the first important section of Leonardo's treatise was intended to deal with proportion and decoration as well as architectural design in urban building, for both sacred and secular structures, the second part was to be devoted to technical problems of construction. For this part as well, Leonardo made intensive preparatory investigations, while individual chapters such as those dealing with the arch and with the causes of structural defects were exhaustively studied. The intended contents of the treatise can be determined with reasonable certainty on the basis of the preserved preliminary studies.

High Renaissance architectural concepts were exemplified in such instruction books as Sebastiano Serlio's treatise, which is an up-to-date version of the traditional pattern book. Leonardo had established the basis for these practical handbooks of building through his development of perspective architectural representation. At the same time, his scientific knowledge enabled him not only to develop a treatise on construction which satisfied all demands of a practical nature but also to make a number of valuable suggestions in the field of statics, which were to be given a systematic exposition only a century later by Galileo in his "Lectures on the Theory of Arches."

Leonardo's artistic and technical gifts were equally reflected in the field of military engineering. His sketchbooks are full of designs for military apparatus of every kind (PL. 118; IV, PL. 268), including various weapons and huge catapults that can be operated by one man despite their enormous size. Equally inventive are his projects for temporary bridges, provisional defensive structures, and offensive scaffolding consisting of easily movable parts that can be rapidly assembled and dismantled. The instructions provided deal with even the smallest details, such as the design of the knots to be used in fastening various parts to one another.

The major part of Leonardo's interest in military engineering was concentrated on the development of firearms (then still a novelty), especially artillery. He designed cannons that can be considered prototypes of the machine gun and other modern firearms. He was active as well in the elaboration of the breech-loading system and the movable gun carriage, which were to improve accuracy in aiming. Leonardo also contributed to the field of ballistics, and the results of his empirical investigations of the trajectory of missiles were applicable not only to artillery but also, and to an even greater extent, to the construction of fortifications. Although his mathematical calculations were inadequate, as a result of his ballistic studies apparently Leonardo became the first person to urge a change from the spherically shaped missile to a conical elongated one able to counteract atmospheric resistance. His designs for such missiles have fins and bear an uncanny resemblance to modern aerial bombs. The significant aspect of these inventions lies in Leonardo's profound insights into problems of ballistics and in the astounding practical application of his theoretical and empirical conclusions, even where the physical premises of his formulations have proved incorrect. This is especially apparent in his designs for fortifications (PL. 118), which show his awareness of new problems facing the military engineer as a result of the introduction of firearms. Aside from the necessary strengthening of the walls, the outstanding feature of Leonardo's defensive structures is the role given to rounded forms. Not only towers but also walls, especially their upper edges, are curved rather than flat and angular in shape. The innovation was an exceptionally intelligent measure intended to minimize the impact of a shot by presenting enemy artillery with an ineffective angle of incidence. Leonardo's ground-hugging forts also were a departure from the tradition of castle fortresses that were high and easily visible from a distance — a farsighted innovation in the light of changing military techniques.

To what extent Leonardo's plans were carried out is not known. The documents connected with his Milanese period show that he was intensively occupied with the fortifications of his patron's city, but the specific accomplishments of this activity can no longer be identified today. It may be assumed that in this branch of architecture, as in others, he functioned primarily in an advisory capacity as a man of considerable reputation. This is shown by his appointment as the chief military engineer and superintendent of fortifications in the service of Cesare Borgia. Leonardo occupied this post for almost a year (1502), traveling throughout the domains of the *condottiere* in Romagna, the Marches, Umbria, and Tuscany in order to inspect his military installations.

In the course of these duties he also executed a series of city plans and topographical maps for Cesare Borgia that greatly enhanced his fame both as a cartographer and as an artist. Having systematically investigated the principles of objective and subjective perspective in his *Treatise on Painting*, Leonardo applied mathematical perspective — and was the first to do so — in cartography, which demands the abstraction of natural vision. Aside from the land-registry maps in common use (schematic plans of entire cities or individual sections of the countryside) or the portolano charts used by mariners, an exact method of cartographic representation was unknown in Leonardo's time. He was apparently first in attempting to combine pictorial and planimetric representation, unifying image and measurement in an important step toward modern cartography. His plan of the city of Imola, which he drew while in the service of Cesare Borgia, is the first city plan to be consistently worked out from an imaginary vantage point. This is no longer the "church-tower perspective" seen in the famous plan of Venice drawn by Jacopo de' Barbari (1500) but a comprehensive view of a landscape. The medieval circular scheme with its division into individual sectors has been retained, but the circle now serves to delimit a real section of landscape as it might be seen from a balloon — a topographical as well as a pictorial entity. In his map of Tuscany, which depicts a watershed primarily, the landscape formation is represented as a flat surface, with elevation shown by gradations of color ranging from the green of the valleys to the dark brown of the mountains. The map would thus fit perfectly into a modern atlas. Another of Leonardo's maps shows a part of Tuscany including Arezzo and Perugia. Mountains and fortified towns are indicated in three dimensions, other elements of the landscape remaining diagrammatic. This method involves a conscious combination of cartographic and pictorial representational devices.

COURT ART. Leonardo produced considerable work as a designer of decorations for courtly festivities. Paolo Giovio called him "a highly admirable inventor and director of theatrical festivals"; many studies for allegorical representations, court festivals, theatrical representations, costumes, and parade weapons show his inventive genius and the variety of tasks of this kind that he frequently set for himself, especially while in the service of the Milanese ruler and at the courts of Louis XII and Francis I. Comprehensive studies, particularly those of Kate T. Steinitz (1961) and Carlo Pedretti (1957), have greatly added to our knowledge of Leonardo as a designer of stage sets and allegories. Of the more restricted studies, one of the most fascinating is Augusto Marinoni's work (1954) on the rebuses, or pictorial charades, which provide insight into that area of Leonardo's thought where verbal and pictorial concepts combined to produce a rich metaphorical content.

While these genial improvisations of Leonardo's, made for specific occasions, have been lost and can be reconstructed only through his sketches, one project of this type has been preserved — the painted decoration of the Sala delle Asse in the Castello Sforzesco in Milan. Badly disfigured by restoration at the beginning of the 20th century, the decoration partially reemerged after a judicious cleaning. It consists of 16 richly foliated trees with their branches artfully intertwined to form a thick leafy vault. The foliage is threaded with a golden cord forming an over-all, netlike pattern of ornamental knots (*gruppi*), a most ingenious combination of naturalistic and abstract elements. In contemporary north Italian painting, both stylized foliage and this type of knot ornament occur frequently, but only on a modest scale, as in a border or on the throne of a Madonna. Bramante also used knots in decoration, and Leonardo himself refers in a note to the "gruppi di Bramante" (Cod. Atlanticus, 225r). The famous engravings of knotted ornament bearing the inscription "Academia Leonardi Vincii" were widely known and prized as models. Dürer made woodcut copies of the entire set. The idea of combining these ornamental motifs in such an imaginative manner, however, was Leonardo's.

The trees in the Sala delle Asse are depicted as rooted in a stony ground from which they seem to burst under the impulse of their own vitality. They are a symbol of the transitory, for the same vitality which brought this artificial bower into being will be the agent of its inevitable destruction. The decorative concept of the Sala is thus not without certain tragic as well as historical implications. This is the first representation of a theme which became central to mannerism — the conflict between natural and artistic form, which was given full expression in the rustic architectural style of the period and in paintings such as those of Giulio Romano in the Palazzo del Te in Mantua. The theme continued on into the work of Buontalenti and, in its theoretical form, appeared in the writings of Vasari and Serlio and finally was expanded in the *Iconologia* of Cesare Ripa.

SCIENTIFIC WORKS. Leonardo's scientific work must be discussed as the accomplishment of an artist. He regarded himself primarily as an artist, and it was through art that he came into contact with science. Leonardo's first comprehensive task which brought together art and science was the *Treatise on Painting*. In the form in which it is presently known, this famous book is not an original work of the master but a compilation based on various manuscripts by Leonardo, made under the supervision of his student and heir, Francesco Melzi, about the middle of the 16th century. The manuscript copy of Melzi's work is preserved in the Vatican Library (Cod. Urbinas lat. 1270). Thus while the contents of Melzi's compilations are taken faithfully from Leonardo's notebooks, the sequence of the subjects was not established by the artist. In addition, this compilation by no means includes all of the numerous comments on painting found in Leonardo's original manuscripts.

The plan of the treatise as Leonardo intended it can be approximately inferred from literary sources and personal remarks of the master. It would have been composed of two principal parts dealing respectively with the theory and practice of painting. The theoretical part was to have dealt with perspective under the subheadings of linear, color, and aerial perspective. A chapter on light and shade was to have followed, presumably with a section on color theory, which is twice explicitly mentioned by Leonardo. The second part of the treatise, elaborating the practical aspects of painting, would have dealt with drawing and color, to be followed by large sections devoted to the human figure (proportion and anatomy) and its motion (physical and spiritual). Both parts of the work would have included rules and advice on composition, as in the earlier treatise of Alberti. These principles concerning the representation of man were to be followed by a discussion of the representation of nature. In this context Leonardo planned to deal with problems in the rendering of cosmic forces, the atmosphere, clouds, water, air, wind, and the structure of the earth and plants. Corresponding to the plan of earlier treatises, Leonardo's work might have been introduced by a comprehensive statement on the meaning of art and an attempt to define its relative significance in the form of a *paragone*, by which it was customary to compare the merits of painting with those of poetry, music, and sculpture. Whether his *precetti* were to have followed directly after the introduction, as in the Codex Urbinas, or to have been relegated to the conclusion, as in Alberti's treatise, is not known but is of no critical importance.

Available sources do not make it possible to define the over-all plan of Leonardo's intended treatise with greater precision. He had not himself, in any case, arrived at a final formulation of the work. This is shown by an analysis of the sequence of his notes for the project, as far as it can be determined in the original manuscripts. These notes stretch from the year 1490 until at least 1513, and thus over much of the artist's career. Just as Leonardo's scientific studies changed considerably during these years, so the treatise as Leonardo intended it toward the end of his life differed considerably from the scheme he had developed as a young man. The earlier plan is reflected in rough form in Manuscript 2038 in Paris (Inst. de France), and considerably later plans for the arrangement of the treatise are recorded in Manuscripts E and G (Paris, Inst. de France), probably conceived between 1510 and 1513.

The treatise should therefore be analyzed chronologically as well as for content. In the light of Leonardo's attempts to give his later theories a broader scope than was developed in earlier treatises, his relationship to the intellectual tradition of late Scholasticism must be considered, especially the concepts of order and value. The *paragone* was written about 1490, at a time when Leonardo's concepts were still in the formative stage. The *precetti* were also for the most part formulated early in his career, in so far as they were concerned with concepts of a general and didactic nature. In later years these principles were altered to some extent, and a more subtle distinction was made between practice and theory. The section dealing with anatomy is the result of considerable experience acquired over a long period of time through persistent study. Leonardo's anatomy lessons for the painter are not contained in the excerpts of the Codex Urbinas and must be reconstructed on the basis of the original manuscripts. His notes and drawings on the subject extended over his entire career, developing, as in the other parts of the treatise, from the purely descriptive to the broader issues of concept and meaning.

Leonardo's treatment of nature as it has been transmitted in the Codex Urbinas is confined to a number of sketchy passages. This section, which was to have dealt with cosmology from the viewpoint of the problems confronting the painter, must therefore also be culled from the original manuscripts.

Leonardo's practical application of his theories was determined by his conviction that by means of his *saper vedere* he must not only express the laws of nature in abstract terms but must also present them concretely. These demands on his sensory and intuitive capacities forced Leonardo to expand his work beyond the bounds of the traditional treatise on painting and led to a veritable encyclopedia of form and representation. One of the most significant aspects of Leonardo's method of exposition was the development of a dynamic and intimate relationship between word and picture, probably meant to be even more closely integrated than the Codex Urbinas would suggest. This is an innovation in art education which has been almost entirely overlooked. A large number of Leonardo's sketches can with certainty, often through the Codex Urbinas, be accepted as illustrations intended for the treatise on painting and can be clearly differentiated both from Leonardo's purely artistic sketches and from specific scientific projects. In the treatise drawings, especially in those of the late years, the two purposes of art and science are inseparable, further indicating how in this work Leonardo's interests are united. The dual allegiance of the treatise is all the more remarkable, considering that the work was created at a time when science and art were both bidding for the claim to greater objectivity.

Mathematics, optics, and mechanics. If there is one unifying principle in the great mass of notes and drawings left by Leonardo, it would seem to be an intention on his part to create nothing less than an encyclopedic exposition of human knowledge. Such an encyclopedia would have included optics as the necessary basis for correct perception, mechanics as the study of the physical forces within organic and inorganic nature, and biology as the study of growth and life, with anatomy as its central theme, and cosmology as the study of the forms and energy active in the universe. Leonardo believed himself qualified to undertake this gigantic task through his education as an artist. Only the artist, he believed, is endowed with *saper vedere*, owing to his dual ability to perceive reality and to transmit his perceptions to others.

"Let no one who is not a mathematician read my work," Leonardo wrote on one of his anatomical studies (Windsor, Royal Lib., 19118v). This statement, which Leonardo presumably meant to elaborate upon in the preface to his treatise on anatomy, must be properly interpreted: Leonardo was not a mathematician in the ordinary sense of the word. He considered mathematics to be the only science equipped with its own means of verification, to be the basis of all scientific thought; he accepted it as the logical foundation of perception. But Leonardo's activity as a mathematician was limited to the consideration of practical problems of a purely objective nature. He hardly concerned himself with arithmetic and concentrated for the most part on geometry, where his interest ranged from the Euclidian theorems to playful speculation. Already in Milan in 1494–98 he had set down in two notebooks the principal propositions of geometry that constituted the fundamentals of perspective for the art of that period and, therefore, the scientific foundation of painting. His main adviser in these matters had been Luca Pacioli, for whose *De divina proportione*, completed in Milan in 1497, Leonardo had provided illustrations. He may also have met mathematicians during his later travels to such places as Urbino.

Pacioli may also have interested Leonardo in the *ludi matematici*, the half-serious, half-playful exercises in mathematical speculation which the Renaissance had taken over from antiquity. These exercises involved problems of applied mathematics primarily: surveying and arithmetical puzzles, geometric combinations of simple ornamental constructions, matters relating to regular surfaces and bodies, the so-called "transformations," the squaring of curved planes, and the cubing of spheroids. Leonardo's manuscripts are full of such exercises. In the later years of his life he composed a work entitled *De ludo geometrico*, which was completed, according to a note, in Rome on July 7, 1514. There Leonardo manifested the same predilection for proportioning and geometric centering that is a dominant element of his artistic compositions. These mathematical fantasies, as they can be called, are the basis not only of much of Leonardo's ornamentation but also of his centralized ground plans, which are freely conceived as geometric configurations rather than constructions in response to specific practical demands. In Leonardo's painting, compositions such as *The Adoration of the Magi* (PL. 117) and, to an even greater extent, *The Battle of Anghiari* are based on geometric principles of organization, the general relationship of parts being governed largely by mathematical considerations.

Mathematical principles played a central role in the artistic theory of the time. Pacioli had divided mathematics into three parts — arithmetic, geometry, and proportion — and this was the conception held by Leonardo. In mathematics Leonardo saw a combination of logic and imagination, of abstract and concrete speculation, which could serve as a bridge between artistic and scientific preoccupations. This type of intuitive mathematical thinking was of constant assistance to him in problems of method and verification. He saw the principles of geometry and proportion as the starting point of every branch of science, as the regulator of nature manifest in the symmetrical structure of plants, sediment, whirlpools, and whirlwinds. All of Leonardo's studies in optics, mechanics, biology, and cosmology are based on this understanding of mathematics. Only through mathematics was he able to formulate the hidden laws of cosmic harmony that played such an important role in his thinking as both artist and scientist. "Proportion," he wrote, "is not only found in numbers and measurements but also in sounds, weights, time, and position, and whatsoever power there may be" (Paris, Inst. de France, Ms. K, 49r).

Of Leonardo's projected work on optical theory, only fragmentary preparatory studies are preserved, but even these show the dedication with which he pursued this inquiry, which was to constitute the foundation of his concept of cognition, just as his theory of vision formed the basis of his concept of art. His theory of vision held that the sense of sight was the most reliable instrument of perception, and in his study of optics he sought to prove this in mathematical terms. Beginning with artistic problems bearing on aerial and color perspective, treated in detail in the *Treatise on Painting*, Leonardo made intensive studies in the field of optical theory. He systematically investigated the formation of shadows in the presence of simple or multiple sources of light and developed a method for measuring the intensity of light (Paris, Inst. de France, Ms. C, 22r). He was aware of the reversal of the image in the human eye and had also arrived at the principle of the camera obscura. His observations on optics are startling. He was fully cognizant of the reflection, refraction, and diffraction of light rays, and even the phenomena of interference and irradiation were familiar to him. He analyzed the spectrum and knew that the kaleidoscopic effects of color in bird feathers, iridescent glass, and oil slicks were caused by the refraction of light. He made a precise description of the diffraction of light around a candle flame, even though his explanation of this phenomenon proved incorrect. He accurately explained the glimmer of starlight as a natural consequence of the mechanism of vision reacting to the circular diffusion of light and thus recognized the interference principle of light rays.

Leonardo's achievement in the field of optics lies more in the discovery of specific natural phenomena than in their explanation. His contribution was made possible by singular powers of perception. Leonardo observed with the naked eye phenomena that even today can be detected only with the help of instruments and with a certain amount of effort. He did not approach nature as a methodically trained scholar but with a great thirst for knowledge that led him to perform countless experiments; lacking a logically consistent procedure, these experiments did not lead to theoretically conclusive results.

Leonardo's studies in mechanics also depended on observation primarily and were based largely on his powers of perception and his ability to present his perceptions in an objective representational form. Here again Leonardo's artistic activity was the point of departure for his interest in a particular branch of science, and his concern with mechanics only gradually developed into a preoccupation for its own sake. To understand this development one must separate Leonardo's interest in mechanics as an engineer and as a theoretician. Until old age, Leonardo remained a brilliantly inventive engineer. His sketchbooks, full of technical studies, show that he was a master of applied mechanics. Models constructed on the basis of his drawings, for the great Leonardo exhibition in Milan in 1939, proved that many of his ideas were thoroughly practical and could be fully realized. Most of Leonardo's drawings of machines — in contrast to earlier, contemporaneous, and, in some cases, later graphic representations of mechanical devices by others — could easily be translated into working models. This is a result not only of their clarity as drawings but also of the application of correct mechanical principles, often merely through intuition.

The historical importance of Leonardo as an inventor, however, stems less from his innumerable designs than from his fundamentally new approach to the machine as a mechanical organism. This new attitude arose in the process of developing a scientific, experimental method based on an orderly progression from practice to theory and on the formulation of general principles as a step beyond the observation of individual phenomena. Leonardo subjected the most varied aspects of mechanics to a precise analysis. On one of the sheets of the Codex Atlanticus, for example, the principal types of cogwheels and threads are drawn side by side; on another, calculations concerning the operation of pulleys are entered. It would appear that Leonardo had intended to compose a compendium of elements of the machine, which would have served as a guide in all types of endeavors connected with construction; such a guide would indeed have been an unprecedented achievement.

All of Leonardo's studies on construction show a common concern with the operation of mechanical forces, a concern which over the years came more and more to the fore. His principal interest, despite great competence as an engineer, was in theoretical rather than applied mechanics. (The material on mechanics was collected and annotated by Arturo Uccelli, 1940.) "Mechanics," Leonardo wrote, "is the paradise of the mathematical sciences because by means of it one comes to the fruits of mathematics" (Paris, Inst. de France, Ms. E, 8v). As the theory of the forces active within nature, mechanics became the focus of his investigations into the laws that govern the universe.

Leonardo had considered bringing together his studies on applied and theoretical mechanics in one large work, and often referred to ideas elaborated in his *Libro del peso*. He was aware of most of the available literature on this subject and stated his position in regard to the two major schools of scientific thought of his day — the dominant qualitative or philosophic doctrines of late Scholasticism and the quantitative and experimental ones of the school of Jordanus Nemorarius: Leonardo was essentially predisposed toward the latter, but being skeptically inclined and self-trained, he jealously guarded his independence and remained aloof from all factions.

Leonardo's experimental method applied to mechanics was also based exclusively on the concept of *saper vedere*. His keen observation permitted him to record the most trifling occurrences in nature, which were then tested through comparison with other material and ultimately visually demonstrated by graphic means. There exist an enormous number of drawings and calculations concerning the lever, the scale, the inclined plane, friction and resistance, and the principle of virtual velocities. Often the same problem is repeated in endless variations, and it seems unclear whether Leonardo had arrived at any logical conclusion. As a rule he was content to demonstrate a particular phenomenon and did not feel compelled to elaborate on its general theoretical implications. When he did formulate concepts of statics and kinetics, he was able to recognize their validity within the total realm of nature. The conformity of natural laws to one principle of order never failed to evoke his wonder. Leonardo expressed this in his famous concept of force (Paris, Inst. de France, Ms. A, 34v), which, although it does not provide a theoretical definition of force, was for the time a significant statement and provides insight into the philosophy of science of this "omo sanza lettere."

Anatomy and physiology. "Arrange it so that the book of the elements of mechanics with examples shall precede the demonstration of the movement and force of man and of the other animals, and by means of these you will be able to prove all your propositions" (Windsor, Royal Lib., Anatomical Ms. A, 10r). These words, written between 1510 and 1513, express the natural connection between Leonardo's views on mechanics and anatomy and, at the same time, point to the new direction which his studies in biology were to take. Leonardo's investigation of anatomy grew out of the practical knowledge of this science common among artists of the period. His earliest drawings, which can be dated in the 1480s, are characterized by an earnest effort to master the structure of the human body, a goal which he was to establish in his *Treatise on Painting* as an important requirement in the training of artists. But apparently the medical practices of his time soon made Leonardo skeptical about the anatomical knowledge available and led to an interest in the subject that was to make him a truly fanatical student of anatomy. In 1498 he composed a plan for a comprehensive treatise on anatomy (Windsor, Royal Lib., Anatomical Ms. B, 20v). In this project the thirty-seven-year-old Leonardo proposed for himself the task of a lifetime: Proportion, physiology, physiognomy, and psychology; these themes, which would absorb his interest throughout his artistic career, were to be dealt with as autonomous subjects of investigation. The mere fact that Leonardo considered anatomy in such a broad sense, embracing the principles of growth of the organism and the study of the mechanism of life itself, raises his efforts far above the scientific concerns of his contemporaries.

Leonardo had to provide his own tools of investigation. According to his testimony he dissected 30 cadavers, an astoundingly high number at that time. He had to improvise entirely new means of representation; contemporaneous scientific practice and literature were of no help. Thus Leonardo's investigations were conducted in two directions simultaneously: toward the intuitive perception of phenomena and toward the discovery of means to illustrate that which is known. To a much greater degree than in his studies on mechanics, Leonardo's aims in the field of anatomy were directed toward the perfection of the image as a carrier of information capable not only of supplementing the written word but also of supplanting it. He felt impelled to place his skill in the service of science and truth and clearly expressed this view in a passage written about 1507, intended for the preface of his anatomical studies (Windsor, Royal Lib., Quaderni d'Anatomia, I, 2r, 13v).

The bulk of Leonardo's anatomical studies (PL. 118; IV, PL. 268) can be distributed within three periods of his life, each representing a stage in his development. One group of notes and drawings was produced in the Milanese period of 1490–1500; another can be attributed to his 1502–07 stay in Florence; a third can be placed in Milan and Rome in the period of 1508–15. In Rome his anatomy studies were interrupted when Pope Leo X, on the basis of slander, denied him access to the death chamber of the Ospedale di Sto Spirito. Yet Leonardo did not fully abandon his studies; until his death he continued to work on his great anatomy treatise.

The early anatomical studies dealt principally with the skeletal frame and musculature. Already in these works there appeared a new type of anatomical representation based upon a scientific method of demonstration. Later the mechanics of the body became the major concern of these studies. That a purely artistic problem was sometimes the stimulus for scientific inquiry is shown in the preparatory drawings for *The Battle of Anghiari*: one study for a fighting man is unexpectedly accompanied by a precise analysis of the function of the shoulder muscles (Windsor, Royal Lib., 12640). Many beautiful examples among Leonardo's analytical drawings show how the same problem was handled (Windsor, 19003v). In these drawings the graphic requirements for scientific illustration are fully developed, including various typical sections, the simplification of forms carried almost to conscious stylization, and representation of the three-dimensional body in full transparency. Leonardo developed these principles in a group of written instruction sheets. While the rules deal only with the principles of scientific illustration, the drawings themselves not only realize these rules but also exhibit Leonardo's artistic genius, which is of primary importance in his anatomical studies.

Leonardo's interest in the life processes of man led him to give special attention to the internal organs, especially the lungs and heart. In a number of fine drawings he recorded the lungs with the bronchial tubes, the larynx, the throat, the soft palate, the windpipe, and the gullet. He minutely investigated the process of vocal production and modulation and the musculature of the tongue and lips. A drawing of the lip muscles (Windsor, Royal Lib., Anatomical Ms. B, 38v) recalls those studies, previously mentioned, comparing the expressions of man and beast. Actually, Leonardo's late drawings of skeletal and muscular anatomy would appear to the true anatomist to be riddled with errors, as in the representation of the spine in one of his last anatomical sketches (Windsor, Royal Lib., 19075v). The apparent inaccuracy, however, was intentional and motivated by Leonardo's desire to represent the muscular system so that the head appears to be supported by the spinal column "like a mast by its rigging." In order to make this comparison clear, Leonardo deliberately represented the trapezius as a series of individual cords, although he had often represented it in its normal form. He was certainly also aware that the muscles are attached to the shoulder blade proper and not to its upper edge. This schematization also must have been suggested by the comparison with the mast. He was not concerned here with the correct representation of anatomical form but rather with the illustration of a mechanical principle and thus was willing to sacrifice accuracy in favor of meaningful stylization. This is a characteristic aspect of what might be called his "speculative physiology," although in his hydraulic and aerological studies, as well as in the purely artistic creations of his last years, similar tendencies may be observed. In his late anatomical studies Leonardo remained faithful to his basic ideal, the visual representation of the forces operative in the organism. This is shown in his treatment of the problems of respiration and movement of the blood and to an even greater degree in his embryological studies, which led him close to the mystery of generation. His analysis of the reproductive organs reflects the keen precision of his powers of observation, even though several errors may be found in his representations. Thus in his famous drawing of the uterus (Windsor, Royal Lib., 19102r) he was led by an erroneous process of analogy to show the cotyledons of the placenta as they appear in the cow, not as they exist in the human female. The position of the embryo and the placement of the umbilical cord, however, are rendered with such accuracy and excellence that this drawing is still found in medical textbooks.

The value of Leonardo's anatomical studies lies in the keenness of his observation and the force of his imagination. When his powers of perception could not be put to use, however, Leonardo's conclusions suffered. His failure to recognize the circulation of the blood, although he had correctly understood nearly all the individual phenomena connected with it, is a prime example of the limitations of his method.

In about 1507 Leonardo came in contact with the Pavian doctor Marc' Antonio della Torre. The close collaboration with this distinguished man was highly rewarding, and through him Leonardo had the opportunity to acquaint himself with the best that contemporary medicine had to offer. In addition to the art of dissection and experimentation on living subjects, he was able to familiarize himself with the current terminology of medicine, much of which went back to Galen.

Zoology and botany. Apart from his general pictorial studies after nature, Leonardo's zoological interests fall mainly within the framework of comparative anatomy. Only two subjects within this area interested him seriously, each for very different reasons: the anatomy of the horse and the flight of birds. It is known from various sources that Leonardo composed a work on the anatomy of the horse, but it is no longer possible to reconstruct its scheme. The work was known to both Dürer and Rubens, probably through copies of individual sheets which must have been widely circulated (cf. New York, Pierpont Morgan Lib., Cod. Huygens, in part derived from Leonardo's work; XI, PL. 348). Today the only remaining evidence for the existence of this work is a number of splendid drawings, for the most part in the Royal Library at Windsor.

The artist's studies on the flight of birds continued throughout his life. At the time that the thirty-year-old Leonardo was offering his numerous inventions and engineering designs to the Duke of Milan, he must have formulated the idea of constructing a flying machine. The early sketches and notations for this project largely concern the adaptation of the principle of the bird wing to human flight. In his anatomical investigations Leonardo identified two principal parts in the structure of the wing: the concave underside, to which he attributed the load-bearing function, and the upper, convex surface, which he associated with motion. He intended to apply these findings in the construction of his flying machine (Milan, Ambrosiana, Cod. Atlanticus, 276, 311). On the evidence of the many surviving drawings the flying devices that Leonardo developed in his Milanese period can be divided into two types. In the first, the flier was strapped in a horizontal position and the flying mechanism was activated by swimming motions made with his hands and feet. In the second, he stood erect and with his hands and feet operated a complicated crank mechanism that reproduced the motion of wings in flight. Both types were unworkable, owing primarily to the great disproportion between the weight of the flier and the amount of motor power he could generate solely by means of muscular exertion. The experiments have great historical value, however, for Leonardo's methodological premises were based on fundamentally sound assumptions concerning the nature of air and its resistance. An indication of Leonardo's clear thinking is that he himself discovered the critical flaw in his invention and sought to rebuild his theory of human flight on an entirely new foundation. The Codice sul Volo degli Uccelli ("Codex on the Flight of Birds," Turin, Bib. Reale), written in Florence about 1500–05, is worked out with systematic clarity. Beginning with the consideration that a heavy body can be maintained in a floating state through aerial resistance, Leonardo studied the motion of birds' wings in windy and calm atmospheric conditions. He analyzed the process of flight itself: gliding flight; motion forward in straight, inclined, and curved patterns; climbing and descent; slowing down in flight and when landing. Through his investigation of the complex mechanical problems associated with flight, Leonardo gained insight into the characteristics of atmospheric behavior, which he later incorporated in his more general consideration of aerological and hydraulic problems. These studies were to be the basis of his cosmology, his study of inorganic nature. When in the last years of his life, about 1513, he once more turned his attention to the flight of birds, he was motivated to do so by purely physical problems. His primary interest at this later point was in the characteristics of air (Paris, Inst. de France, Ms. E). Thus Leonardo's interest in flight passed through the same phases evident in his other work — from the systematic exploration of a problem, to the theoretical analysis of the data gathered, to the practical application of derived principles, and ultimately to the formulation of a comprehensive, speculative theory.

Leonardo's interest was led to the field of botany (PL. 118; IV, PL. 268), as it was to anatomy, through the mediation of painting. In his early paintings and drawings he had exhibited a special fondness for the plant world. At about the age of thirty he had begun to collect plants and was making drawings and wax impressions of leaves in order to study their skeletal structures. From external appearance he proceeded to an analysis of form and organic structure. He was able to make a number of fundamental discoveries which are still valid today, and his work is considered of such importance that he has been designated the founder of the science of botany. Since antiquity the study of plants had been largely the domain of pharmacology and magic, and the sole concern had been with their useful or harmful qualities. Leonardo was the first to conceive of botany as an autonomous biological science. A sheet of studies in the Accademia in Venice, admirably delicate and precisely rendered, is perhaps the earliest example of scientific botanical illustration, even though it was certainly executed as a study of artistic motifs. Leonardo's later drawings reflect his profound understanding of the nature of the plant organism. In his study of a star-of-Bethlehem at Windsor Castle (12424), the living growth of the plant has been beautifully expressed, while the Windsor drawing of the Cyperaceae (12427) could easily be used as an illustration in a modern textbook.

Cosmology and other physical sciences. Many of Leonardo's commissions stimulated his interest in the problems of inorganic nature. In the practice of his craft as a painter, as a military engineer and cartographer, and especially as a hydraulic engineer, he was forced to face these problems. In the course of his studies, however, his interest developed into the independent pursuit of geology. Through a concern with the shape of the earth's surface he gained an insight into its structure. His singularly well-developed powers of observation led him to formulate conclusions which, in this field too, were remarkable for his time and are still to a large extent valid today. According to his own word, he became preoccupied with geological questions as early as his work on the Sforza monument (i.e., before 1500). His notes on the properties of water, which he consigned to a large manuscript (Cod. Leicester, ca. 1500–04, Norfolk, Holkham

Hall, Earl of Leicester Coll.) and to various notebooks (Paris, Inst. de France, Mss. E and F; Milan, Ambrosiana, Cod. Atlanticus), were in large part written only after 1500. In close relation with aerological studies, this interest extended to the end of his life.

Through his own efforts to discover the true origin of fossils, based on the theories of Albert von Helmstedt, Leonardo was able to arrive at a highly precise explanation of various forms of sedimentation. The study of fossils apparently made him conscious of the infinite span of time and of time's all-consuming power. When, however, he believed his own means of perception to be exhausted, he fell back on traditional theories. For a relatively long time he attempted to base his explanation of the behavior of terrestrial bodies on inferences drawn from the observation of the human body. Thus he adhered to the macrocosm-microcosm theory that had been formulated in antiquity, transmitted by the Middle Ages, and ultimately taken over by Renaissance philosophy, especially in the work of Nicholas of Cusa. Similarly Leonardo drew on the theories of ancient writers and commentators to help him formulate a general theory of the earth's origin based on his discoveries in connection with fossils. When he was in a position to make direct geological observations, however, as in studying the Italian peninsula, his opinions became more realistic. In Tuscany Leonardo made a thorough survey of the valley of the Arno and the Apennine chain, and while in Milan he investigated the valley of the Po and the Alpine region.

Observing the broad area watered by the Po, the Alpine rivers and streams, the snow-covered peaks of the great mountains (he had been the first to climb far above the snow line on Monte Rosa), everywhere he saw evidence that water is the dominant force of nature. "Water is nature's carter," he once wrote (Paris, Inst. de France, Ms. K, 2r), and to the study of water he devoted himself tirelessly. While in his geological pursuits Leonardo attempted to grasp the static form of the earth, the aim of his study of water was to seek out its dynamic forces. In Milan Leonardo had the opportunity to learn much that was new from the Lombards, who since ancient times were known for their skill in engineering. His notebooks record the names of many hydraulic engineers from whose practical and theoretical experience he profited. As an independent technician Leonardo first appears in connection with a project that was being considered by the Florentine Signoria between 1502 and 1504, when Leonardo was technical advisor for the Florentines. The project, previously mentioned, was aimed at cutting off the beleaguered city of Pisa from access to the sea. Leonardo's bold plan to divert the waters of the Arno into canals was abandoned because it held no prospect of quick military success. But from this military scheme grew the more productive idea of making the Arno navigable and at the same time opening up large stretches of reclaimed land for agricultural purposes (Cod. Atlanticus, 46r-b). Leonardo's notes and cartographic sketches indicate the farsightedness that characterized his efforts in hydraulic engineering and land reclamation.

A more practical scheme occupied Leonardo during his second Milanese stay — that of making the Adda River navigable in order to connect Milan and Lake Como by a direct waterway (Windsor, Royal Lib., 12399; Cod. Atlanticus, 141v-b). During his stay in Rome Leonardo became involved with a project for reclaiming the Pontine Marshes that was begun in 1515 by Giovanni Scotti da Como, a north Italian. In France Leonardo elaborated a plan for the drainage of the marshes in the Sologne region for Francis I, to make land available for the castle and gardens that the King intended to build at Romorantin (London, Br. Mus., Cod. Arundel, 263, 270v).

The significance of these hydraulic projects lies less in their technical achievement, which can often no longer be defined in detail, than in their theoretical foundation, all the more admirable for having been developed on the basis of personal observation and experience. Leonardo's notes indicate that he intended to write a comprehensive treatise on the nature and characteristics of water, and individual studies from the 1490s as well as the later work in the Codex Leicester bear out this intention. On one of the first leaves of the Codex Leicester he outlined his work as follows: "These books contain in their first part, of the nature of water itself in its motions; the others treat of the effects of its currents, which change the world in its center and shape" (5r). During the 17th century an anthology of his notes was made in an attempt to reconstruct a treatise on the nature of water, after the model of the *Treatise on Painting*. Repeatedly reprinted, this work included only incomplete parts of the extant material in the original manuscripts. The organization of the work also did not conform to what appears to have been Leonardo's far more ambitious outline.

As always, Leonardo separated the concepts of substance and function. In numerous experiments he analyzed water as matter, characterizing it as a flowing mass incapable of either altering its basic substance or of engendering its own motion. He was then led to differentiate the two states of motion that water might exhibit as a result of external conditions: stationary and progressive. The principal subject of his hydromechanical studies was the investigation of the forward motion of water and the principles of its flow. Leonardo was especially fascinated by the movements of eddies, which stirred his artistic sense by their beauty and organization; through them he became conscious of the great variety of effects produced by the behavior of mechanical forces. Leonardo was able to depict clearly the complicated optical phenomenon presented by the swirling vortex (Windsor, Royal Lib., 12680), and his studies of eddies are among his most impressive works of graphic demonstration. In both scientific and purely artistic terms, these drawings are a vivid testimony of Leonardo's remarkable powers of analytical and synthetic observation (Windsor, Royal Lib., 12660v).

In order to assess these drawings properly it is necessary to grasp the intellectual process by which they came into being. Even more remarkable than Leonardo's brilliance in unraveling the complex structure of eddies is his ability to give a clear account of both the formal characteristics and the functional properties of such a piece of "water sculpture." For Leonardo's drawing clarifies not only this fascinating play of forms but also the dynamics of the interplay of forces present in the constantly moving, yet basically unchanging, liquid body.

As in the case of his anatomical and biological studies, Leonardo's investigations of water show the combination of artistic and scientific thinking that characterizes his work. The method of graphic representation exhibited in his drawing of the eddy depends on the same principles followed in his late anatomical drawings — transparency and formal stylization. The conscious schematization by which a simultaneous analytic and synthetic visualization is achieved serves both an artistic and a scientific end. The eddy depicted as an ornament composed of lines of force is intended to express the harmony of form and of function as the effect of natural law.

New considerations growing out of his investigations of water led to Leonardo's return to the study of birds during his later years. He now began to study the air as a medium and bearer of cosmic energy. Leonardo observed that air, in contrast to water, is markedly compressible and expandable and that its density decreases in proportion to its distance from the ground. He devoted special attention to the whirling motion of the wind, its course, and its various forms. He noted that whirling currents and the conditions that produce them occur most frequently in mountainous regions. He compared these natural phenomena with certain similar characteristics in whirlpools. Leonardo had also observed that birds make use of upward currents to keep themselves aloft with a minimum of effort. A late drawing (Paris, Inst. de France, Ms. E, 23v) demonstrates this point in an interesting way: The waves breaking against the cliff stand not only for water but also for air currents, whose direction of motion is used to advantage by the gulls in landing and taking off. The invisible lines of force of the wind currents are thus graphically rendered in much the same way as the currents of water. This sketch shows a method of draftsmanship which is important in Leonardo's last graphic works — that of materializing invisible cosmic forces in the elements in which they operate.

Leonardo was over sixty when he began his final study of the principles of water and air currents. Between 1513 and 1517 he was intensely preoccupied with these problems and instituted various experiments shortly before his death. The conclusions drawn from these experiments moved Leonardo to work on a visual and visionary representation of the ultimate resolution of the forces active in the universe. What emerged was a series of drawings in black chalk called the *Deluge* drawings; they were not intended to represent the Biblical flood but rather the end of the world.

The technique that Leonardo had already employed for the generalized representation of material substances in his scientific illustrations and in his demonstration of upward air currents appears in the *Deluge* drawings as a wholly distinctive method of representation. Through a process of stylization the various materials in nature — stone, water, clouds, air — are rendered virtually undistinguishable from one another and are thus reduced to their common material denominator. Invisible cosmic forces manifest themselves in the substances which they, the forces, motivate, compelling these substances to assume the forms in which they in turn act as prime movers according to fundamental mechanical laws. Thus the basic forces and functions of the cosmos are revealed through the basic cosmic substances. Leonardo's *Deluge* drawings are symbols of these basic forces in their final resolution, destroying what they themselves have brought into being, yet destined even in the final destruction of the universe to conform to the principles of order and harmony. The ultimate conclusions which Leonardo formulated as a scientist were thereby given expression in artistic terms, revealing again the indissoluble bond between his scientific and artistic inclinations.

With this synthesis of scientific reason and artistic imagination, Leonardo pushed to the fullest his powers of visual suggestion. How deeply he was aware of human limitation is reflected in his statement: "Nature is full of infinite causes which were never set forth in experience" (Paris, Inst. de France, Ms. I, 18r). Until the last moments of his life Leonardo remained secure in his belief in the existence of a universal harmony governing all forms and forces, all time and space, which would manifest itself even in the apparent chaos of the end of the world. He sought to discover this harmony in the phenomena which came into the range of his spirit and to bring it into all his own creations through the medium of his art.

Ludwig H. Heydenreich

LEONARDO'S THOUGHT. To attempt to derive an organic vision of life and reality, or indeed a systematic philosophy, from Leonardo's writings would be to misunderstand his work profoundly. His fragments do not constitute a philosophy in the technical sense. Nothing could be more mistaken than the effort that has at times been made to compare them to fragments of the writings of the Greek pre-Socratic philosophers — which are, in fact, scattered remains of what once were integrated works arranged to present a total vision of reality. Leonardo's literary remains are merely hasty notes on technique and construction, artistic memoranda, maxims and aphorisms, and notebooks with words and phrases that interested him. Rational chains of argument and the foundations provided by consciously elaborated principles — the very sinews of philosophy — are missing.

Leonardo's scanty knowledge of Latin precluded direct access to the scientific work of his contemporaries. He was informed on matters that were debated and discussed, but the books he consulted were compilations, often out of date and mediocre in quality — Pliny in the vernacular translation of Landino, Ramusio's *Valturio*, Cecco d'Ascoli's *L'Acerba*, Brunetto Latini's *Trésor*. But this apparent limitation constitutes his strength. Leonardo's lack of access to traditional expositions freed him from the dead weight of a passive inheritance to which he reacted with disdain and scorn. The culture of the universities, the Scholastic tradition, the circumscribed research of the natural scientists as well as the theologians, belonged to a different world; the small part of it that filtered through to Leonardo in vernacular translations and in conversations served to stimulate his curiosity without stifling his originality, even though the gulf between his method of inquiry and the method of the world in which he lived left his efforts without an echo. The more one studies his manuscripts, the more it becomes apparent that Leonardo had only slight cognizance of classic and late medieval science, and this was derived from minor or popular works, public debates, and discussions among the learned and in artists' workshops in such centers of rapid dissemination of ideas as Florence. His many remarks based on a name, a secondhand reference, a word, or a trite question are hardly informative. When not anachronistic, they at most reveal a horizontal culture, a background of problems and doctrines. Leonardo's work cannot be identified with any circumscribed trend, be it Platonism, Cusanism (the philosophy of Nicholas of Cusa), Parisian physical science, or Aristotelianism; one finds throughout his notes an indifference to coordinated, unified argument capable of reconciling differences and contradictions. Yet his thought, which remains perhaps his greatest innovation, is nonetheless based on certain specific points; these form the sole basis for an attempt to isolate his first principles.

The Ariadne's thread that may serve as a guide among so many scattered riches is the constancy of the method imposed on the investigation — a new classification, so to speak, of the arts and their reciprocal connections. Thus one must consider the revolt, common at the time but nonetheless important, against the "authors," against knowledge based on the commentary of a book: "the authors, who by employing only their imagination, wished to make themselves interpreters between man and nature" (Paris, Inst. de France, Ms. I, 102r and v). That Leonardo, in his disdain of "letters," sought to reject the world of the 15th-century Humanists has been often repeated; but it has been less commonly observed that his rejection struck primarily at a science of nature which was largely limited to annotating Aristotle and which insisted on the interposition of an authoritative text "between man and nature." Leonardo wanted to eliminate the concept according to which the only "scientific knowledge is that ... which is born and ends in the mind."

The collection that constitutes the *Treatise on Painting* contains some of the most significant strictures against "the lying sciences of the mind," while the principles of certainty are outlined with precision. For Leonardo the condition of knowledge was the circle from experience to experience, by way of the mind and reason. Leonardo's power and originality reside not in the insistent demand that there be a recourse to sense experience — that is nothing new — but rather in the criticism of the mental sciences and in the method of apprehending the integration of the mind and senses and the integration of experience and mechanical operations. He declared that "those sciences are vain which have not passed through the senses," that "experience [is] the mother of all certainty," and that the investigation into "things which cannot be tested by the senses [such as] the nature of God and of the soul or similar things" is destined to remain subject to perpetual dispute and contention. ("Where reason is wanting, men cry out against each other, which does not happen with certainties.") Thus emerges a clear criterion for discriminating between the spheres of contention and scientific certainty. The "eternal silence" which follows the mathematical proof is contrasted to the eternal clamor of the philosophers. "Where one disputes there is no true science; because the truth has one single end, which being published, argument is destroyed forever" (*Trattato della pittura*, ed. Borzelli, 1924, par. 29; Windsor, Royal Lib., Quaderni d'Anatomia, II, 14r).

The result is a reshuffling in Leonardo's records of the customary hierarchy of disciplines. Those which, precisely because of their separation from the perceivable, held the higher position in the Renaissance view are simply dismissed with an elementary principle: Where the "dispute" is not eliminated either by demonstrable mathematics or by experiment, there is nothing but sophism. "The true sciences are those which have been penetrated by the senses, so that the tongues of argument are silenced; ... [the true sciences] do not nourish on the dreams of investigators but proceed in orderly sequence from the first true and established principles through successive stages to the end" (*Trattato della pittura*, par. 29). And their character is further specified by Leonardo, both for the mathematical fundamentals concerned and for their relationship to things. He tends to consider natural processes as reducible to mathematical fundamentals; and mechanical, "practical," or "manual" operations as an integral part of the very process of scientific knowing. ("These true and exact sciences belong to the mechanical sciences because they cannot be brought to conclusion without manual operations.")

Perhaps this is the most brilliant as well as the most ambiguous of Leonardo's positions: most brilliant if we observe the development of the relationship between theory and practice, of the idea of continuous intervention of the senses (through hand and eye), and of the concept of building "manually," which is present in drawing, painting, sculpture, and in all the natural sciences that are "brought to conclusion" by means of machines and various instruments.

Beginning with the science of painting ("which is first in the mind of the conceiver and cannot come into being without manual activity"), Leonardo posits a new significance for man and his relationship with nature: He holds that natural processes actuate, in concrete experience, a rational necessity for the shortest methods that can be devised (Cod. Arundel, 85v). But man, "the greatest instrument of nature," through experience becomes "an interpreter between resourceful nature and the human species" and may succeed in investigating the cause of these natural processes (Milan, Ambrosiana, Cod. Atlanticus 86r-a). The knowledge of causes, which by necessity guide the creative processes, allows man to insert in nature, which does not vary the ordinary species she has created, the temporal novelty of his own creations. Nature "is concerned only with the production of elementary things," while man "with these elementary things produces an infinite number of compounds [which] change with the passage of time."

While the various "true sciences" with "manual operations" and machines diffuse pragmatic knowledge in every possible direction, the reflection on nature — which has its own "reasons," or rational necessity, and which, as he also recognizes, encompasses the human sphere — constitutes the philosophic nucleus of Leonardo's idea of reflection. Yet while speculations on the "true sciences" present a solid beginning, in the area of "pure philosophy" we encounter only hindrances in the ambiguity of terms and concepts not yet resolved. His discussion of nature constrained to the necessity of laws recalls a historic theme already treated by L. B. Alberti. There is oscillation in meaning in his use of such terms as "spirit," "spiritual," "soul," and "force" — all of which are key concepts. [Opposing interpretations of his terms are given by C. Luporini (1953) and A. Marinoni (1954), for example.] Philosophically it is but one step from a mode of thought that reduces reality to a nature animated by infused "reasons" to a reality that subsumes nature within a spirit that inwardly nourishes the All. Thus Ficino echoed Lucretius, and Leonardo in turn echoed Ficino, although the Leonardian cadence differs: "home" is nature, not heaven; "the chief evil is the suffering of the body" (Milan, Bibl. Trivulziana, Cod. Trivulzio, 2v), not sin; and "the definition of the soul is left to the wisdom of the friars..., who by inspiration know all mysteries" (Windsor, Royal Lib., Quaderni d'Anatomia, IV, 10r). Here, in pragmatic knowledge and in "true science," lies Leonardo's personal quality as a thinker — in the convergence of an ardent naturalistic inspiration and an ambiguous Platonic atmosphere.

Eugenio GARIN

WRITINGS. *a. Codices*: Paris, Inst. de France, Bib., Mss. A, B, C, D, E, F, G, H, I, K (often separated into K¹, K², K³), L, M, 2037 (formerly Ashburnham 1875/1), 2038 (formerly Ashburnham 1875/2) [C. Ravaisson-Mollien, Les manuscrits de Léonard de Vinci de la Bibliothèque de l'Institut de France, 6 vols., Paris, 1881–91; I manoscritti e i disegni di Leonardo da Vinci pubblicati dalla Commissione Vinciana, II: Il Codice A (2172) nell'Istituto di Francia, Rome, 1936; A. Corbeau et al., Léonard de Vinci: Manuscrit B de l'Institut de France, Grenoble, 1960]; Milan, Castello Sforzesco, Arch. Storico Civ., Bib. Trivulziana, Cod. Trivulzio [L. Beltrami, Il codice di Leonardo da Vinci nella Biblioteca del Principe Trivulzio in Milano, Milan, 1891; Comune di Milano, Raccolta Vinciana, testi vinciani, I: Il Codice Trivulziano, ed. N. De Toni, Milan, 1939]; Turin, Bib. Reale, Codex on the Flight of Birds [T. Sabachnikoff and G. Piumati, Codice sul volo degli uccelli e varie altre materie, Fr. trans. by C. Ravaisson-Mollien, Paris, 1893; E. Carusi, ed., I fogli mancanti del Codice di Leonardo da Vinci sul volo degli uccelli, Rome, 1926; J. da Badia Polesine, ed., Il Codice sul volo degli uccelli, Milan, 1946]; Milan, Bib. Ambrosiana, Cod. Atlanticus [G. Piumati, ed., Il Codice Atlantico..., 3 vols., Milan, 1894–1904; G. Galbiati, Dizionario Leonardesco: Repertorio delle voci e cose contenute nel Codice Atlantico, Milan, 1939; G. Semenza and R. Marcolongo, Indici del Codice Atlantico, Milan, 1939; C. Pedretti, Cronologia dei fogli del Codice Atlantico, in S. vinciani (Travaux d'Hum. et Renaissance, XXVII), Geneva, 1957, pp. 264–84; C. Pedretti, Fragments at Windsor Castle from the Codex Atlanticus, London, 1957; C. Pedretti, Spigolature nel Codice Atlantico, Bib. d'Hum. et Renaissance, XXII, 1960, p. 526 ff.]; Windsor Castle, Royal Lib., Anatomy, Folio A, B, Quaderni d'Anatomia I–VI [T. Sabachnikoff and G. Piumati, Dell'Anatomia, Fogli A, Paris, 1898; T. Sabachnikoff and G. Piumati, Dell'Anatomia, Fogli B, Paris, 1901; O. C. I. Vangenstein, A. Fonahn, and H. Hopstock, Leonardo da Vinci: Quaderni di Anatomia, I–VI, Christiania, 1911–16; K. Clark, A Catalogue of the Drawings of Leonardo da Vinci at Windsor Castle, Cambridge, 1935]; London, Br. Mus., Cod. Arundel 263 [Commissione Vinciana, ed., Il Codice Arundel 263, 4 vols., Rome, 1923–30; C. Pedretti, Cronologia del Codice Arundel di Leonardo da Vinci, Bib. d'Hum. et Renaissance, XXII, 1960, pp. 172–77]; London, Vict. and Alb., Cod. Forster I–III [Commissione Vinciana, ed., Il Codice Forster nel Victoria and Albert Museum, 5 vols., Rome, 1930–36]; Norfolk, Holkham Hall, Lib. of the Earl of Leicester, Cod. Leicester [G. Calvi, Il Codice di Leonardo da Vinci della Biblioteca di Lord Leicester in Holkham Hall, Milan, 1909]. *b. Anthologies*: E. Solmi, Leonardo da Vinci: Frammenti letterari e filosofici, Florence, 1925; G. Fumagalli, Leonardo omo sanza lettere, Florence, 1938; E. MacCurdy, The Notebooks of Leonardo da Vinci, 2 vols., London, 1938; J. P. Richter, The Literary Works of Leonardo da Vinci, 2d ed., 2 vols., London, New York, 1939; A. M. Brizio, ed., Scritti scelti di Leonardo da Vinci, Turin, 1952; A. Chastel, Leonardo da Vinci par Lui-même, Paris, 1953. *c. Compilations on various subjects*: Trattato della Pittura di Leonardo da Vinci novamente dato in luce con la vita dello stesso autore scritta da Rafael du Fresne, Paris, 1651 (Editio princeps illustrated by drawings of N. Poussin); Trattato della pittura... sopra una copia a penna di mano di Stefano della Bella, ed. Fontani, Florence, 1792; G. Manzi, ed., Trattato della Pittura di Leonardo da Vinci, Rome, 1817 (1st ed. from Cod. Urbinas, 1270, in the Bib. Vat.); F. Cardinali, ed., Leonardo da Vinci: Del moto e misura dell'acqua, Libri IX, Bologna, 1826; H. Ludwig, ed., Lionardo da Vinci: Das Buch van der Malerei, Vienna, 1882 (critical ed. of the original It. text of the Cod. Urbinas, 1270, with Ger. trans.); E. Carusi and others, ed., Del moto e misura dell'acqua, Bologna, 1923; A. Borzelli, ed., Trattato della pittura di Leonardo da Vinci, Lanciano, 1924; R. Giacomelli, ed., Gli scritti di Leonardo da Vinci sul volo degli uccelli, Rome, 1936; A. Uccelli, ed., I libri di meccanica di Leonardo da Vinci, Milan, 1941; A. Marinoni, ed., Gli appunti grammaticali e lessicografici di Leonardo da Vinci, 2 vols., Milan, 1944–52; A. Marinoni, ed., Leonardo da Vinci: Tutti gli scritti, I: Scritti letterari, Milan, 1952; A. M. Brizio, ed., Delle Acque, in Leonardo: Saggi e ricerche, Rome, 1953, pp. 275–89; A. P. McMahon and L. H. Heydenreich, ed., Leonardo da Vinci: Treatise on Painting, 2 vols., Princeton, 1956 (facsimile of Cod. Urbinas, 1270, and Eng. trans.); K. T. Steinitz, Leonardo da Vinci's Trattato della Pittura: A Bibliography of the Printed Editions, 1651–1956, Copenhagen, 1958; C. Pedretti, Note sulla cronologia del Trattato della Pittura, L'Arte, N.S., XXIV, 1959, pp. 25–39, XXV, 1960, pp. 16–89; A. Chastel, ed., Traité de la Peinture, Paris, 1960.

SOURCES. B. Bellincioni, Rime, Milan, 1493; P. Gaurico, De sculptura, Florence, 1504; L. Pacioli, De divina proportione, Venice, 1509 (ed. C. Winterberg, Vienna, 1889); K. Frey, ed., Il libro di Antonio Billi (1481–1530), Berlin, 1892; F. Albertini, Memoriale di molte statue e pitture della città di Florentia, Florence, 1510 (ed. G. Milanesi and C. Guasti, Florence, 1863); A. de Beatis, Relazione del viaggio del cardinal Luigi d'Aragona (1517–18), ed. L. Pastor, Freiburg im Breisgau, 1905; P. Giovio, De viris illustribus (ca. 1524), in J. P. Richter, The Literary Works of Leonardo da Vinci, 2d ed., I, London, New York, 1939, pp. 2–3; K. Frey, ed., Anonimo Gaddiano o Codice Magliabechiano (ca. 1537–42), Berlin, 1892; M. Bandello, La prima (La seconda, La terza) parte de le Novelle del Bandello, Lucca, 1554; Vasari, IV, pp. 17–90; G. Poggi, Leonardo da Vinci: La vita di Giorgio Vasari, nuovamente commentata e illustrata, Florence, 1919; G. Vasari, Le vite (Ger. ed. by A. Gottschewski and F. Schottmüller), VI, Strasbourg, 1906, pp. 1–26; L. Goldscheider, Leonardo da Vinci, New York, 1943, pp. 5–13 (Eng. trans. of Vasari); Sabba di Castiglione, Ricordi, Venice, 1554 (2d ed., 1559); G. B. Giraldi detto Cintio, Discorsi, Venice, 1554; B. Cellini, La vita scritta da lui medesimo (1558–66), ed. P. Bacci, Florence, 1901; B. Cellini, Della architettura, pub. in I trattati dell'oreficeria e della scultura, ed. C. Milanesi, Florence, 1857; G. P. Lomazzo, Trattato dell'arte della pittura, Milan, 1584; Codex Huygens, ed. E. Panofsky, London, 1940; G. P. Lomazzo, Idea del Tempio della Pittura, Milan, 1590; G. Uzielli, Ricerche intorno a Leonardo da Vinci, I, Florence, 1872, Turin, 1896, II, Rome, 1884; P. Duhem, Etudes sur Léonard da Vinci: Ceux qu'il a lus et ceux qu'l ont lu, 3 vols., Paris, 1906–13 (reprinted 1955); E. Solmi, Le fonti dei manoscritti di Leonardo da Vinci, Turin, 1908; E. Solmi, Nuovi contributi alle fonti dei manoscritti di Leonardo da Vinci, Giorn. storiche della lett. it., LVIII, 1911, pp. 297–357; G. Calvi, Contributi alla biografia di Leonardo da Vinci, Arch. storico lombardo, XLIII, 1916, pp. 417–508; L. Beltrami, Documenti e memorie riguardanti la vita e le opere di Leonardo da Vinci, Milan, 1919; G. Calvi, I manoscritti di Leonardo da Vinci dal punto di vista cronologico, storico e biografico, Bologna, 1925; C. Pedretti, Documenti e memorie riguardanti Leonardo da Vinci a Bologna e in Emilia, Bologna, 1953; C. Pedretti, Studi vinciani (Travaux d'Hum. et Renaissance, XXVII), Geneva, 1957.

BIBLIOG. *Collected bibliogs.*: Raccolta Vinciana, XIV, 1930–34 ff.; E. Verga, Bibliografia vinciana, 2 vols., Bologna, 1931 (rev. by G. Calvi

Arch. storico lombardo, LIX, 1933, pp. 560–68); K. T. Steinitz and E. Belt, Manuscripts of Leonardo da Vinci, Los Angeles, 1948; L. H. Heydenreich, Leonardo-Bibliographie 1939–1952, ZfKg, XV, 1952, pp. 195–200. *General*: C. Amoretti, Memorie storiche sulla vita... di Leonardo da Vinci, Milan, 1804; P. Müller-Walde, Leonardo da Vinci: Lebensskizze und Forschungen, Munich, 1889–90 (incomplete); G. Séailles, Léonard de Vinci: L'artiste et le savant, Paris, 1892; P. Müller-Walde, Beiträge zur Kenntnis des Leonardo da Vinci, JhbPreussKSamml, XVIII, 1897, pp. 92–169, XIX, 1898, pp. 225–66, XX, 1899, pp. 54–116; E. Müntz, Léonard de Vinci: L'artiste, le penseur, le savant, Paris, 1899; E. Solmi, Leonardo, Florence, 1900; W. von Seidlitz, Leonardo da Vinci: Der Wendepunkt der Renaissance, Berlin, 1909 (2d ed., Vienna, 1935); F. Malaguzzi-Valeri, La Corte di Ludovico il Moro, II: Leonardo e Bramante, Milan, 1915; O. Sirén, Leonardo da Vinci: The Artist and the Man, New Haven, 1916; M. Mignon and others, Léonard de Vinci, Rome, 1919; Per il IV Centenario della morte di Leonardo da Vinci, 2 maggio 1919, Bergamo, 1919; P. Valéry, Introduction à la méthode de Léonardo de Vinci, Paris, 1919; W. von Bode, Studien über Leonardo da Vinci, Berlin, 1921; E. Solmi, Scritti Vinciani, Florence, 1924; E. Hildebrandt, Leonardo da Vinci, Berlin, 1927; K. Clark, Leonardo da Vinci: An Account of His Development as an Artist, Cambridge, 1939 (2d ed. 1952); C. Baroni and others, Leonardo da Vinci, Novara, 1939; R. L. Douglas, Leonardo da Vinci, Chicago, 1944; A. E. Popham, The Drawings of Leonardo da Vinci, New York, 1945; L. Venturi, Storia della critica d'arte, Florence, 1948; A. Vallentin, Léonard de Vinci, 2d ed., Paris, 1950 (Eng. trans., E. W. Dickes, New York, 1952); M. Brion, Léonard de Vinci, Paris, 1952; G. Castelfranco, Leonardo da Vinci, Milan, 1952; Atti del Congresso di Studi Vinciani, Florence, 1953; L. H. Heydenreich, Leonardo da Vinci, 2 vols., Basel, 1954 (Eng. trans., 2 vols., London, New York, 1954; bibliog.); Comitato nazionale per le onoranze a Leonardo da Vinci, Leonardo: Saggi e ricerche, Rome, 1954; J. Gantner, Leonardos Visionen von der Sintflut und vom Untergang der Welt, Berne, 1958; A. Marinoni, Leonardo da Vinci, Letteratura italiana (I minori), Milan, 1960. *Exhibition catalogues*: Mostra di Leonardo da Vinci, Milan, 1939; Los Angeles County Museum, Leonardo da Vinci Loan Exhibition, Los Angeles, 1949; Biblioteca Medicea Laurenziana, Quinto centenario della nascita di Leonardo da Vinci: Mostra di disegni, manoscritti e documenti, Florence, 1952; Musée du Louvre, Hommage à Léonard de Vinci, Paris, 1952; Royal Academy of Arts, Leonardo da Vinci: Quincentenary Exhibition, London, 1952; C. Wolters, Über den Erhaltungszustand der Leonardobilder des Louvre, Kchr., V, 1952, pp. 135–44. *Painting*: Venturi, IX, 1, pp. 1–221; A. de Rinaldis, Storia dell'opera pittorica di Leonardo da Vinci, Bologna, 1926; W. Suida, Leonardo und sein Kreis, Munich, 1929; H. Bodmer, Leonardo: Des Meisters Gemälde und Zeichnungen, Stuttgart, 1931; B. Berenson, Italian Pictures of the Renaissance, Oxford, 1932, p. 279; G. Isarlo, L'œuvre de Léonard, Le Combat, May 26, 1952; G. Castelfranco, La pittura di Leonardo da Vinci, Milan, 1956 (Eng. trans., B. Johnson and L. Macellari, New York, 1956); C. Baroni, Tutta la pittura di Leonardo, Milan, 1958; H. von Einem, Das Abendmahl des Leonardo da Vinci, Cologne-Opladen, 1961; J. Shearman, Leonardo's Colour and Chiaroscuro, ZfKg, XXV, 1962, pp. 13–47. *Sculpture*: Venturi, X, 1, pp. 1–66; W. von Bode, Leonardo als Bildhauer, JhbPreussKSamml, XXV, 1904, pp. 125–41; F. Malaguzzi-Valeri, Leonardo da Vinci e la scultura, Bologna, 1922; T. A. Cook, Leonardo da Vinci, Sculptor, London, 1923; R. S. Stites, Leonardo da Vinci, Sculptor, Art S., IV, 1926, pp. 103–09, VI, 1928, pp. 73–77, VIII, 1931, pp. 289–300; J. Pope-Hennessy, Italian Renaissance Sculpture, London, New York, 1958, pp. 67–72 and passim; A. Bovi, L'opera di Leonardo per il Monumento Sforza a Milano, Florence, 1959. *Architecture*: W. Lübke, Leonardo da Vinci als Architekt, in Kunstwerke und Künstler, Breslau, 1888, pp. 217–30; Venturi, XI, 1, pp. 1–49; V. Spinazzola, Leonardo architetto, in Leonardo da Vinci: Conferenze fiorentine, Milan, 1910, pp. 107–36; A. Annoni, Considerazioni su Leonardo da Vinci Architetto, Emporium, XLIX, 1919, pp. 171–80; J. Strzygowski, Leonardo, Bramante, Vignola im Rahmen vergleichender Kunstforschung, Mitt. der kunsthist. Inst. zu Florenz, III, 1919–31, pp. 1–37; L. H. Heydenreich, Die Sakralbaustudien Leonardo da Vincis, Engelsdorf, 1929; I. Calvi, L'architettura militare di Leonardo da Vinci, Milan, 1943; L. H. Heydenreich, Leonardo da Vinci: Architect of Francis I, BM, XCIV, 1952, pp. 277–85; A. Sartoris, Léonard architecte, Paris, 1952; K. T. Steinitz, Les décors de théâtre de Léonard de Vinci, Bib. d'Hum. et Renaissance, XX, 1958, pp. 257–65; C. Pedretti, A Chronology of Leonardo da Vinci's Architectural Studies after 1500, Geneva, 1962. *Science. a. Mathematics, optics, and mechanics*: M. Cantor, Über einige Konstruktionen des Leonardo da Vinci, Festschrift... mathematischen Gesellschaft in Hamburg, Leipzig, 1890, pp. 8–15; F. Schuster, Zur Mechanik Leonardo da Vincis, Erlangen, 1915; I. B. Hart, The Mechanical Investigations of Leonardo da Vinci, London, Chicago, 1925; R. Marcolongo, La meccanica di Leonardo da Vinci, Naples, 1932; R. Marcolongo, Leonardo da Vinci artista-scienziato, Milan, 1939; I. B. Hart, The World of Leonardo da Vinci, London, New York, 1961. *b. Anatomy and physiology*: G. Lesca, Per Leonardo anatomista, Emporium, XLIX, 1919, pp. 115–28; J. P. McMurrich, Leonardo da Vinci the Anatomist, Baltimore, 1930; K. D. Keele, Leonardo da Vinci on Movement of the Heart and Blood, Philadelphia, London, Montreal, 1952; S. Esche, Leonardo da Vinci: Das anatomische Werk, Basel, 1954. *c. Zoology and botany*: A. Baldacci, Leonardo da Vinci botanico e fondatore del metodo sperimentale, Bologna, 1914; G. B. De Toni, Le piante e gli animali in Leonardo da Vinci, Bologna, 1922; G. B. De Toni, Il mondo delle piante in Leonardo da Vinci, Mem. R. Acc. Sc. dell'Ist. di Bologna, 9th ser., VII, 1939–40. *d. Geology*: M. Baratta, Leonardo da Vinci e i problemi della terra, Turin, 1903; A. Favaro, Leonardo da Vinci e le scienze delle acque, Emporium, XLIX, 1919, pp. 272–79; G. de Lorenzo, Leonardo da Vinci e la geologia, Bologna, 1920; R. Weyl, Die geologischen Studien Leonardo da Vincis, Philosophia Naturalis, I, 1950, pp. 243–84. *e. Leonardo's thought*: (Only a few selected works are included): B. Croce, Leonardo filosofo (1906), in Saggio sullo Hegel, Bari, 1913, pp. 213–40; L. Olschki, Geschichte der neusprachlichen wissenschaftlichen Literatur, I, Heidelberg, 1919, pp. 252–413; E. Cassirer, Individuum und Kosmos in der Philosophie des Renaissance, Leipzig, 1927, pp. 162–68; F. M. Bongioanni, Leonardo pensatore, Piacenza, 1935; G. Gentile, Leonardo (1919), in Il pensiero italiano del Rinascimento, 3d ed., Florence, 1940, pp. 117–49; K. Jaspers, Lionard als Philosoph, Berne, 1953; C. Luporini, La mente di Leonardo, Florence, 1953; J. H. Randall Jr., The Place of Leonardo da Vinci in the Emergence of Modern Science, J. H. of Ideas, XIV, 1953, pp. 191–202; A. Marinoni, Una virtù spirituale, in I rebus di Leonardo da Vinci, Florence, 1954, app., pp. 27–120; A. Guzzo, La scienza, Turin, 1955, pp. 160–77; G. Fumagalli, Leonardo ieri e oggi, Pisa, 1959; A. Marinoni, L'essere del nulla, Rinascimento, XI, 1960. See also general works on Renaissance thought, as well as commemorations of the centenary of 1952.

Illustrations: PLS. 115–126.

LESCOT, PIERRE. French architect (b. Paris?, ca. 1515; d. 1578). Traditionally regarded as the first "modern" architect in France, although his known or attributed works give no basis for such a characterization, Lescot can be associated securely only with a small section (southwest corner) of one building — the Palais du Louvre. Of this section, the courtyard façade alone remains relatively unaltered (V, PL. 396); the exterior façades have either been destroyed (south) or significantly remodeled (west). In the extensive documentation for this work (begun 1546), only one reference implies that Lescot actually was the building's "designer"; otherwise, the numerous documents identify Lescot as acting only as the king's "overseer" or "supervisor." He is similarly identified in the document (dated 1544, for work beginning in 1542) pertaining to the only other work with which Lescot is definitely known to have been associated — the altar screen for the Church of St-Germain-l'Auxerrois (dismantled 1745; no representations extant). Documents also give Lescot the titles of court chaplain, royal counselor, and canon (1554) at Notre-Dame, Paris. Ronsard, a fellow court member, describes Lescot as possessing a natural talent for painting and as having studied mathematics and architecture. Lescot's gift for painting is equally praised by Blaise de Vigenère (ca. 1595), who at the same time criticizes Lescot for attempting to direct the work at the Louvre — a building that those "learned in the art" find "filled with errors" — because such important edifices should not be undertaken by novice architects.

Thus, from the contemporaneous evidence, Lescot emerges as a talented amateur, not as an architect by profession: an estimate borne out by the Louvre project itself, where the final design (1551) was determined only after two previous ones (1546–48, 1549–50) had been partially executed. Since in each instance the effect of the façade became increasingly dependent upon a revolutionary use of relief sculpture, its design must have resulted from an intimate collaboration between Lescot and the sculptor-architect Jean Goujon (q.v.), who also had worked on the above-mentioned altar screen (fragments in the Louvre; V, PL. 395). Later writers foster the idea of their collaboration by attributing to Lescot the design of works decorated by Goujon: entrance portal, Hôtel Carnavalet (remodeled), attribution made only by H. Sauval (ca. 1655); Fontaine des Innocents, 1549 (first attributed 18th cent.). Nineteenth-century historians accepted both attributions and added others to substantiate their belief that Lescot was a critical figure in the formation and development of French architecture — a concept gradually being rejected by modern-day historians.

BIBLIOG. C. Bauchal, Dictionnaire des architectes français, Paris, 1887; R. Blomfield, History of French Architecture, 1494–1661, London, 1911; A. Blunt, Art and Architecture in France, 1500–1700, Harmondsworth, 1954.

Bates LOWRY

LE VAU, LOUIS. French architect (b. Paris, 1612; d. Oct., 1670). Although Le Vau directed the majority of the vast building projects initiated by Mazarin, Colbert, and Louis XIV, he has never achieved the artistic fame that such accomplishments would normally bring. In part this fate results from Le Vau's practice of planning and directing numerous undertakings concurrently rather than developing his initial, often brilliant, architectural concepts into carefully refined, final designs. Le Vau aimed principally for a striking over-all effect, with buildings composed of simple but contrasting volumes whose forms are strongly defined by light (manipulated through differentiating surface textures) and by large-scale, simplified membering. Placed within imposing settings (Vaux), Le Vau's work may appear impressive, but the repetition of stock motifs and the disregard for architectonic detailing denies his work the stamp of creative genius that turns buildings into works of art and their designers into esteemed architects.

Essentially, Le Vau was a builder and an organizer who directed a team of artists and relied upon assistants for the working drawings and daily supervision necessary at individual building sites. (This practice allowed one recent writer to claim that the bulk of Le Vau's work was designed by his assistant François d'Orbay.) In this role Le Vau was eminently successful, beginning with a series of town houses designed and built for the residential development of Île Saint-Louis (1638-48). Le Vau's replacement of Jacques Lemercier in 1654 as First Architect of the King opened a decade of extensive building activity: at Vincennes (1654-60); the Hospital of La Salpêtrière (1660); College des Quatre-Nations (1661 on); Hôtel de Lionne (1662); the Louvre (Galerie d'Apollon and adjacent buildings, 1661; south wing, completed 1663); Tuileries (1664 on); and at Vaux-le-Vicomte, where in only four years (1657-61) Le Vau created, with André Le Nôtre and Charles Lebrun (qq.v.), the most sumptuous residence in France (II, FIG. 289).

In 1664, however, upon Colbert's becoming director of the royal building works, Le Vau's artistic domination ended abruptly. Colbert immediately rejected Le Vau's design for the Louvre entrance façade, already under construction, and publicly requested that a better design be found. Colbert's ultimate choice — the Colonnade — was the product of a council (Le Vau, Lebrun, and Claude Perrault), a procedure Colbert favored because buildings so designed became known as the king's work, not as one artist's achievement. Thus, although Le Vau remained First Architect, the fame of the projects he directed (Louvre, Versailles) was not associated with him, since their designer's identity was obscured. Probably because he was more organizer than artist, Le Vau accepted Colbert's dictates, although the decision to destroy his south façade of the Louvre — finished only five years before — must have been a difficult one for Le Vau to concur with.

BIBLIOG. C. Bauchal, Dictionnaire des architectes français, Paris, 1887; A. Blunt, Art and Architecture in France, 1500-1700, Harmondsworth, 1954; A. Laprade, François d'Orbay, Paris, 1960.

Bates LOWRY

LIANG K'AI. Chinese painter, born third quarter of the 12th century, died probably after 1246; also called Po Liang (tzŭ or alternate name) and Liang Fêng-tzŭ (hao or nickname).

Together with Fa-ch'ang (Mu-ch'i, q.v.), Liang was one of the most important painters of the late Southern Sung dynasty. The basic biography from which all subsequent ones are derived is recorded in the T'u-hui pao-chien (preface dated 1365) by Hsia Wên-yen. The artist was a descendant of Liang I (or Liang Hsi), who rose to be chief minister in the feudal principality of T'ung-ping (Shantung prov.) under the Han dynasty. Hsia goes on to say that Liang K'ai was a good painter of human figures, landscapes, Buddhist and Taoist subjects, ghosts, and celestial deities. He was a "follower" (pupil?) of Chia Shih-ku, who was recorded as a "Painter-in-Waiting" (chih-hou) at the court of Kao-tsung (1127-62). Evidently Liang surpassed his master, for in the Chia-t'ai era (1201-04) of the reign of Ning-tsung he was made "Painter-in-Attendance" (tai-chao) and was awarded the Golden Girdle, the highest honor available to a painter of the Imperial Academy. The artist, preferring less official recognition, returned the Girdle and departed. The T'u-hui pao-chien records that Liang was fond of wine and humorously called himself "Liang the Eccentric" (Liang Fêngtzŭ). His remaining paintings, says the standard biography, are sketchy and executed in an abbreviated manner (chien-pi).

A few significant additions can be made to this all too brief outline. Since during the reign of Li-tsung (1225-64) one of Liang's pupils, Yu Hung, was made "Painter-in-Attendance," it may safely be inferred that Liang had pupils and that his teaching was recognized. Two dates referring to Liang give evidence of his life span. One of Liang's lost, but recorded, paintings bore the title The Ch'an Master Miao-fêng Being Carried Out by Four Ghosts at Night. Since the subject of the painting, Miao-fêng, died in 1235, Liang must have lived beyond that time. The reference seems reliable, occurring in the collected literary works of Chung-fêng (d. 1323), a close friend of Chao Mêng-fu (q.v.), the early Yüan painter, scholar, and official. In the collected poetry of Pei-chien, another Ch'an monk (d. 1246), one poem is "presented to the Imperial Attendant Liang of the Court Service" and reads in part (trans., Wai-kam Ho): "Liang K'ai treasured his ink as if it were gold./ But when he got drunk [the valued drops of ink] could suddenly become a downpour. / Sometimes singing, sometimes silent, this heavenly music comes and goes by its own will. / While the ordinary painters could do nothing but [lay down their brushes and] become completely lost." This would indicate that Liang must have lived at least until 1246, since the poem was presented, not dedicated, to him, and that he was still associated with the "Court Service," either in fact or by honor.

Later sources repeat the old biography and often embroider it with clichés. A valuable note in Li Jih-hua's (1565-1635) Tz'ŭ-t'ao-hsuan tsa-cho says (trans., O. Sirén): "He painted Buddhist and Taoist figures with great refinement, including even the smallest details, but the rocks and trees he dotted down quite freely, apparently without intention. Yet, the intention was to increase the effect of life by the free and vigorous brushwork, since the figures were so delicately drawn." Since Liang's master, Chia Shih-ku, is listed in the T'u-hui pao-chien as a 12th-century follower of Li Kung-lin (q.v.), the great Northern Sung painter of the fine-line (pai-miao) style, the words "refinement," "details," and "delicately" are not without significance for Liang's early works. Another late reference in the I-men kuan-tu is quoted in the Nan-sung yüan-hua lu (1721), and notes that Liang painted with wedgelike strokes (pieh-na, strokes like those of the character jên) and with strokes like broken reeds.

A summary of the Chinese historical records referring to Liang K'ai can be ended with a list of some of the titles of paintings by the master, now lost: T'ao Yüan-ming with a Chrysanthemum Flower Standing beneath a Pine Tree; Confucius Dreaming of the Duke of Chou; Chuang-tzŭ Dreaming He Is a Butterfly; Mêng Hao-jan Riding a Donkey on the Pa Bridge; Chung-k'uei the Demon Queller; P'u-t'ai; The Ch'an Master Miao-fêng Being Carried Out by Four Ghosts at Night; Portraits; Frogs Chasing Ants; Withered Lotus; Village Joys; Pen-hsiang or A Pictorial Representation of the Lotus Sūtra. The artist's subjects were varied and ranged over all three of the major faiths of his time and place: Buddhism, Taoism, and Confucianism.

That Liang K'ai in his later years became an artistic rebel, even an outcast, seems evident from his meager biography, from his relatively undistinguished ranking by later Chinese critics, and from the fact that all his extant works except two possible attributions — Immortal in a Loose Gown (Taichung, Formosa, Nat. Palace Mus.) and The Supreme Taoist Master, Chang T'ien-shih, Holding Court (PL. 129) — are to be found in Japan. They have been there since at least the 14th century, when they were imported as part of the massive wave of Ch'an (Jap., Zen) influence from southern China after the troubles at the end of the Southern Sung and the beginning of the foreign Mongol (Yüan) dynasty. Paintings by Liang K'ai are listed in Japanese sources from the Kundaikan Sayuchōki (extant in two versions, 1476 and 1511) on, particularly in later Zen diaries and tea ceremony (cha-no-yu) records. While Liang had little influence on later Chinese painting, such Japanese artists as Sesshū (q.v.; 1420-1506), Yūshō (1533-1615), and Niten (1584-1645) owe much to his style.

This important relation to Japanese art, Zen Buddhism, and the tea ceremony has served to confuse Liang K'ai's place in Chinese art history. He was not a Ch'an painter, though he painted some Ch'an subjects and his later style was most acceptable to the intuitive, irrational, and often psychologically shocking practices of that sect. James Cahill has emphasized the Confucian origins of the various informal and heterodox styles of painting lumped together under the general heading of "literary man's painting" (*wên-jên-hua*). This includes the rough, "splashed ink" manner of Liang K'ai and his contemporary, the Ch'an monk Mu-ch'i. Its origins are to be found in a complex of reasons involving revolt against the herd and officialdom; the demonstration of character to one's equals without appeal to the herd; and the desire to exploit the full possibilities of ink and the Chinese writing and painting brush, the most flexible of all ancient painting instruments.

In Liang's case there is an additional factor — alcoholic inspiration. Two references to Liang's drunkenness have already been noted, and it is surely no coincidence that the two "fathers" of "splashed ink" painting, Wang Mo (d. ca. 805) and Hsiang Yung (late 8th cent.), were also recorded as lovers of wine who painted marvelously and wildly when drunk. It is an ancient belief, not unknown even today, that drunkenness is next to godliness, or at least that it places one nearer the sources of inspiration. Modern psychology at least partially supports this old idea. The power of alcohol to release inhibitions and make the drinker feel that he is elevated or superhuman is generally recognized, but the psychological lift is accompanied by a progressive decline in physical coordination. For the experience to be of value to the painter, the release of inhibitions must slightly overbalance on an esthetic scale the still not crucial loss of physical power. Only a tremendously disciplined talent can profit by these practices. Inebriation cannot bestow a technique; it can only lessen physical control and perhaps release psychic energy from its inhibiting shell of conformity. The vinous school of painting at its best may gain in spontaneity and the intuitive realization of visual images and of significant gestures and movements of the brush. The artist or his friends presumably censored the failures in soberer moments. The works resulting from this selection are surely masterpieces, and their appeal to Ch'an and Zen devotees is readily understandable.

The historical record that Liang K'ai's early style was careful and linear and that he later changed to the rough "splashed ink" manner is confirmed by the remaining works that can reasonably be attributed to him or to his immediate circle. More than any other artist of the Southern Sung dynasty, he proves to be a strong link with the past, as well as the author of a series of stylistically radical works that provide the ultimate exclamation point in the development of Sung painting.

Beginning as a follower of Chia Shih-ku, Liang was a disciplined painter of the by-then academic school of fine-line figure painting, whose greatest name was Li Kung-lin (q.v.). The scroll of *The Supreme Taoist Master* (PL. 129) is a conservative work, even rigidly iconic, in the best Buddhist and Taoist painting tradition. One need only substitute a Buddha for the Master and bodhisattvas for the attendants to obtain an almost typical 12th-century sūtra painting. The carefully controlled, thin, even lines and the repetitive faces, draperies, and clouds are sensitive and sure but still have a religious geometry. As in Italian painting of the late 14th and early 15th centuries, the progressive and esthetically rewarding passages of the painting are to be found in the secondary scenes at the right and left of the central iconic representation. There, in scenes of artisans at work making images, or in pathetic scenes with beggars and ghosts, or in a frightening scene in one of the hells, one finds a freer brushwork, still immature but crackling, bordering on the weird and grotesque — a portent of Liang's later painting style. Other works, now lost, must have been executed in this style, including such recorded works as *Village Joys* or *Scenes of Rice Culture and Sericulture* (known only in a copy reproduced by Tanaka) and such free variations as the scroll by Chêng Chi now in the Freer Gallery, Washington, D.C.

If the *pai-miao* figure style was Liang K'ai's early discipline, he soon mastered the great monumental landscape manner of the Northern Sung dynasty and the lyrical, fragmented, and asymmetrical style of the Southern Sung Academy, best known in the works of Ma Yüan and Hsia Kuei (qq.v.). *Snow Landscape with Two Horsemen Near a Mountain Pass* (PL. 128) combines the rugged monumentality and foliage conventions of Fan K'uan (active ca. 990–1030) with the daring simplification and asymmetry initiated by Li T'ang after the fall of the Northern Sung in 1127 and developed further by the "Ma-Hsia" school. A trace of Liang's beginnings is to be found in the fine and accurate rendition of the gateway guarding the high distant pass. Though Liang lived in the south, this landscape is the conventional rendition of the bare and lonely northern frontier characteristic of much Northern Sung painting associated with Fan K'uan, Li Ch'êng, Kuo Hsi, and others.

Liang must have deserved his official honors because of both his early styles; the *Śākyamuni Descending from the Mountain on His Way to the Bo Tree*, which is comparable with the *Snow Landscape with Two Horsemen* in many respects, bears an inscription that it was painted for the emperor after Liang's promotion to *tai-chao*. The subject, the Buddha-to-be forsaking his fruitless austerities and moving through a grim winter setting toward his final Meditation and Enlightenment beneath the Bo tree, became a standard one for Japanese Zen painters — the *Shussan-no-Shaka*. (Cf. the early 14th-century iconographic sketch, perhaps based on Liang's painting, in the Seattle Art Mus.; S. E. Lee, "Japanese Monochrome Painting at Seattle," *Artibus Asiae*, XIV, no. 1-2, pp. 43-61.) While Liang K'ai's *Śākyamuni* moves in a landscape whose vastness is suggested by expressive fragments — a cliff, a gnarled tree — the figure itself is more carefully painted and recalls Liang's early work. The swirling drapery even goes back to T'ang Buddhist prototypes, notably the "Western" style of drapery derived from northwestern India via Central Asia. It is a deeply moving picture, not only because of the intense concentration depicted in the face but also because of the poignant tension between the rather slight, inwardly focused figure and the rough, almost threatening environment. This great masterpiece must stand near the mid-point of his creative years. Some small album leaves appear to be of a similar nature, notably the *Herons Near a Rocky Bank* (PL. 131), though this particular leaf betrays an impatient freedom that is closely related to the group of "splashed ink" paintings that crown the artist's achievement.

While "splashed ink" painting has been much associated with Ch'an Buddhism, its origins, as mentioned above, are properly placed with the initial stages of Chinese *wên-jên-hua* and are partially connected with the influence of alcoholic inspiration. The two surviving and relatively sure examples of this aspect of Liang K'ai's art are *Hui Nêng, the Sixth Ch'an Patriarch, Chopping Bamboo at the Moment of Enlightenment* (PL. 130) and *The Poet Li Po* (IV, PL. 282). The former is a Buddhist subject emphasizing the irrational and haphazard occurrence of Enlightenment, and the latter is a traditional Chinese subject, largely Taoist in its overtones, stressing the free and independent character of the soul of a noble man. *Hui Nêng Chopping Bamboo* is the more extreme of the two, its brushwork and ink ranging from the wildest scrubbing on the tree trunk to sharp, sword-cut strokes in the draperies and hands and in the joints of the bamboo. Many parts seem to exploit happy accidents in a manner not unlike that of modern "action" or impressionist painters. Accidental splashes of ink resulting from the frenzied, possessed (or, if one prefers, drunken) actions of the artist are to be found on the right thigh of the patriarch and in the bank on the lower left. The over-all impression is one of tremendous strength and inspired rapidity of execution. Rough and brutally direct, the painting has an impact that defies lengthy rational analysis. In this it is unique, since the two famous and related hanging scrolls, *Hui Nêng, the Sixth Ch'an Patriarch, Tearing a Sūtra* and *P'u-t'ai Carrying His Sack*, seem more elegant and contrived, their slighter brushwork and conscious drollery indicating a skillful, even inspired, Japanese copyist. The immense popularity of Liang K'ai and Mu-ch'i among such Zen monk-painters as Sesshū, Kaō, and others inevitably led to much copying, sometimes signed by the copyist (Sesshū in particular has left at least two signed copies of Liang album leaves).

The somewhat damaged but cleverly restored *Li Po* shows the calmer side of inspiration. The dominant brush strokes are long and wet with soft edges. Only in such accents as hair, features, and feet does the artist reveal the sharp and staccato accents of which his brush was capable. Again the initial impact remains memorable. Tranquil nobility of character is revealed in an almost weightless, grave image in slow movement — certainly one of the greatest pictorial expressions of the ideal of the Chinese literary man. It cannot be without significance that numerous tales are told of Li Po's inspired participation in parties where wine flowed endlessly. Seen in this light, the tilt of the poet's head and his open, perhaps singing mouth may indicate that "Liang the Eccentric" had imagined the subject to his liking.

Beyond these examples of "splashed ink" the rational Chinese were loath to go. The Japanese of the Muromachi period (1333–1568) pushed the style, called by them *haboku*, to further extremes. But the Chinese artists during the Yüan dynasty (1280–1368), of both the academic and *wên-jên-hua* persuasion, returned to previous styles for points of departure. Only the monk-painters of the Ch'an monasteries or a few isolated Taoists or amateurs seriously continued the "splashed ink" manner; they could not match the great Liang K'ai and Mu-ch'i, whose works in this style were the proper ending to the development of Sung painting.

WORKS. *a. Probably original*: The Supreme Taoist Master, Chang T'ien-shih, Holding Court; hand scroll in ink on paper. Signed, Liang K'ai; colophon by Wang Chih-têng dated 1568. Formerly, An Kuo Coll. (early Ming collector); now New York, H. C. Weng Coll. - *Śākyamuni Descending from the Mountain on His Way to the Bo Tree*; hanging scroll in ink and faint color on silk. Signed, Painter in the Imperial Presence, Liang K'ai; one identified seal. Formerly, Sakai Coll.; now Tokyo, Coll. E. Shima. - *Snow Landscape with Two Horsemen Near a Mountain Pass*; hanging scroll in ink and faint color on silk. Signed, Liang K'ai; seal of Ashikaga Yoshimasa. Formerly, Akaboshi Coll.; now, Tokyo, Nat. Mus. - *Three Ancient Trees in a Snowy Landscape* (PL. 127); hanging scroll in ink and faint color on silk. Unsigned; seal of Ashikaga Yoshimasa. Formerly, Tokyo, Matsudaira Coll.; now, Tokyo, Nat. Mus. - *Herons Near a Rocky Bank*; oblate circular album leaf in ink on silk. Signed, Liang K'ai. Formerly, Coll. Daté; now, Miyagino, Kanagawa, Japan, Hakone Art Mus. - *Geese and Reeds*; rectangular album leaf in ink on silk (*Liang K'ai*, 1957, pl. 22). Signed, Liang K'ai (later addition?). Formerly, Coll. of the Tokugawa family; now, Coll. K. Yamanouchi. - *Hui Nêng, The Sixth Ch'an Patriarch, Chopping Bamboo at the Moment of Enlightenment*; hanging scroll in ink on paper. Signed, Liang K'ai; seal of Ashikaga Yoshimitsu at lower left. Formerly, Sakai Coll.; now, Tokyo, Nat. Mus. - *The Poet Li Po*; hanging scroll in ink on paper. Signed, Liang K'ai; unidentified seal at upper right. Formerly, Tokyo, Matsudaira Coll.; now, Tokyo, Nat. Commission for the Protection of Cultural Properties. - *Han-shan and Shih-tê*; hanging scroll in ink on paper (*Liang K'ai*, 1957, pls. 13–14). Signed, Liang K'ai (later addition?); seal of Ashikaga Yoshimasa. Formerly, Coll. Isogai; now, Miyagino, Kanagawa, Japan, Hakone Art Mus.

b. Some copies after, or paintings close to, Liang K'ai: Wang Hsi-chih Writing on a Fan; Chinese copy; hand scroll in ink on paper (*Liang K'ai*, 1957, fig. 1). Signature of Liang K'ai and several purportedly Yüan colophons, one dated 1324. Formerly in collection of the emperor Ch'ien Lung and the Manchu Household Coll.; now, Peking, Coll. Bur. Cultural Property Administration. - *Hui Nêng, the Sixth Ch'an Patriarch, Tearing a Sūtra* (traditionally paired with *Hui Nêng Chopping Bamboo*); hanging scroll in ink on paper (*Liang K'ai*, 1957, pls. 6–7). Signature of Liang K'ai. Formerly, Tokyo, Matsudaira Coll.; now, Coll. T. Mitsui. - *P'u-t'ai Carrying His Sack*; early Japanese copy (?), related to *Hui Nêng Tearing a Sūtra*; hanging scroll in ink on paper (*Liang K'ai*, 1957, pls. 10–12). Signature of Liang K'ai; two seals above, one of Ashikaga Yoshimitsu, the other (with a poem) of the Ch'an monk Ta-ch'uan Pu-chi (d. 1253). Formerly, Coll. Marquis Oshu; now, Osaka, Coll. Murayama. - *P'u-t'ai Watching a Cock Fight*; Japanese copy; hanging scroll in ink on paper (*Liang K'ai*, 1957, fig. 6). No signature. Formerly, Odawara, Coll. Masuda; present location unknown. - *Winter Landscape with Birds and Alighting Heron* (somewhat damaged, possibly very close to *Herons Near a Rocky Bank* and *Geese and Reeds*); oblate circular album leaf in ink and faint color on silk (S. E. Lee, *Chinese Landscape Painting*, Cleveland, 1954, no. 22). Signature of Liang K'ai. Formerly, Denman Ross Coll.; now, Cambridge, Mass., Fogg Art Mus. - *A Wandering Poet by the Marsh Land*; oblate circular album leaf in ink and faint color on silk. Signature of Liang K'ai. Formerly, Coll. Chang Ta-ch'ien; now, New York, Coll. J. M. Crawford, Jr. - *Immortal in a Loose Gown*; Yüan copy (?); rectangular album leaf in ink on paper in the album *Ming-hua lin-lang* (*Three Hundred Masterpieces of Chinese Painting in the Palace Museum*, Taichung, 1959, vol. III, no. 118). Signature of Liang K'ai. Formerly in the collection of the emperor Ch'ien Lung; now, Taichung, Formosa, Nat. Palace Mus.

SOURCES. Li Ê, ed., Nan-sung yüan-hua lu (Record of Southern Sung Academic Painters), 1721 (includes all previously known references).

BIBLIOG. A. Waley, Introduction to the Study of Chinese Painting, London, 1923; S. Tani, Critical Studies on Chinese Pictures Imported into Japan in the Kamakura and Ashikaga Periods, Part II, On the Appreciation of Chinese Painting in the Japanese Middle Ages, Bijutsu Kenkyu (J. of Art S.), no. 46, Oct., 1935; W. Speiser, Meisterwerke Chinesischer Malerei, Berlin, 1947; S. Shimada, Ihin Gafu Ni Tsuite (On I-p'in, the "Extraordinary" Style of Chinese Painting), Bijutsu Kenkyu (J. of Art S.), no. 161, 1950; S. Shimada and Y. Yonezawa, Painting of the Sung and Yüan Dynasties, Tokyo, 1952; O. Sirén, Chinese Painting: Leading Masters and Principles, II, London, New York, 1956; I. Tanaka, The Art of Liang K'ai, Bijutsu Kenkyu (J. of Art S.), no. 184, Jan., 1956, pp. 129–49 (text in Jap.); Bijutsu Kenkyu-sho (Inst. of Art Research), Liang K'ai, Kyoto, 1957; J. Cahill, Chinese Paintings, XI–XIV Centuries, New York, 1960; J. Cahill, Chinese Painting, Geneva, New York, 1960.

Sherman E. LEE

Illustrations: PLS. 127–131.

LIBERIA. The Republic of Liberia, independent since 1847, occupies that part of the coastal zone of western Africa between the Mano and Cavally rivers and borders Sierra Leone, the Ivory Coast, and the Republic of Guinea. Geographically varied, the region comprises a narrow strip of marshy coast covered by dense forest, a wide hilly plain (beginning 7–15 miles from the coast), also covered by forests, and a plateau with savanna and woodlands in the interior. It is inhabited by several ethnic groups, of which the best-known are the Kpelle and the Dan (see GUINEAN CULTURES).

At present there is no evidence of prehistoric or archaeological discoveries in the area, although the working of bronze among the Dan-Ngere groups seems to have begun quite early. Today art production, except for bronze casting, is limited to wood sculpture.

The coast is inhabited largely by the descendants of repatriated American slaves, who are so strongly Westernized in culture that they produce no significant art of indigenous inspiration.

Almost nothing is known of the representational sculpture of central Liberia. A few masks undoubtedly from the area reveal a mixture of naturalism and stylization, with long slender face, high round forehead, aquiline nose, and eyes formed by large protruding cylinders in which are set metal plaques. These may derive from similar masks of the Kono tribe of Sierra Leone (q.v.).

Most of the extant art of Liberia is a product of the tribes living on the interior plateau, whose chief form of expression seems to be the mask, although some examples of freestanding sculpture and of the minor arts can be found. Although it is almost impossible to make stylistic distinctions about this interior culture, it can be said that the art of the northwestern groups seems to be particularly related to ancestor worship or to the various secret societies; the northeastern art shows clearly defined stylistic peculiarities but has been mainly inspired by the styles of the Republic of Guinea.

The Gbundi and Toma (or Loma) tribes in the northwestern part of the country make male and female wooden figures, which are shaped like posts and are kept in special huts. More numerous are zoomorphic figures, perhaps connected with totemistic beliefs, which are generally of rather crude workmanship and take the form of elephants, snakes, crocodiles, birds, and fish.

In comparison with the statuary, the masks — especially those connected with the Poro secret society — are of greater variety and esthetic value. The Toma, who move back and forth across the border of the Republic of Guinea, create a flattened and stylized mask, with eyes and nose barely indicated by a line and with hornlike appendages surmounting the upper part. Another northwestern tribe, the Gbande, make game masks worn by both men and women at feasts in honor of the dead.

The Gola people, living farther southwest, toward the coast, have absorbed the style of the Mende (or Mendi; see SIERRA LEONE). This borrowed style is reflected in the masks connected with the Bundu, a female secret society. The two outstanding features of these masks are the real human teeth inserted in the mouth and the lips painted red, contrasting sharply with the black background.

South of the Gola territory the Mende style appears again in large masks produced by the Bassa, a tribe of the Kru group. In both the large masks and the miniature replicas (ht., ca. 3 in.) the eyes are indicated by only a slight swelling without a slit. Like other Kru tribes, the Bassa carve wooden figures; these have large heads in which the small rounded mouth and the facial planes meet at a 45° angle.

The Kpelle, a large group of whom is also settled in the Republic of Guinea, produce their masks in connection with the male

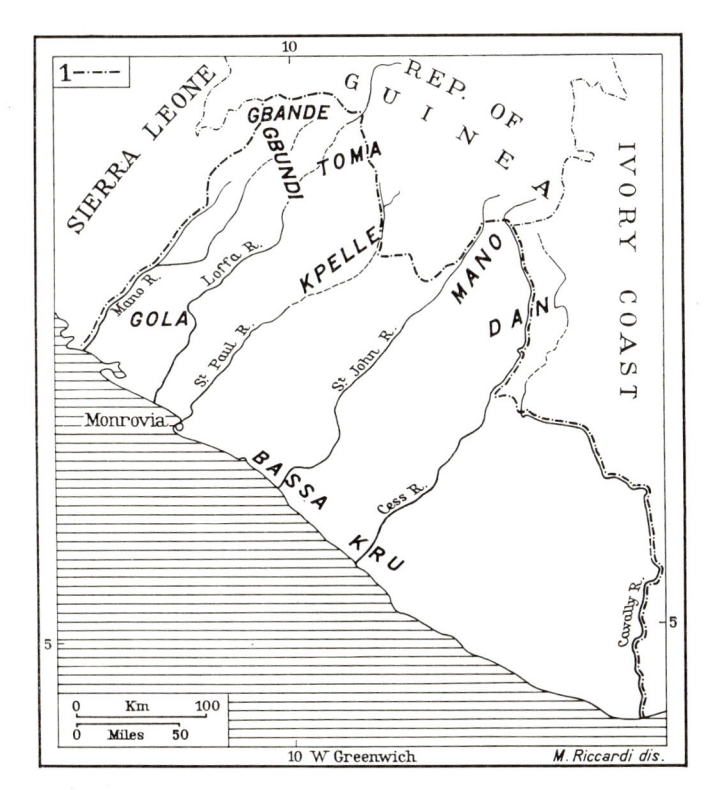

Liberia, distribution of principal tribal groups that produce art (names in heavy capitals). *Key*: (1) Modern national boundaries.

Poro society. Their style recalls that of other Liberian masks, such as those of the Mano, of the Ge, and of the western Ivory Coast. The mask generally represents a human face in the form of an oval with a pointed chin, two circles for the eyes, a wide flattened nose, and a pronounced mouth, sometimes set with human teeth (IV, PL. 175); the chin terminates in a beard of plant fibers, and the top of the head may be covered with a hat. Kpelle craftsmen also make small masks (common among the Mano and the Dan as well) representing ancestors and protectors and occasionally having animal features.

The northeastern tribes are linked to those of the northwest by the Mano people, whose art forms a stylistic bridge. Other northeastern groups of outstanding artistic ability are the Dan, together with their sub- and related groups, the Ge, Gio, Yakuba, and Ngere, or Guere (VII, PLS. 118, 120, 121). All these peoples excel in the art of wood sculpture, a hereditary craft, transmitted from father to son, often carried on in secret. Less important today is the casting of metal (formerly bronze) by the lost-wax process.

The Mano, the Dan and minor groups, and the Kru (who are distributed between Monrovia and the Bandama River in the Ivory Coast) create masks associated with both the male (Poro) and female (Sande) societies; they can be divided into six principal types. The first category consists of carved "portrait" masks, with a spiritualized expression, small eye slits, and vertical scarification from the forehead to the nose (Mano). The second kind is like the first, but with hair and beard of human hair or of plant fibers and with the eyes indicated by white or red paint or by strips of colored cloth (Mano). The third is again of the same type, but with protruding tubular eyes and a forehead often decorated with carving (Mano). The fourth is distinguished by a beak-shaped, occasionally movable, mouth (IX, PL. 356). These four types of mask are produced south of Mount Nimba, in the border area between the Mano and the Dan-Ge territory. Ancestor masks, with the upper part representing the human face and surmounted by horns, comprise another aspect of mask making. To this type belong enormous stylized masks with great hollow triangles or round holes for the eyes (Dan, Ge) and miniature masks, which repeat every type of ancestor mask and are worn by the owner on his person or kept in the home. Finally, a unique category comprises the fantastic ape masks.

Sculpture in the round — once closely connected with ancestor worship but now embracing secular subjects — is dominated by the Kru, who also furnish the Mano and the Dan with their art products. Almost always the sculptor works for a chief, and, since present-day statuettes are mostly female, it seems that he is more or less required to portray the various women in the family of his patron. Generally the works of the groups can be distinguished by the tattoo marks and the headdresses. The sculptural style is rudimentary but relatively naturalistic. Although the faces are usually stylized, each statuette bears the name of the person it represents. At one time these figurines represented tribal ancestors and, on the occasion of festive dances, were anointed with palm oil and sprinkled with animal blood. Other relics of ancestor worship are the one- or two-headed herms (the latter supposedly the older), sometimes of wood but more often of clay. In the shape of monstrous human heads, always crowned by feathers, they guard the huts and their inhabitants.

That working of bronze among the Kpelle, Mano, Dan, and Kru is a fairly ancient art is shown by the use of certain ornamental motifs found in the Cameroons as well, suggesting some relationship with the styles of Nigeria (Schweeger-Hefel, 1948). Today the working of brass is influenced by the neighboring Anyi-Baule of the Ivory Coast and has almost disappeared from native Liberian art. The lost-wax system is used, with a separate casting of the various pieces, which are then soldered together.

The most frequent motifs of freestanding metal sculpture are mothers with children (VII, PL. 121), horsemen, animals, and standing or seated figures, occasionally on stilts. Objects of personal adornment (for which imported aluminum is increasingly replacing brass and bronze) include bracelets, rings, and pendants. These pieces often have fine geometric engravings, which at times signify the grades in the different secret societies.

The rude, utilitarian pottery, handmade by women using the coil technique, is occasionally ornamented with a lozenge, cord, or wave pattern (Mano, Dan).

Among the decorative objects worthy of mention are the ceremonial wooden spoons, which, although carved by Kru women, are found throughout most of Liberia. The handle terminates in a skillfully shaped male head. These spoons are inherited in the female line and are carried by the women when they dance. Other products of the Kru people are their fine carved wooden plates.

The Dan tribes specialize in worked-leather weapon sheaths and gunpowder cases; occasionally they also decorate the interior and exterior walls of their huts with paintings, but these are less esteemed.

Art of colonial derivation is practically nonexistent except in the capital, Monrovia, which was the first civil nucleus. Founded in 1822, the present city of over 80,000 inhabitants includes some very modern buildings (University of Liberia, Capitol). Most of the rest of the country, however, has retained the traditional character of the native village.

BIBLIOG. H. Neel, Deux peuplades de la frontière libérienne, L'Anthropologie, XXIV, 1913, pp. 445-75; D. Westermann, Die Kpelle: Ein Negerstamm in Liberia, Göttingen, Leipzig, 1921; P. M. Gamory-Dubordeau, Notes sur les coutumes des Tomas, B. Comité des ét. h. et sc. de l'A.O.F., IX, 1926, pp. 288-350; P. Germann, Die Völkerstämme im Norden von Liberia, Leipzig, 1933; G. Greene, Journey Without Maps, London, 1936 (2d ed., New York, 1961); E. Becker-Donner, Kunst und Handwerk in NO-Liberia, BA, XXIII, 1940, pp. 45-110; E. Becker-Donner, Überlieferungen aus NO-Liberia, ZfE, LXXI, 1940, pp. 174-200; G. W. Harley, Notes on the Poro in Liberia (Pap. Peabody Mus. for Archeol. and Ethn., XIX, 2), Cambridge, Mass., 1941; E. Becker-Donner, Über zwei Kruvölkerstämme, Wiener Beiträge zur Kulturgeschichte und Linguistik, VI, 1944, pp. 71-108; M. H. Lelong, Libéria intime (L'Afrique noire sans les blancs, I), Paris, Algiers, 1946; R. P. Lassort and M. H. Lelong, Chez les Kpélé du Libéria et les Guérzé de la Guinée française, Et. guinéennes, II, 1947, pp. 9-20; J. Schwab, Tribes of the Liberian Hinterland (Pap. Peabody Mus. for Archaeol. and Ethn., XXXI), Cambridge, Mass., 1947; A. M. Schweeger-Hefel, Afrikanische Bronzen, Vienna, 1948; J. Genevray, Eléments d'une monographie d'une division administrative libérienne, Mem. IFAN, XXI, 1952, pp. 1-135; B. Holas, Mission dans l'est libérien, Dakar, 1952; D. Paulme, Gens du riz, Paris, 1954; E. von Sydow, Afrikanische Plastik, Berlin, New York, 1954; H. and U. Himmelheber, Die Dan: Ein Bauernvolk in westafrikanische Urwald, Stuttgart, 1958.

Ernesta CERULLI

Illustrations: 1 fig. in text.

LI KUNG-LIN. Chinese painter of the late Northern Sung period; also known as Li Po-shih (*tzŭ* or alternate name) and Li Lung-mien (after the Lung-mien Mountains, where he spent his last years). Li Kung-lin was born in Anhwei province, south of the Yangtze River, about 1049. His father was an antiquarian and collector of books, and Li grew up in scholarly and artistic surroundings. After receiving the standard Confucian education, he passed the examination for the *chin-shih* ("Bachelor of Arts") degree in 1070 and embarked on his career as a government official, following the usual course for a man of the educated class (or literati) in China. He attained moderately high rank, becoming a secretary in the Imperial Board of Revision.

More important to his artistic development was the fact that his official post brought him to the capital, Kaifeng, and into its stimulating intellectual circles. Li Kung-lin became one of the luminaries in a brilliant coterie of scholars, officials, poets, and artists, of which the central figure was the great Su Shih, or Su Tung-p'o (1036–1101). Others included several painters — the master of ink bamboo Wên T'ung (active ca. 1049–70), the landscapists Wang Shen (b. ca. 1046, d. after 1100) and Mi Fu (Mi Fei, 1051–1107; q.v.) — and calligraphers such as Huang T'ing-chien (1050–1110) and Su Shih himself. Within this group, just at that time, a new concept of painting was evolving, with a new system of artistic values that rejected traditional criteria of excellence (fidelity to the subject, visual beauty, skill) in favor of unorthodox techniques of brushwork and forms expressive in themselves rather than primarily descriptive. The literati artists sought to capture in their works a special refinement and "literary" flavor that would reflect their own characters as sensitive, literate Confucian scholars. As amateurs, they avoided styles that required high technical finish and implied "professionalism"; as collectors and connoisseurs familiar with old paintings, they imitated antique styles, bringing the factor of conscious archaism into Chinese painting, perhaps for the first time. This was the origin of the school that came to be known as "literati painting" (*wên-jên-hua*), which was eventually to divert the whole course of Chinese painting.

Li Kung-lin followed the main doctrines of this school in his life and art. He collected paintings and took every opportunity to copy famous old works until he felt he had absorbed the best points of the old masters; then he went on to create a style of his own. His declared aim in painting, like that of most other literati artists, was personal expression. Complaining that people were always asking him to paint pictures for them as if he were a professional, he is reported to have said: "I make paintings as a poet composes poems; I lyricize my nature and feeling, and nothing more." The conception of the work was all-important to him, he claimed; the planning of the composition and execution of details were secondary. All this is what one would expect of a scholar-painter. In other ways, however, he was atypical. For one thing, he was evidently an accomplished technician and could, when he chose, paint with great skill. Also, he was concerned with religious subjects to a degree quite unparalleled in the literati school.

When he was about sixty years of age, he lost the use of his right arm through rheumatism but went on painting, using his left. About the same time, in 1100, he retired to a villa in the Lung-mien ("Sleeping Dragon") Mountains and thereafter called himself Lung-mien Chü-shih, "The Retired Scholar of Lung-mien." One of his most famous works, a scroll entitled *Dwelling in the Lung-mien Mountains* (PL. 134), represents the environs of his mountain retreat. He died in 1106.

Li Kung-lin has been regarded by some Chinese writers (e.g., Hsia Wên-yen, the author of the 14th-cent. biographical compilation *T'u-hui pao-chien*) as the greatest of the Sung dynasty artists. This judgment seems extravagant today, and modern authorities are more temperate in their evaluations. It must be remembered, however, that any modern evaluation is hampered by the absence of really reliable works from his hand and by inadequate understanding and appreciation of the kinds of painting in which he excelled. Among Chinese artists of the first rank Li Kung-lin remains perhaps the most complex and problematic. Even if we disregard the adulation accorded him in later times and depend upon reports from writers fairly close to him, who may have known him and seen his genuine works in considerable numbers, it is still difficult to discern any very clear artistic personality. Moreover, there is a similar lack of consistent character in the extant paintings attributed to him.

He is said to have begun as a painter of horses, adopting at first the style of the T'ang master Han Kan (8th cent.) but later developing a more original mode, and also relying heavily on actual observation of horses, especially those of the imperial stables, to which he had access. In order to understand better his equine models, he identified himself with them to a dangerous degree; such, at least, was the opinion of a certain aged Buddhist, who warned him that if he persisted he would end by becoming a horse. Li, who was himself a devout Buddhist, is said to have accepted this warning and turned to religious subjects. In these he displayed a certain unorthodoxy in subject matter, portraying Buddhist figures — especially Kuan-yin (Avalokiteśvara), for whom he had a special predilection — in settings and poses that had no iconographic precedent. Like Wu Tao-tzŭ, his great T'ang predecessor with whom he was often compared, he preferred subjects with secular overtones, such as Vimalakīrti, who could be presented in the guise of a Chinese sage (e.g., *Vimalakīrti and Attendant*; see below), or arhats, the disciples of the Buddha (see below), or the figures of the *Hua-yen Sūtra* (PL. 135).

His copies and imitations of old paintings were often executed in the orthodox mode, in ink line with colors on silk. Liu K'o-chuang, in the early-12th-century *Hou-ts'un t'i-pa* (IV, 8b), describes a Li Kung-lin copy of a horse painted by Han Kan and comments that, although Li ordinarily worked in ink on paper, in this case he used colors on silk because he wanted his picture to resemble Han Kan's as closely as possible. His original works, however, were done in the manner most closely associated with his name, the fine ink-line drawings, usually on paper, in plain (i.e., uncolored) delineation (*pai-miao*). His models for the creation of this style were probably ink sketches in Buddhist iconographic sketchbooks, cartoons for wall paintings, and other works that were not in themselves considered "finished" productions. Occasionally, especially in his landscapes, Li Kung-lin made use of the broader, drier kinds of brushwork characteristic of the literati school. A critic writing shortly after Li's death remarks that, although his detailed paintings in color could be imitated with fair success by common artists, his rough and abbreviated style could never be approached by others.

The paintings attributed to Li Kung-lin that are executed in colors on silk do not seem, on the whole, to have much likelihood of being originals or even close copies. The only possible exception is *Horses Being Driven to Pasture* (see below), which, according to the inscription on it, is a copy of a work by the T'ang dynasty master Wei Yen. This agrees with the statement cited above that Li used this orthodox mode for his copies and imitations of old paintings. A better-known horse painting ascribed to Li Kung-lin, quite possibly an original, is the *Five Horses and Grooms* scroll (PL. 132), formerly in the Kikuchi Collection (Tokyo), but reportedly destroyed during World War II. Painted in ink on paper and, except for some shading on the horses, in the *pai-miao* technique of line drawing, it is the work of a highly accomplished draftsman, whether Li himself or not. The figures, and perhaps the horses also, seem to have antecedents in T'ang paintings but are drawn with greater realism and a special elegance that is of Li's own period.

Another extraordinarily skillful performance in the *pai-miao* technique is the hand scroll illustrating a historical anecdote, *General Kuo Tzŭ-i Receiving the Homage of the Uigurs* (PL. 133). The line, although it is fine and precise, is not of even thickness, but swells and tapers in perfectly controlled rhythms. The figures are expertly characterized, and the drama of the situation is well brought out in their postures and interrelations. This is once again the work of a master draftsman, although it cannot be confidently assigned to Li Kung-lin; the signature is probably an interpolation, and some features of the painting indicate a later date and even a different stylistic school. Probably closer to Li Kung-lin's own style, whether or not a work from his hand (a question that cannot be decided on the basis of reproductions), is the *Dancing Peasants* scroll (also known as *Beating the Ground*; PL. 134). The fluctuating brush line moves more freely and swiftly, seeming less tightly controlled than in the *Kuo Tzŭ-i* scroll, and there is evident that touch of conscious naïveté — partly occasioned by the popular subject, but also an ingredient of the style — that is found in other works ascribed to the master.

The association of Li Kung-lin with the literati school, his penchant for archaism, and the references in early texts to his "rough" style all suggest that technical skill and apparent sophistication in the drawing may not be satisfactory criteria for assessing the reliability of paintings attributed to him. Several works that would have to be rejected immediately on the basis of such criteria may in fact be early productions of his followers, if not his own. The long scroll of illustrations to the *Hua-yen Sūtra* (PL. 135) is one of these. An attitude of conscious primitivism underlies the expressionless faces and stiff postures, the unrealistic drapery drawing, and the decorative clouds. These qualities serve to impart a cool, classical air to the picture and a special dignity to the figures.

A different kind of primitivism, a naïveté with suggestions of amateurism in it, is seen in the scroll of the *Women's Classic of Filial Piety* (see below), a series of small and dark pictures on silk that may well go back to the late Northern Sung period. The inscriptions separating them have been accepted by esteemed authorities as authentic examples of the handwriting of Li Kung-lin. The line used for the figures and architecture is very fine, resembling pen drawing, and the brushwork in other parts, such as the contours of rocks, may give some clue to Li's "rough" style.

The evidence that these elements of primitivism and "roughness" were conspicuous in at least some of Li's works is too strong to be ignored; and it seems clear that they represent an attempt to recapture, or at least to evoke, the unsophisticated charm of archaic painting, but in a new context that in fact makes them quite sophisticated. Li's most renowned landscape composition, *Dwelling in the Lung-mien Mountains* (PL. 134), which exists in several versions, is plainly an archaistic play on such a T'ang landscape type as is seen reflected in extant copies of Lu Hung's *Ten Views from a Thatched Lodge*. (For the best extant version, see *Ku-kung ming-hua san-pai-chung*, 1959. The copy has been ascribed to Li himself, but is more likely later, perhaps 14th-cent.) The artist's intent is, in a sense, as much literary as pictorial. The same is true of the scroll illustrating the "Nine Songs" of Ch'ü Yüan (see below), which appears to be a copy of indeterminate date. In both scrolls certain very symmetrical arrangements of architecture and landscape violate canons of Li Kung-lin's own time; these arrangements, which again are probably references to T'ang designs, are echoed in various other works by Li's followers and were evidently among the distinctive features of the school manner. The distortions of form and space, the violent disproportion between the figures and their setting, and the scratchy brushwork set these pictures far apart from another variety of ink landscape, the abbreviated or "impressionistic" renderings of nature, such as, for example, the *Scenery of the Hsiao-Hsiang Region* (see below), also attributed to Li Kung-lin. This is a picture vastly superior as a landscape, but probably farther in style and taste from the work of Li himself. Nevertheless, there was a tradition in the Southern Sung and later periods connecting such misty river landscapes, done largely in a pointillist technique over graded ink washes, with Li Kung-lin: for instance, the *Panorama of the Upper Yangtze River* (see below), attributed to him but probably 13th-century in date, and the landscapes painted on screens depicted in a scroll by Mou I dated 1240. There was probably some basis for the tradition in Li Kung-lin's own works, as is reasonable in view of his close friendship with Mi Fei, who painted landscapes in a related manner.

The course of the Li Kung-lin school during the Southern Sung period (1127–1279) is represented in works connected with several of his followers. A scroll illustrating Su Shih's ode "Red Cliff," attributed to Li's direct disciple Ch'iao Chung-ch'ang (New York, Coll. J. M. Crawford, Jr.), is one of the most important because of its closeness to the master, as well as for its own high quality (Hsieh Chih-liu, 1957). A series of portraits of arhats in hand-scroll form, attributed to the 12th-century Ch'an Buddhist painter Fan-lung (Washington, D.C., Freer Gall. of Art), is untypical of the school in, for example, the remarkable characterization of the faces, but it displays the *pai-miao* figure drawing of the Li Kung-lin tradition in its finest form (Cahill, 1960). Another scroll (also Freer Gall.), a series of illustrations to the "Odes of Pin" section of the "Book of Odes," or "Songs" (*Shih-ching*), is attributed to the 12th-century court painter Ma Ho-chih; although the landscape elements are close to the style of that master, the figures are in the manner of Li Kung-lin, and the painting may be by some Southern Sung painter who was influenced by both. One of the most valuable of all, since it bears a trustworthy date, is the superb *Making Clothes for the Warriors* scroll by Mou I, dated 1240, formerly in the Palace Collection, Peking (*Ku-kung ming-hua san-pai-chung*, 1959; Sirén, 1956).

At least two paintings attributed to Li Kung-lin himself can be assigned with some assurance to the 13th century through their stylistic affinities with the work of Mou I. One is the famous *Realms of the Immortals*, a long hand scroll representing the Taoist paradise (PL. 136). The fantastic rock formations are clearly derived from the decorative rockeries of Sung gardens; the figures are delicately drawn in hair-thin lines and surrounded with faint ink washes shading outward into the enveloping space, a convention also seen in the Mou I painting but hardly to be met with elsewhere in Chinese painting. These two pictures also have in common a particular manner of outline and shading in the rocks and trees. Something essentially in agreement is seen also in another set of illustrations to the "Odes of Pin," which, like the scroll attributed to Ma Ho-chih mentioned above, represents agricultural occupations of the four seasons (Sickman, 1962, pls. 23–24). The childlike quality of the figures recalls the *Women's Classic of Filial Piety* and other works of the school; the suaveness apparent at some points of the architectural drawing and the *gaucherie* of some others suggest again a conscious primitivism.

The high point of Chinese esteem for Li Kung-lin was in the Yüan dynasty (1280–1368), when such major masters as Chao Mêng-fu (1254–1322; q.v.) and Ch'ien Hsüan (ca. 1235–1300) followed his style in their figure and horse paintings, and critics were unbounded in their praise. His influence declined after that, although a few Ming painters, notably Yu Ch'iu (late 16th cent.) did creditable imitations. Spurious "Li Kung-lins" were produced in abundance during the Ch'ing period, but these labored and tasteless productions preserve almost none of the essential features of the tradition.

WORKS ATTRIBUTED TO LI KUNG-LIN (inferior and obviously unrelated paintings omitted). *Horses Being Driven to Pasture*, after Wei Yen; hand scroll in colors on silk (Sirén, III, pl. 193). Peking, Hui-hua-kuan. Sirén says this may possibly be genuine. – *General Kuo Tzŭ-i Receiving the Homage of the Uigurs*; hand scroll in ink on paper (*Ku-kung ming-hua san-pai-chung*, II, no. 85). Signed. Taichung, Formosa, Nat. Palace Mus. – *Illustrations of the "Nine Songs" of Ch'ü Yüan*; copy after an original by Li Kung-lin (?); hand scroll in ink on paper (Sirén, III, pl. 198). Formerly, Peking, Palace Coll.; published there as a reproduction scroll in 1934. – *Dancing Peasants (Beating the Ground)*; hand scroll in ink on paper; colophon dated 1265 (Sirén, III, pl. 194). Formerly, Peking, Palace Coll. Seen and photographed by Sirén ca. 1930, and judged by him an original. Present location unknown. – *Dwelling in the Lung-mien Mountains*; hand scroll in ink on paper (Sirén, III, pl. 195). Taichung, Formosa, Nat. Central Mus. Conceivably an original, but more likely a close and early copy of this famous composition. Another, greatly inferior version belongs to the Berenson Foundation, Settignano, near Florence (Sirén, II, opp. p. 44). – *Five Horses and Grooms*; hand scroll in ink on paper; colophon by Huang T'ing-chien (*Kokka*, 380; Sirén, III, pls. 191–192). Formerly, Tokyo, Kikuchi Coll.; reportedly destroyed in 1945. Quite possibly genuine. – *Vimalakīrti and Attendant*; hanging scroll in ink on silk (Sirén, III, pl. 199). Hauge Coll.; kept in Tokyo. A Sung work of high quality, but the connection with Li Kung-lin is tenuous. – *Arhats*; two hanging scrolls in ink and colors on silk, from a set of 16 (*Kokka*, 30, 41; S. Tajima, *Tōyō bijutsu taikwan*, VIII, Tokyo, 1908). Tokyo, Academy of Art. Twelfth-century works, perhaps in a stylistic tradition established by Li Kung-lin. Several copies of the whole set exist. – *Scenery of the Hsiao-Hsiang Region*; hand scroll in ink on paper (S. Shimada and Y. Yonezawa, *Painting in the Sung and Yüan Dynasties*, Tokyo, 1952, pl. 28). Tokyo, Nat. Commission for the Protection of Cultural Properties. The signature is evidently spurious; the painting is by another artist with the surname Li, who is mentioned in a 12th-century colophon. – *Illustrations of the "Homecoming" Ode of T'ao Ch'ien*; hand scroll in ink and colors on silk (O. Sirén, *Chinese Painting in American Collections*, Paris, 1927-28). Washington, D. C., Freer Gall. Copy, 14th century or later, of a Sung work perhaps by Li Kung-lin. – *Panorama of the Upper Yangtze River*; hand scroll in ink on paper (*Kokka*, 273). Washington, D. C., Freer Gall. Probably a 13th-century work in the tradition of Li Kung-lin. – *Realms of the Immortal*; hand scroll in ink on paper (Sirén, III, pls. 196-197). Washington, D. C., Freer Gall. Thirteenth century, school of Li Kung-lin. – *The White Lotus Society*; hand scroll in ink on paper. Washington, D. C., Freer Gall. Copy, perhaps by Yu Ch'iu (late 16th cent.), of this famous composition. – *The Cassia and Epidendrum Palace*; hand scroll in ink on paper (Sirén, III, pl. 201). Washington, D. C., Freer Gall. A Ming-dynasty work, unrelated to Li Kung-lin. – *Seven Immortals*; hand scroll in ink and faint color on silk (Royal Ontario Museum, *Loan Exhibition of Chinese Paintings*, Toronto, 1956, no. 4). Ottawa, Nat. Gall. of Canada. – *Metamorphoses of Heavenly Beings According to the Hua-yen Sūtra*; hand scroll in ink and faint color on paper (L. Sickman and A. Soper, *The Art and Architecture of China*, Harmondsworth, 1956, pl. 96). Paris, C. T. Loo & Cie. An old and famous work, probably close to Li Kung-lin in period and style. – *Illustrations of the "Odes of Pin"*; hand scroll in ink on paper. New York, Coll. J. M. Crawford, Jr. Thirteenth century (?). – *The Drunken Monk* (i.e., the 8th-cent. Ch'an Buddhist monk-calligrapher Huai-su); hand scroll in ink and color on paper. Washington, D. C., Coll. Mrs. Eugene B. Meyer. Copy of Yüan period or later (?). – *Women's Classic of Filial Piety*; hand scroll in ink on silk. New York, Coll. C. C. Wang. Probably as early as Li Kung-lin, and possibly by him.

SOURCES. Hsüan-ho hua-p'u (cat. of the collection of Emperor Hui-tsung), preface dated 1120, chap. 7; T'eng Ch'un, Hua chi ("Continuation of Painting"), 1167, chap. 3; Hsia Wên-yen, T'u-hui pao-chien ("Mirror of Painting"), preface dated 1365, chap. 3; P'ei-wên-chai shu-hua-p'u (encyclopedia of calligraphy and painting), 1708, chap. 50.

BIBLIOG. C. Nagagawa, Li Lung-mien and Monochrome Drawing, Kokka, 380, 1912, pp. 327-42; A. E. Meyer, Chinese Painting as Reflected in the Thought of Li Lung-mien (with two portfolios of photographs), New York, 1923; A. Waley, Introduction to the Study of Chinese Painting, London, 1923, pp. 196-200; O. Sirén, Chinese Painting: Leading Masters and Principles, II, London, New York, 1956, pp. 39-52, III, 1956, pl. 312; Kishida Tsutomu, Rikōsin Ronkō, Tōyō Shigaku, XIV, 1956, pp. 1-28; Hsieh Chih-liu, T'ang Wu-tai Sung Yüan ming-chi, Shanghai, 1957, pls. 23-33; Chu Chu-yü, T'ang Sung hua-chia jên-ming tz'ü-tien (Dictionary of Painters of the T'ang and Sung Dynasties), Shanghai, 1958, pp. 103-07; A. Giuganino, La pittura cinese, Rome, 1959, I, pp. 91-92, II, pls. 144-50; Ku-kung ming-hua san-pai-chung (Three Hundred Masterpieces of Chinese Painting in the Palace Museum), I, Taichung, 1959, nos. 5-14, III, no. 119; Chou Wu, Li Kung-lin, Shanghai, 1959; J. Cahill, Chinese Painting, Geneva, New York, 1960, p. 94; L. Sickman, ed., Chinese Calligraphy and Painting in the Collection of John M. Crawford, Jr., New York, 1962, pp. 72-75, 90-93, pls. 15-16, 23-24.

James CAHILL

Illustrations: PLS. 132-136.

LI LUNG-MIEN. See LI KUNG-LIN.

LIMBOURG, POL, HERMAN, AND JEHANEQUIN DE (also called Malouel, Maelwael, Maelweel). Painters, sons of a sculptor (*beeldensnijder*) Arnold van Limburg (also called van Aken or Aachen) and nephews of Jean Malouel, the titular painter of Duke Philip the Bold of Burgundy, the Limbourg brothers were born after 1385 in Nijmegen. Undoubtedly on the recommendation of their uncle, they went to Paris about 1400 to apprentice themselves to a goldsmith. An account of 1402-03 mentions a contract dated Feb. 9, 1402, wherein two illuminators, Pol and Jean, were hired for four years to decorate a "très belle et notable Bible" for Philip the Bold. After the death of Philip on Apr. 27, 1404, nothing is known of them until the names of Pol and his brothers reappear in the accounts of Philip's brother Jean de France, Duc de Berry, in whose service they evidently replaced the painter Jacquemart de Hesdin about 1410. The posthumous inventory of the books of Jean de Berry, made in 1416, mentions "plusieurs cahiers de très riches heures que faisent Pol et ses frères." Their work remained incomplete, since they were all dead by February of 1416, and their patron, Jean de Berry, died on June 15 of the same year.

Leopold Delisle (1884) recognized as the "très riches heures" a volume in the library of the Duc d'Aumale at Chantilly. This fortunate discovery, together with the originality of the Limbourgs' clearly recognizable style, has made it possible to identify others of their works with near certainty.

The Bible executed for Philip the Bold has not been preserved. [A copy of a *Bible moralisée* painted in part by the Limbourg brothers and now in Paris (Bib. Nat., Ms. fr. 166) does not appear to correspond to the one mentioned in the accounts of Philip the Bold.]

Probably after Philip's death the young artists, deprived of their patron, continued to work on the Bible in some studio where they completed their artistic formation alongside fellow artists from the Low Countries who, like themselves, were established in Paris, which at that time attracted many foreign painters. One important workshop there was that of the Master of 1402, which employed Mosan and Rhenish artists. The Limbourg brothers reveal certain affinities with this group, from whom they borrowed numerous artistic formulas and acquired a general preciosity that was to become almost a mannerism toward the end of their careers. Nothing of their work before 1410 can be identified with certainty; two miniatures, however, from the vast Parisian production, may be by one of them, probably Pol, the oldest and apparently the most proficient of the brothers. The first of these, *The Court of Heaven*, formed the frontispiece of a Parisian copy of *The Golden Legend* of Jacobus de Varagine, dated 1404 (Paris, Bib. Nat., Ms. fr. 414, fol. 1); the scene was exactly duplicated by the brothers seven or eight years later in the *Belles Heures du Duc de Berry* (New York, Met. Mus., The Cloisters, 54.1.1., fol. 218). The second, a *Virgin with a Petition*, was painted on the dedication page of a collection of devotional works, also of Parisian origin (Paris, Bib. Nat., Ms. fr. 926, fol. 2), which was given in 1406 to Jean's daughter Marie de Berry by her confessor, the Augustinian brother Simon de Courcy. This miniature later served as the model for two facing pages, of controversial attribution, added to the *Très Belles Heures du Duc de Berry* (*Très Belles Heures de Notre-Dame*; Brussels, Bib. Roy., Ms. 11060-61), which was decorated for the duke before 1410 by Jacquemart de Hesdin. To these two miniatures it is perhaps possible to relate the frontispiece of another *Golden Legend*, of a slightly earlier date (Paris, Bib. Nat., Ms. fr. 242, fol. A). Although very similar in style, it is not necessarily by the same hand as that of Ms. fr. 414 and Ms. fr. 926 nor by one of the Limbourgs. Nevertheless, it does show the harmony of composition and elegant reserve that distinguish the works of the three brothers. The colors, the poses, the facial types have a quality that was to be typical of these extraordinarily gifted illuminators, whose artistic evolution proceeded with astonishing rapidity. The technical differences, due to the lapse of time between the presumed works of 1404-06 and the *Belles Heures du Duc de Berry*, an established work (ca. 1410-13), are not more problematical in this respect than those which distinguish the latter work from the *Très Riches Heures*, on which the Limbourgs were working in 1415 at the latest. The interval between the first two is approximately eight years; between the second and the last it is two or three.

At the court of Jean de Berry from about 1410 the Limbourg brothers found the conditions necessary for the independent development of their artistic personalities. They entered a new period, of which the *Belles Heures*, mentioned in an inventory of 1413, is the first datable evidence. The manuscript contains 94 large double-column miniatures, two-thirds or three-quarters of a column in length; 78 smaller one-column works, one-half the page or more in depth; and numerous initials. The decoration, markedly homogeneous, appears to be the work of one hand, certainly that of Pol, or possibly of two, but distinction between them is difficult. To the usual elements of a Book of Hours (calendar, hours of the Virgin, etc.), with their traditional illustrations, were added seven episodes from the lives of saints, taken from *The Golden Legend* — namely, SS. Catherine, Gregory, Bruno, Jerome, Paul the Hermit, Anthony Abbot, and John the Baptist — as well as the story of the emperor Heraclius. In each of these narratives, illustrated with 2 to 12 miniatures, Pol shows a resourceful imagination and a most unusual sense of documentary detail. His presentation was as factual and historically accurate as he could make it, and the combination of ingenious invention with a degree of realism previously unknown in France foreshadows the marvelous figures of the *Très Riches Heures du Duc de Berry* and, in some respects, the work of Jean Fouquet (q.v.).

This manuscript demonstrates that the Limbourgs, better than anyone before them, understood the new inventions of Italian origin. The Italian derivation is less significant in iconography — even though certain elements are directly borrowed (e.g., tabernacles with figures above the capitals, as in the Cathedral of Milan; procession of Litanies inspired by paintings such as the *Beheading of St. George* in Padua) — than in the treatment of form and space. The Limbourgs' sense of mass and volume indicates a profound study of the Giottesque tradition. Their distances are developed in plains and hollows and are animated with far-off landscapes and shifting skies. An effort toward a consistent perspective construction becomes apparent, reflecting 20 years of trial and error in the Parisian international milieu and prefiguring pictorial discoveries yet to come. The work also reveals original observation, most likely enriched by familiarity with the large collections of Jean de Berry, which are known to have included a wealth of Italian art, paintings, sculpture, furniture, and medals. The *Belles Heures* was acquired in 1416 by Yolanda of Aragon, duchess of Anjou; rebound about 1620; and found, in the second half of the 19th century, in the possession of the Baron d'Ailly. The manuscript passed to the collection of the Baron Edmond de Rothschild, and then, in 1954, to the Metropolitan Museum, New York; it is exhibited in The Cloisters.

One surviving copy of a *Bible moralisée* (Paris, Bib. Nat., Ms. fr. 166), illuminated during the time of the French king Charles VI (1380–1422), was begun by the Limbourgs, no doubt at about the same time as they were working on the *Belles Heures du Duc de Berry* — a deduction justified by the close relationship of the two manuscripts (which makes it unlikely that this was the work commissioned by Philip the Bold). If the Bible was, indeed, intended for Jean de Berry, its omission from the inventories of his library may perhaps be attributed to the fact that it was too incomplete to deserve mention. After the death of the Limbourgs the Bible was continued by various painters, including the Master of Juvénal des Ursins (Master of the Geneva Boccaccio) and other less able artists, who worked on it until the end of the 15th century, but it remained unfinished.

The work of three hands, very close but nevertheless distinct, can be recognized in the decoration of the first three gatherings of the *Bible moralisée*, which were divided among the brothers. The miniatures in the third gathering (fol. 17–24), because of their superiority, may be attributed to Pol, after which follow in order of excellence the first gathering (fol. 1–8) and then the second (fol. 9–16).

The frontispiece, which appears to have been added to the Bible, is contemporaneous in execution and is undoubtedly the work of one of the brothers. This full-page miniature shows St. Jerome, seated at his desk among his books, translating the Bible; his lion is in front of him and his cardinal's hat hangs on the wall. Simpler versions of the same scene are to be found in the *Belles Heures du Duc de Berry* (fol. 187v) and in the initial letter of a Valerius Maximus manuscript in the Vatican Library (Reg. lat. 939), also by the Limbourgs, the text of which was written in Paris by an Italian about 1410; and there are two drawings of it. One of the drawings, in Paris (Louvre, Cabinet des Dessins, RF 423), is very close to that of the Limbourgs but less polished; the other, in Rotterdam (Mus. Boymans–Van Beuningen, Königs Coll.), which contains only the seat and architectural decoration, is no doubt from the Limbourgs' atelier. The theme stems ultimately from Carolingian Evangelist portraits, which were themselves derived from antique author portraits. It reached France from Italy, as witness the portrait of Petrarch in a copy of *De viris illustribus* (Darmstadt, Landesbib., Cod. 101), drawn about 1380, which is comparable in every respect, save that it is surrounded by Italian architectural decoration and furniture, perhaps reproducing a lost mural from the Hall of the Giants (Sala Virorum Illustrium) in the Carrara Palace in Padua. Like the Darmstadt portrait, that of the *Bible moralisée*, completed down to every detail, was intended as a grisaille. The connection with Padua is probably more than coincidental, for it appears also in the Litanies of the *Belles Heures du Duc de Berry*.

The illustration of a luxurious *Book of Hours of Rome Use*, in the possession of Count Antoine Seilern, London (formerly, James de Rothschild Coll.), can without doubt be attributed to one of the Limbourgs, possibly the artist of the second gathering of the *Bible moralisée*, and was painted between 1413 and 1416. It is not known for whom this manuscript was destined, for it contains no coat of arms, nor is it mentioned in the posthumous inventory of Jean de Berry. Unfinished at the death of the Limbourgs, the manuscript was completed by the master who had also been the final contributor to the Brussels *Très Belles Heures*. Apart from the added section, the illustrations are as homogeneous as those of the *Belles Heures du Duc de Berry* and are composed of 5 small (one-third of a column) and 18 full-page miniatures. The work is placed chronologically between the New York *Belles Heures* and the *Très Riches Heures* and marks a distinct stylistic phase between the two. The images are of the traditional type represented in the former, some features of which are closely reproduced. For example, the *Belles Heures* scene (fol. 94v) from the life of St. Bruno, with Raymond Diocrès emerging from his coffin, occurs again in the Seilern Hours (Office of the Dead, fol. 81v), repeating the poses of the frightened monks and the architecture and furnishings, and though Diocrès is absent, it is still an obvious example of copying. The frames of the miniatures are of two types, comprising, like those of the *Très Riches Heures*, an Italian acanthus pattern filled with figures and naturalistically rendered flowers.

Shortly after finishing the *Belles Heures du Duc de Berry*, the Limbourg brothers began the decoration of the manuscript listed in the 1416 inventory as the "très riches heures" (*Très Riches Heures du Duc de Berry*; Chantilly, Mus. Condé, Ms. 65), the second of their works that can be dated with precision and the masterpiece of French International Gothic style. Left unfinished at the death of the Limbourgs, it was completed about 1485 by Jean Colombe of Bourges for Charles I of Savoy and his wife, Blanche of Montferrat, distant cousins descended from Bonne de Berry, the daughter of Jean. The volume contains 129 miniatures, some full-page or three-quarters of a page in two columns, and some smaller, one-third or two-thirds of a page in one column. Of these, 71 were by the Limbourgs, and the rest, some already begun by the brothers, were completed by Colombe.

The pictorial program goes far beyond that of the *Grandes Heures du Duc de Berry* (X, PL. 440; Paris, Bib. Nat., Ms. lat. 919) illustrated by Jacquemart de Hesdin for the same patron. Just as the content of the *Grandes Heures* was complementary to the *Petites Heures* of Jean de Berry (Paris, Bib. Nat., Ms. lat. 18014), so the *Très Riches Heures* complements the *Belles Heures* in a way that indicates for both pairs of manuscripts the editorial assistance of specialists and the preference of the patron himself. The *Très Riches Heures* opens with the usual 12 figures of the calendar, but whereas in the *Belles Heures* these labors of the months conform to traditional themes, here the artist has animated them by providing a realistic and lively setting (VI, PL. 65). In the January page (PL. 137) Jean de Berry personally receives his household for the New Year's dinner. The physical appearance of the duke matches the features on his funeral effigy; the other figures surely must be portraits also. Scenes for other months show a gathering of elegant young people for a rustic betrothal, a May promenade, a hunt, and alert peasants and fresh-faced yeomen laboring in the fields of the prince with one of his châteaux in the background (PL. 8). In the December scene (PL. 138) night falls on an autumnal clearing where a stag lies dead after the hunt. In the background, lit by the last rays of the sun, are seen the high towers of the castle of Vincennes, where Jean de Berry had been born. This dreamlike apparition, so soon to vanish in the night, this recollection of a distant past in the melancholy atmosphere of the closing day and the dying year, evokes in naturalistic terms the idea of death and of man's final end. The painter had found the principal motif (the dogs with their quarry) in some album such as the sketchbook of Giovannino de' Grassi (Bergamo, Bib. Civ., Cod. VII, 14), but the setting in which it is employed in the Jean de Berry calendar envelops the Italian motif in a fairy-tale atmosphere; the real has been transmuted to fantasy.

Precise observers of natural landscape forms, the Limbourgs established a mystic correspondence between the physical universe and the world of the spirit. Far from abstracting forms of nature to reveal their hidden content, they scrutinized the ways of nature to find the revelation of a higher order. The *Coronation of the Virgin* is equally revealing of their poetic genius. The composition, rounded at the bottom in double curves, rises, expands, and melts into the gold and the azure, like a cloud that dissipates the light and the celestial glow. Everything in this ascending rhythm magnifies the glory of the Virgin, but the idea is expressed by representational means, without any tendency toward stylization or abstraction. Similarly, in the glowing red scene of Hell a jet of flame and smoke ceaselessly spews forth the souls of the damned from the gridiron of Lucifer and drops them back again into the volcano of fire. It is a terrifying scene over which hovers the eternity of punishment.

The meticulous documentation — of the local color, for example — appears even more clearly in this manuscript than in the *Belles Heures*. Antiquity, real or imagined, and Italy were again important sources of inspiration. The kneeling Adam in the *Eden and the Expulsion* (PL. 139) has close affinities with an ancient statue of the Pergamene school, of which a copy can be found in Aix-en-Provence (Mus. Granet). Medallions of Heraclius and Constantine, which the duke, believing them to be ancient, had purchased from Italian merchants in 1402, served as models for one of the horsemen of *The Meeting of the Three Kings* (PL. 140) and for the solar chariot of the calendar. (The medallion of Constantine had already been used as a source for the *Belles Heures*.) *The Purification* (fol. 54v) was inspired by a scene similar to *The Presentation of the Virgin in the Temple* by Taddeo Gaddi in Florence (Sta Croce, Baroncelli Chapel).

In the 18th century the *Très Riches Heures* was owned by the Spinola family of Genoa, then by the Serra family, and finally by Baron Felix de Margherita of Turin, who sold it in 1856 to the Duc d'Aumale. The duke bequeathed his collection to the Institut de France.

It is difficult to date with precision several minor works of the Limbourg brothers. One is an excellent *Departure of Jean de Berry on a Journey*, perhaps contemporary with the *Belles Heures du Duc de Berry*, inserted in the *Petites Heures du Duc de Berry* (Paris, Bib. Nat., Ms. lat. 18014, fol. 288v) at the beginning of the prayer "ad capiendam viam suam." As obvious flattery, it makes use of the figure of the guardian angel of the Holy Family from the *Flight into Egypt* (fol. 63) in the *Belles Heures* manuscript. Others are two scenes with rather heavy figures (*Adoration of the Trinity* and *Prayer to the Angels*) that were added to the *Très Belles Heures de Notre-Dame* (Paris, Bib. Nat., Nouv. acq. lat. 3093, pp. 225 and 240; formerly Rothschild Coll.), once the property of Jean de Berry. Finally, the author portrait in the Valerius Maximus manuscript in the Vatican (mentioned above) seems to be a work of commercial character and probably antedates the Limbourgs' entry into the service of Jean de Berry. To the foregoing may be added the initial of a Consecratory Charter of the Ste-Chapelle of Bourges, dated Apr. 18, 1405; since this is known only by a reproduction (A. de Bastard, *Documents manuscrits*, Paris, 1838–69, XII), it is difficult to be sure that it is not a later copy or even whether it is by one of the Limbourgs.

To one of the brothers or their circle, Erwin Panofsky has attributed a *Portrait of a Lady* (Washington, D.C., Nat. Gall.), as well as the original of a profile portrait of John the Fearless known through a copy in the Louvre. Other works have been attributed to them without valid reason. Certainly the marginal decorations of the *Book of Hours* in Oxford (Bodleian Lib., Ms. Douce 144), the paintings in the *Book of Hours of Rome Use* (Br. Mus., Ms. Add. 35311 and Ms. Harley 2897) should not be ascribed to them. More problematic is the beautiful *Madonna of Humility* in the Prayer Book of Philip the Bold (Brussels, Bib. Roy, Ms. 11035–37, fol. 6v; cf. C. Gaspar and F. Lyna, *Les principaux manuscrits à peintures de la Bibliothèque royale*, Paris, 1937, I, pp. 419–23 and pl. XCVIIIa). On the other hand, the *Book of Hours of Paris Use* in Chantilly (Mus. Condé, Ms. 66) is very close to the Seilern Hours.

The brevity of the Limbourgs' career explains not only why we have so few works by them but also the isolation of their position. They were in advance of their time, and their activity, although fairly well documented, became known only slowly and fitfully, at least in France (perhaps because of the historical crises of the times). Their work represents a crucial stage in the development of European art just prior to the Van Eyck brothers (see EYCK), but it is difficult to determine the extent to which these artists, of such boundless curiosity and remarkable sensitivity, can be regarded as innovators and to what extent they adopted the art forms of their own times. The admiration which they aroused is seen in the large number of imitations of their figured scenes in French illuminations. The *Belles Heures du Duc de Berry* furnished a number of themes for the Rohan Hours (Paris, Bib. Nat., Ms. lat. 9471), painted for a member of the Anjou family between 1418 and 1425; for the *Book of Hours of René of Anjou* (Paris, Bib. Nat., Ms. lat. 1156A); and for the *Hours of Angers Use*, formerly in the collection of Martin le Roy (Paris, private coll.). The decoration of the Breviary of John the Fearless included certain motifs derived from the Limbourgs, as did the Oxford Hours and some drawings added, perhaps about 1420, to the Psalter of Henry VI (Br. Mus., Ms. Cotton Domitian A.XVII). Other imitations of the Limbourgs' work — in a *Bible historiale* in Chantilly (Mus. Condé, Ms. 28) and in the Hours of Marguerite d'Orléans (Paris, Bib. Nat., Ms. lat. 1156B) — show the continuing prestige of their style. Finally, the calendar of the *Très Riches Heures du Duc de Berry* served as a model for the famous late 15th- or 16th-century manuscript, the Grimani Breviary (PL. 138; X, PL. 80; Venice, Bib. Marciana, Ms. s.s.), as well as for works of a comparable nature decorated by Flemish painters.

BIBLIOG. L. Delisle, Les Livres d'heures du Duc de Berry, GBA, XXIX, 1884, pp. 97–110, 281–92, 391–405; P. Durrieu, Les très riches heures de Jean de France, duc de Berry, Paris, 1904; F. Winkler, ThB, s.v. Limburg, Paul, XXXIII, 1929, pp. 227–29; R. Schilling, A Book of Hours from the Limbourg Atelier, BM, LXXXI, 1942, pp. 194–97; C. Sterling, Les peintres du Moyen âge, Paris, 1942, pp. 22–23, pls. 19–21; H. Bober, The Zodiacal Miniature of the Très riches heures of the Duke of Berry: Its Sources and Meaning, Warburg, XI, 1948, pp. 1–34; G. Ring, A Century of French Painting, 1400–1500, London, 1949, pp. 199–200; B. Degenhart, Autonome Zeichnungen bei mittelalterlichen Künstlern, Münch. Jhb. der bildenden K., N.S., I, 1950, pp. 93–158; L. Baldass, Jan Van Eyck, London, 1952, pp. 9–16; E. Panofsky, Early Netherlandish Painting, I, Cambridge, Mass., 1953, pp. 61–66; J. Porcher, Les Belles Heures de Jean de France, duc de Berry, Paris, 1953; F. Gorissen, Jan Maelwael und die Brüder Limburg über den Verfasser des Codex Gelre, Bijdragen en meded. der Vereiniging "Gelre," LIV, 1954, pp. 153–221; J. J. Rorimer and M. Freeman, The Belles Heures of Jean, Duke of Berry, Prince of France, New York, 1958; J. Porcher, L'enluminure française, Paris, 1959, pp. 61–65 (Eng. trans., J. Brown, London, New York, 1959, pp. 62–66); M. Meiss, French and Italian variations on an early fifteenth-century theme: St. Jerome and his Study, GBA, Sept., 1963, pp. 147–70; O. Pächt, The Limbourgs and Pisanello, GBA, Sept., 1963, pp. 109–22.

Jean PORCHER

Illustrations: PLS. 137–140.

LIPCHITZ, JACQUES (Lipschitz). Sculptor (b. Druskieniki, Lithuania, Aug. 22, 1891). Son of a Jewish building contractor, Jacques Lipchitz after a routine schooling in various Lithuanian cities went to Paris in 1909, a trip opposed by his father but aided by his mother. There he sought formal training in sculpture, briefly at the Ecole des Beaux-Arts, then at the Académie Julian. His early work includes some portrait heads modeled in clay (1910–11) and a rather academic *Woman and Gazelles* (1912). In 1913 he exhibited several small, dynamically posed and geometrically stylized plaster groups (later cast in bronze), such as *Acrobat on Horseback* and *Woman with Serpent*, perhaps influenced by current sculpture of Archipenko and Duchamp-Villon. In *Sailor and Guitar* (1914) he introduced the flat, overlapping planes of cubist painting. This was followed by a series of severely geometric marionettes, composed of silhouetted, flat wooden panels assembled with dowels, somewhat resembling collage. To the same period (1915–17) belong several bold and austere abstracts in stone, such as *Man with Guitar* (New York, Mus. of Mod. Art). These mark his emergence as a significant modern sculptor and cubist. In addition to many rather large figures of interwoven angular planes (e.g., *Bathers* and *Harlequins*, 1917–19) like the paintings of hermetic cubism, he also executed several reliefs of musical instruments. (Some of these are on the exterior walls of the Barnes Foundation, Merion, Pa.) In the 1920s, after a brief return to portraits (*Gertrude Stein, Berthe Lipchitz*), his cubist figures became more curvilinear. Also, for the first time, he executed life-sized sculpture (*Bather*, 1923–25). Experimenting with the lost-wax technique, he produced a group of small bronze "transparents" (1926–28), so called because of the interplay of solids and voids, some like cardboard cutouts, others like drawings in thick wire. Similar spatial interpenetrations appeared in his larger works such as *La Joie de Vivre* (1927) and *Reclining Nude with Guitar* (1928). One of the most powerful is the totemlike *Figure* (1930; New York, Mus. of Mod. Art).

In the 1930s there occurred a major change both in his subject matter and his style. In place of the impersonal and cubist *Harlequins* and *Bathers*, he turned to subjects which were based on personal experience but which had allegorical or symbolic overtones, such as *Mother and Child* (1930) and *Return of the Prodigal* (1931). His figural style was based on a simplified and enlarged naturalism, probably influenced by Picasso's surrealist figures. He also began to acknowledge a great respect for Rodin, whose work he had previously disliked. One of his most beautiful works of this period is the large *Song of the Vowels*, a blend of ambivalent symbolism and broad cubist forms. Profoundly disturbed by the threatening political events of the 1930s, Lipchitz produced *Prometheus Strangling the Vulture*, a huge allegorical group, commissioned for the Paris Exposition Universelle of 1937, and a more modest but equally forceful *Rape of Europa* (IV, PL. 184). During World War II, Lipchitz escaped to New York, where in the next few years, from 1941 to 1948, he produced some of the most dramatic sculptures of his career: *Mother and Child II, Benediction*, the "Sacrifice" series (I, PL. 131), and a revised version of the monumental *Prometheus* (one example of which is in the Philadelphia Museum of Art, another at the Walker Art Center, Minneapolis). A second series of "transparents" (*Blossoming, Springtime*) is romantic and lyrical in theme and execution. One of the most important commissions of his later career was the large *Notre Dame de Liesse* for the little church of Assy, near Mont Blanc, begun in 1948 and finally installed in 1954. (Other examples are at Iona, Inner Hebrides, and in New Harmony, Ind.) His New York studio destroyed by fire in January, 1952, he built a new studio near his home in Hastings-on-Hudson. His subsequent work has been limited mostly to small sketches, a few portraits, and an interesting series based on "found objects."

BIBLIOG. H. R. Hope, The Sculpture of Jacques Lipchitz, New York, 1954; A. Hammacher, Jacques Lipchitz, New York, 1961.

Henry R. HOPE

LIPPI, FILIPPO AND FILIPPINO. Painters, father and son, among the most interesting and significant personalities of the Florentine Quattrocento.

SUMMARY. Filippo (col. 257). Filippino (col. 261).

FILIPPO. Filippo Lippi was born in Florence about 1406 and died at Spoleto in 1469. In 1421 he took the vows of a Carmelite monk in the monastery of S. Maria del Carmine, Florence, where he remained for over ten years. In 1432 he executed the fresco *The Reform of the Carmelite Rule* (PL. 141), after which he probably left the monastery, since its records no longer mention him after Jan. 1, 1433. In 1434 he worked in the Basilica of S. Antonio in Padua and the Cappella del Podestà of the same city; his paintings in Padua have not survived. The *Madonna and Child* (PL. 143), formerly in the museum in Tarquinia (now Rome, Gall. Naz.), is dated 1437. In the same year the *capitani* of Orsanmichele commissioned him to paint a panel for the Barbadori Chapel in Sto Spirito, Florence (Louvre). It is this work to which Domenico Veneziano alludes in his letter of Apr. 1, 1438, to Piero di Cosimo de' Medici, declaring Filippo to be a "good master," together with Fra Angelico. The *Coronation of the Virgin* (PL. 142) in the Uffizi, commissioned by Canon Francesco di Antonio Maringhi, seems to have been begun in July, 1441, and the final payments were made only in 1447, in which year Filippo's painting *St. Bernard's Vision of the Virgin*, formerly in the Palazzo della Signoria (London, Nat. Gall.), was also completed. In 1450 Fra Filippo was accused and convicted of having falsified a receipt for a sum of money to be paid to the painter Giovanni di Francesco. In April, 1452, the *provveditori* of the Cathedral of Prato invited him to decorate the choir of the Cathedral, on which he began work the following month, together with his assistant, Fra Diamante di Feo da Terranova. This work continued, with many suspensions, until 1464.

In 1452, Fra Filippo was named chaplain to the nuns of S. Niccolò de' Frieri in Florence and painted for Leonardo di Bartolommeo Bartolini a tondo, the Madonna with scenes from the life of the Virgin (PL. 144) now in the Pitti. The *Virgin Enthroned and Two Saints* in the Galleria Comunale at Prato is dated 1453, and *The Adoration of the Child* for the convent of Annalena (Uffizi, No. 8350) was finished about 1455. In May, 1455, Fra Filippo was relieved of his duties as rector of the Church of S. Quirico at Legnaia, near Florence. In the following year, however, he was named chaplain to the nuns of S. Margherita at Prato; it was from this sisterhood that he induced the nun Lucrezia Buti to elope with him. About 1457 Lucrezia bore him a son, Filippo, known as Filippino (see below). In 1458 Fra Filippo was commissioned by the Compagnia della SS. Trinità di Pistoia to complete an altarpiece of the Trinity which Francesco Pesellino had left unfinished at his death; this work (London, Nat. Gall.) was finished by Lippi in 1460. In 1461 the *Ufficiali di Notte e Monasteri* of Florence accused Fra Filippo and a notary of Prato of immoral behavior: Lucrezia Buti and her sister Spinetta, although they had renewed their nuns' vows in 1459, were once again living with the painter. Through the intercession of the Medici, Pius II released Fra Filippo and Lucrezia from their vows, and they were thenceforth recognized as man and wife. About 1463 Filippo painted an *Adoration of the Child* (Uffizi) for Lucrezia Tornabuoni. In 1466 he received the first payments for his frescoes in the apse of the Cathedral of Spoleto. While engaged on these frescoes, the painter fell ill and died in 1469 — on October 8, according to the necrology of the Carmine; on October 10, according to the notarial archives of Spoleto.

Fra Filippo Lippi, who lived in the monastery of the Carmine from 1421 to 1432, undoubtedly saw Masaccio and Masolino at work on the frescoes in the Brancacci Chapel of the monastery church. This experience was of first importance in his artistic formation, as the *Reform of the Carmelite Rule* in the cloister and the contemporaneous *Madonna of Humility* (Milan, Mus. del Castello Sforzesco) attest. In these works we may note a powerful striving for plasticity that derives directly from Masaccio and, at the same time, an attempt to incorporate the clear, pure colors and abstract diffused luminosity characteristic of Masolino.

Also apparent in Fra Filippo's early works are the influence of both Lorenzo Monaco, who had decorated the Bartolini Chapel in Sta Trinita, and Gherardo Starnina, who had worked at the Carmine itself, in the Chapel of St. Jerome. Other works which have been attributed to this phase of Fra Filippo's activity (ca. 1432) include the *Madonna with Saints and Angels* of the Galleria della Collegiata in Empoli, that in the Cini Collection, Venice, and the little *Madonna with Saints* in the

Musée Condé at Chantilly (also attributed to Francesco Pesellino).

After this period the next extant works of the painter are the above-mentioned *Madonna and Child* ("The Tarquinia Madonna"; PL. 143) and other paintings executed between 1437 and 1440. During the intervening years occurred Fra Filippo's Paduan sojourn, from which no works have survived; traces of it, however, are perhaps discernible in the "Tarquinia Madonna," particularly in its color: arbitrary and unusual juxtapositions of dark, hard, almost stony hues that remain unaffected by the surrounding light and have nothing in common with the transparent late-Gothic tonalities of Lippi's pre-Paduan paintings. This change of key, which is generally explained in terms of influences from Lorenzo Monaco, is more probably related to the dark tonalities common in the late-Gothic painting of the Veneto. Among the works associated with the "Tarquinia Madonna" and the period 1437–40 are the *Madonna and Child with Angels and Saints* (XII, PL. 35) formerly in Sto Spirito (Louvre) and its predella (Uffizi); the *Madonna and Child Enthroned* (New York, Met. Mus.) with the two pairs of saints (Turin, Gall. dell'Acc. Albertina) that originally formed a single triptych; and the *Annunciation* in S. Lorenzo, Florence, in which the influences of Paolo Uccello and Donatello are apparent.

The paintings of 1437–40 show a dominant interest in volume, combined with an unusual feeling for the changing play of light over surfaces and an insistence on flowing line. These are the first indications of a departure from the monumental stasis of Masaccio, which became final in Filippo's *Coronation of the Virgin* (PL. 142), executed about 1441–47. In this complex work the thronged figures are disposed symmetrically, one next to the other, about the central group; but the somewhat archaic composition is rendered fresh and immediate by the action of the light which flows over the figures, modifying form and color alike and overcoming any impression of immobility. The value of light is reinforced by that of line, which takes precedence over modeling: a freely flowing, insistent line, well adapted in its decorative character to a sense of space quite foreign to the laws of Brunelleschi.

The Uffizi *Coronation of the Virgin* thus is linked with Filippo's preceding works of 1437–40 and with his works of the 1450s and '60s, rather than with those of the decade of the 1440s, during which it actually was painted. This anomaly indicates that the changing interest of the artist was directed toward other experiments, marking a parenthesis in the natural evolution of his style. Shortly after 1440 Filippo participated in a classicist episode of taste shared by many of the Florentine painters and sculptors of that time. The interest in effects of pure plasticity aroused by Masaccio's works in the 1420s and '30s now gave place to investigations of spatial effects. These investigations — initiated by painters of refined intellect who had arrived at the Renaissance by way of a Gothic education, such as Paolo Uccello and Domenico Veneziano — were taken up by Filippo in the *Virgin Enthroned* formerly in Sta Croce (Uffizi) and the *Virgin and Child* in the Museo Mediceo, Florence, both seemingly painted between 1440 and 1442.

Certain paintings which form a distinct group may be dated between 1442 and 1447: the *Annunciation* in the Galleria Nazionale in Rome, the *Coronation of the Virgin* in the Vatican Museums, the Alessandri altarpiece (New York, Met. Mus.), the *Annunciation* (Munich, Alte Pin.), the *Adoration of the Magi* in the National Gallery, Washington, D.C. (PL. 146), and *St. Bernard's Vision of the Virgin* (London, Nat. Gall.). In these paintings it is clear that Filippo was influenced in the early 1440s by Fra Angelico, from whom he adopted bright, unshaded colors, a decorative line, and an ecstatic sentiment. He did not, however, construct his figures with the light but firm geometric regularity of the older painter; rather, he posed them in attitudes and movements of levity that dispel any sense of mystic contemplation.

After this Angelican interlude Filippo returned to his more customary style in the Madonna and Child with scenes from the life of the Virgin (PL. 144), which, although quite dissimilar in other respects, is directly related to the Uffizi *Coronation of the Virgin* in its intensified linear sensibility and in the harmony of delicate colors infused with light. Close to this singular painting are *The Death of St. Jerome* in the Cathedral of Prato (of which only the lower half is by Filippo, the upper being the work of Fra Diamante) and *The Adoration of the Child* (Uffizi, No. 8350), the earliest of three paintings of this subject, in which suggestions of Angelico are still present in the figure of the Madonna and in the angels.

These paintings date from about 1452, the year in which Filippo began the decoration of the apse of Prato Cathedral, and they reveal a close stylistic connection, not so much with the broadly conceived *Evangelists* (almost in the manner of Andrea del Castagno) in the vault as with the scenes from the lives of John the Baptist and St. Stephen in the choir. The Prato frescoes represent Filippo's most ambitious undertaking, and the problems intrinsic to them are solved with indisputable mastery. Their visual coherence, achieved through a consistent emphasis on line and light, is coupled with a subtle emotional coherence by virtue of which the figures' every state of being is infused with thoughtful melancholy. The scenes representing St. John in the wilderness still seem oriented toward a late-Gothic world, recalling 14th-century representations of the Thebaid (e.g., PL. 7). *The Funeral of St. Stephen* (PL. 145), on the other hand, which an inscription dates as from 1460, following a sojourn in Florence (1457–58), places Filippo definitely in the Renaissance. The ample figures are placed within a spacious, columned interior pervaded with silvery light, against which their own warm colors stand out strongly. Red is used throughout with such freedom and exuberance as to heighten the modeling and vividness of the figures, many of which are portraits. *Herod's Feast* (PL. 145) lacks the solemn spatial equilibrium of *The Funeral of St. Stephen*, but its use of vibrating light and of a free, rhythmic line anticipates the art of Botticelli and even that of Leonardo.

The other autograph works of the late 1450s were executed in Florence, among them the polyptych painted for Alfonso II of Naples; its two surviving lateral panels, *St. Michael* and *St. Anthony*, were formerly in the Cook Collection at Richmond, England. From the late 1450s and early 1460s come the *Madonna Adoring the Child* in Berlin (PL. 146) and the *Annunciation and Seven Saints* painted for the Medici (London, Nat. Gall.). The personal characteristics of the master's late style find their quintessential expression, however, in the famous *Madonna and Child with Angels* in the Uffizi, from which the less successful *Madonna and Child* in Munich (Alte Pin.) derives.

Fra Filippo's artistic activity was concluded with the frescoes in Spoleto Cathedral, executed between 1467 and 1469, depicting scenes from the life of the Virgin (PL. 146). Much of the work on these frescoes he delegated to his collaborator, Fra Diamante. Nevertheless, certain of the autograph sections prefigure, still more clearly than the frescoes in Prato Cathedral, the future development of Florentine painting in the hands of Botticelli and of Filippino Lippi. Of all the Florentine Quattrocento painters, Fra Filippo Lippi can undoubtedly be considered one of the richest in creative possibilities.

An early evaluation of Filippo is that in the letter mentioned above from Domenico Veneziano to Piero di Cosimo de' Medici, dated Apr. 1, 1438: "... there are good masters like Fra Filippo and Fra Giovanni [i.e., Fra Angelico] who have much work to do...." Thus even at that date Filippo was considered the equal of Angelico. Another citation occurs in the *Apologia* prefixed to Cristoforo Landino's 1481 edition of Dante, in which Fra Filippo was named as one of Florence's illustrious artists. He was also mentioned among the outstanding Florentines by Antonio Manetti (*Le Vite di XIV uomini singhulari*), by Antonio Belli in his *Libro*, and by Francesco Albertini in his *Memoriale . . .* (1510). All call his work skillful (*artifitioso*), beautiful (*hornato*), and varied in coloring. These writers furnish the nucleus for a catalogue of Filippo's works.

The first biography of the artist is Vasari's. It seems to contain a sizable admixture of fiction, especially in the expanded second edition of the *Lives* (1568), but it includes an extensive list of paintings, as well as valuable information on Filippo's formative period with his study of Masaccio's works at the Carmine. Vasari's assessment of Filippo's artistic personality, though rather general, is repeated by Borghini (1584) and Baldinucci (1681–1728). Luigi Lanzi (1789) also accepts, with some reservations, Vasari's critical estimate and his biographical data.

The first notable critical discussion of Filippo is supplied by Jakob Burckhardt (1855), who emphasizes both the creative originality of the painter's imagination and his importance as an innovator, though an innovator who built upon the contributions of the past. Somewhat later, Alexis François Rio (1861), scandalized by the behavior of the man, condemned the painter as lacking in those qualities which the portrayal of sacred subjects requires.

A similar moralistic prejudice is discernible in J. A. Crowe and G. B. Cavalcaselle's *New History of Painting in Italy*; they are disinclined to accept Vasari's account of the relationship between Fra Filippo and Lucrezia Buti and regard his art as deriving more directly from Fra Angelico and Masolino than from Masaccio. Nevertheless, Cavalcaselle's chapter on Filippo — carefully documented and not without valuable new ideas, such as the influence of Donatello on the painter — was an important contribution to our knowledge.

Berenson, in 1896, considered Fra Filippo "a high-class illustrator." This judgment is perhaps in part a corollary to the moral prejudice of the period, which paid more attention to the artist's amorous adventures than to his art.

The first monograph on Fra Filippo, by Igino Benvenuto Supino, appeared in 1902. Serious and conscientiously informative, it made some important documentary contributions. On a higher interpretive level was the monograph by Henriette Mendelsohn (1909), notable for the accuracy of its attributions, for its investigation of problems of collaboration (not infrequently present in Fra Filippo's work), and for the consequent revision and augmentation of the catalogue.

Adolfo Venturi's consideration of Fra Filippo in his *Storia dell'arte italiana* is explicitly based on Mendelsohn's book. Venturi, starting with the presupposition of a collaboration between Fra Filippo and Fra Angelico in the Washington *Adoration of the Magi*, postulated a straight-line development for the master, from Gothic to Renaissance, reiterating that concept of stylistic coherence to which so many 19th-century art historians were attached. Especially impressive, for Venturi, were Fra Filippo's inventive freedom and the reconciliation he often accomplished between the aspirations of Fra Angelico and those of Masaccio.

It was Berenson, in 1932, who took the next important step forward in the criticism of Filippo's work. He proposed that the Masaccio phase of the artist's activity was the initial one, not a later episode; that Masaccio's influence, supplemented by other stimuli, continued to be important until about 1442; that just when Fra Filippo was integrating these influences into a coherent personal style, he entered into collaboration with Fra Angelico on the Washington *Adoration of the Magi* and as a consequence took over features from that master's style, not unconsciously and occasionally as he had previously done, but deliberately and systematically; and that after some years in this vein, he returned to his natural style, which culminated between 1452 and 1464 in the frescoes at Prato.

Berenson's thesis, generally accepted, inspired a sudden upsurge in Lippi studies, particularly in 1936, when it was discussed, refined, and made more exact by such scholars as Mario Salmi, Giuseppe Fiocco, Giovanni Poggi, and, most importantly, Georg Pudelko. This view of Fra Filippo's artistic evolution was also fundamental to the monographs of Robert Oertel (1942), André Chastel (1948), and Mary Pittaluga (1949), each of whom added his own deductions, insights, and interpretations.

FILIPPINO. The painter was born at Prato about 1457, the son of Fra Filippo Lippi and Lucrezia Buti, and died in Florence on Apr. 18, 1504. From 1467 through 1469 he was in Spoleto with his father and in 1469, after Filippo's death, received grants in the form of gifts from the Cathedral chapel there. In 1472 he is described in the *Libro Rosso* of the Compagnia di San Luca in Florence as "painter with Sandro Botticelli." In 1482 the Signoria of Florence assigned to him the decoration of a wall in the Palazzo Vecchio, which was never executed, and in 1483 the town of San Gimignano commissioned the *Annunciation* (in two tondos) which, probably finished in the 1490s, is now in the Pinacoteca at San Gimignano. Probably between 1481 and 1483 Filippino worked on the scenes from the life of St. Peter in the Brancacci Chapel of S. Maria del Carmine in Florence, completing the fresco cycle begun by Masolino and Masaccio. The *Madonna Enthroned with SS. John the Baptist, Victor, Bernard, and Zenobius* (PL. 147), painted for the Sala degli Otto di Pratica in the Palazzo Vecchio, dates from 1485. About 1486 Piero di Francesco del Pugliese commissioned Filippino to paint *The Vision of St. Bernard* (PL. 149) for the monastery of the Campora (near Porta Romana, Florence), and in 1487 Filippo Strozzi entrusted him with the fresco decoration of the family chapel in S. Maria Novella, which he completed in 1502. In 1488 he was called to Rome by Cardinal Oliviero Carafa to decorate the Carafa Chapel in S. Maria sopra Minerva; these frescoes were completed, and Filippino returned to Florence between 1489 and 1493. We know also that before September of 1488 Filippino painted two pictures, now lost, for King Matthias Corvinus of Hungary. In 1491 he presented a design in competition for the façade of the Cathedral of Florence. The *Christ Appearing to the Virgin* in the Alte Pinakothek at Munich was finished in 1495. From 1496 until the painter's death in 1504 there is a series of dated pictures comprising *The Adoration of the Magi* for S. Donato a Scopeto (Uffizi, 1496); *The Meeting of Joachim and Anna* (Copenhagen, Statens Museum for Kunst; 1497); the tabernacle containing a *Madonna and Saints* painted for his mother's house on Canto del Mercatale in Prato (Prato, Gall. Comunale; 1498; reconstructed from fragments after World War II); *The Mystic Marriage of St. Catherine* (Bologna, S. Domenico; 1501); the *Madonna with Saints* in the Galleria Comunale of Prato (1503); and the St. Sebastian altarpiece for the Church of S. Teodoro in Genoa (Genoa, Palazzo Bianco; 1503). In 1503 Filippino also began the *Deposition* (Florence, Accademia) for the high altar of SS. Annunziata in Florence, but he died before being able to finish it and it was completed by Perugino.

Filippino Lippi's earliest documented paintings date from 1483. Reconstructions of his prior activity are therefore somewhat conjectural. The Accademia in Florence contains an *Annunciation* generally attributed to the Master of the Castello Nativity, in which Filippino may have had some part about 1475. Attributable to Filippino in the years 1475–80 are most of the paintings given by Berenson in 1899 to an artist he called "Amico di Sandro" and subsequently reattributed to Filippino by Berenson and others. Among these are *Five Female Allegorical Figures* (Florence, Coll. Corsini); *The Madonna and Child with St. Anthony of Padua and a Monk* (Budapest, Mus. of Fine Arts); a *Madonna* (Berlin, Staat. Mus.); *The Virgin and Child with St. John* (London, Nat. Gall.); *The Adoration of the Kings* (London, Nat. Gall.); *Scenes from the Story of Lucretia* (Florence, Pitti; PL. 147); *The Story of Virginia* (Louvre); *The Story of Esther* (divided among Chantilly, Mus. Condé; Paris, Coll. Comtesse de Voguë; Vaduz, Liechtenstein Coll.; and Florence, Fondazione Horne); *The Adoration of the Child* (Uffizi, No. 3249); and *Tobias and the Three Angels* (Turin, Gall. Sabauda).

Such productions must have been well received by the Florentines, since in the early 1480s they entrusted the young painter with the task of completing the fresco cycle of the life of St. Peter in the Brancacci Chapel. In these paintings in the Carmine Filippino's style takes on a breadth quite unknown in the preceding works. The decorative line that associates them with Botticelli and Fra Filippo is here functionally integrated with the representation of mass. An exception is the fresco depicting St. Peter's liberation from prison, clearly Botticellian in character.

The Masaccio phase of Filippino's style is confined exclusively to the Brancacci frescoes. In the contemporaneous *Madonna Enthroned with SS. John the Baptist, Victor, Bernard, and Zenobius* (PL. 147) Filippino took up his accustomed manner with a new security and decisiveness. There are suggestions of Botticelli and even of the young Leonardo in this picture.

For the first time in Filippino's œuvre, Flemish influences — already well assimilated — make their appearance in *The Vision of St. Bernard* (PL. 149), one of the artist's most notable achievements. They are evident particularly in the realm of color. The rather complex composition involves a singular landscape where, in an atmosphere filled with blue-gray-green reflections, one sees an unreal monastic life set amid the rocks that improbably overhang the two principal figures. The saint, of whom there is a drawing in the Uffizi (No. 129E), still recalls Botticelli, but the drapery no longer accompanies the movement of the body as Botticelli's would; rather, it forms a separate decorative entity with linear effects that contrast with the static pose of the figure (M. Fossi).

Whether the connection between Botticelli and Filippino is simply the dependence of Filippino on Botticelli or is that of a parallel evolution arising from their common artistic formation under Fra Filippo and their subsequent association, as Supino suggests, one thing is certain: when Filippino went to Rome to decorate the Carafa Chapel, his development took another direction. The *Annunciation* on the chapel altar is still slightly "Florentine," but the wall frescoes of *The Triumph of St. Thomas Aquinas* (PL. 148) exhibit a striving for novelty and grandeur of style. From a drawing in the British Museum it appears that the scenes must originally have had a greater illusion of depth. The fresco has been cut off at the bottom by an alteration in the chapel structure, so that the buildings towering over the figures now seem less distant. The figures themselves are broadly conceived, with strongly characterized features, and ample, swelling drapery. This striving for monumentality, presaging 16th-century aspirations, appears also in *The Assumption* (PL. 148, 150) and *The Crucified Christ Approving St. Thomas's Work*. The frescoes of the Carafa Chapel, so markedly different in style from other Florentine painting of the time, seem to embody the effect on the painter of "the grandeur that was Rome," perhaps reinforced by influences from such sculptors as Antonio Rossellino, Antonio Pollaiuolo, and, especially, Andrea del Verrocchio. Certainly Filippino made extensive use in his Roman works of ornamental motifs from antique monuments — flowers, candelabra, bucrania — which accorded with his decorative sense.

The paintings Filippino executed after his return to Florence continue to bear the stamp of his Roman sojourn. Important among them are *Christ Appearing to the Virgin* (Munich, Alte Pin.), the *Crucifixion* in Berlin (Staat. Mus.) — which must, according to Scharf, have been flanked by the *St. Mary Magdalene* and *St. John* in the Accademia in Florence — *The Adoration of the Magi* in the Uffizi, and *The Meeting of Joachim and Anna* in Copenhagen (Statens Mus. for Kunst). In painting the Uffizi *Adoration of the Magi* (1496; X, PL. 491), Filippino was clearly aware of Leonardo's treatment of the same subject, but this situation (not unusual for Filippino) did not inhibit his creative spontaneity. It seems rather to have opened to him new fields of interest; his composition appears wrapped in a shadowy penumbra that veils the colors and imparts to the figures an evanescent life. The same stylistic character is shared by the altarpiece (*The Virgin and Child with SS. Jerome and Dominic*) of the National Gallery in London. The *Madonna and Saints* from the tabernacle on Canto del Mercatale, Prato, is set apart from these by its return to the slender and fragile forms of Filippino's youth.

The frescoes, *Scenes from the Lives of SS. Philip and John*, in the Strozzi Chapel of S. Maria Novella in Florence constitute the most complex and significant document of Filippino Lippi's latest style. The four patriarchs in the vault appear enlarged, wrapped as they are in voluminous and convoluted drapery, while the scenes of martyrdom and miracle working on the walls below set an uncontrolled abandon in gesture and movement against architecture strangely inspired by the classical world. Striking examples are the disconcerting *Miracle of St. Philip* and the *Resurrection of Drusiana*, in which the figures are as if caught up in a wind that transforms their garments into whirlpools. (There exists a drawing for the latter composition — Uffizi, No. 186E — light and airy, with reminiscences of Leonardo pleasingly reworked.) These late frescoes, in their irregular and restless compositions, their rotary play of lines and planes, their anxious and intense sentiment, embody Filippino's unmistakable personality, which tried without success to escape the limits of his time. The same sense of uncontrolled bizarreness is present in the coeval *Allegory of Music* (Berlin, Staat. Mus.), a work which must have interested Piero di Cosimo.

Other late paintings, aside from the dated works previously mentioned, include *St. Jerome* (Uffizi), *Christ and the Samaritan Woman* and *Noli me tangere* (both Venice, Seminario Patriarcale), and the *Deposition* (Florence, Accademia) finished by Perugino.

Educated as he was in the circle of Fra Filippo Lippi and Botticelli, Filippino naturally relied on line as his primary expressive means. From the first he used it to quite personal ornamental effect, as can be seen with particular clarity in his drawings (PL. 257; IV, PL. 270). When he came into contact with the Roman world, however, the stylistic environment in which he had grown up must have seemed to him inadequate and old-fashioned (as may be noted in the innovations in his Carafa frescoes). Returning to Florence, he looked searchingly at Leonardo and with new eyes at Botticelli, Ghirlandajo, Signorelli, Perugino, at the sculptors, and at the northern painters, such as Hugo van der Goes, whose Gothic intensity of emotion struck a responsive note in his own anxious spirit.

Filippino Lippi's historical position is important in that he was among the first to feel the conflict between the art of his past and the artistic exigencies of his present, even if he never developed means completely adequate to a new expression. It is precisely this precocious sensibility, never completely resolved in art, that gives his painting its particular fascination.

Filippino's reputation through the centuries has been rather modest. The earliest sources are scanty even of factual data: Albertini in his *Memoriale* ... (1510) cites a few paintings without comment, while a more extensive list occurs in the *Libro* of Antonio Billi. Vasari is the first to show a real interest in Filippino: he calls him "a most excellent talent [that produced] very attractive inventions" and praises him for being the first to paint "grotesques that resemble the antique," for the "strange caprices of his invention," and for the recollections in his work of "the ancient things of Rome." Luigi Lanzi, 250 years later, speaks of him without sympathy, and denies that he was the first to depict "grotesques, trophies, weapons taken from the antique." One must go on to Jakob Burckhardt to find a critical, if succinct evaluation: he declares that Filippino excels Botticelli "in imagination, spirituality, and esthetic sense." Cavalcaselle emphasizes the artistic affinity between Botticelli and Filippino and establishes a solid scholarly foundation for our knowledge of the master's activity.

In 1899 Berenson, as mentioned above, isolated a group of paintings attributed by Cavalcaselle and others to the young Filippino and ascribed them to a hypothetical painter whom he named "Amico di Sandro." In 1932, however, he renounced his earlier creation and reattributed most of these paintings to Filippino, thus amplifying and clarifying the artist's œuvre. Most important was Berenson's systematic investigation — the first to be undertaken — of Filippino's drawings (in *The Drawings of the Florentine Painters*). His view of Filippino's artistic personality is, by contrast, very limited; he characterizes the artist as a "popularizer" of Botticelli.

The first monographic study of Filippino Lippi was that of Supino (1904), who stressed Filippino's originality by casting doubt on Botticelli's influence and by discounting Leonardo's influence in *The Adoration of the Magi*. In 1911 appeared Adolfo Venturi's chapter on Filippino in the *Storia dell'arte italiana*. Firmly documented and rich in critical perceptions, it points out the artist's salient stylistic characteristics. The monograph of Urbain Mengin (1932) is in the scholarly-descriptive tradition of Supino.

In 1935 appeared Alfred Scharf's fundamental monograph, combining the most rigorous and extensive documentary investigation with an attentive study of the artist's personality. Scharf sees summarized in Filippino's painting all the aspirations of the Florentine Quattrocento: the feeling for nature, the interest in spatial perspective, the delight in effects of line and color, the striving for characterization of figures, and the cult of the antique (as seen through 15th-century eyes). He also underlines Filippino's importance as a precursor whose innovations interested even Raphael and Michelangelo, and he sees a significant affinity between Filippino's historical position and that of Piero di Cosimo — an affinity apparent also in the drawings, to which Scharf allots a separate chapter. In 1950 Scharf published a second and briefer monograph, incorporating critical contributions (his own among them) of the intervening years. Important among these is the monograph by Katharine Neilson (1938), well informed and containing some notable ideas.

In 1957 Luciano Berti and Umberto Baldini published a monograph on Filippino Lippi that for the first time gave full value to the final phase of the painter's activity (the Strozzi Chapel frescoes), treating it with originality and critical rigor. The same year also produced intelligent essays on the artist by Cesare Brandi, Roberto Salvini, Valerio Mariani, and Giuseppe Fiocco.

SOURCES. a. *Filippo*: C. Landino, Commento a Dante, Florence, 1481; A. Manetti (?), Vite di XIV uomini singhulari in Firenze dal 1400 innanzi (ca. 1472), in G. Milanesi, Operette istoriche di A. Manetti, Florence, 1887; K. Frey, ed., Il libro di Antonio Billi (1481-1530), Berlin, 1892; F. Albertini, Memoriale di molte statue e pitture della città di Florentia, Florence, 1510; M. A. Michiel, Notizia d'opere di disegno (1521-43), 1st ed., J. Morelli, Bassano, 1800, 2d ed., G. Frizzoni, Bologna, 1884; K. Frey, ed., Anonimo Gaddiano o Codice Magliabechiano (ca. 1537-42), Berlin, 1892; Vasari, II, p. 611; R. Borghini, Il Riposo, Florence, 1584; b. *Filippino*: K. Frey, ed., Il libro di Antonio Billi (1481-1530), Berlin, 1892; F. Albertini, Memoriale di molte statue e pitture della città di Florentia, Florence, 1510; Vasari, II, p. 461.

BIBLIOG. a. *Filippo*: F. Baldinucci, Notizie de' professori del disegno, 6 vols., Florence, 1681-1728; L. Lanzi, Storia pittorica dell'Italia..., Bassano, 1789; F. Baldanza, Le pitture di Fra Filippo nel coro della Cattedrale di Prato, Prato, 1835; F. Baldanza, Descrizione della Cattedrale di Prato, Prato, 1846; B. Gonzati, La Basilica di Sant'Antonio in Padova, I, Padua, 1852, pp. xli-xlii; J. Burckhardt, Der Cicerone, Basel, 1855, pp. 800-01; A. F. Rio, De l'art chrétien, 2d ed., I, Paris, 1861, pp. 356-65; J. A. Crowe and G. B. Cavalcaselle, A New History of Painting in Italy, II, London, 1864, pp. 319-52; G. Guasti, I quadri della galleria e altri oggetti del Comune di Prato, Prato, 1888; H. Ulmann, Fra Filippo und Fra Diamante als Lehrer Sandro Botticellis, Breslau, 1890; B. Berenson, The Florentine Painters of the Renaissance, London, New York, 1896, pp. 43-45, 117-18; E. C. Strutt, Fra Filippo Lippi, London, 1901; I. B. Supino, Fra Filippo Lippi, Florence, 1902; H. Mendelsohn, Fra Filippo Lippi, Berlin, 1909; Venturi, VII, 1, 1911, pp 360-82; L. Fausti, Le pitture di fra Filippo Lippi nel Duomo di Spoleto, Arch. per la storia eccl. dell'Umbria, II, 1915, pp. 1-36; P. Toesca, Una tavola di Filippo Lippi, BArte, XI, 1917, pp. 105-10; G. Gronau, ThB, s.v. Fra Filippo Lippi, XXIII, 1929, pp. 271-74; B. Berenson, Fra Angelico, Fra Filippo e la cronologia, BArte, XXVI, 1932-33, pp. 1-22, 49-66; B. Berenson, Italian Pictures of the Renaissance, Oxford, 1932, pp. 287-89; P. Toesca, Una Madonna di Filippo Lippi, L'Arte, N.S., III, 1932, pp. 104-09; G. Fiocco, Filippo Lippi a Padova, RArte, XVIII, 1936, pp. 25-44; G. Poggi, Sulla data dell'affresco di Fra Filippo Lippi, RArte, XVIII, 1936, pp. 95-106; G. Pudelko, The Early Work of Fra Filippo Lippi, AB, XVIII, 1936, pp. 104-12; G. Pudelko, Per la datazione delle opere di Fra Filippo Lippi, RArte, XVIII, 1936, pp. 45-76; M. Salmi, La giovinezza di Fra Filippo Lippi, RArte, XVIII, 1936, pp. 1-24; B. Berenson, The Drawings of the Florentine Painters, 2d ed., Chicago, 1938, I, pp. 80-84, II, pp. 156-57, III, pls. 166-72; P. Bacci, Documenti e commenti per la storia dell'arte, Le Arti, III, 1940-41, pp. 353-70, 418-31; R. Oertel, Fra Filippo Lippi, Vienna, 1942; M. Pittaluga, Filippo Lippi, Florence, 1949 (bibliog.); C. De Tolnay, Autobiographic Aspect of Fra Filippo Lippi's Virgin, GBA, XXXIX, 1952, pp. 253-64, 295; H. Comstock, The Connoisseur in America: Great Florentine Tondo, Connoisseur, CXXXV, 1955, p. 281; M. A. Lavin, Giovannino Battista: A Study in Renaissance Religious Symbolism, AB, XXXVII, 1955, pp. 85-101; C. Shell, The Early Style of Fra Filippo Lippi and the Prato Master, AB, XLIII, 1961, pp. 197-209. b. *Filippino*: L. Lanzi, Storia pittorica dell'Italia..., Bassano, 1789; J. Burckhardt, Der Cicerone, Basel, 1855, pp. 802-03; J. A. Crowe and G. B. Cavalcaselle, A New History of Painting in Italy, II, London, 1864, pp. 431-52; H. Ulmann, Sandro Botticelli, Munich, 1893; B. Berenson, The Florentine Painters of the Renaissance, London, New York, 1896, pp. 116-17; I. B. Supino, Les deux Lippi, Florence, 1904; P. G. Konody, Filippino Lippi, London, New York, 1905; Venturi, VII, 1, 1911, pp. 643-80; P. Halm, Das unvollendete Fresko des Filippino Lippi in Poggio a Caiano, Mitt. des kunsthist. Inst. in Florenz, III, 1919-31, pp. 393-427; O. H. Giglioli, Disegni sconosciuti di Filippino Lippi e del Pontormo, Dedalo, VII, 1926-27, pp. 777-91; W. R. Valentiner, Leonardo as Verrocchio's Coworker, AB, XII, 1930, pp. 43-89; A. Scharf, Filippino and Piero di Cosimo, Art in Am., XIX, 1931, pp. 59-62; A. Scharf, Studien zu einigen Spätwerken des Filippino Lippi, JhbPreussKSamml, LII, 1931, pp. 201-22; B. Berenson, Italian Pictures of the Renaissance, Oxford, 1932, pp. 284-87; C. Gamba, Filippino Lippi e l'Amico di Sandro, Misc. di storia d'arte in onore di J. B. Supino, Florence, 1932, pp. 461-79; U. Mengin, Les deux Lippi, Paris, 1932; L. Venturi, Contributi a Filippino Lippi, L'Arte, N.S., III, 1932, pp. 418-21; C. Brandi, The First Version of Filippino Lippi's Assumption, BM, LXVIII, 1935, pp. 30-35; A. Scharf, Filippino Lippi, Vienna, 1935; B. Berenson, The Drawings of the Florentine Painters, 2d ed., Chicago, 1938, I, pp. 103-07, 335-39, II, pp. 139-54, III, figs. 222-57; K. B. Neilson, Filippino Lippi, Cambridge, Mass., 1938; A. Scharf, Filippino Lippi, Vienna, 1950; A. M. Frankfurter, Renaissance and Renascence, AN, LI, 3, 1952, pp. 16-19, 59; M. L. D'Otrange Mastai, Drawings of the Morgan Collection at the Pierpont Morgan Library, New York, Connoisseur, CXXXV, 1955, pp. 136-42; M. Fossi, Disegni di Filippino Lippi e Piero di Cosimo (exhibition cat.), Florence, 1955; L. Berti and U. Baldini, Filippino Lippi, Florence, 1957; C. Brandi and others, Saggi su Filippino Lippi, Florence, 1957; U. Middeldorf, Korrecturen Filippino Lippis in einem Bild aus der Werkstatt seines Vaters, Festschrift Kurt Bauch, Munich, 1957, pp. 171-76; F. Gamba, Filippino Lippi nella storia della critica, Florence, 1958.

Mary PITTALUGA

Illustrations: PLS. 141-150.

LI SSŬ-HSÜN (651-716) **and LI CHAO-TAO** (active ca. 700-40). These two painters, father and son, are traditionally considered to have founded, or greatly developed, a technique of landscape painting known in China as *ch'ing-lü-pai* (blue, green, and white) or *chin-pi shan-shui* (gold and blue-green landscape), which became the basis of the "palace style" in later centuries. No authentic works by either artist have survived, and estimates of their style — in which the son followed the father — are based partly on literary evidence and partly on later paintings that seem to accord with their manner as it is described in early texts.

Li Ssŭ-hsün (personal name Chien-chien) was of noble birth, the grandson of the nephew of the first T'ang emperor. He received his first appointment to the capital about the year 680. However, he soon became involved in a scandal and was exiled to Yang-chou (Yangchow). During the usurpation by the empress Wu (684-705) he resigned from office in protest against her ruthless liquidation of members of the imperial family. The restoration brought him back into favor, and he was rewarded for his loyalty with a fief and a state pension, and was given the honorary rank of general in a guards regiment drawn from the sons of the aristocracy. His son Chao-tao, about whom even less is known, also had a fairly distinguished official career, rising to the rank of Vice-President of the Right Grand Secretariat of the Crown Prince. Li Ssŭ-hsün became known to history as Big General Li (Ta Li Chiang-chün); his son was known as Little General Li (Hsiao Li Chiang-chün), although so far as is known he never held military rank. Three other members of the family were also noted painters in their day. Nothing is known about their work, though it seems likely that they were influenced by the style of Li Ssŭ-hsün.

Early texts contain several stories about Li Ssŭ-hsün's achievements as a painter, but because the events occurred in the reign of Ming-huang (713-56) and also concern the great figure painter Wu Tao-tzŭ (ca. 700-60; q.v.) they probably refer to Li Chao-tao rather than to his father. One story, preserved in the *T'ang-ch'ao ming-hua lu* (Record of Famous Painters of the T'ang Dynasty) by Chu Ching-hsüan (ca. 840-45), relates how, during the T'ien-pao era (742-55), Ming-huang summoned Li Ssŭ-hsün to paint a wall and some screens for the palace at Ta-t'ung (Tatung). Later the emperor said to him, "From the screens that you painted, sir, I have heard the sound of water coming at night. Yours is a mastery that partakes of the divine, and your landscapes take first place in this dynasty."

Another version of this story, in the biography of Wu Tao-tzŭ in the same work, says that both Li and Wu painted landscapes in a hall at Ta-t'ung, Wu in a day, Li taking several months. "Ming-huang's comment was, 'Li Ssŭ-hsün's achievement of many months and Wu Tao-tzŭ's work of a single day — both are excellent in the extreme.'" This is taken as illustrating the contrast between the meticulous craftsmanship of the former and the inspired spontaneity of the latter. The *T'ang-ch'ao ming-hua lu* places Li Ssŭ-hsün in the bottom grade of the Inspired Class and his son Chao-tao one rank lower, in the top grade of the Excellent Class.

The *Li-tai ming-hua chi* (Record of Famous Painters of Successive Dynasties) by Chang Yen-yüan (preface dated 847), the most important, and generally the most reliable, source for the early history of Chinese painting, states that "the development of landscape painting began with Wu and was perfected by the two Lis." This would of course have been impossible. Wu Tao-tzǔ was about sixteen when Li Ssǔ-hsün died, and Li Chao-tao is more likely to have derived his landscape style from his father than from the great painter of Buddhist and figure subjects. Wu Tao-tzǔ's reputation as a landscape painter rests chiefly upon this one remark by Chang Yen-yüan, who regarded him with much the same unqualified admiration as Vasari regarded Michelangelo.

In the *Li-tai ming-hua chi* the art of Li Ssǔ-hsün is described in flattering, if very general, terms: "In his painting of landscapes or of trees and rocks, his brush style had an intense forcefulness. His rapids seemed really to be running water; his clouds and vapors added a hazy uncertainty. Sometimes when one looks at [his painting on] the theme of Taoist Immortals, [one senses] dimly all the mystery of cliffs and ranges." He is highly praised in the *T'ang-chao ming-hua lu*: "Ssǔ-hsün's style was lofty and original, and his landscapes were supremely excellent. Birds and beasts, or plants and trees, he always characterized perfectly."

Of Li Ssǔ-hsün's son, Chu Ching-hsüan remarks that "Chao-tao did not equal his father in intelligence and strength of brush, though his depictions of landscapes and of birds and beasts were very detailed and clever." Chang Yen-yüan, however, takes a different view of Li Chao-tao: "He changed his father's style... and even surpassed him in excellence," and notes that he was "the first to do really good seascapes." The early Sung art historian Kuo Jo-hsü, in his *T'u-hua chien-wên chih* ("Record of Things Seen and Heard Regarding Painting"; ca. 1075), says that both father and son were excellent painters, though elsewhere in the book he gives the opinion that had they been active in his own time no one would have paid any attention to them — so much had the art of landscape painting advanced since their day.

The first precise indication of Li Ssǔ-hsün's style is given by Kuo Jo-hsü, who, in discussing the 10th-century painter Tung Yüan, says that he "had a colored style like that of Li Ssǔ-Hsün." A similar note is struck by an entry under Ssǔ-hsün's name in the catalogue of the collection of the Sung emperor Hui-tsung (1101–25), *Hsüan-ho hua-p'u*, compiled in 1302 from authentic records of his reign. "People today," it runs, "who paint mountains in the colored style all follow him, but they cannot equal his marvelous achievements." This is amplified by the *T'u-hui pao-chien* (Precious Mirror of Pictures), a collection of biographies of painters with a preface dated 1365: "He used gold and blue-green (*chin-pi*) in brilliant effect to found a 'family method' (*chia-fa*)."

The painting *Gaily Colored Lotuses in the Imperial Garden* (formerly Manchu Household Coll.) was described by the 17th-century connoisseur Wang Chih-teng in words that convey an excellent idea of what late Ming critics considered to be the authentic manner of Li Ssǔ-hsün: "It contains lofty buildings, temples, houses, gate-screens, costumes, and boats with their oars, all painted with the utmost skill and refinement, including every detail down to the smallest grass-blade. The mountains stand clear and luminous in the light of the setting sun; the billowing waters of the lake reach far beyond the limits [of the view]. Red flowers, rushing streams, green trees, soaring clouds and meandering rivers..." (*Wu-chün tan-ch'ing-chin*).

It seems from the passages quoted above that Chinese art historians became increasingly precise about the Li style the further removed they were from him in time, but there seems no reason to doubt the tradition that he painted in a meticulous miniaturist's technique, making full decorative use of strong mineral colors, often aided by gold outlines. It is unlikely that he invented this style; the ancient metaphor for painting — *tan-ch'ing* (reds and blues) — indicates that a richly colored style must have been in existence long before his time, and, indeed, provincial echoes of it are to be found in landscape details of 6th-century wall paintings at Tun-huang (q.v.). But it is probable that Li Ssǔ-hsün — aristocrat, official, and painter of talent — did, in fact, raise this technique to a new level of prestige and magnificence. On the evidence available, it is not possible to assess the relative contributions to this tradition of Li Ssǔ-hsün and his son or to gauge the accuracy of Chang Yen-yüan's remark in the *Li-tai ming-hua chi* that Li Chao-tao "changed his father's style."

Although nothing survives of the work of either Li, the titles of some of their paintings are preserved in early texts. Among the works of Li Ssǔ-hsün in the collection of Hui-tsung listed in the *Hsüan-ho hua-p'u* are two versions of *The Four Graybeards in a Mountain Retreat* (four famous scholars of the Ch'in dynasty who refused to serve Shih Huang-ti and retired to the hills), *Idly Fishing among the Streams*, *A Multitude of Peaks and Dense Forests*, and *Ming-huang's Excursion in the Imperial Park*. Figure subjects in the imperial collection included one Buddhist deity, one Taoist fairy, and a picture of five palace girls. Later texts and catalogues attribute to him a larger number of landscapes and of palaces and pavilions in landscape settings.

Of the paintings associated with the name of Li Ssǔ-hsün and still, or until recently, in existence, none are works of the early T'ang period. One of the most archaic in style is the *Chiu-ch'êng pi-chu t'u* ("Chiu-ch'êng Summer Palace"), a round fan painting on silk (PL. 152). This depicts the Jên-shou-kung, the former Sui imperial palace, after its transformation into the summer residence of T'ai-tsung of the T'ang dynasty. The palace buildings in the foreground nestle against a group of mountains piling up to the left. The dominant colors are blue and green; the pillars and walls are picked out in vermilion, and the hills are outlined in gold. Although this sumptuous little picture may well derive from an early T'ang original by either Li Ssǔ-hsün or Li Chao-tao, the actual execution, notably in the treatment of the distant mountains, suggests a date not earlier than the Ming dynasty.

More paintings are attributed by early sources to Li Chao-tao than to his father. The *Li-tai ming-hua chi* notes that there was a landscape by Li Chao-tao on the wall of the Wan-an temple in Ch'ang-an. Pictures attributed to him in Hui-tsung's collection include two sunsets (*Lo-ch'ao t'u*), a seascape, and a spring landscape. The sunset theme appears only briefly in the history of Chinese painting. It was used at Tun-huang to illustrate the story of Queen Vaidehi, and examples can be found in versions of the Ingkayō scroll and on the plectrum guard of a *p'i-p'a* (guitar) in the Shōsōin in Nara (Japan), but it went out of fashion after the end of the T'ang dynasty. Hui-tsung's collection also contained a picture by Li Chao-tao entitled *Chê-kua'tu* ("Plucking Melons"), a euphemism for the flight of the emperor Ming-huang from the rebel An Lu-shan, who occupied the capital in 756; the picture derives its name from the fact that one version showed a court lady plucking melons, evidently intended to suggest that this was no more than a leisurely excursion. Several early texts also attribute to Li Chao-tao a version of the *Chiu-ch'êng Summer Palace* (PL. 153).

At least five surviving ancient paintings are more or less closely associated with the name of Li Chao-tao. In the National Palace Museum (Taichung, Formosa) is a large hanging scroll depicting the scenery of the Ch'ü River (*Ch'ü-chiang t'u*). It shows an elaborate complex of palace buildings set in a towering landscape of peaks and rivers. The atmosphere is festive, the style archaistic rather than archaic; it might be a product of the Southern Sung Academy. The richly detailed album leaf in the National Palace Museum, the "Loyang Mansion" (*Lo-yang lo t'u*), preserves his subject matter, but the style is also that of the 12th or 13th century. Closer to the style of his period is a long landscape in gold and blue-green (*Chin-pi shan-shui t'u*) in the Sasakawa Collection in Japan. Though weak in execution, this cold, brooding landscape may well derive from one of his paintings.

The National Palace Museum contains a large landscape with towering peaks, "Travelers in the Mountains in Spring" (*Ch'un-shan hsing-yu t'u*), that is traditionally attributed to Li Chao-tao. It depicts a group of elegantly dressed men and women on horseback winding down through a defile into a clearing in the woods at the base of a triple mass of cloud-ringed peaks. The verticals are deliberately exaggerated; the style, particularly in the painting of the rocks, is precise and somewhat mannered — indeed, rather what might be expected of a court painter of the Sung dynasty attempting to imitate the Li style. This picture is closely related to another much smaller and finer version of the same subject in the National Central Museum (Taichung, Formosa) entitled "Ming-huang's Journey to Shu" (*Ming-huang hsing Shu t'u*). Here the composition is spread out laterally instead of being squeezed into a vertical panel; the figures of the emperor and his entourage, horses, trees, and verdure are painted with minute precision, yet in a freely flowing line; the towering and overhanging peaks glow with soft blues and greens against the white clouds. Although certain details of the landscape and the extraordinary freshness of the colors indicate that this is probably a copy of the Sung dynasty at the earliest, this magnificent picture, more than any other surviving early work, seems to preserve the courtly style of the landscape painting of the 8th century, of which Li Chao-tao was the chief exponent. However, although several pictures of this incident are attributed to him in early texts, it is doubtful whether Li Chao-tao himself ever painted this subject. By 756, when the disastrous flight took place, he would have been a very old man, if indeed he was still living, and it seems unlikely that court painters would have been called upon to record it, in so gay and sumptuous a manner, while the memory of it was still fresh. Some authorities even doubt that this picture depicts the emperor's flight at all, and have suggested that it simply celebrates an imperial picnic. But whatever its subject, and whoever its author, this picture is an important document in the evolution of the green-and-blue "palace style" associated with Li Ssŭ-hsün and Li Chao-tao.

Another and more ancient picture that must closely reflect their style is a short hand scroll, "Travelers in Springtime" (*Yu-ch'un t'u*; PL. 155). It bears an inscription by the emperor Hui-tsung attributing it to the Sui court painter Chan Tzŭ-ch'ien. Here an open landscape is depicted, with a broad river stretching back diagonally between simple humped hills, and with a boat, figures, and blossoming trees. The style is archaic, the composition echoing some of the earliest landscape designs at Tun-huang; the careful drawing and the disposition of the trees along the contour lines are characteristic of the *chung-ku* (middle antiquity) style. Certain sophisticated conventions used in drawing foliage, however, suggest that this may be a late T'ang copy. In spite of the august source of the attribution to Chan Tzŭ-ch'ien, this anonymous painting could well have originated in a work by one of the two Lis.

The importance of Li Ssŭ-hsün and Li Chao-tao in the history of Chinese landscape painting is, like that of Wu Tao-tzŭ, not to be measured in terms of surviving paintings. It is even doubtful that a single authentic specimen of their work survived after the end of the Northern Sung period. But from early accounts of their style and from later pictures that are believed to reflect this style, it can be deduced that they perfected the decorative and meticulous realism that became identified with the "palace style" and was later carried on by Chao Po-chü (early 12th cent.) and a host of chiefly anonymous court painters (PL. 151) up to modern times. The Ming critics Mo Shih-lung (active 1560–82) and Tung Ch'i-ch'ang (1555–1636; q.v.) called this tradition the northern school, in contradistinction to the southern school of monochrome landscape painting, which they held had been founded by the 8th-century poet-painter Wang Wei (q.v.). No such distinction is made in the early records, however, and it seems likely that the style of Wang Wei was not as radically different from that of Li Ssŭ-hsün and Li Chao-tao as Chinese critics since the late Ming period have claimed.

Sources. Chu Ching-hsüan, T'ang-ch'ao ming-hua lu (Record of Famous Painters of the T'ang Dynasty), ca. 840–45 (see BIBLIOG., A. C. Soper, 1958); Chang Yen-yüan, Li-tai ming-hua chi (Record of Famous Painters of Successive Dynasties), preface dated 847 (see BIBLIOG., W. B. R. Acker, 1954 (Eng. trans. of first 4 chapters); Kuo Jo-hsü, T'u-hua chien-wên chih (Record of Things Seen and Heard Regarding Painting), ca. 1075 (see BIBLIOG., A. C. Soper, 1951); Hsüan-ho hua-p'u (Catalogue of Paintings in the Hsüan-ho [Palace]), believed to have been compiled from authentic 12th-cent. records by Wu Wên-kuei in 1302; Hsia Wên-yen, T'u-hui pao-chien (Precious Mirror of Pictures), preface dated 1365; Wang Chih-teng, Wu-chin tan-ch'ing-chin, 1563.

BIBLIOG. A. Waley, Introduction to the Study of Chinese Painting, London, 1923; J. C. Ferguson, Chinese Painting, Chicago, 1927; S. Ise, Kogaishi yori Kei Kō niitaru Shina sansui-ga shi (History of Chinese Landscape Painting from Ku K'ai-chih to Ching Hao), 2 vols., Kyoto, 1934; A. C. Soper, Early Chinese Landscape Painting, AB, XXIII, 1947, pp. 141–64; A. C. Soper, Kuo Jo-hsü's Experiences in Painting (T'u-hua chien-wên chih), Washington, D.C., 1951; W. B. R. Acker, Some T'ang and Pre-T'ang Texts on Chinese Painting, Leiden, 1954; L. Sickman and A. C. Soper, The Art and Architecture of China, Harmondsworth, 1956; O. Sirén, Chinese Painting: Leading Masters and Principles, I: The First Millennium, I–III, London, New York, 1956; Fu Pao-shih, Chung-kuo ku-tai shan-shui-hua shih ti yen-chiu (Researches into the History of Ancient Chinese Landscape Painting), Shanghai, 1958; A. C. Soper, T'ang Ch'ao Ming Hua Lu (rev. trans.), AAs, XXI, 1958, pp. 204–30; T'eng Ku, T'ang Sung hui-hua shih (History of T'ang and Sung Painting), Peking, 1958; T'ung Shu-yeh, T'ang Sung hui-hua t'an-ts'ung (Collected Writings on T'ang and Sung Painting), Peking, 1958 (previously pub. in 1937 as Chung-ku hui-hua shih [History of Painting in Middle Antiquity]); National Palace Museum and National Central Museum of Taiwan, 300 Masterpieces of Chinese Painting in the Palace Museum, 6 vols., Taichung, 1959; J. Cahill, Chinese Painting, Lausanne, 1960; M. Sullivan, The Birth of Landscape Painting in China, Berkeley, Los Angeles, 1962.

Michael SULLIVAN

Illustrations: PLS. 151–155.

LITHOGRAPHY. See ENGRAVINGS AND OTHER PRINT MEDIA.

LITURGICAL AND RITUAL OBJECTS. The types of objects used in religious ceremonies and magico-religious rites are frequently equivalent to those in secular use (see ARMS AND ARMOR; COSTUME; EMBLEMS AND INSIGNIA; FURNITURE; HOUSEHOLD OBJECTS; MASKS; MUSICAL INSTRUMENTS; UTENSILS AND TOOLS; VEHICLES). However, liturgical and ritual objects may be given distinctive form or decoration suitable to their specialized functions (cf. DEVOTIONAL OBJECTS AND IMAGES; ESCHATOLOGY) and reflecting the art traditions inspired by specific religious beliefs (see BUDDHISM; CHRISTIANITY; CONFUCIANISM; HINDUISM; ISLAM; JAINISM; JEWISH ART; MAGIC; SHAMANISM; SHINTOISM; TAOISM; TOTEMISM; ZOROASTRIANISM). While the variety of such objects is enormous, they may logically be grouped into a single broad category because of the many cross-cultural similarities of type and use.

SUMMARY. *Primitive ritual objects* (col. 270): *Function; Form; Production and procedures. Antiquity and Asia* (col. 276): *General observations; The ancient Near East; The classic world; The Iranian world; India, southeast Asia, Nepal, and Tibet; China; Japan. Christian liturgical objects* (col. 289): *The altar and its furnishings: a. Altar; b. Altar frontal (or antependium); c. Altarpiece; d. Candlesticks; e. Cross; f. Altar cards; Other church furnishings. Ritual objects: a. Chalice; b. Paten; c. Pyx; d. Monstrance (ostensorium); e. Ampulla; f. Aquamanile and basin; g. Liturgical spoon; h. Offering basin; i. Reliquary; j. Bell; k. Censer (thurible); l. Incense boat; m. Aspergillum and aspersorium; n. Oil lamp and spirit lamp; o. Flabellum; p. Lectern; q. Faldistory. Vestments and sacerdotal insignia: a. Alb; b. Surplice; c. Rochet; d. Dalmatic; e. Tunicle; f. Girdle; g. Amice; h. Chasuble; i. Cope; j. Maniple; k. Stole; l. Pallium; m. Succinctorium; n. Fanon; o. Rational; p. Miter; q. Tiara; r. Crozier. Jewish ceremonial art* (col. 309): *The Torah scroll and its appurtenances; Lamps; Other Sabbath and festival ritual objects.*

PRIMITIVE RITUAL OBJECTS. The controversial term "primitive" is applied here to the cultures that (unlike literate and more advanced societies) are chiefly dependent on nature — the hunting and gathering peoples, fishermen, and agricultural and pastoral tribes. This discussion of their ritual and sacred objects will exclude the fixed appurtenances and decorative elements of the sacred or cultural premises and treat only those objects utilized during religious ceremonies. These ceremonies assume a variety of forms, including sacrifice and prayer, ritual dances, and processions, as well as numerous observances which, though preponderantly social in character, follow inherently ritual forms and are at times related to the cult of a supreme being — for example, many marriage and funerary rites, initiation rites, and shamanistic practices.

Cult ceremonies consist of various organically related rites that succeed one another in a given order: preliminary and immediate preparations, the central ceremonial action, the participation of the people, and the conclusion. In this procedure there are introduced accessories and equipment which, though they may be ordinary in themselves, take on the sacred character of the ritual. For example, a priest who purifies himself before offering the sacrifice requires a ewer and basin for water, and these objects become ritual equipment because of their association with the sacrifice. In the same way almost any object may become associated with ritual — from an undressed stone to a sculptured figure, from a rattan cord to a woven ceremonial robe, from a simple noisemaker to a stringed instrument, from a feather in the hair to an elaborate mask costume. The distinguishing factor is that objects are classified as ritual only when they are intrinsic and not merely incidental to ritual use.

The place of ritual objects in primitive art as a whole may be arrived at as follows: Within the broad division of sacred (as distinguished from secular) art, the products are either magic or religious. The former are discussed elsewhere (see MAGIC), though it may be pointed out that magic objects on occasion assume the function of cult objects; for example, the sword with which a medicine man vanquishes a disease demon to heal his patient may also be used as a ritual weapon in a ceremony to ward off malign spirits. Religious art, which is the dominating element in primitive art, may take a variety of forms, even occurring as a survival in secular art. Within this field, ritual objects, which are under discussion here, may be classified as "utilitarian," in that they serve specific functions during the cult ritual. The more stationary religious art forms and appurtenances do not fall into the same category, even when they are at hand during the celebration of the rites.

From the definition of ritual objects and equipment as religious utilitarian art two observations follow: First, with their obviously functional nature and religious purpose, these objects constitute the core of primitive art; they are therefore highly indicative of the character peculiar to the art as a whole, for the manifestation of religious art is most intense in the service of the ritual. Second, the interpretation of this ritual art must begin with its function, since the aim of primitive artists is not artistic beauty but suitability to the purpose. This approach is essential to conceptual interpretation, and it applies also to form and design, though the latter may be affected by factors unrelated to function.

Neither in ethnology nor in art history, fields that intersect in the study of primitive art, has there been undertaken a thorough thematic research on sacred objects and cult equipment; such a survey would provide the best means for distinguishing the religious and secular significance of these works of art. There are, of course, a number of studies of individual objects, including the sacred, but with few exceptions they deal primarily with technique or with the form and esthetic aspects of the objects.

Function. Every communal ritual has a twofold aspect: First it is an emotional expression of the community, involving an act of worship of the transcendental powers. Second, it brings the transcendental into the human world of the senses. The ritual centers around the act of worship and the scene of revelation, and is at once a serious act and a sacred game. It may cover the entire gamut of psychic, social, religious, and magical life, embracing mythology and cosmic imagery, but not necessarily in all forms of worship. For example, in ritual drama or dance a representational character predominates, whereas in sacrifice or prayer the cult action itself predominates. The twofold aspect of the common ritual, with the related cult practices, is reflected in the cult objects and furnishings, which may be classified in terms of the functions they serve.

The objects required to fulfill a physical action serve an *instrumental* function; the form they take depends on the immediate purpose. For example, the knife (PL. 157) is used to kill the sacrificial victim, the basin to wash the hands, the sacrificial cup to contain the substance intended for libation.

A *psychological* function is served by objects that arouse an emotional response. The drum may be used to heighten receptiveness to a state of ecstasy; incense predisposes toward trance; music creates an atmosphere of solemnity; monstrous masks inspire fear and hatred of the demons (PLS. 354–359).

The function of cult objects having emblematic significance may be viewed as essentially *social*. The ceremonial costume of the priest sets him apart as the representative of the people; emblems and standards are associated with specific groups or clans; the cult ancestor image intensifies the sense of collectivity; masks disguise the secret cult societies.

When a *magic* function appears within the ritual, implements are used to produce specific effects: sacral weapons banish demons; vessels dispense fecundity; amulets heal the sick who touch them. The magic power may be inherent in the object itself, or it may derive from a particular magic practice employed; in some cases the painted decoration, the form or material of the object, or the blood with which it is sprinkled constitutes the magic element.

The *animistic* function of certain cult objects and accessories is to provide the abode of ghosts or ancestor spirits, who may be consulted for advice, as oracles, judge the acceptability of the sacrifice, or otherwise participate in the rites. Sometimes the spirits manifest themselves by vibrating, making noises, pounding, or the like.

Cult objects also have a *representational* function, which involves both the subject and the manner in which it is realized. Whether artistically fashioned or not, these objects may represent a great variety of things: deities, spirits, demons, ancestors, myths, rites, acts of worship, magical spells, the great beyond, the upper or the lower world, the earth, the men wandering in the beyond. The manner of representation may be purely and intentionally symbolic. For example, a crude post or a magic wand may be identified with the phallus, or a stool with a tiger spirit; or the symbolism may be expressed in motifs such as a zigzag line for thunder, a wavy line for water, an eye for the all-seeing ancestors, a knob for a skull. On the other hand, the subject of the representation may be treated realistically: the serpent of the underworld may be carved on the backrest of a chair, the totemic animal painted on a drum, mythological scenes depicted on ceremonial vestments, or the tree of life represented on ritual fabrics.

The reference to reality is particularly important, because in the primitive concept the beings to whom ritual acts are addressed are not imaginary. This reference may be made in three ways: First, a meaning or fact may simply be conveyed. For example, the design on a shaman's drum may indicate that the shaman, during the trance, ascends to the heavens, without any implication that heaven is immanent in the drum. Second, the "presence" may be made actual in the object or may be represented: the head of a spirit carved on an object attests the spirit's presence therein; the animal painted on a ceremonial staff indicates that the club possesses the animal's strength. The spirit to whom a sacrifice is offered is regarded as being present. Third, according to the primitive concept that things can render actual what they represent, certain objects, usually connected with specific rites, may materialize supernatural beings and events. The shaman's costume (XIII, PLS. 1–3) not only has the effect of rendering him similar to the guardian spirit, but also, by virtue of initiation, can materialize the presence of the spirit and transform the shaman into it. Among the Australians of Arnhemland an entire mythical event is made real by the beating of a drum in which a snake is enclosed. Drum and serpent represent the primordial pair of ancestors, and the beating represents their sexual union. Either the form of objects or their ornamentation can activate the magic force of the things represented. As the bearers or representatives of transcendental powers or beings, cult objects and sacred furnishings often come to be worshiped. The ritual staff, in which a divinity is actually present, transcends itself, becomes identified with the divinity, and is worshiped as such. In some cases, therefore, the cult objects may be considered rudimentary forms of figural "idols," lacking only the development of form.

Frequently objects perform more than one function in a rite, one of which is the principal function, the others being secondary. The primary function may vary according to whether the object is used in a dance, in a procession, for sacrifice, or in some other connection. Objects such as axes or spears sometimes lose their functional nature and become decorative axes or display spears, unsuited by their dimensions or decoration for practical use. The multiple functionality of the objects is a reflection of the beliefs of primitive people, who, in their religion make no rational differentiations but express the whole being of man and his world.

Musical instruments (X, PLS. 224, 225) are as ancient as worship and are rarely absent from it. They serve to mark the rhythm, create moods or excitement, express the feelings of the participants in the rites. Through sound, moreover, they effect contact with the other world. They may have cosmic significance (for example, a gong filled with rice represents the cosmic mountain) or they may symbolize spirits. The harp of the Bambara, with its square shape, symbolizes the mask of Kumabana: the two lateral pieces represent the eyes; the sounding box, the nose; the terminal portion, the mouth and teeth; the eight strings, the words. The high notes symbolize heaven; the low ones, the earth. Particularly rich in significance is the sacred drum. Among the Lovedu (Transvaal) the drum cult is one of the means of controlling nature for beneficent ends; the drum is in mystic relationship with the life of the queen and the people. Among the Woodlands Indians of the United States, the drum of the dream dance represents the Great Spirit. Among the Australians of Arnhemland the drum represents the uterus of the progenitress; in Africa, the mouth of man which opens and sings; among the shamans of Siberia, the world tree (birch) from which it is made. The drum summons or dispels spirits; it is the vehicle by which the shaman flies in the sky. Among the musical instruments, a distinction must be made for the so-called "voice masks" (PL. 156), which perform acoustically the same functions as the facial masks: they disguise the voices of the cult members, representing the utterance of transcendental beings. The bull-roarer (PL. 156) represents the supreme being's voice, but it is also used to ensure fertility, to protect, and to invoke misfortune.

Weapons, basically intended for defense, attack, and killing, are also introduced into ritual. The spear is used to transfix the sacrificial victim, and thus the weapon partakes of the blood's magic. A spear may also symbolize the cosmic tree; it may represent a phallus, or virile strength, or the might of the ruler or god; it may be the emblem of a deity, the abiding place of spirits, or the ancestral spear of the tribe.

The ritual ax in Africa illustrates the variety of functions an object may serve: Of divine origin (fallen from the sky), it is the insignia of the tutelary divinities of the ancestor; as the symbol of lightning, it heals the sick, promotes fertility, punishes injustice; as symbol of the thunder-god, brought to earth by the rainbow serpent, it is itself a thunderbolt; it is the instrument of the peace ceremonies, for it can overcome the strongest resistance; when represented on medicines (curing objects), it effects healing; it serves to sever the umbilical cord; it indicates a state of possession in dancers; and it is a symbol of virile force, the insignia of royal dignity, the accessory of messengers, an attribute of the priest, and so forth. Similarly rich in significance are the bow and arrow used in a ritual athletic contest in Tahiti.

Ceremonial costume serves as the adornment and insignia of rank; often prescribed by the gods and derived from the garb of divinities, it identifies man with god. Even sacrificial animals may be clothed, and costume itself may be a sacrificial offering. Often the costume is nothing more than a symbolic item such as a belt, which embodies the symbolism of binding and loosening, or a woolen cord representing the original woolen garment or the sacrificial animal. The costume of the shamans is a cosmic symbol, a microcosm, or a means of identification with the tutelary spirit, such as a skeleton or an animal.

Banners may represent tribes or serve as emblems of divinity or as the divinity itself. Together with its staff a banner may represent (as among the Dyak) the entire cosmos, since the staff is the tree of life. Banners and various items of apparel or cloth possess magic power, heal the sick, and dispel demons.

Vessels serve primarily to contain lustral water, sacrificial blood, or liquids for libation. Being of earth, however, they also represent the earth and are connected with the fertility complex; they may be symbols of the underworld, of the primordial waters, the water of life (Dyak); filled with rice, they represent the cosmic mountain of precious stone and are the home of spirits. Pottery vessels as soul dwellings are documented in Africa. Pots are also linked to the skull cult, in which head, vessel, and coconut shell are interchangeable elements.

Masks (q.v.) have an extremely important function, and not only as a primary part of the costume; in addition they invoke the presence of transcendental beings, are symbols of divinity, and have magical efficacy in warding off demons, in the prevention and cure of diseases, and so on.

These few examples indicate that an analysis of cult objects is necessarily concerned with their functions, which in practice are continually repeated.

Form. Restrictive factors over which the individual artist has no control are stronger in the ritual art of the primitives than in that of more advanced civilizations. Apart from the criterion of practical usefulness, effective factors are the magico-religious functions and their involvement with tradition, society, and the economy. These operate to determine the style, which accordingly varies from realism to abstraction. Four variations of form may be distinguished: (1) unworked objects left in their natural state, in which the original form is particularly significant (e.g., bones, roots, and stones); (2) objects fashioned in a purely instrumental form, with or without artistic effect, including those examples which have added decoration or organic modeling (e.g., unadorned sacrificial knives as well as painted drums, decorated fabrics, knife handles in the form of lizards, serpent-shaped ceremonial chairs); (3) artistically evolved objects (masks, ceremonial staves, banners); (4) objects combining evolved elements with parts retained in their natural state (e.g., a mask with human hair, a pole terminating in a skull).

The material frequently dominates the form because of its magic power (portions of the human or animal body, bones, skin, and hair have particular efficacy); because of its symbolism (e.g., the hardness of stone); because of its mythical requirements (for instance, the shamanistic drum in Siberia must be of birch, since this tree represents the world tree, and the drumhead must be of deerskin); or because in a given myth the archetype of the object is carved from a specific material, and the tradition cannot be disregarded. Particular apotropaic power is attributed to metals.

The art-critical claims as to the unity and purity of materials in primitive ritual objects are illusory. The materials cannot be tampered with because the determining factor in the art is not esthetic form but rather the practical, magical, and religious purpose. For example, shells set into carved eyes have a definite significance. From the link of purpose and material there also follows automatically a fixed stylistic tradition for particular objects; variations that might result from the use of new materials do not occur.

The technique of shaping varies with the individual arts: woodworking, sculpture in stone, metalworking, weaving, basketry, painting. Evidences of inadequacy in mastery of the technique may be due partly to the primitive nature of the artisan's tools and partly to religious traditionalism, in that ancient techniques continue to be respected even after new methods have come into use in the secular field.

It would be idle to expect a broad repertory of expressive forms such as are found among more technically advanced peoples. The primitive artist adheres more closely to the natural form and surface quality of his material. Thus he limits himself to fundamentals and tends toward abstraction.

The economy naturally influences the selection of materials (e.g., the preference shown for bone and hide among hunting or pastoral peoples), and it may also exert a direct influence on style. The hunters, continually dependent on a close observation of nature, are more inclined toward realistic representation. The sedentary cultivators find inspiration more in ideas and the imagination; their art tends to be ideological and inclined toward abstract forms. In these cultures the function of ritual objects is emphasized by the prominence given to certain parts of the body, for instance, a hand placed on a drum.

The instrumental function gives the object its fundamental form, to which all subsequent elaboration is linked. Dependent on this function are many stylistic peculiarities such as deformation, shortening, adjustment of lines, which adapt the various figures to the form of the object. The primitive artist, who has little or no mastery of the techniques of gluing and fastening, is likely to follow natural forms, as for example, in carving a stool in the natural shape of a branch. Two-dimensional decorations are more easily adapted to the functional shape of the object, but even here a special color symbolism may interfere with purely esthetic composition.

The other functions, especially representation, allow greater freedom, and the cult form may become elaborated. A mask that is used in an initiation will have different features from those on one representing a disease demon. An ancestor figure used in ancestor worship requires a careful and detailed human likeness, whereas a more summary execution and an emphasis on certain features would suffice for its magical function.

In all the aspects of form mentioned the influence of tradition is constantly present. There is also a direct traditional influence on creation, restricting the art product to the ideas of form that prevail in the community. An arbitrary deviation from such ideas is virtually unthinkable; such a rupture with tradition would be considered a profanation, since the forms linked to the cult partake of the absolute nature of the religion. Ritual objects are also intended, from the psychological viewpoint, to produce a specific effect on the spectators; this is achieved only if these objects conform to the generally accepted forms and ideas capable of producing such an effect. Accordingly, a mask should not be altered, since it would otherwise no longer be accepted as genuine. Thus a definite conservatism is evident in religious art objects. Even when modern implements have long been used in secular life, circumcision must be performed with the primordial stone knife, and the sacred fire kindled by striking flints or rubbing pieces of wood together; in the same way, the forms of ritual objects remain unchanged. The study of ritual objects may therefore be of great value in seeking the earliest forms of religion and art.

While ethnological studies have modified several nonhistorical theories on primitive art and have revealed a number of outside influences (such as those originating in the more advanced civilizations in Africa), these migratory influences are felt most strongly where art has lost its religious character. Stylistic changes in the ritual art of primitive peoples do not come from outside; on the contrary, religious art determines the other spheres of art. A change in style occurs usually through the transmission of a living concept, with the development of new forms of religion, whether indigenous or foreign. This distinction is to be observed also in the delimitation of styles and style regions. Ritual art does not readily become a part of a secular stylistic category, although the degree of secularization must be taken into account. Frequently two different styles can be distinguished in the same type of object: one secular and more advanced, the other sacred and conservative. The repertory of forms drawn from the religious background of a people readily leads to fixed types, standardization, and a formal impoverishment in their ritual art, so that the full potential of artistic development cannot be realized.

Production and procedures. Ritual objects are characteristically the work of trained men. Among most peoples women are barred from the production of ritual objects, except for pottery. Only rarely do the artisans work as independent individuals. For the most part, they belong to a group or are priests, magicians, or medicine men. In many places the cult officiant, the shaman for example, must himself make his instruments, his drum, and his iron insignia; in other words, he must know the trade of a blacksmith. The smith holds a special position in the creation of ritual objects. The artists are sometimes of aristocratic origin or have special ties with the chief's family (Congo, Polynesia). The ritual objects are not always produced in the place where they are to be used; certain pastoral groups in East Africa and the Todas of India do not make weapons, even though weapons are employed in their rites.

Since the artist has little freedom of creation and must heed tradition, the son or pupil learns from his father or teacher not only the technique but also the form; this, and not reality, is his model and will remain fixed in his memory. Thus there are established certain family or group schools, in which there is usually no division of labor. A single individual chooses and prepares the material and works on the object through the final stages.

The work is usually in itself an act of devotion. The artist must respect prescribed tenets, sacrifice, pray, purify himself, abstain from certain things, to ensure that the result will be successful. Usually he must even choose a propitious time: for instance, the heads intended for the skull cult must be boiled down and placed inside the sacred containers only during certain phases of the moon. The artist must purify his tools (possibly by fumigation) in accordance with all the magic relating to implements. During the work he often withdraws into a secluded place that is taboo to lay persons; the craftsman himself may likewise be taboo during that period, and it may be dangerous to touch his hands, because they are animated by divine force. At times, after his work, the artist is considered a sort of priest.

Also closely associated with the sacredness of the fabrication is secrecy. Among primitive peoples, the group of craftsmen often has almost the character of a secret society, with its own education, training, and initiation; and this is particularly true of ritual craftsmen. Often the instruction regarding the nature, manufacture, and use of the sacred objects constitutes one of the chief tasks in the secret initiation of the boys. The manufacture may also be linked to the secret traditions of certain tribes or families; in Togoland, for instance, the casting of bronze was usually secret and practiced by members of the Amonikoyi family, natives of Ilorin.

The sacred nature of the objects requires their separation from the secular world by means of a consecration, usually in connection with a sacrifice. The objects are given a ritual bath or are fumigated, smeared with blood or anointed, decked with symbolic ribbons, painted, or decorated with magic appendages. When the object is to have an animistic function, it is animated or opened up to the spirits or ancestral ghosts by being colored red or painted with an eye motif, a circle, or other symbol.

Ritual objects are taboo and therefore are kept in special places, in temples, spirit houses, or priests' homes. They are often forbidden to the sight of women and may not be touched by laymen; frequently they are kept secret and hidden.

Because of their sacredness, their magic power, or their function as the abode of spirits, ritual objects, even when not in cult use, can be worshiped individually, as independent "idols." For example, a priestly garment, a banner, or a ceremonial spear may become the center of a secondary cult, with religious rites or magic powers in divination, evocation of spirits, curing, and so forth. After their consecration ritual objects must be cared for, strengthened, nourished with sacrifices, and reanointed, so that their power does not weaken. Unusable objects that have lost their efficacy or strength usually cannot be converted to secular purposes; they are abandoned to slow decay, taken to some secret place, burned, or buried out of respect for their sanctity.

Dominik Schröder

Antiquity and Asia. *General observations.* The statements in the preceding section basically apply also to ritual objects of the ancient world. Certain fundamental attitudes in religious beliefs and worship, and all the practical consequences of these attitudes, remain unchanged throughout the ages regardless of differences in locale and the evolution of cultures. It may be objected that the combined evidence of primitive cultures and of the oldest historical documents is insufficient to shed light on the genuinely initial phases of religious activity and especially to explain the evolution from these phases to the forms in use among advanced civilizations (a problem that constantly recurs in any study of the genesis of particular aspects of culture and art). From the mute, extremely fragmentary archaeological documentation it seems virtually impossible to determine the facts about prehistoric cults and about the meaning of objects pertaining to them.

Richly decorated *bâtons de commandement*, so-called, from the Magdalenian period (XI, PL. 247), pebbles painted with geometric patterns dating from the Mesolithic era (from Le Mas d'Azil, in France), and many other artifacts of uncertain purpose may be attributed in theory to some unknown ritual requirement, and any attempt at figural representation among prehistoric peoples may fall within the province of religion or magic (see PREHISTORY). Nevertheless, such products cannot be designated, even tentatively, as ritual objects in the sense applicable to certain classes of products from the great religions of antiquity.

The essential factor in the artistic development of any group of sacred objects from the more advanced civilizations is the degree or manner of differentiation in appearance from the objects or furnishings in everyday use, such as containers, knives, tables, and articles of clothing or personal adornment. The distinction may exist in the richness of the material, in the shape of the object or its embellishments, or in the addition of allusive or symbolic details suited to some specialized use; conversely, it may be manifested in the ritual preservation of primitive forms at variance with the material progress of the culture. For example, the stone sacrificial knife was retained in certain sacrificial rites in the classic world, and the form of the tabernacle on the Christian altar perpetuates that of the nomadic tent. There are also, occasionally, completely new types and forms relating to particular ritual requirements.

These processes are obviously directed toward meeting the fundamental requisites of the cult in various forms of religious activity. For sacrificial and purificatory rites there were developed special tables, altars, portable trays, hearths, braziers, tripods, and censers, in addition to vases for offerings, axes, and knives. To accompany the ceremonies there were musical instruments and noisemakers, as well as lamps, torches, and candelabra. To set apart and adorn the celebrants and their attendants, the victims, and the ceremonial sites, there were ornaments, fillets, crowns of flowers, and the like. Certain objects associated with special rites, notably those of the mystery religions, are difficult to interpret.

Unfortunately, archaeological documentation of these categories of objects is extremely scant and incomplete or, in many cases, simply nonexistent, because temple furnishings, with their sacred character or actual value, were more likely to vanish in the course of time than material sealed in tombs. The lack can be supplied to some extent by figural representations of ritualistic scenes and by written sources.

Historically there is a certain unity of traditions and continuity of types in the development of the great polytheistic civilizations of antiquity, from the earliest settlements of agricultural and proto-urban centers in the Near East, in the Mediterranean, and in southern Europe through the entire classic age.

* *

The ancient Near East. The development and use of morphologically differentiated ritual instruments and sacred equipment should certainly be considered as having occurred even before the appearance of written documents (3000–2800 B.C.). This assumption is supported both by finds such as the female votive or cult statuettes in terra cotta in western Asia and the rich deposits of pre- and protodynastic offerings at Hierakonpolis in Egypt (IV, PLS. 322, 324, 325) and by the Mesopotamian religious rituals and the evidence of the pyramids, the conservative nature of which makes it almost certain that a whole set of ritual objects had developed concomitantly with the appearance of the highly developed polytheism characteristic of the peoples of the ancient Near East in the preliterate period.

The obvious difference in character between ritual and non-sacred objects from earliest times is evident, for example, in Mesopotamia, where the presence of a cult altar is sufficient to identify a building (temple of Eridu). Likewise, certain rooms in the autonomous palace complexes of later periods may be identified as chapels by the presence of offertory tables; such is the case with the palace of Mari, in which two rooms were set aside for specific religious functions.

It is essential to make a distinction between the ritual objects of peoples of high sedentary cultures and those of the nomadic and seminomadic peoples from the mountains or desert. The less complex and differentiated cult activities of the nomads did not produce any extensive development of ritual objects and even less of sacred furnishings. The lack of documentation here is only partially offset by the descriptions of certain archaic sacrifices in a few Biblical passages and in the Ugaritic poem of Kerat (I, 62–79), which make it possible to attribute these rites to seminomadic peoples; however, the liturgical objects mentioned (chiefly gold and silver vessels) are not necessarily as ancient as the sacrifices described.

While it is not usually difficult to identify ritual material as such, it is frequently the case, especially in Mesopotamia, that the names of many sacred emblems (e.g., Sumerian *šar-úr*, *šar-gaz*, *an-kár*, *eme-gir*, *mi-ib*, *a-ma-ru*, *ḫa-ra-ib*) and ritual objects (e.g., Sumerian *alal*, *alal-liš*, *pisàn*, *mal*, *zi-da-kù*, *bur-kù*) are known from the abundance of ritual texts, but the morphological nature of these remains unknown because of the comparative scarcity of depictions of ritual scenes; only occasionally do the cuneiform ideograms permit the precise identification of objects. The problem is more easily resolved in respect to Egyptian objects because of the existence of large temple reliefs that give a clear idea of the furnishings of several New Kingdom temples; particularly notable are the accurate representations of the solemnities in honor of the god Min of Coptos. Syria, too, has yielded a considerable number of ritual objects, which can be interpreted only by reference to Biblical texts because, apart from the remarkable list of votive objects from the temple of Ningal in ancient Qatna, there is a dearth of other useful sources. Very few ritual objects have been found in Anatolia and southern Arabia (almost all the examples from these regions being irrelevant), though a study of Hittite rituals might suggest that there had been an extensive development of objects of this sort.

Ritual objects of the ancient Near East have remained morphologically unchanged to an exceptional extent, apparently because of their functions; but despite this immutability, sacred objects can be distinguished from others by the precious materials used for ritual articles and by their fine workmanship (in some cases that of very skilled craftsmen in precious metals). This does not apply to such very common objects as vases, although there are exceptions (e.g., the ritual vase of Uruk; IX, PL. 466).

Certain special materials were customarily used in the different cultural regions of the ancient Near East for objects that were most important in function and size. In Egypt, for example, altars and offertory tables were usually made of stone (or secondarily, but rarely, of brick), while in Mesopotamia altars for burning sacrifices, podia for offerings, and basins for libations were generally built of brick, or occasionally of plaster, even in places close to stone quarries, such as Mari.

Not infrequently certain types of both ritual objects and furnishings came into use beyond the geographic boundaries of the specific cultures, Egyptian and Mesopotamian cultures generally constituting the preponderant influence in such dissemination.

Sabatino MOSCATI

The most important element in ritual furniture of the ancient Near East is the altar. In its simplest form, common to all cultures of that region, the altar appears as a rather small table (usually circular, but occasionally in one of various geometrical shapes) sustained by a support in any one of several different forms. In Egypt this type of altar is documented as far back as the earliest dynasties, and it persisted up to the Ptolemaic period. The support is very high in proportion to the breadth of the table itself, cylindrical in shape and tapering slightly toward the base. Basically similar in form is a table depicted on a relief from Ugarit, in Syria, which differs only in that the lower portions of the support form a tripod, a variant characteristic of the wooden Egyptian prototypes from the archaic period. In the rest of the Asiatic regions, including southern Arabia (where, as in Egypt and Syria, the altar was a table for offerings to the dead), the type of table used for offerings during divine office or in funerary services was indistinguishable from an ordinary table: a table with legs crossed in an X form or forming a tripod or tetrapod (the last type is depicted on the Phoenician sarcophagus of Aḥīrām). The four-legged table was also used in Egypt. Related to this type are Assyrian altars from Khorsabad — one dating from the reign of Ashurnasirpal II (London, Br. Mus.) and two others from the period of Sargon II (Paris, Louvre; and Istanbul, Archaeol. Mus.) — in which the features described above are combined with those of another type: a large circular table of stone, resting on a stone prism with a triangular base, its corners resembling the legs of a bronze support. However, the latter type of altar generally does not occur in the earliest Mesopotamian periods.

A second type of altar, in widespread use throughout Mesopotamia and in adjacent regions, consists of a rather low block of massive stone; in representations it appears cube-shaped or in the form of a parallelepiped, either smooth or, more frequently, fluted toward the top; or it may be cylindrical, widening toward the top or bottom or in both directions. From the 2d millennium B.C. this type of altar, in the shape of a prism, was quite commonly used, to hold various sacred objects, such as symbols of divinity, baetuli, or horned tiaras. There are two variants of this type from Assyria: one has two kinds of protuberances along the upper edges, as seen on two altars of the late 2d millennium; the other, which subsequently came into widespread use in Iran, Anatolia, and Phoenicia, has a series of stepped pinnacles along the upper edges and at the four corners. The small horned altars found in several sites in Palestine may be a variant of this type. Small cubical altars on four pedestals or on truncated pyramids have been found in southern Arabia.

There are other more complex variants that cannot be traced back to a common prototype, even a theoretical one. For instance, stepped altars were in common use in Mesopotamia throughout the Akkadian period and until the beginning of the 2d millennium B.C.; these consisted of two steps, on the first of which a container of flowers or plants was sometimes placed (the prototype of the Syrian "gardens of Adonis"). One terra-cotta example from Ashur looks exactly like those depicted on monuments. In Syria, Palestine, and southern Arabia, stele-altars have been found that seem to carry out the same theme of two steps: a staircase, on which offerings were perhaps placed, projects from under the stele, which bears liturgical symbols. Characteristic of Anatolia is a monumental altar, known from reliefs on two statue bases from Boğazköy and later found in excavations at Beycesultan. The altar consists of a massive cube on which there stood two long poles that curved forward. A relief from Alaca Hüyük shows a king sacrificing before such an altar, which is high and T-shaped, with the lower portion widening toward the base. Highly unusual in its bold and complex structure is the unique Egyptian solar altar that stood in the courtyard of the temple of King Neuserra (5th dynasty). Of monumental size, it consists of a central circular slab of alabaster, flanked by four alabaster blocks with the hieroglyphic sign *ḥtp*.

Certain other ritual furnishings are related to the offertory tables. Most commonly used throughout Mesopotamia in the 2d and 1st millenniums B.C. were tall, slender cylindrical stands widening toward the base. There were also more complex stands, among them two bronze specimens from Kish: one is shaped like a trident resting on the back of a frog; the other, much damaged, is in the form of a cylindrical basket into which a vase was inserted. Stands from the Syro-Palestinian region are more complex. The bronze tripod (PL. 158) found at Ugarit (similar to the altar base depicted on the sarcophagus of Aḥīrām) and the wheeled carts found in Palestine and Cyprus (IV, PL. 92), which correspond to the cart described in the Bible as built by Hiram for Solomon, are expertly wrought in bronze and represent a type that apparently did not exist in Mesopotamia of that period.

From several Palestinian sites come certain objects of undetermined significance, which appear to have had a ritual purpose because of the symbols of divinity (often serpents) with which they are decorated. They are made of terra cotta and are classified as censers or perfume burners because they have slits, although they bear no traces of fire.

Other objects of uncertain function are the small models of sanctuaries and sacred edifices. Some of them might have been connected with funerary rites (e.g., urns in the shape of a hut, from Ugarit), but this is not certain in every case. The articles were in widespread use throughout a region that includes the Syro-Palestine area (Jericho, Hadera, Mari, and Ugarit).

The ritual article that was most widely diffused was the libation vase. The earliest Mesopotamian specimens are either conical or cylindrical, with a foot; there is an example of the latter from Uruk preserved in the Iraq Museum of Baghdad (PL. 466). Of later date is a vase with a long slender spout, a type not confined to this region, however (PLS. 470, 475; IV, PL. 204). In Egypt, besides libation cups, which may have been related to the Palestinian footed chalice, there is documented a ritual sprinkling vessel that remained practically unchanged in form throughout the entire period of the Pharaonic civilization; a narrow, elongated bottle, slightly wider toward the top, occasionally with a large side spout, it was originally produced in terra cotta but was later made in nonprecious metals, such as copper or bronze, and, occasionally, in precious metals, such as gold or silver. Several representations from the New Kingdom show a sprinkling vase patterned on the hieroglyphic sign for "life," a theme that also occurred in Egyptian-inspired Syrian seals. In the Assyrian period in Mesopotamia and in the Saite period in Egypt it became a widespread practice to use bronze pails (situlae) for lustral water. Many of these Egyptian receptacles are decorated with figures of deities and with ritual scenes (PL. 158). In Assyrian reliefs the water seems to be extracted from the pails by means of a cone that served as an aspergillum (PL. 489). In Palestine specimens of multiple vases (kernoi) with circular bases have been found.

In Egypt and in the areas it influenced (Palestine, Syria, and Anatolia) offerings were purified with incense; the incense was put in terra-cotta bowls that were placed in the hand of a wooden model arm. The censer, subsequently made of metal, was still further refined in Egypt by the addition of a second small bowl in the middle of the arm for the pellets of incense. The name of the censer is the equivalent of "incense arm" and, later, "the arm of Horus," because the handle had the hawk-headed form of that god. There are a few bronze specimens of the later type preserved in excellent condition in the British Museum and in the Vatican Museums (PL. 158). In Palestine this type of censer also occurs in stone, and there are huge bronze ladles with handles in the form of female figures.

Although some articles — such as votive objects, foundation treasures, Mesopotamian stone vases, various receptacles, the bed on which the sacred nuptials took place, sacrificial implements, and the priestly insignia borne by the king or priests — played some role in liturgical practice, they will not be treated here, because too little is known for adequate discussion of the types, or they properly fall under other headings. However, several categories of cult instruments should be mentioned, among them the sacred musical instruments. Sacred ceremonies were always accompanied by music, at least in Mesopotamian and Anatolian cultures. In these areas there was but one sacred instrument, the kettledrum, the construction of which is minutely described by a liturgical text. A representation, unfortunately very schematic, can be seen on a fragment of a Sumerian vase in the Louvre: behind the figure of a man in priestly robes two women support a large drum, on which a small figure stands; around the cylinder of the drum there are some semicircles, perhaps jingles. In Egypt the sistrum was used in the worship of the goddess Hathor (PL. 158). The oldest known specimen is a model of a votive sistrum, made of alabaster and bearing the royal protocol of Teti (6th dynasty), now in the Metropolitan Museum of New York. Its finely executed handle is formed like a papyrus stalk, and the sound box is a small temple surmounted by a hawk. This type of sistrum, with jingles suspended in rows, is documented as early as the Ptolemaic period, in stone, bone, or pottery votive models and in wall paintings in temples and tombs. The head of Hathor often appears on both sides of the tip of the handle. With the New Kingdom there came into widespread use another type, without a sound box and with the jingles inserted into an elliptical frame. Sound was produced by small jingling crossrods loosely set into the frame or by disks strung upon fixed crossrods. A great many votive specimens of this second type, dating from the Saite and Ptolemaic periods, still exist.

There were also objects that could be carried in processions. In Egypt there were many such objects, documented principally by temple reliefs (e.g., the relief in Luxor which illustrates the celebration of the feast of Opet), and there is ample testimony in the Harris I papyrus (Br. Mus.) from the reign of Ramses III (first half of 12th cent. B.C.), as well as indications in other texts and from excavations. Of great importance in Egyptian temples was the sacred bark for transporting the divine image during the yearly rites (IV, PLS. 368, 385). An especially magnificent example is the boat of Amen, called *wrs-ḫ3t*, which was made of cedar sheathed with gold, the shrine it bore being of solid gold and precious stones. During feasts small portable shrines, their sides often veiled with curtains, were also used. There is a specimen in Berlin (Staat. Mus.) of one in bronze and wood that had been consecrated by Amasis (mid-6th cent. B.C.). Also displayed in religious ceremonies were the divine insignia, which were carried on long poles topped by small platforms; the symbols called *wp-w3wt* frequently preceded the litter bearing the sacred image in processions.

Statues of Mesopotamian deities were carried on their bases, into which long wooden poles were inserted. The same system was employed for miniature temples, or portable shrines, as well as for the thrones of Anu and Enlil (which did not have cult statues). The structure of the Mesopotamian boats, which are often depicted on seals, is not clearly known; some texts imply that there was a river basin (*apsū*) in the vicinity of every temple, which might explain the representations of large boats that sometimes bear divine figures and an altar.

For the religious objects used by the Israelites, see below, *Jewish ceremonial art*.

Sergio BOSTICCO and Giovanni GARBINI

The classic world. In the religious sphere of Greece and Rome the primitive rites of offering, purification, and sacrifice gradually took on fixed forms, and the establishment of the state brought about a marked difference between private observances and public religious functions. For the latter there were developed increasingly imposing and even spectacular furnishings and implements, while private rites retained more traditional and simpler forms. In Roman houses, for example, the appurtenances for the simple ceremonies of libation, offering, and lustration were limited to the patera, salinum, acerra, and praefericulum. The altar was at first identical with the hearth, and one name (Lat., *focus*; Gr., *eschara*) applied to both; with the later development of the Roman house, this identity was lost, and an actual altar (ara) was placed before the image of the penates.

Public rites called for the use of a great number of accessories, but they may be reduced to a few types.

Of primary importance is the altar (Lat., *ara*; Gr., *bōmos*). Primitive altars were simple masses of shaped stone, and their ornamentation was of a temporary nature; subsequently, however, wreaths, festoons, and sacred fillets were carved directly on the flanks, enriching the altar with a decorative element that was at times remarkably artistic.

Aside from such monumental altars as that of Pergamon or the Roman Ara Pacis (the actual use of which is debatable), there are many examples of altars richly decorated according to the artistic tastes of the time. In spite of great variety in form and dimensions, the essential elements of the altar were substantially the same. However, the altar employed exclusively for blood sacrifices was a large structure, equipped with a step, with grooves and holes for drainage of the victim's blood, while the altar used for simple offerings was usually a smaller unit with more carefully executed decoration.

In Greece the altar, in keeping with the classic linear style of the temple, was of studied proportion and detail, the decoration usually being confined to skillfully designed cornices. In the Roman world, however, a range of types developed, including special funerary, votive, and commemorative aras, as well as certain others varying in significance according to where they were erected (e.g., at the boundaries of fields).

A purpose similar to that of the ara was served by a portable brazier (also called *focus*), on which libations of wine or incense were poured, and by the tripod (Lat., *tripus*; Gr., *tripous*), which took two different forms. In the form of a brazier, a small receptacle on three legs, it substituted for the ara and was often delicately worked. This type may be seen in many historical reliefs (PL. 161). In the form of a table with a flat surface, the tripod held liturgical objects and offerings; an example of this type appears on a relief from Konjic, Yugoslavia, showing a tripod-table prepared for the mystic feast with four crossed loaves of bread and a cup.

The finest tables were placed in the cella of the deity, forming an integral part of temple furnishings; less elaborate in both execution and material were the tables on which instruments and offerings were laid out (*mensae anclabres* or *anclabria*).

The ara and some of its related forms also existed outside the sphere of direct Greco-Roman influence. A ceramic fragment from Numantia bears a religious scene in which the ara is a simple polyhedral mass decorated in a manner suggesting not so much actual sets of ornaments as the free fancy of the decorator. The altar used by the Sardinians seems to have been a simple stone block with a hollow in the center and a drainage channel, but the tripod ara (PL. 432) also appears to have been in use, as well as a cruder form of the offertory table, a roughly circular block with a hollow for the offering. Several pieces of precious metalwork from Crete show the altar in the schematic form of a parallelopiped surmounted by one or more pairs of sacred horns; later, tripod altars and offertory tables were also used in Crete. The great table of Mallia is the most famous example of a long series that excavations have brought to light nearly everywhere in Crete from Pyrgos to Platonos to Pseira. In these specimens it is apparent that an effort was made to achieve an artistic solution or, at least, to attain a certain rhythm in the regular placement of the hollows; and the remarkable variety of form makes it one of the most interesting categories of ritual furnishings. In Etruria there were both very large aras, such as those of Vignanello and Veii, for blood sacrifices, and other, smaller altars, of simple workmanship and adorned only with a molding on the upper portion.

There is a vast number of receptacles designed to contain the liquids for libations (see CERAMICS; HOUSEHOLD OBJECTS), some of these vessels being used only during one particular ceremony; for example, the plemochoe, a sort of covered chalice, was used on the final day of the Eleusinian mysteries, and the chous was used only on the second day of the Anthesteria. There are also special receptacles for decanting the liquid and others to hold the lustral water.

The most sacred receptacle was the phiale, documented in Greece as early as the end of the 6th century; it corresponds exactly to the Latin patera, being a broad cup, without foot or handles and with a raised boss at the center (PL. 161). Indispensable to every ceremony, it was the ritual vessel par excellence; it is often reproduced in bas-reliefs and coins to indicate some religious function or purpose. The decoration of paterae is rather restrained, usually being limited to gadrooning, although there are some with festoons of leaves and fruit, but the material was usually of special value. Another vessel having a like function was the *spondeion*.

Among the instruments used for pouring liquid into the patera was the simpulum (PL. 161), which was at first used for domestic purposes as well but later was replaced by the kyathos, a vessel similar in form but of greater capacity. Since this vessel is frequently mentioned in temple inventories, it is likely that there were finely wrought examples.

The *capedo*, a cup with handles, is an example of the persistence of obsolete objects in rituals, for the prototypes go back to prehistory, but the vessel very early went out of use for everyday purposes. Two other receptacles of this type are the *spondochoe* and the praefericulum, the latter a small bowl — usually made of silver — that, like the patera, was usually very carefully wrought. Again, the decoration is not complex or highly varied, being usually limited to a gadroon on the body of the vessel, with the curve of the handle ornamented only slightly more elaborately, but the vessel had a marked dignity of form, especially during the Roman imperial period.

The liquid for the libation was first poured into a crater, a receptacle documented quite early as having a clearly defined purpose. Both its size and its use in particularly solemn ceremonies indicate that this vessel was one of the most important of the ritual implements. Sources often cite, among the outstanding objects in sanctuary treasuries, magnificent craters of precious materials in the Eastern tradition.

Another type of libation cup, the rhyton, merits special attention. A large number of these vessels have been discovered in Crete. They vary in form, but most typical is an elongated cone, generally of simple design but made of precious material. Some are exceptionally artistic and valuable as documents, among them a rhyton from Hagia Triada (IV, PL. 62).

Of the group of vessels for holding lustral water, undoubtedly the best known is the *lebē*, a basin that varied in capacity, often with the addition of either a conical or tripodal support. The finest examples are those from the Etruscan areas, in particular those from Vetulonia, made of sheet bronze with Orientalizing decoration. Although these vessels were not actually ritual objects, and though the situlae found in that area were made exclusively for tomb furnishings, the characteristics of vases used for ritual purposes can be determined from the form of these objects.

The origins of the situla date back to the Iron Age. Generally a vessel of truncated conical shape, the type was widespread throughout the entire Mediterranean basin, for domestic utilitarian purposes as well as for religious and funerary rites. The situla was carried to the site of the ceremony by means of a rod passed through the handles, as depicted on the sarcophagus of Hagia Triada (IV, PL. 62), the Certosa situla (V, PL. 34), and, later, the Corsini chair (Rome, Mus. Naz.). The examples shown in Cretan painting are polychrome, perhaps indicating damascening, a technique known to the Minoan-Cretan civilization. However, the decoration of Italian and Etruscan situlae was usually limited to repoussé. Little used in the Greek world, the situla was widely employed in Rome, particularly after the introduction of the worship of Isis.

Other containers for purificatory water include the kalpis (VII, PL. 194); the *futile*, a vessel with a pointed base, which was used in special ceremonies in the cult of Vesta; the *ardanion*; and the urceus. The *perirrhanterion* and the labrum were basins placed at the entrances of temples or sacred enclosures for the requisite purification, an ancient usage that still survives in the use of the holy-water font in churches. Lustral water was at first sprinkled by means of a bunch of leaves, but later the aspergillum (PL. 161) — the direct forerunner of the Christian aspergillum, or holy-water sprinkler — came into use for that purpose as an independent instrument with its own special form.

There are also many vases about which little or nothing is known, except that they were used during sacrifices.

Undoubtedly one of the most distinctive receptacles is the kernos, which was very likely a vase for offerings and seems to have been used only in certain mystery ceremonies. This name is generally applied only to a cup-shaped vase, to the sides of which other small receptacles were attached.

Besides the vessels proper there were baskets used to contain both the offerings to the deity and the ritual objects. One of these baskets is the *vannus*, broad and flat in shape, which originally functioned as a sieve to separate the wheat from the chaff. This object was especially important in initiation ceremonies, during which it was placed on the neophyte's head. A very similar receptacle is the *kanes*. The *cista* was a cylindrical basket with a lid used to hold the sacred symbols for the performance of mystery rites. It evolved from the simple container for offerings of classic times to become in a later period an indispensable element in the Greek mystery cults from the East.

A separate group of ritual objects are the sacrificial weapons. These objects may be reduced to two basic types: the ax and the knife.

Among the first group are the dolabra, an ax of rather general use, and the *securis*, the weapon usually represented in scenes of sacrifice, which corresponds completely to the modern ax. The double ax (sacena) of the high priests (PL. 161) seems to have had a more symbolic significance, serving almost as a badge of the highest priestly office, in addition to its sacrificial function.

Among the sacrificial knives are two weapons that were a cross between the sword and the knife, the *kopis* and the *machaira*, the former with a long, slightly curved blade, the other with a slightly wavy blade. In preference to these types, used predominantly by the Greeks, the Romans favored a shorter knife with an iron blade and an ivory handle ornamented with gold and silver. Even in the latter case the knife was not, strictly speaking, an object of artistic value, since the very use of precious material seems to have been considered an almost exceptional decorative element, a point stressed in the sources. Furthermore, the emphasis on function in instruments of this kind, against the background of the archaic and conservative character of the ritual, explains the simplicity and, at times, crudeness of such objects. A special type of knife is the *secespita*, which has a thickset and roughly trapezoidal blade.

Another sacrificial instrument is the *malleus*, a hammer that was sometimes used instead of an ax for slaughtering very large animals.

One of the purifying elements, in addition to water and fire, was incense, which was kept in the acerra (Gr., *libanoutris*), a small chest decorated more or less elaborately for an effect of richness.

Another accessory for incense was the *turibulum* (Gr., *thumiaterion*) or censer, which, in the classic period, was similar to a candelabrum with a simple shaft, surmounted by a small brazier. Depictions from various epochs and places, ranging from the Minoan-Mycenaean civilization to the Etruscan and Roman worlds indicate that it was extensively diffused. Occasionally the censer had the form of a small, low brazier with three or four feet — a type in which the craftsman was free to follow his imagination, producing extravagant creations that disguised the true nature of the object.

Thuribles used in ceremonies were more restrained and functional in design, as indicated by discoveries from excavations of cult sites and sanctuaries in Crete, which yielded thuribles in the form of braziers, as well as others, many of terra cotta, in the shape of a simple column.

The purificatory element of fire was always present; torches, or *faces*, were used in every place of worship and during every religious rite. Their function as illumination was not the major one, for torches were used even in daylight and in the open air and had sacred fillets twined around the shafts.

Accessories that were only occasionally used include the *tensa*, a small two-wheeled cart of costly material and rich decoration, which was used to carry the attributes of the divinity; and the pulvinar, a richly adorned bed on which the images of the gods were deposited to symbolize their direct participation in the ceremony. On the other hand, the armarium and the sacrarium were in constant use; these were small aediculae, with or without doors, in which were placed, respectively, images of the lares and the ritual instruments (V, PL. 429).

The Greek and Latin forms of worship differed considerably in that greater importance was attached to music in Greek ritual. In Rome the use of ancient religious chants was a sporadic phenomenon linked to popular spontaneous expression, while in Greece music was an essential part of the ceremony itself, perhaps as a result of Greece's propinquity to the Oriental world, in which the dance and music took on a very special character and were themselves tantamount to prayer. The aulos, either single or double, and the lyre were the most extensively used of Greek musical instruments. Musical accompaniment with flute and lyre also became customary in Etruscan regions, and the practice spread from there to Rome, where the influence of Hellenic civilization fostered its diffusion. A very common instrument in the pre-Roman world was the tuba, a long, straight trumpet invented, according to tradition, in one of the Etruscan cities. There were also other musical instruments believed to possess prophylactic or apotropaic powers; examples include the sistrum, tintinnabulum, and tympanum (see MUSICAL INSTRUMENTS).

Among liturgical objects there may also be included the lituus, a curved, knot-free stick used by Etruscan priests for bounding the sacred space of the templum (the lituus, originally, was slightly curved at one end, but later it acquired a more complex form with a large three-turn volute); the *mantele*, a small towel borne by the camillus on the left shoulder or arm; and the sacred fillets (vittae, taeniae, infulae) with which sacrificial victims were adorned to indicate their inviolability, this being further defined by the *dorsuale* and *frontale* adorning large sacrificial animals in ceremonies of special solemnity. In addition, wreaths were used to embellish temples, altars, and sacred enclosures on ceremonial days.

Little is known about ritual objects used in the religious ceremonies of the peoples on the periphery of the classic world. The only object known to be peculiar to the Germano-Celtic peoples is the small golden sickle with which the Druids cut the sacred mistletoe on the sixth day of the moon. However, sacrifices were made, and it can be assumed that the weapons used in killing the victims were similar to those used by the Greeks and Romans. The only existing example of an altar is that in Gamla Uppsala, Sweden, under the present parish church on the site of an older temple.

Ritual objects from Iberian cultures are represented in votive statues from Cerro de los Santos and Despeñaperros (PLS. 408, 410) and in the reliefs of Osuna, as well as in a number of scenes painted on pottery from Liria, which show that a double-reed pipe, an ax, a knife, and receptacles for offerings were used.

Giovanna ALVISI

The Iranian world. Since the earliest phases of the Iranian religion, the instrument most frequently and widely used has been the sheaf of twigs referred to in the Avesta as the *baresman* and called *barsōm* in Pahlavi. Representations of it are known from as early as the Luristan phase (e.g., the silver plaque with an image of the god Zurvan; Cincinnati Art Mus.), although there are fewer examples from later periods. However, except as reflected in religious iconography, the *baresman* is intrinsically without artistic merit, as is its modern counterpart in steel wire used in the Parsi ritual. The twigs were bound with a noose (Avestan, *aiwyāṅana*; Pahlavi, *aiwyāhan*; now called *kustī*), but since this was a perishable element, no description can be offered. It is likewise difficult to determine the artistic and esthetic value of such cult instruments as the cup (Pahlavi, *tasht*) for liquid offerings (*zaōthra*), especially milk (cf. *Yasna*, X, 17; *Vīdēvdāt*, V, 39, VII, 73, XIV, 8, XIX, 9); the mortar used not only for crushing the haoma but also for obtaining fruit juice (*Yasna*, XII, 2, XXVII, 7; *Visprat*, X, 2, XI, 2, XII, 2 and 5; *Vīdēvdāt*, XIV, 10, XIX, 9); and the officiant's breastpiece of cloth, mentioned in the *Vīdēvdāt*, XIV, 8, 9 and XVIII, 1, as well as in the *Yashts*, V, 123. Such objects are difficult to identify among others of similar type or in the damaged state in which they have survived. The great stone vase in the R. Lévy Collection, Geneva, may be a large mortar, but many factors tend to refute this identification. The documentation is insufficient to resolve the question. However, it should be noted that the protohistoric period was characterized by the diffusion of long-spouted vessels, at first of terra cotta and later of metal, which have been found among tomb furnishings in various localities. In the beginning these spouts were designed to imitate a bird's beak and presumably had to do with rites of sprinkling the corpse with liquid or grain. The usual types indicate a progressive evolution away from the theriomorphic model (which sometimes has two eyes alongside the spout) toward completely free forms. If they really were connected with funerary rites, these vases offer a minor but interesting bit of information on ritual practices.

Mario BUSSAGLI

India, southeast Asia, Nepal, and Tibet. In the religions of India rituals have always had a fundamental importance. From the Vedic period on, the rites and ceremonies have been very numerous, some connected with the cult of the family and worship of the gods in the shrines, and other more solemn ones connected with the seasonal celebrations and with such special events as the consecration of a ruler (Aśvamedha), a shrine, a symbol, or a statue of a divinity. Since every phase of human life takes on a religious significance, all stages of existence, from before birth to after death, were marked and accompanied by ceremonies. In every shrine and at every hour of the day the symbol or statue of the god (conceived of as his abode) was an object of worship and received offerings. Although in the Vedic period the rites were primarily sacrificial or oblationary, they later became fundamentally significant of homage and veneration (puja) in Hinduism, Buddhism, and Jainism (qq. v.). This continuous veneration was manifested through ablutions; gifts of flowers, fruit, and rice; and offerings of light, music, perfume, and incense. Thus arose the use of ritual objects and sacred ornaments which became fixed in form, function, and symbolism by tradition and were so perpetuated. The cult accessories later spread into the regions of southeast Asia, Nepal (see NEPAL; NEPALESE ART), and Tibet (PLS. 176, 177; see also TIBET; TIBETAN ART), together with the beliefs transmitted from the Indian civilization. However, the ladles, cups, and vases used in the Vedic age for offerings and libations and to contain the sacrificial liquor (*soma*) or the lustral water used in the consecration of the king (Rājasūya) are known to us only from texts. The cup for the *soma* was shaped like a mortar and was placed near the sacrificial fire. The earliest ritual objects surviving to our time are generally connected with Buddhism, and many of these came to light in the excavations at Sirkap (the Parthian site of Taxila) in the Punjab.

Some of the reliquaries used in the cult of the relics of the Buddha or of other religious figures were of crystal, and others were of metal. Among the earliest objects of artistic value may be mentioned the reliquary of repoussé goldwork set with rubies, from Bimaran, Afghanistan (VII, PL. 465; see also BACTRIAN ART), and the bronze reliquary said to be that of the Kushan king Kanishka. Their decoration is related to the Gandharan style (see GANDHARA) of the 2d–3d century, and the execution reveals a high level of technical skill, which may be noted also in miniature stupas and in bronze and copper incense burners.

Many ritual objects dating from a later period are common to the various Indian religions, which, in fact, have very similar ceremonies. Among these objects are ceremonial ladles, the flared vessel and ewer (lota) designed respectively for receiving and pouring the lustral water, bowls of varying depths, and trays used for offerings of flowers, fruits, and sweets. A small container (*arghya pātra*), shaped like an oval pot with rounded base and a spout, and receptacles of other forms may hold grain, sesame, sandalwood powder, or even water, perfumed and sprinkled with colored powder (PL. 177). The temple lamps show a wide range of types, especially in Nepal (PL. 178). Some have single columnar bases, of varying heights, supporting the container for burning oil or camphor. The finest specimens have the form of a many-branched tree; others hang from a chain, so that they can be swung before the idol. At times a series of lamps hangs from a horizontal rod in the hand of a statuette. Incense burners (*dhūpana*) occur in many forms; some, used in Buddhist ceremonies, have long handles, and their shape, which subsequently was used also in the Tarim Basin and Tunhuang, seems to repeat a type used in Iran and western Asia. Censers often take the form of a footed cup with one or two handles. Other ritual objects include the bell (*ghaṇṭā*) with handle, rung to attract the god's attention; the shell (*śaṅkha*), blown for the same purpose or to mark the end of a ceremony; and another sort of shell, which often rests on a decorated, footed cup and is used to pour water over the idol.

A richly ornamented throne supports the image; on domestic altars were placed statuettes of the gods or the linga, symbol of Śiva. Mirrors (*darpaṇa*) were used to reflect the image of the god so that it could be washed and anointed, particularly when the image was of clay. Candleholders, fans, and umbrellas, often sumptuous, were arranged around the statues. The processional cars, which in southern India attained monumental proportions, were sometimes of wood with carved panels (IV, PL. 213). Many musical instruments (q.v.) gradually acquired a ritual nature and constituted indispensable temple accessories; such were the bells, gongs, various trumpets, and other instruments accompanying religious dances and ceremonies. Small tubes containing relics and amulets were for more personal use.

Ritual objects offer proof of the high artistic caliber of the minor arts both in India and in the areas to which Indian types of art spread. The workmanship was particularly painstaking, and the appearance was the product of a long tradition that had fixed the forms in relation to function, the appropriate and harmonious proportions, and the motifs of the rich decoration. Most of the ritual objects are of metal: copper, bronze, sometimes brass, and, for the most precious objects, gold and silver were used. Various techniques of metalworking were adopted, and certain ones became local specialties. The decorative motifs were conventional, symbolic, or drawn from the particular iconography of each religion: representations of the Buddha, the bodhisattvas, and Buddhist emblems, which in Tantrism were augmented by figures of deities and demoniac forms, and depictions of the great gods of Hinduism with the personages of their retinue, *śakti*, vehicles (*vāhana*), secondary gods, and genii.

The Indian types recur in the ritual objects of the southeast Asian countries, as well as in Nepal and Tibet, but every region has individual decorative forms. Silver ritual vases from ancient Champa (see CHAM, SCHOOL OF) have come to light in the treasury of Po Nagar; and the conchs, bells, candlesticks, and other objects from the ancient Khmer empire (see CAMBODIA; KHMER ART) are works of outstanding beauty. In the school of Mahayana Buddhism, new importance attaches to the *vajra*, a four- or eight-branched thunderbolt, sometimes linked to a small bell and a sacrificial knife. In Tibetan Lamaism ritual objects include libation bowls, sometimes carved from human skulls, often mounted in metal and elaborately decorated; ceremonial aprons made of a network of bone beads; magic daggers adorned with demonic shapes; thigh-bone trumpets; and tambourines, some fashioned from two half skulls and shaken to mark the intervals of prayers and incantations. Prayer wheels, consisting of a rotating metal cylinder enclosing a fragment of sacred text, come in all sizes. Like all Tibetan ritual objects, these are very well made and embellished with rich symbolic decoration. There are also altar frontals, miniature stupas, the eight Buddhist emblems and the seven jewels, ceremonial staves, portable altars, and crowns for the celebrants, comprising five panels on which the five supreme Buddhas (*pañcatathāgata*) are depicted. Amulet cases, often of silver set with semiprecious stones, are worn suspended on the chest. The costumes of the Tibetan lamas, of embroidered brocade, are sumptuous, as are the caps, which vary in color and shape according to the sect, and the fabrics and painted banners (tanka) adorning the shrines. Masks (q.v.), marked by their intense expression, are worn during dances, which in Tibet, as well as in Indonesia and Bali, are religious.

Madeleine HALLADE

China. The array of ritual instruments and sacred objects in the religions practiced by the Chinese vary enormously from one period or place to another. As early as the pre-Confucian religion, and later in Confucianism (q.v.), although there was no clearly defined priesthood, the celebrant — whether he were head of a state or only the head of a social or family group — wore different clothing and headgear for the various religious ceremonies, including the rite in commemoration of ancestors and funeral ceremonies. Certain texts dating from the first millenium B.C. indicate that many of these ceremonies were accompanied by the music of flutes, drums, and sonorous stones, generally played by blind musicians. The musical instrument sometimes used to summon the worshiper might also be a liturgical instrument, the music being the means of evoking the spirits or gods for the ceremony. Many bronze vases from the archaic period were sacrificial or ritual vessels (PL. 175). The ruler, when obliged to make special offerings, donned a garment of coarse cloth and swallowed powdered jade, as a symbol of purity. As attested by the *Shih-ching* ("Book of Odes" or "Songs"), the princesses who assisted their husbands in making offerings wore their hair dressed in a particular style (*fu*) with special hairpins.

In addition to the official court religion, the rank and file, particularly in southern China, practiced more elementary forms of religious expression and resorted to the magic services of sorcerers (*hsi*), witches (*wu*), and shamans. Some pre-Han texts tell how, before evoking a given divinity, the witch would wash her face with water in which orchids had been boiled, would put on ceremonial robes (probably the same as those of the spirit invoked) and grasp a long, jade-handled sword; musical instruments, in these invocational rites, were one of the means used by the *wu* to achieve a state of trance. Even in rites of this nature, the *wu*'s clothing and jewelry (particularly the pendants) were changed, depending on the spirit to be evoked or invoked. The exorcists (*fang-hsiang-shih*) made use of various instruments in their work, for example, peach-tree branches and brooms for dispelling maleficent emanations during funerals. Clothing always played a fundamental part in Chinese ritual; it often identified the wearer with the previous deceased owner or with the god. In funeral rites, one person was delegated to mount to the roof of the deceased's home dressed in the latter's clothing in order to evoke his ghost; likewise, in the rites for the deceased, his representative (*shih*) — usually one of the younger family members — would don his clothing to receive offerings and eulogies.

A genuine priesthood arose in China only with the introduction of Buddhism and later, under Taoist influence in imitation of the Buddhist clergy, and with this development the rites and the pertinent instruments, ornaments, and ritual objects were more closely prescribed. Among the Buddhist furnishings and objects were the *fo-k'an*, a niche in which images of the Buddha were placed; the *ling-p'ai*, tablets bearing the names of defunct bonzes, usually placed alongside the *fo-k'an*; the *ho-kuei*, a turtle-shaped candelabra; the *huo-shih*, a perfume still (PL. 159); the *hsiang-lien*, an incense coffer; the *fan* (*fo-fan*), a banner; the *t'ien-kai*, or canopy; the *o-chia-t'ung*, or small copper pail, filled with an essence to be offered to the Buddha; the *ju-i*, or scepter; and the *fu-tzŭ*, the deertail fly whisk. There were also a great many musical instruments, such as the *mu-yü*, or wooden fish, a slit drum beaten with a stick to summon the worshipers; the *pao-lo*, a univalve seashell, played to summon the deva; various drums and scrapers; and the *ling*, or little bell. Many of these instruments or objects, as in the case of the *ju-i*, were of genuine artistic merit.

Taoism attached importance to the color of garments worn during ceremonies, as well as to musical instruments, incense for burning on the special tripods, and the writings containing the magical eight trigrams (*pa-kua*) of the *I-ching* ("Book of Changes"). In certain ceremonies lamps and perfume stills were placed at temple doors to show the way to the spirits summoned; golden dragons placed beside the doors were believed to dominate the four regions of space and the spirits thereof. In other ceremonies the Taoist masters held a bamboo rod with nine joints (nine was the number symbolic of heaven); and in still others, the face was smudged with soot and the forehead with mud (the *t'u-t'an-chai*, or fast of mud and soot). However, the Taoist liturgy and the ritual objects used in it varied with the passage of time and the development of separate sects.

Lionello LANCIOTTI

Japan. Shintoism was originally a religion based solely on magical practices and animistic beliefs, but with the introduction of Buddhism and Chinese culture into Japan, it underwent profound changes and adaptations, engendering an elaborate official cult connected with the political system.

In spite of these changes, the ritual objects for both private and official observances remained virtually identical. While Buddhism, with its elaborate ritual, created countless ritual objects, Shintoism, which did not develop an ethical system, metaphysics, or the concept of an afterlife, made use of a very small number of such objects, because its simple ceremonies are limited to three rites of purification: *harai* exorcism), *misogi* (ablution), and *imi* (abstention). Of these three only the first requires a special ritual object, the *o-musa*, which consists of a wooden pole on an octagonal base, with little strips of paper (sacred symbols) and hemp fibers fastened to the free end. The *o-musa*, held in oth hands by the *iwai-nushi* (master of the rite), one of the officiating *kannushi* (Shintoist priests), is waved over a throng of the worshipers first to the left, then to the right, and then once again to the right. The *kannushi* thus performs the purificatory rite, which is preceded by the reading of prayers (*norito*).

Shortly before the rite of *harai* — which is linked to the myth of the bath taken by the god Izanagi in the river Oto, after his exit from the underworld, and the myth of the expulsion from heaven of the god Susa-no-ō — the worshipers make use of various purification objects, including the *katashiro*. This genuine, although uncommon, ritual object consists of a piece of paper shaped like clothing, on which the penitent writes his own sex, with the month and year of his birth; he rubs it against his own body and breathes upon it so as to transfer to it all impurities. The pieces are taken to the temple, gathered together in bundles, and, after the *harai*, placed on a boat and thrown into a stream or the sea.

During Shintoist religious festivals, use is made of the *gohei* (see DEVOTIONAL OBJECTS AND IMAGES), an object related to the *o-musa*, consisting of a slender stick topped by a strip of white (sometimes black) paper, folded in a special way and in a number of folds which varies according to the sects by which the object is used. In ancient practice the *kannushi* would hold a *gohei* in his hand and touch it during the ceremony in order to induce a state of ecstasy; today a larger version is even carried in processions, attached to the saddle of a richly caparisoned white horse led by a *kannushi*.

Antonio Priori

CRISTIAN LITURGICAL OBJECTS. In its earliest stages, Christianity created no new and distinctive liturgical objects; the developments that did occur were of a symbolic rather than instrumental nature, and even the symbol of the cross can be found in earlier religions. For its ritual Christianity adopted both secular and sacred objects, in part from the Hebrew-Oriental tradition and in part from contemporary Western civilization. The appointments are of three kinds, as outlined below: the immovable fittings of the church (altar, baptismal font, pulpit, lectern, etc.); altar furnishings, including the sacramental implements, and other, less sacred objects (aquamanile, censer, bell, etc.); and the vestments and insignia of the clergy.

With the elaboration of the ritual over the centuries, many objects were added or given more distinctive form and significance, so that certain ones acquired a symbolic value outweighing the purely functional. This is true, for example, of the chalice, the candlestick, and the censer (which, along with the aspergillum, derives from pagan usage). Nevertheless, a large number of liturgical utensils have remained substantially unchanged (despite modification in form and size) since they were introduced into the Christian liturgy. Among them are the sacramental vessels (except for the pyx, for which new and original forms were developed during the Middle Ages), for although taken directly from contemporary secular usage, they remain closely bound by tradition because of their symbolic character. Most of the vestments and sacerdotal insignia have also remained essentially unchanged. Introduced between the 4th and 9th centuries, they were based on the robes of the contemporary upper classes. Their form and color were fixed according to the ritual in which they were used and in accord with hierarchic distinctions. Among the few exceptions is the crosier, which in its form and full symbolic significance was taken over from Judaic patriarchal usage.

The altar is undoubtedly the most important and, along with the enclosure of the presbytery, one of the oldest elements assimilated by Christianity. The early Christian altar was meant to represent the table of the Last Supper and was always associated with the traditional concept of the blood sacrifice. Nevertheless its form, furnishings, and subsidiary structures became similar to those of the altars in contemporary tombs and martyriums, combining the idea of the cult of the martyrs and saints with the divine cult in honor of one of the fundamental principles of the faith, afterlife.

Christianity did introduce genuine new features in the sacred furnishings. Of particular artistic interest are the altarpiece, which was produced during a relatively short period but had a prodigious development; the ambo and pulpit, both designed for preaching; and the confessional, which was a later development in Church usage, not precisely established in the liturgy. Reliquaries and monstrances, of no less importance, were created to satisfy a purely Western desire to make the objects of veneration visible. The particular forms given to these vessels, as well as to the tabernacle, were in part a matter of taste and fashion but also originally an instance of the intent to create a symbolic image of the Church. This was true as well, for a certain period, of the *turibulum* and the sacred vessels, which took on forms from monumental architecture and followed the stylistic evolution from Gothic to baroque. Throughout the 19th century earlier styles, especially the Gothic and baroque, were imitated, but with the emergence of the Liturgical Movement at the end of the century an effort was made to bring the best in contemporary art and design into the service of the Church. Where tradition enters into this style, it often reflects the simple forms of Early Christian pieces. Though not accepted by all, this trend has influenced much that has been made in the 20th century.

Usage and liturgical equipment in the various Protestant denominations varies enormously, from a fairly high degree of similarity to Roman Catholic practices to the complete elimination of all the categories of objects mentioned. The relative paucity of Protestant liturgical art is the logical result of certain doctrinal and procedural changes initiated during the Reformation (see REFORMATION AND COUNTER REFORMATION) and of the democratic revolution that went hand in hand with the establishment of many "dissenting," "separatist," and "protestant" groups. Religious dissent in this phase of history, like many others, tended to be linked with political dissent and anti-authoritarianism. Underlying the history of Protestantism is a reliance on the authority of "the Word," rather than on visual representation of sacred subjects or symbols or on the intermediation of human beings or sacred objects between the worshiper and his God. For this attitude the translation of the Bible into the vulgate and the invention of printing, together with the spread of literacy to the common people, prepared the way. With "the Word" thus widely available, the major doctrinal premises of the Reformation profoundly affected the attitudes and behavior of the laity, and a literal reading and close interpretation of particular passages prompted a deliberate return to earlier and simpler forms of observance modeled on the acts of Christ and the disciples as described in the Gospels.

A major point of Reformation liturgical theory was the rejection of the doctrine of transubstantiation. Variously interpreted by the Protestant denominations, this theological controversy has, in the most extreme form of dissent, resulted in the elimination of the communion rite altogether, with all the objects pertaining to it, including the altar. In the many churches that administer the rite, each with its own doctrinal interpretation, practices differ as to whether it is open to all the congregation or only to the professed believers (the confirmed), whether a single chalice or individual cups are used for the wine, etc. In general, the communion is "of both kinds"; that is, the laity partake of both the bread and the wine, as was done also in the Catholic churches in earlier times. The "altar" is, in some churches, only an altar rail; in others, a simple table; and in still others, an altar in the sense described below, with handsome and precious furnishings.

Another important aspect of the Reformation was the rejection of the veneration of saints and of the Virgin. This fact, along with a strict application of the First Commandment, accounts for the prevailing exclusion of images, reliquaries, and figural representations from Protestant churches. Within the churches decoration of the fixed furnishings and liturgical objects is generally restricted to the symbol of the cross, the monogram of Christ, and Biblical inscriptions, or sober ornamental moldings and the like. Representational art, however, is frequently used in religious publications, where it serves an educational, visual-aids, or graphic-arts purpose unrelated to the liturgy. The books used by the laity in participating in the service (prayerbooks, hymnals, etc.) are usually unadorned.

A third fundamental idea of the Reformation was the rejection of the celibacy of the clergy. This departure from Catholic practice, together with the idea of a return to earlier Christian customs and the leveling desire inherent in the Protestant movement, also led to variations in the usage of the individual denominations. These variations are manifested, for example, in the costume of the clergy both inside the churches and in daily life, so that the dress of the "pastor," "minister," or "preacher" may be identical on all occasions with that of the layman; it may be distinguished only by the clerical collar; or it may include ritual vestments varying according to the ceremonies of the church calendar. The ultimate degree of differentiation is the total elimination of the clergy, with free participation of the congregation in religious observances.

One specific instance of the adherence to original forms is the rite of baptism by immersion, reflecting the baptism of Christ in the Jordan. Certain denominations following this practice retain the early type of baptismal pool in the churches; others follow the Biblical precedent even more literally by holding baptismal ceremonies in rivers. Even in those denominations that practice baptism by aspersion or affusion, particular sentiment is occasionally attached to the use of water procured from the Jordan.

The list of liturgical objects that follows is based on the Catholic rites. It applies to Protestant usage only in part or to a certain degree.

* *

The altar and its furnishings. a. Altar. As a symbolic reproduction of the table of the Last Supper, the altar was originally a simple movable wooden table. Later, with the construction of the first basilicas, fixed altars of stone, marble, or masonry were placed at the end of the nave, at the visual and ritual focal point of the church. Four basic forms can be distinguished: table, hollow coffer or chest, block, and sarcophagus. (The altar as a fixed and integrating element of sacred architecture is discussed in the article STRUCTURAL TYPES AND METHODS.) Examples of portable altars, the use of which was limited though not altogether abandoned during the Middle Ages, include a 7th-century one from the tomb of St. Cuthbert (Durham, Cathedral Mus.). It comprises an oak slab encased in silver plates. Other examples are the Stavelot altar (IV, PL. 409), the one by Master Eilbertus (PL. 168), and the 12th-century wooden altar in S. Maria in Vulturella (Mentorella) near Tivoli. Among the 14th-century altars are the one in S. Maria in Campitelli, Rome, and that in the Cathedral of Capua.

b. Altar frontal (or antependium). The modern altar frontal, or medieval antependium, decorated the front of the block altar and chest altar. Though frontals were later created in a variety of forms and materials, the first ones were carved and decorated stone slabs, such as the one in S. Agnese, Rome, with a depiction of St. Agnes (4th cent.?), and the one in the Cathedral of Pulj (Pola), Yugoslavia, with a cantharus between affronted animals. Other examples include that of Magister Ursus in the Abbey church of S. Pietro, in Ferentillo, and that of Ratchis in the Cathedral of Cividale del Friuli (VII, PL. 373; XI, PL. 326). From the 11th through the 13th century, frontals with mosaic inlay were common in Italy. The decoration generally comprised tondos and friezes around the edges and rarely included figure compositions. There are examples in S. Miniato al Monte, Florence, in the Cathedral of Ferentino, and in S. Maria in Sermoneta, as well as works in Rome by the Cosmati (q.v.), including those in S. Prassede, S. Cesareo, and SS. Nereo e Achilleo. Contemporaneous frontals of precious metals (see GOLD- AND SILVERWORK), ivory, or cloth differ from those mentioned above in that they could be removed. Sumptuous metal ones include the golden altar of S. Ambrogio, Milan, by Wolvinius (III, PL. 63), the chased-gold altar that Henry II (973–1024) gave to the Cathedral of Basel (VI, PL. 263), the partially gilded silver altar donated to Città di Castello by Celestine II in 1143 (PL. 168), and those in the Treasury of the Cathedral of Aachen, in the Abbey church of Klosterneuburg (X, PLS. 315, 318), and in the sacristy of the Cathedral of Ascoli Piceno. Although the only ivory frontal that is still complete is the one in the Treasury of the Cathedral of Salerno, ivory antependia seem to have been fairly common. The use of embroidered or painted fabric for frontals endured longer. Two fine works in the Treasury of the Cathedral of Anagni reveal that Roman embroidery workshops were influenced by the painting of Cavallini. Among the many Tuscan and Venetian works of the 14th century are the frontal in St. Mary, Zadar, and that in the Church of St. Mary, Gdańsk. In Catalonia in the 12th century a distinctive type of painted frontal was developed, on which the figures and decoration are carved of gesso and slightly raised. Generally a figure of Christ enthroned is shown in the center, and both scheme and style reflect the monumental wall paintings of the period.

The silver altar frontal with scenes from the life of John the Baptist, from the Baptistery in Florence (XI, PL. 184), is of great artistic interest, since many leading artists worked on it, including Bernardo di Bartolommeo Cennini, Verrocchio, Michelozzo, and A. Pollaiuolo. Altar frontals embroidered with figures and scenes were common during the Renaissance, and some were made after designs by leading artists. They were primarily of silk or brocade. Noteworthy examples include one by Jacopo di Cambio (Florence, Pitti); one in the Treasury of S. Francesco, Assisi, that may have been designed by A. Pollaiuolo; and others in S. Maria in Vallicella, Rome.

In northern Europe wool was frequently used, and frontals were either in tapestry weave or embroidered. Numerous outstanding examples are found in the major collections of Germany, Switzerland, Belgium, and France. Sixteenth-century frontals reveal a preference for ornate floral patterns rather than figural motifs, a trend that continued in the 17th and 18th centuries, when costly silks and gold and silver threads were used profusely and the raised design was intended to imitate other media (PL. 168).

c. Altarpiece. Used in the West from the 13th century and set up at the back of the altar, the altarpiece, or *ancona*, probably derives its name and function from the medieval *icone*. The earliest ones consisted of a single panel with a figure of the Virgin or a saint, set within a tabernacle or aedicula on the altar. This form was either horizontal or, more commonly, vertical, as in the *Rucellai Madonna* (IV, PL. 286) and in the *Madonna and Child Enthroned* by Guido da Siena (VIII, PL. 185). Many altarpieces were given gables and cusped arches. When the size increased, small subsidiary scenes were added one above the other on either side of the main figure, as in the altarpiece of the Magdalen in the Accademia, Florence, by the Magdalen Master, and the panel of St. Francis in S. Francesco, Pescia, by Bonaventura Berlinghieri (VIII, PL. 181). With the increase in the number of figures and scenes as well as in size, several distinct panels came to be used. They were set on a long narrow projecting base called a "predella," which also had small painted scenes. The altarpiece terminated in a gable or lobed arch. From these beginnings the Italian altarpiece developed along several lines. The Stefaneschi Polyptych (Vat. Mus.), made for St. Peter's in Giotto's workshop, was a prototype that had many varied successors, both of the type in which the central panel predominates, as in the *Annunciation* by Simone Martini (PL. 339), and of the later type made up of many articulated panels, as for example, the back of the Duccio *Maestà* (IV, PL. 285). This type was often given a complex crown, as may be seen in the polyptych of 1319 by Simone Martini (PL. 335).

The basic northern European altarpiece was the triptych with movable wings. Carved wood was used more often than painted panels, especially in German and Flemish works; these became extremely complex, sometimes having several sets of wings, and the scenes were on a small scale, which favored a wealth of figures and detail. Entire cycles of sacred scenes were often included and framed within delicate architectural elements. A fine example is the altarpiece of the Virgin in the Church of St. Mary, Cracow, by Veit Stoss, completed in 1489. In certain works the main scene in the center is carved and the wings are painted, a system employed in the relatively simple mid-14th-century altarpiece of St. Clare in Cologne Cathedral. Here the carved architectural elements of the interior are almost identical with the painted ones on the exterior. The same practice existed in Flanders and France, as evidenced by the altar for the Chartreuse of Champmol, for which Melchior Broederlam painted the wings about 1399 (Dijon, Mus. des Beaux-Arts). In painted altars the rich variety in form and detail may be seen in Lukas Moser's altar of 1431, depicting the story of the Magdalen, in Tiefenbronn, Germany, and in the Van Eyck Ghent Altarpiece, completed in 1432 (PL. 11; V, PLS. 215, 216), the tradition culminating in Grünewald's powerful Isenheim Altar, which has two sets of wings (VII, PLS. 88, 89). A fine metal altarpiece is the Pala d'Oro in S. Marco, Venice (IV, PL. 405).

In Spain the *retablo* (retable, or altarpiece) enjoyed a unique development in the 16th century. Often very tall, it was divided into several scenes, usually three rows of three. Some retables have only painted scenes, while others combine these with polychromed wooden figures in the round (VI, PL. 357). The complex architectural elements and late Gothic ornamentation compete in importance with the painted decoration.

Altarpieces of outstanding artistic quality, of painted wood, glazed terra cotta, and marble, were produced in Italy in the 15th and 16th centuries. Later the practice of placing the altar directly against the rear wall diminished the importance of the altarpiece, which was all but incorporated into the wall decoration of the apse or chapel. A stage in this process of architectural unification is represented in the Piccolomini Altarpiece in the Cathedral of Siena; although this marble altarpiece is still a distinct unit, it is attached to the rear wall and incorporated in the architectural and decorative scheme of the chapel. Once the unification of both elements was achieved, the *ancona* was replaced by a large painting set into an aedicula, often of polychrome marble and enriched with decorative detail. The baroque aedicula had contemporary architectural features, including paired columns, and angels and allegorical figures. The modern trend toward simplicity has led to the elimination of the altarpiece as well as other forms of decoration, even when the altar is freestanding.

d. Candlesticks. Candlesticks, varying in number from two to six, have had a definite place on the altar since the 13th century. In the early liturgy the acolytes at times held the candles in their hands, as may be seen on the ivory cover of the Drogo Sacramentary (III, PL. 62; Paris, Bib. Nat., Ms. lat. 9428) and in the frescoes in the lower church of S. Clemente, Rome. The cross and candlesticks were set up next to the altar during the service. Such must have been the purpose of two bronze candlesticks of the 5th–6th century, with tripod bases carved in the form of animals (London, Br. Mus.; Trieste, Mus. di Storia e d'Arte). Important later examples are the monumental and sumptuously carved pair of 11th-century candlesticks in the Church of St. Magdalena, Hildesheim, with intricately worked human and animal figures; the one in the Hildesheim Cathedral Treasury (both PL. 167); and the bronze Gloucester Candlestick (VI, PL. 252).

The traditional Hebrew seven-branched candlestick was also widely used in Christian churches. Outstanding examples are in the cathedrals of Brunswick (PL. 170), Essen (10th cent.), Milan (13th cent.), and S. Maria in Vulturella (given by the Fortebraccio family ca. 1424). Enamel and gilded bronze candlesticks were produced in large quantities in the workshops of the Meuse and Limoges in the 12th–14th centuries. Sometimes the base had three supports; sometimes it was circular or broad and lobed. The high stem was interrupted by a heavy knop and a round disk beneath the pricket. The collection of the British Museum contains pieces outstanding for their enamelwork. In Gothic examples the decoration of the foot and knop was richly sculptured and at times imitated contemporary architectural forms.

There are many sumptuous and valuable Renaissance altar candlesticks. The Treasury of St. Peter's has a rich collection of 16th-century works by such artists as Benvenuto Cellini, Antonio Gentili (PL. 167), and Valerio Belli, as well as works based on designs by Michelangelo, Carlo Spagna, and others.

At this time there was produced a type of piece consisting of a kneeling or standing angel holding a small candlestick; not all of them were intended for the altar, however. Examples in marble and in bronze, the work of leading contemporary sculptors, include the two marble ones by Niccolò da Bari and Michelangelo beside the tomb of St. Dominic in S. Domenico, Bologna, and those in the Cathedral of Siena.

The practice of depicting candelabra as an ornamental motif in architecture, clearly of classical derivation, was common in the 15th and 16th centuries, but when used in a religious context these depictions had definite symbolic significance. The motif was very common, appearing in almost every work of architecture, in altars, tabernacles, and funerary monuments.

During the 17th and 18th centuries the number of candlesticks on the altar was increased and finally established at six. There was an enrichment of decorative motifs, in which chromatic values began to outweigh the sculptural sense that had characterized 16th-century ornament. Notable 17th-century examples are the bronze candlesticks in St. Peter's. The altar furnishings for the Chapel of São João Baptista in the Church of São Roque in Lisbon, including candlesticks by Antonio Arrighi, are representative of 18th-century work. On the whole, the baroque style continued to be used for altar furnishings until various modern artists began to find significant new forms. Important in this respect are the candlesticks Matisse designed (completed 1951) for the Chapelle du Rosaire of the Dominican nuns in Vence.

The Easter candlestick is known to have been part of the liturgy as early as the 5th century, but no such early examples are known today. In Italy during the Romanesque period monumental marble candlesticks took the form of large columns, carved with scenes and decorated with mosaic inlays and often set on a base made up of two or more animals. There are many outstanding pieces, including two in Rome — the historiated candlestick in S. Paolo fuori le Mura, made by Niccolò d'Angelo and Pietro Vassalletto (III, PL. 477), and one with Cosmati work in S. Maria in Cosmedin — as well as those in the Cappella Palatina, Palermo (VIII, PL. 173), and S. Maria della Pietà, Cori (XII, PL. 259). There are also important candlesticks from the Renaissance period, including that of Doge Cristoforo Moro, of gilded silver (15th cent., Venice, S. Marco); the two by Antonio Pollaiuolo in the Treasury of St. Peter's, Rome; the one by Andrea Briosco (known as Riccio) in S. Antonio in Padua (1507-15), and the two of the early 1520s by Maffeo Olivieri in S. Marco, Venice. Those of the baroque period are noteworthy for their sumptuous ornament and elegant forms (e.g., the silver candlestick, 17th cent., in the Treasury of S. Marco, Venice). The Easter candlestick has kept its traditional form and ornamentation, although those created since the end of the 19th century are usually slightly smaller and simpler.

e. Cross. Along with candlesticks the cross had been given a permanent place on the altar by the 13th century. Previously it had often been set up beside the altar during services and had been carried in processions since early times. As liturgical objects, two types of crosses were important from the 4th century on: the Latin and the Greek. The former, with a long vertical arm and a shorter horizontal one fairly high up, represents the cross of the Crucifixion; because it had a triumphal character, it was often a sumptuous work encased in gold or silver plates and studded with gems. The Greek cross, with equal arms, was fixed on a short handle (as represented in Byzantine ivories from the 5th century on) and was used for benedictions, since it represents the thaumaturgic powers of Christ. Derived from this cross is one that is close to it in proportions but is set on a long pole terminating in a flared foot. It may be seen in mosaics in S. Lorenzo fuori le Mura, Rome.

The Irish processional crosses are exceptionally beautiful, as may be seen in the Cross of Cong (Dublin, Nat. Mus.), dated about 1123, with its intricate metalwork, gold filigree, and enamel bosses. The top of the staff is in the form of an animal head with the cross set into its mouth.

A 9th-century miniature shows an acolyte holding a cross with a knobbed shaft and tripod stand (Autun, Bib. Municipale, Sacramentary of Marmoutier, Ms. 19bis, fol. 1v) and may well be an early representation of an altar cross. In any case, it is believed that the cross appeared on the Byzantine altar before it appeared on that of the Western Church. Considered one of the first examples is the silver repoussé cross (ca. 3 ½ ft. tall) in the Lavra, Mt. Athos, probably dating from the 12th century. Perhaps processional and altar crosses were originally interchangeable, the processional cross merely being set on an appropriate base between the two candlesticks on the altar. As early as the 11th century both types began to bear a relief figure of Christ crucified, as on the two Ottonian Mathilde crosses (Cathedral, Essen, 971–82) and the cross of Bernward (Hildesheim, St. Magdalena). Among the few remaining Italian Romanesque processional or altar crosses in metal are the one in Chiusdino (near Siena) and that in Vigolo Marchese (Emilia), both of which have rectangular terminals similar to those of the large painted crosses suspended above the altar.

In the Gothic period a greater number of altar crosses was produced. The terminals are usually lobed and the foot polygonal or lobed; enamel decoration is common. The stem is longer than before and in many cases is interrupted by a knop, often in the form of a miniature *tempietto*, such as the one on the reliquary of the Tree of the Cross in Lucignano (Mus. Civ.) and that of the Cross in the Casa Comunale, Santa Vittoria in Matenano. The processional cross evolved along similar lines, the forms becoming richer and more varied, as for example, the cross by Andreolo de' Bianchi in the Treasury of S. Maria Maggiore, Bergamo, and that in the Cathedral Treasury, Venzone. Many fine crosses were made in the Abruzzi during the 14th and 15th centuries, including the crosses by Niccolò da Guardiagrele for S. Maria Maggiore, Lanciano (1422), and for the Cathedral of Aquila (VI, PL. 265). Venetian work in the 15th century was noted for processional and altar crosses of rock crystal adorned with miniatures. Because of the high quality of their enamelwork, the finest crosses made in northern Europe are those from Limoges. The Gothic and late Gothic Calvary cross depicts the Crucifixion, and the base is shaped to represent Mount Golgotha (sometimes with the skull of Adam) with the figures of the Virgin and St. John. At times these two figures are set on secondary arms branching out from the high stem, as in the cross in the Cathedral of Salzburg, where these branches are formed to imitate tree branches, and in the 15th-century work for the altar of the Baptistery, Florence (VI, PL. 265).

During the Renaissance niello work and more elaborate sculptural decoration, especially of the foot, characterized the production of crosses. Outlines became simpler, forms more static, and the figure of Christ more realistic, as may be seen in the many altar crosses in the Castello Sforzesco, Milan, and in the Treasury of St. Peter's, Rome. While, in this period and the succeeding one, crosses were brought stylistically closer to the other altar furnishings (e.g., candlesticks), in the baroque period there was a return to a more exuberant use of color through the employment of a wide variety of materials, including crystal, *pietra dura*, and coral. Thereafter, forms and decoration gradually became simpler. A notable example in the contemporary production of sacred art is the cross made by Matisse (completed 1951) for the Chapelle du Rosaire in Vence.

f. Altar cards. Since the 16th century the furnishings of the altar have also included the three altar cards that present to the officiant of the Mass certain passages and prayers in the service. The altar cards are generally placed inside a carved and gilded wooden frame. The frames were particularly rich in ornamental motifs in the baroque period, as for example the 17th-century silver repoussé frames in the sacristy of S. Maria della Steccata, Parma. Today the altar cards, notably simplified, are contained in smooth gilded wooden frames or in brass frames.

Other church furnishings. As was the case with the altar, so other objects connected with Christian worship that were derived from secular furniture soon became fixed elements of sacred architecture. Although some of these appurtenances (e.g., the ambo, pulpit, and choir stalls) fall outside the context of liturgical objects and within that of architecture (see STRUCTURAL TYPES AND METHODS), a few may be briefly mentioned here.

The ciborium is of ancient origin as a symbol of cosmic power. It became part of Christian church furnishings in the form of a flat or vaulted canopylike structure supported on vertical elements, according to the tradition of the Byzantine East, which had employed the ciborium as a symbol of imperial dignity. This symbolic canopy, which soon became a fixed stone structure, was originally used in the tombs of particularly venerated saints and probably also in the martyriums of Near Eastern sanctuaries. Its use over the altar seems to have resulted from the spread of the cult of the martyrs, as well as from the entry of symbols of imperial power into the liturgy. In the East, vaulted ciboria are documented by illustrations in Early Christian and Byzantine manuscripts (Vienna Genesis, Vienna, Nationalbib.; Menologion of Basil II, Vat. Lib.; etc.). The fragments of a ciborium from 514–23 found in S. Clemente, Rome, are evidence of its early use in the West. The Romanesque ones have pyramidal roofs and are often decorated with Cosmati work or with sculpture (I, PL. 462).

The baldachin (a term sometimes used interchangeably with "ciborium") is generally a movable canopy consisting of a wooden structure or a wooden armature over which fine fabric is draped. The earliest reference is in a 12th-century manuscript in the Cathedral of Notre-Dame in Paris. The baldachin became common in Europe during the 13th century, being hung from the ceiling or, if the altar was set against a wall, attached to the wall.

Another type of baldachin is used during processions to protect the priest who carries the Eucharist. It has no frame at the top, so that the cloth is directly attached to the four or six supports. Fine 18th-century silk or velvet baldachins embroidered in gold and silk are the property of many churches, including S. Petronio and S. Domenico, Bologna.

The holy-water font (stoup), a basin on a stand for the holy water, is set near the entrance of a church. The font derives from the cantharus (basin) that stood in the atrium of Early Christian basilicas and was used for the purification of the faithful. In the baroque period the font was attached to the wall instead of having its own base. At this time some movable fonts of precious metal were also made.

The baptismal font originally consisted of a large basin at floor level — usually with marble or mosaic trim — with steps leading down into it. As the practice of immersion baptism was abandoned, the font became progressively smaller, taking the form of a large bowl that was either set directly on the floor or supported by a pedestal. The metal fonts made in northern Europe are most impressive, for example, the brass one by Renier de Huy in St-Barthélemy, Liège, dating from the first quarter of the 12th century. It is cylindrical, covered with reliefs, and supported on 12 bulls (V, PL. 319). The later font in the Cathedral of Hildesheim (PL. 167) is wider at the top than at the bottom and is supported by four kneeling allegorical figures. Also worthy of mention is the 14th-century bronze one formerly in the Church of St. Maria in Wismar. Similar examples in wood and stone are preserved in Sweden.

The official position of the cathedra, or bishop's throne, is at the back of the apse. Its shape derives not from the Greek *kathedra* (seat or bench), as its name would seem to indicate, but from the *thronos* (chair of state), and, like the latter, it has a high back and arm rests. Examples of Early Christian cathedras have been preserved in the Basilica Eufrasiana in Parenzo (Poreč), Yugoslavia, and in S. Sabina, Rome. Since most early cathedras were heavy stone structures, the "throne of Maximian" in Ravenna (V, PL. 432) is unique in that it is made up of carved ivory plaques with figures of saints and Old and New Testament scenes. The Cathedra Petri, in St. Peter's, placed by Bernini in a monumental bronze and stucco setting (II, PLS. 135, 275), goes back, at least in part, to the 8th–9th century. Important cathedras of the Romanesque period include those in S. Clemente, S. Balbina (III, PL. 477), S. Lorenzo fuori le Mura (III, PL. 483), and S. Sabina, Rome, as well as the one by Vassalletto in Anagni. Southern Italian cathedras usually have sculptured decoration and are often supported by animals, including elephants (influenced by Islamic art), as in the one made by Romualdus, in the Cathedral of Canosa di Puglia (VIII, PL. 172); caryatids, as in the Throne of Elia, in S. Nicola, Bari (XII, PL. 261); and lions, as in the cathedra in the Cathedral in Calvi.

From the Gothic period few complete cathedras remain. The greater use of wood rather than stone is a contributing factor, as is the practice of placing the altar at the back of the church. Noteworthy is the cathedra of Nicholas IV (reigned 1288–92) in the cloister of St. John Lateran. The flanking columns are twisted, with bands of mosaic inlay, and there are terminating pinnacles. An example of the late Renaissance cathedra is the one of St. Robert Bellarmine in S. Maria in Via, Rome. Though cathedras became less and less important, some wooden ones upholstered with costly fabrics are known from the 18th and 19th centuries, and there are also simpler later examples.

Ritual objects. a. Chalice. The chalice was originally classified according to the ritual functions of consecration of the wine, of administering the Eucharist, and of giving milk and honey to the baptized. Over the centuries the chalice has varied greatly in form and material. An early type with two handles is seen in the fresco of the *Fractio panis* in the Catacomb of Priscilla, Rome (III, PL. 93). This type usually had a thick foot and a flaring upper part, as in the mosaics in S. Vitale and S. Apollinare in Classe, Ravenna.

A second type, which was first made of glass and later of metal, comprises a hemispherical or almost cylindrical cup, without handles, set directly on a small conical foot; this type is documented by the glass chalices depicted in two floor mosaics in the Bardo, Musée Alaoui, in Tunis, and by several metal chalices found in Syria (Br. Mus.; Louvre), as well as by the Chalice of Antioch (PL. 162), decorated with vine scrolls and figures in relief (though it is not certain that this piece had a liturgical use). For a long time the Byzantine Church used both forms simultaneously. In the Treasury of S. Marco in Venice are examples of both types, dating from the 10th–11th century and showing great variety: cups of glass, crystal, onyx, and agate are set in silver-gilt mounts embellished with enamels, niello work, and precious stones. The splendid late-14th-century chalice of Manuel Palaeologus (1391–1425) in the Vatopedi Monastery, Mt. Athos, is a broad, low onyx cup with elegant dragon-shaped handles revealing the reciprocal influence of the two original types.

In the West, too, both types existed until the 10th century, when the type with two handles disappeared. Outstanding early Western chalices with handles include the one from the Gourdon Treasure (Paris, Cabinet des Méd.), which may be from the 6th century; the Ardagh Chalice, possibly dating from the 9th century (I, PL. 285); and the 10th-century chalice of St. Gauzelin (Cathedral of Nancy).

Derived from the handleless Syrian type are the curious wooden chalice in S. Michele, Pavia; the Tassilo Chalice (I, PL. 287); the chalice of St. Chrodegang (8th cent.) in The Hermitage, Leningrad; and the chalice (ca. 10th cent.) from Trewhiddle, Cornwall (Br. Mus.). Until the 13th century the chalice was rather low, with a broad cup and a conical foot inserted directly in the knop. Subsequently the cup became longer and was set on another element; the stem, usually polygonal, became longer, and the knop more prominent and set farther from the polygonal or lobed foot. Early examples of the new style are the silver-gilt Dolgelly chalice in the National Museum of Wales, Cardiff (mid-13th cent.), signed by Nicholas of Hereford; the 14th-century chalice in Klosterneuburg; the chalice of Agilulf and Theodolinda, with a sapphire bowl, from the 6th century (PL. 163); and some Spanish chalices of the period, executed with great liberty of invention. Noteworthy French and Italian chalices were produced, the former including the chalice of St. Remi (PL. 160). Among the outstanding Italian works are those made in Siena, including the one Guccio di Mannaia executed in 1290 for Nicholas IV (Assisi, S. Francesco, Treasury), one by Cataluccio da Todi (Perugia, Gall. Naz. dell'Umbria), a chalice by Giovanni di Jacopo (Messina, Cathedral), and one by Ciccarello di Francesco (PL. 163). The chalice presented to the Cathedral of Monza by Gian Galeazzo Visconti in 1396 exemplifies an important innovation that was to become comparatively common during the next century: the knop comprises a group of miniature Gothic tabernacles. There are numerous 15th-century chalices characterized by a richer repertory of decorative motifs.

The Renaissance saw the establishment of the conventional chalice — a bell-shaped cup set into a bulb, a tall smooth stem with a knop in a variety of forms, and a flared lobed foot. Decoration of enamel, gems, and other polychrome elements was replaced by sculptural motifs (e.g., foliage, figures) that are an integral part of the metal structure. Outside Italy at this time Gothic elements continued to appear, for example, in the chalices in the Cathedral of Wrocław (Breslau) and in St. Andreas in Düsseldorf.

In 17th-century baroque chalices the emphasis on three-dimensional decorative motifs is much greater, and sometimes color plays an important part, as may be seen in the gold and enamel chalice of the Emperor Ferdinand III in the Abbey of Monserrat. In harmony with the general trends of the 18th century, ornament on chalices became lighter (e.g., the Stuart chalice, in the Treasury of St. Peter's, Rome). Modern works comprise greatly simplified forms, and ornament is reduced to a few traditional Eucharistic symbols such as the wheatstalk and the grape cluster. Noteworthy examples are the chalice designed by Karl Holey in the Abbey of Zwettl (Austria), and the one in the Treasury of St. Peter's, with a spherical bowl decorated with diamonds and rubies, made by Nottbrock in 1933 and presented by the Prince of Wittelsbach.

b. Paten. Chalice and paten form a pair of liturgical objects. The paten is a round, flat plate or shallow vessel with a broad rim. In early times it varied considerably in size, form, and use; this contributes to the difficulty of ascertaining which of the surviving plates were meant for ritual use. Perhaps the earliest examples were glass, as suggested by the 14th-century gilded glass dish from Cologne (London, Br. Mus.) and the few unclear depictions in Ravenna mosaics. Among the earliest metal examples are those from Syria, with crosses, busts, and figures in niello or relief (paten with the Communion of the Apostles, from Stuma; PL. 162), those from Constantinople and Cyprus (two patens with monograms, from the Lampsacus Treasure; London, Br. Mus.), and others from Canoscio, Carthage, and Nicosia. The larger ones, however, were probably intended for the offerings of the congregation and are not true patens. Byzantine art produced notable patens with figural decoration, including the Halberstadt paten (PL. 162), with the Crucifixion depicted; that of Pulcheria, in the Monastery of Xiropotamou, adorned with reliefs in ophite; and numerous others in glass, agate, onyx, and alabaster, with silver settings, adorned with pearls, precious stones, and sacred inscriptions (several in the Treasury of S. Marco, Venice; PL. 162). The Treasury of S. Marco also preserves a curious glass paten (10th–11th century) with a silver handle set with gems. Later the Eastern Church developed a special type of paten set on a high foot or pedestal. This was the panagiarion, used for the holy wafers (PL. 173). In the West the usual form was a round plate with a lobed central section that was frequently decorated with a niello or enamel bust of Christ, the Hand of God, or the Lamb of God. The 10th-century paten of St. Gauzelin in the Cathedral of Nancy is an outstanding example. The *Liber Pontificalis* mentions patens of precious metal that were even hexagonal, and a rectangular paten with a cross in the center and a border of glass paste and other types of stones was found with the Gourdon chalice (Paris, Bib. Nat.). Later, patens were produced as mates to chalices and were decorated with motifs from the same repertory, as in the examples in St. Godehard, Hildesheim, from the late 12th century; in the Cathedral of Worcester, from about 1250, showing the Hand of God; the one belonging to the Dolgelly chalice in the National Museum of Wales, Cardiff, with a figure of Christ enthroned; and the one with a Crucifixion that belongs with the Spanish Pelagius chalice of the 13th century (Paris, Louvre). Most Italian patens of the period are less ornate, and many even lack the lobed area, for example, the mate to the so-called "Chalice of St. Francis," in Assisi, Treasury of S. Francesco, and an enameled one in S. Lorenzo, Scala. More elaborate is the paten that belongs with the chalice by Cataluccio da Todi, in Perugia (Gall. Naz. dell'Umbria). In modern times patens have become smaller and are usually unadorned, as are contemporary chalices.

c. Pyx. The pyx, which holds the reserved Sacrament, has undergone extensive modifications of form over the centuries. Early Christian pyxes were usually small cylindrical boxes (with flat lids) carved of bone or ivory (VIII, PL. 240). Numerous Syrian and Egyptian examples dating from the 4th through the 6th century are known. Also used as pyxes, particularly in the succeeding period, were boxes that were intended to hold incense, decorated with secular scenes. Small silver capsae were also used and, later, so were cylindrical boxes of wood or ivory, of Islamic workmanship. According to the *Liber Pontificalis*, the pyx was kept in a *turres*, of unknown form and origin.

For a time pyxes in the shape of a dove were suspended above the altar by a chain from the ciborium. Perhaps the earliest date from the 10th century. Metal examples are preserved in S. Nazaro Maggiore, Milan (13th cent.), Sto Sepolcro, Barletta (12th cent.), and in Paris (PL. 164), as well as in the Museo Nazionale, Florence, and the monastery in Göttweig, Austria (both 12th cent.). In 11th–12th-century frescoes there are pyxes in the form of two-handled vases suspended over the altar in place of the dove-shaped ones. At the beginning of the 13th century the workshops of Limoges were producing cylindrical pyxes with conical enameled lids. Later in the 13th century the pyx began to resemble the chalice, in that it was given a broader spherical bowl set directly on a conical foot, and either a conical or spherical lid terminating in a small cross or knop. (When the container for the reserved Sacrament is of this kind, it is generally called a "ciborium.") Among the earliest examples are the one from Montmajour, signed by G. Alpais (PL. 171), and one in the British Museum; both are decorated with enamels and gems. During the 15th and 16th centuries the pyx sometimes took the form of the Gothic *tempietto* with features of the monstrances used in the Ambrosian rite. Thereafter, pyxes came to resemble chalices more closely in style and form but retained the crowning cross and large broad bowl.

d. Monstrance (ostensorium). The monstrance is another type of container for the Sacrament and one of the latest additions to the liturgical vessels, having been introduced only in the 14th century with the Feast of Corpus Christi. Most of the few extant medieval examples are shaped like the architectural Gothic reliquary and are supported by a tall stem with a knop and flared foot clearly derived from contemporary chalices. Examples of this first type of monstrance, which was soon discarded and continued in use only in the Ambrosian rite, are in the Cathedral of Seo de Urgel (PL. 166); S. Ambrogio, Milan; the Castello Sforzesco, Milan; and the cathedrals of Rossano and Benevento. In Renaissance monstrances the architectural elements resemble those of the contemporary *tempietto*. Gothic pinnacles, spires, and buttresses are replaced by delicate columns, tympanums, and cupolas, as may be seen in examples in S. Antonio, Peia, and S. Pancrazio, Corlaga. Ambrosian monstrances made in Spain and Sicily in the 14th century are impressive architectural creations that often reach a height of 6 or 7 ft. In the 15th century another type of monstrance was introduced in the Roman liturgy. In place of the *tempietto* its terminal had a glory of golden rays, which was sometimes adorned with enamels and gems. Early examples of this second and extremely popular type are in the Musée de Cluny, Paris; the Museo dell'Opera del Duomo, Siena (both PL. 166); S. Domenico, Palermo; and the Museo Pepoli, Trapani. In many later examples the stem represents saints or angels who support the glory, as may be seen in monstrances in the Residenzmuseum, Munich (PL. 166), S. Luca in Padua, S. Giovanni in Stilo, and the Cathedral of Castel di Sangro. Baroque monstrances are more complex and have more variety in their decorative motifs (II, PL. 219), but the basic forms of both types remain the same. During the 17th and 18th centuries such renowned goldsmiths as Giuseppe Filiberti, Angelo Spinazzi, and Sebastiano Juvara made splendid monstrances with rich plant motifs around the glory and with adoring angels. Outstanding examples of that period are in the Church of S. Alessandro della Croce, Bergamo; S. Lazzaro, Piacenza; Monte Vergine, Messina; and the Museo Diocesano in Palermo. With neoclassicism monstrances became more austere, but the basic scheme of that used in the Roman liturgy remained the same.

e. Ampulla. The cruets for the wine and water, holy oils, and aromatic essences used in the Mass resemble similar contemporary vessels for daily use. They usually have a narrow neck, amphora-shaped body, and a handle. In Early Christian times the wine offered for the sacrifice was kept in amulas, elegant small amphoras, usually of metal. Some silver examples survive that were probably made in Syria and Cyprus. One in the Vatican Museums is decorated with a band of busts in medallions and may date from the 5th century. Other receptacles serving the same function and with similar decoration, though without handles, include a vase from Emesa (mod. Homs; Paris, Louvre) and small rectangular glass flasks with crosses in relief on the sides (e.g., one in London, Br. Mus.). Designed for keeping the holy oils were the *eulogiae*, which were usually small flasks of a squat spherical shape, in silvered lead or terra cotta, with stamped inscriptions; there are many examples from Palestine now in collections in Monza and Bobbio. These flasks, dating from the 6th–7th century, bear depictions of the Crucifixion, the Exaltation of the Cross, the Anastasis, or the Ascension, among others, and are of immense interest for the study of traditions of iconography. Other examples bear the image of a saint with the symbol of martyrdom or with a cross, since the oils held in these receptacles were taken from the lamps that burned at the sepulchers of certain saints. Many Byzantine examples of the 10th and 11th centuries are in S. Marco in Venice. These include pieces made of glass, agate, and onyx with silver mounts. They vary considerably in shape, some being small squat vessels, others elongated ewers of fanciful silhouette. Noteworthy Renaissance examples include a pair in the Louvre, for water and wine; of Venetian workmanship, they are made of crystal with mounts of silver and handles in the form of dragons. In modern times the form and decoration have varied only slightly.

f. Aquamanile and basin. The aquamanile, similar in form to the ampulla, but of different size and material, holds the water for the washing of the priest's hands during the Mass. Its liturgical application is very old, although it is difficult to identify early examples, since secular vessels were probably also employed in the Mass. But it is certain that a heavy, dark bronze amphora from S. Lorenzo, Rome (11th cent.?; Vat. Mus.), is a liturgical object, as is a 10th-century Islamic aquamanile of rock crystal in the Victoria and Albert Museum, London. In S. Marco are preserved fine large Byzantine aquamaniles of crystal, agate, and onyx. In the Romanesque period the Rhine workshops produced aquamaniles in the shape of lions and fantastic animals, and some of them were undoubtedly used in churches, for example, the one from the Cathedral of Grado (Viterbo, Mus. Civ.). The most important workshops were located in the Rhineland, at Limoges, and at Dinant (PL. 164). The aquamanile in the form of a horse with rider was an additional design later introduced by the Dinant workshops. The design of the basin that caught the used water was always comparatively simple. Among the oldest basins is the 15th-century example of German workmanship in the Cathedral of Atri.

In the Renaissance the basin and aquamanile, reserved for pontifical and special Masses, were heavier and were adorned with chased or repoussé floral motifs and figures. Notable examples of basins of the baroque, neoclassic, and modern periods are preserved in the Treasury of St. Peter's, Rome, and in the Museo dell'Opera del Duomo, Siena.

g. Liturgical spoon. The liturgical spoon had various uses in the old liturgy — adding water to the wine in the chalice, taking the Host from its container, filtering the wine from the ampulla into the chalice (in this case, a perforated spoon), and administering the Sacrament. Spoons seem to have been used during Communion in Syria by the 7th century; from there their use spread to Constantinople and became a part of the Greek Orthodox rite. Therefore it is difficult to ascertain the specific function of the many spoons found in the various treasures that have come to light, or even to be certain that all of them had a liturgical use (for example, the spoons found at Kyrenia in Cyprus), although some bear Christian inscriptions (e.g., spoons dated 360–400 in Dorchester, Dorset County Mus.). The handle is usually thin, and the concave part is elongated (e.g., those from Carthage, now Br. Mus.) or elliptical; they bore the names of the apostles (e.g., those from the Lampsacus Treasure, Br. Mus.). Pierced spoons, or strainers, were used until the 17th century. Noteworthy examples include those of gilded silver from the Traprain Treasure (Edinburgh, Nat. Mus. of Antiquities of Scotland). The golden spoon known as the "Coronation Spoon" (perhaps 12th cent.), in the Tower of London, seems to have had a liturgical function. The late medieval examples with the Madonna and apostles depicted on the handle were secular objects and also served as Christmas gifts.

h. Offering basin. As early as the 5th and 6th centuries there were large disk-shaped vessels that, because of their repoussé decoration, cannot be considered plates or patens. They were probably used for collecting the Host. Rather large bronze basins, produced by Rhine workshops in the 12th century, bear holy scenes and stories of the saints (with inscriptions). Many examples are preserved in several German museums and in the British Museum. Also designed to collect offerings (but not strictly related to the liturgy) are vessels of nonprecious metals (e.g., pewter), adorned with repoussé crosses or busts of Christ and saints. These have been produced throughout western and central Europe in modern times.

i. Reliquary. Of various forms and materials, the reliquary, a container for holy relics, owes its origin and extreme popularity to the cult of the martyrs (see DEVOTIONAL OBJECTS AND IMAGES). There are ancient Syrian examples in the form of small stone sarcophagi. These sometimes had holes for oil, which was later distributed among the worshipers. An example is the reliquary of Sokahni (Syria), from which is derived a small urn in the Cathedral museum, Verona; this urn has small arches and is decorated with affronted peacocks (second half of 6th cent.). When reliquaries became smaller, boxes of precious material were used. Some of these were of secular origin and bore pagan depictions of the Roman theater. The most common type of Early Christian reliquary was the small casket or coffer. Among the many extant examples are the ivory casket generally referred to as the "Lipsanotheca of Brescia" (VIII, PL. 240); the 5th-century cylindrical gold container found under the altar in Pulj, and the chased silver casket with busts in medallions and with inscriptions, in the Cathedral of Grado (5th cent.). Fourth-century examples in the form of a cross, elaborately worked, are preserved in the Vatican Museums. Byzantine gold- and silverworkers created the various *staurothekes*, reliquaries in the form of a small richly adorned chest containing a gold cross, inside which is preserved a relic of the Cross (e.g., enameled examples in the cathedrals of Limburg an der Lahn, 10th cent., and Esztergom, or Gran, Hungary).

Smaller but no less admirable are the 13th-century enameled medallions containing relics (e.g., in Washington, D.C., Dumbarton Oaks Coll.). Reliquaries were designed in various forms in the Middle Ages. The most common type in the West was the small chest or coffer of fine metal with repoussé or niello ornamention and decorated with enamels and gems.

In Germany in the 12th–13th century fine reliquaries were produced in the form of miniature temples with Byzantine and Romanesque-Gothic architectural elements. Examples include that of St. Victor, in Xanten (1129), by Master Eilbertus; the so-called "Tower Reliquary" in Darmstadt, Landesmuseum; the Three Kings reliquary (VI, PL. 388; X, PL. 316); and one in the Treasury of the Cathedral of Aachen (completed before 1238). The architectural type of reliquary was also used in Italy, beginning in the 13th century; it had decidedly Gothic elements. Noteworthy examples include the one containing garments of St. Francis (Assisi, Treasury of S. Francesco); the reliquary in the Treasury of S. Nicola, Bari; that in Savona Cathedral; and the Reliquary of the Holy Corporal, in Orvieto (VI, PL. 382). In addition, there are traditional reliquaries in the form of chests and crosses (e.g., in the Treasury of S. Maria Assunta, Padua; the reliquary of the Tree of the Cross, in Lucignano, Mus. Civ.). Another type created in this period, one which enjoyed great popularity later, is the bust reliquary of a saint, with a small aperture on the chest. Bust reliquaries were generally made of gilt and painted wood, sometimes of metal. The most noteworthy include the bust reliquaries of St. Agatha (Catania, Cathedral), St. John Gualbertus (Passignano, Badia), St. Zenobius (Florence, Cathedral), St. Januarius (Naples, Cathedral), St. Ermagora (Gorizia, Cathedral), and St. Donatus (Cividale, Cathedral), in which characteristics of the various regional schools of sculpture are evident. In France bust reliquaries were used at least as early as the 13th century. These were produced in the Limoges workshops and include that of St. Baudime (church at Saint-Nectaire) and others in the British Museum; they are richly enameled. In the metal reliquaries produced in the workshops of the Rhine and the Meuse, the architectural element was ever more important. Later, French influence caused this element to be reduced in favor of figural work. Rectangular or polygonal reliquaries, of ivory or metal, continued to be produced throughout the 15th century (e.g., examples in S. Petronio, Bologna, and S. Nicola, Bari). More common in this period were reliquaries of glass or precious metal in the form of a chalice, or *theca*, supported by angels and ornamented with motifs derived from contemporary architectural forms (e.g., the reliquary of St. Louis, King of France, Florence, Mus. degli Argenti, and many others in the Treasury of S. Marco, Venice).

Reliquaries in the form of a Renaissance *tempietto* or tabernacle, made in Italy during the 15th and 16th centuries, are important in relation to the major artistic trends of the time. Outstanding examples include the reliquary of the "Libretto" (Florence, Mus. dell'Opera del Duomo); the reliquary containing the wedding ring of the Virgin, in the Cathedral of Perugia; and the numerous creations of a certain Pietro of Padua and of Bartolommeo da Bologna. A comparable Spanish piece is the early-16th-century reliquary in the Cathedral of Cádiz. Other types of reliquaries were made in the 16th century, especially "anatomical" ones, such as polychromed busts (e.g., in S. Maria Novella, Florence) and other parts of the body (e.g., arm reliquary of St. Magnus and leg reliquary of St. Theodore, both in Treasury of S. Marco, Venice). During the baroque period small coffers were the most common type, and they were given rich carved and painted decoration. Heavy, ornamented thecas and amphora-shaped reliquaries carried by angels were also common. Later reliquaries were usually in imitation of baroque models, but traditional coffer and urn-shaped reliquaries continued to be produced.

j. Bell. Liturgical bells are here distinguished from other bells on the basis of origin and decorative motifs. The practice of ringing a bell to emphasize certain parts of the Mass became usual during the 13th century, although it must have been fairly common earlier. The oldest bell that is known to have been used in the church services is a bronze bell (12th cent.) in the Cathedral of Reims, bearing the symbols of the Evangelists. Liturgical bells dating from the 15th–16th century are preserved in the Cathedral Treasury, Monza, and in the Castello Sforzesco, Milan. The liturgical bell ranges in shape from a truncated cone (the most common type) to a hemisphere; a few are even square. Various materials were used, including gold, silver, bronze, copper, and iron; there are also examples in glass, porcelain, and terra cotta. A double or multiple bell, a form which is still in use today, is called a *cymbalum*. Good examples of various kinds of bells are in the Museo Nazionale in Florence, the Victoria and Albert Museum in London, and the Treasury of St. Peter's in Rome.

k. Censer (*thurible*). The burning of incense was taken over from pagan cults at an early date. The first Christian censers, small metal containers with or without lids, are known from Early Christian representations. According to the *Liber Pontificalis*, Constantine the Great donated fine metal censers to the Church of St. John Lateran. A cylindrical censer without a lid and hanging by three chains is depicted in the mosaics of S. Vitale, Ravenna (II, PL. 440). Eastern and Byzantine censers are usually potbellied vases on low round pedestals, or small hexagonal containers without feet, and are suspended from chains; an example is the hexagonal 6th-century silver censer from Cyprus (Br. Mus.), with a bust in a medallion on each face. A few censers with long straight handles are also known. In the West very simple censers of geometric form, sometimes spherical, were used until the 11th century. Occasionally censers were made in the form of a human being or imaginary animal, with floral motifs in repoussé; such pieces never had covers. An outstanding 12th-century example of this type is the hemispherical censer in Lille (Mus. B.A.), attributed to Renier de Huy or a follower. In another type that became important during the Romanesque period and continued throughout the Gothic, the lid was transformed into an architectural structure that, according to Theophilus (*Schedula diversarum artium*, III, lx, lxi), is a symbolic allusion to the ideal structures of the Heavenly Jerusalem. Examples of this type, adorned with tympanums and small perforated turrets, and sometimes decorated with plant motifs and the symbols of the Evangelists, were made in the metal workshops of northern Europe. Two elaborate 12th-century censer tops in the British Museum show that the type had also spread to England. All extant examples are of bronze, some gilded, but early inventories indicate that gold and silver censers were also made. From the 13th century on, the covers (set on hemispherical vases) became more decidedly Gothic, with spires and pinnacles, as may be seen in the Ramsey Abbey Censer (PL. 165) and those in the Cathedral Treasury, Mileto (late 14th cent.), in the Cathedral of Rossano (15th cent.), and in S. Antonio, Padua. Censers frequently are depicted in 14th- and 15th-century painting and sculpture: in the tomb sculpture by Arnolfo di Cambio in St. John Lateran (I, PL. 465) an acolyte is seen blowing into one; singing angels are often shown holding them. Censers are also used as decorative motifs on marble sepulchral monuments, altars, and tabernacles. Renaissance architectural elements supplanted Gothic ones by the 16th century, as may be seen in the censer in S. Giovanni, Stilo, and the one attributed to the workshop of Benvenuto Cellini, in the Cathedral of Fidenza. In the baroque period the repertory of architectural and ornamental motifs used in censers was enriched. Noteworthy 17th-century examples are those in the cathedrals of Fidenza and Rossano. The 18th-century censer and incense boat of chased and gilded silver in Bologna (Metropolitana; PL. 165) and the set in S. Maria Maddalena, Norano Calabro, are also of interest. The traditional censer with various kinds of covers and supported on chains is still commonly used in liturgical ceremonies.

l. Incense boat. The incense boat, a metal receptacle for carrying incense, usually accompanies the censer and is decorated with the same motifs. In Early Christian times cylindrical ivory boxes (acerras) of pagan origin and tradition were used as incense boats. Later, long flat metal boxes were used, each with a small foot, first without lids, then with lids. Their resemblance to a boat has led to the suggestion that they symbolize the Church. The earliest extant examples are very simple pieces made of base metals. More interesting are those shown held by angels in many Romanesque reliefs. A fine Byzantine work is the incense boat of sardonyx and mother-of-pearl in the Treasury of S. Marco, Venice. In the Renaissance the form of the incense boat corresponded more and more to that of an actual boat. Some works are faithful to such details as masts and rigging, for example, the 15th-century Venetian incense boat in the Museo Antoniano, Padua, and the early-16th-century gilded-silver and mother-of-pearl boat in the Treasury of the Cathedral of Chartres (PL. 165). This type of incense boat, simplified and adapted to meet practical needs, has continued in use to the present day.

m. Aspergillum and aspersorium. It is one of the oldest Christian rites to sprinkle objects and people with holy water. In the Early Christian period a branch of olive, hyssop, myrtle, or laurel was simply dipped into the holy water, and for certain ceremonies this is still the practice. Metal aspergilla, being more practical and convenient, were gradually adopted. These consisted of a long handle, usually metal, that terminated in either a pierced sphere or a clump of white bristles. This fundamental type continues to be used, having undergone only minor alterations.

Aspergilla from various periods, together with their buckets, have been preserved in the Treasury of the Sé Nova (New Cathedral), Coimbra, Portugal.

The holy water is kept in a bucket (aspersorium) that serves as a portable holy-water font. The oldest extant examples (10th cent.) are of ivory. They are rather squat and round, as is the one in the Treasury of the Cathedral of Milan, with figures of the Virgin and the Evangelists. The 11th-century one, from the time of Otto III, in the Cathedral of Aachen is octagonal with two registers of figures on each face and is decorated with gold mounts. The handles were usually in the form of affronted or addorsed dragons, serpents, and other animals. From the 11th century on, aspersoria were almost always metal (steel, silver, bronze, copper) but occasionally *pietra dura*. Outstanding examples are the bronze bucket in the Cathedral of Speyer (12th cent.); one of glass in the Treasury of S. Marco (13th cent.); and porphyry and jasper buckets in the Louvre and elsewhere. Gothic buckets are larger and more soberly decorated (figural depiction is rare) and are of more varied forms. Many have the shape of small cooking pots and are set on a heavy circular base or on three small feet, sometimes in the form of animal heads or claws; the handles are frequently trilobed. The most common material at this time was brass. There are outstanding 15th-century examples in the Louvre. Precious metals were also used, and a silver bucket has been preserved in the Museo dell'Opera del Duomo, Siena. During the Renaissance especially fine bronze pieces were made in Italy, among them the 16th-century Venetian one in the Museo Nazionale, Florence, and the one of jasper in the Louvre (VI, PL. 267). The baroque employed more complex forms and a greater variety of materials (including majolica), which were set in carved silver mounts. The traditional potbellied metal bucket, however, became the established type and is still in use.

n. Oil lamp and spirit lamp. Various kinds of lamps, suspended on chains or attached to the wall, have been used since early times during liturgical ceremonies. In the Early Christian period the most common type was the *polycandelon* — a large bronze disk, with several holes for glass oil dishes, that was suspended on chains. The British Museum preserves a noteworthy example dating from the late 6th century. In the Museo Archeologico in Florence are numerous 4th–5th-century lamps, for the most part of bronze, including clay oil lamps used in the catacombs; classic oil lamps with handles; box-shaped lamps with a single or double hinge, ornate handles, and several spouts; and more elaborate lamps in the form of a boat with figures of Christ and Moses. Other box-shaped lamps were held on supports very like candlesticks, with feet in the form of animals, a long stem with several knops, and a broad plate with a point in the middle. Their exact use, however, is not known. A curious hemispherical lamp found at S. Martino ai Monti, Rome, may date from the 5th–6th century. Made of silver foil, perforated and with braided decoration, and with holes for suspension chains, it was designed to hold a glass oil vessel. In the Romanesque period the extensive use of metal lamps in the form of vases, amphoras, crowns, and other objects is documented by depictions in frescoes and miniatures, as well as by actual examples that have survived, including a fine 11th-century work in gilded silver and glass in the Treasury of S. Marco, Venice. This collection also contains numerous contemporaneous Byzantine examples in glass and crystal. The unique pieces in the Cathedral of Aachen and in the Church of St. Maurice, Coburg, were inspired by the imaginary architecture of the Heavenly Jerusalem and depict a wall with gates and towers; they may date from the 12th century. The lead lamp in S. Maria Maggiore, Barletta, has the form of a plate with holes and is adorned with palmettes. It derives from the *polycandelon* type, which continued to be used in the Byzantine Church. In the Gothic period suspended lamps were made of finer materials and were more elaborately decorated. The Treasury of S. Marco preserves 13th–14th-century works in glass, alabaster, and ivory set in silver mounts with precious stones, as well as a fine collection of 15th-century Venetian lamps in blown glass and openwork brass. Renaissance lamps, almost always of bronze, were created in a variety of forms. There are examples by excellent artists in the Museo Nazionale in Florence and in S. Marco, Venice. In the 16th century oil and spirit lamps began to be replaced by more efficient chandeliers with several lights. The so-called "chandelier of Galileo" in the Cathedral of Pisa is famous. In modern times lamps continue to be used, although much less extensively because of modern lighting techniques. By specific liturgical requirement, suspended lamps of traditional form continue to burn votive oil in front of altars of the Holy Sacrament. Modern works include the lamp of gold and precious stones by Pio Castellani (1870), in the Treasury of St. Peter's, and the one by Alberto Gerardi (1935) in the Church of Gethsemane in Jerusalem.

o. Flabellum. Another instrument that early entered liturgical use is the flabellum, or fan, a disk on a long handle that was used in order to keep flies away from the Eucharist. The earliest extant examples date from the 9th century, but the flabellum was certainly used earlier. Greek-rite flabella, known as "rhipidions," are all metal, silver for the most part, and cherubim heads are engraved on the disk. The two flabella (12th–13th cent.) in the Cathedral of Seres (Macedonia) were even enhanced with enamels. Metal flabella were also used in the West, for example, those in the Cathedral of Hildesheim, in Angers, and at Kremsmünster. Often the disk was replaced by a piece of silk or linen, by parchment, or, more frequently, by feathers. At the same time carved bone or ivory came to be used for the handle in place of gilded silver. One of the most important ivory-handled examples is the flabellum of Tournus (PL. 174). By the end of the 14th century flabella had nearly gone out of use; in modern times they are used only in pontifical Masses in the Greek and Armenian rites and are of symbolic significance. The modern flabellum consists of a fan of two rows of ostrich and peacock feathers on a long handle covered with crimson velvet and adorned with a gold band.

p. Lectern. In Early Christian times the function of the lectern was served by an inclined slab set on the ambo. In the Romanesque period the function was performed by a support in the shape of the symbolic eagle, incorporated into the pulpit. There was no lectern on the altar, the text being placed directly on the altar. The lectern as a distinct object was adopted only later for common reading and prayer in the monasteries and there formed part of the wooden choir. There were also metal lecterns (iron, bronze) with bases similar to those used for monumental candlesticks. This type of lectern was the specialty of the workshops of Dinant from the late 14th century on; there are examples in many French and German cathedrals. In the Gothic period works of outstanding beauty were created in carved wood, with elegant intarsia, such as those in S. Orso in Aosta and in the Pinacoteca Nazionale in Lucca. In Italy 15th-century lecterns often took on architectural forms, as in the one designed by Baccio d'Agnolo for S. Pietro in Perugia. Renaissance lecterns are more complex in design and decoration (PL. 170); this trend was, of course, more pronounced in the baroque period. In addition to the monumental lecterns in the choir, lighter but no less elaborate ones were also used, for example, the 17th-century one in the Museo Nazionale di Antichità, Parma. In later centuries the large immovable lectern became less common, in part because of the smaller dimensions of later choir books and liturgical texts. More common was the altar lectern, a simpler structure of carved and gilded wood which is still used.

q. Faldistory. The faldistory, or faldstool (from Old High German, *faldstuol*), is a folding chair of metal, wood, or ivory, used as the seat of a bishop within the chancel. The folding chair itself is derived from Roman types known chiefly through reliefs and coins. Notable faldistories include the six examples discovered in the necropolis of Nocera Umbra, as well as the so-called "Throne of Dagobert" (III, PL. 68), and the *sella plicatilis* discovered in Pavia and dated to the 8th–9th century. When the position of the altar was finally established against the rear wall, with the episcopal throne flanking the altar, the faldistory was abandoned. Today it is used only in certain churches for the reading of the litany.

Vestments and sacerdotal insignia. This section will be limited to a short catalogue of the most important liturgical garments and insignia; for further discussion see COSTUME (especially FIG. 45) and EMBLEMS AND INSIGNIA.

a. Alb. The alb is one of the oldest and most traditional liturgical garments. It is a long white linen tunic with long sleeves and derives from the Roman *tunica talaris*, which was especially popular in the eastern provinces. The only changes it has undergone through the years are those in the decoration and some minor variations in the cut. During the Early Christian period it was undecorated. Later it was adorned with bands and rectangles of colored or embroidered cloth called "apparels." At first these were dyed a solid color, most often purple, and consisted of vertical strips called "clavi," one over each shoulder reaching nearly to the hem, as well as edging of gold and silk embroidery at the neck, wrists, and hem. The edging later took the form of rectangular patches. At the same time the body of the alb became fuller (IV, PL. 10). In the 16th century there was a reaction against the colorful embroidery, and it was replaced by white lace. A colored ground matching the vestments of the celebrant is now permitted beneath the appliquéd lace.

b. Surplice. The surplice, a later transformation of the alb, is a white linen or cotton gown, shorter and more ample than the alb, with long wide sleeves. It is worn not only by priests but also by attendants at the Mass. It seems to have been introduced during the 11th century in England, France, and Spain, and later spread to the rest of Europe. During the 16th century it was given ruffles and tucks, and in the 17th lace edging and embroideries were added.

c. Rochet. The rochet is another variation of the alb and differs from the surplice in that it has narrow sleeves. A long unornamented rochet, documented since the 11th century, was worn by all medieval prelates and clerics. During the Renaissance lace was added at the neck and wrists; from that time only the higher clergy were permitted to wear it. It was worn under the mozzetta, a short, hooded cape.

d. Dalmatic. The dalmatic derives from a garment of the same name adopted by Roman patricians during the late-antique period. In the 3d century it became the daily habit of bishops. It was then a loose garment, reaching just below the knee, and had wide sleeves; it also had clavi and bands around the sleeves. When it became a vestment, it was worn by all the clergy, and the clavi and bands were woven in with purple thread. During the early Middle Ages the dalmatic was almost always white, as may be seen in the paintings and mosaics of the period (Ravenna; Milan, S. Maria presso S. Satiro). By the 10th century colored cloth was used in many countries, though in Italy white prevailed. During the Romanesque period the dalmatic became more ample, flaring below the arms, and by the 14th century the sleeves were often wider at the wrist than at the shoulder. At the same time more valuable textiles, rich colors, and embroidery were used (IV, PL. 10). In the late 12th century, when the canonical colors were established, the dalmatic began to be dyed to match the other vestments. The most important Renaissance change was the enlargement of the neck opening and the addition of two tasseled cords to close it. Since then the dalmatic has changed little.

e. Tunicle. The tunicle is a liturgical overgarment derived from the ancient tunic and is similar to the dalmatic but narrower and with longer sleeves. As a liturgical vestment it was distinctive of subdeacons in Rome in the 6th century. Although abolished by Pope Gregory the Great, it was reintroduced in the 8th century to be worn under the chasuble by bishops and the Pope, but it again went out of use at the end of the Middle Ages.

f. Girdle. The girdle is a later version of the belt worn with the ancient tunic and has been used to belt sacerdotal tunics since Early Christian times. Because it was part of the vestments and had been established in the liturgy as a symbol of chastity, it became a precious ornament during the Middle Ages. Usually it was a long silk band studded with gold and gems or richly embroidered. Now it is thought of only as a functional object and is usually merely a cord with tassels at the ends.

g. Amice. The amice is a rectangular piece of white linen worn over the alb, around the neck and shoulders. It is kept in place by two cords passed under the arms, crossed in back, and tied in front. Its origins are not clear, but it has belonged to the liturgical vestments since the end of the 8th century. It is worn during some rites, and in the 13th–16th centuries it also served as a hood. Its border was often richly embroidered and even enhanced with gold and gems, as in the two embroideries, embossed and covered with seed pearls, preserved in the Church of St. Mary, Gdańsk. Although it has not lost its double function, it is now given its simpler early form.

h. Chasuble. The chasuble is an outer garment, a full, calf-length cloak derived from the ancient paenula. It was included among the liturgical vestments in the 5th or 6th century, as may be seen from the mosaics in Ravenna and in S. Agnese, Rome, and from the frescoes in the Catacombs of S. Pancrazio, Rome. From the 12th century on, the officiating priest wore a chasuble. Romanesque chasubles were usually of fine stuffs of solid color with an allover design. Richly embroidered examples from this period have survived, for instance, those in the Treasury of the Cathedral of Bamberg — one of the 11th century with figures in medallions, another depicting the stars and constellations — as well as a later one known as the "Hungarian coronation mantle."

The cut of the chasuble gradually changed. The early type, generally referred to as the "bell chasuble," was made from a semicircular piece of cloth. After the 13th century it became narrower and was open at the sides, giving the arms greater freedom. Finally, it was so narrow at the shoulders that this type came to be called a "fiddleback chasuble." Many different kinds of cloth were used — wool, linen, cotton, silk — and the designs were as varied, the more common being geometric, floral, and even animal motifs (the last introduced from the East). From the 11th century on, the chasuble was decorated with the orphrey, a broad vertical band divided into two or three branches at the top, suggesting a cross. The orphrey is usually richly embroidered, often with religious scenes and with gold and silver threads and even pearls and gems. The present-day chasuble is usually of embroidered silk, and its background color is determined by the colors assigned to the feasts and by the Ordinary of the Mass. Outstanding medieval and Renaissance chasubles are in the church at Sankt Paul im Lavanttal in Carinthia; in the Cathedrals of Erfurt, Halberstadt, Fermo, and Pistoia; in the Cathedral Treasury of Anagni; in St. Mary's, Gdańsk; in the Museo dell'Opera del Duomo, Siena; and in S. Maria in Vallicella, Rome.

i. Cope. The cope is an ample cloak of semicircular shape that is usually richly adorned, often with motifs or figures repeated in an allover pattern. It is known to have been used as a liturgical vestment by the 10th century. Originally it differed from the standard bell chasuble only in that it was open in front and had a hood. There have been almost no changes in its cut. The only alteration was in the hood, which lost its function after the 12th century and, during the 14th and 15th, became a flat ornamental panel; at first this panel was triangular, but later it was shaped like a heraldic shield, usually edged with a gold fringe, and bore a tassel at the bottom. There are outstanding examples in the Victoria and Albert Museum, London; Sankt Paul im Lavanttal, Carinthia; the Schatzkammer, Vienna; and the Museo Civico, Bologna. The cope was closed at the neck by a brooch. During the late Middle Ages and the Renaissance such brooches were often very large and ornate examples of the finest goldsmithery. Frequently religious scenes were illustrated on them, as in a Gothic example with the Annunciation, in the Cathedral in Aachen. Others had only a single figure, often a saint, or heraldic motifs. During the 13th century another sort of fastening was devised for the cope. This was the morse, an embroidered rectangle that was sewn to one side of the cope and fastened to the other.

j. Maniple. The maniple is an embroidered band of cloth which derives from the Roman *mappa*, or *mappula*, a cloth that served as a napkin and as an insigne of office for consuls and other officials. It is recorded as a liturgical item in the early Middle Ages, but neither its form nor its function is certain. During the 8th and 9th centuries the maniple was a folded cloth, but by about A.D. 1000 it was a decorative band. In both cases it was hung over the left forearm, as it is still.

k. Stole. The stole is a long decorated band worn by deacons, priests, and bishops since the 10th century. It is draped across one or both shoulders and sometimes crossed over in front, depending on usage and the rank of the wearer. Little is known about its origins except that it seems to have been worn by the lesser clergy in the East as early as the 4th century. There have been no changes in its form. Medieval and Renaissance stoles are often richly embroidered.

l. Pallium. The pallium is a long band of white wool, worn by popes and archbishops since the 15th century as a circular piece with pendants in front and back. It has been part of the liturgical vestments since the 5th century. It probably derives from the ancient Roman *pallium*, and early mosaics and frescoes show that it was a loose band worn draped over the shoulder, with one loose end hanging down the front and the other down the back.

m. Succinctorium. The succinctorium is similar to the maniple and is worn attached to the girdle on the left side. It is an insigne of the higher clergy, beginning with bishops. Although it is recorded in Rome and Ravenna in the 8th and 9th centuries, little is known about its medieval forms and usage. In modern times it usually has a Lamb of God embroidered in gold at one end and a cross at the other.

n. Fanon. This term is sometimes used for the maniple, but it may also designate a short cape or deep collar covering the shoulders, worn as a papal garment. In use by the 13th century, it has changed little since then.

o. Rational. The rational is a medieval liturgical vestment for bishops. Cut in any of several different ways, all derived from the pallium, it can be Y-shaped, circular (like a large collar), or H-shaped, with or without pendant elements. It almost always has richly embroidered scenes and inscriptions and often is adorned with gems, pearls, small plaques, or brooches. The term "rational" is also used for the large metal plaque hung from a chain around the neck or attached over the chest with a brooch. Neither type was used after the Middle Ages.

p. Miter. The most important liturgical headgear is the miter (PL. 174). Though it came into use comparatively early, its origins are uncertain. It underwent various changes in form, beginning with an almost perfect cone. In the 11th century the crown was often rounded, and later it was frequently indented in the middle. At this time two streamers were added in back. During the Middle Ages this type of miter came to be worn sideways, a practice that became established. During the 16th century the two pointed sides, thereafter separated into front and back panels, took the form of a pointed arch. The miter now worn by bishops, cardinals, and the pope is made of two stiff boards of this shape joined by a cloth so as to form a bellows, and streamers are attached. Through the 16th century the decoration usually consisted of embroidered ornamental bands, figures, and gems. In contrast, the miter used in the Eastern rite has a single bulbous crown and is surmounted by a cross.

q. Tiara. The tiara, the papal diadem or apostolic crown, developed from the miter. Its early form was conical, and an 8th-century description mentions that it was usually white and shaped like a candle snuffer. About the 10th century it was given a broad vertical rim band that symbolized papal authority. Boniface VIII (1294–1303) added a second crown; thus one signified the pope's temporal power and the other his spiritual power. Early in the 14th century either Benedict XI (1303–04) or Clement V (1305–14) added a third; it was then called the "triregnum" and symbolized both the Trinity and the pope's triple jurisdiction as the Vicar of Christ. The circlets are of gold and very like actual crowns. The earlier tiaras were more rounded and usually surmounted by a small cross; those produced since the 16th century have changed little.

r. Crosier. The crosier, or pastoral staff, is a tall staff with a crooked head. It is a liturgical insigne reserved for bishops and mitered abbots. Its origin is unclear, but it seems to derive, at least symbolically, from the staff of the Hebrew shepherds rather than from that of augurs or from the staff used in the investiture of Byzantine officials. Early crosiers were simple wooden staves terminating in a knop, a cross, a crook, or a tau. The early Celtic staves, most of which belonged to saints and were therefore preserved, were very plain, but as objects of veneration they were later encased in elaborately worked gold, silver, or bronze plates, often set with gems (e.g., crosier of Kells, Br. Mus.). In the 11th century the crosier was given a handle terminating in a volute. One of the earliest examples of this type of handle is the staff of St. Erhard in the Louvre. Gothic crosiers show great variety and inventiveness in the designs of the heads. Precious metals (PL. 174), enamels, ivory, or carved, gilded, and painted wood were used. Decorative motifs, animal figures, and even whole scenes appeared on them, as in the many fine crosiers made in Limoges in the 13th century. In these the knop is round and often pierced; in many other Gothic staves, however, the knop takes the form of a Gothic *tempietto*, as in the silver-gilt and enamel staff that belonged to William of Wykeham, Bishop of Winchester (1367–1404), in Oxford, New College. In the 15th and 16th centuries relief replaced polychrome decoration. The volute again underwent a rich development in the baroque period, but subsequently there was greater simplicity in its form and ornament.

Francesco NEGRI ARNOLDI

JEWISH CEREMONIAL ART. Documentation of Jewish ceremonial art begins with the Old Testament. The Israelites carried about with them in their wanderings the Ark of the Covenant, a coffer plated with gold and surmounted by the figures of two cherubim, and the craftsman Bezaleel, who with Aholiab was responsible for the construction of the Tabernacle in the wilderness, is mentioned in terms of high respect. Later the Ark of the Covenant was placed in Solomon's Temple, where it was guarded by two winged cherubs carved in olivewood and gilded; we have descriptions, too, supported by archaeological parallels, of the altar, lamps, lavers, and other Temple appointments, and of the two gigantic freestanding columns with pomegranate (or pomegranate-and-lily) capitals before the porch of the Temple, which were to be a recurrent symbol in Jewish ceremonial art. Yet, owing to the singular history of the Jewish people — and perhaps also to the nature of its religious teachings (see JEWISH ART) — the oldest of the great living religions of the Western world can point to almost no surviving ritual objects that antedate post-medieval times.

The dispersion of the Jewish people throughout the world brought about radical changes in their ceremonial art, as it did in all phases of their lives, but because so few examples have come down to us, little is known about the nature of these changes. Only from the 16th century onward is there enough material extant to enable us to form a clear picture. The diversity of styles that emerges points up the unique linking of the Jews with the culture of the lands in which they live. In the ritual objects of Islamic provenance the styles of the ancient East are reflected, and abstract ornament prevails, as in Islamic art. Jewish ceremonial art of European provenance partakes, in the 17th century, of the splendor of the baroque style, in the 18th century of the delicacy of the rococo; the late-18th- and early-19th-century works conform to the formal neoclassic style, while works of the end of the 19th century reflect the prevailing artistic eclecticism. Today leading artists and craftsmen are interpreting the traditional Jewish symbols in new forms and materials, bringing contemporary design into ritual appurtenances for home and synagogue.

The Torah scroll and its appurtenances. The Torah scroll contains the Pentateuch, the first five books of the Bible, inscribed by hand in accordance with elaborate regulations that have ensured consistency over the centuries. As the Torah is the most sacred possession of the Jew, the Torah scroll is the most sacred object in the synagogue. (The synagogue generally has several scrolls.) The use of the parchment scroll — forerunner of the book — which was general in antiquity, has been maintained to this day, but the Torah scroll is an unusual variant of the ancient form, being wound around two handles rather than one; the tradition of the double scroll for the Torah goes back at least as far as the time of the Second Temple.

The Torah scrolls are kept in the Torah shrine, or Ark (*aron kodesh*, Ark of the Law). The Ark, consisting of a movable wooden structure, was probably an important element of the synagogue by the 2d or 3d century of the present era. Synagogues of the 4th and 5th centuries in Palestine in many cases have apses in which the shrine was placed. By the 4th century, stone shrines and wall niches also often served to house the Torah scrolls (VIII, PL. 333). How the Torah shrines of the Talmudic period appeared can be learned from representations on late-antique mosaic pavements of synagogues from the 5th to the 8th century, as well as on gold glasses and on other examples of the minor arts. Most of these seem to be wooden structures closely resembling the Roman armarium (cupboard), which also served as a bookcase, as can be seen from various Roman reliefs and paintings. Thus the Ark usually has two doors, a low base, often with feet, and a gabled top. In many examples there are two columns with pomegranate capitals suggesting the two columns before the Temple. The Ark shown in the mosaic in the Beth Alpha Synagogue is an especially richly decorated example (VIII, FIG. 915). Of particular interest is the rare representation on a gold glass in the Vatican Museums in which the doors are open to show the shelves crammed with scrolls.

In Europe during the Middle Ages, the Ark, following contemporaneous secular styles, came to look like a fairly large and elaborate two-tiered cupboard (see FURNITURE). A beautiful Gothic example from Modena dated 1505 is in the collection of Musée de Cluny, Paris. With the Renaissance, forms became larger, more architectonic, and imposing, adopting the columns, pediments, carefully profiled moldings, and monumental balance of proportions of contemporary furniture. One of the most famous Torah shrines is the Ark of the Portuguese Synagogue in Amsterdam (1675). By this time the Ark, which had been somewhat eclipsed during the Middle Ages by the large bema (reading platform) in the center of the synagogue, had again become the focal point. In eastern Europe the emphasis was on richer and more colorful decoration rather than on the architectural aspects, and in some of the smaller, wooden synagogues of Poland and Russia this type of work reflected the finest traditions of folk art.

In the lands under Islamic domination, too, the Ark was usually a two-doored wooden structure; forms were influenced by Eastern designs, and Hebrew inscriptions served as decorative elements in much the same way as did Arabic calligraphy in the mosques.

The desire to render beautiful the setting and the ceremonial objects for the service of God, which applied with particular force to the Torah, extended to its various appurtenances, and upon these as well the utmost artistry and the finest materials were lavished. The visible parts of Torah handles, or rollers, when made of wood were often elaborately carved or turned or richly inlaid with ivory or mother of pearl; some were entirely made of ivory.

The Torah scroll is protected by a mantle of fine fabric or a case. The form of the case, dictated by that of the scrolls, is either cylindrical or octagonal, and both wood and metal are used. Most of the cases are of finely worked silver, usually embossed or chased, but some are of other metals, as is the copper one inlaid with silver made by one Master Joseph in Damascus in 1565 (New York, Jewish Mus.). In Persian and other Eastern Jewish communities the case was usually of wood, sometimes embossed with metal, and the Torah scrolls could not be removed from it (examples in the Bezalel Nat. Mus., Jerusalem).

The embellishments of the Torah traditionally include ornaments placed over the upper ends of the handles — either a crown (*keter*) or a pair of finials (*rimmonim*), in a few cases both (VIII, PL. 338). Custom varied in different periods and in different regions. The symbolism of the Torah crown is based on the Rabbinic metaphor referring to the "Crown of the Law." The term *rimmonim* (pomegranates) arises from the fact that in the East an early form was modeled on this fruit, a motif with antecedents going back to the two columns before the Temple of Solomon. Many other forms, some of them architectural (the steeple, the turret), appear, most of them greatly elaborated. Silver and silver-gilt were the metals chiefly used. The earliest examples of finials with small bells (which became a universal feature) are Sicilian, of the 14th or 15th century (Treasury of the Cathedral of Palma, Mallorca).

The so-called "breastplate," another adornment of the Torah scroll, is an essentially rectangular plaque, originally with an interchangeable, central panel bearing an inscription indicating the Sabbath or holiday on which a particular Torah scroll was to be used. Around the inscription there was ample space for a wealth of decoration, and finally the utilitarian function disappeared and only the decorative element remained. This ritual object, too, reflects contemporaneous influence, lending itself particularly to the more delicate chasing of the rococo style. As the name implies, the breastplate took on a symbolical relation to the breastplate of the Biblical high priest, and two of the more common ornamental motifs have a religious significance: two columns, again alluding to the two columns standing before King Solomon's Temple, and the lions, symbolizing the Lion of Judah. How early and how extensively the breastplate was used is not certain.

The pointer used by the reader of the Torah to follow the text, to spare it from being touched by the hand, was traditionally fashioned with the same care as the other appurtenances of the Torah. Innumerable examples have survived from the 18th and 19th centuries, none earlier than the 16th. Silver was the popular material; gold, carved bone, and semiprecious and precious stones were also used. Elaborate designs, with decorations of inlay and filigree work, are common. As a rule the pointer terminates in a miniature hand with the index finger extended; from this feature derives its designation, *yad* (hand).

The artistic workmanship of the gold and silver ritual objects is equaled by the splendor of the textiles used in connection with the Torah. These serve various functions: A fine cover is placed on the table on which the Torah scroll is unrolled to be read. The wrapper, a long, narrow strip of cloth, is used to bind it together when not in use. The mantle that covers the Torah scroll when it is not in use has already been mentioned. A curtain of richly ornamented material (*paroket*) is hung before the Ark. It is known that the artistic development of these textiles was considerable during the European Middle Ages, though few examples have been preserved that antedate the end of the 16th century. One of the earliest examples is not a European piece; it is the Torah curtain dated 1509 in the Samaritan Synagogue in Nablus (anc. Shechem), Jordan. The finest materials — linens, silks, brocades, and velvets — are used; they are richly embroidered in allover patterns and with inscriptions in silk, gold, and silver threads. Much use is made of appliqué. In areas such as Czechoslovakia, where the local textile industry could not supply suitably sumptuous work, fine textiles were imported from Italy, Spain, and elsewhere. These Jewish ceremonial textiles reflect the best in contemporaneous production (see TEXTILES), being distinguished from others only by their ornate Hebrew inscriptions and motifs. The inscriptions are of great historical significance, since they often provide such information as the name of the donor, the place of origin, and the date. A fine example in New York (Jewish Mus.) is dated 1681 and was made in Italy; it is of purple silk, worked with gold and silver appliqué and embroidery. It shows the tablets of the Law appearing at Mount Sinai and the walled city of Jerusalem with the Temple and its Holy of Holies.

One of the richest collections of ceremonial textiles is in the Jewish Museum in Prague, where some 10,000 pieces from Moravian and Bohemian synagogues that have suffered destruction or desertion have been assembled. The importance attached to the Torah curtain can be gathered from the fact that the Pinkas Synagogue in Prague had so many beautiful examples that before World War II a different one was hung up every day of the year.

Lamps. Lights and the act of lighting have an important place in Jewish ritual, whether in the synagogue or in the home: As the Tabernacle in the wilderness had a perpetual fire burning upon the altar, so an everlasting light (*ner tamid*) is suspended before the Ark in the synagogue; the celebration of the Sabbath is inaugurated and closed by the kindling of lights; and the eight days of Hanukkah, or the Feast of Lights, are marked by the successive lighting of the lamps of the eight-branched candlestick — to cite a few examples. The description in Exodus of the seven-branched golden candlestick made for the Tabernacle is believed to apply to the menorah in the Second Temple (built by Herod and sacked by the Romans A.D. 70, after the fall of Jerusalem); this may have been the one depicted in the relief on the Arch of Titus (PL. 161), where the conquerors are carrying it in the triumphal procession. After the destruction of the Temple it was forbidden to make seven-branched candlesticks for use, and no freestanding ones from ancient times have been found. As a symbol the menorah is, of course, one of the recurrent decorative motifs in Jewish ceremonial art.

From ancient times up to the 8th century, oil was used for the Sabbath lights. The hanging Sabbath oil lamp of the Middle Ages is familiar to us from illuminated manuscripts. It had a rich and complex development, incorporating all the diverse metalworking techniques and the regional styles of the Diaspora lands, but the basic form remained comparatively consistent. The oil was contained in a star-shaped bowl with projecting points that served as spouts for the wicks. Frequently there were six points, as in the Star of David, and below the main bowl was a smaller one to catch drippings; the upper part was often made up of a series of knops or of a towerlike structure such as is seen in the 17th-century silver lamp from Frankfurt am Main in New York (Lehman Memorial Coll., Temple Emanu-El). In the 17th century the Sephardic Jews in London and Amsterdam developed a characteristic variant with blunt spouts. Many examples are in silver, some of the finest pieces being attributable to well-known silversmiths; Sabbath lamps were also made in brass and in glass. The Jewish Museum of London contains an example in glass dating from 1694 that looks like a typical mosque lamp except for the Hebrew inscription. In the Near East, as elsewhere, few early works have survived, although in late-antique and early medieval times the Jews were renowned in these parts for their glass and metalwork. During the last two centuries, as candles have replaced oil, lamps have given way to candlesticks.

The Hanukkah lamp, lighted during the holiday commemorating the rededication of the Temple by the Maccabees after their victory over the Syrians in 165 B.C., has two typical forms. The older is the "bench" type, with the eight lights in a row at the bottom and the "servant light" (*shammash*) at the top of the solid back piece. Originally the lamps were, like the Roman oil lamps, of clay; there are also examples in stone and in pottery. During the Middle Ages, when Hanukkah lamps began to be lighted in the synagogue and lamps on a larger scale were in order, the menorah type of lamp was developed, following the description in Exodus and the representations in illuminated manuscripts; smaller versions of the type were created for home use. Metal became the rule — brass, bronze, pewter, and later silver. A few Gothic pieces are extant: a 14th-century Italian lamp in New York (Lehman Memorial Coll., Temple Emanu-El) and a 14th-century French or Italian one in Toronto (private coll.).

Other Sabbath and festival ritual objects. The ceremony proclaiming the holiness of the Sabbath or holiday (kiddush, or sanctification), is recited over a cup of wine before the evening meal. A favorite material for the kiddush cup (which is required to be without flaw) is silver, but other metals are used, and glass as well. These goblets are worked in infinite variety; some of the most striking examples are made for particular festivals, such as Passover. Perhaps the most interesting of the many examples in the Jewish Museum in New York is a gold kiddush cup from Frankfurt am Main dated about 1600. Hebrew inscriptions are entwined among vases with flowers and three cartouches with animals (lion, stag, and unicorn).

In the ceremony concluding the Sabbath (*habdalah*, or "separation," i.e., of the holy day from the other days of the week), a special braided candle is lighted and aromatic herbs and spices are used to symbolize the sweetness of the day. Containers to hold these aromatics have been, over the centuries, a particular challenge to the ingenuity and skill of craftsmen. The majority of the containers are of metal, most often silver, but other materials have been used. One of the most popular forms, both in Europe and in the Near East is the miniature tower: the earliest surviving ones obviously imitate medieval steeples, sometimes being adorned with clocks, small figures, and bells or pennants; in eastern Europe the container often was given the form of a fruit or flower on a curved stem.

Numerous other ceremonial appointments have been and are being produced with that degree of creativity and imagination which places them in the category of art objects; among these are the plate to hold the symbolic foods for the Passover Seder and the cup for Elijah used at the same service, the ram's horn (shofar) blown in the synagogue on the high holy days, the *greger* (noisemaker to anathematize Haman) used in the Purim service, and the box to hold the ethrog (citron) during the celebration of Sukkoth. Cases for the phylacteries (*tefillin*) used in daily prayer and the mezuzah attached to the doorpost of the house are still other characteristic objects that should not be omitted from even a summary treatment of Jewish ceremonial art.

* *

BIBLIOG. *Tribal art*: *a. General works*: E. Wilson, Das Ornament auf ethnologischer und prähistorischer Grundlage, Leipzig, 1914; J. Lehmann, Die Ornamente der Naturvölker und Halbkulturvölker, Frankfurt am Main, 1920; E. von Sydow, Ahnenkult und Ahnenbilder der Naturvölker, Berlin, 1924; E. von Sydow, Kunst und Religion der Naturvölker, Oldenburg, 1926; E. Vatter, Die religiöse Plastik der Naturvölker, Frankfurt am Main, 1926; E. von Sydow, Die abstrakte Gebrauchskunst im Grasland von Kamerun, BA, XV, 1932, pp. 160–80; M. Eliade, Images et symboles, Paris, 1952 (Eng. trans., P. Mairet, London, New York, 1961); O. Eberle, Cenalora, Olten, Freiburg am Breisgau, 1954; F. Herrmann, Um die Interpretation der Bildnerei der Naturvölker, Studium Generale, VII, 1954, pp. 394–409. *b. Special studies*: L. Frobenius, Die Masken und Geheimbünde Afrikas, Halle, 1898; J. Combarieu, La musique et la magie (Et. de philologie musicale, III), Paris, 1909; S. Seligmann, Die Zauberkraft des Auges und das Berufen, Hamburg, 1922; A. Krämer, Die Málanggane von Tombára, Munich, 1925; J. H. F. Kohlbrügge, Tier- und Menschenantlitz als Abwehrzauber, Bonn, 1926; G. Landmann, The Origin of Images as Objects of Cult, Arch. für Religionswissenschaft, XXIV, 1926, pp. 196–208; A. Eichhorn, Alt-Hawaiische Kultobjekte und Kultgeräte, BA, XIII, 1929–30, pp. 1–30; F. Krause, Maske und Ahnenfigur, Ethn. S., I, 1931, pp. 344–65; S. Behn, Schönheit und Magie, Munich, 1932; W. Klingbeil, Kopf- und Maskenzauber in der Vorgeschichte und bei den Primitiven, Bonn, 1933; G. Lindblom, Spears and Staffs with Two or More Points in Africa (Statens Etn. Mus., Smärre Meddelanden, 14), Stockholm, 1937; E. Manker, Die lappische Zaubertrommel (Nordiska Mus., Acta Lapponica), 2 vols., Stockholm, 1938–50; A. Steinmann, Das kultische Schiff in Indonesien, IPEK, XIII–XIV, 1939–40, pp. 149–205; J. Söderström, Die Figuren-Stühle vom Sepik-Fluss in Neuguinea (Statens Etn. Mus., Smärre Meddelanden, 18), Stockholm, 1941; O. Zerries, Das Schwirrholz, Stuttgart, 1942; A. Steinmann, Masken und Krankheit, Ciba Z., VIII, 1943, pp. 3114–52; A. Steinmann, Das Seelenschiff in der Textilkunst, Ciba-Rundschau, LXV, 1945, pp. 2376–2403; M. Loeffler-Delachaux, Le cercle: Un symbole, Geneva, 1947; E. E. Evans-Pritchard, Nuer Spear Symbolism, Anth. Q., N.S., I, 1953, pp. 1–19; E. A. Worms, Australian Ghost Drums, Trumpets and Poles, Anthropos, LIII, 1953, pp. 278–81; K. Goldammer, Die heilige Fahne, Tribus, N.S., IV–V, 1954–55, pp. 13–55; O. Eberle, Die akustische Maske, Actes IVe Cong. int. des sc. ethn. et anth., II (Ethnologica, 1), Vienna, 1955, pp. 74–78; E. Cerulli, L'iniziazione al mestiere di fabbro in Africa, S. e materiali di storia delle religioni, XXVII, 1956, pp. 87–101; P. Wirz, Kunst und Kult des Sepik-Gebietes, Amsterdam, 1959.

Ancient Near East: W. Reimpell, Sumerische Altäre, ZfAssyr, XXX, 1915–16, pp. 79–80; O. Weber, Altorientalische Kultgeräte, O. S. Fritz Hommel, II, Leipzig, 1918, pp. 370–92; K. Galling, Der Altar in den Kulturen des alten Orients, Berlin, 1925; E. Nassouhi, Les autels trépieds assyriens, Rev. d'assyriologie, XXII, 1925, pp. 85–90; H. Gressmann, Altorientalische Bilder zum Alten Testament, Berlin, Leipzig, 1927, pp. 119–34, 147–60, pls. 164–85, 203–20; G. Furlani, Scene sacrificiali hittite, Aegyptus, XI, 1930–31, pp. 301–62; G. Furlani, Sugli altarini fittili dell'Asia occidentale antica, RendLinc, 6th ser., VIII, 1932, pp. 405–21; A. G. Barrois, Manuel d'archéologie biblique, II, Paris, 1953, pp. 375–88; J. B. Pritchard, The Ancient Near East in Pictures Relating to the Old Testament, Princeton, 1954, pp. 192–206; E. D. Van Buren, Akkadian Stepped Altars, Numen, I, 1954, pp. 228–34.

The classic world: R. Paribeni, Il sarcofago dipinto di Hagia Triada, MALinc, XIX, 1908, cols. 5–86; G. Wissowa, Religion und Kultus der Römer, 2d ed., Munich, 1912; E. Mogk, Germanische Religion (Bilderatlas zur Religionsgeschichte, I), Leipzig, 1924; A. Rumpf, Die Religion der Griechen (Bilderatlas zur Religionsgeschichte, XIII–XIV), Leipzig, 1928; W. Krause, Religion der Kelten (Bilderatlas zur Religionsgeschichte, XVII), Leipzig, 1933; F. A. Altheim, History of Roman Religion (trans. H. Mattingly), London, 1938; W. Deonna, Le mobilier délien, Paris, 1938; N. Turchi, La religione di Roma antica (Storia di Roma, XVIII), Bologna, 1939; P. Tacchi-Venturi, Storia delle religioni, 2 vols., Turin, 1944; A. Almagro and A. García y Bellido, Arte prehistórico (Ars Hispaniae, I), Madrid, 1947; M. V. Giuliani Pomes, Cronologia delle situle rinvenute in Etruria, SEtr, XXIII, 1954, pp. 149–94, XXV, 1957, pp. 39–86; C. Zervos, La civilisation de la Sardaigne, Paris, 1954; I. S. Ryberg, Rites of the State Religion in Roman Art (MAARome, XXII), Rome, 1955; C. Zervos, L'art de la Crète, Paris, 1956; H. G. Bucholz, Zum Herkunft der kretischen Doppelaxt: Geschichte und auswärtige Beziehungen eines minoischen Kultsimbols, Munich, 1959; S. P. Marinatos, Crete and Mycenae, New York, 1960.

Asia: K. Florenz, Ancient Japanese Rituals (Tr. As. Soc. of Japan, XXVII, 1), Tokyo, 1899; M. Revon, Le Shinntoïsme, Paris, 1907; K. Florenz, Die historische Quellen der Shintô Religion, Göttingen, 1919; G. B. Sansom, Japan: A Short Cultural History, London, 1931 (rev. ed., New York, 1962); V. M. Narasimhan, Votive Lamps, Mārg, IV, 3, 1950, pp. 39–44. See also the bibliogs. for CHINESE ART; INDIAN ART; INDONESIAN CULTURES; JAPANESE ART; NEPALESE ART; TIBETAN ART.

Christian liturgical objects: R. Garrucci, Storia dell'arte cristiana, 6 vols., Prato, 1873–81; C. Rohault de Fleury, La Messe, 8 vols., Paris, 1883–89; O. M. Dalton, Catalogue of Early Christian Antiquities in the British Museum, London, 1901 (2d ed. 1921); E. Molinier, L'orfèvrerie religieuse et civile, 2 vols., Paris, 1901; J. Lessing, Die Gewerbesammlung des Kunstgewerbe Museum, Berlin, 1905; M. Magistretti, Delle vesti ecclesiastiche in Milano, 2d ed., Milan, 1905; F. Wieland, Mensa und Confessio, 2 vols., Munich, Leipzig, 1906–12; M. Bauer, Der Bildschmuck frühchristlicher Tonlampen, Griefswald, 1907; J. Braun, Die liturgische Gewandung im Occident und Orient, Freiburg im Breisgau, 1907; Cabrol-Leclercq; F. X. Raible, Der Tabernakel einst und jetzt, Freiburg im Breisgau, 1908; F. Bond, Misericords, London, 1910; F. Bond, Woodcarving in English Churches, London, 1910; O. M. Dalton, Byzantine Art and Archaeology, Oxford, 1911 (repr. New York, 1961); C. J. Jackson, An Illustrated History of English Plate, 2 vols., London, 1911; V. Thalhofer, Handbuch der katholischen Liturgik, 2d ed., 2 vols., Freiburg im Breisgau, 1912; H. B. Walters, Church Bells of England, London, 1912; K. M. Kaufmann, Handbuch der christlichen Archäologie, 2d ed., Paderborn, 1913; J. Braun, I paramenti sacri, Turin, 1914; J. C. Cox, Pulpits, Lecterns and Organs in English Churches, London, 1915; P. Batiffol, Le costume liturgique roman, in Etudes de liturgie et d'archéologie chrétienne, Paris, 1919, pp. 32–83; E. Bossi and G. Tebaldini, Storia dell'organo, Milan, 1919; J. Ebersolt, Sanctuaires de Byzance, Paris, 1921; O. von Falke, Kunstgeschichte der Seidenweberei, 2d ed., Berlin, 1921; W. F. Volbach, Metallarbeiten der christlichen Kultes, Mainz, 1921; O. M. Dalton, Catalogue of the Mediaeval Antiquities in the British Museum, London, 1922; W. W. Watts, Catalogue of Chalices and Other Communion Vessels, Victoria and Albert Museum, London, 1922; J. Ebersolt, Les arts somptuaires de Byzance, Paris, 1923; J. Braun, Der christliche Altar, 2 vols., Munich, 1924; M. Rosenberg, Geschichte des goldschmiede Kunst auf technischer Grundlage, I-II, Frankfurt am Main, 1924–25; C. Diehl, Manuel d'art byzantin, 2 vols., Paris, 1925–26; A. Munier, Construction, décoration, ameublement des églises, II: L'église à notre époque, sa décoration, son ameublement, Bruges, Paris, 1926; P. Nørlund, Gyldne Altre, Copenhagen, 1926; G. Migeon, Manuel d'art musulman, 2d ed., 2 vols., Paris, 1927; J. Weingartner, Das kirchliche Kunstgewerbe der Neuzeit, Innsbruck, Vienna, Munich, 1927; G. Lehnert, Geschichte des Kunstgewerbes, 4 vols., Berlin, 1928–31; E. Tyrrell-Green, Baptismal Fonts, London, 1928; A. Goldschmidt and K. Weitzmann, Die byzantinische Elfenbeinskulpturen des X-XII Jahrhunderts, 2 vols., Berlin, 1930–34; E. Roulin, Linges, insignes et vêtements liturgiques, Paris, 1930; M. Fugmann, Frühgotische Reliquiäre, Leipzig, 1931; J. Mannowsky, Der Danziger Paramentenschatz, 5 vols., Leipzig, 1931–38; J. Braun, Das christliche Altargerät, Munich, 1932; V. Casagrande, L'arte a servizio della Chiesa, 2 vols., Turin, 1932–38; D. Duret, Mobilier: Vases, objets et vêtements liturgiques, Paris, 1932; L. Eisenhofer, Handbuch der katholischen Liturgik, I, Freiburg im Breisgau, 1932; M. Accascina, L'oreficeria italiana, Florence, 1933; G. Astorri, Architettura sacra generale, Rome, 1935; A. Morassi, Antica oreficeria italiana, Milan, 1936; H. H. Arnason, Early Christian Silver of North Italy and Gaul, AB, XX, 1938, pp. 193–226; P. B. Cott, Siculo-Arabic Ivories, 2 vols., Princeton, 1939; J. Braun, Die Reliquiäre, Freiburg im Breisgau, 1940; C. Callewaert, De Dalmatica, Sacris Erudiri, Bruges, 1940, pp. 219–22; E. Giovagnoli, Il tesoro eucaristico di Canoscio, Città di Castello, 1940; W. F. Volbach, I tessuti del Museo sacro vaticano, Rome, 1942; H. Jantzen, Die ottonische Kunst, Munich, 1947; T. Klauser, Der Ursprung der bischöflichen Insignien und Ehrenrechte, Krefeld, 1949; M. M. S. Gauthier, Emaux limousins, Paris, 1950; E. Hutton, The Cosmati: The Roman Marble Workers of the 12th and 13th Centuries, London, 1950; H. Norris, Church Vestments: Their Origin and Development, New York, 1950; M. Righetti, Manuale di storia liturgica, 2d ed., I, Milan, 1950; W. F. Volbach, Elfenbeinarbeiten des Spätantike und des frühen Mittelalters, 2d ed., Mainz, 1952; M. D. Anderson, Misericords, Harmondsworth, 1954; F. Rossi, Italian Jewelled Arts, New York, 1954; C. Oman, English Church Plate: 597–1830, London, 1957; Ars Sacra (exhibition cat.), Louvain, 1958; M. Bárány-Oberschall, Baculus Pastoralis, ZfKw, XII, 1958, pp. 13–16; A. Grabar, Les ampoules de Terre Sainte (Monza-Bobbio), Paris, 1958; A. Henze, Neue kirchliche Kunst, Recklinghausen, 1958; E. Kovács, Casula sancti Stephani regis, Acta historiae artium, V, 1958, pp. 181–221; P. Salmon, Mitra und Stab, Mainz, 1960; M. C. Ross, Catalogue of the Byzantine and Early Mediaeval Antiquities in the Dumbarton Oaks Collection, I: Metalwork, Ceramics, Glass, Glyptics, Painting, Washington, 1962.

Jewish ceremonial art: G. Loukomski, Jewish Art in European Synagogues, London, 1947; H. Volavková, The Synagogue Treasures of Bohemia and Moravia, Prague, 1949; S. S. Kayser, A Polish Torah Crown, Hebrew Union College Ann., XXIII, 2, 1950–51, pp. 493–501; R. D. Barnett, ed., Treasures of a London Temple, London, 1951; G. Schoenberger, Pewter Objects in Jewish Ritual Art, Pewter Collectors' Club of Am., III, 1, 1952, pp. 3–11; F. Landsberger, Old Hanukkah Lamps, Hebrew Union College Ann., XXV, 1954, pp. 347–67; F. Landsberger, The Origin of the Ritual Implements for the Sabbath, Hebrew Union College Ann., XXVII, 1956, pp. 387–415; E. L. Ehrlich, Kultsymbolik im Alten Testament und im nachbiblischen Judentum, Stuttgart, 1959; S. S. Kayser and G. Schoenberger, Jewish Ceremonial Art, Philadelphia, 1959; J. Gutmann, The "Second Commandment" and the Image in Judaism, Hebrew Union College Ann., XXXII, 1961, pp. 161–74; C. Roth, ed., Jewish Art, New York, 1961; G. Schoenberger, ed., Synagoga: Jüdische Altertümer, Handschriften und Kultgeräte, Frankfurt am Main, 1961 (exhibition cat.); J. Gutmann, Jüdische Zeremonialkunst, Frankfurt am Main, 1963 (bibliog.); A. Kampf, Contemporary Synagogue Art, Philadelphia, in preparation. See also the bibliog. for JEWISH ART.

Illustrations: PLS. 156–178.

LOCHNER (LOECHENER, LOCHENER, formerly misread LOETHENER), STEFAN. German painter, born at Meersburg on Lake Constance, not earlier than 1410–15, the son of Georg and Alhet Lochner. After his apprenticeship he doubtless went as a journeyman to the Low Countries, where he must have completed his training in the 1430s in the workshop of Robert Campin (the presumed Master of Flémalle) and perhaps been influenced by the art of Jan van Eyck. His stay in Cologne is documented from 1442 to 1451. In June, 1442, he received an order for decorations from the city council, and in October he acquired a house together with his wife Lisbeth. He is mentioned in notes of **indebtedness** of October, 1444, and September, 1448. In 1447 and 1450 he was elected to the council. He died, probably of the plague, between Sept. 22, 1451, and Jan. 7, 1452.

A notice by Dürer of October, 1520, in the journal of his travels in the Netherlands, informs us that Lochner was the author of the most important panel painting ever executed in Cologne: the *Altar of the Patron Saints* (PL. 179), showing the patrons of the city — the Virgin, the Three Kings, St. Gereon, and St. Ursula. Painted in the 1440s for the Town Hall Chapel that was destroyed in 1945, it has been in the Cathedral since 1810.

This work is not dated, but there are two paintings, both Presentations in the Temple, which are: one in Lisbon (Gulbenkian Foundation), of 1445 (the "5," however, is questioned), the other in Darmstadt (PL. 180), of 1447. The prayer book in the Landesbibliothek of Darmstadt, with illustrations ascribed to Lochner, must be of 1450. Paintings or illuminations can be attributed to him solely on the basis of stylistic comparison with his main work, identified by Dürer.

The oldest preserved painting — to judge from the treatment of space, which relates it to the miniatures of the 1420s and the 1430s, and from the unmistakable dependence on Campin — is the *St. Jerome in His Cell* (coll. of the heirs of Edith von Schröder). The archaic formulas still employed by Lochner set forth in effective contrast the lively conception of details and the very personal, soft, and pleasing treatment of surfaces.

Shortly after 1440, probably, Lochner painted *The Last Judgment* (central panel, Wallraf-Richartz-Mus., PL. 180; inner sides of wings, Frankfort on the Main, Städelsches Kunstinst.; outer sides, Munich, Alte Pin., PL. 182). The inner face presents the resurrection of the dead, the Last Judgment, the portal of heaven, hell, and, on the wings, the martyrdom of saints. A meaningful proportion and a pulsing rhythm relate the three large figures of Christ, the Virgin, and John the Baptist to the swelling mass of little people beneath them. By far the greatest portion of the total area is devoted to the deeds and destinies of the wicked. Wedged between them is the small band of the elect entering the narrow gate of heaven, their backs turned to the world. The details of the demonic scenes are in no way inferior in dramatic power to those of Bosch and Bruegel. All the more striking is the soft and radiant beauty of the painting, masterly in its maturity, which lends a captivating glow to skin, hair, garments, and angels' wings. The tension expressed in the contrasts between godliness and ungodliness, calm and turmoil, reflects the trends of thought that followed in the wake of the great German and Netherlandish mystics of the 14th century; it is manifested even more clearly in many details, such as the variously repeated motif of angel and devil struggling for a soul. The outsides of the wings display six tranquil figures of saints wrapped in pure and gentle majesty (PL. 182).

The *Altar of the Patron Saints* (PL. 179) deals with the homage to the Christ child by the city of Cologne — represented not by its terrestrial, temporal dignitaries but by its eternal guardians and mediators. The subject is not the usual episode of the Adoration in the stable but an event of the highest solemnity unfolding in eternity and mirrored in time and space. The kings with their resplendent following who occupy the central panel are joined, on the wings, by the martyrs who, centuries later, gave their lives on the soil of Cologne. On the right is Gereon (the second head to his left may be a self-portrait of the painter); on the left is Ursula with her maidens, her betrothed Aetherius, and the princes of the church who accompany her. The distribution of the masses and the slightly billowing movement are of incomparable artistry. The figures on the wings, closer to the picture edge than those of the central panel, look as if they sought to form a circle around the Child, a circle that could incorporate the small group of city councilors who, before each session, heard Mass at the foot of the altar. In the Christ child the bloom of infancy accompanies a restrained gesture of conscious dominance that makes this figure the focal point of the composition. The color scheme is based on the elementary triad of red, green, and blue (fire, water, and air) over the grayish-brown of the earth and against the gold of the *quinta essentia* in the background. Each of these colors reappears in the richest nuances over the entire surface; in the central group the red of the oldest king, the green of the middle one, and the ultramarine of the Virgin unite the utmost intensity with an unearthly softness.

The outsides of the wings show the Annunciation (PL. 179), whose ordinary setting, a Cologne interior, presents a deliberate contrast to the nobility of the figures — an illustration of the teaching that anywhere, at any moment, God may enter into the soul of the believer.

Probably a little earlier is the *Virgin with the Violet* (Cologne, Erzbischöfliches Diözesan-Mus.). Although exact specifications seem to have been imposed by the donor, the painter's imagination, kindled by mystic love, was powerful enough to make a personal hymn of this work, which stands alone in its time.

From an altarpiece dedicated to the Virgin and apparently completed in 1445 are preserved the *Presentation in the Temple* (Lisbon, Gulbenkian Foundation) and the *Adoration of the Child* (Munich, Alte Pin., on loan), in which a chatty, almost genrelike quality combines with a gentle grace.

The versatility of Lochner's genius and the rapid development of his artistic capacities are demonstrated in the *Presentation in the Temple* of Darmstadt (PL. 180), by the highly personal manner in which he has mastered the dynamics of depth. In Mary he presents the perfect lady of society, surrounded by figures full of life, yet transfigured as by an unearthly light. In the treatment of colors, especially the ultramarine, few paintings of the century approach this one.

The Virgin in the Rose Bower (PL. 181), in which the still, otherworldly figures are larger in scale than their symmetrically balanced surroundings, must have been painted shortly before the artist's death.

In the realm of painting, the mystic movement fundamental to an understanding of German spiritual life in the late Middle Ages found in Lochner its most distinguished exponent before Grünewald. His art was completely personal and had no continuation. Only for a short time, and in the works of insignificant local painters, can traces of his manner be recognized.

BIBLIOG. F. F. Wallraf, Taschenbuch für Freunde altdeutscher Zeit und Kunst, Cologne, 1816, p. 149 ff.; J. F. Böhmer, Meister Stephan, Maler zu Köln, Kunst-Blatt, IV, 1823, p. 31 f.; J. J. Merlo, Nachrichten von dem Leben und den Werken kölnischer Künstler, Cologne, 1850, pp. 437-69; J. J. Merlo, Die Meister der altkölnischen Malerschule, Cologne, 1852, pp. 108-29; L. Ennen, Lochner oder Lothner?, Annalen des historischen Vereins für den Niederrhein, 11-12, 1862, p. 228; E. Firmenich-Richartz, Stephan Lochner, Z. für christliche Kunst, VI, 1893, cols. 193-208; C. Aldenhoven, Geschichte der Kölner Malerschule, Lübeck, 1902, pp. 150-77; H. A. Dickinson, German Masters of Art, New York, 1914, pp. 63-68; H. Reiners, Die Kölner Malerschule, München-Gladbach, 1925, pp. 62-94, bibliog. p. 329 f.; O. H. Förster, Stefan Lochners Bildform, ZfBk, LXII, 1928-29, pp. 241-59; O. H. Förster, Stefan Lochner, Deutsche Kunst, II, 11, Bremen, Berlin, 1936; L. Brand, Stephan Lochners Hochaltar von St. Katharinen zu Köln, Hamburg, 1938; J. H. Schmidt, Zu Stefan Lochners farbiger Gestaltung, Wallraf-Richartz-Jhb., X, 1938, p. 132 ff.; O. H. Förster, Stefan Lochner, ein Maler zu Köln, 3d ed., Bonn, 1952 (1st ed., Frankfort on the Main, 1938, with facsimiles of sources); J. Büchner, Ein Altar aus der Lochner-Nachfolge in Köln, Wallraf-Richartz-Jhb., XXII, 1960, pp. 165-72; H. Lobeck, Stefan Lochner, Stuttgart, 1960.

Otto H. FÖRSTER

Illustrations: PLS. 179-182.

LONGHENA, BALDASSARE. Major Venetian architect of the baroque period (b. Venice, 1598; d. Feb. 18, 1682). Longhena was a pupil of Vincenzo Scamozzi (q.v.), whose Procuratie Nuove (VIII, PL. 214) in the Piazza di S. Marco he helped to complete, and was influenced by Palladio, Sansovino, and Sanmicheli. Much of his work combines baroque richness of surface with the simple massing favored by these Renaissance masters, so that Longhena's effects differ fundamentally from the complexity of his Roman contemporaries Bernini and Borromini. His dependence on Scamozzi is evident in the earliest building attributable to him, the Palazzo Giustinian-Lolin (ca. 1623).

In 1631 Longhena received the commission for his masterpiece, S. Maria della Salute (II, PL. 141), on the Grand Canal. The church, substantially completed about 1648 but not consecrated until 1687, is basically an octagon with a great dome over it, to which are added a choir and sanctuary; the choir has its own, smaller dome, flanked by twin campaniles, and the plan is further complicated by apsidal transepts on either side of the choir. Calling to mind S. Marco, the array of two domes and two towers is splendid and typically Venetian; and the picturesqueness is enhanced by the huge volutes buttressing the larger dome, which have continued to delight painters from Canaletto and Guardi to Sickert and Kokoschka (I, PL. 410). The synthesis of varied elements and the potential of the setting at the edge of the Grand Canal were fully realized and exploited by Longhena. By comparison austere, the interior interest lies in the complex vistas created by eight identical, cleverly disposed piers, surrounded with an ambulatory and chapels except for the entrance unit and, at the opposite end, the separate but related unit composed of the choir and retrochoir.

The same richness of surface combined with Renaissance simplicity of form is apparent in Longhena's two most important palaces, Ca' Pesaro and Ca' Rezzonico (VIII, PL. 226), both also situated on the Grand Canal. The Pesaro was under construction in 1663, and the Rezzonico in the same decade; both were completed by others in the 18th century. The design of both palaces — a rusticated ground floor and two upper floors with columns between the arched window openings — derives from the Venetian palace type established by Sansovino and Sanmicheli. The Venetian baroque of Longhena, with its scenographic integration of space and clear homage to Renaissance precursors, evidences a considered solution of architectural problems rather than mere striving for ornate and external effect.

BIBLIOG. C. Semenzato, L'Architettura di Baldassare Longhena, Padua, 1954; R. Wittkower, Art and Architecture in Italy, 1600 to 1750, Harmondsworth, 1958, pp. 191-96.

Peter MURRAY

LONGHI, PIETRO AND ALESSANDRO. Venetian painters of the 18th century. Pietro gained eminence as a penetrating observer of contemporary society, and his son Alessandro as a portraitist.

SUMMARY. Pietro (col. 318). Alessandro (col. 321).

PIETRO. Pietro Longhi was born in Venice in 1702 and died there on May 8, 1785. His father was Alessandro Falca, a silver caster; the origin of the name Longhi is uncertain. According to the writings of Pietro Guarienti (1753) and to an anonymous author in the *Compendio de' pittori veneziani ...* (1762), Pietro received his earliest instruction from his father, but while still a youth was placed in the school of Antonio Balestra, who "after keeping him with him for several years" advised him to join the studio of Giuseppe Maria Crespi in Bologna. On Sept. 28, 1732, probably after an artistically profitable Bolognese sojourn, he married Caterina Maria Rizzi in Venice. From 1737 to 1773 his name appears in the register of the *fraglia* (guild) of Venetian painters, and from 1740 he lived in the parish of S. Pantalon. On Feb. 13, 1756, he was selected by a committee, presided over by Giovanni Battista Tiepolo, to be among the first members of the Accademia of Venice, where he taught alternate years until 1780. In 1762, with Giovanni Piazzetta and Tiepolo, Pietro drew up the inventory for and estimated the worth of art objects in the Sagredo estate. In 1763 he directed an academy of drawing and printmaking, founded by the Pisani family at their palace in Campo S. Stefano for the education of Almorò Pisani; but the painter was relieved of this duty after the premature death of the young patrician in 1675.

The large canvas of *The Martyrdom of S. Pellegrino* (ca. 1730) in the parish church of San Pellegrino, near Bergamo, and the frescoes depicting *The Fall of the Giants* (Venice, Pal. Sagredo; on the ceiling and walls of the staircase, signed and dated 1734 but necessarily begun some years earlier) furnish evidence that the young Pietro Longhi painted in the "grand manner." Following in the footsteps of his mentor Balestra, Sebastiano Ricci, and Louis Dorigny, Longhi tried to enter into the great decorative tradition through use of the baroque rhetoric; his success in this genre was limited, however, and probably it is not to be regretted that other examples of his courtly style have disappeared. Among these are the following: *Adoration of the Magi* from S. Maria Mater Domini; *Miracle of the Loaves and Fishes*, *The Wedding at Cana*, and *Miracle of the Centurion* from the Scuola S. Pasquale Baylon; *St. John the Baptist* and two other small pictures from the church on Isola della Grazia (mentioned in 1733 by Antonio Maria Zanetti); the *Blessing of St. James* and *Coronation of the Virgin* from the Oratorio di S. Biagio in Verona. Longhi's inability to distinguish himself in the painting of expansive historical and religious subjects — recognized by his contemporaries — was evidently a failing never overcome, as suggested in two wan figures executed late in his career, those of St. Peter and St. Andrew in the Church of S. Pantalon (last chapel on right-hand side; probably painted ca. 1780, contemporary with those done by his son Alessandro).

A notable exception to Pietro's limitations in this style are the fresco decorations he executed within the replica of the Sanctuary of the Holy House of Loreto, added to S. Pantalon in 1744-45. In the fragmentary groups of Madonnas and saints there is a light and delicate touch (reminiscent of and little inferior to the portrait manner of Rosalba Carriera), a distillation of the freshness and poetic intimacy characteristic of his small scenes of Venetian life.

Pietro Longhi's abandonment of the grand manner in favor of a painstaking depiction of contemporary life was in keeping with the cultural climate then fostered by the ideas of the French Enlightenment. In Venice, as elsewhere at the beginning of the 18th century, an acceptance of social realities became current, in contrast with the grandiose pageants of the established cultural tradition. The first evidence of a change in Pietro's interests can be seen in a sheet of three studies (Venice, Mus. Correr) for *The Fall of the Giants*, in which the academic anonymity of the figure types does not agree with the sure delineation of specific details and features, both in objects and in persons. The determining factor in Longhi's change of artistic direction was his familiarity with the art of Crespi, and its wealth of human interest — a familiarity clearly reflected in some pastoral scenes (Rovigo, Mus. del Seminario Vescovile; Bassano, Mus. Civ.) and in other scenes of peasant life (Venice, Ca' Rezzonico and Gall. Querini Stampalia). The first securely dated intimate views of Venetian life — *The Concert* (1741; Venice, Accademia) and others stylistically similar that must have been contemporaneous or not much later in date, such as *The Dancing Master* (PL. 183), *The Toilette* and *The Tailor* (both, Venice, Accademia), *The Introduction* (Louvre), *The Pot Game* and *The Swoon* (both Washington, D.C., Nat. Gall.), *The Awakening* (1744) and *Blindman's Buff* (both Windsor, Royal Colls.) — all testify to a growing artistic maturity and indicate that Longhi was familiar with 17th-century Dutch and Flemish painting and that he knew contemporary genre painting, particularly that of France.

His attainments and rich background are even more evident in the drawings, which are exceptional in their subtle discernment and in the evocative power of his line. The most important group of Pietro's drawings, that in the Museo Correr of Venice, is related less to the Venetian graphic tradition than to examples by Watteau and Nicolas Lancret. It consists of complete compositions, studies of single figures, and details of human figures or objects (occasionally supplemented by notes on proportions and color relationships). Though intended mainly as preliminaries for pictorial construction, these drawings have an extraordinary poetic quality.

Longhi very likely joined in a widespread European current in which artists sought more immediate apprehension of reality, but his means of expression were truly original; indeed, as early as 1753, Guarienti had referred to "his new and personal manner." The refined aristocracy of Watteau, the crude objectivity of Giacomo Ceruti, or the bitter satiric edge of Hogarth — none serves as suitable analogy for the art of Longhi. His *œuvre* comprises an intimate chronicle that captures, with incomparable penetration and with a subtly ironic viewpoint, the low-key, almost bourgeois character of the 18th-century Venetian aristocracy — reflected in the somnolent atmosphere of the old palace interiors themselves, as much as in the festive air of worldly gatherings or in contacts with the life of the common people. Within the scenic arrangement of his pictures, "blocked in" like the action in a play, the life of the characters is depicted frankly and with a warm sympathy. Their expressiveness and charm are heightened by the bright but softly modulated palette, of a pastellike subtlety, that invests the meticulous drawing, and the whole is harmonized with exquisite sensibility in an equally subtle and vibrant chiaroscuro.

Longhi's fresh and varied interpretation of social milieu, which has been compared in intent and effects with the theater art of Carlo Goldoni (confirmed by the dramatist's published statements of his aims, as early as 1750), was at its most comprehensive during the decade in which he painted — to cite only the most conspicuous examples — *The Visit to the Lord* (1746), *The Meeting* (PL. 185), *The Visit*, and *The Letter* (all New York, Met. Mus.), *The Herbseller* (Warminster, Eng., Longleat House, Coll. Marquess of Bath), *The Tooth Puller* (IV, PL. 29), *The Painter in His Studio*, *Family Reunion*, *The Seamstress*, *The Errand of the Negro*, and *Rhinoceros* (1751; cf. PL. 185, a variant of this subject; last-named five all in Venice, Ca' Rezzonico), the portrait of the Sagredo family (ca. 1752; Venice, Gall. Querini Stampalia), and *Excursion on Horseback* (ca. 1755; Ca' Rezzonico).

After about 1755 there occurs still another change in the painting style of Pietro Longhi. His color range favors dense and warmer tones, attuned to the soft chiaroscuro, while his draftsmanship becomes more free and cursive. The artist's outlook remains essentially unchanged, but it seems enriched by more varied and probing examination of his milieu. The *Sacraments* (Venice, Gall. Querini Stampalia) are incomparable vignettes of everyday religious life in 18th-century Venice, done with a lively wit and inspired, at least indirectly, by the famous series of Crespi. Longhi completed his series before 1757, when Marco Pitteri began to engrave them. No less poetic and evocative is the chronicle of the worldly diversions and domestic life of Venetian nobility in such pictures as the *Masked Reception* (St. Louis, Mo., City Art Mus.), the various versions of *The Ridotto* (Venice, Coll. Salom; Gall. Querini Stampalia; Bergamo, Acc. Carrara), *Portrait of the Giant Magrat* (1757), *The Perfume Vendor*, *Visiting Domino*, and *The Puppeteer* (1757; last-named four in Venice, Ca' Rezzonico), as well as in the wonderful series of the Perera Collection, New York.

In the 1760s Longhi returned to moral considerations, with subjects in which shrewd, good-natured observation was on occasion transformed into the open satire of the clergy found in a work dated 1761 or into the disenchanted humor of the *Lion House* of 1762 (both Venice, Gall. Querini Stampalia). The greatest work of this period in Pietro's activity was the series entitled *Hunt in the Valley* (Gall. Querini Stampalia), which was commissioned by the Michiel family and quickly became celebrated through the prints of Pitteri. As he had done in *Luncheon in the Gardens by the Lagoon* (Venice, Ca' Rezzonico) and *Duck Hunting* (PL. 185), slightly earlier in date and also some of his finest work, in the seven episodes of the *Hunt in the Valley* Longhi presented anecdotal landscapes free of any pastoral conventions and in such a straightforward manner as "to presage Gogol" (Roberto Longhi).

In his last works, however, Pietro Longhi began to show signs of weariness. The rustic scenes he produced in increasing numbers rarely avoided a purely mannered aspect, and even the best of these — the four in the Paolucci Collection (Ferrara; one dated 1775) and the two in the Bisacco-Palazzi Collection (Venice; 1779) — do not achieve the vivid honesty of the *Hunt in the Valley* series. The artist could no longer capture the ironic, charmed atmosphere of the *Lion House* when he came to paint the *Elephant* (Venice, Coll. Salom) or the *Bison* and *Lynx* (1770; both Venice, Gall. Querini Stampalia), in which the interest becomes merely illustrative. Nonetheless, he was at times still able to fix with unbiased perceptiveness the human and historical character of his period in scenes of domestic life, such as *The Hand Kissing* (formerly Venice, Coll. Giovanelli), *Visit to Grandmother* (Venice, Curtis Coll.), and *Adriana Giustinian Barbarigo with Her Son* (1779–80; Venice, Mus. Correr), in which the summary definition of silhouettes, the subdued tonality, rendered as if somehow veiled and yet without the customary chiaroscuro, and the stiff array of figures in a single row and in unnaturally immobile poses all contribute to an extraordinary evocation of the static Venetian society of the last days of the republic.

Upon clarification of the stylistic traits of the artist's son Alessandro, and with the consequent sorting out of his production, the catalogue of portraits relegated to the hand of Pietro Longhi has become much more limited. Perhaps the earliest of those remaining is one of an unidentified nobleman (ca. 1750; Cambridge, Mass., Fogg Art Mus.), which was followed by — among his more intense characterizations — *Francesco Guardi* (1764; Venice, Ca' Rezzonico), the full-length *Ludovico Manin* (1764; Udine, Mus. Civ.), *Stefano Querini* (Paris, Coll. M. Cailleux), and *Matilde Querini* (Algiers, Mus. Nat. B. A.). Both of the Querini portraits can be dated 1772. The unique refinement of color and the discerning characterizations of Pietro's portraiture served as a model for the portraits of Alessandro, the only noteworthy successor to his father in the continuation of the style.

ALESSANDRO. Alessandro Longhi was born on June 12, 1733, in Venice, where he died in 1813. As a boy he was sent by his father Pietro to the school of the Venetian portraitist Giuseppe Nogari, whom he succeeded at the Accademia in 1759. In 1762 he supervised a biographical compendium of Venetian painters, *Compendio de' pittori veneziani . . .*, for which he also executed 24 portrait engravings. From 1773 to 1779 he taught at the Accademia, for which he painted the allegory *Painting and Merit* and the portraits of the doges Alvise Mocenigo (1767) and Paolo Renier (1781), as well as the posthumous portraits of Paolo Veronese, Titian, Tintoretto, and Jacopo Bassano, commissioned in 1770 for the galleries of the Accademia. (This last group of portraits of painters has been lost.)

A portrait of Gioacchino Cocchi, Alessandro's earliest known work, which Jacopo Gradenigo recorded as being exhibited on the façade of S. Geminiano on May 24, 1757, is lost. In the datable early works surviving — such as the *Pisani Family* (1758; Venice, Bentivoglio d'Aragona Coll.) or the portraits of Venetian magistrates, *Alvise Renier, Prospero Valmarana*, and *Vincenzo Dona* (1759; Venice, Doges' Palace) — Alessandro demonstrates the gifts of acute observation and the subtle painterly freedom of his father, rather than the luminous chiaroscuro and decorative manner of the portraiture of Nogari. Although such traits of Nogari are echoed in the background and in the allegorical figures of the *Pisani Family*, the most lively and appealing segment of this large painting is the group of adults with their brood of children, which appears quite like an enlargement of the small family portraits of Pietro. The same fine stippling of color and humanity of characterization also mark *Angelo Memmo IV* (1760; Venice, Mus. Correr) and the so-called *Balotin del Doxe* (Belluno, Mus. Civ.), this last probably a fragment of the second large Pisani family portrait mentioned in the *Compendio* of 1762.

Alessandro's paintings of the 1760s, which maintain the exceptional freedom of his father's technique but are more awkward on the surface, are distinguished by careful study of individual physical and psychological characteristics. This discerning character study is evident in the following examples from these years: the masterly engravings for the *Compendio*; *Giulio Contarini da Mula* (ca. 1759; Rovigo, Pin. dell'Acc. dei Concordi), admirable for its delicate modulation of grays; *Carlo Goldoni* (Venice, Casa Goldoni; no. 143); *Antonio Renier,*

Provveditore Generale di Dalmazia e Albania (1765; PL. 186), with deft gradations of flaming red in the costume; the stately *Grand Chancellor Giovanni Colombo* (1766; Venice, Coll. Cini); and the extremely vivid *Painter Urbani* (1766; Mestre, private coll.). All these works share the remarkably delicate sensibility to color apparent also in the allegorical *Painting and Meri* (Venice, Accademia).

Seeking always to vary the style of his father, in the portraits of his mature phase Alessandro often struck a perfect balance between restraint of pictorial means and acuteness of observation, a tone no less effective than that of Ceruti but not so harshly objective. His sitters during these years, for the most part, were churchmen, as in the two portraits of prelates (Venice, I. Brass Coll.; one dated 1777), the *Abbot* (1776; Uffizi), and the *Parish Priest* (PL. 186); or they were representative of the Venetian bourgeoisie and its pursuits, such as the architect *Tommaso Temanza* and the agricultural theorist *Father Carlo Lodoli* (both, Venice, Accademia), the engineer *Bartolomeo Ferracina* (ca. 1770; Venice, Ca' Rezzonico), the doctor *Gian Pietro Pellegrini* (Venice, Ateneo Veneto), *Captain Pietro Budinich* (1781), and *Count Giuseppe Rusteghello* (last two, Venice, I. Brass Coll.). In the contemporaneous full-dress portraits, the grandiloquence of ceremonial portraiture is saved from pure caricature and theatrical color effects by a keen irony that, while suggesting the satiric edge of Goya, has been mitigated by the artist's Venetian good nature. Examples of such formal commissions in these decades include the *Bishop Ganassoni* (Feltre, Seminario) — dated 1774, as is the signed sketch of the same sitter by the senior Longhi (Ca' Rezzonico) — and the portrait of a pompous admiral, *Alvise Foscari* (1782; Venice, Pal. Widmann-Foscari).

In the early 1780s there is apparent a cold academicism in the figures of the apostles Thaddeus and Matthew (1780), the *Justice* and *Prudence*, the *Works of Mercy*, and *Charity* (1782; all Venice, S. Pantalon), all of which testify that Alessandro lacked an affinity for the sacred genre. On the basis of a statement of G. A. Moschini (1815), who mentioned an altarpiece of the Sacred Heart of Jesus in the Oratorio dei SS. Pietro e Paolo as Alessandro's "most recent work," it can be inferred that the artist had returned to such subjects late in his career.

Although little is known of his last works, the arresting naturalism and coloristic refinement of some late signed works, such as the *Capitano Generale del Golfo Giovanni Battista Contarini* (1787; Treviso, Mus. Civ.), *Monsignor Giovanni Piccardi* (1793; Venice, S. Maria del Carmelo), and the so-called *Tappezziere* and *Boy with a Pony* (both, Venice, I. Brass Coll.) indicate that Alessandro Longhi remained essentially outside the neoclassic current prevailing during his final years.

BIBLIOG. A. M. Zanetti, Descrizione di tutte le pubbliche pitture della città di Venezia, Venice, 1733; C. Goldoni, Al Signor Pietro Longhi veneziano celebre pittore, in Componimenti poetici per le felicissime nozze di Sue Eccellenze il Signor Giovanni Grimani e la Signora Catterina Contarini, Venice, 1750, p. 77; P. A. Orlandi, Abecedario pittorico (enlarged ed. by P. Guarienti), Venice, 1753; G. Gozzi, Gazzetta veneta, 55, Aug. 13, 1760; G. Gozzi, L'Osservatore Veneto, IV, Feb. 14, 1761; A. Longhi, ed., Compendio de' pittori veneziani istorici più rinomati del presente secolo, Venice, 1762; P. Gradenigo, Annotations for Sept. 3 and Dec. 20, 1760, and Apr. 30, 1764 (pub. in L. Livan, ed., Notizie d'arte tratte dai Notatori e dagli Annali del N.H. Pietro Gradenigo, Venice, 1942); G. Gradenigo, Poesie in lode del celebre ritrattista veneziano il Signor Alessandro Longhi, Venice, 1770; G. A. Moschini, Guida per la città di Venezia all'amico delle Belle Arti, Venice, 1815; V. Lazzari, Elogio di Pietro Longhi pittore veneziano, Venice, 1862; E. Masi, Carlo Goldoni e Pietro Longhi, S. sulla storia del teatro italiano nel secolo XVIII, Florence, 1891, pp. 239–79; A. C. Dell'Acqua, La Venezia del Canaletto e la Venezia del Longhi, Ateneo Veneto, XVII, 1, 1893, pp. 153–87; E. and J. de Goncourt, L'Italie d'hier: Notes de voyage, 1855–1856, Paris, 1894; U. Monneret de Villard, Note su Pietro Longhi, Emporium, XXI, 1905, pp. 200–11; G. A. Simonson, Guardi and Longhi, BM, X, 1906, pp. 53–54; P. Molmenti, Di Pietro Longhi e di alcuni suoi quadri, Emporium, XXVII, 1908, pp. 31–38; A. Ravà, Guardi e Longhi, L'Arte, XII, 1909, p. 456; A. Ravà, Pietro Longhi, Bergamo, 1909 (2d ed., Florence, 1923); R. Bratti, Ritratti di Pietro e Alessandro Longhi, Arte Nostra, I, 1910, pp. 20–28; G. Fogolari, L'Accademia veneziana di pittura e scultura nel Settecento, L'Arte, XVI, 1913, pp. 241–72; G. Damerini, I pittori veneziani del '700, Bologna, 1928; L. Brosch, ThB, s.v., XXIII, 1929, pp. 355–56; G. Fiocco, La pittura veneziana alla Mostra del '700, Riv. di Venezia, 1929, p. 497; G. Fiocco, La pittura veneziana del Seicento e Settecento, Verona, 1929; V. Moschini, Disegni del '700 alla Mostra di Venezia, Dedalo, X, 1929–30, pp. 301–30; V. Moschini, La pittura italiana del Settecento, Florence, 1931; V. Moschini, Per lo studio di Alessandro Longhi, L'Arte, N.S., III, 1932, pp. 110-47; V. Moschini, Un ritratto inedito di Alessandro Longhi, Dedalo, XII, 1932, pp. 772-80; E. Arslan, Di Alessandro e Pietro Longhi, Emporium, XCVIII, 1943, pp. 51-63; E. Arslan, Inediti di Pietro e Alessandro Longhi, Emporium, CIII, 1946, pp. 59-69; R. Longhi, Viatico per cinque secoli di pittura veneziana, Florence, 1946; E. Bassi, L'Accademia di Belle Arti di Venezia nel suo bicentenario, Venice, 1950; T. Pignatti, I ritratti settecenteschi della Querini Stampalia, BArte, XXXV, 1950, pp. 216-18; F. Valcanover, Postilla su Pietro Longhi "pittori di storia," Arte Veneta, V, 1951, pp. 169-70; R. Pallucchini, La pittura veneziana del Settecento, II, Bologna, 1952; R. Bacchelli and R. Longhi, Teatro e immagini del Settecento italiano, Turin, 1953, pp. 63-94; F. Valcanover, Un nuovo ritratto di Alessandro Longhi, Arch. storico di Belluno, Feltre e Cadore, XXV, 1954, pp. 33-36; V. Moschini, Pietro Longhi, Milan, 1956 (bibliog.); F. Valcanover, Affreschi sconosciuti di Pietro Longhi, Paragone, VII, 73, 1956, pp. 21-26; F. Valcanover, Due ritratti di Pietro Longhi, in Venezia e l'Europa: Atti del XVIII Cong. int. di Storia dell'Arte, Venice, 1956, pp. 362-63; G. M. Pilo, Per la datazione di tre ritratti di Alessandro Longhi, Paragone, VIII, 91, 1957, pp. 45-52; G. Delogu, Pittura veneziana dal XIV al XVIII secolo, Bergamo, 1958; V. Moschini, Un altro Pietro Longhi, Arte Veneta, XII, 1958, pp. 222-23; M. Levey, Painting in 18th Century Venice, London, 1959; T. Pignatti, Due nuovi Alessandro Longhi al Museo Correr, B. Mus. civ. veneziani, 1959, 2, pp. 6-16; F. Valcanover, Un nuovo Alessandro Longhi, B. Mus. civ. veneziani, 1959, 4, pp. 26-28; R. Pallucchini, Pittura veneziana del Settecento, Florence, 1960; F. Valcanover, New Light on Alessandro Longhi's "Balotin del Doxe," The Connoisseur, CXLVIII, 1961, pp. 227-29.

Francesco VALCANOVER

Illustrations: PLS. 183-187.

LOOS, ADOLF. Austrian architect (b. Brno, or Brünn, Dec. 10, 1870; d. Vienna-Kalksburg, Aug. 23, 1933). The son of a sculptor, Adolf Loos was trained at Dresden Polytechnic. During a three-year sojourn in America (1893-96) he became a skilled bricklayer. From 1896 on, his permanent residence was in Vienna, interrupted only by a stay in Paris from 1924 until 1928 and by frequent travel abroad. For several years he conducted a private architectural school. A brilliant critic, Loos wrote numerous penetrating and witty didactic essays on architecture, art, and culture.

Loos gained international repute, and still is best known, for his opposition to ornamentation, as ultimately formulated in *Ornament and Crime* (*Ornament und Verbrechen*; 1908). His attitude, however, has been much misunderstood. To Loos, the disappearance of ornament was not an esthetic postulate but a historic phenomenon; the outcome of a "natural" process within the evolution of human culture, with far-reaching economic implications. The problem of modern architecture, he felt, is not to create "new form" but to build in the "new spirit": more precisely, in the spirit of the culture of modern man. Basically, this means an insistence on the human element — man's nature, life, and requirements — as the essential condition of architecture. Such is the quintessence of Loos's teaching, contained in all his writings, and most clearly and consistently expressed in his architecture.

His unexecuted projects outnumber his actual buildings. The latter are, with one exception, on a comparatively small scale, but all are characterized by elegance, formal clarity, beauty of material and functional logic. Most significant among the earlier works are the Café Museum (1899; Vienna), Villa Karma (1904; Montreux), the Kärntner Bar (1907; Vienna), the monumental Goldman and Salatsch Building (V, PL. 102), and the Scheu house (1913; Vienna), the first modern house with roof terraces. Loos's most decisive and original architectural discovery was the "three-dimensional plan," the organization of the building volume as an integral whole, without continuous horizontal subdivisions; that is, distributing and coordinating rooms of different heights on different levels. First applied in the Goldman and Salatsch Building, this structural principle, revolutionary in its psychological and economic aspects, is dominant in all of Loos's later buildings, for example, the Rufer house (1922; Vienna), Tzara house (1926; Paris), Moller house (1928; Vienna), and Müller house (V, FIG. 231 b). In these structures, in all probability, is found the genesis of contemporary "open planning"; there is spatial flow, but it is typically without the interpenetration of interior and exterior space that was to emerge in the work of others.

The magnitude of Loos's influence on architecture and architectural thought in modern times, the effect of his ascetic doctrine and austere work in his time and since, is as yet far from fully realized.

BIBLIOG. A. Loos, Richtlinien für ein Kunstamt, Vienna, 1919; A. Loos, Ins Leere Gesprochen, Paris, 1921; A. Loos, Trotzdem, Innsbruck, 1931; H. Kulka, Adolf Loos, Vienna, 1931; L. Münz, Adolf Loos, Milan, 1956; Casabella (Numero dedicato ad Adolfo Loos), November, 1959.

Ernest H. BRANDL

LORENZETTI, AMBROGIO AND PIETRO. The Lorenzetti brothers were Sienese painters (Pietro b. ca. 1280, d. 1348?; Ambrogio d. 1348?), their family relationship documented by an inscription ("Hoc opus fecit Petrus Laurentii et Ambrosius eius frater MCCCXXXV"; recorded by Ugurgieri) appearing on frescoes on which they collaborated in the Hospital of S. Maria della Scala, Siena. Pietro was probably the elder of the two, as his name appeared first. His birth date is based on the first piece of documentary evidence concerning him — the record of a payment made to him on Feb. 25, 1306, by the Sienese government for an unknown painting; use of the diminutive form "Petruccio" suggests that Pietro was still a young man, but he must have been at least twenty-five years old to receive payment directly. Nothing is known about the date of Ambrogio's birth. Further records state that Pietro (in 1341 and 1344) and Ambrogio (in 1324) were living in Siena.

Documentary evidence regarding the artistic activities of both is scarce. The earliest certain documentation regarding a work by Pietro is the contract dated Apr. 17, 1320, for the painting of the altarpiece in the Pieve di S. Maria in Arezzo, commissioned by Bishop Guido Tarlati (PL. 191). The next documented work is the altarpiece for S. Maria del Carmine in Siena (PL. 190), signed and dated 1329. Later the altarpiece was dismantled and moved to the town of Sant'Ansano a Dofana and was subsequently reassembled in the Pinacoteca in Siena. The first certain document for a work by Ambrogio is the inscription on the *Madonna* in the Church of Sant'Angelo a Vico l'Abate (near San Casciano in Val di Pesa) in Florentine territory, which bears his name and the date 1319. Since the next document, dated 1321, regards the seizure by creditors of a suit of clothes left in the house of Nuto Vermigli in Florence, it is probable that Ambrogio's first Florentine sojourn took place during the years 1319-21. After a stay in Siena, where he sold a piece of land in 1324, a second Florentine period is attested by Ambrogio's admission as a painter to the Arte dei Medici e Speziali (Guild of Physicians and Apothecaries) in 1327. He must have remained in Florence at least until 1332, the date established for the triptych in the Church of S. Procolo (no longer extant), now reassembled in the Uffizi; possibly Ambrogio lived in Florence even longer.

The activity of the two brothers was united in Siena in 1335, when they both signed the frescoes (now destroyed) in the Hospital of S. Maria della Scala; nor did their collaboration end at this point. The Lorenzettis worked together on a number of projects throughout the years, as they must have also worked together in the Cathedral of Siena. Pietro was commissioned in 1335 for the St. Savinus altarpiece in the Cathedral; he probably worked on this for a long time, because *The Birth of the Virgin* (PL. 192) — proved by Bacci on the basis of an old inventory to have formed part of the altarpiece — is signed and dated 1342. According to the same source, Ambrogio's *Presentation in the Temple* (now Uffizi) was originally on the nearby altar of St. Crescentius in the Cathedral. Other documents show that Ambrogio was at work on the *Presentation* in 1339-40, and it too is signed and dated 1342.

Although in 1335 and 1339 Ambrogio is known to have been engaged on various small works in the Cathedral, during the 1335-45 period he was largely employed by the Sienese government, for which he painted a number of scenes (no longer extant) from Roman history on the exterior of the Signoria rooms in the Palazzo Pubblico (1337). Also in the Palazzo Pubblico, in the Sala della Pace, he painted the celebrated frescoes of the allegories of Good and Bad Government (PLS. 194-

196); payments recorded in 1338 and 1339 may have been for these. In 1340, according to the chronicle of Agnolo di Tura, he painted the fresco of the Madonna in the upper loggia of the Palazzo. In 1344, for the Sala del Mappamondo in the Palazzo Pubblico, Ambrogio did a map of the world on canvas on a rotating frame; the work is now lost, but it has given the hall its name. *The Annunciation*, also 1344 (now Siena, Pin.; PL. 198), was painted for the Sala dei Donzelli, Palazzo Pubblico. Since the attribution of a small painting (dated 1344) in the Sala di Attesa is disputed, *The Annunciation* is the last signed, dated, and documented work by Ambrogio. An *Annunciation* painted in 1344 on the façade of the Church of S. Pietro in Castelvecchio is unfortunately lost; the badly preserved yet still beautiful panels of the Virgin and of various saints now in the neighboring parish house appear to have belonged to the high altar. Ambrogio also painted other figures (about which no further information exists) in 1345. It is known that in 1347 he was a member of the Consiglio dei Paciari.

Concerning Pietro we possess some extremely controversial data relating to the altarpiece with the stories of the Blessed Humilitas (1316 or 1341; painted in Florence for the Convento delle Donne di Faenza; VI, PL. 378) and to the *Madonna and Angels* (probably 1340; originally Pistoia, S. Francesco; X, PL. 488), both now in the Uffizi. In any event, in 1341 Pietro is known to have been in Siena and in a good financial situation, since he was obliged to pay a special tax which the city levied on wealthy citizens. In 1342 he bought some property at Bibbiano for Cola and Martino, orphans (probably minors) of the sculptor Tino di Camaino, and in 1344 he sold them some property in the same town. Near Bibbiano, in the church in Castiglione del Bosco, Brandi has found frescoes of the Annunciation and of saints, dated 1345, which he attributes with great plausibility to Pietro. These would therefore be Pietro's last known works. After 1347 all trace of the brothers vanishes, and biographers have assumed that the Lorenzettis were among the victims of the plague that devastated Italy in 1348.

On the basis of this fragmentary and sparse documentary evidence, art historians have attempted to reconstruct the stylistic development of the two brothers, for the most part without clues to the dates of the large body of works carefully studied. This is an arduous and as yet uncompleted task. Moreover, the controversial chronological data furnished by the two works in the Uffizi, *The Blessed Humilitas* and the *Madonna and Angels* from Pistoia, have proved to be more a hindrance than a help. The importance of finally establishing the dates of these two paintings is enormous: if it could be proved that *The Blessed Humilitas* altarpiece was painted in 1316 and the *Madonna* in 1340, we would have two certain fixed points for the beginning and the end of Pietro's career. But in actual fact the date of the former is provided only by a copy in Roman numerals of a lost inscription, made not earlier than the 19th century, which historians have read as both 1316 and 1341, because of the obscurity of one of the symbols. The *Madonna*, though it has been date dwith more probability, is badly abraded and has been reconstructed on the basis of conjecture. As a result of these uncertainties, several hypotheses for the development of Pietro's art have emerged: If *The Blessed Humilitas* altarpiece is, in fact, a youthful work, Pietro began his career with the full and mature derivation from Giotto evident here; he then moved toward a style substantially Gothic in concept, from which he subsequently receded, finally and gradually resuming Giotto's teachings. Such an inverse progression, however, would appear unlikely, if not impossible. On the other hand, if *The Blessed Humilitas* is a late work, then Pietro's approach to Giotto was a slow development. It has also been suggested, on internal as well as external evidence, that the painting was executed at an approximate midpoint between these two dates. (See below for further discussion.)

Ghiberti, the first of the early writers on the Lorenzettis, strangely ignored Pietro and outlined the development of Ambrogio's artistic personality within the historical framework of a Humanistic evolution of the Gothic in the light of the new premises of Giotto's art. He called Ambrogio "nobilissimo compositore" (very noble composer of pictures) for his frescoes in S. Francesco in Siena, which Ghiberti was the first to ascribe to him, and "nobilissimo disegnatore" (very noble draftsman) in describing Ambrogio's classical orientation in his drawings of an antique statue found in Siena. It was also Ghiberti who first mentioned Ambrogio's Florentine works in Sto Spirito and S. Procolo. Vasari followed Ghiberti and did not realize that Pietro, to whom he devoted a separate "life" under the incorrect name of Pietro Laurati (based on a misreading of the signature on the Pistoia *Madonna and Angels*), was the brother of Ambrogio. Vasari states explicitly that Pietro was a pupil of Giotto and that he was also active in Rome. He provides detailed descriptions of Pietro's works in Arezzo (frescoes, now lost, in the Pieve di S. Maria), followed by a period of activity in Cortona; some of Pietro's Cortona works later came to light. Vasari also attributed *The Hermits* in the Camposanto in Pisa to Pietro, but this attribution was later refuted by Rosini and Supino.

The fact that Pietro and Ambrogio were brothers was first recognized critically by the Sienese writer G. della Valle (1782), despite the fact that their relationship was explicitly stated in the inscription on the frescoes of the Hospital of S. Maria della Scala in Siena. These frescoes had survived until the 18th century, but after the sheltering roof over the works was removed they were obliterated. Della Valle refuted the derivation from Giotto proposed by earlier art historians and advanced a purely Sienese origin and development. It has been left to modern art historians, however, to attempt to trace a clear evolution of the art of both brothers. Cavalcaselle (1864) made a fundamental contribution by attributing to Pietro the cycle of frescoes in the left transept of the Lower Church of the Basilica of S. Francesco in Assisi (PLS. 188, 189; VI, PL. 62). He pointed out that the artist followed certain Gothic trends not easily reconcilable with Vasari's classification of Pietro as a follower of Giotto, or with the stylistic information provided by *The Blessed Humilitas*, which Cavalcaselle had the vision to introduce, even though tentatively, into the Lorenzetti problem. (This altarpiece had hitherto been believed to be the work of the legendary Buffalmacco.) Decisive contributions to Lorenzetti scholarship were made by Berenson, A. Venturi, and especially F. M. Perkins, who, in commenting on Vasari's life of Pietro, first treated the whole of Pietro's activity (1912), as Von Meyenburg had done for Ambrogio (1903).

Fundamental for the study of Ambrogio's art was G. De Nicola's discovery in 1922 of the *Madonna* in Sant'Angelo a Vico l'Abate. This moved the beginning of Ambrogio's known activity back to 1319, at which time he appears to have been so mature that De Nicola thought him older than Pietro, to whom Ambrogio could have directly transmitted innovations from Giotto after his Florentine sojourn (ca. 1319–21). Reconstruction of the Florentine period received a further contribution from the discovery by Perkins and De Nicola of some of Ambrogio's S. Procolo paintings mentioned by Ghiberti. Step by step the problem of the relation of the two brothers with Sienese art and the art of Giotto entered into a phase of more subtle and complex elaboration. Attempts were made to establish a general historical reconstruction by Van Marle (1924), Weigelt (1930), De Wald (1930), Cecchi (1930), and Péter (1933). But their efforts were always hampered by the difficulty of placing in a logical sequence the undated works revealing diverse tendencies and those works showing the influence of Giotto, particularly Pietro's Uffizi paintings and the markedly Gothic cycles by Ambrogio in S. Francesco in Siena and by Pietro in the Lower Church in Assisi. This thorny problem has sometimes been side-stepped by excluding from the œuvre of Pietro the perpetually contradictory *Blessed Humilitas* and by attempts to create autonomous collaborators such as the "Master of Assisi" (Péter, for the Assisi frescoes) or the "Master of Dijon" (De Wald, for the works of Pietro's last period). The tendency to free the two artists from superfluous attributive incrustations has led to the successful transfer of a group of works formerly attributed to Pietro to a master whom Berenson named "Ugolino-Lorenzetti." To this master M. Meiss has now reattributed the works formerly ascribed to De Wald's "Master of the Ovile Madonna." But G. Rowley's identification of as many masters (of Rofeno, of Pompana, of St. Petronilla) as there are evolutionary phases in the course of Ambrogio's activity is an extreme solution. The monograph by G. Sinibaldi (1933), attempting to define the art of the two Lorenzettis, has the undoubted merit of treating both artists, despite their differences, as a single phenomenon in which 14th-century Sienese art came closest to the incipient Florentine Humanism and yet, in its greater freedom and vitality, remained the irreconcilable antithesis.

The direction of recent studies, begun by R. Longhi, has been in reaction to critical excesses. Denying that Florentine 14th-century painting was a sterile academic imitation of Giotto or was totally subservient to Sienese influences, Longhi recognizes in the works of the Florentine painters Maestro Stefano and Maso di Banco a vital elaboration of Giotto's premises into a new kind of painting that contains the seed of the Renaissance; the work of the Lorenzettis can be fitted into the frame of this intense artistic activity. And while Toesca (1951) once again sees the evolution of Pietro, and to a lesser extent of Ambrogio, concluding in the Gothic involution of all the art of the Sienese 14th century, younger scholars such as C. Volpe follow the lines indicated by Longhi, tending more and more to trace the complex relationship between the arts of Siena and Florence through the art of the Lorenzettis.

A survey of the present state of critical opinion regarding the Lorenzettis shows that the two brothers cannot be considered separately, not only because of their collaboration — which, as Toesca believes, was probably closer than the sources and inscriptions indicate — but also because their art reveals a definite trend in the art of 14th-century Siena at the very time when the leading position was held by Simone Martini in succession to Duccio (qq.v.). The primary origin of the Lorenzettis' art in the school of Duccio constantly enters into the works of the two brothers until the last stages of their maturity. It is probable that Pietro, about whom we have the earliest information, however uncertain, pointed the way to an original break from that school. This break may be seen in those of his works which differ from the output by the anonymous mass of Duccio followers, showing a stronger perception of form and an awareness of the new trends marked by Giotto in his Assisi frescoes. (This awareness also appears in Duccio's own last narrative panels for his *Maestà*.) The new trends can be seen less clearly in the *Madonna* of Casole d'Elsa (attributed by De Nicola to Pietro but by Bacci, on better grounds, to Segna di Bonaventura) than in the *Madonna* of the Church of S. Pellegrino, Siena (Siena, Pin., No. 18); before Adolfo Venturi's attribution, the S. Pellegrino *Madonna* was believed to be by an almost unknown Gilio di Pietro. The same trends can also be seen in the complex of panels related to the *Madonna* in the Pinacoteca Comunale in Città di Castello, which Cavalcaselle had attributed to Pietro's early years. (For these questions cf. Brandi, 1933.)

That the foregoing may have been the premises of Pietro's development, even though proof for a definitive exegesis is lacking, is suggested by Pietro's first documented work, the polyptych in the Pieve di S. Maria in Arezzo (PL. 191), painted 1320–21. Here, together with the Byzantinism of certain figures in the manner of Duccio, there are elements reminiscent of Giotto. The plasticity of Pietro's figures in the Arezzo work is obtained by means of harsh contrasts as yet unresolved by a complete blending of colors. This recalls the work of certain collaborators in Giotto's St. Francis cycle in Assisi, in which C. Gnudi (*Giotto*, Milan, 1958) has noted a "free and vivacious sensibility" of Sienese influence. With this in mind, it is well to remember Vasari's reference to a Pietro who was a student of Giotto and active in Rome, where Giotto went after leaving Assisi on the eve of the Jubilee of 1300; but the reference is as yet only a hypothesis for further investigation.

A Florentine product, the *St. Lucy* in the Church of S. Lucia dei Magnoli, may provide important clues to the early works of Pietro. The removal of the complete repainting by Jacopo del Sellaio reveals in the few surviving areas, apart from some tenuous reminiscences of Duccio, a compact plasticity that recalls the early Giotto. This plasticity is encountered in certain parts of the Arezzo polyptych. Various similarities to the work of Giovanni Pisano, which have often been noticed in this work, may be the result of an interest in sculpture stimulated by Pietro's early association with Giotto, in Assisi, or more probably in Florence. However, in the Arezzo work (1320–21) the tense, spiritual quality of the figures is enriched with subtle lyrical accents and tends to be controlled by the harmonic cadences of the Gothic style of Simone Martini, who had returned to Siena from Naples after 1317.

Pietro's youthful experiences would seem to have concluded in 1320 with this orientation. Thus if *The Blessed Humilitas* altarpiece is correctly dated 1316, it would be extremely difficult to include it among Pietro's works, for here is a mature product in which the Giottesque interpretation has already achieved a vigorous pictorial conviction far distant from the influence of Duccio or Gothic tendencies. To achieve this style, from which it probably would have been impossible for the artist to recede, Pietro must have passed through other evolutionary phases, which art historians are attempting to reconstruct.

The gap of nearly ten years between the polyptych of Arezzo and Pietro's next documented work, the 1329 altarpiece painted for S. Maria del Carmine in Siena (PL. 190), has been filled with works either lacking or only partly provided with chronological indications; such works include those found at Cortona (the *Madonna* in the Cathedral and the large *Crucifix*, now Mus. Diocesano), those from the Convento di S. Francesco in Siena, and frescoes in the Lower Church of S. Francesco at Assisi (PLS. 188, 189; VI, PL. 62). Art historians, following Cavalcaselle's suggestion, have attempted to link Pietro's Assisi cycle (particularly *The Crucifixion*, *The Deposition*, and *The Resurrection*, which iconographically follow the *Childhood* and *Adolescence* frescoes by Giotto followers in the opposite arm of the transept) with the large Cortona *Crucifix* and another *Crucifixion* (formerly, Chapter House, Convento di S. Francesco, Siena; now in the Church of S. Francesco, Siena; PL. 191), as well as two scenes from the life of St. Louis of Toulouse (PL. 197) and the scene of the Franciscan martyrs, which since the time of Ghiberti had been regarded as the work of Ambrogio. Here we find ourselves in the very thick of the most controversial Lorenzetti problems, because in nearly all of these works there stand revealed the elements of an idiom totally and lyrically Gothic, with no parallel in either the Arezzo polyptych or the certain later works of Pietro, from the Carmelite altarpiece (1329; PL. 190) to *The Birth of the Virgin* (1342; PL. 192). This anomaly has led to innumerable attempts to arrive at a coherent chronological position for this whole group within the artistic evolution of Pietro, especially for its most important component, the Assisi cycle. These attempts range from early datings for the Assisi frescoes (ca. 1320; Cavalcaselle, 1864), or even earlier (Volpe), to intermediate ones (1325–29; De Wald, Cecchi, Brandi, Carli), to very late, even after 1340 (Péter, Toesca). On the basis of a progressive identification of elaborate Gothic mannerisms, different dates have even been proposed for the two sections of the frescoes: those on the walls of the transept, dominated by the magnificent *Crucifixion*, and the scenes of the Passion in the vault. The two periods may be included within the years 1325 and 1329 (De Wald, Cecchi), or 1325–29 and the years following 1340 (Péter). However, Péter believes, as did Thode and Venturi, that the works of this very late period represented a continuation by assistants, among whom Péter singles out the principal one, designating him the "Master of Assisi."

The dating problem of the Lorenzetti frescoes in Assisi is not clarified by the assumption that they were painted concurrently with the Giottesque frescoes in the crossing and right arm of the transept, because there are no positive dates for those either. The problem has become further complicated, since the first attempts to solve it were made by Thode and P. Schubring, by the recognition of features in common between some of the Giottesque frescoes and the late style of the Lorenzettis, without any indication as to who influenced whom. Up to now the only basis for dating the whole transept is the fact that the decorations of the two chapels at either end were commissioned by the brothers Napoleone and Giovanni Orsini, both cardinals, who had intended these areas as funerary chapels.

Only the chapel in the right transept, commissioned by Giovanni and decorated by followers of Giotto, was ever completed with a monumental tomb; this can therefore be considered earlier. And since in a fresco over the arch of this chapel Giovanni is depicted (as Schubring noted) as a young man without the insignia of the cardinalate, which was conferred on him in 1316, the beginning of the chapel can be determined as somewhat prior to 1316. In the Napoleone chapel at the opposite end of the transept, the work of Pietro is evident in the frescoed triptych of the Madonna between St. John the Baptist and St. Francis, but the touch is more experienced in linear subtleties and chromatic blending than in Pietro's Arezzo polyptych.

By 1326 the Lorenzetti brothers were engaged in frescoing the Chapter House of the Convento di S. Francesco (now the Pontifical Seminary), Siena, in the increasingly Gothic manner that was already apparent in Pietro's works in both Assisi and Cortona. By combining links in a chain of evidence, and bearing in mind certain affinities (as Péter and Volpe noted) in Ambrogio's narrative paintings and his *Madonna* of Sant'Angelo a Vico l'Abate (1319), a partial Lorenzetti chronology for the period 1320–40 can be hypothesized: Pietro, when he had completed his work in Arezzo in 1321, received the commission for the chapel of Cardinal Napoleone Orsini in Assisi, on which he worked more or less concurrently with his paintings in Cortona. The triptych on the terminal wall of the Napoleone chapel has in common with the Cortona works a more mature stylistic development, and it may be supposed that this was the starting point for the subsequent commission for the frescoes in the whole of the left arm of the transept, executed while Giotto's followers were completing the right arm. In these first years of the decade 1320–30, after Ambrogio had returned from Florence (1321), both brothers might have received the commission for the Chapter House of S. Francesco in Siena. It may be assumed that the feverish activity of these years was fostered by the Orsinis: Giovanni, by then a cardinal and apostolic legate in Tuscany, blessed the first stone of the new Franciscan church in Siena in 1326.

The period of about 1321–27, when Ambrogio was in Siena, provides a possible date for the Assisi frescoes, but if they were preceded by Pietro's activity in Cortona and in the Napoleone Orsini chapel, the beginning date might be slightly later than 1321. Further work on the Assisi transept could have been carried out by Pietro at the same time as the Siena Chapter House frescoes (of which the greater portion is by Ambrogio, who may have remained there alone to paint them); the Assisi work could have continued in the following years until its conclusion in the Passion cycle on the vault by assistants, who carried out Pietro's intentions and projects some time after he had reached a further stage in his stylistic evolution, as revealed in the Carmelite altarpiece (1329; PL. 190) and subsequent works. Such a chronological sequence, even if the evidence is circumstantial, could explain how the Gothic elements in Pietro's art (of which the first indications appear in the Arezzo polyptych and which become predominant in Assisi, Cortona, and in S. Francesco in Siena) do not constitute the definitive direction of his artistic development but represent only a phase during which he participated in the general trend of Sienese art. This phase (1320–40) is found simultaneously in the work of Ambrogio. It also corresponds to Simone Martini's return to Siena from Naples, between 1317 and 1321, which marked the end of the predominance of Duccio's style.

Simone, who had absorbed the culture of France while working at the Angevin court of Naples, brought with him the persuasive refinements of the French style, which constituted the synthesis of the very rich heritage of the Middle Ages then spreading from France throughout western Europe. Although art historians have often attempted to discount any link between the Lorenzettis and Simone, such contacts were noticed as early as the late 18th century by Della Valle and are manifest in all the Lorenzetti works dating from the decade when Simone was the dominating artistic figure in Siena and other parts of Italy. Ambrogio's *Madonna* in Sant'Angelo a Vico l'Abate (1319) is free from the plastic harshness of Pietro's Arezzo work because Ambrogio was able to achieve Simone's luminous color and linear fluidity without being obliged, as Pietro was, to overcome the influences of an early training in the school of Giotto. From Giotto, Ambrogio derived only the tone and the diffused calm; the frontal rigidity of the image seems to reflect Simone Martini's *Majestas* (PL. 332; in its original 1315 version, before the 1321 restoration) in the same way that it was repeated in San Gimignano in 1317 (*Maestà*, Palazzo Com.; signed by Lippo Memmi).

The assignment of certain works to this early period of Ambrogio's activity is not wholly convincing, even if their attribution is certain. The *Madonna* in the Brera, Milan, seems rather to reflect the more decisive and complex plastic intentions of later years; the polyptych of the *Crucifixion, Four Saints, Nativity, and Annunciation to Shepherds* (Städelsches Kunstinst., Frankfort) reveals a full spatial mastery not even reached in the S. Francesco, Siena, frescoes. Of the reconstruction of this period, proposed by Volpe, only the *Crucifix* (No. 598) in the Pinacoteca in Siena, attributed by him to Ambrogio, can be accepted. In this work Giotto is once again reflected, by way of Simone. The latter artist inspired Pietro's almost manneristic stylistic effects of the small, pathetic *Crucifix* in Cortona (Mus. Diocesano). This fusion of Simone Martini and Giotto was Pietro's ideal when he painted in Assisi *The Deposition* (PL. 189), *The Entombment, The Resurrection, The Descent into Limbo, The Hanging Judas*, and *St. Francis Receiving the Stigmata*, on the left terminal wall of the transept, and the figures of five Franciscan friars; it also inspired his great *Crucifixion* (PL. 188), in which a whole medieval world (no less romantic and chivalrous than that of Simone's scene of St. Martin) is assembled at the feet of the three crosses, filling without gaps an immense space that extends beyond the limits of perspective. It matters little, so far as the lyric unity of this work is concerned, if alongside the parts painted by the master brush of Pietro there appears — and actually in the Crucifix itself — the hand of the experienced but more trite assistant to whom in subsequent years Pietro was to leave almost the entire execution of the scenes of the Passion, which he had by that time conceived for the vault.

Pietro's Arezzo polyptych (PL. 191) of 1320–21 reveals the transition from the plastic force derived from Giovanni Pisano to the Elysian harmony of Simone Martini, the two great achievements of the Sienese Gothic. A further step in Pietro's evolution is seen in the *Madonna* of Cortona, which Berenson dated 1315 but which, as Carli correctly states, was done shortly after the Arezzo polyptych, as shown by the softer blending of colors, even though the archaic structure contains reflections of Duccio's Maestàs. The Cortona *Madonna* is closely related to the triptych in the Napoleone Orsini chapel, whose progressive stylistic refinement negates the assignment suggested by some historians of an earlier date than any of Pietro's known works. The large Cortona *Crucifix* tends toward the Gothic in its reminiscences of those suffering crucifixes, gaunt in their exaggerated linearity, by such Sienese followers of Giovanni Pisano as Lorenzo Maitani. The softening of the modeling derived from Giovanni Pisano, leading to a lyrical rendering of the image, was the determining factor in the style of the *Crucifixion* in S. Francesco in Siena (PL. 191) and of the fragment with the *Risen Christ*, still in the Chapter House of what is now the Pontifical Seminary in Siena. This softer modeling and lyric tension loses its effect, however, in the draftsmanship of Pietro's assistant in Assisi. But in the second Assisi triptych (above another small crucifix), depicting the Madonna between St. Francis and another saint (probably John the Evangelist), the melodious flow of Simone Martini's line catches the theme of Giovanni Pisano's *Madonna and Child* in a new version, bright with luminous color. This flowing line had already been revealed in the Arezzo polyptych and was here established with absolute mastery as Pietro's new style.

The evolutionary phase of about 1319–26 for both brothers is reflected differently in Ambrogio's style, although the two artists are linked by a common basic idiom. In the ample spatial organization of the two surviving frescoes in S. Francesco in Siena (the complete cycle was described by Ghiberti), as well as the ascribed fragments in London (Nat. Gall.), Ambrogio's prior Florentine experience is clearly recognizable. In Florence Ambrogio came into contact with the mature Giotto and such pupils as Maestro Stefano and Maso di Banco — artists of a very different stature from those whom his brother saw working in the right transept of the Lower Church in Assisi. But the magnificent spatial balance that Giotto achieved after his Paduan frescoes was modified in Ambrogio's work to follow the path indicated by Simone Martini as early as the *Majestas* (1315). Giotto's enclosed unity of time and space was interpreted according to the dictates of Ambrogio's imagination, in which the actual geometric spatial reality could be turned (as in Simone's works) to lyric effects of unlimited space. In this Ambrogio differed from Pietro, who from the start of his artistic career was oriented, through the influence of Giotto and Giovanni Pisano, toward a plastic concept of form which, as a pupil of Duccio, he expressed in terms of color. During the period when the Lorenzettis followed the new Gothic trend established by Simone, they recalled and interpreted the idiom of Giotto, each according to his own lights. Pietro aspired to a deeper pictorial achievement, Ambrogio to a greater control of spatial clarity. Ambrogio's concentration on this most vital aspect of the problem stated by Giotto made him, during these years, the more progressive artist of the two. As De Nicola has pointed out, at this time Ambrogio could have taught something to Pietro.

It is difficult to follow closely the progress of the two brothers in the course of this mature evolutionary phase, since precise chronological data exist only for Ambrogio. Rowley ascribed to a hypothetical "Master of Rofeno" those of Ambrogio's works which most recall the Siena S. Francesco frescoes and those by Pietro on the transept walls in the Lower Church in Assisi (which this author considers contemporaneous). The designation "Master of Rofeno" derives from the most important of these works, the altarpiece with St. Michael, formerly in the Badia a Rofeno (now in the Mus. d'Arte Sacra, Asciano); here the archangel, depicted fighting with the dragon, is entirely surrounded by a wonderful pattern of arabesques in the manner of Simone Martini, while the Madonna in the cusp is clearly a derivation from Pietro's Madonna in the second Assisi triptych. As also in Ambrogio's *Four Saints* (Francis, Mary Magdalene, Catherine, Benedict; now Mus. dell'Opera del Duomo, Siena), which Rowley would have us believe was originally connected with the Rofeno altarpiece, the clear linear quality derived from Simone gives a more concise outline to the Giottesque forms. These same stylistic factors reappear in a complex figural dialectic in Ambrogio's superb *Madonna del Latte* (formerly hermitage of Lecceto; now Siena, Seminario), in frescoes on the façade of the church of Lecceto, and in Florence in Ambrogio's triptych from the Church of S. Procolo of the Madonna between SS. Nicholas of Bari and Proculus (now reassembled in the Uffizi). For the triptych it has been possible to assign the date of 1332, which G. Cinelli (1677) had read in an inscription now lost. It is uncertain whether Ambrogio's frescoed *Crucifixion*, which, according to the sources, was in the monastery of Sto Spirito, can also be assigned a date within these mature years. No trace of the fresco remains other than its echoes in *The Crucifixion* painted several decades later by Orcagna and Nardo di Cione in the adjacent refectory. Ambrogio's presence in Florentine painting is further attested by the evolution of Bernardo Daddi, who more than anyone else must have been close to Ambrogio between 1328 and 1333.

Pietro, who had remained in Siena during Ambrogio's second Florentine period, proceeded from Simone Martini's Gothicism toward the influence of Giotto. He was, however, not exposed to Giotto's Florentine works but rather to their feeble reflection in the art of Giotto's followers painting in Assisi. Pietro's second triptych in the transept of the Lower Church in Assisi seems to be linked with those later works in which he achieved a very delicate balance between a compositional rhythm and the enchantment of a clear color permeated with light. Such works are the *Three Saints* in the Fondazione Horne, Florence; the exquisite female saint in Le Mans (Mus. des B. A.); the *Virgin and Child Enthroned*, Philadelphia (Mus. of Art, Johnson Coll.); the two angels now in the Rabinowitz Collection, Brooklyn, New York (which possibly once flanked the Virgin of the Johnson Collection); and the Madonnas in the Church of SS. Stefano e Degna in Castiglione d'Orcia, in the Serristori Collection in Florence, in the Perkins Collection in Assisi, and in the Church of SS. Leonardo e Cristoforo in Monticchiello. In these works may be read in a clearly defined sequence the steps leading from Pietro's second Assisi triptych to the Carmelite altarpiece in Siena (1329; PL. 190), which it has been possible to reassemble in the Siena Pinacoteca from sections already available and from the recovered central part of the predella that lay beneath a 16th-century overpainting. It is not certain whether the two saints (Peter and John the Baptist) in the Vatican Museums also belonged to this altarpiece, as has been suggested by Brandi; many art historians regard them as very early works of Pietro.

In *The Madonna between Angels and Saints*, which forms the center of this sumptuous altarpiece, the influence of Simone Martini on Pietro is still very strong. It has been recognized that the Carmelite scenes depicted on the predella do not precede Ambrogio's compositions in S. Francesco, Siena, but are derived from them without achieving their monumental spatial coherence (Péter). Pietro, still aware of Duccio, used elaborate structures to form a composition of planes of clear color and set the central group (showing delivery of the Carmelite rule to St. Brocardo) in a vast space like that in which, a year previously, Simone Martini had evoked his Guidoriccio da Fogliano (PL. 334). But one senses the limits of the Gothic experience which had been reached in the Assisi cycle, even though Pietro's assistants in the Passion cycle of the vault continued to paint in this idiom, especially the so-called "Master of Assisi" to whom Péter ascribes the three saints (Bartholomew, Cecilia, and John the Baptist) in the Siena Pinacoteca (Nos. 79, 81, and 82; from S. Cecilia a Crevole; 1332). As Brandi has established, these paintings are not signed by Pietro, as had been believed. It is unlikely that Pietro would have returned to such Gothic subtleties after the new stylistic intentions of the Carmelite altarpiece. Perhaps at about this time he followed in his brother's footsteps and went to Florence, the center of the art of Giotto. This could be established if it were possible to assign a date within these years to the altarpiece of *The Blessed Humilitas* (VI, PL. 378). Cohn (1959) studied this work after the discovery by Meiss of the scattered parts (three cusps with the Evangelists and seven tondos with the dead Christ between the Virgin, St. John, and other saints) and of an 18th-century drawing depicting the altarpiece before its dismembering and the removal of two of the panels to Berlin. Cohn (1959) concluded that 1316 and 1341 were both possible readings of the date copied from a lost inscription, but outside evidence collected by both Cohn and Carli favored an early date; this evidence, however, can be countered. The research of Luisa Marcucci (1961) has brought to light other data indicating the years 1330–32, during which time the Blessed Margherita died. (Margherita is depicted in the altarpiece together with the Blessed Humilitas.) This was also the period in which the canonical text of the legend shown in the various panels was established. Such a date — a little later than the Carmelite altarpiece — would coincide fully with the stylistic phase revealed in the Humilitas work. In the latter, Pietro follows the pictorial interpretation of Giotto, already felt in the Carmelite work, reducing the total narrative to a poetic evocation of the single episodes and avoiding all Gothic linear simplification of structure, rendered through vivid color.

Ambrogio, in his painting of incidents in the life of St. Nicholas for the second altar of the Church of S. Procolo, Florence (now Uffizi), probably done after the S. Procolo triptych, recalled his brother's *Blessed Humilitas*, actually copying certain figures from it and deriving the spatial relationships and strength of color on which the formal construction is based. However, Ambrogio, with his greater mastery of perspective, elaborated the spatial element in the play of an imaginative series of rooms and vastly extended it by adding a seascape. The hypothesis of a period of activity in Florence of both brothers between 1330 and 1335 — Vasari mentions a tabernacle by Pietro in the Piazza Sto Spirito — would go far to explain many details in their subsequent evolution. The group of paintings of evident Florentine structure attributed by De Wald to the hypothetical "Master of Dijon" (after the triptych in Dijon, Mus. B. A.) could be firmly ascribed to Pietro. Related to this group are the small *ancone* of the Museo Poldi Pezzoli in Milan, in the Berenson Foundation in Settignano (rear panel in a private collection in Rome), and in the Walters Art Gallery in Baltimore. Also close to these works, although stylistically more evolved, is Pietro's *Madonna* of the Loeser Collection (Florence, Palazzo Vecchio). The presumed Florentine sojourn of 1330-35 would also support the theory according to which Pietro, returning to Siena with the fresh imprint in his mind of Giotto's chapels in Sta Croce, Florence, was able to begin the frescoes in S. Maria dei Servi, Siena, where rebuilding had begun in 1334; the frescoes were mainly executed by assistants.

In 1335 the two brothers were reunited in Siena, where they painted the frescoes on the façade of the Hospital of S. Maria della Scala. The loss of these works has deprived us of an example of a fundamental phase of the new style of both artists. Iconographic reconstruction attempted by Péter and Marchini (1930, 1938), based on a study of the strong echoes of these works found in all subsequent Sienese painting, indicates how novel and striking the originals must have seemed to the Sienese, still accustomed to the Gothic art of Simone Martini. The two Lorenzettis must have soon supplanted Simone in his official capacity, since they received important commissions from the Opera del Duomo for the altars of St. Savinus (begun 1335) and St. Crescentius. A short time later Ambrogio must have been called to decorate the Palazzo Pubblico, the most important secular building in the city, with his celebrated frescoes in the Sala della Pace (PLS. 194–196).

A small panel now in London (Nat. Gall.), whose subject, identified by Volpe, indicates that it belonged to the St. Savinus altar, reveals Pietro's progress in the mastery of perspective, which was probably achieved about 1335. As also in another fragment, depicting Christ before Pilate (Vat. Mus.), from an unidentified larger complex, Pietro stresses far more profoundly than he did in the various episodes of the *Blessed Humilitas* scenes the value of open spaces between figures moving freely between foreground and background. Although Pietro absorbed Giotto's spatial understanding more slowly than did his brother, he realized more clearly how this might lay the foundations of a truly pictorial organization. On the basis of the evolution of Pietro's new premises, it is possible to assign dates between 1335 and 1340 to paintings that have hitherto been of controversial chronology, such as the two very beautiful saints, *Agnes* and *Catherine* (Siena, Pin.), and the *St. Clare* in the Contini Bonacossi Collection in Florence. The date of the *Crucifixion* (Cambridge, Mass., Fogg Art Mus.), so far regarded as very early, should also be reconsidered; this is a painting of vast spatial concept and intensely fused color. The date of 1340 for Pietro's *Madonna and Angels* (from Pistoia; Uffizi) can be justified, though it is legible only through the work of restorers. Despite excessive cleaning, the work displays notably fine qualities in the luminous harmony of vivid colors.

Pietro thus arrived at a pictorial resolution of spatial construction through an interpretation of Giotto's teachings that was purely Sienese in its use of chromatic values. This resolution can be seen in the admirable *Funeral of a Saint* (Assisi, Perkins Coll.) and in *The Birth of the Virgin* in the Museo dell'Opera del Duomo in Siena (PL. 192). The latter is dated 1342, although it formed part of the St. Savinus altar begun in 1335. The altarpiece has always been regarded as remarkable for its extraordinary homogeneity of perspective, in which the frame of the triptych actually forms the foreground of the space in which the whole scene is organized.

Ambrogio followed a path of development similar to Pietro's. After collaborating with his brother on the frescoes in the Hospital of S. Maria della Scala, he went on to paint the work on which his fame has since rested, namely, the frescoes in the Sala della Pace in the Palazzo Pubblico of Siena (allegories of Good and Bad Government), documentation for which covers the years 1337-39. Toesca rightly pointed out that the St. Nicholas panels in S. Procolo, Florence, seem to be their direct antecedents. To these could perhaps be added the *Allegory of Sin and Redemption* in the Siena Pinacoteca, which reveals the same spatial mastery. Pietro sought, even if he did not achieve, the closed unity of Giotto's narratives; but Ambrogio, although he had been acquainted with the work of Giotto over a far longer period, avoided such limitations. Ambrogio always remained tied to that wonderful Gothic world of multiform variety and figurative effusion; the city, with its narrow alleys and buildings haphazardly crowded together, unexpectedly rising with an aerial embroidery of loggias, terraces, and crenelated towers (PL. 194), and the undulating countryside, with its gentle mountain outlines (PL. 195), formed the setting for the swarming life that Ambrogio saw and painted. The antique statue which, according to Ghiberti, Ambrogio had carefully drawn, was transformed in his allegory into the figures of Peace (PL. 196) and Concordia, depicted in the Gothic idiom and lost in their attention to prophetic inner voices. This emotional intensity infused his Madonnas with the human quality of maternal love.

Ambrogio's works from 1340 onward are pervaded by these "rare sentiments" (Volpe). Thus the Madonnas of Rofeno and of S. Procolo are developed, with a tighter plastic organization, into the *Madonna* of Serre di Rapolano (Siena, Pin.); the *Madonna and Child* of the St. Petronilla triptych (Siena, Pin.), between St. Mary Magdalene and St. Dorothy (PL. 193); the *Madonna* of the Boston Museum of Fine Arts (formerly Platt Coll.); the *Madonna and Child* now in Washington, D.C. (Nat. Gall.); and perhaps the *Madonna* now in the Brera, Milan. The formal composition of the last-mentioned painting seems too advanced in the artist's evolution to be an early work. A careful study of this group of paintings may establish a precise evolutionary sequence more or less contemporaneous with the decoration of the Palazzo Pubblico and culminating with the great frescoed *Madonna* on the upper Loggia there, painted in 1340. It seems as if the pictorial distention of Maso di Banco and Maestro Stefano had only now become clear to Ambrogio. But even though Ambrogio adopted a new idiom in his painting, he still remained purely lyrical in concept, avoiding simple narrative concreteness. And so he continued in all the works that can be dated after 1340. The *Madonna* of the Loggia was the thematic predecessor of the *Madonna Enthroned* in Budapest (Mus. of Fine Arts) and of the *Madonna and Child* in Roccalbegna, Church of SS. Pietro e Paolo, flanked by two monumental saints; Rowley (1958) ascribed the works to different masters, but the subtle figural counterpoint develops a single lyrical concept to its logical conclusion. This series finally led to the altarpiece in Massa Marittima (Mus. Civ.) — a Madonna and Child amid a host of angels, saints, and Virtues — in which the recollections of Giotto are transformed into the typical Sienese composition of the great Maestàs. There is also a frescoed *Madonna with Saints and Angels* by Ambrogio in the chapel at San Galgano, near Monte Siepi, as well as an *Annunciation* in which the angel fills the whole space with his outspread wings. The color characteristic of these frescoes also appears in vivid flaming tones in the *Maestà* of S. Agostino in Siena, the sole surviving portion of a larger work; this color acquires a corporeal density in *The Coronation of the Virgin* (Montefalco, Church of S. Agostino), although the work is damaged and its attribution controversial. Ambrogio's progressive pictorial development culminates in the pyrotechnics of his small *Madonna, Saints, and Angels* in the Pinacoteca in Siena (No. 65), where the perspective of the throne steps painted in various colors seems to form a continuation of the luminous halo surrounding the Virgin.

While Pietro, in his *Birth of the Virgin* (PL. 192) of 1342, achieved an increasingly clear relationship between the figures and their ambient space, Ambrogio in the same year, by means of a similar perspective construction, achieved an infinite and dreamlike quality in the *Presentation in the Temple* (now Uffizi) for the St. Crescentius altar of the Cathedral of Siena. Much has been written about the perspective coherence of Ambrogio's *Annunciation* of 1344 (Siena, Pin.; PL. 198), which is surprisingly modern. But Toesca has correctly pointed out how everything in it departs from and contradicts all intentional rationality. There remains the evocation of a moment — the ecstatic moment of the Incarnation — free from all other intentions, which, as Rowley has clearly demonstrated, has no counterpart in traditional iconography.

The works ascribed to the two Lorenzettis, in a list the extensiveness of which is an indication of the interest the two brothers have aroused among art historians, are far more numerous than those which it has been possible to mention within this article. It is necessary, at least, to cite the following works that have not been discussed here.

Pietro: *St. Leonard* (Brooklyn, Rabinowitz Coll.); *St. Dorothy* (?) (Assisi, Perkins Coll.) and *St. Catherine of Alexandria* (Met. Mus.), both possibly part of the same work; *St. Clare* (Washington, D.C., Nat. Gall.); the small diptych in Altenburg, Lindenau-Museum, the signature of which Toesca regards as dubious. Ambrogio: Well-known paintings such as *The Holy Family* (Zurich, Abegg Coll.); and the two superb landscapes of controversial attribution in the Siena Pinacoteca (Nos. 70, 71).

The brothers' known activity ends in the years 1344–45. Presumably they both died in the great plague of 1348. By 1340 Simone Martini had left Siena, and thus by the middle of the century that city had lost all the great masters who had enabled her to compete with Florence for leadership in Italian art. Once Giotto had died, the great rivalry came to an end. The road of the future was not the Gothic renewal proposed by the Sienese artists but the completely new art being created in Florence. The lyricism of the Lorenzettis became sterile in the interminable series of replicas by their Sienese followers, but in Florence the influence of the production of Giotto and his followers survived to constitute the vital poetic suggestion that was, in the fullness of the Renaissance, once again brought to life by Angelico.

SOURCES. L. Ghiberti, I Commentarii, II, 11–12 (ed. J. von Schlosser, Berlin, 1912); K. Frey, ed., Anonimo Gaddiano or Codex Magliabechiano (ca. 1537–42), Berlin, 1892; Vasari, I, pp. 471–79, 521–35; G. Vasari, Vita di Pietro Laurati (ed. F. M. Perkins, Florence, 1912); F. Bocchi and G. Cinelli, Le bellezze della città di Firenze, Florence, 1677, p. 389; F. Baldinucci, Notizie de' professori del disegno . . . , 2d ed., II, Turin, 1768, pp. 61–63, 79–81; G. della Valle, Lettere senesi . . . , sopra le belle arti, II, Venice, 1782, pp. 201–27; L. Lanzi, Storia pittorica dell'Italia, 3d ed., I, Bassano, 1809, pp. 319–21; K. F. von Rumohr, Italienische Forschungen, I, Berlin, Stettin, 1827 (ed. J. von Schlosser, Frankfurt am Main, 1920, pp. 289–94); G. Milanesi, Documenti per la storia dell'arte senese, I–II, Siena, 1854; S. Borghesi and L. Banchi, Nuovi documenti per la storia dell'arte senese, Siena, 1898; G. Milanesi, Nuovi documenti per la storia dell'arte toscana . . . , Florence, 1901; L. Olcott and W. Heywood, Guide to Siena, London, 1903 (2d ed. by F. M. Perkins, Siena, 1924); A. Grünzweig, Una nuova prova del soggiorno di Ambrogio Lorenzetti a Firenze, RArte, XV, 1933, pp. 249–51; R. G. Mather, Nuove informazioni intorno alle matricole di Giotto, L'Arte, N.S., VII, 1936, pp. 50–64; P. Bacci, Dipinti inediti o sconosciuti di Pietro Lorenzetti in Siena e nel contado, Siena, 1939; P. Bacci, L'elenco delle pitture, sculture e architetture, compilato nel 1625–1626 da Mons. Fabio Chigi, B. senese di storia patria, X, 1939, pp. 197–213, 297–337; W. and E. Paatz, Die Kirchen von Florenz, 6 vols., Frankfurt am Main, 1940–54.

BIBLIOG. J. A. Crowe and G. B. Cavalcaselle, A New History of Painting in Italy, II, London, 1864, pp. 117–47; E. Dobbert, Die sienesische Malerschule, in Kunst und Künstler (ed. R. Dohme), I, Leipzig, 1878, pp. 38–55; H. Thode, Franz von Assisi, Berlin, 1885, pp. 462–72; H. Thode, Studien zur Geschichte der italienischen Kunst des XIV. Jahrhundert, RepfKw, XI, 1888, pp. 1–22; V. Lusini, Storia della Basilica di San Francesco in Siena, Siena, 1894; B. Berenson, The Central Italian Painters of the Renaissance, New York, London, 1897 (repr. in Italian Pictures of the Renaissance, Oxford, 1932); A. Schmarsow, Meister des XIV. und XV. Jahrhundert im Lindenau Museum zu Altenburg, Festschrift zu Ehren des kunsthist. Inst. in Florenz, Leipzig, 1897, pp. 151–52; P. Schubring, Die Fresken im Querschiff der Unterkirche San Francesco in Assisi, RepfKw, XXII, 1899, pp. 1–12; P. Schubring, Das Gute Regiment, ZfbK, XIII, 1901–02, pp. 138–45; P. Schubring, Die primitiven Italianer im Louvre, Z. für christliche K., XIV, 1901, cols. 353–82; G. Cagnola, Di un quadro poco noto del Lorenzetti, Rass. d'arte, II, 1902, p. 143; A. Pératé, Un Triomphe de la Mort de Pietro Lorenzetti, Mél. Paul Fabre, Paris, 1902, pp. 436–45; E. von Meyenburg, Ambrogio Lorenzetti, Zürich, 1903; Burlington Fine Arts Club, Illustrated Catalogue of Pictures of Siena . . . , London, 1904; O. H. Giglioli, L'allegoria politica negli affreschi di Ambrogio Lorenzetti, Emporium, XIX, 1904, pp. 265–82; F. M. Perkins, Di alcune opere poco note di Ambrogio Lorenzetti, Rass. d'arte, IV, 1904, pp. 186–90; F. M. Perkins, The Forgotten Masterpiece of Ambrogio Lorenzetti, BM, XIII. 1904, pp. 81–84; F. M. Perkins, La pittura alla Mostra d'arte in Siena, Rass. d'arte, IV, 1904, pp. 145–53; F. M. Perkins, Scoperte e primizie artistiche, Rass. d'arte, IV, 1904, pp. 190–91; W. Rothes, Die Blütezeit der sienesische Malerei, Strasbourg, 1904; O. Wulff, Zur Stilbildung der Trecentomalerei, RepfKw, XXVII, 1904, pp. 111–12; Michel, II, 2, pp. 858–77; F. M. Perkins, Scoperte e primizie artistiche, Rass. d'arte, VI, 1906, p. 15; D. E. Jacobsen, Die sienesische Meister des Trecento in der Gemäldegalerie zu Siena, Strasbourg, 1907; W. Suida, Alcuni quadri italiani primitivi nella Galleria Nazionale di Budapest, L'Arte, X, 1907, pp. 178–83; Venturi, V, pp. 668–722 and passim; G. Cagnola, Dipinti ignorati, Rass. d'arte senese, IV, 1908, pp. 45–47; P. Misciatelli, Un affresco inedito senese del secolo XIV, Vita d'arte, II, 1908, pp. 114–16; F. M. Perkins, Alcuni appunti sulla Galleria delle Belle Arti di Siena, Rass. d'arte senese, IV, 1908, pp. 48–61; F. M. Perkins, Ancora dei dipinti sconosciuti di scuola senese, Rass. d arte senese, IV, 1908, pp. 3–9; U. Gnoli, Un polittico di Pietro Lorenzetti scoperto a Gubbio, Rass. d'arte umbra, I, 1909–10, pp. 22–25; F. M. Perkins, Dipinti italiani nella raccolta Platt, Rass. d'arte, XI, 1911, pp. 3–4; G. De Nicola, Arte inedita in Siena e nel suo territorio, Vita d'arte, X, 1912, pp. 1–16; L. Gielly, Pietro Lorenzetti — Ambrogio Lorenzetti, Rev. de l'art ancien et mod., XXXI, 1912, pp. 61–72, 142–52, XXXII, 1912, pp. 449–62; B. Berenson, Catalogue of a Collection of Painting . . . (Johnson Coll.), Philadelphia, 1913; M. Carmichael, An Altarpiece of Saint Humility, Eccl. Rev., XLVIII, 1913, pp. 429–44; G. H. Edgell, Un'opera inedita di Ambrogio Lorenzetti, L'Arte, XVI, 1913, pp. 206–07; G. J. Kern, Die Anfänge der zentralperspektivische Konstruktion in der italienische Malerei, Mitt. des kunsthist. Inst. in Florenz, II, 1913, pp. 39–65; F. Bargagli Petrucci, Il mappamondo di Ambrogio Lorenzetti, Rass. d'arte senese, X, 1914, pp. 3–13; B. Kleinschmidt, Die Basilika S. Francesco in Assisi, 3 vols., Berlin, 1915–28; B. Berenson, Essays in the Study of Sienese Painting, New York, 1918; F. M. Perkins, Alcune opere d'arte ignorate, Rass. d'arte, XVIII, 1918, pp. 105–15; G. De Nicola, Studi sull'arte senese: I saggi senesi del Berenson, Rass. d'arte, XIX, 1919, pp. 95–102; E. T. De Wald, The Carmelite Madonna of Pietro Lorenzetti, AJA, XXIV, 1920, pp. 73–76; F. M. Perkins, Some Sienese Paintings in American Collections, Art in Am., VIII, 1920, pp. 195–210; M. Salmi, Note sulla Galleria di Perugia, L'Arte, XXIV, 1921, pp. 155–71; G. De Nicola, Il soggiorno fiorentino di Ambrogio Lorenzetti, BArte, N.S., II, 1922–23, pp. 49–58; E. T. De Wald, The Master of the Ovile Madonna, Art S., I, 1923, pp. 45–54; R. Van Marle, Opere giovanili di Pietro Lorenzetti, Rass. d'arte senese, XVI, 1923, pp. 59–63; Van Marle, II, pp. 321–431; F. Antal, Gedanken zur Entwicklung der Trecento und Quattrocento Malerei in Siena und Florenz, Jhb. für Kw., 1924–25, pp. 207–39; B. Berenson, Notes on Tuscan Painters of the Trecento in the Städel Institut at Frankfurt, Frankfurt am Main, 1926; L. Gielly, Les primitifs siennois, Paris, 1926; G. Rowley, Ambrogio Lorenzetti: Il Pensatore, La Balzana, I, 1927, pp. 211–20; H. Beenken, Dar Urbild der sienesische Assuntadarstellung . . . , ZfbK, LXII, 1928–29, pp. 73–85; E. Cecchi, Trecentisti senesi, Rome, 1928 (Eng. trans., L. Penlock, London, New York, 1931); F. M. Perkins, Alcune tavole neglette di Ambrogio Lorenzetti, La Balzana, II, 1928, pp. 3–10; F. M. Perkins, Nuovi appunti sulla Galleria di Belle Arti di Siena, La Balzana, II, 1928, pp. 99–115, 143–61, 183–203; F. M. Perkins, Two Unpublished Paintings by Ambrogio Lorenzetti, Art in Am., XVI, 1928, pp. 204–10; A. Schmarsow, Italienische Kunst in Zeitalter Dantes, 2 vols., Augsburg, 1928; G. Sinibaldi, Rapporti di Ambrogio Lorenzetti con Simone Martini e con Giotto, L'Arte, XXXI, 1928, pp. 207–12; E. T. De Wald, Pietro Lorenzetti; Art S., VII, 1929, pp. 131–66; G. H. Edgell, Le martyre du frère Pierre de Sienne . . . , GBA, II, 1929, pp. 307–11; P. Hendy, Two Sienese Paintings at Fenway Court, BM, LV, 1929, pp. 109–10; F. M. Perkins, Affreschi poco conosciuti di Ambrogio Lorenzetti, La Diana, IV, 1929, pp. 261–67; G. Rowley, The Gothic Frescoes at Monte Siepi, Art S., VII, 1929, pp. 107–22; G. Sinibaldi, ThB, s.v., XXIII, 1929, pp. 385–88; E. Cecchi, Pietro Lorenzetti, Milan, 1930; E. T. De Wald, Pietro Lorenzetti, Cambridge, Mass., 1930; F. M. Perkins, Pitture senesi poco conosciute, La Diana, V, 1930, pp. 191–94; A. Péter, Pietro és Ambrogio Lorenzetti egy elpusztult fresko-ciklusa (A Destroyed Fresco Cycle by Pietro and Ambrogio Lorenzetti), Budapest, 1930 (rev. G. Marchini, RArte, XX, 1938, pp. 308–14); C. H. Weigelt, Sienese Painting of the Trecento, Florence, New York, 1930, pp. 34–56; C. Brandi, Affreschi inediti di Pietro Lorenzetti, L'Arte, N.S., II, 1931, pp. 332–47; M. Meiss, "Ugolino Lorenzetti," AB, XIII, 1931, pp. 376–97; A. Colasanti, Due dipinti inediti di Simone Martini e di Pietro Lorenzetti, Dedalo, XII, 1932, pp. 659–65; G. H. Edgell, A History of Sienese Painting, New York, 1932; P. Bacci, Una Madonna di Ambrogio Lorenzetti, BArte, XXVI, 1933, pp. 293–94; C. Brandi, La R. Pinacoteca di Siena, Rome, 1933; A. Péter, Contributi alla conoscenza di Pietro Lorenzetti e della sua scuola, La Diana, VIII, 1933, pp. 164–90; G. Sinibaldi, I Lorenzetti, Siena, 1933; A. Péter, Két Sienai Trecento-rajz (Two Sienese Trecento Drawings), Petrovics Elek emlékkönyv (Misc. for A. Petrovics), Budapest, 1934, pp. 52–58; C. Brandi, Lo stile di Ambrogio Lorenzetti, CrArte, I, 1935–36, pp. 61–68; A. Péter, Giotto and Ambrogio Lorenzetti, BM, LXXVI, 1940, pp. 3–8; G. Sinibaldi, Un dipinto del Maestro di Digione . . . , L'Arte, N.S., XII, 1941, pp. 38–43; P. Bacci, Fonti e commenti per la storia dell'arte senese, Siena, 1944; E. Carli, ed., I capolavori dell'arte senese, Florence, 1946; C. Brandi, Ricomposizione e restauro della pala del Carmine di Pietro Lorenzetti, BArte, XXXIII, 1948, pp. 68–77; C. L. Ragghianti, La Collezione Rabinowitz, CrArte, VIII, 1949, pp. 76–80; E. Carli, Le tavolette di Biccherna, Florence, 1950; S. M. Setti, Il "Maestro di Sant'Agostino" e Ambrogio Lorenzetti, Comm, I, 1950, pp. 207–10; R. Longhi, Una Crocefissione di Pietro Lorenzetti, Paragone, II, 23, 1951, pp. 26–27; R. Longhi, Due resti di un paliotto di Ambrogio Lorenzetti, Paragone, II, 13, 1951, pp. 52–54; Toesca, Tr, pp. 554–90; C. Volpe, Ambrogio Lorenzetti e le congiunzioni fiorentino-senesi nel quarto decennio del Trecento, Paragone, II, 13, 1951, pp. 40–52; C. Volpe, Proposte per il problema di Pietro Lorenzetti, Paragone, II, 23, 1951, pp. 13–26; G. Kaftal, Iconography of the Saints in Tuscan Painting, Florence, 1952; M. Gregori, Due opere di Pietro Lorenzetti, Paragone, IV, 47, 1953, pp. 77–80; E. Sandberg Vavalà, Sienese Studies, Florence, 1953; F. Zeri, Reconstruction of a Two-sided Reliquary by Pietro Lorenzetti, BM, XCV, 1953, pp. 244–45; E. Carli, Ambrogio Lorenzetti, Ivrea, 1954; C. Brandi, Chiarimenti sul "Buon Governo" di Ambrogio Lorenzetti, BArte, XL, 1955, pp. 119–23; E. Carli, Dipinti senesi del contado e della Maremma, Milan, 1955; E. Carli, La pittura senese, Milan, 1955, pp. 82–140 (Eng. trans., Greenwich, Conn., 1956, pp. 26–27, 37–47); M. Meiss, Nuovi dipinti e vecchi problemi, RArte, XXX, 1955, pp. 107–45;

E. Carli, Pietro Lorenzetti, Milan, 1956; M. Laclotte, De Giotto à Bellini (exhibition cat.), Paris, 1956 (rev. M. Meiss, RArts, VI, 1956, pp. 139-48); G. Marchini, Le vetrate italiane, Milan, 1956, pp. 30, 225; S. Béguin, La Vierge au baldaquin, Paragone, VIII, 93, 1957, pp. 59-63; L. Neagle Tampieri, Osservazioni sulla Madonna di Vico l'Abate di Ambrogio Lorenzetti, S. in onore di Matteo Marangoni, Pisa, 1957, pp. 146-51; C. Brandi, Pietro Lorenzetti, Rome, 1958; E. Carli, Guida della Pinacoteca di Siena, Milan, 1958; G. Rowley, Ambrogio Lorenzetti, 2 vols., Princeton, 1958 (bibliog.; rev. G. Previtali, Paragone, XI, 127, 1960, pp. 70-74); W. Cohn, Contributo a Pietro Lorenzetti, RArte, XXXIV, 1959, pp. 3-17; R. Offner, Reflexions on Ambrogio Lorenzetti, GBA, LVI, 1960, pp. 235-38; C. Volpe, Nuove proposte sui Lorenzetti, Arte antica e mod., III, 1960, pp. 263-77; L. Becherucci, Il dono di Bernhard Berenson alla Galleria degli Uffizi, BArte, XLVI, 1961, pp. 33-40; L. Marucci, La data della "Santa Humilità" di Pietro Lorenzetti, Arte antica e mod., 13-16 Jan.-Dec., 1961, pp. 21-26; N. L. Cristiani Testi, Ambrogio Lorenzetti e San Miniato, CrArte, VIII, 46, 1961, pp. 37-45.

Luisa BECHERUCCI

Illustrations: PLS. 188-198.

LORENZO MONACO. Painter, born in Siena (1370/71), where he is inscribed as Piero di Giovanni in the books of the civil authorities. He went on to Florence, where he became a Camaldolite monk, Don Lorenzo, of the Monastery of S. Maria degli Angeli on Dec. 10, 1391 ("Memoriale" of S. Maria degli Angeli, Florence, Archivio di Stato). His career may be traced from documents through the early years of the 15th century, when he left the monastery, and he is known to have been living in 1422. If the statement of Vasari that Lorenzo died at the age of 55 is accepted, the year of Lorenzo's death must have been 1425 or 1426.

Though most Lorenzo critics and scholars have in the past tended to consider his earliest works as painting, the present-day tendency is to maintain — on the basis of the commentary by Milanesi — that his first efforts were illuminations. This appraisal is demonstrated by the illuminated "Chorals" preserved in Florence (Bib. Laurenziana, Cod. Cor. Laur. 5 and 8), dated 1394 and 1395 and executed for S. Maria degli Angeli (PL. 201). Moreover, the frescoes of the Oblate Convent in Florence, once considered to be his first productions, have since been justly ascribed by Antal, Pudelko, and Gronau to Mariotto di Nardo. Inherent in these codices, as in the other youthful works, are elements from the Orcagna style, intermingled with others from Spinello Aretino and Niccolò di Pietro Gerini, in accordance with the tradition at S. Maria degli Angeli, where a famed school of miniaturists and illuminators had flourished since the early 14th century. These same elements occur in several of Lorenzo's depictions of the Madonna (Amsterdam, Rijksmus., recently attributed to Lorenzo by Gronau; Cambridge, Eng., Fitzwilliam Mus.; Bologna, Pin. Naz.); in the *Pietà* (dated 1404) and *The Agony in the Garden* (PL. 201), both in the Accademia of Florence; in the triptych at Empoli (dated 1404; Gall. della Collegiata), the cusp of which was erroneously considered by Sirén to be the *Pietà* in the Accademia Carrara, Bergamo (in fact, the dimensions are at variance); and in the *Madonna* (dated 1405) of the Berenson Foundation at Settignano, near Florence. The characteristics of Florentine painting of the second half of the 14th century influenced Lorenzo Monaco and determined some aspects of his stylistic development between 1394 and 1405. Acquaintance with the work of Agnolo Gaddi, as well as knowledge of Sienese art and the Gothic elements that had already entered Florentine art (Giovanni da Milano and the Bolognese artists), enabled him to refine the heavy forms then current in his ambient.

From 1405 until 1413, the middle period of his activity, Lorenzo Monaco created a series of typically Gothic works, infused nonetheless with a sense of the Florentine tradition that prevented his expressing himself in purely calligraphic and decorative forms. This was the period in which the painter Gherardo Starnina returned to Florence from Spain and in which the travels of nobles and merchants fostered contacts with other regions and nations. Such qualities and new sources of inspiration are reflected in Lorenzo's art, in the panel *David Playing the Psaltery* (formerly Kassel, Staat. Gemaldegal.) and in the *St. Peter* in Munich (Lotzbeck Gal.). (These last-named are related works and, according to Sirén, are probably parts of the altarpiece for the Fioravanti Chapel in the former church of S. Pier Maggiore, mentioned by Vasari.) The same development is to be observed in other works of this period in his career: three panels in the Accademia of Florence, depicting the Crucifixion, the Virgin, and St. John (which Milanesi thought to be cusps of the lost panel from S. Jacopo sopr'Arno, the church from which they came); the gilt-glass *Madonna and Child with Saints* dated 1408 (Turin, Mus. Civico); and the pieces reconstructed as a triptych by Meiss (1958), that is, the two Louvre panels, *The Agony in the Garden* and *The Marys at the Sepulcher* (also 1408), and what must have been the central panel, the *Lamentation* in Prague (Nat. Mus.). Although only a few years separate these works from the early production of Lorenzo Monaco, the change was very marked. This can be seen in, among others, one fundamental element: the lighting, which through contrasts of light and darkness creates an aura of unreality.

Beginning in 1409 Lorenzo Monaco also resumed the illumination of manuscripts. Some of those in Choral Codex 3 (dated) of the Biblioteca Laurenziana, also executed for S. Maria degli Angeli, may be attributed to him. In dealing with these works, Ciaranfi and Salmi have suggested contacts with the International Gothic style. Similar inspiration is evidenced in Ghiberti's (q.v.) second door for the Baptistery of Florence, where stylistic and compositional affinities with Lorenzo's painting are evident (even if it is impossible to prove a direct contact between the two artists). Similarities can be noted in the torsion of the bodies, the accentuated movement of the draperies, and the landscape of harsh, angular rocks over which the light plays with a highly evocative effect. Other works of Lorenzo approximately contemporary with these miniatures are an *Annunciation with Saints* (Florence, Accademia), for which Sirén believes a *Nativity* in Worcester, Mass. (Frank C. Smith Coll.), belonged to the predella; *Flight into Egypt* (Altenburg, Lindenau-Mus.); *Adoration of the Magi* and *Visitation* (Gloucester, Eng., Highnam Court, Gambier-Parry Coll.); *Madonna and Child with Saints* (dated 1410; Florence, Mus. dell'Antica Casa Fiorentina); the altarpiece from the Church of S. Bartolomeo at Monte Oliveto, near Florence, for which there survive documents of payment beginning in 1406; the *Annunciation* in Brussels (Stoclet Coll.), which both Pudelko and Van Marle believe to be the altarpiece, known through documents (1398-1400), for the Ardinghelli Chapel of S. Maria del Carmine in Florence; the tempera polyptych *Madonna and Child with Angels and Saints* (Prato, Gall. Com.); *Madonna of Humility with Angels* from S. Ermete in Pisa (1412; Pisa, Mus. Naz.); the miniatures of 1412, documented works for S. Maria Nuova, with payments in 1412-13 (Florence, Mus. Naz., no. H74); *Madonna* (1413; Washington, D.C., Nat. Gall.); and the *Coronation of the Virgin* of the same year for S. Maria degli Angeli (PLS. 200, 202); related to this last is another altarpiece that has been broken up into panels (London, Nat. Gall.; etc.), a work executed for the former monastery of S. Benedetto Porta a Pinti.

A series of Crucifixion subjects dates from 1415 and 1418, such as that with the Virgin and St. John in S. Giovanni dei Cavalieri in Florence (one of the most dramatic and interesting works of the Camaldolite monk); the one in the museum of S. Maria delle Vertighe, at Monte San Savino; the little-known one in S. Marta, Florence, pervaded with a sense of tragic desolation; and also the version with three sorrowing figures that is in New Haven, Conn. (Yale Univ. Art Gall.). Another group of works that can be dated about 1420 constitute the period of Lorenzo's maturity. These include illuminations from S. Maria Nuova (Florence, Mus. Naz., Cod. E70); various Madonnas (Copenhagen, Thorvaldsens Mus.; Kansas City, Nelson Gall. of Art); an *Annunciation* (Vaduz, Liechtenstein Coll.); *Adoration of the Magi* (Poznań, Nat. Mus.); and the *Adoration of the Magi* (PL. 199), which Suida, Sirén, and Pudelko believe to have been the central part of the altarpiece for S. Egidio, Florence (documented in 1422). Here, as in other compositions to be discussed below, elements of the International Gothic style predominate.

It was about this time that the so-called "Master of the Bambino Vispo," a personality still obscure, returned to Florence from Spain (ca. 1416). Longhi, in agreement with Pudelko, discerns the possibility of some artistic exchange between this painter and Lorenzo Monaco and notes in his art a "subtle affected elegance ... a tendency to unrealistic digression very rare in an Italian." If such a relation existed between the two painters, Lorenzo Monaco — as on other occasions — was capable of transforming any influence that proceeded from it, of investing it with a personal touch and a reality of its own. These gifts are evident in the three late cusp panels above the *Deposition* by Fra Angelico (Florence, Mus. di S. Marco); three predella panels showing scenes from the lives of St. Onuphrius and St. Nicholas of Bari (PL. 202); a *Nativity* (Florence, Accademia), related to the preceding panels; and an *Adoration of the Magi* and a *Visitation*, two interesting drawings in Wiesbaden (Städt. Mus.). As in the previously mentioned works of the late phase, the accented verticality and the steep upward tilt of the planes promote an air of fantasy. The figures appear evanescent and unreal because of the singular lighting, which causes them to emerge from the shadows in a refined play of luminous lines.

With the *Annunciation* and the frescoes in the Bartolini Chapel of Sta Trinita, Florence, the artistic activity of Lorenzo Monaco came to an end. In these last works the sculptural force of his figures marks a prelude to subsequent developments in Florentine painting — a direction presaged particularly in the figures of the prophets on the vault.

Lorenzo Monaco produced a vast quantity of works, an indication that his art was highly esteemed and sought after even during his lifetime. His career is also recorded in many works on which he only collaborated, as well as by the production of his students and his circle. Perhaps most notable among the many artists who came under Lorenzo's influence was Fra Angelico, now generally conceded to have been one of his students.

SOURCES. A. Billi, Il libro di Antonio Billi, 1481-1530, ed. K. Frey, Berlin, 1892 (Copia Strozianus, p. 18; Copia Petrei, p. 19); K. Frey, ed., Anonimo Gaddiano or Codex Magliabechiano (ca. 1537-42), Berlin, 1892, p. 95; Vasari, I, p. 373, II, pp. 17-32, VII, p. 50, IX, pp. 252-53; Agostino Fortunio, Historiarum Camaldulensium, Florence, 1575, Pars posterior, Venice, 1579, p. 126; G. Farulli, Istoria cron. del nobile ed antico Monastero degli Angioli di Firenze, Lucca, 1710, pp. 31-36, 86, 145; G. Richa, Notizie istoriche delle chiese fiorentine, Florence, 1754, I, p. 142, II, p. 2, III, pp. 140-69, 1759, VIII, pp. 163, 271, IX, p. 147; F. Baldinucci, Notizie de' professori di disegno..., 2d ed., I, Turin, 1768, pp. 290-91; L. Lanzi, Storia pittorica dell'Italia, I, 2d ed., Bassano, 1795, p. 42; J. W. Gaye, Carteggio inedito..., II, Florence, 1839, p. 40; G. Milanesi, ed., G. Vasari, Le vite..., 9 vols., Florence, 1878-85.

BIBLIOG. J. Burckhardt, Der Cicerone, Basel, 1855, p. 792; G. Toscanelli, Catalogue..., Florence, 1883, pls. VII, VIII, IX, XXV; G. Poggi, La chiesa di Monte S. Bartolomeo a Oliveto, Misc. d'arte, I, 1903, pp. 57-64; P. Toesca, Ricordi di un viaggio in Italia, L'Arte, VI, 1903, pp. 225-50; O. Sirén, Di alcuni pittori fiorentini che subirono l'influsso di Lorenzo Monaco, L'Arte, VII, 1904, pp. 337-55; P. Toesca, Nuove opere di Don Lorenzo Monaco, L'Arte, VII, 1904, pp. 171-74; O. Sirén, Don Lorenzo Monaco, Strasbourg, 1905; O. Sirén, Tre Madonne nel Fitzwilliam Museum di Cambridge, RArte, III, 1905, pp. 245-52; B. Berenson, The Florentine Painters of the Renaissance, 3d ed., London, New York, 1909, pp. 151-54 (cf. also, The Italian Pictures of the Renaissance, Oxford, 1932, pp. 298-301); B. Berenson, Un nuovo Lorenzo Monaco, RArte, VI, 1909, pp. 33-36; O. Sirén, Opere sconosciute di Lorenzo Monaco, Rass. d'arte, IX, 1909, pp. 433-36; Venturi, V, pp. 889-1086, VII, pp. 3-21; T. Borenius, Two Angels Making Music, BM, XXIV, 1913-14, p. 247; P. D'Ancona, La miniatura fiorentina, 2 vols., Florence, 1914; J. A. Crowe and G. B. Cavalcaselle, A New History of Painting in Italy (ed. L. Douglas), II, London, 1923, pp. 296-302; V. Lasareff, Una Madonna di Lorenzo Monaco a Mosca, L'Arte, XXVII, 1924, pp. 124-26; Van Marle, IX, 1926, pp. 107-256; W. Suida, ThB, s.v., XXIII, 1929, pp. 391-93; V. Golzio, Lorenzo Monaco, Rome, 1931; L. Venturi, Pitture italiane in America, Milan, 1931; A. M. Francini Ciaranfi, Lorenzo Monaco miniatore, L'Arte, N.S., III, 1932, pp. 379-99; B. Berenson, The Drawings of the Florentine Painters, II-III, Chicago, 1938; G. Pudelko, The Maestro del Bambino Vispo, Art in Am., XXVI, 1938, pp. 47-63; G. Pudelko, The Stylistic Development of Lorenzo Monaco, BM, LXXIII, 1938, pp. 237-48, LXXIV, 1939, pp. 76-81; R. Longhi, Fatti di Masolino e di Masaccio, CrArte, V, 1940, pp. 145-91; M. Meiss, Italian Primitives at Konopiště, AB, XXVIII, 1946, pp. 1-16; F. Antal, Florentine Painting and Its Social Background, London, 1947; M. Davies, Lorenzo Monaco's Coronation of the Virgin in London, CrArte, VIII, 1949, pp. 202-08; H. Gronau, The Earliest Work of Lorenzo Monaco, BM, XCII, 1950, pp. 213-22; W. M. Milliken, Miniatures by Lorenzo Monaco and Francesco del Cherico, B. Cleve. Mus. of Art, XXXVII, 1950, pp. 43-46; M. Salmi, Problemi dell'Angelico, Comm. I, 1950, pp. 75-81, 146-56; Toesca, Tr, pp. 654-56; L. Berti, Note brevi su inediti toscani: Seguace di Lorenzo Monaco, BArte, XXXVII, 1952, pp. 174-75; S. Vagaggini, La miniatura fiorentina nei secoli XIV e XV, Milan, 1952; G. Muzzioli, Mostra storico-nazionale della miniatura (cat.), Rome, 1953, pp. 224-26, 229; M. Salmi, La miniatura fiorentina gotica, Rome, 1954; U. Baldini, Note brevi su inediti toscani: Lorenzo Monaco: Crocefisso, BArte, XL, 1955, pp. 81-82; M. J. Eisenberg, A Crucifix and a Man of Sorrows by Lorenzo Monaco, AQ, XXVII, 1955, pp. 45-49; M. J. Eisenberg, Un frammento smarrito della Annunciazione di Lorenzo Monaco nell'Accademia di Firenze, BArte, XLI, 1956, pp. 338-39; M. J. Eisenberg, An Early Altarpiece by Lorenzo Monaco, AB, XXXIX, 1957, pp. 49-51; R. Jurlano, L'autoritratto di Lorenzo Monaco in un codice della Biblioteca arcivescovile di Brindisi, L'Arte, N.S., XXIII, 1958, pp. 243-46; M. Levi d'Ancona, Some New Attributions to Lorenzo Monaco, AB, XL, 1958, pp. 175-91; M. Meiss, Four Panels by Lorenzo Monaco, BM, C, 1958, pp. 195-96, 359.

Rosalba AMERIO

Illustrations: PLS. 199-202.

LORRAIN, CLAUDE (Claude Gellée). Landscape painter (b. 1600 at Chamagne, Vosges, in the French part of Lorraine; d. Rome, 1682). At an early age he moved to Rome, possibly by 1613, almost certainly by 1620. He may have been one of the *garzoni* (apprentices) employed by the Cavalier d'Arpino and Agostino Tassi on the decoration (completed 1616) of the Villa Lante at Bagnaia, near Viterbo, but the documents said to mention him there may refer to another artist of the same name. At some stage (1623?) he seems to have worked in Naples with the Flemish artist, Goffredo Wals. His principal master was, however, Tassi, in whose service he was evidently employed during the early 1620s and whose household he is said to have managed (cf. biographies of Claude by Joachim von Sandrart, 1675, and Filippo Baldinucci, 1728; also records of legal proceedings against Tassi dated 1619). In 1625, according to Baldinucci, Claude left the studio of Tassi and went back to Nancy, the capital of Lorraine, where he worked for a time as assistant to Claude Deruet, painting architectural backgrounds for the latter's ceiling decorations in the Carmelite church, now destroyed. At the end of 1626 or the beginning of 1627 he returned once more to Rome, where he remained, with only one recorded absence (in 1660), until his death in 1682.

In 1633 he joined the Accademia di S. Luca and from 1654 held various of its offices. According to Sandrart, his friends in the 1630s included, besides Sandrart himself, Pieter van Laer, Herman van Swanevelt, François Duquesnoy, and Nicolas Poussin, with whom he remained on good terms until Poussin's death in 1665. Brief accounts of visits to Claude's studio are to be found in the Roman journals of A. Félibien des Avaux (1647; Delaporte, 1958) and B. de Monconys (1665-66); his name is also mentioned several times in the correspondence of the collector Antonio Ruffo of Messina (1660-71).

In the conventional sense Claude was uneducated and wrote (badly) in a mixture of French and Italian. Though referred to by his contemporaries as Claudio di Lorena or Il Lorenese, he signed himself Claud (sometimes Claude or Claudio), with or without his surname, Gellée (Gelée, Gille).

No certain work by Claude survives from before 1630, and even up to 1634-35 our knowledge of him is largely indirect. During the early 1630s he seems to have been active chiefly as a painter of fresco decorations, of which three series, all in Rome, are mentioned by Baldinucci: those in the Palazzo Crescenzi near the Pantheon, those in the Palazzo Muti (now Palazzo Balestra) in Piazza SS. Apostoli, and some in another house belonging to the Muti family near Trinità dei Monti. The only ones remaining (assuming they are by Claude) are seven small landscapes in a frieze in the Palazzo Crescenzi, probably the earliest (ca. 1630); the rest are lost. Sandrart refers to only one of the Muti series (he does not say which); he describes it enthusiastically and in detail, however, and it is clear that this was at once Claude's latest and finest work in fresco (it was finished by 1635) and a major factor in establishing his artistic reputation.

In the meantime he had also begun to work in other media. Sandrart states that, after leaving Tassi, Claude set up on his own and painted little landscapes and buildings, a genre of which the canvas, *A View in Rome with the Trinità dei Monti*

(1632; London, Nat. Gall.), may be an example. His earliest dated work is the etching *The Storm* (1630), together with the drawing for it in the British Museum. A small painting on copper, *The Rest on the Flight into Egypt* (Trustees of the late Duke of Westminster), is dated 1631; several other paintings are datable on stylistic grounds to the same year. These were followed in 1633 by the artist's first mythological subject, *The Judgment of Paris* (Bowhill, Scotland, Coll. Duke of Buccleuch), and in 1634 by two dated etchings, *The Rape of Europa* and a *Harbor Scene* (the latter based on a picture in The Hermitage, Leningrad). Still comparatively unknown in 1633, by 1638 Claude was the leading landscape painter in Italy, with commissions to his credit from the pope, several cardinals, and the king of Spain. At the same time his style began to attract the attention of imitators and forgers — there is a documented instance from 1634 involving Sébastien Bourdon — and in 1635, in an effort to safeguard his artistic reputation, Claude began the great record of his compositions known as the *Liber Veritatis*. This book, now in the British Museum, contains 195 drawings, each one a careful copy in Claude's own hand of its corresponding painting; on the back of each is the name of the collector for whom, or the place for which, the painting was destined. The beginning of the record is incomplete, since a few paintings executed by Claude after he had started the book are not included, but the *Liber Veritatis* survives throughout in its original chronological order; from about 1640 on it forms a virtually complete inventory of Claude's pictorial output. It is therefore an invaluable guide, not only to the canon of his authentic paintings and to the size and class (predominantly aristocratic) of his circle of patrons, but also to the development of his style as an artist. (Only in the second half of the book are the drawings actually dated, but the dates of the rest can be interpolated from a sufficient number of dated paintings and etchings.)

PRINCIPAL WORKS (from ca. 1635). Unless otherwise stated, the list is based on the *Liber Veritatis* (L.V.) and its numbers. – 1636: *Campo Vaccino* (L.V. 9; Louvre); *A Seaport* (L.V. 10; Louvre); both for the French ambassador, Philippe de Béthune. – 1637: *Fête Villageoise* (L.V. 13; Lincolnshire, Brocklesby Park, Coll. Earl of Yarborough); *A Seaport* (L.V. 14; Northumberland, Alnwick Castle, Coll. Duke of Northumberland); both for Urban VIII; *A Seaport* (L.V. 28; Uffizi), for Cardinal (probably Giancarlo) de' Medici. – 1636–38: *The Temptation of St. Anthony* (L.V. 32; Prado); *The Magdalen in the Desert* (not in L.V.; Prado); *An Anchorite Saint* (not in L.V.; Prado). – 1640: *The Finding of Moses* (L.V. 47; Prado); *The Burial of St. Serapia* (L.V. 48; Prado); *The Embarkation of St. Paula* (L.V. 49; Prado); *Tobias and the Angel* (L.V. 50; Prado); all seven for Philip IV of Spain. – 1641: *Seaport: The Embarkation of St. Ursula* (L.V. 54; London, Nat. Gall.; PL. 205). – 1643: *St. George* (L.V. 73; Hartford, Conn., Wadsworth Atheneum), both for Cardinal Fausto Poli. – 1646: *The Embarkation of Ulysses*, also called "Harbor in Mist" (L.V. 96; Louvre; II, PL. 200), for a collector in Paris. – 1647: *Pastoral Landscape* (L.V. 109; New York, Met. Mus.); *The Flight into Egypt* (L.V. 110; Dresden, Gemäldegal.); both for Parasson. – 1648: *The Marriage of Isaac and Rebekah*, also called "The Mill" (L.V. 113; London, Nat. Gall.; PL. 203); *Seaport: The Embarkation of the Queen of Sheba* (L.V. 114; London, Nat. Gall.); both for the Duc de Bouillon, but the former, at least, originally intended for Prince Camillo Pamphili. A replica of L.V. 113, and a different pendant, *The View of Delphi with a Procession* (*Sacrifice to Apollo at Delphi*; L.V. 119; Rome, Gall. Doria Pamphili; PL. 203) were painted for Pamphili in 1649–50. – 1655: *The Rape of Europa* (L.V. 136; Moscow, Pushkin Mus.); replica dated 1667 in London, Royal Colls.); *The Fight on the Bridge* (L.V. 137; Moscow, Pushkin Mus.); both for Pope Alexander VII. – 1656: *The Sermon on the Mount* (L.V. 138; New York, Frick Coll.), for François Bosquet, Bishop of Montpellier. – 1661: *Pastoral Landscape with the Arch of Titus* (L.V. 153; Trustees of the late Duke of Westminster), for Lebrun; *The Rest on the Flight into Egypt* (L.V. 154; Leningrad, The Hermitage); this, with L.V. 160, 169, and 181 (see below), forms a group of four pictures of equal size, painted for Henry van Halmale, Bishop of Ypres. – 1662: *Sacrifice to Apollo* (L.V. 157; Cambridgeshire, Anglesey Abbey, Coll. Lord Fairhaven), for Angelo Albertoni. – 1663: *Tobias and the Angel* (L.V. 160; The Hermitage). – 1664: *Psyche* (*The Enchanted Castle*; L.V. 162; Wantage, England, C.L. Lloyd Coll.). – 1666: *The Rescue of Psyche* (L.V. 167; Cologne, Wallraf-Richartz-Mus.); both for the Constable Colonna, who commissioned nine pictures altogether from Claude and was his best patron in the later years of his life; *Jacob at the Well* (L.V. 169; The Hermitage). – 1668: *The Expulsion of Hagar* (L.V. 173; Munich, Alte Pin.); *Landscape: Hagar and the Angel* (L.V. 174; London, Nat. Gall.; PL. 206); both for Count Waldstein. – 1672: *Jacob and the Angel* (L.V. 181; The Hermitage). – 1674: *Perseus, or the Origin of Coral* (L.V. 184; Norfolk, Holkham Hall, Coll. Earl of Leicester), for Cardinal Massimo. – 1675: *The Arrival of Aeneas at Pallanteum* (L.V. 185; Cambridgeshire, Anglesey Abbey, Coll. Lord Fairhaven), for Don Gasparo Altieri.

Altogether more than 200 of Claude's paintings survive, of which about two-thirds, not counting autograph replicas, are represented in the *Liber Veritatis*, as well as nearly a thousand drawings, including those in the *Liber Veritatis*. More than half the drawings are in the British Museum; the Teyler Museum in Haarlem has about a hundred. He also made 44 etchings.

Claude's position in the history of 17th-century French painting is second in importance only to that of Nicolas Poussin, and in the ideal landscape he was one of the greatest masters of all time. Starting from the northern tradition of Elsheimer, Brill (V, PL. 304), and Tassi (in contrast to Poussin, whose sources lay in the work of the Venetians and Annibale Carracci), he developed a style that was neither so heroic nor so classical as Poussin's but was capable of expressing both a more poetic mood and a livelier sense of the variety and beauty of nature. The keynote of this style is the treatment of atmosphere and light: the cool light of early morning, the brilliance of midday, or the calm glow of evening, which Claude had studied intensively in the campagna and represented with a subtlety unparalleled in his time and not excelled before the days of impressionism. The light in his paintings usually emanates from an area of the sky just above the horizon, so that the spectator may be looking directly or almost directly into it, and spreads forward and outward through the composition, permeating the whole landscape with its radiance and linking foreground and background in a continuous spatial unity. In the mid- and late 1630s, Claude tended to carry these effects almost to the point of exaggeration: massed trees in shadow in the foreground are contrasted with a misty sunlit vista, while, in some of the seaport scenes, a "tunnel of light" radiates from the sun, just visible above the horizon. (The earliest example of this treatment is in the *Harbor Scene* of 1634 in The Hermitage; it is also one of the earliest instances in the history of art.) After about 1642, however, Claude's style became calmer and his lighting more diffused, as in *The Marriage of Isaac and Rebekah* (PL. 203) or *Landscape: Hagar and the Angel* (PL. 206). An idyllic, pastoral mood permeates many of Claude's mature landscapes, and his style begins to show the influence of the Carracci-Domenichino tradition. Tall trees against the sky, fragments of classical architecture, farms and villages, distant hills, and winding streams — all these are selected and combined in such a way as to communicate a sense of enchantment and repose. The human figures, too, are in keeping. Whereas in the 1630s Claude had frequently introduced genre figures into his compositions, he now turned to sacred or classical literature for his subject matter and used for his pastoral scenes a conventional type of Arcadian shepherd. In his late work this process of idealization, of setting the imaginary world of the picture more and more at a distance from the actual world of experience, is taken even further. Claude's last paintings, which include some of his masterpieces, represent a fairyland in which the forms are so diaphanous that they hardly seem to interrupt the continuity of the air and in which the light has a mysterious, almost magical power of evocation.

To turn from paintings such as these to Claude's early drawings from nature is to discover a profoundly different mode of artistic expression, though the vision behind both is the same and the experience gained in draftsmanship was of the utmost value for the paintings. The drawings are much more varied in type and often even bolder in treatment than the early pictures. Some are rapid pen sketches of ships or buildings; others, black chalk and wash drawings of trees (PL. 204; IV, PL. 278) — the pines, ilexes, and chestnuts which then grew in the campagna in greater profusion than they do today. But the majority embody some unexpected effect of light which had caught the artist's interest: a tree seen *contre-jour* before a view of the campagna, a prospect of changing light across the Tiber valley, a path through a sunlit wood, a moonlight effect in a Roman garden. Most of these drawings probably date from before about 1645, but there is reason to believe that Claude continued to make drawings from nature at least until the mid-1660s. In later life, however, he concentrated mainly on finished drawings executed in the studio.

Baldinucci states that figures in Claude's paintings were sometimes put in by other artists and names Filippo Lauri in this connection, but this is unlikely except in Claude's early period, when he may occasionally have handed over such an assignment to one of his friends among the Bamboccianti (q.v.). One assistant, Giovanni Desiderii, is known to have worked in his studio from 1634 to 1655, but there is no sign of studio participation in Claude's authentic landscapes. However, he did have many imitators, as well as followers, both during his lifetime and after his death. Claude was regarded as the "prince of landscape painters" by connoisseurs all over Europe (but especially in England) down to the middle of the 19th century.

SOURCES. B. de Monconys, Voyages, IV, Lyon, 1665-66, pp. 471-79; J. von Sandrart, Teutsche Academie..., Nürnberg, Frankfurt am Main, 1675-79 (ed. A. R. Peltzer, Munich, 1925, pp. 32, 184-85, 209-11, 258, 270, 326, 330, 405); F. Baldinucci, Notizie de' professori del disegno..., VI, Florence, 1728, pp. 353-59; A. Bertolotti, Artisti francesi in Roma, Mantua, 1886, pp. 87, 104, 113-22, 223; V. Ruffo, La Galleria Ruffo nel secolo XVII in Messina, BArte, III, 1916, pp. 167, 169, 175, 190, 192, 238, 293, 316; F. Boyer, Les années d'apprentissage de Claude Lorrain, Actes XIIIᵉ Cong. int. h. de l'art, Stockholm, 1933, pp. 174-78; F.-G. Pariset, Les Debuts de Claude Deruet, B. Soc. H. Art Français, 1947-48, pp. 117-22; Y. Delaporte, André Félibien en Italie, GBA, LI, 1958, pp. 205-06.

BIBLIOG. L. Pascoli, Vite de' pittori, scultori ed architetti moderni, I, Rome, 1730, pp. 20-30; A. J. Dézallier d'Argenville, Abregé de la vie des plus fameux peintres, II, Paris, 1745, pp. 266-70; R. Earlom, ed. J. Boydell, Liber Veritatis, 3 vols., London, 1777-1819; L. Caracciolo, ed., Liber Veritatis, 2 vols., Rome, 1815; J. Smith, Catalogue raisonné, VIII, London, 1837, pp. 175-396; E. F. Pattison (Lady Dilke), Claude Lorrain, Paris, 1884; H. J. Scholten, Musée Teyler à Haarlem, Catalogue raisonné des dessins, Haarlem, 1904; R. Bouyer, Claude Lorrain, Paris, 1905; E. Dillon, Claude, London, 1905; L. Ozzola, Claudio Lorenese e il suo studio dal vero, L'Arte, XI, 1908, pp. 293-97; K. Gerstenberg, Claude Lorrain und die Typen der idealen Landschaftsmalerei, Berlin, 1919; W. Friedländer, ThB, s.v. Claude Gellée, XIII, 1920, pp. 366-72; W. Friedländer, Claude Lorrain, Berlin, 1921; R. Fry, Claude, in Vision and Design, London, New York, 1921, pp. 145-52; A. Blum, Les eaux-fortes de Claude Gellée, Paris, 1923; L. Demonts, Les dessins de Claude Gellée (exhibition cat.), Paris, 1923; A. M. Hind, The Drawings of Claude Lorrain, London, 1925; A. M. Hind, Catalogue of the Drawings of Claude Lorrain in the British Museum, London, 1926; P. Courthion, Claude Gellée, Paris, 1932; K. T. Parker, Catalogue of the Drawings in the Ashmolean Museum, I, Oxford, 1938, pp. 208-18; A. Blunt, French Drawings at Windsor Castle, London, 1945; T. Hetzer, Claude Lorrain, Frankfurt am Main, 1947; P. du Colombier, Essai sur les personnages de Claude Lorrain, B. Soc. Poussin, III, 1950, pp. 41-63; J. White, The Landscapes of Claude, BM, XCII, 1950, pp. 43-46; K. Gerstenberg, Claude Lorrain: Landschaftzeichnungen, Baden-Baden, 1952; A. Blunt, Art and Architecture in France, 1500-1700, Harmondsworth, 1953, pp. 195-201; E. Knab, Die Zeichnungen Claude Lorrains in der Albertina, Alte und neue Kunst, II, 1953, pp. 120-60; E. Knab, Der heutige Bestand an Zeichnungen Claude Lorrains im Boymans Museum, B. Mus. Boymans, VII, 1956, pp. 102-40; M. Davies, National Gallery Catalogues: French School, 2d ed., London, 1957, pp. 31-49; M. Kitson, Swanevelt, Claude Lorrain et le Campo Vaccino, RArts, VIII, 1958, pp. 215-20, 259-66; M. Röthlisberger, Les pendants dans l'œuvre de Claude Lorrain, GBA, LI, 1958, pp. 215-28; M. Kitson and M. Röthlisberger, Claude Lorrain and the Liber Veritatis, BM, CI, 1959, pp. 14-25, 328-37, 381-86; M. Röthlisberger, Claude Lorrain, Connaissance des Arts, Jan., 1959, pp. 50-55; M. Röthlisberger, Les fresques de Claude Lorrain, Paragone, IX, 109, 1959, pp. 41-50; M. Röthlisberger, Ein frühes Gemäldepaar von Claude Lorrain, Mitt. (Bern), XXIX, 1959, pp. 1-4; E. K. Waterhouse, Ascanius shooting the Stag of Sylvia, The Listener, LXIII, 1960, pp. 310-11; M. Kitson, The Altieri Claudes and Virgil, BM, CII, 1960, pp. 312-18; Ideal and Classical Landscape (exhibition cat.), Cardiff, 1960; E. Knab, Die Anfänge des Claude Lorrain, JhbKhSammlWien, N.S., XX, 1960, pp. 63-164; Dessins français du XVIIᵉ siècle (exhibition cat.), Paris, 1960, pp. 15-19; A. Chastel, ed., Actes du colloque Nicolas Poussin, 1960, I, pp. 6-10, 22, 45-55, 72, 88, 179-81, 212-14, 221, 234-35, 293, 305, II, pp. 60, 109, 116, 118-19, 122-23, 180, 187, 197-98, 205, 209, 240, 259; M. Röthlisberger, The Subjects of Claude Lorrain's Paintings, GBA, LV, 1960, pp. 209-24; I. Toesca, G. B. Crescenzi, Crescenzio Onofri (e anche Dughet, Claude e G. B. Muti), Paragone, XI, 125, 1960, pp. 51-59; M. Röthlisberger, New Light on Claude Lorrain, Connoisseur, CXLV, 1960, pp. 57-63; I. Toesca, Disegni inediti di Claude, Paragone, XI, 127, 1960, pp. 69-70; M. Kitson, Claude's Books of Drawings from Nature, BM, CIII, 1961, pp. 252-57; M. Kitson, The Relationship between Claude and Poussin in Landscape, BM, CIV, 1961, pp. 142-62; J. J. Morper, Johann Friedrich Graf von Waldstein und Claude Lorrain, MJhb, XII, 1961, pp. 203-17; M. Röthlisberger, Bemerkungen zum zeichnerischen Oeuvre von Claude Lorrain, ZKg, XXIV, 1961, pp. 163-76; M. Röthlisberger, Claude Lorrain, Arts de France, I, 1961, pp. 351-53; M. Röthlisberger, Dessins (Claude Lorrain), L'Oeil, LXXVIII, 1961, pp. 55-59; M. Röthlisberger, Claude Lorrain: The Paintings, New Haven, 1961 (bibliog.); Animal Studies from Nature by Claude Lorrain (exhibition cat.), New York, 1961; M. Kitson, Claude Lorrain, in L'ideale classico del Seicento in Italia e la pittura del paesaggio (exhibition cat.), Bologna, 1962, pp. 221-55; M. Kitson, Three Drawings by Claude, BM, CIV, 1962, pp. 66-69; M. Levey, A Claude Signature and Date revealed after Cleaning, BM, CIV, 1962, p. 390; M. Röthlisberger, Les dessins de Claude Lorrain à sujets rares, GBA, LIX, 1962, pp. 153-65; M. Röthlisberger, Ein Nachtrag zu Claude, Pantheon, XX, 1962, pp. 167-70; M. Röthlisberger, Claude Lorrain, ses plus beaux dessins retrouvés, Connaissance des Arts, CXXX, 1962, pp. 138-47; M. Röthlisberger, The Wildenstein Album, Paris, 1962; H. S. Francis, Claude Gellée: Landscape with Rest on the Flight into Egypt, B. Cleve. Mus. of Art, XLIX, 1962, pp. 230-35; M. Kitson, The Place of Drawings in the Art of Claude Lorrain, Acts XXth Int. Cong. H. Art, Princeton, N.J., III, 1963, pp. 96-112; E. Knab, Stylistic Problems of Claude's Draughtsmanship, Acts XXth Int. Cong. H. Art, Princeton, N.J., III, 1963, pp. 113-17.

Michael KITSON

Illustrations: PLS. 203-206.

LOTTO, LORENZO. Italian painter (b. Venice about 1480, as can be deduced from his will of 1546, which states that he was then about sixty-six years of age; d. Loreto, 1556). The earliest documented data are from 1503-06, when the artist was living in Treviso. On Oct. 18, 1506, he was preparing to leave Treviso, in order to fulfill a commission from the monks of the Church of S. Domenico in Recanati to paint the large polyptych now in that city (completed, 1508; Pin. Civica). In August, 1508, Lotto was again in Treviso to collect the balance of his fees for an altarpiece he had already completed in 1506: *The Virgin and Child with Four Saints* at Santa Cristina al Tivarone (near Treviso). By 1509 he was in Rome painting in the Vatican, together with Sodoma, Bramantino, and Peruzzi, "in cameris superioribus... prope librariam superiorem" (i.e., in the apartment of Julius II) — in the very rooms that Raphael was soon to decorate or, possibly, was already decorating at that time. Two payments totaling 150 ducats were made out to Lotto on Mar. 9 and Sept. 18, 1509, in connection with this work. Although the artist was again in the Marches in 1512, when he signed and dated *The Entombment* at Iesi (PL. 212), there is no actual proof that he had stayed in Rome during the intervening three years; and it is highly probable, to judge from his style at this juncture, that he had visited Tuscany and perhaps had contacts with the art of Lombardy.

Then, on Mar. 13, 1513, Lotto received from Alessandro Martinengo, in Bergamo, the commission to paint the large altarpiece with the Madonna and saints for the Church of S. Stefano (now in the Church of S. Bartolomeo), which he did not complete until 1516. From this time the artist initiated a long period of activity in Bergamo and its environs which lasted, except for short and infrequent absences, until 1526.

Between 1526 and 1529 Lotto lived mostly in Venice, although he may have returned briefly to Bergamo and the Marches. To this period belong the altarpieces *St. Nicholas of Bari in Glory*, in the Church of S. Maria del Carmelo in Venice; *The Virgin Enthroned with SS. Jerome and Joseph*, dated 1526, formerly in the Church of S. Francesco al Monte in Iesi (now Iesi, Pin. Comunale); and *The Assumption*, dated 1527, in the Church of S. Maria Assunta at Celana (near Bergamo). From 1529 to 1539, although still living much of time in Venice, Lotto was again at work in the Marches, where he completed *The Crucifixion*, 1531, for S. Maria in Telusiano at Monte San Giusto, near Fermo; the St. Lucy altarpiece, 1532, in the Pinacoteca Comunale at Iesi (PL. 211); and the altarpiece *The Madonna of the Rosary*, 1539, in S. Domenico at Cingoli.

In 1538, while in Ancona, Lotto started an account book, which he was to keep meticulously up to date almost to the day of his death. This book is vital both for the biographical information it contains and for its accurate recording of the artist's works.

From 1540 to 1542 Lotto lived in Venice in the house of his nephew, Mario d'Armano. Then, at some time during the next three years, he moved to Treviso and stayed with a friend, Giovanni del Saon. However, from 1545 to 1549 he was in

Venice again, because in Treviso he could not earn enough by his art to support himself. But, always restless, he changed his quarters there at least five times. During this period, on Mar. 5, 1548, he drew up a will in which, nullifying a previous donation to Giovanni del Saon, he bequeathed all his possessions to charity and appointed as executors the monks of the Church of SS. Giovanni e Paolo, in Venice, for whom he had painted in 1542 the altarpiece *St. Antoninus of Florence Giving Alms* (PL. 213). In his will Lotto described himself as "alone, without loyal help, and quite troubled of mind."

In the late spring of 1549 he was ready to leave Venice and go once more to the Marches, having been commissioned to execute the altarpiece *The Assumption* for the Church of S. Francesco delle Scale in Ancona (now Pin. Comunale). Before leaving Venice he entrusted a number of paintings and cameos to Jacopo Sansovino in the hope that the latter would sell them for him. (Later Sansovino returned them all to Lotto, unsold.)

From 1549 to 1552 the artist lived in Ancona. In 1550 he tried to put up 30 of his pictures for a raffle, but he succeeded in disposing of only 7. Finally, since he was still besieged by poverty and wished to avoid wandering in his old age, he managed to obtain admission (Aug. 30, 1552) to the Sanctuary of the Holy House of Loreto. On Sept. 8, 1554, he became an Oblate of the Blessed Virgin, turning over all his property and pledging his works to the Sanctuary. The last entry in his account book is dated Sept. 1, 1556, and shortly afterward he died in Loreto.

Lotto's life, restless and vagabond, ended in solitude, poverty, and oblivion, but his artistic creations, rich in fascinating accents of intense modernity, rank among the finest and most original of the Italian 16th century.

Documents do not indicate who was Lotto's teacher. A wanderer even in his youth, he probably never stayed long in any one shop, preferring — curious and impressionable as he was — to explore the more novel and experimental trends of his times. Pioneering in modern Lotto scholarship with his first monograph of 1895, Berenson traced the artist's antecedents to Alvise Vivarini. Later, however, Berenson himself was to revise his initial theory, when he recognized that some pictures he had attributed to Alvise were actually the work of Giovanni Bellini (for example, the beautiful *S. Giustina*; Milan, Coll. Bagatti Valsecchi). Today there is no longer any doubt that the beginnings of Lotto's art are rooted in Bellini, even if they preserve accents derived from Antonello da Messina and an integrity of form rather reminiscent — except for the vibration of cold coruscating lights, so typical of Lotto — of the finished modeling of, for instance, Cima da Conegliano. Also, Jacopo de' Barbari once was considered as a link to explain the German elements which, from the beginning, were conspicuous in Lotto's painting. But this particular hypothesis was discredited when Jacopo's œuvre was stripped of the major works once attributed to him. It is far more probable that the young Lotto turned his attention directly to Dürer when the latter was in Venice in 1505–06. With Dürer's paintings of that time the early works of Lotto show remarkable affinities.

Luigi Coletti has advanced still another theory that removes Lotto's early formation from the Venetian influence altogether. On the basis of a sentence in the document commissioning the Recanati polyptych ("de melioribus picturis que sunt iste que inspiciuntur, facte in juventute vel potius in adolescentia sua"), Coletti reached the conclusion that Lotto must have lived in the Marches when very young and there developed in the milieu of Melozzo da Forlì and Luca Signorelli. This thesis can hardly be sustained, since Venetian elements are by far the more prevalent in Lotto's earliest works, even in the two heralds of the fresco decoration around the tomb of Agostino Onigo (Church of S. Nicolò in Treviso), on which Coletti especially based his hypothesis.

The works dated and signed by Lotto in his early years are the *Virgin and Child with St. Peter Martyr and the Infant St. John*, 1503 (Naples, Museo di Capodimonte), clearly under Bellini's influence; the *Portrait of Bishop Bernardo de' Rossi*, 1505 (PL. 207); *The Assumption*, 1506, in S. Maria Assunta at Asolo (but not the *Pietà* above, nor the landscape in the predella, both of which are part of the frame and the work of a modest craftsman); and the *St. Jerome in the Wilderness*, also 1506, in the Louvre. The altarpiece in the parish church at Santa Cristina al Tivarone (XII, PL. 72) is documented and can also be dated 1505–06. To the same period should be attributed also the heralds of the Onigo tomb, which (despite contrary opinions) certainly appear, in their daring and fresh conception, to be by Lotto; the Bachofen *Madonna* in the Kunstmuseum, Basel (though close to the style of Pennacchi, its quality alone justifies its attribution to Lotto's early period); the *Head of a Youth* in the Accademia Carrara at Bergamo (but not the *Portrait of a Man with a Red Cap* of the Museo Correr in Venice); and the portrait bust of a woman in the Musée des Beaux-Arts at Dijon, strongly marked with Dürer's characteristics.

A chronological parallel can be drawn, almost date by date, between this group of early pictures by Lotto and the works of Giorgione before he had arrived at his "grand manner," and a correct reading of the date in the *St. Jerome* of the Louvre (1506 instead of 1500) has placed Lotto in proper sequence within the development of Venetian painting. The Santa Cristina altarpiece is just about contemporary with Giorgione's altarpiece at Castelfranco Veneto (VI, PLS. 185, 188); the *St. Jerome* with the *Tempest* (VI, PLS. 186, 187); *Bishop Bernardo de' Rossi* with the so-called "Laura" (VI, PL. 194) of the Kunsthistorisches Museum in Vienna. But the two painters, alike in the distinctly modern qualities of their sensibility, otherwise took widely divergent paths. Giorgione's vision, soft and blended in warm enveloping tones, is turned to a contemplation of nature and of enchantment. Lotto's painting, on the other hand, despite the finish and integrity of its forms and the clarity of its cool light, reflects, in its unexpected dislocations and agitated accents, a restless temperament.

The Recanati polyptych (1506–08), although still quite near to the early Venetian works, is painted with a greater freedom; its color is lighter in hue and softened here and there by suffusing shadows. The inspired profile of St. Dominic, raised toward the Virgin, foreshadows the Raphael of a few years later — for example, his portrait of Sigismondo Conti in *The Madonna of Foligno* (IV, PL. 314) — which might indicate that other works (now lost) of Lotto for the Vatican might have influenced Raphael.

To this period of activity in the Marches belong *The Marriage of St. Catherine* (Munich, Alte Pin.); the *Sacra Conversazione* formerly in Kraków (Puslowski Coll.); *The Virgin and Child with Saints* (Rome, Gall. Borghese), strong in German overtones; and the fine *Portrait of a Youth Before a White Damask Curtain* (Vienna, Kunsthist. Mus.).

As documented, Lotto was in Rome in 1509. Exposed to a new, very different milieu, his style emerged completely transformed. Although the strongest influence would appear to have come from Raphael, the nature of Lotto's work brought him more closely into contact with the circle of Peruzzi, Sodoma, Bramantino, and later with Beccafumi, who appears to have been in Rome between 1510 and 1512. This environment, in which elements of totally different origins met, must be recognized as one of the earliest centers of mannerism, and in this center Lotto was an active participant. Certain similarities between Lotto and Sodoma and between Lotto and Beccafumi probably had their source in these early Roman contacts. Lotto's collaboration with the Peruzzi group probably continued, even after their leaving the Vatican, in the works executed for Agostino Chigi in the Villa Farnesina. Similarities to Lotto are clear in the profound change Peruzzi's style underwent in the frescoes of the Sala di Galatea and the Salone delle Prospettive. Moreover, the origin of the Venetian traits assimilated by Raphael must be found, surely, not only in the work of Sebastiano del Piombo but also, and earlier, in that of Lotto.

After his departure from Rome, Lotto probably went to Tuscany. In the *St. Jerome in the Wilderness* (Rome, Mus. Naz. di Castel Sant'Angelo) and in the *Portrait of a Jeweler*, in a private collection in Switzerland, Umbrian and Tuscan accents are clearly apparent. Roman and Tuscan characteristics are also predominant in the works executed on Lotto's return to the Marches: *The Entombment of Christ* (PL. 212), dated 1512, and the three pictures at Recanati (the *St. James the Greater* in S. Maria sopra Mercanti, the *St. Vincent Ferrar* in the Church of S. Domenico, and the *Transfiguration* in the Pin. Civ.); and the two predellas, one of *The Assumption* (Milan, Brera), the other of *Christ Leading the Apostles to Mount Tabor* (Leningrad, The Hermitage).

After his arrival in Lombardy, Lotto was initially attracted to the Leonardesque painters and to Leonardo himself (here, perhaps, are the roots of Lotto's stylistic affinities with the early Correggio). He found in their works elements not unlike those with which he had been familiar in central Italy. Subsequently he was to enter even more deeply the mainstream of the Lombard school. The great local tradition of fresco painting introduced him to a more epic and narrative treatment, with origins in a popular "folk" background.

To this period belong the three large altarpieces in Bergamo: one (1516) in the Church of S. Bartolomeo (predella now in the Accademia Carrara); another (1521) in the Church of S. Bernardino (PL. 210); and the third (1521) in the Church of Sto Spirito. All these sacred compositions are accented by pathetic, fantastic, or worldly touches. *Susanna and the Elders* (1517), in Florence (PL. 209), and *Christ Taking Leave of His Mother* (1521), in the Staatliche Museen of Berlin, are also of this phase. The *Mystical Marriage of St. Catherine* (1523) in the Accademia Carrara in Bergamo and another *Mystical Marriage of St. Catherine* (1524), in the Galleria Nazionale in Rome, are both rich in exquisite psychological insights. This period also includes a fine group of portraits: *Agostino and Niccolò della Torre* (1515) in the National Gallery, London; the *Man with a Rosary* in the Hage Collection, Nivaa (near Copenhagen), suggesting Holbein, although in fact predating him; *The Prothonotary Apostolic Giuliano* in the National Gallery, London; *Micer Marsilio and His Wife* (1523) in the Prado, Madrid; *Lucina Brembate* in the Accademia Carrara, Bergamo; the *Young Man in His Study* (XI, PL. 224) in the Accademia, Venice; the *Youth* in the Castello Sforzesco, Milan; and others.

Also related to this phase are the frescoes (1524) in the chapel of Villa Suardi at Trescore with the legends of St. Clare (PL. 209) and St. Barbara. The St. Barbara subject is pictured in a panoramic setting wherein the saint travels from chapel to chapel on her road to martyrdom. Like those on a Sacro Monte, each stop corresponds to a stage of her own trial and final martyrdom. Before 1524 Lotto had probably visited the Sacro Monte at Varallo and seen Gaudenzio Ferrari's pictures. The frescoes in the Church of S. Giorgio at Credaro and those in the Church of S. Michele al Pozzo Bianco in Bergamo are from 1525; both show, together with a reappearance of German traits, a stylistic kinship with the art of Gaudenzio Ferrari (ca. 1470–1546). The cartoons for the imaginative inlay of the choir stalls of S. Maria Maggiore in Bergamo, with Biblical scenes and ornamental details in an almost surrealistic manner, can be dated between 1523 and 1530; Lotto sent the last few cartoons from Venice. To this period belong the *Sacra Conversazione* of the Kunsthistorisches Museum in Vienna; the *Adoration of the Shepherds* in the Pinacoteca Civica Tosio Martinengo in Brescia; the altarpiece *The Madonna Enthroned with SS. Jerome and Joseph* (1526) in the Pinacoteca Comunale at Iesi; the *Assumption* (1527) in the Church of S. Maria Assunta at Celana; and the polyptych in the Church of SS. Vincenzo e Alessandro at Ponteranica. The succession of fine portraits was uninterrupted, even after Lotto's return to Venice: the *Dominican Steward* (1526) of the Museo Civico at Treviso; *Bishop Tommaso Negri* (1527) in the monastery of Poljud at Split, Yugoslavia; and *Andrea Odoni* (PL. 208). This last, were it not for the date, 1527, and Lotto's signature, would seem to be a work from later in the 16th century because of its pictorial boldness and the highlighted sculptures.

In Venice, after so long an absence, Lotto found a world much changed from the one in which he had so actively participated in his youth during the years 1500–06. This world had evolved a harmonious artistic culture under the leadership of Titian during the time that Lotto had wandered throughout Italy, alert and receptive to varied experiences and schools. He was the first of the great Venetians to be attracted by central Italy and Rome. Lotto was also one of the first to feel the ferment of mannerism, as noted above, and to contribute importantly to its development. His style cannot specifically be contained within any one school, because he always strove for highly personal solutions, at times almost disconcerting in their modernity. He showed a capricious and restless inclination to render his subjects in their least normal and conventional aspects, but with a profound insight into emotional states.

During these Venice years Lotto painted only one altarpiece, *St. Nicholas of Bari in Glory* (1529), in the Church of S. Maria del Carmelo. Too much insistence has been placed on an alleged approach to Titian's manner in this painting; except for a warmth of color in the figures there is no recognizable influence. The panoramic, airy, and remote landscape behind the looming presence of the saints is far from Titianesque; rather it anticipates Dutch 17th-century landscapes.

In 1530 Lotto again worked principally in the Marches, and his style at this point does not appear to have changed much from that of the last Bergamo years. There is hesitancy here and there and a certain unevenness of quality from work to work; yet in the best pictures his touch was, if anything, more free and dramatic, as is evident in the Iesi altarpiece, where the crowd presses around St. Lucy, and in the *Crucifixion* of the Church of S. Maria in Telusiano at Monte San Giusto, and again in the silent, Rembrandt-like intimacy of the St. Lucy predella (PL. 211), where the light, shimmering over mobile shadows, freezes into cool whites and blues.

After his return to Venice, Lotto painted still another masterpiece, *St. Antoninus of Florence Giving Alms*, 1542 (PL. 213), an unusual composition, presented as if from the point of view of the gesticulating crowd of petitioners in the foreground. Although no single figure is more than a head-and-shoulders study, each one, while fused with the group, has the expressive power of an individual portrait. Lotto continued to produce excellent portraits, including examples in the Galleria Borghese, in the Galleria Doria Pamphili, and in the Pinacoteca Capitolina (Conserv.; all Rome); those of *Febo da Brescia*, *Laura da Pola* (1544), and the *Gentleman with Gloves* in the Brera, Milan; the *Family Group* (*Ser Giovanni della Volta and His Family*; 1547) in the National Gallery in London; and many others. All are rendered with a penetrating knowledge of the sitters' essential psychological traits.

At one point during this period, as recorded in one of Aretino's letters, Titian showed an interest in Lotto when he, too, was acquiring his dramatic, impressionistic late manner. However, the art historians of the Renaissance neglected and belittled Lotto's art. Lodovico Dolce judged his S. Maria del Carmelo altarpiece as a "very remarkable example of bad coloring." Vasari, although less negative, did not commit himself to an opinion of Lotto's work as a whole. In his introduction to the lives of Lotto and Palma Vecchio he was content to acknowledge that the craftsmanship of even one or two pictures by Lotto, despite their small size, was sufficient to justify the admiration of viewers. Even the Venetian historians, C. Ridolfi, M. Boschini, and A. M. Zanetti, do not really give Lotto a position of first rank. More interesting is the evaluation made by G. P. Lomazzo of the artist's Bergamo period. The 18th- and 19th-century studies of F. M. Tassi, D. M. Federici, A. Ricci, L. Crico, and others are strictly erudite in character, and only recently has there been a complete and convincing reevaluation of Lotto's work and of its profoundly human and modern meaning. The Berenson monograph of 1895 marks the beginning of the new studies, including almost all the points that later ones have taken up and developed. Since then Lotto's fame has continued to grow, to such an extent that in the process a correct sense of proportion has, at times, been lost. Signs of impatience with Titian's Olympian grandeur have brought about, by contrast, a perhaps excessive emphasis on the elements of pathos in Lotto's painting.

In his last years in the Sanctuary of the Holy House in Loreto, Lotto withdrew further into his meditations and into a world of his own imagination. His production became uneven and his creative powers were dimmed. Yet he succeeded in producing one more masterpiece, *The Presentation of Christ in the Temple* (Loreto, Palazzo Apostolico), in which the clear and delicate color ranges evoke once again the imaginative and poetic spirit of the stories of St. Barbara and St. Lucy.

BIBLIOG. M. Michiel, Notizie di opere di disegno (ca. 1545), ed. J. Morelli, Bassano, 1800, 2d ed. G. Frizzoni, Bologna, 1884; P. Aretino, Lettere (April, 1548), IV, 492, carta 214 v.; L. Dolce, L'Aretino ovvero dialogo della Pittura, Venice, 1557; Vasari; C. Ridolfi, Le meraviglie dell'arte, 2 vols. in 1, Venice, 1648; M. Boschini, La carta del navegar pitoresco, Venice, 1660; A. M. Zanetti, Della pittura veneziana..., Venice, 1771; F. M. Tassi, Vite de' pittori, sculturi e architetti bergamaschi, 2 vols., Bergamo, 1793; D. M. Federici, Memorie trevigiane..., II, Venice, 1803; L. Crico, Lettere sulle belle arti trevigiane, Treviso, 1833; A. Ricci, Memorie storiche della Marca d'Ancona, Macerata, 1834; G. Frizzoni, Lorenzo Lotto e le sue pitture a Trescore, Giorn. di erudizione artistica, IV, 1875, pp. 65–75; G. Bampo, Spigolature nell'archivio notarile di Treviso, Arch. veneto, XXXII, 1886, pp. 169–76; G. Frizzoni, Il Museo Borromeo di Milano, Arch. storico dell'arte, III, 1890, pp. 345–65; G. Frizzoni, Capolavori dell'arte italiana, Arch. storico dell'arte, V, 1892, pp. 9–25; G. Frizzoni, I capolavori della Pinacoteca del Prado in Madrid, Arch. storico dell'arte, VI, 1893, pp. 268–89; B. Berenson, Lorenzo Lotto, London, 1895, rev. ed., London, New York, 1956; A. Venturi, Il "libro dei conti" di Lorenzo Lotto, Gall. naz. it., I, 1895, pp. 115–224; G. Biscaro, Lorenzo Lotto a Treviso, L'Arte, I, 1898, pp. 138–53, IV, 1901, pp. 152–61; G. Frizzoni, La Galleria Hage a Nivaagaard in Danimarca, L'Arte, XIII, 1910, pp. 401–22; G. Frizzoni, Intorno a Lorenzo Lotto, Rass. d'arte, XVI, 1916, pp. 145–50; A. Venturi, Lorenzo Lotto: Ricerche, L'Arte, XXVII, 1924, pp. 153–57; A. Pinetti, Cronistoria artistica di S. Maria Maggiore, V: Il coro ligneo di G. F. Capoferri e i disegni di Lorenzo Lotto per le tarsie, Bergomum, XXII, 1928, pp. 152–84; Venturi, IX, 4, pp. 1–117; B. Berenson, Italian Pictures of the Renaissance, Oxford, 1932; L. Coletti, Lotto e Melozzo, Le Arti, I, 1938–39, pp. 348–57; R. Longhi, Viatico per cinque secoli di pittura veneziana, Florence, 1946; R. Pallucchini, Commento alla Mostra di Ancona, Arte veneta, IV, 1950, pp. 7–32; P. Zampetti, Pittura veneta nelle Marche (exhibition cat.), Bergamo, 1950; A. Banti and A. Boschetto, Lorenzo Lotto, Florence, 1953 (bibliog.); A. M. Brizio, Il percorso dell'arte di Lorenzo Lotto, Arte veneta, VII, 1953, pp. 7–24; L. Coletti, Lorenzo Lotto, Venice, 1953; T. Pignatti, Lotto, Milan, 1953; P. Zampetti, Lorenzo Lotto (exhibition cat.), Venice, 1953; E. Zocca, Le decorazioni della stanza di Eliodoro e l'opera di Lorenzo Lotto in Roma, RIASA, II, 1953, pp. 329–43; A. M. Brizio, Lorenzo Lotto e i primi avvii del Manierismo a Roma, Venezia e l'Europa: Atti XVIII Cong. int. di storia d'arte, Venice, 1955, pp. 262–65; B. Berenson, Lorenzo Lotto, London, New York, 1956.

Anna Maria BRIZIO

Illustrations: PLS. 207–213.

LUCAS VAN LEYDEN. Lucas of Leyden — more correctly, Lucas Hugensz. (son of Hughe) van Leyden — was born in Leiden (Leyden) in 1494, according to the first biographer of Dutch painters, Karel van Mander, and died in the same city in 1533. His name is listed in the register of the Civil Guard of Leiden in 1514, and in 1515 it is found again in a list of crossbowmen, where it remained until 1519. In June, 1521, Lucas van Leyden is known to have met Albrecht Dürer in Antwerp; and Van Mander tells us of a voyage in Zeeland in 1527, during which Lucas encountered the painter Jan Gossaert (Mabuse). The date of Lucas's marriage to the daughter of a magistrate of the town, Lijsbet van Boschuysen, can be fixed about 1515. From Van Mander it is established that the artist's father was a painter of Leiden, whose name was already known there in 1480. Another of the sons, Dirck Hugensz., apparently chose the same profession and was a constant source of vexation to his family, because of his disorderly life.

Since there exist engravings by Lucas van Leyden dating from 1508 that demonstrate a fully developed graphic talent, an attempt has recently been made, through a varying interpretation of Van Mander's text, to advance the birth date of their maker to about 1489. Such redating, however, cannot alone explain the rapidity of Lucas's youthful development as an engraver; rather, there is reason to believe that these were the work of a prodigious talent which revealed itself quite early in life.

According to Van Mander, Lucas received his first formal training in the studio of his father and subsequently in that of another painter of Leiden, Cornelis Engelbrechtsz., whose work apparently had little influence on him; the period spent in his father's studio seems to have left a greater impression on the young boy. This can be deduced from a comparison of the work of the young painter with that of the Master of the St. John Panels (Rotterdam, Mus. Boymans–Van Beuningen; Philadelphia, Mus. of Art, Johnson Coll.), recently identified with Lucas's father, Hughe Jacobsz. The same feeling for landscapes painted with very bright colors and a predilection for squat figures, often with coarse and caricatured faces, is present in both. Other influences to which Lucas was exposed, notably the work of Dürer and of Jan Gossaert, although they left some mark on his work, did not add essentially to the first impulses from which his painting sprang.

The abundance of existing graphic works by Lucas van Leyden — with Dürer's, one of the most important *œuvres* of the 16th century — permits us to follow his development very closely, particularly since most of his production is dated. The first dated engraving is from 1508; the last are from 1530. During the last three years of his life, he does not seem to have occupied himself with engraving. Moreover, the wealth of dated graphic works helps to establish a reasonable chronological order for his paintings (only five of which bear dates).

The fact that Lucas made engravings throughout most of his life assuredly indicates a preference for that medium. On the whole, it might be said that the engraver triumphs over the painter, even if his conception of engraving in the youthful work seemed to borrow more from painting than from the engraving heritage of his predecessors. Van Mander also tells us that in his youth Lucas did paintings on glass, and perhaps there is reason to seek in this type of work, consisting mainly in grisaille, the origin of the very fine and tightly spaced strokes in his engravings.

The engraving *Mohammed and the Monk* of 1508 (Bartsch, no. 126), the subject of which was taken from *The Travels of Sir John Mandeville*, constitutes the true beginning of Lucas's engraving, although one can reasonably date prior to this work (in which the landscape is already done with remarkable finesse) a small series of engravings less well composed, yet nonetheless engraved with an extremely fine point. Examples of these very early efforts include *Adam and Eve* (B.7), *St. Christopher* (B.108), and *Two Pilgrims* (B.149), and possibly even the *Resurrection of Lazarus* (B.42) and *Abraham Repudiating Hagar* (B.17), plates from a larger series that belong among the greatest rarities of print collecting.

By 1509, Lucas showed proof of marked progress, in the medallionlike so-called "round Passion" series (B.57–65; with two replicas, B.66–67), notably in his concept of space and his adaptation to the round format. Still, he did not achieve such fortunate solutions in this series as he had in certain isolated works of 1508, namely, *Susanna and the Elders* (B.33), the landscape of which was copied by Marcantonio Raimondi, and *David Playing before Saul* (B.27). Perhaps more than any, this last-named print furnishes convincing evidence of an observational gift already highly developed, surpassing by far the efforts of his predecessors. None of his paintings equals the standard of these two engravings.

Among Lucas's painted works, on the other hand, there is little that can be attributed to the period of his early youth, without entering the realm of speculation. A small altarpiece, the *Adoration of the Magi* in Philadelphia (Merion, Barnes Foundation), would be virtually the only safe conjecture. However, there might be added to this a scene of an amorous couple with an old woman (Howett Coll.), a *Story of Job* (Richmond, Surrey, Coll. Viscount Lee), and an *Adoration of the Magi*, known through three copies (e.g., Karlsruhe, Staat. Kunsthalle) that could well be the work of the master himself. *The Temptation of St. Anthony* (Brussels, Mus. Roy. des B.A.), dated 1511, despite the fact that it is signed with an "L," seems to have been executed by a hand other than that of the engraver of the round Passion series.

In 1510 Lucas began to create his real masterpieces of engraving, for in that year he completed *The Milkmaid* (B.158; PL. 216), the great *Ecce Homo* (B.71), and *The Return of the Prodigal Son* (B.78), all remarkable for the sureness with which he rendered both individual figures and groupings. Until then, Lucas seems to have resorted to few older models, except for borrowings from Dürer evident in the round Passion scenes.

His compositions, though of great simplicity, lacked nothing in expressive force.

The acquaintance with Dürer's art and with that of Antwerp inspired in Lucas a desire to rival the achievements of the great art centers. He began to modify his compositional schemes, thereafter crowding his prints with figures and closing off the beautiful perspectives of his early work with architectural motifs. This new tendency became noticeable in the work of the years 1512 and 1513, and the large *Adoration of the Magi* (B.37) was the unsatisfying result of the change in approach.

Fortunately Lucas succeeded in freeing himself of the heaviness manifest in his work of that period, for a return to his former finesse of draftsmanship is evident in the years 1517 and 1518, when he created the two admirable prints *Esther before Ahasuerus* (B.31) and *Christ Tempted by the Devil* (B.41). In 1519, *The Dance of the Magdalen* (B.122) marked the reemergence of the ample composition with many figures arranged in small, dispersed groups. These tranquil figures contrast strongly with the agitated hunt scene in the background. In this device he sought a harmony between vertical elements and the frieze of figures, a composition he later learned to develop more ingeniously in his paintings.

Nevertheless, once oriented in the direction of the major currents of art, Lucas could no longer liberate himself completely from a tendency toward mannerism. Certain pieces from the Passion series of 1521 (B.43–56), inspired by Dürer, suffer from a misuse of mannerist effects; but although the art of the great German master made a strong impression on Lucas, it is interesting to follow his departures from an idea taken from Dürer, for example, in the portrait of the emperor Maximilian (B.172). Inspired by a wood engraving of Dürer, Lucas transformed it into a creation entirely his own by using a combination of aqua fortis and engraving. In the process, he evolved a copperplate technique, known later in France as "taille douce," which no engraver before had used with such effectiveness and bold assurance.

Van Mander's account of Lucas's meeting with Gossaert promotes the likelihood of another strong influence on the artist, already apparent in 1523. In that year he executed *The Poet Vergil Suspended in a Basket* (B.136; PL. 216), shortly after the Madonnas of 1523 (B.82, B.84), which again reveal his great admiration for Dürer. From that time on, Lucas sought after a monumentality that produced lifeless and indifferent results. His last engravings, peopled with distorted figures, are reminiscent of the art of Gossaert and Raimondi and retain some value as testimony to a new art; but in them one seeks in vain the spontaneity of the works of his youth. This development is more pronounced in the engravings, destined for wider dissemination, than in Lucas's paintings. In these, for the most part, he conserved an intimate quality and sacrificed it only in the great altarpieces. Even in his first attempts at painting, there is discernible a predilection for narrative motifs, a tendency that made him a genre painter par excellence. This inclination can be noted in *The Chess Players* (V, PL. 292), a painting dating from about 1508; about 1510 there followed two religious paintings, *Susanna before the Judges* (PL. 215) and an episode from the story of Joseph (Rotterdam, Mus. Boymans–Van Beuningen), in which Lucas introduced genre motifs into religious subjects. In this aspect can be recognized the precursor of Rembrandt, whom he equals as a sensitive observer of fact.

Still another bond between Lucas and his great compatriot of the 17th century is the spontaneous manner in which he could render his own features. The *Self-portrait* (V, PL. 299), dating from about 1508, might also be compared with the self-portraits that Dürer executed in his youth. It shows the same avidity for capturing personal traits with astonishing objectivity. Moreover, in it Lucas excels the portraiture of his contemporaries with a liberty of execution not found even in his own later work. Two other portraits — one painted about 1510 (Lugano, Thyssen-Bornemisza Coll.), in which the features of Lucas's father are purportedly recognizable, and another that dates from about 1521 (PL. 214) — can be attributed to him. The latter work is very studied. There are many similarities with a series of drawings in black pencil, some of which are dated 1521. The influence of Dürer's portraiture is quite apparent, and it would seem a reasonable supposition that Lucas sought to emulate the German master after his meeting with him in Antwerp in 1521.

Other paintings indicate little of this influence deriving from Dürer. Certain traces remain, of course, particularly after Lucas's visit to Antwerp, as in the *Virgin and Child, the Magdalen, and a Donor* (PL. 217), a diptych of 1522, in which the somewhat pedantic and dry execution betrays excessive preoccupation with draftsmanship. More evidence of Dürer's ideas is found in individual figures of Lucas's masterpiece, the *Last Judgment* (PL. 218; V, PL. 292), commissioned in 1526. The farther one goes beyond the significant year 1521 in examining his production, the more this influence generally tends to disappear. In Lucas's last work, *The Curing of the Blind Man of Jericho* (Leningrad, The Hermitage; in Van Mander's time in the collection of the engraver Hendrik Goltzius), an altarpiece of 1531, the Dürer inspiration has given way to a more highly developed conception, in which the artist succeeded in reuniting the vivid qualities of his great engravings with a simplicity of composition anticipating the Renaissance style of Jan van Scorel (q.v.).

Already apparent in the *Last Judgment*, the accomplished distribution of figures within convincing space, with an accurate sense of depth, may cause one to forget that Lucas van Leyden began his career in a north European milieu still virtually medieval. (Another version of the same subject in the Museum of the New-York Historical Society is by some attributed to Lucas.) In tracing the development of the painter, an important place must be given to *Moses Striking Water from the Rock* (Boston, Mus. of Fine Arts), dated 1527. Here Lucas, for the first time, placed large figures in the foreground in such a way that they dominated the composition. His imitators did not succeed fully in attempts to copy this disposition of space. Certain among them — for example, Pieter Cornelisz. (called Kunst), one of the sons of Engelbrechtsz. — imitated his style with such proficiency that for a long time the hand of Lucas himself was thought to be evident in paintings attributed to the younger artist; the best known of these deceptive paintings is the *Sermon in the Temple* (Amsterdam, Rijksmus.).

The true Lucas — engraver in his paintings and painter in his engravings, as M. J. Friedländer has remarked — can be studied in a particularly meaningful way in a painting lately added to the collections of the Rijksmuseum, *The Worship of the Golden Calf* (V, PL. 292), which dates from his finest period. The sequence of movement established in this painting is accomplished so felicitously as to obscure the still medieval form of the altarpiece and the division into three parts, for the painter clearly conceived the work as a unified composition. The figures, and even the colors, can be compared with those of Lotto. Both painters, while largely independent of the past, retained in their new vision something of a strained quality of form, which can simply be characterized as a holdover from the medieval style. This quality was strongly current during the 17th century, when the style of Lucas was imitated in scenes from the Scriptures, in order to add a historical accent to such compositions. In the work of Goltzius, and perhaps more clearly in that of Rembrandt when he returns to Lucas for costumes or architectural accessories, the results of such inspiration are evident.

The activity of Lucas van Leyden was not limited to painting and engraving. He took part in the transformation of Dutch book illustration by introducing new motifs, just as he had given fresh impulse to wood engraving by adapting it to the vigorous strokes of his pencil drawings.

It is difficult to determine whether Lucas designed for stained-glass church windows. Some studies for stained-glass windows found in the Groote Kerk of Gouda may be from his hand (Amsterdam, Rijksmus.). Although their style seems close to that of Lucas, however, one hesitates to attribute them to him without the historical documentation confirming such purely stylistic affinity.

Nevertheless, even if Lucas van Leyden cannot be given a secure place in this last medium, his remaining pursuits are sufficient testimony to the amazing creative force he exerted during his short life. He dominated his entire generation, yet he did not open strikingly new perspectives. Having begun to practice his art with a powerful and acute perception of reality, he seems gradually to have forgotten his unique mission under the influence of Dürer and Gossaert, to have become preoccupied with sheer technical feats. Furthermore, the great lesson of the Italian Renaissance was unknown to Lucas, and it was not until the next generation, with Jan van Scorel, that Dutch art was to comprehend such new conceptions.

BIBLIOG. *General works*: K. van Mander, Schilderboek, Alkmaar, 1604; N. Beets, Luca de Leyde, Brussels, Paris, 1913; L. Baldass, Die Gemälde des Lucas van Leyden, Vienna, 1923; F. Dülberg, Lucas von Leyden, 1499–1533, Leipzig, 1924; P. Wescher, ThB, s.v. (bibliog.); M. J. Friedländer, Die altniederländische Malerei, X, Berlin, 1932, pp. 78–113; N. Beets, 16-eeuwsche Kunstenaars, III: Lucas van Leyden, Oud Holland, LI, 1934, pp. 49–59, 151–62, 197–209; N. Beets, Lucas van Leyden, Amsterdam, 1940; N. Beets, De dans om het gouden kalf: Een hervonden triptiek van Lucas van Leyden, Oud Holland, LXVII, 1952, pp. 183–99; W. Wegner, Eine Bildnis von Hugo Jacobsz von seinem Sohne Lucas van Leyden, Oud Holland, LXXII, 1957, pp. 191–94; C. Müller-Hofstede, Das Selbstbildnis des Lucas van Leyden im Herzog Anton-Ulrich-Museum zu Brunswick, Festschrift F. Winkler, Berlin, 1959, pp. 221–37.

Graphic works: A. von Bartsch, Le peintre-graveur, VII, Vienna, 1808; S. Colvin, Eine Sammlung von Handzeichnungen des Lukas van Leyden, JhbPreussKSamml, XLV, 1893, pp. 165–76, 231–32; C. Dodgson, Beschreibendes Verzeichnis der Buchillustrationen Lucas van Leydens, RepfKw, XXXIII, 1900, pp. 143–53; R. Kahn, Die Graphik des Lucas van Leyden, Strasbourg, 1918; M. J. Friedländer, Lucas van Leyden, Leipzig, 1925 (new ed. by F. Winkler, Berlin, 1963); P. Wescher, Eine unbeschriebene Holzschnittfolge des Lukas van Leyden, Pantheon, IV, 1929, pp. 321–23; W. Nijhoff, Nederlandsche Houtsneden 1500–1550, 2 vols., The Hague, 1933–39; C. Dodgson, On the Book-illustrations of Lucas van Leyden, Oud Holland, LII, 1935, pp. 38–40; F. W. H. Hollstein, Dutch and Flemish Etchings, Engravings, and Woodcuts, X, Amsterdam, 1952; Museum Boijmans, Lucas van Leyden en tijdgenoten, Rotterdam, 1952 (cat.); H. G. Wachtmann, Die Bildform in der frühen Graphik des Lucas van Leyden, Münster, 1960.

Karel G. BOON

Illustrations: PLS. 214–218.

LUTYENS, EDWIN LANDSEER. Architect (b. London, Mar. 29, 1869; d. Jan. 1, 1944). Although a pupil of Sir Ernest George, Lutyens was greatly inspired, initially, by the work of Philip Webb and William Morris. He was given a first commission for a small country house in 1889, and on the strength of this he established a practice. Noticed by the energetic garden designer Gertrude Jekyll and helped greatly by her, Lutyens was also aided in his career by his marriage to a daughter of the Earl of Lytton.

Lutyens soon developed into one of the most talented and resourceful designers of country houses. In the style of Richard Norman Shaw (q.v.) and Webb, his residences have prominent roofs and combine Tudoresque with Georgian motifs (Deanery Gardens, Sonning, Berkshire, 1899–1901; The Orchards, Godalming, Surrey, 1899; Tigbourne Court, Witley, Surrey, 1899; Folly Farm, Sulhampstead, Berkshire, 1905, 1912). These buildings confirmed Lutyens's originality and ability in coordinating forms. Very early, however, he was attracted by classicist tendencies, first of a William-and-Mary kind (Crooksbury House, Surrey, east front, 1899; Hestercombe Orangery, Surrey, 1905), then of a more imposing Neo-Georgian type (Nashdom, Taplow, Buckinghamshire, 1905) and a semi-Palladian, semi-English-baroque "Wrenaissance" (Heathcote, Ilkley, Yorkshire, 1906).

Lutyens shared in full the "folie de grandeur impériale" of the Edwardian period, and it made him the ideal architect of England's last crop of truly spectacular country houses (Lindisfarne Castle, Holy Island, Northumberland, 1903, a restoration, originally built ca. 1500; Castle Drogo, Devon, 1910–30) and, of course, for the master plan and designs for New Delhi. His Viceroy's Residence (ca. 1913) has a genuine monumentality and a sense of grandiose display that Sir Herbert Baker never achieved in his buildings for New Delhi.

In the end, however, Lutyens bogged down in classicism. Despite his extreme care for proportion and the oddly impish details into which his former originality retreated, his later commercial buildings, such as Britannic House in London (after 1920) and his branches for the Midland Bank (1924, etc.), remain outside the main stream of European developments. More genuinely original is an early church of Lutyens, the Anglican St. Jude's in Hampstead Garden Suburb (1909–11), which displays a sense of massing very rare in the ecclesiastical architecture of his time.

BIBLIOG. A. S. G. Butler, The Architecture of Sir Edwin Lutyens, 4 vols., London, New York, 1950.

Nikolaus PEVSNER

LUXEMBOURG. The modern territory, bounded by Belgium, Germany, and France, takes its name from the city of Luxembourg, which arose about the castle of Lucilinburhuc or Lützelbourg. The original nucleus of the future grand duchy, formed in the 10th century, has survived the major political upheavals of the modern age intact.

SUMMARY. Cultural and artistic phases (col. 354). Art centers (col. 355).

CULTURAL AND ARTISTIC PHASES. Its limited territorial extent and its geographic position have prevented Luxembourg from evolving autonomous artistic traditions. The oldest traces of life in the area are of the megalithic period, attested by the dolmen near Diekirch. Evidence of prehistoric settlements has been found at Berdorf. The first roads were built at the time of the Gauls, and the Romans laid out their great network of highways between Belgium and the Rhineland along the old Gaulish routes. To the Roman period belong a relief of pagan divinities under the high altar in the church at Berdorf, the castrum of Ricciacum at Dalheim, vestiges of a mosaic pavement at Nennig, the ruins of a 4th-century bridge at Echternach, and the foundations of a pagan temple under the parish church at Christnach. Frankish tombs are found at Dalheim, Schandel, Emmering, and Waldvies. The scant remains do not allow us to recognize a particular cultural physiognomy in the local archaeological finds distinct from those of the adjacent territories.

The Abbey of Echternach, founded in the 7th century, was the center from which Christianity was diffused throughout the region,

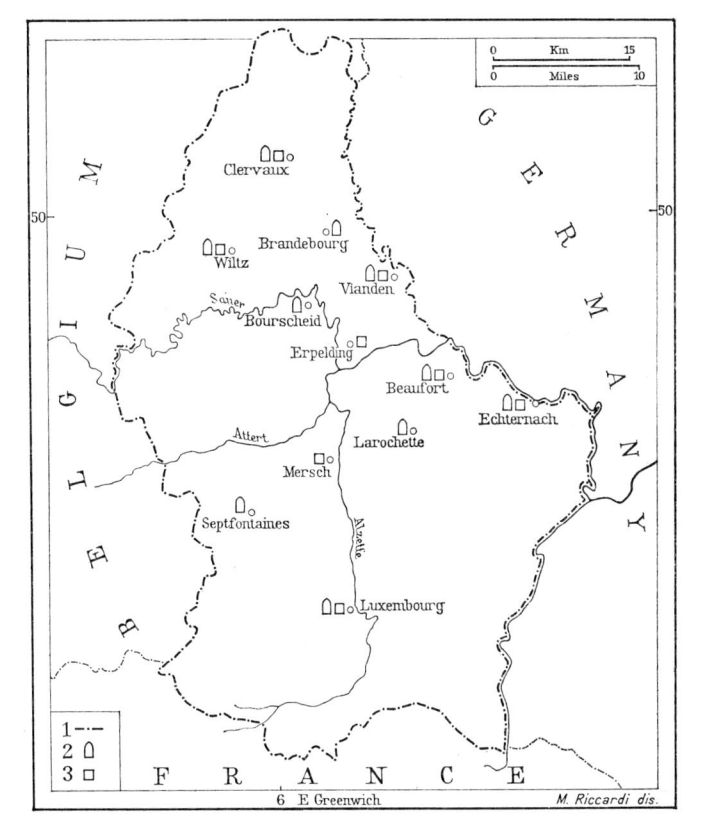

Luxembourg, principal centers of historic and artistic interest. Key: (1) Modern national boundaries; (2) localities with medieval monuments; (3) localities with Renaissance and baroque monuments.

and with it a new cultural impulse. Echternach was one of the important centers of Carolingian learning and art, especially notable for its illuminated manuscripts. When Luxembourg was incorporated into Lotharingia, it became subject to artistic influences from the sphere of the Holy Roman emperors Otto I, II, and III (late 10th–early 11th cent.) and began to participate, in a modest way, in the artistic life of western Europe in that period. During the feudal epoch, when Luxembourg was exposed to the incursions of her warlike neighbors, many fortresses and castles were built (Luxembourg, Larochette, Wiltz, Brandebourg, Vianden, Beaufort, Bourscheid, Septfontaines, Clervaux); these, though mostly in ruins, continue to form a characteristic feature of the landscape. In the Gothic period, French influence was preponderant, particularly in styles of architecture and sculpture. The pronounced Burgundian style of some sculpture (such as the Holy Sepulcher in the church at Septfontaines) can be attributed to the annexation of Luxembourg by the duchy of Burgundy in the mid-15th century. Most of the churches and castles dating from this period have been extensively remodeled, however, and retain slight traces of their original structures. The best example of the architecture of this period is found at Vianden.

Of the Italian Renaissance, there are a few late echoes in isolated decorative elements, such as the portal of Notre-Dame in Luxembourg and carved fireplaces in the castles of Erpelding and Beaufort. In the baroque period many new churches were built, others were remodeled, and fortifications were restored. Some pleasant examples of the rococo, in a fusion of German and French styles, are provided by such buildings as the Pavillon and the Orangerie in the park at Echternach, built by the Mungenasts, a family of Tirolese architects. In the 19th century, French influence again came to the fore, and the noteworthy examples of 20th-century architecture reveal the same inspiration. The popular taste has remained a picturesque juxtaposition of Neo-Gothic, rococo, and Art Nouveau. There has been no discernible local tradition in painting, that is, any tendencies originating in or confined to the grand duchy.

BIBLIOG. A. Wiltheim, Luxemburgum Romanum, Luxembourg, 1842; E. Glaesener, Le Grand-Duché de Luxembourg historique et pittoresque, Luxembourg, 1885; J. Anders, Le Grand-Duché de Luxembourg, Brussels, 1919; N. van Werwecke, Kulturgeschichte des Luxemburgerlandes, Luxembourg, 1926; N. Ries and R. Hausemer, Le beau pays de Luxembourg, Luxembourg, 1928; M. Noppeney, Luxembourg autrefois, 2 vols., Luxembourg, 1936–39; A. Rousseau, Belgique et Luxembourg, Paris, 1948 (Eng. trans., London, 1950); M. Thinnes, La protection des monuments au Grand-Duché de Luxembourg, De Maasgouw, LXIX, 1950, pp. 66–74; Bibliographie succincte sur les arts au Grand-Duché de Luxembourg (excepté l'art musical), établie par la Bibliothèque Nationale, Luxembourg, 1952; R. M. Staud, La renaissance des églises au Grand-Duché de Luxembourg, 1945–1955, L'art d'église, XXIV, 2, 1956, pp. 81–94.

ART CENTERS. Luxembourg. The capital of the grand duchy, the city is situated at the junction of several ancient Roman roads. It grew up around the castle built by Count Siegfried on the Rocher du Bouc, when at the end of the 10th century the nucleus of the present city was founded, probably on the initiative of Siegfried. By the reign of King Wenceslaus IV of Bohemia (1361–1419), who was also Duke of Luxembourg, the city had already achieved importance. Remains of the fortifications, casements, subterranean chambers, and the towers of the city walls of 1393 still exist. In 1554 much of the city was destroyed by the explosion of a powder magazine. It was then rebuilt on a plan conceived by Sebastiaan van Noyen, a scheme incorporating what remained of the old city and retaining the ancient fortifications that over the centuries had defended the city against frequent assaults. Additional fortifications built by Sebastien Vauban in 1684 enhanced the military importance and picturesque character of the city, which remained a citadel between segments of the French and German borders until well into the 19th century. In this century the city has extended its boundaries and has been appreciably modernized. Because of great differences in the level of the terrain (resulting in a variety of panoramas), one of the prominent features of the city is the large number of bridges (64), some of very daring construction. Among the most notable is the Adolphe Bridge, completed in 1903 by the French architect Paul Séjourné.

The Cathedral of Notre-Dame, formerly dedicated to St. Nicholas, was largely built by the brothers Du Blocq, Jesuit architects, between 1613 and 1618, in the prevailing style of the southern Netherlands. Gothic elements are found in the towers flanking the choir, in the vaulting, and in the chapels radiating from the apse. The portal is in Renaissance style, and the interior contains a baroque ambo. The choir was entirely rebuilt and decorated with paintings, sculpture, and stained glass in 1935. St-Michel, a Dominican chapel built in the early 15th century on the ruins of a 10th-century church, has a baroque tower and decorations. The high altar has a frontal, depicting the Assumption, by the Flemish painter Caspar de Crayer (1584–1669). St-Jean Baptiste (1688) is the burial church of the dukes of Luxembourg. The Chapel of St-Quirin, a very ancient structure, is carved from the native rock and has Gallo-Roman foundations. The altar is decorated with crude Romanesque sculpture, and the façade is 14th-century Gothic.

The Grand Ducal Palace was built from designs by the architect Adam Roberti, over the ruins of the old Hôtel de Ville. It reflects the taste for the ornate of the ruling governor, Count Peter Ernst Mansfeld (1517–1604), especially in the Hispano-Moresque façade decorated with relief arabesques. Enlarged and remodeled first in the 18th century, it was again enlarged in the 19th century by Gédéon Bordiau of Brussels. The interior of the Palais de Justice, formerly the seat of the government, dates from the mid-16th-century con-

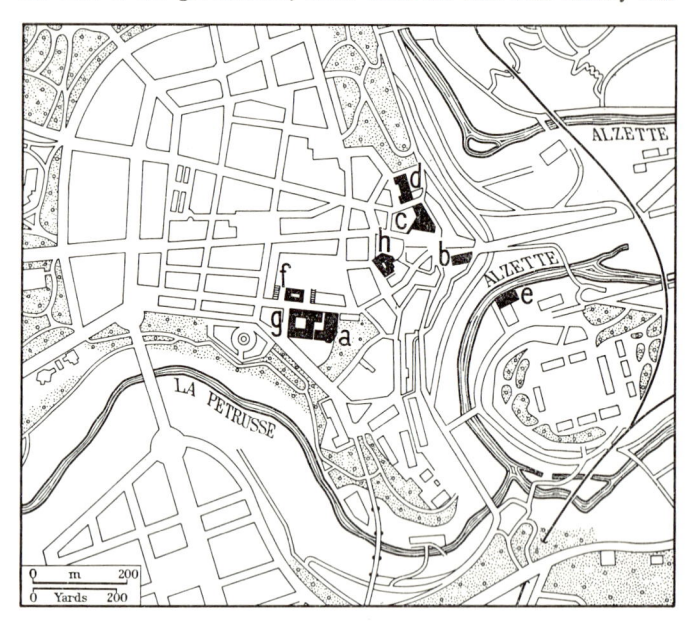

Luxembourg, plan of the center of the city: (a) Notre-Dame; (b) St-Michel; (c) Musée de l'Etat; (d) Palais de Justice; (e) St-Jean Baptiste; (f) Hôtel de Ville; (g) Athénée Bibliothèque; (h) Grand Ducal Palace.

struction, but the neoclassic façade was added in the late 19th century. The palace that houses the Ministry of Internal and Foreign Affairs was built in 1751 over the ancient refuge of St. Maximin of Trier (Trèves). The interior has interesting decorations in the style of Louis XV. Among the noteworthy residences are the "Ancienne Crèche," a picturesque 16th-century house with a 17th-century wing (restored 1956); the Renaissance Maison de Raville; and the medieval "Maison sous les Piliers" (remodeled 1685). Interesting monuments were erected to King William II of the Netherlands, by Antonin Mercié (1884); to Amélie of Saxe-Weimar, by Charles Pêtre, and to the Luxembourg national poets, Dicks and Lentz, by Federspiel (1903).

The Musée de l'Etat (also known as the Musée Pescatore, from the donor of the nucleus of the collection) has several collections: Romanesque reliefs from various churches (carved altar frontals from Rosport); Flemish, German, and Italian paintings; and glass, medals, and silver.

BIBLIOG. N. van Werwecke, La ville de Luxembourg, Luxembourg, 1867; P. Parent, L'architecture des Pays-Bas méridionaux aux XVIe, XVIIe et XVIIIe siècles, Paris, Brussels, 1926; J. Meyers, Le musée de l'État, Luxembourg, 1956; J. Petit, La renaissance d'une vieille maison luxembourgeoise, Luxembourg, 1956; A. Sprunck, Le Palais Grand-ducal à travers les âges, Luxembourg, 1957; J. Harpes, Vieilles demeures, nobiliaires, et bourgeoises de la ville de Luxembourg, Luxembourg, 1959.

Echternach. On the right bank of the Sauer River in a region once under Roman rule (evidenced by a 4th-century bridge), Echternach owes its fame to the abbey founded in the late 7th century by St. Irmina (d. 698) and placed in the charge of St. Willibrord, an English missionary who converted the Frisians. An important center of diffusion for the art of illumination, the monastery produced masterpieces such as the Codex Aureus Epternacensis (1035–40; Nürnberg, Germanisches Nat. Mus.) and the Codex Caesareus (ca. 1050; Uppsala, Univ. Lib., Cod. 93), containing the Gospel according to St. Matthew. The Church of St. Willibrord was rebuilt in 1028, after a fire that had left intact only the crypt of the original church (dated 698); this had been under the Carolingian church, which had choirs at both ends. The crypt, where the sarcophagus of the dedicatory saint rests and where outline paintings of the 12th century have been revealed, was spared by the bombardments that destroyed the Romanesque church in World War II. It lies under the present-day church, which accurately reproduces the previous Romanesque structure, even the Gothic additions in the ogival vaulting. The Corinthian capitals of 1678 also survived the bombing. The parish church of SS. Pierre et Paul, built in Romanesque style in 1220, with a pentagonal choir, was remodeled during the Gothic period and again in the early 18th century.

The monastery underwent major rebuilding in 1732. Later additions within the great park include the Orangerie (1750), designed by the Tirolese Sigmund Mungenast, and the elegant rococo Pavillon (1761–65) by Simon and Paul Mungenast. The Hôtel de Ville (1520–30; restored 1897) has Gothic porticoes and arcades decorated with statues.

BIBLIOG. J. P. Brimmeyr, Geschichte der Stadt und der Abtei Echternach, 2 vols., Luxembourg, 1921–23; N. Goetzinger, Die Gewölbegemälde der St. Willibrorduskrypta in Echternach, Grevenmacher, 1928; R. M. Staud and J. Reuter, Die kirchlichen Kunstdenkmäler der Stadt Echternach, Luxembourg, 1952; R. M. Staud and J. Reuter, Die Kirchlichen Kunstdenkmäler des Dekanats Echternach, Luxembourg, 1953; P. Metz, Das goldene Evangelienbuch von Echternach, Munich, 1956; N. Goetzinger, ed., Willibrordus, Luxembourg, 1958; Treizième centenaire de la naissance de Saint Willibrord 658–1958 (cat.), Luxembourg, 1958; R. M. Staud, Tiroler Steinmetzen in Luxembourg, Ö. Z. für K. und Denkmalpflege, I, 1959, pp. 11–16.

Esch-sur-Alzette. This model workers' city, an important example of urban planning based on contemporary industrial criteria, was built in 1952 from designs by the architects Robert Lentz and Semp Michels.

BIBLIOG. R. Lentz and S. Michels, Cité ouvrière, Arch. d'aujourd'hui, XXIII, 45, 1952, p. 54.

Vianden. An old feudal town on the Our River, dominated by a partly ruined castle (rebuilt several times), Vianden was the seat of a dynasty whose origins date from the 11th century. Among the vestiges of the castle it is still possible to distinguish details of the Hall of the Knights, a Byzantine chamber with trilobed windows decorated with Romanesque capitals. The two-storied decagonal chapel dates from the 13th century, the donjon from the 14th. The church and convent of the Trinité, structures of the Gothic period that have been remodeled, contain the tombs of Marguerite of Spannheim (1400) and Henry of Nassau (1589). The Hôtel de Ville was built in 1579. There is a regional museum of folk art.

BIBLIOG. M. E. Dunan, Étude sur les Châteaux-forts de l'ancien comté de Luxembourg, B. monumental, C, 1941, pp. 5–45, 219–38.

Evelina BOREA

Illustrations: 2 figs. in text.

LYSIPPOS (Λύσιππος, Lysippus). Greek sculptor of the 4th century B.C., a native of Sikyon. His father's name was probably either Lysippos or Lysistratos, as indicated by a recently discovered inscription at Delphi that preserves the first three letters of the patronymic (Marcadé, 1953, p. 66); his brother Lysistratos was also a sculptor (Pliny the Elder, Naturalis historia, xxxv, 153). Though the dates of his birth and death are not specifically established, it is known that he lived to a very old age (Anthologia Palatina, xvi, 332) and that his output was exceptionally prolific (Pliny, op. cit., xxxiv, 37). The following events are important for establishing his dates. Lysippos was the favorite court sculptor of Alexander the Great (ibid., xxxiv, 51, 63), whom he outlived by many years, and was employed by Kassandros no earlier than 316 B.C. (Athenaeus, The Deipnosophists, xi, 784). An inscription found in Rome, now lost (Löwy, IGB, m:o 487, p. 318), seems to indicate that Lysippos made a portrait of Seleukos I Nikator after the latter had assumed the title of king in 306 B.C. He was still active, therefore, in the last decade of the 4th century, but there is no reason to believe that he survived the turn of the century. The above-mentioned inscription at Delphi also refers to a statue of the Theban general Pelopidas, executed by Lysippos no later than 363 B.C. and possibly as early as 369 B.C. Such an important commission could hardly have been awarded him before his twenty-fifth year; thus the date of his birth may be placed in the first decade of the 4th century. Most available knowledge of the life, work, achievement, and style of Lysippos is provided by Pliny (op. cit., xxxiv, 37, 51, 61–67). Because of his method of compiling material from earlier literature, Pliny's accounts are sometimes contradictory and confusing. This does not altogether negate their value as source material, but the order in which this material is presented makes it undependable as a basis for biographical reconstruction. Pliny cannot be relied upon in tracing the stylistic development of an artist such as Lysippos, especially since the sculptor's long career spanned the period during which Greek life and art passed from the postclassic to the Hellenistic phase.

Lysippos spent his early years in the conservative milieu of artisans as apprentice to a coppersmith. Contrary to the prevailing custom, he was not trained in the school of a specific artist. Cicero's assertion (Brutus, lxxxvi, 296) that Lysippos personally considered the Doryphoros of Polykleitos (XI, PL. 189) to be the masterwork he found most instructive illustrates his early conservatism and the heritage he claimed from the classical masters of the 5th century B.C. In apparent contrast stands the endorsement by Lysippos of a famous saying of Eupompos that nature, rather than works of earlier masters, should be imitated. The pronouncements, therefore, must belong to different periods of the artist's life: the first statement indicates artistic idealism; the latter signifies a new spirit of naturalism and a repudiation of earlier models. The two attitudes, however, are not mutually exclusive; they should be interpreted, in the light of Lysippos' stylistic development, as successive expressions of his changing esthetic.

Lysippos often said that other artists represented men as they were, and he, as they appeared to be (Pliny, op. cit., xxxiv, 65). Though this statement is not easily interpreted, it suggests that neither idealism nor naturalism satisfied him as an artistic principle. It can plausibly be understood as a stylistic formula, applicable to a late stage in his life, when he blended human and divine qualities in his portraits of the deified Alexander. These sculptures are well described by such ancient authors as Plutarch and Apuleius and noted in later writings. In this period also Lysippos experimented with the prescribed canon of human proportions, "making the heads smaller than older artists had done, and the bodies slimmer and less muscular, thus increasing the apparent height of his figures" (Pliny, ibid.).

Literary evidence, therefore, seems to support the logical hypothesis that the style of Lysippos underwent a constant development in which at least three different stages are discernible: his early conservative style, the mature style of his middle age, and his late style.

Since no indisputable work of Lysippos now exists, attributions have varied greatly, with little unanimity among scholars in any single case. This disagreement is particularly frustrating because abundant literary reference to his work is available and there is clear evidence of his great influence on his contemporaries and on posterity.

Substantial evidence links to Lysippos the marble figure of Agias (PL. 219) found by the French excavators at Delphi. Agias is one of a group of statues dedicated about 332 B.C. by the Thessalian dynast Daochos II, who that year was hieromnemon at Delphi. It is a copy of a bronze statue erected eight years earlier in Pharsalos, the native town of Daochos, as understood from the identical epigrams inscribed on the two bases. The Pharsalos statue is lost, but its epigram mentions Lysippos as the artist. The Delphian replica can thus be considered a reliable representative of Lysippos' work about 340 B.C., showing in the non-Polykleitan stance of the nude athletic figure the definite abandonment of his early style. The slight advance of one foot in an uncompleted step and the figure's gaze in the same direction forsake the self-contained posture of the Polykleitan models and imply the third dimension. The head of Agias is clearly individualized by nervous tension; its modeling is terse and somewhat dry (cf. Pliny's description, "corpora sicciora"), though vibrant and effective. His limbs are rather slim and his head is somewhat small, but there is no extreme proportional change.

The figure of Agelaos in the same group is so similar in style to that of Agias that it must be the work of the same master. The formulation of the epigram on the plinth associates him directly with Agias and with Telemachos, an intermediary figure whose epigram also links him in turn to Agias. *Telemachos*, *Agelaos*, and *Agias* should, therefore, serve equally as evidence of Lysippos' style. *Telemachos* (sometimes wrongly identified with a fourth statue of the same group, *Sisyphos II*) is obviously contemporary with the two others but seems to display a recurrence of the early style of Lysippos. This assumption is substantiated by the Praxitelean stance of Telemachos, leaning on a herm, his softer, more conservative modeling, and his more solid proportions.

Another athletic victory statue, to which Pliny refers (op. cit., xxxiv, 62), is the famous *Apoxyomenos* (PL. 220), preserved in the Vatican Museums; it is a Roman replica of faithful iconography but mediocre workmanship. In this figure Lysippos' new canon of proportions is fully applied, creating an impression of extreme slenderness. The working of the hair of the *Apoxyomenos* is much more elaborate than in the figures of Agias and Agelaos (cf. Pliny, loc. cit., 65); the right arm is extended forward, while the left is bent in a half circle to meet it at the elbow. Thus, a horizontal plane, enclosed by the two arms, is projected toward the spectator, producing the first truly three-dimensional sculpture in Greek art, a result heightened by the figure's stance and the direction of its gaze. The *Apoxyomenos* may profitably be compared with the so-called "Ilissos stele" in the National Museum, Athens, executed just before 317 B.C. The nude youth on this stele displays the same spatial principles as the *Apoxyomenos* and was probably created under the influence of contemporary Lysippian works. By inference and internal evidence, therefore, the *Apoxyomenos* should be considered representative of the late style of Lysippos about 320–315 B.C.

A Roman copy in Berlin (Staat. Mus., K 233) of the figure of an athlete should be dated, for stylistic reasons, between the *Apoxyomenos* and the Ilissos stele; its original is commonly attributed to the Lysippian circle. Heads of athletic victory statues, stylistically reminiscent of the figures noted above, are the one in Olympia (E. Curtius and F. Adler, eds., *Olympia: Die Ergebnisse der ... Ausgrabung*, II, Berlin, 1797, pl. 54, 3–4), that in the Museo Nazionale Romano, Rome (BrBr, text to nos. 717–18), the so-called "Bardini head" in the Museo Bardini, Florence (BrBr, text to nos. 717–18), and the so-called "Fagan head" in the British Museum. The latter is apparently a replica of the head of a statue usually described as Hermes binding on his sandal (PL. 221), which was ascribed to Lysippos by Christodoros (*Anthologia Palatina*, ii), who saw it in Constantinople. It is more likely an athlete loosening his sandal before joining a contest, and the highly three-dimensional pose and proportions conform to Lysippos' style after 320 B.C. The statue, formerly in the Lansdowne Collection, is now in Copenhagen (Ny Carlsberg Glyptotek).

Literary sources indicate that Lysippos created many cult images and other statues of the Olympian gods. Examples of these are the figures of Zeus in Taras, Sikyon, Argos, and Megara; of Poseidon in the sanctuary of Isthmia near Corinth; of Helios in his quadriga, in Rhodes; of Eros in Thespiai and on the Akrokorinthos; and of Kairos in Olympia. Some of these figures can, no doubt, be vaguely traced through later adaptations, particularly in small bronzes, but none of the surviving specimens presents a reliable picture of this important part of the artist's work. It has been plausibly suggested that the head of Zeus from Otricoli ultimately reflects a Lysippian archetype. The iconography of the Poseidon statue in the Vatican Museums generally corresponds to a Lysippian scheme, but it is an insufficient basis for stylistic comparisons.

Lysippos also frequently portrayed the figure of Herakles. Among such originals were the statues in Taras and Sikyon; the famous *Herakles Epitrapezios*, a seated statue which accompanied Alexander the Great on his campaigns; a Herakles without armor; and a complete group of the Twelve Labors of Herakles erected in Alyzia. Several attempts have been made to trace the lost archetypes of these statues in the great mass of Hellenistic and Roman figures of Herakles which still exist, but such a task is difficult and hazardous and returns only indefinite results. The bronze group of Herakles capturing a deer (PL. 222) in Palermo is commonly attributed to Lysippos. The minuscule mint mark on a tetradrachma of Sikyon, struck near the end of the 4th century B.C. [E. T. Newell and S. P. Noe, *The Alexander Coinage of Sikyon* (*Numismatic Studies, VI*), New York, 1950, p. 28 and pl. 18:27.2] represents Herakles resting on his club, an image in general accord with the iconography of the Farnese *Herakles* in Naples (PL. 226). That statue was executed in the period of the Roman Empire by the Greek sculptor Glykon and is thought to be based ultimately on a Lysippian prototype. The Sikyonian coin renders likely the adaptation of the Farnese *Herakles* from the statue by Lysippos in Sikyon, which was probably erected in the last quarter of the 4th century. Thus, the tragic or weary Herakles is ultimately Lysippos' creation.

Lysippos made many portraits of Alexander the Great, beginning when Alexander was only a boy ("a pueritia eius orsus," Pliny, op. cit., xxxiv, 63). There is reason to believe that these portraits revealed the development of both men during the more than twenty years of their association; the development probably culminated in the heroic portrayal of the features and character of Alexander upon which Plutarch and others commented (*Vita Alexandri*, iv, 1, and *De Alexandri Magni fortuna*, ii, 2). This type is best represented by such portrait heads as that in the Musée d'Art et d'Histoire, Geneva (Johnson, 1927, pl. 45) and is reflected in such Hellenistic adaptations as that in the Museo Barracco, Rome. The inscribed herm in the Louvre from the Azara Collection (PL. 224) is badly worn and of mediocre quality but may well be modeled on a somewhat earlier work of the late 330s B.C. Lysippos made a famous portrait of Alexander with a lance, which might be represented by the small, corroded bronze statuette in the Louvre (Johnson, 1927, pl. 47). Its posture and style are Lysippian, recalling by its heroic nudity and moving stance the figure of Agelaos in the Daochos group at Delphi, and its iconography is clearly that of Alexander, somewhat reminiscent of the "Azara herm."

Alexander's representation in the guise of Herakles on his coinage and on that of his immediate successors is also noteworthy. Good reason exists for the hypothesis that it is based on an original official portrait much like the 4th-century head in the Museum of Fine Arts, Boston (Sjöqvist, 1953, p. 30). This type of portraiture should be dated somewhat before the Alexander with the lance.

As indicated by H. P. L'Orange (*Apotheosis in Ancient Portraiture*, Oslo, Cambridge, Mass., 1947), the creative imagination of Lysippos solved the problem of rendering the features of a deified man, and his solution was perpetuated in modified form throughout the Hellenistic, Roman, and medieval periods.

Lysippos also created a posthumous portrait of Socrates erected in Athens under Lykourgos' administration. Despite recent objections, F. Poulsen's brilliant reconstruction of the work should be accepted (*From the Collections of the Ny Carlsberg Glyptotek*, I, 1931, p. 31 ff., and II, 1938, p. 169 ff.). His combination of the head in the Louvre (ArndtBr, nos. 1038–39) with a seated statue in Copenhagen (PL. 223; ArndtBr, nos. 1126–27) provides a new insight into the art of Lysippos. As a composition it is filled with quiet dynamism. Its drapery is simple and effective in style and is rendered with many strikingly realistic features, as is the aged body. Equally important is the subtle and convincing interpretation of the sublime genius beneath the ugly features of Socrates' face.

On the basis of the preceding identification there is good reason to attribute also to Lysippos or his circle the so-called "Seated Poet" in the Ny Carlsberg Glyptotek, Copenhagen (BrBr, no. 477), the group of Seilenos with the infant Dionysos in the Louvre (PL. 225; BrBr, no. 64), and perhaps the *Marsyas* in the Galleria Borghese (Rome; BrBr, no. 435).

Through his own work and that of his numerous followers and pupils, Lysippos introduced into the history of Greek sculpture a new stage that matured in the Hellenistic period. Yet he should also be considered the last of the great sculptors in the 4th-century tradition. It is thus the dual role of Lysippos both as precursor and conserver which establishes his unique position in the history of ancient art.

WORKS (lost, known from copies or from sources). *Zeus* with the thunderbolt, colossal standing statue, in the agora in Taras. – *Zeus*, probably standing statue, in the agora in Sikyon. – *Zeus Nemeios*, standing, in the agora in Argos. – *Zeus* of Megara, in a temple. – *Muses*, in Megara. – *Poseidon*, in or near Corinth (possibly identifiable with the *Poseidon* in Pausanias, *Description of Greece*, II, i, 7, 9), with the Dioskouroi in relief on the base. – *Dionysos*, on Mount Helikon (possibly identifiable as the bronze *Dionysos* mentioned by Lucian, *Zeus tragoedus*, 12). – *Helios* in a quadriga, in Rhodes. – *Eros*, at Thespiai in Boeotia (PL. 222), mentioned by Pausanias. – *Eros*, in Myndos, then perhaps in the Lauseion in Constantinople, destroyed by fire in A.D. 476. – *Kairos* standing on an astragal, with winged feet and holding a razor, perhaps in Olympia (Lippold), rather than in Sikyon (Kallistratos); later taken to the Lauseion in Constantinople. – *Satyros*, in Athens. – *Herakles*, in the agora in Sikyon. – *Herakles* seated on a basket on which was spread the lion skin: colossal statue on the acropolis of Taras (Bieber, 1955, p. 35; probably between 332 and 326 B.C.), then in Rome (209 B.C.), and in Constantinople (A.D. 325), first in the Basilica there, then in the Hippodrome; destroyed by the Crusaders (1204). – *Herakles Epitrapezios*, seated on a rock, over which was placed the lion skin, and bearing a cup in the right hand and a club in the left, used as a table ornament. – Seated *Herakles*, weary: the god vanquished and disarmed by Eros? – *The Labors of Herakles*, in the Temple of Herakles in Alyzia in Acarnania, then in Rome. – *Hermes* binding on his sandal, attributed to Lysippos by Christodoros (*Anthologia Palatina*, ii; PL. 221). – Portraits of Alexander the Great: Alexander as a child, a statue Nero had gilded. – Alexander with the lance, turning to the left and gazing upward. – Alexander on horseback, over life-size; Caesar replaced Alexander's head with his own portrait and dedicated the statue in the Forum before the Temple of Venus Genetrix. – Group of Alexander menaced by a lion, aided by Krateros, in Delphi (320–315 B.C.), in collaboration with Leochares, erected by the son of Krateros. – Alexander's companions, a series of 25 portrait statues dedicated in Dion for the victory of Granikos (334 B.C.); taken to the Portico of Octavia in Rome in 168 B.C. – *Hephaistion*, Alexander's friend, also attributed to Polykleitos the Younger (Pliny). – Portrait of Seleukos I Nikator; the signed marble base is known through a copy (now lost) in Rome in the 15th century. – *Pythes*, son of Andromachos of Abdera: two athletic statues in Olympia. – *Socrates*, in the Pompeion in Athens, created after the philosopher's death (335–330 B.C.). – *Praxilla*, the poetess, probably in Sikyon, identifiable with the following work. – Drunken flute girl (*temulenta tibicina*). – *Aisopos* (Aesop), shown with the Seven Sages, in Delphi. – *Troilos*, son of Alkinoos of Elis, Olympic victor with biga and quadriga; the base, bearing a metrical inscription, has been found by the excavators at Olympia. – *Cheilon of Patras*, a warrior, an Olympic victor (year unknown), killed in the Lamian War (322). – *Kallikrates* of Magnesia-on-the-Maeander, hoplitodromos, twice victor. – A *pankration* victor, son of Philandridas, from Stratos in Acarnania. – Two statues at Pharsalos: one of Agias, *pankration* victor at Olympia, Nemea, Delphi, and Corinth; fragments of an inscription with the name of the dedicator Daochos II, a Thessalian tetrarch; similar epigram found at Delphi on the base of a statue forming part of a marble group dedicated by Daochos II about 332 (PL. 219; W. Dittenberger, *Sylloge Inscriptionum Graecarum*, 3d ed., Leipzig, 1920, III, 274; IG, IX, 2). – *Koreidas*, *pankration* victor (342 or 338), statue created after 316: an inscription has been found at Thebes on a block also bearing the signature of Polykleitos the Younger (inscription of the late 4th century). – *Apoxyomenos*, later set up before the Baths of Agrippa in Rome (PL. 220). – Quadrigas of many kinds ("multorum generum"), for victories in the games. – Group similar to that of Krateros mentioned above. – Fallen lion at Lampsakos, taken by Agrippa to his baths in Rome, funerary monument for a battle. – Unbridled horse, identifiable with the horse taken to the Hippodrome in Constantinople. – Statue of Pelopidas of Thebes, son of Hippokles, erected by the Thessalians at Delphi; a base with epigram and signature has been found. – Statue at Corinth; a base has been found with traces of feet, of the second half of the 4th century B.C. – Statue at Thermon: a signed base of the second half of the 3d century B.C. has been found, though the original inscription would be earlier. – Bronze statue dedicated by Theramenes, son of Timoxenos; base found in Megara. – Statue in Lindos, Rhodes; base fragment (ca. 325 B.C.). – Terra-cotta vase for the sending of wine to Poteidaia. – Statue with dolphin, with a foot resting on a support, signed by Lysippos, found at Siena, 1334–48, and buried again in Florentine territory, 1357, by the Sienese, who believed that its pagan presence had adversely affected their contest with Florence (recorded by Ghiberti in *Il codice Magliabechiano*, cl. xvii, 33, ed. K. Frey, Berlin). – Bronze dog licking a wound, in the cella of Juno in the Temple of Jupiter Capitolinus in Rome, destroyed in the fire of the Vitellians (A.D. 69).

SOURCES. *a. Life*: Pliny, *Naturalis historia*, vii, 125, xxxiv, 37. 51, 61–67, xxxv, 153; Horace, Epistulae, ii, 1, 237–41; Cicero, Epistulae ad Familiares, v, 12, 7; Valerius Maximus, viii, 11, ext. 2; Arrian, Anabasis, i, 16, 4; Athenaeus, The Deipnosophists, xi, 784 (ed. Loeb, V, 1933, p. 54); Anthologia Palatina, xvi (Planudea App. IV), 344; Petronius, Satyricon, 88; Himerios, Eclogae, xxxi, 2 (ed. Wernsdorf, Göttingen, 1790, p. 286); Plutarch, Vita Alexandri, iv, 1; Plutarch, Morals, 335B. *b. Character*: Quintilian, Institutes, xii, 10, 9; Cicero, *Brutus*, lxxxvi, 296; Varro, De lingua latina, ix, 18; Varro, De re rustica, iii, 2, 5; Propertius, Elegiae, iii, 9; Columella, De re rustica, i, praefatio, 31; Pseudo-Cicero, Ad Herennium, iv, 6; Vitruvius, De Architectura, iii, praefatio, 2; Suidas, Lexicon, s.v. Ἀγαλματοποιοί, χειρουργοί, ἀνδριαντοποιοί (cf. Laterculi Alexandrini, ed. Diels, AbhPreussAk, 1904, p. 7). *c. Works*: Strabo, Geographica, vi, 278, and Scholium, x, 459, xiii, 590; Lucilius, v. 525; Pliny, Naturalis historia, xxxiv, 40; Livy, Ab urbe condita, xxvii, 16, 8; Pausanias, Description of Greece, i, 43, 6; ii, 1, 7, 9; 9, 8; 20, 3; vi, 1, 4; 2, 1; 6, 4–5; 14, 12; 17, 3; vii, 6, 5; ix, 27, 3; 30, 1; Lucian, Zeus tragoedus, 9, 12; Kallistratos, Statuarum descriptiones, vi; Poseidippos, Anthologia Palatina, xvi (Planudea App. IV), 275; Phaedrus, Fabulae, v, 8; Ausonius, Epigrammata, xxxiii; Tzetzes, Epistulae, 70 and 95; Tzetzes, Chiliades, viii, 416–34, x, 266–72, xi, 97–108; Nikephoros Blemmydes, in F. Osann, Kairos des Lysippos, AZ, IX, 1851, cols. 459–61; Plutarch, Fabius Maximus, 22, 6; Suidas, s.v. βασιλική, repeated almost verbatim in Παραστάσεις σύντομοι χρονικαί, cap. 37 (Scriptores originum Constantinopolitarum, ed. Teubner, 1901, I, p. 41); Konstantinos Manasses, Ἕκρατις, I (in L. Sternbach, Beiträge zur Kg., ÖJh, V, Beiblatt, 1902, cols. 65–69); Anonim. in Codinus Excerpta de ant. Const., p. 167, 21, ed. Bonn, 1843; Niketas Choniates, De Alexio Isaaci Angeli Fratre, III, 335 C–D (ed. Bonn, 1835, p. 687); Niketas Choniates, De signis Constantinopolitanis, 5 (ed. Bonn, 1835, p. 858); Martial, Epigrammata, ix, 43; Suetonius, Caesar, 61; Statius, Silvae, i, 1, 84–87; iv, 6; Tullius Geminus, Anthologia Palatina, xvi (Planudea App. IV), 103; Philip, Anthologia Palatina, xvi (Planudea App. IV), 104; Plutarch, De Iside et Osiride, 24; Plutarch, Vita Alexandri, 16, 7; 40, 4; Arrian, Anabasis, I, 16, 7; Justin, Historiae, xi, 6, 12–13; Velleius Paterculus, Historia Romana, i, 11, 3–4; Diogenes Laertius, De vitis philosophorum, ii, 5, 43; Tatian, Adversus Graecos, 33, 6 (Corpus Apologetarum, VI, Jena, 1851, p. 130); Agathias, Anthologia Palatina, xvi (Planudea App. IV), 332; Lucian, Deorum concilium, 12; Philip, Anthologia Palatina, ix, 777; Himerios, Orationes, xiii, 3, xxxi, 23, xlviii, 167, 171, 187 (Scriptores Graeci et Latini Consilio Acad. Lynceorum ed., Rome, 1951); Himerios, Eclogae, xiv, 1 (ed. Wernsdorf, Göttingen, 1790, p. 240); Plutarch, De Alexandri Magni fortuna, ii, 2; Choricius, in J. Förster, Der Praxiteles des Choricius, JdI, IX, 1894, pp. 167–90 at 168; Anthologia Palatina xvi (Planudea App. IV), 120; IG, VII, 38, 2533, XIV, 1206, 1254; Overbeck, SQ, nos. 1443–1512; Löwy, IGB, nos. 93, 94, 476, 477, 487, 506, 534; W. Dittenberger and K. Purgold, ed., Die Inschriften von Olympia (Olympia, V), Berlin, 1897, 166; B. D. Meritt, ed., Greek Inscriptions (Corinth, VIII, 1), Princeton, 1931, 34–35; C. Blinkenberg and K. F. Kinch, ed., Lindos: Fouilles et recherches, II, Berlin, 1941, no. 50, col. 241; J. Marcadé, Recueil des signatures de sculpteurs grecs, I, Paris, 1953, pp. 66–75.

BIBLIOG. M. Collignon, Lysyppe, Paris, 1905; P. Gardner, The Apoxyomenos of Lysippus, JHS, XXV, 1905, pp. 234–59; E. M. Gardiner and K. K. Smith, The Group Dedicated by Daochus at Athens, AJA, XIII, 1909, pp. 447–75; H. Pomtow, Eine neue Signatur Lysipps, JdI, XXXII, 1917, pp. 133–36; F. P. Johnson, Lysippos, Durham, N.C., 1927; E. Will, A propos de la base des Thessaliens à Delphes, BCH, LXII, 1938, pp. 289–304; J. Bousquet, Une statue de Pélopidas à Delphes signée de Lysippe, RA, 6th ser., XIV, 1939, pp. 129–32; M. Bieber, The Portraits of Alexander the Great, Am. Philos. Soc. Proc., XCIII, 1949, pp. 373–427; G. Gullini, Questioni lisippee, I: La statua di Aristotele, AC, I, 1949, pp. 130–48; C. H. Morgan, The Style of Lysippos, Commemorative Studies in Honor of T. L. Shear (Hesperia, Sup., VIII), 1949, pp. 228–34; Lippold, GP, pp. 276–86; E. Loeffler, Lysippos' Labors of Hercules, Marsyas, VI, 1950–53, pp. 8–24; E. Sjöqvist, Alexander-Heracles: A Preliminary Note, BMFA, LI, 1953, pp. 30–33; E. Sjöqvist, The Early Style of Lysippus, Op. Atheniensis, I, 1953, pp. 87–97; G. Kleiner, Der junge Lysipp, in Neue Beiträge zur klassischen Altertumswissenschaft: Festschrift B. Schweitzer, Stuttgart, 1954, pp. 227–42; W.-H. Schuchhardt, Über Lysipp, in Neue Beiträge zur klassischen Altertumswissenschaft: Festschrift B. Schweitzer, Stuttgart, 1954, pp. 222–26; M. Bieber, The Sculpture of the Hellenistic Age, New York, 1955 (rev. ed., 1961); J. Dörig, Lysipps letztes Werk, JdI, LXXII, 1957, pp. 19–43; F. De Visscher, Héraklès Epitrapèzios, L'antiquité classique, XXX, 1961, pp. 67–129.

Erik SJÖQVIST

Illustrations: PLS. 219–226.

MABUSE. See GOSSAERT.

MACCHIAIOLI. The most important school of Italian painters in the 19th century, this group was formed in Florence in the decade 1850–60 to oppose the influence of the Accademia and of the movement called *purismo* (see PRE-RAPHAELITISM AND RELATED MOVEMENTS). The school represents a minor but original aspect of European realism (see REALISM).

SUMMARY. Origin of the movement: theory and history of the macchia (col. 362). The artists (col. 365).

ORIGIN OF THE MOVEMENT: THEORY AND HISTORY OF THE MACCHIA. The name "Macchiaioli" was used for the first time in the *Gazzetta del Popolo*, in an ironic reference to some painters who exhibited at the Florentine Promotrice of 1861 landscapes that they themselves called *macchie* (literally, "spots"), because the pictures were painted in patches of color accenting the contrast of light and dark. Adopted by Telemaco Signorini, the name Macchiaioli eventually was applied, often improperly, to all Tuscan painters of the 19th and early 20th centuries who tended toward realism.

The importance of the Macchiaioli consists in their vigorous return to reality in art—an aspect that the teachings of the Accademia had lost—and in a new esthetic awareness, growing out of the patriotic fervor of 1848 but rooted in earlier cultural developments under Hapsburg-Lorraine rule in Tuscany, which produced a cultured bourgeois class and a moderate liberalism.

The formative period of the Macchiaioli was that of the gatherings and meetings at the Caffè Michelangelo in Florence from 1850 to about 1859, when artistic interests were fused with the democratic ferment developing from the movement toward a liberal and united Italy. According to Signorini, this famous café became the meeting place of almost all the painters who had participated in 1849 in the campaigns of Lombardy and the defense of Rome, Bologna, and Venice, and the amalgamation of ideas and experiences of artists from all parts of Italy that took place there tended to revitalize the figural arts. Along with the original Macchiaioli, not all of whom were Tuscan, various other artists made some impression in Florence — the Neapolitan Domenico Morelli, who had previously rebelled against academic authority; the Roman Nino Costa; Antonio Fontanesi, who by 1855 had abandoned the traditional chiaroscuro in his landscape painting; and even some painters of other nationalities (e.g., Degas).

In the caustic atmosphere of the stormy gatherings at the Caffè Michelangelo modern Italian caricature was born, and here originated the first heated discussions on realism. Here, too, the artistic principles of the group were adumbrated. More completely formulated in the writings of Diego Martelli, Adriano Cecioni, and Telemaco Signorini, these principles were first outlined in the movement's two periodicals, *Gazzettino delle arti del disegno* (1867) and *Giornale artistico* (1873–74), and constituted a theoretical program of realism similar to that embraced contemporaneously in France by Thoré, Champfleury, and Castagnary. In Italy, however, there was a sharper critical attitude toward the artificial literary and rhetorical point of view that had entered even into the field of art. The Macchiaioli stood for the idea of art as a vital and genuine expression of the society in which it arises and the belief that the individual artist can evaluate contemporary society honestly only by a personal interpretation. Accordingly, the entire Italian tradition, having become pedantic and literary, impeded artistic progress. But the iconoclasm of these turbulent habitués of the café was not limited to assaulting either academic art — modestly represented in Florence by G. Bezzuoli, E. Pollastrini, and A. Malatesta — or the more refined but rigid manner of the Purists Luigi Mussini and Antonio Ciseri; it went so far as to deny all values that were linked in any way with academic training. Although such iconoclasm endowed the movement with great vitality, the limitations of the Macchiaioli lie in their very inability to adapt their innovations to a tradition that had produced great results in the line they were following. The resoluteness and the sincerity of their call to life justify the persistent attacks on "men of letters" and "literary critics" with which Signorini, Cecioni, and Martelli filled so many pages; these qualities also clarify the meaning that the *macchia* — the formal solution into which the fundamental requirements of the movement were translated — assumed for Italian painters. In so far as it was limited to immediacy of vision — "truth as it is and as it shows itself" — the *macchia* technique meant an absolute rejection of literary themes, and, as Cecioni said, "a return to the simple truth that figural representations have their origin in the eye" and are therefore nurtured by "the actual visual heritage of the artist." *Macchia* was only an accentuation of pictorial chiaroscuro, a way, as Signorini said, "to emancipate oneself from the primary defect of the old school, in which the solidity and relief of its paintings were sacrificed to an excessive transparency of the bodies." As early as 1854 Signorini himself tried to infuse new strength into his brush stroke, and the arrival in Florence in the same year of the superficial but vigorous Morelli furthered the first attempts of the Macchiaioli in this direction. Most of all, the interest in landscape painting and in the abrupt transition of light and shade adopted by French romanticists in the early decades of the 19th century stimulated the Macchiaioli. They may also have been influenced by English landscape painters who exhibited at the Salon of 1824 and by the landscapists, both Italian and foreign, who painted the countryside around Rome in the 1830s and 1840s. Costa carried out his experiments in that region shortly before the Macchiaioli. The painting of "abridged impressions" (so called by Castelfranco) was widespread in Italy about 1850. Serafino De Tivoli's trip to Paris for the Exposition Universelle of 1855 and the subsequent visit of the Macchiaioli group to the Demidoff collection near Florence were also important stages in this development. In Paris, De Tivoli was more attracted by the work of the landscapists of the 1830s — Corot, the Barbizon school, Troyon, and the Orientalist Decamps — than by the paintings of Delacroix and Courbet. Troyon and Decamps were represented in the Demidoff collection; there, too, the Macchiaioli could have seen some excellent Dutch paintings, as well as a few quick sketches by Delacroix. Costa's arrival in Florence in 1859 and trips to Paris in 1861–62 by Signorini, Costa, and Vincenzo Cabianca reinforced the orientation of the group. It was in romantic landscapes rather than in studio paintings that the Macchiaioli found what they sought: dedication to nature, immediacy of impression, sincerity. Moreover, these artists discovered the freedom of painting in the open, capturing nature in one of its innumerable aspects — as if by surprise — in that instant during which a single effect takes place. They favored distant views, one of their tenets being that the figures in a painting should never exceed 6 inches.

However, something of the romantic spirit disappeared in the Tuscan school, notably the taste for sentiment and mysticism. The Macchiaioli were interested not in abstract concepts but in objects, places, and living persons. They preferred full sun to dusky effects for precise delimitation of objects and chose fragmentary rather than panoramic views, devoting all pictorial means to the achievement of clarity and distinctness. Probably the Macchiaioli had no direct acquaintance with the early Italian landscapes of Corot, and the wonderful simplification by which he joined and contrasted surfaces through the use of light, or with the Italian vistas that Ingres occasionally placed in the background of his portraits. The spiritual affinity of the Macchiaioli with these painters derives from the example of Costa and, above all, the chaste "purist" luminosity of the early drawings of Giovanni Fattori, Silvestro Lega, and Giuseppe Abbati.

After 1860 the *macchia*, which had initially been a splash of chiaroscuro and nothing else, developed into a draftsmanlike latticework, extremely sharp and simple, which has sometimes been compared to 15th-century work, but which actually derives from *purismo*. Like the pieces in a polychrome inlay, the *macchie* assume a natural balance based on tone and color value, serving by their tranquil and lyrical juxtaposition to articulate planes and to suggest volumes and distances. Wrote Cecioni: "The truth is born of spots of color and of light and dark values, each of which has an effect of its own that is measured by means of its relationships. In each spot this relationship is double — as value and as hue. When one says that the color is right in hue but not in value, it means that it is too light in respect to the other tones. For example, in the hue scale, yellow has a greater value than white. But in the scale of light and dark its value may be lower, if the white is in the shade and serves as a background to a sunlit yellow. The color never changes; the light has [only] the property of altering it... because shade does not act like a cloth but like a veil." This elementary theory of visual reality lies at the heart of the best period of this group, which, from about 1860 to 1880, made an unquestionably original contribution to 19th-century European painting.

After 1880 the Macchiaioli gradually lost the unity of inspiration and experimentation that had bound them together, and in consequence the quality of their production declined rapidly. Little by little, the group itself dissolved — Raffaello Sernesi died in 1866, Abbati in 1868, De Tivoli settled in London in 1864, Vito D'Ancona left Italy for a long time, and Signorini, Martelli, and Cecioni (who died in 1886) were away for shorter periods — and soon Italy was pervaded by a new, veristic trend which not even the talents of a Fattori or a Lega could resist. These two artists — isolated, misunderstood, and depressed by the general decline of contemporary culture in Italy — continued to produce works worthy of their best years. Toward the turn of the century Fattori found new accents of pure poetry in the spare and dramatic idiom of etching, in which he expressed powerfully his disillusionment and vexation with Italian society. The vast unified corpus of his 166 etchings fits unmistakably into that climate of harsh naturalism and pessimism which stamped so much of Europe's artistic and literary production during those years.

THE ARTISTS. Against this cultural background the differing personalities of the Macchiaioli group emerge. Nino Costa (1827–1903), fervent patriot and follower of Garibaldi, was only loosely associated with the group, retaining his ties with the Barbizon painters, but he is extremely important as a forerunner of the Macchiaioli, especially because of his contacts with French and English painters; his influence on Fattori was decisive. Among the less representative members of the group were Serafino De Tivoli (1826–92), whose best landscapes (PL. 240) were similar to those of the more advanced painters of the 1830s; Vito D'Ancona (1825–84), whose small studies reveal supple and succulent modeling (PL. 240); Cristiano Banti (1824–1904), a careful and talented, though old-fashioned, painter; and Vincenzo Cabianca (1827–1902), who initially distinguished himself for brutal intensity of light effects (PL. 240) but later passed into obscurity. Because of the wealth and variety of his experience, coupled with his aggressive stance and his qualities as a writer, Telemaco Signorini (1835–1901), a cultivated, talented, and receptive artist, was considered the most prominent figure of the entire group in his time. However, he is no longer so highly regarded, notwithstanding the excellence and animation of some his works (PLS. 234, 235). Among the first to attempt the *macchia*, he often visited Paris, where in 1861 he met Troyon and Corot and later Manet, Zola, and Degas. From Paris he also went to England several times. After 1875 he began to blur his brush strokes in order, like the impressionists, to obtain a maximum of light and air in his works. At times he tended to become merely illustrative, as in his etchings and dry points, for example. Close in style to Signorini was Adriano Cecioni (1838–86). Although he was also a sculptor, Cecioni's best contribution was as a painter and as a critic (PL. 239). His writings, though modest, provide useful documentation for this entire period. Quite different from these artists in artistic temperament was Giuseppe Abbati (1836–68; PLS. 228, 231). A student of Michelangelo Grigoletti in Venice, he worked in Naples in 1856 and went to Florence only in 1860, a veteran of Garibaldi's campaigns. His landscapes and studies of cloisters are marked by a meditative, intense melancholy and are among the finest paintings of the Macchiaioli. Raffaello Sernesi (1838–66; PLS. 229, 237) resembled Abbati in artistic qualities and in temperament. Some of the paintings that reveal his early attempts at *macchia* — in particular, a few delicate landscapes — are of the highest quality and may be placed on a level with those of Abbati. Lovely landscapes and interior views were also produced by Odoardo Borrani (1834–1905), whose extremely unequal work declined greatly after 1880.

The most outstanding figure of the group was Giovanni Fattori (1825–1908), unquestionably the leading Italian painter of the 19th century (PLS. 229, 232, 233, 236). He was not given to artistic discussions, but he had a rare simplicity of feeling, which he communicated directly through his work. He arrived at the *macchia* technique quite late, through the influence of Costa, and it was only in 1861 — the year he painted the *Battle of Magenta* and a magnificent little portrait of his cousin Argia (both, Florence, Gall. d'Arte Mod.) — that his apprenticeship, begun 15 years earlier under Bezzuoli, could be considered finished. The dating of his vast output was established in the Leghorn exhibit of 1953, tracing the development of his style from his first *macchie* of soldiers in 1859 to landscape studies executed with Costa, particularly in 1864–65, and through the period of his best production, in Leghorn and Castiglioncello, during the following 10 years. Several excellent portraits and the *Assault at the Madonna della Scoperta* (1864; Leghorn, Mus. Civ. Giovanni Fattori), a work of greater commitment and scope, also fall within this period. In 1873 Fattori went for the first time to Rome, and in 1875 he journeyed to Paris, where he remained almost a month. The great *Battle of Custoza* (1876–80; Florence, Gall. d'Arte Mod.), a painting with a certain dramatic force, marks a shift to a new inspiration that from this time on reflects his spiritual isolation. Ever more marked by bitterness and pessimism, his art began to reflect the more painful and squalid aspects of the Maremma landscape. This new tendency resulted in the domination of drawing over color and a turn to illustrative inflections, though he reached new heights of achievement in his etchings.

Silvestro Lega (1826–95), who finished his thorough apprenticeship with Mussini only at the age of 35, was the last of this group of artists to take up the *macchia* technique. However, it was precisely this late development that allowed him to make a first-rate contribution to the new idiom after he became one of the dominant personalities — along with Signorini, Abbati, Sernesi, and Borrani — of the Macchiaioli in the Pergentina group, about 1862 (PLS. 227, 230, 238; XI, PL. 444). After 1880 the sharp drawing that had characterized his early paintings occurred only infrequently, while his brush stroke became more forceful and his color vibrant. Like the other Macchiaioli, he was a convinced admirer of Mazzini and interrupted his studies several times to take part in the battles of the Risorgimento. Also connected with the Macchiaioli, although of a younger generation, were Giuseppe De Nittis (1846–84) and Giovanni Boldini (1842–1931; PL. 239), the latter before he established himself in Paris.

The first reliable appraisals of the Macchiaioli are to be found in the writings of Diego Martelli, the only Italian critic to have appreciated fully the impact of contemporary French painting. As early as 1879, in a memorable lecture on the impressionists, he compared the Macchiaioli to them, though granting the difference of relative values. After the turn of the century a real critical interest in these Tuscan artists developed, fostered by *La Voce*. In 1913 a fine check list of Fattori's works was published by Oscar Ghiglia, the first critic capable of singling out the true qualities of the Macchiaioli. Between 1920 and 1927 there followed penetrating articles by E. Cecchi and A. Soffici, which remain basic for the accuracy of their judgments and are important for their attempt to evaluate 19th-century Italian art in relation to contemporaneous European culture. Interest in the Macchiaioli was one example of the taste for the "primitive" manifest in Italy during the 1920s. For instance, Fattori was praised as "illiterate" with a "disinclination to polemics and theory," the "pure painter." Such interpretation of the work of the Macchiaioli was carried to the point of seeing in some of its characteristics (e.g., its elementary content and antiliterary subjects) a sign of a primordial simplicity and purity, almost a suprahistorical essence, capable, according to Tinti, of reaching, through mysterious biological roots, from the paintings of the Macchiaioli to Italian art of the 15th century. Despite the caveats of L. Venturi (1925), critics taking this stand placed greater value on the work of the Macchiaioli than on that of the impressionists, basing their judgments on the alleged "primitive" character of the Tuscan artists. In 1929 Roberto Longhi replied to these exaggerations and errors with a lively controversial sally, expanded later in his "Ragguaglio sull'impressionismo e il gusto degli italiani" (1949). However, he went to the other extreme of belittling excessively the significance of this art that represented, within its limits, an original elaboration of certain aspects of European realism. More recently, critics such as Anna Maria Brizio, Giorgio Castelfranco, Lamberto Vitali, and Corrado Maltese have arrived at a temperate judgment of the contributions of the Macchiaioli, an evaluation supported by several exhibitions of their work, including an exhibit of late-19th-century art that contained some of their works, the VI Quadriennale of Rome (1952); a Fattori show in Leghorn and Florence (1953); and two recent exhibits of paintings by the Macchiaioli, one at the Galleria Nazionale d'Arte Moderna in Rome (1956) and another at the American Federation of Arts Gallery in New York (1963).

SOURCES. T. Signorini, Il Caffè Michelangelo, Il Gazzettino delle Arti del disegno, Florence, May 18, 1867; Giorn. artistico, Florence, 1873-74; T. Signorini, Le 99 discussioni artistiche, Florence, 1877; T. Signorini, Caricaturisti e caricaturati al Caffè Michelangelo (1844-66), Florence, 1893 (2d ed., 1952); A. Franchi, Arte e artisti toscani dal 1850 ad oggi, Florence, 1902 (n. ed. with title: I Macchiaioli toscani, Milan, 1945); A. Cecioni, Scritti e ricordi, Florence, 1905; T. Signorini, Riomaggiore, Florence, 1909 (2d ed., 1942); A. Franchi, G. Fattori, Florence, 1910; 166 Acqueforti di G. Fattori: edizione pubblicata nel Centenario della nascita, Florence, 1925; N. Costa, Quel che vidi e quel che intesi, Milan, 1927; A. Cecioni, Opere e scritti (ed. E. Somarè), Milan, 1932; T. Signorini, Scritti d'arte (ed. E. Somarè), Milan, 1933; M. Borgiotti, I Macchiaioli, Florence, 1946; R. Calzini, 12 opere di G. Fattori nella Collezione Stramezzi, Milan, 1949; R. Calzini, 12 opere di Lega, Milan, 1951; F. Wittgens, 12 opere di R. Sernesi, Milan, 1951; D. Martelli, Scritti d'arte (ed. A. Boschetto), Florence, 1952; L. Vitali, ed., Lettere dei Macchiaioli, Turin, 1953; M. Borgiotti, Poesia dei Macchiaioli, Milan, 1958. Catalogues of private collections of the works of the Macchiaioli are listed in G. Caradente and P. Bucarelli, I Macchiaioli (exhibition cat.), Rome, 1956.

BIBLIOG. U. Ojetti, T. Signorini e I Macchiaioli fiorentini, Rome, 1901; G. Rossetti Agresti, G. Costa: His Life, Works and Times, London, 1904; U. Matini, C. Banti e i pittori Macchiaioli, Florence, 1905; A. Gargiulo, La rivolta realistica in Italia, La Critica, VII, 1909, pp. 233-40; U. Ojetti, Ritratti di artisti italiani, 2 vols., Milan, 1911-23; O. Ghiglia, L'opera di G. Fattori, Florence, 1913; E. Cecchi, G. Fattori, Valori plastici, II, 1920, pp. 1-7; U. Ojetti, Macchiaioli e impressionisti, Dedalo, I, 1920-21, pp. 759-60; A. Soffici, G. Fattori, Rome, 1921; B. Croce, Una teoria della macchia, Problemi di estetica, 2d ed., Bari, 1923, pp. 238-48 (5th ed., 1954, pp. 241-51); L. Venturi, Il gusto dei primitivi, Bologna, 1925, pp. 227-29, 325-26; E. Cecchi, Pittura italiana dell'Ottocento, Rome, 1926 (3d ed., 1946); E. Somarè, T. Signorini, Milan, 1926; M. Tinti, G. Fattori, Rome, Milan, 1926; E. Somarè, Storia dei pittori italiani dell'Ottocento, Milan, 1928 (bibliog.); U. Ojetti, La pittura italiana dell'Ottocento, Florence, Rome, 1929; L. Venturi, Pretesti di critica, Milan, 1929; L. Venturi, Les "Macchiaioli," GBA, X, 1933, pp. 238-54; M. Tinti, Boldini ante Parigi, Emporium, LXXX, 1934, pp. 3-12; L. Vitali, Incisione italiana moderna, Milan, 1934; A. De Witt, Il disegno dei Macchiaioli, Emporium, LXXXVI, 1937, pp. 541-50; A. M. Brizio, Ottocento e Novecento, Turin, 1939 (2d ed., 1944); P. Bargellini, Caffè Michelangelo, Florence, 1944; A. M. Francini-Ciaranfi, Incisioni del Fattori, Bergamo, 1944; F. Russoli, Appunti sui Macchiaioli, ArtiFig, II, 1946, pp. 209-17; F. Russoli, Gli scritti critici dei Macchiaioli, Paesaggio, I, 1946, pp. 93-103; R. Baldaccini, G. Abbati, Florence, 1947; M. P. Cazzullo, La scuola dei Macchiaioli, Florence, 1948; R. Longhi, Ragguaglia sull'impressionismo e il gusto degli italiani, introduction to It. trans. of J. Rewald, History of Impressionism, Florence, 1949, pp. vii-xxix; B. M. Bacci, D. Martelli, Florence, 1952; G. Castelfranco, Pittori italiani del secondo Ottocento, Rome, 1952 (full bibliog.); D. Durbé, G. Fattori (exhibition cat.), Leghorn, 1953 (essential bibliog.); C. L.Ragghianti, G. Fattori, Sele Arte, II, 8, 1953, pp. 33-40; Riv. di Livorno, III, 1953, special no. dedicated to G. Fattori exhibition (bibliog.); P. D'Ancona, Pittura dell'Ottocento, Milan, 1955; G. Delogu, Pittura italiana dell'Ottocento, Bergamo, 1955; G. Caradente and P. Bucarelli, I Macchiaioli (exhibition cat.), Rome, 1956; E. Lavagnino, L'arte moderna, Turin, 1956; M. Pittaluga, Cecioni e De Nittis, Scritti in onore di L. Venturi, II, Rome, 1956, pp. 135-52; M. Giardelli, I Macchiaioli e l'epoca loro, Milan, 1958; D. Durbé, Fattori incisore, Riv. di Livorno, IX, 1959, pp. 263-93; E. Cecchi, Piaceri della Pittura, Venice, 1960 (repr. of his principal writings on the Macchiaioli, 1922-53); C Maltese, Storia dell'arte in Italia, 1785-1943, Turin, 1960; F. Novotny, Painting and Sculpture in Europe: 1780-1880, Harmondsworth, 1960; M. De Micheli, G. Fattori (autobiographical appendix ed. by D. Durbé), Milan, 1961.

Dario DURBÉ

Illustrations: PLS. 227-240.

MACKINTOSH, CHARLES RENNIE. British architect (b. Glasgow, June 7, 1868; d. London, Dec. 10, 1928). One of the most notable pioneers of the modern movement in architecture, Mackintosh was the son of a police superintendent. He was educated at Reid's Public School and Alan Glen's High School, both in Glasgow. Apprenticed to the architect John Hutchinson in 1884, Mackintosh then enrolled as an evening student at the Glasgow School of Art. In 1889 he joined the architectural firm of John Honeyman and John Keppie as draftsman and became a partner in 1904. With three other students — Margaret and Frances MacDonald and Herbert McNair — he formed a group known locally as "The Four" and began to produce remarkably original drawings, posters, craftwork, and furniture. Exhibitions by "The Four" at home and abroad gave international prominence to his work, which in some aspects had an affinity with Art Nouveau.

In 1896 Mackintosh won for his firm the competition for the design of a new Glasgow School of Art. His design, because of its flexibility, spatial concepts, and freedom from historical styles, has come to be recognized as one of the most significant of that period. The first part of the school was constructed between 1897 and 1899, while Mackintosh was working on Queen's Cross Church (an essay in modernized Gothic) and the famous Cranston Tea Rooms, both in Glasgow, and a house for W. R. Davidson at nearby Kilmacolm. In 1900 he married Margaret MacDonald, and was also invited by the Viennese Sezessionists to exhibit in J. M. Olbrich's Sezession Haus in Vienna.

From 1900 to 1906 Mackintosh's reputation as one of the leaders in the new movement was securely established, and he had considerable influence abroad, particularly in Austria. During this period he placed second in an international competition for the design of a "Haus eines Kunstfreundes" held in Darmstadt. He exhibited at Turin in 1902 (I, PL. 468), and elsewhere in Europe, and entered the competitions for the Glasgow International Exhibition (1901) and the Anglican Cathedral of Liverpool (1903). His most notable executed works were Hill House at Helensburgh (1902-03), for W. W. Blackie; Scotland Street School (1904), Glasgow; the Willow Tea Rooms (1904), Glasgow, for Miss Cranston; the interiors of Hous'Hill, Nitshill, Glasgow; and the redesigning of the west wing and library of the Glasgow School of Art. The latter building was completed in 1909, by which time Mackintosh had been elected Fellow of the Royal Institute of British Architects (1907) and Fellow of the Royal Incorporation of Architects in Scotland (1909).

For personal reasons, the Mackintoshes left Glasgow in 1913 and devoted themselves to water-color painting, first in East Anglia and London, then in the French Pyrenees.

BIBLIOG. N. Pevsner, Charles Rennie Mackintosh, Milan, 1950; T. Howarth, Charles Rennie Mackintosh and the Modern Movement, London, 1952.

Thomas HOWARTH

MADERNO (MADERNA), CARLO. The first of the great Roman baroque architects (b. Capolago, Lake Lugano, 1556; d. Rome, Jan. 30, 1629). Maderno was in Rome by 1588, working for his uncle Domenico Fontana, who presumably trained him in the rather arid mannerist style then current. His first major work — and one of the first examples of baroque architecture — was the façade of S. Susanna (II, PL. 137), completed in 1603. This design is clearly based on such famous mannerist prototypes as the Church of the Gesù (IX, PL. 312) by Vignola and Della Porta (qq.v.), most prominently in its vertical articulation; however, the differences between the two are generally held to mark the advent of a new style. Where the elevation of the Gesù is ambiguous and less systematic, S. Susanna is straightforward and simple; the steady progression from pilaster to single column to coupled columns focuses the viewer's attention on the doorway. In the same way, the sculpture is sharply defined within niches, yet given maximum plasticity. This combination of richness of detail and simplicity of articulation is characteristically baroque.

In the same year as his first notable work, Maderno was appointed architect of St. Peter's, where he passed much of his working life. In 1607 he won a competition for the transformation of Michelangelo's central plan into a Latin cross, a modification made necessary partly by lack of space. He added a nave — thereby destroying the basic concept of Bramante and Michelangelo — and, as a necessary corollary, designed a façade as well as the Benediction Loggia required by the new design. He contrived to mask the transept projections of the old central plan behind an extended façade without concealing the dome. His solution was criticized on grounds of proportion, but such adverse judgment failed to consider the difficulties under which he worked, in particular the imposition of towers in 1612 (though never completed). Maderno retained Michelangelo's giant order and decorative details with great skill, but the need for the Benediction Loggia prevented him from developing his façade in depth, with a portico such as Michelangelo had planned: the resulting façade looks rather like a palace. The Maderno additions were consecrated on Nov. 18, 1626.

For S. Andrea della Valle (1608–28), Maderno designed the second largest dome — after that of St. Peter's — in Rome; but much of the church proper is by Carlo Rainaldi. Maderno's principal secular buildings were Palazzo Antici Mattei and Palazzo Barberini, both in Rome. On the whole, the Palazzo Mattei (1598–1618; II, PL. 132) is a simple, well-proportioned edifice of the normal Roman type with a central court; still, it has some features in common with the problematic Barberini, the first of the great Roman baroque palaces. Maderno's final design for the latter residence must have been completed by October, 1628, a few months before his death. It has been convincingly shown that all the new features in the plan (II, FIG. 285), especially the open forecourt (like that of a *villa suburbana*) in place of an enclosed court, are due to him and not to Bernini or Borromini. Borromini, Maderno's kinsman and assistant, remained as assistant to Bernini, who took over after Maderno's death but made few and unimportant changes in his predecessor's design (II, PL. 134).

BIBLIOG. G. Baglione, Le vite de' pittori..., Rome, 1642; N. Caflisch, Carlo Maderno, Munich, 1934; U. Donati, Carlo Maderno, Lugano, 1957; A. Blunt, The Palazzo Barberini..., Warburg, XII, 1958, pp. 256–87; R. Wittkower, Art and Architecture in Italy, 1600–1750, Harmondsworth, 1958.

Peter MURRAY

MAES, NICOLAES. Dutch portrait and genre painter (b. Dordrecht, Nov., 1632; buried Amsterdam, Nov. 24, 1693). The son of a well-to-do soap boiler of Dordrecht, Nicolaes Maes entered Rembrandt's studio in Amsterdam about 1648. He returned to Dordrecht in 1653, married the widow of a preacher in 1654, and bought a house in 1658; he fathered three children. In 1673 he settled in Amsterdam, where he remained to his death.

Maes was one of Rembrandt's most gifted pupils. Like many of the master's students, he began by closely imitating Rembrandt's style. This tendency is most noticeable in his drawings, which often resemble Rembrandt's so strongly that it is difficult to tell the two draftsmen apart. (A large number of Maes's drawings derive from a sketchbook that was broken up and sold at auction in 1922.) His early paintings reflect Rembrandt's style and choice of subject matter of the 1640s.

Maes concentrated on simple themes and favored a treatment of light and shade that created a mood of intimacy, warmth, and domestic quietude. Most of his pictures present women, both young and old, reading, spinning, peeling apples, threading needles, playing with or nursing children, and praying. Attentive to still-life accessories and to local color, Maes gave to his forms a somewhat greater degree of sculptural solidity and distinctness than Rembrandt did during the same period. Besides the inspiration of Rembrandt, Maes owed the compositional schemes of his pictures to such artists as Carel Fabritius and Pieter de Hooch (qq.v.). In his later genre scenes, possibly in response to a demand from his patrons, he stressed anecdotal elements. The subject of a man or a woman eavesdropping on a pair of lovers seems to have enjoyed particular popularity.

During the last decades of his life, Maes devoted himself increasingly to the facile but lucrative practice of portrait painting. His characteristic subjects were middle-class people, placed before curtains or landscape backgrounds to enhance their stature. These portraits are apt to be somber in color and never achieve the elegance of those of Van Dyck; at their best, however, they are dignified and forthright statements of individual personality or frank likenesses.

BIBLIOG. C. Hofstede de Groot, Beschreibendes und kritisches Verzeichnis der hervorragendsten holländischen Maler des XVII. Jahrhunderts, VI, Esslingen, Paris, 1915; W. R. Valentiner, Nicolaes Maes, Berlin, Leipzig, 1924.

Julius S. HELD

MAGIC. In the history of art, magic pertains to a broad category of works intended to interpret, express, or utilize the supernatural. To be sure, it is difficult to isolate theoretically the concept of magic from the beliefs and practices proper to religion, especially in ancient and Oriental cultures and in primitive societies (see COSMOLOGY AND CARTOGRAPHY; DEMONOLOGY; DIVINITIES; ESCHATOLOGY; MONSTROUS AND IMAGINARY SUBJECTS; TERROR IN ART). Nonetheless, in practice the phenomena and attitudes connected with man's manipulation of mysterious forces give rise to the creation of various objects and figures and inspire iconographic types that may be considered apart from religion. From their practical origin, magical concepts have gradually become, especially in the modern world, a fringe aspect of literary and philosophical thought, bordering on the esoteric, the occult, and the symbolic.

SUMMARY. Introduction (col. 370): *Nature of magic; Magic and artistic creation.* Types of relationship between magic and art (col. 373): *Sympathetic magic by means of images; From image to symbol; Unseen art; Sympathetic magic in architecture; Pars-pro-toto magic in art; From the magical to the esthetic.* The iconography of magic from antiquity to the modern West (col. 380): *Prehistory and the ancient Near East; Greece and Rome; Christian art until the end of the Middle Ages; Magic as a "Faustian" subject: a. "Romanticism" about 1500; b. The myth of the magus; c. Homo divinans; d. Astrology; e. Alchemy; f. The mysteries of hieroglyphics; g. Demons; h. Witches; i. Romantic occultism and surrealism.* Aspects of magic in Asia (col. 388).

INTRODUCTION. The term magic (from Gr., μαγεία) was introduced in the classical world to characterize the practices of the Mazdean Magi but was eventually extended to designate the activity of every kind of conjurer whose procedures did not correspond to those of a recognized religion; this more general meaning of magic is that in use in the modern world.

When the scholarly study of comparative religion was begun in the 19th century, the operational distinction between official religious acts and marginal magical activity was applied as well to the abstract concepts of religion and magic. Magic was then regarded as that which differed from the canons of the polytheistic and monotheistic religions inherited from the past and which seemed to be identifiable with certain attitudes "surviving" among the European folk (see FOLK ART) without being displaced by the tenets of Christianity. Such an identification led to the ascription of inferiority, of primitive status, to those religious forms in which magic (or what was called magic) was a major cult expression. With the exception of certain French sociologists (Jean Hubert, Marcel Mauss), who regarded only individual practices as magical, distinguishing them from the common religious activities of the whole people, evolutionary theorists saw in magic a prereligious stage in mankind's intellectual progress. In this stage, of which "primitive" cultures were viewed as an example, man trusted simply in the efficacy of his own acts to achieve his ends, somewhat in the manner of a contemporary scientist (and, in fact, E. B. Tylor, James Frazer, and others spoke of magic as a pseudo science). According to R. R. Marett, however, magic arts served to manipulate an impersonal force (mana) distributed among various elements of nature, man included.

With the dissipation of the predominantly evolutionary climate of thought, the theory of a primitive magical phase in the religious history of mankind was abandoned, but the equivocal identification of magic with all that which seemed to lie "below" the level of "genuine" religion remained. (Religion here was understood as comprising polytheism and monotheism, to which was added W. Schmidt's *Urmonotheismus*, based on the supreme beings of the "primitives.") Thus, manifestations of a magical attitude toward the world were discerned not only where perhaps it was legitimate to do so, as in shamanism (q.v.), or, more broadly, wherever the figures of the magician, wizard, or healer occur, but also in typical ritual forms connected with complex ideologies [e.g., totemism (q.v.), ancestor cults, spirit worship]. Such rituals, not being directed toward "divine" beings, were interpreted as revealing a magical mentality or consciousness or the conviction of the capacity to operate directly without the aid of deities.

Nevertheless, for the purposes of this article, which is to consider the relationships between art and magic both within and beyond the limits of Western civilization and to describe works of art generated by magical concepts, it is useful to consider the possibility of a generic magical mentality or consciousness and to examine the hypothetical character attributable to an artist-magician, for whom ritual realization of supernatural forces plays a greater part than philological abstractions. For further discussion of objects serving religious (and sometimes magical) purposes see LITURGICAL AND RITUAL OBJECTS. For primitive concepts that partake of folklore, religion, and magic, and that include magical ceremonies of apotropaic, curing, divining, fertility, initiation, hunting, and harvest significance, see AFRO-AMERICAN ART; ASIA, SOUTH: TRIBAL STYLES; AUSTRALIAN CULTURES; BANTU CULTURES; CUSHITE CULTURES; GUINEAN CULTURES; and the like.

* *

Nature of magic. Conscious magic presumes the oneness of the physical and the spiritual being; the spiritual is in some way material, although endowed with paranormal characteristics. The magician, or magical type of man (*homo magus*), and the visionary or seer (*homo divinans*) are often eidetic types in the sense described by E. R. Jaensch, who has shown that even today, among children and among some artists, evidence of subjective visual images can be found, and that perceptions of things which have happened, or even only been imagined, can be projected as if they were optically visible. The eidetic type has a tendency to visions and hallucinations and takes his dream life for reality, often even a higher reality. This tendency is linked with an inclination toward autosuggestion or mass suggestion and the hypnotic phenomena that accompany them.

There is a distinction between the more active and the more passive forms of magic. In the narrower sense magic implies an active influence of the magician on the world around him without the mediation of mechanically and causally understandable actions (e.g., without contact or direct hearing and seeing). Such magic depends upon known rites and ceremonies and requires a special kind of self-awareness in the practitioner, a reliance on his own secret spiritual powers; these characteristics distinguish the magical intention (including its *deisidaimonia*, or respect for demons) from the humble attitude of the pious or mystical man of Western tradition. The principal form is the banishing ritual, which includes magic healing and similar phenomena. Sympathetic magic plays a decisive part, and its consequences will be discussed below in relation to the making of works of art. If the intention is harmful, as in the well-known practice of sticking pins into a wax image, the procedure is called "black magic." The power of the image explains the shyness of certain peoples in front of mirrors or any other means of obtaining a likeness, though nowadays the contrary mass suggestion of photography and the cinema has almost eliminated this fear. Opposed to black magic is the tradition of the "white" magician: in contrast to Faust there is Shakespeare's idealized figure of Prospero in *The Tempest*, who uses his power wisely and without the help of demons (or of God either) for the benefit of his fellow men. While the successes of practical magic may all be attributed to the occurrence of hypnosis and autosuggestion, which have been recognized by science but not completely explained, magic remains to some extent effective even for modern man. In the major religions of the Western world magic has been condemned, not because magical relationships were impossible, but because they were misused. Christianity, however, distinguishes between magic and miracles; the latter are attributed to the grace of God through intermediaries, as in the case of blessing, the healing of the sick, and the transformation of the Sacraments.

The results of magic and miracles often appear alike in certain phenomena such as ecstasy or levitation, which occur both in the legends of the saints and in the accounts of sorcerers, and no distinction is made in non-Christian religions. For example, in Indian belief certain deities appear in person as the supreme magician to bring about the materialization of the entire world by an act of immense psychic concentration.

In a wider sense magic includes many passive, or predominantly passive, experiences, for example, intuitive or inspirational receptivity in the seer or clairvoyant, including the interpretation of signs by intuition according to special, definite indications, such as divination (PLS. 252, 253), oracles, and astrology (which, in the form of astromancy, may be compared with the more active magic of alchemy). Also there is often no distinction between magic and a belief in demons or devils, ghosts, and the spirits of the dead. For this reason, and also because of his Faust-like presumption, the more mediumistically talented magician, in trying to redeem himself, incurred the Church's censure on suspicion of Gnostic heresy (see HERETICAL SUBJECTS). In the representation of magic, poetic and artistic freedom of imagination may constitute the last sublimated state of the magical consciousness, making connections with mythology and legend and surviving uncorrupted in the paganism of fairy tales. Language preserves the remains of these relationships in such words as "enchanting," which often carry a transferred esthetic or erotic meaning deprived of the original magical implication.

Magic and artistic creation. The historical relationship between magic and art has been accentuated by the inner affinity, first emphasized by the romantics and then by the surrealists, between artistic creation, with the purely esthetic "enchantment" it evokes, and magical practices. The influence of the subconscious can be traced in both. Faces seen in dreams, and other forms of visions and hallucinations, seem to be of the same nature as the artist's fantasy. It cannot be determined whether the amazing "impressionism" of the late Stone Age cave paintings of animals (PL. 241) is related to the eidetic disposition presupposed in the *homo magus*. The artist's inspiration may be compared both to the trance conditions of the medium and to the visions of religious ecstatics, but the ancients equated singers (or musicians) and seers (*poeta* and *vates*); the Greeks classed the output of artists working with material forms as artisanship, not as art, because of the manual labor and material elements involved. However, painters, sculptors, and architects have also had secret inspirations and miraculous triumphs. The divine revelation of a building site or plan to the architect or donor of a sacred building is a legend common to many cultures, and from such legends there developed complex geomantic rules codified for the use of architects, as occurred in India and China. Perhaps the old Chinese *fêng-shui* also belongs to this category, although it deals not only with visionistic suggestions but also with a whole system of apotropaic, geomantic, and cosmomorphic considerations whereby the proper site for settlements or temples may be determined. In a very broad sense one may include also the fact that there are in mythology a number of gods and demigods who are expressly in charge of the visual arts and inspire artists and craftsmen. Among these are the Indian architect of the gods, Viśvakarma, and two Egyptian architectural gods, Ptah and Khnum. It is noteworthy also that the builder of Zoser's pyramid, Imhotep (q.v.), probably the most ancient architect whose name has survived (if not absolutely the most ancient of all artists known by name), was later mythologized (he was made a son of Ptah) and turned into a great initiate of poetry as well as of the healing art (the Greeks identified him with their medical god Asklepios), a classic case of the union of artist and "white" magician in one person. In Greek mythology there were the hero Prometheus, a magician-sculptor, and the god Hephaistos, who was conceived as a smith.

In this connection it is interesting that among many African tribes the smith is regarded as a wizard, endowed with gifts (or knowledge of arts) that are of a broadly magical character. The making of objects themselves, apart from their intent or final appearance, often presents itself as a magical activity, not only because of the magical symbols and designs which may be associated with them, but also because of the magical power of the material employed (e.g., iron and other minerals, certain plants, hides of certain animals, bones, shells), which only certain persons are permitted to manipulate. The form of the object produced often corresponds to a significant image rather than to a purely practical, utilitarian shape (e.g., the scythe in the form of a crescent moon). The magic involved in creating an object does not necessarily imply that the product must be used in sacred rites; a magically potent material or form may be intended for efficacy in hunting or in harvesting.

Thus it appears that the art object intended for magical purposes is not born from subconscious inspiration; rather, the magical act of creation and its product are closely linked to certain "sacred" techniques, or techniques consecrated by tradition, which only the magician may know and use (his profession is an art as well as a gift). The true artist preserves conscious control over his creative inspiration through his knowledge and understanding of his art. The art products of paranormally gifted persons (mediumistic drawings and so forth) and the paintings of mentally disturbed persons, therefore, generally fall outside the categories under consideration here (see PSYCHOLOGY OF ART).

TYPES OF RELATIONSHIP BETWEEN MAGIC AND ART. Magic, in addition to its connections with religion, cult practices, and the myth-making imagination, may at times be the prime inspiration for the creation of works of artistic worth and purpose in their own right. On the other hand, a work of art may merely represent magical figures and events for illustrative, didactic, or symbolical purposes. In the latter case, magic, with the allied subject of demonology (q.v.), simply constitutes a particular field of artistic iconography. It depends on the point of view whether representations from the enormous field of religious (or mythical, or legendary) miracles should also be regarded as magical. Generally such representations treat paranormal happenings either as cases of mystical transcendence, having no basis of comparison with the natural course of events, or else in a matter-of-fact traditional and dogmatic way. Within the terms of reference here such works would come under consideration only when the miraculous borders on the magical, the supernatural on the occult, the divine on the demonic, the sacraments on thaumaturgy, and the priest on the magician.

Sympathetic magic by means of images. In all parts of the world sympathetic magic offers the broadest scope to artistic expression. If the image of a being is prepared with certain ritual precautions, it is thought to create a certain teleplastic influence on the thing represented. Two principal forms can be distinguished: the first is concerned with the likeness, caught as in a mirror, of anything (men, beasts, and objects) which has once been visibly present; the other kind is concerned with the images of invisible beings. The first group includes everything connected with funerary magic (see ESCHATOLOGY). All over the world, regardless of differences in cultural, racial, and geographical background, men have believed that the preservation of the bodily form of a deceased person with his possessions ensures for both of them some kind of continued existence after death. Even if the ancient practices seem to reveal an invariably causal pattern of thinking, they also reveal an extralogical conviction of the continued existence of the spirit both within the grave, where the form is preserved, and beyond it, in an invisible dimension. Presumably the soul of the deceased, which has in some manner conditioned and formed his personal appearance, can free itself from the body and maintain a shadowy existence if it receives the appropriate magical help by means of its image. Of course, the image, if it is to give this help, must first be equipped with magical spells. This idea played a dominant part in Egyptian life. There the first stage in the magical preservation of life consisted in the preservation (mummification) of the corpse itself with its tangible array of grave gifts (IV, PLS. 449, 454, 460); the second phase was the pictorial representation of the deceased with his belongings, and artistic merit in the representation could redound to the honor and benefit of the deceased (see EGYPTIAN ART).

Just as the form of the image in funerary painting and sculpture was intended to produce results magically for the dead, so it is supposed to have done for the living long before in the period of paleolithic cave art. Animal paintings and relief sculpture executed deep within caves (PL. 241), as well as figures carved into high rocky exterior projections, have generally been interpreted, from the time of the earliest paleoethnologists, as evidence of purely magical intent (see ARCHAEOLOGY; PREHISTORY). It is supposed that the image, through the psychic effort of concentration (perhaps accompanied by ritual dancing) involved in its execution or contemplation, was intended to influence the creature represented and compel it (telepathically or telekinetically) to show itself or to facilitate the hunt. Modern ethnology provides parallels to this procedure. That this was the practical aim seems to be proved by the numerous wounds on the animals represented (PL. 241), but in many prehistoric representations other aims of a more magical or religious sort probably also entered in. In such cases as the famous "Venus" of Willendorf (PL. 247), the aim seems to be fertility and the multiplication of the species. The figural representation was apparently intended to achieve something akin to a solemn placation of the "animal spirit," the "group soul," or a divinity ruling over the animal kingdom. Thus there is implied a transition from a purely magico-utilitarian concept to something specifically religious, from the magic rite to the cult act. Recent studies have emphasized the effective presence of religious elements in combination with (if not even prior or opposed to) the magic factors. Such an opinion is supported by the inaccessibility, obscurity, and consequently sacred character of the galleries deep within the earth. Standing for the animal, the representation must have acquired heightened powers, not through a magic constraint but through prayer, though even a cult of this kind probably preserved many magic elements.

In contrast to a verifiable memorial portrait of the deceased is the imaginary representation, which the artist (priest, shaman, or medicine man) envisions in a dream or trance, and under certain circumstances this imaginary portrait can become established in tradition. By a similar process secret powers in nature, previously unpersonalized, come to be materialized and acquire more personal traits. In the romantic literature of mesmerism and magnetism it is asserted that these powers exist in the form of fluid rays. On the primitive level the manufacture of fetishes is an attempt to turn these powers to use. The need to render visible and tangible the formless powers perceived in the universe is a recognized psychological development.

The objects produced in connection with the fetishistic attitude may be divided into two classes, the fetish object and the fetish idol. The purpose of the first is not the representation of impersonal forces but the control of these forces through a concentration of various elements and signs that may be brought to bear on them. Fetish objects may take the form of stones, sticks, skins, and the like, with incisions and designs, but the typical example is the skin bag containing the various elements prepared by the witch doctor. To this main type belongs the amulet endowed with therapeutic and apotropaic powers (PLS. 243, 248, 249), the use of which is documented from prehistoric times and in both primitive societies and advanced civilizations. A particular type of amulet, often of fine workmanship and valuable material, is the talisman. Instead, the fetish idol (PL. 250) personifies the forces in theriomorphic or anthropomorphic forms, the aim being to reconcile the nonhuman with the human and to make the former approachable and ultimately controllable. These are not likenesses but forms by means of which the shapeless forces are fixed; although understood differently in different cultures, this is the essence of the magic operation. For example, among the Tungus one of the most important functions of the shaman is to induce spirits to enter into wooden forms prepared for them.

The magical aspect of the making of idols sometimes occurs in polytheistic religions, in which the figure is not a fetish but the image of a god. Among the Maya, for example, the craftsmen assigned to carve wooden idols were terrified by the task before them; they accepted it with great reluctance and, assisted by priests, had recourse to fasts, sacrifices, and preparatory rites. In monotheism, which also distinguishes between the god and the image of the god, there sometimes exists the tendency to regard the latter as magically effective in itself. This attitude accounts for the more or less strict rejection of images in the Jewish and Islamic religions, the Byzantine iconoclastic controversy, and the Protestant views on images. Statues in particular presented a special danger to be avoided; the surprising rarity of sculpture in the round in Early Christian and Byzantine art may reflect the widespread belief that demons entered images of this kind to take advantage of an externally holy appearance.

Positive images that partake of numinous power and radiate it include, under numerous transitional forms, those of the world-wide realm of demons. Figures of demons were supposed to ward off other harmful spirits, especially in the material and elementary worlds (fire, water, etc.) as well as to terrorize and banish all human enemies. Of all the magical elements in art this apotropaic pictorial magic has been the best recognized and perhaps one-sidedly overemphasized. The study of non-Christian art (in primitive cultures, in ancient Egypt, in Asia Minor, in India, the Far East, and America, and also among the ancient Nordic, Celtic, and Germanic peoples) has emphasized protective magic (PL. 244) as the reason for the creation of innumerable typically horrific figures, including many fantastic mixtures of man and beast (IV, PLS. 166, 167). Often their original appearance represents some archetypal vision, which in time was taken as a norm. The union of human and animal forms — as exemplified in Mesopotamian art (I, PL. 515), ancient Egyptian art (IV, PLS. 354, 369), Hittite art (I, PL. 523), ancient Nordic and ancient Mexican art (X, PLS. 1, 21, 45), and Romanesque sculpture (IV, PL. 178) — was not originally meant to be interpreted allegorically; rather, it came into being because the subconscious dream symbol thereby appeared to indicate a multiplication or enhancement of the magical emanations (the mana of the South Sea Islanders). In the beginnings of classical antiquity, and in Greek and Etruscan art, as is shown by the abundance of masks, acroteria, and Gorgons' heads (PL. 244; V, PL. 38) in the temples, magic was an active ingredient, and the apotropaic impulse is still to be discerned in Christian architectural sculpture, for example, in Romanesque capitals and Gothic gargoyles.

From image to symbol. It is noteworthy that the earliest surviving art works of presumed magical intention — the often cited Magdalenian cave paintings and rock engravings — represent reality, especially animals, with an exactitude of detail that is not otherwise encountered except at late and highly developed stages of stylistic evolution. (Obscure abstract symbols are sometimes found along with these representations.) On the whole, the magic of art, in the narrower sense described above, is not found where fleeting visual impressions of movement have been caught and fixed with great skill but in the extension of the kind of art which Wilhelm Worringer has described as "abstraction" and has contrasted with "empathy" (*Einfühlung*). It is not known whether the art of Aurignacian man, which by contrast with the Magdalenian already looked old-fashioned, was perhaps followed by a now-lost stage in which the magical purpose was more strongly emphasized and which would have appeared primitive in comparison with the other known stages. Generally the power of fascination, which is of the essence of a magical effect, is lacking in images that convey their meaning by outright imitation. Realistic (or even "idealized realistic") and impressionistic art cannot usually be said to have a truly magical intention, although in certain directions the illustration of magical subjects, as in Far Eastern painting, in Magdalenian art, and in certain primitive areas, arose out of an impressionistic manner of seeing.

In the context of the history of art as a whole, magical works of art, in the sense defined above, appear to use the emblem instead of the picture as an abbreviation, a written or visual formula, for the object that is secretly identified with, works through, or is even concealed in the art works. This difference between realistic and symbolic magical representation arose at the beginning of the Neolithic period. Symbolical representation, though naturally it compressed reality differently in different cases, continued to prevail in the Bronze Age, with its psychological, economic, social, and technical advances.

The range of symbols (including a few isolated magical pictorial formulas dating from the Old Stone Age) extends from crude and awkward drawings to highly advanced representations and involves a number of forms which, as psychological analysis shows, have a suggestive and slightly hypnotic effect on the beholder. Among these forms (in the early archaic period of Egypt and in early Greece) are the stiff, eerie, lifeless, and yet in some way ensouled images of men, demons, or gods. The effect is especially strong when the purpose was (not so much in Egypt and Greece as in the Early Christian, medieval, and Byzantine periods) to represent the actual gaze of the deceased with the hypnotic and magical effect of, first, the evil eye and, later, a suggestion of healing. Besides the stiff frontal aspect, which the Egyptians so often avoided, there occurs an arrangement in monotonously similar rows, a soporific design that suited the Egyptian style of relief, and a heraldic symmetry of arrangement, common in organic and inorganic nature but included in magical art as an effective means of producing a slight spiritual shock by its suggestion of unfriendliness and remoteness from life. As is well known, all these and similar principles of form are used occasionally in pure ornamentation, especially when there are no organic elements drawn from the realm of plants or animals, as was commonly the case in the antique and early Gothic periods. At that stage the naturalistic forms were made to look strange by stylization or by being mingled with demonic signs and figures with an aura of black magic, such as dragons and other fabulous beasts and especially snakes, which so often have a mythical and psychological import. A widespread apotropaic motif is the eye ornament (PLS. 244, 245). In contrast to the antique and even earlier preference for a static style, the decorative arts of the Nordic, Celtic, and Germanic peoples developed, partly in elaboration of Oriental patterns, a new and dynamic style of labyrinthine and monotonous interlaced bands, in which the metamorphosis of inorganic forms into the heads of living animals and demons is quite eerie. These artistic elements, whether used in ornamentation or as separate symbols, were not merely decorative but had originally a magical intention.

In general, magical ornamentation retains an ancient rigidity. This was the case in the early Middle Ages, whereas in the 12th and 13th centuries there was a greater tendency toward a mystical subjective sense of nature. However, the ornamentation of the late northern Gothic style, especially in the great altarpieces and in the church porches, shows a great liveliness, notably in the treatment of draperies. A strange vitality is imparted to naturalistic leaves and branches and, even more, to the broken folds of cloth, which appear to be blown by a magic wind unaffected by the mechanical laws of gravity, and thus the inherently lifeless becomes a vehicle of invisible powers. The style seems to reflect a revitalizing of "Faustian" magic (see below) characteristic of the late Middle Ages. The transparence and immaterial weightlessness of the early Gothic style (see GOTHIC ART), with its mystical impulse, is in contrast to this panentheistic naturalism of about 1500.

In cultural regions where the magical and voluntaristic element is not contrary to the religious attitude, specific influences of this kind can be demonstrated in art works of hieratic style. Thus in Indian yoga and in comparable practices among Taoists individual meditation techniques have had an influence on Asian devotional art.

Unseen art. Magic and magico-religious characteristics are indicated by the fact that in archaic regions many paintings and sculptures (and not only the objects of cult reverence, which would include "ugly" images, but also those which now appear rather decorative and even symbolic) were originally located so as to be almost or entirely out of sight. [However, the difference in Australian cave paintings is notable in this respect. See AUSTRALIAN CULTURES.] In prehistoric cave paintings it is often noticeable that some pictures have been painted over others without any attempt to efface the underlying ones. This fact suggests indifference to the impression of unesthetic confusion that might be conveyed. Apparently the only thing that mattered was the act of painting itself, and, although there was room enough elsewhere, the work was done so far as possible in the same place, as though the place were sanctified by tradition or had some particular efficacy. Furthermore, tomb furnishings, from the extensive and often costly paintings and sculptures in the graves of royal mummies to the simple urn for ashes with a mere indication of a human figure (IV, PLS. 449, 452), were intended to remain visible to the clients and workmen for only a very short time until they disappeared "forever" in the darkness. The same is true of much of the art, generally said to be apotropaic, on sacred buildings. Even when such art is easily visible, as over doorways, the question remains whether the dimensions, sometimes very large, may not have been intended both as a defense against demons and an inspiration to religious fear in men. Many examples of unseen art are provided by Egyptian sculptures and reliefs in tombs or high on the inaccessible tops of obelisks and by the originally almost inaccessible figures of animals, demons, or saints, which were often almost or quite invisible from below, on the upper parts and roofs of Romanesque and Gothic churches. These figures, from their recognizable interpretation, as well as their material costliness and artistic value, were primarily intended to be looked at by the invisibles, that is, by spirits, demons, the gods, or God himself. Art of this kind was not produced in the West after the Renaissance. Later decoration, even if of symbolic and instructive nature or erected in an inaccessible position, is in proportion to the remoteness of the human beholder. The influence of the human observer appears also in the summary treatment of the form, without detail, and in the measurements, which show that the figure is intended to be looked at from below and from a distance with a certain foreshortening. The backs of the images are left more or less unfinished, in contrast to the treatment of unseen parts by the earlier sculptors and stonemasons.

Sympathetic magic in architecture. In addition to the protection of buildings by images of numinous or demonic beings, another method, also derived from the magical attitude to the world, was to create in the building itself analogies with numinous cosmic relationships, thus giving it a share in the eternity of its prototype (see COSMOLOGY AND CARTOLOGY). Evidence of this belief appears from the primitive and archaic stages of the Bronze Age. The monuments may be roughhewn or left almost in natural condition; they may be accurately prepared and finished by stonemasons, as in the case of freestanding monuments, stone circles, gateways, boundary stones, processional ways, and cult places of megalithic and cyclopean type (e.g., V, PLS. 160–165); or they may be architecturally refined buildings, such as temples with closed courts and inner rooms. Besides the powerful effect of size in these colossal or cyclopean works (which were not originally intended to "elevate" in the esthetic sense but rather to create a demonic or numinous shock), there is also a directly magical factor (comparable to that in ancient music) derived from transferring to the architectural proportions of a building the figures and measurements of the geocentric universe (the 7 planets, the 12 signs of the zodiac, the 4 elements, and other mystic numbers). The seven stories of certain step pyramids and ziggurats show this relationship. Cosmic relationships survive in all number mysticism related to building.

Even the orientation of the axes of buildings toward certain significant points in the astronomical sphere, with its calendar symbolism, belongs to the art of magical protection. Examples of this are the orientation to the rising of Sirius, to the position of the zodiac in spring, and to the sun's position at the summer solstice. In Islamic and Christian architecture the orientation, for historical religious reasons, is toward Mecca or toward the Holy Sepulcher, rather than the older cosmic directions.

Another kind of magical insurance is the choice of astrologically favorable moments for laying foundation stones or beginning construction and the casting of horoscopes for individual buildings and towns. This practice is based on the idea that buildings erected by the hand of man will partake of the divine world order. At the time of the early Italian Renaissance, which was influenced by occultism, there was a recrudescence of these "Egyptian" or "Chaldean" ideas, influenced by the writers of late antiquity or perhaps by masonic tradition [cf. Francesco di Giorgio Martini, *Trattato d'architettura* (1482), Turin, 1841].

Besides the astrological guarantees thus given there were also rules of geomantic or geomagical kind. A well-known example is the occult knowledge in the Chinese Taoist *fêng-shui*, the lore according to which certain apotropaic (rather than climatic, hygienic, defensive, or even esthetic) conditions had to be fulfilled in order to determine the right time and the lucky site for the building of a house or settlement. As with astrology, the practice of divination is bound about by traditional, rigid, and complex rules. It has not yet been proved whether in this connection the choice of sites for towns, funerary monuments, and temples was originally influenced by chthonic and magical ideas. In any case, it is noteworthy that many sacred Christian buildings were erected, not, as might be expected, at a conspicuous distance from earlier heathen sanctuaries, but directly on their remains, presumably in order to facilitate conversion by making use of the deep-rooted beliefs of the converts in the sanctity of particular places and regions. Unfortunately, the posthumous survival of number mysticism (Egyptosophy, pyramid mysticism, and the like) from late antiquity to the present, with its fantastic and hasty interpretations, has confused rather than answered the question of magical significance in architecture.

Pars-pro-toto magic in art. Besides similarity to the whole — either as image or in measure and number — another kind of magic that stimulates the creation of art forms is the symbolism of a single part that stands for the whole. The cult of relics (bones, ashes, fragments of the corpse of a hero, saint, or martyr, which are supposed to bring blessing to those who possess and honor them) is in the Catholic churches not entirely reduced to a cult of mementos but in many cases has been related to miracles. Even in classical antiquity, in Buddhism, and in Islam, relics have had an influence that cannot be entirely distinguished from the practices of magic. Primitive practices have a similar aspect in relation to the magical use of bones, teeth, hair, and so on. Purely phenomenologically, it cannot be denied that autosuggestion and mass suggestion (which are characteristic of the magical mentality) have an influence on the belief in the paranormal powers of relics. This kind of faith has many connections with the visual arts. Many shrines, chapels, and churches have been erected over relics. From the 4th century on, altars were erected over the graves, sarcophagi, or remains of martyrs. The growing cult of relics, together with the sacramental function of the altar, had a strong influence on architectural planning and design. Crypts, both subterranean, as the burial places of martyrs in the catacombs, and partly subterranean, as in the east end of the choir of medieval churches, became uncommon in the Gothic period, not only because of changes in religious tenets but also because of a subconscious change of convictions anticipating the Reformation.

No less significant for art, in connection with the belief in the power of relics, was the use of reliquaries for the preservation and exhibition of wonder-working contents. The enormous expenditure of costly materials and the artistic workmanship of dazzling effect express, in the naïve manner typical of the magico-monistic state of mind, the magical and miraculous aspects of religion. A significant symptom of this development, comparable to the disuse of subterranean crypts in the later Middle Ages, is the growing practice of opening reliquaries, from the Gothic period on, to exhibit the contents, which formerly were not visible.

Monstrances, the liturgical receptacles for the consecrated Host, are related to the reliquaries and owe much of their mystical glory to the same half-unconscious attitude. For the same reason early medieval liturgical books were often bound with barbaric splendor and overloaded with glittering semiprecious stones.

From the magical to the esthetic. Comparable to the evolution of the image into the symbol is that of the magical representation to the esthetic level. So long as the magical belief is operative, the artistic products are pertinent to the voluntaristic effort, to the magic action, and to the working techniques. After the magical belief has been superseded, the techniques and the products remain, but the identification with the original meaning is lost or weakened. The symbol that had magical power is transmuted into an emblem. Romantic poetry changes images and moods of magic and wonder into merely fictional fantasy, into the poetry of "as if," eliminating the element of fear and creating a sort of game. In the visual arts, images as a means of conjuring the supernatural powers give way to others in which the powers are no longer thought of as present but are simply honored as implied potencies (as in holy pictures, votive gifts, and devotional objects; see DEVOTIONAL OBJECTS AND IMAGES). However, in the long run, the magical powers are not abolished but are sublimated in various ways; the magical experience survives in the secret miracle of artistic creation. The preservation of the words "magical," "miraculous," and "enchanting," though they may be used esthetically, shows the connection.

The earliest example of a marked supersession of magic in the West comes from ancient Greece, where classical and postclassical art, with its images and myths of the gods, indicates not so much complete secularization as a purified religiosity, from which the magical element has been virtually removed. The recrudescence of "superstition" in late antiquity, which opened the arts to Oriental and perhaps Nordic influences, met in the Early Christian period and the Middle Ages a second wave of magical depotentiation. Later, as will be shown below, magic appeared only in illustrations and allegorical descriptions. In certain forms of modern art (surrealism, tachism, *informel* art, etc.), whose advocates are fond of using the word "magic" in a transferred sense, it often appears that there is an intent to reactivate magic on a new level.

A few examples may illustrate the transformation of magic to the esthetic plane and at the same time will lead on to the questions to be dealt with in the subsequent discussion.

(1) Light and shade: Sunlight has always been regarded as a perceptible revelation from above, from the realm of the superconscious, the holy, and the divine. Darkness, whether the complete darkness of the inner earth (caves) or the darkness above the earth dimly penetrated by the moon, conveys an eerie and demonic impression. The mixture of light and dark — as in the dimensional depth of late Gothic altars, in works such as those of Correggio (q.v.), with his chiaroscuro, and especially of Rembrandt (q.v.), with his acausal lighting — may still remind the observer of the old Gnostic dualism of the kingdoms of light and dark and the struggle between them. On the other hand, Caravaggio (q.v.) and the *tenebrosi* eliminated the secrecy of darkness and made it a mere resource of painting; similarly the French impressionists (most of whom were personally indifferent in matters of religion) neutralized light and made it an object of rational analysis. In the 20th century the repression of the shadow has gone even further, with an overemphasis that may be expected to produce a reaction.

(2) Color: On Chinese funerary vases the color red, as the color of blood, life, and fertility, was supposed to give the deceased some magical help toward resurrection. In many other cultures red has been used as a protection against evil spirits. Red remained an arbitrary symbol of warmth and life, even when no magical power was ascribed to it. Finally, red became the warm hue in the color scale, in contrast to the cold colors, and was used in contexts quite contrary to the magical and symbolic meaning.

(3) Adornment: In primitive societies and ancient cultures parts of the body, for instance the neck and wrists, were magically protected by amulets (PLS. 248, 249). Since these also had a decorative effect, the metals and precious stones used for magical purposes were all the more acceptable because of their beauty and were often elaborately worked for esthetic enhancement. Today the wearing of "charms" is merely a game, though the magic remains in a generalized erotic sense.

THE ICONOGRAPHY OF MAGIC FROM ANTIQUITY TO THE MODERN WEST. *Prehistory and the ancient Near East.* The magician or diviner, with his peculiar states of consciousness, is a favorite theme in the history of the visual arts, not for the purpose of working magic but as illustration or allegory. Naturally this is especially true in religious contexts treating of miracles, for such stories from the Gospels and the legends of saints comprise a large sector of Christian art. However, the iconography of such religious art works is pertinent here only when the miraculous nature of the event is emphasized in a way that presents the paranormal in the magical sense. Thus the principal emphasis here will be placed on representations that fall outside the Christian tradition of miracles and have been of some importance in antiquity or in Western art since the end of the Middle Ages. The Magdalenian cave paintings and rock engravings mentioned above seem to reveal not only a magical and cult purpose but also a certain artistic pleasure in the representation itself and in the skill of execution. The magical motifs so often chosen for illustration are significant: dances (probably with sexual magic) and magicians themselves (comparable to the shamans and medicine men of modern primitive cultures). The magicians appear in animal masks and even in animal costumes to stalk the creatures of the wild, either as part of a mime or in the hunt. These representations are the earliest instance of the ominous and fear-inspiring picture of the magician discharging his proper function, which has always had an exciting influence on the imagination of humanity. Thousands of years later, in the ancient Orient and in Egypt, as in Greek and Roman art, this figure approximated more the idealized type of the priestly sage. An enormous number of images of magical, mythical, and cult significance are encountered in Mesopotamia, with its astrological beliefs, and in ancient Egypt, which was known to the Greeks as the classic land of magic (and later of alchemy) and was revered for its hieroglyphs, which were for centuries thought to be the secret writings of a lost mysterious wisdom. However, most of the images were magical in intent and were not meant for the eyes of the living. In ancient Egypt, for example, the representation of the god Horus as a child, standing upon two crocodiles and suffocating a group of serpents with his hands, is frequently found on healing steles and statues (PL. 250). Mesopotamian objects often bear scenes of exorcism, though the extent of the intended magic factor is not easily determined. One such object is a bronze bell in Berlin (Staat. Mus.) showing a group of exorcists, priests of the god of magic Ea, who hold buckets and are wrapped in curious capes that give the figures a fishlike appearance. Near them appear lion-headed demons and a human figure, possibly a beneficent demon. Another such scene occurs on a terra-cotta slab divided into five strips, with several rows of *orans* figures; the subject of the exorcism lies on a mattress on the earth, while another figure stands upon a boat. The same fundamental motifs are found on a bronze plaque (Paris, Coll. De Clercq). On the reverse side is the back of a demon with the body of a winged lion; his head projects above the plaque, so that it forms the top of the scene shown on the obverse side.

Greece and Rome. In the ancient Near East, stories about sorcerers were less important than the construction of magical instruments, and in ancient Hellas, as discussed above, the magical intention can be fully recognized only in the earliest phases. In the classical centuries magic was only a recollection. On the other hand, the miraculous entered the picture. In Hellenic religion the divine powers were for the first time in human history represented in a bright and cheerful way, but the opposite pole, the nocturnal and sinister, was not absent. The figure of Hecate (of Near Eastern origin) became the focus of everything that was later to survive in folk belief and poetry in connection with ghosts, spirits, the wild hunt, and Thessalian witches. Artemis, Selene, and Persephone, mistress of the underworld, also originated from this complex of ideas. There was also much magic in the Orphic-Dionysiac cycle of myths, with its mysteries, transformations, and representations of the other world in terms of soul birds, harpies, and sirens. Of human warlocks and witches, Medea is the classical prototype. More healthy, but often tragic, is the magic of seers and seeresses, as described by Homer. The belief in the clairvoyant gift of a Calchas, Tiresias, Cassandra, and many others endured throughout the ancient period. In real life, in addition to the renowned oracles that survived for centuries in the face of philosophic and scientific doubts, there were various highly developed methods of interpreting signs, combining definite regulated observations with inspirational means.

Many of these beliefs left their traces in the visual arts of the time, though examples are often missing in many fields today. The gloomy and chthonic element is often strongly in evidence in Etruscan art. In the graves of the late period the horrific side of the classical picture of Acheron and Hades is emphasized, and certain descriptions of the underworld seem like precursors of Christian scenes in hell by Bosch and Grünewald (qq.v.). Commonest are pictures of divination, which are particularly interesting in that many motifs of this kind occur again in the art of the Renaissance.

Illustrations of seers in the ecstatic style that became frequent in the later Middle Ages are rather rare in ancient art. The figures in the Tomb of the Augurs in Tarquinia are probably not those of seers. However, there is no doubt that this subject is intended in a few vase paintings and in the figures of two old men from the east pediment of the Temple of Zeus at Olympia. These figures are especially remarkable because ancient sculpture at that preclassical stage was struggling to express the emotion of the diviner. One of the figures is sunk in a self-searching attitude of meditation, and the alert expression of the other is also to be interpreted as visionary, rather than as the augur's gaze or mantic observation of the flight of birds. At a much later stage the same facial expression of the seer occurs in the enthroned goddess with the child Triton in the Museo Nazionale Romano, Rome. On the basis of coins, this figure has been explained as the *thea sibylla* and therefore a copy, if not the original, of the statue taken to Rome from the tomb of a sibyl in the famous grotto of the sacred well at Erythrae in Asia Minor. The peculiar attitude, and even more the indication of the ecstatic glance (the sculptured pupils), marked the utmost expression of the transcendental in ancient art, because while the enchantment of music was familiar to the period, the transcendental as revealed to the ascetic seer remained closed to it.

Haruspicy, the prophetic observation of entrails and other phenomena, is quite frequently reflected in Etruscan art. As examples there are the bronze sculptures in Piacenza (PL. 253) and in the Vatican Museums, the wall paintings from Golini Tomb II at Porano, near Orvieto, and a magnificent engraved mirror from Tuscania (last two, Florence, Mus. Arch.).

Another favorite subject was catoptromancy, the widespread practice of inhibiting consciousness by staring into reflecting surfaces such as mirrors, crystals, and water vessels and so obtaining true visions from the subconscious (as we should say nowadays) or from gods and demons (as they said then). On an Attic vase of the late 5th century B.C. in Berlin (Staat. Mus.), depicting Themis and Aegeus, this method of divination even appears to replace the Delphic oracle. Lecanomancy is introduced in a Dionysiac scene in the Villa of the Mysteries at Pompeii (PL. 246) and in genre paintings in the frescoes of the House of Livia in Rome. The remarkable examples of divination from mirrors shown on the four reliefs of the silver treasure of Berthouville (Paris, Bib. Nat.) have not yet been reliably interpreted in detail.

The interpretation of the stars and the casting of horoscopes by astrologers were familiar subjects to Hellenistic and Roman artists. There are numerous extant sarcophagus reliefs with such representations: Prometheus, the outline of the career of a high official, the birth and education of a child (e.g., Uffizi, Louvre, and Villa Doria-Pamphili, Rome). The mosaic of the philosopher, from Torre Annunziata, near Naples, with a ball erected on a plinth, must also be mentioned here. The personal horoscope found its most elaborate manifestation in antiquity in the funerary monument of Antiochus I of Commagene at Nimrud Dagh, Anatolia.

Christian art until the end of the Middle Ages. Although within the limits of Christian art an apotropaic undertone was officially no longer allowed, it survived in the earlier Middle Ages in sculpture and ornamentation, especially in Romanesque churches. Moreover, certain pagan and magical elements appeared to an increasing degree, in a manner that combines freely illustrative and old apotropaic intentions.

In the last centuries of the Middle Ages there were an increasing number of representations from the pictorial repertory of the calendar and ancient and Arabian astrology (illuminated manuscripts, frescoes, and tapestries in palaces, town halls, and other public buildings). Originally the traditional signs of the zodiac and occupations of the months, as they appeared on floor mosaics in late Roman, Early Christian, and early Romanesque buildings, and ultimately among the Christian representations on the walls and west fronts of Gothic cathedrals, were merely calendaric; they illustrated the sun's position in the zodiac simultaneously with the relevant occupations on the land and the activities at court.

Magic was involved only in so far as ultimately all representations of stars and constellations from the mysterious Arabian sphere stirred the simple-minded to a pious shudder. In consequence, in engravings and tapestries the zodiac became less and less important, and finally only the agricultural work of the seasons remained. On the other hand, the seven planetary gods provided abundant material for superstitious subjects and symbolism and in the Christian Middle Ages became fantastically garbed demons. The sacred number seven was brought into relationship with other things that went by sevens, such as the liberal arts, the virtues and vices, metals, musical notes, and the ages of man. Examples can be found in the reliefs in the Campanile in Florence (after Giotto), in the Spanish Chapel in S. Maria Novella in the same city, and at the Church of the Eremitani in Padua — all of the 14th century. Giotto, whose interest in this basically non-Christian subject has attracted very little attention, also worked in the Palazzo della Ragione in Padua, the center of the study of astrology as a university subject. One of the professors there was Pietro d'Abano, who has been called "the Paduan Faust of the Middle Ages" (Warburg). Giotto painted, or had painted by his pupils, an enormous compendium of astrology, giving the signs of the zodiac with the corresponding occupations of the months, the supernatural influence of the planets on men born under them, and the Egyptian decans and paranatellons, from which the beholder could read off his fate. Unfortunately the renowned Salone in the Palazzo della Ragione, which was a place of pilgrimage to all interested in magic, was severely damaged by fire not long after its decoration; what remains, with the early-15th-century wall paintings (II, PL. 27) mentioned by Paracelsus, can hardly be regarded as a restoration or even a copy of what has been lost. It is uncertain whether this work should be regarded as a vast horoscope of the city or just a monumental primer of astrology. Perhaps the influence of the stars, because their courses in heaven are unalterable, seemed an especially suitable subject for a hall of justice.

About the same time the sister study of alchemy, which laid more stress upon active magic, was developing its own secret language of hermetic hieroglyphs. The signs were chiefly derived from Arabic prototypes and cannot certainly be traced except in the painted and, later, printed treatises. It is not established whether, as is frequently asserted, certain ecclesiastical sculptures represent not only calendrical subjects but also allusions to the magical (and therefore basically heretical) art of purification.

Christian representations of the early Middle Ages retain remarkable traces of Celtic and early Germanic paganism, which had been repressed into the subconscious. In Irish book illuminations of the 7th and 8th centuries, which are works of fine monastic art, not only the ornamentation (a labyrinthine synthesis of animal motifs, ribbons, and spirals) but also the stylized and imagelike figures of saints seem deliberately intended to arouse feelings of dread (see ANGLO-SAXON AND IRISH ART). This is also true, *mutatis mutandis* and on the crafts level, of much ornamentation of the early Middle Ages (Romanesque capitals; IV, PL. 178). The desire for magical protection survived in combination with the illustration of fables and often came from the heathen world of saga, but it was presented in a way that left open to the beholder a more ecclesiastical and Christian interpretation.

The sculptures, book illustrations, and wall paintings of the early Middle Ages often show on the part of the monastic artists and their patrons a marked preference for stories of miracles (see SAINTS). Tales of healing, exorcism, and the like, taken from the Gospels and the legends of the saints, were presumably chosen because they were especially convincing to people only superficially Christianized. Such pictures usually make the gestures of Christ, the apostles, and saints so emphatic (in blessing, exorcising, and raising the dead) that the distinction between magic and miracles or saint and magician is quite lost. In the early Gothic period this characteristic gave way to pious and mystical devotion, only to recur at the end of the Middle Ages on another level.

There were many transitional stages between the mystical attitude, which was introspective and selfless, and the magical attitude, which was driven by a secret will to power and became more strongly emphasized as the Church's rule became more lax in the 16th century, the period of the German magician Dr. Faustus (Faust). Gothic religious art showed a particular interest in the phenomenon of clairvoyance, which was barely hinted at in the ancient period, developing further the subject of the Old Testament prophets and the pagan sibyls by then adopted into Christian iconography. The best-known example is probably the figure of St. Elizabeth in Bamberg (VI, PL. 360), sometimes called the "Bamberg Sibyl," actually a representation of Elizabeth prophesying to Mary (the Visitation). Giovanni Pisano, Jacopo della Quercia, Claus Sluter, and many wood carvers of the late Gothic period were also masters of the representation of the clairvoyant state. Clairvoyant gifts, which are attributed to Wisdom in the pseudepigraphic Wisdom of Solomon, were also attributed to Prudence, one of the seven virtues. Giotto seems to have been the first to give Prudence (Padua, Scrovegni Chapel), besides the traditional serpent, the attribute of the mirror, not as a sign of self-knowledge but as as a symbol of catoptromancy (see also PL. 255).

Magic as a "Faustian" subject: a. "Romanticism" about 1500. With the general psychological shift that accompanied Humanism, the Renaissance, and the pre-Reformation, there occurred in northern Europe a phase which Wilhelm Pinder called "the romantic period in German art about 1500," but which might be more exactly described as the "Faustian-Paracelsian" period of magic in art (PLS. 254, 258). This conception corresponds to the formal characteristics of the late Gothic period noted above. In the work of Grünewald (q.v.), the younger Cranach, and the Danube school (Altdorfer, Wolf Huber) the mystical golden background was replaced by a new naturalism in the representation of earth, plants, and atmosphere, not only in accurate detail but also with a certain suggestion of animism. Even Biblical miracles and legends of the saints were transmuted into dream and fairy-tale terms, sometimes even into those of panic, demons, and the occult. Grünewald surrounded the resurrected Christ with an unearthly aura (VII, PL. 89), which is perhaps to be understood as implying Docetism; Altdorfer placed Christ's birth in a chthonic cave and made the star of the Wise Men into a cosmic phenomenon (I, PL. 61). These tendencies carry through Adam Elsheimer to Rembrandt, whose mysterious dualism of light and shade, with his clairvoyant understanding of the forgotten world of the Old Testament, suggests that perhaps he personally frequented the company of cabalistic adepts. The mannerist "Monsù Desiderio" (V, PL. 240), with his feverish theater of dreams, was a contemporary of Rembrandt.

b. The myth of the magus. One of the principal symptoms in this mysticism is the image of the philosophical magician, who represents "white magic." This archetype appears in all sorts of costumes and disguises. One of the commonest of these, and a favorite dream of the Renaissance, was that of Orpheus, with his animals enchanted by music. Many "great initiates" of early times appear, including astrologers, geomancers, and alchemists (e.g., Hermes Trismegistus by Giovanni di Stefano in the pavement of the Cathedral of Siena), sometimes in general gatherings (*turbae philosophorum*), sometimes in groups of three, and occasionally singly, as in Rembrandt's well-known etching said to represent Dr. Faustus in his study. There are also the more ambiguous representatives of paganism in late antiquity, such as Hermogenes, Apollonius of Tyana, and the really wicked figures of magic. Dosso Dossi designed at the court of Ferrara a romantic theater based entirely on the cycle of magical symbols and specialized in paintings illustrating the splendor of Circe. Simon Magus (mentioned in the Acts of the Apostles and in the New Testament Apocrypha) was represented in competition with the wonder-working apostles (Bruegel; q.v.). Hieronymus Bosch (q.v.), who was probably the most conspicuous exponent of the new trends in magic and always in the ambiguous position of being partly a critic and partly an unacknowledged member of the circle, put a rather suspect sorcerer in the background of Christ's miracle of the wine and water (*Marriage at Cana*; Rotterdam, Mus. Boymans-Van Beuningen). In his *Temptation of St. Anthony* (Lisbon, Mus. Nacional de Arte Antiga) he included among the ordeals of the saint a Black Mass, as a satanic antithesis to the miracle of transubstantiation of Church doctrine. In addition to these there are many depictions of more trivial kinds of charlatanism of all types, such as Bosch's *Conjurer* (II, PL. 319).

c. Homo divinans. The face of the diviner or clairvoyant, which in antiquity was barely indicated, became in the late Middle Ages fully developed, and the traditional mantic procedures remained of interest as late as the 16th century, when the transcendental interpretation gave way to a no less Paracelsian view of nature. Lucas Cranach (q.v.) provides an excellent example in his attractive early portrait of the Faustian Humanist Johannes Cuspinian (IV, PL. 46). Albrecht Altdorfer, in a work in the Munich Alte Pinakothek, represents the two Johns, the prophetic baptist and the apostle of the Apocalypse, surrounded by miraculously healing herbs, like two masters of natural magic with Paracelsian emblems of the old medical doctrine of signatures. The portrait art of the 15th and 16th centuries is based partly on the study of horoscopic temperaments and partly on the utility of physiognomy as a guide to the intuitive study of mankind (cf. Hans Wechtlin's illustrations to the physiognomical writings of Johannes de Indagine). Crystal gazing and divination by mirrors, as well as lecanomancy, hydromancy, and geomancy, were favorite allegories in Renaissance painting. Examples include works by Giovanni Bellini, Giorgione, and Titian [the sibylline *Vanity* (Munich, Alte Pin.); the so-called "Allegory of Alonso d'Avalos" (Louvre), with reminiscences of I Cor. 12, 13; and the *Sacred and Profane Love* (VII, PL. 382), which is more probably a richly varied version of the subject of the love oracle]. In the 17th century the *homo divinans* took a less conspicuous place. Rembrandt is once more an exception, not only because the atmosphere of dream and divination is found in the whole of his work, but especially because of the famous etching mentioned above, which was described by a contemporary collector as a "practicing alchemist." This description cannot refer to the making of gold, since there is nothing of this to be seen in the etching; it must therefore refer to Rosicrucian or cabalistic esoterism. The connection with Faust was not mentioned until the 18th century. On the other hand, alleged clairvoyants continued for a long time to be satirized. They often appeared in the work of Hieronymus Bosch and later became, with other charlatans, type figures.

d. Astrology. The above-mentioned appearance of astrological subjects in the 14th century was a mere prelude to the expansion of this magical idea during the Renaissance proper.

Of course, the personifications of the planets gradually lost their fantastic and demoniacal magic and mystery when Humanistic logic had liberated them from their half-Oriental, half-Gothic disguise and restored them to their status as classical gods. (See also ASTRONOMY AND ASTROLOGY.) Fifty years after the renovation of Giotto's completely hieroglyphic fresco in the Salone of Padua, the frescoes in the Palazzo Schifanoia at Ferrara were executed for Duke Borso d'Este; they were completed in 1470 by Cosimo Tura, Francesco del Cossa (qq.v.), and others. Here, too, the superstition of being the child of a planet is combined with the zodiacal subject of the occupations of the months, but here the paintings have no magical purpose, as at Padua, but are simply illustration, even though they display much Humanistic-Gnostic learning and make much play with mystery. In the highest register the Olympian gods appear, accompanied by their planetary emblems; their triumphal cars are surrounded by worshipers drawn from the court circle of the Duke, who is himself represented as a child of Venus. The occupations of the months (IV, PLS. 1–3, 5) are represented in the middle register and are rendered in courtly terms, as are those in Burgundian calendar paintings. In the lowest row, however, where the signs of the zodiac appear with the images of their three decans (II, PL. 25), the old-fashioned masquerade and the powers of the planets win out. Raphael shows no knowledge of fancies of this kind in the mosaics in the Chigi Chapel of S. Maria del Popolo in Rome. He simply shows the classical gods of the planets with their guardian angels in flight around the image of God the Father, realizing thereby the ancient ideal of a Christianized astrology. In Germany the same gods, with the personified virtues attributed to them, appear on the façade of the Ottheinrichsbau (1556–59) at Heidelberg; the elector Otto Heinrich himself, as builder, occupies a portrait medallion in the center and has above him as his patrons Charity and Venus, heavenly and earthly love.

Along with learned syntheses, as in Padua, Ferrara, and Rome, the theme of children of the planets, which had occasionally appeared at the end of the Middle Ages, occurred in more popular contexts. In composition the occupations of the months continued to provide the basic scheme, but the zodiacal sign in the sky is replaced by the planetary ruler in his triumphal car, and instead of the terrestrial occupations, the typical destinies and professions of persons born under the relevant planet are shown. Illustrated manuscripts of this kind, usually with explanatory verses, are to be found, for example, in the libraries of Modena, Ulm, Kassel, and Tübingen (where a weird jumble of demoniacal accompanying constellations surrounds the sign of the zodiac that is the "house" of the planet in question). A more aristocratic impression is created by the sketches of the Housebook Master, in which these destinies and activities verge on genre painting. The subject of planetary types [always adapted to the latest fashion and taste, as in woodcuts by Georg (Jorg) Pencz, etchings by Saenredam, and many others] was also popularized in broadsides with woodcuts and etchings illustrating predictions, pestilences, droughts, wars, and peasant revolts to be expected from imminent planetary conjunctions.

Monumental representations were rarer, the best example being, of course, the summarily executed ceiling paintings of Pinturicchio's school in the Borgia Apartments in the Vatican (XII, PL. 34) — a remarkable example of pagan superstition in the papal palace. In the early 17th century the carpetmakers of Flanders sometimes produced, in addition to their favorite theme of the months, carpets illustrating the planets, but then this subject disappeared completely. The influence of the planets on their children was supposed to be strongest in respect to temperament (see CHARACTERIZATION). Frequently, as in the castle at Heidelberg, the personifications of the temperaments were represented in association with the appropriate planetary gods, but the connection is noticeable even when such explicit mention is not made. Thus, in the very popular representations of Melancholy (by Dürer, Cranach, and others), the esoteric Humanists distinguished an elite of Saturnians from the common children of Saturn. Dürer's engraving *Melencolia I* (III, PL. 203) combines the attributes of both the esoteric and exoteric Saturnine influence. The allusion seems to be to the first grade of melancholic divination, as it was distinguished by Marsilio Ficino and Agrippa von Nettesheim (according to Panofsky). Presumably the artist originally intended also to illustrate allegorically the second and third stages. All three grades appear in summarized form in Giorgione's *Three Philosophers* (VI, PLS. 190, 191).

The existence of apotropaic (or horoscopic) zodiacs in Egyptian temples (Dendera) may have become known to the enthusiasts for Egyptian wisdom quite early. The constellations in the small dome above the altar in the Old Sacristy of S. Lorenzo in Florence seem to refer to the stellar configuration on some particular day; so do those of the Pazzi Chapel, though the day indicated was probably not that when the altar was dedicated but more likely that of the Ecumenical Council of Florence (1439). However, even this would be an almost blasphemous combination of Christian and astrological beliefs. Agostino Chigi commissioned Baldassare Peruzzi to paint for him in his summer palace on the Tiber (the Farnesina) a personal horoscope with well-developed astromythological motifs (XI, PL. 119). Probably also the above-mentioned Ottheinrichsbau at Heidelberg contains references to a personal ideal or idealized horoscope of the builder.

Horoscopes as genre painting are found in the work of Giorgione and his imitator Vincenzo Catena, who, perhaps having knowledge of ancient example, painted scenes of this kind in the lofty style of hermetic romanticism, though none survive except a poor copy in Dresden. Similar subjects are found on boxes made for pregnant women, on majolica cups, and in popular woodcuts.

Mythical idealized portraits of the great initiates of astrology and alchemy occur frequently among the representations of *homo magus* and *homo divinans*. The subjects of Giorgione's *Three Philosophers*, for example, are idealized types who possibly represent the three degrees of a secret society. Classic examples are Ptolemy and Zoroaster in Raphael's *School of Athens*.

Examples of portraits with astrological allusions, such as indications of the birth constellations, horoscope schemes in the sky, or even bare indications of the celestial influences, either in the landscape or in amulets worn by the person depicted, are found in the works of Lorenzo Lotto, Dosso Dossi, Giorgione, Wolf Huber (portrait of Otto Heinrich, private coll., U.S.A.), Beham, and Lucas Cranach.

e. Alchemy. Representations of hermetic lore are partly illustrative and partly symbolic (PLS. 259, 260).

(1) Alchemists at work (pictures of men at work, idealized portraits, genre pictures, and satire): As early as the 14th century Petrarch and Chaucer gave satirical descriptions of the activities of adepts, though Gower believed there was a lost truth in alchemy. Thereafter makers of gold were included among the crew of the Ship of Fools. From this use and by way of the woodcut illustrations to Petrarch's *De remediis utriusque fortunae*, the subject of the alchemist soon found its way into drawing and painting. The maniacally obsessed toiler, with his weird concoctions and equipment, surrounded by huge books, his despairing wife, and his pseudolearned adviser, who leaves it to others to dirty their hands at the furnace, is vividly illustrated in a drawing attributed to the elder Bruegel (Berlin, Staat. Mus.). The subject survived for its picturesque value in genre paintings by Jan Steen, Teniers, Ostade, and others. It is also found in the *studiolo* of Francesco I de' Medici in the Palazzo Vecchio at Florence, where the Grand Duke is represented by the Flemish painter Stradanus (Jan van der Straet) as engaged in secret alchemical work; this, of course, has no satirical overtones. In the 17th century Thomas Wyck (Wijck) counteracted the more satirical pictures of his painter colleagues with a more romantic style of Faust representation in duodecimo format.

(2) Symbolism: From the first the adepts concealed the secret of the philosophers' stone behind a variety of metaphors which, in the later Middle Ages, were at first verbal (presumably taken from treatises in Arabic) but later were made visual. Manuscripts and printed treatises on the "royal art" gave secret instructions for hermetic practices and were illustrated

with dream allegories, symbolic figures, and emblems taken from nature, the amorous life, and pagan mythology, as well as occasional Christian subjects. The purification of the *materia prima* was actually compared to the Passion of Christ and His sacrifice (Lapis = Christus). Not many manuscripts have survived from the early period (14th–early 16th cent.): there are a few codices in Florence, the *Aurora consurgens* (Cod. Rhenoviensis, Zurich, Zentralbib.), the *Opera chemica* of Pseudo-Lully (Florence, Bib. Naz.) with illuminations by Girolamo da Cremona, and the *Book of the Holy Trinity* and *Splendor solis* (Berlin, Kupferstichkabinett, and Nürnberg, Germanisches Nat. Mus.). Many survive only in modern imitations, either in the current style of copper engravings or drawn and painted.

(3) Hermetic romanticism: Alchemy stimulated the poetic inspiration of certain painters. In the puzzle-pictures of Hieronymus Bosch, which are the principal evidence for the new encounter between magic and art at the end of the Middle Ages, there are many reminders of the work of the adepts who hoped to hasten the task of nature in their glass retorts. In Venice, too, that semi-Oriental city of mosaicists and glassblowers, painters showed the deepest interest in the mysteries of making gold according to the "royal art." Certain subjects in works by Giorgione and Giulio Campagnola, who was a friend of Giovanni Aurelio Augurello, a writer of alchemical poetry and member of the Florentine Academy, can be explained only in terms of the hermetic feeling for nature combined with a delight in pastoral scenes.

f. The mysteries of hieroglyphics. Dürer provided a set of illustrations for the text of Horapollon, which had been rediscovered as early as the 15th century; the woodcuts illustrating the great novel of initiation which is known as the *Hypnerotomachia Poliphili* (I, PL. 308) originated in the circle of Bellini. The whole study of enigmas, rebuses, and emblems, from the Renaissance on, had its origin in the study of these Egyptian hermetic symbols.

g. Demons. A great deal of folkloristic animism was included in the magical representation of the world, including the belief in benevolent nature spirits and the possibility of dealing with them (as with Ariel in *The Tempest*, and in Goethe's *Faust*). Evil demons, devils, and ghosts, however, were more frequent; the original apotropaic intent of such representations eventually gave way to pure illustration. In Christian sculpture the devil's face, or mask, is the polar opposite to the angelic realm of light. The physiognomy of demons, so amply represented in ancient Etruscan art and in India and the Far East, was most highly developed in Christian art in scenes of the Last Judgment and the Temptation of St. Anthony. In the late Middle Ages there was a whole range of expression which exceeded the normal bounds of fantasy. Bosch owed his reputation as a "faiseur de diables" to his representations of hell, which frequently diverged from the traditional ones; but this subject did not exhaust his invention, since he was at home with all types of esoteric and exoteric magic. This does not imply that he was identified with any obscure sect or took orders from any secret group. His paintings should rather be interpreted as a conscious exposure or as a lampoon of this repressed sphere, even if the artist felt a subconscious "hate-love" or attraction toward it. It is quite likely that Grünewald — whose Isenheim altarpiece depicts the Temptation of St. Anthony (IV, PL. 180) and the Resurrection (VII, PL. 89) mentioned above — had seen pictures by Bosch and just as likely that Giorgione, whose pastoral idylls also had a demonic nocturnal quality, knew Bosch's work.

h. Witches. Representations of women who believe themselves to be possessed by the devil, and hence endowed with magical faculties, must be distinguished from those of enchantresses of a higher type. Witches were depicted as early as Bosch, and the elder Bruegel, in his period, enriched the subject with horrifying references to it, particularly in his etchings. It is hard to understand how such a dangerous subject could become the theme of works of art at the very time when witches were being persecuted. Nevertheless, Dürer's very clever pupil Hans Baldung-Grien made a specialty of depicting witch congresses and Walpurgis Night gatherings, representing his witches as fleshly bacchantes of heathenish abandon (PLS. 255, 257). The subject of witches lasted far beyond Baldung-Grien and Bruegel. In the 17th century Teniers and Salvator Rosa (PL. 256) treated it in a more matter-of-fact manner, and Goya, though intellectually a child of the Enlightenment, as an artist showed a perverse passion for scenes illustrating the witch mania that took so long to die out in his Spanish homeland (IV, PL. 181; XII, PL. 315).

i. Romantic occultism and surrealism. The occult undercurrents that flourished during the century of the Enlightenment (secret societies, Egyptomania, Cagliostro-like frauds, Rosicrucians, Illuminati, and Freemasons) seem to have made an impression on art only in sporadic cases, in contrast with their influence on the novel, the theater, and opera. Tiepolo, in his series of etchings called *Scherzi di fantasia*, found a light and playful subject in the magical practices of Venice; Goya, in his *Disparates*, extended his imagination to the darkest and most gruesome aspects of black magic.

In England at the beginning of the 19th century, the Swiss Fuseli (Johann Heinrich Füssli; q.v.) excelled in ghostly dream scenes of exaggerated pathos. Fuseli's friend William Blake returned again and again to eidetic visionary subjects and magical allusions (X, PL. 252). His Biblical motifs are derived from a peculiar esoteric and theosophical tradition that was often ecclesiastically unorthodox.

In the 19th century, while historical idealism was giving way to a more realistic and impressionistic way of looking at things, the magical undercurrent did not entirely disappear. On the whole the romantic artists, unlike the poets and thinkers, avoided it. Not till the turn of the century did the neoromantic movement begin to employ symbolism and elements drawn from the field of magic, and even then, for the most part, only as esthetic stimulation.

Joseph Péladan and his Rosicrucian revival drew inspiration, though again chiefly esthetic, from the allegorical inventions of Ferdinand Hodler. The inner relationship to magic was more profound in Odilon Redon. A personal friend of the Parisian impressionists, he based his art on dreams and visions (XI, PL. 371), which he nourished with spiritualistic esoterism, especially inclining toward the neo-Buddhist thought of Theosophy. Later his fantasies inspired Alfred Kubin, who tried to appease his neurasthenic anxiety about fate, first with gruesome surrealist allegories, and then later, more successfully, by plunging into traditional German pantheism. The true surrealists, such as Max Ernst (q.v.), turned with interest to Gnostic philosophemes, and show a kinship with the mannerists of the 1600s and their quasi-magical estheticism; with this they mix skepticism, a desperate irony, and agnosticism. The old, traditional subjects, with their demons and other weird ingredients, were thrust aside to make way for a new kind of acausal alienation in which the world of appearances is entirely disintegrated.

Gustav F. Hartlaub

ASPECTS OF MAGIC IN ASIA. In the Asiatic world the division between magic and religion is tenuous; psychological attitudes peculiar to the *homo magus* of the West are essential for the Asian priest, and the gods themselves assume values that are in many respects traceable — sometimes even avowedly so — to magic. What with the techniques of meditation and ecstasy (such as yoga), paranormal experiences, and other less easily definable phenomena, many concepts that form an essential part of Western magical tradition belong to religious tradition in Asia, sometimes with a complete parallelism of techniques, as in the case of the magic formulas (mantra and dharani) adopted by later Buddhism, Saivism, and generally by all the Tantric cults. Thus certain legendary motifs, which in the West never altogether belong to the religious tradition and are closely bound to the tradition of magic, are absorbed in the religious thought of Asia (for example, the characteristic motif of lost objects that must be recovered and kept safe). The Western tradition of the Holy Grail and the Iranian tradition of the *xvarnah* constitute a case in point. With reference to the gods, all the way from Enki of Eridu (magician-god par excellence) to the Vedic Varuṇa (typical dread sovereign of Indo-European mythologies), and to the meaning attributed from the most ancient Indian tradition to sacrifice (which can sway the will of the gods, thereby placing the priest at the summit of universal power), a whole scale of nuances diminishes the difference between magic and religion in Asia. Moreover, the so-called "folk" survivals, reflecting beliefs that coexist within a single society at different social levels, assume in Asia different characteristics from those of the West (see FOLK ART). For this reason, also, the divergence between magic and religion in the Western point of view is considerably attenuated and often disappears completely in the East. Thus the theory of Arnold van Gennep (*Les rites de passage*, Paris, 1909), which regards the magical and the religious as an indivisible unity, distinguishing solely between theoretical (religious) and practical (magical) activities, would seem in its general lines to be valid for the Asiatic world.

In any event, the selection of artistic material pertaining to magic in Oriental cultures depends on the definition of the term "magic." This initial choice of standpoint — however difficult it is made by the variety and persuasiveness of the different theories — must be modified by taking into account the different views held by other civilizations and cultures of what is considered magic, for example, the semantic value of the various words indicating "magic" in the diverse languages.

Broadly speaking, magic may be defined as the use and mastery of those mysterious forces which act by hidden and apparently irrational means. Such forces, often expressing the will of either gods or demons, may be discerned and put to use even by man. Very often the magical element is distinguished from the religious in that the former represents a "wicked" and terrible means of dealing with these hidden forces. An Asian example confirming this interpretation may be found in the *Sakkasaṃyutta*, part of the *Saṃyuttanikāya* (I, 216-40), a well-known Buddhist text in the Pali scriptures, in which Sakka (Skr., Śakra, or Indra) begs Vepacitti, king of the asuras (demons or titans), to instruct him in the magical art, offering to heal him in exchange. Vepacitti, after taking counsel, refuses on the grounds that this art leads those who practice it to the infernal abyss. The episode demonstrates that Buddhist thought long retained Vedic traditions, such as this, for example: that magic was an art belonging to the asuras, opponents of the devas (gods). The refusal of Vepacitti would seem strange, except that the apparent solicitude on the part of the asura king for the salvation of the deva king actually indicates nothing but his determination to keep Sakka out of his personal domain by every means.

Magical objects, in the East as well as in the West, are often at a relatively low level of artistic value. Amulets and talismans, more or less complex geometric figures drawn in ink or by other means, are usually important only for the accuracy of their execution or for the exact inscription of formulas and names. In these, the esthetic interest is secondary, and the workmanship may be hasty and rough, as is the case of the well-known amulets of the Islamic world. The artistic interest of drawn and written talismans lies in the calligraphy applied to magic formulas; here and there, as in the Buddhism of central Asia and northwestern India, magic alphabets were created expressly for composing formulas of evocation. Introduced into China with the expansion of Buddhism, such formulas, especially when they were written in alphabets currently used in India and central Asia, may — by the contrast between the foreign and the Chinese characters — have been impressive to the beholder, but such impressiveness is not truly an esthetic effect; the pleasure derived is rather that of complacency in an occult knowledge reserved to a select few, or the intimation of a supernatural power at the disposal of initiates.

Similarly, the products of the shamans and sorcerers of northern Asia are not intended to have esthetic interest. It is problematical whether the shaman, with his ecstatic techniques and his particular ability to travel in the heavens, in the lower depths, and on the bottom of the sea, should be considered as working solely on the magical level or also on that of religion (see SHAMANISM). The forces sustaining him and which he dominates incline many scholars to prefer the magical view, but it should not be overlooked that the shaman is acting first and foremost on behalf of society. In any case, the shamans' costumes (XIII, PL. 2), which imitate with great imagination the shape of a bird or its skeleton (the Yakut shaman), or have elements derived from birds (the Mongol shaman's wings; the Tungus shaman's boots with claws attached), together with the various ritual objects, all have a magical function, just as do the headdresses and aprons used in certain Tantric rites. The rattle is rarely of artistic workmanship, but the drums bear stylized depictions and ornamental bands (IV, PL. 262), and the magic bells display elements of artistic merit in execution. Chinese and Indonesian bronze drums derived from the shamanic drums and used (in rainmaking) in a function midway between magic and religion are frequently of high esthetic value. Incidentally, the symbols of the world of the dead painted on the magic drums of Lapland (IV, PL. 262) may be derived from the viking iconography of the same world, as seen on certain sculptured stones. The portrayal of shamanistic rites on hide or on birch bark, as well as on imported metalwork (the Sarmatian cup with sgraffitti; Leningrad, The Hermitage), has frequently an ingenuous but not inconsiderable value in its composition. It is not impossible that the Siberian shamanistic practice of attaching metal ornaments, plates, bells, and chains to their vestments may have given rise to armored breastplates and coats of mail, thus influencing the art of arms and armor (q.v.). Certainly, mail vestments and round armor plates remained in use among them until very recent times.

Related to the metal ornaments of the shamans and to their rites of sympathetic magic (linked to hunting and to the animal shapes assumed by the spirits on which shamanistic activities were based) are works of very great esthetic significance, such as those in the animal style, which spread throughout Europe (see ASIATIC PROTOHISTORY). The animal image may have, in certain cases, a perfectly clear symbolic and religious import, as conveyed by the ram in Persia and the bull in prehistoric India (see CERAMICS; INDUS VALLEY ART). In other cases the animal image is related to hunting magic, as in the bronze plaques of Ordos (q.v.; X, PL. 399), in those of Siberia, and in those of the Sarmatian era, which at times display genuine representations of complex hunting scenes.

Part of the metallurgic production of Eurasia has magical significance not only in the figural content but also in the magical function attributed to the artist in the various civilizations and cultures. Metallurgic technique, domain of the few, is by its ritual character often considered close to magic; in China, for example, the smith infuses a soul (that is, a life of its own) into the sword he is shaping. Somewhat similar to this is the Western medieval usage of giving a hero's sword a special name. However, the interpretation of the position of smiths and founders — although they were certainly initiates — is not entirely clear; recent theories tend to regard them as culture heroes, or participants in the process of creation, extraneous to the constituted order of the universe, and, in a certain sense, linked with the primordial chaos. Be that as it may, smiths and their works have a significance that can be defined as magical and derives in part from the magic power attributed to the metals they used. In addition, certain symbolic elements used on the objects (a certain type of Iranian ax, for example, has eyes) must have magical (or religious?) values.

Connected in origin with shamanism is the Tibetan Bon religion, in which magical and necromantic elements seem to prevail. The iconography and symbolism indubitably come from the reorganization undergone by the Bon religion through its contact with Buddhism and pertain, therefore, more to the religious than to the magical aspect. When Tibet, between 763 and 787, was converted to Buddhism (following the edict of K'ri sroṅ lde btsan, who proclaimed it the state religion), the exorcisms of Padmasaṃbhava culminated in the founding of the temple of bSam yas, in sign of his victories over all the deities of mountain and valleys, who form "a sort of sacred geography of Tibet superimposed upon its physical geography and establish the most intimate connection between the land, the clan inhabiting it, and the ancestor from which the clan derives" (Giuseppe Tucci). The temple, reflection and synthesis of the universe, is a symbolic expression of the crushing victory of Buddhism over local religious elements, and therefore one cosmic order over another, which the Buddhists considered to be chaotic and somehow implicated in magic. Naturally, the temple itself displays the symbolism adopted from Buddhism, and thus only the erection of the temple can be considered a reflection of a duel between the "magic" world of Bonism and the religious one of the new faith.

The cult of the god Zhuni, the mysterious deity venerated at Zabul near Ghazni and elsewhere, was regarded by other religions as magical and demoniac in character. Both the Greek tradition of Theodorus Anagnostes, as summarized by Nicephorus Callistus (PG, LXXXVI, p. 202) and by Theophanes (Chronographia, ed. De Boor, Leipzig, 1883–85, pp. 163–79), and the Latin tradition of Victor Tonnennensis (Chronica, Chronicorum minorum, II, p. 194, no. 508, in MGH, Autorum Antiquissimorum, XI) speak of exorcisms accomplished by a Christian priest to assist in the conquest of a temple and its wealth by Kavādh I, a Sassanian ruler. Islamic tradition, too, in recording the conquest of Zabul by 'Abd-al-Raḥmān ibn-Samura, governor of Seistan, mentions the magic power of the castle and temple, although the victory is assigned solely to the Moslem leader's sword.

Within the definition of magic proposed above, it is possible to consider also works which are apparently religious in meaning, but which reflect conceptions that are somewhat at variance with the purely religious vision. For example, the iconography of the halolike xvarnah became, for the Iranians and the peoples under Iranian influence, the expression of royal power, but it may also be seen as an attribute of gods and demons. Another example is the symbolism of flames rising from the shoulders in the iconography of Kushan and other rulers, an element that seems more magical than religious in significance, even though the god of fire is an integral part of the Kushan pantheon. In the Avesta the xvarnah appears either as a personified god or, more often, as a luminous element of power desired and sought after as much by demons as by gods. The ambiguity of magic and religion is, here as in other cases in the Iranian world, not unlike the ambiguity that is at the basis of the word "magic": both the Greek μαγεία and the Latin magia derive from the Persian magavan, which originally stood for the doctrine and science of the Magi (a tribe inhabiting Media, according to Herodotus), well-known in antiquity for their knowledge as well as for their occult practices. Their exact identity has been much discussed by various scholars. According to Alessandro Bausani, the Iranian priests of Parthian and Sassanian times lost their former name of Atharvan (by which they were known in the Avesta) and took on that of mogh, or magus. Thus the magical element seems to merge completely with the religious, since the Magi, whoever they were, present the dichotomy of a highly elevated science and philosophy together with necromantic and peculiarly occult branches of knowledge. In India the symbol of the noose found in images of Kālī and Śiva passed into the iconography of Tantric Buddhism and is linked to the occult power of various deities, becoming the attribute of the "god who binds" and embodying magical power on the divine plane. The above-mentioned passage from the Saṃyuttanikāya shows that the Buddhist world (and previously the Vedic world) took a negative view of magic, relating it to the asuras. In theory, magic is proscribed by Buddhism, but only in so far as it is allied with forces and ideas that Buddhism itself tries to combat. The result is the irrevocable condemnation of all forms of magic related to everyday life and to ordinary wish fulfillment (love philters, magical means of harming others or protecting oneself from them, etc.). Nevertheless, a large number of practices that to Western eyes would seem magical are not only permitted but expounded by the very gods, by the chakravartins (universal rulers), and by kings; such practices come under the heading of ṛddhi, a term which Rhys Davids translated as "mystic wonder" and "magic power." In Buddhism, therefore, the distinction between magic and religion is expressible only in terms of the intent, orthodox or otherwise, that motivates specific acts, and the difference between the yogi and the fakir is only a difference of intent. The yogi is dedicated to attainment of spiritual liberation, while the fakir uses his powers for practical ends. It follows that all rituals concerning optative situations (kāmya), that is, such as are inspired by desires, can be considered magic, including prayers offered up to obtain favors.

In the Chinese world magic assumes a remarkable importance. The concept of magic remained for a very long time one of the essential elements of Chinese thought, and chi and wu (magicians and witches) had a definite place in ancient Chinese society. The denomination chi does not appear outside the oldest texts, but is replaced by that of wu and wu p'o ("sorcerers" and "sorcerers' wives"). The chi and wu most certainly had many points of contact with the shamans of northern Asia. From the art-historical point of view the ideogram t'ao-t'ieh (see ASIATIC PROTOHISTORY; CHINESE ART) may be understood as a depiction (in the shape of a monstrous and imaginary animal; II, PL. 10) of the primordial chaos from which was born the present order of the universe. In this there may be a reelaboration of a shamanic element and hence, as Carl Hentze believes (Zalmoxis, I, 1938, pp. 50–68), a magical significance. The use of jade for amulets is linked partly with qualities attributed to the material itself and partly with magical traditions from the regions where jade was originally procured. Shoulder bones of animals and tortoise shells used for divination, with the magical idea that the future, being revealed, can be corrected by human will, are of artistic interest only as regards the calligraphy of inscriptions. On the other hand, the trigrams and hexagrams mentioned in I-ching ("Book of Changes") could be used as ornamental motifs even in the decoration of architectural structures (for example, the so-called "sūtra pillars" from Turfan, formerly in Berlin, Mus. für Völkerkunde). The trigrams and hexagrams, derived from the cracks in animal shoulder bones and tortoise shells exposed to fire, were also used magically, because their interpretation made it possible to foresee adversities or propitious moments and to avoid the former and exploit the latter. Taoism (q.v.) has accumulated and preserved a remarkable heritage of magical concepts stemming from the communities of sorcerers, conjurers, oracles, and rainmakers which existed even in China's distant past.

The human body and anthropomorphic images may often have magical properties, though they too are difficult to distinguish from religious values. Rather magical than religious are those figures of deities that are considered to be endowed with life by the insertion in their hollow insides of various objects, such as mantras written on slips of writing material and passages from the holy texts. In some instances the wish to "animate" the image goes to extraordinary lengths, for example, in the celebrated Śākyamuni of the Seiryōji (commonly known as the Shakadō) in Kyoto, Japan. A hollow in the back of this figure contained money, other offerings, inscriptions and texts, as well as simulation of the Buddha's own entrails (in silk, with Chinese inscriptions and Sanskrit lettering) filled with various materials (incense, crystals, etc.). Here the effort to confer autonomous life on the statue is altogether clear, but the craftsmanship is of a high order, as for a religious work.

It remains clear that, because of the frequent lack of distinction between magic and religion, the magical purpose of a work influences its style only in certain examples such as the animalistic art of Eurasia and perhaps the composition of the Chinese t'ao-t'ieh. Furthermore the magician operates directly, without intermediaries, or uses the works of others and confers on them his own special powers, in which case there is no relation between style and the magical properties of the work itself; the two aspects are separate or linked in such a way that the esthetic aspect has less importance.

Only in Chinese and in Islamic art is it possible to find portrayals of conjurers at work, for example, the painting of Kuo Hsü, executed about A.D. 1500, which represents Han

Yü watching his nephew perform the peony trick (a variant of the Indian mango trick), and the 18th-century Persian miniature (Seattle, Art Mus.) in which the magician's costume is noticeably Westernized.

Islamic magic in general, called *siḥr* (a term apparently connected with the meaning of hallucination, confused vision, and fright), presents greater similarities to the magic of the West. It is based on the existence of the jinn and is a science revealed (Koran, II, 96) to the Babylonians by two angels who did not stop to think what a temptation this would be for mankind. There arose thereby a very complex theological question: whether and in what cases magic must be proscribed. It is of interest that the Solomon of the Koran tradition employs magical forces at will, and the magician in the *Arabian Nights* is most often a Moor. While magical articles from Islam (amulets, talismans, etc.) are of little esthetic interest, Arabic texts give the most accurate descriptions of magical techniques in use among the various peoples. Ḥajjī Khalīfa summed up the magic methods as follows: "The Indian consists in purification of the soul; the Nabataean in the employment of spells at suitable times; the Greek in compelling the service of the spirits of the spheres and the stars; that of the Hebrews, Copts, and Arabs in mentioning names of unknown meaning — this method being a variety of that by incantation, those who employ it professing thereby to press into their service the angels who have power over the jinn" (Khasf aẕ-Ẕunūn, ed. G. Flügel, London, Leipzig, 1835-58, III, p. 584).

Mario Bussagli

BIBLIOG. The following list is limited to works which directly examine the relationship between magic and the visual arts or which provide indispensable bases for such an examination.

General: J. von Görres, Die christliche Mystik, 4 vols., Regensburg, 1836-42 (new ed. by J. Bernhart, Mystik, Magie und Dämonie, Munich, Berlin, 1927); Hastings' E. of Religions and Ethics, s.v. Magic, VIII, New York, Edinburgh, 1921, pp. 245-321; W. Gundel, Sterne und Sternbilder im Glauben des Altertums und der Neuzeit, Bonn, 1922; L. Thorndike, A History of Magic and Experimental Science, 8 vols., London, 1923-58; J. H. F. Kohlbrugge, Tier- und Menschenantlitz als Abwehrzauber, Bonn, 1926; H. Bächtold-Stäubli, ed., Handwörterbuch des deutschen Aberglaubens, s.vv. Amulett, Horoskopie, Kalender, Maske, Planeten, Sterndeutung, Tierkreis, Berlin, Leipzig, 1927 ff.; E. A. Grillot de Givry, Le musée des sorciers, mages et alchimistes, Paris, 1929; F. Boll and C. Bezold, Sternglaube und Sterndeutung: Die Geschichte und das Wesen der Astrologie, 4th ed., Leipzig, 1931; S. Behn, Schönheit und Magie, Munich, 1932; G. Widengren, Evolutionism and the Problem of the Origin of Religion, Ethnos, X, 1945, pp. 57-96; R. Eisler, The Royal Art of Astrology, London, 1946; K. Seligmann, The History of Magic, New York, 1948; G. F. Hartlaub, Fragen an die Kunst: Studien zu Grenzproblemen, Stuttgart, 1951; G. F. Hartlaub, Das Unerklärliche: Studien zum magischen Weltbild, Stuttgart, 1951; G. F. Hartlaub, Zauber des Spiegels: Geschichte und Bedeutung des Spiegels in der Kunst, Munich, 1951; M. Eliade, Images et symboles: Essais sur le symbolisme magico-religieux, Paris, 1952 (Eng. trans., P. Mairet, New York, 1961); H. Thurston, The Physical Phenomena of Mysticism, London, 1952; M. Eliade, Traité d'histoire des religions, 2d ed., Paris, 1953; L. Hautecœur, Mystique et architecture, Paris, 1954; Rl. für Antike und Christentum, s.v. Bild, II, Stuttgart, 1954, cols. 287-341; W. R. Lethaby, Architecture, Nature and Magic, London, 1956; W. Worringer, Abstraktion und Einfühlung, new ed., Munich, 1959 (Eng. trans., M. Bullock, Abstraction and Empathy, New York, 1953); H. Fischer, Heilgebärden, Antaios, II, 1960-61, pp. 318-47; W. E. Peuckert, Astrologie (Geschichte der Geheimwissenschaften, I), Stuttgart, 1960; Die Religion in Geschichte und Gegenwart, 3d ed., IV, Tübingen, 1960, s.v. Kultus, religionsgeschichtlich, cols. 120-26, s.v. Kunst, cols. 126-61.

Prehistory and primitive peoples: J. G. Frazer, The Golden Bough, 3d ed., 12 vols., London, 1907-15; T. Mainage, Les religions de la préhistoire: L'âge paléolithique, Paris, 1921; H. Bégouen, La magie aux temps préhistoriques, Mém. Acad. des sc., inscriptions et belles lettres de Toulouse, 12th ser., II, 1924, pp. 417-32; T. W. Danzel, Der magische Mensch (homo divinans), Potsdam, 1928; H. Bégouen, The Magic Origin of Prehistoric Art, Antiquity, III, 1929, pp. 5-19; L. Capitan, La préhistoire: La magie quaternaire, Paris, 1931, pp. 123ff.; H. Bégouen, À propos de Vénus paléolithiques, J. de psychologie, XXXI, 1934, pp. 792-97; L. Franz, Religion und Kunst der Vorzeit: Vom vorgeschichtlichen Zauberglauben, Totenkult und Kunstschaffen, Prague, Leipzig, 1937; G. Schwantes, Das magische Ornament in der germanischen Bronzezeit, Forsch. und Fortschritte, XIV, 1938, pp. 85-87; H. Weigert, Die Bedeutung des germanischen Ornaments, Festschrift für W. Pinder, Leipzig, 1938, pp. 81-116; H. Bégouen, Les bases magiques de l'art préhistorique, Scientia, LXV, 1939, pp. 202-16; R. Nougier, Art et magie, Pallas, I, 1953, pp. 223-39; H. Kühn, Das Erwachen der Menschheit: Religion und Denken des Menschen der Eiszeit, Frankfurt am Main, 1954, pp. 149-68; H. Findeisen, Schamanentum, dargestellt am Beispiel der Besessenheitspriester nordeurasiatischer Völker, Stuttgart, 1957; R. Furon, Manuel de préhistoire générale, 4th ed., Paris, 1958, pp. 195-217; E. Holm, Felskunst im südlichen Afrika (Kunst der Welt: Die Steinzeit, vierzigtausend Jahre Felsbilder), Baden-Baden, 1960; K. J. Narr, Weibliche Symbolplastik der älteren Steinzeit, Antaios, II, 1960-61, pp. 132-57.

Egypt and the Near East: A. Wiedemann, Magie und Zauberei im alten Aegypten, Leipzig, 1905; G. Maspero, Les statues parlantes de l'Egypte antique, in Causeries d'Egypte, Paris, 1907, pp. 167-73; A. Moret, Les statues d'Egypte, "images vivantes," Ann. du Mus. Guimet (Bib. de vulgarisation), XLI, 1916, pp. 49-87; P. Lacau, Les statues guérisseuses dans l'ancienne Egypte, MPiot, XXV, 1921-22, pp. 189-209; F. Lexa, La magie dans l'Egypte antique de l'ancien empire jusqu'à l'époque copte, 2 vols., Paris, 1925; M. Weynants-Ronday, Les statues vivantes: Les images animées, Brussels, 1926; J. Vandier, La religion égyptienne, Paris, 1944; E. Dhorme, Les religions de Babylonie et d'Assyrie, Paris, 1945; G. Contenau, La magie chez les Assyriens et les Babyloniens, Paris, 1947; G. Contenau, Manuel d'archéologie orientale, IV, Paris, 1947; G. Roeder, Volksglaube im Pharaonenreich, Stuttgart, 1952; H. Kees, Totenglauben und Jenseitsvorstellungen der alten Ägypter, 2d ed., Berlin, 1956.

Greece and Rome: A. Maury, La magie et l'astrologie dans l'antiquité et au moyen âge, 4th ed., Paris, 1877; A. Bouché-Leclercq, L'astrologie grecque, Paris, 1899; F. Boll, Sphaera, Leipzig, 1903; DA, s.v. Magia, III, 1904, pp. 1494-1521; L. R. Farnell, Magic and Religion in Early Greek Society, Arch. für Religionswissenschaft, 1914, pp. 17-34; C. Clerc, Les théories relatives au culte des images chez les auteurs grecs du II siècle après J.C., Paris, 1915, pp. 63-85; E. Rohde, Psyche: Seelenkult und Unsterblichkeitsglaube der Griechen, 10th ed., Tübingen, 1925 (Eng. trans., W. B. Hillis, Psyche: The Cult of Souls and Belief in Immortality among the Greeks, London, 1950); J. Maurice, La terreur de la magie au IV siècle, CRAI, 1926, pp. 182-88; K. Reinhardt, Kosmos und Sympathie, Munich, 1926; F. Cumont, Les religions orientales dans le paganisme romain, 3d ed., Paris, 1929, pp. 253-304; J. E. Lowe, Magic in Greek and Latin Literature, Oxford, 1929; E. Löwy, Ursprünge der bildenden Kunst, Alm. der Wien. Ak. der Wissenschaften, LXXX, 1930, pp. 275-95; R. Allier, Magie et religion dans la Grèce antique, Rev. de théologie et de philosophie, N.S. XX, 1932, pp. 285-93; A. Delatte, La catoptromancie grecque et ses dérivés, Liège, Paris, 1932; E. Massonneau, La magie dans l'antiquité romaine, Paris, 1934; O. Brendel, Symbolik der Kugel: Astrologischer Beitrag zur Geschichte der älteren griechischen Kunst, RM, LI, 1936, pp. 1-95; M. P. Nilsson, Greek Popular Religion, New York, 1940; S. Eitrem, La magie comme motif littéraire chez les Grecs et les Romains, SymbOsl, XXI, 1941, pp. 39-83; R. Herbig, Θεὰ Εἴβυλλα, JdI, LIX-LX, 1944-45, pp. 141-47; M. P. Nilsson, Geschichte der griechischen Religion, 2d ed., I, Munich, 1955 (Eng. trans., F. J. Fielden, History of Greek Religion, 2d ed., Oxford, 1952); K. Schefold, Griechische Kunst als religiöses Phänomen, Hamburg, 1959.

Middle Ages: F. Saxl, Verzeichnis astrologischer und mythologischer illustrierter Handschriften des lateinischen Mittelalters, 3 vols., Heidelberg London, 1915-53; F. Saxl, Frühes Christentum und spätes Heidentum in ihren künstlerischen Ausdrucksformen, Wien. Jhb. für Kg., II, 1923, pp. 63-121; R. Bernheimer, Romanische Tierplastik und die Ursprünge ihrer Motive, Munich, 1931; J. K. Huysmans, La cathédrale (Oeuvres complètes, XIV), 2d ed., Paris, 1931; W. Überwasser, Von Maass und Macht der alten Kunst, Strasbourg, 1933; K. Prümm, Der christliche Glaube und die altheidnische Welt, 2 vols., Cologne, 1935; W. von Blankenburg, Heilige und dämonische Tiere, Leipzig, 1943; E. Hempel, RlDKg, s.v. Bauhütten, II, 1948, cols. 23-33; Fulcanelli, Le mystère des Cathédrales (preface by E. Canseliet), 2d ed., Paris, 1957; A. A. Barb, The Survival of Magic Arts, in A. Momigliano, ed., The Conflict between Paganism and Christianity in the 4th Century, Oxford, 1963, pp. 100-25.

Late Middle Ages, Renaissance, and modern times: J. Friedrich, Astrologie und Reformation: Die Astrologen als Prediger der Reformation und Urheber des Bauernkrieges, Munich, 1864; E. Schmidt, Faust und das 16. Jahrhundert, Goethe Jhb., III, 1882, pp. 77-131; K. Giehlow, Die Hieroglyphenkunde des Humanismus in der Allegorie der Renaissance, JhbKhSamml-Wien, XXXII, 1915, app. III, pp. 170-224; A. Hauber, Planetenkinderbilder und Sternbilder zur Geschichte des menschlichen Glaubens und Irrens, Strasbourg, 1916; W. Dilthey, Weltanschauung und Analyse des Menschen seit Renaissance und Reformation (Gesammelte Schriften, II), Leipzig, Berlin, 1921, pp. 145-61; F. Saxl and E. Panofsky, Dürers "Melencolia I," Leipzig, Berlin, 1923; L. Volkmann, Bilderschriften der Renaissance, Leipzig, 1923; A. Barzon, I cieli e la loro influenza negli affreschi del Salone in Padova, Padua, 1924; C. Neumann, Rembrandt, 4th ed., Munich, 1924; G. Carbonelli, Sulle fonti storiche della chimica e dell'alchimia in Italia, Rome, 1925; G. F. Hartlaub, Giorgones Geheimnis: Ein kunstgeschichtlicher Beitrag zur Mystik der Renaissance, Munich, 1925; C. de Tolnay, Die Zeichnungen Pieter Breughels, Munich, 1925 (2d ed., Zürich, New York, 1952); H. A. Strauss, Der astrologische Gedanke in der deutschen Vergangenheit, Munich, Berlin, 1926; E. Cassirer, Individuum und Kosmos in der Philosophie der Renaissance (S. Bib. Warburg, X), Berlin, Leipzig, 1927; G. F. Hartlaub, Giorgione und der Mythos der Akademien, RepfKw, XLVIII, 1927, pp. 233-57; H. Schrade, Über Symbol und Realismus in der Spätgotik, D. Vierteljahrschrift für Litteraturwissenschaft und Geistesgeschichte, V, 1927, pp. 78-105; B. Groethuysen, Die kosmische Anthropologie des Bovillus, Arch. für Geschichte der Philosophie, XL, 1931, pp. 66-89; A. Warburg, Bildniskunst und Florentiner Bürgertum, Gesammelte Schriften, I, Leipzig, Berlin, 1932, pp. 89-126, 340-52; A. Warburg, Heidnisch-antike Wahrsagung in Wort und Bild zu Luthers Schriften, Gesammelte Schriften, II, Leipzig, Berlin, 1932, pp. 487-558; A. Warburg, Italienische Kunst und internationale Astrologie im Palazzo Schifanoja zu Ferrara, Gesammelte Schriften, II, Leipzig, Berlin, 1932, pp. 459-81; L. von Renthe-Fink, Magisches und naturwissenschaftliches Denken in der

Renaissance, Darmstadt, 1933; F. Saxl, La fede astrologia di Agostino Chigi, Rome, 1934; A. Greifenhagen, Zum Saturnglauben der Renaissance, Die Antike, XI, 1935, pp. 67–84; H. Priebsch-Closs, Magie und Naturgefühl in der Malerei von Grünewald, Baldung-Grien, Lukas Cranach und Altdorfer, Bonn, 1936; J. Read, Prelude to Chemistry, London, New York, 1936; G. F. Hartlaub, Signa Hermetis: Zwei alchemistische Bilderhandschriften, Z. des d. Vereins für Kw., IV, 1937, pp. 93–112, 144–62; O. Benesch, Der Maler Albrecht Altdorfer, Vienna, 1939; W. Ganzenmüller, Das Buch von der Heiligen Dreifaltigkeit: Eine deutsche Alchemie aus dem Anfang des 15. Jahrhunderts, Arch. für Kulturgeschichte, XXIX, 1939, pp. 167–96; W. Pinder, Die Romantik in der deutschen Kunst um 1500, Das Werk des Künstlers, I, 1939, pp. 3–41; J. Seznec, La survivance des dieux antiques, London, 1939 (Eng. trans., B. F. Sessions, The Survival of the Pagan Gods, New York, 1953); G. F. Hartlaub, Albrecht Dürers "Aberglaube," Z. des d. Vereins für Kw., VII, 1940, pp. 167–96; G. F. Hartlaub, Antike Wahrsagungsmotive in Bildern Tizians, Pantheon, XXVIII, 1941, pp. 250–53; K. A. Laux, Michelangelos Juliusmonument, Berlin, 1943; O. Benesch, The Art of the Renaissance in Northern Europe, London, 1945; A. Chastel, Art et religion dans la Renaissance italienne, Bib. d'humanisme et Renaissance, VII, 1945, pp. 7–61; E. H. Gombrich, Botticelli's Mythologies: A Study in the Neoplatonic Symbolism of His Circle, Warburg, VIII, 1945, pp. 7–60; J. Read, The Alchemist in Life, Literature and Art, London, 1947; W. Fraenger, Die Hochzeit zu Kana: Ein Dokument semitischer Gnosis bei Hieronymus Bosch, Berlin, 1950; G. F. Hartlaub, Giottos zweites Hauptwerk in Padua (Salone), ZfKw, IV, 1950, pp. 19–34; W. Fraenger, The Millennium of Hieronymus Bosch, trans. E. Wilkins and E. Kaiser, Chicago, 1951; E. Castelli, Il demoniaco nell'arte, Milan, 1952; G. F. Hartlaub, Destillieren und Sublimieren in alten Florenz, Werkzeitung der Badischen Anilin und Soda Fabrik (BASF), III, 1953, pp. 8–11; G. F. Hartlaub, Zu den Bildmotiven des Giorgione, ZfKw, VII, 1953, pp. 57–84; G. F. Hartlaub, Romantischer Surrealismus: Edgar Ende, Die Kunst und das schöne Heim, LII, 1953–54, pp. 292–95; G. F. Hartlaub, Chymische Märchen (Splendor solis), BASF, IV, 1954, pp. 47–51; G. F. Hartlaub, Paracelsisches in der Kunst der Paracelsuszeit, Nova Acta Paracelsica, VII, 1954, pp. 132–63; M. Bojanowski, Rembrandts "Faust," D. Vierteljahrsschrift für Literaturwissenschaft und Geistesgeschichte, XXX, 1956, pp. 526–32; G. F. Hartlaub, Die Kunst und das magische Weltbild (Ottheinrichsbau), Ottheinrich-Gedenkschrift, Heidelberg, 1956, pp. 274–95; A. Breton, Art magique, Paris, 1957; J. Combe, Hieronymus Bosch, Paris, New York, 1957; D. Frey, Dämonie des Blicks, Wiesbaden, 1957; G. F. Hartlaub, Hieronymus Bosch: Wege und Abwege seiner Deutung, Das Münster, X, 1957, pp. 374–77; E. Wind, Pagan Mysteries in the Renaissance, London, 1958; W. Andreas, Deutschland vor der Reformation, 6th ed., Stuttgart, 1959; G. F. Hartlaub, Der Stein der Weisen, Wesen und Bildwelt der Alchemie, Munich, 1959; G. F. Hartlaub, Symbole der Wandlung: Eine frühe Bilderhandschrift der Alchemie, BASF, IX, 1959, pp. 123–28; E. Castelli, ed., Umanesimo e esoterismo, Padua, 1960; Fantasmagie: B. trimestriel du Centre int. de l'actualité fantastique et magique, Brussels, 1960 ff.; G. F. Hartlaub, Giorgione im graphischen Nachbild, Pantheon, XVIII, 1960, pp. 76–85; G. F. Hartlaub, Opera chemica: Eine unbekannte Bilderhandschrift der italienischen Frührenaissance (Raimundus Lullus, Opera Chemica), BASF, X, 1960, pp. 97–102; G. F. Hartlaub, Hans Baldung, Hexenbilder, Stuttgart, 1961; E. Iversen, The Myth of Egypt and Its Hieroglyphs in European Tradition, Copenhagen, 1961.

Asiatic and other non-European cultures: J. J. M. De Groot, The Religious System of China, 6 vols., Leiden, 1892–1910); W. Sieroszewski, Du chamanisme d'après les croyances des Yakoutes, Rev. de l'h. des religions, XLVI, 1902, pp. 204–35, 299–338; R. Andree, Scapulimantia, in Anth. Pap. in Honor of Franz Boas, New York, 1906, pp. 143–65; H. Doré, Recherches sur les superstitions en Chine, 18 vols., Shanghai, 1911–38; G. F. Kunz, The Magic of Jewels and Charms, Philadelphia, London, 1915; F. Dornseiff, Das Alphabet in Mystik und Magic, 2d ed., Leipzig, 1925; H. Zimmer, Kunstform und Yoga im indischen Kultbild, Berlin, 1926; H. Maspero, Mythologie de la Chine moderne, in Mythologies asiatiques, Paris, 1928, pp. 227–362; R. Wilhelm and C. G. Jung, Das Geheimnis der goldenen Blüte: Ein chinesisches Lebensbuch, Munich, 1929; A. Waley, Notes on Chinese Alchemy, BSOAS, VI, 1930, pp. 1–24; F. Cumont and J. Bidez, Les mages hellénisés, 2 vols., Paris, 1938; M. Eliade, Metallurgy, Magic and Alchemy, Zalmoxis: Rev. des ét. religieuses, I, 1938, pp. 85–129; U. Harva, Die religiösen Vorstellungen der altaischen Völker, Helsinki, 1938; C. Hentze, Le culte de l'ours ou du tigre et le T'ao-t'ieh, Zalmoxis: Rev. des ét. religieuses, I, 1938, pp. 50–68; J. Marqués-Rivière, Amulettes, talismans et pentacles, Paris, 1938; J. Masson, La religion populaire dans le canon bouddhique pāli, Louvain, 1942; E. De Martino, Il mondo magico, Turin, 1948; M. Eliade, Le "dieu lieur" et le symbolisme des nœuds, Rev. d'h. des religions, CXXXIV, 1948, pp. 5–36; A. E. Jensen, Das religiöse Weltbild einer frühen Kultur, Stuttgart, 1948; G. Tucci, Il libro tibetano dei morti, Milan, 1949; A. J. Festugière, La révélation d'Hermès Trismegiste, 2d ed., I, Paris, 1950; R. J. Forbes, Metallurgy in Antiquity: A Notebook for Archaeologist and Technologist, Leiden, 1950; H. Tegnaeus, Le héros civilisateur, Stockholm, 1950; M. Eliade, Le chamanisme et les techniques archaïques de l'extase, Paris, 1951; R. H. van Gulik, The Mango "Trick" in China: An Essay on Taoist Magic, Tr. of the Asiatic Soc. of Japan, 3d ser., III, 1952, pp. 1–59; E. Lot-Falck, Les rites de chasse chez les peuples sibériens, Paris, 1953; H. Hoppenot, Mexique: Magie maya, Lausanne, 1954; L. Lanciotti, Sword Casting and Related Legends in China, East and West, VI, 1955–56, pp. 106–14, 316–22; M. Eliade, Forgerons et alchimistes, Paris, 1956 (Eng. trans., S. Corrin, London, New York, 1962); D. Strömbäck, The Realm of the Dead on the Lappisch Magic Drums in Arctica, S. Ethn. Upsaliensia, XI, 1956, pp. 216–20; C. Hentze, Cosmogonie du monde dressé debout et du monde renversé, in Le symbolisme cosmique des monuments religieux, Rome, 1957, pp. 91–117; D. Seckel, Buddhistische Kunst Ostasiens, Stuttgart, 1957, pp. 195–209, 225–55; G. Tucci, Il tempio di bSam yas, in Le symbolisme cosmique des monuments religieux, Rome, 1957, pp. 118–23; H. Köster, Symbolik des chinesischen Universismus, Stuttgart, 1958; E. Rouselle, Vom Sinn der buddhistischen Bildwerke in China, Darmstadt, 1958; D. Seckel, Einführung in die Kunst Ostasiens, Munich, 1960, pp. 59–214.

Illustrations: PLS. 241–260.

MAGNASCO, ALESSANDRO. Italian painter (b. Genoa, 1667; d. Genoa, Mar. 19, 1749). He learned his art in the shop of his father Stefano, who was also a painter. Between 1680 and 1682 he went to Milan and stayed with a rich patron, who introduced him to the study of mathematics. Magnasco's inclination toward painting led his patron to apprentice him to the Venetian painter Filippo Abbiati. In this early Milanese period Magnasco painted some successful portraits, now lost. After some time, apparently abandoning portraiture, he turned his efforts to compositions with small figures and, save for a few exceptions such as *The Supper at Emmaus* (for the Convento di S. Francesco di Albaro in Genoa, now in the Palazzo Bianco), he produced this type of work for the rest of his life.

In Milan he met and became a friend of Sebastiano Ricci. In 1705 he left Milan for Genoa, where he attached himself to C. A. Tavella and collaborated with him; from there he went on to Florence, where he became court painter to the Grand Duke of Tuscany. The Florentine sojourn, punctuated by short trips in Tuscany and Emilia, ended in 1711, when Magnasco returned to Milan to remain until 1735, collaborating occasionally with Clemente Spera. Finally he established himself in Genoa and was active there until his death.

Despite the numerous and conscientious studies of Magnasco that have been undertaken, the origins and formation of his style have not been satisfactorily defined. On the basis of C. G. Ratti's statements regarding the painter's long formative residence in Milan and his known associations there, as student or coworker, with Filippo Abbiati and Sebastiano Ricci, the sources of his art have been sought in the Lombard mannerist environment (represented by Procaccini, Morazzone, and Crespi), with possible Venetian influences through the style of Ricci. Yet his Genoese point of departure should not be underestimated, for though Magnasco was quite young when he left for Milan, he must certainly have been exposed, through his father's studio, to the paintings of Valerio Castello, Giovanni Benedetto Castiglione (Il Grechetto), Domenico Piola, and Gregorio de' Ferrari, and probably also to those of Lucas and Cornelis de Wael. Lombard features are undeniably visible in Magnasco's work (perhaps transmitted by way of Ligurian masters, for example, Castello and Piola), but his essential style, allowing for pronounced personal inflections, expresses a Genoese character similar to that of Valerio Castello and Castiglione. Certain late works of Castello (such as *The Dead Christ Mourned by Angels*; formerly Genoa, Moro Coll.) and others by Castiglione (such as *The Crucifixion*; Genoa, Palazzo Bianco) support this hypothesis. The Lombard and Venetian contacts he had in Milan no doubt enriched his background, but they did not change his direction. Of more importance, though undocumented, is Magnasco's supposed encounter with works of El Greco, which he must, by some means or other, have seen. The similarities between the idiom of the two masters, allowing for difference in their temperaments and environments, are too evident to be mere coincidence; in both there is an exaggerated attenuation of the figures, and the spirit of the Counter Reformation inspired both, however diversely. The tone of Magnasco's work, less courtly than El Greco's, has its origins in that of Salvator Rosa and of Jacques Callot, though it is more straightforward and more varied in its poetic sense.

Magnasco's world is ironic and pathetic, bitter and religious, antirhetorical to the highest degree. His subjects include penitent monks and emaciated hermits, debauched gamblers and hungry ragged men, gypsies and nuns, camps and convents, funerals and bacchanals, tribunals and tortures. The setting is generally dark woods or gloomy rooms; flickering light illuminates a humanity that knows no peace. His manner of expression, departing from the traditional norms, seems to prefigure modern painting. He resolved spatial and plastic problems much as Francesco Guardi (q.v.) did later, almost entirely by chromatic means. Colored lights glow and fade in the dark atmosphere from which forms emerge and take shape without distinct outlines, as if born out of, rather than inserted into, the space that contains them. Each form seems to have solidified momentarily from the dark and fluid space as it caught the light and gives the impression that it might quickly dissolve and disappear in space. Thus a disquieting sense of hallucination informs his pictures. The weak residue of Cinquecento mannerism that lingered in Genoa and Milan throughout the 17th century was altogether abandoned by Magnasco; his work laid the ground for 19th-century color values.

More than 400 works worthy of note are attributed to Magnasco. The Genoa exhibition of 1949 afforded so many telling comparisons of his works that it has been possible to attempt a chronology and establish certain milestones for Magnasco's mature period.

The uncertainties about his early Milanese activity remain. The *Old Woman and Gypsies* (X, PL. 510) and *The Tame Crow* (PL. 261) reveal, beneath the flashy brushwork that spreads the forms out into the atmosphere, an underlying solidity which probably places them before 1711, when the artist left Florence. Between 1711 and 1735 his forms became freer; his lighting in this period is luridly dazzling, all substance appears to be permeated by air, and the forms lose their weight. The two paintings of folksingers in the Warsaw National Museum show in their dissolving contours a systematic negation of academic tradition in drawing, while the stormy landscape with fleeing monks (Milan, Brera) and *The Communion of Mary Magdalene* (PL. 263) are marked by a mature and studied handling of accents, for example, the sweep of brown foliage in tremulous lighting against the curving turbulent sky. In the various bacchanals (private collections in Genoa and Milan), despite a rather academic mannerism in the nude figures, painterly means are used to render the sense of space and volume.

Perhaps the highest attainment of the mature Magnasco is represented by his pictures of monks warming themselves by the fire and of monks in a library (formerly Venice, I. Brass Coll.). The wasted dolichocephalic figures produce a sense of restlessness and pathos; they are disposed according to purely rhythmic considerations and consciously abstracted. The cadenced poses of the reading monks and the unstable equilibrium of the little monk dancing in the center of the hall, the fulcrum of all the forms that rotate around him, demonstrate that every trace of intellectual conception has been transformed by the artist's temperament into poetry. Closely related to these are *The Meal* (San Francisco, M. H. de Young Memorial Mus.) and the bold *Don Quixote* (PL. 263) at the Detroit Institute of Arts.

The four very beautiful paintings in the Benedictine monastery of Seitenstetten (Austria) were probably painted between 1720 and 1725 for the Count of Colloredo, then governor of Milan; these are *The Synagogue*, *The Refectory*, a scene of the writing room in a monastery (PL. 264), and *The Preaching of the Christian Doctrine in Milan Cathedral*. In these paintings, particularly in *The Synagogue*, the figures are even further attenuated and immaterial; the air seems to coalesce with objects that have become mere pretexts for the rendering of color and light.

The Gypsy Wedding Feast (Louvre), probably painted during Magnasco's late Genoese sojourn, is executed in the *macchia* (spot) technique by which the forms are not analytically but impressionistically composed. To an equally late period can also be assigned the other *Synagogue* (Cleveland, Mus. of Art), in which the rarefaction is even more extreme, and the breaking up of the forms almost exceeds the limits of figural representation. The ultimate expression of this tendency was reached in Magnasco's masterpiece, the patrician family scene in a garden with panorama (PL. 262); the azure streak of sky, the green lozenges of the plots of land, the black crisscross roads, and the grey zone of unbroken wall establish the setting for the exaggeratedly fashionable and curiously sinister figures of the foreground: powdered ladies and beribboned gallants, abbots, lap dogs, and madrigal singers amid all the glittering clutter of the decadent baroque. In this painting, however, all that remains of the outworn and affected mannerism of the 18th century is the figural content, which serves only as a vehicle for the creative advance of the artist toward formal abstraction.

Toward the end of his life Magnasco's vision grew ever more fantastic, more evocative. The images are ephemeral, phantasmagorical; bodily form, freed of weight, exists only as color. This is the period of the Cézanne-like *Supper at Emmaus* mentioned above, one of the finest of these last works.

Magnasco is now recognized as one of the most imaginative painters of the first half of the 18th century, that productive but chaotic period in Europe. To admirers of the clear classic genius Magnasco's elusive impressionism may not be a congenial style, but by comparison with much of the Italian art of the 17th and 18th centuries, with its stress on academic craftsmanship and its virtuoso showmanship, Magnasco's sincerity, restrained idiom, and incisiveness stand in refreshing contrast.

In all probability Magnasco had no students but only isolated imitators such as Ciccio the Neapolitan and Coppa the Milanese, who are known today only by those names. Giuseppe Antonio Pianca, a painter from Novara who was active in Milan about 1720, was drawn to Magnasco's art but embraced only his manner without ever comprehending the spirit. Sympathetic understanding of Magnasco's artistic goals appeared later, and outside Italy, in the bitter and satirical creations of Goya and Daumier (qq.v.).

BIBLIOG. P. A. Orlandi, Abecedario pittorico..., Venice, 1753; R. Soprani, Le vite de' pittori, scultori ed architetti genovesi, 2d ed. by C. G. Ratti, Genoa, 1768; N. Passeri, Esame ragionato sopra la nobiltà della pittura e della scultura, Naples, 1783; L. Lanzi, Storia pittorica dell'Italia..., II, Bassano, 1795-96, pp. 345-46; G. G. Bottari, Lettere pittoriche, IV, Milan, 1822-25, pp. 36-38; F. Alizeri, Guida artistica per la città di Genova, 2 vols., Genoa, 1846; E. Santarelli, Catalogo della raccolta di disegni autografi donati dal prof. E. Santarelli alla R. Galleria di Firenze, Florence, 1870; F. Alizeri, Guida illustrativa per la città di Genova, Genoa, 1875; N. P. Serra, Catalogo riassuntivo della raccolta di disegni antichi e moderni posseduti dalla R. Galleria degli Uffizi di Firenze, I, Florence, 1890, p. 314; F. Wickhoff, Die italienische Handzeichnungen der Albertina, JhbKhSamml-Wien, XII, 1891, pp. ccv-cccxiv; W. Suida, Genua, Leipzig, 1906; O. Grosso and A. Pettorelli, I disegni di Palazzo Bianco, Milan, 1910; W. R. Valentiner, Stefano Magnasco, ZfbK, XXII, 1910-11, pp. 85-88; T. von Frimmel, Blätter für Gemäldekunde, VI, Vienna, 1911, p. 169 ff.; E. Jacobsen, Gemälde und Zeichnungen in Genua, RepfKw, XXXIV, 1911, pp. 185-223; G. Beltrami, Alessandro Magnasco detto il Lissandrino, Milan, 1913; P. D'Ancona, Alessandro Magnasco detto il Lissandrino a proposito di una recente esposizione delle opere sue, N. ant., CLXX, 1914, pp. 700-03; Exposition des œuvres d'Alexandre Magnasco (cat.), Paris, 1914; B. Geiger, Alessandro Magnasco, Berlin, 1914; B. Geiger, Gesammelte Gedichte, Leipzig, 1914; G. Swarzenski, Magnasco-Glosse, Süddeutsche Mnh., XI, 1914, pp. 634-37; H. Wedderkop, Ein wiederentdeckter Maler des Barock, Alessandro Magnasco, 1667-1749, Munich, 1914; A. Locatelli-Milesi, Alessandro Magnasco, Emporium, XLII, 1915, pp. 421-35; L. Planiscig, Alessandro Magnasco und die romantisch-genrehafte Richtung des Barocco, MnbKw, VIII, 1915, pp. 238-48 (rev. R. Longhi, L'Arte, XX, 1917, pp. 176-77); E. Bernard, Alessandro Magnasco, GBA, LXXXII, 1920, pp. 351-61; E. Bernard, Tintoret, Greco, Magnasco et Manet, Paris, 1920; P. D'Ancona, Alessandro Magnasco detto il Lissandrino, Dedalo, III, 1922-23, pp. 424-49; A. Ferri, Alessandro Magnasco, Rome, 1922; B. Geiger, Beiträge zum Katalog der Werke von Mascagno, Belvedere, I, 1922, p. 35, III, 1923, pp. 29-43; G. Nicodemi, Alessandro Magnasco, Emporium, LV, 1922, pp. 3-27; Pittura italiana del '600 e '700 a Palazzo Pitti (cat.), Florence, 1922; B. Geiger, Alessandro Magnasco, Vienna, 1923; O. Grosso, Le grandi figure nell'opera del Magnasco, B. del Comune di Genova, 1923; O. Grosso, Paesiste genovesi del '600, La Superba, 1923; U. Ojetti, L. Dami and N. Tarchiani, La pittura italiana del Seicento e del Settecento alla Mostra di Palazzo Pitti, Milan, 1924; H. Voss, Die Malerei des Barock in Rom, Berlin, 1924, p. 627; J. Meder and J. Schönbrunner, Handzeichnungen alter Meister aus der Albertina, Vienna, 1925; M. Nugent, Alla Mostra della pittura italiana del '600 e '700, I, San Casciano, 1925, pp. 349-69; A. Arsèn, Alessandro Magnasco, Renaissance de l'art, IX, 1926, pp. 491-98; I. Haumann, Das oberitalienische Landschaftsbild des Settecento, Strasbourg, 1927; D. Castagna-Masini, Guida di Genova, Genoa, 1929; G. Fiocco, La pittura veneziana alla Mostra del '700, Riv. di Venezia, 1929, pp. 497-581; R. Giolli, Il Magnasco delle grandi figure, Poligono, 1929; N. Pevsner, ThB, s.v., XXIII, 1929, pp. 560-65; D. C. Rich, Four Paintings by Alessandro Magnasco, Chicago Art Inst. B., XXIII, 1929, pp. 42-43; Il Settecento italiano (cat.), Venice, 1929; G. Delogu, Pittori veneti minori del '700, Venice, 1930; W. M. Milliken, The Synagogue by Alessandro Magnasco, Cleve. Mus. B., XVII, 1930, pp. 66-68; G. Delogu, Pittori minori liguri, lombardi, piemontesi del Seicento e del Settecento, Venice, 1931; W. Arslan, Appunti su Magnasco, Sebastiano e Marco Ricci, BArte, XXVI, 1932, pp. 209-19; G. Fogolari, Il Settecento italiano, Milan, 1932; R. Buscaroli, La pittura di paesaggio in Italia, Bologna, 1935; E. Scheyer, A Painting by Magnasco, Detroit Inst. of Arts B., XVI, 1936, pp. 34-36; L. Baldass and others, Italienische Barockmalerei (cat.), Vienna, 1937; H. Leporini, Ausstellung italienischer Barockmalerei in Wien, Pantheon, XX, 1937, pp. 213-17; H. Voss, A Rediscovered Picture by Alessandro Magnasco, BM, LXXI, 1937, pp. 171-73; B. Geiger, Beitrag zu Magnasco, Pantheon, XXII, 1938, pp. 283-85; Pittori genovesi del '600 e '700 (cat.), Genoa, 1938; M. Bonzi, "La comunione della Maddalena" del Magnasco, Genova, XXII, no. 2, 1942, pp. 24-25; G. Lorenzetti, La pittura italiana del Settecento, Novara, 1942; B. Geiger, L'autoritratto del Magnasco, Le Tre Venezie, XVIII, 1943, p. 56 ff.; A. Morandotti, Cinque pittori del Settecento, Rome, 1943; B. Geiger, I disegni del Magnasco, Padua, 1945; B. Geiger, Magnasco: Catalogo delle pitture, Venice, 1945 (bibliog.); M. Pospisil, Magnasco, Florence, 1945; M. Bonzi, Saggi sul Magnasco, Genoa, 1947 (2d ed., 1960); M. Bonzi, Una obra maestra de Alessandro Magnasco, Historion, 103, 1947, pp. 862-63; A. Malraux, Psychologie de l'art, I-II, Geneva, 1947-48; A. Morassi, Pittura del Seicento e Settecento in Liguria (cat.), Milan, 1947; B. Geiger, Handzeichnungen alter Meister, Zürich, 1948; G. C. Argan, La peinture de Magnasco à l'exposition de Gênes, Arts plastiques, 1949, 7-8, pp. 303-07; M. Bonzi, I disegni del Magnasco a Palazzo Rosso, Genova, XXVI, 1949, pp. 15-17; B. Geiger, Magnasco, Bergamo, 1949; C. Marcenaro, Magnasco, Genova, XXVI, 1949, pp. 11-17; A. Morassi, Magnasco (cat.), Bergamo, 1949; A. Podestà, La mostra del Magnasco, Emporium, CIX, 1949, pp. 251-70; C. Marcenaro, Una grande figura del Lissandrino, Genova, XXIX, 1952, pp. 14-15; A. Christen, Il Trattenimento d'Albaro, Genova, XXXI, 1954, pp. 7-11; G. Ballo, Da Giambellino a Picasso: Le mostre del dopoguerra, Varese, 1956; V. de Sambricio, De Tiepolo à Goya, Goya, XIII, 1956, pp. 30-37; J. Białostocki and M. Walicki, Europäischen Malerei in polnischen Sammlungen, 1300-1800, Warsaw, 1957; O. Y. Blažíček, Due dipinti inediti del Magnasco, recentemente ritrovati in Cecoslovacchia, Emporium, CXXV, 1957, pp. 152-55; Bosch, Goya et le fantastique (cat.), Bordeaux, 1957; B. Geiger, Memorie di un veneziano, Florence, 1958; R. Longhi, Un tema ambrosiano del Magnasco, Paragone, IX, 101, 1958, pp. 70-71.

Caterina MARCENARO

Illustrations: PLS. 261-264.

MAITANI, LORENZO. Sienese architect and probably also sculptor, son of the sculptor Vitale di Lorenzo (called "Matano"). The appearance of Maitani's name in a *catasto* (tax return) of 1290 places the date of his birth before 1270. On Sept. 16, 1310, he was appointed *Capomastro* (master of works) for the Cathedral of Orvieto, where he spent the last twenty years of his life, except for those rare occasions when he was called elsewhere to serve as an architectural consultant. He gave advice in 1317 and 1319-21 on the repair of the aqueducts at Perugia, in 1322 on the work in progress at the Cathedral of Siena, in 1323 on plans for the castle at Montefalco, and in 1325 on the repair of the castle at Castiglione del Lago. Maitani died in June, 1330.

It appears from the contract of 1310 that Maitani had repeatedly been called from Siena to Orvieto when the transept and apse of the Cathedral of Orvieto threatened to collapse, a danger he averted by erecting buttresses. He also began construction on the roof of the nave and continued this work after his appointment as *Capomastro*. His main occupation at this time was the erection of the west façade. In the Museo dell'Opera del Duomo are preserved two famous drawings on parchment of widely differing projects for this façade. One, showing a single-gable solution (PL. 265), has been dated by most scholars about twenty years earlier than the other, a three-gable solution that largely corresponds to the actual building (VI, PL. 333) and has therefore been universally attributed to Maitani. The earlier plan is strongly influenced by the façade of the south transept of Notre-Dame in Paris (ca. 1260) and could thus be the work of a Sienese master of about 1290 who had been to Paris. The drawing shows part of the decoration of the second pilaster of the façade, on which appears the Tree of Jesse, which was actually executed, and the Madonna with angels in the lunette, which was also executed later but in a vastly different style. These data seem to coincide with what is known about the career of Ramo di Paganello (see GOTHIC ART, VI, cols. 567-68), who was considered a sculptor of great renown in Siena, to which he had apparently returned from France (?; "ex partibus ultramontanis") in 1281. However, the documents in Orvieto indicate only that Ramo was employed there in a subordinate position and may thus have been just one of several Sienese sculptors who were aware of French architectural and sculptural developments; it cannot therefore be proved that he designed the earlier plan for the façade. In the later plan Maitani accepts in principle the older master's solution for the lower part of the façade, that is, the round arch of the central lunette and the framing of the three doors by four wide pilasters. [Since some of the reliefs on the two inner pilasters must already have been *in situ* in 1307 (Fumi, 1891, p. 213), this acceptance was unavoidable.] The French character of the earlier plan, however, is strongly modified; the pediments over the lateral doors are much lower, the rose window of the nave is flanked by narrow panels, and the three-gable system is introduced. All these departures from the French system are found between 1294 and 1302 in Arnolfo di Cambio's (q.v.) plan for the first façade of the Cathedral of Florence, and Maitani may have followed Arnolfo's example.

Most scholars attribute to Maitani a large part of the façade's sculptural decoration, including the six bronze angels flanking the marble Madonna in the central lunette (PL. 267), the three lower rows of the first pilaster, with scenes from Genesis, from the Creation to the Temptation (PL. 268), and the two lower rows of the Last Judgment on the fourth pilaster (PL. 269). Finally, the symbols of the four Evangelists above the four pilasters are also ascribed to Maitani.

The bronze angels are mentioned in documents of 1325, at which time more than six sculptors were preparing models for casting. It does not appear from the documents that Maitani had designed these models; his name is not recorded, and he may have reserved for himself only the role of coordinating the others' work. The style of the bronze angels is close to that of the above-mentioned reliefs on the first and fourth pilasters, but it might be argued that this similarity results not from the identity of the master but from the stylistic derivation of the angels from the reliefs. The scenes from Genesis and the Last Judgment seem superior in quality to the bronze angels; the Genesis scenes in particular seem to be directly developed from the style of those representing the youth of Christ (the Annunciation, the Visitation, the Nativity, and the Adoration) on the third pilaster (PL. 267). These four reliefs are related in composition to Giovanni Pisano's pulpit in the Cathedral of Pisa (1302-10; VI, PL. 213) and in style to a wooden Madonna and Child in the Museo dell'Opera del Duomo in Orvieto (PL. 266), a work that has plausibly been connected with the first drawing for the façade and must therefore be dated about 1300. The reliefs thus can be dated from about 1310 to before 1316, when the Visitation was copied in the silver shrine of the Cathedral of Pistoia. The author of the four reliefs would then be a follower of the master of the wooden statue, who may be identical with the first architect. Therefore Maitani could have been the sculptor of the Genesis and Last Judgment scenes only if he had been a pupil of the master of the four reliefs from the youth of Christ; this is dubious, however, because Maitani had been in Orvieto only occasionally before 1310. It is therefore doubtful that the assistants whom the contract of 1310 permits him to retain for the sculptural work were his own; it is quite possible that they were, rather, the pupils of the master of the four reliefs.

The Genesis and Last Judgment scenes show the combination of a decidedly Sienese Gothic style, which seems to parallel Simone Martini's, with a deep understanding of classical art. The organization of the Genesis scenes reveals the influence of the relief style of the columns of Trajan and Marcus Aurelius in Rome, and heads from Roman sarcophagi are ingeniously adapted in the Last Judgment. The architecture of the second plan for the façade is neither so Gothic nor so classical; in suppressing certain Gothic elements in the first drawing that would not appeal to Italian taste, Maitani did not go back directly to classical sources but to the modified "Tuscan" Gothic of Arnolfo di Cambio. Such a discrepancy between the style of Maitani the architect and Maitani the sculptor is entirely possible; but since the sculptural activity of the master is not clearly documented, the possibility should not be overlooked that the scenes on the lower registers of the first and fourth pilasters were the work of another master. The two beautiful wooden crucifixes in the Cathedral, the crucifix in S. Francesco, the seated Christ blessing in the Museo dell'Opera del Duomo, all in Orvieto and all attributed to Maitani, would then be by one of the masters who continued the work in the upper registers of these pilasters. The symbols of the Evangelists are mentioned in documents of 1329 and stand in the same relation to Maitani as the six bronze angels.

Martin WEINBERGER

The history of Maitani criticism and of the problem of the authorship of the façade of Orvieto Cathedral and its sculptural decoration shows notable differences of opinion.

In the 20th century these questions were considered almost contemporaneously by A. Schmarsow (1926), W. R. Valentiner (1927), and G. de' Francovich (1927-28). Schmarsow, who rejected A. Nardini Despotti Mospignotti's opinion that the two Orvieto Cathedral façade designs preserved in the Museo dell'Opera del Duomo were both drawn by Maitani, assigned the first (PL. 265) to Ramo di Paganello, for whom there exist documentary references of 1281, 1282, 1288, and 1293 but no certain works. To this artist Schmarsow also assigned the Creation scenes of the first pilaster of the façade; to Maitani, then, would belong the reliefs of the other three pilasters, as well as the figures of the Madonna and Child over the central portal and the four symbols of the Evangelists; Maitani would have been responsible also for the second façade project. Valentiner credited Maitani with the two façade projects and the over-all design of the sculptural decoration of the pilasters, which would have been executed by Nicola di Nuto, mentioned in Orvieto documents of 1339 as the sculptor of several wooden figures of the Cathedral choir. Francovich attributed both façade projects to Maitani, who also would have conceived, and in part executed, the entire bronze and marble sculpture decoration of the lower zone of the façade, aided in the execution of the pilaster reliefs by four assistants. Francovich also assigned to Maitani certain wooden sculptures in the Cathedral, in the Museo dell'Opera del Duomo, and in S. Francesco.

H. Keller (1938) again considered the problem of the two drawings for the Cathedral façade, concluding that both were by a single architect, who could only be Lorenzo Maitani. P. Cellini (1939, 1958) maintains that the decoration of the two inner pilasters preceded the inception of Maitani's work on the façade (1310) and connects it with Fra Bevignate, excluding any contribution by Maitani to the execution of the façade sculpture. E. Carli (1947), overlooking Keller's article, returns to the question of the authorship of the two façade projects and is inclined to regard Maitani as responsible for the second one only. Carli, following Cellini, thinks that the decoration of the two inner pilasters was executed before Maitani's arrival and assigns them to the elusive figure of Ramo di Paganello. To Maitani himself — or possibly to a very close follower — Carli attributes the reliefs of the two outer pilasters; a pupil of Maitani would have worked on the central registers of the second and third pilasters and on the two upper registers of the fourth pilaster, while the upper scenes of the first three pilasters would have been executed after Maitani's death (1330). P. Toesca (1951) regards as most convincing the thesis — favored especially by Nardini and Keller — that the two designs are by a single author, probably Maitani. Toesca emphasizes the iconographic and stylistic homogeneity of the whole of the sculptural decoration of the lower zone of the Orvieto façade, "which thus may be regarded as integrally conceived by a single master. This master may well have been the Sienese Lorenzo Maitani, the architect of the façade." In 1959, John White, in a study of the reliefs of the Cathedral façade, expressed the conviction that the documents relating to the façade give a strong impression that the reliefs were executed between 1310 and 1330, when Maitani was master of works of the Cathedral; that nothing on the façade was executed prior to Maitani's appointment as master (1310); that all these reliefs — as Toesca and Francovich had maintained — indicate a fundamental stylistic unity achieved through the over-all direction of a single master, who could have been Maitani; and that this master employed four collaborators, as Francovich had suggested.

* *

BIBLIOG. G. Della Valle, Storia del Duomo di Orvieto, Rome, 1791; G. Milanesi, Documenti per la storia dell'arte senese, I, Siena, 1854; A Rossi, Lorenzo ed Ambrogio Maitani al servizio del Comune di Perugia, Giorn. di erudizione artistica, II, 1873, pp. 57-72; N. Benois, A. Resanoff and A. Krakau, Monographie de la Cathédrale d'Orvieto, Paris, 1877; Vasari, I; L. Fumi, La facciata del Duomo di Orvieto: Lorenzo Maitani e i primi disegni, Arch. storico dell'arte, II, 1889, pp. 327-38; L. Fumi, Il Duomo di Orvieto e i suoi restauri, Rome, 1891; A. Nardini Despotti Mospignotti, Lorenzo del Maitani, Arch. storico dell'arte, VI, 1891, pp. 185-203; A. Brach, Nicola und Giovanni Pisano, Strasbourg, 1904; Venturi, IV, 1906, pp. 320-59; G. Vitzthum and F. Volbach, Die Malerei und Plastik des Mittelalters in Italien, Berlin, 1924; A. Schmarsow, Das Fassadenproblem am Dom von Orvieto, RepfKw, XLVII, 1926, pp. 119-44; G. de' Francovich, Lorenzo Maitani scultore e i bassorilievi della facciata del Duomo di Orvieto, BArte, N.S., VII, 1927-28, pp. 339-72; W. R. Valentiner, Observations on Sienese and Pisan Trecento Sculpture, AB, IX, 1927, pp. 177-220; A. Schmarsow, Italienische Kunst im Zeitalter Dantes, 2 vols., Augsburg, 1928; G. de' Francovich, Un'Annunciazione in legno di Lorenzo Maitani, La Diana, IV, 1929, pp. 171-80; M. Weinberger, Eine Madonna von Giovanni Pisano, JhbPreussKSamml, XLI, 1930, pp. 165-74; E. A. Rose, The Meaning of the Reliefs on the Second Pier of the Orvieto Façade, AB, XIV, 1932, pp. 258-76; P. Cellini, Appunti orvietani, RArte, XV, 1933, pp. 1-20; A. Nava, L'"Albero di Jesse" nella Cattedrale d'Orvieto e la pittura bizantina, RIASA, V, 1935-36, pp. 363-76; H. Keller, Die Bauplastik des Sieneser Doms, Jhb. der Bib. Hertziana, I, 1937, pp. 139-221; M. Weinberger, Nino Pisano, AB, XIX, 1937, pp. 58-91; H. Keller, Die Risse der Orvietaner Domopera und die Anfänge der Bildhauerzeichnung, Festschrift Wilhelm Pinder, Leipzig, 1938, pp. 195-222; P. Cellini, Appunti orvietani, II: Lorenzo Maitani e Nicola di Nuto, RArte, XII, 1939, pp. 229-44; M. Weinberger, The First Façade of the Cathedral of Florence, Warburg, IV, 1940-41, pp. 67-79; E. Carli, Le sculture del Duomo di Orvieto, Bergamo, 1947 (rev. M. Weinberger, AB, XXXIV, 1952, pp. 60-63); Toesca, Tr; A. Watson, The Imagery of the Tree of Jesse on the West Front of Orvieto Cathedral, Various Essays for F. Saxl, London, 1957, pp. 149-64; R. Bonelli, Bevignate architetto o amministratore, CrArte, V, 28, 1958, pp. 329-32; P. Cellini, Appunti orvietani, III: Fra' Bevignate e le origini del Duomo di Orvieto, Paragone, IX, 99, 1958, pp. 3-66; J. White, The Reliefs on the Façade of the Duomo at Orvieto, Warburg, XXII, 1959, pp. 254-302.

Illustrations: PLS. 265-269.

MALAGASY REPUBLIC. The large island of Madagascar, at the southwestern end of the Indian Ocean, took its present name, Malagasy Republic, when it became an independent state in 1960. Its unique ethnic and cultural composition is due both to the proximity of Africa and to its links with southern insular Asia. Migratory movements linking the island with Indonesia may date back as far as two millenniums. Contacts with European culture, mainly through French occupation, were of some importance in the modernization of the country, particularly its capital Tananarive (Antananarivo), but have had little influence on the arts.

SUMMARY. Indigenous cultures (col. 402): *Northern and western area*; *The interior*; *Southern area*. Modern period (col. 406).

INDIGENOUS CULTURES. The population (5,657,601, according to the 1961 census), traditionally subdivided into 19 tribes, shows a relative cultural and linguistic homogeneity, notwithstanding the marked anthropological and environmental differences. This homogeneity testifies to an active circulation of customs and ideas that undoubtedly antedates the attempts at political unification begun by the sovereigns of Imerina (in the central plateau) in the 18th century and completed by the French at the end of the 19th. The art of the country is little known. No systematic prehistoric and archaeological investigations have ever been carried out. There are no monumental complexes nor any visible architectural vestiges of any note belonging to past cultures, autochthonous or foreign. This discussion is therefore restricted to tribal arts of the relatively short period during which they are known to have existed. Malagasy works of art, modest in output, were practically unknown in Europe up to the first half of the 19th century, although the island had been discovered by the Portuguese in 1500, and very little has survived on the island itself because of the perishable materials generally used. With the European penetration these arts declined. In regard to geographical distribution, works of art are relatively scarce in the northern zones and along the eastern coast, while the best are found among the central-southern and southwestern tribes.

Northern and western area. The northern and western areas of the island, from the mouth of the Fanambana River on the Indian Ocean in the northeast to Tulear on the Mozambique Channel in the southwest, are occupied by the large Sakalava group and, farther north, by the linguistically and culturally related Antankarana. These are the ethnic groups most influenced by contacts with the African continent, for the most part by way of Comorian and Makua immigrants or Arab-Swahili merchants from Mozambique and the coastal regions farther north. Conversion to Islam of many groups may have contributed to the disappearance, especially in the north, of preexisting forms of figural art. There are still Arab and Indian colonies in these areas (and to a lesser extent along the southeastern coast and elsewhere on the island), and ruins of buildings attributed to Arab immigrants of undetermined periods are frequent along the coasts and on the numerous small islands off the northern shores. No monuments of artistic value have come to light, but the archaeological finds around Vohemar on the northeast coast are worthy of mention. These consist of tomb furnishings attributed to foreigners of unknown origin, conventionally called "Iharanians" and known to the Sakalava as "Rasikaji." Excavations have yielded "swords, daggers, Chinese bowls and plates, Chinese and Persian trays, extremely fine long-necked Persian bottles, mother-of-pearl spoons, bronze mirrors, amphoras for antimony, glass-bead necklaces, diverse

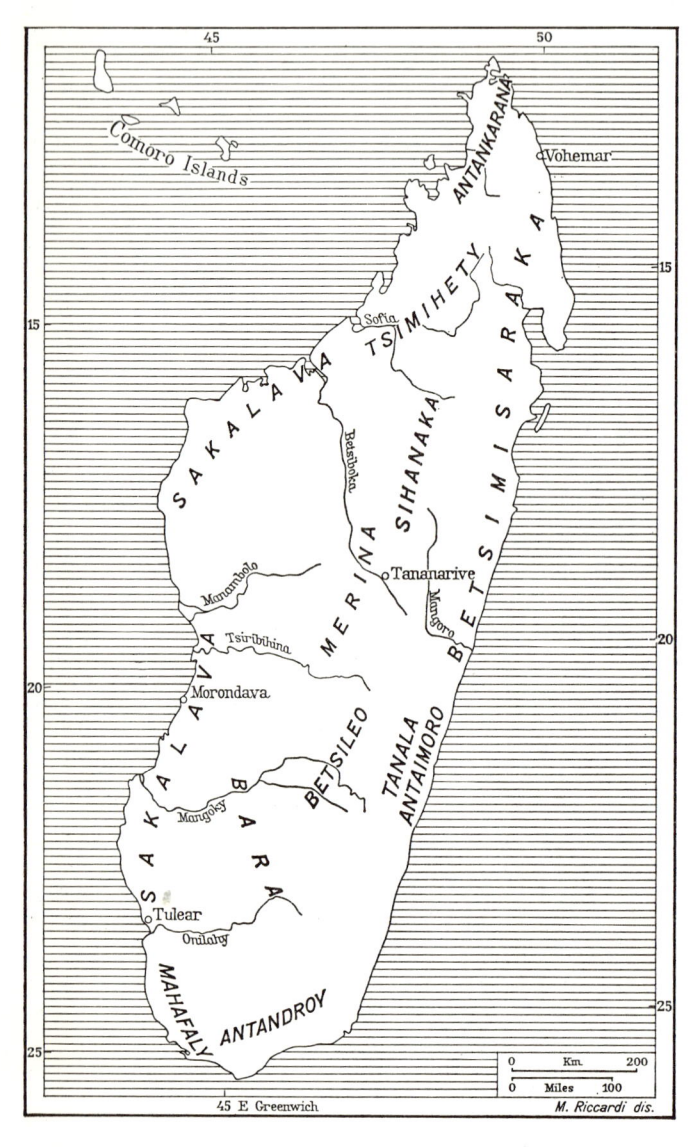

Malagasy Republic, distribution of chief art-producing groups (tribal names in capitals).

pottery" (Deschamps, 1960), as well as unusual tripod pots and locally made basins of soft stone (chlorite schist). The coins, porcelains, and ornaments date back to periods between the 11th and 17th centuries, and the finds as a whole unquestionably indicate an immigrant culture of the Azanian type (see AZANIAN ART). Comparable but less extensive finds have been made in Malaika on the Bay of Ampasindava on the northwest coast.

Other documents of the past include the many menhirs found in almost every part of the island, particularly on the interior plateau. Except in Betsileo country they are unornamented. They have continued to be erected up to the present, and though they have no artistic value, they are of interest with regard to the problem of the relationship between the Malagasy and the south Asian and African megalithic cultures.

The contemporary art of the non-Islamic Sakalava is limited to wood carving for commemorative monuments to the dead and for the decoration of everyday objects. The working of steatite and the decoration of bedboards occur sporadically and probably derive from similar crafts of the Merina (see below). Weaving — which in the Kandreho region produced the attractive rabanna (raffia cloth used for curtains and mosquito nets), with its strange polychrome motifs obtained by a technique similar to that of batik — is a gradually disappearing art.

The traditional Sakalava tombs, to be seen particularly in the zone of Morondava, are enclosed by solid fences surmounted by horizontal beams elaborately carved in high relief with recurrent motifs of a classic Malagasy type: rows of ducks (a symbol of pleasure), cattle pursued by crocodiles, birds. At the fence corners and at the center of the longer sides rise poles topped by stylized figures carved in the round, generally of women (the wives of the deceased) or large ibis. Other Sakalava wood sculptures, also of commemorative character, represent ithyphallic figures. All the sculptures are generally stiff and inexpressive, with triangular faces, arms close to the body, and elaborate coiffures (IX, PL. 250).

In the Maintirano region on the Mozambique Channel the Vezo, a tribe of fishermen living among the Sakalava but distinct from them, produce (or formerly produced) wood sculpture. Their work employs motifs continually recurring in Malagasy sculpture: vertical rows of animals (ox, dog, guinea hen) carved in the round along the shafts of ceremonial staves. Such staves are finished with "tortoise feet." The Vezo motif of the perching bird (decorated on the beak, wings, and base with geometric designs) is rare in Negro sculpture; there are Indonesian parallels, but here the motif seems closer to the steatite birds of Zimbabwe.

The interior. Among the tribes of the central plateaus, the most gifted in the field of decorative arts are the Betsileo, a cattle-breeding tribe. Their most interesting monuments are the *vatolahy*, monolithic steles centered on platforms of gneiss slabs or simply sunk into the ground. At times over 18 ft. high, these monoliths are burial or commemorative monuments of important personages. They are usually rectangular in cross section and surmounted (e.g., at Sabotsy) by amphora-shaped pinnacles or, more frequently, by bucrania. The sides are occasionally carved with geometric motifs in low relief or with superimposed profile figures of zebus in high relief. The largest *vatolahy* used to be erected for the Betsileo rulers as a symbol of their sovereignty over the land. Others were raised in honor of wealthy persons and decorated with bucrania to symbolize the abundance of their herds; in memory of individuals who died far from home or were drowned or assassinated; or in recognition of such important events as floods, hurricanes, council meetings, and gatherings of warriors. The *vatolahy* are also conceived of as dwelling places of manistic spirits and as such are objects of worship and receive offerings and sacrifices.

Equivalent to the *vatolahy* in function and often also in form are the monuments called *teza*, made of single blocks of wood in the form of a high rectangular prism surmounted by a massive rectangular wooden shelf from which emerges a spire or a series of pegs for bucrania. On the early examples still extant the polished sides and the superstructures are decorated with delicate carving of rosettes, concentric circles or rectangles, rows of chevrons or other geometric motifs, palmettes, etc., arranged in alternating bands along the entire height of the monument. These motifs recur through much of the island's decorative art. Robert Heine-Geldern has pointed out their close similarity to corresponding motifs of the Saadang Toradja (Celebes; VIII, PL. 23) and the megalithic monuments of Sumba (VIII, PLS. 24, 25; see INDONESIAN CULTURES). The finial is sometimes carved in the form of a vase.

Other Betsileo funerary monuments consisted of several sculptured pillars of the *teza* type, joined near the top by transverse wooden bars and enclosing in the center a square area (sometimes as much as 7 yd. per side) filled with flat stones. Monumental tombs of this kind were numerous in the region south of Ambositra, especially in Ikiangara, where Louis Catat counted about fifty. Most of these traditional structures, which are no longer built except in crude and simplified forms, have been severely weather-damaged.

Among the minor works of the Betsileo are carved house doors and shutters, sometimes bearing anthropomorphic reliefs, and the so-called "bambou de porteur," adorned with pokerwork of geometric motifs or outlines of cattle. However, much of the decorative repertory of these craftsmen is derived from Tanala art.

The Merina, who occupy the interior plateau north of the Betsileo but also form a dominating minority in almost all other parts of the island, have the largest and the most culturally evolved population. This superiority is not, however, reflected in the quality of their art. On the contrary, their artistic aptitude is inferior to that of other Malagasy ethnic groups, except for two craft forms peculiar to the Merina. One is the working of steatite, from which they turn cylindrical or partly quadrangular monolithic lamps. These are decorated with longitudinal striping on the central portion and with rows of geometric motifs in bands parallel to the base, which is broader, and to the top, which is sometimes carved in the form of a capital. Lamps of similar shape but less painstakingly decorated are also made of pottery covered with graphite, and others are elegantly formed of wrought iron, but all these objects are beginning to go out of use.

More interesting artistically are the bedboards of the Merina, which are now becoming collectors' items. These polished hardwood panels with a fine dark patina, about 2 yd. long by 10–13 in. high, formerly served to hold the straw beds of noble and well-to-do persons (VIII, PL. 39). The entire outer surface is decorated with incised geometric motifs or series of human or zoomorphic figures carved in low relief, in processional ranks or genre scenes. In the oldest examples, which date from the early 19th or the late 18th century, at the earliest, geometric decoration prevails; the motifs are often based on Azanian or similar Indonesian motifs. Contemporary representational subjects — warriors (armed or in battle), horsemen, houses, animals — are seminaturalistic in form or very naïvely stylized. In later examples, datable to the reign of Radama I (1810–28) and the next two or three decades, geometric decoration is used only on the ends of the board, while the center is carved in low relief with gracefully realistic figures (soldiers in the uniform of the period, ladies with umbrellas), genre scenes, plants, and animals (particularly cattle and birds).

The other groups of the interior plateaus, to the north of Imerina, produce little art. The Sihanaka of Andilamena make "talisman-paddles" with triangular handles topped by full-round figures (birds, boars, oxen, horses, etc.) carved in one piece with the object itself. The various colors of the veining in the local varieties of rosewood are skillfully exploited. The Tsimihety, farther north, make staves for the chief or *ombiasy* (witch doctor) that are surmounted by sculptured figures of men, mounted oxen, etc., but such work is not peculiar to this tribe; similar staves or batons are found along the west coast and elsewhere on the island. The Sihanaka, the finest basket-weavers of the island, are renowned for their mats with checkerboard patterns and concentric squares (II, PL. 230).

Southern area. The tribes of the southern areas, which have remained relatively unchanged by European influence, have best maintained the traditions of wood sculpture and various minor arts. The perishability of the materials employed and the lack of historical documentation preclude even conjectural dating of these arts. So far no serious attempt has been made at stylistic comparison to prove, or at least to present as an interesting possibility, affinities with either Bantu or Indonesian sculpture. Although it cannot compare in quality with either of these, the wood sculpture of southern Malagasy presents a wealth of tribal styles, most of which are yet to be studied.

The most noteworthy works of the Antaimoro, whose territory fronts on the Indian Ocean, are the so-called "tomb guardians" (now in Tananarive, Coll. Poirier) found near the royal village of Vohipeno. These are typical examples of anthropomorphic posts, with arms barely indicated and stylized faces. Also from this tribe comes a wooden rice measure (Paris, Mus. de l'Homme) engraved with curious genre scenes, small figures, animals, and houses, and framed by friezes of lozenge and chevron designs.

Among the Tanala, the western neighbors of the Antaimoro, incised geometric decoration (on objects of daily use such as containers, mortars, and doors) prevails. This has been transmitted to the neighboring Betsileo and perhaps even to the Merina. The art of the Bara is more diversified, including wood sculpture in the round (in particular, the so-called "female idols"), figured spoons and combs, and some of the most interesting of the *ody* (the container-amulets common to various Malagasy tribes), with zoomorphic figures in low relief. Peculiar to the Bara is the manufacture of knives with brass handles in the shape of human figures, horsemen, or entwined couples. A tomb found in the Mangoky River region in Bara territory is of interest for the study of the development of Malagasy funerary art. The corpses were placed on biers, the covers of which, shaped like the hull of a boat, are carved on the central rib with motifs of oxen, houses, and canoes. No precise dating can be established, but the tomb is certainly not very old. In spite of its location, it has been attributed to the Sakalava.

The most original art is that of the Mahafaly, who inhabit the southwestern districts of the island. Of particular interest are the *aloalo*, the carved openwork posts surmounting the tombs. They are made of a single trunk of light-colored wood, about 8 in. wide and up to 2 1/2 yd. high, carved with vertical rows of crescents joined on their convex sides, openwork hexagons, lozenges, and ellipses with incised ornament. The post may rest on the head of a slender male or female figure and may be finished at the top with a simple openwork circle or a minute platform bearing an anthropomorphic or birdlike figure, a house, or a horseman. The human figure is rendered with convincing and vigorous realism. Placed in groups above the stones and bucrania that cover the tombs, the *aloalo* exhibit an elegant sense of balance and are unquestionably among the most beautiful of the Malagasy creations. Another form of Mahafaly commemorative art comprises independent anthropomorphic sculptures on which both pyrography and incision are used to emphasize the facial features and an uncommon technique of cross-hatching to render the hair. Outstanding products of the applied arts are the beautiful *ondana* — the almost rectangular wooden headrests decorated in the center with a duck elegantly carved in openwork — and the wooden containers for water and honey, lightly ornamented on the outer surfaces and lids with human and animal figures (crocodiles, cattle, birds) engraved in black and framed by bands of triangles, chevrons, St. Andrew's crosses, and a variety of other geometric motifs.

The Antandroy, eastern neighbors of the Mahafaly and the southernmost tribe of the island, produce harmoniously proportioned three-stringed musical instruments decorated with bovine heads (Coll. Poirier), fine carved wooden plates, and wooden figurines executed to the most minute details (e.g., eyelashes of applied hairs, and nails) in realistic style. One such figurine (Coll. Poirier), said to come from the Ambovombe district, may be considered for its style and harmony of modeling among the finest examples of Malagasy sculpture. The tribal origin of these statuettes is not always certain, and just as it is known that many of the *aloalo* on Antandroy tombs were acquired from Mahafaly craftsmen, so it is also possible that this particular statuette and other similar objects were the work of some Antaisaka sculptor.

BIBLIOG. J. Sibree, Carving, Sculpture and Burial Memorials amongst the Betsileo, Antananarivo Ann., II, 1876, pp. 193–99; A. Jully, Funérailles, tombeaux et honneurs rendus aux morts à Madagascar, L'Anthropologie, V, 1894, pp. 385–401; C. Renel, Les amulettes malgaches Ody et Sampy, B. Acad. malgache, II, 1915, pp. 31–277; E. G. Waterlot, La sculpture sur bois à Madagascar, L'Anthropologie, XXXV, 1925, pp. 133–34; H. Lormian, L'art malgache, Paris, 1929; R. Boudry, L'art decoratif malgache, Rev. de Madagascar, II, 1933, pp. 23–82; R. Decary, L'Androy, II, Paris, 1933; R. Linton, The Tanala, Chicago, 1933; H. Deschamps, Les Antaisaka, Tananarive, 1936; H. M. Dubois, Monographie des Betsileo (Madagascar), Paris, 1938; P. Gaudebout and E. Vernier, Notes à la suite d'une enquête sur les objets en pierre de la région de Vohémar, B. Acad. malgache, XXIV, 1941, pp. 91–99; P. Gaudebout and E. Vernier, Notes sur une campagne de fouilles à Vohémar, B. Acad. malgache, XXIV, 1941, pp. 100–14; C. Poirier, A propos de quelques ruines arabes et persanes, B. Acad. malgache, XXV, 1942–43, pp. 137–39; J. Faublée, L'ethnographie de Madagascar, Paris, 1946; C. Abbadie, Note sur une tombe sakalava au sud de Mangoky, B. Acad. malgache, XXVIII, 1947–48, pp. 21–23; M. Leenhardt, Arts de l'Océanie, Paris, 1947; C. Poirier, Réflexions sur les ruines de Malaika et de Vohémar, B. Acad. malgache, XXVIII, 1947–48, pp. 97–101; R. Decary, Mœurs et coutumes des Malgaches, Paris, 1952; L. Molet, La sculpture malgache, Rev. de Madagascar, I, 1958; H. Deschamps, Histoire de Madagascar, Paris, 1960; A. Lavondès, Art traditionnel malgache, Tananarive, 1961.

Vinigi L. GROTTANELLI

MODERN PERIOD. As a result of the great influx of Europeans to the island's capital during the 19th century, the social and economic life of the country is gradually evolving toward assimilation of Western modes.

Tananarive, capital of the Malagasy Republic, is the only important commercial center of the island. Situated on the Rova, a rocky height on the plateau of Imerina, the city had its first spurt of growth under the Merina dynasty, toward the end of the 17th century. The remains of fortifications of the citadel belong to this period. During the 19th century the city spread out at the base of the cliff. By 1895, the year of the French occupation, Tananarive already had numerous churches, palaces, and other buildings, among them the Cathedral and the Queen's palace (now housing the Mus. des Beaux-Arts). At the beginning of the 20th century it extended northward and, after the construction of the railroad and station, northwest as far as Lake Anosy. In the latter area lies the modern administrative and business quarter, the Zoma, traversed by a wide thoroughfare with modern office buildings and stores, a large covered market, and the post and telegraph offices. In the broad residential areas of the northern zone are the palace of the prime minister, the theater, and the town hall, as well as modern schools, cultural institutions, and parks. An institute of scientific research, surrounded by a park, rises at the edge of the city. There are also historical and folklore collections.

BIBLIOG. C. Robequain, Madagascar et les bases dispersées de l'Union française, Paris, 1958, pp. 317–22.

* *

Illustrations: 1 fig. in text.

MALAYA. The Malay Peninsula south of Thailand is now part of the Federation of Malaysia, which, as established in 1963, also includes Singapore, as well as North Borneo (now Sabah) and Sarawak. (The latter two are discussed in connection with INDONESIA and INDONESIAN CULTURES.) The 11 states of Malaya proper are Johore, Kedah, Kelantan, Malacca, Negri Sembilan, Pahang, Penang, Perak, Perlis, Selangor, and Trengganu. The indigenous population of Malaya and Singapore is made up of the Malays and the Jakun, Samang, and Sakai (or Senoi) tribes. The arts of these tribes remain on a primitive level, while the Malays have been influenced by Indian art in the fields of architecture, sculpture, woodworking, and work in precious metals (see INDIA, FARTHER).

SUMMARY. Prehistoric discoveries (col. 407). Primitive tribal art (col. 407). Malay art (col. 408). Modern centers and developments (col. 409).

PREHISTORIC DISCOVERIES. There have been frequent discoveries of prehistoric artifacts throughout the peninsula. The earliest finds so far were discovered in the gravel of the Perak River valley at Kota Tampan, in 1938, and in Wellesley, a division of Penang. The former belong to the Lower Paleolithic, and the latter to the Upper Paleolithic.

The Hoa-binh culture (ca. 5000–3000 B.C.) belongs to the proto-Neolithic period and is characterized by crudely worked stone tools and by pottery (Perak, Wellesley); from the Neolithic proper (Terembeling; Gua Cha, II, PL. 14; Gua Kepah) come implements of polished stone and fired pottery — ranging from simple round bowls to plates, vases, and jars — decorated with bands impressed by means of a twisted cord; also dating from this period is the ax with rattan handle, akin to the Mongolian ax. Robert Heine-Geldern ("Urheimat und früheste Wanderungen der Austronesier," *Anthropos*, XXVII, 1932, pp. 543–619) believes that this culture, which he calls "the quadrangular adze culture," may derive from northeastern India; other authors, however, argue in favor of southern China and northern Indonesia. The local Neolithic period persisted until about the beginning of the Christian Era, but it has not been possible to establish its initial date. Human remains have not been found in association with the paleolithic deposits. Those found in mesolithic and proto-neolithic sites have Melanesian traits, while those associated with late neolithic deposits exhibit a great many affinities with the present-day Semang.

Of particular interest are the dolmens and menhirs belonging to the megalithic culture. The most important monument, at Berhala Lima (Kota Bahru), consists of a central group of vertical stone slabs, flanked by rows of enormous, aligned blocks; the post of honor for the ancestor spirit to which the entire construction is dedicated, which is north of the central group, is a peculiarity of the Asiatic monuments that is not found in European monuments of this type.

At Slim, Sungkai, and Changkat Mentri (Perak) and at Bukit Jong (Pahang), tomb slabs have been found along with bronze utensils, iron tools, and decorated pottery. While the bronze objects are clearly of Indonesian type, the iron objects are thought to have come from India. At Tembeling and Klang have been found decorated fragments of ceremonial bronze drums of the same type as those found on the Pasemah plateau in Sumatra and, like them, of Dông-so'n derivation (see INDONESIAN CULTURES).

PRIMITIVE TRIBAL ART. The hunting and gathering tribes of the forest, to whom the Malays indiscriminately apply the name *orañ utan*, or wild man, comprise three groups: the Semang, the Sakai, and the Jakun. Their art is limited for the most part to modest decoration of bamboo combs, blowguns, quivers, and other utilitarian objects. The combs, used only by women, are decorated with incised bands, of which the number as well as the sequence of the designs is fixed by tradition. In the six-band combs of the Semang of Perak, the pattern of the second band recurs in the sixth, and that of the third in the fifth; the fourth band, usually larger, must have a different design. The tribesmen attribute to these designs magical powers against disease and the bites of insects and poisonous snakes, and the motifs recur with the same magical significance on ear ornaments, blowguns, and quivers. This amuletic decoration thus provides the primary creative stimulus for the tribal artists, who may either represent an object symbolically or reproduce its form with some realism. For the most part they prefer geometric decoration, and the interpretations of the design are often contradictory. The decorations, generally known as *bunga*, represent plants, flowers, animal teeth or eyes, bird heads, and serpents; the plants depicted are those believed to have magical or medicinal properties.

The combs of the Semang of Perak are preeminent for the beauty of their design and workmanship; those of the Sakai of Kedah and Perak are distinguished by the presence of two small, curved appendages at the sides. The decoration is achieved by removing the outer bark of the bamboo from the parts not covered by the design, so as to make the design stand out in relief. The background is darkened with a special resin (*damar kelulut*) in order to accentuate even more the whitish natural color of the remaining bark. Sometimes the reverse is done: the bark is removed from the design, which is then colored so that it stands out against the light background.

The cave art of the Semang is a modern development, of which notable examples exist. The finest series is found in Gua Badak (Rhinoceros Cave) in northern Perak. Among the subjects most frequently depicted are monkeys, bows and arrows, coconut trees,

Malaya, principal cities and ethnic groups (ethnic names in slanting capitals). *Key*: (1) Modern national boundaries; (2) boundaries between states: (I) Johore; (II) Malacca; (III) Negri Sembilan; (IV) Selangor; (V) Pahang; (VI) Trengganu; (VII) Kelantan; (VIII) Perak; (IX) Penang; (X) Kedah; (XI) Perlis.

men performing various tasks, and automobiles. The figures in black are colored with charcoal, while those in white are obtained by scratching the limestone surface.

Another occupation of these tribal peoples is basketry (mats, containers, nets for capturing wild game, etc.), usually so carefully executed as to rival those of the Malays. The most common materials are the fibers of bamboo, rattan, and breadfruit (*Artocarpus communis*). Clothing is made from the last-named by pounding its fibrous bark. In comparison with the similar production of the Indonesians in Celebes and Halmahera, the workmanship of these garments is rather crude. The belts worn by the women are woven of long, very fine vegetable fibers and wrapped several times around the waist. The Semang of Jeransang (Pahang) make them of rattan fibers and decorate them with crude designs — two species of snake, as well as bees and fish — to which they attribute magical powers that protect the wearer from backaches.

None of the tribes knows the use of fired clay; instead, they use containers hollowed from segments of bamboo.

MALAY ART. Indian civilization has influenced Malay art since the slow process of Hinduization of the peninsula began in the first centuries of the Christian Era. Architecture, sculpture, and the working of wood and precious metals developed under this influence. Conversely, the contribution of Islam (beginning in the late 13th cent.) must be considered minor, since there exist no outstanding Islamic monuments, with the exception of the numerous tombstones of sultans (bearing inscriptions in ancient Malay) such as those of 22 sultans of the Perak dynasty found along the banks of the Pera River. In Kedah, at many sites on the banks of the Sungai Dujang, there are temple ruins dating back to the 5th–6th century; in plan (a solid raised base with a terrace for circumambulation) and in building technique (employing blocks of laterite) they seem to resemble very closely the stupas of southern India. However, the deterioration of the buildings prevents a more detailed comparison. The remains of the principal buildings of an old city on the banks of the same river are of an architecture that can be defined as a peripheral imitation of the Indian.

Also found in Kedah, along the banks of the Sungai Batu Pahat about 2 miles from the village of Merbok, were the ruins of a stone temple, which H. G. Quaritch Wales has assigned to the 7th–8th century and interpreted as a tomb-temple, of the same type as the Javanese candi, built to provide proper burial for deceased rulers. Buildings of this type are very common in Malaya; their shape — tapering toward the top and terminating in a spire — had the symbolic function of connecting the dynasty of the deceased with the world of the gods. Precisely because of this belief, many of these tomb-temples were destroyed by rulers of later dynasties, with the aim of severing the tie between their predecessors and the supernatural world. The plan of the Sungai Batu Pahat structure also exhibits many points of similarity to the temples of southern India but differs in the small dimensions of the building, the material employed, the stone socle of the wooden piers, and the extremely austere decoration. A noteworthy example of a Buddhist temple in Chinese style is the Kek-Lok-Si, with a 7-story pagoda, in Penang.

Sculpture, also of Hindu derivation, is widely used throughout the peninsula in the decoration of temples, tombs, and sacrificial altars. Representations of the Buddha are very frequent. The earliest known image is of bronze and was found, with fragments of pottery from a very large jar, on the banks of the Sungai Dujang (Singapore, Raffles Mus.); it portrays a standing Buddha and has been assigned on stylistic grounds to the Gupta period (5th cent.).

Originality and great refinement have been attained in the working of wood (thrones, furniture, bamboo boxes) and brass (lamps for mosques, lamps in the form of mythological birds for the shadow theater, and articles used in connection with siri, or betel).

Ironwork is very important, chiefly in the manufacture of weapons. The kris — introduced, according to Heine-Geldern (op. cit.), during the Bronze Age — varies widely in ornamentation and size in accordance with very precise standards; the Majapahit variety (named for a medieval kingdom in eastern Java), with blade and hilt formed in a single piece, is the most ancient type still in use.

Pottery is copied from Chinese models, which were imported into Malaya during all periods, as attested by numerous archaeological discoveries. Pasik Durian, in the Tembeling area, is a center of this production. The textile work, with its original designs and striking colors, is also noteworthy.

MODERN CENTERS AND DEVELOPMENTS. With the end of World War II and the subsequent achievement of self-government there began an era of accelerated industrial, urban, and agricultural development, which is rapidly changing the face of Malaya. Business and residential construction continues to contribute to the modern appearance of Kuala Lumpur, long the major city of the peninsula. As capital of Malaya, and of the Federation of Malaysia from the time of its formation, the city also has many government buildings, prominent among them the 18-story Malaysia Parliament and an older structure with a clock tower that houses the Selangor State Secretariat and other government offices. The University of Malaya, founded in 1957, is located here.

Notable examples of industrial and urban development are the new industrial estates or satellite towns, the first of which is Petaling Jaya about 8 miles from Kuala Lumpur. Land set aside by the government for private industrial development is occupied by many factory buildings (built by both foreign and domestic capital, mainly as joint-venture projects). Plans for further residential construction in this new industrial city include some multistoried apartment buildings, as well as other forms of low-cost housing. Other industrial satellite towns are underway at Tesak (Perak), Johore Bahru (Johore), and Butterworth (Penang).

Throughout Malaya public planning and investment have resulted in the modernization and expansion of such facilities as airports, harbors, roads, communication, and other public utilities. Land reclamation projects have involved dam construction, such as that on the Klang River. (Similar programs have been undertaken in Sabah and Sarawak, the less developed states of the Federation of Malaysia. At Jesselton, the capital of Sabah, the traditional waterfront stilt houses are being replaced by new residential structures.)

Singapore. Located on an island of the same name and connected with the mainland by a concrete causeway, the city has about 1,700,000 inhabitants. At the beginning of the 19th century, it was only a village ruled by the sultan of Johore, from whom it was acquired for England in 1819 by Thomas Stamford Raffles, a British colonial officer. Today it is a modern cosmopolitan city and one of the major ports in the Far East. The most characteristic quarter is the Chinese, with a number of temples. Nanyang University was established in 1953 for Chinese-speaking students. The commercial life of the city centers around Raffles Place. Among the notable buildings are the Gothic St. Andrew's Cathedral; the University of Singapore (founded 1949; formerly the University of Malaya); Raffles Museum, with a permanent exhibit of local art objects; Government House; and the Supreme Court building. The Botanical Garden is one of the finest in the world. There are a large number of Christian churches, Hindu temples, and mosques. The city's modern airport is located at Paya Lebar.

BIBLIOG. W. W. Skeat, The Wild Tribes of the Malay Peninsula, JRAI, XXXII, 1902, pp. 124–41; G. B. Cerruti, The Sakais of Batang Patang, Perak, JRAS, Straits Branch, XLI, 1904, pp. 113–17; R. Martin, Die Inlandstämme der malayischen Halbinsel, Jena, 1905; G. B. Cerruti, Nel paese dei veleni, fra i Sakai, Verona, 1906; W. W. Skeat and C. O. Blagden, Pagan Races of the Malay Peninsula, 2 vols., London, 1906; P. Schebesta, Bei den Urwaldzwergen von Malaya, Leipzig, 1927 (Eng. trans., A. Chambers, Among the Forest Dwarfs of Malaya, London, 1929); R. O. Winstedt, History of Malaya, London, 1935; I. H. N. Evans, The Negritos of Malaya, Cambridge, 1937; F. C. Cole, The People of Malaysia, New York, 1945; Anderson Historical Society of Ipoh, Royal Burial Places, Malayan H. J., I, 1954, pp. 76–80; R. Braddell, Malaya's Ancient Past, Malayan H. J., I, 1954, pp. 32–35; G. Sieveking, Gua Cha and the Malayan Stone Age, Malayan H. J., I, 1954, pp. 111–25; R. H. Peacock, The Klang Bronzes, Malaya in H., III, 2, 1957, pp. 120–21; H. G. Quaritch Wales, Prehistory and Religion in South-East Asia, London, 1957; R. Braddell, Most Ancient Kedah, Malaya in H., IV, 2, 1958, pp. 18–40; A. Lamb, The Temple on the River of Cut Stone, Malaya in H., IV, 2, 1958, pp. 2–10; R. O. Winstedt, The Malays: A Cultural History, 5th ed., London, 1958; J. M. Matthews, Rock Paintings near Ipoh, Malaya in H., V, 2, 1959, pp. 22–26.

Olga AMMANN

Illustrations: 1 fig. in text.

MALEVICH, KAZIMIR. Russian painter, founder of suprematism (b. Kiev, Feb. 11, 1878; d. Leningrad, 1935). Malevich was the son of a Polish father and a Russian mother. After study at the Kiev School of Art, he went to Moscow about 1900 and by 1904 was enrolled in the city's Academy of Fine Arts. The impact of contemporary French art turned him toward a radical Fauvist manner about 1910. In 1910–11 he exhibited with the Jack of Diamonds group and thereafter took part in most major exhibitions in Moscow and St. Petersburg. In 1912, after a brief visit to Paris, Malevich began working in a cubist style, and by 1915 he had developed suprematist painting, stressing the primacy of fundamental geometric shapes and pure color (see CUBISM AND FUTURISM; EUROPEAN MODERN MOVEMENTS).

Malevich was a dominant figure during the years 1918–21 and occupied important teaching posts in Moscow and Vitebsk. The official reaction against abstract art in 1921 led him to Leningrad, where, except for a visit to Germany and Poland in 1927, he lived in seclusion until his death. His major works include *The Scissors Grinder* (1912–13; New Haven, Yale Univ., Soc. Anonyme Coll.), *Suprematist Composition* (V, PL. 137), *Large Strong Cross on White* (1916–17; Amsterdam, Stedelijk Mus.), *White on White* (ca. 1918; New York, Mus. of Mod. Art), *Suprematism Form aE* (drawing, 1924; Amsterdam, Stedelijk Mus.).

Like his contemporaries Kandinsky and Mondrian, Malevich devoted himself to the promulgation of a universal artistic language based upon a purified, abstract geometry. His suprematism was a major force in progressive Russian art of the period and, especially through its influence upon constructivism, played an important role in the evolution of Western abstract art.

WRITINGS. Cubism, Futurism, Suprematism, Moscow, 1915; On New Systems in Art, Suprematism, On the Problem of Creative Art, God Is Not Overthrown, Vitebsk, 1920–22; From Cézanne to Suprematism, Moscow, 1921; Die Gegenstandslose Welt (Bauhausbücher 11), Munich, 1927 (Eng. trans., H. Dearstyne, The Non-objective World, Chicago, 1959).

BIBLIOG. A. H. Barr, Jr., Cubism and Abstract Art, New York, 1936; Stedelijk Museum, Kasimir Malevich, Amsterdam, 1957; E. Winter, The Lost Leadership of Malevich, Art News, 57, December, 1958, p. 34 ff.; C. Gray, Kasimir Malevich, London, 1959; C. Gray, Modern Russian Art, London, 1961; C. Gray, The Great Experiment: Russian Art 1863–1922, New York, 1962.

Robert L. HERBERT

MALTA (MALTESE ISLANDS). This small group of islands, comprising Malta (Gr., Μελίτη; Lat., Melita), the principal island, Gozo, and Comino, situated at the intersection of several important maritime routes in the Mediterranean south of Sicily, has come under the influence of various civilizations and cultural currents. Malta was the site of a neolithic civilization that produced original and monumental edifices. In historical times the islands were dominated and culturally influenced first by the Phoenicians and then by the Romans. In the early Middle Ages they passed from the Eastern Roman Empire to the Arabs; later, as part of the Kingdom of Sicily, Malta came under Norman, Angevin, and Aragonese rule. In 1530 Emperor Charles V assigned the islands to the Knights of St. John of Jerusalem (Knights of Malta). From 1814 Malta was a British possession administered, in later years, under various forms of self-government. It received its independence in September, 1964. The art heritage of the islands is particularly rich in prehistoric remains and in Italian baroque art forms and reflects the many changes of sovereignty to which Malta has been subjected.

SUMMARY. Phases of cultural and artistic development (col. 411): *Prehistory; Punic and Roman periods; Medieval and modern periods.* Art centers (col. 414).

PHASES OF CULTURAL AND ARTISTIC DEVELOPMENT. *Prehistory.* The monumental neolithic remains of Malta, known since the 17th century, were at first believed to be Phoenician protohistoric. The discoveries of Sir Themistocles Zammit (whose classifications and theories were disputed by J. D. Evans) and the conclusions drawn from the researches of L. M. Ugolini formerly tended to place Malta on a very high cultural plane, as the focal point of the entire central Mediterranean civilization. The recent trend among archaeologists is to consider the Maltese neolithic as a relatively late offshoot of the Aegean neolithic civilization. The most spectacular remains of the Maltese Neolithic period include Pawla (Paola) and Hal Tarxien, southeast of Valletta, Hagar Qim, Mnajdra (Mnaidra; PL. 426), and, on the island of Gozo, the Ggantija ("Giant's Tower"). All examples of mature and advanced architecture, these religious buildings, with many chambers along a longitudinal axis, are built of huge upright stone slabs with delicately decorated faces; traces of corbeled vaulting remain. The hypogeum of Hal Saflieni, near Pawla, entirely carved within the rock, follows the same architectural scheme, but, being perfectly preserved, it gives an idea of what a complex religious structure was like. The same originality of concept and daring of execution may be seen in small sculptures, such as the so-called "Venus of Malta" and the "Sleeping Lady," both remarkable for their modeling. The neolithic civilization came to an abrupt and mysterious end, probably before the end of the 2d millennium B.C. Compared with its neolithic predecessor, the subsequent Bronze Age civilization, whose origins and contacts with the world outside Malta are better known, represents a cultural regression. Upright stone slabs and dolmens indicate that in the Bronze Age Malta was on the same cultural level as the rest of the Mediterranean (see MEDITERRANEAN PROTOHISTORY).

Punic and Roman periods. Under the Phoenicians (first from Sidon, later from Carthage) Malta entered history, but except for the well-known bilingual cippus of a very late period, a fine anthropoid sarcophagus, and some pottery, the Punic phase left little of interest. The contrary is true of the Roman period, which began in 218 B.C. Cicero, in the second Verrine oration (IV, xlvi), mentions the temple of Juno, which was despoiled of its treasures by Verres. Epigraphical remains and architectural fragments provide evidence of other monumental edifices of Roman Melita. The Museum of Antiquities, housed in a Roman villa discovered in 1881 at Rabat (near Mdina), contains a collection of important architectural fragments, sculpture, and mosaics. A particularly fine piece is a Hellenistic mosaic showing a satyr punished by Bacchae. Also noteworthy are a Hellenistic head of a pugilist and a number of portraits. Roman mosaics are also found in the ruins of the baths of Ghajn Tuffieha, on the west coast. The Roman city of Melita was situated on a hill in the center of the island. It is now known as Città Vecchia or Notabile (from the title conferred on it by Alfonso of Aragon in 1428) or under the Arab name of Mdina (Medina). In the 6th century its Byzantine rulers demolished a part of the city in order to defend it more effectively; they dug a defensive ditch (now the southern boundary of the city) and razed the buildings beyond this limit. Part of the Roman city and its monuments are still buried.

Medieval and modern periods. There are few early medieval and Arabic remains, the only noteworthy piece being the Kufic stele of Maimuna. A few scattered Romanesque capitals provide evidence of buildings belonging to the pre-Gothic period. In the underground chapel of the catacombs of St. Agatha, in Rabat, remains of Byzantine-Romanesque paintings have been found. In the 15th and 16th centuries the painters Pietro Rozzolone, Antonello de Saliba, and Salvo di Antonio worked in the churches of Malta. Alessandro Varotari (also called "Padovanino"), otherwise known only for a single painting (Syracuse, Sicily, Mus. di Palazzo Bellomo), worked in Mdina in the old cathedral, which was destroyed by earthquake in 1693. Antonello Gaggini (1478–1536) executed important sculptures for Malta.

Under the Knights of St. John of Jerusalem (1530–1798) Maltese culture moved out of the confines of Sicilian insular culture into the

Malta and the Maltese Islands (inset). Principal art centers and monuments of archaeological and artistic interest. *Key*: (1) Monuments and settlements of the Neolithic period; (2) Bronze Age sites; (3) towns and monuments of the Roman period; (4) modern cities, towns, and villages.

wider sphere of Italian artistic tradition. After the brief period of late Gothic style, introduced from Rhodes by Niccolò Flavari, the Knights of St. John turned to the Italian courts for new architects. The Knights established headquarters in the coastal town of Borgo del Castello, the name of which was changed to Vittoriosa after the siege of 1565. It was here that Bartolomeo Genga of Urbino built palaces and churches and laid out plans for the new city (as recorded by Vasari, among others). Baldassare Lancia of Urbino, Nicola Bellavante, and Antonio Ferramolino of Bergamo also worked here at this time. Among painters, there were Filippo Paladini, a Tuscan, and Matteo Pérez de Alesio (known as "Matteo da Lecce"), who went to Malta from Rome after he had completed the series of frescoes in the Sistine Chapel.

The most flourishing period in the arts was the 17th century, when Caravaggio (q.v.), Mattia Preti, and Lorenzo and Melchiorre Gafà were active. Lionello Spada and, apparently, the Sicilian Mario Minniti went to Malta after Caravaggio's arrival. Preti, who settled on the island in 1661, was commissioned to decorate the ceiling of the Cathedral of St. John in Valletta. This ceiling may be regarded, since the removal of its 19th-century restorations, as an important and well-preserved example of 17th-century Italian painting. Preti also worked as an architect; it has been definitely established that he designed the Sarria, a church in Floriana.

Melchiorre Gafà, the Maltese sculptor whom Bernini cited as a craftsman capable of surpassing him, left very few works on his native island. The *Baptism* in St. John's Cathedral, a colossal sculpture for which he had been commissioned in 1666, was actually executed by Giuseppe Mazzuoli, the artist who probably also carved the funerary monument of Ramon Perellos in that church. Lorenzo Gafà, younger brother of Melchiorre, was an architect trained in Rome who introduced baroque forms into Maltese architecture.

There were a number of good Maltese architects active in the 18th century. Giovanni Barbara, a daring military engineer and an excellent architect, built the parish church of Lija and the elegant elliptical Church of St. James at Valletta. Giuseppe Bonnici designed the austere Customs House and the Church of St. Barbara at Valletta. Other architects of this period include the two Cachias, Antonio and Domenico. Among painters the dominating figures were two Maltese, Stefano Erardi, an artist of no great originality, and Francesco Zahra, who introduced the style of the Neapolitan school to the island. Toward the end of the century the Sicilian brothers Francesco and Vincenzo Manno and the Frenchman Antoine de Favray worked there, and many followers of Preti and various pupils of Zahra and De Favray were active in this period.

After the departure of the Knights of St. John in 1798, the artistic activity of the island was reduced to very meager proportions. Giorgio Pullicino, a native Maltese who had been sent to Rome, under the patronage of the Knights, to study architecture, returned in the first decade of the 19th century to find the community limited and miserly. In order to eke out a living, he was reduced to painting landscapes for foreign visitors. His fellow countryman, Grognet de Vassé, fared better; he designed and built the parish church, a vast circular edifice, in Mosta (Musta).

Several Maltese painters of the 19th century established their reputations, including Vincenzo and Giovanni Hyzler, trained at the Nazarene community in Rome; Pier Paolo and Raffaello Caruana, both pupils of Tommaso Minardi; Michele Bellanti, a good painter and lithographer; and Giorgio Bonavia, who became a successful portraitist in Paris and London. One of the great engravers of the 19th century, Luigi Calamatta, was a Maltese, although born in Civitavecchia, Italy. His contemporary, Amedeo Preziosi, was a painter of Oriental subjects and a lithographer whose work was fashionable in the European courts. Many painters of the Roman school — including Francesco Grandi, Domenico Bruschi, and Pietro Gagliardi and, somewhat later, V. Monti and A. Palombi — worked in churches in Malta. Two late-19th-century painters were L. Pisani and Gennaro Calì, trained in Rome and Naples respectively. The Maltese sculptor Antonio Sciortino also studied in Rome during the last decade of the 19th century.

Among the established painters of the first half of the 20th century are Gianni Vella and Eduardo Caruana Dingli. There have been many artists of that generation, nearly all of them trained in Rome, who have lived and worked on the island, exhibiting their work in the great international exhibitions of Rome, Venice, and London. The best known of these are the sculptors Vincenzo Apap and Giorgio Borg and the painters Giorgio Preca, Emanuele Vincenzo Cremona, Willy Apap, and Frank Portelli. Maltese architecture, which had remained traditional until the advent of World War II, began to reflect modern trends after that period, but architects still continue to use the square, dressed blocks of local limestone as a structural material within a frame of reinforced concrete.

BIBLIOG. *General works*: J. Quintin, Insulae Melitae descriptio, Lyon, 1536; G. Bosio, Istoria della Sacra Religione Militare di S. Giovanni Gerosolimitano, 3 vols., Rome, 1594–1602; G. F. Abela, Della descrizione di Malta, Malta, 1647; B. dal Pozzo, Historia della Sacra Religione Militare di S. Giovanni, 2 vols., Verona, 1703; R. Aubert de Vertot d'Aubeuf, Histoire des Chevaliers de St. Jean de Jérusalem, 4 vols., Paris, 1726 (Eng. trans., 2 vols., London, 1728); L. de Boisgelin de Kerdu, Ancient and Modern Malta, 3 vols., London, 1804; G. A. Vassallo, Storia di Malta dai primi tempi fino alla dominazione inglese, Malta, 1854. *Prehistoric period*: G. F. Abela and G. Ciantar, Malta illustrata, 2 vols., Malta, 1772–80; J. Houel, Voyage pittoresque des Iles de Sicile, de Malte et de Lipari, 4 vols., Paris, 1782–87; C. Vassallo, Dei monumenti antichi del gruppo di Malta, 2d ed., Malta, 1876; A. A. Caruana, Recent Further Excavations of the Megalithic Antiquities of Hagiar Kim, Malta, 1886; A. Mayr, Die vorgeschichtlichen Denkmäler von Malta, Munich, 1901; G. A. Colini, I monumenti preistorici di Malta, BPI, XXVIII, 1902, pp. 204–33; Valletta Mus. Ann. Rep., 1904 ff.; A. Mayr, Eine vorgeschichtliche Begräbnisstätte auf Malta, ZfE, XL, 1908, pp. 536–42; A. Mayr, Die Insel Malta im Altertum, Munich, 1909; T. E. Peet, Contributions to the Study of the Prehistoric Period in Malta, BSR, V, 1910, pp. 139–63; N. Tagliaferro, The Prehistoric Pottery Found in the Hypogeum at Hal Saflieni, Ann. of Archaeol. and Anthr., Univ. of Liverpool, III, 1910, pp. 1–21; T. Zammit, The Hal-Saflieni Prehistoric Hypogeum, Malta, 1910; T. E. Peet, Prehistoric Painted Pottery in Malta, Ann. of Archaeol. and Anthr., Univ. of Liverpool, IV, 1911, pp. 121–26; T. Ashby and others, Excavations 1908–11 in Various Megalithic Buildings in Malta and Gozo, BSR, VI, 1913, pp. 1–126; T. Ashby, Supplementary Excavations at Hal Tarxien, Malta, in 1921, AntJ, IV, 1924, pp. 93–100; P. F. Bellanti, Studies in Maltese History, Malta, 1924; T. Zammit and C. Singer, Neolithic Representations of the Human Form from the Islands of Malta and Gozo, JRAI, LIV, 1924, pp. 67–100; R. Battaglia, Le statue neolitiche e l'ingrassamento muliebre presso i Mediterranei, IPEK, III, 1927, pp. 131–60; T. Zammit, Prehistoric Malta, Oxford, 1930; G. Patroni, Origine e tipologia delle costruzioni megalitiche di Malta, Rend. Ist. lombardo di sc. e lettere, LXV, 1932, pp. 971–84; L. M. Ugolini, La dormiente di Malta, Dedalo, XII, 1932, pp. 575–85; M. A. Murray, Corpus of the Bronze Age Pottery of Malta, London, 1934; L. M. Ugolini, Malta: Origini della civiltà mediterranea, Rome, 1934; E. De Manneville, La préhistoire méditerranéenne à Malte et les théories d'Ugolini, Rev. de l'art ancien et mod., LXXI, 1937, pp. 85–89; C. Ceschi, Architettura dei templi megalitici di Malta, Rome, 1939; J. B. Ward Perkins, Problems of Maltese Prehistory, Antiquity, XVI, 1942, pp. 19–35; J. D. Evans, The Prehistoric Culture Sequence in the Maltese Archipelago, ProcPrSoc, XIX, 1953, pp. 41–94; J. D. Evans, The Dolmens of Malta and the Origin of the Tarxien Cemetery Culture, ProcPrSoc, XXII, 1956, pp. 85–101; L. Bernabò Brea, Sicily Before the Greeks, London, 1957; D. Woolner, Graffiti of Ships at Tarxien, Malta, Antiquity, XXXI, 1957, pp. 60–67; M. Cagiano de Azevedo, Saggio sul Labirinto, Milan, 1958; L. Bernabò Brea, Malta and the Mediterranean, Antiquity, XXXIV, 1960, pp. 132–37; J. D. Evans, Malta, London, New York, 1960; A. Maiuri, Arte e civiltà nell'Italia antica, Milan, 1960; EAA, s.v. Malta; D. H. Trump, The Later Prehistory of Malta, ProcPrSoc, XXVII, 1961, pp. 253–62; D. H. Trump, The Trefoil Temple at Skorba, ILN, CCXXXIX, 1961, pp. 1144–46. *Punic and Roman periods*: C. A. Barbaro, Degli avanzi di alcuni antichissimi edifizi scoperti a Malta l'anno 1768, Malta, 1794; O. Bres, Malta antica illustrata, Rome, 1816; A. A. Caruana, Ancient Pagan Tombs and Christian Cemeteries in the Island of Malta, Malta, 1898; A. A. Caruana, The Crypt of St. Agatha, Malta, 1899; T. Ashby, Roman Malta, JRS, IV, 1915, pp. 28–80; R. Paribeni, Malta, Bergamo, 1930; T. Zammit, The Maltese Rock-cut Tombs of the Late Pre-Christian Type, Valletta Mus. B., 1931, pp. 103–31; T. Zammit, Roman Villa and Thermae at Ghajn Tuffieha, Valletta Mus. B., 1931, pp. 56–64; C. Psaila, Avanzi archeologici della primitiva comunità cristiana maltese, Ann. della Diocesi di Malta, 1933, pp. 267–74; C. Zammit, I triclini funebri nelle catacombe di Malta, Ann. della Diocesi di Malta, 1934, pp. 129–42; P. C. Sestieri, Sculture maltesi, Arch. storico di Malta, X, 1939, pp. 153–63, 231–38; A. Ferrua, Le catacombe di Malta, Civ. cattolica, 1949, 3, pp. 505–15. *Medieval and modern periods*: S. Zerafa, Discorso sulla storia artistica di Malta, Malta, 1850; L'arte (bimonthly periodical), Malta, 1862–64; C. Promis, Biografie di ingegneri militari dal secolo XIV alla metà del XVIII, Turin, 1874; W. H. Tregellas, Historical Sketch of the Defenses of Malta, J. Royal Engineers, III, 1879, pp. 185–211; G. Calleja, Works of Art in the Churches of Malta, Malta, 1881; A. Ferris, Memorie dell'inclito Ordine Gerosolimitano, Malta, 1885; A. J. Flower, Notes on Renaissance Architecture in Malta, J. Royal Inst. of Br. Arch., 3d ser., V, 1897–98, pp. 25–48; J. Crocker, History of the Fortifications of Malta, Malta, 1920; A. Mifsud, La milizia e le torri antiche di Malta, Arch. Melitense, IV, 1920, pp. 55–100; V. Mariani, Mattia Preti a Malta, Rome, 1929; F. Ashford, Caravaggio's Stay in Malta. BM, LXVII, 1935, pp. 168–74; A. A. Bernardy, Antoine de Favray pittore e cavaliere a Malta, Arch. storico di Malta, I, 1936–37; pp. 58–64; G. C. King, Mattia Preti, AB, XVIII, 1936, pp. 371–86; V. Bonello, La chiesa siculo-bizantina di S. Ciro, Malta, 1937; E. Sammut, Profili di artisti maltesi, Malta, 1937; J. Pratt, Fortifications of Malta, Arch. Rev., LXXXVI, 1939, pp. 37–38; J. B. Ward Perkins, Mediaeval and Early Renaissance Architecture in Malta, AntJ, XXII, 1942, pp. 167–75; H. Braun, An Introduction to Maltese Architecture, Valletta, 1944; H. Braun, Works of Art in Malta, London, 1946; J. Fleming, Malta: Naval Base of the Baroque, Arch. Rev., XCIX, 1946, pp. 169–76; A. St. B. Harrison and R. P. S. Hubbard, Maltese Vernacular, Arch. Rev., CV, 1949, pp. 77–80; H. Luke, Malta, London, 1949 (2d ed., 1960); E. Sammut, Caravaggio in Malta, Malta, 1949; V. Bonello, Il primo architetto dell'Ordine in Malta, Melita h., I, 2, 1952; J. Q. Hughes, The Influence of Italian Mannerism upon Maltese Architecture, Melita h., II, 1, 1953; E. Sammut, Art in Malta, Malta, 1953; J. Q. Hughes, The Building of Malta During the Period of the Knights of St. John of Jerusalem, 1530–1795, London, 1956 (bibliog.); V. Bonello and J. A. Cauchi, L'arte sacra a Malta, Floriana (Malta), 1960.

ART CENTERS. Valletta. Capital of the Maltese Islands, Valletta is situated on the northern coast of Malta, at the tip of a peninsula that lies between Grand Harbour and Marsamuscetto (Marsamxett) Harbour. The city was founded in 1566 by Grand Master Jean de la Valette, from whom the name is derived. The fortifications were designed and built by Francesco Laparelli (1521–70) of Cortona, who also prepared the plan of the city and began its construction, assisted by the Maltese architect Gerolamo Cassar. Valletta, which has streets intersecting at right angles, is one of the earliest examples of modern city planning. The massive fortifications toward the interior, designed by Pietro Paolo Floriani of Macerata, have high sentry towers and deep moats and give the city its characteristic appearance. Valletta has many monumental buildings and dwellings of great architectural merit. The Cathedral of St. John, which contains a number of important works of art, is a fine example of Italian architecture of the late 16th and 17th centuries. It was built in 1573–77 in the Italian mannerist idiom by Gerolamo Cassar, whose local background and training are evident in certain elements and details of the design, such as the slightly pointed arches and the absence of any projecting entablature. In addition to the ceiling decoration by Mattia Preti and the work of Mazzuoli mentioned above, the church contains altarpieces by Mattia Preti, the great tapestries of Peter Paul Rubens depicting scenes from the life of Christ, and paintings by Caravaggio, Andrea Sabatini (called "Andrea da Salerno"), Andrea Piccinelli (called "Andrea del Brescianino"), Matteo Pérez de Alesio, Francesco Potenzano, Stefano Pieri, Lionello Spada, Palma Giovane, Giovanni Francesco Romanelli, Agostino Massucci, and Antoine de Favray. There are also sculptures by Antonello Gaggini, Alessandro Algardi, Massimiliano Soldani (Benzi), Vincenzo Pacetti, Pierre Puget, and Jean Jacques Pradier. The floor is inlaid with about four hundred sections of colored marble depicting the coats of arms, emblems, and deeds of some of the Knights, many of whom belonged to the highest-ranking nobility of Europe. Cassar built several other churches in Valletta and Auberges, or Inns, of the various components, or "tongues" (*Langues*), of the Order. The Auberge d'Italie, a severely styled edifice, is the most noteworthy; built in 1574 and enlarged in 1683, it now houses the Law Courts. The Auberge de Provence, built in 1575, was also expanded later. It is now the National Museum. The imposing Auberge de Castille et León was rebuilt in 1744 by Domenico Cachia. The Palace of the Grand Master (now the Governor's Palace), which was begun about 1572 by Cassar and remodeled in the mid-18th century, survived the despoilments of the 19th century; it contains tapestries, furniture, ceramics, a fine quez), A. Palombi, Vincenzo Hyzler, and Giacomo Ceci. The Jesuit church of St. Mary, by Cassar, contains paintings by Pietro Novelli (called "Il Monrealese"), Antonio Catalano, Pasinelli, Vincenzo Hyzler, and Giuseppe Bonnici. The Church of St. Francis, which was built in 1600 and remodeled in 1681, has been altered and restored in recent times; it contains paintings by Filippo Paladini, Mattia Preti, Pietro Gagliardi, and Gennaro Calì. The Church of St. Augustine, designed by Domenico Cachia, contains some good 19th-century paintings. The large altarpiece in the sacristy is by Lionello Spada.

Valletta, development of the city. Principal monuments: (*a*) Palace of the Grand Master; (*b*) Library of the Knights; (*c*) Cathedral of St. John; (*d*) Auberge d'Italie; (*e*) Auberge de Provence (National Museum); (*f*) Palazzo Parisio; (*g*) Church of Our Lady of Victory; (*h*) Church of St. Augustine; (*i*) Auberge d'Aragon; (*j*) Auberge de Bavière; (*k*) Archbishop's Palace; (*l*) Auberge de Castille et León; (*m*) St. Paul's Anglican Cathedral; (*n*) St. Elmo Fort; (*o*) Ricasoli Fort; (*p*) St. Angelo Fort; (*q*) Manoel Fort; (*r*) Tigne Fort.

armory, and a number of paintings. The rooms were decorated by Matteo Pérez de Alesio, Filippo Paladini, and Nicola Nasoni (or Nasini). The statue of Neptune in the courtyard has been attributed to Giambologna but may perhaps be the work of Leone Leoni. There are many churches of great architectural interest and rich in works of art, the most noteworthy being the Gesù, designed by Filippo Bonamici of Lucca, in the style of the Counter Reformation. It contains paintings attributed to Baldassare Peruzzi and by Romanelli del Battistiello, Mattia Preti, Louis Finson, Romanelli, and Stefano Erardi. Another interesting and richly decorated church is St. Paul's, which has a wood statue by Melchiore Gafà and paintings by Filippo Paladini, Antoine de Favray, Giuseppe Velasco (or Velas-

Among the smaller churches are the Church of All Souls, which has paintings by Mattia Preti, and the Church of St. Catherine of Italy, which contains paintings by Mattia Preti and Benedetto Luti. The Church of St. Ursula has altarpieces by Mario Minniti, Mattia Preti, and Gennaro Calì.

The Library building was designed by the Catanese architect Stefano Ittar, whose rather precious decorative style anticipates neoclassicism. A characteristic feature of Maltese architecture is the overhanging "gallery," of Oriental derivation, which is an element that was introduced by the Knights and incorporated into the designs of Italian architects. The few structures built recently are sober and sometimes elegant. The most interesting contemporary monument is the large fountain at the main gate of the city by the sculptor Vincenzo Apap.

The National Museum has an archaeological section, a numismatic collection, and a painting gallery with works by Tintoretto, Mattia Preti, Salvator Rosa, Alessandro Magnasco, and Giovanni Battista Tiepolo.

The surrounding towns and villages are generally dominated by large parish churches. The parish church of St. Mary in Attard is a good example of High Renaissance architecture; it was designed by the Maltese architect Tommaso Dingli. Also at Attard is the St. Anton Palace, the summer residence first of the Grand Master and later of the Governor. It was begun in 1623 and has a garden in the Italian style. At Birkirkara the Church of the Annunciation (begun by Vittorio Cassar; completed by Dingli) is partly in ruins. The village is dominated by the parish church of St. Helena, begun in 1727. The churches in Naxxar, Zebbug, Qormi, Siggiewi, and Luqa are interesting both for their plan and interior decoration. Zurrieq, a large and very old village, has a church containing many paintings by Mattia Preti, who took refuge in the village during an outbreak of the plague in 1676. In the garden of the parish house there are remains of several ancient buildings of different periods. The parish churches of Balzan and Lija are notable for their elegance. In Zabbar, just outside the fortifications built by Antonio Maurizio Valperga, there is a church with a well-articulated façade. The village of Mosta has a large circular parish church, built in neoclassic style by Grognet de Vassé in the first half of the 19th century. Many of these towns and villages were rebuilt extensively after World War II, some of them in a rather pretentious manner and not always in keeping with the character of the island.

BIBLIOG. A. Ferris, Descrizione storica delle chiese di Malta e Gozo, Malta, 1866; V. Bonello, La chiesa di S. Giovanni, qualche precisazione, Ann. della Diocesi di Malta, 1934, pp. 143–58; V. Bonello, Old Valletta, Valletta Mus. B., 1934, pp. 159–64; J. Pratt, Valletta and Its Architecture, The Builder, 1941, pp. 221–23, 243–45; A. St. B. Harrison and R. P. S. Hubbard, Valletta, Malta, 1945; R. J. L. Wilkinson, The Auberge de Provence, Malta, 1945; E. Sammut, The Co-Cathedral of St. John, Malta, 1950; H. P. Scicluna, The Church of St. John in Valletta, Rome, 1955; V. Bonello, La Chiesa Conventuale di S. Giovanni, Melita h., II, 1956, pp. 48–54; V. Bonello, La Chiesa di S. Giovanni a Malta, Brutium, XXXVI, 1957, pp. 1–5; V. F. Denaro, Houses in Merchants Street, Valletta, Melita h., II, 1958, pp. 158–71; V. F. Denaro, Houses in Kingsway and Old Bakery Street, Valletta, Melita h., II, 1959, pp. 201–15.

Hal Saflieni. This locality near the village of Pawla acquired considerable importance in 1902, when a rock-cut neolithic hypogeum, which had been used for religious ceremonies, was accidentally discovered. Built on three levels, probably over a period of several centuries, the hypogeum is a complex labyrinth of passages, galleries, connecting chambers, and niches, some with doors and ceilings painted in red spiral patterns, as in the oracle chamber (or holy of holies). Several of the chambers are carved to imitate megalithic masonry, façades, corbels, and trilithons. In the hypogeum were found weapons, flint and obsidian tools, pottery with geometric incised decoration, and statuettes in terra cotta and stone, especially female and steatopygous fertility figures. The material is now in the National Museum in Valletta.

Hal Tarxien. This site, not far from Pawla, has an interesting complex of three neolithic temples. These temples are uncovered, but it is not known whether or not they were originally roofed. They consist of a number of interconnecting ellipsoid chambers that are especially noteworthy for their megalithic construction: large, dressed, and carefully joined limestone slabs placed either horizontally or vertically. The decoration consists of reliefs of floral and zoomorphic designs. On a hill above the temple complex there is a Bronze Age cremation necropolis which has given its name to the Bronze Age Tarxien Cemetery culture (ca. 1550–1350 B.C.).

Mdina (Medina; Notabile; Città Vecchia; Melita). A Roman municipium at the time of the Empire and later the capital of the island until the arrival of the Knights of St. John in 1530, this city is still enclosed within the Byzantine walls, which have survived intact, although they were partly restored in the 18th century. It looks like a medieval Sicilian city — with its narrow streets, monasteries with high windowless walls, and houses with graceful galleries of double-arched windows on the upper floors — except for its massive baroque Cathedral and a few 18th-century palaces. The well-preserved Falzan Palace is a noteworthy example of Sicilian-Norman architecture. The palace of the Banca Giuratale has a flavor that anticipates Piranesi's work. The Palace of the Grand Master, with balconies and an imposing portal, was built in the early 18th century. The Cathedral, designed by Lorenzo Gafà, was built in 1697 to replace the Sicilian-Norman cathedral built by Roger II in the 12th century and destroyed in the earthquake of 1693. It contains paintings by 15th-century Sicilian painters, by Mario Minniti, Mattia Preti, Francesco and Vincenzo Manno, and by the 19th-century artists Domenico Bruschi, Francesco Grandi, and Pietro Gagliardi. There are also a crucifix by Fra Innocenzo da Petralia and sculptures by Moschetti and Giuseppe Valenti. The baptismal font, the doors of the sacristy, and the choir stalls (partly restored by Preti) came from the old cathedral. Attached to the Cathedral is a museum containing illuminated manuscripts, drawings, prints, and paintings, including a 16th-century Catalan-Sicilian polyptych. The Church of

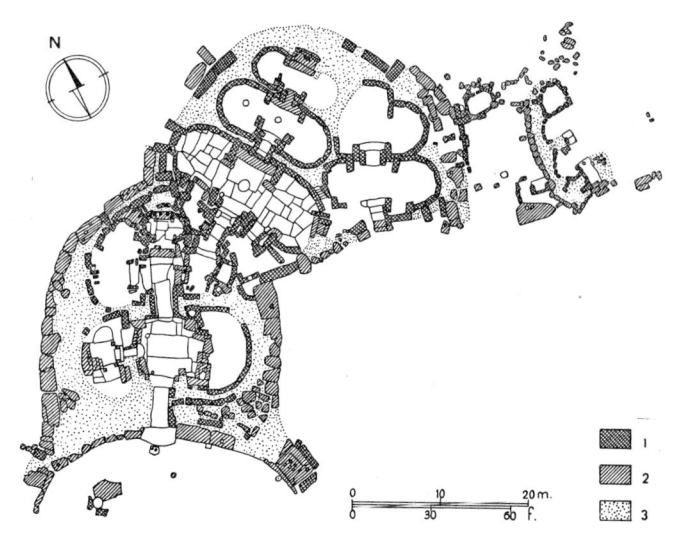

Hal Tarxien, plan of the neolithic temples I, II, and III. Key: (1) Outer walls of vertical stone slabs; (2) inner walls of horizontal blocks, altars, bases, and seats; (3) rubble and earth filling the space between the inner and outer walls (from Ceschi).

St. Benedict contains two panels of a polyptych by Salvo di Antonio (1511) and an altarpiece with a Madonna and saints by Mattia Preti.

In the neighboring suburb of Rabat are the remains of a Roman villa, now housing the Museum of Antiquities. The church of the Minorites contains a *Madonna and Child* and a *Deposition* by Antonello de Saliba and a *Madonna and Child* by Antonello Gaggini (1504). The parish church of St. Paul and the Sanctuary of St. Publius have a single façade. The church contains a *Madonna and Saints* and other paintings by Mattia Preti, works by Stefano Erardi and Francesco Zahra, and a 16th-century wooden crucifix, brought to Malta from Rhodes. Under the church is the Grotto of St. Paul, a highly venerated shrine that was originally a Roman prison where St. Paul is believed to have been held in captivity for three months in the winter of A.D. 60–61. South of Rabat are catacombs with underground chambers that contain circular tables for funeral repasts, couches for reclining, and niched graves. Remains of painted decoration in Byzantine-Romanesque style have been found in the underground chapel in the catacomb of St. Agatha. In the area are the underground oratories of Tal Virtù and the Abbatija tad-Dejr (L-Abatija tad-Deir), which resemble Basilian lauras and retain traces of paintings.

At Boschetto, near Rabat, is the Verdala Palace (built 1581–95), with a chapel containing paintings by Mattia Preti. South of Boschetto stands the 18th-century summer palace of the Inquisitor.

BIBLIOG. V. Bonello, La Notabile, Le vie del mondo, VI, 1938, pp. 591–609.

Vittoriosa. Across from Valletta, on Grand Harbour, is Vittoriosa, originally called Borgo del Castello. Its present name commemorates the defeat of the Turks by the Knights in 1565. During World War II it was heavily bombed. One of the buildings that survived the damage is the Inquisitor's Palace, built at the end of the 16th century and incorporating the 15th-century Castellania with its Gothic cloister. The large church of St. Lawrence, rebuilt by Lorenzo Gafà from an older Sicilian-Norman church, contains paintings by Filippo Paladini, Alessandro Turchi (called "l'Orbetto"), and Mattia Preti. Adjoining the church is a small but interesting museum. The fortifications of Vittoriosa and the neighboring towns of Cospicua (or Burmola) and Senglea are the work of Vincenzo Maculano da Firenzuola and the Piedmontese engineer Antonio Maurizio Valperga. The latter built the Ricasoli Fort (1670), with a monumental gateway that guards the entrance to the harbor. Maculano's fortifications (the Cottonera and Firenzuola), also with massive gates, enclose the three towns within a vast system of defensive walls.

Gozo (Gaudos, Gaulus). A lesser island of the archipelago, Gozo is similar in character to Malta. In Roman times it was a municipium. Near Victoria, in the center of the island, is the ancient citadel, a picturesque medieval town surrounded by high walls dating from antiquity. Set into the wall at the main gate is a great marble block with fragments of a Roman inscription from the Antonine period. The citadel, which now consists almost entirely of ruins and of small cultivated plots, encloses a number of interesting buildings; it is dominated by the majestic Cathedral (designed by Lorenzo Gafà), with a 17th-century façade, and includes the ancient Law Courts, the prisons, the Gozo Museum, a few houses of the Sicilian-Norman period, the ruins of the Bishop's Palace, and some arches in Sicilian-Moresque style. Victoria, the chief town of the island, which lies at the foot of the citadel, has a number of elegant houses with terraces and balconies in finely carved stone. In the parish church are paintings by Mattia Preti.

East of Victoria, near the village of Xaghra (Caccia, or Sciara), are the remains of a large neolithic temple complex, the Ggantija ("Giant's Tower"), which consists of two separate temples surrounded by a common outer wall. The larger (south) temple, built of enormous limestone blocks, is probably the earlier of the two. Nearby are the remains of the so-called "Grotto of Calypso," a huge pile of fallen rocks that originally formed the roof of the cavern. There are some traces of a flight of steps carved from the rock. On the In-Nuffara hill ruins of a Bronze Age village (14th cent. B.C.) have come to light.

BIBLIOG. A. Ferris, Descrizione storica delle chiese di Malta e Gozo, Malta, 1866.

Vincenzo BONELLO

Illustrations: 3 figs. in text.

MAMELUKE ART. The artistic activity that took place in Egypt and Syria under the Mameluke dynasty (1250–1517) was brought about by a religious upheaval: the return to Sunnite orthodoxy after the Scythian interlude under the Fatimids (see FATIMID ART). The effect of this reversion was a renewed interest in religious art and, particularly, architecture; and there was at the same time a remarkable increase in richness and variety of crafts and of the minor arts. The entire period was one of great productivity in the arts, and represents an individual and important aspect of the art of Islam (q.v.).

SUMMARY. Cultural components of Mameluke art (col. 419). Architecture (col. 420): *Religious architecture; Civil architecture; Residential architecture; Architectural elements and features.* Decorative arts (col. 425): *The art of the book; Ceramics; Glass; Metalwork; Rugs and textiles; Woodwork; Ornamentation.*

CULTURAL COMPONENTS OF MAMELUKE ART. The mamelukes (Ar., *mamlūk*, slave or captive) were slaves brought by the Ayyubids, and later by the Mamelukes themselves, from Turkistan, Transoxiana, Persia, Caucasia, and other places to serve as soldiers. They rose to power when, with the death of Sultan aṣ-Ṣāliḥ Najm ad-Dīn and the assassination of his son, the Ayyubid rule of Egypt was virtually ended. The widow of the sultan, the famous Shagar ad-Durr, was elected queen by the Mamelukes, who had brought about a palace revolt; but she could maintain her position only by marrying one of their number, Aybak, and making him a sultan — the first of the Mameluke dynasty. The rise of the dynasty, which was beset throughout its history by struggles for power from within, was accompanied by serious external threats. Crusading expeditions were a continuing danger from the West, but the greater peril was from the Mongols of Central Asia (see ASIA, CENTRAL; MONGOLIAN ART), who had swept over Persia and Iraq and were preparing to invade Egypt through Syria. The Mameluke rulers, well aware of the menace, checked the spread of the Mongol empire with a decisive victory at Ain Jalut (1260), thus securing Syria and establishing their supremacy.

Many refugees from Persia and Iraq, fleeing the Mongol invasion, settled in Mameluke territories; among these were undoubtedly artists and craftsmen who brought with them their native traditions. Evidences of their influence can be seen in inlaid metalwork and enamel-painted glass, which, though its origin has not been fully established, was prized during this period. At the same time Chinese and Central Asian influences were reaching the Mameluke countries, either directly, through exchange of commerce, or indirectly, by way of Persia; these influences can be clearly seen in the decorative motifs of certain Mameluke ceramics. Diplomatic and commercial relations between Egypt and some of the countries of Europe, continuous waves of emigration and pilgrimage by Moslems of the West, and Byzantine and Hellenistic survivals in Syria, too, all made their contributions; but foreign influences, although undeniably important, were minor factors in the larger development of Mameluke art, which was primarily religious in nature. This art evolved locally from the Ayyubid tradition — itself an offshoot of Fatimid art (q.v.), exhibiting a highly individual character in the composition of architectural masses and elements, and also in decoration, in which the depiction of the human figure was almost entirely abandoned in favor of calligraphic and geometric ornamentation.

ARCHITECTURE. The dominant influence in Mameluke architecture was religion, and the majority of the existing monuments are of a religious character: mosques, madrasahs (theological colleges), khankahs (*khānaqāhs*, monasteries), and minor buildings such as the kuttab (or *maktab*), a primary school where boys learned reading, writing, and recitations from the Koran. Most madrasahs and khankahs had mausoleums for their founders attached; these were sometimes built separately.

There were also, however, many structures serving civil purposes erected during this period: hospitals, public baths, bridges, aqueducts, animal drinking-troughs, and so on. Residential architecture was well represented by large and small private houses, the *rab'* (tenement block), and the *wakāla* (Pers., *khān*; hostel or storehouse). One well-preserved example of military architecture of the period survives: the fort of Qāit Bey, in Alexandria, the façade of which exhibits medieval European influences.

Religious architecture. Mosques, especially the congregational ones, were designed mainly as houses of prayer but were sometimes used for teaching. Madrasahs were colleges of religious instruction providing living accommodation for students and teachers and often including space for a kuttab on an upper floor. They also served the function of a mosque in that they were used for prayer by the college residents and the people of the neighborhood. Khankahs served almost the same purpose as madrasahs, except that the residents were Sufis — men, most of them unmarried, who devoted themselves to worship and the deeper teachings and philosophy of Islam.

Mameluke mosques were constructed according to either of two principal plans: the traditional, or *riwāq*, plan; and the cruciform, or liwan, plan, which was used mostly for madrasah-mosques. The *riwāq* plan consists of a four-sided open court (*ṣaḥn*), on each side of which is a series of aisles known as a *riwāq*. The *riwāq* of the *qibla* side (the side oriented toward Mecca) is deeper, having more aisles than the others. An early example of the *riwāq* plan is the Mosque of al-Ẓāhir Baybars (1266–69; VIII, FIG. 341a), which consists of a large open court or *ṣaḥn*, slightly oblong, with a *riwāq* at each side. The *qibla riwāq*, containing the prayer niche, or mihrab, is formed of six aisles parallel to the wall; a square in the center of the three aisles next to the wall was once covered with a dome. Each of the other three *riwāq*s consists of two aisles parallel to its outer wall, but is also cut in half by a transept. The three entrances to the mosque, placed on the axes of the *ṣaḥn*, are of the projecting monumental type, and the main one formerly supported a minaret. The local elements here are the monumental entrance, the transept, and the building material — stone for the outer walls and brick for the arcades. The imported elements are the design of the sanctuary, which probably came from Mayyafariqin in northern Iraq; the buttressed walls, of either Syrian or western Islamic influence; the interlacing frame in the main entrance, which is Syrian; and the small cusps in some of the window grills, which are western Islamic in style. A later example is the Mosque of Sultan al-Mu'ayyad (Cairo, 1415–20) in which there are three aisles in the *qibla riwāq*, parallel to the wall, and two aisles in each of the other three *riwāq*s. The east corner of the building contains the domed mausoleum of the founder, and a remarkable pair of minarets are placed on top of the two towers of the Fatimid Bāb Zuwayla. The angular main entrance (a form of dog-leg) is at the east corner of the main

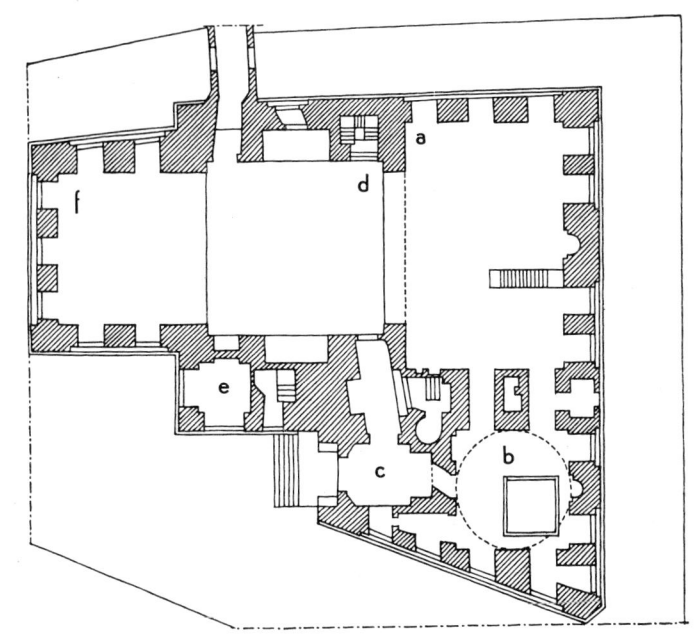

Cairo, plan of madrasah-mosque of Qijmās al-Isḥāqī, 1480–71: (*a*) *qibla* liwan; (*b*) mausoleum; (*c*) vestibule; (*d*) covered *ṣaḥn*; (*e*) *sebīl*; (*f*) liwan.

façade. Some western Islamic influences are exhibited in the ornaments of two stucco blind windows. Connected to the mosque on the northwest side is the bath built by the sultan.

The liwan plan consists of a central open court, usually square, with a wide covered aisle, or liwan, at each side. The full length of the liwan opens onto the court. As the *qibla* liwan is the most important, it is the largest. Mameluke mosques of the pure liwan type are very rare. The mosque of Shaykhū (Cairo, 1349), although basically a liwan plan, is, in fact, a combination of the two types, for each liwan is treated like an arcaded *riwāq*. There is a mausoleum on the south side of the sanctuary, and a minaret rises above the vestibule of the main entrance.

Madrasah-mosques, however, were built exclusively on the liwan plan. A world-famous example is the madrasah-mosque of Sultan Ḥasan (1356–63; PL. 270). Here a vaulted liwan is built on each of the four sides of a large open court, the *qibla* liwan being the largest. The liwans are kept solely for prayer and the corners in between are occupied by four colleges, one for each of the four rites of the Sunnite sect: the Shafiite, the Malikite, the Hanafite, and the Hanbalite. Each college consists of an open small court with a vaulted liwan at one side and rooms above. A huge mausoleum is built behind the *qibla* liwan. The edifice is remarkable for its fine colossal proportions and for the elegance of detail in its architecture and decoration.

In a later, typical, Mameluke example, the madrasah-mosque of Qijmās al-Isḥāqī (1480–81; PL. 270, FIG. 421), the central court is no longer left open but is covered with a wooden ceiling, decorated with painting and gilding, above which is an octagonal skylight. The *qibla* liwan has become a large rectangle parallel to the *qibla* wall; but the opposite liwan retains the old proportions, and the other two have evolved into tall, narrow recesses of shallow depth. The usual elements of the madrasah are present; that is, mausoleum, angular entrance, and *sebīl*.

The madrasah-mosque of Sultan Qalā'ūn (PL. 270) is unusual in that it has only two liwans, a large *qibla* liwan and a smaller one opposite. The other sides of the *ṣaḥn* and the corners are occupied by cells that were used by residents.

The open courts of both *riwāq* and liwan plans were sometimes provided with ablution pavilions in the center.

Khankahs were chiefly built on the liwan plan. The khankah of Baybars al-Gāshankīr (Cairo, 1306–10) consists of an open court, two vaulted liwans, and side halls. The building is provided with several *malqaf*s, or ventilating devices, to catch the cool prevailing wind. The other parts of the building are occupied with cells for the Sufis. A mausoleum is built on the left of the typical angular entrance. The cushion voussoirs in the entrance arch and the acanthus capitals are evidence of Syrian influence.

The khankah of Farag ibn-Barqūq (1400–10) in the group of the Tombs of the Mamelukes, in Cairo, is the largest existing, and is also notable for the two graceful minarets on the northwest façade and the two nearly identical domed mausoleums that flank the *qibla* liwan.

Civil architecture. The Qalā'ūn complex (PL. 270) included a hospital, now in ruins. This building contained wards — quarters, both for men and for women, consisting of cells arranged around courts with fountains in the center; rooms for doctors and assistants; dispensaries; stores and kitchens; and so on.

The Aqueduct of al-Nāṣir Muhammad begins on the Nile with a massive intake tower, hexagonal in plan. Water supplied by underground tunnels was lifted from interior wells by sakiehs (Ar., *sāqiya*), or oxen-driven water wheels. It then flowed through an open channel created by thick walls formed of alternate high pointed arches and stout piers built of rusticated masonry, and the level was further raised by a series of sakiehs and towers until it reached the Citadel of Cairo.

*Sebīl*s, public drinking edifices, are usually attached to madrasahs. An underground cistern supplies a basin in the *sebīl* with water which flows from it down a *salsabīl*, an inclined marble slab carved with decorations, and a channel brings the cooled water to the sill of the outside windows for people to drink from cups. The *sebīl* is usually located at ground level, under an open loggia which is used as a *kuttab*.

Residential architecture. No Mameluke house exists intact, but with the help of Mameluke ruins and houses built on Mameluke traditions surviving from the later Turkish period, it is possible to form an idea of their general design. A typical

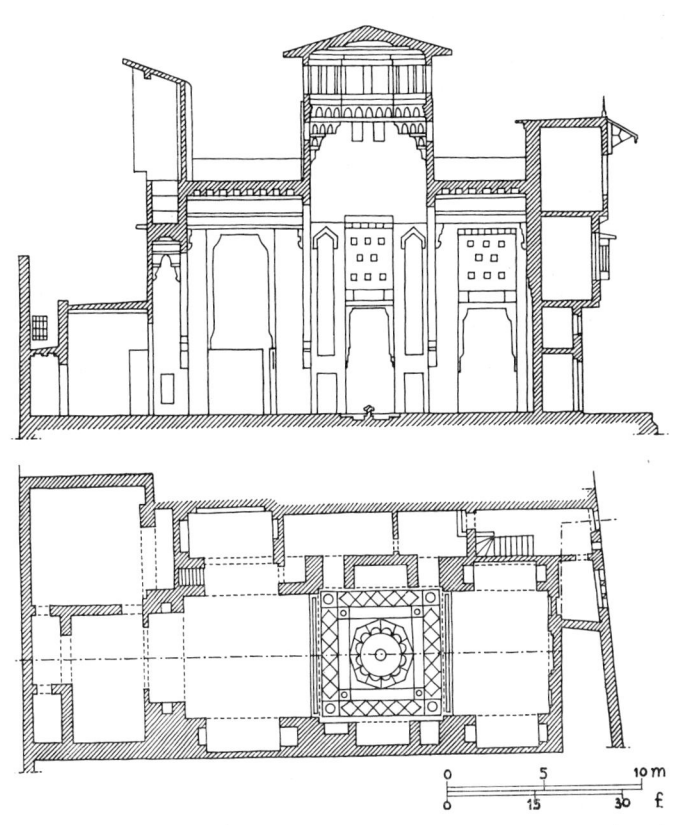

Cairo, Naḥḥāsīn, the *qā'a* (reception hall) of Muḥibb ad-Dīn, 1350: (*above*) section of the building; (*below*) plan.

Mameluke house (FIGS. 422, 423) was a small labyrinth of rooms arranged in levels around a central court that provided light and air. The main reception area was a great hall, or *qāʿa*, formed by a central square space with a skylight. The *qāʿa* often contained a marble mosaic fountain. Two liwans, slightly above floor level, were on opposite sides of this central space, the total height of which was greater than one story; and connected to it was a loggia, or *maqʿad* (PL. 274), overlooking the court and open to it in order to catch the prevailing cool winds. The women's quarters were secluded from the reception hall for men, but connected to it by corridors and stairs. Female members

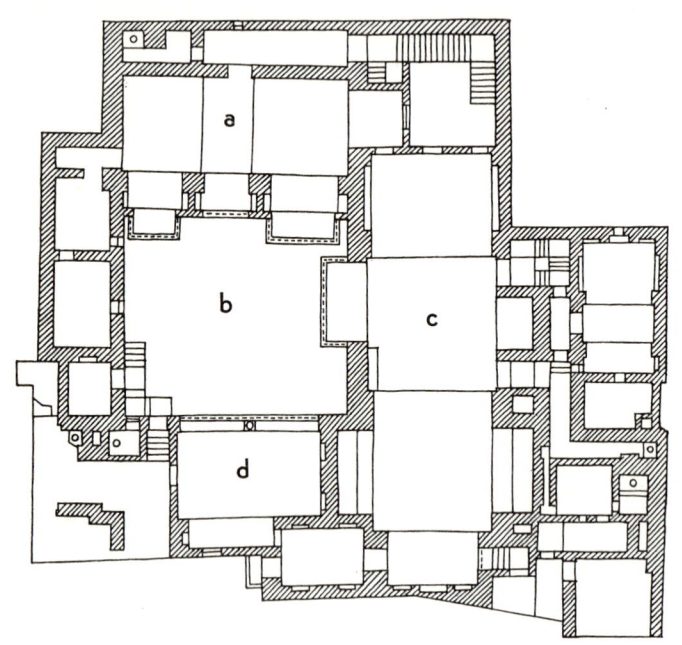

Cairo, plan of the house of Zainab Khātūn: (*a*) The *qāʿa* (reception hall) of the harem; (*b*) main courtyard; (*c*) reception hall for men; (*d*) *maqʿad* (loggia).

of the household could observe festivities held in the *qāʿa* through *mashrabiya*s (grates, or wooden latticework) in the upper floors. *Mashrabiya*s were extensively used, as they assured privacy while admitting light and air. Some houses included bathrooms (preceded by antechambers and supplied with hot water); and stables, storehouses, wells, and cisterns were common features. Building materials included dressed stone for the main walls and façades; and rubble, brick, and wood for the secondary parts of the house. Marble was used for floors and dadoes of main units.

The *rabʿ*, or tenement block for the poorer classes, consisted of a large open court surrounded by storerooms on the ground floor and, above, by corridors leading to apartments. *Khān*s and *wakāla*s were of similar design, but the ground floors contained stores and shops, and the apartments above were usually let to merchants. Each apartment in the *wakāla* of Qāit Bey at Bāb an-Naṣr (PL. 274) consisted of two floors. The lower contained a *qāʿa* with a liwan overlooking the street through a small *mashrabiya*, and on the same floor were a small sleeping cell, kitchen, and lavatory. On the upper floor was a room overlooking the *qāʿa*.

Architectural elements and features. Mameluke religious buildings have various elements and features in common. Façades, in general, are simple and rather flat, with scarcely any bold projections. Most have broad surfaces with slightly sunken panels in series containing rows of arched windows, single or coupled, usually with bull's-eye openings at the top. Windows were filled with decorative stucco grilles and colored glass that gave to the interiors a dim and peaceful effect. The hoods of the façade panels are composed of stepped rows of stalactites, or *muqarna*s (see below), which bring forward the recessed surfaces to the front plane. Main stalactite portals, of Syrian origin, are seldom projecting but consist chiefly of porches set within deep, richly patterned recesses and stepped rows of stalactites enclosed within hooded cusps. Later, courses of alternate colors of stone or marble came into favor for façades, and curved and flat arches were often constructed with colored voussoirs and joggles of elaborate design.

Residential façades were also of plain design. Screened windows and projecting balconies of various sizes and shapes, some of which contained small, elegant receptacles for cooling ceramic water vessels, or *qulla*s, served to break the monotony of the flat surfaces.

Minarets were important elements of religious architecture. Two types were characteristic of the Mameluke period — the *mabkhara*, so called because of the supposed resemblance of its crown to the cover of a *mabkhara*, or incense burner; and the *qulla*, the topmost part of which is shaped like the upper half of the classic water vessel. The *mabkhara* minaret (VIII, PL. 162) consists of a high square base surmounted either by an octagonal pavilion or, more often, by a short shaft, generally octagonal, above which is the top pavilion crowned with a small ribbed cupola (the *mabkhara*). An interior spiral staircase is lighted by openings set in sunken panels with a variety of decorative hoods. The top pavilion is usually a circular shell cut by slender openings. Base, shaft, and pavilion are each crowned by projecting stepped rows of stalactites skillfully arranged in attractive patterns of pendants and alcoves, and the crowns of the base and shaft carry platforms from which the muezzin, or *muʾadhdhin*, chants the call to prayer.

The *qulla* minaret (PLS. 270, 271), purely Mameluke in origin, first appeared in the early part of the 14th century. Its cubiform base, the top corners of which are chamfered or molded, is surmounted by an octagonal shaft, above which there is sometimes placed another, polygonal or circular, shaft. The topmost part consists either of eight graceful columns, sometimes coupled, or of a circular shell pierced by slender openings. It is crowned, in either case, by the *qulla*. All *qulla* tops have two or more bronze finials of torus moldings carrying crescents that face Mecca. Toward the end of the Mameluke period *qulla* tops acquired curious shapes, as can be seen in two in Cairo: the minaret of Sultan al-Ghūri in the Mosque of al-Azhar and that of the Mosque of Qāni Bey, both of which have connected twin pavilions, square in plan and topped by *qulla*s. All Mameluke minarets were built of stone, except for a few early *mabkhara*s of brick construction.

Stalactites are among the most fascinating elements of Islamic architecture developed since the 11th century. Probably originating in the multiplication of small squinched arches, they evolved during the Mameluke period into a variety of wonderful designs, both simple and complex. Stalactites were used as decorative structural elements wherever possible, especially in corbeling (see also ISLAM, col. 349).

Arches are exceedingly various in form: there are the pointed type, struck from two, three, or four centers; the half round; the keel; and the triangular, the straight, the cusped, and the molded (PL. 272). Voussoirs were mostly of plain masonry, sometimes joggled and, in a few cases, decorated with cushions, cusps, and so on. The horseshoe form, which made its appearance and spread throughout Egypt in the early Mameluke period, evidently came from western Islam; it was utilized for pointed and half-round arches. Arches of open arcades were provided with tie beams for reinforcement at the springing line.

Columns of marble and granite were greatly prized, as they have a greater bearing capacity than masonry. Sultans and emirs obtained them, usually by purchase, from older buildings for use in their own monuments. Often a variety of capitals, shafts, and bases of disparate types and sizes were clustered together, and in order to form columns of equal height it was necessary to shorten shafts or add pedestals. Columns of pure Islamic design, however, were also used. One type, evolved from designs of earlier periods, has a bulb-shaped capital and base (PL. 272) and in outline is an upright *cyma recta* acting as a zone of transition between the square abacus and the circular or octagonal shaft. Another form used for capitals, and sometimes for bases, was the stalactite. This seems to have been a Mameluke invention and varied according to the number and form of stalactites used. Capitals bearing the classic acanthus motif were also used: an example can be seen in the entrance to the khankah of al-Gāshankīr. It is unlikely that these capitals were taken from older buildings, as they seem to be designed expressly for the space they occupy. A survival of Hellenistic influence emanating from Syria seems to be a much more likely explanation of the motif. The shafts of Mameluke columns, circular or octagonal in form, are sometimes devoid of ornament and sometimes covered with arabesques, interlacings, zigzags, helicoidal flutes, or grooves.

The mimbar (PL. 272; VIII, PL. 88), a raised platform from which the imam delivered the Friday sermon, or *khutbah*, was also used for announcing official orders and reading documents of public interest. Mimbars were generally made of wood and portable, though marble was sometimes used. They were entered through a framed door opening onto a flight of about ten steps that led to the platform. A pavilion above was supported by four columns that carried molded arches, and above these rose a *qulla* with a bronze finial. Decoration varied according to the material used in construction: wood was decorated almost exclusively in star patterns, but various designs were used for marble.

A feature of religious edifices is the mihrab, or prayer niche, a semicircular alcove on the interior *qibla* wall that directs worshipers toward Mecca. In the mihrab the outer arches of the semidome are carried by columns placed in recessed nooks flanking the niche. Simple examples have stucco decorations, but more complex ones are decorated with rich designs in marble and have joggled voussoirs, panels, and friezes patterned in fine mosaics, and arcades set on blue ceramic columns. Glass mosaic was sometimes used for the hood and spandrels, evidently as a result of Syrian influence.

Domes were used to cover tombs. Though they were all, to a degree, pointed, individual forms varied. Until the 14th century most domes were plain inside and ribbed outside (PL. 271); later, when brick was replaced by stone, the exteriors were covered with zigzag, star, and other geometrical patterns, sometimes combined with arabesques, the chief decorative motif of the late period (PL. 273; VIII, PL. 162). The drum, pierced with windows, is usually circular and of the same diameter as the dome, thus increasing the height of the cylindrical part. Occasionally the dome projected beyond the drum, resting on corbeled stalactites, and was reminiscent of the bulbous forms of Persian domes. Like minarets, domes had bronze finials.

The domed roofing system was more or less reserved for tomb construction, but brick or stone vaulted roofs were used for madrasahs, mosques, and khankahs during the early period of Mameluke architecture and for vestibules, corridors, storehouses, tunnels, stables, and the like throughout the period. These roofs employed tunnel and cross vaults, usually pointed, but during the last half of the 15th century a fanlike cross vault began to be used.

Flat wooden ceilings in many fine designs were constructed for *riwāq*s, liwans, reception halls, and other rooms. One type consisted of a series of joists, rectangular at the ends and with rounded or chamfered undersides — the transition being effected by stalactites. The space between the joists was either filled by stalactites or divided into shallow panels of different shapes. Rectangular corbels supported the joists, which surmounted panels of friezes alternating with stalactites. These ceilings were usually painted and gilded in geometric and floral patterns and were sometimes decorated with inscriptions in relief. Another system involved covering the ceiling with planks, upon which were nailed colored and gilded ornamental patterns, and coffers. A third ceiling design, resembling a honeycomb, was constructed by means of a series of octagonal coffers with gilded and painted decoration — geometrical, floral, and epigraphical.

DECORATIVE ARTS. *The art of the book.* Certain illustrated manuscripts, copied and dated in Cairo, suggest that a Mameluke school of painting had once been developed in Egypt. These illustrations exhibit the traditions of the Baghdad school of painting, and yet they contain clear evidence of Mameluke influence. Manuscripts having some traits in common with those mentioned above can thus be provisionally attributed to the same school. It is also interesting to learn that illustrated playing cards were used in the period. Calligraphy (q.v.) and illumination of manuscripts (see MINIATURES AND ILLUMINATION), especially copies of the Koran, became a favorite activity of artists. Very fine specimens, some of great size, are exhibited in the Egyptian Library in Cairo. The opening pages are often elaborately decorated with geometrical and floral ornaments, gilded and painted in attractive colors. Sura titles, written mostly in Kufic script, and the text of the verses in beautiful Naskhi script are alike set on profusely decorated backgrounds. It was customary for valuable texts to be enclosed within bindings of comparable beauty, and the principal material for this purpose was leather, patterned with blind tooling and stamped floral and geometrical ornament. In some cases the designs were composed of a central medallion with arabesques cut on colored backgrounds. The *doublures* usually bore stamped arabesques (VI, PL. 414).

Ceramics. Ceramics of the Mameluke period fall into two main groups. The first, made of local clay which provides a thick, dark brown body, is covered with a transparent lead glaze. The designs were mainly Naskhi inscriptions of names, titles, and good wishes combined with geometrical ornaments and arabesques of the conventional type. Bird and animal motifs were also employed, sometimes exhibiting exceptional vigor, but human figures were rarely used. Blazons of high officials were frequently represented; these resemble somewhat the heraldic shields of medieval Europe. The second group of ceramics is made of a paste derived from a vitreous composition of ground quartz and white clay and was produced from the beginning of the 12th century. This group includes a type of ceramic ware with polychrome geometrical patterns that is attributed to the second half of the 15th century. Contemporary with this style is another, featuring human figures and faces, animals, and birds. The colors are black, blue, red, and sometimes green. Fragments and wasters of copper luster painting on dark-blue backgrounds have been found at Fostat. These and other pieces believed to come from Syria indicate that this technique (PL. 275) was not abandoned in the early Mameluke period.

A well-known category of the second group is the so-called "Sultanabad" type, in which decoration consists mainly of a central animal or bird figure on a crowded background of plant elements — lotus, trefoil, leaf forms, and so on. Though such motifs were originally Asiatic, the main influence was Persian. The colors under the glaze are tints and shades of green and, rarely, of blue, with outlines drawn in black. This category is attributed to the first half of the 14th century. In the 15th century ceramics with designs in cobalt became predominant, and many pieces of this type bear signatures of the great artists of the Mameluke period — Ghaibī, at-Taurīzī, and Ghazāl. In these pieces backgrounds are clearer and figures more elegant.

Glass. Mameluke glass (see also GLASS) achieved universal fame, owing to the technique of decorating with colored enamel paints and gold. This technique began to spread in Egypt and Syria at the end of the 13th century, but its origin has not yet been established. Enameled glass reached its zenith in the 14th century, during which most of these delicate pieces were produced. Cups, plates, bottles, vase-shaped lamps, and jewelry were among the chief products (VI, PL. 227). Designs consisted of bands and medallions filled with Naskhi formulas of good wishes and with stylized or naturalistic floral motifs. Human and animal figures are very rarely seen on lamps but occur frequently on other products. Such figures were influenced by the Seljuk style of painting (see SELJUK ART) on ceramics and manuscripts. Enamel colors were white, yellow, green, blue, and tomato red. Gold was used for outlines, edges, or backgrounds. In the 15th century glasswork began to decline in quality, and centers of glass manufacture produced only inferior imitations of Mameluke work.

Metalwork. Various metalwork objects were executed in iron, copper, bronze, and, in particular, brass. Hanging lamps of assorted shapes — pyramidal, polygonal, and vase-shaped —

were decorated with incised and perforated designs and provided with pendent glass cups containing oil and wicks. Brass candlesticks of typical Islamic form were much used in public and private buildings; many were elaborately decorated by hammering slices and wires of gold and silver into grooves incised in the metal body — a technique that had become a vogue in Persia and Iraq before the Mongol invasions and then spread to Syria and Egypt, where it reached its zenith during the 14th century. Other objects, such as bowls, trays, plates, tables, and ink boxes, were decorated with inlay (PL. 275). Names and titles of sultans and emirs and expressions of good wishes written in Naskhi script formed part of the decorative composition (PL. 275), together with naturalistic floral motifs, mostly of Asiatic origin. Geometrical designs were relegated to background patterns.

Rugs and textiles. It is now acceptable to consider the group of so-called "Damascus rugs" as late Mameluke work. Usually the warp was of silk and the weft of wool; in a few cases silk was used for both warp and weft. Designs consisted of borders of different widths framing a central field containing one or more medallions formed of angular cusps. Decorative motifs were exclusively geometrical, with even floral patterns represented in abstract angularity. The colors used were red, green, and blue.

The production of textiles followed in the local traditions of the Ayyubid period. A characteristic example is a linen cushion cover embroidered in stripes of lozenges with human figures, animals, and birds executed in angular forms. Printed fabrics were also produced, as were silks exhibiting differing tastes and designs. There exists a group of silkstuffs woven in decorated bands and stripes with Naskhi inscriptions alternating with bands of animal figures, the background being filled with naturalistic floral designs. Another group is decorated with a mixture of Chinese motifs and Mameluke inscriptions and designs.

Woodwork. Work in wood was plentiful and various in application; it was utilized for doors, windows, mimbars, Koran chairs and boxes (PL. 275), dinner tables, cenotaphs, screens, friezes, and ceilings. One of the favored techniques employed was the division of surfaces into geometrical designs. The star pattern, composed of small panels of many shapes and sizes joined by slender molded mullions, was predominant. The panels were decorated with floral ornaments carved in wood or ivory, or inlaid with little slices of bone, ivory, and ebony arranged in patterns. Sometimes large surfaces were covered with inlay (V, PL. 458; VIII, PL. 88). Floral motifs carved in wood were only of the conventional stylized type, never naturalistic. Latticework, or *mashrabiya*, used for screens, balustrades, and to cover windows in residential buildings, is composed of bars, square in section and turned on a simple machine in round beads alternating with small cubes. The bars are then linked together by little beads, and the whole panel is enclosed within a strong frame.

Ornamentation. Geometrical decoration, although favored since early Islamic times in both East and West, achieved its final maturity in the Mameluke period in architecture and the minor arts. Of these geometrical designs the so-called "star pattern" is the most important. It was employed wherever possible in carving, painting, inlay, mosaics, and all kinds of decoration. Another great favorite was the arabesque, highly developed by Moslem artists. It consisted of scrolls and undulating, curved and twisted stems bearing leaves of either stylized or naturalistic variety: traditional Islamic abstract forms of the palmette and split palmette; calyx and split calyx; the naturalistic acanthus and its derivatives, evidently of Syrian origin; and the Asiatic lotus and its relatives. Arabesque was used alone or combined with geometrical decorations and Kufic inscriptions. Kufic script (see CALLIGRAPHY), with its angular and graceful forms, was most suitable for decoration and was often placed on a background of arabesque. A world-famous example exists in the madrasah-mosque of Sultan Ḥasan in Cairo. Animals, birds, and fish were sometimes used in illustrations but were more often employed as decoration; in both cases they usually appear in abstract forms typical of Islamic art. Human figures were included among other decorations and were generally represented in abstract style (see HUMAN FIGURE; IMAGES AND ICONOCLASM).

BIBLIOG. *General works*: E. Prisse d'Avennes, L'art arabe, 4 vols., Paris, 1877; S. Lane-Poole, The Art of the Saracens in Egypt, London, 1886; J. Bourgoin, Précis de l'art arabe, Paris, 1892; G. Migeon, L'exposition des arts musulmans au Musée des Arts Décoratifs, Paris, 1903; M. van Berchem and E. Fatio, Voyage en Syrie (Mém. Inst. fr. d'archéol. o. du Caire, XXXVII), 2 vols., Cairo, 1913-14; S. Lane-Poole, A History of Egypt in the Middle Ages, 2d ed., London, 1914; E. Diez, Die Kunst des islamischen Völker, Berlin, 1915; H. Glück and E. Diez, Die Kunst des Islam, Berlin, 1925; G. Migeon, Manuel d'art musulman, 2 vols., Paris, 1927; R. Koechlin and G. Migeon, Islamische Kunstwerke, Berlin, 1928; L. A. Mayer, Saracenic Heraldry, Oxford, 1933; L. A. Mayer, A New Heraldic Emblem of the Mamlūks, Ars Islamica, IV, 1937, pp. 349-51; L. A. Mayer, A propos du blason sous les Mamluks circasssiens, Syria, XVIII, 1937, pp. 389-93; Zakī Muḥammad Ḥasan, Funūn al-Islām (Arts of Islam), Cairo, 1948; M. S. Dimand, A Handbook of Muhammadan Decorative Art, 3d ed., New York, 1958; R. P. Wilson, Islamic Art, London, 1959. For other general and specific studies see K. A. C. Creswell, A Bibliography of the Architecture, Arts and Crafts of Islam, Cairo, 1961, s.v. Egypt. *Architecture*: P. Coste, Architecture arabe, Paris, 1839; M. Herz, La mosquée du Sultan Hasan au Caire, Cairo, 1899; K. A. C. Creswell, A Brief Chronology of the Muhammadan Monuments of Egypt, BIFAO, XIV, 1919, pp. 39-164; K. A. C. Creswell, The Origin of the Cruciform Plan of Cairene Madrasas, BIFAO, XXI, 1923, pp. 1-54; U. Tarchi, L'architettura e l'arte musulmana in Egitto e nella Palestina, Turin, 1923; M. Briggs, Muhammadan Architecture in Egypt and Palestine, Oxford, 1924; K. A. C. Creswell, The Works of Sultan Bibars al-Bunduqdārī in Egypt, BIFAO, XXVI, 1926, pp. 129-93; E. Pauty, Contribution à l'étude des stalactites, BIFAO, XXIX, 1929, pp. 129-53; L. Hautecoeur and G. Wiet, Les mosquées du Caire, 2 vols., Paris, 1932; E. Pauty, Les palais et les maisons d'époque musulmane au Caire (Mém. Inst. fr. d'archéol. o. du Caire, LXII), Cairo, 1932; E. Pauty, Les hammam du Caire (Mém. Inst. fr. d'archéol. o. du Caire, LXIV), Cairo, 1933; Ḥasan 'Abd al-Wahhāb, Tarīkh al-masājid al-athārīya (History of Classic Mosques), 2 vols., Cairo, 1946; Farīd Shāfi'ī, West Islamic Influences on Architecture in Egypt, B. Cairo Univ. Faculty of Arts, XVI, 2, 1954, pp. 1-49; K. A. C. Creswell, The Muslim Architecture of Egypt, II, Oxford, 1959. *The art of the book*: B. Moritz, Arabic Paleography, Cairo, 1905; F. Sarre, Islamic Bookbindings, Berlin, 1923; L. A. Mayer, Mamluk Playing Cards, BIFAO, XXXVIII, 1939, pp. 113-18; H. Buchthal, Three Illustrated Ḥariri Manuscripts in the British Museum, BM, LXXVI, 1940, pp. 144-52; Ḥasan al-Bāshā, at-Taṣwīr al-Islāmī fi-l- Uṣūr al-Wusṭā (Islamic Painting in the Middle Ages), Cairo, 1959. *Ceramics*: C. Prost, Les revêtements céramiques des monuments musulmans de l'Egypte (Mém. Inst. fr. d'archéol. o. du Caire, XI), Cairo, 1916; Musée de l'art arabe du Caire, La céramique égyptienne de l'époque musulmane, Basel, 1922; A. Abel, Ghaibi et les grands faïenciers égyptiens de l'époque Mamluk, Cairo, 1930; A. Bahgat and G. Massoul, La céramique musulmane de l'Egypte, Cairo, 1930; R. L. Hobson, A Guide to the Islamic Pottery of the Near East, London, 1932; M. Mostafa, Two Fragments of Egyptian Lustre Painted Ceramics from the Mamluk Period, BIE, XXXI, 1949, pp. 377-82; A. Lane, Later Islamic Pottery: Persia, Syria, Egypt, Turkey, London, 1957. *Glass*: G. Wiet, Lampes et bouteilles en verre émaillé, Cairo, 1929. *Metalwork*: L. Massignon, Six plats de bronze de style Mamluk, BIFAO, X, 1912, pp. 79-88; G. Migeon, Lampe de mosquée en cuivre ajouré au Musée du Louvre, Syria, I, 1920, pp. 56-57; G. Wiet, Objets en cuivre, Cairo, 1932; D. S. Rice, Two Unusual Mamlūk Metal Works, BOAS, XX, 1957, pp. 487-500. *Rugs and textiles*: O. Falke Kunstgeschichte der Seidenweberei, 2 vols., Berlin, 1913; A. F. Kendrick, Catalogue of Muhammadan Textiles of the Medieval Period, London, 1924; E. Kühnel, Islamische Stoffe aus ägyptische Gräbern, Berlin 1927; J. H. Schmidt, Damast der Mamluken Zeit, Ars Islamica, I, 1934, pp. 99-100; C. J. Lamm, Some Mamluk Embroideries, Ars Islamica, IV, 1937, pp. 64-77; S. Troll, Damaskus-Teppiche, Ars Islamica, IV, 1937, pp. 201-31; K. Erdmann, Kairener Teppiche, Ars Islamica, V, 1938, pp. 179-206, VII, 1940, pp. 55-81. *Ornamentation*: E. Kühnel, Die Arabeske, Wiesbaden, 1949; E. Kühnel, Die Mamlukische Kassetenstil, Wiesbaden, 1950; E. Neuberg, Islamische Sternflechtornamente, Forsch. und Fortschritte, XXX, 1956, pp. 90-94.

Farīd SHĀFI'Ī

Illustrations: PLS. 270-275; 3 figs. in text.

MANET, EDOUARD. French painter, born in Paris on Jan. 23, 1832, of an old and well-to-do bourgeois family. In 1844 he entered the Collège Rollin, where he distinguished himself only in athletics and drawing. In deference to his father he decided on a naval career, and in 1848, to prepare for admission to the Ecole Navale, he embarked as a cadet on a merchant vessel bound for the South Seas; the voyage lasted six months, of which two were spent in the harbor of Rio de Janeiro. By the time he came back, his notebooks filled with sketches, he had a sure sense of his true vocation. In January, 1850, he enrolled in the studio of Thomas Couture, a painter high in official favor, together with his good friend Antonin Proust, whose recollections provide a vivid and authentic source of information on the artist. From Couture Manet received a solid grounding in his craft, supplemented by visits to the Louvre, two study trips to Italy (1853 and 1856), and a tour of the museums of Holland, Germany, and Austria (1856). He copied some of the great old masters: Titian, Rembrandt, Velázquez; among modern masters he was drawn to Goya, Delacroix, Courbet, and Daumier. He left Couture's studio in 1856.

Manet was still a schoolboy when, commenting on a remark of Diderot's, he expressed what was to be one of his guiding principles: "... we must be of our time and work with what we see." It is with him rather than with Courbet (whose anticipatory role, however, must not be slighted) that modern painting begins — painting free of anecdote and false conventions, painting attuned to the new rhythm of life, bound solely by its own laws. As Matisse recognized, "He was the first to act by reflex and thus to simplify the painter's task ... expressing only what immediately touched his senses." From eye to hand, from sensation to transcription, nothing extraneous, no intervention of the sentimental or the picturesque. The impressionist movement, which Manet inspired but with which he only in part identified himself, derived from him its technical emancipation and its chief characteristics: naturalness and freedom, modern themes, clear light, a direct, instantaneous visual grasp. Yet no artist ever appeared less revolutionary than this accomplished man of the world. Elegant and sociable, steeped in tradition, he aspired to nothing more than official acclaim and the honors of the Salon. It was by no intention of his own that he aroused controversy; the violent reaction of the public to his work surprised and pained him. As if to excuse himself, he said: "It is an effect of sincerity that some works should take on the character of a protest when the painter has merely thought of conveying his impression, simply tried to be himself and not somebody else."

Stress has often been laid on the paradox of Manet's art — highly innovative though enriched by borrowings — and the duality of his nature, a subversive bent masked by the appearance of conformism and the superior detachment of a dandy. Brilliant, witty, cultured, most charming, enamored of music and literature, equally at ease in high society and Bohemia, he was an intimate friend of the two greatest French poets of his time, Baudelaire and Mallarmé.

His personality quickly asserted itself, transcending the diverse influences he assimilated. *The Absinthe Drinker* (Copenhagen, Ny Carlsberg Glyptotek), his first realistic painting, powerful and simplified, Baudelairian in spirit though somewhat melodramatic, failed ignominiously at the Salon of 1859. Only Delacroix, whom he had visited in 1857, voted for him. The spirited *Guitarist* (New York, Met. Mus.), on the other hand, earned him a medal at the Salon of 1861 and, because of its picaresque subject, the enthusiastic praise of Théophile Gautier. The stylistic novelty of this painting, decisive for the evolution of Manet's art and of modern art as a whole, lies in the suppression of half tones and of the traditional chiaroscuro, dependent on a dominant value, in favor of straightforward, bold contrasts. Encouraged by his success, his encounter and friendship with Degas, and the admiration of young artists such as Alphonse Legros and Fantin-Latour, Manet painted an ambitious series of works in 1862. Victorine Meurend, for a long time his favorite model, posed for his *Street Singer* (Boston, Mus. of Fine Arts) and *Mlle Victorine in the Costume of an Espada* (PL. 276). The marriage in 1853 of Napoleon III with a Spanish beauty had revived that fashion for things Hispanic born of romanticism and realism, nurtured by literature and the numerous traveling companies of singers, dancers, musicians, and *toreros*. Manet, very responsive to the fluctuations of fashion, willingly bowed to it in his subjects and technique. He painted the *Ballet Espagnol* (Washington, D.C., Phillips Coll.) in the spacious studio of his friend Alfred Stevens, where he gathered the company after having made preliminary studies at the Hippodrome. The presentation has life and savor, but the figures, remarkable individually, are out of proportion and poorly related to one another. Because of "the fury," as Mallarmé put it, "that flung him onto the empty canvas, confusedly, as if he had never before painted," he sometimes showed, in spite of his virtuosity, unevenness and a difficulty in mastering compositions with several figures. More successful are his single portraits, such as *Lola of Valencia* (IV, PL. 280; V, PL. 120), the "rose and black jewel" celebrated by Baudelaire. Manet's preoccupation with Spanish subjects, which waned in 1863 but revived in 1865, after a trip to Spain, might be dismissed as an exotic phase had it not been supported by a genuine understanding of Spanish masters. In his youth he surely saw the celebrated collections of Louis Philippe and Marshal Soult before they were dispersed and, on his trip to Vienna, the fine examples of Velázquez owned by the Hapsburgs. Moreover, he drew repeatedly on the engravings of Goya, a series of which was published in 1859. His absorption with Spanish and Venetian paintings led Manet to his own direct and simplifying style.

Yet another important work dates from 1862: *La Musique aux Tuileries* (London, Tate Gall.), the first realistic rendering of a contemporary urban scene, painted — without anecdote or allegory — in a sensitive, imaginative manner, in that "open-air *salon*," the Tuileries of Manet's day. Suddenly he discovered the unrecorded spectacle of his city and his time, an enchanting procession of forms and lights; he discovered the poetry of modern life dreamed by Baudelaire, who, in fact, is portrayed in the elegant crowd with the artist's other friends. "With Manet the eye played such a role," Antonin Proust tells us, "that Paris has never known an idler who idled to better purpose"; in a notebook he would take down fleeting impressions, mere nothings — a hat, a profile — in bright and vivid strokes.

After a one-man show at the Galerie Martinet in 1863, Manet became with the *Déjeuner sur l'Herbe* (Paris, Mus. du Jeu de Paume; cf. study, VII, PL. 416) the star of the Salon des Refusés and the rallying point of the young independents in revolt against academicism. This composition, sharply criticized as indecent illustration, is actually in the classicizing tradition of Giorgione and Raphael, but situated, as Manet said, in the "transparency of the atmosphere"; the presentation is nonmythological, bluntly alive and real. Although in 1864 Manet won favor with some still lifes of fruit, fish, and flowers, notably a series of peonies rendered in a highly voluptuous palette, in 1865 the uproar reached a climax when *Olympia* (PL. 278) was exhibited at the Salon. The public was horrified by the subject, took offense at the black cat, whose presence is strictly pictorial; the critics denounced the absence of shadows and of modeling, the use of clear tones — the audacities, the demands of a new style. Manet rightly considered this work his masterpiece. The means are simplified in the extreme; plastic and expressive values are reduced to purely pictorial ones. Crystallized in her whiteness, abstract and yet alive, Olympia appears before us in her unclad majesty, her sovereign indifference, partaking of that life of idols and not of the flesh that style confers on the highest creations of art. The multicolored bouquet held by the black slave foreshadows Fauvism.

Exasperated by the general ill will and incomprehension, Manet took refuge for a few days in Spain, where he met the critic Théodore Duret. He acquired a taste for bullfighting, and he convinced himself that Velázquez was "the painter of painters." On his return he abandoned the elegant Café de Bade and Café Tortoni for the Café Guerbois, to which he attracted avant-garde writers and artists. After some overliteral interpretations of Velázquez, such as *The Tragic Actor* (formerly New York, George W. Vanderbilt Coll.), he executed in 1865-66 three magnificent variations on the theme of bullfighting (Chicago, Art Inst., PL. 276; Tokyo, Matsukata Coll.; Paris, Goldschmidt-Rothschild Coll.) and a brilliant technical feat, *The Fifer* (Paris, Mus. du Jeu de Paume), his most popular and representative painting, which consists of large areas of clear color — like playing cards, Daumier remarked — against a monochrome gray background. No more half tones or modeling; the shadows hug the vibrant contour, which encloses the silhouette without giving it roundness and animates without dissolving it. Here is a bold and original synthesis of the catalyzing influences from Spain and from the Japanese prints discovered with enthusiasm by Manet's whole generation. The novel charm of Japanese art, which in different ways was also to affect Gauguin, Van Gogh, and the Nabis, resided for Manet in its decorative freshness, its rhythmic outlines, its spatial simplifications, its abrupt contrasts of light and dark. Photography — Manet, like Degas, was an amateur photographer — also contributed to the complex formation of his style.

Rejected by the Exposition Universelle of 1867, he organized on Place de l'Alma his own pavilion, opposite Courbet's, and drew the jeers of the multitude and the admiration of the future impressionists. At the Salon of 1868 he exhibited the *Portrait of Zola* (PL. 276); the novelist had been his warm supporter since 1866. Although Manet was hostile to history painting and did not forgive Delacroix's concessions to the genre, current events inspired him on several occasions — a testimony to his humanitarianism and his liberal convictions. In 1867 he painted the *Execution of Maximilian* (Mannheim, Städtische Kunsthalle), an interpretation of sober pathos. In the summer of 1868, while vacationing in Boulogne, where he was to paint several beach scenes the following year, he began *The Luncheon* (Munich, Neue Staatsgalerie), his most harmonious and relaxed composition, accepted at the Salon of 1869 at the same time as *The Balcony* (VII, PL. 433). The second painting was inspired by Goya and concluded Manet's Spanish period, before the succeeding impressionist phase. There are harmonies of extreme boldness here — metallic greens against pearly grays: Manet's hallmark — but the central mass remains indistinct in the gloom of the background, and each of the figures has a life apart. In the foreground is Berthe Morisot, who often served as his model before becoming his sister-in-law in 1874. In the summer of 1872 alone he painted four portraits of her, of which the one in the black hat (Paris, Coll. Mme Ernest Rouart) was particularly valued by Valéry.

After the War of 1870, in which he served as a lieutenant of the Garde Nationale, he joined his family in the Pyrenees, where they had taken refuge. The way home took him by easy stages along the Atlantic coast, and he painted wide fluid marines, of which the finest is the *Harbor of Bordeaux* (Zurich, Heirs of E. Bührle Coll.). Since 1869, doubtless under the influence of Berthe Morisot, he had turned to plein-air scenes. From Berck he brought back a whole group of paintings and aquarelles rich in effects of transparency and vibration. In Paris, under the limpid light of waning summer, he extended his new manner to figure compositions. Victorine Meurend, the model for *Olympia*, posed for *The Railway* (Washington, D.C., Nat. Gall.), a brilliant painting done in a single burst of inspiration in the garden of the painter Alphonse Hirsch. In the *Game of Croquet* (Frankfort on the Main, Städelsches Kunstinstitut) the fusion of figures and atmosphere is even more complete. The movement of reflections and shadows pervades the scene, without, however, impairing the firmness of the contours, a quality peculiar to Manet that contrasts with impressionist evanescence. In 1873 he executed the nocturnal counterpart of *La Musique aux Tuileries: Masked Ball at the Opéra* (New York, Mrs. Doris D. Havemeyer Coll.), according to Mallarmé a work of capital importance in the painter's œuvre, in which the magic of this fete is evoked in all its splendor and its emptiness.

The Salon being the only battleground Manet recognized, he refused to participate in the first exhibition of the impressionists in 1874. But in the summer, during his stay at Gennevilliers on the Seine, he often joined Monet at Argenteuil, on the opposite bank, recognizing without quite adopting the impressionist painter's principles. Manet practiced neither pure landscape art nor the prismatic division of tone. Nonetheless, the richer and more luminous canvases done under impressionist influence in August, 1874, bespeak his rapid absorption of the new style. They include pictures of Monet surprised in his garden or in the boat that served him as a floating studio, two landscapes depicting the banks of the Seine, and two spacious compositions saturated with sunlight, showing pleasure boaters. In these last paintings the same picturesque couple in particolored clothes poses in the forefront — full face and rather stiff in *Argenteuil* (Tournai, Mus. B. A.), in profile in the livelier, more dynamic and unified *Boating* (PL. 277). Drenched in the radiance of the atmosphere, the figures henceforth take form through color, not contour. With almost miraculous ease Manet achieved the synthesis of incompatibles, image and light. From a brief trip to Venice in September, 1875, he brought back two bold paintings (San Francisco, Mrs. William H. Crocker Coll.; New York, Mrs. J. Watson Webb Coll.) in which his individual approach harmonizes with the happiest effects of the impressionists.

His production in later life was more abundant but less even than in his youth. His technical virtuosity remained exceptional, but his work, affected by the contradictory claims of naturalism and worldliness, lost something of its boldness and unity. Whenever he recovered the firmness of his style and drew on his best source of inspiration, that of contemporary life, he still produced some masterly genre scenes. Among these are three characteristic paintings of 1877 — *The Plum* (New York, Arthur Sachs Coll.), *Skating* (Cambridge, Mass., Fogg Art Mus.), *Nana* (Hamburg, Kunsthalle) — and two fine compositions of 1879 — *The Conservatory* (Berlin, Nationalgalerie) and *Chez le Père Lathuille* (Tournai, Mus. B. A.). Before leaving his studio on the Rue de St-Pétersbourg in 1878, Manet wished to preserve the memory of the Rue Mosnier (now Rue de Berne), which his windows faced and which he had had before his eyes for six years. The five successive versions he made, different in details, are his best urban views and his best essays in impressionist style. Immediately after, he devoted an equally felicitous cycle of paintings and drawings to the *brasseries* and café concerts then coming into fashion. Several represent the Cabaret de Reichshoffen on Boulevard Rochechouart, among them *La Servante de bocks* (London, Tate Gall.), notable for the transparency of the lights.

From 1879 onward, overtaken by the first symptoms of the illness that was to cause his death, he often resorted to the more easily handled medium of pastel, whose stylistic and technical possibilities he enlarged, at the same time as Degas, to portray Parisian celebrities and all the pretty women who flocked to his studio on the Rue d'Amsterdam. Summers he spent in the country, in the gardens of Bellevue, Versailles, and Rueil, painting uninterruptedly, with feverish haste, as his paralysis worsened. Early in 1881 he projected four paintings of women symbolizing the seasons. He executed only two, *Autumn* (Nancy, Mus. B. A.), the model for which was Méry Laurent, and *Spring* (New York, Mrs. Harry Payne Bingham Coll.), posed by the young actress Jeanne de Marsy. One of Manet's most radiant portraits and his first popular success, *Spring* was presented at the Salon of 1882 together with *Bar at the Folies-Bergère* (London, Courtauld Inst. Galls.), a vast composition that, drawing on all the resources of his resplendent palette, evokes the whole phantasmagoria of Parisian night life. A sketch of the same subject is in Amsterdam (PL. 279). He dreamed of decorating the Hôtel de Ville with a mural to the glory of Paris and modern civilization, but, confined to his bed, he had strength only to paint the delicate bouquets, roses and lilac, sent him by his charming women friends. He died on Apr. 30, 1883. "He was greater than we thought," said Degas on leaving the little cemetery at Passy where the artist is buried. "To this day," concedes André Masson, "all freshness, all daring, owes him a debt of gratitude."

BIBLIOG. T. Gautier, Salon, Moniteur Universel, July 3, 1861; E. Zola, Mon Salon, Paris, 1866; E. Zola, Edouard Manet: Etude biographique et critique, Paris, 1867 (repub. in Mes Haines, Paris, 1902); E. Zola, Edouard Manet, L'Evénement Illustré, May 10, 1868; S. Mallarmé, Le Jury de Peinture pour 1874 et M. Manet, La Renaissance Artistique et Littéraire, Apr. 12, 1874; G. Jeanniot, Manet, La Grande Revue, Jan., 1882; A. Proust, Le Salon de 1882, GBA, 1882, I, pp. 533-34, II, pp. 145-60; E. Bazire, Manet, Paris, 1884; P. Mantz, Les Œuvres de Manet, Le Temps, Jan. 16, 1884; R. Marx, Edouard Manet et son exposition, Journal des Arts, Jan. 11, 1884; G. Moore, Confessions of a Young Man, London, 1888; J. de Nittis, Notes et souvenirs, Paris, 1895; A. Proust, Souvenirs de Manet, Revue Blanche, 1897; S. Mallarmé, Divagations, Paris, 1898; T. Duret, Histoire d'Edouard Manet et de son œuvre, Paris, 1902; J. Meier-Graefe, Manet und sein Kreis, Berlin, 1902; H. von Tschudi, Edouard Manet, Berlin, 1902; T. Duret, Manet and the French Impressionists, trans. J. E. Crawford Flitch, London, Philadelphia, 1910; W. Pach, Manet and Modern American Art, Craftsman, 1910, pp. 483-92; G. Séailles, Edouard Manet, Revue de Paris, Feb., 1910, pp. 583-602; A. Proust, Edouard Manet: Souvenirs, Paris, 1913; C. Glaser, Edouard Manet, Munich, 1922; G. Severini, Edouard Manet, Rome, 1924; J.-E. Blanche, Manet, trans. F. C. de Sumichrast, London, 1925; P. Jamot, Manet as a Portrait Painter, BM, XLIX, 1926, pp. 302-09; E. Moreau-Nélaton, Manet raconté par lui-même, 2 vols., Paris, 1926; H. Focillon, Manet en blanc et noir, GBA, 1927, pp. 337-46;

P. Jamot, Manet peintre de marines, et autres études, GBA, 1927, pp. 27-50, 381-90; J. Guiffrey, Lettres illustrées d'Edouard Manet, Paris, 1929; E. Manet, Lettres de jeunesse (1848-1849), Paris, 1929; L. Venturi, Manet, L'Arte, XXXII, 1929, pp. 145-64; C. V. Wheeler, Manet: An Essay, Washington, 1930; C. Léger, Manet, Paris, 1931; A. Tabarant, Manet: Histoire cartographique, Paris, 1931; P. Colin, Manet, Paris, 1932; P. Jamot, G. Wildenstein, and M.-L. Bataille, Manet, 2 vols., Paris, 1932 (crit. cat.); R. Rey, Choix de 65 dessins de Manet, Paris, 1932; P. Valéry, Le Triomphe de Manet (preface to the retrospective exhibition at the Musée de l'Orangerie), Paris, 1932 (repub. in Pièces sur l'art, Paris, 1932); L'Amour de l'Art, XIII, May, 1932, pp. 145-84 (articles by P. Jamot, G. Bazin, R. Huyghe); Art Vivant, June, 1932, pp. 273-87 (articles by P. Valéry and others); Formes, 1932 (articles by J. Meier-Graefe and others); E. Lambert, Manet et l'Espagne, GBA, 1933, pp. 369-82; J. Mesnil, Le Déjeuner sur l'herbe, L'Arte, XXXVII, 1934, pp. 250-57; A. Tabarant, Une Correspondance inédite d'Edouard Manet: Lettres du Siège de Paris, Paris, 1935; M. Florisoone, Manet inspiré par Venise, L'Amour de l'Art, XVIII, Jan., 1937; R. Rey, Manet, trans. E. B. Shaw, New York, Paris, 1938; G. Jedlicka, Manet, Erlenbach, Zurich, 1941; M. Guérin, L'Œuvre gravé de Manet, Paris, 1944; I. N. Ebin, Manet and Zola, GBA, 1945, pp. 357-78; J. Thyis, Manet et Baudelaire, Etudes d'Art (Algiers), 1945; Lettres d'Edouard Manet sur son voyage en Espagne, Arts, Mar. 16, 1945; L. Piérard, Manet l'incompris, Paris, 1946; M. Florisoone, Manet, Monaco, 1947; B. Reifenberg, Manet, Bern, 1947; J. Rewald, Edouard Manet: Pastels, Oxford, 1947; A. Tabarant, Manet et ses œuvres, Paris, 1947; J. Alazard, Manet, Lausanne, 1948; J. Leymarie, Manet et les impressionistes au Musée du Louvre, Paris 1948; D. Cooper, Manet, London, 1949; Edouard Manet: Peintures, Paris, 1949 (introd. by F. Mathey); J. Leymarie, Edouard Manet, Paris, 1951; J. C. Sloane, Manet and History, AQ, XIV, no. 2, 1951, pp. 92-106; A. Bento, Manet no Brasil, Rio de Janeiro, 1953; J. Cassou, Manet, Paris, 1954; G. H. Hamilton, Manet and His Critics, New Haven, London, 1954; N. G. Sandblad, Manet: Three Studies in Artistic Conception, trans. W. Nash, Lund, 1954; G. Bataille, Manet, trans. A. Wainhouse and J. Emmons, New York, 1955; J.-L. Vaudoyer, Manet, Paris, 1955; J. Richardson, Edouard Manet, London, 1958; K. Martin, Manet: Water-colours and Pastels, trans. R. Allen, London, 1959; H. Perruchot, La Vie de Manet, Paris, 1959; Portrait of Manet by Himself and His Contemporaries, ed. P. Courthion and P. Cailler, trans. M. Ross, London, 1960; P. Valéry, Degas, Manet, Morisot, trans. D. Cooper, New York, 1960; J. Mathey, Graphisme de Manet, Paris, 1961.

Jean LEYMARIE

Illustrations: PLS. 276-280.

MANICHAEAN ART. Widely diffused in Central Asia and China from the 7th century, Manichaeanism was responsible for a wave of Iranian cultural influence, for which there is ample documentary evidence in the eastern part of Central Asia. Although its impact cannot be compared with that of Buddhism (q.v.), Manichaeanism did influence certain tendencies of the art of Central Asia (see ASIA, CENTRAL), either because of its color symbolism or perhaps because the very reputation of Mani, considered a painter of remarkable talent, brought about a traditional and almost sacred interest in the pictorial arts. The Manichaean miniatures of the Turfan area (see TURFAN) are of special interest to the art historian, not only because of their indisputable esthetic merit, but also because sundry historical factors led to their influencing the development of the Islamic miniature. The Manichaean miniatures were both an immediate source of inspiration and a varied, but not overly dissimilar, link in the chain of transmission of Iranian pictorial tradition. Manichaeanism introduced this Iranianism to the Uigurian Turks, whose art in turn constituted an important factor in the genesis of the Islamic miniature.

SUMMARY. The Manichaean doctrine (col. 433). The spread of Manichaeanism (col. 435). Centers of Manichaean art (col. 436). Frescoes: Bezeklik and Khocho (col. 437). Paintings on silk (col. 439). Paintings on paper and miniatures (col. 439). Dating and characteristics (col. 442).

THE MANICHAEAN DOCTRINE. Mani (Gr., Manes; Lat., Manichaeus) was born in northern Babylonia in A.D. 216/17; he received divine revelations in 228/29, and in 240/41 began the work of preaching his new religion. As to his somewhat obscure relations with the Sassanid rulers, suffice it to say that, accused of heresy by Bahrām I and the Magi, Mani was arrested and condemned. He was executed in chains soon after, on Feb. 26, 277.

His doctrine developed in part out of his journeyings through various regions, including India, from which he gathered and readily assimilated many religious and philosophical influences. Mani actually proclaimed himself the last of the celestial messengers, the supreme revealer, and the seal of the prophets (the latter an appellation also used by Mohammed; Koran, XXXIII, 40), recognizing as his principal predecessors (apart from Adam) Zoroaster, the Buddha, and Jesus. He therefore constituted, as it were, the terminal link in a chain. As the perfect illuminator, and in his capacity as savior, he can be likened not only to the Paraclete of Christian theology, but also — though to a lesser degree — to the Bodhisattva Maitreya. Mani claimed that the word preached by him was of a universal nature and ascribed the limited territorial expansion of preceding doctrines to the fact that they had been based upon an incomplete truth. Hence his assertion: "My hope will go to the West as well as to the East." On this basis of superiority or universality rested the missionary character of Manichaeanism. Its doctrine was contained in seven works which, according to Mani himself, were fundamental to the new religion and, as sacred canons, must remain unaltered; for, in Mani's view, Zoroastrianism, Buddhism, and Christianity (qq.v.) declined precisely because the oral teachings of their respective founders eventually became distorted.

This premise of universality in turn determined the syncretistic character of Manichaeanism, which incorporated various elements of Christian, Zoroastrian, and Buddhist philosophy acknowledged as in harmony with the truth. But Manichaeanism cannot be regarded as merely a syncretistic system. H. C. Puech recognizes in it, above all, a capacity to adapt to the most varied environments without losing any of its soundness ("Manicheismo," Civiltà dell'Oriente, III, 1958, p. 271). On the contrary, adds this French scholar: "The Indian, Iranian, Christian, and Hellenic elements to be found in greater or lesser degree in Manichaean writings appear to be, for the most part, not so much innate components of the system as, rather, subsequent and secondary layers, the result of a conscious and voluntary adaptation." Manichaeanism is, of course, a variation of Gnosticism; despite the criticisms Mani leveled at the systems of Bardesanes and Marcion, the influence of their doctrines is quite unmistakable in several instances. The very structure of Manichaeanism coincides fundamentally with the Gnostic attitude, in its deep-seated dissatisfaction with the human condition, man being perpetually tainted with evil and yet aspiring to supreme good. The problem of evil — resolved by attributing its source to a principle, in itself bad and inferior but as a power opposed to God, who is solely truth and goodness — becomes an essential factor. It is only through an understanding of self and a knowledge of God that man can save himself. The consubstantiality of God and souls, which are luminous particles of the divine substance, constitutes another basic tenet of the Manichaean system; it is precisely the spirit, or intelligence, which can redeem this small portion of the divine essence by releasing it from its momentary state of degradation. In short, only knowledge — gnosis — enables man to recognize his destiny, his mission, and the background and causes of his very contradictory human condition.

This knowledge is of a total nature, embracing at once theology and cosmogony — things divine, terrestrial, and infernal — and develops in terms of mythology. Thus there grew up a gigantic myth — continually expanded by later exegeses — whose eternal protagonists are the decayed human soul and the intellect which strives to free it. The divine, luminous substance is at once savior (in the form of the intelligence) and object of salvation (the soul as such). The myth itself, naturally based on the contrast between good and evil and the various other opposites (spirit and matter, light and darkness, etc.) proceeding from this primeval dichotomy, is divided into three different phases of time: past, present, and future. Hence Manichaeanism is known as the doctrine of the two principles, or roots, and the three ages, or periods. The Realm of Goodness, or Light — presided over by the Father of Greatness, who is sometimes identified with the Zurvan of Mazdaism — is opposed to that of Darkness (matter or evil), ruled by the Prince of Darkness, who is comparable to the Ahriman of Iranian tradition. The former, as Puech observes (op. cit., p. 274), "is pictured as a sphere of light, surrounded by a resplendent ether and consisting of five abodes, or members of God (intelligence, reason, thought, reflection, and will), inhabited by innumerable Aeons. Conversely, the opposing realm consists of five superimposed abysses (starting from the top, the worlds of smoke, or fog; of consuming fire; of air, or destructive wind; of water, or mud; and of darkness), presided over by five regents, or Archons, of monstrous form — bestial or demonic — and crawling with five different sorts of infernal beings." All the attributes of the Realm of Light are the opposite of those of the Realm of Darkness.

According to the myth, the conflict between these two realms reached its climax with the attempt of Darkness to invade the Realm of Light. The Father of Greatness meets his adversary in person by sending to the fray his own soul, personified in his son, who is also Primal Man. Defeated, the latter falls headlong into the abysses, and so a part of the divine soul becomes mixed with matter. In the course of a series of symbolic events, during a second emanation from the Father of Greatness, the Spirit of Life is "awakened" (i.e., created) and descends into the Realm of Darkness to deliver the Primal Man, who is brought back to his place of origin: the Paradise of Light. However, Primal Man, the first being to fall and the first to be saved, has left his soul behind in the Realm of Darkness. Its redemption necessitates the creation of the material universe, an event in which the Spirit of Life, having overcome the demonic Archons, also plays an essential part. The myth — becoming ever more complex and involved, though certainly not without an intensely poetic strain — proceeds through subsequent phases which describe fresh dangers and further conflicts, the rational and almost mechanical ordering of the life of the cosmos, and atrocious apocalyptic scenes, to the redemption of Adam by a savior who is sometimes called "Luminous Jesus." Nevertheless, except for those who practice absolute continence, the decay of souls will not cease before the end of time; the last phase will mark the definitive separation of the light from the darkness.

This forceful effort of imagination and intellect is directed toward proving not only the consubstantiality of man's intelligence and his individual self with God, but also the possibility of redemption. Salvation consists in regaining an understanding of oneself (thanks to Mani's revelations), in order to be able to maintain one's soul in a state of lucidity and to remain perfectly detached from fleshly impurities and material lusts. Only thus will man be able, at his death, to return to the Paradise of Light, there to enjoy the peace of Nirvana.

Finally, the Manichaean doctrine also contains some extremely rigid moral precepts that can be followed in entirety only by the Elect, who are destined to be saved at the end of their earthly existence. For the others, rebirth, conditioned by their respective merits, is inevitable. Furthermore, the belief in the existence of a soul — not only in human beings, but also in animals, plants, the elements, and even in inanimate objects — doubtless constitutes one of the more interesting tenets of Mani's religion, a religion whose missionary spirit and sense of predication and apostolate clearly reflect the spiritual attitude of its founder.

Mario BUSSAGLI

THE SPREAD OF MANICHAEANISM. According to tradition, Mani began his mission with a journey to India, between 240/41 and 242/43, either in order to gain firsthand knowledge of Buddhist beliefs, or because he wanted to follow in the footsteps of the apostle Thomas and convert the Christians of those regions to his own faith. In any case, having returned to Persia, between 244 and 261 he organized a number of missions, one of which won over Bactria and perhaps even Sogdiana. Moreover, in consequence of the founding of important communities in those regions, numerous missionaries went farther and farther east until finally they reached China.

Up to the 10th century the sect was centered in Babylon, but with the establishment of the Abbasside caliphate (see ABBASSIDE ART), this seat was transferred to Samarkand, because Manichaeanism had by then lost most of its adherents in the West, whereas, since the 7th century, it had gained a tremendous following in the East.

Eastward expansion may have been furthered by the conquest of present-day Chinese Turkistan (see ASIA, CENTRAL) by T'ang China (see CHINESE ART) and by the consequent restoration of safety along the routes leading east. The Manichaeans must have founded small communities along the two routes through Serindia, as doubtless the Nestorians (see NESTORIAN ART) also did; in 694, these communities enabled a Manichaean dignitary to reach the court of China. It is also possible that the expansion toward the east was linked with successive waves of Sogdian migrations toward both Semirech'e and Serindia at the time of the Arab invasion, some groups having preferred to abandon Sogdiana rather than renounce their faith. However, these communities presumably would have made only sporadic contributions toward any important artistic developments in Central Asia without the conversion to Manichaeanism, in 763, of the ruler of the Uigurs, whose capital was Kara Balghasun in the Orkhon River region, and, with him, of the great majority of his grandees and his people.

The Uigur empire (see TURKISH ART), established in Outer Mongolia, disappeared without leaving any traces — apart from the famous trilingual inscription carved during the reign of the Khan Ai-Tängridä-qut-Bulmish-alp-Bilgä (808-21) — to show the level of civilization attained by this people. In 840, the invasion and destruction of their empire by the Kirghiz from the region of the Yenisei forced them to settle in the oases of northeastern Serindia, where they came under the influence of the sedentary Indo-European population; it was only then that the Uigurs adopted a way of life propitious to the flowering of an indigenous art. Ousted from their empire in Mongolia, the majority established themselves in 843 at Khocho (Kara-Khōja; Chin., Kao-ch'ang), on the site of present-day Turfan (see TURFAN); farther north at Besh-balik (The Five Cities; formerly Pei-t'ing); at Yen-ch'i, or Agni, which later became Karashahr; and at Kucha (see KUCHA); the remainder settled in the region of Kan-chou in about 860. Only the western group — at least in so far as is known — contributed to the maintenance of certain art forms, adapting them to their Manichaean beliefs; but even this lasted for only a relatively short time, for, in all probability, the Manichaean frescoes of Bezeklik and Khocho date from about the 9th century, while some of the paintings may have been executed at the beginning of the 10th century.

A characteristic aspect of Manichaeanism was its veritable cult of the book. Having perceived that the religions of his time had suffered a rapid decline — in many cases because of differing interpretations and redactions of their scriptures — Mani resolved that his doctrine should be recorded in books written by himself. These books, seven in number, having been long forgotten, are now known, although imperfectly, from fragmentary discoveries made at the end of the 19th century and the beginning of the 20th in the Turfan area and the repository at Tun-huang (q.v.); these finds have since been supplemented by others at Medinet el-Fayum in 1931. The texts found in Central Asia are in such diverse languages as Chinese, Uigur, and the various forms of Iranian — Persian, Parthian, and Sogdian — while those found in Egypt are in Subakhmimic Coptic.

Mani was said to have been a calligrapher and painter — a repute corroborated by discoveries made in Central Asia, for a number of the fragments found there are not only written in elegant calligraphy but also adorned with illuminations and miniatures probably executed in a style that goes back to the founder of the sect (PLS. 281, 282, 284, 287). These manuscripts constitute a series of invaluable documents, together with the records supplied by the Bezeklik and Khocho frescoes, the latter consisting only of a few fragments in very poor condition because of technical deficiencies in their execution. Unfortunately, the Medinet el-Fayum manuscripts have neither illuminations nor miniatures, so that it is impossible to determine whether a uniform Manichaean pictorial tradition existed throughout the regions in which this sect had adherents.

CENTERS OF MANICHAEAN ART. The Turfan oasis comprises such extremely varied sites as the ruined cities of Idikut-shahri and Khocho, ancient capitals of the kingdom of Turfan, and monastic complexes situated at a greater or lesser distance from these cities. A number of fragments of Manichaean manuscripts and works of art were found in Khocho, in two groups of buildings designated with the letters K and α. In addition, a relatively well-preserved page from a manuscript was found in one of the numerous monasteries, temples, and stupas located in the gorge of Senghim (Senghim-aghiz; I, PL. 490), which opens a few miles northeast of the plain in which the two cities rose; several Manichaean frescoes were discovered at Bezeklik, a monastic city situated at the head of the valley and consisting of rock-cut sanctuaries and temple structures; a manuscript with a Manichaean miniature was found at Murtuk, another monastic complex comprising rock-cut sanctuaries and brick buildings, located about 25 miles north of Bezeklik; finally, more manuscripts were recovered about 10 miles east of Khocho, at Toyuk, the site of two very large monasteries.

FRESCOES: BEZEKLIK AND KHOCHO. The Manichaean frescoes that survived at Bezeklik were located in two rock-cut sanctuaries (Caves 17 and 25); these frescoes had been concealed by the Buddhists, who covered them either with a brick wall faced with plaster or simply by means of a coating of mud plaster mixed with chopped straw. It seems reasonable to assume that Bezeklik was first a Buddhist site, for the Buddhist decoration in some of the sanctuaries clearly dates from the early T'ang period (7th cent.); it was not until after the conversion of the Uigurs to Manichaeanism — that is, sometime after 760 — that the decoration in a few of the sanctuaries must have been changed, only to be restored in about 850 to its original, Buddhist character. (Cf. I, PLS. 485, 488, 489.)

Cave 25 is the most noteworthy sanctuary, although some of its Manichaean frescoes, having been "prepared" merely with a thin layer of lime, have succumbed to humidity. When the cave was reconverted upon its recovery by the Buddhists, the rear, which communicated by a passage with Cave 26, was walled off and the front part rededicated to the Buddhist cult. It was in this walled-off area at the back that the Manichaean frescoes remained, those on the right wall being still visible when A. Grünwedel studied them in 1905.

On the upper part of the back wall, which has a slight batter and constitutes a sort of pediment, is one of the most important of the surviving frescoes, although it is badly damaged. Grünwedel, who recognized its non-Buddhist character, gave a compendious description of it, pointing out that the wall had been merely whitewashed, that the treatment of the figures — outlined in India ink without any preliminary sketching — was fairly loose, and that only three colors had been used: bright red, green, and dull yellow. The fresco, a rigidly symmetrical composition, shows twelve figures, six on either side, under a tree with three trunks; the roots are sunk in a small basin, and there are three huge clusters of fruit hanging from either side of it; four figures kneel in the foreground, and two others stand behind them in each of the two groups of figures, which are arranged in absolute symmetry with the trunks of the sacred tree. Many of the details of the garments of these figures recur in compositions found at Turfan and Tun-huang and in the cities of the Tarim Basin. The entire composition is bordered along the lower edge with a wide red band.

Some of the Khocho frescoes were found in a monument designated by German archaeologists as "Ruin K" (a plan of it was made by A. von Le Coq, 1913), which was situated slightly to the south of the center of the city, and others were discovered in a ruined complex, designated as "Ruin α," located in the southwest corner of the city, not far from its fortified outer wall. The latter ruin is the cella of a temple which strongly resembles the open-air Buddhist temples with surrounding galleries and, in fact, may even have been a Buddhist temple.

Ruin K consists of four groups of structures. The north group comprises four square rooms with domed roofs, of Iranian type, arranged on either side of a central alley and flanked by smaller, barrel-vaulted rooms; two beautiful Manichaean miniatures were found in one of these small chambers. The only remains of the east group, which was almost totally destroyed, are a barrel-vaulted passageway, in which two votive banners (PL. 286), pieces of embroidered material, painted silks, and a few book covers were found; a square room — originally with a domed roof and adorned with wall paintings — which was thought to have been a library because of the numerous manuscripts it contained; and a few minor rooms. Nothing was found in the west group, which consists merely of a large, square, domed chamber; but the south group — consisting of a row of three large, rectangular, adjoining halls — yielded two objects of particular importance: a wooden column base, carved in a highly characteristic style, in the north hall, and a large wall painting in the middle hall.

Ruin α contained many manuscripts (among them a page illuminated on both sides, the most beautiful of the miniatures found at Turfan), as well as a wall painting, representing the elect, in a corner of the chamber.

The most important of the Khocho frescoes is one located on the west wall of the hall in the center of Ruin K. It depicts, against a clear gray background, a group of men and women dressed in white (probably the elect), a few lay figures (undoubtedly "auditors"), and, on the left, a much larger figure (according to the German archaeologists who discovered it, probably Mani himself) — only the head and shoulders of which remain — wearing a pale violet-gray miter with red-orange designs (PL. 283).

Of the other fresco fragments found in Ruin K, one shows portions of the heads of three divinities (PL. 285); another is a detail of a garment, of some high ecclesiastical dignitary, apparently; while a third and particularly interesting fragment represents four warriors, armed with bows and long spears and dressed in long, multicolored robes, one of them adorned with green flowers.

Ruin α has also yielded a fragment of a large composition that shows two figures, but only the heads and shoulders have been preserved; the figures closely resemble those in the large fresco of Ruin K, for they are dressed in white, wear white miters, and have Western faces with beards and mustaches.

These murals, the only Manichaean frescoes presently known, exhibit all the characteristics of the Buddhist paintings of the T'ang period in the Turfan region, as well as unmistakable traces of late Sassanian influence. A special technique was used in the frescoes at Bezeklik, but those at Khocho appear to have been executed on a surface similar to that of the earlier Buddhist frescoes of that region.

The influence of Chinese art is reflected in some of the general features — such as the over-all tone of some of the frescoes and the importance accorded the drawing, in which lines add lightness and fluency to the composition. Indeed, many of the frescoes, as well as the paintings on silk banners and the manuscript miniatures, are in a light key, determined partly by the large number of white garments that are often the dominant element in the compositions, and partly by the use of a very pale gray tone for the background. This same tendency seems to prevail in the frescoes at Kumtura, in which Chinese influence predominates (the majority of the paintings adorning the Cave of the Apsaras are in light tones, and those in the Cave of Nirvana also display these same characteristics), whereas it contrasts sharply with that prevailing at Kizil, where bright tones are juxtaposed to the point of constituting almost violent contrasts (I, PLS. 483, 484). Furthermore, the marked affinity with Chinese art that is revealed in the drawing — which is characterized essentially by fluid lines — is even more evident in the long flowing garments with wide sleeves, which are the same as were worn in China during the T'ang period and quite unlike the dress displayed by the figures in the Kizil paintings or in the earliest Kumtura frescoes; the costume depicted in the latter frescoes consists of a tailored jacket with tight sleeves and close-fitting trousers, very similar to the type worn by the Iranians and Sogdians (see COSTUME).

It seems, however, that Chinese art was not the sole influence on the Manichaean frescoes, which may well have some affinity with the painting of Central Asia, for the juxtaposition of bright tones here and there corresponds to the tendency manifest in the frescoes at Kizil, despite a fairly pronounced difference in their reds and blues. The influence of Sassanid Iran is also apparent — in one of the frescoes in Ruin K, for instance, and, specifically, in the detail of a medallion enclosing the representation of a divinity, of which only the haloed head and a raised hand still remain; this medallion is adorned with large beads — a motif undoubtedly derived from Sassanian art, for it also occurs at both Tumshuk and Kizil.

PAINTINGS ON SILK. The surviving fragments of paintings on silk reveal similar tendencies (PLS. 286, 287). The two votive banners found at Khocho are adorned with a male and a female figure, respectively, both drawn to a large scale and doubtless representing Manichaean elect. Another fragment of silk from the same source is adorned with a text and, below this, with an ornamental band on which only the head and shoulders of two helmeted warriors remain; though somewhat coarse, the drawing is extremely interesting. Here the helmets have a plate extending over the forehead, like a kind of nosepiece, recalling those of certain warriors at Shorchuk and comparable to those worn by some figures at Pyandzhikent.

The fragment discovered in Ruin α is equally noteworthy, for both its size and its subject matter. The printing is in a yellow-bistre frame — bounded along its remaining, vertical edge with two thick black lines — and is bordered along the top with a band of geometrical designs on a red-orange background, above which, on a bistre and light-yellow background, there must have been a scene that is now no longer discernible. The painting represented, against a blue background, two rows of five seated Manichaean elect (only four of each row remain), their hands hidden in the wide, flowing sleeves of their white robes. These figures wear a sort of cap made of white material which falls in folds behind the head and over the ears; below this group is a fragment of a halo which must have encircled the head of a divinity or of the principal figure. As in the frescoes representing a similar subject, the drapery is merely indicated by a few brownish lines; the dress as a whole is of a Chinese type, although the figures have decidedly pink complexions — a fact which seems to indicate that they are not Chinese.

The fragments of embroidered silk depict typically Chinese dragons, with elongated and twisted bodies, as well as a cock and lotus flowers. One of the most interesting pieces in this category is a fragment that shows a magnificently attired divinity, accompanied by a few of the elect wearing the usual white robes; each figure stands on a stylized, rather dark, blue and brownish-yellow lotus, clearly derived from Buddhist art.

PAINTINGS ON PAPER AND MINIATURES. The paintings on paper and miniatures adorning manuscripts, of which quite a number have survived, are of extremely varied inspiration. In some — as in the frescoes and in the majority of the paintings on silk — Chinese influence predominates; some proceed from purely Central Asian sources, while others clearly derive from prototypes to be sought in western Asia, if any Sassanian or Manichaean miniatures had survived there. The latter, in fact, most likely contributed toward the evolution of the Arabo-Persian miniatures of the Mongol period, and perhaps even of the pre-Mongol era, which ultimately led to the development of the Indo-Persian miniatures of Moghul India (see MOGHUL SCHOOL).

Among the paintings on paper which reveal Chinese influences is a scroll, found at Khocho, of which only the illuminated title remains (PL. 281); it is possible to discern a few letters of the text, but the title itself, which is set in a vertical rectangle, does not show up in reproductions because the ink is so pale. The rectangular space is a sort of banner (vexillum), suspended from a wooden rod that is adorned at either end with a motif of rising flames and is surmounted by a miter made of fur and/or feathers; two scarves, each tied with a knot at either end of the rod, fall symmetrically on either side of the banner and are held by two divinities. These figures wear Chinese robes and tall headdresses with veils suspended from them; their coiffure — of a rather distinctive type which reappears in some of the miniatures — consists of a few curls on the forehead, the rest of the hair hanging down over the shoulders. They stand on a pedestal in the form of a lotus, and they wear over their robes a Chinese type of armor reminiscent of the kind seen at Tun-huang.

A fragment of a manuscript found in Ruin α shows a few kneeling figures, also dressed in Chinese fashion, who, judging by their positions, must originally have formed part of a group surrounding a central figure, since lost. The long white object they hold in their hands could be a *kuei* (Chinese emblem of dignity), according to Von Le Coq. The only figure whose head is intact wears a sort of cap with a veil hanging from the back of it; Von Le Coq likened this cap to the headdress in the fragment he called the "Gandhara miniature," the latter headdress being, in his opinion, of Sassanian derivation.

Another miniature, from Murtuk, on a page shaped like a *pothī* (Indian manuscript of oblong form), shows a priest with typically Central Asiatic features, dressed in white robes and kneeling on a rug under a tree covered with huge flowers in many colors, his tiara hanging on a branch behind him; perhaps this is a representation of Mani in prayer.

Two miniatures, which doubtless manifest a purely local influence, so closely resemble Buddhist paintings that they may well have been directly inspired by Buddhism. One of these probably depicts a divinity, seated in European fashion on a red throne, his head crowned with a sort of diadem and encircled by a reddish halo. The background, as in most Manichaean miniatures, is blue, and the throne is placed under a red canopy (only one side of which remains), draped with a voluminous red curtain held back by a cord. The figure, the folds of whose garments recall those of the bodhisattvas, raises his right (and sole remaining) hand in the gesture of teaching (see BUDDHISM). The other miniature is probably of a bodhisattva; it shows a haloed figure enclosed in a vast mandorla.

A fragment from Khocho depicts a half-length female figure wearing a tight-fitting and very décolleté tunic-corselet, which has all the characteristics of the garments found in the frescoes at Kizil and Kumtura and on a statuette from Tumshuk. Another fragment from Khocho shows the remains of a vertical band outlined with a motif — derived from Sassanian tradition — of large white beads, as well as the head of some divinity.

The rest of the surviving miniatures constitute a fairly homogeneous group, whose origins should most likely be sought in Iran or in the eastern Mediterranean area. It seems possible to distinguish several different types among the miniatures in this group, which also includes some decorative motifs bordering the manuscripts, a few of these borders having survived with the miniatures, while others are the only remnants of the pages they adorned.

The fragment found at Khocho, called the "Gandhara miniature" by Von Le Coq, shows five ladies of high rank, each wearing a crown of a type similar to that found in Gandharan art (see GANDHARA), according to Von Le Coq; moreover, their dress is not Uigurian, but Iranian, and the name of each figure is written in Sogdian script near her head. In its treatment of the face and hair, this fragment bears a definite relation to two other small fragments from Khocho, also depicting female figures; two additional small fragments of paintings, one of a male and the other of a female figure, are also treated in the same manner. The female figure, in three-quarter view, is wearing a white cap with a curved brim, topped with a golden disk mounted on a low base. The bearded male figure, who has long hair hanging down his back, is of the same type; he is dressed in red and also wears a strange white cap shaped like an inverted flower cup.

A fragment illuminated on both sides, found in Ruin α at Khocho, may be classed in the same category (PL. 284). On one side, in the margin of a text in red Manichaean script, two figures are shown kneeling on a lotus with red petals and a gold center; both have halos and must therefore be divinities, though their features denote a demonic nature. On the other side, a centered miniature shows two beardless figures, nude except for white loincloths, advancing toward a third figure on the very edge of the fragment (on which may also be seen a part of the shoulder of still another figure dressed in green), his left hand raised above his shoulder with the index finger pointing in the air, as if beckoning to the two prisoners to come forward. The latter are separated, above, by a green sheaf and, below, by two footprints (?).

Another type of miniature is represented by two fragments, one of them of a miniature — framed by the text and by red ornamental motifs containing nude, dancing "putti" — showing two figures in Chinese dress kneeling on a rug in prayer before two tall, white, semiobliterated forms wearing white miters; these are seated on another rug. The other fragment is of a miniature depicting six figures — three male and three female — also kneeling on a rug, who are wearing the same brightly colored garments as the many figures in the frescoes of the Uigur period at Turfan; although it is difficult to determine the various influences underlying this composition, the garments are of a Chinese type, especially those of the female figures, whose tall headdresses are typical of the T'ang period. Above this group is a stylized tree with enormous red, lotus-shaped flowers; two of these flowers support bearded figures in white — seated crosslegged — one of whom wears a white miter (the top of the other's head is missing), while somewhat higher, on a flower in bloom, there seems to be a gilded throne on which another figure must have been seated with legs crossed.

Two large fragments belong in this same category. One of these (PL. 287), found in Ruin K at Khocho, is illuminated on both sides, one side depicting two rows of bearded elect in white tiaras, their black hair pushed back behind their ears; each kneels behind a draped writing table, on which a sheet of white paper is spread, and some hold pens and seem to be about to write. The other side consists of a text bordered by flowering boughs and by a miniature — likewise bordered by a branch in bloom — of a row of small, kneeling figures playing on various musical instruments.

The second large fragment, found in Ruin α at Khocho, is far more complex (PL. 282). On one side of it is depicted a scene in a hall with richly decorated walls and floor — probably an assembly convened on the occasion of some feast. The other side has a curious appearance: a central miniature is framed by the text, which is in turn bordered by severely damaged bands of ornamentation. The various figures represented include a Gaṇeśa with a green halo and a divinity with a boar's head haloed in red.

One fragment, in extremely poor condition, is adorned with representations of divinities, on one side with a large figure that has a rather intricate gold halo, and on the other with another large figure flanked, on the right and left, by two smaller figures apparently standing either under an arch or in a niche. In both compositions it is possible to descry a few winged figures whose origins may be traced to the West, for they recall the winged Victories adorning both the monument at Ṭāq-i-Bustan in Iran and the Cave of the Pretas at Kizil (I, PL. 474).

A few other fragments, with illuminations outlined in black on a slightly tinted background, seem not to fit into any group. One shows a bearded figure with huge eyes, wearing an elaborate headdress, seated with legs crossed; another shows a few figures in tall caps, but the figures are damaged and their faces obliterated. The highly stylized decorative motifs, though reminiscent of certain isolated motifs in other fragments, seem to be peculiar to this group.

Floral decoration of the text is as characteristic of Manichaean art as the prominence accorded the inscriptions, usually brightly colored or gilded, that constitute the manuscript titles. Composed of branches of huge fruit, of floral bands, and of flowers of all kinds, the decoration serves as both a frame and a background for the letters, without ever blending into or forming part of them. This mode of decoration seems to be the same as that used in late Coptic manuscripts; in the Manichaean manuscripts of Turfan, however, the decoration projects beyond the heading to border the whole margin of the manuscripts.

There are no written documents on the manner in which these miniatures were executed. Here is an art which survived only among the Uigurs of Turfan, and that under extraordinary circumstances; moreover, the neighboring regions have as yet furnished no similar works which might link this art to artistic manifestations of the same genre in Iran or in the eastern Mediterranean region.

DATING AND CHARACTERISTICS. No criterion for dating these miniatures is really valid. It is possible that some manuscripts were illuminated during a period prior to the settlement of the Uigurs at Khocho; these were executed either by the Uigur Manichaean community established at Khocho before the Uigurs seized control of the region in 840, or they were done at an earlier date by the Manichaean community established at Kara Balghasun in 763 — the year in which the khan of the Uigurs brought the first Manichaean priests from Lo-yang. The problem of dating is indeed insoluble, for Manichaeanism continued to flourish among the Uigurs after the restoration of Buddhism, a fact attested by Islamic writers and in the account of the Chinese envoy, Wang Yen-tê, who visited the Uigurian kingdom between 981 and 984. The period in which these miniatures could have been executed thus extends over at least three centuries, if not longer. The problem of dating is further complicated by the variety of influences manifest in this art and by the fact that it is difficult to distinguish the different elements constituting it, to determine its origins, or even roughly to trace its development.

In the main, the miniatures have one feature in common, the blue background; but this does not seem to constitute a decisive test, for there are a few miniatures not executed in this way that nevertheless appear to have a definite affinity with Irano-Manichaean art, as in the case of the fragment depicting winged Victories. It is possible that not all the miniatures collected by Von Le Coq are Manichaean; however, since many of them are in such poor condition, a definite conclusion cannot be reached. In any case, widely disparate elements went into the making of Manichaean art: Turkestan was at that time characterized by a highly complex aggregation of races and creeds, not only by reason of its geographical position, but also because the religious communities which had become established there maintained close relations with those from which their founders had migrated.

All that can presently be stated is that some of the unusual features seem to have been common to other centers of art. As Von Le Coq pointed out, a link with the West may be found in the technique and decorative motifs of the Turfan bindings, which, according to him, seem to correspond to an analogous technique and similar designs in late Coptic manuscripts. This was confirmed by U. Monneret de Villard, who pointed out that the heart motif described by Von Le Coq is of Irano-Bactrian origin and that it also occurs in a Coptic binding preserved in the Museum für Völkerkunde in Berlin. On the other hand, the theme of the tree exaggerated in width and laden with enormous flowers and clusters of fruit, a motif which occurs in a fresco at Bezeklik as well as in several miniatures found in Murtuk and Khocho, seems also to recur in Tunhuang, where according to J. Hackin, it appears in a votive painting representing the Temptation of the Buddha.

In several of the miniatures, the figures have features resembling those of figures in Coptic painting and wear their hair in curls over the forehead and temples; it also seems that the same type of figure is to be found in the paintings at Miran, which date from the late 3d or early 4th century and are of an unmistakably Western origin that can apparently be traced to coeval Coptic art. Furthermore, since it is believed that Mani himself was the author of the illuminations that adorn the manuscripts written by him, it is probable that, like his writings, the corresponding illuminations were also faithfully copied, in accordance with his injunctions. Some of the Turfan paintings might therefore be distant copies of these originals, a fact which would explain their vague resemblance to the paintings of the 3d century, but that is a very tenuous hypothesis.

In actual fact — apart from the influence of Chinese T'ang painting, which had so marked an effect on the art of the Uigurs in Khocho, and that of northwestern India and eastern Iran, which may have been transmitted through Buddhist painting — Manichaean painting displays elements clearly derived from Sassanian Iran (see SASSANIAN ART), such as the winged Victories and the beaded ornamental bands so characteristic of Sassanian decoration. It also seems possible to establish some affinity with the art of Pyandzhikent, in which traces of Manichaean influence may have appeared in turn; moreover, the facial expressions and coiffures in some of the Manichaean miniatures should perhaps be regarded as reflecting the influence of Coptic painting. One thing seems certain: namely, that the Manichaean clergy of central Asia must have kept in constant touch with Mesopotamia, and later with Sogdiana, hence maintaining relations with the whole of western Asia and perhaps even with Africa.

It is conceivable that Manichaean art reappeared in a disguised form in Iran after the Mongol conquest. Many Uigurian officials were entrusted with the administration of the conquered territories and even held high positions under the Ilkhans (see ILKHAN ART). Doubtless the Uigurs preserved the artistic traditions they had brought into the favorable atmosphere of Iran. There are those who see Sassanian and Manichaean traces in Persian painting; others maintain that the motifs and effects common to both the Manichaean and Persian miniatures were derived from a single source: the Sassanian miniature, of which absolutely nothing is known. There does, indeed, exist an interesting parallel between some of the Manichaean miniatures and the miniatures that adorn the text of Rashīd al-Dīn's great history *Jāmiʿ at-Tavārīkh* (early 14th cent.), Dioscorides' *De materia medica* (copy of 1222), and the manuscript of al-Bīrūnī's *al-Āthār al-Bāqiyah* (copy of 1307) discussed by T. W. Arnold (1924). Arduous research will have to be undertaken before any definite conclusions can be made in this regard. However, it does seem that the decorative border of Manichaean manuscripts was perpetuated in the Persian miniature, and that it reappeared no later than the end of the 13th century, in the bestiary known as *Manāfiʿ al-Ḥayavān* (New York, Pierpont Morgan Lib., M. 500). As to the influence which Manichaean painting may have exerted in the Far East — where numerous Manichaeanist communities were founded, some of them continuing to flourish for a long time in the region of the lower Yangtze — the question has still to be fully explored, but it seems reasonable to suppose that the existence of illuminated books in these communities must have exerted some influence on Chinese book illustration.

BIBLIOG. A. Grünwedel, Altbuddhistische Kultstätten in Chinesisch-Turkistan, Berlin, 1912; A. von Le Coq, Chotscho (Ergebnisse der königlich preussischen Turfan-Expedition), Berlin, 1913; U. Monneret de Villard, L'arte manichea, Rend. Ist. lombardo, di sc. e lett., 2d ser., LVI, 1923, pp. 16-20; A. von Le Coq, Buddhistische Spätantike in Mittelasien, II: Die manichäische Miniaturen, Berlin, 1923; T. W. Arnold, Survivals of Sasanian and Manichaean Art in Persian Painting, London, 1924; J. Charpentier, Manikeiska miniatyrer fran Centralasien, Svenska Orientsällskapets Årsbok, 1924, pp. 73 ff.; J. Hackin, Recherches archéologiques en Asie centrale, RAA, IX, 1935, pp. 124-43, X, 1936, pp. 65-72; U. Monneret de Villard, The Relations of Manichaean Art to Iranian Art, SPA, III, 1939, pp. 1820-28; P. de Menasce and A. Guillon, Un cachet manichéen de la Bibliothèque nationale, Rev. de l'h. des religions, CXXXI, 1946, pp. 81-84; H. C. Puech, Le Manichéisme, son fondateur, sa doctrine, Paris, 1949.

Louis HAMBIS

Illustrations: PLS. 281-287.

MANNERISM. The terms *maniera* (lit., manner or style; historically, the style of the 16th cent.) and "mannerism" have been used since the 16th century to designate and characterize the complex stylistic phenomena occurring in Italy and throughout Europe in the period between the apogee of Renaissance classicism, represented by Leonardo, Michelangelo, and Raphael, and the advent of the new artistic era ushered in by the Carraccis, Caravaggio, and Bernini. These phenomena have in the course of the following centuries been subject to a wide range of critical interpretation — being viewed variously as the final exhaustion, indeed, degeneration of Renaissance artistic premises, as the vital elaboration essential to a new stylistic synthesis, or simply as the expression of a self-sufficient esthetic entity. The last view has dominated the thinking of an active group of modern critics devoted to the restoration of the historical conception of the *maniera*, now elevated to a stylistic category, as mannerism, by means of careful analysis of single phenomena and of their historical interrelation. Since the outcome of this scholarly undertaking is still at issue, it seems useful to review both the history of the new critical formulation of the problem and its consequences for the historical reconstruction of the artistic revolution of the 16th century.

SUMMARY. The problem of mannerism (col. 444). The maniera in its historical setting (col. 453).

THE PROBLEM OF MANNERISM. The term *maniera*, from which "mannerism" derives, goes back to the earliest Italian critical writing. Cennini used it (ca. 1390) to mean individual style; Ghiberti was the first (ca. 1450) to extend its meaning to apply to the style of a period. Its specific application to 16th-century style originated in its use by the greatest of 16th-century critical writers, Giorgio Vasari (q.v.), for whom the term had a variety of clearly differentiated meanings (*Vite...*, 1550 and 1568). Like Cennini, he used it extensively to indicate a habitual mode of artistic expression, that is, the personal manner or style of an individual artist, but he also used it to denote a national or historical style, as had Ghiberti (*maniera greca*, Byzantine style; *maniera moderna*, modern style). However, in Vasari's hands it served too, standing alone, as a term of critical approbation in the absolute sense of *good* style: an artist either had *maniera* or he did not. Here *maniera* contrasted with the objective imitation of nature, which Vasari considered to be the primary characteristic of 15th-century painting, and denoted a quality peculiar to 16th-century painting, the ideal imitation of nature; *maniera* was the decisive factor integrating the achievements of the Renaissance — *regola* (rule), *ordine* (order, or composition), *misura* (proportion, or measure), and *disegno* (design, or drawing). If *disegno*, called by Vasari "the father of the three arts," was the physical expression of "a form, or idea, of all things in nature," the "idea" being identified in contemporary Neoplatonic thought with beauty itself, *maniera*, qualified as *bella maniera*, was the extension of this idea of beauty into a pervasive principle of style. "The artist's manner [*maniera*] becomes then the more beautiful from the practice of frequently drawing the most beautiful things and from adding together the most beautiful hands, heads, bodies, and legs, thus forming from all these beauties a figure more [beautiful] than is possible [that is, than occurs in nature], and making use of it in every work for all the figures; hence it is called *bella maniera*."

The process of study, selection, addition, and projection — of individual judgment and subjective interpretation — constituting the *bella maniera* implied the idea of the intervention of imagination alongside objective intellectual elaboration. In Vasari's view this process of the ideal imitation of nature was the liberating discovery of the 16th century, when art was thus freed from the self-imposed limitations of 15th-century art arising from its attachment to objective reality and was enabled, through this infusion of subjectivity, to surpass in effect the paradigm of the art of antiquity, admired throughout the Renaissance as capable of adhering simultaneously and equally to nature (*similitudo*) and to ideal beauty (*pulchritudo*). Inherent, however, in the very liberating function of the *bella maniera* was a subtle conflict between the desire for definitive rules and the desire for a form of expressive enrichment that made it necessary to transcend them. This tension implicit in 16th-century style was recognized by contemporary writers; Vasari's appreciation of the great creators of the High Renaissance, particularly Michelangelo, was based precisely on this capacity to transcend the established boundaries, especially those of classical example.

The term *maniera*, then, actually indicated by implication and by extension the common basis of all 16th-century style, not only of Vasari's own generation but also, and more particularly, of the golden age itself, which he regarded as an unsurpassable artistic achievement. Vasari recognized this age as already ended; thus, by indirection, the *maniera* as practiced in his own day represented a descent from that height. However, the difference was essentially one of magnitude, not of kind. For G. B. Armenini (*De' veri precetti della pittura*, 1586) too the grandeur of the attainments of the golden age admitted of eclecticism and imitation as the only developmental possibilities.

No real censure of the *maniera* was formulated until 1672, when, in the context of 17th-century classicism, one of its most authoritative spokesmen, Giovanni Pietro Bellori, published the work containing the celebrated definition of the *maniera* as "a fantastic idea based upon studio practice and not upon imitation [of nature or suitable classical examples]" which has served as the starting point for much of the modern discussion of the subject. In the course of less than a century the ideal principle of an entire style had become an empty shell, by Bellori's time persisting only in studio practice, no longer sustained by what had been its point of departure, the observation of nature. It must be remembered, however, that Bellori regarded the *maniera* as the style of the later 16th century (i.e., of Vasari's *Quarta Età*), which differed not only in degree but in kind from that of the High Renaissance, and that his disapproval extended equally to the "naturalistic" innovations of Caravaggio, which he mistakenly regarded as simply the representation of the immediate and accidental aspects of nature. The critical vantage point of Bellori was thus still one of high ideality: artists should "correct nature" so that a form "originating in nature overcomes its origin and is made an original of art." The late followers of the *maniera* were no longer capable of this, for they had become ensnared in the imitation of the great Renaissance masters. It was necessary not to reject the ideal principle of the style but to give it a new foundation, and this was provided by 17th-century classicism. Bellori's disapprobation was thus directed not so much at the artistic principle itself as at the senescence of the style of imitators incapable of understanding the stylistic elements they had borrowed, for whom (as Luigi Coletti has pointed out) the phrase "fantastic idea" has less relation to creative imagination than to empty intellectualism. On this basis the imitators of Raphael and Michelangelo were sharply criticized from this time forward.

The late-17th-century critic Baldinucci, in his *Vocabolario toscano dell'arte del disegno* (1681), gave *maniera* the altogether negative meaning of the individual will of the artist in opposition to the evidence of nature. As such, *maniera* might be variously qualified, but always in the negative sense (crude, washed out, pinched, languid, wooden, imitative, dry, etc.), the severe judgment being mitigated only in the case of *maniera gagliarda* (vigorous, bold, rich manner), which emphasized formal chiaroscuro; in the case of the "Lombard manner" of the north Italian painters, whose color retained its firm attachment to reality; and in the case of the "ideal manner" of those artists who were not so enthralled by reality as to forget what they had observed "in the most beautiful of nature and in the works of the most sublime masters." (But they must be interpreters, not copyists, of these masters, so as not to fall into the "wooden manner," the "vice of musculature," of the 16th-century followers of Michelangelo.) Apparently, even in the language of the workshops and studios, which were Baldinucci's sources, the term *maniera* was by then synonymous with creative inertia and expressed positive meaning only by virtue of a qualifying adjective. "Mannered" (*ammanierato*) was used by Francesco Milizia (1797) to denote artistic dishonesty, and "mannerist" became the term customarily applied to the imitators of Raphael and Michelangelo. This transition in the history of a term from an artistic category to a disparaging adjective sums up the parabola of the Renaissance artistic idiom.

Originating in baroque criticism of the art of the preceding period, the derogatory connotation of *maniera* remained unchanged until modern times. To Lanzi, writing in 1789, "mannerism" signified the decline of art into the inert repetition of formulas. But for the first time it was, by him, given chronological limits as a distinct trend: the golden age of Renaissance art did not survive the Sack of Rome (1527; "after this that capital gradually declined in painting and was finally filled with mannerists"). The same thing had happened in Florence after Vasari, while in Venice the mannerist dissipation of the great coloristic tradition took place only in the 17th century, with Palma Giovane. Furthermore, the 16th century, said Lanzi, in the preface to his treatment of the Bolognese school, had been, at its apogee, so rich in definitive solutions that anyone who came after, "whether he wanted to or not, though he was an imitator of nature must at the same time be [an imitator] of the greatest masters." "Only the way of imitation was open to the human genius to distinguish itself" until the Carraccis (q.v.) — not Caravaggio, who to Lanzi was an isolated figure quite apart from the mainstream — found a new way through which "the painter might divide, so to speak, his glances between nature and art." Mannerism was henceforward to designate, however negatively, the style of a specified period of Italian art. Jakob Burckhardt (1855), limiting it chronologically to the 50 years between 1530 and 1580, traced its origin not only to the inhibiting presence of the great masters but also to social factors such as the final breakdown of the guild system.

The shift in the critical position on mannerism took place at the end of the 19th century and was a consequence of the reassessment of baroque art that followed the long estrangement from neoclassic intellectualism as well as romanticism. The study of the baroque led to the search for its premises and origins in the art of the 16th century, and in the quest, which began in the field of architecture, not only the crystallization of the "classical style" but also its radical transformation began to be discerned. Cornelius Gurlitt (1887) described a "late Renaissance" in which Michelangelo and the architects active in Rome at the end of the 16th century shared in that triumph of personal sentiment over intellectualism basic to both Reformation and Counter Reformation, but Heinrich Wölfflin in his fundamental work *Renaissance und Barock* (1888), rejecting the intermediary period proposed by Gurlitt, traced back to the "classical" maturity of the Renaissance the beginnings of the evolution leading to baroque style, which was in his opinion clearly defined as early as 1580. That artistic change which Gurlitt saw as the consequence of cultural and spiritual factors was defined by Wölfflin in purely formal terms as the shift from closed, "sculptural" form to open, freely pictorial form — a concept he later (1915) fully developed in his *Kunstgeschichtliche Grundbegriffe* (*Principles of Art History*). Renaissance and baroque style thus represent essentially opposed currents of art, the mutually exclusive, though chronologically adjacent, terms of the eternal classic-romantic antinomy. Within the brief period of "classic art," which began with Leonardo and was dominated by Raphael, Michelangelo represented the individual crisis presaging the rise of the baroque — even though the imitation of Michelangelo by the mannerists constituted dross destined to be discarded. The necessity of an intermediary phase between two diverse stylistic phenomena was restated by Alois Riegl (1894–1900; pub. 1908); he identified, besides the evolution leading directly from Michelangelo to the baroque, an architectural current — the optical-coloristic — derived from Raphael's purely pictorial interpretation of Donato Bramante (q.v.), which spread beyond Rome to Venice and the rest of north Italy. This current, which found theoretical expression in the treatise of Serlio, was characterized by a concern with the animation of surfaces rather than with baroque structural innovation. Riegl thus attributed a positive evolutionary character to that gray zone of art which earlier critics had delimited chronologically but had seen only as a crystallized involution. Extending this critical insight from architecture to painting, K. H. Busse discerned, several years later (1911), through his study of the origins of Lodovico Cigoli, that actually the crisis of Renaissance perspective — an essential condition for the free, pictorial space construction of the baroque — had taken place in Florentine mannerism. This marked the beginning of a new critical concentration on mannerist painting, henceforth regarded as a style of crisis, a crisis of liberation: the rational rule of the Renaissance had to be voided to make possible the free development of a new expressive volition. In the course of the inquiry F. Goldschmidt (without, it must be noted, using the word "mannerism") centered attention on Pontormo, Il Rosso, and Bronzino, demonstrating (1911) that in their work, despite their very different personalities, a definitive emancipation from the tyranny of perspective was achieved. Space, both as subjective observation and as rational measure, had, as in Michelangelo, to be constructed through the figures themselves.

Subjectivism, affirming itself in contemporary art through the expressionist movement, by now swayed not only taste but critical perceptions, and criticism veered more and more toward a rebellion against rationality, in which the very concept of the Renaissance, in reaction to its canonization in the 19th century by Burckhardt and Eugène Müntz, became enmeshed. Indeed, as early as 1903, Bernard Berenson, while generally viewing mannerism as a decline, had not only noted the particular appeal of Pontormo to contemporary taste but pointed out his great worth as an esthetic personality. The importance of such factors to the new critical orientation was explicitly recognized by Werner Weisbach, who in 1910 summed up and extended earlier views in a basic article that he called *Der Manierismus* as a positive affirmation of the identity of mannerism as a style — the style in which the Renaissance was at once developed and concluded. "Mannerism exists when forms that originally had a precise meaning and expressive value are taken over and carried to extremes, so that they appear affected, artificial, empty, degenerate." However, the forms, drained of specific meaning, took on an abstract esthetic value that could be embodied in imitation of Michelangelo's heroic style or in an original ideal of grace, evolved from Raphael and Correggio (qq.v.). In particularizing this ideal Parmigianino (q.v.) manifested a creative vein thoroughly responsive to the taste of a new society, which differed from that of the 15th-century *bourgeoisie* in the very refinement of its behavior (as reflected in Baldassare Castiglione's *Il Cortigiano*). True, art was alienated, except in Venice, the true matrix of the baroque, from the vigorous sources of naturalism. It is also true that the Church of the Counter Reformation had no use for an art of moribund though persistent Humanistic content, which had further (like expressionism) succeeded in cutting itself off from any relation to natural verisimilitude and employed natural forms only as the means to new emotional experiences. On the impact of this factor, on either earlier or contemporaneous art, Weisbach reserved judgment.

By the post-World War I period, then, the bases for the revision of all preceding historical constructs had been established. The rehabilitation of baroque style represented a critical victory on a par with the reaction of art against the late-19th-century attachment to physical actuality. Increasingly, in the name of this reaction, the critical attack on the concept of the Renaissance, burdened since the 17th and 18th centuries with the now unforgivable cultural fetishes of rationalism and idealism, took shape. The favor the Renaissance lost accrued to mannerism precisely in proportion to the degree to which the two deviated, and this involved the risk that the new criticism might degenerate into sheer polemic or arbitrary generalization. The appearance in 1920 of Hermann Voss's *Die Malerei der Spätrenaissance in Rom und Florenz* was a call for the return to the close study of specific data. Voss, himself steeped in baroque painting, was opposed to the Wölfflinian view of the Italian 16th century as merely a preparatory stage. Baroque pictorial expression was conditioned by northern Italy, particularly Venice, but it could have become a style only in conjunction with the complex formal evolution of Florence and Rome. Voss traced this process through the various currents of 16th-century painting (one of which, but not the only one, was mannerism), suggesting parallels, but not causal relations, with contemporaneous developments in the other arts, for example, in architecture and music.

The objective viewpoint assumed by Voss put schematic generalizations to the test of individual facts, personalities, and works of art. Virtually concurrent with this historical objectivity was the unreservedly subjective countertendency of Max Dvořák, to whom is attributable the definitive status of mannerism as an autonomous style — a position that remained determinative for later critics. In the celebrated lecture delivered by Dvořák in 1918, *Über Greco und den Manierismus* (pub. 1924), the devaluation of Renaissance art was absolute. Its limitation lay in the submission to natural reality — although it had attempted to idealize this through form. Michelangelo overcame this limitation through an overwhelmingly subjective expression, so far beyond rationality of form that many of his late sculptures were considered unfinished. And through his influence, Tintoretto (q.v.) was able to transform the naturalistic sensualism of the Venetian palette into a free counterpoint of light and color. El Greco (q.v.), inheriting from both, became the great interpreter of that triumph of emotion over reason upon which was based the spiritual revival of Ignatius Loyola and St. Theresa. This profoundly religious resolution was made possible for El Greco, however, by his experience of a similar tendency in the secular world: the individualistic estrangement from rational form, characteristic of mannerism, as perceived in the Fontainebleau school (see FRENCH ART).

Dvořák's thesis was developed more fully in his *Geschichte der italienische Kunst* (based on lectures of 1919 and 1920; pub. posthumously, 1927–29), which must be credited with restoring to critical favor both Michelangelo's late paintings in the Pauline Chapel and the works of artists such as Daniele da Volterra, until then considered sterile imitators. In general, Dvořák discerned the positive aspects of the mannerist evolution more acutely than any other writer. He saw in the pupils of Raphael a revival of monumental painted decoration and the emergence of a new kind of religious painting, in which the dramatic aspect of the image was intensified on the basis of premises entirely opposed to the naturalism and rationalism of the Renaissance. Free movement in space replaced static regularity; poetic content was liberated in *invenzione*; new forms (the *storietta* and the ideal landscape) were invented; drawing, engraving, and book illustration flourished. Immediately on its completion (1541), the *Last Judgment* of Michelangelo dominated the contemporary artistic scene, as the inexhaustible source not only of a universal repertory of solutions to problems of form but also of that ideal conception of a world of metaphysical being before which, as in some vast drama, all rational certainty crumbled.

The Florentine artists Pontormo, Il Rosso, and Bronzino were most keenly aware of the crisis of style implicit in High Renaissance art, and it was in direct consequence of the critical confrontation with the weighty inheritance from the past that the characteristics of this art of formal and spiritual originality of the first generation of mannerists were determined: alongside fanciful caprice, a sadness intensified to the limits of the bearable, to the expression of martyrdom; the search in drawing for the most expressive lineaments of reality, which were then separately exploited in a new mode of representation; the effort, in the portrait, to convey, beyond the depiction of the individual, the essence of a particular social position. And this confrontation was the point of departure for later critics in their subtle individuation of the maddeningly subjective aspects of the new esthetic — the grotesque, the satanic, the saturnine, the ugly, and the absurd — which modern taste has found ambivalent.

The very extremism of Dvořák's premises (the absolute naturalism of the Renaissance, the absolute subjectivity of mannerism) made them useful as working hypotheses for further discoveries, so that they remained effective even though it later became necessary to reformulate them. All confusion between mannerism and protobaroque was now eliminated: mannerism assumed a character of its own and was henceforth studied as an independent style. The distinction was further articulated by Luise Fröhlich-Bum (1921): in the 16th century, besides the baroque direction indicated by Michelangelo and the impressionistic direction set by Venice, there was a new synthesis of old Renaissance data effected by Parmigianino, based on an ideal of grace detached from all but purely esthetic considerations; from this synthesis derived a vigorous style current, in sculpture as well as in painting, discernible in the work of Cellini, Ammanati, and Giambologna in Florence, of Vittoria in Venice, and, beyond the Alps, in such followers of Giambologna as Adriaen de Vries. Mannerism thus extended from painting into all fields of art. Erwin Panofsky, elaborating suggestions made by Gurlitt and Riegl, explored the possibility of a definitely mannerist, not protobaroque, architectural style which fully utilized the formal repertory of the classical style. This point of view was to be systematically developed by E. Michalski (1933), who advanced the thesis that mannerism in architecture consisted in the disruption of Renaissance static equilibrium through irrational inversion of the relations of mass and support, such as was apparent in the work of certain architects until then considered exponents of classicism: Peruzzi, Vignola, Palladio, Galeazzo Alessi, and, north of the Alps, De Vries, Ducerceau, and Frans Floris de Vriendt.

Scholars now attempted to provide the mannerist style, by this time homogeneous in the three arts, with a clear patent of esthetic legitimacy. Margarete Hörner (1924) drew parallels between the development of 16th-century Italian art and that of Greek sculpture from Phidias to Polykleitos, in order to raise the status of mannerism from an empirical historical observation to an ahistorical conceptual category necessarily intermediary between the terms of the Wölfflinian antinomy. Panofsky (1924) sought to establish an original philosophical foundation for the new style through analyzing the treatise of Federico Zuccari (or Zuccaro), *L'Idea de' scultori, pittori e architetti* (1607); he reassigned the subjectivist approach of mannerism to a new position as the philosophical premise on which the Renaissance had been based. The "idea" in which mannerist art originated was no longer of rational and naturalistic origin; it was of a mystical character — a revival of a Neoplatonic concept, in harmony with Counter-Reformation religious thought, according to which the very capacity for artistic expression was attributed to divine grace. Mannerism was thus historically confirmed as the expression of an autonomous current of thought. In a long controversy with Weisbach, who regarded the baroque as the style of the Counter Reformation, Nikolaus Pevsner held (1925) that, on the contrary, the aims of that movement were fully concordant with those of mannerism; he gave positive value to features until then judged negatively as medieval and Gothic elements rejected by the rationalist Renaissance — even to the Counter-Reformation mortification of individuality as an intensification and strengthening of artistic subjectivity.

From what had gone before, it was a natural step to the neat formulation of mannerism as an anticlassical style arrived at by Walter Friedländer and enunciated in his lecture *Die Entstehung des antiklassischen Stiles in der italienischen Malerei um 1520* (1914; pub. 1925). More important, Friedländer was the first to localize the origins of mannerism, not in Rome, as a reaction to or development from Raphael or Michelangelo, but rather in Florence, in the consciously dramatic stand taken by Pontormo and Il Rosso against the art of their masters Fra Bartolommeo and Andrea del Sarto (qq.v.): they broke up into irrational rhythmic freedom the fixed proportional meter of the older masters. The impact of these innovators was so great as to touch even Michelangelo, who was thus not the initiator of but only a participant in the mannerist trend. About 1523, Il Rosso took the new style to Rome, in this way exerting a decisive influence on the Roman development of Parmigianino and, through him, and through his own later work at Fontainebleau, on much of the subsequent artistic history of Europe.

The consistent direction taken by German criticism at the end of the 19th and in the first 30 years of the present century, in identifying mannerism as a countertendency to classicism, produced a total reversal in the view of 16th-century Italian art and the entire Renaissance phenomenon. The vitality of the Renaissance was no longer seen to consist in the elevated stylistic purveyance of a profound knowledge of nature; rather it was seen to consist in the freeing and expression of the more irrational and subjective impulses. The victory of Humanism, which imposed a rational order on the dark forces of nature, was regarded as transitory: the original struggle between it and the Gothic could only seemingly have ended in its favor if even the very height of the newly achieved classicism was marked by a Gothic revival in the form of mannerism. An increasing effort was made to identify mannerism with a new access of Gothicism, that vivifying Germanic element of Western art, seen as in perpetual antithesis to formalistic Mediterranean rationalism. H. Wescher-Kauert (1924) equated with Italian mannerism the resurgent Gothicism of late-15th- and early-16th-century painting — supposing Altdorfer, Grünewald, Baldung-Grien (qq.v.), and Jörg Breu to have constituted a more or less conscious opposition to the classical efforts of Dürer (q.v.). Frederick Antal (1948), in his comprehensive survey, from this viewpoint, of the whole Italian Renaissance, saw Florence, the birthplace of Humanism, as the theater of a continuing unresolved conflict with the Gothic, ultimately culminating in the anticlassical rebellion of the early 16th century, which left a deeper imprint on the character of both Italian and international mannerism than did the estheticism of Parmigianino and of the Fontainebleau school. Similar convictions led Georg Weise to the assiduous phenomenological identification of all the Gothicisms latent in Italian Renaissance art. From this searching inquiry the concept of mannerism as a style emerged as an indisputable historical discovery. Its precise position in the sequence of history was treated by Hans Hoffmann in his *Hochrenaissance, Manierismus, Frühbarock* (1938), in which he compared the stylistic concepts that inform mannerism to those of the High Renaissance and the protobaroque.

In the decade 1920-30 Italian critics were also concerned with the problem of mannerism, not so much in conducting a systematic examination as in measuring the conceptual structure of the German critics against the standard of what was to remain the fundamental premise: the living individuality of the work of art. From this and from the personality of the artist it was possible to re-create the homogeneous continuity of a historical fabric that would not be merely the arbitrary demonstration of a priori concepts. The need to historicize the newly accepted stylistic category also appears in the work of later German writers (e.g., Friedrich Kriegbaum, Ulrich Middeldorf) and, more recently, of American scholars. In Italy the crucial work was that of Roberto Longhi, who, while apparently limiting himself to the consideration of single works or single artists, drew conclusions valid for mannerism as a whole. As early as 1926 a sculpture of Pietro Bernini afforded him the occasion for framing a subtle distinction between abstract mannerist colorism and robust baroque pictorialism; an attribution to Lelio Orsi led to the most penetrating definition of the mannerist esthetic, as representing "Renaissance culture ... in process of becoming once more romantic, without, however, wishing to lose an iota of the science and archaeology of the 16th century — on the contrary reveling in them and adorning itself with them as with borrowed finery." Later (1927), by way of confirming the attribution to Velázquez of a *St. Thomas* in the Musée des Beaux-Arts of Orléans, Longhi formulated a complete historical outline of the diffusion in Spain — by way of the works of late Florentine and, more importantly, Lombard mannerists — of those survivals of a "naturalistic vein that cherished the optical appearance of things" which prepared the way for the acceptance of the naturalism of Caravaggio, the artistic substratum of the new art of Velázquez. Finally (1953), it was his reconstruction of the Italian work of Alonso Berruguete that shed light on the complete interaction of stylistic influences characterizing the early 16th-century Florentine environment in which Pontormo and Il Rosso developed.

Since the decade 1930-40 Italian criticism has similarly centered its concern with mannerism on the reconstruction of individual artistic personalities. At the same time Adolfo Venturi's history of Italian art reached the 16th century. Throughout the immense amount of material there assembled is a wealth of perceptive comment altogether free of any conceptual prejudice. A general effort to define mannerism historically is evident in a series of monographs published in the 1940s (Luisa Becherucci, on 16th-century sculpture and architecture and on the Tuscan mannerists; A. Graziani, on Bartolomeo Cesi; and Giuliano Briganti, on Pellegrino Tibaldi, treated in the framework of a general consideration of mannerism).

Objection to the frequent insinuation that mannerism is to be identified with ambiguous and amoral expressive content was raised by Francesco Arcangeli, who stated that this content could have found expression only through a subtle interplay of mannerism with the continuing formal heritage of the Renaissance: mannerism was, therefore, not so much a concerted artistic trend with its own expressive goals as the manifestation of an irreconcilable crisis. The consequences of this "realistic" revision of the concept of mannerism have been twofold. First, granting that everything that has been called "mannerist" is mannerist, in which case mannerism embraces nearly all of the 16th century, the question arises whether it can legitimately be termed a separate and autonomous artistic current. Secondly, the critical characterization of mannerism as an esthetic nurtured only by such pernicious sources as the absurd, the exaggerated, and the abnormal leads to doubt as to the positive ethical, and hence artistic, value of the entire trend.

On the occasion of the 1940 Mostra del Cinquecento Toscano in Florence, Mario Salmi had pointed out the equivocation implicit in the very term "mannerism," derisive in origin, and proposed a return to designating the trend, and regarding it historically, as a late phase of the Renaissance. In 1950 P. Barocchi posed the question whether the category was valid for artists of great originality, such as Il Rosso, who hardly merited a label bearing the stigma of decadence, which in addition wrongly lumped together phenomena so different as the rebellion against formal academicism and the rhetorical delight in it. Longhi took exception to this sweeping dissent — on the ground of the effective presence, even in Il Rosso, of that particular captious, introverted, imaginative quality which Longhi, more sensitively than anyone else, had observed — but a similar reservation has persisted, more or less explicitly declared, in later discussions of the problem.

The moral ambiguity of mannerism has increasingly concerned writers. G. C. Argan (1942) saw in late-16th-century mannerism the total "dislocation of the ethical certainty that had kept the 15th-century imagination within the bounds of reality"; the problem of truth was evaded in the approximation of verisimilitude, and moral commitment in the moralism propagated by the Counter Reformation. Going further, G. Nicco Fasola (1947) based her definition of the art of Pontormo on a negative valuation not only of mannerism but of the whole Italian Renaissance: Renaissance intellectualism dried up the spontaneity of Italian culture, whereas the northern Reformation revitalized transalpine civilization. Artists who were aware of this cultural malady might arrive at the tortured but vain rebellions of a Pontormo; those who were not could indulge in virtuosity and figural eccentricity, in dangerous dalliance with the abnormal and the terrible, without, however, ever breaking the vicious circle of stultifying intellectualism, which has been ever since the "plague of Latinity." This harsh condemnation was mitigated only in respect to 16th-century Italian architecture, where functional necessity applied the brake to intellectualizing abstraction. In Nicco Fasola's opinion, previous writers had been too much concerned with the formal aspects of mannerism, rather than with the investigation — required for a valid historical judgment — of the spiritual trends underlying artistic expression. In certain respects an excursus of Eugenio Battisti (1960) reveals a similar view; he fully accepts the concept of mannerism as a rebellion against the classicism of the Renaissance but judges it as lacking an adequate moral base, since, like the object of its opposition, it was intellectual in origin rather than the outgrowth of a new moral and religious experience. It was thus a revolt *manqué*, not even supported by contemporaneous society, which, in its spiritually impoverished state, repudiated it out of deep-rooted conservatism. And the Counter Reformation, far from identifying with mannerism, directed its criticism at the expressive extremes of mannerist art. On the social level both mannerism and the High Renaissance have been condemned also by Arnold Hauser (1951) as the expression of an aristocratic and oversophisticated neofeudal class.

This extreme negative view of mannerism both as a style category and as a historical phenomenon is not, however, the prevailing position of contemporary criticism. That position has been expressed by Longhi in his *Ricordo dei Manieristi* (1953): mannerism ought no longer to be spoken of as a programmatic tendency deliberately running counter to the stylistic mainstream of the 16th century. Rather, this modern-day distortion of the term, the product of a one-sided and tendentious critical position, should be rejected, and the definition of the *maniera* as the style of the 16th century itself — as it was used in contemporaneous historical writing, from Vasari on — should be restored. The *maniera* was interpreted with a high degree of originality by "those Florentine hands from boyhood grown weary in transcribing the two cartoons of Leonardo and Michelangelo in the Palazzo Vecchio..." in the same unfettered and whimsical spirit as Florentine artists of the last generation of the 15th century, such as Pollaiuolo, had interpreted naturalistic and classical Humanism. It was this freedom of action within the *maniera* that assured its vitality and gave to it that foundation of solid graphic experience present in even the boldest, most bizarre adventures of the imagination — indexes indeed of an ethical crisis, of a dissatisfaction from which a new future of art was arising. The early-20th-century intellectual movement, in seeking an origin for its own expressionistic and surrealistic graphic extremes, had arbitrarily separated out of the 16th-century context episodes congenial to itself, imposing on them the convenient tailor-made legend of mannerism as the style of the abnormal and the monstrous. The reaction of later critics against this form of expedient conceptualism has been toward a proper historical revision based on the careful study of individual artists and works of art.

That this revision remains a pressing scholarly concern was emphasized by the 1960 congress of the Accademia Nazionale dei Lincei on the theme "Mannerism, Baroque, and Rococo: Concepts and Terms," which thoroughly investigated the contemporary critico-historical situation in regard to the manifestations of these three in literature and music as well as the visual arts. The two basic papers on mannerism in art, given by Weise and Salmi, reexamined the two different approaches in modern criticism. Weise no longer saw in mannerism "a new style in the sense of the other great periods of the history of art"; rather, mannerism was "a shading [of the existing style] accompanied by the continuation of the classicizing vein," and thus "symptomatic of a period of transition and of contrasts between the High Renaissance and the formation of the new baroque synthesis." Salmi persisted in his refusal to use the term at all: mannerism could at most, he held, represent a qualification of one of the terms of the eternal dialectic between the classical and the anticlassical. In connection with the discussion of the boundaries between mannerism and baroque, Salmi cautioned that the individual fact of the work of art ought always to prevail over generalization. In a paper treating the subject from the literary point of view, Raimondi, though recognizing mannerism as a stylistic category of European range "necessary in order to remove the traditional verdict of decadence from the stylistic metamorphosis that overcame the great tradition of Renaissance classicism," noted that its adoption in the works of L. Curtius had virtually compromised the results of visual art criticism by transforming it from a definitive historical trend to a "phenomenon coincident with a style of the unnatural, complementary to classicism in all periods." Faced with this abstract vitiation of the concept of mannerism, Raimondi too advocated a "return to history."

Thus, a discussion that about 1925 had seemed definitively closed has been reopened, and modern scholars are beginning to see that the problem was inadequately framed from the start. Born of the necessity to provide an evolutionary continuity for baroque art, which late-19th-century criticism had construed as a sort of romantic rival to Renaissance classicism, the concept of mannerism as a style never lost its original polemic cast, whether viewed as the liberation of subjective sentiment in opposition to an intellectual stylistic norm, as the resurgence of the Gothic against Humanism, or as the tangible expression of impulses — perhaps ambiguous, but existentially genuine — forbidden expression by the hypocritical moralistic conformity of the Renaissance, reflected in art in an artificial formal idealism. But this persistent antinomy had then been examined in only one of its terms, the other term remaining permanently fixed in the concept of the immutable perfection of a formal style bound by the premises of conformity to nature and to the esthetic principles of classical art in which it had been hypostatized by the criticism of 17th-century classicism and 18th-century neoclassicism. Only in comparison with such a crystallization of the High Renaissance, precluding any later evolution of art, could all the troublesome intolerances and rebellions with which mannerism had, almost symbolically, been burdened have retained any validity. Strangely enough, art historians seem to have been unaware that this antiquated intellectual structure had already received fierce blows from the direction of philosophical inquiry; Ernst Cassirer, as early as 1906, and later in the fundamental *Individuum und Kosmos in der Philosophie der Renaissance* (1927), as the protagonist of reopening the question of knowledge of the principle of form through the unceasing formulation achieved in living works of art, rather than through the speculation of theologians and philosophers, had put the consideration of Renaissance art on a new basis. Through perspective, the invention of artists and the interpretation, and hence the "imitation," of nature were based on the absolute rational certainty of numerical proportion, thus establishing the identity of artistic "form" with the essential "necessity" of nature. However, the development of perspective theory itself gave rise to the complex problems of the infinite proportional relation, and in consequence the concept of space as a measurable quantity evolved into that of space as a "free and ideal ordering function," opening the way to the theory of motion, from which at the end of the Renaissance emerged the new science of Galileo. The essential "form" that art, the standard-bearer of modern science, pursued in all the aspects of nature was not something changeless and static but the dynamic principle of the unending process of becoming. The inner tension thus produced pervaded the new artistic image, whatever its figural components, Humanistic or Gothic, and brought about that *superamento* which Renaissance criticism had already discerned in the pictorial chiaroscuro of Leonardo, in the plastic extremes of Michelangelo, and in the color-light configurations of the Venetians and of Raphael.

This art, whose formal basis was form itself, however, in its rationality — manifestation of the movement which, to Leonardo, was the "causa d'ogni vita" — did not require the opposition of the irrational, of the subjective, to open the way to the most daring experimentation. It could hazard the most perilous adventures without foundering in formlessness, the negation of all expressive power. It was enough — and Longhi clearly recognized this — that the minds of men were overwhelmed by the anxiety, the anguish, the tormenting doubts, the yearnings for transcendental evasions of an era of complex spiritual development such as the 16th century; the mastery of form calmly yielded to the expression of these, capable of embracing all such tendencies within itself.

The investigation of mannerism has thus led to the realization of the need for a more far-reaching analysis of the concept of the Renaissance. This process has already begun, and the new methodology is being applied to its fundamental problems, beginning with perspective. The accumulation of interpretive dross is being discarded and the "classical style" of the 16th century, the analytical consideration of which had been arrested, so to speak, at the impressive but now inadequate definition of Wölfflin, squarely confronted. It is symptomatic that the more subtle students of mannerist estheticism have turned their attention to this problem. Weise seeks its premises in the "heroic ideal" of Humanism (1961); Sidney Freedberg, whose valuable monograph on Parmigianino appeared in 1950, has traced the development of the classical style in the complex dialectic of Leonardo, of Michelangelo, and of Raphael and laid it down as the necessary first principle for the comprehension of Pontormo and Il Rosso (1961). And though mannerism is still seen as substantially different from the High Renaissance, the way is now open to a more coherent grasp of their relation, through which the development of 16th-century style can be assessed at its full historical value.

THE MANIERA IN ITS HISTORICAL SETTING. The painstaking study of the subject of mannerism resulted in a new interpretation of the entire course of the 16th century from a point of view totally at variance with the traditional approach. The focus of attention shifted from the great masters to certain marginal trends hitherto depreciated as constituting an opaque and distorted reflection of their art; here art historians discovered and traced a very energetic treatment of representational elements previously overlooked but fundamental to the historical continuity of the art of this period and capable of attaining — as they did in many cases — to the level of the masterpiece. Even though the legitimacy of regarding it as a style is still *sub judice*, mannerism cannot be denied a place in the historical development of the 16th century, whether regarded as an independent current, as one component of a larger dialectic, as only a nuance, that is, the visual embodiment of an intellectual canon, or even as a mere working hypothesis serving no other purpose than to eliminate the dross of long-standing interpretative accretions. The task of the modern art historian must be to differentiate more and more precisely the various aspects of this whole phenomenon, to trace the dialectic of its development, to evaluate the individual achievement of the artists who, in ever-increasing number, are emerging from the anonymous group of "followers." From such detailed study the continuity of the historical evolution not only of mannerism but of all the art of the 16th century emerges more clearly.

The most important factor, and one that is fundamental to the new approach to the problem of mannerism, was the critical rediscovery of those Florentine artists who had been rejected by the classical taste of the 17th, 18th, and 19th centuries. It was Goldschmidt who first saw in mannerist art the reversal of the premises of naturalistic rationality and perspective which were the basic tenets of the Renaissance tradition. Friedländer found confirmation of this deliberately anticlassicist purpose, the point of departure of a new style which was to have wide dissemination when the fully mature Pontormo made contact with northern art, taking the engravings of Dürer as the model for his *Passion* in the Certosa near Florence (1522–25). Today the tendency is to lay greater emphasis on Pontormo's lifelong study of Michelangelo's art; in works that preceded the Certosa *Passion*, such as the *Veronica* in the Popes' Chapel of S. Maria Novella, Florence (1515), and the lunette in the Medici villa of Poggio a Caiano (IV, PL. 201), there are distinct borrowings from Michelangelo, not so much from the Sistine Chapel ceiling as from such Florentine works as the *Holy Family* (IX, PL. 527). These are not imitations but rather interpretations of what appeared new in a culture whose Humanistic components seemed, by that time, obsolete and remote. Pontormo's Dürer phase does not therefore appear to be such an anomaly as to cause the outcry that it did among his contemporaries: it is almost the consequence (even if carried to the most dangerous extremes) of that revolution in the figural arts which produced, in the battle cartoons executed early in the 16th century by Leonardo and Michelangelo for the Palazzo Vecchio, the great paradigms of a new artistic idiom. This idiom, to which the traditional term "classical" can be applied only in the sense of a higher expressive choice, was the consummation, at the beginning of the 16th century, of the Renaissance mastery of form, which, all its aims achieved, had come to signify the free energy of movement, "the cause of all life" — the universal dynamic relation that was the great discovery of the Renaissance. The expressionistic elements, formal and coloristic, that had characterized "Gothic art" for centuries no longer appeared abnormal, as they had to the early Humanists. On the contrary, they became comprehensible and even congenial in this dynamic liberation of form.

Neither Pontormo nor Il Rosso was going against the stream when he studied the engravings of Dürer and Lucas van Leyden (q.v.): they were boldly yielding to the most vital pressures of their time. If their work represents a deliberate reaction, it is against compositional rationalism, crystallized into harmonic formulas in the iconic and devotional paintings of Fra Bartolommeo and his followers in the Scuola di S. Marco, formulas that even the vivid pictorial imagination of Andrea del Sarto could not manage to surmount. But under the liberating impulse of Michelangelo, Andrea's young disciples succeeded where their master had failed: it accounts not only for the strong draftsmanship of Pontormo but also for that artist's intensity of color as well as his treatment of complementary colors, daring to the point of actual dissonance. Also, it emboldened Il Rosso to carry out the imaginative pictorial reelaborations of Michelangelo's sculptural contrasts in the great works of the years 1521–23: the *Deposition* in Volterra (Pin. Comunale), the altarpiece in the parish church of Villamagna, near Volterra, the S. Lorenzo *Marriage of the Virgin*, and the *Moses* (PL. 290). Art historians, aware of the great difference in the problems these two artists faced, have not always accepted this theory of a decisive influence of Michelangelo. But Michelangelo opened up such immense expressive vistas as to give rise to the most diverse derivative strains: the tormented, morbidly introspective, haunted works of Pontormo as well as the ironic, mordant, and earthy paintings of Il Rosso. Their Florentine spirit was weighed down by disillusionment with a civilization that, in the decadence of its social fabric, was no longer finding nourishment for further great intellectual achievements. The living center of the Renaissance had become the *miserrima civitas* that aroused the distaste of Leo X's retinue when the Florentine pope returned there for a visit in 1515. The subtle romantic turn tinged with bitterness, which, at the end of the 15th century, had been the essence of the works of Filippino Lippi and Piero di Cosimo, developed in the next generation of artists into the hopeless awareness of a disaster from which there could be no escape. But the very sincerity of this avowal was a new element and marked an expansion of the domain of art. The images that Pontormo and Il Rosso painted (and not only in their portraits) of contemporary society gave expression to the marginal zones of the human spirit — to tortuousness, bewilderment, and illusory escapes into irony and mockery. Hence art historians recognized in them the artists of a new idiom, the most authentic interpreters in the whole realm of 16th-century art not only of the end of an epoch but also of the awareness necessary for a reawakening.

But this was not possible in Florence, where the expressive scope of Leonardo and Michelangelo had nothing to sustain it but that merciless self-criticism. The real problems of civilization were no longer the intellectual ones of the Florentine Renaissance. It was now a question of providing a new spiritual basis for every aspect of life through total religious reform such as had assumed diverse aspects in various countries — the great conflicts that harassed Europe throughout the 16th century. In this struggle the Catholic Church engaged all its most active forces, and Rome, the seat of the papacy, rather than Florence, became the arena. Though the basic texts of the new art remained in Florence, it was only in Rome that this art could develop the fullness of its idiom. This was to be the task of Raphael.

It was in his work that the new impulse, the true style of the Italian 16th century, which was termed "*la bella maniera*," achieved definitive expression. The occasion was provided by the frescoing of the Vatican Stanze, in which the glorification of the high points of ecclesiastical history and of Humanist culture (which the Church had by now completely absorbed) brought about the rise of artistic expression to the supreme level of almost emblematic impact. Raphael was able to achieve this sublime "rhetoric" (in the original and positive meaning of the word) because he was still acting from the conviction of that order, that system of universal value, which perspective had constituted for Humanism in art before the crisis of the Florentine concern with the problems of form. Acquired in the artistic circle of Urbino, where the teachings of Piero della Francesca (q.v.) still prevailed, Raphael's conviction had not been shaken by his youthful experiences in Florence. In the presence of this ideally ordering rule, the idiom of the *School of Athens* (XI, PL. 426) and of the *Disputa* (IV, PL. 230) presented a paradigm more universal than the gigantesque dynamism of Michelangelo's Sistine ceiling. What it taught did not burden the imagination but harmoniously disciplined all the elements: it was the foundation of the idiom on whose development the art of the 16th century was wholly centered.

It has come to be recognized that an important role in the development of the Raphael style was played by the circle of assistants — until recently classed together in the colorless anonymity of imitators — who made possible the master's immense *œuvre*. Frederick Hartt in his study of Giulio Romano (1958) went to the heart of this collaboration, which was not limited to the physical execution of Raphael's designs. Giulio Romano and Giovanni Francesco Penni, and, later, Raffaello dal Colle, Giovanni da Udine, and Perino del Vaga, worked out, from the model, ideas barely indicated by Raphael in quick sketches, sometimes even giving visual form to a merely verbal suggestion — preparing the program, as it were, the drawing to which he affixed the final stylistic seal of his color. Thus the collaboration, beyond its immediate practical goals, amounted to an earnest group effort toward the creation of a new artistic idiom: here converged all the various strains of the artistic milieu. Besides giving form to the great celebrative themes of the Vatican decoration, the Raphael workshop developed in the decoration of the Sala di Psiche (1517–18) in the Farnesina, the villa built in Rome between 1508 and 1511 by Baldassare Peruzzi for the wealthy banker Agostino Chigi, the themes of a secular culture for which, since the late 15th century, classicism represented no longer the domination of form but a realm open to the free flight of the imagination (X, PL. 250). The *Metamorphoses* of Ovid provided innumerable occasions for the more nonrealistic *invenzioni*, which Raphael — as is seen in the *Galatea* (III, PL. 392), the only one executed by his own hand — was able to resolve in a now musically refined rhythmic coherence. And Raphael's inspiration burns with lyric intensity in the final undertaking, the decoration of the Vatican Logge, in which the whole by then enormous band of his assistants was involved (II, PL. 291; V, PL. 239; XI, PL. 431). The personal imprints of Giulio Romano, Penni, Perino, Giovanni da Udine, Polidoro da Caravaggio, and perhaps also Baldassare Peruzzi are discernible within this symphonic orchestration of effects, where the vaults open into illusionistic perspectives and where grotesques and stuccowork of attenuated elegance (inspired by the recent archaeological discoveries of the Golden House of Nero and the House of Titus) enframe Biblical scenes — here an almost theatrical representation, vividly mimetic, indifferent to the awesome meanings that Michelangelo had elicited from them in the Sistine ceiling. But this extreme figural elaboration is always contained within the precise metrical clarity by then achieved by Raphael. He had turned to architecture not only because it was required of him by his appointment as master of works of St. Peter's in 1515 but also from a need to deepen his rhythmic sensibility through the exigencies of structural function. Implicit in the buildings he designed, such as the Chigi Chapel in S. Maria del Popolo (XI, PL. 436) and the Palazzo Vidoni (formerly Caffarelli), and in the changes that he made in Bramante's project for St. Peter's (shifting from a central to a longitudinal plan), and explicit in a letter of 1519 to Leo X, is his intention of working toward a complex pictorial enrichment of the severe "classical" style of Bramante.

It is impossible to imagine where this new direction of Raphael's might have led had it not been cut short by his untimely death. The *Transfiguration* (ca. 1517–20; Vat. Mus.), carried on concurrently with the Logge and completed by assistants after Raphael's death, reveals two as yet unreconciled expressive directions (Sergio Ortolani): the elevation of form and content to an ultrareal vision and the descent to a more immediate dramatic historicity — the two lines along which 17th-century art was to develop. Both were beyond the capacity of his immediate followers: they could only continue that elaboration of idiom which, no longer directed by the actual presence of the master, showed a dangerous tendency to slip into the figural virtuosity that gave grounds for the negative assessment of mannerism by critics from the 17th century onward. Regarded without preconceptions, however, the Raphaelesque products of his immediate followers — such as the elegant decoration in Villa Madama conceived by Raphael and executed by Giovanni da Udine and Peruzzi, and the works in the Vatican's Sala di Costantino (1520–25) by Giulio Romano and Penni, testamentary heirs to Raphael's commissions, and in Perino del Vaga's Sala dei Pontifici in the Borgia Apartments of the Vatican (1521) — are admirable for their figural richness, accumulated like some boundless patrimony that could be spent, even squandered, for centuries. It is a tumultuous succession of variations sustained by extraordinarily accomplished draftsmanship and prompted by a body of learning continually enlarged by scholarly research. The artistic imagination seethed with the idea of shaping the new classic learning to the requirements of a stylistic rhythm intensified to the point of the most fanciful nonrealism.

Thus the *bella maniera* became so intellectually supple an expressive instrument that Perino del Vaga, on coming to work in Florence in 1523, dared pridefully to declare it capable of surpassing even the achievements of Masaccio. However, neither he nor the others of his circle were able to employ it poetically. For this, more genuine sources of inspiration were required, and herein lies the historical contribution of artists such as Parmigianino and Il Rosso, who, trained in different environments, arrived at full maturity in the experience of the *bella maniera*.

Beginning with Friedländer, critics have, rightly, recognized the importance of the meeting of these two artists in Rome about 1524, at the time when, after the brief pontificate of the Fleming Adrian VI, who was averse to all outward display, the election of another Medici pope, Clement VII, seemed to reopen to artists their former opportunities. Friedländer attributes a decisive role in the situation to Il Rosso, as having, from Rome, widely disseminated the Florentine anticlassical revolt. Yet further consideration of this meeting, in the light of the individual development of the two artists, would seem to indicate that it resulted not so much in giving rise to a new current, differing in its goals from the *maniera*, as in infusing the *maniera* with the vivifying force of a genuine poetic impulse. Parmigianino, as Freedberg recognized, had, even before going to Rome, drawn from the Pandean abandon of Correggio's art an intensely intellectual grace of Arcadian savor — as in the Diana and Actaeon frescoes in Fontanellato, in which Longhi has divined definite influence from the Sienese Domenico Beccafumi. Parmigianino's encounter with Il Rosso (which occurred, it must be remembered, within the circle of the followers of Raphael) was not, therefore, unilaterally decisive but rather was more akin to a complex interplay of reciprocal influences. This might be clearer to us if the cycle of frescoes in the Via Giulia, jointly executed by the two artists, had been preserved; still, it can be noted both in the nonrealistic emphases of luminary contrasts (showing the influence of Il Rosso as well as Beccafumi) apparent in Parmigianino's work of this time, such as the *Madonna and Child* in the Galleria Doria Pamphili (Rome) and the *St. Catherine* in the collection of the Earl of Normanton (Somerley, Ringwood, Hampshire), and, conversely, in the more continuous and elegant rhythms in Il Rosso's frescoes in S. Maria della Pace, in Rome, which recall Parmigianino. However, these contacts occurred within the framework of the more substantially influential presence of the *bella maniera*, which attracted both artists through the possibilities for the mastery of expressive technique. To it they brought an acute critical discernment, effecting that outpouring of heightened rhythmic power to which the too much and too exclusively stressed unnatural attenuation of figures is incidental. In turn, their effect on the current idiom was one of genuine poetic inspiration, be it the winning grace of Parmigianino or the biting extravagance of Il Rosso. Through them the *maniera* attained those lyric heights which strained even the descriptive powers of Vasari.

The stylistic evolution that began about 1520 in the troubled time preceding the great crises of the Sack of Rome (1527) and the siege of Florence (1529), in which the civilization of the Renaissance seemed to collapse, along with its greatest centers, therefore took the form not so much of the rise and polemical articulation of an anticlassical style as of a renewal of that lyrical trend initiated by Raphael in the Logge. And though this, in diverse guises, appeared in the various currents of Italian art, only in the fullness of the Roman idiom did it find complete expression. This is apparent in the later work of those artists who reached maturity in Rome before 1527. In Parmigianino's post-Roman work *grazia* was redeemed from its own intellectualism as a new revelation of reality. One thinks — along with the subtle stylizations of the so-called "Madonna dal Collo Lungo" (XII, PL. 81) and of the *Amor* (Vienna, Kunsthist. Mus.) — of the liveliness of portraits such as the Naples "Antea" and the young woman in a turban in Parma. And though Il Rosso's inspiration seemed to flag in the labored altarpieces in S. Lorenzo, Sansepolcro, and the Cathedral of Città di Castello, it rose triumphant again at Fontainebleau, where he (in the service of Francis I, from 1530) resolved the Roman decorative repertory into a rich, imaginative pictorial effect, consisting equally of the sprightly *invenzione* of the frescoes and the intense light-created plasticity of the exuberant stucco frames, carved in relief and in the round.

The Sienese Domenico Beccafumi (PL. 295), too, whose development had from youth proceeded through the tortuous ways marginal to the major currents of Florence and Rome, attained through his complete experience of the *maniera* to the enchanted chromatic lyricism that characterizes the masterpieces of about 1530, such as the ceiling of the Palazzo Bindi Sergardi in Siena and the *Birth of the Virgin* in the Pinacoteca in the same city. It was through his art, which then spread to Genoa and Pisa, that the Sienese province came to have a central effect on the course of the 16th century and a final influence on baroque painting on the threshold of the 17th. Meanwhile, Giulio Romano, who had left Rome in 1524 to work for the Gonzagas in Mantua, acting directly on Raphaelesque premises, gave his buildings, the Palazzo Ducale and the Palazzo del Te (XII, PL. 53), and the sumptuous frescoes that lined their interiors, the impress of a romantic emotionalism, in an accent no less lyrical, if lacking in subtle intellectualism. The rugged vitality of nature was imposed on the more elaborate forms of these buildings, where the bossage of the *opus rusticum* became rough rock from which the arch or column appeared to emerge only with difficulty. Painting partook of similar effects, as in the terrifying illusionistic scheme of the Sala dei Giganti (PL. 298) and the sweeping perspectives of the Sala di Troia, works that prefigure the great baroque illusionistic inventions of Pietro da Cortona and Giovanni Battista Tiepolo (qq.v.).

Thus, between 1520 and 1530 the *bella maniera* of Raphael completed an evolution productive of the richest diversification of effects, rhythmic coherence always remaining the basis of its artistic idiom. The new style, to which the term "mannerism" can be applied only in the most conventional sense, was thus different from the sterile imitation to which early criticism reduced it — but likewise from the anticlassical polemic into which modern criticism shaped it. It was on the one hand the ultimate development of the dynamic freedom achieved by Florentine form and on the other the ultimate possibility derivable from Raphaelesque rhythmic design, both basic components of High Renaissance style. The great expressive achievement of a whole civilization was neither discarded nor traduced. Rather, it was redirected; abandoning the Leonardesque crisis of the problems of knowledge that had made art in the two preceding centuries the standard-bearer of the new science, mannerism fostered the poesy that, in the field of art as in the field of literature, was the true goal and glorious achievement of the Italian 16th century.

The stylistic crisis of the decade 1520–30 appears to have been the precise statement of these aims through the mastery by then achieved of an artistic idiom equal to every expressive demand. It was not the crisis of a fettered classicism but the evolution of a new classical tendency, equal to the ancient in elevation of style but with motive forces more various and real. Between 1520 and 1530 the new style became universal, not only because of the exodus of artists from Rome after the Sack of 1527 and the resulting dissemination of Roman style, but also because all bents of inspiration found in this mature artistic idiom the possibility of poetic expression, and Rome became, as Florence had been, the *scuola del mondo*, to which all must go for a necessary formative experience. The rich casuistry of the later *maniera* resulted from this confluence of styles, upon which the *maniera* itself acted as both catalyst and solvent.

What is called "mannerism" was the beginning of this new dialectic, which though it first asserted itself in painting infiltrated the whole domain of art.

For example, Baldassare Peruzzi (q.v.), stimulated by the example of Raphael's architecture, turned away from the still 15th-century regularity of the Farnesina to the fanciful developments of plan, structure, and chiaroscuro effect evident in the Palazzo Massimo alle Colonne (begun 1532; XI, PL. 121; XII, PL. 52) and in his innumerable designs and projects, which are even more revelatory of his eager quest for new expression than those actually built. He seems also to have furnished Sebastiano Serlio (q.v.) the material for the *Regole generali di architettura* (1st ed., Venice, 1537), which appears to be a codification of the workings of a taste that is not yet a style and tries every means of defining a goal. Though Vitruvius (q.v.) remained the enduring paradigm, Serlio betrays also a subtle delight in departing from him in that "bizzarria nelle cose miste, et licentiose" in which he indulged in order to please the "uomini bizzarri, che cercano novità." The preferred model was no longer the severe architecture of Bramante or the Sangallos, but that "copiosa di lumi," pervaded with chromatic effect, which in Venice found a matchless exponent in Jacopo Sansovino and which, elsewhere, in his rich illustration of portals, Serlio, like Giulio Romano, sought instead in the "opera di natura," its bossage like living rock rather than cut stone. Serlio's work does not yet exhibit a mature architectural sense: his complicated designs would be almost impossible to build. The much more radical return to form in the following generation was required for architecture to renew its own true idiom. Explicit in this generation, too, and always under the impetus of Raphael, was the new lyric way, which was still one of aspiration and quest but was capable of being diverted into the most varied areas (and distorted into intellectualism), the contradictions that make it difficult for art historians to extract a single direction for mannerism. Such contradictions are, however, inevitable when not only is the working out of an artistic idiom in process but also the mind of the time is seeking to relieve its own inquietude in the certainty of abundant inspiration.

The clarifying synthesis of a great personality was needed, and this is one aspect of the enormous importance of Michelangelo. Vasari, who formulated the most acute definition of the *maniera*, recognized the aloofness of Michelangelo, who separated himself from what was demiurgic in it. For in him alone the problem of form, as the Renaissance had posed it, maintained the driving impetus of a continuing search. Throughout his long life (1475-1564) he strove with it, though contemporary developments, flowing round him like waves round a rock, drew from his work deductions that never went to the essence of the problem — that essence of which he remained the sole repository. In the decades immediately following Raphael's death, Raphael's influence had determined stylistic development, and Michelangelo increasingly appeared the antithesis of this. Though the Sistine ceiling had been the object of an almost bewildering admiration that had estranged rather than attracted other artists, the very adoption of Michelangelo's motifs had been possible only through Raphaelesque interpretation. But in later years, surviving to tower alone over the artistic scene, Michelangelo seemed the very symbol of the contradiction of it, the awesome standard of comparison between the totality of a problem and partial solution. This contradiction entered all the phases of artistic life that he restlessly undertook and triumphed in; thus he was, perforce, dissociated from the diametrically opposed currents of Florence and of Rome.

In 1522 Michelangelo transferred his base of operations back to his native Florence (which he had left early in the century) because of the commission given him in 1520 by Leo X and Cardinal Giulio de' Medici (later Clement VII) for the family mortuary chapel in the Medici Church of S. Lorenzo. It was in this period — in the Medici Chapel, where the architecture itself assumed a somber emotive tone through the constriction of great classical members within a small space, and the figures of *Dawn* and *Night* (PL. 531) seemed the afflicted prisoners of harmonic rhythms rarefied to an unendurable degree — that this extraordinary artistic individuality shows the effects of the *maniera*. These, however, soon became for him the "aspra catena" ("the harsh bond"), the new bar to the ultimate "superamento," the "non finito" ("unfinished") already foreshadowed in the nearly formless masses of the *Day* and the *Evening* of the Medici Chapel (PL. 530; XII, PL. 60). Other sculptures born of this new expressive phase were the Medici *Madonna*, the *Genius of Victory*, and the *Dying Slaves* (PL. 529) for that ever less realizable project, the tomb of Julius II. But the Florentine artists were not aware that these sculptures achieved in solitude — virtually an artistic testament — would remain forever in that state of unconcluded struggle for liberation. The new Florentine models, replacing the worn-out battle cartoons, were thus those labored reactions of Michelangelo against the *maniera*: the Medici tombs and the projects for colossal figure groups, such as the *Hercules and Antaeus*, the current steps in the deepening of his ever-resurgent concern with structure. These models were a source of confusion to Pontormo, who, with the problems there embodied, complicated a style that had by then reached the heights of his *Supper at Emmaus* (1525) and the S. Felicita *Deposition* (1526-28; PL. 288), tormenting himself with them up to the disastrous outcome of the lost frescoes of S. Lorenzo. They deflected Baccio Bandinelli (1493-1560; PL. 307) from the feeling for chiaroscuro derived from his first Leonardesque master, Giovan Francesco Rustici, to the elegant stylizations but vacuous athleticisms of his sculptured figures. Benvenuto Cellini (q.v.), returned from his post as sculptor and goldsmith at Fontainebleau, was the severe critic of this trend, opposing to it the slender grace of his *Perseus* (Florence, Loggia della Signoria); it was the mannerist critics who recognized his ductile harmony of design as very different from such intellectualistic purism. Yet the residue of this consciousness of form in Florence determined the use of color in the work of Bronzino (q.v.; PLS. 292, 296) to achieve the abstract sublimation of form, the very essence of his remarkable portraits. Cellini made an exception of Bronzino when he pronounced himself in favor of sculpture over painting in Benedetto Varchi's referendum (1546) among the leading artists of the day on which of the two arts held primacy. Among the many answers, only Cellini's specified the true significance of sculpture: he contrasted contemporary painters, "in tra fioralisi, con molte compositioni di vari colori qual sono uno inganna contadini" ("drowned among nosegays and employing themselves with many varicolored compositions which can only cheat the simple"), with the sculptors, whose work could be enjoyed from innumerable points of view in the unfolding beauty of its rhythm — the "figura serpentinata" that was later, for Lomazzo, the mannerist canon par excellence. Thus the intellectualizing dissociation of form and color, no longer reconciled on the evidence of reality, was adumbrated in the comparison of the two arts. Michelangelo, almost annoyed at being called as a witness in a matter that did not concern him, made short shrift of the question, reverting to the Albertian definition of sculpture "per forza di levare" ("by cutting away"), the actual freeing of form from the block.

In Rome Michelangelo had completed his *Last Judgment* (1541; PL. 536), in which form and space unite, carried along by a tremendous figural tension, and the restless, vague, lyrical anxiety of the *maniera* yields before the awesome inspirational power of an individual drama that has found definitive and universal religious motivation. Precisely through understanding the late style of Michelangelo as an ascent, not a retrenchment or a decline, Dvořák interpreted it as an expression of the mystical impulse animating the Counter Reformation, the culmination of that trend — ever imminent in a Renaissance entangled in its own knowledge — which for Dvořák was mannerism. But in Michelangelo it was really the Renaissance that reached the heights of discovery in this free, ideal functionalism of form. It was not one single current but the whole development of art that experienced its catharsis in Michelangelo's late works.

Inevitably, the conclusions drawn from Michelangelo were limited and one-sided. Only the formal and compositional dynamism of the *Last Judgment* was grasped. And from it were derived, in the free play of the *maniera*, plastic attempts which complicated mannerism with abnormal strainings, with an inert heaviness that arrested its animated rhythmic flow, and which were to prove the utter confusion of the followers, that later generation of mannerists most scorned by the critics. Yet in some of the sounder of these artists it inspired a grave and anguished tone that is sometimes lyrically resolved, as in the case of Daniele Ricciarelli, known as Daniele da Volterra (1509–66; PL. 294), whose *Deposition* (Trinità dei Monti, Rome) raises to the threshold of religious tragedy the nonrealistic scheme of Il Rosso's treatment of the same subject in Volterra. Increased severity also pervades the persisting recollection of Raphael's Logge in the decoration of S. Giovanni Decollato, begun in 1535 and carried on until the middle of the century by a group of artists who are currently undergoing scholarly reevaluation: the Florentines Jacopino del Conte (1510–98) and Francesco Salviati (1510–63; PLS. 294, 309), the Venetian Giovanni Battista Franco (ca. 1510–61; PL. 300), and the Neapolitan Pirro Ligorio (1514–ca. 1583). In their work first appeared the expressive pathos that the Counter Reformation, now sure of its direction (until 1545 this was still being formulated by the Council of Trent), began to require of religious painting, directing it to the celebration of the transcendental, a trend which made that anticipatory example, the *Transfiguration* of Raphael, far closer and more comprehensible. And F. Zeri has rightly pointed out (1957) how, at this time especially, the altarpieces of Sebastiano del Piombo (1485–1547), notably the *Birth of the Virgin* in S. Maria del Popolo (ca. 1532), so different in their chromatic emotiveness from the gay nonrealism of the *maniera*, assumed the authority of examples. Plastic effects were intensified with contrasts of chiaroscuro. As A. Venturi recognized, the importance of the Lombard Marcello Venusti (ca. 1512–79) lay in providing, by way of the vestigial Leonardism of his early training, "the chromatic solution to the formal principles of Michelangelo." The new plasticity was also built up by means of color that gained strength in reaching toward the very substance of things, as in the inspired work, already prebaroque, of Pellegrino Tibaldi (1527–96) — especially the decorations that he carried out in the Palazzo Poggio (Palazzo dell'Università) in Bologna (PL. 298; XI, PL. 100) after going there from Rome, which contain the germs of the reform of the Carraccis. External criticism of the *maniera*, which only later took shape in the open hostility of the Counter Reformation, began in this incipient self-criticism. The whimsically pictorial effect was no longer satisfactory if what was sought was to go beyond illusion to dynamic structural reality. And about 1540 the problems that had been felt principally in painting were demanding solution in the field of architecture as well (PLS. 311–314).

The revival of Vitruvian studies was symptomatic. Interest in this canonical text of classicism had been lively throughout the 16th century; as early as 1521 the first printed translation appeared in Venice, followed by that of Francesco Lucio da Castel Durante (1524) and, in 1556, by another, the celebrated rendering by Daniele Barbaro, the Patriarch of Aquileia. While in the Venetian milieu this interest in architecture never lost the character of an aristocratic diversion, in Rome it assumed a more rigorously scientific direction with the foundation, in 1542, of the Accademia Vitruviana, whose program ranged from the production of a critical edition of Vitruvius and a lexiconlike exegesis of his technical terms and a comparison of the Vitruvian text with extant classical monuments to an actual census of all surviving Roman antiquities. A program seemingly antiquarian, it answered a very different esthetic need — to judge from the list of artists (among them some of the greatest of the 16th century, for example, Vignola) who from their youth participated in it — the need, that is, for a new interpretation of the nature of the classical itself in order to base new creations on solid structural experience.

Michelangelo, too, turned to architecture in the years following the *Last Judgment*, but, as always, acting through the motivations of his exceptional personality. He experienced again in the exigency of his own art the common exigency of all artists; he cast it in the lucid form of a problem that is still the Renaissance problem of form. In the realm of pure architectonic abstraction he reaffirmed his concept of form as the ultimate liberation, not now the overcoming of all limitation, the *non finito*, but the revelation of the actual energy of this overcoming — even in the closed balance of the centralized plan on which, from Bramante on, the problem of the construction of St. Peter's had been based. Michelangelo was able to resolve this, thus concluding a half century of discussion, precisely by returning to the clear harmonies of Bramante — divested of the pictorial complications of Raphael and of the compromises of Antonio da Sangallo — and converting them, through the unifying power of the colossal order, to a great block of articulated members culminating in the dome. And the organization of surrounding space itself was, for him, form — as in the Piazza del Campidoglio, unitary and tense with untrammeled dynamism.

This complete mastery of structural reality indicated to architects a surer means than the now totally spent mode of classicism. For this reason, only in architecture was Michelangelo fully understood (and not partially imitated) as representing the new consciousness of form in which stylistic aspiration attained creative power. The final convergence of the tendencies that from the beginning of the century had been polarized in Michelangelo and in Raphael, the ultimate statement of the problem and its articulation in an artistic idiom, the style and the *maniera*, were only now achieved — as they had not been in the encounters of artists between 1520 and 1530 from which mannerism had issued victorious. Mannerism had now fulfilled its purpose as the basis of a new creative idiom. That it attained in architecture to some of the most exalted artistic expressions of the Italian 16th century has frustrated all critical attempts, from Wölfflin to the present, to make of this phase of architecture a secondary or transitional phenomenon in a historical sequence polarized exclusively between the antithetical premises of Renaissance and baroque, or to consider it (by extension of the mannerist formulation in painting) as a separate entity based on the polemical reversal of Renaissance static rationality and therefore doomed to an ambiguous if not flatly negative evaluation. That masters such as Vignola and Palladio have been regarded as mannerists has had the positive virtue of setting them apart from a presumed academic classicism and from a tentative baroque, thus eliminating the inadequate bases of judgment that for centuries had beclouded the comprehension of their art, if not the consistent appreciation of their greatness. But this last is really what places them outside any specific category, at the very center of a style of which they represent the highest reaches. The premises of the *maniera* survived in them, but they directed themselves confidently toward their own goal, ridding it of every vestige of uncertain aspiration, of indecisive procedure, which gradually made it generate differences within the vaguer and more evocative designation of mannerism, to emerge now in the established certainty of style.

Yet, certain isolated manifestations scattered throughout the century must be classified as mannerist concessions to the taste for the fantastic, the exceptional, the abnormal: the Palazzina of Pius IV, built by Pirro Ligorio in the Vatican Gardens (VIII, PL. 429; XII, PL. 89), in which structural clarity is submerged in a mass of relief sculpture; the house ("capriccio poetico") that Federico Zuccari built for himself in 1593 in Rome (now the Biblioteca Hertziana), where doors and windows are the wide-open mouths of horrid monsters (PL. 314); and that obscure assemblage of *invenzioni* of literary inspiration, the park of the Palazzo Orsini, Bomarzo, near Viterbo (X, PL. 137). This classification does not include, as has been said, the work of the greater masters, such as Vignola and Palladio, in whom every ambiguity of this style was resolved in the bold surge of inspiration.

If the weakness of the mannerists lay in the preponderance of illusion over structural reality, they were, on the other hand, powerful creators of structural forms that were to be elaborated but not surpassed for centuries. They achieved this through an experience that for both the Emilian Vignola and the Ve-

MANNERISM

Architectural elements: (*a*, *b*) Rome, Porta Pia (architect, Michelangelo), gateway and window; (*c*) Rome, S. Maria in Aracoeli (architect, J. Sansovino), Bracci monument; (*d*, *e*) Milan, Palazzo Marino, now Municipale (architect, G. Alessi), windows of the façade; (*f*) Mantua, Palazzo del Te (architect, Giulio Romano), detail of façade; (*g*) Florence, Casino Mediceo, now Palazzo della Corte d'Appello (architect, Buontalenti), window of façade.

netian Palladio was possible only in Rome, in the formative confluence of the direct study of the antique and of a basic artistic idiom embracing, besides the *maniera*, the great architecture of Bramante, of the Sangallos, and of Raphael, and, finally, the living example of Michelangelo. As new and original as the interpretation of this background in their buildings is its reflection in theory. In the *Regola delli cinque ordini d'architettura*, published by Vignola in 1562, then in 1570, and countless other times as the canonical text of modern architecture, there is an exhaustive inquiry into the classical law of proportion, the Palazzo Chiericati (XI, PL. 30) in Vicenza and of the organic clarity of the Venetian churches of the Redentore (XI, PLS. 34, 35) and S. Giorgio Maggiore (VIII, PL. 227; XI, PL. 34; XII, PL 49). The villas, open through airy porticoes to the countryside, reveal a sublimation of classical rhythms enlivened by the lyric impulses of the day, as does the Teatro Olimpico of Vicenza (FIG. 465), where the taut classical auditorium is designed like an instrument to vibrate with resonance. Not even Vincenzo Scamozzi (q.v.), the puristic corrector of Palladio, escaped his lyric suggestion when he completed that theater with the diverg-

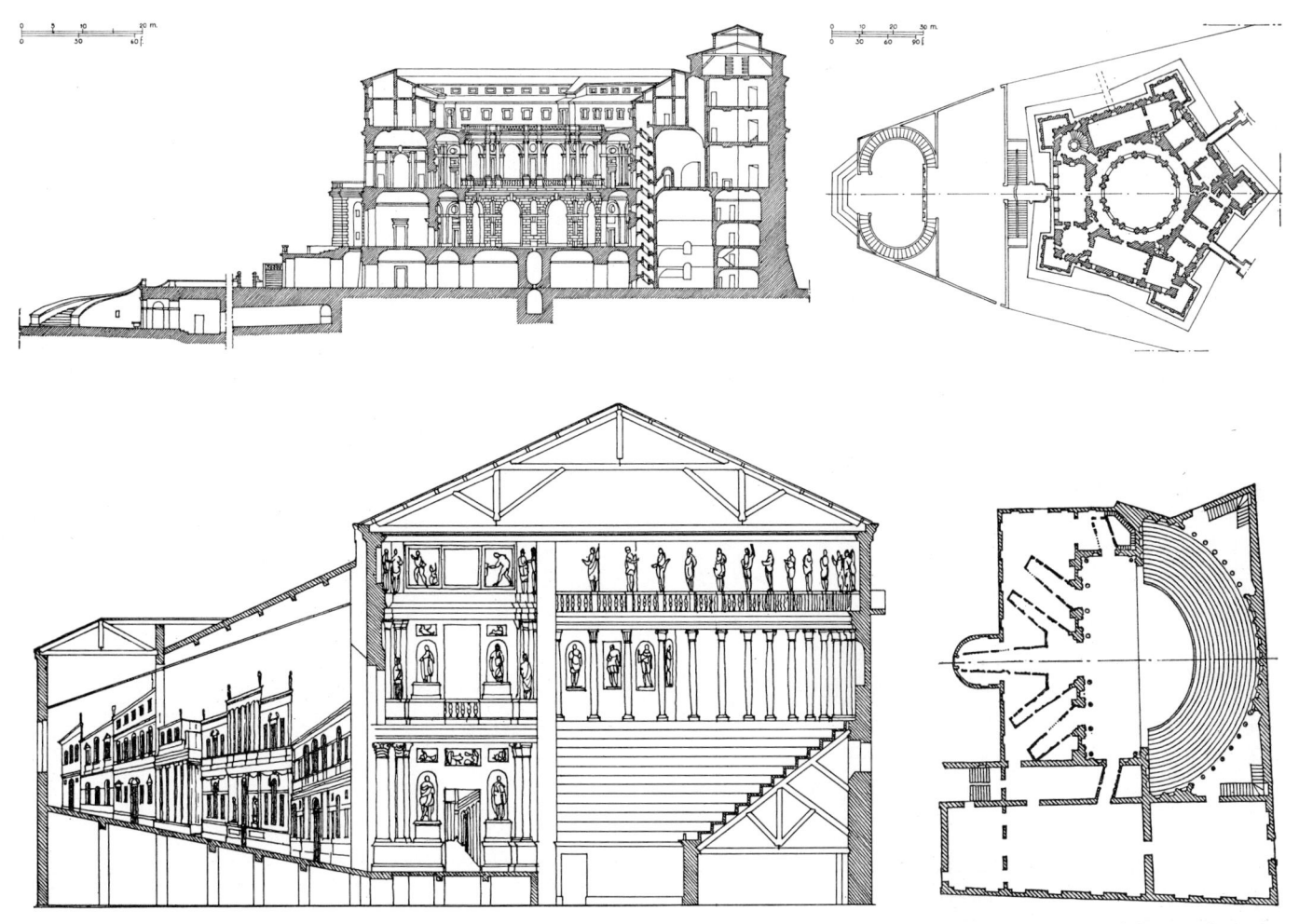

Above: Caprarola, Palazzo Farnese (architect, Vignola), section and plan. *Below*: Vicenza, Teatro Olimpico (architects, Palladio and Scamozzi), section and plan.

but in his view the classical orders were "ornaments" of structure, not a determining factor. Thus the *Regola* is only an exposition of his own architecture — of its foundation on a measured rhythmic flow; it can tell us nothing of the tremendous force of imagination that rendered Vignola able to shape the plastic mass of a wall into the great semicircular exedra of the Villa of Julius III (Villa Giulia; XII, PL. 89), to conceive the magnificent Bramantesque trabeation of the round courtyard of the Palazzo Farnese at Caprarola (FIG. 465; I, PL. 388), and to resolve the great longitudinal space of the Church of the Gesù (1568; PL. 312) through the enormous rhythmic tension in the centralizing force of the dome.

So, too, in *I quattro libri dell'Architettura*, which Palladio published in Venice in 1570, the classical city inspired by Vitruvius was not a scholarly reconstruction but a poetic dream. For that now-distant world of form passed in Palladio into the coloristic vision that was for centuries the architecture of Venice: the opening up of areas of shade between the articulation of the members, the rhythmic punctuation of façades rather than the concentration of solid masses. Here is the source of the Palazzo della Ragione (called the "Basilica") and

ing illusionistic perspectives of an unreal city beyond the space of the actual stage (PL. 312; XI, PL. 36).

Italy was transformed by this new architecture. Vicenza became the near realization of Palladio's ideal city, and Genoa acquired a new aspect through Galeazzo Alessi (ca. 1512–72), not so much by way of the monuments constructed by him — the Church of S. Maria di Carignano, the palaces, and the suburban villas — as by way of the artistic current deriving from him, which took in Giovanni Battista Castello, Rocco Lurago, and Pantaleone and Benedetto Calvi (father and son), the builders, with Alessi, of the palaces with their façades aligned in a fantastic scenic "fugue" along the Strada Nuova (now Via Garibaldi), a prospect admired by Rubens and recalled in his later work. In Milan, Pellegrino Tibaldi, though he was the originator, while in the service of the Counter-Reformation purposes of Cardinal Federigo Borromeo, of austere church structures and palaces such as the Collegio Borromeo (FIG. 467), took note, as a painter working in the Cathedral, of the impressive chiaroscuro of the Gothic building and carried it over into the decoration of the chancel ambulatory and the portals of the façade.

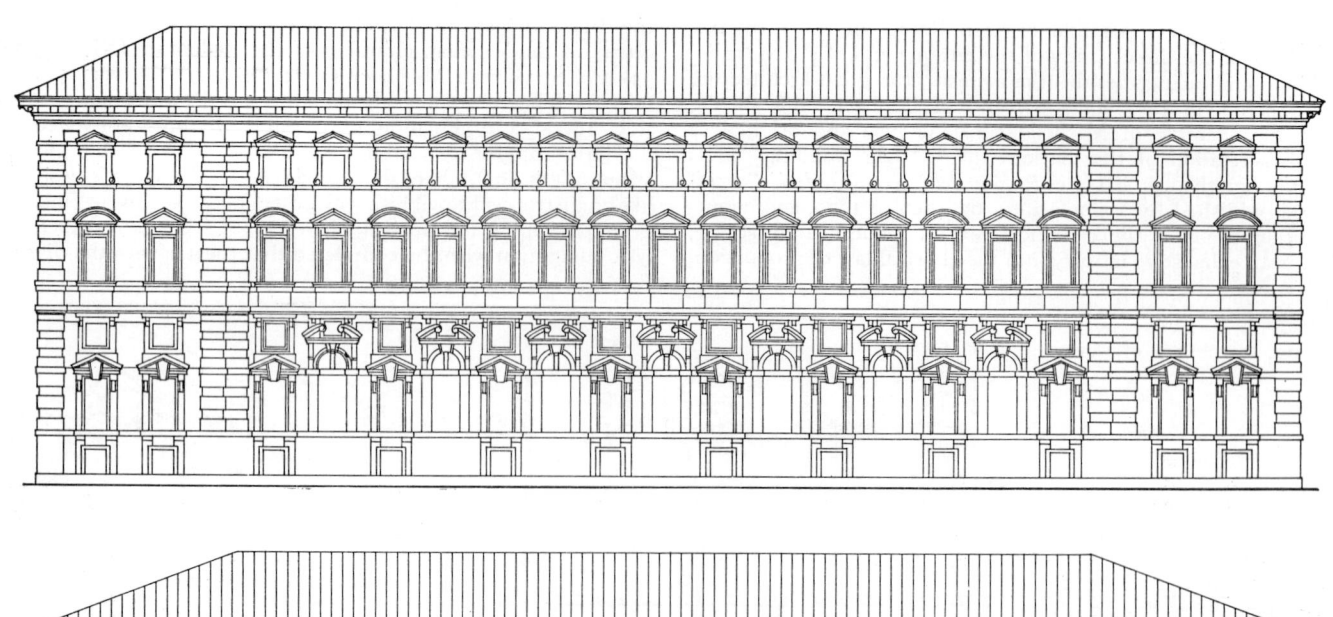

Above: Pavia, Collegio Borromeo (architect, P. Tibaldi), elevation (*from L'Architettura, no. 30*); *Below*: Rome, Palazzo Spada (architect, Mazzoni), elevation (*from P. Letarouilly, Édifices de Rome moderne, V, Paris, 1874*).

The architecture of the second half of the 16th century attained an assured maturity of style equaled only by Venetian painting, which continued in the inexhaustible vein opened up by Giorgione, celebrating the harmony between man and nature, that harmony reached in the course of time which had been the poetic warrant for the great Renaissance invention of tonal painting, the penetration of color by the ever-moving play of light. The hard-won achievements of the *maniera* were readily absorbed into this sureness of principle, accentuating and enriching but not substantially altering it. Mannerist contributions were particularly centered, aside from the sporadic passages through Venice of Florentine and Roman artists — among them Il Rosso and later F. Salviati and Vasari, and, at the end of the century, Federico Zuccari — in the influence of the nearer centers: Mantua, dominated by the impetuous romanticism of Giulio Romano, and Emilia, where the whimsical elaboration of Parmigianino's style appeared in the art of Primaticcio and Lelio Orsi (PL. 301). It is known that the study of Parmigianino's drawings was fundamental for the great Venetian sculptor Alessandro Vittoria (1525–1608), modifying his innate and rather harsh plastic vigor into the almost evanescent elegances of the stuccoes on the ceiling of the Scala d'Oro in the Doges' Palace and also into the strong chiaroscuro of his statues — for example the *St. Jerome* of S. Maria Gloriosa dei Frari (ca. 1565; XII, PL. 86) and the *Daniel* of S. Giuliano (ca. 1584) — in which sculpture too became an expression in the highest degree pictorial. Also following in this direction was the painting of Andrea Medolla, known as Lo Schiavone; later the naturalism of the Bassanos (q.v.) was to emerge. In the painting of Paolo Veronese (q.v.), whose symphonic orchestration of color (so different from the evasive subtleties of the *maniera*) represents the mainstream of Venetian art, the more robust accents of the still Raphaelesque style of Giulio Romano and the example of Palladian architecture are regarded as more influential than the grace of Parmigianino. The sheer simplicity of Veronese, whose painting seems most felicitous in encompassing this color tradition, has caused him always to be compared, and often preferred, to Tintoretto, who drove himself to the adoption in color — the resonant, almost diffused color of the late Titian — of the nonrealistic effects of the *maniera*. But with his program "disegno di Michelangelo e colorito di Tiziano" — too often interpreted as the statement of an eclectic compromise — his work appears impelled far beyond the *maniera* to the point of the intense figural dynamism of the *Last Judgment*, from which derived that heightening of inspiration which made him feel the tonal balance of Giorgione as a restraint to be broken by the apotheosis of light. He created a new Venetian lyricism, no longer the celebration of a Pandean identification with nature but the impassioned vision of another world of ultrareality. This explains why even to Venetian critics Tintoretto's painting seemed an abnormal phenomenon and required for its full acceptance the baroque sensibility of Antonio Maria Zanetti.

In Venetian painting, as in Venetian architecture, the *maniera* represented only the enriching of the existing visual tradition with a new feeling for life necessary to a new classicism of style, differing from that of the early 16th century precisely in the more complex and refined spirituality implicit in it. Thus, the current tendency to circumscribe this central chapter of Italian art within the confines of a mannerism opposed to the Renaissance, down to its very premises, involves the arbitrary dissolution of a synthesis that is, on the contrary, so complete and definitive just because of its reaffirmation of the basic Renaissance premises of organic form. Along with this mainstream of style, the course of the *maniera* was henceforward virtually that of a survival which gradually used itself up, but not without producing consummate elaborations from which the great lyric creations that continued from the 16th into the 17th century could still draw sustenance.

In contrast to this major development, Florence in the second half of the century seemed to withdraw ever further into subtle intellectualism. The *maniera* was not for Florentine artists a means of experimentation toward a new conclusion: rather, it was an end in itself, elaborated to the utmost with all the resources of a high artistic tradition, even though in the provincial isolation of Florentine life, this tended to descend to the level of an artisanlike — if indeed most expert — skill. With Michelangelo in Rome, Pontormo gone from the scene, and Giorgio Vasari, architect of the Grand Dukes from 1555 (FIG. 470), in control of Florentine art, this trend no longer met with any resistance. Vasari covered the walls of the rooms and apartments of the new Medici residence, the Palazzo Vecchio, with the whole repertory drawn from the incredible graphic erudition acquired in his travels throughout Italy (II, PL. 28; VIII, PLS. 102, 103). This display would not have been redeemed as art had he not had working alongside him, in the Sala dell'Udienza, that master of *disegno*, Francesco Salviati. But Vasari was also capable of creations such as the portico of the Uffizi (PL. 312), whose significance lay not so much in the "new classicism" of its forms, hitherto unknown in Florence, as in its character as an original piece of town planning, establishing as it did a new point of view and of interpretation for the Palazzo Vecchio, which was framed by the succession of buildings in an "angle shot," so that the dynamic thrust of the tower (I, PL. 396) was accentuated. By summoning Bartolommeo Ammanati, a skilled designer already expert from long building practice in Venice and in Rome, to work in Florence in 1560, Vasari brought about that other town-planning project, the courtyard of the Palazzo Pitti, the most beautiful of Florentine 16th-century structures, open on one side to the green prospect of the Boboli Gardens (VIII, PL. 429). Vasari's famous corridor over the Ponte Vecchio connected the Palazzo Vecchio and the Palazzo Pitti. Similarly, via Ammanati's Bridge of Sta Trinita, with its marvelous Michelangelesque tensions, the old walled city seemed to reach out, over the river, to the pleasant Tuscan countryside that the patient labor of man had virtually formed into an immense park. This return to the countryside, one of the most characteristic phenomena of 16th-century Florentine life, was in subtle accord with the naturalistic vein that appeared in the architecture itself; however, its force, vivified by a purity of form, was felt especially in sculpture. Niccolò Tribolo and Pierino da Vinci had already given their best in the slender fountains of the Villa di Castello (VIII, PL. 431) and the Villa della Pe-

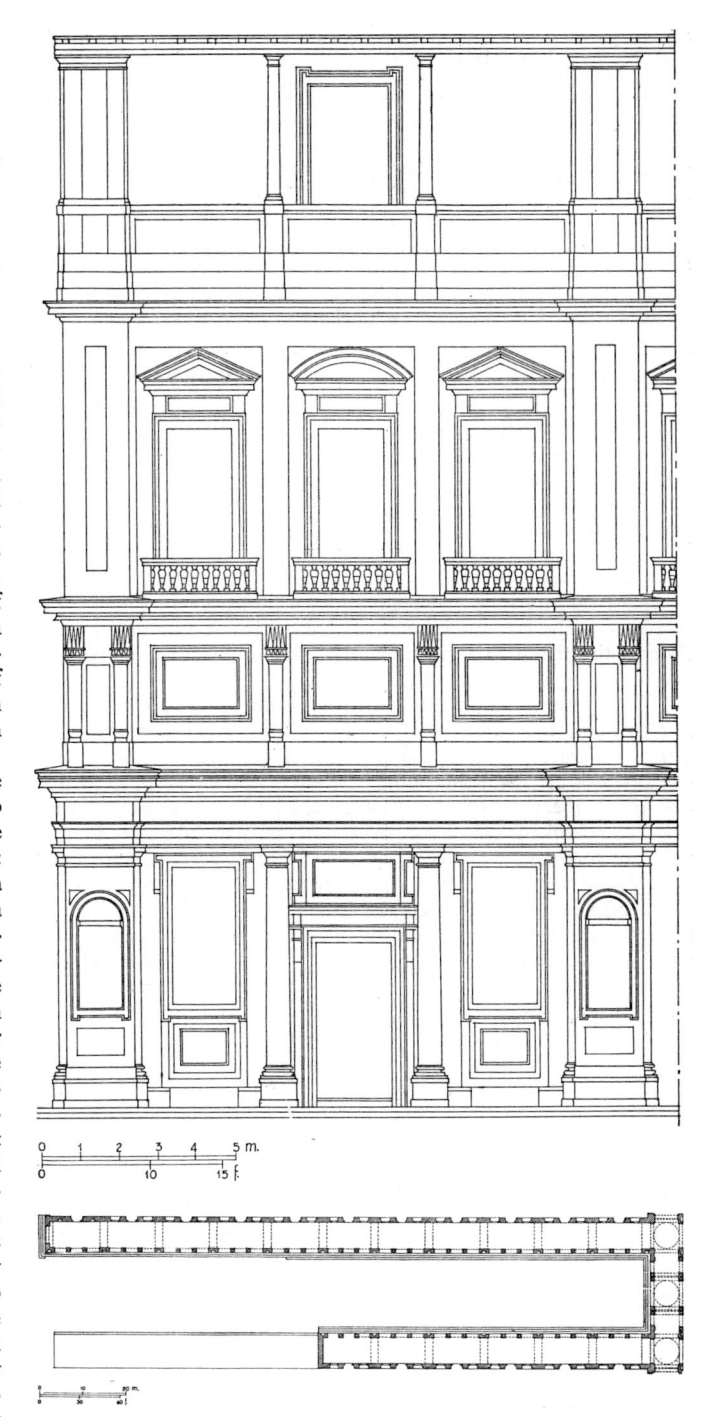

Florence, Palazzo degli Uffizi (architect, G. Vasari), partial elevation and plan (*from A. Haupt, Architettura dei palazzi dell'Italia settentrionale e della Toscana, IV, Rome, Milan, n.d.*).

traia (XII, PL. 57); now Ammanati placed in the fountain before the Palazzo Vecchio the festive group of fauns and naiads, almost bounding on the rim of the basin, thus redeeming the inert gigantism of the Neptune, the "Biancone" of popular irony (VIII, PL. 210). And Giambologna (q.v.), who arrived in Florence proficient in the agile style of Fontainebleau, found in this fresh naturalism a contemporary accent for his virtuoso elaborations of form, such as the great *serpentinato* group of the *Rape of the Sabines* and the *Neptune* (PL. 308). His best works were the *Venus* for the Fontana della Petraia and one for the grotto of the Boboli Gardens built by Bernardo Buontalenti (VIII, PL. 430). His followers, among them Pietro Francavilla, Taddeo Landini (VIII, PL. 206), Valerio Cioli (VII, PL. 384; X, PL. 137), and G. B. Caccini, were to elaborate on this rustic vein, which seemed to revive ancient sources of 15th-century inspiration — suggestions that were to be taken up by 17th-century sculpture.

This Florentine phase of mannerism was significant precisely because of the freedom with which artists worked within it. In the *studiolo* of the Palazzo Vecchio (VIII, PL. 103), designed about 1570 by Vasari, in conformity with the fanciful and romantic taste of the Grand Duke Francesco I, the little scenes painted by a group of artists — besides Vasari himself, Alessandro Allori, Francesco Morandini (Il Poppi), the Fleming Jan van der Straet (Stradanus), and, among the ablest, Mirabello Cavalori and Girolamo Macchietti — reevoked a whole tradition in their subtle variations on themes drawn from human activity, from mythology, and from the new allegory, all held together by the slender thread of an admirable rhythmic coherence. This represents the last residue of the great cult of form, still so deep in the artistic consciousness as to moderate the capricious and the arbitrary. Buontalenti was the creator, again for Francesco I, of the Galleria of the Uffizi, in the decoration of which a group of artists directed by Alessandro Allori (PL. 293) revived the Raphaelesque motif of grotesquerie in a charming fantasia of themes: animals, little figures wittily satirized, small genre scenes. He was also the imaginative author of theatrical interludes, of festival decorations, even of fireworks displays — the last interpreter of that which in mannerism had lighted the flame of lyricism and which in Florence alone still produced a poetical result.

But Florence paid a much greater tribute to the 16th century, not through the practice of art but through art history. The *Vite* of Vasari (1550; 1568) put into focus the events of two centuries of art from the point of view of the *maniera*, in which the great masters of the past seemed unsurpassable. Vasari vividly reevoked the lives of those artists, inspired to the point of torment, who were, as he acutely discerned, not of the 16th century only but had their precursors in the two preceding centuries — an instance of historical perception not diminished by the ceremonious courtesy that makes Vasari do honor, on the other hand, to the members of the Accademia del Disegno founded in Florence through his own efforts in 1562. The formal abstraction of the *maniera* established itself in a secure position there, as in a last stand, popularizing with didactic aim the residue of the great ideal *norma* of the Renaissance. But in Florence this could still be resolved in the cadences of rhythmic design. In Rome, on the other hand, and elsewhere, the dilemma in the *maniera* between extreme abstraction and the progressive return to reality, to which color opened the way, was sharpened.

As early as 1564, the very year of Michelangelo's death, there appeared, in the treatise of G. A. Giglio (see TREATISES), the first denunciation of the *maniera*; it is symptomatic that this opposition was advanced in the name of the religious rigors of the Counter Reformation, which sought in art an instrument to further its purposes. Many art historians have seen in this repressive and total opposition the cause of the final decline of the *maniera*. But, as F. Zeri has with good reason cautioned, the precedents for the artistic events of the end of the century had long existed in purely devotional painting, especially in the severe design and restrained feeling of the new altarpieces, from the time of Sebastiano del Piombo. The reaction to the *maniera* may assuredly have had these motivations, but the most profound causes came from within, now that the idiom evolved from it was spoken in more poetic accents by the great masters. The *maniera* lost, therefore, its active function, retreating into itself and taking on, in varying combinations, all the aspects assumed in its dissemination throughout Italy and beyond. Its greatest exponents — Vasari, for example, and, toward the end of the century, Federico Zuccari — were indefatigable travelers, and from every part of Europe artists flocked to share in the Roman cultural experience. The results of this exchange, the circumstances of which cannot even be outlined within the scope of the present discussion, are to be seen in Rome, where there were innumerable opportunities, in the decoration of palaces and noble villas, for anyone possessed of technical proficiency and versed in the artistic repertory which had never ceased to grow within the rhythmic canon established by Raphael. The practice of art in Rome in the latter half of the century was controlled by the Zuccaris (Taddeo and, after his death in 1566, Federico), the decorators of Caprarola (PL. 310) and later the continuers of the Raphaelesque tradition in the Vatican. The Accademia Romana was founded in 1577 by Federico Zuccari, and he also attempted — in his *Idea de' scultori, pittori e architetti*, a sort of updating of the old Renaissance Platonism in the light of an exclusively religious motivation, in which the influence of the Counter Reformation was crucial — a theoretical justification of contemporary working practices. By now, however, far more valid experiments were taking place in painting: while the Zuccaris and their heir, the Cavalier d'Arpino (d. 1640; PL. 303), were dragging out the *maniera*, by this time merely a decorative system, well into the 17th century, the Carraccis and Caravaggio (q.v.) were already working; it was in comparison with the new directions indicated by them that Giovanni Pietro Bellori formulated his condemnation of the *maniera*.

Roman architecture, on the other hand, in which for some time already a new style had been asserting itself, could never be called mannerist, not even on the basis of those new formal types, the greatest of which was the Gesù of Vignola (1568).

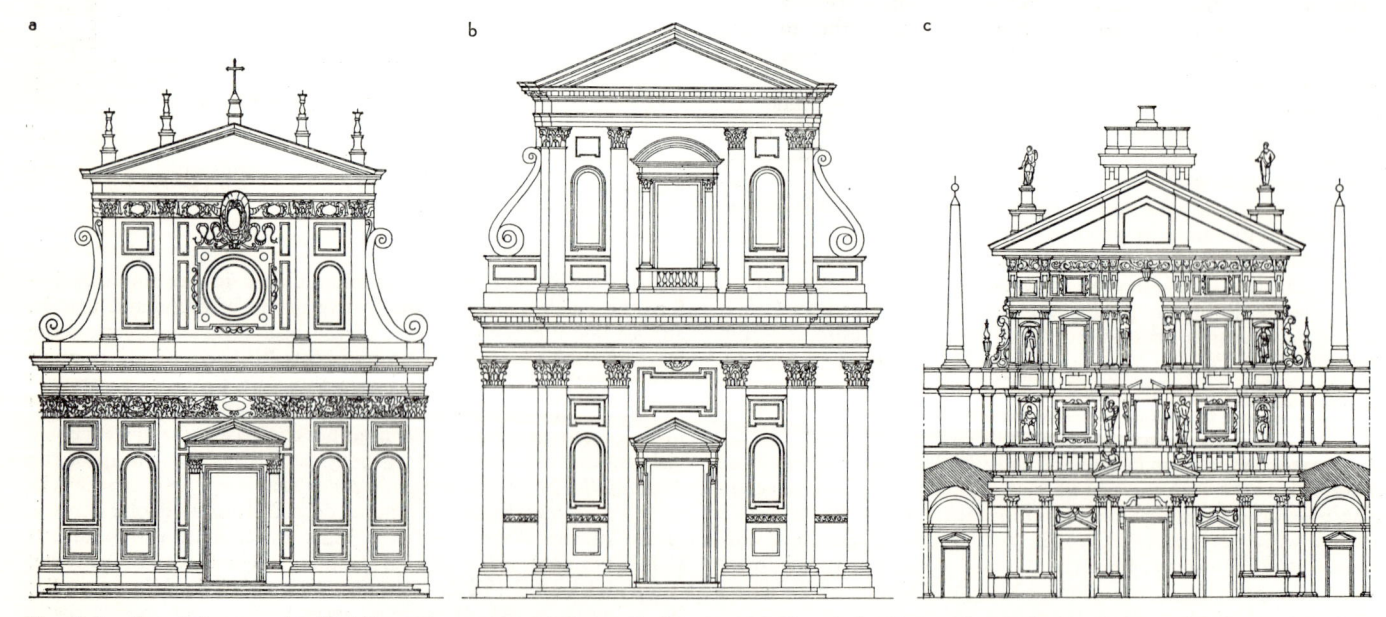

Church façades of the second half of the 16th century: (*a*) Rome, S. Caterina dei Funari (architect, G. Guidetti); (*b*) Rome, Madonna dei Monti (architect, Giacomo della Porta); (*c*) Milan, S. Maria presso S. Celso.

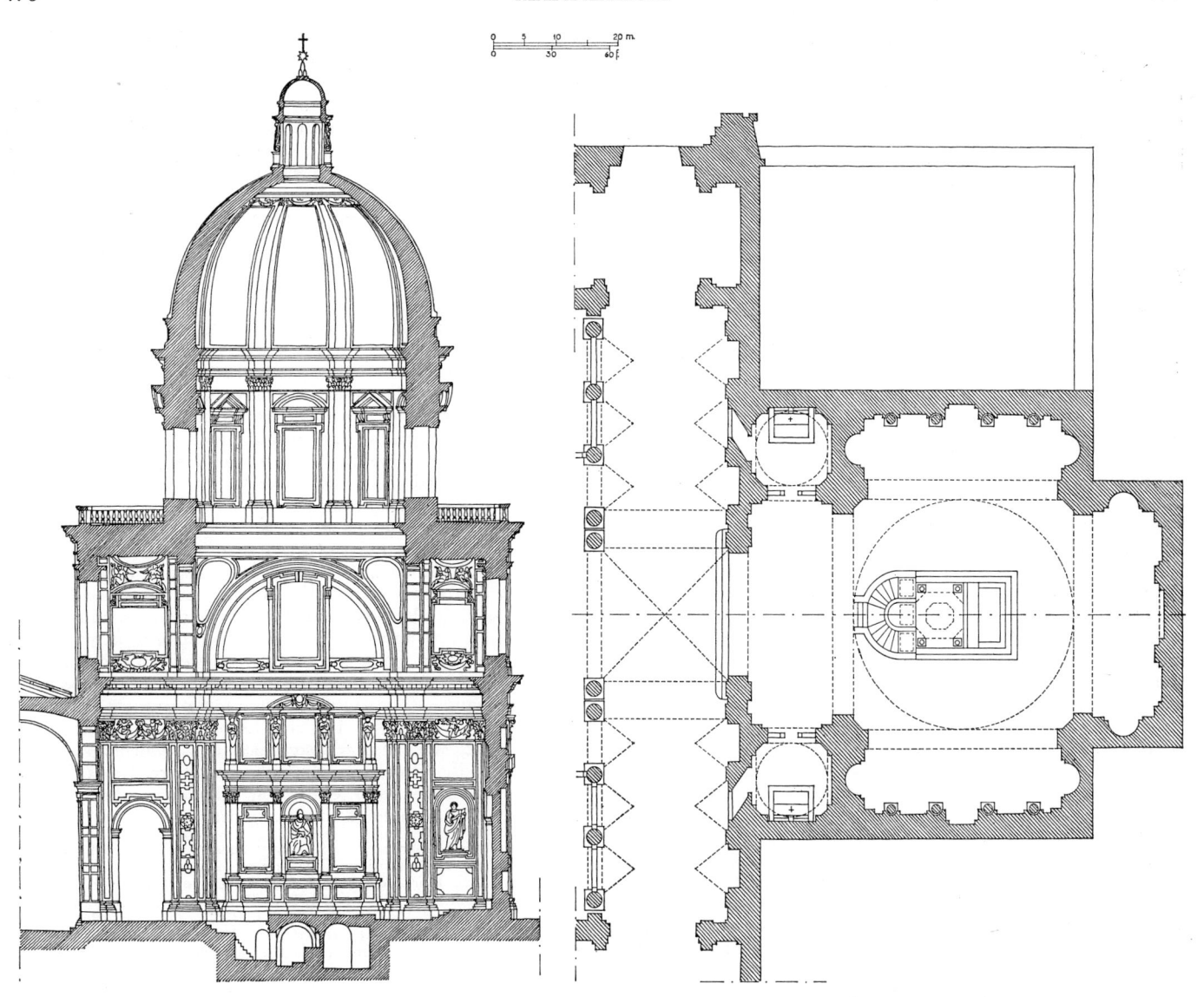

Rome, S. Maria Maggiore, Sistine Chapel (architect, D. Fontana), section and plan (*from P. Letarouilly, Édifices de Rome moderne, V, Paris, 1874*).

The work of Giacomo della Porta (ca. 1537–1602; FIG. 471), who completed the dome of St. Peter's and designed the façade of the Gesù (PL. 312), and of the dynasties of Lombard builders, the Longhis and the Fontanas (FIG. 473), as well as of other able artists, gave to the city its architectural character, not only through the creation of individual monuments but through the organization of the whole, the great city plan that Domenico Fontana laid out for Sixtus V, the implementation of which has been pursued, one might say, down to our day. Here was a new classicism, by this time sure enough of itself to discount the classicism of antiquity, to face unhesitatingly even the possible destruction of the Colosseum when it was a question of the requirements of one of the great axial streets connecting the basilicas.

Thus at the end of the century the Roman and the Florentine course of mannerism appeared vastly different. In Rome mannerism exhausted itself in practical performance, for progressing alongside it by this time was that return to reality which, as a reinvigorated sense of form, had determined the new architecture; in painting, gradually taking on the motivations of the Counter Reformation, mannerism assumed the aspect of a devotional production which, if still illumined by the impetuous fantasy of a Giuseppe Valeriani, had its typical exponent in the God-fearing Scipione Pulzone (PL. 297) and soon ceded to the imminent Caravaggesque reform. In Florence, on the other hand, the late *maniera* remained a style of rarefied lyricism, the harmonic elaboration of a rhythm that found only within itself fitting motives and was even able to gather in other art forms, in that synthesis of representation and music that was shortly to become the opera.

But it was in this extreme lyric outpouring that Florentine art came into accord with developments on the international scene, where the diffusion of Italian mannerism was proceeding on a grand scale. It can be said that only through mannerism was a total unification of artistic idiom achieved — from France to Flanders, to Bohemia, to Germany, to Spain — in lands, that is, where Gothic premises had persisted right up to the 16th century and the Renaissance had never put down solid roots. In some critical circles this has been taken to demonstrate the anti-Renaissance nature of mannerism, which was thus interpreted as the last phase not of Renaissance but of Gothic evolution. This deduction appears less valid when one considers that the artistic idiom of the Renaissance itself originated in the contest of a dialectic between Gothic art and the new problems that had been posed and worked out in Italy. And mannerism was still a comprehensible means of communication, through which distant kinships were rediscovered, permitting Italian and northern European art now to proceed in the same direction. Leonardo and Andrea del Sarto, called to France by Francis I, did not find there a favorable terrain, still less a following, whereas Il Rosso, working from 1530 on at Fontainebleau, was soon surrounded by artists who constituted for decades a genuine stylistic current, the Fontainebleau school (PL. 304; V, PLS. 392, 395, 396; XII, PL. 100).

This was not a question of establishing an Italian colony; it represented the transplanting of an artistic tradition that opened new horizons to French artists. The felicitous convergences that took place in Rome in the years before the Sack of 1527 seemed to be repeated at Fontainebleau when, in 1532, the Bolognese Primaticcio, the most graceful interpreter of the refinement of Parmigianino, joined Il Rosso. He was followed in 1551-52 by the Modenese Niccolò dell'Abate (1509-71; PLS. 299, 301; IV, PL. 415; XII, PL. 81), who maintained the glowing colorism of Ferrarese derivation, and by Luca Penni (d. 1556), pupil of Perino del Vaga. They were joined by Tribolo; Cellini worked there (saltcellar of Francis I, IV, PL. 414; VI, PL. 269; *Nymph of Fontainebleau*, PL. 307); and later Serlio and Vignola were visitors. Thus in France the free stylistic flow of the *maniera* and its great lyric power (so soon opposed and misdirected in Italy through the persistence of Renaissance problems posed by Michelangelo) continued; on the other hand, there was a resurgence, unhindered, of the old Gothic rhythmic heritage, which yielded a profuse artistic production, notable for the work of such figures as Antoine Caron (1515-93; PL. 315) and Jean Cousin the Younger (1522-94) and, above all, for the refined sculpture of Jean Goujon and Germain Pilon (V, PL. 395). When, after an interruption, the Fontainebleau school resumed its activity and renewed its influence, under Henry IV, working there alongside French artists such as Toussaint Dubreuil (1561-1602), Martin Fréminet (1567-1619), and François Bunel the Younger (1522-99) were Flemings such as Ambroise Dubois (1563-1614), who, by contributing a more solid chromatic strength to the elegance of the school, influenced the final evolution of "international" mannerism toward the end of the century.

The controversial question of the effect of the Fontainebleau school on the painting of the Low Countries remains unresolved. F. Antal, differing with H. Kauffmann, has pointed out as more decisive the new contacts arising from the exchanges with Italy: Dutch and Flemish artists flocked there to vary their experience and stayed to work, while, too, Italian artists visited Flanders and Holland (e.g., in 1574, Federico Zuccari). Still under discussion is which of the Italian centers was more influential — Rome with its countless artistic convergences or mannerist Florence of the Vasarian period after the middle of the century. It is difficult to decide, for the Flemings were active in both places; but for some, such as Stradanus and Friedrich Sustris (ca. 1540-99), the Florentine sojourn with Vasari was longer and more decisive. A survey of the activity of the artists at work in the Low Countries — such as Marten de Vos (1532-1603), Hieronymus Francken (1540-1610), and Anthonie van Blocklandt (1532-83), all pupils of the Romanist Frans Floris de Vriendt (1516-70; XII, PL. 98), as well as Abraham Bloemaert (1564-1651; PL. 305), Cornelis Cornelisz. van Haarlem (1562-1638; V, PL. 297), Joachim Wittewael (1566-1638), Hendrik Goltzius (q.v.), and, surpassing all, Bartholomaeus Spranger (1546-1611; PL. 316; XII, PL. 122) — and a comparison with the activity centering in the Medici court in Florence and in the late Humanistic circle of Cardinal Alessandro Farnese in Caprarola, near Rome, reveal a common foundation of artistic idiom in which all the ramifications of mannerism are now combined. It was inevitable that this should happen in the realm of Vasari and the Zuccaris, for whom the *maniera* was an idiom that could by then be taught and learned in the academies, without insistence on its problems, which had now, it seemed, found definitive solutions suited to all expressive occasions. This standardization of the style makes it difficult to assess the relative importance of Florence and Rome, especially since the great arbiters of art traveled freely from one country to another and did not hesitate before any task (even the terrifying one of completing the masterpieces of the Renaissance, as when Vasari and then Federico Zuccari covered the inside of Brunelleschi's dome of the Cathedral of Florence with frescoes, or when the Cavalier d'Arpino prepared the mosaics for the dome of St. Peter's; X, PL. 192).

By this time the artistic idiom was the same in Florence and in Rome, but the Flemish masters, like the Florentine masters of the *studiolo*, in addition to learning it, understood its possibilities not as rhetoric but as poetry of the unreal, of the improbable, which placed on the same plane of whimsical diversion topical matters and legend, erudition and fresh invention, formal purism and the caprices of chromatic dissonance and dazzling luminosity. It was even easier to take this approach outside Italy, where Humanistic culture was not a heritage but a recent acquisition and the persistent Gothic note could freely intervene as a component of that magical interplay. Such was the art of these masters — which the greatest of them, Spranger, raised to the plane of Arcadian, almost 18th-century, poesy. It was he who, called in 1583 to the court of Rudolph II in Prague, made it, on the threshold of the 17th century, the most active center of the style, with Hans von Aachen (1552-1615) and Josef Heintz the Elder (1564-1609), architects as well as painters, Hans Vredeman de Vries (1527-1604?), and Hans Mont working there. Active at the court of Bavaria were L. Sustris and Pieter de Witte (known as Candid). It is understandable that, by using these manifestations as a point of departure and tracing their origins to Rome after the death of Raphael and to the Florence of the first followers of Michelangelo, transalpine critics were led to frame this development in Gothic terms rather than in terms of the Renaissance, whose art was regarded as an art only of rational definition and of *regola*. But at the heart of the Italian origins of this extreme refinement of the *maniera* was the conquest of the *moto [che] è causa di ogni vita*, to which the Humanistic study of form had been devoted in Florence since the 15th century and toward which Leonardo and Michelangelo had consciously striven. The 15th century made use of this conquest in order to pass beyond toward the unknown regions where poetic sense alone can be the guide. The 16th century was the century of Ariosto, Tasso, and Cervantes, and astride its boundaries stood Shakespeare. Alongside their consummate achievements stand, in the realm of the visual arts, the universal utterances of Raphael and of Michelangelo and, even though less lofty, the authentic and genuine utterances of the mannerists.

SOURCES. Schlosser provides a comprehensive account. Of particular importance are: B. Castiglione, Il Cortegiano, Venice, 1527; B. Varchi, Due lezioni..., Florence, 1549; Vasari; L. Dolce, Dialogo della Pittura intitolato L'Aretino, Venice, 1557; J. Barozzi da Vignola, Regola delli cinque ordini d'architettura, Venice, 1562; G. A. Gilio, Due dialoghi... degli errori de' Pittori, Camerino, 1564; B. Cellini, Due trattati: Uno... dell'oreficeria, l'altro... della cultura..., Florence, 1568 (ed. G. Milanesi, Florence, 1857); A. Palladio, I quattro libri dell'Architettura, Venice, 1570; R. Borghini, Il Riposo, Florence, 1584; G. P. Lomazzo, Trattato dell'Arte della Pittura, Milan, 1584; S. Serlio, Settimo Libro di Architettura, Venice, 1584; S. Serlio, Tutte l'Opere d'Architettura... (ed. G. D. Scamozzi), Venice, 1584; G. B. Armenini, De' veri precetti della pittura, Ravenna, 1586; G. P. Lomazzo, Idea del Tempio della Pittura, Milan, 1590; R. Alberti, Origine e Progresso dell'Accademia del Disegno... in Roma, Pavia, 1604; F. Zuccari (or Zuccaro), L'Idea de' scultori, pittori e architetti, 2 vols., Turin, 1607; M. Boschini, La carta del navegar pitoresco, Venice, 1660; G. P. Bellori, Le Vite de' pittori, scultori, ed architetti moderni, Rome, 1672; F. Baldinucci, Notizie de' professori del disegno..., 6 vols., Florence, 1681-1728; F. Baldinucci, Vocabolario toscano dell'arte del disegno, Florence, 1681; L. Lanzi, Storia pittorica dell'Italia..., Bassano, 1789; F. Milizia, Dizionario delle belle arti del disegno, I, Bassano, 1797.

BIBLIOG. Only a selection from the immense bibliography pertaining to mannerism can be included here; preference is given to theoretical studies and works containing bibliogs. J. Burckhardt, Der Cicerone, Basel, 1855 (Eng. trans., London, 1873); C. Gurlitt, Geschichte des Barock-Stiles in Italien, Stuttgart, 1887; H. Wölfflin, Renaissance und Barock, Munich, 1888 (ed. H. Rose, Munich, 1926); H. Wölfflin, Die klassische Kunst, Munich, 1899 (Eng. trans., P. and L. Murray, Classic Art: An Introduction to the Italian Renaissance, London, New York, 1952); E. Cassirer, Das Erkenntnisproblem in der Philosophie und Wissenschaft der neueren Zeit, I, Berlin, 1906; W. Kallab, Vasaristudien, Vienna, 1908; A. Riegl, Die Entstehung der Barockkunst in Rom, Vienna, 1908; J. von Schlosser, Die Kunst- und Wunderkammern der Spätrenaissance, Leipzig, 1908; K. H. Busse, Manierismus und Barockstil, Leipzig, 1911; G. Goldschmidt, Pontormo, Rosso und Bronzino, Leipzig, 1911; M. J. Friedländer, Die Antwerpen Manieristen von 1520, JhbPreussKSamml, XXXVI, 1915, pp. 66-91; H. Wölfflin, Kunstgeschichtliche Grundbegriffe, Munich, 1915 (Eng. trans., M. D. Hottinger, Principles of Art History, London, 1932); F. M. Clapp, Jacopo Carucci da Pontormo: His Life and Work, New Haven, 1916; W. Weisbach, Der Manierismus, ZfbK, N.S., XXX, 1918-19, pp. 161-83; A. E. Brinckmann, Barockskulptur, 2 vols., Berlin-Neubabelsberg, 1919; E. Panofsky, Die Scala Regia im Vatikan und die Kunstanschauung Berninis, JhbPreussKSamml, XL, 1919, pp. 241-78; J. Strzygowski, Norden und Renaissance, ZfbK, N.S., XXXI, 1919-20, pp. 98-103; H. Voss, Die Malerei der Spätrenaissance in Rom und Florenz, 2 vols., Berlin, 1920; L. Fröhlich-Bum, Parmigianino und der Manierismus, Vienna, 1921; H. Kauffmann, Der Manierismus in Holland und die Schule von Fontainebleau, JhbPreussK-

Samml, XLIV, 1923, pp. 184–204; M. Dvořák, Über den geistlichen Voraussetzungen des niederländischen Romanismus, in Kunstgeschichte als Geistesgeschichte, Munich, 1924, pp. 205–25; M. Dvořák, Über Greco und den Manierismus, in Kunstgeschichte als Geistgeschichte, Munich, 1924, pp. 261–76 (Eng. trans., Mag. of Art, XLVI, 1953, pp. 15–23); M. Hörner, Manierismus, Z. für Ästhetik, XVII, 1924, pp. 262–68; E. Panofsky, Idea: Ein Beitrag zur Begriffgeschichte der älterer Kunsttheorie, Leipzig, Berlin, 1924 (rev. ed., Berlin, 1960; It. trans., E. Cione, Idea: Contributo alla storia dell'estetica, Florence, 1952); H. Wescher-Kauert, Das Ende der altdeutsche Malerei und die antiklassische Strömung, Der Cicerone, XVI, 1924, pp. 996–98; W. Friedländer, Die Entstehung des antiklassischen Stiles in der italienischen Malerei um 1520, RepfKw, XLVI, 1925, pp. 243–62 (Eng. trans., Mannerism and Anti-Mannerism in Italian Painting, New York, 1957, pp. 1–43); N. Pevsner, Gegenreformation und Manierismus, RepfKw, XLVI, 1925, pp. 243–62; Venturi, IX–XI, 1925–40; R. Longhi, Precisioni nelle gallerie italiane, I: R. Galleria Borghese, Vita Artistica, I, 1926, pp. 65–72; F. Antal, Zum Problem des niederländischen Manierismus, Kritische Berichte, I–II, 1927–29, pp. 207–56; E. Cassirer, Individuum und Kosmos in der Philosophie der Renaissance, Leipzig, Berlin, 1927; M. Dvořák, Geschichte der italienische Kunst, 2 vols., Munich, 1927–29; R. Longhi, Un San Tomaso del Velasquez e le congiunture italo-spagnole tra il '500 e il '600, Vita Artistica, II, 1927, pp. 4–12; F. Saxl, Antike Götter in der Spätrenaissance: Ein Freskenzyklus und ein Discorso des Jacopo Zucchi (S. der Bib. Warburg, VIII), Leipzig, Berlin, 1927; F. Antel, Un capolavoro inedito del Parmigianino, Pinacotheca, I, 1928–29, pp. 49–56; W. Friedländer, Der antimanieristische Stil um 1590 und sein Verhältnis zum Übersinnlichen, Vorträge der Bib. Warburg, VIII, 1928–29, pp. 214–43 (Eng. trans., Mannerism and Anti-Mannerism in Italian Painting, New York, 1957, pp. 45–83); M. Hörner, Der Manierismus als künstlerische Anschauungsform, Z. für Ästhetik, XXII, 1928, pp. 200–210; N. Pevsner, Die italienische Malerei vom Ende der Renaissance bis zum ausgehende Rokoko, Wildpark-Potsdam, 1928; K. Steinbart, Die niederländischen Hofmaler der bairischen Herzöge, Marburger Jhb. für Kw., IV, 1928, pp. 89–164; W. Weisbach, Gegenreformation, Manierismus, Barock, RepfKw, XLIX, 1928, pp. 16–28; D. Frey, Gotik und Renaissance als Grundlagen der modernen Weltanschauung, Augsburg, 1929; M. Neusser, Die Antikenergänzungen der Florentinischen Manieristen, JhbKhSammlWien, N.S., VI, 1929, pp. 27–42; W. Pinder, Die deutsche Plastik vom ausgehenden Mittelalter bis zum Ende der Renaissance, II, Berlin-Neubabelsberg, 1929; G. C. Argan, Andrea Palladio e la critica neoclassica, L'Arte, N.S., I, 1930, pp. 237–46; E. Panofsky, Das erste Blatt aus dem 'Libro' Giorgio Vasaris: Eine Studie über die Bedeutung der Gotik in der italienischen Renaissance, mit einem Exkurs über zwei Fassadenprojecte Domenico Beccafumis, Städel Jhb., VI, 1930, pp. 25–72 (Eng. trans., in Meaning and the Visual Arts, Garden City, N.Y., 1957, pp. 169–235); L. Hagelberg, Die Architektur Michelangelos in ihren Beziehungen zu Manierismus und Barock, Münch. Jhb. der bildenden K., N.S., VIII, 1931, pp. 264–80; W. Pinder, Zur Physiognomik des Manierismus, in Festschrift Ludwig Klages, Leipzig, 1932, pp. 148–56; E. Michalski, Das Problem des Manierismus in der italienischen Architektur, ZfKg, II, 2, 1933, pp. 88–109; C. L. Ragghianti, I Carracci e la critica d'arte nell'età barocca, La Critica, XXXI, 1933, pp. 65–74, 382–94; C. L. Ragghianti, Il valore dell'opera di Giorgio Vasari, Atti Acc. naz. dei Lincei, 6th ser., IX, 1933, pp. 758–826; H. Wölfflin, Kunstgeschichtliche Grundbegriffe, Logos, XXII, 1933, pp. 210–18; G. C. Argan, EI, s.v. Manierismo, XXII, 1934, p. 126; L. Becherucci, La scultura italiana del Cinquecento, Florence, 1934; W. Weisbach, Zum Problem des Manierismus, Strasbourg, 1934; R. Wittkower, Michelangelo's Biblioteca Laurenziana, AB, XVI, 1934, pp. 123–218; E. H. Gombrich, Zum Werke Giulio Romanos, JhbKhSammlWien, N.S., VIII, 1935, pp. 79–104, IX, 1936, pp. 121–50; L. Becherucci, L'architettura italiana del Cinquecento, Florence, 1936; L. Coletti, Introduzione al Tintoretto, Convivium, X, 1938, pp. 241–51; H. Hoffmann, Hochrenaissance, Manierismus, Frühbarock, Zurich, Leipzig, 1938; A. Graziani, Bartolomeo Cesi, CrArte, IV, 1939, pp. 54–93; E. Panofsky, Studies in Iconology: Humanistic Themes in the Art of the Renaissance, New York, 1939 (2d ed., 1962); G. Rehbein, Malerei und Skulptur des deutschen Frühmanierismus, Würzburg, 1939; M. Riemenschneider-Hörner, Holbein, Erasmus und der frühe Manierismus des XVI, Jahrhunderts, Z. für Ästhetik, XXXIII, 1939, pp. 27–40; A. Blunt, Artistic Theory in Italy, 1450–1600, Oxford, 1940; R. W. Lee, Ut pictura poesis: The Humanistic Theory of Painting, AB, XXII, 1940, pp. 197–269; N. Pevsner, Academies of Art Past and Present, Cambridge 1940; G. Poggi and others, Mostra del Cinquecento toscano (exhibition cat.), Florence, 1940; M. Salmi, La mostra del Cinquecento toscano, Nuova Antologia, CDX, 1940, pp. 75–83; H. Lossow, Zum Stilproblem des Manierismus in der italienischen und deutschen Malerei, in Festschrift für W. Waetzold, Berlin, 1941, pp. 192–208; M. Treves, *Maniera*: The History of a Word, Marsyas, I, 1941, pp. 69–88; G. C. Argan, Cultura artistica della fine del Cinquecento, Le Arti, IV, 1942, pp. 181–84; J. Coolidge, Vignola, and the Little Domes of St. Peter's, Marsyas, II, 1942, pp. 63–123; S. Ortolani, Raffaello, Bergamo, 1942; J. Coolidge, The Villa Giulia: A Study of Central Italian Architecture in the Mid-16th Century, AB, XXV, 1943, pp. 177–225; L. Becherucci, Manieristi toscani, Bergamo, 1944; F. Hartt, Raphael and Giulio Romano, AB, XXVI, 1944, pp. 67–94; G. Briganti, Il Manierismo e Pellegrino Tibaldi, Rome, 1945 (rev. F. Arcangeli, Leonardo, N.S., XV, 1946, pp. 156–60); J. Coolidge, The Arched Loggie on the Campidoglio, Marsyas, IV, 1945–47, pp. 69–79; N. Pevsner, The Architecture of Mannerism, in The Mint, London, 1946, pp. 116–38; O. Benesch, Art of the Renaissance in Northern Europe, Cambridge, Mass., 1947; G. Nicco Fasola, Pontormo o del Cinquecento, Florence, 1947; F. Antal, Florentine Painting and Its Social Background, London, 1948; E. Cassirer, P. O. Kristeller, and J. H. Randall Jr., ed., The Renaissance Philosophy of Man, Chicago, 1948; L. Coletti, Intorno alla storia del concetto di Manierismo, Convivium N.S., I, 1948, pp. 801–11; E. R. Curtius, Europäische Literatur und lateinisches Mittelalter, Berne, 1948 (Eng. trans. W. R. Trask, New York, 1952); W. K. Ferguson, The Renaissance in Historical Thought, Boston, 1948; F. Zeri, Salviati e Jacopino del Conte, Proporzioni, II, 1948, pp. 180–83; R. Zürcher, Stilprobleme der italienischen Baukunst des Cinquecento, Basel, 1948; C.H. Smyth, The Earliest Works of Bronzino, AB, XXXI, 1949, pp. 184–210; R. Wittkower, Architectural Principles in the Age of Humanism, London, 1949 (3d ed., 1962); F. Arcangeli, Mostra di Lelio Orsi a Reggio Emilia, Paragone, I, 7, 1950, pp. 48–52; P. Barocchi, Il Rosso Fiorentino, Rome, 1950 (rev. R. Longhi, Paragone, II, 13, 1951, pp. 58–62); S. J. Freedberg, Parmigianino: His Works in Painting, Cambridge, Mass., 1950; L. Becherucci, Il Convegno internazionale di studi vasariani, Il Rinascimento, II, 1951, pp. 186–91; A. Hauser, The Social History of Art, 2 vols., London, New York, 1951; L. Marcucci, Due disegni di Lelio Orsi, Belle Arti, 1951, p. 60–62; L. Marcucci, Note sulla pittura fiorentina intorno al 1560, Belle Arti, 1951, pp. 63–70; F. Barbieri, Vincenzo Scamozzi, Vicenza, 1952 (rev. L. Becherucci, RArte, XXVIII, 1953, pp. 214–20); F. Bologna and others, Fontainebleau e la Maniera italiana (exhibition cat.), Florence, 1952; G. Castelfranco, Introduzione a Leonardo, Nuova Antologia, CDLIV, 1952, pp. 1–25; N. Ivanoff, Il concetto dello stile nel Poussin e in Marco Boschini, Comm, III, 1952, pp. 51–61 (rev. L. Grassi, Comm, III, 1952, pp. 224–25); F. Kriegbaum, Zur Florentiner Plastik des Cinquecento, Münch. Jhb. der bildenden K., 3d ser., III–IV, 1952–53, pp. 10–67; R. Longhi, Un ritratto del Pontormo, Paragone, III, 35, 1952, pp. 40–41; Studi Vasariani: Atti Conv. int. per il IV centenario ... delle Vite del Vasari (1950), Florence, 1952; G. Weise, Il termine di tardo-gotico nell'arte settentrionale, Paragone, III, 31, 1952, pp. 24–36; R. Longhi, Ricordo dei Manieristi, L'Approdo, II, 1953, pp. 55–59; L. Marcucci, Appunti per Mirabello Cavalori disegnatore, RArte, XXVIII, 1953, pp. 77–98; R. Pallucchini, La vicenda italiana del Greco, Paragone, IV, 45, 1953, pp. 3–39; C. Zupnick, The "Aesthetics" of the Early Mannerists, AB, XXXV, 1953, pp. 77–98; G. S. Adelmann and G. Weise, Das Fortleben gotischer Ausdrucks- und Bewegungsmotive in der Kunst des Manierismus, Tübingen, 1954; N. Ivanoff, Le ignote considerazioni di G. B. Volpato, sulla "maniera," Atti III Cong. int. S. umanistici (Retorica e Barocco), Venice, 1954, pp. 99–107; Pontormo to Greco: The Age of Mannerism (exhibition cat.), Indianapolis, 1954; L. Becherucci, Momenti dell'arte fiorentina nel Cinquecento, in Il Cinquecento, Florence, 1955, pp. 161–83; W. Lotz, Die ovalen Kirchenräume des Cinquecento, Römisches Jhb. für Kg., VII, 1955, pp. 9–99; P. Pirri, Giovanni Tristano e i primordi dell'architettura gesuitica, Rome, 1955; Rijksmuseum, Amsterdam, Le triomphe du maniérisme européen (exhibition cat.; also Dutch ed.), Amsterdam, 1955; P. Barocchi, Il Vasari pittore, Rinascimento, VII, 1956, pp. 187–217; L. Berti and others, Pontormo e del primo Manierismo Fiorentino (exhibition cat.), Florence, 1956; M. Calvesi, Il Sacro Bosco di Bomarzo, in Scritti in onore di L. Venturi, I, Rome, 1956, pp. 369–402; G. Nicco Fasola, Il Manierismo e l'arte veneziana del '500, in Venezia e l'Europa: Atti XVIII Cong. int. Storia dell'arte, Venice, 1956, pp. 291–93; G. Nicco Fasola, Storiografia del Manierismo, in Scritti in onore di L. Venturi, I, Rome, 1956, pp. 429–47; G. R. Hocke, Die Welt als Labyrinth: Manier und Manie in der europäische Kunst, Hamburg, 1957; F. Zeri, Pittura e Controriforma, Turin, 1957; Atti IV Congresso di Studi umanistici (Umanesimo e Simbolismo), Venice, 1958; F. Hartt, Giulio Romano, 2 vols., New Haven, 1958; W. Lotz, Architecture in the Later 16th Century, College Art J., XVII, 1958, pp. 129–39; A. Terzaghi, La nascita del Barocco e l'esperienza europea di F. Zuccari, in Actes XIXe Cong. int. H. de l'art, Paris, 1958, pp. 285–97; G. R. Hocke, Manierismus in der Literatur, Hamburg, 1959; G. Weise, Vitalismo, animismo e panpsichismo nella decorazione del Cinquecento e del Seicento, CrArte, VI, 1959, pp. 375–98, VII, 1960, pp. 85–96; E. Battisti, Rinascimento e Barocco, Turin, 1960; A. Emiliano, Il Bronzino, Busto Arsizio, 1960; C. Pericoli Ridolfini, Le case romane con facciate graffite e dipinte (exhibition cat.), Rome, 1960; G. Weise, La duplice interpretazione dell'antichità classica nel Rinascimento e nel Barocco, Paragone, XI, 121, 1960, pp. 3–14; G. Briganti, La maniera italiana, Rome, 1961; S. J. Freedberg, Painting of the High Renaissance in Rome and Florence, 2 vols., Cambridge, Mass., 1961; G. Weise, L'ideale eroico del Rinascimento ..., Naples, 1961; E. Raimondi, Per la nozione di Manierismo letterario, Manierismo, Barocco, Rococò: Concetti e termini, Convegno int. (Rome, 1960), Rome, 1962, pp. 57–79; M. Salmi, Tardo Rinascimento e primo Barocco, Manierismo, Barocco, Rococò: Concetti e termini, Convegno int. (Rome, 1960), Rome, 1962, pp. 305–17; G. Weise, Storia del termine Manierismo, Manierismo, Barocco, Rococò: Concetti e termini, Convegno int. (Rome, 1960), Rome, 1962, pp. 27–38; F. Würtenberger, Der Manierismus: Der europäische Stil des 16. Jahrhunderts, Vienna, 1962; C. H. Smyth, Mannerism and Maniera, Locust Valley, N.Y., 1963.

Luisa BECHERUCCI

Illustrations: PLS. 288–316; 6 figs. in text.

MANSART, FRANÇOIS AND JULES HARDOUIN. French architects, the two greatest names in a family of French artists active in the 17th and 18th centuries. Like many of the old families of architects, the Mansarts (whose name was frequently written Mansard) formed a veritable dynasty related to other families of architects, painters, and sculptors.

SUMMARY. François (col. 478). Jules Hardouin (col. 481).

FRANÇOIS (b. Paris, Jan. 13, 1598; d. Paris, Sept. 3, 1666). After a brief apprenticeship with his brother-in-law, Germain Gaultier, he became the pupil of Salomon de Brosse, with whom he collaborated at the end of 1618 on the Château of Coulommiers.

Although François was appointed architect to the king in 1636, he worked chiefly for the aristocracy and the rich Parisian bourgeoisie. His style marks the period of transition from Renaissance forms, which had already been appreciably modified by Salomon de Brosse, to those of classicism, which were to triumph in France after 1650. François Mansart's formative period occurred at the beginning of the 17th century, and his earliest works reveal his admiration for the masters of the 16th century. He never went to Rome, but he learned about the great Italians from engravings and books; he knew of Bramante's perspective and his treatment of vaults, and the bulging friezes of Serlio. That he was well aware of the development of the centralized plan can be observed in his Convent of the Visitation, in the chapel at Fresnes, and in the Val-de-Grâce. Mansart also knew Vignola's entablature style and the Palladian taste in the disposition of decorative figures on pediments. He studied the illustrations by Jean Goujon for Jean Martin's translation of Vitruvius and imitated the Corinthian capitals he found there. He was inspired particularly by Philibert Delorme (q.v.) and imitated his rhythmic treatment of bays, his expanded columns, and his hemispherical domes (IV, PLS. 163-165). Mansart also shared Delorme's taste for stereotomic feats, beautiful and involved squinches, sophisticated staircases, and careful masonry.

He maintained the traditional arrangements that he had learned from Salomon de Brosse: the châteaux of rectangular plan, with a triumphal entry on one side; double pavilions; windows with alternating segmented and triangular pediments; embossments; ironwork; and separate roofs over each section of a building.

He was animated, as were so many of his contemporaries, by an enthusiasm for certain baroque traits. He loved decoration, sometimes abundant decoration, and employed types derived from Flemish as well as Italian sources. His was a sculptural *décor*, developed in space, which took advantage of the play of light and shadow. He evidently enjoyed using curves, as may be seen in the plans of his churches and in some oval rooms such as that at the Hôtel de la Vrillière and in the porticoes of the Berny and Blois châteaux. He was fond of perspective effects in, for instance, sequences of rooms in an interior or in the scenographic disposition of buildings articulated on various planes, such as the façade of the Church of the Minims. He opened vertical views and made light burst forth from the tops of domes and staircases.

However, unlike the baroque architects, François Mansart never overdid the decoration, making it subordinate to the architecture as a whole. As he matured he steadily eliminated all superfluous features, reducing, for example, the wings of a château such as that at Maisons-Laffitte (PL. 317) to massive pavilions, as he strove for simplicity and unity of structure. He purified the forms, joined various parts by great horizontals, and covered them with a single roof; he imposed geometric schemes and harmonious proportions on his compositions, dividing them into halves. He was, thus, one of the creators of the classicism that was to reign in France to the end of his life. His influence remained important into the 18th century and came to the fore again when J.-F. Blondel and his friends reacted against the rococo; even in the 19th century the eclectics drew inspiration from his works for building town houses and châteaux.

Works. 1618: Château of Coulommiers (Seine-et-Marne), where he collaborated with Salomon de Brosse and built a staircase. – 1623: Nov. 27, contract with Pierre Brulart, viscount of Puisieux, for the construction of the Château of Berny (Seine). – 1624-29: Paris, portal of the Chapel of the Feuillants, begun by Father Estienne de St-Ignace ca. 1600. – 1630: Paris, Hôtel Bouthillier, near the Hôtel St-Pol, built for Léon Bouthillier, Count of Chavigny. – 1632: Paris, the Convents of the Visitation on the Rue St-Jacques (destroyed) and on the Rue St-Antoine (the chapel of which is now a Protestant church). – 1635: Paris, Hôtel de la Vrillière, built for Louis Phélypeaux de la Vrillière (altered, 1713, by Robert de Cotte; again, after 1870, by C. A. Questel; now Banque de France); additions to the Château of Blois for Gaston d'Orléans, brother of Louis XIII (PL. 317). – 1636: Paris, Hôtel de Macé de la Bazinière on the Quai Malaquais (transformed; now part of École des Beaux-Arts). – 1640: Paris, Chapel of the Dames de Ste-Marie, Chaillot; Paris, his own house in the Rue Payenne. – 1642: Maisons-Laffitte (Seine-et-Oise), Château of Maisons, for the president of the parliament of Paris, René de Longueil (PL. 317; FIG. 479). – 1645: Paris, enlargement of the Hôtel Tubeuf for Cardinal Mazarin. (The building was previously the Hôtel de Chevry, built 1635, by Jean Thiriot; it was sold in 1641 to Jacques Tubeuf, who had it enlarged by Pierre Le Muet and rented it in 1643 to Mazarin. Mansart constructed two superposed galleries and decorated the apartments. Mazarin sold the Hôtel on Aug. 30, 1649. The stables and library are the work of Le Muet. Today the Hôtel is part of the Bibliothèque Nationale.) – 1645-47: Paris, the Val-de-Grâce (II, PL. 151; FIG. 481; the plans were modified by Le Muet in 1654). – 1648: Paris, Hôtel Le Jars on the Rue de Richelieu (destroyed late 18th cent.). – 1640-50: Paris, Hôtel for Charles de l'Aubespine on the Rue Coquillère; and perhaps the Aubespine family tomb in the Cathedral of Bourges; Paris, Hôtel d'Albret on the Rue des Francs-Bourgeois; Paris, Hôtel Fieubet on the Quai des Célestins (now transformed), finished in 1650; Paris, Hôtel de Nevers, remod-

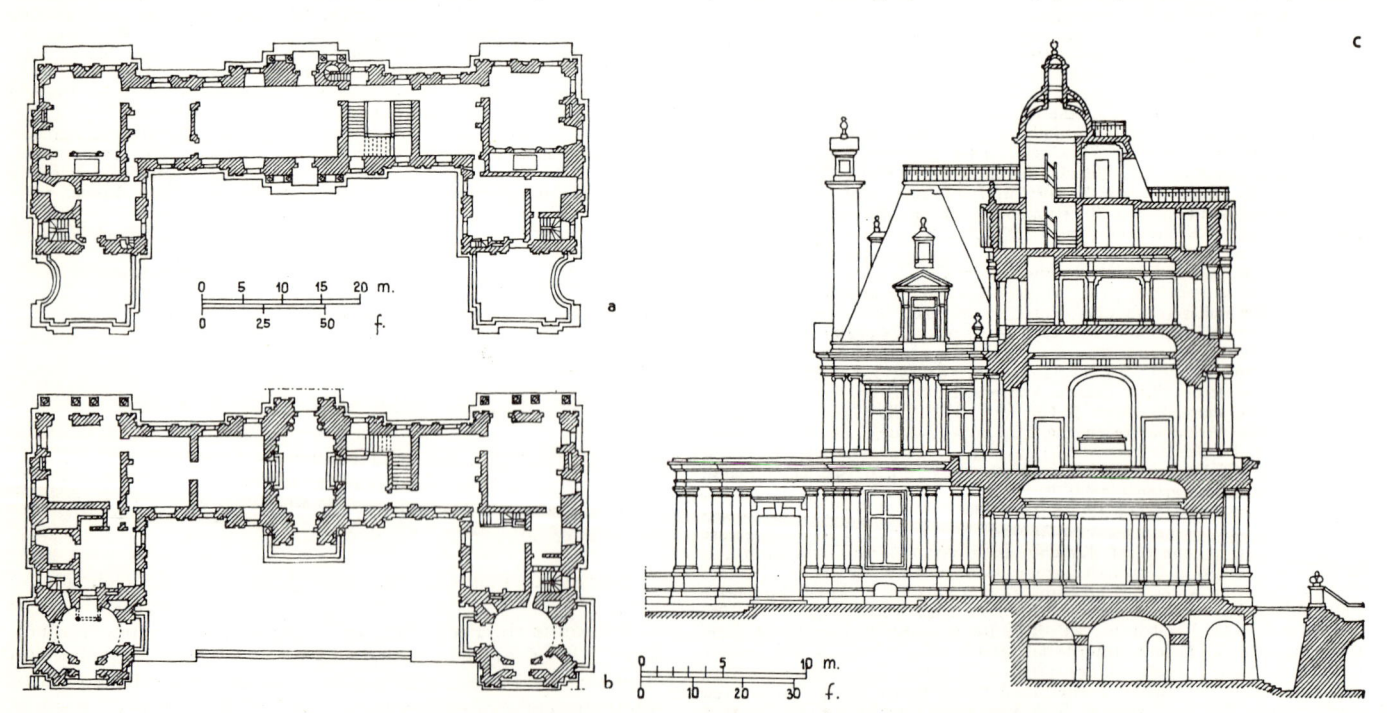

Maisons-Laffitte, the Château of Maisons: (*a*) Plan of second floor; (*b*) plan of ground floor; (*c*) section.

eled for Guénégaud (in 1670 it became the Hôtel de Conti; now the Mint). – ca. 1651: Paris, house for Guénégaud in the Rue du Grand-Chantier; Fresnes (Seine-et-Marne), Château for Guénégaud. – 1655–61: Paris, remodeling of the Hôtel Carnavalet; Paris, remodeling of the Hôtel d'Aumont on the Rue de Jouy (after 1655; originally built by Le Vau before 1649). – 1657: Paris, portal of the Church of the Minims, near the Place Royale (the work was interrupted in 1665 but resumed with modifications by Pierre Thévenot in 1672). – 1664: Projects for the Louvre. – 1665: St-Denis, projects for the Bourbon funerary chapel. – *Uncertain date*: Paris, altar of the Church of St-Martin-des-Champs. – *Unproved or erroneous attributions*: Châteaux at Cany, Chantelou, Daubeuf (Seine-Maritime), Dampierre (Aube), Balleroy (Calvados), La Ferté–Saint-Aubin (Loiret), Chamarande (Seine-et-Oise), and many others.

JULES HARDOUIN (b. Paris, April, 1646; d. Marly, May 11, 1708). He was the grandnephew of François, whose family name he took and with whom he studied for a period; he also studied drawing with Charles Poerson the Elder and architecture with Libéral Bruant. Jules was the favorite architect of Louis XIV, being awarded the titles of Intendant des Bâtiments du Roi (1685), Premier Architecte du Roi (1686), Inspecteur Général des Bâtiments du Roi (1691), Surintendent des Bâtiments du Roi (1699). A great part of his career was dedicated to the completion of the Château of Versailles, the construction of houses for the nobility, and other works of restoration and reconstruction, although his urban projects, the design of various notable squares and parks of Paris, such as the Place Vendôme and the Place des Victoires, and the plan and design of the dome of Les Invalides (PL. 318; II, PL. 150), are no less important.

The style of Jules Hardouin Mansart developed through study of the works of others to an expression that was clearly his own. He certainly remembered the lessons of his great uncle, for at Clagny forms derived from Maisons and Blois are unmistakable. In the first project for the royal chapel of the Château of Versailles François's influence is evident, and in both the plan and the section of the dome of Les Invalides there is a dependence upon François's project for the Bourbon chapel at Saint-Denis, both in the method of drawing and in

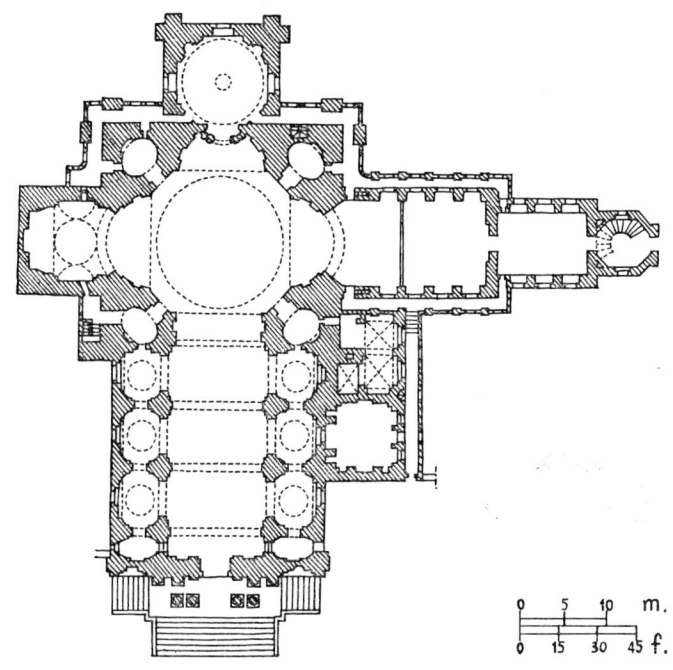

Paris, Val-de-Grâce, plan.

the proportions. At Clagny there are also motifs taken from Le Vau, such as the opening of vestibules onto peristyles. Jules must have collaborated with Lebrun (q.v.) until about 1685; the Hall of Mirrors (Galerie des Glaces) at Versailles (II, PL. 212; V, PL. 409) and the painted façades of Marly were the result. Mansart's taste for scenographic effects and daring perspective may also be the result of this collaboration. Mansart was also faithful to certain long-standing French traditions; for example, he preserved the characteristic château plan at Boufflers, and at Versailles he wished to crown the building with great roofs, a typically French feature. At the Orangerie of Versailles and in the famous flat vault of the Arles city hall,

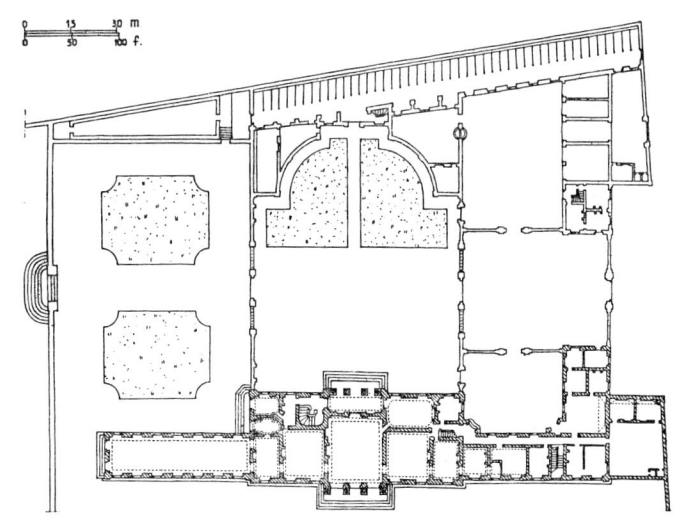

Saint-Germain-en-Laye, Hôtel de Noailles, plan of ground floor from the original project (from J. Mariette, *L'architecture française*, Paris, 1727).

he showed his love for the art of stonecutting, an inheritance from the master craftsmen of earlier times.

Despite his reliance on tradition and receptivity to contemporary architecture, however, Jules Hardouin Mansart, even in his earliest works, was an innovator. At the Château du Val and at the Hôtel de Noailles at Saint-Germain-en-Laye (FIG. 482) he established the type of long, low edifice with horizontal accents that he revived at the Grand Trianon of Versailles. He replaced the rectangular windows of Le Vau with bays topped by semicircular arches, a type which survived until the 18th century; for the Hôtel de Lorges he used bays with depressed arches, an innovation erroneously attributed to Charles-Augustin d'Aviler. In the Place Vendôme (X, PL. 153) he surmounted the arcades of the ground floor with a two-story colossal order, producing an original interpretation of a 16th-century Italian idea.

Jules Hardouin Mansart had a sense of rhythm, symmetry, and grandeur, as well as versatility and variety. From the time of the Château du Val he gave different plans to neighboring rooms. While respecting an underlying geometric arrangement, he abandoned the rigidity of rectangular schemes in favor of polygons, circles, and ovals, which also appear in his great "Places Royales," often imitated in the 18th century. He knew how to unite a taste for majesty with a care for elegance, for example, in the colonnade of the park at Versailles. Like many French architects, Jules respected comfort and created practical arrangements of rooms; he heated various apartments with stoves set in the walls and installed the most compact and ingeniously arranged systems of fireplaces. In the Hôtel de Lorges he provided a covered entryway for guests arriving in carriages. His ability to resolve technical problems arising from his complicated style was already recognized by his contemporaries. Jacques-François Blondel credited Mansart with the distinction of introducing a logical rapport between façades and the surroundings. He designed façades that were almost bare (as Bruant and Pierre Bullet were then doing) and established the building type that in the 18th century inspired his students and the Gabriels. According to his collaborators he was a perfect draftsman.

Jules Hardouin Mansart modified the accepted scheme of interior decoration. While Lebrun, a painter who controlled French taste for many years, loved polychrome, large pictures, tapestries, and rich materials, Mansart, as an architect, limited painted decorations to vaults and domes, and in the Church of Les Invalides and the chapel at Versailles, erected after Lebrun's fall from favor, he left the stone white in order to give to the supporting elements their full architectural value. In salons he devised a similar scheme, using, instead of compartmented wall coverings, arcaded orders surmounted by a cornice, coving, and a ceiling ornamented within a single central rosette. As a result of economic difficulties at the end of the reign of Louis XIV, he replaced gold decorations with light colors or sometimes with natural wood. The invention of the oblique chimney permitted the elimination of vast superstructures, and Mansart developed the type of fireplace that survives to the present, above which a mirror could be incorporated, a feature made possible by technical advances in glassmaking. He used new motifs on a smaller scale and of more charming character, including the scallop shell which later gave its French name *coquille* to the *rocaille* or rococo style. He and Robert de Cotte created a style intended to reconcile baroque grace with classic regularity, a style that triumphed in the 18th century. It was directly continued by his grandson, Jean Hardouin Mansart de Jouy, the designer of the façade of the Church of St-Eustache in Paris, and by Jacques Hardouin Mansart de Levy, who built the Church of St-Louis at Versailles.

WORKS. 1666: Paris, Hôtel de Vendôme in collaboration with Libéral Bruant; Paris, a staircase at the Hôtel de Lasseville in collaboration with his brother, Michel Hardouin (1647–87). – 1671: Versailles, work on the Hôtel de Créqui. – 1674: Saint-Germain-en-Laye, work on the royal Château: in the park he began the Château du Val; in the town the Hôtel de Noailles, finished 1679 (FIG. 482). – 1675: Paris, plan for a pavilion for the Hôtel d'Aligre on the Rue St-Antoine; probably work began on his own house on the Rue des Tournelles and the Hôtel de Lorges on the Rue St-Augustin; designs for the city hall of Arles (Bouches-du-Rhône); a project for an administrative center in Lyons. – 1675–77: Versailles, the Bosquet des Dômes in the park. – 1676–81: Paris, second Hôtel Fieubet on the Quai des Célestins. – 1676–83: Versailles, Château of Clagny for Madame de Montespan. – 1677: Saint-Cloud, the first works for the king's brother. – 1678–79: Works at Fontainebleau. – 1678–81: Versailles, modifications of Le Vau's Cour de Marbre and construction of the south wing of the Château on the park; projects for the Château of Meudon, acquired by the Marquis de Louvois. – 1678–84: Versailles, rebuilding of Le Vau's park façade of the Château and work on the Hall of Mirrors (V, PL. 409) and certain apartments. – 1679–84: Beaucaire (Gard), project for the city hall. – 1679–86: Versailles, construction of the stables and kennels; Marly, Château. – 1680: Paris, model for the dome of Les Invalides (executed 1680–1706; PL. 318); Dampierre (Seine-et-Oise), Château for the Duc de Luynes (PL. 320). – 1680–83: Chantilly, Orangerie. – 1681–86: Versailles, Orangerie. – 1682: Work at Chambord. – 1682–84: Versailles, Grand Commun and the royal garden. – 1684: Paris, projects for the Pont-Royal; Arles, completion of the flat vault in the city hall. – 1684–86: Versailles, colonnade in the park; plan for the city; construction of the Church of Notre-Dame. – 1684–89: Versailles, north wing of the Château on the park. – 1685: Maintenon (Eure-et-Loir), wings of the Château; Moulins (Allier), a bridge. – 1685–86: Paris, Place des Victoires and projects for the Place Vendôme. – 1686: Saint-Cyr, Collège; Dijon projects for the Palais des Etats; Montpellier (Hérault), drawings for a statue of the king; Chantilly, reconstruction of the Château; Châlons-sur-Marne, high altar of the Cathedral of St-Etienne; Navarre (Eure), Château for the Duc de Bouillon. – 1687: Versailles, Grand Trianon (PL. 320); Tours, arch of triumph (demolished, 1774); Grignan (Drôme), wing of the Château. – 1690: Laigle (Orne), Château; projects for a canal from the Marne to the Seine. – 1691: Gaillon (Eure), gallery in the Château for Nicolas Colbert, archbishop of Rouen. – 1692: Paris, work in the royal palace for the king's brother. – 1694: Orléans, jube of the Cathedral of Ste-Croix. – 1695–99: Work at Marly. – 1697–1710: Versailles, royal chapel at the Château (PL. 319). – 1698–1700: Versailles, Zoo, in the park. – 1698–1704: Work on the Château of Meudon, which was bought by the Dauphin. – 1699: Versailles, remodeling of some apartments; Orléans, woodwork in the Cathedral. – 1699–1708: Paris, projects for the choir of Notre-Dame, executed by Robert de Cotte, 1708–14. – 1700: Versailles, remodeling of the Grand Trianon; Lyons, plans for the city hall; Nancy, plans for the archbishop's palace and a palace for the Duc de Lorraine. – 1701: Saint-Omer (Pas-de-Calais), bishop's palace (now Palais de Justice). – 1704: Moulins, new bridge; Versailles, works in the park (Salle des Marroniers, Bosquet des Bains d'Apollon, gardens of Trianon). – 1705: Poissy (Seine-et-Oise), restoration of the abbey; Paris, Chapel of the Virgin in the Church of St-Roch. – 1708: Paris, high altar of the Novitiate of the Jesuits; plans for rebuilding the Collège de France. – *Uncertain date*: Paris, Hôtel de Choiseul-Beaupré on the Rue des Archives; Paris, work on the Hôtel de Cavoye on Rue des Sts-Pères; Paris, Church of St-Paul-et-St-Louis, altar; Bordeaux, Maison Daurade; Pinon (Aisne), Château; Boufflers (Aisne), Château; Plessis-Piquet (Seine), Château, Château du Pin (Orne), constructed (1716–28) after his death; Castres, bishops' palace (now city hall); Saint-Denis, project for the Church of the Annunciation; Châlons-sur-Marne, project for the Convent of the Dames de Ste-Marie. – *Uncertain attributions*: Châteaux of Louvois near Reims (Marne), Montfrin (Gard), Verneuil-sur-Indre (Indre-et-Loire), Yville-sur-Seine (Seine-Maritime), and Serrant (Marne-et-Loire), right wing.

BIBLIOG. *a. General*: J. Marot, Recueil des plans, profils et élévations ... dessinés, mesurés et gravés, Paris, 1664; C. Perrault, Les hommes illustres qui ont paru en France pendant ce siècle, 2 vols., Paris, 1696–1700 (Eng. trans., 2 vols., London, 1704–05); H. Sauval, Histoire et recherches des antiquités de la ville de Paris, 3 vols., Paris, 1724; M. Félibien des Avaux, Histoire de la ville de Paris, 5 vols., Paris, 1725; J. Mariette, L'architecture française, Paris, 1727 (ill. ed. by L. Hautecoeur, 3 vols., Paris, 1927–29); J. Rigaud, Maisons royales, Paris, ca. 1730; A. N. Dézallier d'Argenville, Voyage pittoresque de Paris, Paris, 1749; C. F. Lambert, Histoire littéraire du règne de Louis XIV, 3 vols., Paris, 1751; J. F. Blondel, Architecture française, 4 vols., Paris, 1752–56; A. N. Dézallier d'Argenville, Voyage pittoresque aux environs de Paris, Paris, 1755; J. A. Piganiol de la Force, Description historique de la ville de Paris et de ses environs, 2d ed., 10 vols., Paris, 1765; J. F. Blondel, Cours d'architecture, 9 vols., Paris, 1771–77; A. N. Dézallier d'Argenville, Vie des fameux architectes et sculpteurs depuis la Renaissance des arts, 2 vols., Paris, 1787; A. C. Quatremère de Quincy, Histoire de la vie et des ouvrages des plus celebres architectes, 2 vols., Paris, 1830; G. Bonnefons, Les hôtels historiques de Paris, Paris, 1852; A. Berty et A. M. Tisserand, Histoire générale de Paris, 6 vols., Paris, 1866–97; C. Sauvageot, Palais, château, hôtels et maisons de France du XVe au XVIIIe siècle, 4 vols., Paris, 1866; A. Lance, Dictionnaire des architectes français, 2 vols., Paris, 1872; L. C. Colomb, François Mansart et Jules Hardouin dit Mansart, Paris, 1885; C. Bauchal, Nouveau dictionnaire biographique et critique des architectes français, Paris, 1887; A. de Montaiglon, ed., Correspondance des directeurs de l'Académie de France à Rome, vols. 6–17, Paris, 1887–98; P. Planat, ed., Encyclopedie de l'architecture et de la construction, 6 vols., Paris, 1888–92; A. Schmarsow, Barock und Rokoko, Leipzig, 1897; M. Tourneux, Table générale des documents contenus dans les archives de l'art français, Paris, 1897; H. von Geymüller, Die Baukunst der Renaissance in Frankreich, 2 vols., Stuttgart, 1898–1901; J. Vacquier, Les vieux hôtels de Paris, 12 vols., Paris, 1909–30; R. Blomfield, History of French Architecture, 4 vols., London, 1911–21; H. Lemonnier, L'art français au temps de Louis XIV, Paris, 1911; H. Lemonnier, L'art français au temps de Richelieu et de Mazarin, 2d ed., Paris, 1913; A. E. Brinckmann, Die Baukunst der 17. und 18. Jahrhundert in den romanischen Ländern, Berlin, 1915; H. Lemonnier, L'architecture française au XVIIe siècle, in Michel, VI, 1921–22, pp. 163–200, 535–80; H. Rose, Spätbarock, Munich, 1922; R. Schneider, L'art français: XVIIe siècle, Paris, 1925; E. von Cranach-Sithart, ThB, s.v.; S. F. Kimball, The Creation of the Rococo, Philadelphia, 1943 (enlarged Fr. ed., Le style Louis XV, Paris, 1949); L. Hautecoeur, Histoire de l'architecture classique en France, II, Paris, 1948; Versailles et les châteaux de France (exhibition cat.), Versailles, 1951; P. Moisy, Deux cathédrales françaises: La Rochelle et Versailles, GBA, XXXIX, 1952, pp. 89–102.

b. François Mansart: L'architecture française des bâtiments particuliers, Paris, 1673; J. Bernier, Histoire de Blois, Paris, 1682; J. F. Blondel, Description, plan, élévation et coupe du château de Blois en 1750, Bib. de l'Inst., Ms. 1046; L. E. de Laborde, Le Palais Mazarin, Paris, 1846; A. Dauvergne, Notice sur le château neuf et l'église des Capucins de Coulommiers, B. monumental, XIX, 1853, pp. 597–629; E. Giraudet, Histoire de la ville de Tours, 2 vols., Tours, 1873; A. Félibien des Avaux, Mémoires pour servir à l'histoire des maisons royales (1681), new ed., Paris, 1874; L. de La Saussaye, Histoire du château de Blois, 7th ed., Blois, 1875; V. Ruprich-Robert, L'église et le monastère du Val-de-Grâce, Paris, 1875; G. E. Bertin, Notice sur l'hôtel de La Vrillière et de Toulouse, Mém. Soc. d'h. de Paris, XXVIII, 1901, pp. 1–36; F. Sauve, Histoire de la ville d'Apt, Apt, 1903; C. Sellier, L'hôtel d'Aumont, Paris, 1903; L. Deshairs, Le château de Maisons, Paris, 1907; J. Guibert, Le château de Maisons, Paris, 1907; A. Félibien des Avaux, Vues du châteaux de Blésois (ed. F. P. Lesueur), Paris, 1911; M. Reymond, L'autel du Val-de-Grâce, GBA, V, 1911, pp. 367–94; P. Vitry, Le château de Maisons-Laffitte, Paris, 1912; E. von Cranach-Sichart, Der Baumeister François Mansart, Munich, 1914; P. Dorbec, L'hôtel Carnavalet, Paris, 1916; G. Vauthier, Anne d'Autriche et l'église du Val-de-Grâce, Mél. Jules Guiffrey, Arch. de l'art fr., N.S., VIII, 1916, pp. 146–69; F. P. Lesueur, Le château de Blois, Paris, 1921; L. Hautecoeur, L'origine du dôme des Invalides, L'Architecture, XXXIII, 1924, pp. 353–60; M. Dumolin, Etudes de topographie parisienne, 3 vols., Paris, 1929–30; M. Dumolin, La construction du Val-de-Grâce, B. Soc. d'h. de Paris, LVII, 1930, pp. 92–150; M. Dumolin, Conservation de l'hôtel d'Aumont, Procès-verbaux de la Commission du Vieux-Paris, 1932, pp. 6–7, 35–36; F. Laudet, L'hôtel de Toulouse, Paris, 1932; J. Stern, Maisons, Paris, 1933; A. Blunt, François Mansart, London, 1942; R. A. Weigert, L'hôtel de Chevry-Tubeuf, B. Soc. de l'h. de l'art fr., 1945–46, pp. 18–33; P. Du Colombier, L'église du Val-de-Grâce, Paris, 1948; H. J. Adhémar, The So-called Portrait of Mansart and Claude Perrault, Warburg, XII, 1949, pp. 200–02; E. J. Ciprut, Documents inédits sur l'ancienne église des Minimes de la place Royale, B. Soc. de l'h. de l'art fr., 1954, pp. 151–74; E. J. Ciprut,

Marché entre François Mansart et M. de Puysieux pour le Château de Berny, B. Soc. de l'h. de l'art fr., 1954, pp. 175-81; M. A. Fleury, Le dispositions testamentaires et l'inventaire après décès de François Mansart, B. Soc. de l'h. de l'art fr., 1956, pp. 228-53; E. J. Ciprut, L'église des Feuillants, GBA, L, 1957, pp. 37-52; J. P. Darel, Le maître-autel de Saint-Martin-des-Champs, B. Soc. de l'h. de l'art. fr., 1957, pp. 159-74.

c. *Jules Hardouin-Mansart*: M. Hardouin, Livre de tous les plans, profils, élévations du château de Clagny, Paris, 1680; A. Félibien des Avaux, Description du château de Versailles, Paris, 1696; J. F. Félibien des Avaux, Description de la nouvelle église des Invalides, Paris, 1702; P. Le Pautre, Portes et placarts à lambris desssinés par le sieur Mansart et cheminées à la royale, Paris, n.d. (ca. 1705); J. F. Félibien des Avaux, Description de l'eglise royale des Invalides, Paris, 1706; Harcouet de Longeville, Description des grandes cascades de la maison royale de Saint-Cloud, Paris, 1706; C. N. Cochin, Les excellentes peintures et sculptures de l'hôtel des Invalides, Paris, 1736; J. A. Piganiol de la Force, Description de Versailles, 8th ed., 2 vols., Paris, 1751; G.-L. Perau, Description historique de l'hôtel royal des Invalides, Paris, 1756; J. Duchesne, Notice historique sur la vie et les ouvrages de J. Hardouin-Mansart, Mag. encyclopédique, XI, 1805; D'Avannes, Esquisses sur Navarre, 2 vols., Rouen, 1839-40; C. Sauvageot, Le château de Saint-Germain-en-Laye, Paris, 1856; P. Bonnassieux, Le château de Clagny et Madame de Montespan, Paris, 1881; J. Guiffrey, Comptes des bâtiments du Roi, 5 vols., Paris, 1881-91; E. Auguin, Monographie de la cathédrale de Nancy, Nancy, 1882; A. M. de Boislisle, La place des Victoires et la place Vendôme, Mém. Soc. d'h. de Paris, XV, 1888, pp. 1-272; V. Champier and G. R. Sandoz, Le palais royal, 2 vols., Paris, 1900; M. Fleury, Le palais de Saint-Cloud, Paris, 1902; G. Macon, Les arts dans la maison de Condé, Paris, 1903; A. Peraté, Versailles, Paris, 1904; P. Marcel, Les peintures décoratives de l'église des Invalides et de la chapelle de Versailles, GBA, XXXIV, 1905, pp. 265-80; P. Marcel, Inventaire des papiers de Robert de Cotte, Paris, 1906; G. Brière, Le château de Versailles, 2 vols., Paris, 1907-09; L. Deshairs, Le Grand Trianon, Paris, 1908; A. Hallays, Nancy, Paris, 1908; G. Houdard, Les châteaux royaux de Saint-Germain-en-Laye, 2 vols., Paris, 1909-11; R. Le Nail, Lyon: Architecture et décoration aux XVIIe et XVIIIe siècles, Paris, 1909; A. M. de Boislisle, L'hôtel de Lorges à Paris, B. Soc. d'h. de Paris, XXXVIII, 1911, pp. 199-208; M. Fouquier, De l'art des jardins du XVe au XXe siècle, Paris, 1911; H. Lemonnier, Procès-verbaux de l'Académie royale d'architecture, I-II, Paris, 1911-12; P. de Nolhac, Histoire du château de Versailles, 3 vols., Paris, 1911-18; L. Lambeau, La maison de Jules Hardouin-Mansart, La Cité, XVII, 1917, pp. 204-15; G. Moussoir, Les écuries royales de Versailles, Rev. de l'h. de Versailles, XXI, 1919, pp. 36-63; J. G. Lemoine, Le château de Maison Laffitte, Renaissance de l'art fr., III, 1920, pp. 383-88; P. Gruyer, L'hôtel de Noailles à Saint-Germain-en-Laye, Renaissance de l'art fr., V, 1922, pp. 564-73; J. Robiquet, Evocation artistique de nos maîtres d'œuvre des XVIIe et XVIIIe siècles, Renaissance de l'art fr., VI, 1923, pp. 123-32; C. Mauricheau-Beaupré and E. Hennet de Goutel, Le château de Versailles et ses jardins, Paris, 1924; L. de la Tourrasse Le château du Val dans la forêt de Saint-Germain, Paris, 1924; G. Macon, Chantilly et le Musée Condé, Paris, 1925; L. Meister, Les origines beauvaisiennes et la descendance de J. Hardouin-Mansart, Beauvais, 1925; L. Dimier, L'Hôtel des Invalides, 2d ed., Paris, 1928; P. Marot, J. Hardouin-Mansart et le plan de la primatiale de Nancy, Nancy, 1930; P. Jarry, Conservation de l'hôtel Jules Hardouin-Mansart, Procès-verbaux de la Commission du Vieux-Paris, 1932, pp. 8-13, 34-35; C. Mauricheau-Beaupré, Le Château de Marly, Vieux Marly, I, 1932-40, pp. 17-24; F. Benoit, La voûte de l'Hôtel de ville d'Arles, Mém. Inst. h. de Provence, X, 1933, pp. 163-78; A. Blunt, The Hypnerotomachia Poliphili in 17th Century France, Warburg, I, 1937-38, pp. 117-37; M. de Castelbajac, Le Haras du Pin, Argentan, 1939; A. de la Harpe, Les communs et écuries de Meudon, B. Soc. des amis de Meudon-Bellevue, XVIII, 1940, pp. 321-26; S. F. Kimball, Mansart and Le Brun in the Genesis of the Grande Galerie de Versailles, AB, XXII, 1940, pp. 1-6; A. Marie, Le cabinet du conseil au château de Versailles, B. Soc. de l'h. de l'art fr., 1940, pp. 65-76; P. Lavedan, Histoire de l'urbanisme, II, Paris, 1941; P. Chazaran, Meudon au temps du Grand Dauphin, B. Soc. des amis de Meudon-Bellevue, XXVII, 1942, pp. 532-45, XXVIII, 1942, pp. 561-69; P. Tiersonnier, Les Hardouin-Mansart et le Bourbonnais, B. Soc. d'émulation du Bourbonnais, XLIV, 1942, pp. 294-95; A. Marie, Quelques documents nouveaux sur le Palais-Royal, Beaux-Arts, 112, 1943, p. 5; S. F. Kimball, The Chapels of the Château de Versailles, GBA, XXVI, 1944, pp. 315-32; J. Thuile, L'entrée du Peyrou à Montpellier, Rev. h. du Languedoc, I, 1944, pp. 27-40, 149-62; Marché de 1680 pour Marly, Le Vieux Marly, II, 1945, pp. 12-15; A. Marie, Le Grand Trianon, B. Soc. de l'h. de l'art fr., 1945-46, pp. 88-92; Hardouin-Mansart et son école: Exposition à la Bibliothèque Nationale (exhibition cat.), Paris, 1946; S. F. Kimball and A. Marie, Unknown Versailles, GBA, XXIX, 1946, pp. 85-112; P. Quarré, Le Salon Condé au Musée de Dijon, B. Soc. des amis du Mus. de Dijon, 1946-48, pp. 50-52; P. de Cosse-Brissac, Châteaux de France disparus, Paris, 1947; A. and J. Marie, Marly, Paris, 1947; J. Gérard, Les châteaux de Meudon: Précis chronologique, B. Soc. des amis de Meudon-Bellevue, XLIX, 1948, pp. 844-91; A. Vois, Le Haras du Pin, Cong. Soc. fr. d'archéol., CXI, 1952, pp. 309-16; F. Lucet-Vivier, Asnières et son château, Urbanisme et habitation, XXII, 1955, pp. 15-32; E. J. Ciprut, L'auteur de l'église des Capucines de la place Vendôme, B. Soc. de l'h. de l'art fr., 1956, pp. 259-69; Dijon: Capitale provinciale au XVIIIe siècle (exhibition cat.), Dijon, 1959; P. Bourget and G. Cattaui, Jules Hardouin-Mansart, Paris, 1960; J. M. de la Varende, Le Haras du Pin, Paris, 1960; A. Laprade, N. Bourdel, and J. Lafond, François d'Orbay, Paris, 1961.

Louis HAUTECOEUR

Illustrations: PLS. 317-320; 3 figs. in text.

MANTEGNA, ANDREA. Italian painter and engraver. Because the village in which he was born, Isola di Carturo, belonged at that time to the territory of Vicenza, Mantegna is called Andrea "de Vicentia" in some of the documents of his Paduan period. His birth date, probably 1431, is deduced from an inscription on the lost altarpiece he executed in 1448 for the Church of Sta Sofia in Padua. Transcribed by Bernardino Scardeone, it reads: "Andrea Mantinea Pat. an. septem et decem natus sua manu pinxit MCCCCXLVIII." He died in Mantua in 1506.

Second son of a certain Biagio, woodworker, Andrea was enrolled in the guild of Paduan painters sometime between 1441 and 1445 as the adopted son of the painter Francesco Squarcione, with whom he remained for six years. In 1448, no longer willing to work for someone else, Mantegna left the studio of this curious Paduan master. During his lawsuit against Squarcione in 1455, Mantegna declared before the judges of Padua that his service had brought substantial profit to his master, "to the sum of 400 ducats and more." Although the arbitrated decision recognized Mantegna's right to reimbursement of only 200 ducats, Squarcione opposed it, citing agreements made in Venice on Jan. 26, 1448; the subsequent judgment, however, pronounced by the Quarantia Criminale of Venice on Jan. 2, 1456, recognized the validity of Mantegna's claims and nullified the conditions "deceitfully and cunningly" imposed by Squarcione in the agreement of 1448.

Unfortunately, no evidence of Mantegna's youthful activity in Squarcione's studio remains; but on the basis of his claim, it must have been of considerable importance. Lost also is the Sta Sofia altarpiece mentioned above, depicting the Virgin "and sundry other images," which was probably the first work executed by Mantegna after leaving Squarcione's shop. In its inscription the young man expresses conscious pride in his artistic identity, justified, it seems, for he had already received considerable recognition in Padua. This fact is clearly demonstrated by the commission entrusted to him in the same year together with three well-known and mature masters — Giovanni d'Alemagna, Antonio Vivarini, and Nicolò Pizzolo — to decorate a chapel in the Church of the Eremitani in Padua. Provision for the decoration of this chapel with scenes from the lives of SS. James and Christopher had been made in the will of Antonio Ovetari, drawn up in 1443. An agreement with Ovetari's widow, Madonna Imperatrice, was signed for Andrea, still a minor, by his brother Tomaso on May 16, 1448. It stipulated that half of the chapel was to be decorated by Giovanni d'Alemagna and Antonio Vivarini, while the other half, as well as a sculptured altarpiece, was entrusted to Nicolò Pizzolo and Andrea Mantegna.

The four artists were to have finished the decoration of the Ovetari Chapel by 1450, but Mantegna's personality asserted itself from the very beginning so peremptorily that the program set forth in the original agreement was soon radically changed. Giovanni d'Alemagna and Antonio Vivarini were to have decorated the right wall of the chapel with scenes from the life of St. Christopher and the large vault crossing with the figures of the four Evangelists. Further, these two artists were to paint a large Passion of Christ on the inner wall above the entrance arch, figures of saints in the intrados of the arch, and a frieze on the outer wall. The themes for the other half of the chapel are not stipulated in the contract. A year after work was begun, differences between Pizzolo and Mantegna led to an explicit statement of their respective parts, which were defined by the arbitrator, Pietro Morosini, on Sept. 27, 1449. The first decision concerned the sculptured altarpiece; it may thus be considered one of the chief causes of dissension. Mantegna — who, according to contemporary witnesses (e.g., G. C. Scaligero), was also a sculptor — wanted to participate in this work. In it he would have been able to give expression to his bent toward the direct modeling of figures, a tendency obvious in the emphatic sculptural qualities of his painting style. The decision, however, was in favor of Pizzolo, giving him the right to complete the altarpiece and specifically excluding any intervention on Mantegna's part. As for the frescoes, Pizzolo's task was limited to the execution of the last episode of St. James, the decoration on the right-hand section of the triumphal arch that separates the apse from the main room, and the right-hand side of the apse, except for the figures of SS. Peter, Paul, and Christopher. These had already been partly painted by Mantegna, who was obliged to complete them. Besides these three figures of saints, Mantegna was to execute the decoration of the left-hand portion of the triumphal arch and five of the six scenes from the life of St. James on the left wall.

Actually the decoration of the chapel took a very different course: Of the part entrusted to Giovanni d'Alemagna and Vivarini, only the crossing was executed by them, and the death of Giovanni in 1450 afforded Vivarini an opportunity to free himself of the obligation. His subsequent participation in the chapel was limited to completing the decoration of the crossing left unfinished by Giovanni d'Alemagna, as evidenced in the appraisal made in May, 1450, of the work already executed. Vivarini finished this work before Nov. 27, 1451. Pizzolo executed the altarpiece of the Madonna Enthroned with saints, but of the paintings assigned to him, he completed only the frescoes of God the Father and of St. James, on the conch of the apse, already begun before the decision of 1449, and the four Fathers of the Church in perspective in the oculi. He also decorated the right side of the triumphal arch with a great head, perhaps a self-portrait, like that painted by Mantegna on the other side of the same arch. After Pizzolo's death, when Squarcione and Giovanni Storlato, in February, 1454, appraised the works he had executed, it was found that the last scene of St. James was not even begun. In addition, Pizzolo had left blank the apsidal wall behind the altar, intended for the Assumption, while the Apostles below, which were also to have been done by him, had already been painted by Mantegna. The decorations assigned to Pizzolo were not, however, left incomplete because of his violent death in 1453; he would have had ample opportunity to finish them between June, 1452, the date of his last payment for work in the chapel, and his death. The explanation is, rather, to be found in Mantegna's dominant personality. After having finished the subjects assigned to him in the arbitration (except the fifth episode of the St. James cycle), Mantegna painted, soon after Pizzolo's death, the Apostles, and then the Assumption, and finally the two remaining scenes with St. James.

The St. Christopher series, on the right wall of the chapel, was begun after the death of Giovanni d'Alemagna; the first four episodes must have been completed by Oct. 30, 1451, when Ansuino da Forlì received payment for the fourth scene signed by him, which depicted the preaching of St. Christopher. The third episode, St. Christopher ferrying the Christ child, had already been painted by Bono da Ferrara, who, on July 30, 1451, received final payment for it. The first two scenes, St. Christopher before the king and St. Christopher refusing to follow the Devil (appearing as a king on horseback), were executed toward the end of 1450. They are attributed to Ansuino da Forlì by Fiocco (1927). However, on the basis of their formal character, it seems more likely that they should be assigned to two different artists, as Longhi noted (1926), although his attribution of the scene of St. Christopher before the king to Girolamo di Giovanni da Camerino is not entirely convincing. The third and last register of the cycle of St. Christopher, in which the martyrdom and death of the saint are represented in a single scene, was painted by Mantegna (PL. 324); the date of execution of this great fresco, however, is uncertain.

The chronological problem of the Eremitani frescoes is complex, and the opinions of various historians continue to differ rather sharply, even after the publication of some fundamental documents by E. Rigoni (1949). According to the most recent opinions, the frescoes, begun in 1449, were finished in 1455, the last date mentioned in the list of payments for the Ovetari Chapel. The major disagreement concerns the dating of the last scenes of the St. James cycle and the St. Christopher fresco and arises from differing critical interpretations of the course of Mantegna's stylistic development. According to Vasari, the episodes of the martyrdom and death of St. Christopher were painted last. This view, shared by many scholars, among them Kristeller (1902) and Fiocco, has been reaffirmed by Martin Davies. But other historians — Eisler, Rigoni, Tietze-Conrat (1955), and Pallucchini — maintain that the last scenes painted by Mantegna were those of St. James led to his death and the martyrdom of St. James, on the opposite wall. In their opinion these were not executed before 1454. The fresco of the martyrdom and death of St. Christopher would thus precede the last two of the St. James cycle and would have been completed in 1451 or 1452 (Rigoni, Tietze-Conrat, Pallucchini). Various justifications for such an early dating of the St. Christopher fresco have been offered: its chromatic quality, reminiscent of that of late-14th-century painting (Eisler); the perspective system, which, unlike those of the last episodes of St. James, does not take into account the spectator's point of view (Tietze-Conrat); above all, its striking similarity to Tuscan painting, which does not occur with the same intensity in the subsequent works of Mantegna (Ragghianti). These diverse reasons, formulated from fragmentary though sometimes acute observations, lead to a conclusion that does not seem justified. Vasari, always sensitive to changes of style, was well aware of the substantial difference between the two last scenes of the St. Christopher frescoes and the others. He explained it by relating the famous anecdote concerning Squarcione's spiteful judgment: "these pictures had not the semblance of living things, but of antique statues of marble." Vasari says that Mantegna, in reaction to this criticism, demonstrated in the great St. Christopher fresco "that he knew not less how to extract the good from living and natural things, than from those made by art." Divested of its literary embellishments Vasari's opinion remains valid, and the dating of the St. Christopher fresco as the last of the works in the Ovetari Chapel seems correct. The style is, in fact, much closer to that of the *S. Zeno Altarpiece* (finished in 1459; PL. 322) and even to the works of the Mantuan period than to the other decorations in the Ovetari Chapel.

Unfortunately, almost all the paintings in the Ovetari Chapel were destroyed in World War II. There remain *The Assumption, The Martyrdom of St. Christopher* (PL. 324), and some parts of *The Martyrdom of St. James* (restored; XII, PL. 140). These had been removed for restoration and escaped the fate of the other frescoes.

In the period between 1449 and 1455, during which the decoration of the chapel was executed, Mantegna also painted a little picture, now lost, incorporating portraits of Lionello d'Este and Folco di Villafora, done during a brief stay in Ferrara in 1448. Others of this period include the fresco in the lunette over the main portal of S. Antonio in Padua, depicting SS. Bernardino and Anthony holding the Sacred Name of Christ, signed and dated 1452 (subsequently detached; now Mus. Antoniano); the polyptych of St. Luke for the Church of S. Giustina (Milan, Brera), for which payments were made in 1453–54; and the signed and dated *St. Euphemia* (1454; Naples, Mus. di Capodimonte). After the completion of the Eremitani frescoes, the major work undertaken by Mantegna between 1457 and 1459 was the great altarpiece for the Church of S. Zeno in Verona, the last documented work of the Padua period.

In this first decade of his activity Mantegna's style matured, and in the *S. Zeno Altarpiece* (PL. 322) he realized the extraordinarily incisive concept of form, fully articulated along classical lines, that remains evident in the early Mantuan works. The difference between this artistic idiom and that of the first frescoes in the Ovetari Chapel is truly remarkable. The SS. Peter, Paul, and Christopher, painted in 1449 in the apse of the chapel, possessed a rough spontaneity, but a strained quality was also present, for although the artist established a connection with the studio of Donatello in Padua and although he was influenced by the works of the other great Tuscan artists who had worked in the Veneto — Andrea del Castagno, Filippo Lippi, Paolo Uccello — it was obvious that he had difficulty in assimilating the new style. Yet the violent self-portrait on the left side of the triumphal arch, painted with rapid, sure strokes that suggest the marks of the modeling tool in fresh clay, already fully revealed the sculptural force that is the source of Mantegna's style. The two half lunettes with the calling of James and John and the preaching of St. James, executed almost contemporaneously with the saints in the apse, indicated a similar situation: suggestions of Castagno prevailed in the first, where the strong figures and splintered landscape had the sharp savor of a primeval nature; and the mannerisms of Lippi appeared in the other. The latter was Mantegna's first attempt at an architectonic composition; within it the dramatic movement of the figures appeared to run tangentially in the lower part of the painting.

After these first compositions Mantegna felt the need to discipline his instinctive sense of three-dimensionality by means of rigid formal logic. It is likely that he interrupted the decoration of the chapel for some time, perhaps for a trip to Ferrara, which would have made possible an acquaintance with the works of Piero della Francesca. He had studied antique sculpture in the workshop of Squarcione, and he now acquired a knowledge of classical architecture, stimulated, as Fiocco has noted, by his contacts with Jacopo Bellini. The second register of the St. James cycle is the product — at first sight disconcerting because of its apparent academicism — of the rigorous discipline to which Mantegna subjected himself in this period in order to achieve a calculated compositional relation between sculptural mass and perspective space. The scenes of the baptism of Hermogenes and St. James brought before Herod Agrippa were painted in an experimental interlude, during which Mantegna made a voluntary break from the idiom of the cruder but spontaneous earlier frescoes. These later scenes were dominated by the artist's intellectual pursuit of a perspective structure formed by rhythmic spatial connections between the various compositional elements. The figures had a cold immobility, for they were assimilated into their architectural setting, but some lively details stood out in the midst of the rigid framework. Squarcione's sharp criticism, which must have referred particularly to these frescoes, was not entirely unjustified. Mantegna was aware of the necessities that impelled him toward these researches and could be proud of his accomplishment, for the painters who were working on the other wall quickly took up his classical references, notably Ansuino da Forlì in the preaching of St. Christopher. The program of experiments conducted in these two scenes of the St. James cycle were essential to the development of Mantegna's classicism, which reached full maturity in the fresco showing St. James led to execution. The lowered viewpoint in this painting allowed the artist to give an absolute spatial unity to the composition, and the architectural elements, although grandiose, do not overpower the figures, which are crowded into the foreground as onto a narrow stage. The sudden growth and expansion of the masses in acute foreshortening confers on the images a sculptural power that is reinforced in the vigorous membering of the great barrel vault, itself a vast echo of the heroic dimensions given by Mantegna to the protagonist of these scenes.

In the writer's opinion, this episode of the St. James series should be dated about 1454, shortly after the Apostles in the apse of the Ovetari Chapel. The perspective scheme of these two scenes, in which the viewpoint is below the frame of the composition, was first used in the lunette of S. Antonio in Padua. The fact that the lunette has been considerably repainted makes a quality judgment difficult, but the composition, because of the perfect accord of its elements with the architectural structure, is one of great effectiveness. The upper and lower parts of the altar wall of the Ovetari Chapel were not done at the same time: the Assumption scene above was painted after Squarcione's appraisal in February, 1454, while the Apostles had evidently already been painted by that time, since reference was made to a difficulty that had arisen, probably fomented by Squarcione himself, over the reduced number of Apostles, which Madonna Imperatrice considered a breach of contract. The different perspective viewpoint of the two parts emphasizes the rude sculptural quality of the eight Apostles, a number Mantegna considered sufficient for esthetic purposes.

The *St. Euphemia*, executed in 1454, returns to the scheme of *The Assumption*, but the style seems closer to the intense chromaticism that characterizes the great St. Luke polyptych painted for the Church of S. Giustina in Padua in this same period. (Judgment is difficult, however, because the *St. Euphemia* has been blackened by fire.) The *St. Luke Altarpiece* (now in Milan, Brera) is formed of 12 panels arranged in two registers: In the lower are represented St. Luke in the center, seated on a cathedra and writing; SS. Scholastica and Prosdocimus at the left; and SS. Benedict and Justina at the right. In the upper register are the Dead Christ between the Virgin and St. John in the center; at the left, SS. Daniel and Jerome; and at the right, SS. Augustine and Sebastian. This work, one of the greatest achievements of Mantegna's Padua period, reveals a resurgence of his interest in Tuscan painting, in particular in the works of Andrea del Castagno and Piero della Francesca. Although the *St. Luke Altarpiece* is still basically Gothic in composition (this arrangement appears in the earlier polyptychs of Antonio Vivarini), Mantegna effected a radical change by making the gold ground the equivalent of atmospheric space (as did Piero della Francesca in the *Madonna of Mercy*; XI, PL. 157) and freely disposing the figures along perspective orthogonals converging upon the central figure of St. Luke. The five full-length figures of the lower register stand on a marble pavement that recedes sharply toward a background which, together with the vertical elements of the frame, forms a porticolike architectural setting; the half figures of the upper register are seen slightly from below, as if they were standing at the windows of the same building. The original frame has unfortunately disappeared, but it probably formed the first plane of this architectural structure, to which the orthogonals of the figures were related according to compositional ideas developed in the *S. Zeno Altarpiece*.

The sixth episode of the St. James cycle (XII, PL. 140) in the Ovetari Chapel, representing the death of the saint, was probably executed after the St. Luke polyptych; and the two payments of December, 1454, and January, 1455, which are the last indicated in the memorandum published on the progress of work in the chapel, would then refer to this fresco and to *The Assumption*. This scene is the most intense and exalted in expression of the whole cycle, and its splendid landscape setting, pictorially inspired by Mantegna's interest in the work of Andrea del Castagno and Piero della Francesca but reflecting also a certain northern quality derived from Pisanello, was repeated by Mantegna in the Camera degli Sposi in Mantua.

The last documented work of Mantegna's Padua period was the altarpiece painted between 1457 and 1459 for the Church of S. Zeno in Verona (PL. 322). In this composition, inspired by Donatello's high altar in S. Antonio, there is no trace of the traditional arrangement that had survived in the St. Luke polyptych. Further, the great architectural frame that encloses the altarpiece is so intimately related to the paintings that the term "polyptych" seems inappropriate, so complete is the organic unity. The enthroned Madonna and Child at the perspective center of the composition, with SS. Peter, Paul, John the Evangelist, and Zeno at the left, and Benedict, Lawrence, Gregory, and John the Baptist at the right, are assembled within the open space of an ideal classical temple with richly decorated entablatures resting on stout piers, behind which the luminous depth of the sky appears. To the piers that constitute the first plane of the painted composition are attached the fluted Corinthian columns of the frame supporting the entablature and tympanum of the temple. Thus three-dimensional and pictorial elements are joined in a perspective unity; the architectural structures in relief connect the imaginary space of the painting with real space, thus emphasizing the illusion of depth. In this altarpiece Mantegna fully developed his "archaeological mysticism," which recomposed in Humanistic terms the scattered fragments of the classical world, creating a hallucinatory intellectualized reality. The relation between figures and architecture is precisely measured around the central axis of the Madonna's throne, and the varied placement of the figures in relation to the picture plane, emphasized by strong chromatic contrasts, seems to enlarge and articulate the interior space of the edifice. The near perfection of this masterpiece is sustained by a dramatic stylistic tension derived from vividness of form and a radical approach to modeling that gives the picture surface a lapidary hardness. This quality may be seen particularly in the severity of the composition within the classical temple, but it is also apparent in the three compartments of the predella, which represent the Crucifixion (PL. 323), the Agony in the Garden, and the Resurrection (the two last, Tours, Mus. B.A.). In the first two, which are among Mantegna's most intensely poetic expressions, this violence of style becomes almost inhuman, especially in the tragic immobility of the Crucifixion, where the figures, as if turned to stone by a sudden cataclysm, rise like archaeological remains of a blasted world within a landscape of jagged rocks. The desolation is rendered even more acute by the light that flickers over the empty city on the hill and models the bodies of the crucified, cruelly exposing the most minute details.

The almost unfailingly high quality of Mantegna's pictorial style from this time on precludes a precise chronological arrangement of his numerous undated works. It seems certain, however, that the *St. Sebastian* (Vienna, Kunsthist. Mus.) belongs to the Padua period and was probably painted during the same years as the *S. Zeno Altarpiece*, since the highly sculptural idiom of these two works is identical. *St. Sebastian* was perhaps that small work to which the podesta of Padua, Jacopo Antonio Marcello, referred in his letter to Ludovico Gonzaga of March, 1459, asking that Mantegna be permitted to delay his departure from Mantua by some days, so that he might finish a painting. In January of 1457 Mantegna had agreed to enter the service of the Gonzaga family, but his obligations for the *S. Zeno Altarpiece* and other works had forced him several times to postpone his departure for Mantua. It was not until 1460 that he was finally permanently established there. However, in the second half of 1459 he may have made a brief visit to Mantua to give directions for the architecture of the chapel of the Castello di S. Giorgio, the decoration of which was the first large work commissioned from him by Ludovico Gonzaga. In the years between the completion of the *S. Zeno Altarpiece* and the decoration of the chapel, Mantegna painted a number of small pictures of great intensity, including *The Agony in the Garden* (London, Nat. Gall.), *The Adoration of the Shepherds* (New York, Met. Mus.), *Madonna and Child* (Milan, Mus. Poldi Pezzoli), *Madonna and Child* (Bergamo, Acc. Carrara), *Madonna and Sleeping Child* (Berlin, Staat. Mus.), and the portraits of Cardinal Mezzarota (Berlin, Staat. Mus.) and Cardinal Francesco Gonzaga (XI, PL. 217). The style of these works is characterized by strong chromatic relationships and bold modeling in an incisive, almost Flemish draftsmanship.

The most important work of Mantegna's first years in Mantua was the decoration (now lost) of the chapel of the Castello di S. Giorgio. Some scanty information regarding this decoration is contained in a letter of June, 1458, in which Ludovico asks the artist to come to Mantua to discuss the architecture of the chapel, and in a letter from Mantegna to Ludovico of 1464, stating that the pictures for the "chapeleta" could not be put in place because the gilding of the frames was not yet finished. Thus the decoration of the chapel must have consisted of small panel paintings and not frescoes or large-scale works (as Tietze-Conrat thought). This is also confirmed by Vasari, who, in 1565, referred to the existence in the chapel of a small picture or altarpiece (*tavoletta*) with scenes that were "not very large, but most beautiful." Possibly the decoration took the form of an architectural structure of gilded wood — that contained the painted panels — a structure that would represent an intermediary phase between the compositional ideas of the *S. Zeno Altarpiece* and those later developed in the Camera degli Sposi. Nothing is known about the disappearance of these pictures, which, in 1492, were mentioned by Giovanni Francesco II Gonzaga as among Mantegna's most admirable pictorial accomplishments. It is possible that the loss of the panels and the destruction of the chapel took place in the 16th century, when the interior of the castle was radically transformed by Giulio Romano and his followers.

Some of Mantegna's extant panel pictures — such as the so-called "Triptych" in the Uffizi (consisting of a curved center panel, *The Adoration of the Magi*, flanked by two rectangular panels, *The Ascension* and *The Circumcision*) and *The Death of the Virgin* (PL. 326) — may, however, have come from this chapel. The identical dimensions of the panels of *The Ascension*, *The Circumcision*, and *The Death of the Virgin*, and the curved form of the panel of *The Adoration of the Magi* suggest, in fact, that these formed part of a single decorative complex composed of episodes from the life of Christ and the Virgin and of subjects taken from the Gospels. It is interesting to note, in this connection, the dates of the earliest historical information referring to the panels in the Uffizi and that in the Prado: in 1587, the "Triptych" of the Uffizi was indicated as belonging to Don Antonio de' Medici, while *The Death of the Virgin* was recorded in the list of paintings restored between 1586 and 1588 by Sebastiano Filippi in the chapel of the ducal palace of Ferrara. Thus, this might be the period when any pictures still in the chapel of the Castello of Mantua were quietly dispersed. The three panels of the Uffizi were joined to form a triptych in 1827. It is evident that Mantegna did not intend the present juxtaposition of *The Ascension* and *The Circumcision* with *The Adoration of the Magi*, since there is no direct connection between the figural elements and the perspective structures of the three compositions. Furthermore, as Tietze-Conrat has pointed out, *The Ascension* and *The Adoration of the Magi* seem some years earlier than *The Circumcision*. On the basis of the stylistic data yielded by these works, it could be maintained that the decoration of the chapel was begun about 1460 with *The Nativity*, which would have been very close in style to the *S. Zeno Altarpiece*, and that it was finished, after Mantegna's Florentine sojourn, with *The Circumcision* and other scenes having a related architectural motif, for example, representations of Christ among the doctors, or Christ and the woman of Samaria, both cited among the lost works of Mantegna. Longhi, who has felicitously reunited the Prado *Death of the Virgin* with its missing upper fragment (representing Christ carrying the soul of the Virgin to heaven), which he discovered in the Vendeghini Collection in Ferrara, thought that this panel had once been part of the triptych and that it had subsequently been replaced by *The Circumcision* (which has the same dimensions) either for iconographic reasons or because the lighting came from the wrong direction. This hypothesis, however, is not only iconographically incongruous but is contradicted by the lack of compositional unity among the three paintings.

In the decade between 1460 and 1470, the period of Mantegna's finest small-scale works, often characterized by an unexpected lyric abandon and an unusual serenity, should be placed some pictures that, like *The Circumcision* of the Uffizi, emerged from a vivid renewal of Mantegna's experiences with Tuscan art during his trips to Florence and Pisa in 1466-67. *The Presentation in the Temple* (PL. 321), generally considered a Paduan work of about 1454 (but recognized in 1937 by Fiocco and C. Gamba as belonging to the first decade of Mantegna's activity in Mantua) is perhaps one of the first of Mantegna's pictures to be executed in the new spiritual climate of classic serenity inspired by his contact with great Tuscan masters, whom he met now on equal terms and even with the proud awareness of his own greater modernity. Without losing its incisive strength, his style became broader and simpler. There was more stress on functional compositional relations, as in the lyric meter of the figures in the Berlin *Presentation*. An even more intense lyricism is found in the later *St. George* (Venice, Accademia), one of the most fascinating of Mantegna's works, in which the serene Apollonian beauty of the saint, softened by the gentle luminous tones of the landscape, embodies the artist's most ecstatic and romantic vision of his classical ideal. The compositional relation between the figures of the Berlin *Presentation* and those of the Venice *St. George* and the painted marble frames surrounding them may be the result of Mantegna's study of Castagno's frescoes in the Cenacolo di S. Apollonia (I, PL. 238, 240, 242-44) and in the Villa Pandolfini in Soffiano (I, PL. 245; XII, PL. 27), which are firmly installed within the architectural rhythm of rectangular classical niches.

Also to this period may belong *The Virgin of the Quarries* (Uffizi), although Vasari says that it was painted in Rome about 1489. This painting, almost miniature in size, nevertheless conveys an effect of monumentality because of the relation between the luminous void of the sky and the heaviness of the Virgin and Child, who seem carved from the rocks of the background. Another work of these years, possibly painted in Florence in 1466, is the noble portrait of Carlo de' Medici (Uffizi), one of the first expressions of the spiritual depth that Mantegna's style took on in the portraits of the Camera degli Sposi (PL. 328). This great pictorial cycle is heralded in the *St. Sebastian*, formerly in Notre-Dame, Aigueperse (Louvre, PL. 325), where it must have been taken in 1481 by Chiara Gonzaga when she married Gilbert de Bourbon, Count of Mentpensier. The painting has often been thought to date from the Padua period, but the profound compassion of St. Sebastian's expression and the accord established among the elements of the composition — the body of the saint, the column to which he is bound, and the landscape — seem closer to the narrative power that Mantegna attained later, in the Camera degli Sposi. The early *St. Sebastian* (Vienna, Kunsthist. Mus.), like a chained Prometheus in its exaggerated statuary hardness and angular form, is quite different from the *St. Sebastian* in the Louvre, with its broad bodily articulation and the softer, more vibrant chiaroscuro that creates an almost elegaic quality.

The decoration of the Camera degli Sposi (PLS. 328, 329) in the Palazzo Ducale of Mantua was finished in 1474, according to the date of Mantegna's inscription in which he dedicated this masterpiece of his maturity to Ludovico Gonzaga and his wife, Barbara of Brandenburg. It is not known for certain, however, when he began the work. Some historians believe that it was executed in the extremely brief time of little more than a year. Others believe that it required nearly a decade, because the date 1465 is scratched into the embrasure of a window and supposedly indicates the beginning of the decoration. However, this cycle could not have been done before Mantegna's Tuscan trips of 1466–67, and it is probable that it was executed between 1471 and 1474. A letter written by Ludovico in October, 1471, indicates that Mantegna was already working on this room, which Carlo Ridolfi, accepting a provocative traditional name, called the "Camera degli Sposi," but which is referred to in the old documents as the "Camera picta." In the paintings here Mantegna returned to the compositional theme set forth in the *S. Zeno Altarpiece*, which he must have developed further in the chapel of the Castello di S. Giorgio. Now, however, after direct study of the great Tuscan pictorial cycles, particularly those of Andrea del Castagno and Piero della Francesca, Mantegna's perspective became more dynamic, and all distinction between real and pictorial space was discarded. The perspective orthogonals of all the paintings on the walls of the room are made to converge upon a single point, thus placing the spectator within the unified space formed by these perspective projections. The real architectural space is a square room covered with a coved vault that springs from the walls and is articulated by three lunettes on each side of the room. Two corner windows illuminate two adjacent walls with beams of light, while the opposite two remain in shadow. The finely worked architraves over the two doors, the classical frieze on the mantel, and the corbel brackets on which the vault rests complete the architectural features. The functional connection with the pictorial decoration indicates the explicit instructions furnished by Mantegna as to the kind of structure and plastic elements he required. The artist imagined a pavilion supported by piers joined together in the vault, with three arches on each side. The pavilion was closed on two sides (the shadowed walls) by curtains of gilded leather and open on the other two (the illuminated walls, on which the principal narrative episodes appear) to the free-flowing space of an airy landscape and to a courtyard paved with fine marbles. The surface of the coved vault of the room is transformed by pictorial illusion into a hemispherical calotte.

Against its gold ground stand out in clear illusionistic relief the simulated stucco decoration, ribs, portraits of the Caesars upheld by putti, and scenes with Hercules, Orpheus, Arion, and Periander. From the center of the vault light seems to pour into the interior from a painted oculus, around which drastically foreshortened ladies and putti appear against the luminous background of the sky (PL. 329). The architectural, sculptural, and pictorial elements of the composition form graduated perspective areas, with unexpected passages that give to the space an extraordinary viability and to the persons represented on the walls the tangibility of living beings within the environment of the spectator himself. The two scenes on the main walls, one depicting the Gonzaga family and the other the return of Cardinal Francesco to his family, seem to stand out in bold relief; in view of their representational power, the controversy over their precise meaning in terms of Renaissance court life seems trivial. The portraits of the personages, revealed by Mantegna's incisive vision in their naked human essence, create a flow of internal narrative.

There is little information regarding the artist's activities in the years 1474–85, between the completion of the Camera degli Sposi and the beginning of the pictorial cycle *The Triumph of Caesar*. However, at the end of this decade may be placed the lively and highly sculptural composition *The Madonna and Child with Cherubim* (Milan, Brera). These were certainly difficult years for Mantegna, for during them occurred the death of his favorite son and, one after another, of the nobles who esteemed him and protected him from the enemies made by his difficult personality. The grave moral and material distress of these years led Mantegna to contemplate moving to Florence under the patronage of Lorenzo the Magnificent, who had visited his studio and of whom he was forced to ask financial aid in 1484. These plans, however, were discarded, for with the accession of young Francesco II in 1484 the Gonzaga patronage was revived.

The nine great canvases of *The Triumph of Caesar* (XII, PL. 32), preserved at Hampton Court, were the first fruits of this patronage. Mantegna must have meditated at length on this subject, which was inspired by literary sources, particularly the *De re militari* of Valturius (Verona, 1472). The misfortunes of the Gonzaga family, however, had not permitted him to apply himself to it before 1485. By August of 1486 some parts had already been painted, but the series was not finished before 1492. The episodes of *The Triumph of Caesar*, which present a turbulent succession of trumpeters, bearers of emblems, carriers of booty, sacrificial oxen, elephants, armor bearers, prisoners, musicians, and the triumphal chariot of Caesar, were conceived as a continuous pictorial decoration, seen from below through an architectural structure of piers placed between one canvas and the next. Thus the compositional scheme of the Camera degli Sposi was developed into a dramatic movement through the flow of the triumphal procession, with a unity of form and content that was maintained in the nine canvases without interruption. The strong color (now unfortunately greatly altered) that set the figures in vivid three-dimensional clarity against an extensive landscape, the stately rhythm, and the heroic severity of this great composition combine to produce the most exalted Humanistic expression of Mantegna's art. In spite of the damage these canvases have undergone from the 18th century on, the evocative power of Mantegna's idiom still remains so vivid that one can well understand the great impression the work made on his contemporaries.

From 1488 to 1490 Mantegna must have interrupted work on the *Triumph* to journey to Rome, where he had been called by Innocent VIII to decorate the Pope's private chapel in the Belvedere (destroyed 1780). This little chapel, preceded by a small sacristy painted with cupboards and trompe l'oeil objects, was, according to an early detailed description, extraordinarily rich in figural decoration. Its dome was divided by a latticework of vegetation seen against the luminous background of the sky. This arboreal motif, of which Mantegna's funerary chapel in the Church of S. Andrea in Mantua is a pale reflection, was developed further in the arbor of the *Madonna della Vittoria* (Louvre), which was ordered by Marchese Francesco in 1496 to commemorate the Battle of Fornovo. The heroic figural conception of this *Madonna*, the most important altarpiece of the period, is still that of the *Triumph*, but the relation of the latticework to the pearly tones of the sky (a motif later employed by Correggio in the Camera di S. Paolo in Parma; III, PL. 465) reveals in Mantegna's style a new emphasis, tending toward the tonalism of 16th-century painting. The free disposition of the figures, in a space no longer restricted by the severity of geometric perspective, as well as the volume of the forms and the brilliant glaze of the color, are characteristics of the late style of Mantegna that recur, differently developed but with a similar tonality, in other religious canvases: *The Madonna and Child with Saints and Angels*, painted in 1497 for the Church of S. Maria in Organo in Verona (Milan, Castello Sforzesco); *The Holy Family* (Dresden, Gemäldegal.); and *The Madonna and Child with SS. John the Baptist and Mary Magdalene* and *The Holy Family with St. John* (both London, Nat. Gall.). However, the subjects in which the artist fully expressed the tragic sense of life that emerged from the depths of his experience in this period were those of the *Christ Seated on a Sarcophagus* (Copenhagen, Statens Mus. for Kunst), the *St. Sebastian* of the Ca d'Oro in Venice (PL. 325; IV, PL. 403), and the *Dead Christ* of the Brera (PL. 321). In these works of the last decade of the century Mantegna reached the ultimate development of the original elements of his poetic idiom. The heroic tone of the *Triumph* becomes in the Copenhagen *Christ Seated on a Sarcophagus* an almost Ferrarese hardness of expression; here Mantegna's native sculptural force appears again in full vigor, and the subject is rendered still more pathetic by the livid landscape and by the static balance of the composition. The inspiration of the *St. Sebastian* of the Ca d'Oro is similar. There the theme of pain without respite is developed to its tragic extreme in the contrast between the internal energy manifested by the strained volumes and tortured outlines of the titanic figure and the inexorable geometric rigidity of the restricted architectural space, within which the saint is pierced by arrows crossing the picture plane from all directions.

The dating of the Brera *Dead Christ* is disputed. According to some scholars (Tietze-Conrat, 1955), the invention of this boldly foreshortened composition may date from the early Paduan period (and the *Dead Christ* of the Brera would thus be a late replica), or it may be related to Mantegna's experiments after seeing the works of Andrea del Castagno during his Florentine trip of 1466. On the other hand, a much later and final contact with Castagno is evident in such late works of Mantegna as the Copenhagen *Christ* and the *St. Sebastian* in the Ca d'Oro; and the tragic distortion of the Brera *Dead Christ* — even if it was inspired by Castagno's lost fresco of the Death of the Virgin for S. Egidio in Florence — is more likely a reflection of that sense of stark and absolute truth common to the late works of Mantegna.

In the last years of his life Mantegna painted for the *studiolo* of Isabella d'Este two mythological canvases: the so-called "Parnassus" (1497; PL. 327; X, PL. 249), which really represents, according to an inventory of 1547, "Mars and Venus amusing themselves with a Vulcan and an Orpheus playing, and nine nymphs dancing"; and *Minerva Expelling the Vices from the Garden of Virtue* (1502; PL. 327; III, PL. 211). A third canvas, with the legend of the god Comus (Louvre), was unfinished when the artist died on Sept. 13, 1506, and was completed by Lorenzo Costa. In treating these mythological tales, dictated by the fashionable Humanistic culture of the court of Isabella d'Este, Mantegna achieved a fluency of formal expression and a subtle range of color relationships that were fundamental for the development of 16th-century classicism. If he had satirical intentions toward this world of theatrical artifice, they were diffused in the Pandean spirit of landscape, which is the true subject of these pictures.

The great monochrome *Scipio Receiving Cybele* (London, Nat. Gall.; I, PL. 307), which represents the introduction of the cult of Cybele in Rome, was ordered from Mantegna by the Venetian Francesco Cornaro in 1504. This canvas, which on the master's death remained in the possession of his son Francesco, sums up in its sculptural rhythm, inspired by antique reliefs, the ultimate development of Mantegna's classicism, upon which Giulio Romano and his pupils were to draw extensively. Other monochromes on canvas of this period (conceived as simulated bas-reliefs), in which sculptural figures are usually seen against a background plane of colored marble, represent episodes from the Old Testament and must have been intended as decoration for a specific location. Among these small pictures, the uneven quality of which indicates the participation of studio assistants, are *Samson and Delilah* (PL. 330), *The Sacrifice of Abraham* and *David with the Head of Goliath* (Vienna, Kunsthist. Mus.), *The Judgment of Solomon* (Louvre), a *Judith* in Dublin (Nat. Gall. of Ireland) and another in Montreal (Mus. of Fine Arts), and *Esther and Mordecai* (Cincinnati, Art Mus.). The London *Samson and Delilah* is of particular interest, for its highly refined style is similar in its Humanistic tone and its high quality to that of the "Parnassus." Mantegna treated the Judith theme several times — for instance, in a painting which he probably presented in 1484 to Lorenzo the Magnificent, among whose effects it figured in 1492, and which some historians identify with the little picture in the National Gallery in Washington, D.C. A very beautiful drawing of Judith (1491; Uffizi) reflects a subsequent development of this theme and is considered one of Mantegna's greatest graphic expressions.

The sculptural emphasis of Mantegna's style is directly and forcefully manifested in the exceptional graphic power of his stroke, which gives a clear and sharp relief to his unfortunately rare drawings and to the famous engravings of religious and mythological subjects that became widely known in his time (IV, PL. 424; VII, PL. 379; see ENGRAVINGS AND OTHER PRINT MEDIA).

BIBLIOG. Baptista Mantuanus (G. B. Spagnoli), Opera omnia, Bologna, 1502, fol. 49b; M. Sanudo, Diarii, VI (1504-07), Venice, 1881; Maffeus Raphael Volaterranensis, Commentarii, Rome, 1506, lib. XXI; M. Michiel, Notizie d'opere del disegno (1525-43), ed. G. Frizzoni, Bologna, 1884; G. Vasari, Le vite..., Florence, 1550; B. Scardeone, De antiquitate urbis Patavii et claris civibus patavinis, Basel, 1560; D. Barbaro, La pratica della perspettiva, Venice, 1569; G. P. Lomazzo, Idea del tempio della pittura, Milan, 1590; G. C. Scaligero, Poëmata, in Bibliopolio Commeliniano, n.p., 1600, pp. 119-20; C. Ridolfi, Le meraviglie dell'arte..., 2 vols. in 1, Venice, 1648 (ed. D. von Hadeln, Berlin, 1914-24); M. Boschini, Le ricche minere della pittura, Venice, 1664; M. Boschini, Descrizione di tutte le pubbliche pitture della Città di Venezia, Venice, 1733; A. Taja, Descrizione del Palazzo Apostolico Vaticano, Rome, 1750, pp. 401-07; G. P. Chattard, Nuova descrizione del Vaticano, o sia della sacrosanta basilica di S. Pietro, III, Rome, 1762-67, pp. 130-44; S. Bettinelli, Delle lettere e delle arti mantovane, Mantua, 1774; L. Lanzi, Storia pittorica dell'Italia, Bassano, 1789; P. Brandolese, Pitture, sculture ed altre cose notabili di Padova, Padua, 1795; P. Brandolese, Testimonianze intorno alla patavinità di Andrea Mantegna, Padua, 1805; G. A. Moschini, Delle origini e delle vicende della pittura in Padova, Venice, 1826, pp. 31-60; J. W. Gaye, Carteggio inedito di artisti de' secoli XIV, XV, XVI, 3 vols., Florence, 1839-40; C. D'Arco, Delle arti e degli artefici di Mantova, 2 vols., Mantua, 1857; A Baschet, Documents inédits concernants la personne et l'œuvre d'Andrea Mantegna, GBA, XX, 1866, pp. 318-39; A. Baschet, Recherches de documents d'art et d'histoire dans les Archives de Mantoue, GBA, XX, 1866, pp. 478-91; G. Campori, Raccolta di cataloghi e inventari inediti di quadri dal secolo XV al XIX, Modena, 1870; Vasari; F. Portheim, Andrea Mantegna's Caesar's Triumph (in Mantova), RapfKw, IX, 1886, pp. 266-80; A. Luzio, Disegni topografici e pitture dei Bellini, Arch. storico dell'arte, I, 1888, pp. 276-78; C. Yriarte, Isabelle d'Este et les artistes de son temps, GBA, III, 1895, pp. 382-98 at 393; H. Thode, Mantegna, Bielefeld, Leipzig, 1897; A. Luzio and R. Renier, La cultura e le relazioni letterarie di Isabella d'Este, Giorn. storico della lett. it., XXXIV, 1899, pp. 1-97; B. Berenson, Study and Criticism of Italian Art, London, 1901; M. Cruttwell, Andrea Mantegna, London, New York, 1901; C. Yriarte, Mantegna, Paris, 1901; P. Kristeller, Andrea Mantegna, London, 1901; J. C. Ady, Isabella d'Este, New York, 1903; R. Eisler, Mantegna's frühe Werke und die römische Antike, Monatsberichte für K. und Kw., III, 1903; R. Eisler, Die Hochzeitstruken der letzten Gräfin von Görz, Jhb. der Central-Kommission für Denkmalpflege zu Wien, 1905; B. Berenson, North Italian Painters of the Renaissance, New York, London, 1907; J. Burckhardt, Die Kultur der Renaissance in Italien, 10th ed. by L. Geiger, 2 vols., Leipzig, 1908; S. Davari, L'affresco di Andrea Mantegna nella sala detta "degli Sposi" nel Castello di Mantova e il cronista Stefano Gionta, Atti e mem. della R. Acc. Virgiliana di Mantova, XXIII, 1908, pp. 5-19; G. Gerola, Nuovi documenti mantovani sul Mantegna, Atti R. Ist. veneto di sc., lettere ed arti, LXVIII, 2, 1908-09, pp. 905-15; V. Lazzarini, Documenti relativi alla pittura padovana del secolo XV, Nuovo arch. veneto, XV, 1908, pp. 1-2; A. Hind, A Catalogue of Early Italian Engravings in the British Museum, 2 vols., London, 1909-10; P. Kristeller, Francesco Squarcione e le sue relazioni col Mantegna, Rass. d'arte, IX, 1909, 10, pp. iv-v, 11, pp. iv-v; F. Knapp, Andrea Mantegna, 2d ed., Stuttgart, 1910; F. Schmidt-Degener, Two Drawings by Andrea Mantegna in the Boymans Museum of Rotterdam,

BM, XVIII, 1911, pp. 255-56; E. Berger, Quellen und Technik der Fresko-, Oel-, und Tempera-Malerei des Mittelalters, 2d ed., Munich, 1912; V. Goloubew, Les dessins de Jacopo Bellini au Louvre et au British Museum, 2 vols., Brussels, 1912; E. Bertaux, Le Musée Jacquemart-André: L'art italien, Rev. de l'art ancient et mod., XXXIV, 1913, pp. 413-38; T. Borenius, Four Early Italian Engravers, London, 1913; A. Luzio, ed., La Galleria dei Gonzaga venduta all'Inghilterra, Milan, 1913; Venturi, VII, 3, 1914, pp. 86-262; R. Bratti, Notizie d'arte e di artisti, Nuovo arch. veneto, XXX, 1915, pp. 435-85 at 465; K. Giehlow, Die Hierogliphenkunde des Humanismus in der Allegorie der Renaissance, JhbKhSammlWien, XXXII, 1915, pp. 1-232; L. Testi, Storia della pittura veneziana, II, Bergamo, 1915; G. Frizzoni, Un dipinto inedito del Mantegna nella Galleria Campori di Modena, L'Arte, XIX, 1916, pp. 65-69; E. Tietze-Conrat, Zur höfischen Allegorie der Renaissance, JhbKhSammlWien, XXXIV, 1916, pp. 25-32; G. Frizzoni, Il Mantegna a Roma, Rass. d'arte, XVII, 1917, pp. 195-201; P. Lavallée, Les dessins de l'École des Beaux-Arts, GBA, XIII, 1917, pp. 265-83; R. Schwabe, Mantegna and His Imitators, BM, XXXIII, 1918, pp. 215-16; J. Meder, Die Handzeichnung, Vienna, 1919; W. Weisbach, Trionfi, Berlin, 1919; R. Schneider, Le fantastique de Mantegna, B. Soc. de l'h. de l'art fr., 1920, pp. 94-96; Van Marle, XVII-XVIII, 1923-27; E. Panofsky, Perspective als symbolische Form, Vorträge der Bib. Warburg, 1924-25, pp. 258-330; H. Posse, Meisterwerke der staatliche Gemäldegalerie zu Dresden, 3d ed., Dresden, 1924; A. Venturi, Giambellino: Nuove ricerche, L'Arte, XXVII, 1924, pp. 137-40; D. von Hadeln, Venezianische Zeichnungen des Quattrocento, Berlin, 1925; C. Cottafavi, R. Palazzo ducale di Mantova, BArte, N.S., VI, 1926-27, pp. 136-42; G. Fiocco, Felice Feliciano amico degli artisti, Arch. veneto-tridentino, IX, 1926, pp. 188-99; R. Longhi and G. Fiocco, Lettere, Vita artistica, I, 1926, pp. 127-39, 144-48; S. Brinton, The Gonzaga, Lords of Mantua, London, 1927; M. Dvořák, Geschichte der italienischen Kunst, I, Munich, 1927; G. Fiocco, L'arte di Andrea Mantegna, Bologna, 1927 (2d ed. Venice, 1959); E. Panofsky, Imago Pietatis, in Festschrift für M. J. Friedländer, Leipzig, 1927, pp. 261-308; E. Rigoni, Nuovi documenti sul Mantegna, Atti R. Ist. veneto di sc., lett. ed arti, LXXXVII, 1927-28, pp. 1165-86 (rev. by G. Fiocco, RArte, X, 1929, pp. 141-52); A. Venturi, Un'opera inedita di Andrea Mantegna, L'Arte, XXX, 1927, pp. 31-33; A. Moschetti, Le fonti classiche di una celebre opera di Andrea Mantegna, Atti R. Ist. veneto di sc., lett. ed arti, LXXXIX, 1929-30, pp. 725-29; G. Fiocco, ThB, s.v.; H. G. Beyen, Andrea Mantegna en de verovering der ruimte in de schilderkunst, The Hague, 1931; E. Coudenhove-Erthal, Die Reliquienschreine des Graz-Doms und ihre Beziehung zu Andrea Mantegna (Kunstdenkmäler der Steiermark, II), Graz, 1931; F. Filippini, Di alcune opere attribuite al Mantegna, Il Comune di Bologna, Dec. 12, 1931, pp. 42-44; P. Hendy, Catalogue of the Exhibited Paintings in the Isabella Stewart Gardner Museum, Boston, 1931; R. Longhi, Risarcimento di una Mantegna, Pan, I, 1934, pp. 503-12; J. B. Shaw, A Last Portrait of Mantegna, Old Master Drawings, IX, 1934, pp. 1-7; L. Dussler, Giovanni Bellini, Frankfurt am Main, 1935; E. Tietze-Conrat, Mantegna or Pollaiuolo?, BM, LXVII, 1935, pp. 216-19; I. Blum, Andrea Mantegna und die Antike, Strasbourg, 1936; G. Fiocco, Mantegna, Milan, 1937; C. Gamba, Giovanni Bellini, Milan, 1937; C. L. Ragghianti, Casa Vitaliani, CrArte, II, 1937, pp. 236-52; G. Fiocco, Andrea Mantegna e il Brunelleschi, Atti I Cong. naz. di storia dell'arch. (1938), Florence, 1939, pp. 179-83; G. Fiocco, Andrea Mantegna scultore, RArte, XXII, 1940, pp. 220-28; F. Hartt, Carpaccio's Meditation on the Passion, AB, XXII, 1940, pp. 25-35; A. Luzio and R. Paribeni, Il Trionfo di Cesare di Andrea Mantegna, Rome, 1940 (rev. by G. Fiocco, B. Mus. civico di Padova, XXIX-XXX, 1939-41, pp. 181-91); H. Tietze, The "Cristo in scurto" by Mantegna, Art in Am., XXIX, 1941, pp. 51-56; W. Boeck, Mantegna: Der Meister der oberitalienischen Frührenaissance, Burg bei Magdeburg, 1942; G. Fiocco, Il calco della Madonna della Vittoria di Andrea Mantegna, RArte, XXV, 1942, pp. 90-102; T. Muchall-Viebrock, Andrea Mantegna als Zeichner, Pantheon, XXIX, 1942, pp. 73-78; L. Ozzòla, Il cartone per la Madonna della Vittoria di Andrea Mantegna, Civiltà, VIII, 1942, pp. 67-74; H. Tietze, Mantegna and His Companions in Squarcione's Shop, Art in Am., XXX, 1942, pp. 54-60; F. J. Mather Jr., A Fragment by Mantegna; A Problem in Reconstruction, Art in Am., XXXI, 1943, pp. 21-26; E. Tietze-Conrat, Was Mantegna an Engraver?, GBA, XXIV, 1943, pp. 375-81; G. Fiocco, Mantegna: La Cappella Ovetari nella chiesa degli Eremitani, Milan, 1944; V. Moschini, Gli affreschi del Mantegna agli Eremitani di Padova, Bergamo, 1944; H. Tietze and E. Tietze-Conrat, The Drawings of the Venetian Painters of the 15th and 16th Centuries, New York, 1944; W. E. Suida, Mantegna and Melozzo, Art in Am., XXXIV, 1946, pp. 57-72; J. Lauts, Andrea Mantegna: Die Madonna della Vittoria, Berlin, 1947; R. H. Wilenski, Mantegna and the Paduan School, London, 1947; G. Fiocco, Two Unknown Paintings by Andrea Mantegna, BM, XCI, 1949, pp. 213-14; E. Rigoni, Il pittore Niccolò Pizolo, Arte veneta, II, 1949, pp. 141-48; E. Tietze-Conrat, Mantegna's Parnassus: A Discussion of a Recent Interpretation, AB, XXXI, 1949, pp. 126-30; E. Wind, Mantegna's Parnassus: A Reply to Some Recent Reflexions, AB, XXXI, 1949, pp. 224-31; L. Vertova, Mantegna, Florence, 1950; M. Davies, The Earlier Italian Schools (Nat. Gall. Cat.), London, 1951 (2d ed. 1961); E. Tietze-Conrat, Notes on Hercules at the Crossroads, Warburg, XIV, 1951, pp. 305-09; F. Hartt, Mantegna's Madonna of the Rocks, GBA, XL, 1952, pp. 329-42; F. Landsberger, A New Interpretation of an Old Picture, Cincinnati Art Mus. B., III, 1, 1952, pp. 3-4; L. Coletti, La pittura veneta del Quattrocento, Novara, 1953; G. C. Argan, La peinture dans l'Italie du Nord, Lausanne, 1955; P. Hendy, Art Treasures of the National Gallery of London, New York, 1955; M. Tamassia, Visioni di antichità nell'opera del Mantegna, RendPontAcc, XXVIII, 1955-56, pp. 213-49; E. Tietze-Conrat, Mantegna, London, New York, Florence, 1955; F. Bologna, Ricordi di un Cristo morto del Mantegna, Paragone, VII, 75, 1956, pp. 56-61; R. Cipriani, Tutta la pittura del Mantegna, Milan, 1956; P. D'Ancona, Mantegna, 2d ed., Milan, 1956; G. Paccagnini, Sul disegno della Madonna della Vittoria nel Palazzo ducale di Mantova, BArte, XLI, 1956, pp. 177-82; R. Pallucchini, La pittura veneta del Quattrocento, Bologna, 1956; M. Meiss, Andrea Mantegna as Illuminator: An Episode in Renaissance Art, Humanism and Diplomacy, New York, 1957; G. Paccagnini, Mantegna: La Camera degli Sposi, Milan, 1957; J. White, The Birth and Rebirth of Pictorial Space, London, 1957; G. Fiocco, Il museo imaginario di Francesco Squarcione, Mem. Acc. patavina di sc., lett. ed arti, LXXI, 1958-59, pp. 59-72; A. Mezzetti, Un Ercole e Anteo del Mantegna, BArte, XLIII, 1958, pp. 232-44; L. Coletti and E. Camesasca, La Camera degli Sposi del Mantegna a Mantova, Milan, 1959; P. D. Knabenshue, Ancient and Medieval Elements in Mantegna's Trial of St. James, AB, XLI, 1959, pp. 51-73; M. Meiss, Towards a More Comprehensive Renaissance Paleography, Appendix; Addenda Mantiniana, AB, XLII, 1960, pp. 97-112; G. Paccagnini, La Camera picta da Andrea Mantegna nel Castello di Mantova, Milan, 1960; G. Paccagnini, Il Mantegna e la plastica nell'Italia settentrionale, BArte, XLVI, 1961, pp. 65-100; G. Paccagnini and A. Mezzetti, Andrea Mantegna (exhibition cat.), Venice, 1961; G. Paccagnini and M. Salmi, Andrea Mantegna, Milan, 1961; G. Paccagnini, Appunti sulla tecnica della "Camera picta" di Andrea Mantegna, Scritti di storia dell'arte in onore di Mario Salmi, II, Rome, 1962.

Giovanni PACCAGNINI

Illustrations: PLS. 321-330.

MANUHAR. Indian miniaturist to the court of the Moghul sovereigns, active in the late 16th and the first half of the 17th century. Although he was not included in the list of court artists compiled by Abū'l-Faḍl 'Allāmī, the prime minister of Akbar the Great, Manuhar left many drawings and paintings, which once belonged to the great collections of the palaces of Agra and Delhi and have since been divided among various museums and private collections. His work was done primarily between 1581 and 1620, during the reigns of Akbar, Jahāngīr, and Shah Jahān. An examination of the signed works, as well as those which can almost certainly be attributed to Manuhar, reveals a multiplicity of interests and modes of expression. The greater part of his works are portraits of emperors or courtiers, nocturnal scenes of a fanciful nature, or animal studies. In all of these, the quality of the draftsmanship is exceptional, the details precisely rendered, the colors vivid and brilliant, and the arabesques in the backgrounds or borders extremely fine and often gilded.

His most beautiful portrait subjects include: Akbar, receiving guests in a splendid palace setting; Jahāngīr, holding an antelope by a leash while one of his servants leads a black buck (Br. Mus.); Prince Khurram, the future Shah Jahān, receiving orders from his father, Jahāngīr, in the presence of other dignitaries; and Amīr Mīrzā Gazi Beg, holding a flower in his right hand. The details, especially of the costumes are always scrupulously accurate; for example, in a miniature depicting the Ilkhan sovereign Hūlāgū, a historical figure included among various persons of the court of Jahāngīr, the artist has taken care to dress the Moghul courtiers in the regional garb of the time, while Hūlāgū wears Mongol attire.

At the school of the court of Jahāngīr, in whose service he worked for a lengthy period, even though his name is not among those cited in the memoirs of the emperor, Manuhar and the painter al-Manṣūr were specifically charged with executing studies of animals. The animals, however, were to be represented as court ornaments, not as beasts roaming in their native environment. The conventional limitations imposed upon the artists notwithstanding, the bird studies of Manuhar and al-Manṣūr are excellent examples of careful scientific observation allied with a superb elegance of form. Among animal subjects, Manuhar seems to favor the deer, which recurs very often in his miniatures. A handsome black buck appears in a portrait of Jahāngīr, and two splendid studies of a black buck are preserved in the British Museum and in the Wantage Collection of the Victoria and Albert Museum.

Another recurring theme in the works of Moghul painters is the night scene. A fine example of Manuhar's work in this genre, representing a fairy garden with a prince visited at night by winged genii, was probably painted about 1595 (PL. 331). The delicate gold border designs of this miniature accentuate the dark tones of the garden and of the figures, whose faces are drawn with great finesse and subtlety.

A Manuhar portrait of a bearded man (Louvre) shows clear European influence. The standing figure, treated in a three-quarter view, holds a book. He is dressed in a long garment, fastened by a row of small buttons, and has a belt around his waist; an ample cape and large hat complete the costume, which is certainly not an Oriental fashion. Stchoukine's suggestion (1929) that this might be a Portuguese missionary seems plausible, since the presence of European Jesuits, and especially Portuguese, at the Moghul court has been documented (cf. X, PL. 121). Moreover, in another miniature depicting Jahāngīr surrounded by courtiers, there appears a figure very similar to the one in Manuhar's portrait.

Maclagan (1932) has pointed out that many European paintings were imported into India and copied by the court artists of Akbar and Jahāngīr, under the guidance of Jesuit fathers who made certain that the originals were reproduced faithfully, especially the religious subjects. In this way Indian artists learned chiaroscuro and Western perspective, and among all the painters of the era, it was undoubtedly Manuhar who benefited most from the lessons. He mastered the new techniques to such a degree as to create some works in which the only Oriental element remaining was the subject. Two of his drawings in the Gulistan Museum, Teheran, furnish examples of this style. The first is a pastiche depicting a woman playing a lyre, surrounded by maidens and sheltered by an elaborate structure. Here the theme of the "concert in the garden" so frequent in Indian miniatures has clearly been adapted to a European interior. The maidens' costumes are in the style of the 16th century, and their hair is arranged according to the Western fashion of the period. The second drawing depicts Laylā visiting Majnūn in the desert, and the female figures are similar to the maidens in the other drawing. Majnūn has been reinterpreted along the lines of the European motif of the dance of death. A miniature portrait of Jahāngīr (Dublin, Chester Beatty Lib.) attributed by critics to Manuhar seems to reveal a Dutch influence.

The finest works of Manuhar are undoubtedly the scenes of palace life crowded with figures, each of them clearly distinguishable, the great audiences of the sovereigns, the delicate drawings of gardens in bloom, and the magnificent studies of animals, in which turquoise, blue-green, and bright red are mingled or contrasted with gold backgrounds and blue-gray margins with elegance and incomparable grace.

BIBLIOG. A. K. Coomaraswamy, Indian Drawings, I, London, 1910; F. R. Martin, The Miniature Painting and Painters of Persia, India and Turkey, 2 vols., London, 1912; L. Binyon and T. W. Arnold, Court Painters of the Grand Mogul, London, New York, 1921; C. S. Clarke, Indian Drawings: Thirty Mogul Paintings of the School of Jahāngīr in the Wantage Bequest, London, 1922; E. Kühnel and H. Goetz, Indische Buchmalerei aus dem Jahāngīr-album der Staatsbibliothek zu Berlin, Berlin, 1923; P. Brown, Indian Painting under the Mughals, A.D. 1550–1750, Oxford, 1924; E. B. Havell, Indian Sculpture and Painting, 2d ed., London, 1928; I. Stchoukine, Les miniatures indiennes de l'époque des Grand Moghouls au Musée du Louvre, Paris, 1929; E. Maclagan, The Jesuits and the Great Mogul, London, 1932; L. Ashton, ed., The Art of India and Pakistan (cat.), New York, 1950.

Bianca Maria ALFIERI

Illustration: PL. 331.

MANUSCRIPT ILLUMINATION. See MINIATURES AND ILLUMINATION.

MARC, FRANZ. German painter and graphic artist (b. Munich, Feb. 8, 1880; d. near Verdun, Mar. 4, 1916). A leading member and the cofounder (with Kandinsky) of the Blaue Reiter branch of expressionism (q.v.), Marc began to practice his art about 1900 as an academically influenced painter of naturalistic landscapes and portraits. Soon he was influenced by the decorative qualities of Jugendstil as well. By 1903 he had visited Paris and had made a few impressionist sketches and evidenced his awareness of modern color possibilities; his abiding interest in Oriental philosophy and religious ideas also began to emerge. His first animal drawings appeared in 1905, marking the beginning of his efforts to relate all animal (and human) figures to Nature in a broad pantheistic sense. An increasing emphasis on rhythmic effects, the influence of Jugendstil art, was frequently accompanied by the use of large areas of decorative and symbolic color — the symbolic intent related to the postimpressionism of Van Gogh and Gauguin. To achieve these new ends, color became less naturalistic, more generalized in application, and subjective in choice, always accompanied by flowing linear patterns.

In 1909 he came into contact with a Russian emigré group of nonrepresentational artists living in Munich (including Jawlensky and Werefkin), participants in the recently established Neue Künstlervereinigung (New Artists' Federation). At this time his friendship with Heinrich Campendonk and August Macke also developed. About 1910 he had his first one-man show, and then encountered Kandinsky. The hostile reaction of the newspapers to the second Federation exhibit (1910) persuaded Marc to join the struggle actively in defense of modern art. By 1911 it was quite clear that he had arrived at a personal and mature form of expression, characterized by the already mentioned nonnaturalistic line and nondescriptive (that is, symbolic) color: thus the red, yellow, or blue horses and other animals are expressly emotive, their generous billowing outlines rhythmically and symbolically related to the backgrounds that represent Nature itself. Although continuing the Gauguin-Fauve-Brücke concern with living beings and their relation to Nature, he substituted animals for humans; moreover, he sought to convey a variety of emotions and philosophical ideas through his choice of animals. Thus, in the *Blue Horse* (1911; Berlin, B. Koehler Coll.) a young animal is painted in blue and white, with deep blue shadows — the colors symbolizing belief and infinity, a mood appropriate to this youthful creature. The *Yellow Cow* (1911; Hofheim, Vom Rath Coll.) presents a more joyous note of affirmation, stemming from the new-found happiness of the painter's marriage. Whatever the animal or idea chosen, man no longer played any role in Marc's art. During 1912 he moved toward a more blocklike, geometric formulation under the influence of the facet cubism of Picasso and Braque (V, PL. 209); but the vivid color range was peculiarly his own.

In 1912 there appeared the one and only number of *Der Blaue Reiter*, jointly edited by Marc and Kandinsky, in which Marc set forth his anti-impressionist views. From December, 1911, to January, 1912, the great Blaue Reiter group show was presented; it has since come to be judged an important influence in the history of modern art. In 1912 Marc's visit to Paris, where he met Delaunay, prepared the way for his progression from facet cubism toward analytical cubism. Since this new method involved fragmentation of the various forms, Marc was able to effect a more complete union of his creatures with Nature by literally dissolving them into their backgrounds, yet always retaining his own lambent and symbolic color, such as in the *Deer in the Forest* (V, PL. 127). In 1914 he began to work in an abstract, almost nonobjective, vein of lyricism, in an apparent search for elemental organic forms symbolizing the genesis of all life. This new turn in his art was cut short when Marc, who had enlisted at the outbreak of war, was killed in action on March 4, 1916.

BIBLIOG. A. J. Schardt, Franz Marc, Berlin, 1936; K. Lankheit, Franz Marc, Berlin, 1950; B. S. Myers, The German Expressionists, New York, London, 1957, 1963; P. Selz, German Expressionist Painting, Berkeley, Los Angeles, 1957.

Bernard S. MYERS

MARIN, JOHN. American painter (b. Rutherford, N.J., Dec. 23, 1870; d. Cape Split, Maine, Oct. 1, 1953). Marin's early training was architectural, with one year at Stevens Institute of Technology, Hoboken, and four years as an architectural draftsman. At the age of twenty-nine he began serious study of art at the Pennsylvania Academy of the Fine Arts, Philadelphia (1899–1901), and went on to the Art Students League, New York (1901–03). He was in Paris during most of the period from 1905 to 1911. This European sojourn was important, though Marin remained curiously unaware of many of the significant contemporary European developments and did not even come in contact with the works of Cézanne until his return to the United States. An oil, *The Mills of Meaux*, was purchased by the Musée du Luxembourg of Paris in 1908. Also in 1908, he exhibited in the Salon d'Automne in Paris, and in 1909 at the Salon des Indépendants.

In Paris, during 1909, Marin met Alfred Stieglitz, who from 1909 held annual exhibitions of Marin's work in New York and proclaimed him the greatest American water-colorist. After Marin's return to the United States, he lived in Cliffside, New Jersey, and passed his summers in New England and, less frequently, in Taos and Santa Fe, New Mexico.

Marin's early etchings on architectural subjects, influenced by Whistler, were sensitive and exacting. As early as 1908 his water colors suggested some relationship with the postimpressionists, but Marin seems to have developed independently in this direction. On his return from Europe he soon established the boundaries of his artistic world: the pulsing movement and vitality of New York City and the wind-swept energy of the Maine coast. His buildings turn and topple with uneasy life, as full of angular movement as his figures, qualities exemplified in *Movement — Fifth Avenue* (1912; Chicago, Art Inst.). His method was one of immediate visual contact, and he developed an absolute mastery of the transparent water color and a peculiarly effective kind of symbolic pictorial shorthand. A favorite compositional device plays circular and rectangular rhythms against each other; while often the angular boundaries start a kind of chain reaction, they never seem to be limiting factors. The works are large in their suggestive power though small in actual scale, such as the *Maine Islands* (1922; Washington, D.C., Phillips Coll.). Marin also found stimulating motifs in circus activities and Indian scenes of the Southwest.

In the 1930s Marin returned to the oil medium. Most of these works were also seascapes, in which he realized the tumultuous movement of great masses of water, the tossing lightness of sailboats, and the changing character of clouds. Often a kind of jagged tracery was superimposed on the paintings, as in *Movement — Boat and Sea in Grey* (1952; New York, Joseph H. Hirshhorn Coll.). A curiously personal feature of the late paintings is their carved and colored frames, designed and executed by the artist. Marin's art remained independent and essentially original. Though he reflected many of the preoccupations of the abstract trend, a strong involvement with the specific visual experience was clearly manifest in all his work (I, PL. 118).

BIBLIOG. Museum of Modern Art, John Marin: Watercolors, Oils, Etchings, New York, 1936; J. T. Soby, Contemporary Painters, New York. 1948, pp. 16–21; D. Norman, ed., The Selected Writings of John Marin, New York, 1949; John Marin: Drawings and Watercolors, New York, 1950; D. Norman, John Marin: Conversations and Notes, College Art J., XIV, 1955, 320–31; John Marin, Berkeley, 1956.

Allen S. WELLER

MARINI, MARINO. Italian sculptor (b. Pistoia, Feb. 27, 1901). Trained at the Accademia di Belle Arti in Florence, Marino Marini worked at painting and etching until about 1928, when sculpture became his main interest. From 1929 to 1940 Marini taught at the Villa Reale art school in Monza, then at the Accademia di Belle Arti in Milan. He visited and lived in Paris for long periods, and during World War II he moved to Switzerland. Although he has traveled widely in later years, Milan remains his home. From 1935 onward, Marini began to receive recognition and awards, and since 1946 he has achieved international fame.

With few exceptions, Marini has always worked in clay, with the finished form in terra cotta or bronze. From the beginning his sculpture has been in the great tradition of Rodin and Medardo Rosso — the tradition of impressionistic realism, with its attention to animated pose, textured surface, and the effects of light and shadow on the modeled form. Early in his career, following strong 20th-century trends of classic revival (Maillol, for instance) and toward the archaic and primitive, Marini began to develop a figural style of rounded volume, as in classical torsos, but with rough, broken surfaces.

His early figures, such as the *Juggler* (1933), often have blank facial expressions and an aura of loneliness. Marini seems to have derived the stark, dispassionate quality of his work from Etruscan terra-cotta tomb figures and, perhaps, from certain Roman portrait heads and steles. The double figure group *People* (1929) is clearly inspired by an Etruscan sarcophagus, and the portrait of the sculptor Melotti (1937) is reminiscent of Roman republican sculpture. The *Horseman* (1936), a full-scale representation of a horse and rider, is handled with a remarkable combination of ingenuous naturalism and hieratic rigidity that evokes the magic of a primitive idol. *Pugilist* (1935), a seated nude with head thrown back and one arm crooked over an invisible rope, is an early example of Marini's interest in the dynamic and often contorted pose, which appears in so many of his later male figures, particularly the *Horse and Rider* (V, PL. 143). This subject, for which the sculptor is best known, is treated in a series of works of varying sizes from about a foot high to nearly life size.

His female nudes are usually less distorted, with bodies reminiscent of the Maillol prototype, but generally shorter and plumper and with rough, sketchy texture. In fact, the surface of nearly all Marini's bronzes is subjected to special treatment, making it quite different from the usual patina of bronze. The metal, rough and irregular, shows file marks and grid patterns apparently introduced into the mold deliberately. Fragments of white plaster remain in the incisions, and occasionally there are touches of gold, so that the work has a polychromatic effect. These qualities of texture and color suggest his early interest in painting. His later portraits are powerfully expressive and often distorted, qualities exemplified in the portrait of Stravinsky (1950) and, especially, the head of Curt Valentin (1954).

BIBLIOG. U. Apollonio, Marino Marini, Scultore, Milan, 1953.

Henry R. HOPE

MARTINI, SIMONE. Italian painter (b. Siena, ca. 1284; d. Avignon, July, 1344), son of a certain Martino. His earliest known work is identified by his signature and the date 1315, in his hand, on the great fresco of the *Maestà* (or *Majestas*) in the Palazzo Pubblico in Siena. Probably because of the immediate prestige this fresco procured for Simone, he was shortly afterward summoned to the Angevin court of Naples, where he must have created works of exceptional value, since the king, Robert of Anjou, knighted him and awarded him an annual stipend of 50 ounces of gold, according to a documented receipt dated July 23, 1317. To this period is attributed the signed altarpiece showing St. Louis of Toulouse crowning King Robert (PL. 336; originally in the Church of S. Chiara in Naples, now in the Mus. di Capodimonte), painted about 1317, the year of the canonization of St. Louis.

Simone's stay in Naples probably lasted until he moved to Pisa, where in 1319 he executed, along with other works now lost, the large signed polyptych for the Dominican church of S. Caterina. In Orvieto the following year, again for the Dominicans, Simone painted the polyptych, signed and dated 1320, commissioned by the bishop of Soana, Trasmondo Monaldeschi; five panels of the work are conserved in the Museo dell'Opera del Duomo in Orvieto. In 1321–22 the artist worked in Siena on the restoration of portions of the *Maestà* that had been damaged and painted other works, now lost, including a Madonna for the chapel in the Palazzo Pubblico (1321), some unspecified paintings for the same chapel and for the Loggia of the Palazzo Pubblico (1322), and a St. Christopher with the coat of arms of the podesta in the Biccherna (1322). In 1324 Simone married Giovanna, the daughter of the painter Memmo di Filippuccio and sister of his collaborator, Lippo Memmi.

No dates have been recorded for Simone's sojourn in Assisi, during which he created the frescoes in S. Francesco, or for the stay in Florence noted by Vasari, but many documents give details of his work in Siena before his departure for Avignon, about 1340. They testify to an unspecified painting of 1325 in the Palazzo del Capitano del Popolo; a standard for the

Duke of Calabria in 1326; some work with gilded lilies and lions in 1327; two angels for the chapel altar in the Palazzo Pubblico in 1329; the figure of Marcus Atilius Regulus for the Sala del Concistoro of the Palazzo Pubblico in 1330; the pedestal of a cross for the Consiglio dei Nove in 1332; and a Virgin Enthroned with the Saviour and angels (1335), on the façade of a house — all lost works. The surviving paintings from this period are the fresco of the *condottiere* Guidoriccio da Fogliano (PL. 334), on the wall facing the *Maestà* in the chapel of the Palazzo Pubblico of Siena, executed in 1328; and *The Annunciation* (Uffizi), painted in 1333 in collaboration with Lippo Memmi (the two saints of the side panels are Lippo's) for the Cathedral of Siena.

What little information exists regarding Simone's activity after 1335 refers to his stay in Avignon, the dates of which are generally given as 1339-44. However, the beginning of the period at Avignon cannot be earlier than the end of 1340, inasmuch as two documents published by André Péter (1939), dated May 27, 1340, and Oct. 24, 1340, show that in October of 1340 Simone had not yet left Siena. During his stay in Avignon Simone maintained a close friendship with Petrarch, for whom he executed a miniature with a portrait (now lost) of Laura and the frontispiece of Petrarch's Vergil, (PL. 337), now in the Biblioteca Ambrosiana, Milan. His last surviving signed and dated work is the *Holy Family* (1342) now in the Walker Art Gallery, Liverpool.

Nothing is known of Simone's work during the first thirty years of his life, that is, prior to the *Maestà* in the Palazzo Pubblico of Siena (1315; PL. 332). It is probable that he worked in Siena from the first years of the 14th century, and that he received his early training in the studio of Duccio di Buoninsegna, as maintained by George H. Edgell (1946) and Luigi Coletti (1949). Nevertheless, the question has remained unsolved, even though several paintings have been attributed to this period, such as the *Christ Blessing* (Vat. Mus.), *St. John the Evangelist* (New York, Met. Mus.), *SS. Nicholas and Gregory* (Boston, Mus. of Fine Arts), *Christ Blessing* (Naples, Mus. di Capodimonte), *SS. Catherine and Lucy* (Settignano, Berenson Foundation), the *Maestà* in Massa Marittima (Mus. Civ.), and others. In fact, some of these works were not painted by Simone, while those which can more credibly be attributed to him, such as the *Christ Blessing* in the Vatican and the *St. John the Evangelist* in New York, reveal stylistic traits that would make them of a later date than the *Maestà* of 1315, which therefore remains the earliest authenticated work of the artist. Although the traces of Duccio recognizable in it confirm Simone's early Sienese training, it is fundamentally a mature and original work, markedly different from Duccio's masterpiece, which, just a few years earlier, in 1311, the Sienese had accompanied in a solemn procession from the artist's studio to the Cathedral. A new conception of life and of art is expressed by Simone's *Maestà*; the depth of its composition is in sharp contrast with the architectural hierarchy of the sacred personages in Duccio's *Maestà*, placed in one symmetrically balanced plane flanking the central figure of the Madonna. Simone's fresco is conceived, first of all, as a painting within a splendid framework. There is a vivid naturalistic sense of space in the composition of the work, with the figures arranged in perspective, following the lines of the steps and the poles of the canopy, which recede toward the background of the sky. The space suggested by the canopy set against the sky, the disposal of the figures in a circle round the throne, and the modeling of each separate figure combine to form a harmonious whole in which each part contributes to the rhythmic and spatial relationship. These new compositional values, born of a renewed interest in natural phenomena, are indicative of Simone's affinity, from the time of his first masterpiece, with the popular traits of Giotto.

The most important element in the novelty of style in the Siena *Maestà*, however, is clearly the influence of the French Gothic manner, which is not discernible in the work of any other Italian painter of this period. It is possible that Simone's contact with French culture came about through the wide diffusion of illuminations, textiles, goldsmiths' work and ivories, with their refined and worldly expression of beauty. But the influence is so strongly revealed in Simone's *Maestà* that it renders attractive C. Gnudi's hypothesis (1956) of a direct contact with French culture, possibly made during a trip to France during the undocumented period before 1315, for it was during this period that Simone's style reached the unprecedented maturity of expression so fully consummated in the Sienese masterpiece. Conceivably, during the reign of Clement V, Simone may have gone to the papal court at Avignon in the retinue of some high-ranking art-loving prelate, such as one of the Orsini or the Stefaneschi families, with whom he was later connected. This would better explain the total lack of information about the artist in Siena at the time, as well as the strong impression that his new style must have made, inducing the administrators of the city of Siena to commission from him, rather than from Duccio, the *Maestà* for the Palazzo Pubblico. Moreover, the fact that Simone was called to the Francophile court of King Robert of Anjou in Naples, immediately after he had completed the *Maestà*, is a testimony to the modernity and sophistication of this seminal work, one of the most advanced of its period.

About 1317, in the atmosphere of refined culture engendered by the Angevin court, the artist painted the beautiful predella for the *St. Louis of Toulouse Crowning Robert of Anjou King of Naples* (PL. 336). By the knowing application of diverse techniques, Simone imparted silvery refractions to the colors and a subtle fluidity to the line. Unfortunately, the grave damage suffered by the surfaces of both the *Maestà* of Siena and the *St. Louis* of Naples has forever marred the original chromatic splendor that won Simone immediate fame among his contemporaries as the finest colorist of his day.

However, in the polyptych of the *Madonna and Saints*, executed in Pisa in 1319 for the Church of S. Caterina (PL. 335), the purity of Simone's color is displayed in all its splendor, like some molten, fiery substance. The articulation of the figures in space, almost in opposition to the Giottesque modeling, is achieved by differentiation of the delicate surface texture through the use of shadows in complementary tones and intensification of the pigments adjacent to the flowing contours of the figures. The volumes thus become weightless, with iridescent forms like blown glass, absorbed and reflected in the luminous and incorporeal space of the gold background. There is an acute sensitivity and a severe sense of form in the large figures and in the gentle variations of the predella, with its wonderful chromatic embellishment. The exquisite sensitivity of the figures of Mary Magdalene and St. Catherine in the Pisa polyptych also appears in the lovely *Madonna and Child* discovered at Lucignano d'Arbia by Enzo Carli (1958), who dates it about 1321.

Simone's activity at Orvieto probably began with the polyptych executed in 1320 for the Dominican monastery, the five remaining panels of which depict the Madonna and Child and four saints (Orvieto, Museo dell'Opera del Duomo). It is difficult to evaluate accurately this Orvieto period, since collaboration is clearly evident in the paintings attributed to Simone for these years: the polyptych with SS. Michael, Ambrose, and Augustine in the Fitzwilliam Museum, Cambridge, Eng.; the polyptych with the Madonna and four saints in the Isabella Stewart Gardner Museum, Boston; the *Madonna and Child* in the Museo dell'Opera del Duomo, Orvieto; the *St. Catherine*, formerly in the Liechtenstein Gallery, Vienna; the little *Crucifixion* in the Fogg Art Museum, Cambridge, Mass.; and the *Crucifixion* in the Church of the Misericordia in San Casciano, Val di Pesa. In the autograph works of this period the figures have greater weight and volume in relation to the plane in which they are situated, and a greater compactness of volumes, while the line moves with increased firmness and assurance.

All this points to a renewed exposure to the art of Giotto, as may be seen in such works as the polyptych painted in the early 1330s in Florence, the remaining panels of which are the *St. Stephen* (Florence, Fondazione Horne), *Angel of the Annunciation* (Washington D.C., Nat. Gall.), and the *SS. John the Evangelist and Lawrence* (Chaâlis, Mus. Jacquemart-André). Nothing has survived with which to evaluate Simone's Florentine works discussed amply by Vasari: a Madonna with St. Luke and other saints in the Gondi Chapel of S. Maria Novella has been lost; the scenes of the Passion of Christ frescoed in the chapter house of the Augustinian church of Sto Spirito were destroyed in 1560, according to Vasari; and perhaps the "many fresco works" believed to have been painted by Simone and Lippo Memmi in Sta Croce suffered the same fate. It is highly probable that between 1320 and 1325 the cultural climate of Florence favored a meeting of minds between these two "modern" painters, even though their artistic and moral worlds were as diverse as those of Dante and Petrarch in the contemporary literature.

So far as Simone is concerned, there is no doubt that the spatial structure of the scenes from the life of St. Martin, his greatest and most complex work, constituting the pictorial decoration of the Chapel of St. Martin in the Lower Church of S. Francesco in Assisi, is similar to that in Giotto's frescoes of the Peruzzi and Bardi Chapels in Sta Croce, Florence. For this reason, also, the controversial date of the St. Martin frescoes can be fixed as just subsequent to Giotto's frescoes at Sta Croce (i.e., about 1325–26). The St. Martin frescoes comprise 8 full-length saints on the underside of the entrance arch, the dedication of the chapel on the wall above the entrance arch, 18 busts of saints in the embrasures of three large windows (for which the stained glass was designed by Simone), and 10 episodes from the life of St. Martin, on the two side walls and in the vault. These episodes represent the saint dividing his cloak with the beggar, Christ appearing to St. Martin, the saint armed as a cavalier, St. Martin abandoning his arms (PL. 333), the meditation, the Mass, the saint raising a boy from the dead, the miracle of fire, the death, and the funeral of the saint.

The five busts of SS. Francis, Louis of Toulouse, Elizabeth of Hungary, Clare, and Louis of France, painted by Simone in the transept of S. Francesco, are also stylistically of the same period as the decoration of the Chapel of St. Martin. Apparently belonging to an earlier period is another painting in the transept, the *Madonna and Child between Two Saints*, perhaps executed by Simone upon his return from Naples.

The two last scenes, according to the narrative order of the life of St. Martin, that is, the death and funeral, painted in the vault, were very likely — because of the normal procedure in fresco painting of working from the top toward the bottom — Simone's first works in the chapel. In these frescoes the images are drawn in clearer volumes, set off by the subtle spatial scheme of the lines; the buildings, placed on parallel planes sloping toward the background, give breadth and a sense of perspective; the position of the figures, seen frontally, in profile, and in three-quarter view, the hands painted in perspective, and the roundness of the tonsured heads, all tend to create continuous links in depth among the different planes of the composition. During this period Simone achieved the greatest volumetric emphasis permitted by the intact purity of his planes of color. There is an evident similarity to the broad, careful harmony of style and subtlety of color notable in Giotto's Florentine work of the same years. Simone's modern and receptive spirit could not remain unaffected by the innovations of Giotto, to which he had been attracted since the period of the *Maestà* of Siena and the *St. Louis* of Naples; however, he did challenge Giotto by interpreting his perspective solutions in a completely different manner. Thus, the comparable stratifying of the buildings on parallel planes in Giotto's work sets a solemn tone in the sculptural and spatial unity of the composition, while in Simone's the fluid tapering off of forms toward a distant point leading into the deepest planes creates a serene atmosphere of vision filtered through a poetic memory.

This is the most felicitous period of Simone's art; here, in the decorations of the Chapel of St. Martin, he assumed full command of that cultivated and aristocratic style of up-to-date French traits which had fascinated him since his youthful introduction to the French Gothic. Splendid scenes of an inexhaustible tonal richness, becoming increasingly intense in each succeeding episode, follow one another on these walls, culminating in the ecstatic lyrical concentration of the saint's meditation and the prodigious harmony of the saint armed as a cavalier and the abandoning of arms (PL. 333). In these scenes, the last in temporal and stylistic order, Simone achieved a poetic and human equilibrium of the fundamental tendencies of his spirit: the unfailing regard for formal values; consummate mastery of style; continuing interest in new ways of expression; and, at the same time, a freshness of view, an ever-youthful wonder, that was the source of his abiding gift for pure color and fluid linear grace.

Also attributed to Simone's Assisi period, about 1326, is the small tempera painting of St. Ladislaus, King of Hungary, in the Church of S. Maria della Consolazione at Altomonte (Calabria) — a brief, exquisite lyric, which, in its alternating division of the pictorial passage, suggests the condensed rhythm of a sonnet and achieves the same lofty poetic value as some of the unforgettable images in the Chapel of St. Martin. Closely related stylistically to the *St. Ladislaus* of Altomonte are the two saints, painted on octagonal panels — perhaps part of a predella — in Birmingham (Barber Inst. of Fine Arts) and in Boston (Mus. of Fine Arts), respectively. The large panel in the Church of S. Agostino in Siena, depicting the Blessed Agostino Novello and four of his miracles, was most likely executed directly following the frescoes of Assisi. The accentuated plasticity of the scenes of St. Martin is softened in this new masterpiece, and the fairy-tale space of the small paintings is achieved by the relationship of the planes, limpid and luminous in color. Simone maintains the same lofty lyrical vein in his retelling of the four miracles: the child attacked by a wolf, the child fallen from the balcony, the knight fallen into the ravine, and the child fallen from his cradle. In each he described with inexpressible tenderness the life of the people of his neighborhood. His brush lingers over every detail with the same affectionate attention as he fixes each action and transforms it into a miracle of color.

The poetic feeling for landscape which runs throughout the story of the Blessed Agostino Novello reaches its most intense and solemn expression of those years in the large fresco of 1328, depicting the *condottiere* Guidoriccio da Fogliano (PL. 334), which commemorates the reconquest of the rebel towns of Montemassi and Sassoforte. Simone here displays a vivid, naturalistic power of observation in rendering the encampment, the tents, and the palisades, as well as the banners, lances, and shields that suggest the hidden presence of soldiers in the rugged hills. Etched against the sky, the walls, houses, and empty towers of the besieged fortresses seem immersed in a terrified silence. The solitude of the landscape is permeated by an aura of fantasy and suspense, and the figures of Guidoriccio and his elaborately caparisoned steed are lyrically transfigured into a single equestrian emblem, strange and disquieting; this image seems to ride, phantomlike, in a dark night sky rather than across those bare desert crags, scarcely grazed by the horse's hoofs.

In the emblematic abstraction that confers on the spacious colored surfaces of this fresco the aspect of a large tapestry, the characteristics of Simone's late style make their appearance, but they are fully revealed only after an interval of five years — during which nothing is known of the painter's activities — in the freedom and rhythmic cadence of the Uffizi *Annunciation* (PL. 339), painted in 1333 for the Cathedral of Siena. Certain scholars have been negative in their judgment of this exquisite painting and of others painted by Simone in the last years of his life at Avignon; their extreme purity, to which Simone's style tended from the very beginning, has been unjustly mistaken for a virtuoso emphasis on formalism, in which poetry gave way to decadent mannerism. Petrarch was not of that opinion. In an analysis that is still substantially valid, he perceived in the Avignon works particularly an affinity between his own poetic world and the supreme lyricism of Simone's late style, in which pictorial emotion is expressed in terms of ideal and aristocratic beauty with a serene but ecstatic rhythm. Rarely has another painter achieved the ethereal and radiant lyricism of the Uffizi *Annunciation*, with its angel all iridescent splendor and the shadowy Virgin bowed and withdrawn in her sweet melancholy. The breadth of luminous space in this painting is not that of reality; rather, it is the lyrical internal measure of the images, expressed in the faces and in the liquescent forms and the color cadences of the garments, playing in striking patterns against the over-all vibrant tone of gold.

The contradictory critical evaluations of Simone's work in Avignon are a consequence of the meager and inexact state of knowledge that has continued to the present. A better understanding might be gained from the recovery of the surviving fragments, damaged as they are, of the frescoes he executed in the Cathedral of Notre-Dame-des-Doms. These frescoes, harmoniously enclosed within the beautiful Romanesque architecture of the porch, are still worthy of study. They express a monumental conception skillfully related to the available space. Detachment and restoration of these frescoes would not only save the remaining fragments of the surface but would also uncover the magnificent sinopias that are visible in exposed areas. Irrevocably lost is the St. George killing the dragon, which still existed in 1818 but was destroyed ten years later (Eugène Müntz, 1884). Still surviving are some surface areas of the underside of the entrance arch, decorated with ornamental motifs and angel heads, and other parts of the frescoes above the portal of the church: in the lunette, the Madonna and Child with two kneeling angels (one perhaps representing Cardinal Jacopo Stefaneschi, who died at Avignon in 1341); and in the gable, Christ Blessing, surrounded by six angels.

Other works attributed to the Avignon period include the frontispiece of Vergil in the Biblioteca Ambrosiana (PL. 337); the *Virgin of the Annunciation* in The Hermitage, Leningrad; the *Holy Family* in the Walker Art Gallery, Liverpool; and the dramatically vivid little polyptych of the Passion, its panels now divided among the Musée Royal des Beaux-Arts of Antwerp, the Staatliche Museen of Berlin, and the Louvre. In Antwerp are *The Archangel Gabriel*, *The Virgin of the Annunciation* (PL. 338), *The Crucifixion*, and *The Deposition* (PL. 340); in Berlin *The Entombment*; at the Louvre *The Way to Calvary* (VI, PL. 378), bearing on its reverse side the Orsini family's coat of arms. The stylistic and iconographic relationships of the Passion polyptych seem so close to the Giotto of Assisi and Padua and the Duccio of the *Maestà* that the attribution of this work to Simone's last years seems unjustifiable. It seems instead that in the very novelty of these beautiful compositions — so close in their enamellike purity of color to the predella of the Pisa polyptych — archaic formal modes appear with innovations, while still reflecting the early Duccio training that remained perceptible in Simone's works until the Orvieto period. Moreover, the range of color, in which the figures are bathed in light and shadows of varying iridescent hues — for example, a light yellow with a shadow of rose or blue or brick red, a light red with a violet shadow — is closer to that of the Pisa and Orvieto works than it is to the subtle tonal values of light in the Avignon paintings. Even the minutest linear details, precise as a jeweler's design (e.g., the jewels of the Antwerp *Archangel Gabriel*), resemble those of the polyptych of Pisa or that of the Fitzwilliam Museum. The slender white stem of the lily in the Antwerp Archangel's hand has a subtle line like that of the fragile light rays touching the angels' fingers in the Fitzwilliam Museum work, and the delicate ornamental motifs are cut into the gold instead of impressed with the burin, as in the late works. In the other Avignon paintings the artist's style has a cadence of line and a delicate, airy use of color that create a virtually musical rhythm. The pictorial subtlety of the Vergil frontispiece may reflect something of the quality that elicited Petrarch's enthusiasm for the irrecoverable portrait of Laura painted by Simone for the great poet.

The course of Simone's art reaches its conclusion in the warm colors of the *Holy Family* (Liverpool, Walker Art Gall.), in 1342; its lyric intimacy is conveyed in well-defined, flowing, economical lines that seem already to predict the worldly elegance of the International Gothic style.

SOURCES. L. Fracassetti, ed., Francisci Petrarcae epistulae de rebus familiaribus et variae, III, Florence, 1863; L. Ghiberti, I Commentarii, (ed. J. von Schlosser, Berlin, 1912); Vasari; F. Baldinucci, Notizie de' professori del disegno da Cimabue in qua..., 2d ed., II, Turin, 1768, pp. 5-10; G. della Valle, Lettera senesi..., sopra le belle arti, II, Venice, 1782, pp. 77-101; L. Lanzi, Storia pittorica dell'Italia, Bassano, 1789.

BIBLIOG. J. W. Gaye, Carteggio inedito di artisti..., I, Florence, 1839; G. Milanesi, Documenti per la storia dell'arte senese, I, Siena, 1854; J. Ruskin, Mornings in Florence, London, New York, 1876; E. Müntz, Les peintures de Simone Martini à Avignon, Mém. Soc. nat. des ant. de France, XLV, 1884, pp. 67-92; E. Müntz, Pétrarque et Simone Martini: A propos du Virgile de l'Ambrosienne, Gazette archéol., XII, 1887, pp. 101-07; E. Müntz, Le palais des Papes à Avignon, Paris, 1892; A. Gosche, Simone Martini. Leipzig, 1899; E. Bertaux, L'art siennois à Naples, RA, XXXVI, 1900, pp. 313-21; E. Müntz and V. Masséna (Pr. d'Essling), Pétrarque: Ses études d'art, Paris, 1902; P. Schubring, Ein Passionältarchen des Simone Martini aus Avignon, JhbPreussKSamml, XXIII, 1902, pp. 741-46; C. Ricci, Il Palazzo pubblico di Siena e la Mostra dell'antica arte senese, Siena, 1904; P. Rossi, Simone Martini e Petrarca, B. senese di storia patria, XI, 1904, pp. 160-82; W. Rothes, Die Blütezeit der Sienesischen Malerei, Strasbourg, 1904; E. Bertaux, Gli affreschi di Santa Maria Donnaregina, Napoli nobilissima, X, 1906, pp. 129-33; L. Coletti, Arte senese, Treviso, 1906; G. De Nicola, L'affresco di Simone Martini a Avignone, L'Arte, IX, 1906, pp. 336-44; O. Sirén, Quadri sconosciuti nel Museo Cristiano Vaticano, L'Arte, IX, 1906, pp. 321-35; E. Jacobsen, Sienesische Meister der Trecento in der Gemäldegalerie zu Siena, Strasbourg, 1907; Venturi, V, pp. 589-668; F. Mason Perkins, Gli affreschi di Simone ad Avignone, Rass. d'arte senese, IV, 1908, pp. 87-88; B. Berenson, The Central Italian Painters of the Renaissance, 2d ed., New York, London, 1909; F. Mason Perkins, Un dipinto poco conosciuto di Simone Martini, Rass. d'arte senese, V, 1909, pp. 3-4; G. Cristofani, Due inediti di Simone Martini nella Basilica Inferiore di Assisi, L'Arte, XVI, 1913, pp. 131-35; M. L. Gielly, Les trecentistes siennois: Simone Martini et Lippo Memmi, Rev. de l'art ancien et mod., XXXIII, 1913, pp. 205-20, 253-65; P. D'Ancona, La miniatura fiorentina, II, Florence, 1914; W. D. Schulemburg, Una vetrata di Simone Martini, Rass. d'arte senese, X, 1914, pp. 54-56; O. Sirén, A Descriptive Catalogue of the Pictures in the Jarves Collection Belonging to Yale University, New Haven, 1916; B. Berenson, Essays in the Study of Sienese Painting, New York, 1918; G. De Nicola, Studi sull'arte senese, Rass. d'arte, XIX, 1919, pp. 95-102; R. André-Michel, Avignon: Les fresques du palais des Papes, in Mélanges d'histoire et d'archéologie, Paris, 1920, pp. 19-66; R. van Marle, Simone Martini et les peintres de son école, Strasbourg, 1920; L. Dami, Simone Martini, Florence, 1921; A. De Rinaldis, Tavole di S. Lorenzo Maggiore nel Museo di Napoli: La tavola di Simone Martini, Napoli nobilissima. N.S., II, 1921, pp. 97-104; L. Ozzola, Lippo Memmo collaboratore del padre Memmo e di Simone Martini, Rass. d'arte, XXI, 1921, pp. 117-21; A. Venturi, Un'opera di Duccio di Buoninsegna a Copenhagen e una di Simone Martini a Vienna, L'Arte, XXIV, 1921, pp. 198-201; L. Dami, Il polittico pisano di Simone Martini, Dedalo, III, 1922, pp. 1-14; P. D'Ancona, La miniature italienne, Paris, Brussels, 1925; L. J. Gielly, Les primitifs siennois, Paris, 1926; L. Venturi, Il gusto dei primitivi, Bologna, 1926; A. De Rinaldis, La Regia Pinacoteca del Museo Nazionale di Napoli, Naples, 1927; R. Offner, Italian Primitives at Yale University, New Haven, 1927; G. M. Richter, Simone Martini Problems, BM, LIV, 1927, pp. 166-73; M. Salmi, S. Francesco a Siena, Siena, 1927; E. Cecchi, Trecentisti senesi, Rome, 1928 (2d ed., 1948); G. Sinibaldi, Rapporti d'Ambrogio Lorenzetti con Simone Martini e con Giotto, L'Arte, XXXI, 1928, pp. 207-12; R. van Marle, Quadri senesi sconosciuti, La Diana, IV, 1929, pp. 307-10; L. Venturi, La critica d'arte e Francesco Petrarca, in Pretesti di critica, Milan, 1929, pp. 37-51; T. Borenius, An Early Sienese Crucifixion, BM, LVI, 1930, pp. 255-56; F. Mason Perkins, Pitture senesi poco conosciute, La Diana, V, 1930, pp. 244-61; G. Sinibaldi, La pittura del Trecento, Florence, 1930; C. H. Weigelt, Sienese Painting of the Trecento, Paris, Florence, 1930; M. Micheli, Simone Martini, Turin, 1931; L. Venturi, Pitture italiane in America, Milan, 1931; C. H. Weigelt, Minor Simonesque Masters, Apollo, XIV, 1931, pp. 1-13; A. Colasanti, Due dipinti inediti di Simone Martini e di Pietro Lorenzetti, Dedalo, XII, 1932, pp. 659-65; G. H. Edgell, A History of Sienese Painting, New York, 1932; P. Bacci, Alcuni documenti nuziali di artisti senesi del XIV e XV secolo, Siena, 1934; C. Brandi, Sie Stilentwicklung des Simone Martini, Pantheon, XIV, 1934, pp. 225-30; A. De Rinaldis, Simone Martini, Rome, 1936; F. Mason Perkins, ThB, s.v.; A. Péter, Quand Simone est-il venu en Avignon?, GBA, XXI, 1939, pp. 153-74; P. Bacci, Fonti e commenti per la storia dell'arte senese, Siena, 1944; L. Coletti, I Primitivi, II: I Senesi e i Giotteschi, Novara, 1946; G. H. Edgell, A Crucifixion by Duccio with Wings by Simone Martini, BM, LXXXVIII, 1946, pp. 107-12; E. Carli, Capolavori dell'arte senese, Florence, 1947; G. Paccagnini, An Attribution to Simone Martini, BM, XC, 1948, pp. 75-80; C. Brandi, Catalogo della VI Mostra di Restauri, Rome, 1949; L. Coletti, Gli affreschi della Basilica di Assisi, Bergano, 1949; L. Coletti, The Early Works of Simone Martini, AQ, XII, 1949, pp. 290-308; J. Pope-Hennessy, Three Panels by Simone Martini, BM, XCI, 1949, pp. 193-96; E. Sandberg Vavalà, Simone Martini, Florence, 1950; Toesca, Tr; G. H. Edgell, Two Recently Acquired Sienese Paintings in the Museum of Fine Arts, BMFA, LI, 1953, pp. 7-10; C. Gnudi and J. Dupont, La peinture gothique, Geneva, 1954 (Eng. trans., S. Gilbert, Geneva, 1954); E. Carli, La pittura senese, Milan, 1955 (Eng. trans., Greenwich, Conn., 1956); G. Paccagnini, Simone Martini, Milan. 1955; C. Gnudi, Grandezza di Simone, in Scritti di storia dell'arte in onore di L. Venturi, I, Rome, 1956, pp. 87-100; K. Steinweg, Beiträge zu Simone Martini und seiner Werkstatt, Mitt. des kunsthist. Inst. in Florenz, VII, 1956, pp. 162-68; E. Carli, Una nuova Madonna di Simone Martini, Siena, 1958; E. Carli, La scuola senese, in Medioevo romanico e gotico, Milan, 1959, pp. 75-135; E. Castelnuovo, Avignone rievocata, Paragone, X, 119, 1959, pp. 28-51; E. Carli, Ein neuer Simone Martini, Pantheon, XVIII, 1960, pp. 165-71; Catalogo della IV Mostra di Restauri (exhibition cat.), Naples, 1960; Italian Art in Britain (exhibition cat.), London, 1960; M. Laclotte, L'école d'Avignon: La peinture en Provence aux XIV et XV siècles, Paris, 1960; J. Rowlands, A Hitherto Unknown Panel by Simone Martini, BM, CII, 1960, pp. 67-68; G. Coor, A Further Link in the Reconstruction of an Altarpiece by Andrea di Bartolo, J. of the Walters Art Gall., XXIV, 1961, pp. 55-60; K. M. Birkmeyer, Pietà from San Remigo, GBA, LX, 1962, p. 463; A. Martindale, Italian Art and the International Gothic Style, LXXVI, 1, N.S., 1962, pp. 277-82; A. Blunt, Simone Martini at the Hôtel de Sully, BM, CVI, 732, 1964.

Giovanni PACCAGNINI

Illustrations: PLS. 332-340.

MASACCIO (TOMMASO DI GIOVANNI, called "Masaccio"). Painter (b. San Giovanni Valdarno, Dec. 21, 1401), son of Ser Giovanni di Mone. Masaccio died in Rome, perhaps in the autumn of 1428 "at about the age of twenty-seven," according to the 15th-century writer Antonio Manetti.

On the whole, modern scholarship discounts the reports in 16th-century sources of a formal apprenticeship of the young Masaccio to Masolino. Mario Salmi considers that Masaccio's early formation showed rather close ties with the late Gothic style of Gentile da Fabriano and Arcangelo di Cola da Camerino and even an initial influence from the Arno Valley painters, such as Mariotto di Cristofano. Roberto Longhi, however, asserts that the very nature of Masaccio's genius would have prevented him from benefiting from the achievements of the Gothic artists of his own or earlier periods. There are even some who, bearing in mind considerations of chronology, maintain that the manner of Masaccio can be explained historically by reference to the results already achieved by Brunelleschi and Donatello. Ugo Procacci has ascertained that Masolino came from the same area as Masaccio, a fact that might support the assertions of the 16th-century sources, but any early relationship of Masaccio to Masolino would have been limited to a mere preliminary technical instruction.

Luciano Berti's attribution (1961) to Masaccio of the triptych discovered in the Church of S. Giovanale at Cascia di Reggello seems entirely correct. The triptych, *The Madonna Enthroned with Saints and Two Adoring Angels*, is dated Apr. 23, 1422, the same year in which Masaccio was enrolled in the Arte dei Medici e Speziali in Florence. If this discovery does not fully clarify his artistic formation, it does place it within the broad context of traditional Florentine culture. According to Procacci, Masaccio was already in Florence by about 1417. The Cascia di Reggello triptych reveals certain important facts: there is no influence of Masolino here; instead there appears the common Florentine tradition, along with innovations (from Giotto to Donatello to the perspective of Brunelleschi).

The placement of this triptych at the outset of Masaccio's career seems to dispose of the hypothesis, first advanced by G. Magherini-Graziani (1904), and variously discussed and accepted by art historians, that the fresco *The Enthroned Madonna and Child with SS. Michael and John the Baptist*, in the rural shrine near Montemarciano, is an early work of Masaccio. Rather, comparison with the S. Giovenale altarpiece makes it evident that the Montemarciano fresco must be assigned to Francesco d'Antonio, as Henrik Lindberg (1931) and more recently Longhi (1940), Procacci (1951), and Berti (1961) have concluded. However, the attribution to Masaccio has been upheld by Schmarsow, Berenson, Toesca, Venturi, Somarè, Salmi, and Pittaluga.

With the S. Giovenale triptych as a reference point, a new and more convincing chronology emerges for the Uffizi *Virgin and Child with St. Anne* (formerly, Florence, S. Ambrogio; PL. 341). The date of 1420 proposed by Procacci (1951), who regards it as Masaccio's earliest known work, can no longer be sustained. Since the date would have to follow that of the triptych of 1422, it must then fall during the period of the first collaboration between Masaccio and Masolino in 1424 in S. Maria del Carmine, Florence, as Longhi (1940) discerned. Berti concurred with this view, but restricted the beginning of the collaboration to the period from the end of 1424, when Masolino returned from Empoli, until September of 1425, when Masolino left Florence for Hungary.

Following Vasari, who in the second edition of the *Vite* (1568) attributed the execution of the Uffizi panel to Masaccio, subsequent historians considered the work to be his alone. Only the most recent findings, taking advantage of the extensive restoration of 1935-54, have demonstrated the evidence of a collaboration between Masolino and Masaccio.

In the commentary to his edition of Vasari, Giovanni Masselli had observed (1832) that if the Uffizi painting was actually by Masaccio it must be considered one of his earliest. G. B. Cavalcaselle, beginning the comparative exegesis of the Uffizi panel (1864), found in it an affinity to Masolino's work at Castiglione Olona. Working along the same lines, August Schmarsow (1895) saw a relationship with the fresco in which St. Peter heals a cripple and raises Tabitha (PL. 374) in S. Maria del Carmine and attributed that as well as the other frescoes to Masaccio; but today it is known to be by Masolino. In Berenson's first edition of his lists of Italian painters (1896), the Uffizi work was cited as a Masaccio. Later he used it as a secure basis for eliminating works previously assigned to Masaccio and giving them instead to Masolino.

The first to distinguish in the Uffizi painting "two distinct styles, two completely diverse ways of painting" was Paolo D'Ancona (1903), who separated the "soft and graceful" manner (in the faces of the Madonna and of the angels and in the garment folds) from the "full, rather crude forms" (the Christ child and the St. Anne). Pietro Toesca (1908) did not agree with this distinction that suggested the possibility of a collaboration with Masolino. He concluded that the angels, reminiscent as they are of Masolino in their light coloring and lack of relief and their slender and insubstantial form, are the key to the solution of any attributive controversy; they are the sign of a relatively youthful stage of Masaccio's art, in which he failed to understand Masolino's style, even though he was making use of its formulas.

The question of Masolino's collaboration in *The Virgin and Child with St. Anne* was studied by Adolfo Venturi (1911), K. Escher (1922), and O. H. Giglioli (1921), but always with the conclusion that it was completely by Masaccio. Later (1929) Giglioli held that the resemblances to Masolino in the panel, believed to indicate so marked a difference between the two artists, were superficial and fleeting.

Jacques Mesnil (1927) once again pointed out the influence of Masolino in the type of the angels, with their tapering fingers, in the elongated face of the Virgin, as well in the general tonality, and reconfirmed as Masaccio's innovation the composition conceived as a unified entity. Raimond van Marle had no reservation in assigning the work to Masaccio. But Lindberg (1931), making a detailed comparison of elements, studied the paintings and frescoes of the two artists and concluded that the Uffizi painting was the result of a collaboration. Later Robert Oertel (1933) and Mary Pittaluga (1935) reaffirmed Masaccio's sole authorship.

In 1940 Longhi reexamined the problem. Having studied the Uffizi panel during the cleaning, he attributed the Virgin and Child and the angel in the upper right to Masaccio. The remainder he assigned to Masolino. He considered that Masaccio was an independent assistant to Masolino, from whom the painting had perhaps been commissioned.

Scholars have agreed almost unanimously that a stylistic distinction exists in the Uffizi panel. They disagree only in regard to the figure of St. Anne. Salmi, who had previously noted (1932) the influence of Masolino on Masaccio "for the first and only time" (in the "delicate and pure blond heads of the angels"), expressed (in the second edition of his monograph, 1947) his doubt concerning the St. Anne. This figure establishes an over-all unity with the other figures in the construction of a composition which, he felt, could have been conceived only by Masaccio, so that Masolino's role was subordinate in the esthetic whole. C. L. Ragghianti (1949) considered that the foreshortened head of the angel at the top of the panel should also be attributed to Masaccio.

Procacci, who as early as 1936 had declared that the painting was in part by Masolino, accepted (1946) the distinction made by Longhi regarding the Virgin and Child and the angels but remained uncertain (1951) with respect to the figure of St. Anne, because of its poor state of preservation. However, he held that the conception of the central group of three figures was Masaccio's. Roberto Salvini (1952) associated himself with this view, stating that St. Anne could be the work of Masaccio because of "her hand, which seems to explore the depth of the picture space."

Two Masaccio documents of minor but specific interest — a payment of 2 lire on Oct. 6, 1422, to the steward of the Arte dei Medici e Speziali and the enrollment in 1424 in the Compagnia di S. Luca — are very important in establishing chronology. Another document is the commission by Ser

Giuliano di Colino degli Scarsi da San Giusto for Masaccio to paint a large altarpiece for a chapel in S. Maria del Carmine at Pisa for the sum of 80 florins. The commission is dated Feb. 19, 1426. The execution of the altarpiece, according to the testimony of the various payments on account, including the closing one, continued until Dec. 26, 1426.

The Pisan polyptych was dismembered and dispersed in the 18th century; to date 11 parts have been found and identified in museums and private collections. The discoveries of *The Virgin and Child Enthroned* (PL. 344), now in the National Gallery, London (Berenson saw it in 1907 in the Sutton Collection of Brant Broughton, Lincolnshire, labeled with the name of Gentile da Fabriano), and the *Crucifixion* (PL. 343), now in the Museo di Capodimonte, Naples (Wilhelm Suida, 1906; Venturi, 1911), were essential for the partial reconstruction of the work. The other parts are: *St. Paul* (PL. 342) in the Museo Nazionale, Pisa (related to the polyptych by Cavalcaselle, who, despite the traditional attribution to Masaccio, saw in it the hand of Andrea di Giusto); *St. Andrew*, Lanckoronski Collection, Vienna (Schmarsow); and in Berlin (Staat. Mus.), four small figures of saints (Schubring) and three parts of the predella containing five scenes: *Adoration of the Magi* (PL. 346; Cavalcaselle), *Crucifixion of St. Peter* and *Beheading of the Baptist* (PL. 346), and *Scenes from the Life of St. Julian* and the *Miracle of St. Nicholas* (von Hadeln, with an attribution to Andrea di Giusto).

In the 15th century Antonio Manetti recorded that Masaccio had worked in Pisa, and in his *Vite* Vasari described the work in some detail: "In a chapel in the church of the Carmine at Pisa there is a painting of the Madonna and Child with angels at their feet playing musical instruments. One of them is giving rapt attention to the harmony he is producing. St. Peter and St. John the Baptist are on one side of the Virgin, and St. Julian and St. Nicholas on the other. On the predella beneath are little scenes from the lives of these saints; in the center is an Adoration of Christ. There are horses in this part of the work which are so beautiful that nothing better could be desired. The persons of the train of the three Magi are dressed in the fashionable clothes of the time. Over all are various Saints in several compartments, placed around a Crucifix." Upon this description — which is the only source — is based all research regarding the tentative reconstruction, the location, and the identification of the various parts.

A graphic scheme of the ensemble — made before the discovery of the London *Virgin and Child Enthroned* — was published by Suida in 1906. The most exact and reasoned reconstruction is that of Salmi (1932 and 1947), who has put forth an interesting hypothesis concerning the still missing lateral panels: the SS. Peter and John the Baptist and the SS. Julian and Nicholas. He suggests that an approximate idea of their appearance can be drawn from the two panels in the Museo Bandini at Fiesole by Giovanni del Ponte (Giovanni di Marco), which, in spite of Gothic-Ghibertian accents, are unquestionably inspired by Masaccio, or from the four saints that flank the Virgin and Child in a Louvre terra cotta attributed to Luca della Robbia. With the exception of two predella scenes — the *St. Julian* and *St. Nicholas* in Berlin, which all scholars agree are workshop pieces by Andrea di Giusto or by Scheggia — the extant panels of the polyptych are generally accepted as Masaccio's. Cavalcaselle, Bode, and Poggi, however, assign the *St. Paul* of Pisa (PL. 342) to Andrea di Giusto.

It is important to note that in 1426 Donatello was also in Pisa, where he was working with Michelozzo on the monument of Cardinal Rinaldo Brancacci for the Church of S. Angelo a Nilo in Naples. Documents prove Donatello's presence on July 24 and Dec. 18 of that year, when payments were made to Masaccio for the Carmine polyptych.

Critics have noted various relationships in Masaccio's early work to the sculpture of Donatello. Donatello's influence is certainly a major factor in Masaccio's first experiments with perspective and modeling, from the triptych of S. Giovenale, as Berti has pointed out, to *The Tribute Money* (PL. 348) — from the initial flattened perspective to the open three-dimensional space of the architecture and the grouping in *The Raising of the Son of Theophilus* and *The Trinity* (PL. 345) in the Brancacci Chapel of S. Maria Novella, Florence, with their Brunelleschian perspective.

Donatello's influence, particularly in the central part of the Pisan polyptych and the *Crucifixion* above it, has been pointed out by Salmi, who found a relationship especially in Masaccio's manner of accentuating contrasts in his modeling, frequently stressing the contours with light in the fashion of Donatello. One can see, even in the triptych of 1422, that it was through Donatello that Masaccio entered the Renaissance.

Scholars tend to believe that before the Pisan polyptych Masaccio painted the great fresco of the *Sagra del Carmine* in the cloister of S. Maria del Carmine in Florence. The *Sagra* was destroyed toward the end of the 16th century, when a new cloister was constructed. It represented the consecration of the church on Apr. 19, 1422, and is recorded in the 15th-century sources (Manetti and Billi), as well as by Vasari, who spoke of it as one of Masaccio's masterpieces. There are 16th-century drawings that partially reproduce the groups of figures in the great procession filing by the church. Fiocco believed that an over-all idea of the *Sagra* might be given by *The Consecration of S. Egidio*, which Bicci di Lorenzo painted on the façade of that church in Florence and which, in Fiocco's opinion, was inspired by the *Sagra*. Salmi opposed this hypothesis on the grounds that Bicci's composition failed to demonstrate any relationship between the figures and the space and neglected the principles of perspective so clearly defined in Vasari's description of the Masaccio work. Salmi places the *Sagra* fresco at about 1425 because it included Lorenzo Ridolfi, who was "in those times," according to Vasari, Florentine ambassador to Venice. This dating seems reasonable, although a date of 1424, if not earlier, has also been advanced by Procacci. Berti seems to find in the *Sagra* the most plausible and logical point of departure for the collaboration between Masolino and Masaccio in the Brancacci Chapel.

Three paintings — two portraits and a Madonna — are placed by some scholars in direct relationship with the *Sagra*, both as to date and to the personages portrayed. Others, however, rule these works out of the strict listing of Masaccio's œuvre. The first of the portraits is a young man in profile in the National Gallery, Washington, D.C., first attributed to Masaccio in the 19th century and since renominated by Salmi (Schmarsow proposed Masolino or Paolo Uccello). The second portrait is a profile of a man in the Isabella Stewart Gardner Museum, Boston, first attributed to Masaccio by Berenson. The attribution is accepted by a majority of the scholars, the exceptions being Langton Douglas, Giglioli, and Mesnil; Salmi related it to the two attendants on the left in the fresco *St. Peter Baptizing* (Brancacci Chapel) and suggested, with reference to the *Sagra*, a date of 1425 for its execution. Also from Salmi is the supposition that this portrait is the one cited by Vasari as being in the house of Simone Corsi. The third work, *The Madonna of Humility* in the National Gallery, Washington, D.C., was attributed to Masaccio by Berenson (1929) and dated not later than 1425, that is, before the Madonna of the Pisan polyptych. In general the critics agree that it is by Masaccio and are inclined to date it prior to 1424, as suggested by Salmi. However, L. Venturi placed it closer in time to the fresco of Montemarciano; and Longhi, because of its poor state of preservation and extensive modern restoration, did not attempt to date it. Because of this restoration Procacci stated that no judgment was possible before removal of the repainting which covers the entire surface of the panel. In any case, the elements of its composition seemed, in Procacci's view, to exclude any possibility that it could have been conceived by Masaccio.

The *Scenes from the Life of St. Julian* (Florence, Fondazione Horne), although in bad condition, is nevertheless fairly distinct, and most scholars uphold the attribution to Masaccio. It is the relationship of the *St. Julian* to the Carnesecchi triptych of S. Maria Maggiore in Florence (see MASOLINO) that divides the art historians. Longhi considered the *St. Julian* to be a first version of the same subject for the predella of the Pisan polyptych, later discarded because of the patrons' dissatisfaction.

Salmi rejects this theory, as well as the proposition that it belonged to the S. Maria Maggiore triptych, because it does not completely correspond to the description given by Vasari, and because its dimensions would have necessitated the elimination from the predella of an episode of the legend of St. Nicholas — which, given the presence of this saint in one of the compartments of the triptych, could not have been left out. Procacci returned to the hypothesis propounded by Gamba that credence should be given to Vasari's statement (first edition of the *Vite*) that only the predella of the S. Maria Maggiore triptych was by Masaccio. Among the elements suggested as having belonged to the triptych, some scholars propose the St. Julian predella panel in the Musée Ingres in Montauban, which is a certain work of Masolino.

After the document of Dec. 26, 1426, which records the final payment for the polyptych of Pisa, no other record appears until July 29, 1427, the day on which Masaccio and his brother registered a property declaration. At about this time — some think 1426 and others later — Masaccio began work in the Brancacci Chapel. As previously mentioned, Berti has convincingly proposed a new chronology for the Brancacci Chapel frescoes. He advances the theory that the beginning of the collaboration of Masaccio and Masolino was sometime before August, 1425. Masolino himself may have recommended Masaccio to the monks or to the patron. As Masolino had to leave Florence on Sept. 1, 1425, for Hungary (Procacci), he did not wish to leave the work in the chapel completely abandoned; he had himself already completed the frescoes in the vault and those of the upper sections of the wall. It is probable that the substitution of Masaccio was accepted with good grace by the monks and the patron because, as noted above, he had perhaps already painted the *Sagra* fresco in the cloister. On this assumption the following chronology would result: From the first months of 1425 until August of the same year, Masaccio's work on *St. Peter Baptizing, The Expulsion from the Garden of Eden* (PL. 350), and *The Tribute Money* (PLS. 348, 349) paralleled Masolino's execution of *The Preaching of St. Peter* and *The Original Sin*; and Masolino, aided by Masaccio, painted the fresco of St. Peter healing a cripple and raising Tabitha. From the latter part of 1425 and into 1426 Masaccio painted *St. Peter Healing the Sick with His Shadow* and *SS. Peter and John Distributing Alms* (PL. 347). Masolino was in Hungary the entire year of 1426, not returning to Italy until July, 1427, and Masaccio left the Brancacci Chapel during 1426 to work on the Pisan polyptych. Since the monks of the Carmine also commissioned the polyptych, it was probably easy for Masaccio to obtain permission to leave the Brancacci Chapel. (Salmi has pointed out that the assistant prior of the Pisan monks at that time was a Florentine, Fra Bartolomeo da Firenze.) In 1427 Masaccio worked on *The Raising of the Son of Theophilus*, which was left unfinished.

Except for minor variations, the sequence given above is basically the same as the one first proposed by Salmi and generally accepted. Although Salmi accepted 1425 as the beginning of the collaboration of Masaccio and Masolino, perhaps on one of the wall lunettes, now destroyed, he placed the *St. Peter Baptizing* in 1426, *The Expulsion from the Garden of Eden, The Tribute Money,* and *St. Peter Healing the Sick with His Shadow* in 1427, and *SS. Peter and John Distributing Alms* and *The Raising of the Son of Theophilus* in 1427–28.

Procacci's chronology differs substantially from the proposals of Salmi and Berti. He maintains that until about Sept. 1, 1425, Masolino worked alone on the vault and the upper tier (both destroyed during the redecoration of 1748). Procacci believes that all work on the chapel was suspended during the entire period of Masolino's absence and was not resumed until about August, 1427. Then began the collaboration between Masolino and Masaccio, after which Masaccio continued alone until the autumn of 1428, when he left Florence for Rome. Procacci's theory regarding the fresco sequence also diverges from those of Berti and Salmi. He established the following order: *St. Peter Baptizing, The Tribute Money, The Expulsion from the Garden of Eden* (which seems more logical for technical reasons related to the use of scaffolding and follows a more precise work plan), *SS. Peter and John Distributing Alms, St. Peter Heals a Cripple and Raises Tabitha,* and *The Raising of the Son of Theophilus*. He posits that the first three frescoes were painted by Masaccio — with Masolino working beside him — and the last three by Masaccio after Masolino had left for Rome.

Scholars today are in agreement, barring a few exceptions to be discussed below, as to Filippino Lippi's part in the Brancacci Chapel as distinguished from the work of Masaccio and Masolino. This agreement has been arrived at through a new appraisal of the first edition of Vasari's text, as well as through the undertaking of more precise studies and a resulting increase of knowledge. A definite contribution has been made toward the solution of one of the most debated problems in 19th- and early-20th-century art criticism.

Other divergences of opinion concerning chronology arise over presumed intermediate or antecedent trips to Rome taken by Masaccio with Masolino. Longhi believed that after a period of work together in S. Maria del Carmine in 1424–25, they went to Rome in 1425, during the Jubilee; that they both worked in Rome on the Chapel of St. Catherine in S. Clemente and later on the triptych (painted on both sides) for S. Maria Maggiore. In 1427, according to Longhi, Masaccio returned to Florence to work alone in the Brancacci Chapel.

Although the theories of Schmarsow and Oertel regarding the Brancacci Chapel are inadmissible, their two systematic studies of Masaccio should be mentioned. Schmarsow saw in the Brancacci frescoes a demonstration of two modes of painting, which he explained as a well-defined stylistic evolution in Masaccio's work. Schmarsow believed the whole fresco cycle to be by Masaccio (under Masolino's influence) and dated it before 1422, preceding the other known works, which he arranged chronologically from 1426. Oertel considered Masaccio to be a pupil of Lorenzo Monaco and believed that he painted the *Madonna* of Bremen (Kunsthalle) in 1423 (yet even if the numerous objections by the majority of scholars to this attribution were not sufficient, the publication of the S. Giovenale altarpiece clearly reveals its impossibility). Oertel established the following chronology: 1422–23, the Roman works now generally agreed to be by Masolino (excepting some minor contributions by Masaccio); 1424–25, the early frescoes (actually by Masolino) in the Brancacci Chapel; 1427, completion of the Brancacci Chapel frescoes following Masaccio's return to Florence, after painting the Pisan altarpiece.

The Carmine frescoes, which were noted by all the 15th-century sources, were, according to Vasari, commissioned by Antonio Brancacci, but through documents discovered by modern scholars (M. Amari, D. Catellacci, C. Carnesecchi, H. Brockhaus) the true name of the patron was found to be Felice di Michele Brancacci. Toward the end of the 17th century all the frescoes were in danger of being destroyed as a result of a reconstruction scheme planned for the whole chapel. That they were saved was due to Vittoria della Rovere, widow of Ferdinand II and mother of the Grand Duke Cosimo II, to whom members of the Accademia del Disegno, together with many others, turned for help.

Later, between 1746 and 1748, during the partial redecoration, Masolino's frescoes in the vault and in the lunettes were demolished and replaced by new decorations by Vincenzo Meucci and Carlo Sacconi. A new marble altar was erected, a large rectangular window replaced the former two-lighted window, and the Gothic arch over the entrance, perhaps decorated by Masolino, was modified with a semicircular arch. During the night of Jan. 28, 1771, fire raged in the church (Procacci gives a precise account), but the chapel frescoes were saved, only two pieces of plaster falling from the left wall where *The Tribute Money* and *The Raising of the Son of Theophilus* are located. The frescoes were, however, much blackened by the smoke, a condition recently confirmed when two marble projections were removed from either side of the altar, revealing small areas of the painting as it was originally, in Masaccio's *St. Peter Baptizing* and *The Preaching of St. Peter* by Masolino. In these areas the colors, with their luminous whites, appear much clearer, in striking contrast to the other painted surfaces, which have a rather leaden tonality. Cleaning of the entire chapel should reveal the true chromatic values and luminosity of the frescoes.

The identification of *St. Peter Baptizing* as the first fresco Masaccio painted in the chapel is unquestioned (excluding the previously noted theories of Schmarsow and Oertel and the confusion surrounding Masaccio and Masolino in the 19th century). Longhi and Salmi, however, believed that Filippino Lippi repainted the head of St. Peter, and Longhi would also have included the heads of the two young men behind the saint. Procacci refuted Longhi's theory with persuasive technical reasons. In his view the three heads were painted by Masolino.

The Tribute Money (PLS. 348, 349) is the key fresco, the one that has in general received the highest praise: from Vasari, who stressed the psychological aspect of the personages portrayed, and Cavalcaselle, for whom it marked the opening of the High Renaissance — that is, of the compositional balance of Raphael and Fra Bartolommeo — down to the most recent scholars who have studied it exhaustively for its dating, its innovations, its sources, its achievements, and its connections. Most scholars consider it completely by Masaccio's hand, but Lindberg believed that the figure of St. Peter, seen on the left as he removes the money from the fish's mouth — an area of the highest quality — was the work of Andrea di Giusto. More recently Longhi advanced the theory that the head of Christ, which is less strongly modeled, was the work of Masolino, who painted only this head before he left the work in 1424. Salmi rejected this theory, agreeing with Toesca's earlier opinion that Masaccio had attempted to paint Christ's face in the manner of Masolino but the results only superficially suggest Masolino. Salmi's hypothesis is supported by a technical analysis of the fresco surface and the sequence of the adjacent painted areas, which exclude Longhi's thesis. The fresco depicts in a continuous narrative three episodes of Christ's entrance into Capernaum (Matt. 17:24–27).

The Expulsion from the Garden of Eden (PL. 350) is completely autographic except for the leaves around the loins of the nude figures and a few other areas of retouching and repainting of the surface. There are evident traces of restoration in the architrave and in the lower area of *St. Peter Healing the Sick with His Shadow* (Acts 5:12–16), which is also completely by Masaccio. Vasari stated that the man wearing a red headdress between the saint and the man standing in prayer is a portrait of Masolino, although this has not been proved.

It is also probable that the bearded man between the two saints in *SS. Peter and John Distributing Alms* (PL. 347) is also a portrait of Masolino. This fresco (cf. Acts 4:32–37 and 5:1–6) is also an autographic work. Except for a large part of the figure of Ananias, which has been redone, the fresco is one of the best-preserved in the chapel. Salmi believes the last profile on the right to be that of Masaccio's brother.

The iconography of *The Raising of the Son of Theophilus* with *St. Peter in Cathedra* (PL. 347) is derived from an episode in the *Golden Legend* (xliv), and the separation of the sections painted by Masaccio from those painted by Filippino Lippi has long been a subject of dispute. It was Cavalcaselle who, after Vasari, accurately noted that the central group was painted by Filippino. The group on the left he attributed to Filippino, except for the profile head of the Carmelite, which he gave to Masaccio. Although the group is composed of five figures, only eight feet are shown; this anomaly, together with the strange isolation from the rest of the group of the figure painted by Masaccio, would suggest the acceptance, at least in part, of Brockhaus's theory that the entire scene was painted by Masaccio and that in 1436 the sections containing portraits of the Brancacci were destroyed when the family was declared rebel and exiled by Cosimo de' Medici. It seems more probable, however, that Masaccio, although leaving the fresco unfinished, had painted in this section figures (perhaps portraits of the Brancacci) which were destroyed at a subsequent period and that the space was thereafter filled in by Filippino with other portraits of noted personages.

Filippino's contribution, dated in accordance with Berti as 1481–83 rather than 1484–88, can be readily observed in the rest of the fresco: it consists of the eight figures to the right in the central scene of the miracle, comprising the figures from the Carmelite in profile to the figure in green with the cap; in addition, the lower part of the fresco, which includes the resurrected boy, the child next to him, the clothing of the figure in green, the body of St. Paul and the raised hand of St. Peter, and, probably the paneled wall behind the figures. The head at the extreme right seems to be neither by Masaccio nor Filippino but rather a later addition, perhaps of the early 19th century, or quite possibly painted following the fire of 1771. Filippino's well-placed and unified figures might be explained by Salmi's hypothesis that he used the sinopias drawn by Masaccio on the plaster.

Some scholars give Masaccio a share in sections of the frescoes painted by Masolino. Among several of such theories the most tenable is that of Longhi; reviving a hypothesis of Gamba, he maintained that Masaccio had executed the architectural background of the square and the small figures that enliven it in the scenes where St. Peter heals a cripple and raises Tabitha. Salmi and Procacci (in part) concur in Longhi's attribution. The suggestion is also put forth by Longhi that in *The Preaching of St. Peter* Masaccio painted the figure of the saint and the three young men behind him.

The attribution to Masaccio of *The Birth Plate* (Berlin, Staat. Mus.), was made at a relatively late date, 1834, when the work formed part of the Ciampi Collection at San Giovanni Valdarno. It may be dated about 1427, after the Pisan altarpiece. G. Morelli assigned it to Andrea di Giusto, but E. Müntz reaffirmed the attribution to Masaccio. Not all scholars concur: Brandi gives it to Domenico di Bartolo, Ragghianti to Domenico Veneziano, and Procacci, without specifying an artist, dates it to the fourth decade of the 15th century, that is, after Masaccio's death. Lindberg, accepting the work as by Masaccio, dated it 1425 because the lost Annunciation for S. Niccolò oltr'Arno, which he assigned to the same year, also had a colonnade in perspective (a thesis which, as Salmi states, is impossible to prove). However, the majority of scholars accept Mesnil's dating of 1427.

If Masaccio's conception of perspective in his early frescoes of the Brancacci Chapel, from *St. Peter Baptizing* to *The Tribute Money*, is derived from that of Donatello as exemplified in the bas-relief of St. George (1419; IV, PL. 242) — as Berti has written in his summary of the most noteworthy deductions by scholars on this theme — the last phase of the Brancacci cycle, *The Raising of the Son of Theophilus*, reveals a grasp of perspective that reflects Brunelleschi's theories. This new awareness of perspective found full realization in *The Trinity, with the Virgin, St. John, and Donors* in S. Maria Novella (PL. 345), painted at the culmination of Masaccio's activity in Florence. Salmi dates it 1427, between *St. Peter Healing the Sick with His Shadow* and *SS. Peter and John Distributing Alms* and *The Raising of the Son of Theophilus*. The scholars have generally accepted this date; Procacci, less plausibly, places it before the entire fresco cycle of the Brancacci Chapel.

The *Trinity* fresco was commissioned by Don Lorenzo Cardoni. The work was first mentioned in the *Libro* of Antonio Billi and subsequently by Albertini, Vasari, and others. After the construction of the altars (1570), it was covered by Vasari's *Madonna of the Rosary*. The *Trinity* came to light again in the second half of the 19th century during the course of the restoration of the 16th-century altars. In 1861 the *Trinity* was detached and transferred to the interior wall of the façade on the left of the main entrance of the church.

Statements in the *Libro* of Antonio Billi, in both surviving versions, as well as the Anonimo Magliabechiano, that an image of Death could be seen at the base of the fresco led Procacci to investigate the wall of the third altar on the left, where the fresco had been originally located. His investigation resulted in the uncovering of the lower section of the fresco, which depicts the skeleton of Adam lying on a tomb between paired columns. The perspective employed in this section corresponded to that of the *Trinity*, which was then redetached and returned to its original location. The two parts are separated by a narrow breach made by the insertion of an altar top into the wall. The question that arose when Procacci supervised the relocation of the fresco, of whether Masaccio had intended the insertion of an altar, has not been discussed in print. But it would seem logical that the fresco originally had an altar painted in perspective in accordance with the rest of the work. It would have been a votive altar, rather than an actual altar, although later, and as yet unpublished, documents note that an actual altar, adapted for liturgical rites, existed in the second half of the 15th century. The present writer believes that the altar top was inserted after the death of Masaccio. That Brunelleschi himself assisted Masaccio in painting the architectural elements of the *Trinity* has long been debated. M. Reymond proposed an intervention by Paolo Uccello. Brunelleschi's participation was strongly championed by J. Kern, accepted by H. Wieleitner and K. Frey, but refuted by Mesnil and Oertel. Although today no one accepts this theory, it is apparent that Masaccio was directly influenced by Brunelleschi's architecture (Salmi cited the Barbadori Chapel in S. Felicita) and by the tabernacle of Donatello and Michelozzo in Orsanmichele (as W. Bode has observed).

Returning to the scaffolding of S. Maria del Carmine after completing the *Trinity* fresco, Masaccio began *The Raising of the Son of Theophilus*, but left it incomplete when Masolino — who presumably was already in Rome in the autumn of 1427 — summoned him to Rome.

Although critics have attempted, on the basis of Vasari's attribution, to identify Masaccio's hand in the S. Clemente frescoes in Rome, the results have been inconclusive (for the hypothesis, see MASOLINO). Also Longhi's recent thesis that in 1425 Masaccio helped in the painting of the *Crucifixion* has not been universally accepted.

Longhi, following a proposal of K. Clark, dates, during this conjectural first visit to Rome, Masaccio's assistance in painting the *SS. Jerome and John the Baptist* on the left side of the S. Maria Maggiore triptych, now in the National Gallery, London. Clark believes that the triptych was begun by Masaccio alone in 1425 and finished by Masolino in 1428. The date proposed by Longhi and Clark for Masaccio's work on the triptych follows Vasari's hypothesis that Masaccio was in Rome during the Jubilee of 1425. Salmi rejects this dating and proposes instead that the whole triptych was done during 1428, explaining as concessions to contemporary Roman taste (Gentile da Fabriano) those stylistic characteristics which seem less developed than in the Pisan polyptych. Procacci, although his first judgment was negative, now seems to agree to a limited participation of Masaccio in the triptych, reinforcing his opinion with reasoning based on quite convincing historical considerations. Brandi also concurs in the attribution to Masaccio.

M. Meiss dates Masaccio's part in the triptych 1422–23, with which F. P. Hartt agrees, maintaining that the work was begun in Florence and finished by Masolino in Rome. Rather than Masaccio, Martin Davies sees in the London panel, among other currents, the influence of Fra Angelico. His dating is in agreement with that of Ulrich Middeldorf, who places it about 1435 and sees in it, besides, a pictorial sensibility suggesting Domenico Veneziano.

When Berti turned to the problem of the London panel, he declared his agreement with Salmi that it was Masaccio's last work. In addition to its moral-physical power, Berti saw in the sloping flowered earth, the leg of John the Baptist, and the book in perspective with curling leaves, the extreme refinement that entered Florentine painting much later in the work of Domenico Veneziano, Fra Angelico, and Andrea del Castagno.

Of the vast catalogue of works formerly attributed to Masaccio — and some still attributed to him — those that are no longer seriously considered by the critics are not included here. However, the small *Madonna and Child* exhibited among the art works recovered from Germany should be mentioned, as it is under study. Longhi attributed it to the youthful period.

Reference has been made above to the *Sagra* of S. Maria del Carmine in Florence and the missing panels of the Pisan polyptych (St. Peter and St. John the Baptist, St. Julian and St. Nicholas) and to other figures as works now lost that had been cited by 15th-century sources as well as by Vasari. To this group should be added: a fresco of St. Paul, also from S. Maria del Carmine, lost in 1675 when a new chapel was erected in honor of St. Andrea Corsini; St. Yves of Brittany, a fresco in the Church of the Badia, detached from the wall in 1625 and since disappeared; a panel painting of the Annunciation for the Church of S. Niccolò (its identification with the *Annunciation* in the National Gallery in Washington, D.C., is not convincing, as it does not correspond to Vasari's detailed description); two panels of St. Peter and St. Paul and a birth plate with a combat scene listed in the inventory drawn up at the death of Lorenzo the Magnificent in 1492; a portrait of Bartolomeo Valori and other portraits, cited by Vasari as being in the house of Simone Corsi; a Last Judgment (?) fresco from the monastery of S. Maria degli Angeli, cited by Albertini; a panel of a nude man and woman, cited by Vasari as in the Palazzo Rucellai; a panel depicting Christ healing the possessed man, cited as in the collection of Ridolfo Ghirlandajo (an identification has been suggested with the small panel attributed to Andrea di Giusto in Philadelphia, Mus. of Art, Johnson Coll.).

SOURCES. A. Manetti, Vite di XIV uomini singhulary in Firenze dal MCCCC innanzi, in G. Milanesi, ed., Operette istoriche... di A. Manetti, Florence, 1887, pp. 159–68; L. B. Alberti, A Filippino di Ser Brunellesco: Dedicatoria del Trattato della pittura (Codex Magliabechiano, IV, 38, 1436); A. Billi, Il libro di Antonio Billi, 1481–1530, ed. C. von Fabriczy, ASI, ser. 5, VII, 1891, ed. K. Frey, Berlin, 1892; La Divina Comedia di Dante Alighieri, col commento..., Florence, 1481, c. 5; F. Albertini, Memoriale di molte statue et picture... di Florentia, Florence, 1510; Vasari; R. Borghini, Il Riposo, Florence, 1584; F. Bocchi, Le bellezze della città di Fiorenza, Florence, 1591 (new enlarged ed. by G. Cinelli, Florence, 1677).

BIBLIOG. F. Monti and G. Tancredi, Masaccio, Rome, 1662; P. Coccapani, Descrizione della festa per la solenne traslazione del corpo di Sant'Andrea Corsini, Rome, 1675; F. Deseine, Nouveau voyage en Italie, II, Lyon, 1699; F. Baldinucci, Notizie de' professori del disegno, III, Florence, 1728, pp. 70–86; G. Richa, Notizie istoriche delle chiese fiorentine, X, Florence, 1762; J. Richard, Description historique et critique de l'Italie, III, Dijon, 1766, p. 49; T. Patch, The Life of Masaccio, Florence, 1770; G. Pelli, Elogio di Masaccio, in Elogi degli uomini illustri toscani, II, Florence, 1782, pp. 14–19; V. Fineschi, Il forestiero istruito in S. Maria Novella, Florence, 1790; L. Lanzi, Storia pittorica dell'Italia, 2d ed., I, Bassano, 1795, pp. 51–53; G. Dall'Armi, Le pitture di Masaccio esistenti in Roma, Rome, 1809; J. B. Séroux d'Agincourt, Histoire de l'art par les monuments, III, Paris, 1823, pp. 145–48; K. F. von Rumohr, Italienische Forschungen, Berlin, Stettin, 1827, pp. 243–51 (ed. J. Schlosser, Frankfurt am Main, 1920, pp. 376–81); A. Nibby, Itinerario di Roma, Rome, 1830; M. Valéry, Voyages historiques, III, Paris, 1832, p. 127; F. Gherardi-Dragomanni, Memorie della terra di S. Giovanni nel Valdarno superiore, Florence, 1834; J. W. Gaye, Carteggio, I, Florence, 1839, pp. 115–17, II, Florence, 1840, pp. 469–73; A. M. Jameson, Memoirs of the Early Italian Painters, 2 vols., London, 1845; M. Missirini, Masaccio, Florence, 1846; F. D. Kugler, Handbuch der Geschichte der Malerei, Berlin, 1847, pp. 304–98; C. Milanesi and others, Sulle pitture della Cappella Brancacci, in Le Vite del Vasari, III, Florence, 1848, pp. 165–91; A. Reumont, Kapelle Brancacci: Masaccio und Filippino, Kunstblatt, Stuttgart, Tübingen, 1848, p. 117; E. Breton, Notice sur Tommaso Guidi dit Masaccio, Saint-Germain-en-Laye, 1850; J. Burckhardt, Der Cicerone, Basel, 1855, pp. 798–99 (ed. W. von Bode and C. von Fabriczy, Leipzig, 1910, p. 683); A. H. Springer, Handbuch der Kunstgeschichte, Stuttgart, 1855 (It. ed. by C. Ricci, Bergamo, 1913, pp. 105–14); F. Fantozzi, Nuova guida di Firenze, Florence, 1856, p. 706; P. Selvatico, Storia estetico-critica delle arti del disegno, Venice, 1856, pp. 333–38; G. Milanesi, Le vite di alcuni artefici fiorentini scritte da G. Vasari, Giorn. storico degli arch. toscani, IV, 1860, pp. 194–96; A. F. Rio, De l'art chrétien, I, Paris, 1861, pp. 344–49; A. F. Rio, Interno della Chiesa di S. Maria Novella dopo i restauri fatti nel 1861, Florence, 1861; A. F. Rio, Intorno ai lavori di S. Maria Novella, Florence, 1861, p. 2; M. Amari, I diplomi arabi del R. Archivio fiorentino, Florence, 1863; J. A. Crowe and G. B. Cavalcaselle, A New History of Painting in Italy, I, London, 1864, pp. 519–50 (new ed. by L. Douglas and G. De Nicola, IV, London, 1911, pp. 34–65); A. H. Layard, The Brancacci Chapel, London, 1868; P. Santi Mattei, Ragionamento intorno alla antica chiesa del Carmine di Firenze, Florence, 1869, pp. 40–60; A. Zahn, Masolino und Masaccio, Jhb. für Kw., II, 1869, pp. 155–71; W. Lübke, Masolino und Masaccio, Jhb. für Kw., III, 1870, pp. 280–86; A. Reumont, Die Kapelle der h. Katharina in S. Clemente zu Rom, Jhb. für Kw., III, 1870, pp. 75–79; H. Delaborde, Des oeuvres et de la manière de Masaccio, GBA, XIV, 1876, pp. 369–84; M. Thaussing, Masaccio und Masolino in der Brancacci Kapelle, ZfbK, XI, 1876, pp. 225–38; C. Pini and G. Milanesi, La scrittura di artisti italiani, I, 14, Florence, 1877; J. A. Symonds, Renaissance in Italy: The Fine Arts, London, 1877, pp. 229–31; Vasari, II, pp. 305–25; D. Catellacci, Diario di Felice Brancacci, ASI, VII, 1881, pp. 157–88; A. Woltmann and K. Woermann, Geschichte der Malerei, II, Leipzig, 1882, pp. 138–51; J. P. Richter, Notes on Vasari, London, 1885; W. Lübke, Essai d'histoire de l'art, II, Paris, 1887, pp. 158–60; L. Tanfani-Centofani, Donatello in Pisa, Pisa, 1887; E. Müntz, Les collections des Médicis, Paris, 1888, pp. 58, 62, 86; T. Cole, Masaccio, Century Mag., XVI, 1889, p. 659; E. Müntz, Histoire de l'art pendant la Renaissance, I, Paris, 1889, pp. 336, 612–19; W. J. Stillman, Masaccio, Century Mag., XVI, 1889, pp. 653–59; F. Wickhoff, Die Fresken der Katharinen Kapelle in S. Clemente zu Rom, ZfbK, XXIV, 1889, pp. 301–10; Early Italian Art in the New Gallery (exhibition cat.), London, 1893–94; I. Lermolieff (G. Morelli), Kunstkritische Studien über italienische Malerei, Leipzig, 1893; A. Cocchi, Notizie storiche, Florence, 1894, pp. 57–60; E. Müntz, Les plateaux d'accouchées, MPiot, I, 1894, pp. 203–32; A. Schmarsow, Masaccio-Studien, 5 vols., Kassel, 1895–99; B. Berenson, Florentine Painters of the Renaissance, New York, London, 1896 (2d ed. 1909); A. Philippi, Die Kunst der Renaissance in Italien, I, Leipzig, 1897, pp. 187–205; L. Tanfani-Centofani, Notizie di artisti tratte da documenti pisani, Pisa, 1898, pp. 176–80; W. Bode, Donatello als Architekt und Decorator, JhbPreussKSamml, XXII, 1901, pp. 3–28; M. Creutz, Masaccio, Berlin, 1901; A. Filangeri di Candida, Un quadro acquistato dalla Galleria del Museo Nazionale di Napoli, L'Arte, IV, 1901, pp. 74–75; B. Marrai, Il tabernacolo col gruppo del Verrocchio in Orsanmichele, L'Arte, IV, 1901, pp. 346–52; W. Weisbach, Der Meister des Carrandschen Triptychons, JhbPreussKSamml, XXII, 1901, pp. 35–55; A. Bayersdorfer, Masaccio und Filippino Fresken in der Brancacci Kapelle, Munich, 1902, pp. 56–58; B. Berenson, The Study and Criticism of Italian Art, London, 1902, pp. 77–89; C. de Fabriczy, Ancora del tabernacolo col gruppo del Verrocchio in Orsanmichele, L'Arte, V, 1902, pp. 46–48, 336–40; A. H. Layard, The Italian Schools of Painting, I, London, 1902, pp. 140–46; J. B. Supino and B. Marrai, Ancora del tabernacolo col gruppo del Verrocchio in Orsanmichele, L'Arte, V, 1902, pp. 185–89; I. Wood Brown, The Dominican Church of Santa Maria Novella, Edinburgh, 1902; C. Carnesecchi, Messer Felice Brancacci, in Misc. d'arte, Florence, 1903, pp. 38–40; P. D'Ancona, La tavola di Masaccio ora nella R. Galleria di Belle Arti, Misc. d'arte, Florence, 1903, pp. 174–77; J. Del Badia, Masaccio e suo fratello, Florence, 1903; B. Marrai, Il tabernacolo col gruppo del Verrocchio in Orsanmichele, RArte, I, 1903, pp. 36–38; G. Poggi, La tavola di Masaccio per il Carmine di Pisa, Misc. d'arte, Florence, 1903, pp. 182–89; G. Magherini-Graziani, Masaccio: Ricordo delle onoranze rese in S. Giovanni Valdarno nel dì 25 ottobre 1903, Florence, 1904; M. Marasse, Masaccio und S. Clemente in Rom, Die Kunst-Halle, IX, 1904, pp. 257–90; R. Pantini, La Cappella della Passione in S. Clemente a Roma, Emporium, X, 1904, pp. 31–52; A. Chiappelli, Pagina d'antica arte fiorentina, Florence, 1905, pp. 97–105; V. Leonardi, Affreschi dimenticati del tempo di Martino V, Atti Cong. int. di sc. storiche, Rome, 1905, pp. 286–308; M. Reymond, L'architecture des peintres aux premières de la Renaissance, Rev. de l'art ancien et mod., IX, 1905, pp. 41–42, 48–50; P. Schubring, Cassoni, Leipzig, 1905, pp. 84, 104, 238; G. Sortais, Masaccio et la chapelle Brancacci, Ét., LIV, 1905, pp. 343–71; P. Schubring, Notizie di Berlino, L'Arte, IX, 1906, pp. 384–87; W. Suida, L'Altare di Masaccio già nel Carmine a Pisa, L'Arte, IX, 1906, pp. 125–27; B. Berenson, La scoperta di un dipinto di Masaccio, Rass. d'arte, VII, 1907, p. 139; B. Berenson, La Madonna pisana di Masaccio, Rass. d'arte, VIII, 1908, pp. 81–85; D. F. von Hadeln, Andrea di Giusto und das dritte Predellen Stuck von Pisanischen Altarwerk des Masaccio, Mnh. für Kw., I, 1908, pp. 785–89; F. X. Kraus, Geschichte der christlichen Kunst, II, Freiburg am Breisgau, 1908, pp. 180–84; R. Pantini, Masaccio, The Connoisseur, XIX, 1908, pp. 25–28, 87–90; A. Peraté, Histoire de l'art, III, Paris, 1908, pp. 597–600; P. Toesca, Masolino da Panicale, Bergamo, 1908, pp. 22–36, 70–72; L. Justi, Die italienische Malerei des XV. Jahrhunderts, Berlin, 1909, pp. 13–23; R. Muther, Geschichte der Malerei, I, Leipzig, 1909, pp. 92–98; J. Reynolds, Discours sur la peinture (ed. and trans. L. Dimier), Paris, 1909; Venturi, VII, 1, pp. 86,113–26; A. De Rinaldis, La Pinacoteca del Museo Nazionale di Napoli, Naples, 1911, pp. 14–19; R. Fry, Exhibition of Old Masters at the Grafton Galleries, BM, XX, 1911, pp. 66–77; J. Mesnil, Per la storia della Cappella Brancacci, RArte, VIII, 1912, pp. 34–40; K. Woermann, Masaccio und Masolino (1880), in Von Apelles zu Böcklin und weiter, I, Esslingen, 1912, pp. 41–48; G. J. Kern, Das Dreifaltigkeits Fresko in S. Maria Novella, JhbPreussKSamml, XXXIV, 1913, pp. 36–58; J. Mesnil, La fresque de la Trinité . . . , B. de l'art ancien et mod., XV, 1913, pp. 223–24; J. Mesnil, Masaccio et la théorie de la perspective, Rev. de l'art ancien et mod., XXXV, 1914, pp. 145–56; C. Gamba, Il Palazzo e la raccolta Horne a Firenze, Dedalo, I, 1920, pp. 162–85; H. Wieleitner, Zur Erfindung der verschiedenen Distanzkonstruktionen in der malerischen Perspektive, RepfKw, XLII, 1920, pp. 249–62; W. Bode, Beschreibendes Verzeichnis der Gemälde im Kaiser-Friedrich Museum, Berlin, Leipzig, 1921, pp. 272–73; O. H. Giglioli, Masaccio, Florence, 1921; K. Escher, Malerei der Renaissance in Italien, I, Berlin, 1922, pp. 35–46; W. Bode, Die Kunst der Frührenaissance in Italien, Berlin, 1923, pp. 34–35; S. Popovich, Conception of Space in Old Masters, BM, XLIV, 1924, pp. 222–28; E. Somaré, Masaccio, Milan, 1924; J. Mesnil, Die Kunstlehre der Frührenaissance im Werke Masaccios, Vorträge der Bib. Warburg, 1925–26, pp. 122–46; A. Schmarsow, Neue Beiträge zu Masolino und Masaccio, Belvedere, VII, 1925, pp. 145–57; H. Beenken, Masaccio, Belvedere, IX–X, 1926, pp. 167–78; A. Chiappelli, Un capolavoro antico sotto nuova luce, Marzocco, Florence, June 20, 1926; M. Dvořák, Geschichte der italienischen Kunst, I, Munich, 1927, pp. 47–62; R. Longhi, Piero della Francesca, Rome, 1927, pp. 15–18, 21–22, 75; J. Mesnil, Masaccio et les débuts de la Renaissance, The Hague, 1927 (rev. M. Pittaluga, Belvedere, VIII, 1929, pp. 240–43); O. J. Rusconi, Masolino e Masaccio, Marzocco, Florence, April 15, 1928; A. Schmarsow, Masolino und Masaccio, Leipzig, 1928; Van Marle, X, pp. 251–307; H. Beenken, Zum Werke des Masaccio, ZfbK, LXIII, 1929–30, pp. 112–19, 156–65; B. Berenson, Un nuovo Masaccio, Dedalo, X, 1929, pp. 331–36; O. H. Giglioli. Masaccio, Bergamo, 1929; O. H. Giglioli, Masaccio, B. R. Ist. di Archeol, e Storia dell'Arte, III, 1929, pp. 55–101 (full bibliog.); J. Mesnil, Masolino ou Masaccio?, GBA, I, 1929, pp. 206–09; M. Pittaluga, Masaccio e L. B. Alberti, Rass. it., 3d ser., XXIV, 1929, pp. 779–90; M. Pittaluga, Rinascimento italiano, L'Arte, XXXII, 1929, pp. 90–93; W. Stechow, Zum Masolino-Masaccio Problem, ZfbK, LXIII, 1929–30, pp. 125–127; B. Berenson, A New Masaccio, Art in Am., XVIII, 1930, pp. 45–53; H. Brockhaus, Die Brancacci Kapelle in Florenz, Mitt. des kunsthist. Inst. in Florenz, III, 1930, pp. 160–82; O. H. Giglioli, ThB, s.v.; B. Kleinschmidt, Die Heilige Anna, Düsseldorf, 1930, p. 226; M. Pittaluga, La critica e i valori romantici di Masaccio, L'Arte, N.S., I, 1930, pp. 139–64; A. Schmarsow, Zum Masolino und Masaccio, ZfbK, LXIV, 1930–31, pp. 1–3; L. Venturi, Contributi a Masolino, Lorenzo Salimbeni e Iacopo Bellini, L'Arte, N.S., I, 1930, pp. 166–86; L. Venturi, A Madonna by Masaccio, BM, LVII, 1930, pp. 21–27; H. Lindberg, To the Problem of Masolino and Masaccio, 2 vols., Stockholm, 1931; L. Venturi, Pitture italiane in America, Milan, 1931; H. Beenken, Masaccios und Masolinos Fresken von San Clemente in Rom, Belvedere, XI, 1932, pp. 7–13; J. Mesnil, Vues nouvelles sur l'art de Masaccio, Rev. de l'art ancien et mod., LXII, 1932, pp. 145–62; U. Procacci, L'incendio della chiesa del Carmine, RArte, XIV, 1932, pp. 141–232; M. Salmi, Masaccio, Rome, 1932 (rev. A. Colasanti, Leonardo, III, 1932, pp. 436–38; E. Trenkler, Beiträge zur Masaccio Forschung, Wiener Jhb. für Kg., VIII, 1932, pp. 7–16; A. M. Brizio, L'Arte, N.S., IV, 1933, pp. 147–48; R. W. Kennedy, AB, XVI, 1934, p. 396; 2d ed. Rome, 1947); R. Oertel, Die Frühwerke des Masaccio, Marburger Jhb. für Kw., VII, 1933, pp. 191–289; R. Oertel, Masaccio und der Geschichte der Freskotechnik, JhbPreussKSamml, LV, 1934, pp. 229–40; M. Pittaluga, Masaccio, Florence, 1935; G. Wassermann, Masaccio und Masolino, Strasbourg, 1935; M. Meiss, The Madonna of Humility, AB, XVIII, 1936, pp. 435–64; C. Gamba, Masaccio, Emporium, LXXXIX, 1939, pp. 173–88; R. Longhi, Fatti di Masolino e di Masaccio, CrArte, V, 1940, pp. 145–91; R. Oertel, Wandmalerei und Zeichnung in Italien, Mitt. der kunsthist. Inst. in Florenz, V, 1940, pp. 217–314; M. Salmi, Civiltà fiorentina del primo Rinascimento, Florence, 1943; U. Procacci, Mostra d'opere d'arte trasportate a Firenze durante la guerra e di opere d'arte restaurate, Florence, 1947; K. Steinbart, Masaccio, Vienna, 1948; K. Clark, An Early Quattrocento Triptych from Santa Maria Maggiore, Rome, BM, XCIII, 1951, pp. 339–47; M. Davies, National Gallery Catalogues, London, 1951 (2d ed. 1961); U. Procacci, Tutta la pittura di Masaccio, Milan, 1951 (Eng. trans., P. Colacicchi, New York, 1962); R. Longhi, Presenza di Masaccio nel trittico della Neve, Paragone, III, 25, 1952, pp. 8–16; M. Meiss, London's New Masaccio, AN, LI, 2, 1952, pp. 24–25; J. Pope-Hennessy, The Santa Maria Maggiore Altarpiece, BM, XCIV, 1952, pp. 31–32; M. Salmi, Gli scomparti della Pala di S. Maria Maggiore acquistati dalla National Gallery, Comm, III, 1952, pp. 14–21; U. Procacci, Sulla cronologia delle opere di Masaccio e di Masolino tra il 1425 e il 1428, RArte, XXVIII, 1953, pp. 3–55; U. Baldini, Masaccio, Mostra di 4 Maestri del Primo Rinascimento (exhibition cat.), Florence, 1954; U. Baldini, Restauri dei dipinti fiorentini in occasione della Mostra di quattro maestri del Rinascimento, BArte, XXXIX, 1954, pp. 221–40; C. Brandi, I cinque anni cruciali per la pittura fiorentina del '400, in Studi in onore di M. Marangoni, Pisa, 1957, pp. 169–70; F. Hartt, The Earliest Works of Andrea del Castagno, AB, XLI, 1959, pp. 159–81, 225–36; R. Offner, Masaccio's Classicism, in Studies in the History of Art: Dedicated to W. E. Suida, London, 1959, pp. 66–72; E. Borsook, The Mural Painters of Tuscany, London, 1960; L. Berti, Masaccio 1422, Comm, XII, 1961, pp. 84–107; U. Schlegel, Observations on Masaccio's Trinity Fresco in Santa Maria Novella, AB, XLV, 1963, pp. 19–33.

Umberto BALDINI

Illustrations: PLS. 341–350.

MASKS. There are very few societies, whether ancient or modern, primitive or civilized, in which masks are unknown, for their use springs from instinctive beliefs common to all mankind. For an understanding of the role of masks in art, their meanings and functions must first be known.

The ancient Greek and Latin terms for mask indicate their original classical meaning. The Greek word is *prosōpon* ("face"); the Latin word is *persona* ("mask"), literally, the mask over the face through which (*per-*) the actor sounds forth (*sonat*). The relatively recent word "mask" comes from Italian *maschera*, German *maske*, French *masque*, which derive from Late Latin *masca*, *mascha*, *mascus*, and Arabic *maskharah*. The Arabic word is usually translated "buffoon," but Geoffrey Parrinder states: "The transformation of men into animals is expressed by a special word (*maskh*)" (*Witchcraft*, Harmondsworth, 1958, p. 121). This is of especial interest in the light of the personification, transformation, and identifying function of certain masks, to be discussed below. A mask is frequently called a "false face," but this term applies only to such masks as those worn by members of the Falseface Society of certain northeastern Algonquian Indian tribes and those worn by children for fun, by Halloween merrymakers, at masquerade parties, and the like.

Aside from the meanings of the word "mask" itself, all masks signify whatever they are designed to represent: ancestors, deities, demons, and other supernatural beings, the souls of the dead, spirits of good and evil, spirits of nature, of game animals, of corn and other crops, of rain, of disease, drought, fertility, and abundance, of death. Masks also have represented heroes and characters in drama and story. Funeral masks and theater masks are fully discussed below.

The full meaning of any specific mask, even when one knows what it represents, cannot be revealed or understood apart from its function. The functions of masks might be indicated in general as follows: (1) to evoke certain reactions in the beholder, for instance, awe of the god represented, fear in an enemy, or ecstasy of the wearer, culminating in possession or trance; (2) to cure disease (in men, cattle, crops) by impersonating the supernatural curer, or to dispel disease and evil by exorcising the demons causing them; (3) to impersonate and identify with certain supernatural beings in order to effect some individual or communal good, for instance, fertility (e.g., fecundity of domestic and game animals and of women and crops); (4) to enhance the self, as by wearing the mask of privileged secret societies or by representing clan or family totems or other heraldry; (5) to criticize, and thereby control or alleviate, social wrongs by terrorizing wrongdoers or, by satire and buffoonery, ridiculing them.

SUMMARY. Mythical and ritual origins (col. 521). Antiquity (col. 525): *From the full head to the mask; Heads and masks of deities and other supernatural beings; Funeral masks; Ceremonial masks and ritual masquerades; Theater masks; Apotropaic masks; The fear of masks and death; Ornamental masks.* Folk masks in Europe (col. 530). The modern mask since the Renaissance (col. 538). The Orient (col. 543): *India; China; Japan.* Primitive masks (col. 547): *Africa; South Pacific; The Americas.*

MYTHICAL AND RITUAL ORIGINS. Ceremonial nakedness greatly increases the magico-religious power of woman, and the chief attribute of the Great Mother is her nakedness. In her body, by her body, the goddess reveals the mystery of inexhaustible creation on all levels of life in the cosmos. Every woman shares the essence and the import of the goddess in this archetypal nakedness. The ancient concept involved here has never wholly disappeared, even in very highly evolved religions. For the Hindus, for example, every nude woman incarnates *prakṛti*, nature, matter, the primordial substance, and the prototype of woman.

Man, on the contrary, increases his magico-religious possibilities by hiding his face and concealing his body. When he puts on a mask, he ceases to be himself; at least, he seemingly, if not actually, becomes another. This amounts to saying that, at least after a certain period in history, a man knows himself as a man precisely by changing himself into something other than himself. By wearing a mask he becomes what he is resolved to be: *homo religiosus* and *zoon politikon*. Such behavior has a good deal of bearing on the history of culture.

There are three general kinds of masks with three different purposes: ritual masks, war masks, and masks for spectacles. However, all masks are ritual in origin. War masks are fashioned to frighten and paralyze the enemy; they represent terrifying monstrous faces. Their magical function is unmistakable; it derives from the practice of painting the head and body, the earliest known magico-religious disguise. The cultural origin and function of dance and spectacle masks are plain enough.

Ritual use of masks is extremely varied, but two important classes of marks may be distinguished: those worn by the living and the masks of the dead.

It is worth stressing the almost world-wide diffusion, the antiquity, and the continuity of masks. There are masks attested as early as paleolithic times; in Europe they have a history of more than 30,000 years, and there are villages where masks are to this day worn in ritual. Paleolithic hunters' masks represent wild beasts. The cultural heirs of neolithic man, the modern European peasantry, use, together with masks of stags, wolves, and bears, also masks of domestic animals and (these probably of urban origin) human faces. Certainly the religious role of the mask was different for paleolithic hunters from what it was for neolithic farmers. Still, the cultural role of stag masks and bear masks in central and eastern Europe is a continuation of traditions originating in the religious ideas of paleolithic man.

Some fifty-five paleolithic representations of men in animal disguises are known. From Teyjat in Dordogne there are antlers carved with three figures disguised as chamois; and from Lourdes comes a slate plaque showing a man in deerskin, antlers, and a long horse's tail. But the religious function of the mask in paleolithic hunting cultures is most plainly revealed by the great "sorcerer" of the Trois-Frères cave (X, PL. 133). Thirty inches high, deeply carved in the rock, the sorcerer dominates the many animal figures on the walls. He has a stag's head topped with immense antlers, an owl's face, ears like a wolf's, a long goat's beard, uplifted arms ending in bear paws, and a long horse's tail.

This sorcerer may represent a human being or perhaps a supernatural being, a hunters' god in the guise of a paleolithic sorcerer. A. C. Blanc has compared him to a Melanesian spirit with fish in the place of its head, hands, and feet. This Melanesian spirit is protector both of sea creatures and of fishermen; he fills nets but can also do harm. Whatever the Trois-Frères figure represents, it is certain that paleolithic sorcerer-priests used animal disguises like this for the purpose of raising themselves to a superhuman state.

There are many modern examples of magico-religious transformation brought about by wearing a mask. The Eskimos believe that the wearer is mysteriously impregnated with the spirit represented by the mask: to put on the mask representing a totem is to become that totem. Certain aspects of shamanism contribute to a better understanding of the function of the Trois-Frères sorcerer. In their trances Siberian shamans wear costumes with animal motifs, among others. Along with bird motifs (of an obvious symbolism) appear deer and reindeer antlers. The costumes of Altaic and Tungusic shamans include furs and hides and ribbons and scarves representing serpents. The shaman possesses, among other powers, the ability to identify himself with an animal or magically to transform himself into an animal. In certain places, the shaman represents the Lord of the Beasts, playing an important role in the community hunt.

True masks are rather rare among Siberian shamans, but among the Eskimos, especially in Alaska, where the influence of American Indian cultures is strong, the shamans do use masks. However, shamanic dress is in itself and in origin a mask. Mask or dress, the function is the same: to proclaim the incarnation of a mythological figure — a god, ancestor, or mystic animal. The mask effects the transubstantiation of the shaman, transforming him before everyone's eyes into the supernatural being he is impersonating.

A similar transformation takes place in the ceremonies of certain mask societies, but the magico-religious experience involved here is different from the shaman's or from the paleolithic hunter's. In this case it is bound up with a community rite of ancestor worship. The masks represent the ancestors; by wearing masks the members of the secret society personify the ancestors. By means of masks, the dead return to life. It is no longer the mask-wearers who perform the rite but the mythico-ritual beings whom they have become. For the dead are mythico-ritual beings absorbed into the mythical First Ancestor, the first man to know death. In other words, when members of the secret society wear the masks, they act out a myth of beginnings: how in days primordial the Ancestor met his death — changed his state and became "other" — and afterward revealed to the people the mysteries of death and resurrection through the dramatic ceremonies of initiation. All mask societies are based on origin myths. Therefore the mythical event that gave birth to the secret society is periodically reenacted in its ceremonies.

It is likely that mythico-ritual ceremonies involving the ritual presence of ancestors (represented by masked initiates in the guise of wild beasts) were common among primitive men on a cultural par with paleolithic hunters. In some African initiation ceremonies the officiants are clad in lion and leopard skins, complete with claws, and the circumcision knives are furnished with hooks. Circumcision symbolizes the destruction of the genitals by the animal patron of the initiation. The officiants are sometimes called "lions," and circumcision is expressed by the verb "kill." Afterward the neophytes are themselves "masked," that is, dressed in leopard or lion skins. In other words, they are assimilated to the divine essence of the initiation animal and hence are reborn in him.

The masks — the ancestors — terrify women and the uninitiated and impose severe tests on the neophytes during their initiation. For example, the cruelties of the Duk-duk society of New Britain are well known. The maskers harass, attack, and sometimes kill those whom they meet in their way. The behavior of wild beasts is the model of certain men's societies.

The members enjoy a predatory privilege that associates them with the carnivores. In the secret brotherhoods of the Japanese and of the Germanic tribes of antiquity, the masks, the indescribable uproar, and the barking of dogs (ritually become "wolves") testify to the ancestors' presence, the return of the dead. Because of the terror they inspire, masked brotherhoods sometimes come to have a certain political power. Some carnivorous animal — such as the wolf in central Asia and in Europe, the leopard in Africa — constitutes the model both of the perfect hunter and formidable warrior and of the invincible conqueror and absolute master. It is through masks that this power is constituted and maintained.

Initiation into this sort of secret society necessarily involves, however, the disclosure of the purely human nature of the wearers of the masks. In Ubangi country, this revelation has a dramatic character. An old man, costumed and masked, comes out of the bush, runs and leaps upon the freshly circumcised neophytes, lashes them with a whip, and then disappears. At the close of the rites, the neophytes, encouraged by the leader of the initiation, seize the masked one, take away his whip, unmask him, and recognize the face of an old man of the village. From then on, they know. They have learned not only that the masked one is a human being but how to go about striking terror into the uninitiated. They have learned the secret of incarnating the spirits of the dead by smearing themselves with paint and wearing masks. This knowledge does not do away with the sense of mystery, for even while knowing the nature of his mask, the member of a secret brotherhood continues to look upon the masks of superior members as truly supernatural beings. Moreover, the mask-wearer finally becomes fascinated with his own mask and by the fear that it elicits. "He no longer knows himself, a monstrous cry escapes his throat, the cry of a beast or a god, a superhuman outcry, a pure emanation of battle force, of creative passion, of boundless magic power by which he believes himself — by which he is, in this moment — possessed" (G. Buraud, *Les Masques*, Paris, 1948, p. 101).

The morphology of terror-producing masks is extremely rich. Principal sources of inspiration are the world of nightmares, death myths, demonology, and images relating to the process by which a cadaver is transformed into a skeleton. All these images of terror express the otherness of the dead, the different ways of becoming "other" (cadaver, skeleton, ghost, demon). The masks used in the "devil dances" (Tibet, China, Ceylon) are related both to the ritual for expelling demons (souls of the dead) and to that of initiation. In Tibet masks represent certain demonic beings that the soul meets after death. By attending the ritual dances, onlookers learn to overcome their fear of the death journey; they are prepared for encounters beyond the grave.

Sometimes masks represent superhuman beings not *in concreto* but in spirit. The best-known examples are the Zuñi kachina masks. The kachinas are spirits of the dead, more or less identified with ancestors. According to myth, they periodically used to return to visit the living; and whenever they took their leave, women followed them. The kachinas then decided to come no longer in person but in spirit. They commanded that masks be made resembling the ones they wore themselves in the other world and declared that they would be present in spirit in these masks. The masked dances are a re-creation of mythical times; they reproduce certain deeds performed by the kachinas at the dawn of time. The masks are neither theriomorphic nor terrifying. They are geometrical faces, abstractions. The geometrical design expresses the remote, the nonhuman, the transcendent. This is to say that the kachinas are exemplars, archetypes existing in another world, who, while remaining in touch with our own, transcend it.

The periodic visit of the kachinas has a religious function: they bring rain and bless the harvest. Among farming peoples, masked processions are believed to have a beneficent influence on cattle and crops. The Slavic and Balkan *kolyadi* are groups of young people, sometimes masked, who visit houses, singing and dancing, during the Twelve Days of Christmas. Their songs (*kolyadki*) invoke the harvest's abundance and the cattle's increase. But the association with the spirits of the dead is plain: if they enter a house in which the family has lately lost a member, the *kolyedari* bring news of the departed. In fact, some Bulgarian masks simulate a death's head. The *kolyedari* and their counterparts in other parts of central Europe are masked, carry trappings shaped like goats or horses, and make noise with bells or other instruments. Their masks are theriomorphic (stags, goats, foxes, eagles, and so on) or represent various figures from Christian folklore (the Devil, for example). The procession takes place during the 12 days between Christmas and Epiphany or during carnival.

These masked processions carry animal effigies curiously vestigial of Dionysiac processions, and in so far as elements of cults of the dead and of agricultural religion are present in the Dionysiac tradition, this resemblance in folk custom is easily explainable. But the mask is still more closely linked with the cult of Dionysos, for it played a leading role in the origin of tragedy. In this case the mask is anthropomorphous, but the human element is transfigured by the mask's very structure; the rigidity, the fixity, and immobility of feature do not belong to an ordinary man; only gods or the dead present such immobility of expression, while still being able to speak, to communicate their desires and their thoughts. The context here is that of another cultural sphere, the expression of another level of consciousness. Despite its anthropomorphism, the Greek mask, too, depicts an archetype, an exemplar. The play — whether tragedy or comedy — reenacts a fabulous deed performed by type characters in paradigmatic situations. The actor temporarily loses his identity: he becomes another, he *is* the character he enacts. Masks used in Japanese drama have a like function: they help to transcend earthly space and time and lead the audience into a world where it is not men who move, but types.

Gold funerary masks are attested from as long ago as the 2d millennium B.C. in the Cretan-Mycenaean age (IV, PLS. 73, 449). Perhaps they should be thought of as portraits, specifically death portraits, since the fine gold leaf was surely molded on the dead man's face. The Romans molded faces in wax and painted them in natural colors; these were used during the rites for the dead and were preserved later (see below). But long before molds were employed to preserve a likeness of the dead, there were funerary masks. They are found in gold, silver, bronze, or terra cotta, from Mesopotamia and Phoenicia to England, in the valley of the Danube, and in the Crimea. The idea is everywhere the same: the preservation of the dead person. The means and meaning of the preservation vary from culture to culture. In the Minusinsk region (the Tashtyk culture), plaster masks were made to preserve the individuality of the dead man, along with his soul substance (derived from the ancestors), which was retained in his bones or ashes.

Some death masks were, in fact, supplementary to mummification and later became a substitution for it. In front of or upon the case in which a body was mummified, the ancient Peruvians placed a rude wooden image, fashioned while a man was still alive and usually painted and adorned with human hair or a headdress. In Melanesia the skull itself served as a mask during the sacred dances. Obviously, in this case, it was no longer a matter of making a death mask, a portrait or representation of the dead. The skull itself represented the departed and preserved the essentials. Closer to the idea of a portrait mask are Etruscan funerary urns in the shape of a human face (e.g., those from Chiusi, 7th cent. B.C.; PL. 352; V, PL. 28), a variant of the anthropomorphous urn. The attempt was to preserve the identity of the man's ashes, or, more exactly, to connect them with the face that was shown to his fellows in his lifetime.

Masks, then, are always, in one way or another, bound up with the idea of time. Whatever sort of mask is worn, the wearer transcends earthly time. Whether ritual, funerary, or for any spectacle, the mask is an instrument of ecstasy. He who wears one is no longer himself, since he is projected beyond his personal temporal identity. He becomes "other," even when the mask is his own portrait.

The mask's capacity for existence on another time level perhaps explains its dual function: alienation of the personality (ritual and theater masks), and preservation of the personality (death masks and portraits). Both cases exemplify a reactivation of past time: primordial time in the case of ritual and spectacle masks; historic and personal time in the case of death masks and portraits. Primordial mythological time, reactualized by ritual and spectacle masks, can be *lived*, but only by means of changing the personality and becoming "other." On the other hand, death masks and portraits reactualize historic time, which is not only past but dead, for no one can relive the inner life of anyone else. In either case, the time implied by the mask is ecstatic time, removed from the here and now. Whatever its type, every mask proclaims the presence of some being who does not belong to the everyday world.

Mircea ELIADE

ANTIQUITY: *From the full head to the mask.* As is well known, the detached head, be it human or animal, still covered with skin, embalmed, or stripped of flesh to the skull, has played an important role in universal belief ever since prehistoric times.

In accordance with the principle of *pars pro toto*, it stands for the entire being of which it is the principal part, the seat of life, of the soul and its faculties, of the individual character. Even though dead, the head preserves its properties, which may be exploited by the living. The face (the "mask") especially expresses personality, through the eyes (the "windows of the soul"), through the mouth, by which communication with others is possible, and through the various other features. Once again *pars pro toto*, the face stands for the entire head. One more simplification: the eye, as the most meaningful part, in itself often suffices to represent both the head and the face, as well as the entire person.

To hide the face symbolizes withdrawal from the normal world of the living. In ancient Egypt the face of a criminal being led to execution was veiled, and the order "let his face be covered" was tantamount to the death sentence. The faces of the dying were veiled, and this isolation veil was used in many situations: Cyrenaic funeral busts of dead persons or chthonian deities consisted of a head with hair but without facial features (VII, PL. 406). The dead were also shown without mouths, for they do not speak, with closed eyes, for they do not see; they are eternally mute and blind in the darkness, solitude, and silence of the other world. A face devoid of these features is not of this world.

Examples of this transition from preserved head and skull to artificial masks are still to be found in primitive cultures. Heads are preserved in various ways: the skull is covered with clay or some other substance, which is molded, painted, and decorated in the semblance of a face. The back of the skull may be removed, leaving only the front part, which is covered with clay and shaped into a face, thus turning it into a half-natural, half-artificial mask.

In art forms the same correspondence exists between the whole head, the mask, and the eyes. In Egypt, the custom of laying a mask over the face of the dead body (PLS. 351, 353), which appeared at the beginning of the Middle Kingdom, originated in the ritual practice of placing substitute heads of stone in 4th-dynasty tombs. This progressive simplification may be followed also in the treatment of the Greek Gorgon. It is shown either standing or simply as a head, the gorgoneion; in black-figure vase paintings this mask is reduced to two eyes, eyebrows, and a nose, then to the apotropaic image of two eyes only (PL. 245). These various forms all possess the same virtues and, because of the image's magic power, correspond to the actual being they are meant to represent. (Regarding the identification of the model with its figural representation, see MAGIC.)

Heads and masks of deities and other supernatural beings. Deities may be depicted in the form of isolated heads. The Greek herms consisted of a head set on a pillar which also bore a phallus; it was not a sacred and aniconic stone or pillar that had evolved into an anthropomorphic image, nor was it a statue in a simplified form. The essential element was not the pillar, but rather the two emblems of life, the head and the phallus, of which the pillar was merely the support, as Macrobius pointed out. In the archaic period, Dionysos was often represented by a bearded mask attached to the top of a wooden pole or pillar, hung with robes, into which branches were stuck to signify his role as a god of vegetation and tree god. There are many such examples in Greek vase paintings, and stone masks of the god have also been found. Here too the important thing is not the pillar but the mask; Dionysos appears as a "mask god." Until the end of antiquity, masks of Dionysos were used to decorate reliefs and were applied to vases and to various other objects. Since masks had a ritual function in the cult of the god, his companions, the sileni and satyrs, were also represented by masks. Among many other mythological deities whose masks are known were Acheloos, Oceanus, and Zeus Ammon. In Celtic Gaul, even after it was Romanized, deities were personified by stone heads on busts or large pedestals and by repoussé metal masks mounted on wooden stakes (cf. III, PL. 111). Everywhere masks were also used to represent demonic beings (e.g., in Greece, the gorgoneion; VII, PLS. 38, 52) and spirits of water, trees, mountains, and so forth — in general, the spirits of terrestrial fertility, subterranean spirits, and spirits of the dead. Thus masks embody, beneath the features assigned to them, the innumerable supernatural and invisible beings who surround the living, beings who represent for the living another world, maleficent or benign.

Funeral masks. Dionysos was not only a god of vegetation; he was also a god of the dead, the notions of life and death having always been closely associated. He was commonly represented by a mask, just as everywhere, certainly since paleolithic times, the spirits of the dead, the souls of ancestors, have been represented by masks or appeared as masked beings. Such beings have been worshiped and appeased in rites during which they were personified by masked figures who performed dances or pantomimes. These rites were one of the sources of theatrical representations, for example, in Greece, the Dionysiac rites.

The effigy of a dead person could take the form of a half statue, a bust cut off at the midriff (IV, PL. 339). Such busts appeared to be still half buried in the ground, only partially protruding. This sort of funeral monument always had the same meaning, even in Roman art, where the form was secularized and used to commemorate the living. There were also busts of underworld deities, guardians of the dead, who seemed to rise up out of the earth.

The deceased was frequently represented by the head alone. In Egypt substitute heads of stone were placed in tombs to assure the departed person's continued existence; a stone head of the deceased, as well as a bust, was placed above the false door of the tomb. In Greece gravestones consisted of a human head at the top of a pillar. Among the innumerable examples of funeral masks those of pre-Hellenic Mycenae and of Trebenište (Yugoslavia, 6th cent. B.C.) are notable. The mask may be placed directly over the face of the dead, since it is frequently only a thin sheet of pressed gold foil that covers either the whole face or just the eyes and the mouth. Both kinds have been found in Syrian necropolises such as that in Emesa (mod. Homs), from the 1st century of our era. Masks were buried next to the body, attached to the coffin (Mycenae), or carved and molded on the lid of the sarcophagus over the spot where the head of the body lay (PL. 352; IV, PL. 449). Funeral masks have been interpreted in various ways: because of their durable and sometimes incorruptible material (such as gold), they preserve the features of the deceased, effaced by death; they afford the tangible substitute that is indispensable to funeral rites; they enable the dead person to remain in contact with the living; they help him to exist in the other world, and on his final journey they ward off evil spirits who, failing to recognize him, leave him in peace. A man's funeral mask protects him and, when placed on his face, may take the form of a guardian deity. But the underlying principle, basic to all these various meanings, is that the mask, like the head, is regarded as the seat of life of the soul.

Masks of divinities, of grimacing demons — like the Punic masks — and theater masks were put into the tomb to protect it; they were hung on the door of the vault, on the funeral shrine, or carved on the sarcophagus. From prehistoric Troy through the Roman period, urns with human faces or Etruscan canopic vases surmounted by heads (V, PL. 28) and containing the ashes of the dead represented either the dead person himself or some mortuary deity. Phalli were sometimes molded on the side of the urn, thus uniting, as in the Greek herms, the vital parts, the head and the reproductive organ.

Such masks were not always conventional but were intended to reproduce the real lineaments of the deceased, as is evident as early as some of the Mycenaean gold masks, and especially when they were made by taking a mold of the dead person's face.

Funeral rites as practiced in Rome offer a typical example. A cast was taken of the dead man's face. When the body was laid out in state, the death mask thus obtained was placed over the face; during the funeral procession, it was worn by an actor, who thus took on the identity of the deceased. It was then placed in the tomb. (Two such masks, in wax, were found in a Cumaean tomb along with the remains of skeletons.) After burial a copy of this mask, mounted on a bust, was set up in the atrium together with those of other members of the family who had died before. These latter, worn by actors, were also carried in the funeral procession. The busts formed a gallery of ancestors, the *imagines majorum*, and proud was the family who possessed the *jus imaginum*. This custom of using death masks as mementos and substitutes for the deceased has been observed down to modern times, for example, in the funerals of the French kings. At the death of Henry IV of France, a mold taken of his face was used for casting a wax bust that was fastened to a dummy dressed in the royal robes, laid out in state, then later displayed in the funeral procession. It was also used as a model for numerous portraits of the king. Even today the faces of people one wants to remember are cast in plaster.

Ceremonial masks and ritual masquerades. Just as with the apparel of a god or the skin of a sacred animal, the mask, in accordance with the principle of sympathetic magic, transforms its bearer into whomever it personifies. The being so portrayed temporarily assimilates the wearer and invests him with his powers. So a mask is worn not so much to imitate or to deceive as to take on another identity. This is the origin, in primitive as well as in ancient and modern civilizations, of many ritual masquerades accompanied by dancing, which aroused a state of mystic ecstasy and facilitated this identity with the attitudes and actions of the model, the purpose being to make the model a real presence.

In Greece, the terra-cotta masks in the temple of Artemis Orthia at Sparta, dating from the 7th–6th century B.C., are votive masks but are copied from wooden cult masks. At Pheneos, in Arcadia, the priest of Demeter Kidaria put on the mask of the goddess and beat the ground with a stick to scourge the spirits of the underworld. The mask of Artemis was worn in the Laconian cults of Artemis Korythalia in Sparta, of Artemis Alpheia in Pisatis, and of another Laconian Artemis who took the shape of ugly women. During the Karneia in Sparta, youths would pursue a masked figure who undoubtedly represented Apollo Karneios.

Animal masks caused men to be mystically changed into animals. Masquerades of animal masks are common in primitive cultures and date from prehistoric times. The "sorcerer" of the Trois-Frères cave mentioned above is a good example. Animal masks existed in Mesopotamia, in Egypt, in Greece, both pre-Hellenic (for example, a Mycenaean fresco showing men with donkey heads; on gems) and Hellenic. In Dionysiac rites, masks in human and animal forms (bull and he-goat) were worn to represent the god and his companions, and even at the time of Demosthenes one could take part in Dionysiac processions only if wearing a face mask. These ritual masks were also known to certain Roman cults. Men disguised themselves as animals, but the animals also took on human guises, and it is sometimes difficult to make a clear distinction between the various forms and meanings. Some animals were able to impersonate others. In the tombs of Pazyryk (Altai) horses were given headpieces in the shape of elk and reindeer masks, that they might symbolize these animals as escorts to guide the dead to the other world, or to combine the psychopomp roles of horse and deer.

These masquerades achieved various effects. They honored the beings represented by the masks in either human or animal form; they appeased and propitiated them in the rites of gods or demons and in the offerings to ancestral spirits or to the dead. During the hunt — and this was particularly the case with primitive and prehistoric masquerades — the masks not only identified the wearer with the quarry, thus enabling him to approach it without arousing suspicion, but because of the occult power inherent in the masks, they also acted on the prey, making it easy to kill or causing it to appear in abundance. Masquerades induced fecundity, the vegetal, animal, and human fertility imparted by the god. Those associated with Laconian Artemis cults and the worship of Dionysos were actually vegetation and fertility rites. They also played a role in the rites of probation and initiation of adolescents. They guarded against evil and warded off its power.

Masquerades have survived in Christianity. The Church has accepted some, condemned others as heathen and diabolic; but many maquerades still bear traces of their original meaning, although others have become mere nonreligious pastimes.

Theater masks. In some countries, actors never appeared on stage without masks: in Japan, in Java, in ancient Greece, for tragedies, comedies, and satirical plays, and in Rome, for pantomimes as well (PLS. 360, 361, 364). This practice was everywhere derived from the ritual masquerades discussed above with relation to god cults and the veneration of the dead. In Greece theatrical representations originated in the cult masquerades of Dionysos, as the god of vegetation and of death and resurrection, and in other funeral rites. In Rome theater masks were also related to religious ceremonies; in the autumn festivities of Tellus and Silvanus the peasants would smear their faces with minium or put on masks of bark and amuse themselves by exchanging coarse jokes, as in the Bacchic Comus. With time, the original meaning became obscured, but theater masks continued to be used, divorced from religion, personifying the nonreligious characters required by the action. They nevertheless kept their original apotropaic function and were still used in mortuary decoration.

Apotropaic masks. That the human head, whether whole, in its natural state, or reduced to a skull, a mask, or even the eye, possesses apotropaic powers is one of man's instinctive beliefs; and the human head has fulfilled this function from prehistoric times down through the ages. Artificial masks derived from the head were endowed with the same powers, in addition to those possessed by the particular being represented and to the ritual use to which they were put. Such masks represented gods and other supernatural and mythical beings — Dionysos, sileni and satyrs, or demons, such as the Gorgon — and theatrical identities, tragic (and the term is used here also in the modern sense, pertaining to the terrible and frightening) or comic, which warded off evil through laughter. And there were many, many others. They were used wherever their protection was deemed useful; masks of Gorgons, of sileni, satyrs, and others adorned antefixes, acroteria, and pediments of temples and other religious, funerary, and nonreligious buildings (V, PL. 38). They were placed on tombs and on personal belongings, and in fields and gardens they watched over the harvest. Some masks guarded against and cured illnesses and warded off the evil spirits that caused them, according to a primitive belief by which illness was chased away through the sympathetic, homeopathic practice of reproducing the outward effects of the disease in question. War masks protected warriors by means of the expressions and attributes depicted; they transmitted the powers of the subjects represented and terrorized the enemy. Face helmets, chiefly Roman, and battle and ceremonial arms were also related to funeral masks and placed in tombs; they belong to the same category. There were disciplinary and penal masks — avenging spirits often appeared masked — worn to enforce the observance of social laws. On punitive expeditions the guilty party was forced to wear a mask as a penalty for certain misdemeanors.

The fear of masks and death. Given the relation between masks and deities (especially chthonian deities), demons, and the often malicious spirits of the dead, the fear that masks inspire is understandable, for they evoke a world of mystery and threat. They summon up the idea of death, which they not only represent but can even bring about, like the mask of the Gorgon which turned whoever gazed upon it to stone. They resemble the faces of dead people, possessing the same rigidity, the same set expression, the livid pallor and chalky complexion. For this reason, in the theater Thespis made use of a mask of the same white plaster that was used for death masks, a material serving also in various funeral and mystic initiation rites.

Children, and many adults, are still afraid of masks. According to popular tradition, masks representing demons and souls of the dead frighten children, and parents sometimes resort to them as threats when children are disobedient. Plutarch remarked that when a small child is afraid of masks, his fear can be calmed by placing them in his hand and turning them around to be seen from all sides. On Roman sarcophagi a child is shown completely hidden by a large silenus mask; all that can be seen of the child is his hand sticking out of the mouth, as though he had been eaten. He amuses himself by terrifying a small companion standing in front, trembling with fright. This is not a simple game, for the mask of the man-eating monster symbolizes the annual death and resurrection of the cult of Dionysos. A statue in the Villa Albani, Rome, repeats this motif, and it is undoubtedly funerary. Pliny recounts that the comic actor Marcus Ofilius Hilarius gave a birthday dinner after having scored a great public success; during the meal, he fixed his gaze on the mask he had always worn on stage, removed his festive wreath, and died without anyone realizing it. On gravestones the dead person is shown carrying a theater mask in his hand or gazing at one set up in front of him. On a sarcophagus relief, a young woman is shown on her deathbed, surrounded by relatives and friends in mourning; behind her is a small cupboard containing a theater mask, undoubtedly representing, as a sort of anticipation, the images that would be carried in the procession. In the light of their origins, theater masks often have a funerary meaning, and for this reason often appear alone on many sarcophagi and reliefs and are even placed inside tombs.

Ornamental masks. Like many other objects that in time lost their original meaning, the mask was often used, even in ancient times, as an ornament, a decorative motif (PL. 365), or for entertainment, without thought of the ideas which had produced it.

The artist had numerous possibilities for depicting masks in a wide range of concepts and types, but masks have done more than provide the artist with an abundant repertory; they have influenced the rendering of the human face in art, acting as a vehicle for realism, by differentiating one face from another through individual characteristics of expression, contrary to the idealism that led to a certain uniformity.

Spirits were frequently thought of as hideous and terrifying, an aspect which masks have rendered with sometimes remarkable intensity. In antiquity the masks used in the sanctuary of Artemis Orthia and those found in Punic tombs, and in modern times carnival masks, are examples of this. Masks focus the artist's attention on the ugliness and deformities of the human face, which are no less interesting than its beauties. Theater masks have also contributed to this differentiation process, as is clear from a study of Greek literature and figural monuments. They have not only characterized human types through facial expression, establishing the distinguishing features of sex, age, and social condition, but they have also enabled men to give expression to emotions and passion, from the tragic to the comic, from sadness and despair to effusive joy and laughter. Masks have participated in the trend toward a realism, not only physical but moral, which, so long as idealism reigned supreme in Greek art, showed up only vaguely and was limited to certain specific subjects, until it gained ascendancy and imposed its influence during the 4th century B.C., notably in the Hellenistic period. Death masks stimulated individual realism in portrait sculpture especially through the procedure of making molds of the faces of the deceased, a process known in Egypt, Carthage, and Greece, where its invention was attributed to Lysistratos, the brother of Lysippos. It was also known in Etruria and in Rome, where the image taken from the mold of the dead person's face led to the well-known realism of Roman portraits, some of which seem to have been copied directly from death masks. It is interesting to note that this same process of casting a person's face after death also gave rise to realism in portraiture in the Middle Ages (at the end of the 13th or the beginning of the 14th century) and during the Renaissance.

Waldemar DEONNA

FOLK MASKS IN EUROPE. A knowledge of ancient civilizations and a comparative study of primitive civilizations facilitates understanding of many of the masked ceremonies of European peoples.

Masked folk ceremonies are always held at specific times: at the beginning or the end of the year, according to the dates calculated by the various ancient calendar systems, or at the beginning or end of the cycle of the seasons. From earliest times the intercalary days between the last month of the old period and the first month of the new have been considered a particularly dangerous time. The supernatural world was unleashed. The souls of the dead returned from beyond the grave to punish the misdeeds of the living or to bring good luck. For thousands of years men have chosen this period as a time for ritualistic masquerade. By assuming the forms of demons and the ghosts of their ancestors, they have kept in contact with the supernatural world and at the same time, by their sinister behavior, have managed to intimidate the other members of their clan or social group. The right to masquerade was later taken over by younger people, and this remains true to this day.

The primitive ritual ceremonies, which here and there developed into primitive drama, were aimed at preventing the souls of the dead or other evil spirits from causing harm. At the same time they were intended to win the spirits' favor. That is, the peoples hoped, by means of homeopathic magic, to eliminate evil and assure good for the new period about to begin. It was necessary to do penance in atonement for past misdeeds, and it seems that gifts gathered at the compulsory collection served as propitiatory offerings, and public condemnation of the vices of the community helped to banish evil. Evil itself was often personified and represented by a dummy that might be hanged, buried, or burned. The actions of a symbolic couple — actions which nowadays would be considered obscene, since they imitated coitus in public (*coram publico*) and childbirth — were, in fact, ritualistic magic used to guarantee fecundity. The same idea lay behind the customary sprinkling of water and ashes, the soiling, the blows and beatings, and so on. The costumes assumed to represent the spirits of the dead reflected the popular concepts of beings from the other world. These were terrifying forms that always expressed the numina, whether they represented animals (theriomorphic forms) or purely supernatural beings (usually anthropomorphic), or whether the costume was simply white. The behavior of the maskers tended also to create the impression of supernatural beings: their rhythmic gait or dance, loud noises made with bells or jingles, and utter silence on the part of the figures, who remained mute as silent shades (*umbrae silentes*) or spoke only in a high falsetto.

With the decline of the Roman Empire and of the religious world of antiquity, the old rites, which were a product of pagan mythology, were transformed into playful travesties. The Byzantine mimes advanced this process by standardizing certain typical characters, which were quickly absorbed into folk ceremonies. Thus the Balkan Peninsula, placed midway between the civilizations of the Levant and the Near East and those of western Europe, became the point of departure for influences and ideas which, thanks to the mimes, spread throughout the domain of the ancient Roman Empire. This explains the striking similarities, the same types of characters, the same ritualistic traits that are found all over continental Europe from the Balkans to England and into the Scandinavian countries. However, the majority of peoples have also developed their own variations on these themes, variations related to their own traditions and the conditions created by the Middle Ages, the Renaissance, and even modern times. Everywhere folk masquerades have been the exclusive privilege of men. The intrusion of women is a sign of the breaking up of the tradition. Everywhere the seasonal masked processions revolve around a central character who personifies the past period and who is often replaced by a dummy. Sometimes he is accompanied by a female character (a young man in women's garb).

The Balkans, which were separated from the rest of Western civilization under the Ottoman empire, preserved their ancient forms even when they accepted certain Turkish elements. Archaic forms are preserved up to the present day in the folk ceremonies of Greece, Macedonia, Bulgaria, Serbia, and Romania. They make their appearance during the Twelve Days of Christmas and the end of carnival. Everywhere the participants recall the ancient satyrs. They dress in goatskins and assume anthropomorphic or theriomorphic shapes; bells on the belt are *de rigueur*, and a bag of ashes is frequently carried. The principal character is accompanied by his "spouse." The couple are known in Greece as the Kalogheroi, among the Slavs as the Kuker (or Kuk) and the Kukerica (Ded and Baba; the Old Man and Old Woman). In Romania the Cuci corresponds to the Slavic Kuker. The man's disguise is much the same everywhere: goatskins, mask, or hat-mask with characteristic ornaments (two branches for horns decorated with feathers or perhaps even crows' wings), a belt with cowbells, and a large wooden phallus painted red. Here and there one finds in the group a king and queen, a doctor, a pope, a Jew, and in recent times, Gypsies, brigands, Albanians, Moors, and devils. Among the theriomorphic characters the Bear is very widespread, as is also the Camel, though a little less so. But by far the most interesting is the Goat.

The Goat is a particular characteristic of Romanian processions, but it is also very widespread throughout a large part of northern Europe. In the Romanian version of this seasonal drama, the Goat is called Brezaia but is known also as Turcă or just Capră (Goat). Usually it is accompanied by a hunchback, known as the Old Man (Moş, Moşul). The Brezaia is both goat and wife at the same time and stands out by reason of the bright colors of the costume (neckerchief, blanket), which is sometimes made simply of many-colored rags. These derive from the *centunculus*, or patchwork garment of the ancient Roman *mimus*. The majority of the processions, with their terrific noise of bells and their singing and dancing the *kolo* (a round dance), are associated with taking up a collection, but the maskers also perform their little dramas retaining vestiges of more ancient primitive spectacles. Very often one of the characters is killed in order to be resuscitated by the Doctor. In the eastern Balkans, ritual plowing of the land is also presented. Very often the representations and performances are rather free. Sometimes there are ritual mimes in which quite remarkable battles spring up between certain masked groups when they meet. Originally the dead were buried in a special graveyard, but the killers in this ritual combat were never punished. The wearer of the Brezaia mask in Romania was considered excommunicated for seven years.

One can easily trace the same traditions among the Serbs and Croats. There the two old people, the ritual buffoon couple, are called Djed and Baba, and the processions are often called D(j)edovi. The Turica appears in Dubrovnik and has counterparts in Poland and Romania. He frightens children with his cracking jaw. In Bosnia the Old Man, accompanied by Jews, leads the Goat. On the frontiers of Slovenia and in the Croatian region around Kastav, the maskers are the Zvončari. All these, with goatskins on their backs, bells on their rumps, skin hat-masks on their heads, a cudgel (the old phallus?) in one hand, and a bag of ashes in the other, form a link in the chain of tradition that stretches from the Balkans to beyond the Alps. In the Croatian region of Slavonia ritual plowing takes place on Shrove Tuesday and, as is more often the case, on Ash Wednesday. The custom is the continuation of a ceremony that is well known in Bulgaria and Romania. In Croatia Carnival himself (Pust, Krnjo) is put on trial and, after a satirical defense speech, is condemned to be drowned, hanged, or burned — a cultural trait that must be considered Western rather than Eastern.

In Slovenia there are numerous characters who dress in sheepskin coats worn inside out, with bells hanging from their belts, and wear skin masks that are frequently decorated with horns. The most remarkable are the Kurenti from around Ptuj. These maskers bear a startling resemblance to those called Kukeri in the Balkans. Moreover, they also perform ritual plowing, and a fight breaks out when two rival groups happen to meet. The Laufarji at Cerkno, also in Slovenia, are interesting for their wooden masks; Carnival (Pust), in the guise of the Wild Man, is condemned on the spot and executed. There is usually a funeral for him, and this gives rise to new inventiveness. In masked ceremonies, the Bear and the Horse make their appearance. The Horse is represented by one or often two persons and has various names: Camel (Kamela, Gambela), Horse (Rusa), Doe (Košuta). Masked processions take place during carnival; the Šeme of the Bohinj Valley in the Alps make their rounds during the New Year celebration.

In Slovenian territory, at the extreme west of Yugoslavia, is found a mythical (and carnival) character, Perhta, who is similar to the Italian Befana and seems to be a result of the mingling of two mythological streams: the Illyrian-Slav (basically Greco-Roman) and the Germanic, especially as represented by the Bavarian. From the 8th-century duchy of Carantania, Perhta has spread all along the northern frontier of present-day Slovenian territory and has penetrated the German regions of the eastern Alps (Austria, Bavaria) as far as Bohemia. In folk imagination Perhta is a horrible personage dressed as a terrifying old woman with a frightful mask. On the eve of Epiphany she is chased through the streets by children making as much noise as they can. In northeast Slovenia Perhta takes the form of Lucija or Luca (Lucy), an equally frightening spirit who sets children atremble on St. Lucy's Day. Perhta has thus enriched the folk traditions in central Europe since the Middle Ages (8th cent.?). Another masked character in Slovenia is the famous Green George (Zeleni Jurij), a youth enveloped in green branches, who in the past was led through Slovene villages and neighboring Croat districts on St. George's Day. In olden days the processions of St. Nicholas were very impressive, and bands of singers masked as the Three Kings were numerous.

Slovene masks are a foretaste of the wealth of masked ceremonies that exist in the Alps and still preserve the typology of a common heritage. The Austrian regions (Styria, Carinthia, Salzburg, Tirol), Switzerland, and the German lands (particularly Bavaria) excel in masks. The masquerades take place at carnival, but there are also New Year's maskers who "hunt the Perchten" and maskers in St. Nicholas processions (influenced by the cult of the saint and propagated by St. Gall in Switzerland). Then there are the spectacles presented by singers representing Christmas and the Three Kings.

In the heart of the Alps the Perchten predominate. There are two kinds: ugly and evil ones (Schiachenperchten), and beneficent and beautiful ones (Schönperchten). The ugly ones are personages with frightening wooden masks who wear sheepskins and have many bells hanging from their belts. They create a terrific noise and perform frenzied dances. Perchten are still found in northern Carinthia (Mölltal), though only the ugly ones are known there, but the best-known Perchten are found in Salzburg and the Tirol. In Salzburg the Perchtenlaufen of Pongau and Gastein have become important tourist attractions. The headdresses of the beautiful ones are 4 to 5 ft. tall and are exuberantly decorated with loops, ribbons, and flowers, and their masks have a sweet expression. Along with the Perchten of both types, there are also certain familiar masked characters: the farcical couple, the Bird with the Long Beak (Schnabelpercht), the Hobbyhorse (Schimmelreiter), the Devil, the Quack Doctor, the Capuchin Monk, the Gypsy, the Turk, the Jester (dressed in white), and the Wild Man. Ritual plowing of the land takes place. In the Tirol both the beautiful and the ugly Perchten are assisted by the Huttler, who are dressed in multicolored rags like the *centunculus*, and by Wild Men. In some places other shaggy, running mummers parallel the Perchten: the Klöpfler (Tirol) and the Schemen (Salzburg).

In the German-Swabian territory Perchta is replaced by St. Nicholas, known as Klas or Kläuse in eastern Switzerland. The Klausen stand out by reason of their headdress, a miter, often with ribbons (as in Appenzell) recalling the decorative headdresses of the Perchten. In Glarus canton these headdresses are illuminated. The Germanic-Swiss influence spreads into neighboring Germany (Swabia, Württemberg, Baden), where the ceremony is known as Klausengehen, and to the north, where St. Nicholas is accompanied by Knecht Ruprecht, the German Christmas character, and the Christ child (Christkind). They are assisted by the Horse, the Bear (Erbsenbär, dressed in pea vines), the Goat (she-goat or he-goat), and the Stork. The Swiss-German influence is also felt in Austria. The headdresses of the Glöckler of Aussee (Styria) and of the Salzkammergut (Salzburg) are simply stylizations of the miter of St. Nicholas. After 1850 in some parts of Salzburg and Styria, Perchta was completely replaced by St. Nicholas, and the devil was used only to frighten children. The good saint finds himself in the company of the Deer, the Ox, the Goat, the Fox, and the Bear.

With the coming of carnival, frightening masks make their appearance once again under different names. There are quite a considerable number associated with the ritual plowing in Styria (Unzmarkt) and especially in the Tirol. Here the most important ceremony (Schemenlaufen) takes place at Imst, at Thaur, and at Telfs. The Wild Men, the Harlequins (Huttler, Zottler at Hall), and ritual plowing are recurring elements. Bavaria has the same thing, with the important masquerades of Garmisch-Partenkirchen, the Lake Constance area (Überlingen, with its Hänsele, or harlequins), and Donaueschingen, with Hanseli, Blätzlebue (harlequins), Wild Man, and the Horse. The Horse is the most important character in the carnivals of Württemberg (Tübingen). In the company of the Bear he is killed and then brought back to life (or buried). More or less identical ceremonies exist in Westphalia.

In a few of the most isolated valleys of Switzerland, the old carnival masks have been preserved. The most famous are those of the Roitschäggäten of Lötschental, Valais (Wallis) canton, who are dressed in sheepskins, with their faces hidden by typical frightening wooden masks (PL. 359), and make a loud din with bells tied to their belts. Very similar to these are the masks found in the region near Sargans. Here the harlequins are called Huttli or Plätzlimannli. The types of masquerade found in Einsiedeln (Mummerie, Hörelibajasse, Johee) are characterized by beautiful smiling masks; here also little cakes are distributed to the crowd. Finally, at the cowherd's fair (Älplerkilbi) in the region of Lake Lucerne, people disguise themselves as Wild Men (Tschämeler) and, after a railing criticism of the neighborhood, there is a repast of sweets. Also worthy of note are the masked ceremonies of spring: the Fête Feuillu in Geneva canton and the May Bear (Maibär) of Bad Ragaz, which is like the Slovene Green George.

North Germany seems more austere. However, the Goat, the Bear, and among the Sorbs of Lusatia (Lausitz) the Bear, the Horse, and the Camel still take part in the carnival season.

Impressive carnival observances are held in certain large towns. In Switzerland there is a traditional procession at Basel with the Lion, the Wild Man, and the Griffon. In Germany King Carnival rules not only in Cologne but also in Mainz, Düsseldorf, and elsewhere. The Schönbartlaufen (or Schembartlaufen) of Nürnberg (begun in 1348-49) is a famous, picturesque, and historical carnival, though it is not strictly within the folk category.

Alpine elements spread to the neighboring Slav area and were partly adopted by the Hungarians, who were also subject to Balkan influences. Perchta, for example, went to Bohemia (Perechta, Šperechta), along with her Slovenian counterpart, Lucy. She is characterized by a long beak and white mantle, but she also appears with other terrifying masks and sometimes even with a horse's head. Sometimes she is accompanied by the Goat. Another influence in Bohemia that has come from the West is the St. Nicholas procession. At one time it was an occasion to bring out the full repertory of the masks: the Old Man and the Old Woman, the "Cracker" (either Goat or Horse; each has a mobile, snapping jaw), the Brigand, the Turk, Death, the Hussar, the Dragon, and St. Nicholas with his pageboy. The procession was led by a Herald (Laufr). These same characters can be found outside the St. Nicholas procession, during the Christmas period as well as at carnival. Theriomorphic characters are very frequent and recall the Horse and the Goat (Koza); the Bear is also very popular. The disguise of the Little Singers of the Kings is like that of central Europe. The carol singers make their rounds with a little portable crib (*betlehem*) and enact the roles of the shepherds adoring the Christ child.

A branch of the Alpine elements extends into Hungary, which has its Lucies (though without the assimilation to Perchta) and its St. Nicholas processions. The Kings' Singers are very popular, especially those with the portable crib and, sometimes, masked shepherds. The Hungarians also have adopted the Goat (Koza, Turka), and they enjoy celebrating the funeral of Winter. The Catholic Croatian population of southern Hungary, the Šokci, formerly used wooden masks (Busó) representing anthropomorphic characters, often horned. The carnival ceremonies (loud noises, drum beating, etc.) recall those of the Balkans, but the masks testify to Alpine origins.

The Goat seems to be the most popular mask in Poland. A wooden goat's head, with real horns, bells, and a tow beard, is fixed to the end of a stick. Multicolored cloth, decorated with ornaments, is used to cover a young boy, who bends down and leans on the stick while walking and turning somersaults. One variation of the Goat figure type is called Tur or Turoń, which means urus (*Bos primigenius*). Since this animal became extinct in the 17th century, the mask is very indefinite and variable. Sometimes it resembles the Goat, sometimes the Ox, and sometimes even the Ram. It should be noted that Goat and Tur never appear together in a procession. It is significant that in Poland the archaic mask of the Goat should be associated with the carol singers. A young boy who carries the star and another with the portable crib (*szopka*) are accompanied by a third, who represents the Goat. With the aid of a musician they sing a *kolenda* (carol), and afterward the Goat does some clowning. Often the Bear, led by a Gypsy, also takes part in the procession. In some places the Bear is wrapped up in straw, sometimes even in pea vines, as is the custom in northern Germany. In the evening the older boys come with the Tur, who is led by the Old Man (Dziad) and accompanied by the Jew. The presence of the Tur excludes that of the Bear, a fact that is not without interest. The jokes are vulgar and are aimed particularly at the young girls. Among the Polish masks are found the Crane and the Stork, which occur among all the northern Slavs as far as the Finnish Ostyaks of Siberia. They are masks with long cracking beaks. The Cock, it seems, belongs to the same family. The Horse (Koń, Konik) does not appear except in areas where the Bear is known, and except for the head, his costume is no different from that of the Goat.

It is not difficult to follow the same kinds of masks farther north, across Russia. They are found even among the civilizations of the Caucasus, where Balkan and Near Eastern influences are frequent. The Russian regions have their masked ceremonies generally around the Christmas period. Masks are also found at nuptial feasts. The Goat and the Bear are the characters that are most widespread in White Russia and Little Russia. The Goat appears in the company of the Old Man (Ded) and sometimes a Gypsy. In one short scene, the Goat falls dead and the Old Man brings him back to life. Masking at wedding celebrations is usually limited to blackening the face with soot and wearing clothes of the opposite sex.

The common heritage of masked ceremonies has found full development in Italy, and from there it has spread to influence other neighboring peoples. In Italy, too, the people like to put on disguises at the end of the yearly cycle (Carnevale), or at the end of the cycle of the seasons (Calendimaggio). The central character personifies the past period or represents the chief of the ancestors who have returned from the grave.

The local names of this character differ, but just as the annual cycle superseded the seasonal cycle, so now the name Carnevale is common everywhere. Demonic masks were at first represented in Italy by devil masks. One type, Pulcinella (Punchinello), became for some time the characteristic mask of Italian carnival. (In time Pulcinella became a character of the *commedia dell'arte* and lost his diabolic connotations, but the costume remains; the English Punch, however, is quite a devil.) His black mask, beaked nose, white garb, hood, and stridulous voice were perfectly suited for imitating the soul of a dead man. Later he became localized around Naples, and today southern Italy is his kingdom. Usually he is assisted by other devils, and, as everywhere else, they wear sheepskins and black masks or have their faces made up with soot. They also create a great din with the bells that are hung from their belts. Devils also appear in central Italy (Abruzzi, Molise, the Marches, Tuscany). The islands, too, have demon masks at carnival and Easter. Sicily has some special examples (Mazzamurieddu, Varvarieddu, Zuppiddu), with whom are found devils (*diavolazzi*) and Jews, while groups of Pulcinellas take up the collection. The Mamutones of Sardinia are of particular interest, with their black masks and heavy bells on their belts. The realm of Harlequin is northern Italy and Piedmont. The Harlequin type existed before the *commedia dell'arte*, and because of his character he was the traditional demon par excellence. His costume can be recognized as the stylized form of the ragged suit which was inherited from the *centunculus* and which appeared all over Europe. In Lombardy and the Veneto, there is his counterpart Zanni, who also antedates the *commedia dell'arte*. He wears a red-and-white tunic and a pointed hat decorated with ribbons and cock feathers. His trousers are also red and white, and he has a bell attached to his rump. Generally speaking, the name Carnevale has imposed itself along with the regional and traditional names. Local spirit has often assigned separate proper names to Carnevale: Tomè, Giorgio, Paolinu, Biagio. It is he who undergoes, either in person or in effigy, the trial at which he is condemned to death and either burned or drowned. In northern and central Italy he is often accompanied by a female character: the Old Woman (La Vecchia), Befana, Quaresima (Lent). In the countryside, Carnevale is frequently replaced by the Bear (e.g., in the Friuli and Irpinia areas) and, in Alpine areas, by the Wild Man. The provinces of Italy are also familiar with the other characters of the common tradition: the Goat (Capra, in Monferrato, Mentana, Sicily), the buffoon couple (Lo Sposo and La Sposa), Death (La Morte, in Campania), the horned King with his Queen, the Doctor, the Priest (Corsica). But the *befanate*, or Befana and her husband Befano, and certain other masked characters of the villages are peculiar to Italy. Ritual plowing is customary in the Trentino, where the Zanni pull the plow. Italian maskers take up a collection, too, and claim the right to steal, as do all the maskers of Europe.

In France, folk masking for carnival is on the decline. There are some areas where masks are no longer found (Brittany, Touraine, Poitou, Vendée, Limousin, Berry, Orléanais), or where they are but rarely found (Guyenne, Gascony). "The disguises are simple, atypical and not individualized" (Van Gennep). The remains of an ancient heritage can be recognized in the Horse, which in France is called Bidoche or Bourrique, or else (after the manner of dissimulation) quite simply Échelle (Lyonnais, Languedoc, the Basque provinces, and Provence). The Bear (Pyrénées) and the Wild Man (Homme des Bois) are characters from primitive scenes still generally known. It is also very popular to present different categories of artisans or mock weddings in the processions. There are even the two different types of mask: the beautiful and the ugly, the Reds and the Blacks (Basque provinces). As elsewhere, the maskers take up a collection, soil passers-by, and sprinkle them with ashes, corn, or confetti. Carnival usually appears under the name of Caramantran. Very often he is replaced by an effigy which has to be buried or burned. It sometimes happens, though very rarely, that two groups of maskers will start to fight. As a general rule, however, when the tour has been completed, a communal feast is held. The famous Carnaval of Nice is based on a folk tradition of the Corporation of fishermen, but since 1860 it has became a fashionable manifestation like the carnival of Cologne and others.

The Iberian Peninsula still preserves some folk traditions that will soon be a thing of the past in France. The Spanish and Portuguese countrysides are familiar with the archaic devil masks that are found almost everywhere in Europe. In northeast Portugal the masks are made of wood, metal, and leather and depict anthropomorphic types, always frightening. They are decorated with animal elements, such as horns, hair, and serpents. It is curious, however, that the theriomorphic mask does not appear. The masked processions of the Caretas, the Chocalheiros, and others take place around Christmas time. The people taking part have costumes made of skins or tatters. They wear belts with bells and are armed with sticks with pigs' bladders attached. On the feast of St. Stephen (or at the Epiphany) the young men have their *festa dos rapazes*, when processions of young men dressed in sheepskins and with metal masks pass through the villages giving brief shows and finishing off the celebration with a community feast. On Ash Wednesday two masked figures, the Devil and Death, approach passers-by and force them to kneel down before them. The Spanish processions are more likely to enact the mock marriage ceremony or present spectacles of the death and resurrection of a hero. Once again figures of devils and spirits of the dead play important roles. The burial of the Rey del Mal Humor (King of Evil) is also a feature of Spanish carnival.

Belgium has managed to preserve what France is rapidly losing. This is due primarily to the ancient ceremony of the Big Fire (of Lent), around which center the Walloon mask customs. It appears, though, that the traditional disguises are vanishing. The young people are more and more contenting themselves with a military type of uniform and abandoning real masks. There still exists the tradition of the Old Woman and the Old Man, however, and certain beautiful and ugly characters (Barbençon). The life of the town is criticized in satirical lampoons, and ancient ritualistic battles still take place, though they are infrequent and lack conviction. The climax of all the ceremonies is the burning of an effigy (the Bolome, Jean Caton) suspended from a stake above the pyre. Besides these rustic ceremonies, there are carnivals in two small towns in Wallonia which have become famous: Fosse and, especially, Binche. In Fosse the townspeople have refined the costumes and the headdresses of the Chinels (short for Polichinelles), who are characterized by two humps, one on the back and the other on the chest. The Sapeurs of Fosse, in spite of their white aprons and trousers, show a clear relationship with the Wild Men of Binche by their jackets covered with ivy leaves. The carnival of Binche, with its famous Gilles, is more elaborate and more picturesque, even though it is slightly more sophisticated. The Binche mummers have also developed white costumes of an urban refinement (e.g., splendid headdresses made from ostrich plumes). They have, however, retained the belt with small bells attached to it, a bell on the breast, and the old-style wooden shoes. Tradition preserves the dances accompanied by a drum and hurdy-gurdy (*viole*), just as it preserves the custom of throwing fruit. In these days oranges are used.

In Flanders and the Netherlands, the Klaasen processions recall the St. Nicholas festivals of central Europe. In Flanders the masked processions are reduced to a few wagonloads of clowns (the Hoera, Sintrums, and Gekken) dressed in ragged costumes, who distribute clouts with pigs' bladders to the passers-by and throw confetti. In Brabant the traditional carnival is vanishing. Elsewhere, too, the observance is reduced to youngsters with the *rommelpot* collecting money. There is still the tradition of the right to steal and the burial of an effigy called Jan Poef.

The Baltic countries also share in the common mumming heritage of Europe. In Lithuania, the masked processions are made up of characters dressed in sheepskins and often with straw humps. Dressing in female attire is also very popular. There are grotesque masks made of bark or sheepskin, but for the most part the masks are of wood and are handed down from father to son. Certain masked characters are referred to as "Jews." They pretend to be businessmen and to buy "cows," that is, young girls and women. As they pass they create a terrible noise, cracking whips and so on. In the houses they "steal" whatever they can find, especially food. If two groups happen to meet, there is bound to be a fight. Of the theriomorphic characters, the Horse, the Goat, and the Crane are the most popular. The Bear has vanished, but Death and the Devil are often seen. In general, the processions center around a dummy mounted on a sleigh. Sometimes it represents a woman with large breasts (the Little Mother), and sometimes it is a man (the Old Man or the Uncle). At midnight the dummy is either burned or thrown into the river.

The maskers of Latvia are called in some places Martins (Martini) or Kaladi (Russ., *kolyada*; L., *kalendae*). Masks as such are little used; the face is either blackened or covered with a cloth. Masks of bark occur rarely. The disguises often depict a family whose head is the Old Man, the father. However, it is more popular to have a betrothed couple with their train of Gypsies, Jews, representatives of the various trades, the Devil, Death, and ghosts. The Bear, the Crane, the Horse, and the Goat (he-goat or she-goat) are frequently found. The behavior of the maskers is traditional; they make a great din, steal, hand out blows, and throw water. Obscene jokes and gestures are universal.

The Nordic zone shows some rather particular elements. The Christmas Goat (Julbock) is found most frequently there, while all the rest seems to have faded. In Denmark the ram mask is not much used, even though carnival masquerades are popular in the towns along the sea. In Sweden masked processions are few, but those connected with Christmas are widespread throughout the whole country and are found also in Finland. The main character, the Christmas Goat, or in some places the Ram, has now largely been replaced by Jultomten (Father Christmas). Carnival masquerades take place only in the seaside towns of southern Sweden, a fact which would seem to point to Danish influence. Remaining from the old traditions are the ancient disguises for St. Lucia's Day, when the sexes exchange clothes. The costumes of the young men represent monsters or ghosts (white shirts, straw on the legs and arms — the Staffan is covered all over with straw). The Barber and the Doctor also appear. Bells are still used in northern Sweden, and ritual plowing is still performed in central Sweden. The maskers of St. Knut's Day (Knutsfolk) blacken their faces. Masked characters appear also at wedding festivals. In Norway, masked processions are known only at Christmas. Under the influence of Germany, Father Christmas (Julenisse) was introduced about 1900, and gradually he eliminated the old Christmas Goat. The latter, known as Julbock, was sometimes accompanied by the Christmas she-goat (Julgeita). The Goats wore horns, and their masks were made of skins, birch bark, cloth, or wood.

Beyond the English Channel some of the same characters appear. It is true that the English have not taken over the Continental carnival, but traditional disguises abound, especially around Christmas time and in the month of May. In December, for example, at Haxey in Lincolnshire the kingdom is taken over for one day by a Fool and his 12 companions (Boggins), who are dressed in red, wear high hats decorated with flowers, and have their faces painted black and red. On Plough Monday, in January, ritual plowing is carried out by young men called Plough Stots or Plough Bullocks. They are accompanied by the Fool with his female companion, Bessy (a boy dressed in women's clothes). With the plowing there are often sword dances and other spectacles presented by the mummers. In May, processions are organized with a young couple dressed in flowers (the King and Queen of the May, for example). The English counterpart of Green George is called Jack-in-the-Green. He too is covered with green branches.

The most important theriomorphic character in England is the famous Hobbyhorse. He is prominent in Cornwall; round as a round table, black as the devil, he parades through the village preceded by a choir of young girls and accompanied by the Teaser and his Horse Pairs. In the autumn festivities in Cheshire appears the archaic form of the Horse (the Wild Horse), who has a real horse's head and is covered with a real horsehide. On All Souls' Day, in the procession of the Soulers, there is a character with a ram's head who wears a sheepskin. The most famous instance of theriomorphic elements is to be found in the Abbots Bromley Antler (or Horn) Dance. Six dancers hold before their faces magnificent stag antlers. The rest of the troupe is made up of the Fool with his female companion, along with a Hobbyhorse who makes a cracking sound with his lower jaw. In England masks also appear in the mummers' plays, a form of traditional folk drama not unlike the Balkan Kukeri. Usually the hero, for example St. George, kills his adversary (the Turk), who is then brought back to life by the Fool or the Doctor. Also on stage are devils, a stuffed character (Humpty), the Sweep with his brush, and so on. Another typical English mask is that of the Dragon, but it is in the process of vanishing.

Related to the masquerades discussed above are the folk dances, such as those of the Morris dancers (the English form of the various European *moriscas*), the numerous sword dances, as well as the processional giants which are still paraded in Flanders, are known in Italy, Austria, and Spain, and were once familiar also in France.

Niko KURET

THE MODERN MASK SINCE THE RENAISSANCE. The prevalently religious subject matter of 15th-century painting and sculpture made the theme of the mask relatively rare (PL. 366). It is chiefly in Venetian art, in the late 15th and early 16th centuries, that masks begin to occur in secular and allegorical representations. In a *Ceres* by a follower of Giorgione (Berlin, Staat. Mus.), the head of a ram appears prominently in the foreground on the podium on which the goddess is seated; undoubtedly it has an allegorical function and can be classed as a mask. Similar functions are exercised by the bust of a Roman emperor in Titian's *Christ Crowned with Thorns* (Louvre), by the classic head in the foreground of Lotto's *Portrait of Andrea Odoni* (PL. 208), and by the small skull among the scattered rose petals in the same artist's *Portrait of a Man* (Rome, Gall. Borghese).

Dürer, in the *St. Jerome* (Lisbon, Mus. Nacional de Arte Antiga) and in various engravings, established a clear relationship between the human face and the skull, wherein the former almost assumed the artificial character of a mask.

Important examples of the adoption of the mask with ethico-religious values in the 16th-century art of northern Europe are found in the works of Bosch, and later of Bruegel, in such works as *The Battle between Carnival and Lent* (II, PL. 357).

In mannerist works of an allegorical nature, bucrania and masks appear in pictorial decorations, drawings (e.g., those by Giulio Romano in Turin, Bib. Reale), and in architectural decoration (e.g., the keystones of the arches of Bartolommeo Ammanati's Sta Trinita bridge in Florence — rebuilt after World War II). In the drawings of Luca Cambiaso, masks are a recurrent motif (e.g., *The Masks of Satan*, Brno, Czechoslovakia, Mus.). In an engraving by Agostino Carracci, the actor Giovanni Gabrielli is portrayed with a mask in his hand as the attribute of his profession. By the second half of the 16th century, representations of masks for characters in farces and comedies (Zanni, Pantalone, etc.) appear frequently. Examples include ceiling frescoes by Alexander Paduano (Alessandro Scalzi) in the Castle of Trausnitz, near Landshut, Bavaria, and collections such as the *Habitus variarum orbis gentium* (1581) by Jean Jacques Boissard, with engravings by Julius Goltzius, and the *Diversarum nationum habitus...* (Padua, 1594), with engravings by Pietro Bertelli. (In this last work, the types of masks have a definite relationship with the depiction of various social types, as in the *Arti di Bologna* of Annibale Carracci, 1646.) The Nationalmuseum in Stockholm contains a collection of 44 16th-century engravings depicting Zanni, Pantalone, Franceschina, and others. Zanni is frequently portrayed in the frontispieces of 17th-century editions of *commedia dell'arte* texts. Vignette illustrations in editions of theatrical works became common, especially in the second half of the 16th century (e.g., *Amfiparnasso* of Orazio Vecchi, Venice, 1587). This represents the beginning of a tradition that reached its peak in the 18th-century editions of Molière's plays. In these works the depictions of mimes and masks had an essentially illustrative character without particular allegorical intentions.

Counter Reformation painters regarded the human skull as a mask with an eschatological significance. Through the use of strong realism and dramatic light effects, it often assumed a preeminent role in the composition, for instance, in Caravaggio's *St. Jerome* (Valletta, Malta, Cathedral) or in *The Magdalen with a Night Light* by Georges de La Tour (PL. 91). The skull has the same significance in allegorical scenes such as the *Melancholy* of Domenico Fetti (Louvre). In *The Knight's Dream* by Antonio Pereda (Madrid, Acad. de S. Fernando), a carnival mask and a skull are contrasted symbolically. Depictions of masks of a moralizing and allegoric eschatological character, such as the 17th-century engravings of Giuseppe Maria Mitelli (with legends such as "The comedy is ended"), were derived from the long ecclesiastical polemic of the Counter Reformation against plays and masques, which lasted from the end of the 16th century through the whole of the 17th.

The engravings by Jacques Callot (q.v.) frequently contain types of masks from the contemporary *commedia dell'arte*, such as those in the series of caprices, hunchbacks, and Italian comedians. Masks also often appear in the graphic work of Stefano della Bella (1610–60). Both Callot and Stefano treated them with whimsical significance, fantastic inventiveness, humor, and caprice. The same spirit appears in the *pulcinellate* (buffooneries) of Pier Leone Ghezzi, the comic aspects of which are closely related to caricature in 17th-century art (see COMIC ART AND CARICATURE). In other 17th-century depictions of *commedia dell'arte* masks, such as those of Pantalone and Zanni by J. Honervogt, an interest in social typology and in folk art seems to prevail. The mask as a typical attribute of comedy is shown in Simonin's *Le vray Portrait de M. de Molière en Habit de Sganarelle* (Paris, Bib. Nat.).

The 17th century also saw the use of the mask to indicate duplicity, or a fictitious and illusionary reality superimposed on true reality with the intention of deceiving. An example is the allegorical representation of the activity of the forger Pietro Vecchia in an engraving in *La carta del navegar pitoresco* by Marco Boschini (Venice, 1660). This tendency was fully developed in the 18th century in relation to the increasing interest and research in psychological situations and typology.

The depiction of characters from the Italian *commedia dell'arte*, known all over Europe, is particularly common in 18th-century painting. In the paintings of Alessandro Magnasco, the mask characters (e.g., *Pulcinella Playing the Guitar*, Venice, Coll. Gatti-Casazza heirs) retain the imaginative and free inventive values they had in the works of Callot. In Antonio Cifrondi's work they are depicted with an accentuated characterization (*A Figure from the Commedia dell'Arte*, Milan, Coll. F. Castelbarco Albani). In a not very different way, Claude Gillot repeatedly represented Pulcinella, Arlecchino (Harlequin), Lelio, Tartaglia, and numerous other characters of the Italian comedy (e.g., *Scène "des deux carrosses,"* Louvre). They also appear in the work of Nicolas Lancret (*Les acteurs de la Comédie italienne*, Strasbourg, Mus. B. A.), of François Joullain (*Scene from Italian Comedy*, Paris, David-Weill Coll.), and of Pierre Lacour (*Portrait of an Actor in the Part of Crispin*, 1784; Bordeaux, Mus. B. A.).

In Watteau's works, masks assume a significance related to the psychological analysis found in the contemporary French and English novel. That is, Watteau depicted a human type of mask, revealing the fundamental contradiction between the stereotyped theatrical character and the human feelings of the actor who plays the part, as in *Gilles* (Louvre; XIV, PL. 407). In addition, the mask (even a carnival mask) played an important part in the amorous games of his *fêtes galantes*, as suggested by the poem which forms the caption for an engraved copy by H. S. Thomassin the Younger (1725) of a Harlequin and Columbine by Watteau (London, Wallace Coll.): "Voulez-vous triompher des Belles? | Débitez-leur des bagatelles, | Parlez d'un ton facétieux | Et gardez-vous bien auprès d'elles | De prendre un masque sérieux. | L'Amour demande qu'on l'amuse; | Il est enfant; toute la ruse, | Pour lui plaire est d'être badin, | Et souvent au Sage il refuse | Tout ce qu'obtient un Arlequin."

Masked characters in the work of Giovanni Battista and Giovanni Domenico Tiepolo, and in a different way in the works of Pietro Longhi, present episodes typical of the contemporary social scene. In the Tiepolo drawings the masked scenes are rendered in terms of caricature and comic situation, like the buffooneries of Ghezzi described above. Examples of this are seen in *The Charlatan* (1756) and in *The Ballet* (both, Barcelona, Mus. de Bellas Artes de Cataluña), both painted for the Palazzo Papadopoli in Venice, apparently by Giovanni Domenico Tiepolo, in his frescoes in Ca' Rezzonico (Venice), and in the guest chambers of the Palazzo Valmarana in Vicenza. Examples can also be seen in frescoes by an unknown painter in the Palazzo Grassi in Venice and in the hall of the castle of Krumlov in Czechoslovakia. Here the figures are more or less connected with the characters of the popular theater, especially the plays of Carlo Goldoni. A peculiarity of such characters is that they tend to merge with the spectators, who become part of the action, as Goethe noted in his *Italian Journey* (Oct. 4, 1786).

Characters from the *commedia dell'arte*, very fully illustrated in engravings of the period by Abraham Bosse, Francesco Bartolozzi, and others, frequently appear on 18th-century ornamental objects, especially porcelain figures, such as the series of 16 characters from Italian comedy by Franz Anton Bustelli (second half of 18th cent.), made in the Nymphenburg porcelain factory. (The greater part of this series is in the Bayerisches Nationalmuseum in Munich.) Similar figures were made in Vienna in the factory directed by Claudius Innocentius Du Paquier. Sometimes the masked characters have a satirical intent and refer to social or political events, as in a print of 1797, in which Harlequin proclaims the rights of man in Venice.

The face mask was often used by Watteau to depict human duplicity, reviving the classic motif of the bifront (double face) derived from antiquity. This trend was naturally connected with the study of physiognomy that was so fashionable in the 18th century, by which human character was interpreted from the somatic configuration of the face, which in turn was considered to be determined by the moral nature of the individual. William Hogarth (q.v.) developed his characters along these lines, relying on his own physiognomic observations to create the masks and theatrical characters in his caricatures of the manners and morals of his day (*Masquerades and Operas, A Scene from the Beggars' Opera*, etc.). A new typology of masks was thus evolved, based on the more common physiognomic categories, as promulgated especially by Johann Kaspar Lavater (*Physiognomische Fragmente*, 1775–78). Goya (q.v.) also linked the mask to physiognomy. In pages from the *Madrid Sketchbook*, the word *mascara* ("masked man," "mummer") is used in referring to carnival and burlesque scenes, which take on the value of enlightened criticism of the ethical and natural abnormality of contemporary society. In his *Caprichos* and later in the *Disparates*, the bifront theme reappears, and the mask signifies duplicity and deceit. The *Entierro de la Sardina* (Madrid, Acad. de S. Fernando) demonstrates the irrational popular exaltation of artificiality in a mask. Here, as in the *Disparates*, the theme of the masks and of the ambiguity of the bifront becomes a revelation of the unconscious or preconscious areas of human personality.

Masks appear in the 19th-century Roman carnival scenes (cf. IV, PL. 441) of Bartolomeo Pinelli (Rome, Mus. di Roma; London, Vict. and Alb.), as an exaltation of Roman folklore. In general, however, the neoclassic and romantic movements — except in book illustrations, such as *Scènes de la vie privée et publique des animaux*, by J. I. I. Gérard (Grandville), Paris, 1842 — represented dramatic rather than comic subjects. Moreover, by the second half of the 18th century the *commedia dell'arte* had begun to vanish from the European stage, and in the trend toward realism the old characters were represented with a new, introspective approach, stressing the human side rather than the old emphasis on social typology. Honoré Daumier (q.v.) depicted Pierrot several times (e.g., *Pierrot Chantant*; Winterthur, Switzerland, Oskar Reinhart Coll.); Scapin and Crispin also appear in his graphic works. Similar characters appear in the art of Chardin (q.v.), both in oil and water-color paintings, as well as in various graphic series of the 19th century: *École des Pierrots* (1851), *Manteau d'Arlequin* (1852), *Nuits de Paris* (1862), along with the carnival masks depicted in the series *Dessins de la Mode* (1831), *Carnaval à Paris* (1842), and *Foire des Amours* (1852), in which the true tragic element of carnival is completely revealed. Paul Gavarni's illustrations were a model for the French 19th-century graphic style.

Edouard Manet painted *Le Polichinelle* in 1873 (Paris, Coll. Lecomte), and in the pastels of Hilaire Degas, motifs of mime and mask occur frequently (Harlequin and Columbine, etc.). Cézanne also touched upon this theme in his *Pierrot et Arlequin*, or *Mardi Gras* (Moscow, Mus. of Mod. Western Art). Often during this period, exotic, abnormal, and fantastic values were emphasized (sometimes merely to provide a pretext for color effects). Masks acquire a grotesque fantastic character in works by Gustave Doré such as those in his illustrations to Balzac's *Contes Drolatiques* (1855) and for Cervantes' *Don Quixote* (edition of 1865).

The mask has a fundamental expressive importance in the painting of James Ensor (q.v.), which shows explicit references to Bosch and Bruegel. The mask theme is interwoven with that of the skeleton, signifying unreality and ineluctable decay. Ensor's intent was violent satire against the society of his time, as in *The Entry of Christ into Brussels* (V, PL. 122), which caused such a furore that the painter was expelled from the group of artists called Les XX. This satirical intent is again evident in his *Masks and Death* (1897) and in *Maskers Quarreling over a Hanged Man* (V, PL. 203), which combines skulls with Oriental masks. In his *Portrait of the Artist with a Mask* (1899; Antwerp, Coll. C. Jussiant), Ensor attempted to assimilate the mask to his own features, expressing at the same time a sense of vanity and grotesque exaggeration of appearance.

In symbolist art, masks are also frequent in a complex counterpoint of meaning and allusions, as in the works of Aubrey Beardsley and, in a different way, in those of Odilon Redon, Gustav Klimt, and Egon Schiele. In Alfred Kubin's graphic works the mask is related to presurrealist themes, in an exploration of the zones of the unconscious, as it is also with a definite, but poorer and more circumscribed imagery, in the graphic works of Alberto Martini, which partake of the demonic quality in the work of Edgar Allan Poe, whose stories he illustrated. His form is related to that of the world of Beardsley.

The clowns of the Moulin Rouge and other Parisian cabarets were depicted by Toulouse-Lautrec, both in lithographs (see L. Delteil, *Le peintre-graveur illustré*, X, XI, Paris, 1920, nos. 180, 205, etc.) and in paintings (e.g., *At the Moulin Rouge: The Clown Mlle. Cha-U-Kao*, 1895; Winterthur, Oskar Reinhart Coll.), emphasizing their human values without reference to any moral judgment. Hermengildo Anglada y Camarasa and the young Picasso (e.g., *Au Lapin Agile*, 1904; New York, Coll. Mr. & Mrs. Charles S. Payson) also depicted clowns from this point of view. In the work of Emil Nolde, who took up the forms of Ensor, the mask is charged, in violent and grotesque expressionistic distortion, with mystic significance and with a dramatic social comment (*Still Life of Masks*, 1911, New York, Curt Valentin Coll.; and *Wooden Figure and Mask*, 1913, Basel, Kunstmus.). Other German expressionists, such as Erich Heckel (*Clown and Doll*, 1912; formerly in the collection of the artist) and Ernst Ludwig Kirchner, made similar use of the theme. The primitive mask with its exotic overtones also became subject matter for the expressionists (see EXOTICISM). It had already appeared in the paintings of Paul Gauguin and is found in Nolde's *Wooden Figure and Mask*, already mentioned, and in Max Pechstein's *Still Life* (1913; Mannheim, Städt. Kunsthalle), where it is related to contemporary psychoanalytical research. (Freud's *Totem and Tabu* was published in 1913.) August Macke wrote an article on masks in the *Blaue Reiter Almanac* of 1912.

The themes of Pierrot, of Harlequin, and of the clown had a great vogue in the first decades of the 20th century, frequently as a vehicle for cubist analytical forms and chromatic patterns. Masks played an important part in Dadaism and later in surrealism. Noteworthy examples in Dadaist art are the mechanical mask (1919) by Raoul Hausmann and Sophie Taeuber-Arp's *Dada Head* (1920), a painted wooden hat block. In the art of George Grosz and the works of the left wing of the Neue Sachlichkeit, the mask is directly linked to motifs of social criticism. In surrealist art it assumes the peculiar values of ambiguity and unreality, often having an eschatological significance, as in the work of Salvador Dali, Yves Tanguy, and R. Magritte. In 1929 E. L. T. Mesens created a photomontage, *Mask for Insulting Esthetes*, applying a collage as a mask over a face.

Paul Klee used the mask as a symbolic reduction of the human image to an ideograph for psychological phenomena and the unconscious; in his later works it reveals his own preoccupation with death.

The theme of the human face reduced to a sculptured mask occurs in Picasso's painting in *The Red Tablecloth* (1924; New York, private coll.) and that of the human skull in *Still Life with Skull* (1945; collection of the artist); the same theme appears perhaps in a more decorative sense in the work of Georges Braque.

The reduction of the human face to a mask and the assimilation of one into the other are typical and characteristic of the associative and imaginative process of Chagall (q.v.), as in *I and the Village* (1911; New York, Mus. Mod. Art). He revived with great intensity the theme of the bifront, as in the *Two-Faced Bride* (1927; Bern, private coll.), with allusions of a fantastic, unconscious, and almost ancestral nature, related to the imagery of Russian folk art (see Chagall, *Ma Vie*, Paris, 1957).

In the figural painting of the period between the two World Wars, the clown theme appears frequently, depicted with its various traditional significances, in the works of Walt Kuhn, Jean Metzinger, André Derain, Karl Hofer, and Gino Severini.

In contemporary art, from as early as 1942 in the *Barbara* of Jacques Lipchitz (Northampton, Mass., Smith College Mus. of Art), and especially in abstract art, there has been a tendency toward the complete assimilation of the mask, of the human countenance, and of its entire somatic aspect into a single grotesque concept. No longer is it a question of setting these elements side by side to show their similarities and differences, but rather an effective and unequivocal coincidence and superimposition of the mask and face, as in Willem de Kooning's *Marilyn Monroe* (ca. 1952); Jean Dubuffet's series, *Mirobolus Macadam & Cie.* (1946); and more recent works of A. Jorn and others.

Enrico CRISPOLTI

The cinema has had recourse to the mask in various ways. Its effectiveness for "thrillers" and horror themes has often been exploited, as in *The Laughing Mask*, directed by Louis Gasnier and starring Pearl White; *The Mask of Fu-Manchu* (1932) by Charles J. Brabin; and *The Mystery of the Wax Museum* (1933) by Michael Curtiz. Man Ray satirized the adventure film in 1929 with *Les Mystères du Château de Des*, making use of masked actors. Carnival masks contributed to telling scenes of revelry and confusion in both Jacques Feyder's *Carnival in Flanders* and M. Carné's *Les Enfants du Paradis*, and in the latter the repertory of the popular pantomine was adopted for both comic and tragic effect. Documentary and semidocumentary films have made use of primitive masks both for educational and dramatic purposes, as in Paul Haesaerts' *Sous le masque noir* (1958), on African masks, and the Canadian film *The Loon's Necklace* (1950), on North American Indian masks.

While the trend of the modern theater has not favored the wide use of masks, they have at times been introduced (cf. PL. 368) and have aroused interest in the sphere of art. The Bauhaus included in its study program an investigation of the semantic phenomenology of the mask, and Oskar Schlemmer posed a problem intended to develop a new repertory appropriate for contemporary scenic requirements. During the 1920s the theater masks of W. T. Benda, a Polish-American artist, enjoyed a considerable vogue and were exhibited as a collection.

* *

THE ORIENT. *India.* Masks in India are much less common than might be expected. At present they are found only in areas untouched by Hindu civilization (among the jungle tribes of eastern India, e.g., the Gonds, Konds, Baigas, Murias, Pardhans, Agarias, Bhuiyas) or where its development was arrested at an early date (in the Himalaya, especially Kulu, and in Malabar, Kerala, and Ceylon). Masks are connected with the cults of spirits by whom the masked dancers become possessed. These spirits (yakshas and yakshis: male and female spirits of the soil, fertility, and wealth, local godlings associated with the hills; rakshasas: monstrous devouring demons; nagas and naginis: male and female semihuman water-serpent deities; pretas: spirits of the dead, ghosts; vetalas: evil spirits or ghosts animating corpses) were the object of the cults of the pre-Aryan population from Afghanistan to the far south. They brought droughts, thunderstorms and floods, sterility, diseases, and death, but also wealth and fertility, rich harvests, increase of cattle, and many children. Many spirits acted as incubi or succubi, offering the utmost sexual pleasure but draining away the life of their victims. Their cults required bloody sacrifices (buffalo, goat, cock, even human) and gifts of rice, *yantra*s (mystic geometric diagrams made of thread, straw, and other fibers), magic games, riddles, and ecstatic dances under the influence of narcotics or intoxicants, ending in sexual excesses. On certain occasions images of demons, made of straw, wood, or clay and covered with resin, were burned.

This tradition is best preserved in Ceylon. The yaku (plural of yaka) are spirits of the dead, who in their alien or punitive aspects can represent diseases (Kālu-Yaka, Kālukumāra, Aimāna, Kōla-sanniya, etc.). They can appear in many disguises: as yogi, donkey, snake, wolf, South Indian (enemy of the Singhalese). Others are vampires (e.g., Hiri-yaka, Mahāsōhana, the great cemetery demon, and Aturu-sanniya, the corpse devourer), archaic Hindu deities (Śiva as rakshasa, Skanda or Subrahmanya; Bhairavi as earth goddess), former heroes or heroines who met a tragic end (Paṭṭinī Devī, a wife who committed suicide in order to preserve her chastity), or bastards (e.g., Kālu-Yaka, son of the Indian prince Vijaya, founder of the Singhalese kingdom). All these figures are represented by dancers wearing huge, carved, wooden masks (demon faces with protruding eyes and tongue, surrounded by snakes, subsidiary human or animal heads, and immense crowns and ear ornaments), painted in bright colors (yellow, fire red, and grass green) and varnished.

In Kerala and Malabar similar demons (e.g., Kuttichattān) are represented by the Thaivam dancers, and the bloodthirsty mother goddess Kālī (also known, among her countless names, as Cāmuṇḍā, who destroyed two demons, and as Bhūdevī) is invoked at the Tira festival. Often elaborate crowns are worn here, and the face, instead of being masked, is heavily made up, especially when benevolent deities are represented, for example the goddess Bhāgavatī (the Lady, another epithet of Devī) as Prasanna-Rūpī (she of radiant beauty).

The masks of the jungle tribes of eastern India represent rakshasas and Bhūdevī (the earth goddess) and are somewhat similar to masks in Africa and New Guinea. Among the more Hinduized Bhils of Central India (in the Vindhya Mountains and Maikal Range), the masks have completely degenerated and represent the classic Hindu gods Śiva and Pārvatī.

Dance masks are not known elsewhere in India, but there is indirect evidence that once they must have been common. Literary and archaeological sources show that the yaksha, rakshasa, and naga cults had been very common until at least the 3d-4th century, when Hinduism absorbed most of these godlings as aspects of various Hindu high gods, especially of Śiva and Kālī. Those who could not be transformed were incorporated into the heavenly host of gandharvas, apsarases, *gaṇa*s, and so on, or were reduced to the status of evil spirits and ghosts who could be exorcised only by Tantric magicians. But in Kulu and the adjoining Hindu parts of the Himalaya, where the yaksha cult is still alive, these deities (devatas, called *bīr*s, from Skr. *vīra*, hero; or *brahm*s) are venerated in the form of brass or silver masks mounted on poles and hung with rags. Inscriptions show that some of these deities were regarded as heroes of epic times (e.g., Hiḍimba, an apsaras of the *Mahābhārata*), deceased princes and princesses (e.g., Mujanī Devī, queen of Raja Hemaprakāśa of Nirmaṇḍ, 9th-10th cent.), or even orthodox Hindu gods such as Mahadeo (Śiva) and Cāmuṇḍā-Kālī. To what extent prehistoric funeral masks of bronze and gold, found in Mysore, belong to a similar tradition is uncertain. On the other hand, the mask on the pole seems to have been the prototype of the *mukhalingam*, a rather early representation of the god Śiva. The lingam represents not only the male sexual member — thus depicted until the 4th century — but also, in the form of an erect stone or pole, the seat of the local deity (i.e., yaksha). As an erect stone it has become the orthodox form, the pole type surviving only occasionally, as in the pillar lingam of Draksarama (Godavari delta) or in the Stambheśvarī (Lady of the Pole) cult of Orissa. The face on the lingam dates from the 5th century, when the genital character of the lingam was suppressed. In this form it corresponds to the Greek herm, a combination of a post with a mask and a male genital. Often the face (*mukha*) or four faces (*caturmukha*) form a separate metal cap only temporarily put on the lingam. In the Himalaya a silver mask is put on the face of the idols of Naga temples on the occasion of the Nagapanchami festival. The trance dances once executed by priestess-prostitutes at the yaksha festivals have disappeared, but the Kathak dance of north Indian prostitute-dancing girls has preserved the giddy whirling spin and the stamping footwork met with in such dances among other primitive peoples.

The identification of some of the yaksha godlings with gods or deceased heroes has led to the development of the secular dramatic dance. In Ceylon the demon dancers perform also some epic tales and Jātaka stories and even use, on such occasions, secular masks (king, queen, minister, hero, tradesman, etc.). The Baigas, also perform masked dances on the occasion of the Cherta festival, in which they make fun of their Hindu visitors, especially yogis and tradesmen. Otherwise practically the only masked dramas in northern India are the *Kṛṣṇa-līlā* and especially the *Rām-līlā*. The first celebrates the victories of the young god Kṛṣṇa over the demons sent by the evil King Kansa of Mathura and his love sports with the milkmaids (*gopī*s) at Brindaban. The second dramatizes the victorious campaign of Rāma (incarnation of Viṣṇu) and his brother Lakṣmaṇa to deliver, with the help of devoted monkey and bear tribes, his abducted wife Sītā from the demon king Rāvaṇa of Lankā. In both *līlā*s the heroes appear without masks, but the demons and the monkey and bear characters wear masks. In both cases, however, the masks seem to go back to a now forgotten connection with the yaksha cult. For Kṛṣṇa of Mathura was, in the popular histories of the Purāṇas, the savior and upholder of the mountain Govardhana and later became the Kṛṣṇa of Dwarka. The *Rām-līlā* ends with the burning of a huge effigy of the many-headed Rāvaṇa, a feature unknown in the *Rāmāyaṇa*, on which the story of the drama is based. As the *Rām-līlā* is celebrated in spring, and as the burning of a demon figure in spring is a common feature in many primitive religions (e.g., in some villages in India at the Holī festival), it seems that the *Rām-līlā*, celebrating the victory of the Hindu gods of social order over the yakshas and rakshasas, has superseded an earlier pre-Aryan festival. A similar case seems to be the Kathakāli ballet of the Malabar Coast, the subjects of which are those of orthodox Hindu mythology, its technique borrowed from the classic Bhāratā-nātyam; the quaint make-up of the dancers and their huge circular headdresses and elaborate costumes still survive, although the painted masks are gradually disappearing. Thus it appears that in absorbing the primitive cults, the later Hindus moderated the masked dances connected with them and adapted them to orthodox themes.

Hermann GOETZ

China. Chinese masks have played an important part in artistic and religious activities, in the theater, in myth, and in war. The earliest masks are found on the bronzes of the Chou dynasty (1027-256 B.C.). Some of them, the *tʻao-tʻieh* (known since the preceding Shang-Yin period, 1523-1028 B.C.), probably formed part of the equipment of exorcists or shamans. According to Mircea Eliade's hypothesis, the use of shamanist masks was not widely diffused over the whole Asiatic continent, but it is very probable that they were used in China. There are many Chinese literary references from various periods (the *Chou-li*, the *Shuo-wên*, the *Han-shu*, the *Sui-shu*, and the *T'ang-shu*), which all confirm the custom of wearing masks to exorcise evil spirits or to drive away the influences of pestilences. Such disguises were often protested by orthodox Confucians; for example, the writer Li Yü complains that "people wear masks which depict animals" during the New Year festivities in northern China. Some historical texts also mention the ceremony known as "No," during which each participant wore a special two-colored disguise and a wooden mask (*mu-mien*) with an animal's head.

The use of the disguise or mask was intended to identify the wearer with the figure he represented. In the ceremony of the Pa-cha, for example, the representative of the deceased (*shih*), generally a young close relative, wore a mask reproducing the features of the dead person; in the same ceremony certain animals were also honored and some of the participants were disguised as animals. A Chinese proverb warned that the representative of the deceased must wear the mask because "the soul of the deceased goes wandering and masks are made to hold it." The mask, therefore, in certain cases is the means whereby the soul can be brought back to the world of the living; if the representative were not masked, the rite of evocation might be hindered. Similarly the mask is able to "hold" the animal or supernatural being that it represents.

In China the mask also has an apotropaic value. Even in very remote times, masks of grotesque or hideous appearance were used to drive away pestilences.

According to the heterodox Confucian philosopher Hsün Tzŭ (300–235 B.C.), Confucius had a face similar to the mask of a *fang-hsiang-shih* (exorcist).

The use of apotropaic masks is documented also in peripheral zones. On the island of Hainan, for example, cowhide masks of a type locally called *niu-ma-mien* (ox mask) were used to frighten away both wild beasts and evil spirits. According to another theory, these masks were totemic images similar to those found in certain Indonesian cultures.

In more recent times apotropaic masks have been applied to cuirasses to frighten the enemy.

Recent excavations of certain Manchurian sites have uncovered silver and copper masks. Some authorities believe that they date from the Ch'in (221–206 B.C.) or Han (206 B.C.–A.D. 221) dynasty; others assign them to the Liao dynasty (907–1125; PL. 352). These masks were certainly mortuary, and a text of the Sung dynasty (960–1279), the *Lu-t'ing shih-shih* of Wên Wei-chien, provides proof of this usage.

Masks have had a preponderant part in the Chinese theater. According to some authors the very origins of the Chinese theater are connected with the pantomimes or dances of the shamans and with ceremonies in honor of the souls of the dead. It is probable, therefore, that Chinese theatrical make-up is derived from masks. Moreover, the make-up of the Chinese actor, unlike that in other countries, communicates to the audience the personality of the person he portrays, as well as identifying a particular character in the play. Certain colors and designs of the make-up also have special meaning.

A few specimens of buffoon masks and narrator masks have been preserved. Both are theatrical masks and are sometimes rendered in a grotesque but realistic style, with a second face modeled on the forehead between the eyebrows. This kind of mask is typical of northern China: it has certain similarities to Tibetan masks and is generally made of papier-mâché or painted cardboard.

Lionello LANCIOTTI

Japan. The use of the mask was introduced into Japan from the eastern regions of the Asiatic continent, from China, or more directly, from the Korean peninsula, during the 6th–7th century of our era. Originally it was closely connected with a kind of mime dance performed during Buddhist religious festivities. The oldest masks were those of the Gigaku (PL. 362; VIII, PL. 278), a spectacle generally performed outdoors in front of temples. The varied repertory of these performances required a variety of costumes and masks. The masks were very large, covering all or the greater part of the head. They were carved from wood or made of layer upon layer of lacquer; the earliest ones were probably made by foreign craftsmen, chiefly Koreans. Ancient examples of such masks are preserved in the Shōsōin (Nara) and in some temples, such as the Hōryūji and the Tōdaiji (Nara). The facial features are often caricatured or grotesque, with strongly arched eyes, long noses, large ears with elongated lobes, and mouths with curved beaks. They are highly expressive, often with a leering, grotesque, or ferocious expression. Sometimes these characteristics are combined with a comic zoomorphic effect, as well as certain elements and characterizations of a terseness of description that is a departure from the figural expressions of Far Eastern art. This has led certain scholars to conclude that the origin of these masks is more Western than Chinese, and some think it possible that they may reflect distant Greek and Hellenistic figural motifs.

The Bugaku performances, which probably go back to the 8th century, also consisted essentially of dances of Buddhist religious inspiration, often in courts or temples. The Bugaku masks (VIII, PL. 278) differed from the Gigaku, particularly in their size and form, since they covered only the face. The other differences are chiefly stylistic: a marked symbolism of the images, a tendency toward decorative, highly stylized facial features, and a general idealization of the forms that attenuates even such features as are intentionally realistic. Many examples, however, are derived directly from the Gigaku masks, retaining various similarities in the repertory of characters represented. The oldest are from the 15th century; those of the so-called "twelve deities," preserved in the Tōji (Kyoto), are dated 1486. Some experts believe that the Bugaku masks, too, have an ancient foreign origin.

A special category among masks of the early periods is that of the Gyōdō masks, used in processions and other Buddhist ceremonies. Their resemblance to the iconographical types of religious statuary show them to be directly derived from Buddhist sculpture, which they sometimes reproduce very faithfully.

From the 9th–10th century, masks were increasingly used in the traditional dances and in the ancient Shinto agrestic rites. These merged with certain Buddhist cult rites and ceremonies, thus giving rise to particular types of spectacle from which the No dramas and the comic Kyōgen were derived.

The No and Kyōgen plays and dances had their greatest development after the 13th–14th century. Specific rules were laid down for the use of masks, and the iconographical types conformed to the dramatic repertory, which, through the centuries, remained virtually unaltered. The masks represent male and female characters of different ages and conditions, supernatural beings, divine and demonic, and imaginary and monstrous animals. The old repertory of masks from former times remained in existence, but it became enriched with new types which clearly reveal a new figural concept. In addition to the traditional monstrous, terrible, and grotesque masks, new types with more human expressions were developed. In the No drama (PL. 362) they were pathetic, dramatic, or tragic; in the Kyōgen they were humorous and comic. The place held originally by supernatural beings was taken over by man, and the supernatural itself became transformed, chiefly into an outward expression of an inner state of mind, sentiment, or passion. As they lost their religious significance, masks acquired the function of conveying character by realistic traits, which became progressively more human, though retaining the stylization of types required by their theatrical nature. Such masks sometimes have a stylistic resemblance to certain contemporaneous sculptures — particularly those of the Kamakura period (1185–1333) — in which is evident a search for a less formal and symbolic idiom. Generally, however, masks representing human beings did not represent real types. The idealization of the character required that the mask represent abstract and stylized types; generic physiognomies were rendered with essential features only slightly characterized, and often they were intentionally expressionless but ready to be brought to life by the actor to express the whole gamut of sensations and moods required by the drama. This is the reason for the frequent ambiguity of expression found in certain types of masks, not representing sadness, indifference, or joy, but lending themselves to the expression of any one of these emotions.

The masks cover only the face and are often smaller than the average face. They are carved in wood, then lacquered and painted. They may also be modeled in cloth, covered with lacquer, and then colored. Often the seal of the artist who created them is found inside.

The best specimens of Nō and Kyōgen masks are generally the oldest, dating from the 13th and 14th centuries. They were often the work of great artists such as Shakuzuru, Tatsuemon, Zōami Hisatsugu, and many others, who created types that remained established and almost unvaried for centuries.

Adolfo TAMBURELLO

PRIMITIVE MASKS. Masks have always been conspicuous cultural elements among the majority of primitive peoples the world over. Few Negro tribes in West and Central Africa and few island peoples of the southwestern Pacific Ocean were without them. They were not so ubiquitous, however, among the North American Indians and were relatively unknown on the Polynesian islands in the central and eastern Pacific.

It is not surprising, therefore, to find that primitive peoples have devised a wide variety of masks, in the fashioning of which such materials as wood, shell, bark, leather, bark cloth, cornhusks, bronze, copper, and even the pith of reeds were used. Many masks were life-size, but some were only an inch high, and others were over 3 ft. high. They were often painted, either in a single color or, frequently, with a rich polychromy of three or more bright colors. Various materials, such as shells, seeds, hair, or feathers, were sometimes affixed to masks that were usually worn or used with prescribed costumes. The carved or fabricated face or head was therefore only a part of the total complex of the mask, and to see masks without these attachments and costumes, as they usually appear in museums and collections, gives little idea of how they were intended to appear when in use. Among some primitive peoples a new mask was made whenever one was needed and immediately afterward discarded or even destroyed, whereas other peoples used the same object again and again until it was no longer serviceable. In either case, a diversity of forms, all of them called "masks" in the broad sense, was utilized.

The form shaped to fit over the face was the most commonly used primitive mask. With it was worn a head covering and a costume that further concealed the identity of the wearer. The helmet mask, which completely enveloped the head and was often carved to represent a head, was also a widespread type. In the western Pacific this type developed into a lofty, bizarre creation. However, masks were frequently of a kind that did not hide or cover the features of the wearer, such as the numerous headpieces, carved in various human, animal, or abstract forms, which were supported on the head of a dancer, with or without a costume suspended below them. With the exception of a few exotic shapes, all the major forms of primitive masks fall within these basic types.

The use of masks was associated with all the major cultural focuses: religious, social, economic, and political. Masks usually represented specific beings, such as ancestors, spirits of various kinds, deities, or mythological personages, whose actual presence they symbolized or contained. Some masks were worn at secret rites which could be attended by only a few persons, while others were used in public ceremonials. With few exceptions they must be considered as active, dynamic art forms, since they were usually seen in violent movement with sharp contrasts of strong light and shadow, particularly when worn nocturnally around a flickering fire. In many instances, too, a vitality was given to the mask by the wearer, whose eyes flashed and moved through the perforated eye slits. A further vitality becomes apparent when one considers that many primitive peoples believed in the existence of a power or essence as a fragment of an all-pervading universal force in all animate and inanimate matter. Hence, it was believed, the materials of which the mask was made had an innate energy, and, moreover, the tools that the artist used had a comparable energy. Since this was so, great care and constant prescribed rites had to be observed to create the forms of the mask successfully and safely from these materials. As they took shape under the hands of the sculptor, and as the appearance of the being to be represented or symbolized began to emerge, these forms gave to the basic materials additional power and vitality.

The mask as an esthetic expression must be considered from three points of view: (1) its objective or physical properties, that is, the proportions, relationships, and qualities of its component parts; (2) the meaning and significance of its forms; and (3) the psychological relationships between its exterior forms and their inner content or meaning. The mask is not, therefore, merely an exotic or descriptive appearance; it is, rather, a complex combination of a variety of factors.

Africa. The primitive cultures of Negro Africa were substantially homogeneous, although innumerable differences existed among tribal groups. It is therefore possible to discern the generalized pattern of beliefs and institutions that led to the use of masks in many areas of Africa. A belief in the power of ancestors and of deities and supernatural spirits controlled religious concepts. Through the intervention of these forces, the people derived a sense of protection and general well-being. Certain fundamental needs, while common to all peoples, are particularly evident in the African institutions set up to implement them. These may be considered as (1) the need for security and survival in a world in which uncertainty was always present, and (2) the need for continuity and stability among peoples who had no written historical records and were so loosely organized that integrating elements were essential to them.

African rites involving the use of masks were those enacted to ensure fertility and increase of crops and those performed to obtain protection or health. These rites were substantially motivated by the drive for security and survival. Other ceremonies, which centered around ancestors, the initiation of youth into adulthood of the tribe, and the performance of mythological plays (the great oral literature of Africa), were, on the other hand, directed toward the maintenance of continuity and tribal stability.

All the varied types of primitive masks were used in Africa; wood — with or without polychromy — was the most common material. Costumes were generally worn with the mask, and in some instances extraneous materials were attached to both the mask and the costume, although this was not so common in Africa as in the western Pacific islands. The basic representations were derived from human and animal forms and were sometimes combined in a seminaturalistic or grotesque manner; only in a few cases does the mask approach an abstract design. Throughout Africa certain kinds and styles of masks were standard. A study of those used by related tribes in such large areas as the western Sudan and the central Congo reveals that numerous art elements were shared in common. Although stylistic analogies may be noted in the art forms of peoples far removed from one another geographically, it is nevertheless profitable to classify the mask by broad geographical areas.

Among the largely agricultural tribes of the western Sudan (Mali, Upper Volta, Niger) the spirits of animals and ancestors were closely associated with fertility and the protection of crops. Some animals were of near-totemic character, and their importance for the welfare of human beings stemmed from the days of creation or from later mythological times. In this context, the animal was often a transformation from human form, endowed with human thought and actions and, as such, had either ancestor status or close affinity with the ancestors.

Representative of a form peculiar to this region are the Segoni-kun masks of the Bambara tribes, worn by members of the Tji-wara society. These are three-dimensional sculptures of antelopes attached to round basketry caps and worn on top of the head (XIII, PL. 329). A costume of shredded raffia is suspended from the cap to the knees of the wearer. The numerous differences in these antelope representations, each peculiar to one of the Bambara subtribes, range from a somewhat naturalistic carving of the full animal form to a highly stylized concentration on the neck, mane, head, and horns. During the sowing season Segoni-kun masks are worn in pairs, one depicting a male and the other a female antelope. The dancers imitate the leapings of the animal, which the Bambara believe to be the source and protector of fertility, since it symbolizes the fabulous mythical animal which brought them the knowledge of agriculture.

These masks are usually given a dull black surface, largely by searing with a hot iron, and are intended to be seen as three-dimensional forms moving in space. Their design emphasizes by sweeping curves and contrasts of sharp angles, together with piercing and a volumetric handling of shapes, their dynamic expression and function. Regardless of proportions or the varied shapes involved, stress is placed upon an open form, frequently oriented vertically, in which such characteristic antelope features as the neck, head, ears, and horns are dramatically and freely rendered. The body — if it is expressed — is often shown as a tense, static form of a simple horizontal shape with four stubby vertical supports for the legs. Movement is sometimes implied in the legs by a conventionalized sharp-angled articulation. It is also implicit in the male Tji-wara masks by the upward curve of the neck and mane, which is counterbalanced by the downward thrust of the tapering head. At the junction of the neck and head two ears project upward as sharp diagonals, and above the head long, tenuously curving horns culminate the design.

The artistic effects are achieved by various combinations of a few basic geometric shapes, such as tapering cylinders, long and short curves, short and staccato angles, and long, thin parallel lines. These are rhythmically integrated into a rich and often elaborate design expressive of the selected parts of the animal form and of their vigorous movement in space. The antelope head is particularly significant in the Sudanese style. It is a very tight, contained, almost hieratic form, which often suggests an anthropomorphic rendering. Together with the body, when it is expressed, the head functions as a stabilizing element for the pierced, active forms of the neck, mane, and horns. There is in these masks a close relationship between esthetic forms and the shapes and movement of the animals from which they are derived.

Of the many masks used by Sudanese peoples, animals serve as the inspiration for the majority. The antelope frequently appears, but monkeys, sheep, and birds are not uncommonly represented. Face masks carved with human features are also prevalent. In some parts of the western Sudan, red, black, and white polychromy is characteristic.

South of the western Sudan, in the areas of Liberia, Guinea, Sierra Leone, and Ivory Coast, a profusion of masks appears. The greater number of them are worn over the face with the appropriate costumes and represent or are derived from human features, but they are distinguishable in both style and function (VII, PLS. 120, 125). In Liberia, for example, where the Poro is an all-important male secret society, the mask is worn in the performance of secret initiation rites and in the conduct of diverse public functions of a civic, religious, administrative, or social nature. Poro masks range from a few inches to well over life-size, and from a sensitive, naturalistic representation of human features to a fantastic, sometimes gruesome depiction of animal or combined animal and human forms. They are usually carved by professional sculptors in very hard wood, with the surface smoothed, blackened, and polished until it resembles black marble. When these masks were used, however, the surface was frequently smeared with clay or blood to give the proper power and appearance.

Representative of this Liberian art form is the strongly anthropomorphized bird mask used in public by the judge as he pronounced sentence. Characteristic of the style is the full-volumed handling of the forehead and huge nose, the sculptural double curve that indicates high-arched eyebrows, and the cuboidal contrast of the curving and angled planes of the lower facial area. The dramatic vitality of representation in these masks is enhanced by the glint and movement of the eyes of the wearer through the open eyeholes.

On the western margins of the Ivory Coast and in eastern Liberia, the Dan tribes also often use a refined naturalistic mask. Among them it is a sacred object, which — although worn on some occasions — functions largely as a means of addressing petitions to the ancestors and so to the gods. The masks are therefore doubly symbolic. They are greatly revered and handed down from generation to generation. Dan masks, too, are carved in hard wood and have an extremely high, deep-black polish. The forms tend to be shallow and consist of flowing surface planes that create subtle contrasts of concave and convex areas. The emphasis is frequently on large, empty, round eye sockets and on the high convex curves of the forehead.

Perhaps the best-known African masks are those of the Baule (Baoule) tribes who live in the central Ivory Coast. These masks may be divided into two groups: (1) those based on naturalistic human features, and (2) those derived from animal forms or with animal elements, such as horns, attached to human faces. The first group is by far the more common. Examples range from life-size to almost twice life-size, and frequently the shallowness of their forms and the fluidity of their surface planes relate to the Dan masks; but they differ in their elegant refinement of descriptive detail. For example, a pattern of parallel grooves in deep relief is often used to depict the hairdress; high-arched, parallel relief lines define the eyebrows; and a regularly dentated fringe, meeting below the chin in a pendant, describes a full beard. The basic shape of these Baule masks is an elegant vertical oval, somewhat wider at the top than at the narrowing base. Proportions vary from group to group, so that in some examples the oval is wider or narrower than in others.

The function of Baule masks is incompletely known; it is certain, however, that some of them were worn in religious ceremonies to represent specific deities of an extensive pantheon. For instance, a large naturalistic or stylized oxhead mask was worn at burial ceremonies to represent the deity who accompanied the soul to the hereafter. Apparently a more naturalistic type of mask was used in ceremonies of reverence to ancestors, and other so-called "masks," which were solid unpierced faces, may have been representations of ancestors or deities. When not in use, these sculptures were kept in a sacred house in each village.

At first glance Baule masks seem bilaterally symmetrical, but on closer examination it is apparent that such symmetry does not actually exist. Instead, the arch of one eyebrow is a little higher and longer than the other; the swing of the hairdress dips lower over the temple at one side; the vertical, downward sweep of the nose from the bridge is also slightly to one side; and the mouth is seldom in the exact center of the tapering lower part of the face. This quality of subtle asymmetry gives the Baule mask an esthetic richness and a vitality of expression. Only in a few instances was any color applied to these forms; they were usually monochrome, often black.

The mask was also a prominent art form in southern Nigeria, where among the Yoruba tribes two distinctive types were developed. One type, the Gelede mask, was a somewhat modified helmet form that represented the entire head and was worn horizontally on top of the head (VII, PL. 126). The other, the Epa mask, was a large full-helmet type that covered the head of the wearer and rested on his shoulder; on top of the helmet was carved a composition of several or even dozens of figures (PL. 355). The total height of the Epa masks sometimes reached 4 ft. Both the Gelede, in the central and southern areas, and the Epa, in the northern, were used in comparable dances, which were performed to ensure health and welfare for the community.

Yoruba style is clearly seen in the Gelede masks. Heavy and full-volumed forms are often so closely interrelated as to appear compressed, and facial features, carved in high relief and bold in size and scale, are spread out over the entire face area. Eyes, with heavy upper lids and a large protruding pupil, are described by wide, sharp-pointed ovals, and a short nose terminates in extremely wide, expanding nostrils, below which a full-lipped Negroid mouth protrudes as two parallel shelflike folds that do not meet at the corners. Some Gelede masks have an elaborate, neatly grooved hairdress, and others are topped by a figure or figures, which sometimes represent genre scenes such as a boy climbing a tree for coconuts. This type of mask, unlike the African masks discussed above, is highly polychromed in nonnaturalistic colors which further stress the large scale of the features and the expanding volume of the forms.

Among the major tribes of southeastern Nigeria, the Ibo, Ibibio, and the Ijaw (Ijo), a wide variety of mask forms was developed (VII, PL. 132). In this region masks are used in a great many of the numerous public and secret ceremonies and traditional plays which have social, religious, and political significance. Polychromy — particularly in red, black, and white — is an important feature of these diverse forms and was usually applied afresh each time the mask was used, to emphasize such details as scarification marks, facial features, and hairdress.

Of the many masks of the Ibo, the Mmo, the property of a men's secret society, constitutes a distinctive form. Rituals of this society involved petitions to the ancestors, political duties, and various dance ceremonies performed at village festivals and at members' funerals. Many of these masks are life-size and carved with a thin, shell-like facial area and full cranium, often topped by an elaborate headdress. They are sewed to an enveloping harlequinlike costume, composed of numerous small areas of bright colors, which covers even the hands and feet. The cranium of the mask rests on the head of the wearer, who looks out through the open eye sockets of the carved face. The mask itself is painted red, white, and black; the facial area an over-all white, which is the color used throughout Africa to refer to the dead; lips, eye sockets, and certain scarification marks a bright red; and the hair or headdress a dull black.

The Mmo mask has numerous distinctive Ibo characteristics. The shape, for example, is a wide oval dominated at the top by a high forehead and at the base by a receding chin, above which an open mouth displays teeth. In Mmo masks there is a marked representation of the hard, bony skeletal structure of the face, and the surface is suggestive of skin tightly drawn over fleshless bone. This skeletonlike death's-head appearance is further stressed by the emphasis on empty eye sockets and on the thin, almost fleshless lips. Since the Mmo masks occur among numerous widespread Ibo tribal groups, there is a good deal of variation in both shape and precise details. Among some groups, for example, a single or double rosette appears in front of the ears as a scarification mark in low relief, and crossing diagonals with a bisecting vertical strip are carved on the forehead.

The Ibo celebrate a festival of thanksgiving at the end of the harvest season. At that time numerous plays are performed, including those which culminate the initiation period of the boys. Burlesque performances in some of the plays involve the use of particularly fine and characteristic masks. Such, for example, is the *mba*, an especially well-carved ovoid mask with a trapezoidal palette projecting above the head. The face is painted white, the nose, mouth, and forehead area red, and the hair a flat, dull black; the palette has rich geometric designs, frequently with a pinwheel motif, painted in red, white, and black. These masks are worn in pairs by boys and represent girls, whose behavior they mimic. Ibo style expressed a contained, direct, but not overly dramatic naturalism.

In contrast, the Ibibio masks of the Ekpo men's secret society are fantastic in appearance and dynamic in expression. The function of this society is to propitiate the ancestors for the general well-being of the village and to maintain the political and social status quo. In the past its rituals were so secret that any nonmember who saw them was killed. Of the varied masks used by the Ekpo society, the naturalistic black ones represent ancestors and the more grotesque ones the spirits from the underworld. Each of these spirits was portrayed in the ritual as a dangerous and irresponsible character, which was expressed in the masks by fantastic forms of strikingly malignant appearance. In some, the heavy animal-like tusks and the enormous, concentric circular eyes represent nothing human nor quite animal but successfully convey the impression of evil. Other Ekpo masks might have the lower jaw carved separately and hinged with fiber so that during the rites the mouth could be moved. The sculptured forms in Ibibio masks are large in size and scale and are carved with real mastery in the use of angled planes and contrasts of abrupt projections into space and recessions into depth to a flattened background. The emphasis is entirely upon a bold sculptural statement of shapes and not upon a refinement of line or detail. Many of the Ekpo society masks were remarkably polychromed, at times with such delicate colors as soft gray, yellow, and mauve appearing in juxtaposition. The face and semihelmet masks were by no means the only types used by the Ibo and Ibibio. Both groups had a number of carved figures or combinations of figures which were worn or carried on top of the head.

The Ijaw tribes, who live in the swampy delta of the Niger River, wore masks in the rituals they performed to propitiate the water spirits, important sources of protection and fertility. These are often very large and have grotesque facial structures composed of dynamic combinations of birds, snakes, and crocodiles. In some examples, the animal forms are carved in the round and project considerably above the abstraction of the facial shape. Eyes are rendered as long, protruding, heavy tubular forms which alone suffice to give the mask its bizarre semihuman appearance. The dramatic contrasts of rounded and projecting shapes against the flat or concave background are intensified by the frequently arbitrary bright designs in red, white, and black. These represent still another type of African mask, since they are worn horizontally on top of the head so that the carved and painted designs are exposed to the sky.

Another center of mask development is located in the Cameroun area of West Africa, immediately east of Nigeria. In this region, because of the constant intermingling of small tribes for one reason or another, the art styles have a greater degree of homogeneity than in Nigeria. Three kinds of masks were formerly used in this region: (1) a life-size and fairly naturalistic face type; (2) very large dramatic interpretations of a face or a full-head form, worn either as a helmet or as headgear angled on top of the head (II, PL. 97); and (3) large masks representing animal forms. All three types range in expression from a direct naturalism to a dynamic stylization, at times verging on abstraction, and in treatment from a vigorous sculptural statement of basic expressive shapes to a somewhat more refined and careful delineation of parts. Few of these masks are polychromed; instead they are usually painted either a monochrome dull black or light-red ocher.

In this style, the face or head is interpreted as a full expanding volume, and the large-scale facial features, somewhat as in Yoruba masks, project from but do not break into the volume of the surfaces behind them. Frequently the facial parts are dramatically expressed in a sculptural way so that each feature is a distinct entity. These features are unified either by a strong rhythmic repetition of basic shapes or by a rhythmic adzing of surfaces. Cameroun masks lack the descriptive or decorative details found in other African styles, such as the treatment of the hairdress and scarification marks. The hairdress, for example, is often defined by large and deep parallel grooves that have a marked sculptural quality. This rendition, although it varies somewhat in the depth and scale of the grooves, is found so commonly that it may be considered a characteristic of Cameroun style. Moreover, the rhythms established by the sculptural forms of the hairdress are reechoed in the roundness and contrasting depth of facial features. This is one of the most direct and purely sculptural mask styles found among primitive peoples.

Cameroun masks were largely used by semisecret confraternities of a residual totemic character; many of them had as their emblem an animal with which there was a psychological relationship. The societies, for example, emulated the qualities and powers of the animal, which they believed were accessible to them. The purposes of the societies included the protection and welfare of the group and the punishment of social offenders. The majority of them used masks in many of their secret or public rites. In other societies, masks were used during funeral rites for the propitiation of ancestors and as symbols of societal roles (e.g., the humanoid masks worn in the secret meetings of certain military espionage groups). The precise function of many of these masks is not known, but they constitute one of the distinct features of Cameroun cultures.

To the south, in the Gabon region of equatorial Africa, and especially along the reaches of the Ogooué River, numerous life-size or slightly smaller face masks were used (PL. 356). They represent naturalistic female faces surmounted by crested hairdresses. The facial forms comprise a high, rounded, protuberant forehead, a straight and fairly thin non-Negroid nose, and slanted eyes with both lids often puffy and almost closed, giving the face a rather Oriental appearance. Mouth forms vary, although in many examples the lips are extremely realistic in shape, while the ears, in contrast, are summarily treated. Chins are usually narrow, sometimes almost sharp-pointed, and the eyebrows are carved as distinct arches. Distinctive features of these masks are the remarkably balanced expression of bone structure, the fleshy and muscular form, and the tightness of the covering membrane of skin.

Two categories are distinguishable among them: those with facial scarifications and those without. The facial scars follow a fixed pattern consisting of three rows of three rectangular forms in very high relief in front of each ear and a diamond pattern of similar forms on the forehead just above the bridge of the nose. Hairdresses vary considerably, possibly reflecting the styles of different subtribal groups; but they are all treated in a decorative manner, consisting of carved patterns of parallel lines in low relief. Whether scarified or not, the face was originally painted an over-all white, the lips, scarification designs, and sometimes the eye slits red, and the eyebrows and hairdress a flat black.

These masks were worn by secret societies, especially during the periods of initiation and burial of society members. They represented female spirits, and the rites were sometimes performed with the wearer of the mask mounted on stilts, a feature found not only in this part of Africa but also in some areas of Guinea and Liberia to the west. The purpose of the societies seems to have been to maintain the traditional social relationships through the sanction of the ancestors; hence these masks had a socioreligious significance.

In the western part of the Congo region, especially in the watershed of the Kwango River, numerous masks were used in the secret and public initiation ceremonies when youths received adult status in the tribe. The principal tribes using masks in this area were the Bapende (II, PL. 110), the Bayaka (II, PL. 109), and the Basuku.

Three types of masks were worn: the face, semihelmet, and full-helmet types. But the full-helmet mask, particularly that of the Basuku, may be singled out as the most characteristic. As usual with this type, it comprises a three-dimensional representation of the head and is slightly larger than life-size, so that it can be worn comfortably over the head of the dancer. Basuku examples express the full volume of the head shape by emphasizing rounded surfaces, such as those of the forehead, the half-closed upper eyelids, and the planes of the facial area. The nose and mouth are variable forms, but the nose is characteristically rather short and thin, and the mouth is typically a narrow, open oval with jagged, filed teeth carved within the lips. The hairdress is a flat pattern of lightly carved parallel lines, with a bird, animal, or small human figure represented in the round just above the forehead. These masks were lightly painted with black and red and were worn with an attached costume of shredded raffia. Unlike the Ogooué River masks, which have a calm and contained sobriety of expression, the Basuku masks often combine contradictory expressive elements, such as a detached quietude expressed by the half-closed eyes, and an overt aggressiveness expressed by the conspicuous open mouth with sharp teeth.

The types and styles of masks evolved in the central Congo area are distinguished by a rich coloration (II, PL. 115). The dominant color is a light red obtained by mixing ground camwood with water or oil. Though sometimes used as a monochrome, it is often combined with white, black, and various ochers ranging from yellow to orange.

The eastern branch of the Bapende tribes in this area uses numerous small masks in boys' initiation rites. These are usually much less than life-size, are often marked by sharp, wide oval faces, large heavy-lidded eyes, wide flat noses, and small mouths. The hairdress is built up into a number of knobs or points and is simply described. These masks are frequently carved in hardwood and are rubbed with camwood powder, which gives them a rich red patination. They are stitched to all-enveloping costumes, comparable to those used with the Ibo Mmo masks. The eastern Bapende also wear small face masks with short or long animal horns rising above.

Also characteristic of the central Congo area are very large polychromed masks, sometimes 2 ft. or more in height, used by various groups in socioreligious performances involving mythological characters. They are narrow in proportion to their height, which gives them a conspicuous vertical orientation, and dramatic in appearance, with their features composed of grotesque and nonhuman shapes. The eyes, for example, may be enormous and may project as sharp and long conical forms from a deeply depressed oval eye area. The nose is frequently heavy and blocky, almost cuboid in shape, and the mouth is moderately large, with a roughly ovoid open form. The headdress may be a tight caplike shape, or it may be expanded into other larger broken forms. The facial surfaces are usually a monochrome red; the depressed eye area is white with black stippling; and the eyes are often painted in stripes of yellow, black, and white. Flanking the nose, on either side of the face, there is a zoned design of small triangular geometric elements, sometimes lightly incised on the surface and always richly painted in three or four colors. The total effect is spectacular and weird but arresting in its vibrant contrast of shapes and colors.

The Basonge tribes of the east-central Congo use a unique semihelmet type of mask that has become known as the *kifwebe*. Although they vary considerably in shape and in the precise handling of the features, all *kifwebe* masks have the appearance of combined human and animal features. The design is dominated by wide parallel grooves that cover the entire surface and are painted in white and black or red and black (II, PL. 120). The forehead is often an expanding, heavy, cowl-like form, below which heavy, hooded eyes project. The nose has a cuboidal, triangular shape, and the mouth is a hollow, wide, projecting rectangular form. A long, enveloping raffia costume is suspended from the carving and almost completely covers the body of the wearer. It is said that the forms of these masks are derived from those of lion heads and that they are now used by subversive political groups. Certainly they have a leonine character, but the early accounts of their meaning and function are extremely vague (e.g., "masks used in ceremonies to welcome guests," or "masks used in important secret rites"). They have, in common with other Congo masks, a largeness of scale and a heaviness of carved forms.

The Baluba tribes in the southeastern Congo wore a large, monochrome, dark-brown helmet mask, which expressed, perhaps more successfully than other helmet masks, the contained volume of a full globular shape. The facial features are composed of wide ovoid eyes, with the upper lids sensitively rendered as almost closed, the nose as an undistinguished short blocky form, and the mouth as a protruding rectangular shape. Buffalo horns are carved on the sides of the head and curve upward slightly in front of the face. It is said that these masks were used in initiation rites, but there are no satisfactory data on their function. They constitute, however, in the thinness of the shell of their carving and in the expression of volume, one of the most esthetically appealing of African masks.

As an art form, the mask in Africa appears in a wide range of types and styles, but there is a constant reliance upon sculptured form for descriptive, expressive, or dramatic statement, so much so that color and extraneous materials appended to the mask must be considered of supplementary importance.

The basis for mask forms is deeply rooted in natural forms, both human and animal; even the fantastic and bizarre elements are found, when analyzed, to be not far removed from reality. But it is evident from a study of African masks that the ability and creative interpretation of the individual artist was responsible, as in all art, for the true masterpieces.

South Pacific. The primitive cultures of the island peoples of the central and southwestern Pacific Ocean are, in contrast to those of Negro Africa, varied to the point of heterogeneity. Of the major ethnic divisions of this vast area, only that of Melanesia in the southwestern region used masks extensively; but even in Melanesia, an area peopled by various Negroid stocks, mixed in certain areas with Polynesian and Malay elements, the mask was highly developed in certain regions and entirely absent in others. The main centers of its extensive development are: in New Guinea, the Sepik River and north-central coastal area; the Tami Island region and the central and western shores of the Papuan Gulf; the Torres Strait Islands; New Britain, particularly the northern part; New Ireland; New Hebrides; and New Caledonia.

All types of masks found in Africa were to some degree used in the Pacific, with, perhaps, the face and the helmet types most widespread. Melanesian masks, however, differ greatly from those of Africa in several important ways: in the variety of materials used in their fabrication, in the great array of other materials added to or suspended from them, and in their extremely rich polychromatic effects.

Although wood was the material used almost exclusively in some areas, in others a considerable variety of substances was employed, such as bark cloth, human facial bones or parts of them (which were then modeled or covered with a plastic substance), pith of reeds stitched to a framework in such a way as to resemble basketry, bark, turtle shell, pottery, and very sturdy, finely woven basketry. Surfaces were usually painted, often with a gessolike, transient earth pigment, bright in color, which included all the various ochers from red to yellow, and various clays from white to tinted shades of gray; in some areas, blue-green, mauve, and other delicate tones were obtained from minerals, seeds, and plant juices. Pigments were usually made volatile by mixing them with water, but in a few regions apparently an oil of some kind was used as a binder.

Besides the costume, which was usually of raffia palm, the array of materials attached to the mask included feathers of various types and colors, bright plant seeds, a wide variety of kinds and sizes of shells, fish teeth, and plant leaves. To a considerable extent, in fact, the carved or fabricated face covering accounted for only part of the total appearance of the mask.

The uses of masks in Melanesia may be grouped in diverse functional categories, some more prominent in one area than in others. Masks were almost universally used in both public and private ceremonies, and they were motivated by religious beliefs, social customs, or economic practices. The symbolic importance of the ancestor was extensive, but no great proportion of masks was made for ancestral rites as such; frequently, if the ancestor was invoked, he was of a far-distant, mythological character. Religious belief in numerous supernatural spirits led to their representation or symbolization in the majority of Melanesian masks. During initiation rites of young boys into a tribe or into membership in a secret society, supernatural spirits were frequently in charge of the procedure, specifically spirits represented by masks. Masks were also used in some areas at the harvest season to depict spirits or mythological characters to whom gratitude for a successful crop was due. Masks were used extensively, also, in funerary rites and for terroristic purposes, to maintain a social status quo. In some areas, masks were not worn but functioned as objects in their own right, representing, by large, solidly carved, and unpierced wooden faces, the visages of mythical or supernatural beings. The majority of these forms were extremely sacred objects and could be seen only by members of a restricted group.

In the range of Melanesian mask representation, there is little close reliance on natural proportions, features, and relationships. On the contrary, there is a good deal of expressive stylization of facial shapes and features, which often become grotesque and fantastic. The motivation behind these masks comes not so much from the world of physical reality as from the world of hallucinations, dreams, and states of terror and psychological unbalance. This particular content, in fact, gives to the majority of Melanesian masks their unique and often fabulous appearance.

The region of greatest diversity and richness of mask forms in Melanesia, and in the entire world of primitive peoples, is that of the Sepik River watershed and the north-central coast of New Guinea (q.v.). In this area the masks, which vary from a few inches to over 5 ft. in size, are usually carved in wood, although many remarkable forms are woven in a hard, fine basketry (PL. 442; see MELANESIAN CULTURES). There was in this region of New Guinea such a pronounced fluidity or dispersion of cultural elements that numerous components are shared in common by the many art styles. Three kinds of Sepik masks can be defined on the basis of their function and meaning: those representing (1) ancestors and used at ancestral ceremonies, (2) clan-owned mythological ancestral spirits, and (3) supernatural beings.

Ancestor masks were carved at the death of a man and used in mortuary rites in his honor. They are life-size, with a very tight and narrow ovoid shape in which there is a balanced expression of solid bone structure and of the covering membrane of skin. The forehead and facial areas are rendered in contrasting rounded surfaces and depressed flattened forms. Facial features vary in precise shaping but generally consist of small, open, oval eyes, a pierced, sharp, crescent mouth, and a very long and sometimes fleshy nose. Ears, where they appear, are summary stylizations, frequently placed as tablike forms at either temple. There is often a strong expression of a vertical division of the ovoid shape from the point of the chin to the top of the forehead; this is conveyed by the resultant ridge of the forehead, the consequence of the juncture of its two lateral planes, and is continued downward by the direction of the nose. In some examples the forehead division is a sculptured notched ridge. A realistic detail in all these sculptures is a hole carved through the nasal septum, a feature taken from reality, for these peoples wore nose sticks and other nasal decorations. Many masks were painted a monochromatic red ocher or a dull black; others were painted with the ceremonial facial designs worn by the deceased during his lifetime, thereby associating the sculptured form with a particular person.

Near the mouth of the Sepik River and in the adjacent coastal areas, ancestor masks were carved with combined bird and human forms. The forehead, for example, is shaped like a rounded cranium, the small eyes are given an upward slant, and the nose terminates in a beaklike appendage. Since it was believed that at death the soul departed as a bird, these ancestor masks combine both the physical and spiritual aspects of the deceased (PL. 358).

In the upriver Sepik region, large masks represent clan-owned mythological, ancestral, and supernatural spirits. Many of these forms were not intended to be worn but were suspended along the walls within the men's ceremonial houses as revered objects, to be seen only by the society members. They represent specific spirit beings by the components of their carved forms, by the painted designs and the colors used, and by the numerous appendages attached to them as further iconographical elements. Facial features are often dramatic in shape and in size: the nose, for example, is continued as a beaklike form that terminates in a carved bird's head or a bird figure, and the eyes, shaped like large concentric circular or ovoid forms, convey an intensively of expression. Masks play a prominent role in the extensively developed ceremonialism of this area. Through them, liaison is established with ancestor spirits for protection and general well-being and with supernatural beings for similar benefits.

Another important center of masks in New Guinea is located on Tami Island (PL. 354) and along the shores of the Huon Gulf east of the Sepik coastal area. By comparison, the Tami-Huon masks are restricted both in use and in kind. Two types, closely related in design, were used: a large and often heavy wooden mask and a somewhat smaller construction of bark cloth stretched over a palm-wood frame.

The wooden forms, sometimes over 2 ft. high, have a blocky, vertical, rectangular shape, the rounded surface being only slightly differentiated to indicate separate structural areas. The cranium is a tight, skullcap shape, below which the face is only slightly depressed. The features are connected into a single large design spread out over the facial area; the eyes as loops are joined by a thin, stylized nose with separately articulated nostrils; and the nose, in turn, is attached to the wide, oval mouth below. Characteristic of Tami masks are the triangular-shaped patches tangent to the lower and upper margin of the eyes; the bird- or fishlike forms that are carved to project from the sides of the mask; and a slightly protruding lip plug which fills the open oval of the mouth. The basic color is white, with details painted in bright red and flat black.

The Tami bark-cloth masks are similar to the wooden ones in their over-all shape and facial features, but they lack the tangential pendent forms. Both types were used to represent particular supernatural spirits which were the hereditary property of secret societies. In the past, these spirits visited the villages at ten- or twelve-year intervals for a stay of about a year. Although these masks were religiously motivated and their use brought benefits to the community, they also had strong social and political significance, since the use of them periodically reaffirmed the privileged status of the secret society; thus the use of these religiously inspired forms perpetuated the social and political organization of the people.

In southern New Guinea also, particularly in the central part of the Gulf of Papua area, bark cloth was used in the construction of masks. The bark-cloth mask was, in fact, the only type made in this area. Perhaps to a greater extent than in any other region of Melanesia, these Papuan Gulf forms were a focal element of all aspects of the culture, since they were associated with one vast communal ceremony. The preparations for this ceremony, when the necessary masks were made — and they were made anew for each ceremony — sometimes extended, depending upon the various taboos and other circumstances, over five to ten years or more. The fabrication and wearing of masks was restricted to the adult men in the society. The women, however, collaborated during the period of preparation by producing and storing the surpluses of food which were necessary for the culminating ceremony.

Of Papuan Gulf masks, the conical and the helmet types are comparable to forms found elsewhere in Melanesia, particularly in New Britain; but a third, the *hevehe*, is unique among all masks of primitive peoples. The *hevehe*, like all bark-cloth masks, was made by stretching damp bark cloth over a palmwood armature, to which it was either securely lashed or sewed; when the cloth dried, it fitted tightly over the frame. The *hevehe* consisted of two parts which were inseparable from the point of view of design: a helmetlike head with round eye perforations in the bark cloth, and a long, seemingly crocodile snout of wood attached as a mouth. Above this rose a flattened, ovoid, palette form, ranging from 6 to 15 ft. in height. On the bark-cloth surface covering the front of the palette, narrow strips of cane were sewed to form curvilinear and rectilinear geometrical designs arranged symmetrically on either side of a vertical axis. The designs on this upper part were then painted in very delicate earth and vegetable pigments, the tones frequently being within the gray register but varying from mauve to pink or yellow. The features of the helmet head below were also delineated in color, but these pigments were of a stronger red, black, and white.

The *hevehe* were the most important of the mask forms used in Papuan Gulf ceremonies. They represented first, in the shaping of the head, a supernatural being, and second, in the abstract geometric designs on the palette, mythological elements or events associated with that specific supernatural being. The ceremony in which they were used was one of considerable festivity and rejoicing, since these supernatural beings were of a completely beneficent character and were known to all the clan members, who understood that the purpose of this ceremony was both to honor the spirits and to obtain their continued support. Additional spirits, some of them totemic, were represented by helmet masks, and during the same period the conical bark-cloth masks were worn at the initiation rites of small boys. This spectacular, dramatic ceremony, therefore, had economic, social, political, and religious importance.

On some islands of Torres Strait, which lies between New Guinea and Australia, masks were also a conspicuous cultural expression. Two kinds were made: wooden and turtle-shell forms, which were generally used in harvest fertility ceremonies and in funerary rites (PLS. 251, 358, 441, 442).

The wooden masks represent a large, narrow human face which has in common with other Melanesian masks an aggressive and dynamic expression, achieved by both sculpturing and painting. Small oval eyes with an inlaid seed pupil are placed close to a long narrow nose, the sharp point of which overhangs the wide, open mouth filled with teeth. These features are close-set within the tight limits of the face and are further related by a black painted design above each eye and around the nose and mouth area. The rest of the surface is painted white with details in dark red. Sculpturally, the surface of the face is concave from the forehead to the protruding chin, with only slight modeling. Distinctive are the heavy, looped ear forms placed on a line with the eyes and given open rectangular distensions of the lobe, which in live prototypes accommodated the large ear ornaments worn in this part of the Torres Strait.

Torres Strait turtle-shell masks are a unique type in Melanesia. These were made by steaming, bending, lashing, and stitching together the shell plates. The forms differ greatly, ranging from a life-size, naturalistic human face, to fish and crocodile shapes, and to a number of fantastically elaborate composite forms consisting of human, fish, crocodile, and bird shapes, some of which were 4 ft. or more in length. Shells, seeds, and cassowary feartthers are appended, and the masks are often painted with red ocher and white lime. The turtleshell human face has many of the sharp-featured, aggressive elements seen in the wooden masks; the animal forms are realistically depicted or, in some instances, they dramatize such parts as the open jaws of the crocodile or the wings of the bird. The best examples of these are esthetically arresting and technically rank among the supreme achievements of primitive peoples.

The northern part of the island of New Britain was a center for some of the most fantastic and abstract masks in Melanesia. However, some naturalistic face masks for use in ancestor rites were modeled in a plastic material, consisting of a paste made from mashed parinarium nuts, over the frontal bones of the skulls of deceased members of the tribe. The surfaces were painted dark red, black, and white, presumably following the traditional ceremonial face painting used by the deceased during his lifetime. Several kinds of bark-cloth-covered masks were also made in this area, some in a lofty, conical shape, others in a cylindrical helmet form.

Unique to New Britain are the very large, fantastic masks of the Sulka people (PL. 449). They consist of a bamboo frame over which strips of the pith from reeds are sewed in place. Quite summary human facial features carved in wood are often attached to this surface, but in some examples a mere suggestion or an abstraction of features is worked out in pith. Characteristic of these Sulka compositions is the use of extraordinarily bright colors, such as pink-red, acid green, and yellow, with some white and black. Many of these masks are of a conical type, 3 ft. or more in height, and were worn on top of the head, the wearer looking out through a shredded fiber costume that covered his body. Other examples have a huge circular form impaled at a rakish angle on a conical base, with the undersurface of the circular form elaborately decorated in rich curvilinear designs. Some of these upper circular forms measure as much as 5 ft. in diameter. These masks were the property of secret societies and were worn largely in particularly terrifying and arduous initiation rites.

Of the bark-cloth types found in New Britain, those used by the Baining people in their noctural snake dances are the most spectacular and esthetically arresting (PL. 442). The major mask used in the dances consists of a large and rather fabulous animalistic head worn as a helmet. The forms are dominated by a protruding cowl-shaped forehead and — within the deep concave facial area — by large concentric-circular eyes, which are made by pressing rings of cane over the bark cloth. The face terminates in a long, rather limp protrusion which suggests a tongue. These forms are elegantly painted in symbolic and descriptive designs of white, maroon, and black on the natural tan of the bark cloth. An inverted anchor-shaped design on the forehead is finely outlined in white and black stippling; the eyes are marked by maroon and black; and on the protruding tongue a herringbone design is painted in fine red lines. The true significance and function of these masks are but partly known. Several fieldworkers have agreed that they are used in ceremonies to honor an important visitor. At these dances, long bamboo tubes, also covered with bark cloth, are used by wearers of the masks to blow over the children; other dancers use live snakes somewhat as jumping ropes, a feature which suggests that fertility and apotropaic aims are inherent in such ceremonies.

North of New Britain, in the western part of New Ireland, elaborate mortuary ceremonies required the use of a great number of masks. As indicated in several previous instances, prolonged, elaborate communal rites are characteristic Melanesian cultural phenomena. In New Ireland the mortuary ritual known as the *malanggan* is, together with the *hevehe* ceremony of the Papuan Gulf, among the most spectacular. It was prepared and staged by one of the clans upon which the New Ireland social organization was based. All the design elements were clan-owned, that is, their use was the prerogative of a particular clan whose elders supervised and directed the sculptor as he prepared masks and other art forms.

Several categories of ancestors were honored in the *malanggan*: the original, legendary ancestors, such as the sun and the moon; the mythological ancestors of the remote past; and the more recent clan dead. The carvings are replete with symbols referring to these various ancestors; but since the same or similar forms are given different interpretations, according to the context in which they are found, it is practically impossible for anyone except a clan elder to interpret the full meaning of the sculptures. Basically, but with innumerable variations, the *malanggan* mask is a crested semihelmet form with attached long wings or ears flanking the face on either side. Sizes range from life-size up to nearly 6 ft. in height. Many masks, particularly the largest and heaviest examples, functioned merely as exhibition objects and were placed on shelves in an open-faced shed; some were merely supported by relatives of the deceased, who performed no dance. The life-size mask was worn in pantomimic dances throughout the celebration of the *malanggan*.

An art style unlike that found in any other Melanesian area evolved in New Ireland. This is equally evident in masks, figures, and other art forms and in ceremonial paraphernalia. Distinctive of this style is an intricate over-all openwork pattern. These pierced, three-dimensional designs are substantially sculptural definitions of structure. This, however, is very seldom allowed to remain as a clear esthetic statement. Instead, it is visually denied or even destroyed by the painting of fragmented, small-scale designs upon the structural parts. The coloration on early New Ireland masks is red, dull black, and white. Later, after German contact, some blue, yellow, and other shades of red were used. Typical of this style is the representation of the eye by an inlay of the operculum, or valve-closing plate, of the sea snail, which has swirling colors of green, brown, yellow, and white. The component design elements often combine to give a distinctly surrealistic flavor, when, for example, fish heads protrude as eyes from a grotesque, nonhuman face, and when snake, bird, and pig forms are combined in a single design. These forms exist so completely in an unbounded space as to be termed "aerial."

Prolonged and elaborate Melanesian ceremonies were also performed in the central and northern New Hebrides Islands and marked the advancement of an individual from one grade to another within various secular, religious, and secret societies. A New Ireland clan gained considerable prestige by staging a more elaborate and spectacular *malanggan* than had previously been given. The cultural dynamics in the New Hebrides were even more intensely exacting, since all males from the age of six or seven had to strive constantly to amass sufficient wealth and prestige for advancement within the numerous grade societies. In a culture so motivated, a status quo position was consequently untenable. The main purpose of achieving higher rank was to attain a comparable position in the hereafter, since it was believed that if sufficient rank was not achieved before death, the spirit of the ancestor would face oblivion; thus the continuity between the living and the dead, always a vital matter among primitive peoples, would be broken.

In some of these grade societies, carved, modeled, or fabricated masks indicating the presence of the ancestors were required. One type was face size and carved with close-set scowling eyes, deeply furrowed facial folds, and an open crescent mouth. Some of these, carved in a moderately soft wood, were painted brilliantly in red, white, yellow, or black; others, carved in a hard wood and having a widely looped nose, were painted in a monochrome black. In either case the features were restless and dynamic in expression. Small diamond-shaped masks were modeled over a light palm-wood armature with a compost made largely of cut and mashed vegetable fibers. Some of these were of a helmet type with multifaced sides; others were made of palm spathe and topped with a conical caplike form sometimes covered with spider webbing. In the majority of instances New Hebrides masks have an intense, alert expression and are vividly polychromed with light brick-red, pink, yellow, light mineral-green, blue-black, and white. Long strands of banana fiber or raffia serve as a short costume. The majority of these masks were made by nonprofessional artists, that is, by members of the grade to which a candidate was aspiring. If the "artist" happened to be particularly talented and experienced, the result would obviously be more accomplished and esthetically satisfying. This accounts for the unevenness in the quality of New Hebrides masks.

Two mask types were developed on the large island of New Caledonia (PL. 443). One consisted of a long, narrow, life-size face, which was carved with a handle below the chin so as to be held in front of the face. It was painted simply with black and red as further descriptions of the carved features. Fibers were attached around the edges, and a costume covered the upper body of the dancer. The other type of mask was often larger than life-size and was attached to the base of a cylinder of woven cane which fitted over the head of the wearer, and from both the cylinder and the mask a long wig and beard of human hair were suspended. This mask was worn with a short, thick, black-feather costume reaching slightly below the knees and represented a combination of aquatic and jungle supernatural spirits.

Both types are heavy-featured and menacing in appearance. An open V-shaped mouth is carved with sharp teeth; the nose is of a naturalistic, fleshy, Melanesian type and is usually given a huge beaked or hooked form, the hook sometimes describing a three-quarter circle. The eyes differ in treatment but are usually very large, with an intense expression, and are set beneath scowling brows. Rounded, heavy, protruding forms suggest cheekbone structure, and in the same way the tight treatment of the forehead expresses the hard skull area. These masks are a dull monochrome black, which is occasionally relieved by the use of red or white around the eyes and mouth. They are massive in scale and completely sculptural in their expression of intense and dramatic aggressiveness.

In view of the great diversity in kinds and styles, it is impossible to make any extensive generalizations on Melanesian masks. But it is understandable why these forms, when considered as prerequisite to the implementation of vivid ceremonials which reflected a lack of assurance and deep anxiety, were not derived from physically observed and experienced reality, as they were to a great extent in Africa. Instead, they originated during emotionally disturbed states when fantastic apparitions from an intangible and imaginary world made themselves known. This resulted in a vividly dramatic and richly symbolic art that has always appealed to 20th-century surrealists.

The Americas. Among the Indians of the Americas, the mask was an object of varying importance in the high cultures of pre-Columbian South and Middle America, as well as among the more primitive tribes of historical times. The forms included pierced and unpierced face coverings, hoods or helmets enveloping the entire head, and a costume mask covering the whole body, with or without a face covering. Stone, metal, wood, leather, fibers, basketry, and bark cloth were used in the fabrication of these varied forms.

In pre-Columbian Middle America, stone funerary masks were used at Teotihuacán and elsewhere. Finely carved in a hard stone, they were created in a strong but generalized naturalistic style to symbolize the dead, with the unpierced eyes and mouth cut into the stone in relief. It is believed that these carvings were attached to the burial shrouds of persons of rank. Various relief sculptures, such as the Maya stele on which masked figures represent the gods, furnish evidence that it was the custom to depict the gods in this manner at religious ceremonies.

In the ancient Andean area of South America, human beings wearing animal or bird masks appear on ceramics, textiles, and stone sculpture, and it would seem that these, too, denoted gods and a comparable custom of using masks at religious rites. Masked figures, for example, are prominent on the painted pottery of the Mochica, the textiles of the Nazca, and as running figures with condor masks on the stone reliefs of the famous "Gateway of the Sun" at Tiahuanaco, Bolivia (I, PL. 169). Another form of mask found in various parts of the Andean region consisted of a face made of hammered gold or silver, carved wood, or painted cloth, which was attached to mummy bundles. Larger hammered-gold masks were possibly used in this way by the Quimbaya Indians of Colombia, and small gold masks were used decoratively by persons of rank in various Andean cultures, as, for example, by the Inca, who attached them to the tops of sandals or wore them at the knees or on the shoulders.

Three types of masks are therefore prevalent in the high pre-Columbian civilizations of South America: religious ceremonial forms representing deities; mortuary faces for attachment to mummy bundles; and masks used decoratively for prestige purposes. Like their counterparts in Middle America, deity masks were intended to depict the appearance of gods, with the consequence that a descriptive style was developed in which the distinguishing features of the subject were given distinctly, and often so emphatically as to be a dramatic statement. The mortuary masks, also like those of the north, are merely symbolic forms and thus were rendered in a very simplified style to convey a generic pattern of human features; the small decorative masks stress a refinement of form and an elaboration of detail.

Among the more primitive tribal Indians of South America, some kind of mask or disguise is a culture element common to many areas. The purpose of the mask is usually to establish the identity of a spirit, either by means of face and body coverings or by the use of costume alone. Bark cloth is used extensively as a material for masks, as well as wood, bark, basketry, and hide. Costumes are made of bark cloth, bast, leaves, grasses, feathers, and shell, often in various combinations, which are accompanied, or sometimes replaced, by elaborate body painting in geometric designs. White, black, brown, yellow, and various shades of red are the colors most commonly used both for body decoration and for the painting of the mask proper.

The simplest of South American Indian disguises are the conical bark or hide masks made by the Ona Indians of Tierra del Fuego and their neighbors. These cones fit entirely over the head of the wearer, who peers through narrow rectangular slits marking the eyes, the only features defined. Ona masks are used to impersonate numerous spirits at boys' initiation rites, and they are also worn to keep the women subservient. Esthetically these forms have little to commend them. This is also true of the rudimentary masks worn by the Toba and Pilagá Indians of the Gran Chaco in their victory scalp dance; these consist merely of fiber bags stretched over large, angular wooden frames and tied under the chin to cover the head completely.

A characteristic trait of the Indian cultures of the western Amazon basin is the presence of painted bark-cloth masks. The Witoto Indians in this area wear a simple bark-cloth mask that fits over the head like a bag and hangs loosely around the neck. Facial features are sparse, consisting usually of wide, vertical, oval openings as eyes; some have large loop ears appended at right angles to the sides of the head, and an ill-shaped small slit defines the mouth. The facial area is outlined by a wide, roughly painted band, and a narrow line borders the eye openings. To the top of the mask is often attached a small bird form of bark cloth or a larger abstract open birdlike construction of thin pieces of wood; in some, a wide band of bark cloth hangs down the back. With this mask is worn a tight-fitting sleeveless garment of bark cloth extending from the neck to the hips. It is decorated on the front with large painted dentates, which curve in a sweeping arc from the shoulders to the hips, and on the back with rectangular and curvilinear designs. Although rather limited in esthetic quality, these masks, with their bold red and black surface patterns against the white of the bark cloth, are arresting in appearance. The precise purpose of these forms is not known, but they represent supernatural beings and are worn at festivals associated with planting, harvesting, and housebuilding.

The Tucuna Indians, also of the western Amazon basin, use more varied and fantastic bark-cloth masks to represent demons and animals. These forms are motivated by the need to create arresting effects and are not associated traditionally with any societies or other restraints. They are made and worn by the guests invited to the feasts held during the girls' puberty rites. The disguises consist of sleeveless robes of bark cloth which cover the entire upper part of the body and terminate in a long pliable neck and a crude grotesque head. A fringe hangs from the bottom of the costume to below the knees, and slits at the base of the fabricated neck provide eyeholes for the wearer. Tucuna masks are intended to excite by their fantastic appearance and are entirely the products of some individual's imagination. Their esthetic character therefore results from their melodramatic and exciting aspect.

Bark-cloth masks of a more elaborate and inherently esthetic kind are produced by the tribes of the northwestern Amazon region. Among the Cubeo Indians along the Vaupés River, for example, the disguises worn during mourning ceremonies are distinctive in shape and in their painted surface designs. They cover the upper part of the chest and the head of the dancer, with an attached full fringe of straw hanging down below the knees and a tufted, domical top which is formed by pulling together the upper edge of the bark cloth, as with a drawstring. The arms of the wearer protrude from the sides of this cylinderlike form, which is usually painted in bold geometric designs of lozenges, hatched or solid triangles, and crude frets rendered in black, yellow, and dark red on the white surface of the bark cloth. In some examples, a very simplified human face is painted at the top of the front surface. As is commonly the case among South American Indian tribes, these masks are not made by trained artists. They are worn at mourning ceremonies to represent the actual presence of ancestors, forest monsters, and all the beings of the world, including animals, birds, fish, and insects, all of which are symbolically depicted by abstract painted designs. The purpose of the ceremonies is to assuage grief by the presence of these beings and to drive the ghost of the deceased out of the house.

The numerous tribes of the upper Xingú River, which is south of the Amazon and empties into it in east-central Brazil, used a variety of highly developed masks until the present century. Disguises in this region included: zoomorphic headdresses of carved wood, woven straw, and painted calabashes; flat, oval masks of woven straw, with abstract surface designs painted on them or with stylized human eyes and nose modeled in wax and attached to the surface; and rectangular wooden masks, sometimes with only the forehead and nose carved, but usually with eyes and mouth also rendered, and with a bold geometric design painted across the central facial area. The lower part of the mask usually supported a long beardlike fringe of straw. The Bacaïri Indians wore below the carved mask a huge straw crinoline that covered the entire body and was at times 30 ft. in circumference.

The carved wooden masks of the upper Xingú River are best represented by those of the Mehinacu, Bacaïri, and Auetö Indians. Although these horizontally oriented rectangular forms are shaped as human faces, they depict animals, which can be identified by the abstract geometric patterns painted on the expanded middle area of the face. In the stress on triangles as design elements in their abstract symbolism, these masks bear some analogy to the Cubeo bark-cloth fabrications of the northwestern Amazon area. But, unlike them, the focal point is the carved face mask and not the entire upper part of the body. The Mehinacu and Auetö forms in particular are carefully made, with a marked bilateral symmetry on either side of a short but voluminous nose; small eyes are set high up beneath the slightly overhanging forehead, and frequently no mouth is depicted. The emphasis is clearly on the painted geometric surface pattern. Esthetically these are among the most striking of South American Indian masks. It is said that each village had its own collection and that they were probably worn in various dance cycles; but the significance of the forms and of the dance cycles is not known.

Another center of carved wooden face masks is located on the eastern slopes of the Bolivian Andes, among the Chiriguano and Chané Indians. The concentration here is on a simple representation of the human face devoid of painted surface patterns, unlike the Xingú River masks. The forms are carved in a soft wood, and the face is usually surrounded by a wide flange to hide the head of the wearer; a low rectangular palette sometimes rises behind the head. These masks have a wide horizontal oval shape and seem to fall into two types: those which represent the entire face, including the forehead; and those which are restricted to the area below the forehead. In both types, the facial plane is flat, the eyes are narrow, horizontal rectangular openings, the nose is heavy and straight, and the mouth a tight horizontal slit. When the forehead is included, it is marked off from the features below by a straight horizontal ridge, with the cranium above given as a shallow rounded form. The alignment of strongly marked verticals and horizontals within the tight oval outline of the delimited shape gives these masks a calm, contained, and undramatic expression. They are worn now for purposes of amusement at festivals and carnivals when the masked dancer collects food at the conclusion of his performance. It is believed, however, that these forms originally represented nature spirits or ghosts.

Elaborate costumes composed of grasses, leaves, basketry, bark, and feathers, which completely hide the identity of the wearer, are used alone by many South American tribes to evoke various spirits and mythological beings. Characteristic examples are those worn by the Bororo, Sherente, and Carajá Indians of eastern and central Brazil. Face masks simply cut and shaped from gourds or calabashes are also common and are frequently worn in secular dances. They differ considerably in quality and reflect the variability of skill found among all peoples without trained and professional artists.

Among the American Indians north of Mexico, the mask was an important art form only in the southwestern and eastern areas and on the North Pacific Coast. There are, moreover, no analogies either in style or function between masks from these areas. Although the incidence of masks in prehistoric sites is relatively rare, they nevertheless have been found in various regions. (It may be that they were more common than evidence indicates but were made of fragile materials, such as pottery, cloth, or vegetable fiber, and so have not survived.)

One type of mask, with summarily rendered facial forms cut in shell, was apparently put over the face of the deceased at interment. The size varied from 3 or 4 in. high to more than life-size. In some prehistoric mounds of the Ohio-Mississippi drainage, copper headdresses that fall somewhat within the mask category were discovered, and wooden face masks with carved deer antlers have been found, principally in the Spiro Mound in Oklahoma. In southwest Florida, wooden animal masks, especially of deer and alligator heads, were carved in late pre-Columbian times by the now extinct Calusa Indians. They were smaller than life-size, with clear indications that they had been painted red, white, black, and various shades of gray; shell inlay appears on some of them. Their precise usage is not known, but it seems likely that they functioned as important elements in a ceremonial complex.

A strong center of masks exists in the Pueblo area of the Southwest, especially among the Zuñi and Hopi Indians. In keeping with the general character of American Indian art, diverse materials such as tanned animal skins, wood, feathers, and animal hair are used in the creation of their masks, which are composite in character. The forms consist of a face covering, usually made of leather, to which are attached numerous materials and objects of iconographic significance pertaining to specific gods. A number of colors, including several shades of light green, bright red, blue, yellow, black, and white, are used to paint the different parts, and further polychromatic effects are achieved by the appended multicolored feathers and animal hair.

The face covering is usually designed as an undifferentiated convex surface. Often the eyes and the mouth are simple rectangular, ovoid, or circular openings; the nose is seldom represented. The designs may be elementary but naturalistic interpretations of basic human features, or they may be creations of fantastic shapes with a distorted scaling of elements within the facial area. On still other examples the face covering is treated as an abstract painted design, with unobtrusive narrow slits serving as eyeholes. Thin wooden panels, known as *tablitas*, are attached as surmounting parts to the women's headdresses in the many saints' day dances to which they give their name. These are painted with multiple symbolic forms relative to the character and function of the deity or saint they represent.

The most important masks of the Southwest, the kachinas, represent the beneficent dead (ancestors) as well as gods or supernatural beings who figure prominently in mythology and bring fertility, especially through rain, and long life, together with other benefits. The kachinas are impersonations of these spirits who, it is thought, return to earth at certain regular intervals to participate in prescribed ceremonials. It is believed that the masked kachina dancer is in actuality the supernatural being whom he impersonates.

A unique mask form was used in the southeastern United States, particularly among the Cherokee and other Indian groups of the Carolina region. These masks were carved in wood or were made of animal skins such as beaver or bear. Worn over the face, they were extremely simple and of a completely descriptive nature, representing both animal and human forms. Unfortunately, too few examples from precolonial days have survived to permit a valid characterization of this art.

In the eastern United States, the Iroquois Indians are the best-known mask-producing group, whose activity in this field has been a particular cultural feature from the time of early contact to the present. The types made fall into two categories: (1) the carved wooden forms, called the Falsefaces (PL. 357; X, PL. 361), and (2) those made of braided cornhusks, called the Shuck- or Huskfaces (see NORTH AMERICAN CULTURES). Historical accounts clearly show that both types antedate European contact. The wooden masks follow exactly prescribed patterns of composition, the meaning of which refers to specific mythological characters or supernatural beings, who through the Falseface Secret Society exorcised evil spirits responsible for disease and otherwise protected and aided the Iroquois. The masks are first roughly blocked out on a living tree, from which they are then cut free and finished in their final form. It is believed that the spirit of the tree remains in the finished sculptures, thereby imbuing them with a life essence. Cornhusk masks, made by a plaiting technique, were used at thanksgiving celebrations to promote fertility, particularly of crops.

Iroquois masks have a distinctive style. They are shallow in form with a singular statement of facial elements: the wide-open round eyes are often outlined with tin; in some, the nose is a large crooked shape; and the mouth, huge and thick-lipped, is given varied grotesque expressions. The surface planes of the face are usually broken by series of deep parallel grooves, which are powerful expressive devices. Some of these masks are painted in a monochrome red or black; others have the lateral halves painted red and black.

Among North American Indian cultures, the mask was used most extensively in the North Pacific Coast area, where all the tribes wore masks in their highly elaborate winter ceremonials. These tribes, from southern British Columbia north to southeastern Alaska, are the Kwakiutl, the Bellacoola (Bella Coola), the Tsimshian, the Tlingit, and the Haida Indians of the Queen Charlotte Islands. The sculpture of this entire area is so essentially homogeneous that tribal styles cannot be characterized without first understanding the broadly shared and commonly used art elements. This is particularly evident in the mask, the art form having the widest distribution and yet the closest relationship to individual tribal ideas.

Human, animal, and hybrid human-animal forms, often of fabulous appearance, provided the subject matter for masks. The face mask was common to the whole area, but important differences in this type must be noted. It could be, for example, a monoxylic carving of a contained ovoid shape within a sculpturally expressed outline, broken only by a few modestly projecting parts such as ears. It could also be, in contrast, a composite form, in which the outline of the shape was considerably extended by conspicuous attached parts, including bird beaks, winglike ears, bird or animal heads, or even by attached superposed forms. In addition, this type could be a movable construction, with the lower jaw carved separately and hinged to the upper part of the face so that it could be moved by the wearer; or it could be constructed as a double mask, with the two halves carved separately, hinged, and closed over another mask which remained hidden until, at a specific point in the dramatic ceremony, the wearer pulled a concealed string and revealed it. This was one of the most complex types of mask evolved by primitive peoples, as well as one having the greatest dramatic possibilities. Some of these, in fact, incorporated three representations in their final construction.

An exception to the face type was a very large form, of composite character, in which a series of bird heads of different sizes might be superposed along a vertical axis in such a manner that each head could be moved; or the body of a whale might be depicted with movable fins and tail attached. These masks, of somewhat limited distribution, were not worn but were carried or supported by a person who was concealed entirely by a covering blanket.

Northwest Coast Indian masks are based upon an initial statement of essential planes and shapes which establishes the necessary total structure of the subject represented. A final definition and expression is achieved by the carving of surfaces and by the careful delineation of features and details. Emphasis may be given to the bulk and mass of certain forms by a modeled textural surface treatment, or to their inner content or volume by tight and smooth exterior planes. These facial planes have a prominent lateral curvature and frequently a less emphatic vertical curvature of a similar kind. The sculpturally form-defining surfaces are usually fragmented into many separate and marked-off parts, which are further indicated by outlines and by the application of a flat paint.

The mask design is, therefore, usually composed of a number of clearly separate and distinct parts, such as facial features and surface patterns, which, because of their large scale, give the mask a scale incommensurate with its actual size. A bilateral vertical division, either tangibly represented or strongly implied by the prominent verticality of the nose, creates in most instances an absolute symmetry. Significantly related to this axis is the large inverted triangle which has the horizontal of the eyebrow line as its base and the tapering chin as its apex, and the downward movement of which is counteracted by the vigorous upward thrust of another triangle having its base along the horizontal of the mouth and its apex at the bridge of the nose. The resultant interlocking arrangement of triangles focuses attention on the eyes and the mouth. The sweep of the eyebrows, the emphasized chin, and the prominently sculptured mouth make this interlocking pattern strongly apparent.

Facial features and details are lucid and precise in statement and ample in scale, stressing especially the vigor and integrated character of the design. The eye is defined by a wide oval terminating in sharp points and is represented either by a fine, low-relief line or by an equally fine painted outline. The pupil is carved as a slightly protruding, circular, and pierced shape, the bounds of which are fixed by a painted or a carved relief line. Although the mouth is variously differentiated, it emphasizes the projecting, sculpturally formed lips. Incised and painted surface details, another constant style feature of the masks, are often used independently to delineate symbols, to function in a decorative manner, and to describe further the carved forms.

The use of line, both expressively and esthetically, is of great importance in all the art forms of the Northwest Coast and is particularly evident in the masks. Two types may be discerned: one, a "resultant line," is the consequence of the meeting of two planes of different angle or depth, which are usually painted in contrasting colors; the other is a "pure line," which may be carved in low relief, incised into, or painted on the surface. Pure and resultant lines are sometimes used together to enhance the statement of a given shape or area. The quality varies from fine to moderately heavy. Long, often curved lines, smoothly modulated to the surface plane, predominate and may be punctuated, though rarely, by staccato strokes. Curvilinear elements, sometimes abruptly and dramatically changing their direction, as in the eyebrow design, are an important feature of this style and may be designated as "angular curves." There is a marked tendency to use connective or closely associative linear arrangements, leading to the formation of an over-all pattern distinct from that of the carved forms. The conflict or tension thus produced between lines and sculptured forms contributes dramatically to the expressive power of the masks.

Since color was used extensively as an adjunctive element, delineated or carved surface patterns — whether employed symbolically or descriptively — were usually painted in a flat tone contrasting with that of the surrounding parts. An incised line was often filled in with a color of different shade or intensity from that of the detail or form it surrounded; pure line was also frequently painted on the surface in a conspicuously contrasting hue. Although preferences varied somewhat from tribe to tribe, the most commonly used colors were red, yellow, black, and white.

An emphatic division of form and surface must be regarded as another characteristic of the art of this region. But, whether carved or painted, the forms and surfaces tend to stress and to follow the outline of the mask. An effective unity is achieved by the interaction of carved forms and surface-design elements which are similar in shape or size, thus bringing the sculptured shapes and painted areas into a significant visual and expressive relationship.

To distinguish between the artistic production of tribal groups within the complex of the Northwest Coast, specific and subtle differences in the combinations of design and form that particularize the styles must be sought beyond the generalized pattern of shared elements. In art-historical terms, the Tsimshian mask style may be designated as "classical"; the Haida as "baroque"; the Tlingit as "rococo"; and the Kwakiutl as flamboyant "expressionist." Bellacoola masks have a style that may be considered a modified derivation of the Kwakiutl.

The term "classical," as a characterization of Tsimshian mask style, is based on the moderation and sensitive restraint evident in the interpretation of typical shapes, in the conformation of facial elements, and in the treatment of surface design motifs. Sculptured forms are given a more naturalistic and organic expression than in other styles, and there is a more lucid depiction of design elements, with a strong use of resultant line, and a harmonious unity as the primary basis of quality. This is emphasized by the careful balancing of the inner content or volume with the plasticity of mass and surface. Dramatic effect is, in fact, achieved by the Tsimshian Indians both in spite of and because of their classicism.

The Tlingit, near neighbors of the Tsimshian, have, in contrast, a style in which the smaller and more decorative design elements warrant the appellation "rococo." The scaling of parts as well as the more frequent use of inlays, including abalone shell and copper, point up the more ornate and elaborate design vocabulary (PL. 354). Another particularizing feature of this style is the conspicuous use of a blue-green pigment together with a lighter tone of red than is found elsewhere. Animal masks were used more extensively by the Tlingit than those with human features, but in both instances the stress is placed upon the separate elements that comprise the form, rather than upon its organic unity. Tlingit masks generally emphasize the volume and lightness of forms through undifferentiated treatment of the broad surface planes in which the small and ornate design units are placed.

The Haida "baroque" style is expressed in terms of nearclassical forms, which at times approximate those of the Tsimshian but are given a more dramatic and vigorous interpretation of human and, especially, of animal or animal-human features (PL. 357; X, PL. 357; see NORTH AMERICAN CULTURES). An emphatic rendering of the weight and mass inherent in heavy, bulky forms is prevalent. Combinations of diverse startling shapes and details of forms give to this style its spectacular and, sometimes, even melodramatic effects. The usually large-scale patterns of Haida design are presented in resultant and, more especially, pure line. Colors tend to be dark, although rich and vibrant, with occasional dramatic splashes of bright, contrasting tones. The subject matter inclines toward forceful animal-human representations or fantastic symbolic forms.

The Kwakiutl Indians were undoubtedly the originators of the complex, strikingly theatrical, composite masks, and many of their innovations of form were diffused throughout the whole North Pacific Coast culture area. Kwakiutl artists exploited the full realm of possibilities in the interpretation of dynamic form; vivid delineation of descriptive detail is also implicit in their style. Blatant distortions of both human and animal forms, arranged in spectacular or grotesque combinations of shapes, show an intention to achieve active and dramatic effects. These contribute to a mask style which in its totality is both flamboyant in statement and expressionistic in appearance. Movable parts are common on these masks, particularly on the large superposed types. Their powerful expression is unquestionable evidence of the important role assigned to them in the melodramatic performances characteristic of Kwakiutl dances and ceremonies (X, PL. 357).

Bellacoola mask forms were, in large measure, modified versions of certain Kwakiutl forms. Both the animal and human types which prevailed were often totally lacking in the fantastic character of the Kwakiutl forms. There is, however, a very strong sculptural expression of structural components. Of particular note is the use of a rich brick red and a bright azure blue; the two, often in juxtaposition, differentiate and stress the forms and surfaces, in which boldness of size and scale is strongly felt.

Northwest Coast masks were used largely in the winter ceremonials, when leisure time was amply available because the seasonal run of salmon, the main dietary staple of these people, was over. These rituals, of religious and secular significance, consisted of organized dramatic performances and dances, often motivated by the desire to exhibit the prerogatives of social position or rank. Among the Kwakiutl the religious performances dramatized the original encounters of the ancestors with the supernatural beings, at which time the ceremonial complexes had been learned, the right to wear masks had been granted, and the ability to perform certain sleight-of-hand tricks as supernatural miracles had been acquired. Reenactments of these experiences were performed both as theatrical exhibitions and for the purpose of initiating new members who had inherited the dance as a privilege. The dance groups were graded and, since membership was restricted, functioned as secret societies. The supernatural beings were represented with the features of animals, mythological monsters, and conventionalized human forms.

Among the Haida, Tsimshian, and Tlingit Indians to the north, although religious dances occurred, masks were worn largely to display the crests or insignia of rank at secular occasions. These animal and sometimes human forms depicted the supernatural beings who had originally permitted the wearing of such masks by selected individuals. These forms were also displayed on totem poles, boxes, spoons, and numerous other objects. Bellacoola masks, used during the winter ceremonials, portrayed deities to whom the dramatization of myths referred. They were also used to depict hereditary clan crests and legends.

Northwest Coast masks were, therefore, of great importance in the dramaturgic presentation of religious beliefs and experiences and in the demonstration of social position or rank. In either case, the masks visually manifested their expressive purpose as they were worn in the histrionic revelations of supernatural experiences. They were also powerful agents of religious and social control.

Along the Arctic littoral, the Eskimo developed various ceremonials and entertainments in which mask forms were employed. These were often given composite form with numerous attachments, including wood, bone, feathers, and shell. Many Eskimo masks of Alaska represented evil spirits of specifically therapeutic character. Other types were used as a form of caricature. The majority of Eskimo masks, however, were used either to propitiate or to humor malevolent spirits, such as those of winter and of disease. The differentiation of types and styles is considerable. Many masks are completely surrealistic in their combination of grotesque human, animal, and imaginative forms; nor is it unusual to find masks in which one side of the face is completely unlike the other, with extreme asymmetry. Other masks have the character of mobiles, with projecting or arched forms supporting bits of bone, feather, hide, or other materials in a state of suspension, which create movement when the mask is used. As is true elsewhere, they were used in dramatic performances in combination with one another. Prescribed costumes were worn to coordinate the mask and the ceremony (V, PLS. 5–7).

Any study of masks clearly reveals that very few elements can be found which are common to all of them, either from the point of view of esthetic expression or of content. The recurrence of similar kinds of masks throughout the primitive world has little relevance to a consistency of either motivation or function. Nevertheless, it can be said that the mask, wherever it is found, is basically used to conceal one identity and to create another. In actual fact, many masks are known to be composites of numerous identities associated in mythological or dramatic contexts. Often important, too, is the fact that the mask imparts anonymity to its wearer. Some investigations have revealed that the mask may become a vital or living entity in some ceremonies, at which time viewers and wearers alike experience it as an actual presence. Sometimes it is an inert but nevertheless important symbol, in which case the wearer of the mask or his identity is frequently known. Among primitive peoples, most masks functioned in a strongly dual capacity, as characters in a ceremony or performance and as cathartic agents for the viewers and frequently for the wearers.

In Africa and parts of the western Pacific it is apparent that there was an interchange or diffusion of types and formal elements; within certain limits this is also true of the American Indians. But in all areas there was a good deal of inventive freedom on the part of the artist. While it is true that mask types were dictated or controlled by convention, it was nonetheless possible, as surviving examples reveal, for the artist to give a personal, poignant, and sensitive interpretation to a traditional type.

The mask has been by far the most unifying element in the art of primitive culture groups, since it was tied closely to tradition, hence conservative, and acted as a strong cohesive element among otherwise loosely organized peoples. It must, therefore, be considered as one of the most important cultural and esthetic creations of the primitive world.

Paul S. WINGERT

BIBLIOG. *Mythical and ritual origins*: L. Frobenius, Die Masken und Geheimbünde Afrikas, Halle, 1898; K. Meuli, Handwörterbuch des deutschen Aberglaubens, s.v. Maske, Maskerei, V, Berlin, Leipzig, 1932–33, cols. 1744–852; O. Höfler, Kultische Geheimbünde der Germanen, I, Frankfurt am Main, 1934, pp. 44–46 and passim; K. Meuli, Schweizer Masken, Zurich, 1943; G. Buraud, Les masques, Paris, 1948; R. Bleichsteiner, Masken- und Fastnachtsbrauche bei den Völkern des Kaukasus, Ö. Z. für Volkskunde, N.S., VI, 1952, pp. 3–76; L. Schmidt, ed., Masken in Mitteleuropa, Vienna, 1955; R. Caillois, Les jeux et les hommes, Paris, 1958 (Eng. trans., M. Barash, Man, Play, and Games, New York, 1961).

Antiquity: M. Bieber, RE, s.v. Maske, XXVIII, 1930, cols. 2070–120; W. Klingbeil, Kopf- und Maskenzauber in der Vorgeschichte und bei den Primitiven, Bonn, 1932; M. Murray, Ritual Masking, Mém. Inst. fr. du Caire, LXVI, 1934, pp. 251–55; W. Klingbeil, Kopf, Masken und Maskierungszauber in der antiken Hochculturen insbesondere des alten Orients, Berlin, 1935; G. Montandon, Traité d'ethnologie cyclo-culturelle, Paris, 1935; K. Kerényi, Mensch und Maske, Eranos Jhb., XVI, 1948, pp. 183–208; H. Bonnet, Rl. der ägyptische Religionsgeschichte, s.v. Maskierung, Berlin, 1952, pp. 440–42; H. Seyrig, Antiquités syriennes, 53: Antiquités de la nécropole d'Émèse, Syria, XXIX, 1952, pp. 209–27; F. Behn, Vorgeschichtliches Maskenbrauchtum, Berichte über die Verh. der sächsischen Ak. der Wissenschaften zu Leipzig, Philologisch-historische Klasse, CII, 1, 1955; A. Parrot, Le temple d'Ishtar, Paris, 1956, pp. 156–57; W. S. Smith, The Art and Architecture of Ancient Egypt, Harmondsworth, 1958, p. 206.

Folk masks in Europe: V. S. Karadzhich, Zhivot i obichayi naroda srpskoga (Life and Dress of the Serbian People), Belgrade, 1867; E. T. Kristensen, Gamle folks fortaellinger om det jyske almueliv (Tales of the Elders on the Life of the Jutland Peasantry), 6 vols., Kolding, 1891–94; H. Bragard, Au "Cwarmai" ou Carnaval de Malmédy, Wallonia, VII, 1899, pp. 25–47; E. K. Chambers, The Mediaeval Stage, 2 vols., Oxford, 1903; N. Keyland, Julbröd, Julbockar och Staffanssång (Christmas Bread, Christmas Goats, and the Song of Staffan), Stockholm, 1919; M. Arnaudov, Sbornik za narodni umotvoreniya i narodopis' (Studies on Art and Folk Traditions), Sofia, 1920; S. Trojanović, Maske kod našeg naroda (Masks among Our People), in Strena Buliciana, Zagreb, 1924, pp. 695–99; M. Vulpescu, Les coutumes roumaines périodiques, Paris, 1927; D. Zelenin, Russische (ostslavische) Volkskunde, Berlin, Leipzig, 1927; A. Nicoll, Mimes, Masks and Miracles, London, 1931; J. Janson, Die lettischen Maskenumzüge, Riga, 1933; A. Spamer, Deutsche Fastnachtsbräuche, Jena, 1936; W. Liungman, Traditionswanderungen Euphrat-Rhein (Folklore Fellows Comm., 118–19), 2 vols., Helsinki, 1937–38; M. Gavazzi, Godina dana hrvatskih narodnih običaja (Annual Recurrences in Croat Folk Customs), I, Zagreb, 1939; K. Moszyński, Kultura ludowa Słowian (Slavic Folk Culture), II: Kultura duchowa, Kraków, 1939; C. W. von Sydow, En Småländsk Traditionsgrupp: En Bok om Småland (A Group of Traditions of Småland: A Book on Småland), Stockholm, 1943, pp. 306–17; Z. Szendrey, Jeles napok (Propitious Days), A magyarság néprajza, IV, Budapest, 1943, pp. 269–85; K. Viski, Drámai hagyományok (Traditional Dramatic Legends), A magyarság néprajza, III, Budapest, 1943, pp. 291–323; E. Hoffmann-Krayer, Die Fastnachtsgebräuche in der Schweiz, in Kleine Schriften zur Volkskunde, Basel, 1946, pp. 24–94; A. Van Gennep, Manuel de folklore français contemporain, I, 3: Cérémonies périodiques cycliques, Paris, 1947; H. von Zimburg, Der Perchtenlauf in der Gastein, Vienna, 1947; J. Balys, Fastnachtsbrauche in Litauen, Schw. Arch. für Volkskunde, XLV, 1948, pp. 40–69; A. Dörrer, Tiroler Fastnacht innerhalb der alpenländischen Winter- und Vorfrühlingsbräuche, Vienna, 1949; M. S. Filipovich, Anketa Etnografskog muzeya u Beogradu o igrama pod maskama (Inquiry of the Ethnological Museum of Belgrade into Masked Performances), Muzeyi, III–IV, 1949, pp. 163–66; M. Leach and J. Fried, ed., Funk & Wagnalls Standard Dictionary of Folklore, Mythology, and Legend, 2 vols., New York, 1949–50; K. Ter Laan, Folkloristisch Woordenboek van Nederland en Vlaams België, The Hague, 1949; J. Künzig, Die alemannisch-schwäbische Fasnet, Freiburg im Breisgau, 1950; C. Zíbrt, Veselé chvíle v životě lidu českého (Festivities in the Life of the Czech People), 2d ed., Prague, 1950; R. Marchi, Le maschere barbaricine, Il ponte, VII, 9–10, 1951 (special no. dedicated to Sardinia), pp. 1354–61; R. Wolfram, Die Volkstänze in Österreich und verwandte Tänze in Europa, Salzburg, 1951; V. Alford, Introduction to English Folklore, London, 1952; H. Henningsen, Bådeoptog i danske søkøbstaeder og i Udlandet, Copenhagen, 1953; R. Meurant, Les géants processionnels de Wallonie: Province de Luxembourg, Brussels, 1953; J. Baumel. Le "Masque-Cheval" et autres animaux fantastiques, Paris, 1954; L. Weiser-Aall, Julenissen og Julegeita i Norge (The Christmas Gnome and the Christmas Goat in Norway), Oslo, 1954; N. Kuret, Aus der Maskenwelt der Slowenen, in Masken in Mitteleuropa, Vienna, 1955, pp. 201–20; A. Mais, Die Tiergestalten im polnischen Brauchtum, in Masken in Mitteleuropa, Vienna, 1955, pp. 221–35; P. Toschi, Le origini del teatro italiano, Turin, 1955; Binche, cité des Gilles, B. de la Fédération touristique du Hainaut, special no., Feb. 1956; J. Noël, Les Chinels de Fosse, Fosse, 1956; V. I. Chicherov, Zimnii period russkogo narodnogo zemledel'chescogo kalendarya XVI–XIX vekov (The Winter Season of the Russian Agricultural Calendar of the 16th–19th Centuries), Moscow, 1957; G. A. Megas, Greek Calendar Customs, Athens, 1958; D. S. Pessanha, Mascarados e mascaras populares de Trás-Os-Montes, Lisbon, 1960; R. Pinon, Le nouveau Carnaval de Gozée et les survivances de l'ancien, N. rev. wallonne, XII, 1960, pp. 1–15; R. Pinon and J. Vandereuse, Quelques carnavals curieux de l'Entre-Sambre-et-Meuse, Guetteur wallon, III, 1960.

The modern mask since the Renaissance: F. Wieseler, Das Satyrspiel, Göttingen, 1848; K. F. Flögel, Geschichte der Grotesk-Komischen, 5th ed. by F. W. Ebeling, Leipzig, 1888; F. Hellwald, Urgeschichte des Masken, Leipzig, 1891; J. Lorrain, Histoire de masques, Paris, 1900; E. Cassirer, Philosophie der symbolischen Formen, 3 vols., Berlin, 1923–29; A. Beijer, ed., Recueil de plusieurs fragments des premières comédies italiennes qui ont été représentées en France sous le règne de Henri III, Paris, 1928; R. Eisler, Wörterbuch der philosophischen Begriffe, 4th ed., II, Berlin, 1929, p. 463; Musée Carnevalet, Le théâtre à Paris, XVIIe–XVIIIe siècles (cat.), Paris, 1929; A. Nicoll, Mimes, Masks, and Miracles, London, 1931; Les spectacles à travers les âges: Théâtre, circque, music-hall, cafés-concerts, cabarets artistiques, Paris, 1931; Les spectacles à travers les âges: Musique, danse, Paris, 1932; C. Zervos, Pablo Picasso, I, Paris, 1932; I. Schneider Lengyel, Die Welt der Maske, Munich, 1934; H. H. Borcherdt, Das europäische Theater in Mittelalter und in der Renaissance, Leipzig, 1935; S. Dali, Conquest of the Irrational, New York, 1935; A. H. Barr, ed., Fantastic Art, Dada and Surrealism, New York, 1936; G. Lorenzetti, Le feste e le maschere veneziane, Venice, 1937; R. Pallucchini, Nota sulla mostra di feste e maschere veneziane, Critica d'arte, II, 1937, pp. 260–64; G. Morazzoni, Una raccolta di maschere partenopee e veneziane, Ceramica, I, 1942; C. Sterling, Early Paintings of the Commedia dell'Arte in France, BMMA, N.S., II, 1, 1943, pp. 11–32; J. Adhémar, French 16th-Century Genre Paintings, Warburg, VIII, 1945, pp. 41–46; A. Breton, Le surréalisme et la peinture, New York, 1945; M. Tapié, Mirobolus Macadam & Cie.: Hautepates de J. Dubuffet, Paris, 1946; W. Baumeister, Das Unbekannte in der Kunst, Stuttgart, 1947; M. Praz, La carne, la morte e il diavolo nella letteratura romantica, 3d ed., Florence, 1948; A. Malraux, Saturne: Essai sur Goya, Paris, 1950 (Eng. trans., C. W. Chilton, New York, 1957); R. Motherwell, The Dada Painters and Poets, New York, 1951; A. Kyrou, Le surréalisme au cinéma, Paris, 1953; H. Adhémar, Sur quelques tableaux français représentants la Commedia dell'Arte, XVIe–XVIIIe siècle, R. di s. teatrali, IX–X, 1954, pp. 106–13; R. Bacchelli and R. Longhi, Teatro e immagini del settecento italiano, Turin, 1954; W. Grohmann, Paul Klee, Stuttgart, 1954 (Eng. trans., London, New York, 1954); J. López Rey, Goya's Caprichos: Beauty, Reason, and Caricature, 2 vols., Cambridge, Mass., 1954; H. Thoma, Cinémascope au XVIe siècle, L'Oeil, III, 1955, pp. 13–17; G. R. Hocke, Die Welt als Labyrinth, Hamburg, 1957; V. Pandolfi, La commedia dell'arte, 6 vols., Florence, 1957–61; E. Crispolti, Otto nuove pagine del taccuino di Madrid di Goya ed alcuni problemi ad esso relativi, Comm, IX, 1958, pp. 181–205; A. Grévin, Les nouveaux travestissements parisiens: Dessins inédits, Paris, n.d.

India: E. W. West and N. L. P., Golden Masks, Indian Ant., VII, 1878, pp. 26, 160; J. Burgess, Two Bronze Masks from Mysore, Indian Ant., XIII, 1884, pp. 429–30; H. Sastri, Historical Documents of Kulū, Ann. Rep. Archaeol. Survey of India, 1907–08, pp. 260–76; W. Ridgeway, The Dramas and Dramatic Dances of Non-European Races, Cambridge, 1915; H. L. H. Shuttleworth, Inscribed Mask Discovered at Nirmand, ActaO, I, 1922, pp. 224–29; P. Wirz, Exorzismus und Heilkunde auf Ceylon, Bern, 1941 (Eng. trans., Exorcism and the Art of Healing in Ceylon, Leiden, 1954); V. Elwin, The Tribal Art of Middle India, Oxford, 1951; Moti Chandra, Some Aspects of Yaksha Cult in Ancient India, B. Prince of Wales Mus. in Bombay, III, 1953, pp. 43–62; U. P. Shah, Yaksha Worship in Early Jaina Literature, J. Baroda O. Inst., III, 1953, pp. 54–71; H. Lucas, Ceylon-Masken, Kassel, 1958; Ajit Mookerjee, Indian Primitive Art, Calcutta, Delhi, 1959.

China: P. W. Meister, Chinesische Bronzemasken, OAZ, XIV, 1938, pp. 5–11; L. Lanciotti, Two Bronze Masks of T'ao-t'ieh, East and West, VII, 1956, pp. 247–50; M. Granet, Danses et légendes de la Chine ancienne, 2 vols., Paris, 1959.

Japan: T. Nogami, Masks of Japan: The Gigaku, Bugaku, and Noh Masks, Tokyo, 1935; S. Noma, Nihon kogaku-men (Old Japanese Masks), Tokyo, 1935; L. Kongo, Nōgaku nō-men taikan (Collection of Ancient Noh Masks of Japan), Tokyo, 1941; F. Bowers, Japanese Theatre, New York, 1952; J. Okada, Nihon kōgei zuroku (Illustrated History of Japanese Crafts), Tokyo, 1952; T. Nogami, Nō kenkyū to hakken (Studies and Discoveries concerning Noh), Tokyo, 1953; K. Shigetoshi, ed., Geinō jiten (Dictionary of Spectacles), Tokyo, 1953; R. Sieffert, Japan, in Le masque (exhibition cat.), Paris, 1960, pp. 46–48.

Primitive masks: W. H. Dall, On Masks, Labrets, and Certain Aboriginal Customs, Bur. of Am. Ethn., Ann. Rep., III, 1884, pp. 67–203; A. Krause, Die Tlinkit-Indianer, Jena, 1885 (Eng. trans., E. Gunther, Seattle, 1956); R. Andrée, Die Masken in der Völkerkunde, IAE, XVI, 1886, pp. 477–506; A. B. Meyer, Masken von Neu Guinea und den Bismarck Archipel, Dresden, 1889; F. Boas, The Social Organization and the Secret Societies of the Kwakiutl Indians, Rep. U. S. Nat. Mus., 1895, pp. 311–738 (also pub. separately, Washington, D.C., 1897); A. B. Meyer and R. Parkinson, Schnitzereien und Masken vom Bismarck Archipel und Neu Guinea, Dresden, 1895; O. Reche, Der Kaiserin-Augusta-Fluss, Hamburg, 1913; J. Maes, Aniota-Kifwebe, Antwerp, 1924; A. Krämer, Die Málanggane von Tombara, Munich, 1925; A. Skinner, Some Seneca Masks and Their Uses, Mus. of the Am. Indian, Heye Foundation, Notes, II, 1925, pp. 191–207; R. L. Bunzel, Zuni Kachinas, Bur. of Am. Ethn., Ann. Rep., XLVII, 1932, pp. 837–1086; H. Nevermann, Masken und Geheimbünde in Melanesien, Berlin, 1933; J. Gregor, Masks of the World, London, 1936; R. Eberl-Alber, Die Masken der Männerbunde in Sierra Leone, Ethnos, II, 1937, pp. 38–46; M. Griaule, Masques Dogon, Paris, 1938; H. Himmelheber, Eskimokünstler, Stuttgart, 1938; E. H. Kennard, Hopi Kachinas, New York, 1938; H. Himmelheber, Les masques Bayaka et leurs sculpteurs, Brousse, I, 1939, pp. 19–39; E. Becker-Donner, Kunst und Handwerk in nordost Liberia, BA, XXIII, 1940, pp. 43–110; W. N. Fenton, Masked Medicine Societies of the Iroquois, Smithsonian Inst. Ann. Rep., 1940, pp. 397–429; F. M. Olbrechts, Maskers en dansers in de Ivoorkunst, Louvain, 1940; F. E. Williams, Drama of Orokolo, Oxford, 1940; J. Keppler, Comments on Certain Iroquois Masks, New York, 1941; M. Lantis, Alaskan Eskimo Ceremonialism, New York, 1947; F. H. Lem, Sculptures soudanaises, Paris, 1948; L. Underwood, Masks of West Africa, London, 1948; P. Vandenhoute, Classification stylistique du masque Dan et Gueré de la Côte d'Ivoire occidentale, Leiden, 1948; G. Harley, Masks as Agents of Social Control in Liberia (Peabody Mus. Pap., XXXII, 2), Cambridge, Mass., 1950; B. Holas, Les masques Kono, Paris, 1952; G. Kutscher, Exotische Masken, Stuttgart, 1953; M. Huet and K. Fodeba, Les hommes de la danse, Lausanne, 1954; O. Riley, Masks and Magic, New York, 1955; J. F. Glück, Afrikanische Masken, Baden-Baden, 1956; H. Himmelheber, Die Dan, Stuttgart, 1958; Musée Guimet, Le masque (cat.), Paris, 1959.

Illustrations: PLS. 351–368.

MASO DI BANCO. Italian painter and sculptor. Among 14th-century Florentine painters named Maso, a certain Maso di Banco is to be identified with the artist praised by the sources as a disciple of Giotto. Maso was living in the parish of S. Lorenzo in the year 1341 (not 1346, as Toesca wrote in 1951) when, on Sept. 29, two painted altarpiece panels were confiscated at the instance of Rodolfo de' Bardi and associates, together with various household goods and art materials. Between January and April of 1346 Maso was enrolled in the Florentine Arte dei Medici e Speziali. Since his name does not appear in a memorandum of 1347, listing the major Florentine painters worthy of executing a panel for S. Giovanni Fuorcivitas in Pistoia, it has been conjectured that by then he was dead.

Maso is called a "great master" in a document of 1392 concerning his lost *Deposition* (originally above the cemetery door of S. Pier Maggiore), which was "mended" by Niccolò di Pietro Gerini. Among the sources, Filippo Villani characterizes Maso as "delicatissimus" ("most delicate"), alluding to his pictorial manner, and in referring to his figures declares that he painted "with wonderful and incredible beauty." Ghiberti states that Maso was also a sculptor, citing a statue for the Campanile of the Cathedral (no longer identifiable), and mentions three of his paintings: a Descent of the Holy Spirit in the Augustinian church of Sto Spirito, a depiction of "Our Lady with many figures" in a tabernacle in Piazza Sto Spirito, and the legends of St. Silvester and the emperor Constantine, in a chapel in Sta Croce founded by Gualtiero di Jacopo de' Bardi di Vernio, who died in 1336. Of these works, only the frescoes in the Cappella Bardi di Vernio survive.

Cristoforo Landino mentions Maso, praising him in a general way. In Francesco Albertini's *Memoriale* (Florence, 1510) and in the *Libro* of Antonio Billi, the tabernacle in Piazza Sto Spirito is attributed to a certain Giottino, to whom are also ascribed other works not mentioned in earlier sources. Maso's name reappears in the Anonimo Magliabechiano (or Gaddiano) manuscript, where Ghiberti's list of works is slightly expanded. Finally, Giovanni Battista Gelli, writing between the appearance of the first edition of Vasari's *Lives* (1550) and 1562, briefly treats of Maso "sopradetto" (i.e., called) Giottino.

Vasari himself writes at some length of "Tommaso di Stefano, called Giottino," thus apparently amalgamating Maso with a certain Giottino di Stefano who is recorded as having worked in the Vatican in 1369. Maso's figure remains unclear in much modern art history, which has ascribed to Vasari's Giottino many very disparate works. The finest of these, which seem to belong to a unified group, include a *Coronation of the Virgin* and two scenes from the life of St. Stanislas, in the Lower Church of S. Francesco in Assisi, a *Crucifixion* in the chapter house of the monastery, and other paintings in S. Rufino and in S. Apollinare (now the Educatorio di S. Giuseppe), in Assisi. The *Deposition* from S. Remigio in Florence (Uffizi), attributed to Giottino by Vasari and highly praised by him, is often included in this group, but it was executed by another artist of a younger generation.

To reconstruct Maso di Banco's artistic personality, one must take as a point of departure the frescoes in the Cappella Bardi di Vernio in Sta Croce (PLS. 369, 370, 371). These were probably begun in the 1330s and not yet completed in 1341, which would account for the confiscation mentioned above. The legend is depicted in five scenes, which follow rather faithfully the narration of Jacobus de Voragine in *The Golden Legend*. In the first, a large lunette, Constantine appears in a spectacular chariot, flanked by knights in the foreground, and assures a group of desperate women that he has no intention of butchering 3,000 Christian children and bathing in their blood, a course of action which had been recommended to him as a cure for his leprosy. The painting, in very bad condition and partly effaced, evinces a mastery of space and figural construction that derives from Giotto, as do certain attitudes of grief in the mothers.

The lower register of this wall is occupied by a single rectangular scene, which is cut off by a tall sepulchral niche. This scene shows SS. Peter and Paul appearing to Constantine — who lies in a room constructed in oblique perspective (guards and a page in the foreground accentuate the depth of the scene) — to advise him of the means by which he might be cured. The composition, which some scholars relate to Simone Martini and Ambrogio Lorenzetti, was executed by an artist less robust and less sensitive than Maso but was certainly conceived by him.

The following scene (PL. 370), in the lunette opposite, more elevated in style, is divided into two distinct parts: The first shows Constantine enthroned in a loggia of pre-Renaissance character, solemnly receiving the Pope (St. Silvester), who, followed by a train of cardinals, displays an icon representing SS. Peter and Paul so that Constantine may recognize his visitors of the previous night. In the right-hand scene Constantine, kneeling in a porphyry tub, is baptized by St. Silvester in the presence of prelates and dignitaries, while Christ, whose head appears in a ray of light with the dove of the Holy Spirit, blesses him from above. The setting, a hall faced with marble, has an upper tier like that of the loggia in the adjoining scene, but there the upper section is set back to give spatial variation. Notable here are the balanced composition, the measured dignity of action, and the power of figural representation typical of Maso. However, the hard contrasts of light and dark in the scene showing Constantine enthroned suggest the activity of a collaborator (Toesca, 1951), possibly the painter of the frescoes in the chapter house of Sto Spirito, formerly ascribed to Maso and now to Orcagna.

The legend continues on the broad wall space below. Constantine's mother, Helen, unsympathetic to his rapid conversion, has asked for proof of the sanctity of the new religion. Before Constantine (seated between his mother and an old counselor), and to the amazement of the crowd gathered in the spacious hall, St. Silvester resuscitates with a single gesture of blessing a bull which a Jewish sorcerer had killed by his magic arts. In this scene the space is deeper and completely unified; it is punctuated by two slender columns which establish an interval between the central and the two lateral groups. The clear articulation obtained by disposing the figures in three planes, beginning with the persons in front of the balustrade, represents an expansion and enrichment of the compositional means employed in late works of Giotto and has been ascribed to the influence of Ambrogio Lorenzetti (O. Sirén, *Giotto and Some of His Followers*, I, London, 1917, p. 201), although it is possible that Maso arrived at this elaboration independently. Certainly his color sense, as revealed in this fresco — with its liquid and soft, but not saccharine color, of a purity especially striking in the details — cannot be wholly explained as a derivation either from Giotto or from Sienese artists.

Still more personal is the last composition (PLS. 369, 370, 371). At the left St. Silvester (in a trench, simply but effectively realized among broken walls) binds the jaws of a dragon whose poisonous breath had killed hundreds. At center St. Silvester, again in profile and providing a firm axis for the composition, revives two magicians poisoned by the dragon's breath. The magicians are simultaneously represented stretched out on the ground and revived, kneeling before the saint in a clearly Giottesque pose, while at the right Constantine and his retinue look on. In the figures of this fresco the color, though thinned by overcleaning, is modulated with great subtlety and refinement and impregnated with light to create solid volumes. But Maso's originality here is most apparent in his conception of the setting: wide, deep, and quite untraditional. In the foreground a single column symbolizes the antique world, now in ruins, while crumbling and irregularly disposed buildings create a harmonious spatial whole in which the figures move. The figures themselves are devoid of dramatic excesses; in the context of Maso's deliberate narrative and "delicate" (to use Villani's term) way of painting, they are imbued with a measured and human spiritual fervor.

The decoration of the chapel also includes other elements. In the rear wall a stained-glass window has figures suggesting the style of Maso. There are also frescoed images of saints, subsequently restored in part. The underside of the entrance arch is frescoed with busts in round frames; these were executed with the help of assistants. Within the above-mentioned sepulchral niche Maso painted a Christ in Judgment seated in a mandorla surrounded by angels and, below, the expressive portrait of a risen soul among the barren crags of a desolate valley. In this work, too, there is some evidence of collaboration. The adjacent sepulchral niche (for a female member of the Bardi family) contains a Deposition attributable to Taddeo Gaddi, who worked in the Baroncelli Chapel of Sta Croce between 1332 and 1338, and to whom some scholars attribute the lesser figural ornamentation of the Cappella Bardi di Vernio.

The art of Maso combines the teaching of Giotto with some Sienese influence in composition, both factors being reinterpreted and elaborated with considerable originality. The two elements are integrated by a new way of using color, and this, together with certain perspective solutions of intensified profundity, this author considers traceable to Maso's knowledge of antique painting in Rome and Naples. Such a hypothesis is supported by the fact that Maso's hand can be recognized in the color, the details of form and handling, and the types of eleven heads that have been rediscovered in the window embrasures of the Cappella Palatina of the Castel Nuovo in Naples. Giotto is known to have frescoed this chapel with scenes from the Old and New Testaments between 1329 and 1332, and although these frescoes have entirely disappeared, the few remains in the window embrasures show that Maso numbered among the assistants. Though at this time Maso must have been quite young, he was evidently capable of profiting from the non-Tuscan experiences of his journey.

Maso's work in Naples is somewhat uneven and less refined than the Sta Croce cycle, and there are other paintings that seem to represent stages between the works in Naples and those in the Cappella Bardi di Vernio. One is a frescoed *Coronation of the Virgin*, formerly in the lunette of a side door of Sta Croce (transferred to the church museum). A softer mode of handling is found in a much-damaged polyptych in Sto Spirito (PL. 372) and in another later polyptych in Berlin (PL. 373). Originally a part of the latter was *St. Anthony of Padua*, now in the Metropolitan Museum. The frescoes of the Covoni Chapel in the Church of the Badia, Florence, show close affinities with the Sta Croce cycle, but they reveal also an attenuation of monumental values in favor of greater pictorial softness and therefore must represent the latest phase of Maso's art. These frescoes are preserved only in fragments: a Martyrdom of St. Bartholomew, a Stoning of St. Stephen, a prophet, and a few unidentifiable scene fragments are all that remain visible. Despite the many paintings ascribed to him, no other works are known by Maso. It is possible, however, that ideas derived from the lost Descent of the Holy Spirit are preserved in other 14th-century paintings and miniatures, such as Andrea da Firenze's *Pentecost* in the Spanish Chapel of S. Maria Novella.

Maso di Banco's artistic personality must have emerged and developed rapidly in the Florentine environment. (This is indicated by the presence of assistants in the St. Silvester cycle, a work which represents the full maturity of his art.) Maso, together with Taddeo and Agnolo Gaddi, represents a Florentine artistic tendency capable of development in various directions. On the one hand, Maso continues the powerful formalism of Giotto, which may have been passed on through him to Orcagna; on the other, his achievements in the use of chiaroscuro are reflected in the art of Nardo di Cione, while his coloristic innovations reappear in the work of the various personalities often confused with him, among them Giottino. Maso di Banco's works, then, confirm Ghiberti's statement that this eminent Florentine painter "had many disciples, all very skilled masters."

BIBLIOG. W. Suida, ThB, s.v., (with earlier bibliog.); L. Coletti, Contributo al problema Maso-Giottino, Emporium, XCVI, 1942, pp. 462–77; E. L. Lucignani, Il problema di Giottino nelle fonti, RArte, XXIV, 1942, pp. 107–24; G. Sinibaldi and G. Brunetti, Catalogo della Mostra Giottesca, Florence, 1943, passim; P. Toesca, Gli affreschi della cappella di San Silvestro in Santa Croce a Firenze (Artis monumenta photographice edita, II), Florence, 1944; L. Coletti, Primitivi senesi e giotteschi, Novara, 1945, pp. 40–41; M. Salmi, Maso di Banco a Napoli, Atti e mem. dell'Acc. Colombaria, N.S., I, 1947, pp. 415–21; E. L. Levi, Ricostruzione di un affresco perduto di Maso di Banco, RArte, XXV, 1950, pp. 193–97; Toesca, Tr, pp. 626–34; G. Marchini, Le vetrate italiane, Milan, 1956, p. 32; U. Baldini and L. Berti, Mostra di affreschi staccati (exhibition cat.), Florence, 1957, pp. 47–48.

Mario SALMI

Illustrations: PLS. 369–373.

MASOLINO (TOMMASO DI CRISTOFANO, or CRISTOFORO, FINI, called "Masolino"). Painter (b. Panicale, near Florence, 1383; d. Florence, 1440 or 1447, if one accepts either of the death dates for a Tommaso di Cristofano registered in the Cathedral in Florence). His artistic formation, which remains insufficiently clarified, was certainly influenced by Ghiberti and contemporary sculptors, for there seems to be no evidence to discredit the sources (e.g., Vasari) that refer to Masolino as an assistant of Ghiberti on the doors of the Baptistery. There is a Maso di Cristofano cited in Ghiberti's contracts of 1403 and 1407 with the Arte dei Mercanti di Calimala (Merchants' Guild), but Gaetano Milanesi and Dominic Colnaghi have preferred to identify him with the goldsmith Tommaso di Cristofano di Braccio, who died Jan. 13, 1430. Mario Salmi has suggested that Masolino's relatively late enrollment (1423) in the Arte dei Medici e Speziali (Painters' Guild) may be indirect evidence that he was occupied in work with Ghiberti until that time.

Vasari says also that Masolino studied painting with Gherardo Starnina; since Starnina remains an almost legendary figure, the statement cannot be verified. Other artistic interrelations have been proposed by 20th-century scholars: with Lorenzo Monaco, Arcangelo di Cola da Camerino, and Gentile da Fabriano (Salmi); with Giovanni da Milano (Roberto Longhi); with an artist such as the Master of the Strauss Madonna or the Pseudo-Ambrogio di Baldese (Cesare Brandi).

Masolino's earliest known work is the little *Madonna of Humility* (Bremen, Kunsthalle) of 1423. On its attribution to Masolino (first proposed by August Schmarsow) all scholars agree except Robert Oertel, who gives it to Masaccio. Actually it shows no trace of Masaccio's style; its stylistic connections are with the artists mentioned above, and the iconographic motif is close to types in Sienese art of the Trecento and in the works of Lorenzo Monaco and others.

Probably somewhat later is the Munich *Madonna and Child* (PL. 374). Luciano Berti has proposed the date 1425, which seems probable in view of its connections with Masaccio and with Gentile da Fabriano's Quaratesi polyptych of 1425. Salmi, however, prefers to place it closer in time to the Bremen Madonna; Longhi dates it 1424, at the beginning of Masolino's collaboration with Masaccio and just before the lunette in Empoli; and Oertel dates it about 1435, in the period of the Castiglione Olona frescoes.

Documents published by Giovanni Poggi and by Odoardo H. Giglioli establish Masolino's presence and activity at Empoli in 1424. In the Church of S. Stefano, sinopias and some areas of fresco (on the wainscot, archivolt, and window embrasures) remain of episodes from *The Legend of the True Cross* that Masolino painted in the Chapel of St. Helen; these were rediscovered by Ugo Procacci. Also in S. Stefano are a fragment with a group of adoring children (rediscovered by Procacci) and a lunette depicting the Madonna with angels. In the Galleria della Collegiata di S. Andrea, Empoli, is one of the artist's most impressive works, the *Pietà*, a fresco formerly in the Baptistery.

These works, particularly the lunette, still manifest some indebtedness to Gentile da Fabriano, but their simplification of line and surface — seen especially in the sinopias — is in marked contrast to the virtuoso calligraphy typical of late Gothic painting. Indeed, the paintings at Empoli, the saints in the archivolt, for example, seem to reflect the manner of Masaccio, with whom Masolino must already have been in contact, though these reflections are transformed by Masolino's courtly and refined sensibility. Certainly neither the physical grandeur nor the emotional force of the Christ in the *Pietà* can be explained solely by a familiarity with the sculpture of Ghiberti — an opinion shared by Salmi, Toesca, and Longhi. Berti, although admitting that the two painters must at this point have known each other, doubts the presence of a tangible influence from Masaccio; Oertel, on the other hand, follows Schmarsow in attributing the *Pietà* to Masaccio.

Another important work which appears to be of this period is the Carnesecchi triptych, executed for S. Maria Maggiore in Florence. It was dismembered in the 17th century; the parts that have been identified include the central Madonna, which was stolen from the Church of S. Maria at Novoli shortly after its discovery there by Toesca in 1923, a wing representing St. Julian (Florence, Seminario Maggiore del Cestello), and a predella panel which shows a scene from the life of St. Julian (Montauban, Mus. Ingres). Longhi (1940), Salmi, and Berti date the triptych 1425; Toesca considers it as postdating the Brancacci Chapel; Lindberg proposes the date 1428; and Ruth Kennedy assigns it, with reservations, to the period of the Castiglione Olona frescoes. Oertel attributes the entire altarpiece to Masaccio and dates it 1424–25, but denies that the Montauban predella panel belongs to it.

At the end of 1424 or the beginning of 1425 Masolino began the fresco decoration of the Brancacci Chapel — alone, according to Procacci's persuasive investigations — and executed the *Evangelists* in the vault and the *Scenes from the Life of St. Peter* in the upper lunettes. (These were destroyed when the chapel was redecorated in the 18th century.) After Masaccio arrived on the scene, Masolino executed *The Original Sin, The Preaching of St. Peter*, and the scene of St. Peter healing a cripple and raising Tabitha (PL. 374). Masolino departed for Hungary on Sept. 1, 1425. (For discussion of the collaboration between Masolino and Masaccio, particularly in reference to the Brancacci Chapel, see MASACCIO.) *The Original Sin* has been attributed to Masaccio by G. B. Cavalcaselle, by Schmarsow, by Raimond Van Marle, by Heinrich Brockhaus, and by Oertel. Lindberg was the first to date the Brancacci frescoes as following the paintings in Empoli, a sequence now generally accepted. Procacci is of the opinion that the extant Brancacci frescoes — both Masaccio's and Masolino's — were executed after Masolino's return from Hungary in 1427. Salmi relates the Adam and Eve of Masolino's *Original Sin* to Masaccio's lost picture of "a male and a female nude, life size" which Vasari cited as being in the Rucellai Palace, Florence.

Masolino's departure for Hungary left Masaccio (if one disregards Procacci's thesis) to continue the frescoes of the Brancacci Chapel alone. Masolino returned to Florence in July, 1427, and on July 12 was assigned the decoration of a chapel in the Church of S. Francesco, Figline Valdarno, probably never executed, as Procacci notes. Masolino's name does not appear in any Florentine document after July 20, 1427. Berti — who, like Salmi and most other scholars, does not believe that the Brancacci frescoes were executed after Masolino's return from Hungary — points to this fact in support of his view; he also notes that in the Rome works (excepting the debated *Crucifixion*) Masolino fails to sustain the advances he made in figure painting and perspective as a result of his association with Masaccio in the Brancacci Chapel.

The fresco cycle commissioned by Cardinal Branda Castiglione for the Chapel of St. Catherine in S. Clemente, Rome, has been variously dated. The cardinal was the incumbent of S. Clemente from 1411 to 1431, when he became Bishop of Porto, and a dating between 1427 and 1431 would therefore seem logical. The datings of 1420 (proposed by Wilhelm Lübke and Adolfo Venturi), 1422–23 (Oertel and Emilio Lavagnino), and 1436 (Ernst Trenkler) are unacceptable for stylistic reasons. Improbable also would seem Longhi's dating of 1425 and his hypothesis (based on a suggestion by Carlo Gamba) that Masolino and Masaccio went to Rome for the Jubilee of 1425 and that Masolino finished their joint work between 1428 and 1430. In fact, Masaccio's participation in these works (Vasari attributes to him the entire cycle) is still to be demonstrated, since no attempt to prove it has thus far been convincing.

The frescoes in S. Clemente comprise: in the vault, the *Evangelists and Doctors of the Church*; along the intrados, the *Apostles*, in half-figure; on the side of the entrance arch, *The Annunciation*; on a pilaster, *St. Christopher*; on the walls, scenes from the life of St. Ambrose (*St. Ambrose in His Cradle, St. Ambrose Named Bishop of Milan, A Miracle of St. Ambrose, St. Ambrose's Study, The Death of St. Ambrose*) and from the life of St. Catherine of Alexandria [*St. Catherine Refuses to Worship the Idol, The Conversion and Martyrdom of the Empress, St. Catherine and the Philosophers* (PL. 378), *The Miracle of the Wheel, The Martyrdom of St. Catherine*], and *The Crucifixion*.

Critical speculation has been focused especially on the large and important *Crucifixion* (X, PL. 484). Longhi has ascribed to Masaccio the distant landscape, with its tunnels of illusionistic space, and all the figures in the middle ground, which, with exception of the unsatisfactory figure of the horseman on the right, reinforce and clarify the sense of a precise and complicated spatial circulation. On the other hand, it has been suggested that Masolino was aided here by the young Domenico Veneziano. The present author shares Salmi's opinion that the entire S. Clemente fresco cycle was executed at one time and by one artist, Masolino, and that any elements resembling Masaccio's work are merely reflections of the figural solutions achieved in the Brancacci Chapel.

Another important and much-discussed Roman work is the triptych painted for S. Maria Maggiore. It was, as Schmarsow first suggested, painted on both sides. One side had as its centerpiece *The Founding of S. Maria Maggiore* (PL. 374) and at left and right, respectively, the *SS. Peter and Paul* and *John the Evangelist and Martin*, now in Philadelphia (Mus. of Art, Johnson Coll.). The other side comprised *The Assumption* (Naples, Mus. di Capodimonte), at center, and the *SS. Jerome and John the Baptist* and *SS. Liberius and Matthias* (London, Nat. Gall.), at left and right. The London panels were rediscovered only in 1951. The S. Maria Maggiore triptych is best dated 1428, but several other dates have been suggested. Longhi and Kenneth Clark connect it with Masaccio's supposed Roman sojourn of 1425; Lindberg proposes 1429, a date that would exclude the participation of Masaccio; Oertel suggests about 1423 and assigns the Philadelphia saints to the young Masaccio.

Postdating the frescoes of S. Clemente but lacking their reminiscences of Masaccio is a group of paintings which precedes Masolino's activity at Castiglione Olona. This group includes an *Annunciation* in two panels, formerly in the Kress Collection (Washington, D.C., Nat. Gall.; PL. 377); another *Annunciation*, also in Washington (Nat. Gall.), formerly in the Mellon and Goldman Collections; a fresco, *The Madonna with Two Angels*, in the Church of S. Fortunato at Todi; and a *Madonna of Humility*, formerly in the Contini Bonacossi Collection, Florence. Of these works, only the *Madonna* at Todi is securely dated (Masolino was paid for it on Nov. 1, 1432), but the others can be chronologically ranged, before and after, in the above order, from about 1430 to about 1435. The *Madonna* at Todi is also the only one of these works that recalls Masaccio (in the perspective of the throne, as if seen from below, which Longhi has pointed out). All of them, however, combine the earlier derivations from Gentile da Fabriano and the rhythms of Ghiberti with a perceptible approach to the style of Fra Angelico. In this new combination of elements, Masolino, after his more grandiose Masaccio period, reassumed his essential personality — to quote Longhi, his "character of a late little treasure" — and reintegrated the motifs of his personal poetry.

At Castiglione Olona Masolino painted two important fresco cycles, one in the Collegiata and one in the Baptistery. The frescoes of the Collegiata (comprising *The Annunciation, The Marriage of the Virgin, The Nativity, The Adoration of the Magi*, and *The Coronation of the Virgin*) are in the vault. They were at one time whitewashed but were rediscovered in 1843, and because the *Nativity* is signed, their attribution has never been disputed. What has been argued is their chronological relation to the fresco cycle of the Baptistery (comprising *The Annunciation, The Evangelists, The Doctors of the Church, God the Father with Angels*, and *Scenes from the Life of John the Baptist*), which is dated 1435. This date, on the intrados of the chancel arch, is repainted but plausible and may, as Lindberg suggests, refer to the completion of the work.

The Collegiata frescoes have been dated somewhat later than 1425 (almost contemporary with the consecration of the church) by Schmarsow; about 1423 by Toesca and A. Venturi;

in 1430 by Lavagnino; and about 1432 (just before the Baptistery frescoes) by Salmi. This last opinion is shared by Lionello Venturi, Lindberg, and Oertel. Longhi, however, dates them after the Baptistery frescoes and supposes that they were interrupted by the painter's death, which he places in 1440.

The frescoes in the Baptistery (PLS. 375, 376) have been accepted at face value by most scholars as works of Masolino, from about 1435; the notable dissenters from this opinion are Lindberg, who sees in them the presence of a different hand, and Longhi, who postulates a contribution from Il Vecchietta, by reference to the "rational" perspective of the *Zacharias Inscribing St. John's Name* and in the upper part of the *St. John in Prison*. (Vecchietta may also have worked in the Collegiata, on the wall frescoes of scenes from the lives of St. Lawrence and St. Stephen.)

Lost works by Masolino, besides those previously mentioned, include a frescoed St. Peter in S. Maria del Carmine in Florence, which Vasari cited as a preliminary to the frescoes of the Brancacci Chapel. In the Vatican Museums there is a *Crucifixion* that is at least a product of Masolino's workshop and may be a late work by his own hand; and in the Casa Castiglione in Castiglione Olona is a fresco, of which only two portraits and a fantastic landscape survive, attributed to Masolino by G. Cagnola and Salmi and considered by the latter as belonging among Masolino's latest works in Lombardy.

SOURCES. A. Manetti, Vite di XIV uomini singhulary in Firenze dal MCCCC innanzi, in G. Milanesi, ed., Operette istoriche... di A. Manetti, Florence, 1887, pp. 159–68; Filarete (A. Averlino), Trattato di architettura, ca. 1451–64 (ed. W. von Oettingen, Vienna, 1896); A. Billi, Il Libro di A. Billi, 1481–1530 (ed. K. Frey, Berlin, 1892); F. Albertini, Memoriale di molte statue et picture... di Florentia, Florence, 1510 (ed. H. P. Horne, London, 1909); G. Vasari, Le Vite, Florence, 1550 (2d ed., 1568); R. Borghini, Il Riposo, Florence, 1584 (2d ed., G. G. Bottari, Florence, 1730); F. Bocchi, Le bellezze della città di Fiorenza, Florence, 1591 (2d amplified ed., G. Cinelli, Florence, 1677).

BIBLIOG. P. Coccapani, Descrizione della festa per la solenne traslazione del corpo di Sant'Andrea Corsini, Rome, 1675; G. Richa, Notizie istoriche delle chiese fiorentine, 10 vols., Florence, 1754–62; L. Lanzi, Storia pittorica dell'Italia, Bassano, 1789; J. A. Crowe and G. B. Cavalcaselle, A New History of Painting in Italy, II, London, 1864; A. Zahn, Masolino und Masaccio, Jhb. für Kw., II, 1869, pp. 155–71; W. Lübke, Masolino und Masaccio, Jhb. für Kw., III, 1870, pp. 280–86; A. Reumont, Die Kapelle der heiligen Katharina in S. Clemente zu Rom, Jhb. für Kw., III, 1870, pp. 75–79; J. P. Richter, Notes on Vasari, London, 1885; F. Wickhoff, Die Fresken der Katharinenkapelle in S. Clemente zu Rom, ZfbK, XXIV, 1889, pp. 301–10; A. Schmarsow, Masaccio-Studien, 5 vols., Kassel, 1895–99; G. B. Gelli, Vite d'artisti fiorentini, Florence, 1896; E. Jacobsen, Uber einige italienische Gemälde der alteren Pinakothek zu München, RepfKw, XX, 1897, pp. 425–42; M. Creutz, Masaccio, Berlin, 1901; A. Filangeri di Candida, La pinacoteca di Napoli e il neoriordinamento, Napoli nobilissima, X, 1901, pp. 33–35; B. Marrai, Il tabernacolo col gruppo del Verrocchio in Orsanmichele, L'Arte, IV, 1901, pp. 346–52; B. Berenson, Quelques peintures méconnues de Masolino, GBA, XXVII, 1902, pp. 89–99; B. Berenson, The Study and Criticism of Italian Art, 2d ser., London, 1902; C. de Fabriczy, Ancora del tabernacolo col gruppo del Verrocchio in Orsanmichele, L'Arte, V, 1902, pp. 46–48, 336–40; J. B. Supino and B. Marrai, Ancora del tabernacolo col gruppo del Verrocchio in Orsanmichele, L'Arte, V, 1902, pp. 185–89; B. Marrai, Il tabernacolo col gruppo del Verrocchio in Orsanmichele, RArte, I, 1903, pp. 36–38; G. Cagnola, Un affresco inedito di Masolino, Rass. d'arte, IV, 1904, pp. 75–76; V. Leonardi, Affreschi dimenticati del tempo di Martino V, Atti Cong. int. di sc. storiche, Rome 1905, pp. 286–308; G. Poggi, Masolino e la compagnia della Croce a Empoli, RArte, III, 1905, pp. 46–53; M. Reymond, L'architecture des peintres aux premières de la Renaissance, Rev. de l'art ancien et mod., IX, 1905, pp. 41–42, 48–50; O. Sirén, Notizie critiche sui quadri sconosciuti nel Museo Cristiano Vaticano, L'Arte, IX, 1906, pp. 321–35; F. Mason Perkins, Un dipinto sconosciuto di Masolino, Rass. d'arte, VII, 1907, pp. 184–87; P. Toesca, Masolino da Panicale, Bergamo, 1908; B. Berenson, Florentine Painters of the Renaissance, 3d ed., New York, London, 1909; J. Breck, Dipinti italiani nella raccolta del Sig. Teodoro Davis, Rass. d'arte, XI, 1911, pp. 111–15; Venturi, VII, 1911, pp. 81–112; K. Woermann, Masaccio und Masolino (1880), in Von Apelles zu Böcklin und weiter, I, Esslingen, 1912, pp. 41–48; U. Gnoli, L'affresco di Masolino a Todi, BArte, VIII, 1914, pp. 175–76; G. J. Kern, Der Mazzocchio des Paolo Uccello, JhbPreussKSamml, XXXVI, 1915, pp. 13–38; B. Berenson, The Annunciation by Masolino, Art in Am., IV, 1916, pp. 305–11; T. Borenius, The Annunciation by Masolino, BM, XXIX, 1916, p. 45; R. Offner, Italian Pictures at the New York Historical Society and Elsewhere, Art in Am., VIII, 1920, pp. 7–14; C. F. Rumohr, Italienische Forschungen (ed. J. Schlosser), Frankfurt am Main, 1920, pp. 376–81; O. H. Giglioli, Masaccio, Florence, 1921; B. Berenson, Una predella di Masolino, Dedalo, III, 1922–23, pp. 633–35; R. Offner, Un pannello di Masolino a San Giuliano a Settimo, Dedalo, III, 1922–23, pp. 636–41; W. Bode, Die Kunst der Frührenaissance in Italien, Berlin, 1923; P. Toesca, Frammento di un polittico di Masolino, BArte, N.S., III, 1923–24, pp. 3–6; A. Venturi, L'arte a San Girolamo, Milan, 1924; A. Schmarsow, Neue Beiträge zu Masolino und Masaccio, Belvedere, VII, 1925, pp. 145–57; G. Vitzthum, Ein Stadtbild im Baptisterium von Castiglione Olona, Festschrift P. Clement, Bonn, 1926, pp. 401–11; M. Dvořák, Geschichte der italienischen Kunst, I, Munich, 1927; J. Mesnil, Masaccio et les débuts de la Renaissance, The Hague, 1927; M. Salmi, Gli affreschi di Castiglione Olona, Dedalo, VIII, 1927–28, pp. 227–44; A. Schmarsow, Masolino und Masaccio, Leipzig, 1928; Van Marle, IX, 1928, pp. 257–314; H. Beenken, Zum Werke des Masaccio, ZfbK, LXIII, 1929–30, pp. 112–19, 156–65; O. H. Giglioli, Masaccio, B. R. Ist. di Archeol. e Storia dell'Arte, III, 1929, pp. 55–101 (bibliog.); J. Mesnil, Masolino ou Masaccio?, GBA, II, 1929, pp. 206–09; W. Stechow, Zum Masolino-Masaccio Problem, ZfbK, LXIII, 1929–30, pp. 125–27; B. Berenson, The Italian Painters of the Renaissance, Oxford, 1930; H. Brockhaus, Die Brancacci Kapelle in Florenz, Mitt. des kunsthist. Inst. in Florenz, III, 1930, pp. 160–82; O. H. Giglioli, ThB, s. v., XXIV, 1930, pp. 210–11; M. Salmi, An Unpublished Masolino, Art in Am., XVIII, 1930, pp. 186–205; L. Venturi, Contributi a Masolino, Lorenzo Salimbeni e Iacopo Bellini, L'Arte, N.S., I, 1930, pp. 165–90; H. Lindberg, To the Problem of Masolino and Masaccio, Stockholm, 2 vols., 1931; W. R. Valentiner, Eine Verkündigung Masolinos, Pantheon, VIII, 1931, pp. 413–16; L. Venturi, Pitture italiane in America, Milan, 1931; H. Beenken, Masaccios und Masolinos Fresken von S. Clemente in Rom, Belvedere, XI, 1932, pp. 7–13; B. Berenson, Quadri senza casa: Il Quattrocento fiorentino, Dedalo, XII, 1932, pp. 512–41; J. Mesnil, Vues nouvelles sur l'art de Masaccio, Rev. de l'art ancien et moderne, LXII, 1932, pp. 145–62; M. Salmi, Masaccio, Rome, 1932; E. Trenckler, Beiträge zur Masaccio Forschung, Wiener Jhb. für Kg., VIII, 1932, pp. 7–16; R. Oertel, Die Frühwerke des Masaccio, Marburger Jhb. für Kw., VII, 1933, pp. 191–289; R. Oertel, Masaccio und die Geschichte der Freskotechnik, JhbPreussKSamml, LV, 1934, pp. 229–40; P. Johansen, Masolino, Masaccio und Tabitha, Copenhagen, 1935; M. Pittaluga, Masaccio, Florence, 1935; G. Wassermann, Masaccio und Masolino, Strasbourg, 1935; A. Morassi, Die Fresken des Masolino in Baptisterium vom Castiglione Olona, Pantheon, XIX, 1937, pp. 72–80; H. Horváth, Il Rinascimento in Ungheria, Rome, 1939; R. Longhi, Fatti di Masolino e di Masaccio, CrArte, V, 1940, pp. 145–91; R. Oertel, Wandmalerei und Zeichnung in Italien, Mitt. des kunsthist. Inst. in Florenz, V, 1940, pp. 217–314; P. Toesca, Masolino a Castiglione Olona, Milan, 1946; U. Procacci, Mostra di opere d'arte trasportate a Firenze durante la guerra e di opere d'arte restaurate, Florence, 1947; R. Longhi, Gli affreschi del Carmine: Masaccio o Dante, Paragone, I, 9, 1950, pp. 3–7; K. Clark, An Early Quattrocento Triptych from Santa Maria Maggiore, Rome, BM, XCIII, 1951, pp. 339–47; M. Davies, National Gallery Catalogues: The Earlier Italian Schools, London, 1951; U. Procacci, Tutta la pittura di Masaccio, Milan, 1951 (Eng. trans. P. Colacicchi, New York, 1962); R. Longhi, Presenza di Masaccio nel Trittico della Neve, Paragone, III, 25, 1952, pp. 8–16; J. Pope-Hennessy, The Santa Maria Maggiore Altarpiece, BM, XCIV, 1952. p. 31; M. Salmi, Gli scomparti della Pala di S. Maria Maggiore acquistati dalla National Gallery, Comm, III, 1952, pp. 14–21; U. Procacci, Sulla cronologia delle opere di Masaccio e di Masolino tra il 1425 e il 1428, RArte, XXVIII, 1953, pp. 3–55; U. Baldini, Restauri di dipinti fiorentini in occasione della Mostra di quattro Maestri del Rinascimento, BArte, XXXIX, 1954, pp. 221–40; U. Baldini and L. Berti, Mostra di affreschi staccati (exhibition cat.) Florence, 1957; C. Brandi, I cinque anni cruciali per la pittura fiorentina del '400, in Studi in onore di Matteo Marangoni, Pisa, 1957, pp. 167–75; F. Hartt, The Earliest Works of Andrea del Castagno, AB, XLI, 1959, pp. 159–81; E. Micheletti, Masolino da Panicale, Milan, 1959; E. Borsook, The Mural Painters of Tuscany, London, 1960; L. Berti, Masaccio 1422, Comm, XII, 1961, pp. 84–107; U. Procacci, Sinopie e affreschi, Milan, 1961.

Umberto BALDINI

Illustrations: PLS. 374–378.

MASSYS, QUENTIN (also spelled Matsys or Metsys). Massys was born in Louvain between Sept. 10, 1465, and Sept. 10, 1466; he died in Antwerp between July 13 and Sept. 16, 1530. He spent the first part of his life in Louvain, according to tradition practicing the craft of his father, who was a smith. Karl van Mander asserted that Massys taught himself to paint, but his works indicate that he had formal training, very probably from one of the sons or other followers of the great Dirk Bouts, who served as official painter of Louvain from 1468 until his death in 1475. By 1491 Massys had moved to Antwerp, where he became a member of the painters' guild in that year.

No works by Massys have been definitely assigned to his early period in Louvain, but two Madonnas (Brussels, Mus. Royaux des B. A.), a *St. Christopher* (Antwerp, Mus. Royal des B. A.), and a *Madonna and Child Enthroned* (formerly Malvern, Eng., Dyson Perrins Coll.) have all been associated with this first phase of his career. His most important works are two large altarpieces painted between 1507 and 1511. The first is the St. Anne Altarpiece, or *The Holy Kinship* (Brussels, Mus. Royaux des B. A.), signed and dated 1509, which was commissioned for the Church of St-Pierre in Louvain in 1507. The other is the triptych of the Deposition (Antwerp, Mus. Royal des B. A.), ordered in 1508 by the guild of the joiners in Antwerp for their chapel in the Cathedral and completed by Massys three years later. There are numerous other signed works by Massys, some of them dated, including the *Portrait of an Old Man* (Paris, Mus. Jacquemart-André) and *The Money Changer and His Wife* (VI, PL. 66). He is also believed to have painted a diptych of Erasmus (XII, PL. 98) and Petrus Aegidius (Salisbury, Longford Castle, Coll. Earl of Radnor), both about 1517. He collaborated with the landscape painter Joachim Patinir, providing the figures for the *Temptation of St. Anthony* (Prado). When Dürer went to Antwerp, he visited the house of Massys, which was by then one of the city's notable sights, but he did not meet the master. Two of Quentin's sons, Cornelis and Jan Massys, were also painters; and he influenced many others, particularly Joos van Cleve, Marinus van Roymerswael, and Jan Sanders van Hemessen.

The art of Massys blends the medieval Flemish tradition with the style of the Renaissance. His sweet, graceful, and elegant types display affecting but restrained emotion. His subjects are the conventional ones of his Flemish predecessors in the 15th century. He had a sure mastery of painting techniques and employed a subtle and distinctive range of colors, in which the violets, tawny yellows, and rose are especially pleasing. Soon after finishing the two great altarpieces, he seems to have become acquainted with the art of the Italian Renaissance, and especially the drawings of Leonardo da Vinci. This familiarity is evident in some Leonardesque compositions that he afterward adopted and in his development of a soft chiaroscuro. Architectural settings and richer ornament are also characteristic of his later works. (See also III, PL. 415; V, PLS. 284, 288.)

BIBLIOG. M. J. Friedländer, Die altniederländische malerei, VII, Berlin, 1929; H. B. Wehle and M. Salinger, A Catalogue of Early Flemish, Dutch and German Paintings, New York, 1947, pp. 107–10; L. Mallé, Quinten Metsys, Commentari, VI, 1955, pp. 79–107; K. G. Boon, Quinten Massys, Amsterdam, n.d.

Margaretta M. SALINGER

MATHURA. The name of the city (in recent times also called Muttra), once a great religious center (Μαδούρα ἡ τῶν θεῶν, Ptolemy, *Geography*, VII, i, 50), also designates the school of art that flourished there, a school that systematically and consistently opposed the reworking of classical elements in Gandharan art (see GANDHARA). The winter residence of the Kushan rulers (see KUSHAN ART), Mathura produced works that most likely reflect the taste of the dominant groups in the empire. It acted as a center for the adaptation and Indianization of those few iconographic schemes and pictorial motifs which classical Indian art adopted from the schools of the northwest. Mathura continued to be an important artistic center in the Gupta period (see GUPTA, SCHOOL OF), though its style was gradually diluted by the internationalism that characterized the new art movements. The Mathura school is noteworthy for the quality of its output during the half millennium of its development.

SUMMARY. Religious, geographical, and historical background (col. 579). Pre-Kushan period (col. 581). Kushan period (col. 582). Gupta period (col. 584). Conclusion (col. 585).

RELIGIOUS, GEOGRAPHICAL, AND HISTORICAL BACKGROUND. Situated on the Jamuna River, a sacred tributary of the Ganges, the city of Mathura was for many centuries the home of an influential school of art that owed its rise to, and in turn reflected, the city's importance as a great religious center where a variety of faiths coexisted or succeeded one another. Popular cults persisted alongside Buddhism and Jainism (qq.v.) until these two great faiths were superseded by Hinduism (q.v.), principally through the widespread veneration of Kṛṣṇa; Islam (q.v.), too, left traces, but at a later date. Although there had been some artistic activity in the region before our era, the Mathura school proper flourished from the 1st to the 4th century and remained active through the 6th and even into the medieval period; it owed its development to the number and prosperity of the Buddhist and, to a lesser degree, the Jain establishments.

Geographical and historical factors also contributed to the formation and expansion of the school. Situated on the great trade route linking the Ganges basin with that of the Indus and with regions farther south, the city of Mathura was favorably located for exchanges with other centers near and far. On the one hand, direct communication with cities and religious centers to the east and south encouraged the adoption and perpetuation by Mathura of ancient Indian traditions that had developed in those regions; on the other hand, traffic with the northwestern areas (Punjab and Gandhara) and contacts with important ports along the western seaboard — which in turn communicated with the Iranian and Mediterranean regions — facilitated the introduction of foreign elements that served to renew its art. Thus, Mathura's geographical position, in addition to its importance as a place of pilgrimage, explains not only the diffusion of its works of art — found in places as far apart as Sarnath, Pataliputra (mod. Patna), Sravasti, Sanchi, and Taxila — but also the appreciable influence these works exerted both in India and beyond.

Mentioned as early as the Avadāna of Aśoka (3d cent. B.C.), the city came under the domination of the Śakas about the 1st century B.C. and then fell under the Yüeh-chih, who conquered all of northwest India in the second half of the 1st century of our era and, under Wima Kadphises, founded the powerful Kushan dynasty (see KUSHAN ART). The prosperity of Mathura and its school reflected the fortunes of the Kushan rulers, the most celebrated of whom, Kaniṣka I (2d cent.), extended his empire from the Ganges basin to regions beyond the Oxus (mod. Amu Darya) and the Pamirs. Although a few Buddhist stupas and monasteries had been built under the Śakas, their marked increase was largely due to the patronage of Kaniṣka and his successors (Vāsiṣka, Huviṣka, Vāsudeva), all of whom were favorably disposed toward Buddhism. The city became surrounded with religious establishments, both Buddhist and Jain, since the Kushan rulers tolerated concurrent development of the two great religions. Subsequent devastation, however, has left few vestiges of these buildings.

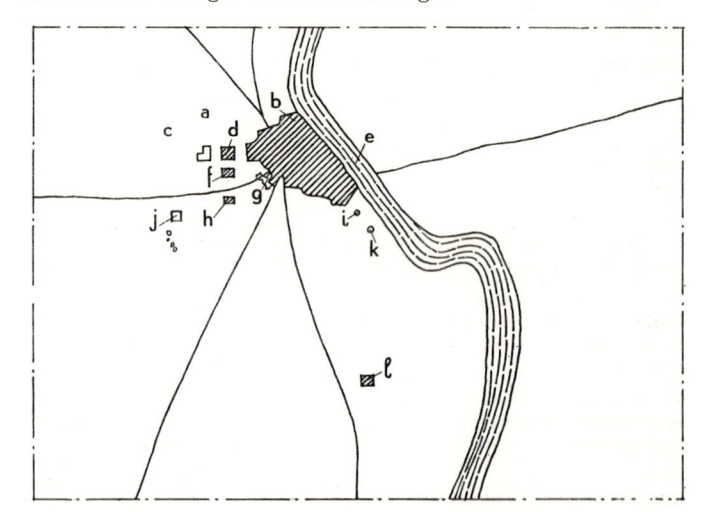

Mathura and environs, principal monuments of archaeological and artistic interest: (*a*) Mahāvidyā Ṭīlā; (*b*) Ambarīkhā Ṭīlā; (*c*) Chaurāsī Ṭīlā; (*d*) Yaśa Vihara, Katra; (*e*) Isapur; (*f*) Bhuteshar; (*g*) Gāyatrī Ṭīlā; (*h*) Vodva Stupa, Kaṅkālī Ṭīlā; (*i*) Dhruv Ṭīlā; *j*) Madhura Vanaka, Chaubara; (*k*) Guha Vihara, Saptarṣi Ṭīlā; (*l*) Huviṣka Vihara, Jamalpur (*from J. P. Vogel, La Sculpture de Mathura, Paris, Brussels, 1930*).

The domination of the region by rulers of foreign origin and the vastness of their empire inevitably affected the art of Mathura; these circumstances not only promoted the establishment of relations with the northwestern provinces, where a different style was developing, but also led to the introduction of beliefs, forms, and themes from diverse areas, as coins, sculptures, and decorative motifs variously attest. Such religious eclecticism is manifest in the variety of divinities and symbols on Kushan coins, as well as in the representation of fire altars and of flames issuing from the shoulders of monarchs. The dress of these monarchs (and that of several donors), which recalls their

Nordic origin, influenced the religious iconography and was thereafter adopted for the sun god Sūrya, known from the Vedic period. In some instances, the rulers' personal taste determined the aspect of the works. Such is the case of the dynastic portrait statues, a genre in itself unusual in India; the sober, rugged mien and the imposing severity of these figures set them apart from the numerous statues of purely Indian tradition. Nevertheless, the fact that these dynastic statues were reproduced almost identically at the two poles of the empire, at Mathura (VIII, PLS. I, 410) and at Surkh Kotal in Bactria (a group was found in the fire temple on this site; II, PL. 89), constitutes a telling demonstration of the success, however temporary, of the Kushans in rallying distant and disparate provinces, thereby briefly uniting cultures and tendencies strongly diversified and in many cases seemingly incompatible.

With the disintegration of the vast Kushan empire, undermined by struggles with the Sassanians (see SASSANIAN ART) in the mid-3d century, the bonds linking Mathura with the provinces of the northwest slackened or were broken. About 319 the province passed into the hands of the Guptas. Despite the avowed adherence of the new dynasty to Hinduism, attested by the inauguration in 380 of a temple dedicated to Śiva, Buddhism continued to flourish throughout the 5th century. On his way through Mathura about the year 400, the Chinese pilgrim Fahsien noted the existence of 20 Buddhist monasteries inhabited by 3,000 monks; Hsüan-tsang, who visited the city in the mid-7th century, counted the same number of monasteries but a great depopulation of the monks: the rest undoubtedly fled before the invasion of the Ephthalites, about A.D. 455. Although the 5th century marked a new era of prosperity for the sculpture workshops, their activity nevertheless seems to have come to a sudden halt toward the middle of that century. The period of flourishing was marked by a stylistic renewal related to that being effected contemporaneously in the eastern part of the country, in religious and artistic centers with which Mathura was then associated.

Although the artistic production of Mathura was most abundant and original during the period of Kushan domination, in the preceding and ensuing periods it was by no means negligible. The works antedating the Christian Era constitute the first steps in the formation of an Indian esthetic, adopted by the Mathura school, whereas those of the late phase witness the flowering of new, and sometimes alien, tendencies that mark a further stage in the evolution of Indian art.

PRE-KUSHAN PERIOD. Although Mathura must have possessed monuments of some importance as early as the Maurya and Śuṅga periods (late 3d–1st cent. B.C.), almost no trace of them remains. All that is worthy of note are a few fragments of railings (vedikas) of the type that surrounded Stupa No. 2 at Sanchi and the stupa at Bharhut (2d cent. B.C.). The medallions adorning the Mathura railings correspond in both style and motifs (lotus rosettes, Buddhist symbols, etc.) to those in low relief at Sanchi and Bharhut. The few sculptures found in the region are more characteristic of the Mathura style. Among the oldest surviving works in stone (ca. late 3d cent. B.C.) are the fragment of a colossal statue from Baroda and the statue found at Parkham (II, PL. 403), both of which are larger than life size, modeled in the round, and frontally presented. Despite its ponderous forms and rigid, archaic aspect, the Parkham image is a typically Indian work in the effect of roundness and mass, in dress (dhoti) and jewelry, and even in the yaksha type it represents. Many figures of ancient Indian art and of the Kushan period at Mathura are derived from this type.

The surviving terra-cotta figurines are far more numerous. Deriving from ancient prototypes of the 3d and 2d millenniums, they link the art of the Kushan period to pre-Vedic traditions and in their predominant type — the female tutelary figure — demonstrate the persistence of archaic beliefs. Frequently represented at Bharhut and Sanchi and perhaps even more often at Mathura, the yakshi was to remain the symbol of abundance and fertility, as the nude goddess (the earth goddess or mother goddess) must have been centuries before. A few of the figurines are of the early period; entirely modeled except for some details added by impress, they retain a certain affinity to those of the Indus Valley (see INDUS VALLEY ART). From the end of the pre-Maurya period until about the 2d century the technique changed and the quality improved. Pleasing, smiling faces were produced from molds, while the bodies of the figurines continued to be fashioned by hand; the hair was dressed with strings of beads and rosettes. During and following the Śuṅga period the figurines were entirely produced from molds, and the nude goddess was gradually superseded by abundantly bejeweled female figures dressed in the dhoti or a tunic. Both male and female figures are very similar to the types in contemporaneous stone statues. The female figures, their broad hips and opulent bosoms contrasting with slim waists, conform to the unchanging Indian ideal of female beauty. Until the beginning of the Christian Era these figures, including the colossal yakshi from Didarganj, continued to be represented frontally; it remained for the Kushan school of Mathura to give them a supple and vivacious movement. The amorous couples (mithuna) represented on terracotta plaques are likewise the precursors of many later works.

KUSHAN PERIOD. The origins of the Kushan school of Mathura, which came into being toward the end of the 1st century and continued to flourish until the 5th, are found in the sculpture of the great Buddhist centers in the neighboring regions of Bharhut, Sanchi, and Bodhgaya. There, between the 2d century B.C. and the 1st century of our era, the great traditions of ancient Indian art had developed, assimilating and transforming certain outside elements through the Gandhara school, which was developing contemporaneously under Kushan domination.

As yet few architectural remains have come to light. Mounds marking the sites of the many Buddhist and Jain establishments have frequently been excavated unsystematically. The monasteries must have corresponded to the Gandharan type of sangharama of the plains. Among the rare surviving structural elements worthy of note are gate pillars and decorated crossbars. Various representations of monuments in relief provide slightly more information, as do some of the small votive stupas. The stupa, both Buddhist and Jain, remained of the ancient central-Indian type. The gateway (torana), with pillars and tiers of crossbars, and the railing enclosing the monument also followed the earlier tradition both in form and in details of joining, which were copied from wooden architecture. The large fragments of railings and of torana crossbars so far brought to light reveal that their decoration resembled that of the earlier works in both distribution and style. At Bhuteshar, however, the railing pillars are somewhat unusually adorned with female figures in high relief (PL. 382). Other buildings and architectural elements shown in relief carvings include an apsidal temple, sanctuaries in the form of storied towers, doorways surmounted by tiers of arches, windows framed in horseshoe arches, and columns of various shapes. Of the columns, the most usual type is that used in the earlier rock-cut monuments of Karli, Kanheri, and Nasik; it is characterized by a vase-shaped base, a polygonal shaft, and a bell-shaped capital of the Persepolitan type surmounted by addorsed animals.

The abundant and varied sculptural production comprises individual figures, steles, figures in high relief on architectural elements, narrative carvings in low relief, and a wealth of decorative carving (PLS. 379–84; VII, PLS. 447, 450). Statuary and relief carvings from Buddhist monuments are the most numerous of these works, but there are also a number of images of both Jain and Hindu dedication and others revealing the persistence of popular cults. Of more unusual inspiration are the royal effigies, which demonstrate the religious significance attached to the dynastic concept. These diversely inspired works of the Mathura school have in common both stylistic qualities and the material from which they were carved — red sandstone streaked with yellow, from the nearby quarries of Sikri. Predominant among the Buddhist works are the images of the Buddha. The question of whether the anthropomorphic (as opposed to symbolic) representations of the Buddha were first produced at Mathura or at Gandhara remains a subject of controversy (see IMAGES AND ICONOCLASM). It seems that each school created its own distinct type for the Master at about the same time. The

Gandharan Buddha type reflects elements of Hellenistic and Roman origin, while the Mathura Buddha remains within the Indian tradition and is immediately distinguishable by the rounded and smiling face and by the gossamer fabric of the clinging garment that clearly reveals the figure (VII, PLS. 134, 453). Both attitudes in which the Master is represented (seated in the Indian fashion and standing) are rigidly frontal. By their vigor and stability the two standing Buddhas from Sarnath and Sravasti, dedicated by the monk Bala at the beginning of Kaniṣka's reign, are the direct descendants of the yaksha of Parkham, despite the quality of their modeling and the skillful treatment of their drapery. The right shoulder and half the chest are bare, and the robe is arranged in a series of narrow pleats over the bent left arm, while a panel of the material is raised gracefully over the left hand. A stele found in an excellent state of preservation at Katra shows the peculiarities of the type devised for the Buddha seated in the Indian fashion (padmāsana). On the upper part of the body the robe is draped in the same way as that of the standing Buddhas. The hair is dressed in a manner that was discontinued later: drawn up on top of the head, it is twisted into a spiral bun which constitutes the cranial protuberance (uṣṇīṣa). The right hand is raised to shoulder level, the palm facing forward, in the gesture of reassurance (abhayamudrā), the only gesture represented in this style and during this period when the iconography was still in a formative stage. The large halo bordered with semicircles is a characteristic feature, and the throne supported by lions (siṃhāsana) is of a type that was already traditional. This stele, with its central Buddha framed by two smaller bodhisattvas and by little flying figures, presents all the characteristics of a composition that was to be maintained. The Master's spiritual eminence is brought out by the greater size of the figure and by the treatment in high relief. Beside these works of local character the later seated Buddhas seem rather clumsy interpretations of Gandharan models. Their monastic robes (saṅghāṭi) cover both shoulders, and the regular pleats are schematically indicated; the short, snail-shell curls covering the head and uṣṇīṣa were to become the general rule. Although nude, some of the Jain images are very similar to those of the Buddha.

Certain bodhisattvas carry on the type of the yakshas of Bharhut and Sanchi. Except for their rounded faces, they closely resemble the Gandharan bodhisattvas, both types being clothed in the princely garb of an Indian raja: a dhoti wrapped around the lower part of the body, a scarf, and a wealth of jeweled ornaments (diadem, necklaces, armlets, bracelets, and a belt). Maitreya, the future Buddha, may be distinguished by his flask (of amṛta, or ambrosia). The Śiva type corresponds to that of the bodhisattvas and is sometimes represented with four arms and addorsed to his phallic symbol (linga). The cult of this Hindu deity, as well as that of Kṛṣṇa, is thus attested in the region as of this period.

Though possibly of less iconographic interest, the female figures of Mathura most clearly illustrate both the progress achieved since the early period in India and the creative genius of the Indian sculptors. These tutelary beings figure mainly on railing pillars and torana brackets; their mythical mount or vehicle (vāhana) and the vegetation in which they are often framed are borrowed from the earlier yakshi tree goddess representations. As symbols of fertility they may be accompanied by a child; for the most part, however, these lush figures with opulent forms and in sensuously inflected attitudes (tribhaṅga) are represented intent on some trivial or mundane occupation, such as clasping a flowering branch, carrying a vase, fingering the end of a scarf, playing with a pet bird, or beautifying themselves. The dhoti (if present) is so transparent as to leave the body seemingly naked, the hips scarcely covered by a wide gold belt set with gems. Among a profusion of jeweled ornaments the heavy bangles around the ankles are a particularly characteristic feature. The somewhat affected charm and sensual beauty of these smiling and vivacious female figures seem to suggest a zest for life and its pleasures far removed from the Buddhist ideal of renunciation (PLS. 382-84; VII, PL. 450).

Huge images of the serpent king (Nāgarāja) indicate the persistence of the popular cult of the tutelary rain spirit. Life-size statues of this divinity were sometimes set up near fountains, as was the case of the Nāgarāja of Chargaon, the best preserved of its kind. He is represented in human form and standing in an inflected posture against a stone slab; his polycephalous reptilian nature is shown by the seven cobra heads forming a halo over him and their coils framing his body. The headless Nāgarāja in the Musée Guimet, Paris, with its supple modeling, its elegant posture, and its decorative arrangement of the cummerbund, is an excellent example of the mastery achieved by the Mathura school. The corpulent dwarf yakshas, generally represented crouching, are also connected with popular cults.

Another group of sculptures reflects the foreign origins of the Kushans. The most characteristic is the huge sculpture of three rulers, two standing and one seated, found on the site of a dynastic temple at Mat, north of Mathura. All three are dressed in Scythian fashion, similar to that of the Parthians, in a belted tunic reaching down to the knees and high, soft leather boots; in the standing image of Kaniṣka the dress is completed by a flared mantle fastened only across the chest. Some of the figures, including a few of the donors, wear high, conical caps. With their rigid posture and the simplicity of their dress — highly unusual in Indian art — the royal effigies of Mat seem related to the heavy and imposing Parthian statuary (see PARTHIAN ART). The large dynastic statues found at Surkh Kotal, which bear so striking an affinity to those of Mathura, are of Iranian origin. Introduced by the Kushans, this Iranian influence is manifest in several images of the solar god Sūrya, who is generally represented seated in a chariot drawn by rearing horses deployed in profile to either side (IV, PL. 221). The fact that the god wears (and was to retain) the Kushan dress demonstrates the importance of the solar cult in the more westerly regions.

The relief carvings on crossbars and railing pillars show less variety than the statuary. Indeed, it is almost as though, at a time when huge images of the Buddha were numerous, representations of scenes from his life and from his former incarnations had ceased to be of interest. Few episodes are illustrated and some, such as Indra's visit, are frequently repeated. The compositions are harmonious and clearly disposed and the figures skillfully handled, but the verve of the early periods has disappeared. For representations of the great Miracles of the Buddha and certain other episodes, many elements were borrowed from the Gandhara school. The decorative motifs show somewhat more variety and are of excellent workmanship; the most recurrent include architectural elements and Jain and Buddhist symbols, as well as real and mythical animals, certain of which are earlier borrowings from Iranian art. The tritons of Hellenistic origin assume a curious aspect, with their bifid tails symmetrically disposed and occasionally transformed into fantastic animals. Moreover, the Indian flora, mainly arranged on undulating boughs, is interspersed with acanthus and vine.

Certain tendencies of the Mathura style are found also in works from other localities and thus may indicate a more or less direct connection with the Mathura school. Among such works are the ivories found at Begram (VIII, PL. 241), which abound in graceful and animated female figures, and the carvings adorning rock-cut temples, such as the opulent couples in the chaitya at Karli and the regal figures at Kanheri. Similarities of dress and jewelry also indicate a certain contemporaneity.

GUPTA PERIOD. Several images of the Buddha, of bodhisattvas, and of various other divinities reveal that Mathura's artistic activity continued uninterrupted through the 5th century and the first half of the 6th. However, the sculpture produced in and around Mathura during this period is merely a by-product of the great Gupta school (see GUPTA, SCHOOL OF) that developed in the Ganges Valley and of which Sarnath was the main center. While the sculptures of the Kushan period had achieved great beauty in the lifelike rendering of flesh, particularly in the female figure and Nāgarāja, the Gupta Buddhas show a different spirit, more in keeping with Buddhist doctrine (II, PL. 380). In accordance with the transformation that occurred at Sarnath, Śākyamuni's anthropomorphic aspect was gradually idealized to suggest the deified Buddha's superhuman essence. All the formal elements tended to be refined, and the image was imbued with a spirituality previously unknown. Anatomical proportions were generally elongated, giving greater elegance to the body, which is clearly visible under the gossamer of the clinging garment. The monastic mantle that covers both shoulders is copied from Gandharan prototypes, but its pleats are so fine and are rendered so schematically as almost to be lost. The shape of the face was changed from round to ovoid, in conformity with the ideal type that was being evolved. The placid visage, with its half-closed eyes, emanates a serenity, a benevolence, and an inward concentration that later artists strove to recapture. A large and richly decorated halo adds a note of refinement to the whole. These images thus established a type of Buddha that was to reappear later with the same drapery, the same snail-shell curls, and even the same two symbolic gestures (especially in standing figures), that of reassurance (*abhayamudrā*), in which the hand is raised with the palm facing forward, and that of giving (*varadamudrā*), with the hand extended toward the worshiper. The images of bodhisattvas and Hindu divinities also reflect a high esthetic standard.

Conclusion. The great importance of the Mathura school in the Kushan period derived from the quality and diversity of its works and the diffusion of its influence. Heir to preestablished Indian traditions, it elaborated them and in turn transmitted them to contemporaneous and later schools. Through its contact with the workshops of Gandhara, Mathura occasionally influenced Gandharan production (as in certain Buddhas whose bodily form is more in evidence, and in the type of the bodhisattva); on the other hand, Mathura adopted, assimilated, and transmitted such Gandharan elements as decorative motifs, iconographic details, and certain specific compositions and forms for scenes from the life of the Buddha. The Mathura school thus constituted a connecting link between the art of the northwestern regions and that of the various provinces of India, in particular Amaravati; in addition, it served as a means for transmitting art forms to more distant regions, such as Serindia. Technical progress during the Kushan period enabled the "makers of forms in stone" (*śailarūpakāra*) to produce works of great dimensions, embodying the inveterate tendencies of Indian esthetics — a sense of volume and modeling, supple rendering of movement, and love of living form. No less far-reaching was the influence exerted by the Gupta school of Mathura; the idealized type of Buddha it created inspired numerous later representations, both in India and, by way of the Pala style of Nalanda (see PALA-SENA SCHOOLS), in distant regions such as Serindia and even in China.

BIBLIOG. G. Bühler, New Excavations in Mathurā, Wiener Z. für die Kunde des Morgenlandes, V, 1891, pp. 59-63; G. Bühler, Dr. Führer's Excavations at Mathurā, Wiener Z. für die Kunde des Morgenlandes, V, 1891, pp. 175-80; G. Bühler, Specimens of Jaina Sculptures from Mathurā, Ep. Indica, II, 1894, pp. 311-23; V. A. Smith, The Jain Stūpa and Other Antiquities of Mathurā (Archaeol. Survey of India, New Imperial Ser., XX), Allahabad, 1901; J. P. Vogel, The Mathurā School of Sculpture, Ann. Rep. Archaeol. Survey of India, 1906-07, pp. 137-60, 1909-10, pp. 63-79; J. P. Vogel, Nāga Worship in Ancient Mathurā, Ann. Rep. Archaeol. Survey of India, 1908-09, pp. 159-63; J. P. Vogel, Catalogue of the Archaeological Museum at Mathurā, Allahabad, 1910; J. P. Vogel, Excavations at Mathurā, Ann. Rep. Archaeol. Survey of India, 1911-12, pp. 120-34; J. P. Vogel, A Statute of King Kaniṣka, J. of the Pañjab H. Soc., II, 1912, pp. 39-49; D. R. Sahni, Catalogue of the Museum of Archaeology at Sārnāth, Calcutta, 1914; A. Foucher, On an Old Bas-relief in the Museum at Mathurā, JBORS, VI, 1920, pp. 470-73; R. P. Chanda, Four Ancient Yakṣa Statues, J. Calcutta Univ. Dept. of Letters, IV, 1921, pp. 47-84; R. P. Chanda, The Mathurā School of Sculpture, Ann. Rep. Archaeol. Survey of India, 1922-23, pp. 164-70; D. R. Sahni, A Mathurā Image of the Nāga Dadhikarṇṇa of the Kushān Period, Ann. Rep. Archaeol. Survey of India, 1924-25, pp. 149-50; A. K. Coomaraswamy, Six Reliefs from Mathurā, BMFA, 144, 1926, pp. 54-60; O. C. Gangoly, A Kuṣāṇa Caryatid from Mathurā, Rupam, XXXI, 1927, pp. 73-74; J. P. Vogel, La sculpture de Mathurā, Paris, Brussels, 1930; D. B. Diskalkar, Some Brahmanical Sculptures in the Mathurā Museum, J. United Prov. H. Soc., V, 1932, pp. 18-57; V. S. Agrawala, Pre-Kushāna Art of Mathurā, J. United Prov. H. Soc., VI, 1933, pp. 81-120; P. Stern, A Nāgarāja from Mathurā, JISOA, III, 1935, pp. 33-35; V. S. Agrawala, Mathurā Terracottas, J. United Prov. H. Soc., IX, 2, 1936, pp. 6-38; V. S. Agrawala, The Wine Motif in Mathurā Art, JISOA, IV, 1936, pp. 130-33; V. S. Agrawala, An Early Brahmanical Relief from Mathurā, J. United Prov. H. Soc., X, 2, 1937, pp. 30-34; V. S. Agrawala, A Short Guide-book to the Archaeological Section of the Provincial Museum of Lucknow, Allahabad, 1940; V. S. Agrawala, A Palace-scene on a Terracotta Panel from Mathurā, JISOA, X, 1942, pp. 69-73; C. C. Das Gupta, Some Terracottas from Mathurā Preserved in the Francis Hopp Museum of Asiatic Art, J. As. Soc. of Bengal, IX, 1943, pp. 211-24; V. S. Agrawala, Palace Scenes on a Mathurā Pillar in the Lucknow Museum, J. United Prov. H. Soc., XIX, 1946, pp. 56-60; V. S. Agrawala, A New Stone Umbrella from Mathurā, J. United Prov. H. Soc., XX, 1947, pp. 65-68; J. E. Van Lohuizen de Leeuw, Two Notes on Mathurā Sculpture, in India Antiqua, Leiden, 1947, pp. 231-39; V. S. Agrawala, Buddha and Bodhisattva Images in the Mathurā Museum, J. United Prov. H. Soc., XXI, 1948, pp. 43-98; K. D. Bajpai, Some New Mathurā Finds, J. United Prov. H. Soc., XXI, 1948, pp. 117-30; V. S. Agrawala, Catalogue of the Brahmanical Images in Mathurā Art, J. United Prov. H. Soc., XXII, 1949, pp. 102-210; V. S. Agrawala, Catalogue of the Mathurā Museum, J. Uttar Pradesh H. Soc., XXIII, 1950, pp. 35-147, XXIV-XXV, 1951-52, pp. 1-160; C. C. Das Gupta, Unpublished Ancient Indian Terracottas Preserved in the Musée Guimet, AAs, XIV, 1951, pp 283-305; A K. Coomaraswamy, Archaic Indian Terracottas, Mārg, VI, 2, 1952, pp. 22-35; C. L. Fabri, Mathurā of the Gods, Mārg, VII, 2, 1954, pp. 8-22; K. D. Bajpai, New Buddhist Finds from Mathurā, Lalit-Kāla, III-IV, 1956-57, pp. 102-04; K. de B. Codrington, Mathurā of the Gods, Mārg, IX, 2, 1956, pp. 41-49; O. Viennot, The Goddess Mahiṣāsuramardinī in Kushān Art, AAs, XIX, 1956, pp. 368-73.

Madeleine HALLADE

Illustrations: PLS. 379-384; 1 fig. in text.

MATISSE, HENRI. French painter and sculptor (b. Le Cateau, Nord, Dec. 31, 1869; d. Cimiez, Nice, Nov. 31, 1954). After studying law in Paris (1887), in 1889 he entered the office of a lawyer at Saint-Quentin. While convalescing from an illness in 1890, he took up painting as a distraction and, drawn to this new activity, decided to dedicate himself to it completely, despite parental opposition. He enrolled at the Ecole Quentin de Latour, directed by Croisé, where he practiced the fundamentals, making academic drawings and paintings. In 1891 he moved to Paris and, in order to prepare for the entrance examinations of the Ecole des Beaux-Arts, attended the Académie Julian. The school was directed by Adolphe William Bouguerau, whose paintings were much in vogue at the time, but who was incapable of rising above a merely academic level, either in his own work or in his teaching. Matisse soon left the school and began to attend the evening classes of the Ecole des Arts Décoratifs, where he met Albert Marquet.

In 1895 Gustave Moreau admitted Matisse to his studio at the Ecole des Beaux-Arts without requiring him to take the entrance examination. It was in Moreau's studio, the most liberal of those in which painting lessons were given, that Matisse met, among others, Georges Rouault, Henri Manguin, and Charles Camoin. In the summer of the same year Matisse went to Brittany for the first time, together with the painter Emile Wéry, whom he had met in Paris and who probably influenced him to brighten his palette. At the Louvre Matisse copied the paintings of Poussin, Philippe de Champaigne, Watteau, and Fragonard, directing his researches toward an increasing emphasis on color. Toward this end, consideration of the works of Chardin played a decisive role and marks the beginning of Matisse's attraction to impressionist and postimpressionist painting. It was in 1895 also that Ambroise Vollard held an important Cézanne exhibition, which Matisse certainly must have attended.

The following year Matisse began to exhibit his works at the Salon of the Société Nationale des Beaux-Arts and sold to the state his *Woman Reading* (Château Rambouillet), which he had painted in 1894, when he was still using darker tones. It was in 1896 that he met Pissarro and entered a long period of meditation on impressionism. His marriage to Amélie Payrayre and visits to England, Corsica, and Toulouse took place in 1898. Returning to Paris in 1899, he left Moreau's studio, the direction of which had been assumed by Fernand Cormon after the death of the master in the preceding year. Matisse next attended the Académie Carrière, where Eugène Carrière gave critiques from time to time. After reading Paul Signac's "D'Eugène Delacroix au Néo-Impressionisme," published in installments in *La Revue Blanche*, he became interested in pointillism, which was to have its effects on his art some time later, about 1904. Matisse's tastes and direction in this period can be deduced from his purchase from Vollard of a painting by Cézanne, *The Three Bathers* (donated in 1936 to Mus. du Petit-Palais,

Paris), and of a plaster portrait bust of Henri Rochefort by Rodin.

Between 1899 and 1904 Matisse executed his first sculptures, which showed first the influence of A. L. Barye and then that of Rodin (*Madeleine*, 1901; *The Slave*, 1900–03). At the beginning of the 20th century Matisse was faced with a succession of financial difficulties, and in order to help him, his wife opened a dressmaking shop. Commissioned by one Jambon, who ran a workshop for theatrical scenery, Matisse and Marquet executed a decorative frieze in the Grand-Palais, on the occasion of the Exposition Universelle of 1900.

In 1901 Matisse met Vlaminck and the critic Roger Marx; the latter presented him to Berthe Weill, in whose gallery he began to exhibit in 1902, with Marquet and Jules-Léon Flandrin. During this period Matisse produced such paintings as *A Glimpse of Notre-Dame in Late Afternoon* (1902; PL. 385), which demonstrates how color may lose its naturalistic connections and function as an independent entity, within a composition in which the buildings and bridge are deprived of all detail and become mere luminous surfaces. Generally, however, during the period 1901–04 Matisse reverted to darker-toned paintings of a considerably more realistic nature. In 1901 his work was exhibited for the first time at the Salon des Indépendants; in 1903 he participated in the first Salon d'Automne and in 1904 held his first one-man show, in the gallery of Vollard, with a presentation in the catalogue by Roger Marx. The show, however, was neither a critical nor a commercial success.

Matisse spent the summer of 1904 at Saint-Tropez in Signac's villa, together with Henri-Edmond Cross, and the contact with these two divisionist painters strongly influenced him. The interests he had held as far back as 1899 were revived; divisionism now seemed to him to have surpassed in chromatic intensity the atmospheric vibration of impressionism and to offer a possible means of arriving at chromatic abstraction, no longer bound by the need to represent the subject literally. The painting which he sent to the Salon des Indépendants, *Luxe, calme, et volupté* (Paris, private coll.), and which was bought by Signac, was executed with the division of the patches of color characteristic of pointillism. It is evident, however, that Matisse tried to avoid not only the schematism of divisionism but also the geometric surface aspect of the images that is inherent in the broken stroke of divisionist paintings. What seems to have interested him more and more was not so much the abstract sensation resulting from this painting device as the possibility of the clash that would result from the juxtaposition of two primary colors. In fact, the composition of the *Pastorale* (1905; Paris, private coll.) is more reminiscent of Cézanne than of Signac; its character is emotional rather than purely geometric.

Although the study for the painting *Joie de vivre* (1905; San Francisco, W. A. Haas Coll.) still reveals vestiges of the pointillist technique, the brush strokes have become fuller, and the final painting (1905–06; Merion, Pa., Barnes Foundation), sent to the Salon des Indépendants of 1906, is completely free of the small dabs of broken color. Color flows over the figures in broad areas, and in the originality of his technique Matisse has achieved complete artistic independence. Clearly, although Matisse had begun with divisionism and had absorbed its principles, he did not linger over variations on it. As early as 1904–05 he had evolved a new treatment of color; in 1905 he exhibited this new style at the Salon d'Automne, along with the works of those artists who were experimenting on similar lines — Braque, Derain, Manguin, Marquet, Louis Valtat, Vlaminck, Othon Friesz, and Rouault — and who comprised the "cage of wild beasts" (see FAUVES).

In this period was born a pictorial conception which was to influence many successive experiments, and which offered to modern art one of the first chances of breaking away not only from naturalistic representation but also from that variation on reality, impressionism (V, PL. 259). Hence, Guillaume Apollinaire was justified in stating, in 1910, that Matisse, along with a few other artists, had succeeded in freeing himself completely from impressionism and that he sought not to imitate nature but to express what he saw and felt through the materials of painting themselves, just as a poet makes use of the words in a dictionary to express his vision of nature and his feelings [*Chroniques d'art* (1902–18), Paris, 1960, p. 74]. It should be acknowledged, however, that experiments such as those of Matisse and the Fauve painters in 1905 would have been inconceivable without the rupture which impressionism itself had brought about in the traditional concept of space and color, even though it was Matisse himself who changed "impression" to "expression." This Fauve, furthermore, was an esthete, and again it was Apollinaire who declared in 1909 (op. cit., p. 65) that Matisse surrounded himself with ancient and modern works of art, with splendid textiles, and with sculptures by the Negroes of Guinea, Senegal, and Gabon, in which the passions of wild nature are depicted with rare purity. This Fauve was not an instinctive painter, however, but "un artiste cartésien."

Apollinaire had written of Matisse as early as 1907 in two articles, one of which appeared in *Je dis tout* on Oct. 12, the other, longer and more important, in *La Phalange* on Dec. 15. In the latter article several of Matisse's works were reproduced: a self-portrait, a portrait of his wife, *La Coiffure*, and *Le Luxe I* (op. cit., p. 452). Apollinaire's interest is particularly significant, not only for its recognition of Matisse's contribution to the avant-garde painting of the period, which was completely transforming the language of painting, but also because the poet centered his attention on the painter at the moment when an order began to appear in Matisse's work — not so rigid as that being created by the cubists in the same years, but certainly far removed from the completely instinctive approach of the Fauve expressionists.

Matisse began to draw away from his fellow artists, as did Braque. Matisse had gone to live in Collioure in 1905, and the strong light of this area was in part responsible for the explosion of color in his paintings. A memento of his visit to North Africa in 1906 is the *Blue Nude*, or *Souvenir de Biskra*, of 1907 (PL. 387), in which the distortions of form and of movement resemble those in certain sculptures executed in Collioure the same year. But gradually his figures became slimmer and subtler, as in the *Still Life with Antique Torso*, of 1908 (PL. 386), and his paintings began to reveal a nonrealistic color spread out in broad areas and a linear style that eliminated all anatomical detail. This tendency is seen in *Le Luxe I* (Paris, Mus. d'Art Moderne) and even more clearly in the second version of the painting (Copenhagen, Statens Mus. for Kunst, Coll. J. Rump). Progressing through *Red Room* and the *Game of Bowls* (both 1908; Leningrad, The Hermitage) and through certain portraits in 1909, the decorative synthesis was finally fully achieved in *The Dance* and *Music* of 1910 (both Leningrad, The Hermitage; cf. study for *The Dance*, 1909–10, PL. 385). This expansion of the chromatic planes, which had begun with the *Joie de vivre*, conferred on the image complete pictorial autonomy and established a principle, primarily regarding the treatment of two-dimensional space, which was absolutely essential to succeeding artists in their search for still greater freedom in representing an object.

In 1907 Matisse visited Italy, where he particularly admired the works of Giotto and Piero della Francesca. At the request of Sarah Stein and Hans Purrmann, in 1908 he formed a group of pupils, giving lessons first in his studio, in the expropriated Couvent des Oiseaux, in rue de Sèvres, and later at the Hôtel Biron, in the former Couvent du Sacré-Coeur. Sarah Stein collected notes from these lessons (included in A. H. Barr Jr., 1951, pp. 550–52), in which the striking element is not so much the program of instruction as the esthetic set down by the artist. For example, on the subject of still life, Matisse recommends: "To copy the objects in a still life is nothing; one must render the emotion they awaken in him. The emotion of the ensemble, the interrelation of the objects, the specific character of every object — modified by its relation to the others — all interlaced like a cord or a serpent." In December, 1908, *La Grande Revue* published Matisse's "Notes d'un peintre," a long article in which he clarified still further the goal toward which he was striving: "What I am after, above all, is expression.... Expression to my way of thinking does not consist of the passion mirrored upon a human face or betrayed by a violent gesture. The whole arrangement of my picture is expressive. The place occupied by figures or objects, the empty spaces around them, the proportions, everything plays a part." And further: "What I dream of is an art of balance, of purity and serenity devoid of troubling or depressing subject matter, an art which might be for every mental worker, be he businessman or writer, like an appeasing influence, like a mental soother, something like a good armchair in which to rest from physical fatigue." Thus, expression is a sublimation of decoration, in which the image must have a vaster and more human significance than usual, and in which the colors should represent sensations. "A work of art," Matisse affirmed, "must carry in itself its complete significance and impose it upon the beholder even before he can identify the subject matter." This is the reason for the importance of style, of the striving for the essential, and of pictorial order, which is an order of style and ideas and therefore not a naturalistic order. On this subject, Matisse later added, in a note published by R. Escholier (1956, p. 95): "When I am in direct accord with my sensations of nature, I always feel entitled to step back from them in order to render more precisely what I feel. Experience has always proved me right."

From 1909 Matisse's fame spread throughout the world. In that year he took up residence in Issy-les-Moulineaux. In 1910 there were Matisse exhibits in New York, Moscow, and Berlin; in 1912 his sculpture was shown in New York. The following year, upon his return to Paris from Africa, where he had visited Morocco with Marquet and Camoin, the Galerie Bernheim-Jeune exhibited his Moroccan paintings and a number of sculptures. In these years a certain cubist influence appeared in Matisse's work; his use of it was original, however, and his paintings retained their intensity of color, but the space began to be ordered more geometrically, assuming a regular and rhythmic pattern. Typical of this new approach are *The Blue Window*, of 1911, and *The Piano Lesson* and *The Moroccans*, both of 1916 (all New York, Mus. of Mod. Art). In the years following — years of decline for a large sector of European painting, of a return to classicism, of the "appels d'Italie" — Matisse remained faithful to the fundamentals of his esthetic and to the brilliant colors of his odalisques (V, PL. 202), even though occasionally a highly charged decoration tended to obscure the relation of figure to background, as in the *Decorative Figure on an Ornamental Background*, of 1927 (PL. 385). In 1920 Matisse designed the settings and costumes for the Diaghilev company's production of the Stravinsky ballet *Le Rossignol*, with choreography by Léonide Massine. The following year he took up residence in Nice; in 1925 he traveled again to Italy; he was awarded first prize at the 1927 Carnegie International Exhibition, Pittsburgh. In 1930 he went to the United States, where he was commissioned by Dr. Albert C. Barnes to decorate the central hall of the Barnes Foundation building with a mural: upon his return to Nice, he began to work out its theme, the dance. Because of an error in calculation, the first version of the decoration (Paris, Mus. d'Art Moderne) turned out to be too large for the building in Merion, and Matisse designed another. At the same time he was working on engravings for the illustrations to the Skira edition of Mallarmé's *Poésies* (1932). In 1933 he went to Merion to supervise the installation of his mural, *The Dance*, at the Barnes Foundation. In 1935 he designed cartoons for the tapestries of Marie Cuttoli and in 1938 created the costumes for the ballet *Rouge et noir*, with music by Shostakovich and choreography by Massine. The *Rose nude*, of 1935 (PL. 388), shows that Matisse had recaptured his great capacity for synthesis. He continued to create illustrations for books, including those for the edition of Joyce's *Ulysses* published by George Macy (1935); and in 1941 he began to work on illustrations for the *Florilège des amours de Ronsard*, published by Skira in 1948, and Henry de Montherlant's *Pasiphaé*, published by Fabiani in 1944. In 1941 he also painted the magnificent *Still Life with Magnolia* (PL. 386), with its rich use of color and its free arrangement of objects.

At the outbreak of World War II Matisse had decided to leave France, but he changed his mind and went south to Nice. He was a member of the Emergency Rescue Committee, and in 1943 he went to live in Vence. Between 1948 and 1951 he worked on the decoration of the Chapelle du Rosaire of the Dominican nuns of Vence, the achievement closest to his heart in the last years of his life. Matisse's final style, his most simplified and abstract, is less evident in the chapel (although these works are executed in a very free style) than it is in the "gouaches découpées," as exemplified by *Zulma* (1950; PL. 386). Here Matisse returned to the rapid and economical delineation of his subject and to that juxtaposition of areas of pure color, the contrasts of which impart a luminous quality. In the final years Matisse's creative capacity remained intact. His freedom of expression (albeit following in a great tradition), the heights to which he raised the use of color, the originality of his views with regard to representation, and above all his constant fidelity to his own principles, in addition to the quality of the works themselves — these are elements which Matisse brought to art. His contribution to the development and enrichment of the language of modern painting is inestimable. (See also IV, PL. 183; V, PLS. 123, 258; VII, PL. 390.)

WRITINGS: From the numerous writings, see in particular the following: Notes d'un peintre, La grande rev., LII, 1908, pp. 731-45; Formes, I, 1, 1930 (autobiog. note); On Modernism and Tradition, The Studio, IX, 1935, pp. 236-39; Divagations, Verve, 1, 1937, pp. 80-84; Notes d'un peintre sur son dessin, Le point, 21, 1939, pp. 104-10; Le chemin de la couleur, Art présent, 2, 1947, p. 23.

BIBLIOG. L. Vauxcelles, Matisse, Gil Blas, Oct. 14, 1904; A. Gide, Promenade au Salon d'Automne, GBA, XLVII, 1905, pp. 75-85; G. Apollinaire, Matisse, La phalange, II, 18, 1907; B. Berenson, Letter to the Editor, The Nation, LXXXVII, 1908, p. 461; G. Stein, Henri Matisse, Camera Work, special no., 1912, pp. 23-25; G. Apollinaire, [Matisse], L'intransigeant, Apr. 28, 1913; M. Sembat, Henri Matisse, Paris, 1920; R. Schacht, Henri Matisse, Dresden, 1922; A. Basler, Henri Matisse, Leipzig, 1924; W. George, Dessins de Henri Matisse, Paris, 1925; F. Fels, Henri Matisse, Paris, 1929; E. Tériade, Visite à Matisse, L'intransigeant, Jan. 14 and 22, 1929; A. Bertram, Matisse, London, New York, 1930; R. Fry, Matisse, New York, 1930; R. Huyghe, Matisse et la couleur, Formes, I, 1, 1930, pp. 5-10, 31-32; G. Poulain, Sculptures d'Henri Matisse, Formes, I, 9, 1930, pp. 9-10; P. Fierens and others, Henri Matisse, CahArt, VI, 5-6, 1931, pp. 229-316; A. C. Barnes and V. De Mazia, The Art of Henri Matisse, New York, 1933; P. Courthion, Henri Matisse, Paris, 1934; R. Kawashima, Matisse, Tokyo, 1936 (in Jap.); R. Escholier, Matisse, Paris, 1937; A. Romm, Matisse, Leningrad, 1937; P. Guéguen, Les sculptures d'un grand peintre, XXᵉ siècle, 4, 1938, pp. 3-13; J. Cassou, Matisse, Paris, 1939; G. Besson, Matisse, Paris, 1943; L. Swane, Henri Matisse, Stockholm, 1944; M. Valsecchi, Disegni di Matisse, Milan, 1944; L. Aragon, Matisse, Geneva, 1946; G. Scheiwiller, Matisse, Milan, 1947; G. Duthuit, Les Fauves, Geneva, 1949 (Eng. trans., New York, 1950); A. H. Barr Jr., Matisse: His Art and His Public, New York, 1951 (full bibliog.); A. H. Barr Jr., Matisse, Picasso and the Crisis of 1907, Mag. of Art, XLIV, 1951, pp. 163-70; G. Diehl, Matisse, Paris, 1954; G. C. Argan, Matisse scultore, La Biennale di Venezia, 26, 1955, pp. 31-35; R. Escholier, Matisse ce vivant, Paris, 1956 (Eng. trans., G. and H. M. Colvile, New York, 1960); W. S. Lieberman, Matisse: 50 Years of His Graphic Art, New York, 1956; G. Rosenthal, Matisse's Reclining Figures: A Theme and Its Variations, Baltimore Mus. N., XIX, 1956, pp. 1-9; P. Reverdy and G. Duthuit, Dernières œuvres de Matisse 1950-1954 (Verve, 35-36), Paris, 1958 (Eng. trans., New York, 1958); C. Gottlieb, Joy of Life: Matisse, Picasso and Cézanne, Coll. Art. J., XVIII, 2, 1959, pp. 106-16; J. Lassaigne, Matisse (Eng. trans., S. Gilbert), Geneva, 1959; J. Leymarie, Le Fauvisme, Geneva, 1959 (Eng. trans., J. Emmons, Geneva, 1959); E. C. Elliott, Some Recent Conceptions of Color Theory, J. Aesthetics, XVIII, 1960, pp. 497-99; M. Wheeler, The Last Works of Henri Matisse: Large Cut Gouaches (exhibition cat.), Garden City, N. Y., 1961; H. Geldzahler, Two Early Matisse Drawings, GBA, LX, 1962, pp. 497-505.

Nello PONENTE

Illustrations: PLS. 385-388.

MA YÜAN. Chinese painter active from about 1190 to sometime after 1225. His *hao* (nickname) was Ch'in-shan; he was also called Ma Ho-chung because he was a native of Ho-chung in Shansi. In the reign of Kuang-tsung (1190-94) Ma Yüan was already a "Painter-in-Attendance" (*tai-chao*), and enjoyed the favor of Ning-tsung (1195-1224). Chou Mi (b. 1232) in his *Ch'i-tung Yeh-yü* mentions a painting of *The Three Religions* (depicting Śākyamuni, Lao-tzu, and Confucius) as "a work by Ma Yüan, the Painter-in-Attendance in the reign of Emperor Li-tsung" (1225-64).

Ma Yüan was the next-to-last and greatest painter of the Ma family. Five generations of this family are recorded:

1. Ma Fên (Pên), *tai-chao* in the Hsüan-ho Academy of the emperor Hui-tsung (r. 1101-26). Two paintings are doubt-

fully attributed to him: *The Hundred Geese* (Honolulu, Acad. of Arts), a hand scroll in ink monochrome on paper, and *Herding the Buffaloes* (formerly Peking, Palace Coll.), a hand scroll with a date of 1095.

2. Ma Hsing-tsu, *tai-chao* in the reign of Kao-tsung (1127–62). Three extremely doubtful paintings attributed to him — two album leaves and a pair of hand scrolls — are given in Sirén's annotated list (1956).

3. Ma Kung-hsien and Ma Shih-jung, both *tai-chao* in the Shaohsing Academy (1131–62) of Kao-tsung. Only one painting by Ma Kung-hsien remains, and that seems to be an autograph work: *The Hermit Yao-shan Talking to the Poet Li Po* (III, PL. 264).

4. Ma Yüan and Ma K'uei (ca. 1150–1224). The most reliable work by Ma K'uei was the fan painting in ink on silk showing a man and a boy in a boat (formerly Magoshi Coll.; destroyed in World War II).

5. Ma Lin, the son of Ma Yüan, active in the mid-13th century, and a "Painter-in-Waiting" (*chih-hou*) in the Academy of Painting. At least 20 works reasonably attributed to Ma Lin are known (see Sirén's list), the most reliable being *Evening Landscape* (III, PL. 270), a silk hanging scroll with a poem and seal of the emperor Li-tsung; *Two Blossoming Plum Branches* (Peking, Hui-hua-kuan); *Branches of Plum Blossoms and Bamboo* (Taichung, Formosa, Nat. Palace Mus.); *Fragrant Spring after Rain*, a silk album leaf in the same collection; *Rocky Shore* (III, PL. 270), showing a scholar on a stag by a lake, a silk album leaf; *Ling-chao Nü in the Snow* (Boston, Mus. of Fine Arts), a silk album leaf; and *Two Birds Sleeping on a Maple Branch* (also in Boston), a silk album leaf.

Ma Yüan was the leading master of the family. His greatness was not fully recognized by many later Chinese critics, although a Ming dynasty writer, Ch'ên K'an, in his *Ta-chiang-tsao-t'ang-chi*, wrote, "Li T'ang, Liu Sung-nien, Ma Yüan, and Hsia Kuei of the Kuang-tsung and Ning-tsung periods were collectively called the Four Great Masters of Southern Sung." Because Ma was considered a member of the "Northern School," antithetical to the accepted scholarly "Southern School," he was often criticized and was not eagerly collected in his native country. However, his works and copies of them were widely collected in Japan, where they greatly influenced Japanese painting from the 15th century on, and since Western knowledge of Chinese painting was first acquired largely from Japanese sources, Ma Yüan's name has always been high on the list of great Chinese painters known to the West. Current indications are that competent Chinese criticism today accepts in large part the Japanese and Western evaluation of Ma's art.

Ma Yüan and Hsia Kuei (q.v.) were the leading masters of their time and were closely related in their style. Hence the appropriate designation "Ma-Hsia" for that style and its followers. An excellent hand scroll in ink on paper, *Snow Landscape*, now in Shanghai, is a significant example of the close stylistic relationship between the two painters. Each section of the scroll has a poem written by the empress Yang, wife of Ning-tsung. Since many of Ma Yüan's works are recorded as having inscriptions of the empress or her younger sister Yang Wa, the Shanghai museum has attributed the work to Ma Yüan, despite the absence of a signature. But from a stylistic point of view the work seems equally close to Hsia Kuei. This is true also of a recorded, but still unidentified, scroll entitled *Returning Boats on a Snowy River*, in which "the master did some diamond-shaped short fences in the luxuriant bamboo grove. There are a few snow-covered houses partly hidden by the woods. The spirit of desolation and coldness is expressed here at its best" (Wang Shih-chêng in *Chü-i-lu*).

The Ma-Hsia style as revealed in the Shanghai scroll and other paintings is based on bold and asymmetrical compositions emphasized by the suppression of complex detail and the full use of contrasts between relatively complex ink areas and open stretches of silk or paper. The effect is romantic, even dramatic, and is markedly different from the monumental, complex, and balanced compositions of the earlier landscape painters, especially those of the great Northern Sung masters. Recent efforts to equate the Ma-Hsia style with Neo-Confucian rationalism seem abortive. Quite the contrary: the very fact that the style was largely derided by the later scholarly painters indicates its antirational and decorative character. This is further confirmed by the Japanese adoption of the style, for Japan's painters have always been torn between the extremes of realism and romanticism and have seldom followed the characteristically rational approach of the Chinese.

The romantic asymmetry characteristic of the Ma-Hsia style has been graphically described by Chinese critics as "one-cornered" (*not* "side-horned"). The sharpest criticism of the style, voiced by Kuo Shun — "What have I to do with their fragments of mountains and left-over streams, productions of ignoble refugees?" — is a good description if one removes the derogatory implications. It should be mentioned here that much of the harshest criticism of Ma and Hsia was due to their association with an "ignoble" dynasty when China's political fortunes were rapidly waning.

The "one-cornered" compositions with their great open spaces of silk or paper have been accepted by Westerners as characteristic of Chinese style in general, but nothing could be farther from the truth. This mistaken concept can be traced directly to the early appreciation of Chinese painting by Westerners through Japanese eyes. The famous work *Scholar Contemplating the Moon* (III, PL. 265), is an excellent example of this aspect of Ma Yüan's art, hence its enormous popularity in the West.

But Ma Yüan seems to have begun, like so many others of his contemporaries, under the towering influence of Li T'ang (d. after 1130; ranking master of the Hangchow Academy). *Rain over Trees on a Rocky Shore* (PL. 392) seems the most conservative of Ma Yüan's works and is in a style much indebted to that of Li T'ang, although ignoring much of the forcefulness of that painter. The composition is much more centralized and monumental and seems to indicate a transitional stage between the art of the earlier master and that of the fully developed Ma Yüan. This rare type of painting by Ma Yüan is known from literary sources. Wang Yü-hsien in the *Shan-shui chia-fa* states: "People say that Ma Yüan painted only one-cornered compositions, because they have not seen many works of his. But in his big paintings, which are to be found in Chekiang, there are steep mountains rising imposingly with streams winding around them and waterfalls between the trees partly hidden and partly visible. At the side of the mountains you see a far-extending lowland with a wide expanse of water and beyond it the faint contours of a pagoda. All this makes perfectly balanced pictures."

The masses of trees and foliage in the lower center of *Rain over Trees on a Rocky Shore* are, however, already painted with Ma's characteristic brush symbols. According to the *Tu-kung t'an tsüan* in *Shu-hua fang*, "His brush manner was severe and regular. He used scorched ink in painting trees and rocks. The branches and leaves are defined by outlines; the rocks he made sharp and angular with wrinkles like the scars made by a large axe, using diluted ink for these parts. Complete views by him are not common; in his small pictures the tops of the high mountains are not visible and the steep cliffs reach down, so that their bases are not seen. The near mountains touch the sky, but the distant mountains are low. He painted a single boat with a lonely man rowing on the moon-lit sea. Such were his one-cornered scenes."

The well-known picture of an angler in Tokyo (PL. 389) cannot be the picture mentioned in this quotation, but it is the finest extant example of that type of subject, rare in Ma Yüan's work. The contrasting textures of the woven boat hood, rush raincoat, wicker hat, smooth planks, hair, and the gently swirling water are as much the subject of the picture as the placement of all this on the bare silk. The original shape of the painting is not known, but it is entirely possible that this is a fragment of a hand scroll by Ma, or at least a very early Japanese copy from such a hand scroll, now lost.

The variety of Ma Yüan's brushwork and the daring nature of his compositions are probably best seen in a hand scroll called *The Four Sages of Shang-shan* (or *The Four White-Headed Ones*; PLS. 390, 391). The subject — the flight of the scholars to a wilderness retreat in the Shang mountains at the time of the fall of the Chin dynasty — is dear to the Chinese scholarly mind, hence the 40 attached colophons, which provide the most important documentary accompaniment to any remaining work by the artist. Further corroborating evidence is provided by genuine seals of such collectors as Hsiang Yüan-pien (16th cent.), and especially the discerning Liang Ch'ing-piao (17th cent.), as well as the more recent seals of the emperor Ch'ien-lung and his successors.

In the figures of the old sages, the naillike strokes described by Chou Li-ching in his *T'ien-hsing tao-mao* are clearly seen: "There are, moreover, eighteen types of line-drawings for the folds of the garments.... The eighth type is like that of Ma Yüan and Hsia Kuei, who used a stump brush for the 'blunt-tip nail' technique." The brushwork of the rocks, trees, and water is described by Lan Ying in *Ch'i-hsiu lei-kao*: "As for Ma Yüan, his mountains are done with 'the big-axe-cut wrinkles' together with the 'nail-head and rat-tail' technique. His pine needles are of the 'cart-wheel' and 'butterfly' type. His water is of the 'fighting-water' type." Wang K'o-yü in the *Shan-hu-wang* has described the bare tree branches in the painting: "There are four types of tree branches: the 'clove-shape' branches of Fan K'uan, the 'bird-claw' branches of Kuo Hsi, the 'flame-shape' branches of Li Tsun-tao, and the 'dragged-down' branches of Ma Yüan."

These brush devices are used in *The Four Sages* as a means of producing a dramatic, crackling composition, which almost overwhelms the frailer figures in the painting. The staccato power of this scroll recalls that of Li T'ang in his hand scroll *The Virtuous Brothers Po I and Shu Ch'i Picking Herbs in the Wilderness* (Coll. Ho Kuan-wu, Hong Kong). Despite some damage and retouching, *The Four Sages* remains one of the most original and most important of Ma Yüan's paintings.

The most numerous examples of the style of Ma Yüan are the album paintings, invariably in ink and slight color on silk, and either rectangular or oblate-circular in shape. This particular type was much imitated by Chinese academic masters or artisans, Japanese painters under Chinese influence, and modern forgers. The most reliable of these album paintings, while quite romantic in mood and composition, show rich ink tones and an abbreviated but firm use of the brush. The often-reproduced and justly famous album leaf *Early Spring: Bare Willows and Distant Mountains* (Boston, Mus. of Fine Arts), despite its extremely subdued and lyrical mood, has brilliant passages of strong brushwork, notably in the far-reaching willow branches, the low-spreading plum to the right, and the bridge over the water. One cannot emphasize enough the consistency of the brushwork in the paintings mentioned above.

Ma Lin, the son of Ma Yüan, was not rated the equal of his father; but the problem of their artistic relationship is not a simple one. According to the *Hua-shih hui-k'ao*, "The artistic tradition of the Ma family, which had been handed down through several generations, reached its fulfillment in Ma Yüan. No other artist could come up to his level. Ma Lin's works were inferior to his father's but Ma Yüan loved him very much and signed such pictures as satisfied him with the name of the son. In this way Ma Lin also became famous and was appointed a *chih-hou* in the Academy."

Among the uneven works by or attributed to Ma Lin, one signed hanging scroll in particular deserves special mention, since its daring composition and suggestive use of empty silk seem to epitomize the innovations of the father. The sketchily (and rather weakly) rendered distant mountains rise above four flying swallows seen from above against gently rippling water. The emperor Li-tsung's ten-character poem, like a hanging screen, seems to mark the near pictorial plane, providing a foil for the distance and far distance below. "The [distant] mountain, in autumn colors, looks near. And for the passing swallows, the setting sun lingers."

The important later followers of Ma Yüan during the Yuan dynasty were Sun Chün-tse, Chang Yüan, and Ting Yeh-fu; during the Ming dynasty, Wang E, Chung (Ch'in)-li, Chu Tüan, and Sun K'o-kung.

Other works by Ma Yüan or convincingly close to him, in addition to those mentioned above, are: National Palace Museum, Taichung, Formosa: *A Man Carrying a Pheasant in the Snow* and *A Scholar beneath a Pine Tree*, album leaves from the *Ming-hua chi-chên*; *Mountains and Tall Pine Trees by a Cottage in the Snow*, hanging scroll; *An Immortal on a Dragon in Clouds and Mist*, hanging scroll; *The Feast of Lanterns*, hanging scroll. Hui-huakuan, Peking: *Ducks in the Water beneath an Overhanging Plum Tree*, album leaf. National Museum, Tokyo: *The Ch'an Monk Tung-shan Wading a Stream*, hanging scroll. Museum of Fine Arts, Boston: *Hsiao Ssu-hua Seated beneath a Tree Playing the Ch'in*, album leaf; *Two Sages and an Attendant beneath a Plum Tree*, album leaf. Formerly C. Edward Wells Collection, New York: *The Scholarly Gathering in the Western Gardens*, silk hand scroll.

BIBLIOG. A. Waley, Introduction to the Study of Chinese Painting, London, 1923 (especially pp. 203-11); W. Speiser, Ma Lin, Festschrift Eduard von der Heydt, Zurich, 1952, pp. 1-12; O. Sirén, Chinese Painting: Leading Masters and Principles, II, London, New York, 1956, pp. 112-19, and annotated list, pp. 74-76, III, 1956, pls. 284-291.

Sherman E. LEE

Illustrations: PLS. 389-392.

McKIM, MEAD & WHITE. American architectural firm. Charles Follen McKim (b. Aug. 24, 1847; d. Sept. 14, 1909) spent one year at Harvard College (1866-67), worked briefly with Russell Sturgis, and attended the École des Beaux-Arts in Paris (1867-70). Following this he worked for Henry H. Richardson (q.v.) for about two years. McKim then practiced independently until 1878, when the firm of McKim, Mead & Bigelow was formed. William Rutherford Mead (b. Aug. 20, 1846; d. June 20, 1928), a graduate of Amherst College in 1867, worked as an engineer and was then employed by Russell Sturgis (1868-71). Mead practiced in New York (1872-78) before entering the partnership. When William Bigelow left the group in 1879, Stanford White became the third partner. White (b. Nov. 9, 1853; d. June 25, 1906) was trained in Richardson's office (1872-78), where his influence as residential designer was discernible. A European trip preceded his association with McKim and Mead.

Both McKim and White were designers, the latter especially gifted in decoration and interior design. Their early work was largely free of historicism and was characterized by the open planning, picturesque massing, and the textured shingle sheathing typical of the "shingle style." The Casino (1879-81) and Isaac Bell, Jr., house (1881-82; I, PL. 85 and FIG. 258), both in Newport, R. I., and the William G. Low house (1887; I, PL. 85) at Bristol, R. I., exemplify this phase. When Joseph M. Wells (1853-90), whose early death deprived the firm of a significant influence, designed the Italianate Villard houses (New York, 1883-85; I, PL. 85), a classical trend was initiated, deriving from Italian Renaissance, 18th-century American, and Roman sources. This academic reaction soon dominated American architecture.

The Boston Public Library (1887-92) marked a transition from residential work to monumental architecture, often involving large-scale planning. Characteristic was the Chicago World's Fair of 1893, where McKim influenced the over-all scheme and designed the Agricultural and New York State buildings. The firm also designed numerous buildings on the campus of Columbia University, beginning in 1893, and was active in the redevelopment of Washington, D.C. (from 1901). Clubs such as the Century, Metropolitan, and University in New York were designed by McKim, Mead & White and typified the nineties, when the firm gained preeminence. McKim was also instrumental in founding the American Academy in Rome, and its quarters were designed by the firm (1913). The period of construction of Pennsylvania Station in New York (1906-10) encompassed White's death and McKim's. Although Mead's retirement in 1919 left the firm without any of its original partners, it continued to exist until 1961.

BIBLIOG. A Monograph of the Work of McKim, Mead, and White, 1879-1915, 4 vols., New York, 1915; C. Moore, The Life and Times of Charles Follen McKim, Boston, New York, 1929; C. C. Baldwin, Stanford White, New York, 1931; V. Scully, The Shingle Style, New Haven, 1955.

Allen BROOKS

MEDIA, COMPOSITE. The term "composite media" is adopted here to distinguish that aspect of 20th-century art in which works of art are created, in part or wholly, by the integration of various substances or objects that were previously foreign to the fine arts and by the intermingling of materials and techniques that formerly characterized a single art or craft, frequently resulting in creations to which such traditional designations as "painting," "sculpture," and "relief" do not apply. The time-honored term "mixed media" — which has served primarily to describe such accepted combinations as oil and tempera or water color and gouache in painting and stone, wood, or metal with adjuncts of other substances in sculpture — seems inadequate to cover the ultimate development of this trend: works in which the artist's function is concerned entirely with the selection and juxtaposition or composition of prefabricated elements into a visual entity. Other more recent labels, such as "collage," "*papier collé*," "assemblage," "combine," "construction," and so on (see below), apply better to one or another of the manifestations of combined materials than to the category as a whole, because of the diversity of methods and materials adopted toward similar ends during the evolution of a new and antitraditional art.

The practice of combining materials in a single work of art is not new; it has been common since ancient times and in widely differing cultures; but only in the 20th century has the act of combining been singled out as a particular means of exploring new avenues of expression or as an art in itself, with a validity independent of conceptual content in the work. Ancient art, folk art, primitive art, and the sophisticated arts of many periods include innumerable examples of objects fashioned of a great variety of materials, chosen and united for specific functional, symbolic, representational, and even purely decorative purposes. However, the motivation of the selection and combination is quite different from that operating in the modern movement. In these other periods and cultures the material was, in general, significant for an intrinsic or symbolic value attributed to it by the society or by the patron, whereas in the modern movement the only value in any material is held to be that conferred upon it by the artist's acceptance and manipulation of it. This change in point of view is the sign of a period in which originality is viewed as the paramount artistic criterion and tradition is cast off as an impediment to the artist's personal and psychological development. Since the early years of the century, when their collages opened a phase of the revolt against traditional media and techniques, the moderns have affirmed the right and freedom of the artist to express himself in whatever materials he chooses.

Many of the materials that came to be adopted by the avant-garde are identical with those found in primitive and folk art — natural substances, such as leaves, straw, sand, pebbles, shells, feathers, butterfly wings, as well as other elements prefabricated for other purposes, such as bits of metal, mirror fragments, burlap and cord, scrap paper, and synthetic products. As in some categories of primitive and folk art, the modern interest often lies in the immediate effect, rather than in the durability of the object created, so that perishability of the materials is of no importance. Certain primitive and folk products (ceremonial objects, festival apparatus, and the like) are intended to be destroyed or discarded after serving their purpose. No doubt, similar ephemeral objects existed also in antiquity, but they have rarely survived. On the other hand, in the preceding sophisticated arts and in the survivals from antiquity it is clear that there was a search for the materials ensuring the greatest degree of permanence for important works of art intended as enduring records or precious possessions. By the frequent choice of perishable materials, without intrinsic value and flexible enough in connotations to be manipulated for the expression of original turns of thought, the modern artists declare the topical and experimental character of their work, the about-face on ideas of beauty, value, and meaning in art.

It cannot be said, therefore, that works fashioned of multiple elements in the past or in other cultures are direct antecedents of the modern composite media. Nevertheless, methods, as well as materials, were occasionally borrowed from primitive and folk art, particularly in the simple and unpretentious manner of joining parts — unconcealed knots, simple lashing, coarse stitching, and unfinished joints. Such indications of poverty of means, either material or technical, were preferred to the studied and polished craftsmanship of the previous sophisticated arts.

Here, however, similarity ends, as a few examples will show. In primitive art a combination of materials usually has (or had originally) a cosmic, magical, or supernatural power that contributed to the function of a particular object (see MAGIC). A ritual mask, for example, might include elements of bone, horn, teeth, feathers, hide, shell, hair, or a human skull (e.g., PLS. 395, 441–443; II, PLS. 109, 115; XIII, PL. 4), each of which, in conjunction with the others, has a special virtue for invoking the power or presence of a supernatural being who can bring rain, cure sickness, ensure fertility, and so on. Nails or mirrors are attached to wooden fetish figures (e.g., II, PL. 103) as elements having a particular physical efficacy, just as do the many attachments of a shaman's costume (XIII, PL. 2). In such art, originality or departure from cultural tradition regarding material, form, or technique would result in the failure of the object to perform its function. That such traditions are still operative, even after long acculturation, is proved by the fact that in 1964 the conservation services of the U. S. Government fulfilled an urgent request from the Pueblo Indians for eagle feathers to be used in ceremonial equipment; laws protecting wild life had deprived the tribes of an indispensable material.

This importance ascribed to specific materials for religious and ritual objects is also characteristic of more advanced societies (see LITURGICAL AND RITUAL OBJECTS). The rarest and most precious materials obtainable have generally been lavished on objects intended for the glorification of a deity, for the embellishment of sacred premises, or for containing sacred offerings or relics (e.g., PLS. 160, 395; IV, PLS. 405, 409; VI, PLS. 260, 261, 263). Similarly, the association of costly and rare materials is symbolic of royalty, political power, social rank, and wealth, so that objects intended as signs of exalted position (see EMBLEMS AND INSIGNIA) or as personal adornment and accessories of royalty are generally elaborate accumulations of precious metals, stones, and products of the jeweler's art (e.g., I, PL. 286; IV, PLS. 361, 391; VI, PLS. 241, 242, 247).

In all these periods and cultures a combination of materials may also have a purely representational value, offering greater verisimilitude in color values, textures, forms, and light effects than any single medium provides. The mimetic factor is present alongside the magical factor in the primitive use of shell eyes, human hair, and so on, when the intent is to create or re-create a being. In ancient statues and late Renaissance and baroque copies of such works, the flesh is rendered in white or black marble, with varicolored stone for clothing, and eyes inset in color. In the application of color to stone, wood, or clay sculpture, a mixture of media has been in use for representational fidelity since ancient times, for example, in Egypt (IV, PLS. 337, 338, 352, 382), in Greece (I, PLS. 337, 351, 361), in China (III, PL. 257), as well as in primitive and folk art.

The mimetic motive is strong in the combination of materials in folk art. The selection of media may be limited by availability, and traditional factors involving remote and forgotten magical concepts may also enter in, but in general the folk artist chooses his means for their representational effectiveness. In paper collage and appliqué, for example, a folk form that long antedates the cubist and Dadaist experiments with this medium, cutouts from a variety of solid-color paper are mounted to form traditional landscapes or naturalistic decorative compositions (e.g., the *Alpfahrt* collages of Switzerland, the elaborate cut-paper certificates of the Rhineland, and the Polish paper work in openwork, silhouette, or appliqué; V, PL. 349). Details are occasionally enhanced by painting, and at times preprinted papers are included. Other composite creations include the Nativity scenes — the *crèches*, *krippen*, and *presepi* — of folk art, for which all manner of materials are adopted to give realism to the figures, costumes, and settings. These scenes are sometimes boxed or framed as permanent units. Similar arrangements, with religious, secular, or even still-life groups are the *kästchen*, the little shadow-box scenes in which flowers, beads, ribbons, buttons, and other decorative objects are combined. Materials used in traditional folk festival masks and costumes are frequently rough natural substances such as straw or pea vines, attached to wood, coarse cloth, or other foundations for the impersonation of specific characters (see MASKS).

Perhaps the most extreme efforts at mimetic effect are exemplified by the combination of media in baroque architectural settings to achieve a trompe l'oeil transition between painted or sculptured works and the architectural elements adjoining them (e.g., II, PLS. 166, 172) and in landscape architecture (q.v.). The latter in certain periods has involved construction of elements in shells, stone, pebbles, and innumerable other materials for the purpose of reducing to the compass of a single garden the many picturesque aspects of natural geographical features in the form of artificial grottoes (PL. 395), fountains, mountains, and so forth.

The artists of the early 20th century were ideologically far removed from all such concerns, either as reasons for creating a work of art or for selecting a congenial medium in which to execute it. Experimenting freely in many directions (see EUROPEAN MODERN MOVEMENTS), they were concerned with new optical, spatial, and psychological concepts and required new means for expressing them. Within the technique of painting, the experiments with composite media in the works of Picasso and Braque (qq.v.) played an integral part in the evolution of cubism (see CUBISM AND FUTURISM). Early in 1912 Picasso incorporated a piece of oil cloth printed with simulated chair caning into his *Still Life with Chair Caning* (Picasso Coll.) and surrounded the picture with rope instead of a frame, creating his first "collage." Later the same year Braque, by pasting three pieces of wood-grained wall paper in the *Compotier et verre* (London, D. Cooper Coll.), executed his first *papier collé* (pasted paper). Within a short time both artists, along with Gris (q.v.; IV, PL. 80), Marcoussis, and other cubist painters, were including certain extraneous materials as integral parts of many of their paintings; postage stamps, playbills, newspapers, strips of cloth, mirrors, playing or calling cards, and metal foil are all to be found in the cubist compositions of 1912–14.

Such materials fulfilled various functions within the cubist paintings. They served to define certain stable planes within compositions which, as a result of the fragmentation of the objects depicted, have foregrounds almost completely filled with many facets held precariously in balance between recession beyond the now-limited depth of the picture and projection forward from its surface. Newspapers and similar printed materials were ready substitutes for the stenciled typographical letters and numbers which had earlier been introduced in cubist paintings for this same purpose. In addition, the subjects, which frequently became unrecognizable, could be made identifiable by the substitution or incorporation of a representational fragment of these objects; for instance, a newspaper on a table is rendered by a piece of newspaper pasted on a strip of wood-grained paper, or a real label is pasted on a painted bottle (PL. 393). The inclusion of a piece of reality within a painting projects it into the world of objects, narrowing the distance between the painting and the spectator. This occurrence is in accord with the cubists' concept of their works as self-contained, constructed objects with weight, solidity, and texture. "It is not enough to make the painted object visible," wrote Braque, "it must also be made tangible."

The adoption of composite media was, however, also a repudiation of the classical tradition of painting, with its emphasis on technical ability and especially on slickness of brushwork. In using nontraditional materials, the artist asserted his freedom to use any technique or medium in his work, opening the way both to the rediscovery of the artistic interest of commonplace objects and to the wide-ranging technical experimentation of the 20th century. Guillaume Apollinaire gave literary weight to the new concept of art by stating, "You may paint with whatever material you please, with pipes, postage stamps, postcards or playing cards, candelabra, pieces of oil cloth, collars, painted paper, newspapers" (*The Cubist Painters*, 1913).

At about the same time as the cubists were experimenting with collage in paintings, the futurists (see CUBISM AND FUTURISM) were producing the first three-dimensional objects made from agglomerations of heterogeneous materials. Similarly opposed to traditional technical criteria, Umberto Boccioni (q.v.), in his *Technical Manifesto of Futurist Sculpture* (1912), declared that futurism should "deny the exclusiveness of one material for the entire construction of a sculptural ensemble. Affirm that even twenty different materials can compete in a single work to effect plastic emotion ... glass, wood, cardboard, iron, cement, horsehair, leather, cloth, mirrors, electric lights, etc., etc." Having become interested in sculpture as it relates to the problems of the continuity of particular forms in space, Boccioni produced, as one of a series of "plastic complexes," the *Fusion of a Head and a Window* (ca. 1912; destroyed), in which he combined a sculptured plastic head, a wooden window frame, metal hardware, and glass panes. Although futurist experimentation along this line was short-lived, Boccioni and other futurist painters such as Severini, Balla (qq.v.), Sironi, and Carrà, influenced by cubism, continued to explore the possibilities of composite media (especially the combination of printed materials) in their collages. Often, however, they were less concerned with the spatial and textural qualities of the materials than with their verbal content, which was chosen for social or propagandistic purposes (Carrà, *Patriotic Celebration*, 1914; Milan, Coll. G. Mattioli) or for topical reasons — the newspaper in Boccioni's *Cavalry Charge* (1914; Milan, Coll. R. Jucker) identifies the battle depicted.

The idea of rebellion against the technique and the illusionism of traditional art inherent in these early uses of composite media was advanced by the Dada movement in its anarchic denial of all accepted standards of producing and judging art. As early as 1913, Marcel Duchamp (see DUCHAMP BROTHERS) had exhibited unaltered industrial objects ("ready-mades") and natural materials (*objects trouvés*, or "found objects") as works of art. Combinations of such objects, as well as scraps and refuse, formed the basis of many collages and constructions displayed at the Dada exhibitions of the years 1917–22, by Arp (q.v.), Duchamp, Man Ray, Picabia, and others.

In the following years, the surrealists Max Ernst, Joan Miró (qq.v.), André Masson, George Grosz, and others exploited the verbal and symbolic content of the materials of collage and related techniques as a direct means of giving form to the fantasies of the subconscious (products of dreams, hallucination, chance, insanity), a primary goal of surrealism (q.v.). The use of these forms liberated surrealist art from traditional technical restrictions and from the vagaries of style, taste, and personal ability. (Even the untutored could externalize the products of their subconscious.) Max Ernst, who had earlier been a Dada artist, was a most prolific creator of collages — even collage novels, such as *Une Semaine de Bonté* ("One Week of Kindness") — incorporating altered technical illustrations, photographs, photoengravings, and anatomical charts. His definition of collage as an exploration of "the fortuitous encounter upon a nonsuitable plane of two mutually distant realities" shows that the material in itself need not have any predetermining influence on the use to which the artist puts it in a collage, and that the only valid relationship between different materials is their juxtaposition within the work itself. Kurt Schwitters, who participated in a highly individualistic way in both the Dada and surrealist movements, conceived of an art form embracing not only many materials but also all the arts — a form called "Merz," after the fragment of a word in one of his collages. As part of this idea, he produced many small "drawings" (primarily pasted papers), larger collage compositions, and three large architectural constructions (*Merzbau*), all composed of imaginative combinations of varied rubbish. These works are primarily juxtapositions of shapes, colors, objects, textures, and substances — with contrasts of wire on wood, metal against paper and canvas (PL. 397), fabrics over printed materials, and so on — resulting in abstract objects of great variety of design and organization.

Works assembled from various ready-made materials are now generally grouped under the name "assemblages," first suggested by the painter Jean Dubuffet. A more comprehensive term than either collage or *papier collé*, it includes these techniques, as well as those of gathering and juxtaposing, constructing and mutilating, pasting and unpasting (*décollage*), photomontage, etc. This broad usage underlines the fact that assemblage has become a new medium with its own techniques, conforming neither to painting nor sculptural categories but falling somewhere between the two. The creative activity in assemblage consists in the gathering and arrangement of the separate objects, and the measure of value and content of the work is based on that creativity rather than on conventional technical proficiency.

The arrangement of the parts of an assemblage can be comprehended on a series of different levels. An artist may dispose his objects with purely formal intentions, a primary concern being the relationship of their sizes, shapes, textures, colors, etc., and the qualities derived from the method of producing them — cutting, tearing, burning (PL. 398), sewing (X, PL. 343), sawing, compressing, nailing, welding. The materials are often devoid of any aspect which would identify them with their previous functions. This approach has become basic to the production of much nonobjective art. Robert Motherwell, working primarily with pasted papers, explained his use of composite media. "One cuts and chooses and shifts and pastes, and sometimes tears off and begins again. In any case, shaping and arranging such a relational structure obliterates the need, and often the awareness, of representation. Without reference to likenesses, it possesses feeling because all the decisions in regard to it are ultimately made on the grounds of feeling." Jean Dubuffet has used a technique of arranging previously painted, cut pieces of paper or canvas; similarly, Corrado Marca-Relli creates, in effect, a second painting from cut-up pieces of an earlier one. John Chamberlain uses automobile parts as painted metal raw material for his abstract reliefs (*Essex*, 1960; New York, L. Castelli Coll.).

An object in assemblage may also be used as a representational device, either representing itself or suggesting the whole of which it is only a part. In Dubuffet's *Landscape with Three Trees* (PL. 398), leaves themselves become the trees, while in photomontages parts of photographs, individually descriptive, become entirely new representations by their unorthodox combinations. In addition to grouping for formal effects, objects may also be combined for symbolic reasons to convey an idea or determine a mood (PL. 394).

Aside from those assemblages which are simply abstract formal arrangements, constructions of recognizable objects, or completely representational compositions, great attention has been aroused in the 1960s by those in which the objects, drawn from the manufactured ephemera and the vast junk heaps of contemporary civilization, retain much of their original shape but little or none of their original function. Often called "factual" or "pop" art, or the "new realism," the works of this type have an ironic humor resulting from a surprise confrontation with diverse fragments of reality. Robert Rauschenberg, whose "combines" have been influential for many "pop" artists, approaches his work as "a matter of just accepting whatever happens, accepting all those elements from the outside and then trying to work with them in a sort of free collaboration." Frequently such assemblages appear to be random combinations, haphazardly packaged — for example, as boxes containing numerous unaltered similar objects [Arman (Fernandez), *Little Hands* (*Ainsi font, font...*), 1960; Great Neck, N.Y., Robert C. Scull Coll.]; as groups of a few isolated objects in boxes, which are then stacked together and painted a uniform color (e.g., works by Louise Nevelson); as a single compartmented box, in which individual or grouped similar objects are doubled by reflection in a mirror [Martial Raysse, *Super Market* (*Hygiène de la vision*), 1961]; or as a single, mirror-compartmented box in which diverse objects are similarly displayed in similar bottles (Joseph Cornell, *Apothecary*, 1950; Houston, Texas, J. de Menil Coll.). In other assemblages the materials may be arranged on or as an adjunct to a canvas. Robert Rauschenberg's *Canyon* (1959 New York, M. Sonnabend Coll.) consists of pasted papers, wood, and oil paint on canvas, a stuffed eagle projecting from it, and a pillow hanging below on a cord tied to it. Raymond Hains's *Affiches Lacérées* are pictures made of torn and weathered posters, removed from walls, and repasted on canvas. On a larger scale,

works in this category may be groupings of the junk remains of heavy industry, among them César's creations of welded or compressed automobile parts and Jean Tinguely's machines, verging on automata (q.v.), of which the spectacular *Homage to New York: A Self-constructing and Self-destroying Work of Art* (1960; made of an upright piano, machine fragments, a weather balloon, bicycle parts, etc.) was a series of continually changing, chance juxtapositions of materials with movement and sound.

The effort to overcome the limitations of traditional materials and techniques has often led to the addition of unfamiliar substances to conventional media in the work of 20th-century painters and sculptors. Along with their collages and *papiers collés*, Picasso and Braque began experiments with mixing foreign materials (ashes, wood shavings, sand, metal filings, soot, and tobacco) with their paints to vary textural quality and to convey color (by then almost absent from cubist compositions) through texture. Similarly, other painters have explored a great variety of effects produced by combinations of paint with other substances: for example, Paul Klee (q.v.) with gesso, gouache, and exposed canvas (PL. 397); André Masson, with oil, sand, and pencil (XIII, PL. 320); Sonia Delaunay-Terk, with oil and wax (*Portuguese Market*, 1915; New York, Mus. Mod. Art); Willi Baumeister, with sand and sometimes pieces of colored substances with paint (X, PL. 499); Jackson Pollock, with oil, aluminum paint, and Duco (X, PL. 342); and Antoni Tàpies, with oil and sand (*Great Painting*, 1958; New York, Solomon R. Guggenheim Mus.). Sculptors too have employed a wide variety of new materials, joined together directly and chosen for their specific properties. The works of Vladimir Tatlin (as early as 1913), Calder, Gabo (I, PL. 132), Pevsner, and Giacometti (XII, PL. 522) have displayed combinations of glass, wire, sheet metal, plastics, paints, and wood, replacing marble or cast bronze as the principal materials of sculpture and fulfilling the goals and prophecy of the futurist manifestos of the early 20th century.

BIBLIOG. L. Aragon and others, Exposition de collages (exhibition cat.), Paris, 1930; T. Tzara, Le papier collé ou le proverbe en peinture, CahArt, VI, 1931, pp. 61–74; C. Zervos and others, L'objet, CahArt, XI, 1936, pp. 3–66; J. Dubuffet, Prospectus aux amateurs de tout genre, Paris, 1946; N. Pevsner, Pioneers of Modern Design, New York, 1949; E. Motherwell, The Dada Painters and Poets: An Anthology, New York, 1951; G. C. Argan, Scultura di Picasso, Venice, 1953; H. Wescher, Les collages cubistes, Art d'aujourd'hui, IV, 3–4, 1953, pp. 33–42; M. Seuphor and others, Collages, Art d'aujourd'hui, V, 2–3, 1954, pp. 1–42; H. Wescher, Aspects nouveaux du relief, Art d'aujourd'hui, V, 7, 1954, pp. 1–7; J. Cassou and others, La matière et le temps dans les arts plastiques, XXe siècle, N.S., V, 1955, pp. 3–68; H. Wescher, Collages and the Breakdown of Optical Unity, Graphis, XI, 57, 1955, pp. 52–59; F. Elgar and others, Le papier collé du Cubisme à nos jours, XXe siècle, N.S., VI, 1956, pp. 3–60; Rose Fried Gallery, International Collage Exhibition (cat.), New York, 1956; J. T. Soby, The Importance of Collage, in Modern Art and the New Past, Norman, Okla., 1957, pp. 82–87; E. Crispolti, Il problema del secondo futurismo nella cultura italiana fra le due guerre, Notizie, II, 5, 1958, pp. 34–51; C. Greenberg, The Pasted-paper Revolution, AN, LVII, 5, 1958, pp. 46–49, 60–61; A. Henze, Über das Basteln in der modernen Kunst, Kunstwerk, XI, 7, 1958, pp. 15–36; J. MacAgy, ed., Collage International: From Picasso to the Present (exhibition cat.), Houston, 1958; J. Golding, Cubism: A History and an Analysis, 1907–1914, New York, 1959, pp. 103–07, 188–89; M. Seuphor, The Sculpture of This Century, New York, 1960; C. Giedion-Welcker, Contemporary Sculpture, 2d rev. ed., New York, 1961; H. Janis and R. Blesh, Collage, New York, 1961; J. Lynch, How to Make Collages, New York, 1961; W. C. Seitz, The Art of Assemblage (exhibition cat.), Garden City, N.Y., 1961 (bibliog.); J. C. Taylor, Futurism (exhibition cat.), Garden City, N. Y., 1961; Sidney Janis Gallery, New Realists exhibition cat.), New York, 1962.

* *

Illustrations: PLS. 393–398.

MEDITERRANEAN, ANCIENT WESTERN. The ancient civilizations of the western Mediterranean islands and of the Iberian Peninsula never reached a development comparable to those of Greece and Italy. Apart from the Greek colonization in the area, which began in the 7th century B.C., the only attempt at unification before the Roman conquest, in the 2d century B.C., was undertaken by Carthage (see PHOENICIAN-PUNIC ART). But what the Carthaginians created, more than anything else, was a politico-economic system of little consequence for the general cultural development of the area, and still less for the arts. Cultural development in the regions of the western

Mediterranean between the end of the Bronze Age and the Roman conquest was therefore heterogeneous and unrelated, the product of individual peoples at different levels of development. To a great extent it was determined by the protohistoric heritage, influenced, with varying degrees of intensity in different localities and in different periods, by the civilizations of the Aegean, of Greece, of the Semitic East, of Italy, and of Rome (see MEDITERRANEAN PROTOHISTORY). Of these, Greek influence was the strongest and most widespread, so much so that the western Mediterranean may be regarded as marginal to the main sphere of Greek art. In any case, the individual areas of greatest interest are nuraghic Sardinia, the Balearic Islands, western Spain, and southern France. In the present article these areas will be considered in succession under separate headings rather than combined within a single unitary treatment. Of the areas under discussion, only Spain achieved a relatively mature and original artistic tradition (see below, *Iberian civilization*).

SUMMARY. The insular civilizations: Sardinia, Corsica, the Balearic Islands (col. 601): *The nuraghic civilization of Sardinia; The megalithic culture of Corsica; The Balearic Islands and the talayotic civilization*. The Iberian civilization (col. 614): *Origins and development of Iberian art; Cultural areas; Principal phases; Architecture and architectural decoration; Sculpture; Painting and ceramics; Minor arts*. The indigenous art of pre-Roman southern Gaul (col. 627): *Provincial Greek architecture and sculpture; Indigenous sanctuaries and sculpture; Minor arts*.

THE INSULAR CIVILIZATIONS: SARDINIA, CORSICA, THE BALEARIC ISLANDS. Sardinia, Corsica, and the Balearic Islands constitute an area of the western Mediterranean in which it is possible to discern, if not an ancient unified and original ethnic substratum, a complex of cultural relations and affinities that make it a distinct provincial strain, with definite characteristics and its own individual products.

There are two principal reasons for these cultural similarities, these common results: on the one hand, the insular nature of the area and, on the other, the ethnic bond between the peoples who from earliest times inhabited it. The former, determining both their mode of life and the forms of their art, tended to produce a sort of spontaneous generation, a creative originality of expression; however, this insularity also limited their contacts and eventually either impoverished their creative impulses and forms of expression or reduced their pristine freedom of expression to the banal and the routine. In Sardinia, Corsica, and the Balearic Islands certain artistic forms are of first quality and full of significance, while other artistic products are "recessive," giving evidence of artistic atrophy or outright disappearance, from lack of cultural give-and-take. In the case of these western Mediterranean islands their insularity has been the common factor determining their cultural recessiveness and compartmentalization; and basically a product of this recessiveness is the phenomenon of megalithic art — a remarkable archaic relic that continued there well into the historical period. This isolation favored the survival of very ancient ethnic elements, relatively free from later admixtures, in which can be glimpsed affinities with the Libyan world and with the peoples of the substratum of the Iberian and Ligurian regions. It is possible that the common ethnic background of the western islands and, even more, the reciprocal contacts in various prehistoric periods may have fostered analogous artistic and monumental forms of expression, of which the megalithic is one of the more obvious manifestations.

The megalithic architecture of Sardinia, Corsica, and the Balearic Islands has substantial ties with that of Malta (q.v.; see MEDITERRANEAN PROTOHISTORY), of Africa, and even of continental Europe (see EUROPEAN PROTOHISTORY), but the relation is not always apparent because of cultural and chronological divergencies. The links that connect the European and the Mediterranean megalithic are the dolmen type of monument and its special funerary function, the dolmenic form, in itself the architectural essence of the trilithon, and the orthostatic form, which gives structure to the symbolic principle of the menhir and which appears everywhere. At the same time, Sardinian-Corsican-Balearic megalithic art is distinct in that it is characterized by the development of tower structures, by the hypaethral nature of the surfaces (exquisitely Mediterranean in feeling and flavor), and by an architectural function essentially connected with the practical necessities of the living, rather than the religious and funerary character of the continental European megalithic. A further differentiation is found in the structural use of blocks and a greater curvilinear articulation of the surface planes, of the supporting elements, and of the roofing. This does not preclude the possibility of the presence in the islands of megalithic structures of the mainland type, persisting as a fairly pure strain alongside the variant insular megalithic architecture as it developed. Indeed, it is clear that onto the main trunk of dolmenic megalithic architecture (of Western origin and function) was grafted a branch of Eastern derivation and style, the prime expression of which is the tholos. This brought with it and developed the elements of curvilinear architecture, which became characteristic of the ancient Sardinian, Corsican, and Balearic peoples and, to a certain extent, of their modern descendants.

Eastern influences are also seen in the figural arts (small Sardinian bronzes, larger Balearic bronzes), in the crafts (ceramics and glass paste, etc., in Sardinia, Corsica, Mallorca, and Minorca), and in certain religious elements (the cult of the Mother Goddess and of the ox in Sardinia and the Balearic Islands). However, apart from certain elements originally imported in very ancient times from the east (Aegean-Anatolian) and certain others of Cretan-Peloponnesian and possibly even Cypriote origin, the basis of the eastern component represents the residue (simplified and bastardized, through the effect of recessiveness) of original acquisitions of the 2d millennium B.C., surviving late into historical times in a peripheral region, unaffected by cultural perspectives that had lost their original meaning and importance.

These western islands, themselves scattered like megaliths, are a striking example of cultures typical of the Bronze Age. They are repositories, outside of time, of civilizations in which the use of bronze continued even when the technique of ironworking was flourishing elsewhere. They are prehistoric manifestations that flourished with a certain rude vitality in the era of the great historic colonization of the West by the Greeks and the peoples who were their rivals. The island civilizations were only in part affected by these colonizing movements: the Greek was effective in a limited way in eastern Sardinia (which accounts for the name and tradition of the town of Olbia), and the Phoenician and Carthaginian in Sardinia and on the island of Ibiza. While present and operative in the western islands, the Phoenician-Carthaginian and Greek cultural influences were much less decisive there than they were in the same period on the coasts of Italy and on the Iberian Peninsula (see below).

The nuraghic civilization of Sardinia. The first genuine civilization in Sardinia, which can be connected with peoples whose names are recorded in historical sources (the Iolei and the Bàlari), and which can thus be called historical even though it left no written records, is the nuraghic, so termed from the nuraghe, the most conspicuous and remarkable monumental expression of proto-Sardinian architecture, as well as the most lasting concrete achievement of the social and politico-economic system of those ancient times. The formative elements of the nuraghic civilization undoubtedly are to be found in the preceding neo-aëneolithic culture of the island (see MEDITERRANEAN PROTOHISTORY). Present knowledge based on modern research suggests that there was no clear-cut division between the two periods; instead, there was a gradual transition, a progressive enrichment, an orderly regeneration. Thus, the nuraghic civilization gives the idea not of spontaneous generation or of importation as a whole, but rather of development from earlier historical and sociological conditions under particularly favorable environmental circumstances. This development was also marked by the influence of foreign elements and motifs on the earlier cultural substratum. The nuraghic civilization (or culture of the Sardinian Bronze–Iron Age) was rooted in a society of shepherds and warriors: the dynamism, the territorial ambitions, and the warlike temper of the pastoral

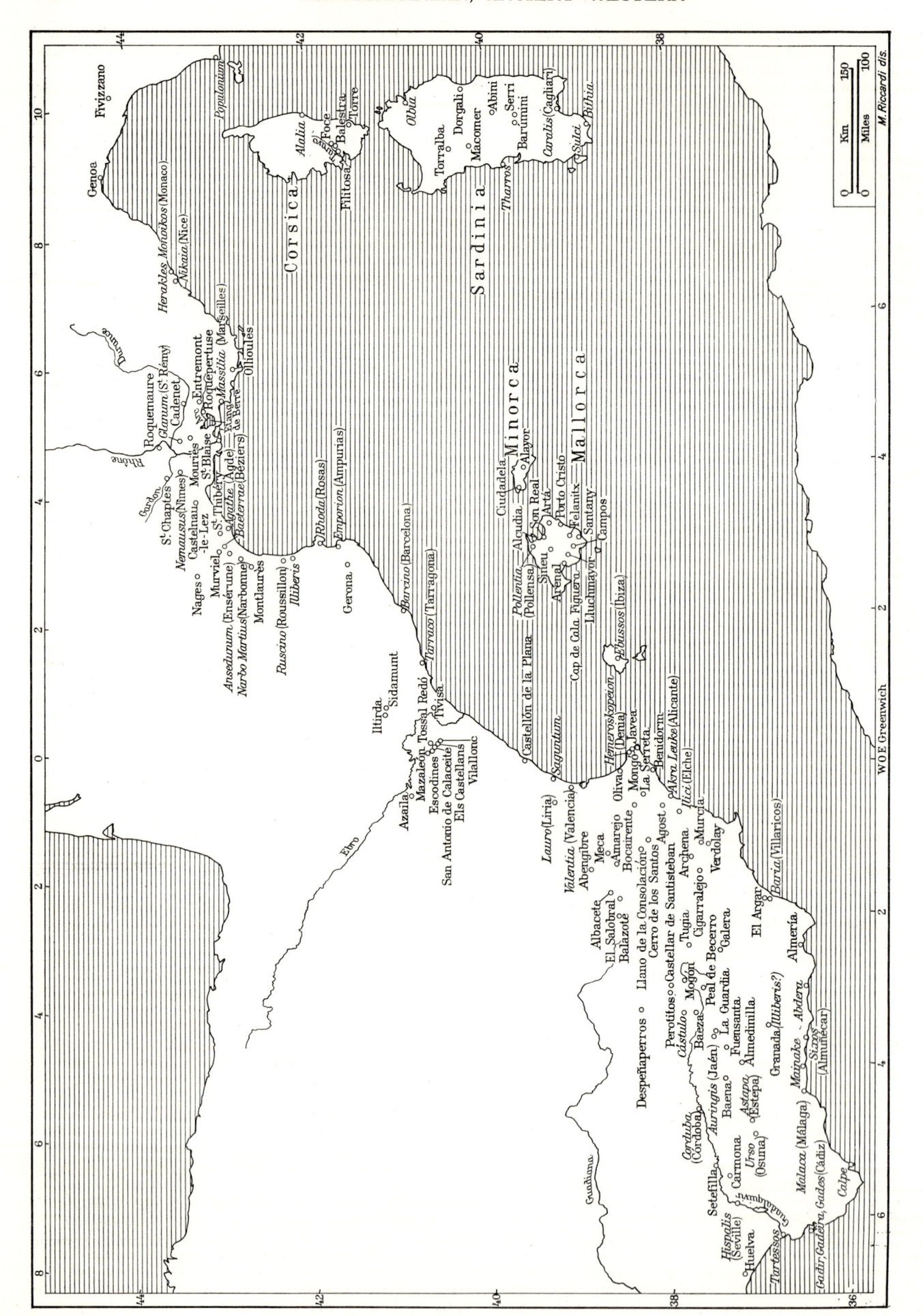

Principal cities and archaeological sites of western Mediterranean cultures (Sardinia, Corsica, Balearic Islands, Iberian Peninsula, southern France).

communities gave this culture its original impetus, determined its structure, and provided continuous incentive and sustenance for a development extending over many centuries. From the territorial fragmentation, the strong tribal antagonisms, prompted by nature — the upland plains cut by deep valleys forming the natural frontiers of small states — the nuraghic civilization derived both its character and its historical limitations, which accounts for the fact that the island people, although always resistant to foreign pressures, have been in almost every period subjected to foreign domination.

The nuraghe (PL. 401), the most tangible and striking product of this civilization, was a form of military architecture, the development of which paralleled the cultural evolution of ancient Sardinia. There are approximately 7,000 such fortresses, large and small, scattered more or less densely throughout the island (FIG. 605). The nuraghe, with its studied and elaborate development of line and volume, is the most complex and evolved protohistoric architectural formula found in the islands — possibly in the whole western Mediterranean area. Gradually, the single isolated tower was surrounded by a complex of smaller towers and concentric circular curtain walls, disposed in a system of terraces on a central plan, as seen in polylobed examples such as the nuraghe Su Nuraxi at Barúmini, the nuraghe Santu Antine at Torralba (PL. 401; FIG. 611), and the nuraghe Orròli at Orrùbiu.

Despite the variety and complexity of structural solutions and additions (FIG. 611), certain constants are to be found in this monumental type of architecture — the tholos, the truncated-cone form, and the continuous curved line, as well as other details and practical accessories.

Two components of the nuraghe belong to the prenuraghic tradition drawn from megalithic island architecture of the beginning of the metal age: the dolmen, or trilithon, exemplified by that form especially widespread in north-central Sardinia; and the technique of laying stones in circular tiers, stepped inward from bottom to the top, as exemplified in monumental form in the great platform (probably of sacred character) of Monte d'Accoddi, near Sassari. The dolmenic component is embodied in the type of nuraghe classified as "corridored," in which the interior of a circular (or more often rectangular or elliptical) structural mass is reduced to one or more narrow corridors with flat walls and ceilings; examples are the nuraghe Fronte (Fonte) e Mola at Thiesi, the nuraghe Séneghe at Suni (FIG. 611), and the nuraghe Peppe Gallu at Uri. The inclined wall composed of courses of superimposed stone blocks diminishing in section is found in both the corridored and the tholos type of nuraghe. The possibility exists that the outside walls meeting at an acute angle, as found in certain corridored nuraghi, are a continuation of prenuraghic rectilinear architecture (the altar of Monte d'Accoddi; hypogeum dwelling-tombs in the Sassari district; etc.). The two components cited denote a historicultural stratum of Western type — the indigenous contribution to nuraghic architecture.

The most outstanding imported component of nuraghic architecture is the tholos. Whether the models for this came from Asia Minor, Cyprus, the Aegean, or the Peloponnesos, the tholos introduced into the Western architectural substratum the curvilinear spatial concept that started nuraghic architecture on the development of its juxtaposed and superimposed spatial forms. On this Eastern component are based the thousands of domed nuraghi, representing almost 99 per cent of the total number on the island. The remaining 1 per cent, of the corridored type, survive mainly in "recessive" areas, subordinate and peripheral to those of intensive cultural development.

Related to nuraghic architecture in technique, details of form and structure, and fundamental style are other funerary and religious structures; among the former are the "giants' graves," and among the latter the domed wells with underground stairs (well-temples) and the megaron temples. The "giants' graves" (PL. 401) are large apsed structures, in which an arched extrados is preceded by an exedra, containing a long and narrow mortuary chamber, in some cases surmounted by a high arched stele with a small postern at the base (Goronna, near Paulilátino). The dolmenic structure of the corridor and the rectilinear profile of the external walls are vestiges of the prenuraghic component, while the projecting outer structures and the curvilinear outline of the apse, of the exedra, and of the stele derive from the nuraghic style. The development of these monumental structures parallels that of the nuraghi: from the simple dolmen to the megalithic tomb without frontal hemicycle (Ena e Muros, Ossi) and finally to the complete form with exedra and stele, certain of them echoing decorative elements found in the Greek or Grecized Punic orbit (e.g., the dentilated cornices in the tombs at Oragiana and Cùglieri and at Nela and Sindìa).

How the type of sacred well, or well-temple, developed from the curvilinear nuraghic form with projecting element is quite apparent (FIGS. 607, 608). The "vaulted" chamber of the nuraghe becomes a tholos cella containing the water springing from the well; in some instances (e.g., S. Anastasia in Sàrdara) the walls of the cella are arranged in the articulated projecting courses of undressed masonry of the nuraghic tholoi, clearly showing the source from which they were derived. In the majority of cases, however, the outer facing of the rim of the well (preceded by a vestibule), the stairway, and the wellhead are of isodomic masonry. In section the domes show a continuous incline, and

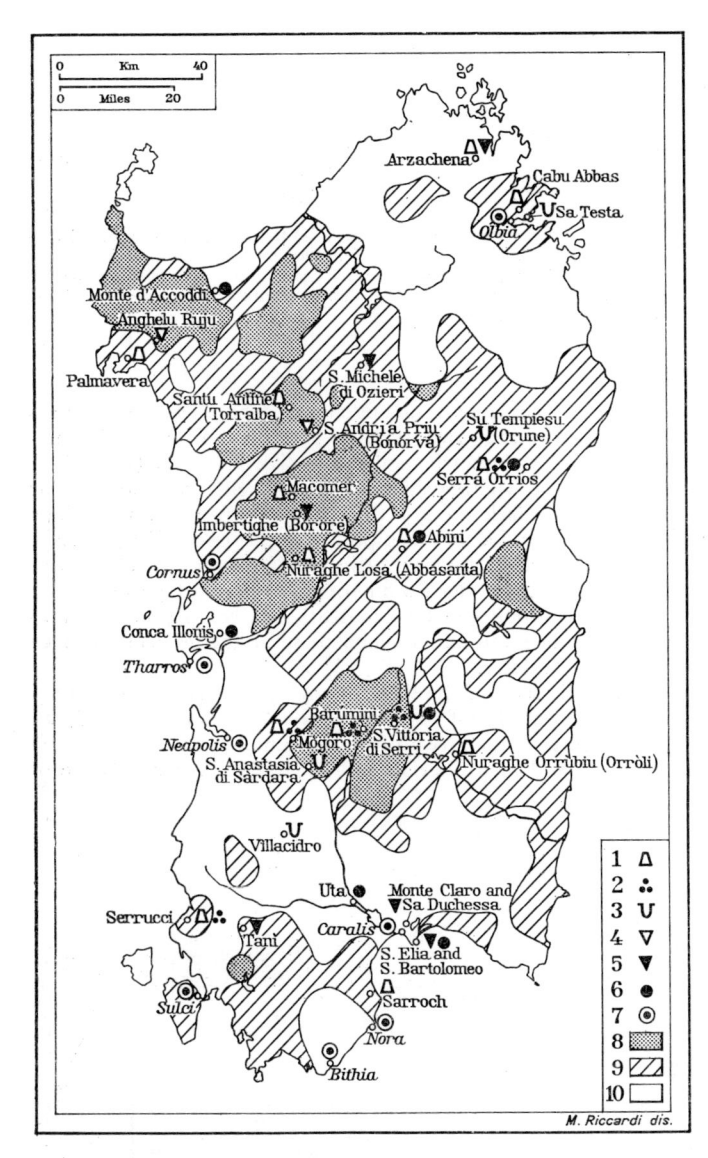

Principal archaeological and monumental sites in pre-Roman Sardinia. *Key*: (1) Nuraghi; (2) nuraghic village; (3) well-temple; (4) necropolis with artificial grottoes (prenuraghic and nuraghic); (5) other necropolises, funerary deposits, and tombs (prenuraghic and nuraghic); (6) other monuments and sites of important finds (prenuraghic and nuraghic); (7) Phoenician-Punic cities; (8) concentration of nuraghi less than 0.1 per sq. km.; (9) concentration of nuraghi 0.1–0.5 per sq. km.; (10) concentration of nuraghi more than 0.5 per sq. km.

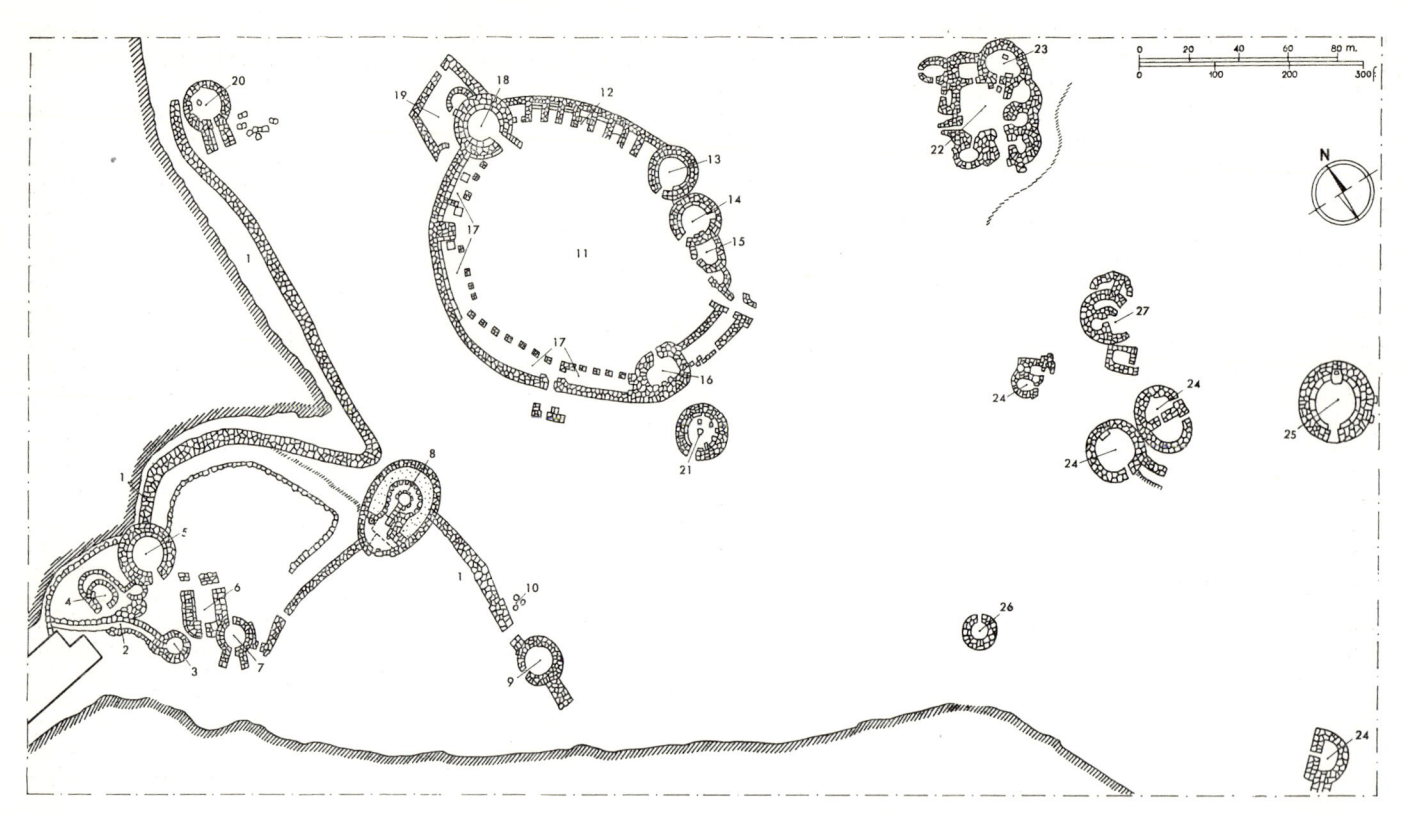

Santa Vittoria di Serri, Sardinia, sanctuary on the acropolis, plan: (1) Walls; (2) corridor; (3) crenelated nuraghic tower; (4) trench; (5) enclosure; (6) rectangular temple; (7) dwelling hut of priest (?); (8) well-temple; (9) hut at entrance; (10) baetuli; (11) enclosure for markets and feasts; (12) banquet area(?); (13) "enclosure of the double-headed ax"; (14) enclosure with seats; (15) house of the hearth; (16) cookhouse; (17) portico with pilasters; (18) foundry(?); (19) sheeppen; (20) large dwelling hut; (21) hut with small altar; (22) square with dwellings; (23) enclosure with double baetulus; (24) huts; (25) large circular edifice, possibly for meetings; (26) hut of caretaker(?); (27) group of dwellings (from Zervos).

the ceilings of the stairs are corbeled, with smooth and symmetrical lines. On the front are added architectonic-decorative elements with bichrome effects (e.g., those at Santa Vittoria di Serri) — animal sculptures (bulls), and symbolic ornaments (bosses, geometric signs). An example is the triangular pediment-shaped element, with a cluster of bronze swords as acroterium, of the recently discovered and excavated small temple of Su Tempiesu (FIG. 608) in the district of Orune (province of Nuoro). These monuments would seem to indicate a certain amount of contact between barbarian and Greek, or Grecizing, cultures.

The influence of Hellenic models, possibly transmitted by way of Phoenician-Punic culture, is also seen in a number of small temples *in antis* (Santa Vittoria di Serri, FIG. 607; Dorgali), especially in the mountain monument of Domu de Orgìa in Esterzìli (FIG. 609). In view of the archaic techniques — megalithic rather than isodomic — the possibility cannot be dismissed that these monuments represent a late echo of the plan of the Anatolian-Peloponnesian megaron. Similarly, a certain type of circular dwelling with central atrium appears to go back to a remote Aegean prototype; this type, which was present in the declining phase of the nuraghic civilization, is seen in Barúmini (province of Cagliari), the village around Su Nuraxi (PL. 401), a form strangely similar to the example of the dwelling at Khamaizi, in eastern Crete (district of Sitia; IV, FIG. 81). The chronological interval is enormous (ca. 1800 B.C. in Crete, 5th cent. B.C. in Barúmini), but it would seem as if the kingdom of Minos had found a last refuge in Sardinia.

Another typical art form of the protohistorical civilization here is the bronze sculpture, some examples of which reach a high artistic level. This noteworthy production was entirely small-scale; large sculpture of human subjects, was unknown among the ancient Sardinians, as was painting. More than 400 such figurines (PLS. 403, 404) have come to light; the majority of them represent warriors, but there are also statuettes of kings, priests, women, peasant folk, and animals, as well as some works of magico-religious significance. These sculptures can be divided into two stylistic groups: the geometric, distinguished by volumetric and decorative elements (Uta-Abini group), and the Mediterraneanizing, freer in form and popular in subject (Barbaricino group). Both groups show reflections of ancient Near Eastern sculptural forms (Anatolian, Syrian, Aegean), and there appear basic motifs from the Geometric art, of Greco-Italic derivation, of the historical period. The bronzes as a group can be dated 8th–6th century B.C., but in certain remote mountain regions these statuettes continued to be made even later.

Geometric style of the linear, nonfigural phase is exemplified also in fine examples of pottery (recovered from the nuraghi, the mountain huts, and above all from the temples, e.g., S. Anastasia in Sàrdara) and in utilitarian and decorative bronzes. Some of

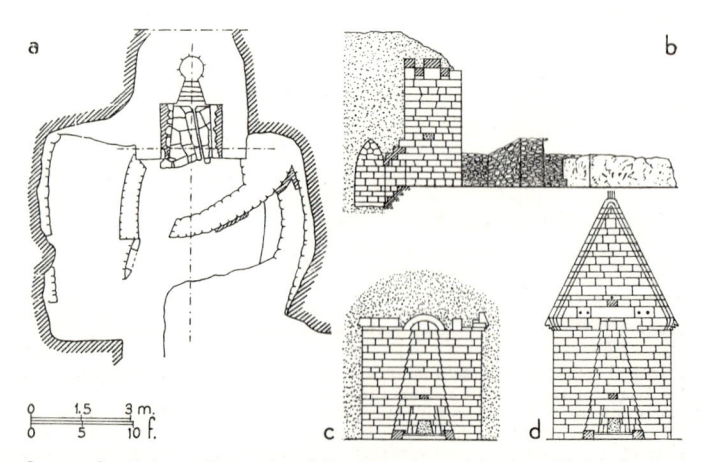

Orune, Sardinia, well-temple of Su Tempiesu: (*a*) Plan; (*b*) longitudinal section; (*c*) cross section; (*d*) hypothetical reconstruction of the front (*from Lilliu, 1955–57*).

the ceramics, as well as certain of the bronze pieces, exhibit interesting parallels to art forms of the Villanovan and early Latin cultures of continental Italy, with significant similarities even in ornamental details (see ETRUSCO-ITALIC ART). There are other ceramic objects, more ancient, of an archaic facies of the nuraghic civilization, the Monte Claro; this pottery is characterized by shapes probably derived from metal prototypes, by a red color, by grooved decoration, and by the persistence of a free and unarticulated decorative style achieved through older techniques drawn from the chalcolithic tradition (examples found in tombs at Cagliari, in the villages of the municipalities of Mógoro and Oristano and in the grottoes of the Súlcis area).

The great chronological extent of the megalithic protohistorical nuraghic civilization accounts for the variety and diversity of the typological, formal, and cultural aspects of its art. The periodic division has lately become clearer from stratigraphic studies of the excavated nuraghe and village of Barúmini. Further chronological data have been furnished by the discovery of the Monte Claro facies mentioned above. To sum up, the nuraghic civilization can be divided into the following periods: Early Nuraghic A (middle Bronze Age), 1500–1200 B.C.; Early Nuraghic B, Monte Claro facies (late Bronze Age), 1200–1000 B.C.; Middle Nuraghic (early Iron Age), 1000–500 B.C.; Late Nuraghic (late Iron Age), 500–200 B.C.

The megalithic culture of Corsica. Sardinia and Corsica, separated only by the Strait of Bonifacio, form, in their basic physical structure, a homogeneous whole. Ethnographic evidence and types of monument common to the two islands (dolmens, menhirs, steles) make it reasonable to assume a certain ethnic uniformity in very ancient times (premegalithic and pre-Bronze Age). Later, with the strengthening of the Libyo-Iberian cultural basis in Sardinia and of the Ligurian in Corsica, this unity gradually dissolved, and the original homogeneous, or almost homogeneous, cultures took separate if not divergent paths. To this separation the differing geographical situations of the two islands contributed, in that Corsica faces toward Europe, while Sardinia extends into the Mediterranean at the crossroads of the routes between East and West.

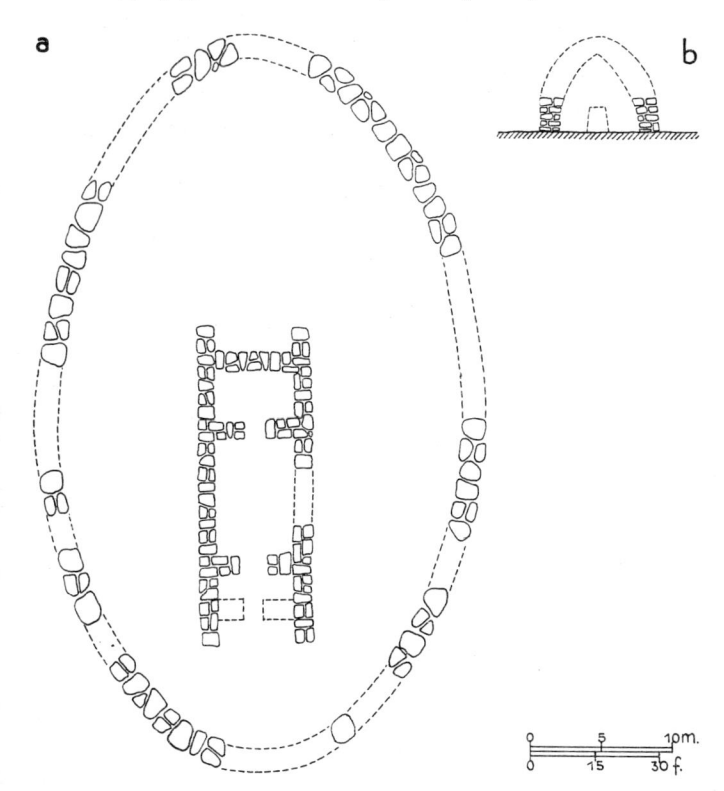

Esterzili, Sardinia, Domu de Orgìa, probably a temple within an elliptical enclosure: (*a*) Plan; (*b*) cross section of the temple (*from Zervos*).

Until a few years ago, Corsica was an archaeological unknown, but research and excavation by French archaeologists have begun to block out a definite character — and it is megalithic. The earlier catalogue of *stazzone, stantare, filarate* (dolmens and menhirs) and some menhir (or "stele") statues, isolated in space and time, has been enriched by a splendid and monumental series of menhir statues, the truly exceptional complex of Filitosa, in the Taravo Valley (PL. 405; XII, PL. 562). Also, Roger Grosjean has published a number of remarkable examples of towered (FIG. 611) and corridored structures which show, in a general way, Mediterranean influences and, more in detail, close connections with both Sardinian and Balearic monuments.

The fifty-odd Corsican menhir statues, of which more than twenty belong to the Filitosa group, are of the anthropomorphous type, ranging from a simple and elemental smooth shaft surmounted by a stylized human head (perhaps a stone version of the totem pole) to the more complex and elaborate form in which the graphic treatment extends to the body of the shaft, indicating anatomical details, ornaments, and weapons. The statues are derived from the aniconic menhir and seem to have had a similar funerary purpose, representing the deceased (possibly also the spirit of the ancestor). Some of the statues are more than 6 ft. high and fit into the northern Italian (Liguria, Alto Adige) and southwestern French type of menhir statue, indicating a common custom. By some, these are all attributed to the Ligurian peoples, who at one time inhabited an area much larger than that of the Liguria of historical times. But the Corsican menhir statues show special characteristics, both in style and in development. In particular, there is a taste for loose and unarticulated composition, unrestricted in movement, showing a more pronounced Mediterranean feeling. Their chronology has not yet been firmly established; the middle of the 2d millennium B.C. has been suggested as the terminal date, but it would be more prudent to suppose (also because they are a form of sacred art) that menhir statues were used until the early Iron Age, particularly those which show representations of a type of dagger that became common in Europe in the early centuries of the 1st millennium (PL. 405).

More than thirty towered structures have been studied in southern Corsica, nine of them in the Taravo Valley, in the ethnographic and cultural area of the menhir statues. Of particular significance among these nine are the towers of Foce, Balestra, and Filitosa (FIG. 611) — to which should be added, as no less interesting, the one at Torre (near Porto-Vecchio). These towers are of two types, or forms: round structures containing, in the first form, a covered circular chamber roofed over in tholos fashion (tholos type); in the second form, rectangular chambers, more or less articulated, and covered with a flat ceiling of stone slabs (corridored type). The Foce and Balestra towers belong to the first type, those at Filitosa and Torre to the second. At Filitosa there are two such corridored towers, one at the center and one at the edge of a vast megalithic wall of polyhedral masonry (425 × 130 ft.) which blocks a rocky spur dominating a large area. The tholos type of tower, of relatively small-sized masonry, is believed to have been funerary and to have served for the cremation of the dead, as did the corridored type (at Filitosa also used for religious rites).

Both types have remarkable correspondences with the Sardinian tholos and corridored nuraghe, which suggests the possibility of a common heritage whose development has followed a course in part parallel and in part divergent as regards chronology, customs, and material culture. The tholos, which in Sardinia was used by the living, retained in Corsica its characteristic Eastern function as a place for the dead — its rudimentary state — while in Sardinia the force of practical necessity brought about development into forms that were enormous and architecturally superior. Sociological conditions, probably similar in the two islands, determined the form of the corridored tower: it was an instrument of hidden warfare, a tower-hideout, inasmuch as it was suitable for the guerilla fighters, who, the ancient writers tell us, continued to live and fight in the wild and inaccessible mountains of the two islands until the Roman republican period. The archaeological material (pottery and bronze) that has come to light in the corridored towers indicates

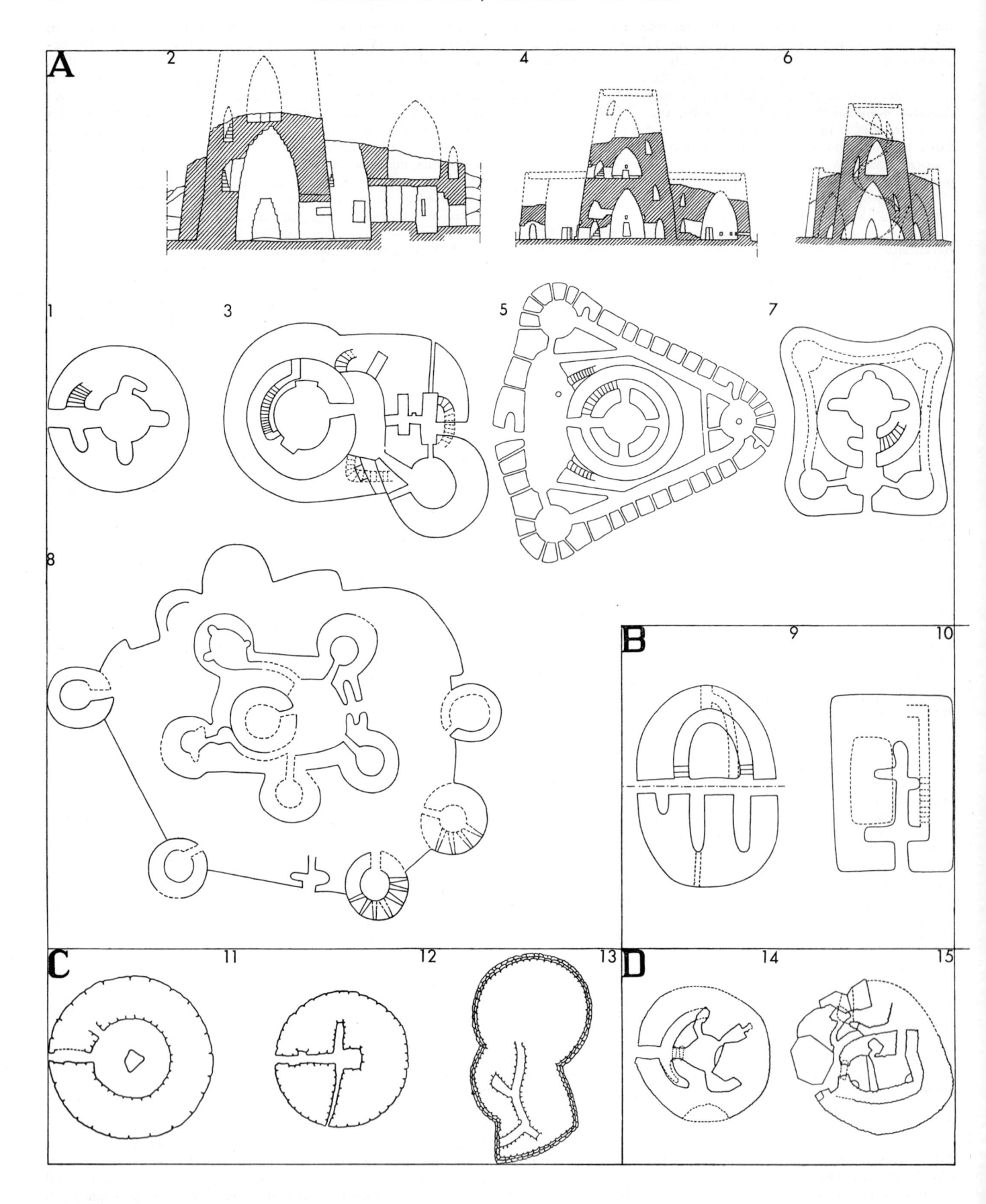

Plans of Sardinian nuraghi, Balearic talayoti, and Corsican tower monuments: (*A*) Nuraghi: (1) Tittirriola (Bolótana); (2 and 3) Palmavera (Alghero), section and plan; (4 and 5) Santu Antine (Torralba), section and plan; (6 and 7) Santa Bárbara (Macomer), section and plan; (8) Orrùbiu (Orròli); (*B*) Corridored nuraghi, or pseudo-nuraghi: (9) Séneghe (Suni); (10) Fronte e Mola (Thiesi); (*C*) Talayoti: (11) Sa Canova (Artá, Mallorca); (12) Rafal-Roig (Mercadal, Minorca); (13) Santa Monica (Mercadal, Minorca); (*D*) Tower monuments: (14) Foce; (15) Filitosa.

customs and events common to the two islands that belong to a relatively late historical period, at any rate to the 1st millennium B.C.

The Balearic Islands and the talayotic civilization. The major Balearic islands, Mallorca and Minorca (anc. Nure), fostered the third, and westernmost, insular megalithic civilization of the western Mediterranean. It is not possible to document a prehistoric Ibero-Levantine ethnic base from which the Balearic megalithic civilization derived, but the infiltration of certain forms, as well as geography itself, makes this a legitimate assumption. Later, in historical times, this substratum acquired the designation Baleari, comparable with that of the Sardinian Bàlari, to whom historical tradition ascribes an Iberian origin. Like the Sardinians and the Corsicans, the inhabitants of the Balearic Islands were a warlike people and formidable wielders of the sling.

The megalithic culture of the Balearic Islands is also highly evolved, imposing, and grandiose, although on a different scale and to a different degree from that of Sardinia. It presents its own individual accent, with modulations more numerous and varied in Minorca, perhaps because of the proximity to the "quasi-continental" island of Sardinia, whence it undoubtedly received a cultural stimulus.

The Balearic megalithic structures, which came to be known as the talayot (FIG. 611), the naveta (or naus), the taula, and the *antigor*, are of dry masonry with cyclopean elements (PL. 406). Most numerous is the talayot (over 1,000 in Mallorca, 267 in Minorca), which served both as dwelling and as fortification, and, in more than one case, as burial vault. The majority of the talayoti are circular in form, with inclined walls that rise, like those of the nuraghi, in horizontal courses of stones diminishing gradually in size. There are also, however, a number of talayoti of elliptical or rectangular plan (the latter with truncated pyramidal section) with the same kind of exterior facing. On the basis of interior plan the talayoti are, like the Sardinian nuraghi and the Corsican towers, classified as of the tholos or of the corridored type, the former being more numerous.

In the tholos type, the true dome is seen as an exception (Son Carlá, Minorca), with the upper part of the projecting walls replaced by a ceiling of wooden beams and stone slabs supported by a central pillar made up of many stones (Sa Canova, in Artá, Mallorca; FIG. 611). Perhaps in ancient times the complete tholos occurred in many talayoti, since examples are still found in a secondary cycle derived from the ancient megalithic forms, in certain rural constructions, particularly in Minorca (*pont de bestiar, barracas*). The central pillar, built of dry masonry of stone blocks that are progressively larger from bottom to top, is a characteristic of the talayot and of other Balearic structures (*navetas*, dwelling houses, hypostyle rooms for funerary or religious use). It suggests an influence stemming from the early megalithic culture, of a stamp that is dolmenic, Mediterranean (Maltese), but, above all, Ibero-Atlantic, in which the flat ceilings of the small dolmens and of the large corridor tombs are supported on orthostats, sometimes consisting of a number of stones. This element of orthostatic and trilithic architecture (of aëneolithic origin), which gives an archaic cast to the Balearic megalithic, obstructed the new fashion of the Eastern dome, hindering, if not its adoption and application, its growth and spread, and furthered the establishment of the corridored talayot as the chief architectural form. The corridored type of talayot is seen in both the circular and the rectangular form, just as in Sardinia. The corridors, which sometimes have an entrance at ground level (Fontredones de Baix, Mercadal, Minorca), are either contained within the interior of the tower, built in the form of a solid mass (Minorca: Santa Monica, FIG. 611; San Cristóbal), or traverse it diametrically like a tunnel (Mallorca: Ses Païsses, Artá).

Both types of tower are sometimes diversified by steep and narrow spiral stairs built within the thickness of the walls, leading to rooms on an upper story or to terraces (Torre Vell d'en Lozano, Ciudadela, Minorca); in other cases they are surrounded by the remains of circular walls which supported external ramps (Ses Païsses), so that they take on the appearance of stepped towers, as in the modern *pont de bestiar* and the Apulian trullo (V, PL. 337), derived from Bronze and Iron Age *specchie*).

Typological and formal connections with Sardinia are met with again in the *naus*, a large structure in the form of an upturned ship, with an apse at the far end, which, apart from having no exedra in front, is related in plan and exterior appearance to the Sardinian "giants' graves." However they differ as to interior space, which is sometimes divided into aisles by a row of pillars of the type described above — even, in exceptional cases, being on two levels, as in the "Naveta dels Tudons" at Ciudadela in Minorca (PL. 406). In the *naus* the dolmenic orthostatic element is much more pronounced than in the "giant's grave," in which the projecting component, derived from the nuraghe, predominates. The function of the *naus* was funerary.

On the other hand, the taulas, vast monuments in trilithic style, peculiar to Minorca, seem to have been temples; the horseshoe form is faintly reminiscent of the Maltese "temples" (as is the great size of the orthostatic structures) and, in a more general way, of the famous megalithic complex of Stonehenge (V, PLS. 164, 165). The term "taula" derives from the gigantic horizontal stone slabs laid horizontally atop the monolithic upright piers in the center of the vast enclosure, the two elements (pier and slab) together forming a T shape, perhaps the aniconic symbol of a deity.

Talayoti and taulas not infrequently form part of settlements on the order of the fortified village, surrounded by massive walls, with gates and towers on the perimeter; the dwellings inside are also megalithic and orthostatic (in some cases the plan is like that of the *naus*, basically a large and monumental dwelling for the dead). Noteworthy among these *poblados*, or villages, are Son Carlá, in Minorca, and, in Mallorca, Els Antigors (Ses Salines), Capocorp Vell (Lluchmayor), and Ses Païsses (Artá). In the unusual necropolis of Son Real, Alcudia, in Mallorca, are to be seen structures, built one against the other, that repeat in miniature and in perfectly regular isodomic masonry the design of the round talayoti and of the *navetas*: this is the refined touch of a less remote locality, freer in outlook, which invested with the Greek spirit the megalithic-cyclopean cultural base of these islands.

On the basis of findings in the recent excavations of the talayot complex of Ses Païsses, the talayotic culture can be subdivided into three distinct phases: (1) Archaic Talayotic period (ca. 1200–1000 B.C.?), which produced the corridored talayoti and corresponds to the oldest phase of Balearic megalithic culture, characterized by the influence, both architectonic and nonarchitectonic, of the civilization of the Iberian Peninsula, admixed with Mediterranean elements, such as artificial rock-cut grottoes; (2) Middle Talayotic period (ca. 1000–500 B.C.), the time of the greatest monumental and cultural expressions of the Balearic peoples, marked by connections with the *floruit* of Sardinian nuraghic architecture and by commercial relations with the southern part of the Iberian Peninsula, and, more remotely and perhaps indirectly, with the Atlanto-European area (as shown by the Huelva and northern bronze artifacts), as well as by Phoenician-Punic influences from the Phoenician colony established at Ibiza (see PHOENICIAN-PUNIC ART); (3) Late Talayotic period (ca. 500 B.C. to the Roman conquest), in which there was a survival of declining older traditions alongside new imported cultural elements — Punic, Hellenistic, Greek, Iberian, and other — eventuating in a notable local production of figural crafts including bronze statuettes and such works as the Costitx bulls' heads (Madrid, Mus. Arqueológico Nacional).

Giovanni LILLIU

THE IBERIAN CIVILIZATION. The topography of the Iberian Peninsula has well-defined features: in the center is a plateau (the Meseta), whose altitude above sea level averages 2,000 ft., flanked by two roughly triangular depressions, the valley of the Ebro on the northeast and the valley of the Guadalquivir on the south; the rest consists of coastal strips. The actual area that was the seat of the Iberian civilization includes only the Mediterranean coastal strip and the two above-mentioned de-

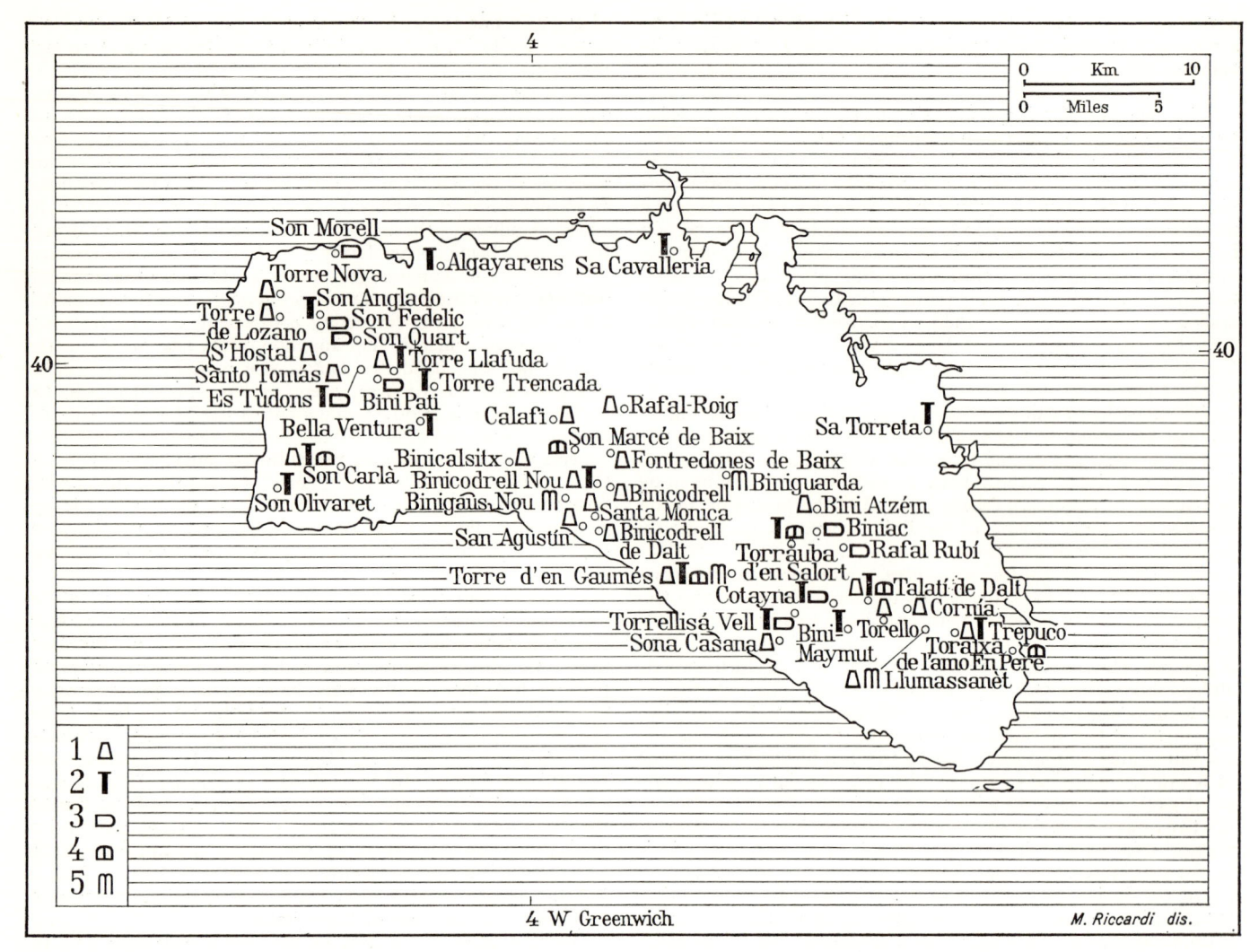

Minorca, principal megalithic monuments. *Key*: (1) Talayoti; (2) taulas; (3) *navetas*; (4) megalithic grottoes; (5) hypostyle halls.

pressions, for the central Meseta and the western portions remained outside the sphere of Mediterranean civilization; not until they were conquered by the Romans in the 2d century B.C. did they become part of the Latin cultural world.

The early Greek geographers and historians called the people who inhabited the Mediterranean side of the peninsula "Iberians"; the inhabitants of the southern part of the peninsula were designated as "Tartessians." Thus was indicated the existence of a shade of difference in the ethnic substratum, a difference that slowly disappeared as cultural development brought about the unification of the area. Consequently, as the region became better known the term "Iberian" was extended to cover an ever-increasing geographical area, and in Greek historiography the term came to designate the whole peninsula, although the difference between the peoples of the eastern and southern parts and those of the interior — the Iberian Celts, or Celtiberians, as they are termed — remained very real.

Two elements enter into this differentiation: a clear racial divergence, and a differing capacity to react to the Mediterranean stimulus. This indicates that the ancient historians recognized the existence of an "Iberian civilization," which was capable of taking its place alongside the other Mediterranean civilizations, in contrast with the uncivilized inhabitants of the interior, who were included in the Greek category of "barbarians." However, there persist in the Iberian region traditions going back to prehistoric times that point to differences, derived from the earlier development of distinct cultural phases, that seem to define two areas; one in the east and the other in the south.

In the south the population was descended from a very ancient people who, already settled in this region in the Neolithic period, gained vigor from the arrival of an ethnic group from the eastern Mediterranean, numerically inconsiderable but of a superior culture and with new religious ideas. This fusion produced, in the course of the 2d millennium B.C., a distinct culture, the Andalusian megalithic civilization, which, although its impulses were Orientalizing, was original in its development and prospered from the great metallic wealth (copper) of the region. A new wave of Mediterranean immigration, probably of Anatolian origin, introduced into the southeast the working of silver, giving rise in the middle Bronze Age to the El Argar culture, which, while it did not follow the religious practices of the older megalithic civilization but deviated in its rites and funerary practices, did not, from the ethnic point of view, differ from its predecessor to any appreciable extent. Being a region poor in metals, eastern Spain did not receive a similar stimulus and, throughout the 2d millennium, continued unchanged in its neolithic traditions, modified by the influence of the Central European neolithic culture, more intensely felt in the territory north of the Ebro. Only the eastern Pyrenees region and the adjacent regions felt the influence of the Mediterranean megalithic civilization, which did not essentially modify the racial character of the population. Thus the Iberian contribution can be considered to have been the indigenous population (see MEDITERRANEAN PROTOHISTORY).

The cultural division between the south and the east became more marked at the end of the 2d millennium B.C. From the Mediterranean coast of southern France the first wave of the Urn-field people arrived in the peninsula, with a largely continental cultural heritage and a new religious concept, which introduced in Iberia for the first time the rite of cremation of the dead. Absorbed by the more numerous indigenous population, this group, concentrated north of the Ebro, succeeded in exercising a certain influence even in the south. Here, immediately preceding the Phoenician colonization, a new and vigorous Mediterranean cultural impulse that must have been a large-scale colonization, from outside, of the lowlands of the Guadalquivir and the Guadiana is already distinguishable under the historical name of Tartessos. While silver had been the great stimulus of the middle Bronze Age culture, it was now western tin that was to determine the success of the westward expansion of Mediterranean civilization. The actual beginnings of the Tartessian component are difficult to establish accurately; data obtained through recent researches point to the Aegean-Cypriote region at the time when the eastern Mediterranean was attempting to regain its economic balance after the crisis familiar to historians as the migrations of the Peoples of the Sea. The Tartessian element in the south and the Urn-field element in the east contributed to the maintenance of the traditional duality already noted between the two regions; southeastern Spain, the point of contact, constituted the most advanced and vital center of Iberian culture.

The Mediterranean colonizations of the Iberian Peninsula and their varied fortunes represent the decisive factor in the formation of the Iberian civilization. The first event was the Phoenician colonization, which, concerned exclusively with commercial activity, affected only the south coast, where even before 1000 B.C. the city of Gadir (mod. Cádiz) had flourished, monopolizing Tartessian metal production and exerting a great influence in the transmission of eastern techniques (chiefly in gold- and silverwork) and religious concepts (lunar cults, worship of Astarte, Kronos, Melkarth, etc.). When, beginning in the 6th century B.C., Carthage achieved political supremacy over the western Semitic world, the influence on southern Spain continued to be more Phoenician than Punic, so that Carthage's attempt to found a territorial empire in Spain in the 3d century B.C. came at a time when Iberian culture had already reached its classic phase (see PHOENICIAN-PUNIC ART).

Geographically far more extensive was the influence of the Greeks. The mineral wealth of Tartessos, monopolized by the Phoenicians, enticed the Greeks to colonize the southern coast in the 7th century B.C. Greek literary tradition recalls the discovery of Tartessos by Kolaios of Samos and of his attempt to settle in that region. Numerous traditions survive regarding contacts with the Iberian coast, but the first genuine colonization is attributed to the Phokaians, who founded Mainake, in an as yet undetermined location on the Málaga coast, Hemeroskopeion (mod. Denia) on the Alicante coast, and Emporion (mod. Ampurias) on the Gulf of Rosas, near the eastern Pyrenees. The ultimate goal of the Greeks was the Tartessian market; but Mainake, surrounded by Phoenician settlements, managed only to establish relations with the interior areas by overland routes. Hemeroskopeion, whose early history is unknown, exerted a powerful influence on the formation of Iberian culture. Emporion was influential in a later period; it must have been founded at the beginning of the 6th century B.C. as a mere port of call on the route to Tartessos (a six-day voyage away). At the end of the 6th century B.C., when the power of Massilia (mod. Marseilles) declined, the center of Tartessian power shifted toward Gadir, and Mainake was abandoned. Emporion then began to make its influence felt in the area north of the Ebro and maintained maritime contacts with Hemeroskopeion, with the southeastern region, and with the Punic world (e.g., via Ibiza). Through its relations with the Greek cities of Magna Graecia, Emporion contributed greatly to the evolution of Iberian culture north of the Ebro (see GREEK ART, WESTERN).

Less important — because later — but no less interesting is the Italic influence on late Iberian culture. From the mid-4th century B.C., Italic imports, probably brought in through Greek trade in immense quantity, completely supplanted Attic products: Campanian ware was extensively and habitually used for the table in the Iberian world until well into the 1st century and was widely imitated by local potters.

A further influence on the Iberian world was exercised by the Celtic inhabitants of the interior of the peninsula. With the discovery of iron in Moncayo and in the Soria area, the Indo-European population of the interior developed a highly original culture, without, however, reaching what could be termed an urban level. Drawn by the superior cultural centers of the Iberian region, the Celtic population of the interior eventually gravitated to them, and eventually it contributed certain aspects of its own artistic heritage — particularly certain decorative motifs — which in turn were absorbed and taken over by the Iberian populace (see CELTIC ART).

Apart from these, so to speak, passive influences affecting the Iberian world, there was another influence, of an active sort, arising from the direct contact of large numbers of Iberian mercenaries serving in the Carthaginian armies during the wars in Sicily. Iberian troops took part in the battle of Himera (480 B.C.) and for two centuries were participants in the Punic expeditions, thus passing through the principal Greek cities of Sicily in peace and war. This experience revealed to the Iberians the Greek civilization in all its splendor, and they returned home filled with new ideas which were to be realized in Iberian art forms.

Origins and development of Iberian art. Built on so heterogeneous a substratum, subjected to such a variety of influences, the formative process of the civilization of the Iberian world was not uniform, in either time or space, and never reached the same level in all regions. Actually, there arose gradually in various areas a development toward a process of cultural unification which in the south and southeast appears to have been complete as early as the 5th century B.C., while in the rest of the eastern region and in Catalonia it was not effected until the 4th century B.C. The first center was that which the ancient writers called "Tartessian": this extended from the region of the Strait of Gibraltar to the extreme western end of the peninsula, thus including the lower basins of the Guadalquivir and the Guadiana. Since in this area the Cypro-Phoenician cultural stimulus had been felt since very ancient times, an urban culture had been achieved as early as the 9th century B.C. But the period of the greatest flowering of the Tartessian culture was the 8th–6th century B.C. After that the entire valley of the Guadalquivir saw the development of an "Iberian" culture constituting a separate area, yet but partially known, in which are encountered the ceramics showing Cypriote influence that were the prototypes of the ware which came to be known as Ibero-Andalusian.

Another center of activity, in the southeast, includes the modern provinces of Alicante, Murcia, Albacete, Jaén, and, in part, Almería and Granada. Its cultural stimulus clearly appears to have been that stemming from the Alicante coast with the beginning of the 6th century B.C. The existence of rich mineral deposits in the provinces of Jaén and Córdoba and the difficulties experienced by the Greeks in their attempts to reach this region by the maritime route, because of Phoenician-Punic control over the zone of the Strait of Gibraltar, impelled the Greeks to seek an overland route from the Alicante coast to the interior. Through this route they exerted so strong an influence over the entire territory that during a certain period the Ionian alphabet was adopted even in the writing of the Iberian texts found in the cities and sanctuaries.

The intensity of Greek influence in the southeast caused this area, richer and culturally and artistically more highly developed, to assume predominance as the Iberian region from which cultural influences spread along the coastal lands as far as the Ebro; there, however, the earth was poor in metals, and development toward an urban culture was much slower.

A third productive center comprised the eastern Pyrenees zone, near the Greek colony of Emporion. Although the city of Emporion was in existence in the 6th century B.C., the cultural development of this area was late, for the indigenous Catalan population, both to the north and to the south of the Pyrenees, powerfully influenced by the Indo-European migration from the Urn-field region, was less open to the Mediterranean stimulus of the Greeks, and their incorporation into the Iberian cultural sphere proper was therefore slower and was effected later than in other areas. Nor did this area ever reach a cultural level comparable to that of the peoples of the southeast; indeed, some of the principal art forms are not found —

sculpture, for example, never having progressed in Catalonia beyond the stage of simple decorative reliefs for architectural use (Ampurias; Ullastret).

The Iberian cultural evolution was a varied and complex process, tending toward unification and crystallization. The cultural unification of the Iberian world began to develop in the middle of the 5th century B.C., stimulated by the political expansion of certain peoples whose existence can be presumed because of archaeological finds but of whom written sources offer no information. At the end of the 5th century B.C. Iberian culture penetrated toward the interior of the peninsula across the basin of the Ebro, gaining a foothold among a population in which, though its ethnic origins were diverse, the Indo-European element already predominated. In the Ebro Valley this gave rise to a mixed culture, which on the technical level coincides with that of the Iberian world but which artistically appears to be more closely tied to the peninsula's Celtic stratum.

Cultural areas. Because of this complicated formative process, the Iberian world, in spite of its geographical unity, remained divided into separate cultural areas, each with its own individual character. The most important are: (1) the Andalusian region, comprising Lower Andalusia (the lower basins of the Guadalquivir and the Guadiana), which coincides with the ancient Tartessian area; (2) the southeast, which extends to the upper valley of the Guadalquivir, the adjacent Mediterranean provinces of Alicante, Murcia, and Almería, the inland provinces of Albacete, Jaén, and in part Granada, with individual settlements as far as the province of Córdoba; (3) the east, comprising the provinces of Valencia, Castellón de la Plana, and Tarragona and reaching inland toward Lérida, Saragossa, and Teruel; (4) the Catalan region, which includes both the southern and northern slopes of the eastern Pyrenees (approximately from the Hérault River, in France, to the Tordera), centering in the provinces of Gerona and Roussillon.

Outside these areas, the Iberian civilization amounted only to a light cultural admixture, arising from the play of economic forces, which did not affect the individual character of the people or its structure. This applies particularly to the district of Numancia (anc. Numantia), in which the Celtiberian culture (see above) developed in a relatively later period. This culture, in certain technical aspects such as vase painting, was in part indebted to Iberian influences that had penetrated via the Ebro basin.

Leaving aside the different gradations in the different areas, one sees in the Iberian world not only a highly original cultural unity but also an ethnic, religious, and linguistic unity. From the *oppidum* of Ensérune to the middle Guadalquivir basin (Cástulo, or Castulon) indigenous inscriptions show the use of a common language and the same onomatology; while a highly original semisyllabic system of writing was developed in the same area, it is interesting that from the middle of the 2d century B.C. this system was also adopted by the Celtic peoples of the interior for writing in another language, which was related to those of the Gaulish (Celtiberian) group. In the lower Guadalquivir basin and in southern Portugal (the region corresponding to the oldest Tartessian boundaries) a different language seems to have been spoken, but its character has not been determined.

Principal phases. The development of Iberian art can be divided into three distinct phases: A "formative" phase, extending from mid-6th to mid-5th century B.C., is characterized by strong archaizing and Orientalizing Greek influence, particularly evident in the development of sculpture; this phase is found only in the southeast, archaeologically the best-known area; it is absent in the others. A second phase, which will be termed "classic," extended from mid-5th to mid-3d century B.C., two centuries that are most important in the development of an Iberian community with a political life of its own, upon which Carthaginian pressures did not yet impinge. The policy of annexation established by the Carthaginian military leaders, Hamilcar Barca and his successors, interrupted the autonomous development of the indigenous community and imposed new political systems and foreign religious beliefs, but Carthage also prevented the formation of centralized Iberian powers capable of providing a stimulus to the already established cultural base and promoting its wider development. Iberian culture thus grew arid and repetitive, and when the territory was occupied by the Romans, it languished, although maintaining a certain originality in many aspects of decorative art, particularly in ceramics. This last phase of Iberian art, which can be termed one of "survival," lasted until the middle of the 1st century B.C.

Architecture and architectural decoration. Iberian civilization, essentially urban in character, supported a threefold development of architecture — civil, military, and funerary — but in many areas it is little known today, because of the insufficiency of excavations of the richer strata, and because of the very fact that in many Iberian cities life continued uninterruptedly throughout the Roman period.

Construction materials used were stone, clay, and wood. The use of clay is typical, in the shape either of the tapia (wall formed in a mold, *tapial*, made of boards) or of adobe (sun-dried brick). Genuine bricks were little used before the Roman conquest. To avoid dampness from the soil the walls were raised on a stone foundation on the order of a socle. Wooden posts and architraves were built into the walls, following the Mediterranean tradition. The clay roofs were supported on lathing resting on wooden frames.

Very little is known about the structure of private dwellings, but the clear demarcation of social classes in the southeast and the south would lead us to suppose that there must have been a great variety. In general, houses were formed of adjoining square or rectangular rooms, in accordance with the particular topography of the location. In the Catalan area, in the east, and in the Ebro basin, the Iberian house was simply a development and elaboration of the type of dwelling peculiar to the region in the early Iron Age — when the houses, built on an elongated rectangular plan, had the hearth in the center and various interior subdivisions, reproducing the general plan of the megaron — with few differences between one and another, for the social structure does not appear to have been so stratified here as it was in the south.

The make-up of the large cities of the south is practically unknown to us. Literary sources tell us that they contained an agora and were encircled by walls. In the east, in Catalonia, and in southern France the urban unit was the *oppidum*, or village, situated on the summit of a hill, surrounded by walls. The houses were built on streets laid out on a grid plan following the topographical conformation.

The greatest architectonic efforts of the Iberians are apparent in military architecture. The cities were surrounded by walls ranging in thickness from 6 to 18 ft. and standing more than 24 ft. high, partly built of cyclopean stone masonry, without mortar: a double range of dressed stone blocks, the intermediate space being filled with earth and stones. This cyclopean technique, while not used in all walls, is typical of the east (Catalan) and southeast; notable examples are at Tarragona and Gerona. There were also smaller walls, of very careful construction, such as those of Ullastret, which show the direct influence of West Greek (Sicilian) models. The walls were punctuated by towers, generally square in plan (a few were circular), and the gates were fortified by very thick bastions. Preoccupation with the military was characteristic of the warlike Iberians.

The very interesting development of funerary architecture can be studied only in a limited part of the southeast, in the provinces of Granada (necropolis of Galera) and Jaén (necropolises of Peal de Becerro, La Guardia, and Los Castellones de Ceal; the last in part unpublished). In these cemeteries, alongside simple pit graves, are true hypogeum structures in which, under a tumulus of earth, are rectangular chambers preceded by a dromos. In some cases the vaults are supported by columns or piers, surmounted by a kind of capital decorated with interlace patterns in relief; the interior walls are painted and stuccoed. Unfortunately the known tombs are in a very bad state of repair and the details of the paintings have been lost, but they appear to have been geometric and floral in design (interlacing and palmettes). The colors were chiefly white and

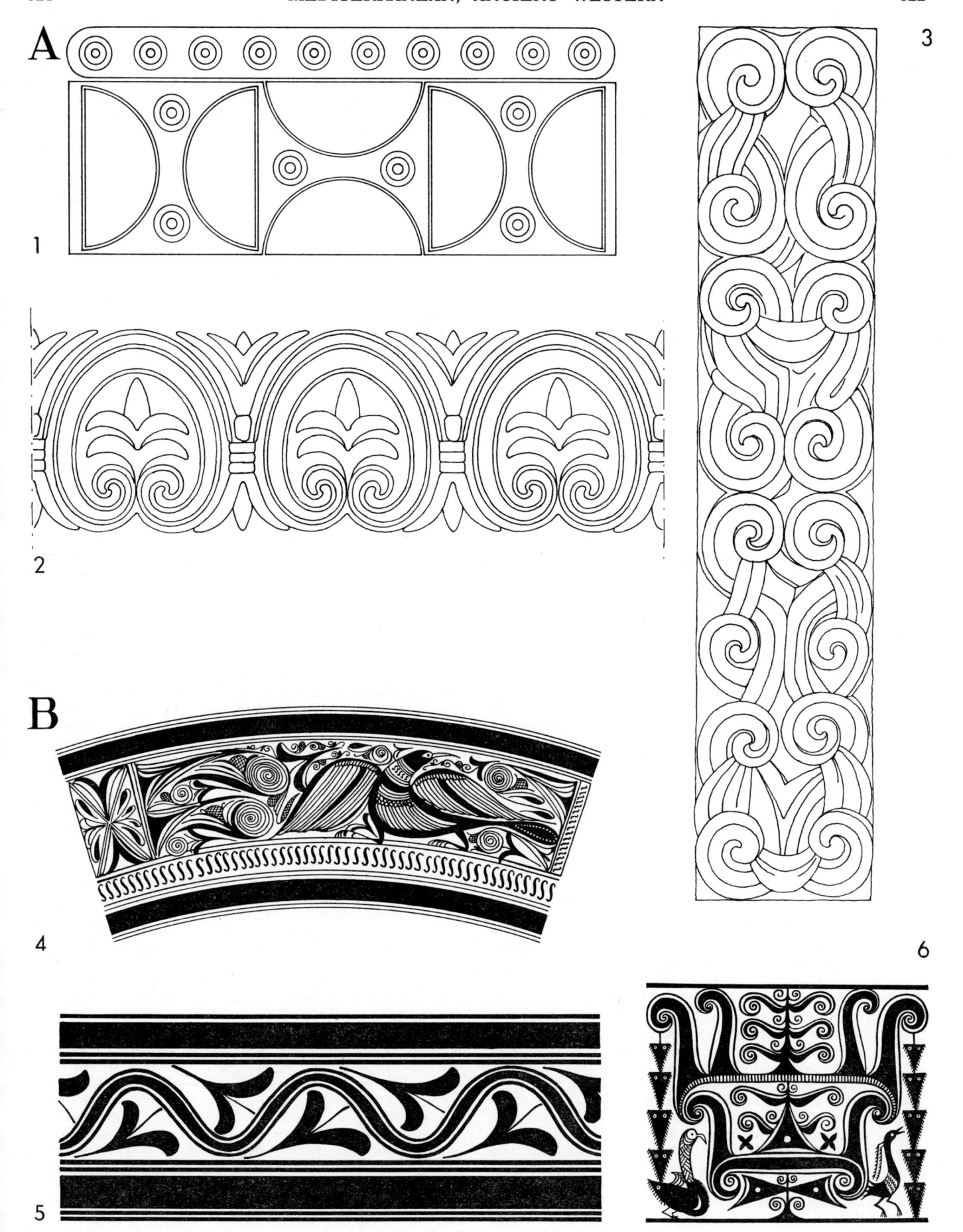

Principal Iberian decorative motifs. (*A*) Architectura /sculptures: (1) Capital from the Cortijo del Ahorcado in Baeza; (2) capital from Elche; (3) architectural element from Osuna. (*B*) Ceramics: (4 and 5) Border designs from Archena; (6) decoration on urn from Azaila (cf. PL. 400).

red. The date of the tombs can be deduced from the presence of Attic craters of the 5th and 4th centuries B.C. The Iberians, like all Mediterranean peoples, were profoundly religious. In every important city or village there rose on the acropolis a sanctuary or a temple to which the faithful made pilgrimages on given days, bringing to the divinity votive offerings of various kinds, in accordance with the specific nature of the shrine. Very little is known of the architecture of these sanctuaries: probably they consisted of a rectangular cella with clay walls, and the architrave and lintels of the doors were of stone, richly carved with floral and geometric designs. Remains of sculptures from such sanctuaries (FIG. 621) have been found at Elche, Cástulo (Castulon; PL. 408), Baeza (Cortijo del Ahorcado), and Osuna. Their artistic inspiration was east Ionian, though the palmettes have been transformed and have a fully independent character. At Osuna there are a number of orthostats and sculptured blocks, which would indicate the existence of religious constructions of importance.

Sculpture. The originality of Iberian art is strongly apparent in the sculpture (stone, bronze, and terra cotta) which is found in the two southern regions, Andalusia and the southeast; in other parts of Spain sculpture is almost totally absent. Iberian sculpture appeared abruptly, without local antecedents, under the direct influence of the archaic Greek world, felt especially in the southeast (provinces of Alicante, Murcia, Albacete, and Jaén). The formative phase is characterized by zoomorphic sculptures, representing fantastic animals, derived from the Orientalizing iconography with which the Iberians became familiar through the Greek art of Sicily. There are sphinxes, either recumbent or sitting on their hind legs, with fine women's heads. These were found chiefly in Agost (Alicante), Llano de la Consolación (Murcia), El Salobral (Jaén), and Haches (Albacete). Then there are griffins, such as the one found at Redován (Murcia), and human-headed bulls, such as the "Bicha de Balazote" (PL. 408). Also from this first phase are a few human figures, such as the seated statue found as reused material in the necropolis of Verdolay (Murcia). The phase of Iberian sculpture to which all these pieces belong began in the second half of the 6th century and extended to the middle of the 5th (in which the greater part of them were doubtless executed). They are of fine workmanship and show a perfected technique that denotes a direct knowledge of Greek sculpture; but they were all found away from their original locations, and their true nature and purpose are not known.

A second phase saw the development of a clear tendency toward regional originality. Art freed itself from Greek influence and became essentially Iberian, gaining in originality what it lost in technique. This is realistic sculpture: the artist depicts the clothed figure with the more significant details minutely rendered. The garb of the priestesses, the overlaid ornamentation of necklaces and earrings, the clothing and arms of the warriors, and the trappings of the horsemen are all represented with great virtuosity. This phase, the most fruitful in the whole development of Iberian art, began in the middle of the 5th century B.C. and lasted until the middle of the 3d, when the Carthaginians, in their wars of conquest, destroyed the greater number of the cities of the southeast. These cities were later rebuilt in large part, but with the lessening of political liberty the originality of Iberian sculpture soon faded.

The works of these two centuries represent a number of distinct schools and greatly varying degrees of artistic excellence, but beyond these, a conceptual unity that stamps the works with a certain baroque aspect is continually present, regardless of the greater or lesser abilities of their authors. A common feature is the exclusively "human" character of this sculpture: it does not depict deities or heroes but men and women from its daily life — priestesses, ladies (perhaps princesses), warriors, and so on. These figures were dedicated to particular deities in sanctuaries and temples.

One of the great artistic centers emerged at Elche (anc. Ilici), undoubtedly in the shade of a famous temple, in which were dedicated a great number of sculptures of male and female figures, gradually being brought to light by excavation. The work that stands out for its high quality among all these sculptures is the famous "Lady of Elche," the masterpiece of all Iberian sculpture (PL. 409). This is the bust of a woman, shown wearing a mantle rendered schematically with flattened pleats to emphasize the intricate character of the triple necklace of heart-shaped pendants and urn-shaped amulets. The head, covered by the characteristic high headdress (the Iberian *peineta*), has hair that is braided and rolled up in two large metal circlets, next to which hang cordons with gold tassels. Everything tends to accentuate the sumptuousness of the lady's attire. The face is one of great delicacy, the features fine and expressive — a long and narrow nose, a regular mouth with fine lips, high cheekbones, and cheeks ever so slightly sunken. The eyes, with prominent brows, contribute to an expression at once gentle and remote, with a slight suggestion of melancholy. Every detail denotes the hand of a great artist. The "Lady of Elche" is not an isolated work, as excavations carried out in recent years in Elche have brought to light numerous other sculptures of superlative quality and great originality. Though unfortunately in a poor state of preservation, they confirm the importance of this artistic center.

Other sources of great sculpture are the sanctuary of Cerro de los Santos and the one near Llano de la Consolación, both close to Yecla (Murcia). From the former come more than 300 pieces, now in Madrid (Mus. Arqueológico Nacional), mainly bearers of offerings — male and female figures, standing or sitting (PL. 408). These hieratic and in many cases crude works are of great interest as documents of classic Iberian sculpture. Their artistic merit varies: alongside pieces of quality — appreciable especially in the heads — are second-rate types, mass-produced and monotonously repeated. The greater part are the products of uninspired workshops, but are perhaps for that very reason highly realistic. Since these sanctuaries continued to be frequented during the centuries of Roman rule, there also appear among the votive offerings toga-clad figures showing the new influence (see HISPANO-ROMAN ART).

The most remarkable of this group in Madrid is the "Lady of Cerro" ("Dama del Cerro"), also known as the "Great Lady" ("Gran Dama"), a standing figure wearing a mantle that hangs from the shoulders, reaching to the ankles, arranged in front in regular graduated folds (PL. 408). Under the mantle she wears a double tunic with pleated border, which reaches to the shod feet appearing beneath its edge. On her head, instead of the characteristic *peineta*, she wears a diadem in Orientalizing style, with a fringe on the forehead and two lateral rosettes, from which hang five jeweled braids. Like the "Lady of Elche," the "Lady of Cerro" is adorned with a triple necklace recalling the Iberian silver torques. In her two hands she holds, at waist height, a ritual urn. Many other figures, both male and female, are depicted in the same attitude; an occasional group comprises two figures. A few wear the tall pointed headdress; all are fairly large, though smaller than life size.

Animal sculpture followed a parallel development in this classic period. Fantastic animals disappeared and their place was taken by representations of bulls, deer, rams, and lions, the last interpreted most freely and imaginatively, and with no great concern for realism. These animal sculptures appear with equal frequency in Andalusia and the southeast, and some seem to have been funerary, placed on tombs as steles.

The Celtic inhabitants of the Meseta later imitated this form of sculpture and developed a somewhat cruder animal art in which bulls, boars, and pigs — the fauna that constituted the economic basis of this pastoral people — are recurrent themes.

In the lower Guadalquivir Valley, a center rich in sculptural activity grew up around Osuna (anc. Urso); among its productions was an important complex of carved stone blocks and orthostats decorated with high reliefs. These pieces, reused later as construction material for the ancient walls, originally belonged to Iberian religious edifices. On the whole these reliefs are of great originality and far superior to the votive statues of Cerro de los Santos. Represented are a flute player, an acrobat, female offering bearers holding urns, warriors, and horsemen. Not all the pieces belong to the same period; some, especially one showing warriors armed with *caetrae* (short Spanish shields), obviously belong to the late Roman period and appear to reflect the military atmosphere of the Lusitanian wars.

In the sanctuary of Cigarralejo (Murcia) the small sandstone votive statues are all of horses, some with magnificently worked trappings. Some of them are in flat relief on stone slabs, but there are many that are freestanding figurines. This sanctuary was undoubtedly dedicated to a tutelary deity of horses.

So far as is known, large sculpture in bronze did not enter into Iberian art, but thousands of cast-bronze figurines were dedicated as votive gifts to sanctuaries in all parts of the Iberian territories (PL. 410). The greater part of these statuettes have come to light as the result of continued plundering by treasure-seekers, over many centuries, of the subterranean vaults of these temples; however, there have been assembled in the Museo Arqueológico Nacional of Madrid a number of important groups of these pieces obtained through more legitimate excavations. Some of these figurines were cast by the lost-wax process; others were cast in sandstone molds. Artistically, they are of uneven quality; their chief interest is iconographic. The male figures depict warriors, either nude or wearing a sagum, holding a curved sword or a lance, and with a shield (caetra) slung over the shoulder; other examples represent horsemen with javelin and shield, wearing either headgear or true helmets. The female figures present a great variety of types: nude (the smallest number) or clad in mantles and with the typical mantilla on the head. They are shown in numerous attitudes — offering bearers with a small bird held in the left hand; others with the right arm extended and the palm of the hand open, in the act of salutation, or with arms open and hands extended in supplication.

From an artistic point of view the quality, as has been said, is as varied as the attitudes. Some are well modeled and realistic, comparable to similar pieces found in Greek temples and distinguishable from the latter only by details of garment or headdress. Others are highly schematized and without originality. Their chronology is uncertain. It may be that their qualitative variation is economic rather than chronological in origin, that is, that the small schematized types which constitute the greater part were produced cheaply for the poorer classes, while the realistic statuettes, all of which are of larger proportions, were destined for the well-to-do. However, the sanctuaries were frequented over many centuries, during which art must naturally have undergone some evolution. Unfortunately the course of this evolution is completely unknown, since the provenance of the majority of the figurines has not been recorded. Together with the human figurines has been found a great number of animal representations, also in bronze, but in general more naturalistic in treatment. All these bronze figurines are small, the majority from 3 to 4½ in. high, the largest between 7 and 8 in. The pieces of larger size are rare exceptions.

Terra-cotta sculpture, too, was produced by the Iberians. This medium was used, as by the Greeks, in architectural decoration (antefixes) and also in the sanctuaries for votive artifacts and for funeral objects such as have been found in the necropolises. In the sanctuary of La Serreta, near Alcoy (Alicante), all the votive gifts were of terra cotta — female figures of very crude workmanship, hollow inside, represented with children in their arms and often accompanied by flute players. There are among these ex-votos more complex groups of several characters, but because of their fragility these have sustained much damage. The workmanship, crude and popular, is comparable to that of the bronze votive offerings.

Painting and ceramics. What remains of the painting is very little, limited as it is to the decorations in burial chambers (see above) and on rectangular cinerary urns such as the one from Galera (Madrid, Mus. Arqueológico Nacional). However, the high artistic level reached in figural ceramic painting warrants the assumption that great mural paintings existed in the temples and sanctuaries.

As for ceramics, these constitute one of the most important elements in the study of Iberian art. From the 6th century B.C. onward, the potter's wheel, which made possible the production of pottery on an industrial scale, was known and used. This production began in the colonial settlements, in imitation of imported Phoenician and Greek pottery in the south, and of Greek pottery throughout the east and in Catalonia. Local production, which imitated Ionian pottery decorated with opaque red bands, began early. From copying, the potters progressed to the creation of new and original forms, which they came to decorate likewise with simple red or purple bands, together with such motifs as circles and semicircles. The quality of the clay and their good firing technique enabled the Iberians even to surpass the imported pottery. Indeed, production soon reached a high degree of development and homogeneity in all the areas of Iberian civilization, the predominant type in the classic period being a ware decorated with a simple geometric pattern of bands. The great innovation of Iberian pottery was the appearance of vases with rich floral decoration and figural representations, at a time when the Mediterranean peoples had for the most part already passed the figural stage and were pursuing beauty in the ceramic art through monochrome glazes. In the southeast, in the neighborhood of Elche and Archena, workshops produced an ornate pottery, with decoration of a baroque type based on plant forms, in which the stems proliferate into sprays, tendrils, and spirals covering the whole surface of the vase. These motifs present a variety peculiar to Iberian art (PL. 399; FIG. 621; III, PL. 137; VI, PL. 106). In this group of ceramics, zoomorphic and human figures make their first appearance: on one vase wild animals of wolflike aspect pursue a strange bird with outspread wings; in a mythological or religious scene appears a goddess with wings in place of arms, or with one wing and one arm, holding a dove — a figure that has been identified, on no very convincing evidence, as a depiction of the goddess Tanith.

Farther north, in the eastern area proper, vase painting, which at Archena had for the first time represented scenes of warriors, underwent marked development in Liria (anc. Lauro), where a very interesting type of pottery was produced, with a variety of scenes from daily life: hunting, fishing, wrestling, religious pilgrimages, bands of musicians. The painters of Oliva attempted even more ambitious subjects, such as the siege of a fortress. The scenes, painted in a purplish red, reveal the varying artistic abilities of the painters. This pottery is not only of artistic interest, for inscriptions in Iberian accompany many scenes. However, these do not as yet contribute to their interpretation, since the language has still to be deciphered.

Similar painted pottery has recently been discovered in Castelillo de Alloza, a village in the province of Teruel; the designs are more schematized and seem to anticipate the abstract representations of Numantine painting. Pottery workshops also developed in the lower Ebro Valley, at Azaila. Here the painting was more severe but of excellent quality (PL. 400); it derived from the work of the centers of production in Lower Urgel and of Sidamunt in the Catalan region. The production of Iberian pottery continued until the 1st century B.C.

There has been much discussion of the chronology of Iberian figural painted pottery. Some experts regard it as simply an imitation of archaic Greek pottery; others, on the basis of certain figural elements, ascribe it to the first centuries of the Roman period. Recent studies of the material with which this pottery is associated stratigraphically warrant the tentative statements that the beginnings of the Elche-Archena ceramic group date from the 3d century B.C., that the Liria group is a little later, and that production continued through much of the 2d century B.C. This would mean that production began at the end of what has been called the "classic" period of Iberian art and, because of the lively market for this ware, persisted for a long time.

Minor arts. The character of Iberian art can be studied in many other manifestations which clearly demonstrate the special decorative spirit that consistently expresses itself through the same elements as are found in sculpture and ceramics. Although the Iberians had less skill in the techniques of working metal than did the Celtiberi of the interior, they were able to master certain technical secrets, such as applying niello work to copper and inlaying gold and silver in bronze and iron. In the making of arms and in their ways of decorating them, they were able to give free play to their exuberant imagination. The typical

Iberian curved swords, pointed, with a single cutting edge, have hilts in the form of birds or equine protomas and are ornamented with niello inlay of plant forms based on spirals, which is similar to the painted decoration of the pottery. Belt buckles, in the form of rectangular bronze plaques, were overlaid with silver foil in a repoussé decoration of motifs inspired by the eastern Mediterranean palmetto.

Gold and silver jewelry constitute another of the art forms of the Iberian world; these have survived in hiding places, or treasures, traces of which were once lost in the wars. In the gold jewelry a strong Greek influence is seen — always with an Orientalizing tinge. A typical piece is the Jávea diadem (Madrid, Mus. Arqueológico Nacional), which shows the interlace and spiral designs found in other art forms. The Iberian, with his taste for display and ornamentation, adorned himself, as is seen in the sculpture, with an abundance of fibulas, necklaces, and earrings which ancient authors described as very rich. The most famous treasures (Mogón, Fuensanta, Perotitos, Marrubial and Los Almadenes) are located in the mineral-rich southeast. Nearly all of them contained silverware, some of which (e.g., the series of plates from Abenjibre) is truly remarkable. An important collection of vases and paterae in gold-plated silver, showing a strong Greek influence, was found at Tivisa (Tarragona). One of the most famous paterae (PL. 407) has an engraved decoration depicting a scene from a now unknown Iberian myth, the elements of which are derived from the Mediterranean orbit, a confirmation of the Mediterranean filiation of all Iberian art.

Finally, another form characteristic of Iberian art is its coinage, which began as an imitation of the drachmas of Emporion, in a style altogether Greek but showed its originality through the introduction of indigenous symbols such as the wolf in the coins of Iltirda (Lérida) and in the inscriptions written in Iberian characters. When, under the Romans, Iberia adopted the Roman denary system, the Iberian denarii remained within the classic Hellenizing current. Particularly noteworthy are the obverses depicting a male head, the closest parallels of which are found in the sculptures of Cerro de los Santos, and the reverses depicting an Iberian horseman, the special symbol of all Iberian civilization (PL. 410).

Juan MALUQUER de MOTES

THE INDIGENOUS ART OF PRE-ROMAN SOUTHERN GAUL. The coast of southern Gaul, from the Alps to the Pyrenees, inhabited by a Ligurian people which from the 5th century onward was subject to Celtic and Iberian infiltration, maintained trade relations, over land routes, with the interior of Gaul from the beginning of the metal age. At the end of the 7th century B.C., and more especially in the 6th century, maritime relations were in effect with Asia Minor, Greece, and Etruria, which established trading stations on the coast in order to acquire the products that they lacked: precious metals, salt, salted fish, and medicinal herbs. The Phokaians founded the colony of Massilia (ca. 600 B.C.) in order to intercept, by way of the Rhone Valley, the traffic in tin coming from Cornwall, which had hitherto been monopolized by the Phoenicians.

Among the goods imported from the eastern Mediterranean the most important were wine amphoras and earthenware accessories for the consumption of wine; the place of origin of this class of pottery, none of it earlier than the end of the 7th century B.C., enables us to trace out the map of the trade relations of Massilia and the other trading stations on the coast, from Nicaea (mod. Nice) to Ruscino (mod. Roussillon), with the Phoenician coast (undoubtedly Tyre, represented exclusively by amphoras), Etruria (amphoras and black bucchero ware), Rhodes, Chios, Phokaia, Miletos, Corinth, Attica, Chalkis, and Laconia.

While — in contrast to the situation in the eastern part of the Iberian Peninsula — the Phoenician connection left no mark on the indigenous art of southern Gaul, its Celto-Ligurian inhabitants came under the twofold influence of eastern Greece and northern Italy. But these influences operated differently in different localities: thus only the Greek colony of Massilia seems to have had, from the 6th century B.C., Greek architectural and sculptural models; not before the 3d century B.C. did the indigenous inhabitants of the coast and of the Rhone Valley draw from Greco-Italian art forms the means of expressing their religious beliefs through architecture and sculpture. Moreover, the intensity of Greek penetration varied from the east to the west bank of the Rhone, and in fact in the sphere of sculpture and pottery the Mediterranean influence made itself felt more strongly in Provence and the lower valley of the Rhone.

Provincial Greek architecture and sculpture. Greek temple architecture is exemplified only by a capital of the Ionic order, carved in the local limestone of Cap Couronne, on the coast between Marseilles and the Étang de Berre, site of a quarry used by the Greeks from the 6th century B.C. The capital, of unusual dimensions (l. 5 ft., 11 in.; ht. at axis, 1ft., 10 in.), belongs to the archaic period (ca. 520 B.C.), as is shown by the proportions of the volutes and of the fluting, and is comparable to the capitals of Phokaia and Ephesos. The provincial imprint is seen in the acanthus that replaces the traditional palmette at the base of the volutes, a peculiarity also found in the Ionic capitals of the pronaos of the Doric temple of Athena (Ceres?) in Paestum. Imitation of the volutes of the Ionic order is found in the barbarian capitals of the columns of certain indigenous dwellings at Constantine, north of the Étang de Berre, and at Ensérune (late republican period). This taste for the Ionic takes on even greater interest from the fact that the Doric order was used for the capitals of the peristyle houses of Glanum (Saint-Rémy-de-Provence) and Ernaginum (Saint-Gabriel), in the Alpilles — these also dating from the late republican period.

The classical profile of the echinus of the Glanum capitals, of stone and Carrara marble, with an Ionic base and a horizontally faceted striated torus of the type found in the Temple of Artemis in Ephesos, shows the same taste for Greek archaism that prevailed in this "Little Greece of the West," as the area delimited by the Étang de Berre, the Rhone, and the Durance was called.

The statues that adorned these temples have not survived; all that has been recovered is a deposit of votive offerings (6th cent. B.C.) from a temple of Artemis, which included a number of steles of local limestone representing the goddess seated in a hieratic pose within a pedimented aedicula, sometimes holding a lion cub on her lap. These steles, which are similar to examples from the Ionian coast (Kyme, Klazomenai) and from Thasos, Rhodes, and Velia (Elea; a Phokaian colony on the Lucanian coast of Italy), are the sole evidence of the Greek art in this region; leaving no echo in indigenous sculpture, nor yet pointing the way for the development of a Massiliote art in the Greek tradition, they nevertheless undoubtedly awakened the sensibility of the Celts to a plastic art that was to express their beliefs in the indigenous pre-Roman sanctuaries.

Indigenous sanctuaries and sculpture. The oldest sanctuary in which human and animal figures are depicted is at Mouriès, on the Caisses plateau; it dates from the end of the Hallstatt period. Menhirs, steles, and some architectural fragments, later reused in the construction of a bastion (4th cent. B.C.), are covered with incised schematic representations of horses, in some cases mounted by horsemen wielding javelins. This stylized art has more affinity with Hallstatt art, and with certain incised carvings found in the Valcamonica (northern Italy), than with Greek art, and it is older than the art in the sanctuaries of the Saluvii — the tribe whose capital was Entremont — in which, under new influences, sculpture in the round unexpectedly makes its appearance.

If the art of these peripheral western provinces could be dated by comparison with Greek and Etruscan art, one would have to attribute to the archaic period a "xoanizing" statue in soft stone found in the sanctuary of the *oppidum* of Courtine at Ollioules. Wrapped in her garment, with arms hieratically pressed to her sides, this figure is related to the Hera of Samos in the Louvre, the votive statue dedicated to the goddess by Cheramyes (I, PL. 356), and even more closely to the Etruscan funerary statues from Chiusi, which comprise a human bust surmounting a figure enclosed in a cylindrical garment. The xoanon of Ollioules, which represents the oldest sculpture of a human figure in the round, was associated with other statues of a more fully evolved style, similar to those found in the sanctuaries of Roquepertuse and Entremont (PL. 411; III, PL. 111).

In the architectural and religious evolution of the Roquepertuse sanctuary, which rises in a rocky semicircle in the valley of the Arc, northeast of the Étang de Berre, is clearly shown the transition from a megalithic culture (represented by rude menhirs and small aniconic steles with chiseled corners, sometimes with cupule-shaped decorations) to an anthropomorphic one. The first sanctuary, an Iron Age structure, was remodeled in the 3d century B.C., the menhirs being reused for the construction of a terrace that supported a portico. It does not seem as if the architectural type of these propylaea was Greek-influenced, since apparently the Mouriès sanctuary already had had a portico, with piers and architraves.

The piers of Roquepertuse were erected with care and decorated with paintings (dentils, stars, horse protomas, birds). They support an architrave above which rises a large bird, sculptured in the round, on the point of taking flight (PL. 412). Another architrave is decorated with incised horse protomas, painted red. These are symbolic portrayals that undoubtedly refer to the ultimate journey (PL. 411).

Lined up in this sanctuary were statues of crouching human figures, on socles in the form of acroteria; though unfortunately they have come down to us headless and without arms, their attitudes can be reconstructed from the statues of Entremont. The question is, are these gods or heroized dead? The sanctuary with menhirs and the one with statues represent the same religious concept: the heroization of the deceased and his survival in the beyond. But these beliefs are expressed with a realism that indicates the persistence of the indigenous religion at the very gates of Massilia. The piers and architraves have niches molded in the shape of a human head, in which were inserted human skulls (doubtless mummified), in accordance with a Gallic custom reported by Posidonius in the 2d century B.C. This custom was prevalent among the Saluvii, as is seen at Entremont. Pillars and architraves with niches have also been found at Saint-Blaise, Saint-Rémy, and Cadenet (on the north bank of the Durance).

The preservation of the skull has the same significance as its sculptured representation: on one of the pillars at Entremont is a group of 12 *têtes coupées* without mouths; on the architrave in Nages (on the west bank of the Rhone) *têtes coupées* alternate with galloping horses; in the sanctuary of Saint-Chaptes (valley of the Gardon) and that of Substantion at Castelnau-le-Lez, near Montpellier, the dead are represented by busts, with the head either covered by a great leather casque or veiled, the eyes closed. Among the Saluvii this macabre realism reached a degree of expression unknown in Greek or Etruscan art and, for the present, unique in sculptural representation. Typical of the statues of Entremont, as well as of those of Roquepertuse, Ollioules, and Glanum, is the *tête coupée* with closed eyes, drawn features, and mouth closed in the last sleep. The hero at Entremont, dressed in leather armor, and the one at Roquepertuse, clad in a scapular decorated with geometric design, both hold in their right hands, poised on the knee, an iron object — either a scepter or the thunderbolt of Taranis, with which the dead man is identified — and each rests the left hand on a human *tête coupée*, a macabre representation of death. Whatever interpretation is given to this cult of the skull, it seems clear that the native peoples meant to preserve, by mummification or by figural representation, the spirit of the deceased residing in the head, from which they hoped to derive benefits in the future life, through the mediation of an ancestral relic or the sacrifice of a prisoner.

These statues show a considerable variety of techniques and styles. Since these cannot be regarded as the evolution of a school of sculpture, we must assume that the sculptors derived their ideas from Greek art of the 4th century B.C. and from Etruscan art. What seems certain is that in carving religious images the artists of the sanctuaries of the Saluvii did not follow a Celtic tradition.

The hair of the Entremont heads is sometimes striated like that of the kouroi, sometimes curled, or rolled into small snail-shaped clusters. Certain of the heads from Mont Garou, in the Bay of Sanary, and from Entremont, with their tightly closed lips and strong chins, recall the archaic heads from Chiusi rather than the idealized heads of Greek art. In the Roquepertuse herm the mouth is represented by a broad slit, in the heads of the heroes from Entremont (PL. 411) it is rendered in a more classical and naturalistic manner, and in a fine female head from Entremont with an oval profile and regular features (Switzerland, private coll.) the mouth is slightly open.

The Romanization of the coast in the republican period, with the consequent destruction of the sanctuaries, caused an abrupt interruption in the production of these statues, and by the time of the foundation of Aix and Narbonne (122–118 B.C.) it had ceased altogether. But the sculptured representation of the crouching hero seems to have survived in the Gallo-Roman art of the Celtic people: it is the prototype of limestone statues of a seated goddess with a ram of Quinssaines (Allier), of the crouching nude hero of the Hechtsheim sanctuary near Mainz (early 3d century of our era), and of the statuettes, in bronze and in terra cotta, representing a seated god, from Bouray (Seine et-Oise; III, PL. 113), from Quilly (Loire Atlantique), and from Vesoul (in the form of Hermes Kriophoros) — all magico-protective funerary images.

Minor arts. The pottery imported into the coastal trading stations and Massilia does not antedate the 7th century B.C. With the exception of a few Phoenician amphoras found with Etruscan amphoras and black bucchero ware, it falls into two groups: fine luxury ware from Rhodes, Chios, Samos, and continental Greece (Corinth, Attica, Chalkis, Laconia) and "colonial ware," decorated with painted bands or made of gray monochrome clay, from Phokaia and the Ionian coast. The only pottery imitated in Massilia and the native settlements of the lower Rhone Valley and of the coast was the colonial ware with late sub-Geometric, chiefly linear, decoration, also met with in Larisa in Aeolis. The thickness of the poorly fired clay, the inferior quality of the glaze and of the decoration, the muddy color, and the lack of slip make it easy to distinguish originals from imitations. The "Little Greece of the West" made no attempt to reproduce either the Attic or the Samos black-glazed ware. Massilia distinguished itself, however, in the creation of a type of wine amphora made of a micaceous clay, without slip; originally potbellied, the form later became ovoid, with a short neck ending in a ringed lip. This amphora was not derived from the Phoenician or Etruscan type with twisted handles attached to the upper part of the belly; rather it was modeled on the Rhodian-Ionian amphoras, shards of which are found in great quantity everywhere on the coast. This indicates that the Greeks had disseminated the art of vine growing and wine making and had provided the Massiliotes, from the 6th century B.C. on, with a new medium of exchange for their commerce with the interior. Viticulture soon spread to the regions of Ensérune and Narbonne, which in the 4th or 3d century B.C. began in turn to export their own wines.

The pattern of diffusion of the imported pottery and of the Massiliote imitations makes it possible, for the first time, to chart the trade routes between the coast and the interior of Gaul. The itineraries followed the valleys of the Rhone and its tributaries as far as Mont Lassois (Vix), Château-Salins, Heuneburg on the upper Danube, the upper Loire Valley (Le Puy Jœuvres), and the valleys of the Hérault, the Orbe, and the Aude. During the whole of the 6th century B.C. the fine bronzes from Rhodes, Samos, and continental Greece were probably transported by the Rhone Valley route: the oinochoai from Vilsingen and Kappel-am-Rhein, the caldron with griffin protomas from the tumulus of La Garenne-Colombes, and the crater from the nearby tumulus of Vix, which, on account of its situation at the confluence of the Saône and the Seine, certainly marks one of the tin routes from Cornwall to Massilia. These trade relations with the interior created, in the second half of the 6th century B.C., what might be described as an Ionian "atmosphere" — civilization is perhaps too strong a term — in a region limited to the coast and to the middle Rhone Valley.

Recent discoveries have revealed a certain number of native settlements where the handmade Hallstatt pottery of dark clay was replaced by a wheel-turned ware, finer in quality, of light-colored clay, with painted decoration derived from the late sub-Geometric pottery made in Larisa and in the Greek cities of the coast of Asia Minor — dentils, rows of dots and flecks (sometimes curvilinear), festoons, wavy lines of zigzag, and cables in relief. These settlements are situated along the Rhone: at Baumes-de-Venisse (Durban), Mourre-de-Séve, Le Pègue, on the east bank; at Nîmes, Roquemaure, and Soyons, on the west bank. There were undoubtedly among the native population Ionian elements who engaged in the transport of goods, and these may have supplied the ceramic craftsmen.

The same Ionian influence is perceptible in Languedoc, in a type of pottery called by turns "pseudo-Iberian" and "pseudo-Ionian." This type was turned on the wheel in reddish clay and has geometric decoration showing the effect of the Iberian influence (Ensérune, Cayla-de-Mailhac, Saint-Thibéry, Ruscino, etc.). This region corresponds roughly to the Roman province of Narbonensis, established under Augustus, differing in many aspects from the Three Gauls, whose capital was to be Lyons (anc. Lugdunum). It was already fully Romanized, over a Greek substratum, at the time of the Gallic wars.

Possibly this limitation of the zone of Ionian influence implies the complete exclusion of Celtic influence. We have seen that the Massiliote trade had carried Ionian pottery as far as the valleys of the Seine, the Doubs, and the Upper Danube. It is certain that the painted sub-Geometric decoration of the pottery found in Vix and in the upper valley of the Seine, dating from the 6th century B.C., is partly derived from Greek influence emanating from the "Little Greece of the West." Handmade or wheel-turned, this pottery was decorated with painted versions of the incised patterns of the Hallstatt ware, plus a series of geometric motifs: zigzags, rows of dots, hourglasses, squaring, and checkerboards, all of which are met with again in the painted pottery of the coast. The association of this pottery with Greek contributions — bronze vessels, Ionian pottery, and Massiliote amphoras — indicates that this region was at the junction of two great currents of civilization: the Hallstatt, issuing from the Alpine hills, and the Mediterranean, from the valley of the Rhone.

Fernand BENOIT

BIBLIOG. *General*: V. G. Childe, The Dawn of European Civilization, 6th ed., London, New York, 1957; G. E. Daniel, The Megalith Builders of Western Europe, London, 1958; G. Sieveking, The Migration of the Megaliths, in E. Bacon, ed., Vanished Civilizations, New York, 1963, pp. 299–322. *Sardinia: a. General*: M. Pallottino, La Sardegna nuragica, Rome, 1950; G. Lilliu, Preistoria sarda e civiltà nuragica, Il Ponte, VII, 1951, pp. 983–98; C. Zervos, La civilisation de la Sardaigne du début de l'énéolithique à la fin de la période nouragique, Paris, 1954; M. Guido, Sardinia, London, New York, 1964. *b. Special studies*: G. Lilliu, Uno scavo ignorato del dottore Ferruccio Quintavalle nella tomba di giganti di Goronna a Paulilatino (Cagliari), S. sardi, VIII, 1948, pp. 43–72; G. Lilliu, Il nuraghe di Barúmini e la stratigrafia nuragica, S. sardi, XII–XIII, 1952–54, pp. 90–469, pls. I–LXXX; G. Lilliu, Nuovi templi a pozzo della Sardegna nuragica, S. sardi, XIV–XV, 1955–57, pp. 197–288; G. Lilliu, Sculture della Sardegna nuragica, Cagliari, 1956; G. Lilliu, La "facies" nuragica di Monte Claro, S. sardi, XVI, 1958–59, pp. 3–266, pls. I–L; G. Lilliu, The Nuraghi of Sardinia, Antiquity, XXXIII, 1959, pp. 32–38; G. Lilliu, The Proto-Castles of Sardinia, Scientific Am., CCI, 1959–60, pp. 42, 62–69; G. Lilliu, I nuraghi: Torri preistoriche di Sardegna, Cagliari, 1962. *Corsica*: R. Grosjean, Corsica Revealed as the Home of the Statue-Menhir, ILN, CCXXX, 1957, pp. 269–71; R. Grosjean, Deux monuments circulaires mégalithiques de la moyenne vallée du Taravo (Corse), Gallia Préhistoire, XVI, 1958, pp. 1–38; R. Grosjean, Torre (île de Corse): Monument mégalithique du Bronze moyen, RA, LIV, 1959, pp. 15–40; R. Grosjean, Filitosa et les monuments protohistoriques de la vallée de Taravo, Promenades archéol., I, Paris, 1960, pp. 5–31; R. Grosjean, Filitosa et son contexte archéologique dans la vallée du Taravo, MPiot, LII, 1, 1961, pp. 1–102. *Balearic Islands: a. General*: J. Maluquer de Motes, La edad del bronce de las Islas Baleares, in R. Menendez Pidal, ed., Historia de España, I, part 1, Barcelona, 1947, pp. 736–51; M. Pallottino, El problema de las relaciones entre Cerdeña e Iberia en la antigüedad prerromana, Ampurias, XIV, 1952, pp. 137–55; J. Camón Aznar, Las artes y los pueblos de la España primitiva, Madrid, 1954, pp. 579–600. *b. Monuments of Minorca*: J. Martìnez Santa-Olalla, L'état actuel de l'archéologie dans l'île de Minorque, Comm. int. pour la préhistoire de la Méditerranée occidentale (1935), Barcelona, 1937, pp. 25–28; W. Fenn, Grafica prehistoria de España y el origen de la cultura europea, Mahon, 1950; J. Mascaró i Pasarius, Els monuments megalitics a l'Illa de Menorca, Barcelona, 1958. *c. Monuments of Mallorca*: P. Bosch Gimpera and J. Colominas Roca, Les fouilles de Majorque et la préhistoire des Iles Baleares, Comm. int. pour la préhistoire de la Méditerranée occidentale (1935), Barcelona, 1937, pp. 17–24; L. R. Amoros, La edad del bronce en Mallorca, Palma, 1952; G. Lilliu, Primi scavi del villaggio talaiotico di Ses Païsses (Artá-Maiorca), RIASA, N.S., IX, 1960, pp. 5–73, figs. 1–93. *Iberian civilization*: P. Bosch Gimpera, Etnología de la Peninsula Ibérica, Barcelona, 1932; G. and V. Reisner, Die Megalithgräber der iberischen Halbinsel: Der Suden, 2 vols., Berlin, 1943; J. Cabré Aguiló, Cerámica de Azaila (Corpus vasorum hispanorum, I), Madrid, 1944; J. Caro Baroja, Los pueblos de España, Barcelona, 1946; E. Cuadrado Diaz, Excavaciones en el Santuario ibérico del Cigarralejo (Mula, Murcia), Madrid, 1950; L. Pericot García, La España primitiva, Barcelona, 1950; C. C. Marquez, G. and V. Leisner, Los sepulchros megaliticos de Huelva, Madrid, 1952 (rev. by S. Piggott, Antiquity, XXVII, 1953, pp. 137–43); F. Alvarez Ossorio, Tesoros españoles antiguos en el Museo Arqueológico Nacional, Madrid, 1954; I. Ballester Tormo and others, Cerámica del Cerro de San Miguel, Liria (Corpus vasorum hispanorum, II), Madrid, 1954; A. García y Bellido, Arte ibérico, in R. Menendez Pidal, ed., Historia de España, I, part 3, Madrid, 1954, pp. 199–338; J. Maluquer de Motes, Los pueblos ibéricos, Madrid, 1954; A. do Paço and E. Sangmeister, Vila Nova de San Pedro: Eine befestigte Siedlung der Kupferzeit in Portugal, Germania, XXXIV, 1956, pp. 211–30; P. Bosch Gimpera, Todavía el problema de la cerámica ibérica, Mexico City, 1958; G. and V. Leisner, Die Megalithgräber der iberischen Halbinsel: Der Westen, 2 vols., Berlin, 1959–60; D. Fletcher, Problemas de la cultura ibérica, Valencia, 1960; Primer symposium de prehistoria de la Peninsula Ibérica (1959), Pamplona, 1960; B. M. Blance, Early Bronze Age Colonists in Iberia, Antiquity, XXXV, 1961, pp. 192–202; A. Arribas, The Iberians, London, New York, 1964. *Gaul*: G. Vasseur, L'origine de Marseille: Fondation des premiers comptoirs ioniens de Massalia vers le milieu du VIIe siècle, Marseille, 1914; M. Clerc, Massalia: Histoire de Marseille dans l'antiquité, 2 vols., Marseille, 1927–29; P. Jacobsthal and E. Neuffer, Gallia Graeca: Recherches sur l'hellénisation de la Provence, Préhistoire, II, 1933, pp. 1–64; J. Böhlau and K. Schefold, Larisa am Hermos, III, Berlin, 1942; F. Benoit, Dès chevaux de Mouriès aux chevaux de Roquepertuse: Recherches sur l'art et le symbolisme funéraire de la vallée du Rhone avant la conquête romaine, Préhistoire, X, 1948, pp. 137–210; H. Rolland, Fouilles de Saint-Blaise (Gallia, sup. 3), Paris, 1951; F. Benoit, Chronique archéologique, Gallia, 1954 ff.; R. Joffroy, Le trésor de Vix, Paris, 1954; L. Lengyel, L'art gaulois dans les médailles, Paris, 1954; F. Benoit, L'art primitif méditerranéen de la vallée du Rhone, 2d ed., Aix, 1955; J. Jannoray, Ensérune: Contribution à l'étude des civilisations de la Gaule méridionale, Paris, 1955; M. Louis, O. and J. Taffanel, Le premier âge du fer languedocien, 3 vols., Bordighera, Montpellier, 1955–60; H. Rolland, Fouilles de Saint-Blaise, 1951–1956 (Gallia, sup. 7), Paris, 1956; A. Varagnac and others, L'art gaulois, Paris, 1956; F. Benoit, Entremont capitale celto-ligure des Salyens, Aix, 1957; J. Moreau, Die Welt der Kelten, Stuttgart, 1958; M. Pobé and J. Roubier, Kelten-Römer, Olten, 1958; H. Rolland, Fouilles de Glanum (Gallia, sup. 11), 2 vols., Paris, 1958; P. M. Duval, EAA, s.v. Celtica, arte, II, 1959, pp. 457–67; G. E. Daniel, The Prehistoric Chamber Tombs of France, London, 1960; R. Joffroy, L'oppidum de Vix et la civilisation hallstattiene finale dans l'est de la France, Paris, 1960; H. Rolland, Glanum, Saint-Rémy, 1960; F. Villard, La céramique grecque de Marseille (VIe–IVe siècle), Paris, 1960; F. Benoit, Céramique peinte de la vallée du Rhone: Le "subgéométrique" rhodanien, Hommages à A. Grenier, I, Brussels, 1962, pp. 274–85.

Illustrations: PLS. 399–412; 8 figs. in text.

MEDITERRANEAN PROTOHISTORY. The origins of Mediterranean civilization and art, the fundament of the entire structure of the classical and the Western world, coincide with the development of the cultures of the Neolithic period and of the metal age in those regions of the Near East that gravitate, to a greater or lesser extent, toward the Mediterranean Sea and in the lands washed by its waters, especially the peninsulas and islands of southern Europe. The character of these cultures differs sharply from the character of the cultures within these areas in the more remote prehistoric period (see PREHISTORY): the progress of human society toward a systematic production of the means of subsistence through agriculture and stock raising gave rise to a sedentary way of life and to the concentration of population in urban centers and hence to the formation of stable traditions in architecture and in the figural arts as well. Since all these innovations had their most ancient focal centers within the Mediterranean area, it is particularly in connection with the Mediterranean world that we can apply the concept of a "prelude to history" — or protohistory — taking in the continental areas that, both to the east and to the north, border on the Mediterranean basin, of which they can be considered from a cultural point of view to be extensions, each with its own individual aspects and phenomena (see ASIATIC PROTOHISTORY; EUROPEAN PROTOHISTORY).

Priority is held by the eastern area, cradle of neolithic civilization, where the development of protohistoric cultures between the 7th and the 3d millennium B.C. reached, in the great historical civilizations of ancient western Asia (see ASIA, WEST: ANCIENT ART) and Egypt (q.v.), a culminating point in advance of all other areas. The Aegean and the Balkans were early exposed to the influences of this development, remaining at this cultural level far into the Bronze Age, when the first historical Greek civilization began to be formed (see CRETAN-MYCENAEAN ART). Cultural development in the countries of the western Mediterranean — the Italian area and Spain — was slower. Here the protohistoric era lasted until the beginning of the Iron Age (see ETRUSCO-ITALIC ART; MEDITERRANEAN, ANCIENT WESTERN). Nevertheless, a basic unity of artistic expression and cultural trends, spanning considerable intervals of time and space, links the various Mediterranean lands; this accounts for a certain well-defined imprint discernible in their artistic concepts, architectural forms, and figural sculpture — a unity that lasted until it was interrupted by the spread of Greek art and civilization in the course of the 1st millennium B.C., that is, until the beginning of the classical world.

SUMMARY. Geographical, chronological, and ethnic background of the early Mediterranean world (col. 633). The Near East, the Aegean, and the Balkans (col. 636). *The Neolithic origins of the Mediterranean cultures and their art forms. Individual neolithic cultural areas: a. Western Asia (Neolithic and Chalcolithic); b. Continental Greece (Sesklo); c. Crete; d. Southeastern Europe. Final phases of the Neolithic: a. Influence of Southeast European Bandkeramik culture in the Aegean area; b. Transition to the age of metals. Aegean-Anatolian cultural unity in the early Bronze Age: a. Anatolia; b. Crete (prepalatial period); c. The Cyclades; d. Continental Greece (Early Helladic); e. Influences in Europe. The middle Bronze Age: a. Anatolia; b. Crete and the Cyclades; c. Continental Greece (Middle Helladic and the beginnings of Greek civilization); d. Late cultural developments in the peripheral areas of the Aegean and in the Balkans. Characteristic elements of protohistoric Mediterranean art and architecture: a. The megaron; b. The tholos; c. Plastic art as represented by statuettes of the fertility goddess; d. Spiral and meander decoration; e. Conclusions.* The central and western Mediterranean (col. 664). *The neolithic cultures: a. Early neolithic; b. Sicily and southern Italy; c. Northern Italy and western Europe. The early age of metals: a. Early phases in Sicily and southern Italy; b. The megalithic civilization of Malta; c. Sardinia; d. Subsequent phases of the early age of metals in Sicily and Malta; e. The aëneolithic cultures and the beginnings of the Bronze Age in Italy; f. Southern France; g. Spain (the Almería and Bell-beaker cultures). The late Bronze Age and the transition to the Iron Age: a. Sicily; b. The Apennine culture; c. End of the Bronze Age and beginning of the Iron Age in Italy; d. The western Mediterranean.*

GEOGRAPHICAL, CHRONOLOGICAL, AND ETHNIC BACKGROUND OF THE EARLY MEDITERRANEAN WORLD. The current division of the periods of the prehistoric and protohistoric era into Paleolithic, Mesolithic, Neolithic, Bronze Age, and Iron Age is valid only in the most general way in the Mediterranean world. Aside from the fact that these periods have no chronological limits that are universally accepted or universally applicable, there are numerous special applications and subnomenclatures, particularly with regard to the Bronze Age. In Mesopotamia the terms "Bronze Age" and "Iron Age" are not generally used, because in this region the periods represented fall within the scope of recorded history; it seems preferable in the historical context to refer to the "Sumerian period" and the "Semitic period." (A parallel situation obtains in Egypt.) In the other regions of western Asia, as well as in the Aegean and Balkan regions, the Bronze Age is subdivided into early, middle, and late. In Crete, the Bronze Age has been broken down by Evans into Early, Middle, and Late Minoan; for continental Greece, Wace and Blegen named the parallel divisions Early, Middle, and Late Helladic. Early, Middle, and Late Cycladic are used for the islands, and for Macedonia, Early, Middle, and Late Macedonian. The majority of these classifications have proved themselves appropriate and useful. The classification for Asia Minor, on the other hand, remains controversial. Here, instead of the early Bronze Age or the Chalcolithic, the early Copper Age is spoken of (rather than Aëneolithic, which is preferred for the central and western Mediterranean areas); although not inappropriate, the term "Copper Age" is not really useful, since in all early Bronze Age cultures copper was only gradually replaced by bronze. For the Bronze Age in Asia Minor, M. J. Mellink favors the designations Early, Middle, and Late Anatolian. It should be borne in mind that the term "Middle Anatolian" is applied to the Cappadocian pottery and Kültepe cultures, as well as the earliest Hittite culture, while Late Anatolian is the period of the Hittite Empire. Moreover, the Minoan palaces belong to Middle and Late Minoan, and, finally, the Late Helladic is the Mycenaean culture and the period is therefore also designated as Mycenaean.

For the western Mediterranean areas (Italy and Spain) the classification and terminology are less clear-cut and are virtually still in a formative stage. Instead of the traditional division into Neolithic, Aëneolithic (for the final phase of Neolithic), Bronze Age, and Iron Age, the tendency (at least as regards Italy) is to use a division into early, middle, and late Neolithic, an early metal age (including the early Bronze Age), late Bronze Age, and an age of transition to the Iron Age.

The interrelations of the main divisions of protohistory as it unfolded in the Mediterranean world are graphically summarized in the table below.

Mesopotamia	Syria	Anatolia	Cyclades	Crete	Continental Greece	Macedonia	Italian Area
Neolithic	Neolithic	Neolithic	Neolithic	Neolithic	Neolithic	Neolithic	Neolithic
Chalcolithic	Chalcolithic	Chalcolithic					
Historical times	Early Bronze Age	Early Anatolian	Early Cycladic	Early Minoan	Early Helladic	Early Macedonian	Early Metal Age (Aëneolithic and early Bronze Age)
	Middle Bronze Age	Middle Anatolian	Middle Cycladic	Middle Minoan	Middle Helladic	Middle Macedonian	
	Late Bronze Age	Late Anatolian	Late Cycladic	Late Minoan	Late Helladic (Mycenaean)	Late Macedonian	Late Bronze Age and transition to Iron Age
			Iron Age				

The chronology of protohistory presents complex problems. In the modern method of dating by radiocarbon (C 14) a rather wide margin of error (up to plus or minus 250 or more years) has to be allowed for. The approximateness of the results is also contributed to by the variety of ways in which the specific materials used for examination are selected and preserved by researchers and by differences in the techniques used in the various laboratories. Thus, at least for the more recent period, the historical method, based on the dates of the rulers of Egypt and of Mesopotamia, remains the surest. The Egyptian sequence places the beginning of the 1st dynasty at about 2850 B.C. For Mesopotamia the list of kings can be traced back as far as 2500 B.C., plus or minus 45 years. Everything belonging to earlier periods (including Egypt and Mesopotamia) must be dated on the basis of criteria derived from the correlation of various stylistic elements or by the radiocarbon method. In Egypt, for the period beginning in 2850, it is possible, on the basis of imports and exports of goods, to establish temporal links with Crete, and from that island with other Aegean locatities; in Mesopotamia such links exist with Asia Minor and the Aegean area. It has thus been possible to establish a series of dates around the Mediterranean basin that enable us to check, from two points of reference, the chronology of the Aegean world.

According to present calculations, and also on the basis of radiocarbon tests, the Neolithic age began, in western Asia and in Egypt, at least as early as the 6th millennium B.C. and possibly even as early as the 7th. At the beginning of the Neolithic age pottery was as yet unknown. The Chalcolithic age in western Asia substantially spans the 4th millennium B.C. The early Bronze Age began in Anatolia perhaps about 2700 B.C., in Crete, toward 2600 B.C., while on the Greek mainland its beginnings are not earlier than 2500. This is because in Asia Minor (especially in the eastern part) metalworking techniques were more advanced than in the other western regions. The middle Bronze Age also began earlier in Asia Minor — about 2200 B.C. — than in the other areas. The Middle Minoan (ca. 2100) similarly anticipated the Middle Helladic (ca. 1950). The late Bronze Age began everywhere about 1600 B.C.; the Iron Age about 1200. For the West there exist only dates synchronous with the eastern Mediterranean chronology (apart from radiocarbon dating). The beginning of the age of metals can be established toward the end of the 3d millennium B.C., the late Bronze Age about 1400 B.C., and the final phase of the Bronze Age and the transition to the Iron Age can be placed at about 1250 B.C.

The oldest ethnic ties within the Mediterranean world can be recognized in the relation between the Basque and Caucasian languages and in the concordance, from Spain to Asia Minor, of a number of place names and nominal suffixes. It is unlikely that these relations were established by later migrations of peoples; they were probably, at least in part, already established in Paleolithic or Mesolithic times. The cultures that rose in the eastern Mediterranean during the Neolithic and the early Bronze Age owe their creation to the initiative of the indigenous populations of eastern Anatolia, Syria, northern Mesopotamia, Palestine, and Egypt. From these regions, beginning in the 5th millennium B.C., cultures spread west and northwest, reaching as far as southern and southeastern and even central Europe. In the 4th millennium B.C. a further stimulus was given to this expansion by the Semitic culture, whose diffusion, however, remained limited to the East. In the 3d millennium B.C. certain elements of the ribbon-decorated-pottery (*Bandkeramik*) culture (see below) were found even in the Aegean area and in certain areas of the Italian peninsula.

From the end of the 3d millennium B.C, the expanding Indo-European peoples gained the upper hand everywhere, and this led, among other developments, to the formation of the Hittite people in Asia Minor, to the earliest Greek beginnings (ca. 1950 B.C.) in Hellas, and to the emergence of the Italic peoples, in the course of the 2d millennium B.C.

Fritz SCHACHERMEYR (with additions)

THE NEAR EAST, THE AEGEAN, AND THE BALKANS. *The Neolithic origins of the Mediterranean cultures and their art forms.* For the early prehistoric periods, Paleolithic and Mesolithic, archaeological evidence in these regions remains scarce, except in Egypt (see PREHISTORY). In Greece the available material is limited to the finds from the banks of the river Peneios and from a cave in Boeotia. Richer material has come to light in Palestine. The researches of R. J. Braidwood have made available abundant material from Kurdistan (some of which has not yet been published).

In the 7th and 6th millenniums B.C. a change of historic portent took place in the Near East: man progressed from the economic stage of food gathering to the stage of systematic production of food by means of agriculture and stock raising. In this new phase of cultural evolution, human groups entered upon a sedentary existence. As food producers, men built permanent dwellings and founded villages, some of which even grew into cities. At the same time, the number of their domestic tools — of stone, bone, and wood — greatly increased. In the social organization the possession of soil and lands assumed importance. From the fact that in the early part of this phase pottery was as yet unknown, whereas the manufacture of stone vessels had reached a very high level, it is sometimes given the designation "stone vessel culture." The most significant documentation of this culture, also termed "prepottery," has been found at Jericho (PL. 413), where it has been possible to establish the existence of solid city walls and towers built with great technical skill. Similar settlements have come to light at Abu Ghosh in Israel, at Ras Shamra (anc. Ugarit) in Syria, and at Jarmo in Iraq (Kurdistan). Even in this very remote epoch we find a few early samples of figural sculpture, chief among them the unbaked clay figurines representing the great fertility goddess (e.g., at Jarmo). In Jericho human skulls, detached from the rest of the skeleton, were worked, in an effort to reproduce the individual features of the deceased, with fine clay to replace the flesh and with bitumen and pieces of shell for eyes (PL. 414). It is interesting to note that in this very early stage of human culture there evolved a type of plastic portraiture and a degree of realism to which much later cultures would return, using, of course, different means.

A parallel transition from the food-gathering to the food-producing level took place (perhaps under West Asian influence) in Egypt and in northern Africa in general. In these regions, however, the development was not so rapid as in western Asia (see EGYPT).

The primacy of the Near East in the transition to agriculture and the raising of animals can be explained in part by the fact that certain types of cereals, and sheep and goats as well, originally came from this region. Crop rotation for the renewal of the soil being as yet unknown, the early agriculturists were obliged continually to seek out virgin soil to clear and bring under cultivation. The agriculture of western Asia was, therefore, of an expanding nature. As it spread, it must have found plentiful sustenance in the rich alluvial soils of western Anatolia, the Balkan Peninsula, and perhaps along the banks of the lower and middle Danube — though the only traces of prepottery agricultural cultures that have so far come to light in these areas are on the Aegean island of Skyros and in Thessaly (Argissa, near mod. Argura; Soufli-Magoula). This diffusion marks the beginnings of that Anatolian cultural movement which, in the 5th and 4th millenniums B.C., brought an ever-increasing number of migrating people — and soon also traders with wares to barter (along with cultural influences) — from western Asia to the Aegean areas and southern Europe. But western Asia was always in the cultural vanguard, while the lands to the west and northwest were at first cultural importers, not cultural exporters. It can be assumed that the appearance in the Aegean area and in southeastern Europe of the agricultural religion of the East, with its Great Mother deity — the Earth Mother, or fertility goddess — and the development, in those regions, of a systematic type of agriculture, with varieties of suitable staple cereals, were connected with these agricultural migrations.

The invention of pottery (see CERAMICS), a great step forward, also occurred in western Asia. Concomitantly, the statuettes of the mother goddess and the clay stamp seals which had hitherto been fashioned in unbaked clay were made more durable by firing. More important was the application of the technique to the manufacture of pottery vessels: the first phase of the Neolithic age — the lithic (stone) phase — gave way to the second, or pottery, phase. The manufacture of clay pottery soon reached a high technical level, as is seen in the quality of the fabric, the skilled firing, the thinness of the walls, and the polished finish. In a few cases a red paint was used. Sometimes the surface decoration was incised, apparently with fingernails, tiny sticks, or some other similar means. Pottery of this type appears, for example, at Mersin in Cilicia; it soon spread from the east toward the Aegean area, being found especially in Thessaly. It is also found in the hinterland of Dalmatia — in the Balkans, along the lower and middle Danube — and at the same time it seems to have appeared in the coastal regions of the central and western Mediterranean (see below, *The central and western Mediterranean: a. Early neolithic*). The typical vessel was the hemispherical bowl, with or without feet. There was also a spherical or oval base with a flaring conical neck, sometimes with circular foot. The figurines of the Great Mother, the representations of the goddess in relief on the sides of clay pots, and the use of clay stamp seals now spread as far as the Danubian territories. In Greece this cultural stage appears as the Proto-Sesklo phase (the term "Pre-Sesklo," in common use, is less satisfactory), in Serbia as the Starčevo I, in Hungary as the Körös, in Bulgaria as the Kremikovci, and in Romania (up to southern Russia) as the Cris. Much later even central Europe was influenced by these cultural currents from the southeast. The art of pottery entered central Europe in the form of the bowls, hemispherical and spherical and without feet, of the *Bandkeramik* culture (see below). Not only was the image of the mother goddess diffused in this region; the religious symbol of the double ax, of Eastern origin, also appears.

Another cultural wave, characterized by incised decoration of pottery and by particular vase forms with spread necks, vertical necks, and so on, seems to have reached Egypt and the other parts of northern Africa at the same time. It affected Crete (see below) and, especially, influenced the central and western Mediterranean, including Sardinia, Corsica, the Balearic Islands, and Spain, and beyond to other areas of western and central Europe.

Individual neolithic cultural areas: a. Western Asia (Neolithic and Chalcolithic). The development of the neolithic cultures of western Asia was a very concentrated and progressive one. It was here that man early learned to use the metal found in great quantities in Asia Minor, Armenia, and Iran; as early as the 4th millennium B.C. gold, silver, and copper appeared, in the shape of wire and jewelry and in other forms. It is the use of metal in western Asia in this period that accounts for the use here of the term "Chalcolithic." Other arts and crafts, such as weaving, basketry, and the decoration of clay pottery with a design of interlaced motifs painted in rich colors emerged contemporaneously. This development began with the Hassuna style — named after the archaeological site in Assyria (mod. Iraq) — and reached its apex in the styles of Samarra on the Tigris (Iraq), and of Tell Halaf on the Khabur (Syria; PL. 416). In the Tell Halaf style, the fertility goddess appears in excellently fashioned statuettes and in reliefs on clay vessels; the finest representations are, however, the polychrome painted decorations on pottery, which constitute a high point in decorative art of all time. There are also some important examples of architecture. In the subsequent al-'Ubaid phase (PL. 415) the potter's craft turned toward more utilitarian and practical designs and mass production, but architecture continued to flourish. Temples that were erected indicate that the builders knew the principles of vaulting. Technical knowledge of fortification was noteworthy. A further stage of evolution was reached early in the 3d millennium B.C. in the Uruk (Warka) phase. By this time the invention of the potter's wheel had caused a decline in the originality of the ceramics, which also suffered from the competition of the newly developed metalworking techniques (see also MESOPOTAMIA).

The styles and cultures of Tell Halaf and of al-'Ubaid spread as far as the Mediterranean; important evidence has come to light at Ugarit and Tell esh-Shaykh (Syria), as well as at Mersin in Cilicia. Even eastern Anatolia — to judge from finds at Malatya (anc. Milid) and Fraktin — seems to have been within this cultural area, as was Armenia (Tilkitepe).

In southwestern Anatolia we find the Hacılar culture, the earliest product of which was a monochrome pottery. Later a painted pottery similar to that of Mersin was produced (PL. 416), and there appears a peculiar tendency toward freely organized grotesque designs, unique in this period. Here, too, the clay figurines of the great fertility goddess reached a high artistic level. At Çatal Hüyük, in southern Anatolia, lively mural paintings representing dances (XI, PL. 297), hunting scenes, and other activities, in a schematic style have come to light; they can be attributed to a neolithic phase earlier than the classic Hacılar phase. Alabaster statuettes and seals (pintaderas) of this earlier phase have also been found. The paintings are the earliest examples of this art form yet found in the eastern Mediterranean region (Mellaart, 1962). A separate province is the Cypriote Neolithic (see CYPRIOTE ART, ANCIENT): in the 4th and 3d millenniums B.C. an original culture developed in Cyprus, with circular dwellings built of stone, surmounted by a tholos (Khirokitia; PL. 413), as well as fine pottery of both the impressed and the painted type (Erimi).

b. Continental Greece (Sesklo). The Sesklo culture, which emerged on the Greek mainland during the 4th millennium B.C., is a continuation of the Proto-Sesklo, the distinction lying in the fact that in the latter, under Eastern influence (as at Mersin and Hacılar), a painted pottery (mainly red) was developed. The most important sites where Sesklo culture finds have been made are in Thessaly, chiefly at Sesklo, Tsangli, Otzaki-Magoula, Arappi-Magoula, and Argissa. In central Greece and in the Peloponnesos similar finds have been made at Halai, Orchomenos, Chaironeia (III, PL. 122), Eutresis, Makri, Marathon (grotto of Pan), Gonia, Corinth, Prosymna, Lerne (PL. 416), and Asea. Because of certain local stylistic differences the term "Sesklo style" is applied in a narrow sense to Thessaly, the style in central Greece being termed "Chaironeian" and in the Peloponnesos "Lerne (Lerna)."

Textiles, pottery, and sculpture figure in the art forms of the Sesklo culture. No original examples of textiles have been preserved, but their decorative motifs, such as interlace, banded, and dentate patterns, appear on the painted pottery. A large, spaced zigzag design, encircling the vessel horizontally is the decoration found on most examples; on others the painting gives the impression of imitating net or lace. As in the Hacılar pottery, the decoration is sometimes divided into vertical panels, suggesting metopes. Curvilinear motifs are virtually unknown; the spiral and the meander do not appear at all. Compared with the vivid ceramic painting found at Hacılar, the decoration of the Sesklo pottery is sober and refined. The same refinement characterizes the very forms of the vessels. The earliest examples were spherical, semispherical, and oval — forms also found in the Proto-Sesklo — but originally of Eastern derivation. The conical or cylindrical neck and foot now assumed an important role in the structure of the base, and splendid wide ribbon handles of fine design appear. While the Tell Halaf style is distinguished by its wealth of ideas and the Hacılar by its imagination, the Sesklo style stands out for its clarity, which can be regarded as classic.

An even more important product of the Sesklo culture is the small-scale sculpture. The majority of the figurines are idols of the great fertility goddess (PL. 423), in which the sex is emphasized and the arms are folded over or just below the breasts. Together with these have been found a number of idols representing a young ithyphallic god, as well as some animal figurines (mostly oxen, a few bulls), probably votive offerings. The Sesklo statuettes present certain peculiar qualities in their elaboration of the female figure. While farther east such statuettes continued to be mass-produced, in Sesklo

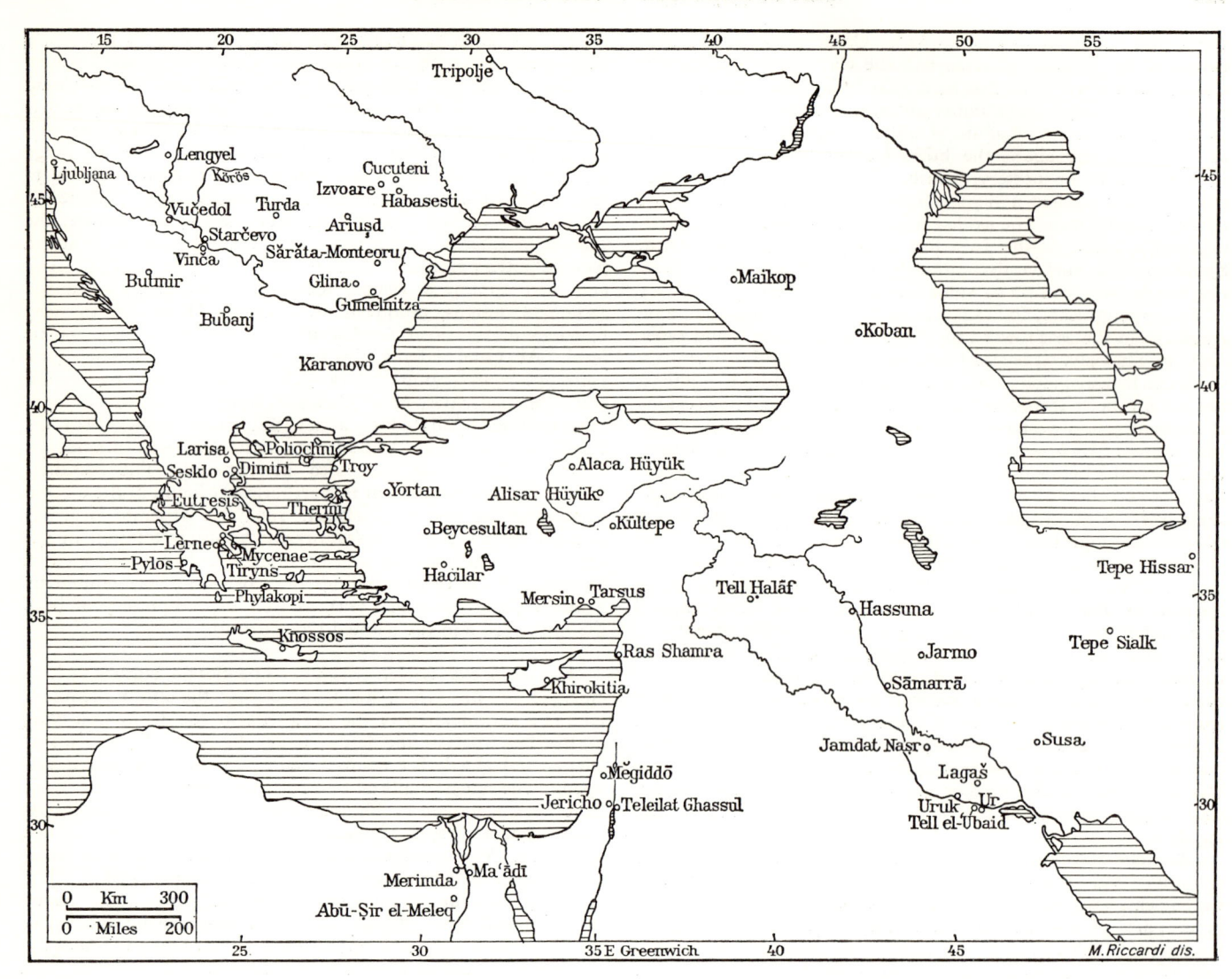

Eastern Mediterranean basin and western Asia, principal archaeological sites and protohistoric art centers.

it would appear that the best pieces were created individually with particular care, no piece being exactly like another. They show an ingenuous naturalism; the artist observes the subject without abstraction but recognizes the existence of a common ideal of female beauty, as is seen particularly in the modeling of the buttocks and the contours of the abdomen. Together with this sculpture in the round, on a high artistic level, are found representations of the mother goddess executed in relief on the sides of clay pots, probably vessels used for religious rites. The majority of these have survived only in fragments. It is possible that the image of the goddess with upraised arms which later became so usual in the Aegean cultural area (especially on vessel walls) had its origins in this period. In architecture, construction with stone or unbaked brick, depending on the availability of the materials, predominates. The commonest type of building is a large square house, with walls buttressed probably for protection against earthquake as well as for subdivision of the interior space. At Otzaki the prototype of the megaron is found.

Metal is very rare in the Sesklo culture, and is found only in small fragments. For this reason the Sesklo culture is considered neolithic, although it is contemporaneous with the Chalcolithic cultures of Hacılar, Mersin, Tell Halaf, and al-'Ubaid. The bearers of the Sesklo cultures were originally inhabitants of Anatolia; their emigration from eastern Asia Minor is placed partly in the Proto-Sesklo period and partly in the Sesklo period proper. Possibly they intermixed with the local paleolithic population. From an art-historical point of view the exceptional importance of the Sesklo culture lies in the fact that its artifacts are the earliest forerunners of the Hellenic art of later times, which was rooted much more deeply in the Mediterranean than in the Indo-European component of the Greek people.

Metal vessels made their first appearance toward the end of the Sesklo period. If not produced locally, these were probably imported from Asia Minor. They affected ceramic styles: a new type of black monochrome pottery showing the influence of metalware was produced (see below). Together with this has been found another type: a ware painted in a brown color over a brown ground, with predominantly vertical decoration. The most beautiful examples of this type come from the grotto of Pan in Marathon.

c. Crete. Crete does not belong to the Sesklo cultural area. Lying between western Asia, Egypt, and Sesklo, it constitutes an autonomous cultural province, not only on account of its geographical position but also on account of its cultural components. A great number of emigrants from eastern Anatolia must have reached the island; in fact, Cretan place names (Tylissos, Knossos, Pyranthos, Rhethymna) share the "Aegean" character of those of Anatolia and continental Greece. Several Cretan ceramic forms show the influence of the Anatolian cultural spread. On the other hand, Crete did not accept painted pottery; the Cretans preferred to imitate the Egyptian type of incised ware with white incrustation. Egyptian influence is also evident in the shapes of the vases; it played a particular part in the formation of a taste for stone vessels; imported at first, these were subsequently imitated locally on the island.

In sculpture there are the same figurines of the Great Mother as appear in western Asia and continental Greece, but they do not equal the artistic maturity of the best Sesklo pieces. The animal statuettes (doves, dogs, cattle), undoubtedly votive, are excellent; they reveal exceptional powers of observation and a definite preference for types rather than emphasis upon the individual. A direct connection exists between this work and the genre type and realistic animal scenes of the Minoan era. In architecture Crete does not seem to have been influenced by western Asia, Sesklo, or Egypt. The layout and plan of the multiple-roomed dwellings that already appear in neolithic Crete show the same internal structural concepts later found in the Minoan palaces. It is in architecture that the earliest purely Cretan artistic expression is revealed. Nevertheless, when viewed as a whole the Cretan neolithic appears to be a less closed culture than the contemporaneous Sesklo. Being more exposed, Crete was affected by numerous influences, and its culture therefore, with the exception of the architecture, had more possibilities for future development. The Egyptian influences on Cretan art can be understood only in the light of that second great cultural movement (mentioned above) which spread from Egypt and the whole of northern Africa along the shores of the Mediterranean.

d. Southeastern Europe. So far as is known, the Sesklo culture spread as far as the mountainous area of southern Macedonia (Servia). A similar culture probably flourished in Macedonia proper (only a few scattered shards have been found), and still farther north — in what is now Bulgaria, Serbia, Hungary, Romania, and southern Russia — flourished the above-mentioned Kremikovci, Starčevo, Körös, and Cris cultures. This is the period of the *Bandkeramik* culture in central Europe. Through the influence of the Hacılar and Sesklo cultures, painted pottery found its way into the Kremikovci, Starčevo, and Cris cultures. It was decorated in black or white, always on a red ground. Farther northwest, painted pottery appeared late and was rare. The Sesklo pottery forms, with their stereotyped division into neck, belly, and foot, appear in all these cultures, at least in the early stages, except the *Bandkeramik*, in which the foot is never, and the neck rarely, seen. Clay stamp seals are found throughout the Aegean world, up to the Körös area. Vases with relief decoration depicting the fertility goddess with upraised arms, as well as female figurines, are found as far north and west as the Austrian and Czechoslovakian zones of the *Bandkeramik* area.

In these more northerly cultural provinces there were certain innovations which appear not to have originated in the southeast but to have been autochthonous. Thus in Romania and Bulgaria a chip-carving technique, originally devised for wooden vessels, is found in pottery, and gradually the products of the new Boian and Vadastra (or corded-ware) cultures supplanted the Cris and Kremikovci types. Throughout the Starčevo, Körös, Cris, and *Bandkeramik* cultural areas is found a vessel characteristic of the region — a typical peasant's receptacle designed to be carried on the back. The spiral and the meander motif appear repeatedly everywhere in this region. They are found in the incised decorations of the *Bandkeramik*, and later also in the pottery of Boian. In the Cris pottery they are painted, in white or black. At Starčevo and Kremikovci the spiral is used less frequently than the meander. The appearance of these two motifs is accompanied by a new feeling for their complementary relations. Designs in which the spiral and the meander replace the zigzag, like those found in the cultures from Tell Halaf to Sesklo, derive from basketry patterns.

This is the first appearance in neolithic art of a mode of decoration which goes back as far as the Paleolithic age (see PREHISTORY) and the development of which was to extend into Minoan, Mycenaean, and ultimately, Greek art.

The diffusion of the latest type of *Bandkeramik*, with large dots suggesting the heads of musical notes (*Notenkopfkeramik*), in the widespread area of the Cris culture and the increased exchange of the spiral and meander styles of southeast Europe created a koine of "Southeast European *Bandkeramik*," which can be subdivided into the following local styles (at least in part coextensive): Bükk in Slovakia (V, PL. 153), Lengyel in Moravia and western Hungary (V, PL. 154), Tisza in eastern Hungary, "West Transylvanian pottery culture," Ariușd (Erösd) in eastern Transylvania, Gumelnitza in Walachia and Bulgaria, Cucuteni in Moldavia (PL. 416; X, PL. 433), and Tripolje in southern Russia (III, PL. 122; V, PL. 167; see also ASIATIC PROTOHISTORY and EUROPEAN PROTOHISTORY). Within this Southeast European *Bandkeramik* zone must be included both the Dalmatian and the Bosnian areas. On the other hand, the Vinča area (in mod. Serbia) shows a fairly autochthonous character: the meander and (at a later date) the spiral appear, but the dominating feature is a polished monochrome pottery imitating metalware.

Final phases of the Neolithic. a. Influence of Southeast European Bandkeramik *culture in the Aegean area.* In the period 2800–2400 B.C., approximately, the bearers of the Southeast European *Bandkeramik* culture began to migrate toward the Aegean Sea. In general this was not so much a large-scale invasion as a series of movements of small groups who joined together either while in transit or on their arrival at their new settlements. Groups from Bükk, the Tisza region, Transylvania, Boian, and Vadastra seem to have taken part in this migration. Their most important goal was Thessaly, where they established a large number of settlements. From Dimini — the best-known of these settlements and one of the most important archaeological sites in Thessaly — the cultural aspect of this migration has taken its name. At Dimini, on the summit of a hill, is a chieftain's megaron, entered from a central court surrounded by several fortified walls (FIG. 655). Between these walls are a number of dwellings for members of the retinue. The pottery produced by the Dimini peoples (III, PL. 122) is not homogeneous in character, for their ethnic origins are diverse. Certain types show the influence of Tisza, or West Transylvanian, ware; others recall the pottery of Boian and Vadastra. The forms of the vessels ("fruit stands" and cups of corded ware and reentrant borders) are of the types found in the Danubian territory, despite the fact that during this period all other pottery forms produced in southeastern Europe as well as in the Aegean area (already partly influenced by metal techniques) were based on Anatolian models. Dimini ware is scarce in central Greece; more of it has been found in the northwestern part of the Peloponnesos (e.g., at Corinth, Prosymna, and Gonia). The other parts of the Greek peninsula were probably never penetrated by the Dimini migrants.

Shortly after the Dimini migrations, other groups reached the Aegean from Gumelnitza. Their culture, in addition to the Boian, embraced chiefly Walachia and Bulgaria. The Gumelnitza peoples migrated to the Thracian and Macedonian coasts of the Aegean. Characteristic of the culture are, among other features, graphite painting and the spiral motif. Another group of migrations seems to have started at the same time from the Lengyel area and from the Dinaric coastal area. It moved, partly overland and partly by sea (perhaps across the Adriatic), toward the Cyclades, where these migrants gave impetus to the Syros culture, with art characterized by recurring and interlaced horizontal spirals. Lengyel influences are also evident in the Rachmani culture in Thessaly, but here they seem to have merged with those from Gumelnitza.

In Anatolia only one isolated instance of *Bandkeramik* influence has so far come to light: in the southeastern part of the peninsula we find the sole evidence of a *Bandkeramik* migration (possibly of Gumelnitza origin) to this area.

In general, we can be sure that the spiral and meander reached the Mediterranean with the migrations from the Danube area. As will be seen, these two decorative elements were to have a particularly rich development in the Mediterranean area.

b. Transition to the age of metals. In Greece and the Balkans, during what is called the Chalcolithic period in western Asia, the cultures were still almost entirely in a neolithic stage. In western Asia the term "metal age" is not properly applied even to the Chalcolithic period, assuming, as this writer does, that the age of metals is entered upon only when metalworking techniques have been developed to the point where the manufacture of utilitarian objects of metal is an activity of the first importance and where metal vessels are fashioned by forging and hammering rather than by the older method of casting. As for types of objects, the age of metals properly begins with the production of pitchers with beaked spouts (*Schnabelkannen*) and other pouring vessels.

Before such a stage was fully reached, in Asia Minor and in the Aegean area, a preliminary phase occurred, lasting approximately from 2900 to 2500 B.C. In Anatolia metal vessels were already being produced, for the most part by casting. They were exported even as far as Greece (Euboea). These vessels, of gold, silver, and copper, exerted an ever-increasing

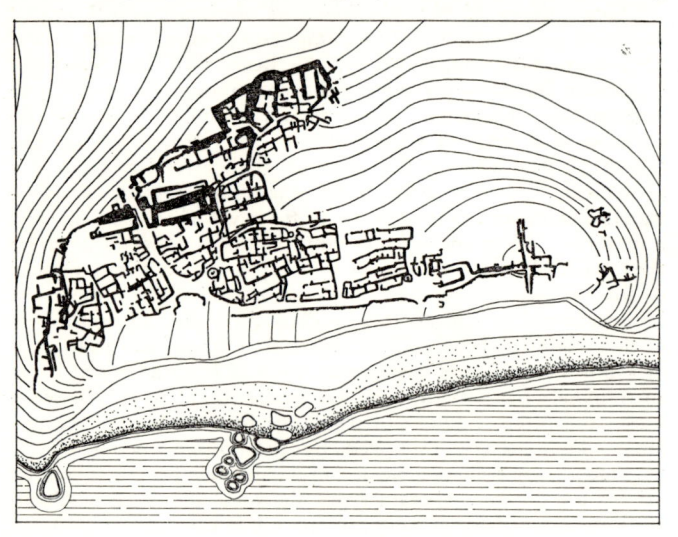

Poliochni (Lemnos), plan (*from BArte, XLII, 1957, p. 194*).

influence on ceramics, stimulating potters to produce a ware in imitation of metal vessels, with rigidly angular forms and a monochrome polished surface. This contributed to the decline of the taste for lively painted decoration; polished black ware was the favorite type of pottery during Phase XII of Mersin, in the late Chalcolithic phase at Alişar (Alishar) in eastern Anatolia, Beycesultan on the Maeander (mod. Menderes), Besiktepe, and Kumtepe in the Troad, as well as in the late Neolithic period in Crete and the Cyclades. In those sectors of continental Greece, Macedonia, and Thrace not reached by the *Bandkeramik* culture (which favored painted spiral and meander decoration) the polished black ware held first place. Ultimately even the *Bandkeramik* immigrants from the north, who merged with the indigenous population, accepted the new type of ware.

The polished black ware spread with the Vinča culture from Macedonia as far as the Danube. In the course of time, however, it was obliged to assimilate *Bandkeramik* influences (spiral and meander decoration applied by incision). The polished Komotini ware (unpublished finds) was produced in Thrace at this time. As in the Vinča culture, the Komotini potters accepted incised decoration and competed with the makers of the Gumelnitza ware, produced in and imported from the north.

Although this polished black ware was basically an imitation of metal with its light-reflecting surfaces, the potters were unable to resist the temptation to apply decoration, especially since between the polished surfaces of the pots sections were left unpolished. On these, bars, crosshatched panels, triangles, and bands of fine white lines (often in the form of a garland), or grooves and button designs were applied. In the Balkans and on the Greek mainland, where *Bandkeramik* influences were stronger, painted decoration was sometimes applied to the polished surfaces after firing.

This polished black ware can be regarded as a universal ceramic form in competition with metalwork. On the important question of whether the diffusion of this type of ware was accompanied by any ethnic movements it is not yet possible to arrive at any definite conclusion. In this connection it should be noted, however, that in the archaeological strata of the dwellings of this period (in Thessaly and at Beycesultan) we find a more primitive type of building than in the preceding period.

Aegean-Anatolian cultural unity in the early Bronze Age. In Anatolia and in the Aegean area the early Bronze Age coincides with the first appearance of the beaked pitcher. This probably occurred in Anatolia between 2800 and 2700 B.C., in Crete about 2600 B.C., and on the Greek mainland about 2500 B.C. In Crete the production of polished black ware overlaps that of early Bronze Age beaked jugs, 2600–2500 B.C.

We can now discern the formation of a unified cultural area comprising Anatolia and the Aegean region. It progressively detached itself from Mesopotamia and Syria but encompassed Cilicia and Cyprus. To the north it gradually included the Macedonian and Thracian coasts but no longer included the interior of the Balkan peninsula. The elements uniting this Aegean-Anatolian community are two: the working of metals, which came from Asia Minor, and the migrations of additional population groups from Asia Minor to the Cyclades, Crete, and the Greek mainland. These peoples also brought with them a more evolved form of urban life, similar to that which had meanwhile developed in Asia Minor. It is possible to distinguish within this Aegean-Anatolian culture five well-defined sectors: Anatolia, the Cyclades, Crete, the Greek mainland, and Macedonia.

a. Anatolia. In the early Bronze Age, Anatolia underwent a series of cultural developments, all of which had artistic consequences. The social structure became more urbanized in comparison with earlier periods, and the number of fixed settlements increased with the foundation of city-states protected by strong walls. City walls also appear in the islands near the Anatolian coast: in Lesbos, at Thermi, and in Lemnos, at Poliochni (FIG. 643). The outstanding example of a royal city is Troy (PL. 418, FIG. 645), founded in the beginning of the early Bronze Age. Levels I–V date from this period. The traits of the period are seen in the massive walls and city gates (Troy I and II), which were constantly restored or rebuilt. Within Troy II there was a central court surrounded by walls. Access was through a large portal; within were megaron-like edifices for princes. It is here that the plan of the megaron, an earlier example of which is found in Dimini, was developed to mature and classic proportions. As for the plastic art forms, minor sculpture was generally in decline; an exception is a sculptured stele (PL. 419) found in Troy I, which is a remarkable work of art. It appears to be a totally isolated example of this form within the Aegean area. Practically nothing is known of the textiles of the period, since their patterns were not reproduced in ceramics, the pottery consisting entirely of monochrome ware. Among the ceramics, which are on the whole of no intrinsic artistic merit, the only noteworthy forms are the urns (often called "face urns") on which the face and the breasts of the fertility goddess are represented, following an ancient tradition; probably such portrayals had a religious purpose.

Metalworking was, however, of the first importance, and metal prototypes provided the inspiration for all kinds of vessels, pottery included. The earliest examples of metal vessels are of gold, silver, electrum, or forged copper or bronze. The forms include beaked pitchers, "sauceboats" (PL. 424), goblets, and teapot vases (PL. 422). Our knowledge of the metal artifacts of this period is not derived entirely from the excavations at Troy and Poliochni; it comes also from the royal tombs at Alaca Hüyük and Horoztepe. These tombs, situated in northeastern Anatolia, show more than one link with the Caucasus and southern Russia, though their metal artifacts are of somewhat coarser workmanship and their style is more original. The usual types of metal vessels are found here; most important are the so-called "standards" (I, PL. 517)

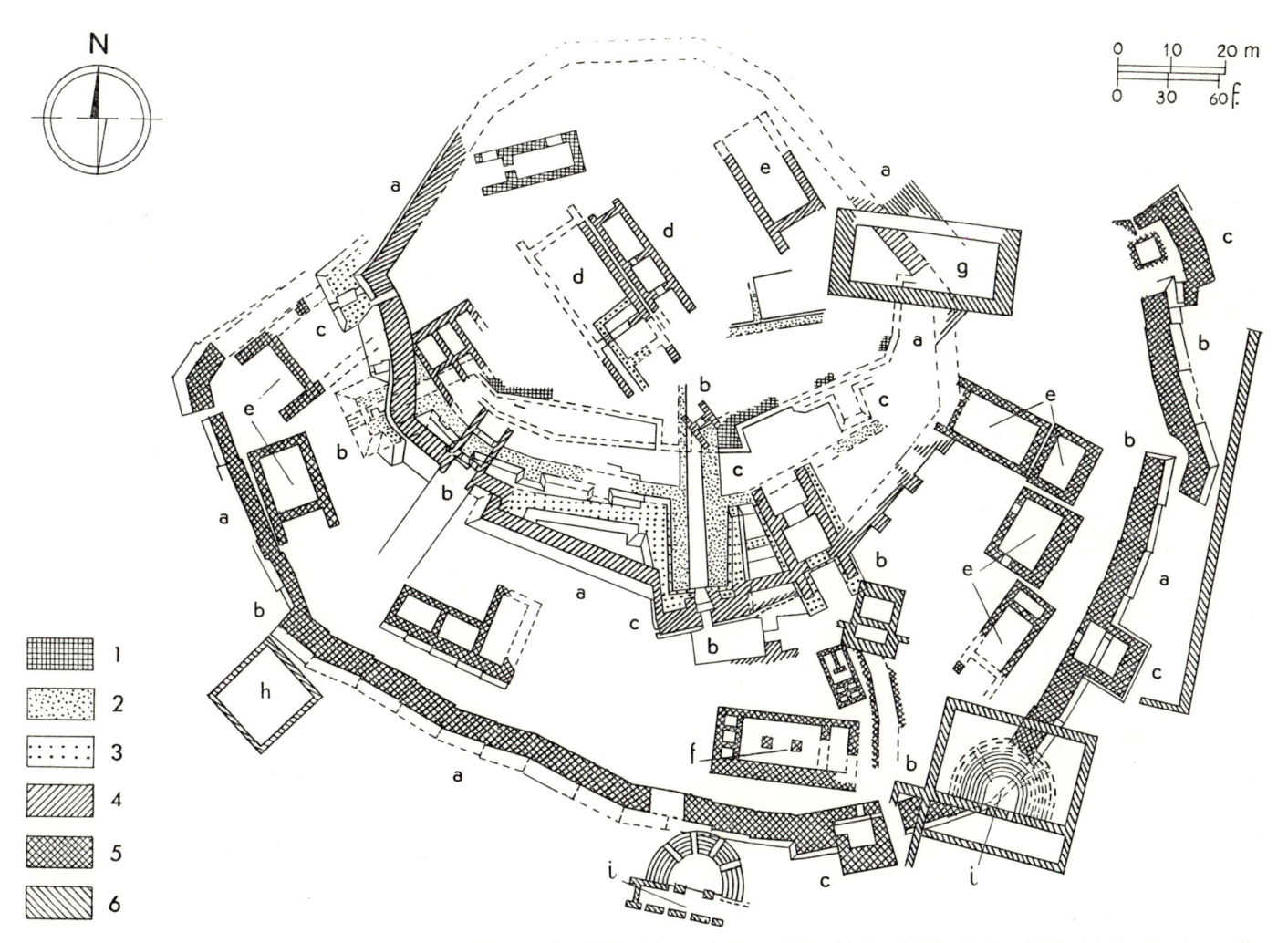

Troy, plan of the citadel. Key: (1) Level I; (2) Level IIa; (3) Level IIb; (4) Level IIc and IIg; (5) Level VI; (6) Level IX. (a) Fortification walls; (b) gates; (c) towers; (d) megara; (e) houses; (f) Pillar House; (g) Temple of Athena; (h) sanctuary; (i) theaters (from Blegen, Caskey, Rawson, and Sperling).

— among them statuettes of sacred animals (especially stags) and religious emblems such as sun symbols — and the necklaces and pins. Particularly characteristic of the region are the bronze statuettes representing human beings and gods. It cannot be claimed that these artifacts represent any very high artistic level; they are, however, enlivened by a spontaneous realism, which is expressed with particular vigor in the bronze statuette found at Horoztepe representing a mother goddess nursing her child (PL. 417). It should be noted that the techniques of metalworking of northeastern Anatolia show very slight ties with the contemporaneous techniques of the Sumerians in Mesopotamia; the artifacts from the royal tombs of Ur (I, PL. 509) are without doubt far more advanced from every point of view. And yet the metal artifacts of the treasure of Troy II (PL. 419) are outstanding for their great delicacy and artistic craftsmanship; in many aspects they are superior to the finds from the royal tombs of Ur. Only in Troy was the production of filigree and granular work, particularly in the exquisite pins, of so high a quality as to tempt one to suggest an attribution to the middle or late Bronze Age.

As the result of the numerous excavations made since Schliemann and Dörpfeld — at Troy by the Americans C. W. Blegen and J. L. Caskey, at Beycesultan and Polatli by English archaeologists, at Alaca Hüyük and many other sites by Turkish expeditions, and at Tarsus by an American expedition under H. Goldman — it becomes evident that in early Bronze Age Anatolia the evolution of the various art forms was neither parallel nor homogeneous. While some forms progressed, others regressed. Clay sculpture and pottery gradually lost in importance and interest because of the advances made in metalworking techniques. In pottery there is another factor of equal weight: with the appearance of the potter's wheel (which existed in Mesopotamia as early as the Uruk phase, ca. 3000 B.C.), for the first time in the course of the history of art the products of the machine compete with handmade work. The result of this first encounter between two methods of manufacture was the decline in the single, handmade artifact in favor of the mass-produced and more anonymous one.

Of course the new machine, the potter's wheel, had not yet, at this time, replaced human hands in the making of pottery; nor had pottery completely lost its old character. But the use of the wheel in a number of workshops in the Uruk period in Mesopotamia was the beginning of a process in which the manufacture of pottery became progressively easier and less demanding of artistic ability, and thus tended to become a handicraft rather than an art. Concurrently with this decline in the ceramic arts there was a corresponding advance not only in metalworking but also in architecture, which achieved a degree of excellence hitherto unknown. About the lithic sculpture of this time, apart from the stele mentioned above, little is yet known.

b. Crete (prepalatial period). In early Bronze Age (prepalatial) Crete we find neither the great innovations nor the unequal levels of productivity found in Anatolia. Metalworking had not yet assumed a leading role, although all the pottery forms were influenced by the forms of metal vessels. Cretan potters attempted to imitate in clay the variegated effect of copper vessels in the so-called "mottled ware." Since Crete has no mineral deposits of consequence, metal had to be obtained from overseas by commercial exchange. The gold ornaments found in the princely tombs of Mochlos show a refined artistic taste reminiscent of Sumerian goldsmiths' work. On the other hand, the technical aspects of this work appear to be rather primitive; filigree and granulation are absent.

Cretan architecture — best studied in the palace of Vasiliki — continued to have a particular importance of its own. In the field of small sculpture, first place is held by the representations of small animals in genre scenes such as the steatite pyxis lid with a sleeping dog found in Mochlos (Heraklion, Archaeol. Mus.). The greatest degree of artistry was achieved in the production of stone vessels; these surpass every other contemporaneous art form. The stimulus came from Egypt, where the creation of stone vessels had reached a very high level, but the Cretan artists were not satisfied to make stone vessels of the same type; they ambitiously attempted to reproduce in stone the new metal vessels such as the beaked pitchers and the teapot and "sauceboat" shapes. Since the stone they used was a delicately flecked material, and they were able to make the walls very thin and fashion graceful handles, their products represent an artistic peak perhaps never again reached anywhere else in the world.

c. The Cyclades. In the early Bronze Age, the Cyclades had a distinct culture, and the Cycladic people was the first in the entire Aegean basin to practice navigation and overseas trade on a large scale. Their ships, with many banks of oars, sailed not only to the Adriatic Sea, Malta, and Sicily, but as far as the Balearic Islands and possibly southern France. The trade in metal between Asia Minor and the Greek mainland, and perhaps Crete, appears to have been a monopoly of the Cycladic seamen. And this enterprising race does not seem to have been content merely with the yield of their maritime trade. Aided by the fact that the islands (especially Paros) were rich in precious marbles, minerals, and clays of excellent quality, they also modeled vases and figurines, some of which were exported.

Among the most typical Cycladic art forms are the marble idols, generally upright female figures which, since they are not shaped so as to stand alone, were probably supported on a base (PL. 421, upper right; VII, PL. 352). The scale varies, ranging up to two-thirds of life size. The anatomy is so highly schematic as to imply a rather superficial workmanship and commercial mass production. Whether these idols represent the great fertility goddess is doubtful; the figure is nude, but the arms are folded and the hands do not touch the breasts. It has not been established that the purpose of the neolithic idols of the Sesklo culture was funerary. That the early Bronze Age Cycladic marble idols likewise had another, perhaps more worldly significance is suggested by the fact that in Cycladic graves statuettes representing musicians are also found. These too, though not so numerous as the female figures, were apparently produced in quantity. To date, two types of musicians have been found, one seated and playing a harp (PL. 420), the other standing and playing the double aulos. These instruments reappear later in the Cretan funerary cult, as represented on the painted sarcophagus from Hagia Triada (IV, PL. 62). Nude male figures are rare.

There are also among the Cycladic artifacts several marble vessels, worked in forms that are also found in pottery versions and were probably executed in metal as well. They are distinguished by their graceful lines, especially of the feet. In the tomb finds marble cosmetic tablets are also fairly frequent. Together with this work, mass-produced yet of high quality, another, cruder type of idol is found, which basically seems to depict a seated or squatting goddess. No anatomical details or limbs appear; curving in at the waist, in the shape of a violin (PL. 421, upper left) or a spade, the idol of this type is a schematic outline of the human torso, neck, and head.

So much for the works in marble. Two types of objects were made of softer stones, especially steatite: pyxides in the shape of a house, and seals. The seals generally show a spiral motif. The pyxides are of great archaeological as well as artistic interest. An example found at Melos reproduces a house with a courtyard: a portal with a cornice leads to the inner courtyard, surrounded by seven round towers. The exterior of the entire piece is decorated with a graceful spiral motif (the infinite curve) in intaglio. Another pyxis, from Naxos, is in the form of an elliptical house with an arched roof. Both the roof and the walls are covered with a fine spiral ornamentation. It is very likely that pyxides were also made of wood, covered with a network of gold spirals; these wooden examples were probably rectilinear. It was presumably the nature of the medium that dictated the rounded forms of the steatite pyxides.

In the early Bronze Age the craft of metalworking was doubtless of no less importance, but unfortunately little of its output survives. Only a silver diadem from Amorgos is worthy of note (Athens, Nat. Mus.). There are also various types of pins, some with a bird or a double spiral at the upper end. Naturally there are also a number of daggers, spearheads, and other similar objects in bronze. All these metal objects seem from their types to be of Anatolian origin, however; they show no elements that entitle them to be classed as original Cycladic works. The only original works coming from these islands would seem to be the wooden pyxides with spiral network of metal mentioned above.

Cycladic pottery of the early Bronze Age is extremely varied. One class, the Pelos pottery, as it is known, shows late neolithic forms and an old-fashioned herringbone pattern. Generally this type of pottery was destined for use as grave goods and was therefore fashioned from clay of inferior quality. Another variety, the Syros pottery, so termed, is distinguished by its spiral decoration based on *Bandkeramik* motifs (Lengyel). The decoration is scratched and incrusted with white; sometimes this is complemented by incised decoration. The vases have pyxis-like forms, sometimes with a graceful foot. A particularly noteworthy type is the so-called "pan-shaped" vessel (or "frying-pan"), flat and circular, with low rim and a single handle (PL. 421). This type undoubtedly had a religious significance, but that such vessels represented the Great Mother, or fertility goddess, as suggested by Zschietzschmann, is unlikely. Some of these "pans" are decorated with spirals and with intaglio designs. The origins of a third ceramic type, the painted pottery (PL. 421), are probably to be found in the woven fabrics which, from eastern Asia Minor, made their way across the trans-Anatolian trade route and finally reached the Cyclades.

What is known about Cycladic architecture is, unhappily, little. Walled cities undoubtedly existed. On the internal layout of the houses, limited data from Melos and Naxos are available, but from the diffusion of the megaron type in the surrounding regions — in Lemnos (Poliochni) and Samos and on the Greek mainland — we can deduce that it was also known in the Cyclades.

Because of their far-flung maritime activity and their commercial expansion, the Cyclades, during the early Bronze Age, exerted considerable influence in the neighboring areas of the Mediterranean world. Cycladic exports are found particularly in Crete (where the spiral eventually gained a place among the principal decorative motifs of Minoan art). Cycladic imports are also found on the Greek mainland and in the Dalmatian islands. The Stentinello culture in Sicily (PL. 428) and the contemporaneous culture of Malta (q.v.) show Cycladic influences. The most distant market for Cycladic exports was probably the Balearic Islands, where a Cycladic pitcher has come to light. On the whole, Cycladic culture was interregional in character, and the radius of its diffusion was very great (later the same could be said of the Phoenicians). The handicrafts were also important in this period, but the products tended to be mass-produced; nor did they have any longer the profundity that had been characteristic of the neolithic cultures.

d. Continental Greece (Early Helladic). The culture that flourished on the Greek mainland between 2500 and 1950 B.C. is known to us chiefly through excavations by the American archaeologists H. Goldman (Eutresis), J. L. Caskey (Lerne), and C. W. Blegen (Korakou and Zygouries); the Swedish archaeologists O. Frödin and A. Persson (Asine), E. Holmberg (Asea), and M. N. Valmin (Malthi); and the Greek archaeologists G. E. Mylonas (Aghios Kosmas) and D. R. Theocharis (east coast of Attica). With the descendants of the neolithic inhabitants had mingled the peoples of the Dimini migrations, and then in the course of the early Bronze Age a number of groups seem to have migrated to the mainland from Asia Minor, reinforcing the older Anatolian influences. Since the Early Helladic is essentially a culture of small cities, architecture held a preeminent place among the arts. In some locations — for example, in Lerne, in Attica, and on Aegina — city walls have been found. The gates and the entry ramps indicate remarkable skill in fortification. This establishes the fact that the science of fortification had reached a high level not only in the Trojan area (including the nearby islands; e.g., sites such as Poliochni in Lemnos and Thermi in Lesbos) and in the Cyclades, but also on the Greek mainland. The cities generally consist of an agglomeration of houses built one next to another and reached through very narrow streets. An occasional structure is built on the megaron plan. Some cities seem also to have served as the seat of a prince or chieftain. A very interesting princely dwelling was discovered at Lerne. The layout does not follow the usual megaron plan; a number of corridors run along the outer walls, and there are two large inner rooms. There may have been an upper story reached from the corridors by means of wooden staircases.

At Tiryns a large and monumental circular construction, some 90 ft. in diameter, has been discovered under the Mycenaean palace. This is believed to have been a large royal residential complex, similar in type to the Sardinian nuraghe; it may, on the other hand, have been a monumental tomb. (The small circular buildings discovered at Orchomenos, in Boeotia, were probably granaries rather than dwellings.)

The suggestion that this large circular structure served as a royal residence seems to this writer of dubious merit. The fact that on the island of Leukas there exist tumulus tombs with circular stone bases of the same period, coupled with the fact that the circular structure of Tiryns stands on the highest point of the hill, leads the writer to suggest instead that this structure is the monumental tumulus tomb of a ruler of that town. Some confirmation of this proposition may be found in the fact that on the summit of the hill in Lerne, when the royal palace which existed on this site was destroyed, a large tumulus with approximately the same diameter as that of the circular structure in Tiryns was covered over by the rubble. The corresponding palace building of Tiryns to which this royal tomb might have belonged is yet to be found.

In the examination of other details of Early Helladic architecture, we find ditches or cisterns (*bothroi*) either within or adjoining the house in almost every case. These probably served for the preservation or fermentation of certain kinds of foods rather than for religious purposes. Another feature is the use of terra-cotta tiles and slate slabs for roofing and street paving. Grooved stones were used for door hinges. The plan of the palace at Lerne, in every detail the work of an experienced architect, shows the high standard that the Early Helladic builders were capable of reaching. The metalworking skills were likewise in evidence in the Early Helladic culture. Mineral ore was brought to the eastern Attic ports, where (as at Raphina) there were metalworking shops that manufactured tools, utensils, weapons, and other objects, both in copper and in bronze. The weapons and utensils show no substantial divergence from the types produced in Asia Minor and the Cyclades, but the hammered metal vessels are different. Two smooth gold "sauceboats" have survived (PL. 424). The form, one that is frequently seen in pottery, is typical of continental Greek art; undoubtedly these are of local manufacture. All the other pottery types may likewise have been patterned after metal models, a possibility that would seem to be confirmed by the facsimile nails found on the handles of a number of clay pots. Symmetrically constructed vessels (jugs, stemmed cups, and bowls with a ring base) as well as asymmetric vessels (askoi, beaked pitchers, "sauceboats") were manufactured. In order to obtain a glossy metallic surface, potters gave the early vessels a high polish; in a later phase vessels were entirely covered with a dark glaze. Only toward the end of the Early Helladic period did the potters return to the colored ornamentation obtained by covering only part of the surface with glaze and decorating the vases with white or dark paint in bands of broken lines and braids. These designs were probably inspired by East Anatolian textiles, which at this time were being exported as far as Greece.

e. Influences in Europe. The early Bronze Age Aegean-Anatolian cultural movement did not penetrate the interior of the Balkan peninsula. Here, as well as in the middle and lower Danubian territory, the *Bandkeramik* cultures were engaged in a mortal struggle with the Indo-European Battle-ax people, by whom they were everywhere defeated. The fusion of the victorious and the vanquished peoples brought forth new populations with a relatively high cultural level. Of these, the most widely diffused were the producers of the *Schnurkeramik* (corded ware).

While the Balkan and Danubian territories were the scene of these upheavals (the effects of which, though lasting for several centuries, were not felt in the Aegean area), the progress achieved in metalworking in the Aegean centers passed on to the rest of Europe. Little by little the European populations learned to obtain and work metals. It is possible to trace the successive stages of the diffusion of the individual metallic forms (e.g., the askos) which reached as far as the Danubian region. The beaked pitcher gradually spread to the whole world. Even the fine ribbon handles of the Baden culture derive from metal originals.

If the influences indicated above have been, up to this point, of a cultural character, it is now possible to establish the occurrence of a series of political counterattacks from the area of the Battle-ax people, events certainly ascribable to migration and violent conquests. Thus, in Troy II, splendid stone double axes, of a type which had long vanished from Anatolia, suddenly appeared. At the same site we also find amphoras of a definitely "tectonic" form, which were found with particular frequency among the *Schnurkeramik* people. Stone double axes and *Schnurkeramik* pottery forms appeared in early Bronze Age Macedonia, and the "tectonic" amphora gradually penetrated to central Greece and the Peloponnesos. Mass migrations of Indo-European populations into Asia Minor did not occur until the end of the period. In approximately 1950 B.C. they also appeared in Greece.

The middle Bronze Age. As has been shown, strong Aegean-Anatolian cultural ties existed during the early Bronze Age. In the middle Bronze Age the various areas of Anatolia, Crete, and the Greek mainland went their separate ways. This came about as a result of the Indo-European invasions of Asia Minor and the Greek mainland.

a. Anatolia. In eastern Anatolia the most important documentation has come from the excavations at Kültepe and Alişar. The middle Bronze Age began somewhat earlier in Anatolia than elsewhere in western Asia; it is marked by the appearance of the painted pottery known as "Cappadocian" (beginning ca. 2200 B.C.). The designs of the painted decoration (partly in the continuous-band and partly in the panel style) were undoubtedly derived from textiles; *Bandkeramik* pottery may have contributed also. Monochrome ware continued to be produced; in contrast to the painted ware, which was handmade, it was made on the wheel. This monochrome ware, as the Kültepe excavations show, gradually evolved into the earliest Hittite pottery, a type distinguished for its sharp edges and daring profiles and curves, which sometimes resulted in singular and even bizarre forms (VII, PL. 290).

Glyptic work reached a high level in the Kültepe culture. Finds include stamp seals with handles (one example is decorated with a continuous spiral design) and also cylinder seals, which clearly were influenced by Mesopotamia. The sculpture too was noteworthy. In stone and clay, statuettes of animals, particularly lions, depicted with a naturalism not lacking in ingenuousness, were favored. Zoomorphic vases (rhytons), which undoubtedly had a religious significance, also appeared. The cast-bronze statuettes, of which the molds have also occasionally come to light, are mainly small figures, draped or nude, of deities; among these is a group of a god and goddess with their child. Eastern Anatolia between 2000 and 1700 B.C. had close ties with the countries to the southeast, with Syria, and especially with Mesopotamia; trade with the last-mentioned was in the hands of the Assyrian commercial colonies that existed on the outskirts of the various Anatolian cities. One colony, which yielded thousands of tablets with cuneiform writing, has been found at Kültepe; another colony has come to light at Bogazköy.

Probably from the middle Bronze Age is the palace at Beycesultan, on the upper Maeander, in western Anatolia

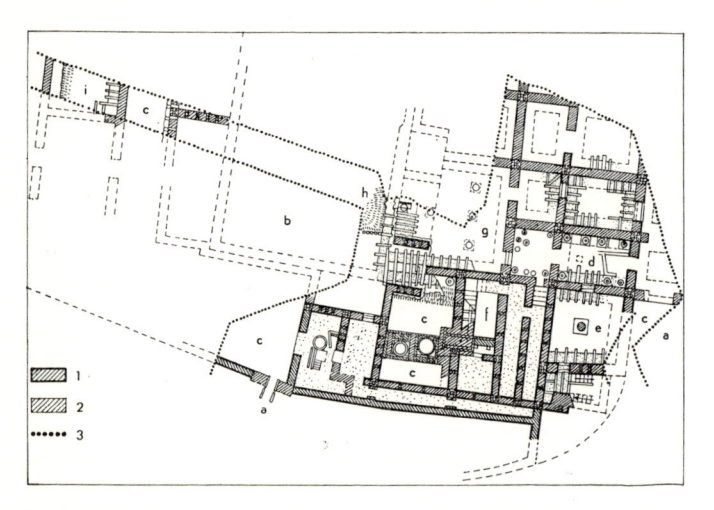

Beycesultan, palace, plan (partly reconstructed). *Key*: (1) Brick walls; (2) ruined foundations; (3) excavated zone: (*a*) entrances; (*b*) central court; (*c*) open areas; (*d*) lustral room; (*e*) "Painted Loggia"; (*f*) stair hall; (*g*) "Painted Hall"; (*h*) level of rushes; (*i*) rush floor (*from Anatolian Studies, 1956, p. 108*).

(FIG. 651). The layout of its interior shows a certain resemblance to the palaces in Knossos (IV, FIG. 85) and Phaistos (FIG. 653), but inasmuch as the excavations at Beycesultan have not yet made clear whether the palace was built around an inner courtyard (as were the Minoan palaces), an assessment of the relations existing between Beycesultan and Knossos would be unwarranted. There is no Cretan equivalent of the use of massive wooden beams found in the palace of Beycesultan, nor is there any visible architectural link between it and the later public edifices of the Hittites (see HITTITE ART) in eastern Anatolia.

The city of Troy V belongs to the transition period between the early and the middle Bronze Age. Troy VI (PL. 418; FIG. 645) was built, probably after a hiatus, in the 19th century B.C. by new colonizers, undoubtedly of Indo-European origin, who in the course of time entered the Aegean cultural sphere and had no further connections with eastern Anatolia. Nevertheless, in the massive fortifications they built around the city (which they had greatly enlarged), the builders of Troy VI remained essentially faithful to the traditions of fortification in Troy II. Only the oldest parts of Troy VI belong to the middle Bronze Age; the later portions were built in the late Bronze Age.

b. Crete and the Cyclades. In Crete, the middle Bronze Age, 2000–1700 B.C., was the floruit of the first palaces (see CRETAN-MYCENAEAN ART), whereas in the Cyclades the middle Bronze Age (Middle Cycladic) was a period of decline. Further, with the development of the Cretan palace culture the Minoan merchant fleet achieved preeminence at the expense of the Cycladic fleet. Minoan influences, as well as Middle Helladic trends from the Greek mainland, made increasingly greater headway in the islands. The production of statuettes and of spiral-decorated pyxides gradually declined, as did the Pelos and Syros pottery. On the other hand, painted pottery maintained its place, along with a monochrome ware, much of it with incised decoration of triangles and the like.

c. Continental Greece (Middle Helladic and the beginnings of Greek civilization). About 1950 B.C. a momentous upheaval took place on the Greek mainland with the arrival of the first groups of Greek-speaking Indo-European peoples to penetrate the peninsula. Violent struggles must have occurred, for the majority of the Early Helladic settlements were destroyed. Some of the cities were completely abandoned, but the majority were rebuilt, at first on a smaller scale and in a simpler architectural style. The indigenous population merged with the newly arrived Indo-European elements, and thus the earliest Greeks came into being.

From the point of view of art history, the arrival of the new people at first caused a serious regression. This not only affected plastic art, which promptly declined, but metalworking as well. Pottery, however, maintained its former level. Two types can be distinguished, the Minyan and the matt-painted wares (*Mattmalerei*). The former (named after the Minyae, since it was found in their city, Orchomenos) was often wheel-made; the monochrome surface varied in color, so that there are gray, black, red, yellow, and other varieties of Minyan ware. In some cases the interior of the vase is of the same color as the outside (presumably owing to consummate skill in firing). Of the various forms, the goblets with graceful stems with horizontal fluting and the wide-mouthed examples (some decorated with the same fluting) are particularly worthy of note. These vase forms seem to have been derived from the silver vessels of eastern Anatolia, although sometimes, in their particularly well-balanced and beautiful form, they surpass their models. The matt-painted ware is also derived from eastern Anatolian models, which undoubtedly reached the Aegean world by the overland route across Anatolia. Both their forms and their decorative motifs are reminiscent of the Kültepe products; the decoration may also have been strongly influenced by the designs of imported textiles.

In architecture a definite regression from the proto-Helladic is perceptible. Some of the buildings have less solid walls, and in general considerably less skill in architecture is in evidence. The most widely diffused type of building is the megaron (often ending in a kind of apse), which is also found in princely dwellings (e.g., Asine and Malthi). Apparently in many cases the cities were surrounded by walls; this can be assumed to have been so in the case, for example, of Malthi, Mycenae (PL. 425), and Tiryns.

In its earlier phases, Middle Helladic culture shows a strong dependence on imports from eastern Asia Minor, and even the production of Minyan pottery appears to parallel the course of the cultures of Chalkis and Troy VI. With the passage of time, cultural exchanges with the Cyclades probably increased, and by the 17th century B.C. Minoan influence seems to have become dominant.

About 1600 B.C., the Middle Helladic culture gave way to the Late Helladic (or Mycenaean) culture, although no ethnic changes seem to have taken place at this time. The Greek ethnic mixture that had been formed in the early phase of the Middle Helladic — which might be termed the "proto–Middle Helladic" — by the merging of Mediterranean and Indo-European peoples continued through the phase of Minoan dominance. The Mycenaean culture came about through the introduction of a great number of Minoan cultural elements from Crete, together with the war chariot from the east. Apparently the Mycenaean princes took advantage of the great earthquake that destroyed Knossos about 1600 B.C. to invade Crete and then continued as far as Egypt. Here, as allies of the Egyptian 18th-dynasty regime, they took part in the expulsion of the Hyksos, and it is here that they may have learned the use of the war chariot. After the earthquake disaster, the Cretans were able to rise again, and a period of peaceful coexistence between Knossos and Mycenae followed. With the beginning of the Mycenaean period the Greek mainland entered the late Bronze Age (see CRETAN-MYCENAEAN ART).

Phaistos, plan of the first and second palaces. *Key*: First palace: (1) walls; (2) foundations; (3) walls reused in second palace. Second palace: (4) walls; (5) foundations; (6) modifications and additions. (*a*) Western square; (*b*) theater area; (*c*) central court; (*d*) eastern square; (*e*) principal entrance; (*f*) propylaea and porticoes; (*g*) warehouses; (*h*) warehouses with pithoi; (*i*) baths; (*j*) cubiculum; (*k*) peristyle; (*l*) court; (*m*) shrine; (*n*) kitchen (?); (*o*) so-called "archives"; (*p*) quadriporticus; (*q*) so-called "men's megaron"; (*r*) so-called "women's megaron"; (*s*) grotto used as cistern (*from L. Pernier and L. Banti, Il Palazzo minoico di Festos, 1935-51, brought up to date*).

d. Late cultural developments in the peripheral areas of the Aegean and in the Balkans. As noted above, east Anatolian and, later, Minoan influences played a rather significant part in the development of Middle Helladic culture. But these advanced cultural influences did not penetrate the mountainous regions to the north and northwest. Until the late Bronze Age, the proto–Middle Helladic culture may be said to have survived in these regions; it is in evidence in Aetolia (Thermon), in Epirus, and in the northernmost part of Thessaly (Argissa). It is possible that these territories were inhabited by the ancestors of the later Dorian and northwestern Greek peoples, who did not fully participate in either the Middle Helladic or the Late Helladic (Mycenaean) culture, having been able to penetrate into Greece only after the destruction of the Mycenaean culture, about the 11th century B.C.

Macedonia also showed a certain retardation in the middle and the late Bronze Age. Actually in the middle Bronze Age the influence of and ties with Anatolia were particularly evident in the Minyan pottery; but matt-painted pottery was absent, and there were no Minoan influences. Incised recurrent spirals were favored in both the panel and the continuous-band styles. In the late Bronze Age, Mycenaean pottery was imported from about 1400 B.C., and there was an increase in the number of imported Mycenaean weapons and other objects. However, incised and painted pottery, with meander, spiral, checkerboard, and zigzag designs, persisted within the orbit of the middle Bronze Age traditions. The same retardative phenomena were operative in the Iron Age from about 1200 B.C.; at this time they seem to have been closely connected with strong Balkan-Illyrian influences ("spectacle" fibulas, etc.), also perceptible, for example, at Trebenište.

Characteristic elements of protohistoric Mediterranean art and architecture: a. The megaron. As an architectural form, the megaron is characterized by an elongated two-roomed plan; the entrance is on one of the shorter sides, and sometimes there is an atrium. In western Asia, only isolated examples of this type of structure are found in the earliest stage of protohistory — at Jericho (PL. 413), Byblos, and Mersin (FIG. 655). In the Sesklo culture a kind of widened megaron, consisting of two rooms but having no atrium, appears at Otzaki-Magoula. The megaron occurs more frequently in the *Bandkeramik* culture of southeastern Europe, but since these megara were

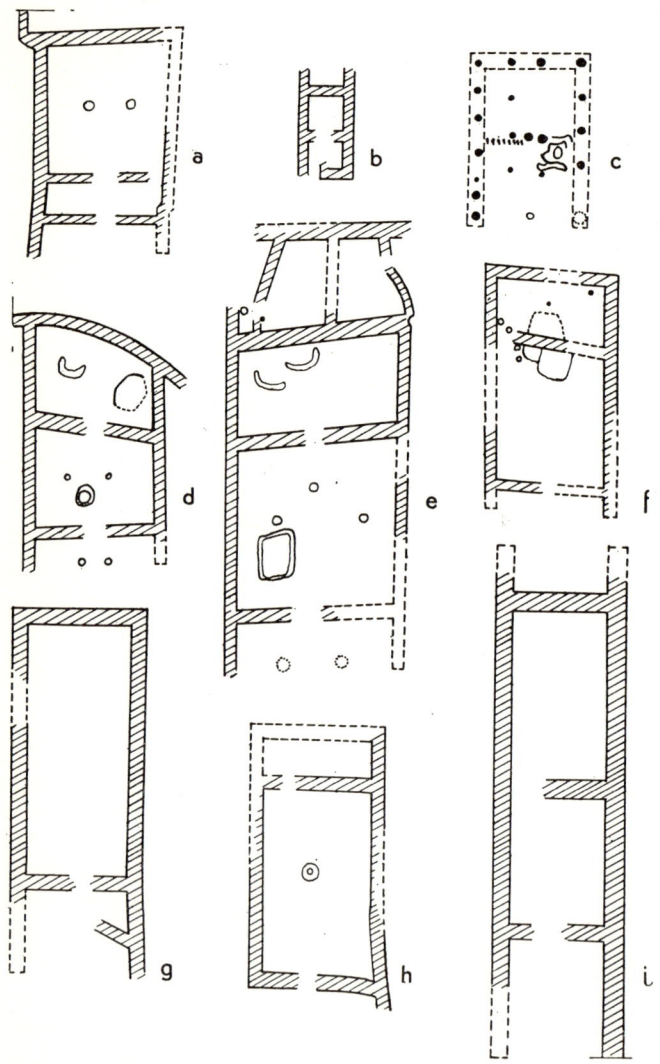

Types of megaron in the eastern Mediterranean: (a) Jericho; (b) Mersin; (c) Erösd; (d) Dimini; (e) Sesklo; (f) Dimini; (g) Troy I; (h) Eutresis; (i) Troy II (*from Schachermeyr, RE, XXII, 1954, cols. 1377-78*).

built of perishable material, the plan is discernible only from the holes dug for the pilasters. In Thessaly, the Dimini people built very beautiful megara, which sometimes served as dwellings for their princes. The megaron appears in Troy I in various structural phases, sometimes with an apse; in Troy II splendid princely megara are found in the inner enclosure reserved for the royal family (FIG. 655). Megara are also found in other early Bronze Age settlements in Anatolia and nearby islands: in Beycesultan they were used for religious purposes; at Poliochni (Lemnos) and Thermi (Lesbos) they served as private dwellings. On the Greek mainland, various types of megara were built during the same period, but from study of the Lerne site it is evident that the megaron was not the dominant architectural form. In the Middle Helladic the megaron assumed considerably more importance: in some cases the end wall is rectilinear, in others the building ends in an apse. Even the royal residences were apparently built on the megaron plan (e.g., at Asine, Malthi). In this period various types of megara

were built in the islands as well. But so far as we know, the megaron was completely unknown in Crete, both in the prepalatial and in the subsequent palace periods; the term cannot be applied to the majestic portico that stands at the head of the famous stairway at Phaistos (IV, PL. 53). On the other hand, in the Mycenaean palaces at Mycenae (IV, FIG. 108), Pylos, and Phylakopi (Melos), for example, the megaron became the great hall par excellence, and it was only by way of Mycenaean emigrants that the megaron was finally brought to Crete. But, again, the throne room of the last phase of the palace at Knossos (IV, FIG. 85; VIII, PL. 92) cannot properly be called a megaron. However, in the postpalatial period, megaron-type houses appeared at Gournia (IV, FIG. 91) and perhaps at Hagia Triada. Later, in their temples, the Greeks adopted the megaron plan for the dwellings of their gods.

b. The tholos. The domed tomb, or tholos, belongs to a type of architecture that had its origins in the North African megalithic culture. There are many indications that originally they were simply circular tombs. Only on structures of moderate size was it possible to erect a dome of overhung concentric courses of masonry. Unfortunately, there has been little research on the North African circular tombs, of which O. Bates (1914) discovered a number in Cirenaica. Circular and domed megalithic structures of north African type appeared in various European areas, assuming the form of the nuraghe in Sardinia (PLS. 401, 402) and of the *naveta* (or *naus*) in the Balearic Islands (FIG. 677). In Spain the megalithic monuments retained their true character of domed tombs (FIG. 677), and from there this type of structure made its way as far north as Britain and Ireland. In Malta (q.v.) circular megalithic chambers are found in the form of underground sanctuaries.

In Crete circular megalithic tombs appeared first at the beginning of the Bronze Age. Particularly in the Mesara district, but in other parts of the island as well, there are circular tombs that are too great in diameter and have walls too thin to support a stone dome. However, small circular tombs with stone domes do occur in scattered locations. All the tombs of this type had a lateral entrance (dromos); an exception is a very small tomb at Krasi, in which the door is blind and the body of the deceased must have been lowered into the grave from above.

During the early Bronze Age the type of megalithic tomb with lateral entrance spread from Crete to the Cyclades and to the coast of Attica (Hagios Kosmas). In Crete itself, within the area of the Palace of Knossos, there are two circular cellarlike chambers hewn from the rock; these evidently belonged to a large princely dwelling built on the site only shortly before it was demolished, about 2000 B.C., to make way for a new palace. The megalithic method of construction with either rectilinear or concentric circular overlapping courses of masonry was widely used in Crete for other types of structures as well. The rectilinear system was used for bridges; an example of the use of the system of concentric rows is the domed springhouse at Arkhanes. The tholos tomb discovered by R. W. Hutchinson (1962) near Knossos undoubtedly belongs to the period 1700–1600 B.C.

The domed tomb at Osman Agha on the Greek mainland is, according to Blegen, of the Middle Helladic period and thus antedates the Mycenaean. It can be assumed that during the Middle Helladic two parallel traditions existed; one spread to Crete and the other to the Greek mainland. At this time, however, the domed tomb did not become the fashion. At the beginning of the Mycenaean period the shaft grave was by far preferred for the burial of kings. The domed tomb came into favor only about 1500 B.C. Later generations of kings (known as Wanaktes) were buried in the splendid tholos tombs of Mycenae, in the no less splendid one at Orchomenos, in the Vaphio tomb, and in the tholos tombs in the vicinity of Pylos, of Tiryns, and of Iolkos. There were also many other smaller tombs, where vassals were sometimes buried. It should be noted that all these edifices had lateral entrances; these dromoi were probably covered with earth and then uncovered for each subsequent burial. Some of these edifices — the so-called "Treasury of Atreus" (IV, PL. 68, FIG. 105), for instance — had portals decorated so sumptuously as to suggest that they must have been left uncovered for the admiration of devout pilgrims. In some cases the lower part of the mounds covering the tholoi was protected by a ring of masonry (*krepidoma*).

It appears probable that in Crete the scattered tholos tombs existed from the time of the very earliest settlements. But, as the excavations at Knossos show, the grander tombs were of the temple type (e.g., the one south of the palace), which was altogether different from the tholos tomb, and of the type of the princely tomb at Isopata, which has walls of rectilinear isodomic rows of masonry and bears some relation in layout to the domestic graves of Ugarit. On the whole it would appear that both the rectilinear and the concentric-circle type were part of the koine of the entire eastern Mediterranean world.

At the time of the great migrations, about the 12th century B.C., the tholos tomb fell into disuse on the Greek mainland. Only in Crete were edifices of this type still built, small in size and with the space beneath the dome sometimes circular, sometimes square. In the Bodrum Peninsula, in Caria, tholos tombs of this period are found under a tumulus surrounded by a *krepidoma*; it is probable that such tombs also existed in other parts of the Aegean area.

In Asia Minor, tumulus tombs without internal masonry structures or lateral entrances made a fleeting appearance. To this category belong the Phrygian tombs at Gordion and the so-called "Tomb of Tantalus," near İzmir (Smyrna), which have an internal well-closed wooden cell, without entrance, and are enclosed by a solid outer facing of stone. To the Lydian period belongs the great tumulus necropolis of Bintepe; some of the tombs there have no means of access, while others have both an entrance and an internal structure of masonry. Beginning in the 4th century B.C., tholos tombs became commoner; in fact they became a veritable fashion, especially in Asia Minor, the Balkans, and southern Russia. One of the largest and most remarkable of these tombs is that of Belevi, near Ephesos.

c. Plastic art as represented by statuettes of the fertility goddess. The small statuettes of the great fertility goddess made of unbaked clay in the prepottery phase of the Neolithic age have already been mentioned as having come to light at Jarmo, among other sites. After the invention of pottery these statuettes, generally squatting female figures, were made in fired clay throughout western Asia. From western Asia, the form penetrated Asia Minor and thence the Aegean area. In the Sesklo culture a variant — the standing figure with the hands raised toward the breast (PL. 423), following a common Oriental form — was preferred. The best of the Sesklo statuettes have real artistic merit; as has been indicated, the early Cretan pieces are not on the same level.

The type was transmitted from Sesklo as far as the region of the middle Danube, but there the arms were generally not worked out in detail, being merely indicated. During the Neolithic age there also appeared, in southeastern Europe and in Greece, the kourotrophos, divine mother and child, a type that, to judge from the material at hand, does not appear in Asia Minor until the early Bronze Age. As early as the beginning of the Neolithic, the representation on pottery (either in relief or painted) of the face and sometimes the breasts of the fertility goddess reached Sesklo from western Asia (Hassuna and Tell Halaf). Similar reliefs on pots found in the middle Danube area would seem to have been derived from the Sesklo type. A type with upraised arms is also found in the middle Danube area. The face of the goddess is represented on the lids of many late neolithic vases from the Vinča culture, in this region. In the early Bronze Age such representations appeared in Troy. But during the early Bronze Age clay sculpture underwent a distinct regression in the Aegean orbit. Only in the Cyclades did stone sculpture maintain its level: here marble statuettes of female figures (it is doubtful whether these represent goddesses) were made for tombs — some executed realistically in great detail, others highly stylized. In Asia Minor, in the early and the middle Bronze Age, cast-bronze statuettes of divinities were of first importance. During the Minoan palace period in Crete (and during the Hittite Empire), there were a great many depictions of the goddess of fertility — in sculpture, in reliefs, in gem carving, and in painting. Toward the end of this period, most particularly in the late Mycenaean age, the ancient types of idols reappeared, both as cult statuettes (particularly the type with upraised arms), and as grave goods. At the beginning of the Iron Age, sculpture was limited in the Aegean world to the production of primitive idols: only in western Asia and Egypt did it maintain a high artistic level.

d. Spiral and meander decoration. Simply coiling a strand or a thread produces a kind of snail-shell spiral pattern; this decorative motif is found, on a stamp seal, as early as the prepottery Neolithic period in Jarmo. However, this is an isolated example, which did not give rise to a spiral-based decorative system. In the Egyptian Neolithic it was for a brief period fashionable to decorate pottery with a number of unconnected snail-shell spirals scattered over the surface. But since not even these offered a spiral pattern capable of development, spirals soon went out of favor, and for a long time they were not used in Egyptian decoration in any form. In the Sumerian period coiled waves were sometimes engraved on cylindrical seals; the rolling of the seal in soft clay produced a spiral pattern of sorts. But since this motif was not adopted in other art forms, no ornamental system based on it was ever developed by the Sumerians. The same is true in the case of one of the phases of the Iranian Neolithic, in the pottery from Tepe Sialk, on which a kind of spiral tree often appeared, and in pottery from Hacılar, on which spiral forms, together with arms and hands, were sometimes used for decoration, without ever really being integrated into a decorative system.

In the beginning of the age of metals, the spiral began to assume a certain importance because the form was easily achieved by the twisting of a wire. In Azerbaijan there now appear on pottery ornaments of one sort or another achieved by means of twisting a cord in plastic relief; the same motifs are found in jewelry from the royal tombs of Ur and in the treasures from Troy II (PL. 419). But these still remain isolated cases. In this period the spiral had not won a permanent place in the ornamental tradition of western Asia or Egypt, nor had it acquired sufficient importance to become an autonomous decorative element. As for the meander, in the early periods of western Asian art it does not appear at all.

Altogether different was the course of the development of the spiral and the meander in Europe. Both appear occasionally as early as the Paleolithic; at Mezen, in northern Ukraine, excellent meander designs have come to light. In the 5th millennium B.C., when pottery reached southeastern and central Europe through the diffusion of western Asian influence, the first vase forms were Aegean-Anatolian, as were the decorative elements — designs incised by the fingernails, short linear segments, and points (impressions made with the serrated edge of the Cardium shell). In the course of time, however, local decorative motifs were applied to ceramics. Thus in the orbit of the *Bandkeramik* culture, textile-derived designs, including the spiral and the meander, were assimilated and were incised on vases. The spiral was generally used in horizontal zones; sometimes it appears in a diagonal design and is then interrupted horizontally or vertically, at need. Zones of meanders used in the same way were popular in Criş (incised) and Boian (painted) pottery in Romania. In Boian and Vadastra the meander is sometimes found along with the spiral. In Starčevo we see only spirals (no meanders), and again in Kremikovci the spiral is dominant. All this variation shows that there were no over-all influences at work; each area drew from its own individual heritage of weaving motifs and adapted to pottery designs derived from fabrics and basketry. Throughout the middle and lower Danube regions spiral and meander designs are found, often entwined and enclosed in panels. But whereas the tendency is to organize the meander in a repeat pattern, the spiral frequently appears in the form of a snail shell or of the letter S. Generally the decoration is applied in bands marked off, for example, by dark or light borders. In southern Russia the spiral was common everywhere; starting from here and spreading through Romania and Bulgaria to the shores of the

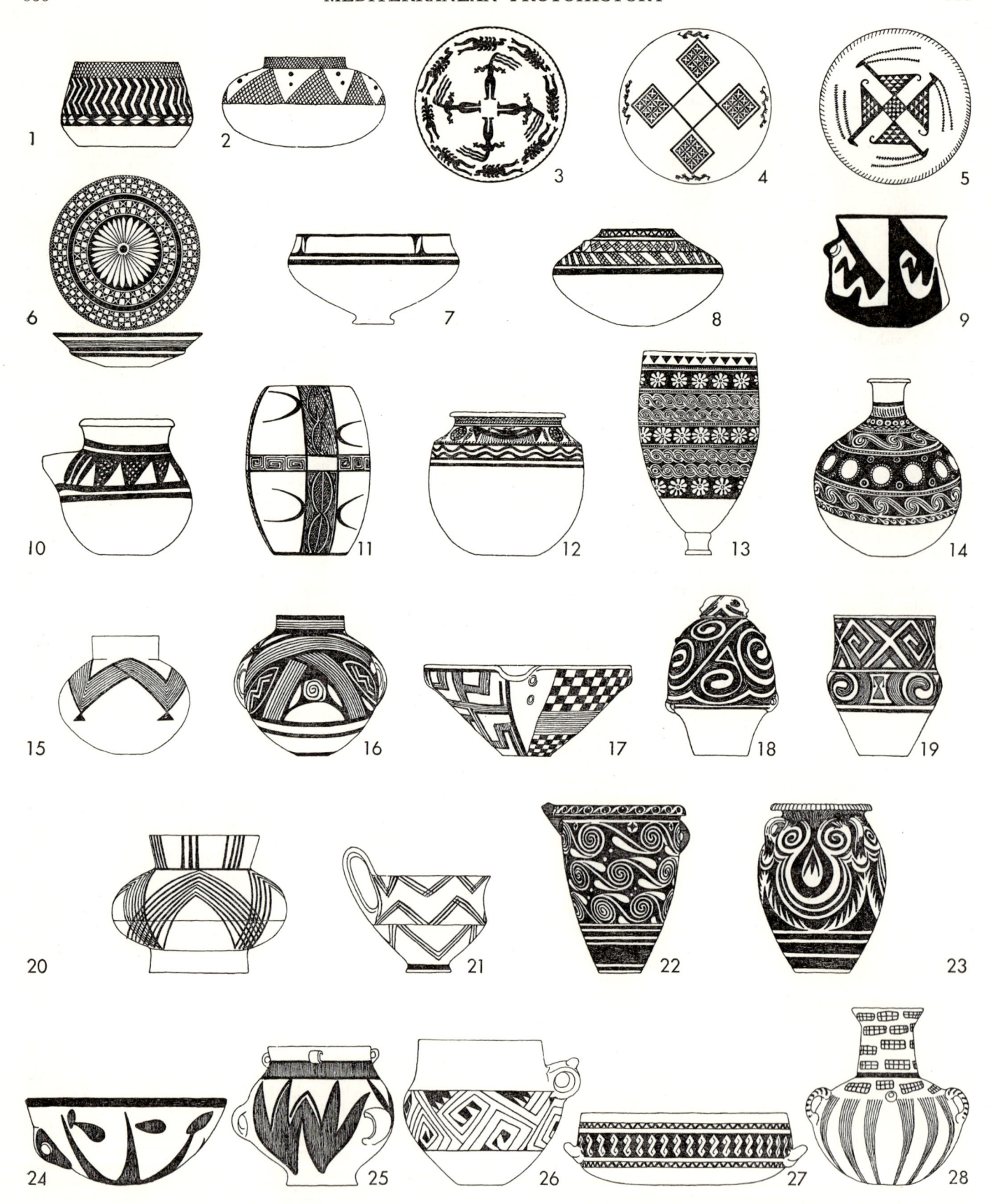

Neolithic and aëneolithic painted ware. (1, 2) Hassuna (Mesopotamia), early 4th millennium; (3, 4, 5) Samarra (Mesopotamia), early 4th millennium; (6) Tell Halaf (Mesopotamia), early 4th millennium; (7, 8) al-'Ubaid (Mesopotamia), 4th millennium; (9) Hacılar (Anatolia), 4th millennium; (10) Jamdat Naṣr (Mesopotamia), early 3d millennium; (11) Erimi (Cyprus), early 3d millennium; (12) Tepe Giyan (Iran), late 3d millennium–early 2d millennium; (13, 14) Tell Atchana (Mesopotamia), mid-2d millennium; (15) Sesklo (Thessaly), 4th millennium; (16, 17) Dimini (Thessaly), first half of 3d millennium; (18, 19) Cucuteni culture (Romania), 3d millennium; (20) Lerne (Greece), second half of 3d millennium; (21) Lerne (Greece), early 2d millennium; (22, 23) Kamares style (Crete), early 2d millennium; (24) Stentinello culture (Sicily), mid-4th millennium; (25) Capri style (Italy), early 3d millennium; (26, 27) Serra d'Alto style (southern Italy), 3d millennium; (28) Serraferlicchio style (Sicily), end of 3d millennium.

Aegean, a particular spiral style was developed which can be described as the flowing spiral or spiral cluster (*Stromlinien-Spiralen*) style.

The migrations referred to earlier carried both the spiral and the meander to the Aegean lands: with the Gumelnitza migration came the flowing spiral and with the Dimini migration the patterns of twisted meander repeats, the meander with spiral hooks, the scattered single spiral (III, PL. 122), and spiral repeats. The Cyclades, on the other hand, were reached only by the horizontal running spiral (sometimes replaced by a horizontal crown of tangential circles), the spiral repeat, and a design of triple and quadruple spirals. So far as is known, the meander did not reach any of the islands, with the exception of Samos.

The spiral and the meander do not seem to have reached western Asia Minor during the transitional period preceding the early Bronze Age, to judge from the finds at Beycesultan, Besiktepe, and Kumtepe. The isolated appearance of the spiral in eastern Asia Minor (prepottery Neolithic, Jarmo) has been mentioned above. In the early Bronze Age in Asia Minor, the spiral appears in the form of wire twisted into ornamentation for jewelry, particularly in Troy; in Mesopotamia, similarly, it is represented in the material from the royal tombs of Ur. On the Greek mainland, spiral ornament was used only on the large pithoi and on ceramic bowls, these designs having been impressed by rollers. In the Cyclades spiral decoration continued to flourish in the local pottery as well as on pyxides covered with a network of gold spirals and on seals.

Toward the end of the early Bronze Age the spiral made its way from the Cyclades to Crete and also to Egypt. In Crete it inspired a veritable revolution, for there it was, from this time on, the principal decorative motif (IV, PL. 53). A strictly stylized recurrent spiral is found thriving contemporaneously with a vegetal spiral in a completely different style; alongside these are spiral vortex designs and entire complexes branching out in multiple spirals, surrounded by a series of vortex designs. The Kamares pottery of the period of the first palaces and the splendid finds at Phaistos furnish the best examples of Cretan spiral-decorated pottery (PL. 422; IV, PLS. 56, 57; X, PL. 432). In the later palace period the vegetal spiral became rare and the stylized spiral came to the fore. In the Minoan palace period the spiral also appeared in glyptic forms. The types most frequently seen are the S spiral and the triple and quadruple spiral group. Contrariwise, the meander never had a prominent place in Cretan art. From the beginning of the period of the first palaces there remain a vase with meander decoration and a few seals with meander repeat pattern.

The diffusion of the spiral in Egypt and the Levant toward the end of the early Bronze Age constitutes an important landmark in the history of art. In Egypt it was adopted for the scarab with enthusiasm; moreover, the spiral was skillfully assimilated into the systems of endless repeats. The Syrian Levant favored the horizontal running spiral and complex spirals, both of which undoubtedly reached the eastern ports with the Minoan silver vases and Kamares pottery. Thence they followed the trade route along the Euphrates. The horizontal running spiral traveled as far as Mari, where it appears in the frescoes of the palace.

In Asia Minor the spiral had a mixed reception. It appears in isolated cases at Kültepe but is more frequent in the glyptics of Kara Hüyük (unpublished), where it either arrived with Cycladic influences or was transported across the Anatolian mainland. In this region, however, the spiral did not, even at this time, become a usual ornamental motif; the interwoven band pattern continued to be preferred.

In the Cyclades the spiral continued in use during the middle Bronze Age, although it was no longer predominant. The first Greek-speaking peoples to migrate to the Greek mainland at the beginning of the middle Bronze Age did not at first appreciate the motif. But later, under the influence of Crete and the Cyclades, they adopted it in certain forms, for example, the S spiral and the recurrent spiral. Of the meander there is no trace.

The Mycenaean pottery of the late Bronze Age assimilated the spiral on the one hand from Crete and on the other from the Cyclades, as well as from the cumulative ornamental heritage of the middle Bronze Age in continental Greece. Thus the spiral, especially in its recurrent form, assumed great importance in ceramics. Spiral repeats also appear frequently, for example, on metal objects. In the later Bronze Age the meander seems to have disappeared almost completely from the Aegean scene. In Macedonia incised and painted spirals appear frequently, the meander only occasionally.

No comprehensive change in decorative style came about until after the great migrations of the 12th century B.C. Curvilinear decoration, and consequently the spiral, gradually lost ground. In its place, a rigorously geometric decoration gained increasing esteem and interest (see GEOMETRIC STYLE). Greek proto-Geometric pottery still made use of concentric circles and semicircles (VI, PL. 93), but these were now traced with the compass. The meander increasingly replaced the spiral, not only in the Greek Geometric style but also in the Phrygian pottery of Asia Minor. Style of ornamentation in both Greece and Asia Minor was more and more determined by architecture, and the meander (VI, PL. 89) was far better adapted to the Phrygian cliff façades (I, PL. 532), for example, and the Greek architectural terra cottas. The spiral had become a purely accessory element in ceramic decoration, being mostly used in scroll-like designs.

e. Conclusions. Summing up, it is clear that the peoples of the eastern Mediterranean had, by the Neolithic and Chalcolithic ages (i.e., in the 4th millennium B.C.), reached a remarkably high artistic level. A further advance, in the Bronze Age, was registered only where the populations were able to remain relatively undisturbed and free of strong influences or migrations from abroad. Such was the case in Egypt from the beginning of the 3d millennium B.C., among the Sumerians in the first half of the 3d millennium, and in Crete in the first half of the 2d millennium. In regions where vast migrations, especially of Indo-European peoples, occurred, an artistic regression is evident at first. Even Hittite and Mycenaean art were not able to check this regression, much less to halt it. It was not until the 1st millennium B.C. that Indo-European peoples — the Persians, the Greeks above all, and finally the Romans — created great new works of art which, in many aspects, surpassed all that had been produced hitherto.

Still, a great many characteristic elements of later Hellenic art in the Aegean area can be traced to the very earliest times. From the Neolithic age on, the population of the Greek mainland showed a remarkable aptitude for sculpture especially in the depiction of the human body. The noble sense of balance that was later to become the most outstanding feature of Greek art is already apparent in the pottery of the neolithic culture of Sesklo, as is the Greek sense of color. On the other hand, Cretan influence is seen in the extraordinary capacity of Greek artists to observe and reproduce genre scenes. The rigorous structural quality that marked the artifacts of the Greek Geometric period was apparent in the "tectonic" amphoras of the Middle European Battle-ax culture, later in the early Bronze Age Aegean culture, and still later in the Minyan ware of the Middle Helladic period. The architectural prototype of the Greek temple may be traced back through the megaron to the Mediterranean Neolithic as well as to the *Bandkeramik* culture. The meander, which was to become such an important motif in Greek decoration, had its roots in the European Paleolithic and was originally introduced into the Aegean area through the Dimini.

Fritz SCHACHERMEYR

THE CENTRAL AND WESTERN MEDITERRANEAN. The neolithic and Bronze Age civilizations of the western Mediterranean do not, on the whole, present outstanding artistic phenomena comparable with those that the preceding paleolithic civilization had produced in the same area (see PREHISTORY), or those that the contemporaneous peoples of the eastern Mediterranean and of the Near East produced (see above).

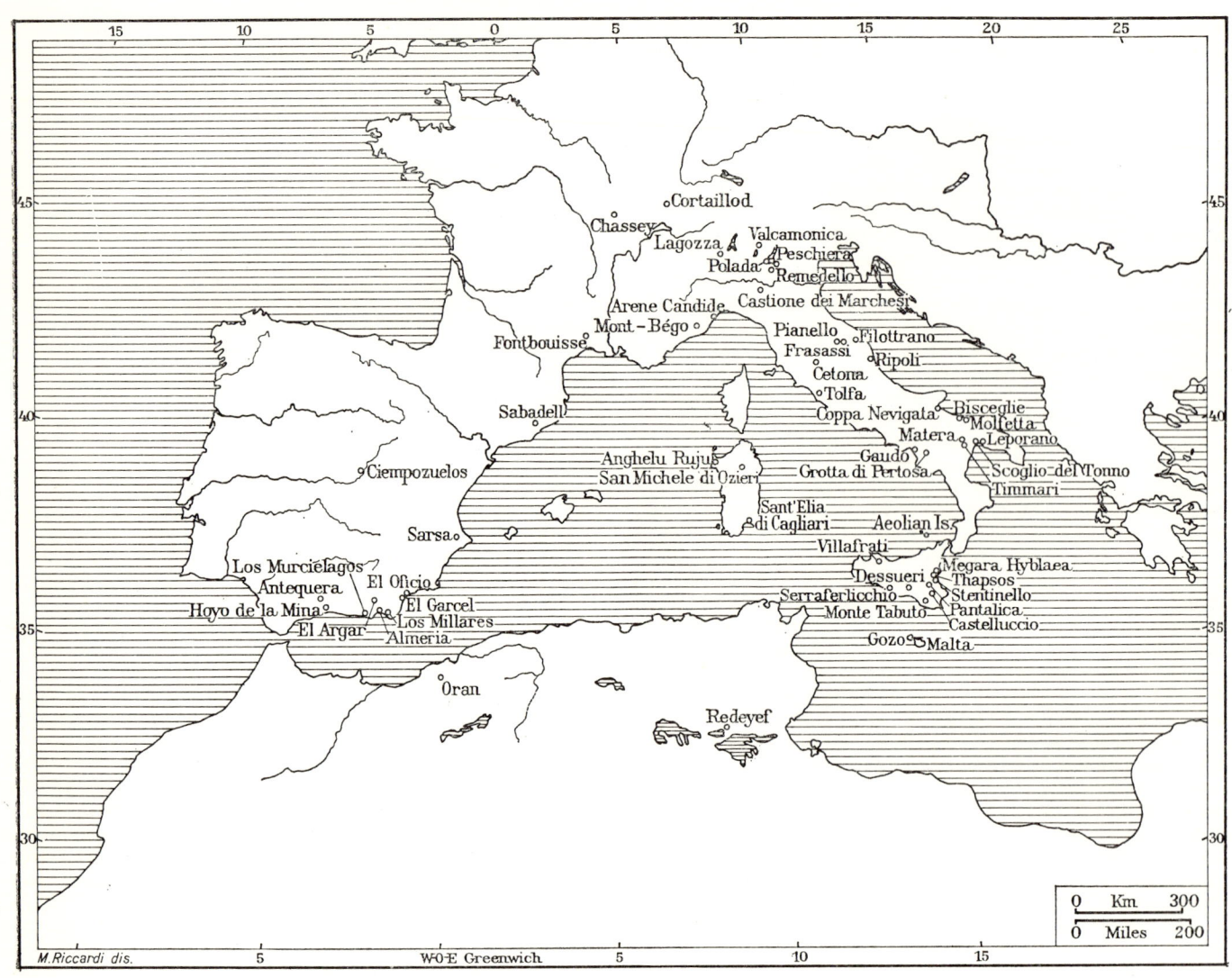

Western Mediterranean basin, principal archaeological sites and protohistoric art centers.

Only Malta (q.v.) and, on a far lesser scale, Sardinia reached an artistic level at the beginning of the age of metals comparable with that of the civilization of the eastern Mediterranean, by which they were undoubtedly influenced. Malta developed not only a very refined type of sculpture, which compares very favorably with Cycladic sculpture, but also an imposing megalithic architecture, which probably formed the basis of all the related architectural forms of the Italian peninsula, of the large Mediterranean islands, of southern France, and of Spain. The hypogeum tombs of Arles, the dolmens in the Málaga region, the megalithic structures of Sardinia and of the Balearic Islands (see MEDITERRANEAN, ANCIENT WESTERN) are artistic expressions having close ties to the Maltese megalithic architecture. But, except for the Arles tombs and the Málaga dolmens, they were achieved at a relatively late period, during the mature or final phases of the Bronze Age or even as late as the Iron Age. To these same late periods belong also the Alpine petroglyphs of Mont-Bégo and of Valcamonica (XI, PL. 294). For the rest, it can be stated that the single field in which the artistic sensitivity of the central and western Mediterranean peoples is revealed to us is their pottery, together with a minor production of clay idols and animal figurines. The great bulk of what constituted the artistic and ethnographic legacy (in many cases undoubtedly extremely rich and varied) of these prehistoric populations has not come down to us because of the perishable nature of its materials (textiles, embroidery, basketry, wood, leather, etc.). Pottery attained a notable degree of grace and stylistic coherence, both in the forms of the vessels and in the decorative style. Thus it is, of all the elements, the one that characterizes and distinguishes the various cultural facies which succeeded each other in space and time, allowing us to observe the concordances, the influences, the expansive and regressive movements, without losing sight of the possibility that the phenomena so observed may also correspond to alignments of an ethnic or political nature.

The succession of the single cultural facies, or — more precisely — of the various styles of ceramic decoration to which they correspond, is shown in a striking and unequivocal manner by certain sites, inhabited over long periods, in which each age has deposited its own testimony overlying those of preceding ages. Among such sites are the grottoes of Arene Candide at Finale Ligure, with deposits that demonstrate the succession of the early, middle, and late Neolithic in northern Italy. The data they furnish are confirmed by other sites, among them the palafitte settlement of the Isolino of Lake Varese, which demonstrates the middle-to-late Neolithic progression; the Agnano cave near Pisa, which shows the succession of late-to-subneolithic cultural phases; and a number of caves in southern France which document the progression from early to late Neolithic (in this region, as we shall see, the middle Neolithic is missing) and the successive subneolithic and early-metal-age facies. The diverse strata of a number of sites in Dalmatia and Herzegovina (Smilčić, Zelena Pećina, Črvena Stijena, etc.) are of great interest because they complement one another and reveal the succession of neolithic and early-metal-age cultures of the Adriatic region. Of particular importance, however, is the stratigraphic sequence offered by the Castello of Lipari in the Lipari (Aeolian) Islands, supplemented by the no less rich but chronologically more limited site in the Diana plain directly below the Castello site. The Aeolian stratigraphic series, even though it lacks an early neolithic facies, is probably the most complete in the entire Mediterranean region because it presents, clearly superposed and hence in a relative chronological sequence that is absolutely reliable, all the successive cultural facies from the beginning of the middle Neolithic up to the dawn of the Iron Age, that is, up to the historical era. Moreover, it permits us to observe the internal evolution of the individual facies. Thus the Aeolian stratigraphy provides us with a means of establishing the chronological position (at least relatively) of the neolithic and the Bronze Age cultures of Sicily and peninsular Italy, whose succession heretofore either had been uncertain or, in some cases, had been erroneously reconstructed. The cultures of the Lipari Islands, with their manifest relations (at least in certain phases) to the Aegean cultures — in some instances attested by the presence of objects undoubtedly imported from the Aegean — likewise enable us to synchronize, step by step, the sequence of cultures in the Italian peninsula and Sicily with that in the eastern Mediterranean and to establish, at least from the 17th century B.C. onward, the first fixed dates of Western prehistory.

The neolithic cultures: a. Early neolithic. The early neolithic is characterized by pottery with decorations impressed on the raw clay — or, at any rate, decoration done with the clay soft, before firing — by diverse objects, often the serrated or smooth edges of shells (usually of the edible Cardium, whence the term "cardial ware"). This type of decoration is found at the beginning of the Neolithic age along the entire extent of the Mediterranean coast — from northern Syria, Cilicia (Mersin), and southern Anatolia to continental Greece (Proto-Sesklo, or Pre-Sesklo, culture of Thessaly), the valley of the Danube and its tributaries (Starčevo and Körös cultures), the Dalmatian coast, the Italian peninsula, and the Mediterranean coasts of France, Spain, and North Africa. This widespread distribution of an almost identical type of pottery in areas where rather diverse mesolithic cultures had previously flourished demonstrates that the advent of neolithic culture was not the outgrowth of an evolution occurring *in loco* but the contribution of new peoples, probably migrating from the Near East; its distribution in coastal areas and its presence even on very small islands show that the diffusion of this neolithic culture must have followed maritime routes.

One of the regions of Italy in which impressed pottery is most widely diffused is Apulia. At first its culture must have produced only impressed pottery, based on a very limited heritage, but at a certain point a type of pottery painted in two colors, whose origins must be sought in the Sesklo culture of continental Greece, began to arrive in the Apulian villages. Locally produced, this painted pottery gradually become more and more diffused, while the impressed type gradually fell into disuse. At the same time there came into circulation a type of pottery scratched with a hard-pointed tool after firing; this is known as "Materan ware" but might more aptly be named "Ostuni ware," since the greatest number of examples, and the finest, have been recovered in the grotto of Sant'Angelo at Ostuni (PL. 434). This technique is also of Eastern provenance; remote prototypes are found in the Neolithic of northern Syria. Thus imperceptibly, by a gradual evolution, the transition is made from the earliest Neolithic, with its impressed pottery, to the middle Neolithic with painted and scratched pottery. It is not, perhaps, an accident that villages of the early Neolithic and of the transitional phases to the middle Neolithic are more numerous in Apulia than in other Italian regions. Apulia, because of its proximity to Greece and the Levant, is the region of Italy which received, before any other, the first wave of neolithic civilization, the bearer of impressed pottery, and then a second wave, bearing painted pottery.

The presence of the earliest neolithic impressed pottery in San Domino, one of the Tremiti Islands, and the discovery of many worked flints in the Palagruža Islands (Split, Yugoslavia, Archaeol. Mus.) may indicate the route by which the early Neolithic reached Italy: the islands of Korčula, Lastovo, Palagruža, Pianosa, and Tremiti form a bridge that lessened the risks of crossing the Adriatic. The characteristics of the impressed-pottery neolithic cultures in Dalmatia and Herzegovina are identical with those of the Italian peninsula and are extremely different from the early impressed-pottery neolithic cultures of the Danube Valley (Starčevo).

From Apulia and the promontory of Mount Gargano this culture spread northward along the Italian Adriatic coast as far as the Marches. Southward it must have spread over the plains bordering the Gulf of Taranto, and evidence of it has come to light at Favella, near Sibari. The mountainous terrain of Calabria may have presented an obstacle to its expansion, but there is reason to think that before long it had reached the Tyrrhenian coast. Unknown in Latium and Tuscany, it presents typical fragments on the island of Elba and in Corsica. We find it again in Liguria, at Finale Ligure, in the lowest neolithic level of the cave of Arene Candide and in the cave of Arma dell'Aquila, and north of the Apennines at Alba in Piedmont.

The same culture was widely diffused in southern France along a coastal strip varying from 30 to 60 miles, approximately, in width. The characteristic cardial pottery of this area shows a decoration chiefly of horizontal bands with impressed borders, which if not unknown is at least rare at Arene Candide, whereas in Catalonia it predominates. At Fontbrégua, Bord de l'Eau, Châteauneuf-les-Martigues, Unang, La Baume-Latrone, and Roucadour the early neolithic stratum lies directly below the late neolithic stratum (Chassey culture); there is no trace of the middle neolithic. This would lead us to suppose that in the west the early neolithic was able to survive for a long time, coetaneously with at least the early stages of Italian middle neolithic.

Similar conclusions can be drawn for the cardial facies of the Neolithic in Catalonia — the Montserrat culture, which takes its name from the principal complex of deposits in the grottoes of Montserrat near Barcelona. At Esquerdade los Roques del Pany, near Torelles de Foix, the Montserrat stratum lies below the stratum characterized by bell-beaker pottery. There are many deposits in Catalonia, in which the pottery, like that of the Levant, is decorated with impressions of the umbo as well as the outer rim of the Cardium shell. Of the deposits in eastern Spain the most important is Cueva de la Sarsa at Bocairente (Valencia). The backwardness of this cultural facies seems evident here and may have lasted beyond the limits of the middle Neolithic of the Italian peninsula. Cardial ware does not seem to have been diffused southward much beyond the provinces of Valencia, Alicante, and Murcia. Scattered examples have come to light in the region of Almería (Velez Rubio, La Gerundia) and of Granada (Alhama de Granada); farther south it is as yet unknown.

b. Sicily and southern Italy. In Sicily the impressed-pottery neolithic culture had a remarkable development, but with characteristics different from those of the peninsular Italian neolithic, being perhaps more evolved and later: this is the Stentinello culture, so named after a village near Syracuse. Like other similar and neighboring sites (Matrensa, Megara Hyblaea, Ognina), Stentinello was fortified, being surrounded by a trench (at Matrensa the trench is discontinuous) some 6 to 12 ft. wide, cut in the soft limestone and reinforced by a rampart of dry stone masonry. Only a few traces of the huts remain on the rock that lies barely below the topsoil. The Stentinello culture flourished in almost every part of Sicily and also in Malta, at Ghar Dalam and Li Skorba. Two classes of Stentinello pottery can be distinguished: a coarse ware, frequently with cardial decoration, which is identical with the impressed pottery found in peninsular Italy, and a much finer ware, richly decorated either by impression or in intaglio, the decoration not infrequently enlivened by a white incrustation not found elsewhere. Two techniques are sometimes associated on the same vessel (Naxos; PL. 428). Among the designs found on the finer ware is the motif of stylized eyes, which undoubtedly had an apotropaic significance. In a few of the Stentinello-culture villages (Megara Hyblaea, Trefontane, etc.) scant fragments of painted pottery have been found, some with two colors (red on a light background; PL. 428) and some (identical with the earliest middle neolithic pottery of Apulia) with three colors (red bordered with black on a light background). Furthermore, nearly all the characteristics observed, beginning with the fortified villages, seem to belong to the middle rather than to the early Neolithic. A few specimens of small idols and clay animal figures appear at Stentinello. In the Stentinello villages obsidian is abundant; it was undoubtedly umported from Lipari. The Stentinello culture, although it grew out of the main stem of the early Neolithic, must actually have developed during the middle Neolithic. So far, no more archaic neolithic stage has come to light in Sicily.

The stratigraphy of Lipari is fundamental to the establishment of the evolutionary sequence of the middle and late Neolithic, since it allows us to recognize four clearly defined successive phases. We have seen that in Apulia there was a gradual evolution from the impressed-pottery early Neolithic to a middle Neolithic characterized by painted pottery in two colors, with red bands or flames on a light ground, with which, for a time, the impressed type continued to coexist. The most typical sites are those around Matera, that is to say, the fortified villages of Murgecchia, Tirlecchia, Murgia Timone, and Serra d'Alto, whose culture is identical with that of the Sicilian Stentinello villages, and two caves, the Grotta Funeraria and the Grotta dei Pipistrelli. The two types of pottery, impressed and painted in two colors, are found in almost equal quantities; only toward the end of this period does a third color appear (the red bands are bordered in black). Relatively common, too, is scratched (graffito) ware, often very graceful. The same elements are found in many caves in Apulia and the Abruzzi.

To this period also belongs the earliest neolithic site in the Lipari Islands, Castellaro Vecchio, on the uplands of the island of Lipari. Here the painted pottery in two colors (a few fragments in three) is associated with the more plentiful brown ware of the Stentinello type. The extraordinary prosperity of Lipari during the Neolithic age was based on the working and export of obsidian. This cultural phase was followed by the first settlement at the Castello of Lipari, with different characteristics. Impressed decoration had now practically disappeared; painted pottery predominated, always in three colors, with red bands or flames, bordered in black on a light ground, often alternating with broken or intersecting clusters of black lines. It is associated with an elegant brown ware, perfectly smooth and polished, often with a sober scratched decoration applied after firing and encrusted with white, or, more rarely, painted with red ocher on a blackish ground. But sometimes the decoration was incised before firing or engraved in intaglio or even carried out in relief; this decoration marks the first appearance of the spiral and meander motifs (not infrequently these cover the entire surface of the vase) that were to become dominant in the following phase.

In southern Italy also appear other classes of pottery painted in three colors (but without spiral and meander designs), which certainly belong to the middle Neolithic; among these is the ware that takes its name from Ripoli, a village in the Abruzzi, which presents a distinctive decorative repertory of bands with large dots and triangles of parallel lines within metope-like panels. The commerce in this type of pottery must have been very extensive, for fragments have come to light in many deposits in southern Italy and also in regions where the painted-pottery neolithic is unknown, such as Emilia, Tuscany, and Liguria; a stray fragment has even been found in southern Spain. In the Grotta delle Felci, on the island of Capri, various vessels of this type have been found, together with others of a style similar to the Lipari pottery (with black-bordered bands and flames) but of a somewhat different quality of clay and a darker brown color. Neither in Capri nor at Ripoli does impressed pottery appear; this type evidently fell into disuse not only in Lipari but also in the Italian peninsula. A third class of three-color painted pottery, different from the other two, shows simple spiral and meander motifs in the technique of black-bordered red bands. It is as yet little known, but excellent examples have come to light (at Scaloria, in the Caverna dell'Erba at Avetrana, in the Ostuni cave, etc.), and it seems to represent a transitional stage leading to the next cultural phase.

A cultural facies with closely similar characteristics also appears at this time on the Dalmatian coast. At Danilo, near Šibenik, and at Smilčić, near Zadar (and also in central Bosnia, at Kakanj) is found a type of three-color painted pottery, without spiral and meander motifs, that is stylistically very near to the Ripoli ware. Associated with it is a brown clay ware — with decoration of spiral and meander motifs, incised or in intaglio, completely covering the surface of the vase — that is identical with the allover decoration at Lipari and has very singular shapes. These are strange objects, probably lamps, with bulging bases shaped like human legs, large oval mouths, and arched handles on the top; they appear also in the Neolithic of Greece, at Drachmani and Corinth. Obviously these similarities are not accidental. A single culture, closely related to continental Greek culture, although with marked provincial differences, was diffused over southern Italy, along the Italian Adriatic shore extending northward beyond Ancona, and on the coast of Dalmatia, opposite.

In Lipari the third phase is characterized by spiral-meander decoration appearing also on the painted pottery, by then a ware of great elegance and delicacy. Qualitatively this is among the noblest products the whole of Italian protohistory has to show. The forms of the vessels are elaborate and sophisticated, frequently heart-shaped; the walls are very thin. The decoration, almost always in miniature, is predominantly formed by complicated derivatives of the spiral and the meander, but checkerboards, lozenges, and, especially, bands of bordered zigzags appear as well. The handles are distinctive: they appear to be made by complicated twistings and turnings of a strip of clay. In Sicily the finds of this ware have been only sporadic. On the other hand, it is typically represented in southern Italy, in the deposit from which it derives its name, situated near the fortified village of Serra d'Alto, near Matera; here it is found in the foundations of the huts, which, it should be noted, are considerably later than the settlement itself. Serra d'Alto ware (PL. 429) is also found in other sites of the Matera district, such as Setteponti, and in Apulia, near Taranto. The same trend also appears farther north, on the Apennine watershed, at Starza di Ariano Irpino; this ware has also come to light on the Tyrrhenian shore at Paestum. Thus it seems to have had a remarkable diffusion.

The fourth phase in Lipari is characterized by the abandonment of painted ceramic decoration. The pottery is now monochrome, of a fine coral-red color, with a glossy finish. The handles also become simpler, being cylindrical or spool shaped. This is the period when the Lipari settlement moved from the Castello to the plain below, the Diana district, an extremely rich site whose name is applied to this ware. In the early stage the shapes of the vessels are still reminiscent of those of the Serra d'Alto styles, with the high rims, flaring lips, and heart-shaped profile. But subsequently the rims become smaller, until they disappear entirely, the profiles gradually become more rigid, until they are carinate, and the handles are reduced to mere symbols. The fine red color of the earlier stages gradually changes to a purplish brown. A fact of great interest is the presence in this phase of the Castello of Lipari of slag from copper smelting, indicating that metalworking techniques were now known and used; it is this that may have determined the change in the color of the pottery, by fostering the taste for a metallic sheen. Numerous deposits and several tombs of this period are known in eastern Sicily. Pottery of the Diana style is also found in Malta, where the painted-pottery middle Neolithic is lacking; it is diffused all over southern Italy and in the central part of the peninsula as well.

On the Dalmatian coast the Danilo-Smilčić culture was replaced by a new facies, of which the richest deposits are those of the Grapčeva, Markova, and Pokrivenik caves on the island of Hvar (Lesina), but which has been reported on other islands, among them Korčula and Lastovo, and at Smilčić (Zadar).

It is characterized by pottery of a brown glazed fabric, the shapes recalling those of the Diana style but incised and painted in red ocher with festoon, half-moon, and spiral motifs; this ware is also found in the valley of the Neretva (anc. Naro), Lisičići, and in the upper strata of Zelena Pećina. On the other hand, this is the time of the culture of Butmir (Sarajevo) in Bosnia, which is also present, but with marked differences, in the Nebo (Travnik) site; its pottery, with an exuberant spiral-meander decoration, either incised or in relief, seems to have stronger connections with the preceding Danilo-Kakanj culture.

There is no question that the neolithic civilization of southern Italy and Sicily shows an uninterrupted continuity of development, whose phases can easily be linked to those of the neolithic in Greece and in the general area of the southern Balkans. Three-color painting and spiral-meander decoration are characteristic of the Greece of the Dimini period, of which the three-color pottery of Lipari, Capri, and Ripoli appears to be a very early derivation, while the Serra d'Alto style represents a later reelaboration with many pronounced local characteristics. The shapes of the Diana ware and its decorative elements (especially the rows of tiny lozenges) seem to correspond rather to the late neolithic ware of such sites as Orchomenos, Eutresis, Larisa, and Corinth, that is, to a period in which the Greek neolithic civilization was undergoing a radical transformation under the influence of other cultures with more advanced metalworking techniques, which were pressing against its borders and making their appearance on the Anatolian shore of the Aegean Sea (see above, *The Near East, the Aegean, and the Balkans; Final phases of the Neolithic*).

c. Northern Italy and western Europe. The characteristics of the middle and late neolithic strata in northern Italy are very different from those in the south. As has been indicated, the sequence rests on the stratigraphy of the cave of Arene Candide at Finale Ligure, where, superposed on the early neolithic, there are rich strata characterized by a brown pottery similar to the type that in southern Italy is associated with the three-color painted pottery. Typical in the beginning of the period are vases with quadrilobed mouth, with square mouth in the fully developed phases; the latter type in particular often shows decoration scratched after firing. From these more evolved phases *pintaderas* of both stamp and cylinder types and small clay idols, generally seated, are among the finds. A few ceramic fragments show spiral-meander decoration and zigzag bands, either incised or carved in intaglio. In the Ligurian caves have been found a few scattered fragments of painted pottery imported from the south, which show that the first phase of the middle Neolithic at Arene Candide corresponds to the period of the three-color painted pottery at Lipari, Capri, Ripoli, and Danilo and that the more evolved phase corresponds to the period of the spiral-meander painted pottery of the Serra d'Alto style.

These two phases appear even more clearly in Emilia, where the pottery has markedly individual shapes; four-handled cups and carinate closed vessels, decorated with small impressions suggesting grains of wheat and with incised festoons, appear. In the second phase, represented chiefly by the Chiozza di Scandiano (Reggio Emilia) site, there are square-mouthed vases with decoration — scratched, incised, or in intaglio — consisting of spiral-meander motifs like those at Arene Candide. But the typically Ligurian tendency, with the square-mouthed pots, is also apparent in some of the oldest palafitte settlements in Lake Varese and in the Veneto, at Quinzano (Verona), as well as in a few lake dwellings of the Val di Marca (Lake Fimon) and of the Val Liona, in the Berici hills, south of Vicenza. To the west, on the other hand, this stylistic tendency does not cross the barrier of the Alps. Nor is there any evidence of it in southern France. A few isolated elements are found in the levels still characterized by impressed pottery (examples at Châteauneuf-les-Martigues) and in the levels similar to those of the Italian Lagozza culture (square-mouthed pots in the *sepulcros de fosa*, or trench graves, of Sabadell, in Catalonia). The middle Neolithic of Tuscany and Latium is less well known, the only important discovery being the tomb in the Patrizi cave at Sasso di Furbara.

At Arene Candide the upper (late) neolithic, or Lagozza, culture overlies the middle neolithic strata. The pottery, undecorated, is generally thin-walled, perfectly smooth, and highly polished; it is black or dark brown in color (in a few cases bright red). The shapes are few and often repeated. Characteristic is the absence of true handles; their place is taken by small perforated lugs. Scratched and incrusted decoration is occasionally found on the bowls. Even before the excavation of the site that gave its name to this culture — Lagozza di Besnate, near Gallarate (approximately 25 miles northeast of Milan) — it was clear that the culture extended to the west and was linked to the coeval cultures of Chassey (France) and of Cortaillod (on the Lake of Neuchâtel in Switzerland). The culture of this horizon is probably also related to the trench-grave culture in Catalonia. Thus it is possible to discern in this period, despite certain regional aspects, a cultural unity of the whole coastal arc of the Mediterranean from the mouth of the Arno to the estuary of the Ebro, including the hinterland — a cultural complex often referred to as the "western neolithic." The type of dwelling and marked differences in the pottery forms and in the stone industry distinguish the Ligurian facies from the Lombard, which is characterized by palafitte lake dwellings, such as those of Lake Varese (Isolino, etc.), Lagozza di Besnate, and Torbiera di Bosisio. The Lagozza culture also appears in peninsular Italy; it is sometimes found (as in Umbria) in association with red pottery of the Diana style, sometimes (as in Tuscany) in association with types of pottery that seem to reflect the influence of the bell-beaker forms. At Pescale di Modena (Emilia), pottery of the Lagozza type is associated with a ware having incised and often also intaglio decoration. This ware, in some of its features and certain of its decorative motifs, can also be related to the late neolithic pottery of the Dalmatian Hvar-Lisičići type, but other features, in particular the intaglio technique, are closer to the "Slavonic" pottery of Vučedol (PL. 416) and of the Ljubljana swamp, representing a culture that succeeded the Hvar and extended over a far greater area toward the Danubian region. All this shows the persistence of this horizon of culture, which lasted beyond the Neolithic age and into the first phases of the age of metals.

As has been noted, the Lagozza facies of the Ligurian caves is found along the entire Mediterranean littoral of France, from the Alps to the Pyrenees, in identical form with the sole exception that a greater quantity of scratched decoration is found in certain deposits. This is the culture which in France took its name from Chassey. The deposits in which the Chassey strata directly overlie those of the impressed-pottery early neolithic are relatively numerous, but there are no traces of the existence of an intermediate facies corresponding to the Italian middle neolithic. It therefore seems likely that beyond the Alps the early neolithic continued to flourish for a long time, concurrently with the Italian middle neolithic; a precocious appearance of the late neolithic in France seems less likely. The Cortaillod culture in Switzerland — the "early lacustrine neolithic" of P. Vouga (1934) — is more closely related to the Lagozza facies of Lombardy, if only for the similarity in the types of palafitte dwellings.

Doubtless also a part of the great late neolithic cultural complex — the "western neolithic" mentioned above — is the Catalan trench-grave culture known too by the name of its most important site, Sabadell; it does not seem to have extended south beyond the mouth of the Ebro. The undecorated pottery of the Sabadell culture is related to the types, generically termed "Western," of Lagozza, Chassey, and Cortaillod, but the presence of ring-shaped handles and of a number of square-mouthed vases seems to recall the Ligurian middle neolithic. Some of the later tombs seem, however, to indicate that the evolution of this culture continued until the dawn of the age of metals. What lay south of the Ebro is, at present, difficult to say, but it seems probable that here the impressed-pottery cultures of very early protoneolithic origin lasted for a very long time; the finds of Cueva de la Sarsa suggest that these cultures, too, continued to flourish until the beginning of the metal age. In fact at Sarsa, in an apparently homogeneous pottery complex, characterized by a cardial decoration far richer, more elaborate, and more exuberant than that found in any other western deposit, there appear isolated elements (vases with beak handles, perforated maceheads, etc.) that reveal their derivation from Aegean-Anatolian prototypes of the same period as those widely diffused in Malta, Sicily, peninsular Italy, and elsewhere. Still farther south, in the region including the provinces of Granada, Málaga, Córdoba, and Seville, there is a noticeably different facies, known chiefly from the discoveries made in a considerable number of caves. In the pottery, which has decoration incised in the raw clay or bears various impressed designs (none cardial), the typical forms are spheroidal cups and, above all, flasks, whose forms, symmetrical triple handles, and raised cord decoration closely

the Neolithic age and the beginning of the age of metals. This was in reality the beginning of the metal age, though metal was probably still a very rare material. A number of new cultural elements made their appearance, among them the horn cult and the collective rock-cut, oven-shaped tombs opening from a small shaft. Following the neolithic Diana style there was a first phase in which a number of different pottery styles seem to have coexisted: the San Cono–Piano Notaro style, the Conzo style, and a polished buccheroid ware. The San Cono–Piano Notaro style, of brown clay decorated with pairs of incised lines often flanked by impressed dots, generally outlining four large panels on each face of the vase, is found in eastern Sicily, on the south coast in the Gela district (at Piano Notaro), and also in the oldest group of oven-shaft tombs in the Conca d'Oro (the area around Palermo). The Conzo style, with similar motifs painted in red and black on a yellowish ground, is, up to now, known

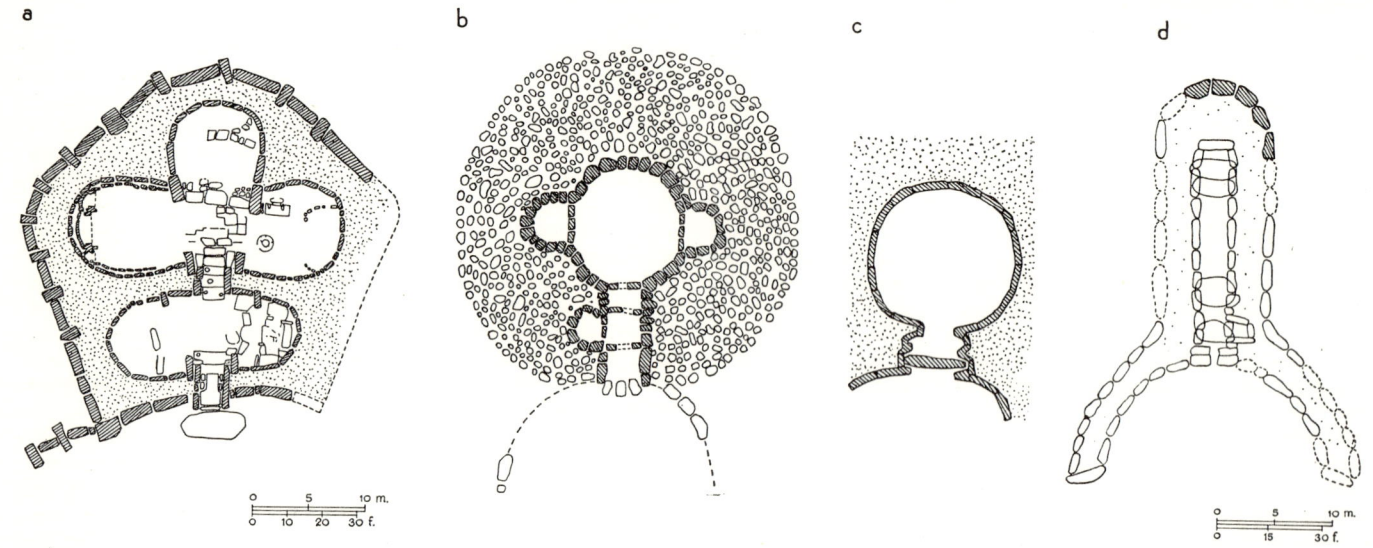

Apsed constructions in the western Mediterranean. (*a*) Gozo (Malta), Ggantija (*from Evans, 1960*); (*b*) Los Millares (Spain), domed tomb (*from V. Gordon Childe, The Dawn of European Civilization, London, 1950*); (*c*) Castelluccio (Sicily), rock-cut tomb (*ibid.*); (*d*) Bultei (Sardinia), "giant's tomb" of Sas Prigionas (*from Zervos, 1954*).

recall the middle neolithic pottery of Arene Candide — of which we are also reminded by certain other artifacts, such as the large-band marble bracelets decorated with horizontal grooves and the stone rings. But in some of the caves the beak-handled vases appear; especially in the cave of Los Murciélagos de Albuñol, which also yielded a very rich hammered-gold diadem; these finds attest the influence of the Aegean-Anatolian cultural stream, bearer to the west of the metal-age civilization.

The early age of metals: a. Early phases in Sicily and southern Italy. A sharp break seems to have occurred at the end of the Diana-style phase in the Aeolian cultural series. The type and forms of pottery that characterize the succeeding Piano Conte culture are entirely new and have no similarity to earlier ones. The ware is rather coarse, glossy, and dark brown to black in color; deep bowls, globular or pear-shaped jars, large closed jars with a type of lugs known as "tunnel handles," and crude cooking pots predominate. A few large basins with rectangular rims also appear. There is only one manner of decoration — bands of shallow parallel grooves, generally horizontal but becoming radial on the borders of the deep bowls — a motif that can be traced in its diffusion from the central part of Anatolia to the shores of the Aegean; this is the decoration found in sheet gold applied to metal vessels, of which excellent examples have been preserved in the tombs of Alaca Hüyük. The Piano Conte culture was diffused all through southern Italy; fragments typical of this culture are found in the Zinzulusa cave at Otranto, in the Ostuni cave, and at La Starza, Ariano Irpino. This period presents a totally different and much more complex situation in Sicily, where there was a radical transformation between the end of

only in the caves of the Syracuse district. A third type is a polished gray buccheroid ware, often decorated with fine striations made with the spatula over the whole surface. In a second phase appears a type of pottery painted with a great variety of motifs in opaque black on a purplish-red ground. The style of this ware is known as Serraferlicchio, after a site near Agrigento. This decorative technique also appears over a wide area of Greece (e.g., Eutresis, Thespiai) at the very end of the Neolithic age, although its origins are much older.

Another complete typological change occurred during the next period in the pottery of the Lipari Islands. This new period takes its name from the Piano Quartara site on the island of Panarea. It appears to have been a period of decline, probably caused by progress in metalworking techniques and the consequent decline in the Aeolian obsidian trade. In Sicily the pottery of this period differs from the Piano Quartara style in that it often has a glossy red surface. The forms, however, are similar and, in some cases, identical; they often recall eastern Aegean prototypes [particularly Troy I, the Green and Red levels of Poliochni, Thermi (Mytilene), together with contemporaneous material from Chios, Samos, and Kalymnos in the Cyclades] approximately synchronous with Early Helladic II, even though, because of the time lag in the spread of cultural currents from east to west, the chronology of this Sicilian culture may have been, to a certain extent, parallel to Early Helladic III. It is relatively easy to follow the evolution of this culture from the Chiusazza–Malpasso–Ticchiara phase, with its almost exclusively red pottery, to the phase in which painted brown decoration on a yellowish or buff ground prevailed. The characteristic shapes of this ware are small single-handled, yellow-toned jugs; small flasks, sometimes with pointed bases and high cylindrical necks cut obliquely to form a mouth; and many other forms which reveal their continuous derivation from Aegean-Anatolian prototypes. The decoration on the belly of the pot consists of separate bands of three lines, each descending vertically; on the neck it consists of a few lines, bands of horizontal segments, or a row of large dots.

b. The megalithic civilization of Malta. The early age of metals in Malta and Sardinia was a period of extraordinary prosperity. Aegean sailors in new types of ships (of which images have been preserved on the Cycladic paterae and the graffiti of the Hal Tarxien temple in Malta) were easily able to reach not only Sardinia but also the Iberian and southern French coasts. Vast new lands now came under the civilizing influence of the Near East. Their natural resources were tapped and exploited; new, flourishing civilizations sprang up and developed along their coasts and spread rapidly throughout the regions of the interior. A thriving commercial traffic passed through the Sicilian channel (between Sicily and Africa), and Malta became an obligatory port of call along this route; hence its extraordinary prosperity.

During the Neolithic period Malta formed part of the Sicilian Stentinello cultural area. Up to now, however, no traces of neolithic painted pottery have come to light, although at Li Skorba there is evidence of late neolithic culture in the form of Diana-style pottery, first brown and later red in color. It was the next period that witnessed the beginnings of the extraordinary megalithic architecture and the construction of the gigantic "temples" which are among the grandest and most imposing creations of Mediterranean prehistoric architecture.

In the field of pottery the sequence of styles was: the Li Skorba (still linked with the Diana style), the Zebbug, Mgarr, Ggantija ("Giant's Tower"), and Hal Tarxien styles. The last two, especially the Hal Tarxien style, represent the apogee of the Maltese megalithic culture, of which the others more or less constitute preparatory phases. However, in spite of the variety of its styles, it can clearly be seen that Maltese pottery is derived from Aegean Cycladic prototypes, as well as from the contemporaneous cultures of Samos, Mytilene, and Lemnos. There are also close ties with the Cretan Early Minoan. Only in the last Maltese phase, that of Hal Tarxien, are there clearly evident relations with the Middle Minoan in Crete and with the Kamares pottery style (see CRETAN-MYCENAEAN ART).

It was John D. Evans who recognized that the Maltese "temples" have their typological origins in the collective rock-cut tombs, sometimes multilobed, which had been built since the beginning of the age of metals under the influence of eastern prototypes, in Malta as well as in Sicily and peninsular Italy. The earliest "temples," built above ground level (e.g., at Mgarr), and the slightly later ones of the simpler type (Kordin III) are, in fact, on a trefoil plan. Each of the three great horseshoe-shaped apses is usually separated from the central rectangular chamber by means of pillars or by masonry forming a gate or balustrade. Sometimes the central chamber is reached through a large trilithic door. Almost all the temples belonging to the more evolved phase (Mnaidra, PL. 426; Hagar Qim; Ggantija, FIG. 671; Hal Tarxien, FIG. 418), already of imposing dimensions, have five apses. In one case (the middle temple at Hal Tarxien) there are seven apses. The central, axial apse, however, generally assumes smaller proportions. The middle gallery is narrow at the point of division between the first and second pairs of apses and is often flanked by a pair of altars. In the older temples the pillars, the thresholds, the posts, and the lintels of the large doorways, and in a few cases also the base blocks of the façade, are great monolithic stone slabs; the rest of the structure, the apses and exterior walls, was of irregular dry masonry. In the later temples there is a carefully constructed plinth of large stone orthostats, often very regular, on which is built the structure of rough-hewn (in some cases perfectly dressed) ashlar in isodomic courses of great technical perfection. In these later phases the interiors of the temples were decorated with magnificent sculptures. The surfaces of the pillars, piers, and lintels are ornamented with a pattern of hammered holes; balustrades and altars are covered with elegant decorations, generally spiral motifs or running spirals in a vine pattern (PL. 427), prototypes of which may be found in the Cycladic steatite pyxides. At Hal Tarxien there are animal friezes depicting sacrificial victims (rams, goats, swine, and oxen; PL. 427). In addition to the temples built aboveground with megalithic techniques, there is a magnificent underground temple at Hal Saflieni, where much the same temple plans and architectural elements are carved in the living rock. It must have served as a place of worship and also for burial.

In addition to temple sculpture, during this period the Maltese also developed a very refined type of small sculpture, generally representing female figures, standing, crouching, seated, or recumbent on a bed. They are sometimes clothed, but more often they are nude, accentuatedly, sometimes even exaggeratedly steatopygous, and almost always vividly realistic (PL. 427). Even though there are some local variations in the ritual position of the arms, these figurines seem closely related to the Cycladic marble idols. The rigid stylization of the latter contrasts, however, with the much looser naturalism of the Maltese statuettes, which are more like the much earlier statuettes that have been discovered in the neolithic strata at Hacılar (Anatolia), at Lerne (Argolis), and at Knossos (Crete). The rigid stylization of Cycladic derivation, on the other hand, is evident in an anthropomorphic stele, found in one of the tombs at Zebbug, which has a remarkable resemblance to a stele from Troy I. This Maltese stele would seem to be one of the links in a chain that joins the distant Anatolian prototypes with the similar, but later, manifestations in Corsica, southern France, and Liguria.

When the megalithic culture of Malta had reached its apogee, it appears to have come to a sudden and violent end. There are no known phases of decadence. Over the ruins of the temples of Hal Tarxien, possibly destroyed by fire, there is a cremation necropolis, belonging to a separate and successive cultural facies. (See below, *Subsequent phases of the early age of metals in Sicily and Malta.*)

c. Sardinia. Sardinia presents a cultural phenomenon similar to that of Malta. There is practically no trace of a Sardinian neolithic culture; at the beginning of the age of metals there developed a flourishing culture which in all its manifestations shows its derivation from the Aegean cultures. The individual phases of its development have not as yet been clearly identified, and it seems probable that the splendors of its terminal phase have obscured those leading up to it. This Sardinian culture is known to us mainly through its tombs, some of which are rich in materials. The predominant type of tomb is cut into the rock in the form of an artificial grotto (known as *domus de gianas*), often grander and more complex than the Sicilian tombs. Some of them (at Anghelu Ruju, Cuguttu, Riu Mulinu, and elsewhere) consist of a number of chambers and sometimes have sculptured decorations of bulls' heads (Anghelu Ruju). Near them are found dolmens, built aboveground of great stone slabs and covered with barrows. While the form of some dolmens (Birori) recalls the rock-cut tombs, others (Su Coveccu, near Bultei; Perdalunga, near Austis; Doli Fichina; S' Enna sa Vacca) show a gradual transition to the *allée couverte* (gallery grave), which developed into the "giants' graves" of the succeeding nuraghic period. The necropolis of Li Muri, near Arzachena (La Gallura), on the other hand, consists of grave circles enclosing cist tombs and smaller cists, perhaps intended to contain cremated remains. Small idols are also found in Sardinia (PL. 433). They are even closer to the Cycladic idols than are the Maltese, but artistically they are greatly inferior to the latter. Many other Sardinian artifacts, such as pierced maceheads (from Li Muri and Macomer), ax-adzes and stone double axes, stone vases (a splendid steatite cup was found at Li Muri), clay tripod vessels (PL. 432) and certain ceramic techniques and decorative motifs, are also of obvious eastern origin. But Sardinia was more open to contacts with the Iberian Peninsula than any other region of Italy, and it is probable that dolmenic architecture was transmitted to Spain from Sardinia. From the Iberian Peninsula, Sardinia (probably in the final phases of this cultural period, which must have lasted for a considerably long time) received the bell beaker and all the other elements generally associated with it, such as buttons with a V-shaped perforation.

d. Subsequent phases of the early age of metals in Sicily and Malta. In a period after those described above, there followed a series of distinct local cultures in Sicily, the Lipari Islands, and Malta. Not only did they differ considerably from one another, but they actually seem to have exerted very little mutual influence. Some of them at least, such as the Castelluccio culture in eastern and southern Sicily, the Capo Graziano culture in the Lipari Islands, and the Hal Tarxien necropolis culture in Malta, have their genesis in, and very close typological connections with, the Middle Helladic cultures in Greece (see above). There seems to have been a colonization of the west by various Middle Helladic peoples, each marked by its own particular character. However, the numerous imports of Early Mycenaean pottery (Late Helladic I and II, ca. 1600–1425 B.C.) in the sites of the Capo Graziano culture show that at least this culture (and probably the other parallel ones also) must have continued to develop at a time when, in the Aegean, the Middle Helladic had given way to the Late Helladic (better known as Mycenaean). These imports provide the earliest definite dates of western Mediterranean prehistory and help to fix the earliest limits of these cultures.

The Castelluccio culture is characterized by pottery painted in a brown or blackish color on a yellowish or reddish ground (PL. 435). It is closely linked, in techniques, decorative motifs, and vase forms, to the matt-painted ware of the Middle Helladic. The Castelluccio people lived in small villages consisting of a few huts, generally situated on high ground at the edges of the richest agricultural zones. The only one of these villages that has been systematically excavated to date is that of Manfria, near Gela, where nine roughly ellipsoid huts (some with lateral niches) have been uncovered. The floors, which are much lower than the level of the ground, are made of beaten clay with a chalk whitewash. The structure is sustained by a central pole and four or more others at the sides. One hut is divided into two sections by five axial pillars and has numerous others around the edge. The interiors are surrounded by small, rough walls. Other important villages include the one at Monte Sallia, near Comiso, and that at Castelluccio, near Noto, which has given its name to this culture. In the adjacent small necropolis of Cava della Signora, the tombs were sometimes closed with sculptured stone portal slabs (PL. 435), which constitute the only examples of prehistoric sculpture in Sicily. The spiral motifs of these sculptures represent the human figure in an extremely schematized form. These same tombs have yielded a number of small bone idols of a singular type, also highly schematized, consisting of a number of globules (PL. 435) with incised decoration. Their greatest interest lies in the fact that they are very similar to idols found in Troy II, in the Peloponnesos (in the first Middle Helladic stratum at Lerne), in southern Italy (Altamura), and in Malta (Hal Tarxien necropolis). No imported Aegean pottery has come to light in the villages of the Castelluccio culture, in contrast to the great quantity found in the coeval strata on the Lipari Islands.

The Castelluccio culture assumes particular and individual characteristics in the various zones of the vast territory it covers. The best-known facies is that of the small villages in the Syracuse area and on the edges of the plains of Vittoria and Gela. In the Agrigento area the pottery from the necropolises of Montedoro, Monte Sara, and Monteaperto, among others, has a much more delicate decoration. The forms that characterize the eastern and southeastern facies, such as hourglass-shaped mugs with one or two handles, do not appear in the Agrigento facies; on the other hand a biconal mug, with or without a foot, is a type unknown in the east and southeast. In the Etna zone the hardness of the lava did not permit the hewing of rock-cut tombs and necessitated a change in the funerary rites. The numerous natural caves and hollows formed by the flowing lava served as burial places. The pottery of the Etna zone often has carinated forms, remarkably similar to the Peloponnesian matt-painted ware. Another facies of the Castelluccio culture has been distinguished in northeastern Sicily (Naxos, Rodì, Tindari) and is characterized by pottery with elongated handles, either in the shape of an ax or bifurcate, with prolongations shaped like equine ears. These types, associated with painted pottery of the Castelluccio type, appear in a tomb at Vallelunga in the central Sicilian province of Caltanissetta.

The Capo Graziano culture takes its name from a promontory of the island of Filicudi, where villages of oval huts have been found. It is documented also by remains on the Castello of Lipari, and evidence is also found in others of the islands (Salina, Panarea, and Stromboli). The huts are not sustained by poles but are surrounded by stout stone walls. During this period the Lipari Islands must have been a prosperous outpost of the Mycenaean maritime commerce with the west. The pottery is of brown clay decorated with incised, frequently wavy, lines and with rows of dots. There is a singular similarity with the richer and more varied Maltese pottery found in the cremation necropolis that extends over the ruins of the Hal Tarxien temples. This necropolis also contains a considerable number of small dolmens.

Northwest Sicily seems during this period to have been oriented toward the west, and it offers evidence of closer relations with the Iberian Peninsula. At La Moarda, Segesta, Villafrati, Isnello, and Torrebigini (near Selinunte) there has been found a particular style of pottery with incised bands, apparently a local derivation of the bell beaker. The center of production and diffusion of this form is believed to have been the Iberian Peninsula; during this period the pottery was widely exported not only throughout the Mediterranean (Sicily, Sardinia, northern Italy, southern France) but also to the Atlantic coast of France, the British Isles, and the Rhine and Danube valleys.

e. The aëneolithic cultures and the beginnings of the Bronze Age in Italy. In peninsular Italy there is evidence of a facies corresponding to the Piano Conte type of deposits. The beginning of the age of metals is, however, best documented by the discovery of the Gaudo necropolis near Paestum. Here the tombs are of the rock-hewn artificial-grotto type, similar to those found in Sicily. The pottery is of monochrome clay and generally undecorated. The most common shapes are flattened spherical flasks with either a cylindrical or truncated-cone neck, askoi of similar shape, but with an eccentric neck, single-handled jugs, twin vessels, and bell-shaped lids. The influence here is evidently Early Helladic. Diverse other objects were found with this pottery, including several large flint daggers, pedunculate arrows, and a small copper dagger. A similar necropolis, discovered on one of the Apennine passes in the district of Santa Maria delle Grazie, near Mirabella Eclano, forms a link between the Tyrrhenian Gaudo facies and the contemporaneous Apulian facies, documented by the collective tombs of Andria, Gioia del Colle, Selva di Matera, and Cellino San Marco, near Brindisi. Here the prevailing types are pear-shaped pots decorated with minute impressions, with rows of small cones in relief, and also with incised patterns, generally arranged in horizontal bands (PL. 434).

Also related to the Gaudo culture is the Rinaldone culture, extending over Latium and Tuscany. It is characterized by rock-hewn artificial grotto tombs at Sgurgola, near Anagni; Alatri; Mandela (formerly Cantalupo); Camerata, near Tagliacozzo; Rinaldone, in the Viterbo district; Bardano, near Orvieto; Ponte San Pietro; and other sites near Lake Trasimeno and on the island of Pianosa. (Farther north, pit graves and stone cist tombs are the prevailing types.) The Rinaldone pottery is like the Gaudo pottery, especially in the forms of the flasks, either plain or decorated with a few slightly raised ribs. The handles differ, however, from the Gaudo type; they are not of the ribbon type, but generally tubular or subcutaneous. Stone battle axes appear, and metalwork is represented by flat adzes, knives studded with small nails, and other objects.

In the lower Po Valley there flourished at this time the Remedello culture, named for a burial ground near Brescia which contains over a hundred tombs. The Remedello people observed the ancient burial rites; bodies were buried singly in a crouching position in a simple pit, nearly always with a rich collection of grave goods. The same facies is found in Emilia. Ornamental objects are numerous and various, including a marble cross and star, small steatite disks, and shell plaques and buttons. The most interesting feature of Remedello pottery is the appearance of the bell beaker. The incised and grooved decoration of some vases includes bands of panels in an alternating arrangement of horizontal and vertical segments. This decoration reappears in other areas where the bell beaker is frequent, such as the Fontbouisse culture in southern France. Less is known about the villages of the Remedello culture. The one to which the Remedello necropolis probably belonged seems to have consisted of huts and was surrounded by a ditch and perhaps also by an inner rampart, like the neolithic villages in southern Italy. Other noteworthy sites are La Sassina, near Verona, where fragments of bell-beaker pottery have come to light, and Colombare di Negrar, where rectangular huts were built agaınt rock cliffs.

It is impossible to separate the Remedello tombs from the villages of the Polada culture, best known for the material recovered from the sites (nearly always lake dwellings and occasionally palafittes) in the natural amphitheater formed by the terminal moraine that bounds Lake Garda on the south, at Polada, Cataragna, Barche di Solferino, Bande di Cavriana, and elsewhere. It has been discovered that the villages of Barche di Solferino and Bande di Cavriana are not built on platforms supported by piles but rather on land reclaimed by covering the sites with tree trunks laid horizontally in crisscross fashion and reinforced by a few small piles on which the huts were probably erected. The pottery is coarse, consisting of cups and jugs; what little decoration there is generally consists of a few horizontal cordons, level with the joints of the handles, or of groups of short vertical ribs. In a finer ware, consisting of blackish vessels with a better and smoother finish, a rather frequent decoration comprises rows of impressed dots and incised geometric motifs; this repertory may have been influenced by prototypes of "Slavonic" pottery. The forms, the types of handles, the techniques, and the decorative motifs closely link the Polada pottery with that of the contemporaneous or earlier cultural facies of peninsular Italy (Ortucchio, Andria, Cellino San Marco) and Sicily (Piano Quartara–Chiusazza and the contemporaneous facies of the Conca d'Oro); this fact demonstrates the peninsular and Mediterranean origins of this cultural complex. The Polada culture undoubtedly had a wide territorial diffusion. In certain areas it lasted even through the subsequent Bronze Age; in a few others it probably lasted until the dawn of the Iron Age.

f. Southern France. The cultural movement that spread from the shores of Anatolia over the whole of the western Mediterranean, bringing with it metal-age civilization, also reached the southern coast of France. It appears likely that it followed a maritime route, passing through Malta and Sardinia. It may also have touched Corsica, an island region hitherto almost entirely unknown from the point of view of prehistory (see MEDITERRAEAN, ANCIENT WESTERN). In southern France, while men continued to dwell in caves, a great number of hut villages sprang up. The best-known of these is Fontbouisse (Salinelles, Gard). The essential funerary symbol of this culture is the anthropomorphic stele, or stele statue, with which must also be associated the aniconic baetuli, possibly originally painted. Caves were used as ossuaries to contain partially cremated skeletons. The cremation rite became common, with the ashes preserved in small cists often associated with sculptured or aniconic steles. In some cases the ashes were placed in natural cracks in rocks and sealed with slabs, but the rock-hewn artificial grotto tomb is also present. The most widely diffused type of tomb, which continued to develop through the successive phases of the Bronze Age, is the megalithic surface monument, built in the form of a simple dolmen, and the *allée couverte*, a number of different groups of which can be identified in southern and western France.

Perhaps one of the oldest, as well as one of the richest, of these groups comprises the magnificent *allées couvertes* of Castellet, near Arles. These are wide galleries carved in the living rock, covered with enormous slabs, and sometimes flanked by funerary cells and surmounted by a barrow with a dolmen. The greatest diffusion of this type of monument is, however, found in the uplands of the Gard and Hérault departments and on the Grands Causses in the departments of Aveyron and Lozère and in the northern part of Hérault. The material found in the tombs does not differ from that found in the villages and caves of the same region. Metal artifacts include adzes, small daggers, olive-shaped or biconical beads, small spirals, and, later, large pins with heads twisted or hammered into disks, trefoils, and other shapes. In the Arles dolmens even gold is found. Pottery shows a great variety of decorative techniques. During the earliest phase there appears to have been a survival of Chassey traditions, including scratched decoration, as well as the initiation of new techniques. These include clusters of grooves or incised lines. The motifs are arranged in simple horizontal bands of lines or in angular groups (chevrons) and in metope panels with alternating clusters of vertical and horizontal segments. Of particular interest is a design of concentric semicircles hanging like festoons, perhaps having a sacred meaning. There are also rows of cones of about the size of a lentil, obtained by boring the wall of the vessel from the inside. Precedents for this technique are found at Orchomenos, at Cellino San Marco (near Brindisi), in Malta, in Sardinia, and elsewhere. The bell beaker, of Iberian origin, is relatively little diffused. A noticeable difference occurs in the large *allées couvertes* of the Audes, which sometimes are as much as 45 ft. long and furnished with very rich grave goods, including gold objects. Here bell-beaker pottery predominates, accompanied by all the artifacts usually found with it. The Aude tombs appear to be an extension of the Iberian cultures. The small dolmens of Roussillon, perhaps much later and less rich, actually form part of the Pyrenean megalithic orbit. Another well-defined group is in the southwest and consists of the *allées couvertes* of La Halliade, Taillan, and other sites,

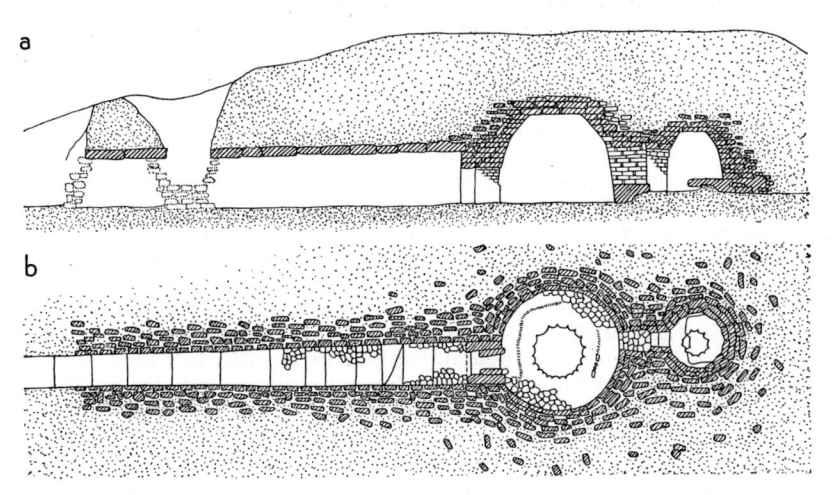

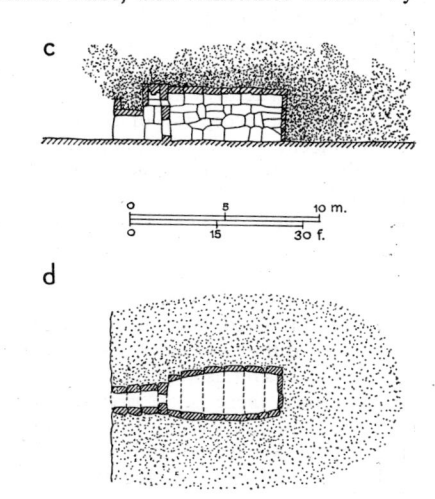

Western Mediterranean megalithic tombs. (*a, b*) Antequera region (Málaga), Cueva del Romeral, plan and section (*from L. Pericot Garcia, La España primitiva, 1950*); (*c, d*) Minorca, Rafal Rubí *naveta* (*from J. Hernandez Mora, Menorca prehistorica*).

containing deep double-cone cups with three, four, or even more small feet (polypedal vases). It is not difficult to follow the route of their diffusion from the eastern Mediterranean via Sardinia. The pottery with eye decoration, from the Peu Richard site in the Charente-Maritime, has clear links to Sardinian and Maltese prototypes.

Luigi BERNABÒ BREA

g. Spain (the Almería and Bell-beaker cultures). The early metal age cultures that spread across the western Mediterranean exhibit some of the same essential characteristics found in the older Aegean-Anatolian Bronze Age cultures in Malta, Sardinia, Sicily, and southern Italy. The chief features are the diffusion of collective rock-hewn or surface graves, more refined stoneworking techniques, and the appearance of copper tools and utensils, as well as the schematic idols. In Spain these developments, undoubtedly of Mediterranean origin, seem to have assumed a preeminence particularly evident in the megalithic technique of building with great stone blocks or slabs placed in juxtaposed and superimposed courses. This construction is found especially in burial galleries and chambers. Such megalithic structures are diffused over almost the entire peninsula, with the exception of the central-eastern region, and have their epicenter in southwestern Iberia, although this is perhaps not their original nucleus, as has been suggested. However, the technique and spirit of these structures are common to a far vaster geographical area, embracing not only the western Mediterranean but the whole of western and northern Europe as far as the British Isles and Scandinavia (see EUROPEAN PROTOHISTORY). Nevertheless, it would not be appropriate to define the Iberian aëneolithic cultures as "megalithic" cultures; it is, moreover, difficult to apply the criterion of megalithic construction as a distinguishing factor among certain cultures.

In Spain there is, at present, no precise method of defining the sequence of cultural phases from the Neolithic to the late Bronze Age or the environmental relationships of the various cultures. The stratigraphic study of inhabited sites has barely begun, and much of the most circumstantial data on the material is provided by the tombs. The Almería zone in the southeast, with its vast, fortified settlements and its grandiose necropolises rich in funerary monuments (particularly Los Millares and Almizaraque), manifests an intensive and relatively well-defined concentration of cultures spanning a long period of development. The earliest innovations that penetrated this region from the east by a maritime route were superimposed on the local neolithic cultures, dominated by the cardial ware mentioned above, and were partly characterized by elements in common with the North African shores of the Mediterranean (whence the term "Hispano-Mauretanian cycle," applied by some authorities to this substratum). The appearance of metalworking, of schematized idols (PL. 432), of incised-bone and terra-cotta plaque-idols, of smooth pottery with predominantly spheroidal shapes, and of pit or cist graves with stone circles characterize the first phase of the Almería culture, represented at El Garcel, at La Gerundia, and in the burial areas of Loma del Jos, La Pernera, and Cerro de las Canteras. This was followed by the first phase of Los Millares, in which funerary architecture was developed into the form of megalithic gallery graves ending in a round cella covered with a false dome (FIG. 671). This type of tomb was undoubtedly inspired by the tholoi of the eastern Mediterranean [see above, *Individual neolithic cultural areas: a. Western Asia (Neolithic and Chalcolithic)*]. Grave furnishings became extraordinarily rich, especially in ornamental objects. A new type of incised pottery appeared, decorated with bands of straight or wavy lines, circles edged by radiating lines, eyes, and schematized figures. There are also protuberances and other elements executed in relief. The high point of the Los Millares phase is characterized by the great increase in size and complexity of the plan of the sepulchers. To this period also belong the monumental pillared gallery tombs found in the Málaga zone and in Andalusia, such as the Cueva de Menga (PL. 431), the expanded form of which anticipates the subterranean and surface *naveta* (or *naus*) tombs of the Balearics. The bell beaker also appears in the Almerian cultural complexes.

The Almería culture extends along the eastern coast of Spain as far as Catalonia, but without the megalithic architecture that is found in the interior and in the western part of the Iberian Peninsula. There it is accompanied by some of the elements found in the Almería zone, especially plaque-idols incised in the unmistakable Geometric style of the Spanish Aëneolithic, together with the eye motif. Another coeval megalithic province exists in the north, in the Pyrenean region, but its characteristics are more archaic and simple than those of the east and south.

At the same time, over the greater part of the peninsula, another very important cultural phenomenon was taking place: the diffusion of the bell beaker, accompanied by certain other elements such as small plaques (probably erroneously believed to have been intended to protect the wrists of archers) and buttons with V-shaped perforations. Bell-beaker pottery is characterized by a rounded base and a flaring mouth. This form is found not only in the beaker (PL. 432) but also in broad, low vessels (*cazuelas*). Simple hemispherical bowls also appear. None of these vessels have handles. The most characteristic element is the decoration of minute impressed or incised lines in straight horizontal or zigzag bands, with dots or cross-hatching, somewhat resembling fine basketry. The prototype of this bell-beaker decoration is undoubtedly to be found in impressed pottery, particularly in the most evolved cardial decoration of the Iberian neolithic substratum, rather than in Almerian incised pottery. Bell-beaker pottery became predominant during the most advanced phase of the Spanish Aëneolithic. In some areas it is associated with megalithic architecture; elsewhere (e.g., in much of the eastern part of the peninsula) it appears independently; but it is diffused over a very wide area even beyond the borders of Spain. In one direction it extends to the Mediterranean, to the Balearic Islands, Sardinia (in the Anghelu Ruju culture), western Sicily, central Italy, and northern Italy (in the Remedello culture). In another direction it spreads north to France, the British Isles, central Europe, and Scandinavia. It has been suggested that this very wide cultural diffusion, presumed to have had its epicenter in Spain, was the result of vast migrations and conquests on the part of the bell-beaker bearers; this hypothesis is as yet unproven (see EUROPEAN PROTOHISTORY). The culminating Bell-beaker phase occurred at the beginning of the 2d millennium B.C.

* *

The late Bronze Age and the transition to the Iron Age: a. Sicily. In the Lipari Islands, the Capo Graziano culture was succeeded about 1400 B.C. by a culture known as Milazzese (from the promontory on Panarea), characterized by villages consisting of oval huts, sometimes with an adjacent rectangular enclosure. The builders of these villages chose locations that were difficult of access but easily defensible (Panarea, PL. 437; Portella on Salina), or they continued to inhabit locations where villages had been built during the preceding era (Castello di Lipari, Capo Graziano on Filicudi), provided these locations seemed strong enough to withstand an enemy attack. Milazzo, on the north coast of Sicily, also belongs to this facies. There a necropolis has been discovered in which the dead were buried in a crouching position within great pithoi, probably covered by stone barrows. This manner of burial had been very widely diffused since the beginning of the Bronze Age in Anatolia and in the Aegean, where the necropolis of Nidri on the island of Leukas provides the closest comparison to the Milazzo necropolis. Finds of Mycenaean pottery (Late Mycenaean IIIa 2, 1400–1300 B.C., and, more rarely, IIIb, 1300–ca. 1230 B.C.), including a small idol, and a necklace of vitreous paste beads (undoubtedly imported) found on Salina provide the proof of continued and active trade relations with the Aegean area. A particularly interesting fact is the presence on local pottery of potters' stamps and marks that sometimes reproduce the symbols of Minoan-Mycenaean linear script. At this time there were also numerous importations of typical Apennine pottery from the Italian peninsula (see below, *The Apennine culture*).

Flourishing in Sicily during this period was a culture known as Thapsos, which succeeded the Castelluccio culture. It is best known from its necropolises of rock-cut oven tombs, identical with those of the preceding phase. The majority of them are found in the country around Syracuse, but the Thapsos culture area also extends to the Etna region (e.g., Naxos and Paternò) and to the Agrigento district (Caldare). In western Sicily only a few traces of the Thapsos culture have been found (Mangiapane cave, near Custonaci). The inventory of the grave goods (e.g., swords, bracelets) shows a much larger diffusion of bronze than in the previous facies. Numerous imported Mycenaean vases are present, and an ivory comb and necklaces of faïence beads have also come to light. These objects belong to the Mycenaean IIIa 2; only a very few pieces may be attributed to Mycenaean IIIb. There are no traces of contacts between Sicily and continental Italy. On the other hand, the necropolises of the Syracuse district contain a great deal of pottery identical with the ware of the Borg in-Nadur culture of Malta. The forms are generally vessels in a truncated-cone shape on a high truncated-cone foot (having, therefore, the form of an hour-glass), single-handled jugs with spherical bellies and strong truncated-cone necks. The clay is reddish in color, and the decoration is rather monotonous, consisting of bands of fine lines incised parallel to the rim or forming large chevron patterns on the walls.

In the course of the 13th century B.C. a radical change occurred in the cultural evolution of Sicily and of the Lipari Islands. The very foundations of the social and economic organization seem to have changed. The relations that had linked these regions with distant Mediterranean countries were apparently broken off. The villages of the Milazzese period were evidently destroyed and never rebuilt. It is probable that these changes were brought about by the arrival of new peoples from the Italian peninsula: the Ausones mentioned by Diodorus Siculus. At the Castello of Lipari there appeared a culture entirely different from its predecessor but similar to the Sub-Apennine culture of continental Italy. The pottery is distinguished by the quantity and variety of terminals or projections (in the form of small upright cylinders, double cylinders, horns, axes, and volutes) on the handles of the carinated bowls. Also very common are situlae decorated with a cordon and four small tongue handles around the rim. This first facies of the Ausonian culture (Ausonian I) seems to have lasted only a short time, probably not longer than a century. The presence of a few rare shards attributable to Mycenaean IIIb establishes the date of the beginning of the facies as not earlier than 1250 B.C. One may suppose that it lasted at least until 1150 or 1100 B.C. The second phase (Ausonian II) presents a far richer and more complex cultural heritage. In the pottery, frequently of a shiny reddish as well as of a blackish color, the projections on the handles disappear almost entirely; only the horned type remains, assuming the form of an animal protoma. New types appear, for example, a cup with an inturned rim and a single arched handle, typically Villanovan features. There is also a type of decoration consisting of grooves, often associated with raised pellets surrounded by semicircular grooves. Two classes of painted pottery appear; one has simple geometric motifs in brown on a yellowish ground; the other has a decoration which may be termed "plumed." The Ausonian period is known from its necropolises as well as from its dwellings. The Lipari necropolis has cremation burials, in which the ashes are preserved in large situlae, always without grave goods, along with inhumation burials consisting of large jars, sometimes enclosing a rich inventory of grave goods: necklaces made of amber, vitreous paste, and rock crystal; gold wire bracelets; and leaf fibulas with either a stilted or a simple bow. A continental type of fibula with a looped bow is related to the fibulas found in the Terramare cultures of the Po Valley, in the Peschiera del Garda palafitte dwellings, and in the proto-Villanovan deposits. In Milazzo, which undoubtedly lay within the Ausonian cultural orbit, a cremation necropolis has also been discovered. It is probably of a more evolved type; the urns, which are covered with pebbles, are of a definitely proto-Villanovan type.

In Sicily, too, after the Thapsos period, the populations abandoned the coastal regions and took refuge in the less accessible hill country. New settlements sprang up at Pantalica (from which the new eastern Sicilian culture took its name), Cassibile, Caltagirone, Monte Dessueri, and elsewhere. Sicilian culture of this period was still based on Mediterranean traditions, and tombs were still of the rock-cut grotto type. At Pantalica, Cassibile, Monte Dessueri, and elsewhere they are gathered in vast necropolises like huge honeycombs cut from the precipitous faces of the cliffs that surrounded the settlements. Household objects such as pottery and bronzes are of types altogether different from the contemporaneous objects of peninsular Italy. In some cases they show close similarities to those of Mycenaean IIIc (ca. 1230–1100 B.C.). The evolution of the Pantalica culture can be traced through several centuries. The first phase (Pantalica Nord, or Pantalica I, ca. 1230–1000) is documented in the north and northwest necropolises of Pantalica, the Caltagirone necropolis, and a number of tombs at Monte Dessueri, by a fine glossy red pottery in which very high tubular feet are common (PL. 437). Some of the forms are of evident Mycenaean derivation; the bronze pieces, too (mirrors, knives, daggers, fibulas with "violin" bows or simple bows), are often of Mycenaean types. In the second phase, which began perhaps about 1000 B.C. (necropolises of Cassibile and Calcarella di Calascibetta, and some of the Monte Dessueri tombs), the red pottery gives way to a painted ware with characteristic "plume" motif. The typical bronze forms include the fibula with a stilted elbow bow and the small knife with a loop handle. Some identical forms are found in the Iberian Peninsula, and some have even come to light on the Atlantic coast of France and in the British Isles. This is the period in which Phoenician commerce dominated the western Mediterranean and extended even beyond the Pillars of Hercules. The third phase (Pantalica Sud, or Pantalica III; Cavetta, and Filiporto necropolises) shows evident influences of the Greek Geometric style. The typical fibula has a small looped bow, which in time is made smaller, while the pin is longer and curved. This phase probably embraced the end of the 9th and the first half of the 8th century B.C. The majority of the tombs in the Finocchito necropolis and all those at Tremenzano and Noto Antica belong to a fourth phase, the Finocchito period, which is contemporary with the foundation of the Greek colonies on the coasts of Sicily. A good many Greek objects (or objects of Greek type), such as small proto-Corinthian vases, now appear. A type of painted pottery developed locally, in imitation of sub-Geometric Greek types. An incised ware was also developed with a Geometric repertory. The fibulas have a long catchplate. Ornamental bronze objects abound, including rings, chains, pendants, and beads for necklaces. And here, for the first time, iron objects appear.

During the Iron Age there developed very profound differences between the cultures of eastern and western Sicily. The southeastern facies of Cassibile, Pantalica Sud, and Finocchito corresponds to a facies in central and western Sicily known as the Sant'Angelo Muxaro culture, named after its largest center, in the province of Agrigento. The town of Sant'Angelo Muxaro may possibly have been the legendary Kamikos, mentioned by Herodotus as the citadel of King Kokalos, where Daidalos found refuge after his flight from Crete and where King Minos, who had pursued him there, met his death. Of the two great ethnic groups, Siculi and Sicani, whom the Greeks found in divided possession of the island in the second half of the 8th century B.C., the Siculi may be recognized as the bearers of the Cassibile, Pantalica Sud, and Finocchito cultures and the Sicani as the bearers of the Sant'Angelo Muxaro culture.

b. The Apennine culture. The term "Apennine" is used to indicate the culture that extended over the entire Italian peninsula, from Apulia to Emilia, probably developing over a long period between the 15th century B.C. and the beginning of the 1st millennium B.C. In its earliest phase, designated as Apennine proper, it is characterized by a type of pottery decorated by incision or intaglio, with bands of dots forming spirals, meanders, lozenges, and crosses. The intaglio is often filled with a colored substance (PL. 438). This type of pottery appears in the Milazzese culture of the Lipari Islands in association with Mycenaean IIIa and b pottery and can, therefore, be dated between 1400 and about 1230 B.C. The next phase is represented predominantly by pottery that is undecorated but has a broad variety of modeled handles. It appears in the Ausonian I period in Lipari and is generally designated as Sub-Apennine. The transition from the decorated Apennine to the undecorated Sub-Apennine, which is seen very clearly in the Lipari Islands, is much less sharply marked in many sites in peninsular Italy, where the settlement continued to flourish without interruption through both phases and through a subsequent transition from the Sub-Apennine to the Iron Age, corresponding to the Ausonian II in Lipari and the first proto-Villanovan urn fields.

A pure decorated Apennine style is found not only in the Milazzese culture of the Lipari Islands but also in the vicinity of Castiglione, on the island of Ischia (where Mycenaean pottery fragments have also been found), and in the Latronico cave (province of Potenza). On the other hand, the late Apennine and the Sub-Apennine are represented in the Nicolucci cave, near Sorrento, and in the Zachito cave (Salerno). The deposits in the Pertosa cave (province of Salerno), at La Starza (Ariano Irpino), and in the Grotta delle Felci on the island of Capri contain material of all these phases as well as post-Apennine. In Apulia the deposit richest in early Apennine material is Coppa Nevigata near Manfredonia. Deposits of the succeeding phase are far more numerous, as at Porto Perone near Leporano (province of Taranto), where Mycenaean IIIc pottery has also been found. Other Apulian deposits include those in the village of Torre Castelluccia, near Pulsano, in the upper layer of the Caverna dell'Erba at Avetrana, in the open-air sites at Bari and Terlizzi, in the Pulo cave at Molfetta, and in the lower levels of Stratum III and in the innermost sections of the Manaccora cave on Monte Gargano. The tombs of this last site have yielded a large number of bronzes. Numerous burials of the Apennine culture have also been discovered in Apulia and in the Matera district. In some cases these are rock-cut tombs, but they are mostly characterized by dolmens. The dolmen appears only in two clearly defined zones on the Adriatic side of the Apennines, and the character of each of these zones is noticeably different. The first group, in the Terra di Bari, comprises a few rather large monuments of the gallery-tomb type, as at Bisceglie (IV, PL. 456), Albarosa, Frisari, Corato, and Cisternino, to which must also be added two dolmens near Taranto, at Leucaspide and Accettulla di Statte. Only the Albarosa dolmen still retains the greater part of the tumulus (specchia) which once covered it. These dolmens have been found to contain Sub-Apennine material. The second group of dolmens is in the Salentine Peninsula; they are generally smaller. Also associated with the megalithic architecture of the Salentine area are the menhirs (*pietrefitte*), although it has been suggested that their origin and use was medieval.

The Apennine culture is found also in the Abruzzi (e.g., in the Valle della Vibrata, in the caves of Sant'Angelo and Salomone, and at Penne). In the Marches the material is very rich, with peculiar forms and decorations. The richest deposit, at Santa Paolina di Filottrano, has yielded some very beautiful decorated ware with the extraordinary and highly complex handles of the older phase, together with Sub-Apennine and post-Apennine material. Pottery of the decorated phase is found at Spineto, at Pievetorina, and especially at Sassoferrato (III, PL. 124). A purely Sub-Apennine deposit is located at Conelle di Arcevia and in the level of the dwellings at Pianello di Genga below the proto-Villanovan necropolis. Later phases are represented in the sites of the Sentino gorges.

On the Tyrrhenian side to the north of Campania, the Apennine and Sub-Apennine cultures have left traces in Latium, in the territories of the Falisci (west of the Tiber) and of the Sabines (east of the Tiber), in Umbria, and in Tuscany. Decorated pottery of the first phase appears in the mountain zone of Tolfa (Pian Sultano) and in the coastal region near Civitavecchia. On the other hand, the Grotta Misa deposit in the Fiora Valley is one of the typical sites of the Sub-Apennine phase. The most important discoveries of the Apennine culture have come to light in the village of Belverde on Monte Cetona, near Chiusi (PL. 438), where it overlies traces of a preceding phase corresponding to the Rinaldone culture, and probably is divided into a series of layers. The stratigraphy, however, is not clear. A considerable amount of pottery appears in various shapes (including large situlae with cordons in relief, large carinated bowls, jars in biconical forms). The decoration is either incised or intaglio and embraces the entire Apennine decorative repertory. Sub-Apennine pottery, with its high handles, is also widely represented. This site was inhabited continuously until the Iron Age (see below).

Farther north the Apennine culture spread up the Adriatic side of the peninsula and extended over Romagna and into the part of Emilia west of the Panaro River. In northern Italy, however, the dominant aspects are those of the Sub-Apennine, which lasted for a very long time and merged with the particular late Bronze Age Terramare and palafitte cultures of these regions.

c. End of the Bronze Age and beginning of the Iron Age in Italy. The situation at Lipari (where the levels of Ausonian I, corresponding to the Sub-Apennine phase on the mainland, lie directly below the completely different culture of Ausonian II) is generally true of the whole of Italy. It was during this period that the rite of cremation became generally diffused. In the cremation burials at Torre Castelluccia, near Taranto, the ashes were preserved in situlae or in biconic jars covered with carinated bowl-shaped lids, also containing bronze objects similar to those found in the necropolis of Lipari. A short distance inland is the necropolis of Timmari (province of Matera), an urn field identical to the one at Milazzo in Sicily and therefore perhaps only very little later than the Torre Castelluccia necropolis. The necropolis of Timmari belongs to the type known as proto-Villanovan, which is diffused over the whole of Italy as far as the Po Valley. This proto-Villanovan type can be recognized in the oldest group of tombs in the Tolfa region (Sasso di Furbara, Tolfa, Allumiere), in the Fiora Valley (Ponte San Pietro), in the Grosseto district (Sticciano Scalo), at Pianello di Genga in the Marches, at Bismantova (province of Reggio Emilia), and at Fontanella di Casalromano (province of Mantua). Information on this culture, especially with regard to bronze household objects, is broadened by the very rich deposit of Coste del Marano in the Tolfa region, including hammered bronze cups with handles in the form of a bull's head and splendid fibulas with leaf bows (PL. 438). The cinerary urns, deposited in small wells and often protected by stone slabs or revetments, are decorated with grooves and cupules; the lids are shaped like a cup with a reentrant rim — a type that was to be widely diffused during the Iron Age. Among the bronze grave goods are fibulas with simple bows and rectangular razors with a double cutting edge.

There is no doubt that the proto-Villanovan culture represents the advent of new elements that were foreign to the preceding Apennine cultures and of European rather than Mediterranean origin. Possibly the arrival of this new culture was connected with contemporary political events, but there is no evidence to suggest that all the elements appeared suddenly or in a single period, or that a clean-cut break occurred between the new culture and the old, nor can it be proved that the proto-Villanovan marks the arrival of a large mass of new people. Nevertheless, the cultural development corresponding to the diffusion of cremation necropolises is reflected in the types of settlements, particularly in the Marches and in Apulia (where production of a type of painted pottery in the Mycenaean tradition and, later, reflecting the Geometric style, continued). At Casa Carletti in the Monte Cetona district, the Sub-Apennine culture also appears to have undergone a transformation. During this period the high raised handles on various types of pots gradually went out of use and handles assumed the shapes of horns or crescents. There was also an increase in the number of figural elements of modeling.

As outlined above, the Sub-Apennine cultural current spread in northern Italy as far as Emilia. Its influence was diffused also across the Po. The palafittes at Peschiera and on the eastern shore of Lake Garda are of particular interest because of the great quantity of bronze objects they contained. These include violin-bow fibulas (one of which is plated with gold), razors, adzes, and many small knives. There is also a wide variety of large pins and hairpins. There is a close connection between these bronze objects and those found, for example, at Scoglio del Tonno near Taranto (of uncertain date because of the lack of stratigraphical data). A comparison with bronzes from Pantalica Nord and from the tombs of Torre Castelluccia and Lipari justifies attribution of the Garda material generically to the Sub-Apennine phase. Nevertheless, the pottery associated with the Garda bronzes, with its grooved decoration, would seem rather to suggest a period at the very end of the Sub-Apennine and close to the time of the diffusion of the proto-Villanovan necropolises.

On the other hand, the identity of types of these bronzes shows that the Peschiera palafittes were contemporaneous with the larger complex of the Terramare, the prehistoric settlements in western Emilia and immediately adjacent territories, where a specialized and more complex structural system, differing from the rest of Italy, existed — or was formerly believed to have existed. These settlements presumably consisted of palafitte dwellings surrounded by a rampart and a moat, laid out on a remarkably regular plan with a fixed orientation. (This was probably the case only in the Castellazzo di Fontanellato site.) A complex pseudohistoric theory, with no sound basis of fact, was evolved about the Terramare, whereby the settlements and their inhabitants were regarded as the forerunners of Italic and Roman civilization. In actual fact the prehistoric sites of the Terramare region (in the provinces of Modena, Reggio Emilia, Parma, Piacenza, and adjacent areas) present a ceramic facies noticeably different from that of the Sub-Apennine sites of eastern Emilia. The handles are more uniformly elevated, the decoration consists of grooves and protuberances, and the technique is generally coarse. This would indicate that the majority of the Terramare material belongs to a chronologically later phase than the Sub-Apennine phase. One cannot, however, exclude the possibility of an earlier development of the Terramare sites, as suggested by the presence in some of them of bronzes than are of earlier types than those of the Peschiera phase (e.g., at Castione dei Marchesi) and especially of pottery of a strictly Sub-Apennine type. Similar occurrences can be noted in Lombardy, where a phase corresponding to the Emilian Terramare overlies the Bronze Age Polada culture. Here, as in the Lake Garda region, palafittes are found.

In the Po Valley, too, one of the most salient characteristics of the late Bronze Age is the diffusion of the new rite of cremation. The oldest group of cremation burials seems to be the one represented by the necropolis of Canegrate near Legnano. The biconical urns, with wide necks generally sharply distinguished from the shoulders and with broad rims, are always decorated with grooves. The decoration is, however, rigidly limited to the shoulder; the motifs of vertical broken lines or of horizontal bands of grooves, sometimes interrupted by small circles or large cupules, clearly differ from the decoration that characterizes the later Terramare and proto-Villanovan production. There is no doubt that this finer and more elegant pottery represents an entirely new element in northern Italy; it gives the impression of an intrusive element from beyond the Alps. In the eastern part of the Po Valley, the earliest burial ground is perhaps the necropolis of Povegliano Veronese, where the dead are inhumed with daggers or long swords at their sides. There are also some cremation tombs. This necropolis is followed, in order of time, by the neighboring necropolis of Bovolone, where cremation prevails with globular groove-decorated urns. Of a similar type are the necropolises of Monte Lonato at Cavriana (province of Mantua) and of Castellazzo di Fontanellato. The adjoining settlements belong to the same period. The necropolises of Ascona (in the Ticino canton, Switzerland) and of Fontanella and Bismantova (ment oned above) are unmistakably proto-Villanovan.

The cultures of the Iron Age in continental Italy show clearly defined regional differences corresponding to the groupings of historic peoples (see ETRUSCO-ITALIC ART). These cultures developed, presumably from the 9th century B.C. onward, on this complex, and not yet entirely clarified, basis of events and currents. In the south the Sub-Apennine tradition, with a few intrusions from the outside, seems to evolve without any noticeable upheavals into the cultural facies of the Iron Age in Apulia, Calabria, and Campania, where inhumation was prevalent. Central and northern Italy underwent a proto-Villanovan type of evolution, relatively uniform throughout its extent, within the increasingly divergent structures of the Villanovan Latian, Umbrian, Atestine, and Golaseccan cremators. This more or less confirms an interpretation of the proto-Villanovan as a phase or as a cultural mode, rather than as an ethnic unity. The counterblows represented by the Greek colonization of southern Italy and Sicily and the rise of a new urban civilization mark the progressive transition from the protohistoric to the historic era.

Luigi BERNABÒ BREA

d. The western Mediterranean. The distribution, sequence, and characteristics of the Bronze Age cultures in the western Mediterranean are, as yet, far from clear. Nevertheless, these phases, with the exception of their final manifestations in Sardinia and in the Balearic Islands, do not seem to present any very significant developments, any remarkable originality, or any particularly creative effervescence in either civilization or art, in comparison with the preceding phases of the beginning of the age of metals. In many places traditions of the earlier period — such as megalithic construction, certain aspects of pottery, the ways of life, and the religious beliefs — seem to have continued long into the second millennium B.C. On the other hand, the influences of Aegean shipping and trade, which, particularly in the late Mycenaean period, acted so strongly on the coast of southern Italy, Sicily, and the Lipari Islands, reached the countries of the western Mediterranean only rarely or indirectly and in some regions not at all. The increasing development of metalworking in the production of weapons and tools was a distinguishing mark of the Bronze Age. This particularly affected the West in two ways. One was the gradual establishment of relations with the Atlantic regions, along the trade route for tin from the British Isles; the other was the presence in Sardinia and in Spain of large deposits of metals, destined to be exploited to an increasing extent, especially during the late Bronze Age and in the historical era.

An initial cultural phase of the Bronze Age, following the Aëneolithic, is only barely noticeable in Sardinia in the middle centuries of the 2d millennium B.C. (Bonnanaro culture). Knowledge of its relationship with the nuraghic culture is still very uncertain. In Corsica, southern France, and Pyrenean Spain, megalithic traditions continued through the early phases of the Bronze Age. In southeastern Spain developed the El Argar culture (PL. 436), the reflections of which are diffused in the Iberian Peninsula and also appear in the Balearic Islands. This culture is characterized by the development of metalworking; fine knives and halberds are the most typical forms. Pottery is glossy black, in imitation of metal; it appears in the shape of rounded ollae, generally without handles, or with very small ones, and footed bowls. Decorated pottery is very rare. Parallels with Italian cultures of the early metal age and Bronze Age are tenuous. It is possible that the El Argar culture represents one of the farthest western offshoots of the early Bronze Age Aegean-Anatolian cultural complex (see above, *The Near East; Aegean-Anatolian cultural unity in the early Bronze Age*).

In the late and final phases of the Bronze Age, in the late 2d and early 1st millennium B.C., there appeared the spectacular development of the insular cultures of Sardinia and the Balearic Islands, particularly in architectural forms. In Sardinia, there was also an advanced production in metalwork with figural works of art (PLS. 403, 404). Undoubtedly there was a link between the two zones, manifest not only in the contemporary and parallel development but more specifically in the similarity of certain monumental types, especially the Sardinian nuraghi and the Balearic talayoti, which represent the most typical elements of the respective architectures. The diffusion of these types of architecture also reached southern Corsica. Nevertheless, a true cultural unity did not exist. The Sardinians elaborated their own structural themes very intensively, notably the false vault and the false dome (PL. 402). In the Balearic archipelago appear peculiar architectural forms (*navetas*, taulas, and hypostyle halls) that are not found elsewhere (PL. 406). It is possible to find prototypes of many of these architectural motifs in both Mediterranean cultural traditions and in western megalithic phases. The essential imprint of both the Sardinian nuraghic and the Balearic talayotic cultures is found in the forms created in the cultures of the Bronze Age. Iron Age features, such as geometric decoration, fibulas, and cremation, are all but unknown in the islands. Chronologically the high point of these cultures must be placed within a period corresponding to the Iron Age and the beginning of historical times, in the Phoenician-Punic and Greek colonizations, between the 9th and 7th centuries B.C. They survived until the periods of Punic domination and the Roman conquest (see MEDITERRANEAN, ANCIENT WESTERN).

The introduction of objects of northern European origin into Spain (during the period of the Atlantic Bronze Age culture, 1100–800 B.C.) and the Balearic Islands in the late Bronze Age can be traced to the commerce, particularly in metals, between the Mediterranean countries and western and northern Europe by continental routes and along the Atlantic coast. The most important development in continental Europe during this period is the diffusion of the urn fields along the French and Spanish Mediterranean coastal regions. This occasioned profound changes, not only in the traditions and rites of the burial of the dead, but also in the types and forms of artifacts, especially pottery and its decoration. The earliest cremation necropolises in these territories are related to the central European phase known as Hallstatt B, dating from the 8th century B.C. Their appearance here is chronologically much later than that of the parallel occurrences in Italy. This may be explained by the greater distance of the southern French and the Iberian regions from the epicenter of the diffusion of the Urn-field culture, the Danubian region of central Europe (see EUROPEAN PROTOHISTORY). In Spain, these new cultural elements, and possibly also new ethnic groups, were introduced through Catalonia, where the oldest cremation burial grounds (Tarrasa type) are found. The eastern and southern coastal regions were, however, soon subjected to other external influences due to Phoenician colonization (apparently particularly early in the south) and Greek colonization (at least from the 7th cent. B.C.), superimposed on the older local cultural traditions. The melding of all these elements marks the beginning of the Iron Age culture in Mediterranean Spain and prepares for the development of the civilization known as Iberian (see MEDITERRANEAN, ANCIENT WESTERN). The continental European elements, represented by the penetration of the Celts, found a particularly favorable and receptive soil for subsequent cultural development in the interior and the western part of the Iberian Peninsula. Here the native and the imported elements combined to constitute one of the most characteristic provinces of Celtic civilization (see CELTIC ART).

* *

BIBLIOG. *Eastern Mediterranean*. *a. General works*: A. Evans, Essai de classification des époques de la civilisation minoenne, London, 1906; A. J. B. Wace and C. W. Blegen, The Pre-Mycenaean Pottery of the Mainland, BSA, XXII, 1916–18, pp. 175–89; H. Frankfort, Studies in Early Pottery of the Near East, II, London, 1927; S. Fuchs, Die griechischen Fundgruppen der frühen Bronzezeit, Berlin, 1937; J. D. S. Pendlebury, Archaeology of Crete, London, 1939; A. Furumark, The Mycenaean Pottery: Analysis and Classification, Stockholm, 1941; H. T. Bossert, Altanatolien, Berlin, 1942; P. Laviosa Zambotti, Le più antiche culture agricole europee, Milan, 1943; C. F. A. Schaeffer, Stratigraphie comparée et chronologie de l'Asie occidentale, I, London, 1948; C. Delroye, Remarques sur la seconde civilisation néolithique du continent grec, BCH, LXXIII, 1949, pp. 29–124; V. Milojčić, Chronologie der jüngeren Steinzeit Mittel- und Südosteuropas, Berlin, 1949; F. Schachermeyr, Die orientalisch-mittelmeerischen Grundlagen der vorgeschichtlichen Chronologie, Prähistorische Z., XXXIV–XXXV, 1949–50, pp. 17–48; K. Bittel, Zur Chronologie der anatolischen Frühkulturen, Reinecke-Festschrift, Mainz, 1950, pp. 13–25; K. Bittel, Grundzüge der Vor- und Frühgeschichte Kleinasiens, 2d ed., Tübingen, 1950; F. Matz and others, HA, II, 1, 1950, pp. 196–230; F. Schachermeyr, Zur Entstehung der ältesten Civilisation in Griechenland, La n. Clio, I, 1950, pp. 567–601; V. Milojčić, Die frühesten Ackerbauer in Mitteleuropa, Germania, XXX, 1952, pp. 313–18; R. W. Ehrich and others, Relative Chronologies in Old World Archaeology, Chicago, 1954; F. Schachermeyr, Dimini und die Bandkeramik, Vienna, 1954; F. Schachermeyr, RE, s.v. Prähistorische Kulturen Griechenlands, XLIV, 1954, cols. 1350–1548; F. Schachermeyr, Die volderasiatische Kulturtrift, Saeculum, V, 1954, pp. 268–91; W. F. Libby, Radiocarbon Dating, 2d ed., Chicago, 1955; P. van der Meer, The Chronology of Ancient Western Asia and Egypt, 2d ed., Leiden, 1955; F. Schachermeyr, Die ältesten Kulturen Griechenlands, Stuttgart, 1955; R. J. Braidwood, Origin of the Village Farming Community, New York, 1956; M. Grbić, Expansion der Butmir-Kultur, Glasnik, N.S., XI, 1956, pp. 237–45; A. Goetze, On the Chronology of the Second Millennium, J. of Cuneiform S., XI, 1957, pp. 53–61, 63–73; V. Milojčić, Zur Anwendbarkeit der C14-Datierung in der Vorgeschichtsforschung, Germania, XXXV, 1957, pp. 102–10; R. Pittioni, Die Bedeutung der Radiokarbon-Methode zur absoluten Datierung urzeitlicher Quellen, Forsch. und Fortschritte, XXXI, 1957, pp. 357–64; R. Pittioni, Die Bedeutung der Radiokarbon-Methode für die Urgeschichte, AnzÖAk, XCIV, 1957, pp. 233–48; F. E. Zeuner, Dating the Past, 4th ed., London, 1958; R. W. Hutchinson, Prehistoric Crete, Harmondsworth, 1962. *b. Origins and the Ancient Near East*: E. Herzfeld, Die vorgeschichtlichen Töpfereien von Samarra, Berlin, 1930; W. Lamb, Schliemann's Prehistoric Finds in the Troad, Prähistorische Z., XXIII, 1932, pp. 111–31; G. Contenau and R. Ghirshmann, Fouilles de Tepe-Giyan, Paris, 1935; M. E. L. Mallowan and J. C. Rose, Prehistoric Assyria: The Excavations at Tell Arpachiyah, London, 1935; M. E. L. Mallowan, The Excavations at Tall Chagar Bazar, Iraq, III, 1936, pp. 1–86; H. H. von der Osten, The Alishar Hüyük: Seasons of 1930–32, 3 vols., Chicago, 1937; R. Ghirshmann, Fouilles de Sialk, II, Paris, 1939; V. Christian, Altertumskunde des Zweistromlandes, I, Leipzig, 1940; D. E. McCown, The Comparative Stratigraphy of Early Iran, Chicago, 1942; M. von Oppenheim, Tell Halaf, I, Berlin, 1943; H. Z. Koşay, Ausgrabungen von Alaca Höyük, Ankara, 1944; S. Lloyd and F. Safar, Tell Hassuna, JNES, IV, 1946, pp. 255–87; C. W. Blegen and others, Troy, 4 vols., Princeton, 1950–58; T. Özgüç, Kültepe kazisi raporu 1948 (Report on the Excavations at Kültepe 1948), Ankara, 1950; R. Pittioni, Beiträge zur Geschichte des Keramikums in Afrika und im Nahen Osten (Prähistorische Forsch., 2), Vienna, 1950; J. du Plat Taylor, M. V. Seton Williams and J. Waechter, The Excavations at Sakce Gözü, Iraq, XII, 1950, pp. 53–138; A. Tobler, Excavations at Tepe Gawra, II, Philadelphia, 1950; S. Lloyd and N. Gökçe, Excavations at Polatli, Anatolian S., I, 1951, pp. 21–75; J. Garstang, Prehistoric Mersin, Oxford, 1953; T. and N. Özgüç, Kültepe kazisi raporu 1949 (Report on the Excavations at Kültepe 1949), Ankara, 1953; H. Goldman, Excavations at Gözlü Kule, Tarsus, II, Princeton, 1956; S. Lloyd, Early Anatolia, Baltimore, 1956; S. Lloyd and J. Mellaart, Beycesultan Excavations, Anatolian S., VI, 1956, pp. 101–35, VIII, 1958, pp. 93–125; M. Mellink, A Hittite Cemetery at Gordion, Philadelphia, 1956; R. J. Braidwood, Jericho and Its Setting in Near Eastern History, Antiquity, XXXI, 1957, pp. 73–81; K. Kenyon, Digging Up Jericho, London, 1957; J. Mellaart, Excavations at Hacilar, Anatolian S., VIII, 1958, pp. 127–56, IX, 1959, pp. 51–65, X, 1960, pp. 83–104, XI, 1961, pp. 39–75; J. Mellaart, The Beginnings of Mural Painting, Archaeology, XV, 1962, pp. 2–12. *c. Greek area*: T. D. Atkinson and others, Excavations at Phylakopi in Melos, London, 1904; A. J. B. Wace and M. S. Thompson, Prehistoric Thessaly, Cambridge, 1912; O. Rubensohn, Die prähistorische und frühgeschichtliche Funde von Paros, AM, XLII, 1917, pp. 1–96; C. W. Blegen, Korakou, New York, 1921; C. W. Blegen, Zygouries, Cambridge, 1928; G. E. Mylonas, Excavations at Olynthos, I, Baltimore, 1929; H. Goldman, Excavations at Eutresis in Boeotia, Cambridge, Mass., 1931; E. Kunze, Orchomenos, II–III (AbhAkMünchen, N.S., V, VIII), Munich, 1931–34; H. Heidenreich, Die vorgeschichtlichen Funde vom Kastro Tigani auf Samos, AM, LX–LXI, 1936, pp. 125–83; W. Lamb, Excavations at Thermi in Lesbos, Cambridge, 1936; C. W. Blegen, Prosymna, Cambridge, 1937; O. Frödin and A. Persson, Asine, Stockholm, 1938; K. Müller, Tiryns, IV: Die Urfirniskeramik, Munich, 1938; W. A. Heurtley, Prehistoric Macedonia, Cambridge, 1939; E. Holmberg, The Swedish Excavations at Asea, Lund, 1944; S. Marinatos, Greniers de l'Helladique ancien, BCH, LXX, 1946, pp. 337–51; S. S. Weinberg, Aegean Chronology, AJA, LI, 1947, pp. 165–82; L. Walker-Kosmopoulos, The Prehistoric Inhabitation of Corinth, Munich, 1948; V. Milojčić, Zur Chronologie der jüngeren Steinzeit Griechenlands, JdI, LXV–LXVI, 1950–51, pp. 1–90; F. Schachermeyr, Die Abfolge der neolithischen Kulturen in Griechenland, Keramopoulos Festschrift, Athens, 1953, pp. 89–104; J. L. Caskey, Excavations at Lerna, Hesperia, XXIV, 1955, pp. 25–49, XXV, 1956, pp. 147–73, XXVI, 1957, pp. 142–62, XXVII, 1958, pp. 125–44; V. Milojčić, Vorbericht über die Ausgrabungen auf der Otzaki-Magula..., AAnz, 1955, cols. 157–231; V. Milojčić, Bericht über die Ausgrabungen auf der Gremnos-Magula bei Larisa, AAnz, 1956, cols. 141–83; L. Bernabò Brea, Recenti scavi a Poliochni, BArte, XLII, 1957, pp. 193–217; D. R. Theocharis, Αἱ ἀρχαὶ τοῦ πολιτισμοῦ ἐν Σεσκλῳ (Beginnings of Social Life at Sesklo), ΠΑΕ, XXXII, 1957, pp. 151–59; C. Zervos, L'art des Cyclades, Paris, 1957; G. E. Mylonas, Aghios Kosmas, Princeton, 1959; H. W. Catling, Cypriot Bronze-Work in the Mycenaean World, Oxford, 1964; see also the bibliog. for CRETAN-MYCENAEAN ART. *d. Eastern Europe*: A. Stocký, La Bohême préhistorique, I, Prague, 1929; F. von Tompa, Die Bandkeramik in Ungarn, Budapest, 1929; I. Nestor, Der Stand der Vorgeschichtsforschung in Rumänien, Bericht der römisch-germanischen Kommission, XXII, 1932, pp. 11–181; H. Schroller, Die Stein- und Kupferzeit Siebenbürgens, Berlin, 1933; W. Buttler, Der donauländische und der westische Kulturkreis der jüngeren Steinzeit, Berlin, Leipzig, 1938; J. Banner, Das Tisza-, Maros-, Körös-Gebiet bis zur Entwicklung der Bronzezeit, Szeged, 1942; I. Kutzian, The Körös Culture, 2 vols., Budapest, 1944–47; J. H. Gaul, The Neolithic Period in Bulgaria, Cambridge, Mass., 1948; L. Arandjelovic-Garašanin, Starčevačka kultura (Culture of Starčevo), Ljubljana, 1954; R. Pittioni, Urgeschichte des österreichischen Raumes, Vienna, 1954; J. Neustupný, Chronologie préhistorique de la Tchécoslovaquie, Prague, 1956; J. Neustupný, Neue Beiträge zum Neolithikum Rumäniens, Slovenska Archaeol., VI, 1958, pp. 257–94.

Characteristic elements. a. Architecture. (1) *Megaron*: C. A. Boethius, Mycenaean Megara and Nordic Houses, BSA, XXIV, 1919–21, pp. 161–84; K. Bitt l, Kleinasiatische Studien, Istanbuler Mitt., V, 1942, pp. 138–50; F. Matz and others, HA, II, 1, 1950, pp. 91–157; B. Schweitzer, Megaron und Hofhaus in der Ägäis, BSA, XLVI, 1951, pp. 160–67; F. Schachermeyr, Die ältesten Kulturen Griechenlands, Stuttgart, 1955, pp. 112–14. (2) *Vaulted tombs*: O. Bates, The Eastern Libyans, London, 1914; S. Xanthoudides, The Vaulted Tombs of Mesara, London, 1924; A. Evans, Palace of Minos, II, London, 1928, pp. 35–44; F. Schachermeyr, Etruskische Frühgeschichte, Berlin, 1929, pp. 89–114; A. J. B. Wace, Mycenae, Princeton, 1949, pp. 26-46, 119-31; C. W. Blegen, An Early Tholos-Tomb in Western Messenia, Hesperia, XXIII, 1954, pp. 158-62. *b. Statuettes of the goddess of fertility*: V. Müller, Die frühe Plastik in Griechenland und Vorderasien, Augsburg, 1929; J. Wiesner, Vorgriechische Idole, AAnz, 1937, cols. 252-65; F. Hančar, Das Problem der Venusstatuetten im eurasiatischen Jungpaläolithikum, Prähistorische Z., XXX-XXXI, 1939-40, pp. 85-156; K. Willvonseder, Die Venus von Drassburg, Germania, XXIV, 1940, pp. 1-5; M. von Oppenheim, Tell Halaf I, Berlin, 1943; K. Bittel, Einige Idole aus Kleinasien, Prähistorische Z., XXXIV-XXXV, 1949-50, pp. 135-44; A. J. B. Wace, Prehistoric Stone Figures from the Mainland, Hesperia, sup. VIII, 1949, pp. 423-26; R. J. Braidwood, Discovering the World's Earliest Village Community, ILN, CCXIX, 1951, pp. 992-95; S. S. Weinberg, Neolithic Figures and Aegean Interrelations, AJA, LV, 1951, pp. 121-33; K. Grundmann, Figürlich Darstellungen in der neolithischen Keramik, JdI, LXVIII, 1953, pp. 1-37; H. Ladenbauer-Orel, Die neolithische Frauenstatuette von Land- Enzersdorf bei Wien, IPEK, XIX, 1954-59, pp. 7-15; J. L. Caskey, A Neolithic Figure from Lerna, Hesperia, XXV, 1956, pp. 175-77; S. Alexiou, 'Η Μινοική θεα μεθ' ὑπωμένων χειρῶν, Hiraklion, 1958; J. Mellaart, Excavations at Hacilar, Anatolian S., VIII, 1958, pp. 144-50; J. Csalog, Anthropomorphe Gefässe und Idolplastiken, ActaA (Budapest), XI, 1959, pp. 7-38; J. Korek, Zu anthropomorphen Darstellungen der Bükker-Kultur, Folia archaeol., XI, 1959, pp. 13-34. *c. Painting, ceramics, and metalwork.* (1) *Spirals and meanders*: M. Hörnes, W. Radimsky and F. Fiala, Die neolithische Station von Butmir, 2 vols., Vienna, 1895-98; G. Wilke, Spiral-Mäander-Keramik, Würzburg, 1910; W. M. Flinders Petrie, Prehistoric Egypt Corpus, London, 1921, pls. 33, 36; F. Matz, Die frühkretischen Siegel, Berlin, Leipzig, 1928; L. Woolley, Ur Excavations, II, London, 1934, pls. 134, 138; H. S. Kantor, The Aegean and the Orient in the Second Millennium B.C., AJA, LI, 1947, pp. 17-108; G. von Kaschnitz-Weinberg, Zur Herkunft der Spirale in der Ägäis, Prähistorische Z., XXXIV-XXXV, 1949-50, pp. 193-215; R. J. Braidwood, Discovering the World's Earliest Village Community, ILN, CCXIX, 1951, pp. 992-95; T. Burton-Brown, Excavations in Azarbaijan 1948, London, 1951; E. Beninger, Spirale und Mäander in der eiszeitliche Bildnerei, Quartär, X-XI, 1958-59, pp. 63-78; J. Mellaart, Excavations at Hacilar, Anatolian S., VIII, 1958, pp. 136-39. (2) *Gold- and silverwork*: W. Dörpfeld, Troja und Ilion, Athens, 1902, pp. 325-43; R. Seager, Exploration in the Island of Mochlos, Boston, New York, 1912, pp. 104-06; L. Woolley, Ur Excavations, II, London, 1934; B. Segall, Katalog der Goldschmiede-Arbeiten der Museum Benaki, Athens, 1938, pp. 11-14, 211-14; H. Z. Koşay, Les fouilles d'Alaca Höyük, Ankara, 1951; L. Bernabò Brea, Recenti scavi a Poliochni, BArte, XLII, 1957, pp. 193-217; T. Özgüç and M. Akok, Objects from Horoztepe, Belleten Türk Tarih Kurumu, XXI, 1957, pp. 211-19; J. Mellaart, The Royal Treasure of Dorak, ILN, CCXXXV, 1959, pp. 754-57.

Central and western Mediterranean. a. General works: P. Vouga, Le néolithique lacustre ancien, Neuchâtel, 1934; P. Laviosa Zambotti, Le più antiche culture agricole europee, Milan, 1943; F. Matz and others, HA, II, 1, 1950, pp. 309-402; H. Müller-Karpe, Beiträge zur Chronologie der Urnenfelderzeit nördlich und südlich der Alpen (Römisch-germanische Forsch., XXII), Berlin, 1959. *b. Italy, including Sicily and Sardinia*: O. Montelius, La civilisation primitive en Italie depuis l'introduction des métaux, 2 vols., Stockholm, 1895-1910; G. A. Colini, La civiltà del bronzo in Italia, BPI, XXIX, 1903, pp. 53-103, 211-23; XXX, 1904, pp. 155-99, 229-304, XXXI, 1905, pp. 18-70; O. Montelius, Die vorklassische Chronologie Italiens, Stockholm, 1912; A. Jatta, La Puglia preistorica, Bari, 1914; U. Rellini, La Grotta delle Felci a Capri, MALinc, XXIX, 1923, cols. 305-406; M. Mayer, Molfetta und Matera, Leipzig, 1924; U. Rellini, La più antica ceramica dipinta in Italia, Rome, 1934; B. Pace, Arte e civiltà della Sicilia antica, I, Milan, 1935; G. Buchner, Nota preliminare sulle ricerche preistoriche nell'isola d'Ischia, BPI, LVI, 1936-37, pp. 65-93; G. Patroni, La Preistoria (Storia politica d'Italia, I-II), Milan, 1937; P. E. Arias, La stazione preistorica di Serraferlicchio presso Agrigento, MALinc, XXXVI, 1938, cols. 693-838; G. Säflund, Le terramare nelle provincie di Modena, Reggio Emilia, Parma, Piacenza (Skrifter utgivna av Svenska Inst. i Rom, VII), Lund, 1939; P. Ducati, Preistoria e protostoria dell'Emilia, Rome, 1942; I. Marconi Bovio, La cultura tipo Conca d'Oro della Sicilia nord occidentale, MALinc, XL, 1944, cols. 1-170; L. Bernabò Brea, Gli scavi nella caverna delle Arene Candide, 2 vols., Bordighera, 1946-56; G. P. Sestieri, La necropoli preistorica di Paestum, RScPr, I, 1946, pp. 245-66, II, 1949, pp. 283-90; L. Bernabò Brea, Le caverne del Finale, Bordighera, 1947; M. Pallottino, La Sardegna nuragica, Rome, 1950; C. Zervos, La civilisation de la Sardaigne du début de l'Enéolithique à la fin de la période nouragique, Paris, 1954; L. Bernabò Brea and M. Cavalier, Culture preistoriche delle Isole Eolie e del territorio di Milazzo, BPI, LXV, 1956, pp. 7-98; L. Bernabò Brea, Sicily Before the Greeks, London, New York, 1957; L. Bernabò Brea and M. Cavalier, Stazioni preistoriche delle Isole Eolie, BPI, LXVI, 1957, pp. 97-151; L. Battaglia, Preistoria del Veneto e della Venezia Giulia, BPI, LXVII-LXVIII, 1958-59, pp. 1-430 (bibliog.); L. Bernabò Brea and M. Cavalier, Mylai, Catania, 1959; R. Peroni, Per una definizione dell'aspetto culturale "Subappenninico" come fase cronologica a sé stante, Atti Acc. naz. dei Lincei, 8th ser., IX, 1, 1959, pp. 1-192; S. Puglisi, La civiltà appenninica, Florence, 1959; L. Bernabò Brea and M. Cavalier, Meligunis Lipara, I, Palermo, 1960; M. Pallottino, Sulla cronologia dell'età del bronzo finale e dell'età del ferro in Italia, SEtr, XXVIII, 1960, pp. 1-47; G. A. Mansuelli and R. Scarani, L'Emilia prima dei romani, Milan, 1961; C. & I. Cafici, RLV, s.v. Cannatello, Isnello Kultur, Monte Tabuto, Pantalica, Sikuler, Sizilien, Stentinello Kultur. *c. Malta*: J. D. Evans, The Prehistoric Culture Sequence in the Maltese Archipelago, ProcPrSoc, XIX, 1953, pp. 41-94; J. D. Evans, The "Dolmens" of Malta and the Origins of the Tarxien Cemetery, ProcPrSoc, XXII, 1956, pp. 85-101; J. D. Evans, Malta, London, New York, 1960. See also bibliog. for MALTA. *d. Western Europe*. (1) *Southern France*: M. Louis, Préhistoire du Languedoc méditerranéen et du Roussillon, Nîmes, 1948; J. Audibert, Le chalcolithique dans le Gard, BSPF, LI, 1954, pp. 443-57; S. Piggott, Le néolithique occidental et le chalcolithique en France: Esquisse préliminaire, Anthropologie, LVIII, 1954, pp. 1-28; G. Bailloud and P. Mieg de Boofzheim, Les civilisations néolithiques de la France dans leur contexte européen, Paris, 1955; N. K. Sandars, Bronze Age Cultures in France, Cambridge, 1957; J. Arnal, G. Bailloud and R. Riquet, Les styles céramiques du néolithique français, Préhistoire, XIV, 1960, pp. 1-211. (2) *Spain*: H. and L. Siret, Les premiers âges du métal dans le sud-est de l'Espagne, Antwerp, 1887; J. Colominas Roca, La prehistoria de Monserrat, Monserrat, 1925; A. del Castillo Yurrita, La cultura del vaso campaniforme, Barcelona, 1928; L. Pericot Garcia, Historia de España, 2d ed., I, Barcelona, 1942; G. and V. Leisner, Die Megalithgräber der pyrenaische Halbinsel, I, Berlin, 1943; J. Martínez Santa-Olalla, Esquema paletnológico de la peninsula hispánica, Madrid, 1946; R. Menendez Pidal, ed., Historia de España, I, Barcelona, 1947; L. Pericot Garcia, Los sepulcros megalitics catalanes y la cultura Pirenaica, 2d ed., Barcelona, 1950; J. San Valero Aparisi, La Cueva de la Sarsa, Valencia, 1950; M. Tarradel, La cultura de los sepolcros de fosa de Cataluña y el problema de sus relaciones con Valencia y Almeria, Saitabi, X, 1960, pp. 5-25; M. Almagro and A. Arribas, Los Millares (in press). *e. Dalmatia*: M. Hörnes, W. Radimsky and F. Fiala, Die Neolithische Station von Butmir, 2 vols., Vienna, 1895-98; R. Schmidt, Die Burg Vučedol, Zagreb, 1945; A. Benac, Prehistorijsko naselje Nebo i problem Butmirske kulture (The Prehistoric Site of Nebo and the Problem of the Butmir Culture), Ljubljana, 1952; A. Benac, Neolitsko naselje u dolini Bile (The Neolithic Site in the Bila Valley), Glasnik, N. S., VIII, 1953, pp. 237-63, pls. I-XIII; G. Novak, Prehistorijski Hvar (Prehistoric Hvar), Zagreb, 1955; S. Dimitrijević, Prilog daljem upoznavanju Vučedolske kulture (Contribution to the Further Understanding of the Vučedol Culture), OpA, I, 1956, pp. 5-56, pls. I-XV.

Illustrations: PLS. 413-438; 10 figs. in text.

MEIDIAS PAINTER. The name of the potter Meidias (Μειδίας), who signed the famous Attic hydria in London with the double-tiered representation of Herakles in the Garden of the Hesperides and Castor and Pollux carrying off the daughters of Leukippos (PL. 439), is also used to designate the anonymous painter of this vase. To the same artist, the most important Greek "mannerist" vase painter, active at the very end of the 5th century B.C., have been definitely attributed fourteen other vases: four hydrias, one pelike, one oinochoe, four lekythoi, two lekanai, and two pyxides. The name of the Meidias Painter is associated with a decorative and linear taste, a refined and somewhat affected style that was taken up by followers more or less direct in their imitation. Not only did this manner of painting lead to the development of an important school of painters around the Meidias Painter, but in effect it also set a decisive pattern for the ensuing Greek vase painting of the 4th century B.C.

At least a hundred vases have been attributed to artists in this red-figure style. Among these, the forms most used are hydria, lebes gamikos (nuptial basin), oinochoe, lekythos, lekane, and pyxis; the calyx-crater (PL. 440) and volute crater are rare. On the whole, the artists of this manner preferred the more complicated and refined shapes, on which the painter could arrange — using a wealth of figures and delineating graceful gestures and poses — those scenes favored by the general taste of the period. The same qualities of delicacy and grace, as well as a love of minute detail, are found on vases not securely attributable to the Meidias Painter himself but clearly very similar to those of the master. Examples of such include a hydria in Karlsruhe (Landesmus.) and an amphora in Arezzo (Mus. Archeol.) representing the story of Pelops and Hippodameia; in these, however, the draftsmanship is less precise.

On those vases attributed with greater certainty to the Meidias Painter, the subjects are predominantly mythological and derive from the realm of Aphrodite, Eros, and Dionysos that had become so popular in late-5th-century Attica, reflecting the decided change in spiritual and cultural values which had taken place there. The London hydria reveals varied mythological inspiration: the rape of the daughters of Leukippos, Herakles in the Garden of the Hesperides, and an array of Athenian heroes that includes Akamas, Philoktetes, and Demophon. But the artist uses these themes chiefly as a point of departure for presenting a diverse group of nymphs and heroes, whose identities have no real significance other than as pretexts for a composition full of charm and serenity. This relaxed tone extends even to the scene of the rape of the daughters of Leukippos, where the sense of drama is lost in a sinuous arabesque. The two hydrias in Florence attributed to the Meidias Painter, with the myths of Phaon (III, PL. 375) and Adonis, illustrate his later tendency toward a more complex decorative scheme. The number of characters is increased, and the figures are placed on different levels, following a system to be linked with the Polygnotan tradition. Lekythoi in the Louvre, Ruvo (Jatta Coll.), and London (Br. Mus.) and a pelike in New York (Met. Mus.) present multiple scenes with Aphrodite and Eros or Adonis according to this same system of superimposed levels. Heads gracefully inclined and arms languidly extended affirm the essential mannerism of pose. As in the wedding scenes on loutrophoroi decorated by artists of the school of the Meidias Painter, the stress is upon elegant detail, a quality of graceful linearity appropriate to the amorous themes to which it is applied. It is a draftsmanship that dwells lovingly on particulars, carefully conveying the most minute details, modeling and emphasizing drapery and anatomy, and often adding arbitrary embellishments.

This mannerist current had already found passing expression in the more modest efforts of the Eretria Painter, a predecessor of the Meidias Painter. The original inspiration came from the drapery style of Phidias's figures on the east pediment of the Parthenon, but in succeeding adaptations the harmonious balance of fluid drapery clothing a firm underlying structure in the Parthenon sculpture was gradually weakened. Between the careers of Phidias and the Meidias Painter falls the art of Parrhasios (q.v.), a highly sophisticated painter from Ephesos, who also lent great elegance of gesture and pose to his figures and gave them a psychological intent previously unknown to Greek painting. The work of the Meidias Painter is clearly more frivolous, on occasion even superficial; nor does this artist have the deep interest in mythology of Parrhasios, who dwelt upon the traditional heroic themes. The Meidias Painter did, however, conserve the same fluidity of contour line and the frequent use of foreshortening.

The mannerism of the Meidias Painter and his school represents one of the more refined manifestations of Greek taste after Phidias. Sculpture after Phidias continued to be well served by such original and substantial artists as Kallimachos and the coin engravers Eukleidas and Kimon, whose work is known from Syracusan coinage. The vase painters instead favored less imposing shapes for the vessels themselves and emphasized the "pathetic" emotional quality of the scenes depicted. These changed aspirations were symptomatic of the spiritual crisis that arose in Athens after the Peloponnesian war. In a sense, the scenes illustrated by the Meidias Painter may be said to have taken inspiration from that cultured, highly refined literary tradition which also constituted the basis for the Platonic dialogues on love.

BIBLIOG. G. Nicole, Meidias et le style fleuri dans la céramique attique, Geneva, 1908; P. Ducati, I vasi dipinti nello stile del ceramista Midia, MemLinc, 5th ser., XIV, 1909, pp. 95–173; P. Ducati, Saggio di studio sulla ceramica attica figurata del secolo IV av. Cr., MemLinc, 5th ser., XV, 1915, pp. 211–368; Pfuhl, II, pp. 592–601; W. Hahland, Vasen um Meidias, Berlin, 1930; Beazley, ARV, pp. 831–41; G. M. A. Richter, Attic Red-figured Vases, New Haven, 1946, pp. 146–49; G. Becatti, Meidias: Un manierista antico, Florence, 1947; Rumpf, MZ, pp. 113–14; P. E. Arias and M. Hirmer, A History of Greek Vase Painting (trans. B. B. Shefton), London, 1962, pp. 212–17.

Paolo Enrico ARIAS

Illustrations: PLS. 439–440.

MELANESIA. Melanesia includes all the archipelagoes and islands lying between Indonesia to the west, Micronesia to the north, Polynesia to the east, and Australia to the south. Discovered as early as the 16th century but explored only in the 18th, particularly during Cook's great voyages, this region was called Melanesia from the Greek μέλας (black) and νῆσος (island) because of the dark skin of its inhabitants, reminiscent of that of the African Negroes. It includes, from north to south and west to east: New Guinea (q.v.), Paramicronesia, the Bismarck Archipelago, the Solomon Islands, the Santa Cruz Islands, the Banks Islands, the New Hebrides Islands, New Caledonia with the Loyalty Islands, and the Fiji Islands; geographically, anthropologically, and culturally, the last group represents an area of transition between Melanesia and Polynesia. In a number of these island groups the traditional art production, which flourished almost to the end of the 19th century, still survives in part, especially in the field of wood sculpture (see MELANESIAN CULTURES). The finest Melanesian art is preserved in the ethnographic museums of Europe, America, and Australia. In the modern period, no metropolitan centers or Occidentalizing art trends worthy of mention have developed.

SUMMARY. Paramicronesia (col. 692). Bismarck Archipelago (col. 692): *New Britain and adjacent islands; New Ireland; Admiralty Islands; Saint Matthias and Tench.* Solomon Islands (col. 694). Santa Cruz Islands (col. 695). New Hebrides and adjacent groups (col. 695). New Caledonia and the Loyalty Islands (col. 695). Fiji Islands (col. 696).

PARAMICRONESIA. Stretching westward from the Admiralty Islands is an archipelago of small low-lying coral islands, called by ethnologists Paramicronesia, to indicate that its light-skinned inhabitants, though belonging to Melanesia, are akin to those of Micronesia and Indonesia, if not to those of Polynesia. In its cultures, also, Micronesian and Indonesian elements are clearly discernible. This archipelago forms part of the Trust Territory of New Guinea, under Australian administration. The principal islands are Wuvulu (Matty) and Aua (Dourour), ethnically homogeneous; the small group of Ninigo; the Luf, or Hermit, Islands; and the Kaniet, or Anchorite, Islands. Evidences of the past are lacking, and contemporary art is rather scant; wood sculpture in the round is rare, being found only on Kaniet and Luf. Many utilitarian objects are outstanding for their nobility of form and attractive pyrographic decoration. In the ornamental carving on Kaniet and Luf appears the spiral motif — sometimes even double — which is very rare in Oceania. Outstanding on Luf in the past were the war canoes with incised (spiral) and painted decoration.

BIBLIOG. K. Hagen, Die Ornamentik von Wuwulu und Aua (Mitt. aus dem Mus. für Völkerkunde, II, 23), Hamburg, 1908.

BISMARCK ARCHIPELAGO. The Bismarck Archipelago, consisting of over 200 islands and islets, was explored by Dampier at the beginning of the 18th century. It is under Australian trusteeship.

New Britain and adjacent islands. This group includes, in addition to New Britain (formerly Neu-Pommern), the island of Umboi (Rooke) and the Siassi Islands, which form the chief link between the cultures of New Britain and New Guinea because of their situation in Dampier Strait, as well as the French Islands. New Britain is inhabited mainly by sedentary cultivators of Melanesian stock, who in the coastal areas engage in fishing and navigation; the island is very little known, with the exception of the Gazelle Peninsula, which was settled by two interesting pre-Austronesian tribes, the Sulka and the Baining, widely known for their rich art production.

Archaeological discoveries are quite numerous: rock carvings have been found on Umboi, together with three large monoliths (*biak*), to which pig's blood is offered in the course of certain ceremonies; also found in the area were stone pestles and club heads. On the island of Watom, off the New Britain coast, square-heeled axes have been found, together with potsherds, qualitatively akin to those from Kunie (Ile des Pins), near New Caledonia. From different parts of New Britain come prehistoric stone artifacts: pestles, pierced stones, a type of pick, and bowls, found chiefly along the western coastal strip; discoveries from the northwest coast, particularly those from the Baining territory, show Polynesian affinities.

The material culture of the Baining, except for those elements borrowed from the coastal Melanesians, belongs entirely to the pre-Austronesian phase and includes, among others, the crude gable-roofed hut, the stone-headed club, the adz with cylindrical stone blade fitted in a special hole in the shaft, the knapsack of knotted cord, and the simple xylophone. As in nearly all New Britain, here, too, pottery is absent. The high point of Baining art is reached in the masks used in the dance and religious ceremonies (PL. 442). The type of mask varies widely in style, technique, and material and differs from all other Melanesian masks (see MASKS). The masks of the Sulka (PL. 449), on the other hand, seem to resemble closely those of the Duk-duk secret society of the coastal population: they are largely conical and made of plant materials. Also noteworthy are the carved and painted shields of the Sulka, of the Mengen, of the tribes of the South Cape, and of the inhabitants of the nearby French Islands.

Sculpture is comparatively rare in New Britain and is limited to the human and zoomorphic figures placed on the Sulka masks and to statuettes of a soft tufflike stone, which on the Gazelle Peninsula serve as cult objects of the Ingiet secret society. The decoration reveals influences from New Guinea; the strongest bonds with this island are discernible on Umboi and in the Siassi Islands, where the art of sculpture and woodcarving extends not only to masks and utensils but also to sculpture incorporated in the structure of the cult houses, on the posts of which are depicted combined human and animal figures, in the style characteristic of the island of Tami (PL. 354; see NEW GUINEA). Outstanding among the minor arts are the dance sticks, a number of which reveal the existence of past ties with the Solomon Islands (Buka), as well as the modeled skulls of the Gazelle Peninsula.

BIBLIOG. P. Bley, Prähistorische Steingeräte aus Baining, Neu-Pommern, Anthropos, IV, 1909, p. 525; O. Meyer, Fund prähistorischer Töpferei und Steinmesser auf Vuatom, Bismarck Archipel, Südsee, Anthropos, IV, 1909, pp. 251–52, 1093–95; P. J. Meier, Steinbilder des Iniet-Geheimbundes bei den Eingeborenen des nördlichen Teiles der Gazelle-Halbinsel, Anthropos, VI, 1911, pp. 837–67; K. Neuhauss, Felszeichnungen auf der Insel Umboi, ZfE, XLVI, 1914, pp. 529–31; C. Laufer, Rigenmucha: Das höchste Wesen der Baining, Anthropos, XLI–XLIV, 1946–49, pp. 497–560.

New Ireland. Forming part of this area, in addition to New Ireland (formerly Neu-Mecklenburg), are the island of New Hanover, or Lavongai, and the smaller islands to the north and east; Tabar, Lihir, Tanga, and Feni. After New Guinea, this is the area of Melanesia where the most outstanding art has been produced.

Evidence of the art of the past is fairly plentiful. In a number of places in New Ireland stone bowls and pestles have been discovered. Figures of sharks, in limestone or volcanic stone, come from the southwest coast and the center of the island and seem to have been used in magic rites connected with fishing. A number of petroglyphs with geometric figures (concentric circles) have been observed at Majom, near Kavieng, in the northern half of the island, while a highly stylized bird motif may have come from southern New Ireland. Bowls and pestles from a very early epoch have also been found on Tabar and Lihir and in several areas on New Hanover. On the last island there are many petroglyphs which, according to the natives, are the work of spirits; the carvings include, besides geometric motifs and prints of human hands and feet, human figures and faces, highly stylized and in the form of masks, showing a strong resemblance to present-day local masks.

The most prized contemporary art in New Ireland is the wood sculpture, both figural and decorative, which reaches its peak in the northern part of the island; the production in the southern part is rather modest. Wood sculptures are known as *malanggan* (PLS. 447, 448; see MELANESIAN CULTURES) and include the anthropomorphic statues called *uli* (PL. 448; see ESCHATOLOGY); various kinds of masks, outstanding among them those called *tatanua*, topped by a high crest of coconut fiber; boards carved in openwork and painted; and a number of zoomorphic figures. In addition, there are dance ornaments and objects intended for ritual or eschatological use, such as the *totok* posts, carved in human form but with a face like the snout of a crocodile. Sometimes carved, at least in part, in an openwork technique that gives them an extraordinary lightness, all these sculptures are further embellished with brilliant colors.

Produced in the southern part of the island are chalk figures, called *kulap*, which are carved in honor of ancestors. In the north, decorative styles predominate, with an abundance of utilitarian objects, ornaments, ornamental house posts, ceremonial planks, and other forms; the principal decorative motifs are the saw tooth, the chevron, and the herringbone, as well as quatrefoil motifs, possibly derived from plants. Deserving special mention are the splendid pectoral ornaments, called *kapkap*, carved from Tridacna (giant clam) and tortoise shells.

BIBLIOG. G. Antze, Ahnenfiguren aus Kreide von Neu-Mecklenburg, Jhb. des städtischen Mus. für Völkerkunde zu Leipzig, IV, 1910, pp. 37–42; A. Krämer, Die Málanggane von Tombara, Munich, 1925; I. Hesse, Die Darstellungen der menschlichen Gestalt in Rundskulpturen Neu-Mecklenburgs, Cologne, 1933; A. Bühler, Neuirland und Nachbarinseln, Basel, 1948; F. Girard, L'importance sociale et religieuse des cérémonies exécutées pour les Malanggan sculptés de Nouvelle-Irlande, L'Anthropologie, LVIII, 1954, pp. 241–67; O. Schlaginhaufen, Muliama: Zwei Jahre unter Südsee-Insulanern, Zürich, 1959.

Admiralty Islands. This group includes a series of smaller islands lying south and east of a main island called Manus, which is also the name of the light-skinned people who live in houses built on piles along the coast and on the reefs. In the interior of the main island are the Usiai, who live in houses on the ground level; the Matankor represent an intermediate stage between the two groups.

Archaeological material is limited to a modest rock art (hand- and footprints, crocodiles, turtles, sun, and moon) near Tingou,
in the interior of Manus, from which also come receptacles made of volcanic stone, spearheads, axes, and other objects.

Contemporary art, of which the Usiai are the real exponents, includes admirable works; the fine workmanship is reminiscent partly of the Tami, partly of the *korwar* style (see NEW GUINEA), but affinities with the Solomon Islands are also present. Preeminent in the field of sculpture in the round are the ancestor figures, of small size and usually naturalistic. The high point of this art is reached in the decorative woodcarving (human figures and crocodiles) and in wooden containers, sometimes of gigantic size and at times in the form of animals, with spiral or anthropomorphic handles in openwork (PL. 452). Also outstanding are the ladles, spatulas, and gourds for betel, with poker work, the ornaments, combs, slit drums, and weapons, and the objects modeled from the pulp of the Parinarium nut. The few pottery vessels are undecorated.

BIBLIOG. H. Nevermann, Die Admiralitäts-Inseln (Ergebnisse der Hamburgischer Südsee-Expedition 1908–1910, II, A, 3), Hamburg, 1934.

Saint Matthias and Tench. Because of their geographic isolation and consequent lack of outside contact, these two islands have retained several archaic cultural traits and have assimilated few important cultural elements from the adjacent archipelagoes. However, a number of manifest similarities prove beyond question the existence of relations with the Admiralty Islands and New Ireland.

Contemporary art excels in the decorative ornamentation of the posts and gables of the chiefs' houses, in zoomorphic sculpture (on Tench, two anthropomorphic figures also have been found), and in the decoration of objects with shell inlay.

BIBLIOG. H. Nevermann, St. Matthias-Gruppe (Ergebnisse der Hamburgischer Südsee-Expedition 1908–1910, II, A, 2), Hamburg, 1933.

SOLOMON ISLANDS. Discovered in 1567 by Álvaro de Mendaña de Neyra, subsequently forgotten, and rediscovered by Bougainville in 1768, this archipelago includes a large number of islands, many of which — Buka, Bougainville, Choiseul, Guadalcanal, Malaita, New Georgia, Nissan — have very distinctive art. The northwestern portion of the archipelago is administered by Australia as the Kieta district of the Territory of New Guinea; the remainder has been a British protectorate since 1893.

Throughout the archipelago there are striking reminders of the past, particularly the stone artifacts (bowls, pestles, and adz blades), figural in some instances, such as two turtle-shaped vessels from Vella Lavella (New Georgia), probably from some pre-Melanesian phase, and the pestles of San Cristobal, some of which terminate in the head of a bird or snake. On this last island can be seen menhirs and dolmens, as well as fine stone sculptures, sometimes of great size, preserved within the meetinghouses; the earliest are of diorite, the later ones of limestone. Outstanding are the sarcophagi carved in bas-relief, discovered on Choiseul (see ESCHATOLOGY; MELANESIAN CULTURES). Because of the vast extent of the Solomon Islands, contemporary art is not homogeneous; even from the anthropological standpoint, the most striking contrasts are apparent between the very dark-skinned Melanesian groups and other lighter-skinned ones who reveal extensive infusion of Polynesian blood. Each island has developed its own type of material culture, but the artistic craftsmanship of each object, even those intended for ordinary use, the weapons, ornaments, and ritual objects, everywhere is of an exceptionally high level. Architectural sculpture is lacking, as is sculpture relating to the cult of the dead; masks are confined largely to the northern islands, from Nissan to Bougainville, and are artistically undistinguished. The shields, found from Choiseul to Guadalcanal, are plaited, those for formal use being inlaid with mother-of-pearl. Anthropomorphic figures are uncommon and are limited to Nissan, Buka, and Bougainville; the depiction of birds (frigate birds) and of fish (bonito; IV, PL. 449) is more widespread. The island of Rubiana is the center for artistically modeled skulls, decorated with delicate inlays of mother-of-pearl.

The working of mother-of-pearl and shells generally, either figurally (VI, PL. 52; see GEMS AND GLYPTICS) for ornamental purposes, or for inlay in wooden figures and containers (PL. 452), attains in the Solomons a perfection reached nowhere else in Melanesia. Geometric motifs are favored in painting, basketry, engraving, mother-of-pearl inlay, and other crafts.

BIBLIOG. H. Balfour, On the Evolution of a Characteristic Pattern on the Shafts of Arrows from the Solomon Islands, JRAI, XX, 1888, pp. 328–32; C. Ribbe, Zwei Jahre unter den Kannibalen der Salomo-Inseln, Dresden, 1903; H. Balfour, Bird and Human Design from the Solomon Islands, Man, V, 1905, pp. 81–83; C. Praetorius, Art in the Solomon Islands, Studio, XXXIV, 1905, pp. 118–24; J. Edge-Partington, Decorated Shields from the Solomon Islands, Man, VI, 1906, pp. 29–30; T. A. Joyce, Forehead Ornaments from the Solomon Islands, Man, XXXIV, 1934, pp. 97–100;

H. A. Bernatzik, Owa Raha, Vienna, 1936; H. Damm, Unbekannte Zeremonialgeräte von Rubiana (Salomo-Inseln), ZfE, LXXIII, 1943, pp. 29–34; F. D. McCarthy, The Shell Inlay Decoration of the Southern Solomon Islands, Australian Mus. Mag., VII, 1943, pp. 154–59.

SANTA CRUZ ISLANDS. An archipelago of volcanic origin, administratively a part of the British Solomons, the Santa Cruz Islands have yielded no traces of prehistoric or archaeological art. Because of the location of this group at the northeastern edge of Melanesia, many foreign, Micronesian, and Polynesian influences are evident in the contemporary art. In sculpture, depiction of the human figure is second to that of animals. The finest local art is the decoration of utilitarian and ornamental objects; in this field the Santa Cruz archipelago has developed a highly individual style, especially in the decoration of the wooden dance sticks, painted white, on which the decorative motifs stand out in red and black, as well as in the *kapkap*. Together with a variety of purely geometric motifs, stylized representations of birds with extended wings and of fish (PL. 242) are frequent.

BIBLIOG. F. Graebner, Völkerkunde der Santa-Cruz-Inseln, Ethnologica, I, 1909, pp. 71–184; F. Speiser, Die Ornamentik von Santa-Cruz, Arch. für Anthr., XIII, 1915, pp. 323–34; W. Foy, Zur Geschichte der Tanzkeulen von der Santa-Cruz-Inseln, Ethnologica, II, 1916, pp. 215–38; F. Speiser and W. Foy, Völkerkundliches von den Santa-Cruz-Inseln, Ethnologica, II, 1916, pp. 153–213; H. G. Beasley, The Tamar of Santa Cruz, Ethnologia Cranmorensis, IV, Chislehurst, 1939, pp. 27–30; F. Curtis, Some Santa Cruz Artifacts, Masterkey, XXXIV, 1960, pp. 62–65; W. Davenport, Red-Feather Money, Sc. Am., CCVI, 3, 1962, pp. 94–104.

NEW HEBRIDES AND ADJACENT GROUPS. Discovered in 1606 by Pedro da Queirós, the New Hebrides, with the Banks Islands, an Anglo-French condominium, includes some forty islands and islets; the chief ones are Malekula, Espíritu Santo, Efate, Ambrim, Oba (Aoba), Eromanga, and Tana. Archaeological finds are outstanding: on Gaua, in the Banks Islands, have been found stone vessels, regarded as sacred by the natives; on Malo, amulets connected with the fertility of pigs, generally with carved male figures, reclining or dancing, which in the earlier pieces were always in low relief; on Achin, near the northeastern coast of Malekula, stones carved into human faces and figures of sharks, used in rain magic; on Malekula are found monoliths, some of which are phallic and others figural. A variety of stone artifacts (bowls, pestles, phalli, pierced stones, etc.) are found on nearly all the islands in the archipelago. The rare petroglyphs are mostly symbolic geometric.

The New Hebrides are inhabited in certain localities by people of small stature, as well as by the tall dark-skinned Melanesians. In several islands, chiefly in the southern part of the archipelago, an obviously Polynesian strain is evident; in the art this is marked by a total absence of figural elements (statuary, masks, and similar expressions). Conversely, the art of the northern and central islands (Malekula and small islands near Ambrim), including the Banks Islands, is not only rich but exhibits a number of distinctive features, particularly the sculpture carved from tree-fern pith, including ancestor images, either naturalistic or stylized, and posts of emblematic significance (Malekula); the modeled skulls of Malekula; statues to which actual human skulls have been attached; and vertical slit drums, generally carved in the likeness of a human face.

The production of masks is one of the activities of the Suque secret society. Among the outstanding art products are the plaited mats, used for clothing and adorned with lozenges or appliqués in relief.

The art of the Banks Islands, quantitatively rather meager, is notable for the formal beauty of its products, both utilitarian and ornamental: basketry, knives with openwork handles, and bamboo ear pendants.

BIBLIOG. W. Flower, On a Collection of Monumental Heads and Artificially Deformed Crania from the Island of Mallecollo in the New Hebrides, JRAI, XI, 1881, pp. 75–81; A. Eichhorn, Neu-hebridische Spinngewerbsmasken, BA, V, 1916, pp. 284–92; F. Speiser, Ethnographische Materialen aus den Neuen-Hebriden und den Banks-Inseln, Berlin, 1923; F. Speiser, Südsee, Urwald, Kannibalen: Reisen in den Neuen-Hebriden und Santa-Cruz-Inseln, Stuttgart, 1924; A. B. Deacon, Geometrical Drawings from Malekula and Other Islands of the New Hebrides, JRAI, LXIV, 1934, pp. 129–75; R. R. C. MacLachlan, Native Pottery of the New Hebrides, JPS, XLVIII, 1939, pp. 32–55; P. O'Reilly, Mégalithes hébridais, une sépulture de chef et deux autres tombes à Nagire, île d'Aoba, JSO, VII, 1951, pp. 175–80; M. Laird, A Small Stone Head from the New Hebrides, JPS, LXII, 1953, pp. 119–22; H. Fischer, Über stehende Schlitztrommeln auf den Neuen Hebriden und am Sepik, ZfE, LXXXII, 1957, pp. 58–65; J. Guiart, Espíritu Santo (Nouvelle Hébrides), Paris, 1958.

NEW CALEDONIA AND THE LOYALTY ISLANDS. Discovered by Cook in 1774, New Caledonia is an overseas territory of France, of which the Loyalty Islands (Lifu, Maré, and Uvéa) are an administrative department. Of all the Melanesian islands, New Caledonia is geographically the most isolated and has therefore had virtually no contact, not even ethnological, with the other cultures of Melanesia. Under these circumstances it has been able to develop and conserve, since remote times, a completely autonomous culture, which in its art reveals both its great antiquity and an exceptional expressive power.

Throughout the island there are many remains of ancient settlements, megalithic dwellings in conjunction with which are found large numbers of stone instruments (which in the eyes of the natives are of magical nature) as well as pottery fragments of diverse styles and epochs; these fragments are similar to the pottery of the present-day inhabitants. There are numerous petroglyphs, mostly of geometric motifs between parallel lines like those of New Hanover and those on the Australian rock carvings and churingas (see AUSTRALIAN CULTURES). The rare figural petroglyphs have peculiar physical characteristics, among them long ears, suggesting that they are the work of a people different from the present inhabitants, and thus from an earlier epoch. More modern in character are the rough anthropomorphic limestone sculptures from the Loyalty Islands, which may derive from Polynesian influences: the spherical head, with the face rather realistic but without relief, is barely separated from the thickset trunk carved in the round; the slender arms, raised upward with the elbows sharply bent, are very sketchily treated. The figures end slightly below the navel in a sort of pedestal.

Of special interest in the contemporary art production are the ornamental carvings of the houses, particularly those of the doors, decorated with human faces with characteristic hooked noses, below which the body is represented in completely abstract fashion. Also worthy of mention are the roof spires, of ceremonial nature, representing mythological symbols or figures. The masks, not connected with secret societies, include a vast range of types, the best-known being that with a gigantic hooked nose, very common in the northern part of the island (PL. 443). A connection can be established between this type of mask and the type of money prevalent in the island, in the form of small carved heads having the features of the masks.

Anthropomorphic sculptures in wood are less common. Peculiar to the island are the bamboo carvings of genre scenes, some of which deal with historical subjects and represent a rudimentary form of writing. Other noteworthy products are the jade and shell ornaments and the beautiful jadeite ceremonial adzes.

BIBLIOG. L. Bonnemère, Les pierres gravées de la Nouvelle Calédonie, B. Soc. d'Anthr. de Paris, 4th ser., VI, 1895, pp. 63–72; M. Archambault, Les mégalithes néo-calédoniens, L'Anthropologie, XII, 1901, pp. 257–68; M. Archambault, Nouvelles recherches sur les mégalithes néo-calédoniens, L'Anthropologie, XIII, 1902, pp. 689–712; M. Archambault, Sur un ancienne ornamentation rupestre en Nouvelle Calédonie, L'homme préhistorique, VI, 1908, pp. 289–318; M. Archambault, Les sculptures et les gravures sur roche de la Nouvelle Calédonie, B. et Mém. Soc. d'Anthr. de Paris, 5th ser., X, 1909, pp. 517–30; M. Archambault, A propos des monuments mégalithiques de la Nouvelle Calédonie, B. et Mém. Soc. d'Anthr. de Paris, 6th ser., IX, 1918, p. 33; G. H. Luquet, L'art néo-calédonien (Trav. et Mém. Soc. d'Anthr. de Paris, II), Paris, 1926; F. Sarasin, Ethnologie der Neu-Caledonier und Loyalty-Insulaner, Munich, 1929; M. Leenhardt, Les masques néo-calédoniens, B. Mus. d'Ethn. du Trocadéro, VI, 1933, pp. 3–21; M. Leenhardt, Gens de la Grand Terre, Paris, 1937; M. Leenhardt, Mawaraba Mapi: La signification du masque en Nouvelle Calédonie, JSO, I, 1945, pp. 29–35; J. Avias, Contribution à la préhistoire de l'Océanie: Les tumuli des plateaux de fer en Nouvelle Calédonie, JSO, V, 1949, pp. 15–50; J. Avias, Poteries canaques et poteries préhistoriques en Nouvelle Calédonie, JSO, VI, 1950, pp. 111–40; P. O'Reilly, Deux sites fortifiés du district de La Roche dans l'île de Maré (îles Loyalty), JSO, VI, 1950, pp. 87–93; G. and M. Lobsiger-Dellenbach, Description de trois bambous gravés de Nouvelle Calédonie, collection M. C. Ratton, JSO, VII, 1951, pp. 105–21; G. and M. Lobsiger-Dellenbach, Dessins réalistes et motifs symboliques gravés sur bambous de Nouvelle Calédonie, Südseestudien: Gedenkschrift zur Erinnerung an F. Speiser, Basel, 1951, pp. 318–30; J. Avias, La préhistoire néocalédonienne, JSO, IX, 1953, pp. 53–63; E. W. Gifford, L'archéologie néo-calédonienne en 1952, JSO, IX, 1953, pp. 64–70; J. Guiart, L'art autochtone de Nouvelle Calédonie, Nouméa, 1953; G. and M. Lobsiger-Dellenbach, Trois bambous gravés de Nouvelle Calédonie, Arch. suisses d'anthr. générale, XXII, 1957, pp. 76–92.

FIJI ISLANDS. The archipelago of the Fiji (or Viti) Islands, discovered in 1643 by A. J. Tasman, includes over 250 islands and islets, only 80 of which are inhabited. Attached to this group, a British colony, is the remote island of Rotuma; the principal islands are Viti Levu, Vanua Levu, Taveuni, and Kandavu. In its geography, anthropology, and culture, the archipelago forms a zone of transition between Melanesia and Polynesia. The inhabitants exhibit predominantly Melanesian physical traits, but naturally in the small eastern islands more Polynesian blood is apparent than in the large western islands, particularly in Viti Levu and Vanua Levu. It is a historically proven fact that in the pre-European period the Fijians were in continuous contact with Polynesia, especially with Tonga; Polynesian influence on local art production seems particularly strong. With the sole exception of pottery, which never penetrated farther east in Oceania, all elements of Fijian art are typically Polynesian; examples are the highly advanced technique and designs of the tapa cloth (PL. 458), the carved motifs on clubs and other instruments, the ornamental bindings of beams and supports in the temples and houses, the style of the ornamental objects, and the extremely rare anthropomorphic figures carved in wood or sperm-whale teeth. On certain islands of the group, petroglyphs have been discovered, some depicting turtles, the significance and age of which are still unknown; the ruins of megalithic structures have also been found. In the contemporary art typical Melanesian products are absent. The carved geometric decoration on the weapons and utilitarian objects is restrained but attractive. The typical local pottery is characterized by individual forms painted in monochrome, usually in a greenish shade, with high luster.

BIBLIOG. C. F. Gordon Cumming, Fijian Pottery, Art J., 1881, pp. 362–65; J. Hornell, The Megalithic Sea Works and Temple Platforms at Mbau in Fiji, Man, XXVI, 1926, pp. 25–32; R. W. Paine, Some Rock Paintings in Fiji, Man, XXIX, 1929, pp. 149–51; R. R. C. MacLachlan, The Native Pottery of the Fiji Islands, JPS, XLIX, 1940, pp. 243–71; E. W. Gifford, Archaeological Excavations in Fiji, Univ. of Calif. Anthr. Records, XIII, 1951, pp. 189–288; E. W. Gifford, Fijian Myths, Legends and Archaeology, Univ. of Calif. Pub. in Semitic Philology, XI, 1951, pp. 166–77; P. A. Snow, Rock Carvings in Fiji, Tr. and Proc. of the Fiji Soc. of Sc. and Industry, IV, 1953, pp. 71–83; P. O'Reilly, Abri sous roche à gravures, Nailou, district de Cakaudrove, Vanua Levu, îles Fiji, JSO, X, 1954, pp. 178–79; E. W. Gifford, Six Fijian Radiocarbon Dates, JPS, LXIV, 1955, p. 240; K. E. Larsson, Fijian Studies, Göteborg, 1960.

Herbert TISCHNER

MELANESIAN CULTURES. In comparison with the other areas of Oceanic art (the Australian, Micronesian, and Polynesian cultures, qq.v.) the art of Melanesia is outstanding in its richness of form and color, figural dynamism, and elaboration of ornament. Superficially it may seem inaccurate to speak of "Melanesian art" as an entity, because each ethnographic region, tribe, or island has developed its own characteristic and unmistakable forms and styles; nevertheless, it is possible to discern in all Melanesian art, despite its infinite variety, a single magico-religious source of inspiration, apparent even in objects such as weapons and implements of a clearly utilitarian nature. Thus the content of the art, even though it is not always readily interpreted, reveals that it has arisen from an integrated cultural milieu. To understand its true meaning, it must be borne in mind that the cultural tradition has been profoundly modified by contact with European civilization. Indigenous Melanesian art is now virtually extinct except in a few isolated or inaccessible places, and even in those a more or less slow process of decadence is taking place.

SUMMARY. General considerations (col. 697). Prehistoric and archaeological art (col. 701). New Guinea (col. 703). Paramicronesia (col. 705). Bismarck Archipelago (col. 707): *Admiralty Islands; New Britain; New Ireland; Saint Matthias and Tench.* Solomon Islands (col. 717). Santa Cruz Islands (col. 719). New Hebrides and the Banks Islands (col. 720). New Caledonia (col. 723). Fiji Islands (col. 726).

GENERAL CONSIDERATIONS. Among the "primitive" arts of the world, that of Oceania was the last to become known and appreciated in the Western world. The delay in this "discovery" (which was precipitated by the interest of avant-garde artists in the modern European movement) was largely due to the difficulty of understanding, from objects exhibited in museums, the intrinsic character of an art that was profoundly bound up with the magico-religious life and was conceived to be seen in movement, in the course of highly dramatic and dynamic ritual acts.

Among the various arts of Oceania, that of Melanesia is distinguished for its dazzling richness of both form and color, the multiplicity of materials, the perfection of the figural sculpture — both independent and architectural — the extraordinary luxuriant ornamentation of surfaces by means of carving, piercing, inlay, or pictorial decoration, and the abundance of embellishment with feathers, shells, leaves, bark, ivory, or other materials. Melanesian art achieves its highest expression in its sculpture, which is characterized throughout by a vigorous dynamism and a particular method of handling the human figure which tends to distort, twist, and combine it in various ways until it may become completely metamorphosed into ornamentation. Examples of figures that are representational but conceived in a unique manner are the *uli* statues of New Ireland (PL. 448), which are bisexual, in conformance with certain supernatural beliefs; certain figurines from New Guinea and Paramicronesia, which combine naturalistic and vigorously modeled heads with bodies that are disproportionately small or barely suggested and appear to serve mainly as supports; and a number of seemingly realistic representations from the Admiralty Islands, in which particular stress is laid on the ornaments (headdress, distended ear lobes, etc.).

In both figural and ornamental sculpture an extremely strong esthetic sense is apparent in the tendency to combine different figures, colors, and materials; this is especially prominent in the *malanggan* style of New Ireland and in the delicate mother-of-pearl inlays in the wooden sculpture of the Solomon Islands. All Melanesian sculpture tends to produce a strong emotional effect, inspiring wonder, consternation, or repulsion, as in the case of certain masks from New Guinea, New Caledonia, and the Gazelle Peninsula (PLS. 442, 443). A compositional harmony prevails both in the independent figures and in group compositions (though the latter are rare; PLS. 444, 445).

Decorative art appears essentially as a supplement to the sculpture. In contrast to the other areas of Oceania (see POLYNESIAN CULTURES) and also to Negro Africa (e.g., see BANTU CULTURES), here the human figure carved in wood, either in the round or in bas-relief, seems almost subordinate to the plethora of ornament that covers the surface, everywhere interrupting the sculptural planes. The planes are apparently regarded primarily as surfaces to be decorated, in accord with a strongly compulsive horror vacui similar to that found in the wood sculpture of the Maoris in New Zealand (q.v.; XI, PL. 205). The few exceptions to this general tendency, with their slender (PLS. 445, 451) or thickset lines (PL. 448) and marked disproportion between head and body (PL. 445), seem to be isolated instances resulting from the personal bent of the sculptor and departing from the traditional lines of Melanesian art as a whole.

The discovery and enthusiastic appreciation of Melanesian art date from the beginning of the 20th century; however, the understanding of the intrinsic values of this art and the analytic and comparative study of the styles of the different island groups followed somewhat later, through the work of specialists. In a way the interpretation of this art was impeded by the wholehearted enthusiasm it aroused among artists (with psychological implications not based on a true understanding of its genesis, evolution, and significance), and also by the tendency of ethnologists to consider it simply another cultural element in primitive art as a whole, quite apart from its own esthetic and ideological values. Only in recent years have efforts been made to perform studies in depth, at once art-historical and cultural, of this multifaceted art. These studies have made it possible to differentiate independent local styles and trace relations between distant archipelagoes, influences from Indonesia, and in some cases the complete evolutionary cycle of a given style or art form. Decisive influences of natural environment, religion, and economic activity, as well as of the racial make-up of peoples producing the art have been recorded. In a number of localities excavations have been undertaken and finds have been made of art from earlier periods that is totally unrelated to the output of the present inhabitants. Moreover, within the proliferation of local styles, it has been possible to discern the existence of two great artistic traditions, one tending toward dramatic effects and a riot of color, especially prominent in central Melanesia (Sepik River region and Gulf of Papua, in New Guinea; the New Hebrides; certain areas in New Britain), and the other highly decorative and at times extremely delicate, found in the Solomon and Admiralty Islands, but also in the Massim area of New Guinea (FIG. 705) and adjacent archipelagoes. Only New Ireland, with its flourishing local development, represents a unique style unrelated to the two foregoing tendencies. An isolated phenomenon within the framework of the Melanesian is the peripheral art of Paramicronisia, New Caledonia, and Fiji; the last is a Polynesian outpost within the Melanesian cultures, of which, however, it is ethnically a part.

Aside from these general stylistic traits, analysis of the objects has revealed affinities of form and content among widely separated islands, sometimes belonging to different racial and cultural milieus. For instance, there can be no question about the kinship between the figural sculpture of the Sepik River and that of the Gulf of Papua (see NEW GUINEA), between certain parts of New Zealand and Easter Island (see POLYNESIAN CULTURES), nor between the artistic production of the Massim and that of the islanders of the eastern Solomons. Indonesian influences (see INDONESIAN CULTURES), especially from the Moluccas (Spice Islands), are evident in northwestern New Guinea, while in the Paramicronesian islands of Wuvulu (Matty) and Aua (Dourour) influences from the Palau Islands (see MICRONESIAN CULTURES) are apparent.

Notwithstanding numerous specific traits, the essential features of Melanesian culture are those common to the other inhabitants of Oceania: ignorance of writing and metallurgy, up to the time of contact with Western civilization; an economy of early neolithic character based on fishing, farming with a digging stick or hoe, and the raising (though not everywhere) of dogs, pigs, and chickens. Hunting, although more intensively practiced than in Micronesia and Polynesia, is decidedly secondary because of the paucity of big game. Hatchets and axes of polished stone or shell are used for cutting trees and building huts and boats, and for all types of woodworking. The knowledge of pottery is general where the raw material has been available. Weaving is limited to a few marginal areas and has been almost entirely replaced by the production of bark cloth (see TAPA), as in Polynesia.

It is difficult to survey the art of Melanesia in terms of its forms, because large numbers of variants exist within single formal categories, which are in turn determined by environmental, anthropological, social, and religious factors; Melanesian art should rather be treated by large geographical sectors.

Aside from a small number of pygmy tribes who live in the mountainous interior of New Guinea and have no outstanding art production, Melanesia is the home of two large native groups, the Papuans and the Melanesians. The former, who were the earlier group to settle there, occupy the greater part of New Guinea and are present in New Britain (the Sulka and Baining) and in Bougainville (Solomon Islands); their language lies outside the large Austronesian, or Malayo-Polynesian, family, to which practically all the other languages spoken in the archipelagoes of Oceania belong. The latter occupy the remaining area of Melanesia; in certain places they have crossed with the Papuans, in others with Polynesian elements, as has happened, for instance, in Fiji.

Certain islands of the Melanesian archipelago were discovered in the first half of the 16th century, but only with the voyages of Tasman (17th cent.), Cook, and Bougainville (latter half of 18th cent.) did their cultural traits begin to become known in Europe. Also dating from the later period of exploration is the first appearance in European museums of art objects and other creations of these remote peoples. The earliest specimens preserved in museums and private collections are qualitatively the best; later examples show increasing signs of decadence. In some islands, after contact with Europeans, either the traditional art disappeared completely or there was a shift to standardized production of inferior items designed for the tourist trade.

It has been noted that the content of Melanesian art derived mainly from the religion, principally from ideas pertaining to the ancestor cult; in order to ensure the presence of his ancestor's ghost, the Melanesian prepares a dwelling for the spirit of the dead relative. As in life, so after death, too, the skull in particular was considered the seat of the soul; accordingly, it was modeled and painted and took on the nature of a portrait, the most faithful one possible (IV, PL. 449; see ESCHATOLOGY). These skulls were preserved in special structures, generally

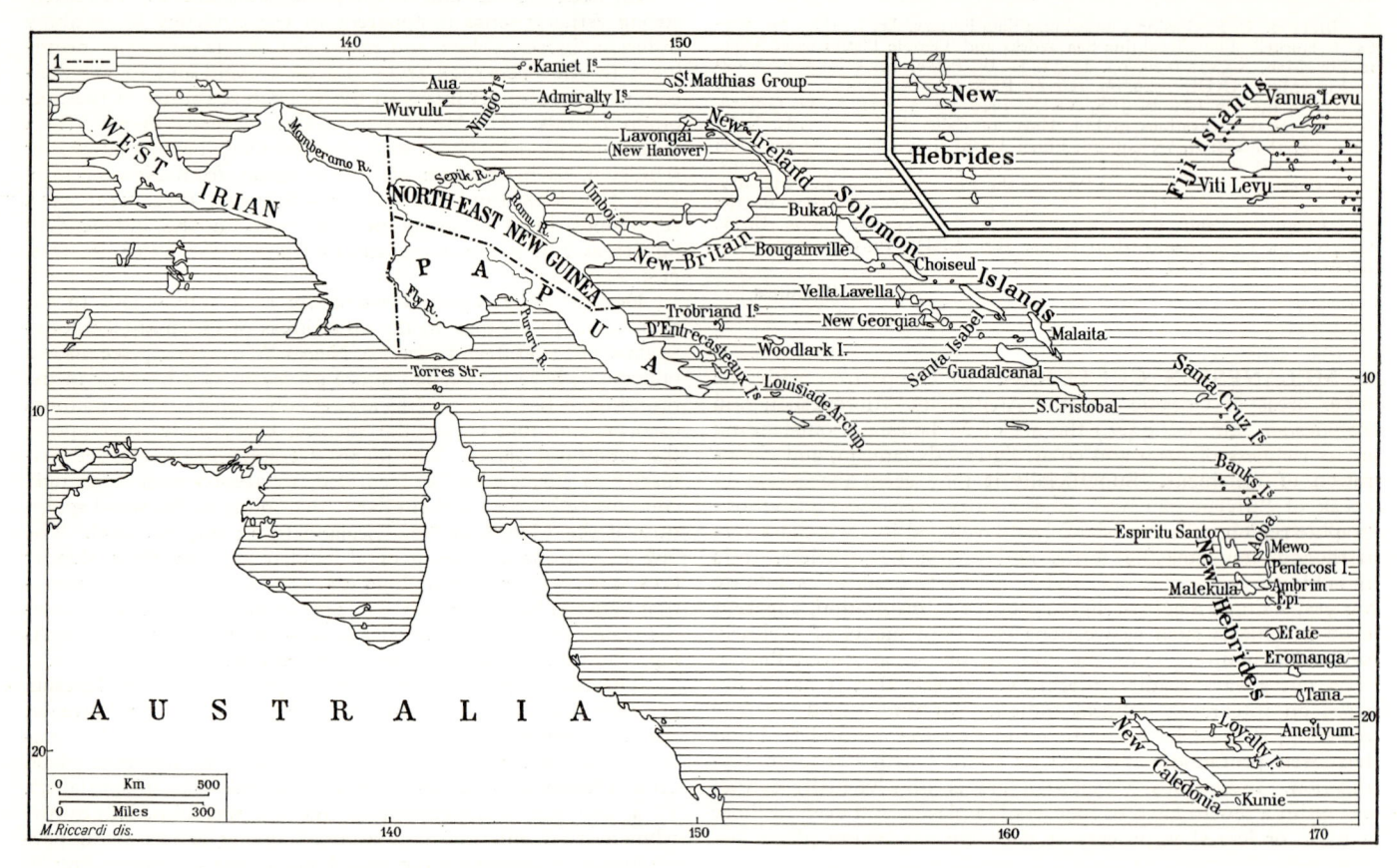

Geographical area showing the diffusion of indigenous Melanesian arts. Key: (1) Modern national boundaries.

inside the men's houses, together with such other ceremonial paraphernalia as masks, sacred flutes, bull-roarers, and drums (see MUSICAL INSTRUMENTS). Even commoner was the full figure of the ancestor, at first consisting of a body of wood or other plant material, to which was attached the skull of the deceased. Later, the entire statue was carved from wood, the pith of tree ferns, limestone, and other materials. The ancestor figure is an outgrowth of the skull cult; there was a gradual departure from the naturalistic reproduction of the human figure, resulting, in certain cases, in purely abstract decorative forms, except for the head. The Melanesians on certain occasions seek to materialize the ghost of the dead in visible and active form. To this end — particularly during the ceremonies of initiation and commemoration of the dead, but on other occasions as well — they employ various types of masks. During the rites the wearer of the mask loses his own identity and embodies the spirit of an ancestor. The existence of this identification is extremely clear in the case of the rare and definitely archaic masks made from actual human skulls. Also a close connection between the use of masks and the institution of the men's societies is evident virtually everywhere.

The application of figural art extends to most of the implements and objects of everyday use. Not even in this case, however, is the ornamentation an idle decorative adjunct or one of purely esthetic nature; rather, it represents the essence of the object itself, for, according to the Melanesian concept, bound up with the decoration are the forces of magic, which are capable of guaranteeing the efficacy of a weapon or the usefulness of a tool. The decoration was handed down from the ancestor in its particular form, and it must not be altered. Fear of the anger of the spirits of the dead and the desire to ensure their aid and beneficent power, their mana, constitute a strong religious tradition throughout all Melanesia.

PREHISTORIC AND ARCHAEOLOGICAL ART. Scientific exploration of the grottoes, caves, and subsoil of Melanesia may yet turn up some surprises that will permit clarification of the traces of the past: heretofore, what has come to light has been the result of chance discoveries and nonsystematic excavations, and only in the immediate past did the contributions of specialists begin.

Even though the natives deny any knowledge of the origins and creators of the art works from their dim past — frequently objects of veneration — it is plain that most of these works are not very old, some antedating the European discovery by only a few decades. Any general effort to establish a chronological order would be premature, however, though it is interesting to observe that many of the present instruments and, in some instances, certain types of decoration still used by the natives stem from archaeological prototypes. According to A. Riesenfeld and certain subsequent authors, all ancient Melanesian art, including the rock art and pottery, should be related to the great body of megalithic art; actually, this art is the product of migratory waves that varied in composition and period: pre-Austronesian, megalithic, Austromelanid, or Melanesian, to the last of which, it is maintained (A. Bühler), most of the art works mentioned are to be ascribed.

Except for New Guinea, where fairly systematic investigations have been conducted, and the Solomons, where prehistoric lithic art appears to be most highly concentrated, finds have been rather infrequent except for isolated manifestations or occasional importations. The findings in Fiji exhibit markedly individual traits.

The rock art of New Guinea is generally scattered along the coasts, with the heaviest concentration around McCluer Gulf (west New Guinea), while the artifacts (pestles, sometimes bird-shaped; cups; axheads; some figure sculpture) are concentrated mostly in the east. The rock carvings show some similarities to those discovered in New Hanover, but the rest of the stone art remains an enigma and for the most part is without parallel elsewhere. Some motifs in the rock art, for instance, certain complicated arabesques, are reminiscent of Indonesia, while others, observed on the dance belts of the present-day Buang (Territory of New Guinea), were probably figural originally but are now completely absorbed into purely ornamental designs. On the other hand, the strange human face that appears in the rock paintings of the McCluer Gulf is reminiscent of present-day examples in the Sepik River region; the group of rock carvings discovered by W. Strong near Port Moresby exhibit, besides ornamental motifs, almost shapeless anthropomorphic figures akin to contemporary ones produced in the region of the Gulf of Papua, while the patterns in the rock art of the D'Entrecasteaux Islands hark back to tattooing and boat decorations. Thus, despite the apparent lack of cultural continuity, the art of the past seems to be linked somehow to that of the present.

The rock carvings of New Hanover, because of the V motif used to indicate the eyes and nose, are reminiscent of the style of Tami Island, in Huon Gulf (see NEW GUINEA). The closest parallels, however, are to be found in the rock art of distant New Caledonia; and there is no lack of influences from New Ireland, nor of points of contact with the geometric-symbolic rock carvings of the New Hebrides. On the other hand, the decorative motifs of New Caledonian rock art (circles; semicircles; Latin, Greek, Maltese, and Lorraine crosses; and spirals) also recur in the incised decoration of bone and bamboo in Portuguese Timor (see INDONESIA) and in European prehistoric art. According to G. Luquet, these motifs presumably derive from the intentionally stylized representation of the human body and, in particular, of the face, and are said to have originated with the ancestors of the present-day Kanakas. Archambault, who studied them on the spot from 1898 to 1922, attributes them to a race with Euro-Asiatic affinities (the Ainus?) and to the same stock responsible for the megalithic mounds and the bird-beak clubs, the latter being repeated in wood by the present-day Kanakas. Sarasin saw in the New Caledonian rock carvings a kinship with those of Australia and with the motifs incised on the churingas (see AUSTRALIAN CULTURES). Moreover, the prehistoric finds of Kunie (Ile des Pins), along the New Caledonia coast, where sizable mounds, signs of the production of stone blades, and potsherds have been observed, show striking similarities to the prehistoric artifacts on the island of Watom, near New Britain.

Compared to the rock art, the other prehistoric creations seem of secondary importance. Stone figures of birds, probably used as pestles, have been discovered in different parts of New Guinea, New Britain (where it seems they were connected with the secret society of Ingiet), and San Cristobal (Solomons). The remarkable stone sculptures of Buka, Choiseul, and San Cristobal (all in the Solomons) show many points of kinship with the stone sculpture, likewise very old, of Oba (Aoba; New Hebrides). At Buka there are erect monoliths, about 6½ ft. high, generally round in section, with geometric and ornamental incised decoration. According to the natives, these stones were erected in very remote times as commemorative monuments on the occasion of the funeral of a chief. According to C. Fox, similar monoliths are also found over tombs on San Cristobal.

In the Basel Museum für Völkerkunde there are two remarkable stone sculptures from Choiseul. One is a crouching human figure about 24 in. high, which has become worn with time; nothing is known of its significance or origin. The other, even more remarkable, consists of the upper portion of a vertical sarcophagus of volcanic stone and a monolith completely hollowed out and filled with bone fragments. The front is adorned with a relief depicting a male figure, with the feet turned inward and the ears singularly protruding and elongated. Underneath can be seen a head treated in similar fashion. The upper portion of the sarcophagus rested on a block of stone about 39 in. square, bearing on the front two relief figures of the same nature. The conception and workmanship of these figures differ, in point of form, from everything presently known in the Solomons and in Melanesia generally; if anything, they are reminiscent of certain Indonesian styles. The natives have been able to furnish only extremely vague information as to their origin. Another sarcophagus, found near the two pieces mentioned above but not transportable, bears signs which, according to the discoverer, are reminiscent of the ideograms of Easter Island (see POLYNESIAN CULTURES). The two figures of limestone or tufa, from Oba, discovered about the 1930s, are thoroughly baffling and unusual. The first, preserved in the Basel Museum für Völkerkunde, represents a boar with tusks, carved in the round; it is about 24 in. long. The other, in the Hamburg Museum für Völkerkunde, is in the form of an outrigger canoe with a bird on the prow. Both these sculptures have rounded wedges on the upper portion, about 2³/₄ in. high and slightly concave, carved out of the rock itself; two of these are located on the concave back of the boar and three on the boat, also concave. Nothing is known of the meaning, origin, or purpose of these sculptures, which have been ascribed to an extinct people; however, the presence and position of the wedges suggest that they served in the ceremonial preparation of kava.

The New Georgian net sinkers, unquestionably very old, are either figural or ring-shaped and show kinship with similar Polynesian implements (Marquesas, New Zealand). Affinities with Polynesia (Marquesas, Tahiti) are also apparent in the remarkable limestone "idols" from Lifu (Loyalty Islands), with spherical heads and lifelike features; these are actually not very old. In substance, the archaeological art indicates the existence of contacts among the various archipelagoes since very early times, and even though the present-day inhabitants seem generally detached from these remote art expressions, many prehistoric styles and motifs persist in the contemporary art.

Ernesta CERULLI

NEW GUINEA. The stylistic areas of New Guinea (q.v.) constitute by far the richest and most important zone in Melanesia. Although in art, as in every other sector of culture, boundaries fluctuate, making it impossible to draw precise limits, specific characteristics and distinct local traits serve to divide the island into nine geographically bounded stylistic areas: the northwestern coastal area, consisting largely of Geelvink Bay, with the islands and islets adjacent to the Vogelkop Peninsula; the northern coastal strip around Humboldt Bay and Lake Sentani; the Sepik River basin; the Huon Gulf area (FIG. 705), with the island of Tami (PL. 354); the Massim area and adjacent archipelagoes; the Gulf of Papua area, principally near the mouths of the Purari and Fly rivers; the Torres Strait Islands; the coast east of Frederik Hendrik Island, inhabited by the Marind-anim, or Tugeri; and the southwestern coastal zone, which coincides approximately with the area of the Mimika and Asmat cultures. In the northwestern zone, art and culture display unmistakable Indonesian influences, especially from the Moluccas.

Except in those zones inhabited by certain mountain or interior tribes, with poor art or almost none, artistic creativity has been lavished on everything, from the gigantic meeting- or community houses to the most modest personal ornament. The wood sculpture, frequently painted in the characteristic colors of black, white, red, and yellow, represents the highest achievement and includes the most striking works of art. Most imposing, certainly, are the ceremonial *bisj* poles of the Asmat, reaching almost 33 ft. and discovered only recently, and the corresponding *bitoro* poles from the Mimika district, which represent human figures harmoniously combined with ornamental rinceaux carved in openwork. Consonant with the native fauna, the most frequent zoomorphic motifs are crocodiles and birds, often used together in the carvings of the ornamental boat prows.

The meeting- or cult houses in the Sepik River area and in the Maprik Mountains on the northern coast, and the *dubudaima* of the Gulf of Papua, noteworthy for their architecture, are veritable temples of art, with anthropomorphic, zoomorphic, or conventional carvings on the beams and posts, multicolored paintings on the gables and interior walls, and numerous objects, mostly of ceremonial nature preserved in them: masks (PL. 358), ancestor figures (PL. 444) and panels (PL. 444; FIG. 704), bull-roarers (PL. 156), flutes, dance drums (see MUSICAL INSTRUMENTS), suspension hooks, and neckrests (PL. 457; V, PL. 426; see FURNITURE). Near the Sepik, these houses also shelter splendid ancestor skulls, realistically modeled with clay and painted; clay figurines, however, are very rare. New Guinea is also the principal zone where war shields are found in quantity; of countless types and forms, generally incised, sculptured, and painted,

they form an essential category in the decorative art (PL. 444; FIG. 705; I, PL. 436). Weapons such as clubs, swords, spears, bows, arrows, and daggers rank second to the shields, though they, too, nearly always bear ornamental or figural motifs. The daggers made from human bones with fine incised decorations are works of art of a high order.

Preeminent among the utilitarian objects are the betel mortars, spatulas, and containers, modeled and decorated in

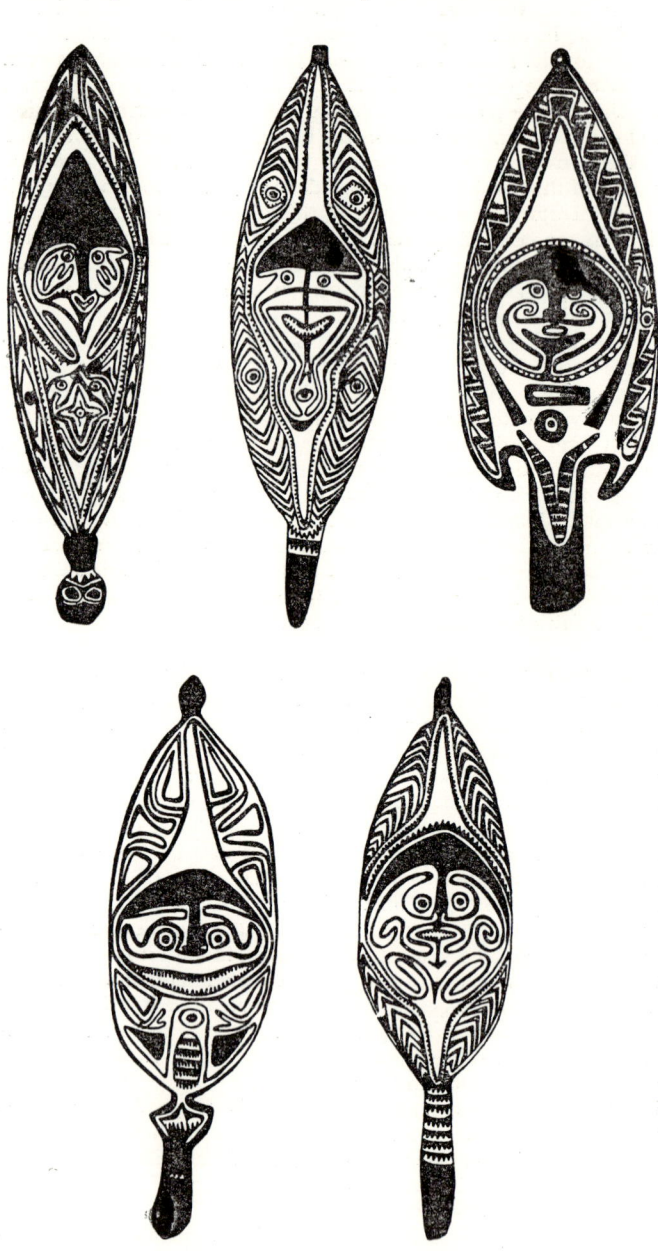

Various types of motifs incised and carved on ancestor panels from the Purari delta, New Guinea (*after A. Buell Lewis, 1931*).

a variety of ways. The containers, usually carved from oblong gourds or, less frequently, from bamboo, are always decorated with pyrography. In the Sepik River area even the lids of the gourd containers, decorated with notable carved motifs of crocodiles and birds, rank among the distinctive achievements in the minor arts, along with the wooden grips of spear throwers, bearing similar motifs.

The New Guinea masks display immense variety in materials, size, and decoration; not always carved from wood, in a number of areas they are made of such materials as rattan or tapa cloth, or even several materials combined, while in the Torres Strait Islands they are nearly always of turtle shell (PLS. 251, 441). Also of turtle shell are the arm bands, about 8 in. wide and with incised bands of ornamentation, typical of the northeastern areas.

Melanesian pottery reaches its peak of technical and artistic perfection in the lower and middle regions of the Sepik River (see CERAMICS), the principal center being the Keram (Potter) River, a tributary on the right bank of the lower Sepik,

niet statues were placed in front of the "temples." Unlike those seen in neighboring zones, they are not painted; their effect is achieved entirely by their simple straight lines and the extraordinary austerity of the bearded heads, elongated and bent slightly forward, which make up nearly half the height of the figures. With the simplest means the sculptures have been given an

Decorative incised and painted motifs from New Guinea: (*a, b, c, d*) Receptacles made of coconut shells, in the Huon Gulf style; (*e*) spiral decoration of a dance shield, in the Massim style, from the Trobriand Islands (*after A. Buell Lewis, 1925*).

named for the activity there in pottery. The earthenware bowls are completely covered with painted ridges (PL. 455), and the huge jars for storing sago, adorned with the pig's-snout or bird's-head motif, are unmatched elsewhere (PL. 453; III, PL. 127).

Among the excellent paintings on tapa cloth, common over wide areas of the island's coast, those in the characteristic Sentani style are outstanding. Some even show figural motifs. New Guinea is the only part of Melanesia in which the inhabitants have produced authentic independent painting; it is of exceptionally high quality, as evidenced by the extraordinary varicolored pictures painted on sago-palm bark lining the inner walls of the cult houses along the Sepik, as well as those which, in the Maprik area, completely cover the triangular gables of the meeting- or ghost houses, to a height of nearly 33 ft. (PLS. 454, 458).

Near the Keram River, a local specialty is the feather mosaic, made from multicolored feathers arranged in definite patterns of figures (PL. 450; see FEATHERWORK); the basketry products (II, PL. 230) are also distinctive.

PARAMICRONESIA. From the anthropological and ethnological viewpoint, Paramicronesia differs sharply from the other Melanesian island groups and cultures, especially in its art. Despite the proximity of differing cultures characterized by a rich and highly developed art of figural wood carving (New Guinea, the Admiralties), in Paramicronesia this art is either completely absent, as in Wuvulu, Aua, Luf, and Ninigo, or present only sporadically, as on Kaniet (PL. 445); here, only a few examples of independent figures have survived, representing ancestors or deities. Their style is so unlike other known works that they must be regarded as local expressions of an indigenous art. According to the sparse accounts from ancient times, the Ka-

exceptionally intense force of expression. The formal characteristics of these figures recur on Kaniet in the paired human heads carved on the handles of wooden combs and occasionally on the handles of the beaters used for making tapa cloth. The abstract depiction of a flying bird on a dance drum from Kaniet is an isolated occurrence.

Individuality of form and skilled workmanship characterize the small boat-shaped wooden containers, also from Kaniet, with ornamental openwork carving on both ends. Suspended from carefully plaited cords, they are used by the men to hold a variety of articles. The tips of the masts of the outriggers of Kaniet are bifid and decorated with a carved double spiral. These are similar to the ones from Luf, but on Kaniet these spirals are turned toward each other, and in Luf they are turned outward.

Many betel gourds and spatulas from Kaniet and Luf resemble one another so closely that they cannot be distinguished; they probably originated on Luf, where the spatulas are small and exquisite works of art (PL. 456). The spiral motif predominates in the wood carving and ornamentation on Luf and is at times repeated in complex combinations, as in the large light-colored wooden spatulas for betel, carved in openwork with the utmost delicacy and refinement.

In the past there were large war canoes on Luf, with rectangular matting sails and magnificent carving on the prow and stern and painting on the sides. The predominant motif was the spiral, painted on the sides in red and white or carved on the slender, high, nearly semicircular bow.

The artistic development of Wuvulu and Aua, whose cultures are homogeneous, represents an autonomous area within Paramicronesia. The art of these two islands differs basically from that of all the other small islands of this archipelago.

23. IX.E.W.A.

Sculpture is completely absent, and there is no painting in bright colors. The implements, weapons, utensils, and boats are distinguished by the elegance and simplicity of their forms. The most notable examples are the food bowls, exquisitely carved from the much-prized dark-red wood of the Calophyllum and decorated with straight and swirling lines combined in various ways. Ornamentation is restricted almost exclusively to pyrography, executed with glowing coconut shell, or to designs stained in with a natural corrosive substance made of chopped areca nuts, betel juice, and lime; all manner of objects were decorated in this way — bowls, clubs, swordlike weapons, and particularly lime gourds. Only the pyrographic decoration of the betel gourds is clearly visible; that obtained by staining is indistinct against the very dark wood and is generally revealed only by close scrutiny. The motifs on lime gourds are predominantly geometric or consist of figures of fish and fishhooks, although even these are reduced to almost abstract decorative forms. The motifs used in the stained decoration on other types of objects comprise human and animal figures (mice, lizards, crocodiles, turtles, birds, and fish), plants, and even landscapes and representations of complete scenes (palm trees with fruit, people dancing, war and harvest scenes, traders with animals loaded on boats, boats surrounded by flocks of birds). All this is very unusual in Melanesia and the South Sea area; unquestionably it indicates a heritage from Micronesia, particularly from Palau (Western Carolines), where, on the coast opposite Indonesia, the famous representational paintings on the gables and beams of the men's houses are an ethnographic curiosity (see MICRONESIAN CULTURES).

BISMARCK ARCHIPELAGO. *Admiralty Islands*. Compared to the islanders of New Guinea the inhabitants of the Admiralty Islands might seem to be only modestly talented in art. They lack a number of those elements which elsewhere in Melanesia produce a very striking impression — the objects of large dimensions, the manner of treatment, the multicolored and grotesque forms. There is no impressive architecture with sculptured elements, nor are there painting, masks, or shields. Nevertheless, the art of the Admiralties is rich and of high caliber; it is restricted largely to the figural or ornamental decoration of utilitarian objects, mostly small and modeled in artistic forms. Such objects include wooden food bowls (PL. 452), ladles, water vessels, boxes, betel gourds and spatulas, dorsal war ornaments (PL. 446), combs with handles, pectoral ornaments (*kapkap*; PL. 457), spears, daggers, and dance headdresses.

There is no stone sculpture; in wood sculpture the commonest and most significant motif, after the human figure, is the crocodile. Ranking first are the ancestor figures, male or female, ranging in height from about 8 in. to 3½ ft.; another group of statues over 4 ft. high (PL. 446) are the tallest in this archipelago. The style of the anthropomorphic sculptures varies little and is intended to be naturalistic. The complete figure is always built up symmetrically with correct proportions; the arms hang loose, with the hands resting on the hips or upper thighs, and the legs are generally slightly flexed at the knee, though not so much as in many figures from New Guinea. The crouching position, typical of the Melanesian and Indonesian islands, is completely absent in the Admiralty Islands. Ancestor figures frequently stand on a cylindrical or conical pedestal cut from the same piece of wood as the figure. Often the feet and lower portions of the legs are fused with the pedestal so that the feet are not represented. Peculiar to this stylistic area are the heads, which are either oval, with a flattened outline around the chin, or rectangular, narrowing toward the bottom. In all cases a pronounced prognathism is apparent, in which the mouth, wide and slightly open (with or without indication of teeth), is placed on the lower margin of the jaw, occupying almost its entire width. The nose, small and straight, widens only slightly toward the base or exhibits a heavy flaring of the nostrils. Some figures have very small close-set eyes; in others, the eyes are almond-shaped and larger, taking up virtually the entire breadth of the face. The ear lobes, often hanging down to the shoulders in a long open ring, faithfully reflect the custom of piercing the ear lobe. In the female figures, the short hair is often realistically represented, while most of the male statues have a chignon carved in the wood, not hanging from the nape, as in life, but standing upright on top of the head. Some large statues, like some of the figurines on the betel spatulas, even have two chignons (PL. 446). The male figures sometimes wear the dorsal war ornament reproduced in wood.

Also found are figures paired back to back, a man and a woman, on a single pedestal. The male figure is identified by the realistically reproduced genital organ, sometimes with the shell penis sheath reproduced in wood, while the female statues are sexually uncharacterized; only rarely are the breasts indicated. All the ancestor figures are covered from forehead to legs with ornamental lines and other designs, sometimes raised, but more often incised and filled with white lime, standing out distinctly against the red background. These lines represent tattooing or sometimes arm and leg bands. Included in this style is all the anthropomorphous sculpture, both the large ancestor figures and those combined with every kind of utilitarian object, such as doorsteps, betel and lime spatulas, spear points, daggers, dorsal war ornaments, canoe prows, and the figural legs of beds. Even the smallest figurines, from 2 to $2^3/_4$ in. high, on the betel spatulas, are excellent pieces of wood carving. The dorsal war ornaments consist of an upper portion of wood representing a human head, two superimposed heads, or a single head surmounted by a bird; inserted vertically beneath the head are sea-eagle feathers, about 12 in. long and with serrated edges (PL. 446); the ornament hangs obliquely across the back.

On the figurally decorated house steps (a stepped beam), the human figure often appears in association with the crocodile motif. The crocodile is the preferred animal motif for ornamental carving throughout the Admiralty Islands. It occurs as an ornamental element, about 2 in. long, on the betel spatulas, and in freestanding figures, about 5 ft. long. It is found on all objects on which the human figure appears, as well as on net floats, wicker or wooden containers, headrests, war swords, water containers made from coconuts, and women's carrying sticks. Other zoomorphic motifs are the pig, dog, turtle, and bird, the last occurring only rarely, on weather vanes and, in highly stylized form, on the carved ornamentation of boat prows. The almost complete absence of the fish motif is probably due to the fact that the Manus, who live on or near the coast, have no carved art of their own. The more artistically gifted Usiai live in the interior.

Preeminent among the artistically decorated utilitarian objects are the wooden food bowls, admirable examples of wood carving, ranging in diameter from about 10 in. to 3 ft. or more. Even the largest specimens are carved from single blocks of wood, except for the attached handles. The bowls, mostly round and only slightly concave, rest on four feet; some have no handles, but many bear along the upper edge a band of carved ornament, and at times the figure of a crocodile or lizard is carved in relief on the convex surface. Many of the finest examples are distinguished by two extremely elegant slender handles carved in an openwork spiral at the ends of the bowl, continuing the swelling line of the container (PL. 452). Many of the smaller containers have two human figures as handles, so designed as to appear to be looking into the container. Less common are the bowls in the form of a dog or a bird. In the last type, the two handles are formed by the head and spread tail feathers, and in the intervening area the wings are indicated in a finely stylized manner.

Of definite artistic merit are the horizontal slit drums (X, PL. 225), often quite large, with handles frequently shaped like the head of an animal (dog?) or like a human being, in which case one end of the drum represents the head and upper portions of the body, and the other end the legs, the whole drum being conceived as a human body. Several bands of ornamentation, emphasizing the curvature, complete the decoration. The wooden handles of the coconut-shell ladles are patterned after a human figure or a crocodile or may be decorated in various other ways.

Peculiar to this archipelago are the figural and ornamental objects modeled from the pulp of the Parinarium nut; before the pulp has completely hardened, the motifs or human figures, in the round or, more frequently, in relief, are modeled upon the handles of combs, obsidian daggers, spears, or coconut-shell water containers, and then painted red, black, and white. Since this pulp is extremely adhesive, it makes a lasting bond between different materials. There are also water containers carved from a single coconut and provided with a small spout affixed with pulp and an ornamental band, also of pulp; other types have ornamentation carved directly into the coconut shell.

The *kapkaps*, characteristic also of New Ireland, are among the finest personal adornments in all Melanesian art (PL. 457). They consist of a thin white disk painstakingly carved from the shell of a Tridacna (giant sea clam), on the upper surface of which is appliquéd a very thin plaque of dark tortoise shell, carved in openwork; the effect is enhanced by the contrast with the dark skin of the natives. The *kapkaps* of the Admiralty Islands, 4 to 8 in. in diameter, are distinguished by the triangular motifs incised around the edge of the disk. Similar incising is noted on the nose plugs, also carved from Tridacna shell and inserted in the pierced nasal septum as an ornament, or perhaps also as an amulet. The arm bands carved from Trochus shell, with similar ornamentation along the outer edge, are purely ornamental. The penis sheaths are carved from the oval white shell of the Ovula snail; these are adorned with incising, and the incised portions are painted black so that the design stands out distinctly. The spherical pottery containers, sometimes with double spout, have only a simple geometric incising.

This part of Melanesia appears to be devoid of rock drawings. Pyrography, on the other hand, is a highly developed art. It is applied mainly to the hourglass-shaped gourds used for holding betel lime, and to the less common lime containers carved from cylindrical sections of bamboo. In addition to the pyrographic decoration applied by means of glowing charcoal, the larger surfaces are usually stained with a natural corrosive substance, probably the same as that employed on the neighboring Paramicronesian islands of Wuvulu and Aua. The motifs on the bamboo containers may be purely geometric forms, regularly arranged over the entire surface or in horizontal rows, or figural motifs (fish, turtles, etc.).

New Britain. From the ethnographic viewpoint, Umboi (Rooke) Island, the Siassi Islands (Dampier Strait), and the French Islands to the north belong to New Britain, the second largest island in Melanesia. Except for the Gazelle Peninsula, in the northeastern part of the island, the exploration of New Britain has so far been inadequate; the interior particularly, covered with dense virgin forest, is still virtually unknown. It is, however, definitely established that the population, like that of New Guinea, is heterogeneous in both race and culture: Melanesian elements are discernible, together with pre-Austronesians more or less intermingled with Papuan tribes, but each tribe, region, or district has specific cultural traits, and the separation of the different cultures is more marked than in other areas of Melanesia. The close proximity and resultant lively traffic with New Guinea explain the correspondences or affinities between certain cultural elements of the two islands. These are naturally more distinct toward the west of New Britain. Among the artifacts common to the two islands are masks and shields, which predominate in the art of New Britain. Unknown in the Gazelle Peninsula, the shield is found only in New Guinea and New Britain, including the French Islands (FIG. 710), except for a few in certain areas of the Solomons. Masks, on the other hand, which are generally associated with the men's secret societies and initiation ceremonies, are a very common element in Melanesia.

Very little is known of the cult life and, consequently, of the masks of most of the New Britain tribes. It is known, however, that here the use of masks is not necessarily connected with the secret societies; there are even secret societies, the Ingiet of the Gazelle Peninsula, for example, in which masks are not used. The most remarkable masks are those created from human skulls by the coastal inhabitants of the Gazelle Peninsula. These bore no relation to secret societies but were worn on such ceremonial occasions as the division of money, the deeper significance of which is unknown. Although the original significance of the skull mask is no longer known to the islanders, it may be considered the oldest form of ghost mask. It consists of the facial portion — including the jawbone — of the skull of an ancestor, modeled in mastic and painted, with human hair glued on, and a modeled beard. The wearer held it in place before his face by gripping a small wooden handle between

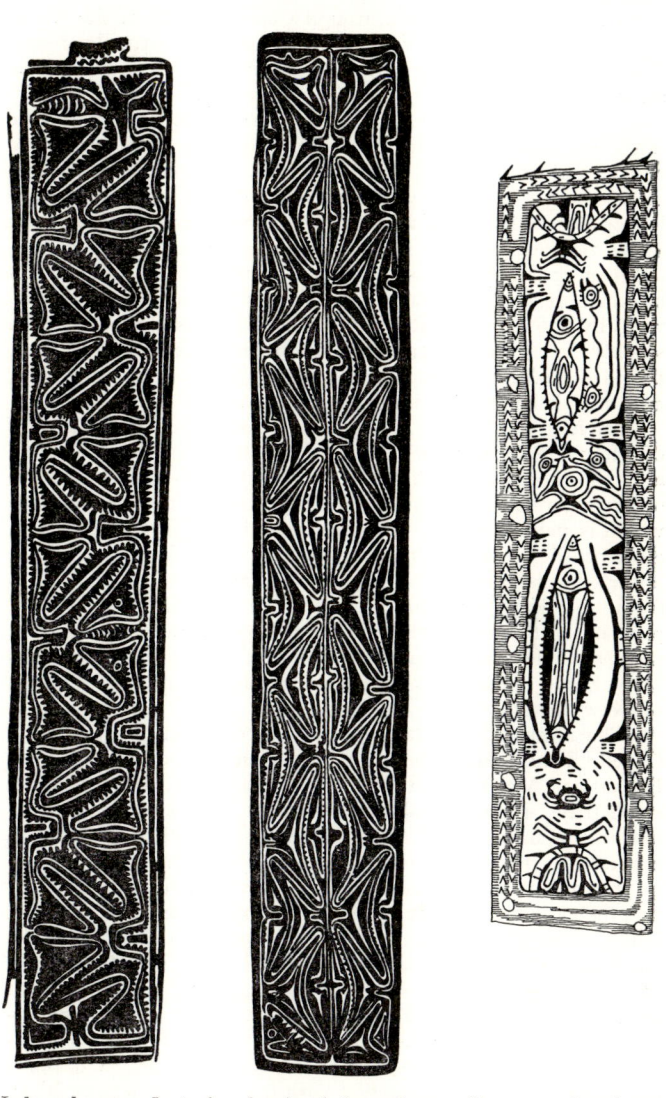

Left and center: Incised and painted decorative motifs on wooden dance shields from the French Islands (Bismarck Archipelago). *Right*: Zoomorphic decoration on an outrigger canoe, from the Siassi Islands, Bismarck Archipelago (*after T. Bodrogi, 1959*).

his teeth. Artistically insignificant, but very popular, are the hat masks of the Duk-duk secret society, also from the Gazelle Peninsula. They probably originated in southern New Ireland and reached New Britain through the Duke of York Islands. Conical headgear about 40 in. high, they are made of netting or wickerwork with various ornaments on the tip; sometimes they also have large round painted eyes and a cloak of leaves hanging from the edges. The *tubuan* masks, also of the Duk-duk, are smaller in size and have a tuft of white cockatoo feathers on the tip. Similarities of form suggest that perhaps a great many other masks of this island are derived from the Duk-duk masks. The *sisu* masks of the Sulka, a tribe living in the southern part of the Gazelle Peninsula, are similar. These consist basically of more or less conical caps on which a face is depicted (PL. 449). Another type of Sulka mask comprises an undecorated conical cap surmounted by a wide variety of human, animal, and spirit figures, in some instances in dramatic poses, in others expressed in simple rounded or elongated images. Since the Sulka masks are of considerable size, they are made of extremely light materials; the framework is of basketry, covered with leaves and the light pith of a species of elder. The animals (e.g., birds with spread wings) and the human figures are carved from wood. Most of the masks are painted in many colors: the major surfaces are red, but black, white, yellow, and a bright green found nowhere else in Oceania are also used. A very unusual type of Sulka mask is the umbrella form produced in the area around Cape Orford; on the tip of the cone concealing the wearer's face is placed a large flat round disk, which may be as much as 58 in. in diameter, made of the same material and painted on the lower portions, in the colors noted above, with typical Sulka geometric motifs. Among the umbrella masks there are many variants; they may even have ornamental and figural additions, such as zoomorphic figures of wood. An example which is unique and of unknown significance is a Sulka mask acquired in 1908, during the Hamburg South Seas expedition. It differs from other such masks in that its gigantic "umbrella" rests on two joined conical masks, each of which represents a face; thus, it is in a sense a twin mask, worn by two dancers. Related to the Sulka masks are the dance shields; flat, thin, and tapering, and as high as 12 ft. or more, they are made of painted bark, with a border of red wood pith, and are shaken by hand during the dance.

Farther west along the southern coast, between the gulf of Montague Island and Moewe Harbor, in the Arue district, are still other kinds of masks. One type consists of an oval piece of bark, bent into a semicircle, which conceals the head and on which is painted a face reduced to an almost purely decorative element; the mask terminates above in a tuft of leaves, while the lower edge is trimmed with grass. Characteristic of the masks from the gulf of Montague Island are animal carvings (fish, birds, pigs) of light wood perched on a small bark cone; hanging from the lower edge is a cloak of leaves that conceals the wearer's body. Some of these sculptures are among the finest art works of New Britain.

The masks of the Baining, pre-Austronesian natives of the Gazelle Peninsula, differ markedly from the others of New Britain and Melanesia in general. The entire art activity of this small tribe, at present almost extinct, is devoted to mask making; in this limited field, however, they have evidenced astounding talent and imagination. Since the Baining represent the most primitive and archaic ethnic element, it must be presumed that they adopted the use of masks from neighboring Melanesian tribes, subsequently developing a completely independent style. All Baining masks are made of painted bark on a framework of small twigs or withes. They vary in shape and size, from about 20 in. for the head masks (PL. 442) to 98 ft. or more for the *hareiga* masks, which are the tallest in the world and must be supported by a number of men with long bamboo poles. The Baining masks have no connection with the secret societies. They are used mainly in the initiation ceremonies; in extremely dramatic celebrations, in which live snakes are also used, they represent ghosts and mythical ancestors. For this reason, the human face is recognizable in only a very small number of such masks; of exaggerated size, they represent fabulous, grotesque, and imaginary creatures, their immense eyes suggesting insects magnified to monstrous proportions. The colors used are always red and black, conspicuous against the natural gray of the bark; for the red, human blood drawn from the tongue is used.

After the masks, the most important art objects are the shields. The main types are those of the Sulka and the Mengen and those from the South Cape district; the shields from the French Islands (FIG. 710) strongly resemble those of the Mengen (Jacquinot Bay). The shields from New Britain are oblong, sometimes rectangular; those of the Sulka are oval. They are carved from a single piece of wood (except those from the South Cape, which are carved from three planks joined vertically), and on the inner face have a handgrip carved out of the thickness of the wood. Often they are partially sheathed with red-painted bark and rattan; they have a plaited border of the same material, which, among the Mengen and on the French Islands, may be decorated with feather appliqués. In most instances both surfaces have carved ornamentation and are painted the usual black, white, red, and sometimes green. A number of the decorative motifs resemble the eye; in the tripartite shields from the South Cape, the spiral predominates. In the French Islands bird figures are sometimes placed in the center of the shields.

Sculpture, including the carved representations on the masks, is moderately developed. The best works, which show the influence of New Guinea, are found on the western islands, on Umboi and the Siassi Islands, where there are fine house posts carved with combinations of human and animal (particularly fish and crocodile) figures. Most unusual is the stone sculpture of the Ingiet secret society of the Gazelle Peninsula, mostly animal figures and less frequently human figures and other motifs. The sculptures are intended as ancestor dwellings and are venerated and kept in secret places.

The remaining art production of New Britain consists of the ornamentation, rarely figural, of utilitarian objects: betel gourds and spatulas, carved coconuts, food bowls, hourglass dance drums, reed flutes decorated with pyrographic designs, net floats, paddles, bull-roarers, bamboo combs, and other ornaments, among which are the finely incised turtle-shell bracelets derived from a New Guinea prototype. On the large outriggers of the Siassi Islanders, who are intrepid sailors, the prows and especially the sides are adorned with carving and painting in a characteristic style showing a close and unmistakable affinity with that of the island of Tami (FIG. 710; see NEW GUINEA). Pottery appears in only a few places; the potbellied spherical containers are either unadorned or have simple scratched designs.

New Ireland. On the long narrow island of New Ireland, separated from New Britain by the narrow Saint George Channel, various racial elements can be distinguished, but they are so thoroughly intermingled that no clear geographic distribution of peoples can be established. In the art, however, a number of distinct stylistic areas have remained isolated by the great length of the island (ca. 230 mi.).

New Ireland, with New Hanover (Lavongai) to the north and the small groups of nearby islands including the Tabar Islands, has long been known as one of the most important art centers in Melanesia. It is the land of those extraordinary art works, the *malanggan*, completely different in style from all other Melanesian objects. By *malanggan* is meant both the rites commemorating the dead and the sculptures used in the ceremonies, including the *uli* statues; the decorative carvings, in the round or on boards; the individual sculptured objects, mostly zoomorphic; a wide variety of masks; and other kindred objects used in religious rites or in the dance. These objects are found within definite geographical areas — the *uli* only in the central district, the decorative *malanggan* and the *malanggan* masks only in the northern third of the island and in the Tabar Islands, and a completely different type of mask in southern New Ireland. The third important stylistic area extends from Namatanai southward to the Rossel Mountains, making up the transitional area between the broad southern section of the island, poor in art, and the central region. In this third area are found the limestone figures, which differ widely from *malanggan* art and are undoubtedly connected with the very similar sculpture of the Gazelle Peninsula. These singular figures, called *kulap*, are carved from a limestone consisting of foraminifera from the Tertiary and calcareous mud. Made to order by specialized artists on the occasion of a death, these ancestor figures are kept in special huts, where food is brought to them. After a certain period they are destroyed. The *kulap* are kept hidden from the women. This complex of ideas, together with stylistic affinities between the limestone figures of New Ireland and those of the Gazelle Peninsula, may be regarded as a clear indication that the two groups are of common origin, although the New Ireland figures, unlike those from the Gazelle Peninsula, never depict animals, but only human figures. They are reproduced in the simplest manner, without adjuncts, and are thus completely different from the *uli* and from the *malanggan*. In the same area as the *kulap* there are also found wooden statues of similar form, equally unconnected with the *malanggan*. The style of the *kulap* is highly uniform, although rigid and angular figures can be distinguished from other softer ones that also show a tendency toward individualization of the facial features. Characteristic of the *kulap* are the cylindrical shape of the torso and the extremities, the exaggeratedly large oval head and flattened facial portion, the large protruding ears, and the heavily marked brow ridge; the face is characterized by large round eyes and a large half-moon mouth. The arms are always bent at the elbow and joined together over the body or on the chest. Face and body are often painted with several series of red, black, and yellow lines to indicate tattooing scars, while sometimes on the upper arm a number of parallel ridges indicate the arm band of Trochus shell, greatly prized in New Ireland. The legs are disproportionately short and slightly bent at the knees. All the *kulap* are nude, and both sexes have greatly enlarged and realistic genitals, while the breasts are barely indicated. Figures of women with infants, evidently commemorating women who died in childbirth, occur infrequently. Figures of men and women, standing back to back or shoulder to shoulder, are more common. The height of the *kulap* ranges from about 8 in. to over 3 ft.; the smaller ones perhaps represent children.

The art production of southern New Ireland is the most modest of the whole island. Toward the north the art becomes gradually richer and multiform, ultimately attaining, in the *malanggan* of the northern area and the Tabar Islands, a particular impressiveness.

Three art products give the central area a special stamp: the *uli*, the large solar *malanggan*, and the extraordinary friction drums and rubbed wood instruments. The last, restricted to the mountaineers of the area, are known under the indigenous names of *livika*, *nunut*, and *lauka*, among others. They consist of an elongated rounded block of wood with an average length of about 20 in., sometimes carved in a zoomorphic shape. According to the natives, this represents a bird, but it looks more like a dog or pig. The terminal portion, generally decorated, clearly represents the head, and the eyes are often enhanced with the gleaming red and green shells of the Turbo snail. Sometimes the back bears geometric ornamentation. The front and hind feet and the tail are fashioned to form three tongue-shaped appendages which, when rubbed with the hand, produce loud sounds of different pitches. The instrument expresses the voice of the spirits (as do the bull-roarers) and is designed to frighten away the women at the time of certain rites, obviously relating to the cult of the dead. More significant as works of art are the solar *malanggan*, round or oval compositions of 5 ft. or more in diameter, made out of branches and small rods held together with tree bark and painted white, yellow, red, and black. The outer edge is surmounted by a radial corona of sticks. Projecting from the center of the "sun" is a composition of leaves, like the calyx of a flower, executed with great artistic skill; this surrounds an aperture in which, at the time of the ceremony, was generally placed the skull of the deceased person being honored. These "suns" were shown in special huts, and women were forbidden the sight on pain of death.

Although to the natives the feast of the solar *malanggan* is more important and sacred than the *uli* ceremonies, the *uli* sculptures are more interesting and significant artistically. The meaning of the word *uli* was known to the natives as late as the 1930s, but it was never revealed and is now irrecoverable. All conjectured interpretations seem highly improbable, and none is confirmed by the natives: for instance, it has been suggested that the name derives from that of the ginger plant (called *uli* in the interior of the island), the stalk of which is used as a brush to paint the figures. The *uli* are ancestor figures, probably of an impersonal collective character appropriate to all important deceased men, such as chiefs, and are venerated during the *malanggan* celebrations. Unlike the "decorative" *malanggan* of the north, the *uli* are not destroyed at the close of the ceremonies but are kept in huts especially built for them. The *uli*, which range in height from about 20 in. to life-size, are the most forceful and expressive of all Melanesian sculpture. They are perfectly symmetrical in structure and have a finished quality that sharply differentiates them from the *malanggan* of the north. Despite the unmistakable unity of concept, it is possible to distinguish at least twelve types, simple or complex, for which the natives employ different terms. The simplest form is that with the arms hanging at the sides and with lateral slats, while other types are distinguished by secondary figures attached on the shoulders; the *uli* may also have another figure above or in front of it. There is one *uli* representing a man astride a pig. Often the *uli*'s face has a beard of plant fibers; the head is always disproportionately large, a trait common to the sculpture of many sections of Oceania, probably to be explained by the importance attributed to the skull; the eyes are often of concave shells. The *uli* wear either a wooden headdress like a rooster's comb, as do the limestone figures from the south, or a triangular headgear very similar to the women's caps of pandanus leaves. A singular characteristic of these statues is their bisexuality, indicated by the representation of both the male genital organ and the breasts. One theory relates the *uli* to the moon, which in New Ireland mythology may be male or female in the same being. It is more likely, however, that the sexual attributes are intended merely to express and accentuate strength and fecundity in general (PL. 448; see ESCHATOLOGY). One type of *uli* is characterized by relief carving of a rope that encircles the neck, crosses the chest, and reaches to the waist; according to A. Krämer, this probably represents the rope used to capture prisoners and thrown around the victim's neck to strangle him. The colors used on the *uli* — red, white, and black — are often renewed, since the statues are exhibited at every celebration; some very old specimens are completely blackened by smoke.

Directly north of the *uli* district, opposite the Tabar Islands, lies the most important art region of New Ireland, that of the decorative *malanggan*, characterized by an enormous variety of forms, a multiplicity of motifs, and a bizarre and extreme dissociation of structural elements. There are three principal groups: independent statues, friezes or figural boards, and masks. The terms that recur in the literature (*totok*, *marandan*, etc.) indicate the individual types of *malanggan*. Most of the freestanding anthropomorphous *malanggan* show unmistakable affinities with the *uli* and vary considerably in the structure, proportions, and composition of the constituent elements. No two pieces are identical, even when the content is similar, but all have in common the dissociation of forms and a complexity of accessories so elaborate as to subordinate the principal figure to the resulting counterforms in space. This is more marked in the freestanding *malanggan* (PLS. 447, 448), in the form of columns which may be over 30 ft. high, than in the friezes or figural planks. The significance of the *malanggan* can no longer be interpreted, since even the natives do not know it. The only certain fact is that the

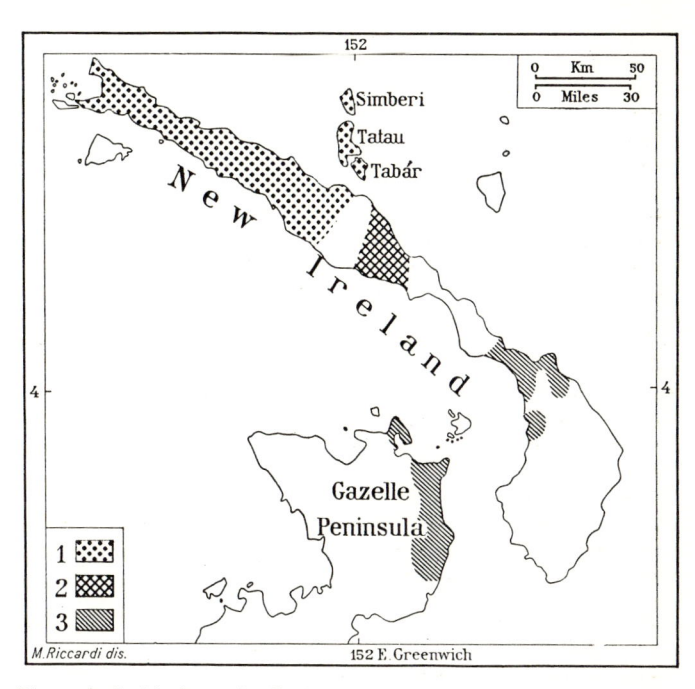

Bismarck Archipelago, distribution of individual sculptural styles. *Key*: (1) Decorative *malanggan* of the north; (2) *uli* figures; (3) limestone statues.

malanggan for the most part represent ancestors, that is, they are human figures, frequently accompanied by animals which, in most cases, may be considered totemic. These animals are the pig, lizard, owl, hornbill, cock, cockatoo, parrot, crow, dogfish, dolphin, snake, and, in a few cases, the butterfly. A considerable number of such animals also appear in individual sculptures; frequent motifs are the bird holding a snake in its beak, or other animals, particularly fish, swallowing a man. The chief element in a considerable number of *malanggan* friezes is a bird with open wings so stylized as to constitute an openwork ornament; the bird often has a human figure standing before it, or the bird may be borne on the head of a man with his arms extended horizontally (this position is also seen in individual statues). The fantastic effect of the *malanggan* is even further intensified by the brilliant painting in red, white, black, and yellow; blue was originally unknown, but in the mid-19th century it was introduced by the Europeans. Unlike the *uli*, the *malanggan* of the north are not considered sacred. Although they are prepared in secret, they are no longer kept hidden after their public exhibition, not even from the women. Since at the close of the celebration they are thrown away, they are made of the soft, light, easily worked wood of the *Alstonia villosa* or *Alstonia scholaris*. Even the most elaborate representations are freely executed: no model is used, and they are carved, with stone or shell tools, from a block of wood on which at most the important reference points have been marked.

The masks of northern New Ireland are of several types. They consist of a face, carved in wood and stylistically similar to the *malanggan*, and a framework, usually of bark or other plant material, that conceals the rest of the head. The most common are those called *tatanua*, in which the cranium, similar to a dragoon's helmet, is made of coconut fiber painted yellow. In masks of this type it is possible to recognize a human face, but in others the face may merge almost completely with the ornamental carving or be replaced by animal forms, such as birds, pig snouts, and the like. In the latter case the masks probably have some totemic significance. Many masks have an extremely high plank-shaped superstructure with incised decoration and gigantic wooden ears (PL. 442) decorated with incising. The masks are brilliantly polychromed and are kept or displayed temporarily in special huts, sometimes splendidly painted, which are destroyed after the celebration.

In the southern area of the island, in the district around Muliama, are found masks of less artistic interest, consisting of a bark framework with elongated protruding eyes. In certain dances masks are replaced by wooden bird figures held erect in the mouth.

The ancestor skulls in New Ireland, unlike those in the Sepik region, were modeled in wax. Some were completely black, and others were painted white, red, blue, and yellow; the eyes were carved out of the green shell of the Turbo snail, a detail which gave them an intense expression. The skulls were burned in the course of certain ceremonies or were kept in special huts. In the central district they were also used in the magic rainfall rites; for this purpose they were sometimes affixed to carved wooden figures.

Other products of the secular art of New Ireland include house posts, ornamentally modeled and at times even decorated with human figures (in the southern area resembling the limestone statues); hourglass dance drums with geometric ornamentation; eating bowls; bamboo combs; betel containers; prow carvings; paddles; and boat paintings. Outstanding among the ornaments are the *kapkaps*, similar (or related) in form to those found on the Admiralty, Solomon, and Santa Cruz islands, but of notable delicacy and variety of modeling. The finest come from Gardner and Fisherman's islands, near the eastern coast of New Ireland. Pottery is unknown on New Ireland. On New Hanover there are petroglyphs rather similar to those on New Caledonia, as noted by Bühler. In addition to geometric designs, such as concentric circles, anthropomorphous figures also appear.

Saint Matthias and Tench. At the beginning of the 20th century the Saint Matthias Group north of New Ireland, which from the ethnological viewpoint includes the islet of Tench, had no contact with the outside world. But a series of elements in its culture are typical of the nearby archipelagoes, showing that in the past the situation must have been different. The closest ties seem to have been with the Admiralty Islands, New Hanover, and New Ireland; also discernible, though to a lesser extent, are Micronesian influences.

Although the art of Saint Matthias contains various elements that correspond exactly to those in the art of the neighboring islands, it lacks certain essential traits of their culture — the masks of New Ireland, the sails and, because of the lack of raw material, the pottery of the Admiralties. Characteristic of Saint Matthias is the house with barrel roof; on Tench even the small shops, built on piles for protection against rats, have roofs of this type. The communal houses of Saint Matthias and Tench, though built accurately and with sound technique, are only modestly ornamented or entirely without ornament, while, as in nearly all Melanesia, the chiefs' houses and men's houses on Saint Matthias (they do not exist on Tench) are distinguished by their rich decoration: painting on the triangular gable, sheathing with carved and painted planks, and carved posts in the interior (IV, PL. 393). The posts perform the important structural function of supporting the horizontal beams, but the planks of the gable are purely ornamental. All the village men participate in the construction of the chiefs' houses and the meetinghouse, each one preparing a decorated plank as well as performing other tasks. Because of the differences in talent and manual skill, the products are of somewhat uneven artistic quality. Some bear simple linear designs, such as triangles, rhombs, or wavy lines, while the planks executed by skilled artists may be decorated with zoomorphic motifs (fish particularly) which, according to the natives, are without totemic significance. It is not known whether the full-round carving on the posts inside the chiefs' houses is merely decorative or whether it has also some religious significance. One post decorated with a human figure represents, according to the natives, the captain of a European sailing ship that visited Saint Matthias about 1900; at most, this may be termed a commemorative image. Only a partial interpretation of the decorative motifs is possible; for instance, the carving known as *laine* represents a very highly stylized fish with the caudal fin raised, while another type suggests such plant forms as star-shaped flowers or cotyledons. According to the natives, the horizontal swellings around the posts are intended to represent arm bands made from the Trochus. Some posts are partially worked in openwork lozenges, in which, as in the center of the floral motifs also, are inserted shells of the Turbo snail, with beautiful dark-green tints. This is a technique typical of New Ireland, where it is used to decorate many objects and to represent the eye on dance masks and *malanggan*. Presumably it was imported from there to Saint Matthias. Aside from the infrequent human figures carved on the house posts, there are also freestanding male and female ancestor figures, averaging in height from 19 to 23 in., with pedestals carved from the same trunk and sometimes decorated with simple wavy lines or similar patterns. The structure of these figures is perfectly symmetrical; the slender arms hang at the sides, the hands touching the hips or, less frequently, resting on the body. The proportion of the limbs is comparatively accurate, and a general tendency toward naturalism is noted. However, the legs are abnormally separated where they are joined to the body; they are rather straight and in profile show a strong accentuation of the calf muscles. The male genitals are clearly represented, while the female ones are indicated simply by a dark coloration; the breasts are not reproduced, but on the male figures the nipples are indicated. The torso is carved in a cylindrical shape, without further modeling. The neck is sharply differentiated from the shoulders. The head is spherical or oblong, the most prominent feature being the chin, which projects obliquely downward; at times a slat, in the form of a crest, runs along the central axis of the cranium, indicating the headgear of a chief. These last characteristics are typical also of New Ireland, especially of the *uli* figures, and the profile of the statues, too, shows unmistakable New

Ireland derivation. The ancestor figures are always carved and painted, the male figures more lavishly than the female. In the former, the face, torso, and thighs particularly are decorated in red and black with zigzag lines, circles, and leaflike designs. The female figures are decorated only on the face and chest. Figures similar to the ancestor statues, but unpainted, also appear on dance sticks and betel spatulas.

The Hamburg South Seas expedition of 1908-10 brought to light two anthropomorphous wood sculptures from Tench, both crudely worked and unpainted. One is a complete standing figure; the other comprises two busts, one larger than the other, placed back to back and joined below. The eyes are indicated by the green shells of the Turbo. The significance of the Tench sculptures is unknown, but they may well be ancestor figures.

The wooden figural sculptures of Saint Matthias and Tench include birds, fish, and turtles; though not numerous, these pieces surpass the ancestor figures in artistic merit. On Saint Matthias, bird figures decorate the ridgepoles of the houses, dance paraphernalia, and the prows of boats, and also serve as toys. The bird figures used as prow ornaments of the large ceremonial boats are fairly naturalistic, while the heron motif on Z-shaped dance sticks is sometimes treated in a highly abstract fashion. A favored motif is the royal kite with a fish in its claws. Definitely derived from this type are the other motifs used in prow ornamentation, so fully assimilated into the decoration as to be undecipherable without reference to the natural model. The head, with the large sharply crooked beak, is still clearly discernible among the abstract forms. In the case of the prow ornamentation, it is therefore possible to reconstruct an entire evolutionary scale, from the naturalistic representation of birds, through the total dissolution of the figures into incomprehensible ornamental forms.

On Tench, even the figures of fish reveal the artist's fine sensitivity and excellent powers of observation; they may be single or coupled, that is, two fish attached by the tip of the tail or by a piece of wood; the latter type is held and shaken during the dance. The type of fish depicted is flat with broad head, long fins, and forked tail. Inserted into the wood, which is unpainted and retains its natural brown color, are the green shells of the Turbo, reproducing fish eyes, and incised in the figure are a number of lines, filled with white lime, which stand out sharply against the background and are probably intended to indicate the bones. Naturalistic wood representations of turtles resemble those of the fish. The pattern of the shell is traced by shallow furrows filled with lime to enrich the general effect. The significance and purpose of these zoomorphic figures — except for the ichthyomorphic dance sticks — are completely unknown.

These are the only types of sculpture found on Saint Matthias and Tench; the remaining art production is purely ornamental but very diverse in material and technique. Painted objects include splendid and often gigantic men's combs with handles, rain cloaks made of palm leaves, and spiral ear ornaments also made of palm leaves. Carving appears on the spears, the dance sticks, the betel spatulas, the coconut scrapers, and ear pendants of tortoise shell. Incised decoration is used on the penis sheaths made of Ovula shells; and etched designs are made by painting with a natural corrosive substance on the bamboo combs and flutes and especially on the hourglass betel-lime gourds. The last, in spite of their different ornamentation, show a close kinship to those of the Admiralty Islands, as do the penis sheaths, indicating the existence of cultural connections between these two island groups.

SOLOMON ISLANDS. The Solomon Islands, despite the early date (1567) of their discovery, remain one of the most inadequately known cultural areas of Melanesia. Their geographic isolation and the notorious warlike spirit of the inhabitants have made it virtually impossible to maintain any consistent lasting cultural contacts with the inhabitants of other islands. Thus their art and culture in general have developed independently and differ markedly from those of nearby New Ireland. Only at the beginning of the colonial period, when the inhabitants of the northern Solomons, Buka especially, were used as a police force and as laborers in the Bismarck Archipelago, did external cultural influences make themselves felt; but these were of little importance in art. The art of the Solomons differs not only from that of other Melanesian regions but also within the archipelago itself, where distinct stylistic regions have developed as a result of the enormous length (ca. 150 mi.) of the double chain of islands and, perhaps primarily, of racial differences. The art is virtually devoid of the monumental features and multicolored decoration that represent the main art activity in other archipelagoes: the sculpture used in conjunction with architecture, ancestor figures, and the secret societies, the masks, and the shields. Although such objects are not entirely absent, they are limited to a few areas and a few types; moreover, they are polychrome only in the northern part of the archipelago, and even there to a limited extent. Masks are employed only in the extreme northern islands, from Nissan to Bougainville, and even there are too uncommon to affect the general panorama of culture and art; nor can they compare with those of other Melanesian areas. Shields, common in several of the large islands between Choiseul and Guadalcanal, are made of basketry, elongated in shape and relatively small but executed with great technical skill. Certain ceremonial or display shields, perhaps intended for the chiefs, are painted or decorated with figural mosaics of mother-of-pearl set in a mastic base; these exhibit such a degree of abstraction and artistic perfection as to rank among the most notable achievements in Melanesian art, but they are quite rare and only a few examples are preserved in museums.

Utilitarian objects — weapons, ornaments, and many objects of everyday use (PL. 452) — are distinguished by elegance and surety of construction, particularly the work in basketry and mosaic.

Disregarding the more subtle differences, it is possible to distinguish in the Solomons two different styles distributed approximately according to the old political division of the archipelago between the Germans and the English: the first is observed in the northwestern islands from Nissan to Bougainville; the second in the other islands, from New Georgia (VI, PL. 52) to San Cristobal and the islets of the south, Owa Raha and Owa Riki, which show strong Polynesian influence. The northwestern section forms a comparatively homogeneous stylistic area; to what extent it is justifiable to include Choiseul and Santa Isabel therein is a problem calling for further study, but these islands probably represent a zone of transition and intermingling between the two styles. Typical of the zone are the paintings on carved surfaces, and the decoration of spears, arrows, clubs, ornaments (combs especially), and other objects with extremely fine plaited work in red and yellow bark. Human figures appear in freestanding wood sculptures, sometimes of uncertain function, as in the case of the extremely uncommon, manifestly male figures of Nissan. Fuller information is available on the statues of Buka; about 40 in. tall, they are carved in soft wood and are used in marriage ceremonies to represent the future daughter of the young bride. In this predominantly matriarchal organization, female offspring are desired. The figure is fairly well proportioned, very rigid, and absolutely symmetrical, with the arms hanging at the sides and hands almost touching the hips; the breasts and vulva are clearly modeled. The elongated head bears a high conical headress. The face, otherwise entirely black, is painted with white lines, and the greatly elongated ear lobes protrude obliquely from the head (PL. 451). Similar statues, male and female, from Bougainville play a special role in that phase of the initiation ceremonies pertaining to the rite of donning and doffing the *upi*, a remarkable large spherical headdress of pandanus leaves. The *upi* is worn by the youths until their hair has grown long enough to fill it completely; then, during the act of initiation, it is cut away together with the hair. Partially painted in widely differing patterns with a red plant sap, these headdresses are now limited to Bougainville, although they were perhaps once used in the more northerly islands as well, including Nissan. On these islands are found many paddles and paddle-shaped dance sticks decorated with human heads or full figures, painted or in relief, wearing a large spherical headdress apparently representing the *upi*. This motif is usually painted in red and black on a white background. The anthropomorphous figures are depicted either standing or crouching, the latter posture being characteristic of the freestanding statues from the central Solomons, in particular Choiseul and New Georgia.

While in the north even the painting of objects is important, the style from New Georgia southward depends not on painting but on form and material, in contrast to neighboring New Ireland and most of the other Melanesian archipelagoes. In the southern style the inlay technique characteristic of these islands reaches its zenith (PL. 457); black-painted figures and other objects — earplugs, head-hunters' boats, the skulls of chieftains, modeled in black — are given added interest by the insertion of small plaques of mother-of-pearl and shell, cut in various shapes. The most admirable objects are the previously mentioned ceremonial shields, found from Guadalcanal to Florida Island, which are veritable mosaic images.

In the anthropomorphous wood sculpture of the southern style the crouching position predominates. A salient feature of these figures is their prognathism, even more pronounced in the small figures than in those of the tall slender prow ornaments of the splendid canoes, representing the guardian spirits of the boat and its crew (PL. 452). These figures, too, are adorned with mother-of-pearl inlay. Outstanding among the other objects are the vessels and bowls, some of finely worked smooth black wood, the majority without inlay but finely incised (PL. 452). These are supported by two small human figures or bear representations of animals, predominantly fish and birds. In the sacrificial vessels, which sometimes are over 6 ft. long, the two animals are combined: the receptacle is the body of the bird, which holds in its beak a fish (probably a whale or dolphin) of diminutive size. In some cases these vessels, decorated with inlay, rest upon pedestals formed by other figures of fish. Less common are the pig-shaped wooden vases. The shark is also effectively represented in large pieces of wood carving, the body hollowed out and used as a case for the chiefs' skulls (cf. IV, PL. 449); they are hung in the sheds where the canoes are kept. There are also huts for the skulls, made of wood or reeds and supported on poles or stones, sometimes of artistic merit; gable ends are made of Tridacna shell, approximately $1\frac{1}{8}$ in. thick, in which openwork figures of dancers or geometric elements are laboriously carved out.

From Rubiana come a few rare and extremely old ceremonial objects, staff-shaped and magnificently adorned with inlay; the principal motif is sometimes a crocodile with open jaws, near which is a standing or crouching human figure, or else a turtle; their meaning is unknown.

Pottery is limited to the northern area, as far as the Shortland Islands, excluding Nissan; it has spread into other parts as well, Choiseul for instance, through trade. The pottery consists of potbellied containers and taller vases with rounded bases (pointed, on the Shortland Islands), of little artistic merit, the decoration being limited to incised geometric designs, triangles grouped in rows, or simple wavy lines on the upper edge of the container; infrequently there is some incising on the lower portion.

SANTA CRUZ ISLANDS. The culture of the Santa Cruz Islands is still inadequately known. Although social and religious aspects of the life are little understood, it is known that there are no male secret societies comparable to that of the Suque of the New Hebrides and no masks, but there are indications of a skull and ancestor cult. Anthropomorphous sculpture seems to be limited to a few wood figurines of no great artistic merit, probably representing spirits or ancestors. Nevertheless, the art of Santa Cruz cannot be considered poor; it includes fine zoomorphic sculpture, and the islanders have developed a distinctive two-dimensional art that shows a keen artistic sensitivity. Characteristic of this art is the ornamentation covering most of the objects, including neck rests, boats, and betel gourds, as well as the three-dimensional representations of fish (PL. 242), birds, and pigs, and the remarkable dance sticks. The last are wooden staves, slightly curved and terminating in a point at the top, the upper decorated portions of which are triangular or semicircular in section. At the end of the rounded grip are fastened rattles made of nutshells or long tufts of plant fibers. According to F. Speiser, these tufts represent bird feathers or wings, and their form is supposed to derive from the figure of a bird, as are nearly all the other formal elements in the ornamentation of the Santa Cruz Islands. The decoration is never carved but merely painted on wood, and the designs in black and red stand out effectively against the painted white surface. Analysis of the ornamental elements found on these islands is enlightening for the study of the entire art production of Oceania, since it shows how the depiction of an animal (in this instance, a bird), realistic at the outset, becomes through continual repetition increasingly stylized until it is a simple abstraction, a mere composite symbol of two crossed lines ending in a hook. Later, when this symbol is no longer understood, the artist begins to play with the motif, combining it or repeating it rhythmically, with the sole aim of filling the surface. However, since man tries to see something familiar in every ornamental element, the original bird form gradually is transformed into a fishlike motif, until eventually the series of transformations comes full circle in a realistic representation, that of a fish. It is not surprising that the bird should be the predominant art motif in the Santa Cruz Islands, since among the animals known to these islanders the bird, as soul bird and as death bird, occupies the most important place in religious thought. The complete abstraction of the bird figure appears clearly in the local pectoral ornament (similar to the *kapkap*), among the most beautiful creations of all Oceania. Against the round white surface of the Tridacna, which may attain a diameter of about 6 in., appears the stylized figure of the frigate bird, carved out of a thin piece of dark turtle shell.

In tattooing, in addition to designs harking back to the bird motif, there are others depicting fish. There are also almond-shaped eating bowls representing fish. One door lintel has been found with two affronted fish carved in relief, but in general few houses have carvings or other decoration. Only the gable of a ghost house was completely covered with vertical rows of black triangles against a white background. Other products include bark cloth with geometric designs, loomed mats for clothing, and knapsacks.

NEW HEBRIDES AND THE BANKS ISLANDS. South of the Santa Cruz Islands stretch the Banks Islands and the New Hebrides, which should be dealt with together, in view of their close cultural affiliation, although the arts are not equally developed in both. Strong Polynesian influence is noted in some of the artistically impoverished southern islands of the New Hebrides: Eromanga, Tana, Aniwa, Futuna, and Aneityum; even in the main island, Espíritu Santo, the art production is rather modest. Areas of outstanding art production are the Banks Islands and the central New Hebrides, especially Malekula, with the adjacent islets of Vao, Achin, and Rano and the larger island of Ambrim.

Among the most striking and ethnologically most distinguished art works of the New Hebrides are the vertical slit drums, characteristic of this archipelago. While undecorated drums are found through the whole territory, the vertical drums are from an area extending from Pentecost Island in the north, across Malekula, Ambrim, and Epi, to Efate in the south, excluding the Banks Islands. Although the vertical drums also occur in simple form, nearly all are distinguished by ornamental carving above or alongside the slit, or by the depiction of human heads, sometimes arranged in rows. Ranging in height from about 3 to 16 ft., the drums play an important role in the ritual of the Suque male secret society. On Ambrim, for example, the type of carving and the number of human faces portrayed indicate the rank of the drum owner, while on other islands this is indicated by the height of the instrument. Certain drums, with a head standing out sharply from the upper part of the trunk, indicate that the entire drum is conceived as a human figure; in a number of specimens the arms are even carved alongside the slit. According to Speiser, the vertical drums derive from a combination of the horizontal drums and the ancestor figures and can thus be considered hollow ancestor figures. They are kept in the dance clearings or nearby, frequently together with other statues indicative of rank; often they form rather dense clusters.

Ancestor figures and the statues indicating rank comprise the bulk of the sculpture of the Banks Islands and the New Hebrides; they are lacking, however, on Espíritu Santo, Oba, Maewo, and the more southerly islands. There are three types of ancestor figures: those of hardwood, those of tree-fern pith, and those capped with skulls. The last are of special interest, as they are a local peculiarity limited to the southern part of Malekula; they are reproductions of the human body, made of plant material, on which are placed the actual skulls of the deceased, modeled in a compost of fibers, clay, and resin. (They are similar to some figures found in the Sepik River region of New Guinea.) Statues of this type, kept in the men's houses, commemorate the deceased who held high rank in the Suque. Certain attributes added to the statues, such as the jawbone of a pig, a conch trumpet, or a particular kind of painting, indicate the rank held in the secret society by the person depicted. The ethnological importance of the statues with skulls stems from the fact that they can be clearly distinguished as the original representations of the ancestor figure; they are the type which preceded the image of wood or tree-fern pith.

Preeminent and typical of the Banks Islands and some parts of the New Hebrides are the ancestor statues and the emblematic poles carved from the pith of tree ferns, a substance that is easily worked, porous but resistant to wear. In order to secure poles of sufficient thickness, the tree is tightly bound at a height of about 5 ft. above the ground, so that the part below the ligature thickens. Several stylistic types may be distinguished: some depict the full human figure, in a plainly naturalistic style, although in most cases the disproportion of the head is emphatic; others depict only the head. Characteristic of Ambrim Island, where only statues of tree-fern pith occur, is the type distinguished by the extraordinarily large eyes, represented by mere cavities or by large flat round or oval plates. The nose and mouth are usually indicated, but the latter is often merged with the chin. The representation of the limbs, if present, is rudimentary, probably because of the fragility of the material. Another type, also from Ambrim, depicts two superimposed figures or a two-faced figure. While in some figures it is impossible to determine the sex, in others this is clearly indicated. In the female statues of the Banks Islands, the breasts are realistically reproduced. In contrast to the rather uniform Ambrim type, the statues of the Banks Islands vary widely. Alongside some quite naturalistic representations can be seen others that are highly abstract or handled in decorative fashion. The head often consists of an elongated acute triangle, the nose is reduced to a line, the eyes to mere dots, and the mouth is remarkably small. Many of the figures from the Banks Islands and Ambrim have crossed legs, while only in those from the Banks does the particular position of the arms sometimes occur in which, instead of resting lightly flexed on the lower part of the body, they are bent slightly upward so that the elbows are held above the chest and the hands horizontally under the head. This position of the arms may be related to R. H. Codrington's observation that ghosts can be recognized by their bent limbs. Also from the Banks Islands are statues that represent only two nearly discoidal faces, surrounded by indented crowns and placed on a slender trunk, above and below which are depicted birds carved from the same block of wood. On Malekula there are emblematic poles of tree-fern pith in which five or six human heads are arranged above a full-length human figure. As in the case of the drums, these statues were executed for persons of the highest rank in the Suque society; the number of faces or heads corresponds to the rank attained.

In style, the sculptural treatment of the wood statues corresponds to that of the statues in tree-fern pith, but in the harder material the details are naturally worked with greater finesse. Within certain limited areas there are widely divergent types of sculpture: for example, a wood statue about 10 ft. high, from eastern Malekula, has the unusual feature of disproportionately long legs, and the head is very small; in another figure of more or less the same height, from the islet of Rano, near the eastern coast of Malekula, the legs are barely indicated by the short thighs, while the elongated almond-shaped head takes up half the length of the entire figure.

All the ancestor and emblematic figures are placed near the men's houses, sometimes in the bush; when they belong to a high dignitary of the Suque society, they stand near the entrance of the person's dwelling. If the figures stand inside the houses, they serve as supports for the ridgepole of the roof. In the Banks Islands and on Vao a representation of a flying bird — evidently the soul bird — forms the end of the beam and extends through the gable. The technique used to make the birdlike figures is simple but ingenious: the sculptors use for this purpose the roots of the tree trunk from which the beam has been hewn, selecting and cutting into the desired shapes two ramifications which between them form the angle necessary to represent the wings, leaving another piece to form the body and removing the rest. Similar soul birds, with their elegant wings from 3 to 6 or 7 ft. long, are found at the acute angle of the terminal points. In a number of areas, such as the Banks Islands and islets adjacent to the northeast coast of Malekula, special huts are built for the ancestor figures. There are very few nonhuman figures; one, surrounded with carved tonguelike projections in superimposed rows, apparently is to be interpreted as a highly stylized representation of a pig jaw. The actual jawbones of sacrificed pigs are hung on poles and preserved near or inside the men's houses, as a visible reminder of the sacrificial ceremonies. In this region of Melanesia, the pig, with artificially deformed teeth, is the most important animal; frequent pig sacrifices lead to increasingly higher rank in the Suque society, ensuring great prestige in life and a happy lot after death. All efforts are therefore directed toward the raising of pigs and, ultimately, toward the Suque society, which has exerted a decisive influence on all art expressions. Where this society does not exist, as in the southern islands, art is absent. To virtually all objects capable of artistic treatment some Suque symbol is applied; foremost are the representations of ancestor spirits, in the form of human faces or full figures; the jawbone of a pig or a single tusk, as a symbol of the sacrifice; birds; and occasionally sharks. These symbols, some realistically depicted and others highly stylized and reduced to mere ornaments, are also found on the clubs used to kill the sacrificial pigs; these are totally unlike the war clubs, the shape being more reminiscent of stone axes. Most of the masks and ritual implements used in the dance and ceremonies, such as dance sticks, hatchets, ornaments, magic stones endowed with mana, and amulets bearing faces like those of the sculpture, all pertain to the Suque ceremonies. Since wherever statues are absent — Espíritu Santo, Malo, Oba, Maewo, Efate, Eromanga, and Tana — masks are also lacking, it is obvious that the whole institution of masks is closely bound up with the cult of spirits, ancestors, and skulls.

At the outset, probably, all Suque masks, with the addition of a cloak of leaves designed to conceal the body, were intended to disguise their wearers as spirits. It was the intention to terrorize the nonmembers of the secret society by means of these sinister masks. The later forms, used in the dance, were designed more to amuse, even though there may not always be a clear-cut distinction between the two types. While the basic type of mask is a human face, horrifyingly deformed in various ways in order to inspire terror, nevertheless, representations of animals, for instance, birds and lizards, are also used for masks. Pigs' tusks may be inserted into masks. Explicitly zoomorphic masks, consisting of a covering of coconut leaves and representing a pig, are found only on Malekula. The great range of mask types in this part of Melanesia shows a lively imagination in the modeling; and since the masks are generally made of perishable materials and are often thrown away after use, it is possible that not all the types are known. Appearing in the southern part of Malekula also is a two-faced mask, and there are even some with four faces, the significance of which is unknown. In the New Hebrides the masks, unlike the statues, are not of a very high artistic level, no doubt because of the use of unsuitable material. This seems to be proved by the fact that the masks of Pentecost and Ambrim islands, the only ones made of hardwood, surpass all other masks in this archipelago (PL. 443). Unique products in the New Hebrides are the masks made in southern Malekula of tree-fern pith and those made partly of spider webs. In order to obtain this unusual material, the natives go into the jungle carrying outspread branches, on which they gather the tough threads of the spider web into a thick mass.

In the Banks Islands, the counterpart of the Suque society is the Tamate secret society. The few specimens preserved indicate that the masks of this society are markedly different in form, material, and ornamentation from the New Hebrides masks; they are of bark or plant fibers, sometimes topped by long appendages which are bent forward and probably derive from fish or bird figures. A notable feature of these masks is their painting: on a white background, aside from large black eyes, there are purely geometric designs and figures, strongly resembling those of Santa Cruz. Even the utilitarian objects exhibit considerable artistic skill: the weapons, especially the clubs and spears, beautiful in form and differing from island to island; the household utensils, including food bowls, knives, and pestles; and the various articles of adornment, outstanding among them the earplugs, with rich incised decoration. The remarkable figural designs on the minor art objects of the Banks Islands strongly resemble tattoo patterns and suggest that even the seemingly nonfigural motifs on the earplugs of Oba and Maewo may have been derived from the human figure. Thus, for the majority of the motifs scratched and incised on a great variety of objects, the inevitable conclusion is that there is an underlying figural significance. This is certainly true of all the motifs indicating rank in the Suque society.

In several islands of this archipelago are found woven mats with highly decorative geometric motifs in red or dark purple, achieved by means of tie dyeing. The parts to be reserved are covered, prior to dyeing, with cords and molds cut from banana wood.

Besides the painting of objects, on the Banks Islands and especially on Gaua, painting exists as a separate art form. Planks, generally with a background of dark red, are painted with white figural representations in simple outline. Since these shapes show an extraordinary likeness to certain statues from the same area, the explanation furnished by the natives appears to be correct; according to them, these are sketches made by the carvers for their sculpture. However, these paintings are also valued in themselves and are used to cover the gables of the ancestor houses and men's houses.

Pottery, completely lacking on the Banks Islands, is found in the New Hebrides only in two villages on Espíritu Santo (VII, PL. 311). Here the women model potbellied containers and ladles; the former often have a distinct raised border, wavy or jagged, while the decoration is almost entirely confined to horizontal or vertical rows of dots, sometimes arranged in zigzags. Although pottery fragments have also been found on other islands of the group, it cannot be assumed that pottery was once produced there also; since all the discoveries were made along the coasts, it is more likely that all came from Espíritu Santo through trade.

NEW CALEDONIA. The small group of the Loyalty Islands — Uvéa, Lifu, and Maré — represents an area of geographic and cultural transition between the southern New Hebrides and New Caledonia. Like the southern New Hebrides, it has been influenced by Polynesia and is artistically poor. It reflects, on a smaller and more modest scale, the culture of New Caledonia, from which its art derives. Masks, which are so typical of New Caledonia, as well as the major forms of sculpture, are absent. The art, like the whole culture of New Caledonia, exhibits an unmistakable autonomy — probably because of its geographic isolation — and indications of remote antiquity. One of the earliest types of artistic expression is the conical-roofed hut, the structural elements of which show New Caledonian carving at its best. The doorframes and the carved ridgepoles are typical of this art. In the interiors the posts are sometimes carved with human faces; in rarer instances a human figure is also carved on the central support.

The doorframes consist of two jambs and a crossbeam, the stylistic peculiarities of which date from early times and reveal no outside influences. The jambs, about 40 to 80 in. high and about 12 to 40 in. wide, are slightly convex in section. They generally adorn the chiefs' houses, and their decoration is almost always the same, representing, more or less recognizably, a man, probably an ancestor. The face is depicted fairly realistically, and in most cases it is characterized by an exaggeratedly long nose and an equally wide mouth. The tongue sometimes protrudes, probably to ward off demons and evil forces; this feature is rather unusual in New Caledonia and in most of Melanesia, being found to a marked degree only in the Sepik River region of New Guinea, where it appears fairly frequently in the masks on the gables of men's houses and on shields. The small eyes of the figures on the doorjambs are almond-shaped or round; they are incised or may protrude like buttons, as do the eyes of certain masks from the same island. (Other variations of style in representation can be ascribed to the island's great length, 248 mi., which has tended to isolate separate stylistic provinces.) Above the foreheads of these figures runs a slender horizontal slat on which zigzag lines are incised; this must surely represent the rope of the slingshot, since the island's discoverers, on Cook's second voyage, noted that the men wore their slingshots tied around their foreheads. The figures are therefore definitely male, contrary to the statement of a native chief that these figures were supposed to represent the wives of the man depicted on the peak of the roof. It is usually hard to see clearly the upper part of the faces of the figures *in situ*, since they are thickly covered by the overhanging thatch roof. The carving below the face, unlike the head, is so highly stylized that if it were considered separately and without knowledge of all the intermediate phases of its development, it would be virtually unrecognizable as a human figure; it is completely abstract, entirely absorbed into an ornamental design composed of rhomboid forms between zigzag lines. Only in a single piece (of uncertain provenance) is it possible to distinguish, beneath the ornamentally carved torso, the legs below the knee, realistically carved in the round. In two other doorjambs, probably originating in the southern part of the island and now preserved in the Museum of Bordeaux, even the faces, represented in superposed rows, assume the form of elongated triangles.

The lintel, nearly 5 ft. above the ground, repeats substantially the same facial motif as the jambs. Formerly the doors of the important huts also had a beam between the doorposts, but its use ceased about the beginning of the present century. One specimen collected by M. Leenhardt is divided into three vertical rectangles, each surrounded by a border and covered with lozenge-shaped carving. The framework of the doors is painted black and red. Near the doorjambs are occasionally observed small slender wooden poles planted in the ground; each is about 39 in. high and bears a small carved head, sometimes with a long drooping beard. No definite information is available regarding the significance of these poles; apparently they are in some way connected with the rank of chief. Occasionally wall posts are made from massive tree trunks about 5 ft. high and bear a carved human face with a long stylized beard. On one particular example on top of the central post of a hut, a very realistic human figure is carved in the round, with the legs extending along the post and the arms, with elbows bent, raised upward.

Sculptures of great variety are placed on the roofs of the circular huts; they are probably symbols or representations of mythical family founders and are ritual in nature, since they are found also on tombs and sacrificial sites and as taboo signs in plantations. Three stylistic types can be discerned among them, which probably developed chronologically: realistic figure sculpture; sculpture in which parts of the human body and stylized accessories are intermingled; and abstract geometric shapes. The commonest figures are evidently intended to represent masked persons, as shown by the large spherical headdress and feathered costume concealing the body, indicated by horizontal rows of indentations. In all these figures the legs are carved separately. Extremely rare is the figure of mother and child, and nude male figures are also uncommon. With a few exceptions, these figures are rigidly symmetrical. In those of the second type, which are mostly in the form of planks, only the faces are recognizable; the S-shaped lateral appendages that frame the face are to be interpreted as legs and arms, as confirmed by the statements of the natives. Also discernible in some sculptures of this group is the decorative slat representing the slingshot cord. To this is joined an ornament in the shape of an inverted heart indicating the spherical headdress. At the tip of the ornament is a slender staff to which are attached large white Triton shells. On the roof sculptures of the third style, in which the face is handled in a purely decorative manner, Triton shells are also found on the terminal pole.

The presence of masks is remarkable, since there is no trace of men's secret societies. The masks are perhaps a secondhand, though not a late, acquisition; this would follow from the fact that the mask represents a sea spirit and, according to tradition, probably reached the island from the north. It seems likely that in New Caledonia the wearing of a mask is a privilege reserved to a few people and that the masks are used on ceremonial occasions, primarily in the *pilu* preceding a declaration of war, and have no ritual use. The individual style and peculiar characteristics of New Caledonian masks suggest that they must have existed there since very remote times. Depending on their origin, different types can be distinguished and classified according to the stylistic treatment of the wooden facial portion; for example, the enormous hooked nose, grotesquely incurved, is typical of the northern part of the island (PL. 443). New Caledonian masks consist substantially of three parts: the face, always carved of dark hardwood; a spherical headdress, often immense, of human hair; and a cloak of Notu-dove feathers knotted into a mesh. Artistic interest attaches only to the facial mask, consisting of a semiovoid piece of wood with the face depicted on the convex portion. In the north of the island, the face is characterized by an immense hooked nose with wide flaring nostrils, a large upturned half-moon mouth, and comparatively small almond eyes. In other parts of the island there are masks with small, strongly protruding round eyes, a broad flat nose, and a small mouth, often horizontal. In all New Caledonian masks the wearer looks out through the open mouth, with its naturalistic teeth, since the mask eyes are always closed. Above, fastened to the wooden part of the mask, is the plaited cylindrical cranial ring, from which rises the spherical headdress of hair, and on the side is the plaited work which encircles the occiput; hanging from the lower edge of the last is the feather cloak, with openings at the sides for the dancer's arms. The face is generally framed at the sides and bottom with tufts of hair and a long beard, also of human hair. The masks are entirely black, and only in a few cases are the nostrils colored red and the teeth white; in one particular type the mouth is bordered with a row of red Abrus seeds, affixed with wax. The person wearing the mask carries a spear in one hand and a club in the other.

There are no other large-scale art works, though numerous smaller objects have decoration of merit. Closely resembling the masks, for instance, are the small wooden heads fastened to the ends of the strings of shell money, which are kept in small wooden boats. Similar small carved heads, and in rarer instances full figures, are found on the light assagais. Of greater importance are the small freestanding wood sculptures representing the human figure; little precise information is available on their meaning. In many cases they may be ancestor figures, perhaps employed in rain magic, as was stated in one case by the natives. Various figures carved in relief on a small wooden board are considered a magical means of obtaining offspring (PL. 247); an infant in a plaited cradle is often depicted. Zoomorphic representations are almost entirely lacking; there is sporadic use of the lizard motif in pottery and on roof gables; one completely isolated specimen is a wooden dove of unknown significance.

A feature peculiar to New Caledonia, but not found in the Loyalty Islands, are the bamboo tubes with incised motifs. Opinions as to their significance and use are divergent: it is thought that they may be emblems of rank. Besides purely ornamental designs, which are probably the prototypes, the bamboo pieces also show a large number of figural representations, many of which are fairly late, including figures of Europeans, persons on horseback, guns, and sailboats. An early observer, E. Lambert, reports that the New Caledonians usually incised on bamboo depictions of the history of their ancestors; many pieces indisputably depict historical events, such as feasts or wars between two villages (see CALLIGRAPHY AND EPIGRAPHY).

FIJI ISLANDS. The art of the Fiji Islands has many characteristics in common with that of central Polynesia, particularly Tonga; there is an almost total absence of independent sculpture on houses and boats, and certain traditional cultural elements, such as masks and shields, are lacking. In complete contrast with Melanesian custom is the tendency not to color art works; even the tapa-cloth ornamentation (PL. 458), in the absence of the most intense and luminous colors, seems almost monochrome. Also almost entirely absent in Fiji are the carved figures which are the predominant expressions in the art of the rest of Melanesia. In a sense, therefore, the art of this archipelago may be regarded as meager. However, in Fiji the epicenter of art production has shifted to other fields. These include the decoration of tapa cloth and pottery (PL. 455) and, less common but nonetheless noteworthy, the ornamental carving of various wooden articles, especially clubs. As in Polynesia, many utilitarian objects are the product of highly skilled workmanship and an exquisite esthetic sense of modeling: examples are the cups for kava and other bowls and plates, the headrests, the splendid pectoral plaques of mother-of-pearl and of sperm-whale teeth, and the carved sperm-whale teeth, with the long tips turned upward; the last, strung on a cord, are the most highly prized ornament of the chieftains. Especially noteworthy among the weapons are the many types of clubs carved in rare wood — the root, pineapple, morning-star, gunstock, paddle (FIG. 727), and lotus-flower clubs, most of which have carved handles (the large head carved as well, in the last two types), often with star- and moon-shaped decorations.

The human figure is found only on the rare wooden suspension hooks and figurines carved of sperm-whale teeth, which are objects of veneration and, according to the Polynesian religion, probably represent divinities rather than ancestors. These ivory carvings were kept in shrines made of plaited coconut-fiber rope, in the great *mbure* cult houses (perhaps temples), and were used by priests for oracular ceremonies. The few surviving specimens suggest that the figures of divinities were not numerous, and since in their severe symmetrical style they are reminiscent of those of Tonga, they may have been imported from this group of Polynesian islands or are the result of influences emanating from there (see POLYNESIAN CULTURES). Two statues of tree-fern pith preserved in the Nationalmuseet of Copenhagen, although found in Fiji, must have been brought there by craftsmen from the New Hebrides; later these figures were adorned with necklaces of sperm-whale teeth typical of Fiji.

Several of the remarkable tree-fern pith statues, about $39^{1}/_{2}$ in. high, are preserved in museums, for example, in the Nationalmuseet of Copenhagen. The relatively late date of their acquisition, together with stylistic details and testimonials that these statues were taken to Fiji by craftsmen from Gaua (Banks Islands), make it virtually certain that these are to be ascribed to a Melanesian influence from the latter islands, where this type of sculpture is very highly developed.

The only class of zoomorphic sculpture (turtles) is evident in the highly developed pottery. Fijian pottery is of special importance, since Fiji is the easternmost point to which pottery spread and also because pottery is the only art of the islanders that has no relation to Polynesia (where pottery is completely absent). It is noteworthy, however, that Fijian pottery bears almost no resemblance to that of Melanesia; it differs in both technique (with a glossy coating of resin, similar to a varnish) and form (PL. 455). Characteristic of Fiji are spherical or potbellied vessels, with or without necks, as well as extremely unusual vessels in the shape of a double boat or of round fruit, two or more pieces of which are joined together by pottery handles. Most of the ornament consists of geometric designs impressed with the fingernail or with a stick.

Decorative ornamentation is applied mainly to bark cloth, with its highly individual motifs often made up of zigzag lines and star-shaped figures (PL. 458). The colors employed against the natural light background of the material are black and a very dark red. Although the making of tapa cloth is a technique not limited to Polynesia, but found also in most of the Melanesian archipelagoes, the Fijian tapa shows a distinctly Polynesian character, in its perfect craftsmanship, decorative technique using dies and matrices, and other features.

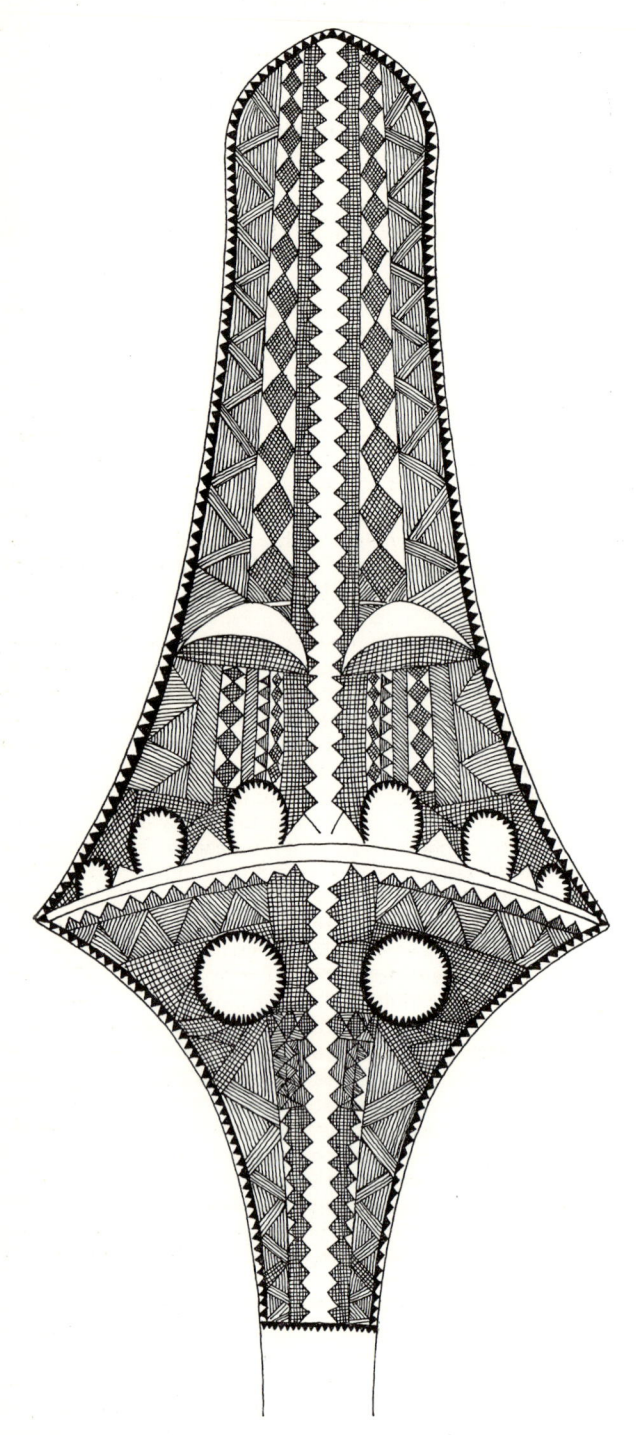

Decorative motifs on a "paddle" club from the Fiji Islands.

BIBLIOG. R. H. Codrington, The Melanesians: Studies in Their Anthropology and Folklore, Oxford, 1891; A. C. Haddon, Evolution in Art, London, 1895; J. Pfeil, Studien und Beobachtungen aus der Südsee, Brunswick, 1899; J. Edge-Partington, Note on the Occurrence of Spiral Ornament in Melanesia, Man, II, 1902, p. 26; R. Parkinson, Dreissig Jahre in der Südsee, Stuttgart, 1907; E. Stephan, Südseekunst, Berlin, 1907; G. Brown, Melanesians and Polynesians, London, 1910; W. H. R. Rivers, History of Melanesian Society, 2 vols., Cambridge, 1914; E. von Sydow, Die Kunst der Naturvölker und der Vorzeit, Berlin, 1923; A. B. Lewis, Decorative Art of New Guinea: Incised Designs (Field Mus. of Nat. H., Anthr. Design Ser., 4), Chicago, 1925; E. Vatter, Religiöse Plastik der Naturvölker, Frankfurt am Main, 1926; C. Zervos and others, L'art des Océaniens, CahArt, IV, 1929, pp. 57–119; M. Schurig, Die Südseetöpferei, Leipzig, 1930; A. B. Lewis, Carved and Painted Designs from New Guinea (Field Mus. of Nat. H., Anthr. Design Ser., 5), Chicago, 1931; G. A. Reichard, Melanesian Design: A Study of Style in Wood and Tortoise Shell Carving, 2 vols., New York, 1932–33; E. von Sydow, Die Kunst der Naturvölker (Samml. Baron Eduard von der Heydt, II), Berlin, 1932; H. Nevermann, Masken und Geheimbünde in Melanesien, Berlin, 1933; H. Nevermann, Südseekunst, Berlin, 1933; F. Speiser, Über Kunststile in Melanesien, ZfE, LXVIII, 1936, pp. 304–69; R. Grunewald, Les industries à faciès préhistorique en Océanie, B. de la Soc. des Océanistes, I, 1938, pp. 33–58; F. Speiser, Kunststile der Südsee, Basel, 1941; H. I. Hogbin, Peoples of the Southwest Pacific, New York, 1945; A. B. Lewis, The Melanesians: Peoples of the South Pacific, 2d ed., Chicago, 1945; A. Bühler, Steingeräte, Steinskulpturen und Felszeichnungen aus Melanesien und Polynesien, Anthropos, XLI–XLIV, 1946–49, pp. 225–74, 577–606; R. Linton, P. S. Wingert, and R. d'Harnoncourt, Arts of the South Seas, New York, 1946; M. Leenhardt, Arts de l'Océanie, Paris, 1947; L. Adam, Primitive Art, London, 1949; P. O'Reilly, Jeunesse de l'art océanien (Mission des Iles, IV, 27), Paris, 1950; A. Riesenfeld, The Megalithic Culture of Melanesia, Leiden, 1950; L'art océanien: sa présence (Le musée vivant, XXXVIII), Paris, 1951; G. Höltker, Die Steinvögel in Melanesien, in Südseestudien: Gedenkschrift zur Erinnerung an F. Speiser, Basel, 1951, pp. 225–66; A. Riesenfeld, Was There a Palaeolithic Period in Melanesia?, Anthropos, XLVII, 1952, pp. 405–46; C. A. Schuster, Prehistoric Stone Objects from New Guinea and the Solomons, Mankind, III, 1952, pp. 247–51; P. S. Wingert, Art of the South Pacific Islands, London, New York, 1953; E. Saccasyn Della Santa, Mélanésie, Brussels, 1954; H. Tischner and F. Hewicker, Kunst der Südsee, Hamburg, 1954; G. Koch, Die Kunst der Südsee, in Kleine Kunstgeschichte der Vorzeit und der Naturvölker (ed. H. Weigert), Stuttgart, 1956, pp. 275–308; R. Biasutti, Razze e popoli della terra, IV, Turin, 1959; T. Bodrogi, Oceanian Art, Budapest, 1959; J. Golson, Archéologie du Pacifique Sud: Résultats et perspectives, JSO, XV, 1959, pp. 5–54; H. Tischner, Kulturen der Südsee, Hamburg, 1959; A. Bühler, T. Barrow, and C. P. Mountford, The Art of the South Sea Islands, New York, 1962 (bibliog.). For regional bibliographies, see MELANESIA and NEW GUINEA.

Herbert TISCHNER

Illustrations: PLS. 441–458; 6 figs. in text.

MELOZZO DA FORLÌ. Italian painter of the Romagna (b. Forlì, 1438; d. 1494). Little is known of his training or of his early style. He is thought to have been trained by Piero della Francesca and possibly through him to have come in contact, at Urbino, with Justus of Ghent and Pedro Berruguete. Actually such hypotheses are undocumented; but in Melozzo's first certified work (VII, PL. 274), a fresco representing the nomination of Platina as prefect of the Vatican Library by Sixtus IV, features of Piero's art are prominent. The assured perspective, the Albertian grandeur of the architecture, the harmony of proportions, the characteristic generalization of specific historical personages, and the fluent equipoise of recession and two-dimensional design all reveal Melozzo's debt to his Umbrian predecessor. Except for the crumpled-drapery style in the figure of Platina, the Humanist custodian of the Vatican Library, no connection with Flemish art — or specifically, with that of Justus of Ghent — is discernible. Another source, however, is significantly present in Melozzo's Vatican fresco: the art of Mantegna. A knowledge of Mantegna, possibly of his Camera degli Sposi of 1471–74 (PLS. 328, 329), one of the earliest group portraits in Italian painting, is suggested by Melozzo's fresco. The low eye level is another feature derived from Mantegna. Seen from below, the figures appear larger and more monumental as a result, while the architecture not only implies recession but also, in filling so much of the picture, forms a strongly decorative element.

Soon after completing the Platina fresco, Melozzo painted the apse of SS. Apostoli in Rome; the surviving fragments of this work, which represented the Ascension, have been detached (Mus. Vat.; Pal. Quirinale). The remaining figures, radically foreshortened and illusionistic in a manner again reminiscent of Mantegna, are among Melozzo's most inventive, and the achievement was highly praised by Vasari. In this fresco, also, the garments are closer in style to the narrow, clinging folds of Mantegna; at the same time, the facial type of Christ and the emphasis on detail may reflect increased awareness of Justus of Ghent. In Melozzo's later work — the frescoes executed in Loreto (VIII, PL. 204) and the designs carried out by Palmezzano at Forlì (XI, PL. 99) — the pliable organic quality of his earlier figures is subordinate in a far greater degree to purely decorative intentions.

Melozzo's distinction lies in his felicitous blending of elements from the art of Piero and of Mantegna. Moreover, the continuing concern of Melozzo with creating monumental decoration, imposing scenes with full-bodied figures in splendid architectural settings, gains him a place as a significant predecessor of High Renaissance painting.

MAJOR WORKS. *Sixtus IV Nominates Platina Prefect of the Vatican Library* (1477; Mus. Vat.). - *The Ascension* (ca. 1477–81; frescoes originally in SS. Apostoli, Rome; fragments, Mus. Vat. and Pal. Quirinale). - *Prophets, Angels, and Cherubs* (ca. 1480–84; frescoed vault, Loreto, Sanctuary of the Holy House), with assistants. - *Prophets and Cherubs* (1493–94, destroyed; vault frescoes, Forlì, S. Biagio, Feo Chapel), execution largely by Marco Palmezzano (d. 1539), pupil of the artist. - *S. Giovanni Battista* and *S. Benedetto* (fragments, Uffizi).

BIBLIOG. A. Schmarsow, Melozzo da Forlì, Berlin-Stuttgart, 1886; O. Okkonen, Melozzo da Forlì und seine Schule, Helsinki, 1910; A. Schmarsow, Joos van Gent und Melozzo da Forlì in Rom und Urbino, Leipzig, 1912; R. Buscaroli, La pittura romagnola del quattrocento, Faenza, 1931, pp. 89–167; R. Buscaroli, Melozzo da Forlì, Rome, 1938; Mostra di Melozzo e del quattrocento romagnolo..., Forlì, 1938 (cat.).

Curtis SHELL

MEMLING, HANS (JEAN, JAN MEMLINC). Painter (b. Seligenstadt, near Frankfurt, ca. 1440; d. Bruges, Aug. 11, 1494). On Jan. 30, 1465, "Jan van Memmelynghe, Harmans Zuene, ghebooren Zaleghenstat" was recorded as a new citizen of Bruges. To judge by the family name, the Memlings probably came from Mömlingen, a small village near Seligenstadt. Memling's German origin is confirmed by Marcus van Vaernewyck (*De historie van Belgis*, Ghent, 1574), who mentions him as "den Duytschen Hans." The Italian historians of the same period altered his name to "Hausse" or "Ausse": this is the case, respectively, with Giorgio Vasari (*Vite*, Florence, 1568) and Lodovico Guicciardini (*Descrittione di tutti i Paesi Bassi*, Antwerp, 1567). Since these historians furnish not the slightest proof of their assertion that Memling learned his art in the studio of Rogier van der Weyden (q.v.), the statement remains questionable. The apparent influence of Rogier on Memling will be discussed below, but it is not in itself sufficient to prove the direct relation of pupil and master. So far Memling's master is not known and neither is the location where he received his professional training. Leaving Seligenstadt he had to pass through Cologne to reach Flanders. He probably spent some time in Cologne, because in his paintings on the St. Ursula shrine (1489; PL. 461) he included some accurate views of that city. However, it would be stretching the evidence to maintain that he was influenced by the school of Cologne; his art has nothing whatever in common with, for example, that of Lochner (q.v.).

The few facts about his life that are known with some certainty support the supposition that he was born about 1440. In 1467 he was received into the painters' guild of Bruges, where he had established residence. His painting must have brought him a considerable fortune, because in 1480 he was obliged (along with 245 other notables) to lend a large sum to the city of Bruges to help Maximilian I cover the enormous costs of his war with France. Yet this contribution far from exhausted Memling's resources; during the same year he bought three houses in the port area. His marriage to Anne de Valkenaere must also have taken place about this time: not much later, because she bore him three sons before she died in 1487, and not much earlier, because the boys were still minors at the painter's death in 1494.

An indirect source made it possible for Henri Dussart to publish in 1891 in the *Annales de la Société d'Émulation de Bruges* the following note relating to the death of Memling by the painter's contemporary Rombout de Doppere, canon of the Collegiate Church of St-Donatien at Bruges: "Die XI augusti [1494], Brugis obit magister Johannes Memmelinc, quem praedicabant peritissimum fuisse et excellentissimum pictorem totius tunc orbis christiani. Oriundus erat Maguncíaco, sepultus Brugis ad Aegidii." This invaluable text furnishes both the date of Memling's death (Aug. 11, 1494) and his burial place, the Church of St-Gilles at Bruges. It also shows the esteem of his contemporaries, who hailed him as "the best painter in all Christendom." However, the statement "Oriundus erat Maguncíaco" ("his origin was Mainz") cannot be taken literally. The most likely explanation is that in those times Mainz was the most important of the cities near Seligenstadt, and Rombout de Doppere meant that he came from the region of Mainz.

The only other facts to be gleaned from contemporary texts relative to Memling's life show that, following the practice of his time, he occasionally took on an apprentice: Jan Verhanneman in 1480, Passchier van der Mersch in 1483, and a certain Louis Boel at an unspecified date. The lives and works of these followers are not known, but it is reasonable to attribute to them as a group, and to various others whose names are unknown to us, the innumerable panels attributed to the studio of Memling which appear in so many churches and museums throughout the world.

The inscriptions and coats of arms found on some authentic panels, along with certain more or less ingenious reconstructions, make it possible to draw up a list of the principal patrons and amateurs who dealt directly with the master. There is no more reliable testimony to the exceptional esteem in which he was held throughout his career, even beyond the borders of the Burgundian Low Countries. Oddly enough, the earliest work of Memling that can be dated with some precision was destined for England, and the very last for Germany. An English lord, Sir John Donne of Kidwelly ordered the *Donne Triptych* (PL. 460) in 1468, while he was in Bruges with his wife, Elizabeth Hastings, and his daughter, to attend the marriage of Charles the Bold, Duke of Burgundy, and Margaret of York. The late (1491) commission for Germany, the Passion triptych (of which the Crucifixion panel is in Lübeck, St. Annen-Mus.), is easily explained by the commercial relations of the port of Bruges with the Hanseatic League towns. Heinrich Greverade, a merchant of Lübeck, chose Memling when he wished to honor the memory of his brother by a painting in the family chapel. There were also Spanish commissions. A diptych, *The Deposition*, and a panel, *The Virgin and Child*, datable about 1475, were in the collection of Isabella I of Castile, and still adorn the Capilla Real in Granada. In addition Memling executed for the organ of the Church of S. María la Real in the Castilian town of Nájera three enormous panels (*Christ Surrounded by Angel Musicians*, Antwerp, Mus. Royal B.A.).

It is understandable that numerous English, German, and Spanish patrons turned to a Flemish painter for lack of masters of equivalent stature in their own countries, but it is surprising that commissions also came steadily from Italy, which was at that time in the midst of a great artistic flowering. Memling enjoyed the patronage of more than one representative of the Medicis at Bruges. The *Last Judgment* (ca. 1473), now in the Church of St. Mary, Danzig, was commissioned by Angelo Tani for a chapel in Florence. Shortly after the marriage of Tommaso Portinari to Maria Maddalena Baroncelli in 1470, a triptych was ordered from Memling (central panel missing; half-figure side panels, showing Tommaso and his wife at prayer, now in New York, Met. Mus.). These patrons also appear in another of Memling's works, *The Passion* (Turin, Gall. Sabauda). In 1487 Memling produced an altarpiece for the Church of S. Maria Novella in Florence; two panels, a St. Benedict and a portrait of Benedetto Portinari, are now in the Uffizi; a panel bearing the portrait of Benedetto's wife is lost; *The Virgin and Child* (Berlin, Staat. Mus.) completed the work. Memling also counted among his customers the Italian medalist Giovanni Candida, who worked for Mary of Burgundy from 1477 to 1479 and of whom Memling painted a portrait (Antwerp, Mus. Royal B. A.).

Naturally Memling worked less often for foreigners than for patrons from his adopted country. Among the latter were, for example, the canon Gilles Joye, a composer attached to the court of Burgundy, who commissioned a portrait in 1472 (Williamstown, Mass., Clark Art Inst.); and Jean Crabbe, a Cistercian abbot from the Abbey of the Dunes at Koksijde to the north of Dunkerque, who commissioned an altarpiece, the parts of which are now dispersed: *The Crucifixion* is in Vicenza (Mus. Civ.); the wings are in New York (Pierpont Morgan Lib.); and the rear panels of the wings are presumably to be identified with two panels in Bruges (Groeninge-Mus.). Two burgomasters of Bruges were also Memling's patrons: Martin van Nieuwenhove, who is represented opposite the Virgin and Child on the diptych of 1487 in the Musée Memling, Bruges (PL. 462); and Guillaume Moreel, who is shown kneeling with members of his family on the *St. Christopher Triptych* (1484; Bruges, Groeninge-Mus.). Here St. Christopher is represented between St. Maurus and St. Giles. Moreel and his wife, Barbara van Vlaenderbergh, are also shown in prayer on the wings of a triptych (ca. 1483), of which the central panel has disappeared (the wings are in Brussels, Mus. Royaux B. A.).

It was for a local institution, the Hospital of St-Jean in Bruges, now housing the Musée Memling, rather than any individual patron, that Memling painted the greatest number of works. The triptych *The Mystic Marriage of St. Catherine of Alexandria* (1479) was donated by the friars Anthonis Seghers and Jacob de Keuninc and the nuns Agnès Casembrood and Clara van Hulsen. The friars Jacob Floreins and Adriaen Reins each donated a triptych, *The Adoration of the Magi* (1479) and *The Lamentation* (ca. 1480). The most celebrated of all these commissions, the St. Ursula shrine (1489; PL. 461; XII, PL. 369), was the gift of two nuns who were also connected with the Hospital, Jocosa van Dudzeele and Anne van den Moortele. This summary of Memling's patrons by no means constitutes an inventory of his works. Nonetheless, it is the nucleus, except for the very numerous panels executed for the rich *bourgeoisie* of Bruges. The names of only a few of these are known, among them the spice dealer Jean du Celier, for whom a diptych, *The Mystic Marriage of St. Catherine of Alexandria* (Louvre), was painted about 1475, and the tanner Pieter Bultync, who commissioned the panel *Scenes from the Life of Christ and of the Virgin* (erroneously called *The Seven Joys of Mary*; Munich, Alte Pin.) about 1480. But the subjects of many bourgeois portraits by Memling, men and women, remain unidentified.

It is striking that Memling seems never to have produced a painting unrelated to his religious beliefs and to those of his clients. This is obvious in the triptychs, diptychs (PL. 462), and single panels representing Biblical subjects. It was consistent with the social and religious tradition of the time to show one or two donors, or whole families of patrons, presented to the Virgin by patron saints (PL. 460). To grasp the religious spirit implicit in the art of Memling, one must note that even individual portraits, usually in the attitude of prayer (PL. 459), were intended for private chapels or served as wings to a central panel (later lost), as in the case of the works for Moreel and Portinari mentioned above. The diptych with Martin van Nieuwenhove (PL. 462) and the panels of St. Benedict and Benedetto Portinari in the Uffizi are rare instances of portrait panels still accompanying their religious counterparts. The hands of all the patrons, joined in prayer or posed in gestures indicating serious meditation, eliminate any possibility that the adjoining panels could have been nonreligious in character.

The whole *œuvre* of the master contains only one work which, from a religious point of view, might disconcert the spectator, the very realistic and beautiful *Bathsheba* (ca. 1485; Stuttgart, Landesmus.), which some prudish collector mutilated by replacing the upper left corner with a much more discreet and ordinary representation of David moved by his adulterous passion. The detached fragment survives in the Nationalmuseum in Stockholm. The panel in its original form transformed the Biblical narrative into a genre scene, throughly intimate, to be sure, but with a healthy candor consistent with the mentality of Memling's time. In spite of the difficulty of representing with delicacy a woman leaving her bath, Memling's nude does not lack dignity, grandeur, or even a certain reserve. The spirit of this painting is such that, in spite of its subject, Memling remains a religious painter.

Too many art historians still assert that this famous painter of Bruges was a patient and careful miniaturist who simply replaced the small page of parchment with a medium-sized oak panel. Certainly this judgment is applicable to a considerable number of Memling's works, from *The Passion* in Turin to the St. Ursula shrine, but to apply it to his work as a whole would be to overlook a radically opposing aspect of his art, the colossal dimensions of some of his triptychs. The Danzig *Last Judgment* (without the frame) measures about 7 ft., 3 ½ in. × 10 ft., 6 in., and each of the three monumental panels formerly in Nájera measures about 5 ft., 6 in. × 21 ft., 8 in. These are extreme cases, but there are other examples such as the Lübeck *Crucifixion*. Furthermore, on more than one of the smaller panels the dimensions of the figures are life-size, including the Stuttgart *Bathsheba*, and the saints and donors of *The Mystic Marriage of St. Catherine* and of the *St. Christopher Triptych* in Bruges.

The great difference in dimensions from one panel to another does not result in two or more techniques or styles according to the surface to be covered. On the contrary, whether the work was monumental or a small portrait such as that of Giovanni Candida, Memling consistently expended the same care, to the minutest detail of the work. From this point of view the term "miniaturist" can appropriately be applied to the master. In addition, the number of figures included in a picture is entirely independent of the dimensions of the panels. For example, on the *St. Christopher Triptych* the three saints, Christopher, Maurus, and Giles, are alone on a large central panel, while on the considerably smaller panel of *The Passion* in Turin there are dozens of figures.

The Passion, certainly the most synoptic of all the paintings, leaves the impression that one can absorb at a single glance all the pages of a manuscript. The painter has narrated here about twenty events from the end of the Saviour's life on earth, from the Entry into Jerusalem to the "Noli me tangere." There can be no doubt of the influence of the medieval theater on the scenes. From contemporary mystery plays Memling borrowed the simple little houses juxtaposed and open on one side toward the spectator. It would be incorrect to assume that this simple device resulted from the painters' inexperience and was discarded later, for the same composition can be found ten years later, in 1480, in the *Scenes from the Life of Christ and of the Virgin* in Munich. It is clear that the scenes on the side of the St. Ursula shrine of 1489 also belong to this anecdotal and synoptic genre, and even the last dated work of the artist, the Lübeck triptych (1491), retains this medieval convention, although the central panel of the Crucifixion is separated from the Biblical narratives, from the Mount of Olives to the Resurrection, which animate the wings.

Comparison of Memling's works reveals a fundamental characteristic: his style presents no marked evolution or logical development; on the contrary, the curious fact is that he perfected his genre at the very outset and thereafter felt no need or found no means to improve on it. His great masterpiece, *The Mystic Marriage of St. Catherine* of 1479 (Bruges), is not greatly superior to the fine *Donne Triptych* of 1468 (PL. 460), nor is it in the least inferior to the Lübeck *Crucifixion* of 1491. In short, the whole group of his mature works must be considered as nuances of a single standard of perfection. That being the case, it is sufficient to enumerate the general characteristics of his style, since they are applicable to practically all his works.

Nothing is more immediately evident than the sweet, celestial, mystical atmosphere of Memling's paintings. While the religious tone may seem to modern eyes to be marked by an excess of tenderness and sweetness, or even mundane bourgeois charm, it is nonetheless the reflection of a natural and confident spiritual fervor, quite different, for example, from the rigorous Spanish asceticism of the same period. At the end of the 15th century in prosperous Flanders, religious faith did not exclude fine clothes, splendid jewels, sophisticated hair styles, or elegant furnishings. Memling's figures are slender with small, rather pretty heads and delicate limbs. The female saints look so much like princesses that serious but unsuccessful attempts have been made to identify some of them with actual persons. The resemblance between King Balthasar in both Adorations of the Magi (Madrid and Bruges) and Charles the Bold of Burgundy is undeniable. The environment of this period is far removed from that of the middle of the 15th century, when the rigorous ideas of the Brethren of the Common Life were imposed on such painters as Dirk Bouts and Hugo van der Goes (qq.v.). The last echo of that past influence is barely noticeable in the extreme reserve, the determined silence, and above all, the physical and spiritual isolation of Memling's figures. Each figure has a life apart from those around it. From each of Memling's works emerges a feeling of sovereign and poetic serenity that is most moving. The sparkling color, still as fresh as the day it was painted, fills each panel with a beautiful luminosity, almost as if it were sunlit. Certain compositions might seem loosely organized but for the lighting that comes from a single source and gives the composition a unified effect, as in the Turin *Passion*. In other more rigid compositions, even those with absolute symmetry of figures and setting, light plays a harmonizing part. Memling applied a nearly constant formula: the foreground and the landscape background, both brightly illuminated, are separated by an intermediate zone immersed in shadow. Constantly striving for a general harmony, the painter always avoided overaccenting, by lighting or other means, any single element in his paintings; instead he strove for equality among all the components of a painting.

In Memling all the most lively tendencies of 15th-century painting are epitomized; an attentive observation of everyday reality in all its aspects provided him with the forms and colors of his settings and his figures, but at the same time he idealized them, transcending the combination of elements to create an extraterrestrial world consistent with his imagination and his faith.

Mention was made above of the hypothesis that Memling served an apprenticeship in the studio of Rogier van der Weyden. It is undeniable that at the beginning of his career Memling often made use of certain angular forms, as in *The Martyrdom of St. Sebastian* (ca. 1470; Brussels, Mus. Royaux B. A.), and even the entire interpretation of certain subjects, as in *The Adoration of the Magi*, that conform to Van der Weyden's types. The fact is, however, that this dependence on Rogier, aside from a few diversions, continued up to the last works of Memling; the group of holy women in the Lübeck *Crucifixion* still shows Rogier's influence. Yet Memling, even in subjects of the same character, never attained, or rather never sought, the same degree of dramatic intensity. In other words, there was no psychological affinity between these two masters. Memling was continually inspired by Rogier but never directly imitated more than his superficial forms.

Toward the end of his life Memling introduced certain decorative elements from the Italian Renaissance into his works: putti discreetly enliven the Washington *Madonna with Two Angels* (ca. 1480–85; Nat. Gall.); they also appear holding heavy garlands of fruits and flowers above the *Madonna with Two Angels* in the Uffizi (ca. 1485) and the Louvre *Resurrection* (ca. 1490). Apart from these small features Memling remained absolutely unaffected by the radical innovations in the Italian art of his time.

In conclusion, the extremely high technical quality of all of Memling's work cannot be overstressed. Considering his abundant output, such consistent quality is extraordinary. Even the occasional small weaknesses are due for the most part to the increasing activity of his collaborators.

Memling's world-wide reputation is founded on two genres of painting, portraits (e.g. XII, PL. 95) and representations of the Virgin. In portraiture he was especially successful with male subjects. The portrait of Guillaume Moreel, which may be considered his best, exemplifies the characteristics common to most of his work in this category: the panel is small; the figure, a three-quarter bust in a pose of meditation or prayer, occupies so much of the available space that the minutely painted background landscape, viewed from a great height, is barely noticeable; and the diffused light does not accentuate the already sufficient relief of the model. Kneeling donors on either side of the central religious subject, usually with their families, are frequent. In the *St. Christopher Triptych*, commissioned by Moreel, the family group occupies the wings. It is not unlikely that some of Memling's saints were modeled after persons known by the artist; the three saints in this triptych would seem to indicate that he followed this practice. The only figure clearly excepted is that of the Virgin. Memling's treatment of the Virgin is the finest aspect of all his work. She is a continually recurring theme, appearing in one manner or another as the principal figure or the focal point of nearly all his religious compositions. Two major types of composition are frequent. In one the Virgin is enthroned, surrounded by a celestial and effulgent choir, in a sumptuous imaginary interior with columns through which can be glimpsed a radiant landscape. In the other type, the small diptych panels (such as the Nieuwenhove diptych, PL. 462), the bust of the Virgin is shown in fullface or with the head slightly inclined, and the donor forms a companion panel. Between the Virgin and the Child there is rarely a strong expression of rapport. Memling's Virgins more often have the hieratic, stiff appearance of the Queen of Heaven than that of the affectionate and attentive mother. This is because the artist invariably gave her the same face — bland, meditative, and spiritual. The art of Memling, despite, its naturalistic aspects, is more one of religious conviction, of poetry, than of earthly realism. Therein lies the secret of its survival.

BIBLIOG. C. Onghena, La châsse de Sainte Ursule gravée par Onghena, d'après Memling, Brussels, 1841; J. A. Crowe and G. B. Cavalcaselle, The Early Flemish Painters, London, 1857 (ed. A. Pinchart and C. Ruelens, 2 vols., Brussels, 1863–65); W. H. J. Weale, Catalogue du Musée de l'Académie de Bruges, Bruges, London, 1861; W. H. J. Weale, Généalogie de la famille Moreel, Le Beffroi, II, 1864–65, pp. 179–96; W. H. J. Weale, Hans Memlinc: Zijn leven en zijne schilderwerken, Bruges, 1871; A. J. Wauters, Sept études pour servir à l'histoire de Hans Memlinc, Brussels 1893; A. J. Wauters, Biographie nat. de Belgique, s.v. Memling, XIV, 1897, pp. 340–56; L. Kämmerer, Hans Memling, Bielefeld, 1899; J. Neve, Le martyre de St. Sébastien: tableau de Memlinc au Musée de Bruxelles, Brussels, 1899; F. Bock, Memling Studien, Düsseldorf, 1900; M. C. Nieuwbarn, Hans Memling, Haarlem, 1900; W. H. J. Weale, Hans Memlinc, London, 1901; K. Voll, Die altniederländische Malerei von Jan van Eyck bis Memling, Leipzig, 1906; K. Voll, Memling: Des Meisters Gemälde, Stuttgart, Leipzig, 1909; M. Jäkel, Zur Komposition des Hans Memling, Leipzig, 1910; O. Rubbrecht, Trois portraits de la Maison de Bourgogne par Memlinc, Bruges, 1910; E. Schenk zu Schweinsberg, Die Illustration der Chronik von Flandern in der Stadtbibliothek zu Brugge und ihr Verhältnis zu Hans Memling, Strasbourg, 1922; E. Torno, Las tablas memlingianas de Najera, del Museo de Amberes: Su primitivo destino, fecha y autor, Mél. Bertaux, Paris, 1924, pp. 300–22; W. Rothes, Hans Memling und die Renaissance in die Niederländen, Munich, 1926; G. Hulin de Loo, Le portrait du médailleur par Hans Memlinc: Jean de Candida et non Niccolò Spinelli, Festschrift für Max J. Friedländer zum 60. Geburstage, Leipzig, 1927, pp. 103–08; G. Hulin de Loo, Hans Memlinc in Rogier van der Weyden's Studio, BM, LII, 1928, pp. 160–77; H. Vollmer, ThB, s.v., M. J. Friedländer, Ein Jugendwerk Memlings, Pantheon, VII, 1931, pp. 185–87; M. J. Friedländer, Die altniederländische Malerei, VI: Memling und Gerard David, Leiden, 1934; J. Held, A Diptych by Memling, BM, LXVIII, 1936, pp. 176–79; M. J. Friedländer, Die altniederländische Malerei, XIV: Pieter Bruegel und Nachträge zu den früheren Bänden, Leiden, 1937, pp. 102–03; P. d'Arschot, L'exposition Memling à Bruges, Brussels, 1939; G. Bazin, Memling, Paris, 1939; M. W. Brockwell, A Document Concerning Memling, The Connoisseur, CIV, 1939, pp. 186–218; J. A. Goris, Hans Memlinc à Bruges, Bruges, 1939; M. Guillaume-Linephty, La châsse de Ste Ursule, Paris, Brussels, 1939; M. Guillaume-Linephty, Hans Memlinc à L'Hôpital St-Jean de Bruges, Paris, Brussels, 1939; P. Lambotte, Hans Memling: Le maître de la châsse de Ste Ursule, Antwerp, 1939; J. Lavalleye, Memlinc, Bruges, 1939; Musée Communal, Exposition Memling (exhibition cat.), Bruges, 1939; J. Muls, Memling, Diest, 1940; F. W., Ein neuer Memling, Pantheon, XXVI, 1940, p. 249; W. Drost, Das Jüngste Gericht des Hans Memling in der Marienkirche zu Danzig, Vienna, 1941; L. von Baldass, Hans Memling, Vienna, 1942; M. J. Friedländer, Noch etwas über das Verhältnis Roger van der Weydens zu Memling, Oud-Holland, LXI, 1946, pp. 11–19; G. H. Dumont, Hans Memlinc ou la fin du monde, Paris, 1947; A. de Schietere de Lophem, Quelques portraits conservés dans les musées de Bruges, B. Soc. royale d'archéol. de Bruxelles, 1947–48, pp. 22–33; M. J. Friedländer, Memling, Amsterdam, 1950; C. G. Heise, Der Lübecker Passionsaltar von Hans Memling, Hamburg, 1950; A. Janssens de Bisthoven and R. A. Parmentier, Le Musée Communal de Bruges: Les Primitifs Flamands (Corpus de la peinture des anciens Pays-Bas méridionaux au XVe siècle, I), Antwerp, 1951; J. Lavalleye, Memlinc à l'Hôpital St-Jean, Brussels, 1953; E. Panofsky, Early Netherlandish Painting, 2 vols., Cambridge, Mass., 1953; M. J. Friedländer, Van der Goes und Memling, Oud-Holland, LXV, 1955, pp. 167–71; C. Johnson, Memling, London, 1955; A. Schouteet, Nieuwe teksten betreffende Hans

Memling, Rev. belge d'archéol. et d'h. de l'art, XXIV, 1955, pp. 81-84; V. Denis, Le théâtre et les primitifs, l'Oeil, 23, 1956, pp. 18-27; J. Muls, Memling: de laat-gotische droom, Hasselt, 1960; F. van Molle, Un portrait de Gilles Joye attribué à Memling (Les Primitifs flamands: Contributions à l'étude des primitifs flamands, 3), Brussels, 1960.

Valentin DENIS

Illustrations: PLS. 459-462.

MENDELSOHN, ERIC. German architect (b. Allenstein, East Prussia, Mar. 21, 1887; d. San Francisco, Calif., Sept. 15, 1953). After study at the Technische Hochschule, first that in Berlin (1908) and then in Munich (1909), where he was in contact with the expressionist artists of the Blaue Reiter group, Mendelsohn graduated and began his own practice in Munich in 1912. Before and during World War I he produced many remarkable and visionary project sketches that were at once expressionist and mechanistic (I, PL. 408). Such imaginative early aspirations were realized in the Einstein Tower (V, PL. 104; FIG. 236) at Neubabelsberg, near Potsdam, designed in 1919 and completed in 1925, among the most remarkable architectural products of the 1920s. Already in 1920 his hat factory at Luckenwalde was of a severe, angular design; and in a series of buildings throughout the rest of the decade — Herpich store, Berlin (1924), Schocken department store, Stuttgart (1926-27; V, FIG. 238); Schocken department store, Chemnitz (1928; V, PL. 105); Metalworkers' Union, Berlin (1929); Columbus Haus, Berlin (1931) — he moved even closer to the dominant "international style" of the period.

Leaving Germany in the early 1930s, Mendelsohn next worked in England, where he built, among other structures, the De La Warr Pavilion at Bexhill (1933-34), in partnership with Serge Chermayeff. From 1934 to 1941 he was in Palestine. His major works there — the Hadassah University Medical Center (1936-38) and the Anglo-Palestine Bank (1937-38), both in Jerusalem — illustrate an imaginative and reasoned response to a hot climate and a different cultural background; the Medical Center is perhaps his finest work. Settling in America, he built the Maimonides Hospital (1946-50) and the Leon Russel residence (1950-51), both in San Francisco. He also designed a series of synagogues and Jewish community centers: B'nai Amoona, St. Louis, Mo. (1946-50); Cleveland (1946-52); Mount Zion, St. Paul, Minn. (1950-54); and Temple Emanuel, Grand Rapids, Mich. (1953). In these something of the expressionist elaboration of form seen in his early work returned.

Recognized from the early 1920s as one of the four or five most important modern architects of Germany, Mendelsohn — like his contemporaries Gropius and Mies van der Rohe — contributed as much or more to world architecture as to the architecture of his homeland. His reputation rose and fell with tides of taste, and to these tides he was not unresponsive. Yet always his work had, as he intended it should, a strongly personal character, and his finest buildings will remain among the landmarks of 20th-century architecture.

BIBLIOG. Structures and Sketches (introd. by Mendelsohn), London, 1924; E. Mendelsohn, Das Gesam Schaffen des Architekten, Berlin, 1930; M. F. Roggero, Il contributo di Mendelsohn alla evoluzione dell'architettura moderna, Milan, 1952; A. Whittick, Eric Mendelsohn, London, New York, 1956; W. von Eckardt, Eric Mendelsohn, New York, 1960.

Henry-Russell HITCHCOCK

MERYON, CHARLES. French etcher (b. Paris, 1821; d. Charenton, Feb. 14, 1868). He was the son of a French dancer, Mlle Pierre Narcisse Chaspoux, and an English physician, Charles Lewis Meryon, who deserted his family a few years after his son's birth. When Meryon was sixteen or seventeen years old his mother died insane. At about this time he entered the French Naval Academy, cruising in the Mediterranean and, in 1842-46, in the South Pacific. In 1847 he resigned because of ill health, but all his life he continued to swab his floors barefoot, sailor-fashion, and kept his room as neat and anonymous as a ship's cabin. He studied painting until, when he put red waves into a picture of the South Seas, it was discovered that he was color blind. He then learned to etch from Eugène Bléry, a mediocre print maker, and copied fifteen 17th-century etchings, being especially influenced by the simple and direct copperplate views of Reinier Zeerman, whom he called "my master and sailor."

In 1850, with his first original etching, Le petit pont, Meryon began the series of 22 Eaux fortes sur Paris, his masterwork, which he etched during the next four years. The lunar hardness of these hallucinatory views of Notre-Dame, the morgue, and the bridges over the Seine fascinated Baudelaire, one of the first writers to discover poetry in the modern city. During 1860 Baudelaire repeatedly offered to write a text for the etchings, but Meryon merely "stared at the ceiling and said nothing." The enthusiasm of a few collectors could not sell these original visions, even at a mere 20 to 40 cents each, or 5 to 6 dollars for all 22.

Meryon's derangement began to be evident in some of his later prints, which show balloons, flights of hawks, sharks, and war canoes invading the skies of Paris. His first violent insanity is said to have been brought on in 1856 by the strain of composing five little daguerreotypes of San Francisco into a panorama of the city; for this work he had to accommodate edges distorted by the primitive camera and reconcile conflicting shadows. During 1857-58 the Duc d'Arenberg induced Meryon to take daguerreotype lessons in order to make views of the duke's château at Enghun, Belgium; but the views were never etched, and the daguerreotypes have never been published. From 1860 to 1866 Meryon was lucid enough to etch from sketches made on his youthful cruise in the South Pacific, but he died in the madhouse of Charenton on St. Valentine's Day, two years later. He had lived for 46 years, had etched for about fifteen, and had crowded the creation of his masterpieces into five.

Meryon used the direct sharpness of 17th-century copperplate techniques to express romantic poignancy. The clarity of his style affected many French etchers, and its influence is apparent in Whistler's Thames Set. Meryon was one of the first to discover that everyday places can haunt and hypnotize, a discovery that became more explicit in the early work of De Chirico and Charles Burchfield. Meryon's manner of working was as individual as all else about him. He drew buildings from the ground up (because that is how they are built) with a sharp, hard pencil on tiny squares of paper concealed in his palm. He then pasted these squares together in his compositions, often combining different points of view.

BIBLIOG. F. Wedmore, Méryon and Méryon's Paris, London, 1879, new ed. 1892; L. Delteil, Catalogue Raisonné of the Etchings of Charles Méryon, ed. and amplified by J. L. Wright, New York, 1924; G. Geffroy, Charles Méryon, Paris, 1926.

A. Hyatt MAYOR

MESOPOTAMIA. The ancient western Asian land of Mesopotamia — "the land between rivers," the Tigris and the Euphrates — was from the end of the 4th millennium until the middle of the 1st the site of a mighty civilization that in antiquity and in duration is comparable only to the other great river-valley civilization of the Near East, that of Egypt (see EGYPTIAN ART). Egyptian art, however, as a result of ethnic homogeneity and geographic autonomy, was relatively isolated and self-contained; whereas Mesopotamian art, sprung from a complex of prehistoric and protohistoric cultures (see ASIATIC PROTOHISTORY; MEDITERRANEAN PROTOHISTORY), drew on a diversity of ethnic elements (Sumerian, Semitic, Indo-European) and underwent great vicissitudes in history, achieving a remarkable variety and manifesting a great power of expansion. This power, which made the art of Mesopotamia the pivot of art development in its area (see ASIA, WEST: ANCIENT ART), was manifest at least from the beginning of the 3d millennium in Elam (see IRANIAN PRE-SASSANIAN ART CULTURES) and to some extent in Egypt itself; at least from the 2d millennium in Anatolia (see ASIA MINOR, WESTERN; HITTITE ART; URARTU) and Syria-Palestine (see SYRO-PALESTINIAN ART; PHOENICIAN-PUNIC ART);

MESOPOTAMIA

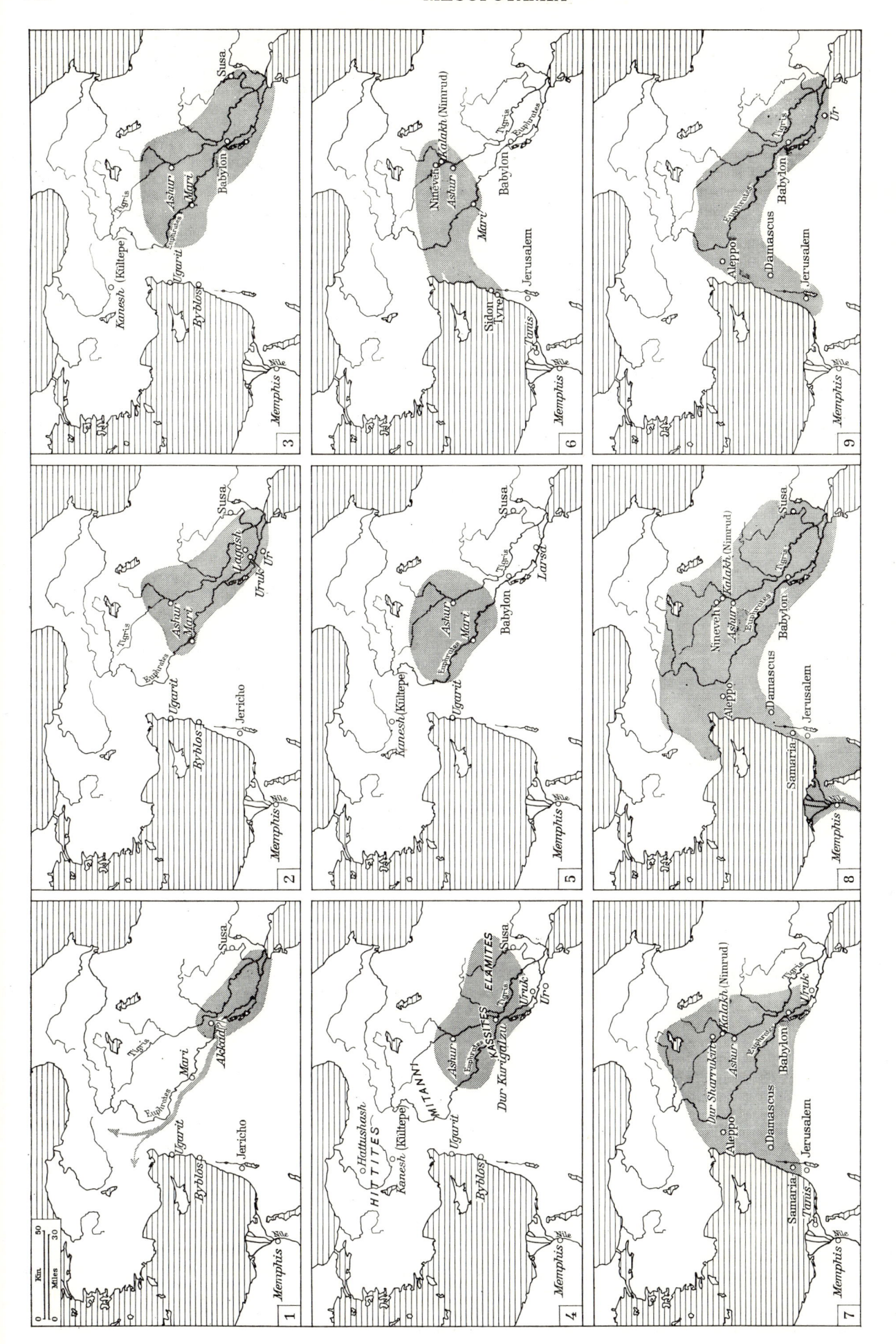

Mesopotamia, the civilizations and reigns of major historical importance from the 3d to the 1st millennium B.C. (shading indicates extent of dominion). (1) State of Akkad (ca. 2350–2150); (2) Neo-Sumerian civilizations (2150–1950); (3) Amorite states in Mesopotamia (first half of 2d millennium); (4) Kassite and Elamite dominion (second half of 2d millennium); (5) Assyria in the reign of Shamshi-Adad I (ca. 1758–1726); (6) Assyrian empire in the reign of Ashurnasirpal II (883–859); (7) Assyrian empire in the reign of Sargon II (721–705); (8) Assyrian empire in the reign of Ashurbanipal (668–626); (9) Neo-Babylonian empire (625–538) (based on Parrot, Sumer 1961, and Arts of Assyria, 1961).

from the 1st millennium in Arabia (see ARABIAN PRE-ISLAMIC ART), in Achaemenid Iran, and in Greece. Thus Mesopotamia appears as the major center of artistic and, more broadly, of cultural irradiation of the ancient Near East, in other words, of the preclassical world.

SUMMARY. Protohistoric periods (col. 739): *Architecture: a. Uruk VI–IVb; b. Uruk IVa; c. Jamdat Naṣr period; Figural Arts: a. Uruk VI–IV; b. Jamdat Naṣr period.* First period of transition and Mesilim period (col. 746): *Architecture; Figural Arts: a. Transition period; b. Mesilim period.* Second transition period and period of Ur I (col. 752): *Architecture; Figural Arts: a. Sculpture in the round; b. Relief.* Akkadian period (col. 756): *Architecture; Figural Arts.* Gutian and Neo-Sumerian period (col. 760): *Architecture: a. Temples of the gods; b. Royal temples and palaces; c. Funerary monuments; Figural Arts: a. Sculpture in the round; b. Relief.* Old Babylonian period (col. 765): *Architecture: a. Cult buildings; b. Palaces; Figural Arts: a. Sculpture; b. Painting.* Middle Babylonian (Kassite) period (col. 768): *Architecture; Figural Arts: a. Architectural sculpture; b. Wall painting; c. Sculpture in the round; d. Relief; e. Glyptics.* Old and Middle Assyrian period (col. 772): *Architecture; Figural Arts.* Neo-Assyrian period (col. 775): *Architecture; Figural Arts.* Neo-Babylonian (Chaldean) period (col. 781): *Architecture; Figural Arts.* Conclusion (col. 785).

PROTOHISTORIC PERIODS. The great creative phase of Mesopotamian art was the protohistoric, called by some scholars "protoliterate," which is linked to levels VI–IV of Uruk (Bib. Erech) and to the period named after the village of Jamdat Naṣr. For about four hundred years (3100–2700 B.C., according to the "short chronology" adopted here) there flourished a monumental architecture and an art of vast dimensions and high quality. Both are related to certain fundamental religious conceptions, sketched at the end of the present section. (See also ASIA, WEST: ANCIENT ART.)

Architecture. The landscape of archaeology in western Asia owes its aspect to the "tell," the mound of ruins built up by the continuous alternation of destruction and reconstruction of villages, cities, or sanctuaries. These alternations early influenced the form of the temple. Through the repeated leveling or transformation of previous constructions in centers of worship there originated the temple on an elevated platform, the prototype of the "high temple" (*Hochtempel*).

The role of antecedent prehistoric structures in the formation of buildings is best illustrated at Eridu, the oldest Sumerian cult city, and at Uruk. There the ruins of E-anna, the "House of Heaven," which are the oldest remains of monumental structures known, show the development of architecture through a first phase (levels VI, V, and IVc–b) and a second one (level IVa); level III belongs to the Jamdat Naṣr period.

a. Uruk VI–IVb. At Eridu, as early as the middle Aëneolithic period, a chapel about 7 × 10 ft. in area was transformed into a temple of characteristic ground plan: a rectangular chamber bordered on the two long sides by subsidiary rooms, one of them a stair room. The remains of three successive temples of this type are preserved there from the al-'Ubaid period. The entrance was always on one of the long sides; stairs led up to a terrace of undetermined height and shape; on one of the short sides there was sometimes a podium and opposite it a hearth or altar. The four corners were accentuated by means of projecting rooms, a device that later fell into disuse. What remained typical, however, was the disposition of sacred edifices along axes diverging about 45° from the main directions of the modern compass. That buildings of the same type were also erected in the Uruk VI–IVb period is proved by the equally impressive sequence of structures under the much later Anu ziggurat of Uruk. Here, too, the rectangular chamber is accompanied by subsidiary rooms.

The examples cited so far show a continuous architectural tradition from the Aëneolithic to the Jamdat Naṣr period. E-anna, the sanctuary of the goddess Inanna at Uruk, on the other hand, was twice fundamentally altered during this time. Level VI has yielded only minor, hardly distinguishable remains of great edifices, but the sanctuary of levels V–IVb (FIG. 740) is largely known. An L-shaped terrace enclosed a court about 7 ft. lower down, with an entrance on the southeast and walls that consisted at first of *Patzen* ("lumps," large unbaked bricks) and later of *Riemchen* ("striplets," small unbaked bricks measuring 2 ³⁄₈ × 2 ³⁄₈ × 6 ¹⁄₄ in.). On the southwest the terrace carried the smaller "Temple A," built of clay, and on the northwest the hall of columns, about 100 ft. in width, with pillarlike supports over 6 ft. in diameter. These supports were covered with a black, white, and red pattern formed by the flat butts of terra-cotta cones embedded in the clay. Similar terra-cotta mosaics covered the walls of the court, the long sides of which were partly resolved into joined half columns (X, PL. 172), while the northwest side formed a kind of platform. The patterns are clearly textile in character and probably derive from the reed mats with which clay walls were once protected.

The largest building of the sanctuary belonging to this phase was the "limestone temple." Given the strict symmetry prevalent in that period, it is possible to reconstruct its ground plan, a rectangle of 230 × 98 ft. enclosing an enormous T-shaped area 203 ft. long and about 38 ft. wide. Since such a width could be bridged only with huge tree trunks, it may be assumed that this area was an open court. The rooms on the long sides

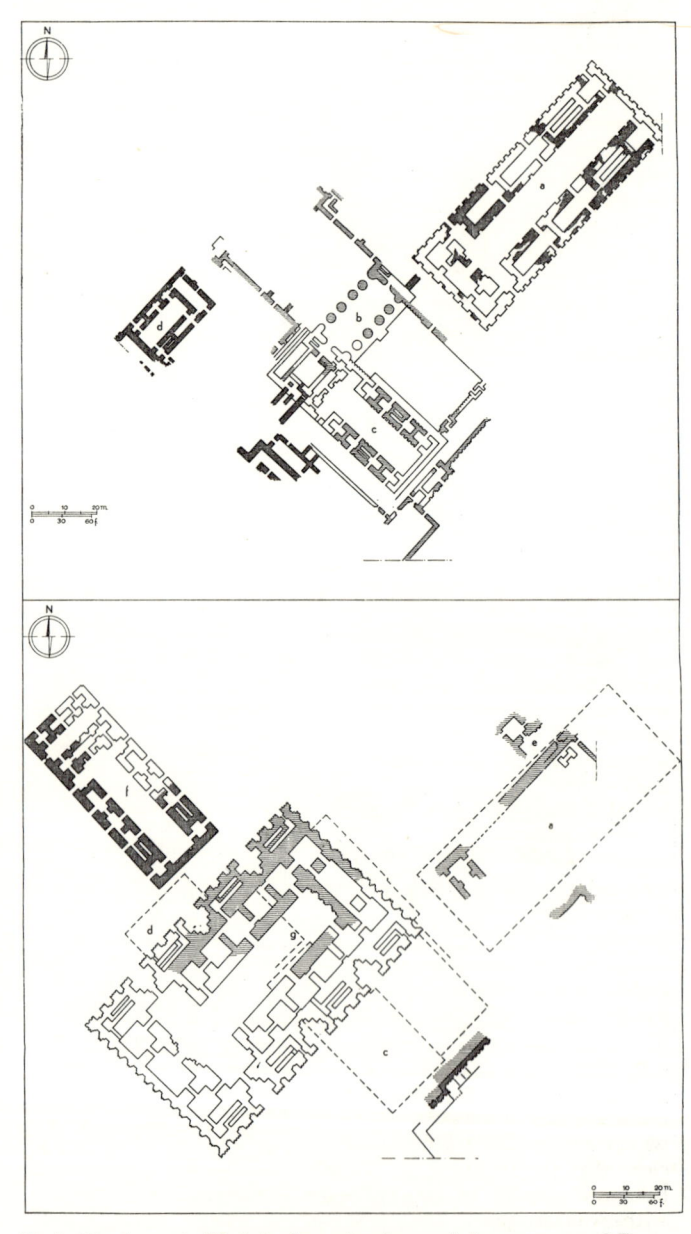

Uruk (Erech, mod. Warka), the early phases of the sanctuary of E-anna. *Above*: First phase (levels V–IVb): (*a*) "limestone temple"; (*b*) hall of columns; (*c*) Temple A; (*d*) Temple B. *Below*: Second phase (level IVa): (*e*) "Red Temple"; (*f*) Temple C; (*g*) Temple D; buildings of the preceding period (*a, b, c, d*) indicated by broken lines (*adapted from Heinrich, 1950*).

were disposed symmetrically, as were the two stairways that led to the flat roof. Most important, no doubt, was the room on the south short side, which was flanked by two small rooms and opened on the court through a wide gateway adorned with niches. Cult niche, altar, and podium are missing, but the sacred character of the building is conveyed by its mighty dimensions and the decoration of the walls with niches — an infallible index of sacred function in western Asia from earliest prehistory through thousands of years. The temple owes its name to the surviving walls of limestone blocks. Their use, of which no instance could be found in the succeeding phase, is exceptional in Mesopotamia, probably because it was not in keeping with the spirit of the architecture rather than because the stone was difficult to obtain; it would have been no more difficult to obtain roofing trunks.

Another method of building more durably than with clay alone is illustrated by a complex at Uruk contemporaneous with E-anna IV, lying between the sanctuaries of Anu and Inanna. There, in a court with terra-cotta cone mosaics, stood a building with wall reinforcements of white alabaster cones and red and black limestone cones. This kind of reinforcement may be an earlier form of the use of terra-cotta cones, an earlier adaptation of reed hangings. Later, this technique, too, was abandoned.

Analogously, it may be supposed that the supports with terra-cotta cones in the hall of columns were derived from stone pillars. Neither stone-block construction nor pillars and columns were to determine the forms of later Mesopotamian architecture, although they were always known — as the arch was shortly to be — as structural elements serving to overcome the force of gravity. Sumerian architecture was not devoted to expressing the functions of load and carry, or tectonics, but rather to artistic effect achieved by decoration of wall surfaces.

b. Uruk IVa. The second protohistoric phase of E-anna marks a peak of artistic development. The sanctuary was thoroughly transformed (FIG. 740). True, there were again two cult buildings of different sizes at right angles to each other, but their position was altered. Where the limestone temple had stood, there was only a big storehouse or administration building. The principal temple, D, assuredly the successor of the limestone temple, covered the whole area previously occupied by the terrace with the hall of columns and Temple A, as well as by the large court with cone mosaics. To the northwest spread Temple C, obviously placed in relation to Temple D and of the same type as the limestone temple. As a matter of fact, it is the best-preserved example of the type. Its ground plan differs solely in that the fore (or westernmost) section was nearly independent of the oblong court complex that lay perpendicular to it in a northwesterly direction. It is noteworthy that no niches appear on the external walls but that the interior compartments of the fore portion were provided with very small niches along their whole extent. Accordingly, it alone may have served cult purposes, and the oblong court complex those of administration.

In Temple D the use of niches both on the external walls and on the interior courtyard walls reached such proportions that it must be regarded no longer as purely ornamental, but rather as a disposition of space. Whereas triple-stepped niches provided a normal articulation of the short sides of the powerful structure — which must have measured 180 × 262 ft. — the niches of the long sides, because of their extreme depth and partly because of their cruciform design, assumed the character of independent rooms. After a group of three niches about 5 ft. deep came a cruciform niche about 20 ft. deep and over 16 ft. wide. However the elevation was carried out in detail, there appears a marked loosening in the masses of brick, of which only a delicate shell, so to speak, remained. It becomes clear that the breaking-up of walls with niches is a transposition into clay of an extremely ancient construction technique with wooden posts.

c. Jamdat Naṣr period. The best-known building of the third protohistoric phase is the so-called "White Temple" at Uruk (PL. 463; I, FIG. 859). It was the product of a centuries-old tradition and corresponds in all details to the type of the Eridu temples. The continuous alternation of destruction and reconstruction made of it, too, a "high temple"; it rises on a terrace, all sides of which slant downward. Its particular importance lies in its good state of preservation. Incasement by a later terrace left the walls standing to a height of 10 ft.

The White Temple can be linked with Temple A of E-anna, also a "high temple," and is perhaps related to the other group, temples C and D and the older limestone temple, through the device of articulation by niches and common features in the spatial disposition of the fore sections. Two similar temples of this time became known in the 1940s: that of Tell 'Uqayr, with its mural paintings, and the "Eye Temple" of Tell Brak in northern Mesopotamia, with a podium decorated on the vertical faces, in true Sumerian style, with gold and colored stones.

The sanctuary of Inanna at Uruk underwent a marked transformation between level IVa and level III, which with two lesser enlargements (IIIa–c) lasted through the Jamdat Naṣr period. The heart of the layout, henceforth, was a terrace on which there probably stood a temple of the same kind as the White Temple, surrounded by numerous buildings for residence and administration, which were frequently altered. It is uncertain whether these subsidiary structures were already connected, as later, to form court complexes and enclosures. By comparison with earlier stages, all clarity and spaciousness have disappeared. Instead of symmetry we encounter confusion of plan in many sections; in others the thick walls of *Patzen* take up more room than the free spaces. Still to be found, however, are the *Riemchen*, though disposed somewhat differently, and the walls with cone mosaics.

To summarize, the Jamdat Naṣr period presents, on the one hand, the continuation of tradition in the architecture of the "high temple," in the decoration with niches, and in the revetments of cone mosaics; on the other hand, something entirely new in the unskillful layout of E-anna. A similar duality may be seen in the other arts of this period.

Figural Arts. Before the turn of the 4th–3d millennium there were but two outlets for figural art in Mesopotamia: polychrome pottery and stamp seals. Whereas pottery in the Aëneolithic era had developed toward abstract ornament, glyptic art for the first time attempted narrative based on observation. Some of the representations were distributed freely on the decorated surface; others were disposed symmetrically, in the manner of mirror images.

a. Uruk VI–IV. Whether seal engraving was the sole form of art practiced during the first phase of the protohistoric period is uncertain; the fact is that no other has been preserved. At Uruk a new kind of seal was devised: the cylinder seal, a stone roller that provides a larger decorated surface than the stamp seal. Although it is not clear how this new shape came into being, there is no doubt that the continuous band of ornament was congenial to the Sumerian spirit. The cycle returning upon itself is the theme of innumerable large and small compositions in ancient western Asia.

Surviving examples consist chiefly of impressions from cylinder seals on the closings of jars; of the seals themselves only a few have been found. Some of the subjects became trend-setting in western Asia: cult processions, sacrifices, battles, and hunts. Others are typical for the protohistoric period: wild beasts running free, domesticated animals, hybrid creatures in heraldic poses. Animals in general already played an important role as symbols of the forces favoring or threatening life. Of fundamental significance, no doubt, was the worship of the gods and of the ruler as warrior and high priest. Human representation was mastered all at once. The distribution of the figures in space remained free of any heraldic arrangement. Observation of nature and symbolic abstraction operated side by side and from the very beginning determined the character of Sumerian art, which attempted both individual pictorial elements and over-all articulation. These two methods of approach, fundamental to all art, preoccupied the artists of western

Asia for centuries, but no valid equilibrium was ever achieved, as it was in Egyptian and in Byzantine art. There exists a series of seal impressions that, from the time of the limestone temple and then increasingly until the following Jamdat Naṣr period, show a preference for symmetrical, unrealistic arrangements of animals and hybrid beings. Nonetheless, the art of this period gives the prevailing impression of a vigorous nature-oriented spirit, not yet aware of a profane world distinct from a holy, suprasensory one. Even where the animals are built up into artificial heraldic groups of symbolic significance, the individual creatures remain strikingly true to nature. It is obvious that the artist strove for round, full, lifelike forms; even his fabulous beings testify to uncommon sharpness of observation in their component parts.

The distinction of two phases of the Uruk VI–IV period in architecture is not possible in glyptics, even though the heraldically composed animal groups came to light predominantly in the later subdivision of level IV.

b. Jamdat Naṣr period. The Jamdat Naṣr period corresponds to levels III and II of Uruk, where Sumerian culture remained centered, although it had by this time extended its influence to Elam, northern Mesopotamia and even the valley of the Nile. The period presents two completely different groups of works: on the one hand, examples of a stylistic continuation of Uruk VI–IV, with a multiplication and enrichment of art forms; on the other, works of a style which, though it seems at first to betoken regression or decadence, was to be of key importance for the future of Sumerian art. The two stylistic trends must have existed simultaneously.

The first group, which preserves the content and the forms of the previous period, marks the zenith of protohistoric art both in the quality and in the diversity of the works. The stone cult vessel particularly inspired the artist. Sometimes it is decorated in low relief, sometimes in high relief, occasionally approximating sculpture in the round in its detachment from the surface of the vase. Vessels in the form of animals, too, were leading to sculpture in the round. The subjects include domestic animals (cattle and sheep) and beasts of prey (lions and eagles), shown individually, aligned, or in combat. Sometimes a naked hero protects the domestic animals, as on the fragment of a limestone vase from Uruk with highly protuberant reliefs (PL. 465). The Sumerian disinclination toward tectonics is here evident once more. Unlike Greek vase painting, for example, the decoration does not emphasize the structure of the vessel, but conceals it. The strict heraldic disposition of the figures tends to be overlooked in the liveliness of the execution.

Totally different in effect are the vases with bas-reliefs, one of the most important of which is a cylindrical alabaster vase from Uruk, adorned with three bands of figures (PL. 466). Doubtless thematically related, the three friezes present in detail a cult procession, condensed versions of which are known from seals of the Uruk IV period. The nearly obliterated figure of the leader in the top register is familiar from numerous seal representations and can be reconstructed from them. He wears a garment of transparent netting and is accompanied by two attendants who carry, one a long cloth sash, the other a basket of fruit. In the middle register naked servants follow one another, bearing baskets, bowls, and libation vases, filled with fruit and beverages. The bottom register displays a file of sacrificial sheep and, underneath, the source of all life, ears of barley and palm shoots aligned over water. The entire procession is met, in the top register, by a woman in a long coat and a pointed, probably horned, headdress. Behind her, two reed bundles indicate the entrance to a temple or storehouse containing sheep, several receptacles with gifts (among them, zoomorphous vases), and a stepped platform with reed bundles; on it stand two human figures, praying and sacrificing.

The reed bundles show that the procession is in honor of the goddess Inanna of Uruk, the embodiment of eternal life. The man in the net skirt must be her lover, the half-mythical king of Uruk, Dumuzi (called Tammuz by the Semites), who personified the dual principle of generation and decay. This vital principle, which ruled the cosmos and linked the world of the gods with the community of men, was the mythic kernel of early Sumerian culture and one of the fundamental tenets of Sumerian culture as a whole.

If the headdress of the main figure indeed carried horns, the scene represents an episode from the myth of Inanna and her lover. The vase would then be the oldest example of anthropomorphic representation of a deity. But it is also possible that the scene depicted is a cult ceremony such as was celebrated every New Year's Day, after the pattern of the myth, by the chief personages of the city and the high priestess. A truer interpretation, however, would eliminate the sharp distinction between myth and reality. The protohistoric Sumerian world was actually in every respect a union of the divine-sacred and the human-profane, of the real and the supernal, of nature and abstraction. Man, not yet dissociated from the community by a consciousness of individuality, achieved through his prince a bond of the utmost closeness with the godhead, gaining thus a share in eternal life. Like an animal or a plant among its kind, he was still living the boundless life of nature and its divine powers.

In a stone trough also from Uruk (PL. 465) the delimitation of the picture areas follows the contours of the receptacle, thus emphasizing its singular form. The narrative sequence of the vase is here replaced by the mirror-image symmetry already familiar from the seals. A group of maned sheep — ram, ewe, and lamb, symmetrically duplicated — stands beside a reed hut. The reed standards on either side of the hut again demonstrate that the scene is a symbolic one related to the cult of Inanna and her sacred herd. As in the heraldic glyptic representations of the preceding phase, the abstract qualities are restricted to the composition; the animals themselves are entirely true to nature.

The images on the short sides of the trough — two reed bundles, two lambs, and two eight-leaved rosettes, symmetrically disposed — can be understood through contemporaneous cylinder seals. For in the glyptic art of the Jamdat Naṣr period too, the sacred herds and sheepfolds and the royal shepherd play a primary role. As in relief sculpture, different artistic principles operate side by side. A comparison of two cylinder seals — one in London (BM 116722; see Frankfort, 1939, pl. 51), the other in Berlin (VA 10537; VI, PL. 33) — on the same subject, the feeding of the sacred sheep of Inanna by a personage in a net skirt, demonstrates that the first exemplifies the narrative approach, the second the symbolic.

Western Asia is indebted to the Jamdat Naṣr period not only for the vase relief but for the relief-adorned stele: the upright stone block bearing reports, at first pictorial, later also written, on the deeds of the kings. From Uruk comes such a stele, about 3 ft. high, on which a king, identified by his diadem, wig, and beard, is shown twice as he combats lions, in the upper register with a spear, in the lower with bow and arrow (Frankfort, 1954, pl. 9a). One side of the stone block was slightly roughhewn to obtain the picture surface, which, however, was not delimited or framed. The two episodes, belonging to different points in time, are depicted one above the other without separation by a strip or even a base line. As for the distribution of the figures, it is not so much free as lawless. This composition is far removed from the abstraction and the orderly narrative of the works considered above. The pictorial field is not yet perceived as an abstraction of space and time allowing the depiction of unfolding events; the stone block itself, the vehicle of the image, has not yet fixed its type.

Approximating sculpture in the round, like the prominent reliefs of some of the stone vases, is a certain kind of wall sculpture of the late Jamdat Naṣr period that includes some of the outstanding animal figures of all time. The animals lie with their bodies along the wall, their heads turned at a right angle. While the bodies are merely scored over to suggest the coat, the heads, especially of the rams, show a sculptural, broad-surfaced treatment of the various parts. The asymmetry of the horns further enhances the verisimilitude, indicating that the artist conceived of the animals not only as elements of nature but also as symbols of a transcendent principle.

Animals provide theme and form for an extraordinarily large

number of amulets — pendants depicting domestic animals and their enemies, beasts of prey, prolific species such as frogs and fish, and even hybrid creatures uniting the qualities of two animals. These amulets, modeled in the round, entered into combination with cylinder seals and stamp seals. They were halved lengthwise, and their flat sides were generally covered with crude signs; or else they were joined to cylinder seals as handles.

Nearly all the stone amulets in the form of quadrupeds represent the animals lying down with their legs folded close to them. Here the capacity of the material to determine style plays its part. The only animal to stand on its legs is a bronze lion from Uruk, one of the few examples of toreutic art preserved from this period (E. Heinrich, *Kleinfunde aus den archaischen Tempelschichten in Uruk*, Leipzig, 1936, pl. 13a). Only small sculptures of bronze, copper, and silver have survived; but large pieces probably existed too, for they would have been produced in the same way, namely by solid casting.

Nothing is so characteristic of Sumerian art as the predilection for piecing together figures from parts made of different materials and thus obtaining color contrasts. Black and white stones were used prevailingly, but lapis lazuli also enjoyed great favor. No less popular was the combination of stone and metal — copper (bronze) as well as silver and gold. In planar work this taste led to inlaid friezes and intarsias; in works in the round, to a technique that thousands of years later, in Greece, reached its ultimate peak in chryselephantine sculpture.

The finest example of a composite animal statuette is the figure of a bull, about 3 in. long, made basically of white limestone ("Siebter vorläufiger Bericht ... Uruk," *AbhPreussAk*, Phil.-Hist. Kl., no. 4, 1935, pl. 24b). The head is perpendicular to the body. At the base of the neck and on the rump are large irregular cavities in which differently colored stone was inserted, doubtless to reproduce the piebald hide of the animal. Hollows in the shape of four-petaled flowers, which must have held colored stones, are found on the loins, back, and neck as well as between the eyes. Of the various extremities — ears, horns, tail, and legs — only the silver hind legs, modeled, like the body, with exceptional realism, have survived. The sculptor's attempt to overcome the limitations of his medium, stone, could be accomplished only with the help of metal. That the organic coherence of the whole suffered thereby did not deter the Sumerian artist, to whom coordination was more congenial than subordination.

To the category of polychrome and composite sculpture belongs a female "mask" of alabaster (PL. 464), discovered, like the small bull just described, at Uruk in a stratum of the Jamdat Naṣr period. It indubitably marks the apogee of all surviving protohistoric art and is most likely the earliest example of truly distinguished sculpture in the round. Nearly life-size, it is not a fragment in the ordinary sense but one part of a female likeness composed of various segments of different materials. The back of the head is missing; the reverse of the face is flat and shows holes for the fastening of other parts; the few planes indicating the hair and the deep indentation of the part were meant to accommodate a gold wig. The eyebrows meeting over the nose must originally have been inlaid with lapis lazuli, and eyeballs of another material were doubtless let into the large sockets between the finely modeled lids. A formal dichotomy is evident in the piece, as in those reliefs in which fully realistic figures are combined in formulas of a heraldic character. There is a striking stylistic contrast between the schematic, generalized upper part of the face and the almost portraitlike austere mouth; the barely suggested folds between the nose and the corners of the mouth produce the kind of expression that can only be taken from an individual. Perhaps it is the tension between likeness and symbol, exemplified by many protohistoric works, that is the source of their value and significance.

The works of the Jamdat Naṣr period considered so far, though some are superior in quality to those of the preceding period, must be regarded, from a stylistic point of view, as outgrowths of the Uruk VI-IV period. There are works of another style, however, that cannot be similarly explained as an evolution from Uruk VI-IV. Nor can these works — any more than the parallel manifestations in architecture — be dismissed with such terms as "poor quality" or "decadence," even though they include many examples of lesser quality, notably a group of cylinder and stamp seals with hastily executed ornamental representations. What these works may well be taken to indicate is a dissolution of the protohistoric style.

Providing a pendant to the female acrolith from Uruk is a female mask from the "Eye Temple" of Tell Brak (*Iraq*, IX, 1947, pl. 1). All realistic touches such as those in the head from Uruk have been avoided in that of Tell Brak in favor of deliberate abstraction. For the first time in the protohistoric period there appears in the depiction of the human figure itself, in this instance the face of a woman, a distortion of nature intended to express the spiritual essence of the subject. A new principle was coming to the fore in the art of the Jamdat Naṣr period; it signified the end of the golden age, but to it belonged the future.

An even clearer example of the new trend is a second stone head from Tell Brak, in which the parts of the face, especially forehead and eyes, are entirely out of proportion — doubtless because the head is that of a deity (ibid., pl. 2). Astonishingly like it in the formation of the eyes is a small fragmental stucco relief with the goddess Ishtar (Inanna), painted black, white, and red, from the archaic strata of the Ishtar Temple at Ashur (W. Andrae, *Die archaischen Ischtartempel in Assur*, Leipzig, 1922, pl. 28c). It presents the goddess frontally, in high relief. She is naked except for heavy jewelry at the neck, breast, and hips. The eyebrows are excessively large; the oval eyes, with their outer corners sharply sunk, almost cover the cheekbones, exactly as in the Tell Brak head.

Painting assumed a greater importance in the Jamdat Naṣr period, although it did not attain the rank of an art form in its own right. Adorning walls, vases, and reliefs, it served architecture, ceramics, and sculpture; it plainly also served as a substitute for other, probably more expensive techniques, such as that of cone mosaics.

It is interesting to observe with what faith and vigor all branches of protohistoric Sumerian art evolved from a central world view, from the idea of an all-creative, all-preserving, ever self-renewing life force existing in immediate relation to the godhead — from the myth of the royal shepherd chosen as the lover and spouse of the queen of heaven, Inanna. The protohistoric repertory of motifs at Uruk centers on the figure of Tammuz, who must die in order to save the goddess from the underworld demons of death. In him is embodied the profound idea that only at the cost and with the help of life can any higher life be preserved. To this idea the early Sumerians joyfully assented, because it held the seed of a higher organization of society and state. Such was the ideological origin of the first monumental temple architecture and of the body of art works that in reality existed solely in its service.

FIRST PERIOD OF TRANSITION AND MESILIM PERIOD. Already in the Jamdat Naṣr period, especially in the last phase of E-anna, architecture was revealing new traits that seemed to consign it to general formlessness — traits contemporaneous with the so-called "decadent style" in glyptics and the sudden appearance of stylization in sculpture. These manifestations point to a new direction, to the reconstruction, after a transitional phase during which all values were disintegrating, of a totally different Sumerian art world in the Mesilim period (ca. 2700–2600 B.C.), named "protodynastic" by some scholars, who take the term to include the Ur I period.

Architecture. In construction the *Patzen* and *Riemchen* typical of the protohistoric period gradually gave way to the so-called "plano-convex" brick, rounded on one of the two large sides. These bricks were laid aslant, alternate rows slanting in opposite directions, with a resulting zigzag pattern. The method of placing foundations also changed. In the protohistoric period temples were almost always erected on a leveled piece of ground; in the Mesilim period the walls were set in deep trenches. Perhaps dedicated to the same idea — fusion of the edifice with the earth — were the foundation figurines that made their appearance. These were pegs or nails with an anthropomorphous upper portion, generally placed at the four corners of the foundation. Their function may also have been to protect the building against subterranean demonic forces.

Another previously unfamiliar idea is expressed in the effort

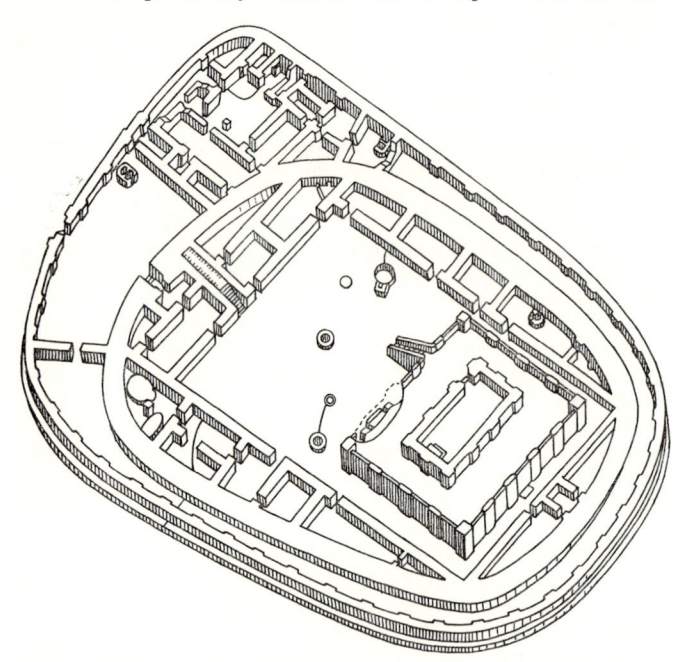

Khafaje, the "oval temple," axonometric reconstruction (*from Parrot, 1946, vol. I*).

to separate the temple as distinctly as possible from its secular surroundings. The entire "oval temple" of Khafaje (FIG. 747), which dates from the height of the Mesilim period, was erected over clean sand filled into an excavation 26 ft. deep. A usage that expresses a similar idea — and one that survived into the Neo-Babylonian era — was to encircle the foundation wall with a second one, the *kisu*, which looked like a thick retaining wall and delimited the building from its immediate surroundings.

Since, unfortunately, no informative remains of temple cellae have been preserved in the heart of the Sumerian territory, their development must be deduced from the well-known sanctuaries of Khafaje, Eshnunna (mod. Tell Asmar), and Tell Agrab, all somewhat peripherally situated in the Diyala region. The connection, difficult to establish, with the type of ground plan exemplified by the White Temple can be made with the least difficulty, comparatively speaking, for the earliest strata of the so-called "Temple of Sin" at Khafaje, which date back to the Jamdat Naṣr period (FIG. 747). But even here the rooms flanking the large central rectangle were already rather exiguous. The entrance, on one of the long sides and placed at a distance from the holy of holies, led to a kind of court of irregular shape. At first not clearly planned, the Temple of Sin in its sixth stratum acquired a definite shape. All the smaller rooms bordered a court, which a gate room and stairway separated from the outside world. The main room, so placed as to make the holy of holies the spot most difficult of access, even from the court, was preceded by an antecella. The freestanding, outward-facing edifice of the protohistoric period, which testified to the bond between the world of the gods and the world of men, became a residence of the god, in which he dwelt in cloistered seclusion, surrounded by those consecrated to his cult. A very similar development can be observed in the various ground plans of the temple of the god Abu at Eshnunna, where numerous superposed levels of construction have been uncovered. In many other Sumerian localities (Ashur, Mari), temples of the same type were built during the transition and the Mesilim period; they show only local divergences and no fundamentally new characteristics.

Today we know two sanctuaries from the Mesilim period, outwardly very different but each in its own way a product of the conceptions of the time and a monumental expression of them: the "oval temple" of Khafaje and the Shara Temple of Tell Agrab. In these sanctuaries not only has the sacred cella attained its new shape, but whole temple complexes with residences for the priests and administrative quarters have been brought into coherent form in accordance with a fixed plan. At Khafaje a "high temple" rose on a terrace 20 ft. in height, within a rectangular court (FIG. 747). The whole was surrounded at first by one oval enclosure wall, later by two. Between the two enclosures was built a priests' residence, akin in ground plan to a section of the great sanctuary at Tell Agrab. But whereas the "oval temple" of Khafaje still employed the rounded enclosure, characteristic during the transition to the Mesilim period, the Shara Temple adopted a nearly square one with buttresses; the wall, many feet thick, enclosed the various parts of the sanctuary according to a well-thought-out plan which joined together several rectangular court complexes.

The sanctuary of Tell Agrab, which attained full flower in the Mesilim period, reveals the end of a protracted development that the Sumerian temple had to undergo after the breakdown of the first great protohistoric civilization. If the separation between sacred and profane is observable in this development, it is not strange that during this period the first evidence of a purely secular state architecture appeared. The palace at Kish is the earliest monumental building that did not belong to a sanctuary. It comprises an older complex to the north, surrounded by a double enclosure, and a monumental gateway preceded by a flight of stairs and flanked by towers. The heart of the palace appears to have been a square court with rectan-

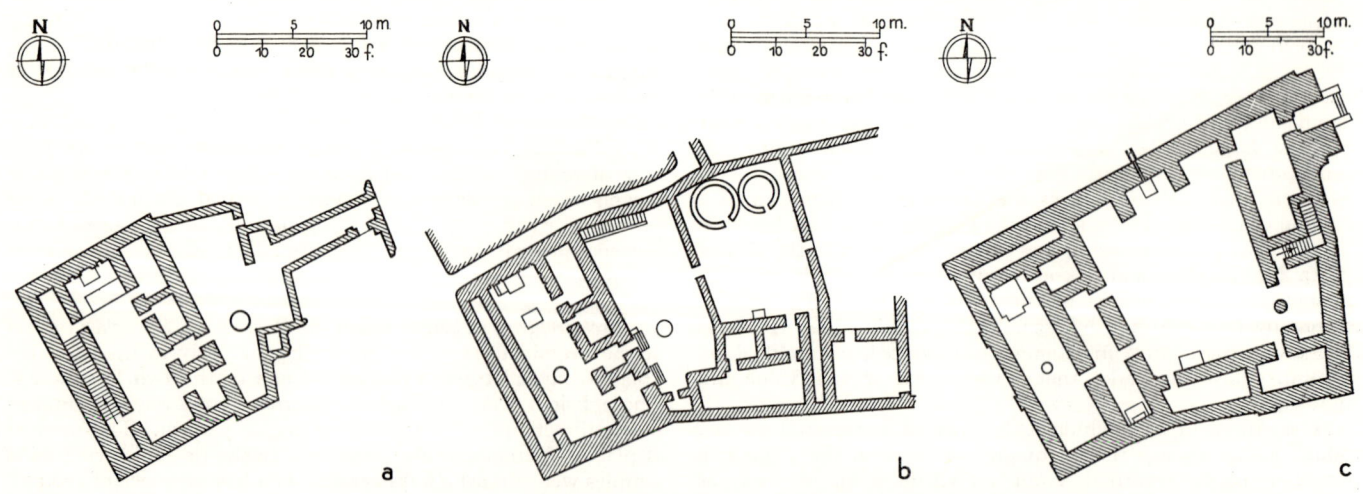

Khafaje, Temple of Sin, ground plans of three successive phases: (*a*) Level II, Jamdat Naṣr period; (*b*) level V, Jamdat Naṣr period; (*c*) level VIII, Mesilim period (*from Frankfort, 1954*).

gular rooms on the north, west, and south and smaller rooms, domestic quarters, on the east. A more recent structure to the south shows two long rectangular rooms in the west; a row of bases following the long axis of the larger room must have carried wooden columns to support the roof. In over-all plan this oldest nonreligious Sumerian edifice differs from everything that preceded it. It is fully turned inward and has many of the features of a fortress. An exact application of the right angle prevails. It is far different from the dissolution of form that had begun in the Jamdat Naṣr period and dominated the time of transition to the Mesilim period.

The first city walls probably began to be built at this time. That of Uruk, in its oldest form, consisted of a double enclosure about 6 miles long. In the Epic of Gilgamesh it is designated as the work of that hero and king of Uruk, who, in contrast to his predecessor Dumuzi, was an enemy of Inanna, the chief divinity of the city. Here too, then, is an expression of the dualism born in the Mesilim period and reflected in architecture by the tendency to separate temple and palace.

Figural Arts. a. Transition period. After all the old artistic principles were relinquished, a process that began in the Jamdat Naṣr period, Sumerian art did not succeed in creating new forms until the height of the Mesilim period. The period of transition was marked by a far-reaching tendency to disorder and confusion, of which the oldest relief from Lagash (mod. Telloh; PL. 467) is an example. The representation, in bas-relief, with an internal scratched design, is of a man in a cross-hatched skirt, presumably of netting, who stands in a posture of salute before two tall maces, symbols of the god Ningirsu. The schematism becomes apparent by comparison with works of the protohistoric period featuring the man in the net skirt: the disposition of the figure and objects in the pictorial field is planless; nor are the elements composing them brought into orderly relation with one another.

The character of the writing helps to place in the transition period a second work, a small stele with reliefs on all sides, probably from Larsa and now in the Metropolitan Museum (*BMMA*, Apr., 1960, fig. 5). It shows in several compartments scenes the encounter between two main figures, one male, the other female, each with followers and separated by an altar or the door of a temple. The women are depicted exactly like the principal female figure on the great alabaster vase from Uruk. The chief male figure, however, is clearly differentiated in posture and apparel from the man in the net skirt. He wears a skirt with a rolled belt and a broad tufted hem. His beard is long and pointed; his hands are folded together on his breast, the elbows jutting out sharply from the body. The skirts of the followers are vertically slit in front, with one side tucked up to allow freedom of movement; this male costume is encountered frequently in the Mesilim period.

The tendencies to a breakdown of forms in the transition period are most noticeable in glyptics. The drill technique applied in the abstractionist ornamental seals of the Jamdat Naṣr period (the group of the so-called "decadent style") continued in use; where animals and plants still occurred, they were broken down into lines and dots. The "seal-impression stratum" under the royal cemetery of Ur has yielded the most examples. Ornamental and figural elements were here used in the same manner; the picture surface no longer represented a space but merely constituted a vehicle for ornament. Signs similar to written characters, but no longer readable, were also employed.

b. Mesilim period. The more recent excavations have yielded a wealth of works of the Mesilim period. The Diyala region, especially, produced an abundant series of statuettes; but important material has also come from Kish, Lagash, Shuruppak, Nippur, Ur, and Mari, which proves that the new style embraced the whole area identified with Sumerian culture. True, the north, subject to a stronger Semitic influence, seems to show a quantitative and a qualitative superiority.

The period owes its name to an inscription, the oldest known, on a relief-decorated macehead that King Mesilim of Kish consecrated at Lagash (PL. 470). The powerful macehead, $7 \frac{1}{2}$ in. high, is decorated along its vertical face with a continuous frieze of lions with heads fullface, each leaping at the one before it. The relief covers nearly the entire vertical surface. The bodies are chiseled out in low relief; the manes, confined within the body outlines, are stylized into groups of short, curved, parallel scratched lines. The animal faces resemble masks with eyes and tongues that were inlaid and angular foreheads on which the ears are planted like handles. By comparison with the full-blooded lions of the preceding period, these appear rather like figments of the imagination. The same is true in even greater measure of the hybrid being depicted on the upper surface of the macehead, a lion-headed eagle presented frontally. The heraldic disposition of the outstretched wings and claws, the masklike lion's head, and the schematic stylization of the feathers endow this figure with the hitherto unknown character of a life-threatening, superior force.

A technique even better suited than bas-relief to convey the incorporeality striven for during this period was line engraving. One of the finest examples of it is to be seen on a bronze spearhead, likewise consecrated at Lagash by a king of Kish (Moortgat, 1935, pl. 15). To judge by its size, it must have been part of the standard of a deity. The rampant lion, engraved in outline with the slightest of interior designs, illustrates the classic Mesilim style. A motif taken from nature has been transformed into a symbol. Dematerialization could go no further, and no greater contrast with the compact, muscular lions of the Jamdat Naṣr period is conceivable.

In addition to the new types of animals and demons there appeared a new type of human figure, illustrated with particular clarity in the remains of inlaid mural friezes from the already mentioned palace of Kish. Among the representations are sheep in walking stance, music-making women, men probably engaged in milking, and warriors with prisoners. The technique of inlaid friezes is known from the Jamdat Naṣr period, but the Mesilim friezes, in which the light-yellow limestone contrasts with the dark surroundings, are different in effect from the works in high relief from Uruk: no appearance of plasticity is intended. Characteristic for the human figures are the meager legs, feet with exaggeratedly high instep, big noses, and long pointed beards.

A form not encountered before the Mesilim period is the square or rectangular stone plaque with a hole pierced in the middle (PL. 470). The function of such plaques is not clear, but they are an excellent source from which to study the development of the relief in this period, and their representations are fundamental to an understanding of a large portion of western Asian art. The central motif is the so-called "symposium" scene: an enthroned woman opposite a man, evidently of lower rank. Both hold drinking cups and often branches in their hands, and a big mixing jar generally stands between them. They are served by attendants and are frequently entertained by musicians and dancers. The second (and often the third) register depicts the bringing of gifts of all kinds and of sacrificial animals. One relief, from the Shara Temple at Tell Agrab (Frankfort, 1943, pl. 63), proves that this motif is connected with the second leading theme of the period, one already known from the protohistoric period: the combat of the hero with the beasts of prey.

That the two themes belong together is also demonstrated by several impressions of double-register cylinder seals of the time. Animal combats, however, furnished the dominant subject of Mesilim seals (PL. 496, second row, left). Many of these, in response to the impetus toward abstraction inherent in the endless ribbon of the cylinder seal, show rampant quadrupeds crossing each other to form the so-called "braided band." The impulse to denaturalization led even further. The trio of the hero subduing two lions underwent a process of abstraction and condensation into a human torso merging below with the bodies of two lions. The "hero" — or is it the upper portion of a bull-man? — grasps the tails of the lions. The component parts of the figures show similar tendencies to simplification: the bodies often become excessively long and stringy; the extremities are reduced to dashes; the face and hair of the "hero" in the fused trio are geometrized into ball ornaments.

Typical for sculpture in the round of the Mesilim period are the many praying figures of stone, one-third life-size at most, which stood in the temple cellae (PLS. 468, 469). They express the chasm between the divine and the human that can be bridged only by prayer and sacrifice. A striking illustration is found in the upward, god-seeking gaze of a bald priest from the hoard of sculptures discovered at level I of the so-called "square temple" dedicated to Abu at Eshnunna (mod. Tell Asmar; I, PL. 501). The two largest pieces by far, a man and a woman, occupy a position apart. In their tiny hands, which bear no relation to the size of the bodies, they hold small cups. Their oversized eyes have inlaid black pupils, likewise abnormally large. The excavator, H. Frankfort, thought the masculine figure was the god Abu, to whom the temple was consecrated. But since it shows none of the marks by which the god was habitually characterized (e.g., a horned cap), it is more probably the likeness of a prince or a high priest, whose function it was to represent the god at the ritual marriage celebrations.

Such worshiper statuettes have been found in many Sumerian cities. They include the whole personnel of the temple, from ministrant to high priest to ruler. Most are men, with long rectangular beards and wigs with a central part or, if they are of lower rank, with heads completely shorn. The clothing is the same as in the reliefs and intarsias: below the bare torso, a half-length skirt with a fringed hem. The hands are folded together on the breast and occasionally hold a cup. The eyeballs and pupils consist of inlays of a different material. The feet and the lower portion of the legs — with or without support, as stability dictates — are worked free from the stone. The elbows are swung sharply outward and pointed. The beard and wig are stylized in horizontal waves or zigzag lines. The hands are generally too small, sometimes altogether atrophied. The back is very often divided into two halves by a sharply etched line. Of this composite picture the innumerable statuettes offer many variants, with marked differences in quality. Common to all, however, is the tendency to stereometric construction.

A variant style is illustrated by a headless statuette from level IX of the Temple of Sin at Khafaje (PL. 468). The skirt is particularly elaborate. The lower portion consists of very long tufts that are deeply modeled, and the upper portion, of several rows of shorter tufts laid in a diamond pattern. At this time, apparently, the form of the skirt underwent a change that was later to gain special significance.

There seems to have been no desire to impart the strongly spiritual cast of the male figures to the statuettes and heads of women, which are generally inferior (PL. 468). The shape of the body in the female figures is concealed by a heavy robe that leaves uncovered only the right arm and shoulder. The fleshy faces under their elaborate crowns of braids appear soft and sensual; only the inlaid eyes look unearthly. Where the robes are overlaid with tufts arranged in rows of scales or scallops, the figures acquire a pleasing quality also present in male statuettes of the same type. In these figures, which doubtless belong to the end of the Mesilim period, there is a beginning of relaxation from the rigid constraints that prevailed in this era.

A group of sculptures from Mari (I, PL. 502; IV, PL. 16) shows that liberation from abstract schemes made considerable progress in the Mesilim period. The Ishtar Temple at Mari has yielded two sculptures bearing the oldest known Akkadian inscriptions; one of them, the seated figure of Ebih-il (I, PL. 503), paleography places in the Mesilim period. This sculpture proves that art was still dominated, as in the Jamdat Naṣr period, by the antinomy of abstraction and observation of nature. There is no purely stereometric treatment of any portion of the statuette. The only particulars that recall the stone worshipers previously described are the hands folded before the chest in a schematic pose and the lower arms that taper off too rapidly from the projecting elbows. All else forms a contrast to such works as those from Eshnunna (I, PL. 501): the soft modeling of the naked torso, as well as the free and natural rendering of the fleece of the skirt; the carefully stylized beard falling in vertical locks spaced by drill holes, as well as the quite normally proportioned skull and the natural-looking eyes inlaid in color. Stylistically inseparable from Ebih-il are two inscribed pieces of Ur-Nanshe (also called Ur-Nina) found in the temple of Ninnizaza at Mari: one a seated figure representing her praying (*Syria*, XXX, 1953, pl. 23), the other a fragment representing her as a harpist (ibid., fig. 9). The fragment in particular, with the harp held free in space, seems a defiance of the stonecutter's craft. But the better-preserved representation of the praying Ur-Nanshe, squatting cross-legged on a cushion — originally, no doubt, with hands folded — likewise conveys in its design the greatest ease and freedom of form.

Similar qualities are revealed by the few remains of contemporaneous bronze sculpture, such as the statuettes found at Khafaje and Tell Agrab, once parts of offering stands. The best examples show begirt, but otherwise naked, male figures, slender and fine-limbed, with hair and beard worn in the fashion of the period (PL. 475). They assume a walking stance, with the torso inclined slightly forward and the head slightly raised, the arms separated from the body, and the hands folded and thrust forward. The whole image, in harmony with the spirit of the Mesilim period, expresses beautifully the fervor of prayer and the humility of surrender to the deity.

A further example shows how toreutic art in this period achieved the liberation of the figure from the mass of the material. The bronze head of a bull in Berlin, one-half life-size, combines, quite in the spirit of the times, the ornamental stylization of natural forms with the attempt utterly to disengage the extremities from the raw material (Zervos, 1935, pl. 154). Mouth and nostrils are double volutes. The magnificently curved horns issue from a tubular extension of the forehead. In comparison with the bulls of the Jamdat Naṣr period, with horns lying along their heads, this work, with its soaring freedom, seems to have shed all cumbrous mass.

SECOND TRANSITION PERIOD AND PERIOD OF UR I. The epoch of the 1st dynasty of Ur (ca. 2500–2350 B.C.) is the first that falls under the full light of history, thanks to the numerous inscriptions of its kings and of the governing priests (*ensis*) of Lagash. The city of Ur now became the center of political and intellectual life. But between the Mesilim period and the Ur I period proper there must have been another period of uncertain length; so much is plain from the clay tablets and cylinder-seal impressions found especially at Fara, the ancient Shuruppak. The second transition period, however, cannot, like the first, have been one of general cultural upheaval. In architecture and monumental art it cannot be strictly delimited and must be regarded as a developmental phase that apparently left behind the ideals of the Mesilim period, yet did not beget any new formulations or ideas. Writing excepted, the only field in which a more precise subdivision is possible is glyptics. Here three phases can be distinguished, of which the first, that of Imdugud-Sukurru, corresponds to the transition period, the second is connected with the Royal Cemetery of Ur, and the third with the later governing priests of Lagash and the kings of the 1st dynasty of Ur.

Architecture. From the second half of the 3d millennium the temples of the Diyala region and of Uruk, Ur, and Ashur were continued, altered, or renewed; but nowhere do fundamentally new plans or forms occur. The plano-convex brick remained in use, where it had been previously employed, until shortly before the end of the Ur I period. Influences emanating from the west (square cella, baetulus) seem to have made themselves felt only at Mari, on the middle Euphrates, in several sanctuaries such as those of Ninnizaza and Ishtarat. Such manifestations, however, were altogether peripheral.

All in all, the types of building, ground plans, and architectural forms remained the same as in the Mesilim period. Only the disappearance of rounded forms — the "oval temple" of Khafaje was transformed into a rectangle — as well as of the plano-convex brick at the end of the period, suggests the relinquishment of certain features that had appeared after the Jamdat Naṣr period.

Figural Arts. In the protohistoric period god and nature were one. When such a unity could no longer be experienced, an effort was made in the Mesilim period to spiritualize nature through art. But the tension inherent in this effort was not one that could be maintained indefinitely. One day a reaction had to set in. Thus sculpture in the round became ever more blocklike; spiritual values, which in the Mesilim period had also dominated bas-relief, yielded to material values; gods turned into men.

a. Sculpture in the round. The praying figure, familiar from the Mesilim period, is also the most widespread type of representation in the succeeding period as well (PL. 474). The inscriptions on these figures indicate that they were supposed to worship the divinity in lieu of the subject and obtain prolongation of his life. In the many male and female seated figures there is apparent toward the end of the period a coarsening and a growing superficiality, despite occasionally good technique. At first, however, as in the statue of the priest Urkisalla from the Temple of Sin, level IX, at Khafaje (PL. 473), the unconstrained style of the Mesilim period continued to hold sway. Still Mesilimic in the geometrization of the naked torso and the separation of the arms from the body is an outstanding figure from Nintu Temple, level VI, at Khafaje, which, although it is quite free from the later blocklike massiveness, yet cannot be placed in the Mesilim period on account of its bald head and its skirt made of many rows of horizontal tufts, a type of garment that became characteristic after this period and remained so until the Akkadian era (Frankfort, 1943, frontis., pls. 19–20). The so-called "Consistorial Councilor" from Ashur (W. Andrae, *Die archaischen Ischtartempel in Assur*, Leipzig, 1922, pl. 30a) unfortunately lacks feet; otherwise this figure would probably give much the same impression. Its small hands and detached arms are still quite Mesilimic, but the fleshy face and the well-fed rounded body do not convey unworldliness. The mass of the heavy tufted skirt begins to dominate the over-all effect. A number of statuettes from Mari belong to the same phase. The transformation into blocklike shapes was not restricted to the lower portions of the body; the torso, too, with the arms cleaving to the sides, became a single unit.

From the period of the governing priests of Lagash, whose line began with Ur-Nina, comes the statuette of King Lamgi Mari of Mari, which, even though the feet in stepping position recall the Mesilim period, exemplifies the new style full-blown (Parrot, *Sumer*, 1961, fig. 145). The fleecy material of the skirt here also covers the left shoulder and arm, and only the right arm emerges from the mass of the stone block. Besides the costume of the Ur I period, there appears here for the first time the hair style of the kings, one magnificently represented by the gold wig from the grave of the younger Meskalam-dug in the Royal Cemetery of Ur (VI, PL. 243): hair parted and waved, a crown of braids held by a diadem, and a knot at the back of the head.

The culmination of the development toward ever blockier forms is illustrated by a diorite figure of Entemena excavated at Ur (*Baghdader Mitt.*, I, 1960, pl. 8, 1). The difficulty of working the stone surely explains, in part, the chunkiness of the figure, which seems to have remained embedded in its medium. The lower portion of the legs and the feet, in high relief — they are not worked free in back from the mass of the stone — are not even on the axis of the body. Clearly the two chief means employed in the Mesilim period to overcome the dead weight of matter — the geometrization of natural shapes and the disengagement of forms from the material — had been utterly relinquished. This marks the end of another epoch, for Entemena may be considered approximately contemporary with A-anni-padda of Ur, the second and last king of his dynasty.

b. Relief. In glyptics it can be well observed how the old motifs — especially the figured frieze, but also the "symposium" scene — were employed in art without the stimulus of new ideas, while figures of schematic aridness were slowly changed back into creatures of flesh and blood; plastic roundness, as far as possible, was brought to all that had been linear, symbolic contractions were rooted out, and the abstract organization of space was gradually loosened up.

The second transition period is represented in glyptics by the seal impressions from Shuruppak that are associated with a piece bearing the inscription of one Imdugud-Sukurru (E. Heinrich and W. Andrae, *Fara*, Berlin, 1931, pl. 44n). In this group men and animals have once more taken on a plastic corporeality; the lions' manes project jaggedly beyond the body outlines; the bison have acquired human faces. Even more exuberant are the animal forms on a big seal of King Meskalam-dug from a grave in the Royal Cemetery of Ur (C. L. Woolley, *Ur Excavations*, II, London, 1934, pl. 196, 55). Finally, we have the impressions from the time of the last governing priests of Lagash and of King Mes-anni-padda of Ur, among which there is a near identity of style. At the end of the Ur I period the artist became sufficiently bold to break up the frieze of intertwined figures and to group men and animals loosely by twos, threes, and fives. He also brought out the musculature of his creatures plastically, with a resulting discrepancy between the spiritual content of the figured frieze, meant to symbolize the cycle of life and death, and the individual figures, overflowing with life and unmistakably of this world. It is important to note that, for example, on one cylinder seal of this period (VA 3878; Moortgat, 1940, no. 144) a god of entirely human shape is presented with decided realism, only the horned cap distinguishing him from his worshipers. Characteristic for the whole history of ancient western Asia, anthropomorphism — the representation of the deity in purely human form — finds complete expression here. Deviations were to be infrequent and transitory.

Also human in aspect are two divinities, one leading the other by the hand, on a little engraved shell plaque from Ur (*AntJ*, V, 1925, pl. 32, 1). Clad in huge bell-shaped skirts, they are equal in girth to the massive figures of the ruling personages of the time. Similar little shell plaques adorn the sound boxes of lyres and harps from the Royal Cemetery of Ur (I, PL. 505). It seems as if even engraving, a technique particularly conducive to effects of immateriality, succumbed to the general striving after compact forms, which produced some of the best works of the period. The engraved silver vase of Entemena from Lagash (I, PL. 504), with its two friezes encircling shoulder and belly — above, a row of squatting oxen; below, lion-headed eagles soaring over lions and goats with heads turned — belongs with the best that exists in vase decoration. The designer succeeded in obtaining that effect dear to the Sumerians, the consecutive frieze returning upon itself, by repeating the motif of the lion-headed eagle above the animals. The difference from the style of the Mesilim period appears only in the individual figures, in the detailed internal design of the feathers and the lavish manes of the lions, which closely resemble those on the seals of Mes-kalam-dug.

The votive plaque with a central hole had been the chief vehicle of the relief in the Mesilim period. It continued to be used in the Ur I period, but what had been until then the most important theme, the "symposium" with a procession of gift bearers, disappeared with only few exceptions (a piece from the Diyala region, two fragments from Mari). Most of the preserved works — from Lagash, Ur, and Nippur — present enthroned gods receiving libations and sacrificial offerings (PL. 475). It is no longer the mystical union between man and the chthonian deity that comes to the fore; dominant now are the luminous gods of the pantheon, whose favor could be won only by constant prayer and sacrifice. The best example of the new type of votive plaque is a little limestone slab found at Ur in the Gig-par-ku (see below), near the sanctuary of the moon god Nannar (IV, PL. 204). The upper frieze carries a libation scene with three priestesses before the enthroned god (note the massiveness of his frame). The lower frieze probably depicts a libation before the temple at the presentation of the bride of the god. She alone in the procession turns her head toward the spectator; her frontal aspect duplicates that of the enthroned goddesses of the period. Here, too, the over-all effect is one of rusticity and squatness. The same applies to a plaque with the high priest Dudu, dating from the time of Entemena (PL. 475).

In this piece, which exactly reproduces the ponderous style of contemporaneous statuettes, the attempt at narrative has been given up; only isolated symbols are presented.

The votive plaques of Ur-Nina (I, PL. 502), the oldest *ensi* of Lagash, are mediocre in quality, but Ur-Nina introduced an otherwise hardly documented theme. On the so-called "family reliefs," in which he had himself portrayed with his wife, his children, and court officials, all identified by name through legends, he appears repeatedly as temple builder with a building basket, containing clay to mold bricks, on his head. The motif of the basket bearer was to have a certain importance in later art.

To De Sarzec's excavations at the beginning of the century we owe a historical and artistic monument that has remained the prime exemplar of the art of relief of its era: the Stele of the Vultures of Eannatum, the greatest *ensi* of Lagash (I, PL. 506). This monument, a sandstone plaque rounded at the top, was placed by Eannatum, in celebration of victory and as a warning, on the boundary between Lagash and Umma, after his god Ningirsu had won back a disputed piece of territory. All four sides were covered with reliefs, the intervening spaces being filled with extensive inscriptions. Only a part of the stele could be reconstructed out of many fragments. From both a pictorial and a literary point of view it is the first sizable composition that succeeded in at once articulating and unifying a comprehensive subject. The main theme, Ningirsu as triumphator, is presented on the obverse. His left hand holds his foes imprisoned in a net, like fish; his right, a club to beat in their heads. On the reverse we see, in the top register, Eannatum at the head of his phalanx of warriors, marching over the corpses of his slain enemies, also pictured in the rounded area above as being torn to pieces by vultures. In the register below he returns victorious from battle, followed by his men, while in the one next below he attends a ceremony of libation and animal sacrifice at the common grave of the fallen heroes. The lowest frieze, unfortunately poorly preserved, must have depicted a further campaign. The reverse, then, is concerned only with happenings in the world of men, while the obverse treats the conquest of Umma symbolically, as a divine action. The dualism of the later Sumerian world here fully reveals itself, even in the style. The bodily compactness of the individual figures, also observable in contemporaneous statuettes, is more pronounced on the reverse, for example in the naked priest of the burial scene. Mass scenes, doubtless in response to the temper of the times, are here for the first time a subject for art.

Unlike the historical stele, which made its first appearance with the fully evolved example just described, the work of art combining different materials played an important role from the earliest times. Many finds of the Ur I period belong to this category, which includes tools, friezes, and sculpture (PL. 471; I, PLS. 505, 509; VI, PL. 5). The pieces of frieze found at the foot of the ziggurat of al-'Ubaid (H. R. Hall and C. L. Woolley, *Ur Excavations*, I, Oxford, 1927, pls. 31–33) must have been linked with the temple of the goddess Ninkhursag that rose on top of it. Among the subjects are birds and cattle, carved in shell or limestone. One strip pictures two heifers coming out of a pen, to the right of which squatting men are milking cows, while to the left other men are busy straining milk and making butter. The light limestone figures rest on dark shale plaques, fastened on wood with bitumen and bordered along top and bottom with bronze strips. The kinship with the sheepfold scenes of the protohistoric period is evident. However, the strongly numinous character of the earlier representations has here become genrelike. The great goddess of life has become a landed proprietress.

The examples of inlay technique from the shaft graves of the Royal Cemetery of Ur are not works of art in their own right, but merely decorations for tools and furnishings. Nonetheless, they are of prime significance, for — like the shaft graves themselves, in which as many as thirty followers of the ruler would join him in death, as though fulfilling a natural condition of their own existence — they testify to the survival of the views on life and death evolved by Sumerian culture in the protohistoric era. The reliefs and sculptures of varicolored materials from the tombs preserve the protohistoric motifs linked with the tree of life and the man in the net skirt, not, however, in the spiritualized form characteristic of the Mesilim period, but with a vivid naturalism heightened by the colors. Animals, since protohistoric times the incarnation of chthonian and magical forces, here are depicted with human features. Indeed, in a reversal of all ideals, they are shown, on the sound box of an instrument, travestying the most sacred ritual, the great feast of the holy nuptials, with banqueting, music, and dancing (I, PL. 505). Death itself, in the guise of a lion, celebrates the feast of life, symbolized by the hero above, who embraces two oxen. These colored incrustations constitute an artistic climax — in their composition, uniting freedom with control, and in their truth to nature, which transcends all stylization.

Part of a piece of furniture was a pair of goats, each upstretched against a shrub (I, PL. 509). The core is carved of wood; the head and legs are gold-plated; the belly is covered with hammered silver plate; horns, beard, and mane are made of lapis lazuli; the coat is carved in shell, with the tufts stylized exactly as in the fleece garments of contemporaneous stone statuettes. The old symbol of life, the tree between feeding animals, has never appeared more joyous.

Finally, it is interesting to compare a gold and lapis-lazuli bull's head of the Ur I period (I, PL. 505) with one from the Mesilim period. Once the representation was a dematerialization of the worldly, an abstraction; now it shows the face of an individual animal sparkling with life, a naturalization of the transcendental, the supernatural drawn into the realm of tangible reality.

It is perhaps no accident that we have found the best examples of composite art where the tradition of the Inanna-Tammuz cult maintained itself with the greatest tenacity: on the one hand, near the temple of a goddess who must have been close in spirit to the Inanna of Uruk; on the other, in the royal tombs of Ur, necessarily connected with the idea of life and death.

AKKADIAN PERIOD. This period spans but two centuries (ca. 2350–2150 B.C.). It is the first in the history of Mesopotamia in which political and religious changes can be traced to the steady infiltration into the isolated Sumerian world of Semitic immigrants from the steppes. For this reason the absence of an unbroken sequence of monuments is particularly regrettable. True, the survival of earlier structures into the Akkadian period has been established at many sites, but of new edifices only very few have survived.

Architecture. Bricks of this period were generally rectangular or square slabs, measuring as much as $20\,^1/_2 \times 20\,^1/_2$ in.; foundations were built in trenches. From such details, however, little can be deduced about the character of a period. Of greater significance seems a transformation such as that undertaken in the ground plan of the ancient Abu Temple at Eshnunna (Tell Asmar). The cella of the so-called "single-shrine Abu Temple" was divided by a wall into cella and antecella. This layout was followed for centuries in the typical Babylonian cult edifice. If it had been possible to excavate the principal cities of the Akkadian empire — Sippar, the city of the sun god Shamash, and the unlocated Akkad, the city of the heavenly Ishtar (Inanna) — the architecture of this period might have revealed the same fundamental changes as are to be seen in fragments of large and small works of art. The plans of some buildings in outlying localities support the inference that, with the king's assumption of divine prerogatives, the palace acquired a greater importance than in Sumerian times, when the temple was dominant.

At Tell Brak the great Naram-Sin, the next to last Akkadian ruler, erected a powerful structure, 120 sq. yd. in area, where the "Eye Temple" had stood in the protohistoric period. The construction of a palace, at once royal stronghold and caravansary, on the sanctified ground of a temple was an enormity of a kind that only a god-king such as Narem-Sin could allow himself. Besides the main court, on the axis of which lay a mighty gate building, the nearly square enclosure, with walls 33 ft. thick, encircled three smaller court complexes. In comparison with the courts, the covered rooms must have taken up a relatively small area. Of the elevation and the interior fittings of the rooms nothing is preserved, but the compactness and clarity of disposition of the ground plan give us some insight into specifically Akkadian characteristics. That the importance of this imposing structure was not merely military and economic is suggested by its resemblance to the original layout of the so-called "Old Palace" at Ashur, which in this writer's view probably dates from the Akkadian period, since an Akkadian clay tablet was found in the foundation trenches, later covered over. This palace at Ashur seems never to have been completed; yet, as witness a number of fragments of basalt statues and a spearhead with an inscription of Manishtusu, the Akkadian rulers were active at Ashur, too.

Figural Arts. The remains of Akkadian figural art works are more numerous than those of architecture. There are a number of pieces securely dated by inscriptions, most of them, however, in a much-fragmented state. Their discovery was due not so much to systematic search as to chance: many were found at Susa, where they had been brought by the Elamites.

From Susa come the fragments of a victory stele of the great Sargon I, the founder of the Akkadian empire (VII, PL. 252). There is no sharp break between it and the reliefs of the Ur I period. It belongs in theme and composition in the immediate succession of the Stele of the Vultures of Eannatum; and if, as seems probable, a fragment representing the enemy imprisoned in a net is part of the Sargon stele, the continuity of the tradition receives further confirmation. Nonetheless, there are clear signs of new tendencies. Sargon, under a parasol, marches as overlord at the head of his fellow combatants; the warrior who slays the prisoners in the net is no god but Sargon himself, for the action takes place before an enthroned divinity, identifiable, by means of the barely preserved symbols on her shoulders, the maces, as warlike Ishtar; the tufts on the garments of the warriors and the goddess are shaped like tongues of flame and lack the internal design found in the Ur I period. These details indicate the altered position of the king in the state, as well as the Akkadian sculptor's rejection of stiff, lifeless forms.

A number of sculptures in the round from Mari, Lagash, and Susa may be grouped with the stele. Bearing a particular resemblance to the enthroned goddess on the stele is a seated goddess from Susa, in the same tufted garment (ibid., fig. 203). A praying figure carrying a sacrificial lamb recurs frequently, as in contemporaneous glyptics.

A limestone relief from Ur (Univ. of Pa., *Mus. J.*, XVIII, 1927, pp. 238, 240) is the most instructive piece of a group of inscribed fragments and sculptures belonging to the period of the sons of Sargon, Rimush and Manishtusu, and his daughter Enkheduanna, divine bride at Ur. The relief, which bears Enkheduanna's votive inscription on one side and a libation scene on the other, gives a conception of the relief technique, the composition, and the costume of the period. Enkheduanna's dress is a many-tiered flounced garment in which each tier consists of vertical tucks made by the incision of wavy parallel lines; on her head she wears the heavy bolsterlike diadem worn by the priestesses and goddesses of the Ur I period. Her two ministrants are a little smaller than she. Strict isocephaly, therefore, does not prevail. The wide spacing between the figures gives an effect of airiness.

Three heads of female statuettes can be stylistically connected with the relief: one from level G of the Ishtar Temple at Ashur (W. Andrea, *Das wiedererstandene Assur*, Leipzig, 1938, pl. 36d–e) and two from Ur (C. L. Woolley, *Ur Excavations*, IV, London, 1956, pl. 43 above). Of these last, one, an alabaster head with a heavy roll-shaped diadem, comes closest to Enkheduanna. The second, a little diorite head, was discovered in the Gig-par-ku at Ur. The inner greatness that it radiates in spite of the miniature scale speaks for its Akkadian origin, as does the entirely un-Sumerian physiognomy. The hair, caught up in back in a chignon, is held by a broad but flat diadem — a hairdress similar to that of the head from Ashur, which, however, is covered with a cap.

The fundamental difference between the Sumerian and the Akkadian worlds is well illustrated by the lower portion of a statue of Manishtusu — the upper part of the body and the head are missing — found at Susa (*Baghdader Mitt.*, I, 1960, pl. 9). This sculpture, for the first time in the history of western Asian art, is not a statuette but a life-size statue. The garment, worn approximately as it was earlier, is made of another fabric than the fleecy material customary in the Ur I period: a firm woollen stuff with a short fringe along the bottom edge and a tasseled border along the vertical edge. In contrast to the Sumerian tufted covering, which deformed the human body into a lifeless block, the fabric here drawn around the body in long slanting folds transforms the inert mass of stone, by the play of light and shadow, into an image of rippling movement which Sumerian sculpture never achieved and, indeed, never attempted.

Another life-size statue of Manishtusu (ibid., pl. 14), made of diorite, was found at Ashur in a stratigraphically undetermined position. Andrae, the excavator, favored attribution of it, as well as of the "Old Palace" at Ashur, to Hammurabi's great rival, Shamshi-Adad I; both style and costume, however, rule out such an attribution. This piece, too, is incomplete, but only the head, hands, and feet are missing. The fabric of the garment is very light, for where it is not draped (on the left arm and shoulder and on the back) it reveals the forms of the body, and the belt is less thick than usual. The disposition of the fabric duplicates that of the statue from Susa; the waves of folds are merely suggested but are essentially the same. The Ashur statue, instructive in that it shows the handling of the musculature, makes all Sumerian sculpture in the round appear schematic by contrast, even though the shoulderblades are treated like small round shields. There were several such statues at Ashur; another example is a torso reconstituted from innumerable fragments found there.

Only a few remains of sculpture in the round have survived from the time of Naram-Sin, the son of Manishtusu. They include the base of a statue from Susa, which shows only the feet, beautifully chiseled, excellent in technique (ibid., pl. 12, 2), and the fragment of a torso with a much-battered surface (ibid., pl. 13). How Naram-Sin was portrayed we learn reliably only from reliefs. On the fragment of a stele in Istanbul (Zervos, 1935, pl. 164) he appears in a long flounced garment like the one worn by Enkheduanna. The narrow pleats of the flounces are merely incised wavy lines. The fabric is so soft and supple that it reveals the curves of the breast. But for the beard and the inscription, the delicate right arm might be taken for that of a woman. Both wrists carry heavy bracelets. In each hand the king holds the haft of a weapon or scepter, unfortunately half broken off. The face is rather battered but shows, nonetheless, a striking resemblance, in all particulars of feature and complicated arrangement of hair and beard, to one of the most important Akkadian works of art, the life-size bronze head of a king brought to light at Nineveh (I, PL. 508). This head is a unique and magnificent testimony to the existence in the Akkadian period of a highly developed art of metal sculpture, sovereign in its mastery of a technique that ranged from hollow casting to the most delicate chiseling. Though not a portrait in our sense of the word, it yet brings before us the countenance of a prince from Sargon's great line of rulers and heroes. The name of this prince cannot be specified with certainty; some have identified him as Sargon himself; but, as already noted, the head (apart from the conical cap in the relief) can be matched feature for feature with the Istanbul relief of Naram-Sin.

A better-preserved stele of Naram-Sin, one more piece carried off to Susa by the Elamites, celebrates his victory over the Lulubaeans, an Iranian frontier tribe (I, PL. 507). It was erected at Sippar, the city of Shamash; whether the eight-pointed stars at the top are in any way connected with this fact is uncertain. The theme is otherwise the same as that of Eannatum's Stele of the Vultures (I, PL. 506). Whereas the Sargon stele retains the old subdivision into horizontal registers separated by strips, the Naram-Sin stele achieves a unified composition in which the movement of the individual figures is communicated to the whole; the victor storming upward and the enemy precipitated downward irresistibly draw along all the figures. The landscape, present here in the true sense for the first time, partakes of this dynamic composition. Four base lines, one above the other, rise in a wavy movement from left to right, carrying trees on the right and crowned by a steep conical hill. At the foot of it stands Naram-Sin, the divine hero with horned helmet, armed with ax and bow and arrow, far bigger than his fellow warriors, trampling his fallen opponents underfoot. He is the focus of the entire composition, from whom all else — the whole scheme — derives its stimulus and significance. A millennium and a half elapsed before similar effects were attempted in Assyrian mural relief.

The glyptic art of the Akkadian period underwent a stylistic development similar to that of the larger sculpture (PL. 496; VI, PL. 33). Although not one of the many Akkadian cylinder seals can be connected with Sargon, good examples survive from the time of his daughter Enkheduanna. The seal of her steward Adda (C. L. Woolley, *Ur Excavations*, II, London, 1934, pl. 212, no. 307) carries a frieze of figures entirely in the Sumerian tradition. Only the degree of modeling and a greater freedom in the composition, as well as certain details of dress, distinguish it from pieces of the Ur I period. The seal of Enkheduanna's scribe Kikudug, on the other hand, is characteristically Akkadian, with a very early example of the typically Akkadian species of cattle, the arna, a buffalo with long curved horns (L. Legrain, *Ur Exacavations*, III, London, 1936, pl. 31, no. 537). The difference in style of later Akkadian glyptics, of the time of Naram-Sin and Shargalisharri, can be seen in the seal of a scribe of the latter ruler, from the De Clercq Collection (Frankfort, 1939, pl. 17c). Over a broad strip, symbolizing a river between mountains, stand two powerful arnas, perfectly symmetrical and turned away from each other, their heads raised to drink from the overflowing vessels held out to them by two naked heroes, presented with head fullface, on bent knee. The space between the horns is occupied by an inscription in eight columns. A classic combination of picture and text, the image forms a decorative entity controlled, and yet not fettered, by the spatial restrictions of the Sumerian period.

There are also cylinder seals on which, as on the great victory stele of Naram-Sin, the figures are so distributed as to give a genuine effect of space. An example is a seal impression from Lagash, dated by the name Shargalisharri (E. de Sarzec, *Découvertes en Chaldée*, I, Paris 1884–1912, p. 282, fig. B). It represents the invocation by a shaman before an enthroned woman, "the beloved of the king," behind whom is a female servant. As the conifer set freely in the space suggests, the scene takes place in the open air. Only occasionally, however, in these small pictures can the movement of the composition compare with that of the Naram-Sin stele: in some hunting scenes, for example, in which the base lines move in large waves and men and women sweep across the pictorial field; one such piece is in Boston (Frankfort, 1939, fig. 36).

Glyptics help fill the gaps left by monumental art in our knowledge not only of form and composition but, even more important, of thematic content. Akkadian seals often show representations drawn from the myths of the great gods, whose deeds and whose trials were doubtless sung in contemporaneous epics. But since such texts are preserved only from later periods, few of the representations can be identified with known mythical episodes. That the seal cutters used such themes is surely due to the inherent importance rather than to the suitability of the scenes to the small format of the cylinder seal. Because of the lack of monuments, the question that naturally presents itself, whether the sculptor of large reliefs availed himself of the epic material, the seals being merely copies of the reliefs, cannot be answered yet. Some of the compositions on cylinder seals, at any rate, can easily be visualized on a monumental scale. On a lapis-lazuli cylinder seal about 1 in. high, excavated at Kish (Parrot, *Sumer*, 1961, fig. 204), the victorious combat of three gods against five others is pictured with such delicacy and spirit, such intrinsic magnitude that execution on a larger scale would seem more fitting. Were the monumental counterparts of such works known, it would be even clearer that Akkadian art, in both form and content, constituted the pinnacle of all ancient western Asian art.

GUTIAN AND NEO-SUMERIAN PERIOD. The empire of the Akkadian dynasty was overrun by savage tribes from the Iranian mountains, the Guti. They seized power in the north and from there tried, under various kings, to substantiate the claim to world dominion of the Akkadian empire. Archaeologically the reign of the Guti is still hardly known. A small group of cylinder seals from Eshnunna (Tell Asmar) that Frankfort attributes to them does not differ thematically from those of the Akkadian period, and the execution is so cursory that no characteristics of style can be deduced. Observing that the Ishtar Temple at Ashur has a quarrystone foundation in only one level, F, the excavator, Andrae, was led to suppose that this type of foundation was Gutian; but other stone foundations have been discovered since which surely date from other periods. New in the time of the Guti, however, is the replacement, among the offerings placed in the foundation, of the earlier "nail figurine" (see col. 747) by a kneeling god with four-horned crown who plants a peg in the ground (G. Contenau, *Les Antiquités orientales*, I, Paris, 1928–30, pl. 27, 1).

The Sumerian south, which was largely spared the devastations of the Guti, was the site of a political and cultural restoration linked to the pre-Akkadian period. During the Gutian dominion Lagash, the city of the god Ningirsu, seems to have grown into a cultural center under the priest-prince Ur-Bau and his son-in-law Gudea. After the expulsion of the Guti, Ur became the political head of the Neo-Sumerian world under the 3d dynasty of Ur. At this time, about 2000 B.C., new immigrants of western Semitic origin began to move into the country and gradually assumed power in a number of city-states, such as Mari, Ashur, Eshnunna, Larsa, Isin, and Babylon. The political end of the Sumerian period can be fixed about 1950 B.C., but art-historically it can be prolonged through certain strata by about a century.

Architecture. a. Temples of the gods. Characteristic for the building technique of this time was the more frequent use of baked bricks for the exterior of buildings — bricks of new dimensions and bearing inscriptions rather than stamps. Two new types of structure seem to have been created in the Neo-Sumerian period: the true ziggurat and the *Tieftempel* or "low temple" (one not elevated on a terrace or ziggurat), with a broad cella (a cella with entrance and altar on the long sides of the rectangle). Neither form has been found earlier; both were to have a long history. It is not possible to deal here with the mass of buildings erected in all Sumerian cities of any importance during the Neo-Sumerian period, which was one of great building activity, especially under Ur-Nammu, the first king of the 3d dynasty of Ur.

At Ur and Uruk are found the best examples of the ziggurat, the artificial substructure about 60–100 ft. high, with sloping or stepped exterior walls, which carried the *Hochtempel* or "high temple" dedicated to the current divinity of the city. The best-preserved ziggurat in Mesopotamia is that of the moon god Nannar at Ur, which owes its relatively good state to Ur-Nammu's having had a thick revetment of bricks laid around the core (I, FIG. 867; III, PL. 485). The four corners are oriented toward the four cardinal points. The revetment is articulated by niches and buttresses. The temple stood on the top stage and was probably reached by means of the straight central stairway; the lateral stairways joined the central one at the first stage.

It was likewise Ur-Nammu who erected upon previously existing terraces the ziggurat of Inanna at Uruk. It was a simpler structure than the ziggurat at Ur: a revetment of unbaked bricks, the outer walls articulated with buttresses but not stepped. Here the inner construction of the ziggurat can be studied more easily than at Ur. Between the layers of sundried bricks of the core, reed matting was inserted at regular intervals to equalize the structure; in the upper sections the matting was replaced by layers of reed straw. In addition, the core was pierced by horizontal channels containing reed ropes as thick as an arm, which doubtless served to anchor the outer walls, counteracting the pressure of the central masses of brick. Nearly square in base (each side ca. 184 ft.), the structure must have been about 46 ft. high, with over-all height of 120 ft. above the plain. Of the temple that crowned it, Loftus still saw some remnants in the mid-19th century.

It is not yet possible to say whether the artificially built-up ziggurat, as known from the time of Ur-Nammu, was the expression of a new religio-cultic idea or whether it was merely continuation of what had previously occurred automatically as temples underwent repeated reconstructions over the centuries: the raising of the main sanctuary on a high platform. Since Ur-Nammu erected the ziggurats of Ur, Uruk, Eridu, and other cities in the very places where the elevated terrace for the main temple had previously risen, it is natural to assume the existence of a religious tradition. If the assumption is correct, our knowledge of the ground plan and interior fittings of the early Sumerian "high temples" (the White Temple of Uruk, the temples of Eridu and Tell 'Uqair) may be correlated with Herodotus' description of the temple on the ziggurat in the late, already post-Babylonian period in Babylon, in order to gain some insight into the significance of the ziggurat. All the ruins mentioned show a temple with an inner chamber having along one of its short walls a kind of stage or podium, well suited by its dimensions to serve as a resting place; next to it, in the middle of the room, is a kind of offering table, made of bricks. According to Herodotus (I, 181), the temple on the ziggurat contained as prime requisites of the cult a bed and a table. He also states that the sacred marriage between Marduk and a selected woman took place in the temple. It would follow that the temple on the ziggurat, or at least one of its parts, was the *gigunu*, often mentioned in cuneiform texts as the place where the marriage was wont to take place; and this, in turn, would explain why, on the bricks employed in a ziggurat at Chuga Zanbil, near Susa, which an Elamite king had erected in the 2d millennium B.C., the *gigunu* is also mentioned as a part of the "high temple."

The second new element of Neo-Sumerian architecture, the broad cella of the "low temple," is illustrated at Ur by two excellent examples, of developed form, with an antecella. In the harbor area, in the southeastern portion of the city, King Bur-Sin (Amar-Sin) dedicated a small temple to the god Enki, in which the features of the new temple are characteristically embodied. The broad cella and the equally large antecella preceding it formed a rectangular central block lying on the main axis of the whole complex; the entrance to this central block, in the middle of one of the long sides of the antecella, was flanked by towers; a customary feature, a niche placed axially on the inner back wall of the cella and probably intended to harbor a representation of the enthroned divinity, has not been discovered here. A rectangular enclosure lined on three sides with connected rooms surrounded the central block, leaving space for a forecourt. An axially placed gate room connected this court with the exterior. The prevailing axiality was deliberate, as was the sequence of gate room, forecourt, antecella, and cella. That the goal of this sequence was the throne niche is proved by the use of the same fundamental scheme in other sanctuaries that otherwise differ in many particulars. The southern portion of the Gig-par-ku at Ur (the conventlike fortified building in which for thousands of years the daughters of kings lived as the consecrated brides of the god Nannar) formed a self-contained temple, of which the nucleus, a broad cella preceded by an antecella of the same proportions, was ringed by a whole complex of rooms. Here the passage through the enclosure was not axial to the niche of the cella but perpendicular to it; from the first forecourt, however, strict axiality prevailed.

b. *Royal temples and palaces.* At Eshnunna the same axial plan, but without antecella, is found in a temple that the governor of the city, Ituria, began for his divinized overlord, King Shu-Sin (Gimil-Sin) of Ur (FIG. 762, *A*). It has been suggested that the royal dwelling in the guise of a temple signified the exaltation of the king to the level of the gods. More likely, however, a reverse process took place: the gods became ever more human, living in grand edifices and surrounded by royal courts; access to them, regulated by court ceremonial, required the intercession of a divine patron. Such humaniza-tion of the gods explains why, from the Neo-Sumerian period onward, presentation to the deity became the central motif of art, relief as well as glyptic. The temple with a broad cella may well be taken as deriving from the idea of a divine audience.

It was a nondivinized prince, Ilushuilia, the son and successor of Ituria and a contemporary of Ibi-Sin of Ur, who built an annex (FIG. 762, *C*) next to the palace of the governors of Eshnunna, west of Shu-Sin's temple. This annex is an exact replica of the temple and must have served for the audiences granted by the prince to the petitioners solemnly brought into his presence. True, the walls are thinner, the rooms some-

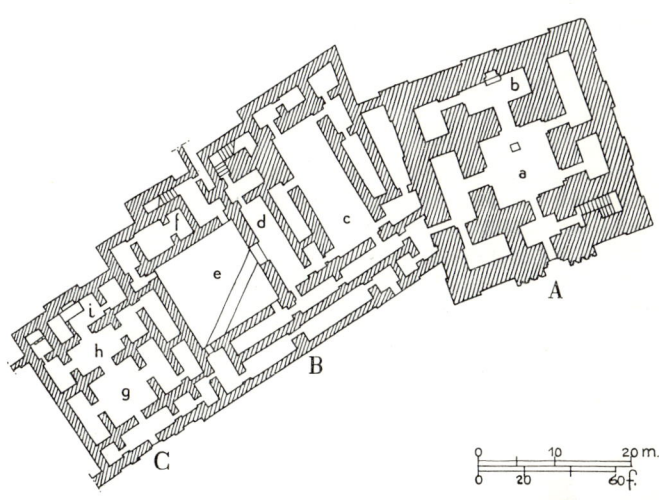

Eshnunna (mod. Tell Asmar), temple of Shu-Sin and the palace of the governors. (*A*) Temple of Shu-Sin: (*a*) court; (*b*) cella. (*B*) Palace of the governors: (*c*) great hall; (*d*) throne room; (*e*) court; (*f*) private rooms. (*C*) Audience building (?): (*g*) court; (*h*) antecella; (*i*) cella (*from Frankfort, 1954*).

what smaller. The difference between god and prince was apparently only one of degree.

The palace of the governors of Eshnunna is the only one of the Neo-Sumerian period that has become known, at least in ground plan (FIG. 762, *B*). Serving residential and administrative purposes, it included an oblong hall of stately proportions (*c*), with a door on the southwest leading to a court (*e*). Unlike the court of the audience annex, that of the palace proper was difficult to reach, being accessible only through a small gate room, long narrow vestibules, and a washroom.

c. *Funerary monuments.* The tombs of the kings of the 3d dynasty of Ur were built in large part of bricks carefully set in bitumen and are therefore relatively well preserved. Architecturally they are vastly superior to the shaft graves of the 1st dynasty of Ur, which are famous chiefly because of the discovery that they harbored the king's following as well as a wealth of offerings. The architectural value of the tomb lies chiefly in the structure erected aboveground, after the elimination of a provisional one, over the subterranean vaulted burial shafts. Excavation has brought to light unequivocal evidence that the underground shafts were opened after a given interval and emptied — not robbed — even before the house, or rather temple, of the dead was erected. The central structure of the 3d-dynasty tombs (VIII, FIG. 294, *k*), which is made of bricks bearing the stamp of King Shulgi (Dungi), is such a temple. However, it does not have the same form as other temples. Its ground plan, as well as that of the more modest annexes on the southeast and northwest, recalls a Babylonian house with central court. Rectangular rooms are disposed along the inner sides of the enclosing wall in such a way as to leave a court free in the middle; on the northwest side five rooms merge into an apartment; two rooms lay in an upper story (nos. 6 and 12; see *AntJ*, XI, 1931, pl. 45). Doors, jambs, and thresholds seem to have been inlaid with gold plate and lapis lazuli; several libation tables were covered with gold plate. The inclination to monumentality manifest in this funerary architecture, as in the architecture of the period generally, is characteristic for other late periods, too.

Figural Arts. a. Sculpture in the round. In sculpture the Neo-Sumerian period is represented by a wealth of examples. The numerous life-size statues of Gudea that De Sarzec found at Lagash (Telloh) toward the end of the 19th century made Sumerian art known to the modern world for the first time. Today the likenesses of the *ensi* of Lagash (PL. 472; I, PL. 511) are regarded no longer as an artistic climax but as a phase in a long development. In content they attain neither the spirituality of the best statuettes of the Mesilim period nor the warmth and life of the Ur I sculptures. They take over from Akkadian art dimensions and material, as well as the costume, with its natural treatment of folds. But a comparison with the fragmentary statue of Manishtusu (*Baghdader Mitt.*, I, 1960, pl. 9) shows that nothing of the inner restlessness and urge to action conveyed by it animates the diorite of Gudea's statues.

Like the artists under the 1st dynasty of Ur, the Neo-Sumerian sculptor sought to exploit the static gravity of the stone block. Hence, no doubt, the esteem for diorite as a medium for the large statues of Gudea, an esteem to which the inscription on statue B in the Louvre (A. Parrot, *Tello*, Paris, 1948, pl. 14c) testifies: "The statue is neither of silver nor of lapis lazuli, neither of copper nor of lead; nor yet has it been fashioned in bronze; it is of diorite . . . ." Hence, too, the striking massiveness of most Gudea statues, with the ponderous head resting almost neckless on the shoulders. In view of the obvious technical virtuosity, such characteristics can scarcely be attributed to the hardness of the stone. A statuette in Copenhagen dedicated to Geshtinanna (Zervos, 1935, pl. 199), though made of a soft stone, steatite, appears as foursquare as many of the other statues. It cannot be disputed, however, that in the course of three generations of *ensis* of Lagash a certain softening took place; witness the so-called "Woman with the Scarf" (PL. 478); or compare the statuette of Ur-Bau, Gudea's father-in-law (ibid., pl. 177), with that of Gudea's son Ur-Ningirsu (PL. 479), who must have been alive when the 3d dynasty of Ur came to power.

The extensive inscriptions that cover large portions of the Gudea statues replace the cartouches bearing the subject's name found on many older monuments. They enumerate the deeds accomplished for the gods by the prince, that in return the gods might grant him life. The sculptures must therefore be regarded not as mere likenesses but as magic substitutes for the worshiper, imbued, through the mouth-opening ceremony, with a life of their own. They bear names and require their own offerings in order to render perpetual service to the deity in their turn. This interpretation of Neo-Sumerian works may be extended both to earlier and to later votive sculpture, for the eternal life these statues solicited was always the goal of humankind in the ancient East.

Little has been preserved of the sculpture of the great kings of the 3d dynasty of Ur; even Shulgi, the mightiest of these kings, is represented only by fragments. In contrast to the much older pieces from Lagash, these remains reveal a predilection for details of dress arrangement and decoration. This deviant style is even more pronounced in some statuettes and statues from Mari, which differ from one another in details of apparel. While the statue of Ishtup-ilum (Frankfort, 1954, pl. 61a) comes closest to the statues of Gudea, the best example of this style is one of Puzur-Ishtar (PL. 485), identified as a contemporary of Ibi-Sin, the last king of the 3d dynasty of Ur; or it might be that of a god-king, Puzur-Ishtar's overlord perhaps, to whom he consecrated the statue. The decorative prominence given the fringes, the indication of arm and chest muscles, the folds of cloth on the upper left arm, all recall Akkadian art, but the execution is dry and schematic. The figure lacks the compactness of the Gudea statues but resembles them in its quadrangular structure.

The finest female statue of the Neo-Sumerian period might well be that of Eannatum (En-ana-tuma), the daughter of Ishme-Dagan of Isin, but erroneous restoration has led to misinterpretation (cf. *AntJ*, VI, 1926, pl. 52a, and Univ. of Pa., *Mus. J.*, XVIII, 1927, pp. 223–29). Better preserved are a number of statuettes from Lagash of female relatives of the *ensis* Gudea, Namakhni, and Urgar; the best piece of the series, however, is without inscription (Zervos, 1935, pls. 206–07). Artistically these pieces offer nothing new; but besides the altered costume they show a new physiognomic type, the male counterpart of which is found in some bald heads (PL. 477) that probably — especially the so-called "White Head" in Berlin — represent Gudea. Whether this type came to Mesopotamia with the Guti and to what ethnic element it belongs are questions still unanswered.

No large-scale bronze sculpture from the Neo-Sumerian period has been found. The only surviving bronze pieces are foundation figurines that continue the tradition of the genre, with the addition of some new types. From the period of Gudea come the kneeling god driving a big conical peg into the ground (Van Buren, 1931, figs. 10–13); the crouching calf on a nail (PL. 480); and, for the first time, the basket bearer as builder, standing on a nail (ibid., fig. 14). From the time of Ur-Nammu we have two variants of the basket bearer. The first variant, also produced under Ur-Ningirsu of Lagash, transforms the lower portion of the body into a conical nail (ibid., fig. 18). The second is completely anthropomorphous: a bald, beardless figure with naked torso and a long belted skirt, holding on its head with both hands a basket resting on a cushion (ibid., fig. 16).

b. Relief. The force of the cultural reaction that followed upon the fall of the dynasty of Sargon is demonstrated even more plainly in relief. Nothing remained of the Akkadian spirit. A considerable number of works from Lagash as well as from Ur itself have survived, most of them fragmentary, yet in a sufficiently good state to give us an idea of the types of relief and their artistic level. It is symptomatic that the vehicles of relief were once more the ancient, pre-Akkadian ones: stone cult vessels (PL. 481), votive plaques with central holes, and cult steles. Thematically the reliefs owe more to the state pantheon than to the gods of life and vegetation. The representations include cult ceremonies, with music and processions of sacrificial animals, and sometimes lower divinities, such as the animal attribute of the god Ningizzida, the patron of Gudea. Votive plaques bear the enthroned Ninsun, mother of Gilgamesh, no doubt receiving a petitioner (PL. 480), or the goddess Bau seated on Ningirsu's knees (A. Parrot, *Tello*, Paris, 1948, fig. 35g) — surely an episode from the feast of the sacred marriage. What is striking in every one of these works is a formal idiom completely without dynamism.

Though the apparel of men and gods is the same as in the Akkadian period, the rigidity with which the figures are bound to the abstract space symbolized by the pictorial field is Sumerian and pre-Akkadian. Men and gods have once more renounced their yearning toward the infinite. Like the Stele of the Vultures (I, PL. 506), the stele of Gudea in Berlin (Parrot, *Sumer*, 1961, fig. 284) and that of King Ur-Nammu in Philadelphia (ibid., figs. 279–82) are divided into several horizontal registers neatly separated by strips; thus once again events are subjected to the constraint of a fixed framework, as before the time of Naram-Sin. Such steles, probably the most important Neo-Sumerian works in relief, were aligned on pedestals in the courts of temples and had fundamentally the same religious function as the statues in the round of priestly rulers and kings. A subject of both steles is the presentation to the deity. The Berlin stele is very effective in the presentation of Gudea, bareheaded and clean-shaven, to the god Ea (Enki) by his tutelary god Ningizzida and a divine herald. The presentation to Nannar and Ningal of Ur-Nammu, wearing a beard and a cap with a brim — an indication of his rank — is the only scene on the Philadelphia stele sufficiently well preserved for continuity to be assured. The similarity of design in the two steles, especially in all details of the gods' apparel — the horned cap, for example — suggests provenance from the same workshop.

The theme of presentation to a god is treated in the same way on many cylinder seals of the period. Presentation to a god-king differs only in details. This ceremony, too, unrolls in broad cellae, where the rulers of the 3d dynasty, enthroned like gods, receive the petitioner with his tutelary deity.

In short, the Neo-Sumerian striving after monumentality took various forms: expansion of building activity, projection of towering ziggurats and mighty temple complexes, copious production of statuary. But this monumentality was not accompanied by a surge of new, creative ideas; nowhere is there a sign that a fresh world view was unfolding. The Neo-Sumerian period was not a classic peak but a late phase.

OLD BABYLONIAN PERIOD. Not long after the fall of Ibi-Sin, the last king of the 3d dynasty of Ur, Mesopotamia was swept by a new wave of western Semitic peoples whose personal names provide the only clue to their nationality and religion. In time the western dynasties came to power at Mari, Ashur, Isin, Eshnunna, and Babylon, bringing forth great rulers such as Shamshi-Adad I of Ashur and Hammurabi of Babylon (ca. 1728–1686 B.C.), after whose dynasty, which endured until about 1550 B.C., the period is named. Unfortunately the Old Babylonian stratum could not be excavated in Babylon itself, the ground-water level being too high, and we are obliged to fall back on other cities for information.

Architecture. a. Cult buildings. At Ishchali, in the Diyala region, excavators uncovered a large complex comprising three temples, of which the chief one must have been consecrated to the Ishtar of the city of Kiti (Ishtar-Kititum). The complex still existed at the time of Ibalpiel II of Eshnunna, a contemporary of Hammurabi, but had already passed through several stages of development during the rule of his three powerful predecessors. Its ground plan formed a rectangle of 262 × 164 ft. In the north and west stood the three temples, each with its own courtyard. In the southeast, on a somewhat lower level, lay a large forecourt that led through a tower-ornamented gateway to the court of the western main temple. A similar gateway gave access to this court from the south; it lay on the same axis as the temple itself, which rose at the opposite end of the court. This temple was virtually a replica of the one with broad cella and antecella previously encountered in the Neo-Sumerian period (see col. 761). On the exterior the antecella was furnished with towers, adorned with fluting. The second temple, which occupied the northeastern corner of the complex, was of the same type, but it lacked an antecella and did not have a gateway on the same axis as the holy of holies. The third temple presented a different aspect. With its rectangular court, it occupied the space between the other two temples on the north side of the complex. A gate flanked by fluted towers on the west side of the court here led not into a broad cella but into an oblong chamber with a deep, narrow niche in its west wall. This form of the cella, not thereafter encountered in Babylonia, may be traceable to western Semitic influences. It can hardly have played a part in the further development of the temple, for the broad cella remained the normal Babylonian form until the 6th century B.C. and at Uruk survived until the Seleucid epoch. Another example of the broad cella in the Old Babylonian period is to be found at Tell Harmal, a ruin in the vicinity of Baghdad.

An odd structure at Eshnunna, the so-called "Audience Hall of Naram-Sin," was dedicated to the cult of the king. It seems to have found no successor in the history of architecture.

b. Palaces. By far the most important architectural monument from this period is the palace at Mari, to which King Zimrilim made the last contributions and which was destroyed by Hammurabi (PL. 483). It is extremely well preserved. On excavation the walls still reached a height of 13–16 ft. Some of the places where the beams for the ceilings were let in could still be recognized.

The palace covered an area of 5–6 acres. The enclosing wall varied in thickness and followed an irregular course, at certain points presenting a fortresslike aspect. In the northwest corner it formed a bastion with casemates; in the southeast, it was rounded. The rooms had no windows; light penetrated through the very tall doorways. The walls were coated with clay or plaster and were richly adorned with paintings. The over-all layout clearly shows that, unlike the palace of Naram-Sin at Tell Brak, for example, this palace was not built according to a unified plan but attained its final shape by slow organic growth.

The design of the whole construction helps to explain the way of life and complex functions of royalty in the Old Babylonian period. Protected by the bastion in the northwest lay the apartment of the king, the supreme war lord, together with a smaller apartment for the queen and rooms for the retinue. Immediately to the south of the royal apartment were the rooms set apart for governmental and administrative purposes, among them some, on the order of schoolrooms and archives, where the scribes worked (PL. 483). In the southwest lay the storerooms; in the southeast, the workshops and other handicraft rooms. West of the workshops was a cluster of rooms that the excavators took to be the remains of a temple; they may also have been part of a funerary monument. The palace was linked with the outside world by a gate building to the northeast that included a gate room, a forecourt, and a caravansary.

The nucleus of the palace consisted of two big courts and the rooms that delimited them. The eastern trapezoid court, the more extensive in area, was connected with the forecourt of the complex through a wide room with nonaligned doors. This large court must have had a special, perhaps ritual, significance, for to the south of it lay one of the most unusual rooms of the palace (no. 132): a rectangular room oriented lengthwise and approached by a semicircular staircase, with a podium against the far short wall and a niche in the east wall, near the entrance. In it were found poorly preserved mural paintings in superposed registers, depicting sacrifices before enthroned deities. The second court (no. 106) could be penetrated only by detours, through a door in the north wall that lay along the north–south axis and permitted a view of the podium in the big transversally oriented room (no. 64) to the south of the court, where the king must have held his large audiences. The south wall of the court bore the most important extant painting of this period (I, PL. 513), the central panel of which represents a kind of investiture of a ruler. Behind what may be identified as the throne room (no. 64) was another court or room (no. 65), with an elevated broad cella to the east. In this part of the palace the conception of kingship must have attained its apotheosis.

Figural Arts. a. Sculpture. In sculpture as in architecture, Babylonia itself yields but little for this period. Information must be derived from finds in outlying areas: the results of the more recent excavations at Mari and Ishchali and especially the discovery in Elam of booty that Shutruk-Nakhunte carried off from Eshnunna and Sippar.

From Susa comes the famous stele inscribed with Hammurabi's legal code; many such steles were set up in the cities of his realm (PL. 486). The crown of the stele (I, PL. 512) consists of a relief in which the king stands before an enthroned god, probably Shamash, in the attitude of the worshiper. Everything in this relief belongs to the Sumero-Akkadian tradition: its inner spirit and the formulation of the theme, even the details, such as Hammurabi's coat, his cap with a border, and his beard, as well as the god's flounced garment and horned headgear and his throne in the form of a temple. The same motif is found on a cylinder seal in Berlin (VA 3330; Moortgat, 1940, pl. 40, 305).

A group of standing and seated statues, likewise from Susa, that are now in Paris (Louvre) bear subsequently added Elamite inscriptions in which they are designated as plunder from Eshnunna. One statue shows remains of the original inscription, which T. Jacobsen would fill out to the name of the *ensi* Ur-Ningizzida of Eshnunna. A seated statue from the same group, with a coat unadorned at the hem and an imposing rectangular beard, is related to the Hammurabi stele (*Baghdader Mitt.*, I, 1960, pl. 22). The clearly projected curving folds, like many iconographic details also noticeable in glyptics, indicate an attempt during this period, at least in some parts of Mesopotamia, to work in the Akkadian tradition.

Noteworthy is a diorite head from Susa in the Louvre, often referred to as "The Aging Hammurabi" (I, PL. 512). Although the cap with a border and the beard are Akkadian — compare the beard with that of the Akkadian bronze head (I, PL. 508) — the individuality and realism of the features are a contradiction of everything known of the Sumero-Akkadian and the later Babylonian-Assyrian mode of representing human beings. Neither the worn features nor the form and stylization of the beard are reconcilable with the known likeness of Hammurabi. Discovered at Susa, the head may be one of the many pieces of plunder found there and originating from the Sumero-Akkadian territory; but it could also be the image of a native Elamite prince. (The Elamites were the only people in the Sumero-Akkadian-Babylonian world who knew genuine portraiture.) Should the head be a Babylonian work after all, its subject might be the old Rim-Sin or his father Kudur-Mabuk, a possibility that suggests itself on account of their Elamite origin.

The life-size statue of the goddess that stood in a court of Zimrilim's palace at Mari as a kind of divine fountain combines grandeur with charm in the expression of the face, softness of sculptural form, and delicacy of surface design with freedom of attitude (PL. 485). Possibly the fragment of a group of two similar figures of uncertain origin in the Louvre is Old Babylonian and not, as has been suggested, Akkadian (*Encyclopédie photographique de l'art*, Paris, 1935, pls. 216–17). Not only is the idea the same as in the statue from Mari, but the neck ornament, with a long counterweight down the back, and the waves with fish on the dress are duplicated too. Also from Mari is the statue of Idi-ilum now in the Louvre (PL. 484).

Old Babylonian toreutic art is known through three unusual pieces. One, from Larsa, shows a genuflecting worshiper on a base decorated with reliefs (PL. 491). Face and hands are covered with gold foil. A votive inscription states that the statuette was dedicated by one Awil-Nannar to the god Amurru for the life of Hammurabi of Babylon. The piece is of value for its theme, because such praying figures did not occur in previous finds. The two other pieces, small bronzes from Ishchali, are even more peculiar. One is a god in a flounced dress, with a long scimitar in his right hand and a flat horned cap on his head, who steps with his left foot on a small crouching ram (IV, PL. 216). The other is a goddess ensconced on a simple stool. She wears a long gown crossed on her breast and holds a flowing vase in both hands (Parrot, *Sumer*, 1961, fig. 352). Her dress is incised with wavy parallel lines running up and down and probably symbolizing water. On her head she wears the same flat cap with horns as the god, but surmounted by a heavy cylinder carrying the design of a temple façade. The cylindrical headgear, characteristic of goddesses in the Syrian domain, here at Ishchali may be one of the motifs imported by the western Semites. What is strangest about the two figures is that each has four faces — a number not encountered elsewhere, even though Janus-faced representations are known, especially of Usumia, the minister of Ea.

b. Painting. The appearance of Sumero-Akkadian painting must be deduced from the motifs transposed to inlay work and vase painting, for only one example has survived: the painting on the podium of the temple of Tell 'Uqayr. From the Old Babylonian period, the palace of Zimrilim at Mari has preserved several types of painting. In many rooms there were remnants of ornamentation painted on plaster. In Room 64, tentatively identified as the throne room, the surface of the podium was treated to simulate marble slabs (A. Parrot, *Mission archéologique de Mari*, II, 2: *Le Palais*, Paris, 1958, pl. 15). Remains of a wooden framework or lattice originally hanging on a wall exemplify another type of plane art (ibid., pl. 3). The excavator, Parrot, assumes that the compartments of this lattice were covered with fabric. It is not certain whether the representations it bore were painted or woven.

The existence of tapestries with figural compositions is attested by the large investiture scene in Court 106 (I, PL. 513). In this painting a wide strip with a spiral pattern frames a field $8^1/_4 \times 5^3/_4$ ft. Two additional borders above and below unmistakably reproduce in stylized form the knotted-fringe tassels of a tapestry; the narrow smooth strips along the short sides copy the selvage. In short, the painting imitates a wall hanging. The organization of its field recalls that of the wooden lattice; the whole composition serves to bring into relief the central investiture scene and to underline its significance.

The less well-preserved murals of Room 132, reconstituted from many fragments to form five superposed registers with figures, seem to have been composed quite differently (ibid., pl. 17). The subjects include porters walking toward the right, a soldier struck by arrows (perhaps from a scene of combat), sacrifices before divinities (on two large bands), and servants carrying fish (on a smaller band). Two aspects of the composition are clearly established: the subdivision into registers and, in several instances, the lack of separation between two apparently unrelated scenes. A comparable want of transition is observable on Syrian seals of the Old Babylonian era and also on Babylonian seals of the period, in which the Neo-Sumerian presentation scene is accompanied by other motifs.

Even freer in composition seems a procession of servants and sacrificial animals, large fragments of which were preserved in Court 106 (PL. 482). The leader of the procession, probably the king himself, in a rich pleated garment with a belt and a double row of fringes, cuts across the two registers into which his followers are grouped; such overlapping, as far as we can tell, was avoided in the other wall paintings. The figures differ from the Babylonian type in their tall caps, short mustaches and beards, and sharp, somewhat pinched profiles. It cannot be determined as yet whether the differences among the wall paintings are attributable to differences in theme — a more or less hieratic content — or to differences in the date of execution.

None of the works that have survived from the Old Babylonian period — except the paintings, which are of particular significance — bespeak a breakthrough of new ideas. A return to Akkadian ideals was balanced by the presumable influences brought to bear by immigrant populations: Elamite influences in the portrait, western Semitic ones in certain architectural elements, in details of costume, and in the beginnings of greater narrative verve in glyptics and the popular art of terra-cotta reliefs.

MIDDLE BABYLONIAN (KASSITE) PERIOD. The Kassites, a mountain people who had threatened Babylon from the time of Samsuiluna, Hammurabi's son (17th cent. B.C.), found their path clear after the transient conquest of Babylon by the Hittite king Mursilis I (ca. 1550). None of the known architectural monuments of Kassite origin, however, dates back further than the 15th century; they continue until the 12th century, when Kassite domination ended. This period, regarded in the past as one of complete decadence, is gradually being revealed, both on a literary and on an artistic plane, as rich in original and fruitful departures. If documentation were not still relatively sparse, such departures would doubtless appear even more striking.

Architecture. Many ancient sanctuaries in the main cities were restored and altered in the Kassite period. One example is the great sanctuary of the moon god Nannar, at Ur, which was entirely in ruins when Kurigalzu I undertook its restoration at the beginning of the 14th century. Generally speaking, he did not make any fundamental changes. The only entirely new structure, and one that is difficult to interpret, seems to have been the Ningal Temple, to the southeast of the ziggurat. The E-dub-lal-makh, a very ancient sacred edifice on the southeastern side of the enclosure of the Nannar sanctuary, Kurigalzu renovated by using the remains of an older structure as the base for the new; this method of setting a temple on a podium is one that appears again among the Kassites. The ruins of E-dub-lal-makh were preserved to an extraordinary height. In one place a high doorway with a fully formed barrel vault was found still standing; this type of vault was presumably common in the Kassite period. It is difficult to make out from the tablets what purpose the edifice served, whether it was a sacred sheepfold with a gate or whether it was a hall of justice. At any rate, it seems to have undergone an unusually thorough transformation in the Kassite period.

Even more characteristic is a small temple in another ancient sanctuary: the Inanna Temple erected by King Karaindash in E-anna at Uruk as early as the end of the 15th century. Though modest in dimensions, this building, both by its ground plan and by its elevation, occupies a position apart. It was a rectangular structure oriented lengthwise; its southwest short side constituted the façade, in the center of which was the entrance gate. The oblong cella with a podium near the inner short wall was preceded by a pronaos and flanked by corridorlike rooms. The four corners of the building were reinforced by bastionlike double towers. Unlike earlier oblong cellae, which formed an integral part of a structure oriented inward toward a courtyard, this oblong temple stood free on all sides, comparable in the effectiveness of its exterior aspects to a Greek temple. The elevation can be reconstructed with considerable probability by reference to the façade, which had a high base of molded bricks forming a frieze of alternating mountain gods and water goddesses, all standing in niches and holding flowing vases (Frankfort, 1954, pl. 70a). This frieze must have encircled the whole structure.

Since Kassite architecture was able to leave its impress at Ur and Uruk, centers of Sumerian tradition, it is not surprising that it should have done so to an even greater degree in places founded by the Kassites themselves. An entirely new conception of this architecture may be gained from the preliminary results of excavations undertaken during World War II at Dur Kurigalzu (mod. 'Aqar Quf), northwest of Baghdad. Kurigalzu I had a new residence erected there, which stood until the late Kassite period (12th cent.). What makes the ruins an attraction to all visitors to Baghdad — the stump of a ziggurat still rising to a height of more than 100 ft. — is not a typical Kassite monument, but one that belongs in the mainstream of Sumero-Babylonian development. However, the temple complex connected with the ziggurat and the palace lying farther to the northwest are characteristic of Kassite architecture. The nucleus of the temple complex seems to have been a rectangular block of sun-dried bricks, the top of which could be reached by a stairway at the northeast corner. Probably the temple itself stood on the block, in the same way as E-dub-lal-makh rose on the remains of an older structure; for Mound A at 'Aqar Quf has yielded a similar block, upon which the outline of the superstructure is still preserved. Close to the block of sun-dried bricks lie several court complexes with nearly square enclosures, in which rooms and doorways, but no cult rooms, are preserved. Between the block and the enclosures, only a very narrow passage was left free — an innovation in plan that, because of the incomplete results of the excavations, cannot as yet be explained.

A new kind of plan is also shown by the palace of Dur Kurigalzu, a little over half a mile from the temple, on Tell Abiad. The structures comprise a central court complex (A), a garland of smaller complexes adjoined all around (B-G), and a later annex (H). The annex differs from the other groups of buildings in that it has many doors in the walls of the court; it must have been built during the very last phase of Kassite dominion, for it lies on a considerably higher level than the remainder of the palace, which subsisted from the time of Kurigalzu I (1380) until that of Mardukapaliddina I (1176–1164). The nucleus of the palace is a square court with one side adjoining a block of sun-dried bricks, which, once again, may be the terrace of a building as yet unexcavated. The groups of rooms on the other three sides are all of the same type. In each instance smaller rooms surround a central rectangular one that must have overtopped them to permit the entrance of light, for the few doors leading from the big court into the smaller rooms could not have admitted enough. The walls are of enormous thickness. To the north and east of the central court complex staircases probably led to the towerlike bastions. The smaller complexes have no wall in common with the central room; the delimiting walls are always clearly separated by a groove.

Kassite architecture, then, although still far from adequately known, reveals a number of characteristic traits, the discovery of which has invalidated the former view that the period was one of stagnation for Babylonia.

Figural Arts. a. Architectural sculpture. This art form in particular must have undergone a signal development in the Kassite period: so much is clear even from the little that has survived. The wall relief composed of molded bricks pressed from a form and then baked must have been widespread. Molded bricks were found at Dur Kurigalzu; at Ur, Woolley came upon something similar in the E-nun-makh of the Kassite period. The best-preserved example, however, is the previously mentioned façade of the Innana Temple at Uruk. The alternating mountain gods and water goddesses, all seen frontally and connected by the stream of the water of life, are perhaps a translation into brick of the stone orthostat with reliefs typical of the architecture of the other mountain peoples. Be that as it may, the frieze of molded-brick reliefs presents a contrast to all that came before. Not an outer layer concealing structure, but true architectural sculpture, it employs structural elements — bricks — with an effect of supporting the building and holding it together.

b. Wall painting. The remains of Kassite wall painting in the palace of Dur Kurigalzu are of two kinds: ornamental patterns, of which scanty remnants were discovered in the older portions of the palace, and figural compositions that imitate wall hangings, as from time immemorial in western Asia. Peculiarly Kassite features are to be sought, perhaps, in the position of the paintings and in the choice of subjects. Rows of striding functionaries or officers depicted on long rectangular fields in ornamental frames decorate the very thick jambs of the doorways, the painting reaching around corners as if to mask the sharp edges, like tapestry (*Iraq*, VIII, 1946, figs. 4–7). The paintings do not reproduce any myth or, it would seem, any religious rite, but record activities once of common occurrence in the rooms where they are found: the coming and going of officials in the fulfillment of their ceremonial duties. With their big heads set almost neckless on their broad shoulders, the figures present a sharp contrast to the elongated ones of the early Kassite period. The evolution from overslender to stocky can be observed over and over in Kassite art, for example, in the stone reliefs of the typically Kassite *kudurru* (boundary stone) and in glyptic art. Although this trend toward the thickset figures of the late Kassite period is surely significant from the point of view of stylistic development, it may also be an indication that the Aramaean element, after steadily gaining ground in Babylonia, was coming into its own.

c. Sculpture in the round. Kassite sculpture in the round was unknown before the discovery of some diorite fragments in the main court of the temple complex at Dur Kurigalzu. Among these was a well-modeled life-size foot, perhaps part of a statue of Kurigalzu, whose name occurs in inscriptions on the fragments. The head of such a statue may perhaps be conceived on the model of a masculine terra-cotta head (ibid., fig. 9) whose expression recalls that of the officials in the palace of Dur Kurigalzu. This technically remarkable piece is partly hollow, partly solid. The eyes are covered with a layer of white stucco, which was probably painted. Hair and beard were painted black. Another piece which appears to be unique, a terra-cotta hyena, is fashioned with striking skill and expressiveness (ibid., fig. 14).

d. Relief. Kassite stone reliefs are best known through the *kudurrus*, on which the king published by word and picture his tax-free gifts of land to individuals and to temples (PL. 486). The examples of greatest importance for the history of art were discovered at Susa, where, like so many other monuments, they had been brought as plunder. Those with extensive reliefs all date from the late Kassite period, a large number from the time of King Melishipak II, who reigned in the early 12th century (II, PL. 20; IV, PL. 203).

A *kudurru* of Melishipak from Susa provides an example of the pure stele form (*Encyclopédie photographique de l'art*, Paris, 1936, pl. 265). It is a stone slab rounded on top, with text on the principal face and the narrow sides. The reverse bears symbols of the gods, not all of them interpretable. In the top register are the lunar sickle, the solar disk, and the star of Venus — the symbols of the three most important celestial bodies: Sin, Shamash, and Ishtar. Below, in the same register, lie the symbols of the three highest Babylonian divinities next to or upon temple-shaped thrones: the horned cap (Anu or Enlil), the ram's head and the goatfish (Ea), and the double volute (Ninmakh). In the register underneath are the symbols of several war gods, followed, in the next register, by those of the younger generation of the gods: a *mushkhush* (or *mushrusshu*, a horned dragon) with a hatchet (Marduk), a *mushkhush* with a tablet and stylus (Nabu), and a dog with a woman's bust (the goddess of health, Gula). Next below we find lightning (Adad), the plow of a god of vegetation, and the lamp of the god of light (Nusku); and, in the lowest register, a shell, a scorpion, and a horned snake, all three doubtless symbols of gods of the underworld. The order followed on this *kudurru* reflects the naïve conception of a cosmos stratified from highest heaven to nether regions. The entire divine hierarchy is here summoned to protect the document. Since the gods are represented only by abstract signs or by their animal attributes — probably symbolizing their vanquished enemies — it is possible that the Kassites felt a repugnance toward the anthropomorphization of divinities.

If such a repugnance existed, however, it was not absolute, as other *kudurrus* of Melishipak demonstrate. On one of them (IV, PL. 203), the record of a gift of land by the king to his daughter, Melishipak is presenting her as a priestess to the goddess Nana (Inanna-Ishtar). Of the symbols of the gods, ordinarily so numerous, there remains only the constellation of Sin, Shamash, and Ishtar. The goddess is shown enthroned. Her garment, somewhat different from the old flounced dress, is made of bands winding aslant around the body. Instead of the horned cap she wears the feather crown customary during the Kassite period. The king appears in a simple belted robe with straps crossing on his chest and a semihigh polos on his head. His daughter carries a harp. All three participants in this ritual scene are stocky, recalling the late Kassite figures in the palace of Dur Kurigalzu.

Other *kudurrus* of Melishipak, employing mythological motifs, are set apart by their design and shape. The base is nearly rectangular. The lower part simulates a fortress with towers at the corners connected by walls, on which the text is generally inscribed; the gods and their symbols often appear on the truncated pyramid above the fortress. The most interesting example of this type, one with an incomplete inscription, comes from Susa and is probably also attributable to Melishipak (ibid., pls. 266–67). Like most of the *kudurrus*, it is crowned by a ringed snake, here surmounted by a crouching bull; at the bottom a second powerful snake supports the fortress. Two friezes of reliefs, one over the other, unroll between the towers and the upper snake. The first is filled with the already familiar symbols of the gods, of which some also appear immediately above the battlements. The second differs from everything else so far known in western Asia. A solemn procession of men marches toward the right, each playing a lute and followed by an animal — a lion, a panther, a goat or a ram, an ostrich. On their heads they have pointed helmets, in some instances bordered with horns, and they wear short skirts with belts hanging down between their legs; on their backs they carry bow and quiver. At the end comes a woman, also carrying a bow and a quiver, who beats a cymbal and dances.

Although the sculptural technique, in a strict sense, is not of the highest quality, it must be conceded that in these reliefs Kassite art attains a spiritual zenith. A "canonization" of the literary heritage — a selection and ordering of epic literature according to ethical criteria — is known to have taken place in the late Kassite period. The same world-ordering spirit is perceptible in the *kudurru* just described. It is a symbolic representation of the cosmos, in which the fortress of the gods bridges the space between the heavenly bull and the chthonian snake, and the two friezes that surmount it evoke the victory over chaos of the luminous gods of light, represented by their symbols, and the subjection of the wild beasts through the power of music.

e. Glyptics. Middle Babylonian glyptic art could not have come into being through the mere preservation of depleted Old Babylonian motifs and compositional schemes. The engravers who produced the cylinder seals in Babylonia from the end of Hammurabi's dynasty until the so-called "2d dynasty of Isin" undoubtedly contributed ideas and formal devices of their own; indeed they brought about a relatively swift and lively development of glyptic style from the 16th to the 14th century. In the period of kings Kurigalzu I and Burnaburiash II most seals (PL. 496) bore a long inscription, a prayer or an invocation to the gods, and a single praying figure of the same exaggerated slenderness as other early Kassite figures, such as the mountain and water divinities of the small temple of Karaindash at Uruk. In time the figures became as heavy-set as those in the late wall paintings of Dur Kurigalzu.

Although at first Kassite glyptic art drew on the past, initiating nothing new, in the 14th century, during the reigns of kings Kurigalzu II and Nazimaruttash II, contemporaries of the great Middle Assyrian kings Ashuruballit I and Adadnirari I, it produced some pieces that are among the supreme examples of western Asian art. It is open to question whether seal engraving could have reached such heights in Babylon without the aid and inspiration of Middle Assyrian glyptics, especially as the themes of these Babylonian pieces center on the tree of life and favor the motifs of a chthonian faith, otherwise restricted in the 2d millennium to the mountain peoples, particularly in the Hurro-Mitannian and Assyrian domain. By a particular stroke of luck these seals are dated with exactitude: their impressions appear on business documents of the old cult capital of Nippur.

OLD AND MIDDLE ASSYRIAN PERIOD. In the 3d millennium B.C. Assyria was culturally a Sumero-Akkadian province. Yet in the first half of the 2d millennium it was the Assyrian people who resisted longest and most vehemently against absorption by the western Semites, and under the dynasty of Ilushuma and Irishum I Assyria seems to have sought independence from the south in cultural matters as well. Not only did the princes of Ashur found their own agencies in Anatolian cities for the delivery of indispensable raw materials; but in these cities of metics the inhabitants recognized Assyrian law, swore by the sword of the god Ashur, knew only the Assyrian calendar and the Assyrian reckoning of years after limmus — officials whose names were given to the years of their magistracy — and they employed a special cuneiform writing and a special Assyrian orthography. Unfortunately not enough of the art and architecture of this period has been recovered to permit definition of Assyrian characteristics. Even in glyptics such an attempt is unsuccessful, although there are numerous cylinder seals and seal impressions on clay tablets from Kültepe (anc. Kanesh) in Anatolia.

When Assyria, too, finally succumbed to the pressure of the western Semites and under the leadership of Hammurabi's great rival, Shamshi-Adad I, became a center of the western Semitic world, one of the effects must have been a great stimulus to art and architecture. Yet almost nothing of significance exists. Only the stele from Mardin in the Louvre (*Rev. d'Assyriologie*, VII, 1910, pl. 5), depicting a triumphant ruler with his foot on a vanquished foe, can be linked with Shamshi-Adad. It is unlikely that Hammurabi in Babylonia would ever have chosen this subject to adorn a stele; Shamshi-Adad in Assyria was able to do so by a direct reversion to Akkadian art. Between the death of Shamshi-Adad and the renewal of Assyrian power under Eriba-Adad I in the first half of the 14th century there elapsed at least three and a half centuries, a period of dependence on the Hurrians and their ruling caste, the Indo-European Mitanni.

Architecture. A number of indications point to a complete transformation of Assyrian architecture and art during this period. The double temple of Sin and Shamash at Ashur, according to the earliest record, dates back to Ashurnirari I. Its ground plan forms an elongated rectangle. In the middle of the monumental northwest side was the gate, flanked by symmetrically stepped-back towers. It led into a large central court, approximately square in shape. The two shrines, which faced each other on the southwest and northeast of the court, consisted of a broad antecella and an oblong cella, a layout typical for all subsequent Assyrian temples. It is not certain whether this plan is truly Assyrian or of Hurro-Mitannian origin, because too little is known about the art and architecture of the Hurro-Mitannian empire at its center and in the period of its greatest flowering. Yet Hurrian architecture must have left its imprint in Assyria. The main hall or court of the palace at Alalakh (mod. Tell Atchana), as rebuilt by Niqmepa in the 15th century, was oriented widthwise. It had a door on one long side and contained a hearth. With some smaller subsidiary rooms it formed the heart of the palace. Such a pattern was to be followed in all Assyrian palaces from the 9th century onward. At Til Barsip (mod. Tell Ahmar), for example, a similar group of rooms formed the core of the residential portion of the palace.

Subsequently, in the 13th century, during the great era of political equilibrium in the western Asian, Egyptian, and Mediterranean orbit, Assyria, under the three great rulers Adadnirari I, Shalmaneser I, and Tukulti-Ninurta I, not only entered into its Hurro-Mitannian heritage in the political realm but succeeded in giving fitting expression to its might in art and architecture. Just as the Sin-Shamash Temple of Ashurnirari I at Ashur revealed a new, specifically Assyrian type of cult building, so the palaces uncovered at Ashur shed light on the beginnings in Assyria of a type of secular edifice that, as an expression of the Assyrian conception of kingship, was almost more important in the next centuries than the temple. The remains of stone foundations belonging to one royal palace most likely date back to Adadnirari I (early 13th cent.). This palace differs from an older one on the same site particularly in that the various court complexes of which it was composed were no longer set into a predetermined regular enclosure, but were joined together at right angles and surrounded by a completely irregular, many-cornered enclosure; the court complex containing the gate and that containing the living quarters constituted separate compartments. Adadnirari seems to have been the first to build this type of palace, which was to remain characteristic throughout Assyrian history.

Adadnirari's grandson, Tukulti-Ninurta I, was a great builder and, like his Babylonian-Kassite contemporaries, transferred his residence from the capital to a city founded by himself, Kar-Tukulti-Ninurta. The results of excavations, however, leave too many gaps to permit a coherent reconstruction of his activities. Remarkable is the Ashur Temple at Kar-Tukulti-Ninurta, a "low temple" with a broad cella leading into a square court and immediately adjoining a ziggurat. By what means the ziggurat was ascended is uncertain.

The remains of Middle Assyrian architecture, fragmentary as they are, show plainly that by the 13th century Assyria had become a culturally independent power in western Asia, in spite of all the bonds of tradition with Sumero-Akkadian and Hurro-Mitannian forms and ideas.

Figural Arts. Art, too, underwent a complete transformation in Assyria between 1500 and 1200, a period in which the formal basis was laid for the monumental wall reliefs of the great royal palaces of the 9th century. The process of transformation can be followed only by a laborious study of the early evolution of the various artistic handicrafts, especially glyptics. Examples of large sculpture in the round and large stone reliefs are very sparse (PL. 487). The most important pieces of applied art, which give us some idea of Assyrian design and relief, come from the large grave No. 14630 at Ashur. Particularly important are two alabaster vases, one with a representation of a half-naked goddess presented fullface, who may continue a Hurrian tradition, the other with a representation of a tree between two bulls (A. Haller, *Die Gräber und Grüfte von Assur*, Berlin, 1954, pl. 32a–b). Comparable to the first vase is the bone statuette of a half-divested goddess from Nuzi (mod. Yorgan Tepe), which in turn reveals a kinship with representations on Syrian seals (e.g., the coat with what looks like a rolled scarf wound several times around the waist) and might therefore be Hurrian (R. F. S. Starr, *Nuzi*, II, Cambridge, Mass., 1937, pl. 101*i*). The palmette tree on the other vase has its parallel in the seals called "Kirkuk tablets," likewise of Hurrian origin. The trees on an ivory pyxis from grave No. 14630 (Haller, op. cit., pl. 29) can be compared with shards of late Nuzi pottery. The form of the alabaster vases is related to Egyptian pieces of the Tell el 'Amarna period.

What the Sin-Shamash Temple of Ashurnirari and the palace of Adadnirari I at Ashur have done for Assyrian architecture — namely, to supply proof that Assyria had sloughed off foreign cultural domination — the 14th-century alabaster and ivory offerings from grave No. 14630 have done for art. Confirmation has come from seal impressions, dated by the inscriptions of the first great independent Assyrian kings, Eriba-Adad I and Ashuruballit I. These show how Assyrian stone engravers drew on a fund of inherited motifs to create strictly ordered forms of their own. In the 14th century, they took a still further step forward, devising a free and natural idiom, which in the 13th century carried Assyrian glyptics to heights not attained since the Akkadian period (PL. 496).

Works of large format comparable in quality to the best examples of seal engraving are unfortunately not preserved. As certain reliefs demonstrate, however, monumental art must have reached a high level in the reign of Tukulti-Ninurta I. A gypsum pedestal, a support for the emblem of a deity, from the Ishtar-Ashuritu Temple at Ashur rebuilt by Tukulti-Ninurta, presents the king, in a single relief, in two phases of prayer before the emblem of the god Nusku (VII, PL. 405). The monument, dated by its inscription, shows that the spatial fusion of different points in time still occurred in the 13th century, as it had in the Jamdat Naṣr period (e.g., the hunting stele from Uruk). The king appears here as an Assyrian high priest, in a wrap-around garment with a rolled belt. A second pedestal is valuable for the relief on its base (unfortunately much battered), which depicts a war episode (W. Andrae, *Die jüngeren Ischtar-Tempel in Assur*, Leipzig, 1935, pl. 29). This piece testifies to the existence of an art form that was to gain increasing importance in Assyrian sculpture: the epic relief. Had the scene on the pedestal vanished completely, the existence of narrative historical reliefs in the 13th century would still have been attested by a small fragment, the cover of a container (Andrae, 1938, pl. 49b). This black marble plate is decorated with a carefully worked relief in two registers that reproduces an incident of war. The composition is utterly free and offers a clear contrast to the nearly contemporaneous murals of Kar-Tukulti-Ninurta (Andrae, 1925, pl. 2). In these paintings, marked by strong Hurro-Mitannian reminiscences, mountain goats were still pictured standing on ornamental branches, without any indication of a base line for the animals. The composition recalls Hurro-Mitannian ones in which the figures are superposed in several tiers, as on the seal of Shaushattar (Starr, op. cit., pl. 118*i*). The reliefs on the pedestals and on the marble cover have gone beyond this stage of composition. By the 13th century Assyrian sculptors had evolved the means to accomplish the great tasks set them from the 9th century onward by the extensive wall plaques in the palaces of the kings.

The history of Assyrian art in the centuries close to the turn of the 2d millennium is but sparsely documented. There is just enough material to show that, besides the mural bas-reliefs of palace halls, two other kinds of relief made their appearance in the Middle Assyrian period: the rock relief and the so-called "obelisk." When in the 9th century, under Ashurnasirpal II, the two great vehicles of the Assyrian idea of kingship, the palace and the wall relief, were united, western Asian art reached its last pinnacle. Beside these, the rock relief and the obelisk, which also served the idea of kingship, have only secondary significance.

In contrast to the rock relief, which had a long history before the Assyrian period, the obelisk — a stele with a rectangular or square base and four faces tapering upward — seems to have been employed only in Assyria from the end of the 2d millennium. The significance, origin, and development of this type of stele have not yet been clarified.

Of all Assyrian obelisks the White Obelisk from Nineveh in the British Museum (E. Unger, *Der Obelisk des Königs Assurnassirpal I aus Ninive*, Leipzig, 1932, pl. 15) is the most important, for it helps fill the gap in the history of the Assyrian relief between the reigns of Tukulti-Ninurta I and Ashurnasirpal II. Each of the four sides of the stone bears eight superposed friezes, some of them carrying the representations around the corners. A heavily damaged inscription on the stepped top mentions a limmu, Ashurnasirpal, identified by B. Landsberger with King Ashurnasirpal II (9th cent.), by Unger with Ashurnasirpal I (11th cent.). Since the date cannot be determined by philological means alone, the representations — the style and the iconographic details — must be taken into account. These militate unequivocally against an attribution to Ashurnasirpal II, from whose reign there survive innumerable wall reliefs from his palace at Kalakh (mod. Nimrud) and also remains of an obelisk. Of particular importance is the fact that on the White Obelisk a number of officials wear a fezlike headdress, whereas on every one of the numerous reliefs of Ashurnasirpal II the fezlike covering with a small conical peak is reserved for the king. The obelisk conforms, in the matter of headgear, to the marble cover of Tukulti-Ninurta I, on which the highest official, the turtan (or tartan), as well as the king, wears a fezlike hat, though without conical crowning. Accordingly, the obelisk must be dated, in any case, before Ashurnasirpal II; and thus it is a bridge between the art of Tukulti-Ninurta I and of Ashurnasirpal II, whose whole stock of motifs it anticipates: sieges of enemy fortresses, armies marching through mountain valleys, receipt of tribute by the victorious king, offering of thanks by the king, victory banquets after the battle, chases of various wild beasts by the king. The importance of the White Obelisk, however, is strictly thematic; the execution betrays not only carelessness in the delineation of the individual figures but also a want of skill in the articulation of the material within the eight registers. The images follow one another around corners and across compartments in unregulated succession, without any accentuation. And it is precisely in the particulars in which these reliefs are deficient that those of Ashurnasirpal II show their masterliness.

NEO-ASSYRIAN PERIOD. Assyrian art attained its peak between the 9th and 7th centuries B.C., at the same time as the empire achieved its greatest political and military power. The great conquering sovereigns demanded magnificent palaces for themselves, and on the walls of courts and state rooms they had their victorious campaigns, hunting scenes, and cult scenes depicted in relief on alabaster slabs over 6 ft. high, following one another without break. Historical narrative never found more glorious expression in ancient western Asia.

Architecture. The two major rulers of the 9th century, Ashurnasirpal II and his son Shalmaneser III, were both great builders, whose annals mention the construction of numerous temples. Shalmaneser seems to have been especially attached to the old capital of Ashur, where he built a new fortification wall with tremendous gates, in which he placed some of his statues. In his cult buildings in that city — reconstructions of the ancient Ishtar Temple and of the Anu-Adad Temple — he strove for the preservation of tradition rather than the creation of new plans. Ashurnasirpal chose Kalakh for his residence. The imposing palace he built there, the so-called "northwest palace," excavated in the 19th century, belongs to the type created by Adadnirari I at Ashur four hundred years earlier. It consisted of several adjoining court complexes. One wing was reserved for public or ceremonial uses, another for dwelling purposes, and a small temple of Ninurta at the foot of a ziggurat was dedicated to the cult. In the public wing, which included a throne room, the lower portions of the walls in the courts and halls were for the first time given a continuous facing of alabaster slabs over 6 ft. high, bearing extensive basreliefs and, again and again, the so-called "Standard Inscription" of Ashurnasirpal. These revetments provided the opportunity for the great development of the Assyrian relief in the 9th century. Their use in a cult building is seen for the first time in the Ninurta sanctuary and a second little temple in its immediate vicinity. The ground plan of the Ninurta Temple comprised an oblong cella preceded by a broad antecella such as Ashurnirari I had introduced in the Sin-Shamash Temple at Ashur. Clearly most of the innovations pertained to external effects, decoration rather than architecture.

Important from a purely architectonic point of view in the northwest palace at Kalakh is the throne room (B), the characteristic form of which was to endure for centuries in Assyria. Situated in the northern part of the palace, it was an elongated rectangular hall of vast dimensions, preceded on one of its long sides by an anteroom (F), which separated it from a court, and flanked on the west short side by a smaller room (C). Its hallmark, found before a shallow wall niche on the east short side, was a podium with two steps, on which must have stood the royal throne. By the decoration of its doorways and walls, and especially of its niche, with sculptures and reliefs, the throne room constituted a first high-water mark in the development of Assyrian architecture and related architectural sculpture in expressing the idea of kingship that dominated people and state.

After Shalmaneser III the great Assyrian kings continued to regard it as a primary task to express the sense of their destiny and might through the construction and pictorial decoration of new palaces — somewhat as the victorious god in the Epic of Creation, after imposing order on the world, erected a new heavenly castle for the gods. Foremost among the palaces of the 8th and 7th centuries was that of Sargon II. This ruler, who brought the Assyrian idea of kingship to its consummation, gave visible form to his concept of world empire by the construction of a royal castle, or rather royal city, of unsurpassed monumentality: Dur Sharrukin (mod. Khorsabad; FIG. 777; I, FIG. 870).

A more varied picture of Assyrian architecture emerges with the attempt to envision the magnificent edifices that Sennacherib had executed in ashlar masonry, probably in imitation of Urartian construction. As crown prince, Sennacherib had been entrusted by his father, Sargon II, with the post of governor in Urartu, where he must have become acquainted with the great canals and aqueducts constructed there. When Nineveh had to be provided with an entirely new system of water conduits, he built the tunnel-canal of Maltay, with its reliefs, and the aqueduct of Jerwan, doubtless on the model of Urartian structures. Yet more important is the fact that Sennacherib for the first time erected structures by the ashlar technique at Ashur itself: a quay wall and the so-called "Mushlalu," probably a stairway for the gods taking part in the New Year's procession. Another ashlar structure was the New Year's festival building, the Bīt Akītu, which Sennacherib had built after the Marduk cult was transferred to Ashur, so that the ritual ceremonies connected with the feast could be carried out. Although the building technique probably came from Urartu, the idea of the Bīt Akītu, the temple in which Marduk fought the forces of chaos, is Babylonian.

Figural Arts. Unlike sculpture in the round (PL. 492), examples of which are few and, for the most part, mediocre, architectural sculpture is well represented and of outstanding quality; but a full century after its rediscovery its themes remain a complex problem. It can be divided into two classes. The first includes the huge stone figures that provided magic protection for doors. Worked partly in relief, partly in the round, these *lamassu*s, genies that gave admittance to the good and drove away evil, combine features of the bull, the lion, the eagle, and man (PL. 488). The second class comprises the various mural reliefs, which in turn can be divided into two groups: (1) those with representations of mythical beings (PL. 489; I, PL. 515; IV, PL. 166), generally winged genies of human aspect, into whose midst the king himself is taken and who are closely linked with the palmette tree, the symbol of life; and (2) narrative reliefs relating the king's exploits in war and on the hunting field. This second type of relief, a species of annals in pictures, first appeared on a significant scale in the White Obelisk mentioned above. Its adoption by Ashur-

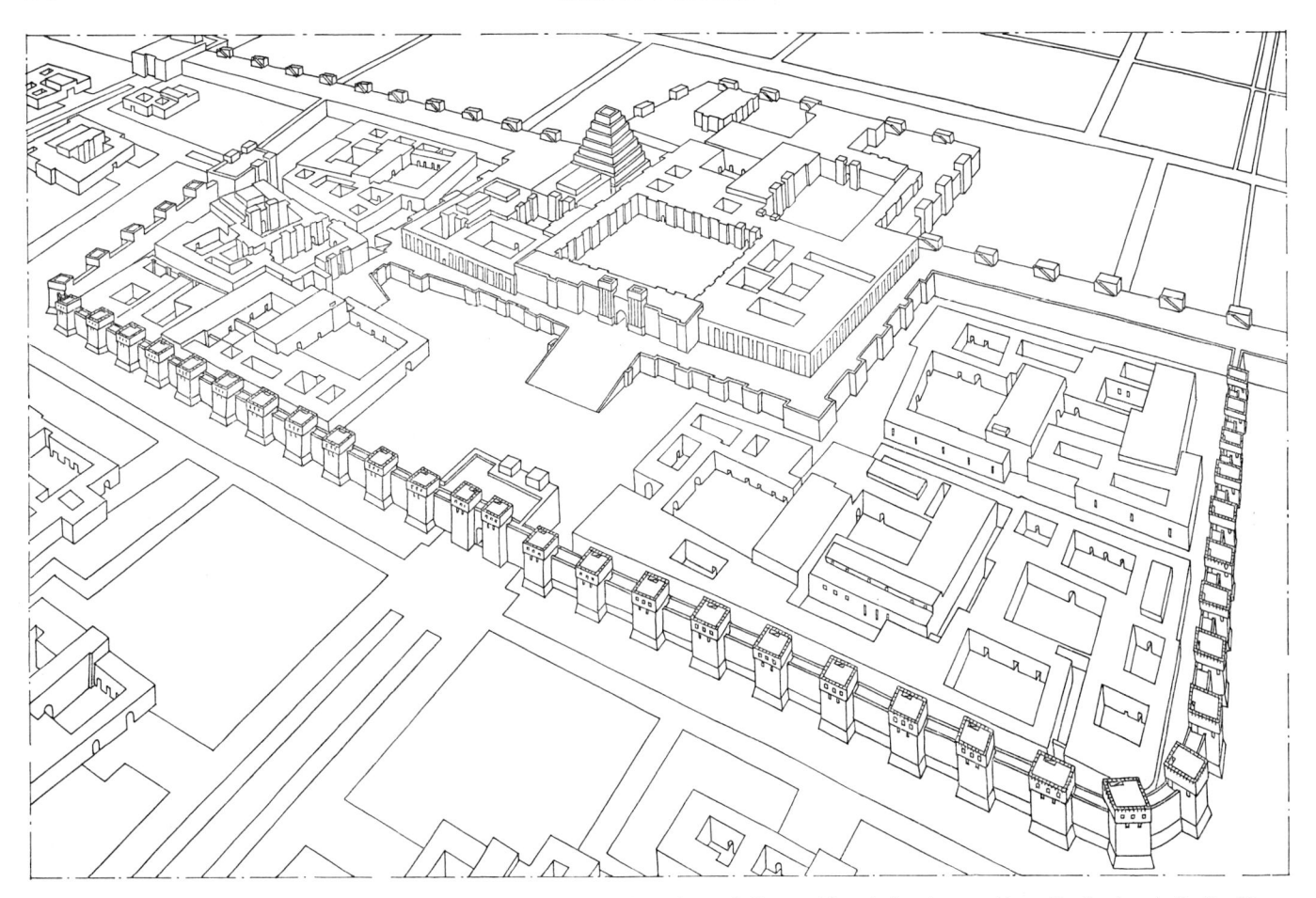

Dur Sharrukin (mod. Khorsabad), reconstruction of the citadel with the palace of Sargon II and the ziggurat (*from G. Loud and C. B. Altman Khorsabad, II: The Citadel and the Town, Chicago, 1938*).

nasirpal II for the walls of the throne room of Kalakh was an important step in the development of the Assyrian relief, and it brought this art to its ultimate heights in the 8th and 7th centuries. Between Ashurnasirpal II and Ashurbanipal — that is, between the 9th century and the end of the 7th — a general shift of emphasis occurred, in the palaces of Kalakh, Dur Sharrukin, and Nineveh, from the mythical to the narrative relief.

In the northwest palace of Ashurnasirpal II at Kalakh, mythical scenes, with figures occupying the full height of the wall plaques throughout, still constituted the great majority. In the throne room the principal scene, the key representation of the entire series of wall reliefs, was recessed into the shallow niche in the east wall, before which sat the king, enthroned on a podium with an extensive inscription referring to the foundation of the palace. The relief, a huge slab of double width, is now in the British Museum (Budge, 1914, pl. 11). In the center is a stylized tree: a palmette-crowned stem under an arch of smaller palmettes tied as by ribbons to one another and to the stem. Poised over the tree is a winged sun containing the upper portion of a bearded god who stretches out both hands. The tree is flanked by two images of the king in the garb of a priest, with a mace in his left hand and his right hand raised. This group, in turn, is framed by two human-headed winged genies, engaged in a ritual act involving little pails and pine cones. The cult of the sacred tree and the cult of the king here seem clearly fused, and this picture immediately brings to mind one of the fundamental motifs of ancient western Asian art: the man in the net skirt with a rosette tree in his hands, the dispenser of life to the tame quadrupeds, the sacred herds. Like this royal shepherd, the Assyrian king undoubtedly symbolizes the preserver of life, of the state, and of the people. The symbolism is of Sumero-Akkadian descent. A second tradition that helped determine the character of Assyrian art, one of Hurro-Mitannian origin, is encountered in the winged sun over the king and the sacred tree. Even in the so-called "Kirkuk tablets," the earliest known Hurrian glyptic, the winged sun over the tree was one of the commonest motifs. In Assyrian art the two great streams of Sumero-Akkadian and Hurro-Mitannian tradition flowed together as into a reservoir, one that was to supply all western Asia during the 1st millennium B.C. The language of the reliefs cannot be grasped without tracing the origin and the original meaning of the motifs. The royal shepherd feeding the animals was also, originally, a martial hero constantly battling evil to protect life; and the Assyrian kings attached such importance to the depiction of their exploits because in combating military opponents and wild beasts they were actually fighting the enemy of life.

In the reliefs from most of the rooms of the northwest palace the wall plaque constitutes the compositional unit, especially in the numerically superior group of mythico-ritual reliefs. Each plaque carries a figure, adapted to it in size and format, of a genius, an official, an officer, or the king. A somewhat different disposition characterizes the small group of plaques of the throne room that deal for the first time with the military and hunting exploits of the king (PL. 493). Here the height of the plaque is halved by a median band with inscriptions, in order to obtain space for two superposed narrative friezes. It is an attempt to free the subject matter from the disposition imposed by the form of the plaque and to evolve new rules of composition suitable to it.

Unfortunately there remains no palace erected by Tiglath-pileser III, actually the military and administrative founder of the Assyrian world empire. But chance has preserved some of the relief-decorated wall plaques from his palace at Kalakh. Several of these clearly show that the wall plaque was relinquished as a compositional unit in his time; individual scenes, even single human or animal figures, overlap from one plaque to the next. Thus the sculptors had overcome one impediment to the representation of space and the organization of elements in space — an impediment that, at the same time, was a source of formal control of the material.

Wall reliefs adorned many of the enormous courts and halls in the palace of Sargon II at Dur Sharrukin (PLS. 489, 490). They picture whole military campaigns, the one against Urartu, for instance, and include cautionary scenes depicting the punishment of renegade allies. On the whole, their superiority to earlier works is one of dimensions rather than of content or expressive power. True superiority was achieved only at Nineveh, in the wall reliefs of Sennacherib in the southwestern palace and those of Ashurbanipal in the northern palace.

Novel and striking among the mythical reliefs with which Sargon adorned the walls of his courts and halls are those in which the heroic shepherd is represented, not with the tree of life, but as a half-naked figure with six locks falling to his shoulders, who restrains a lion with his arm. He is the guardian of tame animals, who had appeared in prehistoric times as a martial hero. At Dur Sharrukin he stood near the entrances of the main halls, a huge guardian of life.

The representations of Sargon's campaigns bespeak an effort to depict events as historical fact rather than half-mythical, as in earlier periods. This effort is evident in the attempt to characterize landscapes and in their frequent identification by inscriptions. The sculptor's aim was not only to rouse the spectator to an awareness of space as such but to transform the ideal space of the picture surface into a particular space. For that reason the wall plaque became ever less binding to him as a compositional unit. In larger pictures he overstepped its limits not only sideways but upward, for he could no longer fit cities, castles, mountains, and seas into a long narrow strip; henceforth he required the full height of the plaque, previously reserved for the single figures of winged genies. The way now lay clear for the ultimate flowering of Assyrian composition under Sennacherib in the southwestern palace of Nineveh, "which has not its equal."

In the wall reliefs of this palace the sculptor seems to have mastered every artifice of composition (see Paterson, 1915). He links together in a simple rhythmic manner the figures of a procession in which the king moves with his following from the palace to the Ishtar Temple; he ingeniously employs the palms of a landscape to give a cadenced, reposeful background to an animated train of tribute bearers or prisoners; he replaces the strip that previously separated the superposed friezes with the wavy lines of a river; by making use of the hilly land rising near Lachish, he imparts the utmost dynamism to a powerful war scene in which the king is enthroned in his tent at the upper right and all lines of the composition lead up to him from the lower left. Yet even these reliefs are not the high point in Assyrian bas-relief composition, which touches its pinnacle in works that nearly achieve perspective representation as they picture armies of workmen transporting immense *lamassu* sculptures for erection in the palace (ibid., pl. 32).

These works were not to be surpassed. When Ashurbanipal, the last great Assyrian king, built his own palace at Nineveh, the dimensions of the wall reliefs were considerably reduced and the sculptors did not attempt to follow the same path as their predecessors. If Ashurbanipal was able to challenge the achievements of the Sennacherib period with something new and original, he succeeded not in the illustrations of the Elamite campaigns, which he had still placed in the southwestern palace, but in the reliefs in his own northern palace at Nineveh; and among these the genuine works of art are not the scenes of war but the symbolic hunting scenes, involving the king (IV, PL. 16).

The reversion to the great beginnings of western Asian art under Ashurbanipal may or may not have been deliberate. That such a reversion occurred, however, can no more be doubted than that an oddly lifelike yet purely artistic idiom distinguishes both the last phase of Assyrian art and that of the protohistoric period. Like the art of the protohistoric period, the reliefs of the northern palace revolve around the royal tamer of animals inimical to life and around the guardian of life and order — hence such themes as the hunting of lions and wild beasts of the steppes. In the well-known garden scene (VIII, PL. 423), which can be linked to the big alabaster vase from Uruk (PL. 466), the old "symposium" receives its last great artistic incarnation. The kinship of feeling toward the universe in the protohistoric period and that of Ashurbanipal emerges with especial clarity in the consummate reliefs from Room E in the northern palace, the so-called "Garden" (Meissner and Opitz, 1940, pls. 10–12). Here, as in a paradise, a harpist soothes the wild beasts through the sound of his playing; good and evil have ended their eternal conflict, as in the golden age, and all of life, in man and beast and plant, has attained full harmony. The conception of a harmonious world has here been brought forth, for the first time in western Asian art, creations inspired by an idea other than the principles of abstraction and truth to nature: the idea of beauty, which, like the application of perspective under Sennacherib, seems as yet but to glimmer in the distance.

It would be erroneous to deduce from the enormous dimensions of Assyrian works, as exemplified by the royal citadel of Dur Sharrukin or the wall reliefs of the southwestern palace of Sennacherib at Nineveh, that the Assyrian sought monumentality in art as an end in itself. Whatever the extent of the layout, whatever the breadth of the composition, he never lost his eye for detail. In battle scenes that cover the walls of entire rooms, the crowning of a tent pole is never forgotten; in the gigantic figures of kings and genies who perform ritual acts by the tree of life, the embroidery that ornaments the garments is drawn in such detail that we not only learn about Assyrian fabrics but enrich our knowledge of Assyrian iconography (PL. 489; I, PL. 514; IV, PL. 16). Indeed the love of detail manifested in the reliefs has made them a major source for the cultural history of the ancient Near East. Nowhere else do we get so much information about the daily life of the Assyrians in war and peace or about their religious and secular activities. The Assyrian predilection for the small form, for detail, also finds expression in various branches of applied art: in polychrome enamel painting on vases and brick walls, in goldsmithing, in glyptics — in which, however, the high level of the Middle Assyrian period was not maintained — and in ivory carving, practiced partly under the influence of Phoenician and Syrian craftsmen, partly in an independent style.

To what degree art and handicrafts, monumental and minor arts, flowed from the same source in Assyria is shown in bronzework. The chamfered bowl of Ashurtaklak, the governor of Ashur, is a masterpiece of its kind (Andrae, 1938, pl. 63c). Some bronze bands, gate revetments of the time of Ashurnasirpal II and Shalmaneser III, originating from Imgur-Enlil (mod. Balawat), are closely related to the contemporaneous wall relief in content, but stylistically they present an interesting divergence (PL. 490). The long narrow strips at the disposal of the artist did not have a limiting effect on the composition, as the wall plaque did on that of the stone reliefs. On the unarticulated bronze strips the narrative proceeds, unaltered by such limitations as its medium might have imposed.

Yet the period of Shalmaneser III, which brought forth the Balawat bronzes, also knew a more disciplined pictorial idiom, as is amply demonstrated by the reliefs of the famous Black Obelisk in the British Museum (PL. 488). The rock reliefs of Sennacherib at Maltay (W. Bachmann, *Felsreliefs in Assyrien*, Leipzig, 1927, pl. 27), which deal exclusively with the adoration of the principal gods of the pantheon by the king, likewise reveal a composition guided by abstract considerations: the figure of the king is duplicated solely on formal grounds — to obtain a balanced group of figures.

Viewed comprehensively, Assyrian art appears unified, notwithstanding its diversity, for in all its manifestations, from the vastest architectural project to the smallest ivory plaque, it served a single idea, that of the king who symbolized in every act the permanence of folk and state. With the fall of Nineveh in 612 B.C., the magnificent synthesis of southern and northern Mesopotamian traditions came to an end, making way for the Aramaean attempt to found a new world empire and give it expression in art.

NEO-BABYLONIAN (CHALDEAN) PERIOD. Two factors contributed to the reemergence of Babylon as the intellectual and cultural center of a western Asian empire after the fall of Assyria in 612 B.C.: the religious power that the city god of Babylon, Marduk, had won in the course of several centuries and the vitality of the Aramaean population, which from the end of the 2d millennium spread over all western Asia and made itself felt with particular rapidity and force in Babylonia. Mardukapaliddina II (721–711 and 703), the tough antagonist of Sargon of Assyria, had tried to found a Chaldean empire in southern Mesopotamia. What he was unable to achieve was brought about effortlessly by Nabopolassar, ally of the Medes against Assyria. At first only a local ruler of Babylon, he received after 612, as booty from the Medes, a part of the region east of the Tigris and territories along the middle Euphrates. His son, the great Nebuchadnezzar II, won the decisive battle against the Egyptian army, and with it supremacy in western Asia. Just as Hammurabi had epitomized the political and cultural fulfillment of the wave of western Semitic peoples that had washed over all western Asia, so Nebuchadnezzar incarnated the triumph of western Asian Aramaeization. Hammurabi and Nebuchadnezzar both looked for the hub of their power in Babylon; both were champions of the Marduk cult — and here lies the difference between Neo-Assyrian and Neo-Babylonian culture and art.

Sennacherib, in his account of the representations adorning the gate of the Bīt Akītu, the New Year's festival building, at Ashur, describes himself as standing with Ashur in the god's war chariot to battle the forces of the underworld; his annals speak the language of the Epic of Creation. With Nebuchadnezzar, he whom Marduk delegated as the prince of peace, the pretext for narrative art — for annals generally, literary and pictorial — fell away. Architecture, in the Neo-Babylonian period, regained the primacy it had had in the Neo-Sumerian and Old Babylonian periods, and temples again took precedence over palaces.

Architecture. Neo-Babylonian architecture did not produce any characteristic new forms. In pursuit of monumentality, it tended to huge dimensions — a hallmark of many late cultures; witness some of the manifestations of Hellenistic and late Roman architecture. Also symptomatic of a late culture is the almost excessive, quasi-archaeological reverence in a ruler such as Nabonidus before edifices of the past, a reverence that he himself expressed in his inscriptions. His great predecessor Nebuchadnezzar and even Ashurbanipal likewise showed themselves faithful, in temple as well as palace, to the Old Babylonian–Neo-Sumerian models. The Neo-Babylonian temples of Babylon — for example, those of Ninmakh (FIGS. 781, 783), of Ishtar of Akkad, and of Ninurta (also known as E-patutila) — are distinguished by a broad cella with a niche for the holy of holies in the middle of the far long wall and a broad antecella on the same axis as the cella. A type thousands of years old, it is exemplified for the Neo-Sumerian period by the Gigpar-ku and the Enki Temple at Ur and by a section of the Old Babylonian sanctuary at Ishchali.

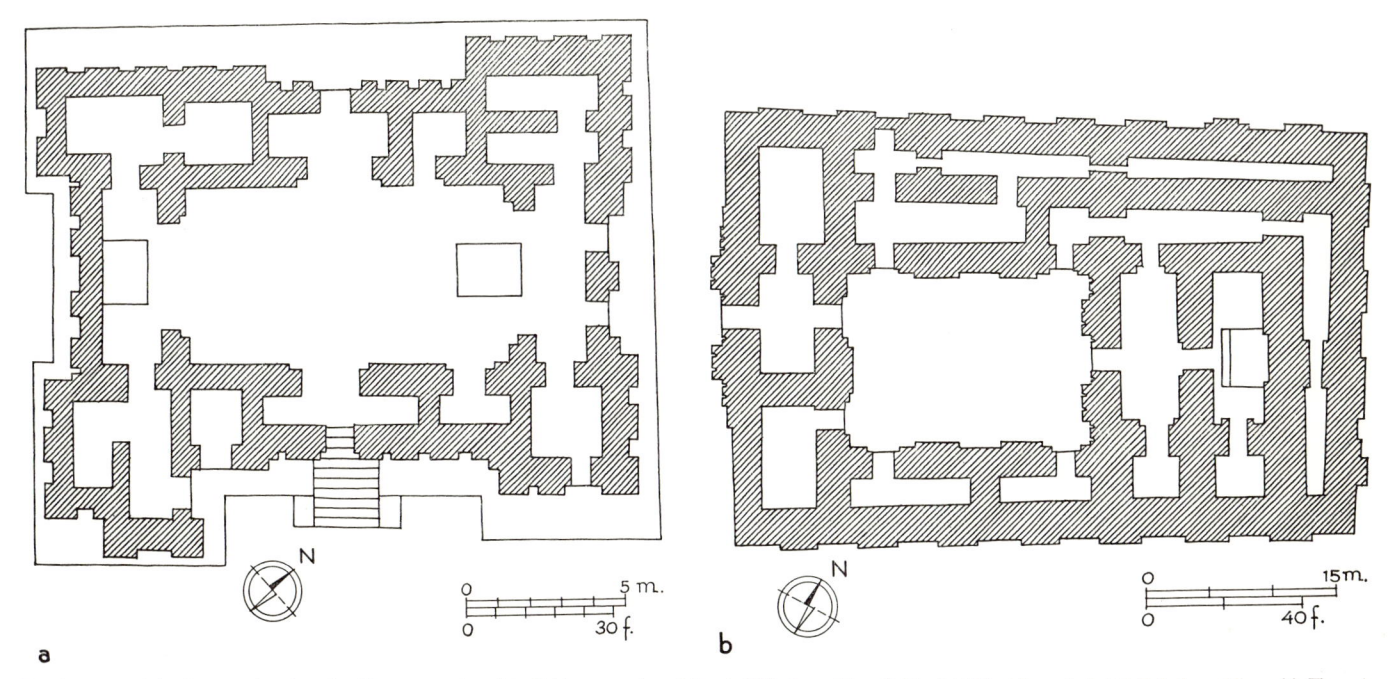

It is not solely the nucleus of the Neo-Babylonian temple that was inherited from the distant past. The most overpowering sanctuaries — for example, E-sagila, the enormous complex of the Marduk sanctuary as reconstructed in Nebuchadnezzar's time — also owe their over-all plan combining several court complexes to an architectonic principle applied, in its essentials, to the sanctuary of the moon god Nannar at Ur, about the time of Ur-Nammu. Indeed even that wonder of the world, E-temen-an-ki, the Tower of Babylon, erected in the Neo-Babylonian period, was in principle nothing but a ziggurat, known in the Neo-Sumerian world, albeit on a smaller scale, since the end of the 3d millennium. Under Nebuchadnezzar, Marduk had a temple on ground level (E-sagila), a "high temple" on its ziggurat (E-temen-an-ki), and a New Year's festival building (Bīt Akītu) outside the city. These structures were but fragmentarily recoverable through the excavations of Koldewey, and they are still as difficult to understand as the great Assyrian wall reliefs. The problem, however, is less an art-historical one than one of religious history.

The Neo-Babylonian palace, unlike the Assyrian, did not foster any significant new architectonic ideas. The palaces of Nabopolassar and Nebuchadnezzar were basically amplified, monumentalized dwellings, in which the court complexes, some with a broad main room on the south side, helped the king fulfill his variegated duties. Artistically the most important part of the palaces in the southern fortress is the broad room (FIG. 783, *e*), of immense size, with a throne niche in the middle of the farther long wall and decorative enamel painting on the exterior front. Here the royal audience took place, a ceremony bordering on the religious since the Old Babylonian period,

Persistence of basic temple plan in Mesopotamia. (*a*) Eridu, temple of level VII, late Aëneolithic (al-'Ubaid) period; (*b*) Babylon, Ninmakh Temple Neo-Babylonian period (*from Frankfort, 1954*).

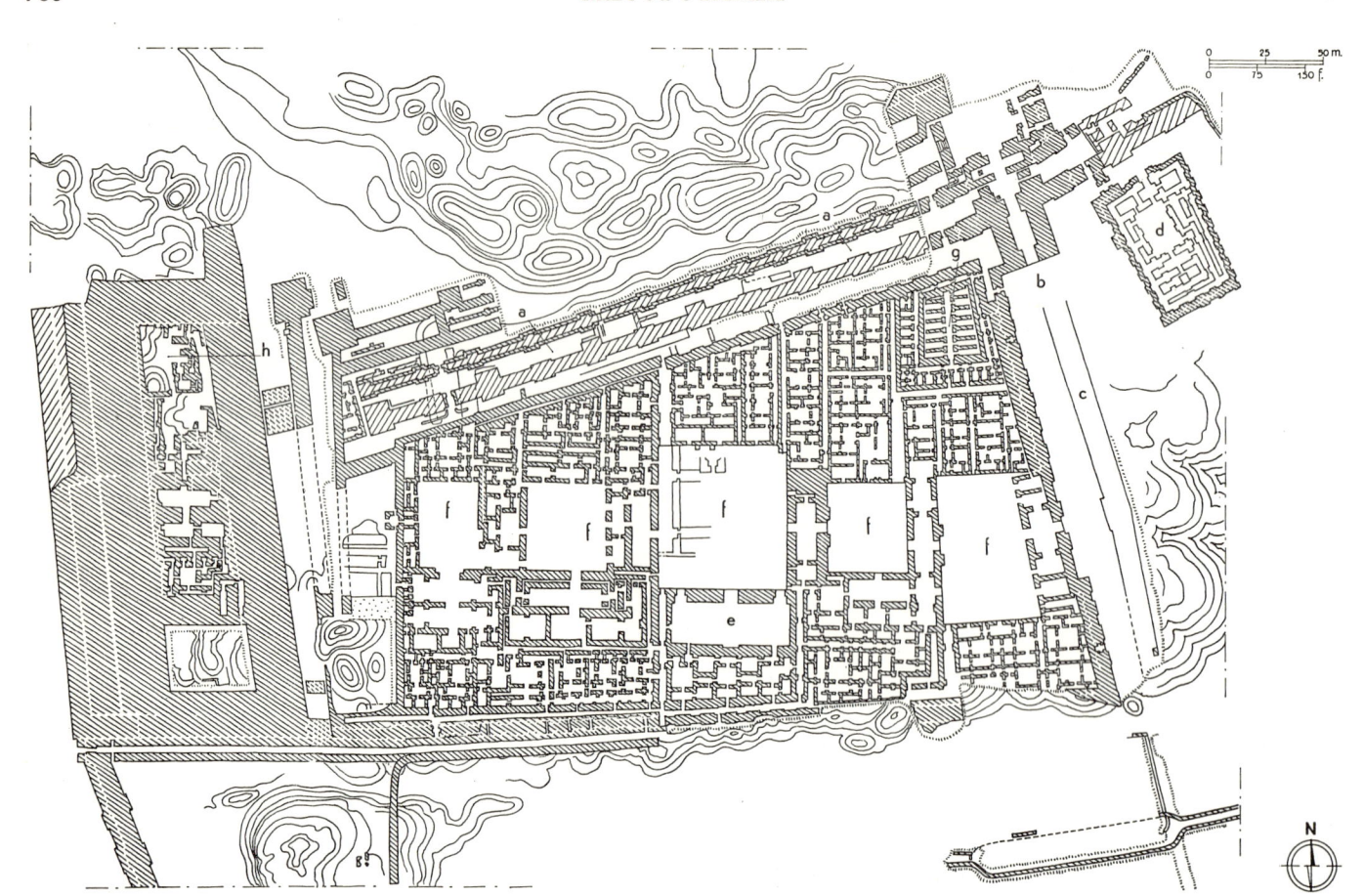

Babylon, plan of the southern fortress. (*a*) City walls; (*b*) Ishtar Gate; (*c*) processional way; (*d*) Ninmakh Temple. (*e-g*) Palaces of Nabopolassar and Nebuchadnezzar II: (*e*) Throne room; (*f*) courts; (*g*) presumed site of the "hanging gardens." (*h*) Fortress on the Euphrates (*from Koldewey, 1925*).

when it unfolded in the rooms leading to Court 106 in the Old Babylonian palace of King Zimrilim at Mari (FIG. 787, *c*).

Figural Arts. The Neo-Babylonian conception of the king as the servant of Marduk, appointed by the god, and as the peaceful shepherd of mankind found adequate expression in the revival of inherited forms and in the increase of dimensions. Unlike the Assyrian conception of kingship, it did not engender an epic art, and the increased size of buildings did not lead to the creation of an architectural sculpture that, like the Assyrian, at once fulfilled its pictorial functions and accentuated the structure of the edifice. The pictorial decoration of Neo-Babylonian architecture can be most easily visualized through the reconstructions in Berlin (Staat. Mus.) of such Babylonian monuments as the processional way, the Ishtar Gate (PL. 494), and the façade of the throne room in the southern fortress. The enamel painting and relief of their brick walls are samples of an ornamental-symbolic art that owes its technical and artistic qualities to the Sumero-Babylonian past, not to an intrinsic creative force of the Neo-Babylonian–Aramaean civilization. Brick relief had already been used on the temple of Karaindash in the E-anna sanctuary of Uruk; as to enamel painting, the Nannar Temple on the ziggurat at Ur must already have had an outer layer of blue glazed bricks. The rows of dragons (*mushkhush*) on the Ishtar Gate, the lions striding over bands of rosettes on the processional way of Marduk, the palmette trees over rows of lions on the façade of the throne room — these images do not illustrate any royal myth, and in neither form nor content are they independent works of art; at most they are stereotyped magic signs without organic connection, repeated in an endless surface pattern. How greatly this type of wall decoration differs from Assyrian architectural sculpture is shown with special force by those palmette trees on the façade of the throne room (see FIG. 785, 7) in which Koldewey still saw an adaptation of columns with volute cap-

itals, supporting an overhang. The Neo-Babylonian glazed-brick revetment is dissociated from the structure of the building, and, like the protohistoric cone mosaics of Uruk, it constitutes a skin, a garment, that conceals rather than emphasizes the supporting framework. Those two artistic principles, the tectonic and the atectonic, were already found side by side in the protohistoric period. Now, after an evolution spanning thousands of years, they confronted each other again with particular bluntness in Neo-Assyrian and Neo-Babylonian art.

The atectonic flow by gentle transitions is more than a formal aspect of Chaldean–Neo-Babylonian art. To see that it is of the very essence of this art, it suffices to compare a Neo-Babylonian with an Assyrian clay vessel. In the Assyrian one there is a clear attempt to differentiate the various functional parts: neck, shoulder, belly, and foot; in the Babylonian one the outline tends to mask the parts. The figures of human beings, too, as exemplified by the few surviving works of Neo-Babylonian sculpture, have the earmarks of structures intended to underplay, to conceal, the supporting elements.

The remains of sculpture in the round — be it the carefully modeled head of a god, of unbaked clay, or an ivory female head — are so few that its principles cannot be deduced with any assurance; but human representations in relief still exist in sufficient number for us to be able to apprehend their distinctive qualities and differentiate them especially from contemporaneous Assyrian ones. These reliefs manifest the survival in the Neo-Babylonian period of the *kudurru* (PL. 495), a type of monument widespread in the Middle Babylonian–Kassite period. Nowhere does the Chaldean–Neo-Babylonian spirit find truer expression than in the *kudurru* of Mardukapaliddina II in Berlin, a black marble stele of exceptional execution (Frankfort, 1954, pl. 120). If the eye follows, say, the outline of the king, who presents his right profile, it will be arrested neither at the neck, nor at the waist, nor at the feet; rather, it will glide along the gentle S line from the tip of the helmet to the toes of the seemingly

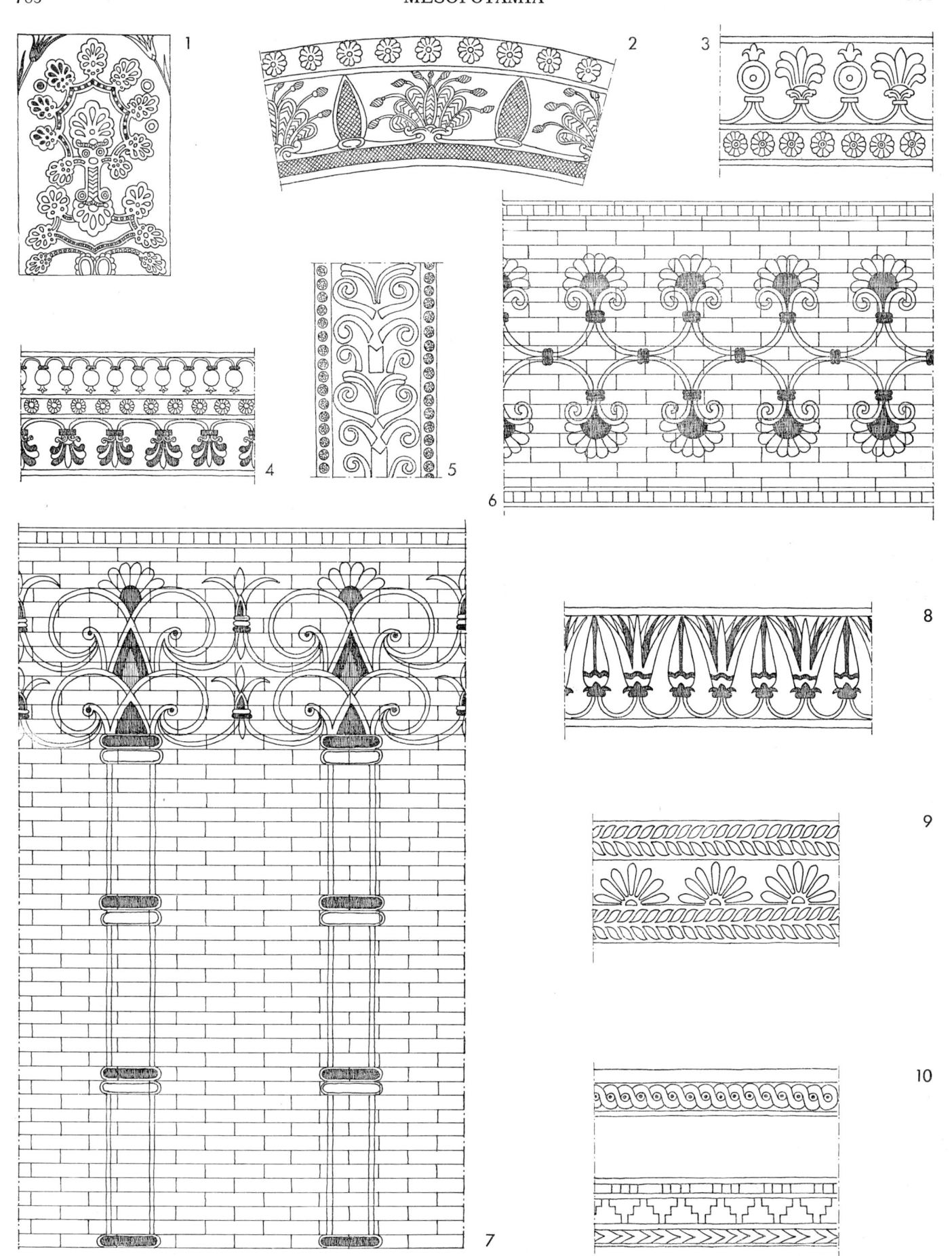

Mesopotamian decorative motifs: (1) Tree of life with palmette leaves; (2) rosettes, palmettes, and pine cones; (3, 4) rosettes, palmettes, and pomegranates; (5) foliated shaft with rosettes; (6) palmettes; (7) palmette tree (columns with volute capitals); (8) lotus flowers and buds; (9) flowers between laurel bands; (10) guilloche, meanders, and chevrons.

boneless, plump body. The broad belt, instead of articulating the form, accentuates its flowing quality. It seems to hold the body together in the long garment as in a sack, much in the same way as the powerful horizontal ropes braced the masses of clay of the ziggurats without constituting a true structural framework. The same softness of form characterizes the female figure surmounting a bronze tripod in Erlangen, Germany

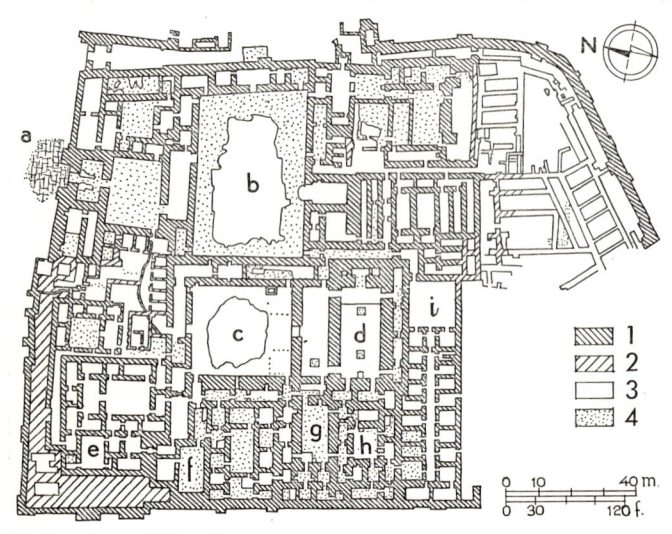

Mari, palace of Zimrilim, ground plan. Key: (1) Well-preserved walls; (2) poorly preserved walls; (3) obliterated walls; (4) remains of brick pavements. (a) Main entrance; (b) main court, leading to Room 132 on the right; (c) court with paintings (No. 106); (d) Room 65 (the throne room, according to the excavator; the author would interpret Room 64, to the left of d, as the throne room); (e) chamber of the king; (f) scribes' room; (g) stewards' offices; (h) oven; (i) court leading westward to the storerooms (*from Parrot, 1953*).

(Frankfort, 1954, pl. 117); and even in a relief that Nebuchadnezzar, like the Assyrian kings, had chiseled out of the rock near the Nahr el-Kelb, a softer contour is noticeable in the human figure, despite the Assyrian model foreign to Neo-Babylonian art.

CONCLUSION. With the fall of Assyria and the extinction of the Chaldean–Neo-Babylonian empire, the historically integrated cultural and artistic complex we call "Mesopotamian" came to an end. The ideas and forms of expression created in the course of about two and a half thousand years were to make themselves felt both eastward and westward far beyond the western Asian orbit and long after the rise of the Achaemenid Persian empire.

The Achaemenid empire, which succeeded the Neo-Babylonian in its sway over Mesopotamia, had its center not there but on the Iranian Plateau. The differences, however, between Achaemenid culture and art and those of the older civilization were not due primarily to the displacement of the political center or to the fact that the new conqueror did not belong to the same ethnic group as the Sumerians and Semites, the twin pillars of the earlier culture. The Achaemenid Persians, who belonged to the Indo-Germanic family of peoples, constituted only one of the innumerable ethnic elements acting as transmitters of culture in Mesopotamia. More important was the incompatibility of the Zoroastrian religion of the Achaemenids with the Sumero-Akkadian and Babylonian-Assyrian religion. Ahura Mazda (Ormazd) did not belong to the class of gods who, as symbols of great natural forces, conducted a victorious contest against the older powers of chaos, who ordered the cosmos according to laws and revealed the destinies of gods and men. He was, rather, a spiritual and ethical power exalted above everything material.

The belief in deities that were agents of order and proclaimers of fate was one of the great "brackets" that held together Mesopotamian culture from Sumerian protohistoric times until the entry of Cyrus into Babylon. The belief in such gods, who became the masters of the Sumerian city-states, determined the consistent development of Sumero-Akkadian and Babylonian-Assyrian temple architecture. This explains the fundamental similarity of form existing, despite all deviations, between the most primitive examples of Mesopotamian architecture, the earliest prehistoric temples of the al-'Ubaid period at Eridu (FIG. 781), and the most fully evolved examples of Neo-Babylonian architecture, the sanctuary of Marduk in Babylon with "high" and "low" temples: E-temen-an-ki and E-sagila.

The other spiritual "bracket" that through the millenniums held together Mesopotamian art was the idea of kingship, the idea of a representative of the divine world orderer, who, like the great forces of nature in the cosmos, defeated the powers of evil, but at the same time constituted a link with a second, probably older group of deities, the powers of life, ultimately sublimated in the great feminine divinity of Uruk, Inanna. The sacred nuptials of this goddess with the battling hero created the bridge between the world of gods and men, the idea that was fundamental to Sumerian culture, with its art and architecture, and laid the basis for a continuous Mesopotamian culture. The unifying conception of kingship explains the identity of theme in the representation of the king as lion killer on a stele of the Jamdat Naṣr period and in the representations of Ashurbanipal in the same role on his reliefs in the northern palace of Nineveh — an identity between works separated by thousands of years of the most intensive development.

In the course of political and social changes the tradition that gave continuity to Mesopotamian art passed from center to center: from the north Mesopotamian villages to south Mesopotamian Eridu, the city of Ea; thence to Uruk, the city of the great goddess Inanna; and from Uruk — as a later myth has it, the city of Dumuzi and Gilgamesh — to Ur, the sanctuary of the moon god. The influence of the Semitic-Akkadian element drew the center of cultural dissemination more toward the north, to Mari, Sippar, and Kish. Doubtless under Akkadian influence, the gods became ever more kingly and the kings ever more godly. The audience with the godlike king, or with the god presiding in state, increasingly dominated the royal and the religious ceremonial and therewith the form of temples and palaces. This trend must have reached its climax at Ur in the period of the 3d dynasty. Then the western Semites, by their wanderings, caused a shift of the cultural center to Babylon. As the might of Assyria came to dominate all western Asia and found its highest artistic expression in the wall reliefs of the palaces, the cultural and artistic center of Mesopotamia shifted once more, to the region of Ashur and Nineveh, where the ancient Hurrian heritage and the Akkadian artistic sense came together. Finally, in the Neo-Babylonian renaissance, Babylon saw the last revival of an art whose origins lay thousands of years back.

BIBLIOG. For monographs on individual sites see bibliogs. IN IRAQ. *Surveys. a. General*: Perrot-Chipiez, II, 1884; F. Reber, Über altchaldäische Kunst, ZfAssyr, I, 1886, pp. 128 ff., 289 ff., II, 1887, p. 1 ff.; L. Curtius, Die antike Kunst, I: Ägypten und Vorderasien, Berlin, 1924; W. Andrae, Die Kunst Vorderasiens, Berlin, 1st ed., 1925, 2d ed., 1930, 3d ed., 1942; L. Speleers, Les Arts de l'Asie antérieure ancienne, Brussels, 1926; G. Contenau, Manuel d'archéologie orientale, Paris, I, 1927, II, 1931, III, 1931, IV, 1947; C. Zervos, L'Art de la Mésopotamie, Paris, 1935; W. Andrae, Vorderasien, HA, 1939, pp. 643–796; V. Christian, Altertumskunde des Zweistromlandes von der Vorzeit bis zum Ende der Achämenidenherrschaft, I, Leipzig, 1940; F. Poulsen, Den Gamle Orients Kunst, Berlin, 1942; A. Parrot, Archéologie mésopotamienne, 2 vols., Paris, 1946–53; A. W. Byvanck, De Kunst der Oudheid, I, Leiden, 1947; W. Speiser, Vorderasiatische Kunst, Berlin, 1952; H. Frankfort, The Art and Architecture of the Ancient Orient, Harmondsworth, 1954; L. Schnitzler, Die Kunst des Alten Orients, Stuttgart, 1957; S. Lloyd, The Art of the Ancient Near East, London, 1961; A. Parrot, The Arts of Assyria, trans. S. Gilbert and J. Emmons, New York, 1961; A. Parrot, Sumer: The Dawn of Art, trans. S. Gilbert and J. Emmons, New York, 1961; J. A. H. Potratz, Die Kunst des Alten Orient, Stuttgart, 1961; C. L. Woolley, The Art of the Middle East, Including Persia, Mesopotamia and Palestine, New York, 1961; M. A. Beek, Atlas of Mesopotamia: A Survey of the History and Civilisation of Mesopotamia from the Stone Age to the Fall of Babylon, trans. D. R. Welsh, London, New York, 1962; J. Hawkes and C. L. Woolley, History of Mankind, I: Prehistory and the Beginnings of Civilization, New York, Evanston, 1963. *b. Architecture*: W. Andrae, Das Gotteshaus und die Urformen des Bauens im Alten Orient, Berlin, 1930; W. Andrae, Die ionische Säule, Bauform oder Symbol?, Berlin, 1933; T. A. Busink, De Babylonische Tempeltoren, Leiden, 1949; H. Frankfort, Town Planning in Ancient Mesopotamia, The Town Planning Rev., XXI, 1950, p. 98 ff. *c. Figural Arts*: B. Meissner, Grundzüge der babylonischassyrischen Plastik, Leipzig, 1915; H. R. Hall, Babylonian and Assyrian Sculpture in the British Museum, Paris, Brussels, 1928; H. Frankfort,

Cylinder Seals, London, 1939; A. Moortgat, Vorderasiatische Rollsiegel, Berlin, 1940; Corpus of Ancient Near Eastern Seals in North American Collections, I: The Collection of the Pierpont Morgan Library, ed. E. Porada, New York, 1948; S. Moscati, Le origini della narrativa storica nell'arte del Vicino Oriente, Rome, 1961. *Sumero-Akkadian period. a. General*: E. Unger, Sumerische und akkadische Kunst, Breslau, 1926; E. Herzfeld, Aufsätze zur altorientalischen Archäologie, Archäologische Mitt. aus Iran, V, 1932, pp. 1–124; C. L. Woolley, The Development of Sumerian Art, London, 1935; P. van der Meer, De Agadeperiode, Kernmomenten der antieke beschaving en haar moderne beleving, Mededeelingen en Verhandelingen van het Vooraziatisch-Egyptisch Gezelschap "Ex Oriente Lux," VII, 1947, pp. 179–241; T. Jacobsen, Early Political Development in Mesopotamia, ZfAssyr, N.S., XVIII, 1957, pp. 91–140. *b. Architecture*: P. Delougaz. Plano-convex Bricks and the Methods of Their Employment, Chicago, 1933; E. Heinrich, Schilf und Lehm, Berlin, 1934; H. J. Lenzen, Die Entwicklung der Zikkurat von ihren Anfängen bis zur Zeit der III. Dynastie von Ur, Leipzig, 1941; E. Heinrich, Die Stellung der Uruktempel in der Baugeschichte, ZfAssyr, N.S., XV, 1950, pp. 21–44; E. Heinrich, Bauwerke in der altsumerischen Bildkunst, Wiesbaden, 1957; H. J. Lenzen, Die beiden Haupteiligtümer von Uruk und Ur zur Zeit der III. Dynastie von Ur, Iraq, XXII, 1960, pp. 127–38. *c. Figural Arts*: F. Thureau-Dangin, Statuettes de Tello, MPiot, XXVII, 1924, pp. 97–111; E. Douglas Van Buren, Foundation Figurines and Offerings, Berlin, 1931; H. Frankfort, Gods and Myths on Sargonid Seals, Iraq, I, 1934, pp. 2–29; H. Frankfort, Early Dynastic Sculptured Mace Heads, Analecta Orientalia, XII, 1935, p. 105 ff.; A. Moortgat, Frühe Bildkunst in Sumer, Leipzig, 1935; M. E. L. Mallowan, The Bronze Head of the Akkadian Period from Niniveh, Iraq, III, 1936, pp. 104–10; H. Frankfort, Sculpture of the Third Millennium B.C. from Tell Asmar and Khafājah, Chicago, 1939; H. Frankfort, More Sculpture from the Diyala Region, Chicago, 1943; L. Le Breton, The Early Periods at Susa, Iraq, XIX, 1957, pp. 79–124; A. L. Perkins, Narration in Babylonian Art, AJA, LXI, 1957, pp. 54–62; M. T. Barrelet, Notes sur quelques sculptures mésopotamiennes de l'époque d'Akkad, Syria, XXXVI, 1959, pp. 20–37; L. Schnitzler, Frühe Plastik im Zweistromland, Stuttgart, 1959; E. Strommenger, Das Menschenbild in der altmesopotamischen Rundplastik von Mesilim bis Hammurapi, Baghdader Mitt., I, 1960, p. 1 ff.; G. Garbini, Le origini della statuaria sumerica, Rome, 1962. *Old Babylonian period. a. General*: A. Parrot, ed., Studia Mariana, Leiden, 1950; A. Parrot, Mari, Neuchâtel, 1953, fig. 80 ff.; H. Schmökel, Hammurabi von Babylon, Munich, 1958, p. 88 ff. *b. Figural Arts*: R. Dussaud, Ex-voto au dieu Amourrou pour la vie d'Hammurabi, MPiot, XXXIII, 1933, pp. 1–10; A. Moortgat, Teppich und Malerei zur Zeit Hammurabis, Bibliotheca Orientalis, IX, 1952, p. 92 ff.; E. Porada, Syrian Seal Impressions on Tablets Dated in the Time of Hammurabi and Samsuiluna, JNES, XVI, 1957, p. 192 ff.; W. Nagel, Glyptische Probleme der Larsa-Zeit, AfO, XVIII, 1957–58, pp. 319–27; R. Opificius, Das altbabylonische Terrakottarelief, Berlin, 1961; M.-L. and H. Erlenmeyer, Vier altorientalische Statuetten, AfO, XX, 1963, pp. 103–08. *Middle Babylonian (Kassite) period. a. General*: A. Moortgat, Bildwerk und Volkstum Vorderasiens zur Hethiterzeit, Leipzig, 1934; A. Götze, Hethiter, Churriter und Assyrer, Leipzig, 1936, p. 124 ff.; E. Porada, On the Problem of Kassite Art, Archaeologica Orientalia in Memoriam E. Herzfeld, Locust Valley, N.Y., 1952, p. 179 ff. *b. Figural Arts*: W. J. Hinke, A New Boundary Stone of Nebuchadnezzar I from Nippur, Philadelphia, 1907; L. W. King, Babylonian Boundary-Stones and Memorial Tablets in the British Museum, London, 1912; A. Moortgat, Die bildende Kunst des Alten Orients und die Bergvölker, Berlin, 1932; E. Herzfeld, Die Kunst des zweiten Jahrtausends in Vorderasien, Archäologische Mitt. aus Iran, VIII, 1937, p. 103 ff.; T. Beran, Die babylonische Glyptik der Kassitenzeit, AfO, XVIII, 1957–58, p. 255 ff. *Assyrian period. a. General*: V. Place, Ninive et l'Assyrie, 3 vols., Paris, 1867–70; E. Unger, Assyrische und babylonische Kunst, Breslau, 1927; A. Götze, Hethiter, Churriter und Assyrer, Leipzig, 1936; W. Andrae, Das wiedererstandene Assur, Leipzig, 1938; B. Meissner and D. Opitz, Studien zum Bīt Ḫilāni im Nordpalast Assurbanaplis zu Ninive, Berlin, 1940. *b. Figural Arts*: E. A. Wallis Budge, Assyrian Sculptures in the British Museum, London, 1914; L. W. King, Bronze Reliefs from the Gates of Shalmaneser, London, 1915; A. Paterson, Assyrian Sculptures: Palace of Sinacherib, The Hague, 1915; O. Weber, Assyrische Kunst, Berlin, 1924; W. Andrae, Coloured Ceramics from Ashur, London, 1925; A. Moortgat, Die Bildgliederung des jungassyrischen Wandreliefs, JhbPreussKSamml, LI, 1930, p. 141 ff.; G. Furlani and E. F. Weidner, Die Reliefs der assyrischen Könige, AfO, X, 1935–36, pp. 204–36; C. J. Gadd, The Stones of Assyria, London, 1936; A. Moortgat, Assyrische Glyptik des 13. Jahrhunderts, ZfAssyr, N.S., XIII, 1942, pp. 50–88; A. Moortgat, Assyrische Glyptik des 12. Jahrhunderts, ZfAssyr, N.S., XIV, 1944, pp. 23–44; R. D. Barnett, A Catalogue of the Nimrud Ivories with Other Examples of Ancient Near Eastern Ivories in the British Museum, London, 1957; T. Beran, Assyrische Glyptik des 14. Jahrhunderts, ZfAssyr, N.S., XVIII, 1957, pp. 141–215; H. G. Güterbock, Narration in Anatolian, Syrian, and Assyrian Art, AJA, LXI, 1957, pp. 62–71; W. Nagel, Meister- und Gesellenarbeit in neuassyrischen Reliefs, Jhb. des Deutschen Archäologischen Inst., LXXIII, 1958, p. 1 ff.; R. D. Barnett, Assyrian Palace Reliefs and Their Influence on the Sculptures of Babylonia and Persia, London, 1960; J. B. Stearns, Reliefs from the Palace of Assurnaṣirpal II, Graz, 1961. *Neo-Babylonian period. a. General*: R. Koldewey, Das wieder erstehende Babylon, 4th ed., Leipzig, 1925; E. Unger, Assyrische und babylonische Kunst, Breslau, 1927; E. Unger, Babylon, Berlin, Leipzig, 1931. *b. Architecture*: T. Dombart, Der babylonische Turm, Leipzig, 1930; J. Jordan, Guide Through the Ruins of Babylon and Borsippa, Baghdad, 1937; O. E. Ravn, Herodotus' Description of Babylon, Copenhagen, 1942; F. Krischen, Weltwunder der Baukunst in Babylonien und Jonien, Tübingen, 1956. *c. Figural Arts*: L. W. King, Babylonian Boundary-Stones and Memorial Tablets in the British Museum, London, 1912; E. Porada, Suggestions for the Classification of Neo-Babylonian Seals, Orientalia, XVI, 1947, p. 145 ff.

Anton MOORTGAT

Illustrations: PLS. 463–496; 10 figs. in text.

METALWORK. The practical use of metal, isolated and shaped by means of hammering or casting, represents a technical conquest made by humanity in a relatively advanced stage of development, only shortly before the invention of writing introduced the historical era. Whether its origin was unique or common to various continents according to the diverse metals available, metalworking was, at first, a strictly functional activity that went hand in hand with the working of wood, stone, bone, and baked earth to produce instruments, weapons, and utensils. Here metal showed new and advantageous qualities of durability, sharpness, resistance, and the possibility of being reused. Only secondarily did metal assume the artistic significance for which its qualities were, in a certain sense, intrinsically predisposed because of the esthetic effect of its luster, the variety of its colors, and its malleability. This manifested itself first in the simplest forms of functional objects and in the use of metals (particularly the precious metals) for personal ornamental objects. Then, always in a more decisive manner, metal became the direct material of decorative and figural artistic expression, lending its surface to design and its mass to modeling in low relief and sculpture in the round. In this sense, wide and definite application was already found in protohistoric civilizations (see ANDEAN PROTOHISTORY; ASIATIC PROTOHISTORY; EUROPEAN PROTOHISTORY; MEDITERRANEAN PROTOHISTORY; MIDDLE AMERICAN PROTOHISTORY).

In the ancient Eastern and Western civilizations metalworking played an essential role in the production of specific classes of objects which merit closer study because of their artistic development (see ARMS AND ARMOR; COINS AND MEDALS; EMBLEMS AND INSIGNIA; GOLD- AND SILVERWORK; HOUSEHOLD OBJECTS; LITURGICAL AND RITUAL OBJECTS; UTENSILS AND TOOLS). Metal is also indirectly involved in other artistic techniques (see ENAMELS; ENGRAVINGS AND OTHER PRINT MEDIA; SEALS) and constitutes the principal means for creating more complex and delicate scientific instruments, which aside from their practical use may also have esthetic qualities (see ASTRONOMY AND ASTROLOGY; AUTOMATA; INDUSTRIAL DESIGN; SCIENTIFIC AND MECHANICAL WORKS; VEHICLES). Lastly, apart from all its functional applications, the working of metal is identified with one of the most preeminent and universally diffused techniques of the visual arts, that of sculpture (q.v.).

With the omission of this last aspect, which must be considered together with the other techniques of sculpture, and with reference to the above-mentioned articles for a more thorough examination of its particular uses, the present discussion is devoted to artistic metalwork in its general and universal framework. Its development is not only concerned with a common technological foundation but is also related to typical forms and decorative elements, which, through their continuity, innovations, transmissions, and characteristics peculiar to each civilization, constitute a history of the art of metalworking.

SUMMARY. *Origins and development of artistic metalwork, with particular attention to the ancient world* (col. 790): *Metals and alloys: a. Gold; b. Silver; c. Copper; d. Bronze; e. Brass; f. Iron. Beginnings of metallurgy. The working and artistic uses of metal in sheets. The casting of copper and bronze. Artistic applications of bronze casting. Ironwork: The blacksmith. Decorative techniques. The artistic production of metalwork in Western civilizations from the Middle Ages to the present* (col. 798): *Bronze and brass; Copper; Lead; Pewter; Wrought iron; Chiseled iron and the art of the locksmith; Cut steel; Damascened iron; Cast iron; Metalwork in contemporary art. Aspects of artistic metalwork in Asia, pre-Columbian America, and Africa* (col. 812): *The Iranian world; Southern and southeastern Asia; China and Japan; Pre-Columbian America; Africa.*

ORIGINS AND DEVELOPMENT OF ARTISTIC METALWORK, WITH PARTICULAR ATTENTION TO THE ANCIENT WORLD. *Metals and alloys. a. Gold.* In nature gold is found in the free, or native, condition. That is, there are nuggets of gold which provide a metal that is ready for use, as distinct from those metals which must be obtained from mineral ores by means of heat and the reduction process. In the Old World, where the quantity of gold nuggets was limited, most gold was probably obtained by washing alluvial sands and deposits from river beds. Such gold dust had to be melted together before it could be used by the goldsmith. Mining for gold occurred at a later period, but there is reason to believe that gold mining was established in Egypt during the 2d millennium B.C. In its natural state gold is always alloyed to some extent with silver, forming a substance called electrum, of which the oldest gold objects were usually made. Analysis shows that a method of purifying gold was discovered during the 1st millennium B.C. Gold is a metal of beautiful appearance, soft, easily worked and cast, and thus ideally suited to artistic work. Indeed, it was almost always used in antiquity for ornamental or artistic objects. It is impossible to determine when gold was first employed, but in some regions of the Old World it may well have been discovered in Neolithic times, even before the discovery of natural copper.

b. Silver. Silver was apparently discovered and used later than gold and copper. It is to be found in the free state and may also easily be smelted from silver ore; neither native silver nor silver ores, however, are abundant in the Old World. According to L. Aitchison (1960), after about 2500 B.C. nearly all silver was extracted from argentiferous lead by means of the cupellation process. Mining for argentiferous lead thus acquired importance in early periods, with a notable center in the great mines at Laurion in classical Greece. Esthetically, and in its working properties, relatively pure silver is an admirable material from which superb objects and ornaments are known to have been fashioned since early in the 3d millennium B.C.

c. Copper. In many parts of Europe and the Near East copper is found in the native state, the form in which it was first used by neolithic peoples. Almost all copper, however, and certainly all copper used in artistic production, was obtained by smelting the various copper ores, a process which may have been discovered in the Near East during the 4th millennium B.C. Copper was the most important metal of remote history chiefly because of its abundance and extensive distribution. Although ore was usually obtainable very near the surface of the ground, true mines were developed from the 2d millennium B.C. onward. Copper also became important because tools and weapons, as well as artistic and ornamental objects, could be made from it.

d. Bronze. The great importance of bronze in metalwork inheres in its superb casting qualities; without it the execution of large-scale metal statues and other works of art since protohistoric times would have been impossible. The metal known as bronze is a copper-tin alloy, which was probably discovered by mixing copper and tin ores in smelting furnaces. Later, but still within the Bronze Age, more skilled metallurgists obtained an improved substance by adding tinstone, and occasionally metallic tin, to liquid copper in a crucible process. This practice continued, advantageously increasing to approximately 10 per cent the amount of tin in bronzes of later periods. Though it is not known what people first discovered the process of making bronze, it is established that the Sumerians used a true bronze, though of irregular composition, during the time of the royal graves at Ur. The use of bronze spread slowly from Sumerian times, and for some centuries its full employment seems to have been generally retarded, probably because of the difficulty of obtaining adequate tin supplies.

e. Brass. The copper-zinc alloy called brass apparently does not date from prehistoric times; its discovery is ascribed to the Romans, who used it considerably in coinage and for other purposes. In antiquity and the Middle Ages brass was made by the calamine method of heating together zinc ore, calamine, and liquid copper. Brass is an excellent casting metal, but the major reason for its popularity with the Romans was probably the range of colors it could provide. By suitably proportioning the amount of zinc in the alloy, brass could be made which, when well polished, resembled gold in color, a feature very useful for coinage purposes.

f. Iron. Presumably, iron was discovered in the Hittite regions of Asia Minor, but, apparently, useful iron was not made in quantity before the middle of the 2d millennium B.C. The process of iron smelting was doubtless found by metallurgists who were experienced in copper smelting. Although iron ores were plentiful, the discovery of this process by prehistoric metallurgists was probably delayed because the iron-smelting furnace produced a dirty lump, of nonmetallic appearance, which did not at all resemble finished iron; ironmaking progressed with the realization that the lump, or bloom, had to be reforged to obtain useful iron. In large measure this discovery laid the foundations of the Iron Age, in which the use of iron and steel greatly expanded. Valuable as a medium for tools, weapons, and structural devices, iron was originally the material of the blacksmith rather than the founder. However, it has also played a considerable role in the field of artistic metalwork.

Beginnings of metallurgy. Although it is certain that toward the end of the 4th millennium B.C. the technique of working copper had attained a high level in Iran, Mesopotamia, and Egypt, it is not known from which center such knowledge spread, or whether it emanated from only one center. According to R. J. Forbes (1950), archaeology and classical tradition indicate the region of northeastern Iran, and beyond, as the source of the earliest metallurgical knowledge, whence it subsequently spread to the Near East. Archaeological excavations have disclosed that copper metallurgy was also known at an extremely early date in Sumer, although it is unlikely that Sumer was the primary center of metallurgy because its copper ore had to be imported from great distances. In the Iranian highlands, however, the ore was readily obtainable, rendering probable Iran's priority over Sumer as the source of the earliest copper metallurgy. Although copper was well established in Egypt in the Gerzean period, metallurgy apparently developed later there than in Iran or Sumer.

From its primary concentration in Iran and Mesopotamia the new art of metallurgy spread outward around the northern arc of the Fertile Crescent, in time reaching the Mediterranean coast, while there was also a strong westward diffusion through Anatolia, eventually reaching the ancient settlement of Troy, which during the 3d millennium B.C. acquired great significance in the history of metals. Metalworkers, traveling metal experts, and merchants established there a focal point whence technical knowledge and metals passed to the islands of the Aegean and beyond. Metals and the knowledge of metals also diffused from Asia Minor by way of the Hellespont and along the well-known Danubian route far into Europe. According to L. Aitchison (1960), "In broad terms, so far as continental Europe is concerned, the influence of Crete was mainly exerted towards the west, in the islands of the Mediterranean such as Sicily and Sardinia, and along the European shores of the sea as far as Spain. Troy and the other centers of influence in Asia Minor and Anatolia were the principal sources of the influences affecting the peoples living along the land routes that had been developed in and around the basin of the Danube. By 2200 B.C., traders from Troy had penetrated into Europe as far as the site of modern Vienna, and to the Erzgebirge [Ore Mountains] in Bohemia."

By the end of the 3d millennium B.C., primitive metalworking cultures had penetrated northward from Danubian lands into south central Europe and westward from the early copper-using cultures of Spain through western Europe. The art of winning copper was probably widely established in Europe by about 2000 B.C. Shortly thereafter began the European Bronze Age, in which the many important trade routes affected the wide exchange of metallurgical knowledge. Ornamental metalwork appeared in Europe, ultimately achieving the skill displayed in this medium by the magnificent art of classical Greece and Rome.

The discovery of copper smelting marked the beginning of true metallurgy and laid the foundations of the present copper and, indirectly, iron and steel industries. Although the origins of copper smelting have not been determined, it is often speculated that the discovery was made by accidentally placing some copper ore in an ordinary fire, perhaps the campfire of a nomadic people. This is theoretically possible because the temperature of a large, hot fire might be sufficient to smelt the ore under favorable conditions. It has been shown experimentally, however, that the discovery of smelting in such a manner is unlikely, because the atmospheric and other conditions of a campfire are not favorable to a reduction of the ore. It is also speculated that this discovery occurred through the more ancient craft of ceramics. If a potter were using a copper-bearing mineral to decorate his pottery, the atmospheric conditions within the kiln could cause an accidental reduction of the mineral to copper. The similarity of some metallurgical furnaces to ancient pottery kilns lends support to this theory. However the discovery of smelting was made, success must have depended upon repeated experiment. Because of the distinctive colors of the oxidized surface deposits of copper ore, it is likely that prehistoric peoples experimented with them, as well as other materials, in their search for copper. The temperature of the melting furnace in which the experiments were probably made would have been more than adequate for reduction to occur; its discovery thus depended upon the correct distribution of fuel and ore in the furnace.

The early primitive smelting furnaces were merely small pits, in which charcoal was used for fuel and a bellows provided an artificial draft. Eventually furnaces rose above ground level. Shaft furnaces, used in classical times, were followed by the Spanish Catalan type and later by the larger medieval furnaces, which were carefully built of stone and less wasteful of fuel and ore.

The introduction of bronze brought about considerable economic changes in the Old World. Of the two metals necessary for making bronze, copper ores were widely distributed, while deposits of tin ores were limited. The principal centers of bronze production were thus located near sources of both ores, in order to avoid transporting materials over great distances. Such specialized conditions appear to have been more frequent in Europe than in Asia, occurring in Cornwall and Bohemia, for example; hence Europe gradually achieved preeminence in bronze metallurgy. The concentration of bronze production in specialized locales led to trade with less favored regions. Such trade was conducted by traveling bronzesmiths, both traders and artisans, whose great bronze hoards have often been found. Because of its diffusion by trade and its superior properties as compared with copper, bronze became the predominant metal in Europe and parts of Asia by about 1500 B.C.

The finest bronzework, such as statuary and ornament, was produced in established settlements where craftsmen worked in permanent shops, often in association with city-states and temples. In contrast, the work of early traveling smiths was essentially limited to utility objects, because they had to carry their materials and build their melting furnaces at the various places where they worked. In either instance, the technical and artistic skill exhibited by early craftsmen, who labored under difficult conditions with only elementary tools (in the early periods they did not even possess tools of iron), was a remarkable achievement, especially that of the metalworkers of the ancient Near East. Tools and methods slowly improved, particularly with the discovery and use of iron, although artistic standards declined in several regions after classical times.

The working and artistic uses of metal in sheets. During prehistoric periods and later, artistic metalwork was the product of the art of the smiths and the metal founders. Smiths of copper, gold, and silver used as their basic material thin sheets of metal, to which various manufacturing techniques were applied. For example, the most obvious and probably oldest way in which to hollow, or "sink," a thin circular disk of metal to form a shallow bowl is to hammer the disk into a depression of the desired shape in a block of wood. This method dates, at least, from predynastic Egypt and Mesopotamia. The use of bronze sheets hammered over wooden molds and then applied to a wooden armature to form a statue was termed *sphyrelaton* by the Greeks; the Heraion of Samos has yielded a statue of this type (PL. 503). Another technique employed by the smith is known as "raising," whereby from a thin metal disk of suitable diameter it is possible to "raise" a vessel until it acquires, for instance, the shape of a beaker or a modern drinking glass. Working from a concentric circle that approximates the diameter of the base of the vessel, the smith gradually hammers the metal disk to the desired form by striking it on the outside surface, using a specially shaped hammer and anvil. A number of vessels found in the cemetery of Ur in Sumer were apparently fashioned by the raising process, thus indicating that the process dates from high antiquity; it was probably widely diffused among the metal-using cultures of the ancient Near East.

Another technique used by early artist-smiths was repoussé work, in which a pattern or design in relief was produced on sheet metal by hammering it either from the back or front (V, PL. 36). Examples of repoussé work from antiquity have also been found at al-'Ubaid and Ur. Other processes used by the smith included the fabrication of such objects as buckets and caldrons from thin plates, which were secured by rivets (PL. 503; V, PL. 34); the decoration of art objects by punching and engraving; and soldering and fusion welding. Turning, spinning, and inlay work were also practiced, probably by specialized artisans. The early craftsmen showed great skill in controlling their raw material while working with it. For example, they had excellent knowledge of the annealing process, by which metal is kept soft and workable, and of forging, casting, riveting, and other techniques.

It may be said that from very early times the work of copper- and bronzesmiths included both the traditional and the new. Bowls and other vessels executed in sheet metal largely imitated ancient pottery shapes and represented the traditional element of copper- and bronzework. Vessels were also made of gold and silver, often being most skillfully decorated, as evidenced by the repoussé work on the gold cups from Vaphio, Greece (IV, PL. 73). Indeed, gold may have been used earlier than copper for objects of art and ornament. Fine goldwork is well known from the royal graves of Sumer. For example, the helmet of Mes-kalam-dug (VI, PL. 243) from Ur, possibly dating from before 2500 B.C., was hammered from a sheet of electrum and ornamented with details in repoussé work; it shows the high standard of craftsmanship attained by early smiths. At Hierakonpolis, Egypt, was found a magnificent head of a hawk, which dates from about 2400 B.C. and is also beautifully fashioned from sheet gold.

An early example of fine silverwork is the vase of Entemena from Telloh (anc. Lagash) in Mesopotamia, dating from the 3d millennium B.C. (I, PL. 504), which was raised in the traditional manner from sheet silver. An outstanding amphora of richly decorated silver (VI, PL. 468), found in a barrow burial at Chertomlyk in southern Russia, was made by Greek silversmiths in about 400 B.C. Silver objects were sometimes decorated with other metals. A silver bowl from Ur is decorated with bands of electrum, and one from Enkomi, Cyprus, dating from about 1400 B.C., is skillfully decorated with inlays of gold and niello.

In addition to traditional work, the artist-smith originated new uses for metal in sculpture and ornament through the fabrication of sheets of copper and gold, for example. Perhaps the finest example of such work is the great Imdugud copper panel, or frieze, from the Mesopotamian site of al-'Ubaid, which dates from the 1st dynastic period of Ur. The frieze portrays Imdugud, the lion-headed eagle of the god Ningirsu of Lagash, between two stags. Its figures are executed in high and low relief and surrounded by a copper-covered wood frame. The entire frieze is covered with copper sheet, hammered to fit over a wood foundation to which the sheeting is secured by copper nails. Also from al-'Ubaid, and equally old, are two copper statues of bulls, which may be the oldest copper statues in existence. They are rather large and are built on a wooden core or foundation, upon which are nailed the separate sheets of thin copper that constitute the animals' various parts. Another remarkable work in copper is the life-size statue of Pepi I, an Egyptian pharaoh of the 6th dynasty, dating from about 2300 B.C. (Cairo, Egyptian Mus.). The statue is made from sheets of hammered copper which are riveted together, but the face, hands, and feet are cast in copper. For technical reasons the casting of copper is not an easy operation, and this work is unusual, if not unique, for its combination of hammered sheet copper, cast copper, and riveting. Because a statue fabricated of copper or bronze sheets, however well made, can hardly be as perfect as one that is cast, statues made from sheet metal almost disappeared with the perfection of bronze casting.

Sheet bronze was used in the same manner as sheet copper for vessels and for repoussé decoration. Examples of such work in sheet bronze include the decoration on a Celtic bucket of the 1st century B.C. from the Aylesford cemetery in Kent, England, and the foundation of the famous Battersea Shield, which was found in the Thames at Battersea, London (I, PL. 289; see GREAT BRITAIN).

The casting of copper and bronze. Copper objects were first cast in simple clay or stone molds. An impression of the object to be cast was molded in a clay block or cut into the surface of a stone block, and the molten metal was then poured into the depression of the so-called "open mold." Hollow "closed molds," resembling modern molds in principle, were developed for more complex articles. Fine objects were cast in bronze from a surprisingly early date, and as metallurgy itself developed and advanced, so also did the founder's technique. Early in the 3d millennium B.C., not only had bronze casting reached a high technical level, but the cire-perdue, or lost-wax, method of casting had been discovered.

The ancient cire-perdue method of casting, which is used for such complicated shapes as statues, where simple molding techniques are not always applicable, has remained unchanged throughout the centuries. It consists, first of all, of making a wax model of the object to be cast. The model is next covered with a layer of fine molding clay, which, in turn, is covered with ordinary clay of sufficient thickness to make a strong mold. The mold is then heated and baked so that the wax runs out leaving a cavity that corresponds exactly to the model. The clay is ready for use when it is hard-baked enough to contain the molten bronze for casting.

Artistic applications of bronze casting. Because of its special properties, bronze was used from the time of its discovery for making weapons (PL. 500) and other objects (PLS. 501, 503–505); this event was so important as to mark the beginning of a new era. The evolution and typology of bronze objects is of considerable interest. In bronze daggers, the flat, almost triangular blades of early copper daggers, which were both ugly and inefficient, evolved into slender and more shapely forms. At the beginning of the Bronze Age swords were developed from these daggers. The hilts of early types of swords were often secured to the blades by rivets, causing a constructional weakness that was later overcome by casting the blade and hilt in one piece. This stronger construction permitted the development of long, heavy blades much closer in proportions to those of a modern weapon. Such heavy bronze swords continued to be used into the early European Iron Age and were copied by the blacksmiths who fashioned the first swords of iron. Typologically, the bronze sword represented an advanced form that could not have been achieved in copper. In early times, a well-made bronze sword was as efficient as an inferior one of iron, if not more so, for it was not until blacksmiths were very advanced technically that the value of iron was fully exploited. The spear developed typologically from crude and weak tanged forms into the much stronger socketed variety which has remained in use through all subsequent periods to the present day.

Elaborate ceremonial weapons, popular in the Middle Ages and after, have also come down to us from prehistoric times. From Luristan come magnificent and highly ornate battle-axes, dating from about the middle of the 2d millennium (I, PL. 437; II, PL. 5; VIII, PL. 122). Some Hungarian battle-axes of the European Bronze Age are also noteworthy both for their design and decoration. In the Russian Kuban very ornate axes were cast after 1500 B.C. A notable battle-ax from Ras Shamra (anc. Ugarit) on the north Syrian coast, dating from about 1300 B.C., has an iron blade and a socket cast of copper and decorated with gold inlay.

Since remote antiquity, bronze has been a leading metal for statuary and works of art in general. A fine, life-size bronze head from Nineveh (I, PL. 508), possibly representing Sargon I, dates from about 2250 B.C. and is probably one of the earliest cast bronzes of this type. Outstanding examples of surviving Greek bronzes include the *Charioteer* from Delphi (III, PL. 346), dating from about 470 B.C.; the *Poseidon* of Artemision (III, PL. 356), belonging to the mid-5th century B.C.; and the *Youth* from Antikythera (III, PL. 377), executed about 340. All these works are life-size or larger. The Etruscans and Romans were also masters of the art of bronze casting. In this connection, it is sufficient to mention the *Capitoline Wolf*, the *Chimera* from Arezzo (V, PL. 40), the "Mars" of Todi (V, PL. 44), the statue of Aulus Metellus (Aule Metelle) from Sanguineto (V, PL. 53), the equestrian statue of Marcus Aurelius on the Capitoline in Rome (X, PL. 148), and the *Colossus* of Barletta (IX, PL. 60).

Great skill was required in the casting of such large statues, and special molding methods were devised. One such technique was piece molding, in which the molds were made in several sections, or pieces, which could be removed from the core in a manner that is impossible with conventional solid molds. This method was advantageous because it made possible the casting of more complex shapes and because the mold did not have to be destroyed after each casting operation. Large, heavy works of bronze were also executed by casting parts of the work separately and fusing them to the main body of the work. It remained, however, a highly skilled task to construct the cores and molds for large statues and to make them strong enough to support the great weight of the casting metal, which had to be melted in special furnaces built for each statue. (Vanoccio Biringuccio and Benvenuto Cellini wrote of these difficulties.)

Bronze has been used from early times for architectural purposes, particularly for ceremonial doors and gateways. The bronze gates of the Assyrian king Shalmaneser III from the palace of Balawat, which date from 845 B.C., were entirely covered with figures in relief (PL. 490). Roman bronze doors that have survived destruction include those in the central portal of St. John Lateran, which were made for the Curia of Diocletian in the Roman Forum, and the door, which is still *in situ*, of the so-called "Temple of the Divus Romulus" in the Forum. Since the 11th century of the Christian Era, large bronze doors have been made for important buildings and churches in Europe, achieving particular magnificence in Italy. In addition to the large works mentioned above, small ornaments and other art objects have always been cast in bronze, those of classical antiquity being of especial merit.

Although the small cast-bronze cups and chalices of ancient Greece and Rome would be difficult to surpass in grace and design, the same fine sense of proportion is often seen in the larger bronze works, for example, the great bronze crater of the 6th century B.C. which was found at Vix, near Châtillon-sur-Seine in France (I, PL. 354). This work is over 5 ft. high and is decorated with finely modeled figures in relief. Among the elaborately decorated mirrors produced by Celtic bronzesmiths in Europe are the Desborough Mirror from Northamptonshire in England, and the Birdlip Mirror from Gloucestershire (I, PL. 289), both of which have beautiful Celtic designs on the back surfaces.

Ironwork: The blacksmith. The traditions and evolution of the iron industry differed from those of bronzework. The blacksmith occupied a special position in primitive and later societies, and his craft traditions were strong and exceedingly conservative. In both Europe and the Near East his craft generated many myths and legends.

Serving principally for the manufacture of tools, weapons, and practical objects, iron was used much less frequently than copper, bronze, gold, and silver for artistic purposes. One of the early uses of iron was in the making of swords. In the field of ironwork technical improvements in strength and quality also led to esthetic advancement, until swords of great beauty were made. The finest swords were made either by "pattern welding" or by damascening, two very different methods. Those made by pattern welding exhibit horizontal bands of ornament running down each side of the blade. This technique may have originated with the Celtic smiths and was certainly known to the Romans. The blade of the damascene sword appears mottled, or watered, because of the composition, method of forging, and heat treatment of the steel. The original material for these swords was a special Indian steel from Hyderabad, which was exported to Persia and Syria as early as the 3d century of the Christian Era; both countries subsequently became famous for the production of fine weapons, particularly in the 13th century and after.

The smelting furnace was the most important element in the iron industry, as it was in the copper industry. It evolved from the small furnace of the early Iron Age, which was merely a hole in the ground, to the large furnace, or *Stückofen*, of medieval times. The early iron smelter was probably also a blacksmith, forging and fabricating the iron after smelting the ore. Although the development of the smelting furnace suggests that specialized craftsmen — separate iron smelters and blacksmiths — soon appeared, strong tradition effected the continuation of primitive methods and equipment in many rural areas. By Roman times iron was mined and produced on a commercial scale in the great centers of the industry. It is difficult to determine when the first associations or guilds of ironworkers were established, but it appears likely that there was a local guild of smiths in republican Rome and possibly in Brescia and Milan.

As late as the 12th century of our era iron was being smelted in many parts of Europe by the same methods that were used in pre-Roman times. After the 12th century there was a marked rise in iron production in Europe. The increased demand for iron products led to further specialization in the blacksmith's work and to the formation of such important craft associations as the historic guilds of the City of London. These guilds, however, existed only in large cities, while by far the greatest proportion of ironwork throughout medieval times was still produced in the traditional manner in country districts served by village or traveling blacksmiths. In medieval England much ironwork was produced in monastic settlements by monks who were highly skilled in the forging and fabrication of iron; in fact, in the Anglo-Saxon Christian period monasteries became the most important centers of ironwork. Although no new metallurgical processes were invented during medieval times, significant progress in increased iron production was accomplished by improved, larger furnaces and chiefly by the introduction of mechanical power in the form of the water wheel to operate the bellows and hammers in foundries and forges.

In quite humble objects for domestic use the smith, especially the Celtic smith, exercised a measure of artistic ability. Firedogs were ornamented with forged terminals in the shape of stylized animal heads; an excellent example is the wrought-iron firedog from Capel Garmon in Wales, dating to the 1st century of the Christian Era. In building construction iron was frequently used. Such use varied from the purely practical, such as tie bars to secure the walls of churches and other buildings, to magnificent wrought-iron grilles and screens in cathedrals. An outstanding example of such work is the superb wrought-iron screen in the Chapel of the Catholic Kings (Capilla Real) in the Cathedral at Granada, which combines vast size with a most delicate effect; for art works of this type iron is a particularly suitable medium. The blacksmith also displayed his art to advantage on grilled enclosures for tombs and shrines of saints.

While the Chinese cast statues and other iron objects from at least the beginning of the present era, the Romans and Greeks apparently made no practical use of cast iron, although it is possible they knew how to obtain it. In Western Europe methods of making and using cast iron have been known only since the 15th century. The ancient and medieval craftsmen found iron an inexpedient metal from which to fashion statuary because it did not readily yield a sound and flawless casting; also, it cannot equal bronze and the precious metals in beauty of finish and color.

Herbert H. Coghlan

Decorative techniques. The decoration of metals is achieved chiefly by means of insertions of metals of different colors. There are two such techniques: damascene and niello. The techniques of granulation and filigree will not be considered here, since these are techniques applied principally in gold- and silverwork (q.v.).

In damascening, thin strips (or even small sheets of foil) of copper, silver, and gold are applied cold (i.e., not fused by heat) on bronze to form ornamental patterns and, sometimes, even depictions. Examples include the famous daggers from Mycenae with lion-hunting scenes (IV, PL. 71). Sometimes the inserted pieces are so wide that they suggest intarsia, as in a late-antique bronze plaque in the Louvre.

In the niello process a black amalgam (*nigellum*; Lat., *nigellus*, dark) of copper, silver, and lead is poured into the grooves hollowed out of the surface to be decorated. This very old technique is particularly adapted to extremely fine and delicate work. Examples include the ceremonial arms from the tomb of Queen Ahhotep (an ax bearing the name of King Ahmose; PL. 497), cups from Mycenae (Athens, Nat. Mus.), and certain cups of the late Roman period. Niello work should not be confused with the oxidized (i.e., black) silverwork that was so highly esteemed in Egypt (Pliny, *Naturalis historiae*, xxxiii, 46, 131).

* *

THE ARTISTIC PRODUCTION OF METALWORK IN WESTERN CIVILIZATIONS FROM THE MIDDLE AGES TO THE PRESENT. *Bronze and brass.* Bronze was used for much the same purposes in the Early Christian period as in antiquity, but large-scale works were less frequently produced. In the Eastern Empire the doors of St. Sophia (PL. 507), some of which date from the 6th century, are the most imposing works in bronze. In the 11th century similar doors of bronze damascened with silver were exported from Constantinople to Italy, where some are still preserved whole or in part, notably in the cathedrals of Amalfi and Salerno. In the 12th and early 13th centuries Italian founders, mostly under Byzantine influence, produced a series of splendid west doors, including those of the cathedrals at Benevento, Monreale (III, PL. 12; XII, PL. 257), and Pisa (PL. 508). The west doors of S. Zeno in Verona (PL. 508), which show northern influence, are ascribed in part to a German founder. The survival of many bronze censers pierced with foliage of Romanesque design indicates the widespread production of small bronzes in 12th-century Italy.

In the West such liturgical objects as oil lamps, censers, and candlesticks were usually made of bronze, the finer examples being gilded. There was a vast production of bronze articles of personal adornment — especially brooches (fibulae) and buckles — which, being small, were usually gilded; these objects have been recovered in large numbers from graves of the Migration period.

Although documentary sources refer to large works of bronze produced between the 5th and 9th centuries, the only surviving examples were cast in Aachen in the foundry established by Charlemagne. Among them were four pairs of doors with lion-mask ring handles (III, PL. 65) based on antique models and the openwork grilles of the triforium in Aachen Cathedral (III, PL. 390). The same foundry also may have created the so-called "Throne of Dagobert" (III, PL. 68).

The flowering of the goldsmith's art in the Ottonian period (q.v.) was paralleled by great advances in the art of casting bronze, centered chiefly in the Rhineland and northern Germany. The Cathedral of Mainz has a pair of bronze doors dating from the late 10th century, each consisting of eight panels with figures from the Old and New Testaments. The pair at Hildesheim was completed in 1015 (X, PL. 467); their design is attributed to Bishop Bernward of Hildesheim. He, or possibly his successor, Bishop Godehard (1022–38), commissioned — probably from the same workshop — the bronze Easter column, nearly 13 ft. high, with cast scenes from the life of Christ, which are spiraled in the manner of the triumphal columns of antiquity. While most of the German Romanesque bronze doors are cast entirely in bronze, those at the Cathedral of Augsburg (PL. 508) are cast in separate panels and affixed to a wooden ground. Another outstanding work is the imperial throne in the Royal Hall at Goslar, Germany, the sides and back of which are covered with sensitively modeled and pierced Romanesque foliage. The German bronze founders were equally successful with such monumental works as the huge coronas at Hildesheim (11th cent.) and Aachen (12th cent.) and with such smaller objects as the holy-water bucket from Mainz in the Cathedral Treasury at Speyer and the imaginative aquamaniles. The aquamaniles were made in naturalistic and grotesque forms, including armored knights on horseback, lions, centaurs, and griffins and other monsters; the handle was shaped as a smaller monster or dragon, and the water could be poured through a spout in the larger animal's mouth or chest. All were made by the cire-perdue process, and no two are identical, though in the late-14th and 15th centuries the designs became more standardized.

Romanesque bronzes were often finished with the care and precision worthy of precious metals, and it is, therefore, not surprising to find in this period a particularly close relationship between goldsmith and bronze founder. Bronzes and articles of precious metal were produced in the same workshops, and some of the most imposing creations of early medieval art were executed in bronze rather than gold or silver (PLS. 167, 511).

During the 12th century bronze foundries in Lorraine (PL. 511) and in such Meuse valley towns as Liège, Huy, and Dinant began to compete with German centers. The presence of plentiful zinc deposits near Liège eventually led the Mosan workers to adopt brass, an alloy of copper and zinc, in preference to bronze, the copper-tin alloy which was generally used elsewhere. Though less expensive as a material, brass was disadvantageous in that it could not be finely chased and did not form a satisfactory ground for gilding. Dinant was so famed for its brassware that in the 15th century the term *dinanderie* was used to describe the brass products of the entire Meuse valley. The oldest surviving and most imposing achievement of the Mosan founders is the great font in the church of St-Barthélemy in Liège (V, PL. 319), which was commissioned by the abbot Hellin (1107-18) from Renier de Huy. The font appears to be of yellow bronze, but the composition of the alloys used in the Middle Ages was not determined scientifically and varied from piece to piece; for this reason, some scholars have preferred to use the term bronze for all Romanesque casting. Among the major achievements of the Mosan founders is the series of huge, seven-branched Easter candlesticks, of which fragmentary examples exist in Reims, in the Church of St. Vitus, Prague, and in the Cathedral of Milan (Trivulzio candlestick, ca. 1200). Exactly where these candlesticks were made is uncertain, but they have been attributed to England and Italy. Large ecclesiastical candlesticks were also made in Essen and Brunswick, Germany, and in England, where only the Gloucester Candlestick (see below) survived the Reformation, however. The most imposing 15th- and 16th-century productions of the Mosan founders included fonts and font covers, such as those in the Church of St. Walburga at Zutphen and the Cathedral of St. John at 's Hertogenbosch; eagle or pelican lecterns; and large chandeliers, which were embellished with figural sculpture and elaborate Gothic tabernacle work. The lecterns were widely exported, mainly to Italy, Spain, and England, in all of which examples still survive.

The term *dinanderie* is usually applied to the smaller articles produced in great quantities in the 15th century: candlesticks, dishes, jugs, and cooking vessels. Various objects for the altar were also made of brass, including figures of the crucified Christ which are often speculatively attributed to Mosan or German founders.

While the production of such large objects as lecterns, fonts, and Easter candlesticks was probably exceptional and therefore confined to a few centers, the smaller Romanesque bronzes were produced in many different places. Numerous superbly modeled crucifix figures have been attributed to Anglo-Saxon bronze founders, but the most significant English contribution is the altar candlestick which was made about 1110 for Gloucester Cathedral and vividly displays the imaginative fantasy of medieval artists (VI, PL. 252). The survival of a fine door knocker at Durham Cathedral and the description of a lost candlestick from the same cathedral as being "as high as the vaults of the aisles" indicate that the Gloucester Candlestick was not an isolated achievement.

The monumental or sepulchral brass, a brass sheet engraved with a representation of the deceased which took the place of a monument, was introduced early in the 13th century. The earliest extant example is the brass of Bishop Iso von Wilpe (d. 1231) at Verden. Originally, such brasses were probably numerous on the Continent, especially in the Low Countries and northwestern Germany, but few survive, many having been destroyed to obtain the metal during the Napoleonic wars. They are much more numerous, however, in England, where over 7,000 survive. Flemish and German brasses were usually large metal plates with diapered backgrounds which set the figures in relief. In England, smaller figures, escutcheons, architectural canopies, and inscriptions were separately inlaid in slabs of gray marble or other stone. Brass was not produced in England until the 16th century, prior to which it had been imported from Dinant and Cologne. After brass production began, some of the English brasses were imported ready-made, but most were cut and engraved in England, probably in London. The earliest surviving English brass is that of Sir John d'Abernon (d. 1277) at Stoke d'Abernon, Surrey, although there is evidence at St. Paul's in Bedford of a monumental brass made in 1208. The designs of the early brasses were two-dimensional; later, in the 15th century, engravers attempted to achieve three-dimensional effects by shading with crosshatching, a method unsuited to the medium. Many English brasses of the 16th century are known to have been reused, because there are traces of earlier designs on the backs. These palimpsest brasses were made from earlier brasses that were removed from the churches during the Reformation; many were also imported from the Low Countries. The use of monumental brasses continued into the 17th century, but later examples were generally small and standardized in design. Near the end of the 14th century Nürnberg became an important brass and bronze center; there, founders produced mortars (PL. 510), sets of weights made to fit into each other and having swing handles decorated with grotesque heads, and the usual range of household utensils. Its most significant artistic productions, however, were bronze fountains, the best of which date from the 16th century. Late Gothic bronze founding in Nürnberg culminated in St. Sebald's Shrine (1519), the chief sculpture of Peter Vischer the Elder (q.v.), located in the church bearing the saint's name. North German bronzework included such masterpieces as the 30-ft. tabernacle of the Marienkirche in Lübeck. Large dishes with stamped ornament and calligraphic inscriptions, which were used as almsdishes and baptismal basins or washbasins, were also produced in Nürnberg and became popular throughout Europe. They were made according to a limited number of stock patterns which were still largely unchanged in the 17th century and constitute an early example of mass production.

Although the sack of Dinant by the troops of Philip the Good in 1466 forced many brass founders to emigrate, the term *dinanderie* was still applied to brasswork. This emigration to other towns in the Meuse valley and to France and England introduced similar brass-founding methods to many towns in western Europe, thus rendering difficult the identification of the exact place of origin of the individual object.

The most numerous surviving objects of the Middle Ages are brass candlesticks for both church and domestic use. From the 13th century on, a large range of types was made, beginning with animal or monster figures supporting the pricket on their backs; these are similar in appearance to the aquamanile (cf. PL. 164), though usually of smaller size. In the 14th century, tripod prickets decorated with octagonal moldings were used. Two main types of brass candlesticks were evolved in the 15th century: the pricket, with a tall, domed base, a molded stem, and a large grease pan immediately below the candle spike; and the socket type, with a tall, trumpet-shaped base, to the upper side of which was attached a wide rim or flange serving as a grease pan. In the latter type, the stem was molded and the socket pierced with a vertical opening, resembling a Gothic window, through which a spike could be inserted to eject the stub. Late medieval candlesticks were generally of uniform design, but local variations appeared in the 16th century, notably in Nürnberg, where an individual type was developed with the stem modeled as a male figure in contemporary dress holding a pricket or socket in each hand (cf. VI, PL. 390).

The brass church furnishings of the Renaissance and later cannot compare with those of the late Middle Ages; one reason for the decline was the increasing use of silver for altar crosses and candlesticks. Apart from the great lecterns that were still made by the brass founders of the Low Countries and such exceptional achievements as the brass choir screen designed by Joannes Lutma in the 17th century for the Nieuwe Kerk, Amsterdam, the most important productions were the many-branched chandeliers for churches. While these were also made in eastern Germany, Poland, and England, the main center of production remained the Netherlands.

Outside Germany and the Low Countries the most important 16th-century works in brass are those known as Venetian-Saracenic because of their mixed origin (VII, PL. 313). The earlier examples of this work, made by Near Eastern masters who had settled in Venice, are hardly distinguishable from those made in their countries of origin, but during the 16th century European elements became more apparent. Among their wares were ewers, dishes, bowls, candlesticks, and incense burners; they were usually Western in form, but the engraved ornament on the earlier examples was composed completely of abstract arabesques. The finer examples were damascened with gold and silver in addition to being engraved. By the mid-16th century, when Italian craftsmen had replaced the Saracenic smiths, figural subjects and floral designs derived from contemporary pattern books were introduced in the ornament. The craft survived the 16th century only in degenerate form.

Bronze plaquettes have been produced as independent works of art for the collector since the 15th century, but they were also employed as elements of other objects, such as the pax used in the Mass, or as decorative additions to furniture, inkstands, lamps, and saltcellars. The first name associated with plaquettes is that of Donatello (q.v.). Most of the famous medalists of the early Renaissance, such as Agostino di Duccio and Bertoldo di Giovanni (qq.v.) are credited with the authorship of plaquettes, but the Paduan masters Moderno and Riccio (VII, PL. 336) were far more productive. Both these masters derived their subjects from classical mythology and Christian legend. Moderno's works are clearly signed and attributions are rather firmly established. During the 16th century most of the great sculptors — among them Sansovino, Benvenuto Cellini, and Giambologna — also made plaquettes. These masters also founded schools, to which many of the plaquettes must be attributed; the main schools were those in Padua, Venice, and Milan. Besides the plaquettes produced by the above-mentioned masters and their schools, there was also a large production of others of slight merit, mostly cast, with religious subjects. After-casts of 16th-century plaquettes were made throughout the 17th and 18th centuries and are, inevitably, of poorer quality than the originals they reproduce. Only the electrotype reproductions of the 19th century achieve the effect of the originals.

About 1500, bronze founders in Italy began to produce a variety of small, useful, and decorative articles in addition to the statuettes, plaquettes, medals, and mortars which had hitherto been their main products. Bronze table candlesticks had appeared in a Gonzaga inventory of 1497, one of which was in the form of an eagle's claw supporting a pricket. The earlier caskets and inkstands were simply rectangular boxes with plaquettes forming the sides, but the inkstands developed into fantastic compositions based on classical vases and surmounted by statuettes. Incense burners and lamps were made in forms that illustrate the exuberant inventiveness of Italian mannerism. At first the lamps reproduced antique forms, but they soon became more extravagant, being made in the form of a foot, a Negro's head, a man with his head between his legs, or quite obscene compositions; some of the most extravagant designs came from the Riccio workshop in Padua. Standing bowls of varying sizes (some roughly finished in the manner of mortars, others superbly chiseled), table bells, firedogs, and door knockers and handles were also made. The bells and door knockers were often decorated with the arms of the owner; the bells were surmounted by statuettes, while the door knockers were often modeled in the form of a human figure. The most original and graceful designs are attributed to Paduan or Venetian workshops. The late-16th-century firedogs were of monumental size and were surmounted by figures. The most important Italian bronzes of the 17th century — other than sculpture — were the great altar candlesticks, many of them based on an original design by Michelangelo.

In the Middle Ages copper had been the preferred ground for enamels, but during the 17th century a cheap form of enameling was introduced in which brass was used as a base. The precise place of manufacture is not known, but the process was very likely not confined to one town or country, probably being practiced in Bavaria, the Meuse Valley, and London. The English type is often misleadingly known as "Surrey enamel." The enamels were of the champlevé type, but, instead of being cut out by hand, the depressions for the enamel were cast in the metal, thus saving a great deal of labor. Such a method was unsuitable for the production of small or fine objects, but it sufficed for such articles as andirons, candlesticks, stirrups, harness bosses, and sword hilts. The range of colors employed in this enameled brassware was usually restricted to blue, red, green, yellow, and white. Somewhat similar enameled brassware was made in Russia, mainly icons and ecclesiastical objects.

In the early 18th century an alloy of copper and zinc, similar to brass but containing a higher percentage of copper, was employed by a London watchmaker, Christopher Pinchbeck (ca. 1670–1732). It had the advantage of resembling gold in color and was, therefore, much used for watchcases, etuis, and cheap jewelry. Though its invention was claimed by Pinchbeck, the same or similar alloys were widely used in 18th-century Europe.

In the 18th century, gilded bronze, which in the previous century had been used mainly for sculpture, was more widely employed. In England the term "ormolu" is normally used to describe useful articles of this material; though the term is of French derivation, it is not used at all in France, where the material is known as "bronze doré." The objects usually made of ormolu in the 18th century included furniture mounts, fireplace furnishings, clockcases, lighting fittings, both candlesticks and chandeliers, sword hilts, and door handles and locks (PL. 517; VII, PL. 346; XII, PL. 181). The fashion for ormolu goes back to the court of Louis XIV of France, and during the century it was produced in the French manner in most European countries, though craftsmen elsewhere rarely achieved the French elegance of design or refinement of finish (V, PL. 444). Ormolu objects were cast, chiseled by hand, and finally fire-gilded; they should be distinguished from those which, though cast from the same molds, were roughly finished in the founder's workshop, instead of being sent to the *ciseleur* for the final process. These last were not gilded, but merely lacquered with a yellow varnish (*mis en couleur d'or*). The quality of ormolu depended on the amount of labor put into the finishing by the *ciseleur*. The finest were almost as expensive as similar articles in precious metal. The most exquisite French ormolu dates from the second half of the 18th century; though lacking the vigor of design of the rococo ormolu, its finish was impeccable. The most distinguished masters of the first half of the 18th century were Jacques Caffieri (1678–1755) and Charles Cressent (1685–1768), who was also an *ébéniste*; Pierre Gouthière, Pierre-Philippe Thomire *fils* (VII, PL. 323), and Etienne Forestier were outstanding during the reign of Louis XVI. Thomire (1751–1843) continued to work during the Napoleonic period, when standards were well maintained. The manufacture of ormolu has continued almost without interruption in France until the present day. Some of the 19th-century work, though not original in design, equaled the quality achieved by the best 18th-century masters and, having been cast from the same molds, can hardly be distinguished; cheaper 19th-century productions were of poor quality in design and finish.

Outside France the bronze founders who produced articles of gilded bronze have mostly remained anonymous. Some of the best work was done during the Napoleonic period in workshops set up under direct French inspiration in the European capitals. In England the firm of Boulton and Fothergill was established in 1761 with the intention of competing with the French bronze founders. The best productions were made after designs supplied by Robert Adam, executed in the attractive Derbyshire fluorspar (blue john); the finish of the Boulton ormolu is never above criticism, however. In the early 19th century, fine ormolu was turned out by such large-scale goldsmith firms as Rundell and Bridge, as a less expensive alternative to gilded silver.

Copper. Pure copper is not used for cast work but, like silver, is worked in the sheet. It formed the ground in the 12th–14th century for both Mosan and Limoges enamels (see ENAMELS) and was used by medieval goldsmiths as an inexpensive substitute for gold and silver. A large proportion of the surviving medieval church plate from the 11th century onward is of gilded copper, not because it was at the time more usual, but because articles of more precious metal have been melted down for conversion to another form or use. Copper formed a very satisfactory substitute for gold, because the red copper provided an excellent ground for gilding. In the 16th and 17th centuries, caskets, clockcases, and scientific instruments were made of copper, engraved with ornament or gilded. Copper was reserved for flat surfaces such as sides of caskets or cases, while those parts which had to be cast were made of bronze. In some countries, including England, the gilding of copper was prohibited, except for church plate, for fear that dishonest persons would sell the product as pure gold. In Germany, however, flagons, tankards, and standing cups were made of gilded copper in the same way and on the same designs as those of silver. In Italy, inkstands, incense burners, and lamps were made of gilded copper on the same designs as those of precious metal and, because of the mass destruction of the latter, form a valuable source of information about Italian Renaissance goldwork.

Copper was also widely used for cooking utensils on the folk-art level. Some 16th-century Italian ewers and basins were finely engraved, while in the 17th and 18th centuries vessels were roughly embossed with bold floral ornament.

A new use for copper was discovered before the middle of the 18th century in England with the invention of Sheffield plate. In this process a copper ingot was fused between two thick silver plates and then rolled out into a thin composite "sandwich," from which objects having the appearance of solid silver could be made. The process was industrialized on a large scale by the firm of Boulton and Fothergill of Birmingham, and the Sheffield plate found a ready export market. The early and better designs were neoclassic in character, but the high relief of the later Empire style could not be effectively executed in Sheffield plate, and the industry lost its earlier advantage over the goldsmiths. It survived until the mid-19th century, when electroplating on nickel silver took its place as a yet cheaper substitute for silver.

The electrotyping industry, which enjoyed a brief prosperity during the second half of the 19th century, made use of copper which was deposited electrically. Its main function was the inexpensive and exact reproduction of earlier metalwork, mostly goldwork. There has been little demand for such reproductions in the 20th century.

Lead. The low melting point of lead and its freedom from contraction when it cools render it a material particularly well suited for casting; it has generally been employed as an inexpensive substitute for bronze or precious metal. Its most important medieval use was for fonts, of which several Romanesque examples survive in England. They are usually cast with arcades enclosing seated figures. The few surviving examples in Germany and France date from the 14th and 15th centuries. A group of 14th-century French wooden caskets — all of similar design, covered with lead tracery and gilded to resemble precious metal — have survived in church treasuries. Their decoration, consisting of coats of arms within pierced tracery, suggests that they were originally secular in purpose, but they have been preserved because they were used as reliquaries in poorer religious institutions which could not afford silver or gold.

Another medieval use of lead was in the production of pilgrims' signs, small badges that were distributed to pilgrims at the various shrines of medieval Europe and worn subsequently on the hat or person as evidence that the pilgrimage had been completed; they usually bore some allusion to the saint at whose shrine they were obtained. The best-known is the shell of St. James of Compostela in Spain, while the most popular in England was that of St. Thomas à Becket in the Cathedral of Canterbury.

During the 16th century, a number of medallions and plaquettes were produced in lead. It is not quite certain whether these were made as inexpensive substitutes for those of precious metal or bronze or as models for the use of goldsmiths. There is, however, no doubt that after-casts have been made in lead from medals and plaquettes at all times; these after-casts can usually be recognized as such, but it is not as a rule possible to date them. The Renaissance fashion for elaborate ornament of a sculptural nature required a competence in modeling that did not lie within the reach of the average goldsmith. As a result, there grew up among the German patternmakers, such as Peter Flötner, Jonas Silber, and the master H. G. (Hans Jamnitzer), the practice of making lead casts from their models, which they sold to goldsmiths all over Europe. The goldsmith could make a mold from the lead pattern and apply the appropriate ornament to the vessel he was working on. Lead plaquettes seem also to have been used by goldsmiths as patterns for the decoration of *tazze* or of dishes with an embossed subject. In this case, the lead model solved the problem of translating the subject being represented from a flat graphic design to one in relief. The use of lead models accounts for the repetition of the same subject or relief on pieces made by different goldsmiths. (An extensive collection of these lead models is preserved in the Historisches Mus., Basel.) In the 15th century an effective use was found for lead in the making of heads for rainwater pipes. Examples from the 16th century are cast with Gothic tracery and decorative ciphers. In the 17th century lead casts became important features of external architectural ornament, bearing the coat of arms of the owner of the house and the date of erection. The most important external use of lead was for garden statuary (see SCULPTURE). Here it suffices to mention the lead vases and urns which decorated the gardens of most 18th-century mansions. Large numbers were made for Versailles and the many German palaces which imitated it, but the most impressive were the two vases, 15 ft. high, modeled by the Frenchman Jacques Villemotte (d. 1746) for the castle at Schleissheim. Lead was used for sarcophagi from the Middle Ages on. Medieval examples were undecorated, but large, freestanding sarcophagi of classical design were introduced in the course of the 16th century. The most significant are those by Balthasar Moll (1717–85) for the Hapsburg tombs in the Kapuzinerkirche, Vienna, and those by Andreas Schlüter (1660–1714) for the Hohenzollern tombs in Berlin.

Pewter. Pewter is an alloy of tin with copper, antimony, or lead. Since the Middle Ages it has been made in two qualities: The first, known as "fine pewter," does not contain lead and is used for plates, bowls, and flatware; the second and lower quality, into which a percentage of lead has been introduced, is used for hollow ware, such as measures, tankards, candlesticks and other objects which by reason of their forms can withstand rough usage.

The earliest surviving medieval pewter dates from the 14th century and shows a pleasing octagonal form, probably derived from similar vessels made of precious metals or of brass. Pewter was used at first by the richer classes in place of wood, leather, and horn, which remained in use among the poor. Inventories of the household goods of the nobility and the rich clergy in the later Middle Ages contain long lists of pewter vessels, most of which were employed in the kitchens of their vast establishments. Pewter was also used for ecclesiastical vessels in the poorer churches of the Middle Ages and for the funeral chalices which were made for burial with simple priests. From the late 16th century, pewter flagons were not uncommon in Protestant churches. As time passed, its use became more widespread, until by the mid-17th century there was scarcely a single household vessel that was not made of pewter. Little early pewter has survived; being a very soft metal, it soon became worn in use, whereupon it was returned to the pewterer for melting and remaking in more modern forms.

The earliest surviving English vessels are ecclesiastical, but a number of very fine guild flagons of Silesian origin show that the craft flourished in Germany in the late 15th century. These flagons, which are tall, polygonal, and engraved with figures of saints within elaborate tabernacle work, show the typical elegance of late Gothic design. Tall, baluster-shaped flagons made in the 15th and 16th centuries for the use of the members of German town and city councils rank among the most original creations of the craft. The German city guilds continued to use large pewter flagons long after the members of city councils had acquired vessels of precious metals. These were often extremely large and intended as much for display as for use at guild functions. While the German guild flagons are of excellent proportion, the standing cups modeled on those of precious metals have little merit. Both flagons and cups were made as long as the guilds existed.

The decoration on German guild plate was restrained, and common domestic plate was undecorated; but in the second half of the 16th century a fashion arose for show plate of a type of pewter known as *Edelzinn*. Such vessels were decorated all over with cast ornament and were meant for display on the cupboards and dressers that were a feature of 16th-century dining halls. The designs, based on those of the silver vessels displayed by the very rich, were cast from copper molds, with intaglio made by a specialized craftsman called a *Formschneider*, whose production fell within the province neither of the pewterer nor the goldsmith, but of the medal die cutter. The molds remained in use for many generations, so that designs were repeated in pewter dishes made over considerable intervals of time; they must have been among the most expensive of the articles that were tools of the pewterers' trade.

Edelzinn was produced in Germany, France, and the Low Countries. Its most prominent master was François Briot of Montbéliard (ca. 1550–after 1616), who designed and executed the models for the "Temperantia" dish, so called after the subject of its central panel. The design is much influenced by the mannerist style of the school of Fontainebleau and is notable for the sensitive modeling of its numerous elongated figures. A companion ewer and another dish (the Mars) are also attributed to Briot, who was otherwise occupied as medalist to the Duke of Württemberg. His designs were copied by the Nürnberg *Formschneider* Caspar Enderlein (1560–1633), who also produced a number of original models in the same late mannerist style. However fine the models from which this show pewter was cast, the decoration soon became rubbed if the vessels were used. During the 17th century pewter reverted to its former and only practical function as a material for domestic plate, and those who wished to make a display on their sideboards used silver.

Domestic pewter of the 16th and 17th centuries did not follow contemporary silver design but was made in simple forms more closely resembling those of pottery. The second half of the 17th century was the peak period of pewter in Europe: flagons, candlesticks, tankards, basins, ewers, and saltcellars were all made in bold, simple forms admirably suited to the nature of the material. In England, and to a lesser extent in Holland, a different form of engraving was introduced during the 17th century. The design was deeply cut into the metal in a zigzag line, producing a pattern that was far more resistant to wear than the raised, cast ornament of *Edelzinn*. The engraving was evidently carried out by the pewterer himself and was a form of popular art.

The 18th century marked a general decline in the craft. In England, silver forms were copied and embellished with a simplified version of the decoration appropriate to the precious metal; in France and Germany pewter was sometimes silverplated, and in Holland it was often japanned. Other materials (e.g., britannia metal) which performed more efficiently the purposes that pewter had served for nearly four hundred years were produced on a large scale.

Pewterers' guilds were in existence by the 14th century, and as early as 1300 an ordinance of the Holy Roman Empire laid down the proportion of lead that might be introduced. At a later date, control marks were stamped on pewter vessels as a guarantee that they were of the necessary hardness and that the proportion of lead was not excessive. In England a statute of 1503 required all pewterers to put makers' marks on the vessels they sold; these consisted of the pewterer's name or initials, or a device. In addition, a quality mark in the form of the letter X with crown or of a crowned rose was introduced, but did not come into general use before the 18th century. On the Continent three marks were used: the town mark, the maker's mark, and the quality mark, which usually consisted of an angel for the first quality or a crowned rose for the second quality.

The mid-19th century indulged in monstrous versions of Renaissance goldsmith's work which were cast in zinc, but pewter returned to favor in the last decades of the century.

Wrought iron. Though iron was used from an early date in the production of weapons and armor, it was not until the 11th century, at the earliest, that any artistic intention can be recognized in the working of it. A number of church doors with elaborately scrolled hinge work of the 12th century survive in England; also, Romanesque weathercocks are illustrated in manuscripts of the period. Several English cathedrals retain 12th-century screenwork, the finest being the St. Swithin grille (ca. 1100) at Winchester Cathedral. In the 13th century, however, the French ironworkers achieved the summit of technical mastery and artistic quality in the hinge work of the west doors of the Cathedral of Notre-Dame in Paris. The design is extravagantly rich, representing the terrestrial paradise, its foliage inhabited by innumerable birds, dragons, and other fantastic beings. Much of the detail of the Notre-Dame doors was produced by the stamping method, first introduced in the 13th century, by which the smith struck hot iron into prepared steel dies, as wax is pressed into a seal; minute detail could thus be achieved with a minimum of effort. Though the process was known and used in England, it suddenly appeared in full magnificence in the Île-de-France. German ironworking in the 13th century was far less ambitious; little or no use was made of stamping, and the smiths were satisfied if they fulfilled their practical function of rendering chests and doors secure from thieves. The best example, from the late 13th century, is the ironwork on the doors of the Church of St. Elizabeth at Marburg. In the 14th century German smiths developed the art of working the cold metal by sawing and chiseling it. New methods were paralleled by new designs, and ironwork was increasingly influenced by contemporary architectural forms. In place of the early Gothic foliate scrolls, geometric forms were adopted, the characteristic grille of the 14th century being a trellis with quatrefoils filling the spaces between the bars.

The earliest Italian grilles, dating from the 13th century, are made up of an iron framework grooved to receive sheet-iron panels. Subsequently, geometric patterns were arrived at by the simple process of riveting straps of iron together. During the 14th century screens composed of quatrefoils became the standard form in Italy; examples of this type of work can be seen in the Cathedrals of Siena and Orvieto, but the most famous are the grilles on the Scaliger tombs in Verona. On the richer grilles the panels of quatrefoils were built into a massive iron framing and surmounted by a frieze of foliage and armorial bearings in bent and cut sheet iron, as in a grille dating from the mid-15th century in the Palazzo Pubblico, Siena, on the frieze of which heraldic shields and the Roman wolf were introduced.

The blacksmiths of the 15th century delighted in copying in iron the elaborate tabernacle work which contemporary stonemasons had, in turn, taken over from the wood carver. Flamboyant tracery could easily be sawed out of sheet iron, and effects of molding achieved by using several thicknesses of sheet. Late Gothic tabernacles were customarily protected by grilles of great delicacy, some of the finest of which are located in the churches and chapels of the Tirol (VI, PL. 389). Outstanding work was also done in this manner in England; the most notable is the pair of gates from the tomb of Edward IV in St. George's Chapel at Windsor Castle, by an English smith, John Tresilian.

During the 16th century the best ironwork was produced in Germany, Austria, and Spain (PLS. 510, 518). Besides door mounts, hinge work, and grilles, which were also made in the Middle Ages, blacksmiths now made choir and chapel screens, staircase railings, and — particularly in the area of Teutonic culture — wellhead screens. The patterns were usually made up of spiral scrolls and trelliswork, in which the bars were interwoven in a manner recalling the elaborate scrolls and flourishes of contemporary calligraphy. The German Renaissance style can be seen at its best in the enclosure of the tomb of Emperor Maximilian I in the Hofkirche at Innsbruck, completed in 1573. The work of Jörg Schmidhammer of Prague, it has 20 panels, each of different design, introducing naturalistic foliage, with an angel holding a shield of arms included in the alternate panels; the effect is heightened by red and gold coloring. The Renaissance spirals continued to provide the basic pattern of German screenwork until the late 17th century; a particularly pleasing example, dated 1678, in the Cathedral of Schleswig introduces a variety of auricular forms into the spirals. During the second half of the 17th century the perspective screens first made their appearance; this favorite baroque device for giving the illusion of greater length appears in a number of the great baroque monastic churches, such as those at Ellwangen and Weingarten (VI, PL. 142), and in the Church of SS. Ulrich und Afra in Augsburg.

The vast screens (*rejas*) in the Spanish cathedrals are the most important 16th-century contributions to the art of ironwork. They were constructed in two or more tiers and reached up to the roof of the nave, a height of 45 ft. or more. At first the uprights were of square section, but spindled balusters of iron, hammered to shape with immense labor, were introduced in the 16th century. Sometimes, as at Toledo, the balusters were heavily plated with silver. The tiers were separated by cornices with chiseled or embossed friezes, and the whole screen was surmounted by a cresting of cut and bent foliage. Spain is so rich in these screens that it is difficult to choose the most significant; the Cathedrals of Toledo, Burgos (VI, PL. 306), and Seville all have outstanding examples.

French blacksmiths set the standards that were followed elsewhere in the 17th and 18th centuries (PL. 519). A French Huguenot *émigré*, Jean Tijou, who made the ironwork for St. Paul's Cathedral in London, completely transformed wrought-iron work in England and raised it from the low standard to which it had fallen during the 17th century. The French smiths succeeded in combining stability of construction with splendid ornament, and their work survives in great quantity, not only in the courtyards of palaces but also surrounding the choirs of Gothic cathedrals (e.g., Amiens and Bourges). Outstanding examples of 17th-century ironwork are the superb staircases of the Palais Royal and the Bibliothèque Nationale by Antoine Lemaître and the Escalier du Roi at Fontainebleau. In the second half of the century the most important commissions were those given by Louis XIV for his palace at Versailles, for which the gates and screen of the Cour d'Honneur cost 32,500 livres. The influence of French wrought-iron work was spread by the numerous pattern books compiled by Louis XIV's court designers, such as Jean Lepautre, Jean and Daniel Marot, and Jean Bérain. The Louis XIV style was based on a combination of interlacing bars with graceful foliate ornament, elements which readily lent themselves to rococo designs. During this period wrought iron for interior use was sometimes finished with a bright polish — as on the famous doors to the Galerie d'Apollon in the Louvre (PL. 520) — instead of with the customary black finish. There are innumerable examples of French wrought iron in the Louis XV style, but the most famous work of the century, executed in the independent duchy of Lorraine, was the gates and screenwork of the Place Stanislas at Nancy, erected for Stanislas I Leszczyński, former king of Poland. In the latter part of the century, screenwork, such as that of the courtyard of the Palais de Justice in Paris, became so massive that the execution presented the greatest difficulty to the smith but could be accomplished with ease by the founder. The polished iron stair rail of the Petit Trianon at Versailles is enriched with chased and gilded-brass foliage. In the 19th century cast iron generally replaced wrought work, and not until the end of the century, under the combined influence of the Arts and Crafts movement and the Jugendstil, did wrought iron return to favor.

Chiseled iron and the art of the locksmith. Pierced and sawed work, similar in character to that applied to tabernacles and grilles, was adopted by the locksmith and used to adorn the whole range of his productions: hinges, locks, knockers, caskets, and clockcases. First appearing in the first half of the 15th century, this style continued well into the 16th, its latest manifestations being found on the wrought-iron clockcases made in the late 16th century by the Swiss clockmaking family of Liechti. The finest work was that of the French locksmiths, though more attention was paid to the decorative features of the locks than to their technical efficiency. The face of the lock was divided by pinnacled buttresses into compartments, each of which was filled with layers of Gothic tracery of varying design, and the ground was covered with scarlet cloth known as *marouflage*. The more elaborate Gothic locks are usually identified as French, but fine work was also done by German and Spanish smiths, the style of the latter being based on German models.

Medieval caskets were made of iron or wood, the latter being supplied with elaborately cut and chiseled iron mounts. It was not until the end of the Middle Ages that recognizable national types appeared. One French type was entirely of iron with an arched lid; the Gothic examples have applied tracery ornament, while the later ones have etched or damascened ornament. The Spanish type was almost rectangular in section, but with slightly curved walls, and made of wood covered with one or more layers of tinned sheet iron pierced with Gothic ornament. The medieval key was of simple design, with the bow in the form of a trefoil or quatrefoil and the shank of plain circular section.

In the late Middle Ages, blacksmiths made a variety of articles of ecclesiastical and domestic furniture. Among them were door knockers roughly chiseled out of iron in the form of an animal or monster and having backplates pierced with Gothic flamboyant tracery; firedogs; hanging chandeliers; font cranes, of which the finest examples were produced in the Netherlands; lecterns; and standing candelabra.

Locksmiths were strongly conservative in their choice of ornament, and it was not until the mid-16th century that Gothic decorative designs were displaced by Renaissance elements. An important development in the history of the lock was the practice, introduced in the late 16th century, of placing the lock mechanism on the inside, rather than the outside, of the chest or coffer. This change diverted attention from the ornament to the mechanism, which became more complex. The German smiths showed particular ingenuity in devising complicated locks and padlocks. A specialty was the lock fixed on the underside of the lids of iron coffers; these shot as many as twelve bolts, all activated by a single key. Nürnberg was the center of fine locksmith work in Germany; there were produced many iron caskets with all-over etched and gilded ornament, similar in pattern to the decorated armor of the period and probably executed by the same masters. While German locksmiths used embossed or etched ornament, that on the French locks of the same period was usually chiseled from solid metal, though in a somewhat coarse manner. However, French locksmiths executed fine door hardware for the châteaux at Fontainebleau and Anet; but even more remarkable than the locks are the keys, which represent the highest peak of the locksmith's art. During the 17th century the French locksmiths' guilds required apprentices to submit an elaborate masterpiece lock, and the finest examples of this period were thus intended less for use than to display the proficiency of their makers.

French locks of the 17th century were unrivaled; the trades of gunsmith and locksmith were always closely associated, and it is no coincidence that the florescence of French locksmithing coincided with the best period of French gunmaking. Engraved decoration now accompanied the chiseling, but the locksmiths were less skilled with the burin than with the hammer and chisel. Brass lock plates were introduced toward the end of the 17th century, and in the following century they became universal. The locksmith now found himself confined to the making of the lockwork, as cast and chased lockcases were obtained ready-made from the founder. In England some fine door hardware was made to the design of Robert Adam, probably at the Birmingham factory of Matthew Boulton, but the locksmith's trade succumbed to the mechanical methods of production introduced in the 19th century.

The iron chiselers were mostly occupied with the adornment of such small articles as casket mounts, sword hilts, and locks and keys, but they occasionally received commissions to produce larger objects. Most important of the latter is the chiseled iron throne (now in Salisbury, Wiltshire, Longford Castle, Coll. Earl of Radnor) made by Thomas Rucker (ca. 1532–1606) of Augsburg for presentation by the city council (*Stadtrat*) to the Holy Roman Emperor Rudolph II. Signed and dated 1574, it is chiseled with numerous figures in the round and 130 medallions with small figural subjects. The laborious practice of chiseling figures in the round out of iron was continued in the 17th century by the Sadeler family, which worked for the Bavarian court, and by Gottfried Leigebe (1630–83), medal die cutter for the court of the Elector of Brandenburg. Leigebe's most important works are two equestrian statuettes of Emperor Leopold of Austria (Dresden, Albertinum, Grünes Gewölbe) and of King Charles II of England (Copenhagen, Rosenborg Castle), each of which is carved out of a single block of iron. These follow on a small scale the customary baroque monumental style.

Some of the most exquisite chiseled work of the 17th century was executed in northern Italy, in and around Brescia, and by the members of the Acquafresca family of Bargi, near Bologna. Their products included snuffboxes, tweezers, and other small, useful articles. The Brescian wares were ornamented with bold, scrolled foliage in a somewhat rustic version of the contemporary baroque style, while the Acquafrescas mastered a more sophisticated, Louis XIV manner.

Iron chiseling was always a subsidiary craft in the fine arms industry, from which both method and style of ornamentation were taken over. In the 18th century the craftsmen who decorated small swords with chiseled figures of classical deities against a mat-gold ground applied similar ornament to a variety of small luxury articles, ranging from chatelaines to etuis, shuttles, and snuffboxes. The finest work in this genre was done in Paris, but French *émigré* workmen introduced the craft to most European capitals.

Cut steel. Cut steelwork was introduced in England during the 18th century; its manufacture was exploited by the same Matthew Boulton who had set up the manufacture of ormolu in Birmingham. Similar work was done in France and, on a particularly ambitious scale, in the Russian town of Tula, near Moscow (VII, PL. 345). In this technique, a large number of steel studs with faceted and highly polished heads were applied to a metal background. It was used most successfully in cheap jewelry, because the faceted steel reflected the light more effectively than the marcasite which it replaced. In France toilet tables and workboxes of finely figured woods were studded with cut steel, while in Russia furniture and even large mantelpieces were adorned in this way. The steel studs were given their high polish by women who rubbed them with bare hands.

Iron chiseling was revived in the mid-19th century in the capital cities of Europe, mainly for the decoration of weapons, notably firearms. There was also a not inconsiderable production of spurious 16th-century works of art in chiseled steel by Parisian and Milanese craftsmen who, for obvious reasons, have remained anonymous.

Damascened iron. Damascening is the art of decorating one metal with incrusted ornament of another metal. In Europe it has usually involved the decoration of iron with gold or silver, but in Italy brass and copper were decorated in a similar way in the 16th century. The usual process was to roughen the surface of the metal to be decorated, using a file, thereby giving purchase to the precious metal, which was then hammered on in the form of wire or foil. By another, more laborious technique, a groove was cut in the surface to be decorated, and crosscuts were made at intervals; the gold or silver wire was then hammered into the groove. The former technique is commonly known as "false damascene" and the latter as "true damascene." Damascened ornament was widely applied in Europe in the Migration period, particularly on iron sword hilts and belt buckles and clasps; but it fell into disuse in the high Middle Ages, only to be reintroduced into Europe in the early 16th century through Italian, probably Venetian, contact with the Near East. Even when the technique had been fully mastered in Europe, arabesque designs of Oriental origin continued to be employed. Such masters as Hans Holbein (q.v.), Peter Flötner, and Virgilius Solis produced innumerable Moresque designs to be copied by the engraver and damascener. At first applied only to weapons, damascene was soon found suitable for all kinds of iron objects (e.g., mirror frames, caskets, and instrument cases) and was even applied to such large articles as tables and chairs, for which its minute scale made it inappropriate. The main center of the art in the 16th century was Milan (see ARMS AND ARMOR). Draftsmen who had emigrated from Milan were probably responsible for the finest damascening that was done elsewhere; thus the Milanese master Francesco Negroli is believed to have executed the fine damascening on the armor of Henry II of France. Benvenuto Cellini (q.v.) mentions in his *Autobiography* that he had mastered the art. Although later Italian damascening shows the inevitable drawbacks of large-scale production, earlier examples, such as the stirrups of Emperor Charles V by Bartolommeo Campi of Pesaro (Madrid, Armería Real), equal the finest Near Eastern work. After the 16th century, damascening was confined mainly to the decoration of arms, but there was a revival of the art in the 18th century in the south Russian town of Tula. The specialty of the Tula craftsmen was to incrust burnished steel not only with gold and silver but with platinum and copper as well. Like the 16th-century Milanese artists they indulged their ambition to the extent of producing large articles, including tables, chairs, and fireplace furnishings, the most important examples of which are preserved in The Hermitage, Leningrad.

In the 19th century, damascening was revived along with the other arts of the Renaissance. The most remarkable work was done by Eusebio de Zuloaga at Toledo, where the industry revived by this craftsman has survived to the present day. He made caskets, weapons, and clockcases which in style faithfully followed Renaissance prototypes but were unmistakably 19th century in spirit.

Cast iron. Though the technique of iron casting was mastered in Europe by the 14th century, it was not until the very end of the Middle Ages that cast-iron products began to show any artistic merit. Apart from objects of warfare, the main use of the material was in the production of fireplace furnishings; in the 15th century, firebacks, firedogs, and stove plates were made of cast iron. The only known Gothic cast-iron stove is preserved in the Veste Coburg (Castle of Coburg), where it was installed in 1501 by Frederick III (the Wise), Elector of Saxony. A number of 15th-century firebacks have been preserved, however, the finest examples of which come from the Eifel region of Germany. These firebacks were cast from molds that were formed by pressing a wood panel carved with the subject to be reproduced on the fireback into a bed of fine sand; the esthetic merit of the result thus depended on the skill of the wood carver. The finest cast-iron work was, therefore, produced in those regions which had both a supply of the raw material and a tradition of wood carving. This explains the relatively poor quality of late Gothic English firebacks in comparison with those cast in Lorraine and the Tirol. In the 16th century the iron-casting industry of Germany was particularly flourishing; some of the finest designs, derived from contemporary graphic art, were carved by Philipp Soldan (ca. 1500–69) of Frankenberg, Hesse.

Both monumental plaques and graveyard crosses were cast in iron during the 16th century and later; some of the plaques, cast with heraldic ornament and inscriptions, are of considerable artistic merit, in spite of the coarse nature of the material. The 16th century was the best period for cast-iron stove plates in Germany. Subsequently, in the 17th and 18th centuries, they were no longer decorated with finely modeled figural subjects, but with ornament of a somewhat abstract nature that was intended to conform to the decorative scheme of the room for which they were destined. In 18th-century England the increasing use of coal instead of wood fuel led to the introduction of the dog grate and the obsolescence of the fireback.

Improvements in casting technique during the 18th century made it possible to extend the uses of cast iron, particularly in architecture. The delicately pierced cast-iron gates at Schloss Pommersfelden, near Bamberg, date from 1718. Cast-iron railings were produced on a large scale in England during the 18th century, the earliest examples being those erected in 1714 around St. Paul's Cathedral in London. Cast iron was also used for the bases, capitals, and balusters of wrought-iron gates and screens, but not until the neoclassic period, in the last quarter of the 18th century, was cast iron regarded as a worthy substitute for wrought iron. It is not surprising that England with her great mineral wealth should have been foremost in exploiting the possibilities of cast iron. The first cast-iron bridge was erected near Coalbrookdale in 1779, and the material was used extensively in late-18th-century architecture. The long rows of terrace houses, which were so typical of late-18th-century English town architecture, required miles of railing of repetitive design, a need which could be met most economically with cast iron.

Cast iron was also used for grates and stoves; some of the neoclassic stove designs were of great elegance. Because the black tone of cast iron made it an acceptable substitute for the far more expensive bronze, in the early 18th century many small objects that would previously have been made of bronze were produced in iron; among these objects were paperweights, doorstops, lamps, and vases, which were of good design in the earlier examples but became increasingly fussy toward the middle of the century. Cast iron was also used in sculpture ranging from small statuettes to life-size figures. The mid-19th-century founders' success in producing fine castings led them to make articles in which delight in elaboration for its own sake is apparent. Some of the worst examples were to be seen at the Great Exhibition of 1851, where furniture and mantelpieces of cast iron with a riot of pierced ornament in a degraded Gothic or Renaissance style were much in evidence.

John F. Hayward

Metalwork in contemporary art. In the late 19th century the followers of Art Nouveau (q.v.) contributed to a remarkable expansion in the employment of iron and other less traditional materials in the arts — not only for railings and balusters (I, PL. 468) and for decorative architectural elements, such as the cast-iron ornamentation of façades by Louis Sullivan (I, PL. 469), but also for furniture (q.v.) and other household objects (q.v.). Early in the 20th century the architect Henri Van de Velde (q.v.) predicted "a great future" for iron, lead, and aluminum. Beginning in 1919, the Bauhaus movement gave added impetus to the use of metals in architecture and in domestic objects, with its buildings of metal and glass, with its furniture workshop (whose director, Marcel Breuer, first introduced steel tubing in the construction of furniture; V, PL. 456), and with its development of functional lamp designs. Only in post-World War II industrial design (q.v.), however, have metals found almost universal application in the production of vehicles, scientific and mechanical works, and utensils and tools (qq.v.).

With the emergence of cubism in the first decade of the century the use of metals in art began to assume the totally new characteristics that have become so typical of our age (see CUBISM AND FUTURISM). Such cubist-inspired works in metal as Picasso's *Female Head* (V, PL. 128), Raymond Duchamp-Villon's *Horse* (IV, PL. 82), and Jacques Lipchitz' *Sailor* (XII, PL. 513) retained the mass of traditional cast sculpture, but thin sheet metal also became an important medium for the rendering of the form-dissecting planes of cubism, as seen, for example, in the *Bust* (1916) by Naum Gabo and in works by Antoine Pevsner (qq.v.; V, PL. 137).

As a result of the impact of cubism and subsequent modern movements on sculpture (see EUROPEAN MODERN MOVEMENTS), modeling and representation have lost their supremacy to the quality of the material and its technical possibilities. Metal is often accepted in a coarse state, either as a beautiful form of nature or because it is considered to have a greater emotional intensity. On the other hand, nickel-plating and other methods of treating metal surfaces against corrosion have contributed to the achievement of purity of design, with an almost complete dematerialization of the object, as seen in works by Brancusi, Arp (qq.v.), and many others.

A large and important group of sculptors have adopted industrial and mechanical techniques for working directly in the metal, whereas in the past the artist usually made only the model from which the final work was cast by a founder. The Spanish artists Pablo Gargallo (1881–1934) and Julio González (1876–1942), both of whom created sculpture in wrought iron, were the forerunners of contemporary sculptors who execute their works with the tools of the smith, among whom are the American artists Theodore Roszak and Seymour Lipton (I, PL. 131; see AMERICAS: ART SINCE COLUMBUS).

In the years following World War II metal has generally been used less as a merely constructional element of sculpture and more for its colors and, above all, for its particular material qualities (PL. 521). The roughness of the surface is emphasized, left-over traces of the casting or soldering process remain, and dark, corroding varnishes are used to simulate aging. Iron, in particular, has proved to be a material that readily adapts itself to the creation of highly stylized sculptural images rich in symbolic references. This characteristic of iron as a sculptural medium can be seen, for example, in works of David Smith (I, PL. 132), Eduardo Chillida (V, PL. 146), and Lynn Chadwick.

The chromatic richness of metal resulting from certain surface coatings or from spontaneous aging has also stimulated pictorial compositions that are almost, if not actually, two-dimensional. These may be composed mainly of soldered or even cast panels, as in works by the French artist César (b. 1921), or of sheet metal freely juxtaposed and superimposed, as in Alberto Burri's 1957–60 series of "Irons." Lucio Fontana has used polished tin in place of canvas for compositions consisting of holes and cuts. Metal, especially iron, is also used extensively in the realization of "Neo-Dada" art forms, such as the assemblages of Richard Stankiewicz (b. 1922), which are made primarily of used machine parts, and those of John Chamberlain (b. 1927), which are composed of automobile fragments. (See also MEDIA, COMPOSITE; NONOBJECTIVE ART.)

* *

ASPECTS OF ARTISTIC METALWORK IN ASIA, PRE-COLUMBIAN AMERICA, AND AFRICA. *The Iranian world.* The vast and varied metalworking activity of pre-Islamic Iran was of some importance in almost all the phases of this period, sometimes setting its mark on particular artistic developments and indirectly but persistently influencing the work of later periods (see IRANIAN PRE-SASSANIAN ART CULTURES). The coherent evolution of Iranian art is partially linked to this consistent activity, which profoundly affected the development of style, as can be seen more clearly in diverse aspects of other activities. The Iranian area, like the areas between Anatolia and the Caucasus, was rich in cupriferous metals, and when the use of copper became common, toward the end of the 4th millennium, the sources of the Sumerian supply of this metal were found in Elam, as well as in Asia Minor and Armenia. The metal was extracted by washing alluvial deposits, and its source has been determined by the correspondence between its impurities and those of the washed sands.

In the Assyrian period the source of supply for the western regions of the Near East was more or less the same. The written records, which distinguish "good copper" from the less pure, emphasize the wealth of both raw mineral and copper products to be found in the Urartu, another very important area for ancient metalwork. The deposits of the Caucasus, which supplied the tribes of the Caspian steppes and other more distant areas (e.g., the valley of the Danube), were also of some importance. The diffusion of stanniferous minerals was responsible for a rapid acquaintance with bronze, to such an extent that one may doubt the existence of a prolonged Copper Age in Iran. According to some authorities, copper was replaced by bronze that contained a small quantity of tin. Classical tradition and archaeological data indicate, nevertheless, that northwestern Iran was the center of an ancient metalworking society, as well as an area of diffusion for the related technical skills. Archaeological and artistic data prove that Elam (the region around Susa) was an equally important area. Here, the first phase of metal production is marked by a predominance of copper pins with the clasp in animal form. These works, which exploit the animal motif so dear to the terra-cotta vase painters, are stylistically linked in various ways to the later productions of the north and already seem clearly Iranian in character. In the following phase, corresponding to the so-called "Royal City" at Susa and dating from the beginning of the 3d millennium, the characteristic types of work done in metal became more varied. There are vases with long, open beaks (derived from clay models), cups, spoons with the bowl divided into five parts, mirrors with handles, pins with terminal bulls' heads, axes, javelins, short sabers, and reinforcing nails for shields. Goldwork became considerably important, possibly because of contact with Mesopotamia, but it differs greatly from that of Mesopotamia, not only in the forms but also in the preference for settings of lapis lazuli (also found in copper objects) and its combined use with bone.

In the north, setting aside Anau, a notable wealth of metal objects corresponding to strata IIIb and IIIc has been found at Tepe Hissar. Copper, bronze, gold, silver, and even lead were used lavishly in goldsmith's work, as well as in functional objects, such as pins, weapons, spiral ornaments, and scepters. The discovery of a considerable quantity of unfinished objects — probably the warehouse of a foundry — has given clear evidence of technical skill and has brought to light other types of work, including small human figures and pins with heads of animals. The working of thin metal plates suggested to the artists of Tepe Hissar the stylized representation of a goat's head as seen from the front; the frontal design, which transforms the large horns of the animal into an almost spiral ornamental motif, was later to be used by the metalworkers of Luristan for similar but much heavier ornaments (II, PL. 6). The working of the metal plates and the stylization of the Tepe Hissar works may also have spread to and reacted by diffusion on the work of India (e.g., the anthropoid figure of copper plate from Bisauli, Uttar Pradesh). There was close contact with the Caucasus and Talish, although the incised decoration differed in the Iranian territory. Nevertheless, certain forms are derived from those of the Caucasus and Talish, such as the daggers and swords with central ribs and a crescent-shaped reinforcement at the base of the blade and with a hollowed-out handle for the grooved inlay work of wood or bone.

The metalcraft of Iran reached its highest point of development in the period of the Elam kingdom. The famous bronze statue of Queen Napirasu, consort of Untash-Huban (Untash-Gal; ca. 1250 B.C.) is sufficient to demonstrate the technical skill achieved by the Elam founders (VIII, PL. 121). Cast in two parts (anterior and posterior), the statue was later soldered with liquid metal that filled it completely, so that, although parts of it are missing, it still weighs about 3,850 pounds. The care with which the figure was executed, the accuracy of the details, the naturalistic vitality of the hands crossed at the waist, the contrast between the softness of the bust and the rigid stylization of the gown, all give this work great creative value, very different from the works of Mesopotamia. Various fragments show that it was a general practice in Elam to use metal bas-reliefs for decorating buildings of importance. The bronze "gates" that were intended to close the entrance to the cella of the fire temple at Susa demonstrate, in their technical skill and dimensions, the ability of the Elamite metalworkers at the time of King Shilhak-Inshushinak (1165–1151 B.C.). An ax from the "treasure" of the same king constitutes a prototype for the image of the griffin which later appeared in the Scythian and Central Asian world. At the same time, this ax, together with the one bearing the name of Untash-Huban discovered by R. Ghirshman at Chuga Zanbil, is undoubtedly an earlier example of the "zoomorphic joint" (a beast's head with wide-open jaws that hold the blade) used by the Scythians and in Luristan. The original source of the zoomorphic joint — characteristic of this metal production — is probably Syrian. Also from the so-called "Treasure of Shilhak-Inshushinak," the dove of lapis-lazuli paste with its collar formed of gold buckles shows the tendency to use polychrome materials and demonstrates the combined use of precious metals with hard and semiprecious stones. A silver hand and a mask from the same place, the surviving parts of a wooden statue of a divinity, show the particular taste and technical skill of the Elamite world. The bronze heads from Hamadan — and particularly the one in the Metropolitan Museum, New York — demonstrate the artist's great effort to translate into metal not only the physical aspect of the subject but, with an acute psychological study apparently of Elamite inspiration, his spirit as well (see PORTRAITURE).

The northern centers, such as Amlash, Hasanlu, and Khurvin (9th–8th cent. B.C., according to the recent chronology), do not seem to have produced monuments nor to have engaged in such a varied activity as that of Elam, but they follow a true decorative sense which shows itself in some exceptional creations of stylistic and compositional ability (II, PL. 5). The qualities of the metal are fully exploited by the sensitivity and technical skill of the artists, and the animal motif is always prevalent. The differences from the corresponding productions in terra cotta, in which the interest in volume is predominant, show that the same taste manifests itself even where the quality of the material necessitates diverse forms. The gold cups of Hasanlu and Amlash, like the well-known one of Kalar Dasht (VI, PL. 249), reveal a mixture of Iranian and Hittite and Syro-Hittite elements. At the same time, it is easy to distinguish those which are purely symbolic-decorative from those which reveal greater involvement and more ambitious intentions. Minor details, such as the triple line indicating the joints of animal limbs and certain other conventional forms, link the production of these northern centers to that of the Luristan bronzes, a production that is certainly more abundant and better known. Divided into two schools or types, that of the mountain tombs and that characterized by large votive pins with round heads (VIII, PL. 123), the production of Luristan also presents noteworthy stylistic variations and, by way of the Caucasus, assimilated influences from Central Asia and China (see ASIATIC PROTOHISTORY). The extensive use of the frontal depiction common to other Iranian centers, such as Geoy Tepe, the ribbon-like stylization of the animal figures, their frequently illogical and monstrous forms (see MONSTROUS AND IMAGINARY SUBJECTS), the highly descriptive quality of the compositions, and the preference for the corded motifs also found at Hasanlu, all are characteristic and distinguishable elements as compared with other works that are more realistic, or conceived on swollen and heavy lines — often of bestial monstrosity — typical of another important aspect of the Luristan production. Differences of time and place are hidden behind these variations, which exploit the qualities of the material by using the most varied techniques, from casting by the lost-wax process to incising and repoussé. Without doubt the artists preferred metal, not only for its esthetic qualities and permanence, but also for the effects that they were able to draw from it. In fact, while the prevalence of iron was later to drain the creative powers of the Iranian metalworkers, it is easy to see how the pottery work of some localities, such as Sakkiz, adapted details derived from the metalwork and used them as decorative elements. The shapes of the clay and the metal vases are also reciprocally related, without the marked differences in style that often occur in the work of other civilizations. The problematical production of Zawiyeh (VIII, PLS. 124, 125) occupies a separate position and acts as a link between the northern centers, Luristan, Central Asia, and Urartu (see IRANIAN PRE-SASSANIAN ART CULTURES).

The Achaemenian phase inherited the use of smaller statuary, as well as an interest in cups and vases, from the preceding Iranian schools. Some echoes of the Assyrian style, already present at Amlash and Zawiyeh, do not alter the autonomous character of the work, and gold, silver, bronze, and iron were used with great ability. The decorative tendency appears somewhat reduced and modified, though the inclination to use polychrome, especially by means of inlaid steelwork or damascene, still persists. From the stone reliefs of Persepolis and Susa it is possible to confirm the important role that Iranian metalwork sustained in this period as well, and perhaps the detailed descriptiveness of the great Achaemenian works can be traced to the minute work of the goldsmiths, who were accustomed to treating every detail of their figures with great care.

The metalwork of those areas where late cultures and nomadic groups predominated is largely responsible for the vast extension of influence, in different periods and diverse styles, from Achaemenid Iran to a considerable part of Eurasia from the Ural regions to the Altai, and from Central Asia to the India of the Maurya dynasty. It is the metalwork, in fact, that testifies to the presence of this influence in the Ural region (e.g., metal plates of the Iranian-Scythian type found in the valley of Yuryuzan' in Bashkiria, from the 6th–5th cent. B.C.; a bronze Achaemenian plate from the Kama River basin; and vases with Aramaic inscriptions and a sword with a handle of enameled gold from the tombs of Prokhorovka); the style of the few metal ornaments found at Pazyryk confirm the stylistic derivation from Achaemenid Iran of the small works of wood certainly inspired by the Achaemenian figural designs. As R. Ghirshman has noted (1961, p. 103), Achaemenian art is connected with the preceding Iranian currents by the continual use of the animal motif so dear to the nomadic people of Eurasia. The new religious and social ideas that animated the first world empire in history, with the severity of its style, naturally limited the creative imagination of the artists. It is in the minor works of metal, full of force and vitality, that the patterns and ideas of the old schools take on new forms, enriched by the artistic experience of the Medes and the Scythians, the Assyrians and the people of Urartu (VIII, PLS. 138–140). One is reminded of Zawiyeh or Kalar Dasht in the details of the silver plates with various repoussé decorations and incised and damascened geometric motifs, in the rhytons terminating in goats' heads, in the protomas of bulls or winged lions, and in the vases of complex structure. At the same time, certain figural conventions persist (e.g., in some representations of lions) that seem to be connected to the ornamentation of Urartu. The wide variety of Achaemenian gold- and silverwork seen in the gold and silver bracelets, small figurines of lions, sumptuous swords, necklaces, rings, and earrings confirms the Iranian founders' and artists' complete absorption in the working of metal.

In the Parthian period, the production of metal remained very intensive. The large bronze statue from Shami (ht., 6 ft., 3 in.), the head of which was cast separately from the body and completed by chiseling, is sufficient evidence of the continued preference for metal (VIII, PL. 141). The technique of separately casting the two parts of the statue is responsible for a lack of balance in the proportions, which suggests that the head may have come from another place, whereas the body was certainly cast at the site. Minor works, also in bronze, indicate an intensive production of metal in Fars, and although there is a lack of archaeological data concerning the Parthian period, the production and working of metal seem to have been an important activity in the rest of the area. The effect of contacts with the classical world is occasionally revealed by some detail of the small statues, perfume stills, gold and silver bowls, rhytons, plates, ornamental plaques, diadems, necklaces, and earrings (some in clusters). Seen together, however, these works remain exquisitely Iranian and are always inspired by a profound ornamental sense, which the chromatic effects of damascening, inlay, and enamels often enliven. The animal motif remained vital in gold- and silverwork as well as in the bronzes. At the same time, with new technical processes, special use was more frequently made of metal (chain mail, breastplates of superimposed sheets, etc.), and a noteworthy development began with the minting of coins.

When the Sassanians came to power, Iranian gold- and silverwork reached perhaps its greatest development, especially in the working of silver taken from the rich deposits of the territory. The style and forms naturally changed, and the plates, bowls, vases, and bottles often came from craft shops whose work served political purposes, since these much-admired creations were then sent as gifts and signs of friendship to foreign kings and chiefs. This explains the enormous diffusion of these works, which reached as far as Japan (e.g., the lobed bowls in the Shōsōin, Nara), coming from Poland by way of Siberia and China.

The high nobility also had craftsmen at their disposal, who produced silver articles for the personal use of their patrons. In such cases, as Ghirshman points out, the image of the reigning king, often used as the central figure of the design, is a sign of the noble's faithfulness to the supreme sovereign. The stylistic evolution of Sassanian silverwork, which was paralleled by a reduced bronze production and some goldwork, goes from moderate relief toward flat and stylized forms that are very effective. The decorative tendencies remain, and polychromy is obtained mostly through damascening. The remarkable exception to this is the so-called "Cup of Khusrau" (XII, PL. 395), with three circular rows of glass medallions of three colors set in a framework of solid gold, with a rock-crystal medallion at the center bearing the incised image of the king. These works, as well as the silks and other fabrics, account for the widespread influence of Iranian art of the Sassanian period. Still more important, it is easily demonstrated how the large rock sculptures commemorating the ascension to the throne or the undertakings of the Sassanian kings are also animated by a descriptive and compositional sense closely related to that of the silverwork. Once again, therefore, the Iranian decorative sense triumphs through the art of metal production, influencing almost all the plastic art forms (even gigantic works) of the period. The widespread influence of the Iranian creations in the field of gold- and silverwork is truly enormous; it is not only the dancing figures impressed into the molded, terra-cotta floor tiles from the monastery of Harwan in Kashmir (VIII, PL. 359) and the stylized mountains of the Chinese Buddhist paintings of Tun-huang that prove this. In fact, many of the pictorial compositions of Central Asia show the effects of the spatial conceptions of Iranian plastic art, and it is difficult to establish whether these derive from the large rock sculptures or the small compositions in silver. It is certain that in some cases — for example, the painting of Kucha (q.v.) — the attempt to achieve illusionistic relief is replaced by a flattening of the forms. This corresponds to the stylistic development of Sassanian toreutic work. Even after the fall of the empire, the Iranian toreutic tradition continued in "Outer Iran," with works of noteworthy importance created in the western regions of Central Asia, especially in Sogdiana (q.v.). Only a careful examination could define these works as post-Sassanian. On the other hand, both the stylized forms of the last Sassanian works and the likewise stylized works of somewhat later date from Outer Iran eventually inspired the daring and curiously modern compositions of the Islamic ceramists of the vital and fertile center of Nishapur. In their work — more than in the working of metal, which was by now partially modified — are found the last echoes of Sassanian and Central Asian toreutic work.

Mario BUSSAGLI

Southern and southeastern Asia. In the northwestern part of the Indian peninsula the working of metals is of very ancient origin. Precious objects of fine craftsmanship, such as jewels in burnished gold, silver vessels, and a few bronze or copper figurines (II, PL. 7), are among the vestiges of the Indus Valley civilization from the 3d to the first half of the 2d millennium B.C. (see ASIATIC PROTOHISTORY, INDIAN ART, INDUS VALLEY ART). It is known that the advance of the Aryans in the 2d millennium B.C. was facilitated by the superiority of their weapons and of their metalworking in comparison to that of an adversary which remained at the level of the Stone Age. In central India silver ornaments and, sometimes, small gold plaques with repoussé work of the protohistoric period have come to light. The documentary sources compiled in the 1st millennium B.C. (Veda, the great epopees, etc.) show, however, that iron was worked at an early period, at the same time as gold, silver, lead, and tin. These texts reveal the sumptuousness already achieved in gold- and silverwork (q.v.) and in jewelry, a taste which has survived in India. Steelmaking was also known before the Christian Era; from that time on, steel was exported from India to regions to the west. Quintus Curtius Rufus reported that the chiefs of the Punjab presented 100 talents of steel to Alexander the Great during his campaign in the Indus Valley.

The ancient texts also recall the importance of the corporative associations, among which those of the metalworkers held a position of some prominence. Each craft guild was headed by a chief or president, who was regarded as a man of high standing at the court of the sovereign. The crafts and the knowledge which they required were generally transmitted from generation to generation within the same family. Frequently several of these families joined together to form production centers for their own specific crafts, founding villages of potters, of carpenters, of smiths, and of other specialized craftsmen, in which traditions were formed and transmitted. Because of this gradual development of techniques and forms, the art of metalworking, like so many other fields of artistic endeavor, has taken its values from and remained faithful to the spirit of Indian art, even if certain techniques and influences have been absorbed from outside. The hereditary office of goldsmith was one of particular importance, and highly placed families retained one or more members of this corporation in their service, thereby assuring themselves of their products.

From the last centuries before our era (principally from the 2d century B.C.) sculpture and painting offer evidence of the abundance of artifacts produced by the various categories of metalworkers, of the most popular forms, and of the richness of the decoration. Depictions of jewels, weapons, and a diversity of other objects indicate the variety of types. The very rare extant samples from about the beginning of the Christian Era document the ability achieved by these craftsmen; the reliquaries, bowls and goblets in gold, silver, or copper are generally worked in repoussé and are sometimes incrusted with precious stones (VII, PL. 465). The jewels and the majority of the artifacts have come to light at Taxila, Pakistan (VI, PL. 256); they testify to the great variety of techniques then in use, which have survived until the present day. In India, gold and other metals are incised, open-worked, repoussé, chiseled, filigreed, granulated, or incrusted with gems, pearls, and other materials. The cloisonné process was already known, and chains of extremely fine links were made in very early times. Although the high quality of the coins of the Greco-Bactrian princes (3d–2d cent. B.C.) was not sustained (see COINS AND MEDALS), the issues of the Indo-Greek kings retained their traditions. These were still reflected in the coinage of the Kushan and Gupta dynasties, which for a short time reacquired an artistic value, only to vanish after the 5th century (see GUPTA, SCHOOL OF; KUSHAN ART).

The perfect knowledge acquired in the casting of iron during the early centuries of our era is evidenced by the surprising creation of works of considerable massiveness. At Dhar there is an iron column, or lat, more than 40 ft. high, which was raised in about 321. Before the Quwwat-ul-Islām Mosque in Delhi there stands the Iron Pillar, about 23 ft. high, bearing inscriptions of the Gupta king Candragupta II and dating from the beginning of the 5th century; its double capital was intended to be crowned with a statue. The quality of the material and the workmanship were such that neither the pillar nor the inscriptions on its surface have been attacked by rust. Moreover, iron and bronze have been used frequently in Indian architecture as fixing anchors or as clamps to connect stone in masonry. In the Sūrya temple at Konarak, incompletely soldered iron beams replace the usual crossed stone beams that support the great slabs which form the ceiling.

Metal was also used in harnesses (gold rings, elephant hooks, etc.), in the construction and ornamentation of carts, chariots, and boats, and in the decoration of palaces; according to a 16th-century writer, a room in the palace of Vijayanagar was "completely lined with gold."

Although few ancient objects have survived, more recent examples are numerous, and the craftsmen, because of their traditionalism, have often preserved the processes and forms through many centuries, in spite of the partial renewal of techniques and decoration that occurred after the arrival of the Moghuls in the 16th century (see MOGHUL SCHOOL). Precious metals (gold and silver) as well as the base metals (iron, tin, and particularly copper) have been used singly, alloyed, or associated according to various techniques. Certain combinations are peculiar to India or to some of its regions. One is bidri, an alloy of lead, zinc, and tin incrusted with silver; the surface of bidri is blackened to bring out the contrast of values. In similar work from Kashmir a floral decoration is traced deeply on a gilded silver object to create a delicate effect of contrast by allowing the silver to show beneath the gilding. Damascening is now used to decorate domestic articles; it was very much favored for the decoration of arms and armor under the rule of Akbar (I, PL. 454) and of his successors and under the Rajput princes (see RAJPUT SCHOOL). Copper, like brass, has been used for a great variety of purposes and worked in all manner of ways, with openwork, niello, repoussé, or gilt, and by being hammered, chiseled, incised, perforated, and even incrusted with silver. The brass of Benares has a gold luster which has never been equaled. The casting of bronze by the lost-wax process has been used for statuettes and other objects, both in India and in the regions whose culture is Indianized. A remarkable example of this process, which has been known for a very long time, is the colossal copper Buddha of Sultanganj of the Gupta period (5th–6th cent.; Birmingham, Eng., City Mus. and Art Gall.).

The art of metalworking flourished in the regions near India (Nepal, Tibet, Burma, Ceylon) and in the areas of southeastern Asia, where Indian traditions were established early and similar techniques often employed. However, although the same taste for jewelry and sumptuous work in precious metals is fairly widespread, and although the same careful craftsmanship was observed in the manufacture of ritual and sacred objects, local tendencies have nevertheless made themselves felt, and the ornamentation of the artifacts is related to that found on architectural monuments. In Tibet, metalwork — in bronze, especially — has been most widely used for religious purposes in the fashioning of liturgical objects of remarkable quality (PLS. 176, 178). In Burma and Thailand silver, in particular, has been worked with great ability (filigree, repoussé, niello, cloisonné). The craft traditions of Cambodia have survived to the present day, the same careful workmanship being applied to gold, silver, and bronze artifacts, with a similar refinement to be seen in the forms. Although ancient objects have survived (e.g., bells, basins, rings and hooks for litters and palanquins), the reliefs of Angkor Wat and of the Bayon have also contributed to our knowledge of the complexity and refinement of the ornamentation and of the sumptuousness and elegance of personal ornaments and ritual and utilitarian objects. Metal has also played an important part in Khmer architecture (see KHMER ART), in which iron anchors with double dovetail joints and clamps were soldered with lead into the stone in masonry construction; also, bronze plaques, which must have served as facings for the decoration of interiors, have come to light. Even though there are no samples of iron used in Indonesian monuments, Indonesian reliefs recall the ancient forms of metal objects. The surviving lamps, vessels, goblets, gongs, bells, and caskets in bronze and precious metals reveal the beauty of the work and the harmony of the ornamentation, as the jewelry still does. Ironwork reached the peak of its perfection in the hands of the armorers, especially in the manufacture of the kris, or Javanese dagger. By means of a special technique (*pamor*) the blade was made of alternate layers of iron and nickel iron, while the handle, made of diverse materials, was richly decorated.

Madeleine HALLADE

China and Japan. The high technical and artistic standards of the bronzes dating from the Shang dynasty (ca. 1500–ca. 1028 B.C.) found at An-yang and other cities indicate a long development. The lack of evidence for a primitive stage of Chinese bronzes is regarded by many scholars as proof of the migration of a bronze culture to China from the west or northwest. According to this interpretation, the Chinese learned how to produce and cast bronze from other peoples but perfected these techniques to a degree which has never been equaled. Currently, however, there is a tendency among Chinese and Western scholars to minimize the importance of external influence in favor of an indigenous evolution.

An-yang, the royal capital of the late Bronze Age was opened to scientific study through excavations at Hsiao-t'un, from 1928–37 and in the 1950s, which led to the discovery of many weapons and vessels characteristic of this period (ca. 1300–ca. 1028 B.C.). Excavations at Chêng-chou (Chengchow), south of An-yang, and bronzes found at Hui-hsien, still farther south, have augmented finds at Hsiao-t'un, disclosing the Bronze Age culture (ca. 1500–ca. 1300 B.C.) before the capital was moved to Hsiao-t'un. Although the vessels from these sites are more primitive in casting and artistic rendering than the classical bronze art of An-yang, they are still of much higher quality than is usual for products of a new art. They need not, in fact, be regarded as direct predecessors of the An-yang sacrificial bronzes, since they may have been made for secular use. In any case, they do not explain the rapidity with which the Chinese achieved the excellence in bronze casting manifested by the An-yang vessels.

According to a local tradition the copper and tin ores necessary for bronze products were once mined in the mountains northwest of An-yang, the old capital. The crucibles, molds, and other tools found there indicate that all the work involving smelting, refining, and casting could be done at workshops in the capital itself. The proportions of copper and tin or lead are not standardized in Chinese bronze, which shows a tin content ranging from 5–20 per cent and a smaller but varying lead content, differing in this respect from the bronze of the Near East and Europe.

The methods of casting can be divided into three types: single-mold, for articles with one flat side (weapons and decorative plaques); valve-mold, for articles which are symmetrical on both sides; and multimold, with the occasional use of internal cores. The third method has been described as either direct casting with molds and core or as an indirect method, in which piece-molds are used only to prepare for cire-perdue casting. Recent conclusive studies on this subject convincingly show that direct casting with molds and core was used, although H. G. Creel and many other scholars have accepted the cire-perdue method. The problem will not be definitely solved, however, until the fragments of molds found at An-yang and Chêng-chou are fully studied.

The earliest bronzes excavated at Chêng-chou and Hui-hsien show a great variety, which is even more noticeable at An-yang. They can be grouped as follows: food, wine, and water vessels; musical instruments; military weapons; tools; and miscellaneous. Of these categories, the sacrificial vessels have been of special interest to the Chinese at least since the Sung period, mainly because of their inscriptions. While the inscriptions on the Shang-Yin bronzes are short, those on bronzes of the early and middle Chou periods (ca. 1028–ca. 600 B.C.) are more informative. Since antiquity various vessels have had special Chinese names, and each type of vessel has had a somewhat standardized decoration of zoomorphic and unique geometrical forms (see III, cols. 474–77, 481–86). The dominant motif is that of the *t'ao-t'ieh*, a monster mask with large, protruding eyes, heavy nose-ridge, saw teeth, horns, and, occasionally, clawed feet, but lacking a lower jaw; the mask can also be read as a pair of opposed dragons with joined heads (II, PL. 10, FIG. 26). These dragons, *k'uei*, also appear individually in borders around the vessels. Also occurring in vessel decoration are cicadas, snakes, birds, bovine masks, deer masks, elephants, and, more rarely, human heads, while some vessels are themselves shaped like elephants, owls, or rams. The background of the zoomorphic patterns is always geometrical, with hooks and spirals in circular and square shapes, the so-called "thunder pattern."

Bernhard Karlgren has closely studied these patterns, classifying them in two main styles, A and B, and providing a key to the identification of the various patterns. Style A is characterized by the high relief of the masks, dragons, and naturalistic animal heads that cover the main surfaces of the vessels. Dominant in the early Chou period, the secondary Style B dissolves the animal motifs of Style A, making the patterns more geometrical and concentrating them within narrow bands which encircle the vessels; also, the relief is much lower than in Style A. In the Shang-Yin period, together with the incised and relief decoration, turquoise was used as inlay and the geometrical design might be filled with a black paste, the exact composition of which is not known.

The defeat of the Shang dynasty by the Chou kings resulted in the relocation of the capital to present-day Sian (Hsi-an), and the entire bronze culture successively underwent a great change, most obvious in the middle Chou period. Many types of vessels were discontinued, and only a few new types were introduced. The shapes of the latter were generally heavier and the casting much coarser. The *t'ao-t'ieh* masks and dragons were dissolved and simplified, and most naturalistic animal heads disappeared. The patterns, predominantly geometrical, were confined to broad, flat bands and included such motifs as horizontal fluting, scale pattern, and undulating meander. The middle Chou bronzes have been found at many places in China and show local variations of style and decoration.

Revived in the 7th century B.C., the art of bronzework subsequently attained new heights in richness of design and technical skill. At that time there appeared a new hybrid style that combined elements from the Shang-Yin and early Chou periods and borrowed elements from the nomadic art of the western tribes, which was transmitted through the Ordos (q.v.) region. Floral patterns were introduced for the first time, and sacrificial vessels ceded their prominence to such small, everyday bronzes as mirrors, dress hooks, horse and chariot mountings, weapons, tools, and other objects such as the bells found in the graves of rulers (PL. 498). The style of the period, which flourished in parts of China from about 600 to 206 B.C., the beginning of the Han period, has been called the "Huai style" (B. Karlgren) after the Huai River, where the first bronzes representative of this period were initially found; the term covers the late Chou, Warring States, and Ch'in periods, which, until now, have been difficult to separate more definitely on a stylistic basis. Characteristic of the style is the almost "baroque" tendency to cover the entire surface with intricate patterns of *t'ao-t'ieh* masks, dragons, birds, and animals against a background of spiral hooks or "grain pattern." For the first time gold and silver were used in great quantities as inlay (see GOLD- AND SILVERWORK); the inlay was made by hammering thin wires of the precious metal into the cavities. The precious metals were also incrusted with turquoise, jade, and other stones and sometimes affixed to the bronzes with lacquer (see LACQUER). It is likely that many small bronzes were produced at this time by the cire-perdue method, which was probably introduced from India about the middle of the 1st millennium B.C. In the period of the Huai style the art of bronzeworking flourished and dominated artistic metalwork to a degree that has never since been equaled.

During the Han dynasty (206 B.C.–A.D. 221) bronze was used mainly for practical purposes. Small bronze mirrors, still of fine quality, were made of so-called "white bronze," an improved alloy with a greater percentage of tin and silver, which gave a better reflection and has been used in China ever since, most frequently during the T'ang period (618–906).

Bronze casting was revived in the 4th and 5th centuries with the introduction of Buddhism into China and the resulting need for sculptures of Buddha, bodhisattvas, and other symbolic figures for the temples. Altar sets of varying sizes were also cast in bronze by the cire-perdue method and gilded, and some are of high artistic and technical quality.

In the Sung period (960–1279) the first careful studies of archaic bronze vessels were undertaken, followed by a great interest in archaizing art. Ancient sacrificial bronzes were copied in free versions, sometimes with skillfully inlaid patterns of gold and silver. The imitation of old bronze vessels continued but declined in quality after the Ming period.

Ironwork, which in China never equaled the importance of bronzework, is infrequently discussed in classical texts and is thought to have been mentioned first in 512 B.C., a very late date in comparison with other Eurasian cultures of antiquity. Though it was first employed in weapons which resulted in great military success for the Ch'in state in the West, iron was used almost exclusively for such agricultural tools as plowshares and spades, which were cast, like bronze objects, rather than forged. The most significant finds of iron tools from the period of the Huai style were found in the Hui-hsien tombs. Cast iron was not suitable for swords and spearheads, and sharp weapons continued to be cast in bronze until the Chinese learned to forge iron. The technique was probably introduced from the south, since many forged swords, daggers, knives, and spearheads dating from the 4th century B.C. have recently been found at Ch'ang-sha in Hunan.

In the Han period the iron industry acquired great importance and ironmasters were "richer than the princes"; as a result the industry became a state monopoly in 120 B.C. Excavations of Han tombs have yielded a rich variety of objects, including not only agricultural tools and weapons but also dress hooks, mirrors, chariot mountings, and horse trappings. The iron was sometimes inlaid with gold and silver or incrusted with plaques of jade (on dress hooks), and iron mirrors were covered with decorative sheet gold. Iron ornamented with gold also occurred much later, during the Ming and Ch'ing periods, for example. Iron has also been used in Buddhist and Taoist sculpture since the T'ang period.

Some sacrificial vessels of the Shang-Yin period were cast in lead, which was also used for tomb furnishings, as evidenced by the so-called *ming-ch'i* of the Han and later periods (see CHINESE ART).

Bo GYLLENSVÄRD

In Japan metalworking, which was probably introduced by the Yayoi culture, has not been traced further back than the 3d century B.C. Since bronze and iron appeared there simultaneously, a Bronze and an Iron Age cannot be distinguished. During most subsequent periods, until contact with the West was first established in the 16th century and renewed in the mid-19th century, Chinese art forms and techniques exerted great influence on all fields of Japanese art; for example, it is difficult to discern whether the metal objects of the Nara period in the Shōsōin of the Tōdaiji were made by Chinese or Japanese craftsmen, although an octagonal openwork lantern (PL. 514) is undoubtedly of Japanese origin. The introduction of Buddhism in the mid-6th century stimulated metalworking because of the demand for ceremonial implements and temple ornaments, most of which were made of bronze (PL. 515); in fact, until the 20th century, most Japanese sculpture was Buddhist in motifs. However, the swords and sword fittings (PL. 515), which were produced from the 8th century onward by a complicated technique and in accordance with an elaborate ritual, remain the finest and most characteristic type of Japanese metalwork. For more detailed discussion of this and other areas of Japanese metalwork, see ARMS AND ARMOR, JAPAN, and JAPANESE ART.

* *

Pre-Columbian America. In the Americas before the arrival of the Europeans the knowledge and use of nonprecious metals were remarkably limited compared to the technical and ornamental richness of the gold- and silverwork. The latter were used extensively in the production of jewels and household articles, particularly in the great Mexican and Andean civilizations (see ANDEAN PROTOHISTORY; GOLD- AND SILVERWORK; MIDDLE AMERICAN PROTOHISTORY). Notwithstanding the presence of iron in the American soil, the native peoples of the two continents did not know of or make use of it. Only quite late did they learn how to use and work copper and bronze; in the Americas there was no Bronze Age comparable to that of the Old World.

Bracelets and other articles from the mounds testify to an ancient knowledge of copper among the Indians in the area of the United States (see AMERICAN CULTURES; NORTH AMERICAN CULTURES). These finds show that the metal was worked by cold-hammering (a method still used by the Copper Eskimos), indicating a separate line of development from the other areas of the continent. Native copper, more frequently alloyed with tin in bronze or with gold in *tumbaga*, was worked mainly in the Andean cultural area, including the surrounding dependent areas of Ecuador, Colombia, northwestern Argentina, and northern Chile (PL. 499; I, PL. 212). The period of its maximum diffusion coincides with that of the Inca hegemony, as is demonstrated by the similarity of technical methods found in the entire area constituting the empire of Tahuantinsuyu.

In Mexico and Central America the importance of nonprecious metals, at least from a quantitative point of view, is completely secondary. There, however, and in the Andean region, gold leaf was employed on copper objects, which were either welded autogenously or joined by soldering.

In the Andean region copper was worked by cold- and hot-hammering and by casting with the lost-wax process. Simple instruments were used, including melting furnaces of fired clay, with an opening at the base for ventilation, blowpipes, crucibles, and molds. In ornamental work, techniques used in gold- and silverwork were employed, such as repoussé work, stamping, *mise en couleur* (by which an alloy is made to look like gold), and filigree work.

Naturally, given the quality of the metal, the copper objects seldom rival in beauty those of the precious metals. Peru, however, has yielded beautiful objects of copper and bronze, such as ceremonial knives (*tumi*); large pins having heads decorated with geometric and figural elements; and openwork clips with figures or scenes in delicate frames, which usually consist of juxtaposed spiral motifs. All these objects have particular importance because recent studies (Heine-Geldern, 1954) have shown their surprising affinity to objects of the same materials found in Asia in the sphere of the Dông-s'on civilization (see INDONESIAN CULTURES). A careful analysis has brought to light not only clear formal and stylistic relationships but identical working techniques as well. If other proofs eventually verify this fascinating hypothesis, it would signify that pre-Columbian metalwork does not represent a local development completely independent of the techniques used in the Old World, as hitherto maintained, but that it was imported from southeastern Asia in the period identified, at least for the Peruvian coast, with the Mochica civilization (4th cent. B.C. – 4th cent. of our era). This would mean that metalworking was introduced at about the beginning of our era, which coincides with other datings obtained from northwest Argentina and Ecuador.

In Middle America metalwork was certainly of later origin than in the central Andes. According to our present knowledge, copperwork appeared there in the late classic or even the postclassic period and already had the characteristics of a mature technique. This leads one to believe in its introduction, by way of the sea, from Peru. The articles produced were essentially utilitarian, except for some bracelets of particular value from the famous Tomb 7 of Monte Albán in Mexico. A unique example is a vigorously modeled mask representing the god Xipe which comes from western Mexico (q.v.; PL. 499).

Among the works that the North American Indians produced by hammering copper in a cold state, worthy of mention are the plaques of painted copper used as money on the northwest coast (III, PL. 416; see COINS AND MEDALS) and an interesting rattle from the same region (PL. 522). On some ornaments recovered from the tumuli of Ohio one can observe the technique of *mise en couleur*, which was undoubtedly obtained by hammering the metal in a hot state.

Ernesta CERULLI

Africa. In tribal art much of the character of the finished work usually derives from the raw material and the processes which have been used to make it. Metalworking techniques are of importance for the present discussion only in so far as they elucidate works of art. It is therefore convenient to distinguish mainly between those techniques in which metal is treated as malleable stone, so to speak, and those which exploit its potentialities as a liquid. The latter, the techniques of casting, are vastly more important for the production of works of art, while the former have been of greater value in most periods for the manufacture of tools and weapons, which are relevant here only in their ceremonial forms.

Most of the metals used in Africa (see BANTU CULTURES; GUINEAN CULTURES; SUDANESE CULTURES) could be beaten or cast; iron, however, could be worked only by hammering because the temperatures required to render it completely liquid could not be attained with the techniques available in the tribal world. In Africa, ironworking first appeared on the west coast late in the 1st millennium B.C., following directly upon the Neolithic period without the intervention of a Copper or Bronze Age; the transitional phase revealed in the Nok culture of northern Nigeria may thus be termed "siderolithic," as opposed to the chalcolithic of western Asia. Nevertheless, there is no evidence of the use of this predominantly utilitarian metal for artistic purposes until fairly recent times, although rust has probably destroyed many earlier works, dating perhaps from the early years of our era. It is likely that the earliest extant iron sculptures, and surely among the most interesting, are two figures about 8 in. high from the Bakuba tribe of the Congo, attributed to King Miele, a great smith who reigned in about the early 16th century (PL. 522).

The massive drop-shaped forging of iron in the shrine of Ogun at Ife, western Nigeria, is also noteworthy; this possibly dates from about the 14th century, but, although not a utilitarian work, it is doubtful if it can be classified as a work of art.

The principal manifestations of the blacksmith's art in Africa are found in the ceremonial axes of the Basonge (Songe; III, PL. 416) of the eastern Congo, in the openwork blades of which from 2 to 82 stylized human heads may be skillfully forged; in the iron standards surmounted by forged birds, chameleons, and other figures, which were used by the Yoruba of western Nigeria chiefly in the cult of Osanyin, the spirit of "medicine" or the life force; in some chiefs' staffs, surmounted by human figures, recently discovered among the Bambara, east of Bamako; and above all in the unique effigy from Dahomey, said to represent the Fon god of metal and war, Gu (the Yoruba Ogun), a "constructivist" masterpiece assembled in the 19th century (PL. 523). The forms of iron sculpture in Africa are conspicuous examples of the influence of technique upon style, being impressively stylized in terms of bent rods and surfaces and differing greatly from products of techniques which involve liquid metal.

The remaining metals may be fashioned either by hammering or casting techniques. The latter are by far the more versatile and important in sculpture, but hammering and related techniques, which are used in Africa more for decorative than sculptural effects, will be considered first.

As with objects of wrought iron, the most impressive works in beaten nonferrous metals have come from the royal court of Dahomey, in the form of human and animal figures from the treasure of the last king Behanzin (Gbehanzin). Outstanding among them is the large, rather naturalistic figure of the war god in sheet brass, the softness of its forms contrasting markedly with the more "abstract" version in iron, and the equally famous lion of finely embossed silver sheets over a wooden core (both, Paris, Charles Ratton Coll.). The Dahomean court style was apparently devised in the 18th and 19th centuries by the newly aggrandized regime through a combination of borrowings from the Europeans and from other African sources of high prestige. One of these sources seems to have been the court art of the neighboring Ashanti and Baule kingdoms; though casting was the principal technique there, some good repoussé work was done in brass (grease pots, or *forowa*) and in gold (some of the soul bearers' badges, or *akrafokonmu*). This syncretistic origin is strikingly reflected in the emphasis on "metallurgical joinery" which is so uncharacteristic of indigenous African work. (The metalwork of the flourishing tourist industry of Abomey, consisting of a combination of casting and sheet-brass work, is derived from this court art).

The Nupe of Nigeria are famed for their skill in making tinned-brass bowls, water vessels, and coffeepots, the forms and motifs of which strongly evidence Near or Middle Eastern origins some centuries ago. The central Yoruba make fine ritual fans of beaten and incised brass for the cult of the river goddess, Oshun. The Ibibio women of Calabar formerly did excellent repoussé work on imported brass dishes; and certain northern Ibo women wore brass anklets with enormous decorative flanges.

The Marka, a Bambara subtribe, and some other groups in the western Sudan use sheet brass to enhance their dance masks. Finally, a closer approach to a sculptural use of sheet (and strip) brass and copper is made by the Bakota, north of the lower Congo, whose ancestral shrine figures may be regarded as metal sculptures in low relief with wood backing; these highly stylized works have exerted a notable influence on modern artists (II, PL. 101).

There remains to be considered the casting process, by which the metal sculptors of the world have realized most of their finest imaginative conceptions. Casting, in this context, means the lost-wax technique, which was invented early in the European Bronze Age and flourished in every continent except Australia until it was largely superseded by the "sandbox" (bivalve or multivalve) technique of modern industry, which has now revived and developed the lost-wax process for finer work. No other single invention has been of such fundamental importance in the history of art, or, it may be added, in the development of Western industrial civilization, if only because of the great acceleration of the rate of technical progress through quantity production of tools and weapons that this technique made possible in the Bronze Age. Its special value for both industry and art inheres in its great versatility, which enables the founder to produce in metal almost any form which can be fashioned in wax.

The lost-wax process is essentially a method of mechanically translating a wax form into a metal one, during which the work of art may be considered to have passed through three states. In the first, it is a wax form exactly corresponding to that which the artist wishes to produce in metal; at this point, therefore, his creative work is already complete, even to the decoration, if any, of the surface. In all but very small castings the form has normally been modeled on a previously prepared core of clay, with the proportions suitably reduced to allow for the layer of wax. In the second state, the work has become a void: the wax has been enclosed in a clay envelope or investment, then liquefied by heat, and completely removed; the work has in fact ceased to exist, except as a negative impression inside the clay mold, and is recoverable only by a successful pour, since the impression is subsequently destroyed in breaking open the mold. In the third state, the casting is complete within the mold, the liquefied metal having been poured into it to take the form of the void. Now it remains only to remove the investing clay and the metal rods which have replaced the pouring channels and, if necessary, to finish the surface.

Cast metal sculpture in Africa is practically confined to the Niger basin. It may well be as old as the Christian Era, but the earliest known examples are the incomparably modeled, though rather static and expressionless, brass heads and figures of ancient Ife (VII, PLS. 107, 109, 115; see GUINEAN CULTURES), of which 25 major examples have been found. Thought to have been made by the Yoruba about six centuries ago, they are remarkably naturalistic, although it is not certain that they are actually portraits. It is believed that about A.D. 1400 this style was transmitted to Benin, about 160 miles southeast of Ife, as numerous bronze heads from the ancestral altars of the Bini kings can be arranged in a chronological series dating from the 15th century to 1933, when the last set was cast. In the earliest group the vigorously humanistic treatment of Ife style is still evident, although some features are much more stylized than others; the thin male heads and the best heads of queen mothers (probably of the 16th cent.) show a technical mastery equal to that of the Ife founders (VII, PL. 111). In the middle and still more in the late periods, however, the sensitive humanism was gradually replaced by an increasingly heavy and unimaginative stylization; L. Underwood suggests that, as the tradition of Ife was forgotten, the more schematic form of the clay core came to dominate the outer surface as well as the inner.

The great series of about 800 rectangular plaques dates from the middle period, probably the 17th century (IV, PL. 20; VII, PL. 113). There were at least one or two more centers of bronze casting, not yet identified, in the region of lower Nigeria. The best works of this group, such as the hunter carrying an antelope (Br. Mus.), express a creative dynamism which is absent in those of Ife-Benin tradition, although very evident in Yoruba castings for the Ogboni secret society. Related to this group are the famous bronzes of Jebba and Tada (see GUINEAN CULTURES), including the four largest castings ever found in Africa; with the sole exception of the sitting figure in the Ife style, they may be tentatively attributed to Idah (see SUDANESE CULTURES). The Igbo brasses, remarkable for their virtuosity, also belong to this complex, and may further be linked with the castings of the Tiv and Jukun of the Benue Valley (PL. 156), of the ancient Sao in the Lake Chad region and perhaps of the Cameroons Grasslands, although the latter may be a more recent phenomenon (PL. 523; II, PL. 99).

In Ghana, apart from the charming little brass weights for gold dust (PL. 523; VII, PL. 128) and brass ritual vessels (VII, PL. 127), and much gold jewelry, there are only a few major works of art (VII, PL. 124), such as a gold trophy head (damaged; London, Wallace Coll.) and two bronze heads found in an excavation in the Bron country. Farther west, among the Dan-Ngere tribes in the Ivory Coast and Liberia, the production of excellent brass figures (VII, PL. 121) was an industry of major importance.

William FAGG

BIBLIOG. *Antiquity*: G. Bapst, Les métaux dans l'antiquité et au moyen âge: L'étain, Paris, 1884; G. M. A. Richter, Greek, Etruscan and Roman Bronzes, New York, 1915; F. Schottmüller, Bronze statuetten und geräte, 2d ed., Berlin, 1921; G. de Manteyer, Les origines de l'étain nécessaire au bronze antique, Aix-en-Provence, 1924; L. Planiscig, Die bronze Plastiken, Statuetten, Reliefs, Geräte und Plaketten, Vienna, 1924; W. Lamb, Greek and Roman Bronzes, New York, London, 1929; G. A. Wainwright, The Occurrence of Tin and Copper near Byblos, JEA, XX, 1934, pp. 29–32; W. A. von Jenny, Keltische Metallarbeiten aus heidnischer und christlicher Zeit, Berlin, 1935; W. Deonna, Le mobilier délien, 2 vols., Paris, 1938; D. M. Robinson, Excavations at Olynthus, X: Metal and Minor Miscellaneous Finds, Baltimore, 1941; G. Bruns, Antike Bronzen, Berlin, 1947; R. J. Forbes, Metallurgy in Antiquity, Leiden, 1950; J. Werner, Slawische Bronzefiguren aus Nordgriechenland, Berlin, 1953; R. J. Forbes and others, A History of Technology, Oxford, I, 1954, pp. 572–662, II, 1957, pp. 41-61, 449–84; U. Jantzen, Griechische Greifenkessel, Berlin, 1955; G. Roeder, Ägyptische Bronzefiguren, Berlin, 1956; B. Svoboda, Neue Denkmäler antiker Toreutik, Prague, 1956; J. Charbonneaux, Les bronzes grecs, Paris, 1958; H. Drescher, Der Überfangguss, Mainz, 1958; U. Jantzen, Griechische Griff-Phialen, Berlin, 1958; G. H. Karo, Zwei etruskische Wundervögel, Baden-Baden, 1958; H. C. A. Kuethmann, Untersuchungen zur Toreutik des zweiten und ersten Jahrhunderts vor Christus, Basel, 1959; L. Aitchison, A History of Metals, 2 vols., London, 1960; J. Deshayes, Les outils de bronze, 2 vols., Paris, 1960; Situlenkunst zwischen Po und Donau: verzierte Bronzearbeiten aus dem ersten Jahrtausend vor Christus (cat.), Vienna, 1962.

Medieval and modern periods: F. G. H. Price, Old Base Metal Spoons, London, 1908; J. T. Perry, Dinanderie: A History and Description of Mediaeval Art Work in Copper, Brass and Bronze, London, New York, 1910; E. Dumonthier, Les bronzes du mobilier national, Paris, 1911; J. Robiquet, Gouthière: Sa vie, son œuvre, Paris, 1912; A. Byne and M. Stapley, Spanish Ironwork, New York, 1915; H. Schmitz, Berliner Eisenkunstguss, Munich, 1917; E. Hintze, Die deutschen Zinngiesser und ihre Marken, 7 vols., Leipzig, 1921–31; J. S. Gardner, Ironwork, 2 vols., London, 1922-27; A. Bonnin, Tutenag and Paktong, Oxford, 1924; A. Goldschmidt, Die deutschen Bronzetüren des frühen Mittelalters, Marburg, 1926; A. Pettorelli, Il bronzo e il rame nell'arte decorativa italiana, Milan, 1926; F. Stuttmann, Deutsche Schmiedeeisenkunst, 5 vols., Munich, 1927–30; H. R. D'Allemagne, Les accessoires du costume et du mobilier, 3 vols., Paris, 1928; H. H. Cotterell, Old Pewter: Its Makers and Marks in England, Scotland, and Ireland, London, 1929; J. S. Gardner, English Ironwork of the 17th and 18th Centuries, London, 1930; A. Kippenberger, Die deutschen Meister des Eisengusses im 16. Jahrhundert, Marburg, 1931; Theophilus Presbyter, Diversarum artium schedula (ed. W. Theobald), Berlin, 1933; H. Clouzot, Les arts du métal, Paris, 1934; O. Falke and E. Meyer, Bronzegeräte des Mittelalters, Berlin, 1935; H. R. D'Allemagne, Les anciens maîtres serruriers, 2 vols., Paris, 1944; H. Jantzen, Ottonische Kunst, Munich, 1947; J. Gloag and J. Bridgewater, A History of Cast Iron in Architecture, London, 1948; O. Homburger and M. Hürlimann, Die Trivulzio Kandelaber, Zürich, 1949; E. B. Frank, Old French Ironwork, Cambridge, Mass., 1950; S. Collon-Gevaert, Histoire des arts du métal en Belgique, Brussels, 1951; Musée des arts décoratifs, Trésors d'art de la vallée de la Meuse (exhibition cat.), Paris, 1951; H. Clouzot, ed., Le fer forgé, Paris, 1953; H. W. Macklin, Monumental Brasses, 7th ed., London, 1953; O. Kastner, Eisenkunst im Lande ob der Enns, Linz, 1954; W. Hentschel, Kursächsischer Eisenkunstguss, Dresden, 1955; H. Kohlhaussen, Geschichte des deutschen Kunsthandwerks, Munich, 1955; R. Michaelis, Antique Pewter of the British Isles, London, 1955; J. F. Hayward, English Cutlery, Victoria and Albert Mus., London, 1956; J. Leisinger, Romanesque Bronzes: Church Portals in Mediaeval Europe, London, New York, 1956; G. Schiedlausky, Essen und trinken, Nürnberg, 1956; A. J. Verster, Brons in den Tijd, Amsterdam, 1956; G. Zarnecki, Romanesque Lead Sculpture, London, 1957; Tardy, Les étains français, 3 vols., Paris, 1957–59; C. Boucaud, Les pichets d'étain, 3d ed., Paris, 1958; H. Landais, Les bronzes italiens de la Renaissance, Paris, 1958; L. Schmidt, Heiliger Blei in Amuletten, Votiven und anderen Gegenständen des Volksglaubens in Europa und im Orient, Vienna, 1958; A. J. Verster, Old European Pewter, London, 1958; J. Harris, English Decorative Ironwork from Contemporary Source Books, 1610–1836, London, 1960; E. Lassen, Knives, Forks and Spoons, Copenhagen, 1960; R. Lister, Decorative Cast Ironwork in Great Britain, London, 1960; E. G. Robertson, Victorian Heritage, Melbourne, 1960; E. Basserman-Jordan and H. von Bertele, Uhren, 4th ed., Brunswick, 1961; O. Höver, Wrought Iron (Eng. trans., A. C. Weaver), 2d ed., New York, 1962; P. Vogt, Standplastiken aus Stahl, Düsseldorf, 1962; G. Ferrari, Il ferro nell'arte italiana, 3d ed., Milan, n. d.

Iran: A. Godard, Les bronzes du Luristan, Paris, Brussels, 1931; K. Erdmann, Die sasanidischen Jagdschalen: Untersuchung zur Entwicklungsgeschichte der iranischen Edelmetalkunst unter der Sasaniden, JhbPreussKSamml, LVII, 1936, pp. 193–232; A. Godard, Les statues parthes de Shami, Āthār-e-Irān, II, 1937, pp. 285–305; SPA, I, 1958, passim; H. Seyrig, La grande statue parthe de Shami et la sculpture palmyrénienne, Syria, XX, 1939, pp. 177–83; G. Contenau, Arts et styles de l'Asie Antérieure, Paris, 1948; C. F. A. Schaeffer, Stratigraphie comparée et chronologie de l'Asie occidentale, I, London, 1948; M. Rutten, Arts et styles du Moyen-Orient Ancien, Paris, 1950; M. Bussagli, Arte iranica (exhibition cat.), Milan, 1956; R. Ghirshman, Argenterie d'un seigneur sassanide, Ars Orientalis, II, 1957, pp. 77–82; J. Deshayes, Marteaux de bronze iraniens, Syria, XXXV, 1958, pp. 284–93; L. Vanden Berghe, Archéologie de l'Iran ancien, Leiden, 1959; R. Ghirshman and G. Wiet, 7000 ans d'art en Iran (exhibition cat.), Paris, 1961.

South and southeastern Asia: G. Birdwood, Industrial Arts of India, 2 vols., London, 1880; W. Egerton, Illustrated Handbook of Indian Arms, London, 1880; C. de Ujfalvy, L'art des cuivres anciens au Cachemire et au Petit Thibet, Paris, 1883; C. de Ujfalvy, L'art des cuivres anciens dans l'Himalaya occidental, Paris, 1884; T. N. Mukharji, Art-manufactures of India, Calcutta, 1888; W. W. Rockhill, Notes on the Ethnology of Tibet, Washington, 1893; T. H. Hendley, Metal Work, JIAI, IV, 1894, pp. 17–24; T. N. Mukharji, Brass and Copper Manufactures of Bengal, Calcutta, 1894; B. H. Baden-Powell, Indian Arms and Armours, JIAI, VI, 1896, pp. 103–06; E. J. Rapson, Indian Coins, Strasbourg, 1897; W. Rosenhain, Notes on Malay Metal-work, JRAI, N.S., IV, 1901, pp. 161–66; H. Cousens, The Iron Pillar at Dhar, Ann. Rep. Archaeol. Survey of India, IV, 1902–03, pp. 205–12; H. Parmentier and E. M. Durand, Trésors des rois Chams, BEFEO, V, 1905, pp. 1–46; V. A. Smith, Catalogue of the Coins in the Indian Museum, 3 vols., Calcutta, London, 1906–08; A. K. Coomaraswamy, The Indian Craftsman, London, 1909; I. H. Burkhill, Fashion in Iron Styles, J. Asiatic Soc. of Bengal, N.S., VI, 1910, pp. 1–18; G. E. Gerini, Siam and Its Productions, Arts and Manufactures (exhibition cat.), Hertford, 1912; R. Hadfield, Sinhalese Iron and Steel of Ancient Origin, J. Iron and Steel Inst., LXXXV, 1912, pp. 134–72; I. E. Lester, Indian Iron, Staffordshire Iron and Steel Inst., Stourbridge, 1912; A. K. Coomaraswamy, Arts and Crafts of India and Ceylon, London, Edinburgh, 1913; W. S. Hadaway, Illustrations of Metalwork in Brass and Copper, Mostly South Indian, Madras, 1913; J. Allan, Catalogue of the Coins of the Gupta Dynasties, British Museum, London, 1914; P. Nevgi, Iron in Ancient India, Calcutta, 1914; R. B. Whitehead, Catalogue of the Coins in the Pañjāb Museum, 3 vols., Lahore, Oxford, 1914–34; S. C. Clarke, Dravidian 16th Century Swords, BM, XXIX, 1916, p. 168; O. C. Gangoly, Southern Indian Lamps, BM, XXIX, 1916, pp. 141–48; O. C. Gangoly, On Some Nepalese Incense Burners, Rūpam, VII, 1921, pp. 13–15; G. Groslier, Objets cultuels en bronze dans l'ancien Cambodge, Art et archéol. Khmèrs, I, 1921–23, pp. 221–28; G. Groslier, Recherches sur les Cambodgiens, Paris, 1921; M. Bernanose, Les arts décoratifs du Tonkin, Paris, 1922; C. J. Brown, The Coins of India, Cambridge, 1923; G. Coedès, Bronzes Khmèrs, Paris, 1923; W. A. Graham, Siam, 2 vols., London, 1924; A. Silice, Exemples d'art cambodgien contemporain: l'orfèvrerie, Art et archéol. Khmèrs, II, 1924–26, pp. 241–52; W. Stutterheim, Een belangrijke Hindo-Javaansche Teekening op Koper, Djawa, V, 1925, pp. 247–52; A. Durier, Dekorative Kunst in Annam, Stuttgart, 1926; W. Stutterheim, Pictorial History of Civilization in Java, Weltvreden, 1926; A. K. Coomaraswamy, History of

Indian and Indonesian Art, New York, London, 1927; T. J. Bezemer, Indonesian Arts and Crafts, The Hague, 1931; Les collections khmères et le Musée Albert Sarraut de Phnom Penh, Paris, 1931; P. Holstein, Contribution à l'étude des armes orientales: Inde et archipel Malais, 2 vols., Paris, 1931; W. H. Rassers, Inleiding tot een bestudeering van de Javaansche kris (Meded. K. Ak. van Wetenschappen, Afdeeling Letterkunde, N.S., I, 8), Amsterdam, 1938; K. K. Ganguly, Early Indian Jewellery, Indian H. Q., XVIII, 1942, pp. 46–59, 110–27; H. Marchal, Architecture comparée dans l'Inde et l'Extrême-Orient, Paris, 1944; A. Mookerjee, Folk Art of Bengal, rev. ed., Calcutta, 1946; S. Granesley, The New Galleries of Oriental Arms and Armors, AB, XVI, 1950, pp. 241–51; V. M. Narasimhan, Votive Lamps, Mārg, IV, 3, 1950, pp. 39–44; J. Auboyer, Arts et styles de l'Inde, Paris, 1951; J. Marshall, Taxila, 3 vols., London, 1951; A. L. Basham, The Wonder That Was India, London, New York, 1954; J. Bhushan, Indian Jewellery, Ornaments and Decorative Designs, Bombay, 1954; S. Swarup, Arts and Crafts of India and Pakistan, Bombay, 1957; A. J. Bernet Kempers, Ancient Indonesian Art, Cambridge, Mass., 1959; A. Mookerjee, Indian Primitive Art, Calcutta, 1959; F. A. Wagner, Indonesia, London, 1959; JIAI, passim.

Far East: *a. China*: W. P. Yetts, The George Eumorfopolous Collection: Catalogue of the Chinese and Korean Bronzes, Sculpture, Jade, Jewellery and Miscellaneous Objects, I, London, 1929; S. Umehara, Shina kōdō seika (The Flower of Ancient Chinese Bronzes), 7 vols., Osaka, 1933–35; B. Laufer, Chinese Muḥammedan Bronzes, Ars Islamica, I, 1934, pp. 133–46; H. Plenderleith, Technical Notes on Chinese Bronzes with Special Reference to Patina and Incrustation, Tr. O. Ceramics Soc., XVI, 1938–39, pp. 33–55; W. P. Yetts, The Cull Chinese Bronzes, London, 1939; B. Karlgren, A Catalogue of the Chinese Bronzes in the Alfred F. Pillsbury Collection, Minneapolis, 1952; M. Loehr, Chinese Bronze Age Weapons, Ann Arbor, 1956; W. C. White, Bronze Culture of Ancient China, Toronto, 1956; J. Needham, The Development of Iron and Steel Technology in China, London, 1958; N. Barnard, Bronze Casting and Alloys in Ancient China, Canberra, Tokyo, 1961; W. Watson, China: Before the Han Dynasty, London, New York, 1961; W. Watson, Ancient Chinese Bronzes, London, 1962 (bibliog.). *b. Japan*: Y. Kuwabara, Chōkin-ka nempyō (Chronology of Metalwork), Tokyo, 1905; Tosen Hirose, Wakyō Shuei (Fine Mirrors in Japanese Style), 2 vols., Kyoto, 1919–21; S. Umehara, Dōtaku no kenkyū (A Study of Bronze Bells), Tokyo, 1927; Hozuma Katori, Nippon kindō-shi (History of Japanese Metalwork), Tokyo, 1932; M. Suenaga, Ancient Weapons of Japan, Tokyo, 1943 (text in Jap.); National Museum of Tokyo, Pageant of Japanese Art, IV, Tokyo, 1958; B. W. Robinson, The Arts of the Japanese Sword, London, 1961; M. Feddersen, Japanese Decorative Art (trans. K. Watson), London, New York, 1962, pp. 95–147 (bibliog.).

Pre-Columbian America and Africa: E. Schmidt, Die prähistorischen Kupfergeräte Nordamerikas, AfA, XI, 1878, pp. 65–106; M. Uhle, Costaricanische Schmuckgeräte aus Gold und Kupfer, Globus, LX, 1891, pp. 163–65; F. H. Cushing, Primitive Copper Working: An Experimental Study, AmA, VII, 1894, pp. 93–117; O. T. Mason, Overlaying with Copper by the American Aborigines, U.S. Nat. Mus. Proc., XVII, 1894, pp. 475–77; F. Boas, A Bronze Figurine from British Columbia, B. Am. Mus. of Natural H., XIV, 1901, pp. 51–52; J. B. Ambrosetti, El bronce en la región calchaquí, Anales Mus. Nacional de Buenos Aires, XI, 1904, pp. 163–314; A. Baessler, Altperuanische Metallgeräte, Berlin, 1906; A. de Mortillet, Le bronze dans l'Amérique du Sud avant l'arrivée des Européens, Cong. préhistorique de France, Ier Session (Périgueux, 1905), Paris, 1906, pp. 443–49; C. W. Mead, Prehistoric Bronze in South America, APAmM, XII, 1915, pp. 15–52; D. A. Cadzow, Native Copper Objects of the Copper Eskimo (Mus. of the Am. Indian, Indian Notes and Monographs, 8), New York, 1920; H. Arsandaux and P. Rivet, Contribution à l'étude de la métallurgie mexicaine, JSAm, XIII, 1921, pp. 261–80; E. Nordenskiöld, The Copper and Bronze Ages in South America (Comparative Ethn. S., IV), Göteborg, 1921; J. Jijón y Caamaño, La edad del bronce en América del Sur, B. Ac. nacional de h., IV, 1922, pp. 119–26; G. B. Phillips, The Primitive Copper Industry of America, AmA, XXVII, 1923, pp. 284–89; H. Labouret, Le pouvoir magique des métaux, L'Anthropologie, XXXVI, 1926, pp. 127–29; G. Antze, Metallarbeiten aus dem nördlichen Peru (Mit. Mus. für Völkerkunde, XV), Hamburg, 1930; J. Maes, La métallurgie chez les populations du Lac Leopold II — Lukenie, Ethnologica, IV, 1930, pp. 68–101; A. Clément, Contribution à l'étude de la métallurgie précolombienne, JSAm, XXVII, 1935, pp. 417–58; P. Bergsøe, The Gilding Process and the Metallurgy of Copper and Lead among the Pre-Columbian Indians, Copenhagen, 1938; P. Rivet and H. Arsandaux, La métallurgie en Amérique précolombienne, Paris, 1946; A. H. Schweeger, Afrikanische Bronzen, Vienna, 1948; L. Underwood, Bronzes of West Africa, London, 1949; R. A. Mauny, Essai sur l'histoire des métaux en Afrique occidentale, BIFAN, XIV, 1952, pp. 545–95; R. von Heine-Geldern, Die asiatische Herkunft der südamerikanischen Metalltechnik, Paideuma, V, 1954, pp. 347–423; Bamenda Brass, Nigeria, 55, 1957, pp. 344–55; P. Dark, Benin Art, London, 1960.

Illustrations: PLS. 497–523.

METSU, GABRIEL. Dutch painter of genre scenes (b. Leiden, Jan., 1629; buried Amsterdam, Oct. 24, 1667). His father was a Flemish immigrant painter who died young. Little is known of Metsu's early career, not even who his master was. At the age of fourteen he signed a petition, along with other Leiden artists, to establish a painters' guild and became one of its first members when the guild was founded in 1648. In 1654 he was still in Leiden. His presence is recorded in Amsterdam in 1657; he married there on Apr. 12, 1658, and remained there until his death. Little esteemed during his life, Metsu was greatly admired by collectors in the 18th century, and his works were reproduced in engravings and mezzotints.

With Terborch, Van Mieris, De Hooch, and Vermeer, Metsu depicted middle-class subjects in which action is less important than the mood of comfort and contentment. Besides showing people talking, eating, making music, writing, or reading letters, Metsu also painted bakers and blacksmiths, market scenes, portraits, and occasionally even religious, mythological, and allegorical scenes. Like Jan Steen, who was also from Leiden, Metsu stressed the anecdotal element; but in action and sentiment his figures are much more reserved than Steen's boisterous characters. Metsu's seem complacent, even phlegmatic in comparison; they harmonize well with the subdued light and mellow colors he preferred.

Metsu's technique at its best is as supple and accomplished as any found in Dutch genre, but his compositions are apt to be somewhat crowded. He was particularly adept in painting still-life detail in his scenes of kitchens and markets. Occasionally he painted night scenes that show the influence of Rembrandt. Appearing in some of his pictures is a white background — a feature he may have derived (as did Vermeer) from Carel Fabritius. Metsu's career, indeed, strikingly parallels that of Vermeer, who was three years his junior. Both did their finest work in the years just before and after 1660, and in their later works both followed the prevailing tendency toward elegance and sophistication. However, although Metsu's life was five years shorter than Vermeer's, his total output was much larger; more than a hundred of his paintings survive.

MAJOR WORKS. *The Sick Child*, Amsterdam, Rijksmus. (V, PL. 316). – *The Letter Received*, London, Coll. Alfred Beit. – *The Visit to the Nursery*, New York, Met. Mus. – *The Vegetable Market at Amsterdam*, Paris, Louvre. – *The Man Selling Poultry*, Dresden, Gemäldegal., Alte Meister. – *The Young Woman Selling Poultry*, Dresden, Gemäldegal., Alte Meister.

BIBLIOG. Hofstede de Groot, Beschreibendes und kritisches Verzeichnis der Werke der hervorragendsten Holländischen Maler des XVII. Jahrhunderts, Esslingen, Paris, I, 1907, pp. 255–336.

Julius S. HELD

METSYS. See MASSYS.

MEXICO. The Federal Republic of Mexico (Estados Unidos Mexicanos) occupies the southernmost part of North America and includes the Isthmus of Tehuantepec, which is sometimes considered part of Central America. These areas, especially to the south and along the coasts, were the seat of some of the most advanced indigenous civilizations that flourished on either of the American continents and certainly the most highly developed that existed in pre-Columbian Central and North America (see AMERICAN CULTURES; MIDDLE AMERICAN PROTOHISTORY). By the time the subjugation of Mexico began with the overthrow of the Aztec empire by Hernán Cortés in 1519, the indigenous civilizations, such as that of the highly refined Mayas, were already extinct, while others, such as that of the Aztecs, were violently destroyed during the conquest. Spanish colonial civilization, superimposed on that of the native peoples, flourished to a remarkable extent, particularly during the baroque period, and influenced the local scene (see SPANISH AND PORTUGUESE ART). The art of modern Mexico has come to exhibit a pronounced national character and has assumed an influential position in the development of international art trends (see AMERICAS: ART SINCE COLUMBUS).

SUMMARY. Pre-Columbian cultures and artistic periods (col. 829): *The sequence of artistic periods in the Huaxtec area; The classic civilization of Veracruz; The Olmec culture; Phases of the Maya civilization; The Zapotec and Mixtec cultures of the Oaxaca area; The Puebla-Tlaxcala area; The Morelos area; The Valley of Mexico from the preclassic to the Aztec period; The Guerrero cultures; The pottery-producing cultures of western Mexico; The preclassic civilizations and*

Tarascan styles of Michoacán; The north central region. Colonial and modern periods (col. 837): *Hispano-Mexican art of the 16th century; Baroque and neoclassic styles of the 17th–19th century; Contemporary art.* Art centers and archaeological sites (col. 843): *Mexico City; Chihuahua; Coahuila; Nuevo León; Zacatecas; San Luis Potosí; Nayarit; Aguascalientes; Jalisco; Guanajuato; Querétaro; Hidalgo; Veracruz; State of México; Colima; Michoacán; Federal District; Tlaxcala; Morelos; Puebla; Guerrero; Oaxaca; Tabasco; Chiapas; Campeche; Yucatán; Quintana Roo.*

PRE-COLUMBIAN CULTURES AND ARTISTIC PERIODS. Of the some 760,000 square miles that constitute the area of the Mexican Republic, more than half — all of the northern and part of the central sections — was inhabited in pre-Columbian times by peoples of an inferior culture, whose artistic contribution is generally insignificant. On the other hand, some of the great indigenous civilizations of the Americas developed in southern Mexico and along the coasts, which with the present territory of Guatemala, El Salvador, British Honduras, and the western part of Honduras (qq.v.) formed a historical unit in which Middle American civilization was born and developed (see MIDDLE AMERICAN PROTOHISTORY). Of that culture area only the part included within the confines of present-day Mexico is dealt with below.

The historical and artistic periods usually recognized by scholars are the following: "preclassic," from the origins to A.D. 50 (broken down into three epochs — the preceramic, the origins of which are still unknown and which extends to 1500 B.C.; the archaic, 1500–500 B.C.; and the formative, 500 B.C.–A.D. 50); "classic," 50–650; and "postclassic," 650–1540 (subdivided into three epochs — the intermediate, 650–900; the Toltec, 900–1200; and the final, 1200–1540).

It is extremely difficult to pursue synoptically and comparatively the unfolding of the different phases within Mexico. In fact, the territory seems to be divided into a series of zones or culture and art areas, which in certain cases are unquestionably interrelated but still possess their own characteristics, as in the case of the similarities and differences occurring among the nations of Europe. Also, in many areas the scantiness of excavation and research makes any documentation fragmentary and our knowledge very incomplete.

For these reasons, it is best to follow the succession of the artistic phases within the individual zones. Naturally, the subdivisions are arbitrary to a certain extent; this must be so, not only because often we do not know the names of the peoples who brought in the individual cultures (thus entailing a certain disparity in the names given to the various areas, which are in some cases ethnic, in others cultural, and in others geographic), but also because there were contacts, exchanges, and overlappings of populations and cultures between areas. Thus, for example, the Maya area can be identified geographically as well as culturally, but this does not change the fact that at the beginning of the postclassic period the Toltecs established themselves in some of its zones and left behind conspicuous artistic evidence of their presence. On the other hand, the differentiation of the cultures of western Mexico is artistic and cultural, inasmuch as we do not know the name of the peoples who created the pottery that characterizes this area. The Oaxaca region is, instead, only a geographic entity, in which the Mixtecs succeeded the Zapotecs. This also happened in the case of the Valley of Mexico, the center of development of the indigenous culture: there the earliest cultural and artistic evidence dates back to the archaic period, but we do not know who was responsible for it. Subsequently, at the outset of the classic period, and perhaps even prior to it, the advanced culture of Teotihuacán developed there, with an extraordinary flourishing of religious architecture; and in the postclassic period the warrior civili-

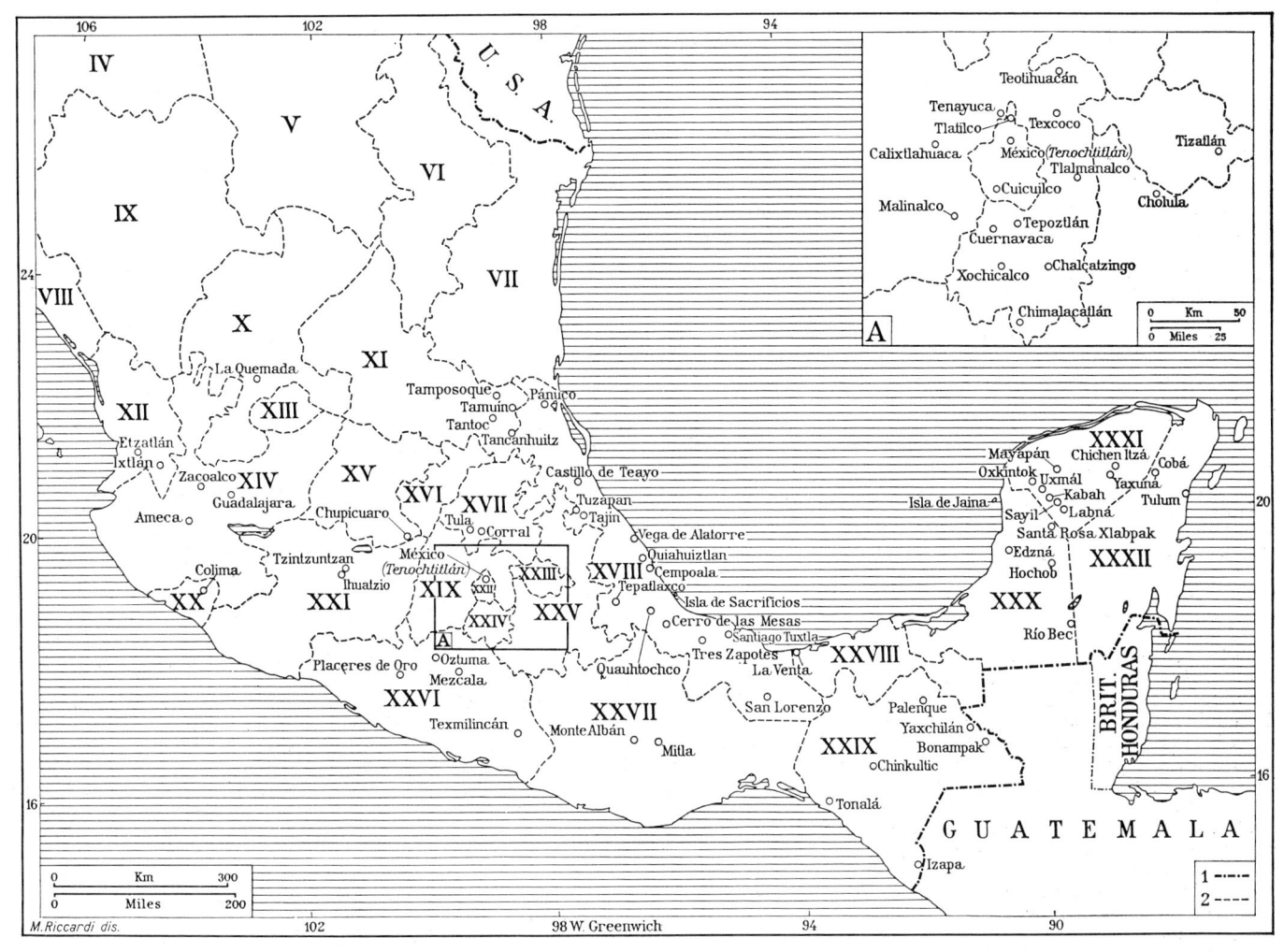

Principal pre-Columbian centers and archaeological monuments in Mexico. *Key*: (1) Modern national boundaries; (2) internal boundaries. States: (IV) Chihuahua; (V) Coahuila; (VI) Nuevo León; (VII) Tamaulipas; (VIII) Sinaloa; (IX) Durango; (X) Zacatecas; (XI) San Luis Potosí; (XII) Nayarit; (XIII) Aguascalientes; (XIV) Jalisco; (XV) Guanajuato; (XVI) Querétaro (XVII) Hidalgo; (XVIII) Veracruz; (XIX) México; (XX) Colima; (XXI) Michoacán; (XXII) Federal District; (XXIII) Tlaxcala; (XXIV) Morelos; (XXV) Puebla; (XXVI) Guerrero; (XXVII) Oaxaca; (XXVIII) Tabasco; (XXIX) Chiapas; (XXX) Campeche; (XXXI) Yucatán; (XXXII) Quintana Roo.

zations of the Toltecs and, later, the Aztecs flourished in the region until they were destroyed by the Spanish conquistadors.

With all the limitations indicated above, the subdivision into areas and the treatment of the sequence of the artistic periods within the individual zones are made necessary, on the one hand, by the extent of our knowledge and the requirements of exposition and, on the other hand, because the most interesting esthetic features and styles are thus grouped in a rather coherent and orderly manner.

The sequence of artistic periods in the Huaxtec area. Geographically, the Huaxtec (Huastec) area includes the southeast part of Tamaulipas, the eastern part of San Luis Potosí, the northern part of Veracruz, and the adjacent regions of the states of Querétaro, Hidalgo, and Puebla. The eastern section is low and torrid, while the plateau enjoys a temperate climate. The present-day Huaxtecs occupy only a small part of the territory which was inhabited by that tribe in ancient times; even as early as the Spanish Conquest essentially nomadic tribes had partially occupied the Huaxtec region where they left no significant cultural remains. In the artistic production that characterizes the Huaxtec region certain stylistic differences are noticeable, but present knowledge does not permit any accurate subdivisions, and thus it is preferable to discuss the area as a whole.

R. S. MacNeish (1954) has identified some dwellings that date back to the 8th millennium B.C. However, the first pottery cultures with an artistic production are not encountered earlier than the 12th century B.C. It is likely that they occupied almost all this area, but they have been studied and defined in only one typical spot, Pánuco. The first three periods — Pavon, Ponce, and Aguilar — and the Pánuco I and II phases are typically preclassic and reflect local variants of the great archaic style present throughout all Middle America. The Pánuco III and IV phases are classical and are principally related to the Teotihuacán and Tajín cultures.

During the Pánuco V and VI phases the characteristic Huaxtec style flourished; nonetheless, it had precedents in the previous period. The extremely original architecture does not exhibit the refinements found in the southern areas. There are tumuli — circular, rectangular, horseshoe-shaped, in the shape of a truncated cone, in combinations of these various forms, with rounded corners, and in odd shapes — and buildings joined together on platforms. The construction is generally of rough stone, but often it is only of clay covered with stucco. The flights of steps, which are double at times and without parapets (the latter appear very late in this region), the side slopes, the facing, and the cornices recall the typical Middle American style. These buildings make up planned groups, which are sometimes intersected by streets.

Some of the most important sculptures of ancient Mexico come from this area, such as the figure of the adolescent boy from Tamuín (X, PL. 49), the magnificent Tzontemoc of Tepetzintla (Mexico City, Mus. Nacional de Antropología), and the numerous sculptures encircling the pyramid of Castillo de Teayo. They reflect many styles, but among the characteristic aspects are the cone-shaped caps, the "fans" on the napes of the necks of the female figures, the hands crossed over the stomach, and the large ears. Although they are sculptured in the round, they give more the impression of being bas-reliefs; in some cases, they bear glyphs with dates, which demonstrate a knowledge of writing and the calendar.

The known examples of Huaxtec mural painting include a pavement with a geometric design in black and red, used perhaps for a game, and, above all, those at Tamuín, where there is a frieze, painted in red against a natural background, around a stucco altar in the shape of a truncated cone. It is about 15 ft. long and represents a procession of 12 elaborately decorated and clothed personages; of the Toltec period, it probably belongs to the 11th century of our era.

The ceramic finds, chiefly from the Pánuco VI phase, are of the black-on-white type and exhibit many interesting shapes in a style that is unique in Middle America. In the final two phases beautiful cast windlasses, pipes, and copper objects are often found.

Among the many other products of this region, attention should be called to the splendid pendants of carved shell and the very important little animals in the form of toys with wheels, which are similar to those, also of the Toltec period, already known from Tenenepango (Tenenepanco) and Tres Zapotes, for example. (There is no need to emphasize the theoretical importance of this use of the wheel.)

The Huaxtec area, like much of Middle America, is covered with archaeological ruins.

The classic civilization of Veracruz. The Totonac region in central Veracruz is bounded on the north by the Río Cazones and on the south by the Río Papaloapan, thus including the great coastal plain and the eastern watershed of the cordillera.

From the end of the preclassic archaic period, and particularly during the formative period, there appears in this area a culture rich in clay objects, such as vases with effigies; human figures with fat, bulbous legs; animals; and fruit. Many of these are of considerable artistic merit. Among the finds are standing and seated figures, some of which are rather flattened out, with great broadened faces and wide-open eyes, while others show a commendable realistic style, as seen in examples from Remojadas (X, PL. 25).

In the classic "horizon" painted ceramics representing both men and gods are found. The most notable type is the so-called "smiling figurine," having a face of serene beauty illumined by a smile, an expression very rarely found in pre-Hispanic art. Both the classic and postclassic epochs produced notably fine examples of modeling in clay (e.g., the heads; X, PL. 24).

Partly contemporary with these figurines is a group of stone sculptures of high quality, among them the so-called "yokes" (which bring to mind those used on horses in ancient times), ceremonial axes, and stones in palmate form and in bizarre shapes, almost all of which show admirable workmanship (X, PL. 23). Hooks, either in echelon formation or interlaced, constitute a recurring fretlike motif; between the hooks or at the center of them appear human figures, animals, and other motifs represented in a distinctive style.

Remains of many cities of the classic period exist in the region, and numerous stone steles, sculptures, and bas-reliefs have been found. Especially beautiful, for example, are the ball-game (pelota) markers at Vega de Alatorre, representing the sacrifice of a defeated player, and the stele at Tepatlaxco.

In classic Tajín and in other later centers remains of mural paintings have been found, though in a poor state of preservation. This epoch produced sculpture inferior to that of Tajín, but, on the other hand, some very lovely polychrome ceramics, such as those from the Isla de Sacrificios. A magnificent collection of artifacts found on this island is located in the British Museum, while another is housed in the Museo Regional de Veracruz at Jalapa. Finely worked small alabaster vases are common, as well as numerous personal ornaments made of various materials.

The Olmec culture. In the territory that lies between the Río Papaloapan and the Río Grijalva (composed, except for the mountains in the area of San Andrés Tuxtla, of a hot coastal plain that is frequently inundated) a high level of culture developed from the beginning of the archaic period and continued in certain cases up to the beginning of the classic period. It was perhaps the original culture of Middle America and has commonly been called the "Olmec" culture from the name that later inhabitants gave to the region ("the land of rubber"). During subsequent periods the zone does not present any special artistic interest.

The features of the Olmec style are not limited to the Mexican region that is being considered here; rather, they are found with varying degrees of frequency over a vast area that extends from the Mexican plateau to Guatemala and even farther south. As for Mexico, it must be remembered that, in addition to the centers to be examined below, Tlatilco in the Valley of Mexico and Cerro de la Cantera in Morelos state are also clearly Olmec. In the region under consideration only three sites of considerable artistic importance have been explored: La Venta, Tres Zapotes, and San Lorenzo Tenochtitlán, where there are some monuments and colossal heads (X, PL. 2).

While Olmec architecture is inferior to that of other cultures, their sculpture includes some of the most remarkable art objects of ancient Mexico, such as the famous athlete, or wrestler, from Uxpanapán (X, PL. 3), one of the extremely rare objects of indigenous art that shows concern with the beauty of the human body; the statue at San Martín Pajapán; and the stele at Alvarado. Besides these monumental pieces, the Olmecs produced numerous small sculptures of light-blue jade or of stone in an unequaled style, marked by pear-shaped heads representing artificial cranial deformation, mouths with drooping corners, anthropomorphic "axheads," semihuman and semifeline masks, simple and sexless bodies, and frequent depictions of deformities, such as hunchbacks or monsters with muscles realistically highlighted, which are often naked and devoid of superfluous details; in addition, there are animals, boats, and other forms.

Also characteristic of Olmec art are the representations of the jaguar-man, the local divinity, in which the features of serpents or of birds are very often combined. Monumental sculptures and tiny figurines of hard stone were fashioned in the same style.

Phases of the Maya civilization. The Maya area not only occupies all of southeastern Mexico, beginning at the Río Grijalva, and much of the Chiapas plateau, but also includes all of Guatemala and British Honduras and parts of Honduras and El Salvador. The part of the Maya area that is situated in Mexico can easily be subdivided into subareas, because the same types of artifacts are not found everywhere, and because the salient characteristics of northern Yucatán, for example, are different from those of the Chiapas plateau.

The area covers the calcareous plain of Yucatán, which is hot and arid with sparse vegetation; the two large Chiapas mountain ranges; the high, wooded, rainy areas of the Usumacinta basin; and the large forest region of Quintana Roo. The population of the Maya territory is just as varied as its terrain.

Even though monuments of the formative period exist in Yucatán, such as the great pyramid of Yaxuná, and some from the first half of the classic period, most of the artistic manifestations begin in a later period. Starting with the 3d century of our era, the centers with large monuments become more numerous. Various architectural styles can be distinguished in the peninsula. The first is perhaps the one termed "ancient Petén," found in centers such as Oxkintok, which repeats the style of northern Guatemala without any originality (see GUATEMALA; MIDDLE AMERICAN PROTOHISTORY).

More important is the "Puuc" style, characterized by walls faced with stone, barrel vaults, decorated cornices, roundish columns flanking the doors, friezes of rounded moldings, and the very extensive façade decoration of stone mosaics with large masks, serpent motifs, frets, shutters, and huts (X, PLS. 9, 12). Only the upper part is decorated, while the lower part is plain, thus giving an impression of repose. The Puuc cities are generally of imposing dimensions, with large buildings having adequate space between them; the most important of these city sites are Uxmal, Kabah, Sayil, and Labná (X, PLS. 8, 9, 11). They do not spread out around a large plaza, as the central Mexico sites do; although temples are found here, the major buildings are of the civil type. Large, vaulted entranceways with tall arches in the Maya style are frequent. In some cities there are steles bearing long narrative inscriptions. Most probably this style disappeared in the 8th century. Many other Puuc cities, of less importance and still unexplored, also exist. There are others which, even with distinct differences, are comparable to the Puuc style, such as Chichén Viejo. Of the mural painting in the Puuc buildings, which is scarce and of secondary importance, only a few fragments have been preserved.

Other cities, to the south of the Puuc cities, exhibit what is known as the "Chenes" style. Chenes architecture is characterized by an excess of façade decoration, although this feature is not common to all the buildings. Very often the doors are composed of the gaping jaws of the celestial dragon, surrounded by heavy stucco masks. Hochob is perhaps the most characteristic ruin in the Chenes style.

Other cities are similar in some ways to those of the above-mentioned style; the most characteristic is Río Bec. The Río Bec style may be regarded as midway between the Puuc and Chenes styles, since it presents masks with mouths serving as doors, along with *décor* based on Puuc features. The decoration does not, however, cover all the façade, but, unlike that of the Puuc, covers only the lower part of the buildings. Here, too, masks, small mortised columns, and the fret motif are found.

Some stone and rock towers, purely decorative and without any apparent function, are peculiar to Río Bec and some similar sites, such as Xpuhil. Imitating the pyramids, they have false stairways in front, a temple, and even an ornamental *fronton*, all of which create an illusion of size. If this feature of Río Bec architecture is not a particularly happy one, the facing of the buildings is, on the other hand, the most perfect in the entire Maya area; the stones are so painstakingly squared and fitted together that they did not have to be mortared.

The cities of the valley of the Usumacinta and of eastern Chiapas state, such as Palenque (X, PLS. 7, 10, 14–18) and Yaxchilán, belong to the classic period, as do the beautiful clay figurines, both male and female, of the island of Jaina, which are modeled with great mastery and feeling (X, PL. 18). Beginning in the 10th century, with the Toltec invasion of northern Yucatán, the styles of the classic Maya period in that region were followed by a new stylistic period, the "Maya-Toltec," characterized by the fusion of Maya and Toltec features; Chichén Itzá is a splendid example of this style (X, PLS. 34–37).

The plateau region and the Chiapas coast, which are little known at present, show strong Maya influences, but with different features that suggest the possibility of a separate subarea. Among the authentic works of art from this area are the steles at Izapa, the buildings constructed of enormous blocks and the fine sculptures at Chinkultic, the monuments at Tonalá, and numerous objects of various materials that reflect almost all styles, from the Olmec to the Maya and the Toltec.

The Zapotec and Mixtec cultures of the Oaxaca area. In the state of Oaxaca, principally on the Sierra of Ixtlán and in the region of the Isthmus of Tehuantepec, the culture of the Zapotecs of the classic period was followed by the postclassic civilization of the Mixtecs. The area was also inhabited by other ethnic groups whose artistic contribution is of little interest, at least in the present state of our knowledge.

Although the culture of the Zapotecs occupied a very extensive area, there is adequate archaeological data only for the great central Oaxaca Valley, which is about 5,000 ft. above sea level and has a temperate climate and sparse vegetation. Although the principal centers are Monte Albán and Mitla, there are other ruins in the valley that are quite interesting but little known. The most ancient buildings of Monte Albán I date back to the formative period, and their style, like that of contemporary monochrome ceramics with human and animal figures, recalls that of the Olmecs. During the Monte Albán II phase other peoples moved into that city and blended their imported style with that of the preceding period; new styles appeared in the pottery, in the fresco painting (red motifs against an orange background), etc. The Monte Albán III phase belongs to the classic period, by the end of which the city was completely built up. Dating back to this period are the great painted tombs and the clay urns representing divinities, the latter constituting the most typical feature of Zapotec art. The magnificent pectorals and other necklaces of jade recall the style of the Mayas. At the end of the classic period Monte Albán became less important. Artistically, the last phase was decadent and characterized by mass production.

Beginning with the end of the classic period, the Mixtecs introduced a very refined culture into this area. Little is known about their architecture, and they did not make large stone sculptures or mural paintings, but the production of small objects was important. Among the finds are splendid polychrome ceramics with predominantly ritual motifs and all kinds of jewelry, such as necklaces, bracelets, rings, diadems, anklets, and nose rings; these sometimes have moving parts (e.g., skulls with jaws that open and shut). The jewelry, which constitutes the principal Mixtec production, is of gold, silver, or copper and laminated, filigreed, or cast by the cire-perdue process; it may be included among the most perfect and exquisite metalwork of ancient Mexico. The examples from Tomb 7 at Monte Albán belong to this culture.

There also exist wooden objects overlaid with a mosaic of turquoise and jade, such as masks (X, PL. 44), spear throwers, spoon handles, helmets, shields, and ornaments; pectorals of jade and of other rare stones; objects of rock crystal or of polished obsidian, representing skulls, deities, animals, or vases; finely worked bone with glyphs, etc.; and goblets of sculptured and incised alabaster. The majority of these jewels and precious objects have been lost, though they were extremely famous throughout Europe beginning with the 16th century.

Most of the painted books of ancient Mexico that have come down to us were produced by the Mixtecs. The most beautiful codices are the Nuttall (London, Br. Mus.; VII, PL. 259), the Vindobonensis (Vienna, Nationalbibliothek), the Cospianus, and the Bodleian (Oxford, Bodleian Lib.); from nearby — probably Tlaxcala — comes the Codex Borgia (Rome, Vat. Lib.; X, PLS. 54, 56, 64), perhaps the most artistic of all the surviving manuscripts. Here, as in the frescoes, the colors are laid on in flat planes, without perspective, but with a great color sense and refinement in design. Some of the animal figures are striking.

The very refined Mixtec culture had a great influence on later periods and, among other things, was one of the sources drawn upon by 15th-century Aztec art.

The Puebla-Tlaxcala area. This is an area abounding in monuments, few of which have been studied. The great pyramid of Cholula, the largest in ancient Mexico, was built and enlarged over a long period of time. In Tizantlán, one of the villages of Tlaxcala, a temple of a later period has been explored, revealing rather unusual architectural features.

The Morelos area. The art documentation from this region is rather abundant. From earlier times there are the Olmec-style clay objects discovered at Gualupita, a quarter of Cuernavaca, and the contemporaneous bas-reliefs of Chalcatzingo, which are sculptured in natural rock and represent human figures in profile, wearing strange garments and hats and bearing various objects in their hands. Although they are fashioned in low relief, they show the same sensitive modeling found in the sculptures at La Venta. This region also possesses important archaeological centers, such as the ruins of Xochicalco (X, PL. 32).

The Valley of Mexico from the preclassic to the Aztec period. Because of its importance as the center of elaboration of the indigenous culture, this area has been explored more intensively than other regions and is therefore better known.

Tlatilco is the most important of the archaic centers from an esthetic standpoint. There are no architectural remains, but there are many ceramics and figures which are closely related to the Olmec style. Some of the most outstanding finds are vases in the shape of fish, armadillos, and *tlacuaches* (opossums) and large bottles in the shape of acrobats, doves, and other figures. These vases are often incised with abstract or geometric motifs of hands or animals.

The Olmec-style clay figurines, seated or standing, are particularly interesting, both for the quality of modeling and for their subjects. Images of dancers, acrobats, magicians, and women with two heads and a single body, all painted in several colors and full of life and movement, and also human or animal masks are abundant in the tombs (VI, PL. 53; X, PL. 1).

Cuicuilco has not yielded any important artistic objects, but it contains some of the oldest known buildings in Middle America. The classic period in the valley begins with Teotihuacán, the first great city of pre-Columbian Mexico. Besides the remains of impressive buildings, the wall paintings, and the sculpture, the Teotihuacán culture produced remarkable stone masks with serene human faces of admirable workmanship (X, PL. 39), as well as figurines and other artifacts made of jade and diorite. The pottery, admired for its form and fine texture, is sometimes painted with ritual motifs and sometimes with figures of deities (X, PL. 5).

Tula, the capital of the Toltecs, was located in the northern part of the valley. Although the Tula style has much in common with that of Teotihuacán, it possesses various distinctive features that also recur at Chichén Itzá in the Maya area. Typical of the Toltec style are the atlantes that support the altars or serve as columns (X, PL. 32); columns shaped like serpents, with the head resting on the ground and the tail forming the architrave; decorative bas-reliefs depicting processions of warriors on the walls or benches; rows of jaguars (or tigers) in motion, also in bas-relief, sometimes alternating with eagles or with other motifs; colonnades adjacent to buildings or supporting an access portico to a pyramid; courtyards surrounded by Coatepantli, which are walls decorated with stone serpents in bas-relief and surmounted by battlements (X, PL. 31); large halls around open courtyards; statues of a reclining deity, called "Chac-Mool," with elbows on the ground and knees flexed; ceramics decorated with a glossy paint that gives a glazed effect. The pyramid at Tenayuca, northeast of Mexico City, belongs to the final period.

In Mexico City there are still some remains of the great temple of Tlatelolco, with its stone walls, and that of Tenochtitlán, as well as some sculptured serpents and bas-reliefs.

Sculpture was the most important of all the arts practiced by the Aztecs. Many fine examples of sculptured work in the Aztec style, dating from the middle of the 15th century to the first part of the 16th century, are preserved in the Museo Nacional de Antropología in Mexico City. Among the most famous are the Aztec Calendar Stone, or Stone of the Sun, an enormous monolith sculptured in bas-relief with the sun and other symbols representing the elements and units of time; Coatlicue, the Earth Mother, realistically fashioned in its details and singularly abstract in its totality, and the statue of Yolotlicue, having the same style and proportions; the Stone of Tizoc (VII, PL. 259), an enormous cylinder sculptured all over, with scenes representing the victories of this emperor around the rim; a large lifelike jaguar with very simple lines, having in its back a circular cavity in which were placed the hearts of sacrificial victims; a porphyry head, with plumes and a human face, representing Quetzalcoatl; the tablet of a temple, bearing the date of dedication; numerous coiled serpents, some of which are abstract in a modern manner; a seated statue of the deity Xochipilli, from Tlalmanalco; the strikingly realistic head of an Eagle Knight (X, PL. 42); and many smaller objects, including a remarkable vase, from Texcoco, of polished obsidian and representing a monkey, a diorite squash, and a carnelian grasshopper.

Among the smaller pieces found in this and other collections, attention should be called to the finely finished objects of rock crystal, such as the skull in the British Museum, animal figures, and vases, as well as articles of alabaster and artistic wood intaglios.

The art of featherwork (q.v.) was highly developed, as is attested by the headdress of Montezuma (Vienna, Mus. für Völkerkunde) and some shields preserved in the ethnological museums in Mexico City, Vienna, Stuttgart, and Madrid. A magnificent Aztec painted manuscript, the Codex Borbonicus, is preserved in the Bibliothèque of the Palais Bourbon in Paris.

Aztec art, original in many respects, has its roots in Toltec and Mixtec art and combines their features to some extent.

The Guerrero cultures. The Guerrero region, potentially very rich, is as yet largely unexplored. A series of subareas apparently exists there, with different styles that have not yet been defined. Along the banks of the Río de las Balsas there are the ruins of many cities, some of them of considerable size. Sculpture, both of a very primitive but expressive type and of a much more advanced type, has been found there. Some of the latter type from Placeres del Oro are reminiscent of the Peruvian Chavín style; others, such as the numerous columns, steles, tablets, and sculptures in the round, are more "Mexican" because of their formal character.

Along the coast there are numerous sites, which can be dated from the formative period up to the Aztec period, where many sculptures, rings for the pelota game, and other objects in a style influenced by the Toltecs have been found. Farther south, in the Ometepec region, there are fine sculptures that reflect the style of Oaxaca. Artifacts of gold and various other materials from Texmilincán attest to a well-developed culture.

In a large area around Mezcala it has been possible to define a style more clearly on the basis of small stone objects: figurines and masks, animals and various other items, such as the customary ornaments, all produced by a technique that seems to have been mechanical and in a rough but vigorous geometric style. Other finds from this region recall both the Olmec style and the classic style of Teotihuacán.

On hills in this area there are numerous fortresses. Some (e.g., Oztuma) have walls and moats that indicate considerable skill in building such defensive works.

The pottery-producing cultures of western Mexico. In the western regions — Nayarit, Colima, and Jalisco — only a few architectural works are known, among which the circular Temple of Ixtlán is noteworthy.

Tombs generally consist of a more or less deep shaft excavated in rock and permitting access to one or more chambers. There is no construction, properly speaking. The best-known tomb found thus far is that of El Arenal near Etzatlán. Near the city of Colima lies the pyramidal monument of Chanal, in the central Mexican style. Ixtepete, an enormous building now being explored, lies near the city of Guadalajara.

While the architecture and sculpture of this vast region are not remarkable, and mural painting seems to have been unknown, the ceramic art developed to an extraordinary degree.

In an ancient period, which is perhaps contemporary with the classic period in the rest of the Middle American area, a large number of clay figures were produced here. Hollow and highly burnished, they are excellently styled and well modeled, showing an extraordinary variety of themes and a naturalism and a mastery of the plastic art that are seldom encountered (X, PLS. 27, 29). Others represent plants, shells, fruit, and frequently animals: parrots, fish, crabs, and the especially well-known little dogs. These last are life-size, in red or brown, with smooth surfaces, and represent examples of a breed that was fattened for use as food (X, PL. 28).

Even the vases are frequently unusual, supported by caryatids or by animals, decorated with human heads, or modeled in strange shapes, such as drums, skulls, and temple bases.

There are also many other smaller solid figurines: musicians (X, PL. 29), acrobats, women grinding corn on metates, sick persons, women giving birth to children, groups of dancers, dignitaries in palanquins borne by four slaves, and many other subjects — realistically depicted or caricatured, comic or abstract — representing human figures, flora and fauna, family or collective life, and popular holidays. In decided contrast to the art of the rest of Mexico, there is no trace of the religious or ceremonial.

The Nayarit figures are coarser, sometimes brutal, if not outright monstrous, in the simplification or in the exaggeration of their features (X, PL. 27). There are numerous large, hollow, naked female figures with enormous feet and very slender arms; individuals so thin that their ribs show; hunchbacks and syphilitics; as well as group subjects. Aside from these figures, which are characteristic of Ixtlán, we find animated scenes representing houses with their inhabitants and animals (X, PL. 26), temples, and pelota games. There are many clay figures of warriors, musicians playing various instruments, dwarfs, women carrying children or vessels, and various persons busy with their daily tasks. All in all, they comprise a lively and often satirical display of the life of these peoples.

Among the outstanding pieces is a parrot made of leaded clay covered with gold leaf, which is now preserved in the American Museum of Natural History in New York.

In Jalisco, the most interesting items are human figurines from the Ameca-Zacoalco region: seated women of hieratic aspect, with large breasts, or warriors holding clubs in their hands, all admirably finished and polished, in an unmistakable style with elongated heads, rounded eyes, and thin, sharp noses. The same general style found in Nayarit and Jalisco also prevails in Colima, where it is generally much more refined.

The regions of Sinaloa and of northern Nayarit do not seem to have been inhabited by sedentary peoples until a very late period, at least. Accordingly, objects of artistic interest appear only shortly before the Toltec period. There are some large polychrome ceramics with ritual or geometric motifs, highly stylized human figures, metal objects, gourds lacquered by a process still used today, and some alabaster vases — all in a Toltec style or in an even later one deriving from Central Mexico.

The preclassic civilizations and Tarascan styles of Michoacán. From an archaeological point of view, Michoacán state is notable only for the central part around its lakes and for some sites near the Río Lerma which overlap into nearby Guanajuato state.

The numerous vases and clay figurines found at Chupícuaro (Guanajuato) probably belong to the formative period. Very carefully finished, they are covered with a brilliant red luster and frequently decorated with geometric motifs in black and white. The figurines represent small standing women, with facial features and ornaments created by means of the superposition of minute clay fillets; other larger ones belong to the style of the red ceramics with black and white motifs.

From the classic period there are magnificent spheroidal terracotta pots painted with friezes of figures in various colors, objects of rare stones fashioned in an archaic style (in at least one case with jade eyes), and stone representations of the fire god in a Teotihuacán style. The Chac-Mool figures, with their primitive style and finish, belong to a later date, but they certainly have the same meaning that the Toltec Chac-Mool had.

Architecture is represented chiefly by the so-called "yácatas," ceremonial monuments of unsquared stones accurately fitted over each other but not cemented by mortar. Generally, only the outer surface is faced with stone slabs. The yácatas are long, high, rectangular platforms linked by means of a corridor to a circular building. In some instances the top is so narrow that the possibility of its having supported a temple must be excluded. The most interesting ones are those at Tzintzuntzán, the ancient Tarascan capital, and those at Ihuatzio; they all seem to belong to the final period.

From the final or Tarascan period, properly speaking, there are a great number of metal objects, among them, for example, the remarkable copper mask in the Museo Regional Michoacano, Morelia, and the gold or gold-plated copper jewelry from the excavations at Tzintzuntzán. Besides these and various tools, there are a tortoise-shaped rattle with a small turtle on its back, richly decorated tweezers, bracelets, and some admirably fashioned obsidian ornaments, sometimes encrusted with gold or turquoise. A magnificent sculpture from Ihuatzio, representing a coyote god, has the body of a naked man and the head of the animal. There are also some stone seats in the shape of coyotes. Tarascan ceramics are of excellent quality and include a series of shapes which are not common in the rest of Mexico.

The north central region. In this vast area, which includes the modern states of Zacatecas, Aguascalientes, and San Luis Potosí, there is a series of sites adjacent to the Middle American region of some artistic interest. However, this area is generally far inferior in every respect to the others and presents a series of cultures that are much less developed than those of Middle America proper. The isolated centers of considerable interest include those of La Quemada, Toluquilla, Ranas, and La Magdalena, all of which show a similar type of construction. This region also produced painted ceramics in splendid animal shapes.

Ignacio BERNAL

COLONIAL AND MODERN PERIODS. *Hispano-Mexican art of the 16th century.* The earliest manifestations of Hispano-Mexican art are found in monastery architecture. In fact, the Franciscan and Augustinian monasteries always possessed their own special characteristics; the monastery church generally had a single aisle, with a barrel vault, buttresses, and a polygonal or semicircular apse. One vault, usually a barrel vault built against the upper interior front, supported the choir, forming with its intrados a vestibule in the Spanish style. Since the principal function of a monastery was the catechization of the indigenous peoples, the "patio," a large enclosed atrium facing the church, was especially important. The entire monastery complex was intended to serve a defensive purpose. Also, the building material was suited to the surroundings; in the poorer buildings, ordinary bricks and sun-baked bricks (adobe) were used, while the more important projects were built of stone, sometimes rough-hewn and sometimes squared into matching blocks, and a variety of colored volcanic rock (*tezontle*), as well as precious woods. The originality of this first Mexican architecture reflects the occupation of the builders, who were for the most part monks rather than architects — hence with old-fashioned, still platersque, tastes — and, also, the use of native workmen who, while possessing an innate decorative sense in keeping with the Aztec tradition, did not know European building methods. The monastic orders, especially the Franciscans, Augustinians, and Dominicans, engaged in a great deal of building activity. Two of the oldest Franciscan buildings are the monasteries at Huejotzingo (1531-70) and Tepeaca (1530), near Puebla; the one at Cholula was built by Toribio de Alcaráz, one of the few well-known architects of the 16th century. Juan de Alameda, a Spanish friar who came to Mexico, perhaps in 1530, deserves the credit for the monasteries at Cálpan (ca. 1550) and Tula (1550), which in the simplicity of their planning, in their plateresque ornamentation, and in the enlarged modules are evidence of the originality of Mexican architecture compared with that of Spain. More generous in proportion and richer in decoration are the Augustinian monasteries at Yuriria púndaro, designed by Pedro del Toro, with roughly plastered, massive walls in sharp contrast with the commonplace decoration of the façade; at Cuitzeo, perhaps built by Fray Juan de Utrera, with an entrance loggia, the church façade on pure Renaissance lines, and a patio with Gothic ribbing inscribing a double row of arches in the plateresque style; at Acolmán (1539), with the appearance of a fortress, softened by the plateresque façade of the church and by the elegant cloister; and at Actopan (1550), the work of Fray Andrés de Mata, perhaps the most imposing, with a Moorish-style keep, two patios, and a sturdy entrance loggia in the Lombard Renaissance style (I, PL. 139). The most remarkable Dominican monasteries are those at Tepoztlán (1559) and Yanhuitlán. In the 16th century and the beginning of the 17th the influence of Juan de Herrera (q.v.), the exponent of Spanish Renaissance purism, is notable; this style is found in the Cathedral of Mérida (second half of 16th cent.), by Juan Miguel de Agüero, and the Cathedral of Puebla (II, PL. 163), erected under the direction of Francisco Becerra. Some of the oldest examples of Mexican civil architecture are the Royal and Pontifical University (now the National University), founded in the mid-16th century, and the Hospital de Jesús, both in Mexico City; the Palacio de Cortés in Cuernavaca (begun ca. 1530, with many restorations); the Palacio de Gobierno at Tlaxcala (extensively remodeled 17th-18th cent.); the Casa de las Monjas and Casa del Adelantado de Montejo, in plateresque style, in Mérida; and the portal of the "Casa del que mató al animal" (House of the One Who Killed the Beast) in Puebla. The less important civil architecture generally followed the Mediterranean custom of locating rooms around a patio, a tradition preserved up to the 19th century.

The most interesting remains of 16th-century painting, exclusively religious in subject and European in style, are the frescoes in white, black, and gray tones found in the monasteries at Acolmán and Actopan; they were painted by skilled artists acquainted with Spanish and Flemish painting of the middle of the century. Among the well-known painters of the 1500s are Rodrigo de Cifuentes and Andrés de Concha. Sculpture has an essentially architectural function and reveals the indigenous taste, which is always closely linked to local tradition. All the 16th-century churches contain examples of this "creole" sculpture (e.g., the open chapel at Tlalmanalco, Mexico state).

Baroque and neoclassic styles of the 17th-19th century. Spanish influence, enriched by frequent direct contacts with Rome, and the indigenous culture evident in the exuberant ornament are essential features of the Mexican baroque period. Building activity continued to be very intense.

The most challenging baroque building is the Cathedral of Mexico City. Begun in the 16th century, perhaps according to plans by Alonso Pérez de Castañeda or by Claudio de Arciniega, who designed the Cathedral of Lima, it was modified in 1615 by Juan Gómez de Mora and was not finished until 1813. The faces, of a volcanic stone (*chiluca*) with a polished surface, exhibit sculptured ornament of some elegance; on the interior, with its immense central nave, the choir is situated opposite the high altar, following a Spanish tradition based on an Arabic compositional concept that does not emphasize perspective. Many churches modeled on the Cathedral were built in Mexico City during the 17th century. Remarkable for their rich ornamentation, especially on the outside, are S. Domingo (XIII, PL. 153), La Profesa, S. Lorenzo, Sta Veracruz, S. Inés, and the Chapel of the Conception, which is in the Cathedral.

Aside from the chromatic variety of the materials (e.g., gray stone for articulated and sculpured elements, red volcanic stone for the smooth surfaces), the baroque churches of this period and later are also distinguished by the predominance of mass over space; they generally have barrel vaults, lunettes, and octagonal cupolas on triangular corbels. This restricted sense of space is probably an inheritance from the pre-Cortés culture, in which the temple was a nonpublic cell isolated from the faithful. Another common feature is the concentration of interior and exterior ornamentation at the points of greatest interest, such as the retable with its paintings and sculptures, the secondary altars, doors, cupolas, and portals. In Puebla, decoration won out over structural clarity; examples are the Rosario Chapel of S. Domingo (XIII, PL. 152) and the churches of S. María Tonantzintla and S. Francisco Acatepec, which are particularly rich because of the use of a variety of materials, such as stucco for the figures and floral motifs, stone of various colors, and *azulejos*, the small polychrome ceramic bricks of Puebla, as well as the wealth

Principal modern centers of artistic interest in Mexico. Key: (1) Modern national boundaries; (2) internal boundaries. States: (I) Baja California; (II) Baja California Sur; (III) Sonora; (IV) Chihuahua; (V) Coahuila; (VI) Nuevo León; (VII) Tamaulipas; (VIII) Sinaloa; (IX) Durango; (X) Zacatecas; (XI) San Luis Potosí; (XII) Nayarit; (XIII) Aguascalientes; (XIV) Jalisco; (XV) Guanajuato; (XVI) Querétaro; (XVII) Hidalgo; (XVIII) Veracruz; (XIX) México; (XX) Colima; (XXI) Michoacán; (XXII) Federal District; (XXIII) Tlaxcala; (XXIV) Morelos; (XXV) Puebla; (XXVI) Guerrero; (XXVII) Oaxaca; (XXVIII) Tabasco; (XXIX) Chiapas; (XXX) Campeche; (XXXI) Yucatán; (XXXII) Quintana Roo.

of paintings covering the walls. Similar is S. Mónica at Guadalajara, one of the earliest of the 18th-century churches. The Bishop's Seminary at Guadalajara (1693–1701) is among the better examples of civil architecture of the period; the only concessions to baorque taste are an occasional ornament in the portals and the use of colored stone for the massive columns of the patio. The Tribunal of the Inquisition (now the National School of Medicine) in Mexico City is a severe building, dating from the first half of the 18th century, which has an elegant cloister with late Renaissance columns. In Mexico City there are also many fine houses of Spanish noblemen, such as that of the Condes de Santiago de Calimaya (18th cent.).

The 18th century was particularly fortunate in architecture of the school that may more properly be termed "late baroque" than "Churrigueresque," the term commonly used by art historians. Annexed to the complex of the Cathedral of Mexico City, the Sagrario Metropolitano (1749–68) is the work of Lorenzo Rodríguez, founder of the school of late baroque architecture, who felicitously blended the façade with that of the Cathedral itself (XIII, PL. 152); the Church of SS. Trinidad is also attributed to Rodríguez. The decorated façade of the Church of S. Francisco, also in Mexico City, is a quite restrained example of this style. The Capilla del Pocito (Chapel of the Well; 1779–91) at Guadalupe is a typically late baroque work by Francisco Guerrero y Torres, which has undulating lines and chromatic contrast in the *azulejos* that cover its façade and cupola. In the still beautiful patio of the Monastery of La Merced in Mexico City the decoration, arranged in flat planes, cancels every sense of motion. Other centers of late baroque architecture are Querétaro, with the Monastery of S. Agustín (now the Palacio Federal) and the churches of S. Rosa and S. Clara; Guanajuato, with the churches of S. Francisco, La Compañía (de Jesús), and S. Cayetano (called "La Valenciana"); and Taxco, with the Church of SS. Sebastián y Prisca (known as S. Prisca).

While a touch of provincialism may be noticed in the occasional formal differences found in this group of churches, this cannot be said of the Sanctuary of Our Lady of Ocotlán at Tlaxcala (I, PL. 140), in which the components of the Mexican baroque style — the European influence and the decorativism of the pre-Cortés civilization — are perfectly blended. The unknown architect, who possessed broad learning and was receptive to international tastes, has rendered here a Mexican interpretation of the baroque, particularly in the marked contrast between the red of the bases of the bell towers and the whiteness of the stucco of the façade, which is repeated in the filigreed belfries.

Some remarkable examples of late-baroque civil architecture may be found in several patrician residential buildings of traditional type in Mexico City, such as the house of the Conde de Heras y Soto, the house of the Marquis del Jaral de Berrio (erected by Francisco Guerrero y Torres), and the house of the Condesa del Valle de Orizaba, popularly known as Casa de los Azulejos (House of the Tiles) because of its facing of blue glazed tiles, which was added in 1735. In Puebla, the Palacio de los Herreros and the Casa del Alfeñique (almond-cake house), covered with polychrome tiles and with sculpture, are very original.

In the baroque period the large number of churches, economic prosperity, and the diffusion of the technique of painting on canvas and on copper (which was easier to transport) did not compensate for a certain poverty of expression. European influences are clearly recognizable: first, the predominant contributions of Zurbarán and Ribera; later, the superimposition of the manner of Rubens, which was more in keeping with the opulent tastes of the colony; and, lastly, the more conventional contribution of Murillo. Noteworthy Mexican painters of this period are Baltasar de Echave the Elder (d. ca. 1620), Baltasar de Echave Ibía the Younger (ca. 1583–ca. 1640; cf. I, PL. 144), Alonso Vázquez (d. 1608), Luis and José Juárez (both, 17th cent.), Miguel Cabrera (1695-1768), and Antonio Pérez de Águílar (late 18th cent.).

Sculpture, which was always regarded as an architectural complement in church façades and as a decorative feature in retables, remained even more anonymous than the painting. The folk art found in the churches and chapels of the small centers is perhaps more interesting. The oldest sculpture was oriented toward the tragic and realistic Spanish style, either exaggerating it in gestures — at times, to the point of caricature — or confining it to the tritest academicism. Among the most famous sculptors are members of the Cora family from Puebla — José Villegas, Zacarías, and José — who were active up to the early 1800s.

Reaction against the baroque began in 1791 with the arrival of the sculptor and architect Manuel Tolsá (1757-1816), a master from the Academia de S. Carlos in Valencia, who, along with Francisco Eduardo Tresguerras (1759-1833), was the greatest exponent of neoclassicism. Tolsá was responsible for the design of the School of Mining (Colegio de Minería) in Mexico City, which shows great compositional clarity, and for the completion of the Cathedral (1813), with its central cupola and sculptured ornamentation, as well as for numerous works in other centers. Tresguerras was born in Celaya (Guanajuato state), where his most important work, the Church of the Carmen, is located. With a few exceptions, such as the Hospice of Guadalajara, Mexican neoclassicism, which lasted until about 1840, was generally rather uninspired in all its manifestations.

Contemporary art. In the second half of the 19th century, under the influence of European eclecticism, an artistic production without national traits or creative personalities developed in Mexico. In the first part of the 20th century, Italian and French architects and engineers made a considerable contribution to the construction of various public works, which were built in the most diverse styles, ranging from Neo-Gothic to Art Nouveau (e.g., the Palacio de Bellas Artes in Mexico City, by Adamo Boari and Federico Mariscal). Acquaintance with European architecture and with its construction methods (especially the use of reinforced concrete) contributed to the training of that group of Mexican architects and engineers which was responsible for the affirmation of modern Mexican architecture, which is highly original and endowed with remarkable personalities, such as José Villagrán García, Ramón Marcos, Enrique de la Mora, Pedro Ramírez Vázquez, Enrique del Moral, Augusto H. Alvarez, Mario Pani, Carlos Lazo, Raúl Cacho, Guillermo Rossell, and Félix Candela. The theoretician Villagrán García argued against the latest manifestations of eclecticism in the name of purer European rationalism. This latter school was, in turn, reelaborated by the succeeding generation with a sense of imagination at times bordering on exuberance, ready to avail itself of the most diverse materials, ranging from iron to cement to those of local origin. The principal characteristics of contemporary Mexican architecture are summed up in the monumental complex of University City in Mexico City (1949-57), which is comprised of works by an outstanding array of architects, including Mario Pani, Enrique del Moral, Salvador Ortega, Carlos Lazo, Pedro Ramírez Vázquez, Augusto Pérez Palacios, Luis Barragán, Juan O'Gorman, Gustavo Saavedra, and Juan Martínez de Valasco.

With the exception of some popular painters, such as José María Estrada (d. 1873), 19th-century Mexican painting, first identified with neoclassicism and then with realism, affords a rather uninteresting panorama. Only in the revolutionary period, beginning in 1910, did new and original forces come into play, such as those found in the work of the engraver José Guadalupe Posada (1851-1913) and, on a more cultivated artistic level, in that of José Clemente Orozco (q.v.), whose work, along with that of Diego Rivera and the younger David Alfaro Siqueiros and Rufino Tamayo (qq.v.), brought Mexican painting into the mainstream of contemporary world art.

Carlo KOVACEVICH

BIBLIOG. *Pre-Columbian period: General works:* A. Peñafiel, Monumentos del arte mexicano antiguo, 3 vols., Berlin, 1890; G. B. Gordon and J. A. Mason, eds., Examples of Maya Pottery in the Museum and Other Collections, 3 vols., Philadelphia, 1925-43; E. P. Dieseldorff, Kunst und Religion der Mayavölker, 3 vols., Berlin, Hamburg, 1926-33; T. A. Joyce, Maya and Mexican Art, London, 1927; A. Basler and E. Brummer, L'art précolombien, Paris, 1928; A. Caso, Thirteen Masterpieces of Mexican Archaeology, Mexico City, 1938; P. Kelemen, Medieval American Art, 2 vols., New York, 1943; S. Toscano, Arte precolombino de México y de la América Central, Mexico City, 1944; J. A. Vivo, ed., Arte prehispánico de Mexico, Mexico City, 1946; I. Bernal, Compendio de arte mesomericano, Mexico City, 1950; P. Westheim, Arte antiguo de México, Mexico City, 1950; I. Marquina, Arquitectura prehispánica, Mexico City, 1951; D. F. Rubín de la Borbolla, México: Monumentos históricos y arqueológicos, 2 vols., Mexico City, 1953; J. Fernández, Coatlicue: Estética del arte indígena antiguo, Mexico City, 1954; I. Groth-Kimball and F. Feuchtwanger, The Art of Ancient Mexico, London, 1954; W. Krickeberg, Altmexikanische Kulturen, Berlin, 1956; P. Westheim, La escultura del México antiguo, Mexico City, 1956; M. Covarrubias, Indian Art of Mexico and Central America, New York, 1957; S. K. Lothrop and others, Pre-Columbian Art: The Robert Woods Bliss Collection, New York, 1957; P. Westheim, Ideas fundamentales del arte prehispánico en México, Mexico City, 1957; G. Kubler, The Art and Architecture of Ancient America, Harmondsworth, 1962, pp. 23-208 (bibliog.).

Single areas or cultures: a. Huaxtec area: J. Meade, La Huasteca, Mexico City, 1942; W. Du Solier, Estudio arquitectónico de los edificios Huastecos, Anales Ist. Nacional de antr. e h., I, 1945, pp. 121-46; W. Du Solier, Primer fresco mural huasteco, Cuadernos am., V, 1946, pp. 151-59; J. Meade, Arqueología de San Luis Potosí, Mexico City, 1948; G. Stresser-Péan, Les indiens huastèques, Rev. mexicana de est. antr., XIII, 1952-53, pp. 213-34; R. S. MacNeish, An Early Archaeological Site near Panuco, Vera Cruz, Tr. Am. Philosophical Soc., XLIV, 1954, pp. 539-641. *b. Veracruz area:* H. Strebel, Alt-Mexiko: Archäologische Beiträge zur Kulturgeschichte seiner Bewohner, 2 vols., Hamburg, Leipzig, 1885-89; J. W. Fewkes, Certain Antiquities of Eastern Mexico, ARSI, 1907, pp. 221-84; J. L. Melgarejo Vivanco, Totonacapan, Jalapa, 1943; M. W. Sterling, Stone Monuments of Southern Mexico (B. Bur. of Am. Ethn., CXXXVIII), Washington, 1943; J. García Payón, Sinopsis de algunos problemas arqueológicos del Totonacapan, El México antiguo, VI, 1947, pp. 301-32; T. Proskouriakoff, Scroll Patterns of Veracruz, Rev. mexicana de est. antr., XIII, 1952-53, pp. 389-401; T. Proskouriakoff, Varieties of Classic Central Veracruz Sculpture, in Carnegie Inst. of Washington, Pub. 606, 1954, pp. 61-94. *c. Olmec culture:* Mayas y olmecas, Mexico City, 1942; M. Covarrubias, El arte olmeca o de la Venta, Cuadernos am., V, 1944, pp. 153-79; M. Covarrubias, Mexico South, New York, 1946. *d. Maya civilization:* J. L. Stephens, Incidents of Travel in Central America, Chiapas and Yucatan, 2 vols., New York, London, 1841; J. L. Stephens, Incidents of Travel in Yucatan, 2 vols., New York, London, 1843 (new ed., 2 vols., Norman, Okla., 1962); E. Förstemann, ed., Codex Dresdensis, Leipzig, 1880 (Eng. trans., S. Wesselhoeft and A. M. Parker, Peabody Mus. Pap., IV, 2, Cambridge, Mass., 1906); W. H. Holmes, Archaeological Studies among the Ancient Cities of Mexico, I: Monuments of Yucatan, Chicago, 1895; C. P. Bowditch, ed., 24 Papers... Translated from the German (B. Bur. of Am. Ethn., XXVIII), Washington, 1904; H. J. Spinden, A Study of Maya Art, Cambridge, Mass., 1913 (rev. ed., Maya Art and Civilization, Indian Hills, Colo., 1957); G. O. Totten, Maya Architecture, Washington, 1926; The Maya and Their Neighbors, New York, London, 1940; D. de Landa, Relación de las cosas de Yucatan (ed. and trans., A. M. Tozzer), Cambridge, Mass., 1941; J. E. S. Thompson, A Survey of the Northern Maya Area, AmA, XI, 1945, pp. 2-24; T. Proskouriakoff, An Album of Maya Architecture (Carnegie Inst., Pub. 558), Washington, 1946; R. Redfield, The Folk Culture of Yucatan, Chicago, 1948; T. Proskouriakoff, A study of Classic Maya Sculpture (Carnegie Inst., Pub. 593), Washington, 1950; J. E. S. Thompson, Maya Hieroglyphic Writing: An Introduction (Carnegie Inst., Pub. 589), Washington, 1950 (2d ed., Norman, Okla., 1960); E. N. Ferdon, Tonalá: An Archaeological Survey, Santa Fé, 1953; P. Rivet, Cités maya, Paris, 1954 (Eng. trans., M. and L. Kochan, London, 1960); J. E. S. Thompson, The Rise and Fall of Maya Civilization, Norman, Okla., 1954; S. G. Morley, The Ancient Maya, 3d ed., Stanford, Calif., 1956; J. E. S. Thompson, A Catalog of Maya Hieroglyphs, Norman, Okla., 1962. *e. Oaxaca area:* A. Caso, Las estelas zapotecas, Mexico City, 1928; J. A. Mason, Zapotec Funerary urns from Mexico, Penna. Univ. Mus. J., XX, 1929, pp. 176-201; A. Caso, Reading the Riddles of Ancient Jewels, Natural H., XXXII, 1932, pp. 464-80; A. Caso, Exploraciones en Oaxaca: Quinta y sexta temporadas, Tacubaya, 1938; S. Linné, Zapotecan Antiquities and the Paulson Collection in the Ethnographical Museum of Sweden, Stockholm, 1938; I. Bernal, Exploraciones en Coixtlahuaca, Rev. mexicana de est. antr., X, 1949, pp. 5-76; A. Caso and I. Bernal, Urnas de Oaxaca (Mem. Inst. nacional de antr. y h., II), Mexico City, 1952; B. Dahlgren de Jordan, La Mixteca, Mexico City, 1954. *f. Puebla-Tlaxcala area:* A. Caso, Las ruinas de Tizatlán, Rev. mexicana de est. h., I, 1927, pp. 139-72; E. Guzman, Los relieves de la roca del Cerro de la Cantera, Jonacatepec, Anales Mus. nacional de arqueología, V, 1, 1934, pp. 237-51. *g. Morelos area:* G. C. and S. B. Vaillant, Excavations at Gualupita, APAmM, XXXV, 1, 1934, pp. 1-135. *h. Valley of Mexico:* S. Linné, Mexican Highland Cultures, Stockholm, 1942; M. Covarrubias, Tlatlico: El arte y la cultura preclásica del Valle de México, Cuadernos am., IX, 1950, pp. 149-62; M. N. Porter, Tlatlico and the Preclassic Cultures of the New World (VFPA, XIX), New York, 1953; R. Piña Chan, Las culturas preclásicas de la Cuenca de México, Mexico City, 1955; L. Sejourné, Burning Water (trans. I. Nicholson), New York, London, 1957; R. Piña Chan Tlatlico, 2 vols., Mexico City, 1958. *i. Guerrero cultures:* J. García Payón, Estudio preliminar de la zona arqueológica de Texmelincan, El México antiguo, V, 1941, pp. 341-43; P. R. Hendrichs Pérez, Por tierras incógnitas, 2 vols., Mexico City, 1945-46. *j. Western Mexico:* I. Kelly, Excavations at Chiametla, Sinaloa (Ibero-Americana, XIV), Berkeley, Los Angeles, 1938; G. Medioni and M. T. Pinto, Art in Ancient Mexico, New York, 1941; G. F. Ekholm, Excavations at Guasave, Sinaloa, APAmM, XXXVIII, 2, 1942, pp. 23-139; I. Kelly, The Archaeology of the Astlán-Tuxcacuexco Area of Jalisco (Ibero-Americana, XXVI-XXVII), 2 vols., Berkeley, Los Angeles, 1945-49; I. Kelly, Excavations at Culiacán (Ibero-Americana, XXV), Berkeley, Los Angeles, 1945; Arte precolombino del Occidente de México, Mexico City, 1946; J. Corona Núñez, Tumba de El Arenal, Etzatlán, Mexico City, 1955. *k. Michoacán area:* D. F. Rubín de la Borbolla, Orfebrería Tarasca, Cuadernos am., III, 1944, pp. 127-38; I. Kelly, Excavations at Apatzingán (VFPA, VII), New York, 1947. *m. North central area:* E. Noguera, Ruinas arqueológicas del Norte de México, Mexico City, 1930; E. Noguera, Vestigios de cultura Teotihuacana en Querétaro, Anales Mus. nacional de Arqueología, 5th Ser., III, 1945, pp. 71-82.

Colonial and modern period: S. Baxter, Spanish Colonial Architecture in Mexico, 10 vols., Boston, 1901; M. Toussaint and J. R. Benitez, Iglesias de México, 6 vols., Mexico City, 1924-27; Republic of Mexico Dept. of Education, Three Centuries of Mexican Colonial Architecture, New York, 1933; C. Mérida, Modern Mexican Artists, Mexico City, 1937; L. Schmeckebier, Modern Mexican Art, Minneapolis, 1939; H. Leipziger, Architectonic City in the Americas, New York, 1944; F. Violich, Cities of Latin America, New York, 1944; D. Angulo Iñiguez, Historia del arte hispánoamericano, I-II, Barcelona, 1945-50; P. Calders, Acólman, Mexico City, 1945; F. Chueca Goitia, Invariantes castizos de la arquitectura española, Madrid, 1947; G. Kubler, Mexican Architecture of the 16th Century, 2 vols., New Haven, 1948; M. Toussaint, Arte colonial en México, Mexico City, 1948; P. Kelemen, Baroque and Rococo in Latin America, New York, 1951; I. E. Myers, Mexico's Modern Architecture, New York, 1952; B. S. Myers, Mexican Painting in Our Time, New York, 1956; 4000 años de arquitectura mexicana, Mexico City, 1956; J. Fernández, Arte mexicano, Mexico City, 1958; A. M. Read, The Mexican Muralists, New York, 1960; V. C. Chipway, The Mexican House, New York, 1960; J. A. Baird, The Churches of Mexico, 1530–1810, Berkeley, Los Angeles, 1962; J. Charlot, Mexican Art and the Academy of San Carlos, 1785–1915, Austin, Texas, 1962; J. Fernández, El hombre: Estética del arte moderno y contemporáneo, Mexico City, 1962; J. Charlot, The Mexican Mural Renaissance, 1920–25, New Haven, 1963.

ART CENTERS AND ARCHAEOLOGICAL SITES. The following survey is arranged by states (including the territory of Quintana Roo) and proceeds continuously from the northwest to the southeast. Mexico City will be considered first.

Mexico City (México, D. F.). Capital of the Republic of Mexico and of the Federal District, the city is located on a high plateau, which is about 7,500 ft. above sea level and surrounded by lofty mountains. Founded in about 1325 by the Mexica-Aztec tribe and named Tenochtitlán, it became the capital of the Aztec kingdom. In 1521, Hernán Cortés, after besieging and destroying the Aztec city, founded the new Mexico City on a regular orthogonal plan and furthered its development by draining the nearby swamps and by building new causeways. The major buildings and the Spanish quarter were built around the Plaza Mayor (officially the Plaza de la Constitución; also known as the Zócalo), covering the area of the large Aztec temple at the geographic center of the pre-Cortés city (see FIG. 844).

The imposing Cathedral, which faces the Plaza Mayor on the north, was begun in the second half of the 16th century, probably on the basis of a plan of Alonso Pérez de Castañeda. After an interruption of work, the construction of the Cathedral was resumed in 1615, under the direction of Juan Gómez de Mora (ca. 1580–1648), with a modified plan. The mixed neoclassic and baroque façade has two orders of columns and is decorated with statues and low reliefs. The interior is cruciform with a nave and two side aisles, both of which are flanked by chapels containing some fine examples of Churrigueresque decoration. The Altar de los Reyes, located to the rear of the high altar, is a particularly notable work in the Churrigueresque style. The Sagrario Metropolitano (1749–68), adjoining the Cathedral, is a work of Lorenzo Rodríguez; it has the form of a Greek cross and is elaborately decorated, both inside and out, in a late-baroque manner (XIII, PL. 152).

Other architectural monuments of the colonial period adjacent to the Plaza Mayor are the Palacio Nacional, originally a residence of the viceroys, which was rebuilt in the early 18th century, and the Palacio Municipal, also rebuilt after the early building was almost totally destroyed in 1692, with additions dating from the early 20th century. Among the earliest surviving examples of colonial architecture are the Church of S. Lorenzo (1650); the former Church of S. Agustín (completed 1692), which is now the Biblioteca Nacional; and the Hospital de Jesús (founded 1527), of which only the patio and staircase remain in somewhat their original state.

Examples of baroque civil and religious structures dating from the 17th and 18th centuries are the churches of Sta Veracruz, S. Hipólito, and S. Inés; the National Preparatory School (formerly the Colegio de S. Ildefonso) and "Las Viscaínas" (Colegio de la Paz); the houses of the Condes de Santiago de Calimaya and the Conde de Heras y Soto, as well as the so-called "Casa de los Mascarones" (House of the Masks); and the patio of La Merced, practically all that survives of the original monastery. Other notable examples of colonial baroque are the Church of SS. Trinidad, designed by Lorenzo Rodríguez; the Church of La Profesa; the Church of S. Francisco, once part of a large monastery complex; the Church of S. Domingo, which was rebuilt in the early 18th century (XIII, PL. 153); the National School of Medicine, built in the first half of the 18th century, which once served as the Tribunal of the Inquisition; the "Casa de los Azulejos," so called for its white and blue tile façade; and two former residential structures designed by Francisco Guerrero y Torres, the Palacio de Iturbide and the house of the Condesa San Mateo Valparaiso (now the Banco Nacional de México).

Throughout the 18th century the city was enriched by many new public and private buildings, some of which have been listed above, and, also, by new steps forward in city planning. Under the viceroy Gálvez, existing streets were improved and new streets were built; under the viceroy Revilla Gigedo, the public park (the Alameda) was opened, and new aqueducts, baths, and fountains (XIII, PL. 153) were constructed.

Also dating from this period are the School of Mining, designed by Manuel Tolsá (1757–1816) and the Castle at Chapultepec (begun 1783), which now houses the Museo Nacional de Historia. After

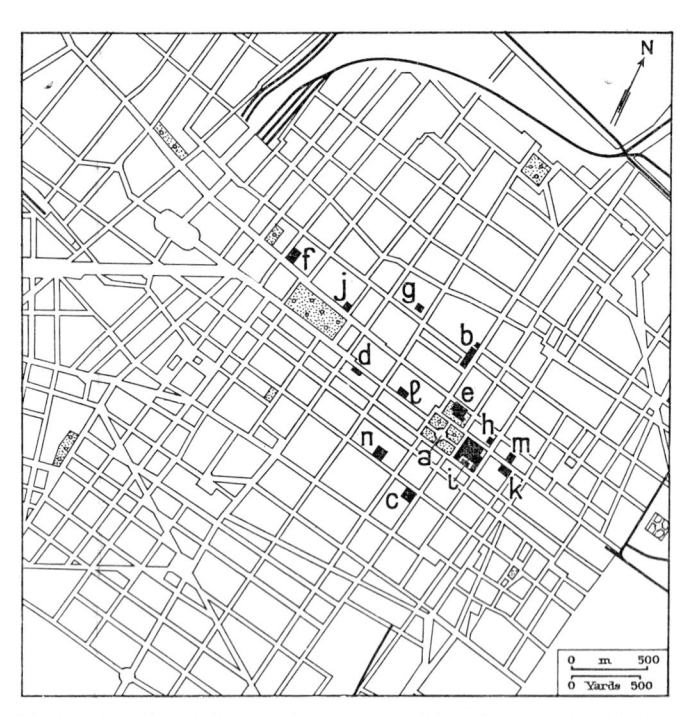

Mexico City, plan of the central zone of colonial settlement. *Key*: (*a*) Plaza Mayor (Plaza de la Constitución; known as the Zócalo); (*b*) S. Domingo and the National School of Medicine; (*c*) Hospital de Jesús and the house of the Condes de Santiago de Calimaya; (*d*) S. Francisco, S. Felipe Neri de Jesús, and the Casa de los Azulejos; (*e*) the Cathedral; (*f*) S. Hipólito; (*g*) S. Lorenzo; (*h*) S. Inés; (*i*) Palacio Nacional; (*j*) Sta Veracruz; (*k*) Escuela Nacional de Bellas Artes (formerly the Academia de S. Carlos); (*l*) Church of La Profesa and Palacio de Iturbide; (*m*) SS. Trinidad; (*n*) Biblioteca Nacional (formerly the Church of S. Agustín).

a period of inactivity, urban development resumed toward the end of the 19th century. A notable early-20th-century structure is the Palacio de Bellas Artes (1904–34), designed in a European eclectic style by Adamo Boari and Federico Mariscal.

Since 1940 a continuous surge of construction activity and development has changed the face of the city proper and its suburbs. In Mexico City the distinctive style of modern Mexican architecture can be seen in the private houses and the commercial and public buildings designed by such prominent architects as Juan O'Gorman, Enrique de la Mora, José Creixell, Enrique Yáñez, Pedro Bustamente, José Arnal, Vladimir Kaspé, Juan Sordo Madaleno, Carlos Lazo, Pedro Romírez Vázquez, Augusto Alvarez, Mario Pani, and Salvador Ortega. University City, about 10 miles from the center of Mexico City, incorporates Indian, Spanish, and modern elements in its numerous buildings, which have attracted international attention (I, PL. 141).

BIBLIOG. M. Orozco y Berra, Memoria para el plano de la Ciudad de México, Mexico City, 1867; J. M. Marroqui, La ciudad de México, 3 vols., Mexico City, 1900–03; J. Galindo y Villa, Historia sumaria de la Ciudad de México, Mexico City, 1925; M. Toussaint and J. R. Benitez, Iglesias de México, II–IV, Mexico City, 1925–27; M. Sola, Historia del arte hispanoamericano, Barcelona, 1935; L. R. Ruiz, Monografía de la catedral de México, Mexico City, 1939; A. Sartoris, Gli elementi dell'architettura funzionale, Milan, 1941; D. Angulo Iñiguez, Historia del arte hispanoamericano, II, Barcelona, 1950, pp. 495–628; Cité universitaire de Mexico, Arch. d'aujourd'hui, XXI, 34, 1951, pp. 82–87; M. Pani, Conservatoire national de musique, Mexico, Arch. d'aujourd'hui, XXII, 38, 1951, pp. 49–52; M. Carrera Stampa, Guía artistica de la ciudad de México y sus delegaciones, Mexico City, 1955; A. Persitz, ed., Architecture mexicaine, Arch. d'aujourd'hui, XXVI, 59, 1955, pp. 2–97; J. Fernández, Arte mexicana, Mexico City, 1958; L. González Obregón, Epoca colonial: México viejo, 2d ed., Mexico City, 1959.

Chihuahua. Chihuahua. Located in the center of a mining region, the city was founded by the Franciscans in about 1705 and developed with a regular street plan. In the old center there are some remarkable examples of baroque and neoclassic architecture, such as the Cathedral (1717-89), which is dedicated to St. Francis, and the Palacio de Gobierno (1908-09), built around the old tower in which Miguel Hidalgo y Costilla, leader in the fight for Mexican independence, was imprisoned before his execution in 1811. An 18th-century aqueduct still supplies water to the city.

Bibliog. E. C. Creel, El Estado de Chihuahua, Mexico City, 1928.

Coahuila. Saltillo. Founded in 1586, on a gridiron plan, its colonial character is still preserved in part. The late-baroque Cathedral, the Church of S. Esteban, and the magnificent 18th-century parks, along with the more recent Palacio de Gobierno, are notable.

Bibliog. M. Toussaint and J. R. Benitez, Iglesias de México, IV, Mexico City, 1927, p. 115; M. Alessio Robles, Perfiles del Saltillo, 2d ed., Mexico City, 1937.

Nuevo León. Monterrey. Although the city was chartered in 1596, Monterrey presents a predominantly modern aspect, having straight streets and large plazas. Among the oldest monuments are the Cathedral, with its baroque façade and austere interior, which was begun in 1630 but remained unfinished until the beginning of the 19th century, and the Bishop's Palace (El Obispado Viejo) with its domed chapel, dating from 1785. Other prominent buildings in the city are the Palacio Municipal (1853) and the Palacio de Gobierno (1908).

Bibliog. M. Toussaint and J. R. Benitez, Iglesias de México, IV, Mexico City, 1927, p. 118; C. Garza, Nuevo León, in Historia mexicana, I, Mexico City, 1952, pp. 494, 515.

Zacatecas. La Quemada. This well-preserved archaeological site, probably the Aztec city of Chicomoztoc, was already abandoned when it was discovered by the Spaniards in 1535. The buildings are constructed of stone slabs, often held together by a mortar of red clay and corn husks. A paved road leads past a series of small pyramids, beyond which stands a quadrangular building with a central patio surrounded by thick stone columns which may have formed a portico. An unusual pyramid, without tiers or a stairway, which is, perhaps, unique in all Mexico, still rises to a height of about 36 ft.; it is not possible to determine whether it was originally pointed or truncated. On the slopes of the hill on which the city is located there are ruins of great stone walls, which give the appearance of an imposing fortress.

Bibliog. A. Hrdlička, The Region of the Ancient "Chichimecs" with Notes on the Tepecanos and the Ruin of La Quemada, Mexico, AmA, N.S., V, 1903, pp. 385-440.

Zacatecas. Founded in 1546 by Juan de Tolosa in the center of a rich mining and farming region, it was accorded the status of a city in 1585 by Philip II of Spain. Irregular and narrow streets give the city a medieval appearance. Of note are the baroque Cathedral (begun 1612; completed and dedicated 1752; XIII, PL. 154), which has a very richly carved façade and a large, tiled dome; S. Juan de Dios; S. Domingo, known as "La Compañía" (mid-18th cent.); and Nuestra Señora de Guadalupe, which contains paintings by Antonio Torres. There is also an imposing 18th-century aqueduct.

Bibliog. M. Toussaint and J. R. Benitez, Iglesias de México, IV, Mexico City, 1927, p. 87; L. Chávez Orozco, Bibliografía de Zacatecas, Mexico City, 1932; J. R. Benitez, Las catedrales de Oaxaca, Morelia y Zacatecas, Mexico City, 1934; D. Kuri Breña, Zacatecas: Civilizadora del norte. Mexico City, 1944 (2d ed., 1959).

San Luis Potosí. San Luis Potosí. Built by the Spaniards on a regular plan, with straight streets, broad plazas, and public gardens, the city retains a baroque appearance. To that period belong the Cathedral (completed and dedicated 1737), which was built on the site of an earlier church, and the churches of S. Miguelito, S. Agustín, S. Francisco, and Nuestra Señora del Carmen, with its tiled domes and delicately carved façade.

Bibliog. J. Betancourt, San Luis Potosí: Sus plazas y calles, San Luis Potosí, 1921; M. Toussaint and J. R. Benitez, Iglesias de México, IV, Mexico City, 1927, pp. 87, 116; J. Meade, Guía de San Luis de Potosí, 2d ed., Mexico City, 1946.

Tamuín. This Huaxtec center covers 20 acres, only part of which has been explored. The largest structure is a platform formed of two low rectangular tiers, with stairways and plain balustrades; in front of it there is a much lower platform, extended by an unusual long, narrow corridor with two conical altars, one located in the middle and the other at the end. One of the altars is decorated with murals of red, green, and white, showing a procession of deities. A statue of an adolescent boy (Mexico City, Mus. Nacional de Antr.; X, PL. 49) was found on the larger platform.

Bibliog. G. Kubler, The Art and Architecture of Ancient America; the Mexican, Maya, and Andean Peoples, Harmondsworth, 1962, p. 80 f.

Tancanhuitz. The buildings of this Huaxtec center are distributed symmetrically. The main structure is low and circular, with a maximum diameter of about 40 ft.

Bibliog. G. Kubler, The Art and Architecture of Ancient America: the Mexican, Maya, and Andean Peoples, Harmondsworth, 1962, p. 80.

Tantoc. This site, which is still unexplored, has the largest tumuli in the Huaxtec area. The largest rises to a height of about 230 ft., while another is about 200 ft. high; both appear to be similar in form to the pyramid at Cholula in Puebla state (see below).

Nayarit. Ixtlán. This archaeological center has a circular temple with five access staircases of finely squared stones. On the upper platform, which is paved with stone and surrounded by a parapet with openings in the shape of a Latin cross, there are two altars with small stairways.

Bibliog. E. W. Gifford, Surface Archaeology of Ixtlán del Río, Nayarit, Univ. of Calif. Pub. in Am. Archaeol. and Ethn., XLIII, 1950, pp. 183-301; J. Corona Núñez, El Templo de Quetzalcoatl en Ixtlán, Anales Inst. nacional de antr. e h., 6th ser., IV, 32, 1952, pp. 45-49.

Aguascalientes. Aguascalientes. Founded in 1575, the city later became a missionary center and retains many features from the colonial period. Among the monuments of this period are numerous 18th-century churches, such as the baroque Cathedral and the Church of Nuestra Señora de Guadalupe.

Bibliog. A. R. González, Historia del Estado de Aguascalientes, Mexico City, 1887; M. Toussaint and J. R. Benitez, Iglesias de México, IV, Mexico City, 1927, pp. 91-110, 135; J. Bernal Sánchez, Apuntes históricos, geográficos y estadísticos del Estado de Aguascalientes, Aguascalientes, 1928.

Jalisco. Guadalajara. Founded in 1531, the city has been the seat of the bishopric of western Mexico since 1549. In the Plaza Mayor are the Cathedral (1571-1618), with its richly decorated façade and interior, and the baroque Palacio de Gobierno (17th cent.). Also notable are the baroque Church of S. Mónica (1720-33), with sculptured foliation on its façade; Nuestra Señora de Guadalupe (XIII, PL. 153), S. Felipe de Jesús, and numerous other churches and monasteries; the neoclassic Hospicio Cabañas; the Guadalajara Museum, housed in an early-18th-century seminary building, which contains valuable paintings, a library, and some archaeological finds; and the Teatro Degollado, an impressive neoclassic edifice dating from the mid-19th century.

El Ixtepete, a pre-Columbian structure from the classic period, is located near the city.

Bibliog. J. Romo, Guadalajara, Mexico City, 1888; M. Toussaint and J. R. Benitez, Iglesias de México, IV, Mexico City, 1927, pp. 66-99, 135; J. Cornejo Franco, Gvadalaxara colonial, Guadalajara, 1938; A. Chávez Hayher, Guadalajara de ayer, Guadalajara, 1956; J. Cornejo Franco, Reseña de la Catedral de Guadalajara, Guadalajara, 1960.

Guanajuato. Celaya. Founded in 1570 by 16 Basque families, it contains many works by the architect, sculptor, painter, and poet Francisco Eduardo Tresguerras (1759-1833), who was born and died there. His principal work is the Church of Nuestra Señora del Carmen (1803-07), which has an exceptionally beautiful dome, decorated with green and gold glazed tiles, and in which there are notable sculptures and paintings by the architect. Tresguerras also designed altars for the Church of S. Francisco, in which he is entombed, and the tower of the Church of S. Agustín.

Bibliog. M. Romero de Terreros, El arquitecto Tresguerras, Anales Mus. nacional de arqueol., h. y etn., 4th ser., V, 1927, pp. 326-45; Homenaje al insigne arquitecto D. Francisco Eduardo Tresguerras en el primer centenario de sa muerte, Guanajuato, 1933; F. de la Maza, Dibujos y proyectos de Tresguerras, Anales Inst. de investigaciones estéticas, V, 18, 1950, pp. 27-33.

Guanajuato. This state capital, built on a site occupied before the conquest by the Tarascan people, became a major mining center under the Spaniards. Situated in a narrow mountain gorge, its streets are very winding and narrow. In appearance Guanajuato has retained its colonial characteristics. Important religious structures from the colonial period are the parish church of S. Francisco (1671-96); the Jesuit church, La Campañía (ca. 1747-65), the work of Felipe de Ureña and Fray José de la Cruz; S. Cayetano (dedicated 1788), called "La Valenciana" after the famous silver mine nearby; and S. Diego (founded 1679; rebuilt ca. 1760), which has a fine Churrigueresque façade. Among the other important buildings are the house of the Condes de Rul y de Valenciana, designed by the architect

Francisco Eduardo Tresguerras; the Colegio del Estado, which houses a mineral collection; and the Teatro Juárez. An important historical landmark is the fortresslike Alhóndiga de Granaditas (1798–1808), now a museum, which was built as a public granary and became the scene of a famous massacre in the Mexican war for independence. Also of interest is the Panteón, the public cemetery, with its catacombs.

BIBLIOG. P. González, Algunos puntos y objetos monumentales de Guanajuato, Guanajuato, 1895; M. Toussaint and J. R. Benitez, Iglesias de México, IV, Mexico City, 1927, p. 87; A. Cortés, Casas históricas de la ciudad de Guanajuato, Guanajuato, 1939.

Querétaro. Querétaro. The city was founded by the Otomi and conquered for Spain in 1531. Almost all of its monuments date from the 18th and 19th centuries, during which it became one of the most important centers in Mexico. The Cathedral (formerly the Church of S. Francisco), dating from the early years of the Spanish occupation, has been modified many times, almost completely in 1727. The baroque churches of S. Clara (founded 1607), S. Rosa (dedicated 1752), and S. Agustín (mid-18th cent.) have highly ornate interiors. Other notable examples of religious architecture are the former monastery of S. Francisco, which now houses a museum; the Capuchin monastery (early 19th cent.); the monastery and Church of La Cruz (founded 1682); the Convent of S. Teresa, or "Teresitas" (1803), a neoclassic work by Tresguerras; and the former monastery of S. Agustín (18th cent.), now the Palacio Federal.

The great aqueduct, about 5 miles long and rising to a maximum height of about 75 ft., was built in the second quarter of the 18th century and brings water to the city's many public and private fountains, among which the Fountain of Neptune (1797; rebuilt 1848) is notable.

BIBLIOG. A. Peñafiel, Ciudades coloniales y capitales de la República Mexicana, Mexico City, 1911; J. Gaxiola, Guide to Queretaro, Mexico City, 1938; R. A. Echavarri, Bibliografía histórica y geografica de Querétaro, Mexico City, 1949; Plano y Guía de la ciudad de Querétaro, Querétaro, 1959.

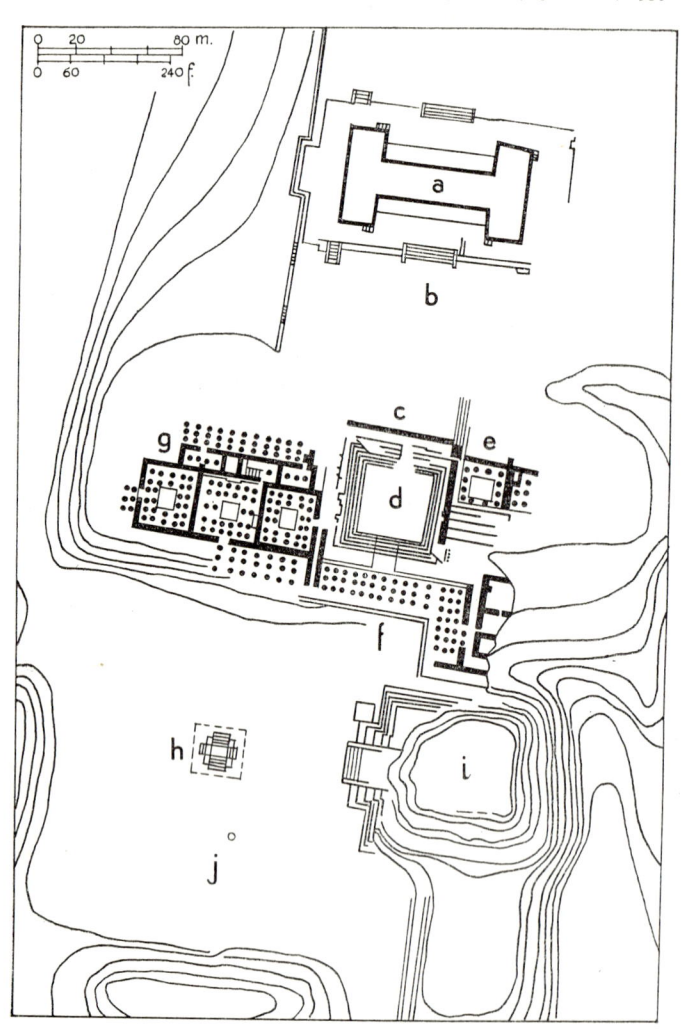

Tula (Tollán), plan of the archaeological zone. *Key*: (*a*) Ball Court; (*b*) the small plaza; (*c*) "wall of serpents" (Coatepantli); (*d*) Temple of Tlahuizcalpantecuhtli (or of Quetzalcoatl, or Mound B); (*e*) Building 1; (*f*) colonnaded portico; (*g*) Building 3; (*h*) altar; (*i*) pyramid; (*j*) the central plaza.

Hidalgo. Tula (Tollán). The principal monument of this Toltec site, located west of the modern town of the same name, is the Temple of Tlahuizcalpantecuhtli (or of Quetzalcoatl, or Mound B), a pyramid with five tiers, which is about 33 ft. high (X, PL. 31). The outer walls, faced with thin stone slabs, are carved with alternate rows of eagles devouring human hearts and heads and processions of jaguars. The roof of the temple was supported by four monumental atlantes, about 15 ft. high, and by piers with warrior figures in low relief (X, PL. 32), while the lintel, in keeping with the Toltec style, was supported by two serpents. These sculptures, almost completely preserved to this day, are among the most important documents of Toltec art. The freestanding "wall of serpents" (Coatepantli), with friezes in low relief (X, PL. 31) and crenelation, lies parallel to the north side of the pyramid. The colonnade on the south side is L-shaped, and a bench which runs its entire length is decorated with a procession of warriors carved in low relief and painted in lively colors. On the west side there are remains of large colonnaded chambers with benches around a central impluvium. To the east, remains of a palace can still be seen; a Chac-Mool was found in one of the rooms. There is also a museum with sculptures, ceramics, and other Toltec objects.

Not far from Tula lies the so-called "Corral" building ("the building of the courtyard"), which has a circular center and quadrangular exterior. Some bas-reliefs in the Toltec style were also found here.

BIBLIOG. J. R. Acosta, Exploraciones en Tula, Rev. mexicana de est. antr., IV, 1940, pp. 172–94; J. R. Acosta, Los últimos descubrimientos arqueológicos en Tula, Rev. mexicana de est. antr., V, 1941, pp. 239–48; J. R. Acosta, La tercera temporada de exploraciones en Tula, Rev. Mexicana de est. antr., VI, 1944, pp. 125–57; J. R. Acosta, La cuarta y quinta temporadas de excavaciones en Tula, Rev. mexicana de est. antr., VII, 1945, pp. 23–64; B. P. Dutton, Tula of the Toltecs, El Palacio, LXII, 1955, pp. 195–246; J. R. Acosta, Resumen de las exploraciones arqueológicas en Tula, Hidalgo, durante las VI, VII y VIII temporadas, 1946–1950, Anales Inst. nacional de antr. e h., VIII, 1956, pp. 37–115; G. Kubler, Chichén-Itzá y Tula, in Estudios de cultura maya, Mexico City, 1961, pp. 47–80.

Veracruz. Castillo de Teayo. This Huaxtec-style pyramid, in a perfect state of preservation, is composed of three almost vertical tiers; a large flight of steps on its west side leads to the upper temple, the walls of which are still standing. Important pieces of sculpture from the surrounding area have been placed around the monument.

BIBLIOG. J. García Payón, Castillo de Teayo: Noticias sobre su arqueología, Uni-Ver, II, 1950, pp. 155–64.

Cempoala. The Totonac capital at the time of the Conquest, this site includes many important stone monuments, which are grouped within low crenelated walls. All the structures are covered with stucco, which is sometimes painted. The most important groups are the Great Temple, the Temple of the Chimneys, and the Temple of the Wind God (Quetzalcoatl-Ehecatl); the first two are rectangular, while the third rises from a round base (FIG. 849).

BIBLIOG. J. García Payón, Restos de una cultura prehistórica encontrados en la región de Zempoala, Veracruz, Uni-Ver, II, 1950, pp. 90–130; J. García Payón, La Ofrenda del Altar de la Gran Pirámide, Zempoala, El México antiguo, VIII, 1955, pp. 57–65; F. del Paso y Troncoso, Las rovinas de Cempoala y del Templo de Tajín, n. p., n. d.

Cerro de las Mesas. Some remarkable stone steles depicting seated or standing personages, with the heads in profile and the bodies in frontal view in the early classic Maya style, have been found here. Other remains reflect pronounced influences from the central Mexican plateau and the Olmec region.

BIBLIOG. P. Drucker, Ceramic Stratigraphy at Cerro de las Mesas (B. Bur. of Am. Ethn., CXLI), Washington, 1943; P. Drucker, The Cerro de las Mesas Offering of Jade and Other Materials (B. Bur. of Am. Ethn., CLVII), Washington, 1955.

El Tajín. The principal monument of this Totonac center, located just north of Papantla, is a six-level pyramid, rising to a height of about 70 ft. (III, PL. 485). On each of its four sides there are niches which create extraordinary effects of light and shadow and, perhaps, had a wider significance, as the number of niches is thought by some to represent the days of the year. A large flight of steps decorated with fretwork (*xicalcoliuhqui*) leads to the top platform, on which the temple once stood (X, PL. 22). In one of the ball courts there is a bas-relief in the characteristic Totonac style, the central scene of which depicts the sacrifice of the losing player by the winner. Many other sculptured objects are found in the region, such as enormous serpent columns and the bas-reliefs or friezes on various buildings. Some roofs are constructed with a kind of cement so thick and solid that columns are not required to support surfaces as large as 90 sq. yd.

BIBLIOG. E. S. Spinden, The Place of El Tajín in Totonac Archaeology, AmA, XXXV, 1933, pp. 271–87; J. García Payón, La ciudad arqueológica del Tajín, Jalapa, 1951; J. García Payón, Exploraciones en El Tajín, Mexico City, 1955.

Pánuco. In the extreme northern end of the Veracruz state, this is an archaeological site of primary importance for our knowledge of Huaxtec art. The architectural remains consist of buildings on platforms with flights of access steps.

BIBLIOG. G. F. Ekholm, Excavations at Tampico and Panuco in the Huaxteca, APAmM, XXXVIII, 1944, pp. 319–512; R. S. MacNeish, An Early Archaeological Site near Panuco, Vera Cruz, Tr. Am. Philosophical Soc., N. S., XLIV, 1954, pp. 539–641.

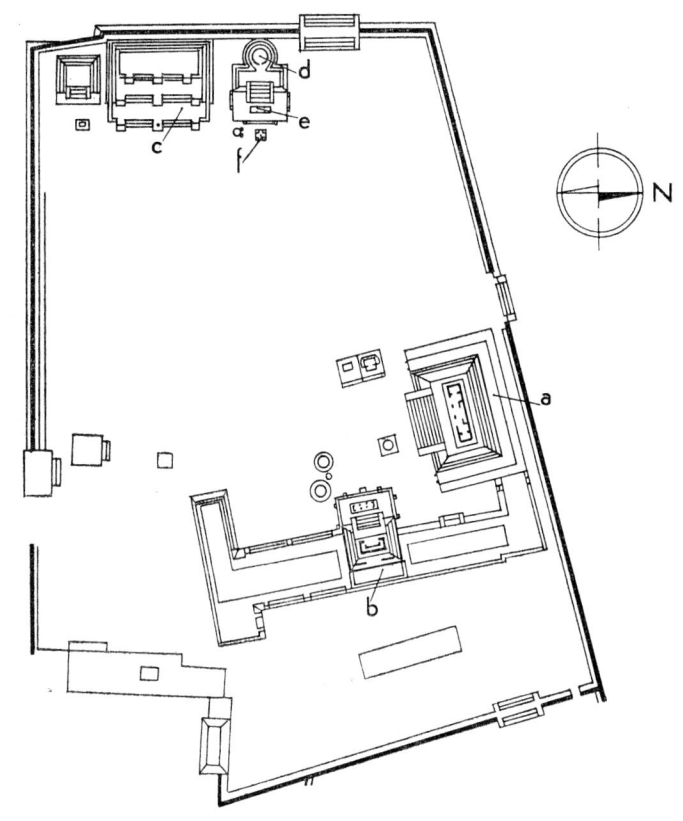

Cempoala, plan of the temple enclosure. *Key*: (*a*) the Great Temple; (*b*) Temple of the Chimneys; (*c*) terraced construction; (*d*) Temple of the Wind God (Quetzalcoatl-Ehecatl); (*e*) Temple of Xolotl; (*f*) the fire altar (*from W. Krickeberg, 1956*).

Quauhtochco. At this Totonac center there are remains of a temple atop a pyramid with four tiers, which is reminiscent of the Aztec style, even though it lacks the characteristic double stairway and the two upper temples.

BIBLIOG. A. Medellín Zenil, Exploraciones en Quauhtochco, Jalapa, 1952.

Quiahuiztlán. This site of a Totonac fortress town contains the well-known types of mausoleum also to be found in other sites of this area. They are small-scale reproductions of a temple — with base, mortuary, chamber for worship, roof, and stairs — and are grouped to form cemeteries in the European style.

Tuzapán. This Totonac center has paved streets, an elaborate drainage system, and pyramids, which have sloping sides but lack the usual projecting cornices.

Veracruz. This port city was founded in 1519 by Hernán Cortés, who named it La Villa Rica de Vera Cruz; the settlement was later abandoned and was resettled in 1599. Today, it is a hybrid city architecturally because of the mixture of the old and the modern. Among the principal monuments are the Church of Nuestra Señora de la Asunción (La Parroquia; dedicated 1734) and the fort on the island of San Juan de Ulúa (begun 1528).

BIBLIOG. L. E. Villaseñor, El puerto de Veracruz, Mexico City, 1890; J. Ramírez Cabañas, La ciudad de Veracruz en el siglo XVI, Mexico City, 1943; M. B. Trens, Historia de Veracruz, 6 vols., Mexico City, 1947–50.

State of México. Calixtlahuaca. This ancient archaeological site, which is situated about 5 miles from the city of Toluca, covers an area of several square miles. The original inhabitants of the site were probably the Matlatzincas; in 1476, during the reign of Ahuitzotl, it was captured by the Aztecs. The noteworthy Temple of Quetzalcoatl-Ehecatl (X, PL. 38) is circular with four tiers. From a rectangular platform that juts out from the base on the east side a broad stairway with a balustrade ascends to the top of the cylindrical temple. The Temple of Tlaloc (the god of rain) is cruciform, with a semicircular forepart built of small squared stones of red and black *tezontle* (pumice) and decorated with parallel rows of skulls made of the same material (X, PL. 38); the structure may have been a Tzompantli, a repository for the skulls of sacrificial victims. Close to the Temple of Quetzalcoatl-Ehecatl are the remains of a building with many small rooms surrounding a terraced courtyard, which was probably a priestly school (*calmecac*).

BIBLIOG. J. García Payón, Zona arqueológica de Tecaxic Calixtlahuaca, I, Mexico City, 1936; Calixtlahuaca: Guía oficial, Mexico City, 1960.

Malinalco. This Aztec center, dating from the final period, is extraordinary among pre-Columbian sites for its buildings carved out of living rock. The layout reveals such precise planning as to anticipate even the minute details of the rock-cut statues. The principal temple, cut from a ledge, has a pyramidal base with two steeply sloping tiers. Two statues of seated jaguars, also carved from the rock, flanked the stairway at the front, in the center of which there is a kind of podium. The circular room at the top is entered through an opening outlined by two deeply incised serpent profiles, which are arranged in such a way that the doorway itself represents a serpent's mouth, with the fangs forming a low podium before the threshold. To the right of the opening there is a serpent's head surmounted by a squat figure, of which the top is missing, and to the left a drum on which there once stood the figure of a Jaguar Knight, of which only the feet remain. A bench which extends around the inner wall of the circular chamber is decorated with carvings of a jaguar pelt and eagles with outspread wings. A large eagle with wings half spread, in the center of the chamber, faces toward the entrance. Aside from this building there are others of less importance, one of which was not completed because of the coming of the Spaniards. One of these buildings contains the remains of a wall fresco, which depicts a procession of warriors, with elaborate headdresses, carrying spears and shields in their hands. A large wooden drum from Malinalco, now in the Museo Nacional de Antropología, Mexico City, is carved with dancing figures of eagles and jaguars, symbolizing the warrior knights of the cults of the Eagle and the Jaguar.

BIBLIOG. H. Larsen, The Monolithic Rock Temple of Malinalco, Mexico, Ethnos, III, 1938, pp. 59–63; J. García Payón, Los monumentos arqueológicos de Malinalco, Mexico City, 1947; J. García Payón, Síntesis de las excavaciones en Malinalco, Rev. mexicana de est. antr., XIV, 1956–57, pp. 161–65.

Tenayuca. The terraced pyramid at Tenayuca, only 6 miles from Mexico City, dates back to about 1200 and shows signs of a number of remodelings and enlargements, evidence of which can be seen in a tunnel which has been excavated through the structure. The double staircase, separated by broad ramps in the Chichimec-Aztec style, covers nearly all of one face of the pyramid and projects about 45 ft. beyond the base (X, PL. 41). Almost nothing remains of the twin temples on the summit, which, in accordance with Aztec practice, were dedicated to the war god, Huitzilopochtli, and the rain god, Tlaloc. A "wall of serpents" (Coatepantli), with sculptured heads and masonry bodies, stretches along the low platform at the base of three sides of the pyramid; traces of painted stucco are still visible on some of the serpents. Remains of wall paintings showing skulls and crossbones are preserved.

BIBLIOG. R. J. Ceballos Novelo and others, Tenayuca (Dept. de monumentos, Pub.), Mexico City, 1935.

Teotihuacán (San Juan Teotihuacán). Probably the first great city of the indigenous people and of the classic period in the Valley of Mexico, this site is as remarkable for its plan as for its monuments and their decoration. The ceremonial nucleus of the city was built along a central axis, the road called "Avenue of the Dead," which begins on the plaza of the Pyramid of the Moon at the north and extends to the south beyond the Temple of Quetzalcoatl. The road is flanked on both sides with both single structures and building complexes, such as that of the Pyramid of the Sun (X, PL. 6).

This pyramid, at present nearly 220 ft. high, is the largest monument in Teotihuacán and one of the largest in Mexico. It has five sloping tiers and served as the base for a temple which once stood on the upper platform. The structure has lost its stucco facing, but excavation has revealed that the core is adobe covered with stone. An adjacent building of later construction was covered with magnificent stone slabs decorated with carved serpents. On the north, south, and east sides, the pyramid is surrounded by a platform. On the west side, eight smaller temples, symmetrically positioned in a large plaza, stood between the pyramid and Avenue of the Dead.

The Pyramid of the Moon, a slightly smaller structure than the Pyramid of the Sun, was also placed in a large plaza, which was the northern terminus of the Avenue of the Dead. Near its base was recovered the enormous monolithic statue of the "Water Goddess" (Mexico City, Mus. Nacional de Antr.), probably the best example of the archaic sculptural style of Teotihuacán, in which the human figure is stylized along geometric lines.

The numerous structures which stand at either side of the Avenue of the Dead, though generally in a very poor state of preservation, are well planned and well constructed and have restrained but excellent decoration, all typical features of the Teotihuacán style.

A little farther south is the so-called "Ciudadela" (Citadel), a vast quadrangle enclosed by a series of platforms and temples, at the center of which stands the Temple of Quetzalcoatl, a five-tiered structure with a wide central stairway. Its splendid, rather "baroque" decoration of sculptured stone represents feathered-serpent heads alternating with other heads that probably symbolize the rain god, Tlaloc (X, PL. 6). This is undoubtedly the most impressive detached structure in central Mexico.

All around this ceremonial area there is a vast zone covered with the ruins of palaces, temples, and dwellings. The latter are made up of central quadrangular patios surrounded by rooms; a number of these units could have formed a large palace with numerous chambers, patios, and connecting passages.

The many well-preserved mural paintings found in the area of Teotihuacán (X, PL. 19) may also be seen in reproductions in the Museo Nacional de Antropología, Mexico City, where most of the major finds from the zone are now kept. The local museum houses many objects found in regional excavations.

BIBLIOG. A. Peñafiel, Teotihuacán: Estudio histórico y arqueológico, 2 vols., Mexico City, 1900; M. Gamio, La población del Valle de Teotihuacán, 3 vols., Mexico City, 1922; S. Linné, Archaeolog cal Researches at Teotihuacán, Stockholm, 1934; A. Caso, El paraíso terrenal en Teotihuacán, Cuadernos am., VI, 1942, pp. 127–36; A. Villagra Caleti, Teotihuacán: Sus pinturas murales, Anales Inst. nacional de antr. e h., V, 1952, pp. 67–74.

Tepozotlán. The Seminary of S. Martín, founded by the Jesuits in 1582, is a remarkable example of ecclesiastical architecture from the colonial period. Especially notable among the seminary buildings is the church (completed 1762), with its Churrigueresque façade and towers and its sumptuous interior (I, PL. 140), in which there are some fine retables (XIII, PL. 154).

BIBLIOG. M. Toussaint and J. R. Benitez, Iglesias de México, III, Mexico, 1925, pp. 78–95; A. von Wuthenau, Tepotzotlán, Mexico City, 1941.

Colima. Colima. At El Chanal, an archaeological site a short distance from the town, a monument in the central-Mexican style has been reconstructed. It consists of a pyramidal base with a wide flight of stone steps, which are decorated in low relief, with the face of a god as the principal motif.

BIBLIOG. C. O. Sauer, Colima of New Spain in the 16th Century (Ibero-Americana, XXIX), Berkeley, Los Angeles, 1948.

Michoacán. Ihuatzio. At this village, south of Tzintzuntzán (see below), there are some Tarascan yácatas which are attributed to the final period.

Morelia. Founded in 1541 by the viceroy Antonio de Mendoza and given the name Valladolid, the city, now the capital of Michoacán state, was renamed in 1828 for José María Morelos, a hero of the struggle for Mexican independence. The Cathedral (1640–1744), which stands between the Plaza de la Paz and the Jardín de los Mártires, has a plateresque façade, twin towers, and a dome; facing it stands the Palacio de Gobierno (begun 1732; XIII, PL. 153), which was formerly a seminary and now houses the state library (Biblioteca del Estado). Another notable architectural monument of the city is the University of S. Nicolás de Hidalgo (founded ca. 1540). An old aqueduct (1785–89) with 254 arches brings water to the city through terra-cotta pipes.

BIBLIOG. J. R. Benitez, Las catedrales de Oaxaca, Morelia y Zacatecas, Mexico City, 1934; J. R. Benitez, Morelia, Mexico City, 1935; F. Benitez, Morelia, Mexico City, 1948.

Tzintzuntzán. This village, the ancient capital of the Tarascan kingdom, has five interesting yácatas. These ceremonial platforms, which belong perhaps to the final period, are T-shaped with stairs on every side. Tombs containing human remains and objects have been found among the yácatas.

BIBLIOG. D. F. Rubín de la Borbolla, Exploraciones arqueológicas en Michoacán; Tzintzuntzan, Temporada III, Rev. mexicana de est. antr., V, 1941, pp. 5–20.

Federal District (Distrito Federal). Cuicuilco (San Cuicuilco). At this archaeological site in the Valley of Mexico there is a circular monument which probably dates to the formative period. It is thought to be the oldest surviving example of monumental architecture in America. The structure, which was probably a temple base, is massive, having a maximum diameter of approximately 400 ft. at the base and rising in four stages to its present height of about 75 ft. The exterior facing of unhewn volcanic rocks is tightly packed against the interior fill of sand and rubble. Excavations have revealed several periods of construction. Access to the upper platform is provided by a staircase that rises between the terraces on one side and a ramp on the opposite side. Other lesser ruins have also been explored at this site.

BIBLIOG. B. C. Cummings, Cuicuilco: The Oldest Temple Discovered in North America, Art and Archaeol., XVI, 1923, pp. 51–58; B. G. Cummings, Cuicuilco and the Archaic Culture of Mexico, Univ. of Ariz. B., IV, 8, 1933, pp. 1–56; E. Noguera, Excavaciones en Cuicuilco, Int. Cong. of Americanists, Proc., II, 1939, pp. 210–21.

Tlaxcala. Tizatlán (San Esteban de Tizatlán). A very late pre-Columbian temple with quite unusual architectural features has been explored in this village near the town of Tlaxcala. It is one of the very rare sites where fired bricks were used as a building material. Two of the altars are decorated with frescoes, executed in a style very similar to that of the Codex Borgia (Rome, Vat. Lib.; cf. X, PLS. 54, 56, 64), in which there are symbolic motifs and, in particular, a magnificent representation of the god Tezcatlipoca and of the god of the planet Venus.

BIBLIOG. A. Caso, Las ruinas de Tizatlán, Rev. mexicana de est. h., I, 1927, pp. 139–72.

Tlaxcala. This small town was a pre-Columbian center which enjoyed great prestige during the colonial period, mainly because its people had opened their city to Cortés and joined him in the conquest of Mexico. Built in 1521, the Church of S. Francisco, with its beamed and paneled ceiling, is perhaps the oldest Christian structure in Mexico. The famous Sanctuary of Our Lady of Ocotlán (I, PL. 140), with its elaborately carved façade and red-tile towers, is a notable example of the Churrigueresque.

BIBLIOG. D. Camargo Múñoz, Historia de Tlaxcala, Tlaxcala, 1892; J. G. Montes de Oca, Tlaxcala: La ciudad morta, Mem. y Rev. Soc. A. Alzate, XLVII, 1927, pp. 161–205; M. Tousaint and J. R. Benitez, Iglesias de México, IV, Mexico City, 1927, p. 23; G. Kubler, Architects. and Builders in Mexico, 1521–50, Warburg, VII, 1944, pp. 7–19.

Morelos. Cuernavaca. The Pyramid of Teopanzolco, which is about all that remains of the Aztec city, consists of two superimposed structures, the earlier of which was covered by another of similar shape. As is typical of Chichimec and Aztec monuments, two flights of stairs lead to the upper platform, on which there once stood two temples, so that separate access to either one of the gods was possible.

The modern city, now capital of Morelos state, developed in the colonial period; Cortés himself lived there for a time. Among the oldest and most important monuments are the Palacio de Cortés (begun 1530, with many later additions), a massive castellated structure with loggias on its façades, which now contains murals by Diego Rivera; the Cathedral (begun 1529), an excellent example of the austere early Franciscan style of Mexico, with a cruciform interior, low dome, and lofty tower; and the Capilla de la Tercer Orden de S. Francisco, situated in a corner of the Cathedral yard and about as old as the Cathedral itself, which has an elaborately carved baroque façade.

BIBLIOG. M. Toussaint and J. R. Benitez, Iglesias de México, IV, Mexico City, 1927, p. 25; R. J. Ceballos Novello, Guía para visitar las principales ruinas arqueológicas de Morelos, Tepoztlán y Teopanzolco, Mexico City, 1929; F. Gómez de Orozco, El convento Franciscano de Cuernavaca, Mexico City, 1943.

Tepoztlán. On the top of Cerro del Tepozteco, a height overlooking the village of Tepoztlán, there are ruins of a temple of the Aztec period. The sanctuary stands upon a two-level base and consists of a porch with benches along the sides and an inner chamber, in which there is a pedestal for a statue of the deity (most likely the local god Tepoztecatl), which was destroyed in the 16th century. Both the piers at the entrance and the benches are decorated with figures and frets in low relief. A number of glyphs have been found among the ruins; some of them are dated, and one bears the hieroglyph of the Aztec ruler Ahuitzotl.

The interesting Dominican monastery and church in the center of the town date from the 16th century.

BIBLIOG. M. H. Saville, The Temple of Tepoztlan, Mexico, B. Am. Mus. of Natural H., VIII, 1896, pp. 221–26; E. Seler, Die Tempelpyramide von Tepoztlan, Globus, LXXIII, 1898, pp. 123–29; M. Toussaint and J. R. Benitez, Iglesias de México, VI, Mexico City, 1927, p. 45 f.; R. Redfield, Tepoztlan, Chicago, 1930; P. C. Gante, Tepoztlán, Mexico City, 1958.

Xochicalco. The very impressive remains of this important Toltec city, which dates from the end of the classic period, occupy the top of a large hill and parts of the surrounding hills. The principal monument that has been explored so far is a pyramid on a quadrangular base, with two sloping tiers, a large entablature, and an upper platform, on which stand the lower walls of a spacious hall that was probably a temple. The most remarkable feature of the monument is the revetment of perfectly fitted squared stones, which are entirely covered with reliefs (X, PL. 32). Large serpents constitute the principal motif; the coils of their bodies enclose seated personages, which are executed in a style reminiscent of the Maya, as well as glyphs and fire symbols. All these motifs were once painted in bright colors. The Ball Court is almost identical in its proportions to the one at Tula. From the court a broad street leads to La Malinche, a mound which has not yet been explored. On a nearby hill there are some ruins of what appears to have been a fortress.

BIBLIOG. M. H. Saville, Bibliographic Notes on Xochicalco, Indian Notes and Monographs, VI, 1928, pp. 185–207; E. Noguera, Exploraciones en Xochicalco, Cuadernos am., IV, 1945, pp. 119–57; E. Noguera, Cerámica de Xochicalco, El México antiguo, VI, 1947, pp. 273–98; C. A. Burland, In the House of Flowers: Xochicalco and Its Sculptures, Ethnos, XVII, 1952, pp. 119–29.

Puebla. Cholula. This town near Puebla was a flourishing city when the Spaniards captured and finally destroyed it. One can still see the great mass of an ancient pyramid (more than 175 ft. high), the largest in Mexico, on the summit of which stands the Church of Nuestra Señora de los Remedios, which was built in the colonial period and subsequently enlarged. Excavations in the remains of the pyramid, which now resembles a natural hill, have shown that it was built and enlarged over a long period in many different styles. At one point the pyramid was decorated with interesting mural paintings of stylized insects. Among the oldest remaining churches of the colonial period are S. Francisco, in Franciscan Gothic style; the Capilla Real, in *mudéjar* style, with 47 cupolas; and S. Gabriel, in the austere Franciscan Gothic style of the early colonial period.

BIBLIOG. M. Toussaint and J. R. Benitez, Iglesias de México, IV, Mexico City, 1927, p. 23; E. Noguera, El Altar de los craneos esculpidos de Cholula, Mexico City, 1937; E. Noguera, La cerámica arqueológica de Cholula, Mexico City, 1954; F. de la Maza, La ciudad de Cholula y sus iglesias, Mexico City, 1959.

Puebla. Founded in 1531 by the Franciscan friar Toribio de Benavente, who was known as Father Motolinia, the city was named Puebla de Los Angeles and developed rapidly from the early days of its settlement. In the 17th century it already boasted 60 churches, with glazed tile domes that dominate the city's sky line, as well as a great many palaces. The city, which lies in the center of a vast plain, has continued to expand harmoniously on the basis of its original grid plan. In the center of the city there are still some imposing buildings from the colonial period: the Church of S. Domingo, which contains the famous baroque Rosario Chapel (completed 1690; XIII, PL. 152); the 16th-century Church of S. Francisco; the "Casa del que mató al animal" (House of the One Who Killed the Beast), so called because of the sculpture over its portal; the ornate Casa del Alfeñique (now a museum), with its exterior decoration of white stucco and blue and white azulejos; and the huge Cathedral (consecrated 1649; II, PL. 163), which has delicate sculptural decoration on its façade, a dome covered with green and yellow tiles, and a richly furnished interior.

Interesting examples of 16th-century architecture in the environs of Puebla are the monastery at Cálpan and the fortresslike church adjoining the Franciscan monastery at Huejotzingo (1531–70), which may have been designed by Fray Juan de Alameda. Also located in the vicinity of Puebla are the churches of S. María Tonantzintla, with its notably exuberant interior, and S. Francisco Acatepec, which has a tiled façade that contrasts sharply with the austere massiveness of the structure.

The Academia de Bellas Artes in Puebla houses a gallery of Mexican painting from the colonial period.

BIBLIOG. A. Martínez, Puebla: Colonial Relicarium of America, Puebla, 1939; J. V. Medel, La capilla del Rosario, Puebla, 1940; J. V. Medel, El Convento de Santa Mónica, 2d ed., Puebla, 1940; M. Toussaint, La catedral y las iglesias de Puebla, Mexico City, 1954.

Guerrero. Cerro Oztuma. At this site in the north of the state there is a fortress with interesting walls and moats, which reveal a fairly advanced knowledge of the building of defensive works.

BIBLIOG. R. H. Lister, Cerro Oztuma, El México antiguo, V, 1941, pp. 209–17; P. Armillas, Oztuma, Rev. mexicana de est. antr. VI, 1942–44, pp. 165–75.

Oaxaca. Mitla. This archaeological center dates from a later period than Monte Albán (see below), from which its artistic style is partly derived. There still remain groups of palaces composed of large rooms; their façades and, in some cases, also the interior walls are decorated with stone mosaics with geometric motifs (X, PL. 47). Each stone is cut so as to fit exactly in its place and thus form part of an over-all design. Along the center of the main hall of one of these palaces there stands a row of enormous monolithic columns that once supported a flat roof. A cruciform tomb built of large blocks of stone admirably fitted together and decorated with the characteristic stone mosaics has been found beneath one of the buildings. Traces of mural paintings in the style of the codices can still be seen.

BIBLIOG. M. H. Saville, The Cruciform structures of Mitla and Vicinity, New York, 1909, pp. 151–90; A. Caso and D. F. Rubín de la Borbolla, Exploraciones en Mitla, 1934–35 (Inst. Panamericana de Geog. e H., Pub., XXI), Mexico City, 1936; E. C. Parsons, Mitla: Town of the Souls, Chicago, 1936.

Monte Albán. In the formative period the first inhabitants settled on this elevation near the present city of Oaxaca, where they began to build, on an incomparable site, one of the most extraordinary cities of pre-Columbian Mexico (FIG. 855). The large stone platforms, which belong to Phase I of the formative period have on their façades large clay panels with reliefs of human figures in motion, the so-called "danzantes" (X, PL. 2); these are reminiscent of the Olmec style, as are almost all the other artistic features of Phase I at Monte Albán. These first settlers also built simple stone tombs and began to urbanize the large central plaza.

During Phase II other peoples who settled on Monte Albán mixed their imported styles with the local style of Phase I. The main plaza was laid out in the form of a huge rectangle with temples and palaces on all sides and another group of temples (Mound H) at the center. The inhabitants built vertical walls of large blocks of stone; those of Mound J were carved with glyphs and various figures. At the same time, the tombs became more spacious and acquired porches, and new pottery styles appeared. The bases and temples of Phase III, which corresponds to the classic period, are decorated with scapular-shaped frets that are repeated indefinitely, thus creating a deliberate monotony that does not mar the over-all view of the plaza. The fact that the peripheral walls of the temples on the west side of the plaza were brought forward to achieve perfect symmetry is a sign of great refinement. Some of the large and complex tombs are decorated with frescoes depicting processions of gods and other motifs. At the end of this phase, during which the minor arts reached their maximum development, Monte Albán declined as an active culture, and the cities in the valley attained greater importance with Phase IV, which lasted until the Conquest. Probably in the 14th century, the Mixtecs occupied part of the valley and left, among other things, the magnificent treasure of metal ornaments (Oaxaca, Mus. Regional) which was found by Alfonso Caso in Tomb 7 in the vicinity of Monte Albán.

BIBLIOG. L. Batres, Exploraciones de Monte Albán, Mexico City, 1902; A. Caso, Las exploraciones en Monte Albán, Temporada 1931–1932 (Inst. Panamericano de Geog. e H., Pub., VII), Mexico City, 1932; A. Caso, Monte Albán: Richest Archaeological Find in America, Nat. Geog. Mag., LXII, 1932, pp. 487–512; A. Caso, Las exploraciones en Monte Albán, Temporada 1934–1935 (Inst. Panamericano de Geog. y H., Pub., XIX), Mexico City, 1935.

Oaxaca. The city's most remarkable architectural monument is the former monastery of S. Domingo (founded 1575), a massive structure with fortresslike walls and a now badly scarred façade. The baroque interior of the monastery church is one of the richest in Mexico; of special interest is the polychrome stucco tree of Jesse in the choir vault. The Cathedral, which was begun in 1553 and completed about two centuries later, has a plateresque façade with niches in which there are some fine statues of saints and apostles (I, PL. 139). Also architecturally notable are the Church of La Soledad, which has a 17th-century baroque façade, and the 18th-century churches of S. Felipe and S. Agustín.

The Museo Regional de Oaxaca is a repository of finds from the nearby ruins of Monte Albán.

BIBLIOG. M. Toussaint and J. R. Benitez, Iglesias de México, IV, Mexico City, 1927, pp. 23, 49, 63; R. García Granados, La ciudad de Oaxaca, Mexico City, 1933; J. R. Benitez, Las catedrales de Oaxaca, Morelia y Zacatecas, Mexico City, 1934; A. F. Ramírez, Hombres notables y monumentos coloniales de Oaxaca, Mexico City, 1948; J. F. Iturribarría, Oaxaca en la historia, Mexico City, 1955.

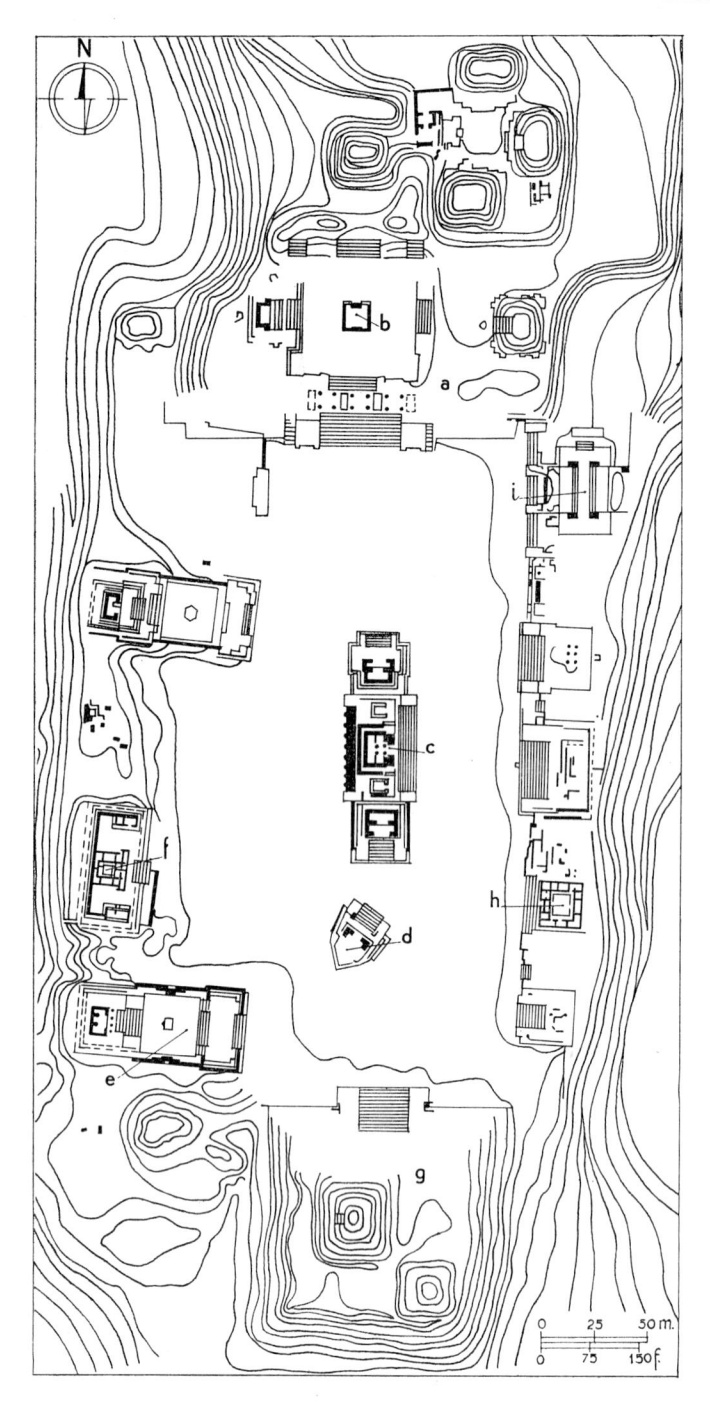

Monte Albán, plan of the archaeological zone. Key: (a) the north platform; (b) sunken court; (c) the central complex (Mound H); (d) Mound J; (e) Group M; (f) platform of the "danzantes"; (g) the south platform; (h) the palace (Mound S); (i) Ball Court (from W. Krickeberg, 1956).

Yagul. The archaeological zone here consists of a fortress — natural for the most part — at the base of which there was an enormous palace composed of various patios surrounded by rooms, as well as a ball court and several temples and dwellings. Many objects in both the Zapotec and Mixtec styles have been found here.

BIBLIOG. J. Paddock, The First Three Seasons at Yagul, Mesoamerican Notes, IV, 1955, pp. 25-47; C. Wicke, The Ball Court at Yagul, Oaxaca: A Comparative Study, Mesoamerican Notes, V, 1957, pp. 37-76.

Tabasco. La Venta. This Olmec center is situated on an island surrounded by swamps. A large central patio flanked by basalt columns and encircled by platforms of reddish clay constitutes the main architectural element. From a later date comes a large tomb with stone columns that are, perhaps, representations of tree trunks. The rather numerous structures are built of earth and adobe; here, in contrast to later cities, stone was used as a building material hardly at all, although there are stone mosaic floors with a motif of grotesque jaguar heads. The most striking features of La Venta are the large stone sculptures, among which there are colossal human heads, quadrangular altars decorated on all sides, deformed human figures, steles, and sarcophagi (X, PL. 2). All the stone used in these monumental sculptures was quarried more than 60 miles away.

BIBLIOG. P. Drucker, La Venta, Tabasco: A Study of Olmec Ceramics and Art (B. Bur. of Am. Ethn., CLIII), Washington, 1952; P. Drucker, R. F. Heizer and R. J. Squier, Excavations at La Venta, 1955 (B. Bur. of Am. Ethn., CLXX), Washington, 1959.

Chiapas. Bonampak. The frescoes found at this classic Maya center near Yaxchilán are generally regarded as the most extraordinary to survive from pre-Columbian times in all America. Three rooms are completely decorated with depictions of religious ceremonies, battles, and sacrifices (IV, PL. 396; X, PL. 20). In these murals — some of which abound in movement, while others are fairly static — hundreds of human figures are represented; there are also many hieroglyphics, and still untranslated inscriptions run along the bottom of certain scenes. The Museo Nacional de Antropología in Mexico City has color copies of the Bonampak frescoes. A fine low relief depicting a human figure in profile is found near the building that contains the murals.

BIBLIOG. A. Villagra Caleti, Bonampak: La ciudad de los muros pintados, Mexico City, 1949; K. Ruppert, J. E. S. Thompson and T. Proskouriakoff, Bonampak, Chiapas, Mexico (Carnegie Inst., Pub. 602), Washington, 1955; A. T. Arai, La arquitectura de Bonampak, Mexico City, 1960; R. Piña Chan, Bonampak, Mexico City, 1961.

Palenque. One of the most important and best-known Maya sites of the classic period, the city, like most Maya cities, does not appear to have been laid out in accordance with an over-all plan, but there are large architectural complexes. The most important building is the Palace, a vast and approximately rectangular structure whose rooms are grouped around patios (X, PL. 7). From it rises a tower, a unique structure in pre-Columbian America, which is about 50 ft. high and divided into three stories with an interior staircase. The Temple of the Inscriptions, named for the panels with hieroglyphics in low relief that decorate its interior, is even more famous for the large crypt discovered there in 1952. This tomb is a large vaulted chamber, profusely decorated with fine stuccoes and connected with the temple above by a stairway. The body was placed in a magnificent stone sarcophagus with a beautifully decorated monolithic top. Many valuable and interesting objects found in the crypt are now in the Museo Nacional de Antropología, Mexico City (X, PL. 17). The temples of the Sun and the Foliated Cross (X, PL. 7) and that of the Cross are three small jewels with triple entrances and sloping roofs that are decorated with stuccoes and ornamental cresting. Although many other interesting buildings are found here, Palenque is noted not only for its architecture but also for the splendid sculptures, principally of stucco, with which it was richly decorated, and for the stone tablets adorned with figures and glyphs, some of which are the most beautiful and important produced by the Maya culture. Very little remains of the Palenque mural paintings.

BIBLIOG. A. Ruz L'Huillier, Exploraciones en Palenque, 1950-1951, Anales Inst. nacional de antr. e h., 6th ser., IV, 1952, pp. 79-110; A. Ruz L'Huillier, La pirámide-tumba de Palenque, Cuadernos am., XIII, 1954, pp. 141-59; A. Ruz L'Huillier, Exploraciones arqueológicas en Palenque, 1953, 1954, 1956, Anales Inst. nacional de antr. e h., 6th Ser., X, 1958, pp. 69-299.

Yaxchilán. Dating back to the classic period, this center on the banks of the Usumacinta has many imposing buildings. Outstanding among them is House K (or Structure 33), which stands on a base and has three entrances. The walls are bare, but the frieze is decorated with human figures seated on thrones, and above it rises a huge ornamental crest, or roof comb, with a large figure in the center. A large number of steles bearing extremely ancient dates have been found, as well as tablets and beautifully sculptured lintels (X, PLS. 15, 16).

BIBLIOG. S. G. Morley, Report of the Yaxchilan Expedition, Carnegie Inst. of Washington, Yb., XXX, 1931, pp. 132-39.

Campeche. Edzná. This Mayan center has an enormous chambered pyramid in the Puuc style, with five tiers and a flying façade.

BIBLIOG. A. Ruz L'Huillier, Campeche en la arqueología Maya (Acta anthr., I, 2-3), Mexico City, 1945, pp. 52-61.

Hochob. The most remarkable ruin here is a Chenes-style temple with a single entrance and a façade entirely decorated with a huge mask and flanked by two protruding buttresses, each of which bears a human figure. At the sides of the main temple there are symmetrical wings, both of which are decorated with masks, the open mouths of which are the entrances.

BIBLIOG. A. Ruz L'Huillier, Campeche en la arqueología Maya (Acta anthr., I, 2–3), Mexico City, 1945, pp. 33–35.

Río Bec. The Río Bec style is intermediate between the Puuc and Chenes styles. There are buildings with large stuccoed masks whose mouths form entrances. Only part of the façade is decorated in accordance with the Puuc style, in contrast with which, however, the decoration occurs on the lower part of the façade, while the upper part remains unadorned. The characteristic towers are purely decorative in function.

on one wall of the east wing there is a representation of the celestial dragon, whose mouth serves as the door, thus recalling the Chenes style. The so-called "Iglesia" has a large flying façade in the Puuc style (i.e., the front wall rises above the level of the roof, thus serving as an ornamental cresting and adding height to the façade). The building called the "Akab-Dzib" (Writing in the Dark), with its unadorned façade, also dates from this period, as it shows no trace of the Toltec style. A particularly fine example of pre-Toltec architecture, because of its perfect proportions, is the Temple of the Three Lintels, which is located at the nearby site of Chichén Viejo (Old Chichén); the lower wall, with three doorways, is smooth, while the upper part has groups of small mortised columns separated by panels of stone latticework and masks at the corners.

In the Maya-Toltec period many new buildings were erected

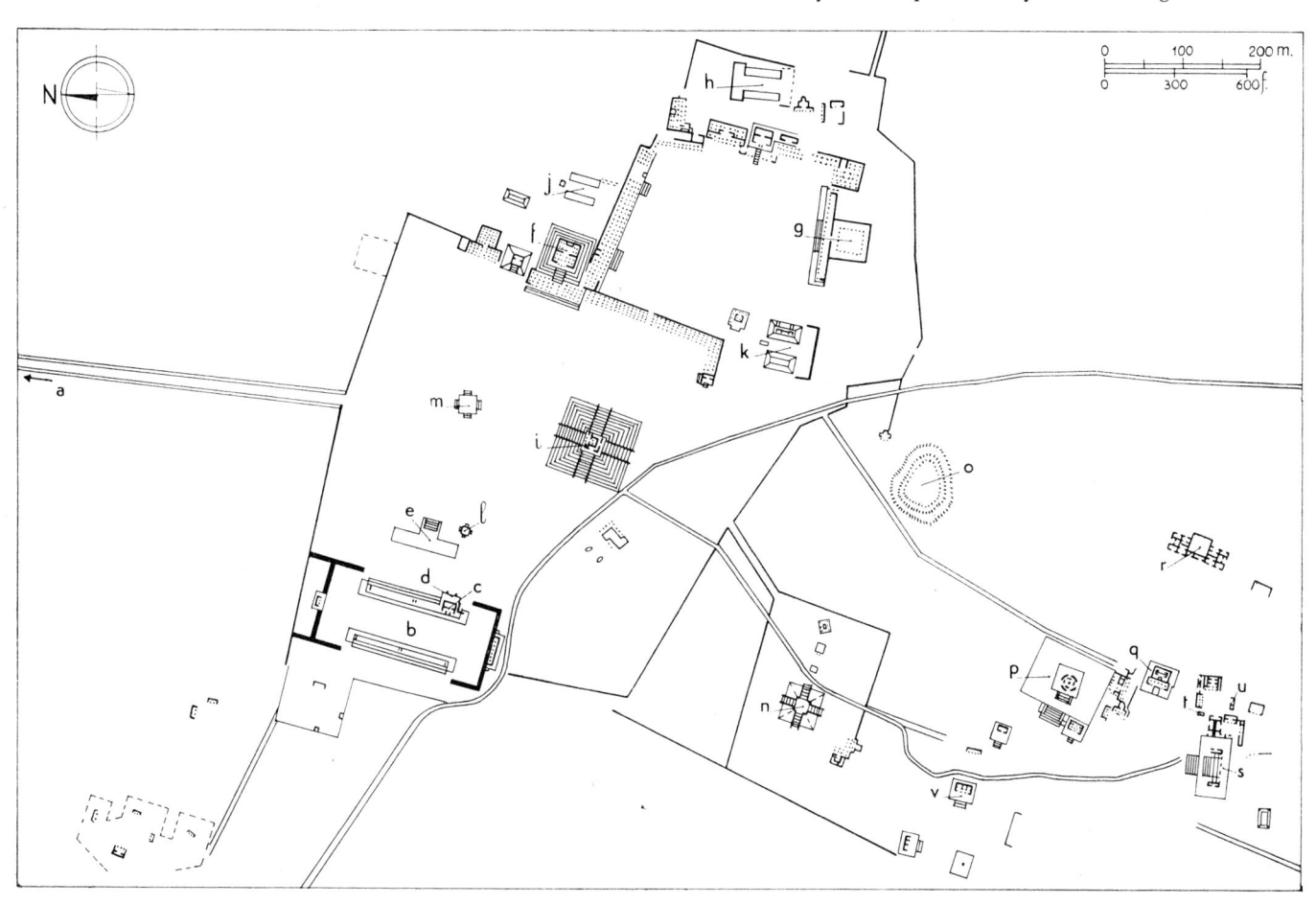

Chichén Itzá, plan of the central archaeological zone. Key: (a) the large *cenote* (Well of Sacrifice); (b) Ball Court; (c) Temple of the Jaguars (or Tigers); (d) lower chamber of the Temple of the Jaguars (or Tigers); (e) Tzompantli (skull rack); (f) Temple of the Warriors and Group of the Thousand Columns; (g) the "Market" (Mercado); (h) Ball Court; (i) Castillo; (j,k) ball courts; (l) Platform of the Eagles; (m) Platform of Venus; (n) tomb of the High Priest; (o) the Xtoloc *cenote*; (p) the Caracol; (q) Temple of the Wall Panels; (r) Akab-Dzib; (s) Casa de las Monjas; (t) the "Iglesia"; (u) annex to the Casa de las Monjas; (v) Red House, or House of the Deer (*from S. G. Morley, 1956*).

BIBLIOG. C. L. Hay, A Contribution to Maya Architecture, Natural H., XXXVI, 1935, pp. 29–33; K. Ruppert and J. H. Denison, Archaeological Reconnaissance in Campeche, Quintana Roo and Peten (Carnegie Inst., Pub. 543), Washington, 1943, pp. 29–36; A. Ruz L'Huillier, Campeche en la arqueología Maya (Acta anthr., I, 2–3), Mexico City, 1945, pp. 21–23.

Santa Rosa Xlabpak. The principal building here is an imposing three-story structure, in the Chenes style, with 42 rooms and two staircases.

BIBLIOG. A. Ruz L'Huillier, Campeche en la arqueología Maya (Acta anthr., I, 2–3), Mexico City, 1945, pp. 37–38.

Yucatán. Chichén Itzá. The buildings of this important Maya center date from the classic Maya and the Maya-Toltec periods. The pre-Toltec style of Chichén Itzá is very similar to the Puuc style, although such features as triple entrances, mortised columns, the small stone "huts," serpents in profile, and revetments of cut stone are rare or nonexistent here. One of the principal monuments of the classic Maya period is the Casa de las Monjas (X, PL. 9), which has three recessed tiers and an L-shaped wing decorated with masks;

at Chichén Itzá, as the city became the most important center in Yucatán. One of the principal Maya-Toltec buildings is the Castillo (or Temple of Kukulcan), a pyramid about 80 ft. high with nine tiers. The temple on the top platform is entered through a doorway with two columns carved in the form of serpents, with the heads at the base and the tails at the top. A large flight of steps flanked by serpent heads ascends each of the four faces of the pyramid. Inside the Castillo, another earlier but similar structure contains a Chac-Mool figure and a throne shaped like a jaguar, which is painted red and inlaid with jade. Above the throne there was once a turquoise mosaic in the form of a solar disk. The Caracol (X, PL. 34), which seems to have been used as an observatory, is a cylindrical structure which stands on a square platform; the substructure shows elements of the Puuc style, while the present building most certainly belongs to the early Maya-Toltec period. The Temple of the Warriors (X, PL. 35) stands at the center of a vast complex. It is approached through a colonnade, which has pillars sculptured with warrior figures. At the top of the access stairway, before the entrance to the temple, there is a Chac-Mool statue. The three entrances are separated by serpent columns like those found in the Castillo, and the walls are decorated with masks in the early Maya style and with

Toltec motifs (X, PL. 36). The temple proper is divided into an antechamber and a sanctuary, toward the back of which there remains an altar supported by close rows of atlantes. Beneath this temple there survives an older temple, which is supported by sculptured pillars. The Group of the Thousand Columns, which forms a vast plaza at the base of the Temple of the Warriors, and the so-called "Market" (Mercado), situated at the south end of the complex, constitute an ensemble very much like the one at Tula. The main Ball Court (X, PL. 36), located northwest of the Castillo, is important not only architecturally but also because it still has the large stone rings through which the players attempted to pass the ball, as well as benches decorated in low relief with themes relevant to the game and the sacrifice of the loser. At the end of one of the lateral platforms of the Ball Court stands the splendid Temple of the Jaguars (or Tigers; X, PL. 37), which contains murals depicting battle scenes and, in another chamber, polychrome reliefs representing a procession of warriors and priests. Numerous other less important structures of the Maya-Toltec period still survive in Chichén Itzá, such as the Tzompantli (skull rack), the Platform of the Eagles, and the Platform of Venus (see FIG. 857).

BIBLIOG. E. H. Morris, J. Charlot and A. A. Morris, The Temple of the Warriors at Chichen Itza (Carnegie Inst., Pub. 406), 2 vols., Washington, 1931; K. Ruppert, The Caracol at Chichen Itza (Carnegie Inst., Pub. 454), Washington, 1935; K. Ruppert, The Mercado, Chichen Itza, Contributions to Am. Anthr. and H., VIII, 1943, pp. 223–60; S. K. Lothrop, Metals from the Cenote of Sacrifice, Chichen Itza (Peabody Mus. Mem., X, 2), Cambridge, Mass., 1952; K. Ruppert, Chichen Itza: Architectural Notes and Plans (Carnegie Inst., Publ. 595), Washington, 1952; A. M. Tozzer, Chichen Itza and Its Cenote of Sacrifice (Peabody Mus. Mem., XI–XII), 2 vols., Cambridge, Mass., 1957.

Kabah. Located near Uxmal, this Mayan city in the Puuc style has not been fully explored, and only a few of its buildings are known. The most important one is the Codz-Pop (or Palace of the Masks), whose four sides were decorated from top to bottom with close rows of masks; the principal façade alone bears about 300 of these sculptures (X, PL. 12). The nose of one large interior mask serves as a step between two chambers. Another building here is decorated only with a frieze composed of small columns. An arch, similar to the one at Labná (see below), has been restored and now serves as the main entrance to the site. There is also an enormous pyramid, as well as various other buildings.

BIBLIOG. P. Kelemen, Medieval American Art: Masterpieces of the New World before Columbus (1 vol. ed.), New York, 1956, p. 77 f.

Labná. At this center, which flourished in the classic Maya period, there are two notable building complexes: the portal group and the Palace. Above Structure XI of the portal group rises a building, sometimes called the "Mirador" (X, PL. 11), with four rectangular rooms and a simple façade, on which there are large figures of maltha which rest on modillions. The flying façade at the top of this building once had at least six horizontal rows of rectangular perforations, before which there were figures. The gateway that connects the courtyard of the portal group with that of the Palace is decorated at the top with a frieze of stepped zigzags, stone latticework "shutters," and "huts," which are replicas of the adobe and thatch houses of the people. The Palace is a very large building of several stories, which was probably built in several stages without an over-all plan; although it consists of a series of distinct sections, the general effect is harmonious. A large part of the building is profusely decorated with characteristic motifs of the Puuc style.

BIBLIOG. E. H. Thompson, The Chultunes of Labna, Yucatan (Peabody Mus. Mem., I, 3), Cambridge, Mass., 1897.

Mayapán. The city, which belongs entirely to the Maya-Toltec period, was the successor of Chichén Itzá as the administrative and ceremonial center of the Mayas in Yucatán. It is surrounded by a rather low wall, which is over 5 miles long, in which there are nine gates. Many of the buildings had colonnades both in front and in back, which were generally covered by flat roofs, rather than the vaulted roofs of Chichén Itzá. In general, the construction is of poor quality, with hardly any trace of the lovely squared stonework of the preceding periods.

BIBLIOG. T. Proskouriakoff, Mayapán: The Lost Stronghold of a Civilization, Archaeology, VII, 1954, pp. 96–103; E. M. Shook, The Temple of Kukulcan at Mayapán, Carnegie Inst. of Washington, Current Rep., XX, 1954, pp. 89–108; E. M. Shook and W. Irving, Colonnaded Buildings at Mayapán, Carnegie Inst. of Washington, Current Rep., XXII, 1955, pp. 127–67; H. E. D. Pollock, ed., Mayapán, Yucatan, Mexico (Carnegie Inst., Pub. 619), Washington, 1962.

Mérida. The city was founded in 1542 by Francisco de Montejo the Younger on the site of the earlier Maya city of T'Ho. Among its oldest buildings are: the plateresque Casa del Adelantado de Montejo (mid-16th cent.), built for the city's founder; the massive Convento de las Monjas (early 17th cent.); and the Cathedral, which was completed in the late 16th century by the architect Juan Miguel de Agüero.

The local archaeological museum houses relics from the numerous Mayan sites in Yucatán.

BIBLIOG. M. Toussaint and J. R. Benitez, Iglesias de México, IV, Mexico City, 1927, p. 62; J. García Preciat, La catedral de Mérida, AEArt, XI, 1935, pp. 73–93; G. Ferrer de Mendiolea, Nuestra ciudad: Mérida de Yucatán, Mérida, 1938; J. I. Rubio Mañé, La casa de Montejo en Mérida de Yucatán, Mexico City, 1941.

Sayil. A Maya center of the classic period, this site has many monuments, of which the most interesting is the Palace (X, PL. 8), a huge building, over 200 ft. long, with a rectangular plan and three stories. The first floor, which is poorly preserved, formerly contained a double series of rooms, as did the second level, which is set back from the first. The striking use of columns on the exterior of the first and second stories is not repeated on the simpler top level. Another noteworthy monument is the "Mirador," a structure which stands on a high pyramid.

BIBLIOG. P. Kelemen, Medieval American Art: Masterpieces of the New World before Columbus (I vol. ed.), New York, 1956, p. 74 f.

Uxmal. This center is probably the most important Maya city in the Puuc style. The tallest of its structures, the so-called "Pyramid of the Soothsayer" (El Adivino), was rebuilt or remodeled five times; only parts of it remain. Outstanding elements in its very complex structure are the immense west staircase, the upper temples, and the large ornamental masks of the Maya rain god (Chac-Mool). An inner temple has magnificent low reliefs depicting a personage surrounded by plants and fish. The Nunnery Quadrangle (X, PLS. 8, 9) consists of four separate buildings, which contain, in all, about 90 vaulted chambers. The four inner façades are profusely decorated with a frieze of stone mosaic, with a different motif on each building thus avoiding an impression of monotony; among the motifs are large stretched-out or coiled serpents, large rain-god masks, stone latticework "shutters," "huts," and sculptures in the round. The carved decoration over the central entrance of the west building shows a throne with a splendid "feather" canopy, above which there is a figure with the body of a tortoise and a human face. Access to the entire complex of the Nunnery Quadrangle is provided by a flight of steps that leads to a magnificent arch with a corbeled, or false, vault in the center of the south buildings. The third large building is the beautiful Palace of the Governor (X, PL. 9), which stands on a series of vast tiered platforms. The central section is flanked by two wings, which are separated from it by passages with monumental corbeled arches (X, PL. 9). The main part consists of two wide central halls with four smaller rooms at each end. The façade begins with a low base decorated with small columns, above which rises a plain wall, which, in turn, is surmounted by a vast and profusely decorated frieze, in which large rain-god masks are repeated and combined in an extremely harmonious manner. The House of the Turtles is decorated only with small columns between the cornice and the architrave and with small turtles, which give the structure its name, in full relief on the upper fillet. Close to the Palace of the Governor are the unexcavated ruins of the House of the Doves, on which a high serrated roof comb is still visible.

BIBLIOG. S. G. Morley, A Group of Related Structures at Uxmal, Mexico, AJA, XIV, 1910, pp. 1–18; S. G. Morley, Ancient Temples and Cities of the New World: Uxmal, The City of the Xius, Pan-Am. Union B., XXXII, 1911, pp. 627–42; M. H. Saville, Bibliographic Notes on Uxmal, Yucatan, Indian Notes and Monographs, IX, 1921, pp. 55–131.

Quintana Roo. Cobá. The most important city of the classic Maya period in northeastern Yucatán, the site is famous as the hub of a system of causeways (*sachbeob*). The existing fragments of these roads show that they had an average width of about 15 ft. The most remarkable, and the only one which has been completely surveyed, connected Cobá with Yaxuná, a distance of approximately 62 miles.

BIBLIOG. J. E. S. Thompson, H. E. D. Pollock, and J. Charlot, A Preliminary Study of the Ruins of Coba, Quintana Roo, Mexico (Carnegie Inst., Pub. 424), Washington, 1932; A. Villa Rojos, The Yaxuna-Cobá Causeway, Contributions to Am. Archaeol., II, 1934, pp. 187–209.

Tulum. This Maya city, which is situated on a high cliff at the edge of the Caribbean, has numerous buildings, some of the Maya-Toltec period and others of a later period; on its three landward sides the city is surrounded by a high, thick wall, in which there are five gates. The Castillo, which is the principal building, stands approximately in the center of the walled area; a wide stairway ascends to the upper temple, which is entered between two serpent columns in the Toltec style. The façade is characteristic of the Tulum style, with walls inclined slightly outward toward the top, a narrow unornamented frieze, and niches over the lintel of the portico. The front of Temple V is decorated with a stucco high relief of a descending god above the entrance. The Temple of the Frescoes has large stucco masks on its corners and bears, as its name indicates, the remains of murals depicting gods or priests on both the interior and exterior walls; these frescoes, in which red and blue predominate, are executed in a less realistic style than that of Chichén Itzá. Tulum was probably the first Mexican city sighted by the Spaniards.

BIBLIOG. S. K. Lothrop, Tulum: An archaeological Study of the East Coast of Yucatan (Carnegie Inst., Pub. 335), Washington, 1924; M. A. Fernández, Las ruinas de Tulum, Anales Inst. nacional de antr. e h., 6th Ser., I, 1945, pp. 95–120.

* *

In the treatment of individual centers the contribution of Ignacio BERNAL for pre-Columbian material and Francesco NEGRI ARNOLDI for material relating to the modern era is acknowledged.

Illustrations: 7 figs. in text.

MICHELANGELO BUONARROTI (Michelagniolo di Lodovico di Lionardo di Buonarroto Simoni). Sculptor, painter, architect, and poet [b. Caprese (now Caprese Michelangelo, Italy), Mar. 6, 1475; d. Rome, Feb. 18, 1564]. He wrote his name Michelagniolo, or Michelangiolo Buonarroti; he signed only one of his works, the *Pietà* in St. Peter's, with the words MICHAEL ANGELUS BONAROTUS FLORENTIN FACIEBAT. Even during his lifetime he was considered the greatest genius of modern art, the equal or even the superior of the masters of antiquity; contemporaries saw in him the culmination of the development of Italian art from Cimabue on.

A knowledge of Michelangelo's life is important for the understanding of his artistic personality, even though he kept the two far apart: his works of art did not directly mirror his daily life, and he never tried to adapt his manner of living to his artistic ideals. In his art he created a heroic, superior world; in his life he remained the Florentine artist-artisan, leading a sober bourgeois existence.

The following factors in his life seem to be most important for an understanding of the character of his art: his birth in Tuscany; his youth in Florence; and his descent from an old Florentine family. His art is essentially Tuscan, though, from his youth on, he separated himself radically from the fashionable Florentine art trends of the day; but he did this only to reach the deeper roots of the monumental Tuscan tradition. He is a Florentine in his passionate, audacious being, full of pride but restrained by sobriety and severity. In the inner tension of his figures enveloped in seeming calm, in the precise yet musical contours, and in the penetrating, almost scientific intensity with which he grasped the inner structure of plastic forms, although always subordinating them to a total vision of impressive unity, his art is essentially Florentine. Even later, when he expanded his Florentine idiom into a universal language, and in his last works when he fused the individual forms, the Tuscan character remained predominant.

It is important to know that his mother, Francesca di Neri di Miniato del Sera, died when he was six years old, because this may explain the sibylline type of woman depicted in the Virgins of his youth, in which motherly tenderness seems lacking. His father, Lodovico, and his four brothers were unworthy of him. Since the oldest brother, Fra Leonardo, had entered the Dominican order, Michelangelo was regarded as the oldest and, as a consequence, from early youth had to shoulder responsibility for the entire family. Actually he wanted through his art to raise the social level of his line. He worked not so much for his own fame or advancement as for that of the Buonarroti. This goal seems to have been one of the reasons for the astonishing physical endurance which permitted him to create his gigantic works. He succeeded in his admitted aim of raising the family to the upper classes through the marriages of his niece Francesca and his nephew Leonardo to the noble Florentine houses of Guicciardini and Ridolfi.

His strong Florentine sentiments manifested themselves in his youth and maturity in a Florentine patriotism. His political views, his republicanism, he inherited from his Guelph family. (For details of his political views, see Tolnay, 1949, p. 9 ff.) He gave artistic expression to it in his marble *David* (Florence, Acc.) and, later, in his *Brutus* (Florence, Mus. Naz.), both incarnations of the normative moral forces on which, according to Florentine views, the "buon governo" should be based.

His patrons played an important role in his life, often acting as ideal "father," sometimes severe like Julius II, and sometimes kindly like Lorenzo de' Medici and, later, Paul III and Julius III. Although Michelangelo did not allow his patrons to influence the conception of his works, except perhaps in the earliest stages, nevertheless the enormous opportunities afforded by their commissions spurred him on to his extraordinary achievements. He wanted to satisfy his patrons, not by courtly flattery, but by the quality and scale of his works.

Of his friends only two seem to have played an important role in the inspiration of his art and spirit: Tommaso Cavalieri and Vittoria Colonna. The former, a Roman nobleman of extraordinary beauty, moved the sixty-year-old Michelangelo to a more exalted conception of earthly beauty as the image of the "divine idea." Vittoria Colonna, descendant of one of the oldest Italian noble families, became Michelangelo's spiritual guide in his late religious "conversion."

Two spiritual trends of the period, in particular, left their mark on Michelangelo's thought, art works, and poetry: Platonism (and Neoplatonism), in which he found the metaphysical justification of his passion for Cavalieri — the love of corporeal beauty being but a vehicle for the adoration of the "divine idea" shining through it. The Neoplatonic doctrines inspired some of Michelangelo's great works of art and many of his poems. Platonism (and Neoplatonism) probably came to Michelangelo through his early acquaintance with Poliziano, Marsilio Ficino, Pico della Mirandola, and Girolamo Benivieni at the house of Lorenzo de' Medici, and also through the poetry of Dante, Petrarch, and Lorenzo de' Medici, which he knew well. (For discussion of Platonism in Michelangelo, see: Tolnay, *L'Arte*, 4th ser., V, 1934, pp. 5–44; *BArte*, 3d ser., XXIX, 9, 1936, pp. 389–408; and A. Chastel, *Marsile Ficin et l'art*, Geneva, 1954.) Secondly, ideas of the Catholic reform, which touched him in his youth in the preachings of Savonarola, decisively influenced him in later years in the form of Juan de Valdés' doctrine of justification by faith alone, which he may have known through Vittoria Colonna. (On the development of Michelangelo's religious ideas, see Tolnay, 1949, p. 61 ff.)

Autobiographical allusions appear in his work, always indirectly in a generalized, sublimated manner. In spite of their completely objective and ideal aspect, his works are more personal than anything done in Tuscany before him. His pride and righteous anger are embodied in the faces of the *St. Proculus* (Bologna, S. Domenico), the *Moses* (Rome, S. Pietro in Vincoli), the marble *David*, and the *Brutus*; it is his spiritual raptus which is in the prophets and sibyls of the Sistine ceiling. In the God the Father of the same work the limitless, absolute creative force for which he himself yearned can be recognized. The suffering of the corporeal chains expressed in the slaves for the tomb of Pope Julius II (both, Paris, Louvre; PL. 529) and the torpor, melancholy, or anger of the Allegories of the Medici tombs (Florence, S. Lorenzo, New Sacristy), all express Michelangelo's own world of feeling. The spiritualization of the *capitani*, the seated figures of the Medici Chapel, parallels his own yearning as expressed in poems written to Cavalieri. His striving for liberation from earthly bonds found touching embodiment in three compositional drawings of the Resurrection of Christ (PL. 539; Paris, Louvre; Windsor, Royal Lib.; Br. Mus.; cf. Tolnay, 1943–60, III, figs. 144, 145, 146). It is Michelangelo's own "conversion" which is depicted in *The Conversion of St. Paul* (PL. 537) and his own suffering of the human condition which finds expression in the *Crucifixion of St. Peter* (PL. 534).

His works may almost always be regarded as spiritual self-portraits — sometimes conscious and sometimes subconscious.

In his *Last Judgment* (PLS. 533, 536) and in the late *Pietà*, or *Deposition* (PL. 526), in the Cathedral of Florence he expressed the autobiographical allusions more directly, but even here he disguised them. In the *Last Judgment* he depicted his own damnation in a self-portrait on the skin held by St. Bartholomew (identified by La Cava, *Il volto di Michelangelo scoperto nel Giudizio Finale*, Bologna, 1925), and in the late *Pietà*, or *Deposition*, the head of Joseph of Arimathea is, according to Vasari, an idealized self-portrait of the artist. In fact, he did this latter work for his own tomb. Since the Hellenistic period the subjective sentiment, the lyric *état d'âme* of an individual, had not been expressed with such intensity in works of art. Nevertheless, the subjectivity of sentiment becomes of universal value in Michelangelo's hands. Michelangelo never speaks in the first person in his works; he does not seem to express individual spiritual experiences or moods but only universal truths in typical general forms. His works demand recognition of their objective validity; but the material of the experiences from which he distills these universally valid truths is deeply personal.

The extraordinary success and fame of Michelangelo during his lifetime had the effect of creating among his contemporaries two contrary images: His friends, admirers, and younger followers made of him a mythical figure, deified him as an artist and as a man, and called him "divino"; others attacked and even defamed him, fabricating an image — which became a cliché, often repeated later — of Michelangelo as an antisocial character, a somber and avaricious man, and a heretic. The incorrectness of this image was definitely revealed, first, in 1863, by the publication of his poems in authentic form and then, in 1875, by the publication of his letters, showing the generosity and nobility of his heart; in popular opinion, however, the legend still lives on.

The first indications of a real "cult of Michelangelo" appear about 1540. The fictional dialogues by Donato Giannotti (ca. 1545), Francisco de Hollanda (1548), and Anton Francesco Doni (1552), in which Michelangelo is one of the protagonists, are early signs. Benedetto Varchi's *Due Lezioni* (1549), with the interpretation of two of Michelangelo's poems, also belongs to this group. Incidentally, Varchi's is the first printed volume on Michelangelo. Then, in 1550, followed the biography by Vasari, partly based on that by the Anonimo Magliabechiano (ca. 1535-40), and, in 1553, that of Condivi; in 1568, Vasari published the second edition of his biography, in which he incorporated facts reported by Condivi and information from other sources. Mention should also be made of Varchi's *Funeral Oration* of 1564, containing another biography, this time a short one (P. Barocchi, *Trattati d'Arte*, Bari, 1960). Vasari's biography of Michelangelo appears at the end of his great work on the lives of Italian artists as the summit of the whole artistic development of Italy from Cimabue on; his is the liveliest and richest contemporary portrait, although Condivi's is the more reliable because it was probably partly written to Michelangelo's dictation. Both Vasari and Condivi cast Michelangelo's personality in a heroic mold, which remained the model for many later biographies until our time. As an artist his works aroused admiration at a very early date, and he was only twenty-nine years old when the first printed appreciative mention of him appeared in Pomponius Gauricus' *De sculptura* in 1504; here his name appears in a list of the best Tuscan sculptors, and it is mentioned that he is "etiam pictor." Vasari praises him as triumphing not only over the great artists of the Renaissance but also over those of antiquity, and even over Nature herself. Michelangelo's spirit is "godlike" (*divino*), says Vasari, and his works are not only the creations of a great genius but the absolute esthetic canon of all art. The opinions of the other contemporaries mentioned above and those of Tommaso Cavalieri and Vittoria Colonna are similar. Thus the highest appreciation of his art he was ever to receive came from contemporary writers and friends.

Equally high in this circle, which was close to him during his lifetime, was the appreciation of Michelangelo as a man. He was even raised by his contemporaries to a social and human esteem that is unique in the history of art. Condivi treats him in his introduction as an equal of the reigning pope, Julius III, and Vittoria Colonna went even further, comparing his goodness with that of the Saviour.

The reaction against this great acclaim began with Paulus Giovius' short biography (ca. 1525), which reflected the reservations of the court of Leo X against Michelangelo's "untamed nature." The attacks on Michelangelo because of the supposed irreligiousness of his works, which, so it was said, contradicted the traditional sacred iconography, began about 1540. The first signal for these attacks was given by the cynical Pietro Aretino, himself completely irreligious. He denounced Michelangelo's *Last Judgment* in a letter of 1545, actually written as a kind of blackmail, with the intention of getting more drawings as gifts from the master. The arguments of this letter — impiety, illicit license in the use of iconography, and the inappropriateness of his treatment to a holy place — were used against him a short time later by priests under the impact of the Counter Reformation. Gilio da Fabriano (*Due dialoghi... degli errori de' Pittori...*, Camerino, 1564) condemned Michelangelo's *Last Judgment* and the frescoes of the Pauline Chapel for supposed inaccuracies in the representation of Biblical scenes. It is interesting to note that at the same time in more liberal Venice the Inquisitor on the occasion of Paolo Veronese's trial upheld Michelangelo's nude figures in the *Last Judgment* as correct, because on the Last Day humanity appears naked before Christ the Judge.

His artistic style was criticized by Lodovico Dolce (*Dialogo*, 1557), who found his nudes monotonous and contrasted his art with the manifold beauties in the works of Raphael; this comparison was repeated throughout the 17th, 18th, and 19th centuries, especially in academic circles.

Also, from about 1546 on, the boldness of Michelangelo's style in architecture was severely attacked as contradicting the classical rules of Vitruvius. These attacks came from the "setta Sangallesca," namely the followers of Antonio da Sangallo the Younger, who after his death wanted to procure for themselves his great architectural commissions, which the Pope, however, preferred to give to Michelangelo.

During the 17th and 18th centuries Michelangelo's artistic greatness was never doubted, but he was often rejected as a "corrupter of art" (G. P. Bellori, *Le Vite de' pittori, scultori et architetti moderni*, Rome, 1672; R. Fréart de Chambray, *Idée de la perfection de la peinture*, Mans, 1662; A. Félibien, *Entretiens sur les vies et sur les ouvrages des plus excellens peintres anciens et modernes*, Paris, 1666-68; R. de Piles, *Abrégé de la vie des peintres*, Paris, 1699; Anne Claude Philippe, Comte de Caylus, *Nouveaux sujets de peinture et sculpture*, Paris, 1755; J. J. Winckelmann, *Gedanken über die Nachahmung der griechischen Werke in der Malerei und Bildhauerkunst*, Heilbronn, 1755; F. Milizia, *Principi d'architettura Civile*, Finale, 1781; and, in the mid-19th century, even Burckhardt). Michelangelo's passionate, serious, and powerful style would obviously not suit the taste of the Roman and French classicists; on the other hand, Bernini's appreciation of him as an architect ("Michelangelo era grande come scultore e pittore, ma veramente divino come architetto") is noteworthy at this period.

A new positive appreciation of Michelangelo began in about 1770, probably under the impact of the Storm and Stress movement, whose first heralds were Reynolds and Fuseli in England and Goethe in Germany. It was bound up with the new cult of genius. These artists tried to describe the effect of Michelangelo's works on them and to define objectively the features of his "grand style." This trend culminated, during the French romantic movement, in writings by Stendhal (*Histoire de la peinture en Italie*, Paris, 1817) and Delacroix (*Rev. de Paris*, XV, 1830, pp. 41-58, XVI, 1831, p. 165; *Rev. des deux Mondes*, XI, 1837, pp. 337-43). Stendhal's glowing picture of Michelangelo's greatness and Delacroix's image of his solitary and passionate being are based on an inner affinity and are the results of their own experience and of their self-identification with the master. These writings are great examples of the force of creative intuition by which the personality and processes of creation of Michelangelo are evoked. They are invaluable as the first visions of the totality of his genius, which they see in its unique essence, but as isolated from the world surrounding it.

Almost all the biographies of the second half of the 19th and beginning of the 20th century follow more or less consciously this romantic pattern; but the historical material has been appreciably enlarged since the late 19th century (especially since 1875). The biographies of H. Grimm (1860–63), A. Gotti (1875), J. A. Symonds (1893), C. Justi (1900, 1909), H. Thode (1902–13), and R. Rolland (1907) are much richer in their documentation than the previous writings, but by this very fact the outline of the image of Michelangelo's genius is somewhat weakened and blurred in them, except in Rolland's.

A new phase in the conception of Michelangelo began with the more intense investigation of the relation of his individual personality and the style of his works to the historical context of which they form a part. This new trend appeared first in the detailed monographic treatment of Michelangelo's youthful works by H. Wölfflin (*Die Jugendwerke Michelangelos*, 1891). This was followed by the monographic treatment of his great cyclic works: the tomb of Julius II, by C. Justi (1900); the Sistine ceiling and the *Last Judgment*, by E. Steinmann (1901–05); the Medici Chapel, by A. E. Popp (1922); the Pauline frescoes, by F. Baumgart and B. Biagetti (1936); and the monographs of Tolnay (1943–60) and H. von Einem (1959). They reveal that even a spiritual and artistic giant like Michelangelo is bound to the historical context of his time and that his originality can be grasped more precisely by investigation of the connection of his works with those which may have influenced him.

In earlier writings about him Michelangelo's individual works were not analyzed in themselves but were used as illustrations of his life or "explained" by his life. Often his works were regarded as expressions of his formal virtuosity alone; this is the point of view of Vasari and Condivi, and also of the biographies of the 19th and early 20th centuries. Only at the end of the 19th century — for the first time in H. Wölfflin's monograph of 1891 — were Michelangelo's works of art analyzed in themselves and recognized as embodiments of essential features of his creative personality. But these analyses were confined to the formal structure of the works, and they were not concerned with the spiritual ideas that Michelangelo expressed.

The newest trend is characterized by the view that the formal structure is conceived as the expression of a spiritual *concetto*. The critic tries to grasp in their entirety the spiritual and formal qualities of the work and to distinguish in them the traditional and original features.

It becomes evident that Michelangelo's works are a language of expression into which the artist infused his own individual world of feelings. The theory (Thode) that Michelangelo's style is an expression of "the deep dualism between pagan form and Christian soul" seems to be oversimplified. There is no contradiction between pagan and Christian elements in Michelangelo, since the "soul" expressed in his works is not specifically Christian but generally human. It is the "human condition" against which the soul in his works rebels, and this conflict is appropriately clothed in the timeless style of antiquity.

The historical place of Michelangelo was defined by the French Romantics, who identified themselves with him and saw in him their spiritual ancestor, the master who broke with the Middle Ages and who "heralded a new world" (Michelet), and with whom "modern art actually began" (Delacroix). On the other hand, more recent writers and artists, such as Worringer, Rodin, Simmel, Dvořák, saw in him the last Gothic master. "Il est l'aboutissement de toute la pensée gothique. Il est l'héritier des imagiers du treizième et du quatorzième siècle" (Rodin). Although both of these opinions contain valuable observations, neither seems to grasp the historical problem.

This becomes clearer when Michelangelo is compared with his contemporary Leonardo da Vinci (q.v.). The scattered scientific tendencies in the art of the 14th and 15th centuries were synthesized, broadened, and greatly advanced by Leonardo. What mattered most to him was to penetrate the visible world around him, without religious prejudice, by empiric observation and experience of the phenomena of nature. He pointed out the analogies in these phenomena and speculated with an admirable freedom of spirit about their common causes. With Michelangelo, on the contrary, appeared a man of moral and religious preoccupation, who turned away from the shining beauty of the visible world to concentrate on the interior images of his spirit. He was the forerunner of the coming century, but at the same time his moral preoccupations can be seen to revive those of the Duecento, elevated to the level of Humanistic thought, which embraces Christianity and antiquity alike, and deepen them according to the exigencies of a solitary, virile, and profound soul. Yet Michelangelo expressed also, and most perfectly, the spiritual preoccupations of his own historical moment.

Michelangelo transferred the linear-sculptural rigor of the Tuscans from a "realistic" level to an ideal sphere. His personality dominated the 16th and 17th centuries. His influence reinvigorated the plastic sense of the leading High Renaissance masters, such as Leonardo da Vinci, Raphael, Fra Bartolommeo, Andrea del Sarto, Correggio, Titian, and J. Sansovino. The new decorative concept of the nude in motion, with rhythmic outlines freely arranged in space and no longer bound to earth, as expressed in the Sistine ceiling, freed younger artists from the tyranny of classical canons — from Pontormo to Il Rosso and Parmigianino, and from Benvenuto Cellini to Vincenzo Danti and Giambologna. After 1541, the date of the unveiling of the *Last Judgment*, Europe was pervaded by a taste for "sublime" art and for "gigantic" form in composition and in depicting figures, as seen in the works of Vasari, Salviati, Tibaldi, Allori, Baccio da Montelupo, Montorsoli, and, in northern Europe, Scorel, Heemskerck, F. Floris de Vriendt, and others. Toward the end of the 16th century Michelangelo's plastic-dynamic sense became eclectically mixed with elements derived from Raphael, Correggio, and Titian. This mixture of elements is evident in the work of such artists as the Carraccis, Domenichino, and Guido Reni.

But the message of Michelangelo was assimilated in a more creatively original manner in Venice by Jacopo Tintoretto, who managed to achieve a synthesis of Venetian color with the rigor of Michelangelo's plastic design. In Flanders, the great Pieter Bruegel succeeded in integrating Michelangelo's monumental sculptural sense with his own northern realism. Later, in Rome, Caravaggio accomplished a synthesis of Michelangelo's plastic sensitivity with an interest in naturalistic detail and contrasts of light and shade. The late style of Michelangelo was a guide for the ecstatic visions of El Greco (Dvořák). All the great European masters of the 17th century admired, studied, and borrowed ideas from the art of Michelangelo. Rubens took up the lesson of Michelangelo in nudes that were animated by vital inner currents. Velázquez posed many of his figures after the manner of Michelangelo. Even in Rembrandt and Poussin there are echoes of Michelangelo. Bernini and Pietro da Cortona (the latter most particularly in the vault of the Palazzo Barberini, Rome) introduced ideas and motifs of Michelangelo in their new triumphal and optimistic view of art. Although his influence diminished in the first half of the 18th century (except in architecture), his "sublime" style was revived first in England, in the work of Reynolds, Blake, and Fuseli, and more strongly in the two masters of French romanticism, Géricault and Delacroix. Rodin, Degas, and Cézanne also admired and studied his work. It can be said that every period and every artist have been attracted by some particular aspect of Michelangelo's work and that this is true even today.

The most varied styles — from the classical style of the Renaissance to mannerism, the baroque, and romanticism — can be seen in relation to the art of Michelangelo, which itself goes beyond any category of style. His starting point and the base of his art was the Florentine Renaissance; but Michelangelo employed Renaissance elements in a decidedly personal manner, using them in new combinations and giving them a dynamism previously unknown. He created expressive symbolic images of his own inner tensions. Consequently Michelangelo's message could never be completely transmitted.

The known facts about Michelangelo's earliest period are mostly those reported by Vasari and Condivi. Though he was born in Caprese, where his father was podestà for six months, he was taken as an infant to Settignano, near Florence; therefore, Caprese played no role in his memory.

His father, Lodovico, had inherited a bit of land with a house in Settignano and rented an apartment on Via dei Bentaccordi, in the Sta Croce quarter of Florence. Michelangelo continued to live in this quarter whenever he was in Florence and later bought several building lots and houses there. His father put the boy into the grammar school of a certain Francesco da Urbino, but, according to Varchi (and to Condivi and Vasari), "the boy preferred to go into the churches, and draw from paintings instead of going to the grammar school to study; often he played truant from school to go where he could watch others painting." There is no reason to doubt this anecdote, which reveals the early emergence of his vocation. His father finally acceded to Michelangelo's wish to become an artist and, probably on the advice of Francesco Granacci (cf. G. Fiocco), placed him in the workshop of the brothers Domenico and Davide Ghirlandajo in April, 1488, when Michelangelo was thirteen years old. The father's record of the contract with the Ghirlandajos, for a three-year apprenticeship, is given in Vasari. Thus Michelangelo began as a painter. At that time, the Ghirlandajos were executing the fresco cycle in the choir of S. Maria Novella, and there Michelangelo most likely learned the elements of drawing and, perhaps, of fresco painting. Also, the crosshatching technique in his earliest drawings may derive from that of Domenico Ghirlandajo's drawings, although with Michelangelo the technique became less pictorial and much more precise in modeling. It is likely that the young apprentice was advised to study ancient works, since this was a practice of the Ghirlandajo workshop (cf. Cod. Escurialensis). The relationship between Domenico Ghirlandajo and the young Michelangelo was tense. Michelangelo did not like his master, who seems to have been jealous of the talent of his pupil and "sbigottito" (dismayed) by the new manner in which Michelangelo made his pen drawings in this early period. On the basis of the existing material there seems to have been no direct stylistic influence of Ghirlandajo on the works of the young Michelangelo.

None of the earliest drawings mentioned by Vasari and Condivi are in existence. These were outlines of a pen drawing, representing clothed women, from the Ghirlandajo workshop; a drawing of the scaffolding in S. Maria Novella; a copy of Martin Schongauer's *Temptation of St. Anthony* (such a copy turned up recently in England, a small tempera in the style of Ghirlandajo, for which an attribution to Michelangelo cannot be supported by positive proofs); copies after works of older masters (perhaps Giotto and Masaccio); and a copy of a head after Ghirlandajo. On the other hand, there are five drawings by the young Michelangelo, which are copies of frescoes by Giotto and Masaccio (F. Portheim, *RepfKw*, XII, 1889, pp. 140–58). Whether they were done as early as 1488, while he was with the Ghirlandajos, or a short time later is a question that cannot be resolved. However, Cellini's *Autobiography* tells us that Michelangelo made copies after Masaccio when he was still a boy.

Three theories concerning the initial phase of Michelangelo's formation have been proposed:

1. The theory that as a pupil of the Ghirlandajos he was strongly influenced by his master. This theory, first expressed by Vasari, has been followed by K. Frey (1907), C. E. Gilbert (*GBA*, 6th ser., XXXIV, 1948, pp. 389–404), and G. Marchini (*BM*, XCV, 1953, pp. 320–31), who attributed to the young Michelangelo three figures of the frescoes in S. Maria Novella.

2. The theory that Michelangelo was initiated into art by Francesco Granacci, a close friend who helped the boy, and not by Ghirlandajo, whom he disliked. This opinion was first expressed by Condivi and taken up by G. Fiocco (*RArte*, XII, 2, 1930, pp. 193–209, XIII, 1–2, 4, 1931, pp. 109–31, XXVI, 1950, pp. 149–55; *CrArte*, II, 4, 1937, pp. 172–75; *Le Arti*, IV, 2, 1941–42, pp. 5–10), who supported Condivi by showing for the first time that Granacci was six years older than Michelangelo and therefore able to advise him. Fiocco attributed to the young Michelangelo several paintings of the Virgin, which are very much in the style of Granacci, and tried to demonstrate by this that the latter directly influenced the former. The attribution of these paintings to Michelangelo remains problematical; according to other authors, they are by Granacci himself (R. Longhi, *Le Arti*, IV, 2, 1941–42, p. 136) or by the Master of the Manchester Madonna (F. Zeri, *Paragone*, IV, 43, 1953, pp. 15–27). Longhi (*Paragone*, IX, 101, 1958, pp. 59–64) has published the fragment of a panel of John the Evangelist, which he attributes to the young Michelangelo, although it is in the style of Granacci. Colin Eisler has suggested (in a lecture) the young Michelangelo as the painter of the tondo in the Museum at Budapest, usually attributed to Granacci, which shows St. John the Evangelist on Patmos.

3. A third theory that the boy Michelangelo was a strong personality, essentially independent of both Ghirlandajo and Granacci (cf. Tolnay, 1943–60, I). On the basis of the material still extant, his earliest drawings are seen to be free copies of those great Tuscan masters of the past with whom he felt an affinity, rather than reflections of contemporary Florentine paintings.

He completed his copies of Giottos and Masaccios by direct observation of nature and gave his prototypes an even more monumental effect by a new conception of volume, weight, attitude, and movement of the body and its relation to drapery. Thus Michelangelo seems to have been essentially self-taught, although he must have learned the techniques from his master, Ghirlandajo. His earliest works manifest a highly independent personality and contain the essential features of his later work.

Probably the penchant for sculpture emerged in Michelangelo at this early age, which may partly explain why he left the Ghirlandajo workshop after one year (although the contract was for three). He entered the "school" in the garden of Lorenzo de' Medici, near the Monastery of S. Marco, which contained a rich collection of ancient sculpture, and the overseer of which was Donatello's pupil Bertoldo di Giovanni (A. Chastel, *Studi Vasariani*, Florence, 1952, pp. 159–67). Bertoldo seems to have given Michelangelo his first instruction in sculptural techniques. However, according to M. Lisner (*ZfKw*, XII, 3–4, 1958, pp. 141–56), Michelangelo received his first practical instruction in sculpture from Benedetto da Maiano before he entered the Garden School. All the works done in the Garden School are lost. According to the earliest biographers Michelangelo made small terra-cotta figures after Bertoldo and a marble head of a faun (lost) after an ancient model, which Lorenzo de' Medici admired (cf. Tolnay, 1943–60, I, fig. 253).

After having worked about a year in the Garden School, Michelangelo was invited by Lorenzo de' Medici, who was enchanted with his talent, to live in his palace on Via Larga, where the artist remained until Lorenzo's death in April, 1492. There he met Poliziano, the court poet and Humanist, who probably introduced him to the ideas of Marsilio Ficino's "Platonic Academy." During this time, according to the earliest biographers, the artist executed two small marble reliefs, *Virgin of the Stairs* and *The Battle of the Lapiths and the Centaurs* (PLS. 524, 525). In neither did Michelangelo attempt an exact imitation of ancient prototypes, but he rendered rather free and personal paraphrases instead.

His *Virgin of the Stairs* is a small, flat relief, of extraordinary monumentality in conception; its style may be defined as that of Donatello remodeled after the antique. From Donatello comes the profile of the Virgin's head, the motif of the steps, and the technique of *rilievo schiacciato* (very low relief), but this is ennobled by inspiration drawn from pagan steles, such as the idea of the whole figure and the veil-like clothing. The Virgin seems absorbed in her thoughts about the future Passion of the Child and seems oblivious to her surroundings; this complete solitude will be characteristic of Michelangelo's later figures. The motif of the Child turning his athletic, muscular back to the beholder is also new and derives from the same conception of solitude. The prophetic anticipation of Christ's death in the Child's pose and in the children with the shroud in the background is a device that will be found in the future works of the master. Michelangelo's Virgin is less graceful but more serious, more distant, and more monumental than those of Leonardo, who preceded him in the tendency to ennoble the representation of the Virgin. In the vague modeling (the hands), in the inaccuracies of the perspective (the steps), in the somewhat awkward manner in which the background of the relief is filled with small motifs, the work of the beginner can be recognized. Nevertheless, R. Longhi (*Paragone*, IX, 101, 1958, pp. 59–64) dates the relief after 1492.

The *Battle of the Lapiths and the Centaurs* is done in *mezzo rilievo* in three parallel planes. It is unfinished, with a zone of rough marble at the top. The relief, which is crowded with nudes in movement, is in contrast to the calm composition of the *Virgin of the Stairs*. It seems as if the young Michelangelo wanted to show that he was master of two idioms: In the *Virgin* he is "classical," in the stillness of the main figure and its closed silhouette, and in the subordination of space to the figure; in the battle scene the swirling mass of the figures, their bodies animated by fluctuating forces from within, anticipates the baroque (Rubens copied this relief in two drawings). The use of these two styles at about the same time is not unlike the methods of contemporary poets who wrote, according to their subject, in either the popular ("volgare") or sublime style. The theme of the relief is the rape of Hippodameia by the centaur Eurytion, as described in Ovid's *Metamorphoses*, but for the young artist this was only a pretext for representing a struggling mass in movement. Although the compositional pattern of the relief is geometric, consisting of two intersecting triangles with two lateral axes, this scheme is almost obscured by a revolving movement around the main figure in the center, an important feature of Michelangelo's later compositions up to the *Last Judgment* and the Pauline frescoes. The movement of the rounded and full athletic bodies is no longer conceived as a mechanical displacement of the limbs (Pollaiuolo) but as the result of an organic unfolding of forces, flowing from within. The technique of the carving seems to be derived, directly or indirectly, from the reliefs of Giovanni Pisano (see VI, PL. 212); the unity of the substance is kept, and even the forms in the foreground are not completely detached from the background. Again Michelangelo fused the ancient inspirations from battle sarcophagi (Tolnay, 1943–60, I) with Tuscan proto-Renaissance traditions. This was not an archaeological interest in antiquity, as with the masters of the second half of the Quattrocento, nor was it a transformation of ancient influences according to a Neo-Gothic pattern, as with Botticelli and Pollaiuolo; it was a direct continuation of the ancient and Tuscan art tradition, which Michelangelo seems to have felt was an uninterrupted stream leading to him. (On Michelangelo's conception of antiquity, see Tolnay, *JhbPreussKSamml*, LIV, 2, 1933, pp. 95–122; Tolnay, 1943–60, I, p. 134; J. Wilde, *Mit. des Kunsthist. Inst. in Florenz*, IV, 1932–34, pp. 41–64; H. von Einem, *Antike und Abendland*, I, 1944, pp. 55–77. See also G. Kleiner, *Die Begegnungen Michelangelos mit der Antike*, Berlin, 1950; A. von Salis, *Antike und Renaissance*, Zurich, 1947; F. Kriegbaum, *MJhb*, III–V, 1952–53, pp. 10–36.)

Both of these earliest works are surprising for the time (ca. 1490–92) and show the sudden bursting forth of Michelangelo's genius; they are full of anticipations of his later works.

After the death of Lorenzo de' Medici, Michelangelo returned to his father's house, where he remained until October, 1494. During this period he seems to have followed, in the Cathedral of Florence, the ardent preachings of the Dominican prior Savonarola (1493–94), which impressed him profoundly and determined his religious conceptions (cf. G. Poggi in *Michelangiolo Buonarroti nel IV Centenario del Giudizio Universale*, Florence, 1942, p. 113 ff.). This was his first contact with the ideas of an inner reform of the Church, which were to play such a great role in his late period, from the *Last Judgment* on. The sources mention two works done during this period, again one with a Christian and the other with a pagan subject.

A smaller-than-life-size wooden crucifix was made for the prior of Sto Spirito, who had given Michelangelo the opportunity to study anatomy by dissecting corpses. This work was rediscovered a few years ago in the cloister of Sto Spirito by M. Lisner (*Kunstchronik*, Jan., 1963, p. 1 ff.). The work has been cleaned of old overpainting, and reveals the original coloring. It is of the quality and shows the manner of modeling of the young Michelangelo. (Some other scholars, however, are doubtful of this attribution.) In this crucifix he seems to have made the attempt to synthesize both expression of suffering and beauty of pose. Michelangelo introduced, probably for the first time in a crucifix, a *contrapposto* between head and legs, thereby conferring an almost classic beauty upon the expressive figure. The importance of this innovation seems to have been immediately recognized by his fellow artists in Florence. A. Parronchi (*Studi Urbinati*, XXXV, 1961, pp. 1–37) attempted to identify as the crucifix of Sto Spirito a crucifix in the Church of S. Rocco in Massa Carrara. However, it is larger than life-size, in contradiction to Condivi, and in the 17th century it was attributed, with more likelihood, to Felice Palma by Filippo Baldinucci. The other work executed during these years was a *Hercules*, larger than life-size (ht., ca. 7 ft., 7 in.). The statue, acquired in 1529 by Francis I, was exhibited at Fontainebleau and has been lost since 1713. An etching by Israël Silvestre of the Jardin de l'Esang at Fontainebleau shows the *Hercules* of Michelangelo, in a rear view, on a pedestal bearing the monogram of Henry IV (cf. Tolnay, 1943–60, I, fig. 152). A pen drawing by Rubens, in the Louvre, shows Michelangelo's *Hercules* in frontal view (identified and published by Tolnay, in *The Art and Thought of Michelangelo*, New York, 1964 and in *GBA*, 6th ser., LXIV, 1964). This first larger-than-life-size nude figure in marble by Michelangelo directly anticipated the marble *David*.

Before Oct. 14, 1494, divining the political trouble that soon led to the fall of the Medici, Michelangelo took flight from Florence. He went first to Venice, where he remained only a short time, and then to Bologna, where he stayed about a year, until the end of 1495, as a guest of Gianfrancesco Aldovrandi. He busied himself there with literary studies, reading the great poets of the vernacular — Dante, Petrarch, and Boccaccio; his own first poems probably date from this time. Michelangelo's artistic activity was limited to the completion of the tomb of St. Dominic (Bologna, S. Domenico), which was unfinished at the death of Niccolò dell'Arca (da Bari) in 1473. Michelangelo had to supply three missing statuettes: an angel (to balance that of Niccolò), a St. Petronius, and a St. Proculus. He had to subordinate his ideas to an already existing structure. These small figures show the influence of Jacopo della Quercia, with whom Michelangelo had a deep artistic affinity. (Cf. Stefano Bottari, *L'Arca di S. Domenico in Bologna*, Bologna, 1964.) Roberto Longhi (*Ampliamenti nell'Officina Ferrarese*, 2d ed., Florence, 1956) sees Ferrarese influences: that of Ercole de' Roberti in the St. Proculus statue and that of Cosimo Tura in the St. Petronius; but, because the Ferrarese style is harder and more angular in the folds, the influence of Della Quercia is more obvious. According to J. Q. van Regteren-Altena (in a verbal communication), the relief of a Virgin of the Annunciation, on the left outside wall of the choir in the Church of S. Petronio, Bologna, may be a work by Michelangelo from this period. The invention is elevated, but the execution is rough and clumsy, and more probably by a pupil and dating from about 1545.

The situation in Florence was consolidated by the formation of the republic of Savonarola; at the end of 1495, Michelangelo returned there. However, he remained in Florence only until June, 1496, probably because he did not get commissions. While there he executed only two statuettes of children, a *S. Giovannino* and a *Sleeping Cupid* (both lost). The *S. Giovannino* has been identified with several statues, but none of the identifications is convincing. (The name Giovannino can be applied to St. John as an infant or as a youth.) There does exist a sketch by Michelangelo of a child (Louvre; cf. Tolnay 1943–60, I, fig. 110) in a *contrapposto* position, with one arm reaching across his breast, a pose reminding us of Leonardo's *Leda*. As A. E. Popp has shown, this motif was copied in the St. John of the so-called "Manchester Madonna" (*The Madonna and Child, St. John and Angels*; London, Nat. Gall.), and it could therefore be a reflection of Michelangelo's lost statuette. The same motif can be found in several statuettes, of St. John as a boy, from the late 16th and early 17th centuries (cf. Tolnay, 1943–60, I, figs. 163–165). According to W. R. Valentiner (*Kunstchronik*, III, 1950, p. 199), a statuette of St. John as a boy, in the Pierpont Morgan Library, New York, may be identified with Michelangelo's work. This is rather in the style of Silvio Cosini. Longhi (*Paragone*, IX, 101, 1958, pp. 59–64) has tried to identify the figure with a statuette of St. John in S. Giovanni dei Fiorentini, Rome; A. Parronchi (*Studi Urbinati*, 1960, p. 3 ff.), with a statue in the Museo Nazionale, Florence, that is sometimes attributed to Donatello and sometimes to Francesco da Sangallo (H. Kauffmann, *Donatello*, Berlin, 1935); and F. de' Maffei (*Michelangelo's Lost St. John*, New York, 1964) — in a study containing some valuable observations — with a statue which is now a property of the dealer Piero Tozzi. The attempts at reconstruction of the lost *Sleeping Cupid* have not been any more successful. The most likely hypothesis still seems to be the identification of the motif with the cupid in Tintoretto's *Vulcan Surprising Venus and Mars* (Munich, Alte Pin.), or with that in Giulio Romano's *Childhood of Jupiter* (London, Nat. Gall.; Tolnay, 1943–60, I, figs. 167, 168). Both representations revert to an ancient sculpture of which several copies are in existence. W. R. Valentiner (*Comm*, VII, 1956, pp. 236–48) and P. F. Norton (*AB*, XXXIX, 1957, pp. 251–57) trace the history of the statuette in England; the former takes up again the hypothesis of K. Lange, according to which the *Cupid* in the Museo di Antichità, Turin, should be identified with Michelangelo's.

The *Sleeping Cupid* became the external reason for Michelangelo's first sojourn in Rome. The statuette was sold to Cardinal Raffaello Riario by a dealer as an ancient work; however, Riario discovered the forgery, and the figure was returned to Michelangelo. According to Condivi, Michelangelo went to Rome partly because of his anger at this.

From the end of June, 1496, until the spring of 1501, Michelangelo was in Rome for the first time. He was in contact with Cardinal Riario; with the banker Jacopo Galli, who bought his *Bacchus*, and for whom Michelangelo made an *Apollo*, or *Cupid* (lost); and with Jean Bilhères de Lagraulas, the French cardinal for whom he executed the *Pietà* in St. Peter's. It was Galli who became his chief patron during his Roman sojourn, and in whose house he may have lived. He made a cartoon of St. Francis receiving the stigmata (lost) for S. Pietro in Montorio. The fresco in the first chapel to the left in this church, representing the same subject, and attributed to Giovanni de Vecchi, may be a reflection, in its centralized composition, of this lost cartoon by Michelangelo. No contact seems to have existed between the artist and the court of Pope Alexander VI. What probably most attracted Michelangelo in Rome were the ancient works of art which he could study in several large collections of antique sculptures there.

Contemporaries chiefly appreciated the lifelike quality and grace of ancient works, in contrast to the dry and angular manner of the Florentine masters of the 15th century. In Michelangelo's *Bacchus* (Florence, Mus. Naz.) his attempt to follow the ancients in this respect can be observed, but the fruits of his study of the works of antiquity in Rome were to become more visible in the works executed after his return to Florence. The lost Galli *Apollo*, or *Cupid*, was previously identified with the crouching *Cupid* in the Victoria and Albert Museum, London. This figure has been attributed to Vincenzo Danti by F. Kriegbaum (*JhbKhSammlWien*, N.S., III, 1929, pp. 247–57); J. Pope-Hennessy (*BM*, XCVIII, 1956, pp. 403–11) considers it an ancient statue, completed in the 16th century.

Of the two extant works of this first Roman period, one has a pagan, the other a Christian subject. Condivi describes the *Bacchus* (Florence, Mus. Naz.) in a detailed way, declaring that the statue corresponds to the conceptions of the ancient writers. It is actually a pseudoantique statue made by Michelangelo, probably for Jacopo Galli's "antique garden," which would explain why the figure has multiple views (the position of the figure and the form of the base) rather than the usual one main view of his sculpture. A drawing by M. van Heemskerck (X, PL. 207) shows the figure as the most important piece among the ancient fragments and sarcophagi of the Galli garden. In the drawing the right hand is missing; today the figure has a right hand holding a goblet, similar to that in a drawing (no. 133) in the Albertina, Vienna, and some of the old bronze copies: one, by Pietro da Barga, is in the Museo Nazionale, Florence, and another, anonymous, is in the Kunsthistorisches Museum, Vienna (cf. Tolnay 1943–60, I, figs. 171, 172). Therefore it is unlikely that it is a "clumsy modern restoration" (E. Wind, *Pagan Mysteries in the Renaissance*, London, 1958). Although the right hand is less well executed than the other, the old restoration seems to have followed the original design. The main motif, in which at the side of the god there is a satyr stealing the grapes, reverts to antiquity (e.g., *Bacchus*, Rome, Torlonia Coll.). The soft, full forms are also ancient in inspiration, giving the figure the aspect of a hermaphrodite. Nevertheless, Michelangelo does not follow a precise antique model and rejects the stereotyped *contrapposto*. Here the relaxed leg is on the same side as the raised arm, while the hanging arm is on the side of the supporting leg, giving the figure the unstable stance of a drunken man. The sinuous S line of the profile view still seems to derive from the late-Gothic tradition of Della Quercia (cf. Tolnay, 1943–60, I, fig. 22). It is not the joyful leader of the Bacchanalia that Michelangelo represents here, but the inebriated god. The group seems to symbolize the cycle of decline, in Bacchus and the animal mask, and rebirth, in the satyr. The life-giving grapes are related to the death symbol of the mask. The conception approximately corresponds to the description of Bacchus as a "cosmic god" in Boccaccio's *De genealogia deorum*. The hypothesis that connects the figure with the Bacchic mysteries of Plato's Phaedrus (E. Wind, *Pagan Mysteries in the Renaissance*, London, 1958, p. 147 ff.) seems to be rather far-fetched.

The other work executed in Rome, the *Pietà* in St. Peter's (PL. 526), was commissioned in the autumn of 1497, but the contract dates from August, 1498 (Milanesi, 1875, p. 613). It was probably intended for the tomb of Cardinal Jean Bilhères de Lagraulas, who ordered it (H. von Einem, 1959). The Virgin, youthful in feature, looks neither at the beholder nor at Christ, but, bowing her head slightly, supports the body of Christ and makes a gesture of silent acceptance of the divine will with her left hand. The composition of the group reverts to a type created in the 13th century, probably in the north, which was known in Italy in 14th-century Byzantine painting and in 15th-century Italian sculpture and painting. Longhi (*Ampliamenti nell'Officina Ferrarese*, 2d ed., Florence, 1956) indicates a strong Ferrarese influence, especially that of the Pietàs of Ercole de' Roberti, but Roberti's represent the *Compassio Mariae*, while Michelangelo's shows a solitary Mary accepting the will of God. The technique of the work is much closer to the fine taste of the Florentine Quattrocento sculptors working in Rome than to that of ancient art. The relieflike conception of the group corresponds also to the Florentine tradition: the group is relatively flat but gives the effect of more depth. It is carved from a block, originally oval in depth, as can be seen from the base. The surface is carefully polished, and the modeling is extremely delicate. In the folds on the breast a transition between Della Quercia's animated drapery and the sharp Florentine manner can be observed. The model for the folds on the legs has been traced by J. Wilde (*BM*, XCV, 1953, pp. 65–77) to early drawings of Leonardo. In the faces there are also similarities with a nearly contemporary cartoon by Leonardo (PL. 123; London, Nat. Gall.; formerly Royal Acad. of Arts). H. Wölfflin (1891) observed that the gesture of the Virgin's left hand and of her bent head are probably inspired by Leonardo's Christ in his *Last Supper*.

The first great creative period of Michelangelo's youth was marked by his sojourn in republican Florence, probably from the spring of 1501 until the spring of 1505. The young artist was already famous; his glory was established, and his name appeared for the first time in a book. He was republican in feeling and by tradition, and his commissions came from the Florentine republic (the Gonfaloniere Pietro Soderini was his friend), the Opera del Duomo, and the powerful corporation of the Arte della Lana. During this time Michelangelo developed his classic style in the heroic figures of the marble *David* (1501-04; Florence, Acc.), the Bruges *Madonna* (ca. 1501; Church of Notre-Dame); the Doni Tondo (1504; PL. 527), and the cartoon for *The Battle of Cascina* (1504).

At that moment Leonardo was the most popular artist in Florence, where he exhibited in April, 1501, the first great work of his new style, the cartoon for the *St. Anne* (lost). When Michelangelo returned to Florence, about one month later, he could not have remained insensible to the successes of Leonardo's art. In a series of works, mostly of the Virgin or the Holy Family, executed during this period, Michelangelo's reaction to Leonardo's style can be traced. In a drawing now in the Ashmolean Museum, Oxford (cf. Tolnay, 1943-60, I, fig. 81), he paraphrased Leonardo's *St. Anne*, the influence of which can also be seen in the Bruges *Madonna*; in the tondo for Bartolommeo Pitti (Florence, Mus. Naz.); in a drawing of the Holy Family (Louvre); in the tondo for Taddeo Taddei (London, Royal Acad. of Arts); and in the Doni Tondo. If in his bronze *David* for Pierre de Rohan Michelangelo followed that of Donatello, it was because the contract required it.

Without abandoning exactitude and richness of detail, Michelangelo now subordinates them to his vision of the whole. His artistic language becomes more austere and monumental, and the austerity of the form corresponds to that of the spirit. The passive figures of Bologna and Rome are supplanted by a heroic race. They are no longer victims of forces out of their control but seem to be masters of their own fate.

The Bruges *Madonna* was probably begun in the spring of 1501 (Tolnay, 1943-60, I, p. 158; V. Mariani, *BArte*, XXXIX, 1954, pp. 43-50). The precise work in the details of the folds, rich in realistic observation, seems to indicate that the group was begun not long after he finished the *Pietà*. However, the artist seems to have progressed slowly in executing the work, and this may explain why the Child seems to be more developed in treatment than the Virgin. The solemnity of the group is accentuated by the axial pose of the Virgin, by the vertical and symmetrical folds on the breast, by the veil covering her head in an almost architectural manner, and by the regular, classical features of her face, inspired by Leonardo's types. Contrary to the Florentine tradition the Child is not seated on the Virgin's knees, but is standing between her legs, surrounded by the draperies of her mantle, as if protected in a kind of niche. The *contrapposto* pose reverts to antiquity (cf. Tolnay, 1943-60, I, fig. 203). The Child still seems to be within the Virgin's body, about to free himself from the maternal womb. While the Virgin's face reveals both anxiety and yet stoic determination to accept her fate, the face of the Child, by contrast, wears an innocent smile. The idea of representing the Child as if in the womb of the Virgin may have been inspired by the Byzantine Platytera, who was depicted with the Child in her womb, or from later Virgins deriving from this Byzantine type — for example, the Virgin by Donatello on the high altar in S. Antonio, Padua, and the Virgin of Cosimo Tura in the National Gallery, Washington, D.C. A new feature in Michelangelo seems to be the contrast between the stern attitude of the Virgin and the hesitating passive pose of the Child. A rapid pen sketch representing the same motif, but with nude figures, is in the British Museum (cf. Tolnay, 1943-60, I, fig. 10). The sketch may have been made in 1506, at the time when Michelangelo was about to sell the group to the Mouscron (or Moscheroni) in Bruges (Milanesi, 1875, p. 6; Gotti, 1875, II, p. 51). According to other scholars, such as Dussler, it is a preparatory sketch.

The two marble tondos of this period show a departure from detailed refinement in the treatment of forms and reveal a tendency toward a more synthetic, monumental, and massive style. The artist left both tondos unfinished, and this vagueness in the detail serves to heighten the suggestive power of the whole. Michelangelo here transformed Leonardo's ideas in a manner related to Roman antiquity and worked classic motifs directly into his compositions.

The marble tondo made for Bartolommeo Pitti (PL. 525) was probably executed about 1503-04, at the same time that Michelangelo was working on the marble *David*. According to other authors it may have been made even later (H. von Einem, 1959). It still resembles the Bruges *Madonna*, especially in the contrasting expressions of the Virgin and Child — the former serious and aware, the latter infantile and innocent — though the bodily forms are more broadly and massively treated. The type and the expression of the Virgin's head and face recall the face of the *David*. The Virgin, seated on a low stone block, partly envelops the naked child in her cloak with a sudden gesture, as if to protect him. She raises her head and gazes into the distance, as though prepared for foreseen danger. Her prophetic faculties are also given symbolic expression by a cherub on her forehead, which signifies the gift of higher knowledge. The Child leans wearily on one arm, which rests on an open book, probably the Virgin's prayer book. He seems to be unaware of his destiny. His pose is almost exactly that of an ancient mourning genie (e.g., the Phaedra Sarcophagus, Pisa, Camposanto; cf. Tolnay 1943-60, I, fig. 218). The head of the Infant St. John seems to have been inspired by antique heads of youthful satyrs or centaurs. The three heads form a triangle, a compositional pattern reverting to Leonardo (early drawing in Windsor, Royal Colls., 12276R); this compositional pattern assumes great importance in the works of both Michelangelo and Raphael. There is a preparatory sketch for the figure of the Virgin in the Musée Condé, Chantilly (cf. Tolnay, 1943-60, I, fig. 98).

Quattrocento artists treated the tondo as a round window, and for this reason half-length figures appear in them. Michelangelo represents whole figures within the confines of the circle, as Luca Signorelli did before him (*The Holy Family*; Florence, Uffizi). By means of recurring curves in the lower half Michelangelo emphasizes the circular silhouette of the group; thus the form of the tondo becomes its natural limit.

The drawing *St. Anne with the Madonna and Child* in the Louvre (PL. 539) is probably a preparatory design for an unexecuted marble tondo. The theme reverts again to Leonardo, though the position of the Virgin's arms was inspired by one of Giovanni Pisano's sibyls on the pulpit of S. Andrea, Pistoia (Wilde).

The other marble tondo (London, Royal Acad. of Arts), made for Taddeo Taddei, is dated before the Pitti tondo by some scholars. However, the quality of execution and the size, almost twice as large as that of the Pitti tondo, speak for a later date. A few details in the folds over the Virgin's left arm seem to have been reworked by an apprentice. Here the three figures are bound together by one action: St. John, playing with a bird, probably a goldfinch, approaches Jesus, who is frightened and seeks refuge in his mother's lap, while the Virgin wards off St. John with her barely sketched right hand. The movement of Jesus is inspired by a child from the ancient Medea sarcophagus type (W. Horne, Panofsky). Studies for the St. John are preserved on a sheet in the British Museum (cf. Tolnay, 1943-60, I, fig. 109).

The only authentic panel by Michelangelo, *The Holy Family* (Doni Tondo; PL. 527), is also a tondo and may be considered from the point of view of the composition as the culmination of this series of tondos inspired by Leonardo. It seems to have been made on the occasion of the marriage of Agnolo Doni and Maddalena Strozzi, at the end of 1503 or the beginning of 1504 (G. Poggi, *Jahresbericht des Kunsthist. Inst. in Florenz*, 1906-07, p. 10). The hard, somewhat abstract forms are still reminiscent of the Bruges *Madonna*, although the grouping of the figures, describing a spiral, seems to go beyond the two marble tondos; for this reason some scholars (Wilde, for instance) date it about 1506. Here the Virgin is a heroic mother who raises her child onto her shoulder with her bare muscular arms. The three figures seem to be formed from a cylindrical block, and the spectator's eye is invited to follow the curving spiral that rises from the right leg of the Virgin and finishes in the upper ring formed by the arms of Jesus. The motif of a figure standing on the shoulders of another is an age-old symbol of the victory of a new principle over an older one which has prepared the way for it. By birth the Virgin and St. Joseph belong to the Old Testament, but by their relationship to Christ they are of the New. With Jesus placed high on his mother's shoulder, Michelangelo apparently wished to show that the principle embodied in Christ, while dependent on that of Mary and Joseph, at the same time surpasses it. On the Child's head there is a band, probably signifying victory, as in ancient statues of victorious athletes. In the background of the composition Michelangelo added nude youths of supple beauty, who are seated or leaning against a low wall, describing a hemicycle. Behind them emerges a bare, mountainous landscape. The ephebic figures seem to symbolize the pagan world *ante legem*, as in Signorelli's tondo in the Uffizi, which was the model for Michelangelo's painting; some scholars, such as Wilde, have interpreted them as angels. The little St. John behind the first wall is the link between the pagan and the Judaeo-Christian world. The unfinished apse in the background could be an allusion to an unfinished ancient temple which will provide a foundation for the new Church of Christ; other scholars have interpreted it as an allusion to the choir of the new St. Peter's (1506). The contrast between the holy scene in the foreground and the pagan world in the background seems to have been fashionable at the end of the 15th and in the early 16th century, as is attested by Leonardo's *Adoration of the Magi* (PL. 117) and that of Hieronymus Bosch (Madrid, Prado; II, PL. 318). From the point of view of color the Doni Tondo is perhaps the earliest 16th-century example of the brightening of the palette and of the use of changing colors, devices which were to be followed by the first two generations of mannerists (Pontormo, Il Rosso, Salviati, Vasari).

In his early Virgins, Michelangelo transformed the traditional devotional image into a philosophicoreligious cult image. Made for private devotion, they do not suppose a believer who is kneeling before the Virgin in prayer but a cultivated Florentine citizen who stands before the image in meditation, finding therein philosophical comfort and edification. This Humanistic and religious conception of the early Virgins set the standard for Michelangelo's religious works of the following periods, up to and including the *Medici Virgin* (Florence, S. Lorenzo, New Sacristy).

Michelangelo's other chief preoccupations during this Florentine period were the problems of the draped standing figures and of the standing or moving nudes. The earliest examples of a change in the conception of draped figures are the statuettes on the Piccolomini Altar (Siena, Cathedral), which were commissioned while he was in Rome (Milanesi, 1875, p. 615 ff.), but which he only began to execute in Florence in 1501. The commission from Cardinal Francesco Todeschini-Piccolomini (later Pius III) called for 15 statuettes by Michelangelo to fill empty places on the altar by Andrea Bregno, which was originally intended to be combined with the tomb of the Cardinal. Michelangelo delivered only four of these statuettes, in 1504 — those of St. Peter, St. Paul, St. Pius, and St. Gregory; a fifth, of St. Francis, was made by Pietro Torrigiani. A letter by Michelangelo's father (1510) suggests that Baccio da Montelupo worked on these figures, which were made after drawings of the master. In 1537 the heir of Pius III transferred his right to the hundred ducats that Michelangelo owed from the advance for the work he never did. About sixty years after the commission, in 1561, Michelangelo's conscience was still troubled, and he wrote to his nephew that he had decided to settle this affair. From these documents it can be deduced: that the statuettes were not actually made by him but by Baccio; that Michelangelo only began to carve the statuettes and left the final execution to Baccio; or that Michelangelo made only some of the figures and the rest were done by Baccio. The problem of the authenticity of these statuettes has been a matter of discussion for more than a half century. In 1940 the statuettes were cleaned, and F. Kriegbaum (*JhbPreussKSamml*, LXIII, 1942, p. 97 ff.) attempted to prove that all four figures are by Michelangelo's own hand; but only in SS. Peter and Paul can the hand of the master be recognized, and the two other figures were probably executed by Baccio. The style of SS. Peter and Paul fits well into the beginning of the Florentine period: The folds of Della Quercia, seen in the SS. Petronius and Proculus of the tomb of St. Dominic, have been replaced by hard, linear folds. In the St. Paul the influence of Donatello is obvious; the head of this figure seems to be a kind of idealized self-portrait of the artist. Longhi (*Ampliamenti nell'Officina Ferrarese*, 2d ed., Florence, 1956) attributes the harder idiom of the folds to the influence of Ercole de' Roberti. A drawing of this monument by Giovanni Antonio Dosio shows in the top center niche a naked resurrected Christ (E. Luporini, *CrArte*, 1958, V, pl. 10). The hypothesis that the Bruges *Madonna* was planned by Michelangelo for this niche (W. R. Valentiner, *AQ*, V, 1, 1942, pp. 3–44) seems to be untenable, because, according to the documents, a Christ flanked by figures of St. Thomas and John the Evangelist should have been located in this niche.

The two most important standing nude figures of this period are the bronze *David* and the marble *David*. Although Michelangelo began work on the bronze *David* about a year later than he began his marble *David*, it is closer to the Florentine tradition than the latter. This can be explained by a stipulation in the contract of Aug. 12, 1502 (Milanesi, 1875, p. 624), which says that Michelangelo's figure should be like Donatello's bronze *David* in the courtyard of the Palazzo Vecchio (Palazzo della Signoria). This was the request of Pierre de Rohan, for whom the Signoria ordered the figure. The statue, still unfinished in 1508, was finally completed in 1509 by Benedetto da Rovezzano. It was then sent to France — first to Blois and then to Bury — and has been lost since the mid-17th century; according to Varchi, it was a life-size figure. The most likely hypothesis is that the David sketch in the Louvre (cf. Tolnay 1943–60, I, fig. 93) is a preparatory sketch for this work. A small bronze *David* in the Louvre (formerly Pulszky Coll.) is regarded by several scholars as a preparatory model for this work (cf. W. Boeck, *Mit. des Kunsthist. Inst. in Florenz*, VIII, 1959, pp. 131–38).

About the last version nothing certain can be said. In the engraving of the courtyard of the Château de Bury by J. A. Ducerceau the figure is too tiny (cf. Tolnay, 1943–60, I, fig. 210); but it seems to represent David holding the head of Goliath as a trophy in his raised right hand, while in the left he is holding a sword. It is not impossible that Cellini's *Perseus* (Florence, Loggia della Signoria), in a similar pose, is a reflection of the final version of Michelangelo's lost bronze *David*.

The block from which Michelangelo had to model the marble *David* (VII, PL. 383; Florence, Acc.) had been worked on forty years earlier (1463) by Agostino di Duccio, who left it incomplete. The block belonged to the Opera del Duomo and was originally destined for the decoration of one of the exterior buttresses of the Cathedral (G. Poggi, *Il Duomo di Firenze*, Berlin, 1909). Agostino began a "giant," probably a David, but he abandoned the work. Since that time the authorities of the Cathedral had been trying to find an artist capable of finishing the block. They found this master in September, 1501, in the person of Michelangelo, who between then and April, 1504, succeeded in producing a figure from the block without recourse to other pieces of marble. It cannot be seen from the front that another artist had previously worked on the block. Only the narrow lateral views indicate that the block was not chosen by Michelangelo, who would certainly have selected a thicker one. The virtuosity with which Michelangelo overcame the difficulties that had baffled others for half a century assured him of an enormous success.

The pose of the figure seems to be calm, but it is full of inner tension; this *David* is ready for action. The contrast between the two sides of his body is marked. All the weight reposes on the right leg, and this side is strictly vertical and closed. The other side, with the silhouette broken by the raised arm, is open. This contrast corresponds, as Wilde has observed, to a moral distinction that was established in the Middle Ages: the right side, under divine protection, is assured; the vulnerable left side is exposed to the powers of evil. Michelangelo repeated this differentiation of the two sides later — in his *Moses*, for example.

This *David* differs from the Florentine tradition of the victorious boy and is inspired in its pose by a type of Hercules on ancient sarcophagi (Tolnay, *JhbPreussKSamml*, LIV, 1933, pp. 95–122), known also in the Middle Ages (Nicola Pisano,

Fortitude, pulpit of the Baptistery, Pisa). Michelangelo's own early *Hercules* had followed this type and therefore anticipated this *David*. This identification of the *David* with Hercules may have its explanation in Michelangelo's desire to embody in the figure, which he conceived as a political symbol, the two principal civic virtues of the Renaissance, *fortezza* and *ira*. Just as Hercules was the symbol of strength in classical antiquity, so David was considered *manu fortis* during the Middle Ages. It is not surprising that Michelangelo fused the two in a monument designed to embody the civic virtues — all the more because Hercules and David had been honored as patrons of Florence since the end of the 13th century and the beginning of the 15th century, respectively. Vasari testifies that the statue was already considered by contemporaries as a representation of the political ideal of the republic: "Just as he [David] had defended his people and governed with justice, whoever was governing that city [Florence] should defend it bravely and govern it justly." The *David* of Michelangelo had to fulfill a concrete function in the life of republican Florence: to remind Florentine citizens, as they stood in front of the Palazzo Vecchio, of the virtue of courage necessary to defend the republic against its enemies. (For a discussion of the meeting called to decide the location of the statue, see Tolnay, 1943–60, I, p. 152 f.)

From 1508 on, the government of the Florentine republic desired to have erected in front of the Palazzo Vecchio, near the entrance, a second gigantic statue group that would make a pair with the marble *David*. This was also to be executed by Michelangelo and to represent Hercules and Antaeus, since, as Vasari said, David, as well as Hercules, was "an emblem of the Palazzo." The block was ordered in May, 1508, by Pietro Soderini, but in 1525 Clement VII gave the block to Baccio Bandinelli, although the Signoria still wanted to entrust Michelangelo with its execution. At that time, in 1525, Michelangelo may have made his red-chalk sketches for the proposed group (Oxford, Ashmolean Mus.; Br. Mus.; cf. Tolnay, 1943–60, III, figs. 139, 140). After the fall of the Medicis, in August, 1528, the Signoria decided to take the already half-worked block from Bandinelli and to give it again to Michelangelo. According to Vasari, Michelangelo at that moment abandoned the proposed Hercules and Antaeus and decided to make a Samson with two Philistines. To this version probably corresponds the original model in clay in the Casa Buonarroti, Florence (Panofsky, 1939, p. 231 ff.; Tolnay, 1943–60, III, pp. 98 ff., 183 ff.). According to Wilde (*Michelangelo: The Group of Victory*, London, Oxford, 1954), however, this is the model for the counterpart of the *Victory* now in the Palazzo Vecchio, both of which were intended for the tomb of Julius II.

The highest expression of the young Michelangelo's mastery of the nude human body was probably the cartoon (lost) for a mural depicting the Battle of Cascina. In autumn, 1503, when the Signoria originally decided to decorate the large Council Hall of the Palazzo Vecchio with murals representing Florentine victories, they contracted with Leonardo to do this work (May, 1504); he began, in the spring of 1505, a painting representing the Battle of Anghiari, the Florentine victory over the Milanese. After this, Gonfaloniere Pietro Soderini also commissioned Michelangelo to paint a mural in this hall, which was to represent the Florentine victory over the Pisans near Cascina. He began the cartoon in November, 1504, seven months after the contract with Leonardo, whose original commission was possibly reduced in favor of Michelangelo; the cartoon was finished between April and November, 1506 (H. Thode, 1902–13; H. von Einem, 1959). The Council Hall at that time offered scope for large murals only on the longitudinal east wall (the other walls being perforated by too many windows), on which there were originally three areas separated by two windows. The original shape of the hall was reconstructed by J. Wilde (*Warburg*, VII, 1944, pp. 65–81), according to whom the central area was not suitable for painting, but his argument seems questionable. Michelangelo seems to have considered this commission as a competition with Leonardo. There are three sketches by Michelangelo representing cavalry battles (one in the Br. Mus.; two in Oxford, Ashmolean Mus.; cf. Tolnay, 1943–60, I, fig. 106, III, figs. 142, 143). It may be deduced that at the beginning he tried to harmonize his composition with Leonardo's *Battle of Anghiari*; but he seems to have realized he could not compete in this field, so he decided to confine himself to the representation of nudes, at which he was a master. In the last version there appear to have been no horsemen, or, if there were, they must have been in the background (copy, Br. Mus.; cf. Tolnay, 1943–60, I, fig. 234). The central scene consists of Florentine soldiers on the banks of the Arno at a moment when the chief of the Florentine army had given the signal of alarm because of the imminent attack of the enemy.

The lost cartoon can be reconstructed on the basis of a grisaille (Holkham Hall, Norfolk, Earl of Leicester Coll.), which is probably the copy by Bastiano da Sangallo mentioned by Vasari (cf. W. Köhler, *Jhb. der k. k. Zentralkommission*, I, Vienna, 1907, pp. 115–72). The prototypes for Michelangelo's composition were Florentine representations of the battles of nudes, like those by Pollaiuolo and by Verrocchio (lost). Michelangelo's composition is reminiscent of a high relief composed in three planes carved from a trapezoid block. The bodies are modeled in the manner of the marble *David*, but the movements of the figures seem fixed, as if they were frozen in the significant poses of ancient statues. From this point of view his work seems to be inferior to Leonardo's, if a judgment on the basis of the copy is possible. The nudes in the cartoon seem to have been transitions from the unarticulated but dynamically conceived nudes of *The Battle of the Lapiths and the Centaurs* to the synthetic monumentality of the nudes on the Sistine ceiling. Certain features of the composition, which is closed at the left and open at the right, may have been determined by the location of the fresco on the left area of the east wall of the hall (Tolnay, 1943–60, I, p. 217; J. Wilde, *Warburg*, VII, 1944, pp. 65–81). This compendium of poses of nude human bodies became the model to be copied by many of the younger Florentine artists; its influence was still perceptible in the 17th century (in Rubens, for example).

Under the pontificate of Julius II, who had an inner affinity with Michelangelo by virtue of the boldness of his conceptions and his seething temperament (*terribilità*), a new period began for the artist and for Renaissance art in Rome. This great Maecenas gathered around him the best artists of Italy, and his attention was soon attracted by the talent of Michelangelo, who was perhaps pointed out to him by Giuliano da Sangallo, Vatican architect and Michelangelo's friend. In March, 1505, the Pope invited Michelangelo to Rome to execute his funerary monument, which was to surpass the ancient mausoleums. The artist began this work with great enthusiasm, making many designs, of which one was chosen. He spent eight months in Carrara having the necessary marble extracted. In December, 1505, he returned to Rome, awaiting with impatience the arrival of the marble blocks. His workshop was near St. Peter's, behind the small church of S. Caterina.

Meanwhile, the Pope had changed his mind. He was now thinking of having the new St. Peter's erected by Bramante and temporarily abandoned the commission for the mausoleum. It seems that, as a compensation, Julius II wanted to commission Michelangelo to execute the decoration of the ceiling of the Sistine Chapel, a project mentioned as early as May, 1506 (E. Steinmann, 1901–05, II, p. 695). Michelangelo wanted to continue the mausoleum, but he was not received at the papal court when he asked for the necessary money for the monument. Offended, he took flight to Florence on Aug. 17, 1506, the day before the laying of the first stone of the new St. Peter's, designed by Bramante. From Florence he offered the Pope, through Giuliano da Sangallo, an arrangement whereby he would work on the blocks in Florence, but it was rejected.

The project for the tomb of Julius II, which occupied Michelangelo's mind for 40 years (1505–45) — and the design of which he changed at least six times — he felt duty bound to complete. He himself said that he was bound (*legato*) to it and that it disturbed his peace of mind. Michelangelo was unable to execute this work, chiefly because of adverse external circumstances. However, it should not be overlooked that with each new reduced design he tried to save the monumental artistic effect, and possibly to enhance it, in spite of the reduction in the number of figures and in the size of the architectural framework. Only in the last version, part of which was not executed by him, did he give up his struggle. Then it seems that he himself, as a consequence of his religious "conversion" and the resulting change in his spiritual orientation, lost interest in the triumphal monument that he had originally conceived. Now he transformed it into a relatively modest religious monument. The reason for the "lamentable final result" seems to lie not in Michelangelo's own "tragic guilt" (as Justi supposed) but chiefly in the hampering power politics of his patrons, Clement VII and Paul III, who wanted his services reserved for their own commissions, and, in the very last version, in Michelangelo's own new spiritual outlook.

The tomb of Julius II was Michelangelo's first cyclical monumental project. For the first time the artist had to execute not only an assembly of statues and reliefs but also a corresponding architectural framework. He had to conceive a total work of art in which sculptures, reliefs, and architecture would form a kind of symphony. The project was originally planned on a gigantic scale with more than forty larger-than-life-size figures. He promised to finish it within five years.

The 1505 design (FIG. 881) of the monument is not known from primary sources; the reconstructions are based on the descriptions of Condivi and Vasari (1568), on later drawings and contracts, and on monuments probably executed under the influence of the lost project. It was to be a freestanding monument, about 24 ft. wide and 36 ft. deep, consisting of three zones, one above the other. The height of the second and third zones is not known. In the bottom zone there were three bays, separated by four herm-pilasters. In the lateral bays there were niches for statue groups called "Victories." The central bay was probably a door which opened to an oval-shaped *tempietto*, probably domed, in the center of which a sarcophagus for the body of the Pope was planned. In front of the herm-pilasters there were chained male figures, the slaves or prisoners; in the second zone, above the niches, there were four large seated figures, two at the front and two at the back. From this platform the monument rose like a truncated pyramid, at the top of which there was a second sarcophagus (a cenotaph) supported by two allegorical figures, which Condivi referred to as Cybele and Caelus and which Vasari designated as angels.

It is still possible to reconstruct the bottom zone on the basis of drawings in the Kupferstichkabinett, Berlin, and in the Uffizi, which seem to have been made either for the model or copied after it (Tolnay, *MJhb.*, N.S., V, 1928, p. 70; E. Panofsky, *AB*, XIX, 1937, pp. 561–79). C. A. Isermeyer (*Kunstchronik*, VII, 1954, pp. 268–69) gave the measurements for the reconstruction of the lower zone of the monument.

The inconsistencies in the profiles and in the composition between the two zones in these drawings speak for the supposition that the lower zone was conceived for two alternative superstructures. The Uffizi drawing indicates that the central niche was originally wider. The supple proportions of the slave figures recall Michelangelo's style of about 1505, rather than that of 1513, the date of the second model. It may be concluded that the drawings are connected with one of the 1505 design, with the central niche and the top part altered, which he seems to have presented again in 1513 to the Pope's heirs. The articulation of the lateral façades of the freestanding monument is problematical. The most likely supposition is that there were three bays (Panofsky) and not two, as in the 1513 project.

There exist only two attempts at reconstruction of the upper zones (E. Panofsky, *AB*, XIX, 1937, pp. 561–79, and Tolnay, 1951; 1943–60, IV). The height of the second zone of the truncated pyramid is determined by the height of the putti, but the height of the third zone is problematical. Probably it was behind the heads of the seated figures, as in the Berlin drawing, rather than above their heads. The most important differences in the two attempts at reconstruction concern the top zone. Panofsky supposed that the Pope was represented seated on a *sella gestatoria*, which supposedly was supported by two angels. This supposition is based on the erroneous interpretation of the word *bara* (Vasari), which is not a *sella gestatoria*, but a bier or sarcophagus. The reconstruction with a *sella gestatoria* is also unsatisfactory from an esthetic point of view, because the seated figure of the Pope would have risen above the monument without being formally connected with the top platform; finally, the angel behind the Pope cannot be seen, either from the front or from the back. The *bara* is probably a sarcophagus with the recumbent figure of the Pope, as he appears also in the project of 1513 and in the last version. The allegorical figures were to be seated on the right and left of the sarcophagus on the base of the *bara*. One of the projects for Michelangelo's catafalque by Zanobio Lastricati (Milan, Ambrosiana) seems to reflect Michelangelo's freestanding monument for Julius II, as the inscriptions on the sheet state. If the top zone is reconstructed on the basis of this drawing, an esthetically satisfying shape is arrived at, because the sarcophagus with the recumbent statue of the Pope is organically connected by the allegorical figures with the rest of the monument. Also, the silhouette is reminiscent of 15th-century Florentine church façades, such as that of S. Maria Novella. However, Michelangelo's proportions are much more compact, and the bays of the three zones correspond strictly to one another. The idea of substituting figures for volutes appears, before Michelangelo, in Leonardo's sketches for the Trivulzio monument (Windsor, Royal Lib., 12353) and, after Michelangelo, in the monument of Il Bambaja (Agostino Busti) for Lancino Curzio (Milan, Castello Sforzesco). Michelangelo's later designs for the Julius tomb — those of 1516, 1532, and 1542 — were inspired by his own project for the façade of S. Lorenzo.

As for the location of the monument, Michelangelo first seems to have thought of erecting it in the Rossellino choir of the old St. Peter's (Condivi), but Giuliano da Sangallo proposed to erect it in a special, probably central-plan chapel outside St. Peter's (Vasari). Finally, Michelangelo had the idea of locating it in St. Peter's itself, which would then have been rebuilt with a central plan. This seems to have been his own idea, and not that of Julius II, as is usually supposed. Therefore, the idea of a freestanding monument seems to have engendered the idea of the new St. Peter's as a central-plan structure in the tradition of the martyrium. If Vasari's contention that Michelangelo wanted to locate the monument in St. Peter's is correct, then it is likely that the artist planned to put the monument above the "confession" of St. Peter, in the center and below the dome of the projected new church (Tolnay, 1951, p. 94 ff.; H. von Einem, in *Festschrift f. H. Jantzen*, Berlin, 1951, pp. 152–68). The tomb of Julius II may therefore have been intended as a double monument, a memorial to the Apostle Prince as well as to the Pope. However, Michelangelo's monument, if placed below the dome of the new St. Peter's, would have been much too small, and, therefore, it may be supposed that the artist intended to enclose it in a central-plan chapel above the confession. At this place, in 1507, Bramante actually erected a building, the so-called "aedicula," to protect the shrine of St. Peter's tomb. This building was not, as was supposed, a provisional structure, but a chapel which was used by the pope when he came to St. Peter's to say Mass. It is a kind of "Holy Sepulcher" and may have been built there precisely in order to prevent the erection of Michelangelo's central-plan chapel. According to F. Wolff Metternich (*Studies in Western Art*, II, Princeton, 1963, p. 70 ff.), the first project for the tomb of Julius II was intended for the northwest lateral chapel of Bramante's St. Peter's. Metternich accepts the tomb reconstruction of this author.

Shortly before his death Julius II issued a brief (Feb. 19, 1513) in which a Cappella Giulia dedicated to the Nativity of the Holy Virgin is mentioned. (The author's attention was called to this *breve* by Mrs. S. Dijkraaf-Galema.) The Pope wished to be buried in this chapel, which was on the south side of St. Peter's; he seems to have reverted in this instance to the above-mentioned idea of Giuliano da Sangallo. The document does not mention the designer of the tomb that the Pope desired to have executed for the Cappella Giulia in 1513.

Compositional designs for the tomb of Julius II, according to reconstructions by C. de Tolnay (drawn by Denise Fossard): (*a*) Version of 1505; (*b*) version of 1513; (*c*) version of 1516; (*d*) version of 1532 *(from C. de Tolnay, 1951)*.

Possibly he was no longer thinking of Michelangelo, but it is also possible that by that time he again wanted to have Michelangelo's monument in this chapel and that his heirs, when they recommissioned Michelangelo to make a new design shortly after, were thinking of this location.

The point of departure for the iconographical program for the lower zone of the first project was probably Antonio Pollaiuolo's tomb of Sixtus IV in St. Peter's; here, around the recumbent figure of the dead Pope, are allegorical figures of the Liberal and Plastic Arts and the Virtues (L. D. Ettlinger, *Warburg*, XVI, 1953, pp. 239–74). All of Pollaiuolo's figures are feminine; in Michelangelo's designs they become masculine. It seems, however, that this program was soon superseded by a new one, in which the slaves were no longer personifications of the Arts and Sciences, "which become prisoners of death" through the Pope's death (Condivi), but allegories of the human soul imprisoned in the body, as they appear earlier in Antonio Federighi's holy-water basin in the Cathedral of Siena. Instead of extolling the Pope's reign, which may have been the original program, Michelangelo created allegories of the human condition in its earthly existence. In the niches he planned groups representing victories of the Virtues over the Vices (Psychomachiae), anticipating the freedom of the soul from earthly bonds, the theme of the second zone. For the platform of the second zone four larger-than-life-size seated figures were planned, representatives of the purely spiritual, intelligible existence of man: Moses and Paul and the Active and the Contemplative Life. On the top of the monument, above the cosmic allegories of Cybele and Caelus (Vasari), was the dead Pope in the empyrean. Therefore the whole of the monument was conceived as a cosmic building, containing, one above the other, three main spheres of existence, which correspond to three conditions of the human soul.

The connection of an architectural structure with sculptural decoration reverts to an ancient tradition, which lived on during the whole of the Middle Ages and in the early Renaissance — for example, in the pulpits of Nicola and Giovanni Pisano. Here, too, the old idea of the hierarchy of the spheres is present. Other influences may have come from Roman sarcophagi (in the bottom zone; Panofsky); from Leonardo's sketches for the Trivulzio monument, where the freestanding structure and the motif of the slaves are anticipated; and, finally, from the *carri dei trionfi*, in which a similar structure and similar elements, such as slaves, are found (Tolnay, 1943–60, IV). A structural relationship with the Holy Sepulcher has also been suspected (H. von Einem, 1959).

The unfinished *St. Matthew* (PL. 529) is connected with a commission from the consuls of the Arte della Lana, in April, 1503, for larger-than-life-size marble statues of the Twelve Apostles for the Cathedral of Florence. Michelangelo was to have delivered one statue a year, but the master did not have the time to dedicate himself to the fulfilling of this commission and obtained release from his contract in December, 1505. It can be supposed that in 1503 he at least made drawings for these Apostles, which are lost with the exception of one (Br. Mus.; cf. Tolnay, 1943–60, I, fig. 103). According to O. Ollendorf (*JhbPreussKSamml*, 1895, pp. 359–68), Michelangelo was working on the *St. Matthew* in the summer of 1506, when he was in Florence (letter from Pietro Soderini). If this dating is right, then the *St. Matthew* is separated from the marble *David* by Michelangelo's important period in Rome and Carrara, when he worked on the designs for the tomb of Julius II. Although this chronology seems likely on stylistic grounds, it is contradicted in a letter written 18 years later (Milanesi, 1875, p. 426), in which Michelangelo states that he ceased work on the commission for the Apostles in March, 1505, when he went to Rome, and that by that time one of the figures had been begun.

In any case, the twisted position of the body and the pathetic emotion in the face of the *St. Matthew* give the impression of his being bound by invisible chains, against which he is rebelling. Amazing for a representation of an Apostle, this figure may better be explained by the supposition that Michelangelo was realizing here a conception intended for one of the slave figures for the Julius tomb. The body of this figure is surprisingly massive and large in comparison with the more slender forms of the marble *David*. Influences of Jacopo della Quercia and of Donatello (the motif of the thumb stuck in the belt) are fused here with inspirations probably coming from the *Laocoön* and the so-called "Pasquino" (G. de' Francovich).

The unfinished *St. Matthew* illustrates Michelangelo's method of working in marble. He attacked the front of the block and worked inward in parallel planes; Vasari uses the analogy of water running out of a bathtub. Michelangelo called this method "per forza di levare" (i.e., by means of successively taking away the superfluous marble without adding any marble to the original block). Although unfinished, the figure expresses the whole artistic idea, and finishing it in more detail would probably have lessened, if not destroyed, its dynamic and expressive qualities. For discussion of the problem of the "non finito" in Michelangelo, see Vasari, Condivi, and Bocchi-Cinelli (quoted in Tolnay, 1943–60, I and III); A. Bertini (*L'Arte*, N.S., I, 2, 1930, pp. 121–38; N.S., II, 2, 1931, pp. 172–74); H. von Einem (*Das Unvollendete als künstlerische Form*, Munich, 1959); J. Gantner (*Rodin und Michelangelo*, Vienna, 1953); P. Barocchi (*Arte Antica e Moderna*, III, 1958, pp. 221–35).

In November, 1506, a reconciliation between Julius II and Michelangelo took place in Bologna, which had been recaptured by the Pope from the Bentivoglio family. The artist was commissioned to execute the model of an enormous seated statue in bronze of Julius II for the façade of S. Petronio. The wax model was ready in April, 1507, the casting done in July, 1507, and February, 1508, and the statue put in place in February, 1508; but it had already been destroyed in May, 1511. Michelangelo seems to have regarded this commission as a compensation for the unexecuted large seated figures he had planned for the platform of the pontiff's tomb. About the same time the Pope also commissioned, for the Palazzo degli Anziani, a stucco statue of himself, also seated and larger than life-size, the motif of which was identical with the bronze statue, having a key in the left hand and giving benediction with the raised right hand. It may be supposed that the stucco statue was also made from a small model, perhaps as a test for the bronze figure.

The lost work can be reconstructed only approximately on the basis of old descriptions, which show that it was a prestige statue of the Pope, probably following the type of Antonio and Piero Pollaiuolo's statue of Innocent VIII in St. Peter's. In a few later prestige statues, or drawings for them, there are reflections of the lost work (e.g., Nicolas Cordier's statue of Paul V, in Rimini, Piazza della Fontana; Baccio Bandinelli's drawing of Clement VII, in the Louvre). The violent movement of the raised arm seems to have been a gesture of condemning, instead of blessing, according to the sources. In all probability this dramatic figure anticipates the prophets and sibyls of the Sistine ceiling and the 1515 version of the *Moses*. The large coat of arms of Julius II, below the niche of the statue, has been hypothetically identified with the one that is in the Museo Civico, Bologna (cf. Tolnay, 1943–60, I, fig. 251).

In March or April, 1508, Michelangelo was in Rome, where he was commissioned by Julius II to execute a new ceiling decoration for the Sistine Chapel (PLS. 528, 535; I, PL. 381; II, PL. 291; for a discussion of the symbolic significance of the Sistine Chapel, see E. Battisti, *Comm*, VII, 1957, pp. 96–104). He accepted the commission reluctanctly at the beginning. The original plan preserved in a drawing (Br. Mus.; cf. Tolnay, 1943–60, II, fig. 230) is rather modest, with the Twelve Apostles represented on the pendentives of the low-pitched barrel vault and a system of framed compartments of different shapes in the vault. This system reverts to ancient ceiling decoration (cf. Schulz, *Warburg*, XXV, 1–2, 1962, p. 51 ff.). The second and third drawings (Detroit, Inst. of Art; Br. Mus.; cf. Tolnay, 1943–60, II, figs. 231, 232) reveal the successive simplification and unification of the system, in which the bays and pilasters of the walls are taken into account. After these attempts Michelangelo, realizing they would turn out to be a "cosa povera," seems to have persuaded the Pope to give him permission to paint also the spandrels and lunettes. The Pope gave him a free hand (Milanesi, 1875, p. 427; Maurenbrecher, 1938, p. 69). In the executed work, which he began in May, 1508, the system of framed compartments was fused into a unified architectural trellis; figures exclusively, instead of ornaments, were used as decoration, and figural compositions were planned for the areas inside the frames. Michelangelo secured an independent existence for the ceiling (now separated from the walls by standing putti) by making it appear to float above the chapel. It may be supposed that the 15th-century decoration of the barrel vault by Pier Matteo Serdenti d'Amelia, with a blue sky and golden stars, played a role in Michelangelo's last project; this too was conceived as a "sky" over the chapel.

The Sistine ceiling is the masterwork of Michelangelo's early maturity. The aspirations of his youth converge, clarify themselves, and find a definite place in this monumental work, which unites in a hierarchic system their manifold tendencies. His earlier works now become a repertory for him, from the accumulated treasures of which he draws in his new work.

The relationship of the architectural framework and the figures is developed from the first version of the tomb for Julius II. Through a renewed study of natural models and of ancient art (E. Gombrich, *Warburg*, 1937, p. 69) Michelangelo was able to formulate in a more monumental and harmonious way the different categories of figures which he had previously created. He drew further inspiration from the reliefs of Jacopo della Quercia in S. Petronio, Bologna, and in one instance, *The Expulsion*, from Masaccio's fresco on the same theme in the Church of the Carmine, Florence; all these borrowings are assimilated in a new style, characterized by fullness of form and enlivened by rhythmic outlines, which is concrete in details, yet synthetic in its whole.

The new structure of the ceiling decoration may be defined as consisting of three distinct zones, one above the other: the bottom zone of the lunettes and spandrels forms a kind of base; next is the intermediate zone of the prophets, sibyls, and *ignudi* (nude figures) placed in front of the painted attic and stone trellis; and, behind the latter, the highest zone with the "histories," which are seen as if through windows. Within this structure the artist assembled figures belonging to different categories in size and in function, appearing to be of bronze, marble, or flesh, and ranging from architecturally confined to free figures. In the attic zone (the second) he used figures of the most different scales side by side (e.g., the seers and the small putti), while in the upper zone the scale is the same in every scene. The links between these different categories are the *ignudi* (XII, PL. 74), with their ambivalent function as crowning motifs of the thrones of the prophets and the sibyls and, at the same time, framing the stories. All these elements combine to give the effect of a powerful polyphony, dissonant in the second zone and achieving harmony at the top.

The subdivision of the ceiling was inspired by the 15th-century floor decoration of the Sistine Chapel, which was divided, according to liturgical requirements, into a space for the laity, separated by a *cancellata* or screen (moved toward the entry ca. 1573) from the *quadratura* of the cardinals and from the altar space. By projecting the division of the floor and the corresponding arcs of the niches containing frescoed figures of popes on the upper walls (J. Wilde, in *Proc. Br. Acad.*, 1958, 1959, p. 61 ff.) onto the curved surface of the vault, Michelangelo created the rhythmically alternating bays on the ceiling. Within this structure the artist distinguished in composition and iconography between those bays which are above the space for the laity and those above the presbytery; above the former he painted stories with many small figures, in which humanity is the prisoner of sin, while above the latter he painted stories with a few large figures, in all of which God appears. It is important to note that the figure of God the Father appears only in the frescoes which are inside and above the presbytery (E. Steinmann, 1901-05, II, p. 220).

Michelangelo took the whole surface of the ceiling as a unity, to which even the pendentives with the prophets and sibyls belong, whereas it was customary to separate the pendentives and to form a border around the vault of the ceiling, including the spandrels. Michelangelo obviously wanted to use a maximum of surface for his frescoes and to unify the curved vault of the ceiling by his decoration.

The pictorial decoration of the vault was not intended as a simple decorative covering of the surface; nor was the decoration intended as merely illusionistic, to be seen from below, which would have nullified the effect of the form of the actual ceiling. It is a plastic-dynamic decoration directly inspired by the mass and surface of the vault and by tension inherent in the very structure of the vault. Michelangelo treated the vault as if it were an enormous block already containing those forces which he expressed in architectural forms, as well as those weights that are personified by the figures. The prophets and sibyls, which are of larger proportions than the *ignudi* above and which, unlike them, have closed outlines, ideally serve to generate the curvature of the vault.

The iconographical program of the earlier versions is not known exactly, except that the Apostles were planned instead of the later prophets and sibyls (PL. 538; I, PL. 381). Nevertheless, it may be supposed that from the beginning the whole of the decoration signified the heavens, following an old tradition of ceiling decoration that reverts to antiquity. The last version may be also considered a new kind of representation of heaven — a sort of Old Testament Olympus peopled by prophets and sibyls, instead of by the Greek gods. Such an interpretation indeed prevailed in several ceiling decorations of the late 16th century, which are actually paraphrases of the Sistine ceiling but represent the mythological Olympus (those of the Zucchis, Giulio Mazzoni, Annibale Carracci, etc.).

The series should be read from the entrance toward the altar, although the chronological sequence of the stories is reversed. In this, Michelangelo was bound by the two already existing cycles in the chapel. The Quattrocento cycles represented in typological order the story of humanity *sub lege* (i.e., the story of Moses) and, facing it, the story of humanity *sub gratia* (i.e., the story of Christ). When Michelangelo decided to decorate his ceiling with histories, there remained no other choice for him but to paint the history of humanity *ante legem* (i.e., Genesis). However, in order to reconcile this tradition with the new demands of the beholder, Michelangelo created a sequence which can be read from the entrance to the altar. He also introduced a new meaning into the historical scenes. The whole ceiling was conceived for the solemn entry of the pope and his entourage into the chapel. The pope could experience, as he proceeded step by step toward the altar, the revelation of the creative power of the highest Being, who, appearing at the beginning in human aspect, takes on a cosmic form. The whole cycle, as seen from the entrance, is thus a gradual theophany in the direction of the altar. It is also a kind of ascension of the human soul to God, *ritorno a Dio*, or *deificatio*.

The histories in the central axis are conceived by the artist as the visions of the prophets and the sibyls, who frame them on the right and left, and the impact of these visions is reflected also in the *ignudi* surrounding them. The figures in the spandrels and lunettes, representing the ancestors of Christ, seem to be excluded from this higher world and unaware of the revelation of God. They seem to be oppressed and to wait aimlessly and without hope, unaware of the coming of the Messiah. The four corner spandrels belong to this same lower sphere; they represent the miraculous deliverance of the chosen people. However, Michelangelo represented the scenes as anonymous events which did not enter into the consciousness of humanity.

In the most recent attempts at interpretation (F. Hartt, *AB*, XXXII, 1950, pp. 115-49, 181-218, XXXIII, 1951, pp. 267-73; E. Wind, *GBA*, LXXVI, 1944, pp. 211-46; H. von Einem, 1959) the tendency has been to discard the above interpretation, although the first two scholars cited here accept this author's theses that the prophets and sibyls are spiritually connected with the histories, which are their visions, and that the spiritual sequence of the series proceeds from the entrance to the altar. Some scholars believe that Michelangelo was inspired by theological writings [according to Hartt, by Vigerio; to Wind, by Sante Pagnini; to H. B. Gutman (*ZfKg*, XVIII, 1955, pp. 74-76), by Nicholas of Lyra; to H. von Einem, by an anonymous theologian] and that the content of the whole plan is not Michelangelo's idea; they hold that he illustrated a program drawn up by theologians, according to which there is a hidden typological meaning in the histories and in the ancestors, so that, in their opinion, the Old Testament scenes represented allude to New Testament scenes not represented. (See E. Wind in *Warburg*, I, 1937-38, pp. 322-30; *Measure*, 1950, p. 411 ff.; and *Renaissance Studies*, London, 1960, p. 312 ff., with woodcut prototypes for four of the medallions on the ceiling from the Malermi Bible of 1490.) But the simplicity of the spiritual idea of the whole, namely the relationship between the finite beings and the infinite Being, as well as the gradual theophany of the latter, does not necessitate the supposition of an erudite program. The typological interpretation of the scenes would seem not to be necessary, because the typological correspondence had already been carried out in the two 15th-century cycles on the chapel walls, and it would have been a pleonasm to repeat this relationship between the Old and the New Testament. The only exceptions are the prophet Zechariah above the entrance, predicting the entry of Christ into Jerusalem — possibly an allusion to the entry of the pope into the Chapel — and the choice of Jonah, the prophet of the Resurrection of Christ, for depiction above the altar. The histories of the ceiling, however, do not seem to allude to the future coming of Christ (E. Wind, *AB*, XXXIII, 1951, pp. 41-47), but they reveal rather the presence of God. Just as Michelangelo's ceiling is an autonomous work, independent of the rest of the chapel, it may also be regarded as such from a spiritual point of view. Some important observations concerning the structure and chronology of the Sistine ceiling can be found in a paper by J. Wilde, "The Decoration of the Sistine Chapel" (*Proc. Br. Acad., 1958*, 1959, p. 61 ff.).

The preparation of the Sistine ceiling was begun on May 10, 1508, the date of the contract (lost). Until the beginning of January, 1509, the artist probably made sketches and studies and prepared the cartoons, and only then did he begin to paint. By the middle of September, 1509, he had completed the first section; this probably comprised the three stories of Noah, with the accompanying five prophets and sibyls, the corresponding eight *ignudi*, and the spandrels with David and Judith, as well as the first two of the spandrels that were to contain the ancestors of Christ. The second, smaller section was most likely done between the middle of September, 1509, and the end of September, 1510 — the date of Michelangelo's journey to Bologna to obtain the necessary money from the Pope; this section probably included the stories of the original sin and the creation of Eve, as well as Ezekiel and the Cumaean sibyl, with the corresponding four *ignudi* and the two spandrels. The third section was probably executed between January and Aug. 14, 1511, the date of the first unveiling; this section probably included the last four stories, the last five prophets and sibyls, as well as the last eight *ignudi*, four spandrels with the ancestors, and the corner spandrels with the crucifixion of Haman and the bronze serpent. The fourth section — probably executed between October, 1511, and Oct. 31, 1512, the date of the unveiling of the whole ceiling — comprised all of the lunettes. (The cartoons for the first eight lunettes seem, however, to have been executed as early as Jan.-Aug., 1511.) The differences of style, composition, and color among these four sections are clearly visible. The figures in each succeeding section become larger in size and reduced in number, making the compositions more monumental and easier to see from a distance. The outlines, pronounced at the beginning, become less and less important, while the colors become softer and the chiaroscuro richer in its transitions. In the lunettes changing colors are introduced. (For more details concerning the chronology proposed here, see Tolnay, 1943-60, II, p. 105 ff.; a slightly different view is expressed by J. Wilde, *Proc. Br. Acad., 1958*, 1959, p. 61 ff.)

The Sistine ceiling was unveiled on Oct. 31, 1512. The four years during which Michelangelo had labored on this immense work, almost without help, were solitary ones dedicated almost exclusively to his work. (In the same period Raphael executed the Stanza della Segnatura and transformed his own style under the influence of Michelangelo's ceiling.) Now he was anxious to resume work on the tomb of Julius II, though from one of Michelangelo's letters it is evident that Julius II was not anxious to let him continue. However, after the Pope died suddenly in February, 1513, a new contract was drawn up between Michelangelo and the executors of the Pope's will (Cardinal Aginensis and Lorenzo Pucci) on May 6, 1513 (Milanesi, 1875, p. 635 ff.; Maurenbrecher, 1938, p. 296). Although the architectural dimensions were somewhat reduced from the first project, the number of the figures was increased, the time of execution prolonged from five to seven years, and the price raised. Indeed, in later letters (Milanesi, 1875, pp. 428, 489) Michelangelo spoke of an enlargement of the monument. The artist rented a house on the Macello dei Corvi near Trajan's Forum, a house which he later acquired and in which he died. He had all the marble blocks brought there, and he made a contract in July, 1513, with Antonio da Pontassieve to execute the ornamental blocks for the architectural structure. Most of these blocks are still in existence and were used in the lower zone of the final version (Tolnay, 1928).

Michelangelo worked until the spring of 1516 on three figures for the monument and executed the two *Slaves* in the Louvre and the *Moses*. He mentions that he worked on the *Rebellious Slave* in 1513, and he seems to have begun the *Moses* in 1515 (Milanesi, 1875, pp. 115, 391).

The project of 1513 (FIG. 881) can be reconstructed on the basis of the contract and Michelangelo's notes concerning it (Milanesi, 1875, p. 636 f.; Maurenbrecher, 1938, p. 296), the subcontract between Michelangelo and Antonio da Pontassieve (Milanesi, 1875, p. 640), and the drawings in the Kupferstichkabinett, Berlin, and in the Uffizi. No longer a freestanding monument, it was now to be attached to the wall on one side. The *tempietto* in the interior of the lower zone was abandoned. Whereas the lower zone seems to have been essentially identical with that of 1505, except for the figures, the upper zone is completely different. The Pope's sarcophagus stands on the platform surrounded by four figures. In the lateral bays of the platform six larger-than-life-size figures, instead of four, were planned. Behind the sarcophagus rises a very high *cappelletta*, terminating in a semicircular arc, in which Michelangelo intended to place five new figures. It is problematical as to whether the *cappelletta* was meant to be a wall decoration or a projecting structure. Consequently there are different reconstructions (cf. E. Panofsky, *AB*, XIX, 4, 1937, pp. 561-79; Tolnay, 1951, fig. 204). In any case, it is obvious that this project is a compromise between the freestanding monument and the traditional wall tomb, except that Michelangelo introduced in the *cappelletta* the dynamic tension he had already achieved in the painted "trellis" of the Sistine ceiling. The iconographical program also seems to have been a compromise between the original triumphal symbolism of the lower zone and the traditional religious representation of the Virgin and the saints in the upper zone. (The full-length figure of the Virgin floating in a mandorla seems to have influenced Raphael's *Sistine Madonna*.) The drawing in Berlin may revert to 1505 and may have been an alternative version for the monument; this would explain why the figures have the character of Michelangelo's style of circa 1505 and why the architectural measurements and the motifs of the figures do not correspond to the stipulations of the 1513 contract. The differences between the measurements in the contract and in the subcontract are explained by C. A. Isermeyer (*Kunstchronik*, VII, 10, 1954, pp. 268-70) by the difference between the Roman and the Florentine palmo.

Michelangelo made new projects for all the slave figures, six of which exist in sketches on a sheet in the Ashmolean Museum, Oxford (cf. Tolnay, 1943-60, IV, fig. 110); all these sketches are for the corner figures. The sketch for the *Rebellious Slave* can be recognized here; he is clearly defined as a soldier, because he has his armor beside him, which will disappear in the final version. Therefore, the *Rebellious Slave* (Louvre) must be considered a corner figure, in all probability destined to decorate the left front corner. The expression of suffering in the face and the movement seem to have been inspired by the *Laocoön* (O. Ollendorf); possibly Leonardo's St. Sebastian drawing (Hamburg, Kunsthalle) may also have influenced Michelangelo. The *Dying Slave* (PL. 529) is for one of the central pilasters of the front, probably the left one. It is not clear whether it is a dying, sleeping, or awakening figure, but, in any case, the gesture of the right hand suggests he is trying to liberate himself from a nightmare. Both of the *Slaves* are accompanied by small unfinished apes (cf. E. Panofsky, 1939).

The *Moses* (ca. 1515-16) was planned originally for the right corner of the first platform, and the figure is indeed more impressive when seen from below. This gigantic seated marble figure is a further development of the bronze *Julius II* and of the prophets Joel and Daniel; at the same time, the influence of Donatello's seated *St. John the Evangelist* (Florence, Mus. dell'Opera del Duomo; IV, PL. 240) is also obvious. The figure seems to be animated by the righteous anger of a chosen spirit confronted with the baseness of this world. The whole is conceived as a cosmic cataclysm depicted in human form; the passion of his soul seems to unleash the elements of the cosmos, in the flowing beard (water), in the flamelike tongues of hair (fire), and in the cloak spreading like lava over the legs (earth). Perhaps the doctrine of "cosmic man," conceived in the Middle Ages, still lives on, but here the anger is controlled and the whole figure epitomizes the birth, culmination, and death of passion. The *Moses* has always been considered an ideal portrait of the artist, but some scholars (e.g., Grimm) believe it is at the same time an image of Julius II. In his last version of the tomb, Michelangelo moved the figure to the central niche at the bottom zone, indicating that he must have come to consider it the most important piece of the whole monument.

The political conflicts that arose in the summer of 1516 between Leo X and the house of Della Rovere were of consequence for the history of the tomb of Julius II as well. Michelangelo felt that he should enter the service of the reigning Pope, and he himself expressed his wish to have the commission for the façade of S. Lorenzo, the church of the Medicis. In spite of this, in a later letter of Michelangelo's and in Condivi it is stated that the initiative came from the Pope. It was obvious that under such conditions the tomb project would have to be reduced. On July 8, 1516, a new contract was signed (Milanesi, 1875, p. 646; Maurenbrecher, 1938, p. 8). On the bottom zone (FIG. 881) the front remained identical, because the stones for it had already been completed, but the lateral façades were reduced to simple *risvolti*. The upper zone now extends across the whole width of the lower zone. It is articulated by half-columns on ornamented bases, and in the center of it there is a niche called a *tribunetta*. At the top, the whole structure is closed by a large entablature, on which four large candelabra were probably to be placed. It is not certain whether the entablature above the *tribunetta* was horizontal or arched (see the reconstruction by J. Wilde, *Michelangelo: The Group of Victory*, London, Oxford, 1954). In spite of this reduction in the architecture and in the number of figures, it is obvious that Michelangelo tried to save the monumental aspect of the façade by enlarging the architectural forms and by unifying the silhouette of the monument. He tried here, in the two stories of equal width and in the proportional relationship of their heights, to use his ideas for the façade of S. Lorenzo. He suppressed the architrave above the herm-pilasters, thereby making the lower zone even more massive for greater contrast with the very high upper zone.

For the niches of the lower zone he now planned isolated figures instead of groups, and in the central field of this zone, there was to be a bronze relief. Four, instead of six, large seated figures — two at the front and one at each small side (*risvolti*) — were intended for the upper zone, with a bronze relief above each of them. The sarcophagus was now to stand parallel to the façade of the monument, while the statue of the dead Pope was to be held by two figures, in the manner of compositions of the entombment of Christ or of the Pietà. (The author's reconstruction of this part of the tomb is based on an original drawing in the Casa Buonarroti; cf. Tolnay, 1943–60, IV, fig. 122.) Above the Pope there was to be a full-length, standing figure of the Virgin with the Child. When Michelangelo decided to settle again in Florence in 1518, he had the unfinished blocks for the monument sent there. However, he left the finished statues and architectural blocks in Rome. Still his work on the tomb did not go forward, mainly because he spent much of his time between 1516 and 1519 in the marble quarries of Carrara and Seravezza, where he was busy with the excavation of marble for the façade of S. Lorenzo. These years were almost lost from the point of view of creative activity. On Mar. 10, 1520, the Pope annulled the contract for the façade of S. Lorenzo (Milanesi, 1875, p. 581). Michelangelo felt this to be a "very great insult" (*vituperio grandissimo*). In the same year he accepted the commission for the burial chapel of the Medicis in S. Lorenzo, and could not spend time on the Julius tomb. Nevertheless, the contract of 1516 remained in force until 1532.

During the short pontificate of Adrian VI (Jan., 1522–Sept., 1523) the wheel of fortune turned in favor of the Della Roveres. Francesco Maria della Rovere, who in 1516 was deprived of his duchy by Leo X, reinstalled himself in Urbino and, supported by Adrian, requested in April, 1523, that Michelangelo execute the tomb according to the plan of 1516 or repay all the money he had received for it (Milanesi, 1875, p. 421 f.); but, as a consequence of the death of Adrian and the election of Cardinal Giulio de' Medici as Clement VII, the hopes of the Della Roveres receded again, and there was no longer the immediate danger of a lawsuit against Michelangelo. The artist had to continue work on the figures for the Medici Chapel and was unable to concentrate on the tomb of Julius II, from which he wished to be completely liberated (Milanesi, 1875, p. 454). In 1525 there emerged the idea of reducing the monument to a small and modest wall tomb, in the manner of the 15th-century tombs of Paul II (Vatican, Grotte Nuove) and Pius II (Rome, S. Andrea della Valle; cf. Milanesi, 1875, pp. 447, 450). Possibly the design mentioned in October, 1526 (K. Frey, 1899, p. 289), is a project for this greatly reduced monument. In any case, a group of sketches has been identified by the author with this project; these, up till now, have been considered studies for the Medici tomb (Br. Mus.; Florence, Casa Buonarroti; cf. Tolnay, 1943–60, III, p. 77, IV, p. 51 f.). However, this design seems to have been immediately discarded.

In 1527, with the incarceration of Clement VII, Michelangelo stopped work on the Medici monuments and, according to A. E. Popp (1936), resumed work on the Julius tomb. After the victory of the Medicis over the Florentine republic, and after Clement VII's magnanimous pardon for Michelangelo, he tried again to rid himself of the tomb of Julius II. The long drawn-out discussions between the Pope and the Della Rovere heirs finally led to a compromise in April, 1532, and a new contract was drawn up which reverted to that of 1516 (Milanesi, 1875, p. 702 f.), but the monument was reduced by the abandonment of the lateral *risvolti* with their figures. Michelangelo obligated himself by making a new model or drawing; by delivering six figures wrought by himself, which were then in his workshops, either in Florence or in Rome; and by finishing all the architectural blocks. Which six figures were ordered is a matter of conjecture. Probably the question was left open on purpose, to give Michelangelo a free hand in his choice. They were most likely either the *Moses* and the Louvre *Slaves*, along with a Virgin, prophet, and sibyl, or the *Moses*, the four so-called "Boboli Slaves" (or "Prisoners"), and a Victory (Tolnay, 1943–60, IV, p. 53); all the other figures could be executed after his drawings by pupils. Now it was decided that the monument should be erected in S. Pietro in Vincoli, the titular church of Julius II. No models or drawings of this new project exist; there is, however, a drawing for the upper zone by Bastiano da Sangallo which reverts to the 1516 project (Florence, Uffizi; cf. Tolnay, 1943–60, IV, fig. 98).

The dating of the four so-called "Boboli Slaves" (Florence, Acc.; I, PL. 381) is a much-discussed problem. According to some scholars, they were begun in 1516 (J. Wilde and H. von Einem); according to others, in 1519, because four figures for the monument were promised for the summer of that year at the urging of the Pope's heirs (Frey, 1899, p. 135; this is also Justi's opinion). The years 1527–30 have been proposed by A. E. Popp (1936) and 1532–34 by the author (1943–60, IV, p. 51), but each dating presents difficulties. However, stylistically they seem to herald the figures of the *Last Judgment*, and, therefore, the later dates seem more likely. These are actually new enlarged versions of the 1513 figures, two of them being for the front and two for the corners of the tomb façade. They could have been placed on the lower zone of the 1532 version (Tolnay, 1943–60, IV, fig. 206). Another opinion is that of J. Wilde (*Michelangelo: The Group of Victory*, London, Oxford, 1954), according to whom the new architecture for which these figures were intended had been planned by Michelangelo in the mid-1520s — an unlikely hypothesis in view of the fact that in 1525 a reduced monument, similar to those of Paul II and Pius II, had been discussed; the figures must belong rather to an enlarged project, which could have been identical with the new design of 1532. The *Victory* (Florence, Palazzo Vecchio) appears also to belong to the 1532 project and seems to have been intended for the left niche of the lower zone of the monument.

During this period (1518-34) Michelangelo executed two independent marble sculptures, a *Christ with the Cross* and an unfinished *Apollo*. *Christ with the Cross* (Rome, S. Maria sopra Minerva) is a second version of a 1514 commission from Metello Vari (Milanesi, 1875, p. 641). Because of a vein in the marble block Michelangelo abandoned the figure in 1516 and later gave it to Vari as a gift. He began a new figure in 1519-20, which he sent in 1521 to Rome, where it was partly reworked and finished by his pupil Pietro Urbano. According to a letter by Vari (Gotti, 1875, I, p. 143), it represents the resurrected Christ, but actually it is a combination of the resurrected Christ and the Man of Sorrows, who holds the instruments of the Passion in his hand. He is represented as victorious over death, an Apollonian nude hero who, instead of showing his suffering, hides it in front of the vulgus. The only feature which is reminiscent of the traditional type of Christ is the bearded face. The *contrapposto* position, with the arm crossing the breast and the head turned in the opposite direction, reminds one of Leonardo's *Leda*. Although the conception seems to be very close to that of ancient statuary, Michelangelo must also have had a concrete religious aim when he made this figure — possibly the idea of erecting the statue of the "true Christ" in the secularized papal city. This is all the more likely since S. Maria sopra Minerva is the Dominican church of Rome, and Michelangelo was a great admirer in his youth of Savonarola.

The other figure is the unfinished *Apollo* (Florence, Mus. Naz.), the history of which is not yet completely clarified. According to Vasari, Michelangelo made, in the autumn of 1530, an Apollo for Baccio Valori, the hated leader of the victorious papal and imperial army and at that time regent of Florence; but in the inventory of the art treasures of Cosimo I de' Medici the figure is described as a David. It may be supposed that this figure, which Michelangelo began (ca. 1525) as a David for the Medici tombs (Popp, 1922), was transformed by him in 1530 into an Apollo. The motif of the figure could be interpreted in both ways. The figure, with its *contrapposto* and the arm crossing the breast, takes up the pose of the *Christ* of S. Maria sopra Minerva, but, since the right leg and the arm across the breast are raised higher, the effect is that of a continuous spiral; it is one of the first *figure serpentinate*. In the sensitive modeling of the surface and in the diffuse distribution of the light and shade, it is one of the master's most harmonious achievements, made in the spirit of the allegories of the Medici tombs. The pose anticipates that of the *Victory*.

The Medici Chapel, or New Sacristy, is situated on the north side of S. Lorenzo (FIG. 892; PLS. 530, 531; IV, PL. 459). In all probability its lower zone dates to the time of Brunelleschi (q.v.). The outside walls of both the second zone and the drum also seem to have been erected before the commission of Michelangelo, under whom — apart from the whole articulation of the interior walls of the chapel — only the cupola and the lantern were executed. However, this dating of the walls (Tolnay, 1943-60, III, p. 27 ff. and p. 124) has been contested (Wilde, *Warburg*, XVIII, 1-2, 1955, pp. 54-66). According to the latter opinion, Michelangelo was the architect of the whole building. The thesis that the chapel was constructed prior to Michelangelo is supported by the observations that the masonry of the exterior on the east and north sides is identical in the lowest zone with that of Brunelleschi's church; that there is no correspondence between the interior design and the exterior (the entablatures are at different levels, the window frames of the drum are higher on the outside than on the inside, etc.); and, finally, that Michelangelo's red-chalk plan of the New Sacristy in the Archivio Buonarroti (identified by Tolnay, *MJhb*, 1928; cf. Tolnay, 1943-60, III, fig. 79) does not yet show the shallow niches, but a chapel with straight walls, the ground plan of which corresponds to that of the Old Sacristy.

Michelangelo deliberately planned the interior of the chapel so as to follow the design of Brunelleschi's Old Sacristy, a fact reported by Vasari. However, it can be seen in the red-chalk drawing that he transferred the articulation of the choir wall, with its three bays, to all four walls and that he disposed the tombs and doors symmetrically. What was still haphazard in Brunelleschi's Old Sacristy here became a system conceived according to the laws of symmetry and correspondence. Michel-

Florence, S. Lorenzo, cross section of the New Sacristy (*from H. von Geymüller, Die Architecktur der Renaissance in Toscana, Munich, 1904*).

angelo went even further in this tendency to symmetrical composition in his final version, in which he made further innovations with respect to the Old Sacristy. He inserted shallow niches in the central bays of the lateral walls and of the entrance wall, thereby creating more room for the sculptured tombs, and added an intermediate zone between the lower zone and that of the lunettes, essentially increasing the height of the chapel. The New Sacristy became a slender, relatively small space, high above which is the cupola. A consequence of these innovations was the transformation of the lighting; the Medici Chapel is filled with a diffused light from above, in contrast to the dimly lighted Old Sacristy. Instead of a "Gothic" dome with ribs of the Brunelleschi type, he erected a hemispherical dome with coffers in the style of the Pantheon.

The *pietra serena* (gray sandstone) order, completed by plain bands of the same material beside the pilasters, served Michelangelo only as a framework into which he inserted fantastic architectural structures of white marble, which seem to be in conflict with the *pietra serena* order. A rational and an irrational conception of space are here contrasted, as in Roman and Pompeian wall paintings. The irrational tomb façades are seen as if through openings in the walls; the role of the painted architectural trellis of the Sistine ceiling is taken over here by the *pietra serena* order. The effect would have been enhanced if the wall paintings had been executed as planned. They would probably have had the function of the tomb façades, that is, they would have served as a contrast to the *pietra serena* order in the second and third stories and would perhaps have conferred on the whole space a new meaning.

It seems that Michelangelo had intended to create in the Medici Chapel an abbreviated image of the universe, a kind of cosmic structure with its spheres arranged hierarchically, one above the other. The lowest zone with the tombs stands for the realm of the departed souls; the intermediate zone with the originally planned stories (Popp) was probably intended to represent the terrestrial sphere; and the zones of the lunettes and the light-filled dome, with its partly completed decoration of garlands (later whitewashed), was to have alluded to the celestial spheres. Thus the whole chapel was conceived as a sacred place where men could communicate directly with the transcendent spheres.

[Concerning the sequence of Michelangelo's designs for the tombs, see Tolnay, 1943–60, III, p. 33 ff., and J. Wilde, *Warburg*, XVIII, 1–2, 1955, pp. 54–66. On the history and dating of the tombs and statues, see Köhler, *Kunstgeschichtliche Anzeigan*, IV, 1907, pp. 90–109; Popp, 1922; Tolnay, 1943–60, III, p. 58 ff.; H. W. Frey, *ZfKg*, XIV, 1951, pp. 40–96. The differing opinion of F. Kriegbaum (*Michelangelo Buonarroti*, Berlin, 1940) is followed only by W. Gramberg (*Mit. des Kunsthist. Inst. in Florenz*, VII, 1953–56, pp. 151–60) and is contested by the author (Tolnay, 1943–60, III, p. 131). Concerning the casts in the Accademia di Belle Arti in Perugia, see G. N. Fasola, *Comm*, VI, 1955, pp. 164–72; in the opinion of this author the casts are only copies by Vincenzo Danti.]

The configurations of the sarcophagi, the allegorical figures, and the seated figures in the niches show that here the relationship between sculpture and architecture is newly defined (PL. 530). The architectural structure is no longer a skeleton for the assembly of figures, but the figures now form an autonomous triangle in front of the architecture. The disposition of the figures expresses the meaning that Michelangelo wanted to communicate. Only a few known facts help us to interpret the spiritual content of the chapel. It was intended as a funerary chapel and was dedicated to the resurrection of Christ; therefore, death and resurrection must have played an essential role in the program. Michelangelo himself indicated the program of the tombs on a sheet with an early plan of the tomb of Lorenzo the Magnificent: "Fame holds the epitaphs of the dead; she moves neither forward nor back, because they are dead and their labor is at a standstill." This indicates that Michelangelo meant that with death the Duke reached eternity, but the allusion to the allegorical figure of Fame suggests that his concept is connected with the idea of triumph, perhaps in the sense of the worldly glorification of the Medicis. This seems to have been the point of departure for Michelangelo in the earlier stage of the program. In fact, the paraphrases of the lost projects of Michelangelo (e.g., those in the Louvre) express this worldly glorification in the form of pagan apotheosis: The *capitani* are enthroned and hold scepters; war trophies decorate the structure, which is inspired by the ancient triumphal arch; and at the feet of the *capitani* a semicircle symbolizes the mourning globe.

On another sheet, Michelangelo wrote as follows: "Heaven and Earth [i.e., the two figures planned for the smaller niches to the right and left of the Dukes], Day and Night speak and say: We led the Duke Giuliano to death by one swift current. It is therefore just that he take revenge for this, as he does; and the revenge is this: since we have killed him, so he took our light in dying, and closed our eyes with his closed eyes, so that they no longer shine over the earth. What would he have done with us had he remained alive?" Although the last sentence is obscure and sounds like a play on words, it is clear that Michelangelo wanted to express here the idea of the spiritual triumph of the soul of the dead over the forces of transience symbolized by Day and Night (PLS. 530, 531; XII, PL. 60). Several of his poems express the same idea, and Condivi also interprets the four allegories as expressions of all-devouring time.

The fact that the allegories of Time and the river gods (the latter planned but never executed; original model, Florence, Acc.) were intended to surround the sarcophagi containing the ashes of the dead expresses the ideas of transience and of mourning. The fact that the images of the *capitani* are placed above the level of the allegorical figures and the sarcophagi signifies their spiritual victory over death. The opening at the top of the sarcophagus allows the souls of the dead to ascend to the higher sphere. Thus the transition from an existence determined by matter to an existence in absolute liberty is plastically expressed. Since the glances of both *capitani* are directed toward the statue of the Virgin, it may be said that in the afterlife their souls live in eternal contemplation of the Virgin. The spiritual center of the whole composition is thus the Virgin and Child, with the statues of the two patron saints of the Medicis, SS. Cosmas and Damian. At the entrance to the choir there is an altar, from which the officiant must also face the figure of the Virgin. Thus the relationship of the other walls to the wall of the *Virgin* created a spiritual unity that was completely new in a funerary chapel. Like the first Virgin sculptured by Michelangelo, the *Medici Virgin* is a *madonna lactans*, but the sibylline expression of the early work becomes an expression of maternal love in the latter.

The Medici Chapel was the first funerary chapel to be conceived, artistically and spiritually, as a complete unity in which the tombs were integrated into the architecture of the chapel and the sculpture into the structure of the tombs. Michelangelo's new conception of the funerary chapel as a spiritual and artistic unity inspired numerous 17th- and 18th-century chapels in which the faces of the sculptured figures of the dead on the side walls are turned toward the altar. The Medici Chapel is the first and only funerary chapel of the Renaissance in which pagan and Christian concepts are completely fused. Michelangelo succeeded in achieving a true synthesis, creating an artistic language for the expression of the fundamental truths — pagan as well as Christian — about life, death, and afterlife. The conception that the soul lives after the death of the body, that it is victorious over matter, that its true life begins after its separation from the body, and that this new life consists in the contemplation of supreme truth is identical in ancient philosophy and Christian belief. There is no conflict between Plato's ideas on death and the afterlife and the text of the Requiem; therefore, the objection that the author's interpretation contradicts the doctrines of the Church is hardly valid. Michelangelo seems to have tried to create a new realm of departed souls, a kind of Christian Hades. The Medici Chapel is indeed inspired by the ancient portrayals of Hades, with its four rivers, with the departed souls in ancient armor contemplating the supreme truth instead of praying, and with doors reminding us of the entrance to that realm. The Christian other world is also reflected in the chapel, which was to have centered on the Virgin, the altar, and the fresco depicting the resurrection of Christ, planned but never executed. From the fusion of pagan ideas and Christian doctrines comes Michelangelo's universal language of art. This interpretation was first expressed by this author (*L'Arte*, N.S., V, 1, 1934, pp. 5–44) and, later, by E. Panofsky (1939), who completed it with the doctrine of the temperaments. On the other hand, an interpretation of the Medici Chapel as "an allegory of the princely and papal power of the Medici and their apotheosis" was proposed — on the basis of Vasari, Condivi, and Varchi — by F. Hartt (*Essays in Honor of Georg Swarzenski*, Chicago, 1951, pp. 145–55; *AB*, XXXII, 1951, pp. 115–49, 181–218). Interpretations based on the liturgy of the Requiem are given by H. Brockhaus (*Michelangelo und die Medici-Kapelle*, Leipzig, 1909) and H. von Einem (1959).

Michelangelo's style changes noticeably with the undertaking of the figures for the Medici tombs. The artist now looks at the spectacle of life as if from a distance. He contemplates the universal creative power, of which the individual beings are only the expressions. The forms become more elongated;

melancholy or passive suffering appears on the faces. Michelangelo begins to concentrate on death. It was a fortunate circumstance that the commission for the funerary chapel offered him the occasion to express his philosophy of death.

In May, 1527, Rome was sacked by the imperial army, and Clement VII was imprisoned. In the same month the Medici faction in Florence was forced out and a republican regime was once more instituted. Michelangelo, republican by tradition, put himself at the disposal of the republic and interrupted his work on the Medici Chapel. In 1528 he mourned the death of his favorite brother, Buonarroto. In January, 1529, he was elected to the Nove della Milizia and, in April, became governor general of the fortifications erected against the united armies of the Pope and the Emperor. He was sent (July–Aug., 1529) on a mission to study the celebrated fortifications of Ferrara, where Duke Alfonso d'Este received him with honors and asked him for a work; Michelangelo executed a cartoon for a Leda (ca. 1530; lost, but known through several copies; J. Wilde, in *Fritz Saxl Memorial Essays*, London, 1957, pp. 270–80). Foreseeing the betrayal of the republic by its governor general, Malatesta Baglioni, he took flight from Florence at the end of September, 1529, going to Ferrara and Venice, after which the Florentine republic declared him a rebel. In November, Michelangelo returned to Florence, under siege by the united armies of the Pope and the Emperor, during which he behaved in a courageous manner. Betrayed by Baglioni, the Florentine republic capitulated on Aug. 12, 1530, and Clement VII once more became master of the city. The artist hid in the tower of S. Niccolò (Vasari), but Clement VII soon pardoned him, asking only that he resume his work on the Medici Chapel. From the summer of 1530 until 1534 he was again at work on the figures for the Medici tombs, but the decoration was left unfinished when he departed for Rome in 1534.

Probably in the summer of 1532, in Rome, Michelangelo met for the first time Tommaso Cavalieri, the young nobleman whose beauty was celebrated by his contemporaries. Passion for him rejuvenated Michelangelo, and he wrote love letters and moving love poems inspired by the Platonic doctrine of love (Frey, 1897, nos. XLIII–XLVI, L–LII, LV, LXIV, LXV, LXXVI, LXXIX). As gifts for Cavalieri he executed drawings with mythological subjects, which are at the same time symbols of his love: *Ganymede* (known only through copies: Cambridge, Mass., Fogg Art Mus.; Windsor, Royal Colls.); *Tityus* (Windsor, Royal Colls.); *The Fall of Phaëthon* in three versions (PL. 539; London, Br. Mus.; Venice, Acc.); and *Archers* and *Bacchanal of Children* (both Windsor, Royal Colls., probably copies). This friendship persisted until the death of the artist. From the beginning of this passion Michelangelo no longer wished to live in Florence and decided to stay permanently close to Cavalieri in Rome. His voluntary exile in Rome may have had political motives as well as sentimental ones; the old republican did not want to live in a Florence transformed into a grand duchy of the Medicis. Later, he would feel morally obligated to remain in Rome until the completion of St. Peter's. A return to Florence was, nevertheless, among his projects at the end of his life; in 1554 he expressed the desire to be buried in his native city at the side of his father. Clement VII favored this transfer from Florence to Rome and promised him an important commission in the Vatican, but only two days after Michelangelo's arrival the Pope died (Sept. 26, 1534).

Michelangelo's late style in sculpture and painting was for a long time considered an expression of the tragic debacle of Michelangelo as a man. More recently the opinion has grown that he acquired complete freedom of expression only in his last period and that his late works reflect a reconciliation with destiny and a revelation of divine grace (Dvořák, Tolnay). This last period is characterized chiefly by his religious conversion, as a consequence of which the form, function, and meaning of his works changed. This change occurred in two stages. The works of the first 15 years of the last period, approximately until the death of Vittoria Colonna in 1547, are still conceived in powerful forms which correspond to the ideals of the Italian High Renaissance, although the content and the aim have already changed. In the last decade Michelangelo freed himself from these esthetic norms and developed a completely personal style. Made for the most part, without a commission, for the artist himself, his works of that time may be called subjective confessions. Without regard to the opinions of patrons and without taking into account his own artistic past, he now seemed to follow his inner voice alone. He rejected the fully developed, ideally beautiful natural form of the human body as a vehicle for the expression of his thoughts and tended to express the movement of his soul directly, that is, by disregarding the rational unity and beauty of the human body. In the forms, which now became elongated and fused together, he succeeded in expressing that supreme peace for which he yearned.

During the pontificate of Paul III Farnese (1534–49), a new period of high productivity opened for Michelangelo. Paul III admired and loved the master and raised him to the highest social level. This Farnese pope was a cultivated Humanist and a great patron of the arts, like his Renaissance predecessors; he was also a religious spirit inclined to the inner reform of the Church. He elevated men of high culture and great moral probity to cardinalships (Sadoleto, Contarini, Carafa, etc.). In confirming the institution of the Jesuits (1540) and in establishing a supreme tribunal against heretics (1542), he was the initiator of the Inquisition and of the Counter Reformation, which remained moderate under his pontificate, however. The serious atmosphere of the papal court was reflected also in the works of art executed during his reign.

Taking up an idea of his predecessor, Paul III commissioned Michelangelo to decorate the two end walls of the Sistine Chapel with frescoes, depicting the fall of the rebellious angels on the entrance wall (never executed) and a Last Judgment on the altar wall. Originally Clement VII seems to have thought of putting a representation, of modest dimensions, of the resurrection of Christ on the wall above the old altar, for which several drawings are still extant (PL. 539; Br. Mus.; Windsor, Royal Colls.; Tolnay, 1943–60, V). The motif of the movement of the resurrected Christ, with his Apollonian naked body and beardless face, anticipates the Christ in the *Last Judgment*. Therefore, the gigantic project of the *Last Judgment* seems to have originated from a much more modest project of a Resurrection mentioned in a letter of 1534. A. Perrig (*ZfKg*, XXIII, 1, 1960, pp. 19–41) has attempted to demonstrate that these drawings represent Christ in Limbo, but this is untenable because in them the tomb from which Christ has risen is also shown. Also untenable, it seems to the author, is the hypothesis of M. Hirst (*Warburg*, XXIV, 3–4, 1961, p. 178 ff.), which tries to connect all of Michelangelo's Resurrection drawings with the plans of Sebastiano del Piombo for the altar of the Chigi Chapel in S. Maria della Pace, Rome.

According to the original program for the decoration of the Sistine Chapel, a Last Judgement does not seem to have been planned. Two 15th-century frescoes, the altar by Perugino (also frescoed), and two lunettes painted by Michelangelo himself had to be destroyed to make way for his *Last Judgment*. In the earliest design (Florence, Casa Buonarroti) he kept the old altar (J. Wilde, *Die Grafischen Künste*, I, 1936, pp. 7–11), but the work was finally executed without taking into account the earlier decoration, including his own frescoes. In composition, in the proportions of the figures, and in color, he invented his *Last Judgment* as an independent work (though Sauer and Wilde do not agree with this opinion). The important thing for Michelangelo seems to have been the immediate impact of this work on the beholder, as an actual event taking place, and this may explain why he excluded a frame for it. The work is an expression of the spirit of the inner reform of the Church. The *Last Judgment* is on the west wall (altar wall) of the Sistine Chapel, as was traditional with this scene.

Michelangelo finished the cartoons for the *Last Judgment* in August, 1535. He began the execution of the work with the two top lunettes in the spring of 1536, and the whole work was finished in October, 1541, and unveiled on All Saints' Day (PLS. 533, 536; IV, PL. 179). The development of the idea of the composition can be reconstructed in part on the basis of the few existing drawings. There are published documents by H. Pogatscher, in Steinmann, 1901-05, II, and by G. Mercati, in D. Redig de Campos, *Il Giudizio Universale*, 1944.

The structure of the final composition has been misunderstood since it was described by Vasari and Condivi; they saw in it the traditional horizontal zones, one above the other, but overlooked the dynamic revolving currents that are the most essential innovation in this composition (Tolnay, *AQ*, III, 1940, pp. 125-46). Like Dante's *Divina Commedia*, Michelangelo's *Last Judgment* contains several meanings at once. The most obvious one is its eschatological meaning: the Second Coming of Christ and the Last Judgment. All the figures seem to depend on a single condemning gesture of Christ, and this dramatic unity is one of the chief innovations of the artist. Into the eschatological drama of humanity Michelangelo has also woven his own personal feeling of damnation; his self-portrait appears on the skin held by St. Bartholomew (La Cava, *Michelangelo scoperto nel Giudizio Finale*, Bologna, 1925). Some of his friends (e.g., Vittoria Colonna, Cavalieri) and some of his enemies (e.g., Biagio da Cesena, Aretino) may be depicted.

Beside its eschatological meaning, Michelangelo's *Last Judgment*, seen as a whole, is a cosmic vision, revealing humanity fatally subjugated to the revolving forces of the universe. It is the first artistic representation of a "heliocentric" system (anticipating Copernicus), with the Apollonian Christ as the Sun (*Sol Novus*), around which the constellations revolve, magically attracted and held at a distance at one and the same time (Tolnay, *AQ*, III, 1940, pp. 125-46; H. von Einem, *Kunstchronik*, VIII, 4, 1955, pp. 89-91). However, this cosmic aspect did not interest Michelangelo scientifically — as it would have Leonardo — but only to the extent to which it made the fate of humanity more palpable; it was the moral aspect that fascinated him. However, his contemporaries admired, above all, his unlimited virtuosity in the representation of the nude human body and his mastery in rendering physical movements and psychological expressions (Vasari, Condivi).

Interpretations of the groups and of the single figures of the *Last Judgment* have been proposed by W. Kallab (*Beiträge zur Kg. F. Wickhoff...*, 1903, pp. 138-53); E. Steinmann (1901-05); H. Thode (*Michelangelo, Kritische Untersuchungen über seine Werke*, Berlin, 1908-13); D. Redig de Campos (*RendPont Acc*, XIX, 1942-43, pp. 390-405); R. Feldhusen (*Ikonologische Studien zu Michelangelo's J. G.*, unpub. thesis, Hamburg, 1953); and H. von Einem (1959).

During the execution of the *Last Judgment* Michelangelo carved a bust of Brutus (III, PL. 389) for Cardinal Niccolò Ridolfi, another Florentine exile, at the instigation of the artist's friend, the Florentine republican Donato Giannotti. The year of Giannotti's entry into the Cardinal's service, 1539, is the earliest possible date for the bust, the style of which is close to certain heads in the upper zone of the *Last Judgment*. The influence of the ancient busts of Caracalla is obvious (A. E. Brinckmann). In the fibula on the shoulder there is a small relief of a head in profile, which is like those of Brutus on ancient coins (Tolnay, *BM*, LXVII, 1935, pp. 23-29; 1943-60, IV, fig. 92). Michelangelo's conception of Brutus is clearly expressed in the heroic disdain and indignation, obviously for the enemies of liberty, conveyed in the head of the bust. This was Michelangelo's idea, as expressed in Donato Giannotti's *Dialogues* (cf. D. J. Gordon, in *Fritz Saxl Memorial Essays*, London, 1957). At the same time, the *Brutus* is an "ideal portrait" of Michelangelo's own spiritual attitude as he had expressed it earlier in the *St. Proculus*, the *David*, and the *Moses*. The bust was finished by Tiberio Calcagni (Vasari); A. Grünwald (*Florentiner Studien*, Prague, 1914) distinguished Michelangelo's own work from that of his pupil.

During the execution of the *Last Judgment* (in 1536 or, more probably, 1538) Michelangelo became acquainted with Vittoria Colonna, widow of Fernando Francisco de Ávalos, Marqués de Pescara. His friendship with this extraordinary woman, who was so full of religious fervor, inflamed and deepened his own religious faith and led to his conversion (cf. Tolnay, 1949, p. 71 ff.). Vittoria Colonna was acquainted with the ideas of Juan de Valdés and was connected with his circle, which included Bernardino Ochino, Cardinal Reginald Pole, Giulia Gonzaga, and Pietro Carnesecchi. It was probably through Vittoria Colonna that Michelangelo adopted the doctrine of justification by faith alone, as shown by certain of his letters and poems. The conversations between her and the artist in the Church of S. Silvestro a Monte Cavallo (al Quirinale), in 1538, are reflected in the *Dialogues* of the Portuguese painter Francisco de Hollanda. Michelangelo addressed a series of gripping religious poems to her and made for her several drawings (presentation sheets) with religious subjects, including a *Crucifixion* (Br. Mus.); a *Pietà* (Boston, Isabella Stewart Gardner Mus.); and a *Christ with the Samaritan Woman* (lost, but known through copies). A drawing representing the Holy Family, entitled *Il Silenzio* (Duke of Portland's Coll.), may also have been made for Vittoria Colonna (C. Gould, *BM*, XCIII, 1951, pp. 279-82).

After finishing the *Last Judgment* Michelangelo wanted to return to work on the tomb of Julius II, but Paul III refused to allow him the time and charged the master with the decoration of his new private chapel, the Pauline Chapel, which had recently been erected by Antonio da Sangallo the Younger; Michelangelo was to paint frescoes in the central bays of the lateral walls. The first fresco was begun in 1542 and finished in 1545; the second was begun in 1546 and finished probably at the beginning of 1550. (For documents and analyses, see F. Baumgart and B. Biagetti, 1934.) From the style it can be deduced that the *Conversion of St. Paul* (PL. 537), on the left wall, is the first, and the *Crucifixion of St. Peter* (PL. 534) the second. Michelangelo conceived both compositions in relation to the architecture of the chapel, as they are both animated by movements in the direction of the altar. Both frescoes are conceived as personal confessions rather than as representations of historical events. (Cf. M. Dvořák, *Geschichte der Italienischen Kunst im Zeitalter der Renaissance*, II, Munich, 1928; Tolnay, 1951; H. von Einem, *Festschrift K. Bauch*, 1957.)

The *Conversion of St. Paul* derives from a Tuscan type of representation of the 15th century (H. van Dam van Isselt, *BArte*, XXXVII, 1952, pp. 315-19). In the figure of St. Paul, who suddenly seems to see the errors of his whole life in the moment of his blindness, Michelangelo probably expresses the moment of his own "conversion." The groups around him are symmetrically disposed, but within the symmetry each figure is contrasted to the figure opposite; the whole is animated by a revolving movement, beginning with the figure of Christ at the top left, continuing in the curve of St. Paul's body, and going up again to the top right, a device which is a further development of the similar movement in the *Last Judgment*.

In the *Crucifixion of St. Peter* Michelangelo tried to reconcile tradition, according to which St. Peter was at his own request crucified upside down, with the artistic exigencies of clear expression. For this reason he represented St. Peter's cross in a diagonal position at the moment of its erection. The figures in this fresco do not participate directly in the action, seeming, instead, to be involuntary witnesses who have come from various directions. They file past the cross without completely understanding what has happened; only the saint seems to be fully aware of the terrible crime of humanity. (A fragment of the cartoon is preserved in Naples, Mus. di Capodimonte.) The style and composition are a continuation of those of the *Last Judgment*, the monochromatic colorism of which he here transformed into a soft polychromy, indicating a return to the colors of the Sistine ceiling and, perhaps, the inspiration of Venetian painting.

In 1542-45, simultaneously with the first Pauline fresco, Michelangelo hastily finished the tomb of Julius II. He suppressed the slave figures and the Victories; instead of the latter he made two allegorical figures — a Rachel (or Contemplative Life) and a Leah (or Active Life) — thereby transforming the program of the triumphal mausoleum into a purely religious one. Of the figures executed earlier he kept only the *Moses*, which was placed in the lower central bay.

Julius III (1550-55), successor of Paul III, was an ardent admirer of the Jesuits and, at the same time, a hedonist in the manner of the great popes of the Renaissance. During his pontificate, Michelangelo made Ignatius Loyola an offer to make the plans and model for the Gesù (1554), the mother church of the Jesuits, out of devotion alone. He also made the designs for the completion of the Cortile del Belvedere in the Vatican, which served for the great festivals of the papal court. He also executed for himself the *Deposition* (PL. 526), which he wanted to have erected on his tomb in S. Maria Maggiore (Vasari). This group, begun before 1550, was abandoned in 1555 (H. von Einem, *JhbPreussKSamml*, LXI, 2-3, 1940, pp. 77-99) and, in the mid-17th century, transferred from Rome to Florence. The figure of Mary Magdalene had been reworked by Tiberio Calcagni. This work reverts to a traditional type of Pietà, an example of which is that of Fra Filippo Lippi in the Musée Henry, Cherbourg. The body of Christ is being supported vertically from under the arms by the Virgin and Mary Magdalene, while Joseph of Arimathea, behind Christ, dominates the group. The disposition of the four figures is about the same as that in the *Pietà* Michelangelo drew for Vittoria Colonna, but without the rigid and abstract symmetry of this earlier composition. In the *Deposition* the group is full of life and suppleness, with the figures drawn closer together, forming an elongated cone. According to Vasari, Joseph of Arimathea is an idealized portrait of the artist himself.

Under Paul IV Carafa (1555-59) nothing remained of the Humanist spirit of the papal courts of the past. This pope perfected the Inquisition and infused it with an inflexible rigor in the persecution of those whom the church considered heretics. A dry and prudish spirit reigned over the art of this period. During this pontificate Michelangelo himself was denounced as a heretic — a "Lutheran" — and the figures of the *Last Judgment* were partly repainted by Daniele da Volterra with loincloths to hide their nudity. Michelangelo probably executed at this time the second version of the *Rondanini Pietà*.

A reaction against the severe regime of the Carafa pope set in under Pius IV (1559-65). The new pope surrounded himself with a brilliant court and alarmed the population by his secular behavior. Nevertheless, he consolidated the Counter Reformation by reconvening the Council of Trent (1560-63) and by approving the Index Librorum Prohibitorum. He also gave the aged Michelangelo important architectural commissions (see below).

The *Rondanini Pietà* (PL. 532) is mentioned in the second edition of Vasari (1568), who tells us that, after having mutilated and abandoned the *Deposition* now in the Cathedral of Florence, the artist once again took up a marble in which he had already begun a Pietà. This first version probably dates from 1552-53 (F. Baumgart, *JhbPreussKSamml*, LVI, 1, 1935, pp. 44-56; D. Frey in *H. Kauffmann Festschrift*, 1956, pp. 208-32), and to it belongs the detached right arm of Christ and the still visible fragment of the Virgin's head (Tolnay, *BM*, LXIV, 1934, pp. 146-57). From this period come the three sketches on a sheet in the Ashmolean Museum, Oxford, that permit the reconstruction of the first version, which was inspired by a type of Trinity (cf. Tolnay, 1943-60, V, figs. 365-369). The second version was begun in 1555, and to it probably belong the polished legs of Christ, which are more elongated in proportion than the fragmentary arm of the first version. According to Daniele da Volterra (G. Daelli, 1865, no. 34), Michelangelo was reworking this group again only six days before his death. He seems to have destroyed the upper body of the Christ of the earlier versions, in order to carve it now from the body of the Virgin, and to have changed the position of the latter's head so that it faces forward, as does the head of Christ. Now the Virgin, instead of supporting the body of Christ, is leaning on it, and the two bodies seem to be fused together. The forms of these bodies appear deprived of all physical beauty; their silhouettes are angular, and their surfaces (except for those parts that belong to the first and second versions) are roughhewn. He used this device to obtain a diffused light and to attenuate the contrast of light and shade.

The late religious drawings of Michelangelo are a new attempt to evoke directly Christ's suffering; they have about them the intimate character of prayer. The series representing the Crucifixion with the Virgin and St. John, which Michelangelo originally drew as designs for a larger-than-life-size marble group (cf. Tolnay, 1943-60, IV, fig. 174), shows the sacrifice of Christ and its effect on the human soul and conscience (IV, PL. 276; London, Br. Mus.; Oxford, Ashmolean Mus.; London, Seilern Coll.; Louvre; Windsor, Royal Colls.; Rome, Vatican Lib.). In the Virgin and St. John are revealed the mourning, guilt, and remorse of humanity in confrontation with Christ's sacrifice. Michelangelo obviously tried to incarnate his own sentiments of guilt and remorse in relation to Christ's sacrifice, a bold innovation in place of the traditionally more objective conception. At the end of the series, however, the Virgin and St. John lean against the Cross as if to seek its protection (Br. Mus.; cf. Tolnay, 1943-60, V, fig. 231). Other subjects treated in his late drawings are the Expulsion of the Money-changers from the Temple (probably an allusion to the purification of the Church), Christ on the Mount of Olives, and the Annunciation (cf. Tolnay, 1943-60, V, figs. 208, 235-247). Perhaps the latest of the surviving drawings is a *Virgin and Child* (Br. Mus.) in which the Madonna is standing, while the Child is embracing her. There remain none of the attributes of the Virgin found in traditional representations; her clothes have become a transparent veil, and the theme is completely humanized into a moving expression of love. (For further discussion of the technique and dating of the late religious drawings, see Tolnay, *RepfKw*, XLVIII, 1927, pp. 157-205; R. Wittkower, *BM*, LXXVIII, 1941, pp. 159-60; J. Wilde, 1953; L. Dussler, 1959; Tolnay, 1943-60, V, p. 72 ff.)

Michelangelo died in Rome on Feb. 18, 1564, in the presence of Cavalieri, Daniele da Volterra, and two doctors. On February 19, his body lay in state in SS. Apostoli. In accordance with Michelangelo's wishes, his body was taken to Florence by his nephew Leonardo; this was done secretly, because the Romans wished to keep the body. On March 12, he lay in state in Sta Croce, the church of his quarter of Florence. On July 14, 1564, the funeral took place in S. Lorenzo; the membership of the Accademia (except for Cosimo I de' Medici and B. Cellini) was present. A description of the funeral can be found in the contemporary book *Esequie del divino Michelagnolo* (1564; see also *The Divine Michelangelo*, a facsimile ed., with trans. by R. and M. Wittkower, London, 1964). Of the funeral orations, those of B. Varchi, L. Salviati, and G. M. Tarsia were published in separate pamphlets in 1564. The tomb in Sta Croce was erected according to a design by Vasari, with the collaboration of the best of the younger sculptors; none of the master's own sculptures was integrated into it.

MICHELANGELO THE ARCHITECT. Michelangelo's approach to architecture was that of a sculptor; he associated buildings with living things. Instead of the traditional mathematical conception of architecture, his was essentially organic and consequently dynamic. He used the architectural members created originally for the "mathematical" conception, but he had to modify them to suit his own. Even in his lifetime his departure from the traditional Vitruvian canons was often decried as purely arbitrary, though it appears completely coherent and logical if one understands the new dynamic functions with which he was investing his architecture. In Michelangelo's works columns and pilasters, entablatures and architraves, walls and empty spaces are formed as if animated. Sometimes the tensions which he wants to express are so strong that they seem to break the traditional architectural unities (e.g., broken segments and tympanums); sometimes several designs of the same architectural *concetto* are juxtaposed, creating a new unity and amplifying the effect. Thus his architectural forms often evoke an actual emotional response in the beholder. Moreover, many of his architectural works symbolize an idea-content which determines, to a certain degree, the treatment of the forms.

According to Michelangelo, the character of architecture is organic and anthropomorphous: "It is certain that the parts of a building correspond to the parts of the [human] body" (Milanesi, 1875, p. 554); the same idea was also expressed by Vitruvius (*De architettura*, III, ch. 1), but in a different sense (cf. Tolnay, 1949, p. 95).

Scholarly research on Michelangelo as architect began with the great work of H. von Geymüller (1904) and gained new vigor in the work of D. Frey (1920). Special problems have been treated in articles by Tolnay (from 1927 on), R. Wittkower (1933, 1934), and H. Siebenhüner (from 1952 on). A recent monograph is J. S. Ackerman's *The Architecture of Michelangelo* (London, 1961).

From 1505, the date of his first project for the tomb of Julius II, Michelangelo designed architectural and figural ensembles in which the relationship between the sculpture and the architectural framework was newly determined. The geometrical lines of the architectural structure and the organic forms of the figures are combined into a whole. Such a compositional system is further developed in the Sistine ceiling, in which the painted architectural members are treated as dynamic entities. The figures do not always respect the lines of the painted architectural trellis: the *ignudi* overlap them. Nevertheless, the figures seem bound to their places and do not yet unite into an autonomous whole in front of the architecture. This was finally realized in the Medici tombs, where the figures together comprise an autonomous composition and the architecture serves as background. There results a juxtaposition of two contrary systems, the figural and the architectural, which play simultaneously one against the other, resulting in the effect of a kind of polyphony. In these three works Michelangelo subordinated the architectural to the sculptural forms. Vasari notes that the master fitted the architecture to the figures, rather than the figures to the architecture.

The marble exterior of the Chapel of Leo X in Castel Sant'Angelo, erected in 1514, is a work attributed to Michelangelo as early as the mid-16th century (drawing by Bastiano da Sangallo, Lille, Mus. des Beaux-Arts). That it is an early work becomes evident from the placement of the two window openings to the right and left of the central axis, an early Renaissance arrangement. In this case, however, the windows have broad proportions and horizontal, rather than arched, frames.

More original is the design of the *finestre inginocchiate* which Michelangelo made (ca. 1517) for the ground floor of the Palazzo Medici. The original drawing (Florence, Casa Buonarroti, 101) gives a more authentic idea of his intentions than the actual windows, in which the inner window frames are of a Quattrocento type, probably to conform to the style of the façade. In the drawing the inner frame seems to be subjugated by the outer frame, and the whole seems to suggest a conflict of forces.

At about the same time Michelangelo made his first sketches for the ground plan of the Palazzo Altopascio. A sketch in the Casa Buonarroti is on the back of a letter dated 1518. However, the drawings for the same project in the Casa Buonarroti (117A, 118A) should be dated later. This palace was intended for the Cavalieri dell'Altopascio and was actually to be the hospital of this confraternity, rather than a private palace.

His first designs for a major architectural work were those for the façade of S. Lorenzo (I, PL. 406), the parish and family church of the Medicis, a design which he entered in the competition of 1515 (Vasari). After the initial difficulties of getting the commission, Michelangelo began the work with enthusiasm, declaring in a letter: "I will do the most beautiful work that has ever been done in Italy." He executed at least three designs and four models. On the basis of the last model a contract was drawn up in January, 1518, but was annulled by the Pope two years later, before the execution could begin. For the rest of his life Michelangelo felt this to be a serious insult.

Several sketches and one wooden model are still in existence (Florence, Casa Buonarroti). A series of block sketches with measurements for the façade have been identified by this author (cf. Tolnay, 1943–60, IV, figs. 145–166), on the basis of which J. S. Ackerman has reconstructed the façade, concluding that it must have corresponded to the model. The authenticity of the wooden model in the Casa Buonarroti is proved by a still-preserved base (previously unnoticed) for one of the seated figures in the mezzanine on the narrow right flank of the façade. The sketches show that Michelangelo was inspired by the façade projects of his elderly friend Giuliano da Sangallo, whose designs (Florence, Uffizi) derived from the traditional Tuscan type of basilican church façades. Though Michelangelo's first projects have the same silhouette as Sangallo's drawings, he transforms the tectonic structure, which consists of three superimposed zones, into one conflict-filled, dynamically animated mass. He accentuates more strongly than Sangallo the central and the lateral parts, thereby creating a tension in the horizontal and in the vertical. The last design by Michelangelo, in which the whole façade is three stories high, is also inspired by a drawing of Giuliano da Sangallo's. Michelangelo first inserted a double mezzanine between the lower and upper stories, so that the weight of the mass was augmented. On the other hand, the continuing lines of the columns and *lesene*, which seem to play the role of buttresses or ribs, gave greater coherence to the orders. Michelangelo transformed the static and distinct forms of Sangallo into a united body, held together by a trellis of architectural members and heightened by the unity of the statuary program, which was to have included the most outstanding saints of Italy and the patron saints of the Medicis. The artist himself summed up the program in a letter, when he said that the façade would be "architecturally and sculpturally the mirror of all Italy." The aim of this program extended beyond the glorification of the Medici family and of Florence, and claimed to be universal by including the saints of papal Rome. (For further details on the façade, see Tolnay, *GBA*, 6th ser., XI, 1934, pp. 24–42; Ackerman, 1961.)

Clement VII, successor of Leo X, had an even greater appreciation of Michelangelo's art. Two of his main Florentine works were executed during this pontificate: the New Sacristy, or Medici Chapel, in S. Lorenzo, and the Biblioteca Laurenziana. During this period he developed his personal architectural language, based on the bichromatic architectural style of 15th-century Florence; in its hard and finely chiseled profiles the Florentine love for precision is recognized. However, Michelangelo's forms express a conflict between an inner energy and a passive outerframe which imprisons it, as the body imprisons the soul in the Louvre *Slaves*.

The first negotiations about the plans for a new library to house the manuscripts and books of the Medicis seem to go back to the autumn of 1523. The idea of locating the library within the cloisters of S. Lorenzo perpetuates the tradition of the Middle Ages. In the history of Renaissance architecture, the Biblioteca Laurenziana is the first library to be conceived in accordance with its secular purposes, rather than with the canonic forms of religious architecture. The execution began in the summer of 1524 and was suspended about two years later, once more to be resumed in 1530 and suspended in 1534. In 1550 the idea of finishing it was again put forward, but only ten years later was the staircase (PL. 540) from the vestibule to the reading room actually executed by Ammanati (q.v.). (For further details on the history of the library, see Tolnay, *MJhb*, N.S., V, 1928; R. Wittkower, *AB*, XVI, 2, 1934, pp. 123–218; Tolnay, *GBA*, 6th ser., XIV, 1935, pp. 95–105; and Ackerman, 1961.)

Michelangelo conceived the vestibule (*ricetto*) as a "preludium" to the reading room, a kind of transition between the outer world and the library itself (FIG. 903). It is a small but very high room with a curious order of encased *pietra serena* (gray sandstone) columns and a dim filtered light that penetrates from above (I, PLS. 381, 418). The visitor entering this room was meant to be separated suddenly from the noises of everyday life and enclosed in a solemn and higher sphere, preparing him for the spiritual work to be done in the library.

The original plan of the stairs was different, calling for a double flight against the lateral walls. This arrangement is seen in sketches preserved in the Archivio Buonarroti, in the Casa Buonarroti (89A), and in Haarlem, Teylers Museum (A33v), and also in a drawing in the Casa Buonarroti, showing the structure of one of the lateral walls. An early project for the library room (Casa Buonarroti, 42A) shows a wall structure similar to that of the vestibule.

The individual architectural forms of the vestibule are not explicable by normal standards. The stairway, instead of leading upward, seems to flow downward like a cascade of lava; the recessed columns do not appear to support any weight, but seem to pull vertically in both directions against the mass of the wall, and the resulting downward pressure is symbolized in the volutes. The motif of the "imprisoned" columns may have been inspired by ancient Roman buildings, such as one of the tombs on the Via Appia, which Giuliano da Sangallo drew in his sketchbook, now in the Vatican Library (Cod. Barb. lat. 4424, fol. 70v). But even here the recessed column still has its supporting function. It was Michelangelo who gave this motif the new meaning of tension.

Between the columns there are ten *pietra serena* tabernacle-niches with hard profiles, as if cast from metal. Because there is a base in each of them, it should be supposed that they were intended for a series of larger-than-life-size statues. Nothing is known of the program of the statues, but it seems likely that a series of *uomini illustri* was intended (i.e., a kind of pantheon of the greatest poets and philosophers of antiquity and of Italy since Dante).

Originally the master planned a secret library of triangular shape at the end of the reading room. Two ground-plan sketches for this room are still preserved. They show that its architecture was to resemble that of the vestibule, with its six recessed columns and nine niches for larger-than-life-size statues. The light would have come from a dome and from the oculi of the attic. The concept of the room as a kind of sacrarium brings to mind the apse of a church.

Aside from the Biblioteca Laurenziana, Clement VII wanted from Michelangelo a ciborium design for the main altar of S. Lorenzo in October, 1525. Actually this was to have been a stone canopy placed above the altar and supported by four antique columns; the ground plan is in the Casa Buonarroti, and a sketch of the whole project is preserved in the Archivio Buonarroti (identified by Tolnay, *MJhb*, N.S., V, 1928, pp. 377–476). This project was abandoned.

About 1531–32, Michelangelo designed a tribune for the

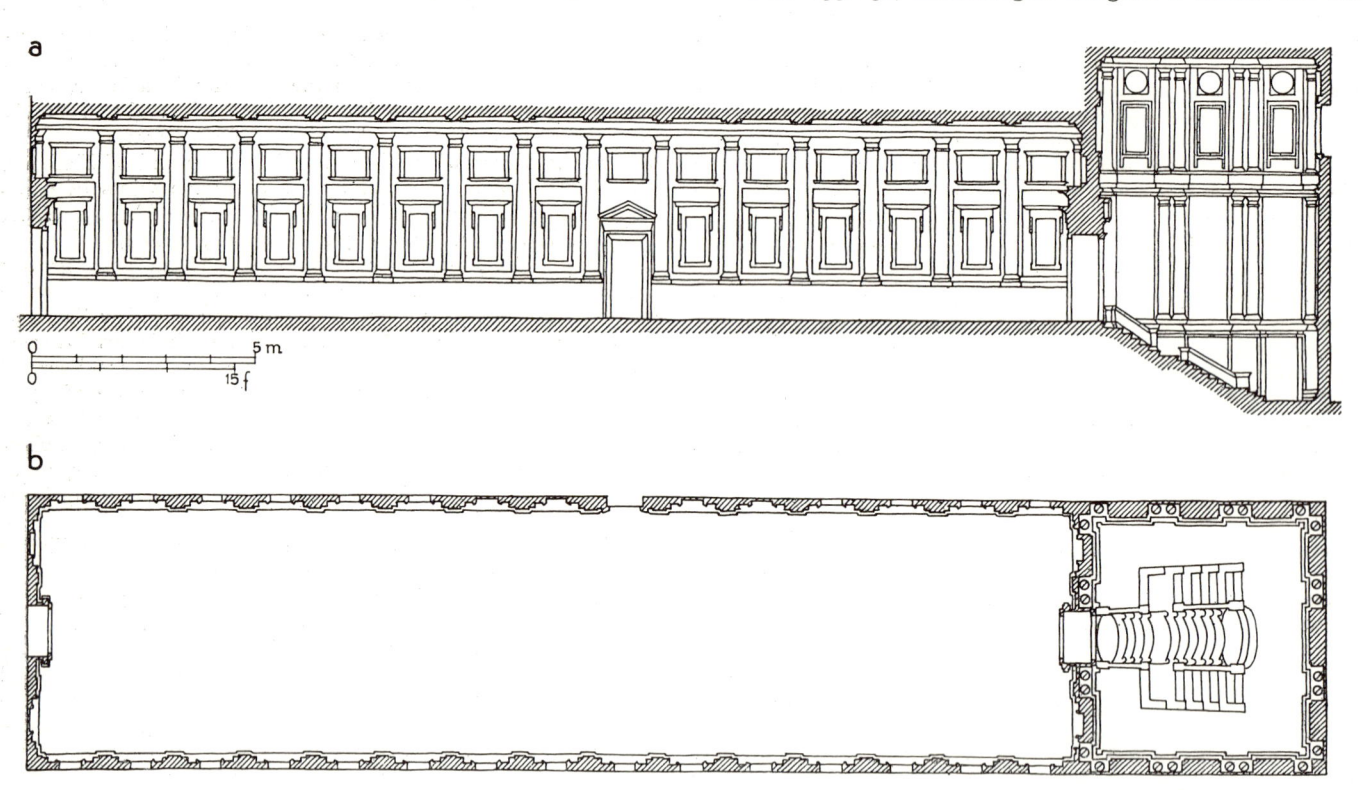

Florence, Biblioteca Laurenziana. (a) Longitudinal section; (b) plan (*from I monumenti italiani raccolti a cura della R. Accademia di Italia, Rome, 1934*).

This vestibule is the earliest enclosed space with a free-standing staircase in its center, and it became the model for the many monumental stairways in halls of the 17th and 18th centuries. The doorway at the top of the stairs opens into an extremely long and relatively low rectangular room, the reading room. Here the traditional three naves are abolished. A residuum of this motif of church architecture is retained, however, in the articulation of the wooden ceiling and in the floor. A sketch for the ceiling by Michelangelo has been identified by this author (Oxford, Ashmolean Mus.; cf. Tolnay, *CrArte*, N.S., II, 1954–55, pp. 237–49). The order of the pilasters comprises a kind of "metallic trellis," which is completed by the beams of the ceiling and the corresponding lines on the floor, forming a kind of "cage." The forms of the pilasters and of the windows are of utmost simplicity. Everything is done to give the room a serious aspect, propitious to the concentration of the user. Bright but diffused lighting is assured by the many windows on both longitudinal walls. Michelangelo's use of such contrasting effects in the vestibule and the reading room was obviously not a simple play of imagination. He wanted to express thus, in the last versions, the different functions of the two rooms.

Medici reliquaries on the inner side of the façade of S. Lorenzo, just above the entrance portal. Several drawings for it are still in existence. This is a delicate balcony of white marble with a rhythmically articulated balustrade. An enormous marble coat of arms of the Medicis in the central axis below the reliquary tribune seems to function as a kind of supporting console; it has the form of a stylized bucranium, and its unusual design should also be attributed to Michelangelo. The three doors of the tribune are small and framed, with utmost simplicity, in white marble. A balcony for the exterior façade was planned but never executed. The entrance door of *pietra serena* leading to this reliquary tribune from the second-floor loggia of the cloister of S. Lorenzo has herm-pilasters and anticipates the tabernacle doors of the Palazzo dei Conservatori on the Capitol in Rome.

At the beginning of 1529, the republican government of Florence, fearing that Clement VII might try to regain power there, decided to complete the fortifications of the city. Michelangelo was nominated Governatore Generale e Procuratore delle Fortificazioni della Città. Still preserved in the Casa Buonarroti are 23 drawings for this task (XII, PL. 87; cf. Tolnay, *AB*, XXII, 1940, pp. 227–37; 1951). In them Michelangelo reveals himself as a bold innovator of fortification designs.

Instead of the traditional geometric (square or triangular) bastions, he gave them zoomorphic shapes, reminiscent of cross sections of crustacea with long antennae and *orecchioni*. These fantastic and beautiful projects were, at the same time, highly practical, having been designed in accord with the recent development of heavy artillery. The curved shapes of the fortifications would prevent the enemy from approaching the city gates and would also allow an active artillery defense from within. The drawings reveal that Michelangelo busied himself with fortification plans for all the city gates, and not only that of S. Miniato as Vasari reports. These drawings are probably not studies for permanent fortifications in masonry and stone; their fantastic forms suggest, rather, that they were intended as temporary structures of packed earth (Vasari). During the siege, there was no time to build them in a more durable material. Their influence on future fortifications was considerable, however; Vauban, the greatest 17th-century engineer of fortifications, was influenced by them.

Michelangelo's most intensive activity as an architect began in his old age; not until he was seventy-one years old did he turn definitely to architecture. This switch was made, first of all, for practical reasons: Since the carrying out of architectural works lay in the hands of other artists and artisans, the aged Michelangelo could confine himself to making drawings for the projects and to directing their execution. He may also have had the reason that the abstract language of architecture corresponded to the inclination toward reasoning and synthesis of his old age (D. Frey, 1920).

With the pontificate of Paul III a new period of high productivity opened for the aged master. The Farnese pope was a great admirer of Michelangelo and appreciated fully his capacities as an architect. He commissioned him for the largest and most significant architectural tasks existing at that time in Europe — the reconstruction of the religious and civic centers of the Eternal City, St. Peter's and the Capitol (FIGS. 906, 907). Both these projects gave a new aspect to the physiognomy of Rome. Finished after the death of the artist, their style is quite distinct from that of Michelangelo's Florentine works. They are characterized by the simplification of lines and masses, by the rejection of the bichromatic style, and by the use of colossal orders executed in travertine, which appear for the first time in Michelangelo's architecture.

In September, 1546, shortly after the death of Antonio da Sangallo the Younger, Paul III appointed Michelangelo to direct the work on St. Peter's. At first he was reluctant to accept, but, when he finally agreed, he began to execute the designs with fervor and later even considered the carrying out of this commission as a kind of religious mission. He directed this undertaking for 17 years, during which the work advanced more than it had in the preceding 40 years. Successive changes in the building plan had been made by his predecessors: Bramante's central-geometrical plan was superseded by Raphael's longitudinal plan, and a compromise between these two plans was followed by Antonio da Sangallo the Younger. Michelangelo rejected the latter's project, with its towers of many shapes, its diverse orders of columns, its atrium, and its ambulatory, which took the light from the interior. Grandeur, simplicity, and majesty were lacking in the project of his immediate predecessor, and Michelangelo resolutely returned to Bramante's conception, which he thought to be superior because it was "clear, straightforward, luminous, and isolated from the Vatican Palace all around" (Milanesi, 1875, p. 535 f.). He gave the plan an even greater clarity by shortening the arms of the Greek cross, by suppressing the corner towers of Bramante (q.v.), and by reducing the size of the four spaces in the diagonal axes; thus the main dome became more dominant (FIG. 906). To consolidate the building he had to reinforce both the four innermost pillars, which support the dome, and the walls. To give a greater unity to the composition of the building he added to its outer walls the same order of colossal pilasters his predecessors had already planned for the interior and placed them in a rhythmic alternance.

Michelangelo made four models for this work. The first was a small clay model of the whole building (Sept.–Nov., 1546), perhaps recorded in a drawing attributed to E. du Pérac (Feltrinelli Coll.; formerly Dyson Perrins Coll.). On the basis of this model a larger wooden model of the whole building was made in 1546–47. This second model is probably the one

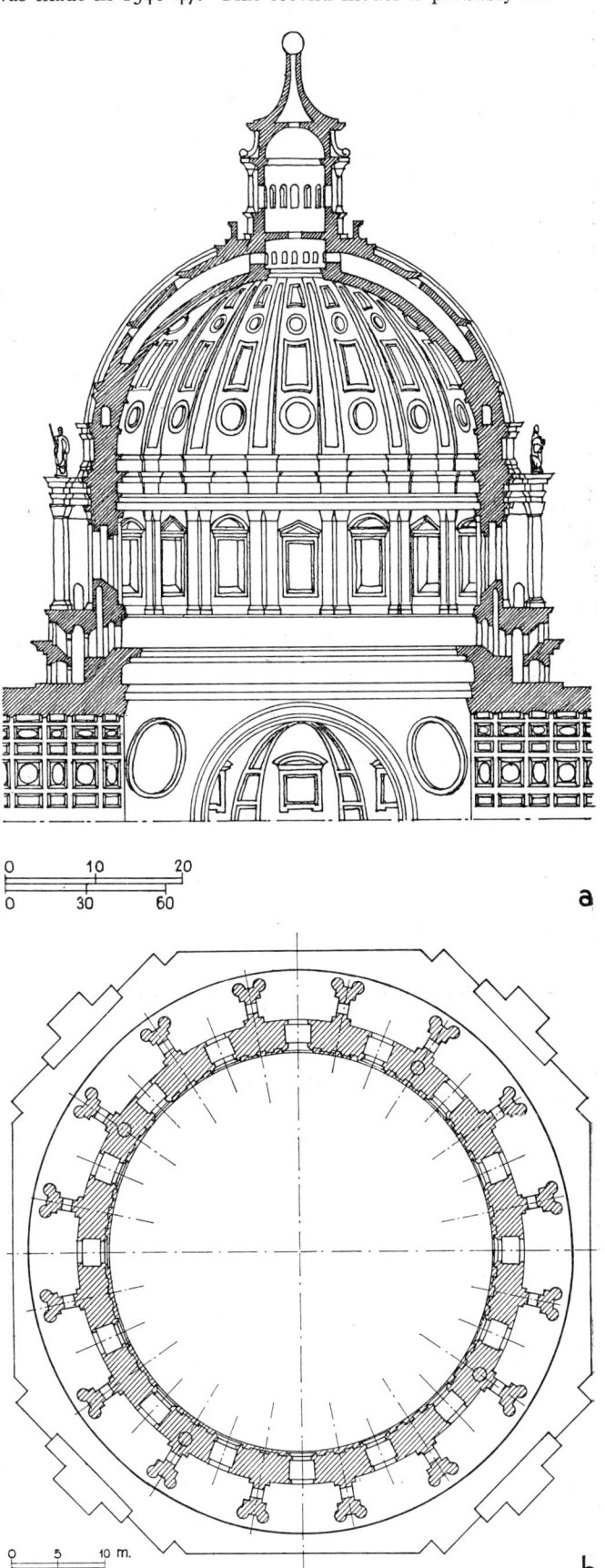

Rome, St. Peter's. (*a*) Cross section of the dome (from a print by E. du Pérac); (*b*) cross section of the drum (*from A. Schiavo, 1954*).

that appears in a painting by Passignano (Florence, Casa Buonarroti). In July, 1557, he made a clay model of the drum and the dome. Finally, between November, 1558, and November, 1561, a larger wooden model of the drum and the dome was constructed. This last model is probably identical in its drum and inner shell with the model still in the Vatican, formerly in the Museo Petriano (IV, PL. 193; cf. W. Körte, *JhbPreussKSamml*, LII, pp. 90–112; R. Wittkower, *ZfKg*, II, 1933, pp. 348–70). The outer shell was reworked later, supposedly by Giacomo della Porta or by Vanvitelli.

If one stands in the center of the space below the dome, it is still possible to realize the intentions of Michelangelo's design. When the expanding forces that radiate from the center through the four arms of the Greek cross reach the apses, they reverse themselves along the arches and seem to

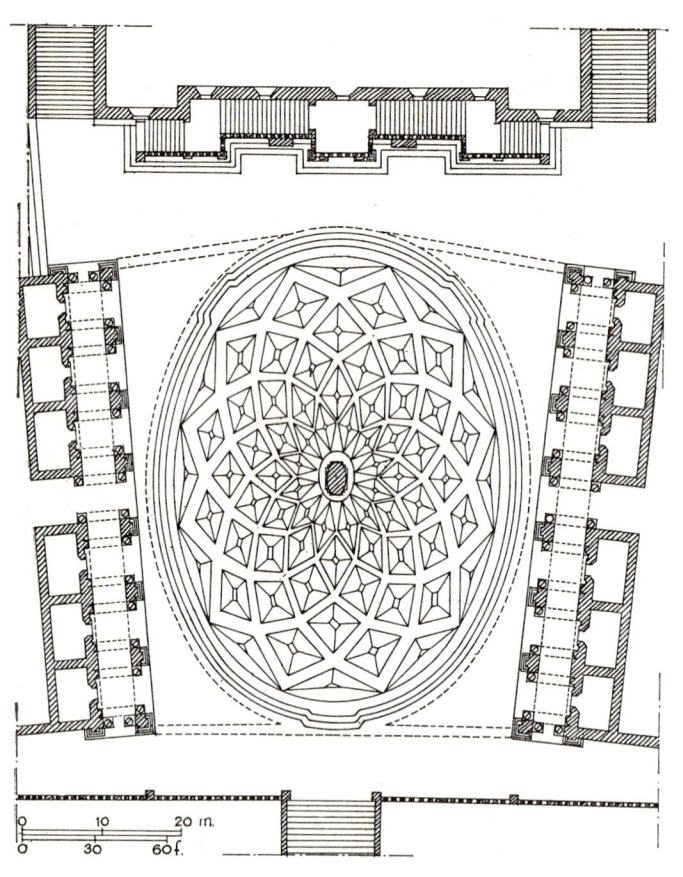

Rome, Piazza del Campidoglio, plan after an engraving of 1567 (*from C. de Tolnay, 1951*).

contract in the four colossal pillars; from there they ascend along the pendentives to the dome. The whole is like a grandiose organism animated by alternating movements of expansion and contraction. The centrally planned building, conceived until that time as immobile, became with Michelangelo a dynamic space.

From the west side (PL. 541) the body of the building appears as one enormous mass. Michelangelo accentuated the ascending forces by means of colossal pilasters in alternating rhythm — a rhythm which is repeated in the attic and in the double columns of the drum. The dome does not seem to rest on these columns but seems, rather, to rise from within the circle of the drum, as from a crater, and appears to be hovering above the building. Finally, at the summit of the cupola in the lantern, the motif of the double columns reappears on a smaller scale. Instead of the Renaissance principle of grouping geometric bodies, there is here the successive sublimation of one unified organism. It is still a much-discussed problem as to whether the elevated curve of the outer shell of the dome as we see it today really corresponds to the intentions of Michelangelo (cf. D. Frey, H. R. Alker, E. Panofsky, L. Beltrami, Tolnay, W. Körte, R. Wittkower, J. Coolidge, D. Gioseffi, J. Ackerman). The fact is that all the original drawings by Michelangelo (Lille, Mus. des Beaux-Arts; Haarlem, Teylers Mus.; Oxford, Ashmolean Mus.) show an elevated profile in the outer shell; on the other hand, this outer shell is shown in the engravings by Étienne du Pérac as a hemisphere. The late Oxford sketch of the lantern (1557–61), with a small section of the top of the dome, still shows several dome profiles and reveals that Michelangelo had not yet definitely decided which to use. Probably Michelangelo's last version was intended to be higher than the hemispherical dome of Du Pérac, but somewhat lower than the version seen in his earlier drawings in Haarlem and Lille (ca. 1546). In any case, the inspiration for the elevated outline of the dome came from Brunelleschi's dome of Florence Cathedral.

Michelangelo's façade design for St. Peter's was not followed. The project seems to have developed in his mind from a portico similar to that of the Pantheon, with six columns carrying a pediment (cf. sketch, Cod. Vaticanus 3211, fol. 92, identified by Tolnay, *RepfKw*, XLVIII, 1927, 157–205; Feltrinelli Coll.; formerly Dyson Perrins Coll.), to a more monumental portico with ten columns rhythmically grouped and a protruding central part with four columns in front of the ten (cf. Du Pérac's ground plan of 1569 and reconstructions based on it by H. R. Alker, V. Mariani, and J. Coolidge).

Perhaps Michelangelo's whole building implied a symbolism of the universe. According to tradition, the dome indicated the heavenly sphere, and it was this idea that Michelangelo expressed plastically in the hovering form of the dome and in the decoration he planned for the interior. The lower part of the building is conceived as a symbol of the earth, with its four apses corresponding to the four cardinal points. This "universal" meaning was appropriate to the double function of St. Peter's as martyrium of St. Peter and mother church of Christianity.

For further details about St. Peter's, see also the works by D. Frey; H. R. Alker; A. E. Brinckmann; E. Panofsky; L. Beltrami (*La Cupola Vaticana*, Vatican, 1929); Tolnay (*JhbPreussKSamml*, LI, 1930, pp. 1–48, LIII, 1932, pp. 231–53); G. Giovannoni (*Saggi sull'architettura del Rinascimento*, 2d ed., Milan, 1935); W. Körte (*ZfKg*, N.S., I, 1932, pp. 161–62); R. Wittkower, (*ZfKg*, N.S., II, 1933, pp. 348–70); J. Coolidge (*Marsyas*, II, 1942, pp. 63–123); G. Marchini (*BArte*, XLI, 1956, pp. 313–17); Ackerman (1961).

The other large commission that Paul III gave to Michelangelo was for the monumental rebuilding of the Capitol. During antiquity and the Middle Ages, the Capitol was associated with a universal idea; it was the center of the political life of Rome, the place from which the city and the imperium (i.e., the world) were governed. The idea of its importance remained always alive and seems to have inspired Michelangelo's designs.

When he received the commission from Paul III, the square of the Capitol lacked artistic unity; only on the west side did it have architectural links with the city below it. Michelangelo's idea was to transform this irregular agglomerate into an ensemble of three symmetrically disposed buildings which would frame a closed, oval piazza (FIG. 907). By means of a flight of steps, the *cordonata*, he joined this piazza at its central axis to the city below. Anyone ascending this majestic approach from the formerly small, cramped streets of the city found at the top a solemn and ordered world. Since 1538 the equestrian statue of Marcus Aurelius had stood on a temporary rectangular base in the center of the piazza. When Michelangelo decided to give the piazza an oval plan, he designed a new oval base for the statue (X, PL. 148). The oval in the center of the trapezoid area formed by the three buildings and by the balustrade on the fourth side produces the effect of two spaces, one inside the other. While the oval, decorated by a star ornament, symbolizes the centrifugal forces, centripetal forces seem to act on the buildings — another instance of the conflict between the expanding forces and the limits that contain them. The first project for the whole piazza seems to date from about 1546 (Tolnay, 1951; Ackerman, 1961), and not from 1561–63 as has been proposed by H. Siebenhüner (*It. Forsch.*, 3d ser., I, Munich, 1954). The oval is convex, probably meant to be the idealized shape of the Capitoline hill, the top of which suggests a pole of the earth. The globe may signify the earth, or perhaps the celestial globe, in which case Michelangelo would be reverting to an old tradition of symbolizing the celestial sphere, well known in ancient floor mosaics. The idea of Rome as *caput mundi* seems also to have guided him in his choice of ancient statues to decorate the piazza. The ensemble would thus illustrate the idea of Rome as eternal and universal. This meaning of the Capitol was first indicated by this author (*JhbPreussKSamml*, LI, 1930, pp. 1-48, LIII, 1932, pp. 231-53) and was later taken over by F. Saxl (*Lectures*, London, 1957, pp. 200-14). On the other hand, H. Sedlmayr (*JhbPreussKSamml*, LII, 1931, pp. 176-81) rejected any symbolic interpretation of the Capitol on a purely formalistic basis.

The only palace on the Capitoline hill dating from Michelangelo's lifetime is the Palazzo dei Conservatori (PL. 542), on which construction began in 1563. Sketches for it have been identified by the author (Oxford, Ashmolean Mus.; Tolnay, *BM*, XCVIII, 1956, pp. 379-80). It has in the lower story a portico with columns that support a second story with aedicula windows; this is surmounted by a large cornice reminiscent of that of St. Peter's. A colossal order of *lesene* and pilasters binds together the mass of the building. Under the pressure of such a gigantic yoke the columns of the portico seem to be pushed apart and the Ionic capitals seem to curl forcefully. Projects for the stairway of the Palazzo dei Senatori are on a sheet in the Casa Buonarroti (cf. Tolnay, 1943-60, III, fig. 125); this type of double staircase with two opposite flights of steps is anticipated in sketches by Leonardo (e.g., Ms. B., fol. 15b). Documents concerning the history of the Capitol in Michelangelo's time were discovered and published by this author (*JhbPreussKSamml*, LIII, 1932, pp. 231-53) and republished, with other documents, by P. Pecchiai (*Il Campidoglio nel Cinquecento*, Rome, 1950).

Mention should be made here of the Cathedral of Padua, the choir of which was designed by Michelangelo, according to documents in the archives. Originally, the entire building was designed by Jacopo Sansovino, but in January, 1551, the Cathedral chapter chose the drawing and model of the choir made by Michelangelo, which was then executed with the assistance of Andrea della Valle. The building was begun in May, 1552, and almost finished by about 1570; the first Mass was held there in 1582 (cf. *Due Lettere sopra la fabbrica della Cattedrale di Padova*, Padua, 1794, published anonymously, the author of which is Canonicus F. S. Dondi Orologio).

The colossal order of Corinthian pilasters is in the style of those of the palaces on the Capitol and of St. Peter's, but executed with less care. The forms of the windows in the choir and the transept remind us of Brunelleschi's in Sto Spirito, Florence. The whole building is impressive in its monumentality. However, its ground plan, with two transepts, is north Italian in origin and may revert to the design of Jacopo Sansovino. (Concerning the choir of the Cathedral of Padua, see the author's article in *Festschrift Herbert von Einem*, 1964/65.)

The building of the Palazzo Farnese was begun almost thirty years before Paul III appointed Michelangelo to complete it, in the autumn of 1546. Its architect was originally Antonio da Sangallo the Younger, who made his first designs for Cardinal Alessandro Farnese from 1517 on. He enlarged the first project after the election of the Cardinal to the papacy in 1534. (For the early history, see F. de Navenne, *Le Palais Farnèse et les Farnèse*, Paris, 1914; also, recent research has been done by W. Lotz. For further details of the history of Palazzo Farnese, see Tolnay, *JhbPreussKSamml*, LI, 1930, pp. 1-48; 1951; also H. Siebenhüner, *Wallraf-Richartz-Jhb.*, XIV, 1952, pp. 144-64; Ackerman, 1961.)

The following parts were executed in accordance with Michelangelo's plans:

1. On the façade, above the main portal, the great window with four green-marble columns and the Farnese coat of arms (XII, PL. 56). Sangallo had already planned a central window with freestanding and applied columns, the drawing of which is in Munich (identified by Tolnay, *JhbPreussKSamml*, LI, 1930, pp. 1-48). Michelangelo transformed Sangallo's arches into a horizontal lintel and added a pair of marble columns behind the outer ones. He gave the window greater depth and crowned it with a monumental coat of arms.

2. The monumental cornice at the top of the façade, of which Michelangelo first made a wooden model in the spring of 1547, and parts of which he finished in July of the same year (F. de Navenne). This cornice was bitterly criticized by followers of Antonio da Sangallo the Younger, whose opinion was expressed in a letter that S. Meller (*JhbPreussKSamml*, XX, 1909, pp. 1-8) attributed to Battista da Sangallo, which is known through a copy made later by Michelangelo.

3. According to Vasari, he enlarged the *sala grande* in the left corner of the façade, a room which is two stories high, the wall decoration of which was never finished.

4. He also made the design for the *ricetto* (vestibule) in front of the *sala grande*, which has a flattened barrel vault in the form of a half oval (Tolnay, 1951, PL. 243). Vasari expressly emphasizes the novelty of this innovation, which had an enormous success, especially in French architecture of the 17th and 18th centuries; it made possible the insertion of a mezzanine for servants' quarters above. This flattened barrel vault is reminiscent of the flattened oval arches of the bridge of Sta Trinita in Florence, which reverts to a design of Michelangelo, according to a 1560 letter of Vasari's (F. Kriegbaum, *RArte*, XXIII, 1941, pp. 137-44).

5. The travertine frieze on the upper story of the courtyard reverts also to Michelangelo, according to Vasari.

6. Inside the courtyard Michelangelo designed a new upper story. The piano nobile, a remodeling of Sangallo's with open arches, has windows that can hardly be attributed to Michelangelo on stylistic grounds. The authentic form of the courtyard is preserved in the engraving published by Antoine Lafréry in 1560, which probably reverts to the model. The engraving by P. Ferrerio — dated 1545, but published in 1650 — shows the piano nobile of the courtyard at the back of the façade with all the arcades open; this is, therefore, an independent engraving, probably reverting to the model or to an earlier drawing after it. The uppermost story of the courtyard is treated by Michelangelo as a heavy attic, in contrast to the Vitruvian tradition, according to which each upper story should be lighter than the one below it. The windows of the upper story (Oxford, Ashmolean Mus., 333) formulate again, and more forcefully, the motif of the subjugation of the inner frame by an outer frame.

7. According to the Lafréry engraving, Michelangelo left open three arches at the back of the courtyard and five outer arches facing the Tiber — a transparent loggia rather than a closed wing (Sangallo). He probably intended this loggia to be a kind of belvedere looking out on the garden, in the center of which he meant to put the just-discovered "Farnese Bull" (XII, PL. 121) as a fountain, and on the axis of which he planned a bridge across the Tiber (Vasari). This would have been one of the early examples of landscape composed as a prospect and would have shown how Michelangelo tried to combine the building with the environment.

During the pontificate of Julius III, Michelangelo offered, in 1554, to execute for Ignatius Loyola, out of devotion alone, the plans and model for the Church of the Gesù; also, the artist made plans, in 1552, to finish the Cortile del Belvedere, the scene of the great feasts of the papal court. The plan for the Gesù, perhaps preserved in a drawing in the Uffizi which was discovered by A. E. Popp (*MJhb*, N.S., IV, 1927, pp. 389-477), shows a longitudinal church consisting of a very large nave, thought to be barrel-vaulted, with four chapels on each side and a choir. This plan — perhaps inspired by that of L. B. Alberti for S. Andrea in Mantua — became the model for Vignola, who 14 years later actually began the construction of the Gesù.

Concerning Michelangelo's projects for the Cortile del Belvedere, see J. S. Ackerman, *The Cortile of the Belvedere*, Vatican, 1954. Vasari, says that Michelangelo replaced Bramante's circular flight of steps in front of the exedra by straight steps (II, PL. 346), similar to those he designed for the Palazzo Senatorio on the Capitol. (The balustrades of the exedra steps were rebuilt in the 18th cent.) A ground plan made after Michelangelo's steps is in the Scholz Scrapbook in the Metropolitan Museum, New York (No. 49.92.72). It seems more likely, however, that Michelangelo's idea of transforming the composition of this courtyard embraced more than these steps. Although the general disposition of the terraces with three flights of steps already existed in Peruzzi's project (Windsor, Royal Lib.), each flight was nevertheless treated as an entity in itself, and it seems likely that it was Michelangelo's idea to unify the three flights by identical balustrades ornamented by spheres (drawing, now Feltrinelli Coll.; formerly Dyson Perrins Coll.). In the mid-16th century the Cortile was called "Teatro di Palazzo" or "Teatro Vaticano." The stage for the representations was the lower courtyard, and the terraces and steps served as the auditorium. The most impressive view was from the Vatican Palace, facing the large exedra, and Michelangelo's steps served to crown the whole composition.

The idea of the foundation of a national church of the Florentines in Rome, S. Giovanni dei Fiorentini, dated back to the pontificate of Julius II, but it was only under Julius III that this idea was revived and the commission for it given to Michelangelo. In 1559 the Florentines of Rome asked him for a drawing and a model. Several extant drawings for this church show a central-plan building with what seems to be a baptismal font in the center. Since the church was to be dedicated to John the Baptist, Michelangelo seems to have conceived it as a baptismal church. The earliest sketches show that he followed a plan by Antonio da Sangallo (Florence, Uffizi), but in later designs he freed himself from this geometric scheme, arriving at a dynamic plan that is a more concentrated version of St. Peter's. A drawing by G. A. Dosio, representing the lost model, has been discovered by C. L. Ragghianti and published by E. Luporini (*CrArte*, XXIV, 1957, p. 458).

The chronology of the three drawings for the ground plan (K. Frey, 1909–11, 296, 295, 294) was established by A. E. Popp. D. Frey identified a drawing in the Casa Buonarroti (36A) as belonging to S. Giovanni dei Fiorentini. Another drawing on the verso of Frey 295 was identified by the author in 1932. There were probably two models: One with segmented entablatures was copied in the prints by J. Lemercier (1607) and V. Régnard (1684); another with triangular entablatures was copied by Dosio. Also, the interior articulation of the dome is slightly different in Dosio's drawing than it is in the other two prints.

The pontificate of Pius IV was characterized by a secular tendency. During this period, the last of Michelangelo's life, the artist developed his last architectural style. He now created a style no longer characterized by the conflict between dynamic space and walls, but by the dematerialization of walls and by the fluctuation of space. These tendencies in his last architectural designs correspond to those in his latest sculptures and drawings.

When Pius IV gave the Baths of Diocletian to the Carthusians for conversion into a church and monastery in 1561, Michelangelo was charged with the designs for this work. He transformed the tepidarium into the Church of S. Maria degli Angeli, which was redecorated in the mid-18th century by Vanvitelli. The most important information about Michelangelo's transformation of the baths into a church comes from a contemporary chronicle published by P. Pasquinelli (cf. *Roma*, III, 1925, pp. 349–56, 395–407), which was used by this author (*JhbPreussKSamml*, LI, 1930, pp. 1–48), who also published a view of the interior of the church as it appeared in 1703, about forty years before Vanvitelli's redecoration. H. Siebenhüner (*MJhb*, 3d ser., VI, 1955, pp. 179–206) adopted these conclusions. The old views show that the artist tried to conserve the ancient character of the enormous hall by keeping the eight colossal columns and reconstructing the primitive vaults. The latter seem to swell like sails and to be held back by the columns. They express perhaps the ancient concept of the "celestial tent" or the "heavenly canopy" mentioned in the Old Testament (Isaiah 40:22). The effect of the mass of the walls was eliminated by leaving large open rooms, transformed into chapels, on the sides of the main room.

Michelangelo's last architectural work, the Sforza Chapel in S. Maria Maggiore, was actually executed by a pupil, Tiberio Calcagni — a fact that is quite visible in the dry profiles and ornaments. The ground plan, which is Michelangelo's, has a surprising originality, however. Its effect is based on the contrast between the plastic pillars with columns and the development of the rounded walls. The pillars are placed diagonally so that the dimensions of the space cannot be controlled. Again the vault suggests the "heavenly tent." Michelangelo also designed a small façade, or entrance, for the Sforza Chapel, which was destroyed in 1748. An 18th-century drawing, made before its destruction, is in Paris, Bibliothèque Nationale, Cabinet des Estampes (identified and published by Tolnay, in *Urbanisme et Architecture, Mélanges Lavedan*, Paris, 1954, pp. 361–62). The idea of this little façade is a further development of that of the Chapel of Leo X in Castel Sant'Angelo.

Pius IV also asked Michelangelo to redesign the gates of Rome, and Vasari states that the artist made numerous drawings for them, but only Porta Pia was built, from 1561 on (PL. 542). The present upper story is a 19th-century addition. The original design is preserved in a 1568 engraving by B. Faleti (cf. Tolnay, *JhbPreussKSamml*, LI, 1930, p. 44). In the center of the yellowish-pink, crenelated brick wall rises an enormous travertine portal; its curious forms suggest ascending forces in the lateral pilasters and in the broken segment, which is subjugated by a triangular tympanum. The portal seems to symbolize the tragic splitting asunder of vital forces, and the whole city gate becomes a kind of *memento mori*. It is obviously composed to be seen in the perspective of the long straight road leading to it, which Pius IV had built. An unpublished drawing of the 16th century (Paris, École des Beaux-Arts) seems to indicate that the upper floor of Porta Pia was not finished at that time. There are also two unpublished drawings after Porta Pia in the Scholz Scrapbook, in the Metropolitan Museum, New York (No./49.92.56r and v). The development of Michelangelo's idea can be followed through the drawings (Florence, Casa Buonarroti; one in Haarlem, Teylers Mus.; one in Windsor, Royal Lib.); also, an earlier version can be seen on a medallion of Pius IV, the design of which is in the Casa Buonarroti (106A.r.).

The probable scenographic inspiration of the composition can be seen in a Vatican fresco in which there is a view of Via Pia, at the end of which emerges Porta Pia (cf. E. B. MacDougall, *JSAH*, XXIX, 1960, pp. 97–108).

MICHELANGELO THE POET. During his lifetime Michelangelo's poetry was known only to the small circle of his friends. Although Luigi del Riccio and D. Giannotti planned to publish the poems, they were actually printed the first time, in revised form, by Michelangelo's grandnephew in 1623. The poems were rediscovered during the romantic period, between 1820 and 1850, from which time date the first translations in French and in German (1826). The first appreciation of his poems as intimate confessions appeared anonymously, in 1833, under the title *Essai sur Michel-Ange considéré comme poète*, the author of which was Lambruschini (cf. E. Dörken, 1936, p. 80 ff.).

Since the middle of the 19th century the essence of Michelangelo the man has often been defined entirely on the basis of his poems (Quinet, Michelet, Romain Rolland, etc.). This is one of the reasons why the late period of Michelangelo has been seen only as a kind of spiritual debacle. The publication of the poems in their authentic form by C. Guasti (1863) and by K. Frey (1897) was of great importance. A recent critical edition of these poems by E. N. Girardi (1960) also contains a new chronology. The essential analyses of his poetry are those of Friedrich Gundelfinger (Gundolf), Georg Simmel, Thomas Mann, and Benedetto Croce. (See also N. A. Robb, *Neoplatonism of the Italian Renaissance*, London, 1935, p. 239 ff.)

Michelangelo was not a poet by profession, and he did not reach in his poems the perfection he achieved in the plastic works of his youth and maturity. Nevertheless, even in his lifetime, he was known as a poet. Proofs of this are his portrait as poet in Raphael's *Parnassus* (I, PL. 307; identified by Tolnay, in *Friedrich Gerke Festschrift*, Baden-Baden, 1961, pp. 167–72) and the first published book about him, Varchi's *Due Lezioni* (1549), which had as its subject two of his poems.

It can be said that Michelangelo applied sculptural methods to his poetic creations, because they seem to be carved with effort from the rough matter of the language. In his poems the Tuscan language has a forcefulness reminiscent of Dante and is distinguishable from the sweet melodious language of contemporaneous Tuscan poets. As in his plastic works of art, he omitted external descriptive details, such as landscape, and only the intensity of his sentiments was allowed to manifest itself. This subjective immediacy and intensity raised Michelangelo's poetry above its models (Petrarch, Poliziano, Lorenzo de' Medici), probably making it the earliest purely lyrical expression in European literature.

The themes of his poems are love, art, and faith. The inspiration came directly from personal experience, but, especially in his youth, he expressed himself in the conventional metaphors of the Petrarchists. Later, the influence of Dante became more important, and at the end he arrived at a poignant personal language. In his poems of his youth his eroticism was not yet sublimated; in his maturity he expressed the tragic fatefulness of love, in his verses written to Cavalieri, and spiritualized his passion for physical beauty, in which he saw the way to the Divine Idea. Then came the poems to Vittoria Colonna, which were written as expressions of an almost religious adoration of this beloved woman. Finally, in his late, religious poems he expressed his doubts about the sincerity of his own faith, imploring the divine mercy to justify himself and invoking directly God the Saviour. The succesive spiritualization of the objects of his love is similar to that of Dante and Petrarch, but with the difference that with Michelangelo the objects change at each level — the "beautiful and cruel lady" (*donna bella e crudele*), Cavalieri, Vittoria Colonna, God. His way to catharsis was not an ascent free of struggle but a continuous conflict between his sensuality and his spiritual yearning.

SOURCES. *a. Literature of art*: F. de Hollanda, De pintura antigua, 1548 (ed. J. de Vasconcellos, Porto, 1918); B. Varchi, Due Lezioni, Florence, 1549; Vasari; A. F. Doni, I Marmi, 4 vols., Venice, 1552-53; A. Condivi, Vita di Michelagiolo Buonarroti, Rome, 1553; L. Dolce, Dialogo della pittura intitulato l'Aretino, Venice, 1557; J. Giunti, Esequie del Divino Michelagnolo Buonarroti, Florence, 1564; L. Salviati, Orazione nella morte di Michelagnolo Buonarroti, Florence, 1564; G. M. Tarsia, Oratione o vero discorso fato nell'esequie del divino Michelagnolo Buonarroti, Florence, 1564; B. Varchi, Orazione funerale fatta e recitata da lui pubblicamente nell'esequie di Michelangiolo Buonarroti in Firenze, Florence, 1564; B. Cellini, Due trattati, Florence, 1568 (Eng. tr., C. R. Ashbee, London, 1898); B. Cellini, Vita (ed. O. Bacci, Florence, 1901); D. Giannotti, Dialogi de' giorni che Dante consumò nel cercare l'Inferno e il Purgatorio (ed. D. Redig de Campos, Florence, 1939). *b. Letters and documents*: J. W. Gaye, Carteggio inedito d'artisti dei secoli XIV, XV, XVI, II-III, Florence, 1840; G. Daelli, Carte Michelangiolesche inedite, Milan, 1865; G. Milanesi, Le lettere di Michelangelo Buonarroti, Florence, 1875; G. Milanesi, Les correspondants de Michel-Ange, I: Sebastiano del Piombo, Paris, 1890; K. Frey, Sammlung ausgewählter Briefe an Michelangiolo Buonarroti nach der Originalen des Archivio buonarrotiano, Berlin, 1899; G. Vasari, Literarischer Nachlass (ed. K. and H. W. Frey), 3 vols., Munich, 1923-40; R. Wolf, Ismeretl aen Michelangelo-Iratok, Rome, Budapest, 1931; W. Maurenbrecher, Die Aufzeichnungen des Michelangelo Buonarroti im Britischen Museum in London und im Vermächtnis Ernst Steinmann in Rom, Leipzig, 1938; E. H. Ramsden, The Letters of Michelangelo, 2 vols., Stanford, 1963. Other letters and documents are published in the monographs of Grimm, Gotti, Steinmann, Baumgart, Redig de Campos, Symonds, and Tolnay.

BIBLIOG. *General works*: *a. Bibliography*: E. Steinmann and R. Wittkower, Michelangelo Bibliographie 1510-1926, Leipzig, 1927; E. Steinmann, Michelangelo im Spiegel seiner Zeit, Leipzig, 1930, pp. 65-94; E. Dörken, Geschichte des französischen Michelangelobildes von der Renaissance bis zu Rodin, Bochum, 1936, pp. 166-70; P. Cherubelli, Supplemento alla bibliografia Michelangiolesca, 1931-1942, in Michelangelo Buonarroti nel IV centenario del Giudizio Universale, Florence, 1942, pp. 270-304; P. Barocchi, in Vasari, La Vita di Michelangelo, I, Milan, 1962, pp. 341-76 (bibliog.). See also the following works. *b. Monographs*: H. Grimm, Leben Michelangelos, 2 vols., Hanover, 1860-63 (Eng. trans., F. E. Bunnett, 2 vols., Boston, London, 1865); A. Gotti, Vita di Michelangelo Buonarroti narrata con l'aiuto di nuovi documenti, 2 vols., Florence, 1875; A. Springer, Michelangelo in Rom, Leipzig, 1887; J. A. Symonds, The Life of Michelangelo Buonarroti, 2 vols., London, 1893; C. Justi, Michelangelo, Leipzig, 1900 (2d ed., Berlin, 1909); H. Thode, Michelangelo und das Ende der Renaissance, 3 vols. in 4, Berlin, 1902-13; R. Rolland, La vie de Michel-Ange, Paris, 1907 (Eng. trans., F. Lees, New York, 1912); H. Mackowsky, Michelagniolo, Berlin, 1908 (6th ed., 1939); E. Carli, Michelangelo, Bergamo, 1942; C. de Tolnay, Michelangelo, 5 vols., Princeton, 1943-60; G. Papini, Vita di Michelangiolo nella vita del suo tempo, Milan, 1949; C. de Tolnay, Werk und Weltbild des Michelangelo, Zürich, 1949; C. de Tolnay, Michelangiolo, Florence, Paris, 1951; H. von Einem, Michelangelo, Stuttgart, 1959; C. H. Morgan, The Life of Michelangelo, New York, London, 1960; R. J. Clements, Michelangelo's Theory of Art, New York, 1961. *Single works or periods*: *a. Youth*: H. Wölfflin, Die Jugendwerke Michelangelos, Munich, 1891; K. Frey, Michelangelo Buonarroti: Sein Leben und sein Werke, I, Berlin, 1907. *b. Sistine Chapel*: E. Steinmann, Die Sixtinische Kapelle, 2 vols., Munich, 1901-05; A. Bertini, Michelangelo fino alla Sistina, Turin, 1942; D. Redig de Campos and B. Biagetti, Il Giudizio Universale di Michelangelo, Vatican City, 1944. *c. Tomb of Julius II*: C. Justi, Michelangelo, Leipzig, 1900; A. E. Popp, Two Torsi by Michelangelo, BM, LXIX, 1936, pp. 202-13; K. A. Laux, Michelangelos Julius-monument, Berlin, 1943. *d. Medici Chapel*: A. E. Popp, Die Medici-Kapelle Michelangelos, Munich, 1922. *e. Pauline Chapel*: F. Baumgart and B. Biagetti, Gli affreschi di Michelangelo e di L. Sabbatini e F. Zuccari nella Cappella Paolina in Vaticano, Vatican City, 1934. *f. Architecture*: H. von Geymüller, Michelangelo Buonarroti als Architekt, Munich, 1904; D. Frey, Michelangelo Studien, Vienna, 1920; A. Schiavo, La vita e le opere architettoniche di Michelangelo, Rome, 1953; A. Schiavo, Santa Maria degli Angeli alle Terme, B. Centro di S. per la storia dell'arch., 8, 1954, pp. 15-42; J. S. Ackerman, The Architecture of Michelangelo, 2 vols., London, 1961. *g. Drawings*: B. Berenson, The Drawings of the Florentine Painters, 2 vols., London, New York, 1903 (I disegni dei Pittori Fiorentini, 3d ed., Milan, 1961); K. Frey, Die Handzeichnungen Michelangiolo Buonarroti, 3 vols., Berlin, 1909-11 (cf. Nachtrag zu Karl Frey, ed. F. Knapp, Berlin, 1925); A. E. Popham and J. Wilde, The Italian Drawings of the 15th and 16th Centuries ... at Windsor Castle, London, 1949; J. Wilde, Italian Drawings in the Department of Prints and Drawings in the British Museum: Michelangelo and His Studio, London, 1953; K. T. Parker, Catalogue of the Collection of Drawings in the Ashmolean Museum, II, Oxford, 1956; L. Dussler, Die Zeichnungen des Michelangelo, Berlin, 1959; P. Barocchi, Michelangelo e la sua scuola: I disegni di Casa Buonarroti e degli Uffizi, 2 vols., Florence, 1962. *h. Poetic works*: C. Guasti, Le Rime di Michelangelo Buonarroti, Florence, 1863; K. Frey, Die Dichtungen des Michelangelo Buonarroti, Berlin, 1897; E. N. Girardi, Le Rime di Michelangelo Buonarroti, Bari, 1960 (with a new chronological arrangement).

Charles de TOLNAY

Illustrations: PLS. 524-542: 5 figs. in text.

MICHELOZZO (Michelozzo di Bartolommeo, sometimes known as Michelozzo Michelozzi). Italian bronze caster, sculptor, and architect (b. Florence, 1396; buried in S. Marco, Florence, Oct. 7, 1472). First mentioned as a bronze caster at the Florentine mint in 1410, Michelozzo worked from 1417 to 1424 as assistant in Ghiberti's studio, employed on the north Baptistery doors and the statue of St. Matthew for Orsanmichele (Florence). From 1425 on, Michelozzo shared a workshop with Donatello, and they collaborated on various works until 1438. The two artists are mentioned together for the marble tabernacle for the statue of St. Louis of Toulouse (Orsanmichele), the reliefs for the Siena Baptistery font, and for the exterior pulpit of the Cathedral of Prato. In these works Michelozzo's share is generally considered to have been confined to the casting and the architectural parts, probably on Donatello's designs. On the other hand, in the two important tombs they executed together — that of the antipope John XXIII (Baldassare Coscia) and the Brancacci monument — it is difficult to establish the extent of Michelozzo's participation in the designs. The Coscia monument (XII, PL. 16) is important as the prototype of the Renaissance tomb. Here, and in the Brancacci tomb (Naples, Sant'Angelo a Nilo), the new classicizing spirit is introduced into a form that is still Gothic, while the reliefs and statues of the dismantled tomb of Bartolomeo Aragazzi (III, PL. 391; London, Vict. and Alb.) illustrate the transformation to the completely classical style that was to be a lasting influence on later Renaissance tombs.

Beginning in 1417, and for thirty years thereafter, Michelozzo received frequent commissions from Cosimo de' Medici, whom he accompanied in the latter's exile in Venice in 1433-34 and for whom he rebuilt the Medici villas around Florence: Careggi, Castello di Trebbio, and Cafaggiolo (VIII, PL. 191). In this last, Michelozzo made a decorative feature of the fortress character of the building and introduced windows and details typical of the rather austere style of the Florentine Renaissance.

Michelozzo's earliest religious architecture is believed to have been the rebuilding of the Monastery of S. Francesco in Mugello (also known as Bosco ai Frati); the sacristy of Sta Trinita in Florence has also been attributed to him. In the 1430s Michelozzo redesigned the façade of the Church of S. Agostino in Montepulciano (VIII, PL. 191), which is Renaissance in form but has Gothic traits in its niches and the architectural frame of the lunette. In Florence he modified and extended the Monastery of S. Marco, also for Cosimo, and won the commission for the Medici (Riccardi) Palace (XII, PL. 4). These works, perhaps Michelozzo's most famous, characterize his mature style, which was strongly influenced by Brunelleschi. The architecture of S. Marco (cloisters, refectory, cells), however, is reminiscent of the architectural forms found in the predella panels of Fra Angelico. The library, in particular, recalls Angelico's delicate white structures, and its linear rhythms and volumetric clarity are far from the typical concentration of Brunelleschi. S. Marco was to become the model for many later monastic buildings in Tuscany, and the Medici Palace, with its combination of grandiosity, elegance, and technical accomplishment, remained the standard palace design for the new ruling class.

For almost forty years Michelozzo was employed on the rebuilding of SS. Annunziata (Florence). Although it was largely transformed in the 17th century and later, the plan has remained intact, as have also the Chiostrino dei Voti, the sacristy, and the shrine of the Annunciation. Several works in and around Florence have been attributed to Michelozzo as designer, if not actually carried out by him, such as the Convent of S. Maria Maddalena in Pian di Mugnone (I, PL. 388), which illustrates the characteristic simplicity and sobriety of his style. His other principal Florentine works are the Chapel of the Novitiate in Sta Croce, the shrine of the Crucifix in S. Miniato al Monte, and the silver statue of St. John the Baptist for the Baptistery (Florence, Mus. dell'Opera del Duomo). Michelozzo succeeded Brunelleschi as *capomastro* of the Cathedral of Florence in 1446, but in the last years of his life most of his work was done outside Florence.

In Milan, the Portinari Chapel in S. Eustorgio (XII, PL. 3) and the Medici bank are traditionally attributed to him, although of the latter only the portal is now accepted as his (XII, PL. 3). In Pistoia he designed S. Maria delle Grazie, a plan strongly influenced by Brunelleschi, and in 1462 he is recorded in Ragusa (now Dubrovnik, Yugoslavia), where he was commissioned to rebuild the Palace of the Rectors, which had been damaged by fire.

Sculpturally Michelozzo's style is transitional from Gothic to Renaissance via an interpretation of classic art that sometimes verges on academism. His earliest sculptures are reminiscent of Ghiberti, with traces of the great sculptors of the 14th century. The Aragazzi monument is perhaps his most individual work and is characterized by a somewhat severe classicism, with the accent on strong forms rather than on refinement of detail. Psychologically he is far less subtle than Donatello, but his works have a strength and character of their own.

As an architect, Michelozzo is much more important, for he extended the influence of the Renaissance style and helped spread the new Humanist principles enunciated by Brunelleschi and Leon Battista Alberti (qq.v.). Although Michelozzo seems scholastic by comparison and his interpretation is characterized by a closer adherence to medieval tradition, especially in his religious works, he nevertheless contributed to the diffusion of these principles by applying them practically and creating a simple, economical, and functional style.

BIBLIOG. O. Morisani, Michelozzo architetto, Turin, 1951; V. Martinelli, Donatello e Michelozzo a Roma, Comm 8, 1957, pp. 167-94, 9, 1958, pp. 3-24; J. Pope-Hennessy, Italian Renaissance Sculpture, London, 1958.

Marco CHIARINI

MICRONESIA. Constituting one of the four principal divisions of Oceania, Micronesia comprises an estimated 2,500 islands with a combined land area of less than 1,500 square miles. The insular fragments are almost lost in the vast reaches of the western Pacific Ocean.

Major geographic subdivisions include the volcanic Marianas, which extend north from Guam toward Japan; the west-east-oriented Carolines, with their numerous low-lying atolls, dominated by the high islands of the Palaus, Yap, Truk, Ponape, and Kusaie; and the widespread Marshall and Gilbert groups, the latter astride the equator and both of them constituted entirely of coral atolls.

SUMMARY. General characteristics (col. 916). Mariana Islands (col. 916). Caroline Islands (col. 916). Marshall Islands (col. 917). Gilbert Islands (col. 918).

GENERAL CHARACTERISTICS. At least eleven subcultural areas are recognized within Micronesia's bounds. Distinctions among them in art, religion, language, social organization, and technology have their roots in the prehistoric origins of island immigrants. The several cultures have undergone centuries of adaptation to local differences of habitat. Other modifications have resulted in historic times from the varied influences of customs introduced by Europeans and from other sources outside the islands.

The islands lie wholly within the tropics, a condition which obviates any serious anxiety about clothing and shelter. The high islands provide a fair range of resources for craft work, including basaltic lavas and a wider variety of woods and fibers than is usually present on the atolls. The latter are composed almost entirely of coral limestone. In both environments some combination of gardening and fishing is the basis of economic life.

In aboriginal times possibly 150,000 people lived in the area. New diseases brought in by Europeans contributed to an alarming decline in population for many years. In the 20th century the death rate was curbed, and a continuing high birth rate resulted in rapid expansion; by mid-century there were more than 100,000 Micronesians. Non-Micronesians were few, except on Guam, where a transient population supported various military facilities. Island communities rarely number more than a few hundred individuals. While the high islands are only sparsely settled, density of population in the more crowded atolls rises to 1,000 persons per square mile.

The older technology manifested a quite direct dependence on the immediate environment. While interisland trading augmented the resources to a degree, most artifacts were fashioned from locally available materials. In social intercourse the bonds of kinship and community played a predominant role and provided the framework for economic and political organization. Micronesians viewed the supernatural as an idealized extension of their earthly existence. Ancestral ghosts advised them on demand, and high gods and unnamed nature spirits were placated in simple ritual.

Marked changes in Micronesian living followed the introduction of European institutions. Time-honored crafts and skills gave way under the pressure of trade imports and the copra industry. Social patterns suffered less, except in port towns and adjacent areas. Although Protestant and Catholic mission practice displaced the formal aspect of island religions, many beliefs of old survived with remarkable vigor and blended with the new.

MARIANA ISLANDS. Ancient Chamorro stonework is known from a wide range of ground stone implements and from the capped uprights, foundations of communal *latte* houses, which have been uncovered in ruins on Guam, Saipan, Tinian, and Rota (see MICRONESIAN CULTURES, *Prehistoric sites*). Associated pottery remains date back to 1500 B.C. and suggest an affinity with older Philippine ceramics. Descendants of the ancient Chamorros long ago abandoned the traditional island crafts, and several centuries of Spanish rule served to create a Hispaniolized colonial culture. Such handiwork as is now produced — some wood carving and shell-ornamented accessories — is primarily for the tourist market. On Saipan a well-established Carolinian colony is responsible for the principal manufacture of mats and other trade items of fiber.

CAROLINE ISLANDS. The Palau Islands (Western Carolines) unquestionably produced the virtuosos of Micronesia, artisans who worked in wood, stone, tortoise shell, and clay. Skilled carpenters constructed magnificent meetinghouses, on the beams and gables of which were carved and painted lively scenes depicting favorite legends (PL. 543). Finely finished bowls and boxes sparkled with mother-of-pearl inlay (PL. 548). Stone monoliths featured a stylized human face suggestive of Sepik River wood art found in New Guinea (q.v.). Dishes and ornaments cut and pressed from tortoise shell showed better control of technique than did the plain ware and modeled lamps of clay (PL. 546). Modern production is limited mainly to "story-boards," on which the decorative storytelling art of the meetinghouse is capsuled in a dimension designed to attract the tourist.

Yap's position, geographically, and esthetically as well, is intermediate to the Palaus, the Marianas, and the atolls lying to the east. The art reflects much of the old Palauan and Chamorro work in stone, wood, and clay. The men's house, raised on a stone foundation and with timbers decorated in a style reminiscent of Palauan, derives additional appeal from artfully arranged sennit lashings and decorative reed wall panels. In tattooing, loom weaving, and canoe design, Yap has more in common with the low islands, since these were crafts in which Palauans (and possibly Chamorros) were less adept. The arts of the Yap region, including the atolls, have survived in modern times as a result of the islands' relative isolation.

A marine flavor pervaded the traditional arts of the Truk Islands, where sea-bird forms and designs symbolizing fish were carved on dance sticks, hair combs, outrigger parts, and canoe-house timbers. A similar style appeared in tattooing and weaving. The Trukese, to an unusual extent, loaded themselves with heavy earrings and necklaces cut from marine and coconut shells. Although the art of Truk cannot compare as a whole with that of Yap or the Palaus, Micronesia's only masks (PL. 545) came from atolls in the vicinity; versions of these dance masks are now mass-produced as souvenirs in the Mortlock (Nomoi) Islands.

The peoples of Ponape (formerly Ascension) and Kusaie surpassed all other Micronesians in the weaving of complexly designed girdles from banana fiber. The geometric motifs of these loomed fabrics appeared also in the carving on their dance paddles, in tattooing, and in the sennit wrappings of outrigger parts. Ancient settlements at Nan Matol on Ponape and at Lele on Kusaie (FIG. 921), which had walled structures and planned waterways constructed from massive lengths of columnar basalt, now lie in ruin. The modern arts of the eastern Carolinians are limited in general to the plaiting of admirable hats and baskets from processed coconut leaf, a 20th-century cottage industry.

As for the two outlying islands, god figures (PL. 547), lacking in anatomical detail yet striking in their formal simplicity, were conspicuous among Nukuoro's generally unpretentious artifacts. Attractive saddle stools served as coconut graters; in recent times the type has been introduced into Kapingamarangi (PL. 544), where such graters are now made in miniature as souvenirs. On both atolls loom-woven fabrics of hibiscus fiber and plaited pandanus-leaf mats were of notable quality, although their artistic appeal depended solely on technique.

MARSHALL ISLANDS. Here weaving found a substitute in handwork utilizing fine pandanus leaf, particularly for dress mats with decorative borders reminiscent of Ponapean loom work. As in tattooing, the mat designs had to do with the sea, fish and bird life, and navigation cues (cf. III, PL. 499). Flowers and shells provided the basis for a refined personal adornment. In modern times traders have encouraged handicrafts utilizing processed coconut leaf in forms quite foreign to aboriginal practice.

GILBERT ISLANDS. In the Gilbert Islands, Ocean Island (Banaba), and Nauru the proficiency achieved in fiber crafts resembled that of the Marshallese, though tattooing and mat decoration showed generally less development. On Nauru, however, plaited fiber aprons of intricate design, suggesting an affinity with Marshallese clothing mats, were worn by pregnant women (PL. 548). The checkerwork basketry was not unlike that of western Polynesia. World-famous are the ancient inventions of sennit-corded armor and shark-toothed weapons, which, in later years, became elaborated to the point of inutility.

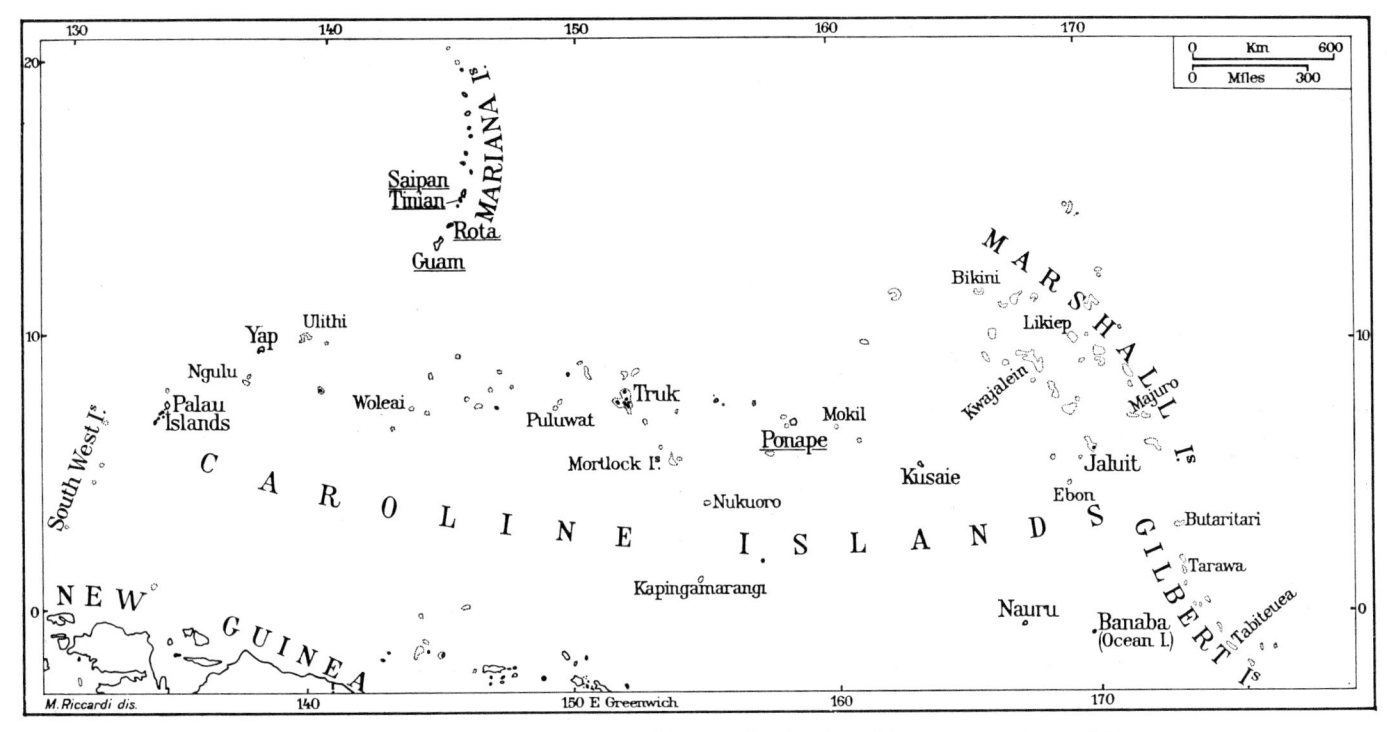

Micronesia, diffusion of indigenous arts. (Centers of archaeological interest are underscored.)

BIBLIOG. O. Finsch, Ethnologische Erfahrungen und Belegstücke aus der Südsee, III: Mikronesien (West-Oceanien), Vienna, 1893; R. Linton and P. S. Wingert, Arts of the South Seas, New York, 1946; O. W. Freeman, ed., Geography of the Pacific, New York, 1951. See also the bibliog. for MICRONESIAN CULTURES.

Leonard MASON

Illustration: 1 fig. in text.

MICRONESIAN CULTURES. The term Micronesia (q.v.) while basically geographic in meaning, serves also as a designation for the various Oceanic cultures and societies that are not otherwise identified as Polynesian, Melanesian, or Indonesian.

The arts and crafts of Micronesia depend fundamentally upon a few traits that are almost universal throughout the area and probably date from the period of earliest Micronesian settlement. Characteristic forms include tattoo patterns, plaited mats and baskets, ornaments of shell, plain wooden bowls, and the functional design of outrigger canoes. To this heritage were added introductions from Indonesia and Melanesia which, however, had not diffused into all or even most of Micronesia before the arrival of Europeans altered the course of developments. In this category we find loom weaving, as practiced in most of the Carolines, pottery and megalithic constructions in the Palaus, Yap, and the Marianas, and representations in wood of human and bird forms in the western and central Carolines. Elaboration of many of these crafts developed as local innovations; examples are the stylized wood art of the Nukuoro-Mortlock-Truk region, the woven belts and stone structures of Ponape and Kusaie, the dress mats of Nauru and the Marshalls, and the style of communal buildings in the Palaus, Yap, and the Gilberts. In general, the more typical Micronesian arts functioned in the Carolines from Yap to Truk; marginal areas marked by idiosyncratic practices were the Palaus, the Marianas, and the several island groups from Ponape eastward. The aboriginal crafts continued until the 20th century but have now almost disappeared. Trade handicrafts, utilizing local wood and fiber resources, have in part replaced them, but these reflect a general lowering of quality.

SUMMARY. General considerations and cultural affinities (col. 919). Prehistoric sites (col. 920). Architecture (col. 921). Three-dimensional art in wood (col. 923). Three-dimensional art in stone and shell (col. 924). Decorative carving and painting (col. 925). Pottery (col. 925). Shell ornaments (col. 926). Tattooing (col. 926). Weaving (col. 928). Plaiting (col. 929).

GENERAL CONSIDERATIONS AND CULTURAL AFFINITIES. The small and scattered land fragments of Micronesia have, over the past four or perhaps five thousand years, felt the tread of multiple migrations from west and south and southeast. From the Palaus to the Gilberts differences in climate, topography, and soil fertility provoked endless experiment by immigrant peoples in the process of adapting their customs to varying conditions. Vast stretches of open sea isolated one island or atoll from the next and contributed further to cultural differentiation within the bounds of Micronesia. The relatively poor resources held to a minimum the size of local populations and provided little economic basis for such elaboration of social and political custom as marked societies in the larger and more hospitable lands of the Pacific basin. Micronesian religious practice, which revolved around a personalized relationship with ancestor and nature spirits, was likewise subject to only moderate formalization.

Micronesian art in general lacks the more spectacular aspects of that known from Melanesia and Polynesia, or from Indonesia and the Asian mainland. Yet the esthetic manifestations of each of Micronesia's subcultures bear a distinctive character, apparent in the ancient Chamorro arts of the north-lying Marianas, in the varied Carolinian styles, and in the atoll crafts of the Marshallese and Gilbertese.

Within Micronesia the most widely distributed art forms, and undoubtedly the oldest, were geometric and nonrepresentational. In the creation of personal ornaments artists revealed their fascination with number and rhythm as they manipulated the size, shape, and color of shell beads and disks. Tattooing designs, derived basically from the diagonal check and twill of plaited mats and baskets, showed a similar preoccupation, and the same array of triangles, chevrons, diamonds, and zigzags appeared in Carolinian carved and painted wood surfaces. Almost the only organic forms realistically represented in tattooing and wood decoration were sharks and porpoises.

Loom weaving has been well documented as an introduction from Indonesia. The decorative motifs in most Carolinian textiles bore an obvious relationship to local plaiting designs, despite the differences encountered in technique. Micronesians found it easy to integrate weaving with their existing art traditions. Wood sculpture, for which evidence points to Melanesia as the source, proved more difficult to master. Essential to the art as it emerged in the Carolines west of Ponape was the representation of human and bird forms in more or less realistic fashion. The absence of sculptured sharks and porpoises and the dearth of surface decoration on sculptured bowls, prow ornaments, and human images suggest the need to distinguish two separate traditions in Micronesian woodworking. The one, suggested as earlier, dealt solely with geometric decoration of wood surfaces (e.g., house beams and canoe hulls). The other, introduced later, was associated with undecorated three-dimensional forms. Only in the Palaus did artists manage successfully to combine the two traditions, notably in the shell ornamentation on wooden utensils and the storytelling scenes carved and painted on meetinghouse gables.

The types of communal houses found in the Palaus, Yap, and the Marianas, while strongly reminiscent of Indonesia and Melanesia, may well have developed locally from a dwelling plan widespread in Micronesia. However, the unusual mastery of carpentry techniques by Palauans was without Micronesian precedent. Ceramics and massive stonework were restricted to the same three groups in western Micronesia (Ponapean stone structures were not in this tradition) and were probably diffused from Indonesia.

The role played by Yap in the evolution of Micronesian art poses an ethnographic problem. In practices common in both Yap and the atolls to the east, for example, weaving, tattooing, and shell decoration, the Yapese frequently took second place. In crafts shared with Palauans and Chamorros, they failed to measure up to the standards of those groups but showed a skill not possessed by the atoll peoples. Although in many ways subject to influences from the nearby Palaus and Marianas, the Yapese leave the impression of having been at the same time an outpost of the atoll region. Thus Yap stood at the crossroads of artistic exchange in western Micronesia.

There remains the possibility of cultural influence from Polynesia. In the context of art the evidence is not convincing. The Micronesian groups accepted on other grounds as being most "Polynesian" are those of the outlying islands of Nukuoro and Kapingamarangi and of the Gilbert Islands. Comparative analysis of art forms indicates that Kapingamarangians and Gilbertese, sharing very little with neighboring Micronesians, could hardly have been carriers of Polynesian media and motifs to the western archipelago. Nukuoro tended to be linked with Truk and the Mortlocks as a result of diffusion from those islands, rather than the reverse. A simplified naturalism and the use of ornamentation issuing from technique and function have often been cited as traditions that associated the central Carolines (and Fiji) with western Polynesia. This resemblance must be interpreted as a common heritage preserved in locally variant forms from earlier times.

Ponape, Kusaie, Nauru, and the Marshalls, marginally situated in eastern Micronesia, lacked many of the artistic refinements of more versatile peoples to westward. Yet within this very region occurred some of the truly exciting inventions in Micronesian art, such as the belt weaving and the tattooing styles in Ponape and Kusaie and the dress mats plaited by Marshallese and Nauruans. Every one of these local innovations can be traced back to the generalized Micronesian art of old, which provided a foundation more directly for the later achievements of the west-central Carolinians.

PREHISTORIC SITES. Double rows of stone columns with hemispherical capstones indicate the location of many ancient Chamorro villages on Tinian, Saipan, Guam, and Rota. These *latte*, as they are known locally, were the roughly cut foundations for large structures of wood and thatch, used as the men's house, the chief's domicile, or as dwellings for an extensive family. The capped uprights, quarried from coral limestone with basalt adzes, stood as high as 16 ft. and covered an area of up to 60 × 15 ft. *Latte* sites were inhabited from the mid-9th century until the 16th-century occupation of the Marianas by the Spanish. Hans G. Hornbostel in the 1920s reported several hundred *latte* locations on the four islands. Most prominent were ruins at Taga, on the southwest coast of Tinian, and at Agingan, similarly situated on Saipan, with 18 and 12 house units respectively. Subsequent colonization by Japanese as well as military activity during World War II resulted in extensive deterioration or destruction of *latte* sites. At the present time the best-preserved include the House of Taga, central and only surviving unit of the Taga group; the Blue site, a mile to the south, excavated in 1950 by Alexander Spoehr; the Gongna Cove group at the north end of Tumon Bay, on Guam, restored in 1946 by Douglas Osborne; the As Nieves quarry, with several unfinished shafts and caps, in eastern Rota; and the Laulau site on Magicienne Bay, on Saipan.

A quite different megalithic tradition is preserved in the jungle-covered ruins of Nan Matol off the eastern shore of Ponape. Here on the reef legendary builders from northern Ponape created more than fifty artificial islets. In an 11-sq.-mi. area, protected by a stone breakwater, walled enclosures were erected from natural blocks of columnar basalt, rafted from the northern part of the island, and built up to heights of 40 ft. in a cribwork filled with coral limestone. The basalt and coral components, all carefully assembled in a kind of dry masonry, show little or no evidence of cutting or shaping. These structures and an associated network of canals served as the seat of a dynastic line that ruled the Ponapeans for many generations until overthrown, with aid from Kusaiens, prior to European discovery. Nan Towas, the outstanding ruin, consists of two high-walled rectangles, one within the other, in the center of which is a capacious vault said to have held the remains of the last ruling chief. Surveys of the ruins were undertaken by Johannes Kubary, F. W. Christian, and Paul Hambruch around the turn of the present century. A similar though less elaborate project was executed in prehistoric times at Lele on the eastern coast of Kusaie, 250 mi. east of Ponape, where reef and sand provided a foundation for an extensive layout of walled courts and canals (FIG. 921).

Dwellings of Ponapeans and Kusaiens are still built on low platforms walled and paved with basalt and coral rock. Elsewhere in Micronesia house platforms and stone-paved yards and roads exist only in the Palaus, Yap, and a few neighboring atolls. Palauans, utilizing andesite boulders, extended this type of construction to piers, drains, causeways, and fresh-water bathing pools.

ARCHITECTURE. Despite regional differences in design, Micronesian housing was basically rectangular in ground plan, with corner posts supporting tie beams and plates on which rested a light, large, and well-constructed saddle roof. Gable ends commonly extended far beyond the floor area and provided additional working space. Pandanus leaf and coconut and other palm leaves were converted into roof thatch. Space under the low-hanging eaves frequently remained clear, although, when necessary, the exposed sides were protected by matting from rain and wind. Wood planking or panels made of reeds served for more permanent enclosure. The types of flooring varied from bare earth to sturdily built platforms of planks or poles.

One widespread solution for ridgepole support depended on the erection of a king post above each tie beam. In the Marshalls, the Gilberts, and Nauru these beams, bridged by numerous slender poles, formed a floor for secluded sleeping quarters just under the roof. In dwellings of many eastern Carolinians only the crossed rafters of the roof carried the ridgepole. Palauans, at the other end of the Carolines, achieved an unusual strength of construction by utilizing their consummate skill in carpentry. The lofty gabled ends of their 50-ft.-long meeting houses (*bai*, PL. 543) represented a composition of carefully hewn planks fitted horizontally behind framing batten boards. The entire roof frame was firmly mortised to wall and corner posts.

The *falu*, or men's house, on Yap, as still constructed today, reflects another principle of roof support. Seven unhewn logs, selected for their superlative dimensions and symmetry of form, are planted deep in the ground along the center line of an elevated platform and rise grandly to meet the ridgepole 30 ft. above. The natural beauty of these timbers, lashed to untrimmed beams and rafters with sennit plaited in artistic patterns, compares favorably with the sophisticated woodworking of the neighboring Palauans. A companion feature of Yapese housing is the hexagonal floor plan resulting from a triangular extension of roof and walls at each end. The same architectural characteristics, although of more modest proportions, distinguish the larger shelters of atoll communities to the south and east, where Yapese influence has penetrated. Building design in this part of Micronesia is possibly related to a need for withstanding the gale winds and typhoons that annually visit the region.

Only superficially similar to the *falu* is the spectacular *maneaba*, or council house, of the Gilbert atolls. This is simply a huge gabled roof of pandanus thatch held up by several rows of coconut-log columns, those under the ridgepole mounting upward to 50 ft. The ground covered by one such public building on Butaritari (Makin) was reported to be 114 × 250 ft. All timbers in the structure are made secure with sennit lash-

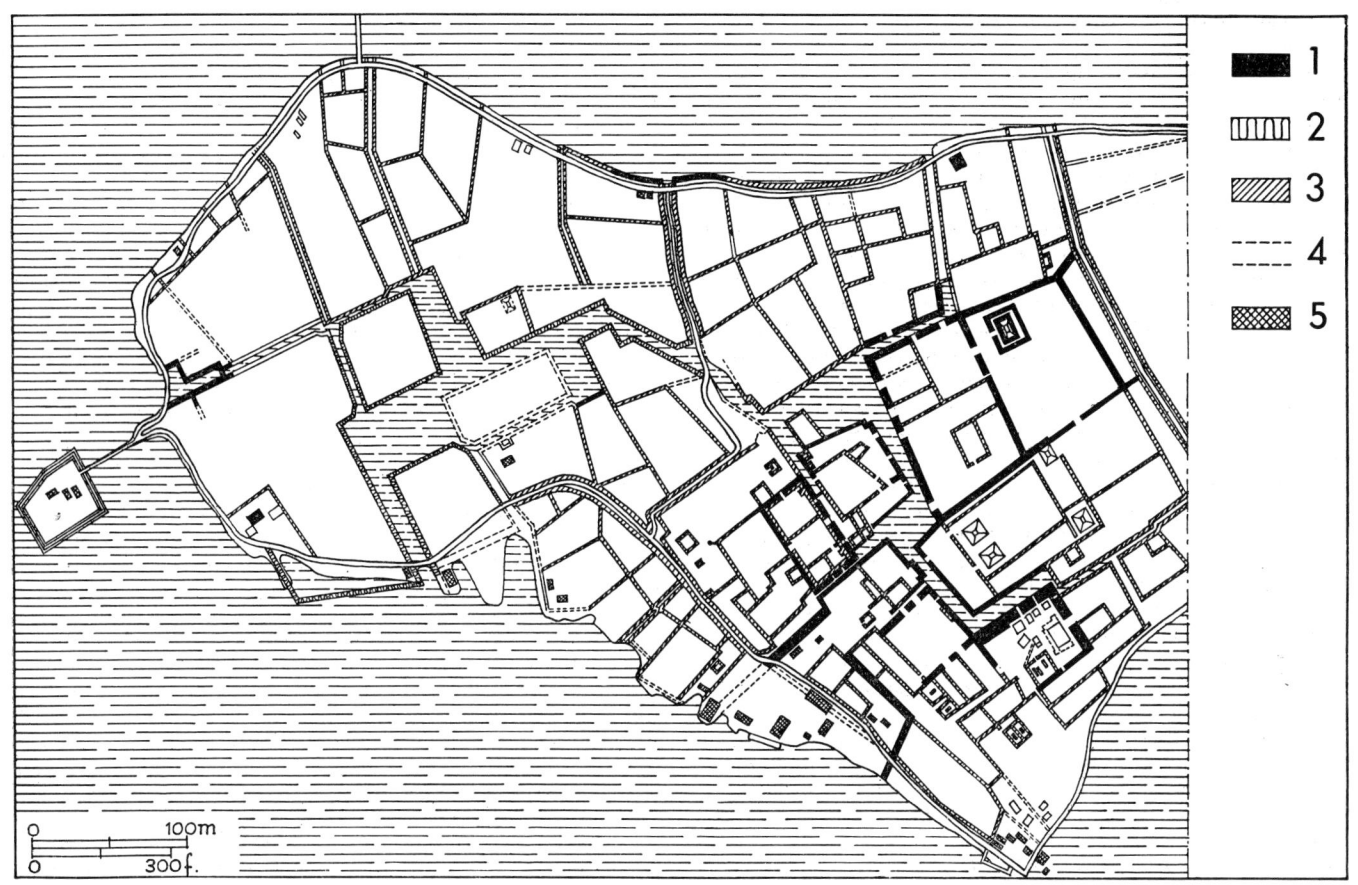

Plan of the ancient settlement at Lele, Caroline Islands. *Key:* (1) Basalt walls; (2) walls of coral limestone; (3) basalt walls in ruins or incomplete; (4) walls of coral limestone in ruins or incomplete; (5) dwellings (from *G. Thilenius, IV, 1919*).

ings. Eaves reach nearly to the ground and the space beneath is left open to lagoon breezes.

THREE-DIMENSIONAL ART IN WOOD. Early European visitors to the Marianas commented favorably on the wood art of the natives but made only very general references to objects produced (e.g., bowls, spears, field implements, and images). Specific statements about the sculptural ability of these people (the Chamorros) must be omitted in a discussion of regional specialties, since the local crafts did not long survive Spanish rule.

The most extensive and, therefore, most typical three-dimensional work in wood was produced in the area from the Palaus to Nukuoro. The artifacts — human images, canoe ornaments, and variously shaped boxes, bowls, and dishes — were not large and were painted sparingly, if at all, in white and black. Artisans preferred the wood of breadfruit trees with its medium-coarse grain, which could easily be shaped with shell-bladed adzes. Representation was limited to human and sea-bird models almost exclusively. Adherence to realism diminished from west to east.

Canoe ornaments in this area were of several types. From Yap to the Mortlocks, bow and stern pieces of sail canoes were terminated by a conventionalized representation of the forked tail of the frigate bird. The endpieces of small canoe models, cult objects which possibly preserved a more ancient form of decoration, terminated in a crescent-moon shape with tips pointed upward. *Aten* figures decorated the ends of the Truk paddle canoes. Bound with sennit cord atop each peaked prow, this carving in its upper portion represented a pair of affronted sea swallows, their beaks in contact and their tails raised pertly behind. The birds are not recognizable to the untutored eye, and the total effect of the symmetrical *aten* design is quite abstract.

As for containers (PL. 548), artisans in Palau and Yap created a greater variety of forms than is to be found elsewhere in Micronesia, in addition to unique four- and six-legged trays, or small tables (PL. 544). From Palau to Puluwat a common artifact was a plain but well-proportioned storage box, lidded and equipped with a cord for suspension from a house beam. Also made to hang were small bowls or dishes that represent the frigate bird by means of realistic duplication of the bird's beaked head and forked tail. In the same region, and in Truk and the Mortlocks, a deep elliptical bowl was part of every household inventory. Rim decorations at both ends, serving as handles and carved in exceedingly stylized fashion, reputedly portrayed the human face with a long straight nose surmounted by a projecting forehead.

Food graters, as a rule crudely made from a bent branch, evoke little esthetic interest. One exception existed in the remarkable bird form conceived by Nukuorans for grating their ripe coconut. Its two sturdy legs and foot-high saddle seat blended gracefully with the outstretched neck of the bird; at the top a toothed shell blade was lashed. Today the people of Kapingamarangi have taken over the Nukuoran form and ably manufacture scores of the product both for trade and for their own use (PL. 544).

The best of Micronesian sculpture depicted the human body. Figures of both sexes, full-length and freestanding, rarely more than a foot or two in height, served as ritual artifacts in the Palaus and Yap. These images are carved in lifelike proportions, with a minimum of detail, and have a moderately rough surface on which adz marks still show. Yapese also incorporated such representations into house posts and window hooks. Tobi, the atoll nearest New Guinea, has become famous in modern times as the source of small squatting male figures, carved in brown hardwood, polished, and fitted with large staring eyes of inlaid mother-of-pearl.

From Yap to Puluwat, where atoll navigators undertook long and dangerous voyages at sea, the sculptured human form appeared as a doll-like fetish to be brandished by canoe captains in the face of oncoming storm clouds. The wooden image was all but obscured by coconut leaflets, knotted about the arms and waist, which enhanced the magical effect. The arms hung straight at the sides; the head was carved simply, with long straight nose, eyes that were usually mere slits, overhanging brow, and small mouth. The hair and beard were painted black, and a woody stump with several projecting spines from a sting ray substituted for the lower limbs. Alternatively, some weather fetishes had two nearly complete torsos, joined at the back and Janus-headed.

Stylistically the famed Mortlock masks and the *tino* images of Nukuoro may well have developed, along with the fetish figure, from a single Caroline Islands tradition. The same basic design of the face in the fetishes was apparent on the slightly convex plane of the heavy Mortlock dance mask (PL. 545). Dominating the 2-ft.-high mask was a T formed by the long straight nose and black-painted eyebrows, both in strong relief, the latter being reminiscent of the wings of a frigate bird in flight. Eyes were frequently omitted, and a small pouting mouth was drawn in black on the lime-coated surface of the mask. Essentially the same facial representation also characterized the normally proportioned head carved as part of the king post on the front gable of men's canoe houses.

Nukuoran sculptors designed their *tino* images (PL. 547) with a long trunk, arms at the sides, short legs tapering into a circular base, and an egg-shaped head, pointed at the chin but otherwise featureless or virtually so. The unrelieved planes of the body lent the figure an anonymous, timeless quality. Life-sized variants of the smaller images (ca. 15 to 20 in.) had faintly perceptible ears and nose and carried a pattern of tattooing on neck and shoulders. Nukuorans lacked the seafaring tradition of other atoll Carolinians and maintained their god-figures in shrines ashore. These fine examples of stylization were more than matched by the abstract forms of a few weather fetishes made in the atolls west of Truk, which consisted simply of a knob "head" connected by two "arms" to a base from which the familiar ray spines protruded.

Wood sculpture in eastern Micronesia scarcely merits the name. Apart from a few distinctive canoe-prow ornaments and a pleasingly proportioned hourglass drum, there were undecorated but nonetheless well-shaped food servers and mixing bowls. The Gilbert Islanders produced only the latter. Equally impoverished in aboriginal times were the residents of Kapingamarangi, on the southern fringe of the Carolines, although (as already noted) they later borrowed a few woodcraft ideas from their neighbors on Nukuoro.

THREE-DIMENSIONAL ART IN STONE AND SHELL. Human or animal representations in materials other than wood seldom occur in aboriginal Micronesian art and never in modern times. From Yap are reported three human heads roughly carved on the face of coral limestone blocks and set into building foundations. The ruins on Kusaie have yielded a human figure in basalt. Sculptures from Palau are more numerous but exhibit only slightly better quality. These andesite monoliths, standing from 2 to 7 ft. aboveground, are carved as conventionalized human heads, sometimes in association with realistic lizard or crocodile forms. They stand near the corners of house platforms or at ceremonial centers in the villages and symbolize spiritual beings. They feature large eyes and, often, prominent noses, but further generalization is not possible because of stylistic differences and indistinctness of details. One quite skillful representation of a life-size human face is preserved in shell material from the giant *Tridacna* clam.

The famed money wheels of Yap are flat-sided disks of aragonite which measure up to 12 ft. in diameter and have center holes by which they can be transported on carrying poles. These fine white limestone pieces were quarried in the Palau Islands, laboriously shaped with stone tools, and rafted across several hundred miles of ocean to the Yap villages. There they still line roadways and lean against clubhouse platforms — repositories of value in the native system of exchange.

Other principal stone artifacts are those used for mashing taro and breadfruit. In the Marianas, Kusaie, and Ponape they were pecked and ground from hard basalt. A more easily worked coral limestone sufficed in the rest of the islands, and in some places wood was substituted. Ancient Chamorro and Marshallese pounders have rather stubby cylindrical forms. Elsewhere these implements bear some resemblance to the Truk type, which is truly a work of art. Stylistically related to Polynesian poi pounders, the Truk artifact averages about 6 in. in height and is beautifully proportioned. Its bell shape is enhanced by a shallow hemispherical base and a flaring ringed top, on the flat surface of which are carved one or more peaked projections in a symmetrical design. Regional variants possess straighter sides and flatter bases and are unornamented.

Techniques for shaping stone worked equally well for processing the thick, heavy shell of the giant *Tridacna* clams. Everywhere in the islands this material was preferred for making adzes, chisels, and gouges. Adz blades, originally lashed with sennit to bent wooden handles, appear in triangular, trapezoidal, and quadrangular forms. In western Micronesia, principally on Guam, archaeologists have also recovered tools made of basalt, although these are limited in number. From *Tridacna* shell, Marshall Islanders once fashioned smoothly finished beaters, employed in preparing pandanus leaf for dress mats. Still in use and greatly valued as family heirlooms, these unique artifacts possess a translucent quality and pleasantly curving outline that imparts a genuine artistic merit.

DECORATIVE CARVING AND PAINTING. Micronesians employed several techniques for decorating the surface of wood constructions and artifacts. In the Marianas and Carolines, particularly from the Palaus to Truk, some manner of painting was practiced. Colors were usually black with white or red, or all three, and in a few islands also yellow; they were applied with brushes of coconut-husk fiber. The resulting decoration, most frequently seen on house posts, beams (PL. 543), rafters, and canoe hulls, had a rough and untutored character that betrayed a relative lack of skill with the medium. In most of these same islands artists at times combined painting with a cutting away of thin sections of surface wood — a technique which was not true low relief but was nonetheless an effective means of emphasizing certain parts of a design. In the Palaus such excised portions on smaller articles were inlaid with mother-of-pearl instead of being painted with a contrasting color.

The people of Yap and of the atolls as far east as Puluwat used sharp mussel shells to incise delicate linear designs on bamboo tobacco containers. On other wood artifacts incising appeared only sporadically — on dance sticks in Truk, on paddles in Ponape, and on the warping benches of Kusaien weavers. White lime was generally rubbed in to heighten the effect of line decoration. House posts carved in relief (PL. 544) are to be found on Yap. Islanders east and southeast of the Carolines paid almost no attention to the potentialities of ornamental carving and painting of wood surfaces; however, they used a patterned covering of tightly plaited pandanus-leaf fiber to enhance, for example, their dance sticks.

Geometric motifs dominated Micronesian wood art. Straight lines appeared in a multitude of combinations with triangles, diamonds, and zigzags, which, in each region, bore a strong resemblance to local patterns of tattooing and weaving. Curved lines were rare, and attempts to represent nature were limited almost entirely to fish forms. To the above statements one important exception must be noted: Natives of the Palau Islands developed the practice, unique in the artistic traditions of Oceania, of embellishing the planked gable ends and squared roof timbers of their grand meetinghouses. In addition to using the familiar geometric signs of other Carolinians, they created complex storytelling scenes dominated by conventionalized human figures, which, in the company of fishes, birds, and reptiles, frolicked in settings replete with trees, houses, canoes, and sea waves. These panels (PL. 543) were executed in the cutaway technique described above and were further enlivened by painting in four colors.

POTTERY. The only Micronesians to be credited with a knowledge of ceramics are Palauans, Yapese, and pre-Spanish Chamorros. Women of Yap and the Palaus continued to make cooking pots well into the 20th century. Their wares, hemispherical in form and with incurved rims, were coarse and friable. Surfaces lacked decoration and were undistinguished by slip or glaze. The method of manufacture combined coiling and molding, the coils being smoothed out with paddle and stone. Palauans also made curious oil lamps (PL. 546), the rims of which are surmounted by crudely modeled figures of seated women, often shown nursing their babes. The antiquity of pottery in the western Carolines is not known beyond the fact that it predated European contact. Extensive excavations have been conducted in the Palaus by Douglas Osborne and on Yap by E. W. Gifford.

Chamorro pottery styles have been studied by Laura Thompson and Alexander Spoehr from shard collections made in Guam, Saipan, and Tinian. The craft did not survive the Spanish conquest of the Marianas in the 17th century. The *latte* builders produced an abundance of undecorated ware of varying quality and color. Vessel forms and technique cannot be reconstructed with any certainty. Some shards of the same period show fine incised lines, cord marks, and other surface decoration. In earlier cultural levels there occurs a distinctive ware of much better quality, thin, hard, and red-slipped, which is associated with the earliest remains of human occupancy in the Marianas (mid-2d millennium B.C.).

SHELL ORNAMENTS. Shell necklaces, ear pendants, girdles, bracelets, and finger rings, used in varying degree, enhanced the individual's appearance throughout Micronesia. Truk Islanders held first place in personal adornment, and they strongly influenced others all the way from the Mortlocks to Yap. In this region the principal materials consisted of white *Conus* and *Trochus* and orange-red *Spondylus* marine shells, black coconut shell, and the beautifully patterned shell of sea tortoises. Esthetic effects were largely achieved by skillfully combining numerous pieces of contrasting color, size, and shape into a total composition. The artisans' preoccupation with geometric order parallels their play with number in the arrangement of wefts when plaiting mats and baskets.

Basic components of design included disks, $1/4$–1 in. in diameter, each of which was roughed out as a flat-sided blank from *Conus* or coconut shell, drilled through the center with a small hole, strung with others on a sennit cord, and reduced to circular form and unit size by rubbing on a rough stone. Larger, less carefully shaped beads of *Spondylus*, a material valued highly because of its scarcity, were interspersed in some necklaces at patterned intervals among white and black disks. Wide belts or girdles consisted of multiple strands, numbering as many as twelve; wood or shell connectors held each strand an equal distance from the next and maintained a flat plane for the entire piece. Among ornaments intended to hang from pierced earlobes were commonly found rings of *Conus*, coconut, and tortoise shell, looped together in chains that often fell below the shoulder line. Earrings and necklaces were sometimes elaborated with pendant triangles of *Spondylus*, large rings of *Conus* and *Trochus*, or elongated immature coconuts. Stylized fishhooks, rings, and triangles were cut from tortoise shell; from Truk and certain atolls to the west have come curious pendants of this material, which resemble the wheel parts of a clock mechanism.

Micronesians east of Truk employed fewer and simpler shell ornaments. Disks of central-Carolinian appearance were strung more often in a longitudinal series rather than face to face. Shells of *Natica*, *Melampus*, and *Cypraea*, attached to strips of hibiscus bast or braided pandanus leaf, were favored for belts, headbands, and necklaces. At the other end of Micronesia, the Palauans used very few personal ornaments and, from archaeological evidence, the same appears to have been true in the Marianas.

TATTOOING. Most Micronesian peoples practiced some form of tattooing; only in the Marianas was it apparently quite absent. Masters of the craft employed a toothed, adzlike bone implement, held above the skin and briskly tapped with a wooden mallet. Soot mixed with water provided coloring. Patients ordinarily underwent the first operation before puberty and in later years extended the tattooed area according to the custom in each locality. Women tended to limit tattooing to hands, arms, and legs; on males the bluish-black markings were frequently applied to the torso as well.

Style varied from island to island. The most complete body design, still extant among older adult males, originated in Ulithi and Yap and was common throughout the western Caroline atolls as far as Woleai and Tobi. Two sets of rays rising above the nipples dominated a vertical composition of dark rectangles which extended to the groin; the back was covered with a symmetrical pattern of curving dark fields that joined along the backbone and terminated on the buttocks. Women in these islands, together with those in the atolls eastward to Truk, displayed a quite different style of tattooing; the decoration, concentrated on the thighs, consisted of an unframed arrangement of fishes, crosses, triangles, and chevrons, set off by bands of crosshatching or rows of parallel diagonals. Men in the eastern part of this area were tattooed much like the women. (See FIG. 927.)

Tattoo patterns in the Caroline Islands. (a) Ulithi; (b) Lamotrek.

The Palauans manifested a third style. Hands, arms, and legs of both sexes (though of women, more than men) were tattooed. Long stripes made up of crosses, chevrons, zigzags, or other symbols, repeated infinitely between confining lines, typically covered the lower limbs.

Among eastern Micronesians a distinctive decoration existed in each linguistic region. In the Gilberts, where tattooing was not important, one common design represented the fronds of a coconut tree. Women in the Marshall Islands favored a pattern of barbed lines and zigzag connectives across the shoulders, and tattooed their limbs with a comb design and further use of zigzag lines. The men extended these motifs to the entire chest and back, and even to the face, where it was a mark of chiefly status. Perhaps the most complex tattooing in all Micronesia existed in Ponape, in the decoration of women's hips, waists, and thighs. Apparently of indigenous origin, this artistry recalls the Ponapean virtuosity in loom weaving, the patterns in both media being remarkably alike.

Micronesian tattooing is essentially geometric and nonrepresentational. The principal motifs are triangles, chevrons, crosses, straight or zigzag lines, and rows of short lines in vertical, diagonal, or crosshatched patterns. Most of the motifs had names, nevertheless, relating them to fish, shellfish, birds, heavenly bodies, and canoes — things that were valued highly by the islanders. The only truly realistic portrayals are those of sharks and porpoises. The spacing of design elements varied widely from the random and discrete to the creation of an integrated composition adapted to the body area being decorated. Curvilinear elements are exceedingly rare and occur mainly as outlines of the dark areas noted in back tattooing among the males of Ulithi, Yap, and Woleai.

WEAVING. Carolinians, with the exception of Palauans and a few atoll communities near Truk, wove quality textiles on simple backstrap looms. Fabrics fashioned from the split fibers of banana stalks were usually worn by men as loincloths; those made from inner bark fiber of the hibiscus tree were favored by women as sarongs. Loom width, which determined cloth width, ranged from 1 to 2 ft. in the central and western Carolines; the length of the finished product was ordinarily three to five times as much. Black, rust, red, and yellow plant dyes were used to alter the light natural color of bast fiber. In some of the atolls where weaving has survived, commercial dyes in blue, purple, red, and green have been substituted.

The ring method of warping was practiced in preparing the loom. Weavers knotted the warp threads end to end and wound them in a continuous spiral around the two beams. The warp-face weaves lent themselves admirably to longitudinal stripe decoration. Color, width, and number of stripes, as preferred according to local custom, were controlled by preplanned knotting of appropriate fibers during production of the warp spiral. Although seven was a favorite number, from one to eight stripes might appear. Wide stripes, combined with narrow ones, were often distinguished by introducing color-contrasting warps to break up the monotone. In striped fabrics, the wefts remained undyed and were incorporated in a plain weave (under one, over one). Ratio of warps to wefts averaged about 60 to 25 per square inch.

Most Carolinians also decorated their cloth by adding dyed wefts of hibiscus in one to a dozen patterned bands across the stripes at both ends of the material. In some places the only decoration was of this type. The extra wefts, commonly paired with the basic undyed wefts, were floated across the warps by using additional heddles or were laid in with pattern sticks, while the undyed wefts were combined with the warps in plain weave. The resulting decoration appeared on the surface of the cloth as rows of geometric forms, including triangles, diamonds, chevrons, and crosses, with a complementary design on the opposite side of the cloth. Many of the design elements were similar to those employed in local tattooing and, in like manner, were named for features valued in the island environment.

The atolls from Ulithi to Satawal formed a fairly homogeneous area in regard to weaving process and design. Ulithians had taught their craft to women on Yap, but Yapese men, constructing a very long loom, also wove a special cloth that was a form of native money. Certain innovations and less conformity to a common style characterized the east-central Carolines, dominated by Truk and including the two Polynesian outliers. Fabrics were shorter and wider; stripes were broader and close together, and the internal design was more complex. Kapingamarangi weavers attempted no decoration at all in their loom cloth.

Among Carolinian weavers, Kusaiens and Ponapeans must be accounted superlative. They produced belts no more than 6 or 7 in. wide from banana fibers so fine that 87 warps per inch have been counted. Kusaiens, especially, achieved ingenious patterns of varicolored warp striping with each stripe only a few threads wide. The effect of transverse bands of decoration was obtained by the careful knotting-in of different colored warps, some only an inch or two long, when the loom was first set up. Weft threads played only a very small role in Kusaien design and served mainly as binder for the warps. Ponapeans not only handled warp knotting with skill but elaborated the ornamental use of extra wefts (brocading) far beyond that achieved elsewhere in the Carolines. Furthermore, they incorporated hundreds of small beads and disks of white, black, and orange shell as part of the brocading process, to produce a surface encrustation that is an integral part of the textile. The remarkable accomplishments of Ponapean and Kusaien weavers represent the masterly conclusion of a few basic Micronesian techniques, namely, ring warping, warp-face weave, and knotted warps.

PLAITING. Micronesians of both sexes continue to manifest their traditional skill in fashioning field baskets and coarse mats from freshly cut coconut leaves. The leaflets, still attached to a split frond, are crossed diagonally to right and left in plain check design.

Most island women in former times knew, although few do nowadays, how to prepare pandanus leaves for making a variety of bags, pouches, baskets, sleeping mats, floor mats, and certain dress items. The green leaves had first to be rid of their thorny edges and midribs. After drying in the sun or over hot coals they were rolled up and softened by repeated blows with wood or shell beaters. Finally the broad leaves were slit lengthwise to desired plaiting widths. Plaiters employed the same diagonal check as in coconut-leaf work but usually doubled the wefts for durability.

Twilled plaiting, less common than check, characterized both pandanus and coconut-leaf products among many Micronesians. The variations from a simple under-one, over-one technique offered infinite possibilities for surface design without recourse to colored wefts. Palauans excelled at twilled work of this kind. Throughout the atolls of eastern Micronesia the decoration of mats and other twilled or checked artifacts was achieved by manipulating light and dark strips of pandanus leaf; the contrasting colors resulted from differences in leaf maturity before processing. In Kusaie, Nauru, and the Marshalls, island artisans produced more sharply defined patterns by laying in strips of black-dyed hibiscus bast on selected pandanus wefts.

Nauruans made mats of a unique type, about 15 in. square, which were traditionally worn by pregnant women (PL. 548); the plaited designs bore a marked resemblance to the warp-face weaving in Kusaien belts. The Nauruan plaiting was distinctive in that wefts ran parallel to the sides, rather than diagonally. Most pieces were executed in plain check with double wefts, though a few mats included some twill. The natural hue of pandanus contrasted nicely with the black, red, or brown of dyed hibiscus fiber. In Carolinian loomed fabrics, vertical wefts were variously arranged in color and number after the manner of warps, while horizontal wefts usually alternated in color. This technique yielded patterns in which unbroken vertical lines and short horizontal dashes predominated. When both horizontal and vertical wefts were ordered in complex rhythms of number and color, practically limitless innovation in rectilinear design was possible.

The finest mat work in Micronesia came from the Marshalls. Women's dress mats, a pair worn front and back covering the body from waist to ankles (PL. 548), bore a superficial likeness to Nauruan pregnancy mats. Double wefts paralleled the edges of the square mats just as on Nauru, and both types had ornamental borders. Marshallese mats, however, were twice as large, with wefts eight to an inch instead of four. They featured the borders rather than the centers, which remained in plain check of brown pandanus. The borders consisted of from three to seven decorative bands in parallel, each plaited intricately in pandanus, black- or yellow-dyed hibiscus, and a dark-brown fiber from the sun-dried inner bark of a creeping beach vine. Unlike the Nauruans, who preferred rectilinear design, the Marshallese stressed diamonds, lozenges, triangles, and chevrons in developing band decoration. This play with diagonal line produced patterns remarkably similar to those in the brocaded transverse bands of finely woven Ponapean belts. The plaiting in both the Marshalls and Nauru suggests a unique attempt to duplicate selected features of eastern-Carolinian loom weaving without adopting the loom itself.

BIBLIOG. J. Kubary, Ethnographische Beiträge zur Kenntnis des Karolinen Archipels, 3 vols., Leiden, 1889–95; F. W. Christian, The Caroline Islands, London, 1899; J. Edge-Partington, Note on the Occurrence of Spiral Ornament in Micronesia, Man, II, 1902, p. 26; A. Krämer, Der Haus- und Bootbau auf den Marshallinseln, Archiv für Anthr., N.S., III, 1905, pp. 295–309; G. Thilenius, ed., Ergebnisse der Südsee-Expedition, 1908–10, II-B: Ethnographie (Mikronesien), 10 vols., Hamburg, 1914–38; A. Matsumura, Contributions to the Ethnography of Micronesia, Tokyo, 1918; L. M. Thompson, The Native Culture of the Marianas Islands, Honolulu, 1945; P. H. Buck, Material Culture of Kapingamarangi, Honolulu, 1950; E. K. Reed, General Report on Archaeology and History of Guam, Washington, 1952; S. H. Riesenberg and A. H. Gayton, Caroline Island Belt Weaving, Southwestern J. of Anthr., VIII, 1952, pp. 342–75; E. G. Burrows and M. E. Spiro, An Atoll Culture, New Haven, 1953; H. Hijikata, Report on Consecrated Stone Images and Other Stone Works in Palau, Micronesia, Minzokugaku-kenkyu, XX, 1955, pp. 103–55 (in Jap., Eng. summary); A. Spoehr, Marianas Prehistory, Chicago, 1957; E. W. and D. S. Gifford, Archaeological Excavations in Yap, Anthr. Records, XVIII, 1959, pp. 149–224; M. Pellett, Marianas Archaeology, JPS, LXX, 1961, pp. 321–25; J. H. Brandt, Nan Matol: Ancient Venice of Micronesia, Archaeology, XV, 1962, pp. 99–107.

Leonard MASON

Illustrations: PLS. 543–548; 2 figs. in text.

PLATES

Pl. 1. *Above*: Pond in a garden, painting from the tomb of Nebamun, Thebes, Egypt, ca. 1400 B.C. London, British Museum.
Below: Village in Punt, relief in the temple of Queen Hatshepsut, Deir el-Bahri, near Thebes, ca. 1480 B.C.

LANDSCAPE IN ART

Pl. 2. *Above*: Tribute ferried from Tyre, relief from the palace gates of Balawat, Assyria, 9th cent. B.C. Bronze, ht., ca. 11 in. London, British Museum. *Center*: Prisoners of war among palm trees, relief from the palace of Ashurbanipal, Nineveh, 7th cent. B.C. Stone. Paris, Louvre. *Below*: Seascape with diver and fishermen, Etruscan wall painting, Tomb of Hunting and Fishing, Tarquinia, Italy, ca. 520 B.C.

Pl. 3. Nile landscape with hippopotamus hunt, from the Maccarani vineyard on the Aventine hill, Rome, 1st–2d cent. Polychrome mosaic, 10 ft., 9 in. × 10 ft., 10 in. Rome, Museo Nazionale Romano.

LANDSCAPE IN ART

Pl. 4. *Above*: Landscape with buildings and bridge, from the House of the Farnesina, Rome, Augustan period (31 B.C.–A.D. 14). Stucco. Rome, Museo Nazionale Romano. *Below*: Landscape, from Pompeii, 1st cent. Wall painting, 11×15 in. Naples, Museo Nazionale.

Pl. 5. *Above*: View of a port (Puteoli?), from Castellamare di Stabia (anc. Stabiae), Italy, 1st cent. Wall painting, 9½ × 10¼ in. Naples, Museo Nazionale. *Below*: Relief representing a city and environs, from the Fucino basin, Abruzzi, Italy, 1st cent. Marble, ht., 25⅝ in. Rome, Museo della Civiltà Romana (cast; original, Coll. Torlonia).

LANDSCAPE IN ART

Pl. 6. *Above*: Rebecca at the well, illumination from the Vienna Genesis, 6th cent. Vienna, Nationalbibliothek (Cod. vindob. theol. graec. 31, fol. 13). *Below, left*: The division of the land from the waters, 12th cent. Mosaic. Palermo, Sicily, Cappella Palatina. *Right*: Scene from the *Viśvantara Jātaka* with background of exotic foliage, late 5th cent. Wall painting. Ajanta, India, veranda of Cave XVII.

Pl. 7. *Above*: T. Gaddi, episodes in the life of Joachim, ca. 1330–40. Fresco. Florence, Sta Croce, Cappella Baroncelli. *Below*: G. Starnina (ca. 1354–1413), The Thebaid, detail. Panel; full size, 2 ft., 5½ in. × 6 ft., 10 in. Florence, Uffizi.

LANDSCAPE IN ART

Pl. 8. *Left*: Pol de Limbourg, July page (fol. 7v) of the *Très Riches Heures du Duc de Berry*, ca. 1409-15. Illumination. Chantilly, France, Musée Condé. *Right*: Battue, frontispiece (left side) of the *Shāh-nāma* by Firdausī executed for Baysunqur, Timurid school, ca. 1430. Illumination. Teheran, Gulistan Palace, Imperial Library.

Pl. 9. A. Lorenzetti (d. 1348 ?), view of a city. Panel, 9 1/8 × 13 1/8 in. Siena, Italy, Pinacoteca.

Pl. 10. H. van der Goes, the Portinari Altarpiece, detail of right wing showing landscape background, ca. 1475. Panel; size of wing, 8 ft., 3 1/2 in. × 4 ft., 7 1/2 in. Florence, Uffizi.

Pl. 11. *Above*: H. and J. van Eyck, Adoration of the Holy Lamb, central panel of the Ghent Altarpiece (completed 1432), detail of V, PL. 216. Panel; full size, 4 ft., 6 in. × 7 ft., 11¼ in. Ghent, St-Bavon. *Below*: Piero della Francesca, Allegorical Triumph of Federigo da Montefeltro, detail, ca. 1465. Panel; full size, 18½ × 13 in. Florence, Uffizi.

LANDSCAPE IN ART

Pl. 12. *Above, left*: F. Francia (ca. 1450–1517), Madonna Land Child in a Rose Garden, detail. Panel; full size, 5 ft., 9 in. × 4 ft., 4 in. Munich, Alte Pinakothek. *Right*: D. Dossi (1479–1542), Circe, detail. Canvas; full size, 5 ft., 9 1/2 in. × 5 ft., 8 1/2 in. Rome, Galleria Borghese. *Below, left*: J. Patinir (ca. 1480–1524), The Passage of the Styx, detail. Panel; full size, 25 1/4 × 40 1/2 in. Madrid, Prado. *Right*: J. Gossaert (Mabuse), St. Jerome Penitent, upper portion of one panel, ca. 1512. Panel; full size, 33 3/4 × 10 in. Washington, D.C., National Gallery.

Pl. 13. *Above*: P. Brill (1554–1626), River Landscape. Oil on copper, 10×11½ in. Madrid, Prado. *Below*: A. Elsheimer (1578–1610), Tobias and the Angel. Oil on copper, 7½×10¾ in. London, National Gallery.

LANDSCAPE IN ART

Pl. 14. *Above, left*: A. van der Neer, Ice Scene, 1655. Panel, 10×14½ in. The Hague, Mauritshuis. *Right*: J. van Ruisdael (1628/29–82), Winter Landscape. Canvas, 16½×19½ in. Amsterdam, Rijksmuseum. *Below, left*: J. van Goyen, The Haarlem Lake, 1656. Panel, 15½×21¼ in. Frankfort on the Main, Städelsches Kunstinstitut. *Right*: A. Cuyp (1620–91), Herdsman with Cows by a River. Panel, 17¾×29 in. London, National Gallery.

LANDSCAPE IN ART

Pl. 15. *Above, left*: Domenichino (1581–1641), Landscape. Canvas, 5 ft., 5 in. × 6 ft., 11½ in. *Right*: N. Poussin, Landscape with Orpheus and Eurydice, ca. 1650. Canvas, 4 ft., 1 in. × 6 ft., 6¾ in. Both, Paris, Louvre. *Below, left*: C. Lorrain, Landscape with Country Dance, ca. 1640. Canvas, 3 ft., 10½ in. × 4 ft., 10½ in. Woburn Abbey, Bedfordshire, Coll. Duke of Bedford. *Right*: G. Dughet (G. Poussin, 1615–75), Landscape. Tempera on canvas, 4 ft., 6 in. × 5 ft., 5 in. Rome, Galleria Colonna.

LANDSCAPE IN ART

Pl. 16. S. Rosa (1615-73), St. John the Baptist in the Wilderness. Canvas, 5 ft. 8¼ in. × 8 ft. 6½ in. Glasgow, Art Gallery and Museum.

LANDSCAPE IN ART

Pl. 17. *Left*: N. (or C.) P. Berchem, Italian Landscape, 1656. Canvas, 35×27½ in. Amsterdam, Rijksmuseum. *Right, above*: A. Locatelli (1695–1741?), Landscape. Canvas, 10¼×26 in. *Below*: J.F. van Bloemen (1662–1749), View of the Caelian Hill. Canvas, 23¼×28¾ in. Last two, Rome, Palazzo Pallavicini-Rospigliosi.

LANDSCAPE IN ART

Pl. 18. *Left, above*: B. Bellotto, View of Munich, 1761 (?). Canvas, 26½×46½ in. Washington, D.C., National Gallery. *Below*: G. van Wittel (G. Vanvitelli), Ponte and Castel Sant'Angelo, 1683. Tempera on vellum, 10¼×18½ in. Rome, Galleria Nazionale. *Right*: G. P. Pannini (1691-1765), Roman Ruins. Canvas, 48½×36 in. Naples, Museo di Capodimonte.

LANDSCAPE IN ART

Pl. 19. P. P. Rubens, Landscape, with peasants returning from the fields, ca. 1637. Panel, ca. 4 ft. × 6 ft, 4 in. Florence, Pitti.

LANDSCAPE IN ART

Pl. 20. J. Vermeer, View of Delft, ca. 1658. Canvas, 38¾ × 46 in. The Hague, Mauritshuis.

Pl. 21. *Above, left*: M. Ricci (1676–1729), Landscape with Stream and Figures. Canvas, 4 ft, 6 in. × 6 ft, 5½ in. *Right*: G. Zais (1709–84), River Landscape with Bridge. Canvas, 3 ft, 2¼ in. × 4 ft, 8¼ in. *Below, left*: F. Zuccarelli (1702–88), The Rape of Europa. Canvas, 4 ft, 8 in. × 6 ft, 10 in. *Right*: M. Marieschi (1696–1743), Imaginary View with Obelisk. Canvas, 21½ × 32¼ in. All, Venice, Accademia.

LANDSCAPE IN ART

Pl. 22. *Left*: C. J. Vernet (1714–89), Roman Street. Canvas, 10 ft, 9 in. × 4 ft., 4¼ in. Rome, private coll. *Right, above*: P. H. de Valenciennes (1750–1819), Ruins of the Orti Farnesiani (Rome). Oil on paper, 10¼ × 15¼ in. *Below*: T. Rousseau, Edge of the Forest at Fontainebleau, 1848. Canvas, 4 ft., 7 in. × 6 ft., 6½ in. Last two, Paris, Louvre.

Pl. 23. J. Constable, Dedham Mill, ca. 1819. Canvas, 21×30¼ in. London, Tate Gallery.

LANDSCAPE IN ART

Pl. 24. *Above*: A. Sisley (1839–99), Road at Louveciennes. Canvas, 18×22 in. Nice, Musée Masséna (dépôt de l'État).
Below: G. Seurat, Gravelines, 1890. Panel, 6¼×9¾ in. London, Courtauld Institute Galleries.

LANDSCAPE IN ART

Pl. 25. *Above*: V. Van Gogh, Thatched Cottages at Cordeville, 1890. Canvas, 28³/₄×36¹/₄ in. Paris, Louvre.
Below: O. Kokoschka, Montana (Switzerland), 1947. Canvas, 35¹/₂×47¹/₄ in. Zurich, Kunsthaus.

Pl. 26. China. *Above*: Kuo Hsi (attrib.), Clearing Autumn Skies over Mountains and Valleys, detail of hand scroll, 11th cent. Ink and slight color on silk; ht., 10¼ in. Washington, D.C., Freer Gallery of Art. *Below, left*: Wang Fu (attrib.), A Mountain Gorge, late 14th cent. Ink on paper, 4 ft., 10 in. × 14½ in. Stockholm, Nationalmuseum. *Right*: Hsü Lin, Winter Landscape with Travelers, early 16th cent. Ink on silk. Yokohama, K. Hara Coll.

LANDSCAPE IN ART

Pl. 27. China. *Above*: Fan Ch'i, River Landscape, detail, 17th cent. Ink and color. Berlin, Museum für Völkerkunde. *Below, left*: Yün Hsiang, Landscape, 17th cent. Ink. Hamburg, Museum für Kunst und Gewerbe. *Right*: Shih-t'ao (Tao-chi, ca. 1630–1707), Landscape. Ink. China, private coll.

Pl. 28. Tani Bunchō (1763–1842), The Poet T'ao Yüan-ming, Japan, Edo period. Color on silk. Tokyo, Muromachi Coll.

LAOTIAN ART

Pl. 29. *Above*: Wat Ban Phong, Tranninh, after 15th cent. *Below*: Wat Xieng Thong, Luangprabang, first rebuilt, 1561.

Pl. 30. Wat Mai, Luangprabang, interior of the pagoda, 1796.

LAOTIAN ART

Pl. 31. *Left*: Wat Mai, Luangprabang, central portal, 1796. *Right*: Walking Buddha, after 15th cent. Bronze. Hanoi, North Vietnam, Museum.

Pl. 32. *Above*: Wat Phra Keo, Vientiane, 16th cent. *Below*: Candelabrum, after 15th cent. Gilded bronze. Hanoi, North Vietnam, Museum.

Pl. 33. Rome, Curia, reconstructed under Diocletian, Roman Forum, early 4th cent.

Pl. 34. Spalato (mod. Split, Yugoslavia), Diocletian's Palace, early 4th cent. *Above*: Forecourt of vestibule. *Below*: Northern gate (so-called "Golden Gate").

LATE ANTIQUE AND EARLY CHRISTIAN ART

Pl. 35. Rome. *Above*: Arch of Constantine, north side, 312–15, incorporating elements from older monuments. (Cf. PL. 54.) *Below*: Arch of Janus, early 4th cent.

Pl. 36. Rome, Basilica of Maxentius or of Constantine, first half of 4th cent., exterior (*above*) and interior view of remaining north aisle.

Pl. 37. *Above*: Rome, so-called "Temple of Minerva Medica," nymphaeum of the Horti Liciniani (?), second half of 3d cent. (?). *Below, left*: Rome, Baths of Diocletian, detail of open-air frigidarium, early 4th cent. *Right*: Trier, Germany, so-called "Imperial Baths," view from the west, first half of 4th cent.

LATE ANTIQUE AND EARLY CHRISTIAN ART

Pl. 38. Rome, S. Costanza, ca. mid-4th cent., exterior and interior view.

LATE ANTIQUE AND EARLY CHRISTIAN ART

Pl. 39. Rome, S. Stefano Rotondo, interior, variously dated, late 4th – early 6th cent.

LATE ANTIQUE AND EARLY CHRISTIAN ART

Pl. 40. Rome. *Above*: S. Maria Maggiore, interior, first half of 5th cent. (ceiling, ca. 1500). *Below*: S. Sabina, interior, first half of 5th cent.

LATE ANTIQUE AND EARLY CHRISTIAN ART

Pl. 41. Rome, Temple of Romulus, son of Maxentius, in the Roman Forum, detail with portal, early 4th cent.

LATE ANTIQUE AND EARLY CHRISTIAN ART

Pl. 42. The "Barberini Goddess," Rome, 307–12. Wall painting. Rome, Museo Nazionale Romano.

Pl. 43. Milan, S. Lorenzo Maggiore, rebuilt (late 16th cent.) preserving the quatrefoil plan of the 5th cent.

Pl. 44. Salonika, Greece, St. George, late 3d cent., with late 4th-cent. mosaics. (Cf. PL. 62.)

Pl. 45. Ravenna, Italy, Baptistery of the Orthodox, 5th cent. (Cf. details, PLS. 66, 72; X, PL. 441.)

Pl. 46. Spoleto, Italy, S. Salvatore, façade, late 4th cent. with subsequent alterations.

Pl. 47. Ruins of Qal'at Sim'ān, northwest of Aleppo, Syria, Church of St. Simeon Stylites, 5th cent. *Above*: Narthex of southern basilica. *Below*: Interior view of eastern basilica from the octagonal court.

Pl. 48. Emperor Diocletian (r. 284–305), from Nicomedia (mod. İzmit, Turkey). Marble, ht., 15 3/8 in. Istanbul, Archaeological Museums.

LATE ANTIQUE AND EARLY CHRISTIAN ART

Pl. 49. *Above*: Reliefs on the south pier of the Arch of Galerius, Salonika, Greece, late 3d–early 4th cent. Marble. *Left*: Emperor addressing the troops, detail of XII, PL. 198. *Right*: Detail of battle scene. *Below*: Emperor making libations, relief on a column base called the "Base of the Decennials," Roman Forum, ca. 303. Marble, w., 5 ft., 11 in.

LATE ANTIQUE AND EARLY CHRISTIAN ART

Pl. 50. Constantine the Great, 317–30 (on a modern plinth). Marble, ht. of figure, 10 ft., 8 in. Rome, St. John Lateran, atrium.

LATE ANTIQUE AND EARLY CHRISTIAN ART

Pl. 51. Colossal head, Constantius II (?), ca. 360. Bronze, ht., 5 ft., 9½ in. Rome, Palazzo dei Conservatori.

LATE ANTIQUE AND EARLY CHRISTIAN ART

Pl. 52. Mosaic portrait in the corridor of the Great Hunt, Roman villa at Casale, near Piazza Armerina, Sicily, ca. second half of 4th cent.

Pl. 53. Constantine the Great, head of a colossal statue, from the Basilica of Maxentius or of Constantine, Rome, ca. 313 (?). Marble, ht. of face, 4 ft., 5 1/8 in. Rome, Palazzo dei Conservatori.

Pl. 54. Reliefs on the Arch of Constantine (PL. 35), Rome. *Above*: Medallion with Selene sinking into the sea and frieze with triumphal procession, ca. 312–15, west side. *Below*: Medallions with hunting and sacrificial scenes, Hadrianic period, and frieze with distribution of gifts, 312–15, north side.

Pl. 55. Porphyry sarcophagi, first half of 4th cent. *Above*: Vintaging putti, sarcophagus of Constantina. Full ht., 7 ft., 4½ in. *Below*: Roman horsemen with barbarian captives, supposed sarcophagus of Empress Helena (partly remade, late 18th cent.). Ht., 7 ft., 11 in. Both, Rome, Vatican Museums.

Pl. 56. Group of the Tetrarchs, early 4th cent. Porphyry, ht., 4 ft., 3 1/8 in. Venice, S. Marco, exterior.

LATE ANTIQUE AND EARLY CHRISTIAN ART

Pl. 57. *Above, left*: Julian the Apostate, ca. 361–63. Marble, ht., 5 ft., 9 in. Paris, Louvre. *Right*: Aelia Flaccilla, from Cyprus, ca. 400. Marble, ht., 30¾ in. Paris, Cabinet des Médailles. *Below*: Emperor presiding over ceremonies, relief on the base of the obelisk (Column of Theodosius) in the Hippodrome, Istanbul, ca. 390.

LATE ANTIQUE AND EARLY CHRISTIAN ART

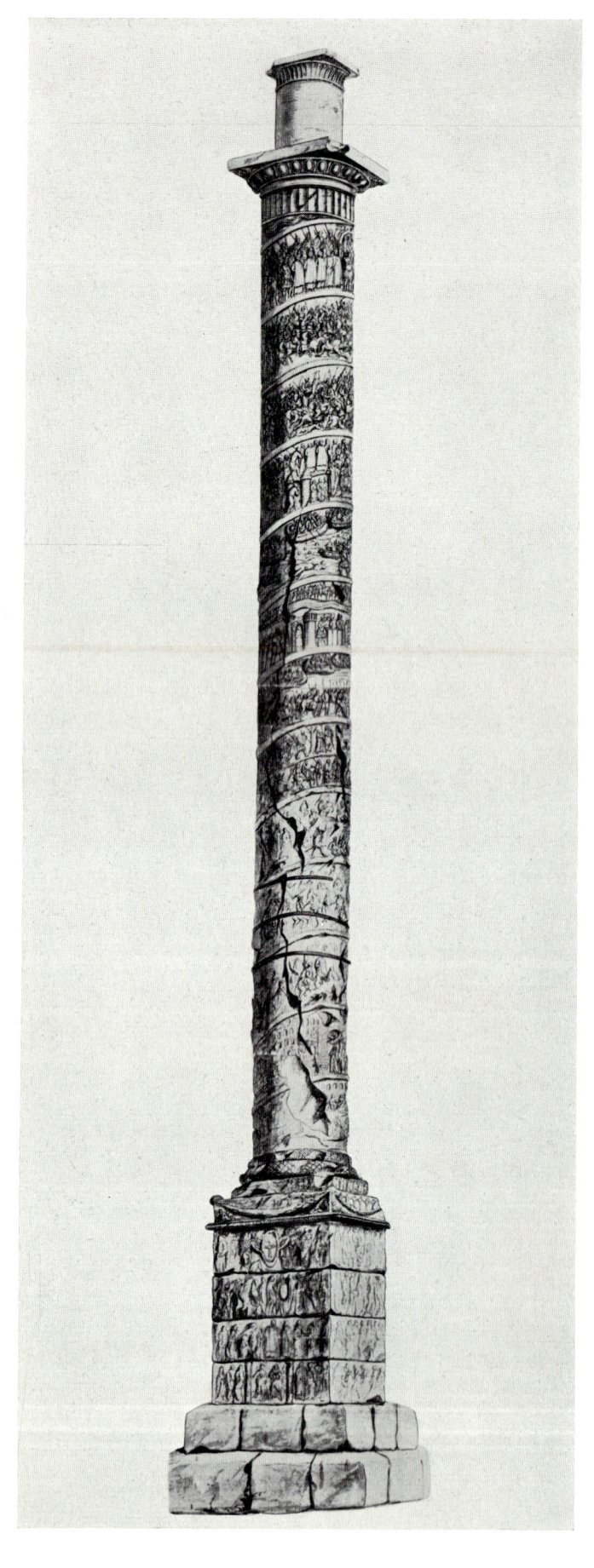

Pl. 58. *Left, above*: Imperial portrait, so-called "Honorius," 5th cent. (on a later bust). Marble. Paris, Louvre. *Below*: Arcadius (?), found at Bayazıt, Turkey, late 4th–early 5th cent. Marble, ht., 12³/₄ in. Istanbul, Archaeological Museums. *Right*: The Column of Arcadius in Constantinople (destroyed ca. 1719), depicted in a drawing, ca. 1670. Paris, Bibliothèque Nationale.

LATE ANTIQUE AND EARLY CHRISTIAN ART

Pl. 59. *Above, left*: So-called "Eugenius," perhaps Theodosius II, mid-5th cent. (bust of later date). Marble, ht. of face, 7¹/₈ in. Paris, Louvre. *Right*: Roman empress, late 5th–early 6th cent. Marble, ht., 9¹/₂ in. Rome, Palazzo dei Conservatori. *Below*: Statues of magistrates, late 4th–early 5th cent. Marble. *Left*: From Rome. Ht., 7 ft., 9 in. Rome, Palazzo dei Conservatori. *Right*: From Aphrodisias, Turkey. Ht., ca. 6 ft. Istanbul, Archaeological Museums.

LATE ANTIQUE AND EARLY CHRISTIAN ART

Pl. 60. The Colossus of Barletta, imperial statue of disputed date. Bronze; ht. of original part (knee to head), 11 ft., 7³/₄ in. Barletta, Italy, outside Sto Sepolcro.

LATE ANTIQUE AND EARLY CHRISTIAN ART

Pl. 61. Detail of mosaic with symbol of the Evangelist Matthew, 5th cent. Naples, Baptistery (S. Giovanni in Fonte).

LATE ANTIQUE AND EARLY CHRISTIAN ART

Pl. 62. Section of mosaic frieze with SS. Cosmas and Damian, late 4th cent., dome of St. George (Pl. 44), Salonika, Greece.

LATE ANTIQUE AND EARLY CHRISTIAN ART

Pl. 63. *Left*: Orpheus surrounded by beasts, 4th cent. Marble, ht. of figure, 26 3/8 in. Istanbul, Archaeological Museums. *Right, above*: Sarcophagus with the Traditio Legis, detail, mid-4th cent. Marble. Rome, Vatican Grottoes. *Below*: Sarcophagus with the Good Shepherd and vintage scenes, from the Catacomb of Praetextatus, second half of 4th cent. Rome, Lateran Museums.

Pl. 64. *Above*: Sarcophagus, formerly called "of Stilicho," showing Elijah's ascent into heaven (end) and Christ teaching the apostles, late 4th cent. Marble, w., 4 ft., 11 1/8 in. Milan, S. Ambrogio. (Photo from cast.) *Below*: Sarcophagus with Christ and apostles, ca. 400 (?). Marble, l., 6 ft., 9 1/2 in. Ravenna, S. Francesco.

LATE ANTIQUE AND EARLY CHRISTIAN ART

Pl. 65. *Above, left*: The Onesti sarcophagus, detail with the Traditio Legis, early 5th cent. Ravenna, S. Maria in Porto Fuori. *Right*: The Isaac sarcophagus, detail with Madonna and Child, early 5th cent. Ravenna, S. Vitale. *Below*: The Rinaldo sarcophagus, front depicting Christ with Peter and Paul, ca. mid-5th cent. Ravenna, Cathedral.

LATE ANTIQUE AND EARLY CHRISTIAN ART

Pl. 66. Reliefs with saints, Baptistery of the Orthodox, Ravenna, Italy, 5th cent. Stucco. (Cf. PL. 45.)

Pl. 67. Fragmentary semicircular ambo with reliefs depicting the Adoration of the Magi, from Salonika, Greece, late 5th cent. (?). Marble, ht., 5 ft., 11 in. (Cf. II, PL. 470.) Istanbul, Archaeological Museums.

Pl. 68. Catacomb paintings. *Left*: Christ among the apostles, detail, late 3d cent. Rome, Catacomb of the Jordani. *Right, above*: So-called "Susanna and the elders," late 3d cent. Rome, Catacomb of SS. Peter and Marcellinus. *Below*: Nebuchadnezzar and the three children of Babylon, 4th cent. Rome, Catacomb of Marcus and Marcellinus.

Pl. 69. Painted tomb of Aelia Arisuth, at Gargaresc, near Tripoli, Libya, 4th cent.

Pl. 70. Junius Bassus in his consular chariot, wall facing in *opus sectile*, from the Basilica of Junius Bassus, Rome, 4th cent. Polychrome marble with glass paste and mother-of-pearl, w. 3 ft., 7 3/4 in. Rome, formerly Palazzo del Drago (awaiting relocation).

Pl. 71. Symbolic lamb, panel from the ancient choir of S. Ambrogio, late 4th cent. Marble and glass paste, 3 ft., 9¼ in. × 4 ft., 7 in. Milan, Museo di S. Ambrogio.

LATE ANTIQUE AND EARLY CHRISTIAN ART

Pl. 72. Ravenna, Italy, Baptistery of the Orthodox, mosaics in the dome showing the Baptism of Christ, apostles, and architectural motifs with altars and thrones, 5th cent. (Cf. PL. 45.)

LATE ANTIQUE AND EARLY CHRISTIAN ART

Pl. 73. *Above*: Mosaic with hunting scene and figures of Summer and Spring, ca. 4th cent., from the Constantinian villa at Daphne-Harbie, Antioch, Turkey. Paris, Louvre. *Below*: Roman villa of Casale, near Piazza Armerina, Sicily, detail of floor mosaic with subjects of the Labors of Hercules, 4th cent.

LATE ANTIQUE AND EARLY CHRISTIAN ART

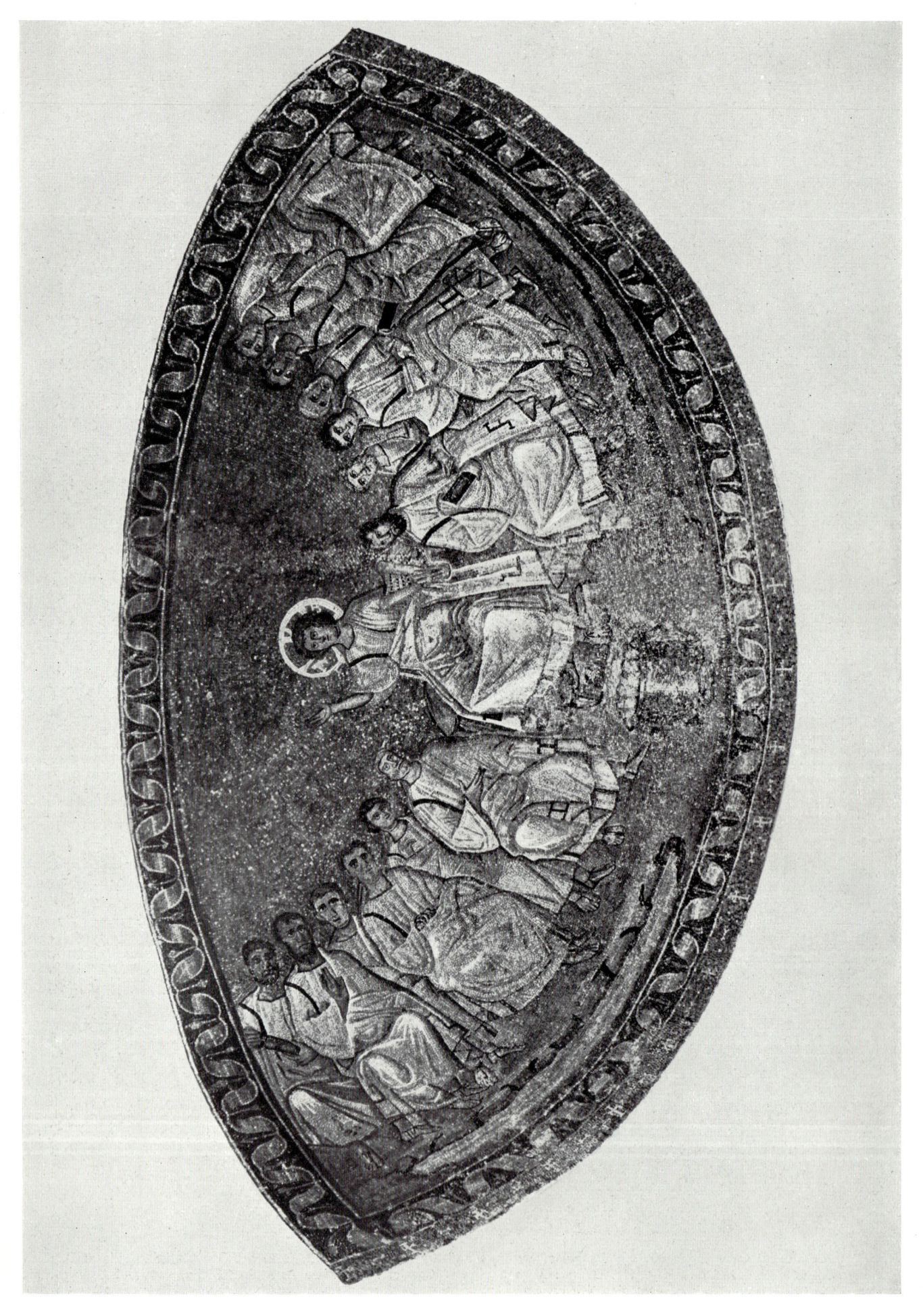

Pl. 74. Milan, S. Lorenzo Maggiore, Chapel of St. Aquilinus, southeast conch, Christ among the apostles, second half of 4th–5th cent.

LATE ANTIQUE AND EARLY CHRISTIAN ART

Pl. 75. Rome, SS. Cosma e Damiano, mosaics of the apse and triumphal arch, 526-30.

LATE ANTIQUE AND EARLY CHRISTIAN ART

Pl. 76. *Left, above*: Mosaic detail with floral motif, from Torre da Palma, Alentejo, Portugal, 4th cent. Lisbon (Belém), Museu Etnológico. *Below*: Ptolemaïs (mod. Tolmeta, Libya), mosaic detail with lions and vase, in the great peristyle near the colonnaded palace, 6th cent. *Right*: Mosaic of the Beribboned Parrots, detail, from Daphne-Harbie, near Antioch, Turkey, mid-3d–5th cent. Paris, Louvre.

LATE ANTIQUE AND EARLY CHRISTIAN ART

Pl. 77. *Left*: Funerary mosaic of the bishop Pelagius, from Thabraca, Tunisia, ca. 5th cent. Ht., 39³/₈ in. *Right*: Medallion representing Autumn, detail of mosaic pavement from the church of St. Christopher, Kabr Hiram, Lebanon, 6th cent. Both, Paris, Louvre.

LATE ANTIQUE AND EARLY CHRISTIAN ART

Pl. 78. Vergilius Vaticanus, the Miracle of Ascanius, scene from *The Aeneid*, Book II, 680 ff., ca. early 5th cent. Illumination. Rome, Vatican Library (Vat. Lat. 3225, fol. 22r).

LATE ANTIQUE AND EARLY CHRISTIAN ART

Pl. 79. The Vienna Genesis. The saving of Lot and the destruction of Sodom, 6th cent. Illumination. Vienna, Nationalbibliothek (Cod. vindob. theol. graec. 31, fol. 9).

LATE ANTIQUE AND EARLY CHRISTIAN ART

Pl. 80. Gold glass, 4th cent. *Above, left*: Portrait medallion. Diam., 2¼ in. Arezzo, Italy, Museo Archeologico. *Right*: Married pair with figure of Hercules, probably the bottom of a plate. Diam., 3¼ in. London, British Museum. *Below*: Medallion with family group. Diam., 1⅞ in. Rome, Vatican Library.

LATE ANTIQUE AND EARLY CHRISTIAN ART

Pl. 81. Joseph pardoning his brothers, back of a reliquary casket, north Italian, late 4th cent. Part-gilded silver, repoussé; ht., 7 in. Milan, S. Nazaro Maggiore.

Pl. 82. Coptic textile with Dionysos, 4th–6th cent. Vienna, Kunsthistorisches Museum.

Pl. 83. The ascent of Elijah, panel of the wooden doors of S. Sabina, Rome, first half of 4th cent.

LATE ANTIQUE AND EARLY CHRISTIAN ART

Pl. 84. Ivories. *Above, left*: Serena late her son, left leaf of the diptych of Stilicho and Serena, ca. 400, 12³/₄ × 6³/₈ in. Monza, Italy, Cathedral Treasury. *Right*: Supposed diptych of Magnus (consul in 518), right leaf, cut down and reworked for church use, from Constantinople, 10³/₈ × 5¹/₈ in. Milan, Castello Sforzesco. *Below*: Christ and two apostles, detail of a reliquary casket, northern Italy (?), third quarter of 4th cent. L., 12⁷/₈ in. Brescia, Italy, Museo Cristiano.

Pl. 85. Ivories. *Above, left*: The Healing of the Man Sick of the Palsy, detail of the so-called "Andrews Diptych," northern Italy, third quarter of 5th cent. W., $3^{7}/_{8}$ in. London, Victoria and Albert Museum. *Right*: Apostle, northern Italy, early 5th cent., $4^{3}/_{4} \times 2^{3}/_{4}$ in. Paris, Louvre. *Below, left*: Bellerophon, panel formerly on a book cover, third quarter of 5th cent. (?), $8^{3}/_{8} \times 3^{1}/_{2}$ in. London, British Museum. *Right*: Emperor Anastasius I (?), leaf of the so-called "Barberini Diptych," late 5th–6th cent., $13^{3}/_{8} \times 10^{1}/_{2}$ in. Paris, Louvre.

Pl. 86. *Above*: Bridal casket of Projecta, lid panel with the *deductio* of the bride, from the Esquiline Treasure, Rome, late 4th–5th cent. Embossed silver, partly gilded; w., 23³/₄ in. *Below*: Decorative panel, 4th cent., found in Asia Minor. Gold, ht., 2 in. Both, London, British Museum.

Pl. 87. Missorium of Aspar Ardabur, 434 (in modern frame). Embossed and engraved silver, diam., 16½ in. Florence, Museo Archeologico.

LATE ANTIQUE AND EARLY CHRISTIAN ART

Pl. 88. *Above*: *Diatreta* glass. *Left*: The Lycurgus Cup, made in Italy (?), second half of 4th–early 5th cent. (metal rim and base, ca. 17th cent.). Olive green and yellowish glass, changing to ruby red and amethyst by transmitted light; diam., 5½ in. London, British Museum. *Right*: Fragmentary cup, from Daruvar, Yugoslavia, ca. 4th cent. Diam., 3½ in. Vienna, Kunsthistorisches Museum. *Below, left*: The so-called "Rubens Vase," with vines and satyrs' heads in high relief, ca. 400 (gold rim, 19th cent.), from Constantinople. Honey-colored agate, ht., 7½ in. Baltimore, Walters Art Gallery. *Right*: Situla with Dionysiac scene, 5th cent. Engraved blue-violet glass with gilded-silver handle; ht., 7⅞ in. Venice, Treasury of S. Marco.

LATE ANTIQUE AND EARLY CHRISTIAN ART

Pl. 89. *Above, left*: Bust of Constantine (?), 4th cent. (mounted in a scepter with arms and drapery added, 15th cent.). Chalcedony, ht., 3 3/4 in. Paris, Cabinet des Médailles. *Right*: Hercules and the Erymanthian boar, from Egypt, ca. 300. Rock crystal, ht., 3 in. Baltimore, Walters Art Gallery. *Below, left*: Equestrian statuette of Constantine, ca. 310–25. Bronze, ht., 4 3/8 in. Vienna, Kunsthistorisches Museum. *Right*: Lamp in the form of a boat with Christ and an orant (or Peter and Paul?), found in Rome, 4th cent. Bronze, ht., 13 3/8 in. Florence, Museo Archeologico.

LATE ANTIQUE AND EARLY CHRISTIAN ART

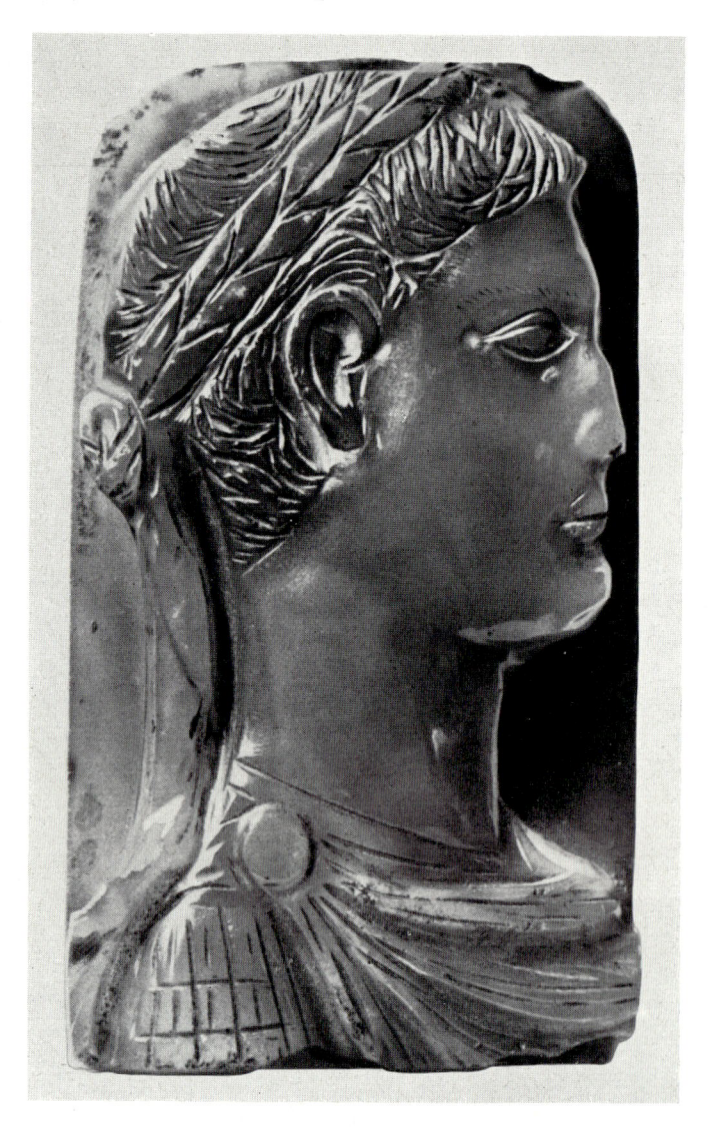

Pl. 90. Imperial portraits on coins and gems. *Above, left*: Obverse of an aureus with Diocletian, 284–305. Rome, Museo Nazionale Romano. *Right*: Cameo, 3d–4th cent., 29×10 mm. Lyons, France, Musée des Beaux-Arts. *Below, left*: Amethyst, 4th cent. (?), 20×15 mm. Leipzig, Germany, Museum des Kunsthandwerks. (Cast.) *Right*: Obverse of an aureus with Valentinian III, 425–55. Rome, Museo Nazionale Romano.

LA TOUR, GEORGES DE

Pl. 91. Magdalen with the Night Light. Canvas, 4 ft., 2 3/8 in. × 3 ft., 1 in. Paris, Louvre.

LA TOUR, GEORGES DE

Pl. 92. St. Sebastian Mourned by St. Irene. Canvas, 5 ft., 3 in. × 4 ft., 2³/⁴ in. Berlin, Staatliche Museen.

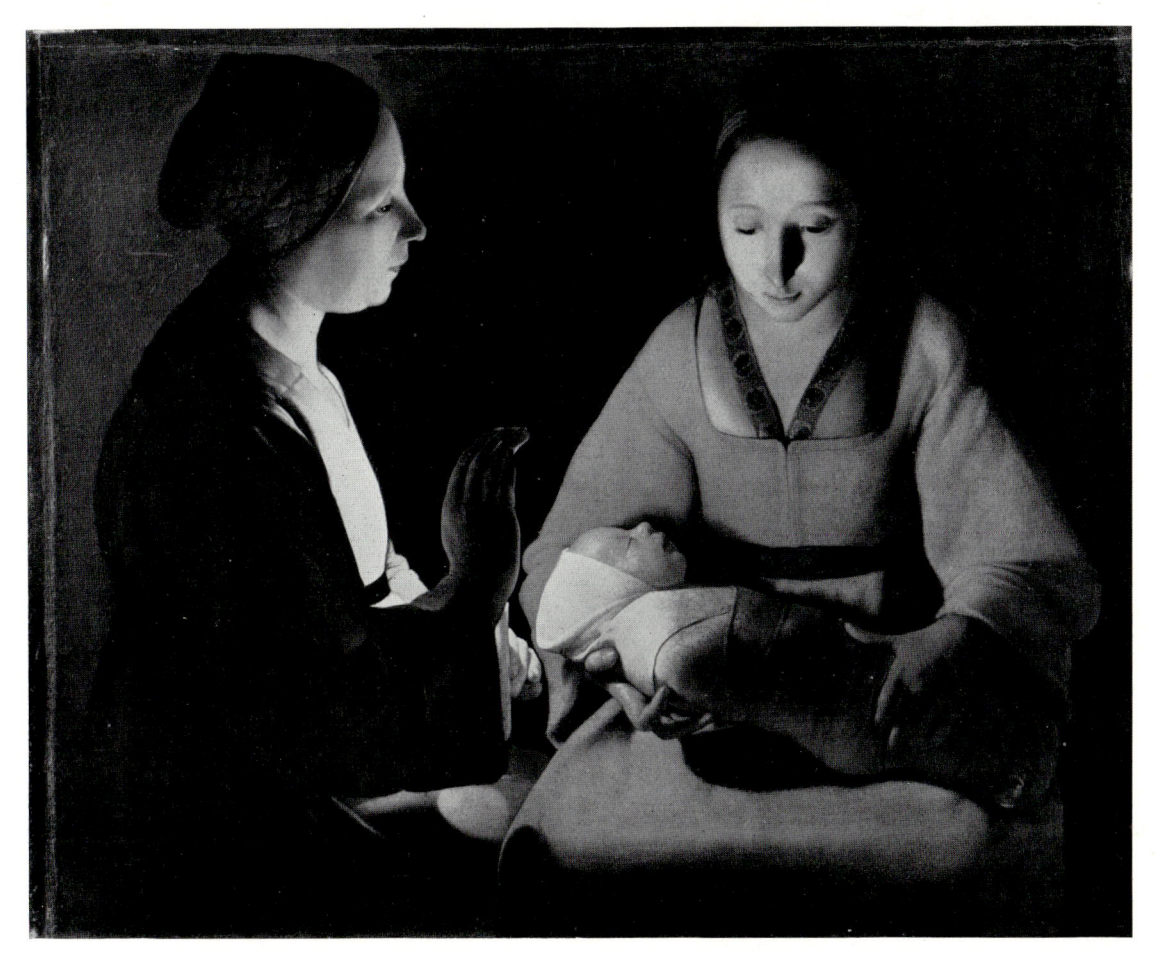

Pl. 93. *Above*: The Denial of St. Peter. Canvas, 3 ft., 11 1/4 in. × 5 ft., 3 in. Nantes, France, Musée des Beaux-Arts. *Below*: The Newborn. Canvas, 29 7/8 × 35 7/8 in. Rennes, France, Musée des Beaux-Arts.

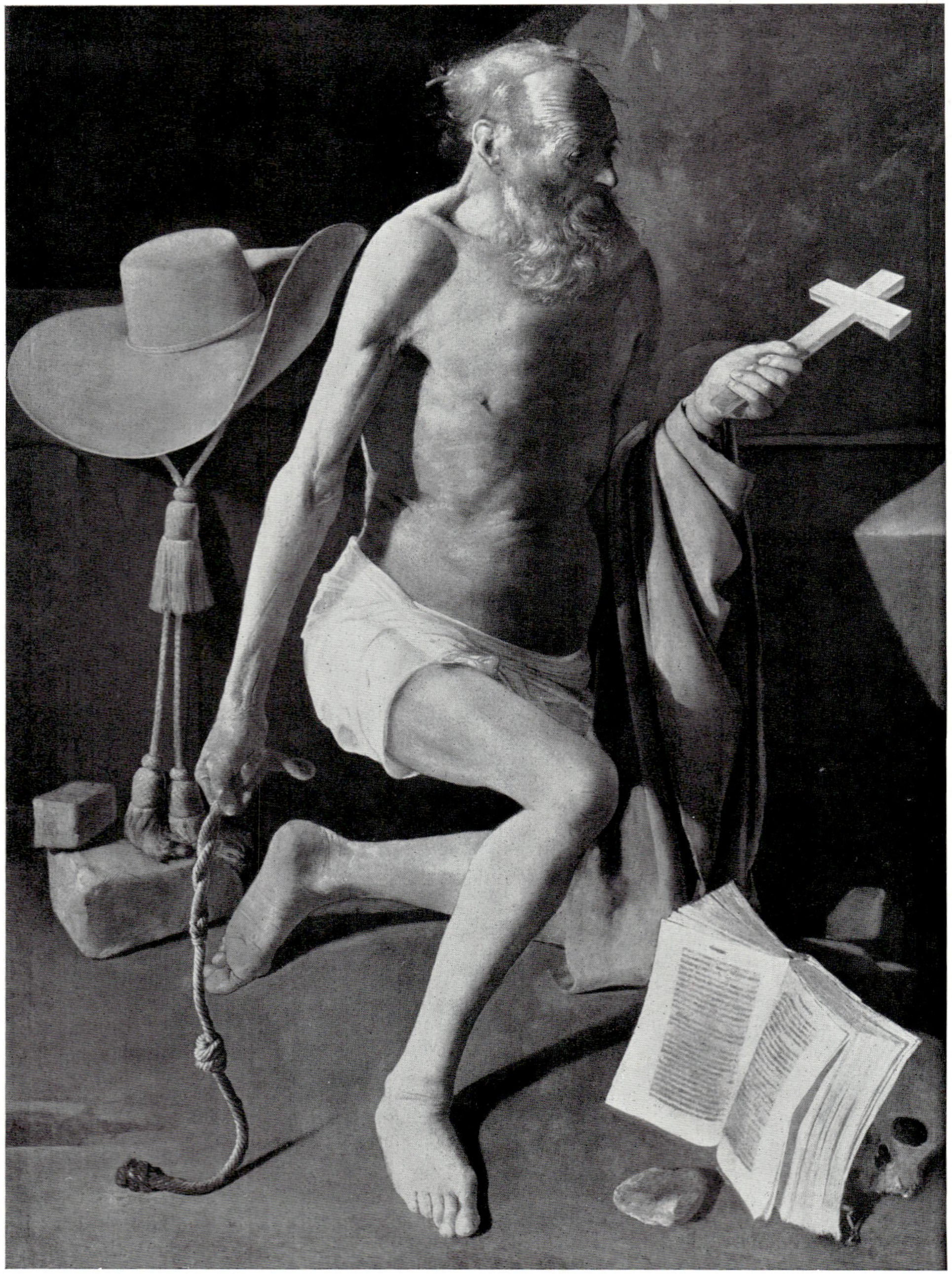

LA TOUR, GEORGES DE

Pl. 94. *Left*: St. Jerome. Canvas, 4 ft., 11⅞ in. × 3 ft., 6⅞ in. Stockholm, Nationalmuseum. *Right*: The Hurdy-gurdy Player. Canvas, 5 ft., 3¾ in. × 3 ft., 5⅜ in. Nantes, France, Musée des Beaux-Arts.

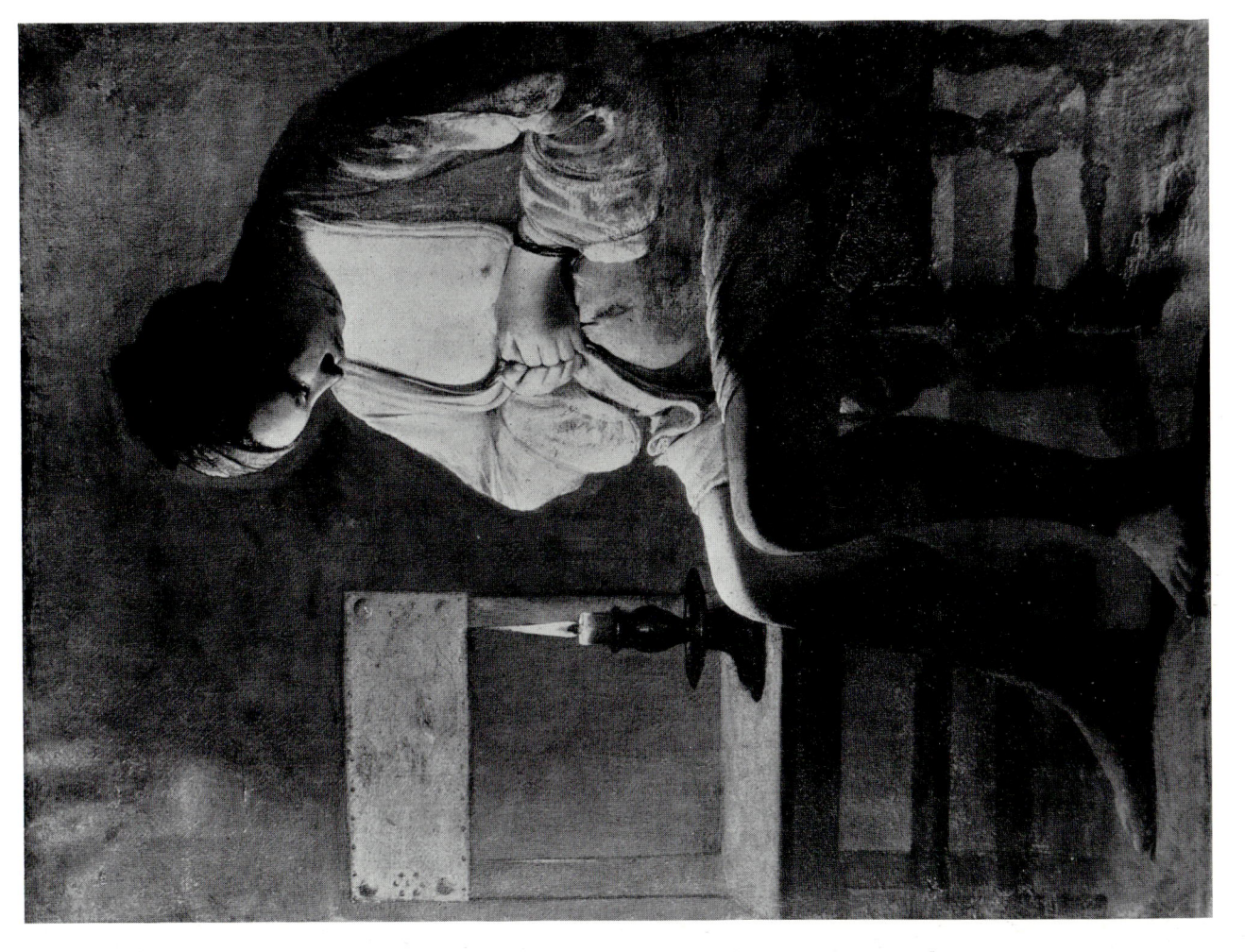

Pl. 95. *Left:* The Discovery of the Body of St. Alexis. Canvas, 5 ft., 2⁵/₈ in. × 3 ft., 8¹/₂ in. *Right:* The Servant with the Flea. Canvas, 47¹/₄ × 34⁵/₈ in. Both, Nancy, France, Musée Historique Lorrain.

Pl. 96. Urbino, Italy, Palazzo Ducale, west façade with towers.

LAURANA

Pl. 97. Urbino, Italy, Palazzo Ducale. *Above*: Throne Room. *Below, left*: Spiral stairway inside one of the towers. *Right*: Entrance to the *studiolo* of Duke Federigo da Montefeltro.

LAURANA

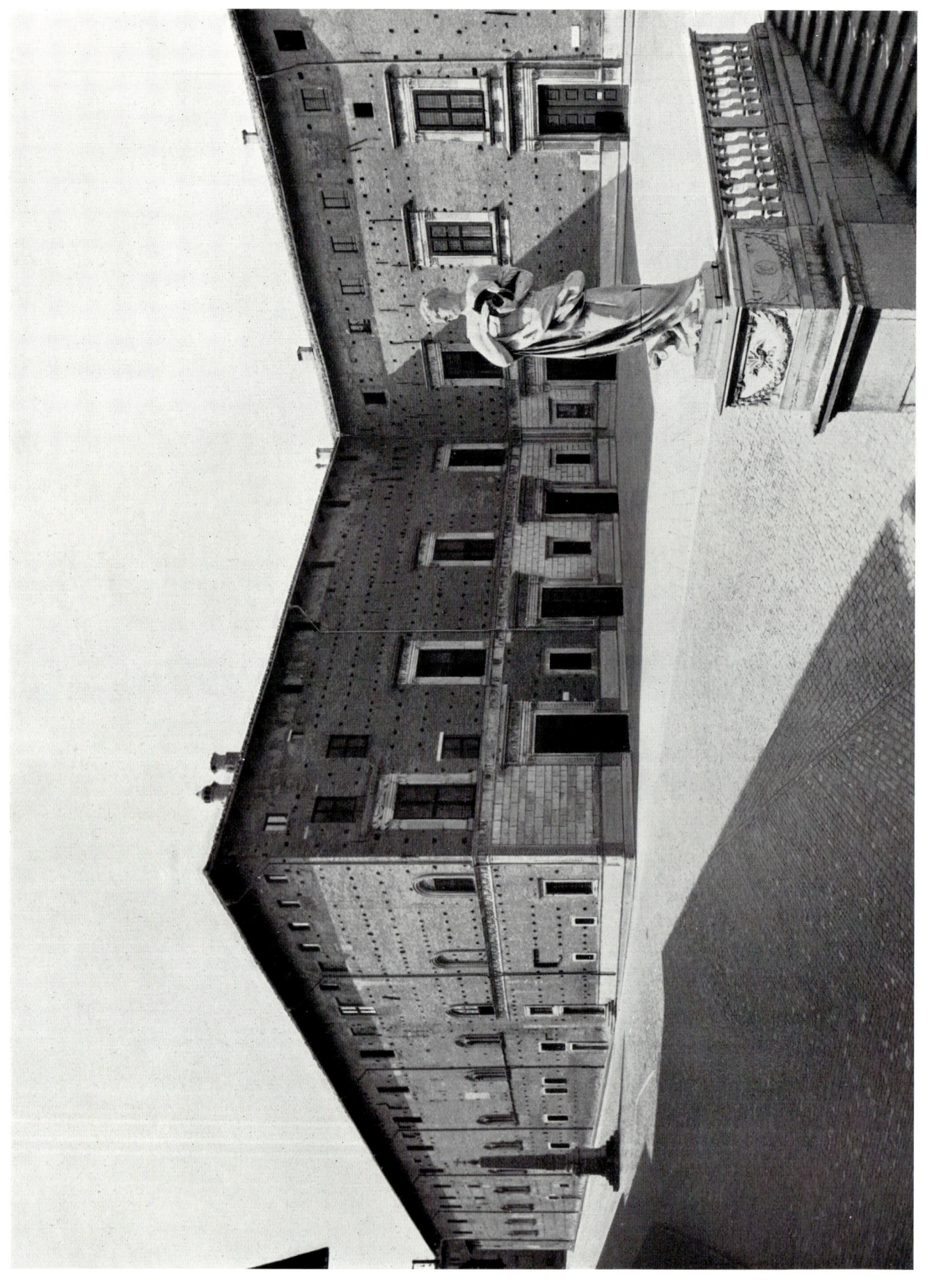

Pl. 98. Urbino, Italy, Palazzo Ducale, view from Piazza Duca Federico.

Pl. 99. Urbino, Italy, Palazzo Ducale, main courtyard.

Pl. 100. Detail of courtyard, PL. 99.

Pl. 101. Alexander the Great Entering Babylon, detail, 1660–68. Canvas; full size, 14 ft., 9 in. × 23 ft. Paris, Louvre.

LEBRUN

Pl. 102. The Chancellor Séguier, 1661. Canvas, 9 ft., 8 in. × 11 ft., 6 in. Paris, Louvre.

LEBRUN

Pl. 103. *Left, above*: Pietà, 1642–46. Canvas, 4 ft., 9½ in. × 7 ft., 3⅜ in. Paris, Louvre. *Below*: Louis XIV Visiting the Gobelins. Tapestry from a design by Lebrun. Canvas, 15 ft., 9 in. × 8 ft., 8⅜ in. Lyons, Musée des Beaux-Arts. *Right*: Louis XIV Adoring the Risen Christ, 1674. Versailles, Palace.

Pl. 104. *Above*: Sceaux, Colbert's château, Pavillon de l'Aurore, interior of the dome, showing decorations by Lebrun. *Below*: Lebrun, J. H. Mansart, and A. Coysevox, Palace of Versailles, Salon de la Guerre, begun 1678.

LE CORBUSIER

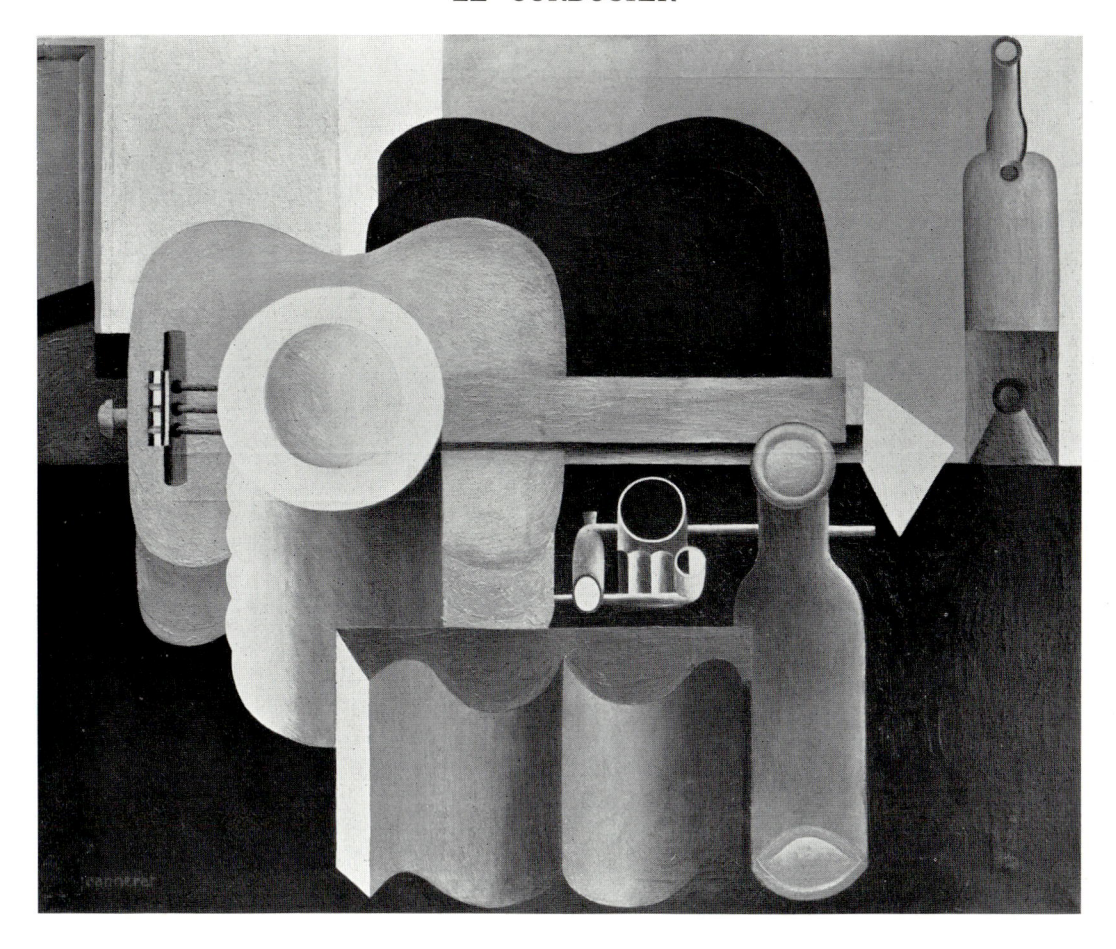

Pl. 105. *Above*: Still Life, 1920. Canvas, 31 7/8 × 39 1/4 in. New York, Museum of Modern Art. *Below*: Stuttgart, house in Weissenhof quarter, 1927. (Cf. V, PL. 109.)

LE CORBUSIER

Pl. 106. *Above*: Poissy, France, Savoye house, 1929–31. *Below, left*: Paris, Cité Universitaire, Swiss Hostel, 1931–32. *Right*: Model for so-called "Cartesian skyscraper," 1935.

LE CORBUSIER

Pl. 107. *Above*: Marseilles, housing unit (*unité d'habitation*), 1946–52. *Left*: Roof terrace. *Right*: View of the *pilotis*. *Below*: Ahmadabad, Gujarat, India, Shodhan house, south wing, 1955–56.

Pl. 108. Chandigarh, India, High Courts of Justice, detail of façade, 1951-56.

Pl. 109. L. Le Nain. *Above*: The Dairywoman's Family. Canvas, 20×23¼ in. *Below*: The Visit to Grandmother. Canvas, 22⅞×28¾ in. Both, Leningrad, The Hermitage.

LE NAIN

Pl. 110. M. Le Nain, The Backgammon Players. Canvas, 35 3/8 × 47 1/4 in. Paris, Louvre.

LE NAIN

Pl. 111. L. Le Nain. The Cart. Canvas, 22 × 28 3/8 in. Paris, Louvre.

LE NAIN

Pl. 112. A. Le Nain, Family Gathering. Copper, $12^{5}/_{8} \times 14^{5}/_{8}$ in. Paris, Louvre.

LE NAIN

Pl. 113. M. Le Nain, Peasants' Meal. Canvas, 30¾×37 in. Leningrad, The Hermitage.

LE NAIN

Pl. 114. L. and M. Le Nain, Venus in Vulcan's Forge. Canvas, 59 × 45 1/4 in. Reims, Musée des Beaux-Arts.

LEONARDO DA VINCI

Pl. 115. St. Jerome. Panel, 40½×29½ in. Rome, Vatican Museums.

LEONARDO DA VINCI

Pl. 116. The Annunciation. Panel, 3 ft., 2 5/8 in. × 7 ft., 1 3/8 in. Florence, Uffizi.

LEONARDO DA VINCI

Pl. 117. *Left*: The Adoration of the Magi. Panel, 7 ft., 11⁵/₈ in. × 8 ft., ⁷/₈ in. Florence, Uffizi. (Cf. IV, pl. 266.) *Right*: Study for the Adoration of the Magi. Pen and ink, 11 × 8¹/₄ in. Paris, Louvre.

LEONARDO DA VINCI

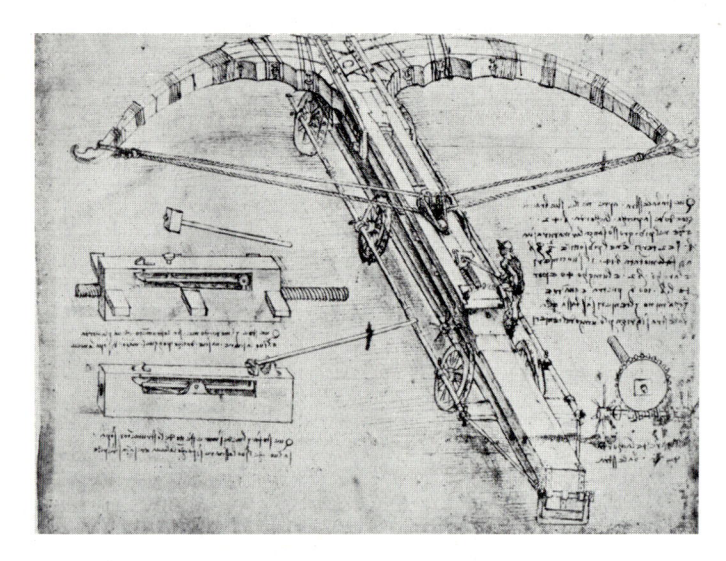

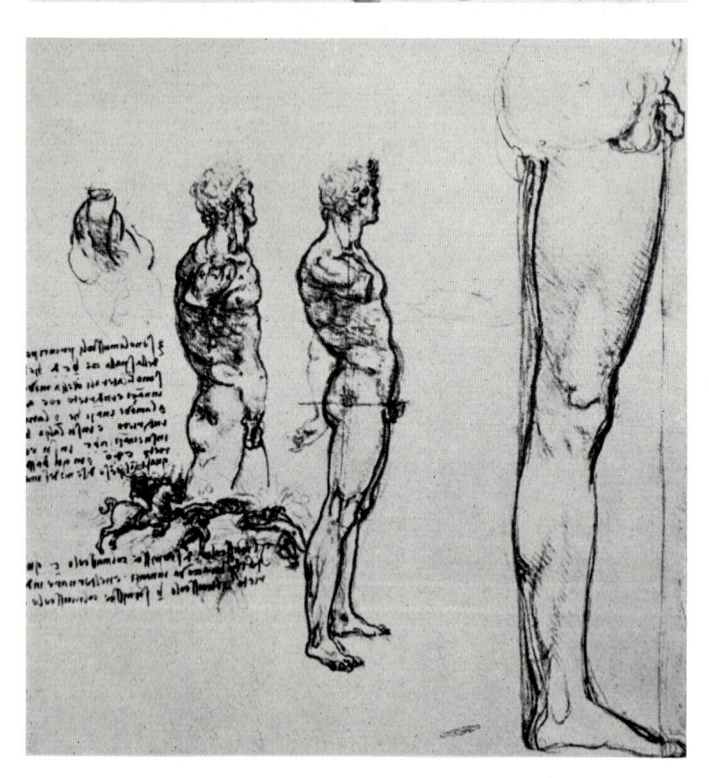

Pl. 118. Drawings. *Left, above*: Giant crossbow. Pen and wash. *Center*: Project for fortifications. Pen. Both, Milan, Biblioteca Ambrosiana (Cod. Atlanticus, fols. 53v-b and 43v-a). *Below*: Nude studies. Red chalk and pen. *Right, above*: Studies for equestrian monument. Pen and bister. *Below*: Botanical study. Red chalk. Last three, Windsor, England, Royal Library.

LEONARDO DA VINCI

Pl. 119. Drawings. *Above*, 1
24³/₄ × 18¹/₈ in. Paris,
Below: Detail of The of the Rocks. Panel transferred to canvas, 6 ft., 6 in. × 4 ft., ¹/₂ in. Paris, Louvre.

LEONARDO DA VINCI

Pl. 122. The Virgin and Child with St. Anne. Panel, 5 ft., 6 1/8 in. × 4 ft., 3 1/4 in. Paris, Louvre.

LEONARDO DA VINCI

Pl. 123. The Virgin and Child with St. Anne and the Infant St. John, cartoon. Charcoal heightened with white, on brown paper, 4 ft., 6³/₄ in. × 3 ft., 3³/₈ in. London, Royal Academy of Arts.

LEONARDO DA VINCI

Pl. 124. *Left*: The Lady with an Ermine (Cecilia Gallerani). Panel, 21¼ × 15⅜ in. Cracow, Poland, Czartoryski Museum. *Right*: John the Baptist. Panel, 27⅛ × 22½ in. Paris, Louvre.

LEONARDO DA VINCI

Pl. 125. The Last Supper, detail. Oil tempera on wall; full size, 15 ft., 1 1/8 in. × 28 ft., 10 1/2 in. Milan, Refectory of the Convent of S. Maria delle Grazie.

LEONARDO DA VINCI

Pl. 126. Mona Lisa, or La Gioconda. Panel, $30^{1}/_{4} \times 20^{7}/_{8}$ in. Paris, Louvre.

LIANG K'AI

Pl. 127. Three ancient trees in a snowy landscape. Ink and faint color on silk. Tokyo, National Museum.

Pl. 128. Snow Landscape with Two Horsemen Near a Mountain Pass, hanging scroll. Ink and faint color on silk, 40 3/4 × 19 3/4 in. Tokyo, National Museum.

Pl. 129. The Supreme Taoist Master, Chang T'ien-shih, Holding Court, whole and detail of hand scroll. Ink on paper. New York, H. C. Weng Coll.

LIANG K'AI

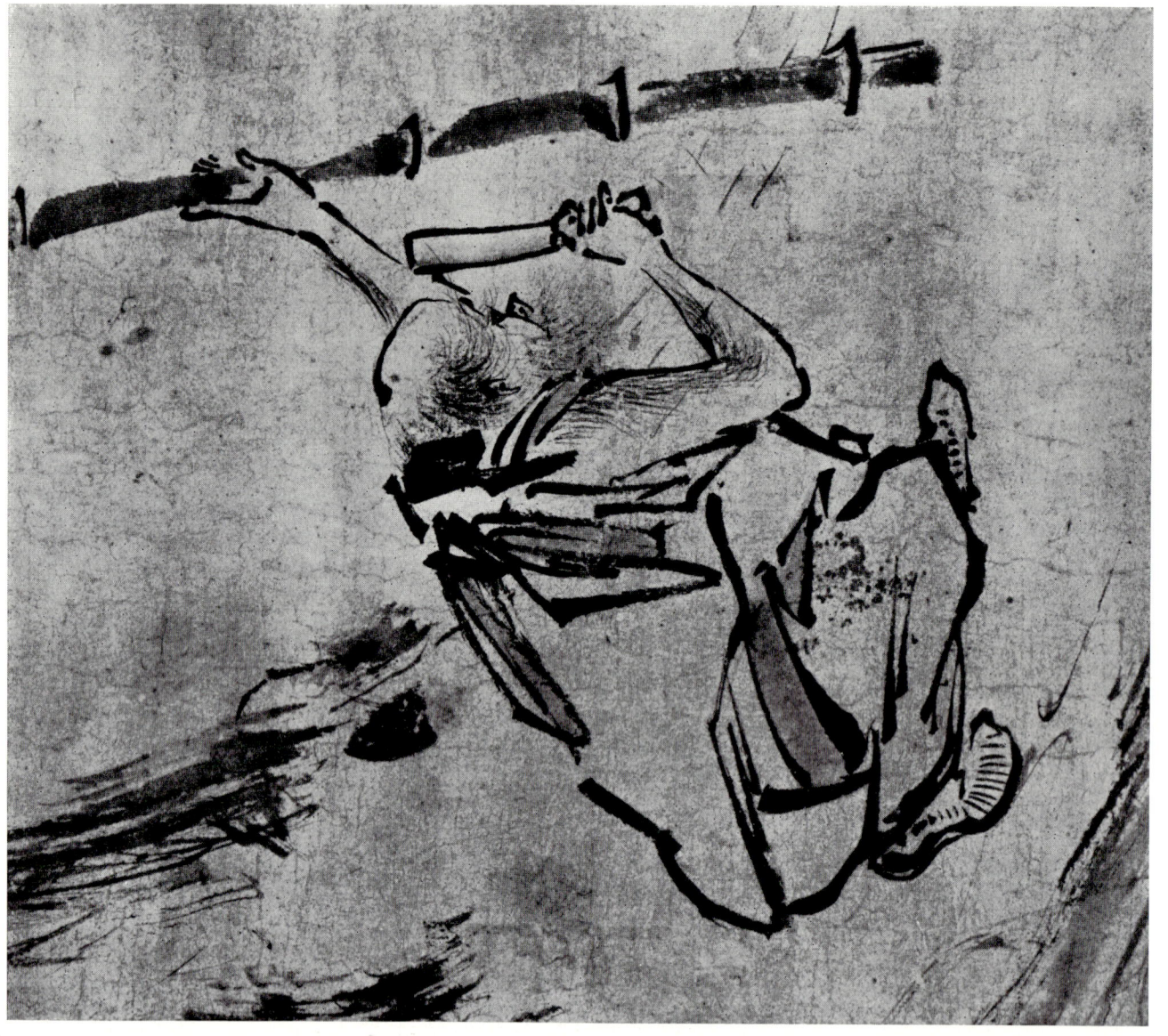

Pl. 130. Hui Nêng, the Sixth Ch'an Patriarch, Chopping Bamboo at the Moment of Enlightenment, hanging scroll, whole and detail. Ink on paper, 28⅝ × 12⅜ in. Tokyo, National Museum.

LIANG K'AI

Pl. 131. Herons Near a Rocky Bank, album leaf. Ink on silk. Miyagino, Kanagawa, Japan, Hakone Art Museum.

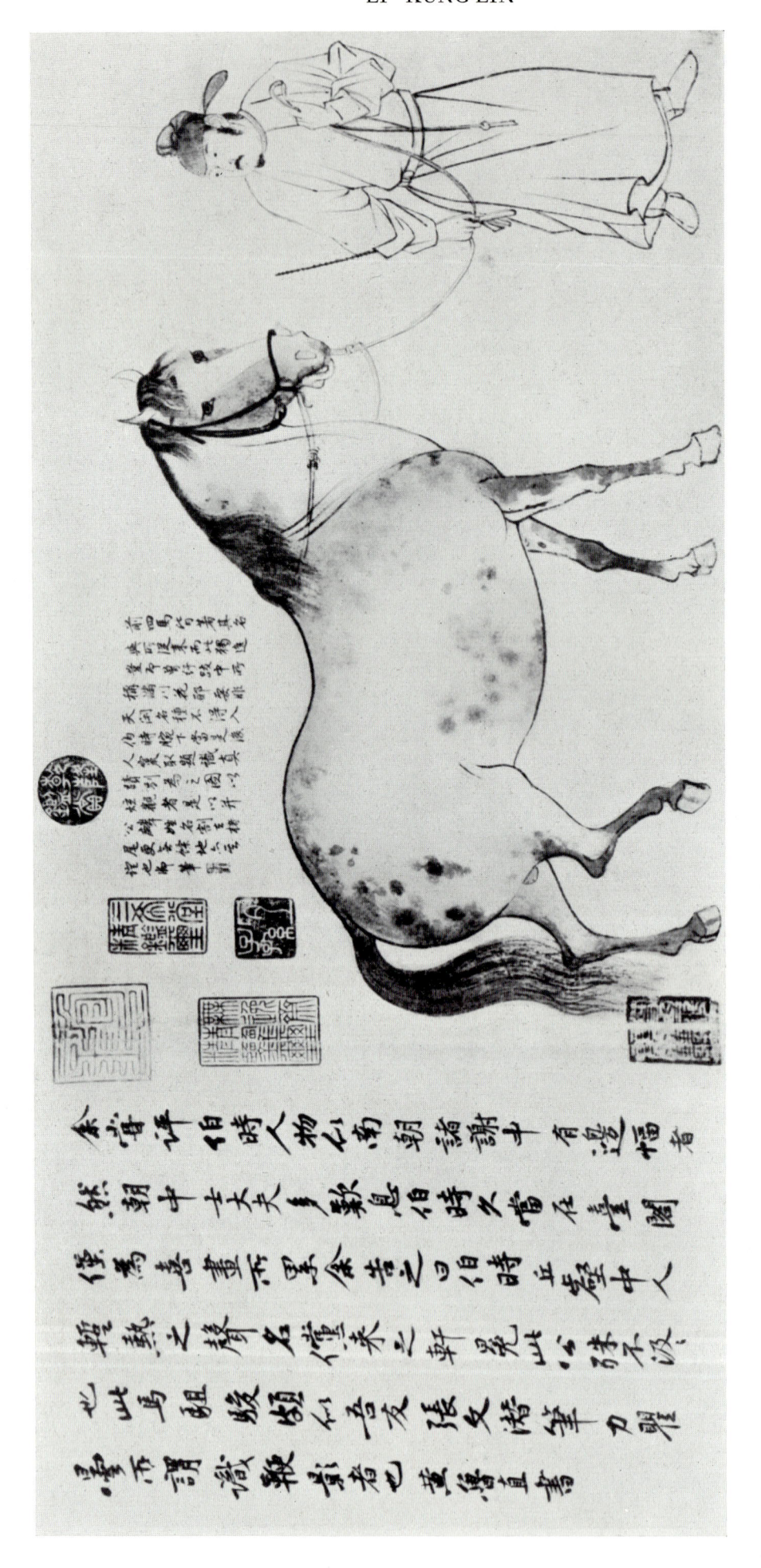

Pl. 132. Horse and groom, from the Five Horses and Grooms hand scroll. Ink on paper; complete scroll, 11¾ in. × ca. 6 ft. (Destroyed, 1945.)

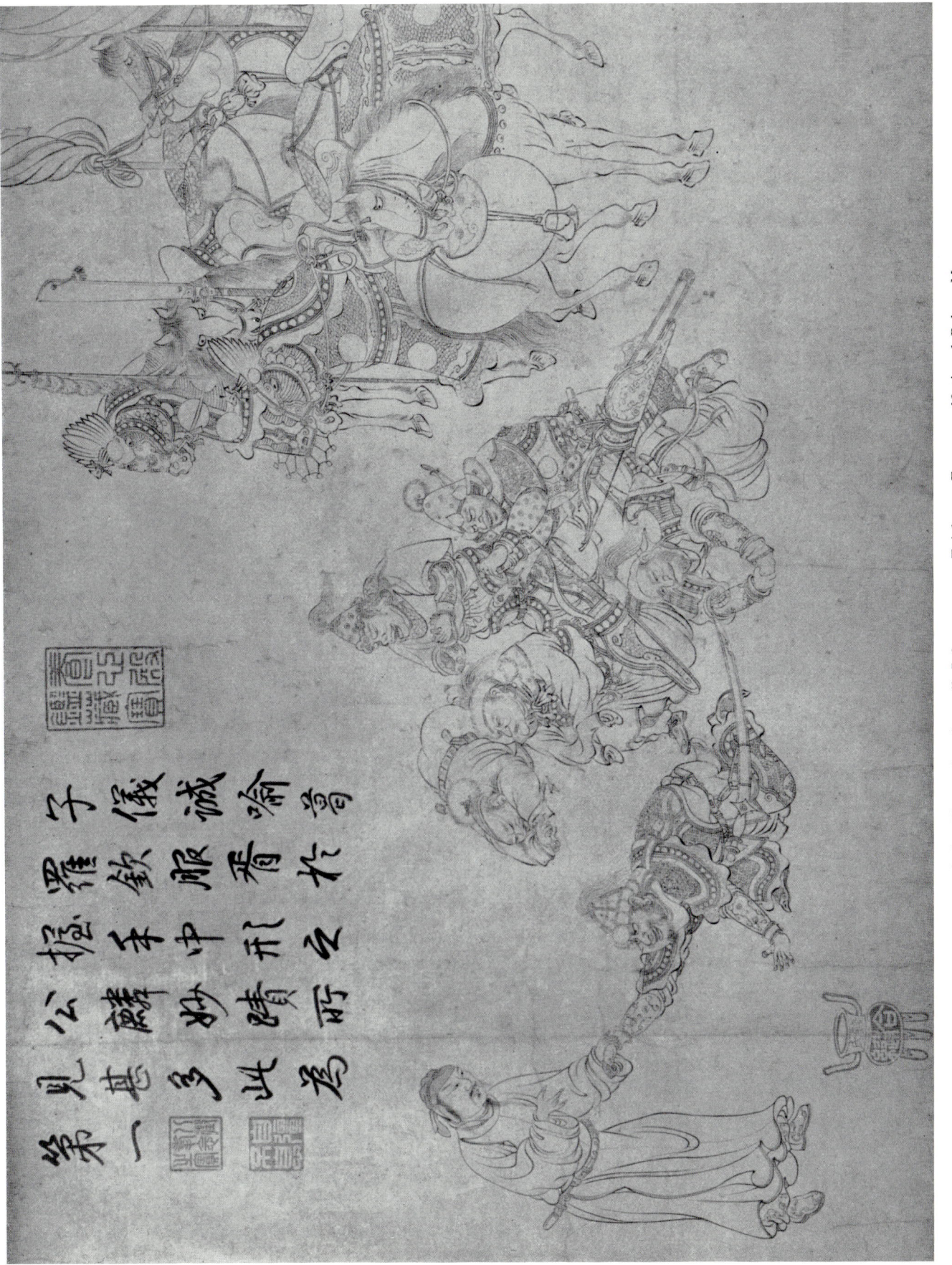

Pl. 133. General Kuo Tzŭ-i Receiving the Homage of the Uigurs, hand scroll. Ink on paper. Taichung, Formosa, National Palace Museum.

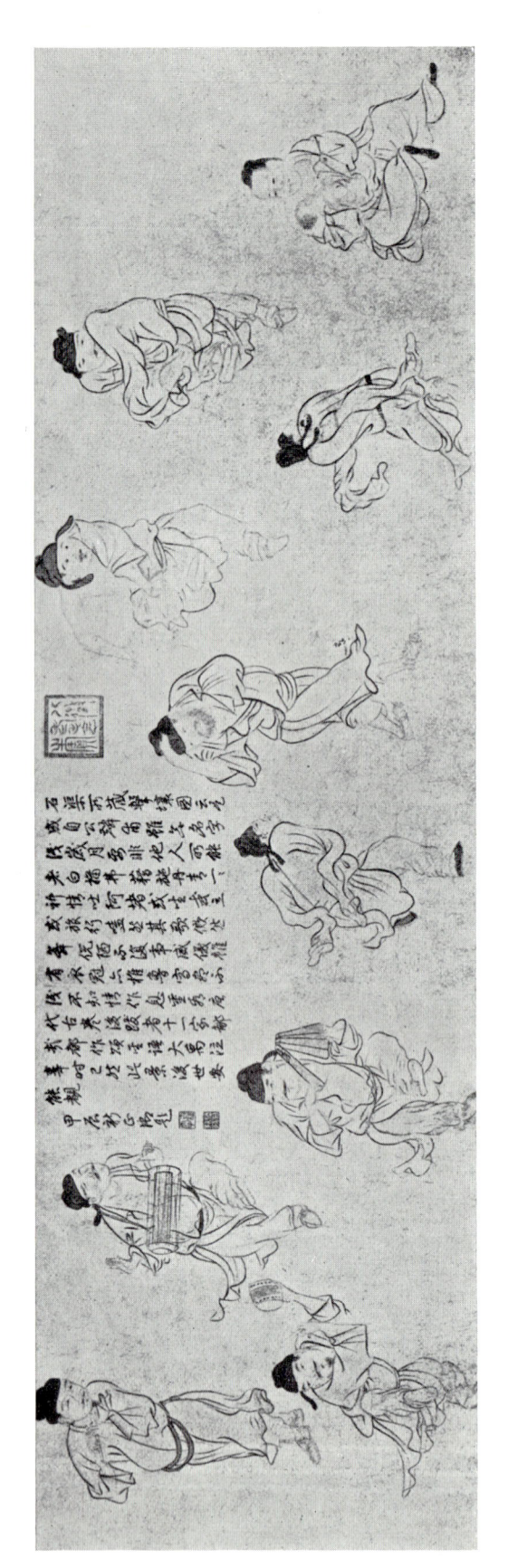

Pl. 134. *Above*: Dancing Peasants (Beating the Ground), detail of hand scroll. Ink on paper. Formerly, Peking, Palace Collection. *Below*: Dwelling in the Lung-mien Mountains, detail of hand scroll. Ink on paper. Taichung, Formosa, National Central Museum.

LI KUNG-LIN

Pl. 135. Metamorphoses of Heavenly Beings According to the Hua-yen Sutra, detail of hand scroll. Ink and faint color on paper; full size, 13 3/4 in. × 36 ft., 6 in. Paris, C. T. Loo & Cie.

LI KUNG-LIN

Pl. 136. Realms of the Immortals, detail of hand scroll. Ink on paper. Washington, D.C., Freer Gallery of Art.

Pl. 137. January page, the Duc de Berry at table, detail, from the *Très Riches Heures du Duc de Berry*. Illumination. Chantilly, France, Musée Condé (fol. 1v).

LIMBOURG

Pl. 138. December page, boar hunt, from the *Très Riches Heures du Duc de Berry*. Illumination. Chantilly, France, Musée Condé (fol. 12v).

Pl. 139. Eden and the Expulsion, from the *Très Riches Heures du Duc de Berry*. Illumination. Chantilly, France, Musée Condé (fol. 25v).

LIMBOURG

Pl. 140. The Meeting of the Three Kings, from the *Très Riches Heures du Duc de Berry*. Illumination. Chantilly, France, Musée Condé (fol. 51v).

Pl. 141. Filippo Lippi, Reform of the Carmelite Rule, detail. Fresco. Florence, S. Maria del Carmine, cloister.

LIPPI

Pl. 142. Filippo Lippi, Coronation of the Virgin, whole and detail. Panel, 6 ft., 6 3/4 in. × 9 ft., 5 in. Florence, Uffizi.

Pl. 143. Filippo Lippi, Madonna and Child ("The Tarquinia Madonna"). Panel, 44 7/8 × 25 5/8 in. Rome, Galleria Nazionale.

Pl. 144. Filippo Lippi, Madonna and Child with scenes from the life of the Virgin, detail. Panel, full diam., 4 ft., 5 in. Florence, Pitti.

Pl. 145. Filippo Lippi, frescoes in the choir of the Cathedral, Prato, near Florence. *Above*: Funeral of St. Stephen. *Below*: Herod's Feast.

LIPPI

Pl. 146. Filippo Lippi. *Above, left*: Adoration of the Magi. Panel, diam., 54 in. Washington, D.C., National Gallery. *Right*: Madonna Adoring the Child. Panel, 50×45⅝ in. Berlin, Staatliche Museen. *Below*: Coronation of the Virgin. Fresco. Spoleto, Italy, Cathedral.

LIPPI

Pl. 147. Filippino Lippi. *Above*: The Death of Lucretia. Panel, 1 ft., 4 1/8 in. × 4 ft., 1 5/8 in. Florence, Pitti. *Below, left*: Madonna Enthroned with SS. John the Baptist, Victor, Bernard and Zenobius. Panel, 11 ft., 7 3/4 in. × 7 ft., 4 5/8 in. Florence, Uffizi. *Right*: St. Philip casting out the demon from the temple of Mars, detail. Fresco. Florence, S. Maria Novella, Strozzi Chapel.

Pl. 148. Filippino Lippi. *Above*: Martyrdom of St. Philip. Fresco. Florence, S. Maria Novella, Strozzi Chapel. *Below*: Frescoes in the Carafa Chapel, S. Maria sopra Minerva, Rome. *Left*: Assumption of the Virgin, detail. *Right*: Triumph of St. Thomas Aquinas, detail.

Pl. 149. Filippino Lippi, The Vision of St. Bernard. Panel, 6 ft., 10½ in. × 6 ft., 4¾ in. Florence, Church of the Badia.

Pl. 150. Filippino Lippi, Assumption of the Virgin, detail. Fresco. Rome, S. Maria sopra Minerva, Carafa Chapel.

Pl. 151. Palaces among Mountains (in style of Li Ssŭ-hsün), 16th cent. Color and gold on silk, 4 ft., 3¼ in. × 2 ft., 1⅛ in. Washington, D.C., Freer Gallery of Art.

Pl. 152. Li Ssŭ-hsün (attrib.), The Chiu-ch'êng Summer Palace, 11th cent. (?). Fan painting, ink and color on silk. Peking, Palace Museum.

Pl. 153. Li Chao-tao (attrib.), Summer Palace. Ink and color on silk. Boston, Museum of Fine Arts.

LI SSŬ-HSÜN AND LI CHAO-TAO

Pl. 154. Landscape (copy after Li Ssŭ-hsün), detail. Ink and color on silk. Washington, D.C., Freer Gallery of Art.

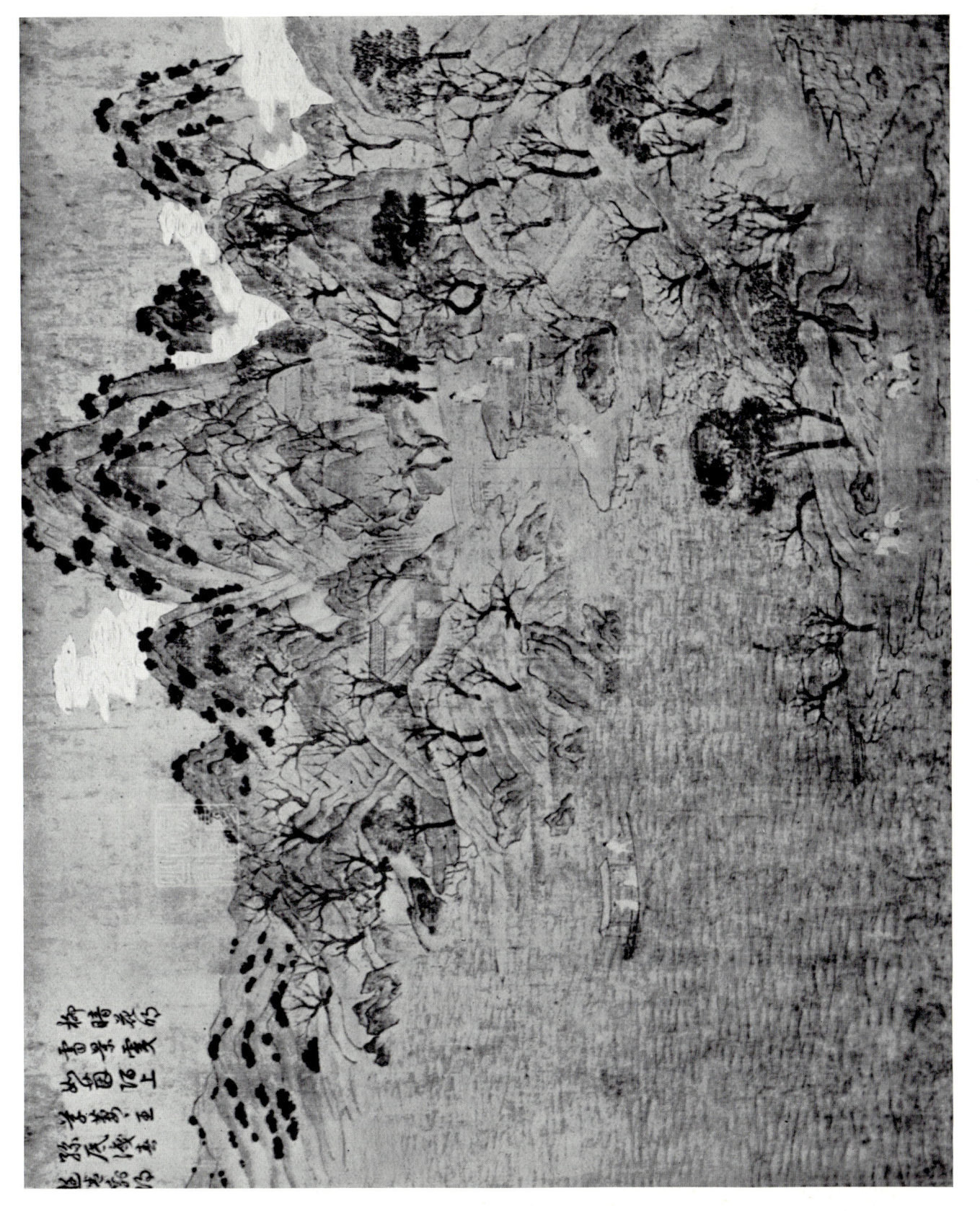

Pl. 155. Chan Tzǔ-ch'ien (attrib.), Travelers in Springtime, detail of hand scroll, T'ang dynasty. Ink and color on silk. Peking, Hui-hua-kuan.

LITURGICAL AND RITUAL OBJECTS

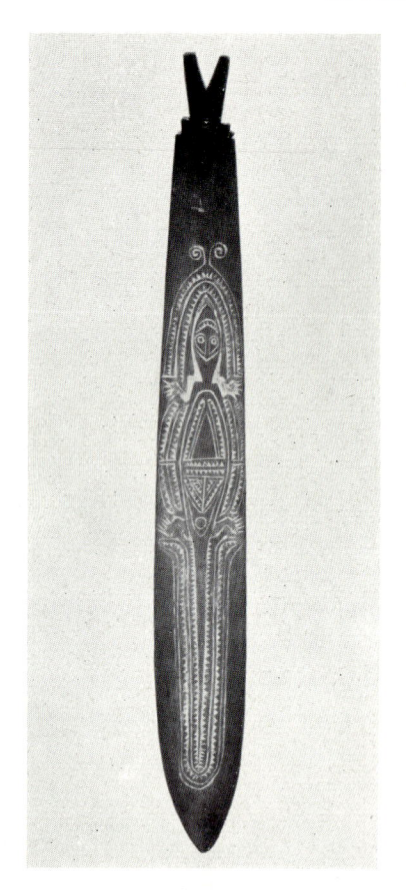

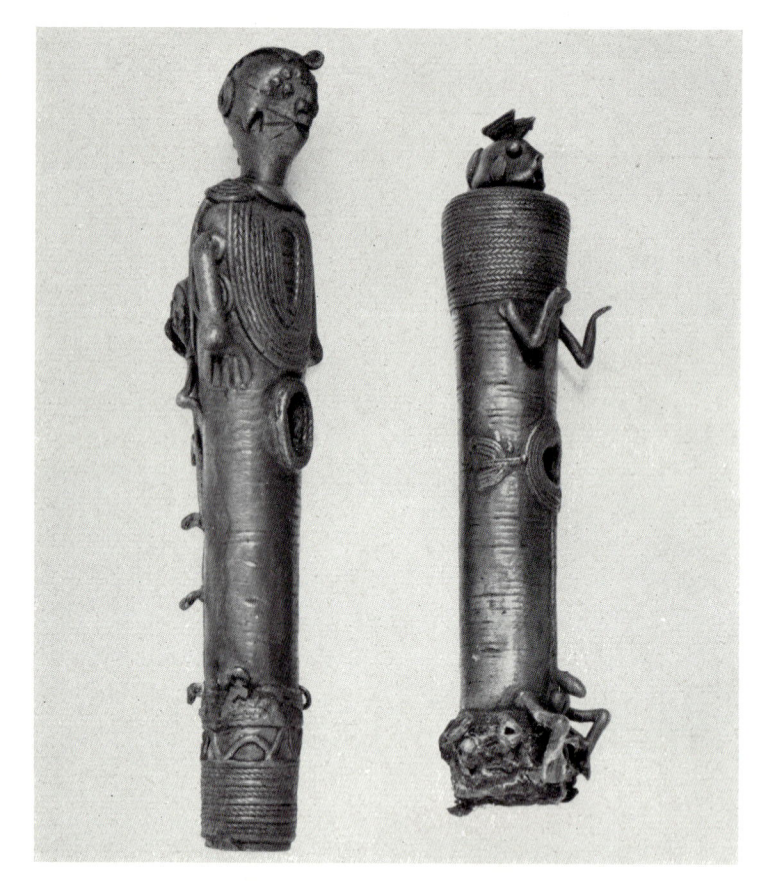

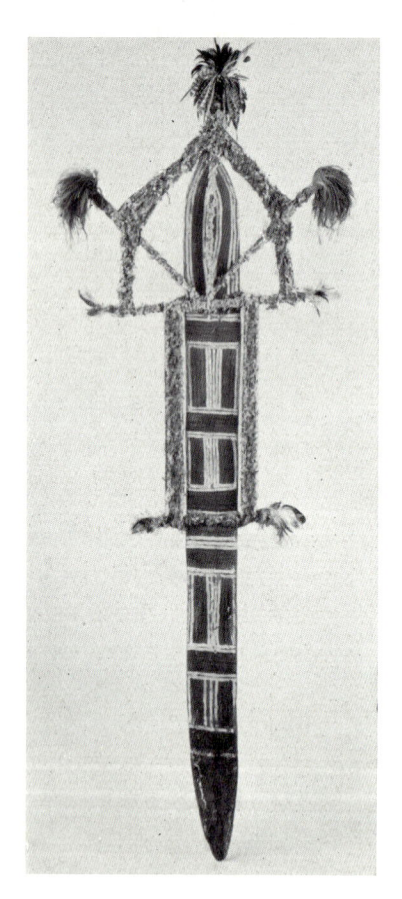

Pl. 156. *Above, left*: Decorated bull-roarer, Elema tribe, Gulf of Papua, New Guinea. Wood, l., 16 in. London, British Museum. *Right*: Voice disguisers (*imborivungu*), Tiv tribe, Benue, Nigeria. Cast bronze; l. of taller, 8¼ in. Oxford, England, Pitt Rivers Museum. *Below, left*: Thread cross, central Australia. Wood, feathers, and hair. Hamburg, Museum für Völkerkunde. *Right*: Shaman's drum, Lapland. Wood and painted hide, 16⅞ × 14¼ in. Copenhagen, Nationalmuseet.

LITURGICAL AND RITUAL OBJECTS

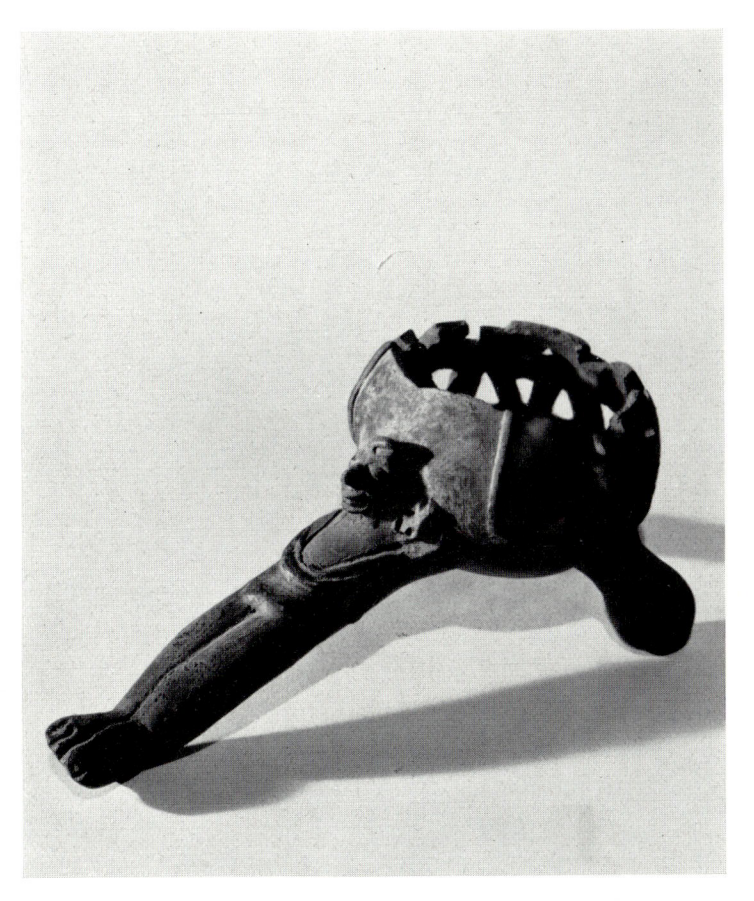

Pl. 157. Mexico, pre-Columbian period. *Above, left*: Ceremonial or votive ax in the form of a temple, Guerrero. Stone, ht., 5 in. Vienna, Museum für Völkerkunde. *Right*: Mixtec incense spoon with anthropomorphous handle, Totonpec, Oaxaca. Reddish-brown clay, l., 8¼ in. Munich, Museum für Völkerkunde. *Below*: Aztec sacrificial knife with handle representing an Eagle Knight. Chalcedony, jade, turquoise, malachite, and shell; l., 11 in. London, British Museum.

LITURGICAL AND RITUAL OBJECTS

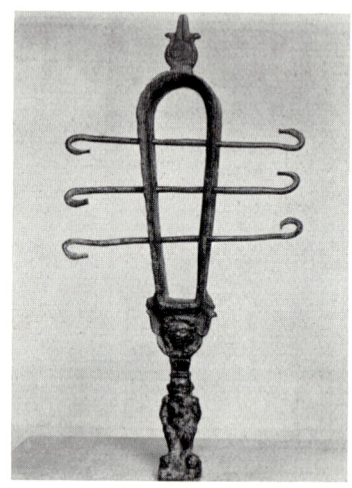

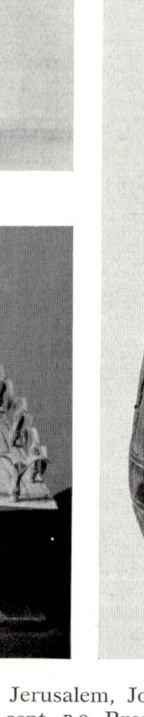

Pl. 158. *Above*: Libation tray, Tell Beit Mirsim, 13th cent. B.C. Limestone; 11×11½ in. Jerusalem, Jordan, Palestine Archaeological Museum. *Left, center*: Phoenician tripod, Ras Shamra (anc. Ugarit), 15th–14th cent. B.C. Bronze, ht., 4¾ in. Paris, Louvre. *Below*: Etruscan incense burning cart, Cerveteri (anc. Caere), ca. mid-7th cent. B.C. Ht., 8⅝ in. Rome, Vatican Museums. *Right, above*: Egyptian incense burner in the shape of an arm, Middle Kingdom. Bronze, l., 20⅛ in. Rome, Vatican Museums. *Middle*: Egyptian sistrum, Greco-Roman period. Bronze, ht., 11⅜ in. Formerly, Berlin, Staatliche Museen. *Below*: Egyptian situla, Ptolemaic period. Bronze, ht., 8⅝ in. Turin, Museo Egizio.

LITURGICAL AND RITUAL OBJECTS

Pl. 159. Perfume still, China, T'ang dynasty. Bronze inlaid with gold, ht., 20 in. London, British Museum.

LITURGICAL AND RITUAL OBJECTS

Pl. 160. Chalice of St. Remi (Remigius), France, 12th cent. Gold and precious stones. Reims, Cathedral Treasury.

LITURGICAL AND RITUAL OBJECTS

Pl. 161. *Above*: Detail of trabeation, showing bucrania, albogalerum, aspergillum, praefericulum, colter, patera with umbilicus, sacena, and simpulum, from the Temple of Vespasian in the Roman Forum, ca. A.D. 81–96. Marble. Rome, Tabularium. *Center*: Sacrificial scene, relief on the Arch of Trajan, Benevento, Italy, A.D. 114. Marble. *Below*: Seven-branched candelabrum from the Temple at Jerusalem, detail of relief on the Arch of Titus in the Roman Forum, ca. A.D. 81–96. Marble.

LITURGICAL AND RITUAL OBJECTS

Pl. 162. *Above, left*: Paten with the Communion of the Apostles, from Stuma, 6th cent. Silver. Istanbul, Archaeological Museum. *Right*: The Chalice of Antioch, 4th–5th cent. Partially gilded silver. New York, Metropolitan Museum, The Cloisters. *Below, left*: Paten with the Crucifixion, 11th–12th cent. Gilded silver. Halberstadt, Germany, Cathedral. *Right*: Paten, 10th–11th cent. Alabaster, gilded silver, precious stones, and enamel; diam., 13 3/8 in. Venice, Treasury of S. Marco.

LITURGICAL AND RITUAL OBJECTS

Pl. 163. *Above, left*: Chalice of Agilulf and Theodalinda, 6th cent., with Gothic mounting. Sapphire and gold. Monza, Italy, Cathedral Treasury. *Right*: Chalice, from the Abbey of St. Trudpert, Freiburg im Breisgau, 1225–50. Gilded silver, niello, and gems. New York, Metropolitan Museum, The Cloisters. *Below*: Ciccarello di Francesco, chalice and paten, early 15th cent. Gilded silver and enamel. Sulmona, Italy, Cathedral Treasury.

LITURGICAL AND RITUAL OBJECTS

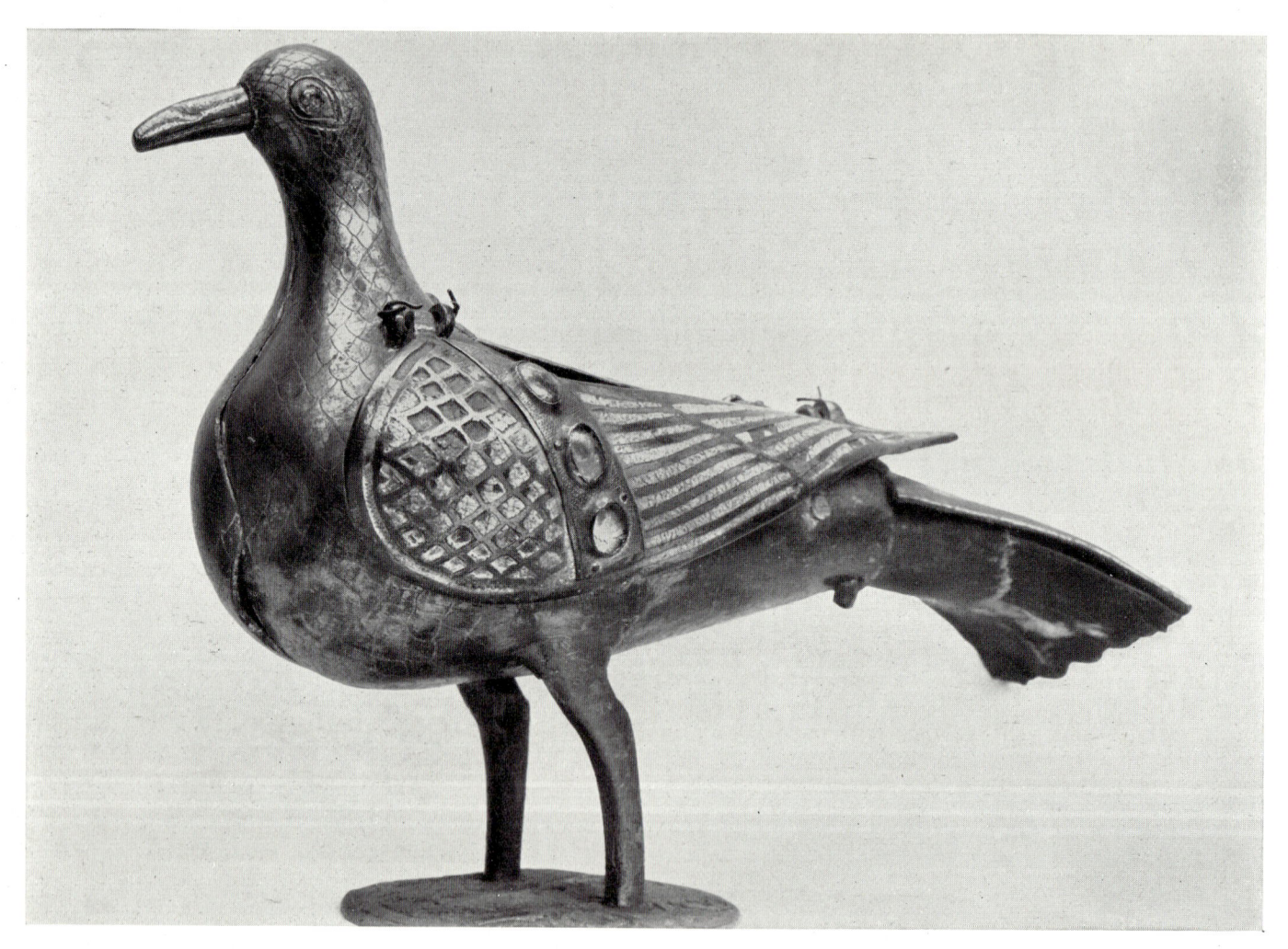

Pl. 164. *Above, left*: Ampulla with the Ascension, Palestine, ca. 600. Silver. Monza, Italy, Cathedral Treasury. *Right*: Aquamanile in the form of a winged monster, Mosan school, early 13th cent. Gilded bronze, silver, and niello; ht., 7$^{3}/_{8}$ in. London, Victoria and Albert Museum. *Below*: Eucharistic dove, Limoges, 13th cent. Gilded copper and champlevé enamel, l., 10$^{1}/_{4}$ in. Paris, Musée de Cluny.

LITURGICAL AND RITUAL OBJECTS

Pl. 165. *Above, left*: The Ramsey Abbey Censer, England, mid-14th cent. Gilded silver, ht., 10¾ in. London, Victoria and Albert Museum. *Right*: Incense boat, France, early 16th cent. Gilded silver and mother-of-pearl. Chartres, Cathedral Treasury. *Below*: Incense boat and thurible, 18th cent. Gilded silver. Bologna, Metropolitana.

LITURGICAL AND RITUAL OBJECTS

Pl. 166. *Above, left*: Pyx-monstrance, 15th–16th cent. Seo de Urgel, Lérida, Spain, Cathedral. *Right*: Monstrance, Germany or Italy, 15th cent. Gilded copper and enamel, ht., 18 1/8 in. Paris, Musée de Cluny. *Below, left*: Monstrance, Italy, 15th cent. Siena, Italy, Museo dell'Opera del Duomo. *Right*: Monstrance, Germany, before 1600. Gold, ht., 21 7/8 in. Munich, Residenzmuseum.

LITURGICAL AND RITUAL OBJECTS

Pl. 167. *Above, left*: Baptismal font, ca. 1220. Cast bronze, ht., 71 in. Hildesheim, Cathedral. *Right*: Master of the Stavelot Portable Altar, candlestick, mid-12th cent. Partially gilded bronze with silver inlay, ht., 7 in. Hildesheim, Cathedral Treasury. *Below, left*: Candlestick, Hildesheim, ca. 1000. Gilded silver. Hildesheim, Church of St. Magdalena. *Center*: Fra Giovanni da Verona, candlestick. Gilded wood. Verona, Italy, S. Maria in Organo. *Right*: A. Gentili, candlestick, 1581. Gilded silver. Rome, St. Peter's, Treasury.

LITURGICAL AND RITUAL OBJECTS

Pl. 168. *Above, left*: Eucharistic veil (air), 11th–12th cent. embroideries mounted on 18th-cent. cloth. Venice, Treasury of S. Marco. *Right*: Altar frontal with story of Christ, 1140. Partially gilded silver. Città di Castello, Italy, Museo Capitolare. *Below, left*: Master Eilbertus, portable altar with figures from the Old Testament, 1150–60. Enamel. Berlin, Staatliche Museen. *Right*: Altar frontal of St. Gregory, 17th cent. Gold-embroidered silk. Messina, Sicily, Museo Nazionale.

Pl. 169. G. L. Bernini, altar and ciborium, 1673–75. Gilded bronze. Rome, St. Peter's, Chapel of the Sacrament.

LITURGICAL AND RITUAL OBJECTS

Pl. 170. *Above, left*: High altar, showing retable and baldachin, 14th cent. Silver plates and enamel. Gerona, Spain, Cathedral. *Right*: Pontile and choir screen, Renaissance, and stalls, 13th cent. Wood. Notre-Dame-de-la-Roche, France, church. *Below, left*: Seven-branched candelabrum, second half of 12th cent. Bronze. Brunswick, Germany, Cathedral. *Right*: Riccio (B. Neroni), lectern, ca. 1568. Carved wood. Siena, Italy, Cathedral.

LITURGICAL AND RITUAL OBJECTS

Pl. 171. G. Alpais, pyx, from the Abbey of Montmajour, France, first half of 13th cent. Gold, enamel, and precious stones. Paris, Louvre.

LITURGICAL AND RITUAL OBJECTS

Pl. 172. Pax in the form of a tabernacle, northern Italy, early 16th cent. Gilded silver and enamels. Milan, Museo Poldi Pezzoli.

LITURGICAL AND RITUAL OBJECTS

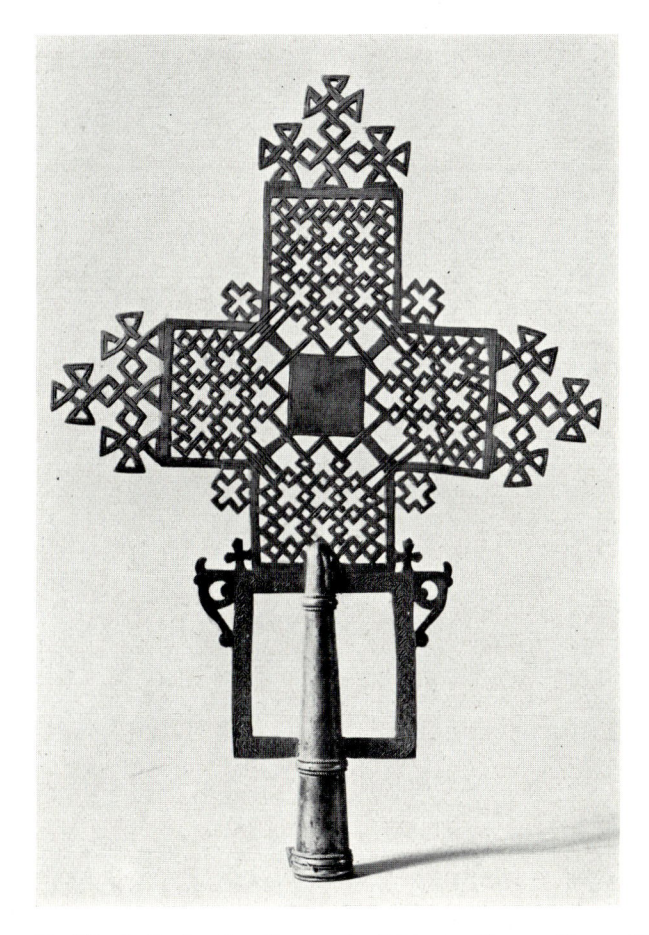

Pl. 173. *Left*: Coptic silverwork, Ethiopia. Rome, Museo Pigorini. *Above*: Censer. *Below*: Cross. *Right, above*: Flabellum, Zarzma, U.S.S.R., first decade of 11th cent. Gilded silver. Tbilisi, U.S.S.R., Museum. *Below*: Ivan Aminj, panagiarion, 1436. Novgorod, U.S.S.R., Cathedral.

LITURGICAL AND RITUAL OBJECTS

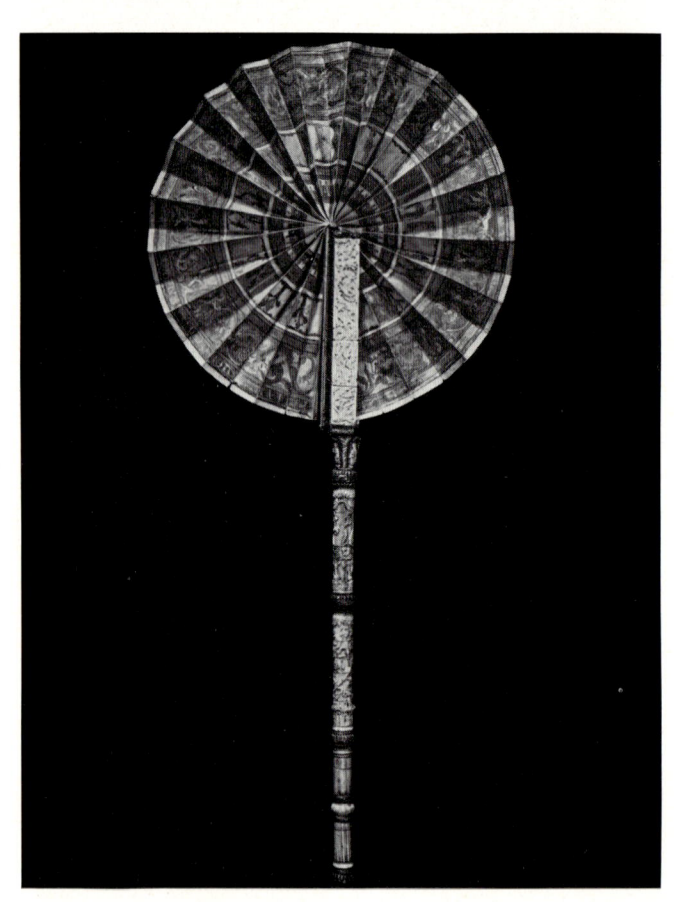

Pl. 174. *Left, above*: A. Arditi, miter of the reliquary bust of St. Zenobius, 1331. Gilded silver with precious stones and enamel. Florence, Cathedral. *Below*: Flabellum, Tournus, France, 9th cent. Illuminated parchment and ivory. Florence, Museo Nazionale. *Right*: Hugo d'Oignies, crozier, Mosan school, ca. 1220. Gilded bronze and crystal. London, British Museum.

LITURGICAL AND RITUAL OBJECTS

Pl. 175. Chinese ritual vessels. Bronze. *Above, left*: Wine vessel of the *yu* type, Chou dynasty. Ht., 9³/₄ in. *Right*: Wine vessel of the *ku* type, Chou dynasty. Both, property of the Chinese Government. *Below, left*: Food vessel of the *ting* type with cover, Warring States period. Paris, Louvre. *Right*: Water vessel of the *i* type, Warring States period. Ht., 7¹/₄ in. Property of the Chinese Government.

LITURGICAL AND RITUAL OBJECTS

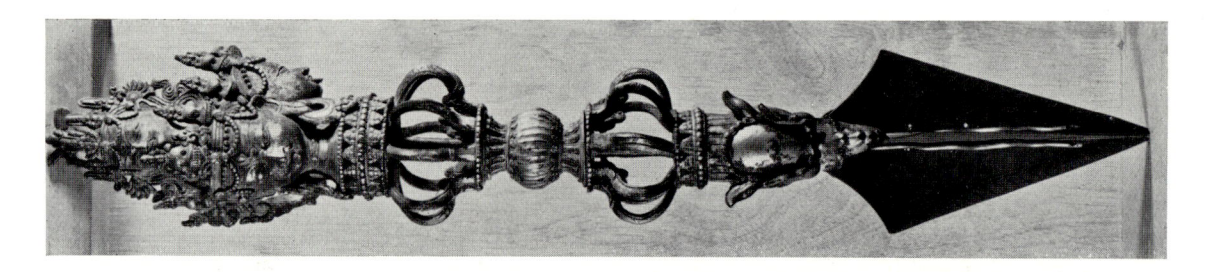

Pl. 176. Tibet, 18th-19th cent. Gilded bronze. Paris, Musée Guimet. *Left:* Bell. *Center:* Ax. *Right:* Ritual knife (*p'ur-bu*).

LITURGICAL AND RITUAL OBJECTS

Pl. 177. *Left*: Ritual vessel, India, 19th cent. Brass. Berlin, Museum für Völkerkunde. *Right*: Ritual vessel, Tibet, 19th cent. Brass. Paris, Musée Guimet.

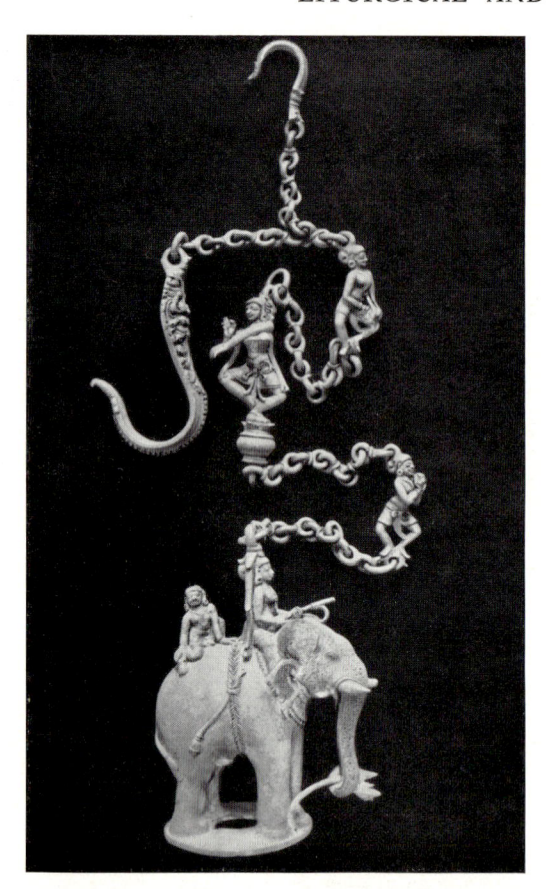

LITURGICAL AND RITUAL OBJECTS

Pl. 178. Ritual objects, 18th–19th cent. Bronze. *Above, left*: Chain for lamp, India. Bombay, Prince of Wales Museum. *Right*: Lamp with representation of sun-god, Nepal. *Below, left*: Censer, Nepal. Last two, Berlin, Museum für Völkerkunde. *Right*: Candlestick, Tibet. Paris, Musée Guimet.

LOCHNER

Pl. 179. Altar of the Patron Saints. Panel; full size, 7 ft., 9³/₄ in. × 15 ft., 6⁵/₈ in. Cologne, Cathedral. *Above*: St. Ursula (*left*); Adoration of the Magi (*center*); St. Gerion (*right*). *Below*: Exterior of wings, Annunciation.

LOCHNER

Pl. 180. *Above and below, left*: The Last Judgment, full view and detail. Panel; full size, 4 ft. × 5 ft., 9¼ in. Cologne, Wallraf-Richartz-Museum. *Right*: Presentation in the Temple. Panel, 4 ft., 6¾ in. × 4 ft., 1⅝ in. Darmstadt, Germany, Landesmuseum.

LOCHNER

Pl. 181. The Virgin in the Rose Bower. Panel, 20 1/8 × 15 3/4 in. Cologne, Wallraf-Richartz-Museum.

LOCHNER

Pl. 182. St. Anthony Abbot, Pope Cornelius, Mary Magdalene, and a donor. Panel, 47 1/4 × 31 1/2 in. Munich, Alte Pinakothek.

Pl. 183. P. Longhi, The Dancing Master. Canvas, 23 5/8 × 19 1/4 in. Venice, Accademia.

LONGHI

Pl. 184. P. Longhi, The Visit. Canvas, 24 × 19¼ in. Bergamo, Accademia Carrara.

Pl. 185. P. Longhi. *Above, left*: The Meeting. Canvas, 24×19½ in. New York, Metropolitan Museum. *Right*: Exhibition of a Rhinoceros at Venice. Canvas, 23¾×18½ in. London, National Gallery. *Below*: Duck Hunting. Canvas, 22×28⅜ in. Venice, Galleria Querini Stampalia.

LONGHI

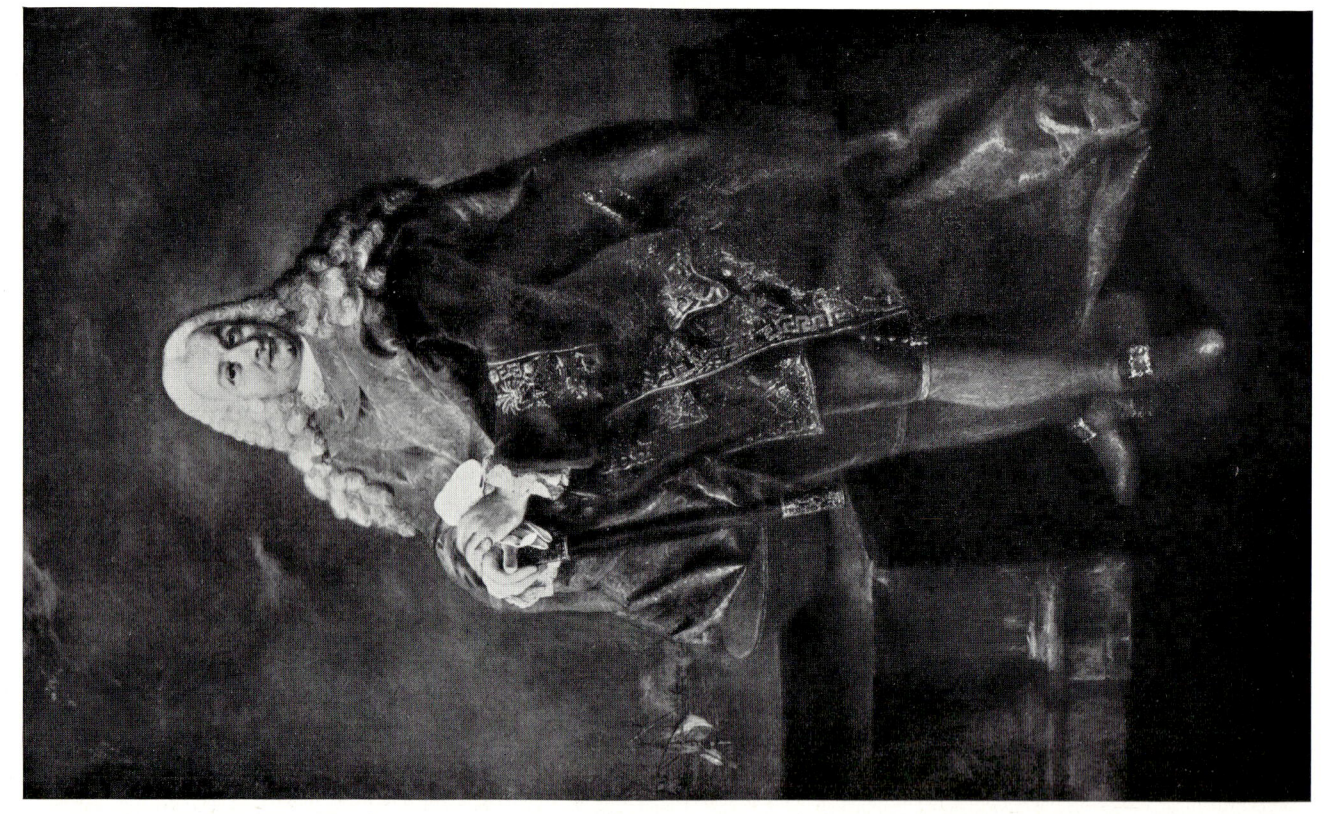

Pl. 186. A. Longhi. *Left*: Portrait of a parish priest. Canvas, 4 ft., 2¼ in. × 3 ft., 1 in. Venice, Church of S. Vidal. *Right*: Portrait of Antonio Renier, Provveditore Generale di Dalmazia e Albania. Canvas, 7 ft., 7¾ in. × 4 ft., 6 in. Padua, Museo Civico.

Pl. 187. P. Longhi, Family Concert. Canvas, 19 3/4 × 24 3/8 in. Milan, Brera.

Pl. 188. P. Lorenzetti, The Crucifixion, detail. Fresco. Assisi, S. Francesco, Lower Church.

LORENZETTI

Pl. 189. P. Lorenzetti, The Deposition, detail. Fresco. Assisi, S. Francesco, Lower Church.

Pl. 190. P. Lorenzetti, scenes of History of the Carmelites, details of predella from the Carmelite altarpiece. Panel, ht., 14 5/8 in. each. Siena, Pinacoteca.

Pl. 191. P. Lorenzetti. *Above*: Polyptych with Madonna and Child, Saints, Annunciation, and Assumption. Panel, 9 ft., 9½ in. × 10 ft., 1½ in. Arezzo, Pieve di S. Maria. *Below*: The Crucifixion. Fresco. Siena, S. Francesco.

Pl. 192. P. Lorenzetti, The Birth of the Virgin. Panel, 6 ft., 2 in. × 6 ft. Siena, Museo dell'Opera del Duomo.

Pl. 193. A. Lorenzetti, St. Dorothy, detail of a wing of the triptych from the Convent of St. Petronilla. Panel; full size of triptych, 4 ft., 10 in. × 7 ft., 5½ in. Siena, Pinacoteca.

Pl. 194. A. Lorenzetti, Good Government, detail. Fresco. Siena, Palazzo Pubblico. (Cf. III, pl. 299.)

Pl. 195. A. Lorenzetti, Good Government, detail. Fresco. Siena, Palazzo Pubblico. (Cf. III, PL. 12 and VI, PL. 378.)

Pl. 196. A. Lorenzetti, Peace, detail of Good Government. Fresco. Siena, Palazzo Pubblico.

Pl. 197. A. Lorenzetti, Boniface VIII receives St. Louis as a novice, detail. Fresco. Siena, S. Francesco.

Pl. 198. A. Lorenzetti, The Annunciation. Panel, 47 1/2 × 45 1/2 in. Siena, Pinacoteca.

LORENZO MONACO

Pl. 199. Adoration of the Magi, detail of an altarpiece. Panel; full size, 4 ft., 8 3/4 in. × 5 ft., 9 5/8 in. Florence, Uffizi.

LORENZO MONACO

Pl. 200. Adoration of the Magi, scene on the predella of the Coronation of the Virgin, pl. 202.

LORENZO MONACO

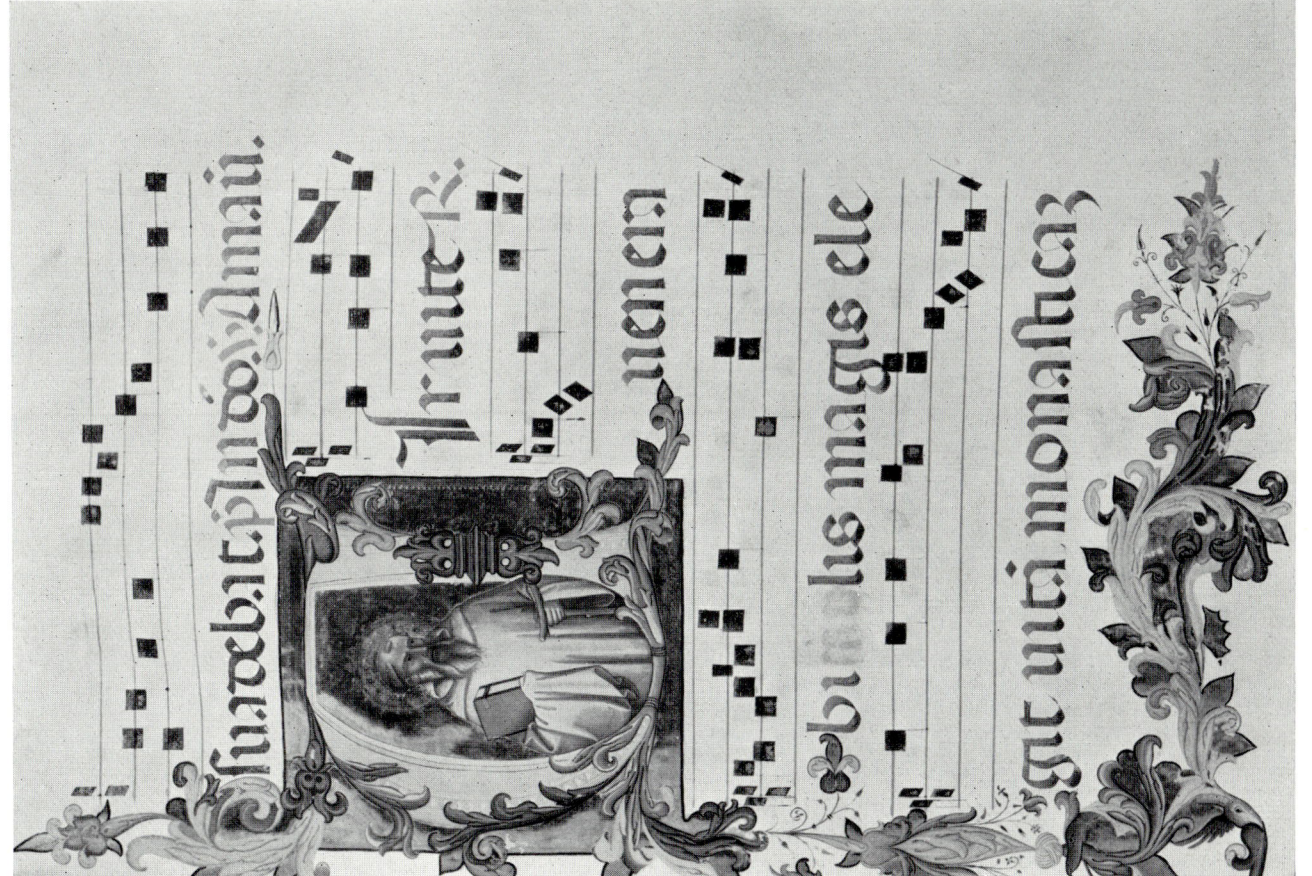

Pl. 201. *Left*: St. Romuald. Illumination. Florence, Biblioteca Laurenziana (Cod. Cor. Laur. 8, fol. 76r). *Right*: The Agony in the Garden. Panel, 6 ft. 3¼ in. × 3 ft. 8⅛ in. Florence, Accademia.

Pl. 202. *Above*: Coronation of the Virgin. Panel, 8 ft., 1¼ in. × 12 ft., 2½ in. Florence, Uffizi. *Below*: Predella depicting St. Nicholas preventing a shipwreck. Panel, 8¼ × 21¼ in. Florence, Accademia.

LORRAIN

Pl. 203. *Above*: The Marriage of Isaac and Rebekah ("The Mill"). Canvas, 4 ft., 10¾ in. × 6 ft., 5½ in. London, National Gallery. *Below*: Sacrifice to Apollo at Delphi. Canvas, 4 ft., 11 in. × 6 ft., 6¾ in. Rome, Galleria Doria Pamphili.

LORRAIN

Pl. 204. On the slopes of the Janiculum. Pen and ink drawing with bister wash shading, $8^{5}/_{8} \times 12^{1}/_{2}$ in. Rome, Gabinetto Nazionale delle Stampe.

Pl. 205. Lorrain: Seaport: The Embarkation of St. Ursula. Canvas, 3 ft., 8½ in. × 4 ft., 10½ in. London, National Gallery.

Pl. 206. Landscape: Hagar and the Angel. Canvas mounted on wood, 20³/₄ × 17¹/₄ in. London, National Gallery.

Pl. 207. Portrait of Bishop Bernardo de' Rossi. Panel, 21 1/4 × 16 1/8 in. Naples, Museo di Capodimonte.

LOTTO

Pl. 208. Portrait of Andrea Odoni. Canvas, 39 3/4 × 44 7/8 in. Hampton Court, England, Royal Colls.

LOTTO

Pl. 209. *Left*: Susanna and the Elders. Canvas, 26 3/8 × 19 3/4 in. Florence, Coll. Contini Bonacossi. *Right*: St. Clare taking her vows. Fresco. Trescore, Italy, chapel in the grounds of Villa Suardi.

LOTTO

Pl. 210. Madonna enthroned with Christ and angels, between SS. Joseph, Bernardino, John the Baptist, and Anthony Abbot. Canvas, 9 ft., 10 in. × 9 ft. Bergamo, Italy, S. Bernardino.

LOTTO

Pl. 211. Details of the predella of the St. Lucy altarpiece. Panel; each, $12^{5}/_{8} \times 27^{1}/_{8}$ in. Iesi, Italy, Pinacoteca Comunale. *Above*: St. Lucy before the judge and the attempt to drag her away. *Below*: The procession of the oxen.

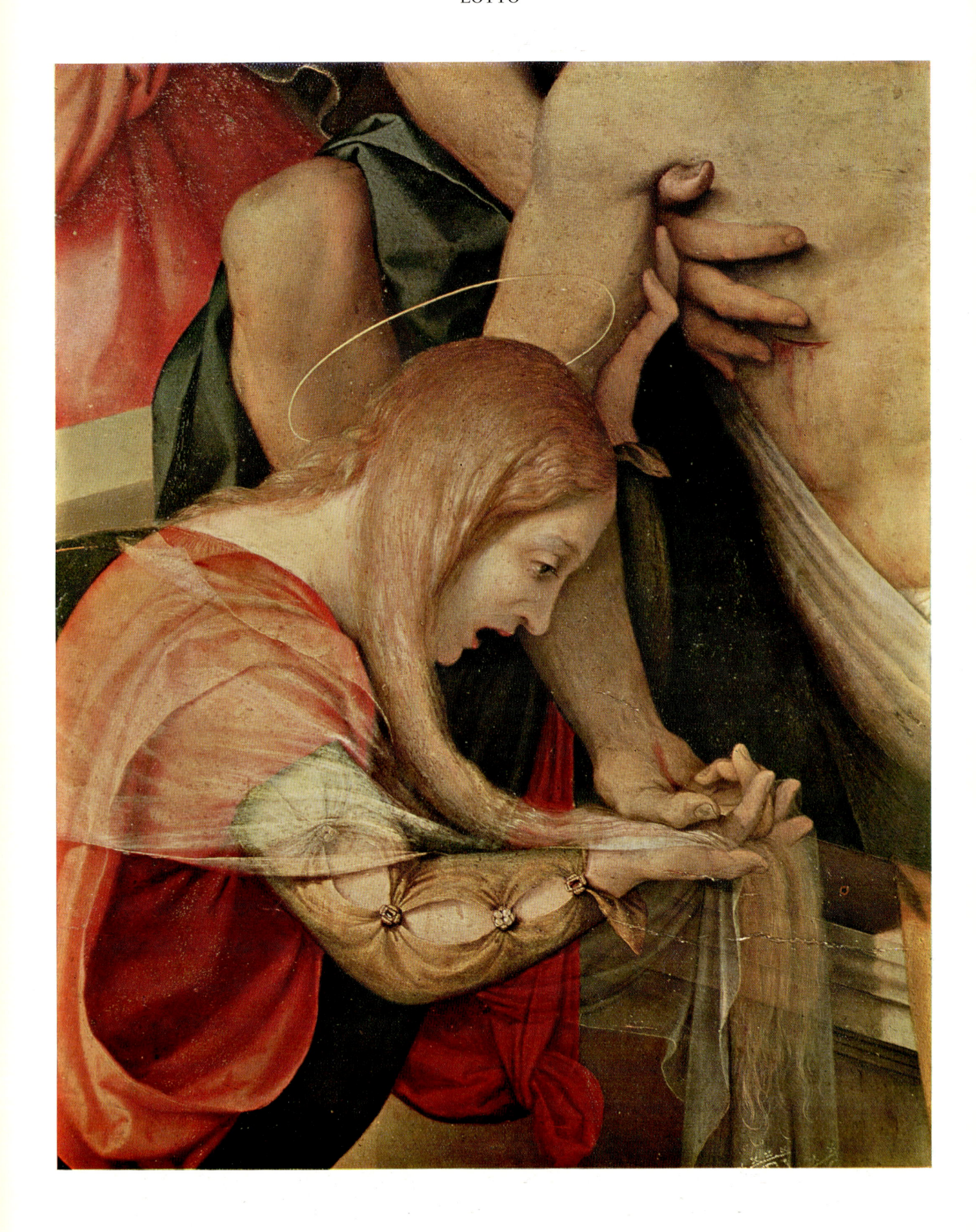

Pl. 212. The Entombment of Christ, detail. Panel; full size, 9 ft., 9 in. × 6 ft., 6 in. Iesi, Italy, Pinacoteca Comunale.

Pl. 213. St. Antoninus of Florence Giving Alms. Canvas, 10 ft., 10¾ in. × 7 ft., 8½ in. Venice, SS. Giovanni e Paolo.

LUCAS VAN LEYDEN

Pl. 214. A Man Aged 38. Panel, 18¾ × 16 in. London, National Gallery.

LUCAS VAN LEYDEN

Pl. 215. *Above*: St. Jerome. Panel, 10⅝ × 12¼ in. Berlin, Staatliche Museen. *Below*: Susanna Before the Judges. Panel, 13⅜ × 18⅛ in. Bremen, Kunsthalle.

LUCAS VAN LEYDEN

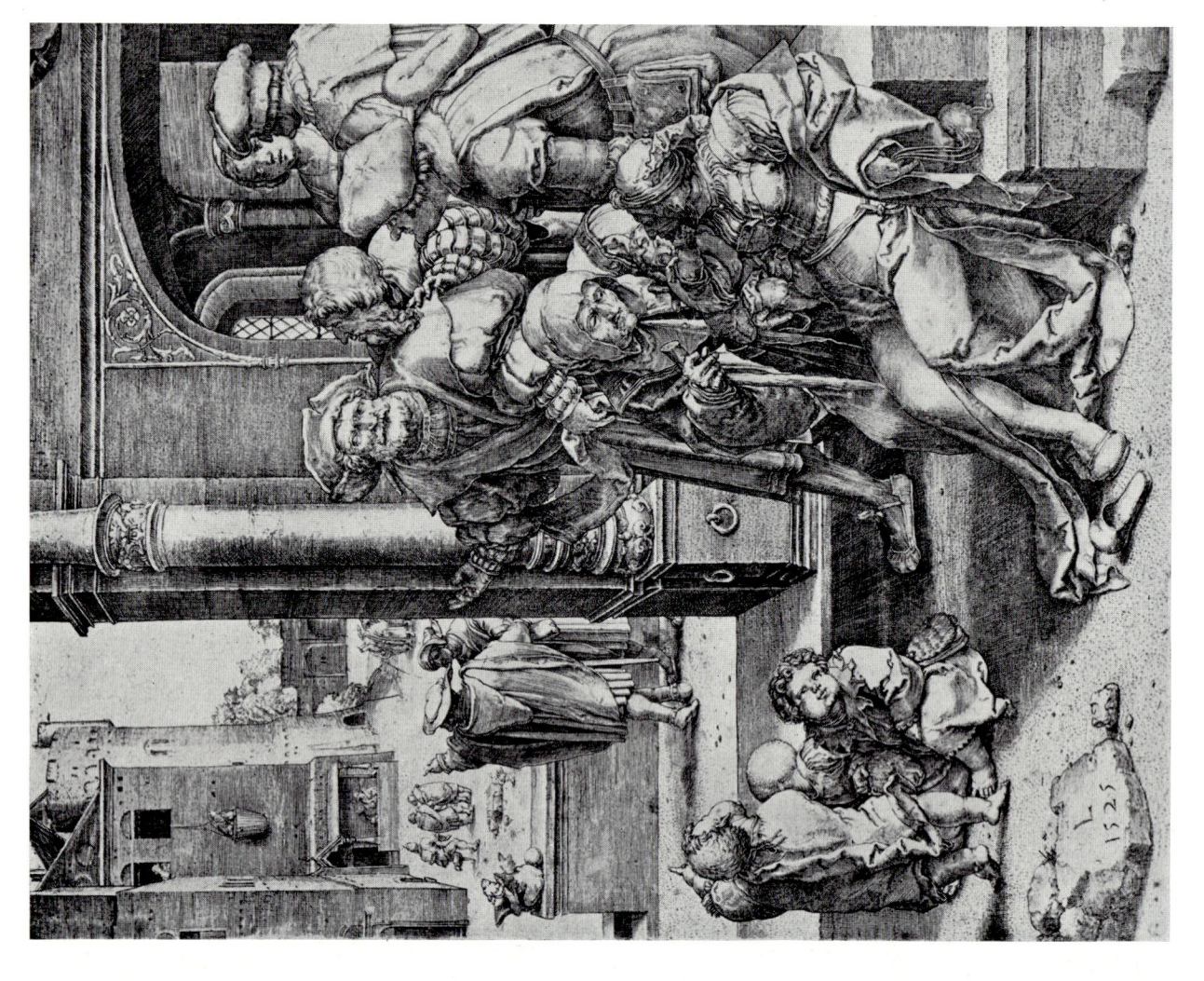

Pl. 216. Engravings. Rome, Gabinetto Nazionale delle Stampe. *Left, above*: The Milkmaid, 4½ × 6⅛ in. *Below*: Golgotha, 11⅛ × 16¼ in. *Right*: The Poet Vergil Suspended in a Basket, 9⅝ × 7½ in.

LUCAS VAN LEYDEN

Pl. 217. Virgin and Child, the Magdalen, and a donor. Panel, 19⅞×26¾ in. Munich, Alte Pinakothek.

LUCAS VAN LEYDEN

Pl. 218. Triptych with Last Judgment, detail of central panel. Panel; full size, 8 ft., 10³/₄ in. × 6 ft., ⁷/₈ in. Leiden, Stedelijk Museum "De Lakenhal." (Cf. V, PL. 292.)

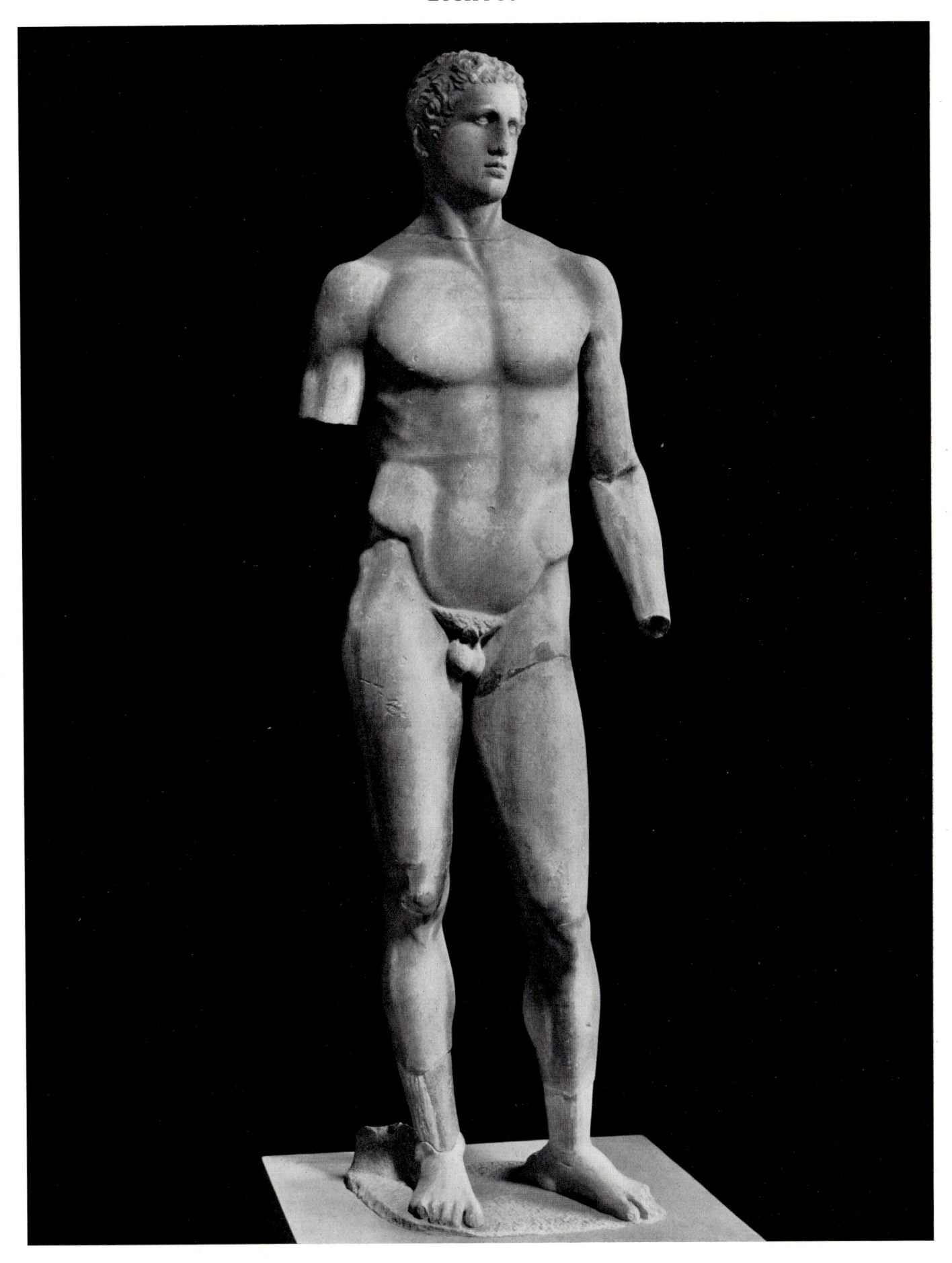

Pl. 219. Agias, contemporary copy. Marble, ht., 6 ft., 5½ in. Delphi, Greece, Archaeological Museum.

LYSIPPOS

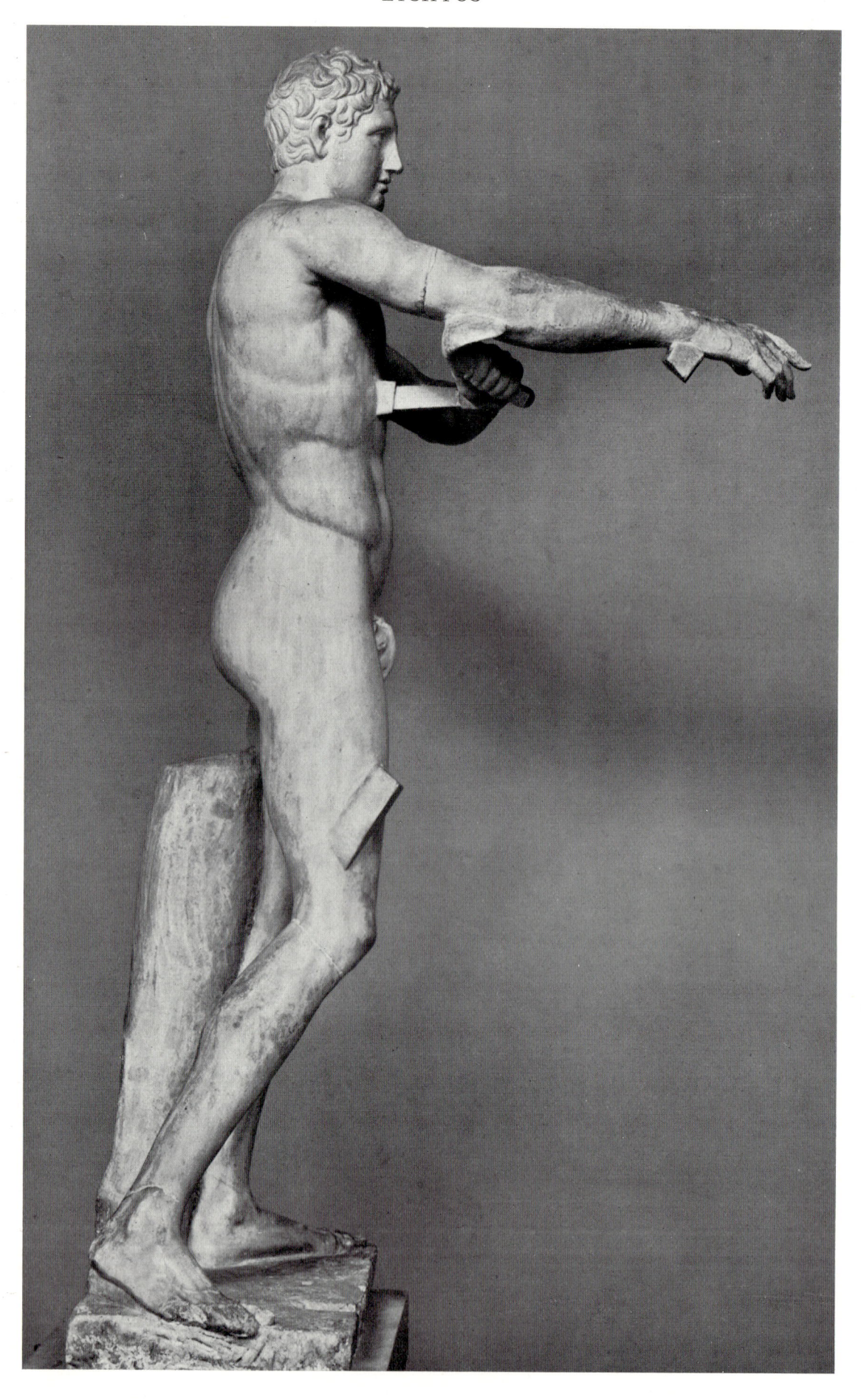

Pl. 220. Apoxyomenos, Roman copy. Marble, ht., 6 ft., 6¾ in. Rome, Vatican Museums. (Cf. III, PL. 382.)

Pl. 221. Hermes binding on his sandal, Roman copy. Marble, ht., 5 ft., 5/8 in. Copenhagen, Ny Carlsberg Glyptotek.

LYSIPPOS

Pl. 222. *Left*: Herakles capturing a deer, Roman copy. Bronze, ht., 23¼ in. Rome, Capitoline Museum. *Right*: Eros with bow, Roman copy. Marble, ht., 48½ in. Palermo, Sicily, Museo Nazionale Archeologico.

LYSIPPOS

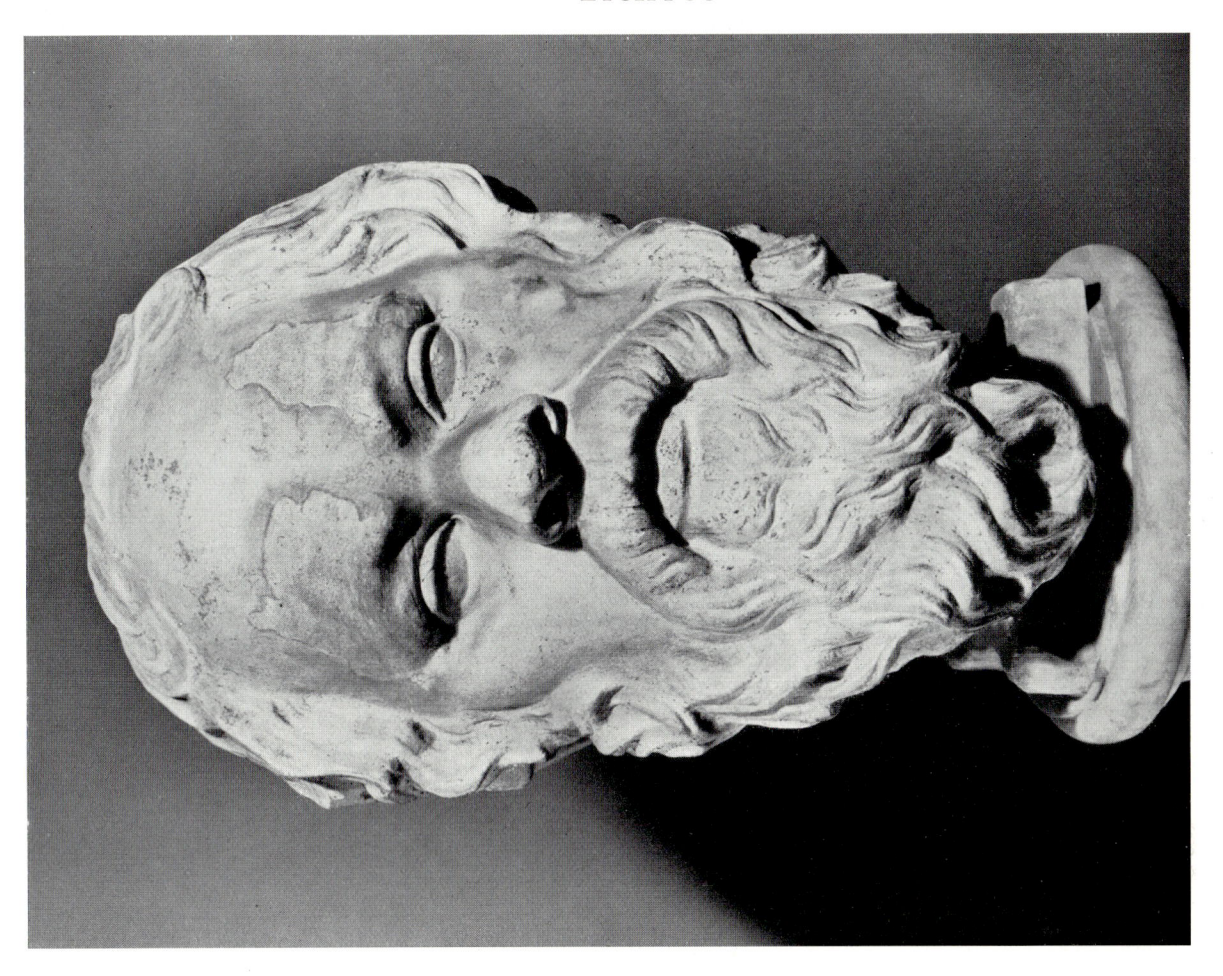

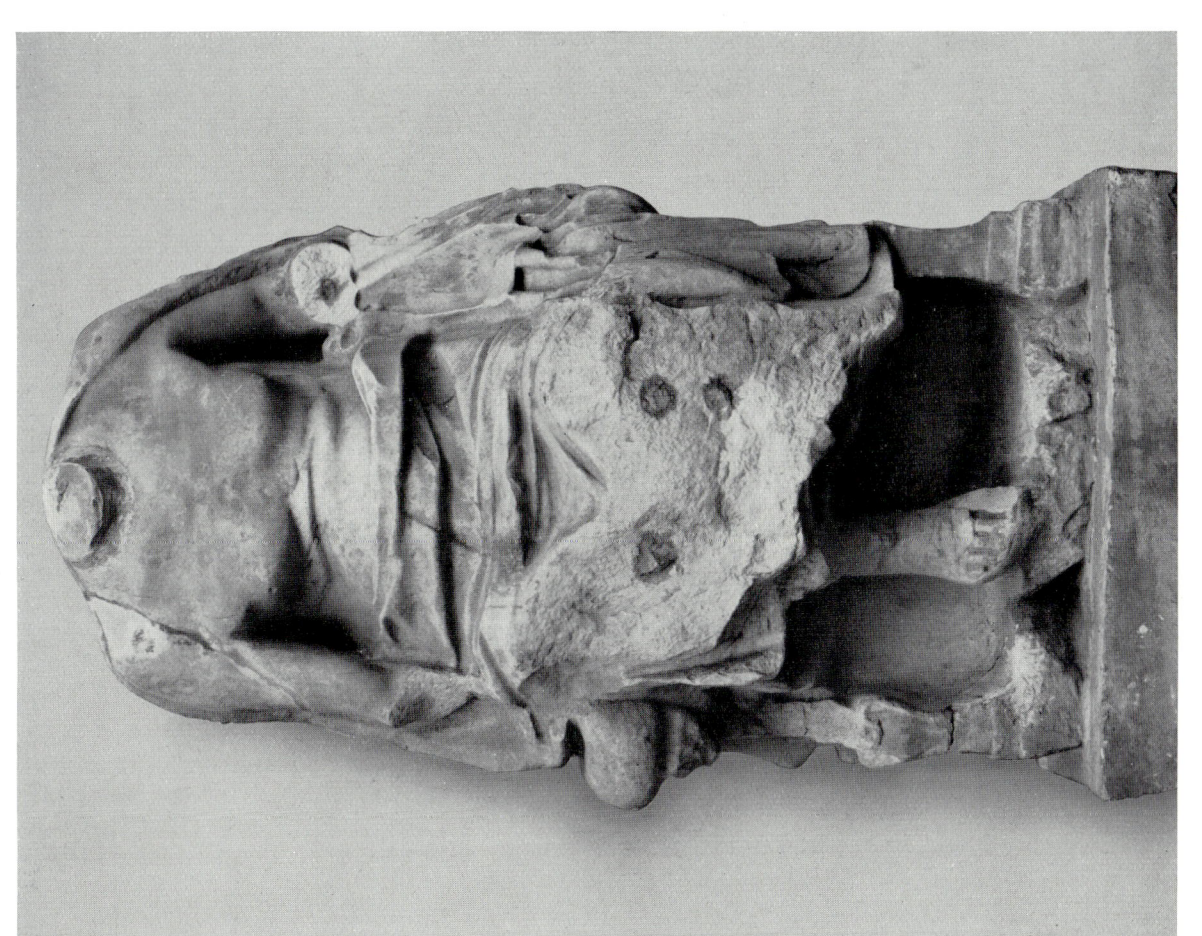

Pl. 223. Portrait of Socrates seated, Roman copies after the same original. *Left*: Marble, ht., 4 ft., 11½ in. Copenhagen, Ny Carlsberg Glyptotek. *Right*: Head. Marble, ht., 11¾ in. Rome, Museo Nazionale Romano.

Pl. 224. Portrait of Alexander (the "Azara herm"), Roman copy. Marble, ht., 25 5/8 in. Paris, Louvre.

Pl. 225. Seilenos with the infant Dionysos, Roman copy. Marble, ht., 6 ft., 2 3/4 in. Paris, Louvre.

Pl. 226. Farnese Herakles, work of the Roman period signed by Glykon of Athens, probably derived from a Lysippean prototype. Marble, ht., 10 ft., 2 in. Naples, Museo Nazionale.

MACCHIAIOLI

Pl. 227. S. Lega, Signorina Tommasi. Panel, 9 1/2 × 5 7/8 in. Crema, Italy, Coll. Stramezzi.

MACCHIAIOLI

Pl. 228. G. Abbati, Sunny Road. Panel, $10^{5}/_{8} \times 9^{1}/_{8}$ in. Milan, Coll. Jucker.

MACCHIAIOLI

Pl. 229. *Above*: G. Fattori, The Palmieri Rotunda. Panel, 4¾×10¼ in. Florence, Galleria d'Arte Moderna. *Below*: R. Sernesi, Roofs in the Sun. Panel, 4¾×7½ in. Rome, Galleria Nazionale d'Arte Moderna.

MACCHIAIOLI

Pl. 230. S. Lega, The Visit. Canvas, 12 1/4 × 23 5/8 in. Rome, Galleria Nazionale d'Arte Moderna.

MACCHIAIOLI

Pl. 231. G. Abbati. *Left*: The Painter Stanislao Pointeau. Panel, 13¾×8¼ in. Milan, Coll. Cavallini. *Right*: Lady in Gray. Panel, 10¼×5½ in. Florence, Galleria d'Arte Moderna.

MACCHIAIOLI

Pl. 232. G. Fattori. *Left, above*: Diego Martelli at Castiglioncello. Panel, 5 1/8 × 7 7/8 in. Milan, Coll. Jucker. *Below*: Southwest Gale. Panel. Florence, Galleria d'Arte Moderna. *Right*: Buttero (Maremma Herdsman). Panel, 15 3/8 × 11 3/8 in. Milan, Coll. Falck.

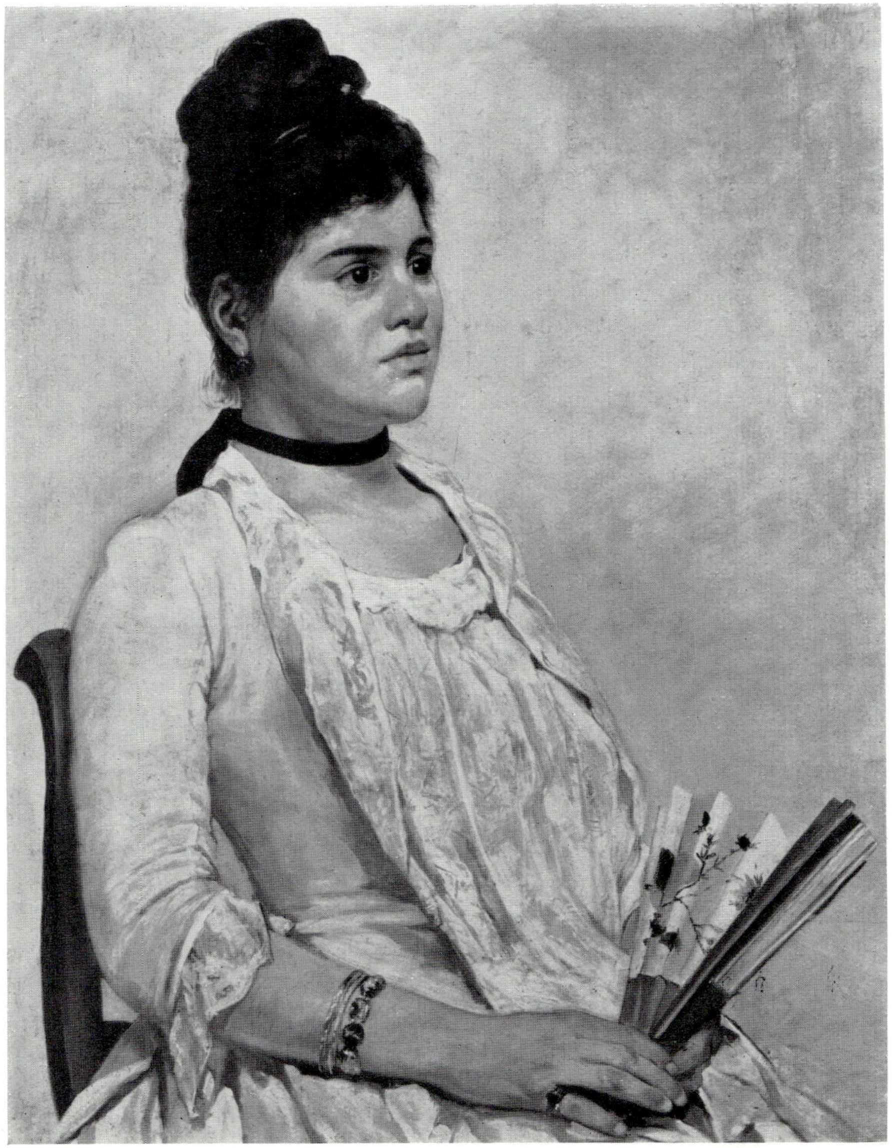

MACCHIAIOLI

Pl. 233. G. Fattori. *Left*: Portrait of the Artist's Stepdaughter. Canvas, 27¹/₂ × 21⁵/₈ in. Florence, Galleria d'Arte Moderna. *Right*: Self-portrait. Canvas, 27¹/₂ × 21⁵/₈ in. Rome, Coll. Giustiniani-Scola-Camerini.

MACCHIAIOLI

Pl. 234. T. Signorini, Girl Writing. Panel, 5½ × 10¼ in. Florence, Coll. Ojetti.

MACCHIAIOLI

Pl. 235. T. Signorini, Square in Settignano. Canvas, 12⁵/₈ × 20⁷/₈ in. Crema, Italy, Coll. Stramezzi.

MACCHIAIOLI

Pl. 236. G. Fattori, Black Horse in the Sun. Panel, 9½ × 13⅜ in. Milan, Coll. Jucker.

MACCHIAIOLI

Pl. 237. R. Sernesi, Lake Trasimeno. Canvas, $12^{5}/_{8}\times31^{7}/_{8}$ in. Milan, Coll. Jucker.

MACCHIAIOLI

Pl. 238. S. Lega, Curiosity. Canvas, 27 1/8 × 19 3/4 in. Milan, Coll. Jucker.

MACCHIAIOLI

Pl. 239. *Above*: G. Boldini, The Painter Lanfredini. Panel, 10¹/₄×10⁵/₈ in. Milan, private coll. *Below*: A. Cecioni, Interior with Figure. Canvas, 11×13³/₄ in. Rome, Galleria Nazionale d'Arte Moderna.

MACCHIAIOLI

Pl. 240. *Above*: S. De Tivoli, Landscape. Canvas, 19³/₄×25⁵/₈ in. *Below, left*: V. Cabianca, Peasant Woman in Montemurlo. Canvas on cardboard, 9⁷/₈×5¹/₈ in. Both, Rome, Galleria Nazionale d'Arte Moderna. *Right*: V. D'Ancona, In the Garden. Cardboard, 5¹/₂×4 in. Florence, Coll. Nardini.

MAGIC

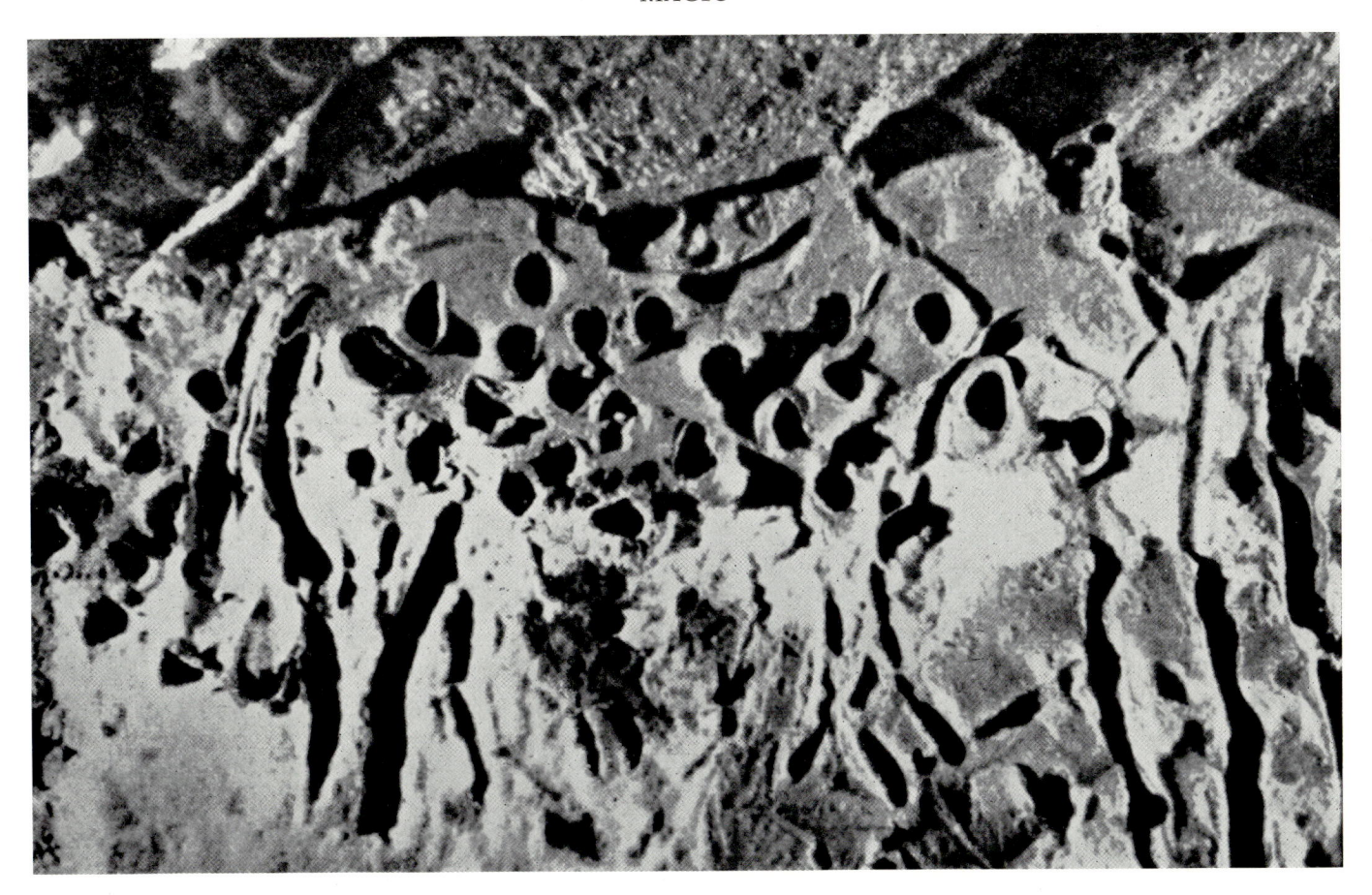

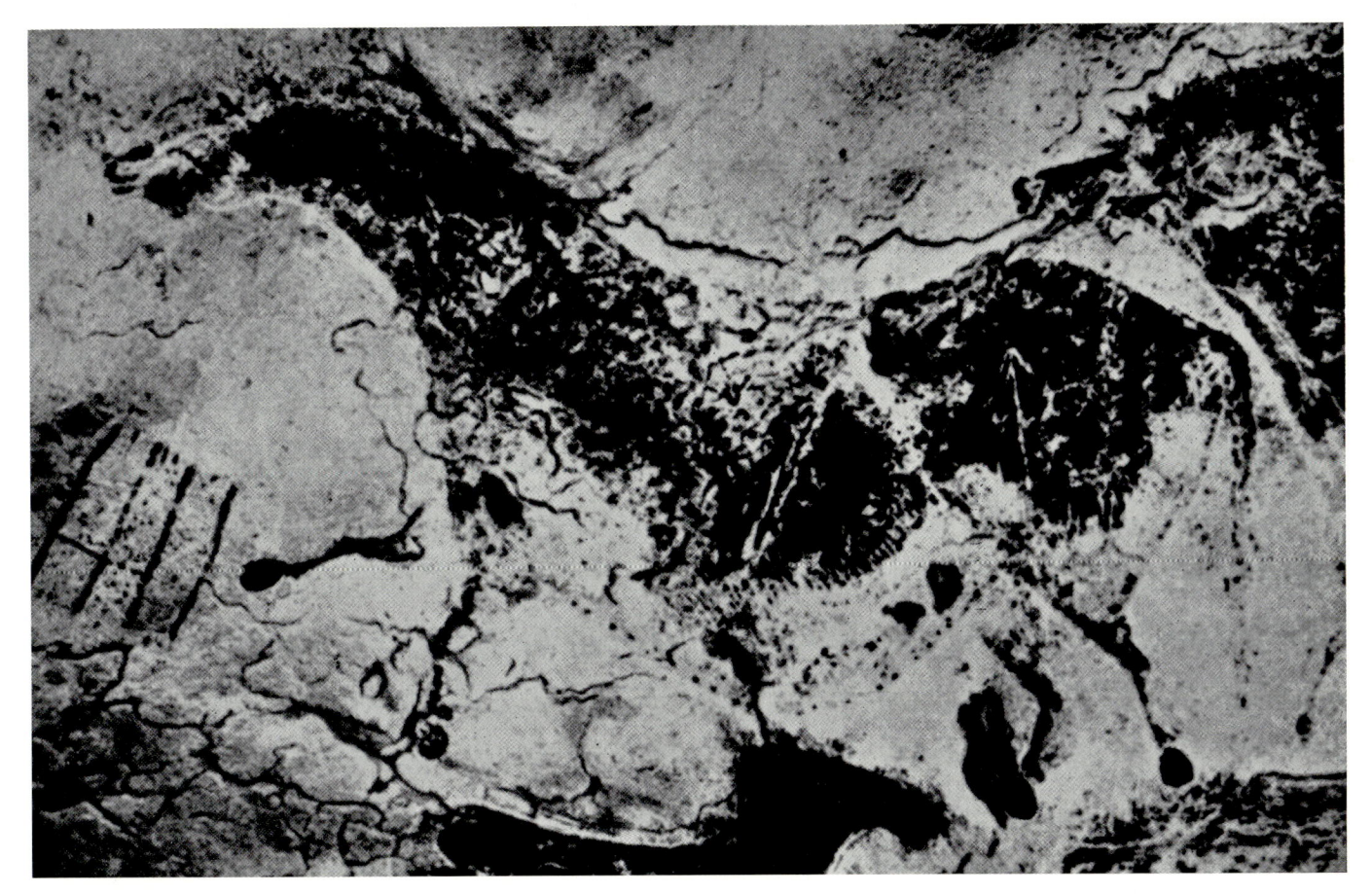

Pl. 241 Hunting magic, Upper Paleolithic period. *Above*: Horse incised on clay, riddled with spear holes. Ht., 11³/⁴ in. Montespan Cave, Haute-Garonne, France. *Below*: Horse painted and engraved on rock, struck by an arrow. Ht., 43¹/⁴ in. Lascaux Cave, Dordogne, France.

MAGIC

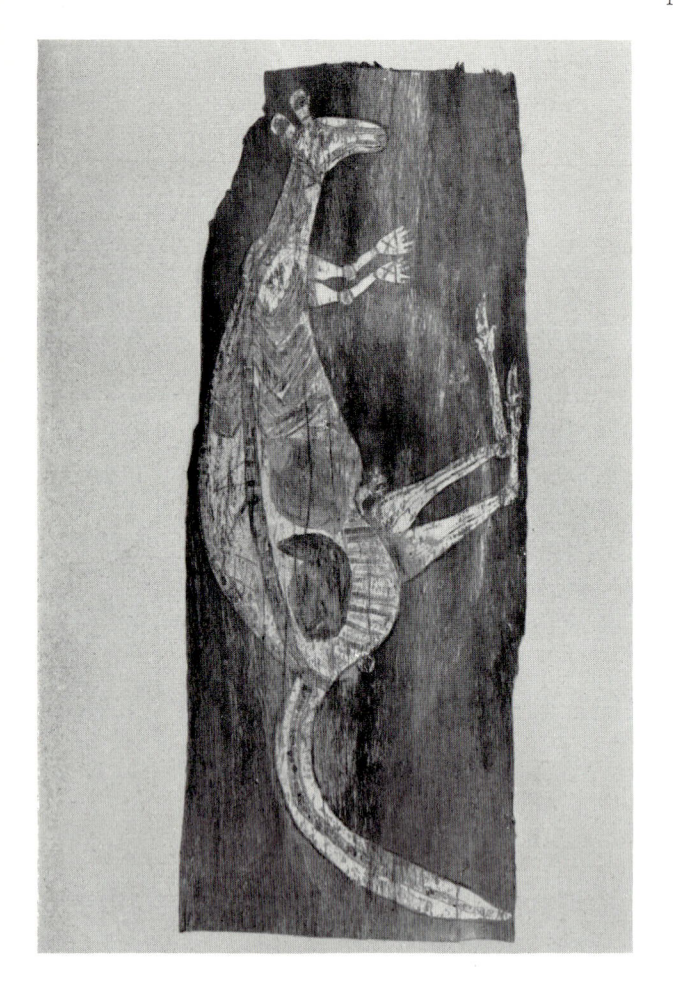

Pl. 242. Hunting and fishing magic. *Left*: Bushman rock painting representing two antelope-masked hunters. Giant's Castle Game Reserve, Natal, Union of South Africa. *Right, above*: Representation of a kangaroo in X-ray style, Arnhemland, Australia. Painting on bark. *Below*: Fish carved and painted with ornamental motifs, Ndeni, Santa Cruz Islands, Melanesia. Wood; l. of longer, 25¼ in. Last two, Basel, Museum für Völkerkunde.

MAGIC

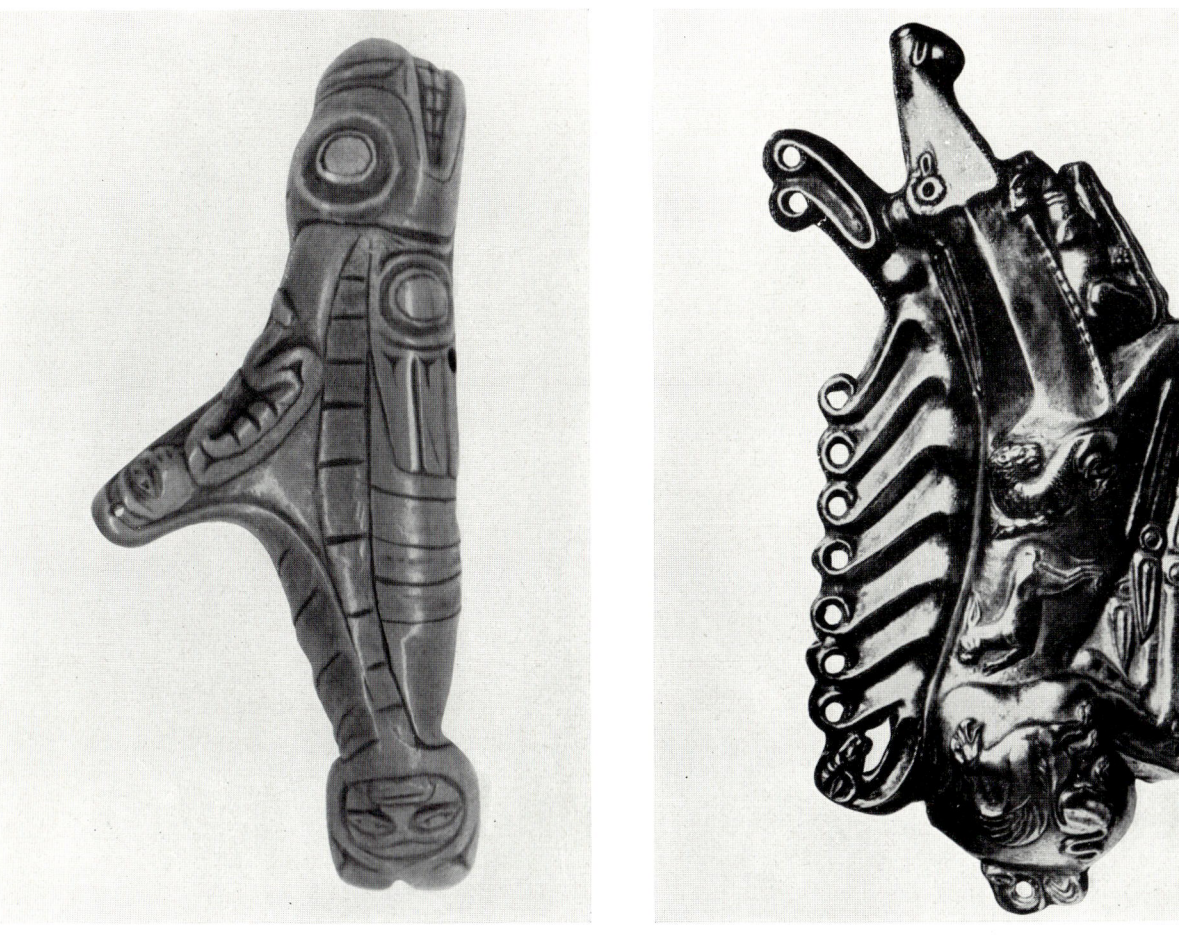

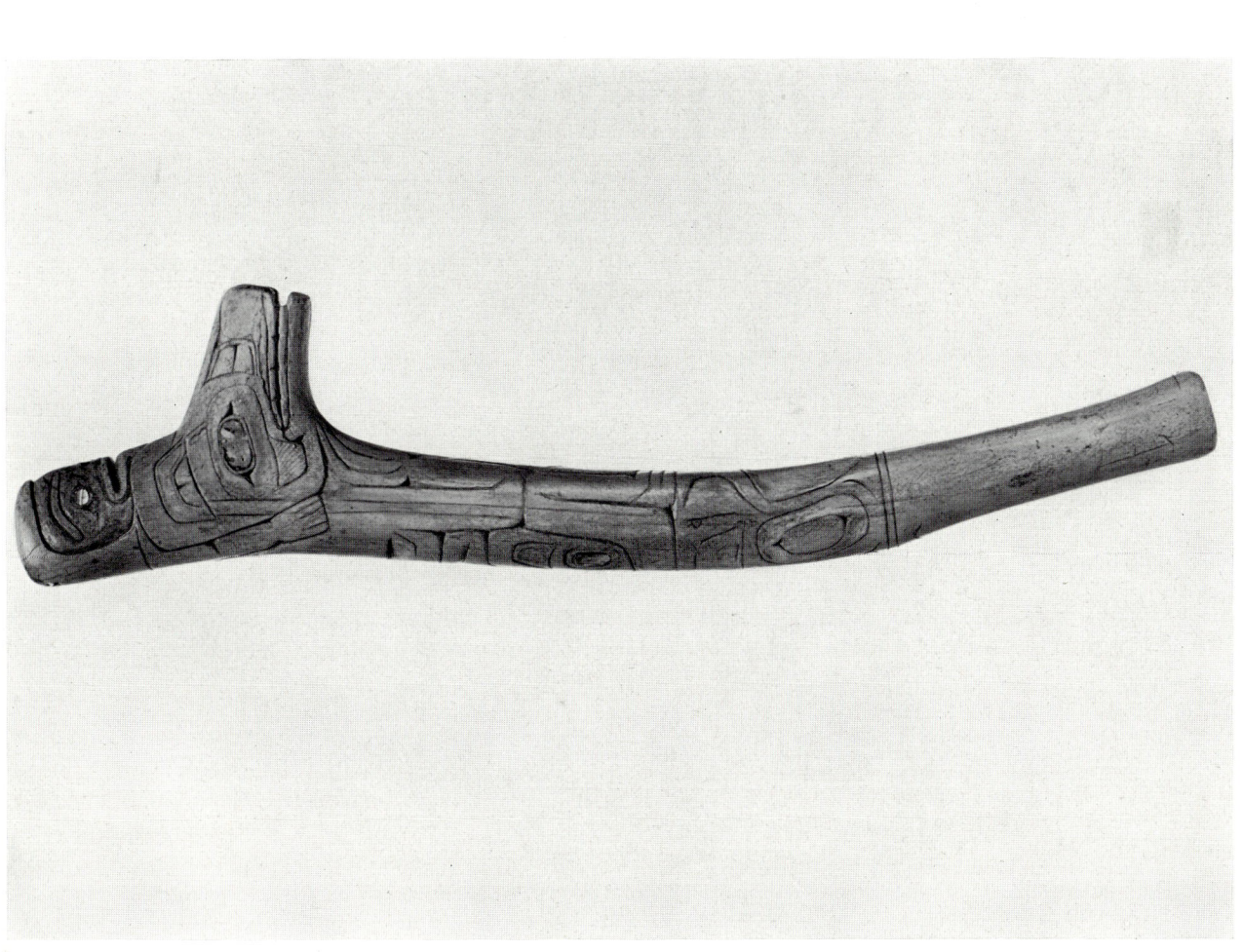

Pl. 243. Hunting and fishing magic. *Left*: Tsimshian war club carved with wolf's head, British Columbia, Canada. Caribou horn. New York, American Museum of Natural History. *Right, above*: Tlingit amulet carved in the form of a whale with human figures, Alaska. Bone. Seattle, Washington State Museum. *Below*: Deer, Kul Oba, Crimea, 4th cent. B.C. Gold, l., 11¾ in. Leningrad, The Hermitage.

MAGIC

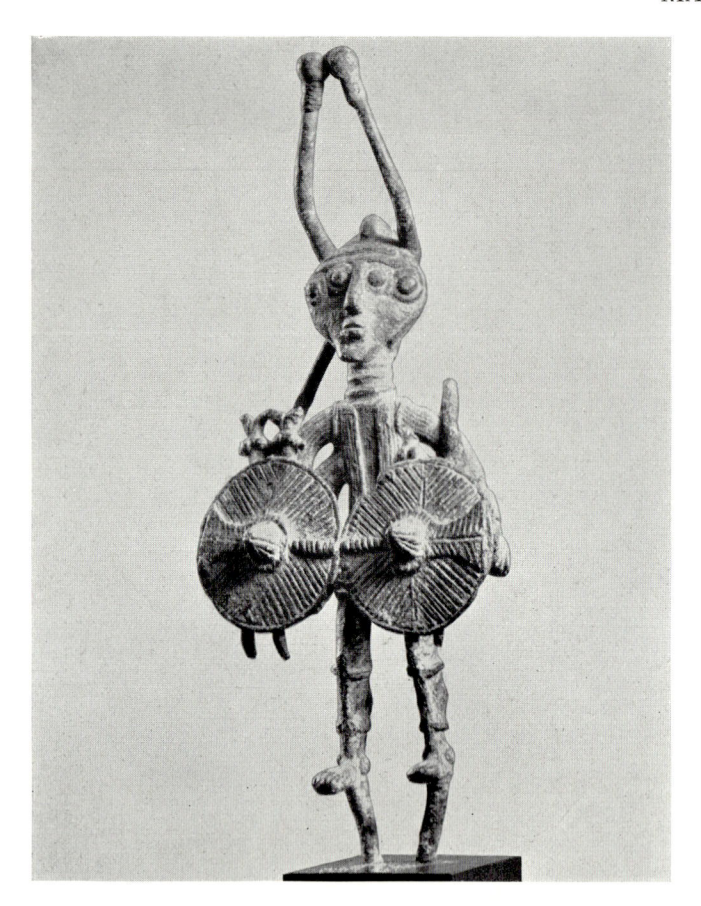

Pl. 244. War magic and apotropaic motifs. *Left, above*: Warrior with four eyes and four arms, Abini deposit, Teti, near Nuoro, Sardinia, 8th–6th cent. B.C. Bronze, ht., 7½ in. Cagliari, Museo Archeologico Nazionale. *Below*: Painted shields with apotropaic masks, Kenyah Dayak and Long Iram tribes, Borneo. Wood; l. of longer, 4 ft., 4 in. Copenhagen, Nationalmuseet. *Right, above*: Etruscan helmet with apotropaic eyes, second half of 5th cent. B.C. Bronze. Berlin, Staatliche Museen. *Center*: The Berlin Painter, shield with gorgon and fantastic animals, detail of an Attic amphora, ca. 490 B.C. Basel, A.G. Ciba Foundation. *Below*: Apotropaic mask, China, Ch'ien-lung period. Colored woodprint.

MAGIC

Pl. 245. Ionic amphora with representation of serpents and dolphin between two apotropaic eyes, second half of 6th cent. B.C. Ht., 13 3/8 in. Leiden, Netherlands, Rijksmuseum.

MAGIC

Pl. 246. Lecanomantic scene, detail of wall painting, mid-1st cent. B.C. Ht., 5 ft., 3¾ in. Villa of the Mysteries (Villa Item), Pompeii.

MAGIC

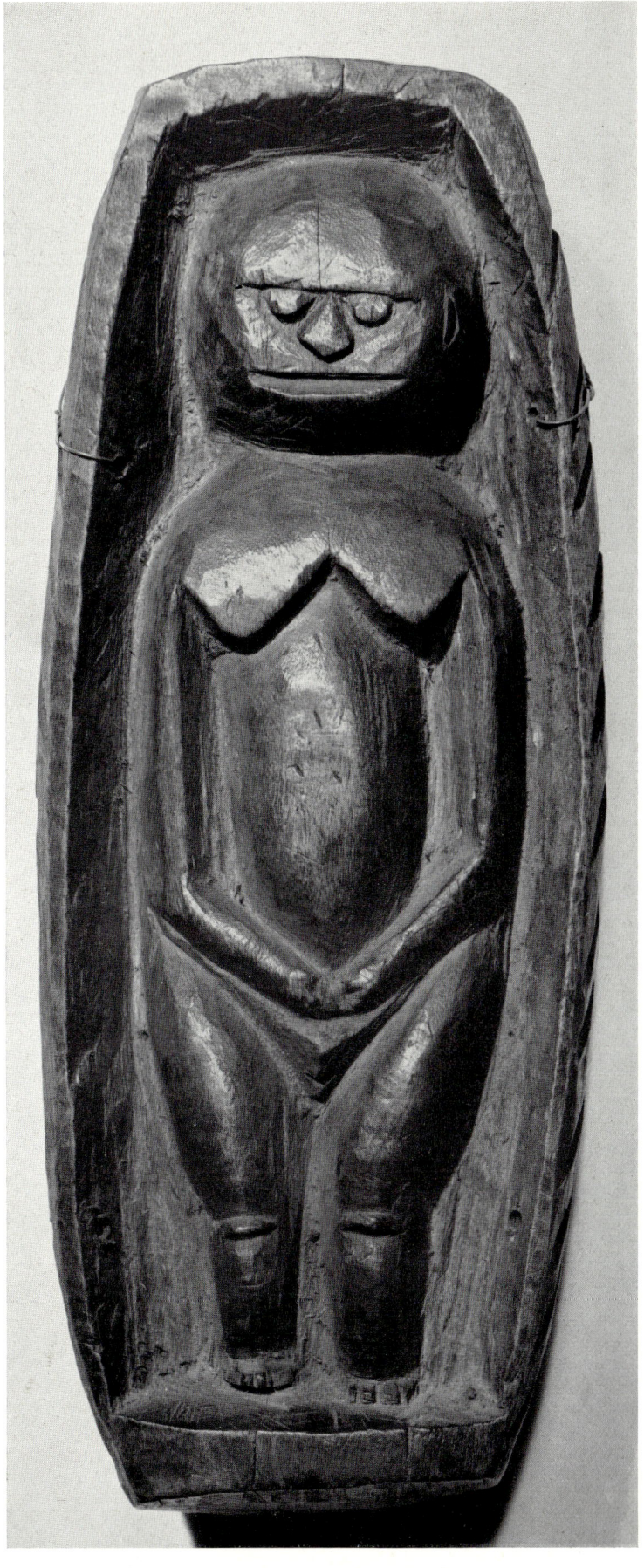

Pl. 247. Fertility and oracular figures. *Left, above*: The Willendorf "Venus," Austria, Upper Paleolithic period. Limestone, ht., 4 3/8 in. Vienna, Naturhistorisches Museum. *Below*: Ancient idol used as fertility spell and oracle, Liberia or Sierra Leone. Stone. Hamburg, Museum für Völkerkunde. *Right*: Female oracular figure (*hwainangi*), Oubatche, New Caledonia. Wood, ht., 11 3/4 in. Cambridge, England, University Museum of Archaeology and Ethnology.

MAGIC

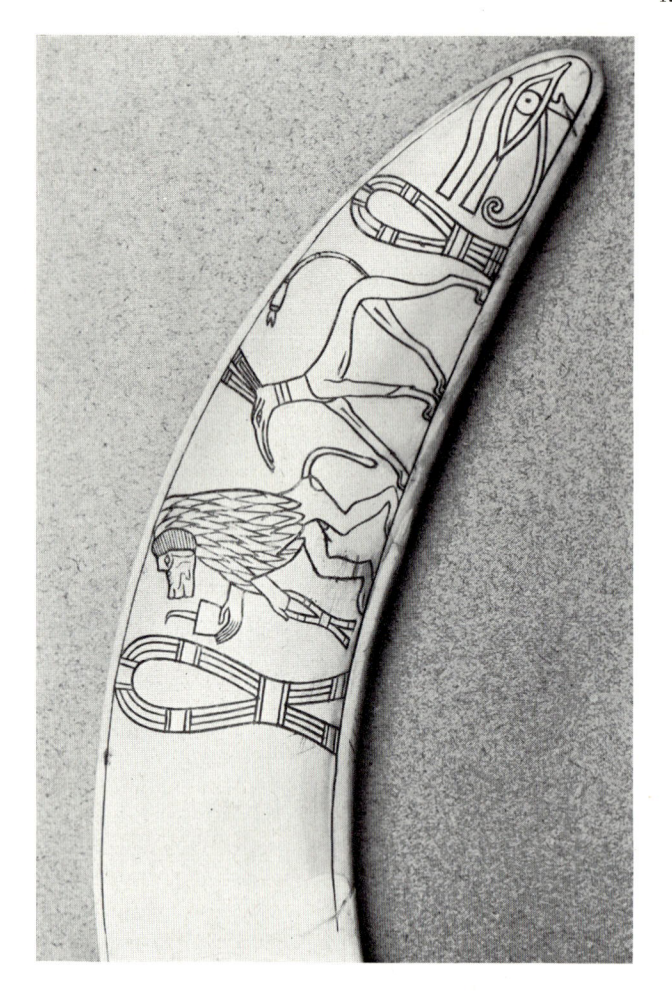

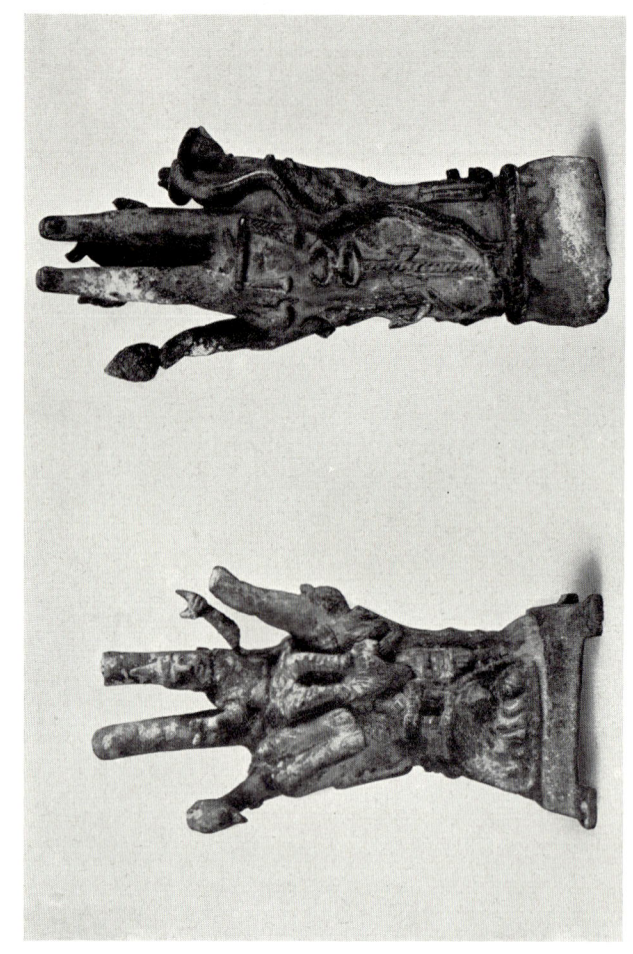

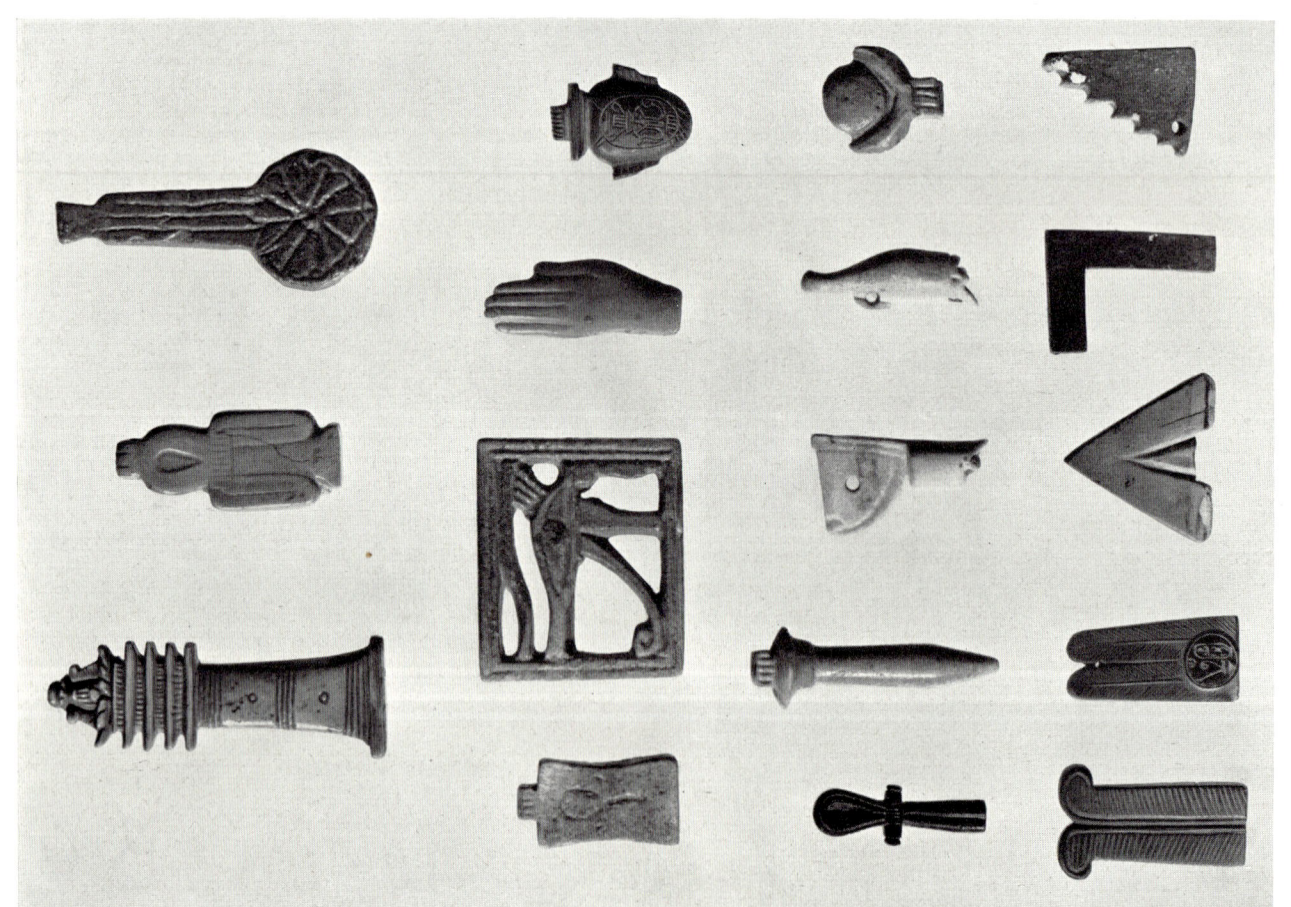

Pl. 248. Amulets. *Left:* Egyptian amulets. Ceramic and *pietra dura*; max. ht., 2 1/8 in.; min., 1 3/4 in. Turin, Museo Egizio. *Right, above:* Egyptian magic knife, probably against serpent bites, detail, Thebes (?), 12th dynasty. Ivory, full l., 5 7/8 in. Edinburgh, Royal Scottish Museum. *Below:* "Votive hands" with Sabazian symbols, Pompeii, 1st cent. Bronze; ht. of hand, ca. 7 1/8 in. Pompeii, Antiquarium.

MAGIC

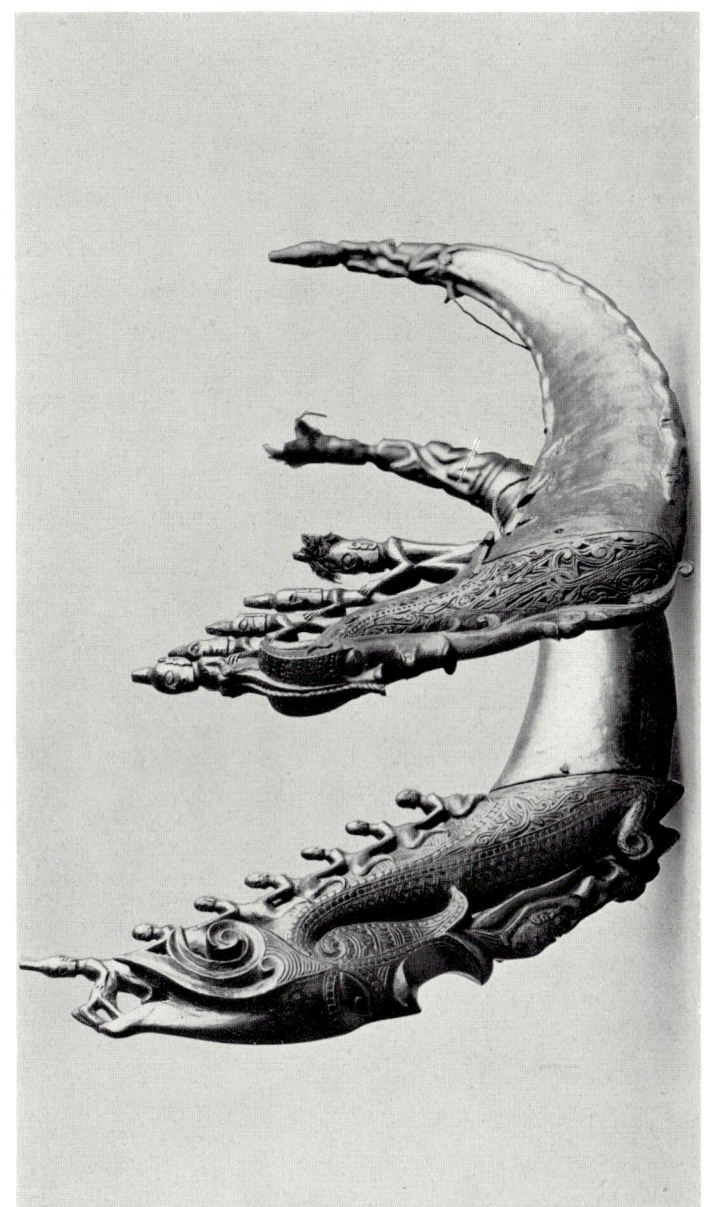

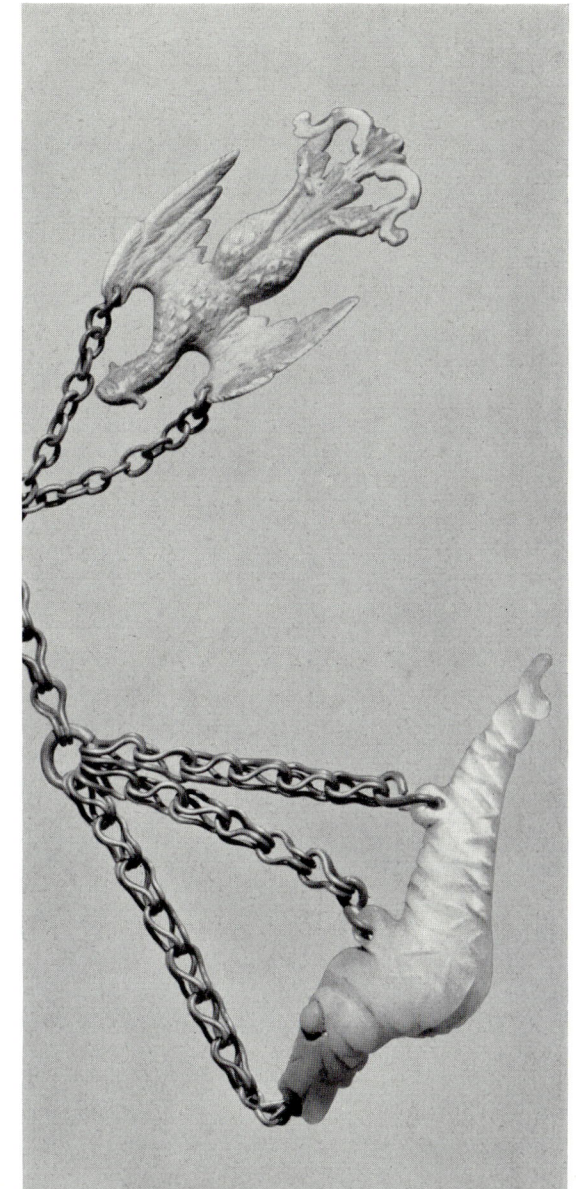

Pl. 249. Amulets. *Above, left*: Bapende amulet mask, Congo. Ivory, 2¼×1¼ in. Tervueren, Belgium, Musée Royal de l'Afrique Centrale. *Right*: Toba Batak containers for magical remedies, Sumatra. Horn and wood. Amsterdam, Koninklijk Instituut voor de Tropen. *Below*: Italian folk charms. Rome, Museo Nazionale delle Arti e delle Tradizioni Popolari. *Left*: Half-moons. Silver. *Right*: Fish and eagle. Coral and silver.

MAGIC

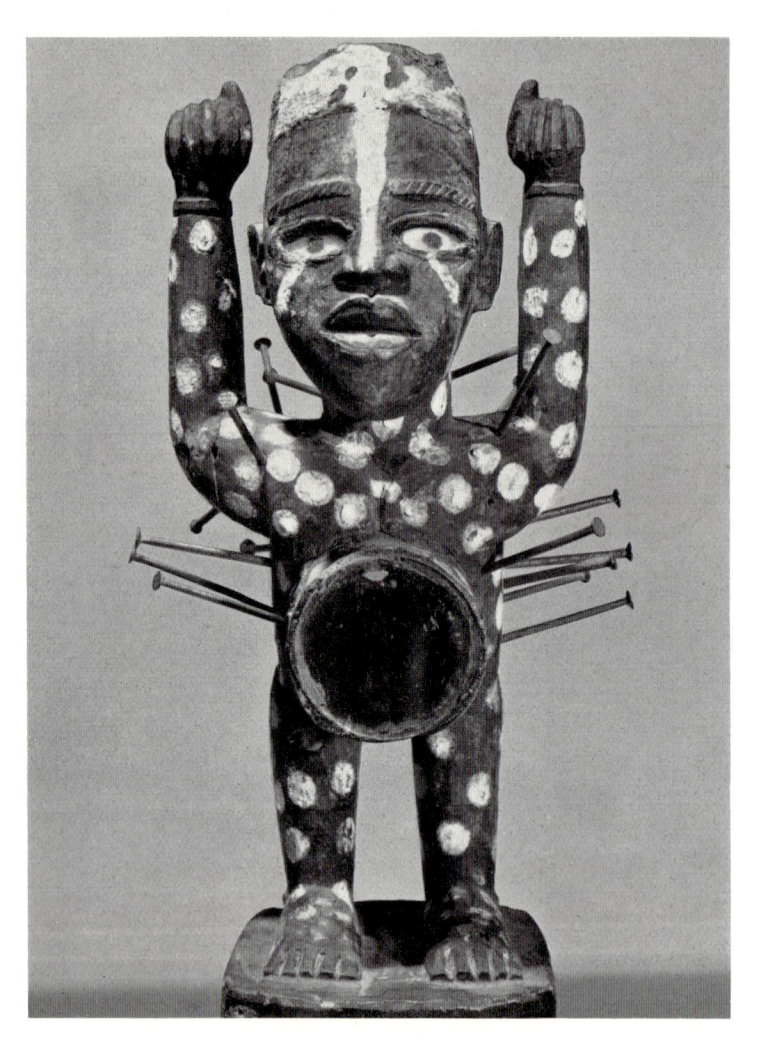

Pl. 250. Statuettes for magical practices or with healing powers. *Left, above*: Sakalava figurines used in magical rites, Madagascar. Wood. Paris, Musée de l'Homme. *Below*: Nail fetish with mirror, lower Congo. Wood. Rome, Lateran Museums. *Right, above*: Egyptian "execration figure," Saqqara, late 12th–early 13th dynasty. Terra cotta, ht., 13 in. Brussels, Musées Royaux d'Art et d'Histoire. *Below*: Egyptian "healing" statue with a "pillar of Horus upon the crocodiles," 30th dynasty. Black basalt, ht., 26 3/4 in. Paris, Louvre.

MAGIC

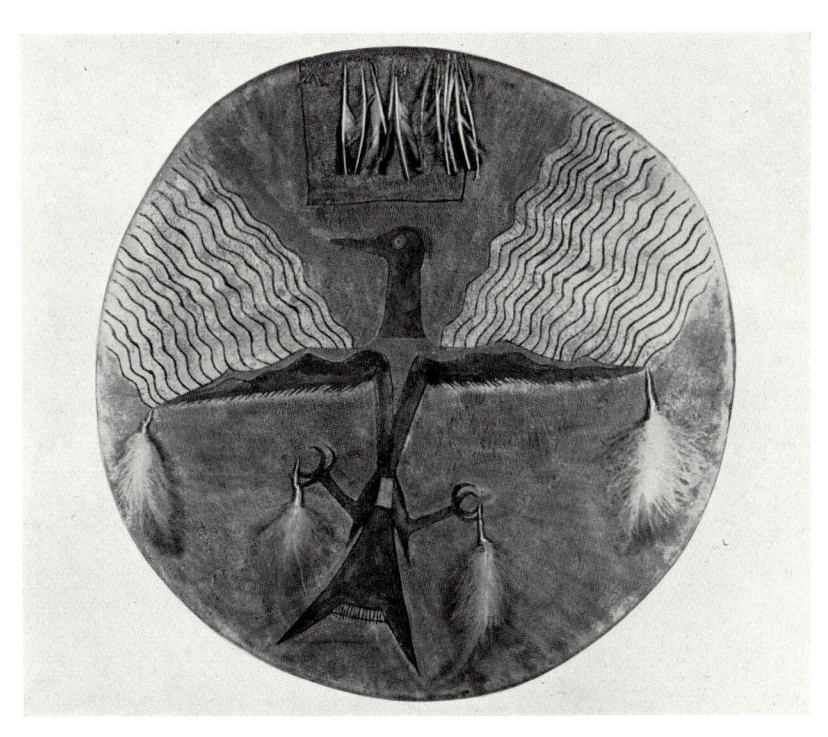

Pl. 251. *Above, left*: Shepherd-priest (*archiboukolos*) of the cult of Dionysus for the fertility of the fields, Ostia, Italy, 2d cent. Marble, ht., 17½ in. Rome, Vatican Museums. *Right*: Sioux shield with the thunderbird and wavy lines symbolizing sound of thunder, U.S.A. Painted hide. Denver, Art Museum. *Below*: Ceremonial dance mask, Torres Straits, New Guinea. Turtle shell on wood, feathers, and shells; l., 4 ft. London, British Museum.

MAGIC

Pl. 252. Divination. *Above*: Mashona divining objects, Southern Rhodesia. Wood and ivory. London, British Museum. *Below, left*: Basonge divining instrument (*katatora*), Congo. Wood, ht., 7¼ in. Tervueren, Belgium, Musée Royal de l'Afrique Centrale. *Right*: Yoruba oracle board used in the Ifa cult, Nigeria. Wood. Hamburg, Museum für Völkerkunde.

MAGIC

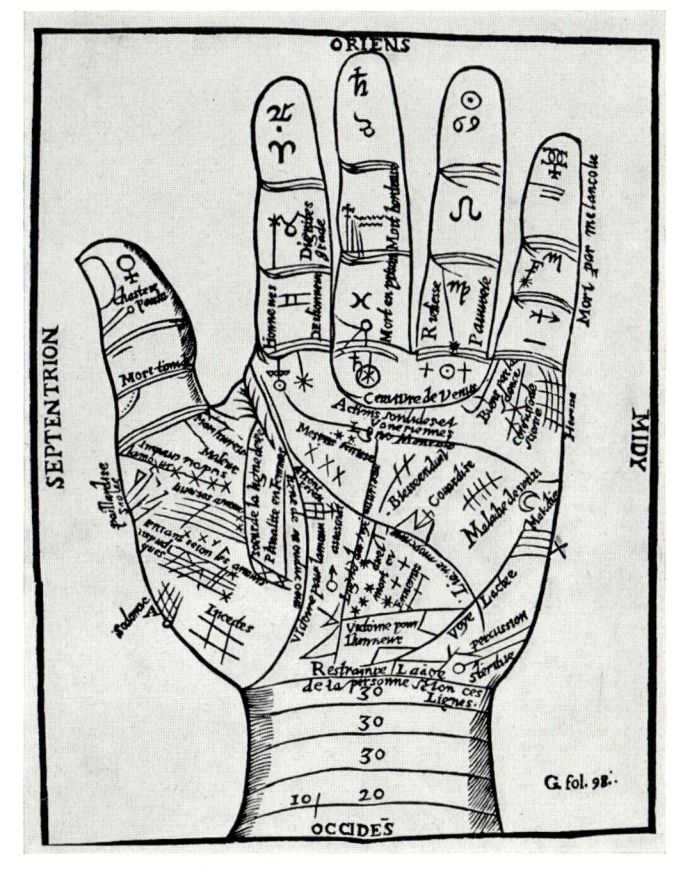

Pl. 253. Divination. *Above*: Batak book with spells, Sumatra. Bark. London, British Museum. *Below, left*: Model of a sheep's liver for divining, with names of Etruscan divinities, 4th–3d cent. B.C. Bronze, l., 5 in. Piacenza, Italy, Museo Civico. *Right*: Hand with explanatory diagram for chiromantic reading, from J. Belot, *Œuvres*, Lyons, France, 1649. Woodcut.

MAGIC

Pl. 254. Lower Rhenish master, The Love Spell, 15th cent. Panel, 9½ × 7⅛ in. Leipzig, Museum der bildenden Künste.

MAGIC

Pl. 255. H. Baldung-Grien, allegorical figure (Prudence?) with divining mirror, 1529. Panel, 32 1/2 × 14 in. Munich, Alte Pinakothek.

MAGIC

Pl. 256. S. Rosa (1615–73), Witch. Canvas, $16^{1}/_{8} \times 12^{1}/_{4}$ in. Rome, Palazzo dei Conservatori, Pinacoteca Capitolina.

MAGIC

Pl. 257. Witches. *Above, left*: Witch riding a demon, Germany, late 15th cent. Woodcut. Berlin, Kupferstichkabinett. *Right*: Types and works of witches. Woodcut from U. Tengler, *Der neu Lajenspiegel...*, Augsburg, 1511. *Below, left*: H. Baldung-Grien, The Meteorologic Witches, 1523. Panel, 25⅝ × 17¾ in. Frankfort on the Main, Städelsches Kunstinstitut. *Right*: Filippino Lippi (ca. 1457–1504), two witches. Drawing. Florence, Uffizi, Gabinetto dei Disegni e Stampe.

MAGIC

Pl. 258. Magical rites and exorcism. *Left*: The necromancers John Dee and Edward Kelly, from E. Sibly, *A New and Complete Illustration of the Occult Sciences*, London, 1807. Engraving. *Right*: Master of the Oberaltaicher Schmerzensmannes (?), St. James exorcising the demons, 1518. Panel, 38¾ × 33½ in. Nürnberg, Germanisches National-Museum.

MAGIC

Pl. 259. Allegories with reference to magic and alchemy, 16th cent. *Left*: T. Stimmer, Death the Alchemist, from the *Altersstuffen des Weibes* series. Woodcut. Basel, Kunstmuseum, Kupferstichkabinett. *Right*: H. Burgkmair the Elder, "How the young white king learned black magic," from the *Weisskunig* series. Woodcut. Vienna, Albertina.

MAGIC

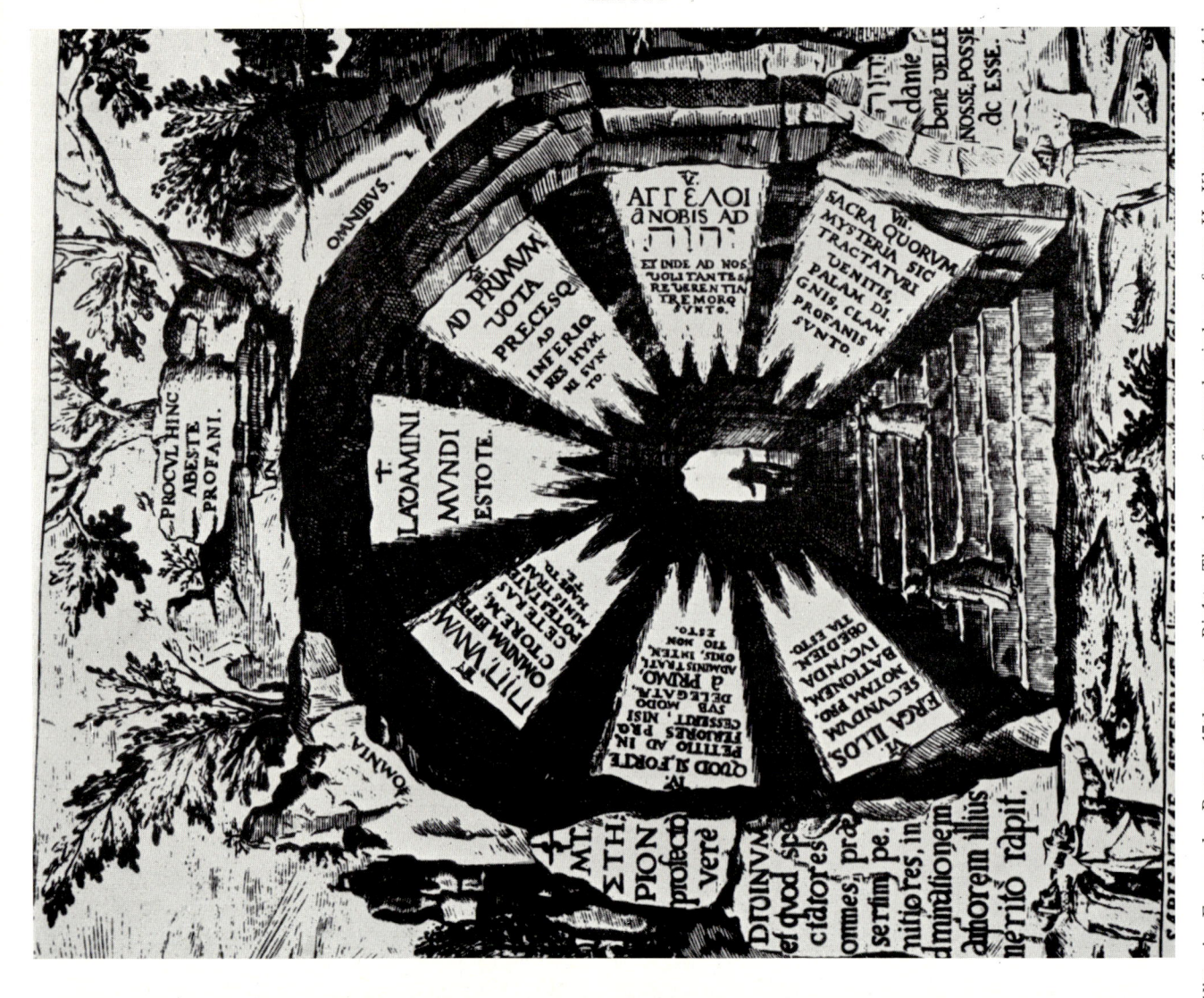

Pl. 260. Alchemic-esoteric symbolism. *Left*: Magical-alchemic door, Piazza Vittorio Emanuele, Rome, 17th cent. *Right*: The door of eternal wisdom, from H. Khunrath, *Amphitheatrum Aeternae Sapientiae*, Hanau, Germany, 1609. Engraving.

MAGNASCO

Pl. 261. The Tame Crow. Canvas, 18½ × 24 in. Florence, Uffizi.

MAGNASCO

Pl. 262. Patrician family scene in a garden with panorama, detail. Canvas; full size, 2 ft., 5 7/8 in. × 6 ft., 6 in. Genoa, Galleria di Palazzo Bianco.

MAGNASCO

Pl. 263. *Left*: Don Quixote. Canvas, 29 1/8 × 23 5/8 in. Detroit, Institute of Arts. *Right*: The Communion of Mary Magdalene. Canvas, 44 1/8 × 33 1/2 in. Formerly, Genoa, Coll. G. Delmonte.

MAGNASCO

Pl. 264. *Above*: The Baptism of Christ. Canvas, 46¼×57¾ in. Washington, D.C., National Gallery. *Below*: Writing room in a monastery. Canvas, 36¼×52⅜ in. Seitenstetten, Austria, Benedictine monastery.

Pl. 265. Ramo di Paganello or L. Maitani (attrib.), first design for the façade of the Cathedral of Orvieto. Drawing on parchment, ca. 43×30³/₄ in. Orvieto, Italy, Museo dell'Opera del Duomo.

Pl. 266. Madonna and Child. Wood, ht., 31½ in. Orvieto, Italy, Museo dell'Opera del Duomo.

Pl. 267. Orvieto, Italy, Cathedral. *Above*: Madonna and Child, lunette of the main portal. Marble and bronze. *Below*: Adoration of the Magi, detail of third pilaster of the façade. Marble.

MAITANI

Pl. 268. Scenes from Genesis. Marble. Orvieto, Italy, Cathedral, first pilaster of the façade.

Pl. 269. Orvieto, Italy, Cathedral, façade. Marble. *Above*: The Creation, detail of first pilaster. *Below*: Hell and the damned, detail of Last Judgment, fourth pilaster.

Pl. 270. Cairo. *Above, left*: Complex of Sultan Qalā'ūn, façade of the mausoleum, 1284–85. *Right and below, left*: Madrasah-mosque of Sultan Ḥasan, 1356–63, ablution fountain and *qibla* liwan; portal. *Below, right*: Mosque of Qijmās al-Isḥāqī, 1480–81.

Pl. 271. Cairo, Mausoleum of Yūnus ad-Dāwadār, before 1382.

MAMELUKE ART

Pl. 272. *Above, left*: Cairo, Mosque of Aq Sunqur, 1346–47, mimbar and mihrab. *Right*: Cairo, drinking fountain of Qāit Bey, before 1495, detail showing molded arch and bulb capital. *Below*: Fountain from a Mameluke *qā'a* (reception hall), 14th cent. Cairo, Museum of Islamic Art.

Pl. 273. Cairo, Mosque of Khairbak, 1502.

MAMELUKE ART

Pl. 274. Cairo. *Above, left*: Naḥḥāsīn, the *qāʿa* (reception hall) of Muḥibb ad-Dīn, 1350. *Right*: Bāb an-Naṣr, an apartment in the *wakāla* of Qāit Bey, 1480–81. *Below*: Maqʾad (loggia) of Māmāi as-Saifī, 1496.

MAMELUKE ART

Pl. 275. *Above, left*: Ewer bearing the name of Sultan Shihāb ad-Dīn Aḥmad, 1342. Brass inlaid with silver. Cairo, Museum of Islamic Art. *Right*: Albarello with copper luster painting on dark-blue background, 13th–14th cent. London, Victoria and Albert Museum. *Below*: Box for the Koran, from the Mosque of Sultan al-Ghūrī, 14th cent. Wood with brass plaques inlaid with silver and gold. Cairo, Museum of Islamic Art.

Pl. 276. *Above, left*: Mlle Victorine in the Costume of an Espada. Canvas, 5 ft., 5 in. × 4 ft., 2³/₄ in. New York, Metropolitan Museum. *Right*: Portrait of Zola. Canvas, 4 ft., 9 in. × 3 ft., 7¹/₄ in. Paris, Louvre. *Below*: Bullfight. Canvas, 17⁷/₈ × 23⁷/₈ in. Chicago, Art Institute.

MANET

Pl. 277. *Above*: Boating. Canvas, 38¼×51¼ in. New York, Metropolitan Museum. *Below*: Portrait of Mme Manet on a Blue Couch. Pastel, 19¼×23⅝ in. Paris, Louvre.

MANET

Pl. 278. Olympia. Canvas, 4 ft., 3 in. × 6 ft., 2¾ in. Paris, Louvre.

MANET

Pl. 279. Bar at the Folies-Bergère, formerly known as "Cafe-Concert, Bar." Canvas, 18 1/2 × 22 in. Amsterdam, Stedelijk Museum.

MANET

Pl. 280. La Blonde aux seins nus. Canvas, 24 3/8 × 20 1/4 in. Paris, Louvre.

MANICHAEAN ART

Pl. 281. Illuminated title of a scroll (*volumen*), from Khocho, China, 9th–10th cent. (?). Paper, ca. 12×8⅝ in. Berlin, Museum für Völkerkunde.

MANICHAEAN ART

Pl. 282. Front and back of an illuminated page, from Khocho, China, 9th–10th cent. (?). Paper. Berlin, Museum für Völkerkunde.

MANICHAEAN ART

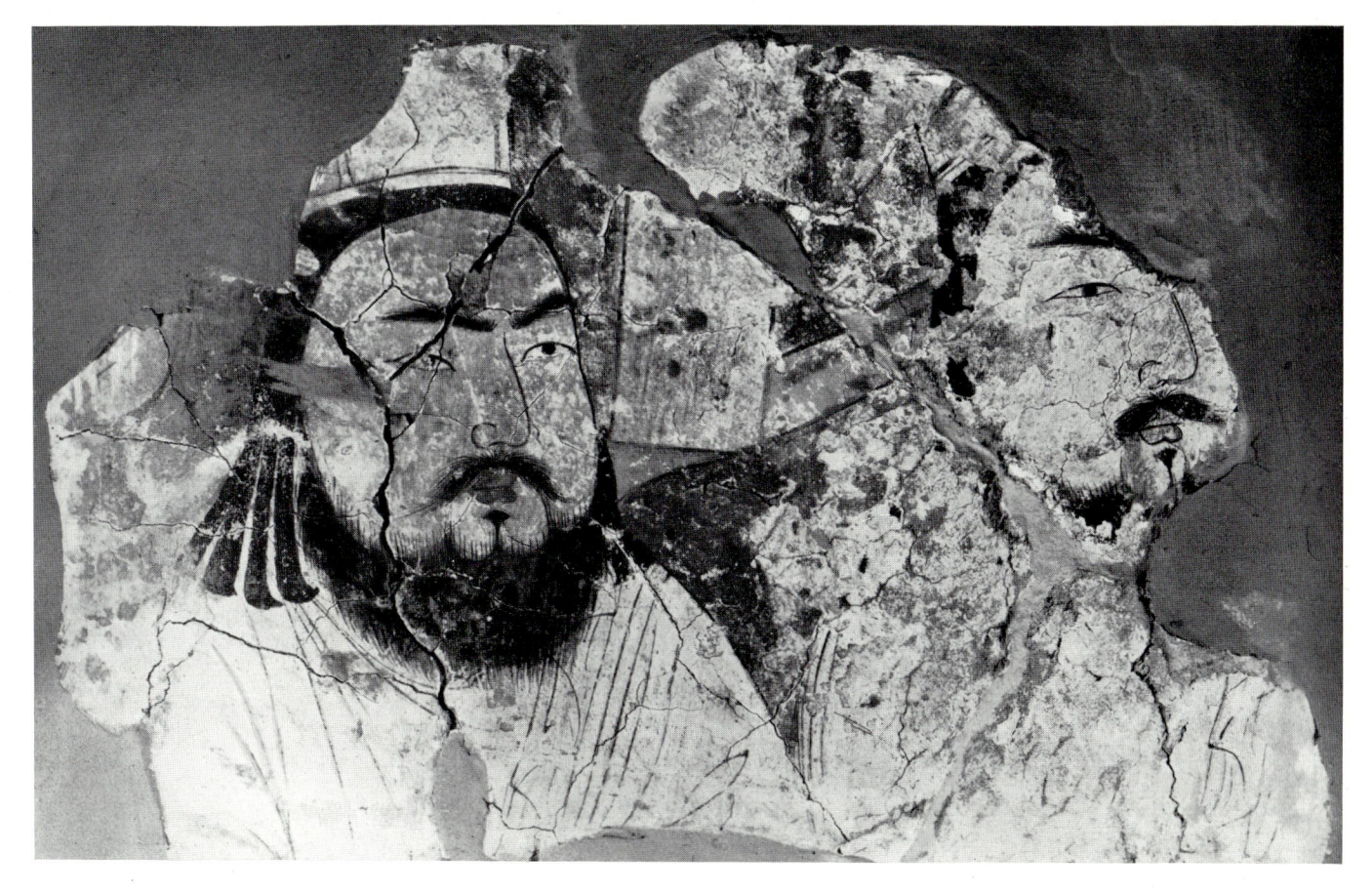

Pl. 283. *Above*: Presumed portrait of Mani surrounded by the elect, from Khocho, China, 8th–9th cent. (?). Wall painting, 2 ft., 10 5/8 in. × 5 ft., 6 3/8 in. *Below*: Two of the elect, from Khocho, 8th–9th cent. (?). Wall painting, 10 5/8 × 13 3/4 in. Both, Berlin, Museum für Völkerkunde.

MANICHAEAN ART

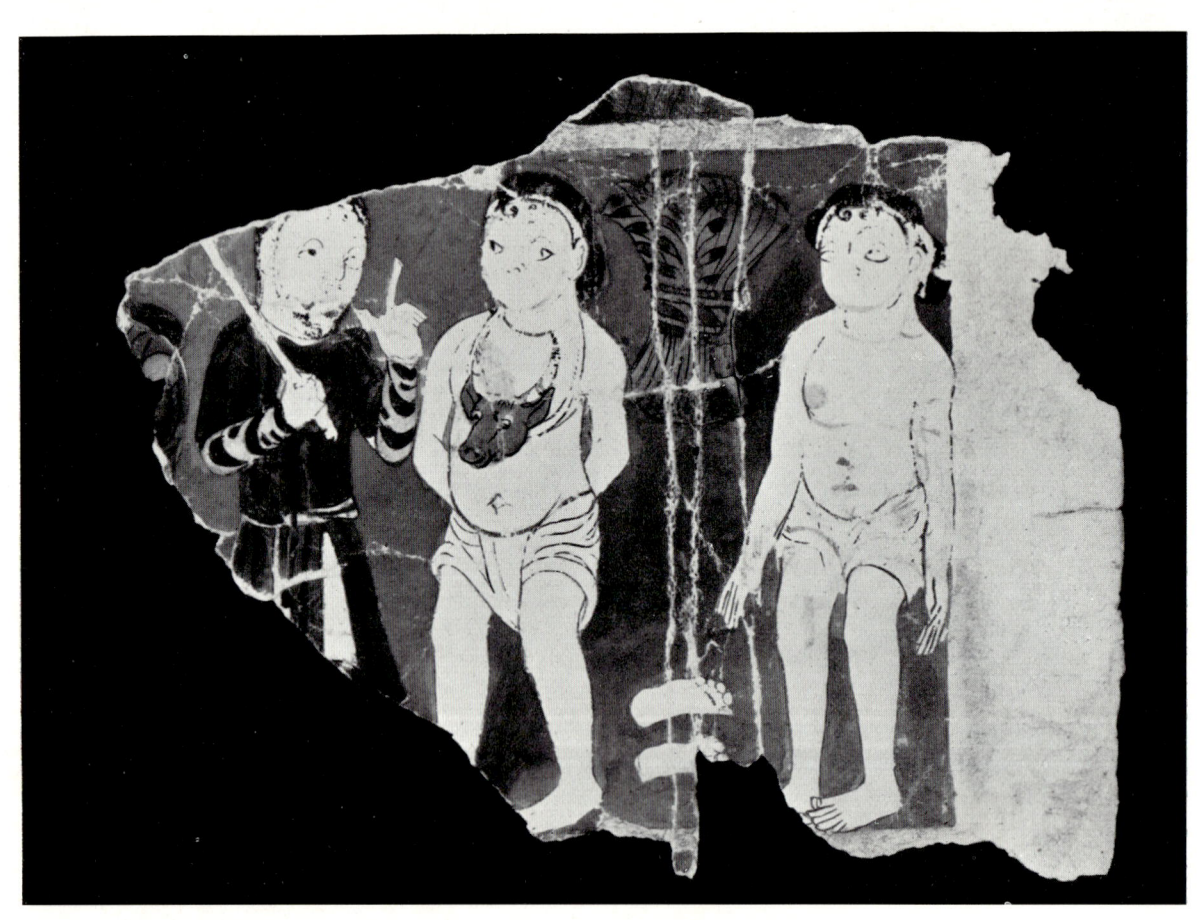

Pl. 284. Front and back of an illuminated page, from Khocho, China, 9th cent. (?). Paper, 3¼×4⅜ in. Berlin, Museum für Völkerkunde.

Pl. 285. Three divinities, from Khocho, China, 9th–10th cent. (?). Wall painting, ht., 11 in. Berlin, Museum für Völkerkunde.

MANICHAEAN ART

Pl. 286. Temple banner with portrait of the donor, from Khocho, China, 9th–10th cent. (?). Painted silk. Berlin, Museum für Völkerkunde.

MANICHAEAN ART

Pl. 287. *Above, left*: The elect, from Khocho, China, 9th-10th cent. (?). Painted silk, 11¾×7⅞ in. *Right*: Illuminated page, from Khocho, 9th cent. (?). Paper, 4⅞×2½ in. *Below*: Front and back of illuminated page, from Khocho, 8th-9th cent. (?). Paper, 6¾×4¾ in. All, Berlin, Museum für Völkerkunde.

Pl. 288. Pontormo, Deposition. Panel, 10 ft., 3 in. × 6 ft., 3 in. Florence, S. Felicita.

MANNERISM

Pl. 289. Pontormo, Madonna and Child with Infant St. John. Panel, 35×28 3/4 in. Florence, Uffizi.

MANNERISM

Pl. 290. Il Rosso, Moses and the Daughters of Jethro. Canvas, 5 ft., 3 in. × 3 ft., 10 in. Florence, Uffizi.

MANNERISM

Pl. 291. *Above*: Il Rosso, Pietà. Panel transferred to canvas; 4 ft., 7/8 in. × 5 ft., 2 5/8 in. Paris, Louvre. *Below*: The Fountain of Youth, 16th-cent. French tapestry after a cartoon by Il Rosso. Vienna, Kunsthistorisches Museum.

MANNERISM

Pl. 292. Bronzino, Venus, Cupid, Folly, and Time. Panel, 57 1/2 × 45 3/4 in. London, National Gallery.

MANNERISM

Pl. 293. *Above, left*: A. Allori, Allegory of Life, after a drawing by Michelangelo. Copper, 15×10⁵/₈ in. Florence, Uffizi. *Right*: J. Zucchi, Coral Fishing. Copper, 21⁵/₈×17³/₄ in. Rome, Galleria Borghese. *Below*: Perino del Vaga, Jove hurling thunderbolts at the giants. Fresco. Genoa, Palazzo Doria Pamphili.

MANNERISM

Pl. 294. *Above*: F. Salviati, Pope Eugenius IV entrusts his troops to the command of Ranuccio Farnese. Fresco. Rome, Palazzo Farnese. *Below*: Rome, Vatican, Sala Regia; architecture by Antonio da Sangallo the Younger, with frescoes by L. Agresti, Daniele da Volterra, G. Vasari, L. Sabatini, and others.

MANNERISM

Pl. 295. D. Beccafumi, Expulsion of the Rebel Angels. Panel, 11 ft., 4$^{5}/_{8}$ in. × 7 ft., 4 in. Siena, Pinacoteca.

MANNERISM

Pl. 296. Bronzino, Eleanor of Toledo (?). Panel, 42⁷/₈ × 33¹/₂ in. Turin, Galleria Sabauda.

MANNERISM

Pl. 297. *Above, left*: A. Sánchez Coello, Prince Don Carlos. Canvas, 43 × 37 3/8 in. *Right*: A. Mor, Catherine, wife of John III of Portugal. Canvas, 42 1/8 × 33 1/8 in. Both, Madrid, Prado. *Below, left*: S. Pulzone, Cardinal Ricci. Panel, 25 5/8 × 19 3/4 in. Rome, Galleria Nazionale. *Right*: B. Passarotti, The Astrologer. Canvas, 39 3/8 × 32 1/4 in. Rome, Galleria Spada.

MANNERISM

Pl. 298. *Above*: Giulio Romano and Rinaldo Mantovano, The Fall of the Giants. Fresco. Mantua, Italy, Palazzo del Te. *Below*: P. Tibaldi, Ulysses Blinding Polyphemus. Fresco. Bologna, Palazzo dell'Università, Accademia delle Scienze.

MANNERISM

Pl. 299. N. dell'Abate, The Conversion of St. Paul. Canvas, 5 ft., 9⁵/₈ in. × 4 ft., 2³/₈ in. Vienna, Kunsthistorisches Museum.

MANNERISM

Pl. 300. G. B. Franco, The Arrest of John the Baptist, detail. Fresco. Rome, S. Giovanni Decollato, oratory.

MANNERISM

Pl. 301. *Above, left*: L. Orsi, Martyrdom of St. Catherine of Alexandria. Canvas, 34⁵/₈×26 in. Modena, Italy, Galleria Estense. *Right*: G. Mazzola-Bedoli, The Conception. Canvas on wood, 11 ft., 11³/₄ in. × 6 ft., 10⁵/₈ in. Parma, Galleria Nazionale. *Below*: N. dell'Abate (attrib.), The Story of Aristaeus. Canvas, 6 ft., 2¹/₂ in. × 7 ft., 9¹/₂ in. London, National Gallery.

MANNERISM

Pl. 302. *Above, left*: Pordenone, Crucifixion, detail. Fresco. Cremona, Italy, Cathedral. *Right*: L. Cambiaso, Pietà. Canvas. Genoa, S. Maria Assunta di Carignano. *Below, left*: Giulio Campi, Martyrdom of St. Agatha. Canvas. Cremona, S. Agata. *Right*: C. Procaccini, The Nativity. Canvas, 10 ft. × 6 ft., 7 in. Bologna, Pinacoteca Nazionale.

MANNERISM

Pl. 303. *Above*: Federico Barocci, Burning of Troy. Canvas, 5 ft., 10½ in. × 8 ft., 3⅝ in. Rome, Galleria Borghese. *Below*: G. Cesari ("Cavalier d'Arpino"), prophets and sibyls, detail of frescoes in the vault of the Cappella Olgiati. Rome, S. Prassede.

MANNERISM

Pl. 304. School of Fontainebleau, portrait of Diane de Poitiers. Panel, 43 3/4 × 38 5/8 in. Basel, Öffentliche Kunstsammlung.

MANNERISM

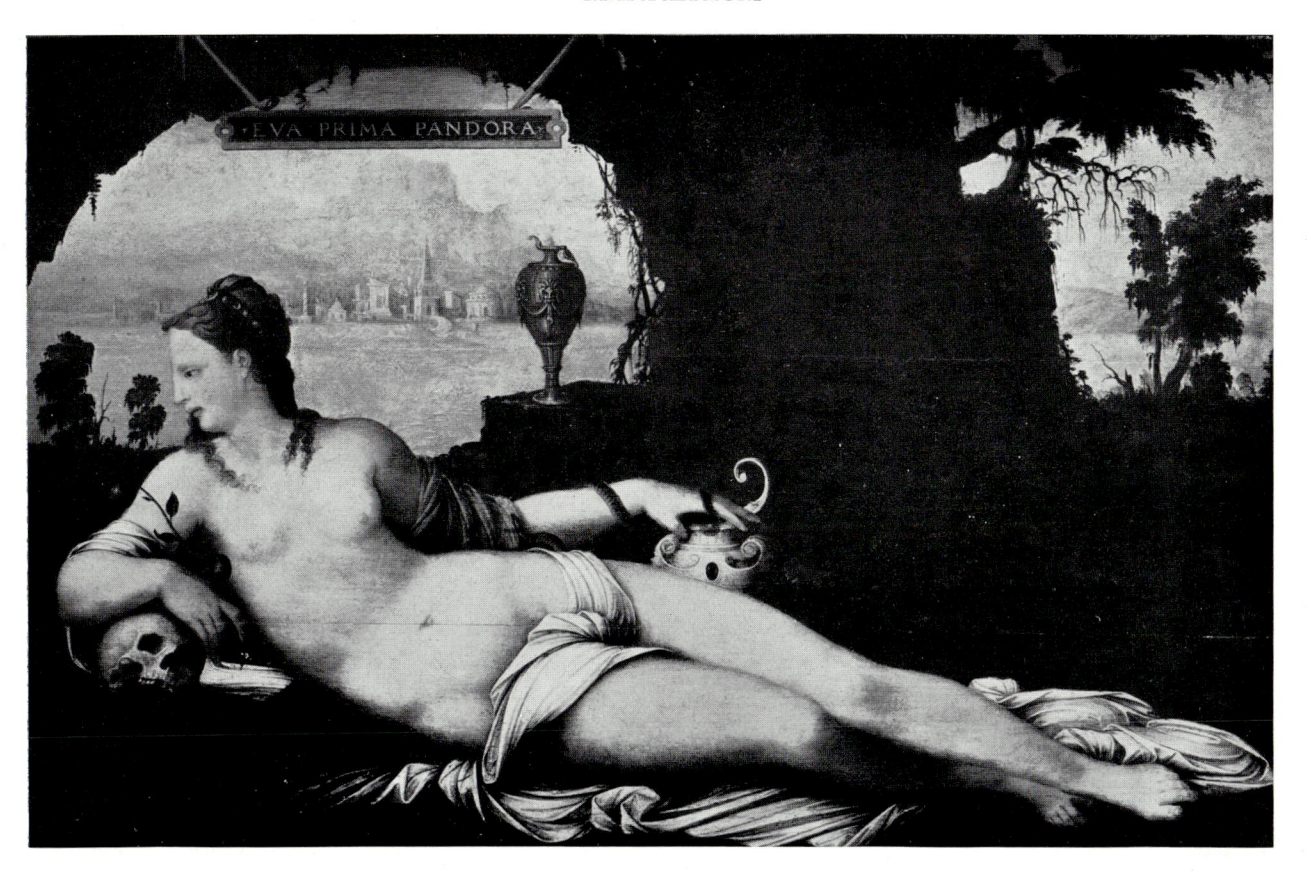

Pl. 305. *Above*: J. Cousin the Elder, Eva Prima Pandora. Panel, 38 3/8 × 59 in. Paris, Louvre. *Below*: A. Bloemaert, Sermon of John the Baptist. Canvas, 4 ft., 6 3/4 in. × 6 ft., 2 in. Amsterdam, Rijksmuseum.

MANNERISM

Pl. 306. *Above*: M. van Heemskerck, Venus and Cupid. Panel, 3 ft., 6 1/2 in. × 5 ft., 1 3/4 in. Göteborg, Sweden, Coll. G. Trädgårdh. *Below*: L. Sustris, Venus and Cupid. Canvas, 4 ft., 4 3/4 in. × 6 ft., 7/8 in. Paris, Louvre.

MANNERISM

Pl. 307. *Above*: B. Cellini, The Nymph of Fontainebleau. Bronze, 6 ft., 8¾ in. × 13 ft., 5 in. Paris, Louvre. *Below, left*: B. Bandinelli, nude, detail of screen for the high altar of the Cathedral, Florence. Marble. Florence, Museo dell'Opera del Duomo. *Right*: V. Danti, Honor Conquers Deceit. Marble. Florence, Museo Nazionale.

MANNERISM

Pl. 308. *Above, left*: Giambologna, Neptune, model for fountain. Bronze. Bologna, Museo Civico. *Right*: A. de Vries, Psyche. Bronze, ht., 6 ft., 1⁵/₈ in. Stockholm, Nationalmuseum. *Below, left*: P. Tacca and assistants, sea monsters, detail of fountain. Bronze. Florence, Piazza della SS. Annunziata. *Right*: W. Jamnitzer, Spring. Gilded bronze, ht., 28 in. Vienna, Kunsthistorisches Museum.

MANNERISM

Pl. 309. F. Salviati, The Visitation, detail. Fresco. Rome, S. Giovanni Decollato, oratory.

MANNERISM

Pl. 310. T. Zuccari, Francis I receives Charles V in Paris. Fresco. Caprarola, Italy, Palazzo Farnese.

MANNERISM

Pl. 311. Rome. *Left*: Palazzo Ricci, façade, monochrome frescoes by Maturino da Firenze and Polidoro da Caravaggio. *Right*: G. di Carpi and G. Mazzoni, Palazzo Spada, courtyard.

MANNERISM

Pl. 312. *Left, above:* G. Vasari, portico of the Uffizi, Florence. *Below:* A. Palladio and V. Scamozzi, stage of the Teatro Olimpico, Vicenza, Italy. *Right, above:* A. Lippi, Villa Medici, Rome. *Below:* Giacomo della Porta, G. B. Tristani, and G. de Rosis, façade of the Church of the Gesù, Rome.

MANNERISM

Pl. 313. *Left*: P. Ligorio, Palazzina of Pius IV, corner façade with fountain by B. Ammanati, Rome. *Right*: P. Ligorio, Organ Fountain, Villa d'Este, Tivoli, Italy.

MANNERISM

Pl. 314. *Left*: F. Zuccari, Palazzetto Zuccari, portal in Via Gregoriana, Rome. *Right*: B. Buontalenti, Porta delle Suppliche, Uffizi, Florence.

MANNERISM

Pl. 315. A. Caron, Augustus and the Tiburtine Sibyl. Canvas, 4 ft, 2 in. × 5 ft, 7 in. Paris, Louvre.

MANNERISM

Pl. 316. B. Spranger, Hercules, Deianira, and the Dead Centaur Nessus. Canvas, 44 1/8 × 32 1/4 in. Vienna, Kunsthistorisches Museum.

Pl. 317. F. Mansart. *Above*: Maisons-Laffitte, Seine-et-Oise, France, Château. *Below*: Blois, Loir-et-Cher, France, Château, façade of Orléans wing.

Pl. 318. J. Hardouin Mansart, Paris, Les Invalides, Eglise du Dôme, detail of the interior.

Pl. 319. J. Hardouin Mansart, Versailles, Palace, interior of the chapel.

MANSART

Pl. 320. J. Hardouin Mansart. *Above*: Versailles, Grand Trianon. *Below*: Dampierre, Seine-et-Oise, France, Château.

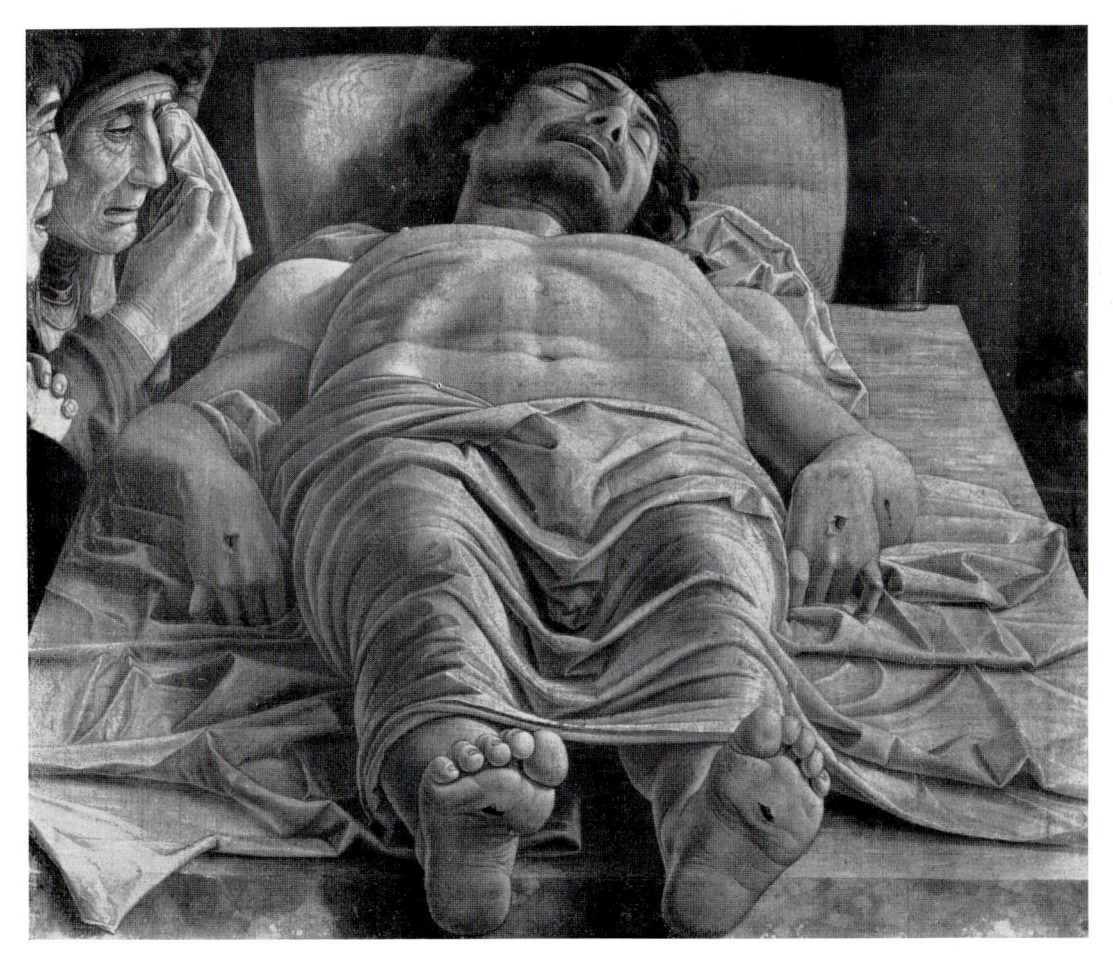

Pl. 321. *Above*: The Presentation in the Temple. Canvas, 26 3/8 × 33 7/8 in. Berlin, Staatliche Museen. *Below*: The Dead Christ. Tempera on canvas, 26 3/4 × 31 7/8 in. Milan, Brera.

MANTEGNA

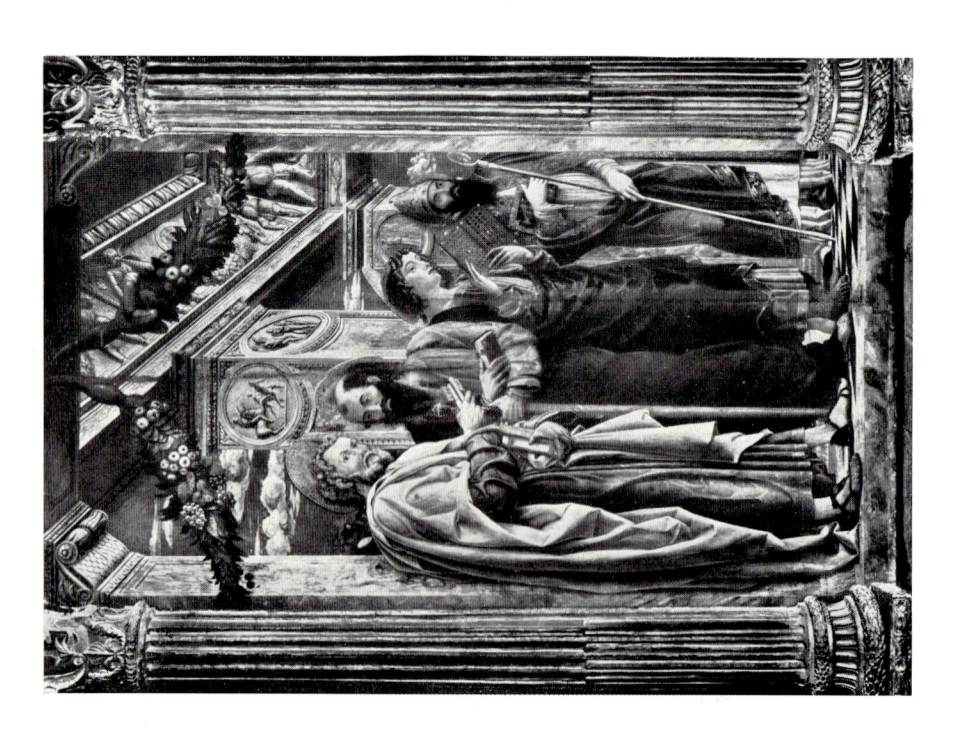

Pl. 322. The S. Zeno Altarpiece: Madonna Enthroned with Angels and Saints. Panel, ht. 7 ft., 2 5/8 in. Verona, S. Zeno.

MANTEGNA

Pl. 323. Crucifixion, central scene of the predella from the S. Zeno Altarpiece. Panel, 26×35 3/8 in. Paris, Louvre.

MANTEGNA

Pl. 324. The Martyrdom of St. Christopher, detail. Fresco. Padua, Church of the Eremitani, Ovetari Chapel.

MANTEGNA

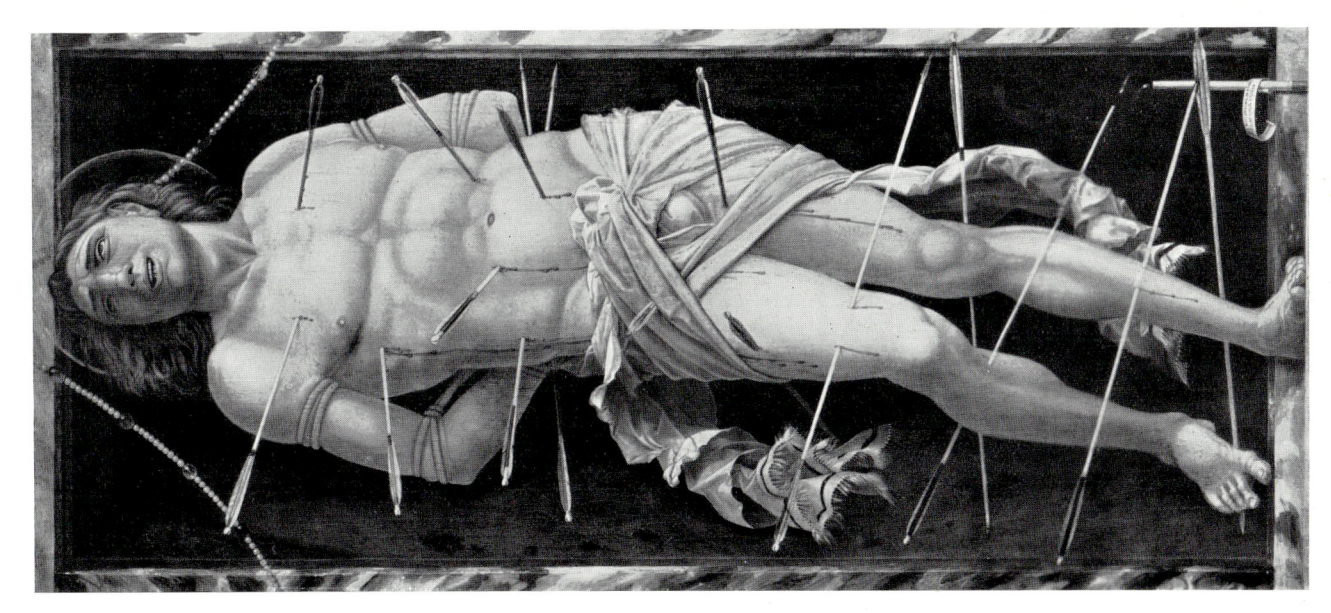

Pl. 325. *Left*: St. Sebastian. Canvas, 6 ft., 10½ in. × 3 ft. Venice, Ca' d'Oro. *Right*: St. Sebastian, detail. Canvas; full size, 8 ft., 5¼ in. × 4 ft., 8 in. Paris, Louvre.

MANTEGNA

Pl. 326. Death of the Virgin. Panel, 21¼×16½ in. Madrid, Prado.

MANTEGNA

Pl. 327. *Above*: Minerva Expelling the Vices from the Garden of Virtue. Canvas, 5 ft., 3 in. × 6 ft., 3⅝ in. *Below*: Parnassus, detail. Canvas; full size, 5 ft., 3 in. × 6 ft., 3½ in. Both, Paris, Louvre.

MANTEGNA

Pl. 328. Frescoes of the *Camera degli Sposi*, Palazzo Ducale, Mantua. *Above*: Putti with dedicatory inscription. *Below*: The Gonzaga Family, detail.

Pl. 329. Ceiling fresco of the *Camera degli Sposi*, Palazzo Ducale, Mantua.

MANTEGNA

Pl. 330. Samson and Delilah. Canvas (?), 18½ × 14½ in. London, National Gallery.

Pl. 331. A prince visited by genii from Paradise, from the *Khamsa* of Amir Khusrau Dihlavi. Miniature. New York, Metropolitan Museum (gift of Alexander Smith Cochran, 1913).

Pl. 332. Majestas. Fresco. Siena, Palazzo Pubblico.

Pl. 333. St. Martin abandoning his arms, detail showing soldiers receiving their pay. Fresco. Assisi, S. Francesco, Lower Church, Chapel of St. Martin.

MARTINI

Pl. 334. Guidoriccio da Fogliano. Fresco. Siena, Palazzo Pubblico.

Pl. 335. Madonna and Saints. Panel; full size, 7 ft., 6½ in. × 11 ft., 2 in. Pisa, Museo Nazionale.

MARTINI

Pl. 336. St. Louis of Toulouse Crowning Robert of Anjou King of Naples. Panel, 6 ft., 6 3/4 in. × 4 ft., 6 1/4 in.; predella, 19 3/4 in. × 6 ft., 8 3/4 in. Naples, Museo di Capodimonte.

Pl. 337. Frontispiece of Vergil, illuminated for Petrarch. Milan, Biblioteca Ambrosiana.

Pl. 338. The Virgin of the Annunciation. Panel, 9½ × 5½ in. Antwerp, Musée Royal des Beaux-Arts.

MARTINI

Pl. 339. The Annunciation, central scene. Panel; full size, 10 ft., 1 in. × 8 ft., 8 3/4 in. Florence, Uffizi.

MARTINI

Pl. 340. The Deposition. Panel, 9⅝×6⅛ in. Antwerp, Musée Royal des Beaux-Arts.

MASACCIO

Pl. 341. The Virgin and Child with St. Anne. Panel, 5 ft., 9 in. × 3 ft., 4½ in. Florence, Uffizi.

MASACCIO

Pl. 342. St. Paul, from the polyptych formerly in S. Maria del Carmine, Pisa. Panel, 24 × 13 3/8 in. Pisa, Museo Nazionale.

MASACCIO

Pl. 343. Crucifixion, from polyptych formerly in S. Maria del Carmine, Pisa. Panel, 30¼×25¼ in. Naples, Museo di Capodimonte.

MASACCIO

Pl. 344. The Virgin and Child Enthroned, central panel from the polyptych formerly in S. Maria del Carmine, Pisa. Panel, 53 1/4 × 28 3/4 in. London, National Gallery.

MASACCIO

Pl. 345. The Trinity, with the Virgin, St. John, and donors. Fresco. Florence, S. Maria Novella.

MASACCIO

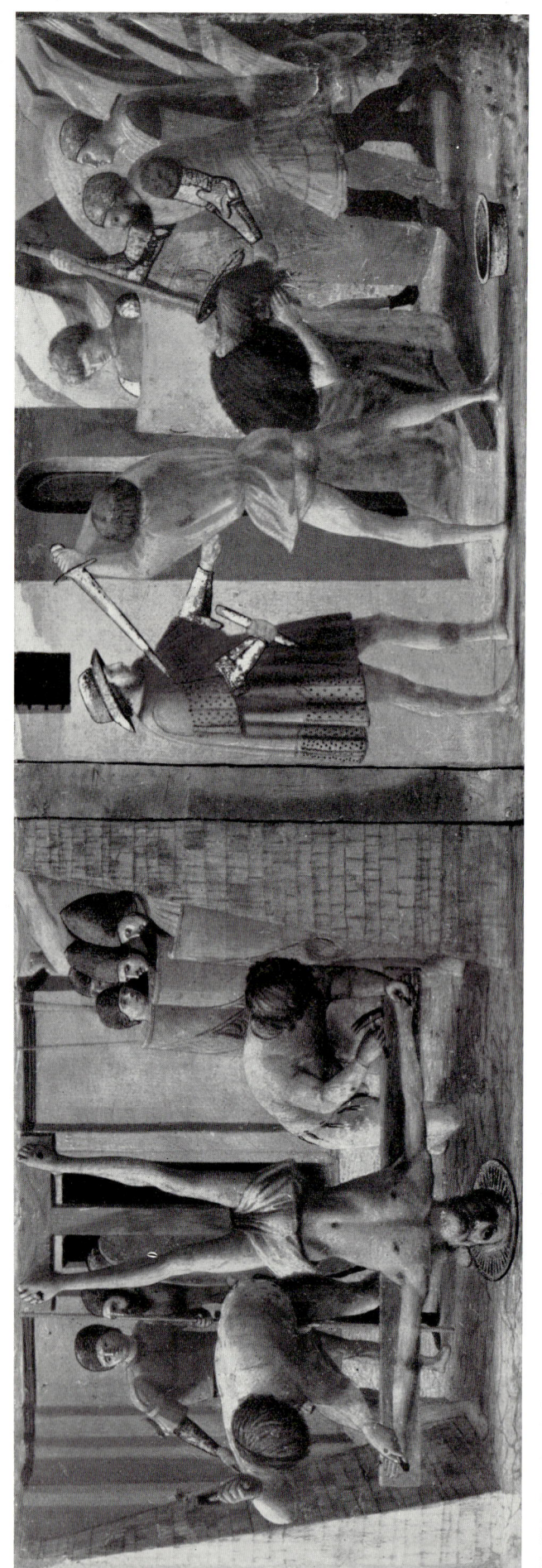

Pl. 346. Panels of the predella from the polyptych formerly in S. Maria del Carmine, Pisa. Each, 8¼×24 in. Berlin, Staatliche Museen. *Above*: Adoration of the Magi. *Below*: Crucifixion of St. Peter, and the Beheading of the Baptist.

MASACCIO

Pl. 347. *Left*: St. Peter in Cathedra. Fresco. *Right*: SS. Peter and John Distributing Alms and Death of Ananias. Fresco. Both, Florence, S. Maria del Carmine, Brancacci Chapel.

MASACCIO

Pl. 348. The Tribute Money. Fresco. Florence, S. Maria del Carmine, Brancacci Chapel.

MASACCIO

Pl. 349. Detail of Pl. 348.

MASACCIO

Pl. 350. The Expulsion from the Garden of Eden. Fresco. Florence, S. Maria del Carmine, Brancacci Chapel.

MASKS

Pl. 351. Funerary mask of Tutankhamen, Thebes, ca. 1350 B.C. Gold, colored glass, and stones, ht., 19¾ in. Cairo, Egyptian Museum.

MASKS

Pl. 352. Funerary masks. *Above, left*: Etruscan, from Chiusi, Italy, 7th cent. B.C. Bronze, ht., 10 1/8 in. Munich, Staatliche Antikensammlungen. *Right*: Chinese, from northern Manchuria, Liao dynasty. Silver, ht., ca. 8 1/2 in. New York, Minkenhof Coll. *Below, left*: Phoenician, Hellenistic period. Gold, ht., 7 7/8 in. Paris, Louvre. *Right*: Chibcha, from Guatavita, Colombia, pre-Columbian period. Terra cotta. Paris, Musée de l'Homme.

MASKS

Pl. 353. Egyptian funerary mask, Ptolemaic period. Cloth, stuccoed and painted; ht., 19 1/4 in. Turin, Museo Egizio.

MASKS

Pl. 354. *Left*: Tlingit medicine man's mask, from Alaska. Painted wood, ht., 19½ in. Basel, Museum für Völkerkunde. *Right*: Mask, from Tami Island, New Guinea. Painted wood, ht., 11⅜ in. Cambridge, Mass., Peabody Museum.

MASKS

Pl. 355. *Left*: *Epa* mask of the northeastern Yoruba, Nigeria. Painted wood. London, British Museum. *Right, above*: Suku mask, from the Congo. Wood and raffia, 17 3/8 × 7 7/8 in. Tervueren, Belgium, Musée Royal de l'Afrique Centrale. *Below*: Bamum mask-headdress for the dance, from Cameroons Grasslands. Plant fibers and beads. Vienna, Museum für Völkerkunde.

MASKS

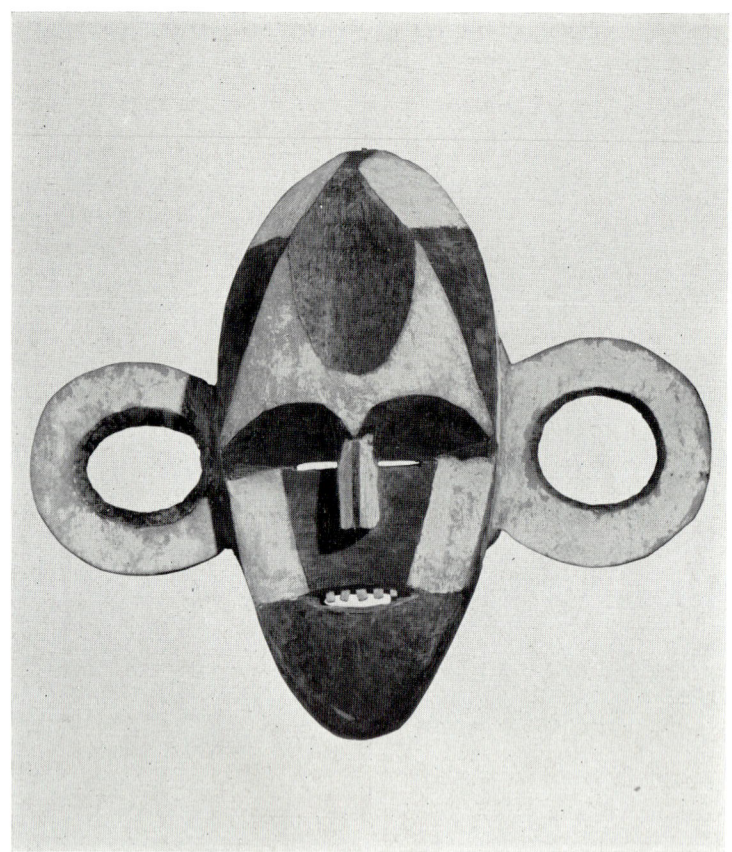

Pl. 356. *Above, left*: Mano mask, from Liberia. Wood, ht., 19½ in. Cambridge, Mass., Peabody Museum. *Right*: Boa mask, from the Congo. Wood, painted black and white; 11¾ × 13¾ in. Tervueren, Belgium, Musée Royal de l'Afrique Centrale. *Below, left*: Bobofign dance mask, Mali. London, British Museum. *Right*: Mpongwe mask, from the Ogooué River region, Gabun. Painted wood, ht., 15 in. Basel, Museum für Völkerkunde.

MASKS

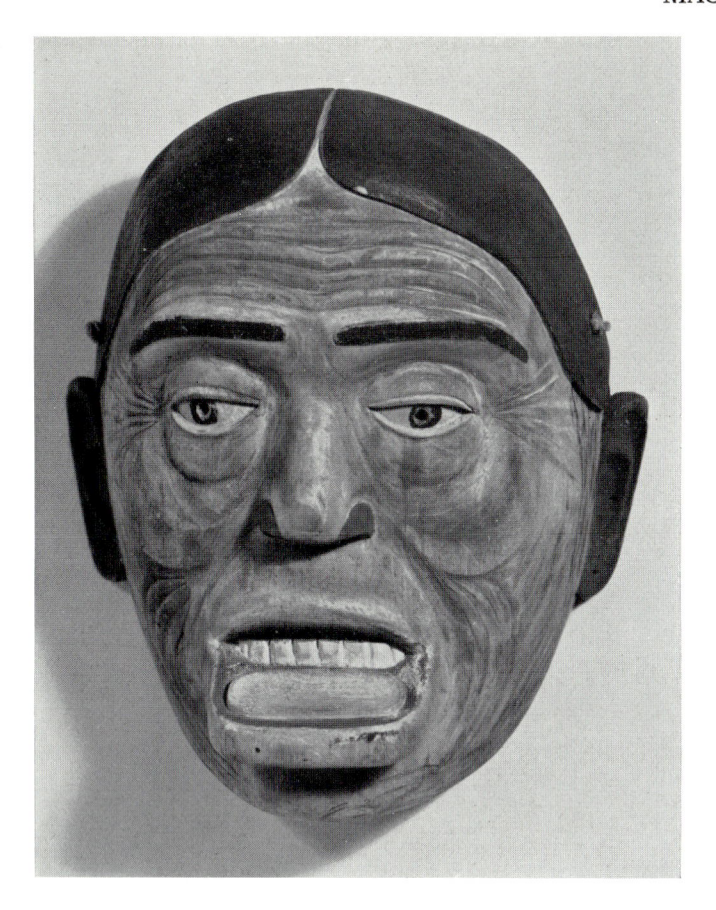

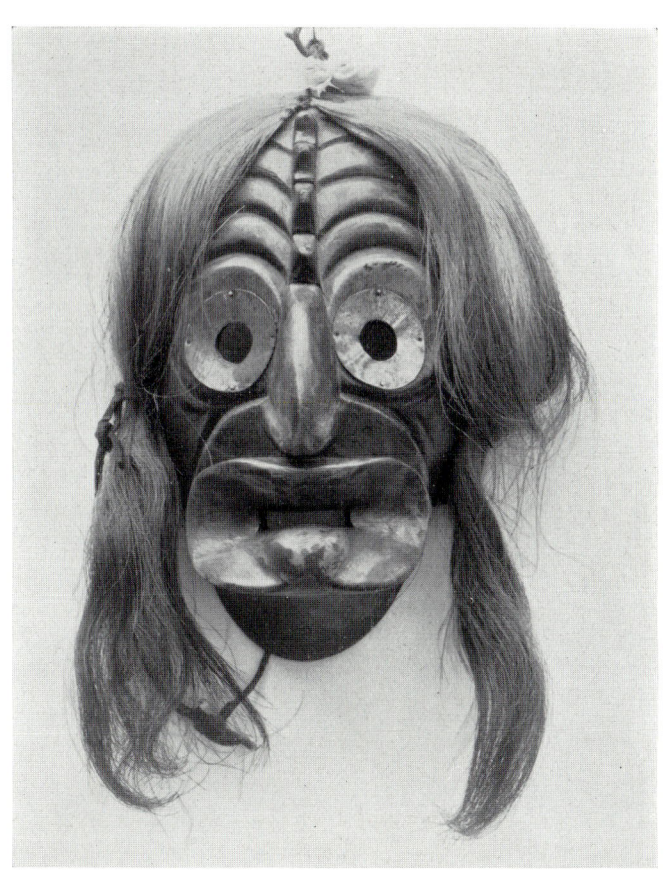

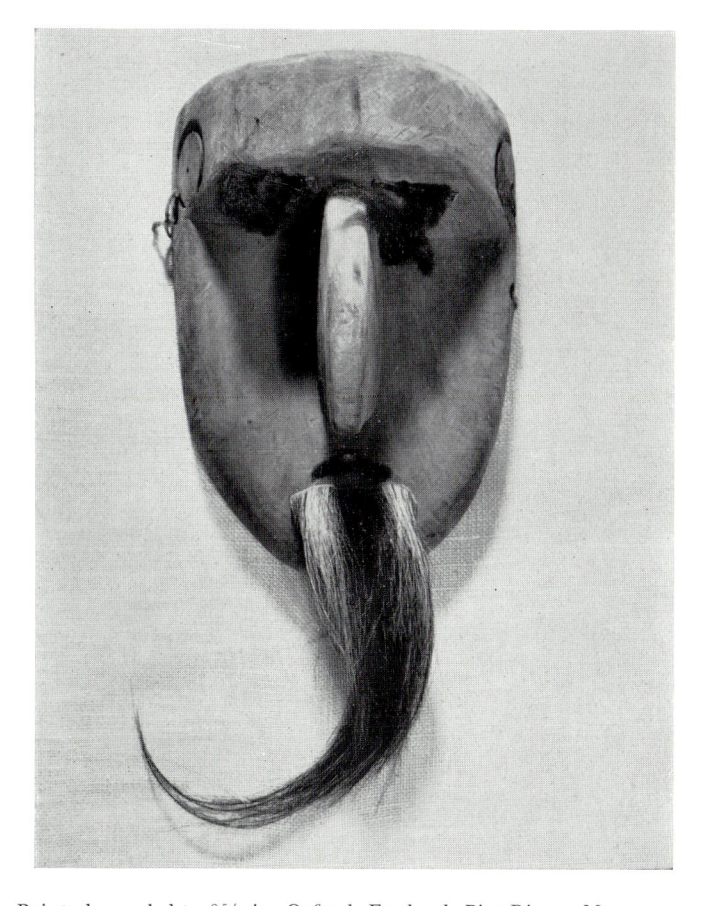

Pl. 357. *Above, left*: Haida mask with lip plug, British Columbia. Painted wood, ht., 8 5/8 in. Oxford, England, Pitt Rivers Museum. *Right*: Kwakiutl dance mask, British Columbia. Wood and hair, ht., 9 1/2 in. Stockholm, Statens Etnografiska Museum. *Below, left*: Seneca mask of the Falseface Secret Society. Wood, metal, and hair; ht., 10 1/2 in. New York, Museum of the American Indian, Heye Foundation. *Right*: Araucanian dance mask, Chile. Unpainted wood and horse hair, ht., 12 7/8 in. Göteborg, Sweden, Etnografiska Museet.

MASKS

Pl. 358. *Left, above*: House gable mask, from the Sepik River region, New Guinea. Painted wood, ht., 26½ in. Hamburg, Museum für Völkerkunde. *Below*: Mask, from Dewar Island, Torres Strait, New Guinea. Wood, plant pods, and raffia; ht., 13¾ in. Copenhagen, Nationalmuseet. *Right*: Dance mask, from southern New Britain. Bark cloth and feathers on frame of palm-leaf ribs, ht., 29½ in. Bern, Historisches Museum.

MASKS

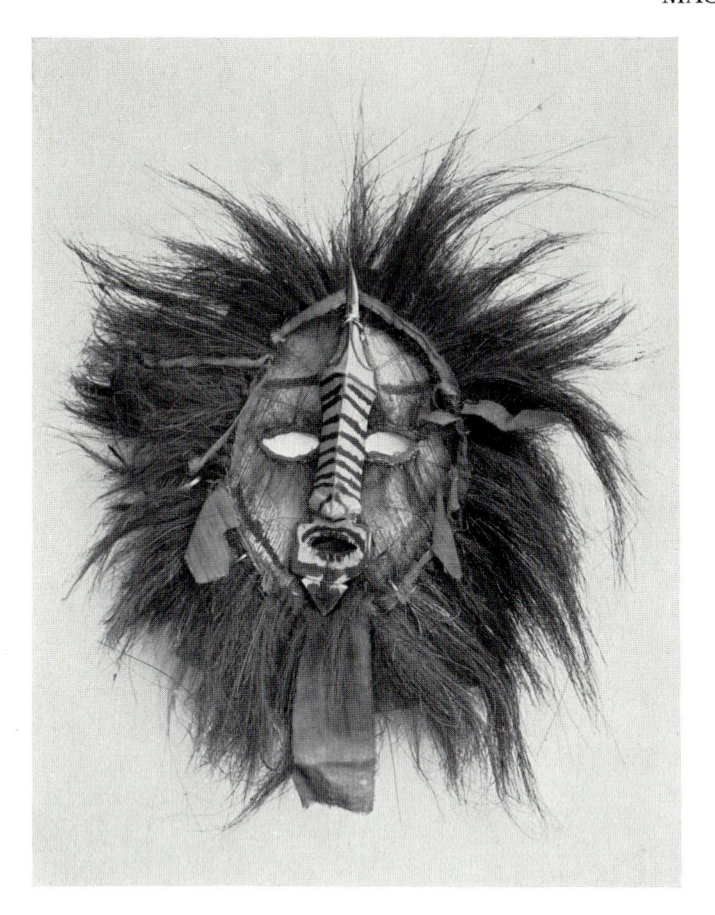

Pl. 359. *Above, left*: Ancestor mask, from Nias Island, Indonesia. Bark and coconut fiber, ht., 9¹/₈ in. Florence, Museo Nazionale di Antropologia e Etnologia. *Right*: Nepalese ritual mask, 19th cent. Painted wood. Rome, private coll. *Below*: Swiss folk carnival masks. Wood, cloth, and fur. Basel, Schweizerisches Museum für Volkskunde.

MASKS

Pl. 360. Greek and Roman theater masks. *Above, left*: *Phlyakes* comedy mask, from Tarentum (mod. Taranto), Italy, Hellenistic period. Terra cotta, ht., 13 3/4 in. Taranto, Museo Nazionale. *Right*: Actor with comic mask, detail of a *trapezophoros*, from Tralles (mod. Aydın), Turkey, 2d cent. Marble, full ht., 43 1/4 in. Istanbul, Archaeological Museum. *Below*: Masked actors in a comedy scene, relief, from Pompeii, 1st cent. Marble, 17 3/4 × 20 7/8 in. Naples, Museo Nazionale.

MASKS

Pl. 361. Aedicula with actors' masks, 9th cent. Illumination from manuscript of Terence. Rome, Vatican Library (Cod. Vat. lat. 3868, fol. 77r).

MASKS

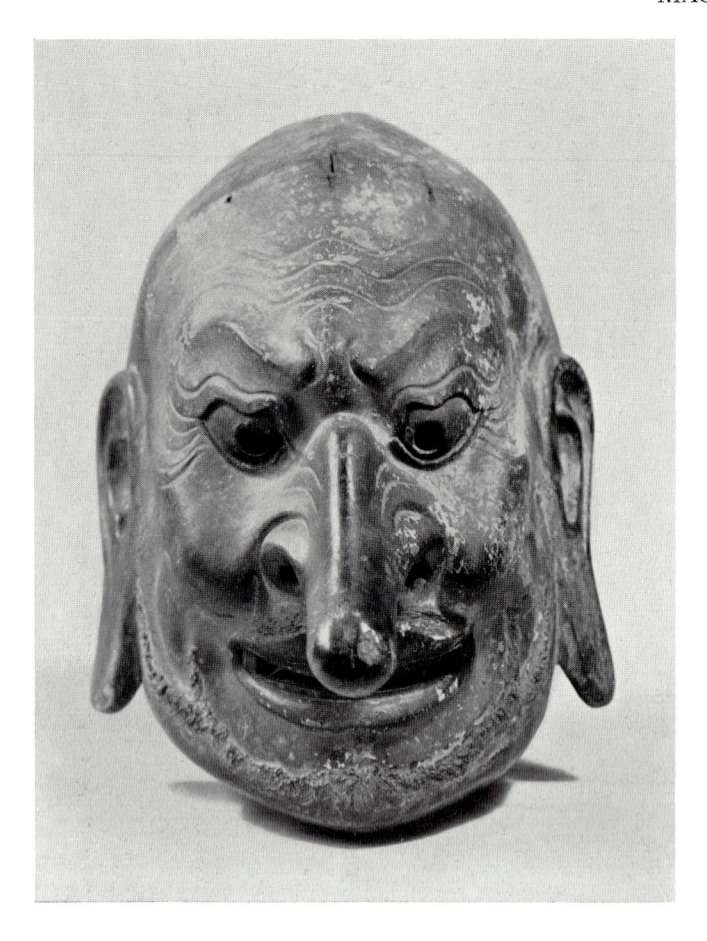

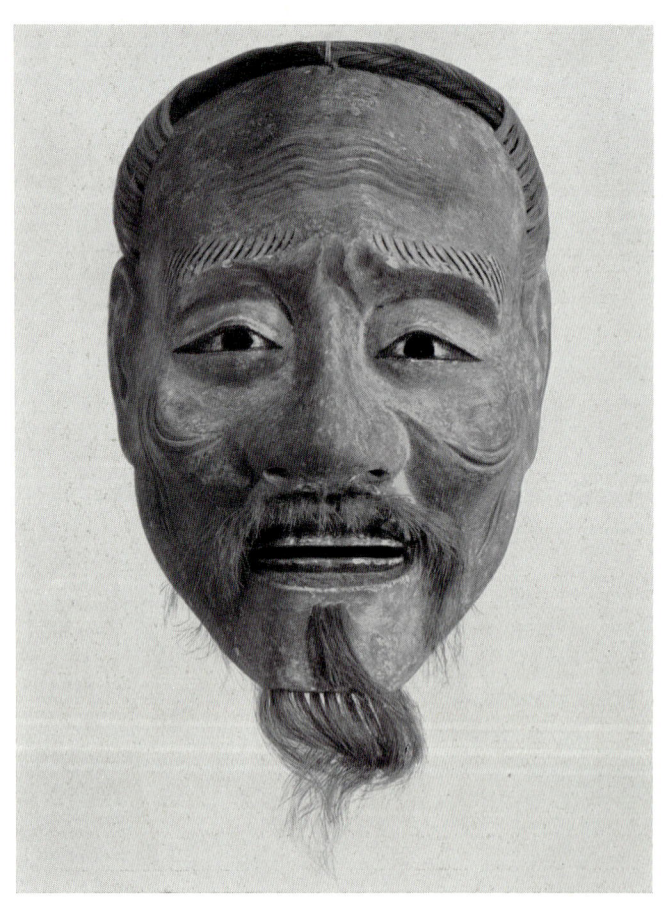

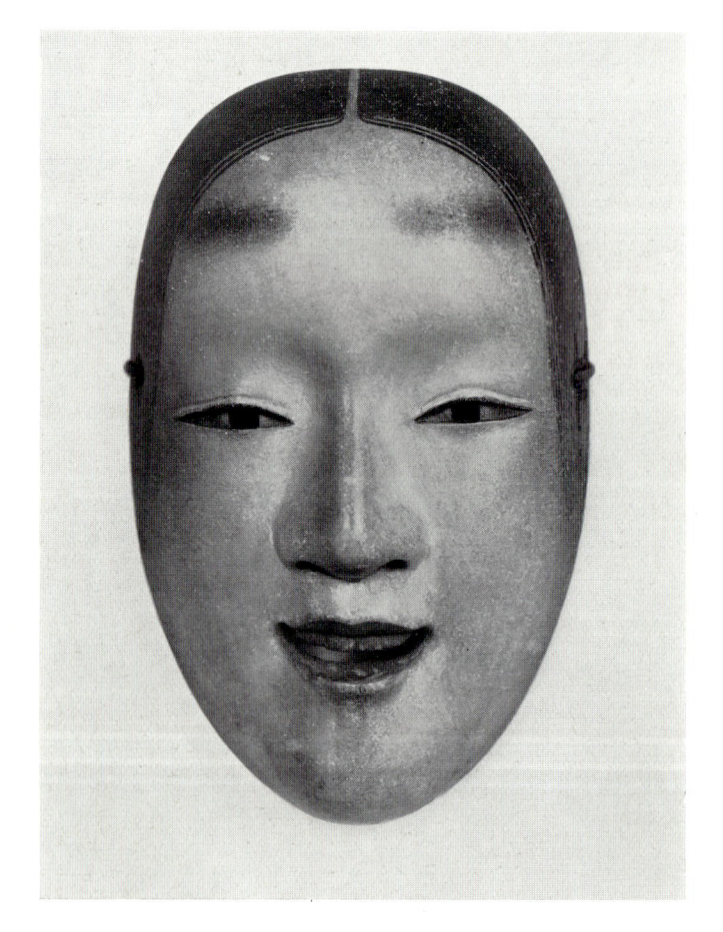

Pl. 362. Japanese theater masks. *Above, left*: Gigaku mask, Asuka period. Wood. *Right*: Gigaku mask, Nara period. Wood. *Below*: Two No masks, Muromachi period. Wood. All, Tokyo, National Museum.

MASKS

Pl. 363. Drama mask of the witch Rangda, from Bali, 19th cent. Amsterdam, Koninklijk Instituut voor de Tropen.

MASKS

Pl. 364. Roman theater masks, tragic and comic, from the Aventine, Rome, 3d cent. Mosaic, 29 1/8 × 35 7/8 in. Rome, Capitoline Museum.

MASKS

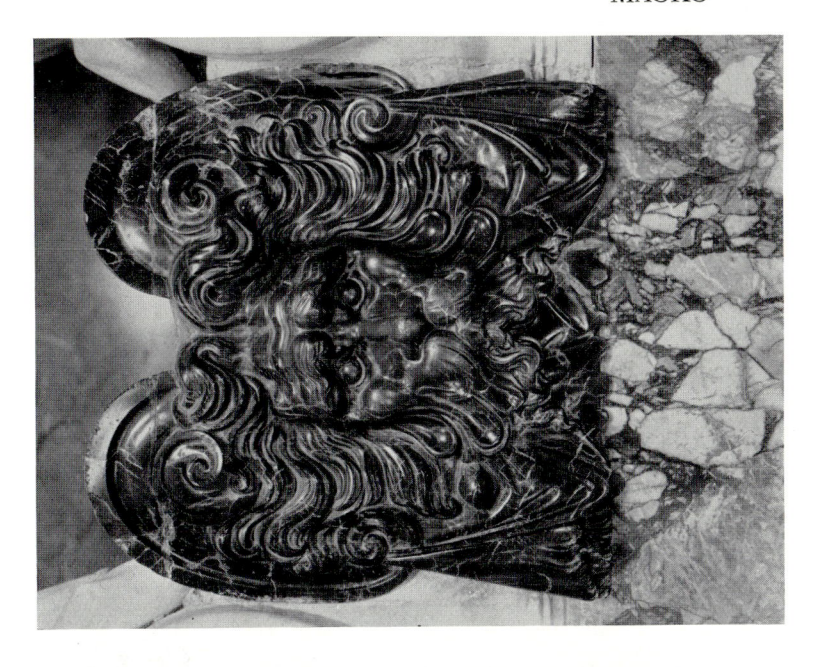

Pl. 365. The mask as a decorative and architectural motif. *Above, left*: Satyr, 2d cent. Marble, ht., 21⁵/₈ in. Rome, Capitoline Museum. *Center*: The so-called "Bocca della Verità," 2d–3d cent. Marble, diam., ca. 4 ft. 3 in. Rome, S. Maria in Cosmedin. *Right*: Guglielmo della Porta, tomb of Pope Paul III, detail. Marble. Rome, St. Peter's. *Below, left*: Michelangelo, detail of cornice. Florence, S. Lorenzo, New Sacristy. *Right*: Khmer decorative panel, from Cambodia, ca. 12th cent. Stone. Paris, Musée Guimet.

MASKS

Pl. 366. *Above*: L. Liédet, knight putting on a devil's costume for a religious play, from *Renaud de Montauban*, 15th cent. Illumination. Paris, Bibliothèque de l'Arsenal (Cat. no. 5072–75). *Below*: Bolognese school (?), *commedia dell'arte* scene representing Signora Lucia and Trastullo, 17th cent. Canvas. Milan, Museo Teatrale alla Scala.

MASKS

Pl. 367. L. Burnacini, comic costumes for a court masquerade. Water color. Vienna, Nationalbibliothek, Theatersammlung.

MASKS

Pl. 368. A. Sartori, mask for the character of Vanna Scoma in Pirandello's *La favola del figlio cambiato* (Piccolo Teatro di Milano, 1957). Painted leather. Padua, property of the artist.

Pl. 369. St. Silvester binding the dragon, detail of PL. 370 (*below*).

MASO DI BANCO

Pl. 370. Florence, Sta Croce, Cappella Bardi di Vernio. Frescoes. *Above*: St. Silvester and Emperor Constantine. *Below*: Miracles of St. Silvester.

MASO DI BANCO

Pl. 371. St. Silvester healing two magicians, detail of PL. 370 (*below*).

Pl. 372. Madonna and Child, central panel of the Sto Spirito polyptych. Panel; full size, 3 ft., 10½ in. × 7 ft., 2⅝ in. Florence, Sto Spirito.

MASO DI BANCO

Pl. 373. Madonna and Child. Panel, 31½×18½ in. Berlin, Staatliche Museen.

MASOLINO

Pl. 374. *Above, left*: Madonna and Child. Panel, 37⁷/₈ × 22¹/₂ in. Munich, Alte Pinakothek. *Right*: Founding of S. Maria Maggiore, from the triptych formerly in S. Maria Maggiore, Rome. Panel, 56³/₄ × 29⁷/₈ in. Naples, Museo di Capodimonte. *Below*: St. Peter heals a cripple and raises Tabitha. Fresco. Florence, S. Maria del Carmine, Brancacci Chapel.

MASOLINO

Pl. 375. Herodias receiving the head of John the Baptist, detail of Herod's Feast. Fresco; full size, 15 ft., 6¼ in. × 12 ft., 5⅝ in. Castiglione Olona, Italy, Baptistery.

MASOLINO

Pl. 376. The Baptism of Christ. Fresco, 10 ft., 3 in. × 7 ft., 5½ in. Castiglione Olona, Italy, Baptistery.

MASOLINO

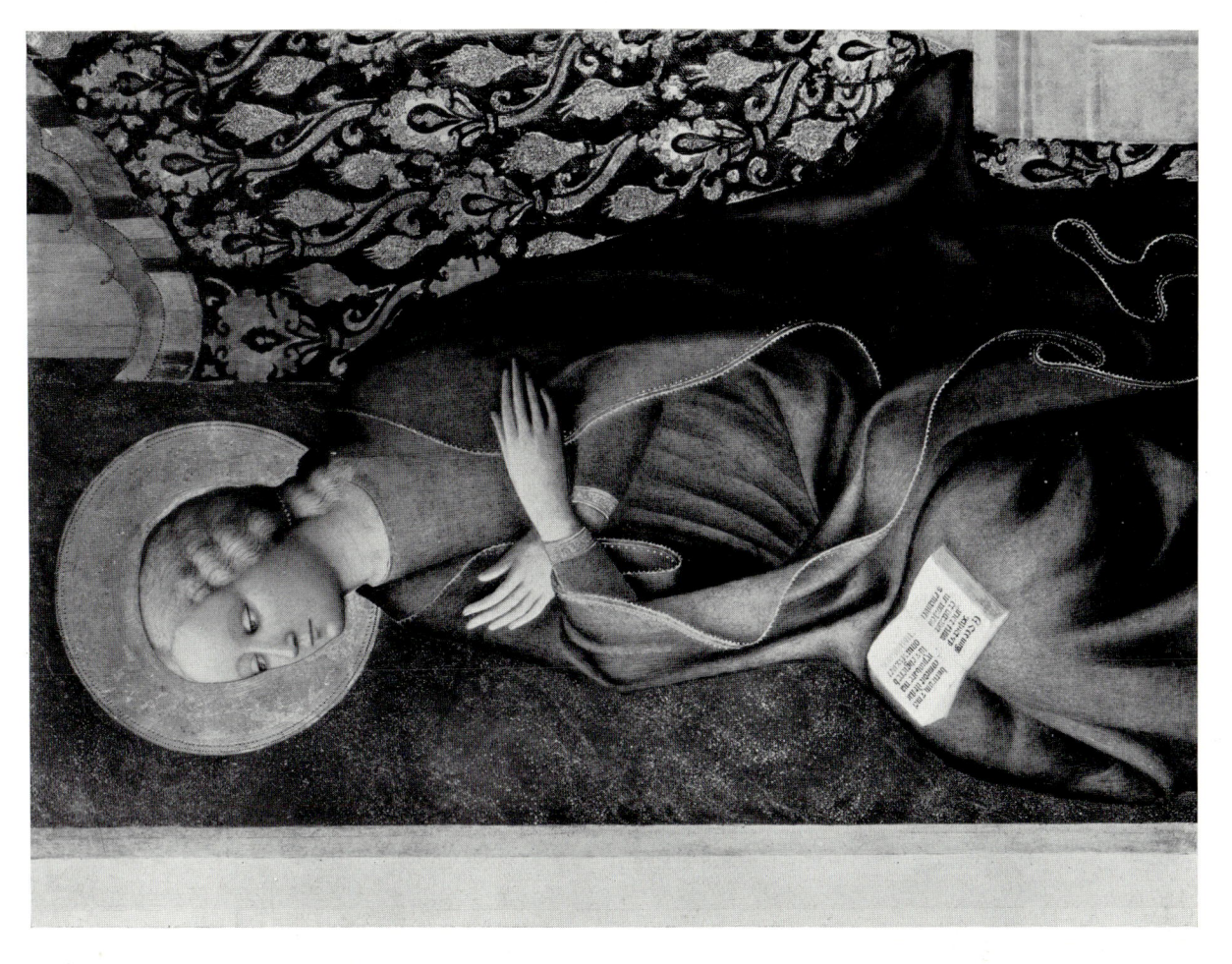

Pl. 377. *Left*: The Archangel Gabriel. Panel, 30 1/8 × 22 5/8 in. *Right*: The Virgin Annunciate. Panel, 30 × 22 5/8 in. Both, Washington, D.C., National Gallery.

MASOLINO

Pl. 378. St. Catherine and the Philosophers. Fresco. Rome, S. Clemente.

Pl. 379. Male head, Mathura, ca. 2d cent. Mottled red sandstone, ht., 10 5/8 in. New Delhi, National Museum of India.

MATHURA

Pl. 380. Statue originally of Maitreya, later converted into a Vaishnava cult image, Mathura, 1st–3d cent. Red sandstone, ht., 5 ft., 9 1/4 in. Mathura, Archaeological Museum.

MATHURA

Pl. 381. Jātaka scene, from a stupa railing pillar, Bhuteshar, ca. 2d cent. Red sandstone, w., 7½ in. Calcutta, Indian Museum.

MATHURA

Pl. 382. Yakshis standing on the backs of dwarfs, from a stupa railing pillar, Bhuteshar, ca. 2d cent. Red sandstone, ht., 4 ft., 7 in. Calcutta, Indian Museum.

MATHURA

Pl. 383. *Above*: Pair of lovers, from a stupa railing pillar, Bhuteshar, ca. 2d cent. Red sandstone, w., 7½ in. Calcutta, Indian Museum. *Below*: Architectural fragment with a woman feeding a parrot, Mathura, 1st–3d cent. Yellow sandstone, ht., 6¾ in. Mathura, Archaeological Museum.

MATHURA

Pl. 384. Female figure in *sālābhañjikā* attitude, Mathura, 1st–3d cent. Red sandstone, ht., 4 ft., 2 3/8 in. Mathura, Archaeological Museum.

MATISSE

Pl. 385. *Above, left*: A Glimpse of Notre-Dame in Late Afternoon. Canvas, 28 1/2 × 21 1/2 in. Buffalo, N.Y., Albright-Knox Art Gallery. *Right*: Decorative Figure on an Ornamental Background (Odalisque with a Straight Back). Canvas, 51 1/8 × 38 5/8 in. Paris, Musée d'Art Moderne. *Below*: The Dance. Canvas, 9 1/8 × 16 1/8 in. New York, Coll. W. P. Chrysler, Jr.

MATISSE

Pl. 386. *Left, above:* Still Life with Antique Torso. Canvas. Paris, Coll. Fukushima. *Below:* Still Life with Magnolia. Canvas, 29 1/8 × 39 in. Paris, Musée d'Art Moderne. *Right:* Zulma. Collage, 7 ft., 9 3/4 in. × 4 ft., 4 3/8 in. Copenhagen, Statens Museum for Kunst.

MATISSE

Pl. 387. Blue Nude (Souvenir de Biskra). Canvas, 36¼×55⅛ in. Baltimore, Museum of Art, Cone Coll.

MATISSE

Pl. 388. Rose Nude. Canvas, 26×36½ in. Baltimore, Museum of Art, Cone Coll.

MA YÜAN

Pl. 389. Angler, fragment of a hand scroll (?). Ink on silk. Tokyo, National Museum.

MA YÜAN

Pl. 390. The Four Sages of Shang-shan, hand scroll, detail. Ink and faint color on paper; full size, 1 ft., 1¼ in. × 10 ft., 1 in. Cincinnati, Art Museum.

MA YÜAN

Pl. 391. The Four Sages of Shang-shan, detail to right of that in Pl. 390.

Pl. 392. Rain over Trees on a Rocky Shore, hanging scroll. Ink and faint color on silk. Tokyo, Seikado Foundation.

MEDIA, COMPOSITE

Pl. 393. P. Picasso, La Bouteille de Suze, 1913. Paper collage with charcoal, 25 1/4 × 19 5/8 in. St. Louis, Coll. Washington University.

MEDIA, COMPOSITE

Pl. 394. J. Arp, abstract composition, 1915. Paper and cloth collage, $9 1/4 \times 7 7/8$ in. Basel, Coll. Marguerite Arp-Hagenbach.

MEDIA, COMPOSITE

Pl. 395. *Above, left*: Ekoi headdress, Nigeria. Wood, antelope skin, bone, and fibers; ht., 28 3/8 in. Paris, Musée de l'Homme. *Right*: Fountain, 1st cent. Marble, glass-paste mosaic, and shells. Pompeii, House of the Great Fountain. *Below, left*: The Virgin's Grotto, 11th–12th cent. (?). Gilded-silver statuette in rock-crystal niche; base, gilded silver with turquoises, garnets, pearls, and cloisonné enamels; ht. of statuette, 3 1/2 in. Venice, Treasury of S. Marco. *Right*: A. Penna, after design by P. Posi, monument of Princess Odescalchi Chigi (d. 1771). Marble and bronze. Rome, S. Maria del Popolo.

MEDIA, COMPOSITE

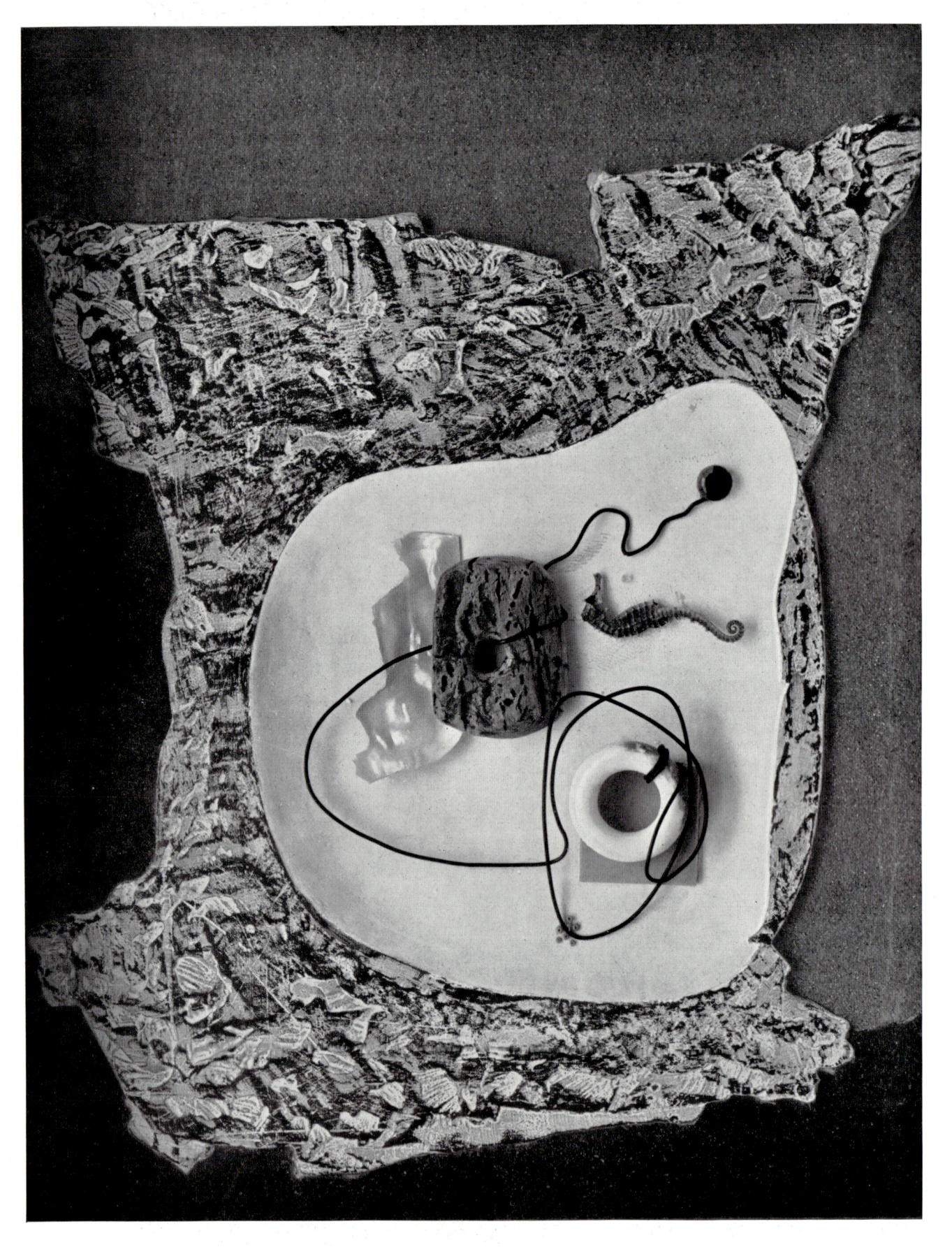

Pl. 396. E. Prampolini Stato d'Animo Plastico Marino, 1937. Colored sand, cork, glass, wire, sea horse, etc., on wood; $12^{5/8} \times 16^{1/8}$ in. Rome, private coll.

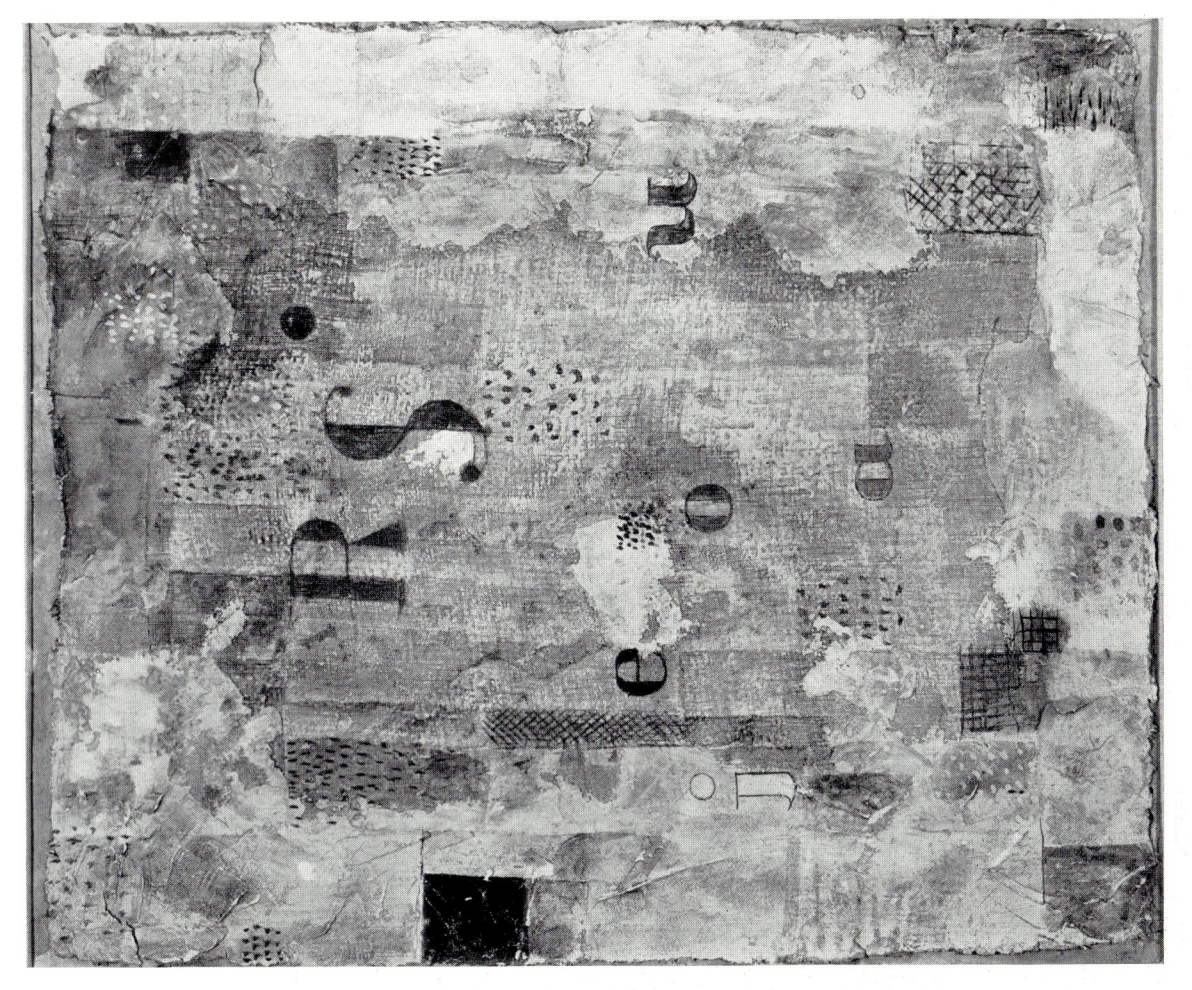

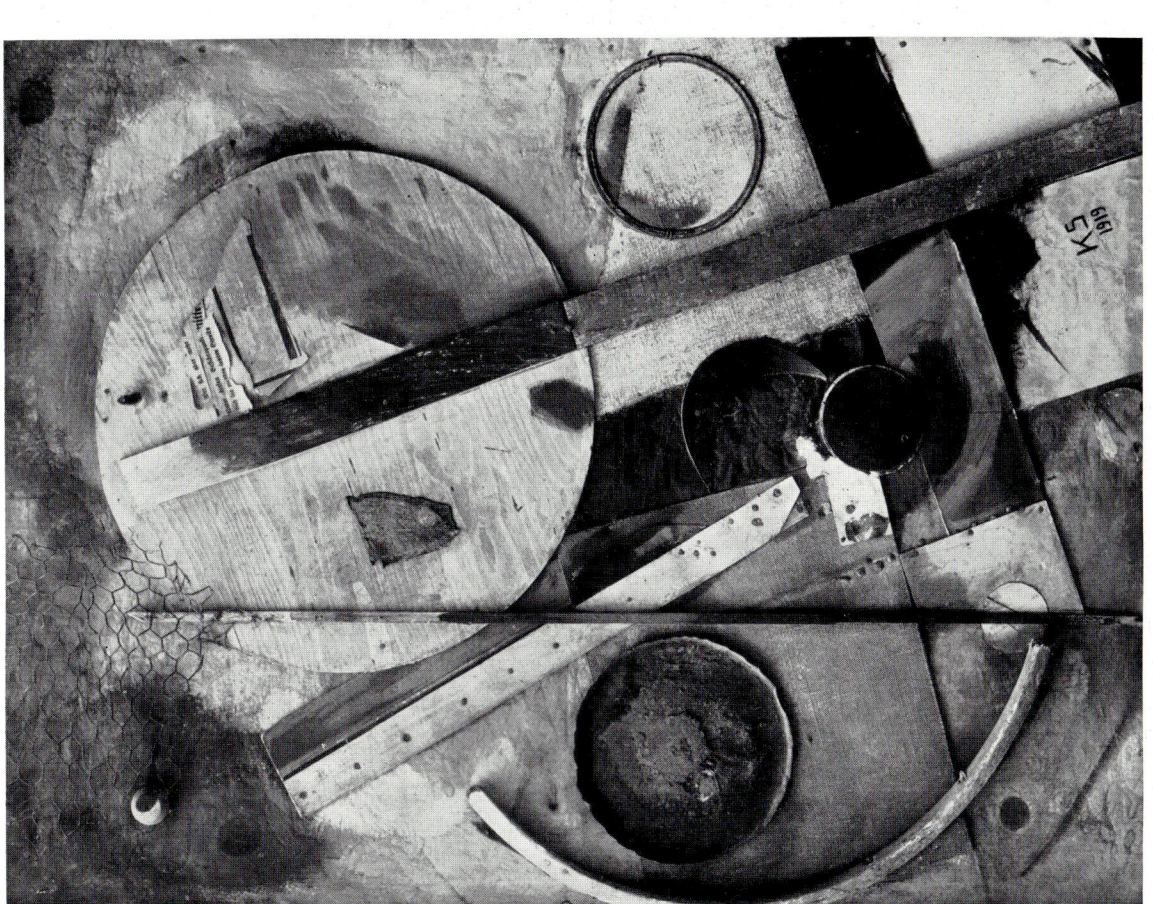

Pl. 397. *Left*: K. Schwitters, Das Arbeiterbild, 1919. Wood, paper, metal, and canvas; 49¼×35⅞ in. Lysaker, Norway, private coll. *Right*: P. Klee, Vocal Fabric of the Singer Rosa Silber, 1922. Gouache and gesso on canvas, 20¼×16⅜ in. New York, Museum of Modern Art.

MEDIA, COMPOSITE

Pl. 398. *Above*: E. Prampolini, Forme–Forze Magmatiche, 1954. Oil, coal, and sand on canvas; 31$^{1}/_{2}$×39$^{3}/_{8}$ in. Monza, Italy, Coll. M. Modorati. *Below, left*: A. Burri, Wood Combustion, 1958. Charred wood and paint on canvas, 6 ft., 6$^{1}/_{2}$ in. × 6 ft., 3 in. Chicago, A. Maremont Coll. *Right*: J. Dubuffet, Landscape with Three Trees, 1959. Collage of plant elements, 23$^{1}/_{4}$×22$^{1}/_{2}$ in. Paris, Coll. D.B.C.

MEDITERRANEAN, ANCIENT WESTERN

Pl. 399. Fragment of Iberian vase, from Elche, near Murcia, Spain, 3d cent. B.C. Madrid, Museo Arqueológico Nacional.

MEDITERRANEAN, ANCIENT WESTERN

Pl. 400. Iberian urn, from Azaila, Teruel, Spain, 2d–1st cent. B.C. Madrid, Museo Arqueológico Nacional.

Pl. 401. Sardinia. *Above*: Barùmini, nuraghe and village of Su Nuraxi. *Below, left*: Torralba, Nuraghe Santu Antine. *Right*: Borore, stele of one of the so-called "giant's graves." Ht., 12 ft., 5½ in.

MEDITERRANEAN, ANCIENT WESTERN

Pl. 402. Ísili, Sardinia, Nuraghe is Paras, interior detail of the false dome.

MEDITERRANEAN, ANCIENT WESTERN

Pl. 403. So-called "tribal chief," from Santa Vittoria di Serri, Sardinia, 8th–6th cent. B.C. Bronze, ht., 11 3/8 in. Cagliari, Sardinia, Museo Archeologico Nazionale.

MEDITERRANEAN, ANCIENT WESTERN

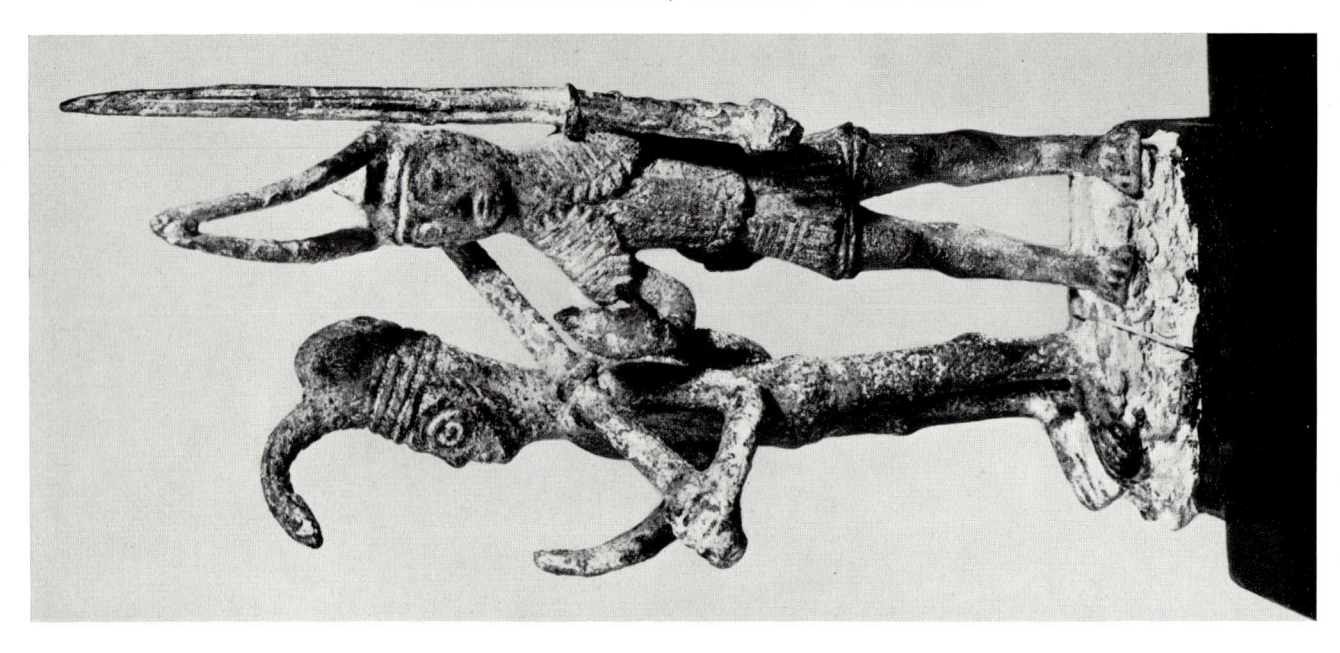

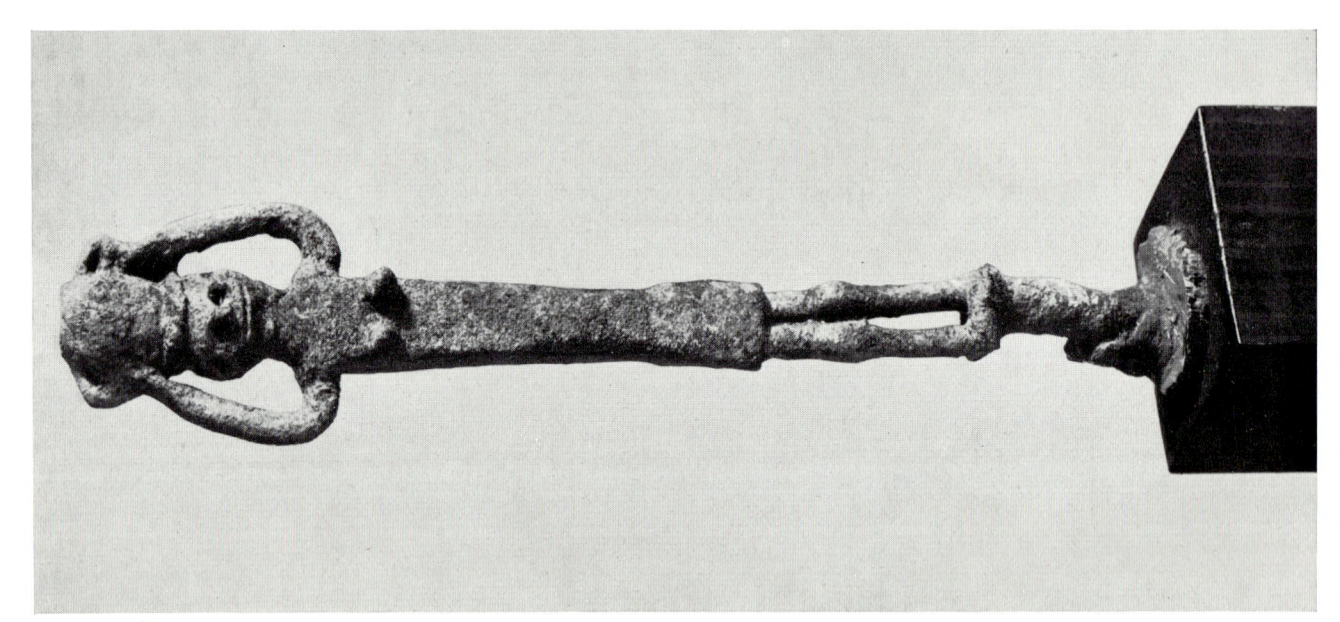

Pl. 404. Nuraghic bronzes, Sardinia, 8th–6th cent. B.C. *Left*: Mother with her dead child (?), from Nuragus, near Nuoro. Ht., 4 in. *Center*: Woman with amphora, from Olbia. Ht., 7¼ in. *Right*: Warriors, from the Abini deposit, Teti, near Nuoro. Ht., 5½ in. All, Cagliari, Museo Archeologico Nazionale.

MEDITERRANEAN, ANCIENT WESTERN

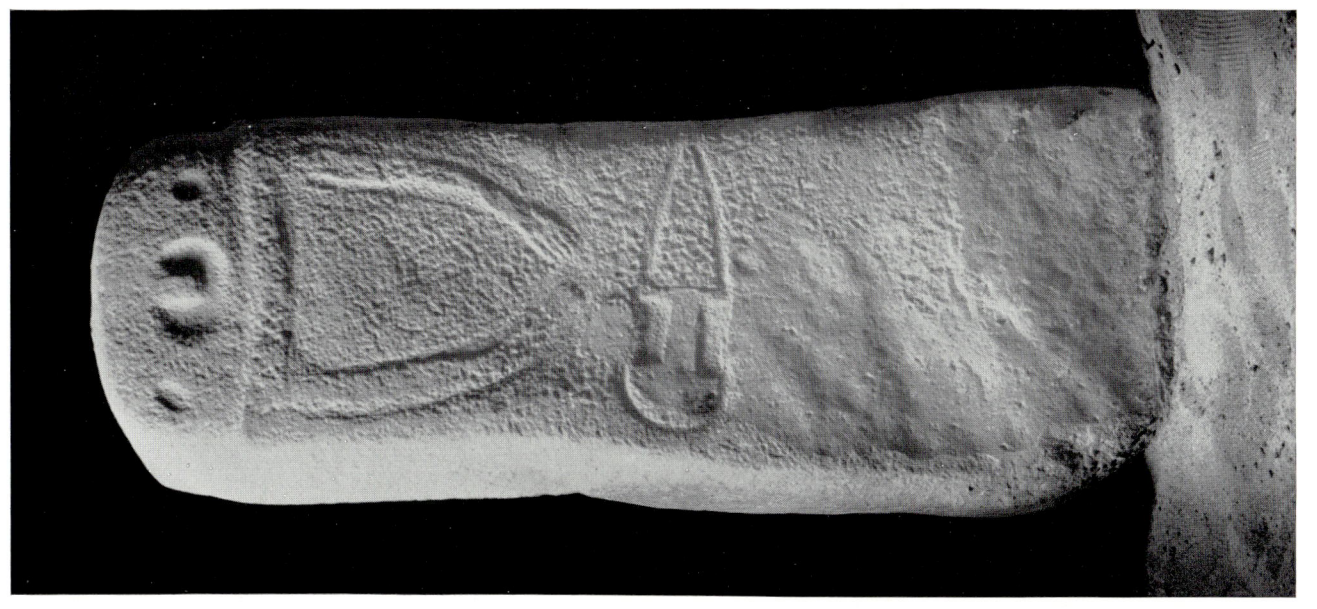

Pl. 405. Menhir statues, mid 2d–early 1st millennium B.C. Stone. *Left and center*: Filitosa, Corsica. *Right*: From Fivizzano, Italy. Ht., ca. 39½ in. La Spezia, Italy, Museo Archeologico Lunense.

MEDITERRANEAN, ANCIENT WESTERN

Pl. 406. Megalithic monuments (taula and talayot) in the Balearic Islands, Bronze Age. *Above*: Mahón, Minorca, detail of a sanctuary known as "Taula de Talatí de Dalt." *Below*: Ciudadela, Minorca, tomb known as "Naveta dels Tudons."

MEDITERRANEAN, ANCIENT WESTERN

Pl. 407. Patera with mythological scene and wolf's-head umbo, from Tivisa, Tarragona, Spain, 3d cent. B.C. Silver engraved and covered with gold leaf; diam., 6 1/2 in. Barcelona, Museo Arqueológico.

MEDITERRANEAN, ANCIENT WESTERN

Pl. 408. Spain. *Above, left*: Architectural element, from Castulon, Jaén, 5th–4th cent. B.C. Stone. *Right*: Human-headed bull known as the "Bicha de Balazote," detail, from Albacete, 5th cent. B.C. Stone, full ht., 28 3/4 in. *Below*: Votive statues, from Cerro de los Santos, Albacete, 4th–2d cent. B.C. Stone. *Left*: The "Great Lady," ht., 4 ft., 5 in. *Right*: Seated woman. All, Madrid, Museo Arqueológico Nacional.

Pl. 409. "The Lady of Elche," detail, Spain, 5th–4th cent. B.C. Stone, full ht. of bust, 22 in. Madrid, Prado.

MEDITERRANEAN, ANCIENT WESTERN

Pl. 410. Spain. *Above*: Hunting scene, detail of vase, from Ampurias, Gerona, 5th–4th cent. B.C. Barcelona, Museo Arqueológico. *Below, left and center*: Votive bronzes, 5th–3d cent. B.C. Female figurine (*left*), from Despeñaperros, Jaén. Ht., 4³/₈ in. Horseman (*center*), from a sanctuary in southern Spain. Ht., 2³/₄ in. Both, Madrid, Museo Arqueológico Nacional. *Right*: Denarii of Segobriga (mod. Segorbe, Castellón de la Plana), 2d cent. B.C. Silver. Barcelona, Gabinete Numismático de Cataluña.

MEDITERRANEAN, ANCIENT WESTERN

Pl. 411. Sculpture in stone, Bouches-du-Rhône, France, 3d–2d cent. B.C. *Above*: Architectural element engraved with horse heads, from the sanctuary at Roquepertuse. Ht., 13 in. *Below, left*: Face from a double herm, from Roquepertuse. Ht., 8¼ in. Both, Marseilles, Musée Archéologique. *Right*: Male head, from Entremont. Ht., 11 in. Aix-en-Provence, Musée Granet.

MEDITERRANEAN, ANCIENT WESTERN

Pl. 412. Statues of warrior-heroes and pillar porch with *têtes coupées*, from Roquepertuse, Bouches-du-Rhône, France, 3d–2d cent. B.C. (reconstruction). Marseilles, Musée Archéologique.

Pl. 413. Dwellings, 7th–4th millennium B.C. *Above*: Jericho, remains of a house. *Below*: Khirokitia, Cyprus, remains of a tholos.

MEDITERRANEAN PROTOHISTORY

Pl. 414. Human skull with face modeled in clay and shell eyes, Jericho, 5th millennium B.C. Amman, Jordan, Museum.

Pl. 415. Figurines, 4th millennium B.C. *Left*: From Mamariyya, Egypt. Painted pottery, ht., 11½ in. New York, Brooklyn Museum. *Right*: Al-'Ubaid culture, Ur. Clay with bitumen wig, ht., 6½ in. London, British Museum.

MEDITERRANEAN PROTOHISTORY

Pl. 416. Painted and incised pottery. *Left, above*: From Hacılar, Turkey, 4th millennium B.C. Ankara, Archaeological Museum. *Center*: From Tell Halaf, Syria, early 4th millennium B.C. *Below*: From Jamdat Naṣr, Iraq, early 3d millennium B.C. Paris, Louvre. *Right, above*: From Lerne, Greece, Sesklo culture, late 4th–early 3d millennium B.C. Athens, National Museum. *Center*: From Traian-Dealul Fîntînilor, Romania, Cucuteni culture, second half of 3d millennium B.C. Bucharest, Archaeological Museum. *Below*: From Vukovar, Yugoslavia, Vučedol culture, late 3d–early 2d millennium B.C. Zagreb, Archaeological Museum.

MEDITERRANEAN PROTOHISTORY

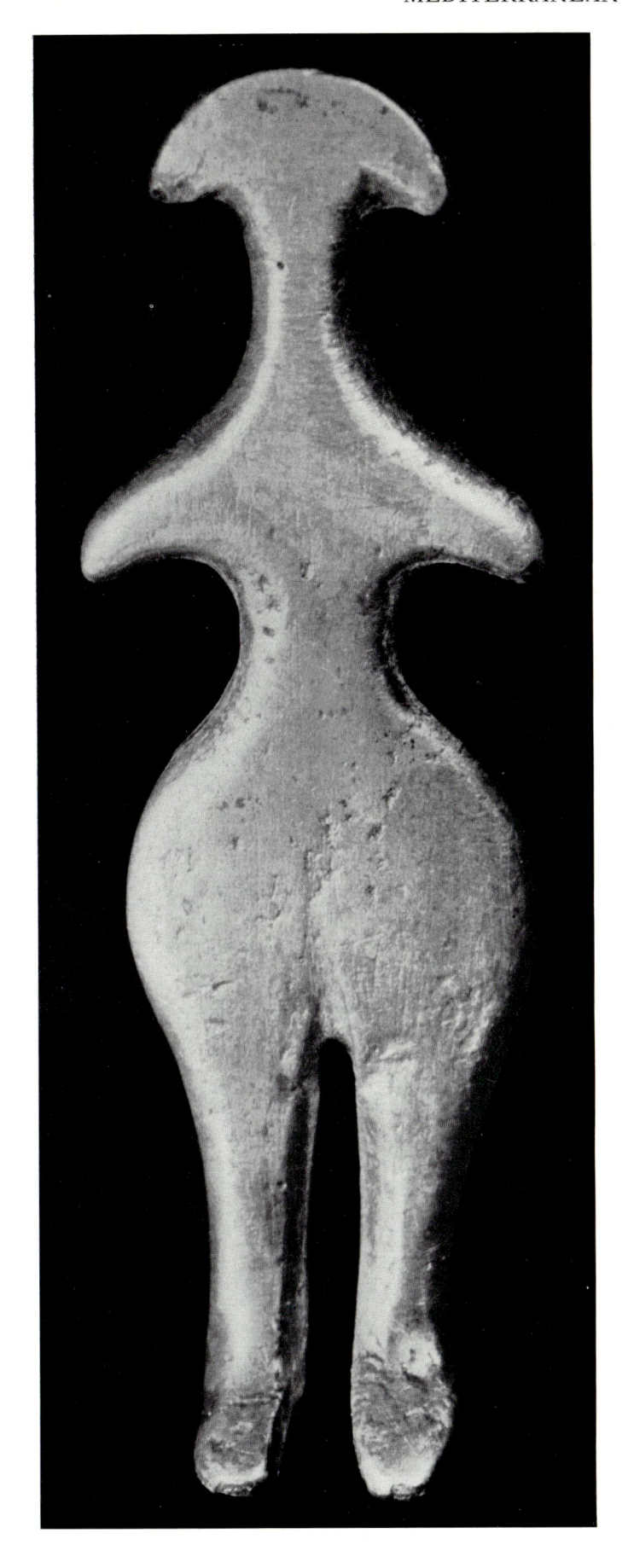

Pl. 417. Anatolian statuettes, second half of 3d millennium B.C. Ankara, Archaeological Museum. *Left*: From Alaca Hüyük. Electrum, ht., 2³/₄ in. *Right*: From Horoztepe. Bronze, ht., 8¹/₂ in.

Pl. 418. Troy (mod. Hissarlik), Turkey. *Above*: View of the city from the southwest with city walls of Troy II, 3d millennium B.C., and Troy VI, 2d millennium B.C. *Below*: View of the tower and east wall of the citadel from the southeast, Troy VI.

MEDITERRANEAN PROTOHISTORY

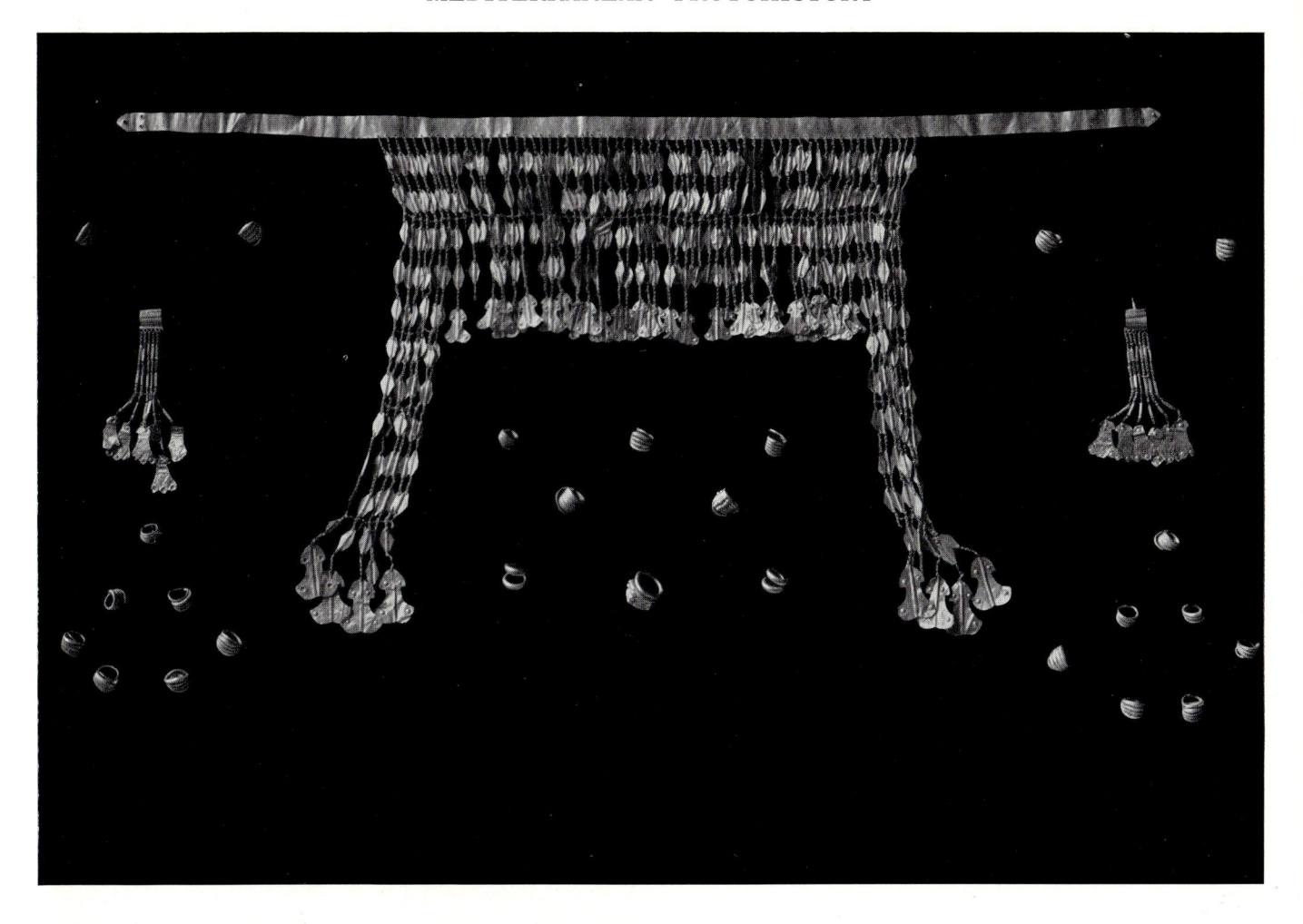

Pl. 419. Trojan culture, 3d millennium B.C. *Above*: Diadem, ear pendants, and curl spirals, from the "treasure of Priam," Troy II. Gold, max. l., 21 1/4 in. Formerly, Berlin, Museum für Völkerkunde. *Below, left*: Sculptured stele, Troy I. Limestone, ht., ca. 39 3/8 in. *Right*: Two-handled cup (*depas amphikypellon*), Troy III. Ht., 11 3/4 in. (Partially restored.) Rome, Museo Pigorini.

MEDITERRANEAN PROTOHISTORY

Pl. 420. Lyre player, Keros, Cyclades, ca. 2000 B.C. Marble, ht., 8⅞ in. Athens, National Museum.

MEDITERRANEAN PROTOHISTORY

Pl. 421. Cycladic culture. *Above, left*: Violin-shaped idol, Paros, second half of 3d millennium B.C. Marble, ht., ca. 4 in. Paris, Louvre. *Right*: Idol, Naxos, second half of 3d millennium B.C. Marble, ht., 3 1/2 in. Oxford, Ashmolean Museum. *Below, left*: "Pan-shaped" vessel, Syros, ca. 2000 B.C. Terra cotta, diam., 11 3/4 in. Paris, Louvre. *Right*: Painted pitcher, Lerne, Greece, 1700–1400 B.C. Ht., 12 1/8 in. Athens, National Museum.

MEDITERRANEAN PROTOHISTORY

Pl. 422. Cretan culture. Heraklion, Archaeological Museum. *Above*: Twin idols of Cycladic type, Tekes, Heraklion, 2500–2000 B.C. Steatite, ht., 2 in. *Left, center*: Teapot vase in Vasiliki style, 2300–2000 B.C. Ht., 7½ in. *Below*: Askos in the form of a bull with acrobats between the horns, Koumasa, 2300–2000 B.C. Terra cotta, l., 8⅛ in. *Right*: Pithos in Kamares style, Phaistos, 1800–1700 B.C. Ht., ca. 19¾ in.

MEDITERRANEAN PROTOHISTORY

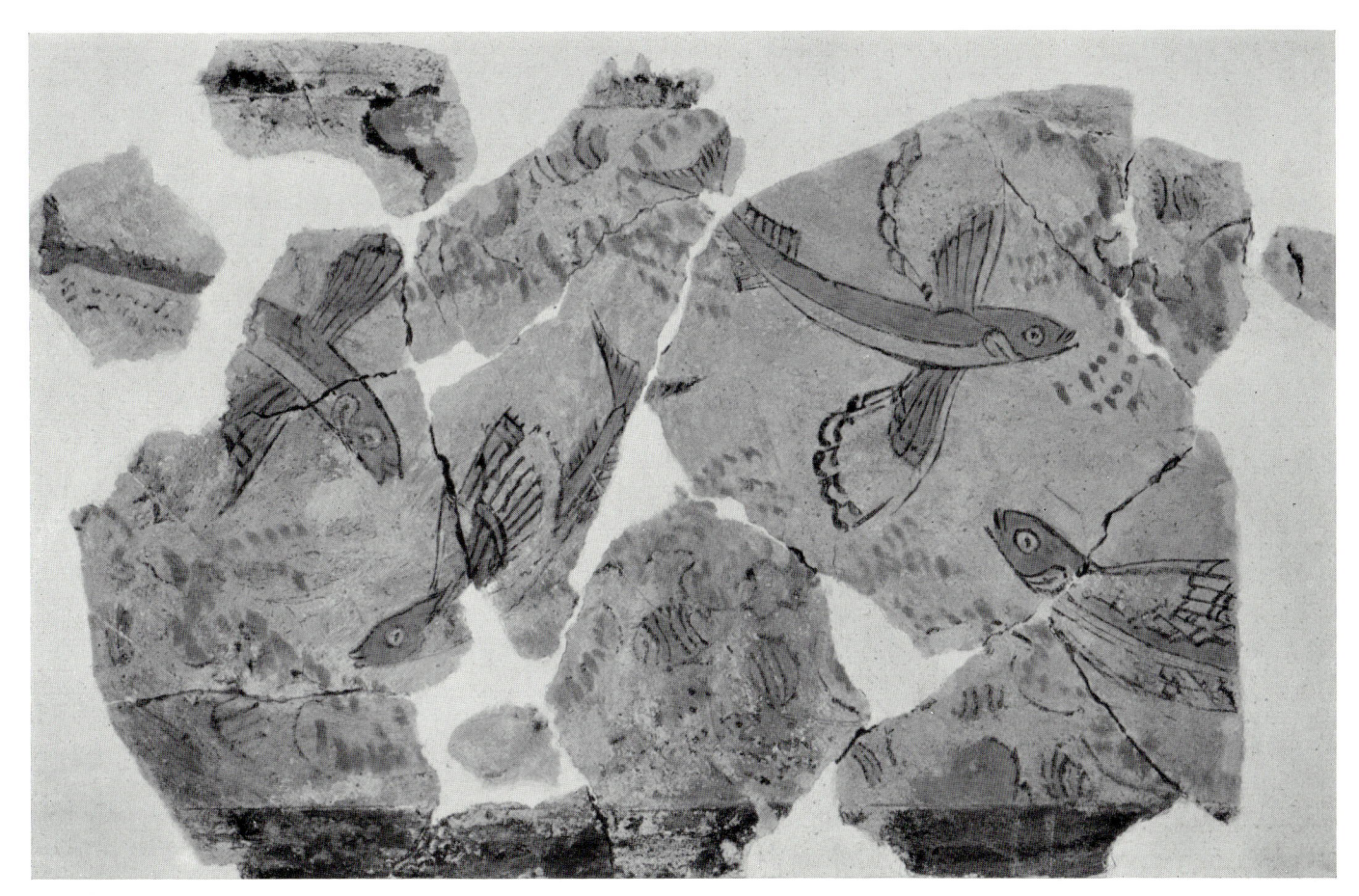

Pl. 423. *Above, left*: Statuette, Sesklo culture, Lerne, Greece, early 3d millennium B.C. Terra cotta, ht., 7 1/8 in. Corinth, Archaeological Museum. *Right*: Female figurine, Lerne, second half of 3d millennium B.C. Terra cotta, ht., 4 3/8 in. *Below*: Fragment of wall painting with flying fish, Phylakopi, Melos, second half of 3d millennium B.C. Ht., 9 1/8 in. (After a water-color reproduction.) Last two, Athens, National Museum.

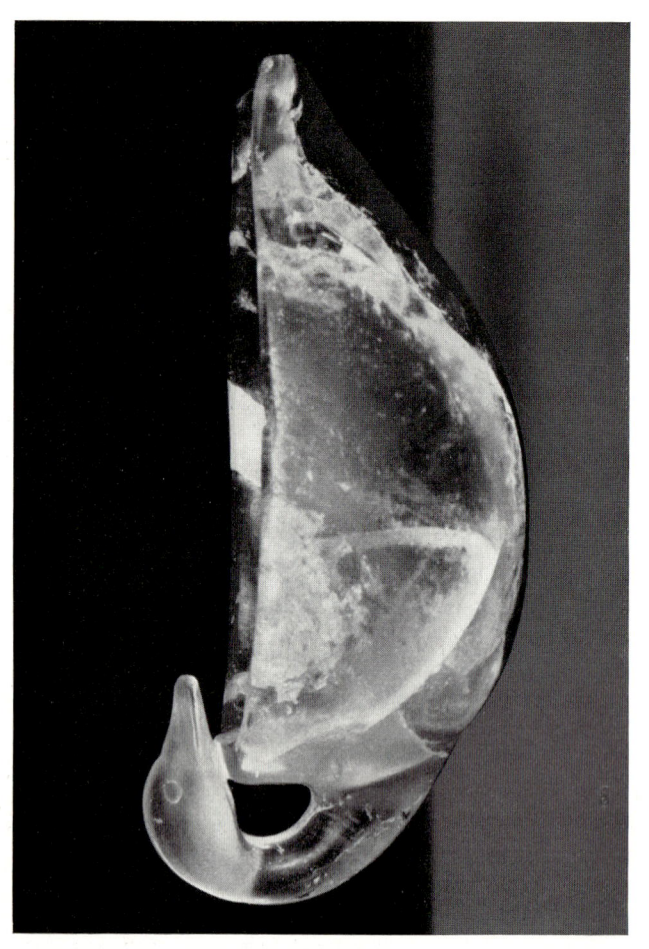

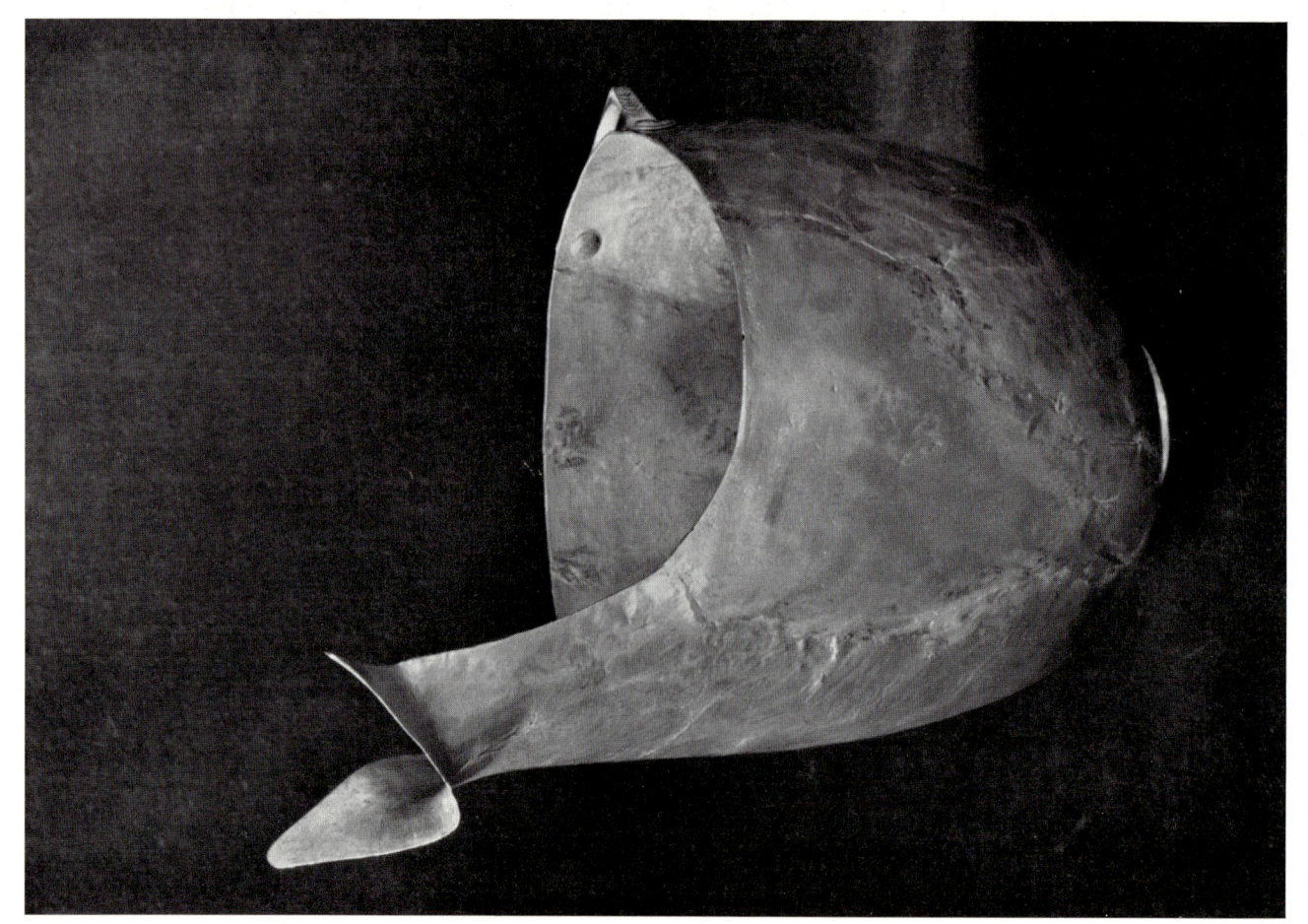

Pl. 424. Helladic culture. *Left*: "Sauceboat," Mycenae, ca. 2500–1950 B.C. Gold, ht., 8 5/8 in. Paris, Louvre. *Right, above*: Matt-painted cup, Lerne, ca. 1950–1700 B.C. Ht., 4 7/8 in. *Below*: Toilet vase in the shape of a duck, Mycenae, 1600–1500 B.C. Rock crystal. Last two, Athens, National Museum.

Pl. 425. Mycenae, royal tomb circle from the northeast, 1600–1500 B.C.

Pl. 426. Malta, Mnaidra, entrance of a megalithic "temple," second half of 3d millennium B.C.

MEDITERRANEAN PROTOHISTORY

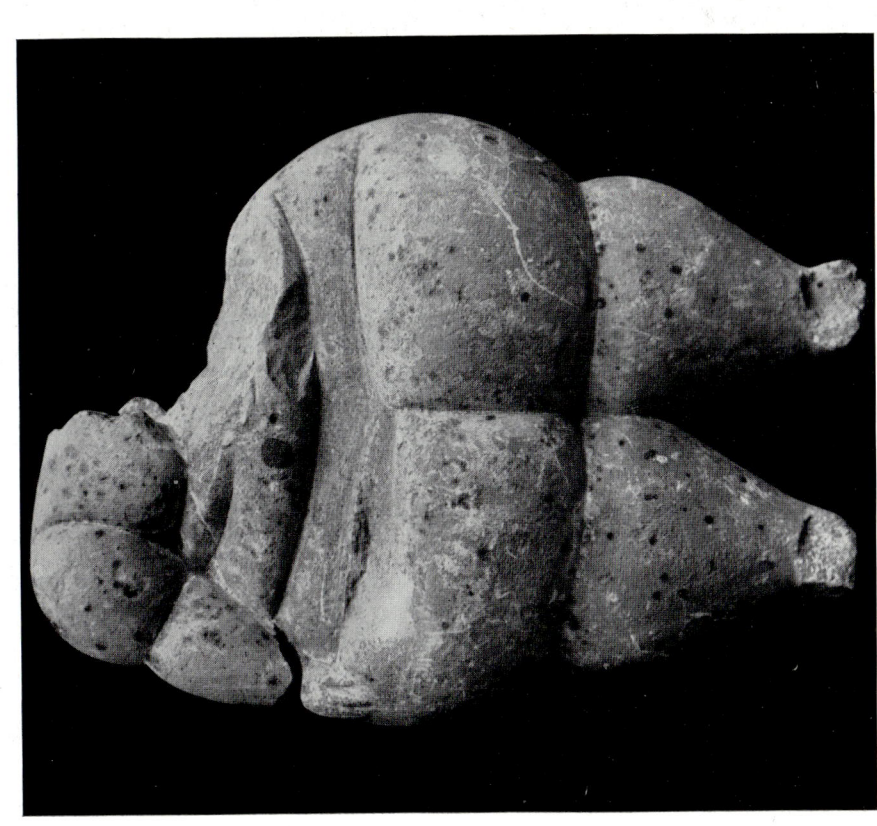

Pl. 427. Maltese culture, second half of 3d millennium B.C. Valletta, Museum. *Above:* Architectural relief with animals, Hal Tarxien. Limestone. *Below, left:* Idol, from the hypogeum of Hal Saflieni. Limestone. *Center:* Architectural relief with spiral decoration, Hal Tarxien. Limestone. *Right:* Architectural element with spiral decoration, Bugibba, St. Paul's Bay. Limestone.

Pl. 428. Pottery in Stentinello style, Sicily, mid-4th millennium B.C. Syracuse, Sicily, Museo Archeologico Nazionale. *Above*: Vase with impressed decoration, Naxos, near Messina. Diam., 8½ in. *Below*: Painted cup, Megara Hyblaea. Diam., 7½ in.

MEDITERRANEAN PROTOHISTORY

Pl. 429. Painted pottery, Serra d'Alto, near Matera, Italy, 3d millennium B.C. Matera, Museo Nazionale. *Above*: Ht., 4 3/8 in. *Below*: Ht., 6 3/8 in.

Pl. 430. "Fruit stand," Vallelunga, near Caltanissetta, Sicily, ca. 1700–1400 B.C. Syracuse, Sicily, Museo Archeologico Nazionale.

MEDITERRANEAN PROTOHISTORY

Pl. 431. Antequera, near Málaga, Spain, megalithic sepulcher known as Cueva de Menga, interior gallery, 2200–1500 B.C.

MEDITERRANEAN PROTOHISTORY

Pl. 432. Iberian Peninsula and Sardinia. *Above, left*: Idol with schematized human figure, from a megalithic tomb in Estremadura, second half of 3d millennium B.C. Alabaster, ht., 7⅞ in. *Right*: Two views of a bowl, from Los Millares, near Almería, Spain, late 3d–early 2d millennium B.C. Both, Madrid, Museo Arqueológico Nacional. *Below, left*: Bell beaker, from Brichs, Spain, late 3d–early 2d millennium B.C. Solsona, Spain, Museo Diocesano. *Right*: Tripod, from the cave of S. Bartolomeo at Capo Sant'Elia, near Cagliari, Sardinia, late 3d–early 2d millennium B.C. Ht., ca. 4 in. Rome, Museo Pigorini.

Pl. 433. Schematic female statuette, Senorbì, near Cagliari, Sardinia, early 3d millennium B.C. Limestone, ht., ca. 17 in. Cagliari, Museo Archeologico Nazionale.

MEDITERRANEAN PROTOHISTORY

Pl. 434. Pottery, Italy. *Above*: Fragment of a bowl with impressed and sgraffito decoration, from the grotto of Sant'Angelo at Ostuni, near Brindisi, late 3d millennium B.C. Taranto, Museo Nazionale. *Below, left*: Vase painted in Serraferlicchio style, Agrigento, late 3d millennium B.C. (?). Ht., 9¹/₂ in. Agrigento, Museo Civico Archeologico. *Right*: Vessel, Mirabella Eclano, near Avellino, first half of 2d millennium B.C. Ht., 8⁵/₈ in. Mirabella Eclano, Antiquario.

MEDITERRANEAN PROTOHISTORY

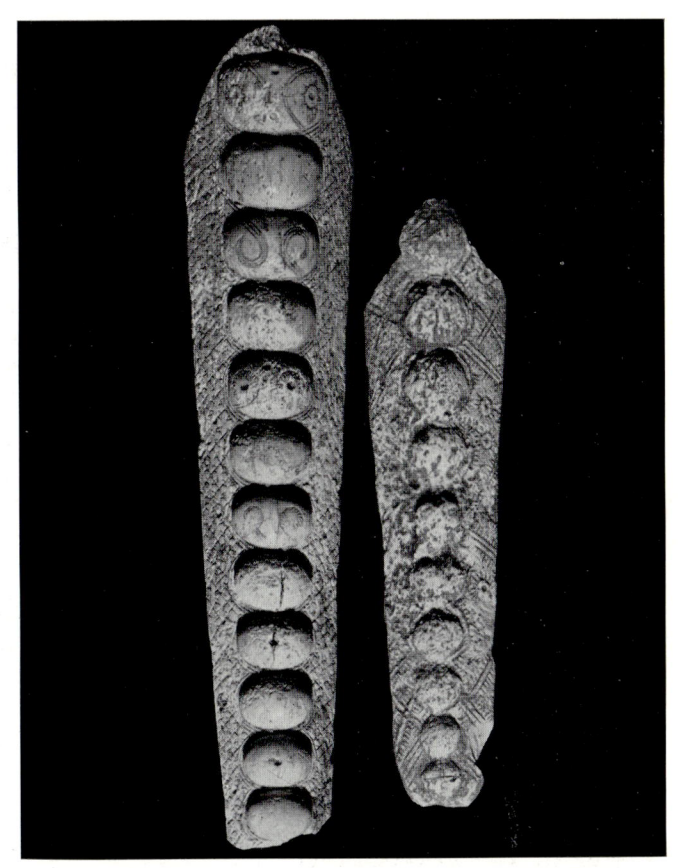

Pl. 435. Sicily. *Above, left*: Painted vase in Castelluccio style, Monte Tabuto, near Comiso, 1800–1400 B.C. Ht., 13 3/8 in. *Right*: Bossed bone objects, Castelluccio, near Noto, ca. 1800–1400 B.C. Ht. of longer, 6 1/2 in. *Below, left*: Carved door slab from a rock-cut tomb, Castelluccio, ca. 1800–1400 B.C. Limestone, ht., 39 3/8 in. All three, Syracuse, Sicily, Museo Archeologico Nazionale. *Right*: Cassibile, near Syracuse, entrance of a rock-cut tomb, ca. 1000–850 B.C.

MEDITERRANEAN PROTOHISTORY

Pl. 436. Spain. *Above*: Pottery, El Argar culture, El Oficio, 1500–1000 B.C. Barcelona, Museo Arqueológico. *Below*: Funerary stele, Solana de Cabañas, Logrosán, 1000–800 B.C. Stone. Madrid, Museo Arqueológico Nacional.

Pl. 437. Lipari Islands and Sicily. *Above*: Panarea Island, remains of a village, ca. 2000–1300 B.C. *Below, left*: High-footed vase of monochrome red ware, from Pantalica, 1200–1000 B.C. Ht., 42 1/2 in. Syracuse, Sicily, Museo Archeologico Nazionale. *Right*: Pitcher, Ausonian II culture, Lipari, ca. 1150–850 B.C. Ht., 13 in. Lipari, Museo Eoliano.

MEDITERRANEAN PROTOHISTORY

Pl. 438. Central Italy. *Above*: Vase in Appennine style, Belverde, near Chiusi, second half of 2d millennium B.C. Ht., 2³/₈ in. Perugia, Italy, Musei Civici. *Center and below*: Coste del Marano, near Tolfa, early 1st millennium B.C. Bronze. Rome, Museo Pigorini. *Center*: Fibula. L., 10⁷/₈ in. *Below*: Bowl. Diam., 5⁷/₈ in.

MEIDIAS PAINTER

Pl. 439. Hydria, with the rape of the daughters of Leukippos, Herakles in the Garden of the Hesperides, and Athenian heroes, ca. 420–400 B.C. Ht., 20½ in. London, British Museum.

MEIDIAS PAINTER

Pl. 440. Phaon and nymph, detail of calyx-crater, 420–400 B.C. Full ht., ca. 15 3/4 in. Palermo, Sicily, Museo Nazionale Archeologico.

Pl. 441. Mask, from Dewar Island, Torres Strait, New Guinea. Turtle shell with pod and shell decoration, partly painted red; ht., 33 1/2 in. Copenhagen, Nationalmuseet.

MELANESIAN CULTURES

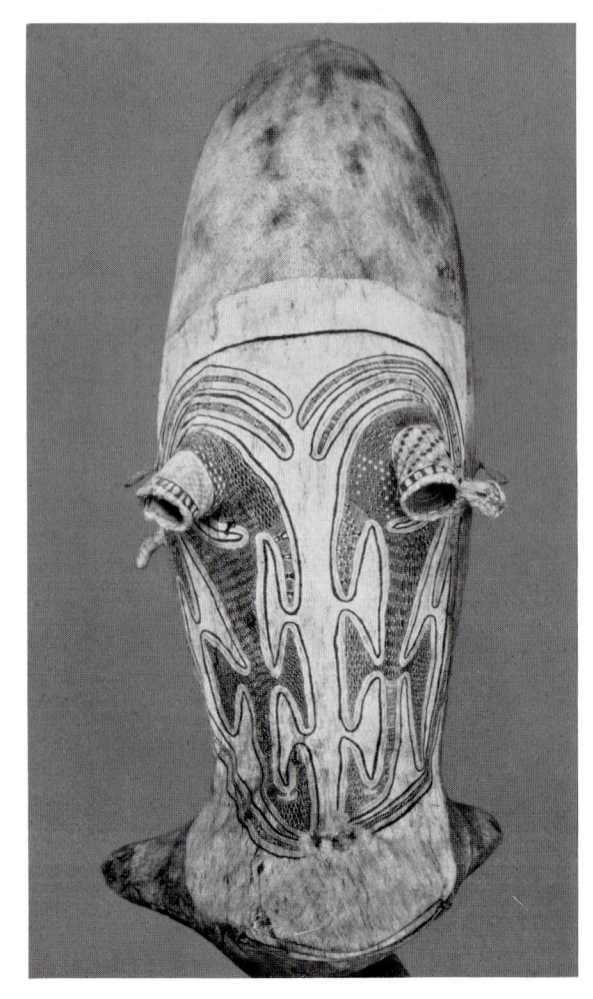

Pl. 442. *Above, left*: Mask, from Sepik River area, New Guinea. Rattan, human hair, palm leaf strips; ht., 29 7/8 in. Basel, Museum für Völkerkunde. *Right*: Ceremonial mask, from Torres Strait Islands, New Guinea. Painted wood, red cloth, artificial hair; ht., 18 1/2 in. London, British Museum. *Below, left*: Winged mask, New Ireland. Painted wood, ht., 25 5/8 in. *Right*: Baining mask, New Britain. Painted tapa. Last two, Hamburg, Museum für Völkerkunde.

MELANESIAN CULTURES

Pl. 443. *Left*: Dance mask, from New Hebrides. Wood with boar tusks. *Right*: Ceremonial mask, from New Caledonia. Wood (wig and beard of human hair). Both, Hamburg, Museum für Völkerkunde.

MELANESIAN CULTURES

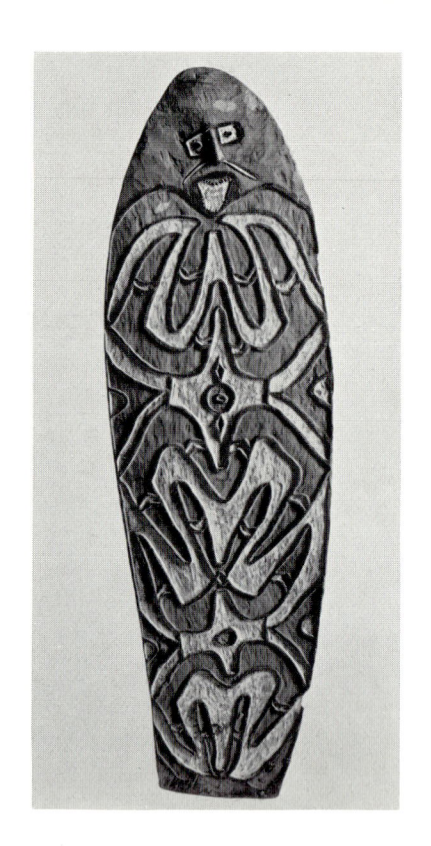

Pl. 444. *Above, left*: Tshuosh openwork figure (perhaps representing a sago beetle), used in funeral ceremonies, from Sepik River area, New Guinea. Wood. Cambridge, England, University Museum of Archaeology and Ethnology. *Center*: Shield with anthropomorphic reliefs, from New Guinea. Wood, l., 48 7/8 in. Rome, Museo Pigorini. *Right*: Panel with stylized human figure, from New Guinea. Wood. *Below*: Human figure with birds, from Sepik River area. Last two, Rome, Lateran Museums.

Pl. 445. *Left*: Fertility charm, from Torres Strait area, New Guinea. Wood, ht., 10¹/₄ in. London, British Museum. *Right*: Image of a divinity, from Kaniet Islands. Wood, ht., 31⁷/₈ in. Bremen, Übersee-Museum.

Pl. 446. *Left*: Ancestor figure with characteristic Admiralty Islands hairdress. Wood, ht., 4 ft., 6⅞ in. *Right*: Dorsal war ornament, from Admiralty Islands. Wood and sea-eagle feathers, l., 20⅞ in. Both, Bremen, Übersee-Museum.

Pl. 447. *Malanggan* sculpture, from New Ireland. Painted wood. Hamburg, Museum für Völkerkunde.

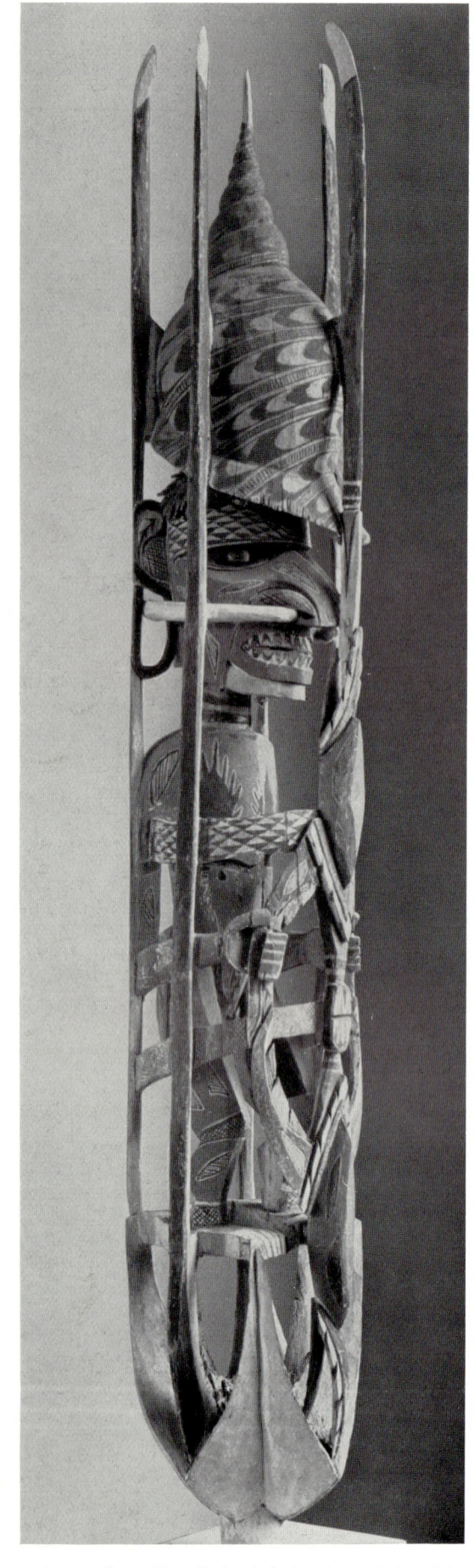

MELANESIAN CULTURES

Pl. 448. *Left*: *Uli* sculpture, from New Ireland. Painted wood. *Right*: *Malanggan* sculpture, from New Ireland. Painted wood, ht., 4 ft., 5 in. Both, Hamburg, Museum für Völkerkunde.

MELANESIAN CULTURES

Pl. 449. Sulka ceremonial mask, from Gazelle Peninsula, New Britain. Reed pith on bamboo frame, with leaf fringe; ht., 24 in. London, British Museum.

Pl. 450. Feather mosaic, from a ghost house, Middle Sepik area, New Guinea. Rome, Lateran Museums.

MELANESIAN CULTURES

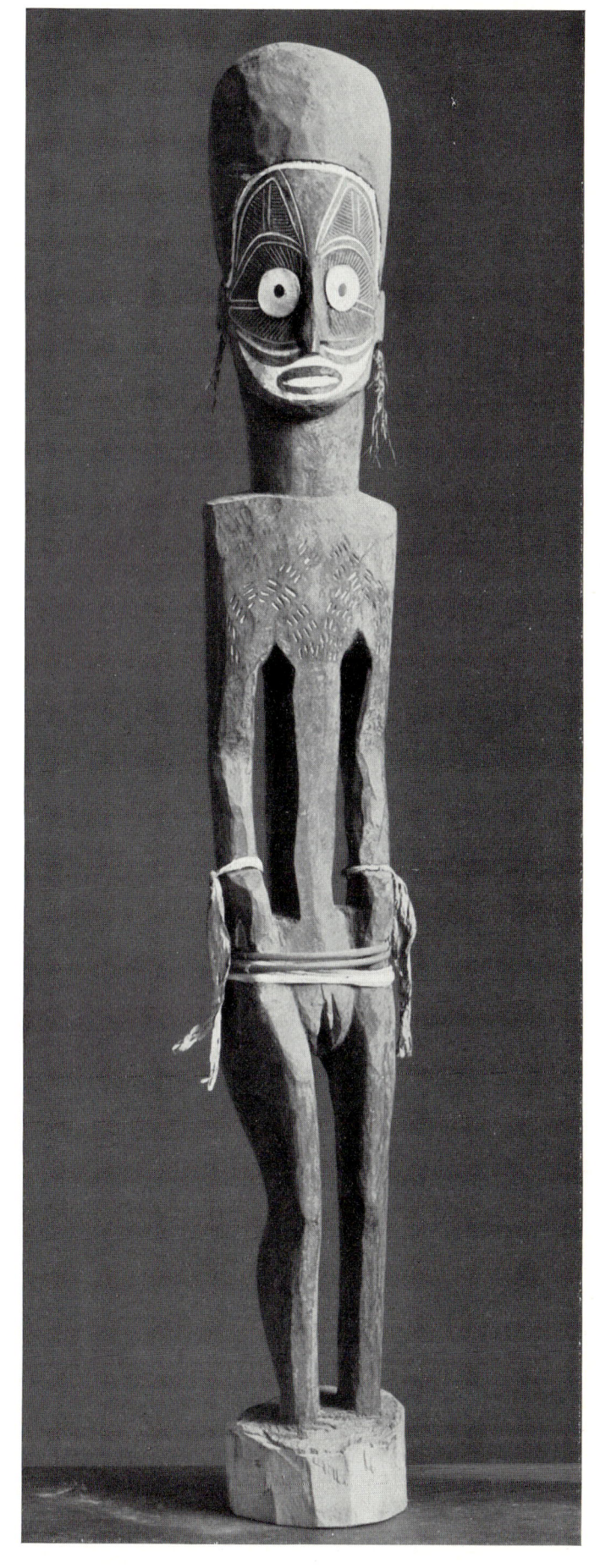

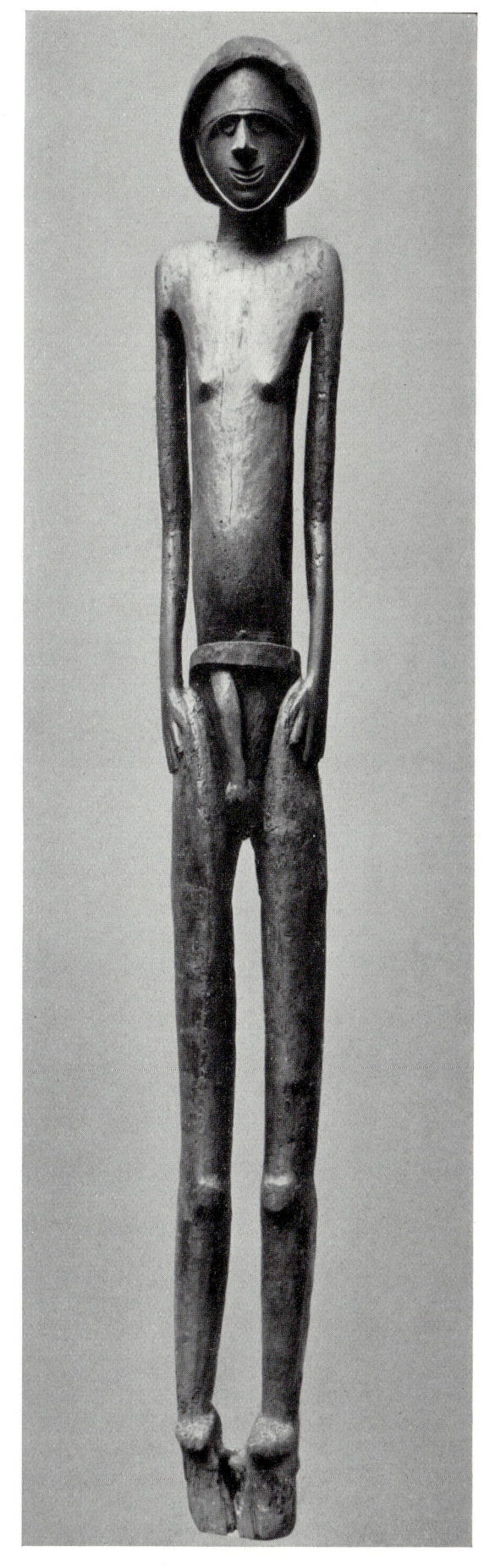

Pl. 451. *Left*: Female figure, from Solomon Islands. Wood, ht., 3 ft., 10³/₄ in. Bremen, Übersee-Museum. *Right*: Achin ancestor figure, from New Hebrides. Wood, 8 ft., 6³/₈ in. Basel, Museum für Völkerkunde.

MELANESIAN CULTURES

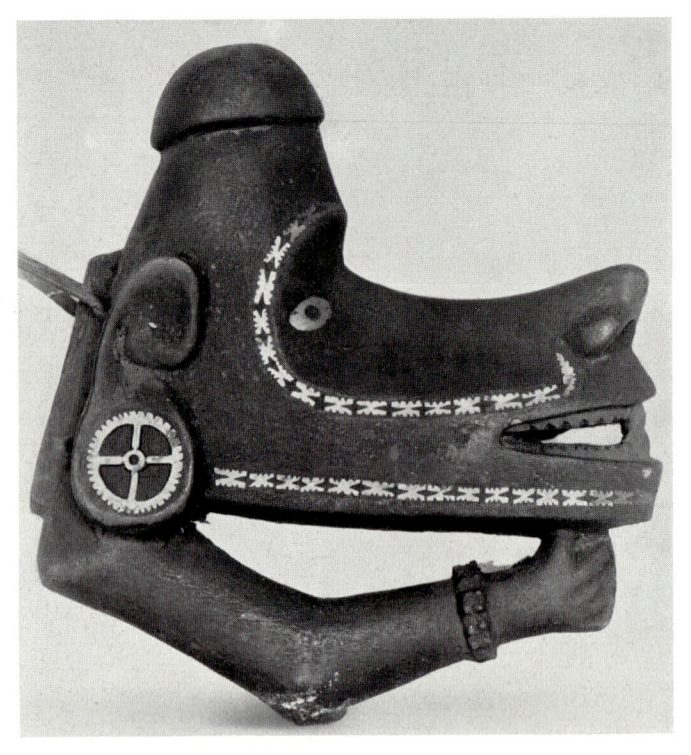

Pl. 452. *Above, left*: Food bowl, from Solomon Islands. Wood, with pearl-shell inlay; ht., 9 in. London, British Museum. *Right*: Marovo prow ornament from a war canoe, New Georgia, Solomon Islands. Wood with mother-of-pearl inlay, ht., 6⅞ in. Basel, Museum für Völkerkunde. *Below*: Food bowl, with openwork ornamentation, from Admiralty Islands. Wood. Hamburg, Museum für Völkerkunde.

MELANESIAN CULTURES

Pl. 453. Jar for storing sago, from Sepik River area, New Guinea. Painted clay, ht., 27½ in. Basel, Museum für Völkerkunde.

MELANESIAN CULTURES

Pl. 454. Painting from a ghost house, south Maprik area, New Guinea. Palm-leaf sections on bamboo frame, 52 × 25¼ in. Basel, Museum für Völkerkunde.

MELANESIAN CULTURES

Pl. 455. *Above*: Bowl, from Sepik River area, New Guinea. Clay, incised and painted, diam., 9¼ in. London, British Museum. *Below, left*: Gable ornament, from Sepik River area. Painted clay, ht., 12¾ in. Salem, Mass., Peabody Museum. *Right*: Water container, from Fiji Islands. Clay with vegetable varnish, ht., 7⅛ in. Paris, Musée de l'Homme.

MELANESIAN CULTURES

Pl. 456. Handles of betel-lime spatulas, from Luf Island. Wood. Hamburg, Museum für Völkerkunde.

MELANESIAN CULTURES

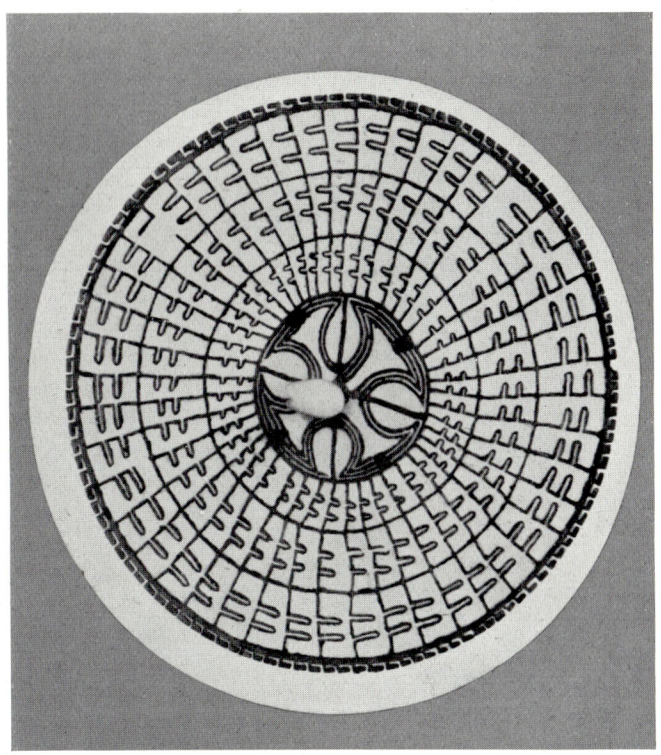

Pl. 457. *Above*: Two pectoral ornaments (*kapkap*). *Left*: From Admiralty Islands. Turtle shell, diam., 4⁷/₈ in. Bremen, Übersee-Museum. *Right*: From Solomon Islands. Tridacna and turtle shell. Rome, Museo Pigorini. *Below*: Neckrest, from Sepik River area, New Guinea. Wood. Formerly, Rome, Museo Pigorini.

MELANESIAN CULTURES

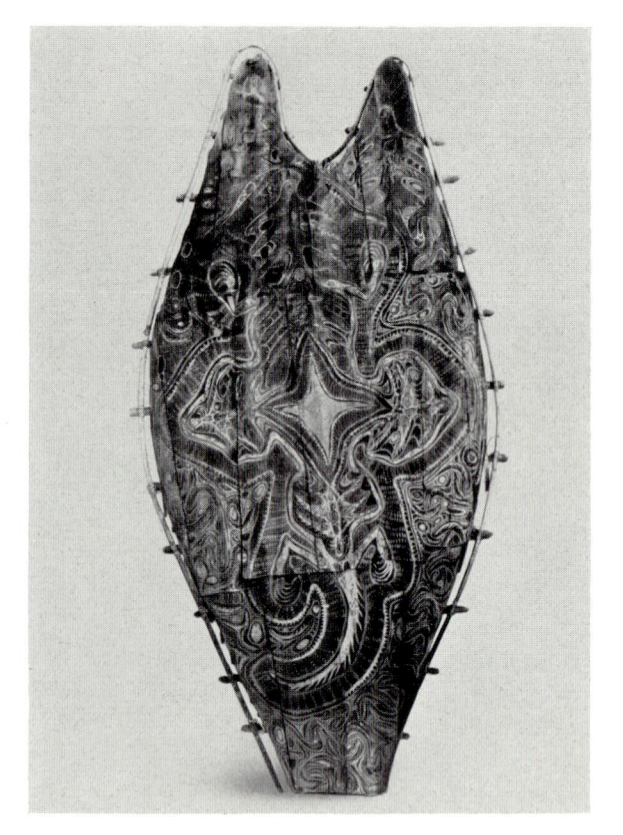

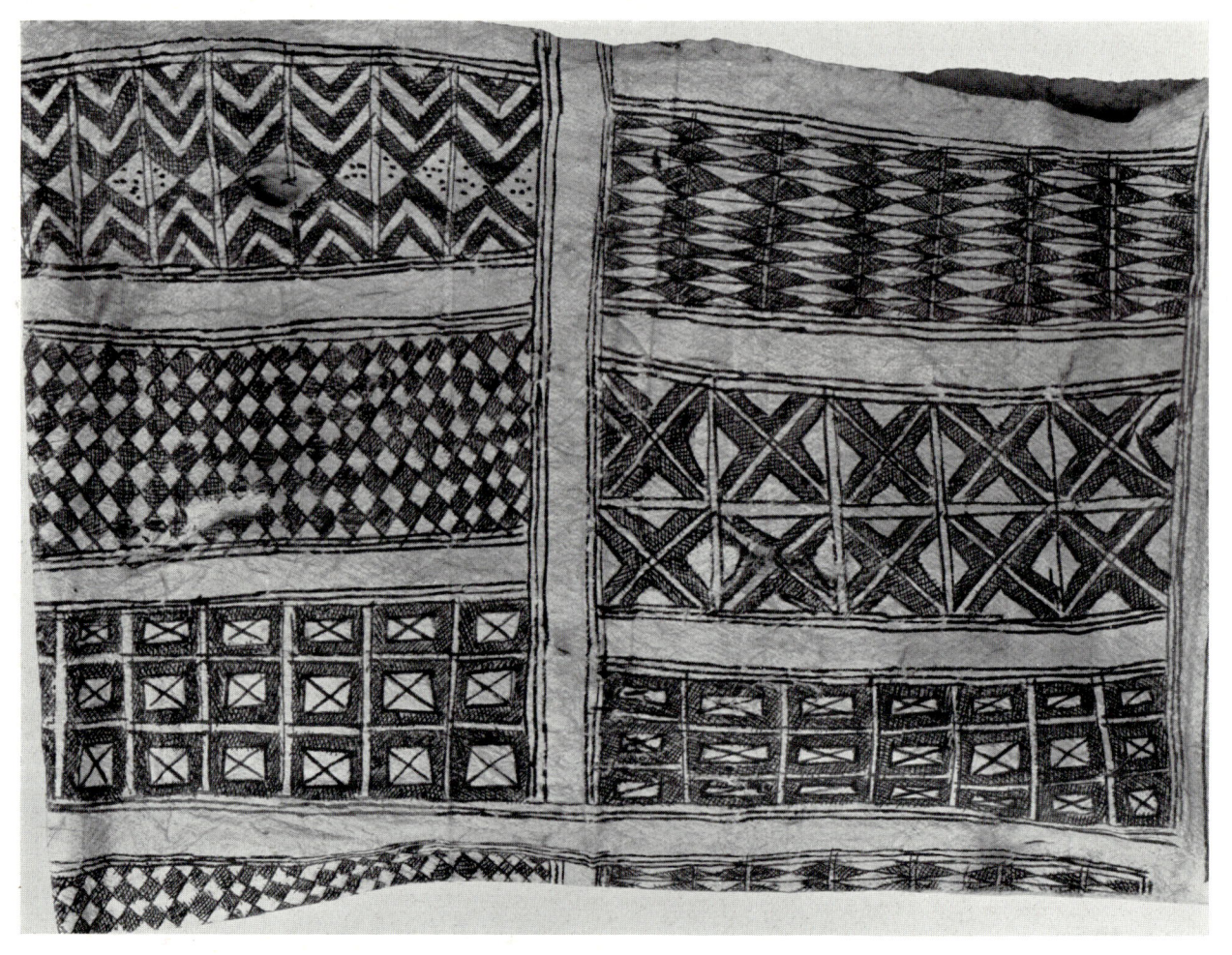

Pl. 458. *Above*: Paintings from ceremonial houses, Sepik River area, New Guinea. Palm-leaf sections on wood and bamboo frames; 3 ft., 4½ in. × 3 ft., 2⅝ in. and 9 ft., 10 in. × 5 ft., 3 in. Basel, Museum für Völkerkunde. *Below*: Tapa with geometric motifs, from Fiji Islands. Florence, Museo Nazionale di Antropologia e Etnologia.

MEMLING

Pl. 459. Portrait of a man. Panel, 11 3/4 × 8 5/8 in. The Hague, Mauritshuis.

MEMLING

Pl. 460. Virgin and Child with Saints and Donors, from the Donne Triptych. Panel, 28×27 in. London, National Gallery.

MEMLING

Pl. 461. St. Ursula shrine. Gilded and painted wood, ht., ca. 31½ in. Bruges, Musée Memling.

MEMLING

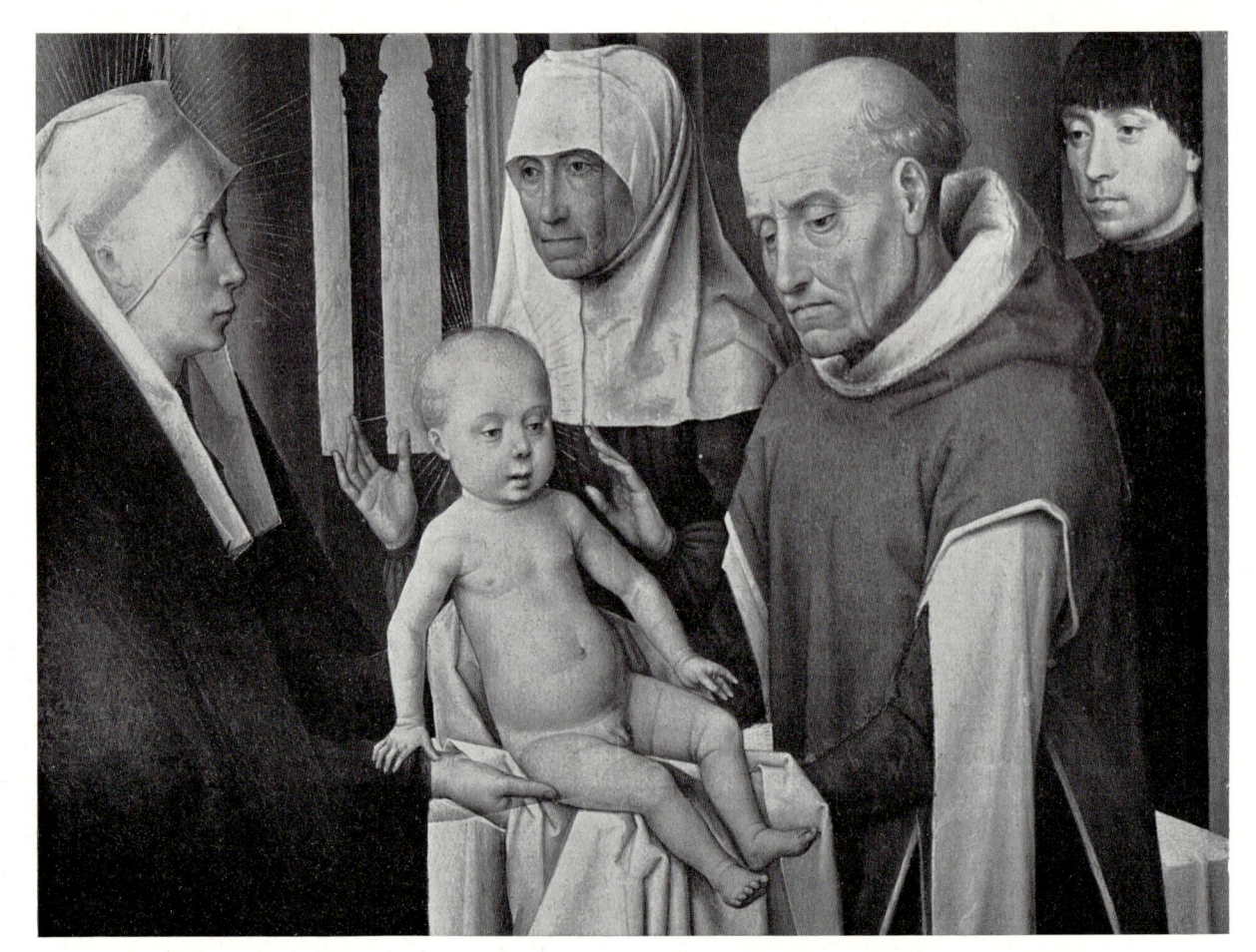

Pl. 462. *Above*: Diptych with the Virgin and Child and the donor Martin van Nieuwenhove. Panel, each 17 3/8 × 13 in. Bruges, Musée Memling. *Below*: The Presentation, detail of triptych with the Nativity, the Adoration of the Magi, and the Presentation. Panel; full size of wing, 37 3/8 × 24 3/4 in. Madrid, Prado.

MESOPOTAMIA

Pl. 463. Erech (Uruk). *Above*: The "White Temple" on the archaic ziggurat, Jamdat Nasr period. *Below*: The ruins of the city to the southwest, from the top of the ziggurat, 3d millennium B.C.

MESOPOTAMIA

Pl. 464. Female head, from Erech (Uruk), Jamdat Nasr period. Alabaster, ht., ca. 8½ in. Baghdad, Iraq Museum.

MESOPOTAMIA

Pl. 465. *Above, left*: Fragment of mace head, from Sippar, Jamdat Nasr period. Brown limestone, ht., 6¼ in. *Right*: Sumerian libation vase, from Erech (Uruk), Jamdat Nasr period. Gray limestone, ht., 4⅞ in. *Below*: Trough, from Erech, Jamdat Nasr period. Limestone, ht., 6¼ in. All, London, British Museum.

MESOPOTAMIA

Pl. 466. Vase with scenes of offerings to the goddess Inanna (Ishtar), from Erech (Uruk), Jamdat Nasr period. Alabaster, ht., 43¼ in. Baghdad, Iraq Museum.

MESOPOTAMIA

Pl. 467. Figure with plumed headdress, from Lagash (mod. Telloh), first half of 3d millennium B.C. Limestone, ht., 7¹/₈ in. Paris, Louvre.

MESOPOTAMIA

Pl. 468. *Left*: Female figure, from Khafaje, Mesilim period. Limestone, ht., 5¾ in. *Right*: Male statuette, from Khafaje, Mesilim period. Yellow stone, ht., 3 in. Both, Baghdad, Iraq Museum.

MESOPOTAMIA

Pl. 469. *Left*: Male "adorant" figure, from Khafaje, Mesilim period. Gray limestone, ht., 9¼ in. *Right*: Male figure from Khafaje, Mesilim period. Gypsum, ht., 10¼ in. Both, Philadelphia, University Museum.

MESOPOTAMIA

Pl. 470. *Left*: Nude priest pouring libation before a goddess, from Lagash (mod. Telloh), Mesilim period. Limestone, ht., 7½ in. *Right*: Head of King Mesilim's mace, from Lagash, Mesilim period. Limestone, 6¾ × 5⅞ in. Both, Paris, Louvre.

MESOPOTAMIA

Pl. 471. So-called "Standard" of Ur, with scenes of war, mid-3d millennium B.C. Panel inlaid with shell, lapis lazuli, and red limestone, 8 × 19 in. London, British Museum. (Cf. VIII, PL. 77.)

MESOPOTAMIA

Pl. 472. Head of a statue of Gudea (known as the "head with a turban"), from Lagash (mod. Telloh), Neo-Sumerian period. Diorite, ht., 9 1/8 in. Paris, Louvre.

MESOPOTAMIA

Pl. 473. Priest, from Khafaje, Mesilim-Ur I transition period. Limestone, ht., 23⁵/₈ in. Baghdad, Iraq Museum.

MESOPOTAMIA

Pl. 474. *Above, left*: Female head, from Lagash (mod. Telloh), Mesilim-Ur I transition period. Alabaster, ht., 3 1/8 in. *Right*: Male head, from Umm el-Agareb, Ur I period. Limestone, ht., 2 3/4 in. *Below, left*: Torso of a statuette, from Lagash, Ur I period (?). Limestone; ht., 6 5/8 in. All three, Paris, Louvre. *Right*: Statuette of an official, from al-'Ubaid, Ur I period. Tufa, ht., 14 3/4 in. London, British Museum.

MESOPOTAMIA

Pl. 475. *Above, left*: Support in shape of male figure, Khafaje, Mesilim period. Copper, ht., 21 7/8 in. Baghdad, Iraq Museum. *Right*: Plaque with libation scene, from Nippur, Ur I period. Slate, ht., 7 1/2 in. Istanbul, Archaeological Museums. *Center*: Plaque with Dudu, priest of the god Ningirsu, from Lagash (mod. Telloh), Ur I period. Bituminous stone, ht., 9 7/8 in. Paris, Louvre. *Below*: Fragment of frieze with reclining bull, from al-'Ubaid, Ur I period. Copper, ht., ca. 10 1/2 in. London, British Museum.

Pl. 476. Head of a divinity, from Lagash (mod. Telloh), Akkadian period. Terra cotta, ht., 4 in. Paris, Louvre.

MESOPOTAMIA

Pl. 477. Male head, from Lagash (mod. Telloh), Neo-Sumerian period. Steatite, ht., 2³/₈ in. Paris, Louvre.

MESOPOTAMIA

Pl. 478. The so-called "Woman with the Scarf," from Lagash (mod. Telloh), Neo-Sumerian period. Steatite, ht., 6³/₄ in. Paris, Louvre.

MESOPOTAMIA

Pl. 479. Ur-Ningirsu, from Lagash (mod. Telloh), Ur III period. Alabaster, ht., 18 1/8 in. Paris, Louvre.

MESOPOTAMIA

Pl. 480. *Above, left*: Nail-shaped foundation figurine of a calf, from Lagash (mod. Telloh), Neo-Sumerian period. Bronze, ht., 10¼ in. *Right*: Fragment of a relief with the goddess Ninsun, Neo-Sumerian period. Black steatite, ht., 5½ in. *Below*: Lamp cover, from Lagash, Neo-Sumerian period. Steatite, w., 2¾ in. All, Paris, Louvre.

MESOPOTAMIA

Pl. 481. Libation vase, from Lagash (mod. Telloh), Neo-Sumerian period. Dark-green steatite, ht., 8 5/8 in. Paris, Louvre.

MESOPOTAMIA

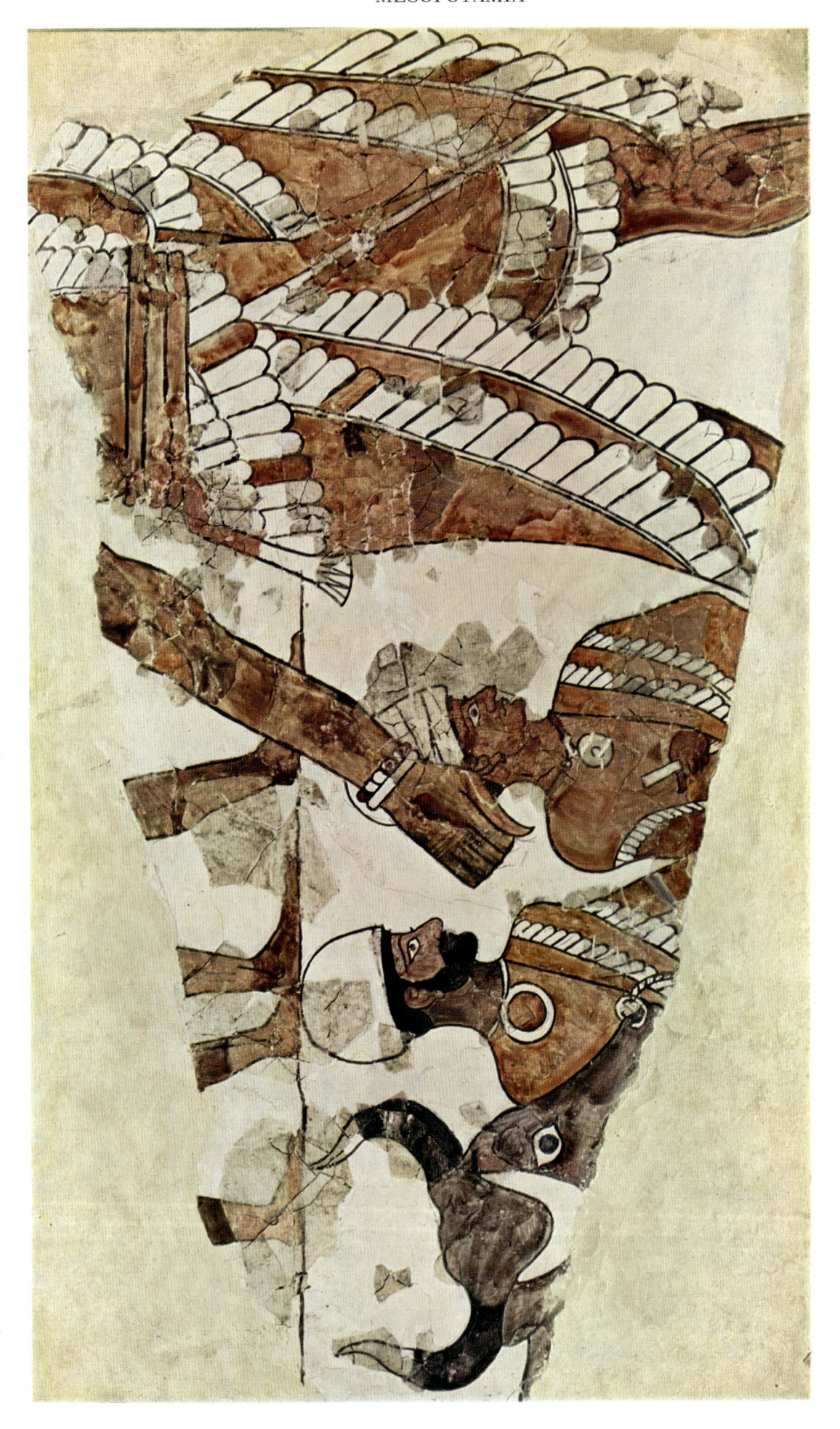

Pl. 482. Fragmentary sacrificial scene, from Zimrilim's palace in Mari, 1st half of 18th cent. B.C. Wall painting, 2 ft., 8 in. × 4 ft., 5 in. Paris, Louvre.

MESOPOTAMIA

Pl. 483. Mari, Zimrilim's palace, 1st half of 18th cent. B.C. *Above*: General view. *Below, left*: Throne room. *Right*: Scribes' room.

MESOPOTAMIA

Pl. 484. The ruler Idi-ilum, from Mari, early 2d millennium B.C. Steatite, ht., 16 1/8 in. Paris, Louvre.

MESOPOTAMIA

Pl. 485. *Above, left*: Goddess with flowing vase, from Mari, early 2d millennium B.C. White limestone, ht., 4 ft., 10⅝ in. Aleppo, Syria, Musée National. *Right*: Puzur-Ishtar, governor of Mari, from Babylonia, early 2d millennium B.C. Diorite, ht., 5 ft., 8⅛ in. Berlin, Staatliche Museen (reconstruction with original head and a cast of the body, which is preserved in Istanbul, Archaeological Museums). *Below, left*: A god killing a fiery "Cyclops," from Khafaje, early 2d millennium B.C. Terra cotta, 4½×3½ in. Baghdad, Iraq Museum. *Right*: Wrestlers, from Eshnunna (mod. Tell Asmar), early 2d millennium B.C. Terra cotta, ht., 4¼ in. Paris, Louvre.

MESOPOTAMIA

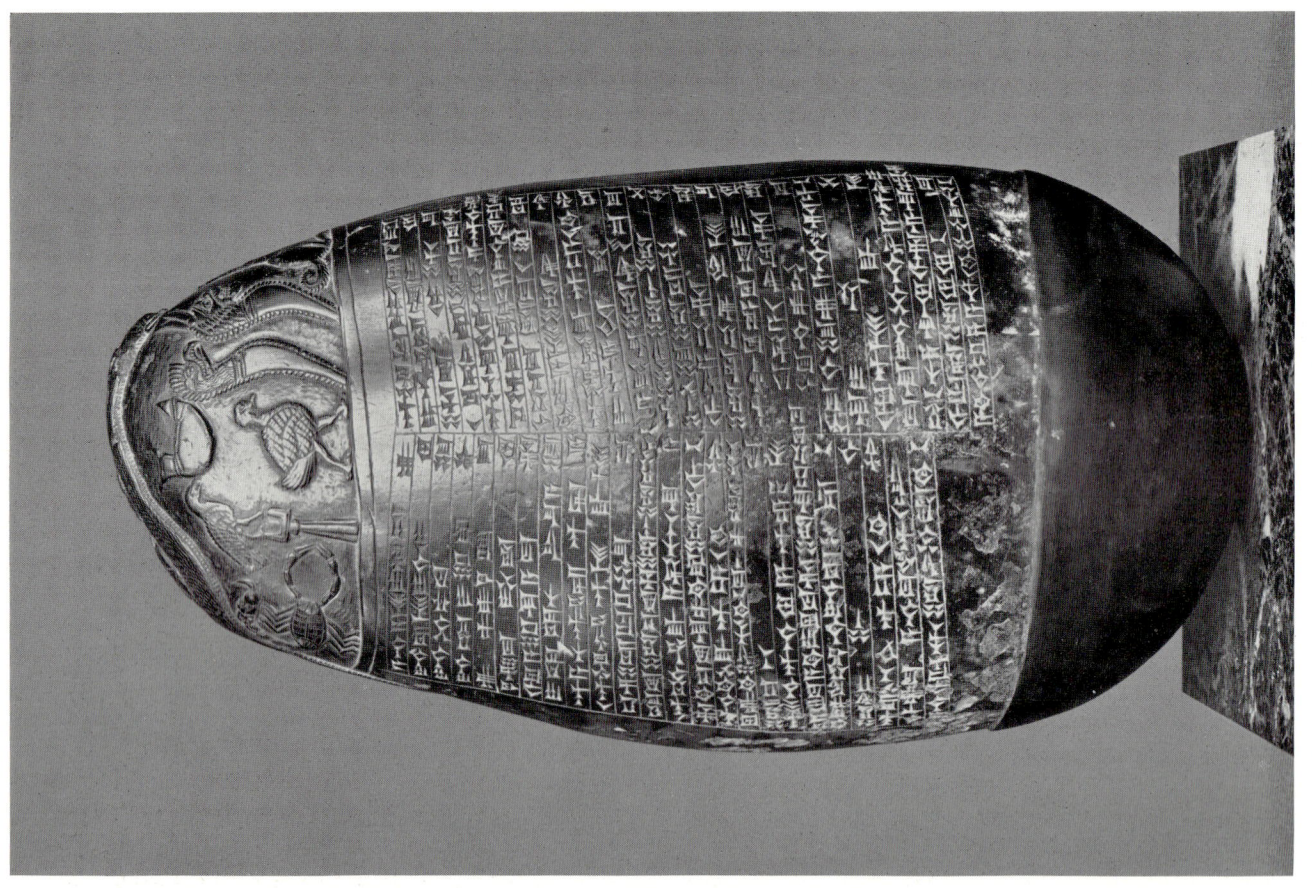

Pl. 486. *Left*: Top of a stele, with a worshiper before a seated god, from Susa, Old Babylonian period. Basalt, ht., 26 3/8 in. Paris, Louvre. *Right*: So-called "Michaux Stone," a boundary stone (*kudurru*), Kassite period. Diorite, ht., 17 3/4 in. Paris, Cabinet des Médailles.

MESOPOTAMIA

Pl. 487. *Left*: God of vegetation, from Ashur, Old Assyrian period. Chalk alabaster, ht. 4 ft., 5½ in. Berlin, Staatliche Museen. *Right*: The goddess Ishtar with dedication of King Ashurbelkala, from Nineveh, 11th cent. B.C. White limestone, ht. 37 in. London, British Museum.

MESOPOTAMIA

Pl. 488. *Left*: Human-headed winged bull, from the palace of Sargon II in Dur Sharrukin (mod. Khorsabad), 8th cent. B.C. Chalk alabaster, ht. 13 ft, 9 3/8 in. Paris, Louvre. *Right*: The Black Obelisk of Shalmaneser III, from Nimrud, 9th cent. B.C. Marble, ht. 6 ft, 8 3/4 in. London, British Museum.

MESOPOTAMIA

Pl. 489. *Left*: Human-headed winged genius, from the palace of Sargon II in Dur Sharrukin (mod. Khorsabad), 8th cent. B.C. Chalk alabaster, ht., 10 ft. *Right*: Eagle-headed winged genius, from Dur Sharrukin, 8th cent. B.C. Chalk alabaster, ht., 45¼ in. Both, Paris, Louvre.

MESOPOTAMIA

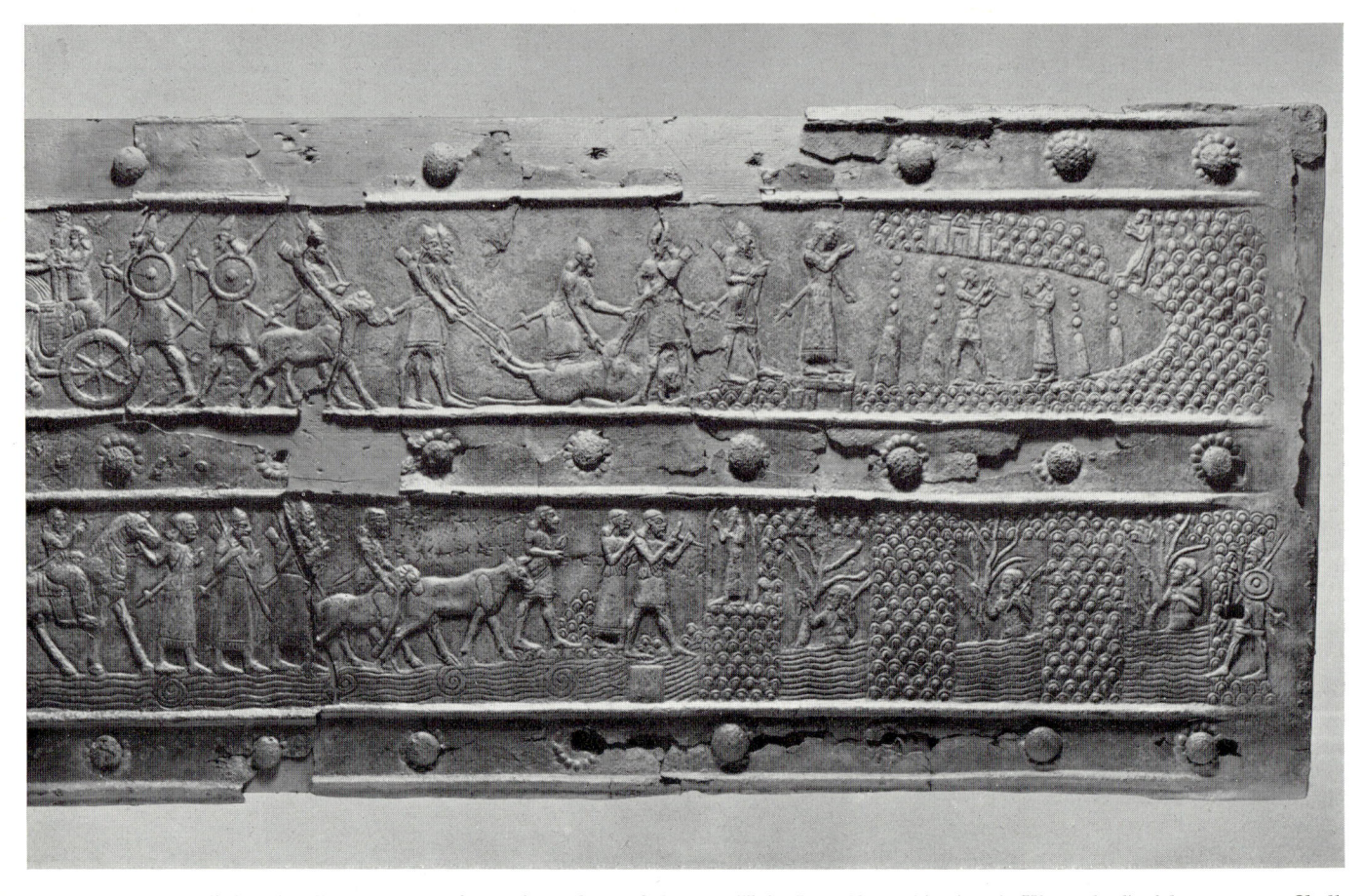

Pl. 490. *Above*: Relief with tribute bearers, from the palace of Sargon II in Dur Sharrukin (mod. Khorsabad), 8th cent. B.C. Chalk alabaster, ht., 5 ft., 3³/₄ in. Paris, Louvre. *Below*: Shalmaneser III's expedition to the source of the Tigris, detail of the reliefs from the palace gates of Balawat, 9th cent. B.C. Bronze, ht., ca. 11 in. London, British Museum.

MESOPOTAMIA

Pl. 491. *Above*: Lion doorkeeper from the temple of Dagan, Mari, early 2d millennium B.C. Bronze and stone, l., 27 1/2 in. *Below, left*: Kneeling worshiper, from Larsa, period of Hammurabi. Bronze and gold leaf, ht., 7 3/4 in. *Right*: Addorsed ibexes, from Larsa, period of Hammurabi. Bronze and gold, ht., 8 7/8 in. All, Paris, Louvre.

MESOPOTAMIA

Pl. 492. Assyrian king, 9th cent. B.C. Amber, ht., 9½ in. Boston, Museum of Fine Arts.

MESOPOTAMIA

Pl. 493. *Above:* Fugitives swimming with the aid of wineskins, from Nimrud, 9th cent. B.C. Alabastrine limestone, ht., 39 in. *Center:* Hunting scene with Ashurnasirpal II, from Nimrud, 9th cent. B.C. Alabastrine limestone, ht., 39 in. *Below:* Relief fragment, with scenes of animal life, from the palace of Ashurbanipal in Nineveh, 7th cent. B.C. Alabastrine limestone, 39×49 in. All, London, British Museum.

Pl. 494. The Ishtar Gate of Nebuchadnezzar II, from Babylon (Koldewey reconstruction), Neo-Babylonian period, 6th cent. B.C. Enameled bricks, ht., ca. 50 ft. Berlin, Staatliche Museen.

MESOPOTAMIA

Pl. 495. Nabupaliddina before the god Shamash, from Sippar, Neo-Babylonian period, mid-9th cent. B.C. Stone, 11 1/2 × 7 1/8 in. London, British Museum.

MESOPOTAMIA

Pl. 496. Cylinder-seal impressions. *Top row, left*: "Brocade" pattern, from Ashur, Jamdat Naṣr period. Serpentine, ht., 1³/₄ in. *Right*: Worship of a divinity, Old Babylonian period. Iron mineral, ht., 1 in. *Second row, left*: Animals and fantastic beings, from Shuruppak (mod. Fara), ca. 2600 B.C. Gray limestone, ht., 1¹/₂ in. All three, Berlin, Staatliche Museen. *Right*: Prayer to the god Marduk, Kassite period. Ht., 1¹/₄ in. London, British Museum. *Third row, left*: Human figures and human-headed bulls, 2500–2350 B.C. Rock crystal, ht., 1 in. Berlin, Staatliche Museen. *Right*: Running deer and tree, from Ashur, Middle Assyrian period. Chalcedony, ht., 1¹/₈ in. New York, Pierpont Morgan Library. *Bottom row, left*: Battle between mythical beings, Akkadian period. Serpentine, ht., 1³/₄ in. Paris, Bibliothèque Nationale. *Right*: Worship of the goddess Ishtar, Neo-Assyrian period. Greenish chalcedony, ht., 1⁵/₈ in. London, British Museum.

METALWORK

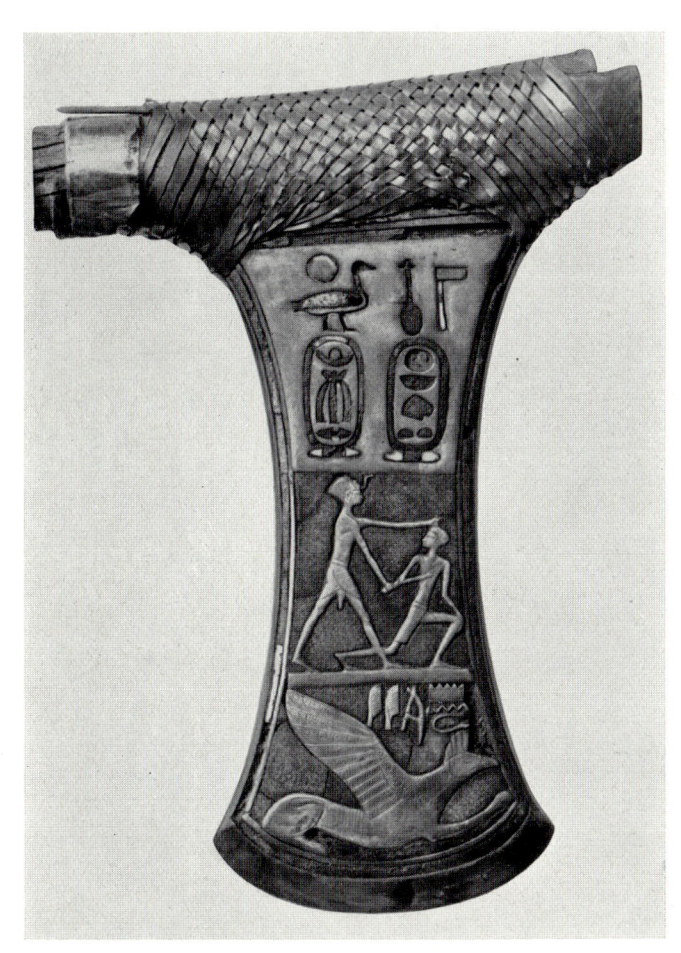

Pl. 497. *Above, left*: Bull's head, Erech (Uruk), first half of 3d millennium B.C. Bronze, 9×7½ in. Berlin, Staatliche Museen. *Right*: Finial, Luristan, late 2d–early 1st millennium B.C. Bronze. Teheran, Foroughi Coll. *Below, left*: Ax with name of King Ahmose, Thebes, early 18th dynasty. Bronze, gold, and lapis lazuli; l. of blade, 5³⁄₈ in. Cairo, Egyptian Museum. *Right*: Winged centauress, part of an Urartian throne, Toprak Kale, 8th–7th cent. B.C. Bronze, ht., ca. 8 in. London, British Museum.

METALWORK

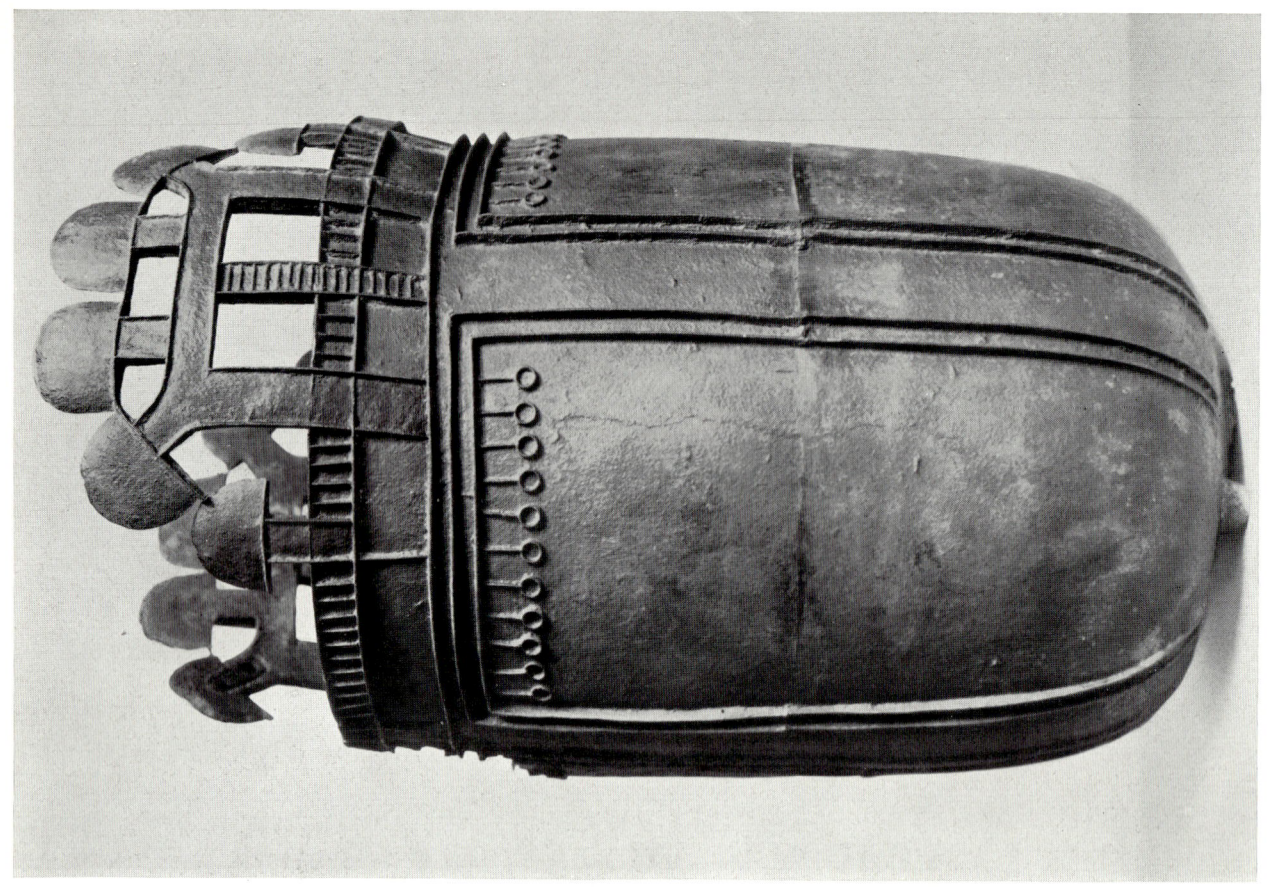

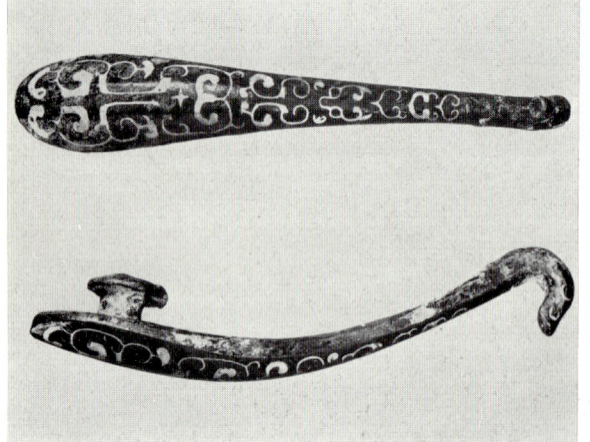

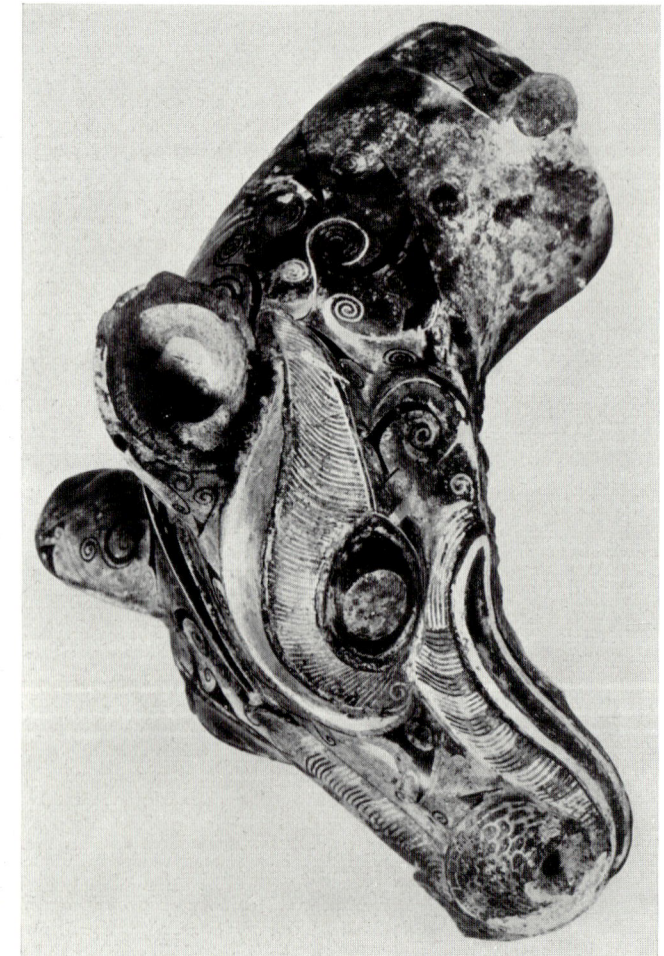

Pl. 498. *Left, above*: Bell (*chung*), from Shou-chou, Anhwei, China, Spring and Autumn period (722–481 B.C.). Bronze, ht., 11 in. *Center*: Girdle (?) hooks, from Chao-ku-ts'un, near Hui-hsien, Honan, China, Warring States period (5th cent.–221 B.C.). Bronze inlaid with gold; l., 3 5/8 in. *Below*: Chariot ornament, from Liu-li-ko, near Hui-hsien, Warring States period. Bronze, l., 5 1/4 in. All three, property of the Chinese Government. *Right*: Hunnish caldron with Chinese influences, from Törtel, Hungary, 4th–5th cent. Budapest, National Museum.

METALWORK

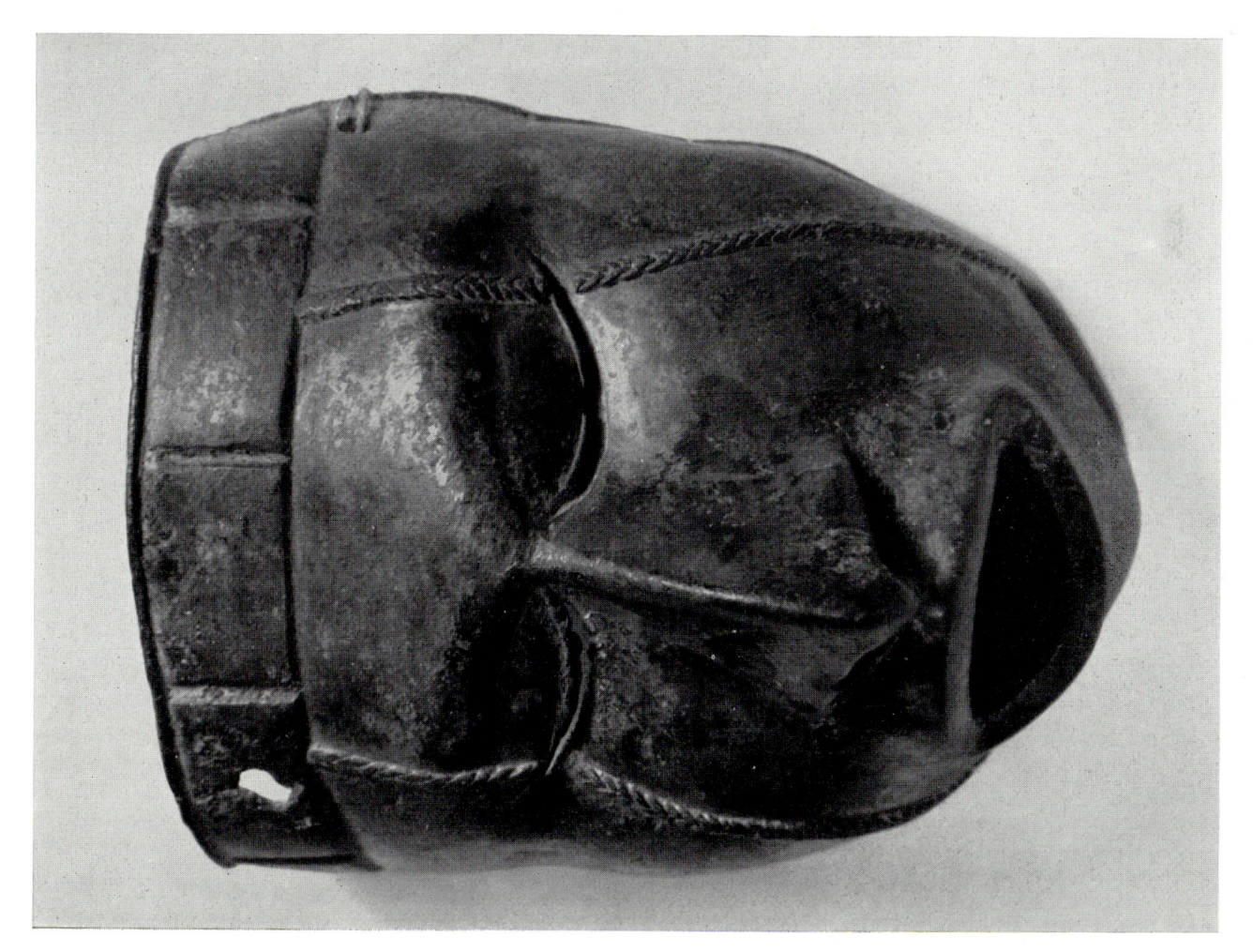

Pl. 499. *Left*: Tarascan mask representing the god Xipe, western Mexico. Copper. Mexico City, Museo Nacional de Antropología. *Right*: Diaguita axhead, northwestern Argentina. Bronze, l., 8½ in. Vienna, Museum für Völkerkunde.

METALWORK

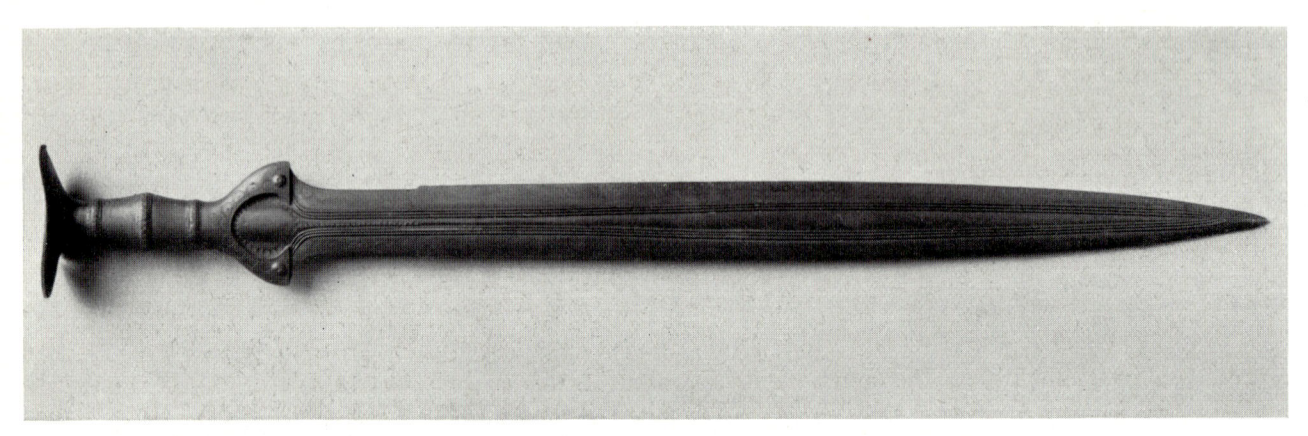

Pl. 500. *Left*: Sword, Hungarian type, late Bronze Age. Bronze, with incised and punctured ornament; l., 21½ in. New York, Metropolitan Museum. *Right, above*: Cretan double ax, ca. 1500 B.C. Bronze. Heraklion, Crete, Archaeological Museum. *Below*: Helmet of Corinthian type, 6th–5th cent. B.C. Bronze. Athens, National Museum. (Cf. I, Pl. 438.)

METALWORK

Pl. 501. Vessel with figurines, from Bisenzio (anc. Visentium), 7th cent. B.C. Bronze, sheet decorated in repoussé; ht., 9 7/8 in. Rome, Museo di Villa Giulia.

METALWORK

Pl. 502. Embossed disk (shield umbo?) showing Scythian influences, 1st cent. B.C. – 3d cent., probably from eastern Celtic lands, found in Helden, Netherlands. Gilded silver, diam., 8 5/8 in. Leiden, Netherlands, Rijksmuseum.

METALWORK

Pl. 503. *Above, left*: Tripod, from Olympia, 8th cent. B.C. Bronze, ht., 27 1/2 in. Olympia, Greece, Archaeological Museum. *Right*: Statuette, from the Heraion, Samos, early 6th cent. B.C. Bronze, made by *sphyrelaton* technique; ht., 5 3/4 in. Vathy, Samos, Museum. *Below*: The "situla of Vače," detail showing reliefs of hunting scenes, from Vače, near Litija, Yugoslavia, late 6th–early 5th cent. B.C. Bronze, full ht., 9 3/8 in. Ljubljana, National Museum.

METALWORK

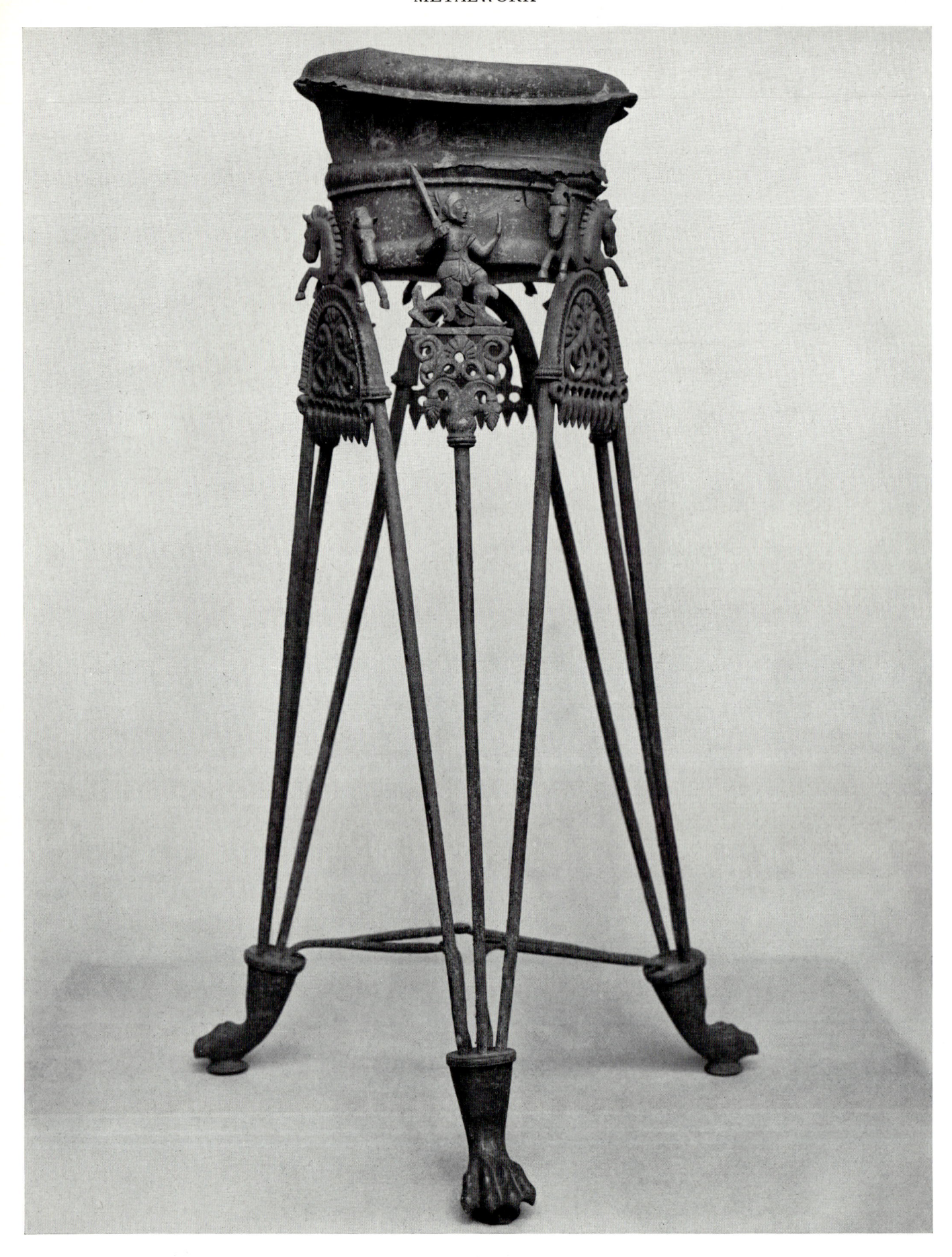

Pl. 504. Etruscan tripod, from Vulci, late 6th cent. B.C. Bronze, ht., 26¾ in. London, British Museum.

METALWORK

Pl. 505. *Above, left*: Greek mirror, ca. mid-5th cent. B.C. Bronze, ht., 19 3/4 in. Athens, National Museum. *Right*: Etruscan oil lamp, underside, mid-5th cent. B.C. Bronze, diam., 23 5/8 in. Cortona, Museo dell'Accademia Etrusca. *Below, left*: Cist, from Palestrina (anc. Praeneste), second half of 4th cent. B.C. Bronze, ht., 24 3/4 in. Rome, Museo di Villa Giulia. *Right*: Hydria with appliqué of Ariadne and Dionysos, eastern Greece (?), 4th–3d cent. B.C. Bronze, ht., 20 1/8 in. Chantilly, France, Musée Condé.

METALWORK

Pl. 506. Drunken silenus as a lamp bearer, from Pompeii, copy of a Hellenistic original of 2d–1st cent. B.C. Bronze, ht., 24 in. Naples, Museo Nazionale.

METALWORK

Pl. 507. Istanbul, St. Sophia, detail of the fifth door from the north in the west wall of the esonarthex, ca. 840. Bronze.

METALWORK

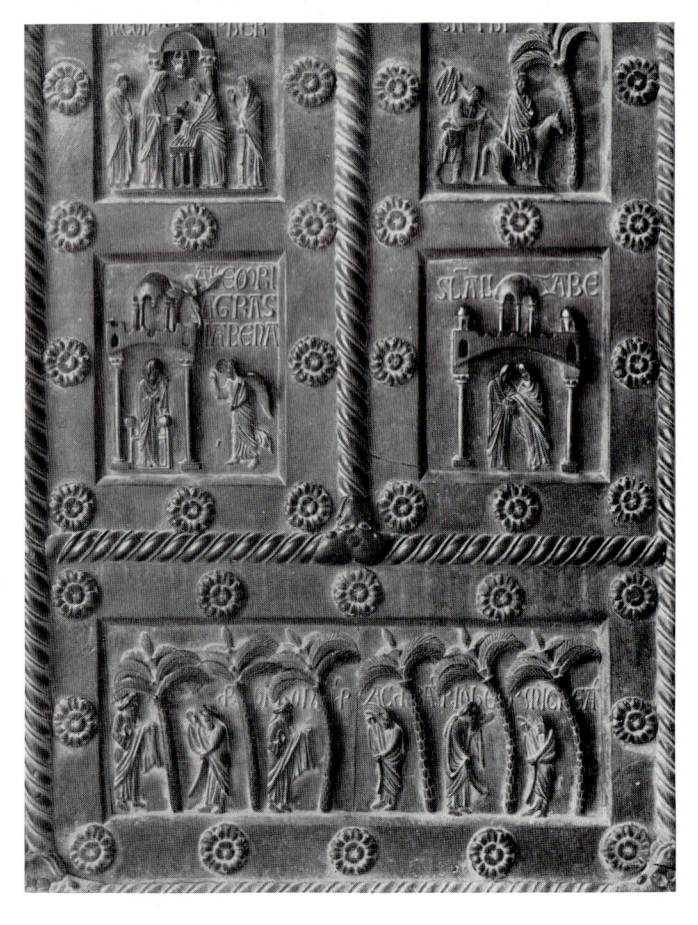

Pl. 508. Bronze door leaves, details. *Above, left*: Augsburg, Cathedral, south side, 11th cent. *Right*: Verona, S. Zeno, west side, 11th–12th cent., partly German work (?). *Below, left*: Trani, Italy, Cathedral, central door, by Barisanus of Trani, second half of 12th cent. *Right*: Pisa, Cathedral, Porta di S. Ranieri, by Bonannus of Pisa, 1180.

METALWORK

Pl. 509. Paris, Notre-Dame, hinge work of the western doors, detail, 13th cent. Wrought iron with stamped details.

METALWORK

Pl. 510. *Above, left*: Measure, mortar, and weight, southern Germany, 15th cent. Bronze. *Right*: Lock and key, southern Germany, ca. 1500. Iron. All, Munich, Bayerisches Nationalmuseum. *Below, left*: Knocker on the entrance door of Hôtel Jacques-Cœur, Bourges, France, 15th cent. Iron. *Right*: Padlock, southern Germany, 17th cent. Iron, ht., 9 1/8 in. Nürnberg, Germany, Germanisches National-Museum.

METALWORK

Pl. 511. *Above, left*: Moses with the Tablets of the Law, Lorraine, late 12th cent. Bronze, ht., 9¼ in. Oxford, Ashmolean Museum. *Right*: Reliquary head, Lower Saxony, from the church in Fischbeck on the Weser, Germany, 13th cent. Gilded bronze, with silver eyes and niello inlay; ht., 12¼ in. Hanover, Kestner-Museum. *Below*: Baptismal font, detail of cover, ca. 1220. Bronze; full ht., 5 ft., 11 in. Hildesheim, Germany, Cathedral. (Cf. IX, PL. 167.)

METALWORK

Pl. 512. *Above*: Hispano-Moresque aquamanile in the form of a lion, 11th cent. Bronze. *Below, left*: Ewer, Iran, 12th–13th cent. Bronze. Both, Paris, Louvre. *Right*: Cuirass, Iran, 13th–14th cent. Bronze. Florence, Museo Stibbert.

METALWORK

Pl. 513. Benin pendant mask, Nigeria. Bronze, ht., 7 1/8 in. Stockholm, Statens Etnografiska Museum.

METALWORK

Pl. 514. Japan, Nara period. *Above*: Amida triad with screen and halo, from the Tachibana shrine, ca. 710. Bronze; screen, 34¼×20⅛ in. Nara, Hōryūji. *Below, left*: Ewer with phoenix head, 8th cent. Gilded silver. Tokyo, National Museum. *Right*: Octagonal lantern, with low relief of bodhisattvas making music. Bronze. Nara, Tōdaiji.

METALWORK

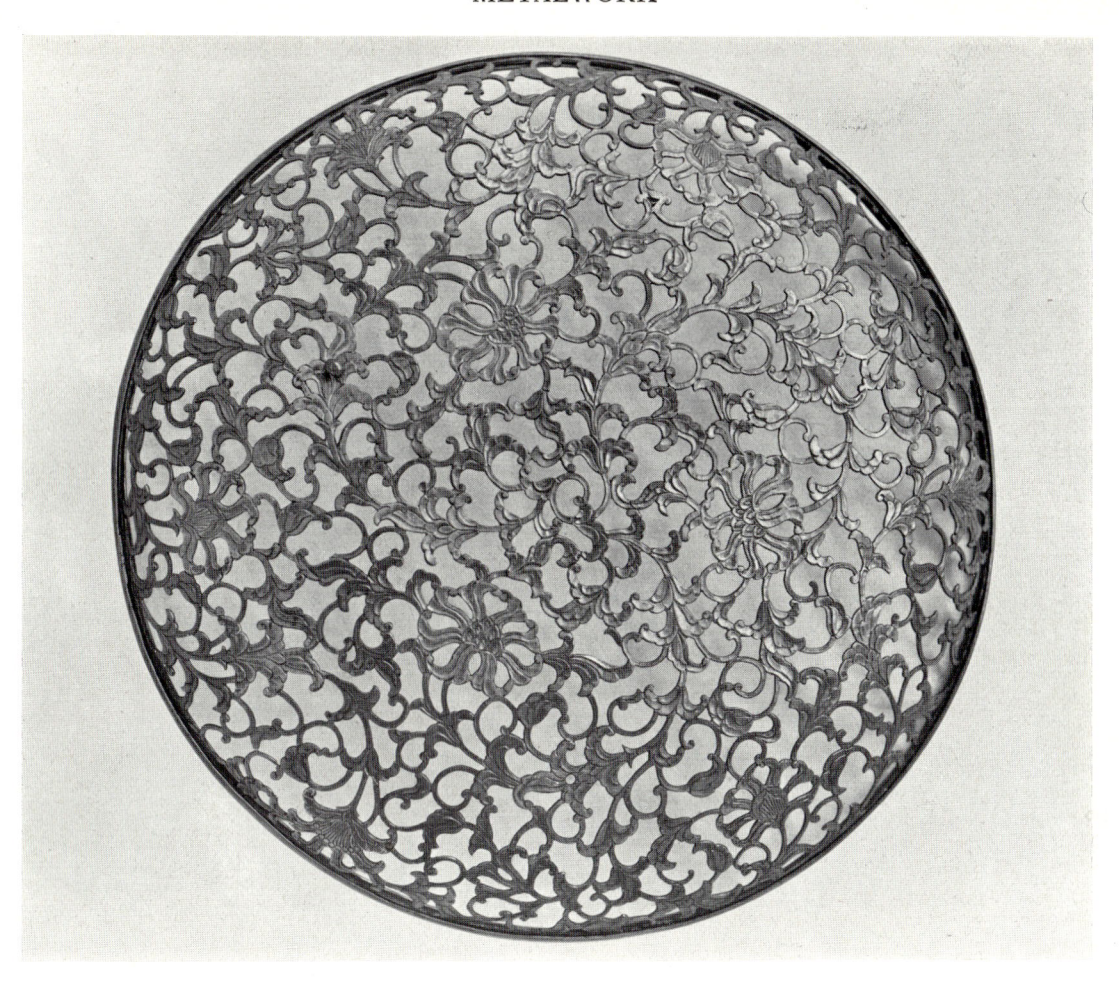

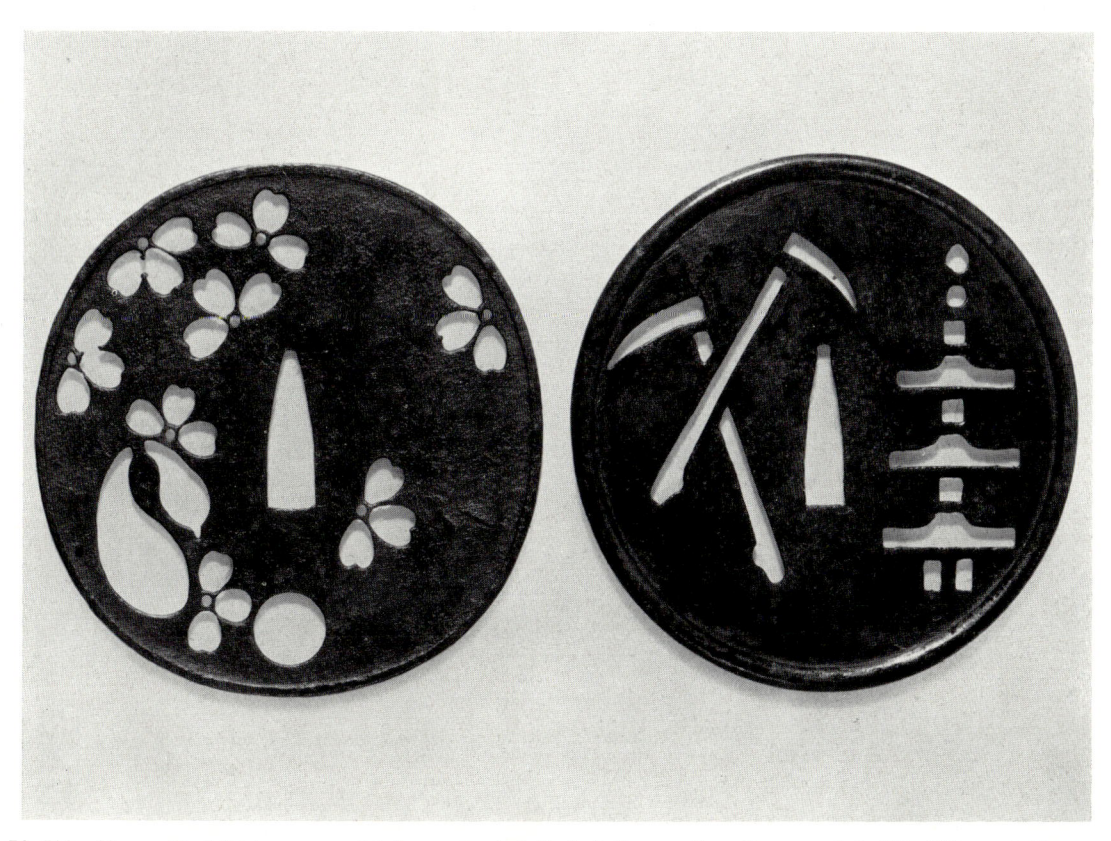

Pl. 515. *Above*: Buddhist ceremonial flower basket (*koko*), Japan, Kamakura period, 12th–14th cent. Bronze with gold and silver plating. Shiga, Jinshoji. *Below*: Tsubas (sword guards), with openwork designs of cherry blossoms and gourd (*left*), sickles and pagoda (*right*), Japan, Muromachi period, 14th–16th cent. Iron. Tokyo, National Museum.

METALWORK

Pl. 516. *Above, left*: Catalan Gothic candelabrum, 15th cent. Wrought iron. Sitges, Barcelona, Spain, Museo del Cau Ferrat. *Right*: Bracket for pitch torches, Palazzo Strozzi, Florence, by N. Grosso, called Caparra, 1500. Wrought iron. *Below, left*: Italian cornucopia-shaped lamp, by G. Serafini of Aquila, 16th cent. Wrought iron. Florence. Museo Nazionale. *Right*: French candelabrum, 18th cent. Bronze. London, Wallace Coll.

METALWORK

Pl. 517. *Above, left*: Door knocker, executed in Paris, 18th cent. Chased bronze. *Right*: Lock plate, France, 18th cent. Gilded bronze. *Below*: Decorative appliqué, France, first half of 19th cent. Gilded bronze. All, Paris, Musée des Arts Décoratifs.

METALWORK

Pl. 518. *Above*: Fire screen, Spain, ca. 1520. Wrought iron. Paris, Louvre. *Below*: Gates with allegorical figures and the Lion of St. Mark, balustrade of the Loggetta di S. Marco, Venice, by A. Gai (cast by I. Romano), 1734.

METALWORK

Pl. 519. *Above*: Railing of Casa Cellesi, Arezzo, Italy, 17th cent. Wrought iron. *Below, left*: Window grating, Germany, late 18th cent. Wrought iron. London, Victoria and Albert Museum. *Right*: Window grating of a house in Winklerstrasse, Nürnberg, Germany, 1772. Wrought iron.

METALWORK

Pl. 520. Gates of Galerie d'Apollon, Louvre, made for Château de Maisons, Maisons-Laffitte, France, ca. 1650. Wrought iron.

METALWORK

Pl. 521. Gate, by Mirko, in the World War II memorial park of the Fosse Ardeatine, Rome. Bronze.

METALWORK

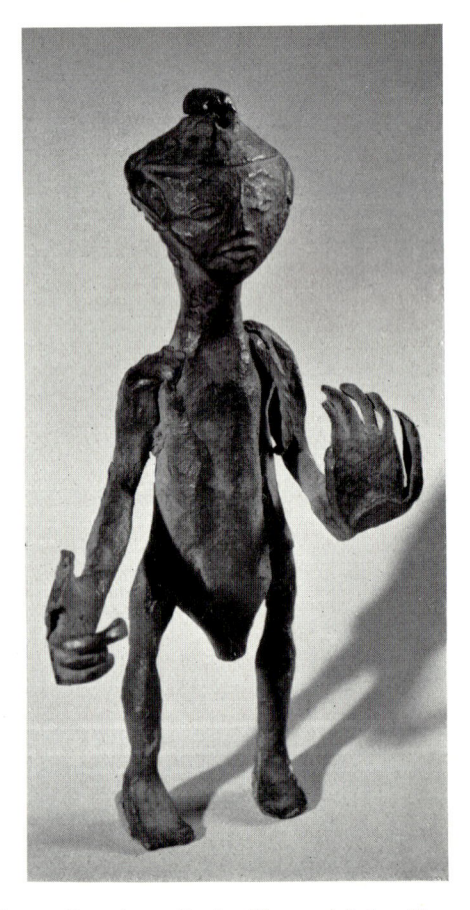

Pl. 522. *Above*: Spanish firedog, of folk workmanship. Wrought iron. Sitges, Barcelona, Spain, Museo del Cau Ferrat. *Below, left*: Northwest Coast Indian rattle, British Columbia, Canada. Copper. Colorado Springs, Fine Arts Center, Taylor Museum. *Right*: Bakuba male figure, Congo, ca. early 16th cent. Iron, ht., 7⁵/₈ in. Antwerp, Ethnografisch Museum.

METALWORK

Pl. 523. *Above, left*: Bamun pipe with human figures and lizards, Cameroons. Brass, lost-wax process, with clay bowl; l., 5 ft., 11⁵/₈ in. Berlin, Museum für Völkerkunde. *Right*: Gu, Fon god of metal and war, Dahomey, 19th cent. Iron, including European scrap. Paris, Musée de l'Homme. *Below*: Ashanti gold weights, Ghana. Brass, lost-wax process. Rome, Lateran Museums.

MICHELANGELO

Pl. 524. Virgin of the Stairs. Marble, 21⁵/₈ × 15³/₄ in. Florence, Casa Buonarroti.

MICHELANGELO

Pl. 525. *Above*: The Battle of the Lapiths and the Centaurs. Marble, 33 1/8 × 35 3/8 in. Florence, Casa Buonarroti.
Below: Madonna and Child with the Infant St. John. Marble, diam., ca. 33 in. Florence, Museo Nazionale.

MICHELANGELO

Pl. 526. *Left*: Pietà. Marble, ht., 5 ft., 8½ in. Rome, St. Peter's. *Right*: Deposition. Marble, ht., 7 ft., 5 in. Florence, Cathedral.

MICHELANGELO

Pl. 527. The Holy Family (the Doni Tondo). Tempera on panel, 35 7/8 × 31 1/2 in. Florence, Uffizi.

MICHELANGELO

Pl. 528. The Creation of Adam, detail. Fresco. Rome, Vatican, Sistine Chapel.

MICHELANGELO

Pl. 529. *Left:* St. Matthew. Marble, ht. 8 ft., 10 3/4 in. Florence, Accademia. *Right:* Dying Slave. Marble, ht. 7 ft., 6 1/8 in. Paris, Louvre.

MICHELANGELO

Pl. 530. Tomb of Giuliano di Lorenzo de' Medici, duke of Nemours. Marble. Florence, S. Lorenzo, New Sacristy.

MICHELANGELO

Pl. 531. Florence, S. Lorenzo, New Sacristy. *Above*: Night, detail of PL. 530. *Below*: Two details of the tomb of Lorenzo di Piero de' Medici, duke of Urbino. Marble. *Left*: Evening. *Right*: Dawn.

MICHELANGELO

Pl. 532. The Rondanini Pietà. Marble, ht., 6 ft., 4³/₄ in. Milan, Castello Sforzesco.

MICHELANGELO

Pl. 533. The Last Judgment, detail. Fresco; full size, 55 ft., 9 in. × 43 ft., 7 in. Rome, Vatican, Sistine Chapel.

MICHELANGELO

Pl. 534. Crucifixion of St. Peter, detail. Fresco; full size, 20 ft., 6 in. × 21 ft., 8 in. Rome, Vatican, Pauline Chapel.

MICHELANGELO

Pl. 535. Rome, Vatican, Sistine Chapel, ceiling frescoes. *Above*: The Creation of the Sun and Moon. *Below, left*: The Erythraean sibyl, detail. *Right*: Isaiah, detail. (Cf. III, PL. 312.)

MICHELANGELO

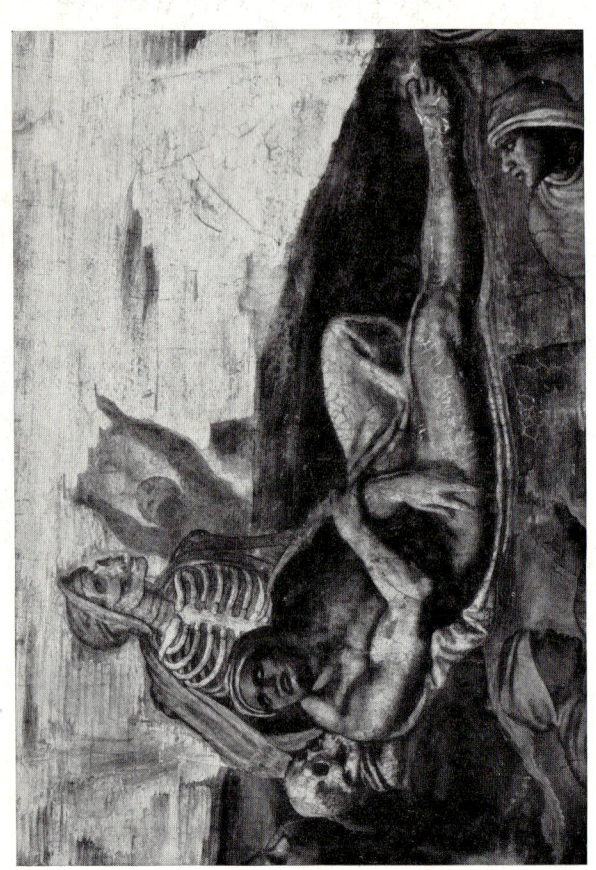

Pl. 536. The Last Judgment, details. Fresco; full size, 55 ft. 9 in. × 43 ft. 7 in. Rome, Vatican, Sistine Chapel. *Left, above*: One of the resurrected assisted by two skeletons. *Below*: Charon's boat. *Right*: The damned.

MICHELANGELO

Pl. 537. The Conversion of St. Paul. Fresco, 20 ft, 6 in. × 21 ft, 8 in. Rome, Vatican, Pauline Chapel.

MICHELANGELO

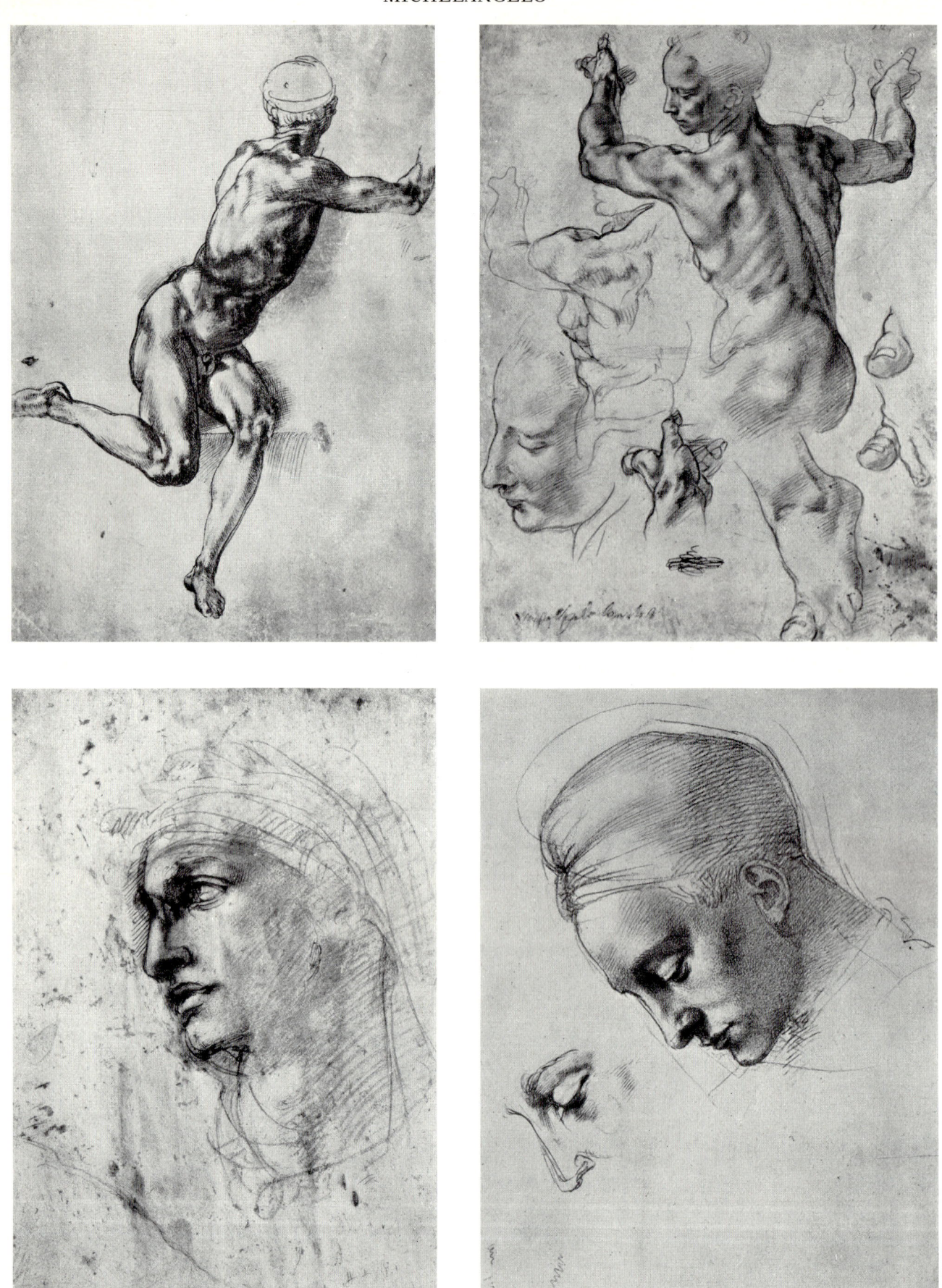

Pl. 538. Drawings. *Above, left*: Study for a male figure. Pen heightened with white lead, 16½×11 in. London, British Museum. *Right*: Studies for the Libyan sibyl. Red chalk, 11³/₈×8¼ in. New York, Metropolitan Museum, Joseph Pulitzer Bequest 1924. *Below, left*: Study of a head. Charcoal, pen, and bister; 13×8¼ in. London, British Museum. *Right*: Study of a head. Red chalk, 13³/₄×10⁵/₈ in. Florence, Galleria Buonarroti.

MICHELANGELO

Pl. 539. Drawings. *Above*: Resurrection of Christ. Black chalk, 11×12⁵/₈ in. London, British Museum. *Below, left*: St. Anne with the Madonna and Child. Chalk and pen, 12⁵/₈×10¹/₄ in. Paris, Louvre. *Right*: The Fall of Phaëthon. Black chalk, 12¹/₄×8¹/₄ in. London, British Museum.

MICHELANGELO

Pl. 540. Florence, Biblioteca Laurenziana, vestibule (cf. I, pls. 381, 418).

MICHELANGELO

Pl. 541. Rome, St. Peter's, view of the apse and dome.

MICHELANGELO

Pl. 542. *Above*: Rome, Porta Pia. *Left*: The gate in an etching of 1568. Rome, Gabinetto Nazionale delle Stampe. *Right*: Detail of a window. *Below*: Palazzo dei Conservatori, Rome, detail of the façade.

Pl. 543. *Above*: Palau Islands, a meeting house (*bai*) with carved and painted beams. *Below*: Storytelling panel, from Palau Islands, detail. Wood, painted and chiseled. Honolulu, R. Sparks Coll.

Pl. 544. *Left, above*: Table for offerings, from Palau Islands. Wood, inlaid with shell; l., 19 in. London, British Museum. *Below*: Coconut grater, from Kapingamarangi, Caroline Islands. Breadfruit wood (with toothed blade), ht., 19 in. Honolulu, L. Mason Coll. *Right*: Post of a men's house, with zoomorphic reliefs, from Yap, Caroline Islands. Wood, ht., 11 ft. Hamburg, Museum für Völkerkunde.

MICRONESIAN CULTURES

Pl. 545. Mask, from Mortlock Islands, Caroline Islands. Wood covered with a layer of lime, ht., 27 1/8 in. Stuttgart, Linden-Museum.

Pl. 546. Oil lamp, from Palau Islands. Baked clay, ht., 9⅝ in. Stuttgart, Linden-Museum.

MICRONESIAN CULTURES

Pl. 547. *Tino* image, from Nukuoro, Caroline Islands. Wood, ht., 13 3/4 in. Paris, Musée de l'Homme.

MICRONESIAN CULTURES

Pl. 548. *Above, left*: Plaited mat worn by pregnant women, from Nauru Islands. Pandanus and black-dyed hibiscus fibers, trimmed with shells; 16 in. square. Honolulu, Bernice P. Bishop Museum. *Right*: Plaited dress mat, from Jaluit, Marshall Islands. Pandanus fiber, 28 3/4 in. square. *Below*: Covered containers, from Palau Islands. Wood with shell inlay, ht., 7 1/4 in. and 8 1/4 in. London, British Museum.